MICROSOFT

Office 2000

Introductory Concepts and Techniques

ENHANCED EDITION

Microsoft Office 2000 Introductory Concepts and Techniques — Enhanced Edition

Gary B. Shelly
Thomas J. Cashman
Misty E. Vermaat

Contributing Authors
Steven G. Forsythe
Jodi L. Groen
Mary Z. Last
Philip J. Pratt
James S. Quasney
Susan L. Sebok
Denise M. Woods

COURSE TECHNOLOGY
25 THOMSON PLACE
BOSTON MA 02210

SHELLY
CASHMAN
SERIES®

Australia • Canada • Denmark • Japan • Mexico • New Zealand • Philippines • Puerto Rico • Singapore
South Africa • Spain • United Kingdom • United States

Asia (excluding Japan)
Thomson Learning
60 Albert Street, #15-01
Albert Complex
Singapore 189969

Japan
Thomson Learning
Palaceside Building 5F
1-1-1 Hitotsubashi, Chiyoda-ku
Tokyo 100 0003 Japan

Australia/New Zealand
Nelson/Thomson Learning
102 Dodds Street
South Melbourne, Victoria 3205
Australia

Latin America
Thomson Learning
Seneca, 53
Colonia Polanco
11560 Mexico D.F. Mexico

South Africa
Thomson Learning
Zonnebloem Building,
Constantia Square
526 Sixteenth Road
P.O. Box 2459
Halfway House, 1685
South Africa

Canada
Nelson/Thomson Learning
1120 Birchmount Road
Scarborough, Ontario
Canada M1K 5G4

UK/Europe/Middle East
Thomson Learning
Berkshire House
168-173 High Holborn
London, WC1V 7AA United Kingdom

Spain
Thomson Learning
Calle Magallanes, 25
28015-MADRID
ESPANA

For more information, contact Course Technology, 25 Thomson Place, Boston, MA 02210.

Or visit our Internet site at www.course.com

PHOTO CREDITS: **Microsoft Windows 98** *Project 1, pages INT 1.2-3* Cardinal, computer, rose, tree, Courtesy of International Microcomputer Software, Inc.; **Microsoft Word 2000** *Project 2, pages WD 2.2-3* Space photograph, Courtesy of Digital Stock; *Project 3, pages WD 3.2-3* Classified listing, pen and glasses, hand on mouse, woman in business suit, Courtesy of PhotoDisc, Inc.; Albert Einstein and signature, Courtesy of the American Institute of Physics; **Microsoft Excel 2000** *Project 1, pages E 1.4-5* Background swirls, building doorway, business man photo, circuit board, hand, library, man at ATM, man talking on telephone, people with groceries, stack of books, student on steps, student with books, woman at computer, woman holding garment, Courtesy of PhotoDisc, Inc.; parking meter, Courtesy of KPT Metatools; *Project 2, pages E 2.2-3* Bike helmet, coffee cup, moon, mountain bike, Courtesy of Corel Corporation; *Project 3, pages E 3.2-3* Money, stacks of bills, house, Courtesy of PhotoDisc, Inc.; **Microsoft Access 2000** *Project 1, pages A 1.4-5* Children in school, log wheels, man painting, ship, teacher at chalkboard, woman and child, woman at computer, Courtesy of PhotoDisc, Inc.; Trojan horse, Courtesy of Corel Professional Photos CD-ROM Image Usage; *Project 2, pages A 2.2-3* Children on puzzle pieces, child on milk carton, Courtesy of PhotoDisc, Inc.; Web pages, Courtesy of the National Center for Missing and Exploited Children; **Microsoft PowerPoint 2000** *Project 1, pages PP 1.4-5* COMDEX/Canada, COMDEX/Las Vegas, conference presentation, Courtesy of 2D Events; IBM computer, Courtesy of International Business Machines; First Apple computer, Courtesy of Apple Computer, Inc.; portable computer, Courtesy of Compaq Computer Corporation; *Project 2, pages PP 2.2-3* Business meeting, man and woman working on laptop computer, woman next to desk, Courtesy of PhotoDisc, Inc.; **Microsoft Outlook 2000** *Project 1, pages O 1.4-5* Business meeting, courtyard, Egyptian image, old book, people at conference table, stars behind moons, stop watch, trees, Courtesy of PhotoDisc, Inc.; **Microsoft Office 2000 Integration** *Project 1, pages I 1.2-3* Doctor, faces, laptop computer, people working at computer, surgeon in operating room, x-ray image, Courtesy of PhotoDisc, Inc.

ISBN 0-7895-6251-0 (Perfect bound)
ISBN 0-7895-6250-2 (Spiral bound)

1 2 3 4 5 6 7 8 9 10 BC 05 04 03 02 01

CONTENTS

Essential Introduction to Computers

Windows 2000 and Office 2000

PROJECT 1

An Introduction to Windows 2000 Professional and Office 2000

Microsoft Word 2000

PROJECT 1

Creating and Editing a Word Document

PROJECT 2

Creating a Research Paper

PROJECT 2

FORMULAS, FUNCTIONS, FORMATTING, AND WEB QUERIES

PROJECT 3

What-If Analysis, Charting, and Working with Large Worksheets

WEB FEATURE

Creating Static and Dynamic Web Pages Using Excel

Microsoft Access 2000

PROJECT 1

Creating a Database Using Design and Datasheet Views

PROJECT 2

Querying a Database Using the Select Query Window

PROJECT 3

Maintaining a Database Using the Design and Update Features of Access

WEB FEATURE

Publishing to the Internet Using Data Access Pages

Microsoft PowerPoint 2000

PROJECT 1

Using a Design Template and AutoLayouts to Create a Presentation

PROJECT 2

Using Outline View and Clip Art to Create a Slide Show

WEB FEATURE

Creating a Presentation on the Web Using PowerPoint

Microsoft Outlook 2000

PROJECT 1

Schedule and Contact Management Using Outlook

Microsoft Integration 2000

PROJECT 1

Integrating Office 2000 Applications and the World Wide Web

Preface

The Shelly Cashman Series® offers the finest textbooks in computer education. We are proud of the fact that our Microsoft Office 4.3, Microsoft Office 95, Microsoft Office 97, and Microsoft Office 2000 textbooks have been runaway best-sellers. Each edition of our Office textbooks has included innovations, many based on comments made by the instructors and students who use our books.

Because of the delay in the release of Office XP, the increased emphasis on the Microsoft Office User Specialist (MOUS) Certification, and many instructor requests for new laboratory exercises, we decided to publish an Enhanced Edition of our best-selling textbook, *Microsoft Office 2000 Introductory Concepts and Techniques*. This *Enhanced Edition* continues with the innovation, quality, and reliability that you have come to expect from the Shelly Cashman Series. *Microsoft Office 2000 Introductory Concepts and Techniques, Enhanced Edition* includes the following enhancements:

- New Laboratory exercises for each project
- What's New in Microsoft Office XP
- MOUS Expert Level Quick Summary that shows how to complete Office 2000 tasks using the mouse, menu, shortcut menu, and keyboard
- New Learn It Online exercises
- Introduction to Windows 2000
- Completely updated *Introduction to Computers* section that presents the necessary computer concepts for success with the Office 2000 applications

In this *Enhanced Edition*, you will find an educationally sound and easy-to-follow pedagogy that combines a step-by-step approach with corresponding screens. All projects and exercises in this book are designed to take full advantage of the Office 2000 features. The popular Other Ways and More About features offer in-depth knowledge of Office 2000. The project openers provide a fascinating perspective on the subject covered in the project. The project material is developed carefully to ensure that students will see the importance of learning Office 2000 applications for future course work.

Objectives of This Textbook

Microsoft Office 2000: Introductory Concepts and Techniques, Enhanced Edition is intended for a course that covers Microsoft Word 2000, Microsoft Excel 2000, Microsoft Access 2000, Microsoft PowerPoint 2000, and Outlook 2000 with an overview of Windows. No experience with a computer is assumed, and no mathematics beyond the high school freshman level is required. The objectives of this book are:

- To teach the fundamentals of Microsoft Office 2000
- To expose students to practical examples of the computer as a useful tool
- To acquaint students with the proper procedures to create documents, workbooks, databases, and presentations suitable for course work, professional purposes, and personal use

COURSE TECHNOLOGY
THOMSON LEARNING
SHELLY CASHMAN SERIES®
MICROSOFT
Office
Introductory Concepts and Techniques
2000
Shelly/Cashman/Vermaat
ENHANCED EDITION
Word 2000
Excel 2000
Access 2000
PowerPoint 2000

- To develop an exercise-oriented approach that allows students to learn by example
- To encourage independent study, and help those who are working alone in a distance education environment

Approved by Microsoft as Courseware for the Microsoft Office User Specialist Program – Core Level

This book, when used in combination with the companion textbook *Microsoft Office 2000: Advanced Concepts and Techniques* in a two-semester sequence, has been approved by Microsoft as courseware for the Microsoft Office User Specialist (MOUS) program. After completing the projects and exercises in this book and its companion book, students will be prepared to take the Core level Microsoft Office User Specialist Exams for Microsoft Word 2000, Microsoft Excel 2000, Microsoft Access 2000, and Microsoft PowerPoint 2000. By passing the certification exam for a Microsoft software application, students demonstrate their proficiency in that application to employers. This exam is offered at participating centers, participating corporations, and participating employment agencies. See Appendix D for additional information on the MOUS program and for a table that includes the Word 2000, Excel 2000, Access 2000, and PowerPoint 2000 MOUS skill sets and corresponding page numbers where a skill is discussed in the book or visit the Web site www.mous.net.

The Shelly Cashman Series Microsoft Office User Specialist Center Web page (Figure 1) has more than fifteen Web pages you can visit to obtain additional information on the MOUS Certification program. The Web page (www.scsite.com/off2000/cert.htm) includes links to general information on certification, choosing an application for certification, preparing for the certification exam, and taking and passing the certification exams.

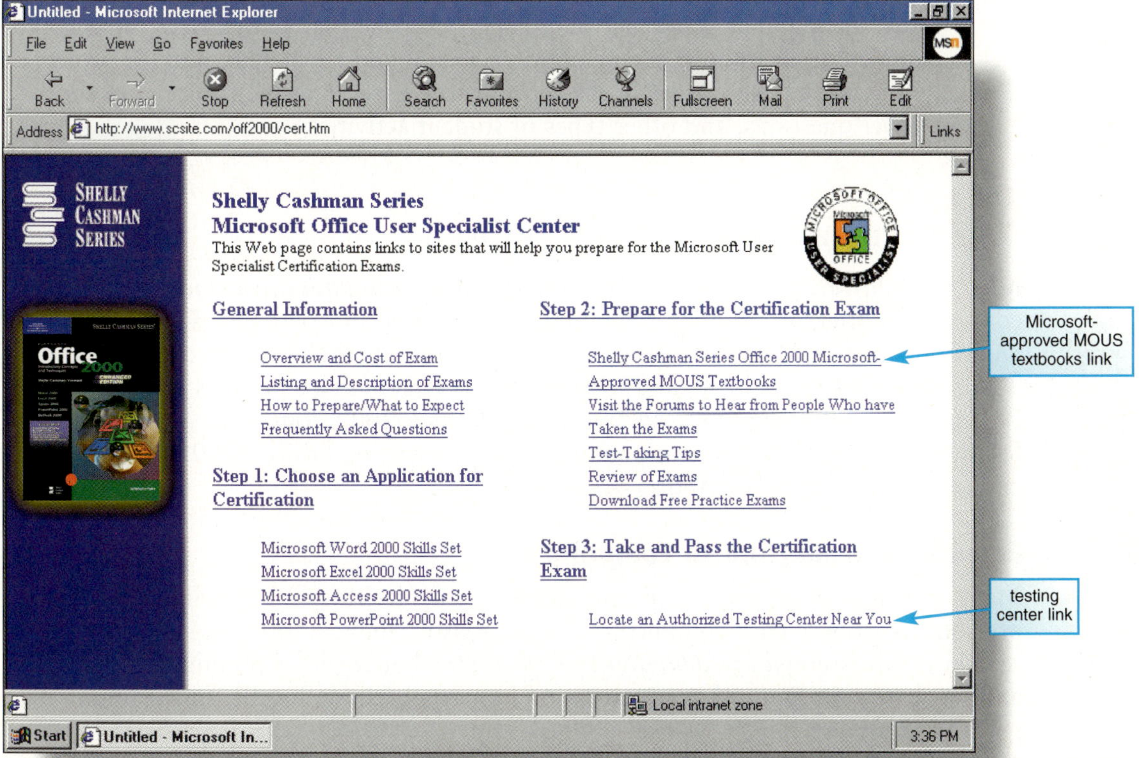

FIGURE 1

The Shelly Cashman Approach

Features of the Shelly Cashman Series Office 2000 books include:

- **Project Orientation:** Each project in the book presents a practical problem and complete solution in an easy-to-understand approach.
- **Step-by-Step, Screen-by-Screen Instructions:** Each of the tasks required to complete a project is shown using a step-by-step, screen-by-screen approach. The steps are accompanied by full-color screens.
- **Thoroughly Tested Projects:** Every screen in the book is correct because it is produced by the author only after performing a step, resulting in unprecedented quality.
- **Other Ways Boxes and Quick Reference Summary:** Office 2000 provides a variety of ways to carry out a given task. The Other Ways boxes displayed at the end of most of the step-by-step sequences specify the other ways to do the task completed in the steps. Thus, the steps and the Other Ways box make a comprehensive reference unit. In addition, a Quick Reference Summary, at the back of this book and also available on the Web, summarizes the ways application-specific tasks can be completed.
- **More About Feature:** These marginal annotations provide background information that complements the topics covered, adding depth and perspective to the learning process.
- **Integration of the World Wide Web:** We have integrated the World Wide Web into the students' Office 2000 learning experience in different ways. For example, we have added (1) More Abouts that send students to Web sites for up-to-date information and alternative approaches to tasks; (2) a MOUS information Web page and a MOUS map Web page so students can better prepare for the Microsoft Office Use Specialist (MOUS) Certification examinations; (3) an Office 2000 Quick Reference Summary Web page that summarizes the ways to complete tasks (mouse, menu, shortcut menu, and keyboard); and (4) project reinforcement Web pages in the form of true/false, multiple choice, and short answer questions, and other types of student activities.

Other Ways

1. Click New Record button on Database window toolbar
2. On Insert menu click New Record

Organization of This Textbook

Microsoft Office 2000: Introductory Concepts and Techniques, Enhanced Edition consists of a brief introduction to computers, a project on Microsoft Windows with an introduction to Microsoft Office 2000, three projects each on Microsoft Word 2000, Microsoft Excel 2000, and Microsoft Access 2000, two projects on Microsoft PowerPoint 2000, one project on Microsoft Outlook 2000, four short Web Features following each application, and one project on integrating Office 2000 applications and the Web. A short description of each follows.

More About 2000

Navigation

For more information on selecting cells that contain certain entries, such as constants or formulas, visit the Excel 2000 More About Web page (www.scsite.com/ex2000/more.htm) and click Using Go To Special.

Essential Introduction to Computers

Many students taking a course in the use of Microsoft Office 2000 will have little previous experience with computers. For this reason, the textbook begins with a section titled *Essential Introduction to Computers* that covers computer hardware and software concepts and information on how to purchase, install, and maintain a personal computer.

An Introduction to Windows 2000 and Microsoft Office 2000

In this project, students learn about user interfaces, Windows 2000, Windows Explorer, and each Office 2000 application. Topics include using the mouse; minimizing, maximizing, and restoring windows; sizing and scrolling windows; launching and quitting an application; displaying the contents of a folder; creating a folder; selecting and copying a group of files; renaming and deleting a file and a folder; using Windows 2000 Help; and shutting down Windows 2000. Topics pertaining to Office 2000 include a brief explanation of Word 2000; Excel 2000; Access 2000; PowerPoint 2000; Publisher 2000; FrontPage 2000; PhotoDraw 2000; and Outlook 2000 and examples of how these applications take advantage of the Internet and World Wide Web.

Microsoft Word 2000

Project 1 - Creating and Editing a Word Document In Project 1, students are introduced to Word terminology and the Word window by preparing an announcement. Topics include starting and quitting Word; entering text; checking spelling while typing; saving a document; selecting characters, words, lines, and paragraphs; changing the font and font size of text; centering, right-aligning, and formatting text in bold and italic; undoing commands and actions; inserting clip art into a document; resizing a graphic; printing a document; opening a document; correcting errors; and using the Word Help system.

Project 2 – Creating a Research Paper In Project 2, students use the MLA style of documentation to create a research paper. Topics include changing margins; adjusting line spacing; using a header to number pages; entering text using Click and Type; first-line indenting paragraphs; using Word's AutoCorrect feature; adding a footnote; modifying a style; inserting a symbol; inserting a manual page break; creating a hanging indent; creating a text hyperlink; sorting paragraphs; moving text; finding a synonym; counting words in a document; and checking spelling and grammar at once.

Project 3 – Using a Wizard to Create a Resume and Creating a Cover Letter with a Table In Project 3, students create a resume using Word's Resume Wizard and then create a cover letter with a letterhead. Topics include personalizing the resume; adding color to characters; setting and using tab stops; collecting and pasting; adding a bottom border; creating and inserting an AutoText entry; creating a bulleted list while typing; inserting a Word table; entering data into a Word table; and formatting a Word table. Finally, students prepare and print an envelope address.

Web Feature – Creating Web Pages Using Word In the Web Feature, students are introduced to creating Web pages. Topics include saving the resume created in Project 3 as a Web page; creating a Web page using the Web Page Wizard; resizing a Web page frame; editing a hyperlink; and editing a Web page from your browser.

Microsoft Excel 2000

Project 1 - Creating a Worksheet and Embedded Chart In Project 1, students are introduced to Excel terminology, the Excel window, and the basic characteristics of a worksheet and workbook. Topics include starting and quitting Excel; entering text and numbers; selecting a range; using the AutoSum button; copying using the fill handle; changing font size; formatting in bold; centering across columns; using the AutoFormat command; charting using the ChartWizard; saving and opening a workbook; editing a worksheet; using the AutoCalculate area; and using the Excel Help system.

Project 2 – Formulas, Functions, Formatting, and Web Queries In Project 2, students use formulas and functions to build a worksheet and learn more about formatting and printing a worksheet. Topics include entering formulas; using functions; verifying formulas; formatting text; formatting numbers; conditional formatting; drawing borders and adding colors; changing the widths of columns and rows; spell checking; previewing a worksheet; printing a section of a worksheet; and displaying and printing the formulas in a worksheet. This project also introduces students to accessing real-time data using Web Queries and sending the open workbook as an e-mail attachment directly from Excel.

Project 3 - What-If-Analysis, Charting, and Working with Large Worksheets In Project 3, students learn how to work with larger worksheets, how to create a worksheet based on assumptions, how to use the IF function and absolute cell references, charting techniques, and how to perform what-if analysis. Topics include assigning global formats; rotating text; using the fill handle to create a series; deleting, inserting, copying, and moving data on a worksheet; displaying and formatting the system date; displaying and docking toolbars; creating a 3-D Pie chart on a chart sheet, enhancing a 3-D Pie chart; freezing titles; changing the magnification of worksheets; displaying different parts of the worksheet using panes; and simple what-if analysis and goal seeking.

Web Feature - Creating Static and Dynamic Web Pages Using Excel In the Web Feature, students are introduced to creating static Web pages (noninteractive pages that do not change) and dynamic Web pages (interactive pages that offer Excel functionality). Topics include saving and previewing an Excel workbook as a Web page; viewing and manipulating a Web page created in Excel using a browser; and using the Spreadsheet Property Toolbox.

Microsoft Access 2000

Project 1 - Creating a Database Using Design and Datasheet Views In Project 1, students are introduced to the concept of a database and shown how to use Access to create a database. Topics include creating a database; creating a table; defining the fields in a table; opening a table; adding records to a table; closing a table; and previewing and printing the contents of a table. Additional topics include using a form to view data; using the Report Wizard to create a report; and using the Access Help system. Students also learn how to design a database to eliminate redundancy.

Project 2 - Querying a Database Using the Select Query Window In Project 2, students learn to use queries to obtain information from the data in their databases. Topics include creating queries; running queries; and printing the results. Specific query topics include displaying only selected fields; using character data in criteria; using wildcards; using numeric data in criteria; using various comparison operators; and creating compound criteria. Other related topics include sorting; joining tables; and restricting records in a join. Students also use computed fields, statistics, and grouping.

Project 3 - Maintaining a Database Using the Design and Update Features of Access 2000 In Project 3, students learn the crucial skills involved in maintaining a database. These include using Datasheet view and Form view to add new records, change existing records, delete records, and locate and filter records. Students learn the processes of changing the structure of a table; adding additional fields; changing characteristics of existing fields; creating a variety of validation rules; and specifying referential integrity. Students perform mass changes and deletions using queries; create single-field and multiple-field indexes; and use subdatasheets to view related data.

Web Feature - Publishing to the Internet Using Data Access Pages In the Web Feature, students learn to create a data access page to enable users to access the data in a database via the Internet. Topics include creating a data access page using the Page Wizard; previewing a data access page from within Access 2000; and using a data access page.

Microsoft PowerPoint 2000

Project 1 - Using a Design Template and AutoLayouts to Create a Presentation In Project 1, students are introduced to PowerPoint terminology, the PowerPoint window, and the basics of creating a multi-level bulleted list presentation. Topics include selecting a design template; increasing font size; changing font style; ending a slide show with a black slide; saving a presentation; viewing the slides in a presentation; checking a presentation for spelling and style errors; changing line spacing on the Slide Master; printing copies of the slides; and using the PowerPoint Help system.

Project 2 – Using Outline View and Clip Art to Create a Slide Show In Project 2, students create a presentation in outline view, insert clip art, and add animation effects. Topics include creating a slide presentation by promoting and demoting text in outline view; changing slide layouts; inserting clip art; changing clip art size; adding slide transition effects; adding text animation effects; animating clip art; running an animated slide show; printing audience handouts from an outline; and e-mailing a slide show from within PowerPoint.

PowerPoint Web Feature – Creating a Presentation on the Web Using PowerPoint In the Web Feature, students are introduced to saving a presentation as a Web page. Topics include saving an existing PowerPoint presentation as an HTML file; viewing the presentation as a Web page; editing a Web page through a browser; and viewing the editing change.

Schedule and Contact Management Using Outlook 2000

In this project, students discover the benefits of desktop information management systems by using Outlook to create a schedule of classes, study time, and meetings. Students learn how to enter both one-time and recurring appointments and events. Topics include starting and quitting the Calendar, Contacts, and Tasks folders in Outlook. Other topics include generating and managing daily, weekly, and monthly schedules; printing and saving a calendar; generating a list of contacts; creating and printing tasks; and creating, importing, and exporting personal subfolders.

Integrating Office 2000 Applications and the World Wide Web

In this project, students are introduced to the seamless partnership of the Microsoft Office 2000 applications, which allows the sharing of information among Word, Excel, PowerPoint, Access, and the World Wide Web. Topics include embedding an Excel chart into a Word document; creating a Web site home page from a Word document; creating a Web page from a PowerPoint presentation; creating a data access Web page from an Access database; and creating hyperlinks from the home page to the PowerPoint and Access Web pages as well as an e-mail link.

Appendices

Appendix A presents a detailed step-by-step introduction to the Microsoft Office Help system. Students learn how to use the Office Assistant, as well as the Contents, Answer Wizard, and Index sheets in the Help window. Appendix B describes how to publish Office Web pages to a Web server. Appendix C shows students how to reset the menus and toolbars in any Office application. Appendix D introduces students to the Microsoft Office User Specialist (MOUS) Certification program and includes a MOUS map that lists a page number in the book for each of the MOUS activities.

What's New in Microsoft Office XP

This section gives an overview of What's new in Microsoft Office XP and describes the new features.

Learn It Online Exercises

Included in this section for each project are online practice tests, learning games, short answer questions, and Web-related exercises that help expand and solidify the students' understanding of Office 2000. The learning games include *Who Wants to Be a Computer Genius?*, *Wheel of Terms*, and the *Crossword Puzzle Challenge*.

Office 2000 Enhanced Exercises

Following the Microsoft Office 2000 Preview are eleven pages of new In the Lab Exercises. Included are two-to-three exercises per project for Word, Excel, Access, and PowerPoint. Samples of what the student creates in the exercises are available on the World Wide Web at www.scsite.com/off2000enh/labs.htm.

Microsoft Office 2000 MOUS Expert Level Quick Reference Summary

This book concludes with a detailed MOUS Expert Level Quick Reference Summary. In the Microsoft Office 2000 applications, you can accomplish a task in a number of ways, such as using the mouse, menu, shortcut menu, and keyboard. The Quick Reference Summary provides a quick reference to each task presented in this textbook.

End-of-Project Student Activities

A notable strength of the Shelly Cashman Series Office 2000 books is the extensive student activities at the end of each project. Well-structured student activities can make the difference between students merely participating in a class and students retaining the information they learn. The activities in the Shelly Cashman Series Office 2000 books include the following.

- **What You Should Know** A listing of the tasks completed within a project together with the pages where the step-by-step, screen-by-screen explanations appear. This section provides a perfect study review for students.
- **Project Reinforcement on the Web** Every project has a Web page accessible from www.scsite.com/off2000/reinforce.htm. The Web page includes true/false, multiple choice, and short answer questions, and additional project-related reinforcement activities that will help students gain confidence in their Office 2000 abilities.
- **Apply Your Knowledge** This exercise requires students to open and manipulate a file on the Data Disk for the Office 2000 books. To obtain a copy of the Data Disk, follow the instructions on the inside back cover of this textbook.
- **In the Lab** Three in-depth assignments per project require students to apply the knowledge gained in the project to solve problems on a computer.
- **Cases and Places** Up to seven unique case studies that require students to apply their knowledge to real-world situations.

Shelly Cashman Series Teaching Tools

A comprehensive set of Teaching Tools accompanies this textbook in the form of a CD-ROM. The CD-ROM includes an Instructor's Manual and teaching and testing aids. The CD-ROM (ISBN 0-7895-4636-1) is available through your Course Technology representative or by calling one of the following telephone numbers: Colleges and Universities, 1-800-648-7450; High Schools, 1-800-824-5179; and Career Colleges, 1-800-477-3692. The contents of the CD-ROM are listed below.

- **Instructor's Manual** The Instructor's Manual is made up of Microsoft Word files. The files include lecture notes, solutions to laboratory assignments, and a large test bank. The files allow you to modify the lecture notes or generate quizzes and exams from the test bank using your own word processing software. Where appropriate, solutions to laboratory assignments are embedded as icons in the files. When an icon appears, double-click it and the application will start and the solution will display on the screen. The Instructor's Manual includes the following for each project: project objectives; project overview; detailed lesson plans with page number references; teacher notes and activities; answers to the end-of-project exercises; test bank of 110 questions for every project (25 multiple-choice, 50 true/false, and 35 fill-in-the-blank) with page number references; and transparency references. The transparencies are available through the Figures in the Book. The test bank questions are numbered the same as in Course Test Manager. Thus, you can print a copy of the project test bank and use the printout to select your questions in Course Test Manager.

- **Figures in the Book** Illustrations of the figures and tables in the textbook are available in Figures in the Book. Use this ancillary to create a slide show from the illustrations for lecture or to print transparencies for use in lecture with an overhead projector.
- **Course Test Manager** Course Test Manager is a powerful testing and assessment package that enables instructors to create and print tests from the large test bank. Instructors with access to a networked computer lab (LAN) can administer, grade, and track tests online. Students also can take online practice tests, which generate customized study guides that indicate where in the textbook students can find more information for each question.
- **Course Syllabus** Any instructor who has been assigned a course at the last minute knows how difficult it is to come up with a course syllabus. For this reason, sample syllabi are included for each of the Office 2000 products that can be customized easily to a course.
- **Lecture Success System** Lecture Success System files are for use with the application software, a personal computer, and projection device to explain and illustrate the step-by-step, screen-by-screen development of a project in the textbook without entering large amounts of data.
- **Instructor's Lab Solutions** Solutions and required files for all the In the Lab assignments at the end of each project are available.
- **Lab Tests/Test Outs** Tests that parallel the In the Lab assignments are supplied for the purpose of testing students in the laboratory on the material covered in the project or testing students out of the course.
- **Project Reinforcement** True/false, multiple choice, and short answer questions, and additional project-related reinforcement activities for each project help students gain confidence in their Office 2000 abilities.
- **Student Files** All the files that are required by students to complete the Apply Your Knowledge exercises are included.
- **Interactive Labs** Eighteen hands-on interactive labs that take students from ten to fifteen minutes each to step through help solidify and reinforce mouse and keyboard usage and computer concepts. Student assessment is available in each interactive lab by means of a Print button. The assessment requires students to answer questions.

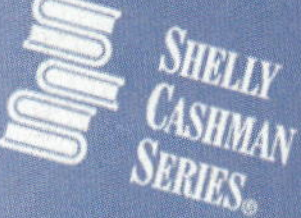

Microsoft Office 2000 Workbook

This highly popular supplement (ISBN 0-7895-4690-6) includes a variety of activities that help students recall, review, and master Office 2000 concepts and techniques. The workbook complements the end-of-project material with a guided project outline, a self-test consisting of true/false, multiple choice, short answer, fill-in, and matching questions, an entertaining puzzle, and other challenging exercises.

MyCourse.com

MyCourse.com is an online syllabus builder and course enhancement tool. Hosted and developed by Course Technology, MyCourse.com adds value to your course by providing content that corresponds with your text and is designed to reinforce what you are already teaching.

MyCourse.com is flexible; customize the online material for your course, or, if you prefer, direct your students to mycourse.com, where they can enter the ISBN of the text and start learning from a pre-assembled course that is organized by chapter!

MyCourse.com provides the following content:

- Objectives from your Course Technology text
- Topics reviews (short summaries of the objectives)
- Case projects (one to three per chapter)
- Practice tests (two to three questions per objective)
- Related Web links

MyCourse.com allows you to do the following:

- Build your class syllabus
- Choose how to organize the material, by date, by session, or by chapter
- Add class announcements
- Include content from more than one text into one course
- Add your own material, including course objectives, hyperlinks, topic reviews and case projects

MyCourse.com is easy-to-use. Go to mycourse.com/instructor to start building your class today!

Acknowledgments

The Shelly Cashman Series would not be the leading computer education series without the contributions of outstanding publishing professionals. First, and foremost, among them is Becky Herrington, director of production and designer. She is the heart and soul of the Shelly Cashman Series, and it is only through her leadership, dedication, and tireless efforts that superior products are made possible. Becky created and produced the award-winning Windows series of books.

Under Becky's direction, the following individuals made significant contributions to these books: Doug Cowley, production manager; Ginny Harvey, series specialist; Ken Russo, senior Web designer; Mike Bodnar, associate production manager; Mark Norton, Web designer; Meena Moest, production editor; Christy Otten, Michelle French, Stephanie Nance, Chris Schneider, and Hector Arvizu, graphic artists; Jeanne Black and Betty Hopkins, Quark experts; Nancy Lamm and Lyn Markowicz, copy editors; Marilyn Martin, Mary Steinman, Kim Kosmatka, proofreaders; Cristina Haley, indexer; Sarah Evertson of Image Quest, photo researcher.

Special thanks go to Richard Keaveny, associate publisher; Jim Quasney, series consultant; Lora Wade, product manager; Erin Roberts, associate product manager; Francis Schurgot, Web product manager; Marc Oullette, associate Web product manager; Rachel Vankirk, marketing manager; and Erin Runyon, associate product manager.

Gary B. Shelly
Thomas J. Cashman
Misty E. Vermaat

Shelly Cashman Series – Traditionally Bound Textbooks

The Shelly Cashman Series presents the following computer subjects in a variety of traditionally bound textbooks. For more information, see your Course Technology representative or call 1-800-648-7450. For Shelly Cashman Series information, visit Shelly Cashman Online at **www.scseries.com**.

COMPUTERS	
Computers	Discovering Computers 2002: Concepts for a Digital World, Web Enhanced, Complete Edition Discovering Computers 2002: Concepts for a Digital World, Web Enhanced, Introductory Edition Discovering Computers 2002: Concepts for a Digital World, Web Enhanced, Brief Edition Discovering Computers 2001: Concepts for a Connected World, Web and CNN Enhanced Discovering Computers 2001: Concepts for a Connected World, Web and CNN Enhanced, Brief Edition Teachers Discovering Computers: Integrating Technology in the Classroom Exploring Computers: A Record of Discovery, Fourth Edition Study Guide for Discovering Computers 2002: Concepts for a Digital World, Web Enhanced Essential Introduction to Computers 4e (32-page)
WINDOWS APPLICATIONS	
Microsoft Office	Microsoft Office 2000: Essential Concepts and Techniques (5 projects) Microsoft Office 2000: Brief Concepts and Techniques (9 projects) Microsoft Office 2000: Introductory Concepts and Techniques, Enhanced Edition (15 projects) Microsoft Office 2000: Advanced Concepts and Techniques (11 projects) Microsoft Office 2000: Post Advanced Concepts and Techniques (11 projects) Microsoft Office 97: Introductory Concepts and Techniques, Brief Edition (6 projects) Microsoft Office 97: Introductory Concepts and Techniques, Essentials Edition (10 projects) Microsoft Office 97: Introductory Concepts and Techniques, Enhanced Edition (15 projects) Microsoft Office 97: Advanced Concepts and Techniques
Microsoft Works	Microsoft Works 6: Complete Concepts and Techniques[1] • Microsoft Works 2000: Complete Concepts and Techniques[1] • Microsoft Works 4.5[1]
Microsoft Windows	Microsoft Windows 2000: Complete Concepts and Techniques (6 projects) Microsoft Windows 2000: Introductory Concepts and Techniques (3 projects) Microsoft Windows 2000: Brief Concepts and Techniques (2 projects) Microsoft Windows 98: Essential Concepts and Techniques (2 projects) Microsoft Windows 98: Complete Concepts and Techniques (6 projects)[2] Introduction to Microsoft Windows NT Workstation 4 Microsoft Windows 95: Complete Concepts and Techniques[1]
Word Processing	Microsoft Word 2000[2] • Microsoft Word 97[1] • Microsoft Word 7[1]
Spreadsheets	Microsoft Excel 2000[2] • Microsoft Excel 97[1] • Microsoft Excel 7[1] • Microsoft Excel 5[1] • Lotus 1-2-3 97[1]
Database	Microsoft Access 2000[2] • Microsoft Access 97[1] • Microsoft Access 7[1]
Presentation Graphics	Microsoft PowerPoint 2000[2] • Microsoft PowerPoint 97[1] • Microsoft PowerPoint 7[1]
Desktop Publishing	Microsoft Publisher 2000[1]
PROGRAMMING	
Programming	Microsoft Visual Basic 6: Complete Concepts and Techniques[1] Microsoft Visual Basic 5: Complete Concepts and Techniques[1] QBasic • QBasic: An Introduction to Programming • Microsoft BASIC Java Programming: Complete Concepts and Techniques[1] • Structured COBOL Programming, Second Edition
INTERNET	
Browser	Microsoft Internet Explorer 5: An Introduction • Microsoft Internet Explorer 4: An Introduction Netscape Navigator 6: An Introduction • Netscape Navigator 4: An Introduction
Web Page Creation and Design	HTML: Complete Concepts and Techniques[1] • Microsoft FrontPage 2000: Complete Concepts and Techniques[1] • Web Page Design: Introductory Concepts and Techniques • Netscape Composer 6 JavaScript: Complete Concepts and Techniques[1]
SYSTEMS ANALYSIS	
Systems Analysis	Systems Analysis and Design, Fourth Edition
DATA COMMUNICATIONS	
Data Communications	Business Data Communications: Introductory Concepts and Techniques, Third Edition

[1]Also available as an Introductory Edition, which is a shortened version of the complete book

[2]Also available as an Introductory Edition, which is a shortened version of the complete book and also as a Comprehensive Edition, which is an extended version of the complete book

Learn By Series — Web and CD-ROM Computer-Based Training

With the many different learning styles encountered in the classroom, it simply is not possible to provide one-on-one lectures tailored to each student's learning style. With the Learn By Series (Figure 1), students can create their own unique program for mastering Microsoft Office 2000 computer skills. By choosing one activity or a combination of activities, students Learn By Reading, Learn By Listening, Learn By Observing, and Learn By Stepping. These activities and all the navigation and menus are accessible using the Left Navpad.

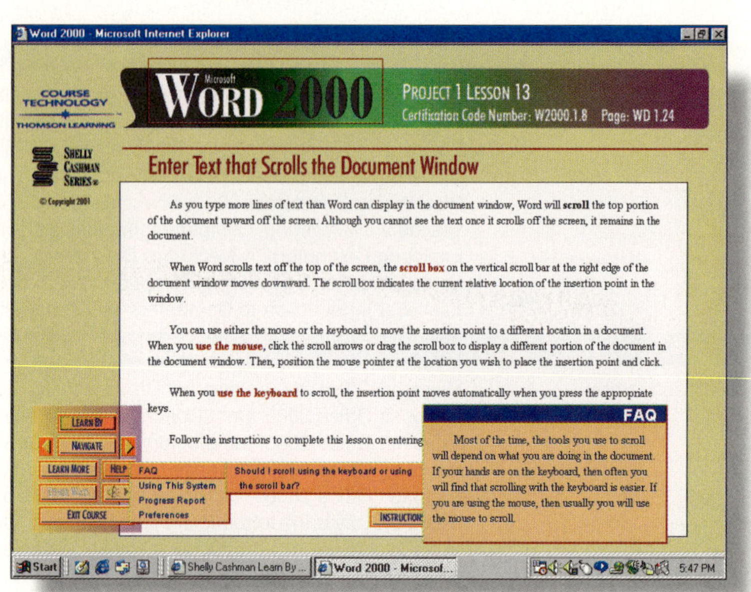

FIGURE 1

LEARN BY READING Visual learners experience learning that parallels reading a textbook, but with greater interactivity. Pointing to a Picture button for a step produces a full-screen graphic of the application window illustrating the result of performing that step.

LEARN BY LISTENING Auditory learners gain knowledge as if they are listening to a lecturer explain and demonstrate a specific skill. Computer animation illustrates completion of the tasks, explanations display on the screen, and recorded sound explains what is taking place.

LEARN BY OBSERVING For students who learn best by watching, this activity provides an experience similar to watching another person demonstrating each step. Computer graphics show the tasks being accomplished, and animations illustrate mouse and keyboard usage.

LEARN BY STEPPING With its hands-on interactivity, this self-paced learning environment is ideal for the tactile learner. Students click the Arrow buttons in the step boxes to execute each step in a detailed animated sequence. Step boxes display strategically to draw students' eyes to the action being performed.

OTHER WAYS, LEARN MORE, AND FAQS The Other Ways feature shows students the variety of ways to carry out a given task in Microsoft Office 2000. Selecting Other Ways on the Left Navpad displays the additional ways. The Learn More feature helps students develop a comprehensive understanding of the application. Pointing to the Learn More button displays topics related to the skill being taught. To give students a well-rounded perspective of how and when they might use the skills they learn in a lesson, the FAQ feature is available by pointing to Help on the Left Navpad.

Using the Learn By Series

The Learn By Series is designed for use with the Shelly Cashman Series *Microsoft Office 2000* textbooks or as a stand-alone learning tool, making it a perfect component of both traditional and distance learning courses. The course is organized as follows:

- When using a Learn By Series course, either with or without the accompanying textbook, students receive a CD-ROM containing the entire course for which they have registered and a password to the LearnBy.com Web site, that provides access to the entire course over the Internet.
- Each Learn By Series course is organized in a project/lesson sequence of multiple lessons, with each lesson teaching a specific application software skill. The projects and lessons correspond one for one with the projects in the *Microsoft Office 2000* books.
- Navigation is easy. Students navigate to any lesson in their course by pointing to the Navigate button on the Left Navpad and then using a menu or by clicking the right or left arrow next to the Navigate button.
- The Learn By Series course is available in project/lesson or certification code sequence by selecting Preferences on the Help menu.

For more information about how to use the Learn By Series and to try it, visit **learnbyseries.com**.

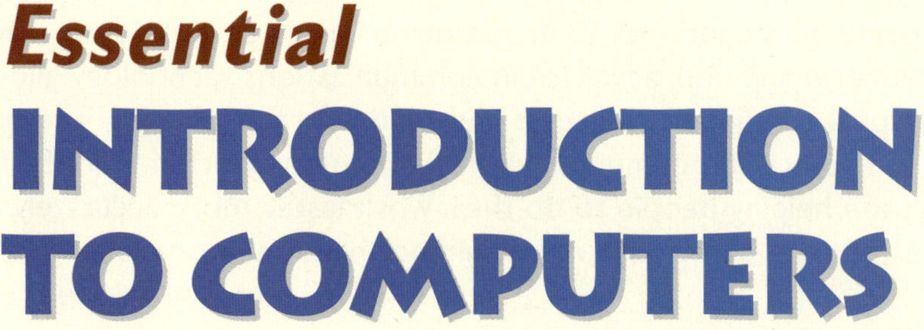

Essential
INTRODUCTION TO COMPUTERS
and How to Purchase, Install, and Maintain a Personal Computer

Objectives

After completing this material, you will be able to:

- Define the term computer and discuss the four basic computer operations: input, processing, output, and storage
- Define data and information
- Explain the principal components of the computer and their use
- Describe the use and handling of floppy disks and hard disks
- Discuss computer software and explain the difference between system software and application software
- Identify several types of personal computer application software
- Discuss computer communications channels and equipment and the Internet and World Wide Web
- Explain how to purchase, install, and maintain a personal computer, a notebook computer, and a handheld computer
- Define e-commerce

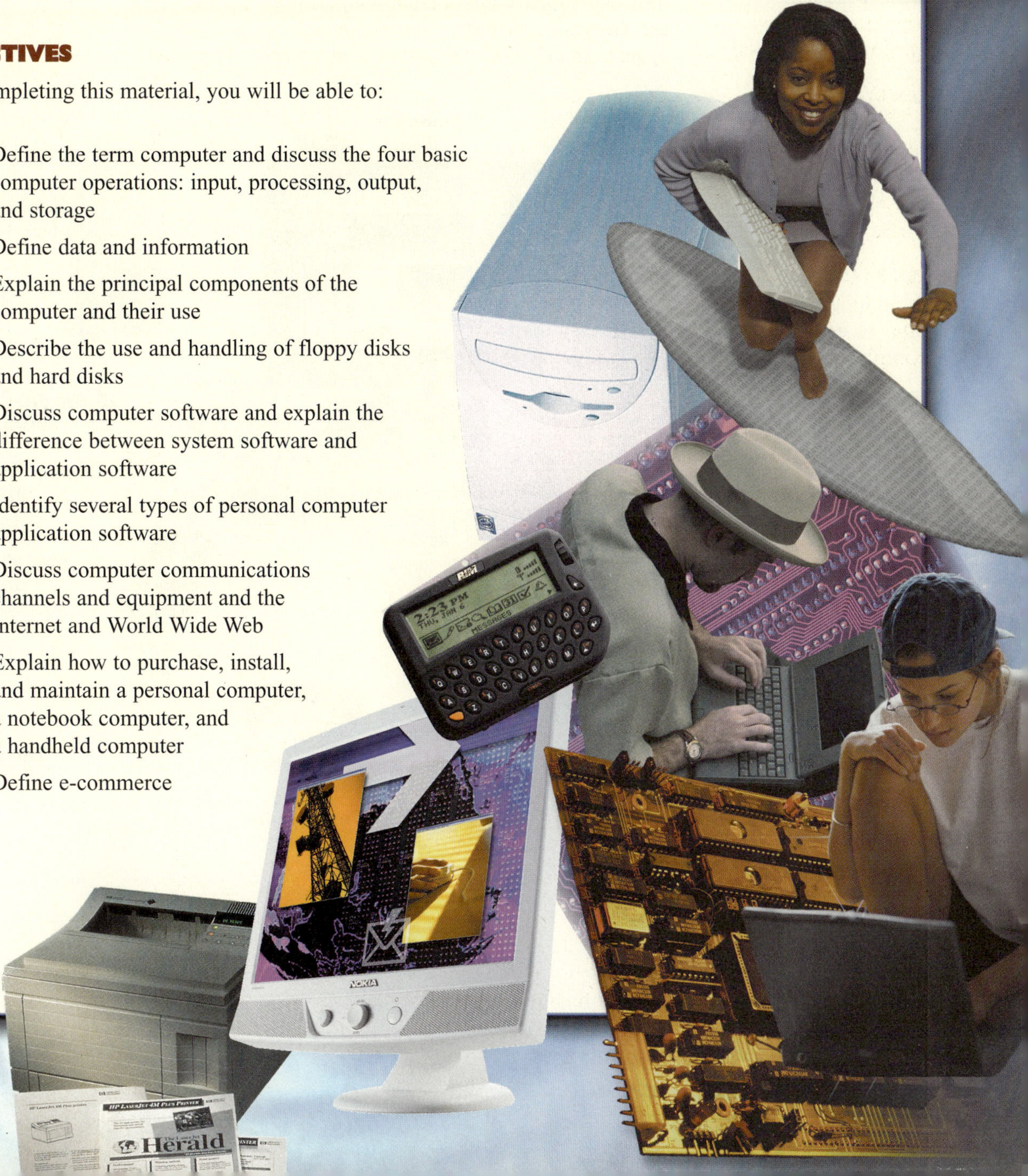

Computers are everywhere... at home, at work, and at school. Every day, computers impact how individuals work and how they live. The use of personal computers continues to increase and has made computing available to almost anyone. In addition, advances in communications technology allow people to use personal computers to access and send information easily and quickly to other computers and computer users. At home, at work, and in the field, computers are helping people to do their work faster, more accurately, and in some cases, in ways that previously would not have been possible.

Web Link

For more information on computers, visit the Introduction to Computers WEB LINK page (scsite.com/ic4/weblink.htm) and click **Computers**.

WHAT IS A COMPUTER?

The most obvious question related to understanding computers is, *What is a computer?* A **computer** is an electronic device, operating under the control of instructions stored in its own memory unit, that can accept data (input), manipulate the data according to specified rules (process), produce information (output) from the processing, and store the results for future use. Generally, the term is used to describe a collection of devices that function together as a system. An example of the devices that make up a personal computer is shown in Figure 1.

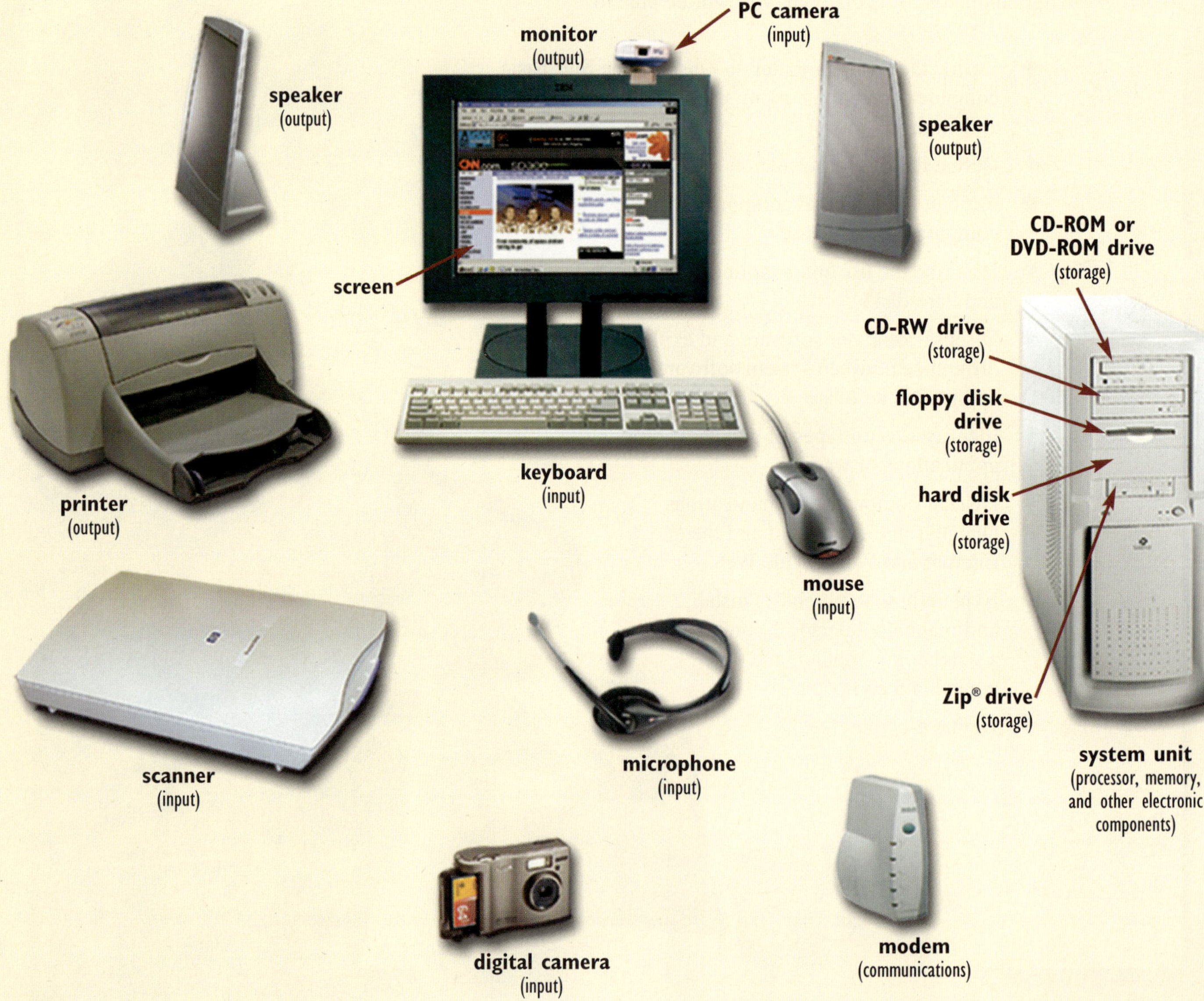

Figure 1
Devices that comprise a personal computer.

What Does a Computer Do?

Whether small or large, computers can perform four general operations. These operations comprise the **information processing cycle** and are input, process, output, and storage. Collectively, these operations describe the procedures a computer performs to process data into information and store it for future use.

For more information on information, visit the Introduction to Computers WEB LINK page (scsite.com/ic4/weblink.htm) and click **Information**.

All computer processing requires **data**. Data is a collection of raw facts, figures, and symbols, such as numbers, words, images, video, and sounds, given to a computer during the input operation. Computers manipulate data to create information. **Information** is data that is organized, meaningful, and useful. During the output operation, the information that has been created is put into some form, such as a printed report, a paycheck, an invoice, a Web page, or spoken words. The information also can be placed in computer storage for future use.

These operations occur through the use of electronic circuits contained on small silicon chips inside the computer (Figure 2). Because these electronic circuits rarely fail and the data flows along these circuits at close to the speed of light, processing can be accomplished in billionths of a second.

People who use the computer directly or use the information it provides are called **computer users**, **end users**, or sometimes, just **users**.

Figure 2
Inside a computer are chips and other electronic components that process data in billionths of a second.

Why Is a Computer so Powerful?

A computer derives its power from its capability to perform the information processing cycle with amazing speed, reliability (low failure rate), and accuracy; its capacity to store huge amounts of data and information; and its ability to communicate with other computers.

How Does a Computer Know What to Do?

For a computer to perform operations, it must be given a detailed set of instructions that tells it exactly what to do. These instructions are called a **computer program**, or **software**. Before processing for a specific job begins, the computer program corresponding to that job is stored in the computer. Once the program is stored, the computer can begin to operate by executing the program's first instruction. The computer executes one program instruction after another until the job is complete.

Web Link

For more information on computer programs, visit the Introduction to Computers WEB LINK page (scsite.com/ic4/weblink.htm) and click **Computer Programs**.

What Are the Components of a Computer?

To understand how computers process data into information, you need to examine the primary components of the computer. The five primary components of a computer are input devices, the central processing unit (control unit and arithmetic/logic unit), memory, output devices, and storage devices as shown in Figure 3. The next five sections describe these primary components.

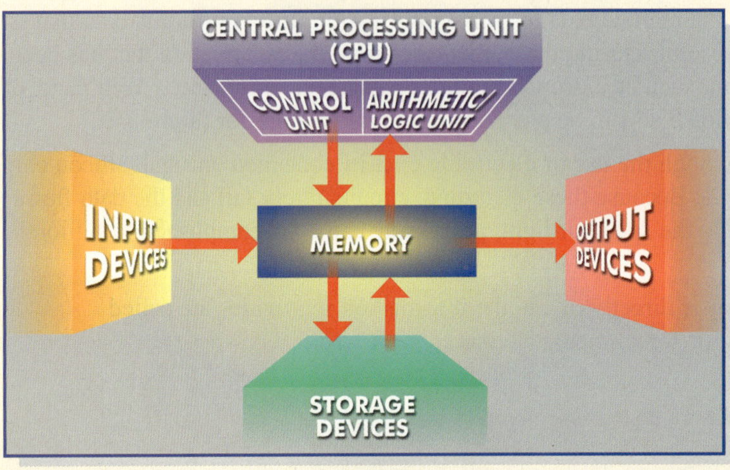

Figure 3
A computer is composed of input devices through which data is entered into memory, the central processing unit (CPU) that processes data stored in memory, output devices through which the results of the processing are made available, and storage devices that store data for future processing.

Web Link
For more information on input devices, visit the Introduction to Computers WEB LINK page (scsite.com/ic4/weblink.htm) and click **Input Devices**.

Input Devices

An **input device** is any hardware component that allows you to enter data, programs, commands, and user responses into a computer. Depending on your particular application and requirement, the input device you use may vary. Popular input devices include the keyboard, mouse, digital camera, scanner, and microphone. The two primary input devices used are the keyboard and the mouse. This section discusses both of these input devices.

The Keyboard

A keyboard is an input device that contains keys you press to enter data into the computer. A desktop computer keyboard (Figure 4) typically has 101 to 105 keys. Keyboards for smaller computers, such as notebooks, contain fewer keys. A computer keyboard includes keys that allow you to type letters of the alphabet, numbers, spaces, punctuation marks, and other symbols such as the dollar sign ($) and asterisk (*). A keyboard also contains other keys that allow you to enter data and instructions into the computer.

Figure 5 shows an onscreen keyboard available with Microsoft Office XP. You use a mouse to select keys on an onscreen keyboard.

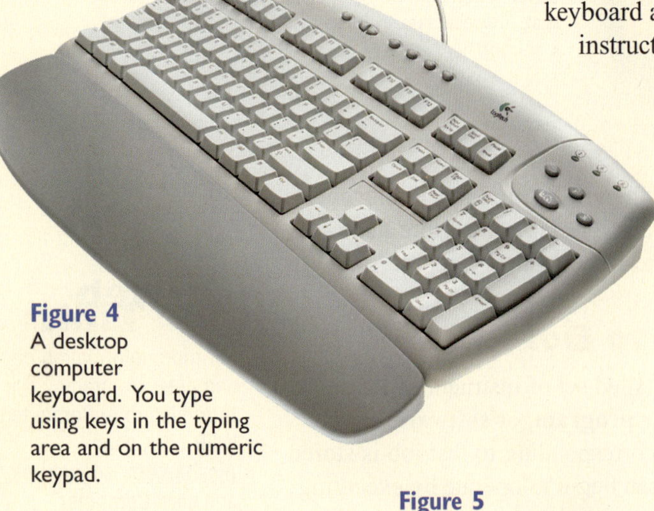

Figure 4
A desktop computer keyboard. You type using keys in the typing area and on the numeric keypad.

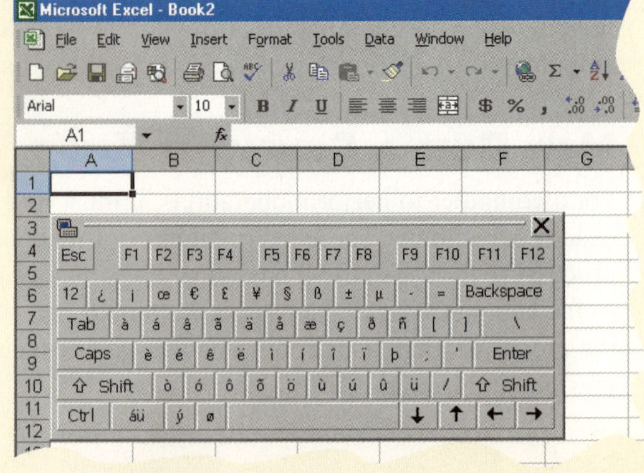

Figure 5
The Microsoft Office XP onscreen keyboard allows you to enter numbers and text using a mouse.

Most handheld computers (left in Figure 6) use an onscreen keyboard. With handheld computers, you use a stylus to select keys on the onscreen keyboard. A notebook computer (right in Figure 6) has the keyboard built into the top of the unit.

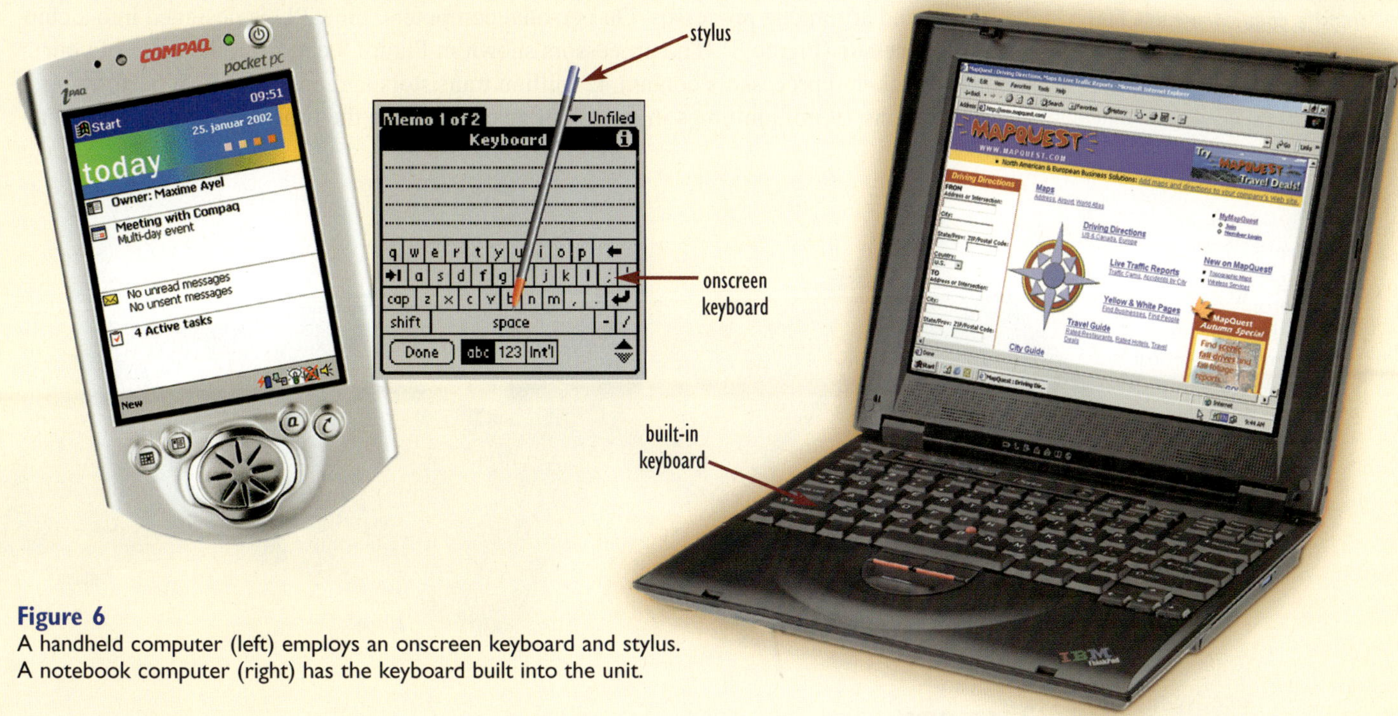

Figure 6
A handheld computer (left) employs an onscreen keyboard and stylus. A notebook computer (right) has the keyboard built into the unit.

The Mouse

A **mouse** (Figure 7) is a pointing device that fits comfortably under the palm of your hand. With a mouse, you control the movement of the pointer, often called the mouse pointer, on the screen and make selections from the screen. A mouse has one to five buttons. The bottom of a mouse is flat and contains a mechanism that detects movement of the mouse.

Notebook computers come with a pointing device built into the keyboard so that you can select items on the screen without requiring additional desktop space.

Web Link
For more information on a mouse, visit the Introduction to Computers WEB LINK page (scsite.com/ic4/weblink.htm) and click **Mouse**.

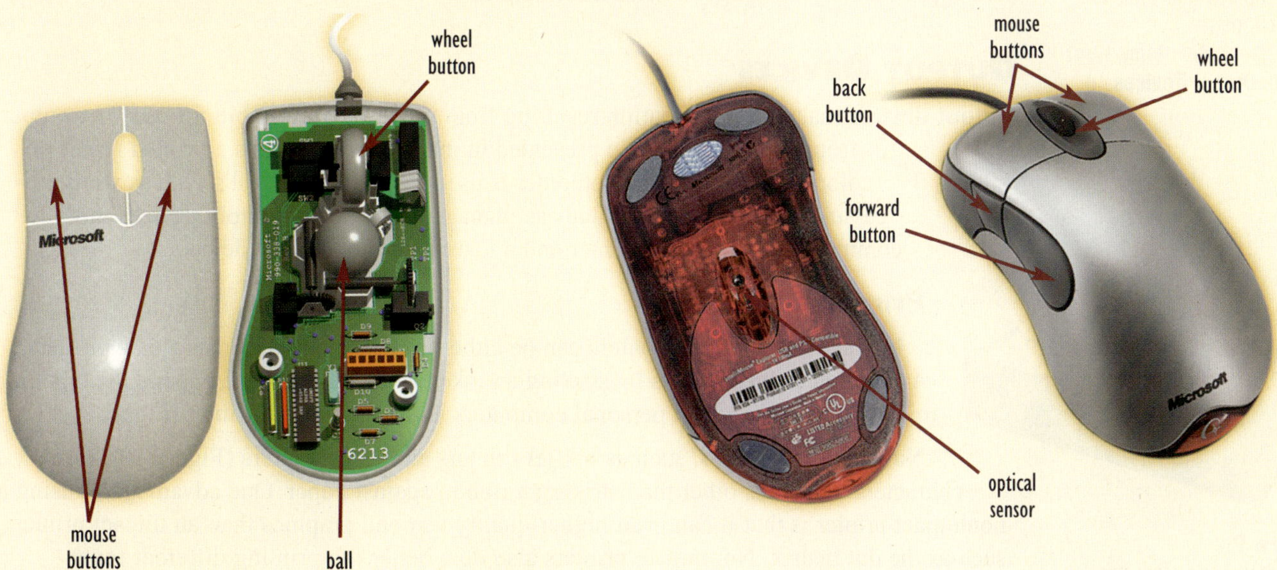

Figure 7
A mechanical mouse (left) contains a small ball. An optical mouse (right) uses an optical sensor, rather than a ball.

The Central Processing Unit

Web Link
For more information on CPUs, visit the Introduction to Computers WEB LINK page (scsite.com/ic4/weblink.htm) and click **CPUs**.

The **central processing unit** (**CPU**) contains the electronic circuits that cause processing to occur. The CPU is made up of the **control unit** and **arithmetic/logic unit** (see Figure 3 on page COM4). The control unit interprets the instructions. The arithmetic/logic unit performs the logical and arithmetic processes. On personal computers, the CPU is designed into a chip called a **processor** (Figure 8). The processors shown in Figure 8 can fit in the palm of your hand. The high-end processors contain 42 million transistors and are capable of performing some operations 10 million times in a tenth of a second, or in the time it takes to blink your eye.

Figure 8
Basic personal computers have a Celeron™ or Duron™ processor. Higher-performance personal computers use Athlon™ and Pentium® processors.

Memory

Memory, also called **random access memory**, or **RAM**, consists of electronic components that store data including numbers, letters of the alphabet, graphics, and sound. Any data to be processed must be stored in memory. The amount of memory in computers typically is measured in kilobytes or megabytes. One **kilobyte** (**K or KB**) equals approximately 1,000 memory locations and one **megabyte** (**M or MB**) equals approximately one million memory locations. A **memory location**, or **byte**, usually stores one character. Therefore, a computer with 96 MB of memory can store approximately 96 million characters. One megabyte can hold approximately 500 pages of text information.

Web Link
For more information on output devices, visit the Introduction to Computers WEB LINK page (scsite.com/ic4/weblink.htm) and click **Output Devices**.

Output Devices

Output devices make the information resulting from processing available for use. The output from computers can be presented in many forms, such as a printed report or color graphics. When a computer is used for processing tasks such as word processing, spreadsheets, or database management, the two output devices more commonly used are the printer and a television-like display device.

Printers

Printers used with computers can be either impact printers or nonimpact printers. An **impact printer** prints by striking an inked ribbon against the paper. One type of impact printer used with personal computers is the dot matrix printer (Figure 9).

Nonimpact printers, such as ink-jet printers and laser printers (Figure 10), form characters by means other than striking a ribbon against paper. One advantage of using a nonimpact printer is that it can print higher-quality text and graphics than an impact printer, such as the dot matrix. Nonimpact printers also do a better job printing different fonts (Figure 11), are quieter, and can print in color. The popular and affordable ink-jet printer forms a character or graphic by using a nozzle that sprays drops of ink onto the page.

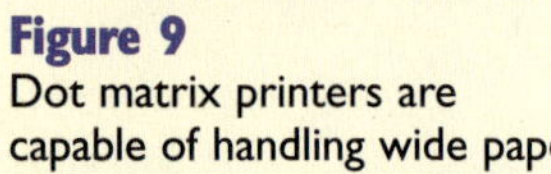

Figure 9
Dot matrix printers are capable of handling wide paper and printing multipart forms.

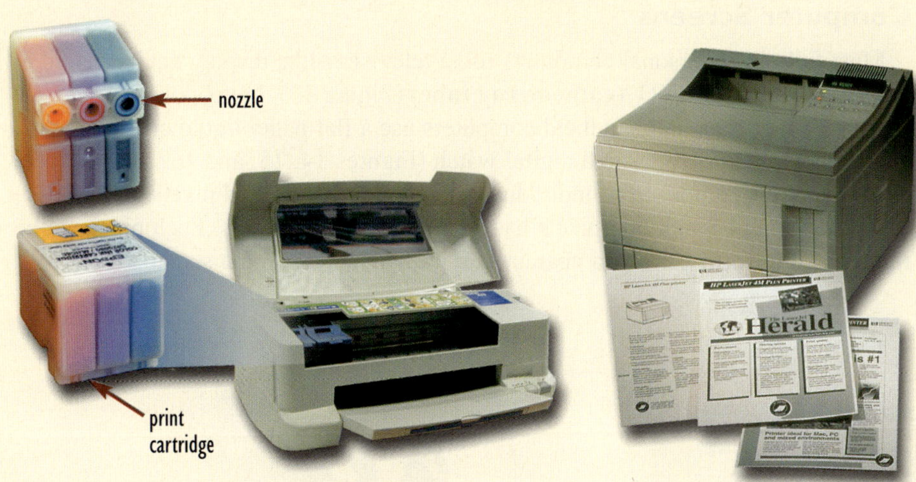
nozzle
print cartridge

Figure 10
Two types of nonimpact printers are the ink-jet printer (left) and the laser printer (right). Nonimpact printers are excellent for printing work that includes graphics.

Ink-jet printers produce excellent images. The speed of an ink-jet printer is measured by the number of pages per minute (ppm) it can print. Most ink-jet printers print from one to eight pages per minute. Graphics and colors print at the slower rate.

Laser printers work similarly to a copying machine by converting data from the computer into a beam of light that is focused on a photoconductor drum, forming the images to be printed (Figure 12). The photoconductor attracts particles of toner that are fused by heat and pressure onto paper to produce an image. Laser printers produce high-quality black-and-white or color output and are used for applications that combine text and graphics such as desktop publishing. Laser printers for personal computers can cost from several hundred dollars to several thousand dollars. The more expensive the laser printer, the more pages it can print per minute.

Courier
Helvetica
Script
Times New Roman

Figure 11
A variety of typefaces (fonts) are commonly available on personal computers.

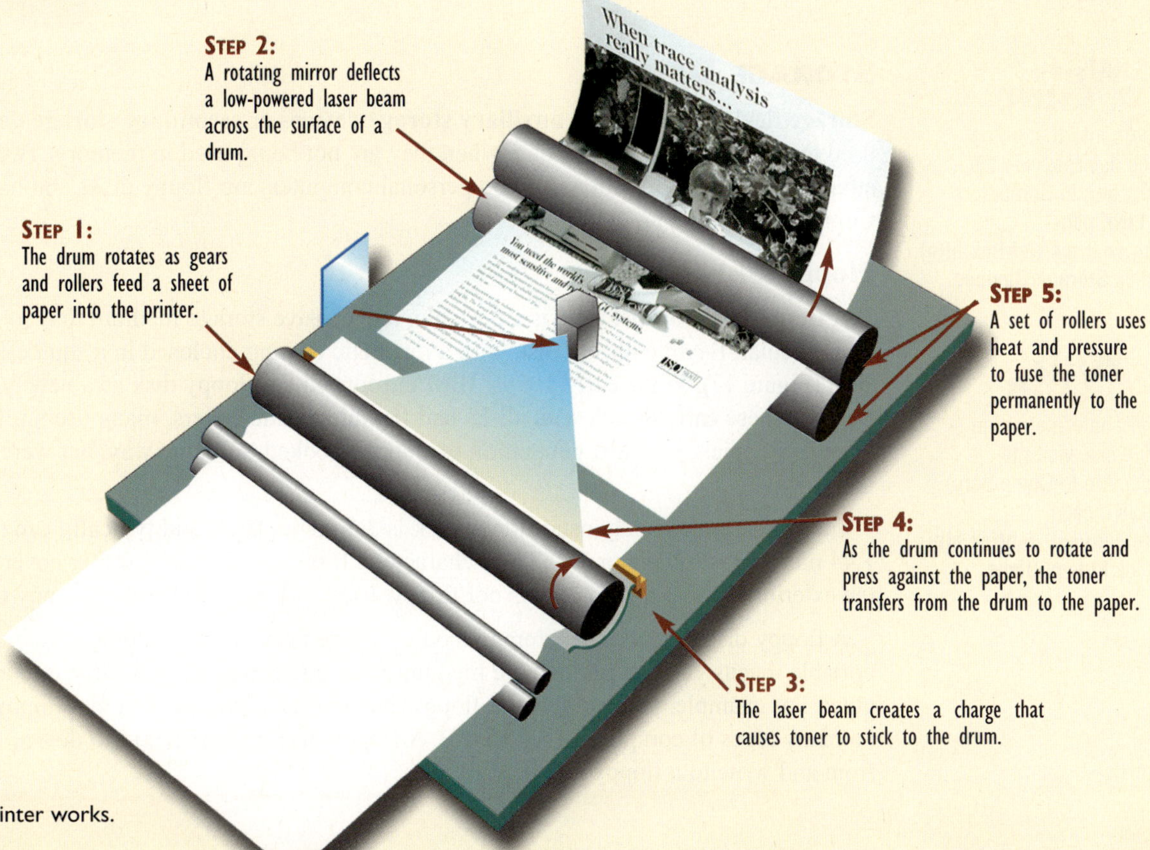
STEP 2:
A rotating mirror deflects a low-powered laser beam across the surface of a drum.
STEP 1:
The drum rotates as gears and rollers feed a sheet of paper into the printer.
When trace analysis really matters...
STEP 5:
A set of rollers uses heat and pressure to fuse the toner permanently to the paper.
STEP 4:
As the drum continues to rotate and press against the paper, the toner transfers from the drum to the paper.
STEP 3:
The laser beam creates a charge that causes toner to stick to the drum.

Figure 12
How a laser printer works.

Computer Screens

Figure 13
The core of many desktop monitors is a cathode ray tube (CRT).

Most full-sized personal computers use a television-like display device called a **screen**, **monitor**, or **CRT** (**cathode ray tube**) (Figure 13). Notebook computers, flat screen displays, and handheld computers use a flat panel liquid crystal display (LCD) technology similar to a digital watch (Figures 14, 15, and 16). The surface of the screen is composed of individual picture elements called pixels. A screen set to a resolution of 800 x 600 pixels has a total of 480,000 pixels. Each pixel can be illuminated to form parts of a character or graphic shape on the screen.

Figure 14
Most notebook computers use a liquid crystal display (LCD) display because it is lightweight and thin.

Figure 15
An LCD monitor is much thinner than a CRT monitor.

Figure 16
Handheld computers use LCD displays.

Web Link

For more information on storage devices, visit the Introduction to Computers WEB LINK page (scsite.com/ic4/weblink.htm) and click **Storage Devices**.

Storage Devices

Storage devices, also called **auxiliary storage** devices or **secondary storage devices**, are used to store instructions and data when they are not being used in memory. Two types of auxiliary storage more often used on personal computers are floppy disks and hard disks. Compact discs also are common.

Web Link

For more information on floppy disks, visit the Introduction to Computers WEB LINK page (scsite.com/ic4/weblink.htm) and click **Floppy Disks**.

Floppy Disks

A **floppy disk**, or **diskette**, is a portable, inexpensive storage medium that consists of a thin, circular, flexible plastic disk with a magnetic coating enclosed in a square-shaped plastic shell (Figure 17). In the early 1970s, IBM introduced the floppy disk as a new type of storage. Because these early 8-inch wide disks had flexible plastic covers, many users referred to them as floppies. The next generation of floppies looked the same way, but were only 5.25 inches wide.

Today, the most widely used floppy disk is 3.5 inches wide and typically can store up to 1.44 megabytes of data or 1,457,664 characters. It has a rigid plastic outer cover. Although the exterior of the 3.5-inch disk is not floppy, users still refer to them as floppy disks.

A floppy disk is a portable storage medium. When discussing a storage medium, the term portable means you can remove the medium from one computer and carry it to another computer. For example, you can insert a floppy disk into and remove it from a floppy disk drive on many types of computers (Figure 18). A floppy disk drive (FDD) is a device that can read from and write to a floppy disk.

A floppy disk is a type of a magnetic disk, which means it uses magnetic patterns to store items such as data, instructions, and information on the disk's surface. Most magnetic disks are read/write storage media; that is, you can access (read) data from and place (write) data on a magnetic disk any number of times, just as you can with an audiocassette tape. Most floppy disks that you purchase are already formatted. If they are not formatted, then before you can write on a new floppy disk, it must be formatted.

Formatting is the process of preparing a disk (floppy disk or hard disk) for reading and writing by organizing the disk into storage locations called tracks and sectors (Figure 19). A **track** is a narrow recording band that forms a full circle on the surface of the disk. The disk's storage locations then are divided into pie-shaped sections, which break the tracks into small arcs called sectors. A **sector** is capable of holding 512 bytes of data. A typical floppy disk stores data on both sides and has 80 tracks on each side of the recording surface with 18 sectors per track.

Data stored in sectors on a floppy disk must be retrieved and placed into memory to be processed. The time required to access and retrieve data is called the **access time**. The access time for floppy disks varies from about 175 milliseconds (one millisecond equals 1/1000 of a second) to approximately 300 milliseconds. On average, data stored in a single sector on a floppy disk can be retrieved in approximately 1/15 to 1/3 of a second.

Figure 17
In a 3.5-inch floppy disk, the thin circular flexible film is enclosed between two liners. A piece of metal called a shutter covers an opening to the recording surface in the rigid plastic shell.

Figure 18
On a computer, you insert and remove a floppy disk from a floppy disk drive.

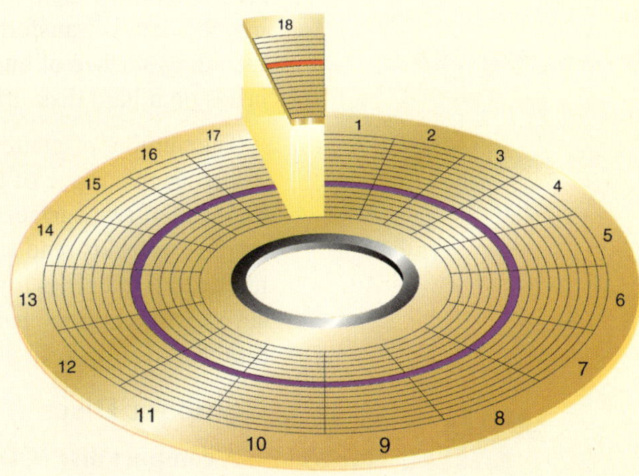

Figure 19
A track is a narrow recording band that forms a full circle on the surface of a disk. The disk's storage locations then are divided into pie-shaped sections, which break the tracks into small arcs called sectors.

For more information on hard disks, visit the Introduction to Computers WEB LINK page (scsite.com/ic4/weblink.htm) and click **Hard Disks**.

Hard Disks

Another form of auxiliary storage is a **hard disk**. A hard disk consists of one or more rigid metal platters coated with a metal oxide material that allows data to be recorded magnetically on the surface of the platters (Figure 20). Although hard disks are available in removable cartridge form, most disks cannot be removed from the computer. As with floppy disks, the data is recorded on hard disks on a series of tracks. The tracks are divided into sectors when the disk is formatted.

Figure 20
The hard disk in a desktop computer normally resides permanently inside the system unit. That is, it is not portable.

The hard disk platters spin at a high rate of speed, typically 5,400 to 7,200 revolutions per minute. When reading data from the disk, the read head senses the magnetic spots that are recorded on the disk along the various tracks and transfers that data to memory. When writing, the data is transferred from memory and is stored as magnetic spots on the tracks on the recording surface of one or more of the disk platters. When reading or writing, the read/write heads on a hard disk drive do not actually touch the surface of the disk.

The number of platters permanently mounted on the spindle of a hard disk varies. On most drives, each surface of the platter can be used to store data. Thus, if a hard disk drive uses one platter, two surfaces are available for data. If the drive uses two platters, four sets of read/write heads read and record data from the four surfaces. Storage capacities of internally mounted fixed disks for personal computers range from one billion characters to more than seventy-five billion characters. One billion bytes are called a **gigabyte** (**GB**). Typical hard disk sizes range from 10 GB to 75 GB.

For more information on compact discs, visit the Introduction to Computers WEB LINK page (scsite.com/ic4/weblink.htm) and click **Compact Discs**.

Compact Discs

A **compact disc** (**CD**), also called an optical disc, is a flat, round, portable, metal storage medium that usually is 4.75 inches in diameter and less than 1/20 of an inch thick. Just about every desktop computer and notebook computer includes some type of compact disc drive installed in a drive bay. These drives read compact discs, including audio discs.

On these drives, you push a button to slide out a tray, insert your compact disc with the label side up, and then push the same button to close the tray (Figure 21). Other convenient features on most of these drives include a volume control button and a headphone jack so you can use stereo headphones to listen to audio without disturbing others nearby.

Compact discs are available in a variety of formats, including CD-ROM, CD-R, CD-RW, and DVD-ROM.

CD-ROMs

A **CD-ROM** (pronounced SEE-DEE-rom), or **compact disc read-only memory**, is a compact disc that uses the same laser technology as audio CDs for recording music. In addition to audio, a CD-ROM can contain text, graphics, and video. The manufacturer writes, or records, the contents of standard CD-ROMs. You can only read the contents of these discs. That is, you cannot erase or modify their contents — hence the name read-only.

A typical CD-ROM holds about 650 MB of data, instructions, and information. This is about 450 times more than you can store on a 3.5-inch floppy disk.

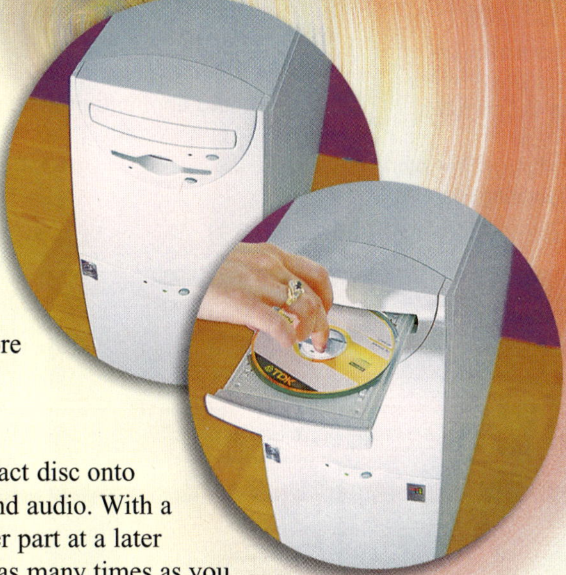

CD-R and CD-RW

A **CD-R** (**compact disc-recordable**) is a multisession compact disc onto which you can record your own items such as text, graphics, and audio. With a CD-R, you can write on part of the disc at one time and another part at a later time. Once you have recorded the CD-R, you can read from it as many times as you wish. You can write on each part only one time, and you cannot erase the disc's contents. Most CD-ROM drives can read a CD-R.

Figure 21
CD-ROM drives allow the user to access tremendous amounts of pre-recorded information — more than 600 MB of data can be stored on one CD-ROM.

A **CD-RW** (**compact disc-rewritable**) is an erasable disc you can write on multiple times. Originally called an erasable CD (CD-E), a CD-RW overcomes the major disadvantage of CD-R discs, which is that you can write on them only once. With CD-RWs, the disc acts like a floppy or hard disk, allowing you to write and rewrite data, instructions, and information onto it multiple times.

DVD-ROMs

Although CD-ROMs have huge storage capacities, even a CD-ROM is not large enough for many of today's complex programs. Some software, for example, is sold on five or more CD-ROMs. To meet these tremendous storage requirements, some software companies have moved from CD-ROMs to the larger DVD-ROM format — a technology that can be used to store large amounts of text and even videos (Figure 22). A **DVD-ROM** (**digital video disc-ROM**) is a very high capacity compact disc capable of storing from 4.7 GB to 17 GB — more than enough to hold a telephone book containing every resident in the United States.

Web Link
For more information on DVD-ROMs, visit the Introduction to Computers WEB LINK page (scsite.com/ic4/weblink.htm) and click **DVD-ROMs**.

Figure 22
A DVD-ROM is an extremely high-capacity disc capable of storing 4.7 GB to 17 GB.

Computer Software

Computer software is the key to productive use of computers. With the correct software, a computer can become a valuable tool. Software can be categorized into two types: system software and application software.

Web Link

For more information on operating systems, visit the Introduction to Computers WEB LINK page (scsite.com/ic4/weblink.htm) and click **Operating Systems**.

System Software

System software consists of programs to control the operations of computer equipment. An important part of system software is a set of programs called the operating system. Instructions in the **operating system** tell the computer how to perform the functions of loading, storing, and executing an application program and how to transfer data. For a computer to operate, an operating system must be stored in the computer's memory. When a computer is turned on, the operating system is loaded into the computer's memory from auxiliary storage. This process is called **booting**.

Today, most computers use an operating system that has a **graphical user interface (GUI)** that provides visual cues such as icon symbols to help the user. Each icon represents an application such as word processing, or a file or document where data is stored. Microsoft Windows (Figure 23) is a widely used graphical operating system. Apple Macintosh computers also have a graphical user interface operating system.

icon

My Computer window

Figure 23
A graphical user interface such as Microsoft Windows makes the computer easier to use. The small pictures, or symbols, on the screen are called icons. Icons represent a program or data the user can choose. A window is a rectangular area of the screen that is used to display a program, data, and/or information.

Application Software

Application software consists of programs that tell a computer how to produce information. The different ways people use computers in their careers or in their personal lives are examples of types of application software. Business, scientific, and educational programs are all examples of application software.

Personal computer users often use application software. Some of the more commonly used applications are word processing, electronic spreadsheet, presentation graphics, database, communications, and electronic mail software. Some software packages, such as Microsoft Office, also include access to the World Wide Web as an integral part of the application.

Web Link

For more information on word processing software, visit the Introduction to Computers WEB LINK page (scsite.com/ic4/weblink.htm) and click **Word Processing Software**.

Word Processing

Word processing software (Figure 24) is used to create, edit, format, and print documents. A key advantage of word processing software is that users easily can make changes in documents, such as correcting spelling, changing margins, and adding, deleting, or relocating entire paragraphs. These changes would be difficult and time consuming to make using manual methods such as a typewriter. With a word processor, documents can be printed quickly and accurately and easily stored on a disk for future use. Word processing software is oriented toward working with text, but most word processing packages also can include numeric and graphic information.

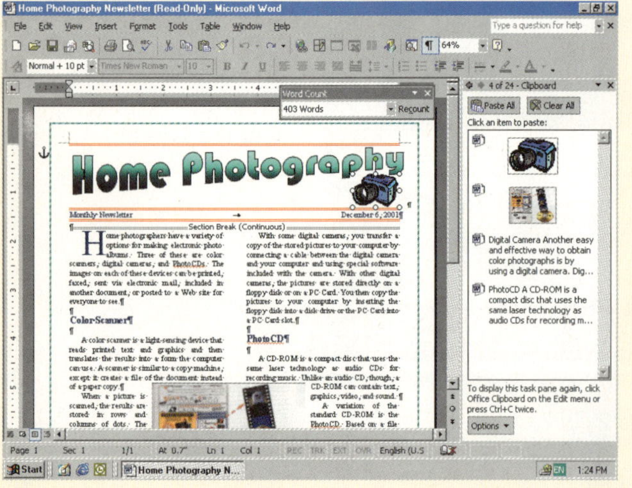

Figure 24
Word processing software is used to create letters, memos, and other documents.

Spreadsheet

Electronic spreadsheet software (Figure 25) allows the user to add, subtract, and perform user-defined calculations on rows and columns of numbers. These numbers can be changed, and the spreadsheet quickly recalculates the new results. Electronic spreadsheet software eliminates the tedious recalculations required with manual methods. Spreadsheet information frequently is converted into a graphic form, such as charts. Graphics capabilities now are included in most spreadsheet packages.

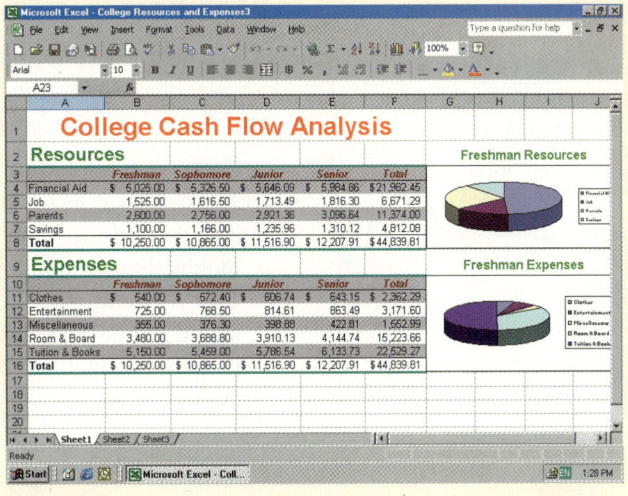

Figure 25
Electronic Spreadsheet software frequently is used by people who work with numbers. The user enters the data and the formulas to be used on the data, and the computer calculates the results.

Web Link

For more information on spreadsheet software, visit the Introduction to Computers WEB LINK page (scsite.com/ic4/weblink.htm) and click **Spreadsheet Software**.

Database

Database software (Figure 26) allows the user to enter, retrieve, and update data in an organized and efficient manner. These software packages have flexible inquiry and reporting capabilities that let users access the data in different ways and create custom reports that include some or all of the information in the database.

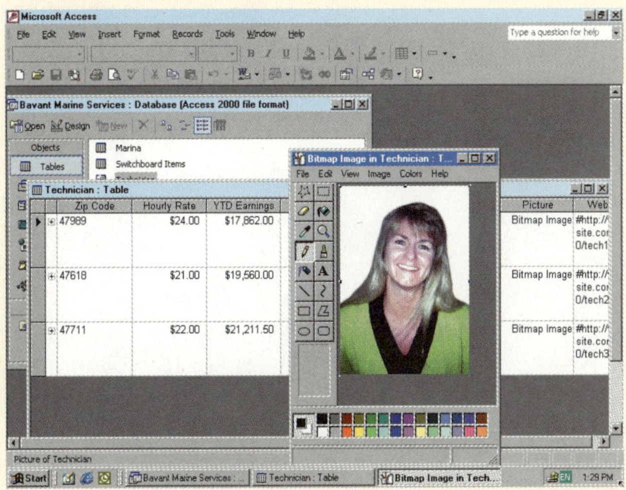

Figure 26
Database software allows the user to enter, retrieve, and update data in an organized and efficient manner.

Web Link

For more information on database software, visit the Introduction to Computers WEB LINK page (scsite.com/ic4/weblink.htm) and click **Database Software**.

Presentation Graphics

Presentation graphics software (Figure 27) allows the user to create documents called slides to be used in making presentations. Using special projection devices, the slides are projected directly from the computer.

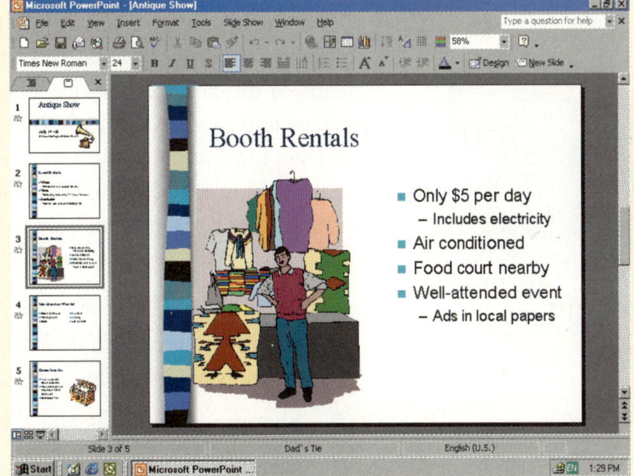

Figure 27
Presentation graphics software allows the user to create documents called slides for use in presentations.

For more information on presentation graphics software, visit the Introduction to Computers WEB LINK page (scsite.com/ic4/weblink.htm) and click **Presentation Graphics Software.**

Networks and the Internet

A **network** is a collection of computers and devices connected via communications media and devices such as cables, telephone lines, modems, or other means.

Computers are networked together so users can share resources, such as hardware devices, software programs, data, and information. Sharing resources saves time and money. For example, instead of purchasing one printer for every computer in a company, the firm can connect a single printer and all computers via a network (Figure 28); the network enables all of the computers to access the same printer.

Figure 28
This local area network (LAN) enables two separate computers to share the same printer.

Most business computers are networked together. These networks can be relatively small or quite extensive. A network that connects computers in a limited geographic area, such as a school computer laboratory, office, or group of buildings, is called a **local area network (LAN)**. A network that covers a large geographical area, such as one that connects the district offices of a national corporation, is called a **wide area network (WAN)** (Figure 29).

Figure 29
A network can be quite large and complex, connecting users in district offices around the country (WAN).

The Internet

The world's largest network is the **Internet**, which is a worldwide collection of networks that links together millions of computers by means of modems, telephone lines, cables, and other communications devices and media. With an abundance of resources and data accessible via the Internet, more than 360 million users around the world are making use of the Internet for a variety of reasons (Figure 30). Some of these reasons include the following:

- Sending messages to other connected users (e-mail)
- Accessing a wealth of information, such as news, maps, airline schedules, and stock market data
- Shopping for goods and services
- Meeting or conversing with people around the world
- Accessing sources of entertainment and leisure, such as online games, magazines, and vacation planning guides

Figure 30
Users access the Internet for a variety of reasons: to send messages to other connected users, to access a wealth of information, to shop for goods and services, to meet or converse with people around the world, and for entertainment.

Most users connect to the Internet in one of two ways: through an Internet service provider or through an online service. An **Internet service provider** (**ISP**) is an organization that supplies connections to the Internet for a monthly fee. Like an ISP, an **online service** provides access to the Internet, but it also provides a variety of other specialized content and services such as financial data, hardware and software guides, news, weather, legal information, and other similar commodities. For this reason, the fees for using an online service usually are slightly higher than fees for using an ISP. Two popular online services are America Online and The Microsoft Network.

Web Link

For more information on the Internet, visit the Introduction to Computers WEB LINK page (scsite.com/ic4/weblink.htm) and click **Internet**.

The World Wide Web

One of the more popular segments of the Internet is the **World Wide Web**, also called the **Web**, which contains billions of documents called Web pages. A **Web page** is a document that contains text, graphics, sound, and/or video, and has built-in connections, or hyperlinks, to other Web documents. Web pages are stored on computers throughout the world. A **Web site** is a related collection of Web pages. You access and view Web pages using a software program called a **Web browser**. A Web page has a unique address, called a **Uniform Resource Locator** (URL).

Web Link

For more information on the World Wide Web, visit the Introduction to Computers WEB LINK page (scsite.com/ic4/weblink.htm) and click **World Wide Web**.

As shown in Figure 31, a URL consists of a protocol, domain name, and sometimes the path to a specific Web page or location in a Web page. Most Web page URLs begin with **http://**, which stands for hypertext transfer protocol, the communications standard used to transfer pages on the Web. The domain name identifies the Web site, which is stored on a Web server. A **Web server** is a computer that delivers (serves) requested Web pages.

STEP 1:
Use your computer and modem to make a local telephone call to an internet service provider.

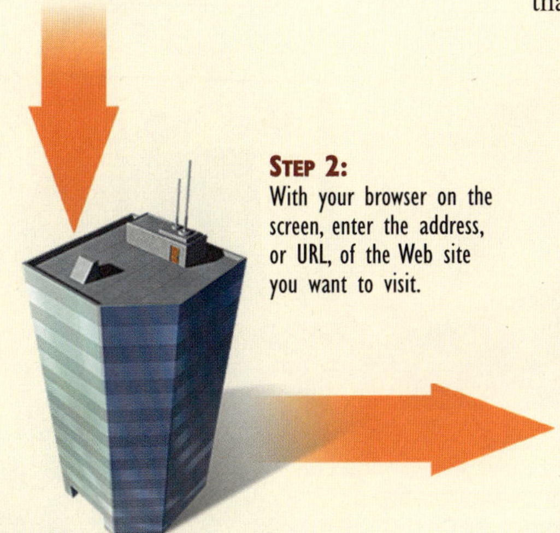

STEP 2:
With your browser on the screen, enter the address, or URL, of the Web site you want to visit.

STEP 3:
The Web browser locates the Web site for the entered address and displays a Web page on your screen.

Figure 31
One method of connecting to the Web and displaying a Web page.

Electronic Commerce

When you conduct business activities online, you are participating in **electronic commerce**, also known as **e-commerce**. These commercial activities include shopping, investing, and any other venture that represents a business transaction. Today, three types of e-commerce exist: business to consumer, consumer to consumer, and business to business. **Business to consumer** (**B2C**) involves the sale of goods to the general public. **Consumer to consumer** (**C2C**) involves one consumer selling directly to another. **Business to business** (**B2B**) provides goods and services to other businesses.

Web Link

For more information on e-commerce, visit the Introduction to Computers WEB LINK page (scsite.com/ic4/weblink.htm) and click **E-Commerce**.

HOW TO PURCHASE, INSTALL, AND MAINTAIN A PERSONAL COMPUTER

The decision to buy a personal computer is an important one — and finding and purchasing a personal computer suited to your needs will require an investment of both time and money. As with many buyers, you may have little computer experience and find yourself unsure of how to proceed. The following guidelines are presented to help you purchase, install, and maintain a desktop computer. These guidelines also apply to the purchase of a notebook computer or handheld computer. Purchasing a notebook computer or handheld computer also involves some additional considerations, which are addressed later.

How to Purchase a Desktop Computer

Web Link

For more information on desktop computers, visit the Introduction to Computers WEB LINK page (scsite.com/ic4/weblink.htm) and click **Desktop Computers**.

1 **Determine what application products you will use on your computer.** Knowing what application products you plan to use will help you decide on the type of computer to buy, as well as to define the memory, storage, and other requirements. Certain application products, for example, can run only on Macintosh computers, while others run only on a personal computer with the Windows operating system. Further, some application products require more memory and disk space than others, as well as additional input/output and storage devices. For example, if you want to efficiently create copies of CDs with your computer, then you will need to include two CD drives: one that reads from a CD, and one that reads from and writes to a CD.

When you purchase a computer, it may come bundled with several software products. At the very least, you probably will want software for word processing and a browser to access the World Wide Web. If you need additional applications, such as a spreadsheet, a database, or presentation graphics, consider purchasing a software suite that offers reduced pricing on several applications, such as Microsoft Works or Microsoft Office.

Before selecting a specific package, be sure the software contains the features necessary for the tasks you want to perform. Many Web sites and magazines, such as those listed in Figure 32, provide reviews of software products. These Web sites frequently have articles that rate computers and software on cost, performance, and support.

2 **Before buying a computer, do some research.** Talk to friends, coworkers, and instructors about prospective computers. What type of computers did they buy? Why? Would they recommend their computer and the company from which they bought it? You also should visit the Web sites or read reviews in the magazines listed in Figure 32. As you conduct your research, consider the following important criteria:

- Speed of the processor
- Size and types of memory (RAM) and storage (hard disk, floppy disk, CD-ROM, CD-RW, DVD-ROM, Zip® drive)
- Input/output devices included with the computer (e.g., mouse, keyboard, monitor, printer, sound card, video card)
- Communications devices included with the computer (modem, network interface card)
- Any software included with the computer

Type of Computer	Web Site	URL
PC	Computer Shopper	zdnet.com/computershopper/edit/howtobuy
	PC World Magazine	pcworld.com
	Byte Magazine	byte.com
	Smart Business for New Economy	zdnet.com/smartbusinessmag/
	PC Magazine	zdnet.com/pcmag
	Yahoo! Computers	computers.yahoo.com
	FamilyPC Magazine	familypc.zdnet.com
	Microsoft Network	eshop.msn.com
	Dave's Guide to Buying a PC	css.msu.edu/pc-guide.html
Macintosh	TechWeb News	www.techweb.com/wire/apple
	ZDNet News	zdnet.com/mac
	Macworld Magazine	macworld.zdnet.com
	Apple	apple.com

For an updated list of hardware and software reviews and their Web sites, visit scsite.com/dc2002/ch8/buyers.htm.

Figure 32
Hardware and software reviews.

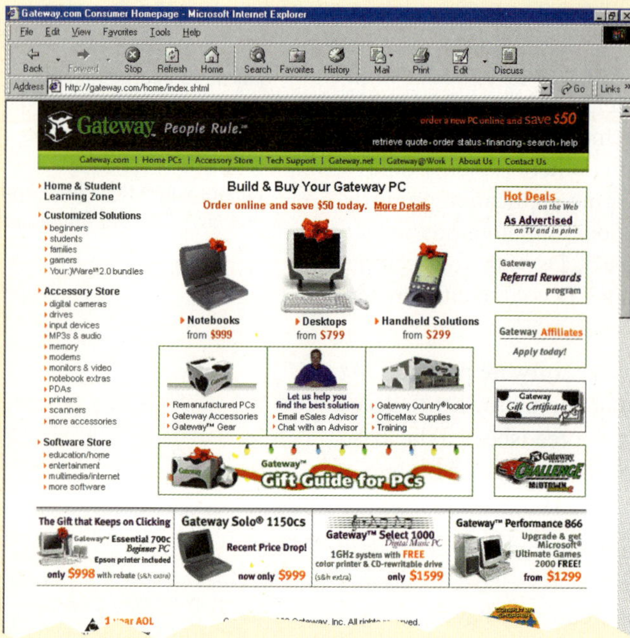

Figure 33
Some mail-order companies, like Gateway, sell computers online.

3 Look for free software. Many computer vendors include free software with their systems. Some sellers even let you choose which software you want. Remember, however, that free software has value only if you would have purchased the software even if it had not come with the computer.

4 If you are buying a new computer, you have several purchasing options: buying from your school bookstore, a local computer dealer, a local large retail store, or ordering by mail via telephone or the World Wide Web. Each purchasing option has certain advantages. Many college bookstores, for example, sign exclusive pricing agreements with computer manufacturers and, thus, can offer student discounts. Local dealers and local large retail stores, however, more easily can provide hands-on support. Mail-order companies that sell computers by telephone or online via the Web (Figure 33) often provide the lowest prices but extend less personal service. Some major mail-order companies, however, have started to provide next-business-day, onsite services. A credit card usually is required to buy from a mail-order company. Figure 34 lists some of the more popular mail-order companies and their Web site addresses.

5 If you are buying a used computer, stick with name brands. Although brand-name equipment can cost more, most brand-name computers have longer, more comprehensive warranties, are better supported, and have more authorized centers for repair services. As with new computers, you can purchase a used computer from local computer dealers, local large retail stores, or mail order via the telephone or the Web. Classified ads and used computer brokers offer additional outlets for purchasing used computers. Figure 35 lists several major used computer brokers and their Web site addresses.

Type of Computer	Company	URL	Telephone Number
PC	Computer Shopper	computershopper.com	Not Available
	Compaq	compaq.com	1-800-888-0220
	CompUSA	compusa.com	1-800-266-7872
	dartek.com	dartek.com	1-800-531-4622
	Dell	dell.com	1-800-678-1626
	Gateway	gateway.com	1-800-846-4208
	Micron	micron.com	1-800-964-2766
Macintosh	Apple Computer	store.apple.com	1-800-795-1000
	Club Mac	www.clubmac.com	1-800-258-2622
	MacConnection	macconnection.com	1-888-213-0260
	MacExchange	macx.com	1-888-650-4488

For an updated list of new computer mail-order companies and their Web sites, visit scsite.com/dc2002/ch8/buyers.htm.

Figure 34
New computer mail-order companies.

Company	URL	Telephone Number
American Computer Exchange	www.amcoex.com	1-800-786-0717
Custom Edge, Inc.	bocoex.com	1-617-625-7722
U.S. Computer Exchange, Inc.	www.uscomputerexchange.com	1-800-711-9000
eBay	ebay.com	Not Available

For an updated list of used computer mail-order companies and their Web sites, visit *scsite.com/dc2002/ch8/buyers.htm*.

Figure 35
Used computer mail-order companies.

6 **Use a worksheet to compare computers, services, and other considerations.** You can use a separate sheet of paper to take notes on each vendor's computer and then summarize the information on a spreadsheet, such as the one shown in Figure 36. Most companies advertise a price for a base computer that includes components housed in the system unit (processor, RAM, sound card, video card), disk drives (floppy disk, hard disk, CD-ROM, CD-RW, and DVD-ROM), a keyboard, mouse, monitor, printer, speakers, and modem. Be aware, however, that some advertisements list prices for computers with only some of these components. Monitors, printers, and modems, for example, often are not included in a base computers price. Depending on how you plan to use the computers, you may want to invest in additional or more powerful components. When you are comparing the prices of computers, make sure you are comparing identical or similar configurations.

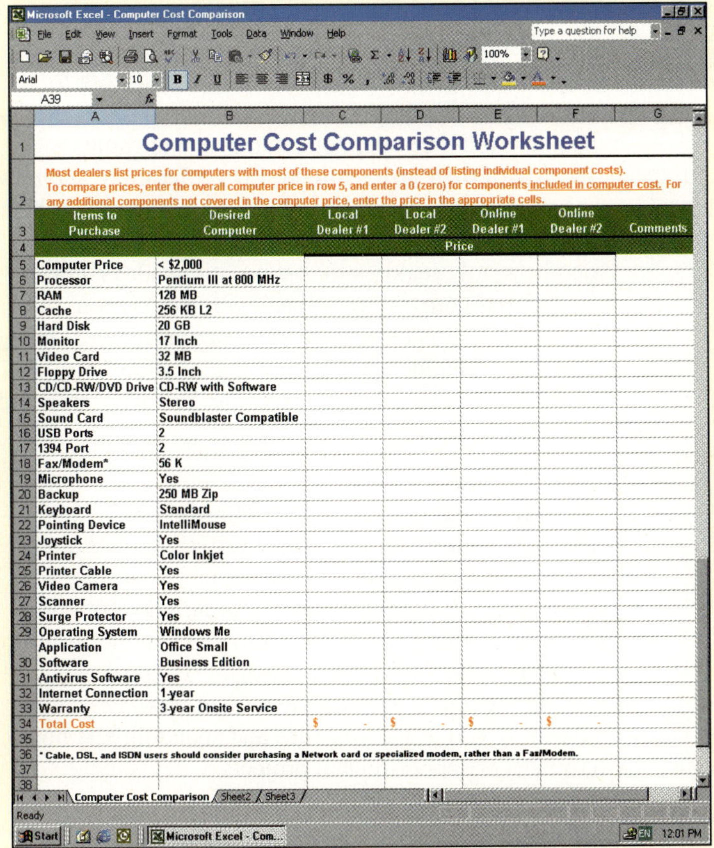

Computer Cost Comparison Worksheet

Most dealers list prices for computers with most of these components (instead of listing individual component costs). To compare prices, enter the overall computer price in row 5, and enter a 0 (zero) for components included in computer cost. For any additional components not covered in the computer price, enter the price in the appropriate cells.

Items to Purchase	Desired Computer	Local Dealer #1	Local Dealer #2	Online Dealer #1	Online Dealer #2	Comments
		Price				
Computer Price	< $2,000					
Processor	Pentium III at 800 MHz					
RAM	128 MB					
Cache	256 KB L2					
Hard Disk	20 GB					
Monitor	17 Inch					
Video Card	32 MB					
Floppy Drive	3.5 Inch					
CD/CD-RW/DVD Drive	CD-RW with Software					
Speakers	Stereo					
Sound Card	Soundblaster Compatible					
USB Ports	2					
1394 Port	2					
Fax/Modem*	56 K					
Microphone	Yes					
Backup	250 MB Zip					
Keyboard	Standard					
Pointing Device	IntelliMouse					
Joystick	Yes					
Printer	Color Inkjet					
Printer Cable	Yes					
Video Camera	Yes					
Scanner	Yes					
Surge Protector	Yes					
Operating System	Windows Me					
Application Software	Office Small Business Edition					
Antivirus Software	Yes					
Internet Connection	1-year					
Warranty	3-year Onsite Service					
Total Cost		$ -	$ -	$ -	$ -	

* Cable, DSL, and ISDN users should consider purchasing a Network card or specialized modem, rather than a Fax/Modem.

Figure 36
A spreadsheet is an effective tool for summarizing and comparing the prices and components of different computer vendors. A copy of the Computer Cost Comparison Worksheet is available via the Web Link on this page. You must use Microsoft Internet Explorer 5 (IE5) or greater to view it.

Web Link
For more information on computer cost comparisons, visit the Introduction to Computers WEB LINK page (scsite.com/ic4/weblink.htm) and click **Computer Cost Comparisons**.

7 **Be aware of hidden costs.** Before purchasing, be sure to consider any additional costs associated with buying a computer, such as an additional telephone line, an uninterruptible power supply (UPS), computer furniture, floppy disks and paper, or computer training classes you may want to take. Depending on where you buy your computer, the seller may be willing to include some or all of these in the computer purchase price.

8 **Consider more than just price.** The lowest cost computer may not be the best buy. Consider such intangibles as the vendor's time in business, the vendor's regard for quality, and the vendor's reputation for support. If you need to upgrade your computer often, you may want to consider a leasing arrangement, in which you pay monthly lease fees but upgrade or add on to your computer as your equipment needs change. If you are a replacement buyer, ask if the vendor will buy your old computer; an increasing number of companies are taking trade-ins. No matter what type of buyer you are, insist on a 30-day, no-questions-asked return policy on your computer.

Company	Service	URL	Telephone Number
America Online	OSP	aol.com	1-800-827-6364
AT&T Data and IP Services	ISP	att.com/wss	1-800-288-3199
CompuServe	OSP	compuserve.com	1-800-848-8990
Earthlink Network	ISP	www.earthlink.com	1-800-395-8425
Juno	Free OSP	juno.com	1-888-829-5866
MCI	ISP	mciworldcom.com	1-800-888-0800
Microsoft Network	OSP	msn.com	1-800-386-5550
NetZero	Free OSP	netzero.com	Not Available
Prodigy	ISP/OSP	prodigy.com	1-800-776-3449

For information on local ISPs or to learn more on any ISPs and OSPs listed here, visit The List™ at thelist.internet.com. The List™ — the most comprehensive and accurate directory of ISPs and OSPs on the Web — compares dial-up services, access hours, and fees for over 9,000 access providers.

For an updated list of ISPs and OSPs, visit *scsite.com/dc2002/ ch8/buyers.htm*.

Figure 37
National ISPs and OSPs.

9 **Avoid restocking fees.** Some companies charge a restocking fee of 10 to 20 percent as part of their money-back return policy. In some cases, there is no restocking fee for hardware, but there is for software. Ask about the existence and terms of any restocking policies before you buy.

10 **Select an Internet service provider (ISP) or online service provider (OSP).** You can access the Internet in one of two ways: via an ISP or an OSP. Both provide Internet access for a monthly fee that ranges from $5 to $20. Some OSPs offer free Internet access. Local ISPs offer Internet access through local telephone numbers to users in a limited geographic region. National ISPs provide access for users nationwide (including mobile users), through local and toll-free telephone numbers and cable. Because of their size, national ISPs offer more services and generally have a larger technical support staff than local ISPs. OSPs furnish Internet access as well as members-only features for users nationwide. Figure 37 lists several national ISPs and OSPs. Before you choose an Internet access provider, compare such features as the number of access hours, monthly fees, available services (e-mail, Web page hosting, chat), and reliability.

11 **Buy a computer compatible with the ones you use elsewhere.** If you use a personal computer at work or in some other capacity, make sure the computer you buy is compatible. For example, if you use a PC at work, you may not want to purchase a Macintosh for home use. Having a computer compatible with the ones at work or school will allow you to transfer files and spend time at home on work- or school-related projects.

12 **Consider purchasing an onsite service agreement.** If you use your computer for business or are unable to be without your computer, consider purchasing an onsite service agreement through a local dealer or third-party company. Most onsite service agreements state that a technician will come to your home, work, or school within 24 hours. If your computer includes onsite service only for the first year, think about extending the service for two or three years when you buy the computer.

13 **Use a credit card to purchase your new computer.** Many credit cards now offer purchase protection and extended warranty benefits that cover you in case of loss of or damage to purchased goods. Paying by credit card also gives you time to install and use the computer before you have to pay for it. Finally, if you are dissatisfied with the computer and are unable to reach an agreement with the seller, paying by credit card gives you certain rights regarding withholding payment until the dispute is resolved. Check your credit card for specific details.

14 **Avoid buying the smallest computer available.** Computer technology changes rapidly, meaning a computer that seems powerful enough today may not serve your computing needs in a few years. In fact, studies show that many users regret they did not buy a more powerful computer. Plan to buy a computer that will last you for two to three years. You can help delay obsolescence by purchasing the fastest processor, most memory, and largest hard drive you can afford. If you must buy a smaller computer, be sure you can upgrade it with additional memory and auxiliary devices as your computer requirements grow. Figure 38 includes minimum recommendations for each category of user discussed in this book: Home User, Small Business User, Mobile User, Large Business User, and Power User. The Home User category is divided into two groups: Application Home User and Game Home User.

Web Link

For more information on base components, visit the Introduction to Computers WEB LINK page (scsite.com/ic4/weblink.htm) and click **Base Components**.

BASE COMPONENTS						
	Application Home User	Game Home User	Small Business User	Mobile User	Large Business User	Power User
HARDWARE						
Processor	Celeron at 600 MHz	Pentium 4 at 1.4 GHZ	Pentium III at 1 GHZ	Pentium III at 700 MHZ	Pentium 4 at 1.4 GHZ	Pentium 4 at 1.4 GHZ
RAM	96 MB	128 MB	128 MB	128 MB	384 MB	512 MB
Cache	256 KB L2	512 KB L2	512 KB L2	512 KB L2	512 KB L2	2 MB L2
Hard Drive	10 GB	20 GB	20 GB	10 GB	80 GB	80 GB
Video Graphics Card	32 MB	64 MB	32 MB	16 MB	64 MB	64 MB
Monitor	17"	19"	17"	15" active matrix	19"	21"
DVD/CD-ROM Drive	48X CD-ROM	12X DVD with Decoder Card	48X CD-ROM	6X DVD	48X CD-ROM	12X DVD with Decoder Card
CD-RW 2nd Bay	Yes	Yes	Yes	Not Applicable	Yes	Yes
Floppy Drive	3.5"	3.5"	3.5"	3.5"	3.5"	3.5"
Printer	Color inkjet	Color inkjet	8 ppm laser	Portable inkjet	24 ppm laser	8 ppm laser
Fax/Modem or Network Card	Yes	Yes	Yes	Yes	Yes	Yes
Sound Card	Soundblaster Compatible	Soundblaster Compatible	Soundblaster Compatible	Built-In	Soundblaster Compatible	Soundblaster Compatible
Speakers	Stereo	Full-Dolby surround	Stereo	Stereo	Stereo	Full-Dolby surround
TV-Out Connector	Yes	Yes	Yes	Yes	Yes	Yes
USB Port	Yes	Yes	Yes	Yes	Yes	Yes
1394 Port	No	Yes	No	No	Yes	Yes
Pointing Device	IntelliMouse or Optical Mouse	Optical mouse and Joystick	IntelliMouse or Optical Mouse	Touchpad or Pointing Stick and Optical Mouse	IntelliMouse or Optical Mouse	IntelliMouse or Optical Mouse and Joystick
Keyboard	Yes	Yes	Yes	Built-In	Yes	Yes
Backup Disk/Tape Drive	250 MB Zip	1 GB Jaz	1 GB Jaz and Tape	250 MB Zip	2 GB Jaz and Tape	2 GB Jaz and Tape
SOFTWARE						
Operating System	Windows ME	Windows ME	Windows 2000 Professional	Windows 2000 Professional	Windows 2000 Professional	Windows 2000 Professional
Application Software Suite	Office Standard	Office Standard	OfficeSmall Business Edition	Office Small Business Edition	Office Premium	Office Premium
Internet Access	Cable, Online Service, or ISP	Cable, Online Service, or ISP	Cable	Online Service or ISP	LAN/WAN (T1/T3)	LAN
OTHER						
Surge Protector	Yes	Yes	Yes	Portable	Yes	Yes
Warranty	3-Year Limited, 1-Year Next Business Day On-Site Service	3-Year Limited, 1-Year Next Business Day On-Site Service	3-year on-site service	3-Year Limited, 1-Year Next Business Day On-Site Service	3-year on-site service	3-year on-site service
Other		Headset		Docking Station		
				Carrying case		
Optional Components for all Categories						
digital camera						
multifunction device (MFD)						
scanner						
uninterruptable power supply						
ergonomic keyboard						
network interface card						
TV/FM tuner						
video camera						
IrDa port						
mouse pad/wrist rest						

Figure 38
Base computer components and optional computer components. A copy of the Base Components Comparison Worksheet is available via the Web Link on this page. You must use Microsoft Internet Explorer 5 (IE5) or greater to view it.

How to Purchase a Notebook Computer

If you need computing capability when you travel, you may find a notebook computer to be an appropriate choice. The guidelines mentioned in the previous section also apply to the purchase of a notebook computer (Figure 39). The following are additional considerations unique to notebook computers.

Figure 39
A notebook computer.

1 Purchase a notebook computer with a sufficiently large active-matrix screen. Active-matrix screens display high-quality color that is viewable from all angles. Less expensive, passive-matrix screens sometimes are difficult to see in low-light conditions and cannot be viewed from an angle. Notebook computers typically come with a 12.1-inch, 13.3-inch, 14.1-inch, or 15.4-inch display. For most users, a 14.1-inch display is satisfactory. If you intend to use your notebook computer as a desktop replacement, however, you may opt for a 15.4-inch display. If you travel a lot and portability is essential, consider that most of the lightest machines are equipped with a 13.3-inch display. Regardless of size, the resolution of the display should be at least 800 x 600 pixels.

2 Experiment with different pointing devices and keyboards. Notebook computer keyboards are far less standardized than those for desktop computers. Some notebook computers, for example, have wide wrist rests, while others have none. Notebook computers also use a range of pointing devices, including pointing sticks, touchpads, and trackballs. Before you purchase a notebook computer, try various types of keyboard and pointing devices to determine which is easiest for you to use. Regardless of the pointing device you select, you also may want to purchase a regular mouse unit to use when you are working at a desk or other large surface.

Web Link

For more information on notebook computers, visit the Introduction to Computers WEB LINK page (scsite.com/ic4/weblink.htm) and click **Notebook Computers**.

3 Make sure the notebook computer you purchase has a CD-ROM or DVD-ROM drive. Loading software, especially large software suites, is much faster if done from a CD-ROM, CD-RW, or DVD-ROM. Today, most notebook computers come with an internal CD-ROM drive. Some notebook computers even come with a CD-ROM drive and a CD-RW drive or both a DVD-ROM drive and a CD-RW drive. Some users prefer a DVD-ROM drive to a CD-ROM drive. Although DVD-ROM drives are more expensive, they allow you to read CD-ROMs and to play movies using your notebook computer.

4 If necessary, upgrade memory and disk storage at the time of purchase. As with a desktop computer, upgrading your notebook computer's memory and disk storage usually is less expensive at the time of initial purchase. Some disk storage is custom designed for notebook computer manufacturers, meaning an upgrade might not be available a year or two after you purchase your notebook computer.

5 If you are going to use your notebook computer on an airplane, purchase a second battery. Two batteries should provide enough power to last through most airplane flights. If you anticipate running your notebook computer on batteries frequently, choose a computer that uses lithium-ion batteries (they last longer than nickel cadmium or nickel hydride batteries).

6 Purchase a well-padded and well-designed carrying case. An amply padded carrying case will protect your notebook computer from the bumps it will receive while traveling. A well-designed carrying case will have room for accessories such as spare floppy disks, CD-ROMs, a user manual, pens, and paperwork (Figure 40).

7 If you travel overseas, obtain a set of electrical and telephone adapters. Different countries use different outlets for electrical and telephone connections. Several manufacturers sell sets of adapters that will work in most countries (Figure 41).

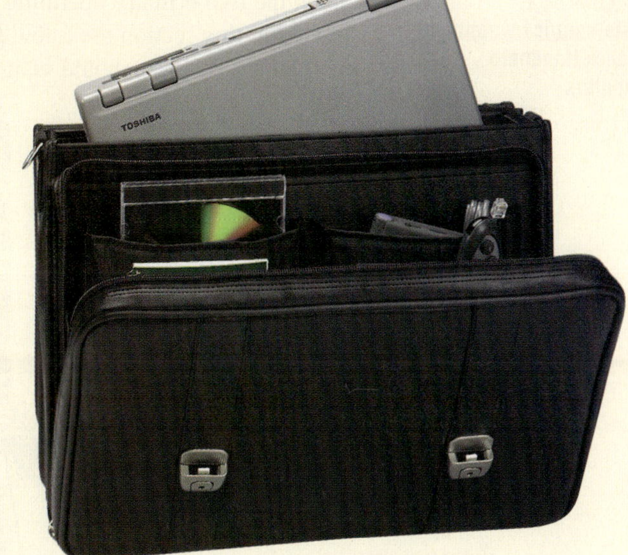

Figure 40
Well-designed carrying case.

Figure 41
Set of electrical and telephone adapters.

8 If you plan to connect your notebook computer to a video projector, make sure the notebook computer is compatible with the video projector. Some notebook computers will not allow you to display an image on the notebook computer and projection device at the same time (Figure 42). Either of these factors can affect your presentation negatively.

Figure 42
Video projector.

Web Link

For more information on handheld computers, visit the Introduction to Computers WEB LINK page (scsite.com/ic4/weblink.htm) and click **Handheld Computers**.

How to Purchase a Handheld Computer

If you need to stay organized when you are on the go, then a lightweight, palm-size or pocketsize computer, called a handheld computer, may be the right choice. Handheld computers typically are categorized by the operating system they run. Although several are available, the two primary operating systems are Palm OS (Figure 43) and Pocket PC (Figure 44). Listed in this section are a few points you will want to consider when purchasing a handheld computer. You also should visit the Web sites listed in Figure 45.

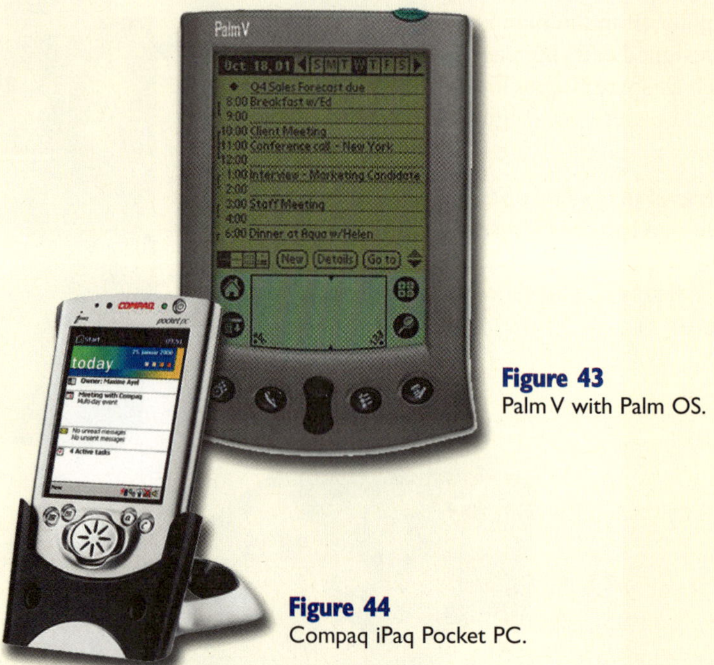

Figure 43
Palm V with Palm OS.

Figure 44
Compaq iPaq Pocket PC.

1 **Determine the applications you plan to run on your handheld computer.** All handheld computers can handle basic organizer-type applications, such as calendar, address book, and notepad. The availability of other applications is dependent on the operating system you choose. With more than 5,000 applications, the depth of software applications for the Palm OS is unmatched. Handheld computers that run Pocket PC have fewer applications available, but they do run a Windows-like operating system and applications you probably are familiar with, such as Word and Excel.

2 **What do you want to pay?** The price of handheld computers runs from $100 to $1,000, depending on their capabilities. In general, Palm OS devices are at the lower end of the cost spectrum and Pocket PC devices are at the higher end. The average selling price for handheld computers is in the $300 to $500 range. For the latest handheld computer prices, capabilities, and accessories, visit the Web sites listed in Figure 45.

Web Site	URL
Compaq	compaq.com/products/handhelds
Computer Shopper	computershopper.com
Handspring	handspring.com
Microsoft	pocketpc.com
Mobile Computing	mobilecomputing.com
Palm	palm.com
PDA Buyers Guide	pdabuyersguide.com
smaller.com	smaller.com
Wireless Developer Network	wirelessdevnet.com

For an updated list of handheld computer Web sites, visit *scsite.com/dc2002/ch8/buyers.htm*.

Figure 45
Reviews and information on handheld computers.

3 **Practice with the touch screen and handwriting recognition before deciding on a model.** You use a pen-like stylus to handwrite on the screen. The handheld computer then translates the handwriting into a computerized font. You also can use the stylus as a pointing device to select items on the screen and enter data using a transparent onscreen keyboard. Some handheld computers are easier to use than others. You can buy third-party software to improve a handheld computer's handwriting recognition.

4 **Decide if you want a color screen.** Pocket PC devices have color screens (as many as 65,536 colors), while most Palm OS devices have monochrome screens (4 to 16 shades of gray). More colors result in greater detail. Resolution also influences the quality of the display.

5 **Compare battery life.** Any mobile device is good only if it has the power to run. Palm OS devices with black-and-white screens tend to have a much longer battery life than Pocket PC devices with color screens. To help alleviate this problem, both Palm OS and Pocket PC devices have incorporated rechargeable batteries, but this only works if you are near a recharger.

6 **Check out the accessories.** You need to consider what accessories you want for your handheld computer. Handheld computer accessories include carrying cases, portable keyboards, removable storage, car chargers, GPS systems, dashboard mounts, replacement styli, synchronization cradles and cables, and more.

7 **Decide if you want additional functionality.** You will find that off-the-shelf Pocket PC devices have broader functionality than Palm OS devices. For example, voice-recording capability, e-book player, MP3 (music) player, and video player are standard on most Pocket PC devices. If you are leaning towards a Palm OS device and still want these additional functions, they can be added later if you find you really need them.

For more information on handheld computer accessories, visit the Introduction to Computers WEB LINK page (scsite.com/ic4/weblink.htm) and click **Handheld Computer Accessories**.

8 **Is synchronization of data with other handheld computers, personal computers, or printers important?** Most handheld computers come with a cradle that connects to the USB or serial port on your computer so that you can synchronize data. An infrared port, however, allows you to synchronize data with any device, including other handheld computers that have a similar infrared port.

9 **If you travel often, then consider e-mail and Web access from your handheld computer.** Some handheld computers come with a modem that can send and receive data across telephone. Other handheld computers allow you to connect to your cellular telephone and use it as a modem. More expensive handheld computers have wireless capabilities built in. In either case, for a monthly network connection fee you can access your e-mail, company Web sites, and any other information on the World Wide Web from anywhere.

Web Link

For more information on installing computers, visit the Introduction to Computers WEB LINK page (scsite.com/ic4/weblink.htm) and click **Install Computers**.

How to Install a Personal Computer

It is important that you spend time planning for the installation of your computer. Follow these steps to ensure your installation experience will be a pleasant one and that your work area is safe, healthy, and efficient.

1 **Read the installation manuals before you start to install your equipment.** Many manufacturers include separate installation instructions with their equipment that contain important information. You can save a great deal of time and frustration if you make an effort to read the manuals.

2 **Do some research.** To locate additional instructions on installing your computer, review the computer magazines or Web sites listed in Figure 46 to search for articles on installing a computer.

WEB SITE	URL
Getting Started/Installation	
Computers 101	newsday.com/plugin/c101main.htm
HelpTalk Online	helptalk.com
Ergonomics	
Ergonomic Computing	cobweb.creighton.edu/training/ergo.htm
Healthy Choices for Computer Users	www-ehs.ucsd.edu/ergo/ergobk/vdt.htm
Video Display Terminal Health and Safety Guidelines	uhs.berkeley.edu/Facstaff/Ergonomics

For an updated list of reference materials, visit *scsite.com/dc2002/ch8/buyers.htm*.

Figure 46
Web references on setting up and using your computer.

3 **Set up your computer in a well-designed work area, with adequate workspace around the computer.** Ergonomics is an applied science devoted to making the equipment and its surrounding work area safer and more efficient. Ergonomic studies have shown that using the correct type and configuration of chair, keyboard, monitor, and work surface will help you work comfortably and efficiently, and help protect your health. For your computer workspace, experts recommend an area of at least two feet by four feet. Figure 47 illustrates additional guidelines for setting up your work area.

Web Link

For more information on ergonomics, visit the Introduction to Computers WEB LINK page (scsite.com/ic4/weblink.htm) and click **Ergonomics**.

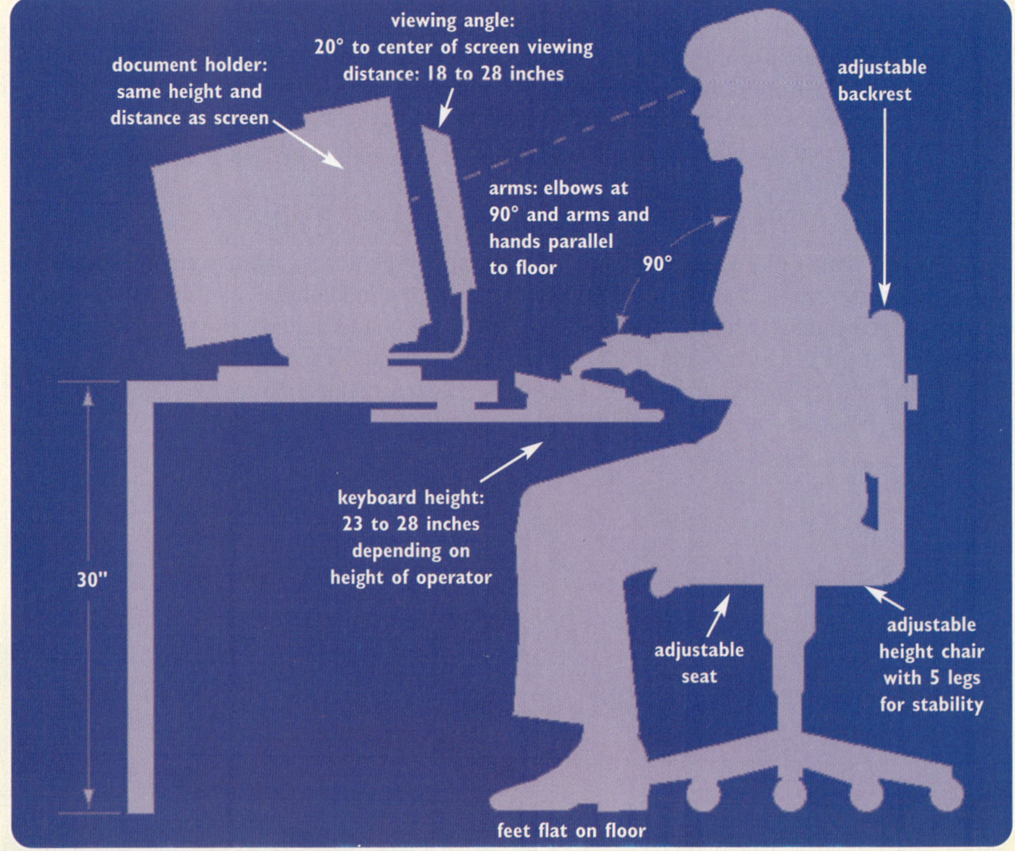

Figure 47
A well-designed work area should be flexible to allow adjustments to the height and build of different individuals. Good lighting and air quality also are important considerations.

Install bookshelves. Bookshelves above and/or to the side of your computer area are useful for keeping manuals and other reference materials handy.

5 **Have a telephone outlet and telephone or cable connection near your workspace so you can connect your modem and/or place calls while using your computer.** To plug in your modem to dial up and access the World Wide Web, you will need a telephone outlet or cable connection close to your computer. Having a telephone nearby also helps if you need to place business or technical support calls while you are working on your computer. Often, if you call a vendor about a hardware or software problem, the support person can talk you through a correction while you are on the telephone. To avoid data loss, however, do not place floppy disks on the telephone or near any other electrical or electronic equipment.

6 **While working at your computer, be aware of health issues.** Working safely at your computer requires that you consider several health issues. To minimize neck and eye discomfort, for instance, obtain a document holder that keeps documents at the same height and distance as your computer screen. To provide adequate lighting that reduces eye strain, use non-glare light bulbs that illuminate your entire work area. Figure 48 lists additional computer user health guidelines.

7 **Obtain a computer tool set. Computer tool sets include any screwdrivers and other tools you might need to work on your computer.** Computer dealers, office supply stores, and mail-order companies sell these tool sets. To keep all the tools together, get a tool set that comes in a zippered carrying case.

8 **Save all the paperwork that comes with your computer.** Keep the documents that come with your computer in an accessible place, along with the paperwork from your other computer-related purchases. To keep different-sized documents together, consider putting them in a manila file folder, large envelope, or sealable plastic bag.

Computer User Health Guidelines

1. Work in a well-designed work area. See Figure 16 on the previous page.
2. Alternate work activities to prevent physical and mental fatigue. If possible, change the order of your work to provide some variety.
3. Take frequent breaks. Every fifteen minutes, look away from the screen to give your eyes a break. At least once per hour, get out of your chair and move around. Every two hours, take at least a fifteen-minute break.
4. Incorporate hand, arm, and body stretching exercises into your breaks. At lunch, try to get outside and walk.
5. Make sure your computer monitor is designed to minimize electromagnetic radiation (EMR). If it is an older model, consider adding EMR reducing accessories.
6. Try to eliminate or minimize surrounding noise. Noisy environments contribute to stress and tension.
7. If you frequently use the telephone and the computer at the same time, consider using a telephone headset. Cradling the telephone between your head and shoulder can cause muscle strain.
8. Be aware of symptoms of repetitive strain injuries: soreness, pain, numbness, or weakness in neck, shoulders, arms, wrists, and hands. Do not ignore early signs; seek medical advice.

Figure 48
Following these health guidelines will help computer users maintain their health.

For more information oncomputer health issues, visit the Introduction to Computers WEB LINK page (scsite.com/ic4/weblink.htm) and click **Computer Health Issues**.

9 **Record the serial numbers of all your equipment and software.** Write the serial numbers of your equipment and software on the outside of the manuals packaged with these items. As noted in Figure 49, you also should create a single, comprehensive list that contains the serial numbers of all your equipment and software.

10 **Complete and send in your equipment and software registration cards.** When you register your equipment and software, the vendor usually enters you in its user database. Being a registered user not only can save you time when you call with a support question, it also makes you eligible for special pricing on software upgrades.

11 **Keep the shipping containers and packing materials for all your equipment.** Shipping containers and packing materials will come in handy if you have to return your equipment for servicing or must move it to another location.

12 **Identify device connectors.** At the back of your computer, you will find a number of connectors for your printer, monitor, mouse, telephone line, and so forth (Figure 49). If the manufacturer has not identified them for you, use a marking pen to write the purpose of each connector on the back of the computer case.

13 **Install your computer in an area where you can maintain the temperature and humidity.** You should keep the computer in an area with a constant temperature between 60°F and 80°F. High temperatures and humidity can damage electronic components. Be careful when using space heaters, for example, as the hot, dry air they generate can cause disk problems.

14 **Keep your computer area clean.** Avoid eating and drinking around your computer. Also, avoid smoking. Cigarette smoke can damage the floppy disk drives and floppy disk surfaces.

15 **Check your home or renter's insurance policy.** Some renter's insurance policies have limits on the amount of computer equipment they cover. Other policies do not cover computer equipment at all if it is used for business. In this instance, you may want to obtain a separate insurance policy.

Figure 49
Inside the system unit and the connectors at the back.

How to Maintain a Personal Computer

Even with the most sophisticated hardware and software, you will need to do some type of maintenance to keep everything working properly. You can simplify and minimize the maintenance by following the steps listed below.

For more information on maintaining computers, visit the Introduction to Computers WEB LINK page (scsite.com/ic4/weblink.htm) and click **Maintain Computers**.

1 **Start a notebook that includes information on your computer.** Keep a notebook that provides a single source of information about your entire computer, both hardware and software. Each time you make a change to your computer, such as adding or removing hardware or software or altering computer parameters, record the change in your notebook. Include the following items in your notebook:

- Vendor support numbers from your user manuals
- Serial numbers of all equipment and software
- User IDs, passwords, and nicknames for your ISP or OSP, network access, Web sites, and so on
- Vendor and date of purchase for all software and equipment
- Trouble log that provides a chronological history of equipment or software problems
- Notes on any discussions with vendor support personnel

Web Link

For more information on passwords, visit the Introduction to Computers WEB LINK page (scsite.com/ic4/weblink.htm) and click **Passwords**.

Figure 50 provides a suggested outline for the contents of your notebook.

PC OWNER'S NOTEBOOK OUTLINE

1. Vendors
   Vendor
   City/State
   Product
   Telephone #
   URL

2. Internet and online services information
   Service provider name
   Logon telephone number
   Alternate logon telephone number
   Technical support telephone number
   User ID
   Password

3. Web site information
   Web site name
   URL
   User ID
   Password
   Nickname

4. Serial numbers
   Product
   Manufacturer
   Serial #

5. Purchase history
   Date
   Product
   Manufacturer
   Vendor
   Cost

6. Software log
   Date installed/uninstalled

7. Trouble log
   Date
   Time
   Problem
   Resolution

8. Support calls
   Date
   Time
   Company
   Contact
   Problem
   Comments

9. Vendor paperwork

Figure 50
To keep important information about your computer on hand and organized, use an outline such as this sample outline.

2 **Before you work inside your computer, turn off the power and disconnect the equipment from the power source.** Working inside your computer with the power on can affect both you and the computer adversely. Thus, you should turn off the power and disconnect the equipment from the power source before you open a computer to work inside. In addition, before you touch anything inside the computer, you should touch an unpainted metal surface such as the power supply. Doing so will help discharge any static electricity that could damage internal components.

3 **Keep the area surrounding your computer dirt and dust free.** Reducing the dirt and dust around your computer will reduce the need to clean the inside of your computer. If dust builds up inside the computer, remove it carefully with compressed air and a small vacuum. Do not touch the components with the vacuum.

4 **Back up important files and data.** Use the operating system or utility program to create an emergency or rescue disk to help you restart your computer if it crashes. You also regularly should copy important data files to disks, tape, or another computer.

Web Link

For more information on viruses, visit the Introduction to Computers WEB LINK page (scsite.com/ic4/weblink.htm) and click **Viruses**.

5 **Protect your computer from viruses.** A computer virus is a potentially damaging computer program designed to infect other software or files by attaching itself to the software or files with which it comes in contact. Virus programs are dangerous because often they destroy or corrupt data stored on the infected computer. You can protect your computer from viruses by installing an antivirus program.

6 **Keep your computer tuned.** Most operating systems include several computer tools that provide basic maintenance functions. One important tool is the disk defragmenter. Defragmenting your hard disk reorganizes files so they are in contiguous (adjacent) clusters, making disk operations faster. Some programs allow you to schedule maintenance tasks for times when you are not using your computer. If necessary, leave your computer on at night so it can run the required maintenance programs. If your operating system does not provide the tools, you can purchase a stand-alone utility program to perform basic maintenance functions.

Web Link

For more information on diagnostic tools, visit the Introduction to Computers WEB LINK page (scsite.com/ic4/weblink.htm) and click **Diagnostic Tools**.

7 **Learn to use diagnostic tools.** Diagnostic tools help you identify and resolve problems, thereby helping to reduce your need for technical assistance. Diagnostic tools help you test components, monitor resources such as memory and processing power, undo changes made to files, and more. As with basic maintenance tools, most operating systems include diagnostic tools; you also can purchase or download many stand-alone diagnostic tools.

LEARN IT ONLINE

Instructions

To complete these exercises, start your browser, click the Address box, and then enter `scsite.com/off2002/exs.htm`. When the Introduction to Computers Web page displays, follow the instructions in the exercises below.

1. Project Reinforcement - True/False, Multiple Choice, and Short Answer

Click Project Reinforcement. Print the quiz by clicking Print on the File menu. Answer each question. Write your first and last name at the top of each page, and then hand in the printout to your instructor.

2. Practice Test

Click Practice Test. Answer each question, enter your first and last name at the bottom of the page, and then click the Grade Test button. When the graded practice test displays on your screen, click Print on the File menu to print a hard copy. Continue to take practice tests until you score 80% or better. Hand in a printout of the final practice test to your instructor.

3. Who Wants to Be a Computer Genius?

Click Computer Genius. Read the instructions, enter your first and last name at the bottom of the page, and then click the PLAY button. Submit your score to your instructor.

4. Wheel of Terms

Click Wheel of Terms. Read the instructions, and then enter your first and last name and your school name. Click the VERY HIGH SCORES link to see other student scores. Close the HIGH SCORES window. Click the PLAY button. Submit your score to your instructor.

5. Crossword Puzzle Challenge

Click Crossword Puzzle Challenge. Read the instructions, and then enter your first and last name. Click the PLAY button. Work the crossword puzzle. When you are finished, click the Submit button. When the crossword puzzle re-displays, click the Print button. Hand in the printout to your instructor.

6. Using the Web Guide

Click Web Guide. Click the Computers and Computing link, and then take a tour of the Virtual Museum of Computing. When you are finished, close the window, and then use your word processing program to prepare a brief report on your tour. Visit four other Web sites listed in the Web Guide and print the main page of each. Hand in the printouts to your instructor.

7. Visiting Web Link Sites

Click the Web Link link. Visit 10 of the 33 Web Link sites. Print the main Web page for each of the 10 Web sites you visit and hand them in to your instructor.

8. Scavenger Hunt

Click Scavenger Hunt. Print a copy of the Scavenger Hunt page; use this page to write down your answers as you search the Web. Hand in your completed page to your instructor.

9. Search Sleuth

Click Search Sleuth to learn search techniques that will help make you a research expert. Hand in your completed assignment to your instructor.

INDEX

PHOTO CREDITS

Figure 1-3b Courtesy of Intel Corporation; *Figure 1-3c* Courtesy of Labtec, Inc.; *Figure 1-3d* Courtesy of Gateway, Inc.; *Figure 1-3e* Courtesy of Eastman Kodak Company; *Figure 1-3f* Courtesy of Thomson Multimedia; *Figure 1-3g* Courtesy of Microsoft Corporation; *Figure 1-3h* Courtesy of Labtec, Inc.; *Figure 2* Scott Goodwin Photography; *Figure 5* Courtesy of Microsoft; *Figure 6a* Courtesy of Compaq Computer Corporation; *Figure 6b* Courtesy of International Business Machines; *Figure 8* Courtesy of Intel and Amd, Inc.; *Figure 9* Scott Goodwin Photography; *Figure 10* Courtesy of Eastman Kodak Company; *Figure 14* Courtesy of Toshiba America Information Systems, Inc.; *Figure 15* Courtesy of ViewSonics Corporation; *Figure 16* Courtesy of Palm, Inc.; *Figure 17* Scott Goodwin Photography; *Figure 18* Scott Goodwin Photography; *Figure 20* Courtesy of Seagate Technology; *Figure 22* Courtesy of Pioneer Electronics; *Figure 39* Courtesy of Compaq Computer Corporation; *Figure 40* Courtesy of Toshiba America Information Systems, Inc.; *Figure 41* Courtesy of Xirom Corporation; *Figure 42* Courtesy of InFocus Corporation; *Figure 43* Courtesy of Palm, Inc.; *Figure 44* Courtesy of Compaq Computer Corporation; *Figure 49* Courtesy of Compaq Computer Corporation and PhotoDisc, Inc.

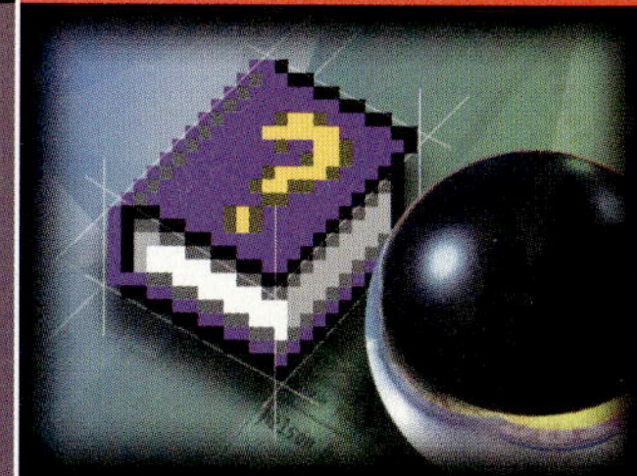

Microsoft Windows 2000 and Office 2000

An Introduction to Windows 2000 Professional and Office 2000

OBJECTIVES

You will have mastered the material in this project when you can:

- Describe the Microsoft Windows 2000 user interface
- Identify the objects on the Microsoft Windows 2000 desktop
- Perform the basic mouse operations: point, click, right-click, double-click, drag, and right-drag
- Open, minimize, maximize, restore, scroll, and close a Windows 2000 window
- Move and resize a window on the desktop
- Understand keyboard shortcut notation
- Launch and quit an application program
- Identify the elements of the Exploring window
- Create, expand, and collapse a folder
- Select and copy one file or a group of files
- Rename and delete a folder or file
- Quit Windows Explorer
- Use Windows 2000 Help
- Shut down Windows 2000
- Identify each application in Microsoft Office 2000 Premium Edition
- Define the Internet, the World Wide Web, and an intranet
- Explain how each Microsoft Office 2000 application uses the Internet
- Understand the Microsoft Office 2000 Help system

Windows 2000

Leads the Way in the New Millennium

In the twenty-first century, the Microsoft Windows 2000 operating system leads the way with its advanced and improved software technology, making it easier, more cost-effective, and enjoyable for people and businesses to use computers. Microsoft Corporation under the leadership of Bill Gates has been a continuous source of innovative products.

Bill Gates's computing efforts began when he was in grade school, when he and classmate, Paul Allen, learned the BASIC programming language from a manual and programmed a mainframe computer using a Teletype terminal they purchased with the proceeds from a rummage sale. In high school, Gates and Allen had a thirst for more computing power. They wrote custom programs for local businesses during the summer and split their $5,000 salaries between cash and computer time. They also debugged software problems at local businesses in return for computer use.

In Gates's sophomore year, one of his teachers asked him to teach his computer skills to his classmates. In 1972, Gates and Allen read an article in *Electronics* magazine about Intel's first microprocessor chip. They requested a manual from Intel, developed a device that experimented with pushing the chip to its limits, and formed the Traf-O-Data company; an endeavor that ultimately would lead to the formation of something much larger.

In 1973, Gates entered Harvard and Allen landed a programming job with Honeywell.

They continued to communicate and scheme about the power of computers when, in 1975, the Altair 8800 computer showed up on the cover of *Popular Electronics*. This computer was about the size of the Traf-O-Data device and contained a new Intel computer chip. At that point, they knew they were going into business. Gates left Harvard and Allen left Honeywell.

When they formed Microsoft in 1975, the company had three programmers, one product, and revenues of $16,000. The founders had no business plan, no capital, and no financial backing, but they did have a product – a form of the BASIC programming language tailored for the first microcomputer.

In 1980, IBM approached Microsoft and asked the company to provide an operating system for its new IBM personal computer. The deadline? Three months. Gates purchased the core of a suitable operating system, dubbed Q-DOS (Quick and Dirty Operating System). Microsoft's version, MS-DOS, would become the international standard for IBM and IBM-compatible personal computers. Riding the meteoric rise in sales of IBM-compatible computers and attendant sales of MS-DOS, Microsoft continued to improve its software stream of revisions. At a significant branch of the family tree, Windows made its debut, providing an intuitive graphical user interface (GUI). Similarly, Windows 95, Windows 98, and Windows NT provided further advances.

The Microsoft Windows 2000 operating system family expands the possibilities even further with the Windows 2000 Server, Windows 2000 Advanced Server, Windows 2000 Data Center, and Windows 2000 Professional designed for use on a server in a computer network. The Windows 2000 Professional can be used on computer workstations and portable computers.

Microsoft Windows 2000
and Office 2000

An Introduction to Windows 2000 Professional and Office 2000

PROJECT 1

CASE PERSPECTIVE

After weeks of planning, your organization finally switched from Microsoft Windows 98 to Microsoft Windows 2000 Professional and installed Microsoft Office 2000 on all computers. As the computer trainer for the upcoming in-house seminar, you realize you should know more about Windows 2000 Professional and Office 2000. Since installing Windows 2000 Professional and Office 2000, many employees have come to you with questions. You have taken the time to answer their questions by sitting down with them at their computers and searching for the answers using the Microsoft Help system.

From their questions, you determine the seminar should cover the basics of Windows 2000 Professional, including basic mouse operations, working within a window, launching an application, performing file maintenance using Windows Explorer, and searching for answers to employees' questions using Windows 2000 Help. In addition, the seminar should familiarize the participants with each of the Office 2000 applications. Your goal in this project is to become familiar with Windows 2000 Professional and the Office 2000 applications in order to teach the seminar.

Introduction

Microsoft Windows 2000 Professional is a widely used version of the Microsoft Windows operating system designed for use on computer workstations and portable computers. A **workstation** is a computer connected to a network. Microsoft Windows 2000 Professional is an easy-to-use program that allows you to control your computer and communicate with other computers on a network.

In this project, you will learn about Microsoft Windows 2000 Professional and how to use the Windows 2000 graphical user interface to organize the manner in which you interact with your computer, simplify the process of working with documents and applications, and use your computer to access information on both the Internet and on an intranet.

In the first part of this project, you will work with the desktop and the windows available on the desktop, learn the basic mouse operations, and launch an application program. Using Windows 2000 Explorer, you will learn to create and view the contents of folders, select and copy a file or group of files, rename and delete files and folders, and use Microsoft Windows 2000 Help.

Microsoft Office 2000, the latest edition of the world's best-selling office suite, is a collection of the more popular Microsoft application software products that work similarly and together as if they were a single program. Microsoft Office 2000 integrates these applications and combines them with the power of the Internet so you can move quickly among applications, transfer text and graphics easily, and interact seamlessly with the World Wide Web. An explanation of each of the application software programs in Microsoft Office 2000 is given at the end of this project.

What Is Microsoft Windows 2000 Professional?

An **operating system** is the set of computer instructions, called a computer program, that controls the allocation of computer hardware, such as memory, disk devices, printers, and CD-ROM and DVD drives, and provides you with the capability of communicating with your computer. The most powerful Microsoft operating system is the **Microsoft Windows 2000 family of operating systems** consisting of the Microsoft Windows 2000 Server, Microsoft Windows 2000 Advanced Server, Microsoft Windows 2000 Data Center, and Microsoft Windows 2000 Professional. The operating system of choice for computer workstations and portable computers is **Microsoft Windows 2000 Professional** (called **Windows 2000** for the rest of this book).

Windows 2000 is an operating system that performs every function necessary to enable you to communicate with and use your computer. Windows 2000 is called a **32-bit operating system** because it uses 32 bits for addressing and other purposes, which means the operating system can address more than four gigabytes of RAM (random-access memory) and perform tasks faster than older operating systems. Windows 2000 includes **Microsoft Internet Explorer** (**IE**), a browser software program developed by Microsoft Corporation that integrates the Windows 2000 desktop and the Internet. Internet Explorer and allows you to work with programs and files in a similar fashion, whether they are located on your computer, a local network, or the Internet.

Windows 2000 is designed to be compatible with all existing **application programs**, which are the programs that perform an application-related function such as word processing. To use the application programs that can be launched under Windows 2000, you must know about the Windows 2000 user interface.

Microsoft Windows 2000

Microsoft Windows 2000 combines the best business features of Windows 98 with the strengths of Windows NT 4.0. Windows 98, designed for use on personal computers, is the most popular operating system for personal computers. Windows NT 4.0, designed for use on a computer network, is the most widely used version of Windows NT.

What Is a User Interface?

A **user interface** is the combination of hardware and software that you use to communicate with and control your computer. Through the user interface, you are able to make selections on your computer, request information from your computer, and respond to messages displayed by your computer. Thus, a user interface provides the means for dialogue between you and a computer.

Hardware and software together form the user interface. Among the hardware devices associated with a user interface are the monitor, keyboard, and mouse (Figure 1-1). The **monitor** displays messages and provides information.

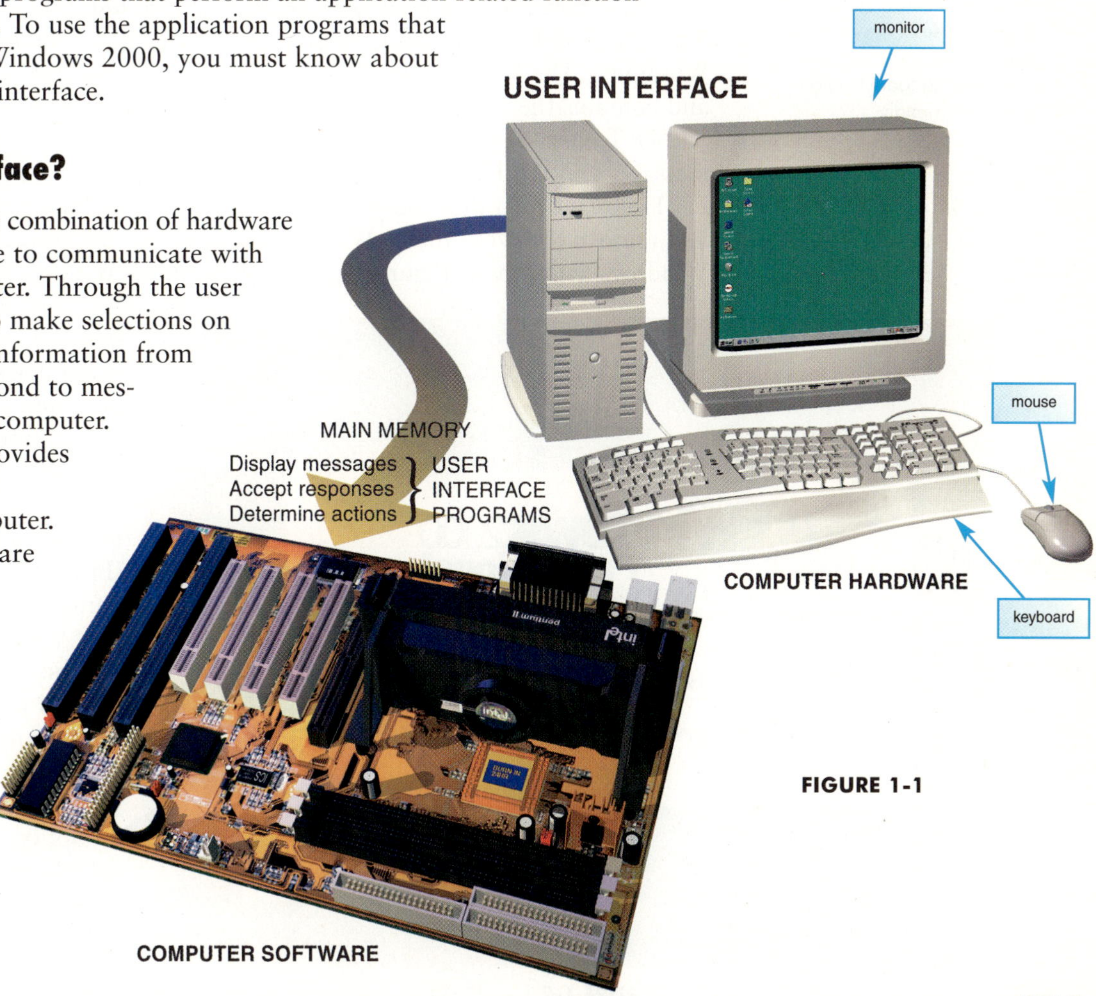

FIGURE 1-1

Windows 2000

For additional information about the Windows 2000 operating system, visit the Office 2000 More About Web page (www.scsite.com/off2000/more.htm) and then click Windows 2000.

The Windows 2000 Interface

Some older interfaces, called command-line interfaces, required that you type keywords (special words, phrases, or codes the computer understands) or press special keys on the keyboard to communicate with the interface. Today, graphical user interfaces incorporate colorful graphics, use of the mouse, and Web browser-like features, making today's interfaces user friendly.

You respond by entering data in the form of a command or other response using the **keyboard** or **mouse**. Among the responses available are responses that specify which application program to run, which document to open, when to print, and where to store data for future use.

The computer software associated with the user interface consists of the programs that engage you in dialogue (Figure 1-1 on the previous page). The computer software determines the messages you receive, the manner in which you should respond, and the actions that occur based on your responses.

The goal of an effective user interface is to be **user friendly**, meaning that the software can be used easily by individuals with limited training. Research studies have indicated that the use of graphics can play an important role in aiding users to interact effectively with a computer. A **graphical user interface**, or **GUI** (pronounced gooey), is a user interface that displays graphics in addition to text when it communicates with the user.

The Windows 2000 graphical user interface was designed carefully to be easier to set up, simpler to learn, faster and more powerful, and better integrated with the Internet than previous versions of Microsoft Windows.

Launching Microsoft Windows 2000 Professional

When you turn on the computer, an introductory screen containing the words, Microsoft Windows 2000 Professional, and the Please Wait... screen display momentarily followed by the Welcome to Windows dialog box (Figure 1-2). A **dialog box** displays whenever Windows 2000 needs to supply information to you or wants you to enter information or select an option. The **title bar**, which is at the top of the dialog box and blue in color, identifies the name of the dialog box (Welcome to Windows). The Welcome to Windows dialog box displays on a green background and contains the Windows logo, title (Microsoft Windows 2000 Professional Built on NT Technology), keyboard icon, instructions (Press Ctrl-Alt-Delete to begin.), a message, and the Help link.

Holding down the CTRL key and pressing the ALT and DELETE keys simultaneously will remove the Welcome to Windows dialog box and display the Log On to Windows dialog box (Figure 1-3). The Log On to Windows dialog box contains the User name and Password text boxes, Log on to box, Log on using dial-up connection check box, and four command buttons (OK, Cancel, Shutdown, and Options). A **text box** is a rectangular area in which you can enter text. Currently, the user name (Brad Wilson) displays in the User name text box, a series of asterisks (*****) displays in the Password text box to hide the password entered by the user, and the computer name, BRADWILSON (this computer), displays in the Log on to box. The **check box** represents an option to log on using an established dial-up Internet connection. The **command buttons** allow you to perform different operations, such

FIGURE 1-2

as accepting the user name and password or displaying additional options. If you do not know your user name or password, ask your instructor.

Entering your user name in the User name text box and your password in the Password text box and then clicking the OK button will clear the screen and allow several items to display on a background called the **desktop**. The default color of the desktop background is green, but your computer may display a different color.

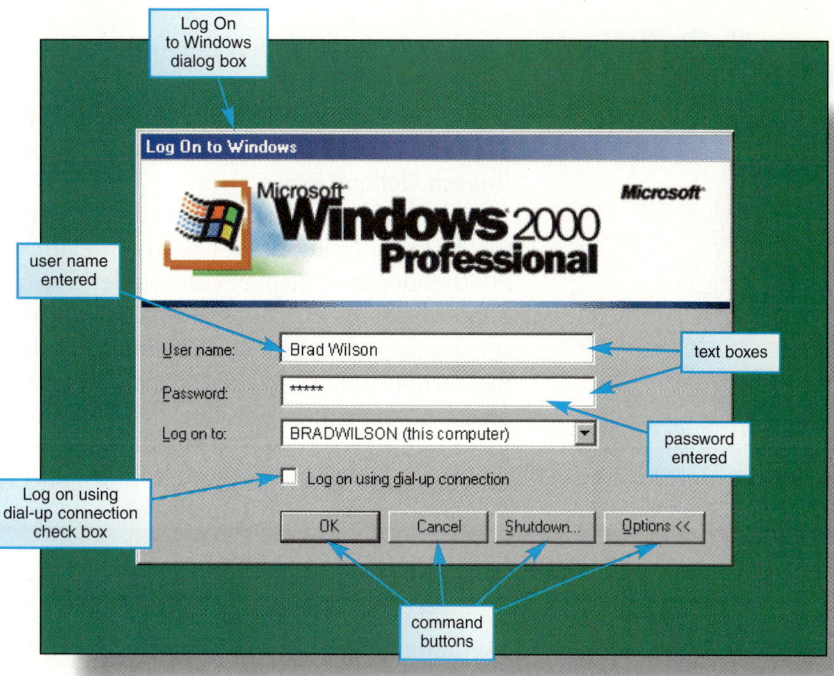

FIGURE 1-3

The items on the desktop in Figure 1-4 include five icons and their names on the left side of the desktop and the taskbar at the bottom of the desktop. Using the five **icons**, you can store documents in one location (**My Documents**), view the contents of the computer (**My Computer**), work with other computers connected to the computer (**My Network Places**), discard unneeded objects (**Recycle Bin**), and browse Web pages on the Internet (**Internet Explorer**). Your computer's desktop may contain more, fewer, or different icons because you can customize the desktop of the computer.

The **taskbar** shown at the bottom of the screen in Figure 1-4 contains the Start button, Quick Launch toolbar, taskbar button area, and tray status area. The **Start button** allows you to launch a program quickly, find or open a document, change the

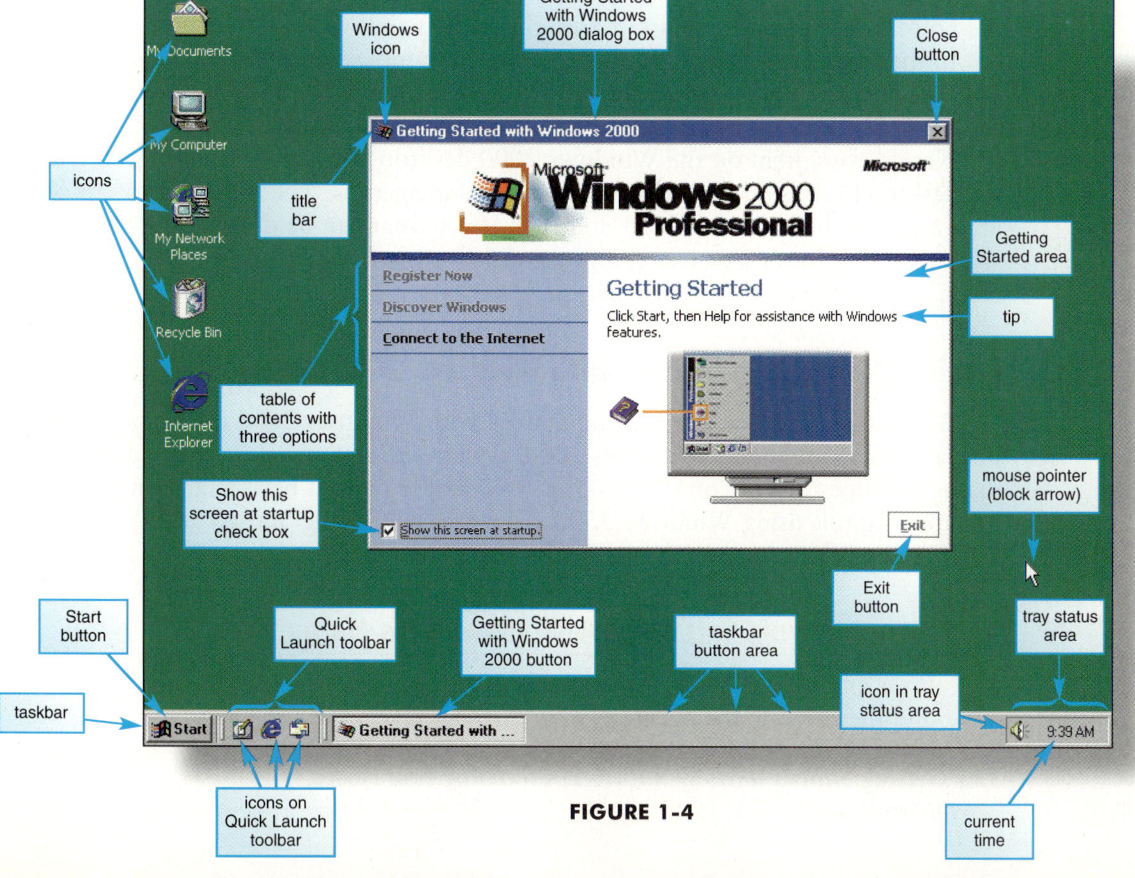

FIGURE 1-4

The Windows 2000 Desktop

Because Windows 2000 is easily customized, the desktop on your computer may not resemble the desktop in Figure 1-4 on page INT 1.7. For example, the icon titles on the desktop may be underlined or objects not shown in Figure 1-4 may display on your desktop. If this is the case, contact your instructor for instructions for selecting the default desktop settings.

Windows 2000 Tips and Tricks

For Windows 2000 tips and tricks, visit the Office 2000 More About Web page (www.scsite.com/off2000/more.htm) and then click Windows 2000 Tips and Tricks.

Windows 2000 Performance

To improve Windows 2000 performance, visit the Office 2000 More About Web page (www.scsite.com/off2000/more.htm) and then click Windows 2000 Performance.

The Mouse

The mouse, though invented in the 1960s, was not used widely until the Apple Macintosh computer became available in 1984. Even then, some highbrows called mouse users "wimps". Today, the mouse is an indispensable tool for every computer user.

computer's settings, shut down the computer, and perform many other tasks. The **Quick Launch toolbar** contains three icons. The first icon allows you to view an uncluttered desktop at anytime (**Show Desktop**). The second icon launches Internet Explorer (**Launch Internet Explorer Browser**). The third icon launches Outlook Express (**Launch Outlook Express**).

The **taskbar button area** contains buttons to indicate which windows are open on the desktop. In Figure 1-4 on the previous page, the Getting Started with Windows 2000 dialog box displays on the desktop and the Getting Started with Windows 2000 button displays in the taskbar button area. The **tray status area** contains a speaker icon to adjust the computer's volume level. The tray status area also displays the current time (9:39 AM). The tray status area on your desktop may contain more, fewer, or some different icons because the contents of the tray status area change.

The Getting Started with Windows 2000 dialog box that may display on your desktop when you launch Windows 2000 is shown in Figure 1-4. The **title bar** at the top of the dialog box, which is dark blue in color, contains the Windows icon, identifies the name of the dialog box (Getting Started with Windows 2000), and contains the Close button to close the Getting Started with Windows 2000 dialog box.

In the Getting Started with Windows 2000 dialog box, a table of contents containing three options (Register Now, Discover Windows, and Connect to the Internet) and the Getting Started area containing constantly changing helpful tips about Windows 2000 display. The options in the table of contents allow you to perform different tasks such as registering the Windows 2000 operating system, learning Windows 2000 using the Discover Windows 2000 tour, and connecting to the Internet.

Pointing to an option in the table of contents replaces the contents of the Getting Started area with an explanation of the option. Clicking an option starts the task associated with the option.

A check box containing a check mark displays below the table of contents. The check mark in the check box represents an option to display the Getting Started with Windows 2000 dialog box each time you launch Windows 2000. The **Exit button** at the bottom of the Getting Started area closes the window.

In the lower-right corner of the desktop is the mouse pointer. The **mouse pointer** is the shape of a block arrow. The mouse pointer allows you to point to objects on the desktop and may change shape as it points to different objects.

Nearly every item on the Windows 2000 desktop is considered an object. Even the desktop itself is an object. Every **object** has properties. The **properties** of an object are unique to that specific object and may affect what can be done to the object or what the object does. For example, one of the properties of an object may be its color, such as the color of the desktop.

Closing the Getting Started with Windows 2000 Dialog Box

As previously noted, the Getting Started with Windows 2000 dialog box may display when you launch Windows 2000. If the Getting Started with Windows 2000 dialog box does display on the desktop, you should close it before beginning any other operations using Windows 2000. To close the Getting Started with Windows 2000 dialog box, complete the following step.

TO CLOSE THE GETTING STARTED WITH WINDOWS 2000 DIALOG BOX

1. Press and hold the ALT key on the keyboard, press the F4 key on the keyboard, and then release the ALT key.

The Getting Started with Windows 2000 dialog box closes.

The Desktop as a Work Area

The Windows 2000 desktop and the objects on the desktop were designed to emulate a work area in an office or at home. You may think of the Windows desktop as an electronic version of the top of your desk. You can move objects around on the desktop, look at them and then put them aside, and so on. In this project, you will learn how to interact with the Windows 2000 desktop.

Communicating with Microsoft Windows 2000

FIGURE 1-5

The Windows 2000 interface provides the means for dialogue between you and your computer. Part of this dialogue involves your requesting information from your computer and responding to messages displayed by your computer. You can request information and respond to messages using either a mouse or a keyboard.

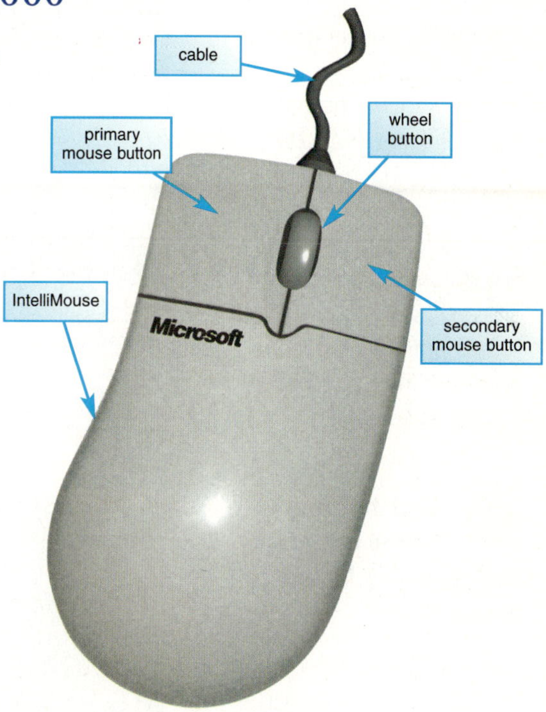

Mouse Operations

A **mouse** is a pointing device that is attached to the computer by a cable. Although not required when using Windows 2000, Windows supports the use of the **Microsoft IntelliMouse** (Figure 1-5). The IntelliMouse contains three buttons: the primary mouse button, the secondary mouse button, and the wheel button between the primary and secondary mouse buttons. Typically, the **primary mouse button** is the left mouse button and the **secondary mouse button** is the right mouse button, although Windows 2000 allows you to switch them. In this book, the left mouse button is the primary mouse button and the right mouse button is the secondary mouse button. The functions the **wheel button** and wheel perform depend on the software application being used. If the mouse connected to your computer is not an IntelliMouse, it will not have a wheel button between the primary and secondary mouse buttons.

Using the mouse, you can perform the following operations: (1) point; (2) click; (3) right-click; (4) double-click; (5) drag; and (6) right-drag. These operations are demonstrated on the following pages.

Point and Click

Point means you move the mouse across a flat surface until the mouse pointer rests on the item of choice on the desktop. As you move the mouse across a flat surface, the movement of a ball on the underside of the mouse (Figure 1-6) is sensed electronically, and the mouse pointer moves across the desktop in the same direction.

Click means you press and release the primary mouse button, which in this book is the left mouse button. In most cases, you must point to an item before you can click it. To become acquainted with the use of the mouse, perform the following steps to point to and click various objects on the desktop.

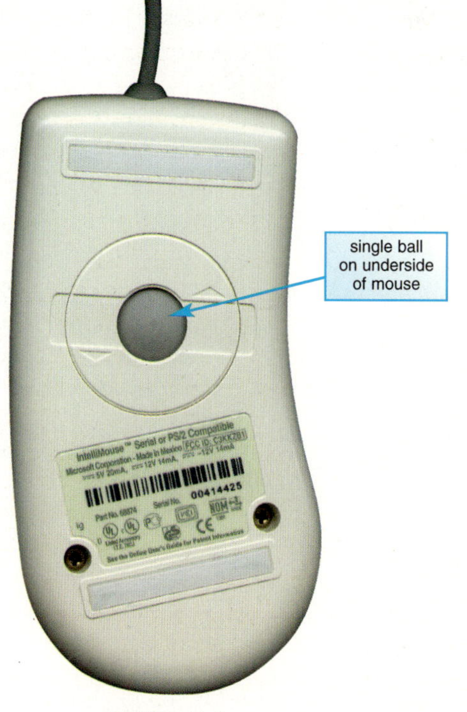

FIGURE 1-6

To Point and Click

1 Point to the Start button on the taskbar by moving the mouse across a flat surface until the mouse pointer rests on the Start button.

The mouse pointer on the Start button displays a ScreenTip (Click here to begin) (Figure 1-7). The ***ScreenTip****, which provides instructions, displays on the desktop for approximately five seconds. Other ScreenTips display on the screen until you move the mouse pointer off the object.*

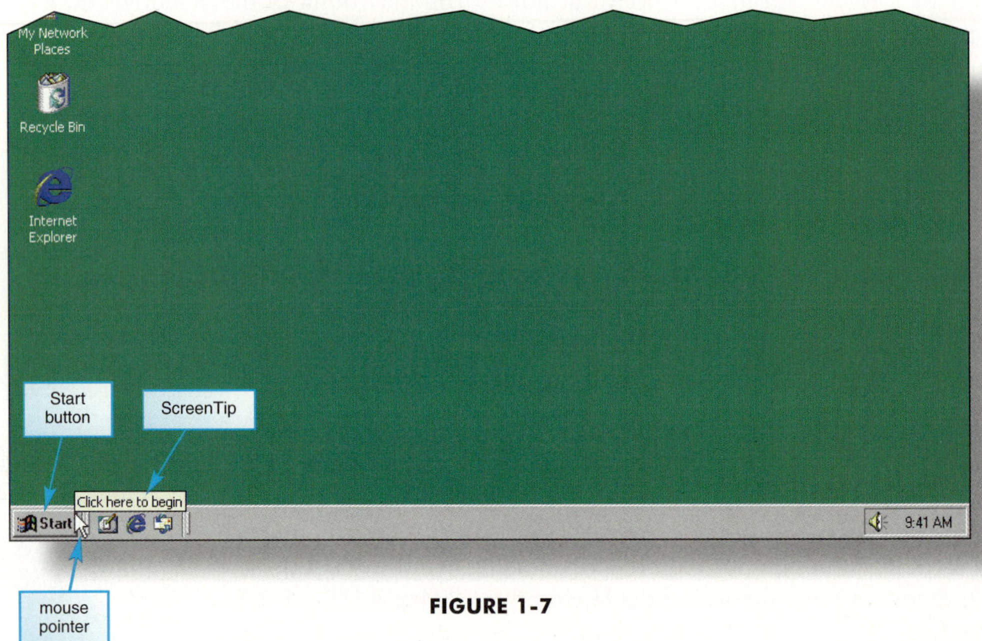

FIGURE 1-7

2 Click the Start button by pressing and releasing the left mouse button.

The Start menu displays and the Start button is recessed on the taskbar (Figure 1-8). A ***menu*** *is a list of related commands. A* ***command*** *directs Windows 2000 to perform a specific action such as shutting down the operating system. Each command on the Start menu consists of an icon and a command name. A* ***right arrow*** *follows some commands to indicate pointing to the command will open a submenu. Two commands (Run and Shut Down) are followed by an* ***ellipsis*** *(...) to indicate more information is required to execute these commands.*

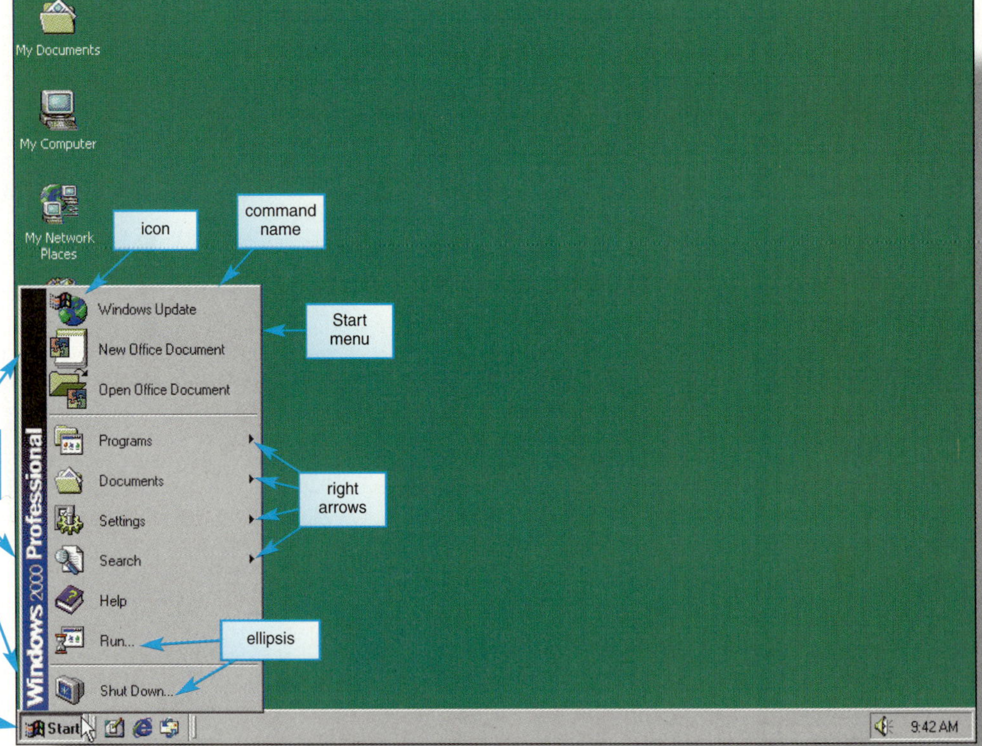

FIGURE 1-8

3 Point to Programs on the Start menu.

When you point to Programs, Windows 2000 highlights the Programs command on the Start menu and the Programs submenu displays (Figure 1-9). A ***submenu****, or* ***cascading menu****, is a menu that displays when you point to a command that is followed by a right arrow. Whenever you point to a command on a menu, the command is highlighted.*

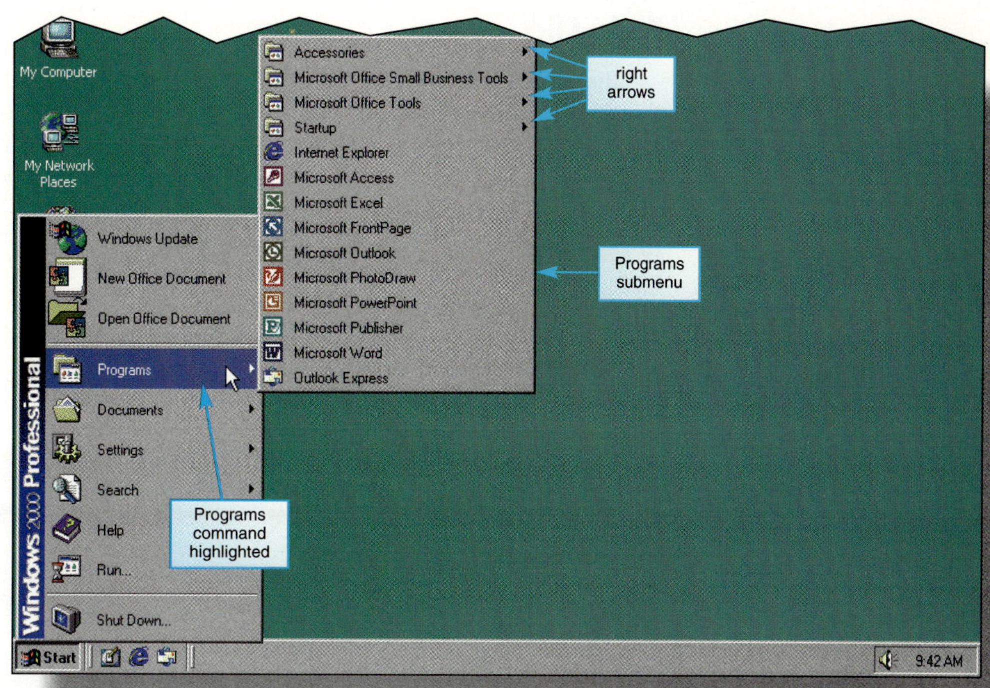

FIGURE 1-9

4 Point to an open area of the desktop and then click the open area.

The Start menu and Programs submenu close (Figure 1-10). The mouse pointer points to the desktop. To close a menu anytime, click any open area of the desktop except on the menu itself. The Start button is no longer recessed.

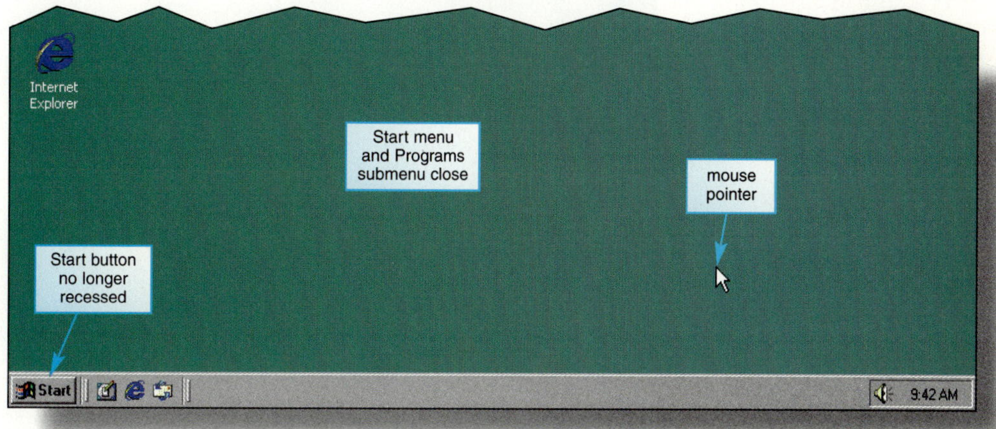

FIGURE 1-10

The Start menu shown in Figure 1-8 is divided into three sections. The top section contains commands to launch the Windows Update application (Windows Update) and create a new or open an existing Microsoft Office document (New Office Document and Open Office Document); the middle section contains commands to launch an application, work with documents or Web sites, customize options, search for files, obtain Help, or run a program from an auxiliary drive (Programs, Documents, Settings, Search, Help, and Run); and the bottom section contains a basic operating task (Shut Down).

When you click an object, such as the Start button, you must point to the object before you click. In the steps on the next page, the instruction that directs you to point to a particular item and then click is, Click the particular item. For example, Click the Start button means point to the Start button and then click.

Buttons

Buttons on the desktop and in programs are an integral part of Windows 2000. When you point to them, their function displays in a ToolTip. When you click them, they appear to indent on the screen to mimic what would happen if you pushed an actual button. All buttons in Windows 2000 behave in the same manner.

Right-Click

Right-click means you press and release the secondary mouse button, which in this book is the right mouse button. As directed when using the primary mouse button for clicking an object, normally you will point to an object before you right-click it. Right-clicking an object, such as the desktop, opens a **shortcut menu** that contains a set of commands specifically for use with that object. Perform the following steps to right-click the desktop.

To Right-Click

1 Point to an open area of the desktop and then press and release the right mouse button.

A shortcut menu displays (Figure 1-11). This shortcut menu consists of eight commands. When a command on a menu appears dimmed, such as the Paste and Paste Shortcut commands, that command is unavailable.

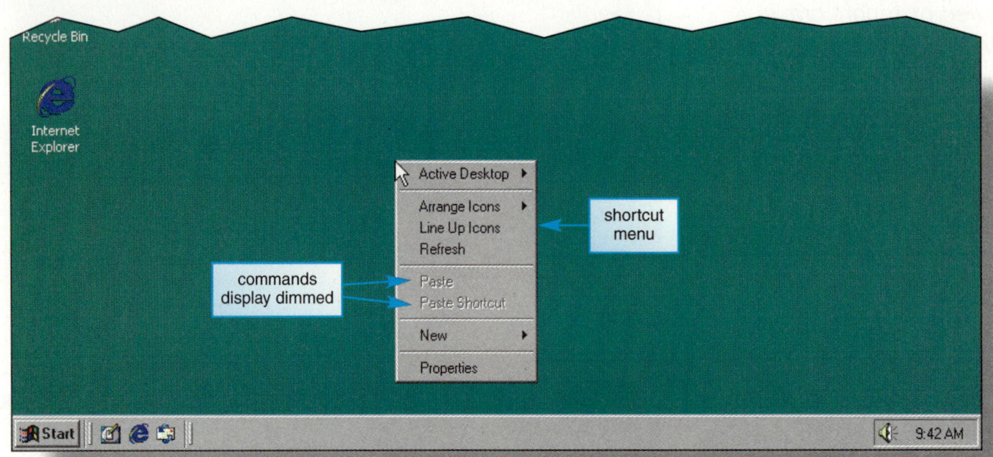

FIGURE 1-11

2 Point to New on the shortcut menu.

When you move the mouse pointer to the New command, Windows 2000 highlights the New command and opens the New submenu (Figure 1-12). The ***New submenu*** *contains a variety of commands. The number of commands and the actual commands that display on your computer may be different.*

3 Point to an open area of the desktop and then click the open area to close the shortcut menu and the New submenu.

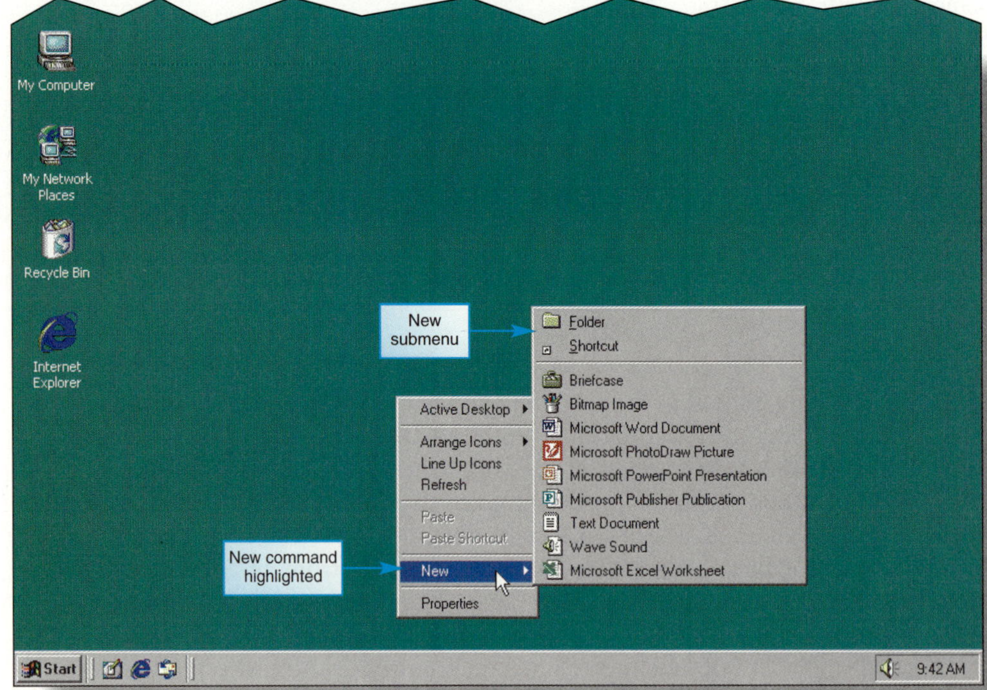

FIGURE 1-12

Whenever you right-click an object, a shortcut menu (also referred to as an **object menu**) will display. As you will see, the use of shortcut menus speeds up your work and adds flexibility to your interface with the computer.

Right-Clicking

Right-clicking an object other than the desktop will display a different shortcut menu with commands useful to that object. Right-clicking an object is thought to be the fastest method of performing an operation on an object.

Double-Click

To double-click, you quickly press and release the left mouse button twice without moving the mouse. In most cases, you must point to an item before you double-click. Perform the following step to open the My Computer window on the desktop by double-clicking the My Computer icon.

To Open a Window by Double-Clicking

1 Point to the My Computer icon on the desktop and then double-click by quickly pressing and releasing the left mouse button twice without moving the mouse.

The My Computer window opens (Figure 1-13). The recessed My Computer button is added to the taskbar button area.

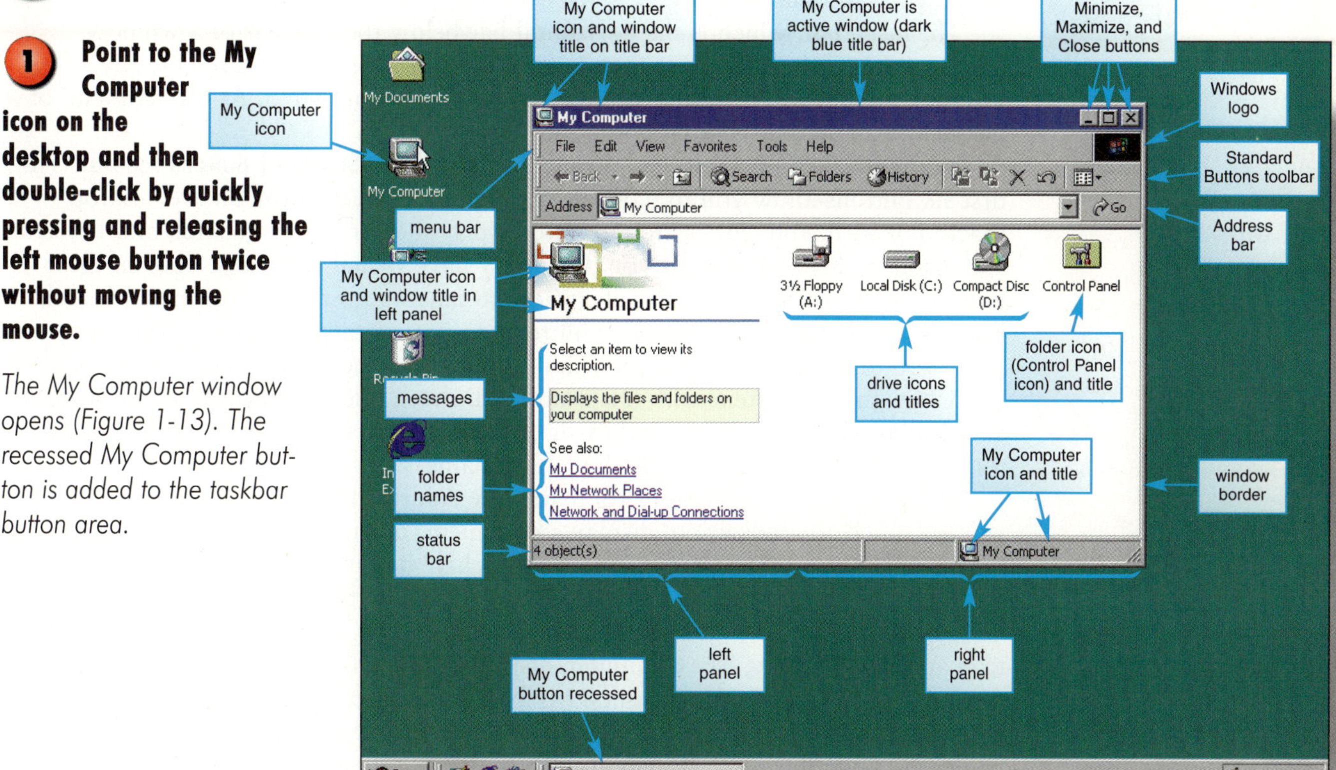

FIGURE 1-13

The My Computer window, the only open window, is the active window. The **active window** is the window currently being used. Whenever you click an object that can be opened, such as the My Computer icon, Windows 2000 will open the object; and the open object will be identified by a recessed button in the taskbar button area. The recessed button identifies the active window.

The contents of the My Computer window on your computer may be different from the contents of the My Computer window illustrated in Figure 1-13.

Double-Clicking

Double-clicking is the most difficult mouse skill to learn. Many people have a tendency to move the mouse before they click a second time, even when they do not want to move the mouse. You should find, however, that with a little practice, double-clicking becomes quite natural.

My Computer

The trade press and media have poked fun at the icon name, My Computer. One wag said no one should use Windows 2000 for more than five minutes without changing the name (which is easily done). Microsoft responds that in their usability labs, beginning computer users found the name, My Computer, easier to understand.

My Computer Window

Because Windows 2000 is easily customized, the My Computer window on your computer may not resemble the window in Figure 1-13 on page INT 1.13. If this is the case, check the commands on the View menu by clicking View on the menu bar. If a check mark precedes the as Web Page command, click the as Web Page command. If a large dot does not precede the Large Icons command, click the Large Icons command.

My Computer Window

The thin line, or **window border**, surrounding the My Computer window shown in Figure 1-13 on the previous page determines the window shape and size. The **title bar** at the top of the window contains a small icon that is the same as the icon on the desktop and the **window title** (My Computer) that identifies the window. The color of the title bar (dark blue) and the recessed My Computer button in the taskbar button area indicate the My Computer window is the active window. The color of the active window on your computer may be different from the dark blue color shown in Figure 1-13 on the previous page.

Clicking the icon at the left on the title bar will display the **System menu**, which contains commands to carry out the actions associated with the My Computer window. At the right on the title bar are three buttons, the Minimize button, the Maximize button, and the Close button, that can be used to specify the size of the window or close the window.

The **menu bar**, which is the horizontal bar below the title bar of a window (Figure 1-13 on the previous page), contains a list of menu names for the My Computer window: File, Edit, View, Favorites, Tools, and Help. At the right end of the menu bar is a button containing the Windows logo.

Below the menu bar, eleven buttons display on the **Standard Buttons toolbar**. The first six buttons allow you to navigate through an open window on the desktop (Back, Forward, and Up); search for and display files or folders (Search and Folders); and display a list of Web sites you previously have visited (History). Four of these buttons contain a **text label** that identifies the function of the button (Back, Search, Folders, and History). The last five buttons do not contain text labels. These buttons allow you to move and copy text within a window or between windows (Move To and Copy To); delete text within a window (Delete); undo a previous action (Undo); and display the icons in the window in different formats (Views). Pointing to a button without a text label displays the button name.

Below the Standard Buttons toolbar is the Address bar. The **Address bar** allows you to launch an application, display a document, open another window, and search for information on the Internet. The Address bar shown in Figure 1-13 on the previous page contains the My Computer icon and window title (My Computer).

The area below the Address bar is divided into two panels. The My Computer icon and window title, My Computer, display in the left panel. Several messages and three folder names (My Documents, My Network Places, and Network and Dial-Up Connections) display below the icon and title in the left panel. The three folder names are underlined and display in blue font. Underlined text, such as the folder names, is referred to as a **hyperlink**, or simply a **link**. Pointing to a hyperlink changes the mouse pointer to a hand icon, and clicking a hyperlink displays the contents of the associated folder in the window.

The right panel of the My Computer window contains four icons. A title below each icon identifies the icon. The first three icons, called **drive icons**, represent a 3½ Floppy (A:) drive, a Local Disk (C:) drive, and a Compact Disc (D:) drive. The fourth icon is the Control Panel folder. A **folder** is an object created to contain related documents, applications, and other folders. A folder in Windows 2000 contains items in much the same way a folder on your desk contains items. The **Control Panel folder** allows you to personalize the computer, such as specifying how you want the desktop to look.

Clicking a drive or folder icon selects the icon in the right panel and displays information about the drive or folder in the left panel. Double-clicking a drive or folder icon displays the contents of the drive or folder in the right panel and information about the drive or folder in the left panel. You may find more, fewer, or different drive and folder icons in the My Computer window on your computer.

A message at the left on the **status bar** located at the bottom of the window indicates the right panel contains four objects (Figure 1-13 on page INT 1.13). The My Computer icon and title display to the right of the message on the status bar.

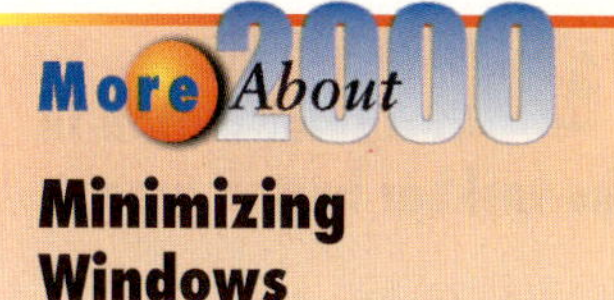

Minimizing Windows

Windows management on the Windows 2000 desktop is important in order to keep the desktop uncluttered. You will find yourself frequently minimizing windows and then later reopening them with a click of a button in the taskbar button area.

Minimize Button

Two buttons on the title bar of a window, the Minimize button and the Maximize button, allow you to control the way a window displays or does not display on the desktop. When you click the **Minimize button** (Figure 1-13 on page INT 1.13), the My Computer window no longer displays on the desktop and the recessed My Computer button in the taskbar button area changes to a non-recessed button. A minimized window still is open but it does not display on the screen. To minimize and then redisplay the My Computer window, complete these steps.

To Minimize and Redisplay a Window

1 Point to the Minimize button on the title bar of the My Computer window.

The mouse pointer points to the Minimize button on the My Computer window title bar (Figure 1-14). A ScreenTip displays below the Minimize button and the My Computer button in the taskbar button area is recessed.

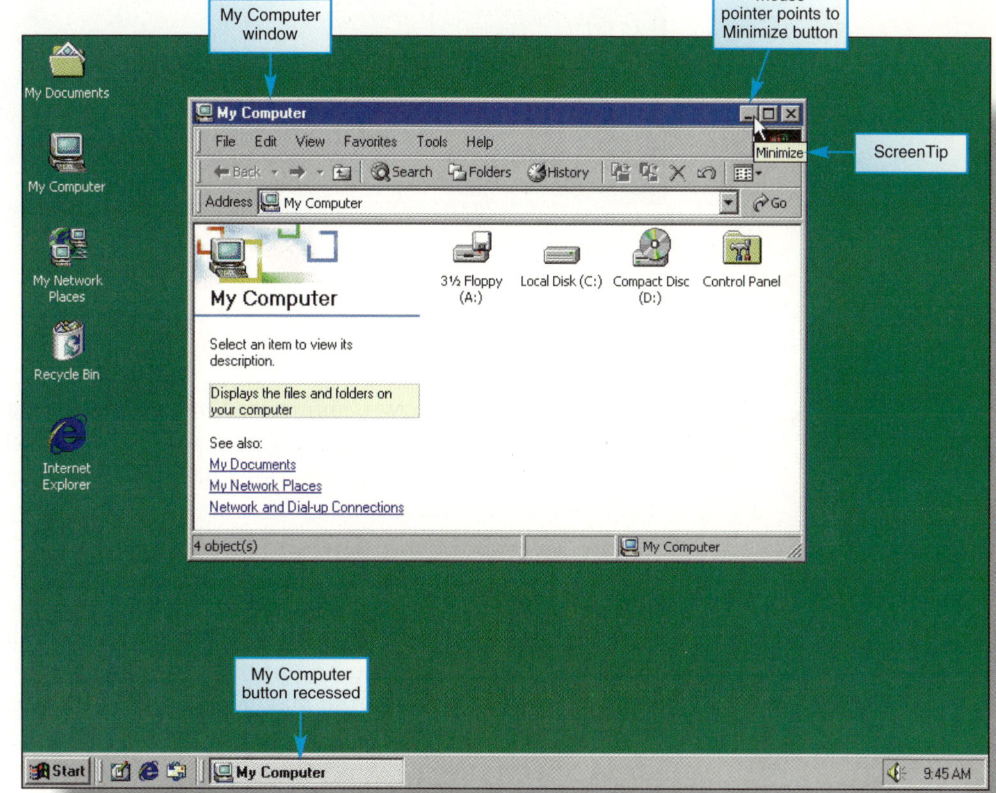

FIGURE 1-14

2 Click the Minimize button.

When you minimize the My Computer window, Windows removes the My Computer window from the desktop and the My Computer button changes to a non-recessed button (Figure 1-15).

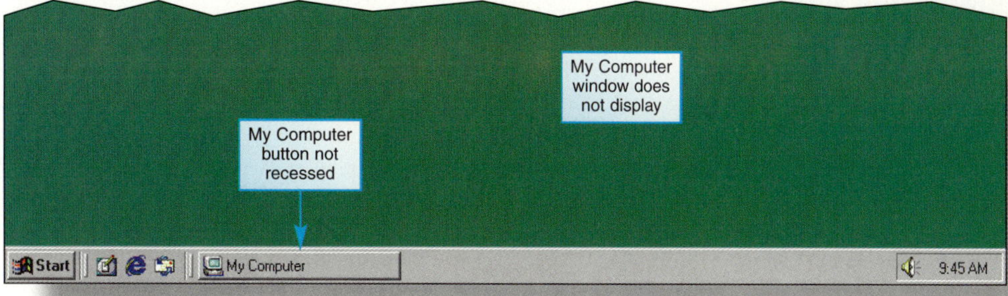

FIGURE 1-15

3 **Click the My Computer button in the taskbar button area.**

The My Computer window displays on the desktop in the same place and size as it was before being minimized (Figure 1-16). In addition, the My Computer window is the active window because it contains the dark blue title bar, and the My Computer button in the taskbar button area is recessed.

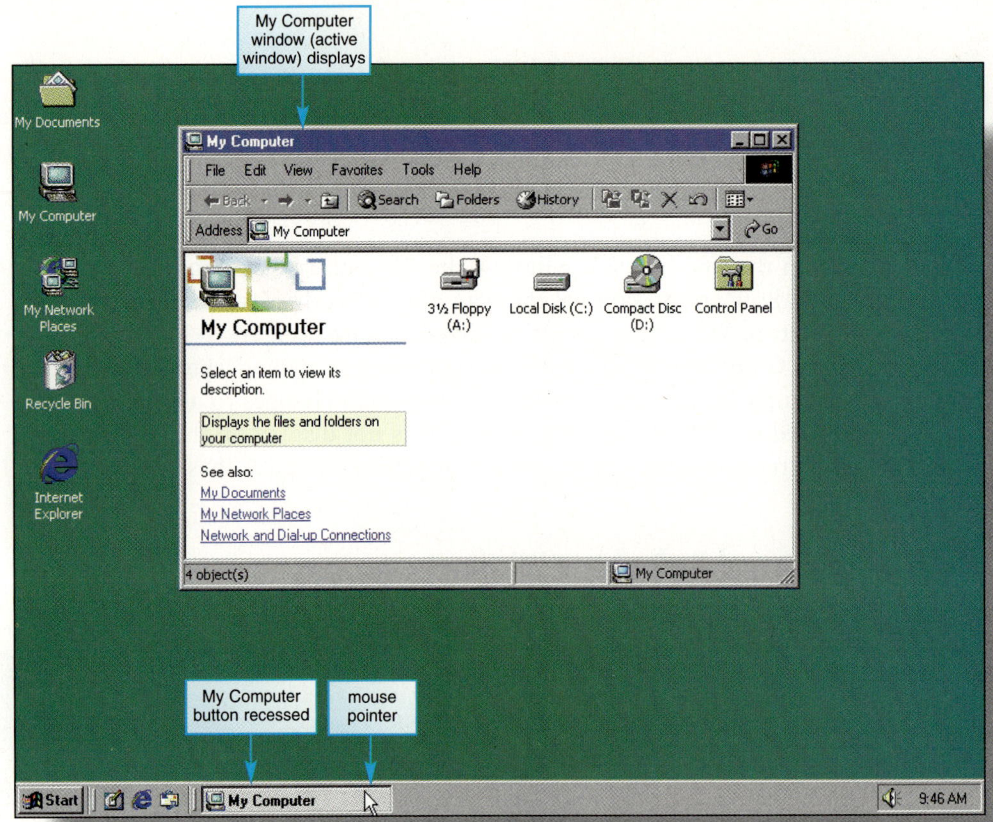

FIGURE 1-16

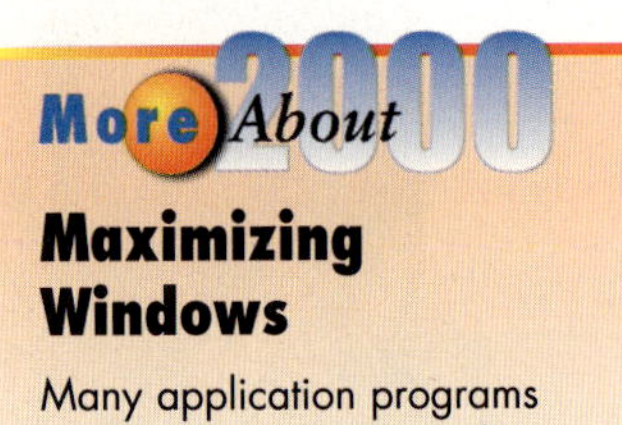

Maximizing Windows

Many application programs run in a maximized window by default. Often you will find that you want to work with maximized windows.

Minimizing and Maximizing Windows

Many users believe it is easier to double-click the title bar to minimize or maximize a window instead of clicking the Minimize and Maximize button on the title bar.

Whenever a window is minimized, it does not display on the desktop but a non-recessed button for the window does display in the taskbar button area. Whenever you want a minimized window to display and be the active window, click its button in the taskbar button area.

Maximize and Restore Down Buttons

Sometimes when information is displayed in a window, the information is not completely visible. One method of displaying the entire contents of a window is to enlarge the window using the **Maximize button**. The Maximize button maximizes a window so that it fills the entire screen, making it easier to see the contents of the window. When a window is maximized, the **Restore Down button** replaces the Maximize button on the title bar. Clicking the Restore Down button will return the window to its size before maximizing. To maximize and restore the My Computer window, complete the following steps.

To Maximize and Restore a Window

1 Point to the Maximize button on the title bar of the My Computer window (Figure 1-17).

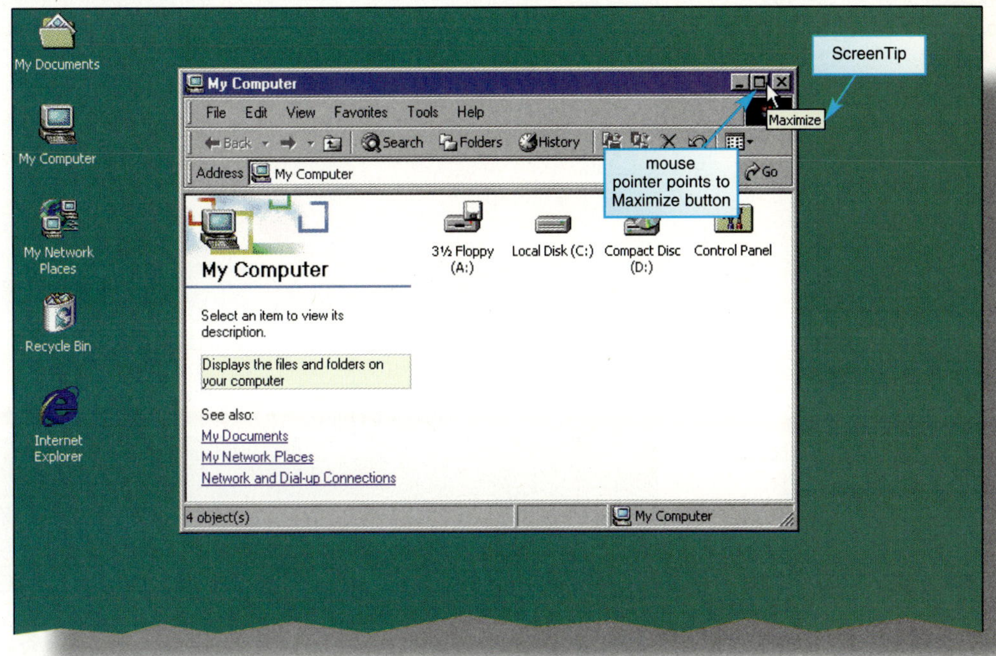

FIGURE 1-17

2 Click the Maximize button.

The My Computer window expands so it and the taskbar fill the entire screen (Figure 1-18). The Restore Down button replaces the Maximize button and the My Computer button in the taskbar button area remains recessed. The My Computer window still is the active window.

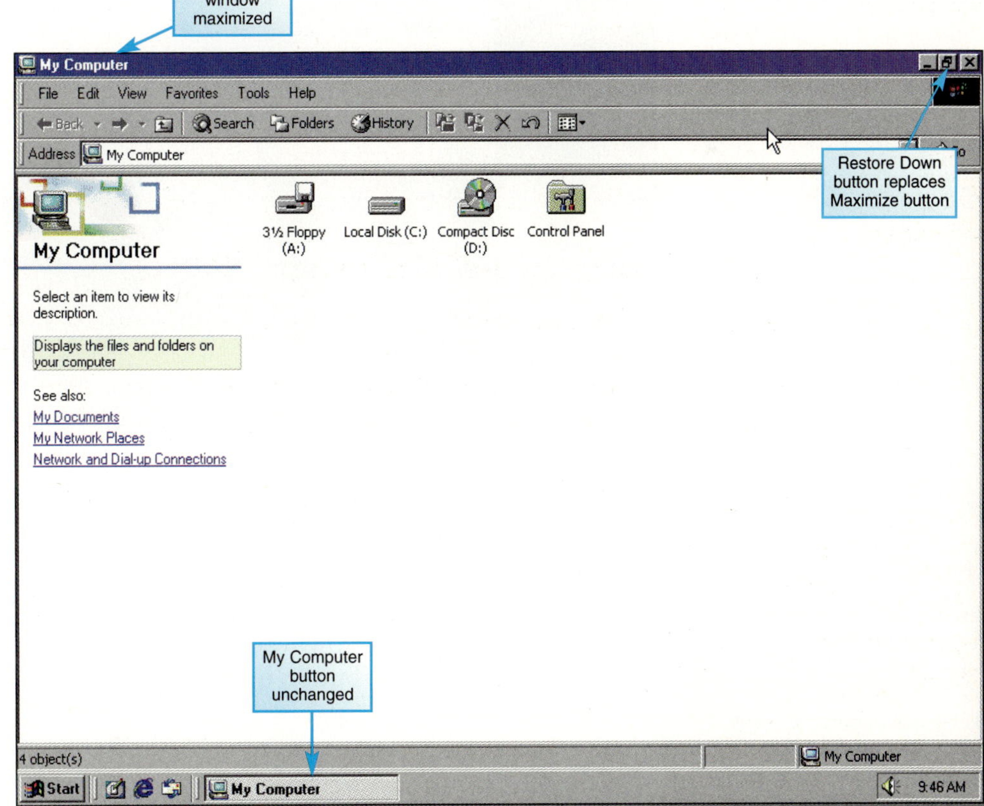

FIGURE 1-18

3 **Point to the Restore Down button on the title bar of the My Computer window (Figure 1-19).**

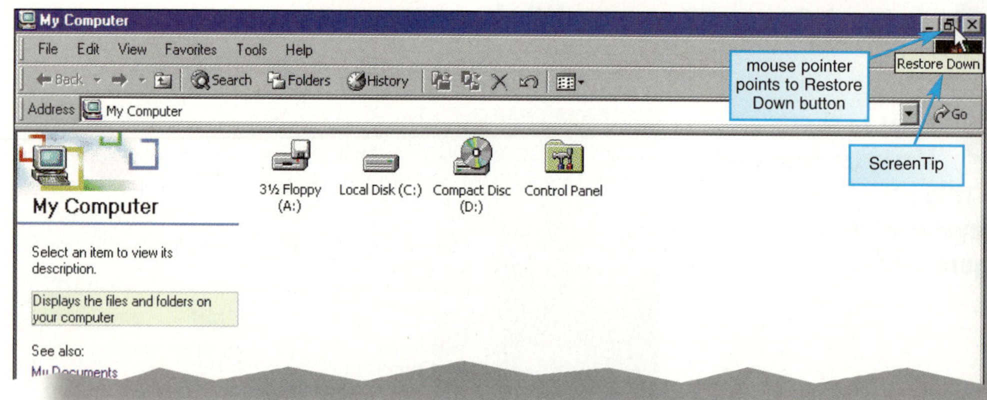

FIGURE 1-19

Click the Restore Down button.

The My Computer window returns to the size and position it occupied before being maximized (Figure 1-20). The My Computer button does not change. The Maximize button replaces the Restore Down button.

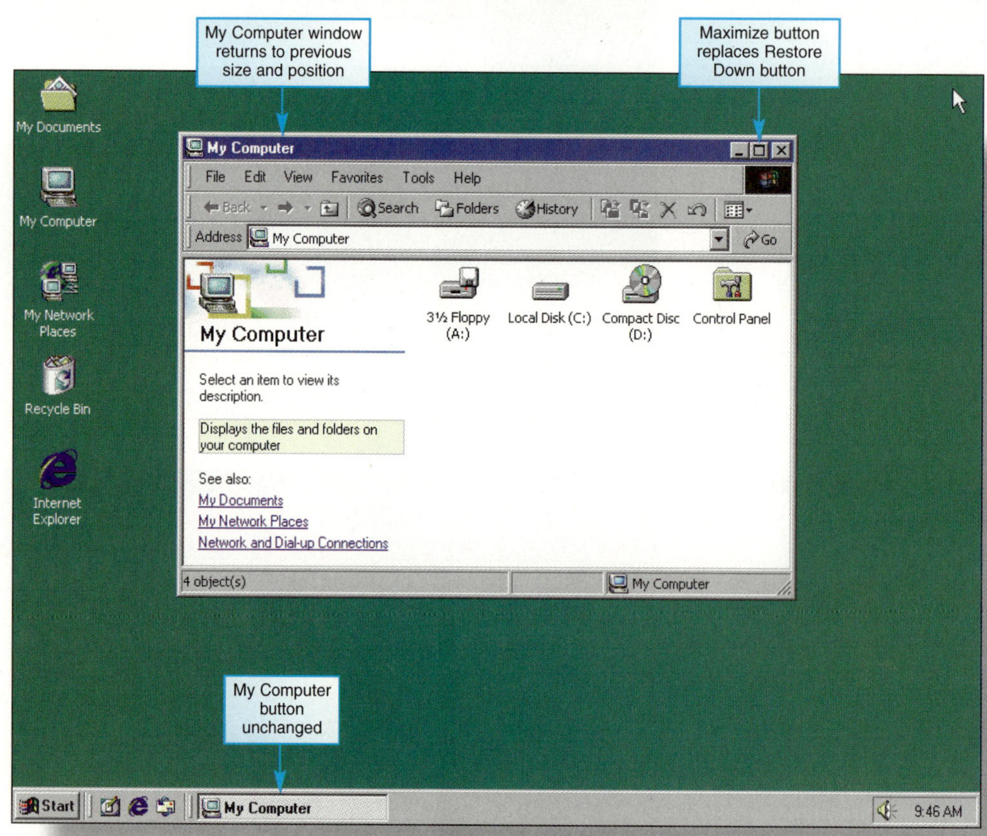

FIGURE 1-20

The Close Button

The Close button was a new innovation in Windows 95. Before Windows 95, the user had to double-click a button or click a command on a menu to close the window. As always, the choice of how to perform an operation such as closing a window is a matter of personal preference. In most cases, you will want to choose the easiest method.

When a window is maximized, as shown in Figure 1-18 on the previous page, you can minimize the window by clicking the Minimize button. If, after minimizing the window, you click its button in the taskbar button area, the window will return to its maximized size.

Close Button

The Close button on the title bar of a window closes the window and removes the window button from the taskbar. To close and then reopen the My Computer window, complete the following steps.

To Close a Window and Reopen a Window

1 Point to the Close button on the title bar of the My Computer window (Figure 1-21).

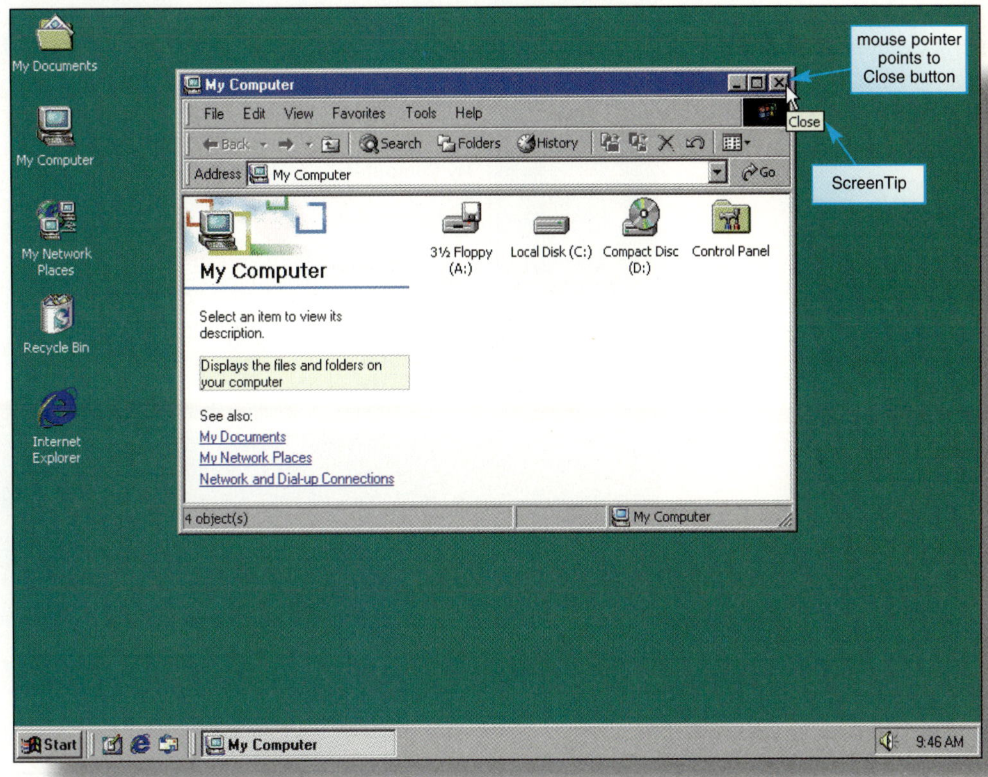

FIGURE 1-21

2 Click the Close button.

The My Computer window closes and the My Computer button no longer displays in the taskbar button area (Figure 1-22).

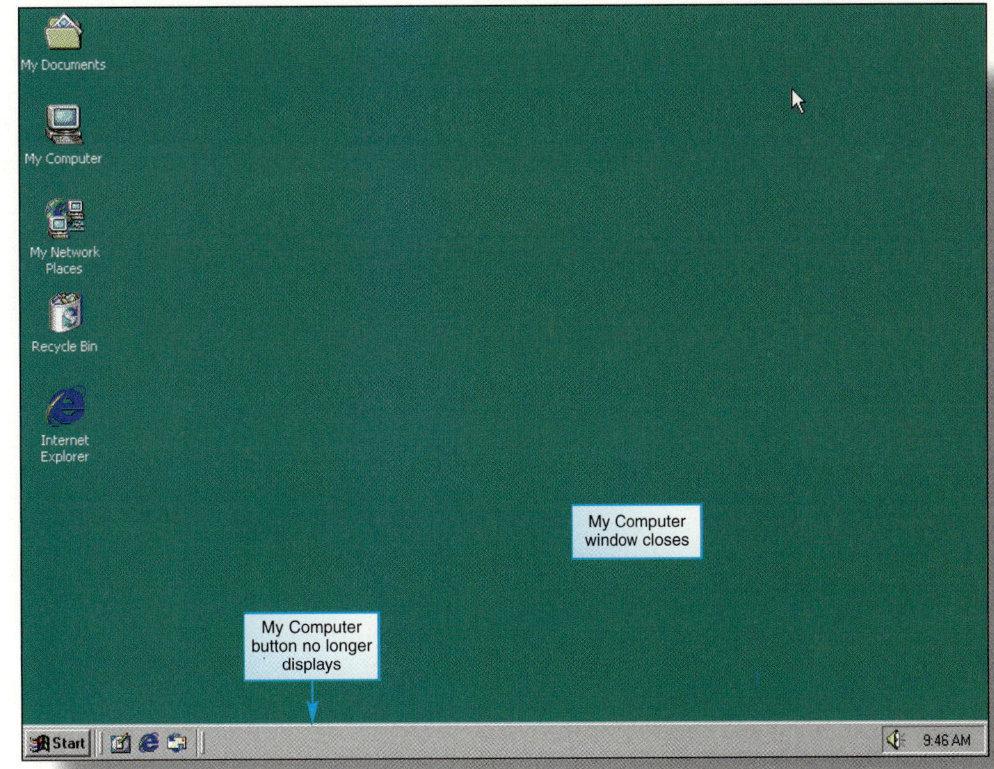

FIGURE 1-22

3 Double-click the My Computer icon on the desktop.

The My Computer window opens and displays on the screen (Figure 1-23). The My Computer button displays in the taskbar button area.

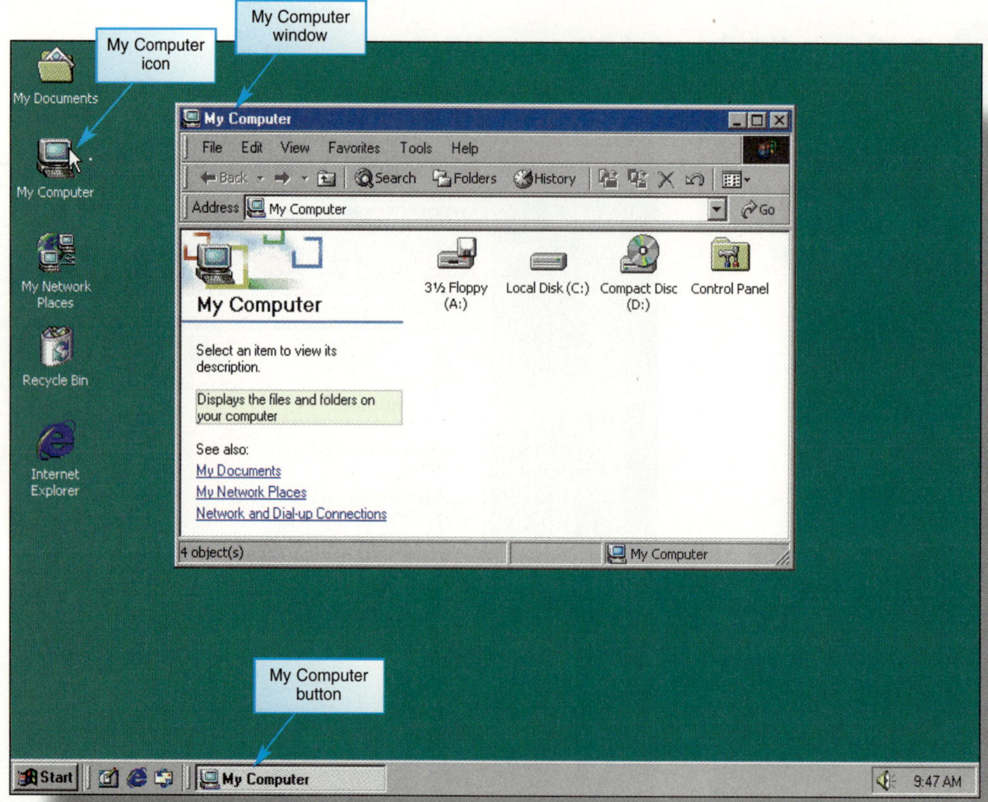

FIGURE 1-23

Dragging

Dragging is the second-most difficult skill to learn with a mouse. You may want to practice dragging a few times so you are comfortable with it.

Drag

Drag means you point to an item, hold down the left mouse button, move the item to the desired location, and then release the left mouse button. You can move any open window to another location on the desktop by pointing to the title bar of the window and dragging the window. To drag the My Computer window to another location on the desktop, perform the following steps.

To Move an Object by Dragging

1 Point to the My Computer window title bar (Figure 1-24).

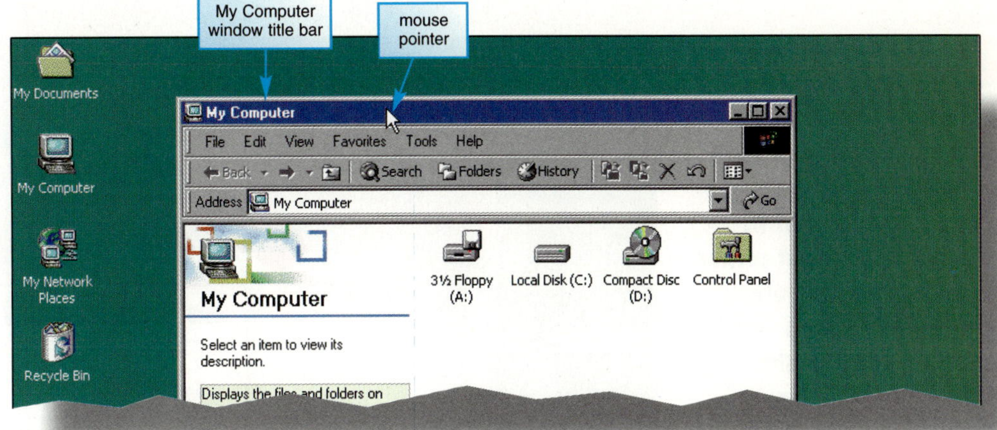

FIGURE 1-24

2 Hold down the left mouse button, move the mouse so the window moves to the center of the desktop, and then release the left mouse button.

As you drag the mouse, the My Computer window moves across the desktop. When you release the left mouse button, the window displays in its new location (Figure 1-25).

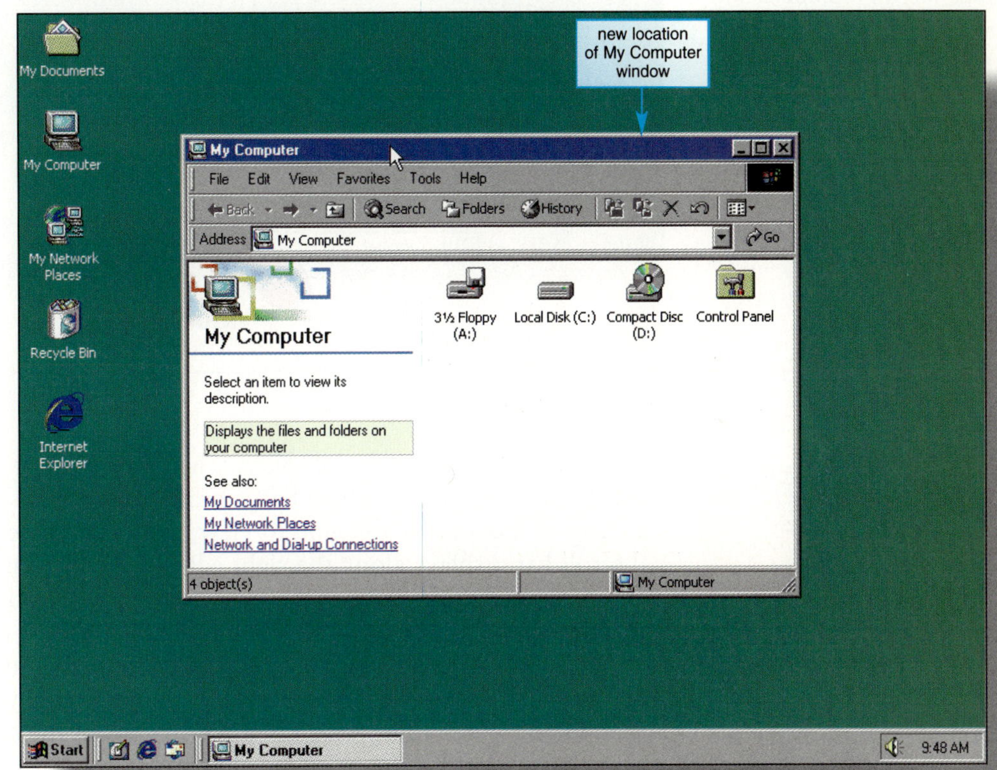

FIGURE 1-25

Sizing a Window by Dragging

You can use dragging for more than just moving an object. For example, you can drag the border of a window to change the size of the window. To change the size of the My Computer window, perform the step on the next page.

To Size a Window by Dragging

1 Position the mouse pointer over the lower-right corner of the My Computer window until the mouse pointer changes to a two-headed arrow. Drag the lower-right corner upward and to the left until the window on your desktop resembles the window shown in Figure 1-26.

As you drag the lower-right corner, the My Computer window changes size, the icons in the right panel display in two rows, a vertical scroll bar displays in the left panel, and a portion of the text in the left panel is not visible (Figure 1-26).

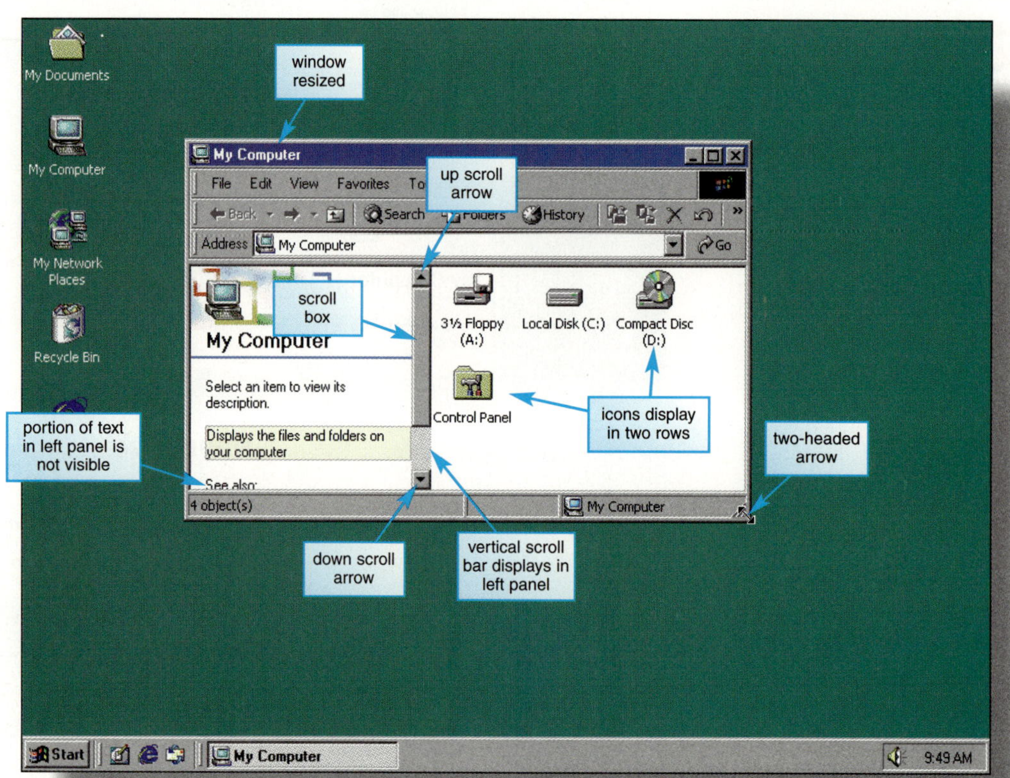

FIGURE 1-26

Window Sizing

Windows 2000 remembers the size of the window when you close the window. When you reopen the window, it will display in the same size as when you closed it.

A **scroll bar** is a bar that displays when the contents of a window are not completely visible. A vertical scroll bar contains an **up scroll arrow**, a **down scroll arrow**, and a **scroll box** that enable you to view areas that currently are not visible. A vertical scroll bar displays along the right edge of the left panel of the My Computer window shown in Figure 1-26. In some cases, vertical scroll bar also may display along the right edge of the right panel of a window.

The size of the scroll box is dependent on the amount of the panel that is visible. The larger the scroll box, the more of the panel that is visible. In Figure 1-26, the scroll box occupies approximately three-fourths of the scroll bar. This indicates that approximately three-fourths of the contents of the left panel are visible. If the scroll box were a tiny rectangle, a large portion of the panel would not be visible.

In addition to dragging a corner of a window, you also can drag any of the borders of a window. If you drag a vertical border, such as the right border, you can move the border left or right. If you drag a horizontal border, such as the bottom border, you can move the border of the window up or down.

As mentioned earlier, maximizing a window is one method of enlarging a window and displaying more information. Dragging a window to enlarge the window is a second method of displaying information in a window that is not visible.

Scrolling

Most people will either maximize a window or size it so all the objects in the window are visible to avoid scrolling because scrolling takes time. It is more efficient not to have to scroll in a window.

Scrolling in a Window

Previously, two methods were shown to display information that was not completely visible in the My Computer window. These methods were maximizing the My Computer window and changing the size of the My Computer window. A third method uses a scroll bar.

Scrolling can be accomplished in three ways: (1) click the scroll arrows; (2) click the scroll bar; and (3) drag the scroll box. Perform the following steps to scroll the left panel of the My Computer window using the scroll arrows.

To Scroll a Window Using Scroll Arrows

1. **Point to the down scroll arrow on the vertical scroll bar (Figure 1-27).**

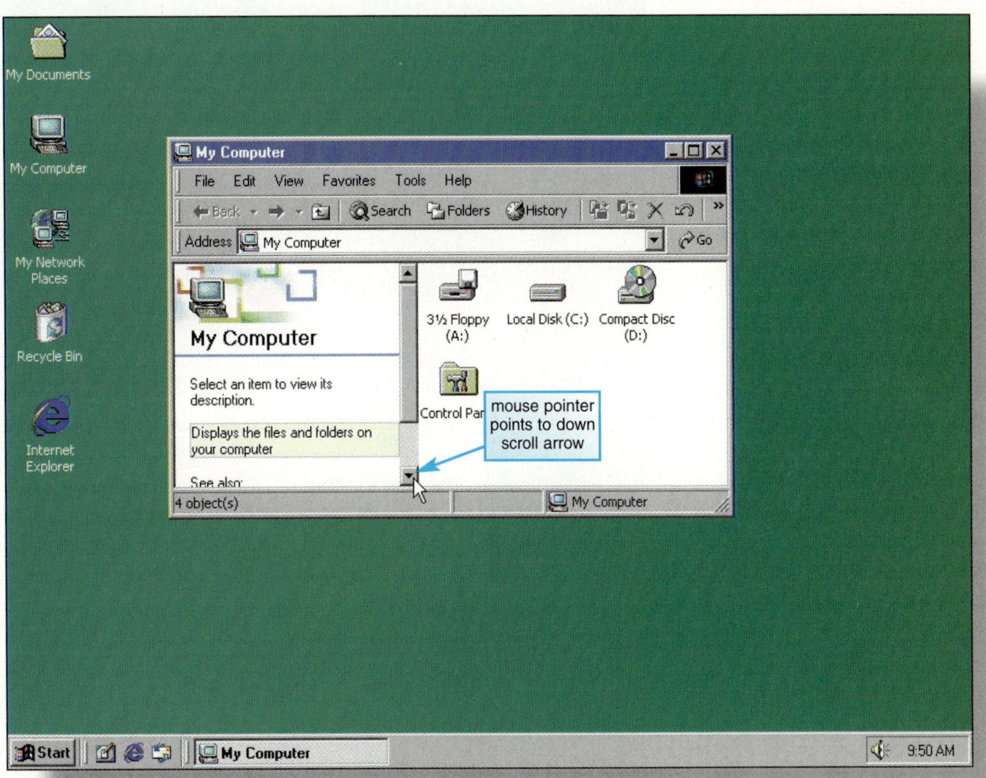

FIGURE 1-27

Click the down scroll arrow one time.

The left panel scrolls down (the contents in the left panel move up) and displays text at the bottom of the left panel that previously was not visible (Figure 1-28). Because the size of the left panel does not change when you scroll, the contents in the left panel will change.

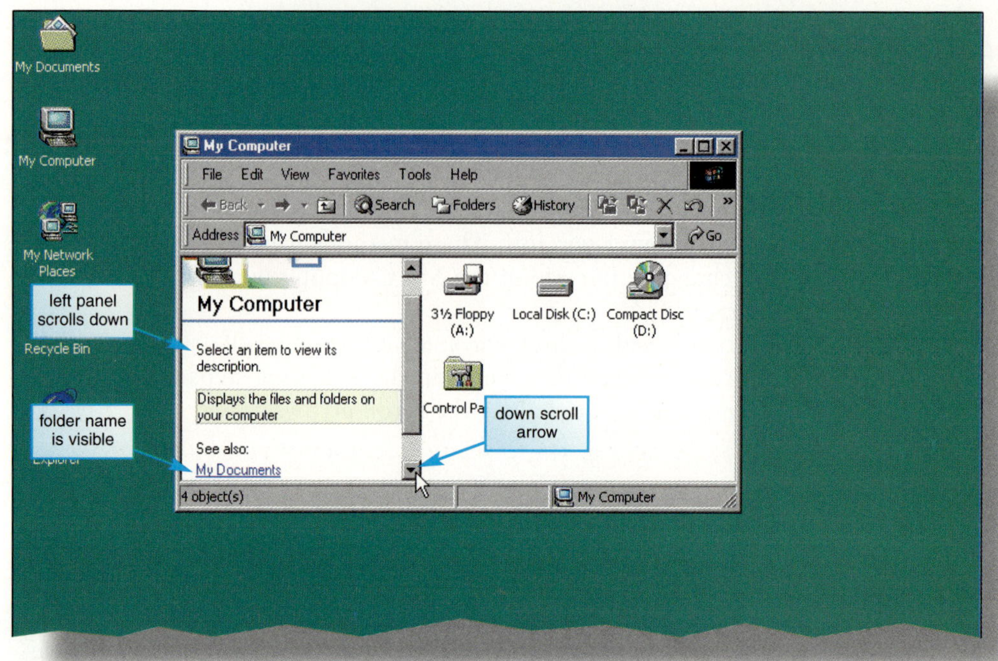

FIGURE 1-28

Click the down scroll arrow two more times.

The scroll box moves to the bottom of the scroll bar and the remaining folder names in the left panel display (Figure 1-29).

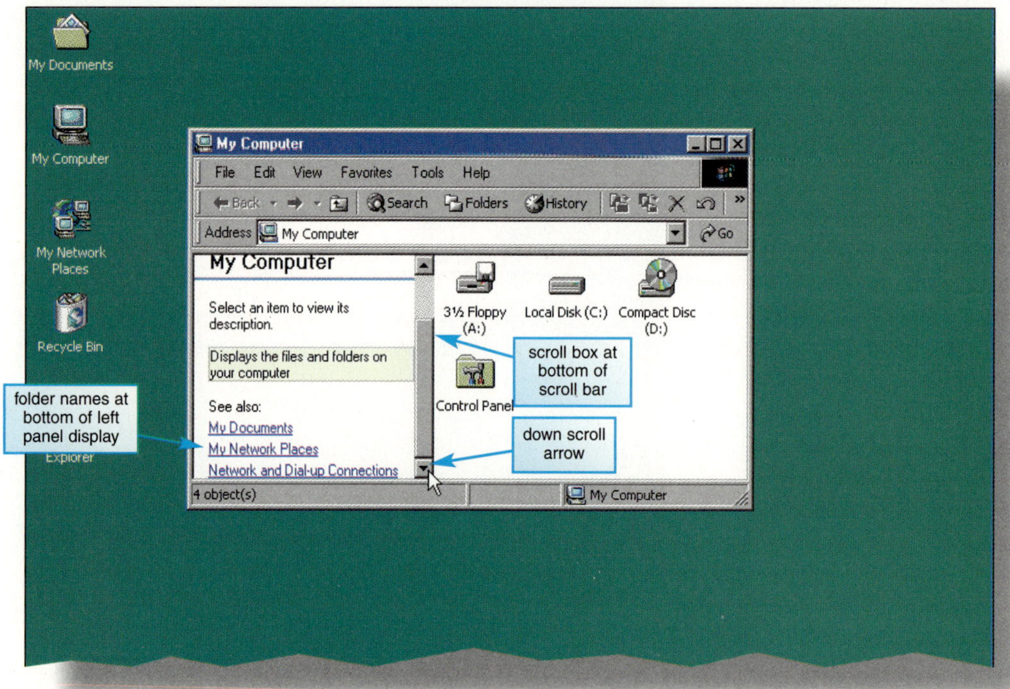

FIGURE 1-29

You can scroll continuously using scroll arrows by pointing to the up or down scroll arrow and holding down the left mouse button. The area being scrolled continues to scroll until you release the left mouse button or you reach the top or bottom of the area. You also can scroll by clicking the scroll bar itself. When you click the scroll bar, the area being scrolled moves up or down a greater distance than when you click the scroll arrows.

The third way in which you can scroll is by dragging the scroll box. When you drag the scroll box, the area being scrolled moves up or down as you drag.

Being able to view the contents of a panel by scrolling is an important Windows 2000 skill because in many cases, the entire contents of a panel are not visible.

Resizing a Window

After moving and resizing a window, you may wish to return the window to approximately its original size. To return the My Computer window to about its original size, complete the following steps.

TO RESIZE A WINDOW

1. Position the mouse pointer over the lower-right corner of the My Computer window border until the mouse pointer changes to a two-headed arrow.
2. Drag the lower-right corner of the My Computer window until the window is the same size as shown in Figure 1-25 on page INT 1.21, and then release the mouse button.

The My Computer window is approximately the same size as it was before you made it smaller.

Closing a Window

After you have completed your work in a window, normally you will close the window. To close the My Computer window, complete the following steps.

TO CLOSE A WINDOW

1. Point to the Close button on the right of the title bar in the My Computer window.
2. Click the Close button.

The My Computer window closes and the desktop does not contain any open windows.

Right-Drag

Right-drag means you point to an item, hold down the right mouse button, move the item to the desired location, and then release the right mouse button. When you right-drag an object, a shortcut menu displays. The shortcut menu contains commands specifically for use with the object being dragged. To right-drag the Launch Outlook Express icon on the Quick Launch toolbar below the icons on the desktop, perform the steps on the next page. If the Launch Outlook Express icon does not display on the Quick Launch toolbar, choose another icon and follow the procedure in the steps.

More About 2000

The Scroll Bar

In many application programs, clicking the scroll bar will move the window a full screen's worth of information up or down. You can step through a word processing document screen by screen, for example, by clicking the scroll bar.

More About 2000

The Scroll Box

Dragging the scroll box is the most efficient technique to scroll long distances. In many application programs, such as Microsoft Word, as you scroll using the scroll box, the page number of the document displays next to the scroll box.

More About 2000

Scrolling Guidelines

General scrolling guidelines: (1) To scroll short distances (line by line), click the scroll arrows; (2) To scroll one screen at a time, click the scroll bar; and (3) To scroll long distances, drag the scroll box.

More About 2000

Right-Dragging

Right-dragging was not available on some earlier versions of Windows, so you might find people familiar with Windows not even considering right-dragging. Because it always produces a shortcut menu, however, right-dragging is the safest way to drag.

To Right-Drag

1 Point to the Launch Outlook Express icon on the Quick Launch toolbar, hold down the right mouse button, drag the icon below the other icons on the desktop, and then release the right mouse button.

The dimmed Launch Outlook Express icon and a shortcut menu display on the desktop (Figure 1-30). A dimmed Launch Outlook Express icon remains at its original location. The shortcut menu contains four commands: Copy Here, Move Here, Create Shortcut(s) Here, and Cancel. The Move Here command in bold (dark) type identifies what would happen if you were to drag the Launch Outlook Express icon with the left mouse button.

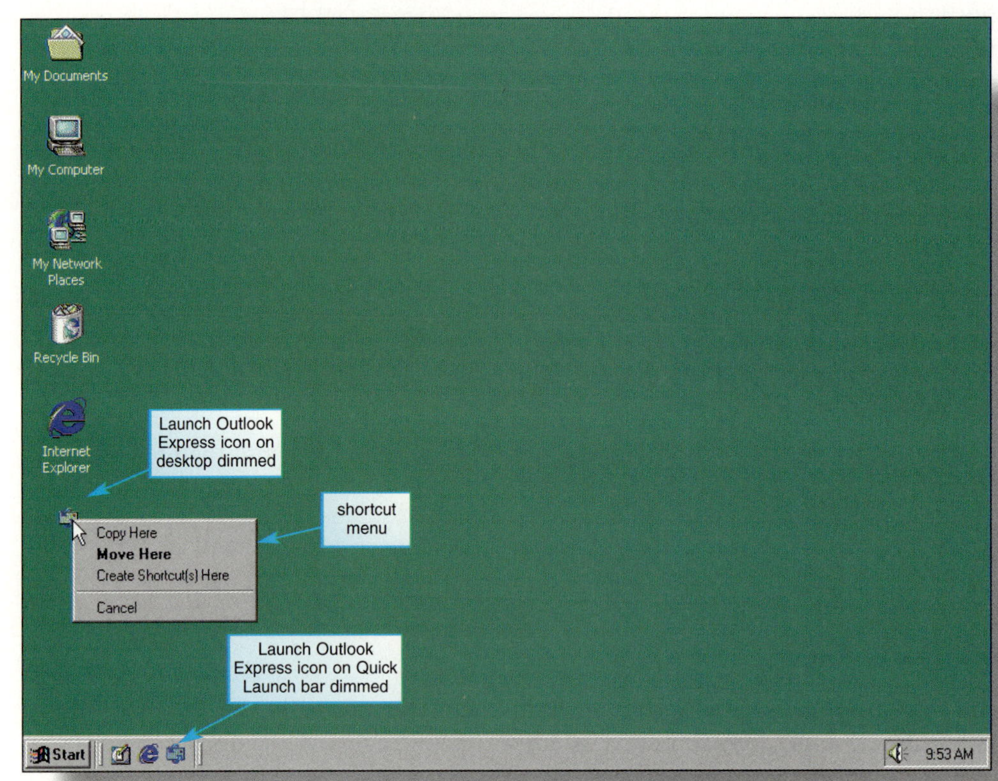

FIGURE 1-30

Point to Cancel on the shortcut menu.

The Cancel command is highlighted (Figure 1-31).

Click Cancel.

The shortcut menu and the dragged Launch Outlook Express icon disappear from the desktop.

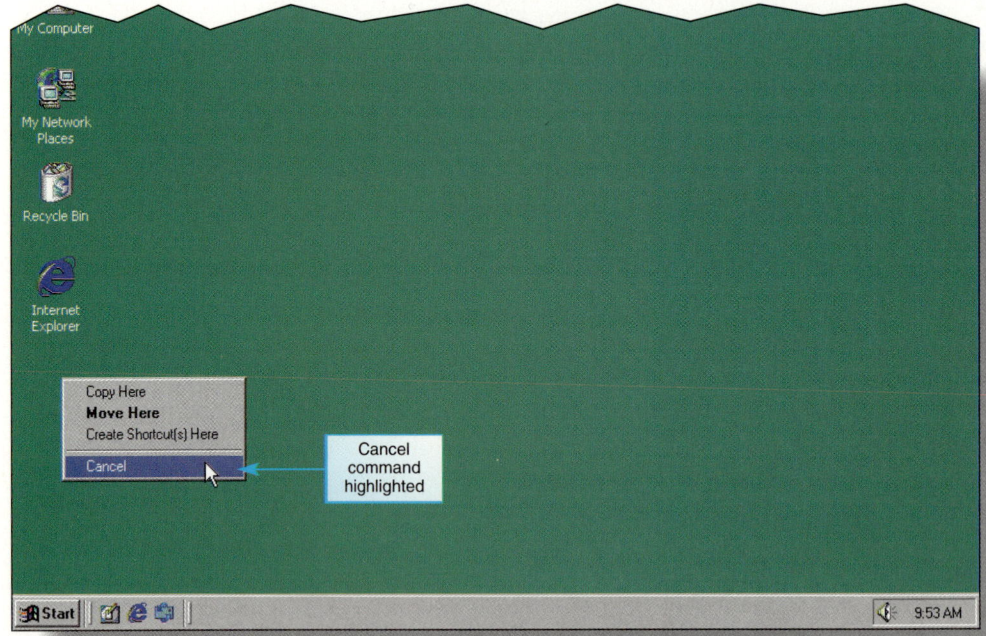

FIGURE 1-31

Whenever you begin an operation but do not want to complete it, you can click Cancel on a shortcut menu or click the Cancel button in a dialog box. The **Cancel** command will reset anything you have done in the operation.

If you click **Move Here** on the shortcut menu shown in Figure 1-30, Windows 2000 will move the icon from its current location to the new location. If you click **Copy Here**, a special object called a shortcut will be created on the desktop and the original icon will display on the Quick Launch toolbar. If you click **Create Shortcut(s) Here**, a shortcut also will be created on the desktop.

Although you can move icons by dragging with the primary (left) mouse button and by right-dragging with the secondary (right) mouse button, it is strongly suggested you right-drag because a menu displays and you can specify the exact operation you want to occur. When you drag using the left mouse button, a default operation takes place and the result may not be what you want.

The Microsoft Keyboard

The Microsoft keyboard in Figure 1-32b not only has special keys for Windows 2000, but also is designed ergonomically so you type with your hands apart. It takes a little time to get used to, but several authors on the Shelly Cashman Series writing team report they type faster with more accuracy and less fatigue when using the keyboard.

Summary of Mouse and Windows Operations

You have seen how to use the mouse to point, click, right-click, double-click, drag, and right-drag in order to accomplish certain tasks on the desktop. The use of a mouse is an important skill when using Windows 2000. In addition, you have learned how to move around and display windows on the Windows 2000 desktop.

The Keyboard and Keyboard Shortcuts

The **keyboard** is an input device on which you manually key, or type, data. Figure 1-32a shows the enhanced IBM 101-key keyboard, and Figure 1-32b shows a Microsoft Natural keyboard designed specifically for use with Windows. Many tasks you accomplish with a mouse also can be accomplished using a keyboard.

FIGURE 1-32a

FIGURE 1-32b

To perform tasks using the keyboard, you must understand the notation used to identify which keys to press. This notation is used throughout Windows 2000 to identify **keyboard shortcuts**.

Keyboard shortcuts consist of: (1) pressing a single key (press the F1 key); or (2) pressing and holding down one key and then pressing a second key, as shown by two key names separated by a plus sign (CTRL+ESC). For example, to obtain Help about Windows 2000, you can press the F1 key; to open the Start menu, hold down the CTRL key and then press the ESC key (press CTRL+ESC).

Often, computer users will use keyboard shortcuts for operations they perform frequently. For example, many users find pressing the F1 key to launch Windows 2000 Help easier than using the Start menu as shown later in this project. As a user, you probably will find the combination of keyboard and mouse operations that particularly suit you, but it is strongly recommended that generally you use the mouse.

More About 2000

Application Programs

Some application programs, such as Internet Explorer, are part of Windows 2000. Most application programs, however, such as Microsoft Office, Lotus SmartSuite, and others must be purchased separately from Windows 2000.

Launching an Application Program

One of the basic tasks you can perform using Windows 2000 is to launch an application program. A **program** is a set of computer instructions that carries out a task on your computer. An **application program** is a program that allows you to accomplish the specific task, or tasks, for which that program is designed. For example, a **word processing program** is an application program that allows you to create written documents; a **presentation graphics program** is an application program that allows you to create graphic presentations for display on a computer; and a **Web browser program** is an application program that allows you to search for and display Web pages.

The most common activity on a computer is to launch an application program to accomplish tasks using the computer. You can launch an application program in a variety of ways. When several methods are available to accomplish a task, a computer user has the opportunity to try various methods and select the method that best fits his or her needs.

Launching an Application Using the Start Button

One method of launching an application program is to use the Start menu. Perform the following steps to launch Internet Explorer using the Start menu and Internet Explorer command.

To Launch a Program Using the Start Menu

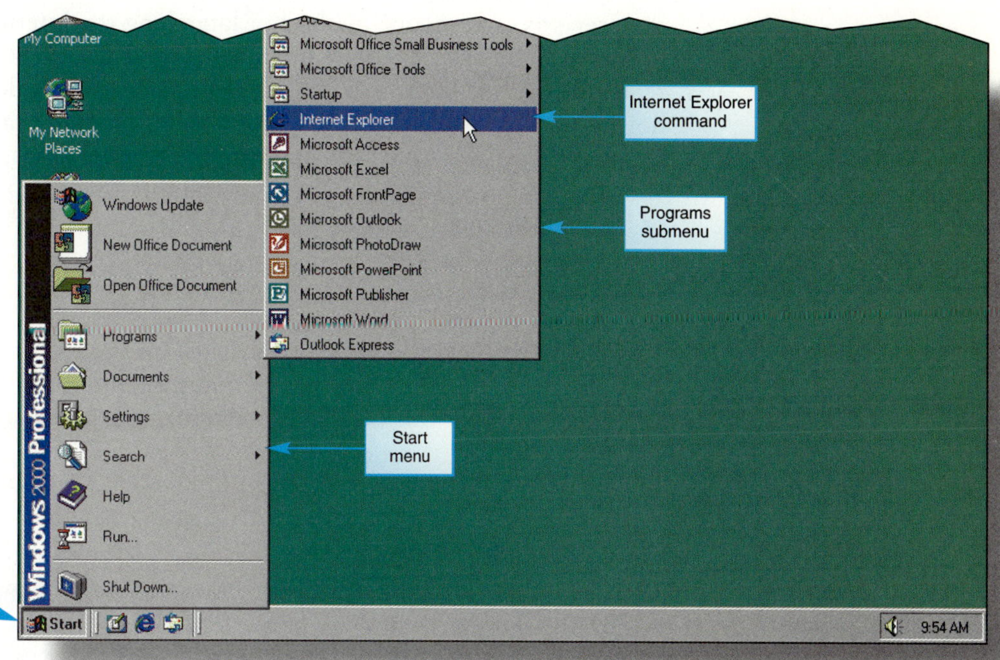

FIGURE 1-33

1 **Click the Start button on the taskbar, point to Programs on the Start menu, and then point to Internet Explorer on the Programs submenu.**

The Start menu and Programs submenu display (Figure 1-33). The Programs submenu contains the Internet Explorer command to launch the Internet Explorer program. You might find more, fewer, or different commands on the Start menu and Programs submenu on your computer.

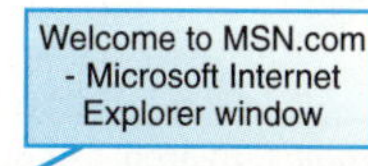

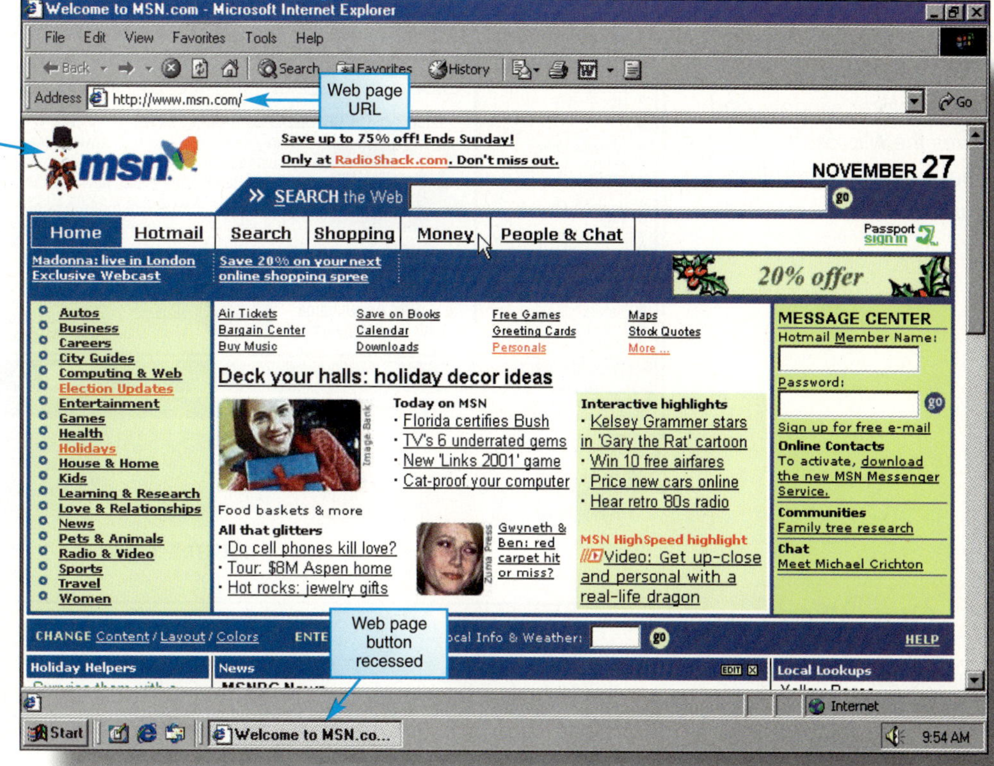

FIGURE 1-34

2 **Click Internet Explorer.**

Windows 2000 launches the Internet Explorer program by opening the Welcome to MSN.com window on the desktop, displaying the MSN Web page in the window, and adding a recessed button to the taskbar button area (Figure 1-34). The URL for the Web page displays on the Address bar. Because Web pages change frequently, the Web page that displays on your desktop may be different.

Other Ways

1. Click Launch Internet Explorer Browser icon on Quick Launch toolbar
2. Double-click Internet Explorer icon on desktop
3. Press CTRL+ESC, press P, press I

After you have launched Internet Explorer, you can use the program to search for and display different Web pages.

Windows 2000 provides a number of ways to accomplish a particular task. In the previous section, one method of launching the Internet Explorer program was illustrated, and then alternate methods were listed in the Other Ways box. The remainder of this book will use the same format: a single set of steps will illustrate how to accomplish a task; and if you can perform the same task using other methods, the Other Ways box will specify the other methods. In each case, the method shown in the steps is the preferred method, but it is important for you to be aware of all the techniques you can use.

Quitting a Program

When you have completed your work using a program, you should quit the program. Perform the following steps to quit the Internet Explorer program.

To Quit a Program

1 Point to the Close button in the Internet Explorer window (Figure 1-35).

2 Click the Close button.

Windows 2000 quits Internet Explorer, closes the Microsoft Internet Explorer window, and removes the Microsoft Internet Explorer button from the taskbar.

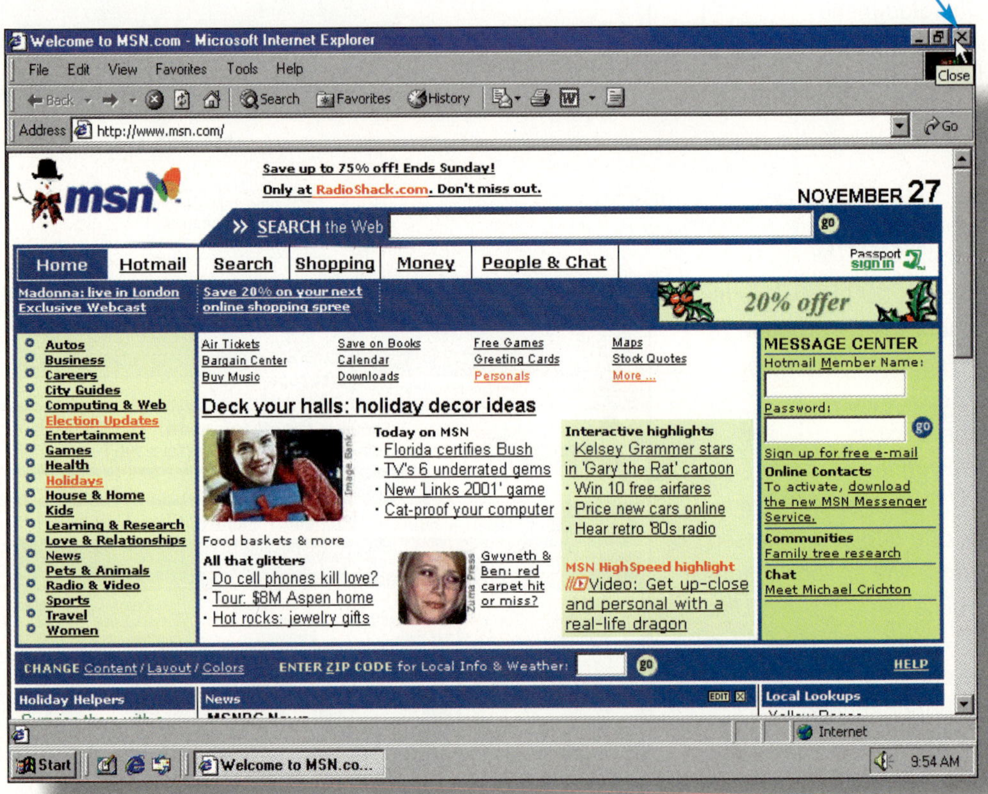

FIGURE 1-35

Other Ways

1. Double-click Internet Explorer logo at left on title bar
2. On File menu click Close
3. Press ALT+F4

In the preceding sections, you launched Internet Explorer and then quit the Internet Explorer program. In the next section, you will launch the Windows Explorer application program.

Windows Explorer

Windows Explorer is an application program included with Windows 2000 that allows you to view the contents of the computer, the hierarchy of folders on the computer, and the files and folders in each folder.

Windows Explorer also allows you to organize the files and folders on the computer by copying, moving, and deleting the files and folders. In this project, you will use Windows Explorer to (1) work with the files and folders on your computer; (2) select and copy a group of files between the hard drive and a floppy disk; (3) create, name, and delete a folder on a floppy disk; and (4) rename and delete a file on a floppy disk. These are common operations that you should understand how to perform.

Starting Windows Explorer and Maximizing Its Window

To explore the files and folders on the computer, launch Windows Explorer and maximize its window by performing the following steps.

To Start Windows Explorer and Maximize Its Window

1 Right-click the My Computer icon on the desktop and then point to Explore on the shortcut menu.

A shortcut menu displays (Figure 1-36). The Explore command will launch Windows Explorer.

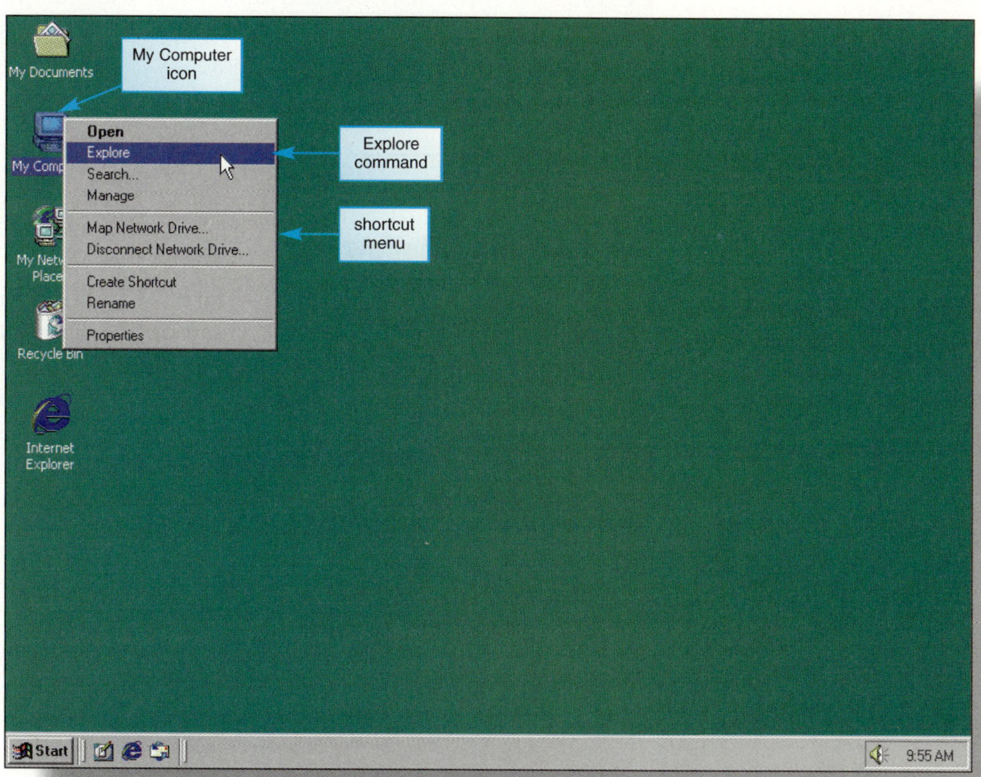

FIGURE 1-36

2 Click Explore and then click the Maximize button on the My Computer title bar.

The My Computer window opens and is maximized. The recessed My Computer button is added to the taskbar button area (Figure 1-37).

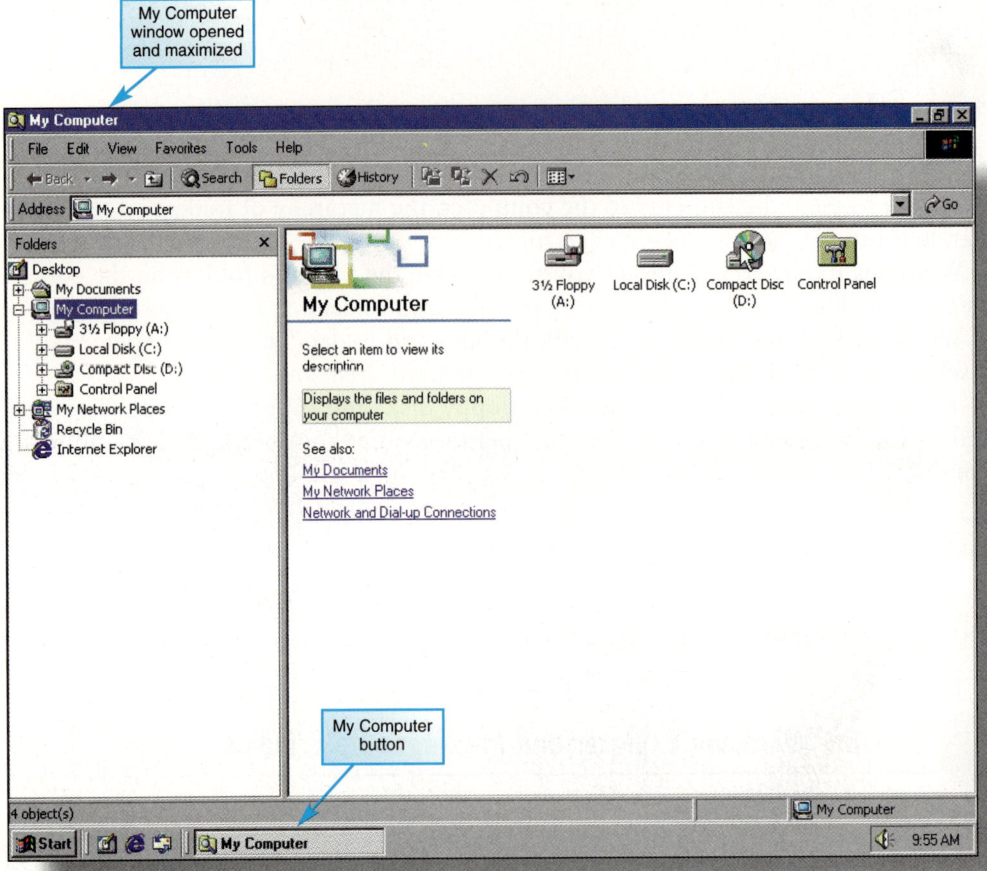

FIGURE 1-37

Other Ways

1. Right-click Start button or any icon on desktop (except Internet Explorer), click Explore on shortcut menu
2. Click Start button, point to Programs, point to Accessories, click Windows Explorer
3. Double-click My Computer icon, click Folders button on Standard Buttons toolbar

The Exploring Window

When you launch Windows Explorer by right-clicking the My Computer icon and then clicking the Explore command on the shortcut menu, Windows 2000 opens the Exploring window (My Computer window) shown in Figure 1-38. The title bar in the window is the same as seen in other windows, and the menu bar contains the File, Edit, View, Favorites, Tools, and Help menu names. These menus contain commands to organize and work with the drives on the computer and the files and folders on those drives. The Standard Buttons toolbar and Address bar display respectively below the menu bar.

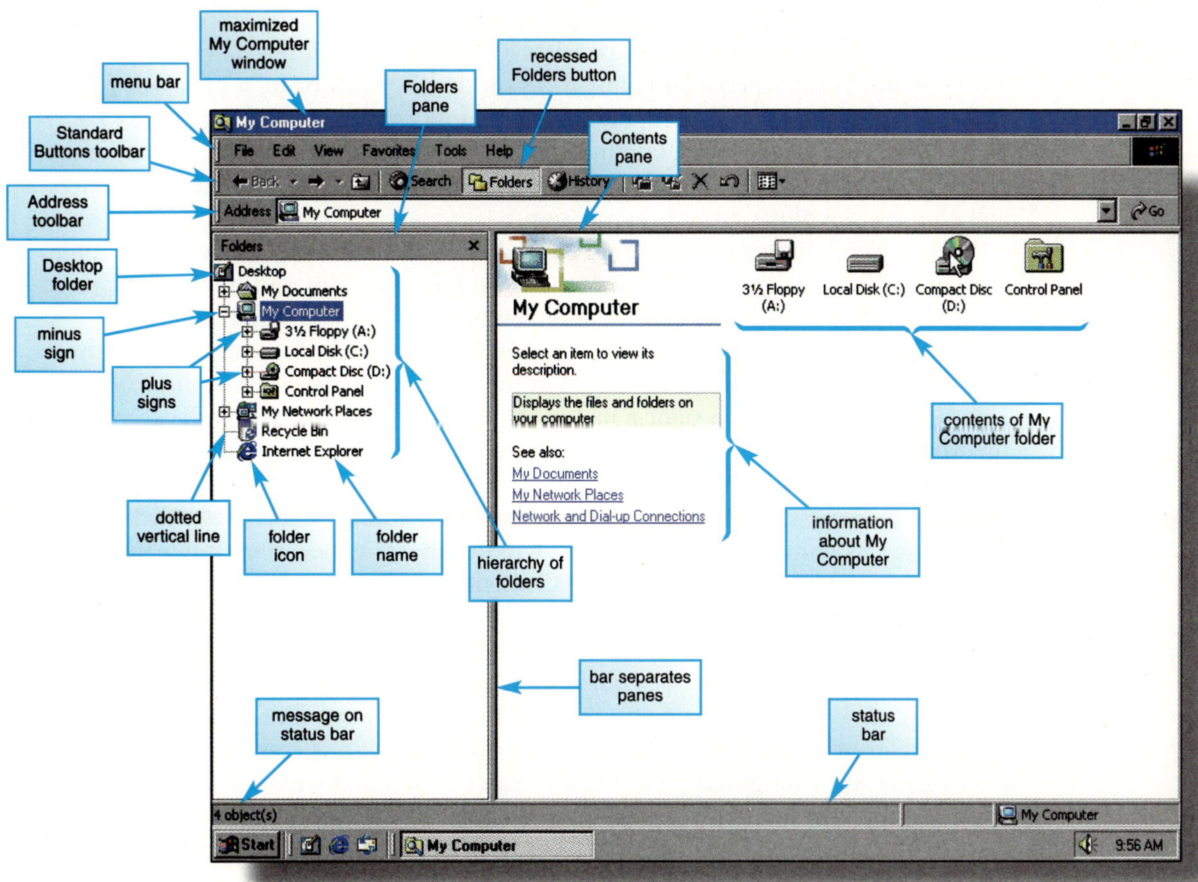

FIGURE 1-38

The main window consists of two panes – the Folders pane on the left and the Contents pane on the right. A bar separates the panes. You can change the size of the Folders and Contents panes by dragging the bar that separates the two panes.

In the **Folders pane**, Explorer displays in **hierarchical structure**, the icons and folder names on the computer. The top level in the hierarchy is the Desktop. Connected by a dotted vertical line below the Desktop are the icons that display on the desktop (My Documents, My Computer, My Network Places, Recycle Bin and Internet Explorer). Your computer may have other icons. Clicking the recessed Folders button on the Standard Buttons toolbar removes the Folders pane from the window, making the My Computer window identical to the My Computer window shown in Figure 1-18 on page INT 1.17.

Windows 2000 displays a **minus sign** (–) in a small box to the left of an icon in the Folders pane to indicate the corresponding folder contains one or more folders that are visible in the Folders pane. These folders, called **subfolders**, are indented and aligned below the folder name. In Figure 1-38, a minus sign (–) precedes the My Computer icon, and four subfolders are indented and display below the My Computer folder name. The four subfolders (3½ Floppy (A:), Local Disk (C:), Compact Disc (D:), and Control Panel) are the four subfolders in the My Computer folder and correspond to the four folders in the Contents pane. Clicking the minus sign, referred to as **collapsing the folder**, removes the indented subfolders from the hierarchy of folders in the Folders pane and changes the minus sign to a plus sign.

A Hierarchy

One definition of hierarchy in *Merriam Webster's Collegiate Dictionary Tenth Edition* is, a division of angels. While no one would argue angels have anything to do with Windows 2000, some preach that working with a hierarchical structure as presented by Explorer is less secular (of or relating to the worldly) and more spiritual (of or relating to supernatural phenomena) than the straightforward showing of files in windows. What do you think?

Windows 2000 displays a **plus sign** (+) in a small box to the left of an icon to indicate the corresponding folder consists of one or more subfolders that are not visible in the Folders pane. In Figure 1-38 on the previous page, a plus sign precedes each of the four icons indented and aligned below the My Computer name (3½ Floppy (A:), Local Disk (C:), Compact Disc (D:), and Control Panel). Clicking the plus sign, referred to as **expanding the folder**, displays a list of indented subfolders and changes the plus sign to a minus sign.

If neither a plus sign nor a minus sign displays to the left of an icon, the folder does not contain subfolders. In Figure 1-38, the Recycle Bin and Internet Explorer icons are not preceded by a plus or minus sign and do not contain subfolders.

The **Contents pane** is identical to the My Computer window shown in Figure 1-18 on page INT 1.17. The left panel in the Contents pane contains information about My Computer. The right panel in the Contents pane contains the contents of the My Computer folder (3½ Floppy (A:), Local Disk (C:), Compact Disc (D:), and Control Panel). These icons may be different and display in a different format on your computer.

The status bar at the bottom of the My Computer window indicates the number of folders, or objects, displayed in the Contents pane of the window, 4 object(s). Depending on the objects displayed in the Contents pane, the amount of disk space the objects occupy and the amount of unused disk space also may display on the status bar. If the status bar does not display in the My Computer window on your computer, click View on the menu bar and then click Status Bar.

In addition to using Windows Explorer to explore your computer by right-clicking the My Computer icon, you also can use Windows Explorer to explore different aspects of your computer by right-clicking the Start button on the taskbar or the My Documents, My Network Places, and Recycle Bin icons on the desktop.

Displaying the Contents of a Folder

In Figure 1-38, the right panel of the Contents pane contains the contents of the My Computer folder. In addition to displaying the contents of the My Computer folder, the contents of any folder in the Folders pane can be displayed in the Contents pane. Perform the following steps to display the contents of the Local Disk (C:) folder.

To Display the Contents of a Folder

1 **Point to the Local Disk (C:) folder name in the Folders pane of the My Computer window (Figure 1-39).**

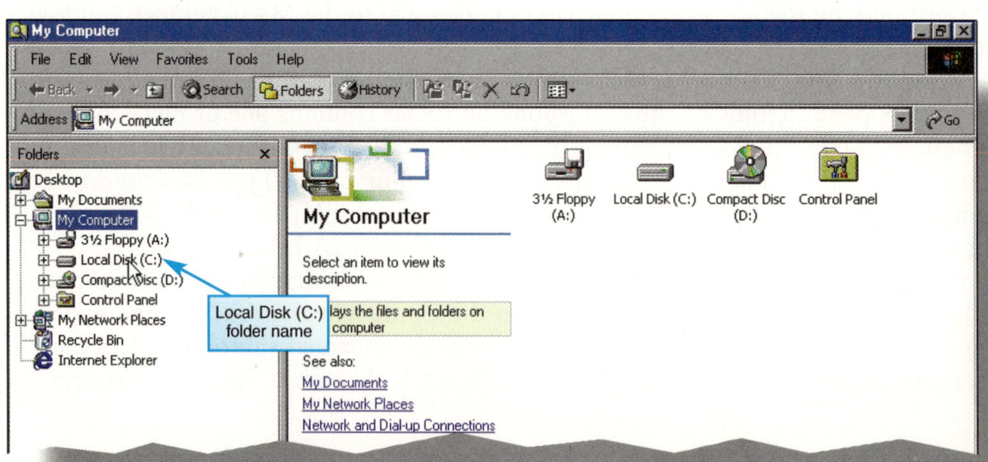

FIGURE 1-39

Click the Local Disk (C:) folder name.

The Local Disk (C:) folder name displays highlighted in the Folders pane, the window title and button in the taskbar button area change to reflect the folder name, and the messages on the status bar change (Figure 1-40). The left panel of the Contents pane contains information about Local Disk (C:) and the right panel contains the contents of the Local Disk (C:) folder. Notice that all the folder icons display first and then the file icons display.

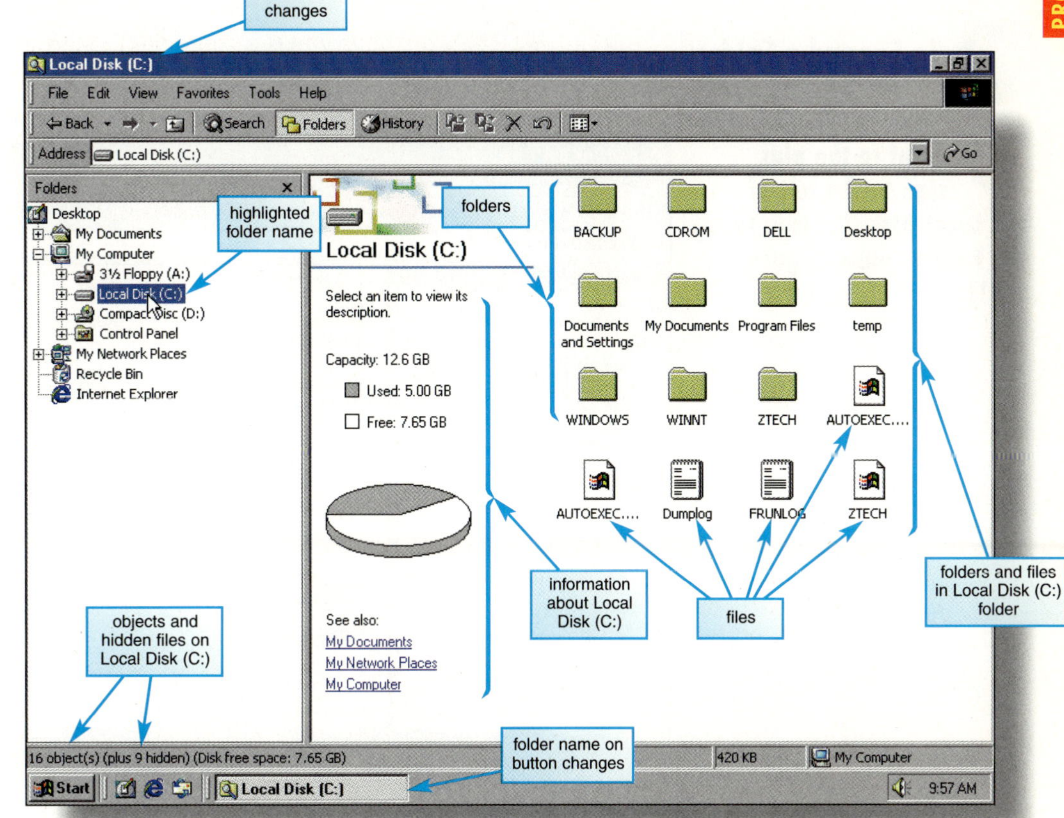

FIGURE 1-40

The status bar in Figure 1-40 contains information about the folders and files displaying in the right panel of the Contents pane. Sixteen objects display in the panel plus nine hidden files that do not display in the panel. The contents of the Local Disk (C:) folder may be different on your computer.

In addition to displaying the contents of the Local Disk (C:) folder, you can display the contents of the other folders by clicking the corresponding icon or folder name in the Folders pane. Information about the folder and the contents of the folder you click then will display in the Contents pane of the window.

Other Ways

1. Double-click Local Disk (C:) icon in Contents pane
2. Press TAB to select any icon in Folders pane, press DOWN ARROW or UP ARROW to select Local Disk (C:) icon in Folders pane
3. Press TAB to select any drive icon in Contents pane, press LEFT ARROW or RIGHT ARROW to select Local Disk (C:) icon in Contents pane, press ENTER

Expanding a Folder

Currently, the Local Disk (C:) folder is highlighted in the Folders pane of the My Computer window, and the contents of the Local Disk (C:) folder display in the right panel of the Contents pane. Windows 2000 displays a plus sign (+) to the left of the Local Disk (C:) icon to indicate the folder contains subfolders that are not visible in the hierarchy of folders in the Folders pane. To expand the Local Disk (C:) folder and display its subfolders, perform the steps on the next page.

More About 2000

Hidden Files

The status bar may or may not indicate that a folder contains a hidden file. Hidden files usually are placed on your hard disk by software vendors such as Microsoft and often are critical to the operation of the software. Rarely will you designate a file as hidden. You should almost never delete a hidden file.

To Expand a Folder

1 Point to the plus sign to the left of the Local Disk (C:) icon in the Folders pane (Figure 1-41).

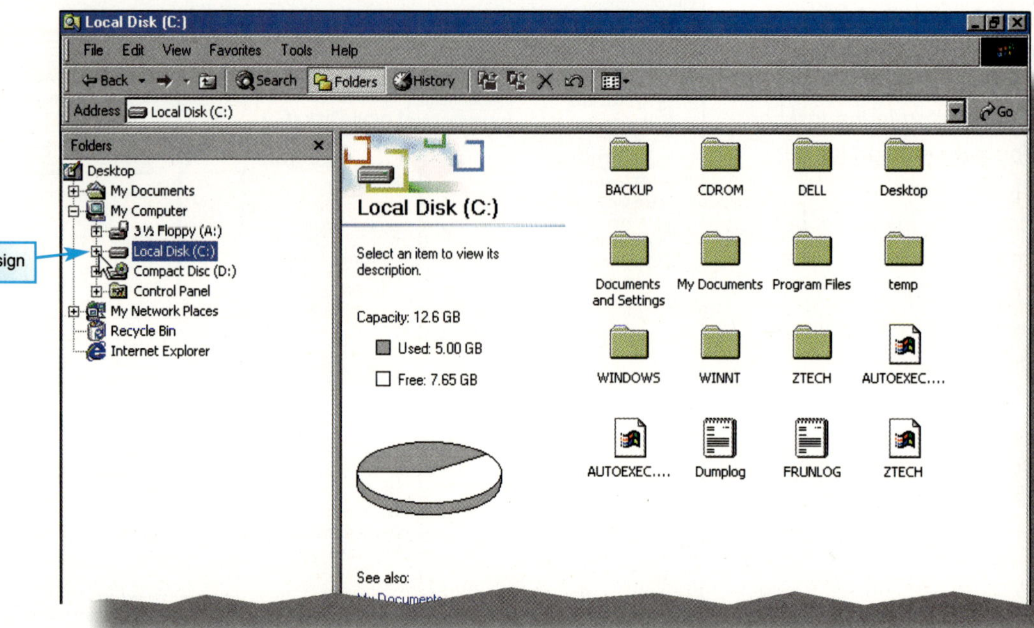

FIGURE 1-41

2 Click the plus sign to display the subfolders in the Local Disk (C:) folder.

The hierarchy below the Local Disk (C:) icon expands to display the folders contained in the Local Disk (C:) folder and a minus sign replaces the plus sign preceding the Local Disk (C:) icon (Figure 1-42).

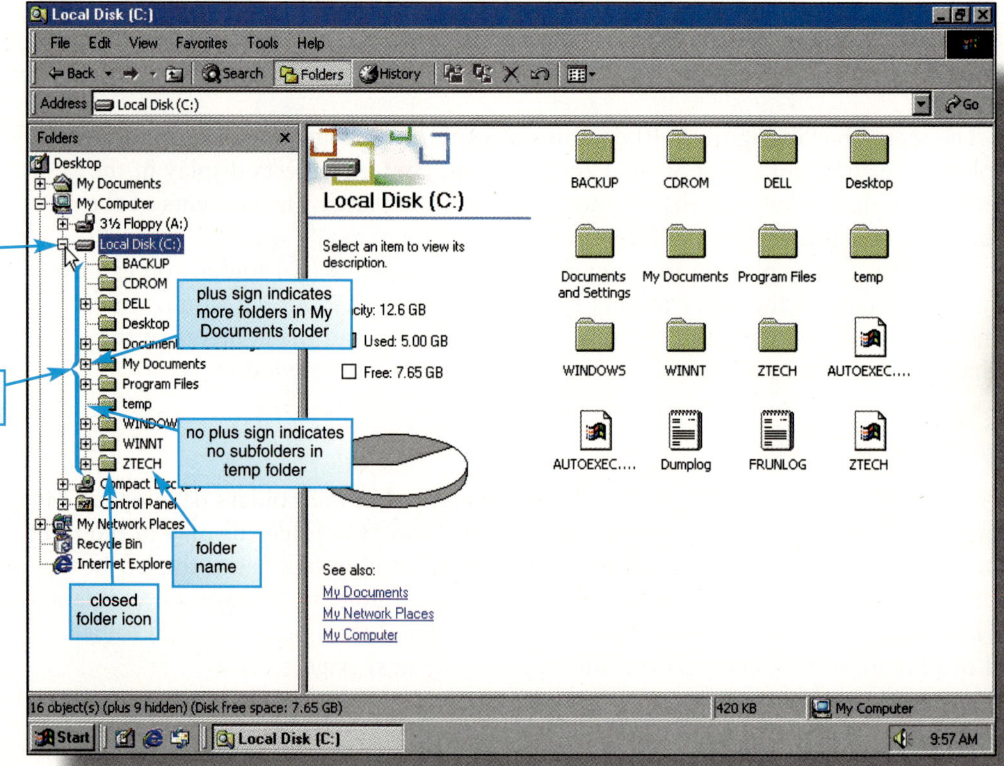

FIGURE 1-42

Other Ways

1. Double-click folder icon
2. Select folder icon, press PLUS SIGN on numeric keypad (or RIGHT ARROW)

The subfolders in the expanded Local Disk (C:) folder shown in Figure 1-42 are indented and aligned below the Local Disk (C:) folder name. A closed folder icon and folder name identify each folder in the Local Disk (C:) folder. A subfolder with a plus sign to the left of it contains more folders. A subfolder without a plus sign contains no more folders. The window title and the files and folders in the Contents pane remain unchanged.

Collapsing a Folder

Currently, the subfolders in the Local Disk (C:) folder display indented and aligned below the Local Disk (C:) folder name (see Figure 1-42). Windows 2000 displays a minus sign (–) to the left of the Local Disk (C:) icon to indicate the folder is expanded. To collapse the Local Disk (C:) folder and remove its subfolders from the hierarchy of folders in the Folders pane, perform the following steps.

To Collapse a Folder

1. **Point to the minus sign to the left of the Local Disk (C:) icon in the Folders pane (Figure 1-43).**

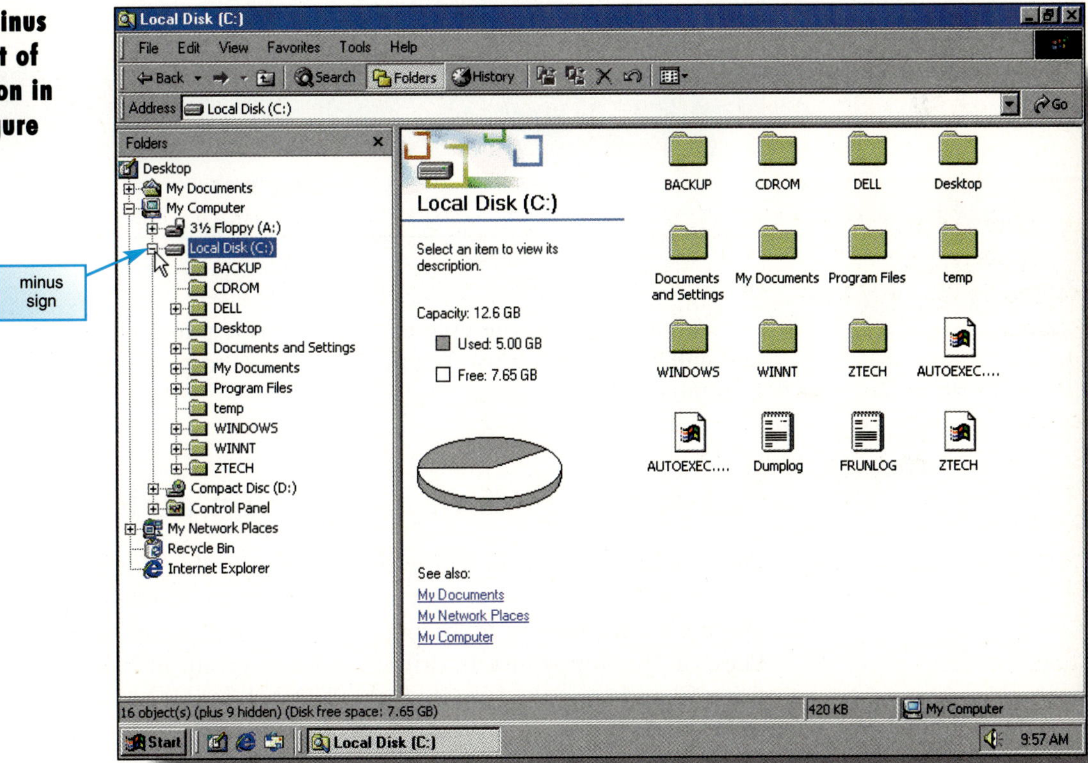

FIGURE 1-43

2 Click the minus sign to display the Local Disk (C:) folder without its subfolders.

A plus sign replaces the minus sign to the left of the Local Disk (C:) icon and the subfolders in the Local Disk (C:) folder are removed from the hierarchy of folders (Figure 1-44).

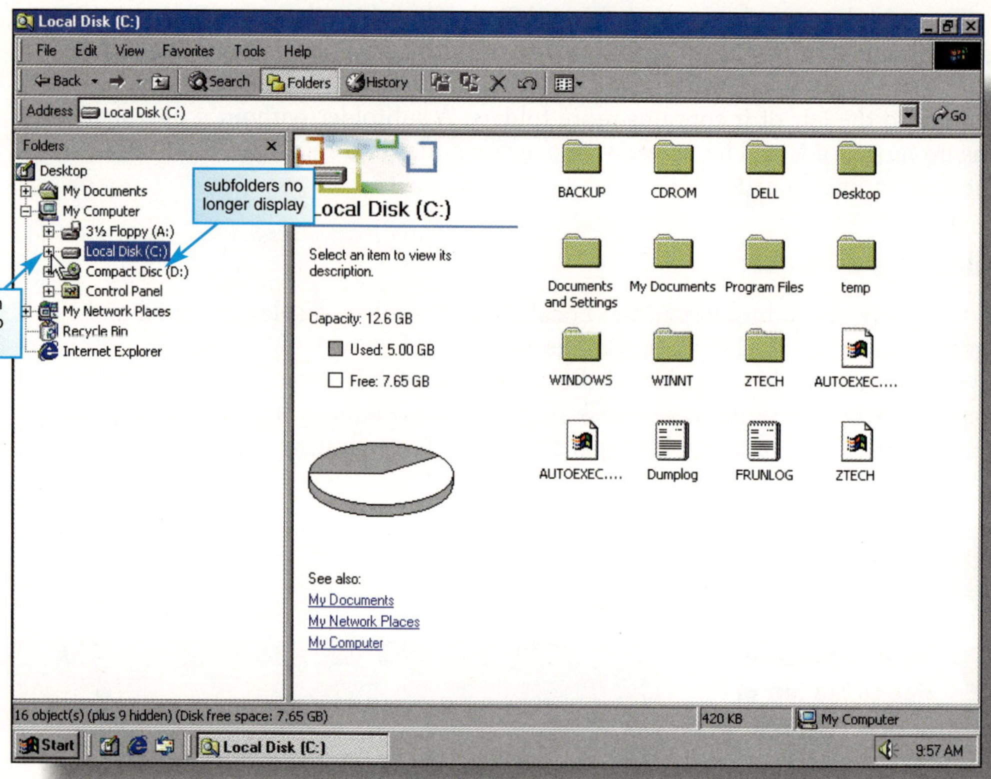

FIGURE 1-44

Other Ways

1. Double-click folder icon
2. Select folder icon, press MINUS SIGN on numeric keypad (or LEFT ARROW)

Moving through the Folders and Contents panes is an important skill because you will find that you use Windows Explorer to perform a significant amount of file maintenance on the computer.

Copying Files to a Folder on a Floppy Disk

One common operation that every student should understand how to perform is copying a file or group of files from one disk to another disk or from one folder to another folder. On the following pages, you will create a new folder, named My Files, on the floppy disk in drive A, select a group of files in the WINNT folder on drive C, and copy the files from the WINNT folder on drive C to the My Files folder on drive A.

When copying files, the drive and folder containing the files to be copied are called the **source drive** and **source folder**, respectively. The drive and folder to which the files are copied are called the **destination drive** and **destination folder**, respectively. Thus, the WINNT folder is the source folder, drive C is the source drive, the My Files folder is the destination folder, and drive A is the destination drive.

Creating a New Folder

In preparation for selecting and copying files from a folder on the hard drive to a folder on the floppy disk in drive A, a new folder with the name of My Files will be created on the floppy disk. Perform the following steps to create the new folder.

To Create a New Folder

1 Insert a formatted floppy disk into drive A on your computer.

2 Click the 3½ Floppy (A:) folder name in the Folders pane and then point to an open area of the Contents pane.

The 3½ Floppy (A:) folder name is highlighted, information about and the contents of the 3½ Floppy (A:) folder display in the Contents pane, and the messages on the status bar change (Figure 1-45). The 3½ Floppy (A:) folder name displays in the window title and on the button in the taskbar button area. Currently, no files or folders display in the Contents pane. The files and folders may be different on your computer.

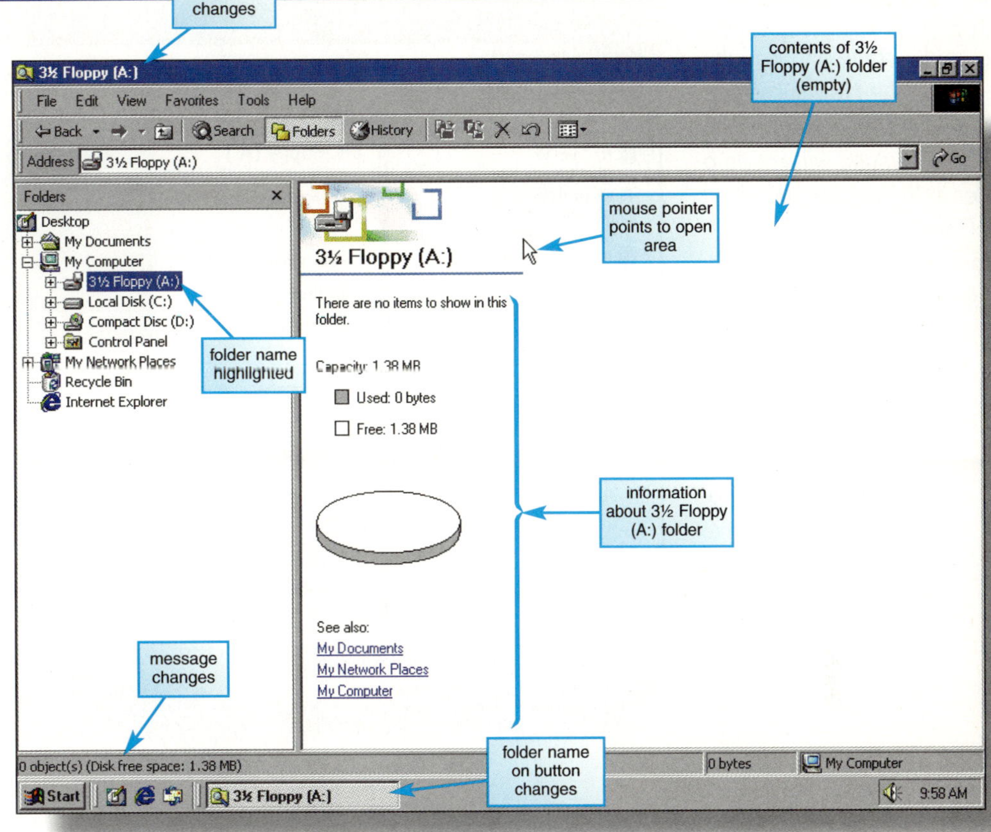

FIGURE 1-45

3 Right-click the open area and then point to New on the shortcut menu.

A shortcut menu and the New submenu display and the New command is highlighted on the shortcut menu (Figure 1-46). Although no subfolders display in the right panel of the Contents pane, a plus sign precedes the 3½ Floppy (A:) icon.

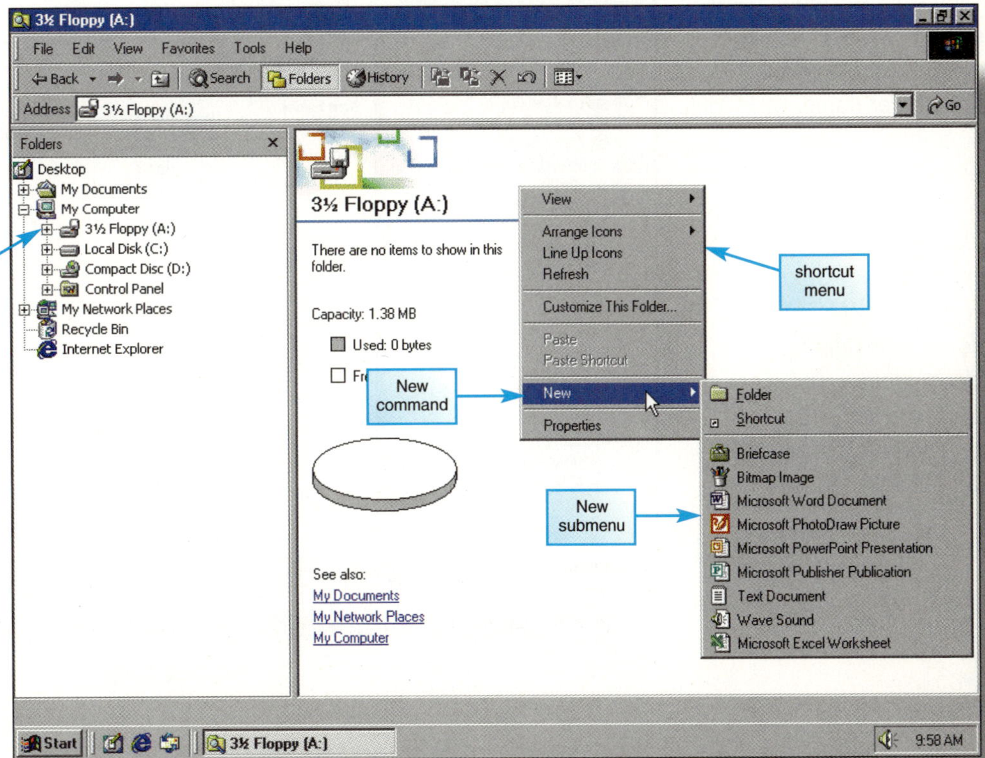

FIGURE 1-46

Point to Folder on the New submenu.

The Folder command is highlighted on the New submenu (Figure 1-47). Clicking the Folder command will create a folder in the right panel of the Contents pane using the default folder name, New Folder.

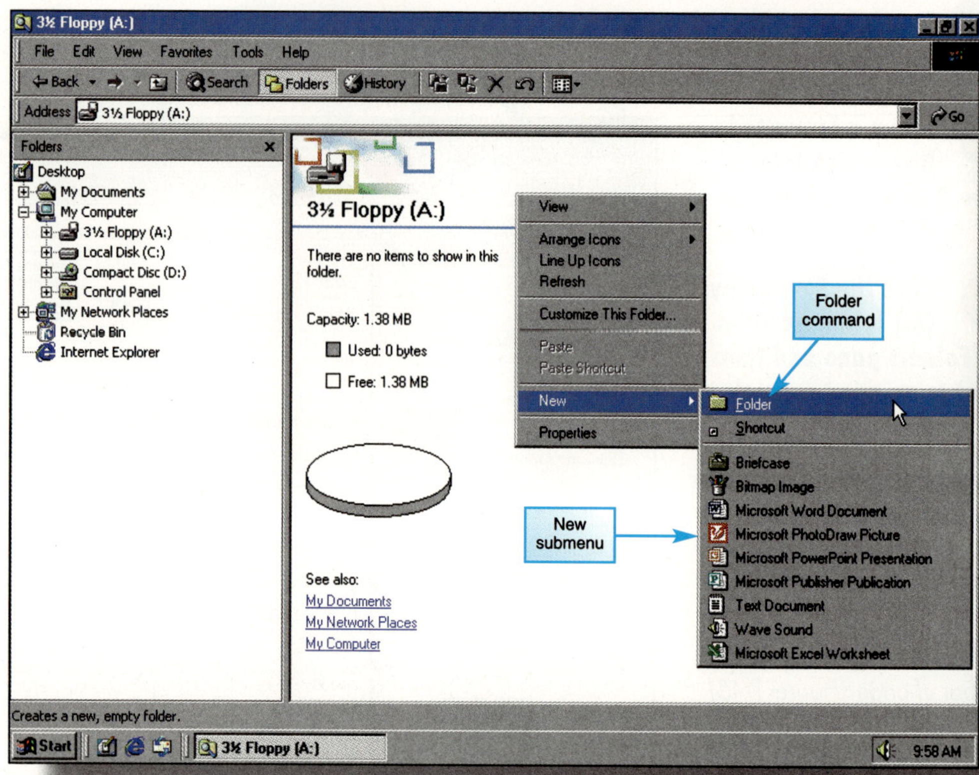

FIGURE 1-47

Click Folder.

The New Folder icon displays in the right panel of the Contents pane (Figure 1-48). The text box below the icon contains the highlighted default folder name, New Folder, and an insertion point. A plus sign continues to display to the left of the 3½ Floppy (A:) icon in the Folders pane to indicate the 3½ Floppy (A:) folder contains the New Folder subfolder. The message on the status bar indicates one object is selected in the Contents pane.

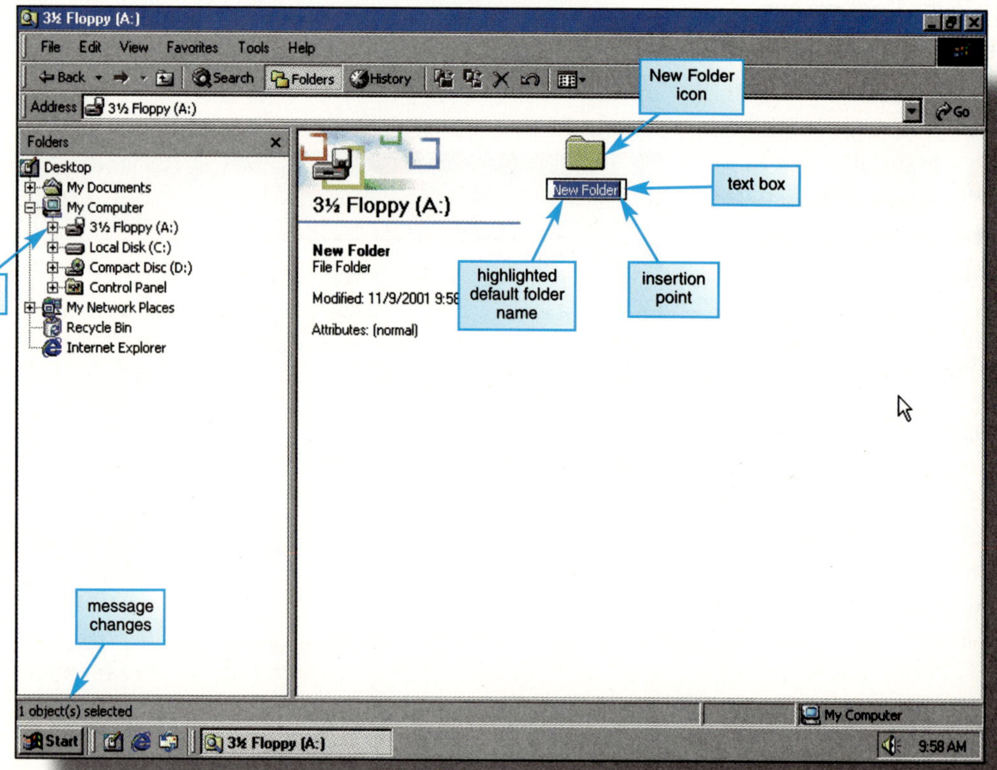

FIGURE 1-48

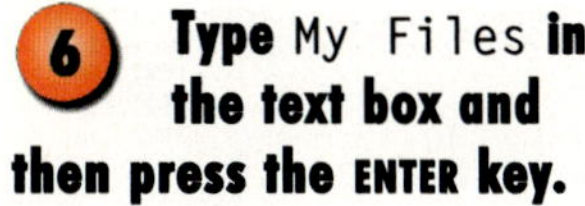

6 Type `My Files` **in the text box and then press the ENTER key.**

The new folder name, My Files, is entered and the text box is removed (Figure 1-49).

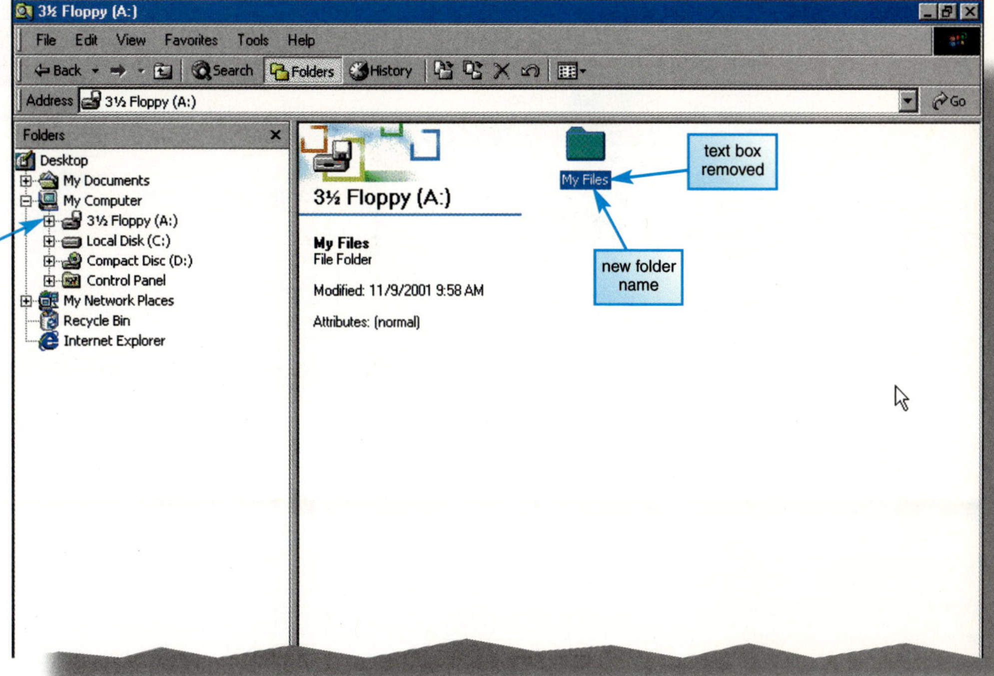

FIGURE 1-49

Other Ways

1. Select drive in Folders pane, on File menu point to New, click Folder on New submenu

After creating the My Files folder on the floppy disk in drive A, you can save files in the folder or copy files from other folders to the folder. On the following pages, you will copy a group of files consisting of the Prairie Wind, Rhododendron, and Santa Fe Stucco files from the WINNT folder on drive C to the My Files folder on drive A.

Displaying the Destination Folder

To copy the three files from the WINNT folder on drive C to the My Files folder on drive A, the files to be copied will be selected in the right panel of the Contents pane and right-dragged to the My Files folder in the Folders pane. Prior to selecting and right-dragging the files, the destination folder (My Files folder on drive A) must be visible in the Folders pane, and the three files to be copied must be visible in the Contents pane.

Currently, the plus sign (+) to the left of the 3½ Floppy (A:) icon indicates the folder contains one or more subfolders that are not visible in the Folders pane (Figure 1-49). Perform the following steps to expand the 3½ Floppy (A:) folder to display the My Files subfolder.

TO EXPAND A FOLDER

1. Point to the plus sign to the left of the 3½ Floppy (A:) icon in the Folders pane.
2. Click the plus sign to display the subfolders in the 3½ Floppy (A:) folder.

A minus sign replaces the plus sign to the left of the 3½ Floppy (A:) folder, the folder name is highlighted, and the My Files subfolder displays in the 3½ Floppy (A:) folder, aligned below the 3½ Floppy (A:) folder name (Figure 1-50 on the next page).

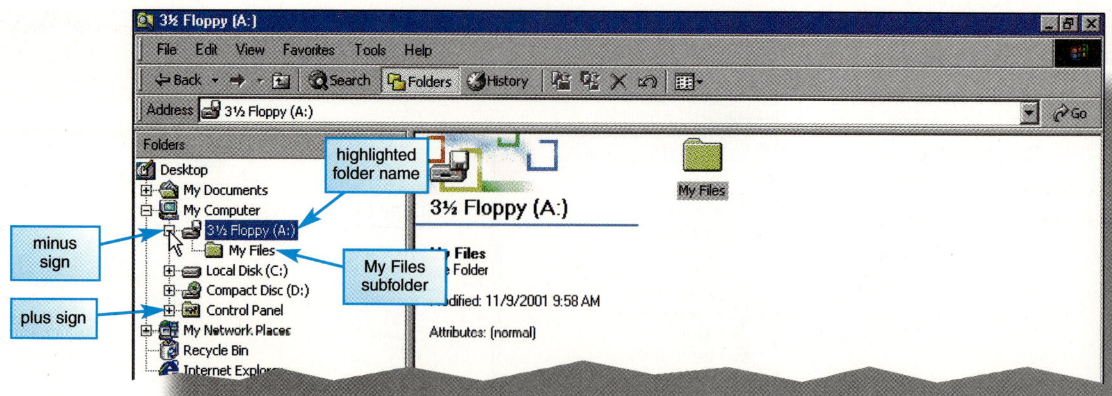

FIGURE 1-50

The WINNT Folder

WINNT is an abbreviation for Windows NT, an older operating system designed for businesses with networks. Because Windows NT used the WINNT folder and Windows 2000 contains many of the features of Windows NT, Microsoft decided to use the WINNT folder name. Some think Microsoft should have used Windows 2000.

Displaying the Contents of the WINNT Folder

Currently, the My Files folder displays in the right panel of the Contents pane of the 3½ Floppy (A:) window. To copy files from the source folder (WINNT folder on drive C) to the My Files folder, the WINNT folder must be visible in the Folders pane and the contents of the WINNT folder must display in the Contents pane. To accomplish this, you must expand the Local Disk (C:) folder in the Folders pane and then click the WINNT folder name in the Folder pane to display the contents of the WINNT folder in the right panel of the Contents pane.

The WINNT folder contains programs and files necessary for the operation of the Windows 2000 operating system. As such, you should exercise caution when working with the contents of the WINNT folder because changing the contents of the folder may cause the programs to stop working correctly. Perform the following steps to display the contents of the WINNT folder.

To Display the Contents of a Folder

1 Click the plus sign to the left of the Local Disk (C:) icon in the Folders pane and then point to the WINNT folder name.

*A minus sign replaces the plus sign to the left of the Local Disk (C:) icon and the subfolders in the Local Disk (C:) folder display (Figure 1-51). In addition to folders and other files, the WINNT folder contains a series of predefined graphics, called **clip art files**, that can be used with application programs.*

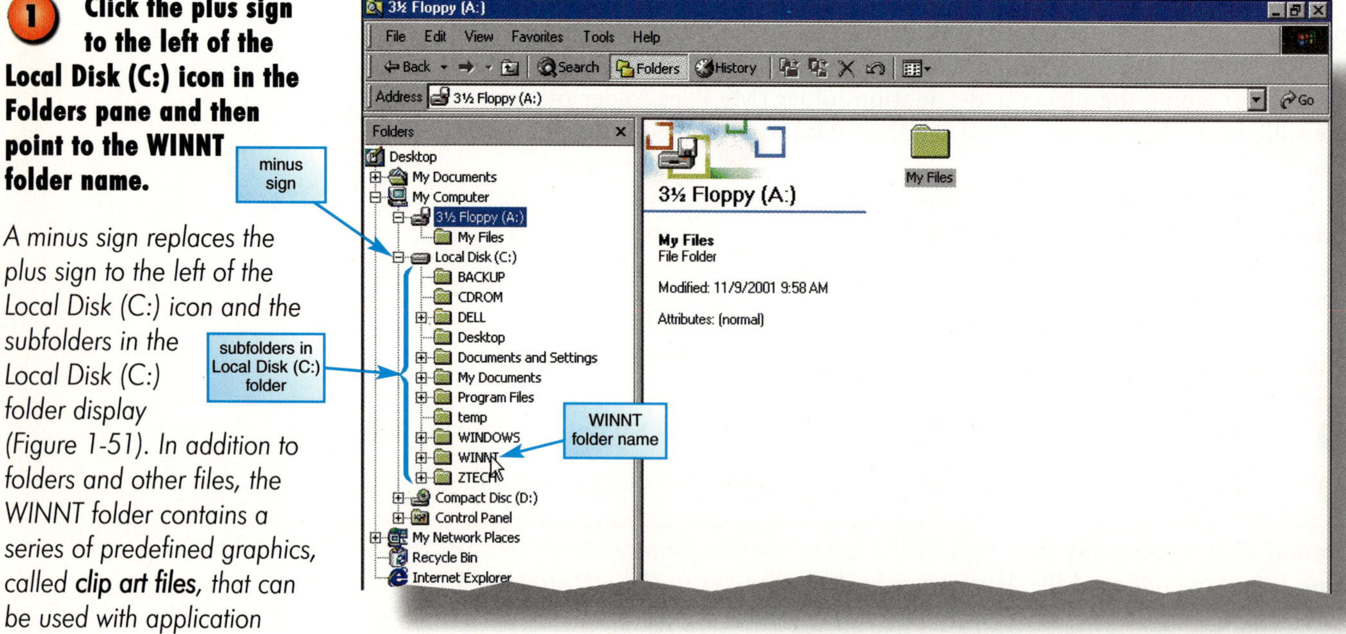

FIGURE 1-51

2 Click the WINNT folder name and then point to the Show Files link.

The WINNT folder name is highlighted in the Folders pane, the closed folder icon preceding the WINNT folder name changes to an open folder icon, and the WINNT button replaces the 3½ Floppy (A:) button. Information about the WINNT folder and the Show Files link display in the left panel of the Contents pane and a graphics image displays in the right panel (Figure 1-52). The mouse pointer changes to a hand and the message in the status area changes.

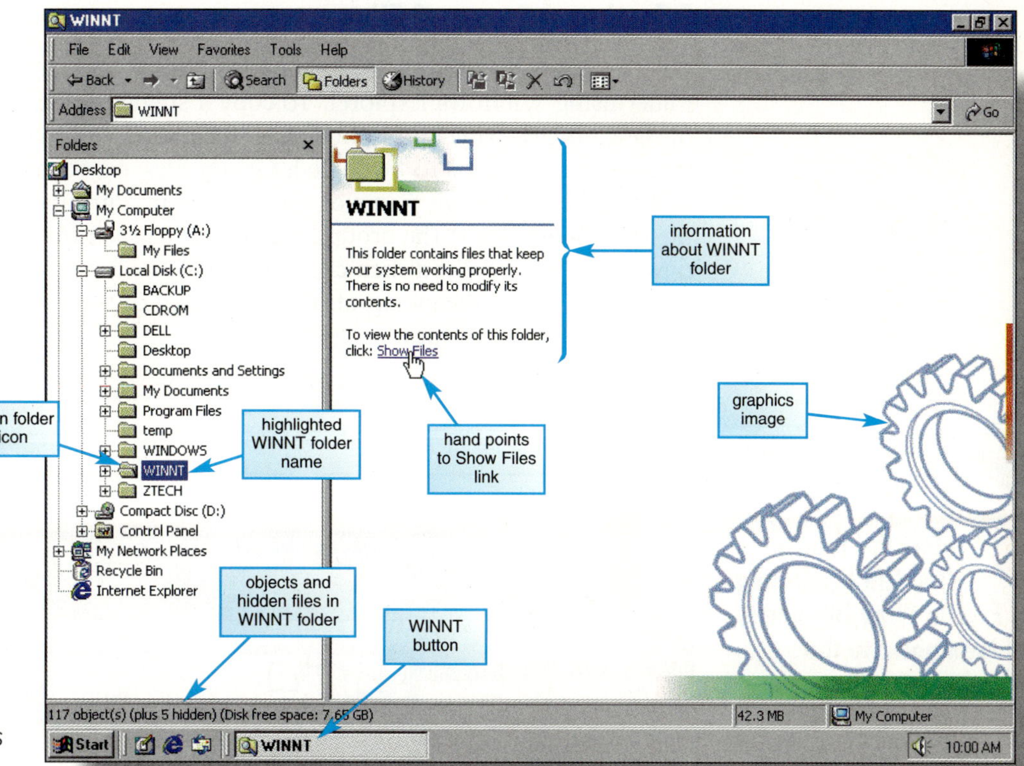

FIGURE 1-52

3 Click Show Files. Scroll the Contents pane to make the Prairie Wind, Rhododendron, and Santa Fe Stucco files in the WINNT folder visible.

The files and folders in the WINNT folder display in the right panel of the Contents pane and the right panel scrolls to display the Prairie Wind, Rhododendron, and Santa Fe Stucco files (Figure 1-53). The files and folders in the WINNT folder may be different and file extensions may display as part of the file names on your computer.

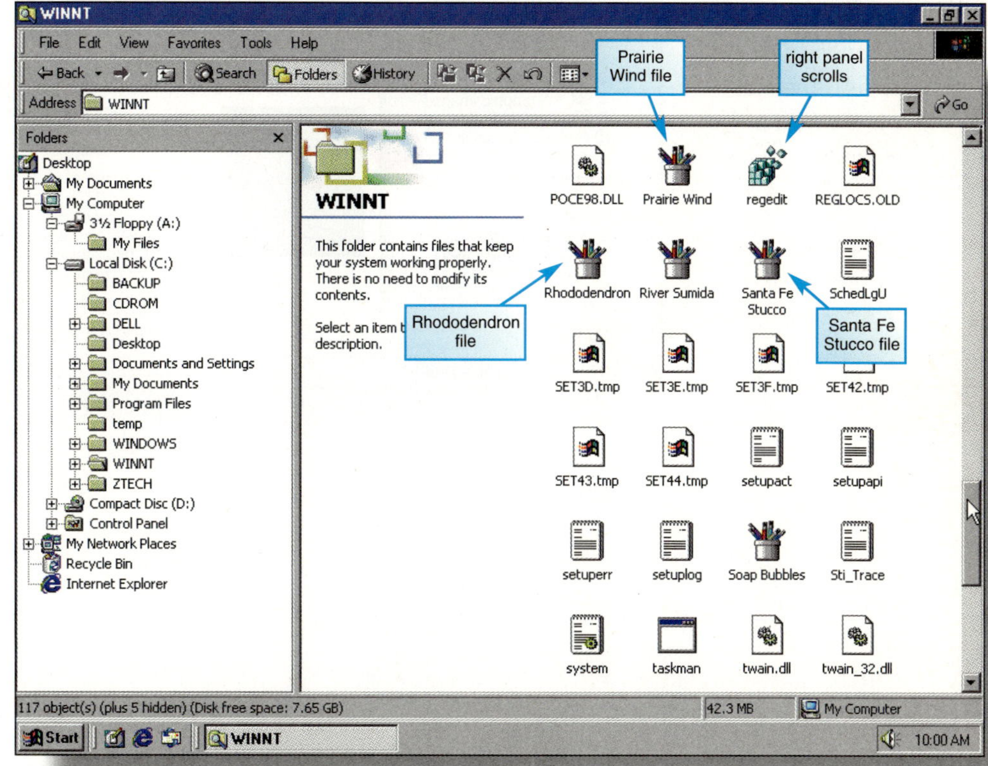

FIGURE 1-53

Selecting a Group of Files

You easily can copy a single file or group of files from one folder to another folder using Windows Explorer. To copy a single file, select the file in the right panel of the Contents pane and right-drag the highlighted file to the folder in the Folders pane where the file is to be copied. Group files are copied in a similar manner by clicking the icon or file name of the first file in a group of files to select it. You select the remaining files in the group by pointing to each file icon or file name, holding down the CTRL key, and then clicking the file icon or file name. Perform the following steps to select the group of files consisting of the Prairie Wind, Rhododendron, and Santa Fe Stucco files.

To Select a Group of Files

1 Select the Prairie Wind file by clicking the Prairie Wind file name, and then point to the Rhododendron file name.

The Prairie Wind file is highlighted in the right panel of the Contents pane, information about and a graphic image of the file displays in the left panel, and two messages display on the status bar (Figure 1-54). The messages indicate the type of file selected (Bitmap Image) and the size of the file (64.4 KB).

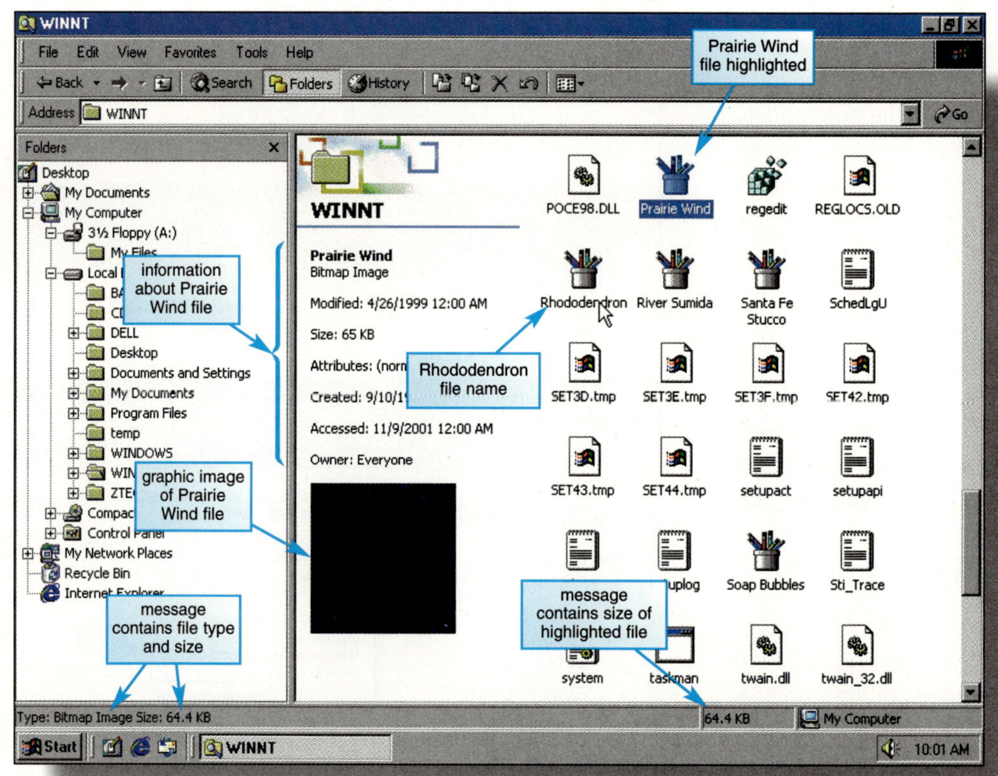

FIGURE 1-54

2 Hold down the CTRL key, click the Rhododendron file name, release the CTRL key, and then point to the Santa Fe Stucco file name.

The Prairie Wind and Rhododendron files are highlighted, information about the two files displays in the left panel of the Contents pane, and the two messages on the status bar change to reflect the additional file selected (Figure 1-55). The messages indicate two files are selected, 2 object(s) selected and the size of the two files, 81.3 KB.

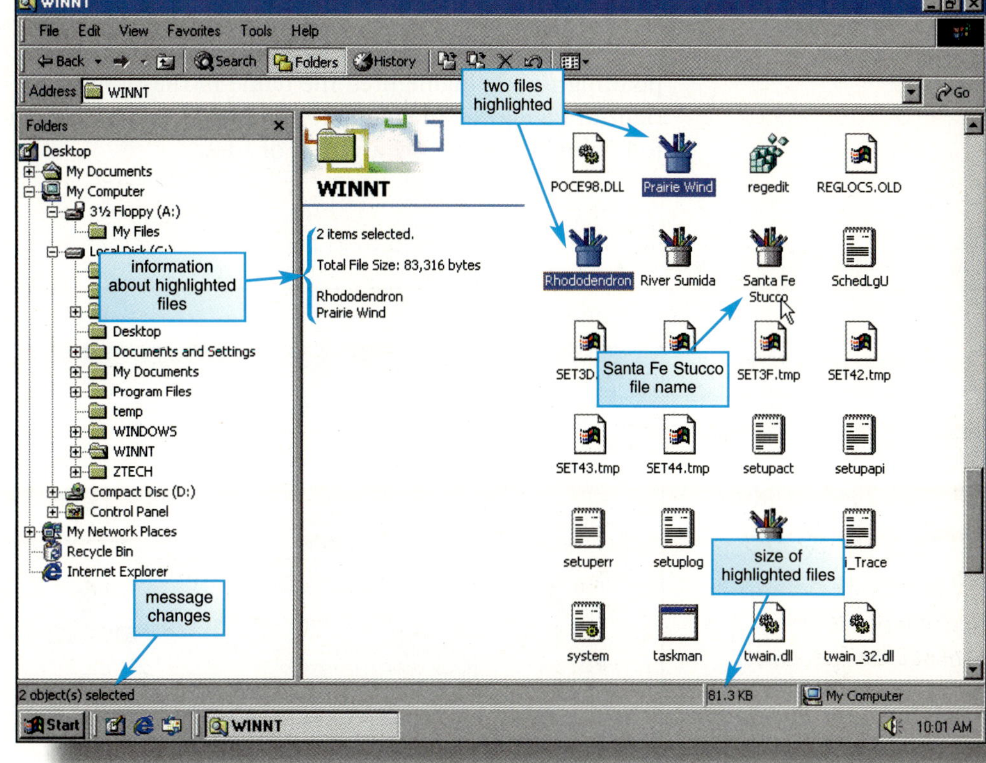

FIGURE 1-55

3 Hold down the CTRL key, click the Santa Fe Stucco file name, and then release the CTRL key.

The group of files consisting of the Prairie Wind, Rhododendron, and Santa Fe Stucco files is highlighted, information about the three files displays in the left panel of the Contents pane, and the messages on the status bar change to reflect the selection of a third file (Figure 1-56). The messages indicate three files are selected, 3 object(s) selected and the size of the three files, 145 KB.

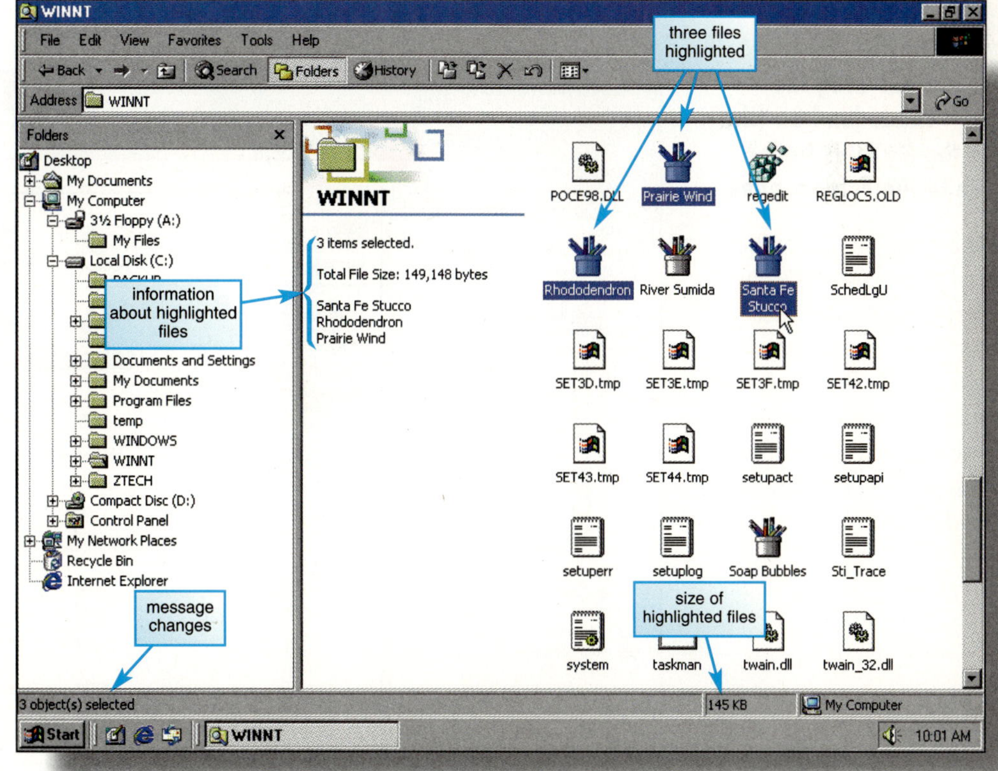

FIGURE 1-56

Other Ways

1. To select contiguous files, select first file name in Contents pane, hold down SHIFT key, click last file name
2. To select all files, on Edit menu click Select All, click OK button

Copying a Group of Files

After selecting a group of files, copy the files to the My Files folder on drive A by pointing to any highlighted file name in the right panel of the Contents pane and right-dragging the file name to the My Files folder in the Folders pane. Perform the following steps to copy a group of files.

To Copy a Group of Files

1 **If necessary, scroll the Folders pane to make the My Files folder visible. Point to the highlighted Rhododendron file name in the Contents pane.**

The pointer points to the highlighted Rhododendron file name in the Contents pane and the My Files folder is visible in the Folders pane (Figure 1-57).

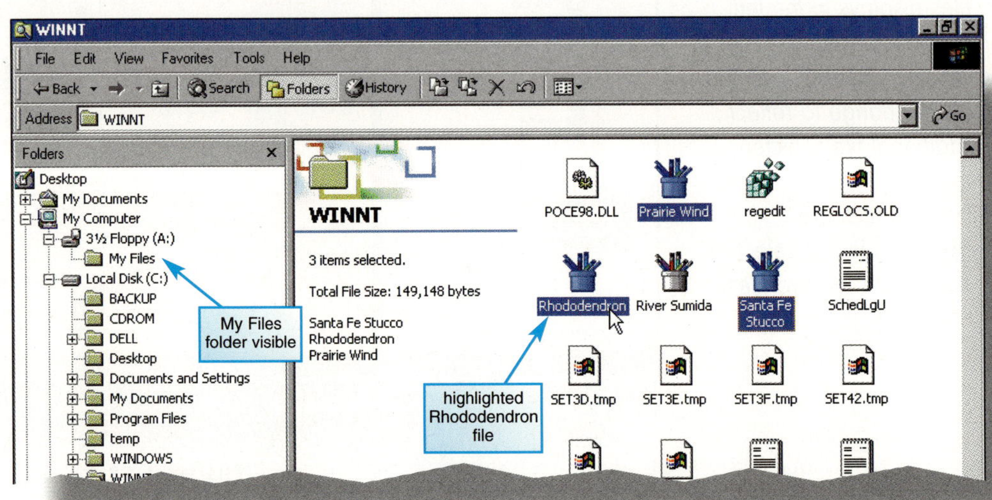

FIGURE 1-57

2 **Right-drag the Rhododendron file over the My Files folder name in the Folders pane.**

As you drag the file, an outline of three dimmed icons displays and the My Files folder name is highlighted (Figure 1-58). The mouse pointer contains a plus sign to indicate the group of files is being copied, not moved.

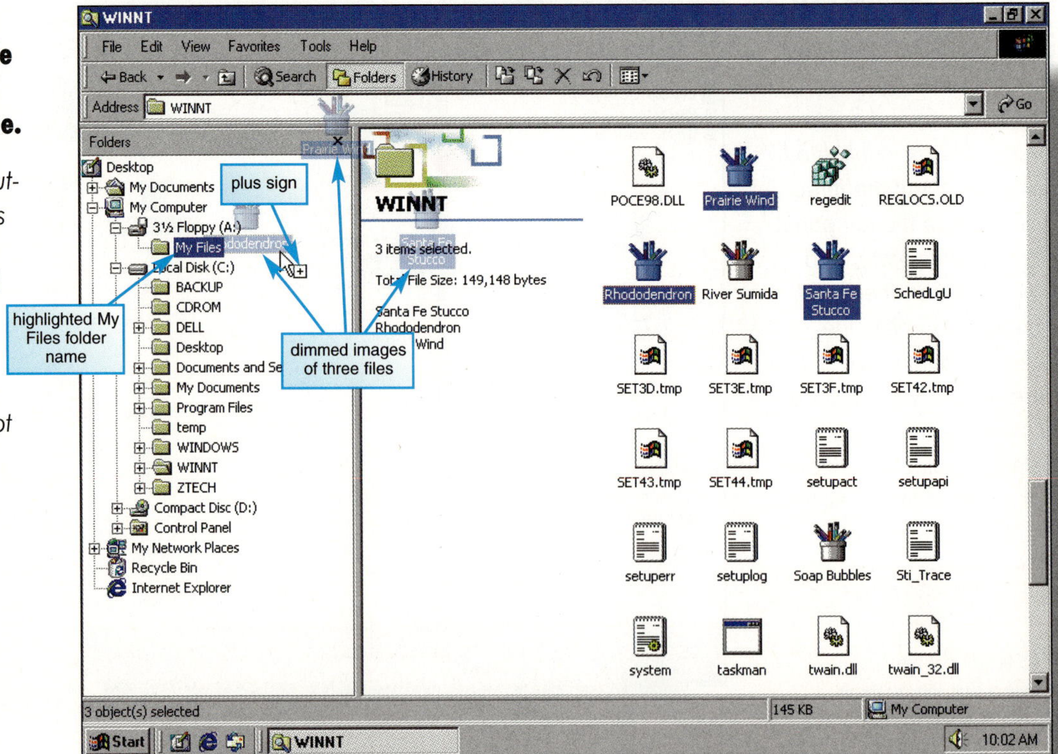

FIGURE 1-58

3 **Release the right mouse button and then point to Copy Here on the shortcut menu.**

A shortcut menu displays and the Copy Here command is highlighted (Figure 1-59).

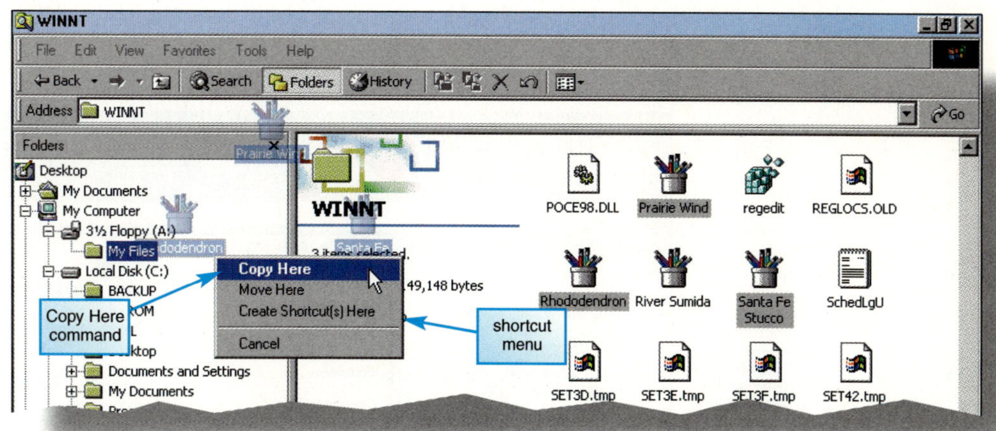

FIGURE 1-59

4 **Click Copy Here.**

The Copying dialog box displays and remains on the screen while each file is copied to the My Files folder (Figure 1-60). The Copying dialog box indicates the Santa Fe Stucco.bmp file is being copied from the WINNT folder to the My Files folder and ten seconds remain in the copy process.

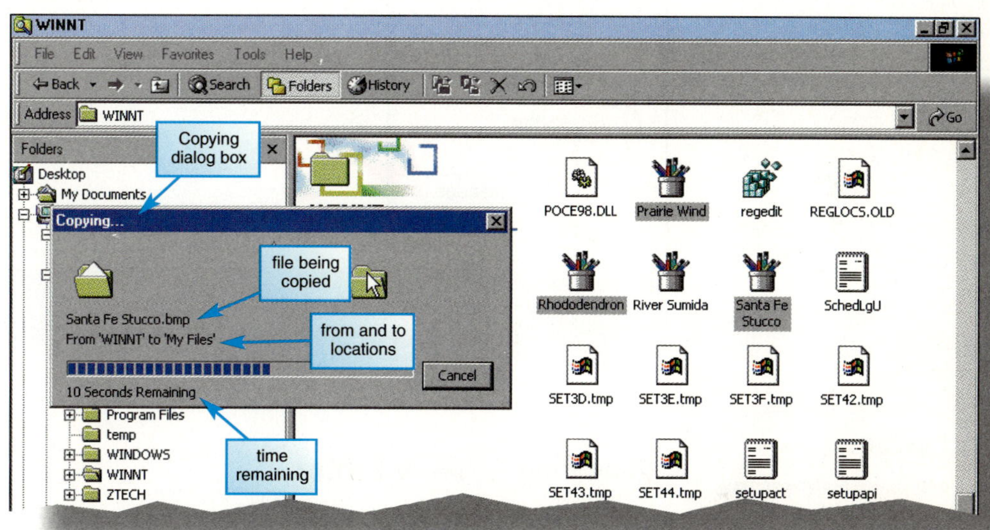

FIGURE 1-60

Displaying the Contents of the My Files Folder

After copying a group of files, you should verify the files were copied into the correct folder. To view the files that were copied to the My Files folder, perform the following steps.

TO DISPLAY THE CONTENTS OF A FOLDER

1. Point to the My Files folder name in the Folders pane.
2. Click the My Files folder name.

The highlighted My Files folder name displays in the Folders pane, the open folder icon replaces the closed folder icon to the left of the My Files folder name, the contents of the My Files folder display in the right panel of the Contents pane, and the message on the status bar changes (Figure 1-61 on the next page). The message on the status bar indicates the amount of free disk space on the floppy disk in drive A, Disk free space: 1.24 MB.

Other Ways

1. Select file to copy in Contents pane, click Copy To button on Standard Buttons toolbar, select folder icon in Browse For Folder dialog box, click OK button
2. Select file to copy in Contents pane, on Edit menu click Copy, select folder icon in Folders pane to receive copy, on Edit menu click Paste
3. Select file to copy in Contents pane, press CTRL+C, select folder icon to receive copy, press CTRL+V

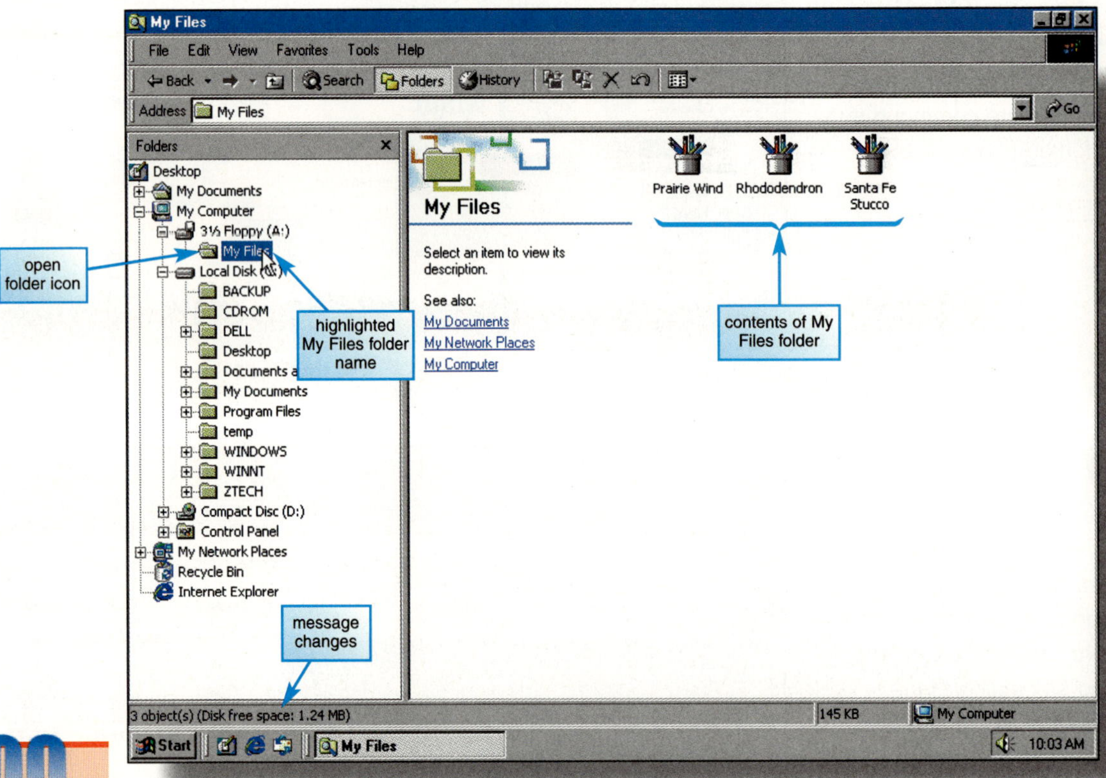

FIGURE 1-61

More About

Renaming a File or Folder

A file or folder name can contain up to 255 characters, including spaces. But, they cannot contain any of the following characters: \/:*?"<>|.

Renaming a File or Folder

For various reasons, you may wish to change the name of a file or folder on a disk. Perform the following steps to change the name of the Santa Fe Stucco file on drive A to Arizona Stucco.

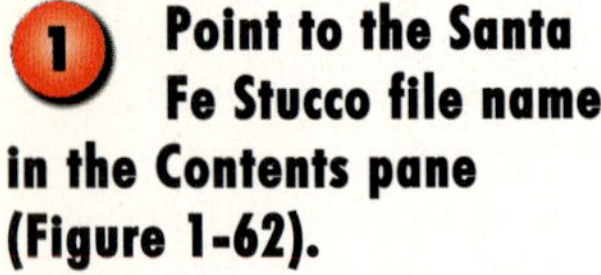

Steps To Rename a File

1 Point to the Santa Fe Stucco file name in the Contents pane (Figure 1-62).

The mouse pointer points to the Santa Fe Stucco file name.

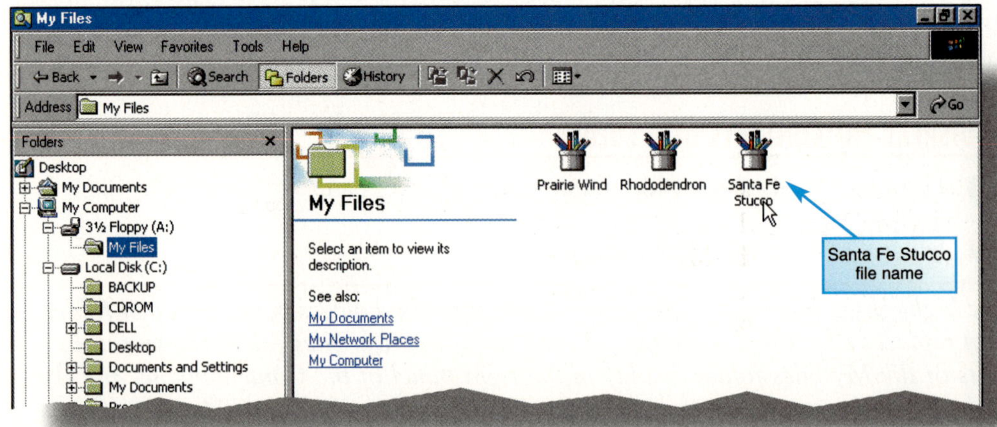

FIGURE 1-62

2 Click the Santa Fe Stucco file name twice (do not double-click the file name).

A text box containing the highlighted Santa Fe Stucco file name and insertion point displays (Figure 1-63).

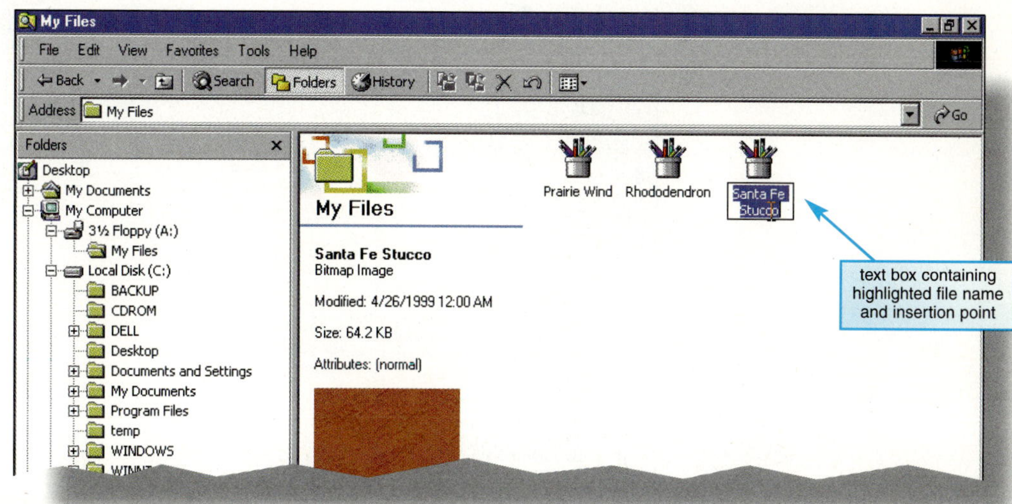

FIGURE 1-63

3 Type `Arizona Stucco` **and then press the ENTER key.**

The file name changes to Arizona Stucco and the text box surrounding the file name is removed (Figure 1-64).

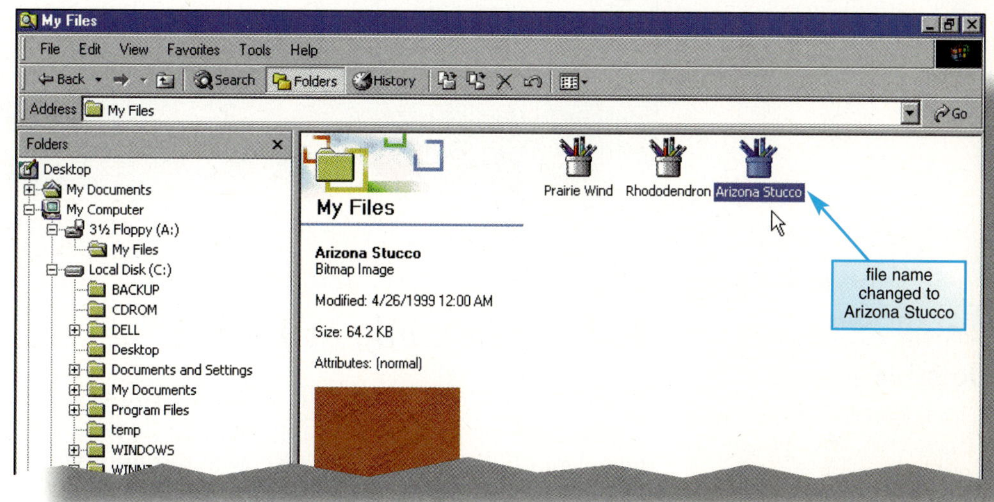

FIGURE 1-64

Other Ways

1. Right-click file name, click Rename on shortcut menu, type new name, press ENTER
2. Select file name, on File menu click Rename, type new name, press ENTER
3. Select file name, press F2, type new name, press ENTER
4. Select file name, press ALT+F, press M, type new name, press ENTER

Follow the same procedure to change a folder name. The following steps change the name of the My Files folder to Clip Art Files.

TO RENAME A FOLDER

1. Point to the My Files folder name in the Folders pane.
2. Click the My Files folder name twice (do not double-click the folder name).
3. Type `Clip Art Files` and then press the ENTER key.

The folder name changes to Clip Art Files and the text box surrounding the folder name is removed (Figure 1-65 on the next page). The new folder name replaces the old folder name in both the window title in the left panel of the Contents pane and on the button in the taskbar button area.

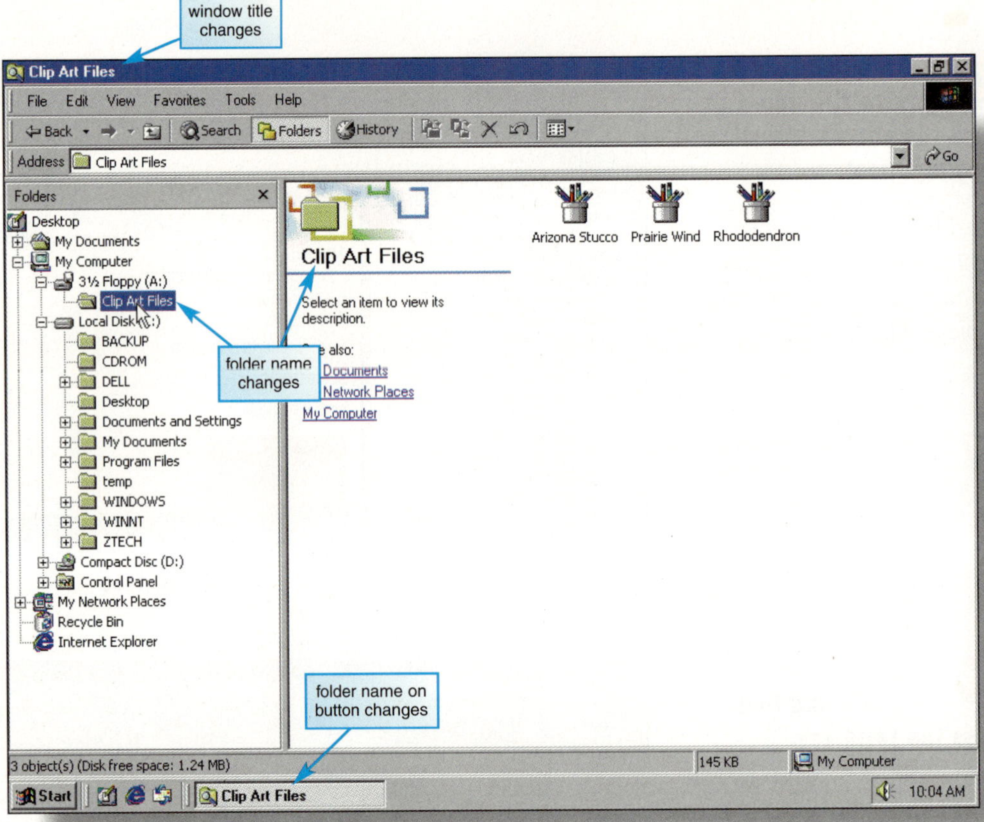

FIGURE 1-65

Deleting Files

A few years ago, someone proposed that the Delete command be removed from operating systems. It seems an entire database was deleted by an employee who thought he knew what he was doing, resulting in a company that could not function for more than a week while the database was rebuilt. Millions of dollars in revenue were lost. The Delete command is still around, but it should be considered a dangerous weapon.

Deleting a File or Folder

When you no longer need a file or folder, you can delete it. When you delete a file or folder on the hard drive using the Recycle Bin, Windows 2000 temporarily stores the deleted file or folder in the Recycle Bin until you permanently discard the contents of the Recycle Bin by emptying the Recycle Bin. Until the Recycle Bin is emptied, you can retrieve the files and folders you have deleted previously by mistake or other reasons. Unlike deleting files or folders on the hard drive, when you delete a file or folder located on a floppy disk, the file or folder is deleted immediately and not stored in the Recycle Bin.

Deleting a File by Right-Clicking Its File Name

Right-clicking a file name produces a shortcut menu that contains the Delete command. To illustrate how to delete a file by right-clicking, perform the following steps to delete the Rhododendron file.

To Delete a File by Right-Clicking

1 Right-click the Rhododendron file name in the right panel of the Contents pane and then point to the Delete command on the shortcut menu.

The Rhododendron file name is highlighted in the Contents pane and a shortcut menu displays (Figure 1-66). The Delete command is highlighted on the shortcut menu.

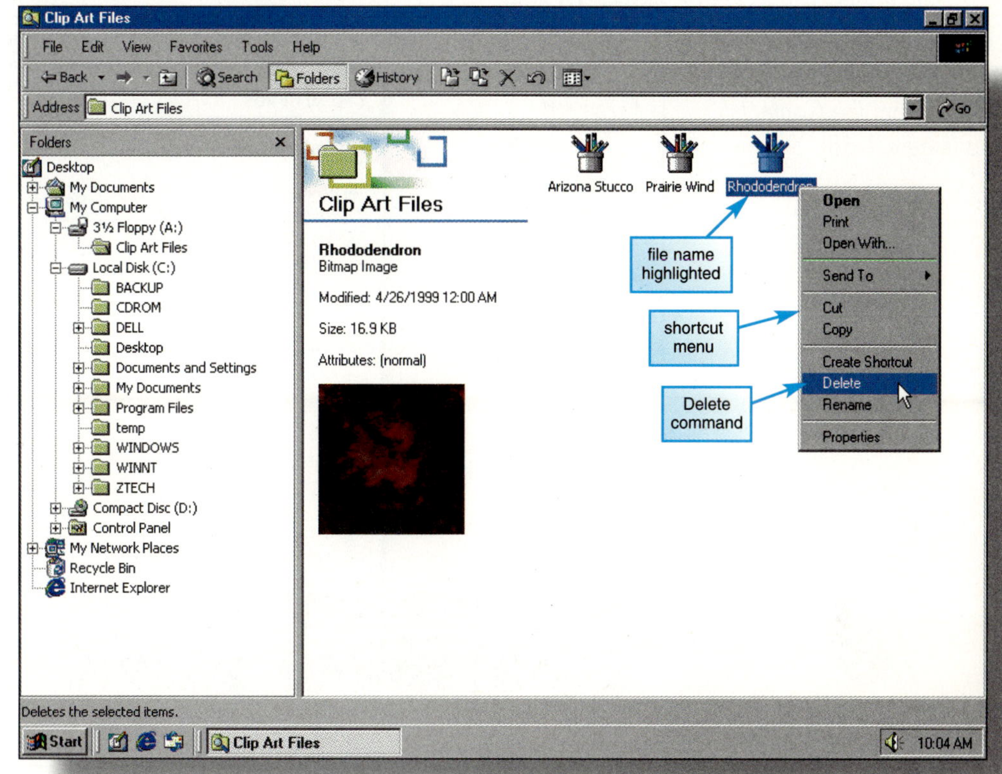

FIGURE 1-66

2 Click Delete. When the Confirm File Delete dialog box displays, point to the Yes button.

The Confirm File Delete dialog box displays (Figure 1-67). The dialog box contains a confirmation message, Are you sure you want to delete 'Rhododendron'?, and the Yes and No command buttons.

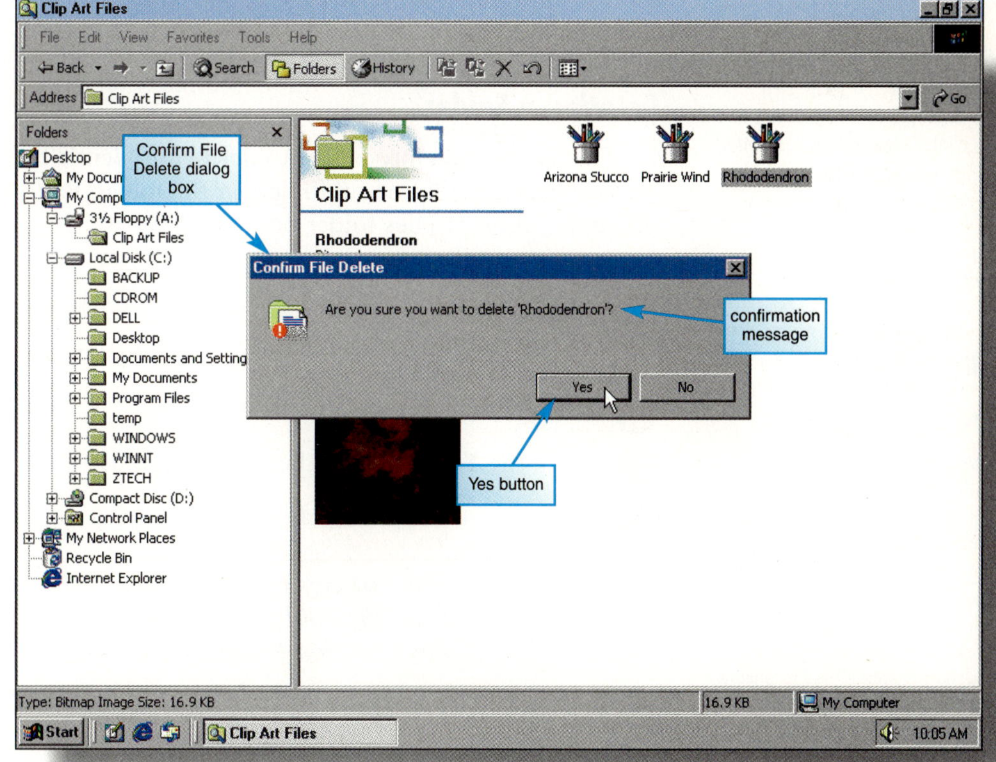

FIGURE 1-67

Click the Yes button.

A Deleting dialog box displays while the file is being deleted, and then the Rhododendron file is removed from the Contents pane (Figure 1-68).

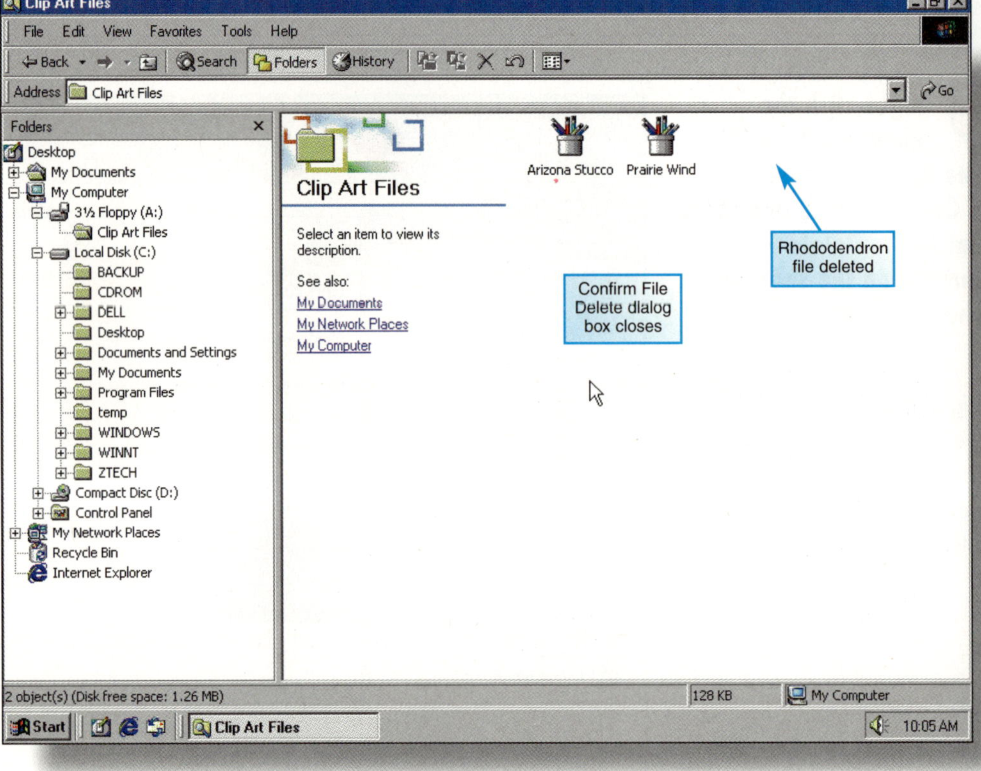

FIGURE 1-68

Other Ways

1. Click file name, click Delete button on Standard Buttons toolbar, click Yes button
2. Right-drag file name over Recycle Bin icon, click Move Here, click Yes button
3. Drag file name over Recycle Bin icon, click Yes button
4. Right-click file name, click Delete, click Yes button
5. Click file name, on File menu click Delete, click Yes button
6. Select file name, press ALT+F, press D, press Y

You can use the file selection techniques illustrated earlier in this project to delete a group of files. When deleting a group of files, click the Yes button in the Confirm Multiple File Delete dialog box to confirm the deletion of the group of files.

Deleting a Folder

Follow the same procedure to delete a folder. When you delete a folder, Windows 2000 deletes any files or subfolders in the folder. Perform the following steps to delete the Clip Art Files folder on drive A.

TO DELETE A FOLDER

1. Right-click the Clip Art Files folder name in the Folders pane.
2. Click Delete on the shortcut menu.
3. Click the Yes button in the Confirm Folder Delete dialog box.
4. Remove the floppy disk from drive A.

A Deleting dialog box displays while the folder is being deleted, the Clip Art Files folder is removed from the Folders pane, and a plus sign replaces the minus sign preceding the 3½ Floppy (A:) icon (Figure 1-69).

More About 2000

Deleting Files

Warning! This is your last warning! Be EXTREMELY careful when deleting files. Hours and weeks of hard work can be lost with one click of a button. If you are going to delete files or folders from your hard disk, consider making a backup of those files to ensure that if you accidentally delete something you need, you will be able to recover.

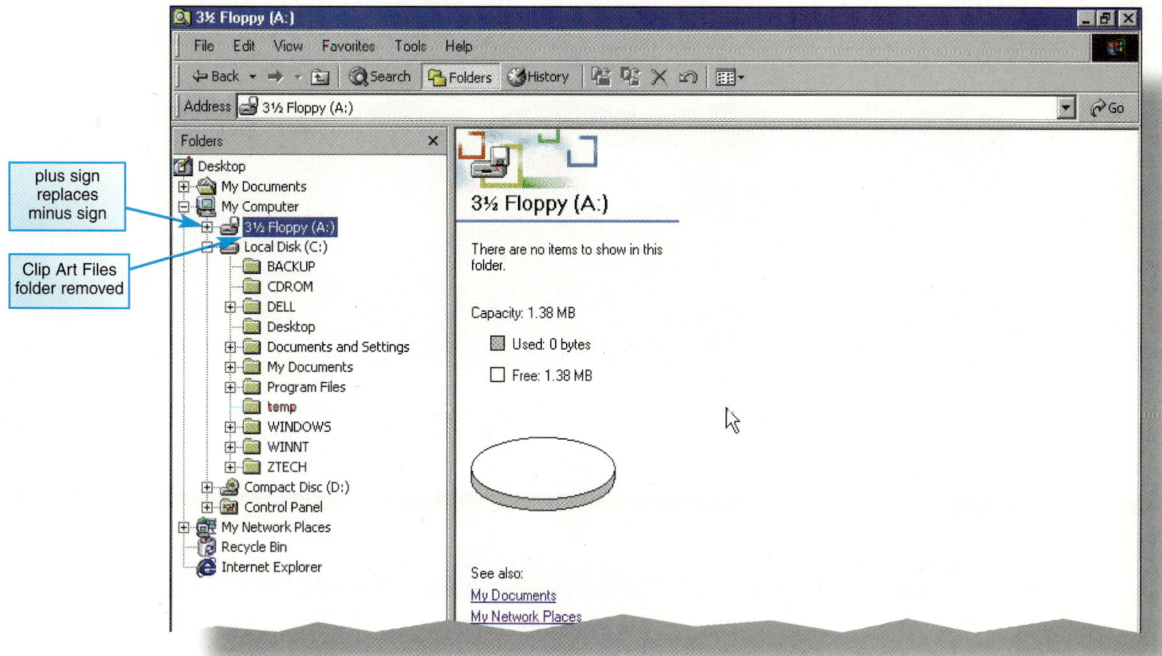

FIGURE 1-69

Quitting Windows Explorer

After completing your work with Windows Explorer, you should quit Windows Explorer. Perform the following steps to quit Windows Explorer.

TO QUIT A PROGRAM

1. Point to the Close button on the Exploring window title bar.
2. Click the Close button.

Windows 2000 closes the Explorer window and quits Windows Explorer.

Using Windows Help

One of the more powerful application programs for use in Windows 2000 is Windows Help. **Windows Help** is available when using Windows 2000, or when using any application program running under Windows 2000, to assist you in using Windows 2000 and the various application programs. It contains answers to many questions you may ask with respect to Windows 2000.

Contents Sheet

Windows Help provides a variety of ways in which to obtain information. One method of finding a Help topic involves using the **Contents sheet** to browse through Help topics by category. To illustrate this method, you will use Windows Help to determine how to find a topic in Help. To launch Help, complete the steps on the next page.

More About 2000

Windows 2000 Help

If you purchased an operating system or application program five years ago, you received at least one, and more often several, thick and heavy technical manuals that explained the software. With Windows 2000, you receive a skinny manual less than 100 pages in length. The online Help feature of Windows 2000 replaces reams and reams of printed pages in hard-to-understand technical manuals.

To Launch Windows Help

1 Click the Start button on the taskbar. Point to Help on the Start menu (Figure 1-70).

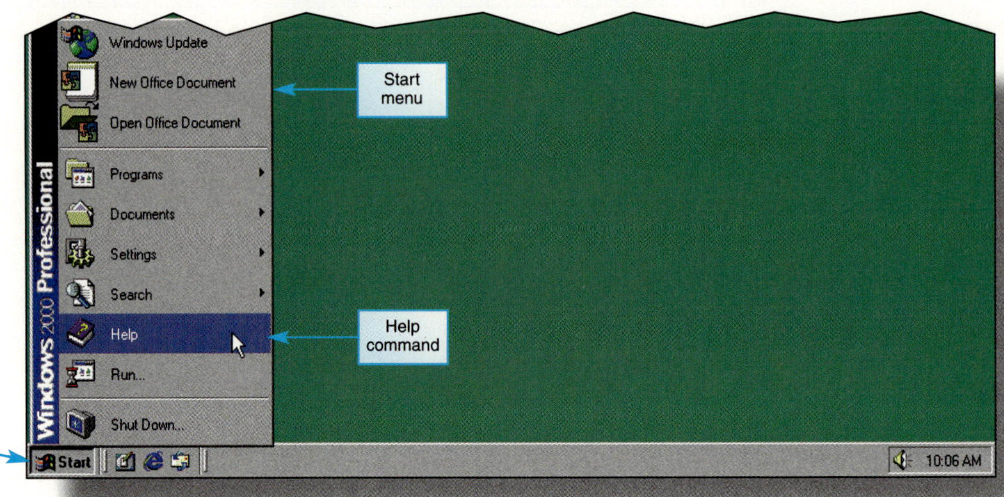

FIGURE 1-70

2 Click Help. Click the Maximize button on the Windows 2000 title bar. If the Contents sheet does not display, click the Contents tab.

The Windows 2000 window opens and maximizes (Figure 1-71). The window contains the Help toolbar and two panes. The left pane, called the ***navigation pane,*** *contains four tabs. Clicking the Contents tab displays the Contents sheet. The right pane, called the* ***topic pane,*** *contains the Start Here screen, containing the Microsoft 2000 Professional title and Start Here table of contents.*

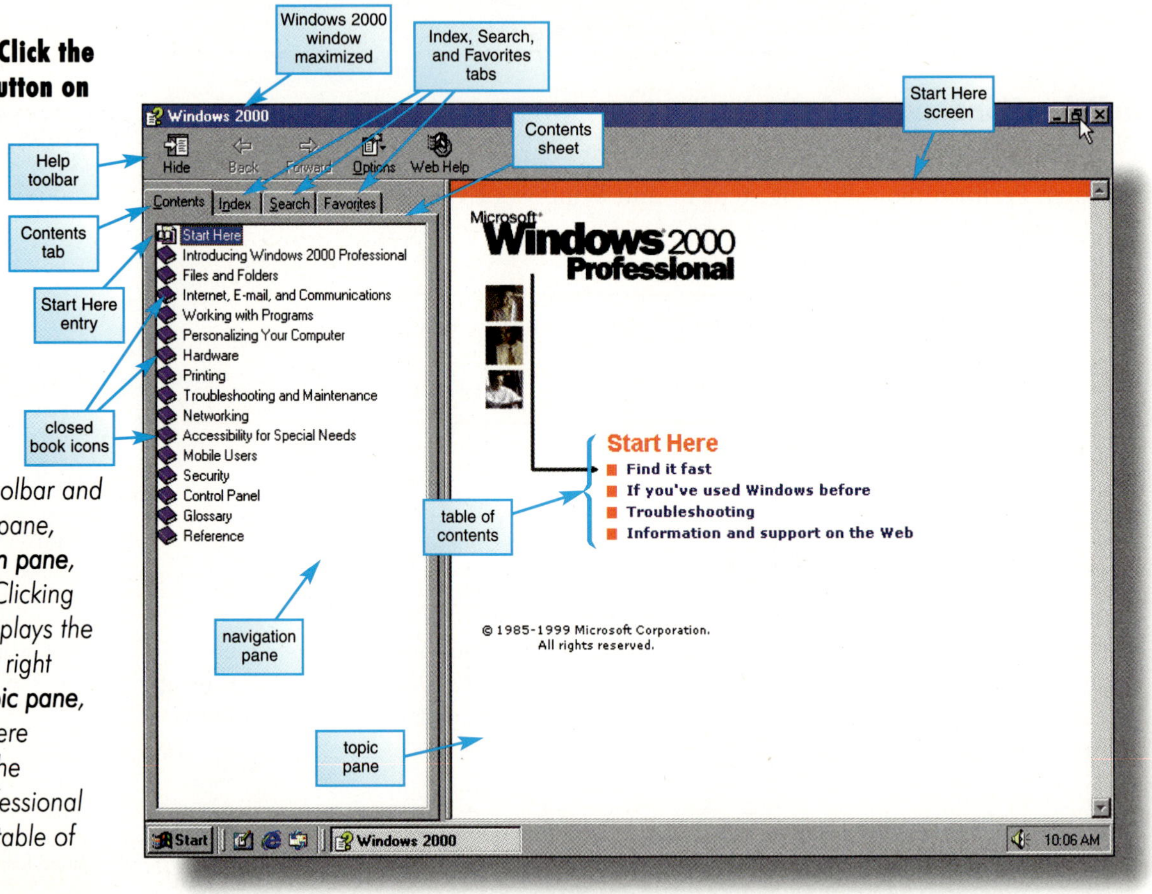

FIGURE 1-71

Other Ways

1. Click open area of desktop, press F1
2. Press WINDOWS+F1 (WINDOWS key on Microsoft Natural keyboard)

The Contents sheet in the navigation pane contains 16 entries. The first entry is identified by an open book and document icon, and the highlighted Start Here name. The **open book and document icon** indicates additional information or an overview is available for the entry. The Start Here entry is highlighted to indicate additional information about the entry displays in the topic pane. The topic pane contains the **Start Here screen**. The Start Here screen contains a table of contents consisting of four items (Find it fast, If you've used Windows before, Troubleshooting, and Information and support on the Web).

A closed book icon precedes each of the remaining 15 entries in the Contents sheet. The **closed book icon** indicates that Help topics or more books are contained in a book but do not display in the Contents sheet. Clicking the Index tab, Search tab, or Favorites tab in the navigation pane displays the Index, Search, or Favorites sheet, respectively.

In addition to launching Help by using the Start button, you also can launch Help by clicking an open area of the desktop and pressing the F1 key.

After launching Help, the next step is to find the topic in which you are interested. Assume you want to find information about locating a Help topic. Perform the following steps to find the topic that describes how to find a topic in Help.

To Use Help to Find a Topic in Help

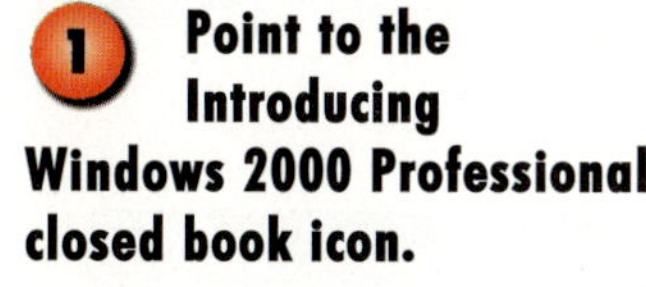

1 Point to the Introducing Windows 2000 Professional closed book icon.

The mouse pointer changes to a hand when positioned on the icon and the Introducing Windows 2000 book name displays in blue font and underlined (Figure 1-72).

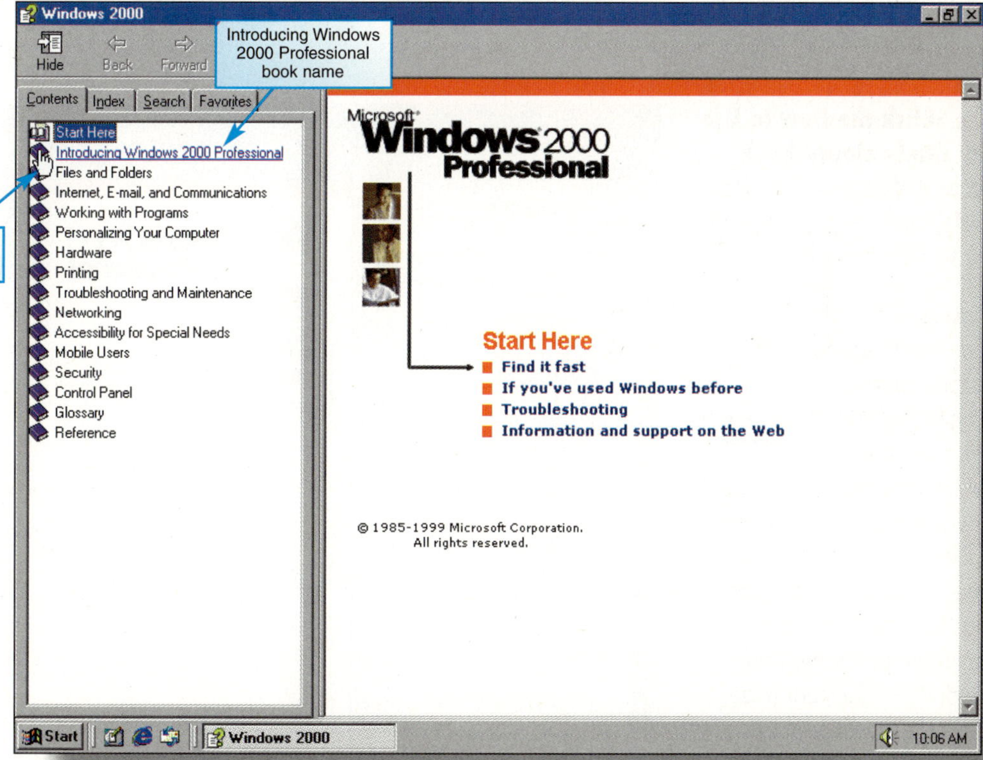

FIGURE 1-72

2 Click the Introducing Windows 2000 closed book icon and then point to the How to Use Help closed book icon.

Windows 2000 opens the Introducing Windows 2000 Professional book, changes the closed book icon to an open book icon, highlights the Introducing Windows 2000 Professional book name, underlines the How to Use Help book name, and displays the name and underline in blue font (Figure 1-73). The **open book icon** *indicates that Help topics or books contained in the book display indented below the book.*

open book icon

closed book icon

book name highlighted

How to Use Help book name

FIGURE 1-73

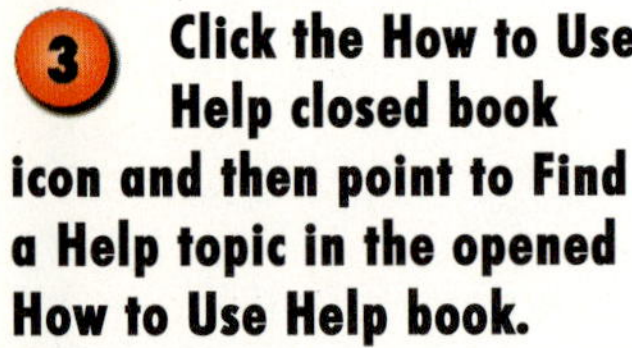

3 Click the How to Use Help closed book icon and then point to Find a Help topic in the opened How to Use Help book.

Windows 2000 opens the How to Use Help book, changes the closed book icon to an open book icon, highlights the How to Use Help book name, underlines the Find a Help topic name, and displays the topic name and underline in blue font (Figure 1-74). The **question mark icon** *indicates a Help topic without further subdivisions. Clicking the* **Help overview** *icon displays an overview of the Help system.*

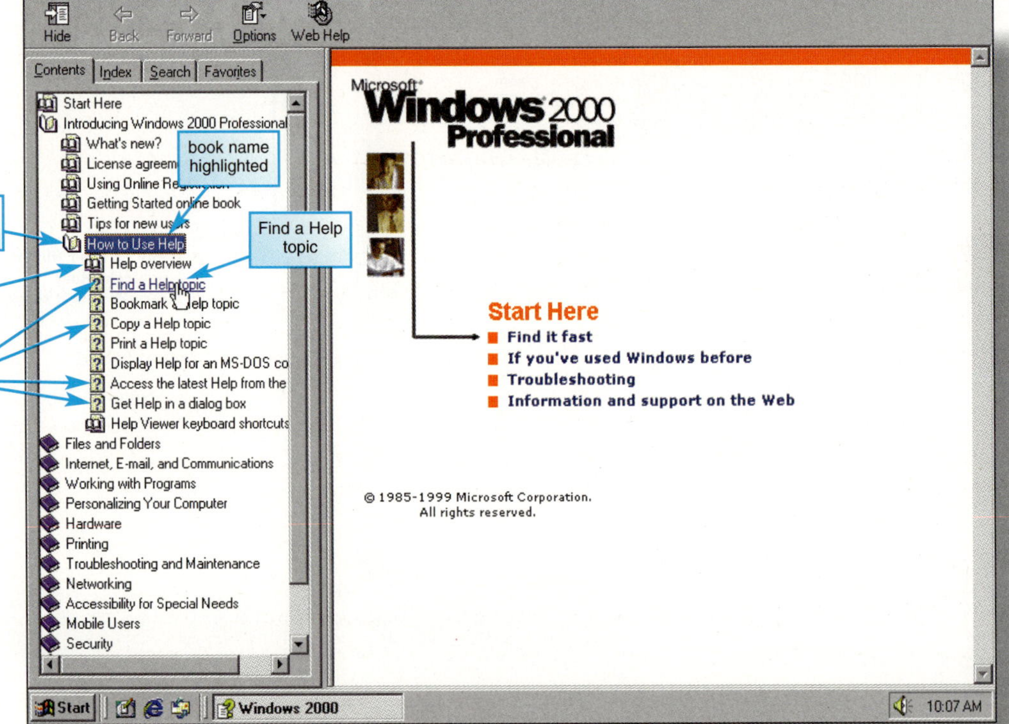

FIGURE 1-74

4 Click Find a Help topic. Read the information about finding a Help topic in the topic pane.

Windows 2000 highlights the Find a Help topic name and displays information about finding a Help topic in the topic pane (Figure 1-75). Clicking the plus sign in the small box to the left of the Contents tab, Index tab, Search tab, or Favorites tab entries in the topic pane displays additional information about the entry.

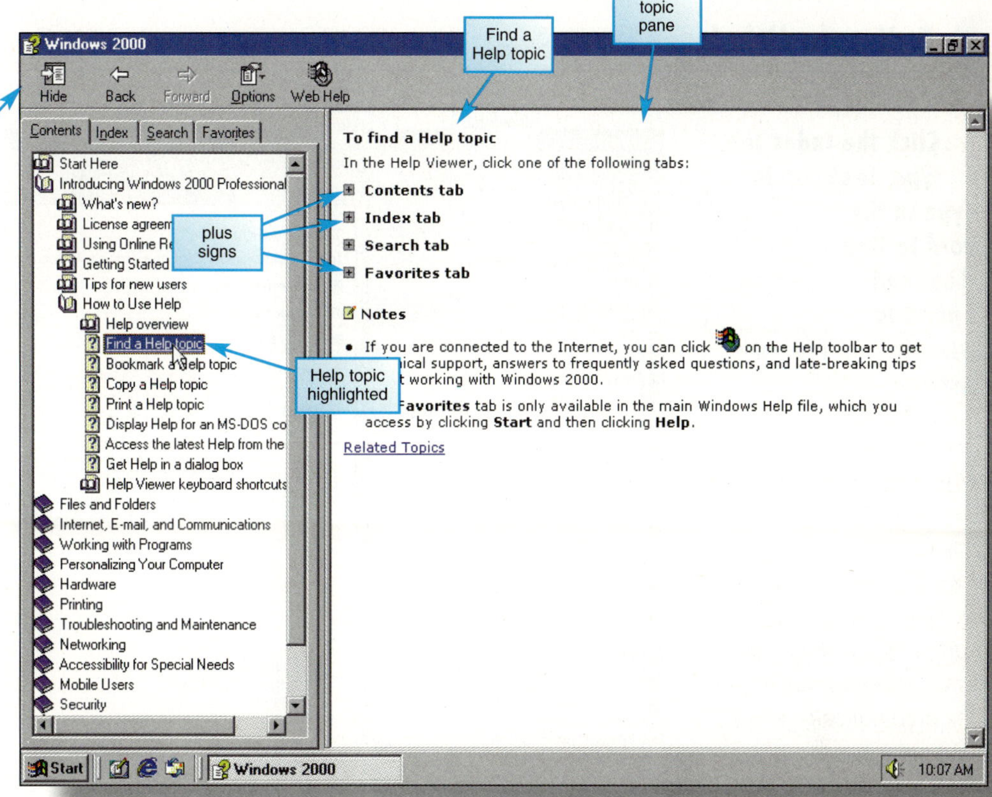

FIGURE 1-75

In Figure 1-75, the Help toolbar contains five icons. If you click the **Hide button** on the Help toolbar, Windows 2000 hides the tabs in the navigation pane and displays only the topic pane in the Windows 2000 window. Clicking the **Back button** or **Forward button** displays a previously displayed Help topic in the topic pane. Clicking the **Options button** allows you to hide or display the tabs in the navigation pane, display previously displayed Help topics in the topic pane, stop the display of a Help topic, refresh the currently displayed Help topic, access the Internet options, access Web Help, and print a Help topic. The **Web Help command** on the Options menu and the **Web Help button** on the Help toolbar allow you to use the Internet to obtain technical support, answers to frequently asked questions, and tips about working with Windows 2000.

Notice also in Figure 1-75 that the Windows 2000 title bar contains a Minimize button, Restore Down button, and Close button. You can minimize or restore the Windows 2000 window as needed and also close the Windows 2000 window.

Index Sheet

A second method of finding answers to your questions about Windows 2000 or application programs running under Windows 2000 is to use the Index sheet. The **Index sheet** contains a list of index entries, each of which references one or more Help screens. Assume you want more information about the desktop and the objects on the desktop. Perform the steps on the next page to learn more about the desktop and the objects on the desktop.

Other Ways

1. Press DOWN ARROW key until book name is highlighted, press RIGHT ARROW (or ENTER), continue until Help topic displays, press ENTER, read Help topic

More About 2000

The Index Sheet

The Index sheet probably is the best source of information in Windows Help because you can enter the subject you are interested in. Sometimes, however, you will have to be creative to discover the index entry that answers your question because the most obvious entry will not always lead to your answer.

To Use the Help Index Sheet

1 Click the Index tab, type desktop **in the Type in the keyword to find text box, and then point to overview in the list.**

The Index sheet, containing the Type in the keyword to find text box, a list box, and Display button, displays (Figure 1-76). When you type an entry in the text box, the list of index entries in the list box automatically scrolls and the entry you type (desktop) is highlighted in the list. Several entries display indented below the desktop entry. The indentation indicates they pertain to the highlighted entry.

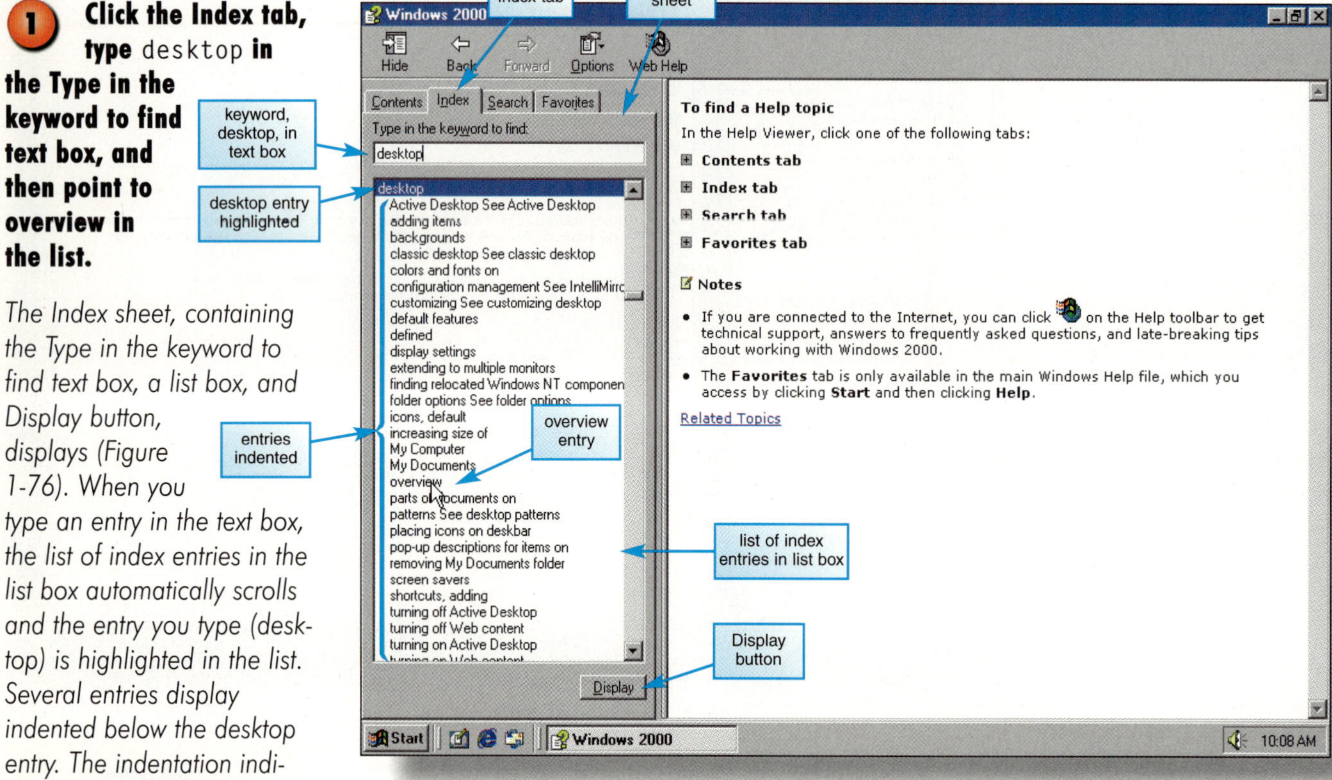

FIGURE 1-76

2 Click overview and then point to the Display button at the bottom of the Index sheet.

Windows 2000 displays the desktop, overview entry in the text box and highlights the overview entry in the list (Figure 1-77).

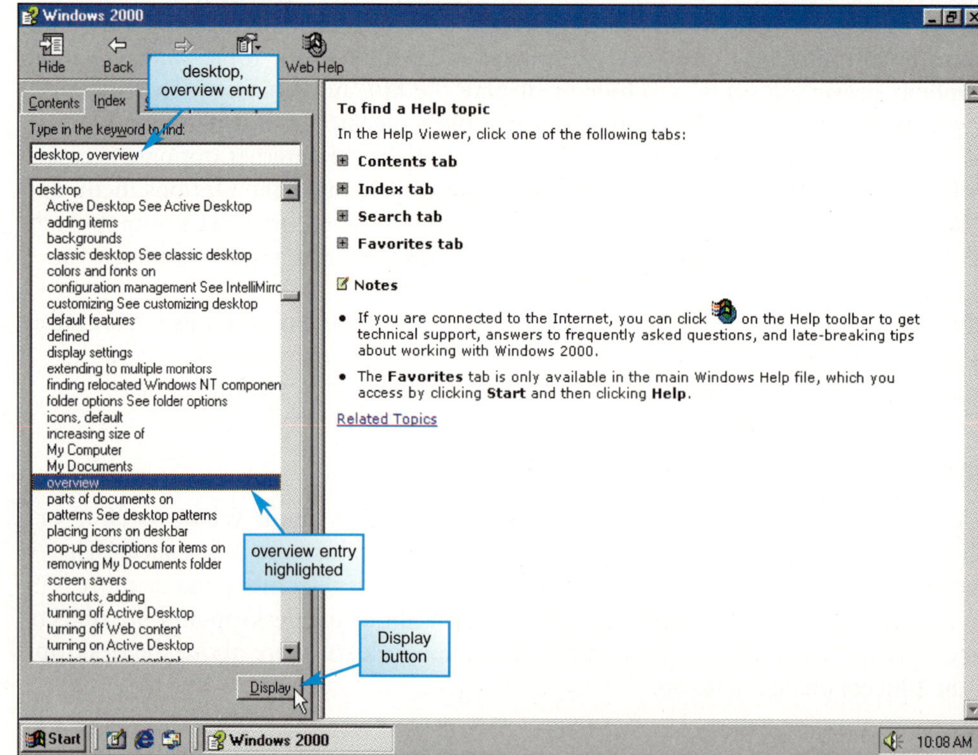

FIGURE 1-77

Click the Display button.

The Desktop overview topic displays in the topic pane (Figure 1-78). The topic contains an overview of the desktop, a list of desktop features, and several links (shortcuts, programs, active content, channel, Windows 2000 Professional Getting Started, and Related Topics). Clicking the plus sign in the small box to the left of a desktop feature displays additional information about that feature.

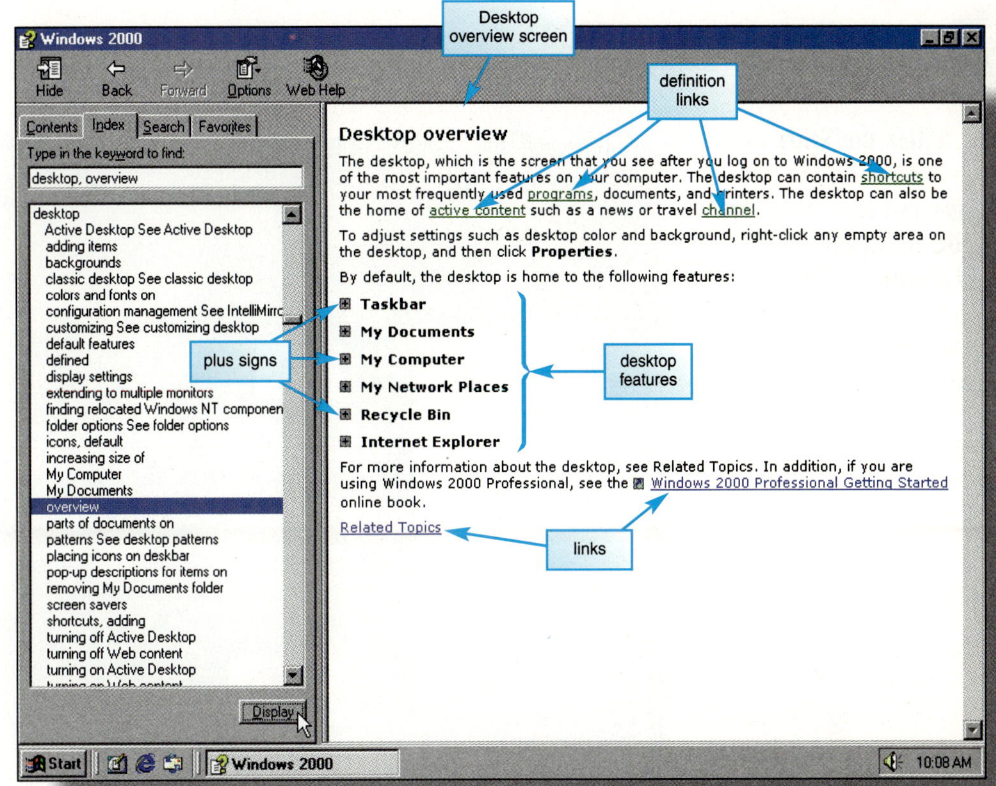

FIGURE 1-78

Other Ways

1. Press ALT+N, type keyword, press DOWN ARROW until topic is highlighted, press ALT+D (or ENTER)

In Figure 1-78, the shortcuts, programs, active content, and channel links are underlined and display in green font to indicate that clicking a link will display its definition. Clicking anywhere off the definition removes the definition.

The Windows 2000 Professional Getting Started and Related Topics links are underlined and display in blue font. Clicking the Windows 2000 Professional Getting Started link displays the Getting Started online book that helps you install Windows 2000, use the desktop, learn about new features, connect to a network, and find answers to commonly asked questions. Clicking the Related Topics link displays a pop-up window that contains topics related to the desktop overview topic.

After viewing the index entries and selecting those you need, normally you will close Windows Help. To close Windows Help, complete the following step.

TO CLOSE WINDOWS HELP

Click the Close button on the title bar of the Windows 2000 window.

Windows 2000 closes the Windows 2000 window.

Shut Down Procedures

Some users of Windows 2000 have turned off their computers without following the shut down procedure only to find data they thought they had stored on disk was lost. Because of the way Windows 2000 writes data on the disk, it is important you shut down Windows properly so you do not lose your work.

Shutting Down Windows 2000

After completing your work with Windows 2000, you may want to shut down Windows 2000 using the Shut Down command on the Start menu. If you are sure you want to shut down Windows 2000, perform the steps on the next page. If you are not sure about shutting down Windows 2000, read the steps without actually performing them.

To Shut Down Windows 2000

1 Click the Start button on the taskbar and then point to Shut Down on the Start menu (Figure 1-79).

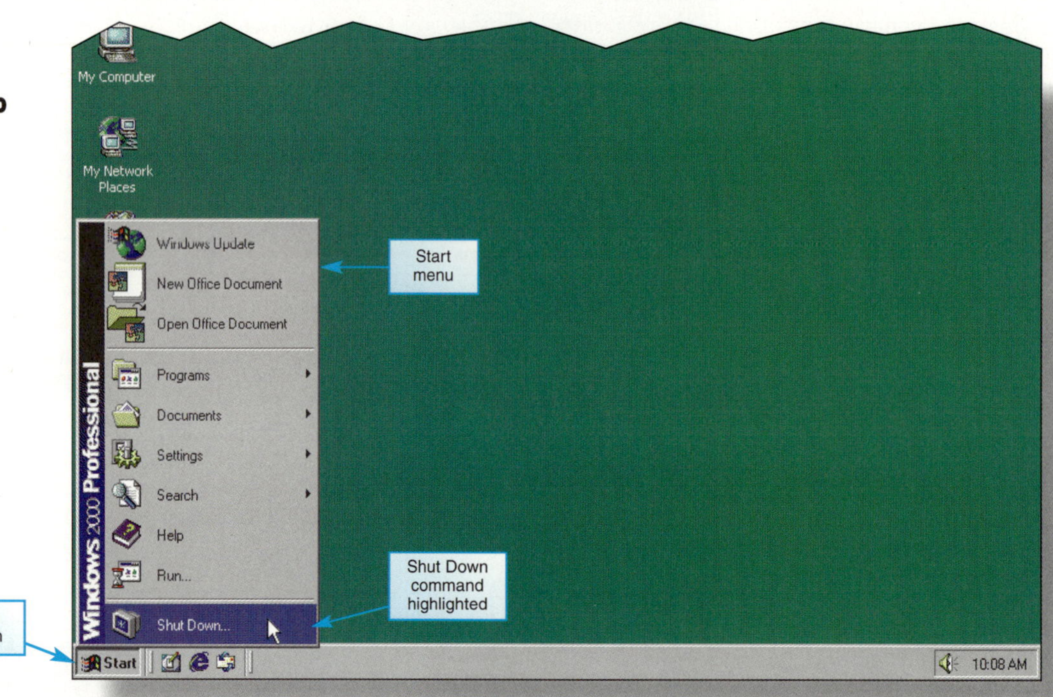

FIGURE 1-79

2 Click Shut Down. Point to the OK button in the Shut Down Windows dialog box.

The desktop darkens and the Shut Down Windows dialog box displays (Figure 1-80). The dialog box contains the What do you want the computer to do? box and three command buttons. The highlighted command, Shut down, displays in the box.

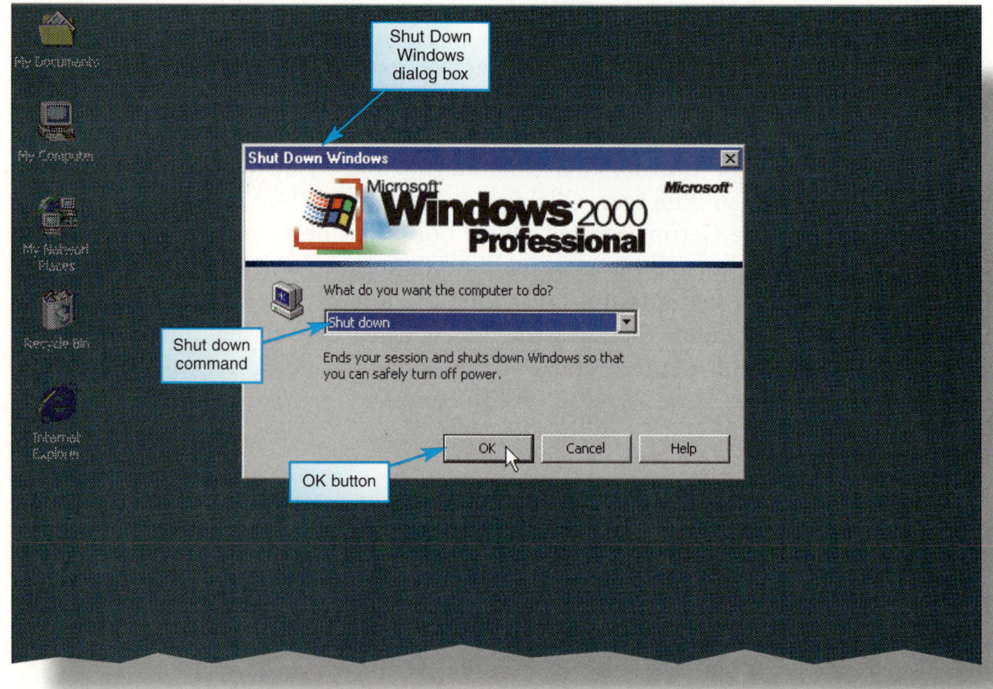

FIGURE 1-80

3 Click the OK button.

Windows 2000 is shut down.

Other Ways

1. Press CTRL+ESC, press U, press ARROW keys to select Shut down, press ENTER
2. Press ALT+F1, press ARROW keys to select Shut down, press ENTER

While Windows 2000 is shutting down, two dialog boxes display momentarily on a blue background. First, the Please Wait dialog box containing the Windows

2000 logo, Windows 2000 name, and the text, saving your settings, displays momentarily. Then, the Shutdown in Progress dialog box, containing the text, Please wait while the system writes unsaved data to disk, displays. At this point you can turn off the computer. Some computers are programmed to turn off automatically at this point. When shutting down Windows 2000, you should never turn off the computer before these two dialog boxes display.

If you accidentally click Shut Down on the Start menu and you do not want to shut down Windows 2000, click the Cancel button in the Shut Down Windows dialog box to return to normal Windows 2000 operation.

What Is Microsoft Office 2000?

Microsoft Office 2000, the latest edition of the world's best-selling office suite, is a collection of the more popular Microsoft application software products. Microsoft Office 2000 is available in Standard, Small Business, Professional, Premium, and Developer editions. The **Microsoft Office 2000 Premium Edition** includes Microsoft Word 2000, Microsoft Excel 2000, Microsoft Access 2000, Microsoft PowerPoint 2000, Microsoft Publisher 2000, Microsoft FrontPage 2000, Microsoft PhotoDraw 2000, Microsoft Outlook 2000, and Internet Explorer. Microsoft Office 2000 allows you to work more efficiently, communicate better, and improve the appearance of the documents you create.

One of the CD-ROMs that accompanies Microsoft Office 2000 contains a clip art gallery that you can use in any of the applications to enhance the appearance of a document. The gallery contains over 16,000 clip art images, sounds, photographs, animations, themes, and backgrounds. In addition, thousands of additional images are available from the Microsoft Clipart Gallery Live found on the Microsoft Web site. Hundreds of new images are added each month to this collection.()

Menus and toolbars adjust to the way in which you work. As Microsoft Office detects which commands you use more frequently, these commands display at the top of the menu, and the infrequently used commands are placed in reserve. A button at the bottom of the menu allows you to expand the menu in order to view all its commands. More frequently used buttons on a toolbar display on the toolbar, while less frequently used buttons are not displayed.

Microsoft Office applications are self-repairing. If you accidentally delete a file that is needed to run an Office application, the Self-Repairing Application feature automatically finds the deleted file and reinstalls the file. This feature reduces the number of calls to technical support and increases user productivity.

In addition, Microsoft Office 2000 integrates its applications with the power of the Internet so you can share information, collaborate on projects, and conduct online meetings.

More About 2000

Office 2000

For more information about any Microsoft Office 2000 application, click Help on the menu bar of any Office 2000 application window, and click Office on the Web. Explore a Web page by clicking a hyperlink. After clicking a hyperlink, click the Back button to display the last Web page.

The Internet, World Wide Web, and Intranets

Microsoft Office 2000 allows you to take advantage of the Internet, the World Wide Web, and intranets. The **Internet** is a worldwide network of thousands of computer networks and millions of commercial, educational, government, and personal computers. The **World Wide Web** is an easy-to-use graphical interface for exploring the Internet. The World Wide Web consists of many individual Web sites. A **Web site** can consist of a single **Web page** or multiple Web pages linked together. The first Web page in the Web site is called the **home page** and a unique address, called a **Uniform Resource Locator** (**URL**) identifies each Web page. Web sites are located on computers called Web servers.

A software tool, called a **browser**, allows you to locate and view a Web page. One method of viewing a Web page is to use the browser to enter the URL for the Web page. A widely used browser, called **Microsoft Internet Explorer**, is included with Microsoft Office 2000. Another method of viewing Web pages allows you to click a hyperlink. A hyperlink is colored or underlined text or a graphic that, when clicked, connects to another Web page.

An **intranet** is a special type of Web that is available only to the users of a particular type of computer network, such as a network used within a company or organization for internal communication. Like the Internet, hyperlinks are used within an intranet to access documents, pages, and other destinations on the intranet.

More About 2000

Microsoft Office 2000

To subscribe to a free Office 2000 weekly newsletter delivered via e-mail, visit the Office 2000 More About Web page (www.scsite.com/off2000/more.htm) and then click Office 2000 Newsletter.

Microsoft Office 2000 and the Internet

Microsoft Office 2000 was designed in response to customer requests to streamline the process of information sharing and collaboration within their organizations. Organizations that, in the past, made important information available only to a select few, now want their information accessible to a wider range of individuals who are using tools such as Microsoft Office and Microsoft Internet Explorer. Microsoft Office 2000 allows users to utilize the Internet or an intranet as a central location to view documents, manage files, and work together.

Each of the Microsoft Office 2000 applications makes publishing documents on a Web server as simple as saving a file on a hard disk. Once the file is placed on the Web server, users can view and edit the documents, and conduct Web discussions and live online meetings.

An explanation of each Microsoft Office 2000 application software program in the Premium Edition along with how it is used to access an intranet or the Internet is given on the following pages.

Microsoft Word 2000

For more information about Microsoft Word 2000, click Help on the menu bar of the Microsoft Word window, and click Office on the Web. Explore a Web page by clicking a hyperlink. After clicking a hyperlink, click the Back button to display the last Web page.

Microsoft Word 2000

Microsoft Word 2000 is a full-featured word processing program that allows you to create many types of personal and business communications, including announcements, letters, memos, business documents, and academic reports, as well as other forms of written documents. Figure 1-81 illustrates the top portion of the announcement that students create in one of the exercises in Project 1 of the Microsoft Word section of this book. The steps to create an announcement are shown in Project 1 of Microsoft Word 2000.

The Microsoft Word AutoCorrect, Spelling, and Grammar features allow you to proofread documents for errors in spelling and grammar by identifying the errors and offering corrections as you type. As you create a specific document, such as a business letter or resume, Word provides wizards, which ask questions and then use your answers to format the document before you type the text of the document.

The Collect and Paste feature allows you to cut or copy as many as 12 objects (text, pictures, e-mail messages, and so on) and collect them on the Office Clipboard. Then you can paste them into the same document or different documents. Collect and Paste can be used within a single Office 2000 application or among multiple Office 2000 applications.

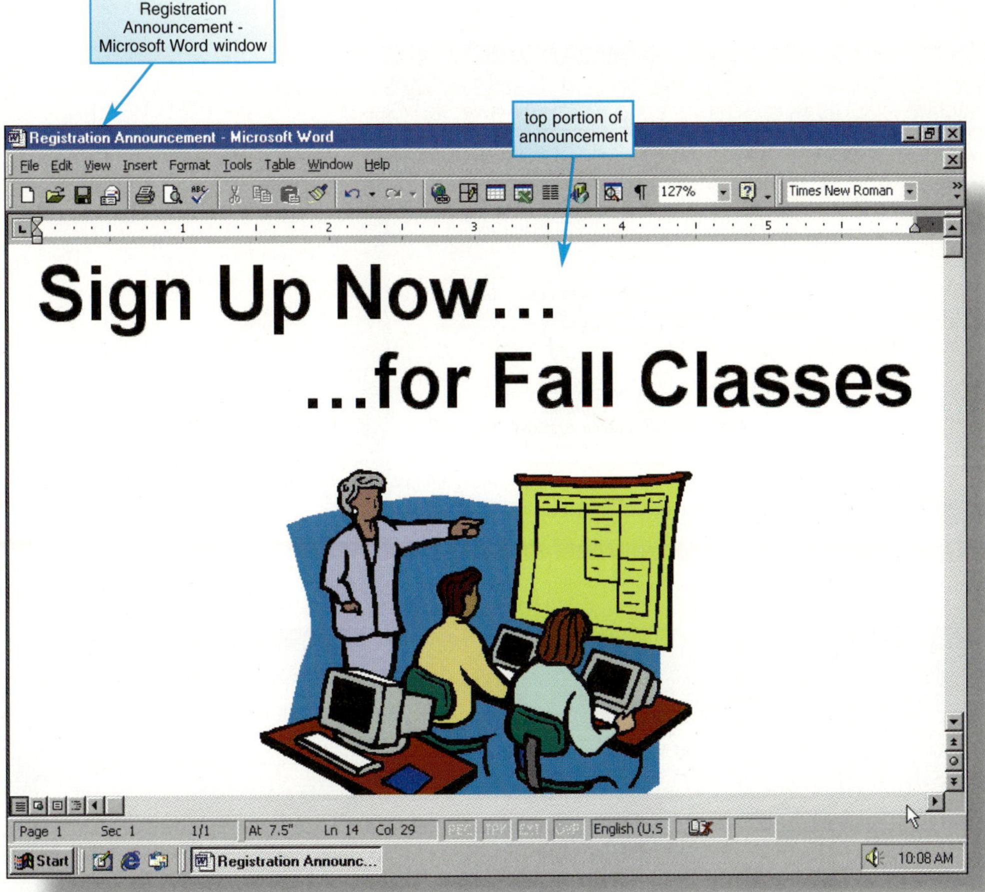

FIGURE 1-81

Microsoft Word automates many often-used tasks and provides you with powerful desktop publishing tools to use as you create professional-looking brochures, advertisements, and newsletters. The drawing tools allow you to design impressive 3-D effects by including shadows, textures, and curves. Floating tables permit you to position a table in an exact location on a page and then wrap text around the table.

Microsoft Word 2000 and the Internet

Microsoft Word makes it possible to access Web pages and search for information, design and publish Web pages on an intranet or the Internet, insert a hyperlink to a Web page in a word processing document, and retrieve pictures from other Web pages. Figure 1-82 on the next page illustrates the top portion of a cover letter that contains a hyperlink (e-mail address) that allows you to send an e-mail message to the sender.

Clicking the hyperlink starts the Microsoft Outlook mail program and allows you to send an e-mail message to the author of the cover letter. In Figure 1-83 on the next page, the Resume and Cover Letter - Message [Rich Text] window that allows you to compose a new e-mail message contains the recipient's e-mail address (brandon@lenox.com), subject of the e-mail message (Resume and Cover Letter), and a brief message.

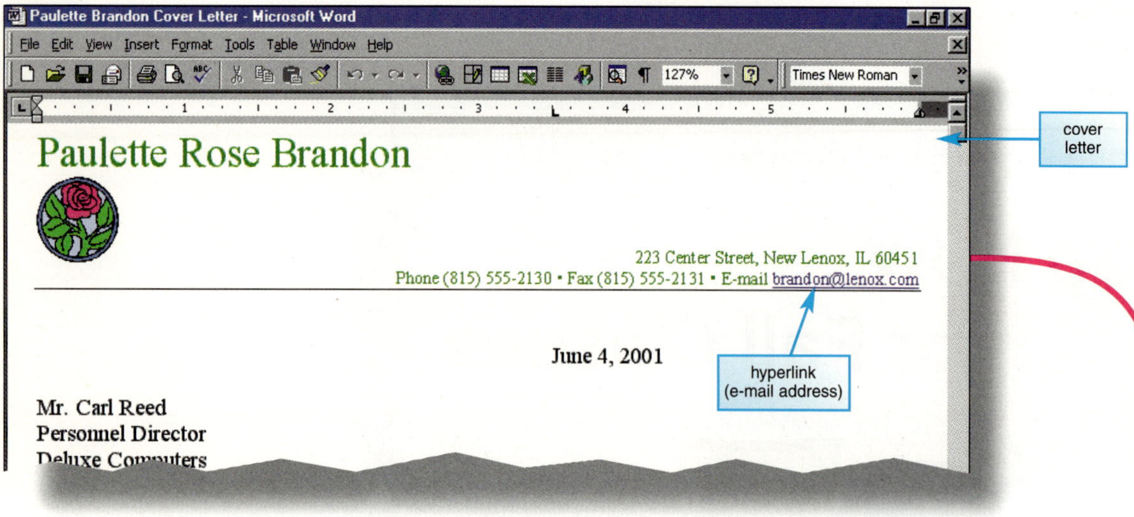

FIGURE 1-82

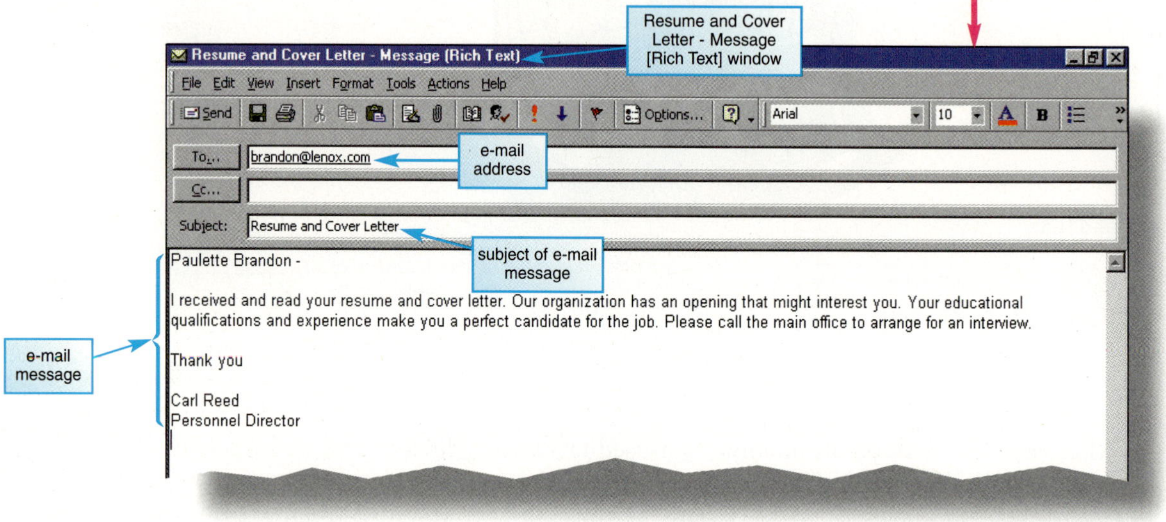

FIGURE 1-83

Microsoft Excel 2000

Microsoft Excel 2000 is a spreadsheet program that allows you to organize data, complete calculations, make decisions, graph data, develop professional-looking reports, publish organized data on the Web, and access real-time data from Web sites. Figure 1-84 illustrates the Microsoft Excel window that contains the worksheet and 3-D column chart created in Project 1 of the Microsoft Excel section of this book.

Microsoft Excel 2000

For more information about Microsoft Excel 2000, click Help on the menu bar of the Microsoft Excel window, and click Office on the Web. Explore a Web page by clicking a hyperlink. After clicking a hyperlink, click the Back button to display the last Web page.

Microsoft Excel 2000 and the Internet

Using Microsoft Excel, you can create hyperlinks within a worksheet to access other Office 2000 documents on the network, an organization's intranet, or the Internet. You also can save worksheets as static and dynamic Web pages that can be viewed using your browser. Static Web pages cannot be changed by the person viewing them. Dynamic Web pages give the person viewing them many Excel capabilities in their browser. In addition, you can create and run queries to retrieve information from a Web page directly into a worksheet.

Figure 1-85 illustrates a worksheet created by running a Web query to retrieve stock market information for two stocks (CMGI, Inc. and America Online, Inc.).

Microsoft Excel - Fun-N-Sun Sojourn 1st Qtr Sales window
Microsoft Excel - Fun-N-Sun Sojourn 1st Qtr Sales
Fun-N-Sun Sojourn 1st Qtr Sales
Mail
Campus
Telephone
Web
Total
Bahamas Repose $ 52,978.23 $ 38,781.35 $ 37,213.45 $ 29,998.65 $158,971.68
Daytona Delight 28,234.50 48,401.53 27,034.56 42,911.16 146,581.75
Key West Haven 62,567.25 72,516.12 24,354.86 77,019.32 236,457.55
South Padre Del Sol 28,567.15 69,777.64 49,976.60 32,019.45 180,340.84
Total $172,347.13 $229,476.64 $138,579.47 $181,948.58 $722,351.82
worksheet
$80,000.00
$60,000.00
$40,000.00
$20,000.00
$-
Mail
Campus
Telephone
Web
Bahamas Repose
Daytona Delight
Key West Haven
South Padre Del Sol
3-D column chart

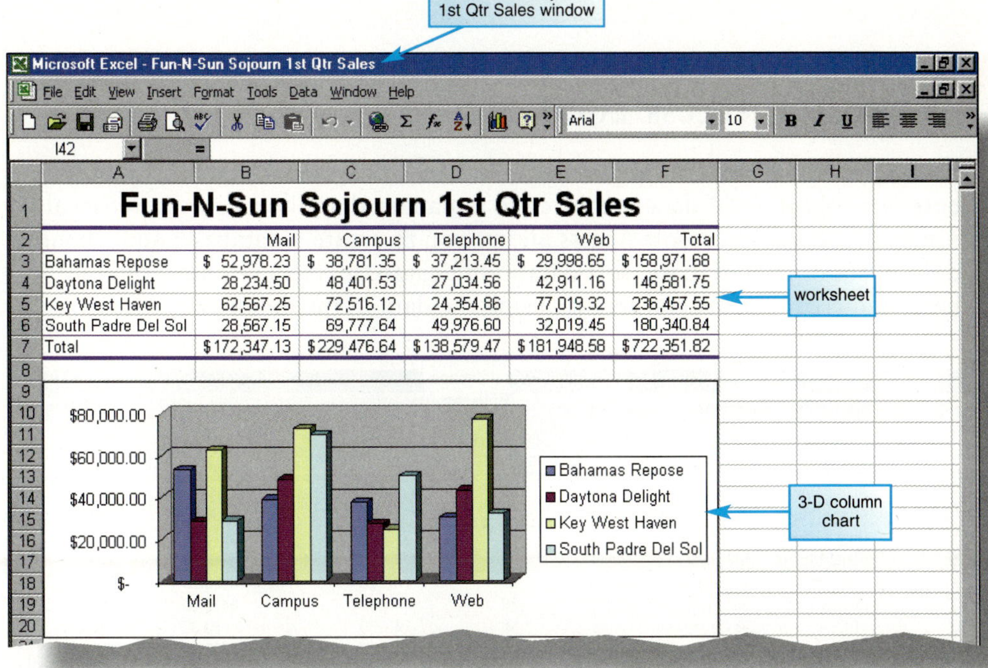

FIGURE 1-84

The two hyperlinks were created using the Insert HyperLink button on the Standard toolbar, and the information in the worksheet was obtained from the Microsoft Investor Web site. The Refresh All button on the External Data toolbar allows you to update the last price of the stocks (Last).

Clicking the Refresh All button locates the Microsoft Investor Web site, retrieves current information for the stocks in the worksheet, and displays the updated information in the worksheet (Figure 1-86). Notice that the stock prices and information in this worksheet differ from what was displayed in the worksheet in Figure 1-85.

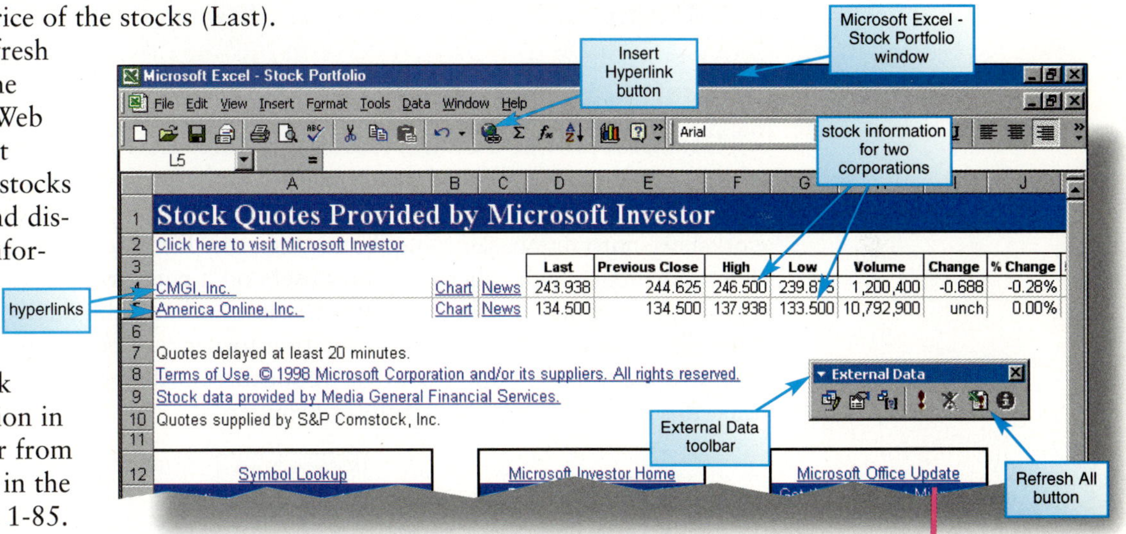

Microsoft Excel - Stock Portfolio window
Insert Hyperlink button
stock information for two corporations
Microsoft Excel - Stock Portfolio
Stock Quotes Provided by Microsoft Investor
Click here to visit Microsoft Investor
Last Previous Close High Low Volume Change % Change
CMGI, Inc. Chart News 243.938 244.625 246.500 239.875 1,200,400 -0.688 -0.28%
America Online, Inc. Chart News 134.500 134.500 137.938 133.500 10,792,900 unch 0.00%
hyperlinks
Quotes delayed at least 20 minutes.
Terms of Use. © 1998 Microsoft Corporation and/or its suppliers. All rights reserved.
Stock data provided by Media General Financial Services.
Quotes supplied by S&P Comstock, Inc.
External Data
External Data toolbar
Symbol Lookup
Microsoft Investor Home
Microsoft Office Update
Refresh All button

FIGURE 1-85

Microsoft Excel - Stock Portfolio
updated last price
updated stock information
Stock Quotes Provided by Microsoft Investor
Click here to visit Microsoft Investor
Last Previous Close High Low Volume Change % Change
CMGI, Inc. Chart News 229.375 229.563 236.000 223.500 1,839,200 -0.188 -0.08%
America Online, Inc. Chart News 129.875 125.250 131.250 125.500 16,070,400 +4.625 +3.69%
Quotes delayed at least 20 minutes.

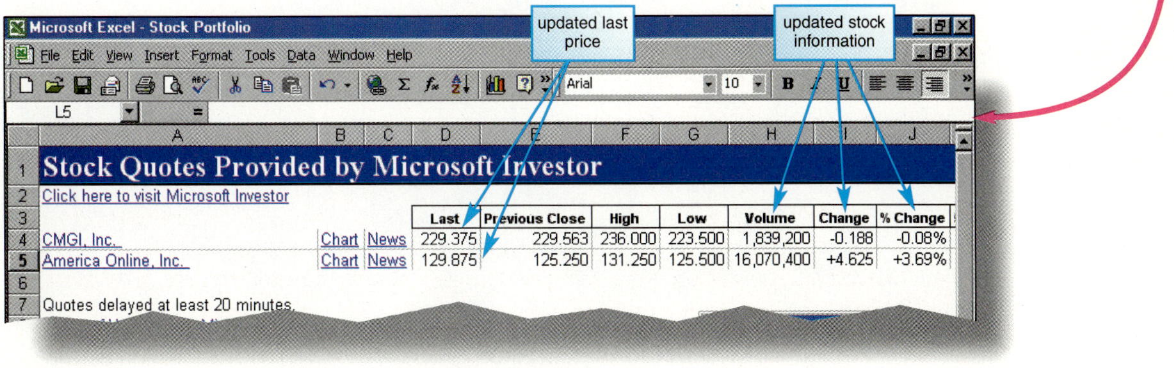

FIGURE 1-86

Microsoft Access 2000

Microsoft Access 2000 is a comprehensive **database management system** (**DBMS**). A **database** is a collection of data organized in a manner that allows access, retrieval, and use of that data. Microsoft Access allows you to create a database; add, change, and delete data in the database; sort data in the database; retrieve data from the database; and create forms and reports using the data in the database.

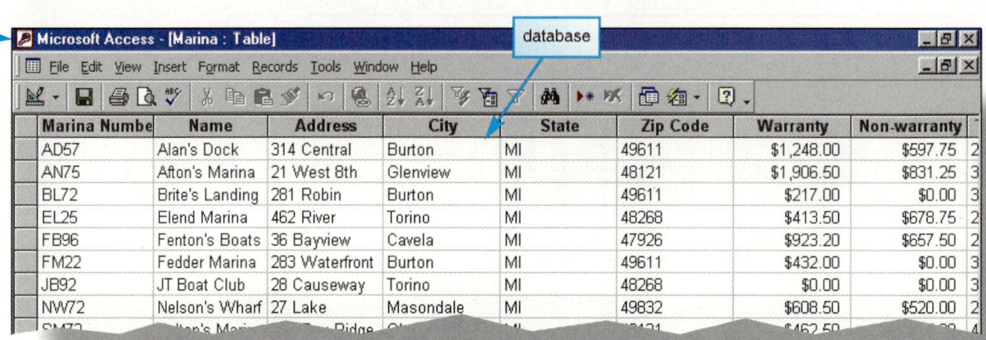

Marina Numbe	Name	Address	City	State	Zip Code	Warranty	Non-warranty
AD57	Alan's Dock	314 Central	Burton	MI	49611	$1,248.00	$597.75
AN75	Afton's Marina	21 West 8th	Glenview	MI	48121	$1,906.50	$831.25
BL72	Brite's Landing	281 Robin	Burton	MI	49611	$217.00	$0.00
EL25	Elend Marina	462 River	Torino	MI	48268	$413.50	$678.75
FB96	Fenton's Boats	36 Bayview	Cavela	MI	47926	$923.20	$657.50
FM22	Fedder Marina	283 Waterfront	Burton	MI	49611	$432.00	$0.00
JB92	JT Boat Club	28 Causeway	Torino	MI	48268	$0.00	$0.00
NW72	Nelson's Wharf	27 Lake	Masondale	MI	49832	$608.50	$520.00

FIGURE 1-87

The database created in Project 1 of the Microsoft Access section of this book displays in the Microsoft Access - [Marina : Table] window illustrated in Figure 1-87. The steps to create this database are shown in Project 1 of Access.

Microsoft Access 2000 and the Internet

Databases provide a central location to store related pieces of information. Microsoft Access simplifies the creation of databases with a wizard that can build one of more than a dozen types of databases quickly. You also can transform lists or worksheets into databases using Access wizards. Data access pages allow you to share a database with other computer users on a network, intranet, or over the Internet, as well as allowing the users to view and edit the database. The database shown in Figure 1-88 contains information (order number, customer number, order date, product number, and quantity) about three orders entered over the Internet using the Microsoft Internet Explorer browser.

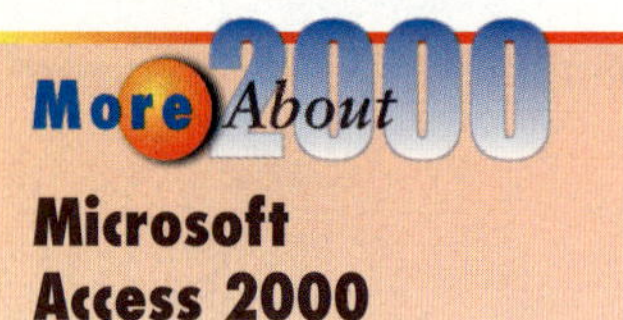

Microsoft Access 2000

For more information about Microsoft Access 2000, click Help on the menu bar of the Microsoft Access window, and click Office on the Web. Explore a Web page by clicking a hyperlink. After clicking a hyperlink, click the Back button to display the last Web page.

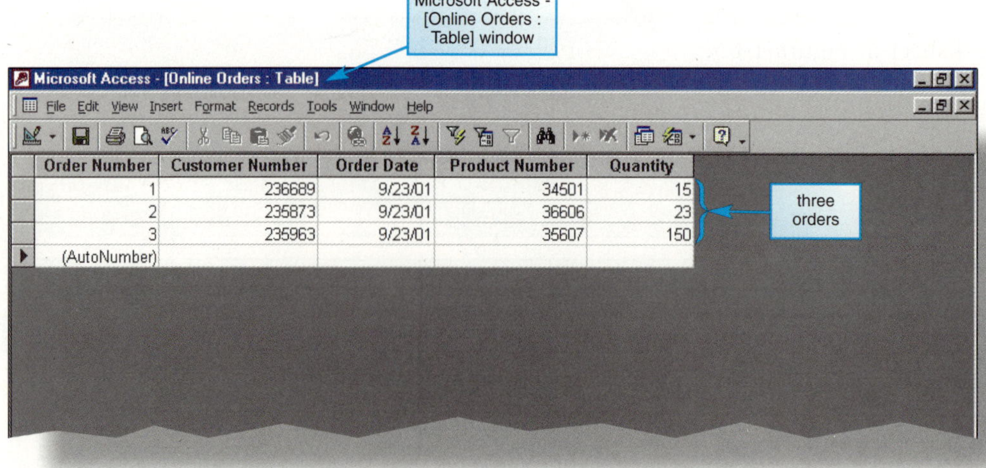

Order Number	Customer Number	Order Date	Product Number	Quantity
1	236689	9/23/01	34501	15
2	235873	9/23/01	36606	23
3	235963	9/23/01	35607	150
(AutoNumber)				

FIGURE 1-88

Figure 1-89 illustrates a simple online order form created to enter order information into the database shown in Figure 1-88. The order form, containing information about order number 4, displays in the Online Orders - Microsoft Internet Explorer window.

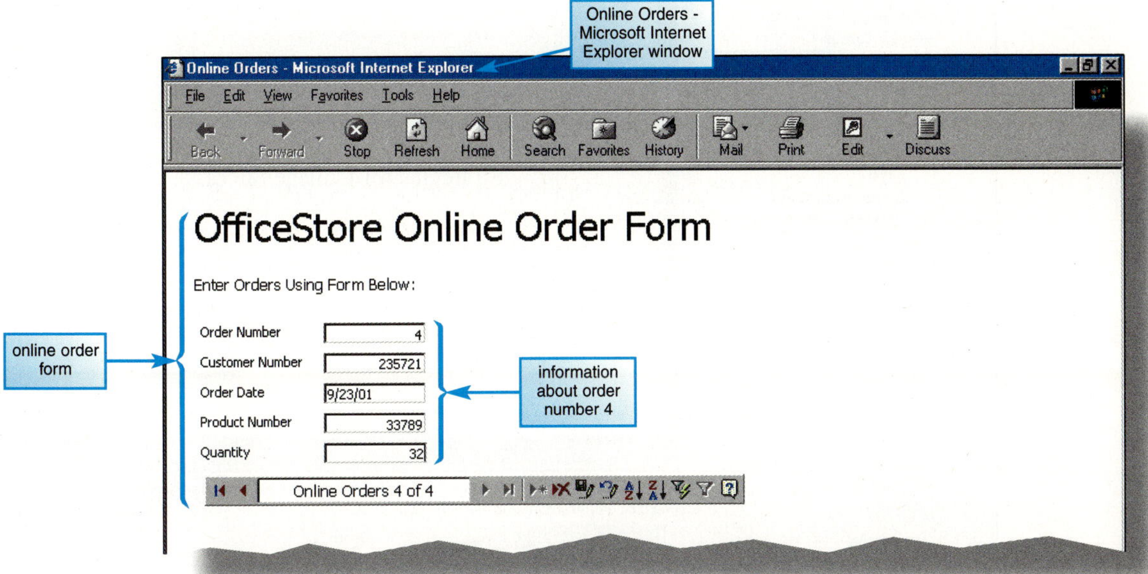

FIGURE 1-89

Microsoft PowerPoint 2000

Microsoft PowerPoint 2000 is a complete **presentation graphics program** that allows you to produce professional-looking presentations. PowerPoint gives you the flexibility to make informal presentations using overhead transparencies, make electronic presentations using a projection device attached to a personal computer, make formal presentations using 35mm slides, or run virtual presentations on the Internet.

In PowerPoint 2000, you create a presentation in Normal view. Normal view allows you to view the outline pane, slide pane, and notes pane at the same time. The first slide in the presentation created in Project 1 of the Microsoft PowerPoint section of this book displays in the Microsoft PowerPoint - [Studying] window illustrated in Figure 1-90 on the next page. The window contains the outline pane with the presentation outline, the slide pane displaying the first slide in the presentation, and the note pane showing a note about the presentation. The steps to create this presentation are shown in Project 1 of PowerPoint 2000.

Microsoft PowerPoint allows you to create dynamic presentations easily that include multimedia features such as sounds, movies, and pictures. PowerPoint comes with templates that assist you in designing a presentation that can be used to create a slide show. PowerPoint also contains formatting for tables, so that you do not have to create the tables using Excel or Word. The Table Draw tool used in Word to draw tables also is available in PowerPoint.

Microsoft PowerPoint 2000

For more information about Microsoft PowerPoint 2000, click Help on the menu bar of the Microsoft PowerPoint window, and click Office on the Web. Explore a Web page by clicking a hyperlink. After clicking a hyperlink, click the Back button to display the last Web page.

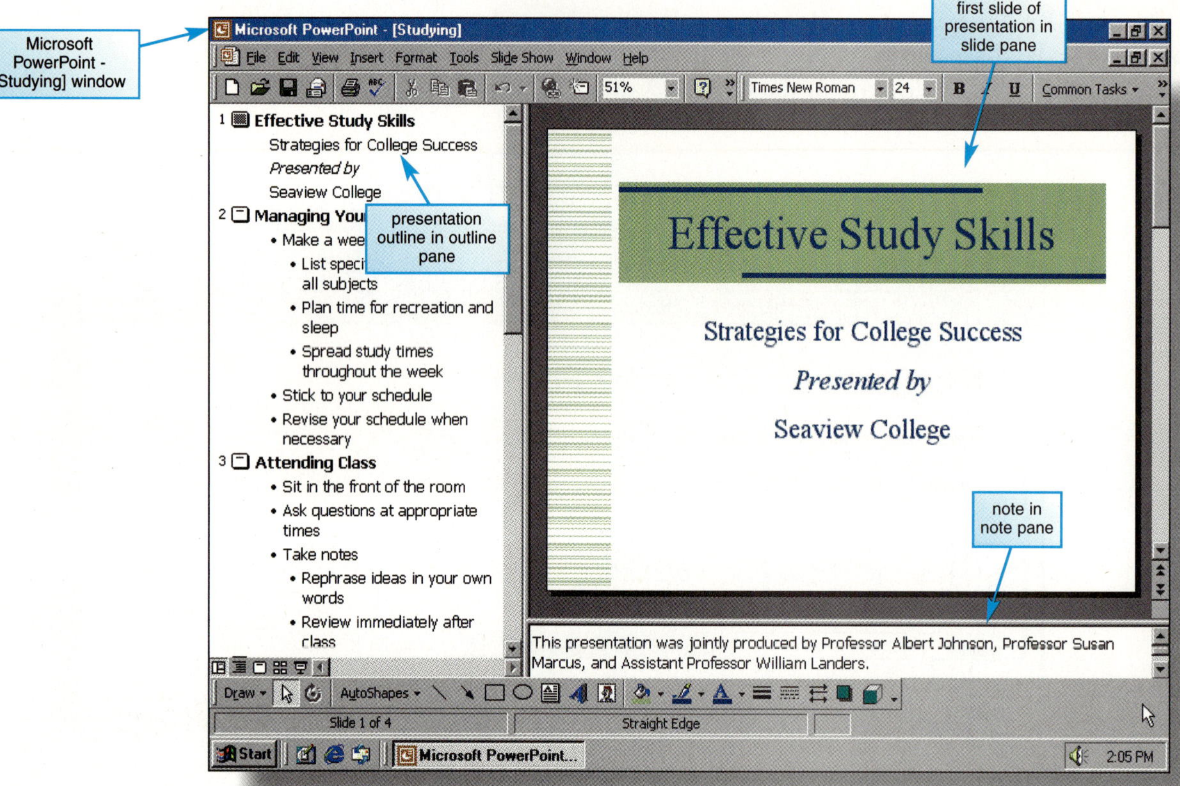

FIGURE 1-90

Microsoft PowerPoint 2000 and the Internet

PowerPoint allows you to publish presentations on the Internet or an intranet. Figure 1-91 illustrates the first slide in a presentation to be published on the Internet. The slide displays in Slide view and contains a title (Microsoft Office 2000), subtitle (Guide to Office Applications), and creation date (Created: October 2001). The additional slides in this presentation do not display in Figure 1-91.

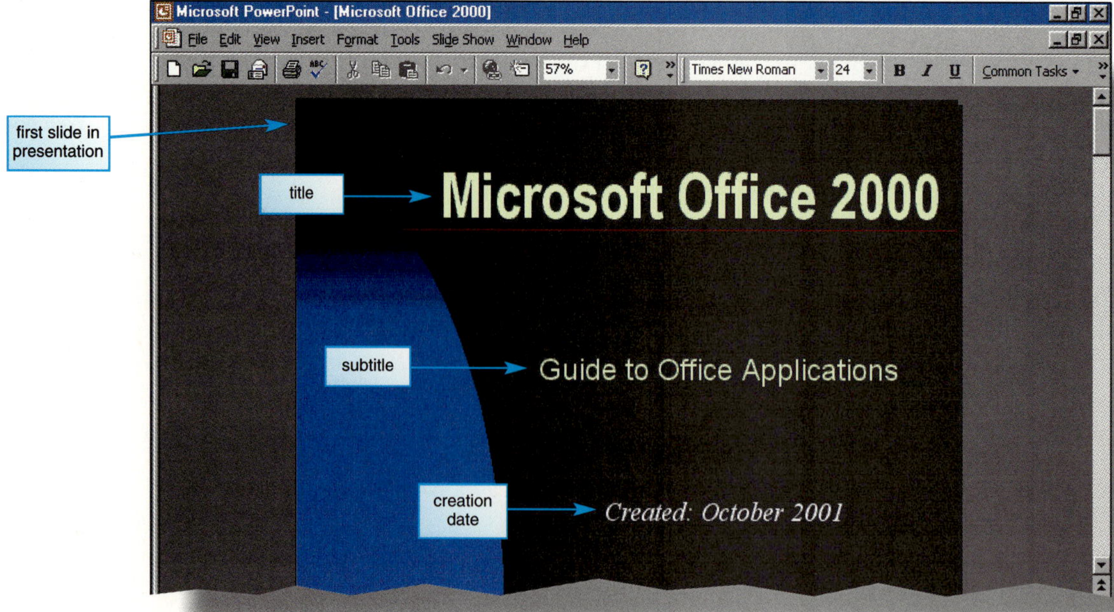

FIGURE 1-91

Figure 1-92 shows the first Web page in a series of Web pages created from the presentation illustrated in Figure 1-91. The Web page displays in the Microsoft Office 2000 - Microsoft Internet Explorer window. Navigation buttons below the Web page allow you to view additional Web pages in the presentation.

FIGURE 1-92

The Web Toolbar

The easiest method of navigating an intranet or the Internet is to use the Web toolbar. The Web toolbar allows you to search for and open Microsoft Office 2000 documents that have been placed on an intranet or the Internet. The Web toolbar in the Paulette Brandon Cover Letter - Microsoft Word window shown in Figure 1-93 on the next page is available in all Microsoft Office 2000 applications except Microsoft Publisher, Microsoft PhotoDraw, and Microsoft FrontPage. Currently, a Word document (cover letter) displays in the window, and the path and file name of the document display in the text box on the Web toolbar.

The buttons and text box on the Web toolbar allow you to jump to Web pages you have viewed previously, cancel a jump to a Web page, update the contents of the current Web page, or replace all other toolbars with the Web toolbar. In addition, you can view the first Web page displayed, search the Web for new Web sites, and add any Web pages you select to the Favorites folder, so you can return to them quickly in the future.

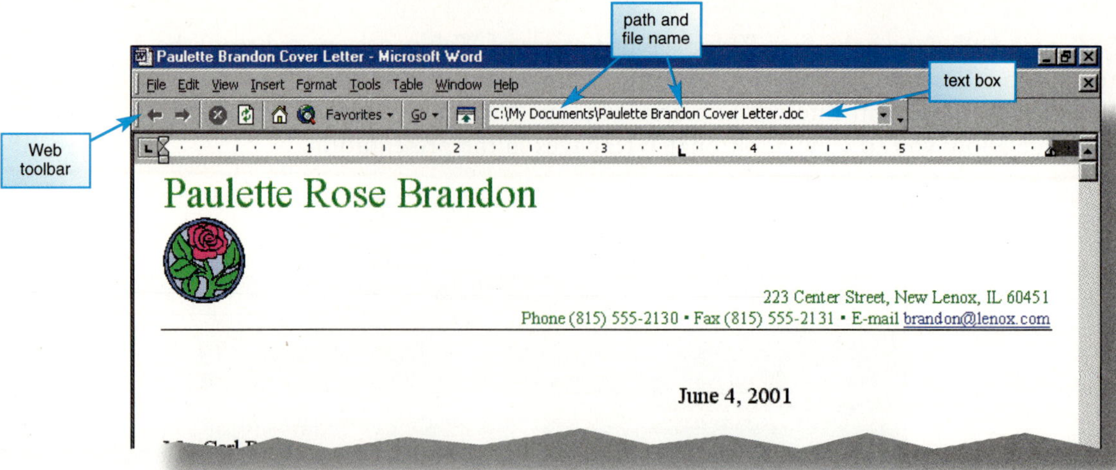

FIGURE 1-93

Microsoft Publisher 2000

Microsoft Publisher 2000 is a **desktop publishing** (**DTP**) **program** that allows you to design and produce professional-quality documents (newsletters, flyers, brochures, business cards, Web sites, and so on) that combine text, graphics, and photographs. Desktop publishing software provides a variety of tools, including design templates, graphic manipulation tools, color schemes or libraries, and various page wizards and templates. For large jobs, businesses use desktop publishing software to design publications that are **camera ready**, which means the files are suitable for production by outside commercial printers.

Publisher allows you to design a unique image, or logo, using one of more than 1,600 professional-looking design sets. This, in turn, permits you to use the same design for all your printed documents (letter, business cards, brochures, and advertisements) and Web pages. Microsoft Publisher includes 60 coordinated color schemes, more than 10,000 high-quality clip art images, 1,500 photographs, 1,000 Web-art graphics, 175 fonts, 340 animated graphics, and hundreds of unique Design Gallery elements (quotations, sidebars, and so on). In addition, you can download an additional 100 images from Microsoft Clipart Gallery Live on the Microsoft Web site each month.

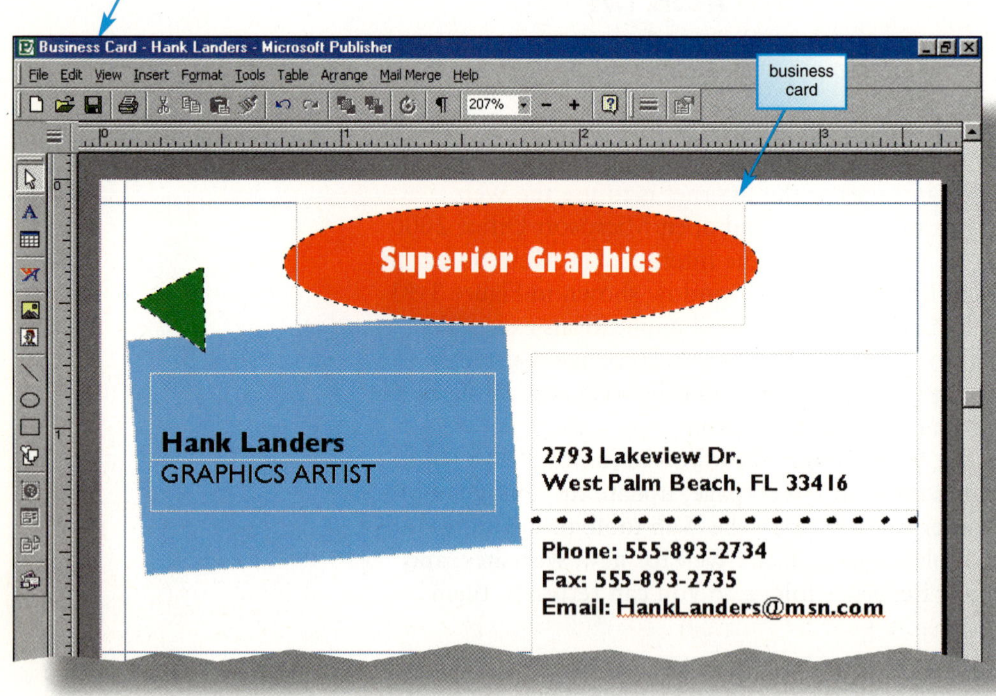

FIGURE 1-94

In the Business Card - Hank Landers - Microsoft Publisher window shown in Figure 1-94, a business card that was created using the Business Card wizard and the Arcs design set displays.

Microsoft Publisher and the Internet

Microsoft Publisher allows you to easily create a multi-page Web site with custom color schemes, photo images, animated images, and sounds. Figure 1-95 illustrates the Superior Graphics - Microsoft Internet Explorer window displaying the top portion of the home page in a Web site created using the Web page wizard and Arcs design set.

The home page in the Superior Graphics Web site contains text, graphic images, animated graphic images, and displays using the same design set (Arcs) as the business card illustrated in Figure 1-94.

More About 2000

Microsoft Publisher 2000

For more information about Microsoft Publisher 2000, click Help on the menu bar of the Microsoft Publisher window, and click Office on the Web. Explore a Web page by clicking a hyperlink. After clicking a hyperlink, click the Back button to display the last Web page.

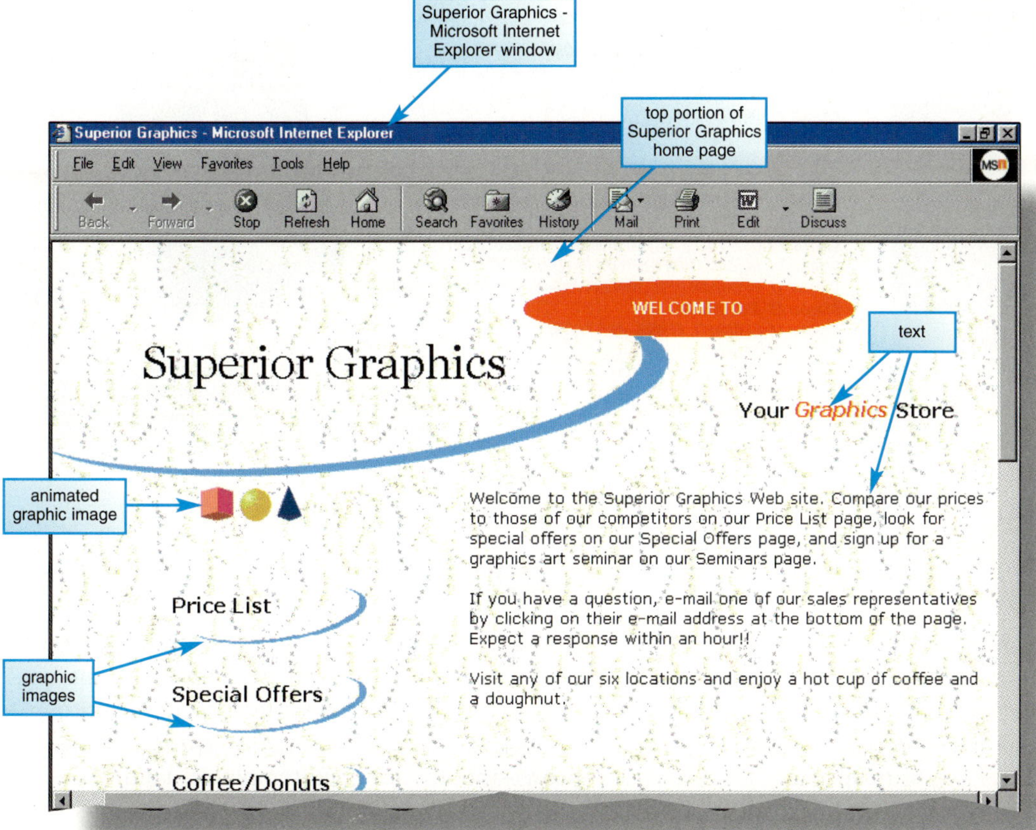

FIGURE 1-95

Microsoft FrontPage 2000

Microsoft FrontPage 2000 is a Web page authoring and site management program that allows you to create and manage professional-looking Web sites on the Internet or an intranet. You can create and edit Web pages without knowing HyperText Markup Language (HTML), view the pages and files in the Web site and control their organization, manage existing Web sites, import and export files, and diagnose and fix problems. A variety of templates, including the new Workgroup Web template that allows you to set up and maintain the basic structure of a workgroup Web, are available to facilitate managing a Web site.

Figure 1-96 on the next page illustrates the top portion of a Web page created using Microsoft FrontPage 2000 that contains information about the Discovering Computers 2000 textbook published by Course Technology. It displays in the Discovering Computers 2000 - Microsoft Internet Explorer window.

Microsoft FrontPage 2000

For more information about Microsoft FrontPage 2000, click Help on the menu bar of the Microsoft FrontPage window, and click Office on the Web. Explore a Web page by clicking a hyperlink. After clicking a hyperlink, click the Back button to display the last Web page.

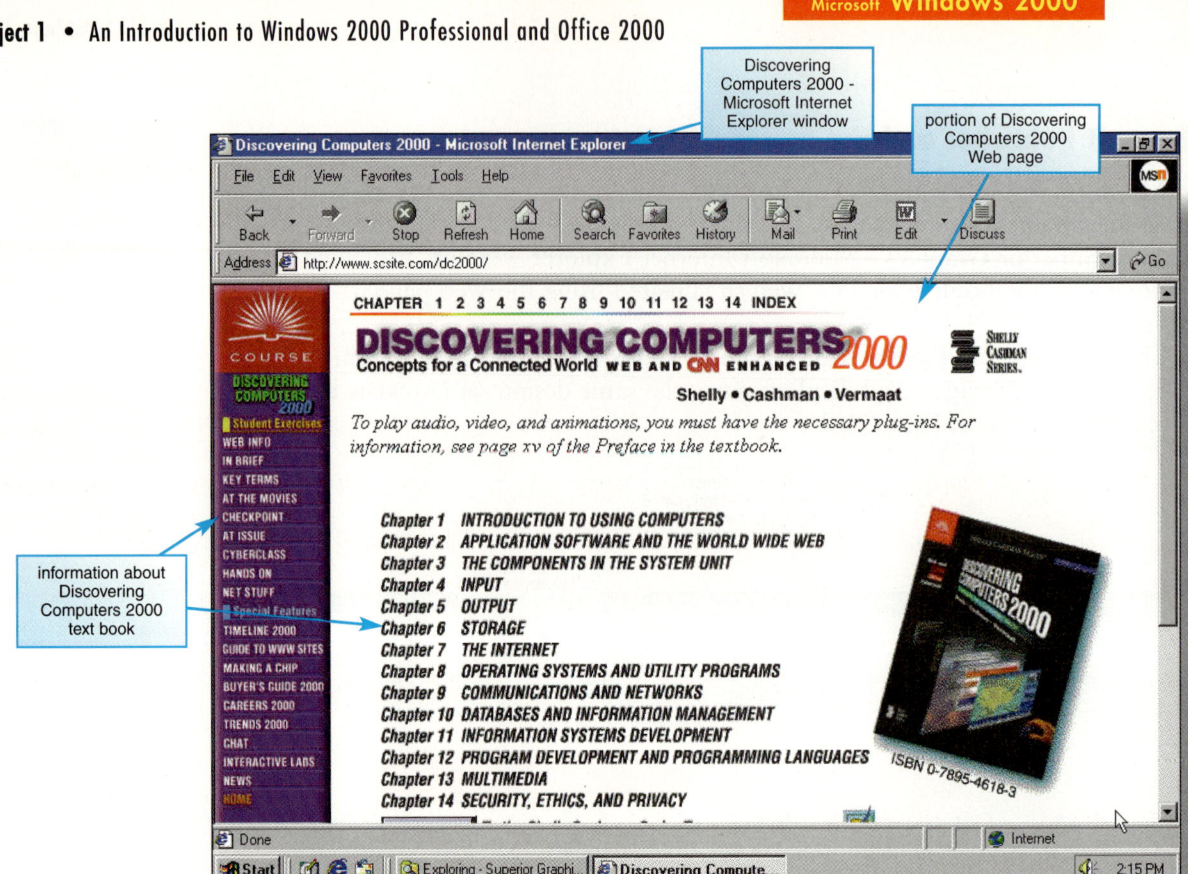

FIGURE 1-96

More About

Microsoft PhotoDraw 2000

For more information about Microsoft PhotoDraw 2000, click Office on the Web on the PhotoDraw Help menu. Explore a Web page by clicking a hyperlink; click the Back button to display the last Web page.

Microsoft PhotoDraw 2000

Microsoft PhotoDraw 2000 is a business graphics software program that allows you to create eye-catching business graphics to be used in documents and presentations on the Web. Microsoft PhotoDraw contains over 20,000 professional images (photos, logos, three-dimensional text, and Web banners), a complete set of graphics tools, 200 built-in special effects, and 300 professionally designed templates. Figure 1-97 illustrates the Microsoft PhotoDraw - [Mystery Falls] window displaying an enhanced, or retouched, photograph that has been outlined using the Soft Edges tool.

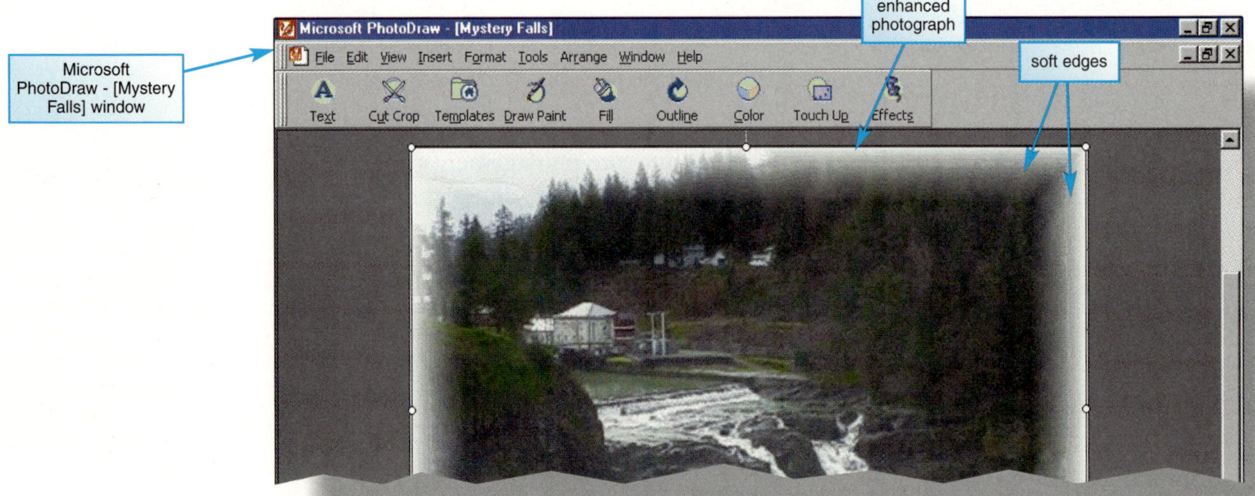

FIGURE 1-97

Microsoft Outlook 2000

Microsoft Outlook 2000 is an integrated **desktop information management** (**DIM**) program that helps you organize information on the desktop and share information with others. Microsoft Outlook allows you to manage personal and business information such as e-mail, appointments, contacts, tasks, and documents, and keep a journal of your activities. Outlook organizes and stores this information in folders on your desktop.

When you start Microsoft Outlook, the Inbox - Microsoft Outlook window displays and the contents of the Inbox folder (your e-mail messages) display in the window (Figure 1-98).

The Inbox icon, representing the Inbox folder, displays on the Outlook Bar on the left side of the window and the information viewer displays on the right side of the window. The contents of the Inbox folder (one highlighted e-mail message and three e-mail messages) display at the top of the information viewer. Summary information (From:, To:, Subject:, and Cc:) and the text of the highlighted e-mail message display at the bottom of the information viewer. Also visible on the Outlook Bar are the Outlook Today, Calendar, Contacts, Tasks, and Journal icons. Clicking an icon on the Outlook Bar displays the contents of the associated folder in the information viewer.

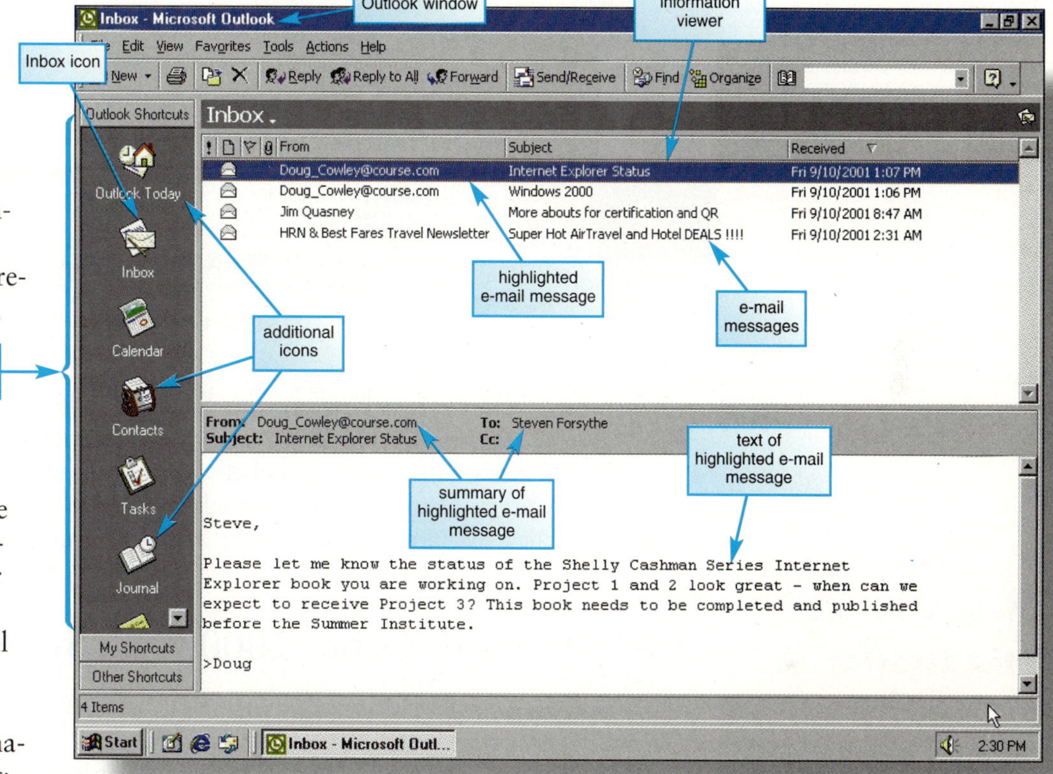

FIGURE 1-98

When you click the Outlook Today button on the Outlook Bar, the Personal Folders - Microsoft Outlook window displays (Figure 1-99 on the next page). The window contains the current date (Monday, September 10, 2001); a list of scheduled events, appointments, and meetings for the week; a list of tasks to perform; and a summary of the e-mail messages.

Microsoft Outlook 2000

For more information about Microsoft Outlook 2000, click Help on the menu bar of the Microsoft Outlook window, and click Office on the Web. Explore a Web page by clicking a hyperlink. After clicking a hyperlink, click the Back button to display the last Web page.

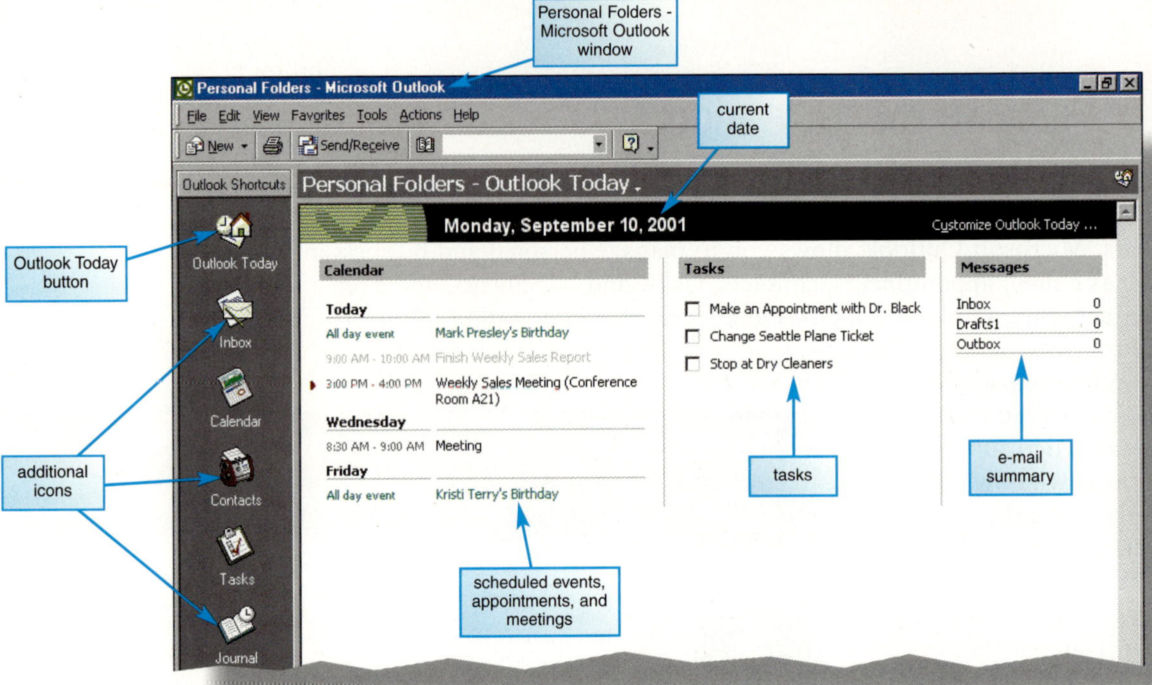

FIGURE 1-99

Microsoft Outlook also allows you to click the Calendar icon to schedule activities (events, appointments, and meetings), click the Contacts icon to maintain a list of contacts and e-mail addresses, and click the Tasks button to view a detailed list of tasks. In addition, you can click the Journal button to view a log of your Outlook activities and click the Notes icon to make and review electronic reminders, or notes.

More About 2000

Office Assistant

To change the Office Assistant, right-click the Office Assistant window, click Options on the shortcut menu, if necessary click Gallery tab, click Next button to select Office Assistant, and click the OK button.

The Microsoft Office 2000 Help System

Anytime you are using one of the Microsoft Office 2000 applications, you can interact with the Help system for that application and display information on any topic associated with the application. Several categories of help are available. One of the easiest methods to obtain help is to use the Office Assistant. The **Office Assistant** answers your questions and suggests more efficient ways to complete a task. The Office Assistant and balloon display whenever you start any Microsoft Office 2000 application. The Office Assistant and balloon that display in the Notes - Microsoft Outlook window are illustrated in Figure 1-100.

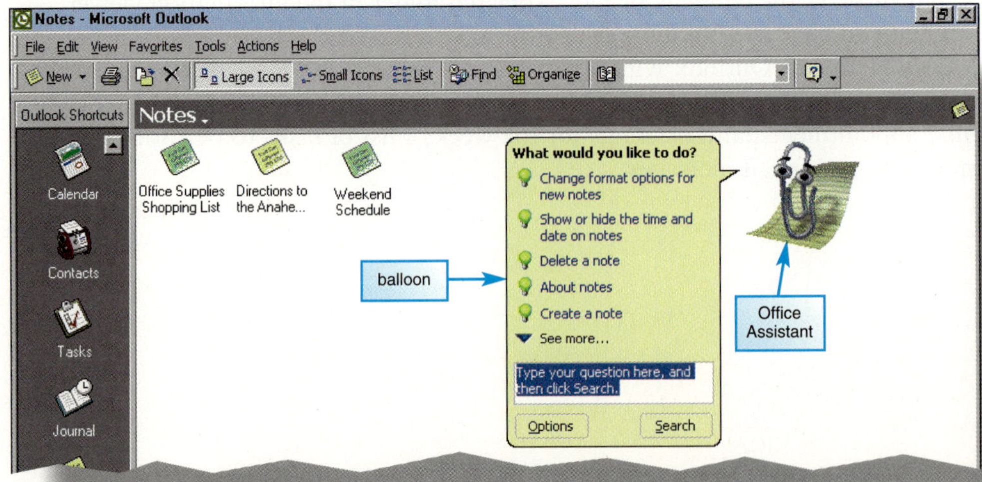

FIGURE 1-100

The Office Assistant (an animated two-dimensional paper clip) is completely customizable so you can select one of nine Office Assistants and the options that best suit the way you work. Detailed instructions for using the Office Assistant and the other categories of Help are explained in Appendix A of this book.

CASE PERSPECTIVE SUMMARY

While continuing to answer questions about Windows 2000 Professional and Office 2000 in the workplace, you spent nearly every free moment in the next two weeks learning about the newly installed operating system and application software. Then, the daily training sessions kept you busy for the following three months. You taught 35 workshops and trained all of the 462 employees in the company. Your supervisor, who attended the Windows 2000 Professional and Excel 2000 seminars, complimented your success by giving you a sizeable pay raise and time off to attend the Shelly Cashman Institute at Purdue University.

Project Summary

Project 1 illustrated the Microsoft Windows 2000 graphical user interface and the Microsoft Office 2000 applications. You started Windows 2000, learned the components of the desktop and the six mouse operations. You opened, closed, moved, resized, minimized, maximized, and scrolled a window. You used Windows Explorer to select and copy a group of files, display the contents of a folder, create a folder, expand and collapse a folder, and rename and delete a file and a folder. You obtained help about using Microsoft Windows 2000 and shut down Windows 2000.

Brief explanations of the Microsoft Word, Microsoft Excel, Microsoft Access, Microsoft PowerPoint, Microsoft Publisher, Microsoft FrontPage, Microsoft PhotoDraw, and Microsoft Outlook applications and examples of how these applications interact with the Internet, World Wide Web, and intranets were given. With this introduction, you are ready to begin a more in-depth study of each of the Microsoft Office 2000 applications explained in this book.

What You Should Know

Having completed this project, you now should be able to perform the following tasks:

- Close a Window *(INT 1.25)*
- Close a Window and Reopen a Window *(INT 1.19)*
- Close the Getting Started with Windows 2000 dialog box *(INT 1.8)*
- Close Windows Help *(INT 1.59)*
- Collapse a Folder *(INT 1.37)*
- Copy a Group of Files *(INT 1.46)*
- Create a New Folder *(INT 1.39)*
- Delete a File by Right-Clicking *(INT 1.51)*
- Delete a Folder *(INT 1.52)*
- Display the Contents of a Folder *(INT 1.34, INT 1.42, INT 1.47)*
- Expand a Folder *(INT 1.36, INT 1.41)*
- Launch a Program Using the Start Menu *(INT 1.29)*
- Launch Windows Help *(INT 1.54)*
- Maximize and Restore a Window *(INT 1.17)*
- Minimize and Redisplay a Window *(INT 1.15)*
- Move an Object by Dragging *(INT 1.21)*
- Open a Window by Double-Clicking *(INT 1.13)*
- Point and Click *(INT 1.10)*
- Quit a Program *(INT 1.30, INT 1.53)*
- Rename a File *(INT 1.48)*
- Rename a Folder *(INT 1.49)*
- Resize a Window *(INT 1.25)*
- Right-Click *(INT 1.12)*
- Right-Drag *(INT 1.26)*
- Scroll a Window Using Scroll Arrows *(INT 1.23)*
- Select a Group of Files *(INT 1.44)*
- Shut Down Windows 2000 *(INT 1.60)*
- Size a Window by Dragging *(INT 1.22)*
- Start Windows Explorer and Maximize Its Window *(INT 1.31)*
- Use Help to Find a Topic in Help *(INT 1.55)*
- Use the Help Index Sheet *(INT 1.58)*

1 Improving Your Mouse Skills

Instructions: Use a computer to perform the following tasks.

1. If necessary, start Microsoft Windows 2000.
2. Click the Start button on the taskbar, point to Programs on the Start menu, point to Accessories on the Programs submenu, point to Games on the Accessories submenu, and then click Solitaire on the Games submenu. If you cannot find the Games command on the Accessories submenu, ask your instructor if the games have been removed from your computer.
3. Click the Maximize button in the Solitaire window.
4. Click Help on the Solitaire menu bar and then click Contents.
5. If the Contents sheet does not display, click the Contents tab.
6. Review the Play Solitaire and Choosing a scoring system topics in the Contents sheet.
7. After reviewing the Help topics, close the Solitaire window.
8. Play the game of Solitaire.
9. Click the Close button on the Solitaire title bar to close the game.

2 Using the Discover Windows 2000 Professional Tour

Instructions: To use the Discover Windows 2000 tutorial, you will need a copy of the Windows 2000 Professional CD-ROM. If this CD-ROM is not available, skip this lab assignment. Otherwise, use a computer and the CD-ROM to perform the following tasks.

1. If necessary, start Microsoft Windows 2000.
2. Insert the Windows 2000 Professional CD-ROM in your CD-ROM drive. If the Microsoft Windows 2000 CD window displays, click the Close button on the title bar to close the window.
3. Click the Start button on the taskbar, point to Programs on the Start menu, point to Accessories on the Programs submenu, point to System Tools on the Accessories submenu, and then click Getting Started on the System Tools submenu.
4. Click Discover Windows in the Getting Started with Windows 2000 dialog box to display the Discover screen (Figure 1-101 on the next page). The word, Discover, at the top of the screen identifies the Discover screen. The left side of the Discover screen contains a message to click a category on the right side of the screen. The right side of the screen contains the four categories in the Discover tour (Easier to Use, Easier to Manage, More Compatible, and More Powerful).
5. Click Easier to Use on the right side of the Discover screen. The five topics in the Easier to Use category display on the left side of the screen, a summary of the Easier to Use category displays on the right side, and a bar containing the four categories in the Discover tour display above the topics and summary. The Easier to Use category is highlighted on the bar.
6. Click Work with Files on the left side of the Discover screen to display the subtopics in the Work with Files topic.
7. Click and read each subtopic in the Work with Files topic. When available, click the Play Animation button to view an animation of the topic. When the animation stops, click the Back button.

8. Click each of the remaining four topics in the Easier to Use category and then click and read each subtopic in each topic.
9. Click Easier to Manage on the bar at the top of the Discover screen. Click and read each of the topics and subtopics in the category.
10. Click the More Compatible category on the bar at the top of the Discover screen. Click and read each of the topics and subtopics in the category.
11. Click the More Powerful category on the bar at the top of the Discover screen. Click and read each of the topics and subtopics in the category.
12. When you have finished, click the Exit link in the lower-left corner of the Discover screen.
13. Click the Exit link in the lower-right corner of the Getting Started with Windows 2000 dialog box.
14. Remove the Windows 2000 Professional CD-ROM from your CD-ROM drive.

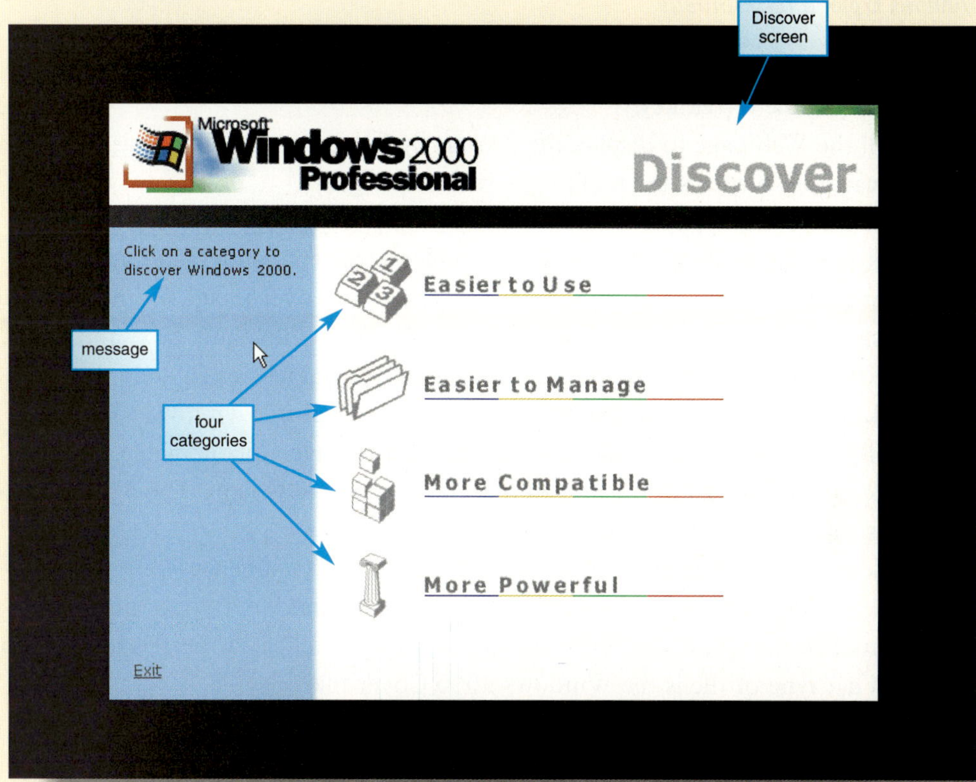

FIGURE 1-101

3 Windows Explorer

Instructions: Use a computer to perform the following tasks.

1. Start Microsoft Windows 2000 and connect to the Internet.
2. Right-click the Start button on the taskbar, click Explore on the shortcut menu, and then maximize the Start Menu window.
3. If necessary, scroll to the left in the Folders pane so the Start Menu and Programs icons are visible.
4. Click the Programs icon in the Start Menu folder.
5. Double-click the Internet Explorer shortcut icon in the Contents pane to launch the Internet Explorer application. What is the URL of the Web page that displays in the Address bar in the Microsoft Internet Explorer window? ______________________________

(continued)

Windows Explorer *(continued)*

6. Click the URL in the Address bar in the Internet Explorer window to select it. Type `www.scsite.com` and then press the ENTER key.
7. Scroll the Web page to display the Browse by Subject area containing the subject categories. Clicking a subject category displays the book titles in that category.
8. Click Operating Systems in the Browse by Subject area.
9. Click the Microsoft Windows 2000 Complete Concepts and Techniques link.
10. Right-click the Microsoft Windows 2000 textbook cover image on the Web page, click Save Picture As on the shortcut menu, type `Windows 2000 Cover` in the File name box, and then click the Save button in the Save Picture dialog box to save the image in the My Pictures folder.
11. Click the Close button in the Microsoft Internet Explorer window.
12. Scroll to the top of the Folders pane to make the drive C icon visible.
13. Click the minus sign in the box to the left of the drive C icon. The 3½ Floppy (A:) and My Documents icons should be visible in the Folders pane.
14. Click the plus sign in the box to the left of the My Documents icon.
15. Click the My Pictures folder name in the Folders pane.
16. Right-click the Windows 2000 Cover icon and then click Properties on the shortcut menu.
    a. What type of file is the Windows 2000 Cover file? ______________________________
    b. When was the file last modified? ______________________________
    c. With what application does this file open? ______________________________
17. Click the Cancel button in the Windows 2000 Cover Properties dialog box.
18. Insert a formatted floppy disk in drive A of your computer.
19. Right-drag the Windows 2000 Cover icon over the 3½ Floppy (A:) icon in the Folders pane. Click Move Here on the shortcut menu. Click the 3½ Floppy (A:) icon in the Folders pane.
    a. Is the Windows 2000 Cover file stored on drive A? ______________________________
20. Click the Close button in the 3½ Floppy (A:) window.

4 Using Windows Help

Instructions: Use Windows Help and a computer to perform the following tasks.

Part 1: Using the Question Mark Button

1. If necessary, start Microsoft Windows 2000.
2. Click the Start button on the taskbar, point to Settings on the Start menu, and then click Control Panel on the Settings submenu.
3. Double-click the Folder Options icon in the Control Panel window.
4. If the General sheet does not display, click the General tab in the Folder Options dialog box.
5. Click the Question Mark button on the title bar. The mouse pointer changes to a block arrow with a question mark (Figure 1-102).

6. Click the icon in the Active Desktop area in the Folder Options dialog box. A pop-up window displays explaining the Active Desktop area. Read the information in the pop-up window.
7. Click an open area of the General sheet to remove the pop-up window.

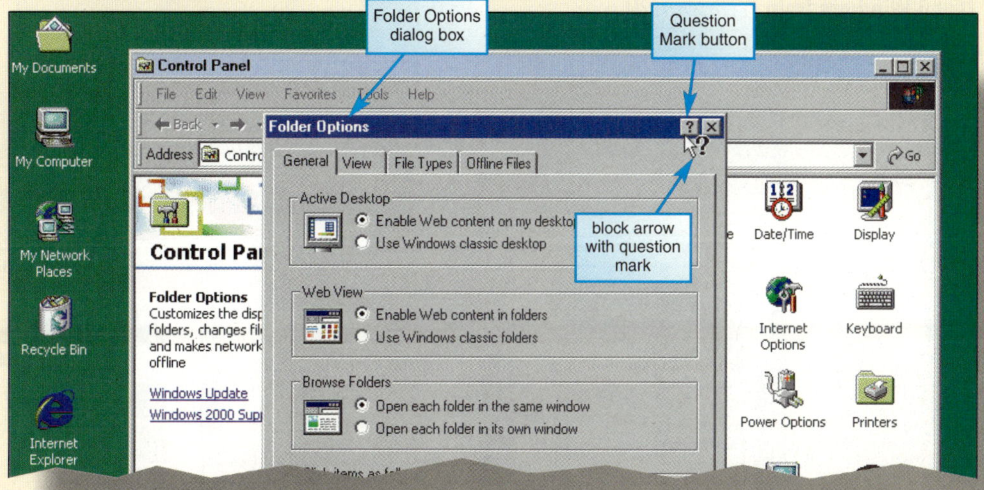

FIGURE 1-102

8. Click the Question Mark button on the title bar and then click the Enable Web content on my desktop option button. A pop-up window displays explaining what happens when you select this option. Read the information in the pop-up window. Click an open area on the General sheet to remove the pop-up window.
9. Click the Question Mark button on the title bar and then click the Use Windows Classic desktop option button. A pop-up window displays explaining what happens when you select this option. Read the information in the pop-up window. Click an open area on the General sheet to remove the pop-up window.
10. Click the Question Mark button on the title bar and then click the Restore Defaults button. A pop-up window displays explaining the function of the button. Read the information in the pop-up window. Click an open area on the General sheet to remove the pop-up window.
11. Summarize the function of the Question Mark button. ______________________________

    ____
12. Click the Close button in the Folder Options dialog box.
13. Click the Close button in the Control Panel window.

Part 2: ***Finding What's New in Windows 2000 Professional***

1. Click the Start button and then click Help on the Start menu.
2. Click the Maximize button on the Windows 2000 title bar.
3. If the Contents sheet does not display, click the Contents tab. Click the Introducing Windows 2000 Professional closed book icon.
4. Click Tips for new users in the Introducing Windows 2000 Professional open book.
5. Click Find a file or folder in the topic pane of the Windows 2000 window.
6. Click the Step-by-step procedure link and read the steps to search for a file or folder.
7. Click the Options button on the Help toolbar to display the Options menu and then click Print.
8. Click the OK button in the Print Topics dialog box to print the steps.

Part 3: ***Reading About the Online Getting Started Manual***

1. Click the Getting Started online book closed book icon in the navigation pane.

(continued)

Using Windows Help *(continued)*

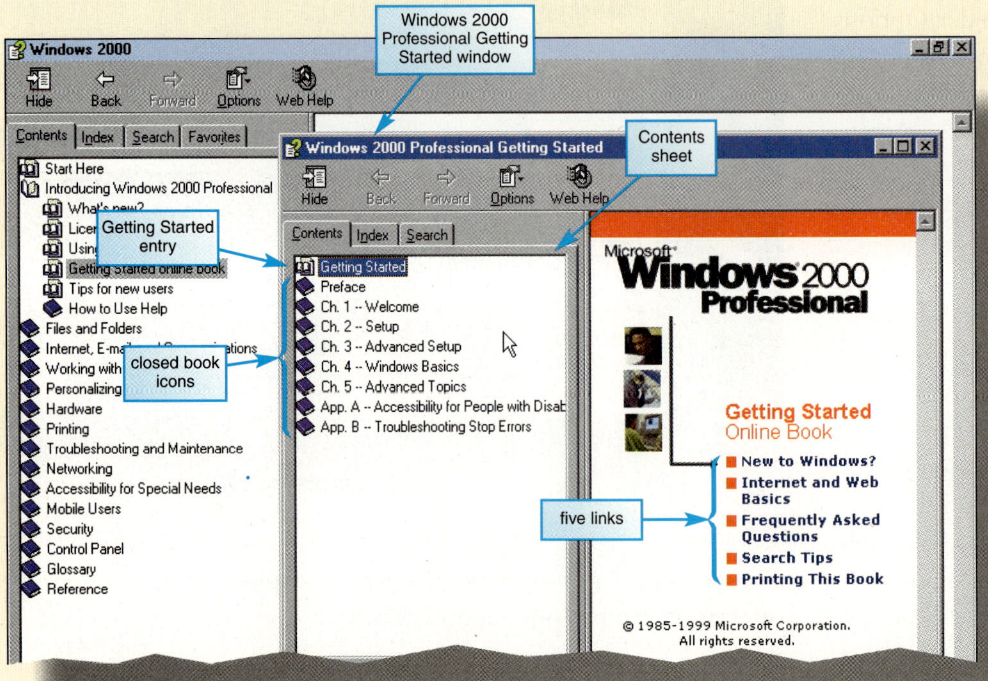

FIGURE 1-103

2. Click the Windows 2000 Professional Getting Started link in the topic pane to open the Windows 2000 Professional Getting Started window (Figure 1-103). The Contents sheet containing the Getting Started entry and eight closed book icons displays in the navigation pane of the window. Five links display in the topics pane of the window.
3. If the Contents sheet does not display, click the Contents tab.
4. Click the Preface closed book icon.
5. Click the How to Use Getting Started topic.
6. Click the Options button on the Help toolbar, click Print, and then click the OK button to print the information about the How to Use Getting Started topic.
7. Click the Ch. 1 -- Welcome closed book icon. Three Help topics and two closed book icons display beneath the entry when the book is opened. Click and read the Windows 2000 Professional at a Glance and If You're New to Windows topics.
8. Click the Where to Find Information closed book icon.
9. Click the Resources Included with Windows 2000 closed book icon.
10. Click the Troubleshooters topic. Read the information about the topic.
11. Click the Options button on the Help toolbar, click Print, and then click the OK button to print the topic.
12. Click the Introducing Windows 2000 Professional closed book icon. Click and read the nine topics in the open book.
13. Click the Close button in the Windows 2000 Professional Getting Started window.
14. Click the Close button in the Windows 2000 window.

MICROSOFT

Word 2000

Microsoft Word 2000

Creating and Editing a Word Document

OBJECTIVES

You will have mastered the material in this project when you can:

- Start Word
- Describe the Word window
- Zoom page width
- Change the default font size of all text
- Enter text into a document
- Check spelling as you type
- Scroll through a document
- Save a document
- Select text
- Change the font of selected text
- Change the font size of selected text
- Bold selected text
- Right-align a paragraph
- Center a paragraph
- Undo commands or actions
- Italicize selected text
- Underline selected text
- Insert clip art into a document
- Resize a graphic
- Print a document
- Open a document
- Correct errors in a document
- Use Microsoft Word Help
- Quit Word

Wobbling Words

Help for the Spelling Challenged

*"My spelling is Wobbly.
It's good spelling, but it Wobbles,
and the letters get in the wrong places."*
Winnie-the-Pooh

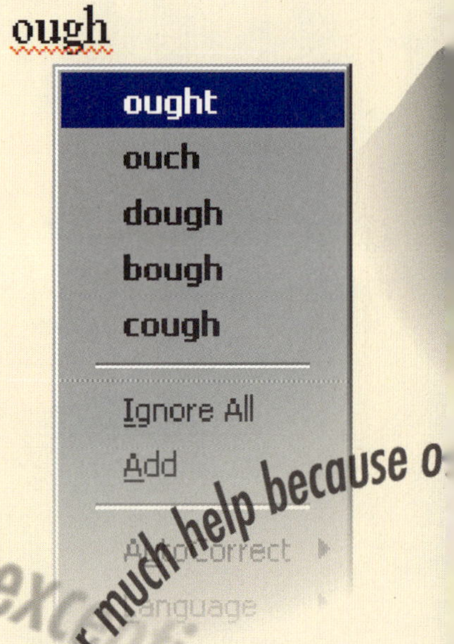

No wonder Pooh has a difficult time trying to spell words correctly. If he pronounces the words bough, cough, rough, though, and through, he realizes that despite the fact they all end with the letters, ough, they all are pronounced quite differently.

If you share Pooh's spelling dilemma, you are not alone. Most people have difficulty remembering how to spell some words. One study reports 20 percent of writers do not spell well because they cannot visualize words. Even remembering the simple rules such as, i before e except after c, does not offer much assistance because of the slew of exceptions such as the words, weird science.

A spelling error in a flyer distributed on campus, a resume sent to a potential employer, or an e-mail message forwarded to an associate

could lessen your credibility, cause a reader to doubt the accuracy of your statements, and leave a negative impression. In this project, Microsoft Word will check your typing for possible spelling errors as you create an announcement for the Student Government Association's upcoming winter break ski trip at Summit Peak Resort.

If you type a word that does not appear in Word's dictionary, Word will flag the possible error with a wavy red underline. If the spelling is correct, you can instruct Word to ignore the flagged word. If it is misspelled, the spelling feature will offer a list of suggested corrections. Despite this assistance from the spelling checker, one study indicates college students repeatedly ignore or override the flagged words.

Word's spelling checker is a useful alternative to a dictionary, but you must not rely on it 100 percent. It will not flag commonly misused homophones, which are words that are pronounced alike but are spelled differently. For example, it is easy to confuse the homophones in the sentence, The Web site contains an incorrect cite to the reference materials discussing regaining sight after experiencing blindness.

Then what is a spelling-challenged writer to do? English teachers emphasize that you can learn to spell better, but not by strictly memorizing long lists or having someone mark all the errors in a paper. Instead, you need to try the following strategies to improve awareness of spelling difficulties.

First, identify error patterns. For example, do you misspell the same words repeatedly? If so, write them in a list and have a friend dictate them to you. Then write the words again. If you involve your senses, hear the words spelled correctly, and then visualize the words, you increase your awareness of the problem.

Next, always consult a dictionary when you are uncertain of a word's spelling. Note the word's etymology — its origin and history. For example, the word, science, originated from the Latin word, scientia, a form of the verb to know.

As you proofread, read from right to left. Use a pencil to point at each word as you say it aloud.

Using Microsoft Word's spelling checker and a good dictionary should enhance your spelling skills, and stop your words from *Wobbling*.

Microsoft Word 2000

Creating and Editing a Word Document

CASE PERSPECTIVE

Jackie Peterson is this year's Activities Chairperson for the Student Government Association (SGA) at Hilltop Community College. Each year, the Activities Chairperson coordinates vacation plans for the winter break and then prepares fliers announcing the exciting plans. SGA members post these announcements in locations throughout the school, print them in the school newspaper, and mail them to each student.

Because of Jackie's avid love of skiing and snowboarding, she attempts to locate a ski resort in the Midwest designed to accommodate all tastes and budgets. She succeeds! Summit Peak Resort has over 5,200 acres of groomed slopes and pristine lakes for skiing, sledding, snowboarding, ice skating, and ice fishing.

As a Marketing major, you have learned the guidelines for designing announcements. Jackie asks for your assistance with this assignment. You recommend using large, bold characters for the headline and title. To attract attention to the announcement, you suggest including a graphic of a skier sailing down the slopes. Together, you begin designing the announcement.

What Is Microsoft Word 2000?

Microsoft Word is a full-featured word processing program that allows you to create professional looking documents such as announcements, letters, resumes, and reports, and revise them easily. You can use Word's desktop publishing features to create high-quality brochures, advertisements, and newsletters. Word also provides many tools that enable you to create Web pages with ease. From within Word, you even can place these Web pages directly on a Web server.

Word has many features designed to simplify the production of documents. With Word, you easily can include borders, shading, tables, graphics, pictures, and Web addresses in your documents. You can instruct Word to create a template, which is a form you can use and customize to meet your needs. While you are typing, Word can perform tasks automatically. For example, Word can detect and correct spelling and grammar errors in a variety of languages. Word also can format text such as headings, lists, fractions, borders, and Web addresses as you type them. Word's thesaurus allows you to add variety and precision to your writing. Within Word, you can e-mail a copy of your Word document to an e-mail address.

Project One — Summit Peak Announcement

To illustrate the features of Word, this book presents a series of projects that use Word to create documents similar to those you will encounter in academic and business environments. Project 1 uses Word to produce the announcement shown in Figure 1-1.

Feel the Thrill...
...Seize the Slopes!
headline
graphic of skier
body title
SUMMIT PEAK RESORT
Summit Peak is the largest ski resort in the country. Breathtaking mountains provide more than 5,200 acres of groomed slopes and pristine lakes for skiing, sledding, snowboarding, ice skating, and ice fishing.
Summit Peak offers a range of vacation packages for every taste and budget, from traditional ski lodges to luxurious condominiums. Add transportation, meals, lift tickets, gear, and lessons for an exceptional value.
body copy
Call (970) 555-SNOW for reservations.

FIGURE 1-1

More About

Word 2000

For more information on the features of Microsoft Word 2000, visit the Word 2000 More About Web page (www.scsite.com/wd2000/more.htm) and then click Microsoft Word 2000 Features.

The announcement informs students about exciting vacation packages offered by Summit Peak Resort during winter break. The announcement begins with a headline that is followed by a graphic of a skier. Below the graphic of the skier is the body title, SUMMIT PEAK RESORT, followed by the body copy that consists of a brief paragraph about the resort and another paragraph about the vacation packages. Finally, the last line of the announcement lists the resort's telephone number. The appearance of the text and graphic in the announcement is designed to catch the attention of the reader.

Starting Word

Follow these steps to start Word, or ask your instructor how to start Word for your system.

To Start Word

1 Click the Start button on the taskbar and then point to New Office Document.

The programs on the Start menu display above the Start button (Figure 1-2). The New Office Document command is highlighted on the Start menu. A ***highlighted command*** *displays as light text on a dark background.*

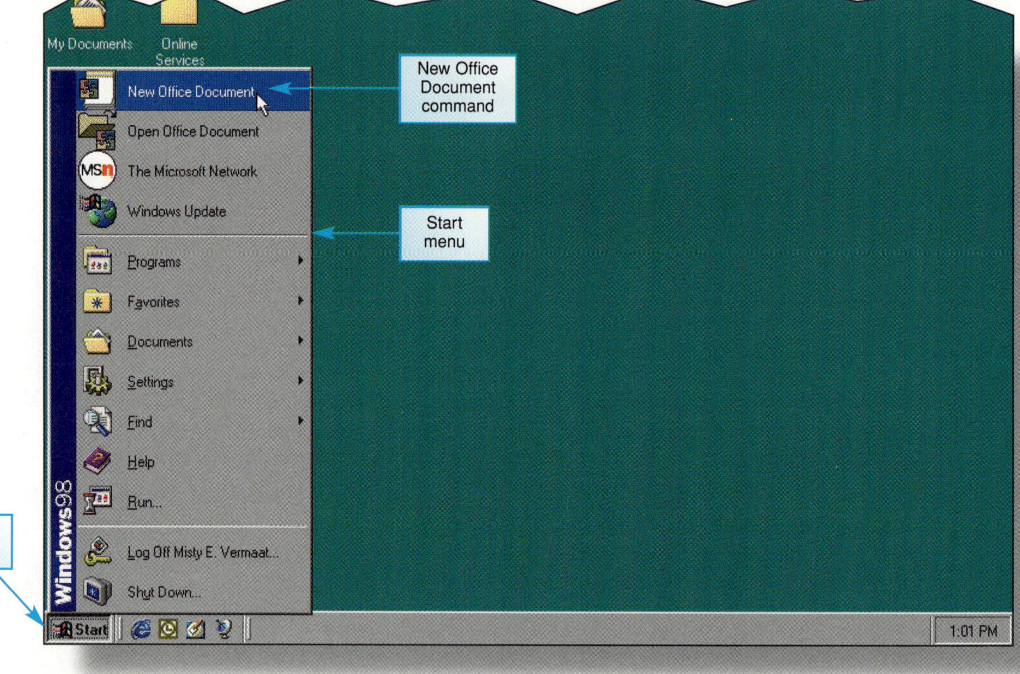

FIGURE 1-2

2 Click New Office Document. If necessary, click the General tab when the New Office Document dialog box first displays. Point to the Blank Document icon.

Office displays several icons in the General sheet in the New Office Document dialog box (Figure 1-3). The icons are large because the Large Icons button is selected. Each icon represents a different type of document you can create in Microsoft Office.

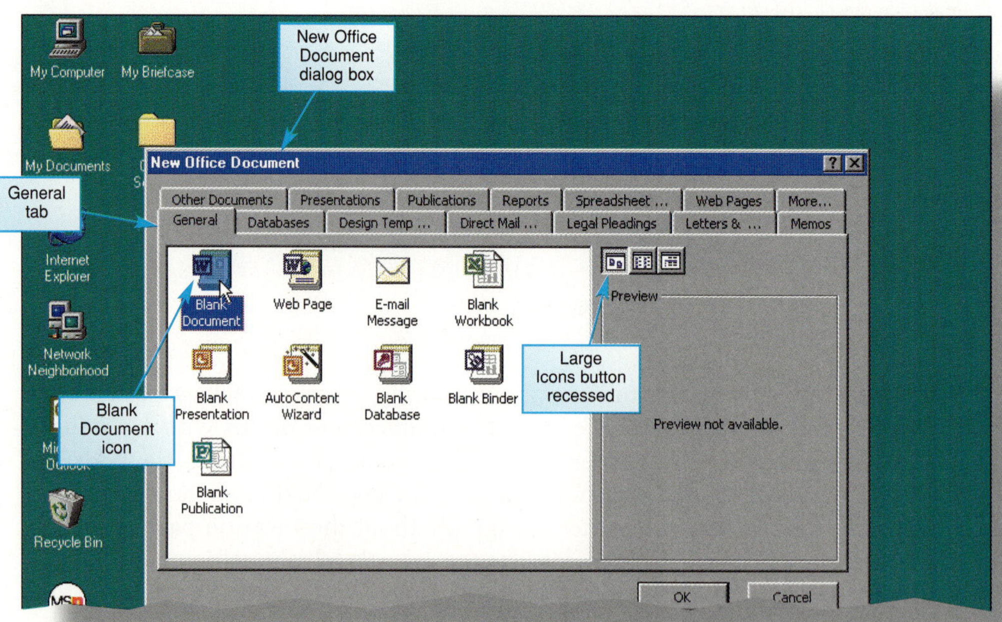

FIGURE 1-3

3 Double-click the Blank Document icon.

Office starts Word. While Word is starting, the mouse pointer changes to the shape of an hourglass. After a few moments, an empty document titled Document1 displays in the Word window (Figure 1-4).

4 If the Word window is not maximized, double-click its title bar to maximize it. If the Office Assistant displays, right-click it and then click Hide on the shortcut menu. If your screen differs from Figure 1-4, click View on the menu bar and then click Normal.

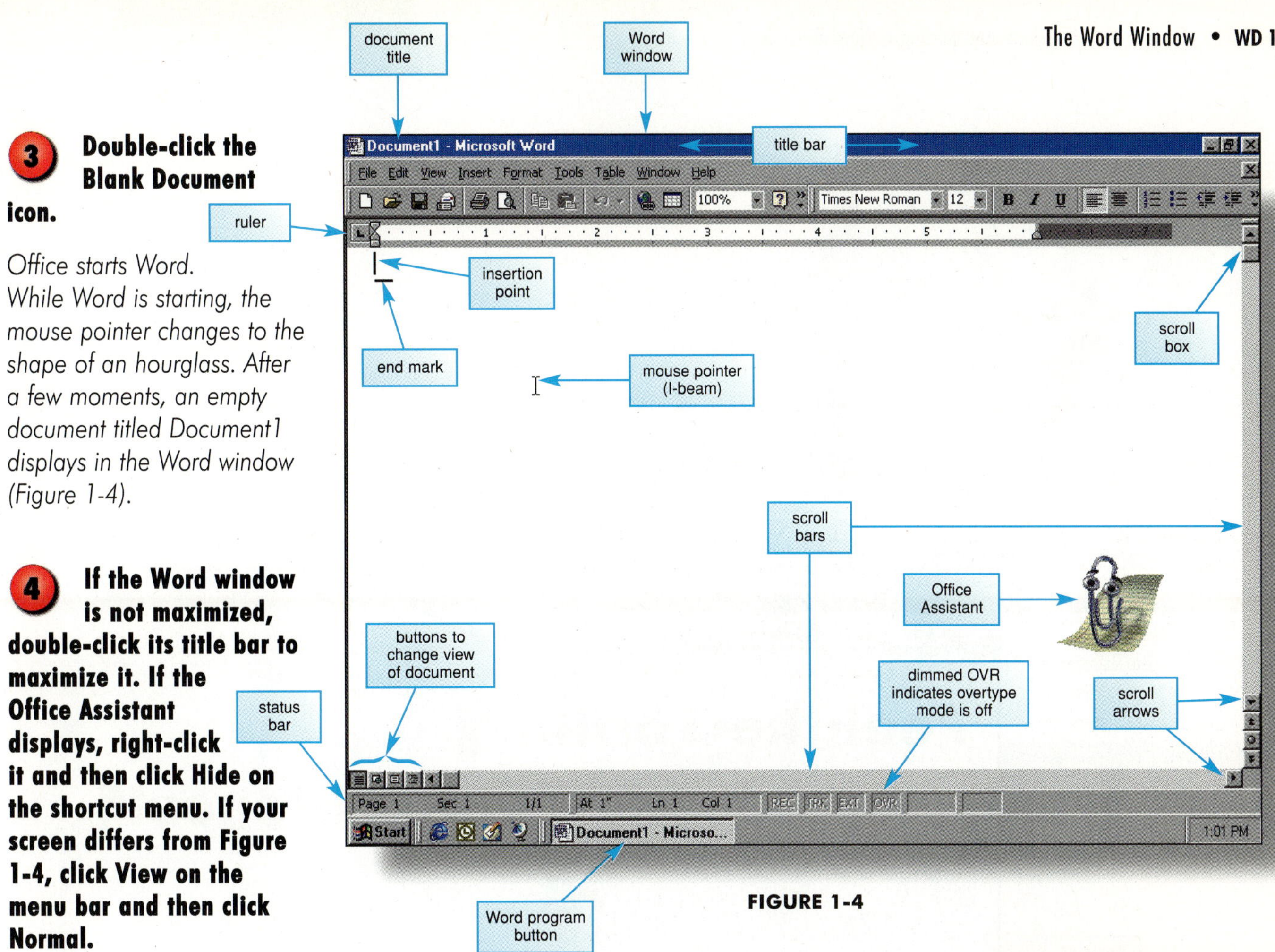

FIGURE 1-4

Other Ways

1. Right-click Start button, click Open, double-click New Office Document, click General tab, double-click Blank Document icon
2. Click New Office Document button on Microsoft Office Shortcut Bar, click General tab, double-click Blank Document icon
3. On Start menu point to Programs, click Microsoft Word

The Windows taskbar at the bottom of the screen displays the Word program button, indicating the Word program is open.

The Word Window

The **Word window** (Figure 1-4) consists of a variety of components to make your work more efficient and documents more professional. The following sections discuss these components.

Document Window

The document window displays text, tables, graphics, and other items as you type or insert them into a document. Only a portion of your document, however, displays on the screen at one time. You view the portion of the document displayed on the screen through the **document window** (Figure 1-5 on the next page).

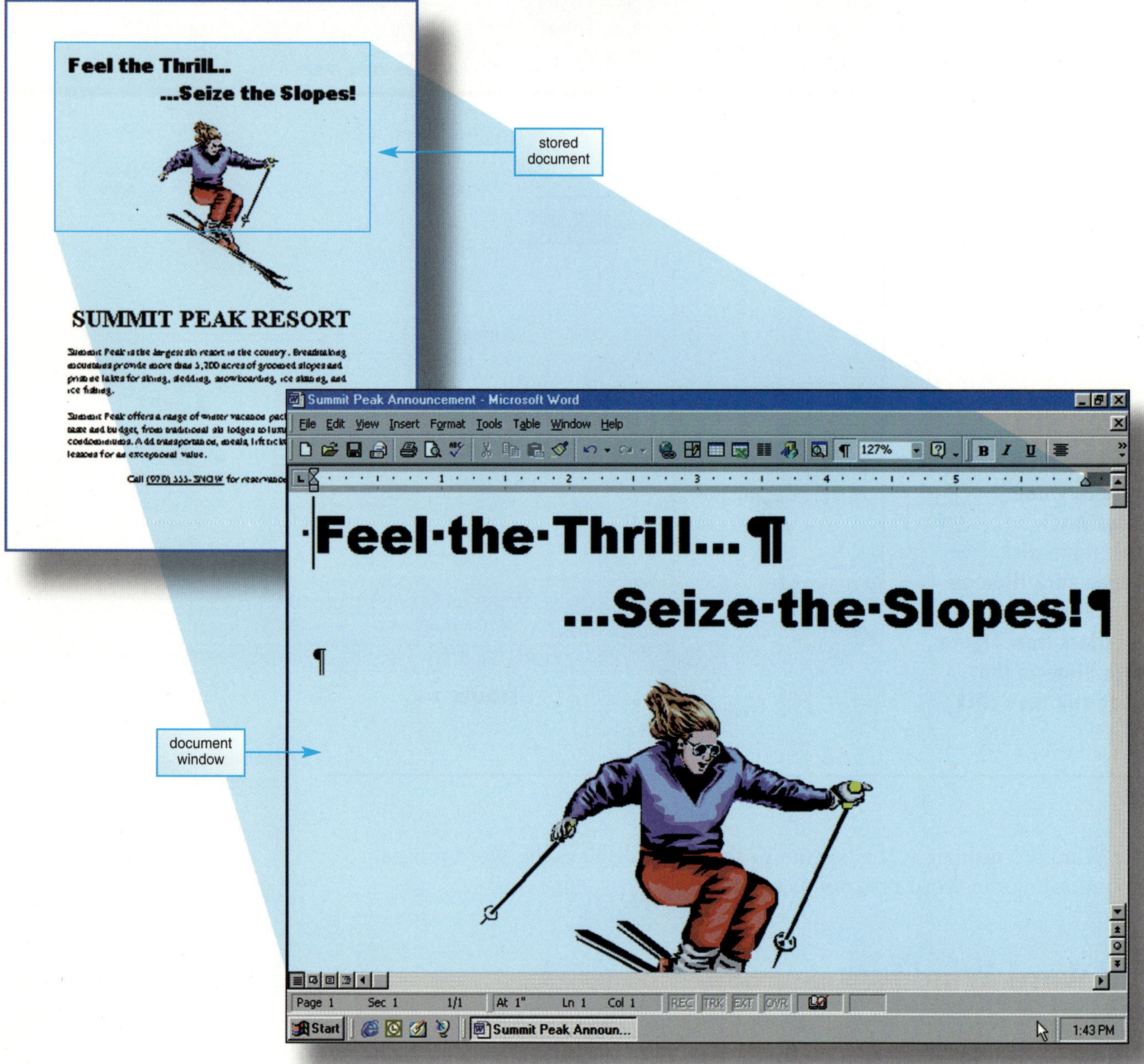

FIGURE 1-5

The document window contains several elements commonly found in other applications, as well as some elements unique to Word. The main elements of the Word document window are the insertion point, end mark, mouse pointer, rulers, scroll bars, and status bar (see Figure 1-4 on the previous page).

INSERTION POINT The **insertion point** is a blinking vertical bar that indicates where text will be inserted as you type. As you type, the insertion point moves to the right and, when you reach the end of a line, it moves downward to the next line. You also can insert graphics, tables, and other items at the location of the insertion point.

END MARK The **end mark** is a short horizontal line that indicates the end of your document. Each time you begin a new line, the end mark moves downward.

MOUSE POINTER The **mouse pointer** becomes different shapes depending on the task you are performing in Word and the pointer's location on the screen. The mouse pointer in Figure 1-4 has the shape of an I-beam. Other mouse pointer shapes are described as they appear on the screen during this and subsequent projects.

The Horizontal Ruler

If the horizontal ruler does not display on your screen, click View on the menu bar and then click Ruler. To hide the ruler, also click View on the menu bar and then click Ruler.

RULERS At the top edge of the document window is the **horizontal ruler**. You use the horizontal ruler, sometimes simply called the **ruler**, to set tab stops, indent paragraphs, adjust column widths, and change page margins.

An additional ruler, called the **vertical ruler**, sometimes displays at the left edge of the window when you perform certain tasks. The purpose of the vertical ruler is discussed as it displays on the screen in a later project. If your screen displays a vertical ruler, click View on the menu bar and then click Normal.

More About

Scroll Bars

You can use the vertical scroll bar to scroll through multi-page documents. As you drag the scroll box up or down the scroll bar, Word displays a page indicator to the left of the scroll box. If you release the mouse button, Word displays the page referenced by the page indicator in the document window.

SCROLL BARS You use the **scroll bars** to display different portions of your document in the document window. At the right edge of the document window is a vertical scroll bar, and at the bottom of the document window is a horizontal scroll bar. On both the vertical and horizontal scroll bars, the position of the **scroll box** reflects the location of the portion of the document displaying in the document window.

On the left edge of the horizontal scroll bar are four buttons you use to change the view of your document, and on the bottom of the vertical scroll bar are three buttons you can use to scroll through a document. These buttons are discussed as they are used in later projects.

STATUS BAR The status bar displays at the bottom of the document window, above the Windows taskbar. The **status bar** presents information about the location of the insertion point, the progress of current tasks, as well as the status of certain commands, keys, and buttons.

From left to right, the following information displays on the status bar in Figure 1-5: the page number, the section number, the page containing the insertion point followed by the total number of pages in the document, the position of the insertion point in inches from the top of the page, the line number and column number of the insertion point, followed by several status indicators. If you perform a task that requires several seconds (such as saving a document), the status bar displays a message informing you of the progress of the task.

Language Mode

If system support for multiple languages was installed on your computer, the status bar also displays the Language mode indicator, which shows the name of the language you are using to create the document.

You use the **status indicators** to turn certain keys or modes on or off. Four of these status indicators (REC, TRK, EXT, and OVR) display darkened when on and dimmed when off. For example, the dimmed OVR indicates overtype mode is off. To turn these four status indicators on or off, double-click the status indicator. These status indicators are discussed as they are used in the projects.

The next status indicators display icons as you perform certain tasks. When you begin typing in the document window, a Spelling and Grammar Status icon displays. When Word is saving your document, a Background Save Status icon displays. When you print a document, a Background Print Status icon displays.

When you point to various areas on the status bar, Word displays a ScreenTip to help you identify it. A **ScreenTip** is a short descriptive name of a button, icon, or command associated with the item to which you are pointing.

Menu Bar and Toolbars

The menu bar displays at the top of the screen just below the title bar (Figure 1-6a on the next page). The Standard toolbar and Formatting toolbar are preset to share a single row that displays immediately below the menu bar.

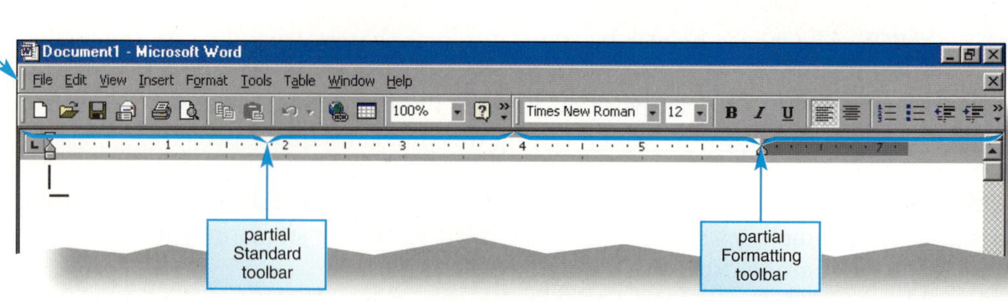

FIGURE 1-6a

More About

Shortcut Menus

Right-clicking an object displays a shortcut menu (also called a context-sensitive or object menu). Depending on the object, the commands in the shortcut menu vary.

MENU BAR The **menu bar** displays the Word menu names. Each menu contains a list of commands you can use to perform tasks such as retrieving, storing, printing, and formatting data in your document. When you click a menu name on the menu bar, a **short menu** displays that lists your most recently used commands (Figure 1-6b). To display a menu, such as the View menu, click the menu name on the menu bar. If you point to a command on a menu with an arrow to its right, a submenu displays from which you choose a command.

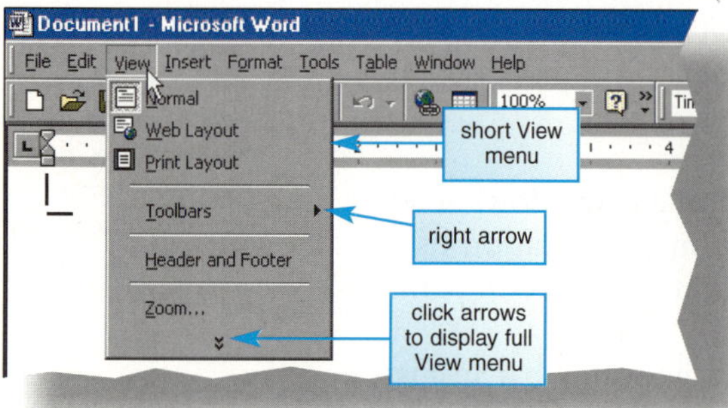

FIGURE 1-6b

If you wait a few seconds or click the arrows at the bottom of the short menu, it expands into a full menu. A **full menu** lists all the commands associated with a menu (Figure 1-6c). You also can display a full menu immediately by double-clicking the menu name on the menu bar. In this book, when you display a menu, always display the full menu using one of these techniques:

1. Click the menu name on the menu bar and then wait a few seconds.
2. Click the menu name and then click the arrows at the bottom of the short menu.
3. Click the menu name and then point to the arrows at the bottom of the short menu.
4. Double-click the menu name.

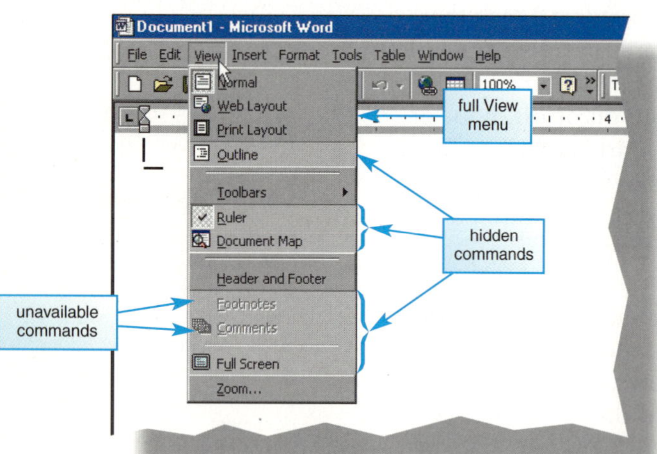

FIGURE 1-6c

When a full menu displays, some of the commands are recessed into lighter gray background and some also are unavailable. A recessed command is called a **hidden command** because it does not display on a short menu. As you use Word, it automatically personalizes the short menus for you based on how often you use commands. That is, as you use hidden commands, Word *unhides* them and places them on the short menu. An **unavailable command** displays dimmed, which indicates it is not available for the current selection.

TOOLBARS Word has many pre-defined, or built-in, toolbars. A **toolbar** contains buttons, boxes, and menus that allow you to perform tasks more quickly than using the menu bar and related menus. For example, to print a document, you click the Print button on the toolbar. Each button on a toolbar displays an image to help you remember its function. Also, when you point to a button or box on a toolbar, a ScreenTip (the item's name) displays below the mouse pointer (see Figure 1-10 on page WD 1.15).

Two built-in toolbars are the Standard toolbar and the Formatting toolbar. Figure 1-7a illustrates the Standard toolbar and identifies its buttons and boxes. Figure 1-7b illustrates the Formatting toolbar. Each button and box is explained in detail as it is used in the projects throughout the book.

The Standard toolbar and Formatting toolbar are preset to display docked on the same row immediately below the menu bar. A **docked toolbar** is one that is attached to the edge of the Word window. Because both of these toolbars cannot fit entirely on a single row, a portion or all of the Standard toolbar displays on the left of the row and a portion or all of the Formatting toolbar displays on the right (Figure 1-8a). The buttons that display on the toolbar are the more frequently used buttons.

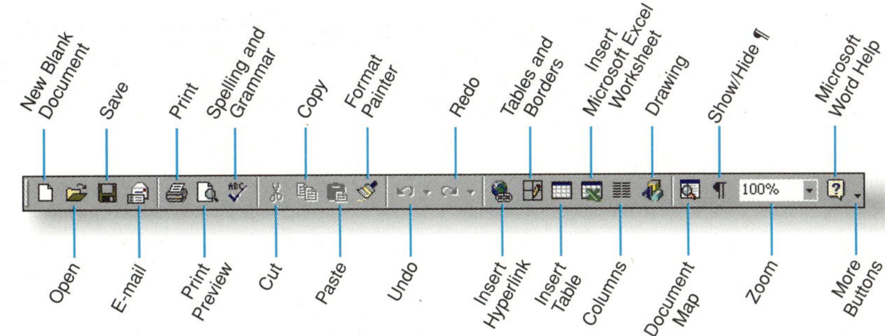

FIGURE 1-7a Standard Toolbar

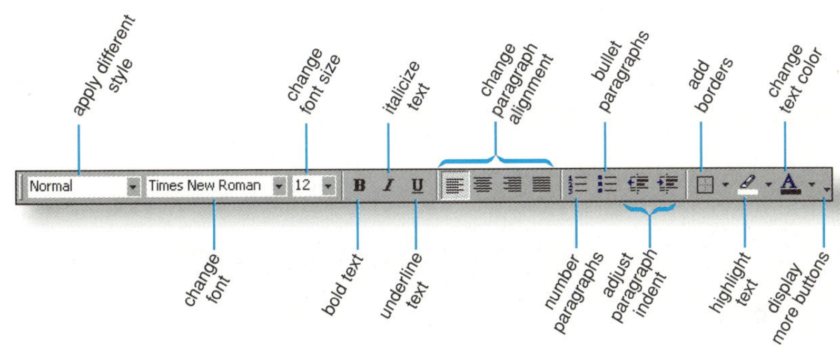

FIGURE 1-7b Formatting Toolbar

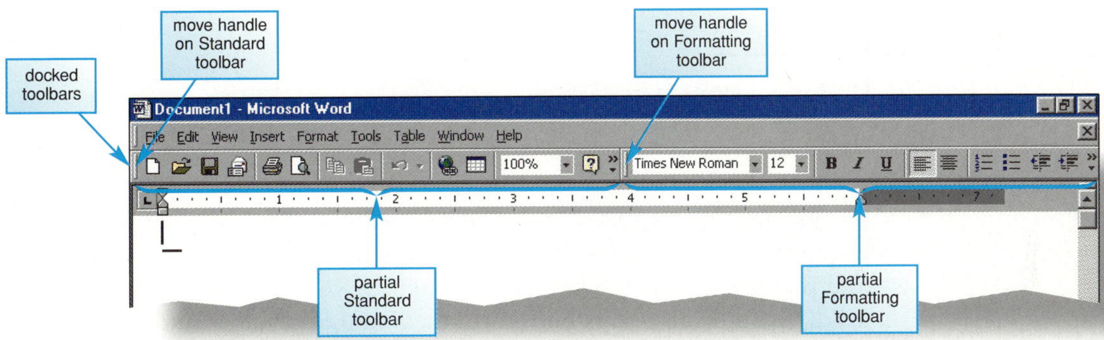

FIGURE 1-8a

To display the entire Standard toolbar, double-click its **move handle**, which is the vertical bar at the left edge of a toolbar. When you display the complete Standard toolbar, only a portion of the Formatting toolbar displays (Figure 1-8b). To display the entire Formatting toolbar, double-click its move handle. When you display the complete Formatting toolbar, only a portion of the Standard toolbar displays (Figure 1-8c on the next page).

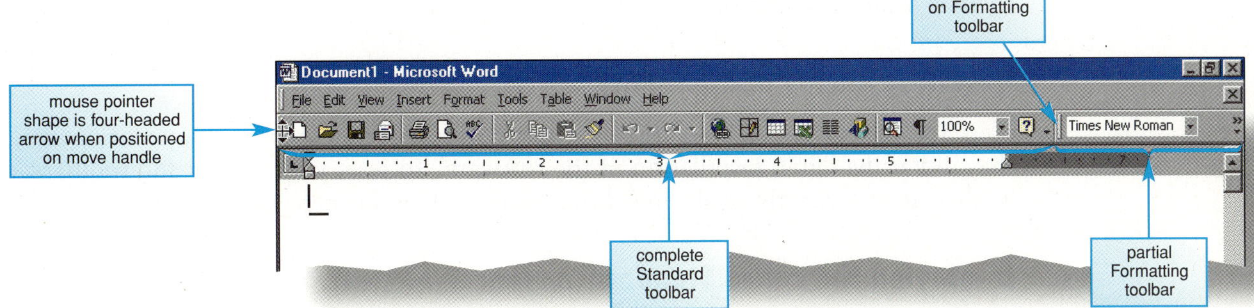

FIGURE 1-8b

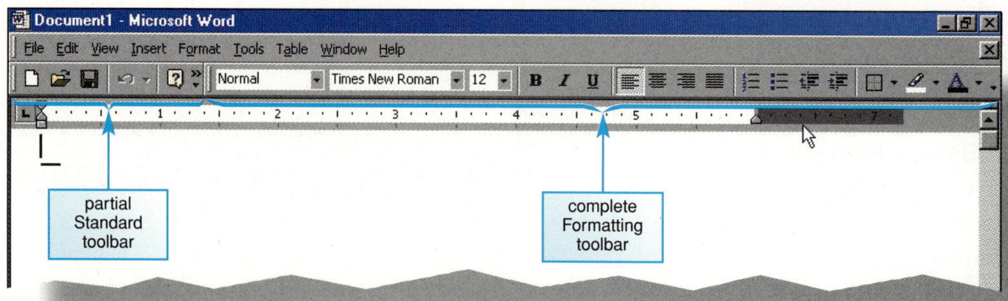

FIGURE 1-8c

An alternative to double-clicking the move handle to display an entire toolbar is to click the More Buttons button at the right edge of the toolbar. When you click a toolbar's **More Buttons** button, Word displays a **More Buttons list** that contains the toolbar's hidden buttons (Figure 1-8d).

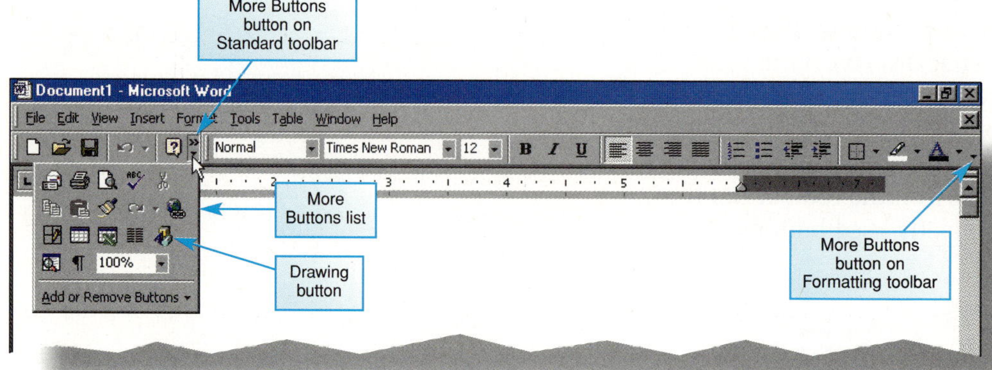

FIGURE 1-8d

As with menus, Word personalizes toolbars. That is, once you click a hidden button in the More Buttons list, Word removes the button from the More Buttons list and places it on the toolbar. For example, if you click the Drawing button in Figure 1-8d, Word displays this button on the Standard toolbar and removes a less frequently used button to make room for the Drawing button. By adapting to the way you work, this intelligent personalization feature of Word is designed to increase your productivity.

Additional toolbars may display on the Word screen, depending on the task you are performing. These additional toolbars display either stacked below the row containing the Standard and Formatting toolbars or floating in the Word window. A **floating toolbar** is not attached to an edge of the Word window. You can rearrange the order of docked toolbars and can move floating toolbars anywhere in the Word window. Later in this book, steps are presented that show you how to float a docked toolbar or dock a floating toolbar.

Resetting Menus and Toolbars

Each project in this book begins with the menu bars and toolbars appearing as they did at the initial installation of the software. To reset your menus and toolbars so they appear exactly as shown in this book, follow the steps in Appendix C.

Displaying the Entire Standard Toolbar

Perform the following step to display the entire Standard toolbar.

To Display the Entire Standard Toolbar

1 Double-click the move handle on the Standard toolbar.

Word displays the entire Standard toolbar (Figure 1-9).

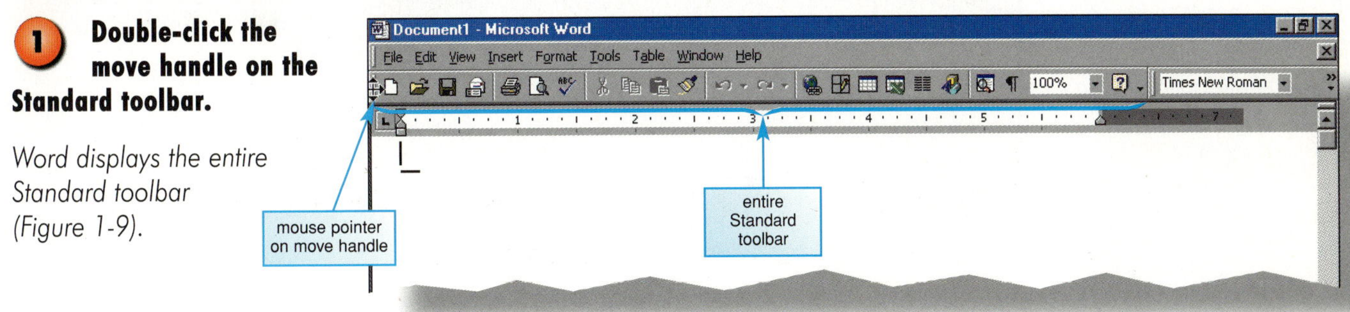

FIGURE 1-9

Zooming Page Width

Depending on your Windows and Word settings, the horizontal ruler at the top of the document window may show more inches or fewer inches than the ruler shown in Figure 1-9. The more inches of ruler that display, the smaller the text will be on the screen. The fewer inches of ruler that display, the larger the text will be on the screen. To minimize eyestrain, the projects in this book display the text as large as possible without extending the right margin beyond the right edge of the document window.

Two factors that affect how much of the ruler displays in the document window are the Windows screen resolution and the Word zoom percentage. The screens in this book use a resolution of 800 x 600. With this resolution, you can increase the preset zoom percentage beyond 100% so that the right margin extends to the edge of the document window. To increase or decrease the size of the displayed characters to a point where both the left and right margins are at the edges of the document window, use the **zoom page width** command as shown in the following steps.

To Zoom Page Width

1 Point to the Zoom box arrow on the Standard toolbar.

The mouse pointer shape is a left-pointing block arrow when positioned on a toolbar button or box (Figure 1-10). When you point to a toolbar button or box, Word displays a ScreenTip.

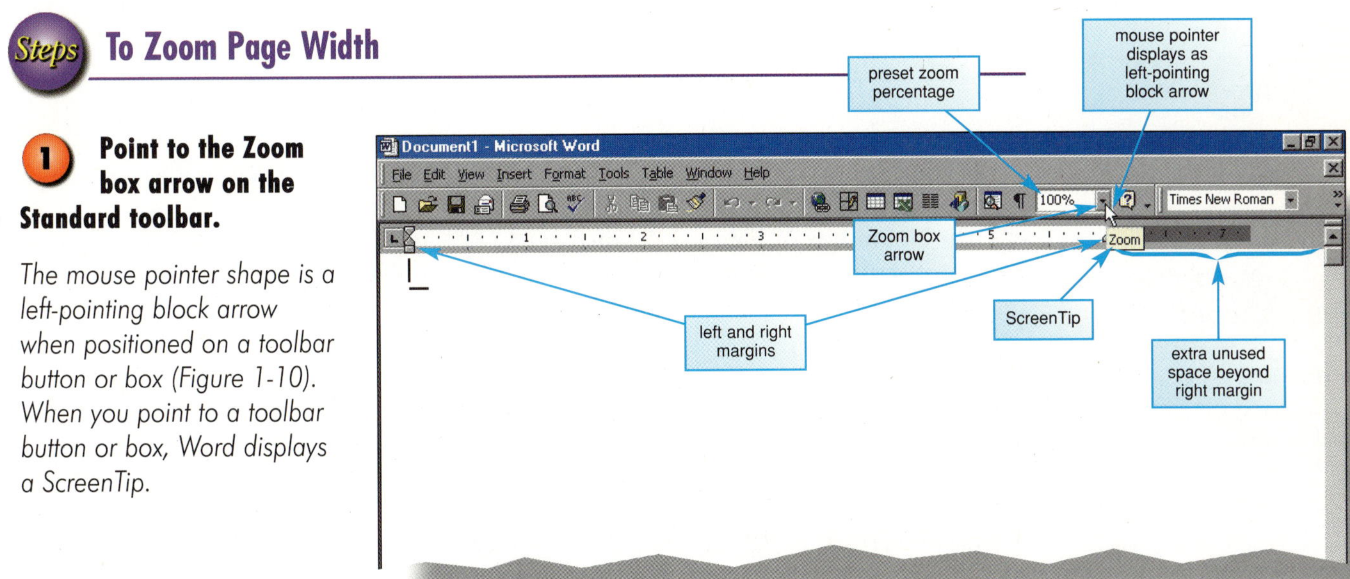

FIGURE 1-10

2 Click the Zoom box arrow.

Word displays a list of available zoom percentages and the Page Width option in the Zoom list (Figure 1-11).

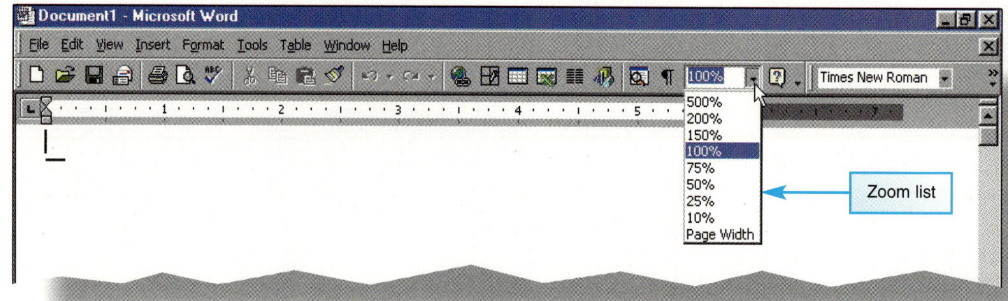

FIGURE 1-11

Point to Page Width in the Zoom list.

Word highlights Page Width in the Zoom list (Figure 1-12).

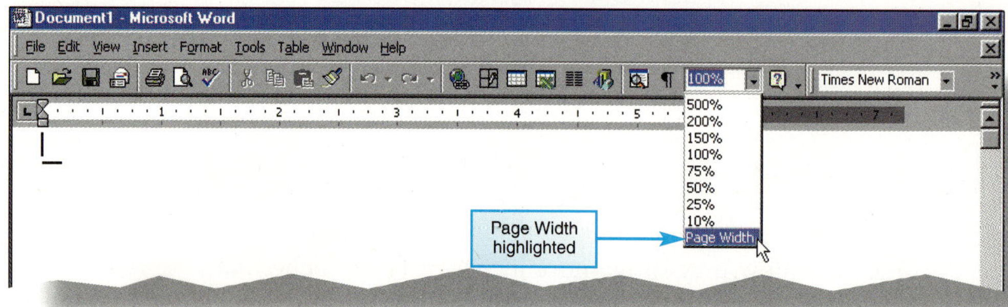

FIGURE 1-12

Click Page Width.

Word extends the right margin to the right edge of the document window (Figure 1-13).

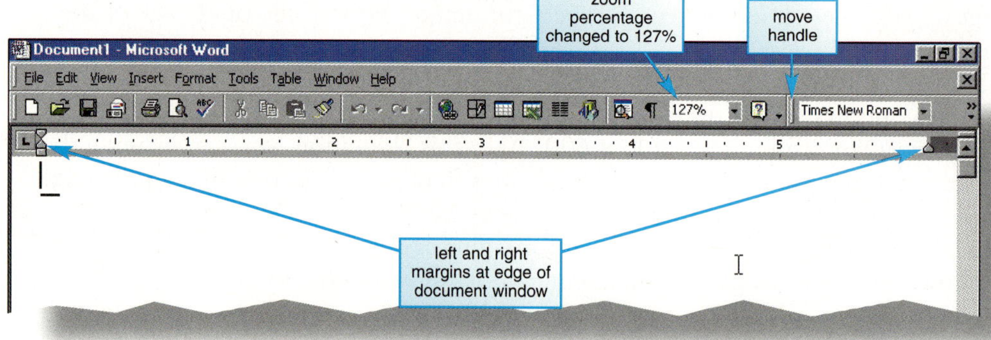

FIGURE 1-13

Other Ways

1. On View menu click Zoom, select Page Width, click OK button

More About 2000

Zooming

If you want to zoom to a percentage not displayed in the Zoom list, you can click the Zoom box on the Standard toolbar, type the desired percentage, and then press the ENTER key; or click View on the menu bar, click Zoom, and then enter the desired zoom percentage.

If your Zoom list (Figure 1-12) displayed additional options, click View on the menu bar and then click Normal.

The Zoom box in Figure 1-13 displays 127%, which Word computes based on a variety of settings. Your percentage may be different depending on your system configuration.

Changing the Default Font Size

Characters that display on the screen are a specific shape, size, and style. The **font**, or typeface, defines the appearance and shape of the letters, numbers, and special characters. The preset, or **default**, font is Times New Roman (Figure 1-14). **Font size** specifies the size of the characters. Font size is determined by a measurement system called points. A single **point** is about 1/72 of one inch in height. Thus, a character with a font size of ten is about 10/72 of one inch in height.

If Word 2000 is installed on a new computer, then the default font size most likely is 12. If, however, you upgrade from a previous version of Word when installing Word 2000, your default font most likely is 10.

If more of the characters in your document require a larger font size than the default, you easily can change the default font size before you type. In Project 1, many of the characters in the announcement are a font size of 16. Follow these steps to increase the font size before you begin entering text.

More About 2000

Font Size

Many people need to wear reading glasses. Thus, use a font size of at least 12 in your documents. Because an announcement usually is posted on a bulletin board, its font size should be as large as possible so that all potential readers can see the announcement easily.

To Increase the Default Font Size Before Typing

1 Double-click the move handle on the Formatting toolbar to display the entire toolbar. Click the Font Size box arrow on the Formatting toolbar and then point to 16.

A list of available font sizes displays in the Font Size list (Figure 1-14). The available font sizes depend on the current font, which is Times New Roman.

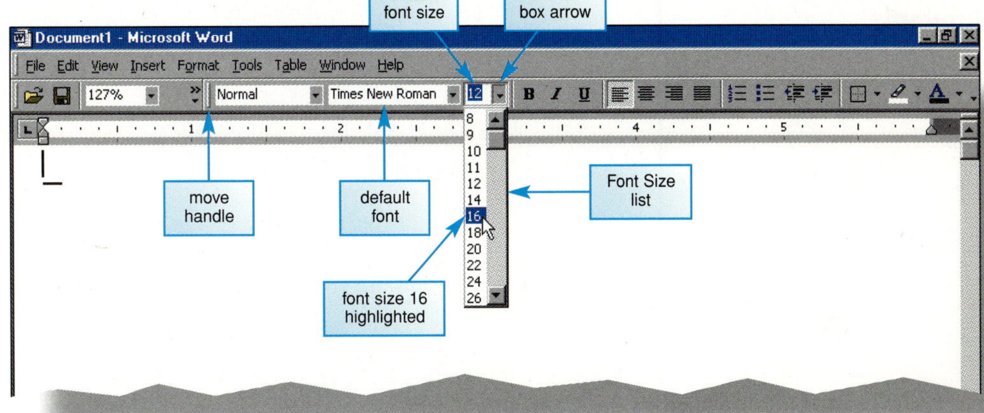

FIGURE 1-14

2 Click 16.

The font size for characters in this document changes to 16 (Figure 1-15). The size of the insertion point increases to reflect the new font size.

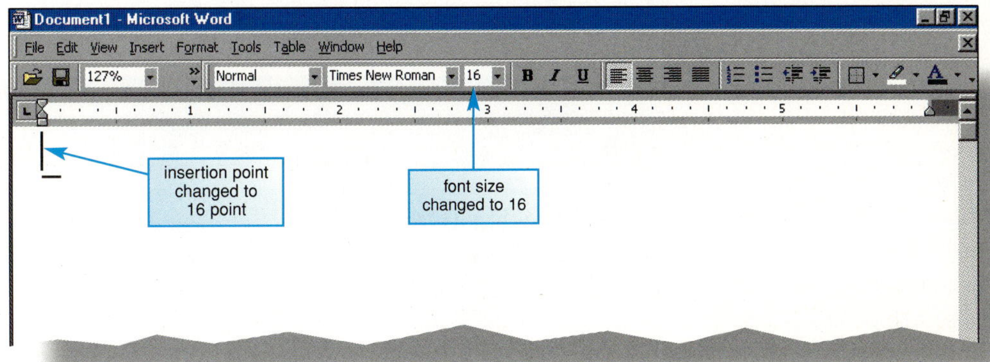

FIGURE 1-15

Other Ways

1. Right-click above end mark, click Font on shortcut menu, click Font tab, select desired font size in Size list, click OK button
2. On Format menu click Font, click Font tab, select desired font size in Size list, click OK button
3. Press CTRL+SHIFT+P, type desired font size, press ENTER
4. Press CTRL+SHIFT+>

The new font size takes effect immediately in your document. Word uses this font size for characters you type into this announcement.

Entering Text

To create a document that contains text, you enter the text by typing on the keyboard. The example on the next page explains the steps to enter both lines of the headline of the announcement. These lines will be positioned at the left margin. Later in this project, you will format the headline so that both lines are bold and enlarged and the second line is positioned at the right margin.

To Enter Text

1 **Type** `Feel the Thrill` **and then press the PERIOD key (.) three times. If you make an error while typing, press the BACKSPACE key until you have deleted the text in error and then retype the text correctly.**

As you type, the insertion point moves to the right (Figure 1-16).

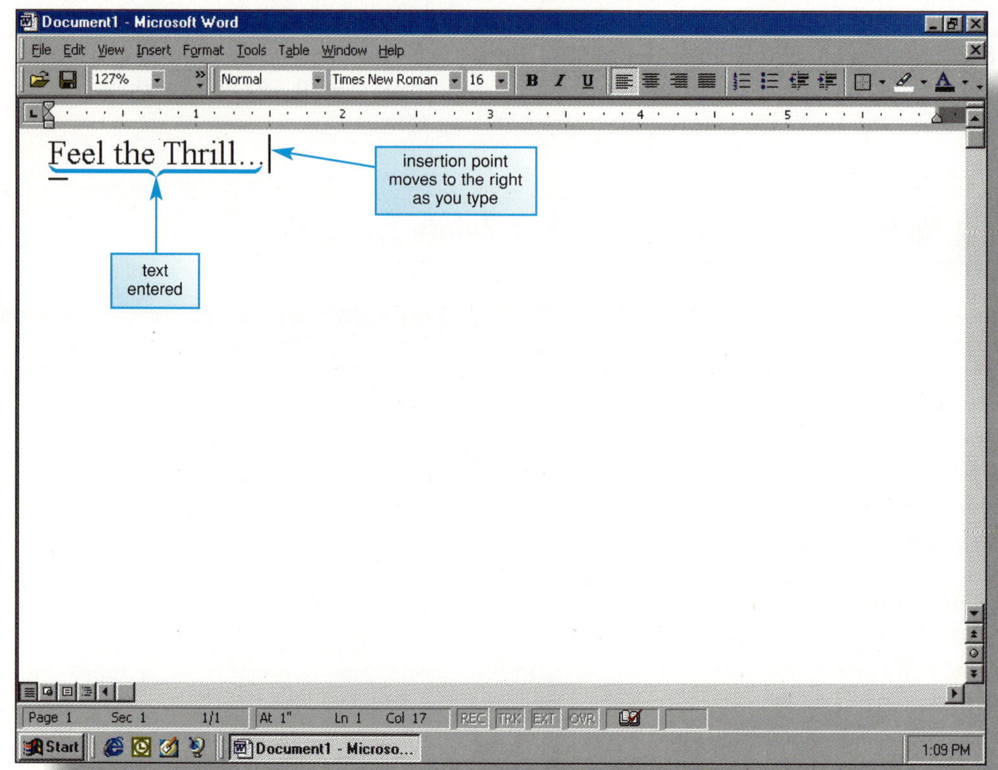

FIGURE 1-16

2 **Press the ENTER key.**

Word moves the insertion point to the beginning of the next line (Figure 1-17). Notice the status bar indicates the current position of the insertion point. That is, the insertion point currently is on line 2 column 1.

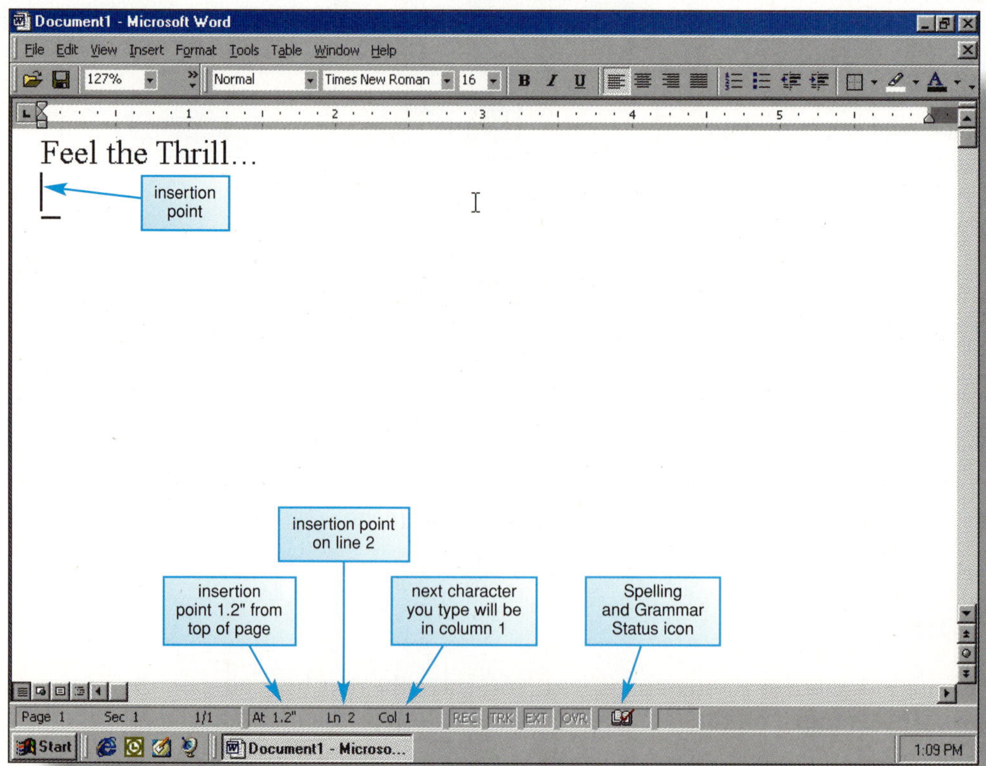

FIGURE 1-17

3 **Press the PERIOD key three times and then type** `Seize the Slopes!` **Press the ENTER key.**

The headline is complete (Figure 1-18). The insertion point is on line 3.

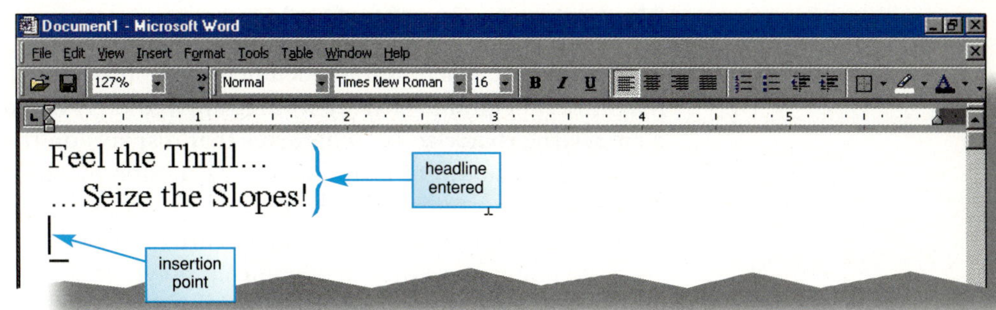

FIGURE 1-18

When you begin entering text into a document, the **Spelling and Grammar Status icon** displays at the right of the status bar (Figure 1-17). As you type, the Spelling and Grammar Status icon shows an animated pencil writing on paper, which indicates Word is checking for possible errors. When you stop typing, the pencil changes to either a red check mark or a red X. In Figure 1-17, the Spelling and Grammar Status icon displays a red check mark.

In general, if all of the words you have typed are in Word's dictionary and your grammar is correct, a red check mark displays on the Spelling and Grammar Status icon. If you type a word not in the dictionary (because it is a proper name or misspelled), a red wavy underline displays below the word. If you type text that may be grammatically incorrect, a green wavy underline displays below the text. When Word flags a possible spelling or grammar error, it also changes the red check mark on the Spelling and Grammar Status icon to a red X. As you enter text into the announcement, your Spelling and Grammar Status icon may show a red X instead of a red check mark. Later in this project, you will check the spelling of these words. At that time, the red X will return to a red check mark.

More About 2000

Entering Text

In the days of typewriters, the letter l was used for both the letter l and the numeral one. Keyboards, however, have both a numeral one and the letter l. Keyboards also have both a numeral zero and the letter o. Be careful to press the correct keyboard character when creating a word processing document.

Entering Blank Lines into a Document

To enter a blank line into a document, press the ENTER key without typing any text on the line. The following example explains how to enter three blank lines below the headline.

To Enter Blank Lines into a Document

Press the ENTER key three times.

Word inserts three blank lines into your document below the headline (Figure 1-19).

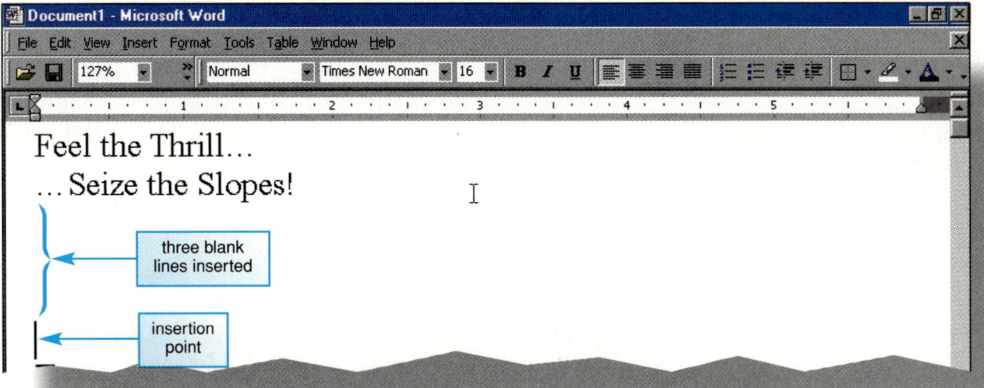

FIGURE 1-19

Displaying Formatting Marks

To indicate where in the document you press the ENTER key or SPACEBAR, you may find it helpful to display formatting marks. A **formatting mark**, sometimes called a **nonprinting character**, is a character that displays on the screen but is not visible on a printed document. For example, the paragraph mark (¶) is a formatting mark that indicates where you pressed the ENTER key. A raised dot (•) shows where you pressed the SPACEBAR. Other formatting marks are discussed as they display on the screen.

Depending on settings made during previous Word sessions, your screen may already display formatting marks (see Figure 1-21). If the formatting marks are not already displaying on your screen, perform the following steps to display them.

To Display Formatting Marks

1 Double-click the move handle on the Standard toolbar to display the entire toolbar. Point to the Show/Hide ¶ button on the Standard toolbar (Figure 1-20).

FIGURE 1-20

2 If it is not already recessed, click the Show/Hide ¶ button.

*Word **recesses**, or pushes in, the Show/Hide ¶ button on the Standard toolbar and displays formatting marks on the screen (Figure 1-21).*

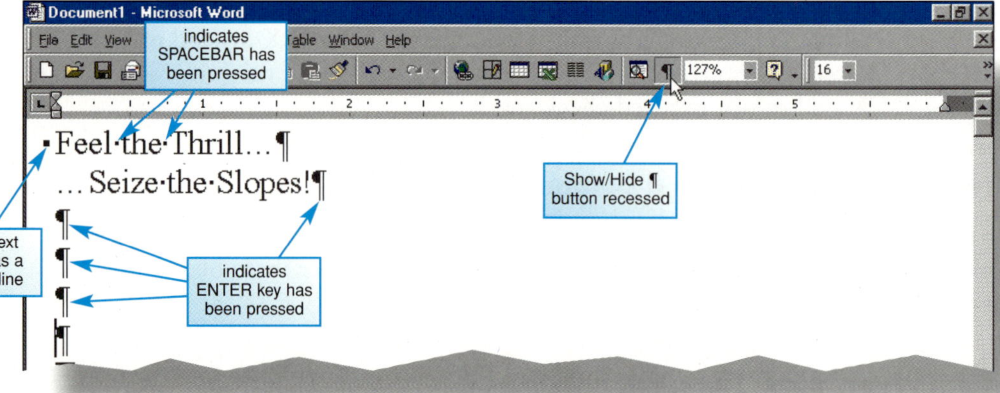

FIGURE 1-21

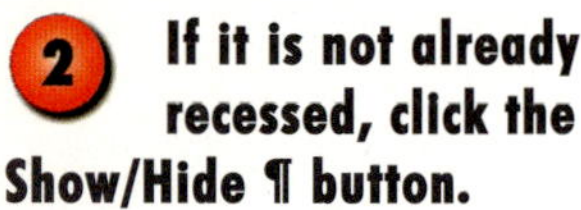

Other Ways

1. On Tools menu click Options, click View tab, click All, click OK button
2. Press CTRL+SHIFT+*

Notice several changes to your Word document window (Figure 1-21). A paragraph mark displays at the end of each line to indicate you pressed the ENTER key. Each time you press the ENTER key, Word creates a new paragraph. Because you changed the font size, the paragraph marks are 16 point. Notice Word places a paragraph mark above the end mark – you cannot delete this paragraph mark. Between each word, a raised dot appears, indicating you pressed the SPACEBAR. A small square at the beginning of the first line in the announcement indicates it is formatted using the Heading 1 style. Styles are discussed in a later project. Finally, the Show/Hide ¶ button is recessed to indicate it is selected.

If you feel the formatting marks clutter your screen, you can hide them by clicking the Show/Hide ¶ button again. It is recommended that you display formatting marks; therefore, the document windows presented in this book show the formatting marks.

Entering More Text

The body title (SUMMIT PEAK RESORT) in the announcement is capitalized. The next step is to enter this body title in all capital letters into the document window as explained below.

TO ENTER MORE TEXT

1. Press the CAPS LOCK key on the keyboard to turn on capital letters. Verify the CAPS LOCK indicator is lit on your keyboard.
2. Type `SUMMIT PEAK RESORT` and then press the CAPS LOCK key to turn off capital letters.
3. Press the ENTER key twice.

The body title displays on line 6 as shown in Figure 1-22 below.

Using Wordwrap

Wordwrap allows you to type words in a paragraph continually without pressing the ENTER key at the end of each line. When the insertion point reaches the right margin, Word positions it automatically at the beginning of the next line. As you type, if a word extends beyond the right margin, Word also positions that word automatically on the next line with the insertion point.

Thus, as you enter text using Word, do not press the ENTER key when the insertion point reaches the right margin. Because Word creates a new paragraph each time you press the ENTER key, press the ENTER key only in these circumstances:

1. To insert blank lines into a document
2. To begin a new paragraph
3. To terminate a short line of text and advance to the next line
4. In response to certain Word commands

Perform the following step to become familiar with wordwrap.

More About

Wordwrap

Your printer controls where wordwrap occurs for each line in your document. For this reason, it is possible that the same document could wordwrap on different words if printed on different printers.

To Wordwrap Text as You Type

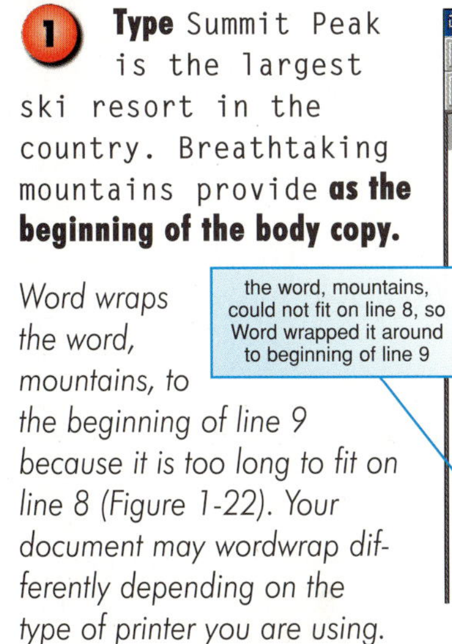

1. **Type** `Summit Peak is the largest ski resort in the country. Breathtaking mountains provide` **as the beginning of the body copy.**

Word wraps the word, mountains, to the beginning of line 9 because it is too long to fit on line 8 (Figure 1-22). Your document may wordwrap differently depending on the type of printer you are using.

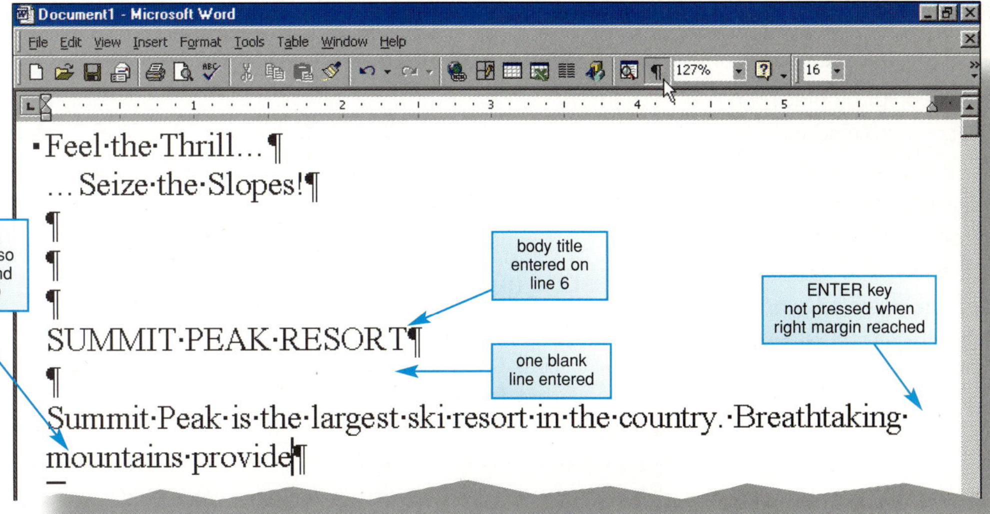
Document1 - Microsoft Word
File Edit View Insert Format Tools Table Window Help
127%
16
Feel·the·Thrill…¶
…Seize·the·Slopes!¶
SUMMIT·PEAK·RESORT¶
Summit·Peak·is·the·largest·ski·resort·in·the·country.·Breathtaking·
mountains·provide¶
the word, mountains, could not fit on line 8, so Word wrapped it around to beginning of line 9
body title entered on line 6
one blank line entered
ENTER key not pressed when right margin reached

FIGURE 1-22

Checking Spelling Automatically as You Type

As you type text into the document window, Word checks your typing for possible spelling and grammar errors. If a word you type is not in the dictionary, a red wavy underline displays below it. Likewise, if text you type contains possible grammar errors, a green wavy underline displays below the text. In both cases, the Spelling and Grammar Status icon on the status bar displays a red X, instead of a check mark. Although you can check the entire document for spelling and grammar errors at once, you also can check these errors immediately.

To verify that the check spelling as you type feature is enabled, right-click the Spelling and Grammar Status icon on the status bar and then click Options on the shortcut menu. When the Spelling & Grammar dialog box displays, be sure Check spelling as you type has a check mark and Hide spelling errors in this document does not have a check mark.

When a word is flagged with a red wavy underline, it is not in Word's dictionary. A flagged word, however, is not necessarily misspelled. For example, many names, abbreviations, and specialized terms are not in Word's main dictionary. In these cases, you tell Word to ignore the flagged word. As you type, Word also detects duplicate words. For example, if your document contains the phrase, to the the store, Word places a red wavy underline below the second occurrence of the word, the. To display a list of suggested corrections for a flagged word, you right-click it.

In the following example, the word, sledding, has been misspelled intentionally as sleding to illustrate Word's check spelling as you type feature. If you are doing this project on a personal computer, your announcement may contain different misspelled words, depending on the accuracy of your typing.

Entering Sentences

Word processing documents use variable character fonts; for example, the letter w takes up more space than the letter i. With these fonts, it often is difficult to determine how many times the SPACEBAR has been pressed between sentences. Thus, the rule is to press the SPACEBAR only once after periods, colons, and other punctuation marks.

Steps To Check Spelling as You Type

1. **Press the SPACEBAR once. Type** `more than 5,200 acres of groomed slopes and pristine lakes for skiing, sleding,` **and then press the SPACEBAR.**

Word flags the misspelled word, sleding, by placing a red wavy underline below it (Figure 1-23). Notice the Spelling and Grammar Status icon on the status bar now displays a red X, indicating Word has detected a possible spelling or grammar error.

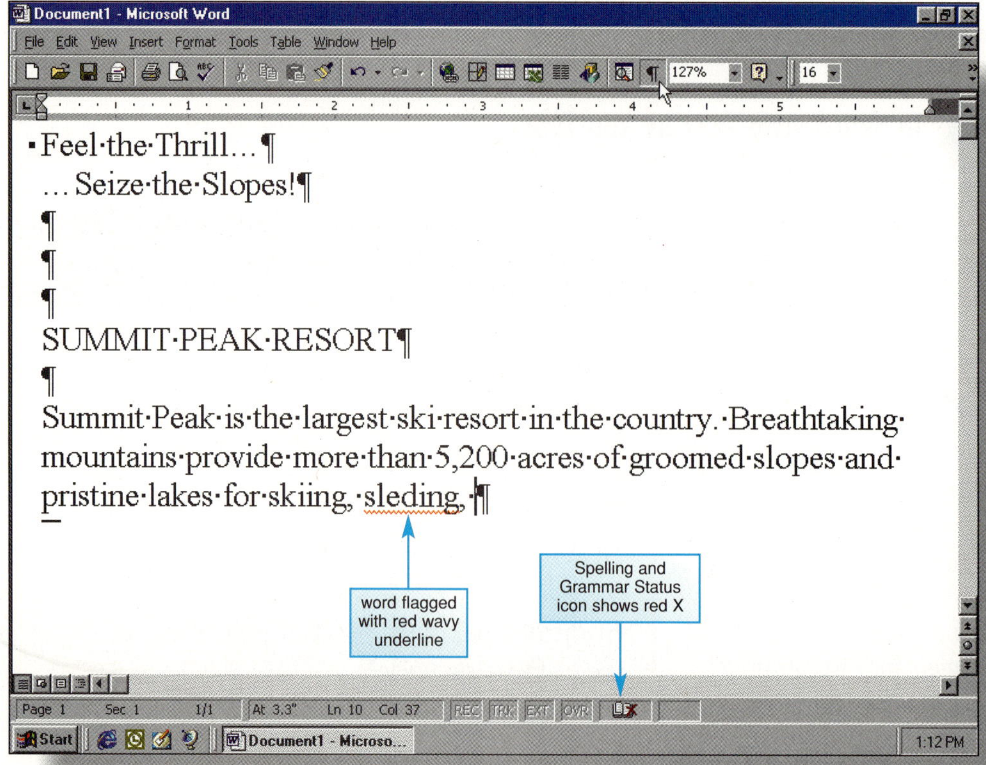

FIGURE 1-23

2 Position the mouse pointer in the flagged word (sleding, in this case).

The mouse pointer's shape is an I-beam when positioned in a word (Figure 1-24).

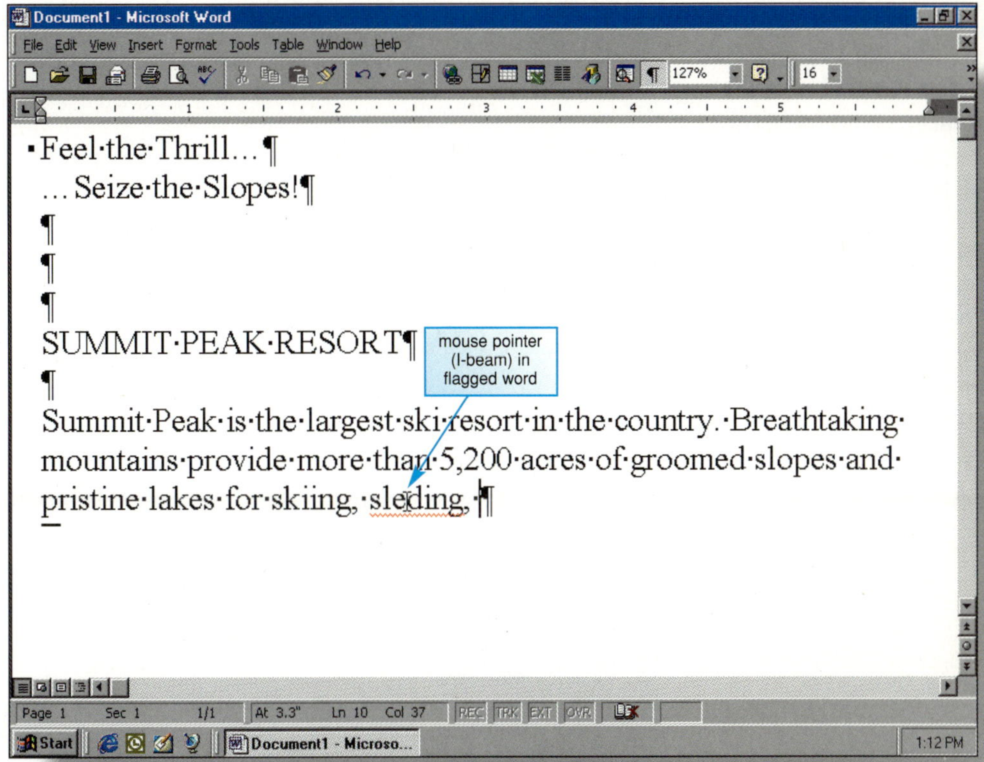

FIGURE 1-24

3 Right-click the flagged word, sleding. When the shortcut menu displays, point to sledding.

Word displays a shortcut menu that lists suggested spelling corrections for the flagged word (Figure 1-25).

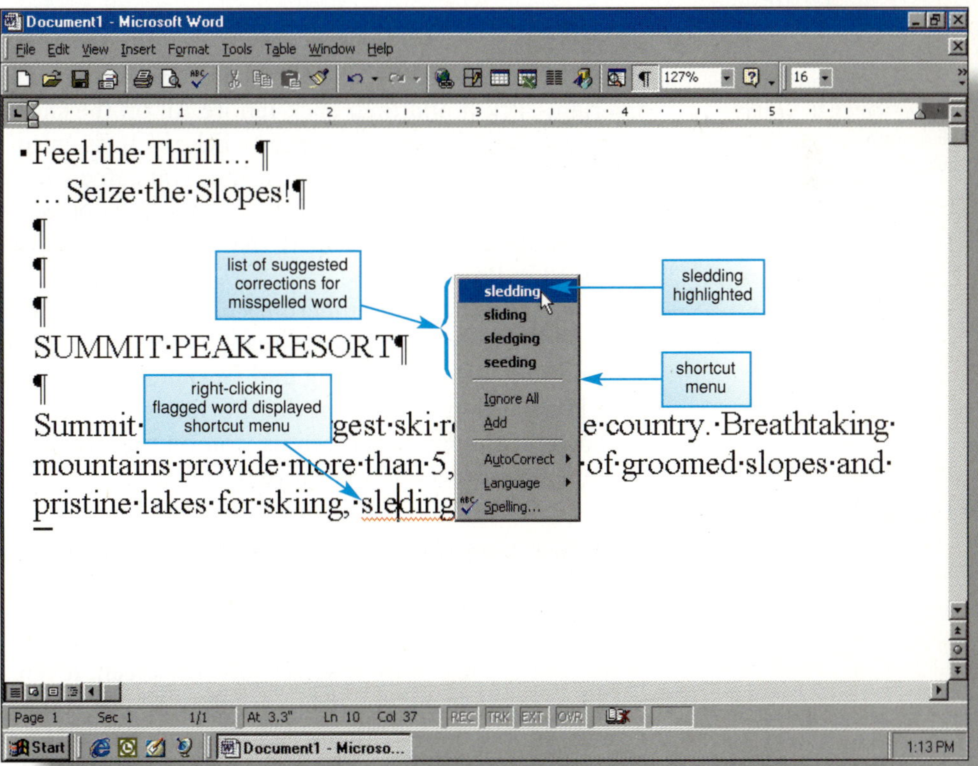

FIGURE 1-25

4 **Click sledding. Press the END key and then type the remainder of the sentence:** `snowboarding, ice skating, and ice fishing.`

Word replaces the misspelled word with the selected word on the shortcut menu (Figure 1-26). Word replaces the red X with a check mark on the Spelling and Grammar Status icon.

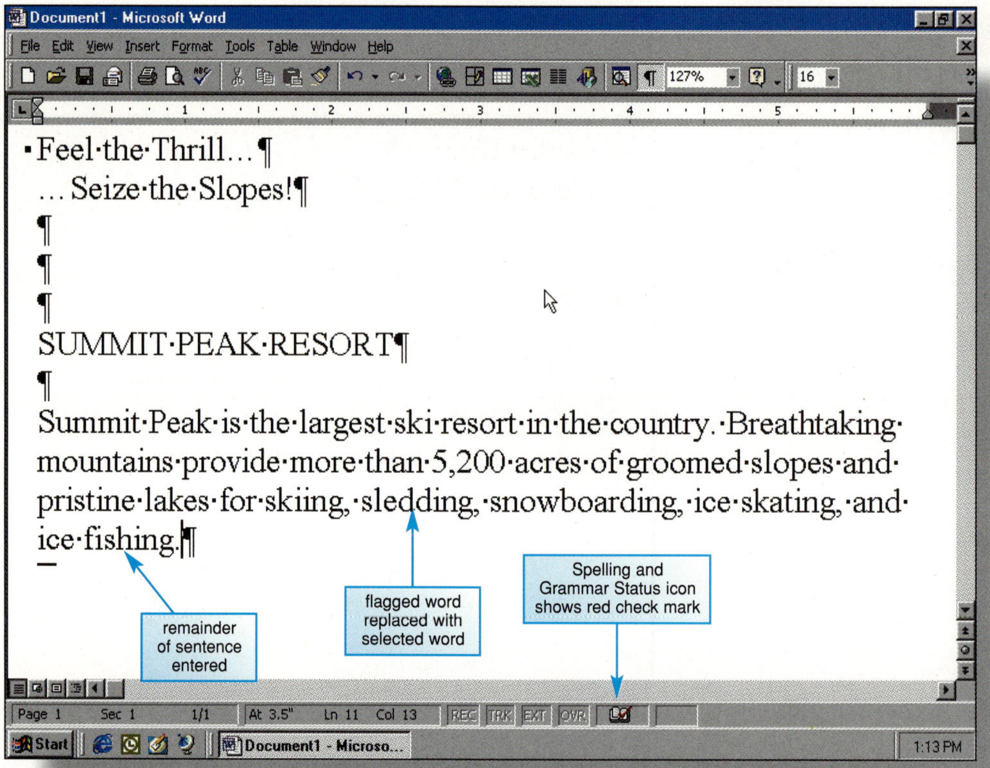
Document1 - Microsoft Word
Feel·the·Thrill…¶
…Seize·the·Slopes!¶
SUMMIT·PEAK·RESORT¶
Summit·Peak·is·the·largest·ski·resort·in·the·country.·Breathtaking·mountains·provide·more·than·5,200·acres·of·groomed·slopes·and·pristine·lakes·for·skiing,·sledding,·snowboarding,·ice·skating,·and·ice·fishing.¶
remainder of sentence entered
flagged word replaced with selected word
Spelling and Grammar Status icon shows red check mark
Page 1 Sec 1 1/1 At 3.5" Ln 11 Col 13
Start
Document1 - Microso...
1:13 PM

FIGURE 1-26

Other Ways

1. Click flagged word, double-click Spelling and Grammar Status icon on status bar, click correct word on shortcut menu

If the word actually is spelled correctly and, for example, is a proper name, you can right-click it and then click Ignore All on the shortcut menu (Figure 1-25 on the previous page). If, when you right-click the misspelled word, your desired correction is not in the list on the shortcut menu, you can click outside the shortcut menu to make the menu disappear and then retype the correct word, or you can click Spelling on the shortcut menu to display the Spelling dialog box. The Spelling dialog box is discussed in Project 2.

If you feel the wavy underlines clutter your document window, you can hide them temporarily until you are ready to check for spelling errors. To hide spelling errors, right-click the Spelling and Grammar Status icon on the status bar and then click Hide Spelling Errors on the shortcut menu. To hide grammar errors, right-click the Spelling and Grammar Status icon on the status bar and then click Hide Grammatical Errors on the shortcut menu.

More About 2000

Scrolling

Computer users frequently switch between the keyboard and the mouse during a word processing session, which places strain on the wrist. To help prevent wrist injury, minimize switching. If your fingers are already on the keyboard, use keyboard keys to scroll; if your hand is already on the mouse, use the mouse to scroll.

Entering Text that Scrolls the Document Window

As you type more lines of text than Word can display in the document window, Word **scrolls** the top portion of the document upward off the screen. Although you cannot see the text once it scrolls off the screen, it remains in the document. You have learned that the document window allows you to view only a portion of your document at one time (Figure 1-5 on page WD 1.10).

Perform the following step to enter text that scrolls the document window.

To Enter Text that Scrolls the Document Window

1 **Press the ENTER key twice. Type** `Summit Peak offers a range of vacation packages for every taste and budget, from traditional ski lodges to luxurious condominiums. Add transportation, meals, lift tickets, gear, and lessons for an exceptional value.` **Press the ENTER key twice. Type** `Call (970) 555-SNOW for reservations.`

Word scrolls the headline off the top of the screen (Figure 1-27). Your screen may scroll differently depending on the type of monitor you are using.

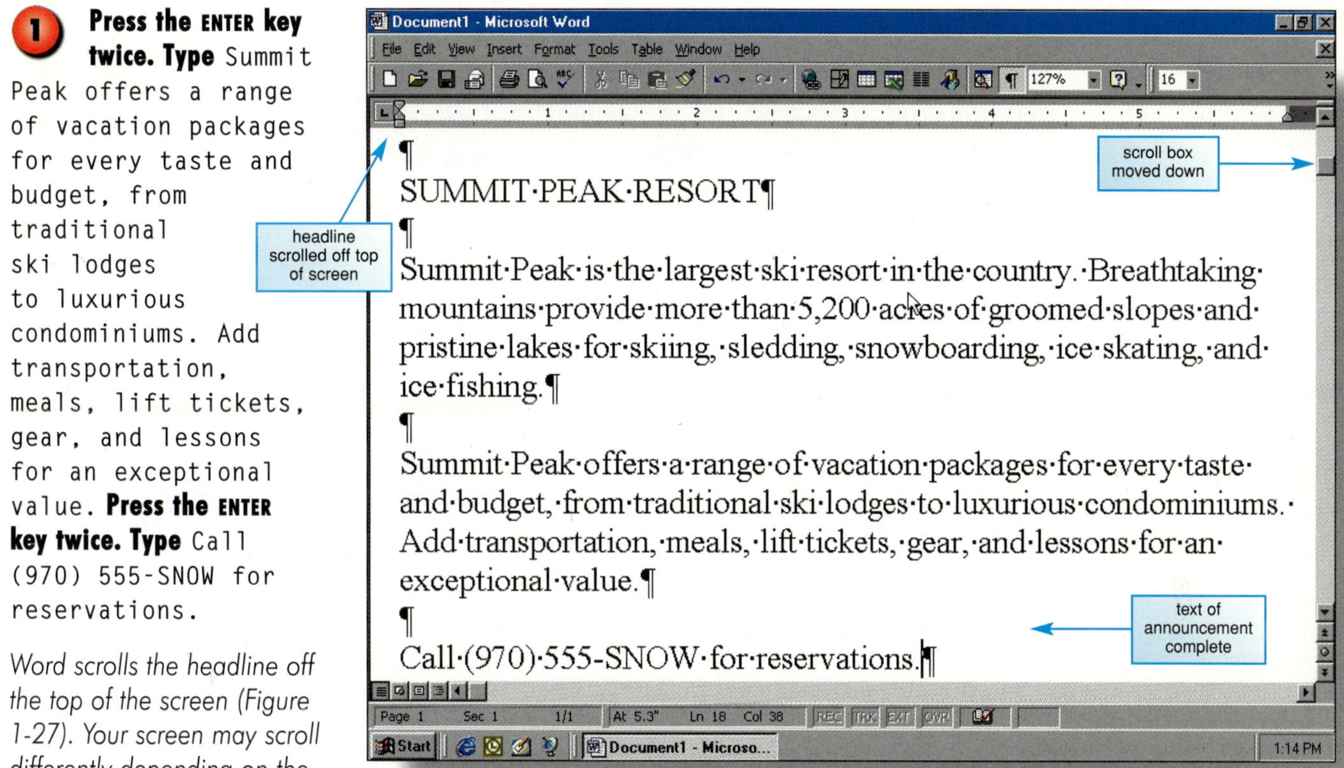
Document1 - Microsoft Word
File Edit View Insert Format Tools Table Window Help
scroll box moved down
headline scrolled off top of screen
¶
SUMMIT·PEAK·RESORT¶
¶
Summit·Peak·is·the·largest·ski·resort·in·the·country.·Breathtaking·mountains·provide·more·than·5,200·acres·of·groomed·slopes·and·pristine·lakes·for·skiing,·sledding,·snowboarding,·ice·skating,·and·ice·fishing.¶
¶
Summit·Peak·offers·a·range·of·vacation·packages·for·every·taste·and·budget,·from·traditional·ski·lodges·to·luxurious·condominiums.·Add·transportation,·meals,·lift·tickets,·gear,·and·lessons·for·an·exceptional·value.¶
¶
Call·(970)·555-SNOW·for·reservations.¶
text of announcement complete
Page 1 Sec 1 1/1 At 5.3" Ln 18 Col 38
Start
Document1 - Microso...
1:14 PM

FIGURE 1-27

When Word scrolls text off the top of the screen, the scroll box on the scroll bar at the right edge of the document window moves downward (Figure 1-27). The **scroll box** indicates the current relative location of the insertion point in the document. You may use either the mouse or the keyboard to move the insertion point to a different location in a document.

With the mouse, you use the scroll arrows or the scroll box to display a different portion of the document in the document window, and then click the mouse to move the insertion point to that location. Table 1-1 explains various techniques for vertically scrolling with the mouse.

More About
2000

Microsoft IntelliMouse®

For more information on the scrolling with the Microsoft IntelliMouse, visit the Word 2000 More About Web page (www.scsite.com/wd2000/more.htm) and then click Microsoft IntelliMouse.

Table 1-1 Techniques for Scrolling with the Mouse

SCROLL DIRECTION	MOUSE ACTION
Up	Drag the scroll box upward.
Down	Drag the scroll box downward.
Up one screen	Click anywhere above the scroll box on the vertical scroll bar.
Down one screen	Click anywhere below the scroll box on the vertical scroll bar.
Up one line	Click the scroll arrow at the top of the vertical scroll bar.
Down one line	Click the scroll arrow at the bottom of the vertical scroll bar.

When you use the keyboard to scroll, the insertion point moves automatically when you press the appropriate keys. Table 1-2 outlines various techniques to scroll through a document using the keyboard.

Table 1-2 Techniques for Scrolling with the Keyboard

SCROLL DIRECTION	KEY(S) TO PRESS	SCROLL DIRECTION	KEY(S) TO PRESS
Left one character	LEFT ARROW	Down one paragraph	CTRL+DOWN ARROW
Right one character	RIGHT ARROW	Up one screen	PAGE UP
Left one word	CTRL+LEFT ARROW	Down one screen	PAGE DOWN
Right one word	CTRL+RIGHT ARROW	To top of document window	ALT+CTRL+PAGE UP
Up one line	UP ARROW	To bottom of document window	ALT+CTRL+PAGE DOWN
Down one line	DOWN ARROW	Previous page	CTRL+PAGE UP
To end of a line	END	Next page	CTRL+PAGE DOWN
To beginning of a line	HOME	To the beginning of a document	CTRL+HOME
Up one paragraph	CTRL+UP ARROW	To the end of a document	CTRL+END

Saving

When you save a document, you use meaningful file names. A file name can be up to 255 characters, including spaces. The only invalid characters are backslash (\), slash (/), colon (:), asterisk (*), question mark (?), quotation mark ("), less than symbol (<), greater than symbol (>), and vertical bar (|).

Saving a Document

As you create a document in Word, the computer stores it in memory. If you turn off the computer or if you lose electrical power, the document in memory is lost. Hence, it is mandatory to save on disk any document that you will use later. The following steps illustrate how to save a document on a floppy disk inserted in drive A using the Save button on the Standard toolbar.

To Save a New Document

1 Insert a formatted floppy disk into drive A. Click the Save button on the Standard toolbar.

Word displays the Save As dialog box (Figure 1-28). The first line from the document displays highlighted in File name text box as the default file name. With this file name selected, you can change it by immediately typing the new name.

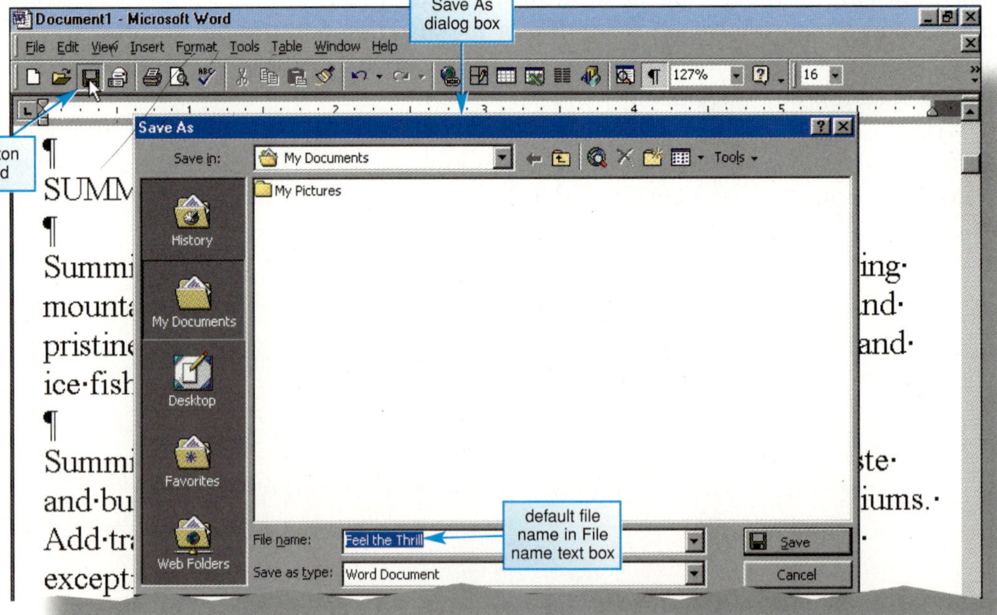

FIGURE 1-28

2 **Type** `Summit Peak Announcement` **in the File name text box. Do not press the ENTER key after typing the file name.**

The file name, Summit Peak Announcement, displays in the File name text box (Figure 1-29). Notice that the current save location is the My Documents folder. A ***folder*** *is a specific location on a disk. To change to a different save location, you use the Save in box.*

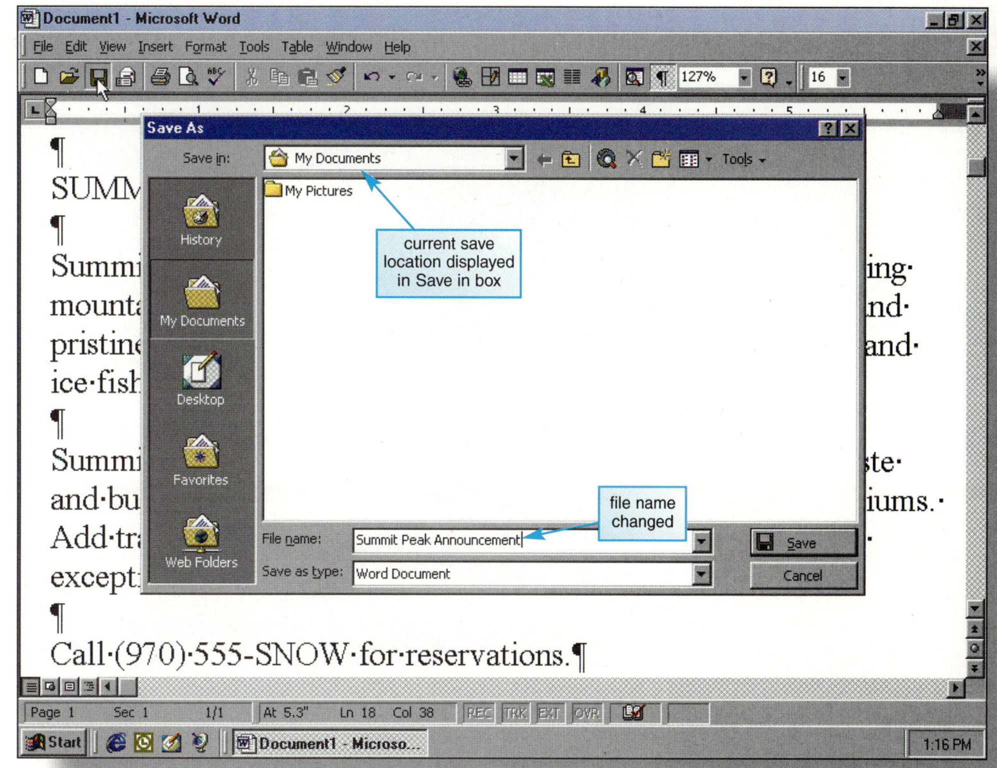

FIGURE 1-29

3 **Click the Save in box arrow and then point to 3½ Floppy (A:).**

A list of the available save locations displays (Figure 1-30). Your list may differ depending on your system configuration.

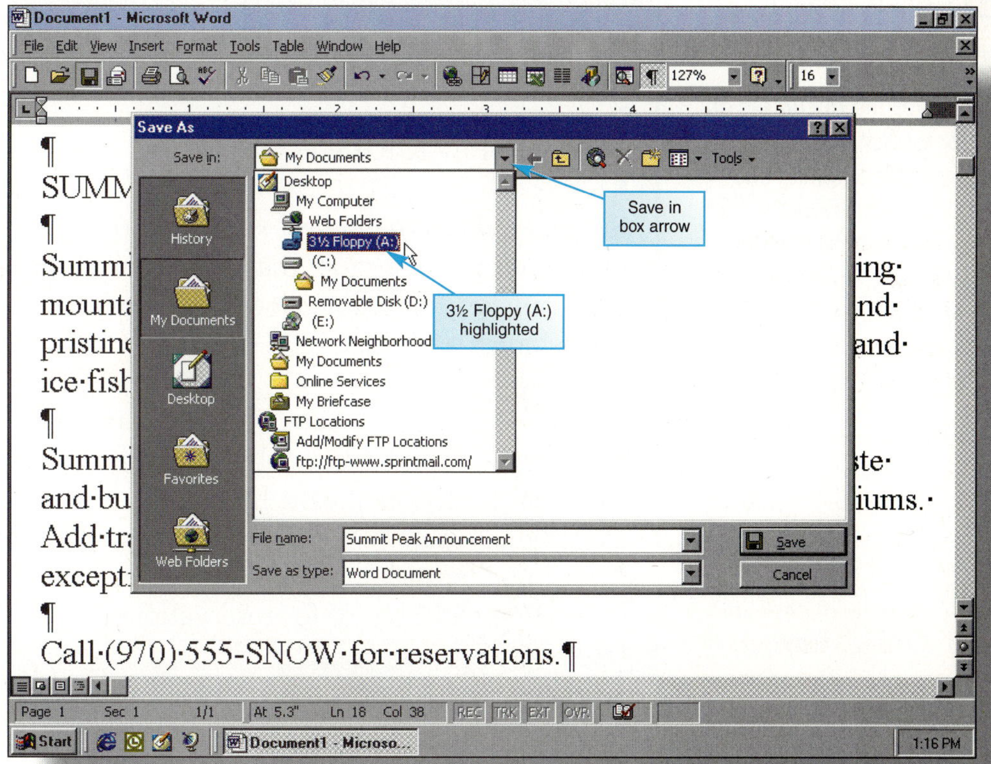

FIGURE 1-30

4 **Click 3½ Floppy (A:) and then point to the Save button in the Save As dialog box.**

The 3½ Floppy (A:) drive becomes the save location (Figure 1-31). The names of existing files stored on the floppy disk in drive A display. In Figure 1-31, no Word files currently are stored on the floppy disk in drive A.

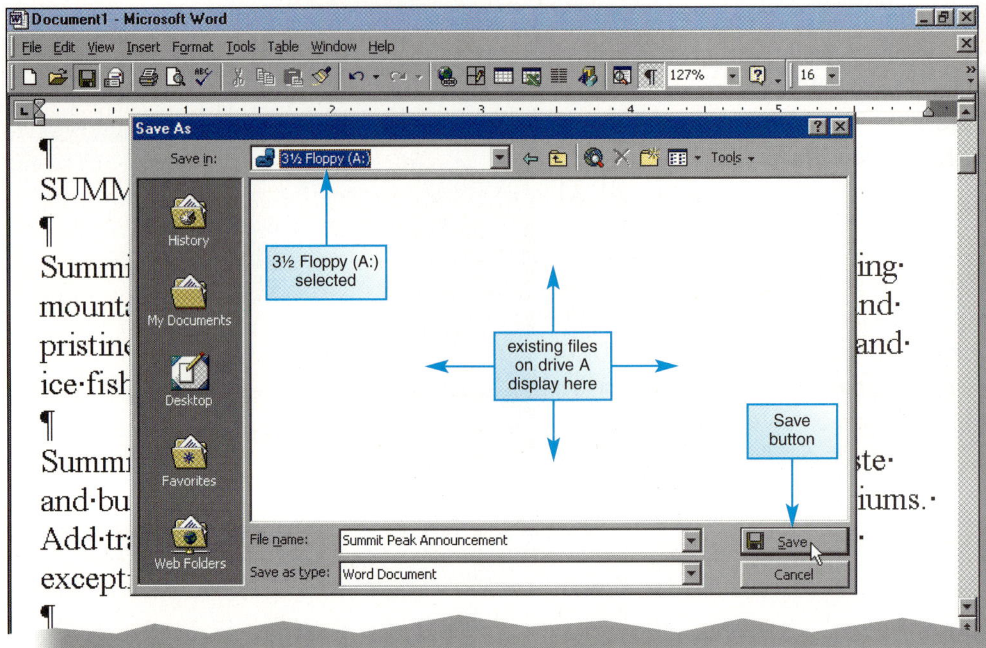

FIGURE 1-31

5 **Click the Save button in the Save As dialog box.**

Word saves the document on the floppy disk in drive A with the file name Summit Peak Announcement (Figure 1-32). Although the announcement is saved on a floppy disk, it also remains in main memory and displays on the screen.

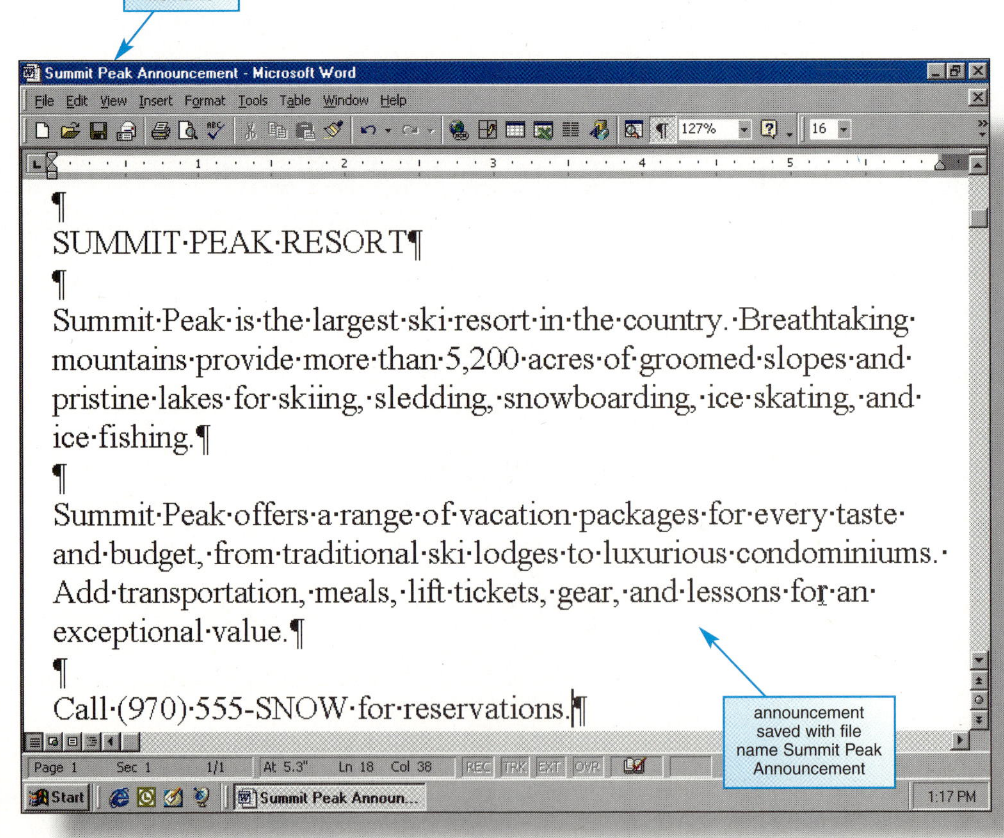

FIGURE 1-32

Other Ways

1. On File menu click Save, type file name, select location in Save in box, click Save button in dialog box
2. Press CTRL+S, type file name, select location in Save in box, click Save button in dialog box

Formatting Paragraphs and Characters in a Document

The text for Project 1 now is complete. The next step is to format the characters and paragraphs in the announcement. Paragraphs encompass the text up to and including a paragraph mark (¶). **Paragraph formatting** is the process of changing the appearance of a paragraph. For example, you can center or indent a paragraph.

Characters include letters, numbers, punctuation marks, and symbols. **Character formatting** is the process of changing the way characters appear on the screen and in print. You use character formatting to emphasize certain words and improve readability of a document.

With Word, you can format before you type or apply new formats after you type. Earlier, you changed the font size before you typed any text, and then you entered the text. In this section, you format existing text.

Figure 1-33a shows the announcement before formatting the paragraphs and characters. Figure 1-33b shows the announcement after formatting. As you can see from the two figures, a document that is formatted not only is easier to read, but it looks more professional.

More About 2000

Formatting

Character formatting includes changing the font, font style, font size; adding an underline, color, strikethrough, shadow, outline; embossing; engraving; making a superscript or subscript; and changing the case of the letters. Paragraph formatting includes alignment; indentation; and spacing above, below, and in between lines.

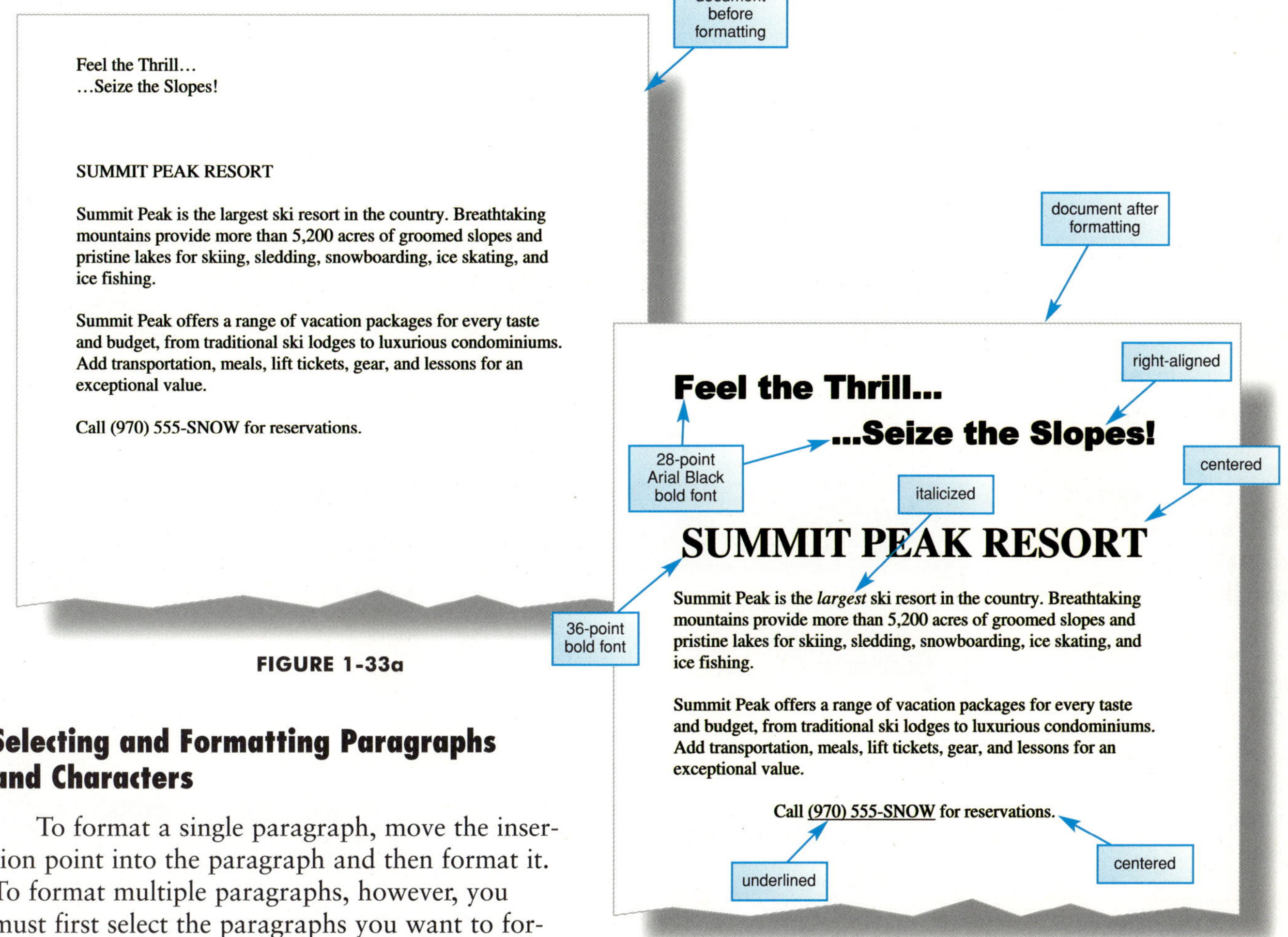
document before formatting
Feel the Thrill…
…Seize the Slopes!
SUMMIT PEAK RESORT
Summit Peak is the largest ski resort in the country. Breathtaking mountains provide more than 5,200 acres of groomed slopes and pristine lakes for skiing, sledding, snowboarding, ice skating, and ice fishing.
Summit Peak offers a range of vacation packages for every taste and budget, from traditional ski lodges to luxurious condominiums. Add transportation, meals, lift tickets, gear, and lessons for an exceptional value.
Call (970) 555-SNOW for reservations.
document after formatting
right-aligned
Feel the Thrill…
…Seize the Slopes!
28-point Arial Black bold font
centered
italicized
SUMMIT PEAK RESORT
36-point bold font
Summit Peak is the largest ski resort in the country. Breathtaking mountains provide more than 5,200 acres of groomed slopes and pristine lakes for skiing, sledding, snowboarding, ice skating, and ice fishing.
Summit Peak offers a range of vacation packages for every taste and budget, from traditional ski lodges to luxurious condominiums. Add transportation, meals, lift tickets, gear, and lessons for an exceptional value.
Call (970) 555-SNOW for reservations.
underlined
centered

FIGURE 1-33a

FIGURE 1-33b

Selecting and Formatting Paragraphs and Characters

To format a single paragraph, move the insertion point into the paragraph and then format it. To format multiple paragraphs, however, you must first select the paragraphs you want to format and then format them. In the same manner, to format characters, a word, or words, you first must select the characters, word, or words to be formatted and then format your selection.

Selected text is highlighted. That is, if your screen normally displays dark letters on a light background, then selected text displays light letters on a dark background.

Selecting Multiple Paragraphs

The first formatting step in this project is to change the font of the characters in the headline. The headline consists of two separate lines, each ending with a paragraph mark. You have learned that each time you press the ENTER key, Word creates a new paragraph. Thus, the headline actually is two separate paragraphs.

To change the font of the characters in the headline, you must first **select**, or highlight, both paragraphs in the headline as shown in the following steps.

To Select Multiple Paragraphs

1 Press CTRL+HOME; that is, press and hold the CTRL key, then press the HOME key, and then release both keys. Move the mouse pointer to the left of the first paragraph to be selected until the mouse pointer changes to a right-pointing block arrow.

The mouse pointer changes to a right-pointing block arrow when positioned to the left of a paragraph (Figure 1-34). CTRL + HOME positions the insertion point at the top of the document.

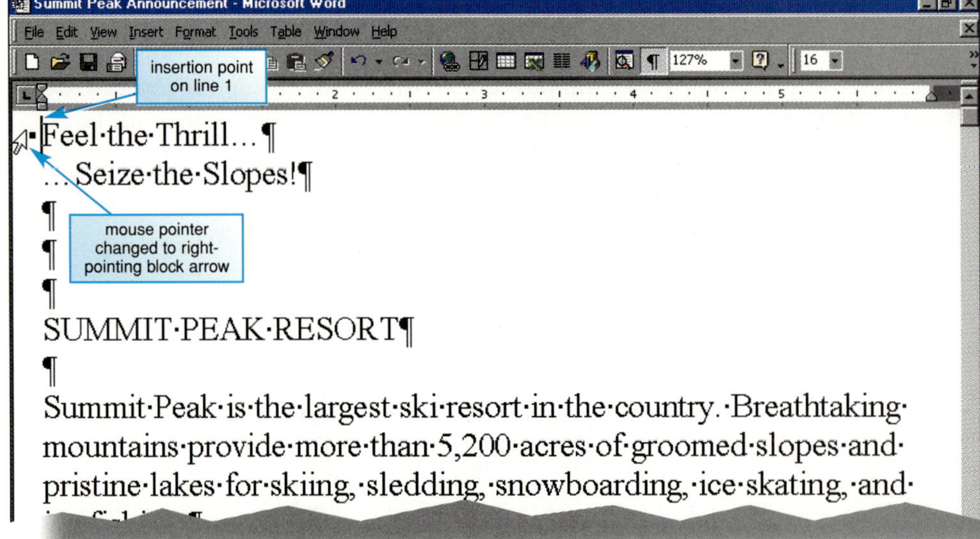
Summit Peak Announcement - Microsoft Word
insertion point on line 1
Feel·the·Thrill...¶
...Seize·the·Slopes!¶
mouse pointer changed to right-pointing block arrow
SUMMIT·PEAK·RESORT¶
Summit·Peak·is·the·largest·ski·resort·in·the·country.·Breathtaking·
mountains·provide·more·than·5,200·acres·of·groomed·slopes·and·
pristine·lakes·for·skiing,·sledding,·snowboarding,·ice·skating,·and·

FIGURE 1-34

2 Drag downward until both paragraphs are highlighted.

Word selects both of the paragraphs (Figure 1-35). Recall that dragging is the process of holding down the mouse button while moving the mouse and finally releasing the mouse button.

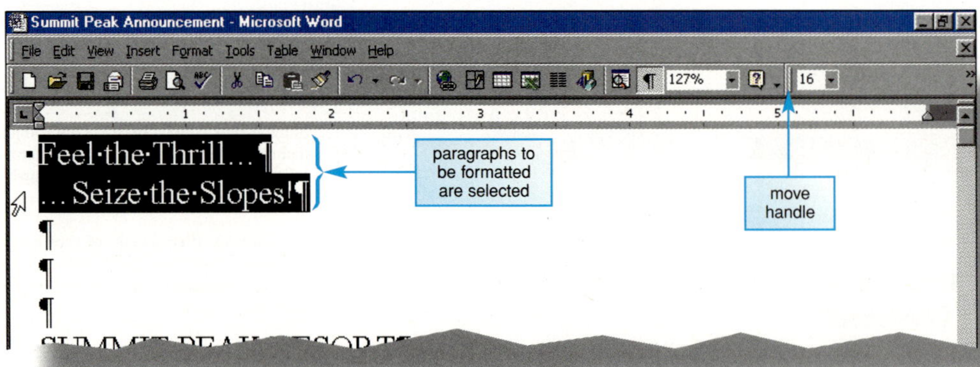
Summit Peak Announcement - Microsoft Word
Feel·the·Thrill...¶
...Seize·the·Slopes!¶
paragraphs to be formatted are selected
move handle

FIGURE 1-35

Other Ways

1. With insertion point at beginning of first paragraph, press CTRL+SHIFT+DOWN ARROW repeatedly

Changing the Font of Selected Text

You have learned that the default font is Times New Roman. Word, however, provides many other fonts to add variety to your documents. Thus, change the font of the headline in the announcement to Arial Black as shown in these steps.

To Change the Font of Selected Text

1 Double-click the move handle on the Formatting toolbar to display the entire toolbar. While the text is selected, click the Font box arrow on the Formatting toolbar, scroll through the list until Arial Black displays, and then point to Arial Black.

Word displays a list of available fonts (Figure 1-36). Your list of available fonts may differ, depending on the type of printer you are using.

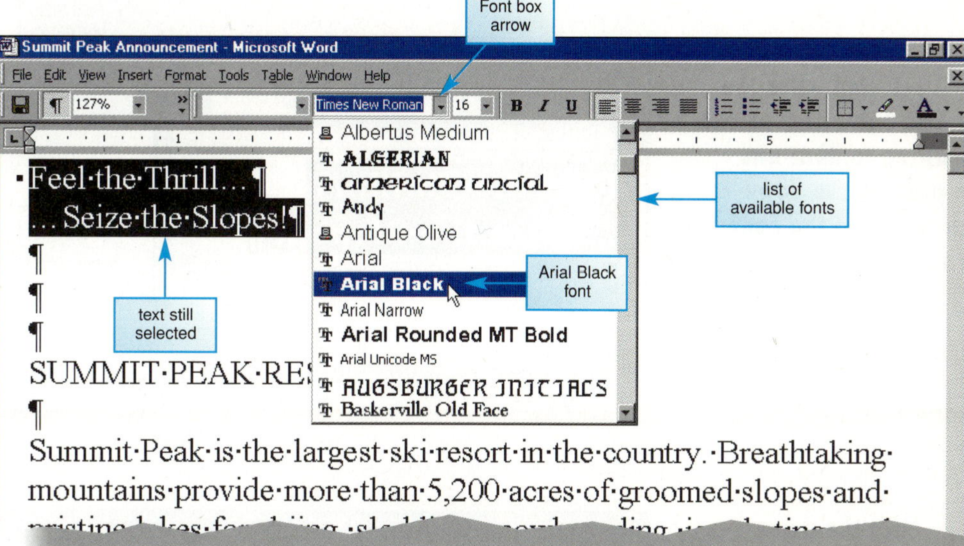

FIGURE 1-36

2 Click Arial Black.

Word changes the font of the selected text to Arial Black (Figure 1-37).

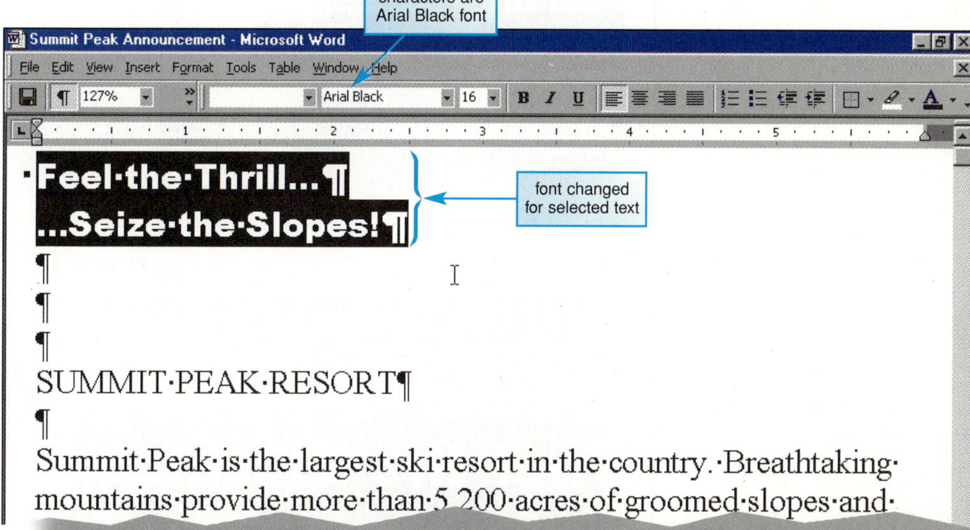

FIGURE 1-37

Changing the Font Size of Selected Text

The next step is to increase the font size of the characters in the selected headline. Recall that the font size specifies the size of the characters. Earlier in this project, you changed the font size for characters in the entire announcement to 16. To give the headline more impact, it has a font size larger than the body copy. Follow the steps on the next page to increase the font size of the headline from 16 to 28 points.

Other Ways

1. Right-click selected text, click Font on shortcut menu, click Font tab, select desired font in Font list, click OK button
2. On Format menu click Font, click Font tab, select desired font in Font list, click OK button
3. Press CTRL+SHIFT+F, press DOWN ARROW key until desired font displays, press ENTER

To Change the Font Size of Selected Text

1 While the text is selected, click the Font Size box arrow on the Formatting toolbar and then point to the down scroll arrow on the Font Size scroll bar.

Word displays a list of the available font sizes (Figure 1-38). Available font sizes vary depending on the font and printer driver.

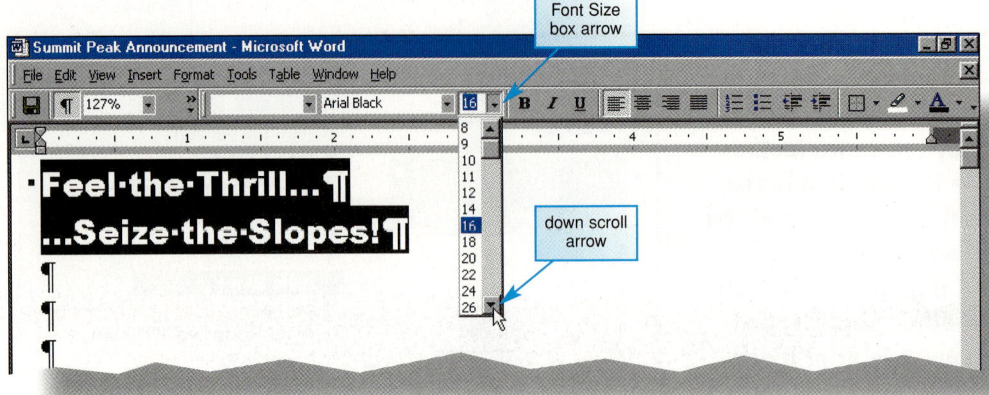

FIGURE 1-38

2 Click the down scroll arrow on the scroll bar until 28 displays in the list and then point to 28.

Word highlights 28 in the list (Figure 1-39).

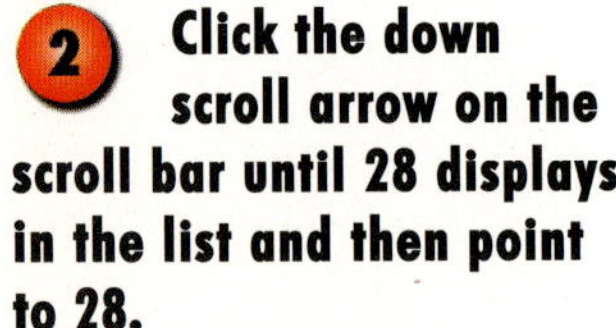

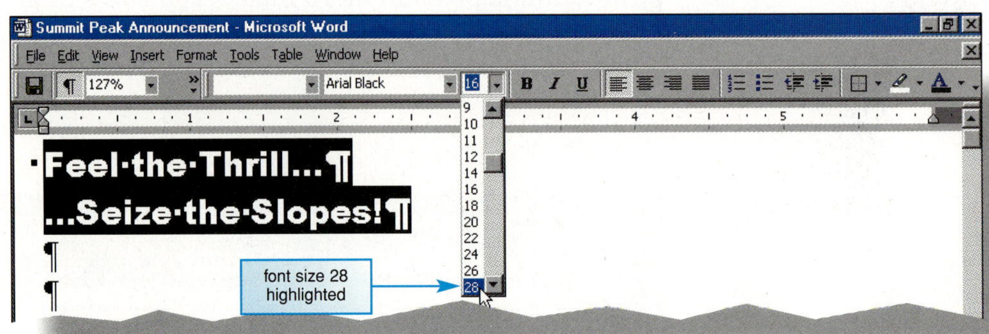

FIGURE 1-39

3 Click 28.

Word increases the font size of the headline from 16 to 28 (Figure 1-40). The Font Size box on the Formatting toolbar displays 28, indicating the selected text has a font size of 28.

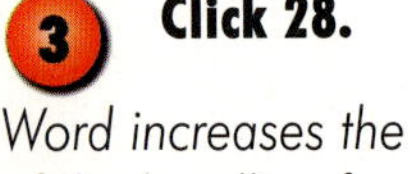

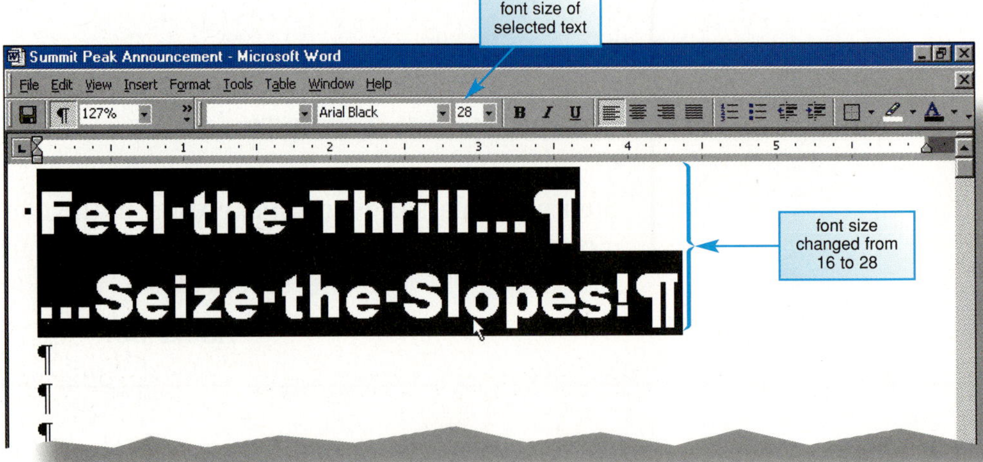

FIGURE 1-40

Other Ways

1. Right-click selected text, click Font on shortcut menu, click Font tab, select desired point size in Size list, click OK button
2. On Format menu click Font, click Font tab, select desired point size in Size list, click OK button
3. Press CTRL+SHIFT+P, type desired point size, press ENTER

Bold Selected Text

Bold characters display somewhat thicker than those that are not bold. To further emphasize the headline of the announcement, perform the following step to bold its characters.

To Bold Selected Text

1 While the text is selected, click the Bold button on the Formatting toolbar.

Word formats the headline in bold (Figure 1-41). The Bold button is recessed.

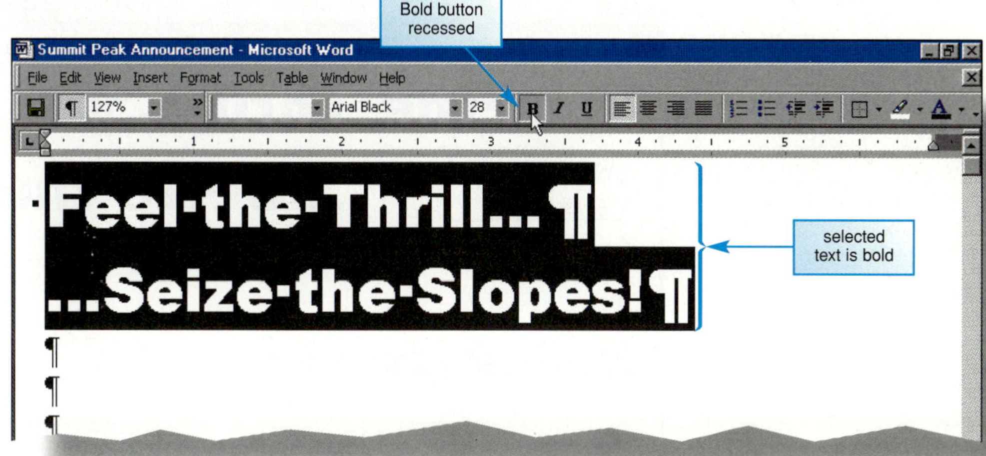

FIGURE 1-41

Other Ways

1. Right-click selected text, click Font on shortcut menu, click Font tab, click Bold in Font style list, click OK button
2. On Format menu click Font, click Font tab, click Bold in Font style list, click OK button
3. Press CTRL+B

When the selected text is bold, the Bold button on the Formatting toolbar is recessed. If, for some reason, you wanted to remove the bold format of the selected text, you would click the Bold button a second time.

Right-Align a Paragraph

The default alignment for paragraphs is **left-aligned**; that is, flush at the left edge of the document with uneven right edges. In Figure 1-42, the Align Left button is recessed to indicate the current paragraph is left-aligned.

The second line of the headline, however, is to be **right-aligned**; that is, flush at the right edge of the document with uneven left edges. Recall that the second line of the headline is a paragraph and that paragraph formatting does not require you to select the paragraph prior to formatting. Just position the insertion point in the paragraph to be formatted and then format it accordingly.

Perform the following steps to right-align the second line of the headline.

To Right-Align a Paragraph

1 Click somewhere in the paragraph to be right-aligned. Point to the Align Right button on the Formatting toolbar.

Word positions the insertion point at the location you clicked (Figure 1-42).

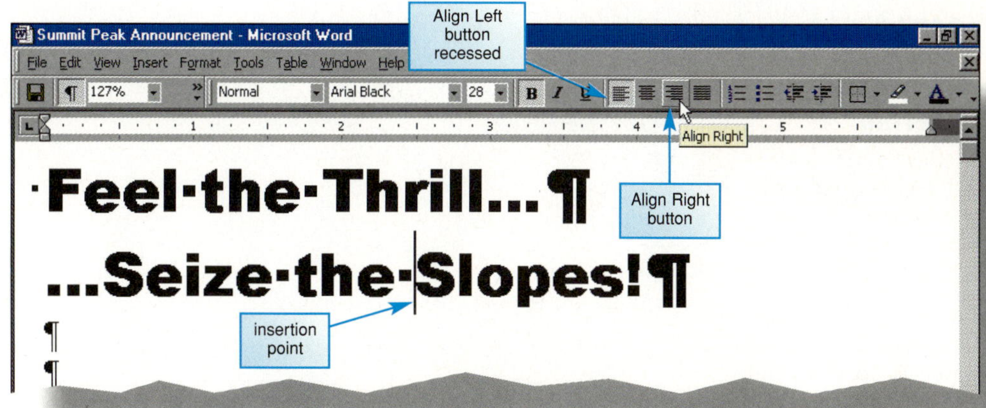

FIGURE 1-42

Click the Align Right button.

The second line of the headline is right-aligned (Figure 1-43). Notice that you did not have to select the paragraph before right-aligning it; paragraph formatting only requires the insertion point be positioned somewhere in the paragraph.

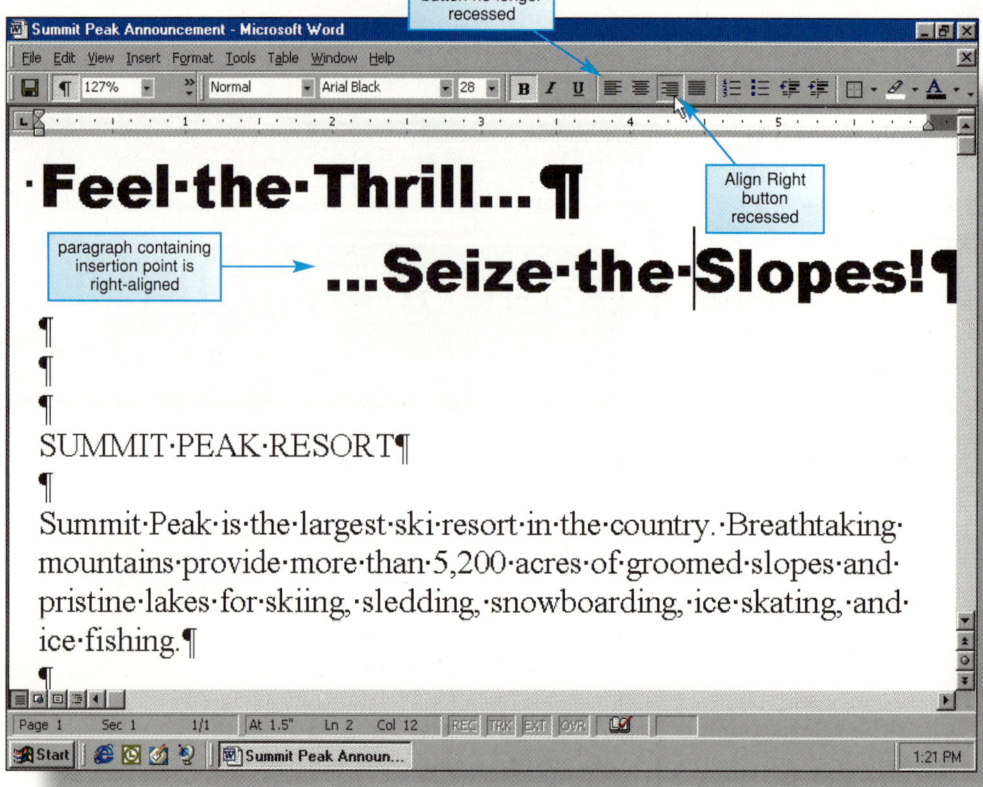
Align Left button no longer recessed
Align Right button recessed
paragraph containing insertion point is right-aligned
Summit Peak Announcement - Microsoft Word
Feel·the·Thrill...¶
...Seize·the·Slopes!¶
SUMMIT·PEAK·RESORT¶
Summit·Peak·is·the·largest·ski·resort·in·the·country.·Breathtaking·mountains·provide·more·than·5,200·acres·of·groomed·slopes·and·pristine·lakes·for·skiing,·sledding,·snowboarding,·ice·skating,·and·ice·fishing.¶

FIGURE 1-43

1. Right-click paragraph, click Paragraph on shortcut menu, click Indents and Spacing tab, click Alignment box arrow, click Right, click OK button
2. With insertion point in desired paragraph, on Format menu click Paragraph, click Indents and Spacing tab, click Alignment box arrow, click Right, click OK button
3. Press CTRL+R

When a paragraph is right-aligned, the Align Right button on the Formatting toolbar is recessed. If, for some reason, you wanted to return the selected paragraphs to left-aligned, you would click the Align Left button on the Formatting toolbar.

Center a Paragraph

The body title currently is left-aligned. Perform the following step to **center** it, that is, position the body title horizontally between the left and right margins on the page.

More About Centering

The Center button on the Formatting toolbar centers text horizontally. You also can center text vertically between the top and bottom margins. To do this, click File on the menu bar, click Page Setup, click the Layout tab, click the Vertical alignment box arrow, click Center in the list, and then click the OK button.

To Center a Paragraph

1 Click somewhere in the paragraph to be centered. Click the Center button on the Formatting toolbar.

Word centers the body title between the left and right margins (Figure 1-44). The Center button on the Formatting toolbar is recessed, which indicates the paragraph containing the insertion point is centered.

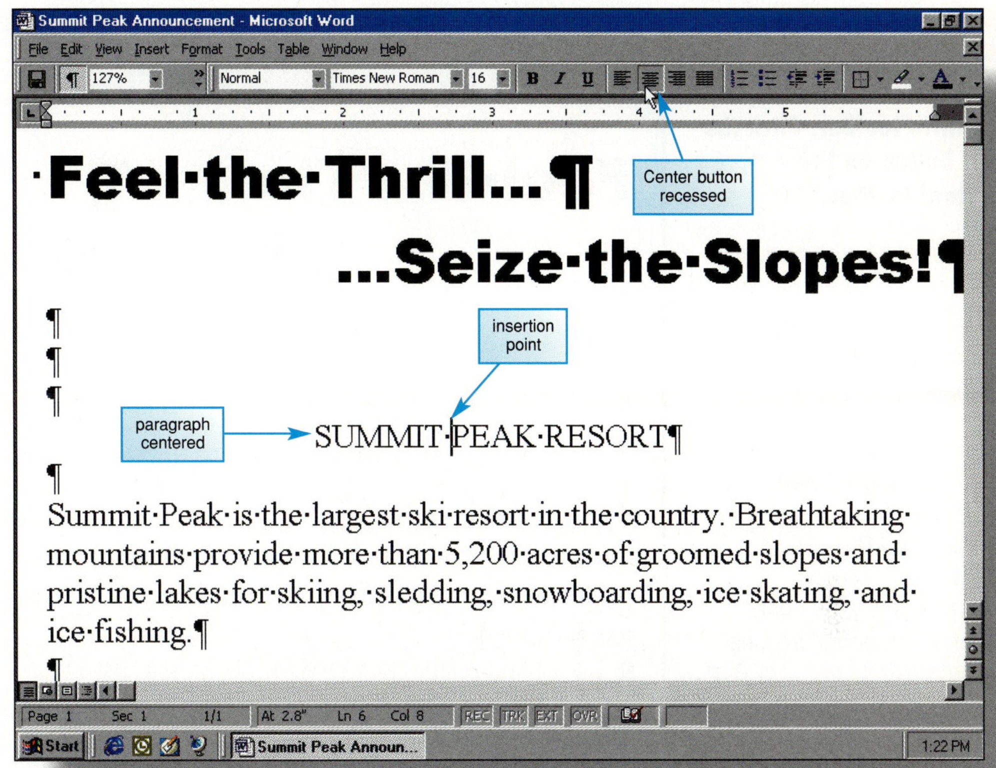
Summit Peak Announcement - Microsoft Word
Center button recessed
Feel·the·Thrill...¶
...Seize·the·Slopes!¶
insertion point
paragraph centered
SUMMIT·PEAK·RESORT¶
Summit·Peak·is·the·largest·ski·resort·in·the·country.·Breathtaking·mountains·provide·more·than·5,200·acres·of·groomed·slopes·and·pristine·lakes·for·skiing,·sledding,·snowboarding,·ice·skating,·and·ice·fishing.¶

FIGURE 1-44

Other Ways

1. Right-click paragraph, click Paragraph on shortcut menu, click Indents and Spacing tab, click Alignment box arrow, click Centered, click OK button
2. On Format menu click Paragraph, click Indents and Spacing tab, click Alignment box arrow, click Centered, click OK button
3. Press CTRL+E

When a paragraph is centered, the Center button on the Formatting toolbar is recessed. If, for some reason, you wanted to return the selected paragraphs to left-aligned, you would click the Align Left button on the Formatting toolbar.

Undoing Commands or Actions

Word provides an **Undo button** on the Standard toolbar that you can use to cancel your recent command(s) or action(s). For example, if you format text incorrectly, you can *undo* the format and try it again. If, after you undo an action, you decide you did not want to perform the undo, you can use the **Redo button** to undo the undo. Some actions, such as saving or printing a document, cannot be undone or redone.

Perform the steps on the next page to *uncenter* the body title and then re-center it.

To Undo an Action

1. **Double-click the move handle on the Standard toolbar to display the entire toolbar. Click the Undo button on the Standard toolbar.**

   Word left-aligns the body title (Figure 1-45). Word returns the body title to its formatting prior to you issuing the command to center it.

2. **Click the Redo button on the Standard toolbar.**

   Word re-applies the center format to the body title (see Figure 1-46).

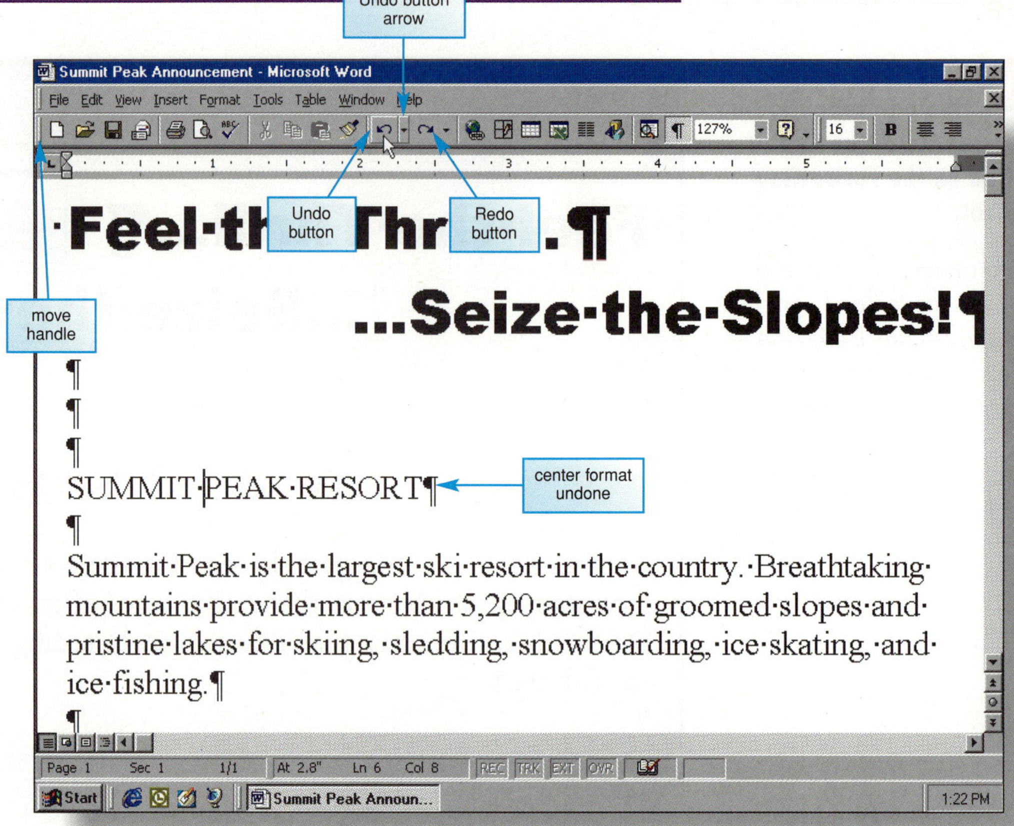
Undo button arrow
Undo button
Redo button
move handle
center format undone
Summit Peak Announcement - Microsoft Word
Feel-the-Thrill.¶
...Seize-the-Slopes!¶
SUMMIT·PEAK·RESORT¶
Summit·Peak·is·the·largest·ski·resort·in·the·country.·Breathtaking·mountains·provide·more·than·5,200·acres·of·groomed·slopes·and·pristine·lakes·for·skiing,·sledding,·snowboarding,·ice·skating,·and·ice·fishing.¶

FIGURE 1-45

Other Ways

1. On Edit menu click Undo
2. Press CTRL+Z

You also can cancel a series of prior actions by clicking the Undo button arrow (Figure 1-45) to display the undo actions list and then dragging through the actions you wish to be undone.

Whereas undo cancels an action you did not want to perform, Word also provides a **Repeat command**, which duplicates an action you wish to perform again. For example, if you format a paragraph and wish to format another paragraph the exact same way, you could click in the second paragraph to format and then click Repeat on the Edit menu.

Selecting a Line and Formatting It

The next series of steps selects the body title, SUMMIT PEAK RESORT, and formats the characters in it. First, you select the body title. To select the body title, perform the following step.

To Select a Line

1 Move the mouse pointer to the left of the line to be selected (SUMMIT PEAK RESORT) until it changes to a right-pointing block arrow and then click.

The entire line to the right of the mouse pointer is highlighted (Figure 1-46).

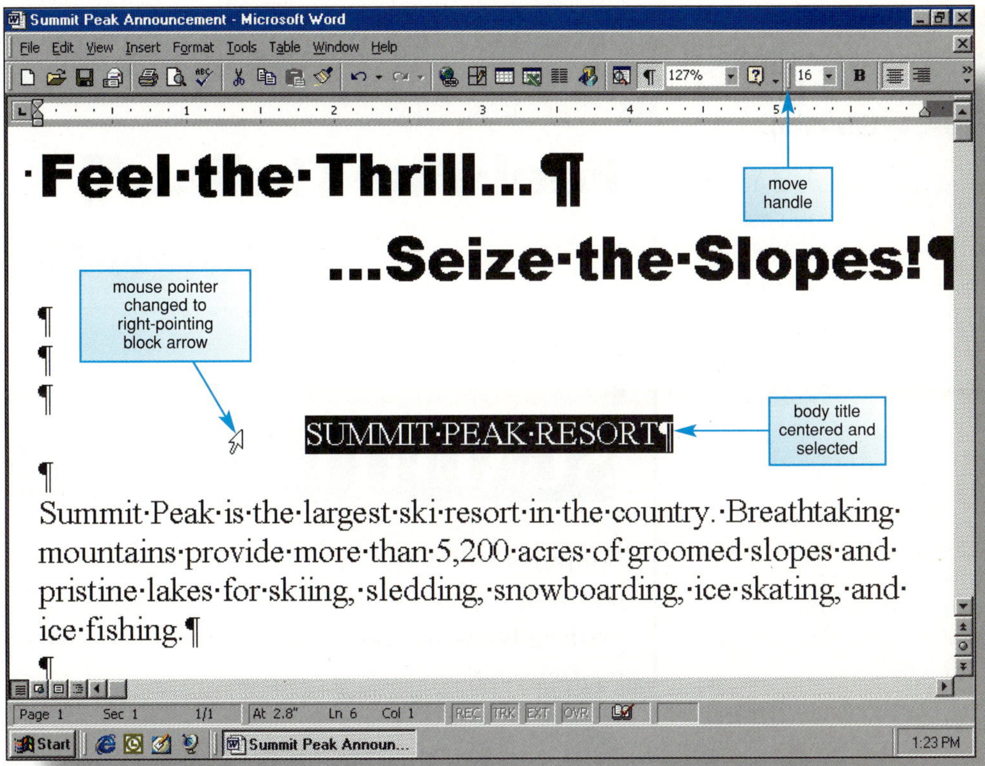
Summit Peak Announcement - Microsoft Word
File Edit View Insert Format Tools Table Window Help
·Feel·the·Thrill...¶
...Seize·the·Slopes!¶
move handle
mouse pointer changed to right-pointing block arrow
SUMMIT·PEAK·RESORT¶
body title centered and selected
Summit·Peak·is·the·largest·ski·resort·in·the·country.·Breathtaking·mountains·provide·more·than·5,200·acres·of·groomed·slopes·and·pristine·lakes·for·skiing,·sledding,·snowboarding,·ice·skating,·and·ice·fishing.¶
Page 1 Sec 1 1/1 At 2.8" Ln 6 Col 1
Start
Summit Peak Announ...
1:23 PM

FIGURE 1-46

Other Ways

1. Drag through the line
2. With insertion point at beginning of desired line, press SHIFT+DOWN ARROW

The next step is to increase the font size of the selected characters to 36 point and bold the selected characters, as explained in the following steps.

TO FORMAT A LINE OF TEXT

1. Double-click the move handle on the Formatting toolbar to display the entire toolbar. While the text is selected, click the Font Size box arrow on the Formatting toolbar and then scroll to 36 in the list. Click 36.
2. Click the Bold button on the Formatting toolbar.

The characters in the body title are enlarged and bold (Figure 1-47 on the next page).

More About 2000

The Formatting Toolbar

Many of the buttons on the Formatting toolbar are toggles; that is, click them once to format the selected text; and click them again to remove the format from the selected text. For example, clicking the Bold button bolds selected text; clicking the Bold button again removes the bold.

Selecting a Word

To format characters in a word, you must select the entire word first. Follow the steps on the next page to select the word, largest, so you can italicize it.

To Select a Word

1 Position the mouse pointer somewhere in the word to be formatted (largest, in this case).

The mouse pointer's shape is an I-beam when you position it in unselected text in the document window (Figure 1-47).

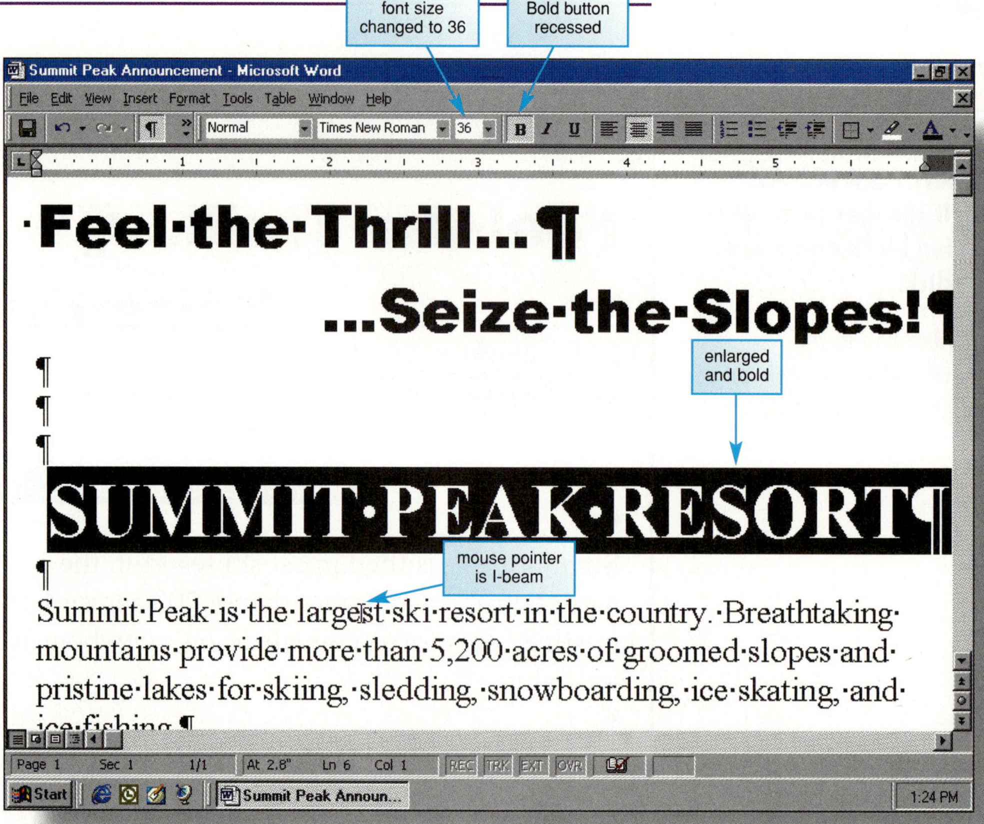
font size changed to 36
Bold button recessed
Summit Peak Announcement - Microsoft Word
File Edit View Insert Format Tools Table Window Help
Normal
Times New Roman
36
·Feel·the·Thrill...¶
...Seize·the·Slopes!¶
enlarged and bold
SUMMIT·PEAK·RESORT¶
mouse pointer is I-beam
Summit·Peak·is·the·largest·ski·resort·in·the·country.·Breathtaking·
mountains·provide·more·than·5,200·acres·of·groomed·slopes·and·
pristine·lakes·for·skiing,·sledding,·snowboarding,·ice·skating,·and·
Page 1 Sec 1 1/1 At 2.8" Ln 6 Col 1 REC TRK EXT OVR
Start
Summit Peak Announ...
1:24 PM

FIGURE 1-47

2 Double-click the word to be selected.

The word, largest, is highlighted (Figure 1-48). Notice that when the mouse pointer is positioned in a selected word, its shape is a left-pointing block arrow.

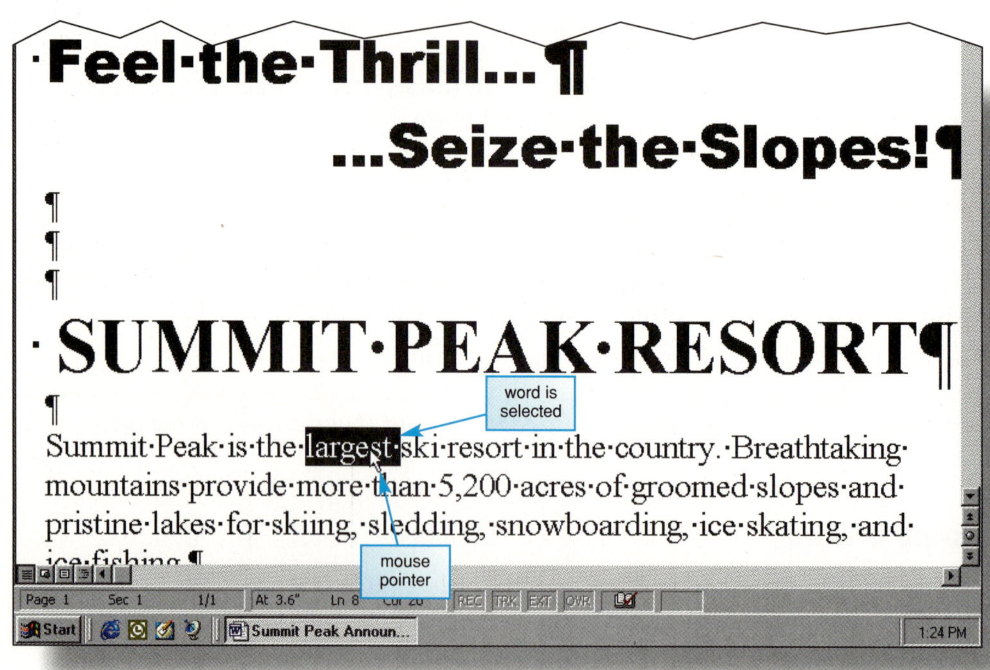
·Feel·the·Thrill...¶
...Seize·the·Slopes!¶
SUMMIT·PEAK·RESORT¶
word is selected
Summit·Peak·is·the·largest·ski·resort·in·the·country.·Breathtaking·
mountains·provide·more·than·5,200·acres·of·groomed·slopes·and·
pristine·lakes·for·skiing,·sledding,·snowboarding,·ice·skating,·and·
mouse pointer
Page 1 Sec 1 1/1 At 3.6" Ln 8 REC TRK EXT OVR
Start
Summit Peak Announ...
1:24 PM

FIGURE 1-48

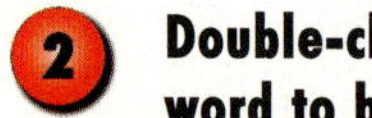

Other Ways

1. Drag through the word
2. With insertion point at beginning of desired word, press CTRL+SHIFT+RIGHT ARROW

Italicize Selected Text

To italicize the word, largest, perform the following step.

To Italicize Selected Text

1 With the text still selected, click the Italic button on the Formatting toolbar.

Word italicizes the text (Figure 1-49). The Italic button on the Formatting toolbar is recessed.

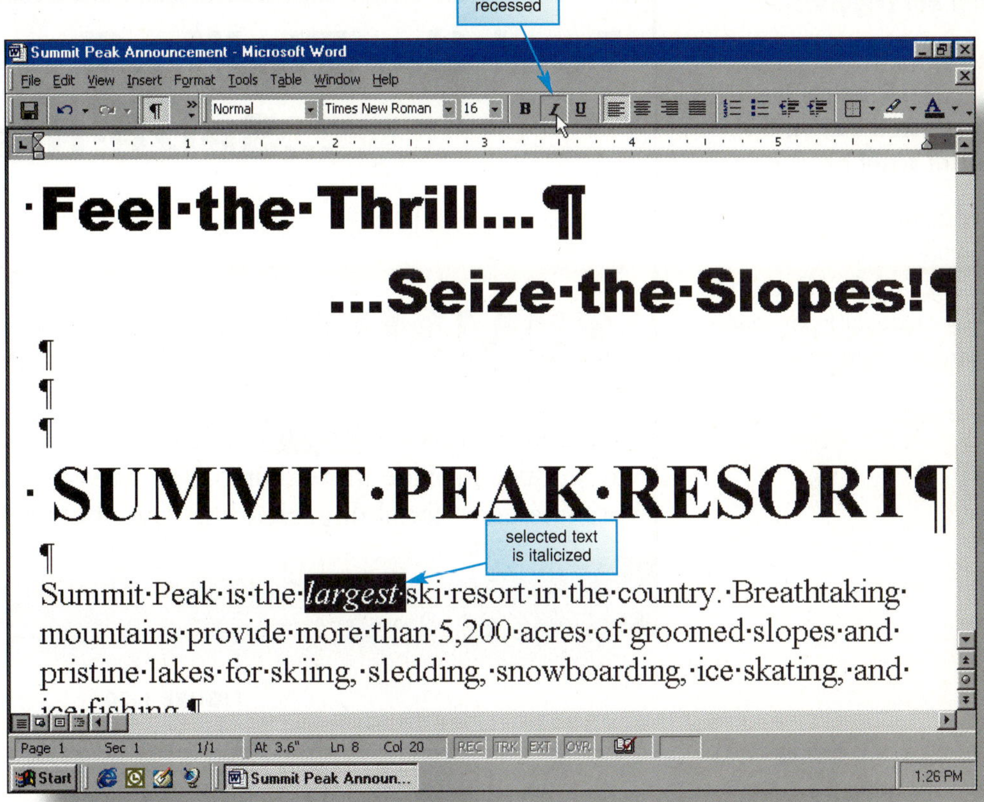
Italic button recessed
Summit Peak Announcement - Microsoft Word
File Edit View Insert Format Tools Table Window Help
Normal
Times New Roman
16
·Feel·the·Thrill...¶
...Seize·the·Slopes!¶
·SUMMIT·PEAK·RESORT¶
selected text is italicized
Summit·Peak·is·the·largest·ski·resort·in·the·country.·Breathtaking·mountains·provide·more·than·5,200·acres·of·groomed·slopes·and·pristine·lakes·for·skiing,·sledding,·snowboarding,·ice·skating,·and·
Page 1 Sec 1 1/1 At 3.6" Ln 8 Col 20
Start
Summit Peak Announ...
1:26 PM

FIGURE 1-49

Other Ways

1. Right-click selected text, click Font on shortcut menu, click Font tab, click Italic in Font style list, click OK button
2. On Format menu click Font, click Font tab, click Italic in Font style list, click OK button
3. Press CTRL+I

When the selected text is italicized, the Italic button on the Formatting toolbar is recessed. If, for some reason, you wanted to remove the italics from the selected text, you would click the Italic button a second time, or you immediately could click the Undo button on the Standard toolbar.

Scrolling

Continue formatting the document by scrolling down one screen so the bottom portion of the announcement displays in the document window. Perform the steps on the next page to display the lower portion of the document.

To Scroll Through the Document

1 **Position the mouse pointer below the scroll box on the vertical scroll bar (Figure 1-50).**

2 **Click below the scroll box on the vertical scroll bar.**

Word scrolls down one screenful in the document (see Figure 1-51). Depending on your monitor type, your screen may scroll differently.

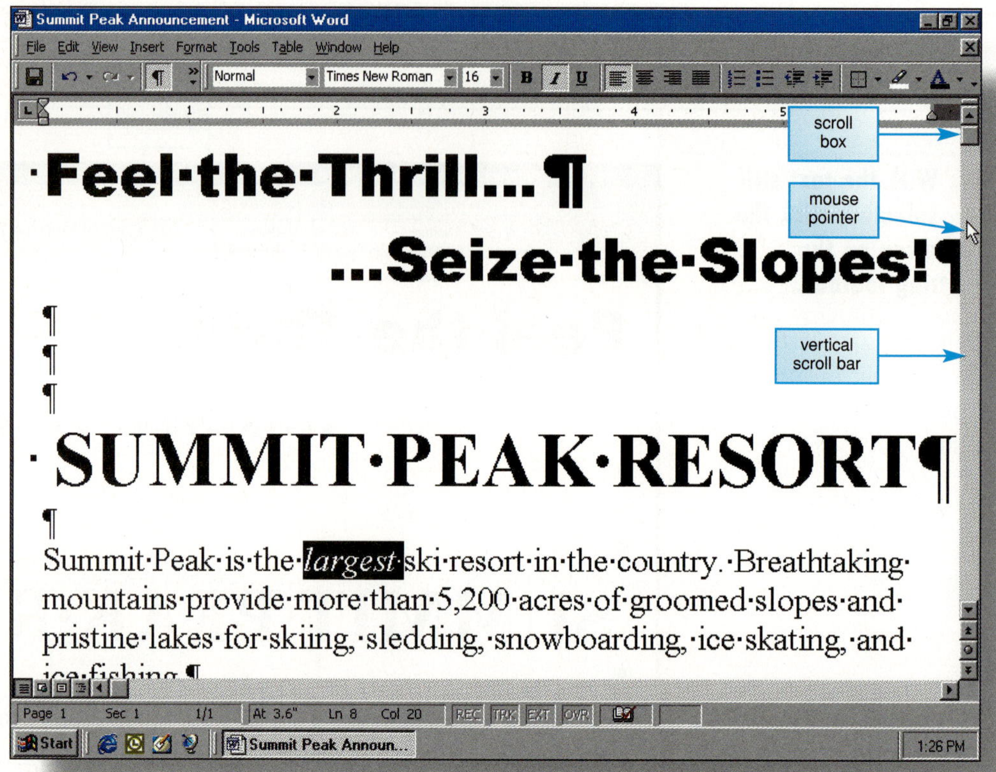

Summit Peak Announcement - Microsoft Word
scroll box
mouse pointer
vertical scroll bar
Feel the Thrill...
...Seize the Slopes!
SUMMIT PEAK RESORT
Summit Peak is the largest ski resort in the country. Breathtaking mountains provide more than 5,200 acres of groomed slopes and pristine lakes for skiing, sledding, snowboarding, ice skating, and

FIGURE 1-50

Other Ways

1. Drag scroll box on vertical scroll bar
2. Click scroll arrows on vertical scroll bar
3. Press PAGE DOWN or PAGE UP
4. See Tables 1-1 and 1-2 on pages WD 1.25 and WD 1.26

The next step is to center the last line of the announcement as described in the following steps.

TO CENTER A PARAGRAPH

1. Click somewhere in the paragraph to be centered.
2. Click the Center button on the Formatting toolbar.

Word centers the last line of the announcement (see Figure 1-51).

Selecting a Group of Words

The next step is to underline the telephone number in the last line of the announcement. Because the telephone number contains spaces and other punctuation, Word considers it a group of words. Thus, the telephone number is a group of words. Select the telephone number by performing the following steps.

To Select a Group of Words

1 Position the mouse pointer immediately to the left of the first character of the text to be selected.

The mouse pointer, an I-beam, is to the left of the parenthesis in the telephone number (Figure 1-51).

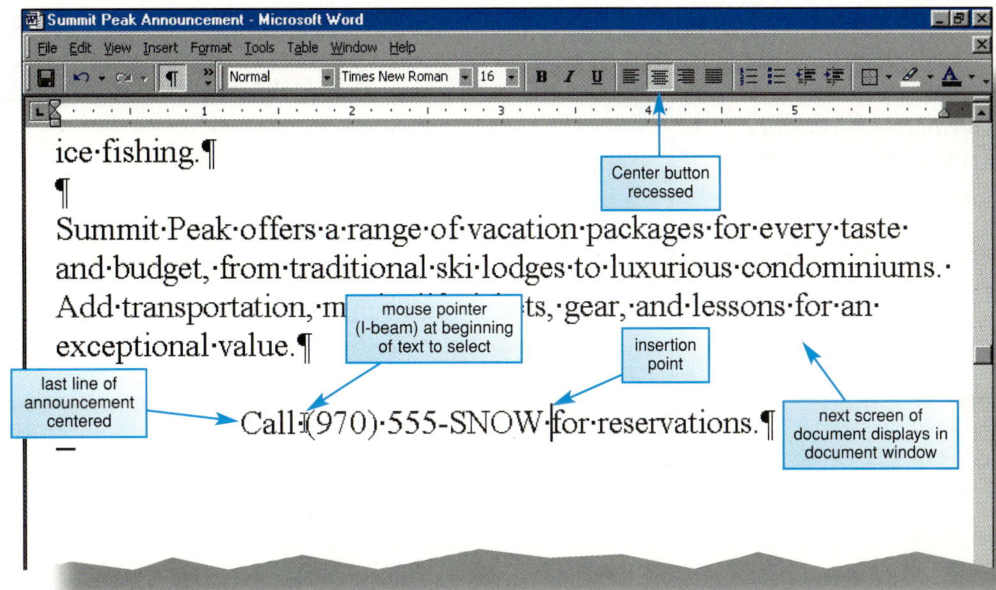
Summit Peak Announcement - Microsoft Word
Center button recessed
ice·fishing.¶
Summit·Peak·offers·a·range·of·vacation·packages·for·every·taste·and·budget,·from·traditional·ski·lodges·to·luxurious·condominiums.·Add·transportation,·m ts,·gear,·and·lessons·for·an·exceptional·value.¶
mouse pointer (I-beam) at beginning of text to select
insertion point
last line of announcement centered
Call·(970)·555-SNOW·for·reservations.¶
next screen of document displays in document window

FIGURE 1-51

2 Drag the mouse pointer through the last character of the text to be selected.

Word highlights the telephone number (Figure 1-52).

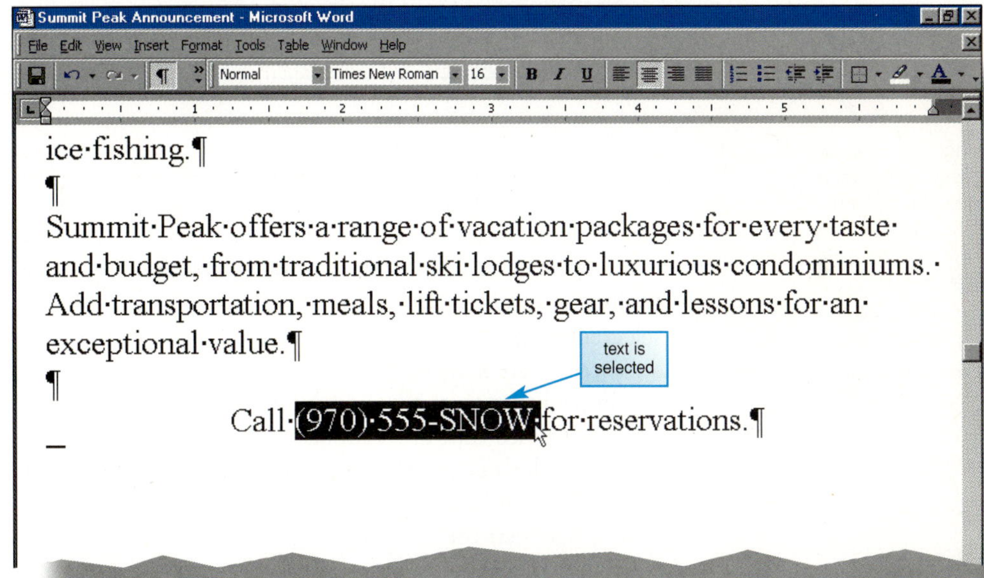
Summit Peak Announcement - Microsoft Word
ice·fishing.¶
Summit·Peak·offers·a·range·of·vacation·packages·for·every·taste·and·budget,·from·traditional·ski·lodges·to·luxurious·condominiums.·Add·transportation,·meals,·lift·tickets,·gear,·and·lessons·for·an·exceptional·value.¶
text is selected
Call·(970)·555-SNOW·for·reservations.¶

FIGURE 1-52

1. With insertion point at beginning of first word in the group, press CTRL+SHIFT+RIGHT ARROW until words are selected

Underlining Selected Text

Underlined text prints with an underscore (_) below each character. Like bold, it used to emphasize or draw attention to specific text. Follow the step on the next page to underline the selected telephone number.

To Underline Selected Text

1 With the text still selected, click the Underline button on the Formatting toolbar. Click inside the selected text to remove the highlight.

Word underlines the text and positions the insertion point inside the underlined text (Figure 1-53). When the insertion point is inside the underlined text, the Underline button is recessed.

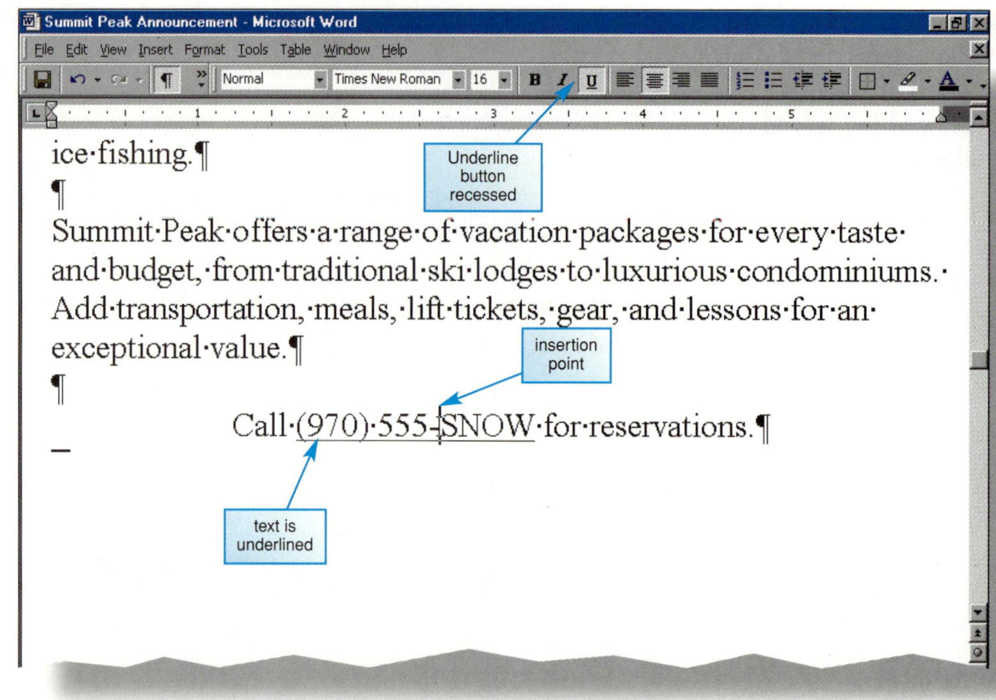
Summit Peak Announcement - Microsoft Word
Underline button recessed
insertion point
text is underlined
ice·fishing.¶
Summit·Peak·offers·a·range·of·vacation·packages·for·every·taste·and·budget,·from·traditional·ski·lodges·to·luxurious·condominiums.·Add·transportation,·meals,·lift·tickets,·gear,·and·lessons·for·an·exceptional·value.¶
Call·(970)·555-SNOW·for·reservations.¶

FIGURE 1-53

Other Ways

1. Right-click selected text, click Font on shortcut menu, click Font tab, click Underline style box arrow, click desired underline style, click OK button
2. On Format menu click Font, click Font tab, click Underline style box arrow, click desired underline style, click OK button
3. Press CTRL+U

More About 2000

The Font Dialog Box

If a character formatting operation is not available on the Formatting toolbar, use the Font dialog box to perform the operation. To display the Font dialog box, click Format on the menu bar and then click Font.

To remove a highlight, click the mouse. If you click inside the highlight, the Formatting toolbar displays the formatting characteristics of the characters and paragraphs containing the insertion point.

When the selected text is underlined, the Underline button on the Formatting toolbar is recessed. If, for some reason, you wanted to remove the underline from the selected text, you would click the Underline button a second time, or you immediately could click the Undo button on the Standard toolbar.

In addition to the basic underline shown in Figure 1-53, Word has many decorative underlines that are available in the Font dialog box. For example, you can use double underlines, dotted underlines, and wavy underlines. You also can change the color of an underline and instruct Word to underline only the words and not the spaces between the words.

The formatting for the announcement is now complete. The next step is to insert a graphical image into the document and then resize the image.

Inserting Clip Art into a Word Document

Files containing graphical images, also called **graphics**, are available from a variety of sources. Word 2000 includes a series of predefined graphics called **clip art** that you can insert into a Word document. Clip art is located in the **Clip Gallery**, which contains a collection of **clips**, including clip art, as well as photographs, sounds, and video clips. The Clip Gallery contains its own Help system to assist you in locating clips suited to your application.

Clip Galleries

For more information on the clip galleries available for purchase, visit the Word 2000 More About Web page (www.scsite.com/wd2000/more.htm) and then click Clip Galleries.

Inserting Clip Art

The next step in the project is to insert a graphic of a skier into the announcement. Perform the following steps to insert a graphic into the document.

To Insert Clip Art into a Document

1 **To position the insertion point where you want the clip art to be located, press CTRL+HOME and then press the DOWN ARROW key three times. Click Insert on the menu bar.**

The insertion point is positioned on the second paragraph mark below the headline, and the Insert menu displays (Figure 1-54). Remember that a short menu initially displays, which expands into a full menu after a few seconds.

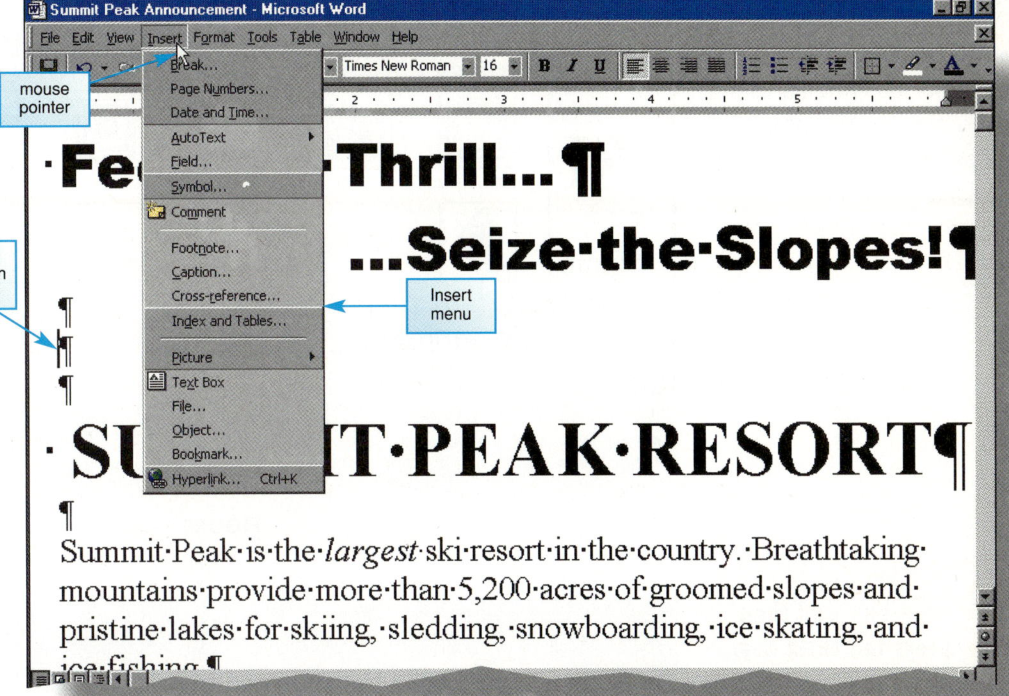

FIGURE 1-54

2 **Point to Picture and then point to Clip Art.**

The Picture submenu displays (Figure 1-55). You have learned that when you point to a command that has a small arrow to its right, Word displays a submenu associated with that command.

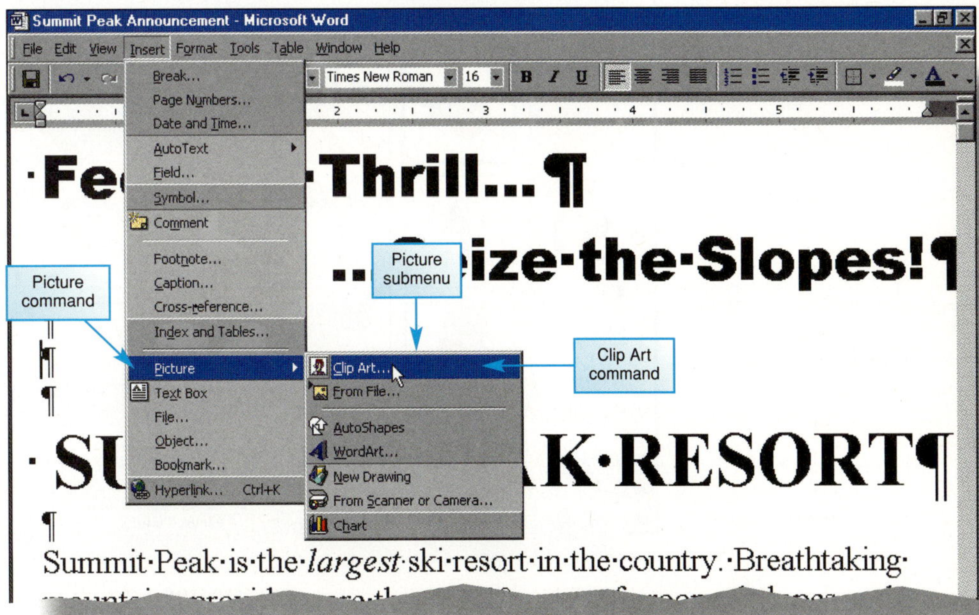

FIGURE 1-55

3 Click Clip Art. When the Insert ClipArt window opens, click the Search for clips text box.

Word opens the Insert ClipArt window (Figure 1-56). The text in the Search for clips text box is highlighted. When you enter a description of the desired graphic in this text box, Word searches the Clip Gallery for clips that match the description.

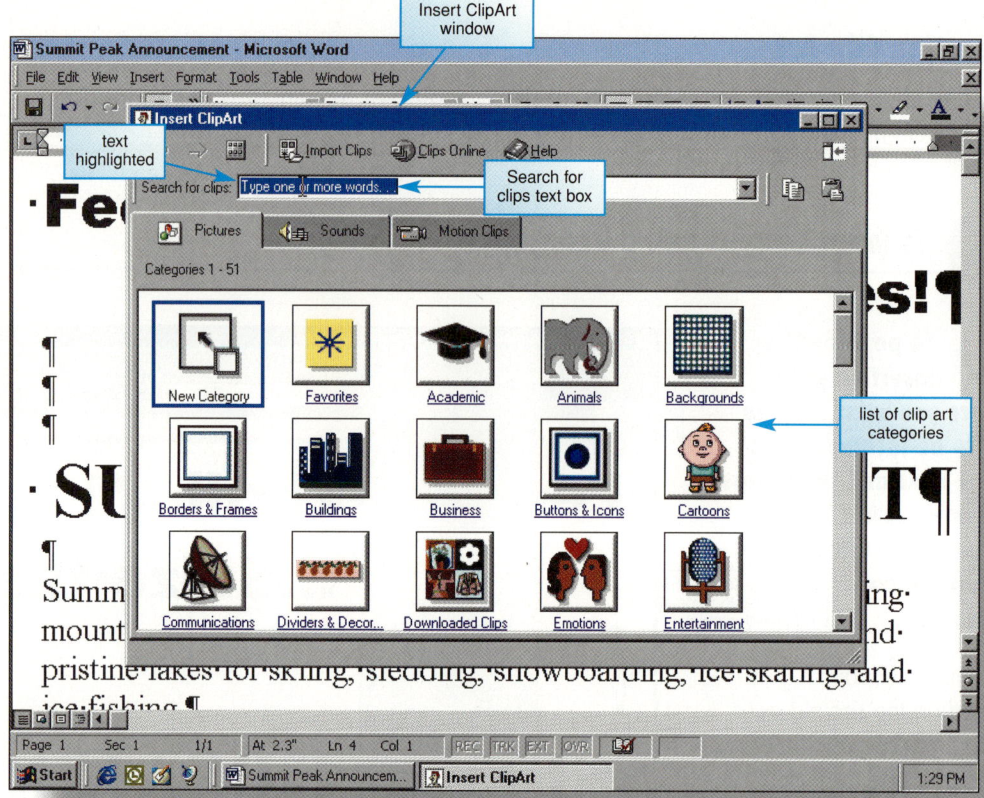

FIGURE 1-56

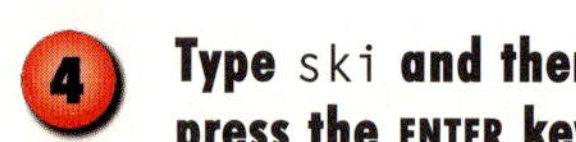

4 Type ski **and then press the ENTER key.**

A list of clips that match the description, ski, displays (Figure 1-57).

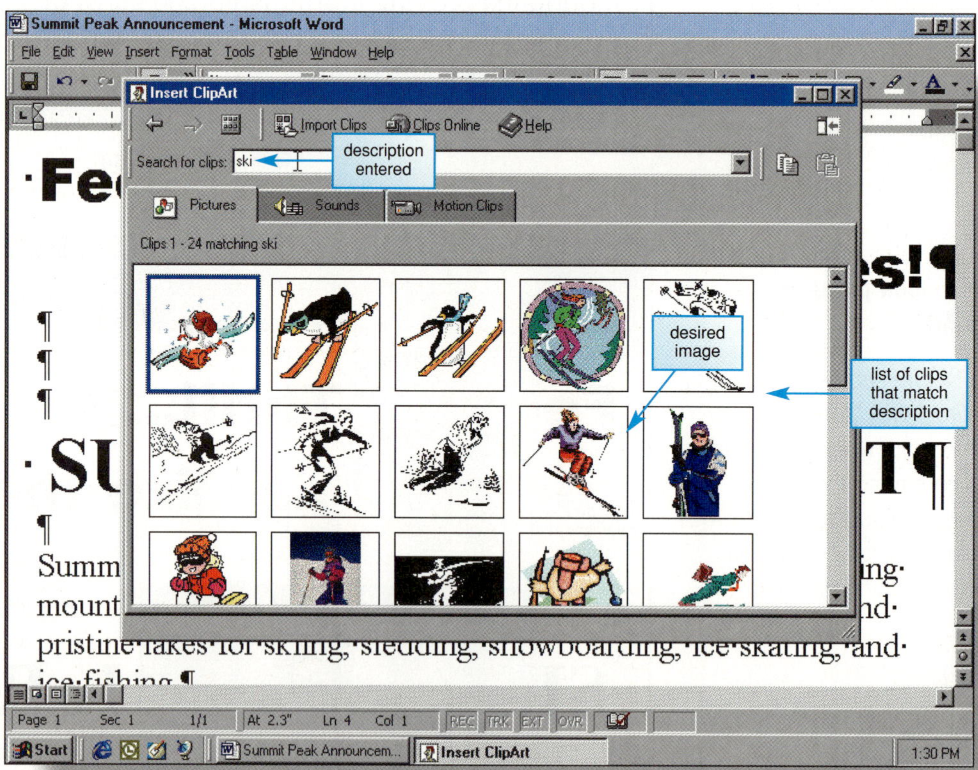

FIGURE 1-57

5 Click the desired image and then point to the Insert clip button on the Pop-up menu.

Word displays a Pop-up menu (Figure 1-58). The Pop-up menu contains four buttons: (1) Insert clip, (2) Preview clip, (3) Add clip to Favorites or other category, and (4) Find similar clips.

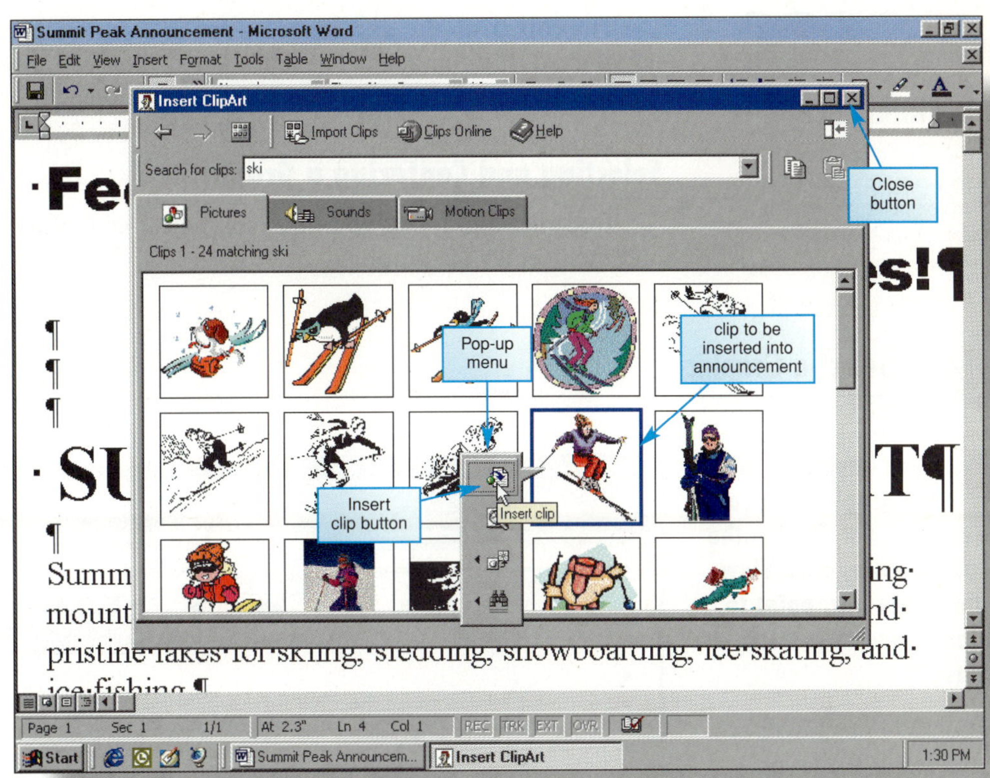

FIGURE 1-58

6 Click the Insert clip button. Click the Close button at the right edge of the Insert ClipArt window's title bar. Press the UP ARROW key twice to display part of the headline.

Word inserts the clip into the document at the location of the insertion point (Figure 1-59). The graphic of the skier displays below the headline in the announcement.

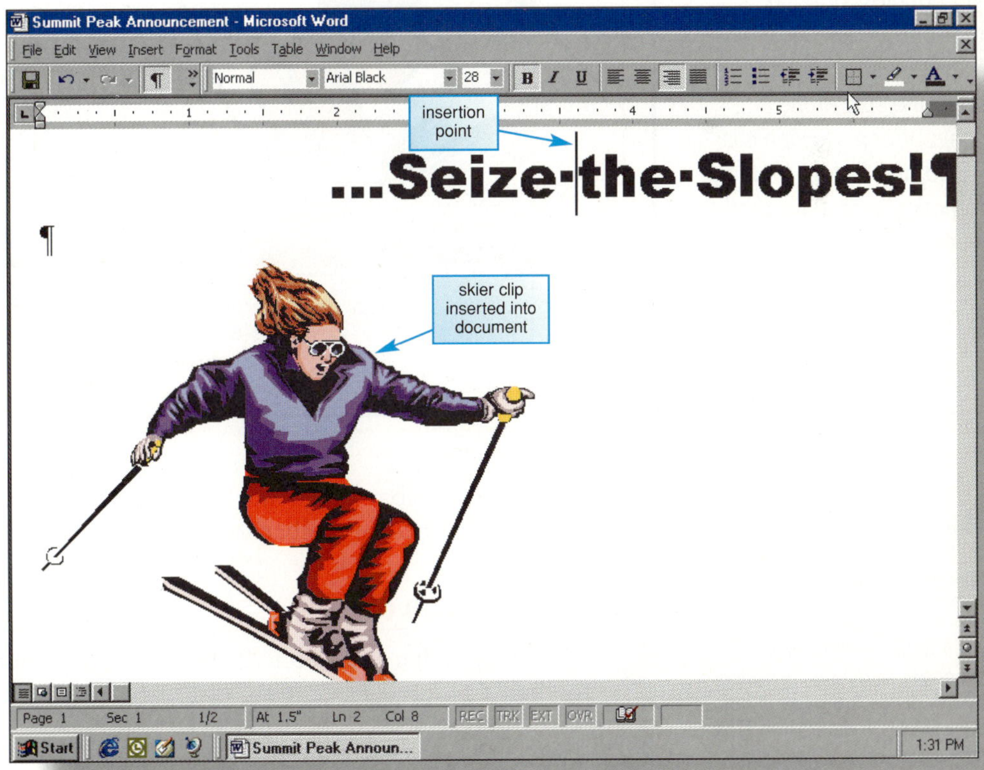

FIGURE 1-59

Obtaining Graphics

If you have a scanner or digital camera attached to your computer, Word can insert a graphic directly from these devices.

The clip art in the document is part of a paragraph. Because that paragraph is left-aligned, the clip art also is left-aligned. You can, however, use any of the paragraph alignment buttons on the Formatting toolbar to reposition the clip art.

Selecting and Centering a Graphic

To center a graphic, you first must select it. Perform the following steps to select and then center the graphic.

To Select a Graphic

1 Click anywhere in the graphic. If your screen does not display the Picture toolbar, click View on the menu bar, point to Toolbars, and then click Picture.

Word selects the graphic (Figure 1-60). A selected graphic displays surrounded by a ***selection rectangle*** *that has small squares, called* ***sizing handles****, at each corner and middle location. You use the sizing handles to change the size of the graphic. When a graphic is selected, the Picture toolbar automatically displays on the screen.*

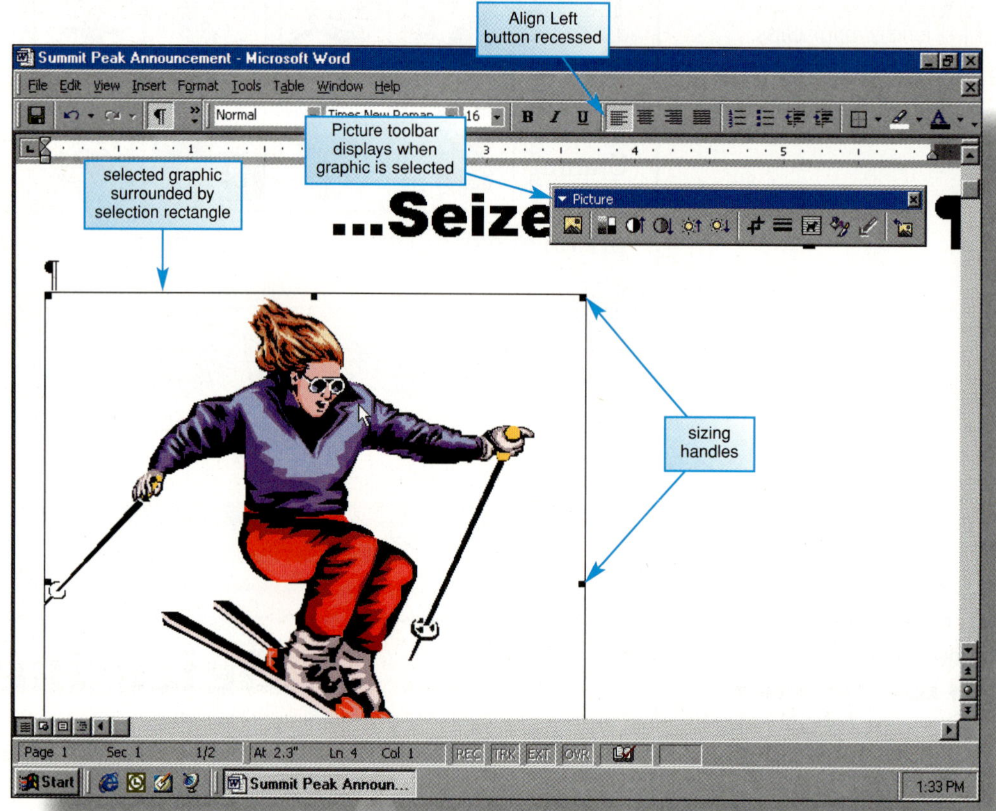

FIGURE 1-60

Graphics

Emphasize a graphic by placing it at the optical center of the page. To determine optical center, divide the page in half horizontally and vertically. The optical center is located one third of the way up the vertical line from the point of intersection of the two lines.

If the Picture toolbar covers the Standard and Formatting toolbars you can drag the title bar of the Picture toolbar to move the toolbar to a different location.

TO CENTER A SELECTED GRAPHIC

 With the graphic still selected, click the Center button on the Formatting toolbar.

Word centers the selected graphic between the left and right margins of the document (see Figure 1-61). The Center button is recessed.

When you center the graphic, Word may scroll down so the graphic is positioned at the top of the document window. The graphic is a little too large for this announcement. The next step is to resize the graphic.

Resizing a Graphic

Once you have inserted a graphic into a document, you easily can change its size. **Resizing** includes both enlarging and reducing the size of a graphic. To resize a graphic, you first must select it. The following steps show how to resize the graphic you just inserted and selected.

Resizing Graphics

When you drag the sizing handles to resize a graphic, you might distort its proportions. To maintain the proportions of the graphic, press the SHIFT key while you drag a corner sizing handle.

Steps To Resize a Graphic

1 With the graphic still selected, point to the upper-left corner sizing handle.

The mouse pointer changes to a two-headed arrow when it is on a sizing handle (Figure 1-61). To resize a graphic, you drag the sizing handles until the graphic is the desired size.

FIGURE 1-61

2 Drag the sizing handle diagonally toward the center of the graphic until the dotted selection rectangle is positioned approximately as shown in Figure 1-62.

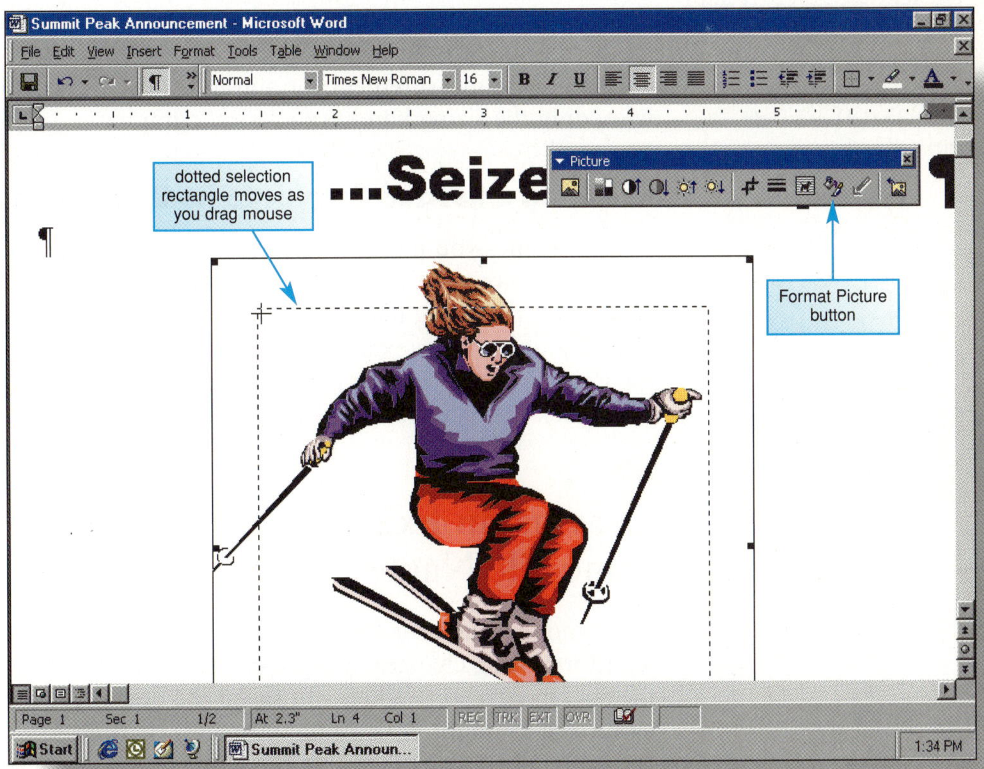

FIGURE 1-62

Release the mouse button. Press CTRL+HOME.

Word resizes the graphic (Figure 1-63). When you click outside of a graphic or press a key to scroll through a document, Word deselects the graphic. The Picture toolbar disappears from the screen when you deselect the graphic.

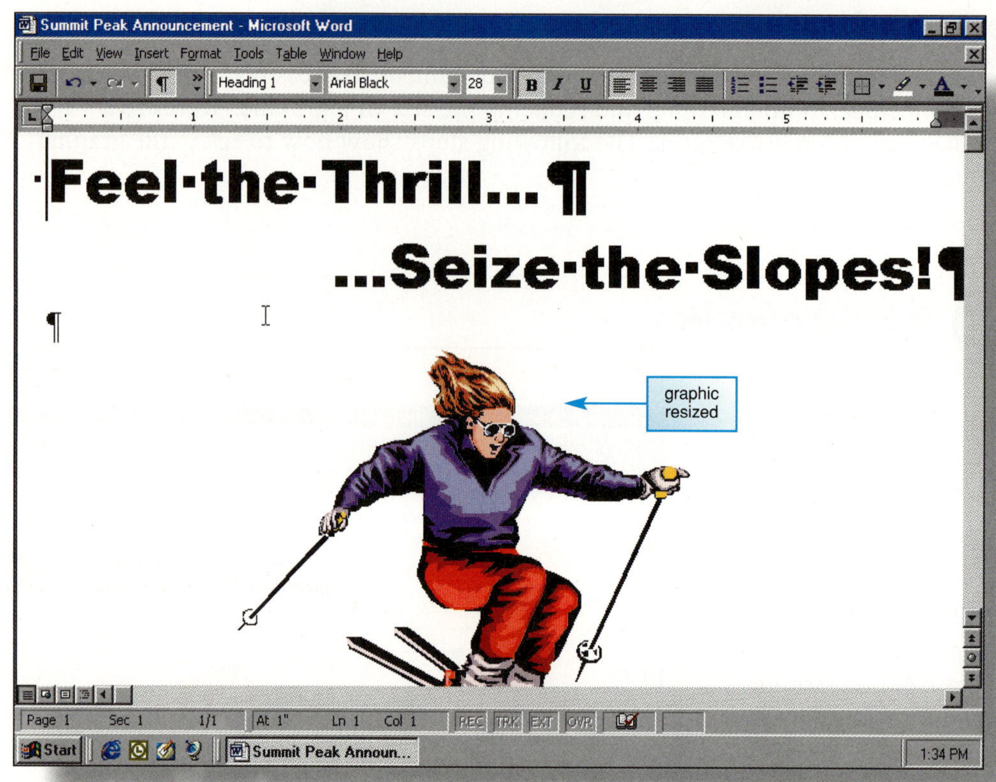

FIGURE 1-63

Other Ways

1. Click Format Picture button on Picture toolbar, click Size tab, enter desired height and width, click OK button
2. On Format menu click Picture, click Size tab, enter desired height and width, click OK button

Instead of resizing a selected graphic with the mouse, you also can use the Format Picture dialog box to resize a graphic by clicking the Format Picture button (Figure 1-62 on the previous page) on the Picture toolbar and then clicking the Size tab. Using the Size sheet, you enter exact height and width measurements. If you have a precise measurement for a graphic, use the Format Picture dialog box; otherwise, drag the sizing handles to resize a graphic.

Restoring a Resized Graphic to Its Original Size

Sometimes you might resize a graphic and realize it is the wrong size. In these cases, you may want to return the graphic to its original size and start again. You could drag the sizing handle until the graphic resembles its original size. To restore a resized graphic to its exact original size, click the graphic to select it and then click the Format Picture button on the Picture toolbar to display the Format Picture dialog box. Click the Size tab and then click the Reset button. Finally, click the OK button.

Saving an Existing Document with the Same File Name

The announcement for Project 1 now is complete. To transfer the modified document with formatting changes and graphic to your floppy disk in drive A, you must save the document again. When you saved the document the first time, you assigned a file name to it (Summit Peak Announcement). If you use the following procedure, Word automatically assigns the same file name to the document each time you subsequently save it.

To Save an Existing Document with the Same File Name

Double-click the move handle on the Standard toolbar to display the entire toolbar. Click the Save button on the Standard toolbar.

Word saves the document on a floppy disk inserted in drive A using the currently assigned file name, Summit Peak Announcement (Figure 1-64).

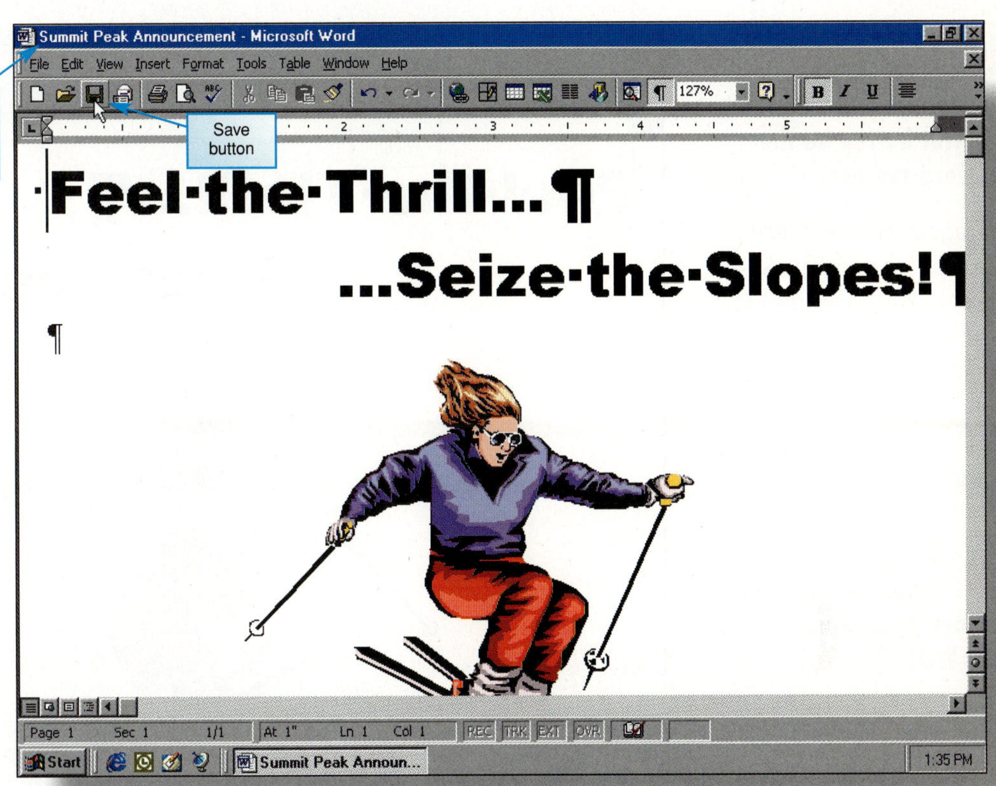

FIGURE 1-64

1. On File menu click Save
2. Press CTRL+S

While Word is saving the document, the Background Save Status icon displays at the right edge of the status bar. When the save is complete, the document remains in memory and on the screen.

If, for some reason, you want to save an existing document with a different file name, click Save As on the File menu to display the Save As dialog box. Then, fill in the Save As dialog box as discussed in Steps 2 through 5 on pages WD 1.27 and WD 1.28.

Save As

In the Save As dialog box, you can create a new Windows folder by clicking the Create New Folder button. You also can delete or rename files by selecting the file and then clicking the Tools button arrow in the Save As dialog box. To display the Save As dialog box, click File on the menu bar and then click Save As.

Printing a Document

The next step is to print the document you created. A printed version of the document is called a **hard copy** or **printout**. Perform the steps on the next page to print the announcement created in Project 1.

To Print a Document

1 **Ready the printer according to the printer instructions. Click the Print button on the Standard toolbar.**

The mouse pointer briefly changes to an hourglass shape as Word prepares to print the document. While the document is printing, a printer icon displays in the tray status area on the taskbar (Figure 1-65).

2 **When the printer stops, retrieve the printout (see Figure 1-1 on page WD1.7).**

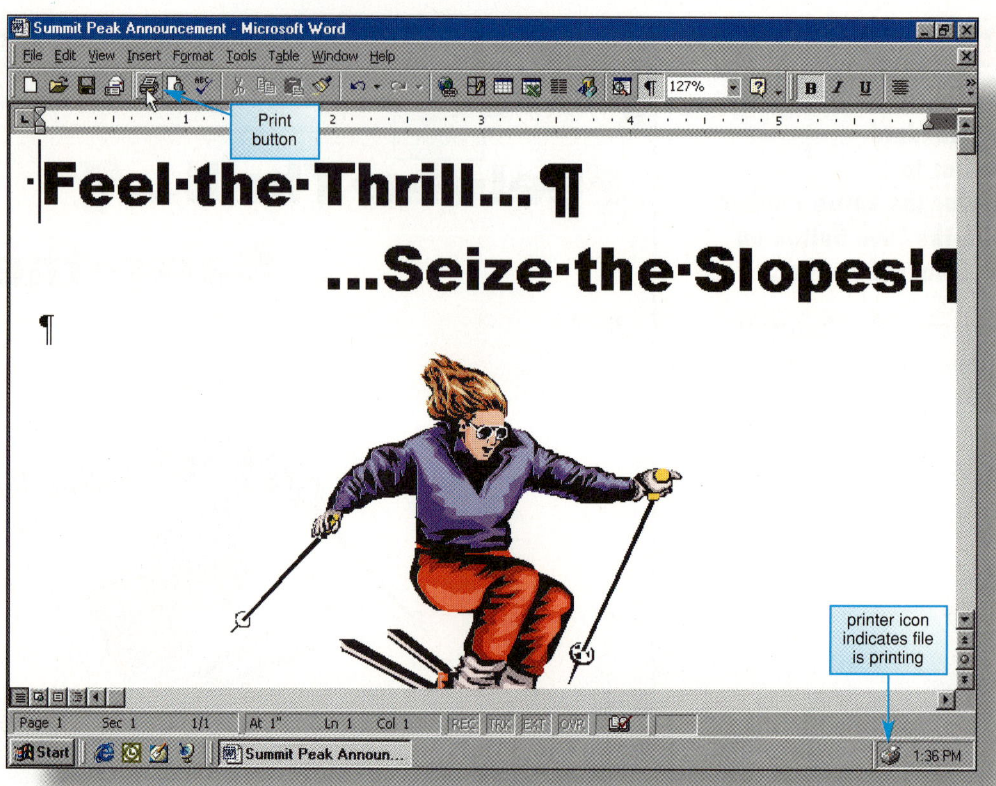

FIGURE 1-65

Other Ways

1. On File menu click Print, click OK button
2. Press CTRL+P, press ENTER

When you use the Print button to print a document, Word prints the entire document automatically. You then may distribute the hard copy or keep it as a permanent record of the document.

If you wanted to print multiple copies of the document, click File on the menu bar and then click Print to display the Print dialog box. This dialog box has several printing options, including specifying the number of copies to print.

If you wanted to cancel your job that is printing or one you have waiting to be printed, double-click the printer icon on the taskbar (Figure 1-65). In the printer window, click the job to be canceled and then click Cancel Printing on the Document menu.

Print Preview

To view a document before you print it, click the Print Preview button on the Standard toolbar. To return to the document window, click the Close Preview button on the Print Preview toolbar.

Quitting Word

After you create, save, and print the announcement, Project 1 is complete. To quit Word and return control to Windows, perform the following steps.

To Quit Word

1 **Point to the Close button in the upper-right corner of the title bar (Figure 1-66).**

2 **Click the Close button.**

The Word window closes.

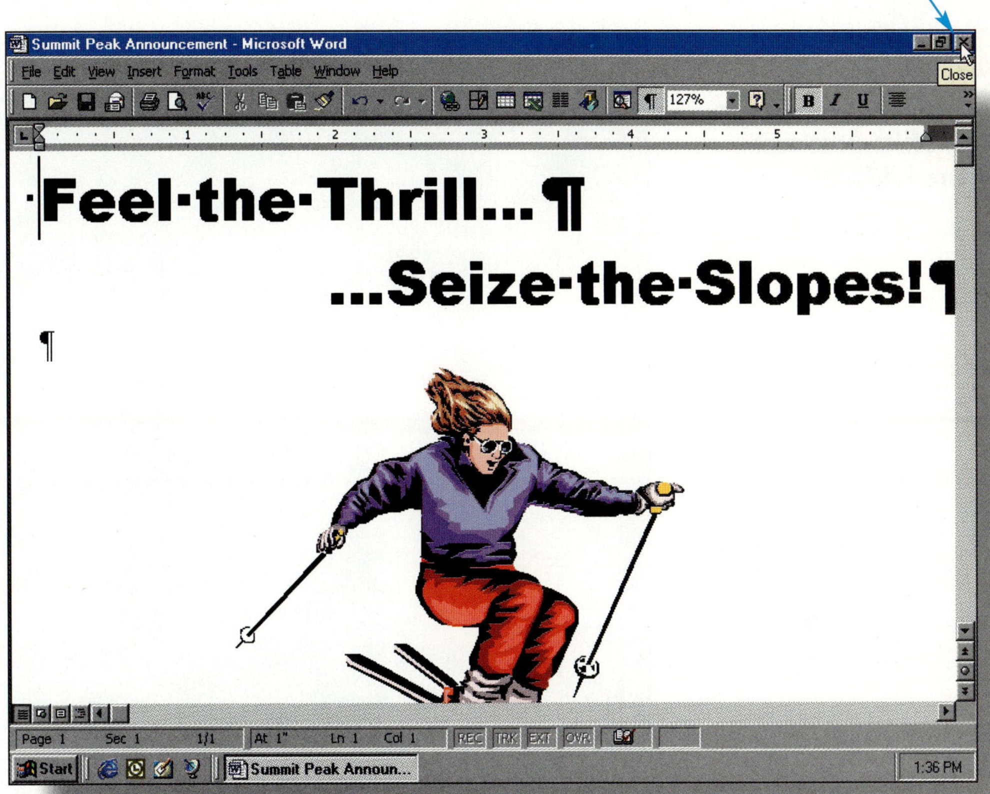

FIGURE 1-66

Other Ways

1. On File menu click Exit
2. Press ALT+F4

If you made changes to the document since the last save, Word displays dialog box asking if you want to save the changes. Clicking the Yes button saves the changes; clicking the No button ignores the changes; and clicking the Cancel button returns to the document. If you did not make any changes since you saved the document, this dialog box does not display.

You created and formatted the announcement, inserted clip art into it, printed it, and saved it. You might decide, however, to change the announcement at a later date. To do this, you must start Word and then retrieve your document from the floppy disk in drive A.

Opening a Document

Earlier, you saved the Word document created in Project 1 on a floppy disk using the file name Summit Peak Announcement. Once you have created and saved a document, you often will have reason to retrieve it from the disk. For example, you might want to revise the document or print it. The steps on the next page illustrate how to open the file Summit Peak Announcement.

More About 2000

Opening Files

In Word, you can open a recently used file by clicking File on the menu bar and then clicking the file name on the File menu. To instruct Word to show the recently used documents on the File menu, click Tools on the menu bar, click Options, click the General tab, click Recently used file list, and then click the OK button.

To Open a Document

1 **Click the Start button on the taskbar and then point to Open Office Document (Figure 1-67).**

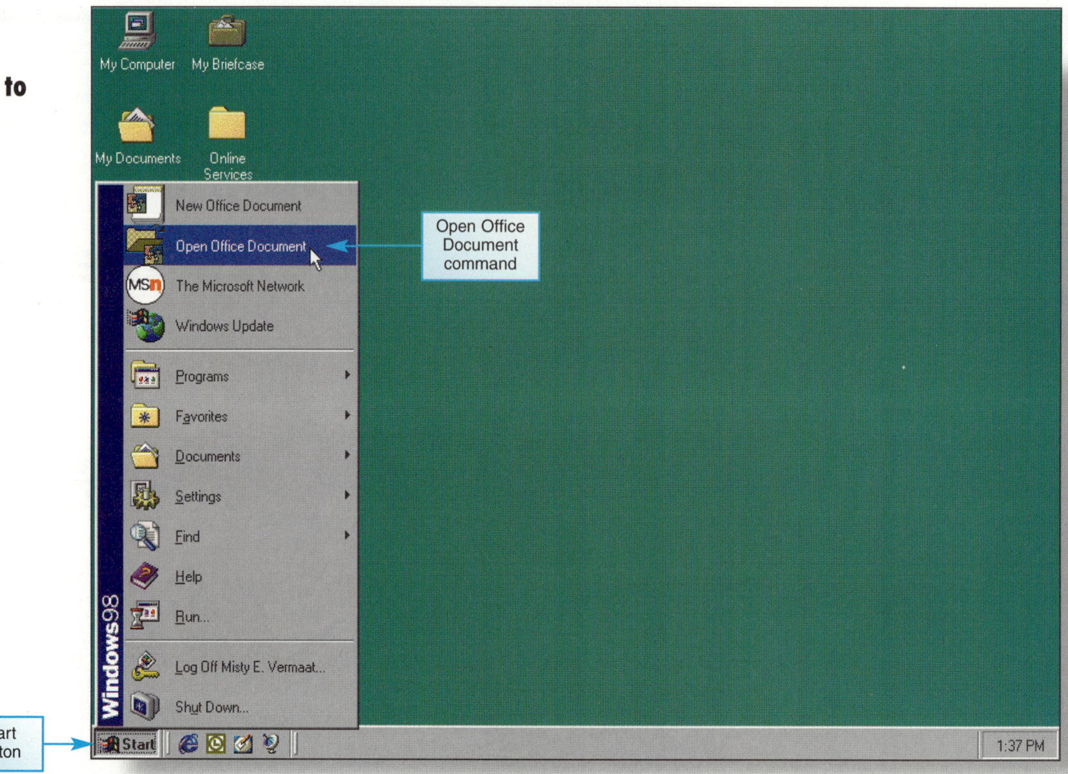

FIGURE 1-67

2 **Click Open Office Document. If necessary, click the Look in box arrow and then click 3½ Floppy (A:). If it is not selected already, click the file name Summit Peak Announcement. Point to the Open button.**

Office displays the Open Office Document dialog box (Figure 1-68). Office displays the files on the floppy disk in drive A.

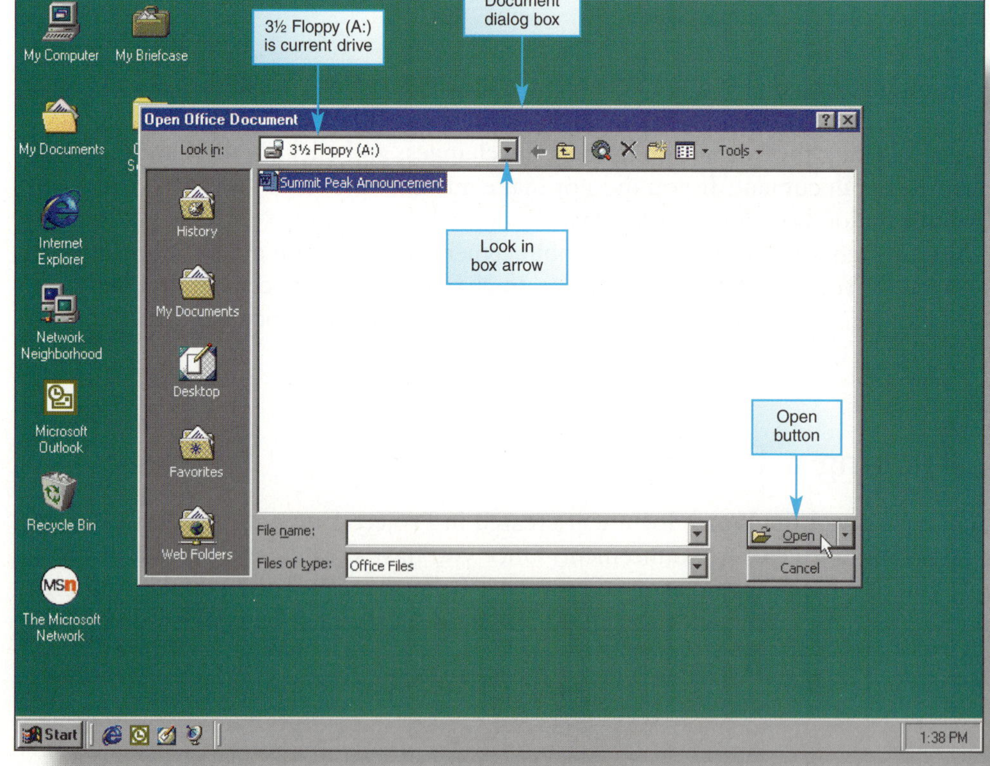

FIGURE 1-68

Click the Open button.

Office starts Word, and then Word opens the document, Summit Peak Announcement, from the floppy disk in drive A and displays the document on the screen (Figure 1-69).

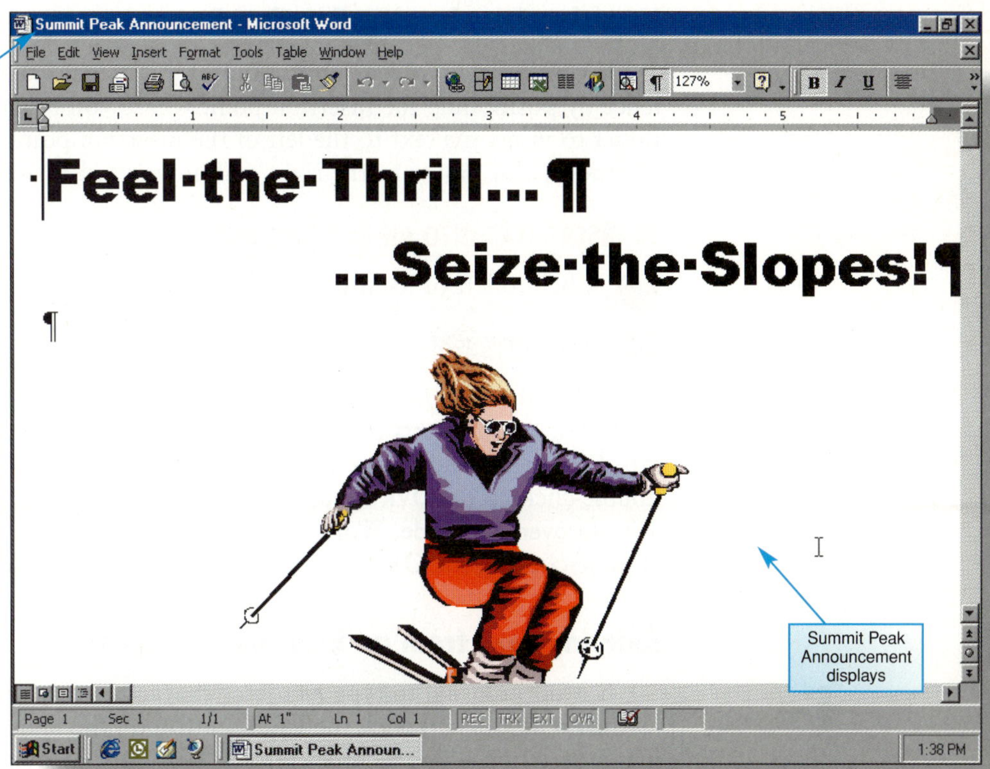

FIGURE 1-69

Other Ways

1. In Microsoft Word, click Open button on Standard toolbar, select file name, click Open button in dialog box
2. In Microsoft Word, on File menu click Open, select file name, click Open button in dialog box
3. In Microsoft Word, press CTRL+O, select file name, press ENTER

Correcting Errors

After creating a document, you often will find you must make changes to it. Changes can be required because the document contains an error or because of new circumstances.

Types of Changes Made to Documents

The types of changes made to documents normally fall into one of the three following categories: additions, deletions, or modifications.

ADDITIONS Additional words, sentences, or paragraphs may be required in a document. Additions occur when you omit text from a document and want to insert it later. For example, you may want to insert the word, winter, in front of vacation packages to differentiate winter packages from summer packages.

DELETIONS Sometimes, text in a document is incorrect or is no longer needed. For example, the resort might remove transportation from their package deals. In this case, you would delete the word, transportation, from the list.

MODIFICATIONS If an error is made in a document or changes take place that affect the document, you might have to revise the word(s) in the text. For example, the resort might purchase more land and have 6,500 acres of slopes and lakes; thus, you would change the number from 5,200 to 6,500.

Word provides several methods for correcting errors in a document. For each of the error correction techniques, you first must move the insertion point to the error.

Inserting Text into an Existing Document

If you leave a word or phrase out of a sentence, you can include it in the sentence by positioning the insertion point where you intend to insert the text. Word is preset to insert the text to the left of the insertion point. The text to the right of the insertion point moves to the right and downward to accommodate the new text.

TO INSERT TEXT INTO AN EXISTING DOCUMENT

1. Click to left of location to insert new text.
2. Type new text.

In Word, the default typing mode is insert mode. In **insert mode**, as you type a character, Word inserts the character and moves all the characters to the right of the typed character one position to the right. You can change to overtype mode by double-clicking the **OVR status indicator** on the status bar (see Figure 1-4 on page WD 1.9). In **overtype mode**, Word replaces characters to the right of the insertion point. Double-clicking the OVR status indicator a second time returns you to insert mode.

Deleting Text from an Existing Document

It is not unusual to type incorrect characters or words in a document. You have learned that you can click the Undo button on the Standard toolbar to undo a command or action – this includes typing. Word also provides other methods of correcting typing errors. For example, you may want to delete certain letters or words.

TO DELETE AN INCORRECT CHARACTER IN A DOCUMENT

1. Click next to the incorrect character.
2. Press the BACKSPACE key to erase to the left of the insertion point; or press the DELETE key to erase to the right of the insertion point.

TO DELETE AN INCORRECT WORD OR PHRASE IN A DOCUMENT

1. Select the word or phrase you want to erase.
2. Right-click the selected word or phrase, and then click Cut on the shortcut menu; or click the Cut button on the Standard toolbar (Figure 1-7a on page WD 1.13); or press the DELETE key.

Closing the Entire Document

Sometimes, everything goes wrong. If this happens, you may want to close the document entirely and start over. You also may want to close a document when you are finished with it so you can begin your next document.

TO CLOSE THE ENTIRE DOCUMENT AND START OVER

1. Click File on the menu bar and then click Close.
2. If Word displays a dialog box, click the No button to ignore the changes since the last time you saved the document.
3. Click the New Blank Document button (see Figure 1-7a on page WD 1.13) on the Standard toolbar.

You also can close the document by clicking the Close button at the right edge of the menu bar.

Word Help System

At any time while you are using Word, you can get answers to questions by using the **Word Help system**. Used properly, this form of online assistance can increase your productivity and reduce your frustrations by minimizing the time you spend learning how to use Word.

The following section shows how to obtain answers to your questions using the Office Assistant. For additional information on using help, see Appendix A.

More About

Help

If you purchased an application program five years ago, you probably received one or more thick technical manuals explaining the software. With Microsoft Word 2000, you receive a small manual. The online Help feature of Microsoft Word 2000 replaces the reams and reams of printed pages in complicated technical manuals.

Using the Office Assistant

The **Office Assistant** answers your questions and suggests more efficient ways to complete a task. With the Office Assistant active, for example, you can type a question, word, or phrase in a text box and the Office Assistant provides immediate help on the subject. Also, as you create a document, the Office Assistant accumulates tips that suggest more efficient ways to do the tasks you completed while creating a document, such as formatting, printing, and saving. This tip feature is part of the **IntelliSense technology** that is built into Word, which understands what you are trying to do and suggests better ways to do it. When the light bulb displays above the Office Assistant, click it to see a tip.

The following steps show how to use the Office Assistant to obtain information on changing the size of a toolbar.

Steps To Obtain Help Using the Office Assistant

1 If the Office Assistant is not on the screen, click Help on the menu bar and then click Show the Office Assistant. With the Office Assistant on the screen, click it. Type `change toolbar size` **in the What would you like to do? text box. Point to the Search button (Figure 1-70).**

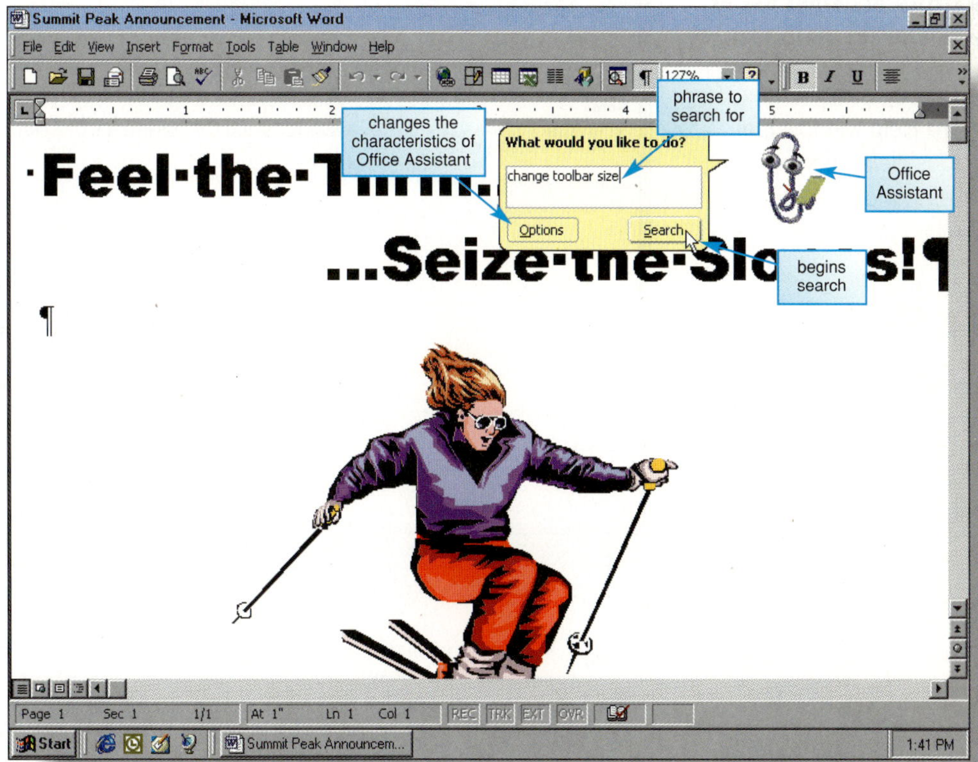

FIGURE 1-70

2 **Click the Search button. Point to Resize a toolbar in the list of topics.**

The Office Assistant displays a list of topics relating to the typed question, change toolbar size (Figure 1-71). The mouse pointer changes to a pointing hand.

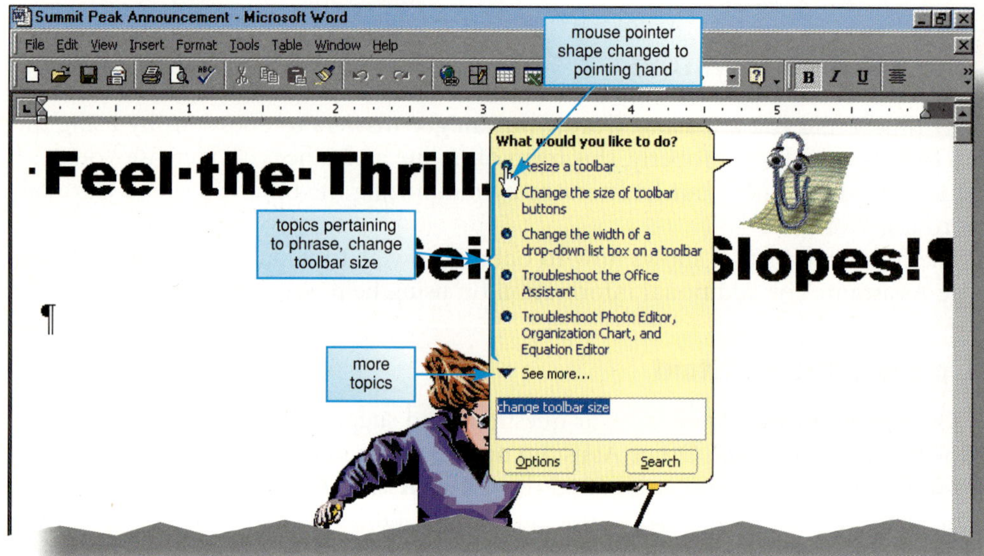

FIGURE 1-71

3 **Click Resize a toolbar. When Word opens the Word Help window, click its Maximize button. If necessary, drag the Office Assistant out of the way of the Help text.**

The Office Assistant opens a Word Help window that provides Help information on resizing toolbars (Figure 1-72).

4 **Click the Close button on the Word Help window title bar.**

The Word Help window closes and the Word document window again is active.

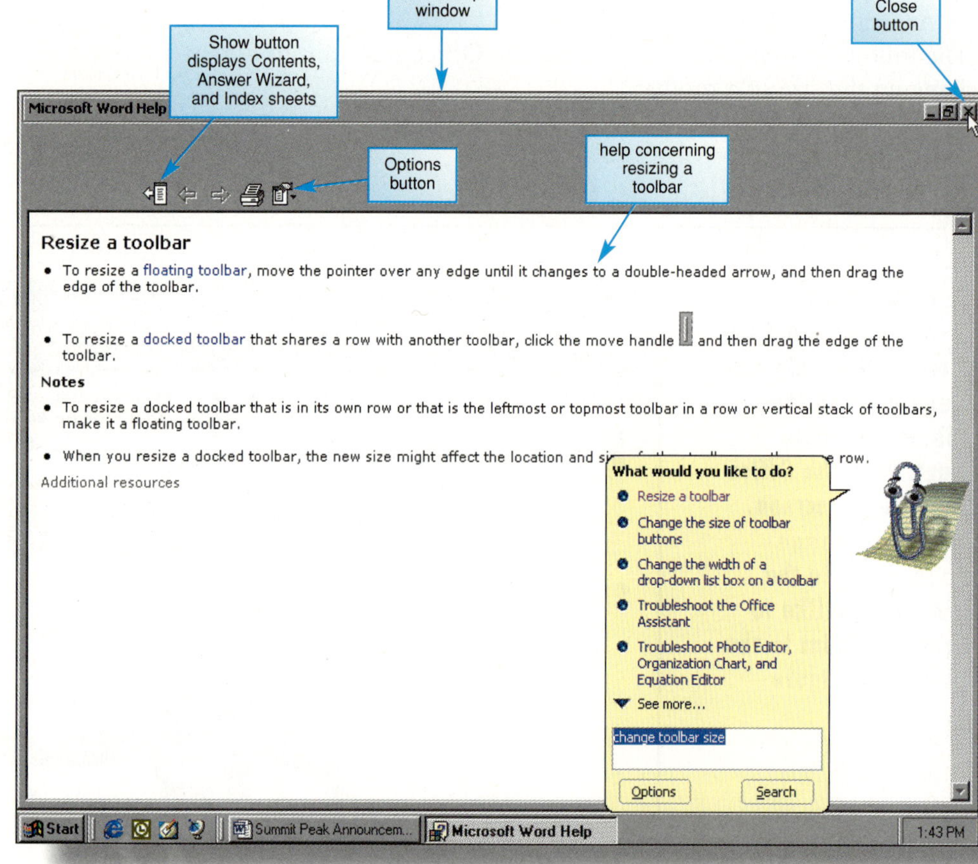

FIGURE 1-72

Other Ways

1. If the Office Assistant is on, click Microsoft Word Help button or click Microsoft Word Help on the Help menu

You can use the Office Assistant to search for Help on any topic concerning Word.

Table 1-3 summarizes the nine categories of help available to you. Because of the way the Word Help system works, please review the right-most column of Table 1-3 if you have difficulties activating the desired category of help.

Table 1-3 Word Help System

TYPE	DESCRIPTION	HOW TO ACTIVATE	TURNING THE OFFICE ASSISTANT ON AND OFF
Answer Wizard	Similar to the Office Assistant in that it answers questions that you type in your own words.	Click the Microsoft Word Help button on the Standard toolbar. If necessary, maximize the Help window by double-clicking its title bar. Click the Answer Wizard tab.	If the Office Assistant displays, right-click it, click Options, click Use the Office Assistant to remove the check mark, click the OK button.
Contents sheet	Groups Help topics by general categories. Use when you know only the general category of the topic in question. Similar to a table of contents in a book.	Click the Microsoft Word Help button on the Standard toolbar. If necessary, maximize the Help window by double-clicking its title bar. Click the Contents tab.	If the Office Assistant displays, right-click it, click Options, click Use the Office Assistant to remove the check mark, click the OK button.
Detect and Repair	Automatically finds and fixes errors in the application.	Click Detect and Repair on the Help menu.	
Hardware and Software Information	Shows Product ID and allows access to system information and technical support information.	Click About Microsoft Word on the Help menu and then click the appropriate button.	
Index sheet	Similar to an index in a book; use when you know exactly what you want.	Click the Microsoft Word Help button on the Standard toolbar. If necessary, maximize the Help window by double-clicking its title bar. Click the Index tab.	If the Office Assistant displays, right-click it, click Options, click Use the Office Assistant to remove the check mark, click the OK button.
Office Assistant	Answers questions that you type in your own words, offers tips, and provides Help for a variety of Word features.	Click the Microsoft Word Help button on the Standard toolbar or double-click the Office Assistant icon. Some dialog boxes also include the Microsoft Word Help button.	If the Office Assistant does not display, click Show the Office Assistant on the Help menu.
Office on the Web	Used to access technical resources and download free product enhancements on the Web.	Click Office on the Web on the Help menu.	
Question Mark button and What's This? command	Used to identify unfamiliar items on the screen.	In a dialog box, click the Question Mark button and then click an item in the dialog box. Click What's This? on the Help menu, and then click an item on the screen.	
WordPerfect Help	Used to assist WordPerfect users who are learning Microsoft Word.	Click WordPerfect Help on the Help menu.	

The final step in this project is to quit Word.

TO QUIT WORD

Click the Close button in the Word window.

The Word window closes.

Quick Reference

For a table that lists how to complete the tasks covered in this book using the mouse, menu, shortcut menu, and keyboard, visit the Shelly Cashman Series Office Web page (www.scsite.com/off2000/qr.htm) and then click Microsoft Word 2000.

CASE PERSPECTIVE SUMMARY

Jackie is thrilled with the completed announcement. The characters in the headline and body title are large enough so students can read them from a distance and the graphic is quite eye-catching. She takes the announcement to the school's Promotions Department and receives approval to post it in several locations around campus, have it printed in the school newspaper, and mailed to each student's home. Members of the SGA assist Jackie with these activities.

Project Summary

Project 1 introduced you to starting Word and creating a document. Before entering any text in the document, you learned how to change the font size. You also learned how to save and print a document. You used Word's check spelling as you type feature. Once you saved the document, you learned how to format its paragraphs and characters. Then, you inserted and resized clip art. You learned how to move the insertion point so you could insert, delete, and modify text. Finally, you learned one way to use Word Help.

What You Should Know

Having completed this project, you now should be able to perform the following tasks:

- Bold Selected Text *(WD 1.33)*
- Center a Paragraph *(WD 1.35 and WD 1.40)*
- Center a Selected Graphic *(WD 1.46)*
- Change the Font of Selected Text *(WD 1.31)*
- Change the Font Size of Selected Text *(WD 1.32)*
- Check Spelling as You Type *(WD 1.22)*
- Close the Entire Document and Start Over *(WD 1.54)*
- Delete an Incorrect Character in a Document *(WD 1.54)*
- Delete an Incorrect Word or Phrase in a Document *(WD 1.54)*
- Display Formatting Marks *(WD 1.20)*
- Displays the Entire Standard Toolbar *(WD 1.15)*
- Enter Blank Lines into a Document *(WD 1.19)*
- Enter More Text *(WD 1.21)*
- Enter Text *(WD 1.18)*
- Enter Text that Scrolls the Document Window *(WD 1.25)*
- Format a Line of Text *(WD 1.37)*
- Increase the Default Font Size Before Typing *(WD 1.17)*
- Insert Clip Art into a Document *(WD 1.43)*
- Insert Text into an Existing Document *(WD 1.54)*
- Italicize Selected Text *(WD 1.39)*
- Obtain Help Using the Office Assistant *(WD 1.55)*
- Open a Document *(WD 1.52)*
- Print a Document *(WD 1.50)*
- Quit Word *(WD 1.51)*
- Resize a Graphic *(WD 1.47)*
- Right-Align a Paragraph *(WD 1.33)*
- Save a New Document *(WD 1.26)*
- Save an Existing Document with the Same File Name *(WD 1.49)*
- Scroll Through the Document *(WD 1.40)*
- Select a Graphic *(WD 1.46)*
- Select a Group of Words *(WD 1.41)*
- Select a Line *(WD 1.37)*
- Select a Word *(WD 1.38)*
- Select Multiple Paragraphs *(WD 1.30)*
- Start Word *(WD 1.8)*
- Underline Selected Text *(WD 1.42)*
- Undo an Action *(WD 1.36)*
- Wordwrap Text as You Type *(WD 1.21)*
- Zoom Page Width *(WD 1.15)*

More About 2000

Microsoft Certification

The Microsoft Office User Specialist (MOUS) Certification program provides an opportunity for you to obtain a valuable industry credential — proof that you have the Word 2000 skills required by employers. For more information, see Appendix D or visit the Shelly Cashman Series MOUS Web page at www.scsite.com/off2000/cert.htm.

1 Checking Spelling of a Document

Instructions: Start Word. Open the document, Meeting Announcement, on the Data Disk. If you did not download the Data Disk, see the inside back cover for instructions for downloading the Data Disk or see your instructor.

As shown in Figure 1-73, the document is a meeting announcement that contains many spelling and grammar errors. You are to right-click each of the errors and then click the appropriate correction on the shortcut menu.

You have learned that Word flags spelling errors with a red wavy underline. A green wavy underline indicates that Word has detected a possible grammar error. *Hint:* If your screen does not display the grammar errors, use the Word Help System to determine how to enable the check grammar feature. Perform the following tasks:

Meeting Notise

All Employees

NEW HEALTH INSURANCE PLAN

Effective Januery 1, Kramer Enterprises will be be switching to a new insurance providor for major medical coverage. At that time, all employees must begin submitting claims and directing all claim-related questions to ofr new provider, Health America.

Representative's from Health America will be visiting our office on Friday, December 1, to discuss our nesw insurance plan. Please plan to attend either the morning session at 9:00 a.m. or the afternoon session at 2:00 p.m. Both session will be in the lunchroom.

insurance cards will be distributed at these meetings!

FIGURE 1-73

1. Position the insertion point at the beginning of the document. Right-click the flagged word, Notise. Change the incorrect word, Notise, to Notice by clicking Notice on the shortcut menu.
2. Right-click the flagged word, Januery. Change the incorrect word, Januery, to January by clicking January on the shortcut menu.
3. Right-click the flagged word, be. Click Delete Repeated Word on the shortcut menu to remove the duplicate occurrence of the word, be.
4. Right-click the flagged word, providor. Change the incorrect word, providor, to provider by clicking provider on the shortcut menu.
5. Right-click the flagged word, ofr. Because the shortcut menu does not display the correct word, click outside the shortcut menu to remove it from the screen. Correct the misspelled word, ofr, to the correct word, our, by removing the letter f and replacing it with the letter u.
6. Right-click the flagged word, Representative's. Change the word, Representative's, to its correct plural by clicking the word, Representatives, on the shortcut menu.
7. Right-click the incorrect word, nesw. Change the incorrect word, nesw, to new by clicking new on the shortcut menu.
8. Right-click the flagged word, session. Change the incorrect word, session, to its plural by clicking sessions on the shortcut menu.
9. Right-click the flagged word, insurance. Capitalize the word, insurance, by clicking Insurance on the shortcut menu.
10. Click File menu on the menu bar and then click Save As. Save the document using Corrected Meeting Announcement as the file name.
11. Print the revised document.

1 Creating an Announcement with Clip Art

Problem: The Director of the Harbor Theatre Company at your school has requested that each student in your Marketing 102 class prepare an announcement for auditions of its upcoming play. The student that creates the winning announcement will receive five complimentary tickets to the play. You prepare the announcement shown in Figure 1-74. *Hint:* Remember, if you make a mistake while formatting the announcement, you can click the Undo button on the Standard toolbar to undo your mistake.

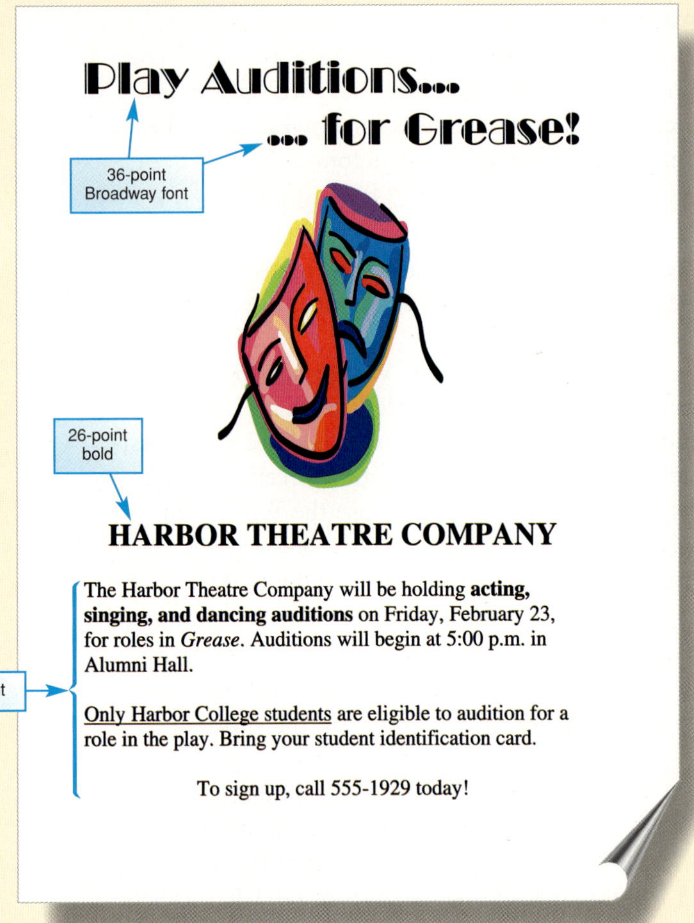

FIGURE 1-74

Instructions:

1. Change the font size from 10 to 18 by clicking the Font Size box arrow on the formatting toolbar and then clicking 18.
2. If necessary, click the Show/Hide ¶ button on Standard toolbar to display formatting marks.
3. Create the announcement shown in Figure 1-74. Enter the document first without clip art and unformatted; that is without any bold, underlined, italicized, right-aligned, or centered text. If Word flags any misspelled words as you type, check the spelling of these words and correct them.
4. Save the document on a floppy disk with Grease Announcement as the file name.
5. Select the two lines of the headline. Change their font to Broadway, or a similar font. Change their font size from 18 to 36.
6. Click somewhere in the second line of the headline. Right-align it.
7. Click somewhere in the body title line. Center it.
8. Select the body title line. Increase its font size from 18 to 26. Bold it.
9. In the first paragraph of the body copy, select the following phrase: acting, singing, and dancing auditions. Bold the phrase.
10. In the same paragraph, select the word, Grease. Italicize it.
11. In the second paragraph of the body copy, select the following phrase: Only Harbor College students. Underline the phrase.
12. Click somewhere in the last line of the announcement. Center it.
13. Insert the graphic of the drama masks between the headline and the body title line. Search for the text, drama, in the Clip Gallery to locate the graphic.
14. Click the graphic to select it. Center the selected graphic.
15. Save the announcement again with the same file name.
16. Print the announcement.

2 Creating an Announcement with Resized Clip Art

Problem: You are an assistant for the Marketing Manager at Taylor Business School. She has asked you to prepare an announcement for Fall Registration. The announcement must include clip art. You prepare the announcement shown in Figure 1-75. *Hint:* Remember, if you make a mistake while formatting the announcement, you can click the Undo button on the Standard toolbar to undo your mistake.

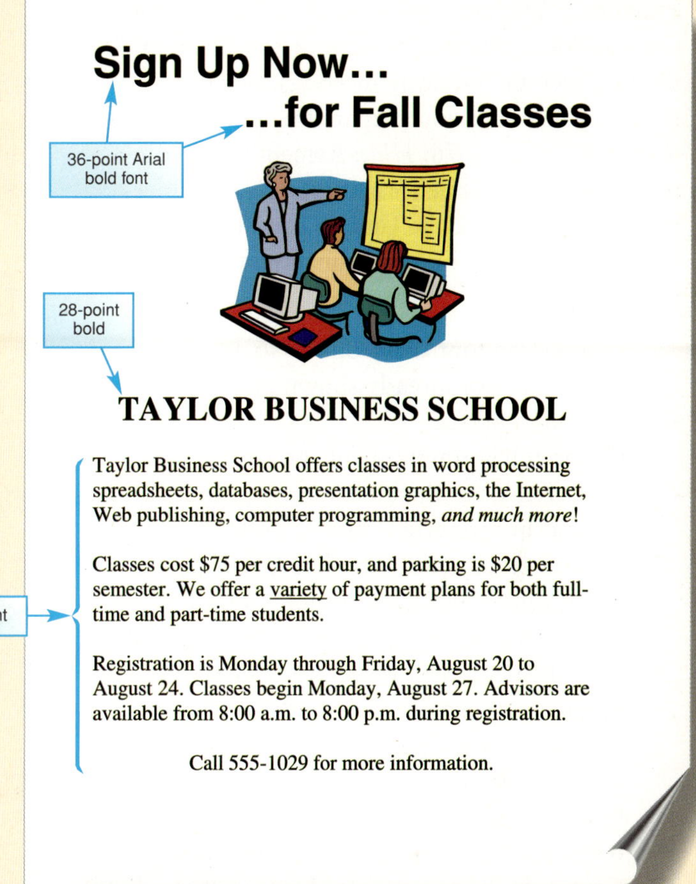

FIGURE 1-75

Instructions:

1. Change the font size from 10 to 18 by clicking the Font Size box arrow on the Formatting toolbar and then clicking 18.
2. If it is not already selected, click the Show/Hide ¶ button on the Standard toolbar to display formatting marks.
3. Create the announcement shown in Figure 1-75. Enter the document first without the clip art and unformatted; that is without any bold, underlined, italicized, right-aligned, or centered text. If Word flags any misspelled words as you type, check the spelling of these words and correct them.
4. Save the document on a floppy disk with Registration Announcement as the file name.
5. Select the two lines of the headline. Change their font to Arial, or a similar font. Change their font size from 20 to 36. Bold both lines.
6. Click somewhere in the second line of the headline. Right-align it.
7. Click somewhere in the body title line. Center it.
8. Select the body title line. Increase its font size from 18 to 28. Bold it.
9. Select the words, and much more, in the first paragraph of the body copy. Italicize the words.
10. Select the word, variety, in the second paragraph of the body copy. Underline it.
11. Click somewhere in the last line of the announcement. Center it.
12. Insert the graphic of the classroom between the headline and the body title line. Search for the text, classroom, in the Clip Gallery to locate the graphic.
13. Enlarge the graphic of the classroom. If you make the graphic too large, the announcement may flow onto two pages. If this occurs, reduce the size of the graphic so the announcement fits on a single page. *Hint*: Use Help to learn about **print preview**, which is a way to see the page before you print it. To exit print preview and return to the document window, click the Close button on the Print Preview toolbar.
14. Click the graphic to select it. Center the selected graphic.
15. Save the announcement again with the same file name.
16. Print the announcement.

3 Creating an Announcement with Resized Clip Art and a Bulleted List

Problem: You are the secretary of The Computer Club at your school. One of your responsibilities is to announce the monthly meetings. For the February meeting, you prepare the announcement shown in Figure 1-76. *Hint:* Remember, if you make a mistake while formatting the announcement, you can click the Undo button on the Standard toolbar to undo your mistake.

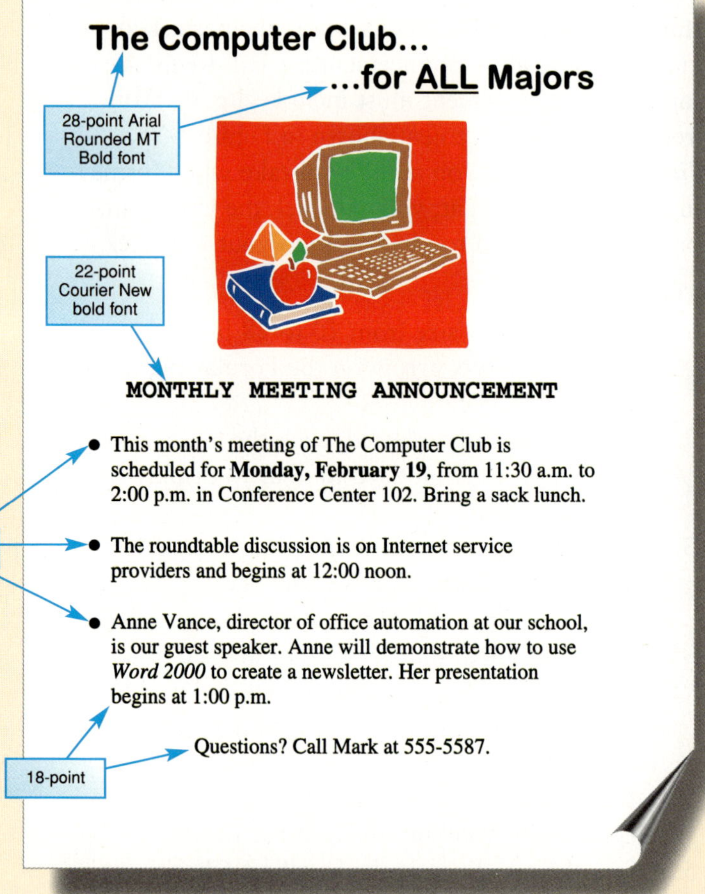

FIGURE 1-76

Instructions:

1. Change the font size from 10 to 18.
2. If they are not already showing, display formatting marks.
3. Create the announcement shown in Figure 1-76. Enter the document first without the clip art and unformatted; that is without any bulleted, bold, underlined, italicized, right-aligned, or centered text. Check spelling as you type.
4. Save the document on a floppy disk with February Announcement as the file name.
5. Format the two lines of the headline to 28-point Arial Rounded MT Bold or a similar font.
6. Right-align the second line of the headline.
7. Center the body title line. Format the body title line to 22-point Courier New bold or a similar font.
8. Add bullets to the three paragraphs of body copy. A **bullet** is a symbol positioned at the beginning of a paragraph. In Word, the default bullet symbol is a small darkened circle. A list of paragraphs with bullets is called a **bulleted list**. *Hint*: Use Help to learn how to add bullets to a list of paragraphs.
9. Bold the date, Monday, February 19, in the first paragraph of the body copy.
10. Italicize the phrase, Word 2000, in the third paragraph of the body copy.
11. Center the last line of the announcement.
12. Insert the graphic of the computer between the headline and the body title line. Search for the text, academic computer, in the Clip Gallery to locate the graphic.
13. Enlarge the graphic of the computer. If you make the graphic too large, the announcement may flow onto two pages. If this occurs, reduce the size of the graphic so the announcement fits on a single page. *Hint*: Use Help to learn about **print preview**, which is a way to see the page before you print it. To exit print preview and return to the document window, click the Close button on the Print Preview toolbar.
14. Center the graphic.
15. Save the announcement again with the same file name.
16. Print the announcement.

Cases and Places

The difficulty of these case studies varies:
◗ are the least difficult; ◗◗ are more difficult; and ◗◗◗ are the most difficult.

1 ◗ You have been assigned the task of preparing an announcement for Starport Airlines. The announcement is to contain a graphic of an airplane from the Clip Gallery. Use the following text: first line of headline – Fly With Us…; second line of headline – … We Have Your Ticket; body title – Starport Airlines; first paragraph of body copy – For the month of October, we are offering flights to 25 cities nationwide for the unbelievable rate of $100 per person round trip.; second paragraph of body copy – Take advantage of these low, low rates and make your travel arrangements now for a vacation, a business trip, or a family reunion.; last line – For reservations, call 555-9898. Use the concepts and techniques presented in this project to create and format this announcement. Ask your instructor if you should bullet the list of paragraphs of the body copy.

2 ◗ You have been assigned the task of preparing an announcement for the Lake Shore Carnival. The announcement contains a graphic of a carnival from the Clip Gallery. Use the following text: first line of headline – It's Time…; second line of headline – …for Our Carnival; body title – Lake Shore Carnival; first paragraph of body copy – Join us for fun, food, entertainment, crafts, contests, and rides at the Lake Shore Carnival on the weekend of July 21 and 22.; second paragraph of body copy – Admission is $10 per adult and $5 for children under 10 years old. Gates open at 8:00 a.m. each day and close at midnight.; last line – For information, call 555-9383. Use the concepts and techniques presented in this project to create and format this announcement. Ask your instructor if you should bullet the list of paragraphs of the body copy.

3 ◗◗ Your Uncle John, a graduate of Eagle High School, will be celebrating his twenty-fifth high school reunion this year. He has asked you to prepare an announcement that can be sent to each member of the graduating class. He asks that you include a graphic of the school's mascot, an eagle. The reunion will be held at Fisher Country Club and will feature live entertainment by The Jazzicians, a local band. The reunion will be held on Saturday, October 27. The doors open at 6:00 p.m. with dinner at 7:00 p.m., followed by entertainment from 8:00 p.m. until 11:00 p.m. Cost is $50 per person. Guests will have the opportunity to reminisce about old times, catch up on current projects, and share future plans. More information can be obtained by calling Sue Nordic at 555-9808. Use the concepts and techniques presented in this project to create the announcement. Ask your instructor if you should bullet the list of paragraphs of the body copy.

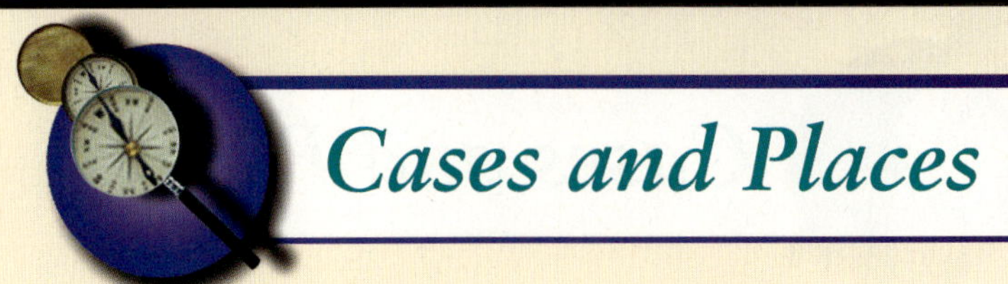

Cases and Places

4 ▶▶ Your parents own a campground called Quiet Oaks. With the new season just around the corner, they have asked you to prepare an announcement for their campground. Located at the intersection of I-293 and SR-35 in southern Louisiana, Quiet Oaks is a secluded campground situated in wooded, rolling hills. It has 75 paved pull-through sites and 46 gravel sites. All have city water and electric hook-ups. Facilities include restrooms, showers, dump, security, laundry, public telephone, and a data port. Recreation includes lake fishing, swimming pool, playground, horseshoes, and a game room. The campground is open from April 1 through October 31. Rates begin at $15 per night. Call 555-9393 for more information. Use the concepts and techniques presented in this project to create the announcement. Be sure to include an appropriate graphic from the Clip Gallery. Ask your instructor if you should bullet the list of paragraphs of the body copy.

5 ▶▶ You have a part-time job as the assistant to the Marketing Director at a new office supply store called Office World. The Director has asked you to prepare an announcement for the store's grand opening. Office World stocks thousands of office products including supplies, furniture, electronics, and computer software. Office World's low price guarantee states it will refund double a customer's money if the customer finds a comparable product for a lower price within ten days of purchase. Customers can purchase at the store, via fax or telephone, or on the Web at www.officeworld.com. Fax number is 555-2982 and telephone number is 555-2983. For purchases over $45.00, delivery is free. For a catalog, customers or potential customers can call 555-2900. Use the concepts and techniques presented in this project to create the announcement. Be sure to include an appropriate graphic from the Clip Gallery. Ask your instructor if you should bullet the list of paragraphs of the body copy.

6 ▶▶▶ Schools, churches, libraries, grocery stores, and other public places have bulletin boards for announcements and other postings. Often, these bulletin boards have so many announcements that some go unnoticed. At one of the above-mentioned organizations, find a posted announcement that you think might be overlooked. Copy the text from the announcement. Using this text, together with the techniques presented in this project, create an announcement that would be more likely to catch a reader's eye. Format the announcement effectively and include a bulleted list and suitable graphic from the Clip Gallery.

7 ▶▶▶ Advertisements are a company's way of announcing products or services to the public. You can find advertisements in printed media such as newspapers and magazines. Many companies also advertise on the World Wide Web. Find a printed advertisement or one on the Web that you feel lacks luster. Copy the text from the announcement. Using this text, together with the techniques presented in this project, create an announcement that would be more likely to catch a reader's eye. Format the announcement effectively and include a bulleted list and suitable graphic from the Clip Gallery.

Microsoft Word 2000

Creating a Research Paper

OBJECTIVES

You will have mastered the material in this project when you can:

- Describe the MLA documentation style for research papers
- Change the margin settings in a document
- Adjust line spacing in a document
- Use a header to number pages of a document
- Enter text using Click and Type
- Apply formatting using shortcut keys
- Indent paragraphs
- Use Word's AutoCorrect feature
- Add a footnote to a research paper
- Modify a style
- Insert a symbol automatically
- Insert a manual page break
- Create a hanging indent
- Create a hyperlink
- Sort selected paragraphs
- Go to a specific location in a document
- Find and replace text
- Move text
- Find a synonym for a word
- Count the words in a document
- Check spelling and grammar at once
- Display the Web site associated with a hyperlink
- E-mail a copy of a document

Elvis and Aliens Abound

Research Net Sources Carefully

The checkout line at your local grocery store is longer than the conga line at your best friend's wedding. You grab a cola and a bag of pretzels off the strategically placed displays. Then, as you shuffle to the registers, you decide to peruse the headlines of the magazines on display. You learn that two-headed aliens have abducted Elvis, that researchers are coming closer to finding a cure for the common cold, and that the Chicago Cubs are in contention for the National League pennant. Which stories do you believe? And what criteria do you use to make these decisions?

These questions are relevant not only at the grocery store but also in the computer lab. When you sit down and surf the Internet for the latest

news, celebrity sightings, sports scores, and reference sources, you make decisions on which sites to visit and which sites to avoid.

Not so long ago, students relied on books and magazines in the library for the bulk of their research material. These permanent sources were professionally evaluated and edited. Not so with the Internet. The Net is chock full of everything from reliable research to fictitious opinions. No one performs quality control checks to verify accuracy and reliability. Anyone can build a Web site and fill it with any content imaginable. And this content can be updated before your eyes.

In this project, you will create a research paper on the topic of Web publishing, which is the method of developing, maintaining, and posting Web pages. You will include a hyperlink that will permit you to navigate to a specific Internet site. Your Works Cited page will list the three sources used to obtain information for the paper. Two of these sources are books; one is an article available on the Shelly Cashman Series Web site (www.scsite.com). How can you judge the reliability of these materials, particularly the article posted on the Web? Just remember the three S's: structure, source, and style.

Structure – Does the information seem objective or biased? Are authorities used as sources? When was the site created or updated? Is a contact person listed so you can verify information? Are working hyperlinks provided that refer you to additional sources?

Source – Examine the Web address to find out the site's sponsor. Is it a nonprofit organization (.org), a school (.edu), the government (.gov), or a commercial business (.com)? Is the purpose of the site to provide information or to make a profit?

Style – Does the site look organized and professional? Can you navigate easily with a minimum of mouse clicks? Does it contain an index and the capability of searching for specific information?

William Miller, a former president of the Association of College and Research Libraries, says that on the Web, “Much of what purports to be serious information is simply junk – not current, objective, or trustworthy.” And by following the three S’s, you will be able to decide that neither Elvis’s abduction nor the Cubs’s pennant seems likely.

LYCOS.C
YAHOO.CO
NFOSEEK.C

Microsoft Word 2000

Creating a Research Paper

PROJECT 2

CASE PERSPECTIVE

Rick Williams is a full-time college student, majoring in Communications. Mr. Claremont, the instructor in his introductory computer class, has assigned a short research paper that must have a minimum of 425 words. The paper must discuss some aspect of computers and must be written according to the MLA documentation style, which specifies guidelines for report preparation. The paper must contain one footnote and three references – one of which must be obtained from the World Wide Web.

Rick's Internet service provider recently announced that all subscribers are entitled to 6 MB of free Web space for a personal Web page. Rick plans to publish his own Web page, so he decides to write the research paper on Web publishing. Rick intends to review computer magazines at the school's library, surf the Internet, contact his Internet service provider, and interview the Webmaster at his school for information on Web publishing. He also plans to use the Internet to obtain the guidelines for the MLA style of documentation. Because you are familiar with the Internet, Rick has asked you to assist him with the Web searches.

Introduction

In both academic and business environments, you will be asked to write reports. Business reports range from proposals to cost justifications to five-year plans to research findings. Academic reports focus mostly on research findings. Whether you are writing a business report or an academic report, you should follow a standard style when preparing it.

Many different styles of documentation exist for report preparation, depending on the nature of the report. Each style requires the same basic information; the differences among styles appear in the manner of presenting the information. For example, one documentation style may use the term *bibliography*, whereas another uses *references*, and yet a third prefers *works cited*. Two popular documentation styles for research papers are the **MLA** (**Modern Language Association of America**) and **APA** (**American Psychological Association**) styles. This project uses the MLA documentation style.

Project Two – Web Publishing Research Paper

Project 2 illustrates the creation of a short research paper describing Web publishing. As shown in Figure 2-1, the paper follows the MLA documentation style. The first two pages present the research paper and the third page lists the works cited alphabetically.

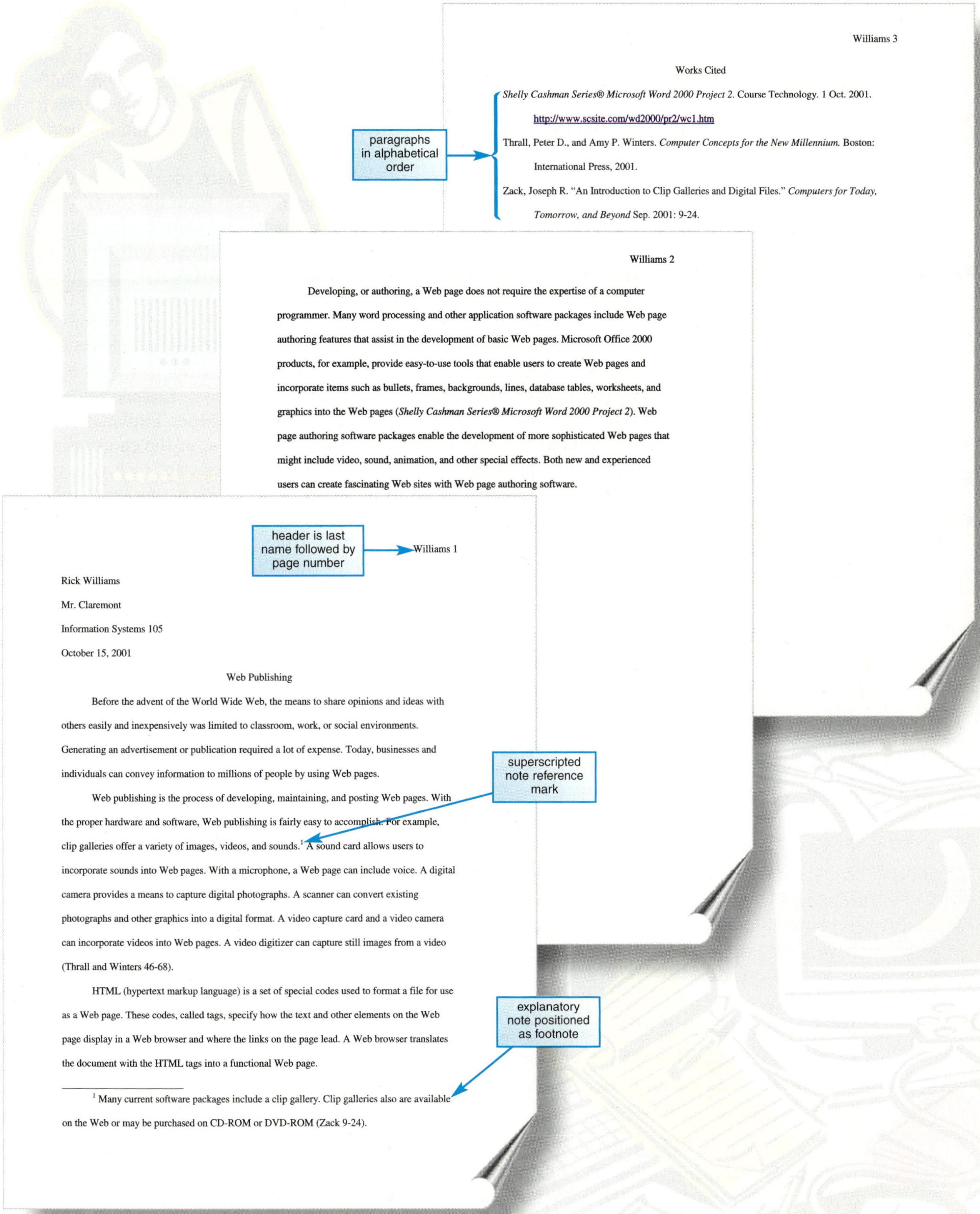

Williams 3

Works Cited

Shelly Cashman Series® Microsoft Word 2000 Project 2. Course Technology. 1 Oct. 2001. http://www.scsite.com/wd2000/pr2/wc1.htm

Thrall, Peter D., and Amy P. Winters. *Computer Concepts for the New Millennium.* Boston: International Press, 2001.

Zack, Joseph R. "An Introduction to Clip Galleries and Digital Files." *Computers for Today, Tomorrow, and Beyond* Sep. 2001: 9-24.

paragraphs in alphabetical order

Williams 2

Developing, or authoring, a Web page does not require the expertise of a computer programmer. Many word processing and other application software packages include Web page authoring features that assist in the development of basic Web pages. Microsoft Office 2000 products, for example, provide easy-to-use tools that enable users to create Web pages and incorporate items such as bullets, frames, backgrounds, lines, database tables, worksheets, and graphics into the Web pages (*Shelly Cashman Series® Microsoft Word 2000 Project 2*). Web page authoring software packages enable the development of more sophisticated Web pages that might include video, sound, animation, and other special effects. Both new and experienced users can create fascinating Web sites with Web page authoring software.

header is last name followed by page number

Williams 1

Rick Williams

Mr. Claremont

Information Systems 105

October 15, 2001

Web Publishing

Before the advent of the World Wide Web, the means to share opinions and ideas with others easily and inexpensively was limited to classroom, work, or social environments. Generating an advertisement or publication required a lot of expense. Today, businesses and individuals can convey information to millions of people by using Web pages.

Web publishing is the process of developing, maintaining, and posting Web pages. With the proper hardware and software, Web publishing is fairly easy to accomplish. For example, clip galleries offer a variety of images, videos, and sounds.[1] A sound card allows users to incorporate sounds into Web pages. With a microphone, a Web page can include voice. A digital camera provides a means to capture digital photographs. A scanner can convert existing photographs and other graphics into a digital format. A video capture card and a video camera can incorporate videos into Web pages. A video digitizer can capture still images from a video (Thrall and Winters 46-68).

superscripted note reference mark

HTML (hypertext markup language) is a set of special codes used to format a file for use as a Web page. These codes, called tags, specify how the text and other elements on the Web page display in a Web browser and where the links on the page lead. A Web browser translates the document with the HTML tags into a functional Web page.

explanatory note positioned as footnote

[1] Many current software packages include a clip gallery. Clip galleries also are available on the Web or may be purchased on CD-ROM or DVD-ROM (Zack 9-24).

FIGURE 2-1

MLA and APA

The MLA documentation style is the standard in the humanities, and the APA style is preferred in the social sciences. For more information from the MLA about its guidelines, visit the Word 2000 More About Web page (www.scsite.com/wd2000/more.htm) and then click MLA. For more information from the APA about its guidelines, visit the Word 2000 More About Web page (www.scsite.com/wd2000/more.htm) and then click APA.

APA Style

In the APA style, double-space all pages of the paper with 1.5" top, bottom, left, and right margins. Indent the first word of each paragraph .5" from the left margin. In the upper-right margin of each page, place a running head that consists of the page number double-spaced below a summary of the paper title.

MLA Documentation Style

When writing papers, you should adhere to some style of documentation. The research paper in this project follows the guidelines presented by the MLA. To follow the MLA style, double-space text on all pages of the paper with one-inch top, bottom, left, and right margins. Indent the first word of each paragraph one-half inch from the left margin. At the right margin of each page, place a page number one-half inch from the top margin. On each page, precede the page number by your last name.

The MLA style does not require a title page; instead, place your name and course information in a block at the left margin beginning one inch from the top of the page. Center the title one double-space below your name and course information.

In the body of the paper, place author references in parentheses with the page number(s) where the referenced information is located. The MLA style uses these in-text **parenthetical citations** instead of footnoting each source at the bottom of the page or at the end of the paper. In the MLA style, footnotes are used only for explanatory notes. In the body of the paper, use **superscripts** (raised numbers) for **note reference marks**, which signal that an explanatory note exists.

According to the MLA style, explanatory notes are optional. **Explanatory notes** are used to elaborate on points discussed in the body of the paper. Explanatory notes may be placed either at the bottom of the page as footnotes or at the end of the paper as endnotes. Double-space the explanatory notes. Superscript each note reference mark, and indent it one-half inch from the left margin. Place one space following the note reference mark before beginning the note text. At the end of the note text, you may list bibliographic information for further reference.

The MLA style uses the term **works cited** for the bibliographical references. The works cited page alphabetically lists works that are referenced directly in the paper by each author's last name, or, if the author's name is not available, by the title of the work. Place the works cited on a separate numbered page. Center the title, Works Cited, one inch from the top margin. Double-space all lines. Begin the first line of each entry at the left margin; indent subsequent lines of the same entry one-half inch from the left margin.

Starting Word

Follow these steps to start Word or ask your instructor how to start Word for your system.

TO START WORD

1. Click the Start button on the taskbar.
2. Click New Office Document on the Start menu. If necessary, click the General tab when the New Office Document dialog box first displays.
3. Double-click the Blank Document icon in the General sheet.
4. If the Word window is not maximized, double-click its title bar to maximize it. If the Office Assistant displays, right-click it and then click Hide on the shortcut menu.

Office starts Word. After a few moments, an empty document titled Document1 displays in the Word window (Figure 2-2 on page WD 2.8). If your screen differs from Figure 2-2, click View on the menu bar and then click Normal.

Resetting Menus and Toolbars

To set the menus and toolbars so they appear exactly as shown in this book, you should reset your menus and toolbars as outlined in Appendix C or follow these steps.

TO RESET MENUS AND TOOLBARS

1. Click View on the menu bar and then point to Toolbars. Click Customize on the Toolbars submenu.
2. When the Customize dialog box displays, click the Options tab, make sure the top three check boxes have check marks and then click the Reset my usage data button. When the Microsoft Word dialog box displays, click the Yes button.
3. Click the Toolbars tab. Click Standard in the Toolbars list and then click the Reset button. When the Reset Toolbar dialog box displays, click the OK button.
4. Click Formatting in the Toolbars list and then click the Reset button. When the Reset Toolbar dialog box displays, click the OK button. Click the Close button.

Word resets the menus and toolbars.

More About

Writing Papers

The World Wide Web contains a host of information, tips, and suggestions on writing research papers. College professors and fellow students develop many of these Web pages. For a list of Web links to sites on writing research papers, visit the Word 2000 More About Web page (www.scsite.com/wd2000/more.htm) and then click Links to Sites on Writing Research Papers.

Displaying Formatting Marks

As discussed Project 1, it is helpful to display **formatting marks** that indicate where in the document you pressed the ENTER key, SPACEBAR, and other keys. Follow this step to display formatting marks.

TO DISPLAY FORMATTING MARKS

1. Double-click the move handle on the Standard toolbar to display the entire toolbar. If the Show/Hide ¶ button on the Standard toolbar is not already recessed, click it.

Word displays formatting marks in the document window, and the Show/Hide ¶ button on the Standard toolbar is recessed (Figure 2-2 on the next page).

Changing the Margins

Word is preset to use standard 8.5-by-11-inch paper, with 1.25-inch left and right margins and 1-inch top and bottom margins. These margin settings affect every page in the document. Often, you may want to change these default margin settings. You have learned that the MLA documentation style requires one-inch top, bottom, left, and right margins throughout the paper.

The steps on the next page illustrate how to change the margin settings for a document when your screen is in normal view. To verify your screen is in normal view, click View on the menu bar and then click Normal.

Changing Margins

In print layout view, you can change margins using the horizontal and vertical rulers. Current margin settings are shaded in gray. The margin boundary is located where the gray meets the white. To change a margin, drag the margin boundary. Hold down the ALT key while dragging the margin boundary to display the margin settings.

Steps To Change the Margin Settings

1 Click File on the menu bar and then point to Page Setup (Figure 2-2).

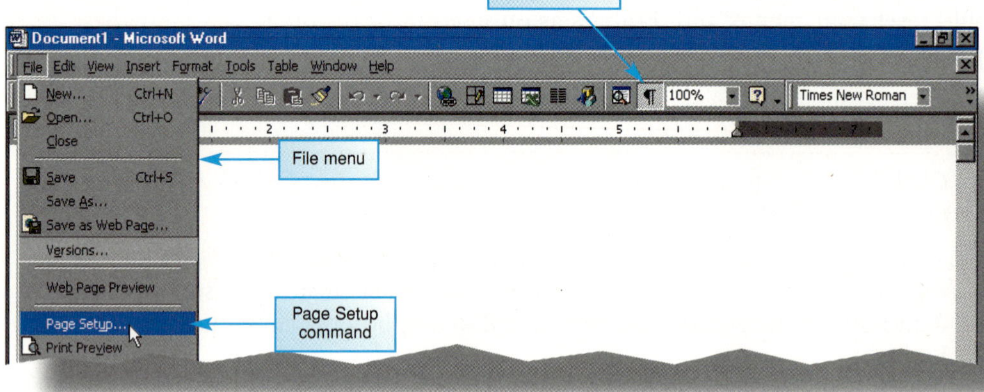

FIGURE 2-2

2 Click Page Setup. If necessary, click the Margins tab when the Page Setup dialog box first displays.

Word displays the Page Setup dialog box (Figure 2-3). Word lists the current margin settings in the text boxes.

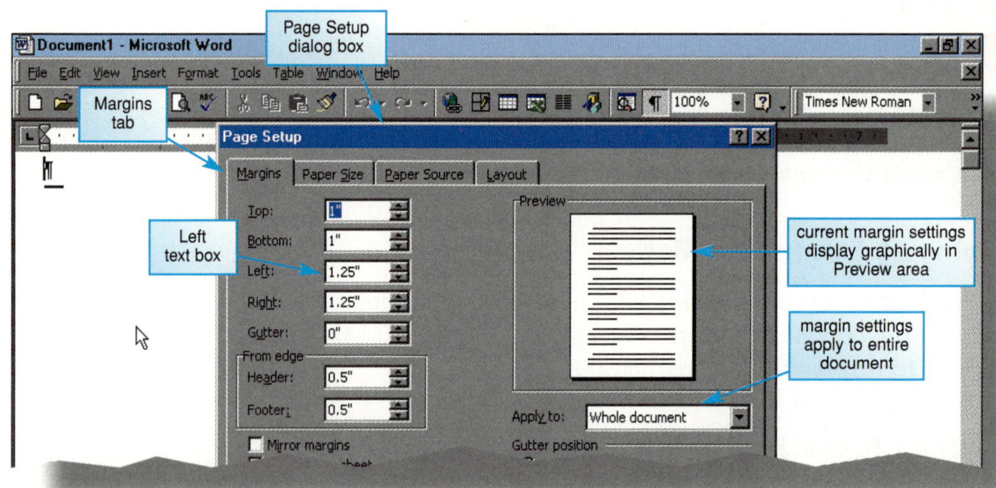

FIGURE 2-3

3 Drag through the text in the Left text box to highlight 1.25". Type 1 and then press the TAB key. Type 1 and then point to the OK button.

The new left and right margin settings are 1 inch (Figure 2-4).

4 Click the OK button.

Word changes the left and right margins.

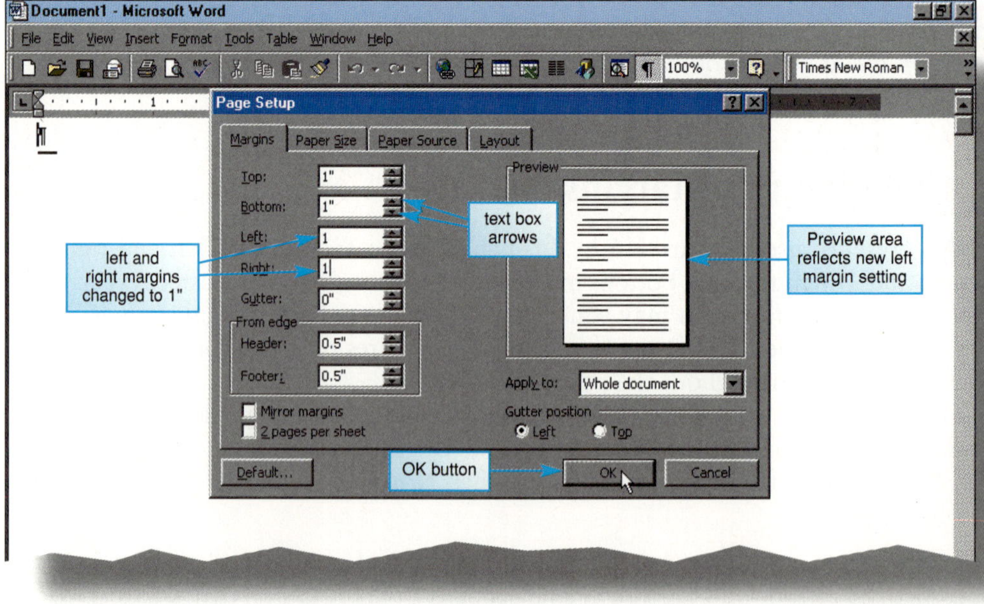

FIGURE 2-4

Other Ways

1. In print layout view, drag margin boundary(s) on ruler

The new margin settings take effect in the document immediately, and Word uses these margins for the entire document.

When you change the margin settings in the text boxes in the Page Setup dialog box, the Preview area (Figure 2-4) does not adjust to reflect a changed margin setting until the insertion point leaves the respective text box. That is, you must press the TAB or ENTER key or click in another text box if you want to view the changes in the Preview area.

Zooming Page Width

As you learned in Project 1, when you **zoom page width**, Word displays text on the screen as large as possible without extending the right margin beyond the right edge of the document window. Perform the following steps to zoom page width.

TO ZOOM PAGE WIDTH

1. Click the Zoom box arrow on the Standard toolbar.
2. Click Page Width in the Zoom list.

Word extends the right margin to the right edge of the document window (Figure 2-5). Word computes the zoom percentage based on a variety of settings. Your percentage may be different depending on your system configuration.

Line Spacing

Sometimes, the top of characters or a graphic is chopped off. This occurs when the line spacing is set to Exactly. To remedy the problem, change the line spacing to Single, 1.5 lines, Double, or At least in the Paragraph dialog box, all of which accommodate the largest font or graphic.

Adjusting Line Spacing

Line spacing is the amount of vertical space between lines of text in a document. Word, by default, single-spaces between lines of text and automatically adjusts line height to accommodate various font sizes and graphics. The MLA documentation style requires that you **double-space** the entire paper; that is, one blank line should display between each line of text. Thus, you must adjust the line spacing from single to double as described in the following steps.

Steps To Double-Space a Document

1. **Right-click the paragraph mark above the end mark in the document window. Point to Paragraph on the shortcut menu (Figure 2-5).**

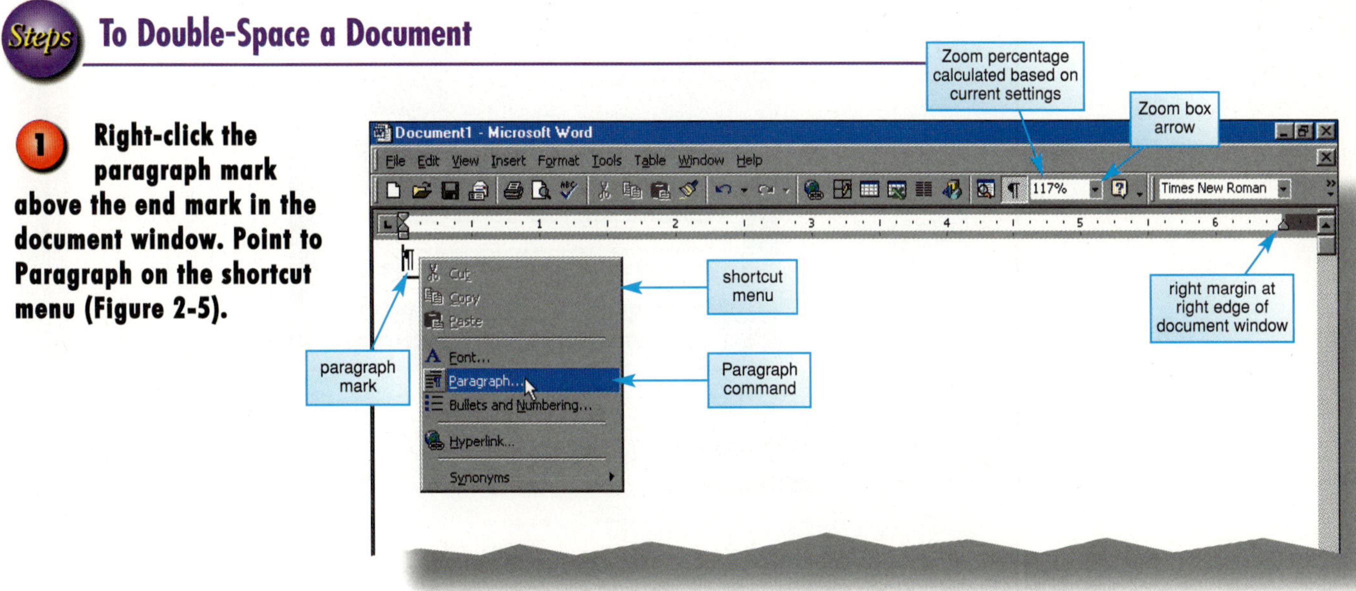

FIGURE 2-5

Click Paragraph. If necessary, click the Indents and Spacing tab when the Paragraph dialog box first displays. Click the Line spacing box arrow and then point to Double.

Word displays the Paragraph dialog box, which lists the current settings in the text boxes and displays them graphically in the Preview area (Figure 2-6). A list of available line spacing options displays.

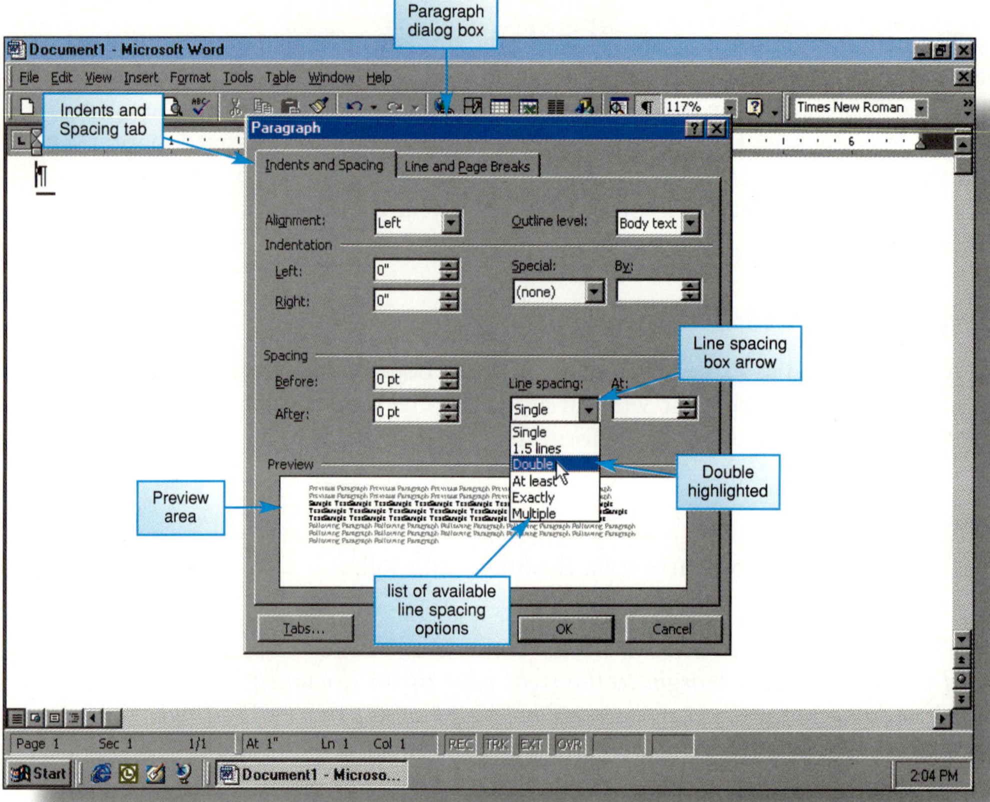

FIGURE 2-6

3 **Click Double. Point to the OK button.**

Word displays Double in the Line spacing box and graphically portrays the new line spacing in the Preview area (Figure 2-7).

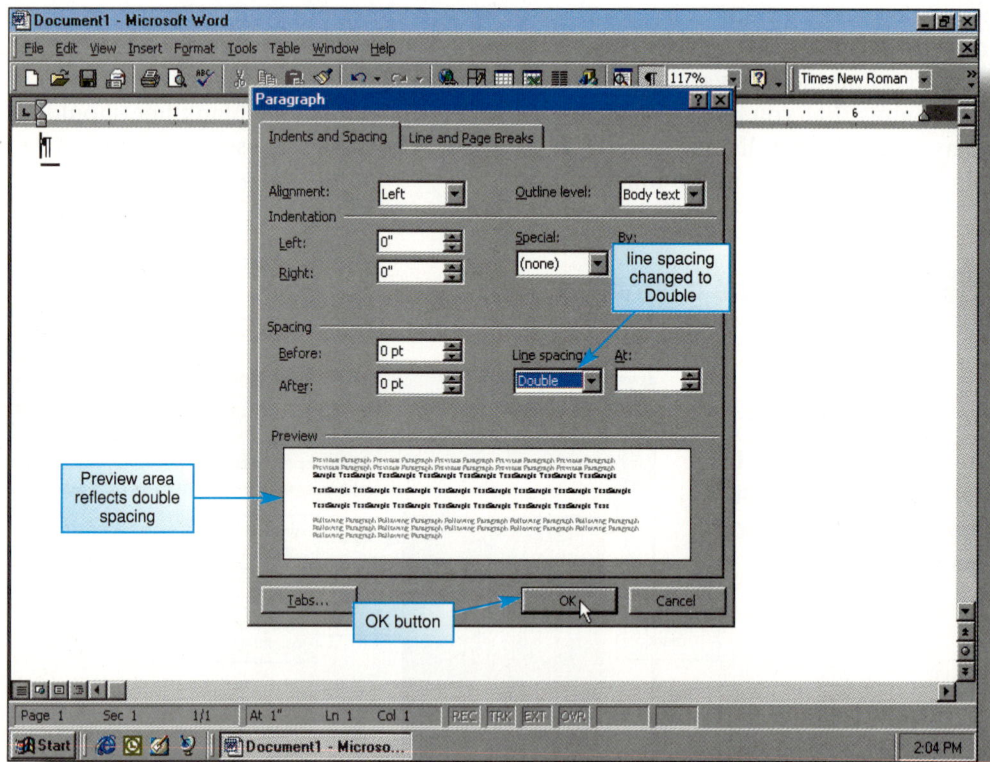

FIGURE 2-7

Click the OK button.

Word changes the line spacing to double in the current document (Figure 2-8).

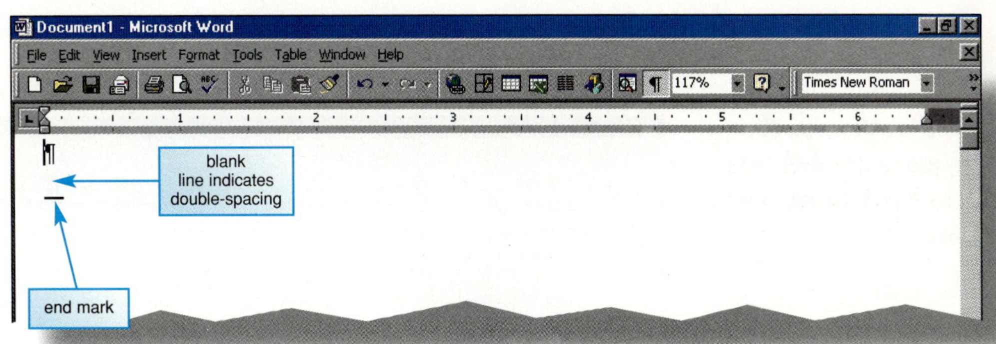

FIGURE 2-8

Notice that when line spacing is double (Figure 2-8), the end mark is positioned one blank line below the insertion point.

The Line spacing list (Figure 2-6) contains a variety of settings for the line spacing. The default, Single, and the options 1.5 lines and Double instruct Word to adjust line spacing automatically to accommodate the largest font or graphic on a line. The next two options, At least and Exactly, enable you to specify a line spacing not provided in the first three options. The difference is that the At least option instructs Word to increase the designation if necessary, whereas the Exactly option does not allow Word to increase the specification to accommodate larger fonts or graphics. With the last option, Multiple, you enter a value, which represents a percentage by which Word should increase or decrease the line spacing. For example, with the number 1 representing single-spacing, a multiple of 1.3 increases the line spacing by 30 percent and a multiple of .8 decreases the line spacing by 20 percent.

Other Ways

1. On Format menu click Paragraph, click Indents and Spacing tab, click Line spacing box arrow, click Double, click OK button
2. Press CTRL+2

Data and Statistics

When researching for a paper, you may need to access data, graphs of data, or perform statistical computations on data. For more information on statistical formulas and available data and graphs, visit the Word 2000 More About Web page (www.scsite.com/wd2000/more.htm) and then click Data and Statistics.

Using a Header to Number Pages

In Word, you can number pages easily by clicking Insert on the menu bar and then clicking Page Numbers. Using the Page Numbers command, you can specify the location (top or bottom of page) and alignment (right, left, or centered) of the page numbers. You cannot, however, place your name as required by the MLA style in front of the page number with the Page Numbers command. To place your name in front of the page number, you must create a header that contains the page number.

Headers and Footers

A **header** is text you want printed at the top of each page in the document. A **footer** is text you want printed at the bottom of every page. In Word, headers are printed in the top margin one-half inch from the top of every page, and footers are printed in the bottom margin one-half inch from the bottom of each page, which meets the MLA style. Headers and footers can include text and graphics, as well as the page number, total number of pages, current date, and current time.

In this project, you are to precede the page number with your last name placed one-half inch from the top of each page. Your name and the page number should print right-aligned; that is, at the right margin.

To create the header, first you display the header area in the document window and then you can enter the header text into the header area. Use the procedures on the following pages to create the header with page numbers according to the MLA documentation style.

To Display the Header Area

1 Click View on the menu bar and then point to Header and Footer (Figure 2-9).

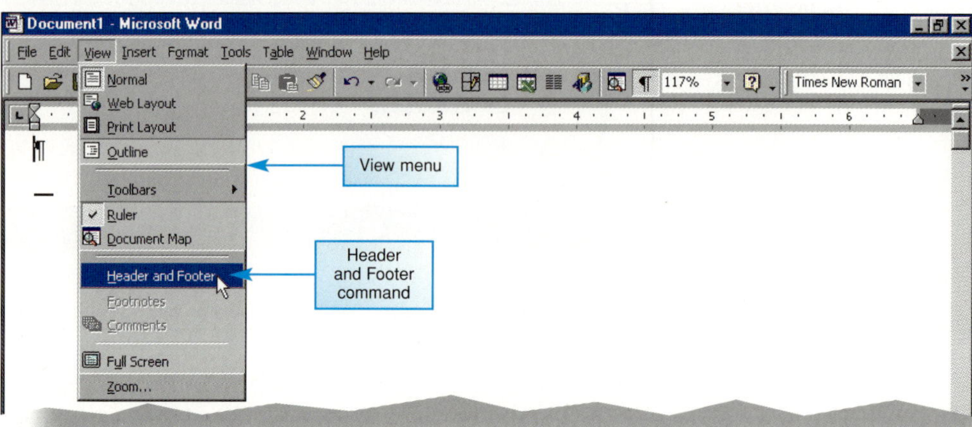

FIGURE 2-9

2 Click Header and Footer.

Word switches from normal view to print layout view and displays the ***Header and Footer toolbar*** *(Figure 2-10). You type header text in the* ***header area****.*

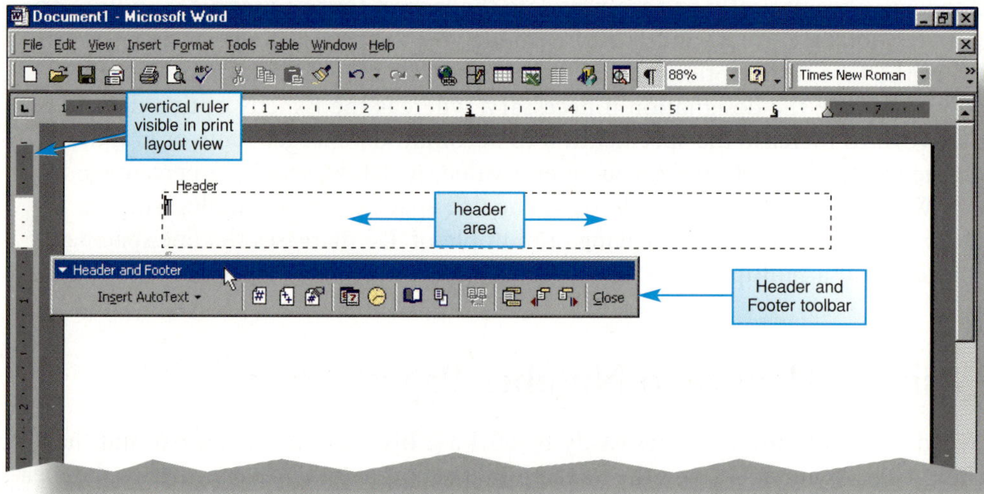

FIGURE 2-10

More About

Print Layout View

You also can switch to print layout view by clicking the Print Layout View button on the horizontal scroll bar. Print layout view shows the positioning of headers, footers, and footnotes. To move forward or backward an entire page, click the double arrows on the bottom of the vertical scroll bar.

The Header and Footer toolbar initially floats in the document window. To move a floating toolbar, drag its title bar. You can **dock**, or attach, a floating toolbar below the Standard and Formatting toolbars by double-clicking the floating toolbar's title bar. To move a docked toolbar, drag its move handle. Recall that the move handle is the vertical bar to the left of the first button on a toolbar. If you drag a floating toolbar to an edge of the window, the toolbar snaps to the edge of the window. If you drag a docked toolbar to the middle of the window, the toolbar floats in the Word window. If you double-click between two buttons or boxes on a docked toolbar, it floats in its original floating position.

The header area does not display on the screen when the document window is in normal view because it tends to clutter the screen. To display the header in the document window with the rest of the text, you must display the document in print preview, which is discussed in a later project, or switch to print layout view. When you click the Header and Footer command on the View menu, Word automatically switches to **print layout view**, which displays the document exactly as it will print.

Entering Text using Click and Type

When in print layout view, you can use **Click and Type** to format and enter text, graphics, and other items. To use Click and Type, you double-click a blank area of the document window. Word automatically formats the item you enter according to the location where you double-click. Perform the following steps to use Click and Type to right-align and then enter the last name into the header area.

Click and Type

Click and Type is not available in normal view, in a bulleted or numbered list, or in a document formatted into multiple columns.

To Click and Type

1 Point to right edge of the header area so a right-align icon displays next to the I-beam.

As you move the Click and Type pointer around the window, the icon changes to represent formatting that will be applied if you double-click at that location (Figure 2-11).

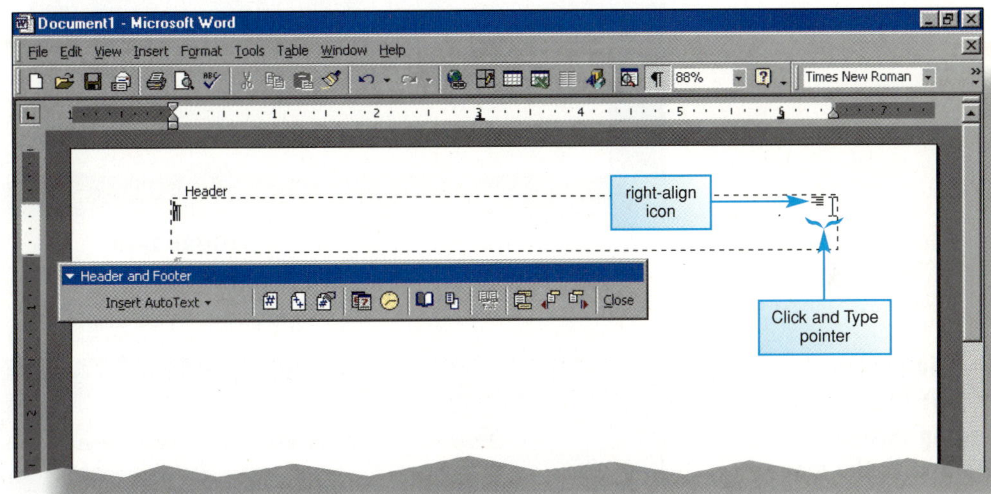

FIGURE 2-11

2 Double-click. Type `Williams` and then press the SPACEBAR.

Word displays the last name, Williams, right-aligned in the header area (Figure 2-12).

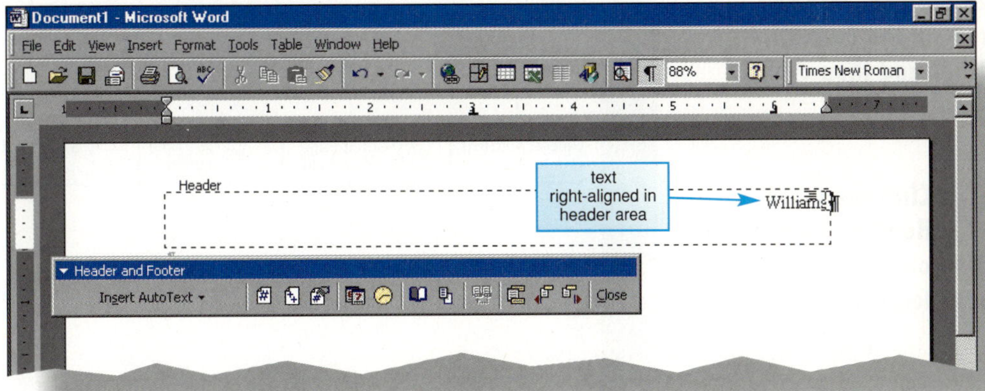

FIGURE 2-12

The next step is to enter the page number into the header area and then format it.

Entering a Page Number into the Header

Word formats the text in the header area using the current font size. Perform the steps on the next page to enter a page number into the header area and then, if necessary, format the entire line of text to 12 point.

To Enter and Format a Page Number

1 Click the Insert Page Number button on the Header and Footer toolbar.

Word displays the page number 1 in the header area (Figure 2-13).

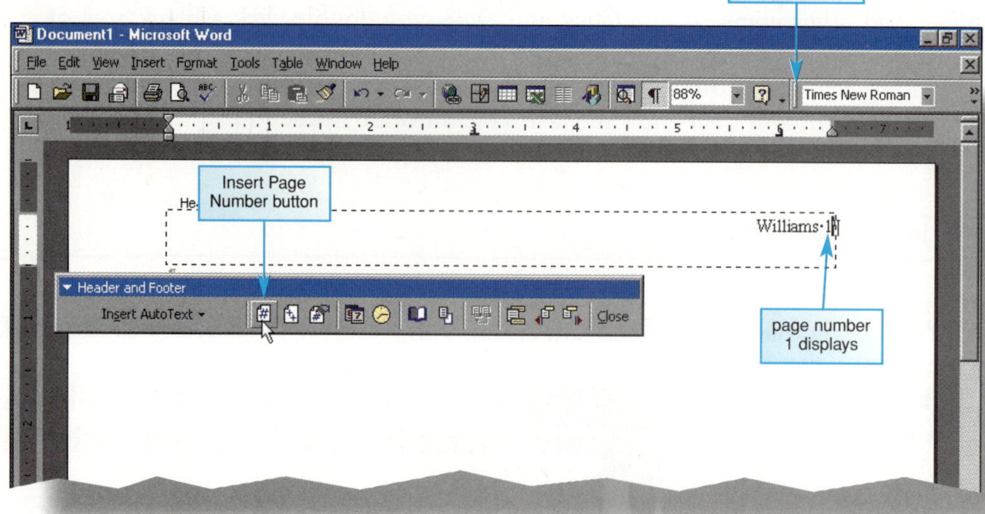

FIGURE 2-13

2 Select the text, Williams 1, by dragging through it. Double-click the move handle on the Formatting toolbar to display the entire toolbar. If necessary, click the Font Size box arrow on the Formatting toolbar and then click 12 (Figure 2-14).

3 Click the Close Header and Footer button on the Header and Footer toolbar.

Word closes the Header and Footer toolbar and returns the screen to normal view (see Figure 2-15 on page WD 2.16).

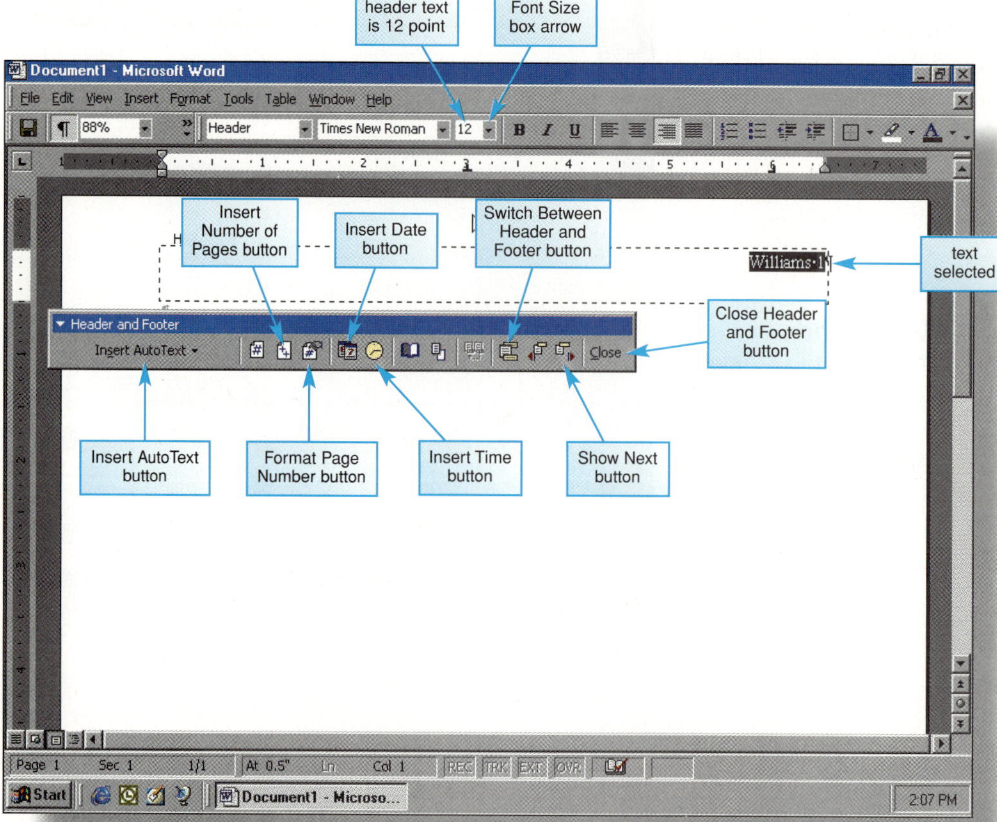

FIGURE 2-14

Other Ways

1. On Insert menu click Page Numbers, click OK button

Just as the Insert Page Number button on the Header and Footer toolbar inserts the page number into the document, three other buttons on the Header and Footer toolbar (Figure 2-14) insert items into the document. The Insert Number of Pages button inserts the total number of pages in the document; the Insert Date button inserts the current date into the document; and the Insert Time button inserts the current time.

To edit an existing header, you can follow the same procedure that you use to create a new header. That is, click View on the menu bar and then click Header and Footer to display the header area; or switch to print layout view by clicking the Print Layout View button on the horizontal scroll bar and then double-click the dimmed header. If you have multiple headers, click the Show Next button on the Header and Footer toolbar (Figure 2-14) until the appropriate header displays in the header area. Edit the header as you would any Word text and then click the Close Header and Footer button on the Header and Footer toolbar.

To create a footer, click View on the menu bar, click Header and Footer, click the Switch Between Header and Footer button on the Header and Footer toolbar, and then follow the same procedure as you would to create a header.

Writing Papers

When preparing to write a paper, many students take notes to keep track of information. One method is to summarize, or condense, the information. Another is to paraphrase, or rewrite the information in your own words. A third method is to quote, or record, the exact words of the original. Be sure to use quotation marks when directly quoting a source.

Typing the Body of the Research Paper

The body of the research paper encompasses the first two pages in Figure 2-1 on page WD 2.5. The steps on the following pages illustrate how to enter the body of the research paper.

Changing the Default Font Size

You learned in Project 1 that depending on how Word 2000 was installed on your computer, your default font size might be either 10 or 12. A font size of 10 point is difficult for some people to read. In this project, all characters in all paragraphs should be a font size of 12. If your default font size is 10, perform the following steps to change it to 12.

TO CHANGE THE DEFAULT FONT SIZE

1. If necessary, click the Font Size box arrow on the Formatting toolbar.
2. Click 12.

Word changes the font size to 12 (Figure 2-15 on the next page).

APA Guidelines

APA guidelines require a title page as a separate page of a research paper, instead of placing name and course information on the paper's first page. The running head (a brief summary of the title and the page number) also is on the title page, along with the page number 1.

Entering Name and Course Information

You have learned that the MLA style does not require a separate title page for research papers. Instead, place your name and course information in a block at the top of the page at the left margin. Thus, follow the step on the next page to begin entering the body of the research paper.

Steps To Enter Name and Course Information

1 **Type** `Rick Williams` **and then press the ENTER key. Type** `Mr. Claremont` **and then press the ENTER key. Type** `Information Systems 105` **and then press the ENTER key. Type** `October 15, 2001` **and then press the ENTER key.**

The student name displays on line 1, the professor name on line 2, the course name on line 3, and the paper due date on line 4 (Figure 2-15).

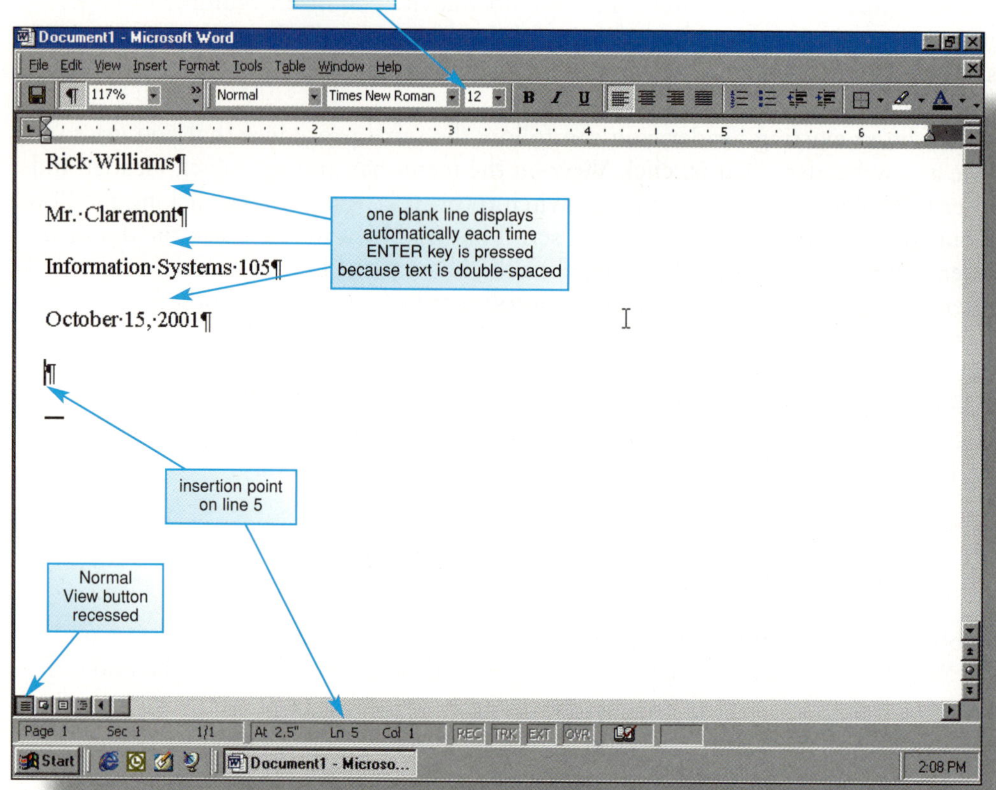

FIGURE 2-15

Notice in Figure 2-15 that the insertion point currently is on line 5. Each time you press the ENTER key, Word advances two lines on the screen, but increments the line counter on the status bar by only one because earlier you set line spacing to double.

If you watch the screen as you type, you may have noticed that as you typed the first few characters in the month, Octo, Word displayed the **AutoComplete tip**, October, above the characters. To save typing, you could press the ENTER key while the AutoComplete tip displays, which instructs Word to place the text of the AutoComplete tip at the location of your typing.

> **More About 2000**
>
> **Shortcut Keys**
>
> To print a complete list of shortcut keys for formatting, do the following. Click the Office Assistant, type `formatting keys` and then click the Search button. Scroll through the list and then click Format characters and paragraphs. In the Help window, click the Print button and then click the OK button.

Applying Formatting Using Shortcut Keys

The next step is to enter the title of the research paper centered between the page margins. As you type text, you may want to format paragraphs and characters as you type them, instead of entering them and then formatting them later. In Project 1, you typed the characters in the document and then selected the ones to be formatted and applied the desired formatting using toolbar buttons. When your fingers are already on the keyboard, it sometimes is more efficient to use **shortcut keys**, or key z board key combinations, to format text as you type it. Perform the following steps to center a paragraph with the CTRL+E keys and then left-align a paragraph with the CTRL+L keys. (Recall from Project 1 that a notation such as CTRL+E means to press the letter E while holding the CTRL key.)

To Use Shortcut Keys to Format Text

1 Press the CTRL+E keys. Type `Web Publishing` **and then press the ENTER key.**

Word centers the title between the left and right margins (Figure 2-16). The paragraph mark and insertion point are centered because the formatting specified in the previous paragraph is carried forward to the next paragraph.

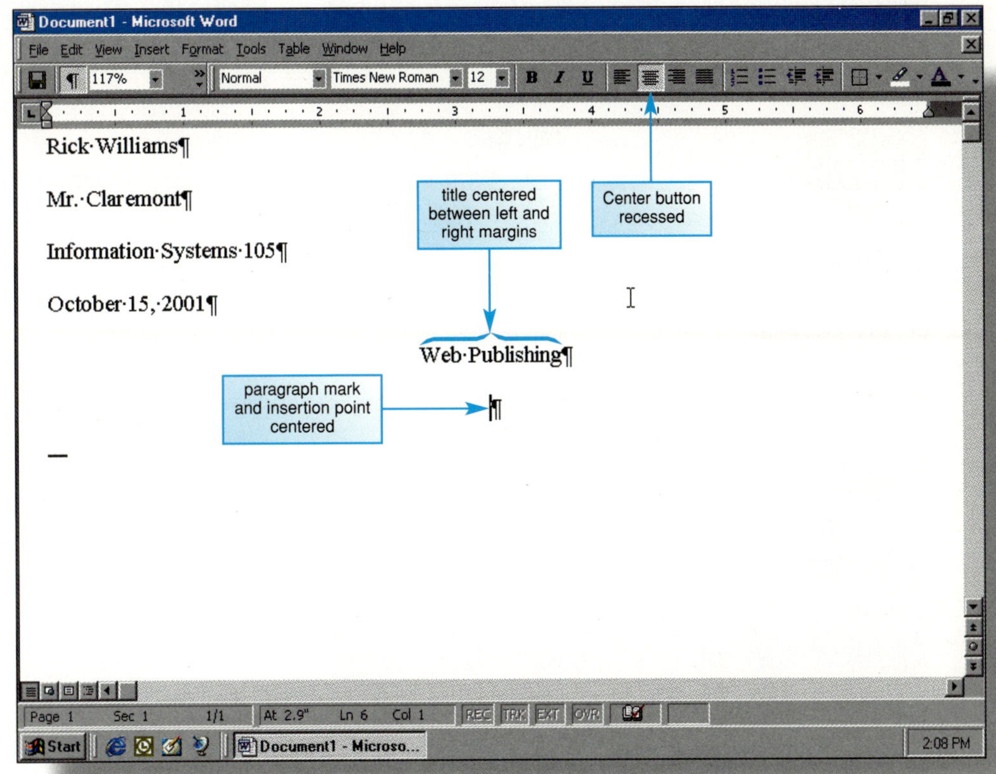

FIGURE 2-16

Press the CTRL+L keys.

Word positions the paragraph mark and the insertion point at the left margin (Figure 2-17). The next text you type will be left-aligned.

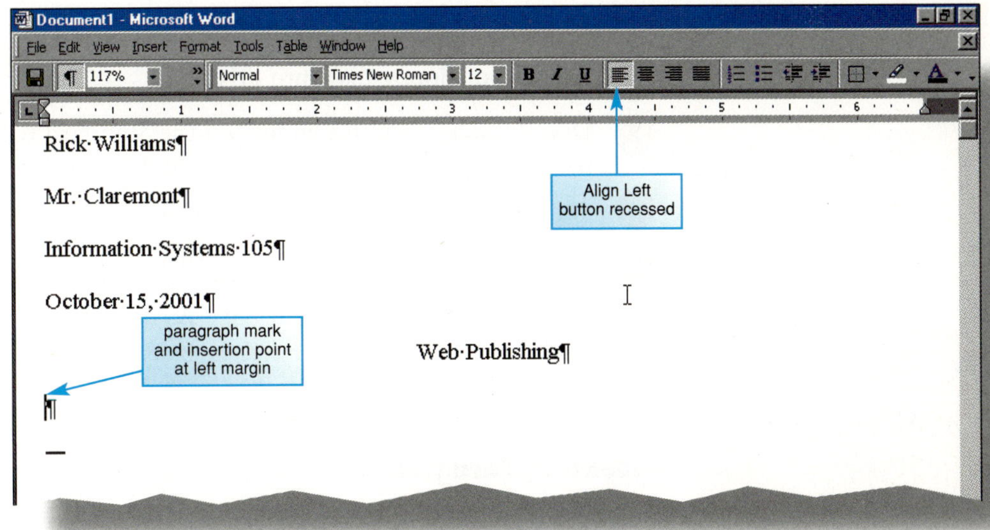

FIGURE 2-17

Word has many shortcut keys for your convenience while typing. Table 2-1 on the next page lists the common shortcut keys for formatting characters, and Table 2-2 on the next page lists common shortcut keys for formatting paragraphs.

Table 2-1 Shortcut Keys for Formatting Characters

CHARACTER FORMATTING TASK	SHORTCUT KEYS
All capital letters	CTRL+SHIFT+A
Bold	CTRL+B
Case of letters	SHIFT+F3
Decrease font size	CTRL+SHIFT+<
Decrease font size 1 point	CTRL+[
Double-underline	CTRL+SHIFT+D
Increase font size	CTRL+SHIFT+>
Increase font size 1 point	CTRL+]
Italic	CTRL+I
Remove character formatting (plain text)	CTRL+SPACEBAR
Small uppercase letters	CTRL+SHIFT+K
Subscript	CTRL+=
Superscript	CTRL+SHIFT+PLUS SIGN
Underline	CTRL+U
Underline words, not spaces	CTRL+SHIFT+W

Table 2-2 Shortcut Keys for Formatting Paragraphs

PARAGRAPH FORMATTING TASK	SHORTCUT KEYS
1.5 line spacing	CTRL+5
Add/remove one line above	CTRL+0
Center paragraph	CTRL+E
Decrease paragraph indent	CTRL+SHIFT+M
Double-space lines	CTRL+2
Hanging indent	CTRL+T
Increase paragraph indent	CTRL+M
Justify paragraph	CTRL+J
Left-align paragraph	CTRL+L
Remove hanging indent	CTRL+SHIFT+T
Remove paragraph formatting	CTRL+Q
Right-align paragraph	CTRL+R
Single-space lines	CTRL+1

Saving the Research Paper

You should save your research paper. For a detailed example of the procedure summarized below, refer to pages WD 1.26 through WD 1.28 in Project 1.

TO SAVE A DOCUMENT

1. Insert your floppy disk into drive A.
2. Double-click the move handle on the Standard toolbar to display the entire toolbar. Click the Save button on the Standard toolbar.
3. Type the file name `Web Publishing Paper` in the File name text box.
4. Click the Save in box arrow and then click 3½ Floppy (A:).
5. Click the Save button in the Save As dialog box.

Word saves your document with the name Web Publishing Paper (Figure 2-18).

First-Line Indent

You may be tempted to use the TAB key to indent the first line of each paragraph in your research paper. Using the TAB key for this task is inefficient because you must press it each time you begin a new paragraph. First-line indent is a paragraph format; thus, it is carried forward automatically each time you press the ENTER key.

Indenting Paragraphs

According to the MLA style, the first line of each paragraph in the research paper is to be indented one-half inch from the left margin. This procedure, called **first-line indent**, can be accomplished using the horizontal ruler. The **First Line Indent marker** is the top triangle at the 0" mark on the ruler (Figure 2-18). The small square at the 0" mark is the **Left Indent marker**. The Left Indent marker is used to change the entire left margin, whereas the First Line Indent marker affects only the first line of the paragraph. Perform the following steps to first-line indent the paragraphs in the research paper.

Steps To First-Line Indent Paragraphs

1 With the insertion point on the paragraph mark in line 6, point to the First Line Indent marker on the ruler (Figure 2-18).

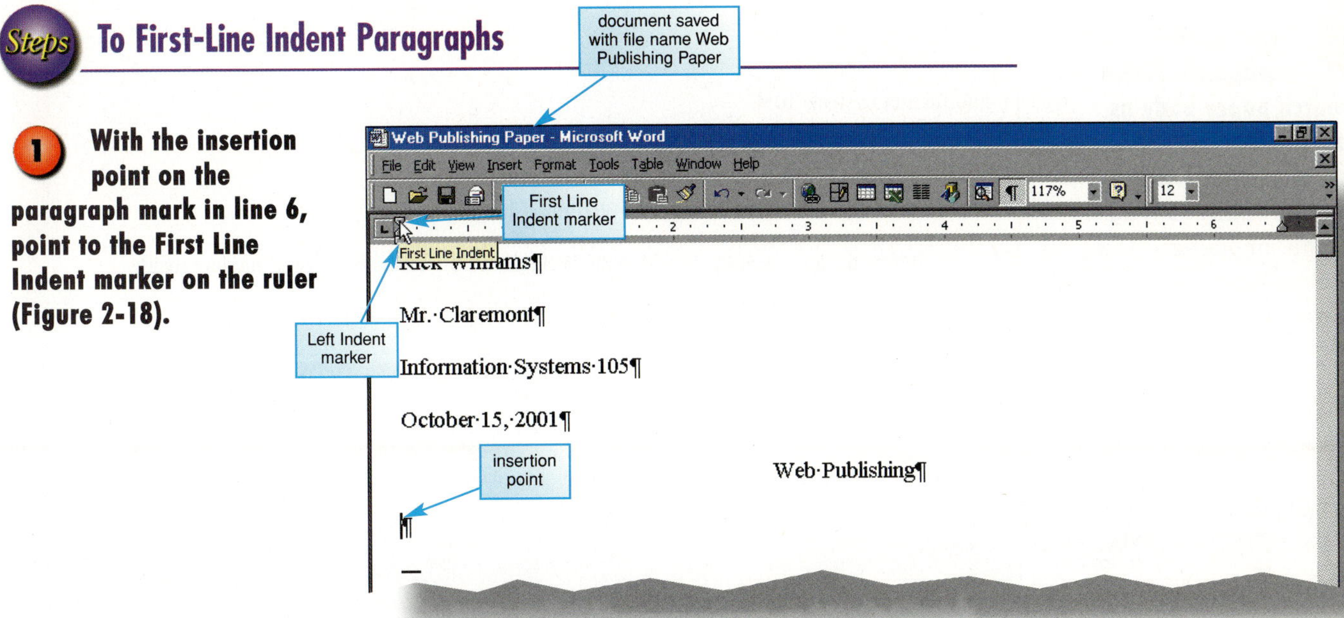

FIGURE 2-18

2 Drag the First Line Indent marker to the .5" mark on the ruler.

As you drag the mouse, a vertical dotted line displays in the document window, indicating the proposed location of the first line of the paragraph (Figure 2-19).

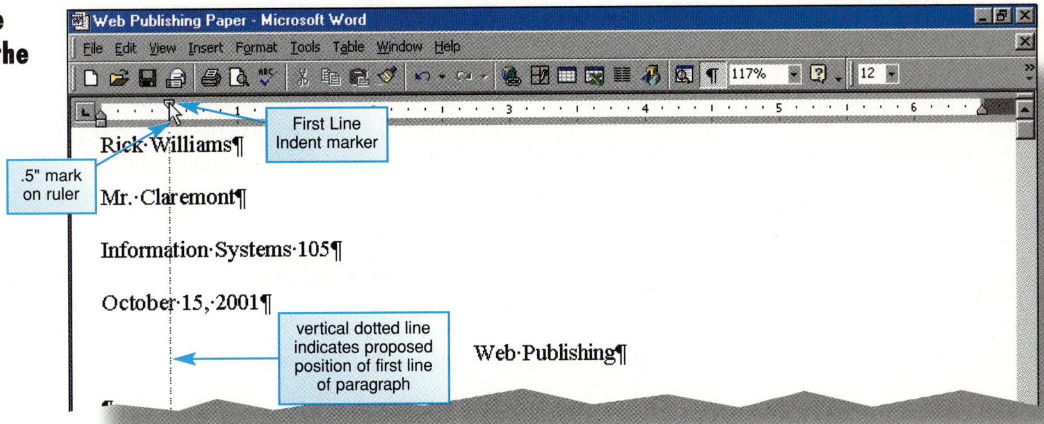

FIGURE 2-19

3 Release the mouse button.

The First Line Indent marker displays at the .5" mark on the ruler, or one-half inch from the left margin (Figure 2-20). The paragraph mark containing the insertion point in the document window also moves one-half inch to the right.

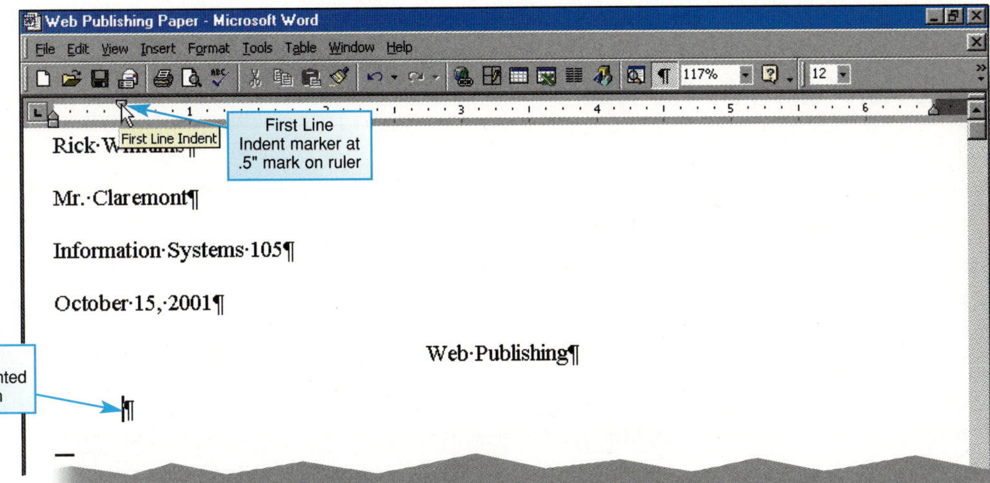

FIGURE 2-20

4 **Type the first paragraph of the research paper body as shown in Figure 2-21. Press the ENTER key. Type** `Web publishing is the process of developing, maintaining, and posting Web pages.`

Word automatically indents the first line of the second paragraph by one-half inch (Figure 2-21).

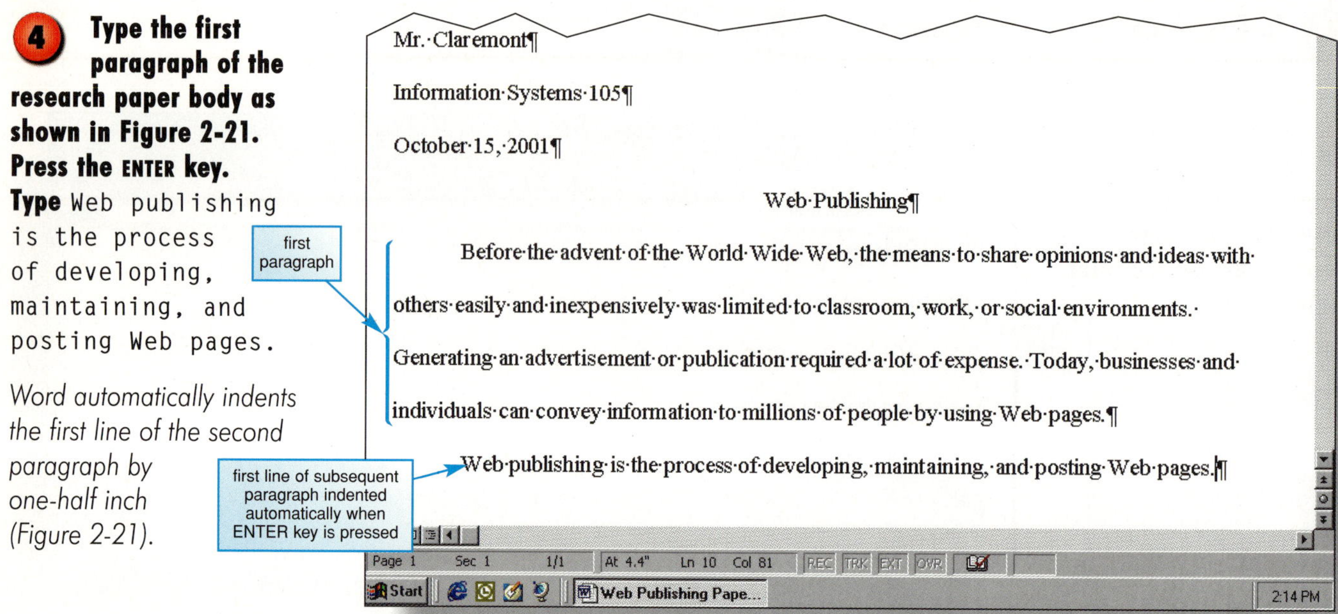

Mr. Claremont
Information Systems 105
October 15, 2001
Web Publishing
Before the advent of the World Wide Web, the means to share opinions and ideas with others easily and inexpensively was limited to classroom, work, or social environments. Generating an advertisement or publication required a lot of expense. Today, businesses and individuals can convey information to millions of people by using Web pages.
Web publishing is the process of developing, maintaining, and posting Web pages.
first paragraph
first line of subsequent paragraph indented automatically when ENTER key is pressed
Page 1 Sec 1 1/1 At 4.4" Ln 10 Col 81
Start
Web Publishing Pape...
2:14 PM

FIGURE 2-21

Other Ways

1. Right-click paragraph, click Paragraph on shortcut menu, click Indents and Spacing tab, click Special box arrow, click First line, click OK button
2. On Format menu click Paragraph, click Indents and Spacing tab, click Special box arrow, click First line, click OK button

Recall that each time you press the ENTER key, the paragraph formatting in the previous paragraph is carried forward to the next paragraph. Thus, once you set the first-line indent, its format is carried automatically to each subsequent paragraph you type.

Using Word's AutoCorrect Feature

Because you may make typing, spelling, capitalization, or grammar errors as you type, Word provides an **AutoCorrect** feature that automatically corrects these errors as you type them into the document. For example, if you type the text, ahve, Word automatically changes it to the word, have, for you when you press the SPACEBAR or a punctuation mark key. Word has predefined many commonly misspelled words, which it automatically corrects for you. Perform the following steps to use the AutoCorrect as you type feature.

To AutoCorrect As You Type

1 **Press the SPACEBAR. Type the beginning of the next sentence and misspell the word, accomplish, as follows:** `With the proper hardware and software, Web publishing is fairly easy to acomplish` **as shown in Figure 2-22.**

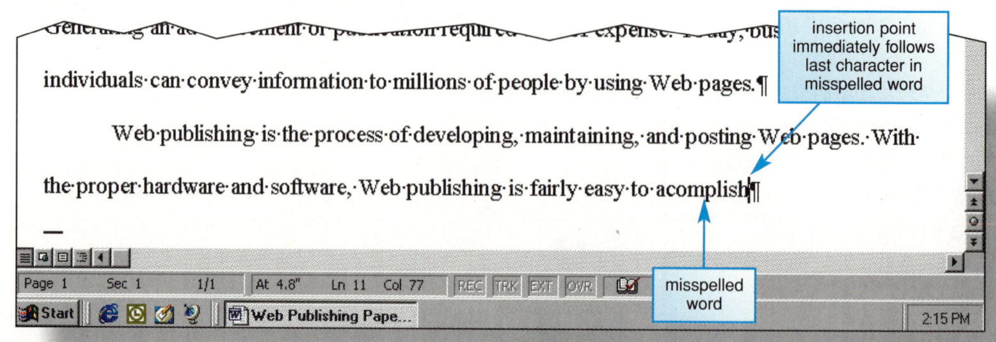

FIGURE 2-22

Press the PERIOD key.

As soon as you press the PERIOD key, Word's AutoCorrect feature detects the misspelling and corrects the misspelled word (Figure 2-23).

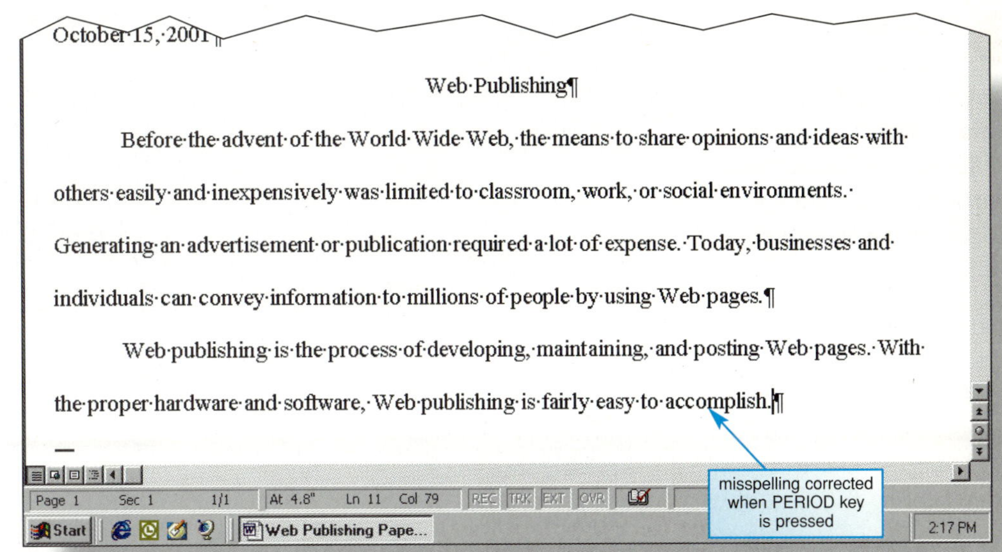
October 15, 2001
Web Publishing¶
Before the advent of the World Wide Web, the means to share opinions and ideas with others easily and inexpensively was limited to classroom, work, or social environments. Generating an advertisement or publication required a lot of expense. Today, businesses and individuals can convey information to millions of people by using Web pages.¶
Web publishing is the process of developing, maintaining, and posting Web pages. With the proper hardware and software, Web publishing is fairly easy to accomplish.¶
misspelling corrected when PERIOD key is pressed
Page 1 Sec 1 1/1 At 4.8" Ln 11 Col 79
Start
Web Publishing Pape...
2:17 PM

FIGURE 2-23

Word has a list of predefined typing, spelling, capitalization, and grammar errors that AutoCorrect can detect and correct. In addition to the predefined list, you can create your own AutoCorrect entries to add to the list. For example, if you often misspell the word, camera, as canera, you should create an AutoCorrect entry for it as shown in these steps.

To Create an AutoCorrect Entry

1 Click Tools on the menu bar and then point to AutoCorrect (Figure 2-24).

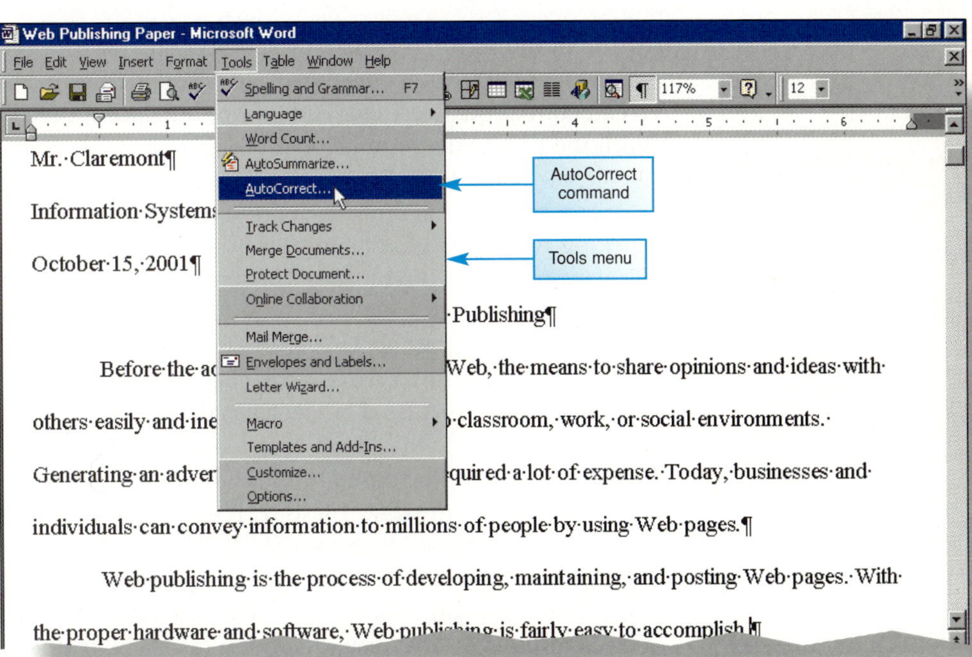
Web Publishing Paper - Microsoft Word
File Edit View Insert Format Tools Table Window Help
Spelling and Grammar... F7
Language
Word Count...
AutoSummarize...
AutoCorrect...
Track Changes
Merge Documents...
Protect Document...
Online Collaboration
Mail Merge...
Envelopes and Labels...
Letter Wizard...
Macro
Templates and Add-Ins...
Customize...
Options...
AutoCorrect command
Tools menu
Mr. Claremont¶
Information Systems
October 15, 2001¶
Publishing¶

FIGURE 2-24

2 Click AutoCorrect. When the AutoCorrect dialog box displays, type `canera` **in the Replace text box. Press the TAB key and then type** `camera` **in the With text box.**

Word displays the AutoCorrect dialog box. The Replace text box contains the misspelled word, and the With text box contains its correct spelling (Figure 2-25).

3 Click the Add button. (If your dialog box displays a Replace button instead, click it and then click the Yes button in the Microsoft Word dialog box.) Click the OK button.

Word adds the entry alphabetically to the list of words to correct automatically as you type.

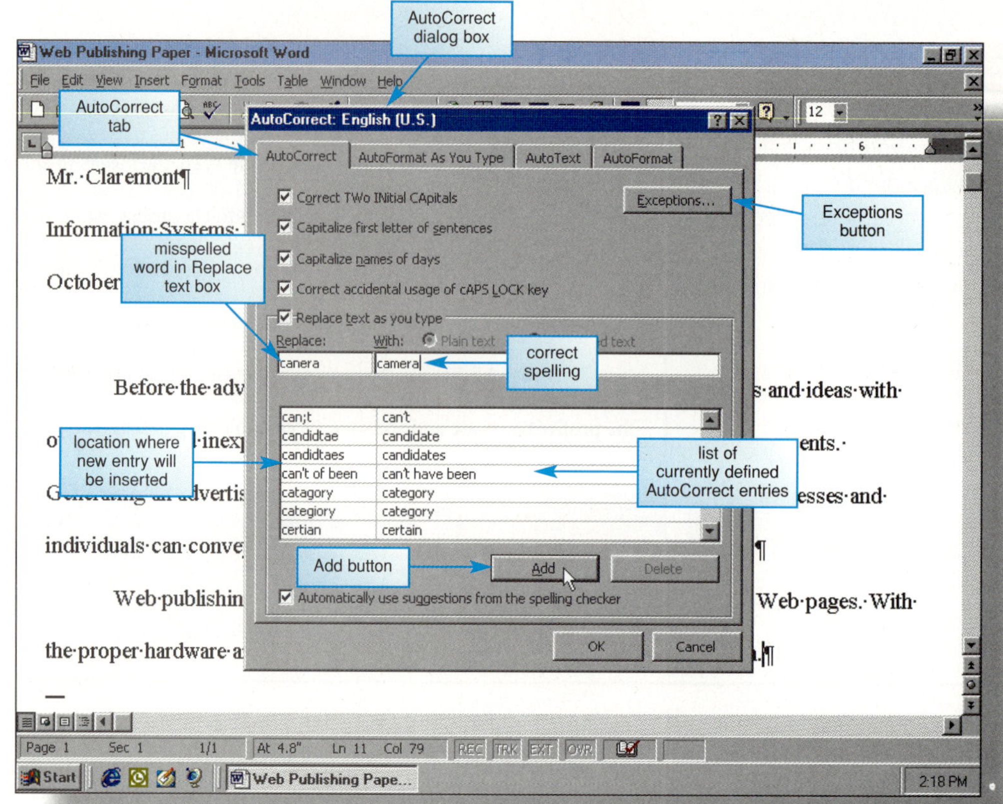

FIGURE 2-25

AutoCorrect

If you have installed the Microsoft Office 2000 Proofing Tools and have enabled editing for another language, Word automatically can detect the language you are using to create the document - as you type. These Proofing Tools provide fonts and templates, check spelling and grammar, and include AutoCorrect lists.

In addition to creating AutoCorrect entries for words you commonly misspell, you can create entries for abbreviations, codes, and so on. For example, you could create an AutoCorrect entry for asap, indicating that Word should replace this text with the phrase, as soon as possible.

If, for some reason, you do not want Word to correct automatically as you type, you can turn off the replace as you type feature by clicking Tools on the menu bar, clicking AutoCorrect, clicking the AutoCorrect tab (Figure 2-25), clicking the Replace text as you type check box to remove the check mark, and then clicking the OK button.

The AutoCorrect sheet (Figure 2-25) also contains four other check boxes that correct capitalization errors if the check boxes are selected. If you type two capital letters in a row such as TH, Word makes the second letter lowercase, Th. If you begin a sentence with a lowercase letter, Word capitalizes the first letter of the sentence. If you type the name of a day in lowercase such as tuesday, Word capitalizes the first letter of the day, Tuesday. Finally, if you leave the CAPS LOCK key on and begin a new sentence such as aFTER, Word corrects the typing, After, and turns off the CAPS LOCK key.

Sometimes you do not want Word to AutoCorrect a particular word or phrase. For example, you may use the code WD. in your documents. Because Word automatically capitalizes the first letter of a sentence, the character you enter following the period will be capitalized (in the previous sentence, it would capitalize the letter i in the word, in). To allow the code WD. to be entered into a document and still leave the AutoCorrect feature turned on, you need to set an exception. To set an exception to an AutoCorrect rule, click Tools on the menu bar, click AutoCorrect, click the AutoCorrect tab, click the Exceptions button in the AutoCorrect sheet (Figure 2-25), click the appropriate tab in the AutoCorrect Exceptions dialog box, type the exception entry in the text box, click the Add button, click the Close button in the AutoCorrect Exceptions dialog box, and then click the Close button in the AutoCorrect dialog box.

Adding Footnotes

You have learned that explanatory notes are optional in the MLA documentation style. They are used primarily to elaborate on points discussed in the body of the paper. The style specifies that a superscript (raised number) be used for a note reference mark to signal that an explanatory note exists either at the bottom of the page as a **footnote** or at the end of the document as an **endnote.**

Word, by default, places notes at the bottom of each page. In Word, **note text** can be any length and format. Word automatically numbers notes sequentially for you by placing a **note reference mark** in the body of the document and also in front of the note text. If you insert, rearrange, or remove notes, any subsequent note text and reference marks are renumbered according to their new sequence in the document. Perform the following steps to add a footnote to the research paper.

MLA and APA

Both the MLA and APA guidelines suggest the use of in-text parenthetical citations, as opposed to footnoting each source of material in a paper. These parenthetical acknowledgments guide the reader to the end of the paper for complete information on the source.

To Add a Footnote

1 **Press the SPACEBAR and then type** `For example, clip galleries offer a variety of images, videos, and sounds.` **Click Insert on the menu bar and then point to Footnote.**

The insertion point is positioned immediately after the period following the end of the sentence (Figure 2-26).

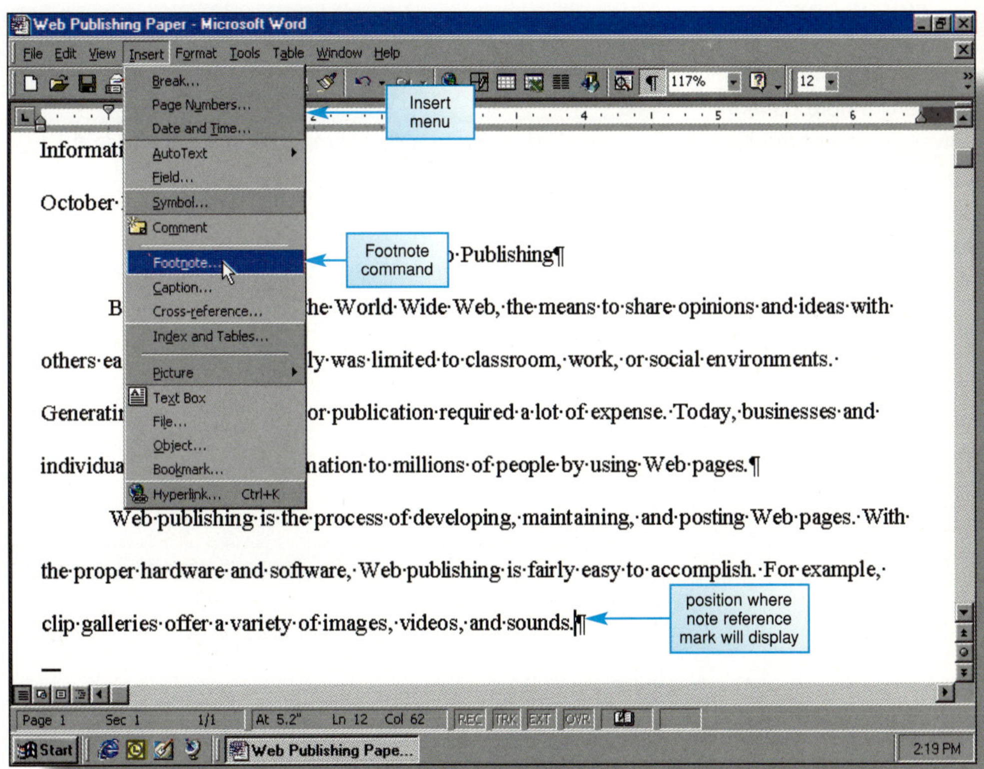

FIGURE 2-26

2 Click Footnote. When the Footnote and Endnote dialog box displays, point to the OK button.

Word displays the Footnote and Endnote dialog box (Figure 2-27).

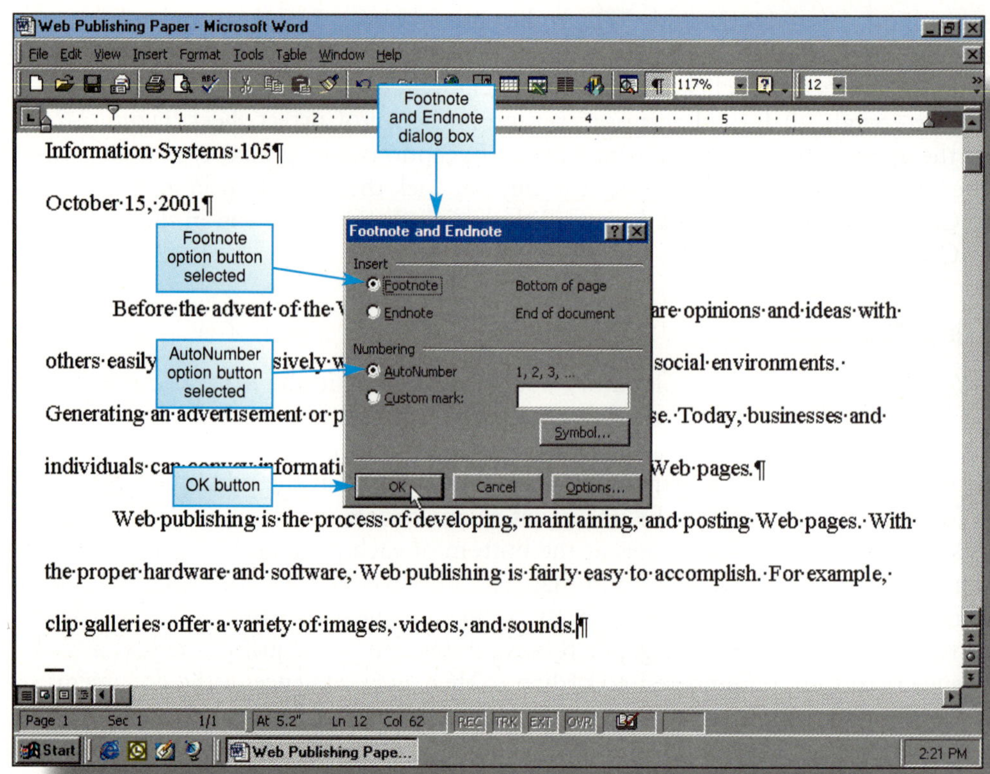

FIGURE 2-27

3 Click the OK button.

Word opens a ***note pane*** *in the lower portion of the Word window with the note reference mark (a superscripted 1) positioned at the left margin of the note pane (Figure 2-28). The note reference mark also displays in the document window at the location of the insertion point. Note reference marks are, by default, superscripted; that is, raised above other letters.*

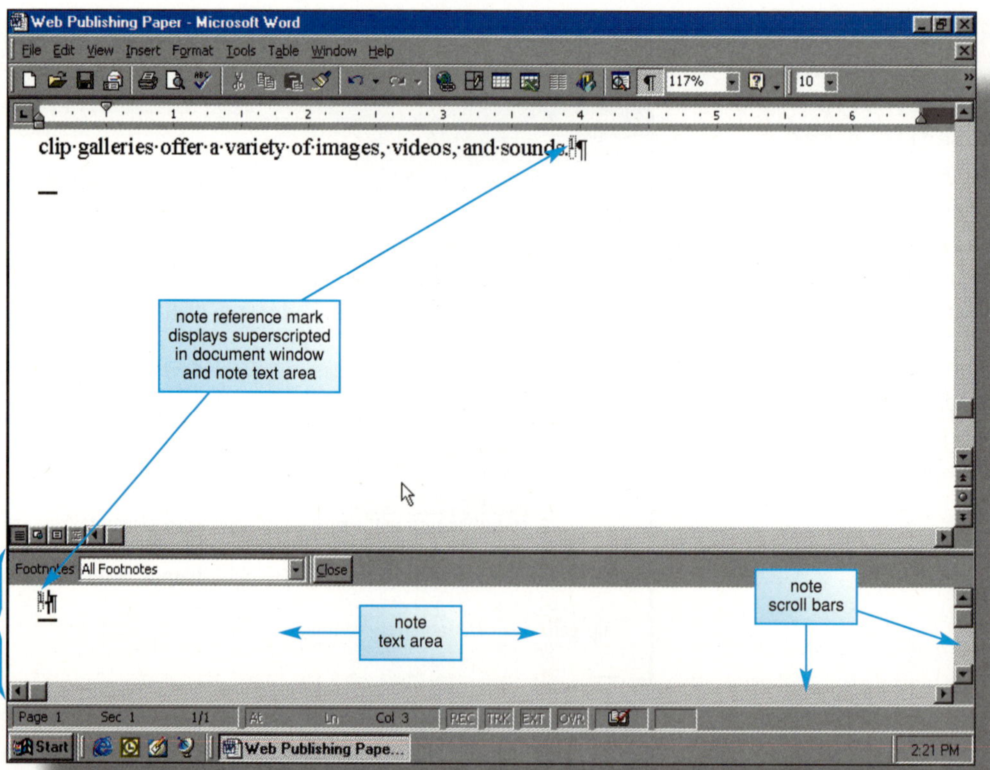

FIGURE 2-28

4 **Type** `Many current software packages include a clip gallery. Clip galleries also are available on the Web or may be purchased on CD-ROM or DVD-ROM (Zack 9-24).`

Word enters the note text in the note pane (Figure 2-29).

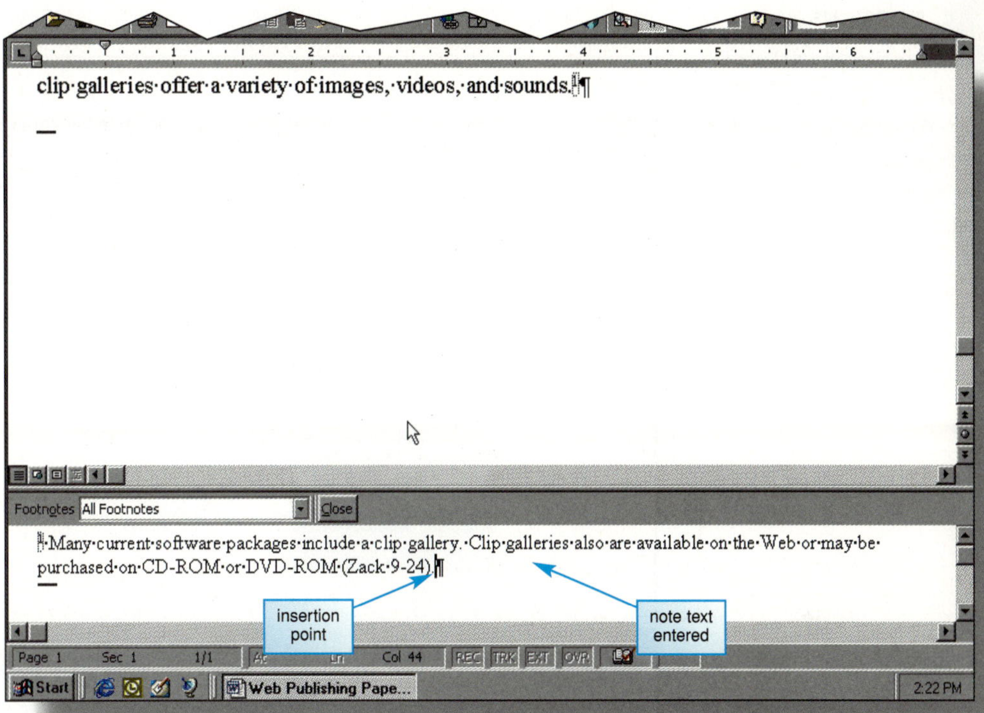

FIGURE 2-29

The footnote is not formatted according to the MLA style. Thus, the next step is to modify the style of the footnote.

Modifying a Style

A **style** is a customized format that you can apply to text. The formats defined by a style include character formatting such as the font and font size, and paragraph formatting such as line spacing and text alignment. Word has many built-in, or predefined, styles that you may use to format text. You can modify the formatting associated with these styles, or you can define new styles.

The base style for new Word documents is called the **Normal style**, which for a new installation of Word 2000 more than likely uses 12-point Times New Roman font for characters and single-spaced, left-aligned paragraphs. Recall from Project 1 that when you upgrade to Word 2000 from a previous version of Word, the default point size more than likely is 10 instead of 12.

In Figure 2-29, the insertion point is in the note text area, which is formatted using the Footnote Text style. The Footnote Text style is based on the Normal style. Thus, the text of the footnote you entered is single-spaced and left-aligned.

You could change the paragraph formatting of the footnote text to first-line indent and double-spacing as you did for the text in the document window. If you use this technique, however, you will have to change the format of the footnote text for each footnote you enter into the document. A more efficient technique is to modify the format of the Footnote Text style so paragraphs based on this style are double-spaced with a first-line indent format. Thus, by changing the formatting associated with the Footnote Text style, every footnote you enter will use the formats defined in this style. Perform the steps on the next page to modify the Footnote Text style.

More About 2000

Styles

The Style box on the Formatting toolbar displays the name of the style associated with the location of the insertion point. Click the Style box arrow on the Formatting toolbar to view the list of styles associated with the current document. To apply a style, select the text to format, click the Style box arrow, and then click the desired style name in the list.

To Modify a Style

1 **Click Format on the menu bar and then point to Style (Figure 2-30).**

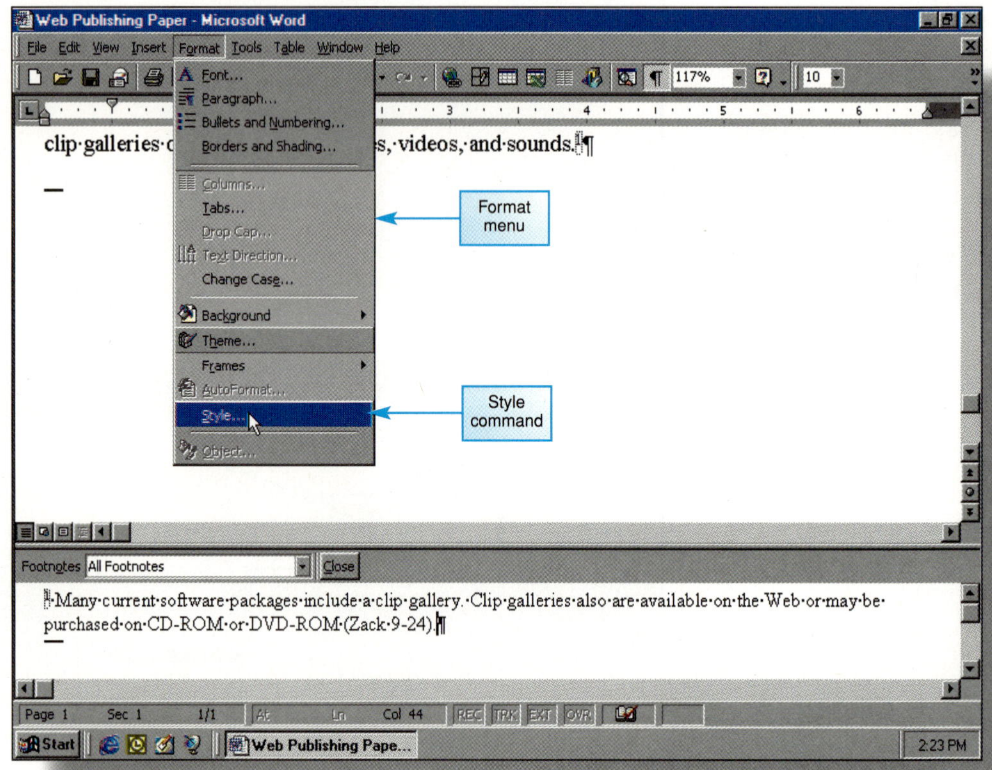

FIGURE 2-30

2 **Click Style. When the Style dialog box displays, click Footnote Text in the Styles list, if necessary, and then point to the Modify button.**

Word displays the Style dialog box (Figure 2-31). Footnote Text is highlighted in the Styles list. The Description area shows the formatting associated with the selected style.

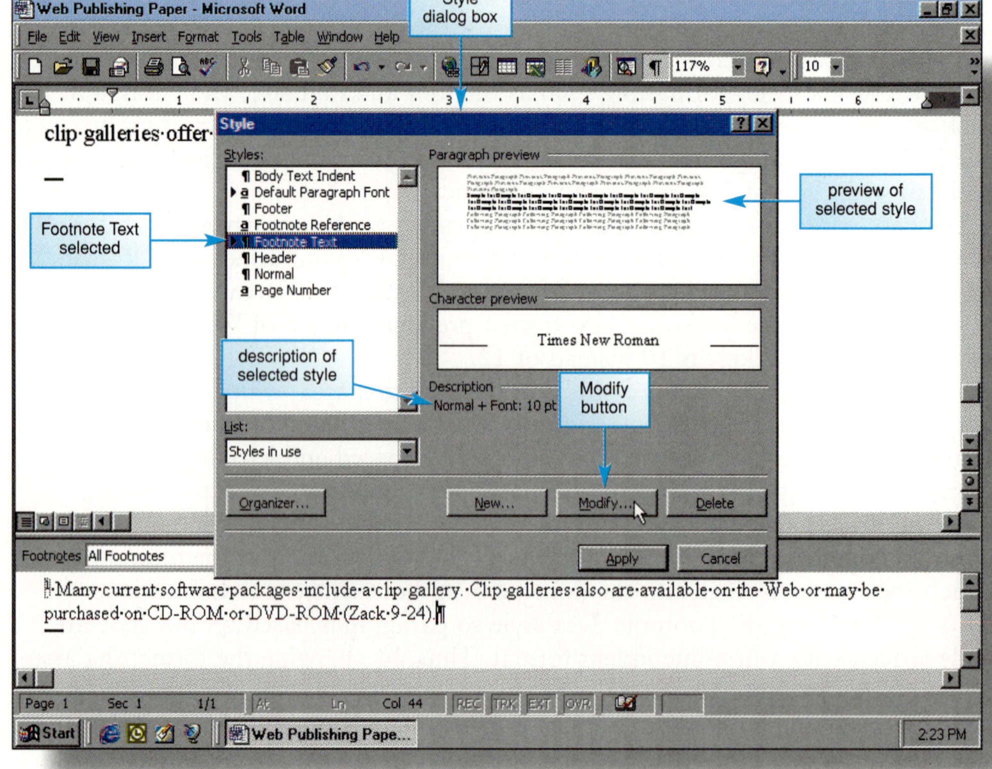

FIGURE 2-31

3 Click the Modify button. When the Modify Style dialog box displays, click the Format button and then point to Paragraph.

Word displays the Modify Style dialog box (Figure 2-32). A list of formatting commands displays above or below the Format button.

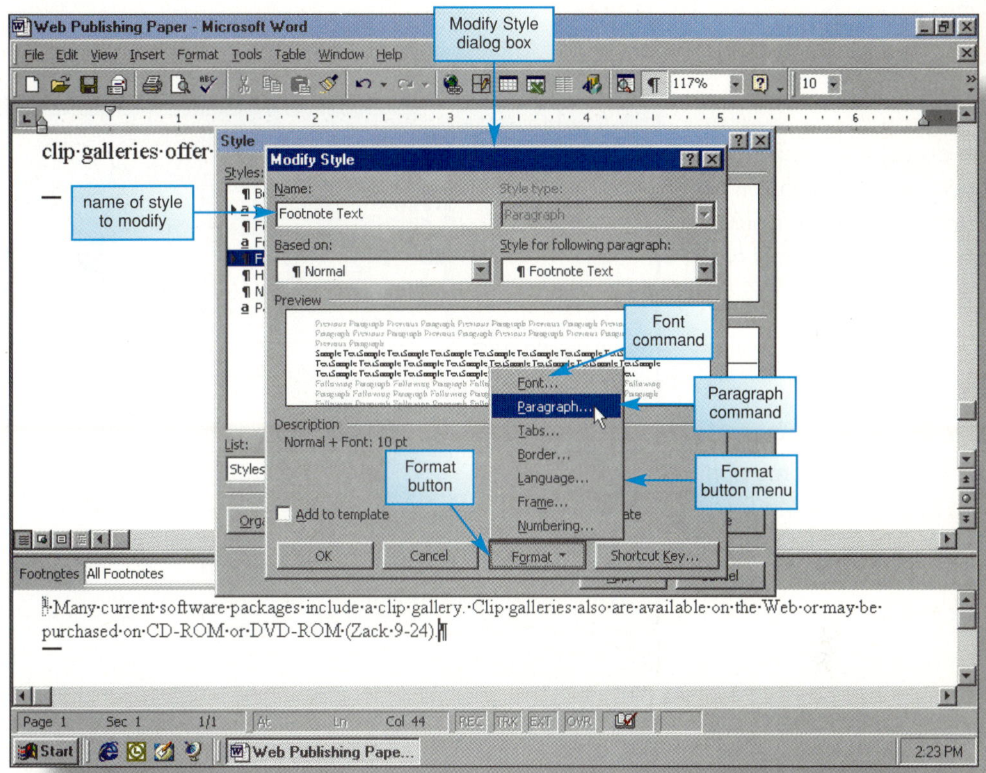

FIGURE 2-32

4 Click Paragraph. When the Paragraph dialog box displays, click the Line spacing box arrow and then click Double. Click the Special box arrow and then point to First line.

Word displays the Paragraph dialog box (Figure 2-33). The Preview area reflects the current settings in the Paragraph dialog box.

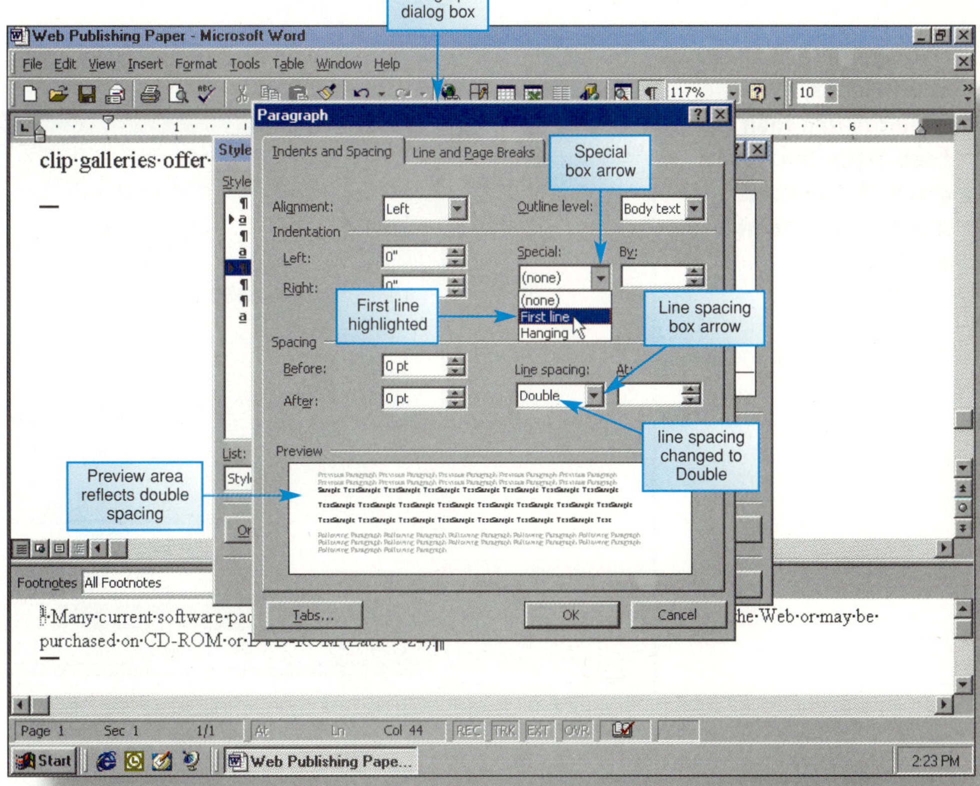

FIGURE 2-33

5 Click First line. Point to the OK button.

Word displays First line in the Special box and Double in the Line spacing box (Figure 2-34). Notice the default first-line indent is .5".

6 Click the OK button.

Word removes the Paragraph dialog box, and the Modify Style dialog box (see Figure 2-32 on the previous page) is visible again.

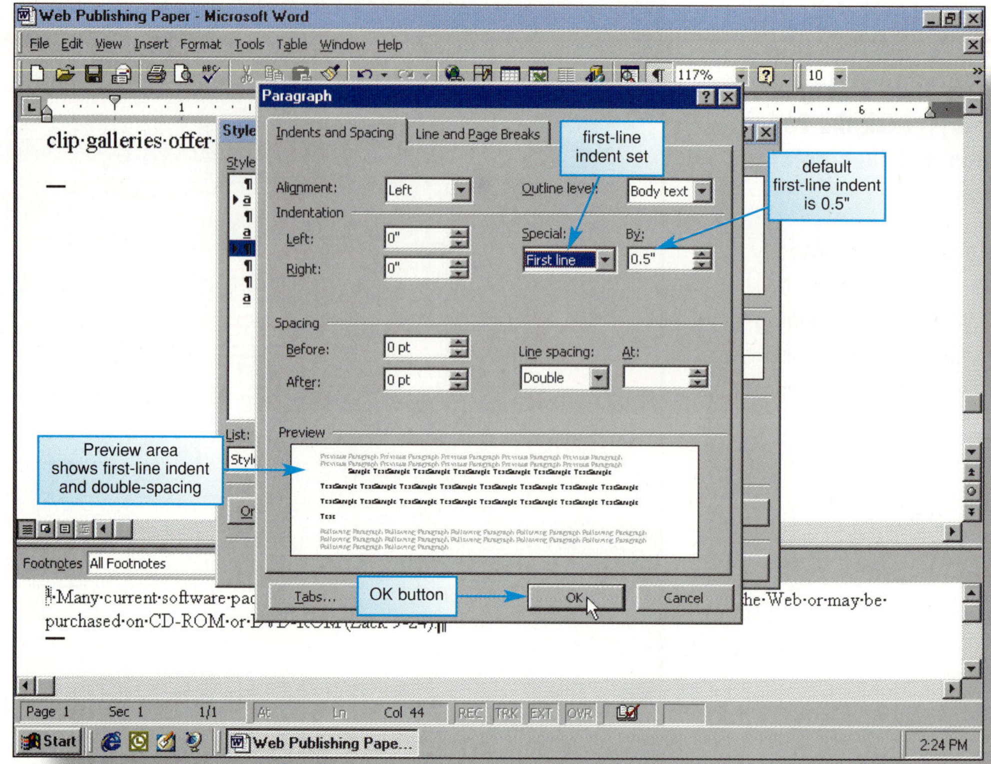

FIGURE 2-34

7 In the Modify Style dialog box, click the Format button and then click Font. When the Font dialog box displays, click 12 in the Size list. Point to the OK button.

Word displays the Font dialog box (Figure 2-35). Depending on your installation of Word 2000, the Size box already may display 12.

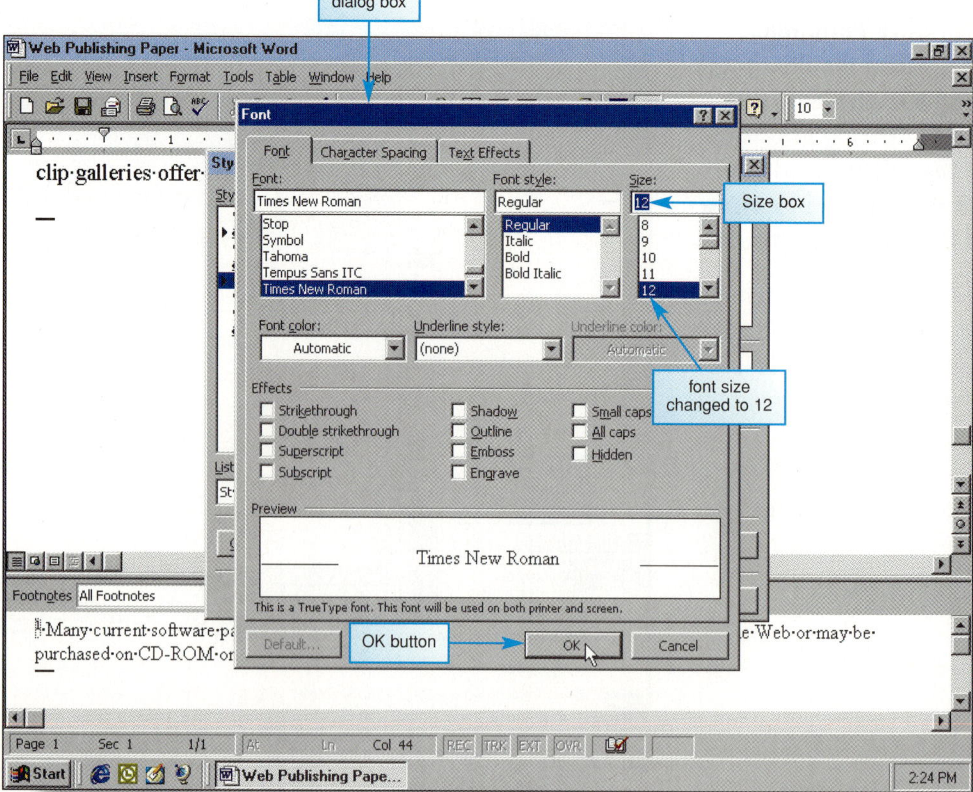

FIGURE 2-35

8 Click the OK button. When the Modify Style dialog box is visible again, point to the OK button.

Word removes the Font dialog box, and the Modify Style dialog box is visible again (Figure 2-36). Word modifies the Footnote Text style to a 12-point font with double-spaced and first-line indented paragraphs.

9 Click the OK button. When the Style dialog box is visible again, click the Apply button. Click the note pane up scroll arrow to display the entire footnote.

Word indents the first line of the note by one-half inch and sets the line spacing for the note to double (Figure 2-37 below).

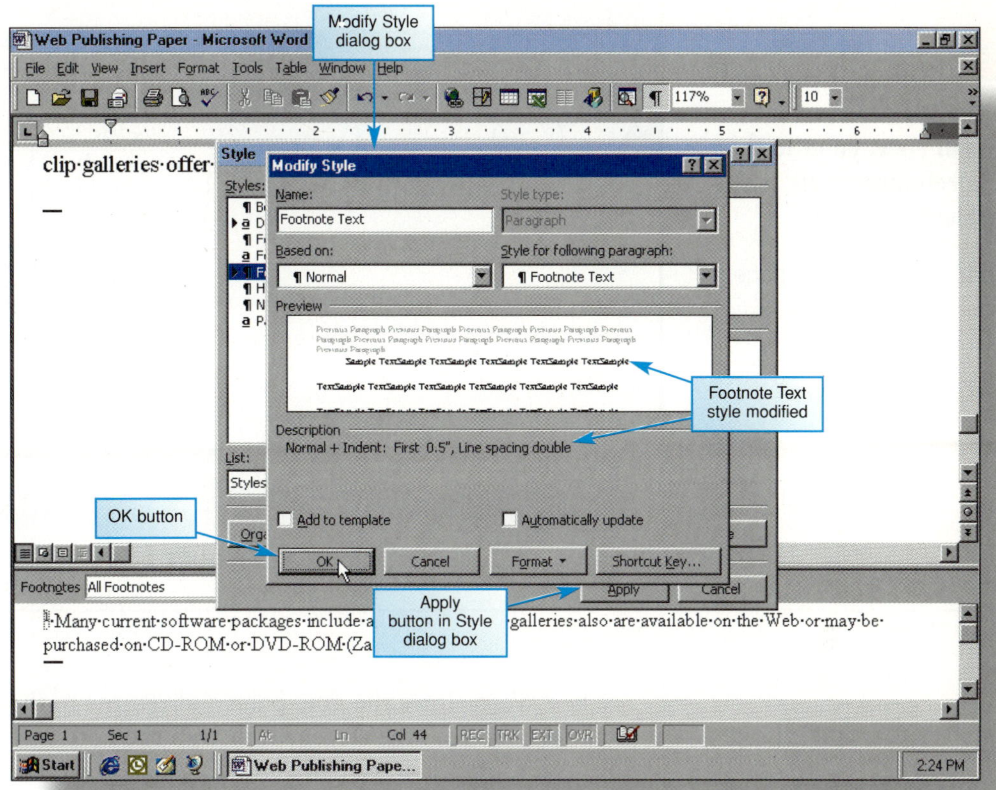

FIGURE 2-36

Any future footnotes entered into the document will use a 12-point font with first-line indented and double-spaced paragraphs. The footnote is complete. The next step is to close the note pane.

To Close the Note Pane

1 Point to the Close button in the note pane (Figure 2-37).

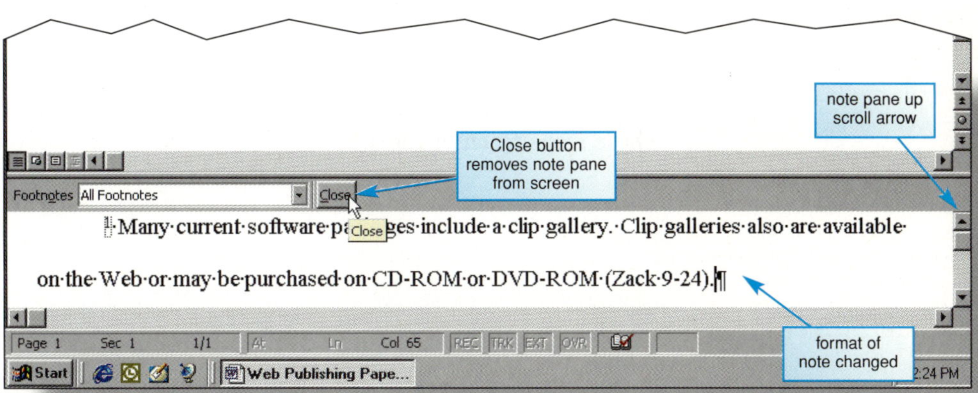

FIGURE 2-37

2 **Click the Close button. If you want to see the note text in normal view, point to the note reference mark in the document window.**

Word closes the note pane (Figure 2-38).

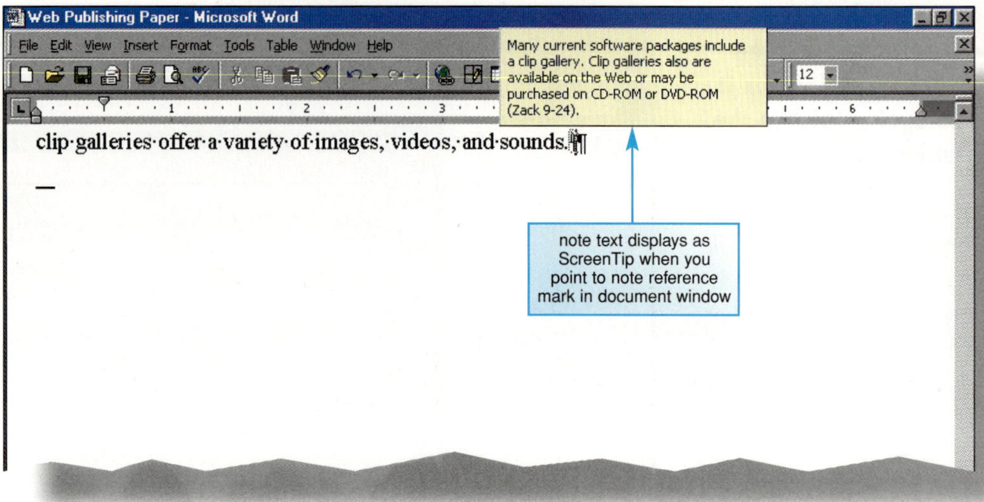

FIGURE 2-38

When Word closes the note pane and returns to the document window, the note text disappears from the screen. Although the note text still exists, it usually is not visible as a footnote in normal view. If, however, you point to the note reference mark, the note text displays above the note reference mark as a **ScreenTip** (Figure 2-38).

To delete a note, you select the note reference mark in the document window (not in the note pane) by dragging through the note reference mark and then clicking the Cut button on the Standard toolbar. Another way to delete a note is to click to the right of the note reference mark in the document window and then press BACKSPACE key twice, or click to the left of the note reference mark in the document window and then press the DELETE key twice. To move a note to a different location in a document, you select the note reference mark in the document window (not in the note pane), click the Cut button on the Standard toolbar, click the location where you want to move the note, and then click the Paste button on the Standard toolbar. When you move or delete notes, Word automatically renumbers any remaining notes in the correct sequence.

You edit note text using the note pane at the bottom of the Word window. To display the note text in a note pane, double-click the note reference mark in the document window or click View on the menu bar and then click Footnotes. Edit the note as you would any Word text and then click the Close button in the note pane. If you want to verify that the note text is positioned correctly on the page, you must switch to print layout view or display the document in print preview. These views are discussed later.

The next step is to enter more text into the body of the research paper. Follow these steps to enter more text.

Notes

To convert current footnotes to endnotes, click Insert on the menu bar and then click Footnote. Click the Options button in the Footnote and Endnote dialog box. Click the Convert button in the Note Options dialog box. Click Convert all footnotes to endnotes and then click the OK button in each of the dialog boxes.

TO ENTER MORE TEXT

1. Press the SPACEBAR. Type the remainder of the second paragraph of the paper as shown in Figure 2-39.
2. Press the ENTER key. Type the third paragraph of the paper as shown in Figure 2-39.

The second and third paragraphs are entered (Figure 2-39).

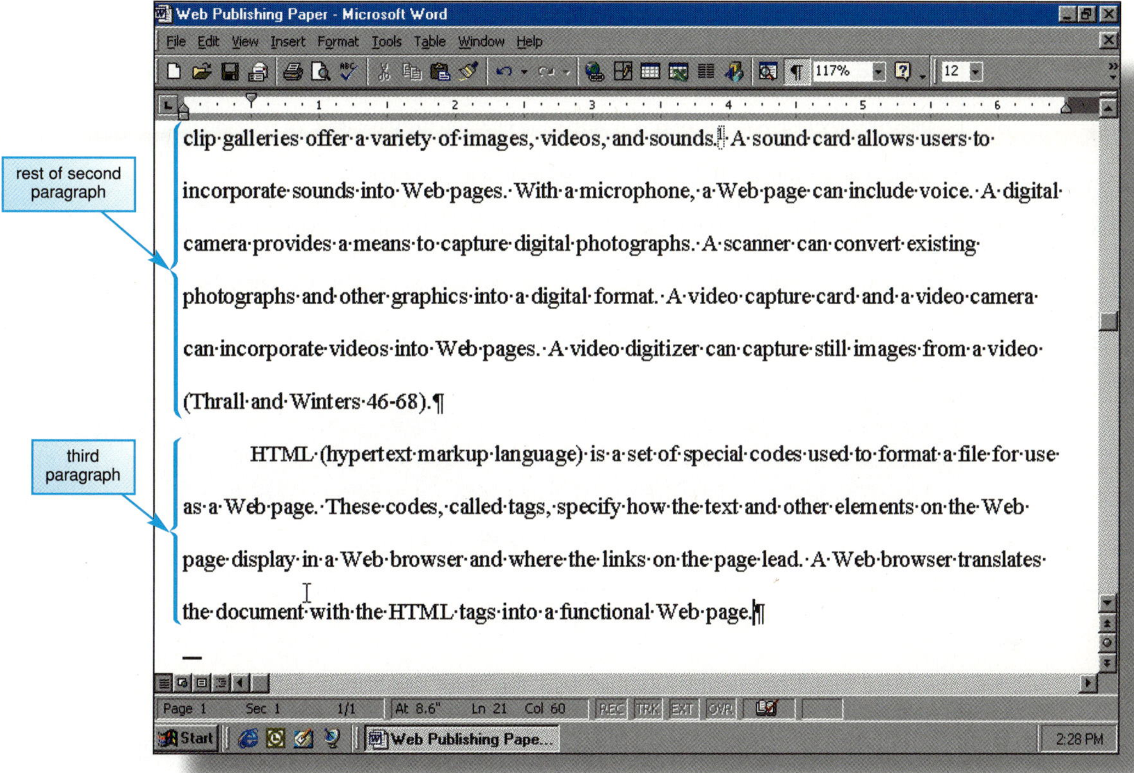

FIGURE 2-39

Automatic Page Breaks

As you type documents that exceed one page, Word automatically inserts page breaks, called **automatic page breaks** or **soft page breaks**, when it determines the text has filled one page according to paper size, margin settings, line spacing, and other settings. If you add text, delete text, or modify text on a page, Word recomputes the position of automatic page breaks and adjusts them accordingly. Word performs page recomputation between the keystrokes; that is, in between the pauses in your typing. Thus, Word refers to the automatic page break task as **background repagination**. In normal view, automatic page breaks display on the Word screen as a single dotted horizontal line. Word's automatic page break feature is illustrated in the step on the next page.

APA and MLA Documentation Styles

The World Wide Web contains a host of information on the APA and MLA documentation styles. College professors and fellow students develop many of these Web pages. For a list of Web links to sites on the APA and MLA styles, visit the Word 2000 More About Web page (www.scsite.com/wd2000/more.htm) and then click Links to Sites on the APA and MLA Styles.

To Page Break Automatically

1 Press the ENTER key and then type the first two sentences of the fourth paragraph of the paper, as shown in Figure 2-40.

As you begin typing the paragraph, Word places an automatic page break between the third and fourth paragraphs in the paper (Figure 2-40). The status bar now displays Page 2 as the current page.

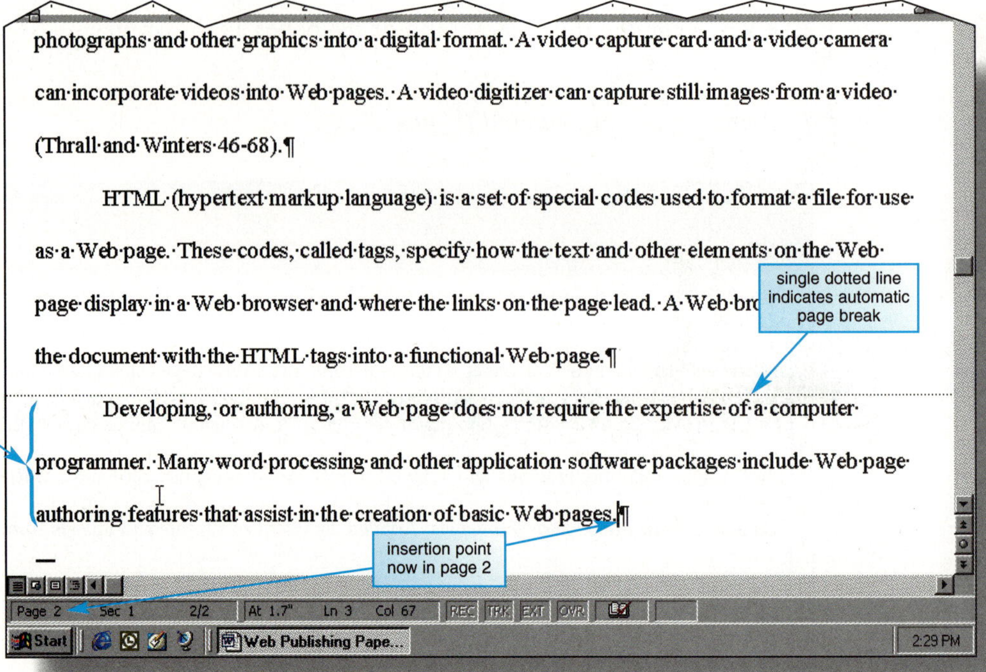

FIGURE 2-40

Your page break may occur at a different location, depending on your printer type.

The header, although not shown in normal view, contains the name Williams and the page number 2. If you wanted to view the header, click View on the menu bar and then click Header and Footer. Then, click the Close button on the Header and Footer toolbar to return to normal view.

Word, by default, prevents widows and orphans from occurring in a document. A **widow** is created when the last line of a paragraph displays by itself at the top of a page, and an **orphan** occurs when the first line of a paragraph displays by itself at the bottom of a page. You turn this setting on and off through the Paragraph dialog box. If, for some reason, you wanted to allow a widow or an orphan in a document, you would right-click the paragraph in question, click Paragraph on the shortcut menu, click the Line and Page Breaks tab in the Paragraph dialog box, click Widow/Orphan control to select or deselect the check box, and then click the OK button.

The Line and Page Breaks sheet in the Paragraph dialog box also contains two other check boxes that control how Word places automatic page breaks. If you did not want a page break to occur within a particular paragraph, you would right-click the paragraph you wanted to keep together, click Paragraph on the shortcut menu, click the Line and Page Breaks tab in the Paragraph dialog box, click Keep lines together to select the check box, and then click the OK button. If you did not want a page break to occur between two paragraphs, you would select the two paragraphs, right-click the selection, click Paragraph on the shortcut menu, click the Line and Page Breaks tab in the Paragraph dialog box, click Keep with next to select the check box, and then click the OK button.

Inserting Arrows, Faces, and Other Symbols Automatically

Earlier in this project, you learned that Word has predefined many commonly misspelled words, which it automatically corrects for you as you type. In addition to words, this built-in list of **AutoCorrect entries** also contains many commonly used symbols. For example, to insert a smiling face into a document, you type :) and Word automatically changes it to ☺. Table 2-3 lists the characters you type to insert arrows, faces, and other symbols into a Word document.

You also can enter the first four symbols in Table 2-3 by clicking Insert on the menu bar, clicking Symbol, clicking the Special Characters tab, clicking the desired symbol in the Character list, clicking the Insert button, and then clicking the Close button in the Symbol dialog box.

If you do not like a change that Word automatically makes in a document, undo the change by clicking the Undo button on the Standard toolbar; clicking Edit on the menu bar and then clicking Undo; or pressing CTRL+Z.

The next step in the research paper is to enter a sentence that uses the registered trademark symbol. Perform the following steps to insert automatically the registered trademark symbol into the research paper.

Table 2-3 Word's Automatic Symbols

TO DISPLAY	DESCRIPTION	TYPE
©	copyright symbol	(c)
®	registered trademark symbol	(r)
™	trademark symbol	(tm)
…	ellipsis	...
☺	smiley face	:) or :-)
😐	indifferent face	:| or :-|
☹	frowning face	:(or :-(
→	thin right arrow	-->
←	thin left arrow	<--
➔	thick right arrow	==>
⬅	thick left arrow	<==
⇔	double arrow	<=>

To Insert a Symbol Automatically

1 **With the insertion point positioned as shown in Figure 2-40, press the SPACEBAR. Type** `Microsoft Office 2000 products, for example, provide easy-to-use tools that enable users to create Web pages and include items such as bullets, frames, backgrounds, lines, database tables, worksheets, and graphics into the Web pages (` **as the beginning of the sentence. Press CTRL+I to turn on italics. Type** `Shelly Cashman Series(r` **as shown in Figure 2-41.**

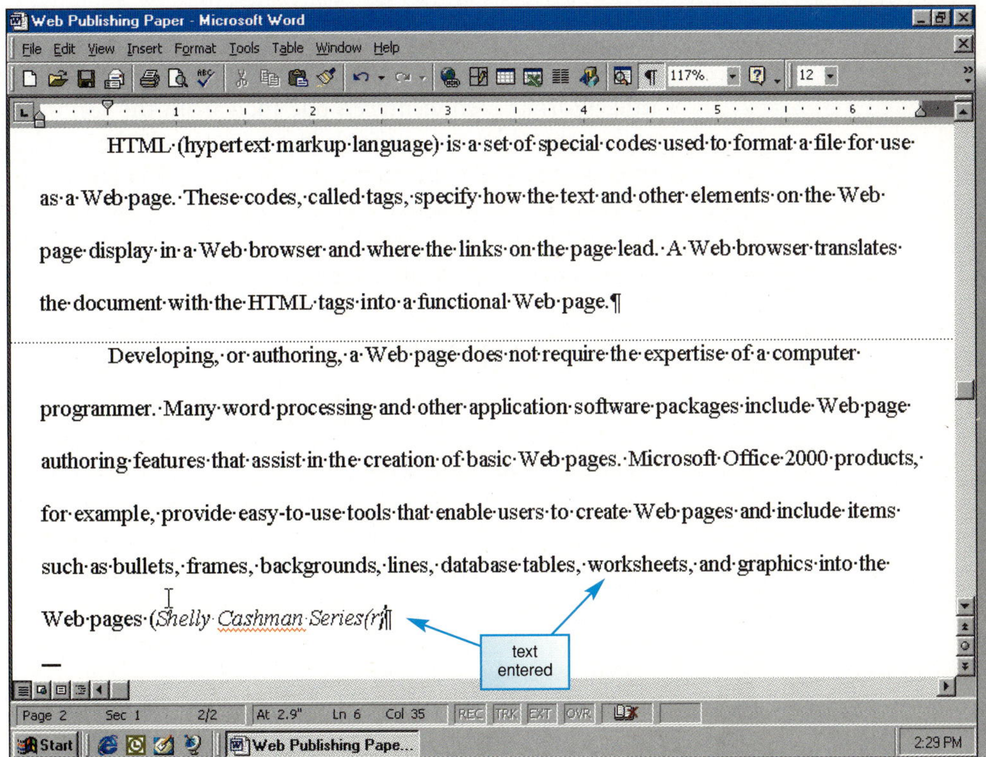

FIGURE 2-41

2 **Press the RIGHT PARENTHESIS key.**

Word automatically converts the (r) to ®, the registered trademark symbol.

3 **Press the SPACEBAR. Type** `Microsoft Word 2000 Project 2` **and then press CTRL+I to turn off italics. Press the RIGHT PARENTHESIS key and then press the PERIOD key. Press the SPACEBAR. Enter the last two sentences of the research paper as shown in Figure 2-42.**

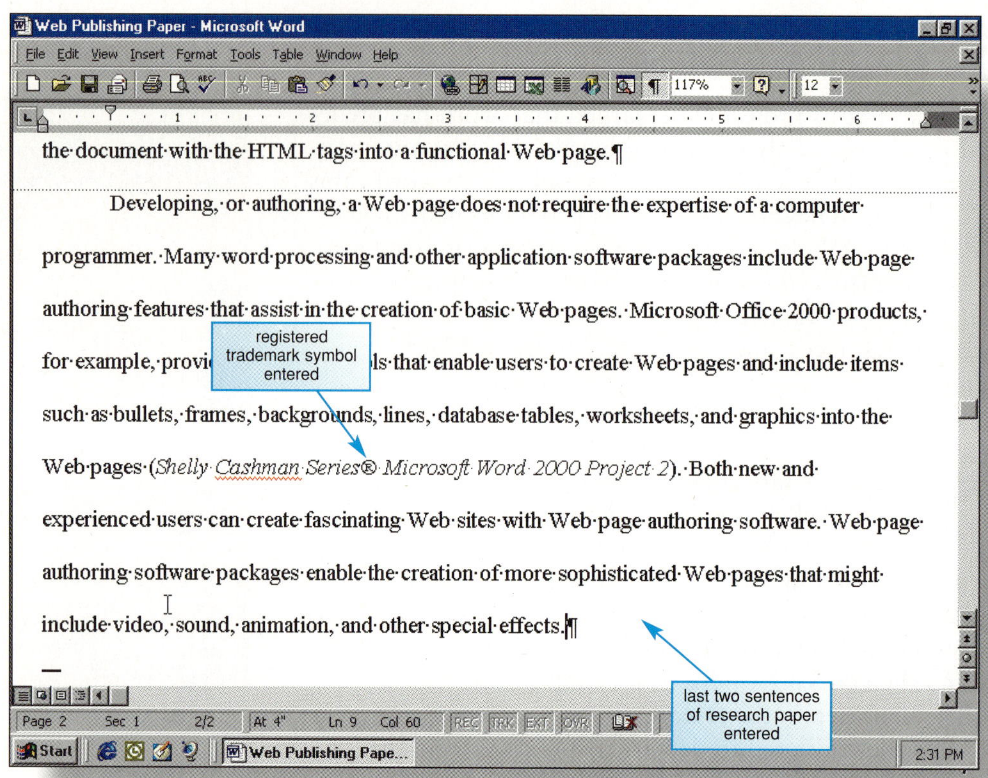
Web Publishing Paper - Microsoft Word
File Edit View Insert Format Tools Table Window Help
the document with the HTML tags into a functional Web page.
Developing, or authoring, a Web page does not require the expertise of a computer programmer. Many word processing and other application software packages include Web page authoring features that assist in the creation of basic Web pages. Microsoft Office 2000 products, for example, provi ls that enable users to create Web pages and include items such as bullets, frames, backgrounds, lines, database tables, worksheets, and graphics into the Web pages (Shelly Cashman Series® Microsoft Word 2000 Project 2). Both new and experienced users can create fascinating Web sites with Web page authoring software. Web page authoring software packages enable the creation of more sophisticated Web pages that might include video, sound, animation, and other special effects.
registered trademark symbol entered
last two sentences of research paper entered
Page 2 Sec 1 2/2 At 4" Ln 9 Col 60
Start
Web Publishing Pape...
2:31 PM

FIGURE 2-42

Creating an Alphabetical Works Cited Page

According to the MLA style, the **works cited page** is a bibliographical list of works you reference directly in your paper. The list is placed on a separate page with the title, Works Cited, centered one inch from the top margin. The works are to be alphabetized by the author's last name or, if the work has no author, by the work's title. The first line of each entry begins at the left margin; subsequent lines of the same entry are indented one-half inch from the left margin.

The first step in creating the works cited page is to force a page break so the works cited display on a separate page.

Manual Page Breaks

Because the works cited are to display on a separate numbered page, you must insert a manual page break following the body of the research paper. A **manual page break,** or **hard page break,** is one that you force into the document at a specific location. Manual page breaks display on the screen as a horizontal dotted line, separated by the words, Page Break. Word never moves or adjusts manual page breaks; however, Word does adjust any automatic page breaks that follow a manual page break. Word inserts manual page breaks just before the location of the insertion point. Perform the following step to insert a manual page break after the body of the research paper.

To Page Break Manually

1 With the insertion point at the end of the research paper, press the ENTER key. Then, press the CTRL+ENTER keys.

The shortcut keys, CTRL+ENTER, instruct Word to insert a manual page break immediately above the insertion point and position the insertion point immediately below the manual page break (Figure 2-43). The status bar indicates the insertion point is located on page 3.

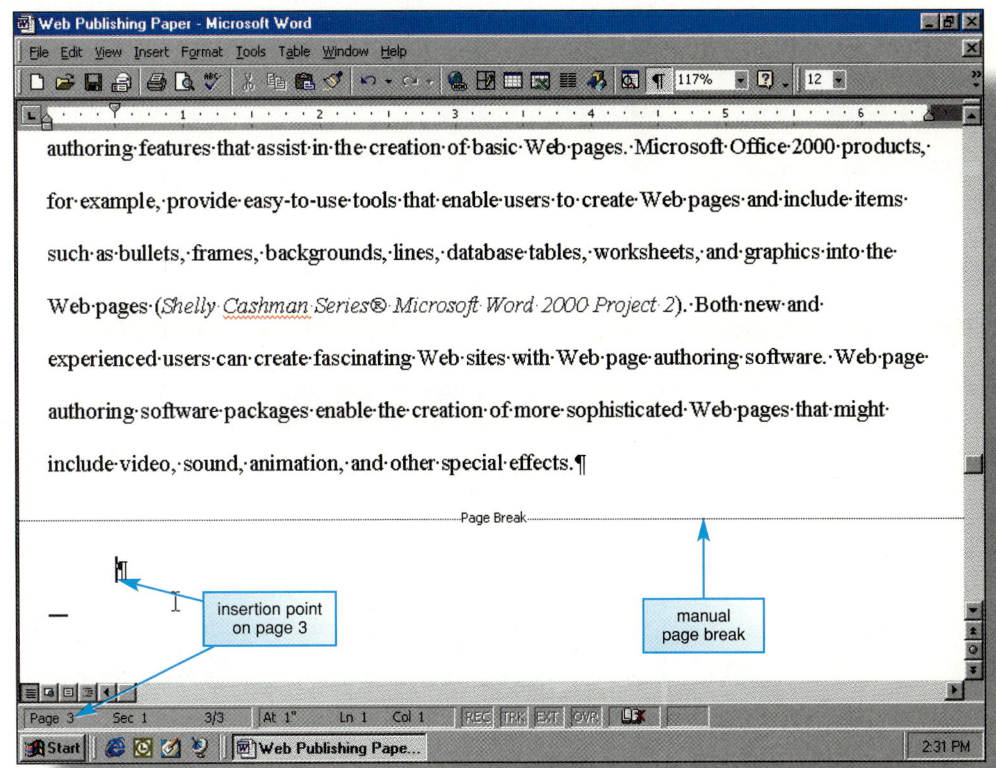
Web Publishing Paper - Microsoft Word
authoring features that assist in the creation of basic Web pages. Microsoft Office 2000 products, for example, provide easy-to-use tools that enable users to create Web pages and include items such as bullets, frames, backgrounds, lines, database tables, worksheets, and graphics into the Web pages (Shelly Cashman Series® Microsoft Word 2000 Project 2). Both new and experienced users can create fascinating Web sites with Web page authoring software. Web page authoring software packages enable the creation of more sophisticated Web pages that might include video, sound, animation, and other special effects.¶
Page Break
insertion point on page 3
manual page break
Page 3 Sec 1 3/3 At 1" Ln 1 Col 1
Start
Web Publishing Pape...
2:31 PM

FIGURE 2-43

Other Ways

1. On Format menu click Insert, click Break, click OK button

The manual page break displays as a horizontal dotted line with the words, Page Break, in the middle of the line. The header, although not shown in normal view, contains the name Williams and the page number 3. If you wanted to view the header, click View on the menu bar and then click Header and Footer. Then, click the Close button on the Header and Footer toolbar to return to normal view.

If, for some reason, you wanted to remove a manual page break from your document, you must first select it by double-clicking it. Then, press the DELETE key; or click the Cut button on the Standard toolbar; or right-click the selection and then click Cut on the shortcut menu.

Centering the Title of the Works Cited Page

The works cited title is to be centered between the margins. If you simply click the Center button on the Formatting toolbar, the title will not be centered properly; instead, it will be one-half inch to the right of the center point because earlier you set first-line indent at one-half inch. Thus, the first line of every paragraph is indented one-half inch. To properly center the title of the works cited page, you must move the First Line Indent marker back to the left margin before clicking the Center button as described in the steps on the next page.

More About 2000

Documentation Styles

The MLA documentation style uses the title *Works Cited* for the page containing bibliographical references, whereas the APA style uses the title *References*. APA guidelines for preparing the reference list entries differ significantly from the MLA style. Refer to an APA handbook for specifics.

TO CENTER THE TITLE OF THE WORKS CITED PAGE

1. Drag the First Line Indent marker to the 0" mark on the ruler.
2. Double-click the move handle on the Formatting toolbar to display the entire toolbar. Click the Center button on the Formatting toolbar.
3. Type `Works Cited` as the title.
4. Press the ENTER key.
5. Because your fingers are on the keyboard, press the CTRL+L keys to left-align the paragraph mark.

The title displays centered properly and the insertion point is left-aligned (Figure 2-44).

> **More About**
>
> **Formatting**
>
> Minimize strain on your wrist by switching between the mouse and keyboard as little as possible. If your fingers are already on the keyboard, use shortcut keys to format text; if your fingers are already on the mouse, use the mouse to format text.

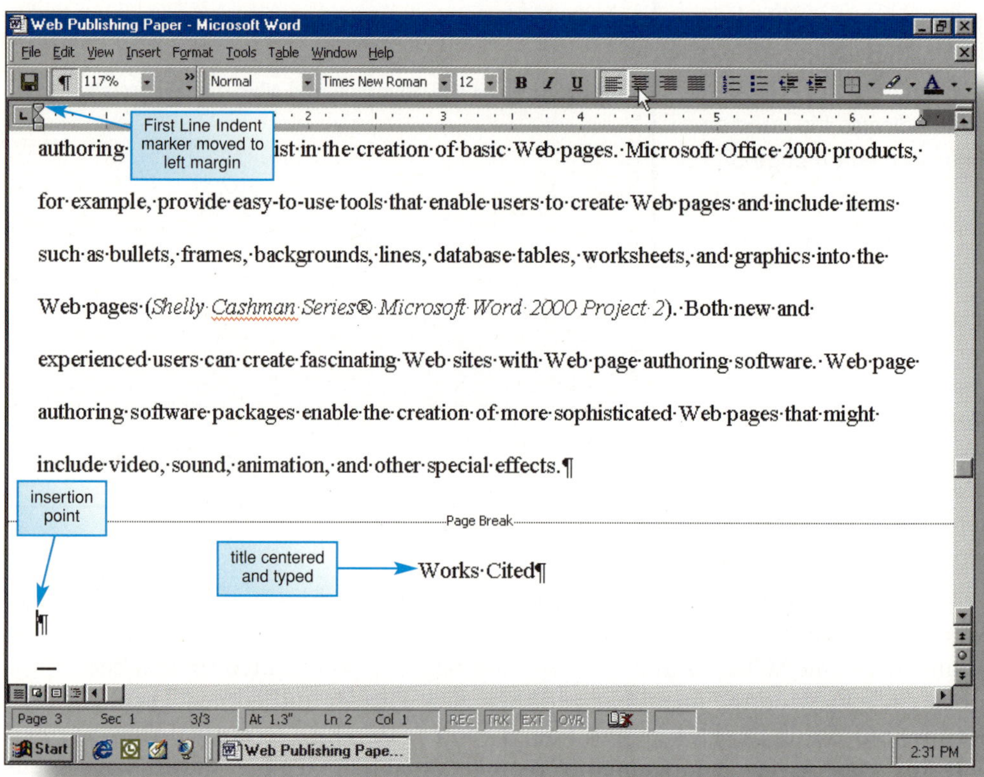
Web Publishing Paper - Microsoft Word
First Line Indent marker moved to left margin
authoring· ist·in·the·creation·of·basic·Web·pages.·Microsoft·Office·2000·products,·
for·example,·provide·easy-to-use·tools·that·enable·users·to·create·Web·pages·and·include·items·
such·as·bullets,·frames,·backgrounds,·lines,·database·tables,·worksheets,·and·graphics·into·the·
Web·pages·(Shelly·Cashman·Series®·Microsoft·Word·2000·Project·2).·Both·new·and·
experienced·users·can·create·fascinating·Web·sites·with·Web·page·authoring·software.·Web·page·
authoring·software·packages·enable·the·creation·of·more·sophisticated·Web·pages·that·might·
include·video,·sound,·animation,·and·other·special·effects.¶
insertion point
Page Break
title centered and typed
Works·Cited¶
Page 3 Sec 1 3/3 At 1.3" Ln 2 Col 1
Start
Web Publishing Pape...
2:31 PM

FIGURE 2-44

Creating a Hanging Indent

On the works cited page, the first line of each entry begins at the left margin. Subsequent lines in the same paragraph are indented one-half inch from the left margin. In essence, the first line *hangs* to the left of the rest of the paragraph; thus, this type of paragraph formatting is called a **hanging indent**.

One method of creating a hanging indent is to use the horizontal ruler. The **Hanging Indent marker** is the bottom triangle at the 0" mark on the ruler (Figure 2-45). You have learned that the small square at the 0" mark is called the Left Indent marker. Perform the following steps to create a hanging indent.

> **More About**
>
> **Crediting Sources**
>
> When writing a research paper, you must acknowledge sources of information. Citing sources is a matter of ethics and honesty. Use caution when summarizing or paraphrasing a source. Be sure to avoid plagiarism, which includes using someone else's words or ideas and claiming them as your own.

To Create a Hanging Indent

1 With the insertion point in the paragraph to format (see Figure 2-44), point to the Hanging Indent marker on the ruler (Figure 2-45).

FIGURE 2-45

2 Drag the Hanging Indent marker to the .5" mark on the ruler.

The Hanging Indent marker and Left Indent marker display one-half inch from the left margin (Figure 2-46). When you drag the Hanging Indent marker, the Left Indent marker moves with it. The insertion point in the document window remains at the left margin because only subsequent lines in the paragraph are to be indented.

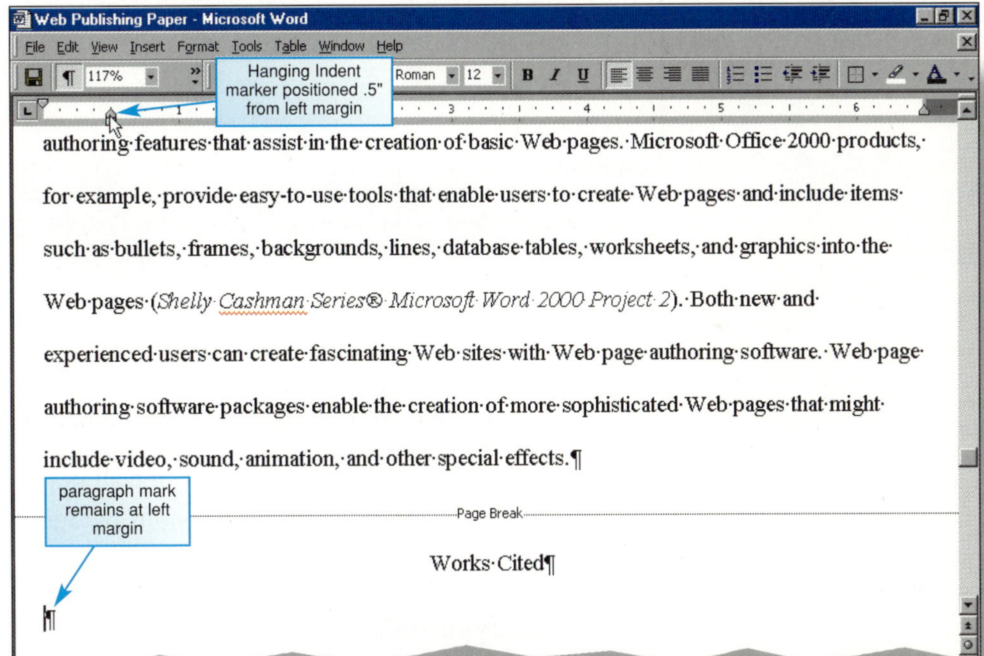
Web Publishing Paper - Microsoft Word
Hanging Indent marker positioned .5" from left margin
authoring·features·that·assist·in·the·creation·of·basic·Web·pages.·Microsoft·Office·2000·products,·
for·example,·provide·easy-to-use·tools·that·enable·users·to·create·Web·pages·and·include·items·
such·as·bullets,·frames,·backgrounds,·lines,·database·tables,·worksheets,·and·graphics·into·the·
Web·pages·(Shelly·Cashman·Series®·Microsoft·Word·2000·Project·2).·Both·new·and·
experienced·users·can·create·fascinating·Web·sites·with·Web·page·authoring·software.·Web·page·
authoring·software·packages·enable·the·creation·of·more·sophisticated·Web·pages·that·might·
include·video,·sound,·animation,·and·other·special·effects.¶
paragraph mark remains at left margin
Page Break
Works·Cited¶

FIGURE 2-46

To drag both the First Line Indent and Hanging Indent markers at the same time, you drag the Left Indent marker on the ruler.

Enter the first two works in the works cited as explained in the steps on the next page.

Other Ways

1. Right-click paragraph, click Paragraph on shortcut menu, click Indents and Spacing tab, click Special box arrow, click Hanging, click OK button
2. On Format menu click Paragraph, click Indents and Spacing tab, click Special box arrow, click Hanging, click OK button
3. Press CTRL+T

Citing Sources

Information that commonly is known or accessible to the audience constitutes common knowledge and does not need to be listed as a parenthetical citation or in the bibliography. If you question whether certain information is common knowledge, you should cite it – just to be safe.

TO ENTER WORK CITED PARAGRAPHS

1. Type `Thrall, Peter D., and Amy P. Winters.` Press the SPACEBAR. Press CTRL+I. Type `Computer Concepts for the New Millennium.` Press CTRL+I. Press the SPACEBAR. Type `Boston: International Press, 2001.` Press the ENTER key.
2. Type `Zack, Joseph R. "An Introduction to Clip Galleries and Digital Files."` Press the SPACEBAR. Press CTRL+I. Type `Computers for Today, Tomorrow, and Beyond` and then press CTRL+I. Press the SPACEBAR. Type `Sep. 2001: 9-24.` Press the ENTER key.

The first two works cited paragraphs are entered (Figure 2-47).

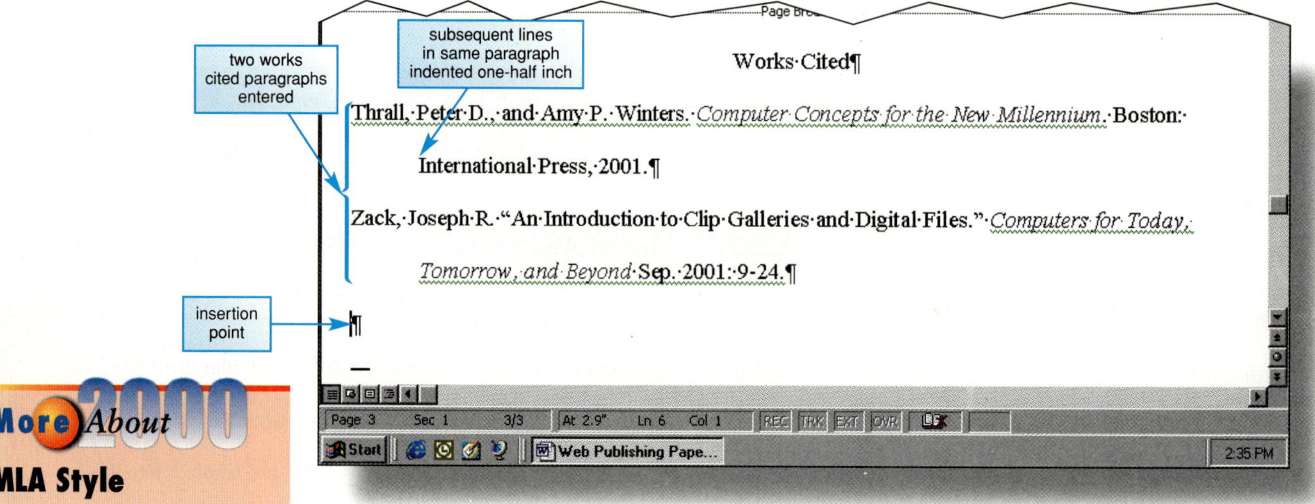
two works cited paragraphs entered
subsequent lines in same paragraph indented one-half inch
insertion point
Works·Cited¶
Thrall,·Peter·D.,·and·Amy·P.·Winters.·Computer·Concepts·for·the·New·Millennium.·Boston:·
International·Press,·2001.¶
Zack,·Joseph·R.·"An·Introduction·to·Clip·Galleries·and·Digital·Files."·Computers·for·Today,·
Tomorrow,·and·Beyond·Sep.·2001:·9-24.¶
Page 3 Sec 1 3/3 At 2.9" Ln 6 Col 1
Start
Web Publishing Pape...
2:35 PM

FIGURE 2-47

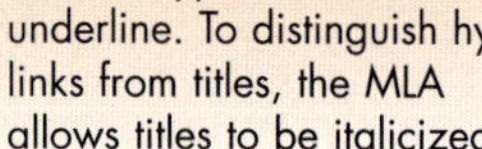

MLA Style

Titles of books, periodicals, and Web sites typically are underlined when a research paper is submitted in printed form. Some instructors require that Web addresses be hyperlinks for online access. Word formats hyperlinks with an underline. To distinguish hyperlinks from titles, the MLA allows titles to be italicized, if approved by the instructor.

When Word wraps the text in each works cited paragraph, it automatically indents the second line of the paragraph by one-half inch. When you press the ENTER key at the end of the first paragraph of text, the insertion point returns automatically to the left margin for the next paragraph. Recall that each time you press the ENTER key, the paragraph formatting in the previous paragraph is carried forward to the next paragraph.

Creating a Hyperlink

In Word, you can create a hyperlink simply by typing the address of the file or Web page to which you want to jump and then pressing the SPACEBAR or the ENTER key. A **hyperlink** is a shortcut that allows a user to jump easily and quickly to another location in the same document or to other documents or Web pages. **Jumping** is the process of following a hyperlink to its destination. For example, by clicking a hyperlink in the document window, you jump to another document on your computer, on your network, or on the World Wide Web. When you close the hyperlink destination page or document, you return to the original location in your Word document.

In this project, one of the works cited is from a Web page on the Internet. When someone displays your research paper on the screen, you want him or her to be able to click the Web address in the work and jump to the associated Web site for more information. If you wish to create a hyperlink to a Web page from a Word document, you do not have to be connected to the Internet. Perform the following steps to create a hyperlink as you type.

More About

Hyperlinks

To verify that Word will automatically convert your Web addresses to hyperlinks, click Tools on the menu bar, click AutoCorrect, click the AutoFormat As You Type tab, verify that the Internet and network paths with hyperlinks check box contains a check mark, and then click the OK button.

To Create a Hyperlink as You Type

1. **Press CTRL+I. Type** `Shelly Cashman Series(r) Microsoft Word 2000 Project 2.` **Press CTRL+I. Press the SPACEBAR. Type** `Course Technology. 1 Oct. 2001. http://www.scsite.com/wd2000/pr2/wc1.htm.`

The insertion point immediately follows the Web address (Figure 2-48).

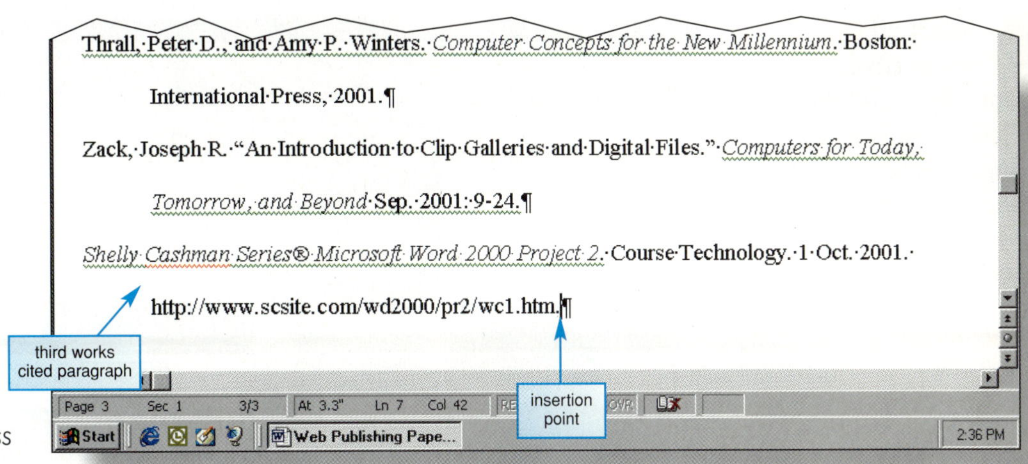

FIGURE 2-48

2. **Press the ENTER key.**

As soon as you press the ENTER key after typing the Web address, Word formats it as a hyperlink (Figure 2-49). That is, the Web address is underlined and colored blue.

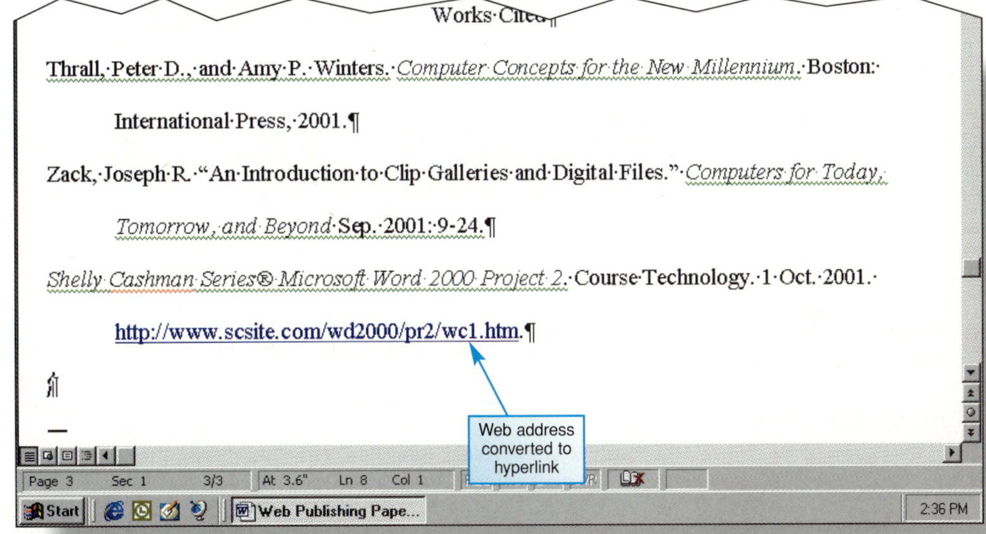

FIGURE 2-49

Other Ways

1. Right-click text, click Hyperlink on shortcut menu, click Existing File or Web Page in the Link to list, type Web address in Type the file or Web page name text box, click OK button
2. Click text, click Insert Hyperlink button on Standard toolbar, click Existing File or Web Page in the Link to list, type Web address in Type the file or Web page name text box, click OK button

Later in this project, you will jump to the hyperlink destination.

Sorting Paragraphs

The MLA style requires that the works cited be listed in alphabetical order by author's last name. With Word, you can arrange paragraphs in alphabetic, numeric, or date order based on the first character in each paragraph. Ordering characters in this manner is called **sorting**. Arrange the works cited paragraphs in alphabetic order as illustrated in the steps on the next page.

To Sort Paragraphs

1 Select all the works cited paragraphs by pointing to the left of the first paragraph and dragging down. Click Table on the menu bar and then point to Sort.

Word displays the Table menu (Figure 2-50). All of the paragraphs to be sorted are selected.

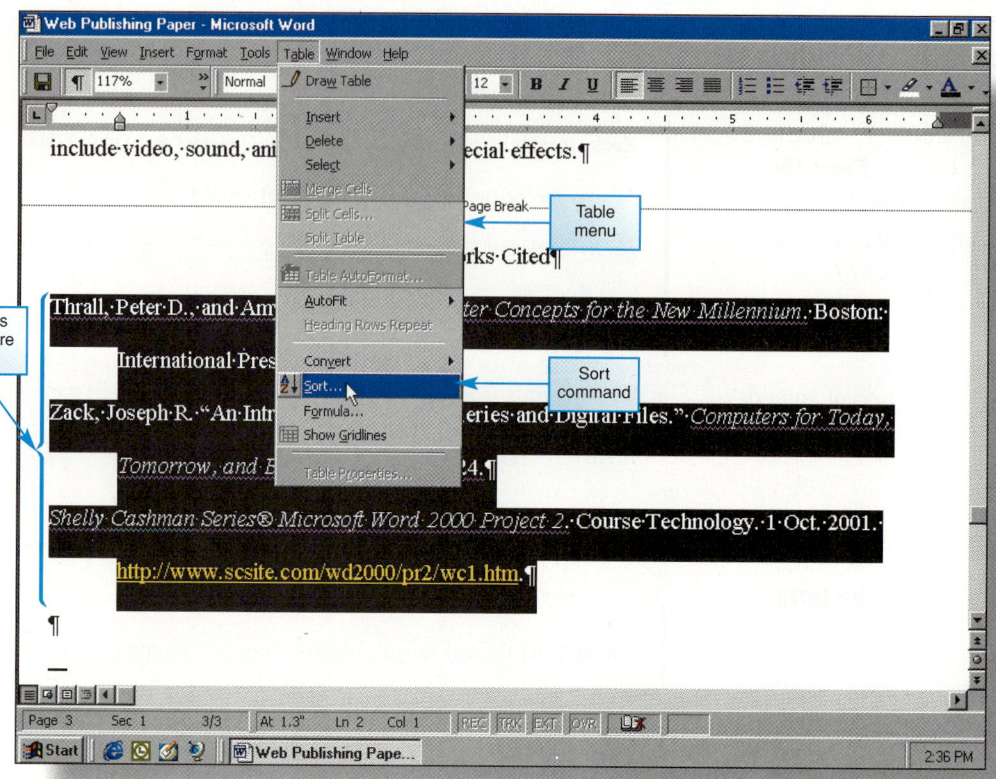

FIGURE 2-50

2 Click Sort. Point to the OK button.

Word displays the Sort Text dialog box (Figure 2-51). In the Sort by area, Ascending is selected. Ascending sorts in alphabetic, numeric, or earliest to latest date order.

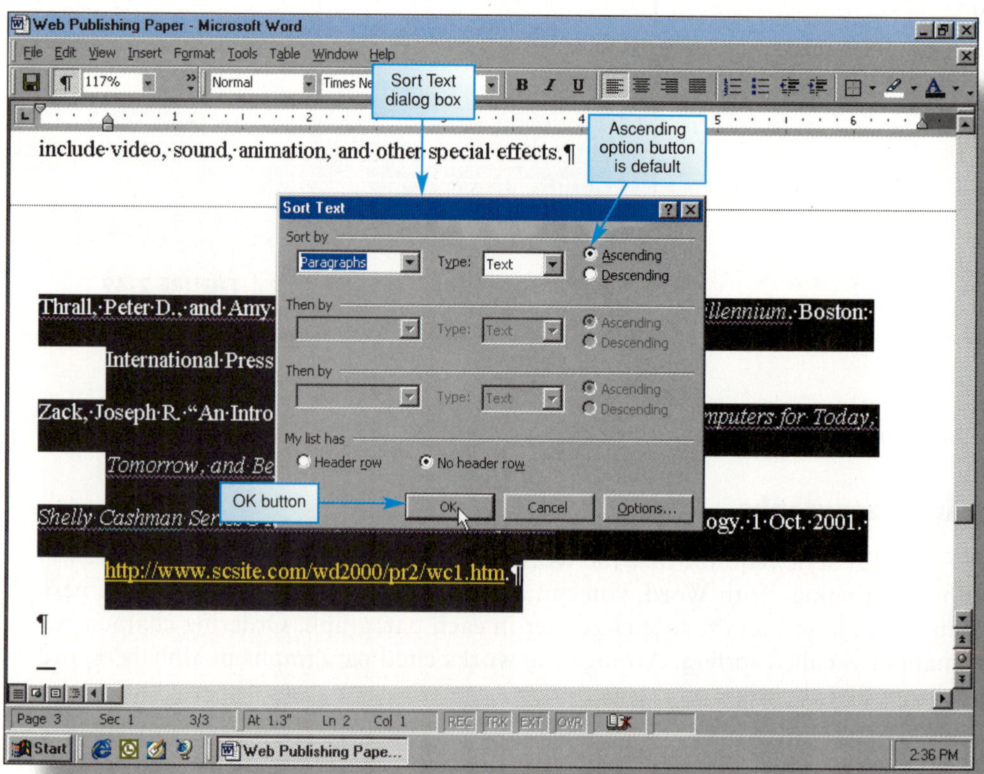

FIGURE 2-51

3 **Click the OK button. Click outside of the selection to remove the highlight.**

Word sorts the works cited paragraphs alphabetically (Figure 2-52).

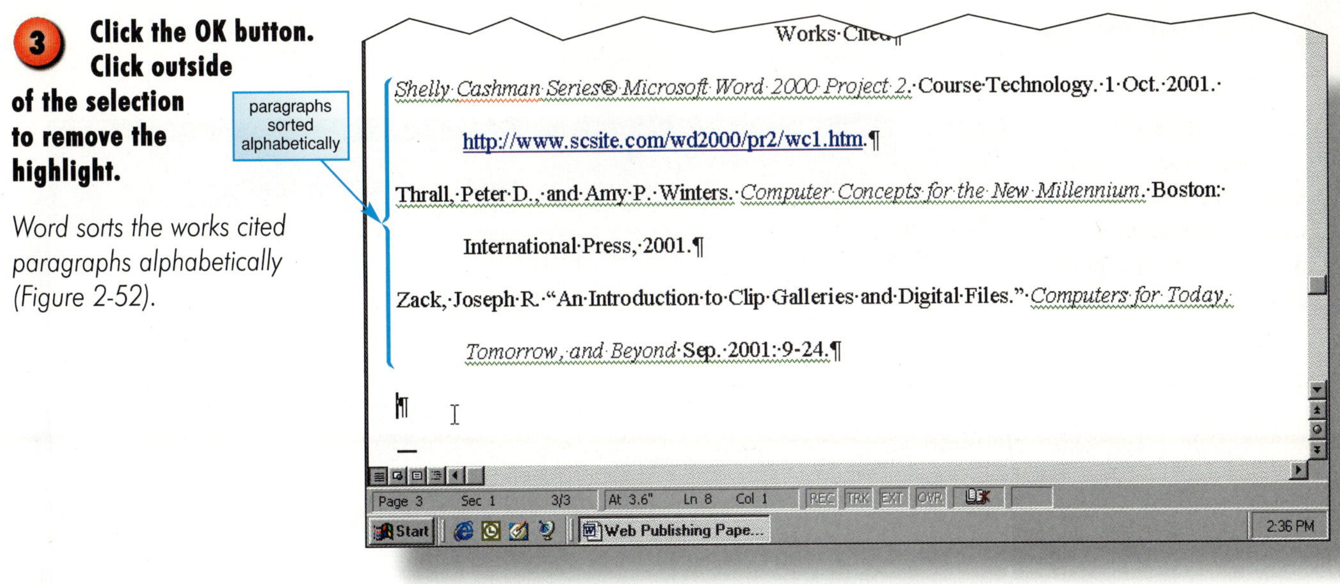

paragraphs sorted alphabetically
Works·Cited¶
Shelly·Cashman·Series®·Microsoft·Word·2000·Project·2.·Course·Technology.·1·Oct.·2001.·
http://www.scsite.com/wd2000/pr2/wc1.htm.¶
Thrall,·Peter·D.,·and·Amy·P.·Winters.·Computer·Concepts·for·the·New·Millennium.·Boston:·
International·Press,·2001.¶
Zack,·Joseph·R.·"An·Introduction·to·Clip·Galleries·and·Digital·Files."·Computers·for·Today,·
Tomorrow,·and·Beyond·Sep.·2001:·9-24.¶
Page 3 Sec 1 3/3 At 3.6" Ln 8 Col 1 REC TRK EXT OVR
Start
Web Publishing Pape...
2:36 PM

FIGURE 2-52

If you accidentally sort the wrong paragraphs, you can undo a sort by clicking the Undo button on the Standard toolbar.

In the Sort Text dialog box (Figure 2-51), the default sort order is Ascending. By default, Word orders in **ascending sort order**, which means from the beginning of the alphabet to the end of the alphabet, smallest number to the largest number, or earliest date to the most recent date. For example, if the first character of each paragraph to be sorted is a letter, Word sorts the selected paragraphs alphabetically.

You also can sort in descending order by clicking Descending in the Sort Text dialog box. **Descending sort order** means sorting from the end of the alphabet to the beginning of the alphabet, the largest number to the smallest number, or the most recent date to the earliest date.

Proofing and Revising the Research Paper

As discussed in Project 1, once you complete a document, you might find it necessary to make changes to it. Before submitting a paper to be graded, you should proofread it. While **proofreading**, you look for grammatical errors and spelling errors. You want to be sure the transitions between sentences flow smoothly and sentences themselves make sense. Very often, you may count the words in a paper to meet minimum word guidelines specified by an instructor. To assist you in this proofreading effort, Word provides several tools. These tools are discussed in the following pages.

Proofreading

When proofreading a paper, ask yourself these questions: Is the purpose clear? Does the title suggest the topic? Does the paper have an introduction, body, and conclusion? Is the thesis clear? Does each paragraph in the body relate to the thesis? Is the conclusion effective? Are all sources acknowledged?

Going to a Specific Location in a Document

Often, you would like to bring a certain page, footnote, or other object into view in the document window. To accomplish this, you could scroll through the document to find the desired page, footnote, or item. Instead of scrolling through the document, Word provides an easier method of going to a specific location via the **Select Browse Object menu**. Perform the steps on the next page to go to the top of page two in the research paper.

To Browse by Page

1 Click the Select Browse Object button on the vertical scroll bar. When the Select Browse Object menu displays, point to Browse by Page.

Word displays the Select Browse Object menu (Figure 2-53). As you point to various commands on the Select Browse Object menu, Word displays the command name at the bottom of the menu.

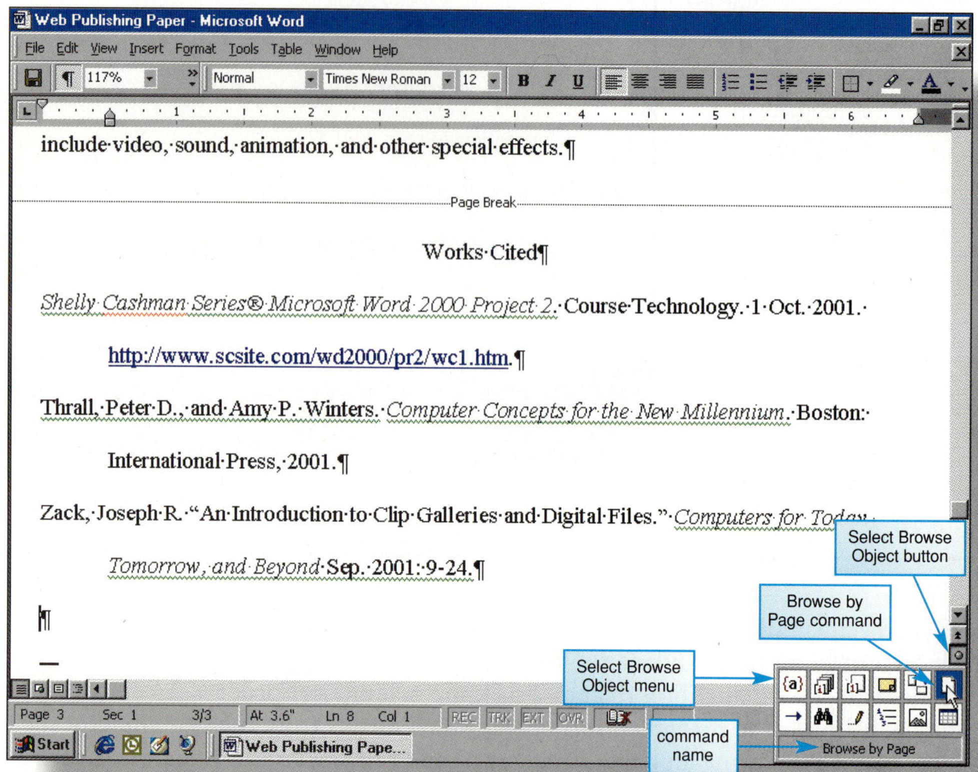

FIGURE 2-53

2 Click Browse by Page. Point to the Previous Page button on the vertical scroll bar.

Word closes the Select Browse Object menu and displays the top of page 3 at the top of the document window (Figure 2-54).

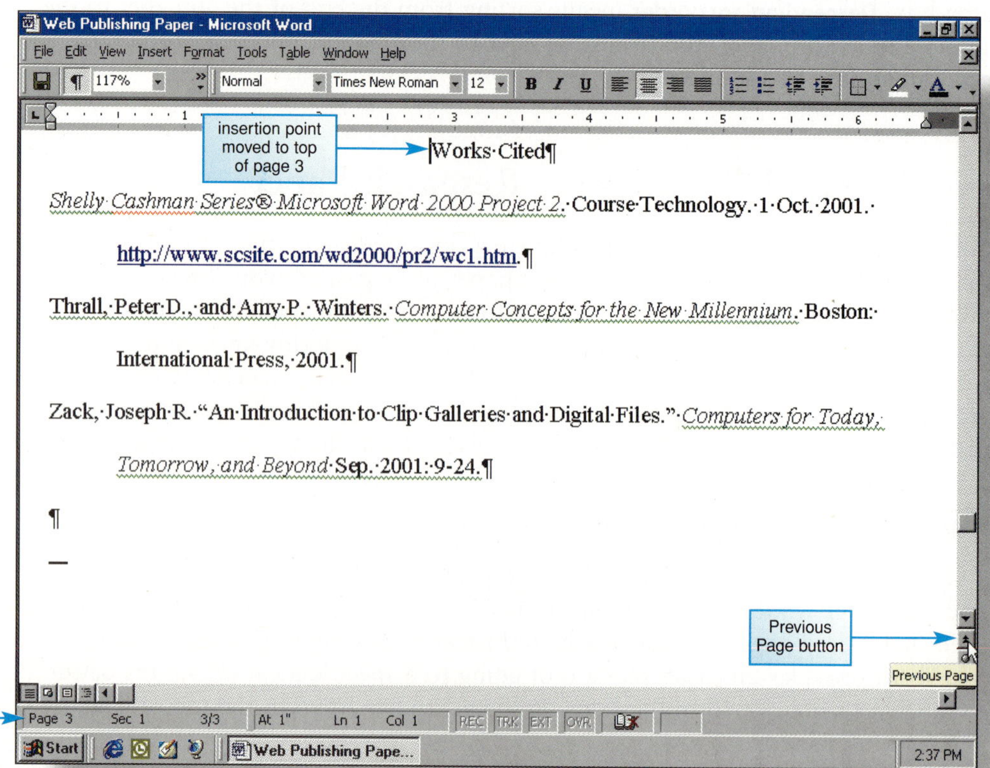

FIGURE 2-54

Click the Previous Page button.

Word places the top of page 2 (the previous page) at the top of the document window (Figure 2-55).

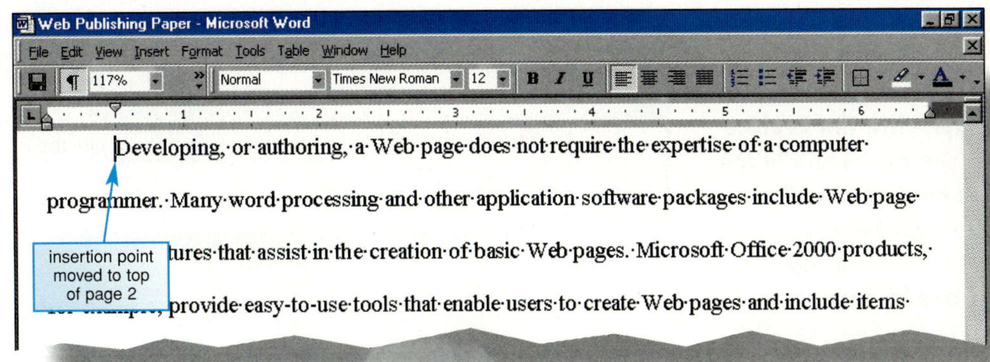
Web Publishing Paper - Microsoft Word
File Edit View Insert Format Tools Table Window Help
117%
Normal
Times New Roman
12
Developing, or authoring, a Web page does not require the expertise of a computer
programmer. Many word processing and other application software packages include Web page
tures that assist in the creation of basic Web pages. Microsoft Office 2000 products,
provide easy-to-use tools that enable users to create Web pages and include items
insertion point moved to top of page 2

FIGURE 2-55

Other Ways

1. Double-click page indicator on status bar (Figure 2-54), click Page in Go to what list, type page number in Enter page number text box, click Go To button, click Close button
2. On Edit menu click Go To, and then proceed as described in 1 above starting with click Page in Go to what list
3. Press CTRL+G, and then proceed as described in 1 above starting with click Page in Go to what list

Depending on the command you click in the Select Browse Object menu, the function of the buttons above and below the Select Browse Object button on the vertical scroll bar changes. When you select Browse by Page, the buttons become Previous Page and Next Page buttons; when you select Browse by Footnote, the buttons become Previous Footnote and Next Footnote buttons, and so on.

Finding and Replacing Text

While proofreading the paper, you notice that it contains the word, creation, more than once in the document (see Figure 2-56 below); and you would rather use the word, development. Therefore, you wish to change all occurrences of the word, creation, to the word, development. To do this, you can use Word's find and replace feature, which automatically locates each occurrence of a specified word or phrase and then replaces it with specified text as shown in these steps.

Steps To Find and Replace Text

1 Click the Select Browse Object button on the vertical scroll bar. Point to Find on the Select Browse Object menu (Figure 2-56).

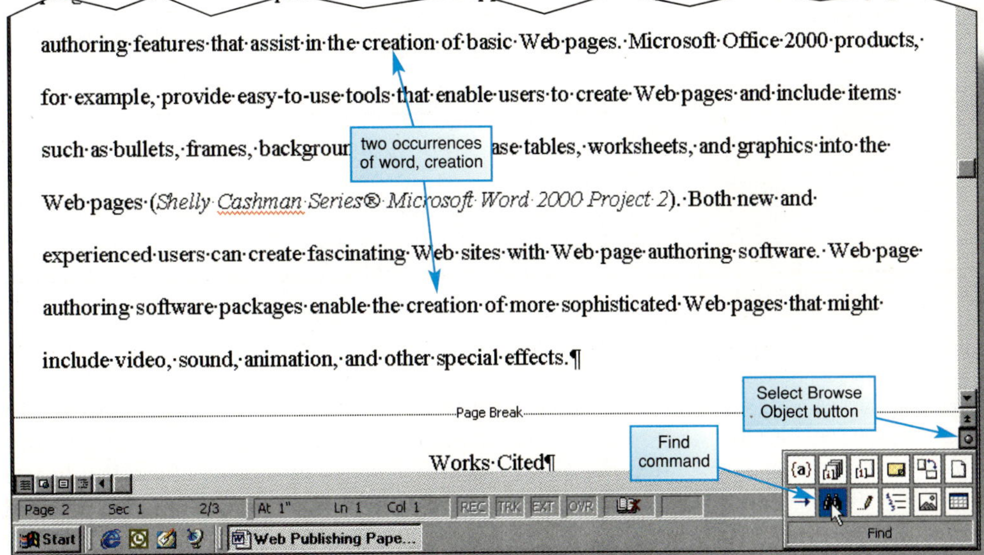
authoring features that assist in the creation of basic Web pages. Microsoft Office 2000 products,
for example, provide easy-to-use tools that enable users to create Web pages and include items
such as bullets, frames, backgrour ase tables, worksheets, and graphics into the
Web pages (Shelly Cashman Series® Microsoft Word 2000 Project 2). Both new and
experienced users can create fascinating Web sites with Web page authoring software. Web page
authoring software packages enable the creation of more sophisticated Web pages that might
include video, sound, animation, and other special effects.¶
Page Break
Works Cited¶
two occurrences of word, creation
Select Browse Object button
Find command
Find
Page 2 Sec 1 2/3 At 1" Ln 1 Col 1 REC TRK EXT OVR
Start
Web Publishing Pape...

FIGURE 2-56

2 **Click Find. When the Find and Replace dialog box displays, click the Replace tab. Type** `creation` **in the Find what text box. Press the TAB key. Type** `development` **in the Replace with text box. Point to the Replace All button.**

Word displays the Find and Replace dialog box (Figure 2-57). The Replace All button replaces all occurrences of the Find what text with the Replace with text.

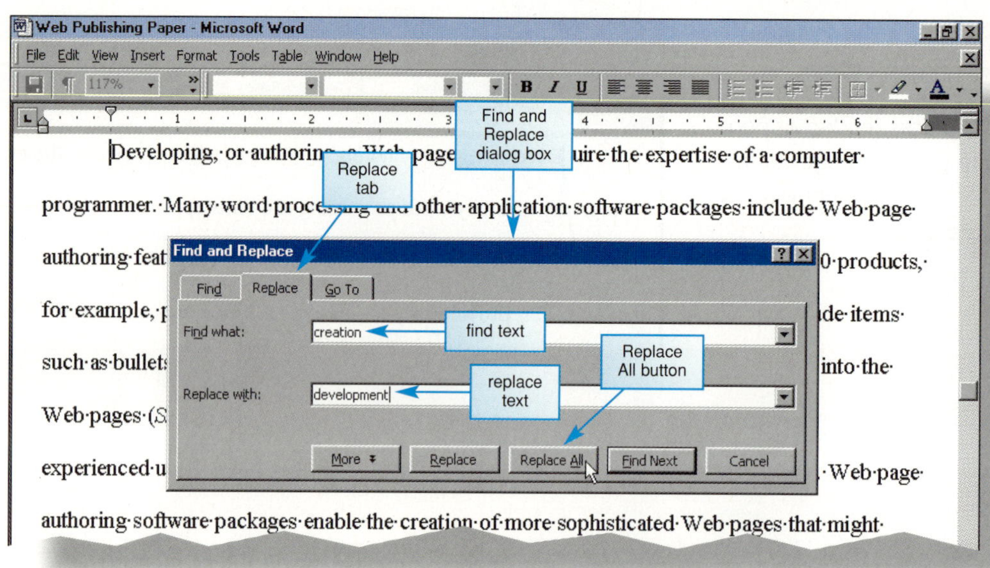

FIGURE 2-57

3 **Click the Replace All button.**

A Microsoft Word dialog box displays indicating the total number of replacements made (Figure 2-58).

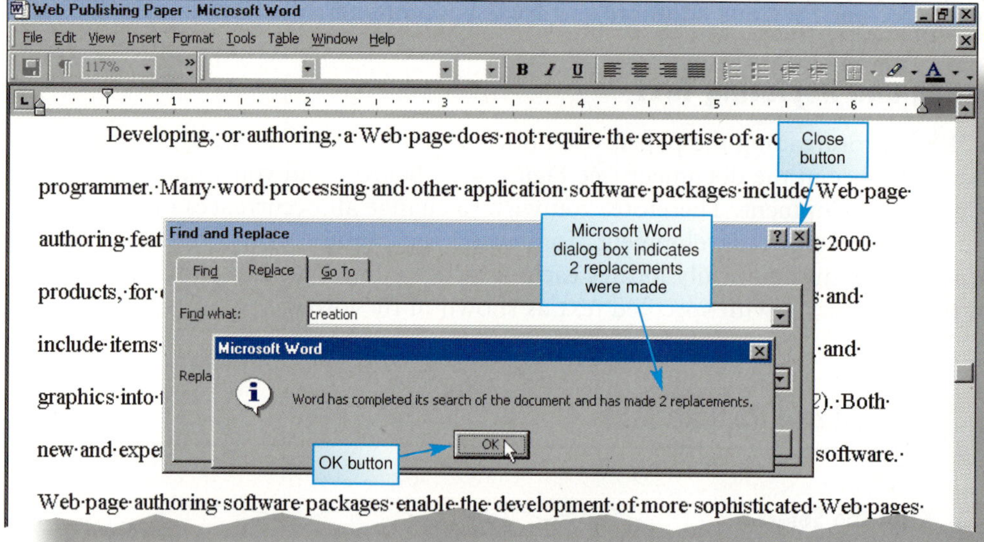

FIGURE 2-58

4 **Click the OK button. Click the Close button in the Find and Replace dialog box.**

The word, development, displays in the document instead of the word, creation (see Figure 2-59).

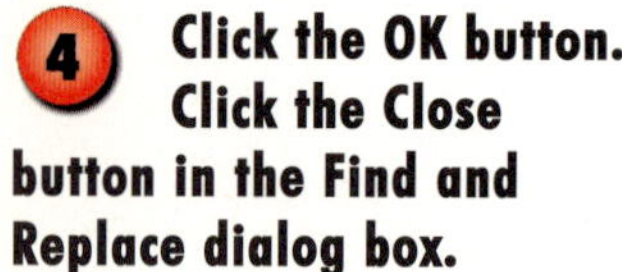

Other Ways

1. Double-click page indicator on status bar, click Replace tab, type Find what text, type Replace with text, click OK button, click Close button
2. On Edit menu click Replace, and then proceed as described in 1 above starting with type Find what text
3. Press CTRL+H, and then proceed as described in 1 above starting with type Find what text

In some cases, you may want to replace only certain occurrences of the text, not all of them. To instruct Word to confirm each change, click the Find Next button in the Find and Replace dialog box (Figure 2-57), instead of the Replace All button. When Word locates an occurrence of the text, it pauses and waits for you to click either the Replace button or the Find Next button. Clicking the Replace button changes the text; clicking the Find Next button instructs Word to disregard the replacement and look for the next occurrence of the Find what text.

If you accidentally replace the wrong text, you can undo a replacement by clicking the Undo button on the Standard toolbar. If you used the Replace All button, Word undoes all replacements. If you used the Replace button, Word undoes only the most recent replacement.

Finding Text

Sometimes, you may want to find only text, instead of find *and* replace text. To search for just a single occurrence of text, you would follow these steps.

More About 2000

Finding

To search for formatting or special characters, click the More button in the Find dialog box. To find formatting, click the Format button, select the formats you want to search for, then click the Find button. To find a special character, click the Special button, click the special character you desire, and then click the Find button.

TO FIND TEXT

1. Click the Select Browse Object button on the vertical scroll bar and then click Find on the Select Browse Object menu.
2. Type the text to locate in the Find what text box and then click the Find Next button. To edit the text, click the Close button in the Find and Replace dialog box; to find the next occurrence of the text, click the Find Next button.

Moving Text

While proofreading the research paper, you might realize that text in the last paragraph would flow better if the last two sentences were reversed. That is, you want to move the fourth sentence in the last paragraph to the end of the paragraph.

To move text, such as words, characters, sentences, or paragraphs, you first select the text to be moved and then use drag-and-drop editing or the cut-and-paste technique to move the selected text. With **drag-and-drop editing**, you drag the selected item to the new location and then insert, or drop, it there. **Cutting** involves removing the selected item from the document and then placing it on the **Office Clipboard**, which is a temporary storage area. **Pasting** is the process of copying an item from the Clipboard into the document at the location of the insertion point.

Use drag-and-drop editing to move an item a short distance. To drag-and-drop a sentence in the research paper, first select a sentence as shown below.

More About 2000

Cutting and Pasting

To move text a long distance (from one page to another page), the cut-and-paste technique is more efficient. When you paste text into a document, the contents of the Office Clipboard are not erased.

Steps

To Select a Sentence

1. Position the mouse pointer (an I-beam) in the sentence to be moved. Press and hold the CTRL key. While holding the CTRL key, click the sentence. Release the CTRL key.

Word selects the entire sentence (Figure 2-59). Notice the space after the period is included in the selection.

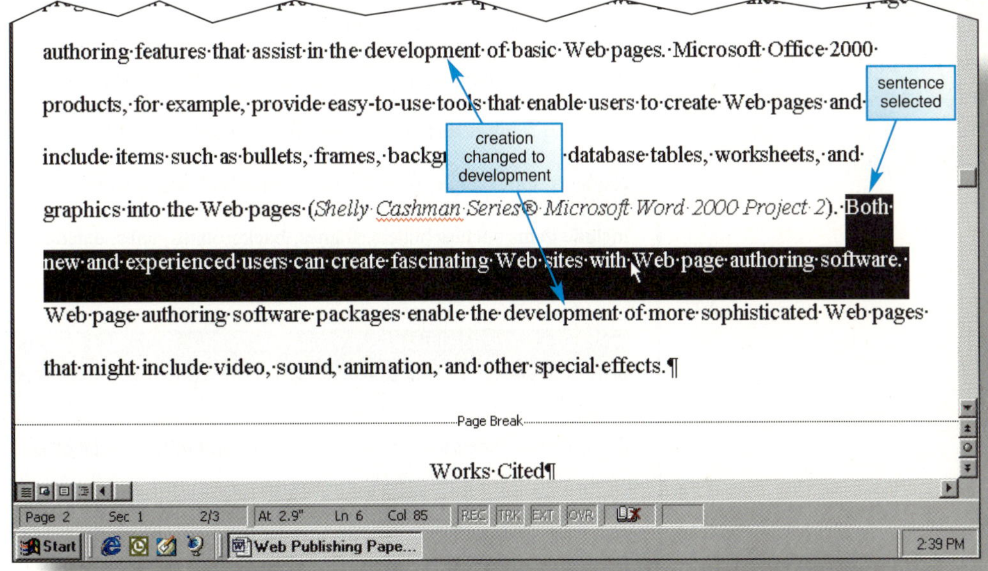
authoring·features·that·assist·in·the·development·of·basic·Web·pages.·Microsoft·Office·2000·
products,·for·example,·provide·easy-to-use·tools·that·enable·users·to·create·Web·pages·and·
include·items·such·as·bullets,·frames,·backg
database·tables,·worksheets,·and·
graphics·into·the·Web·pages·(Shelly·Cashman·Series®·Microsoft·Word·2000·Project·2).·Both·
new·and·experienced·users·can·create·fascinating·Web·sites·with·Web·page·authoring·software.·
Web·page·authoring·software·packages·enable·the·development·of·more·sophisticated·Web·pages·
that·might·include·video,·sound,·animation,·and·other·special·effects.¶
Page Break
Works·Cited¶
sentence selected
creation changed to development
Page 2
Sec 1
2/3
At 2.9"
Ln 6
Col 85
REC
TRK
EXT
OVR
Start
Web Publishing Pape...
2:39 PM

FIGURE 2-59

Other Ways

1. Drag through the sentence

Table 2-4 Techniques for Selecting Items with the Mouse

ITEM TO SELECT	MOUSE ACTION
Block of text	Click at beginning of selection, scroll to end of selection, position mouse pointer at end of selection, hold down SHIFT key and then click
Character(s)	Drag through character(s)
Document	Move mouse to left of text until mouse pointer changes to a right-pointing block arrow, then triple-click
Graphic	Click the graphic
Line	Move mouse to left of line until mouse pointer changes to a right-pointing block arrow, then click
Lines	Move mouse to left of first line until mouse pointer changes to a right-pointing block arrow, then drag up or down
Paragraph	Triple-click paragraph; or move mouse to left of paragraph until mouse pointer changes to a right-pointing block arrow, then double-click
Paragraphs	Move mouse to left of paragraph until mouse pointer changes to a right-pointing block arrow, double-click, then drag up or down
Sentence	Press and hold CTRL key, then click sentence
Word	Double-click the word
Words	Drag through words

Throughout Projects 1 and 2, you have selected text and then formatted it. Because selecting text is such a crucial function of Word, Table 2-4 summarizes the techniques used to select various items with the mouse.

With the sentence to be moved selected, you can use drag-and-drop editing to move it. You should be sure that drag-and-drop editing is enabled by clicking Tools on the menu bar, clicking Options, clicking the Edit tab, verifying a check mark is next to Drag and drop text editing, and then clicking the OK button. Follow these steps to move the selected sentence to the end of the paragraph.

To Move Text

1 With the mouse pointer in the selected text, press and hold the mouse button.

When you begin to drag the selected text, the insertion point changes to a ***dotted insertion point*** *(Figure 2-60).*

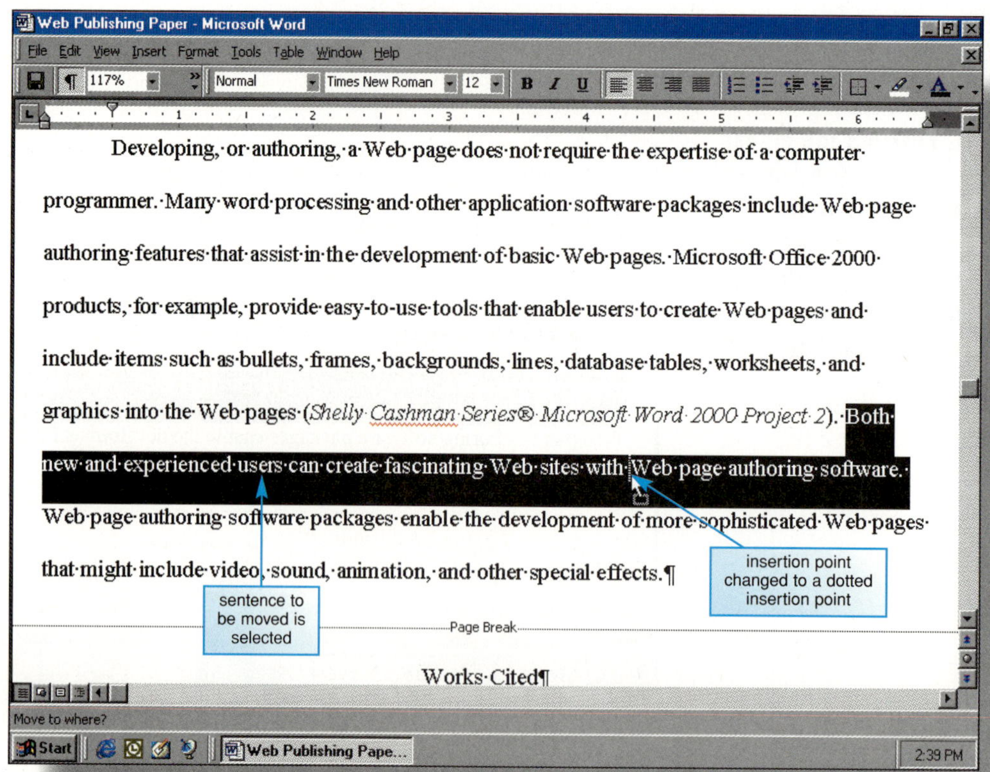
Web Publishing Paper - Microsoft Word
Developing, or authoring, a Web page does not require the expertise of a computer programmer. Many word processing and other application software packages include Web page authoring features that assist in the development of basic Web pages. Microsoft Office 2000 products, for example, provide easy-to-use tools that enable users to create Web pages and include items such as bullets, frames, backgrounds, lines, database tables, worksheets, and graphics into the Web pages (Shelly Cashman Series® Microsoft Word 2000 Project 2). Both new and experienced users can create fascinating Web sites with Web page authoring software. Web page authoring software packages enable the development of more sophisticated Web pages that might include video, sound, animation, and other special effects.¶
sentence to be moved is selected
insertion point changed to a dotted insertion point
Page Break
Works Cited¶
Move to where?
Start
Web Publishing Pape...
2:39 PM

FIGURE 2-60

2 **Drag the dotted insertion point to the location where the selected text is to be moved.**

The dotted insertion point is at the end of the paragraph (Figure 2-61).

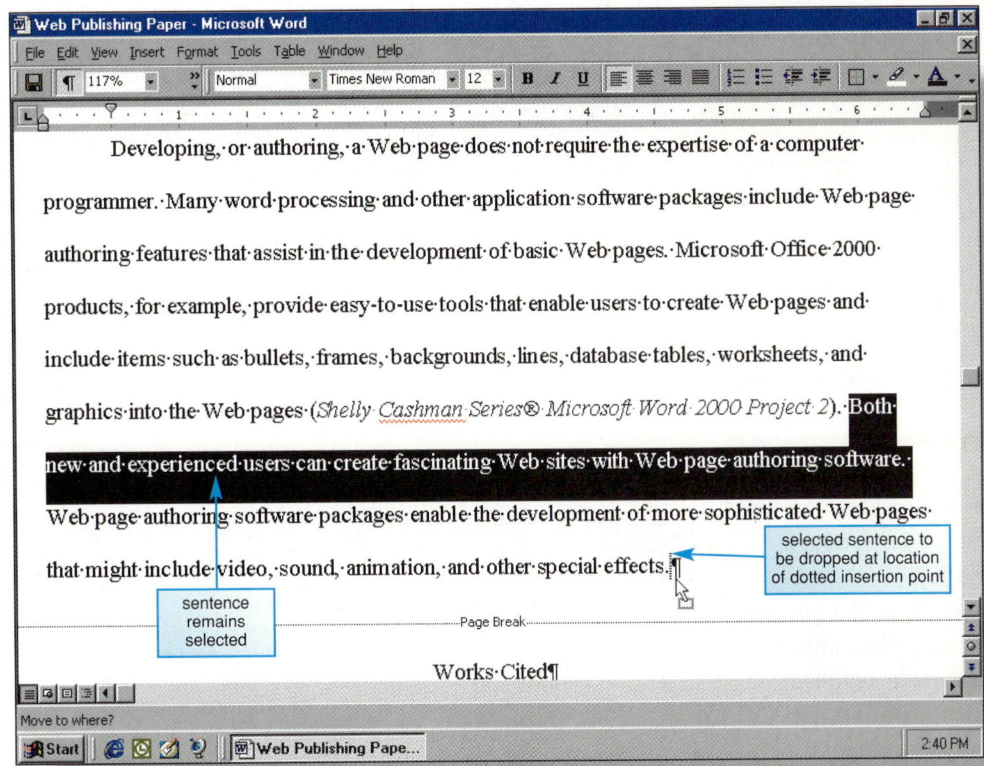
Web Publishing Paper - Microsoft Word
File Edit View Insert Format Tools Table Window Help
Developing, or authoring, a Web page does not require the expertise of a computer programmer. Many word processing and other application software packages include Web page authoring features that assist in the development of basic Web pages. Microsoft Office 2000 products, for example, provide easy-to-use tools that enable users to create Web pages and include items such as bullets, frames, backgrounds, lines, database tables, worksheets, and graphics into the Web pages (Shelly Cashman Series® Microsoft Word 2000 Project 2). Both new and experienced users can create fascinating Web sites with Web page authoring software. Web page authoring software packages enable the development of more sophisticated Web pages that might include video, sound, animation, and other special effects.
selected sentence to be dropped at location of dotted insertion point
sentence remains selected
Page Break
Works Cited
Move to where?
Start
Web Publishing Pape...
2:40 PM

FIGURE 2-61

3 **Release the mouse button. Click outside selection to remove the highlight.**

Word moves the selected text to the location of the dotted insertion point (Figure 2-62).

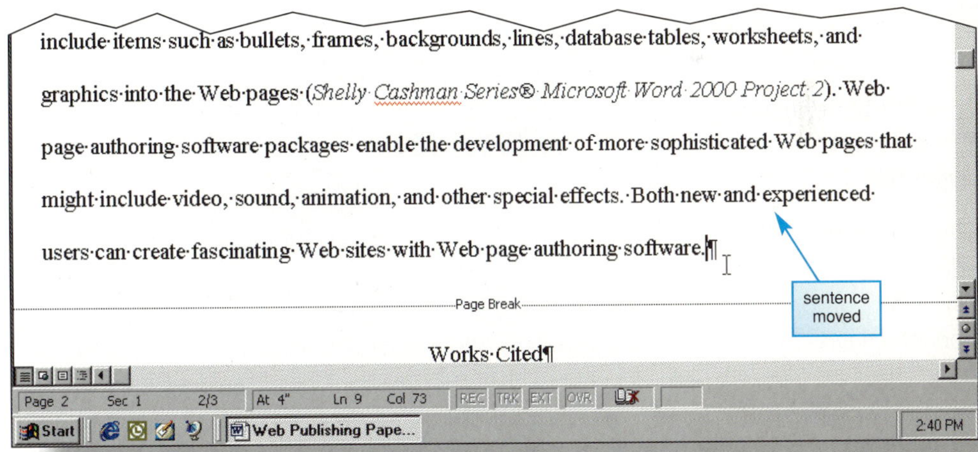
include items such as bullets, frames, backgrounds, lines, database tables, worksheets, and graphics into the Web pages (Shelly Cashman Series® Microsoft Word 2000 Project 2). Web page authoring software packages enable the development of more sophisticated Web pages that might include video, sound, animation, and other special effects. Both new and experienced users can create fascinating Web sites with Web page authoring software.
sentence moved
Page Break
Works Cited
Page 2 Sec 1 2/3 At 4" Ln 9 Col 73
Start
Web Publishing Pape...
2:40 PM

FIGURE 2-62

You can click the Undo button on the Standard toolbar if you accidentally drag text to the wrong location.

You can use drag-and-drop editing to move any selected item. That is, you can select words, sentences, phrases, and graphics and then use drag-and-drop editing to move them.

If you hold the CTRL key while dragging the selected item, Word copies the item instead of moving it.

Other Ways

1. Click Cut button on Standard toolbar, click where text is to be pasted, click Paste button on Standard toolbar
2. On Edit menu click Cut, click where text is to be pasted, on Edit menu click Paste
3. Press CTRL+X, position insertion point where text is to be pasted, press CTRL+V

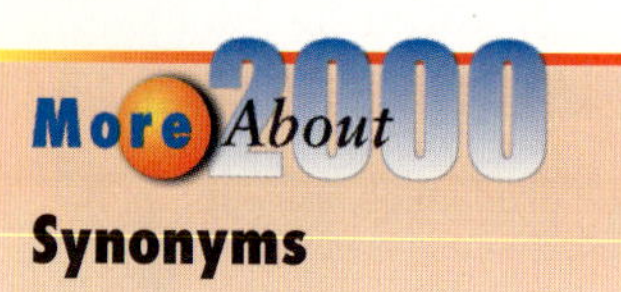

Synonyms

For access to an online thesaurus, visit the Word 2000 More About Web page (www.scsite.com/wd2000/more.htm) and then click Online Thesaurus.

Finding a Synonym

When writing, you may find that you used the same word in multiple locations or that a word you used was not quite appropriate. In these instances, you will want to look up a word similar in meaning to the duplicate or inappropriate word. These similar words are called **synonyms**. A book of synonyms is referred to as a **thesaurus**. Word provides synonyms and a thesaurus for your convenience. In this project, you would like a synonym for the word, include, in the middle of the last paragraph of the research paper. Perform the following steps to find an appropriate synonym.

To Find a Synonym

1 Right-click the word for which you want to look up a synonym (include). Point to Synonyms on the shortcut menu and then point to the appropriate synonym (incorporate) on the Synonyms submenu.

Word displays a list of synonyms for the word containing the insertion point (Figure 2-63).

2 Click the synonym you want (incorporate).

Word replaces the word, include, in the document with the selected word, incorporate (Figure 2-64).

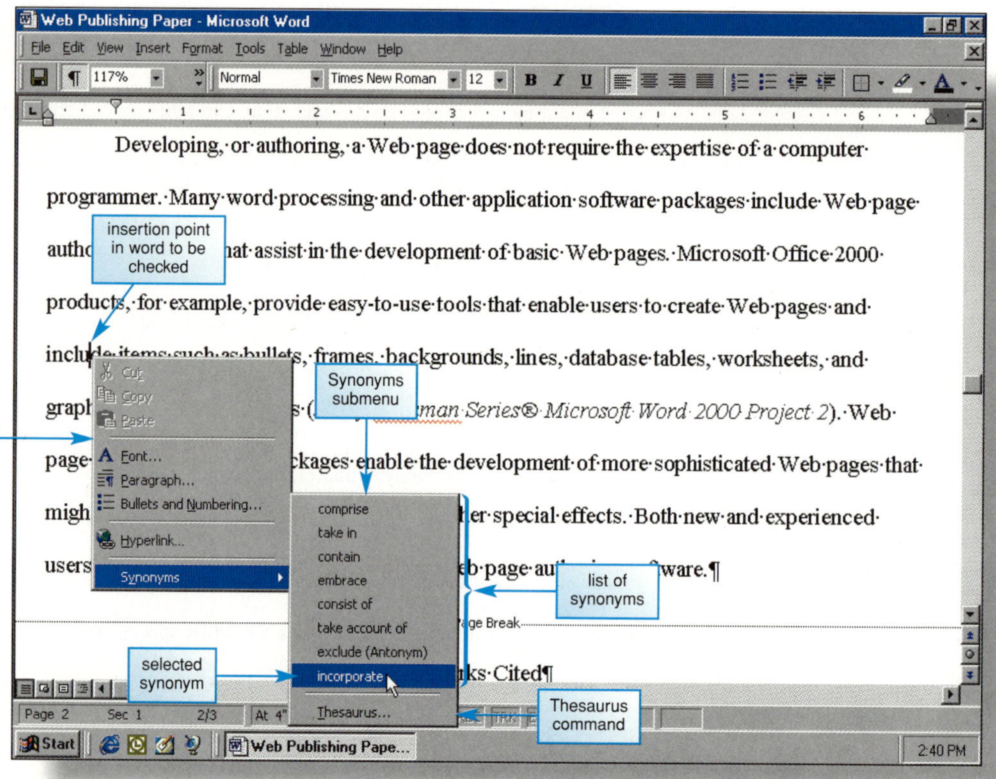

FIGURE 2-63

1. Click word, on Tools menu point to Language, on Language menu click Thesaurus, click appropriate meaning in Meanings list, click desired synonym in Replace with Synonym list, click Replace button
2. Click word, press SHIFT+F7, click appropriate meaning in Meanings list, click desired synonym in Replace with Synonym list, click Replace button

If the synonyms list does not display an appropriate word, you can display the Thesaurus dialog box by clicking Thesaurus on the Synonyms submenu (Figure 2-63). In the Thesaurus dialog box, you can look up synonyms for a different meaning of the word. You also can look up **antonyms**, or words with an opposite meaning.

Using Word Count

Often when you write papers, you are required to compose a paper with a minimum number of words. The requirement for the research paper in this project was a minimum of 425 words. Word provides a command that displays the number of words, as well as the number of pages, characters, paragraphs, and lines in your document. Perform the following steps to use word count.

To Count Words

1 Click Tools on the menu bar and then point to Word Count (Figure 2-64).

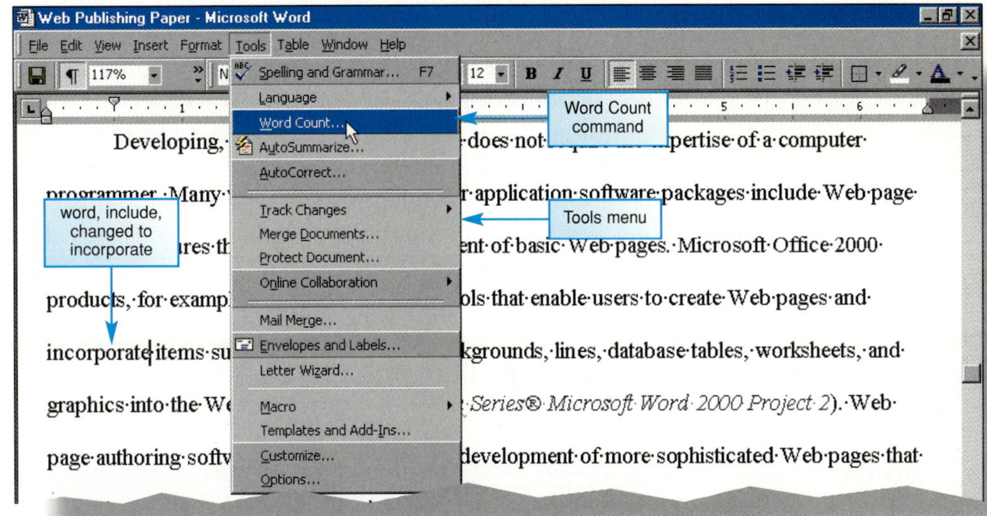

FIGURE 2-64

2 Click Word Count. When the Word Count dialog box displays, if necessary, click Include footnotes and endnotes to select the check box.

Word displays the Word Count dialog box (Figure 2-65).

3 Click the Close button in the Word Count dialog box.

Word returns you to the document.

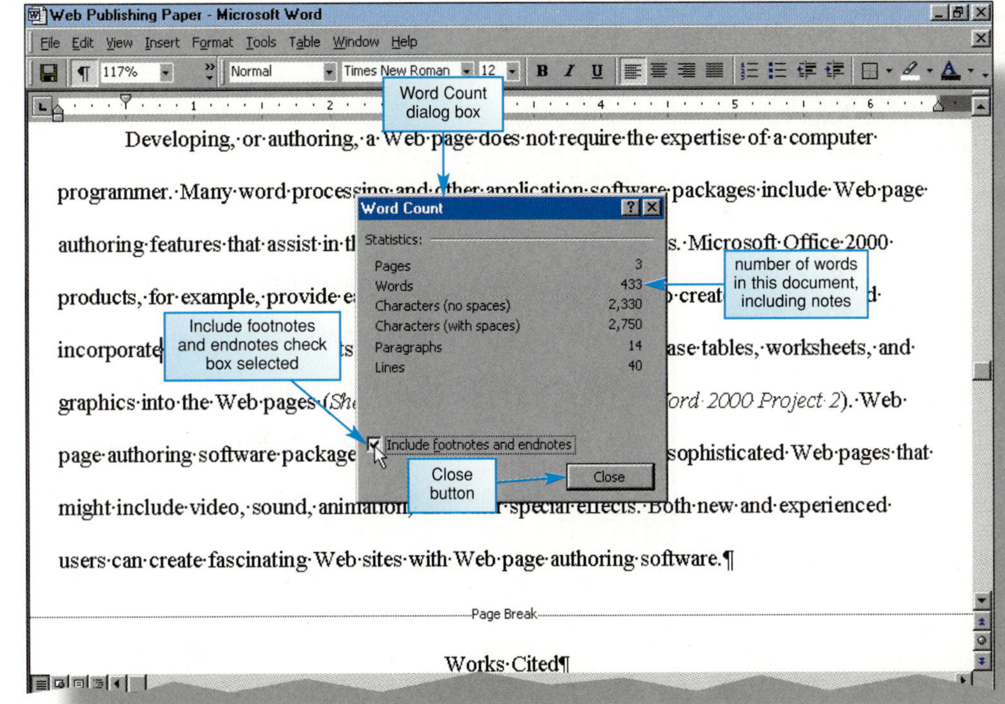

FIGURE 2-65

Other Ways

1. On File menu click Properties, click Statistics tab, click OK button

The Word Count dialog box presents a variety of statistics about the current document, including number of pages, words, characters, paragraphs, and lines (Figure 2-65). You can choose to have note text included or not included in these statistics. If you want statistics on only a section of your document, select the section and then invoke the Word Count command.

Flagged Words

If you right-click a word, a shortcut menu displays. Recall that commands in a shortcut menu differ depending on the object that you right-click. If you right-click a word flagged with a red or green wavy underline, the shortcut menu displays spelling or grammar corrections for the flagged word.

Checking Spelling and Grammar at Once

As discussed in Project 1, Word checks your spelling and grammar as you type and places a wavy underline below possible spelling or grammar errors. You learned in Project 1 how to check these flagged words immediately. You also can wait and check the entire document for spelling and grammar errors at once.

The following steps illustrate how to check spelling and grammar in the Web Publishing Paper at once. In the following example the word, maintaining, has been misspelled intentionally as maintining to illustrate the use of Word's check spelling and grammar at once feature. If you are doing this project on a personal computer, your research paper may contain different misspelled words, depending on the accuracy of your typing.

To Check Spelling and Grammar At Once

1 **Press the CTRL+HOME keys to move the insertion point to the beginning of the document. Double-click the move handle on the Standard toolbar to display the entire toolbar. Point to the Spelling and Grammar button on the Standard toolbar.**

Word will begin the spelling and grammar check at the location of the insertion point, which is at the beginning of the document (Figure 2-66).

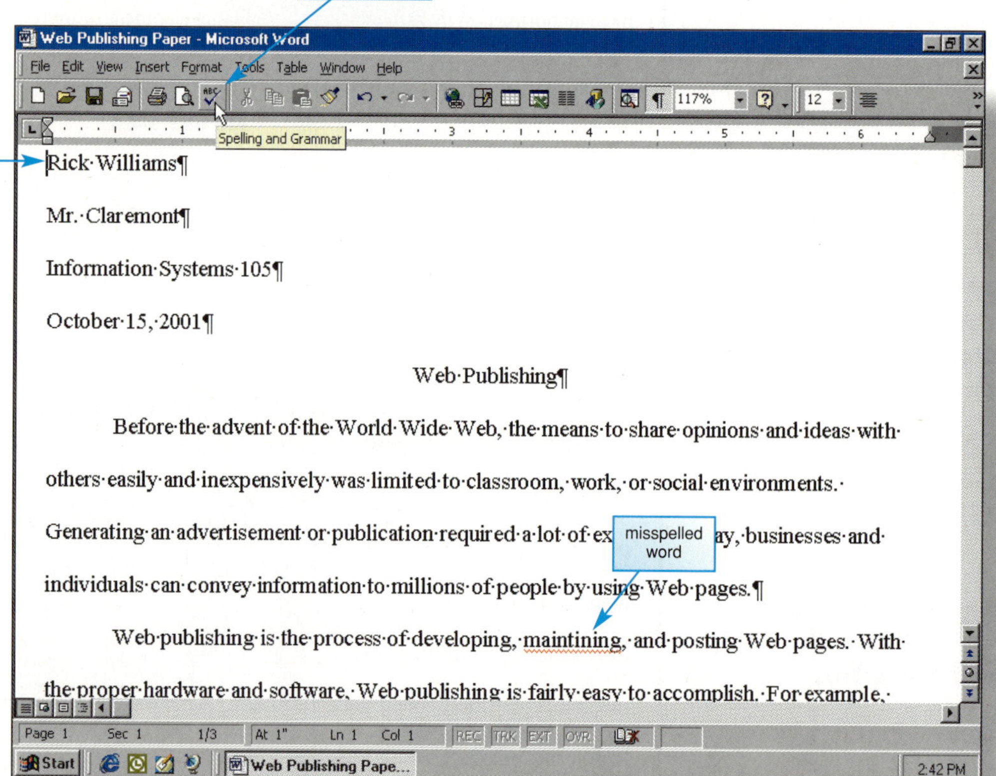
Spelling and Grammar button
insertion point
misspelled word
Web Publishing Paper - Microsoft Word
File Edit View Insert Format Tools Table Window Help
Spelling and Grammar
Rick·Williams¶
Mr.·Claremont¶
Information·Systems·105¶
October·15,·2001¶
Web·Publishing¶
Before·the·advent·of·the·World·Wide·Web,·the·means·to·share·opinions·and·ideas·with·
others·easily·and·inexpensively·was·limited·to·classroom,·work,·or·social·environments.·
Generating·an·advertisement·or·publication·required·a·lot·of·ex
ay,·businesses·and·
individuals·can·convey·information·to·millions·of·people·by·using·Web·pages.¶
Web·publishing·is·the·process·of·developing,·maintining,·and·posting·Web·pages.·With·
the·proper·hardware·and·software,·Web·publishing·is·fairly·easy·to·accomplish.·For·example,·
Page 1 Sec 1 1/3 At 1" Ln 1 Col 1
Start
Web Publishing Pape...
2:42 PM

FIGURE 2-66

2 Click the Spelling and Grammar button. When the Spelling and Grammar dialog box displays, click maintaining in the Suggestions list and then point to the Change button.

Word displays the Spelling and Grammar dialog box (Figure 2-67). Word did not find the misspelled word, maintining, in its dictionary. The Suggestions list displays suggested corrections for the flagged word.

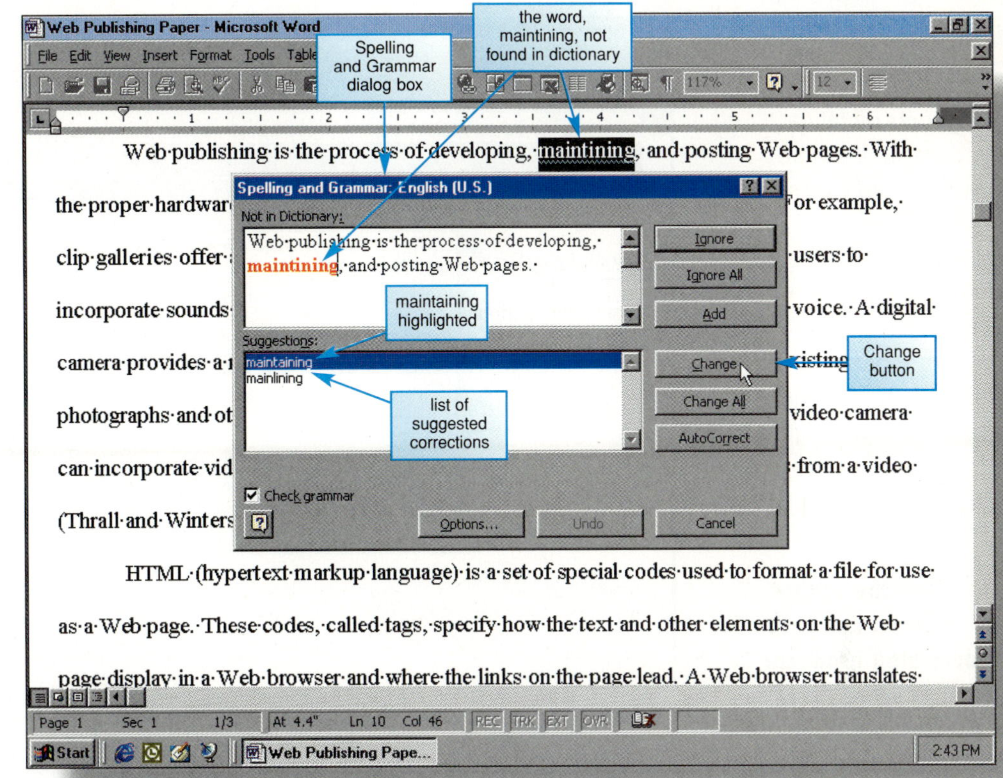

FIGURE 2-67

Click the Change button.

Word continues the spelling and grammar check until it finds the next error or reaches the end of the document (Figure 2-68). Word did not find Cashman in its dictionary because Cashman is a proper name. Cashman is spelled correctly.

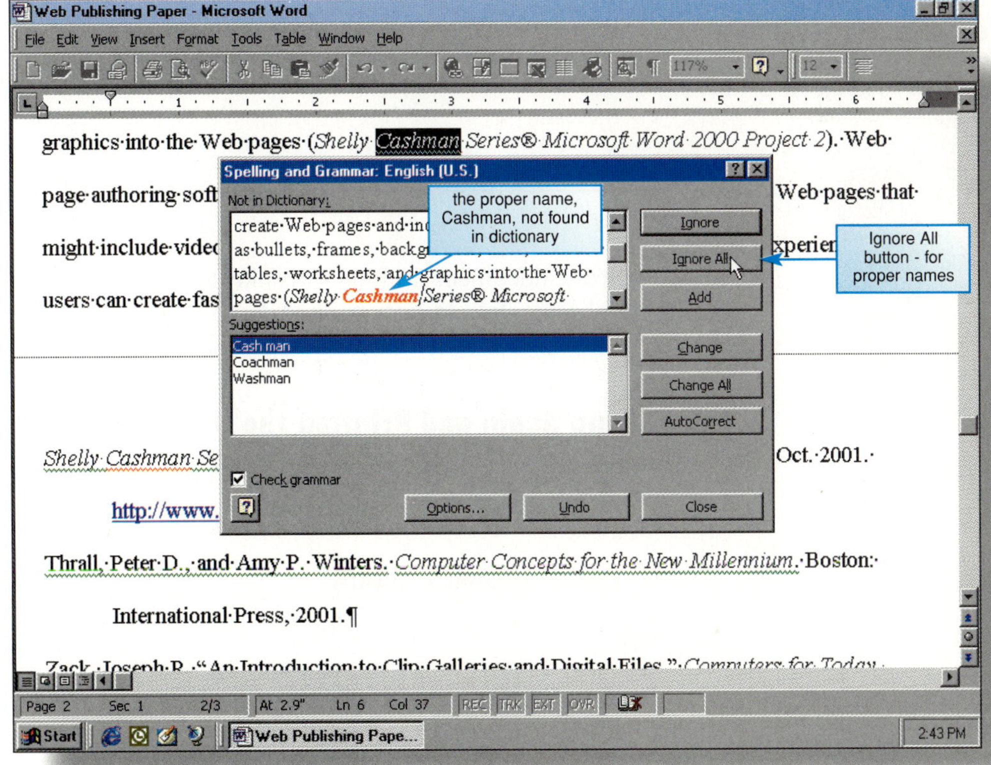

FIGURE 2-68

4 Click the Ignore All button.

Word ignores all future occurrences of the word, Cashman. Word continues the spelling and grammar check until it finds the next error or reaches the end of the document. Word flags a grammar error on the Works Cited page (Figure 2-69). The works cited is written correctly.

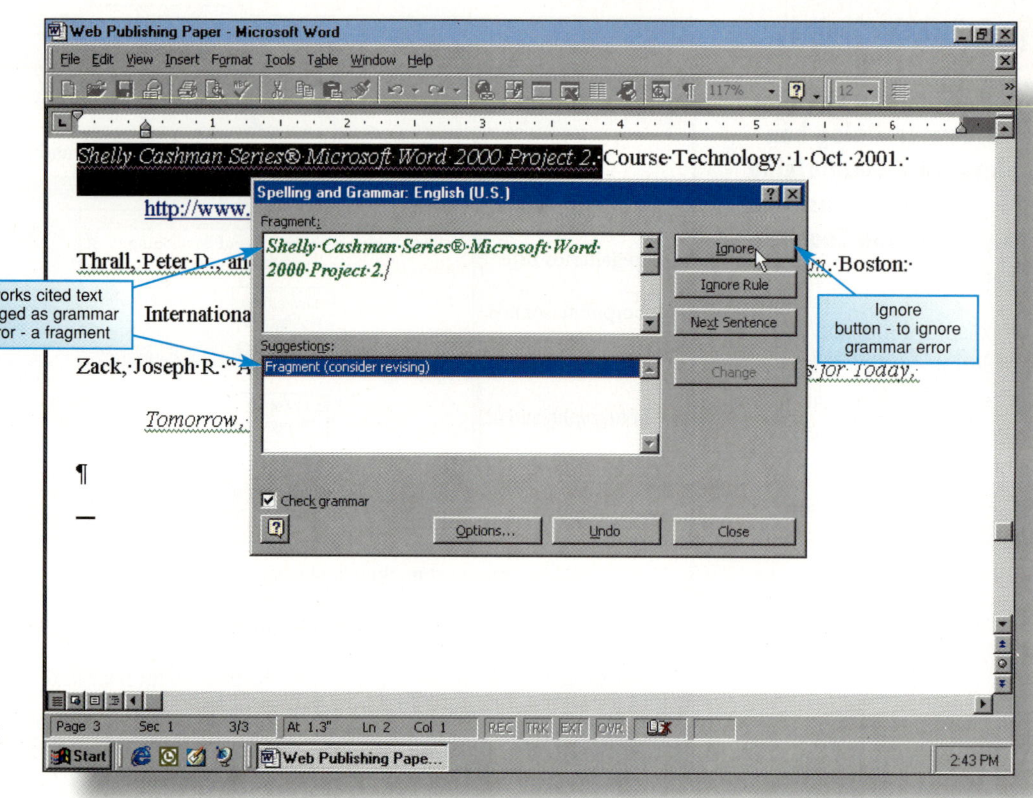

FIGURE 2-69

5 Click the Ignore button. For each of the remaining grammar errors that Word flags on the Works Cited page, click the Ignore button. When the Microsoft Word dialog box displays indicating Word has completed the spelling and grammar check, click the OK button.

Word returns to the document window.

1. Right-click flagged word, click Spelling on shortcut menu
2. On Tools menu click Spelling and Grammar
3. Press F7

Your document no longer displays red and green wavy underlines below words and phrases. In addition, the red X on the Spelling and Grammar Status icon has returned to a red check mark.

Saving Again and Printing the Document

The document now is complete. You should save the research paper again and print it, as described in the following steps.

TO SAVE A DOCUMENT AGAIN

1. Click the Save button on the Standard toolbar.

Word saves the research paper with the same file name, Web Publishing Paper.

TO PRINT A DOCUMENT

1. Click the Print button on the Standard toolbar.

The completed research paper prints as shown in Figure 2-1 on page WD 2.5.

Navigating to a Hyperlink

Recall that one requirement of this research paper is that one of the works be a Web site and be formatted as a hyperlink. Perform the following steps to check your hyperlink.

To Navigate to a Hyperlink

1 Display the third page of the research paper in the document window and then point to the hyperlink.

When you point to a hyperlink in a Word document, the mouse pointer shape changes to a pointing hand (Figure 2-70).

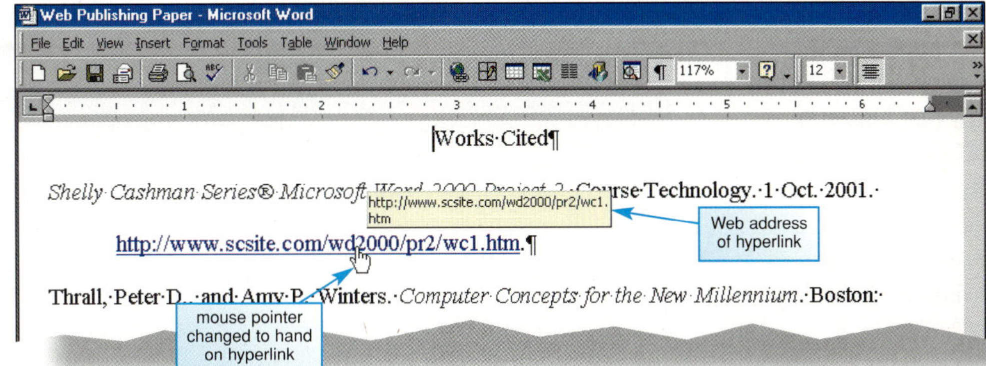

FIGURE 2-70

2 Click the hyperlink.

If you currently are not connected to the Web, Word connects you using your default browser. The www.scsite.com/wd2000/pr2/wc1.htm Web page displays (Figure 2-71).

3 Close the browser window. If necessary, click the Microsoft Word program button on the taskbar to redisplay the Word window. Press CTRL+HOME.

The first page of the research paper displays in the Word window.

FIGURE 2-71

E-mailing

To e-mail a document as an attachment, click File on the menu bar, point to Send To, and then click Mail Recipient (as Attachment).

E-mailing a Copy of the Research Paper

Your instructor, Mr. Claremont, has requested you e-mail him a copy of your research paper so he can verify your hyperlink. Perform the following step to e-mail the document from within Word.

To E-mail a Document

1 Click the E-mail button on the Standard toolbar. Fill in the To text box with Mr. Claremont's e-mail address and the Subject text box (Figure 2-72) and then click the Send a Copy button.

Word displays certain buttons and boxes from your e-mail editor inside the Word window. The document is e-mailed to the recipient named in the To text box.

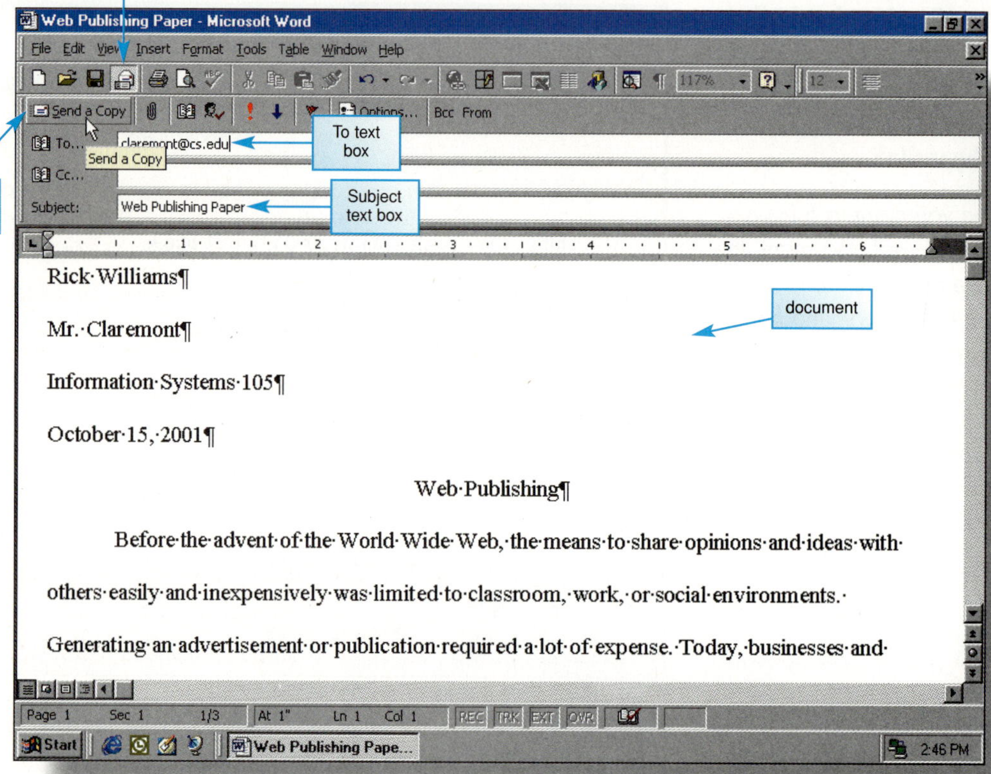
E-mail button
Send a Copy button
To text box
Subject text box
document
Web Publishing Paper - Microsoft Word
claremont@cs.edu
Web Publishing Paper
Rick·Williams¶
Mr.·Claremont¶
Information·Systems·105¶
October·15,·2001¶
Web·Publishing¶
Before·the·advent·of·the·World·Wide·Web,·the·means·to·share·opinions·and·ideas·with·
others·easily·and·inexpensively·was·limited·to·classroom,·work,·or·social·environments.·
Generating·an·advertisement·or·publication·required·a·lot·of·expense.·Today,·businesses·and·

FIGURE 2-72

1. On File menu point to Send To, on Send To menu click Mail Recipient

Quick Reference

For a table that lists how to complete the tasks covered in this book using the mouse, menu, shortcut menu, and keyboard, visit the Office 2000 Web page (www.scsite.com/off2000/qr.htm) and then click Microsoft Word 2000.

If you want to cancel the e-mail operation, click the E-mail button again. The final step in this project is to quit Word, as described in the following step.

TO QUIT WORD

 Click the Close button in the Word window.

The Word window closes.

CASE PERSPECTIVE SUMMARY

Rick accomplished his goal – learning about the basics of Web publishing while completing Mr. Claremont's research paper assignment. Now he is ready to create a personal Web page and publish it to a Web server. Rick decides to use Word's Web Page Wizard to create his Web page. He also contacts his Internet service provider to set up his free 6 MB of Web space. After receiving his personal Web site address from his Internet service provider, Rick publishes his Web page for the world to see. (For more information on publishing Web pages to a Web server, see Appendix B.) He shows Mr. Claremont the Web page, who in turn shows Rick's classmates.

Project Summary

Project 2 introduced you to creating a research paper using the MLA documentation style. You learned how to change margin settings, adjust line spacing, create headers with page numbers, and indent paragraphs. You learned how to use Word's AutoCorrect feature. Then, you added a footnote in the research paper. You alphabetized the works cited page by sorting its paragraphs and included a hyperlink to a Web page in one of the works. You learned how to browse through a Word document, find and replace text, and move text. You looked up a synonym and saw how to display statistics about your document. Finally, you navigated to a hyperlink and e-mailed a copy of a document.

What You Should Know

Having completed this project, you now should be able to perform the following tasks:

- Add a Footnote *(WD 2.23)*
- AutoCorrect As You Type *(WD 2.20)*
- Browse by Page *(WD 2.42)*
- Center the Title of the Works Cited Page *(WD 2.36)*
- Change the Default Font Size *(WD 2.15)*
- Change the Margin Settings *(WD 2.8)*
- Check Spelling and Grammar at Once *(WD 2.50)*
- Click and Type *(WD 2.13)*
- Close the Note Pane *(WD 2.29)*
- Count Words *(WD 2.49)*
- Create a Hanging Indent *(WD 2.37)*
- Create a Hyperlink as You Type *(WD 2.39)*
- Create an AutoCorrect Entry *(WD 2.21)*
- Display Formatting Marks *(WD 2.7)*
- Display the Header Area *(WD 2.12)*
- Double-Space a Document *(WD 2.9)*
- E-mail a Document *(WD 2.54)*
- Enter and Format a Page Number *(WD 2.14)*
- Enter More Text *(WD 2.30)*
- Enter Name and Course Information *(WD 2.16)*
- Enter Works Cited Paragraphs *(WD 2.38)*
- Find a Synonym *(WD 2.48)*
- Find and Replace Text *(WD 2.43)*
- Find Text *(WD 2.45)*
- First-Line Indent Paragraphs *(WD 2.19)*
- Insert a Symbol Automatically *(WD 2.33)*
- Modify a Style *(WD 2.26)*
- Move Text *(WD 2.46)*
- Navigate to a Hyperlink *(WD 2.53)*
- Page Break Automatically *(WD 2.32)*
- Page Break Manually *(WD 2.35)*
- Print a Document *(WD 2.52)*
- Quit Word *(WD 2.54)*
- Reset Menus and Toolbars *(WD 2.7)*
- Save a Document *(WD 2.18)*
- Save a Document Again *(WD 2.52)*
- Select a Sentence *(WD 2.45)*
- Sort Paragraphs *(WD 2.40)*
- Start Word *(WD 2.6)*
- Use Shortcut Keys to Format Text *(WD 2.17)*
- Zoom Page Width *(WD 2.9)*

More About 2000

Microsoft Certification

The Microsoft Office User Specialist (MOUS) Certification program provides an opportunity for you to obtain a valuable industry credential – proof that you have the Word 2000 skills required by employers. For more information, see Appendix D or visit the Shelly Cashman Series MOUS Web page at www.scsite.com/off2000/cert.htm.

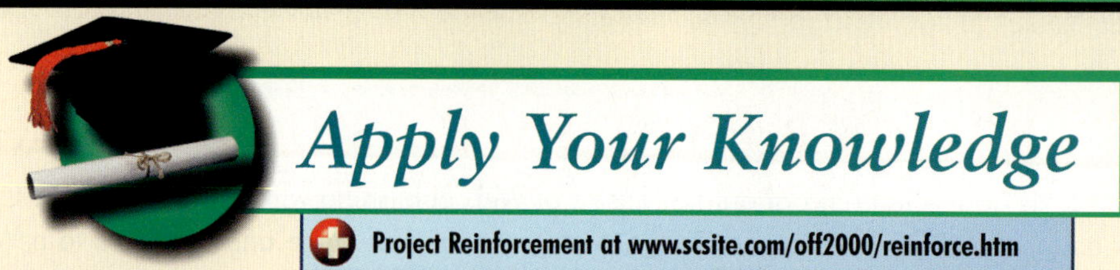

1 Revising a Document

Instructions: Start Word. Open the document, Internet Paragraph, on the Data Disk. If you did not download the Data Disk, see the inside back cover for instructions for downloading the Data Disk or see your instructor.

The document is a paragraph of text. You are to move two sentences in the paragraph and change all occurrences of the word, Web, to the phrase, World Wide Web. The revised paragraph is shown in Figure 2-73.

Although many people use the terms World Wide Web and Internet interchangeably, the World Wide Web is just one of the many services available on the Internet. The World Wide Web actually is a relatively new aspect of the Internet. While the Internet was developed in the late 1960s, the World Wide Web came into existence less than a decade ago – in the early 1990s. Since then, however, it has grown phenomenally to become the most widely used service on the Internet.

FIGURE 2-73

Perform the following tasks:

1. Press and hold the CTRL key. While holding the CTRL key, click in the third sentence, which begins, The Web actually is..., to select the sentence. Release the CTRL key.
2. Press and hold down the left mouse button. Drag the dotted insertion point to the left of the letter W in the second sentence beginning, While the Internet was..., and then release the mouse button to move the sentence. Click outside the selection to remove the highlight.
3. Click the Select Browse Object button on the vertical scroll bar and then click Find on the Select Browse Object menu.
4. When the Find and Replace dialog box displays, click the Replace tab. Type `Web` in the Find what text box, press the TAB key, and then type `World Wide Web` in the Replace with text box. Click the Replace All button.
5. Click the OK button in the Microsoft Word dialog box. Click the Close button in the Find and Replace dialog box.
6. Click File on the menu bar and then click Save As. Use the file name, Revised Internet Paragraph, and then save the document on your floppy disk.
7. Print the revised paragraph.

1 Preparing a Research Paper

Problem: You are a college student currently enrolled in an English composition class. Your assignment is to prepare a short research paper (400-425 words) about digital cameras. The requirements are that the paper be presented according to the MLA documentation style and have three references (Figures 2-74a through 2-74c shown below and on the next page). One of the three references must be from the Internet and formatted as a hyperlink on the Works Cited page.

Thornton 1

Anne Thornton

Ms. Baxter

English 105

March 12, 2001

Digital Cameras

Digital cameras allow computer users to take pictures and store the photographed images digitally instead of on traditional film. With some digital cameras, a user downloads the stored pictures from the digital camera to a computer using special software included with the camera. With others, the camera stores the pictures directly on a floppy disk or on a PC Card. A user then copies the pictures to a computer by inserting the floppy disk into a disk drive or the PC Card into a PC Card slot (Chambers and Norton 134). Once stored on a computer, the pictures can be edited with photo-editing software, printed, faxed, sent via electronic mail, included in another document, or posted to a Web site for everyone to see.

Three basic types of digital cameras are studio cameras, field cameras, and point-and-shoot cameras (*Shelly Cashman Series® Microsoft Word 2000 Project 2*). The most expensive and highest quality of the three, a studio camera, is a stationary camera used for professional studio work. Photojournalists frequently use field cameras because they are portable and have a variety of lenses and other attachments. As with the studio camera, a field camera can be quite expensive.

Reliable and lightweight, the point-and-shoot camera provides acceptable quality photographic images for the home or small business user. A point-and-shoot camera enables these users to add pictures to personalized greeting cards, a computerized photo album, a family

FIGURE 2-74a

(continued)

Preparing a Research Paper *(continued)*

Thornton 2

newsletter, certificates, awards, or a personal Web site. Because of its functionality, it is an ideal camera for mobile users such as real estate agents, insurance agents, and general contractors.

The image quality produced by a digital camera is measured by the number of bits it stores in a dot and the resolution, or number of dots per inch. The higher each number, the better the quality, but the more expensive the camera. Most of today's point-and-shoot digital cameras are at least 24-bit with a resolution ranging from 640 x 480 to 1024 x 960 (Walker 57-89). Home and small business users can find an affordable camera with a resolution in this range that delivers excellent detail for less than $400.

FIGURE 2-74b

Thornton 3

Works Cited

Chambers, John Q., and Theresa R. Norton. *Understanding Computers in the New Century.* Chicago: Midwest Press, 2001.

Shelly Cashman Series® Word 2000 Project 2. Course Technology. 5 Mar. 2001. http://www.scsite.com/wd2000/pr2/wc2.htm.

Walker, Marianne L. "Understanding the Resolutions of Digital Cameras and Imaging Devices." *Computing for the Home* Feb. 2001: 57-89.

FIGURE 2-74c

Instructions:

1. If necessary, click the Show/Hide ¶ button on the Standard toolbar. Change all margins to one inch. Adjust line spacing to double. Create a header to number pages. If necessary, change the font size of all characters to 12 point. Type the name and course information at the left margin. Center and type the title. First-line indent all paragraphs in the paper.
2. Type the body of the paper as shown in Figure 2-74a on the previous page and Figure 2-74b. At the end of the body of the research paper, press the ENTER key and insert a manual page break.
3. Create the works cited page (Figure 2-74c).
4. Check the spelling of the paper at once.
5. Save the document on a floppy disk with Digital Camera Paper as the file name.
6. If you have access to the Web, test your hyperlink by clicking it.
7. Print the research paper. Above the title of your printed research paper, handwrite the number of words in the research paper.

2 Preparing a Research Report with Footnotes

Problem: You are a college student currently enrolled in an English composition class. Your assignment is to prepare a short research paper in any area of interest to you. The requirements are that the paper be presented according to the MLA documentation style and have three references. One of the three references must be from the Internet and formatted as a hyperlink on the works cited page. You decide to prepare a paper on virtual reality (Figures 2-75 below and on the next page).

Jameson 1

Casey Jameson

Mr. Brookfield

English 105

September 14, 2001

Virtual Reality

Virtual reality (VR) is the use of a computer to create an artificial environment that appears and feels like a real environment and allows users to explore a space and manipulate the environment. In its simplest form, a VR application displays what appears to be a three-dimensional view of a place or object, such as a landscape, building, molecule, or red blood cell, which users can explore. For example, architects can use VR software to show clients how a building will look after a construction or remodeling project.

In more advanced forms, VR software requires that users wear specialized headgear, body suits, and gloves to enhance the experience of the artificial environment (Vance and Reed 34-58). The headgear displays the artificial environment in front of a user's eyes.[1] The body suit and the gloves sense motion and direction, allowing a user to move through, pick up, or hold items displayed in the virtual environment. Experts predict that eventually the body suits will provide tactile feedback so users can experience the touch and feel of the virtual world.

Many games, such as flight simulators, use virtual reality. In these games, special visors allow users to see the computer-generated environment. As the user walks around the game's electronic landscape, sensors in the surrounding game machine record movements and change the view of the landscape accordingly.

---

[1] According to Vance and Reed, patients in one dental office wear VR headsets to relax them during their visit with the dentist.

FIGURE 2-75a

(continued)

Preparing a Research Report with Footnotes *(continued)*

Jameson 2

Companies increasingly are using VR for more practical commercial applications, as well. Automobile dealers, for example, use virtual showrooms in which customers can view the exterior and interior of available vehicles. Airplane manufacturers use virtual prototypes to test new models and shorten product design time. Many firms use personal computer-based VR applications for employee training (*Shelly Cashman Series® Microsoft Word 2000 Project 2*). As computing power and the use of the Web increase, practical applications of VR continue to emerge in education, business, and entertainment.[2]

[2] Henry Davidson, a developer of VR applications, predicts that in the future, moviegoers will be able to pretend they are one of a movie's characters. In this environment, the VR technology will link the moviegoer's sensory system (sight, smell, hearing, taste, and touch) to the character's sensory system (Holloway 46-52).

FIGURE 2-75b

Part 1 Instructions: Perform the following tasks to create the research paper:

1. If necessary, click the Show/Hide ¶ button on the Standard toolbar. Change all margin settings to one inch. Adjust line spacing to double. Create a header to number pages. If necessary, change the font size of all characters to 12 point. Type the name and course information at the left margin. Center and type the title. First-line indent all paragraphs in the paper.
2. Type the body of the paper as shown in Figure 2-75a on page WD 2.59 and Figure 2-75b. At the end of the body of the research paper, press the ENTER key once and insert a manual page break.
3. Create the works cited page. Enter the works cited shown below as separate paragraphs and then sort the paragraphs.
   (a) *Shelly Cashman Series® Microsoft Word 2000 Project 2*. Course Technology. 3 Sep. 2001. http://www.scsite.com/wd2000/pr2/wc3.htm.
   (b) Holloway, April I. "The Future of Virtual Reality Applications." *Computers for Today, Tomorrow, and Beyond* Sep. 2001: 46-52.
   (c) Vance, Dale W., and Karen P. Reed. *The Complete Book of Virtual Reality*. Dallas: Worldwide Press, 2001.
4. Check the spelling of the paper.
5. Save the document on a floppy disk with Virtual Reality Paper as the file name.
6. If you have access to the Web, test your hyperlink by clicking it.
7. Print the research paper. Above the title of your printed research paper, handwrite the number of words, including the footnotes, in the research paper.

Part 2 Instructions: Perform the following tasks to modify the research paper:

1. Use Word to find a synonym of your choice for the word, eventually, in the second paragraph.
2. Change all occurrences of the word, artificial, to the word, simulated.
3. In the second footnote, change the word, link, to the word, connect.
4. Convert the footnotes to endnotes. You have learned that endnotes appear at the end of a document. *Hint:* Use Help to learn about converting footnotes to endnotes.
5. Modify the Endnote text style to 12-point font, double-spaced text with a first-line indent. Insert a page break so the endnotes are placed on a separate numbered page. Center the title, Endnotes, double-spaced above the notes.
6. Change the format of the note reference marks from Arabic numbers (1., 2., etc.) to capital letters (A., B., etc.). *Hint*: Use Help to learn about changing the number format of note reference marks.
7. Save the document on a floppy disk with Revised Virtual Reality Paper as the file name.
8. Print the revised research paper.

3 Composing a Research Paper from Notes

Problem: You have drafted the notes shown in Figure 2-76. Your assignment is to prepare a short research paper from these notes. Review the notes and then rearrange and reword them. Embellish the paper as you deem necessary. Add a footnote elaborating on a personal experience you have had. Present the paper according to the MLA documentation style.

Productivity software makes people more efficient and effective in their daily activities. Three popular applications are (1) word processing, (2) spreadsheet, and (3) database.

Word Processing: Widely used application for creating, editing, and formatting text-based documents such as letters, memos, reports, fax cover sheet, mailing labels, and newsletters. Formatting features include changing font and font size, changing color of characters, organizing text into newspaper-style columns. Other features include adding clip art, changing margins, finding and replacing text, checking spelling and grammar, inserting headers and footers, providing a thesaurus, developing Web pages, and inserting tables. Source: "Evaluating Word Processing and Spreadsheet Software," an article in Computers Weekly, January 12, 2001 issue, pages 45-78, author Kimberly G. Rothman.

Spreadsheet: Used to organize data in rows and columns in a worksheet. Data is stored in cells, the intersection of rows and columns. Worksheets have more than 16 millions cells that can hold data. Cells can hold numbers, formulas, or functions. Formulas and functions perform calculations. When data in cells changes, the formulas and functions automatically recalculate formulas and display new values. Many spreadsheet packages allow you to create macros, which hold a series of keystrokes and instructions – a real timesaver. Most also include the ability to create charts, e.g. line charts, column charts, and pie charts, from the data. Source: same as for word processing software.

Database: Used to collect data and allow access, retrieval, and use of that data. Data stored in tables, which consists of rows (records) and columns (fields). Data can contain text, numbers, dates, or hyperlinks. When data is entered, it can be validated (compared to a set of stored rules or values to determine if the entered data is correct). Once the data is stored, you can sort it, query it, and generate reports from it. Sometimes called a database management system (DBMS). Source: Understanding Databases, a book published by Harbor Press in Detroit, Michigan, 2001, pages 35-56, authors Mark A. Greene and Andrea K. Peterson.

Microsoft Word 2000 is word processing software; Microsoft Excel 2000 is an example of spreadsheet software; and Microsoft Access 2000 is a database software package. Source: a Web site titled Shelly Cashman Series® Microsoft Word 2000 Project 2 sponsored by Course Technology; site visited on March 12, 2001; Web address is http://www.scsite.com/wd2000/pr2/wc4.htm.

FIGURE 2-76

Instructions: Perform the following tasks:

1. Change all margin settings to one inch. Adjust line spacing to double. Create a header to number pages. If necessary, change the font size of all characters to 12 point. Type the name and course information at the left margin. Center and type the title. First-line indent all paragraphs in the paper.
2. Compose the body of the paper from the notes in Figure 2-76. Be sure to include a footnote as specified. At the end of the body of the research paper, press the ENTER key once and insert a manual page break. Create the works cited page from the listed sources. Be sure to sort the works.
3. Check the spelling and grammar of the paper. Save the document on a floppy disk with Software Research Paper as the file name. Print the research paper. Above the title of the printed research paper, handwrite the number of words, including the footnote, in the research paper.

Cases and Places

The difficulty of these case studies varies:
▶ are the least difficult; ▶▶ are more difficult; and ▶▶▶ are the most difficult.

1 ▶ Project 1 of this book discussed the components of the Word document window. These components include the menu bar, toolbars, rulers, scroll bars, and status bar. In your own words, write a short research paper (400-450 words) that describes the purpose and functionality of one or more of these components. Use your textbook, Word Help, and any other resources available. Include at least two references and one explanatory note. Use the concepts and techniques presented in this project to format the paper.

2 ▶ Having completed two projects using Word 2000, you should be comfortable with some of its features. To reinforce your knowledge of Word's features, write a short research paper (400-450 words) that discusses a few of the features that you have learned. Features might include items such as checking spelling, inserting clip art, adding text using Click and Type, sorting paragraphs, and so on. Use your textbook, Word Help, and any other resources available. Include at least two references and one explanatory note. Use the concepts and techniques presented in this project to format the paper.

3 ▶▶ A pointing device is an input device that allows a user to control a pointer on a computer screen. Common pointing devices include the mouse, trackball, touchpad, pointing stick, joystick, touch screen, light pen, and graphics tablet. Using the school library, other textbooks, magazines, the Internet, or other resources, research two or more of these pointing devices. Then, prepare a brief research paper (400-450 words) that discusses the pointing devices. Include at least one explanatory note and two references, one of which must be a Web site on the Internet. Use the concepts and techniques presented in this project to format the paper.

4 ▶▶ A utility program, also called a utility, is a type of software that performs a specific task, usually related to managing a computer, its devices, or its programs. Popular utility programs are file viewers, file compression utilities, diagnostic utilities, disk scanners, disk defragmenters, uninstallers, backup utilities, antivirus programs, and screensavers. Using the school library, other textbooks, the Internet, magazines, or other resources, research two or more of these utility programs. Then, prepare a brief research paper (400-450 words) that discusses the utilities. Include at least one explanatory note and two references, one of which must be a Web site on the Internet. Use the concepts and techniques presented in this project to format the paper.

Cases and Places

5 ▶▶ Communications technologies have changed the way individuals interact, by allowing for instant and accurate information transfer, 24 hours a day. Today, uses of communications technology are all around and include e-mail, voice mail, fax, telecommuting, videoconferencing, groupware, global positioning systems (GPSs), bulletin board systems (BBSs), the Internet, the World Wide Web, e-commerce, and telephony. Using the school library, other textbooks, the Internet, magazines, or other resources, research two or more of these communications technologies. Then, prepare a brief research paper (400-450 words) that discusses the communications technologies. Include at least one explanatory note and two references, one of which must be a Web site on the Internet. Use the concepts and techniques presented in this project to format the paper.

6 ▶▶▶ In today's technology-rich world, a great demand for computer and information systems professionals exists and continues to grow. Career opportunities are available in many different areas including an information systems department, education and training, sales, service and repair, and consulting. Select an area of interest and research it. Obtain information about job titles, job functions, educational requirements, experience requirements, and salary ranges. Look through the classified section of a newspaper for job listings. Visit the career development and placement office at your school. Search the Web for employment opportunities at major companies. Then, prepare a brief research paper (400-450 words) on the career opportunities available. Indicate which ones you would pursue. Include at least two explanatory notes and three references, one of which must be a Web site on the Internet. Use the concepts and techniques presented in this project to format the paper.

7 ▶▶▶ The decision to purchase a personal computer is an important one – and finding and purchasing the right computer requires an investment of both time and money. In general, personal computers fall into three types: desktop computers, laptop computers, and handheld computers. Select one of these types of computers and shop for the best package deal. Many retailers offer software or additional hardware as part of a package deal. Visit or call a computer store. Search the Web for an online store. Look through newspapers or magazines for retailers, and obtain prices for their latest computer package deals. Then, prepare a brief research paper (400-450 words) on the various computer deals and recommend the one you feel is the best buy for the price. Include at least two explanatory notes and three references, one of which must be a Web site on the Internet. Use the concepts and techniques presented in this project to format the paper.

Microsoft Word 2000

Using a Wizard to Create a Resume and Creating a Cover Letter with a Table

OBJECTIVES

You will have mastered the material in this project when you can:

- Create a resume using Word s Resume Wizard
- Identify the Word screen in print layout view
- Zoom text width
- Identify styles in a document
- Replace selected text with new text
- Insert a line break
- Use print preview to view, reduce the size of, and print a document
- Open a new document window
- Add color to characters
- Set and use tab stops
- Switch from one open Word document to another
- Collect and paste
- Insert a symbol
- Add a bottom border to a paragraph
- Identify the components of a business letter
- Create an AutoText entry
- Insert a nonbreaking space
- Insert an AutoText entry
- Create a bulleted list as you type
- Insert a Word table
- Enter data into a Word table
- Format a Word table
- Prepare and print an envelope address
- Close all open Word documents

Personalized Letters and Résumés

Get You the Job!

"Young physicist seeks teaching position at the university level. Ph.D. thesis submitted, awaiting acceptance. Works include papers on particle theory, quantum theory, and special theory of relativity. Family man, enjoys playing the violin and sailing. Contact A. Einstein."

Yes, *that* A. Einstein, who, in 1905, wrote by hand literally dozens of letters seeking employment as a teacher while he labored in relative obscurity at the Swiss patent office. The same year, he published three studies that set the world of science on its ear. Fame eventually helped, but persistence in his search paid off when he finally landed a teaching appointment at the University of Zurich after years as a patent clerk.

No one can tell whether Einstein might have met his goals more quickly if he would have had the benefit of modern word processing software, but certainly Microsoft Word would have made his life easier.

As you embark on your professional life, you have the advantage of using Word to prepare a resume and a personalized cover letter. In this project, you will learn these skills. Because employers review many resumes, the content of your resume is very important and its design and detail should represent you as the best candidate for the job. Providing a personalized cover letter with each resume enables you to elaborate on positive points in your resume and gives you an opportunity to show a potential employer your written communications skills.

Using the Résumé Wizard creates a resume that is tailored to your preferences. The Wizard provides the style, formats the resume with appropriate headings and spacing, and makes it easy for you to present your best qualities.

> *"Be studious in your profession, and you will be learned.*
> *Be industrious and frugal, and you will be rich.*
> *Be sober and temperate, and you will be healthy.*
> *Be in general virtuous, and you will be happy.*
> *At least you will, by such conduct, stand the best*
> *chance for such consequences."*
>
> Benjamin Franklin

If good guidelines exist for doing something, then why not use them? This same practicality is built into the Résumé Wizard. Word provides the tools that eliminate the need to start from scratch every time, while you provide responses and supply the substance.

To understand the importance of using these guidelines, consider the meaning of the word represent: to bring clearly before the mind. When creating letters and résumés, which are two elements of business life that are fundamental to success, it is critical to bring a favorable image to mind. These documents must be crisp, to the point, and good-looking, because usually they are the first glimpse a prospective employer gets of a job-seeker.

Even if an individual's personal trip through the universe does not include physics or violins, a good résumé and cover letter may be the launch vehicles that start the journey.

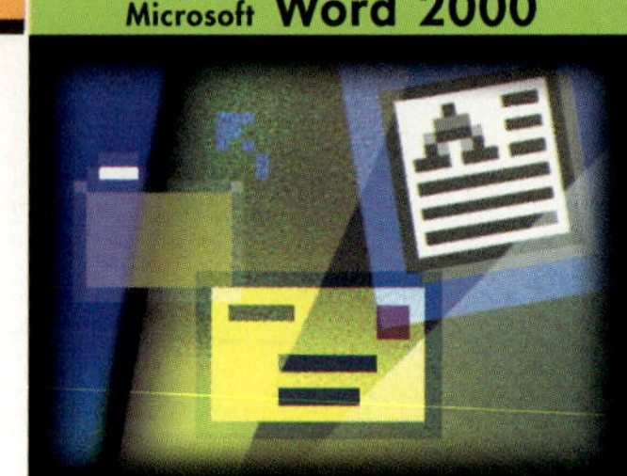

Microsoft Word 2000

Using a Wizard to Create a Resume and Creating a Cover Letter with a Table

CASE PERSPECTIVE

Paulette Rose Brandon recently graduated from Illinois State College with a B.S. in Management, specializing in Marketing. She also has an A.S. in Business and an A.S. in Computer Technology. Ready to embark on a full-time career in computer sales management, Paulette knows she needs a resume and an accompanying cover letter to send to prospective employers. Because you work as an intern in the school's Office of Career Development, she has asked you to help her create a professional resume and cover letter.

While reading through the classified section of the *Chicago Times*, Paulette locates a computer sales management trainee position at Deluxe Computers that sounds perfect for her.

Paulette will use Word's Resume Wizard to create a resume. She will compose the cover letter to Mr. Carl Reed, personnel director at Deluxe Computers, being certain to include all essential business letter components. With her strong business sense and your resume writing expertise, you create an effective package that should ensure Paulette's success in obtaining the position.

Introduction

At some time in your professional life, you will prepare a resume along with a personalized cover letter to send to a prospective employer(s). In addition to some personal information, a **resume** usually contains the applicant's educational background and job experience. Because employers review many resumes for each vacant position, you should design your resume carefully so it presents you as the best candidate for the job. You also should attach a personalized cover letter to each resume you send. A **cover letter** enables you to elaborate on positive points in your resume; it also provides you with an opportunity to show a potential employer your written communication skills. Thus, it is important that your cover letter is written well and follows proper business letter rules.

Because composing documents from scratch is a difficult process for many people, Word provides templates and wizards to assist you in preparing documents. A **template** is similar to a form with prewritten text; that is, Word prepares the requested document with text and/or formatting common to all documents of this nature. By asking you several basic questions, a **wizard** prepares and formats a document for you based on your responses. Once Word creates a document from either a template or a wizard, you then fill in the blanks or replace prewritten words in the document.

Project Three — Resume and Cover Letter

Paulette Rose Brandon, a recent college graduate, is seeking a full-time position as a computer sales manager. Project 3 uses Word to produce her resume shown in Figure 3-1 and a personalized cover letter and envelope shown in Figure 3-2 on page WD 3.6.

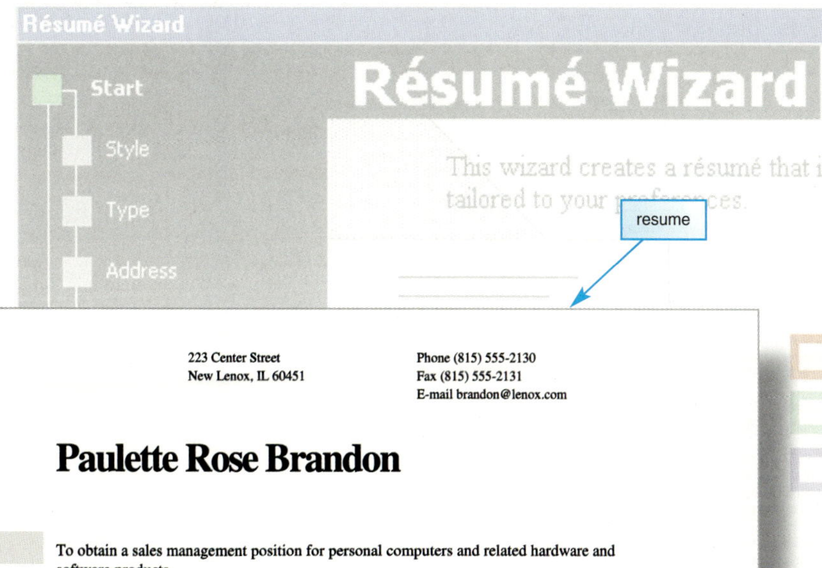

223 Center Street
New Lenox, IL 60451

Phone (815) 555-2130
Fax (815) 555-2131
E-mail brandon@lenox.com

Paulette Rose Brandon

Objective

To obtain a sales management position for personal computers and related hardware and software products.

Education

1997 - 2001 Illinois State College Springfield, IL

Marketing Management

- B.S. in Management, May 2001
- A.S. in Business, May 1999
- A.S. in Computer Technology, December 1999

Computer experience

Software Applications: Microsoft Word, Microsoft Excel, Microsoft Access, Microsoft PowerPoint, Microsoft Outlook, Microsoft FrontPage, Microsoft Publisher, Microsoft Project, Microsoft Money, Corel WordPerfect, Broderbund Print Shop, Intuit Quicken, Intuit TurboTax, Visio Technical

Hardware: IBM and compatible personal computers, Apple Macintosh personal computers, DEC Alpha minicomputer, IBM mainframe, laser printers, ink-jet printers, scanners, tape backup drives, Jaz® and Zip® drives, digital cameras, fax machines, modems, surge protectors, uninterruptible power supplies

Programming Languages: BASIC, Visual Basic, COBOL, C, C++, RPG, SQL, JavaScript, HTML, XML

Operating Systems: Windows, Mac OS, UNIX, Linux, VMS

Awards received

Dean's List, every semester
Top Seller in Student Government Association Fund-raiser, 2001
Carmon Management Scholarship, 1997-2001
MOUS certification: Word and Excel

Interests and activities

The Marketing Club, 1999-2001
Student Government Association, 1998-2001
Plan to pursue Master's degree beginning fall 2002

Work experience

1999 - 2001 Illinois State College Springfield, IL

Help Desk Consultant

- Assist faculty and staff with software questions
- Log hardware problems
- Conduct software training sessions

Volunteer experience

Assist in various fund-raising events for school, church, and the community. Examples include phone-a-thons, magazine sales, car washes, and used equipment sales.

FIGURE 3-1

More About 2000

Resumes and Cover Letters

The World Wide Web contains a host of information, tips, and suggestions on writing resumes and cover letters. For a list of Web links to sites on writing resumes and cover letters, visit the Word 2000 More About Web page (www.scsite.com/wd2000/more.htm) and then click Links to Sites on Writing Resumes and Cover Letters.

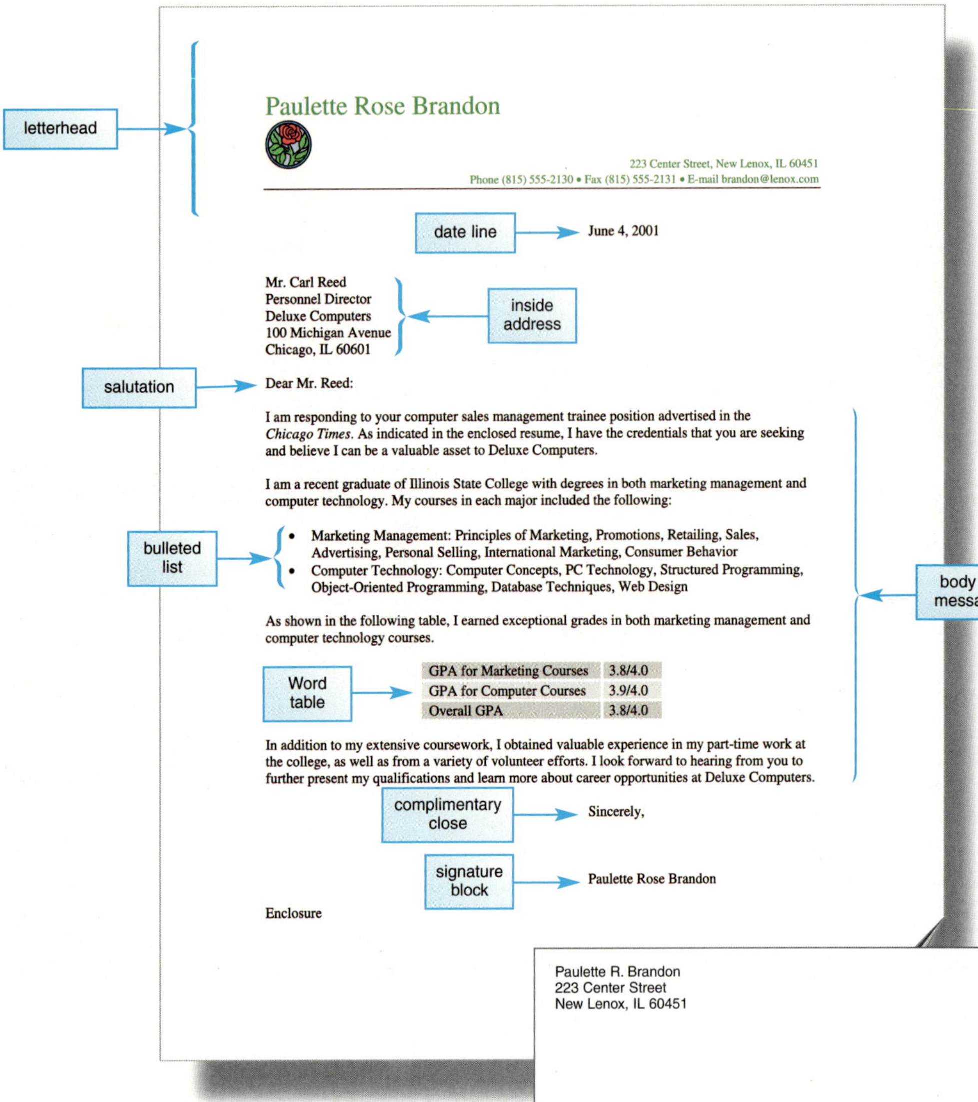

letterhead

Paulette Rose Brandon

223 Center Street, New Lenox, IL 60451
Phone (815) 555-2130 • Fax (815) 555-2131 • E-mail brandon@lenox.com

date line

June 4, 2001

Mr. Carl Reed
Personnel Director
Deluxe Computers
100 Michigan Avenue
Chicago, IL 60601

inside address

salutation

Dear Mr. Reed:

body or message

I am responding to your computer sales management trainee position advertised in the *Chicago Times*. As indicated in the enclosed resume, I have the credentials that you are seeking and believe I can be a valuable asset to Deluxe Computers.

I am a recent graduate of Illinois State College with degrees in both marketing management and computer technology. My courses in each major included the following:

bulleted list

- Marketing Management: Principles of Marketing, Promotions, Retailing, Sales, Advertising, Personal Selling, International Marketing, Consumer Behavior
- Computer Technology: Computer Concepts, PC Technology, Structured Programming, Object-Oriented Programming, Database Techniques, Web Design

As shown in the following table, I earned exceptional grades in both marketing management and computer technology courses.

Word table

GPA for Marketing Courses	3.8/4.0
GPA for Computer Courses	3.9/4.0
Overall GPA	3.8/4.0

In addition to my extensive coursework, I obtained valuable experience in my part-time work at the college, as well as from a variety of volunteer efforts. I look forward to hearing from you to further present my qualifications and learn more about career opportunities at Deluxe Computers.

complimentary close

Sincerely,

signature block

Paulette Rose Brandon

Enclosure

FIGURE 3-2a Cover Letter

Paulette R. Brandon
223 Center Street
New Lenox, IL 60451

Mr. Carl Reed
Personnel Director
Deluxe Computers
100 Michigan Avenue
Chicago, IL 60601

FIGURE 3-2b Envelope

Business Letters

A finished business letter should look like a symmetrically framed picture with even margins, all balanced below an attractive letterhead. In addition, the contents of the letter should contain proper grammar, correct spelling, logically constructed sentences, flowing paragraphs, and sound ideas.

Using Word's Resume Wizard to Create a Resume

You can type a resume from scratch into a blank document window, or you can use the **Resume Wizard** and let Word format the resume with appropriate headings and spacing. Then, you can customize the resulting resume by filling in the blanks or selecting and replacing text.

When you use a wizard, Word displays a dialog box with the wizard's name in its title bar. A wizard's dialog box displays a list of **panel names** along its left side with the currently selected panel displaying on the right side of the dialog box (see Figure 3-4). Each panel presents a different set of options, in which you select preferences or enter text. You click the Next button to move from one panel to the next within the wizard's dialog box.

Perform the following steps to create a resume using the Resume Wizard. Because a wizard retains the settings selected by the last person that used the wizard, your selections initially may display differently. Be sure to verify that your settings match the screens shown in the following steps.

Steps To Create a Resume Using Word's Resume Wizard

1 Click the Start button on the taskbar and then click New Office Document. If necessary, click the Other Documents tab when the New Office Document dialog box displays. Click the Resume Wizard icon.

Office displays several wizard and template icons in the Other Documents sheet in the New Office Document dialog box (Figure 3-3). Icons without the word, wizard, are templates. If you click an icon, a sample of the resulting document displays in the Preview area.

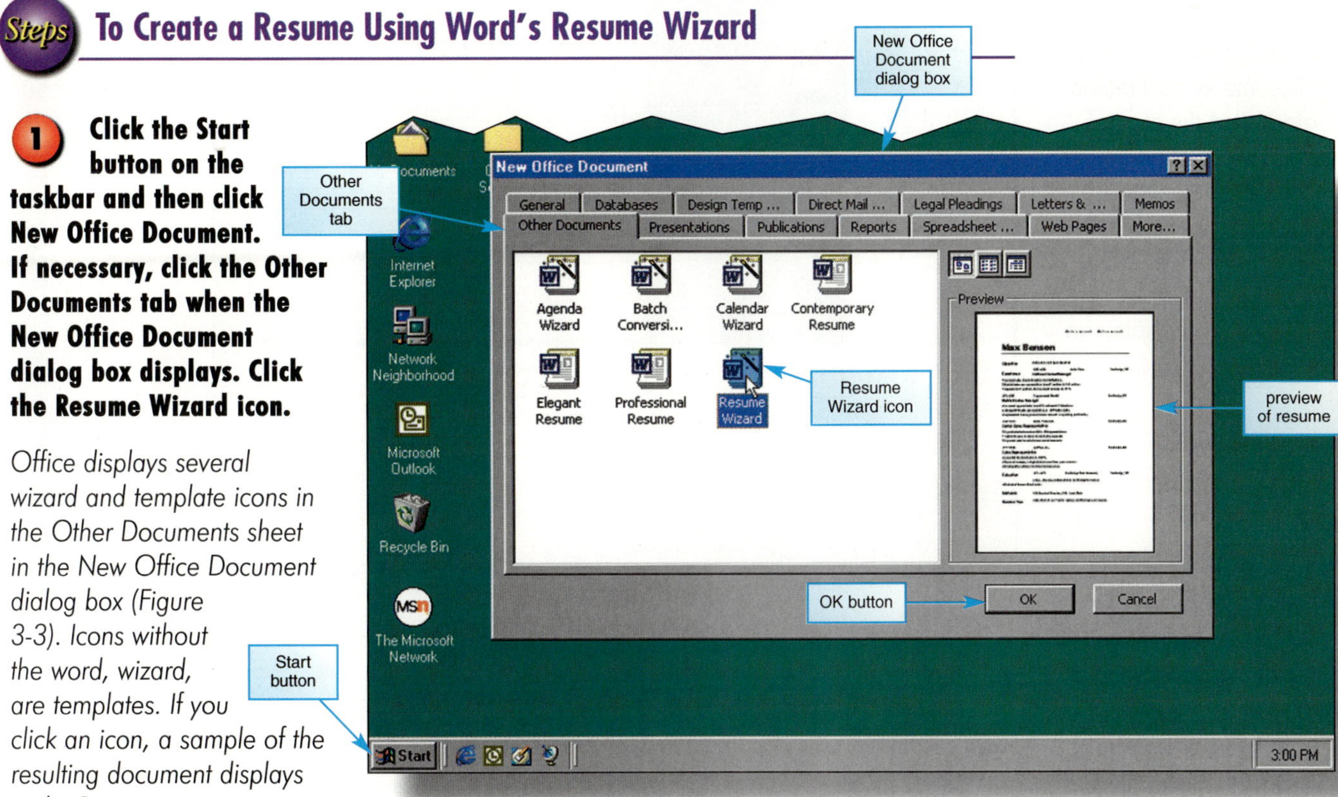

FIGURE 3-3

2 Click the OK button. When the Resume Wizard dialog box displays, point to the Next button.

*After a few seconds, Word displays the **Start panel** of the Resume Wizard dialog box, informing you the Resume Wizard has started (Figure 3-4). Notice this dialog box has a **Microsoft Word Help button** you can click to obtain help while using this wizard. Depending on your system, the Word window may or may not be maximized behind the Resume Wizard dialog box.*

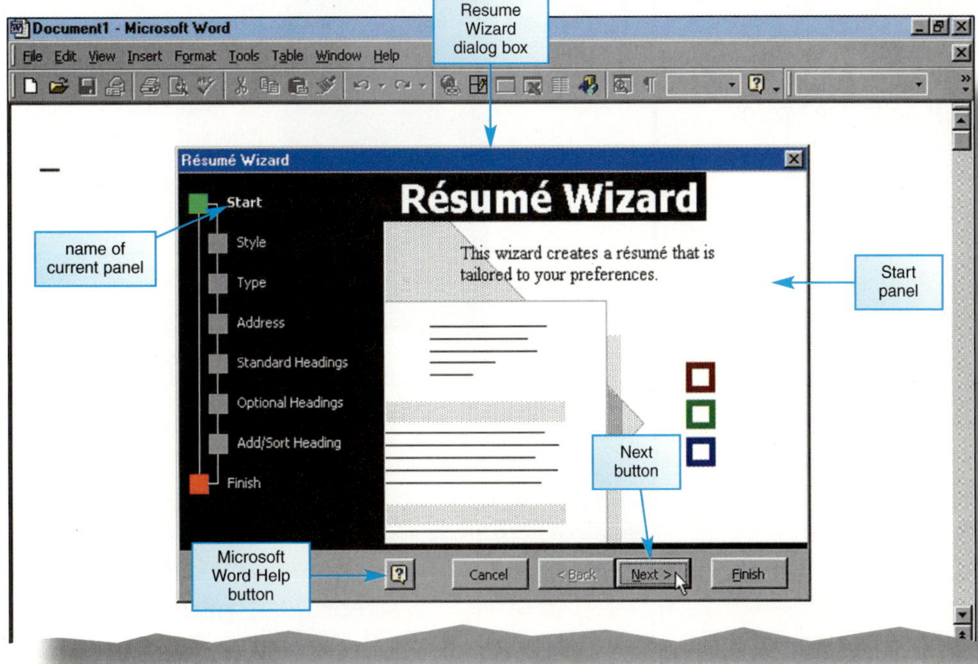

FIGURE 3-4

3 Click the Next button. When the Style panel displays, click Contemporary, if necessary, and then point to the Next button.

*Word displays the **Style panel** in the Resume Wizard dialog box, requesting the style of your resume (Figure 3-5). Word provides three styles of wizards and templates: Professional, Contemporary, and Elegant. A sample of each resume style displays in this panel.*

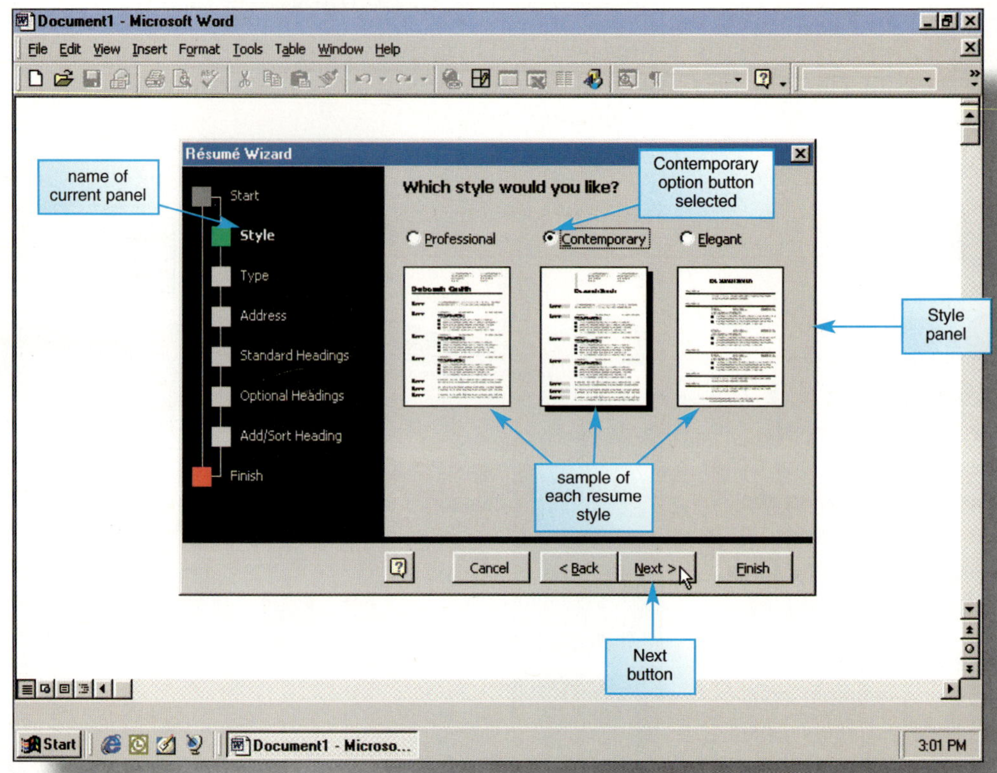

FIGURE 3-5

4 Click the Next button. When the Type panel displays, click Entry-level resume, if necessary, and then point to the Next button.

*Word displays the **Type panel** in the Resume Wizard dialog box, asking for the type of resume that you want to create (Figure 3-6).*

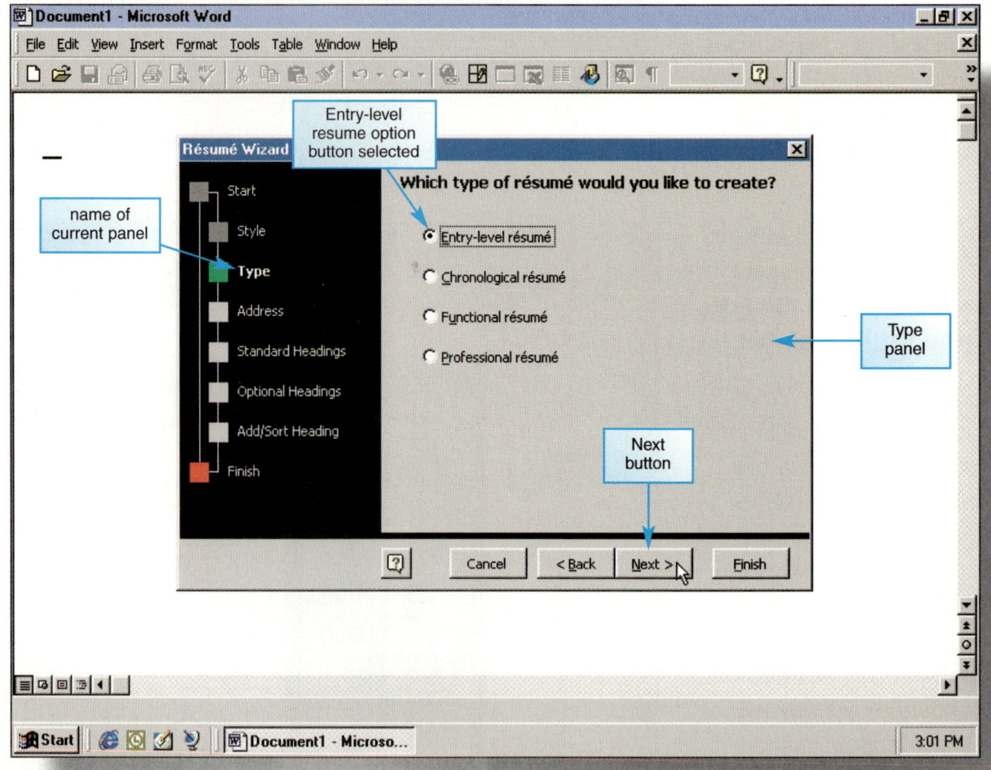

FIGURE 3-6

5 Click the Next button.

Word displays the **Address panel** *in the Resume Wizard dialog box, with the current name selected (Figure 3-7). The name displayed and selected in your Name text box will be different, depending on the name of the last person using the Resume Wizard.*

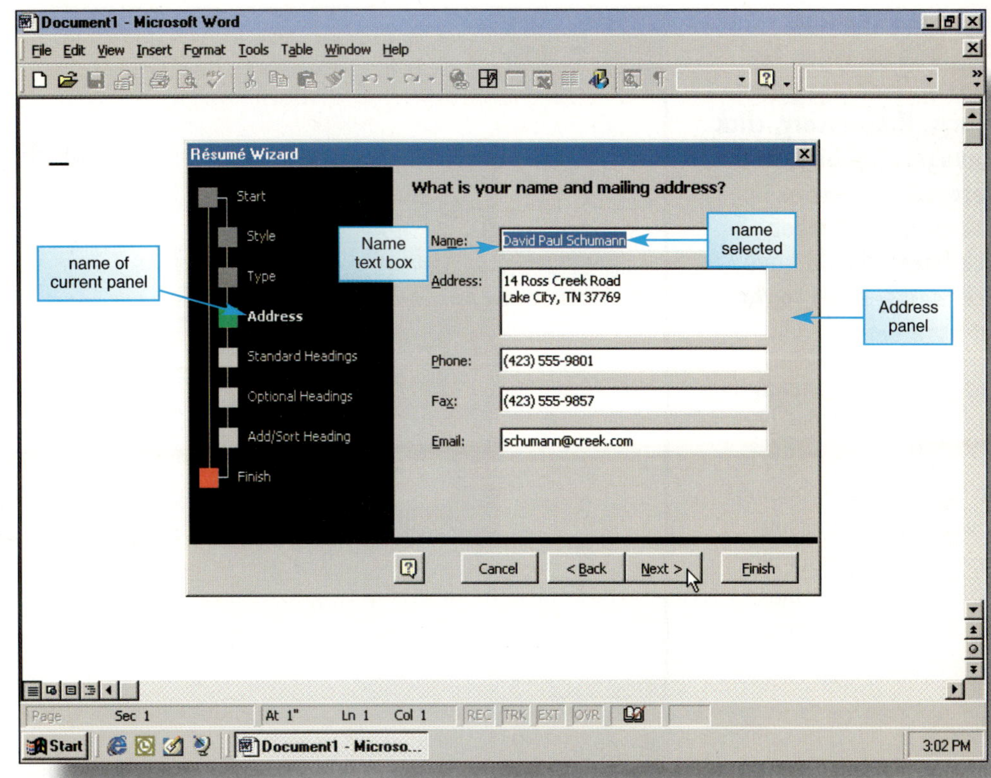

FIGURE 3-7

6 With the name in the Name text box selected, type `Paulette Rose Brandon` **and then press the TAB key. Type** `223 Center Street` **and then press the ENTER key. Type** `New Lenox, IL 60451` **and then press the TAB key. Type** `(815) 555-2130` **and then press the TAB key. Type** `(815) 555-2131` **and then press the TAB key. Type** `brandon@lenox.com` **and then point to the Next button.**

As you type the new text, it automatically replaces the selected text (Figure 3-8).

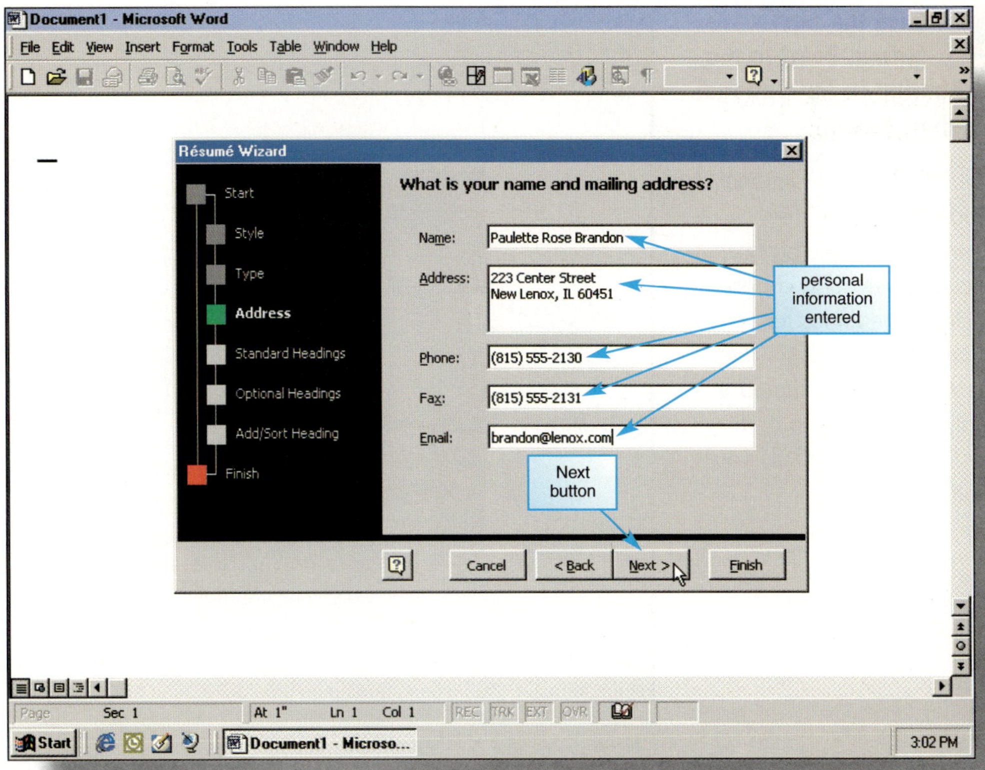

FIGURE 3-8

7 **Click the Next button. When the Standard Headings panel displays, if necessary, click Languages, Hobbies, and References to remove the check marks. All other check boxes should have check marks. Point to the Next button.**

*Word displays the **Standard Headings panel** in the Resume Wizard dialog box, which requests the headings you want on your resume (Figure 3-9). You want all headings, except for these three: Languages, Hobbies, and References.*

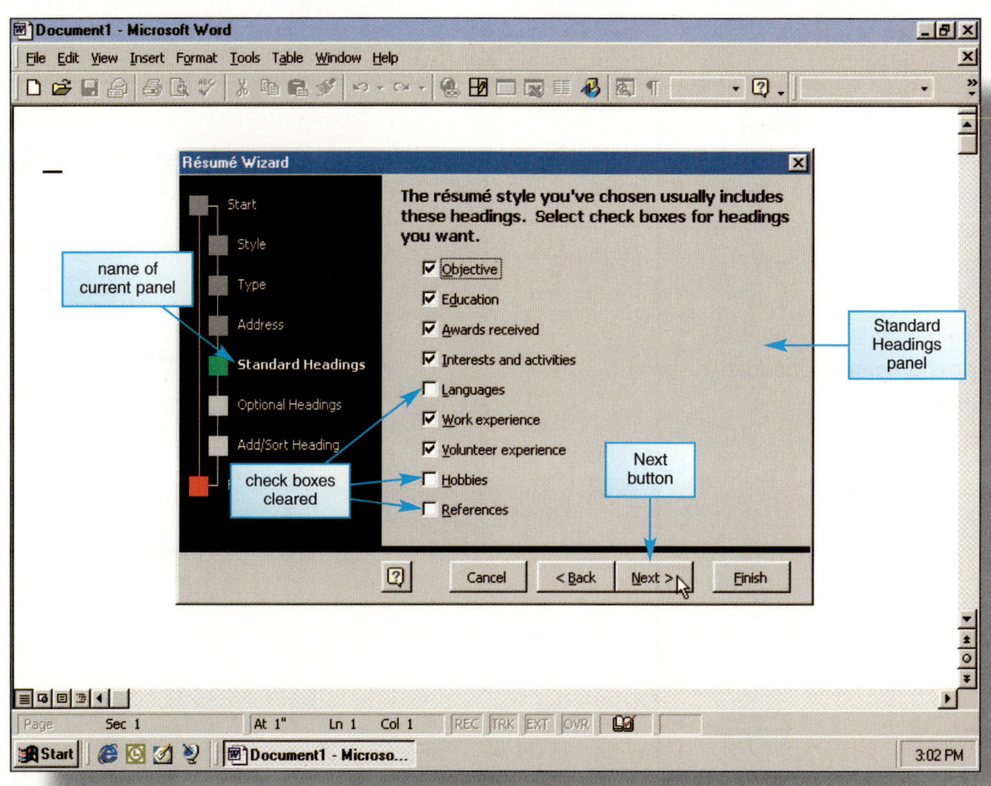

FIGURE 3-9

8 **Click the Next button. Point to the Next button in the Optional Headings panel.**

*Word displays the **Optional Headings panel** in the Resume Wizard dialog box, which allows you to choose additional headings for your resume (Figure 3-10). All of these check boxes should be empty because none of these headings is required on your resume.*

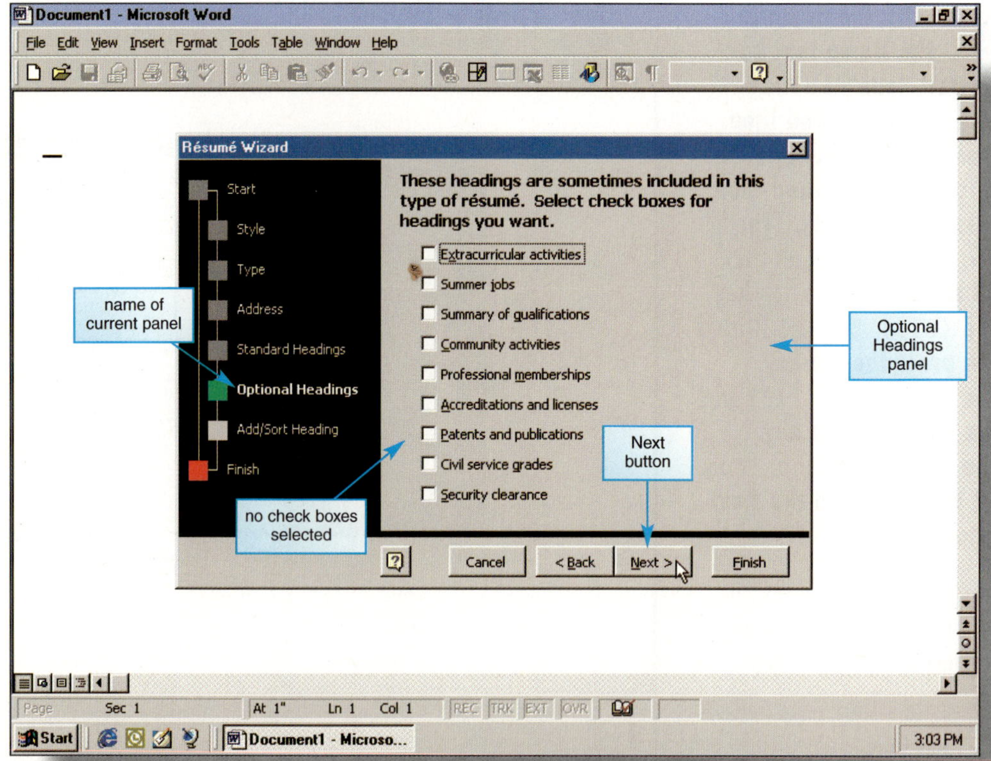

FIGURE 3-10

9 Click the Next button. When the Add/Sort Heading panel displays, type `Computer experience` **in the additional headings text box. Point to the Add button.**

Word displays the ***Add/Sort Heading panel*** *in the Resume Wizard dialog box, which allows you to enter any additional headings you want on your resume (Figure 3-11).*

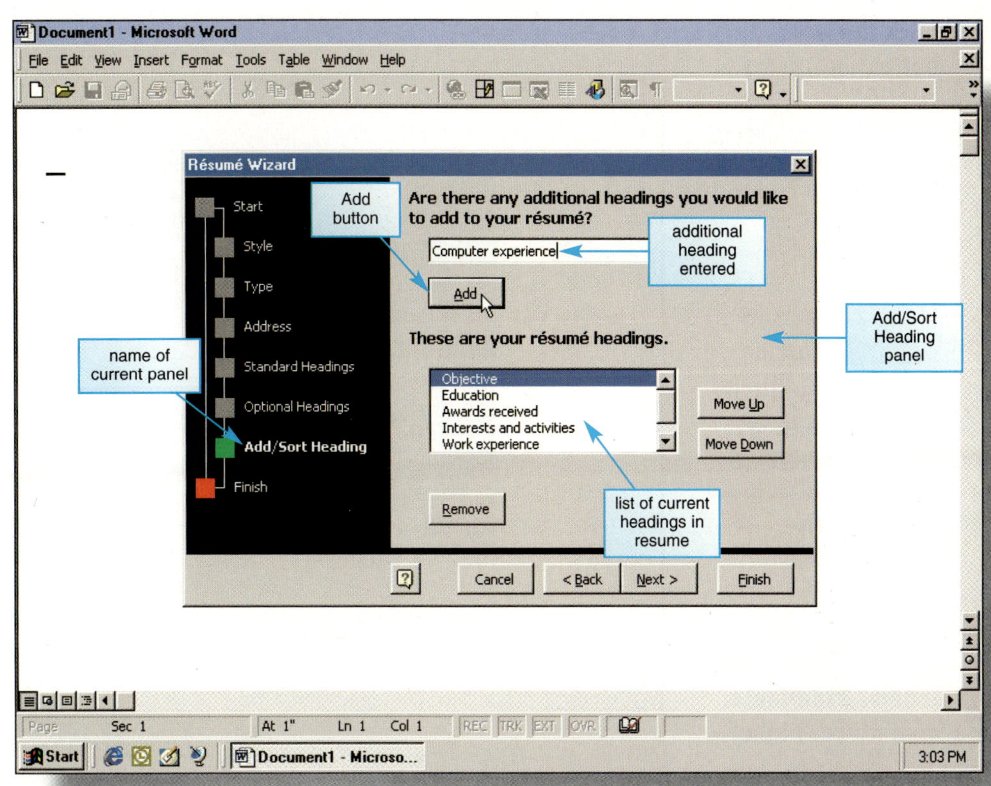

FIGURE 3-11

10 Click the Add button. Scroll to the bottom of the list of resume headings and then click Computer experience. Point to the Move Up button.

The Computer experience heading is selected (Figure 3-12). You can rearrange the order of the headings on your resume by selecting a heading and then clicking the appropriate button (Move Up button or Move Down button).

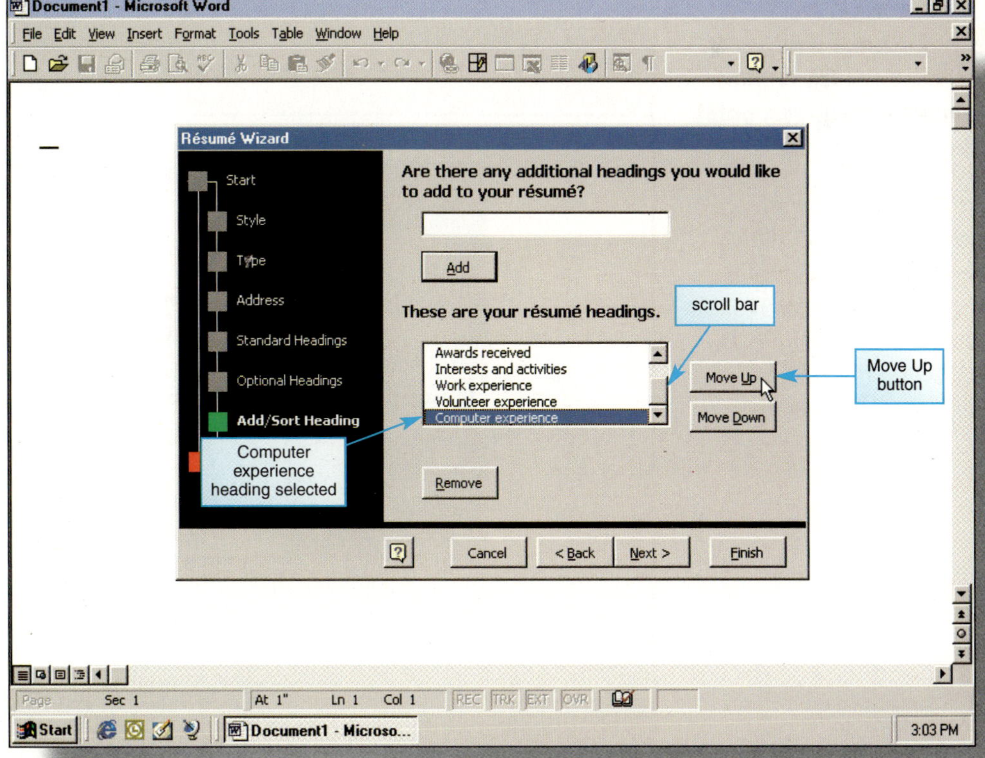

FIGURE 3-12

11 Click the Move Up button four times.

Word moves the heading, Computer experience, above the Awards received heading (Figure 3-13).

12 If the last person using the Resume Wizard included additional headings, you may have some unwanted headings. Your heading list should be as follows: Objective, Education, Computer experience, Awards received, Interests and activities, Work experience, and Volunteer experience. If you have an additional heading(s), click the unwanted heading and then click the Remove button.

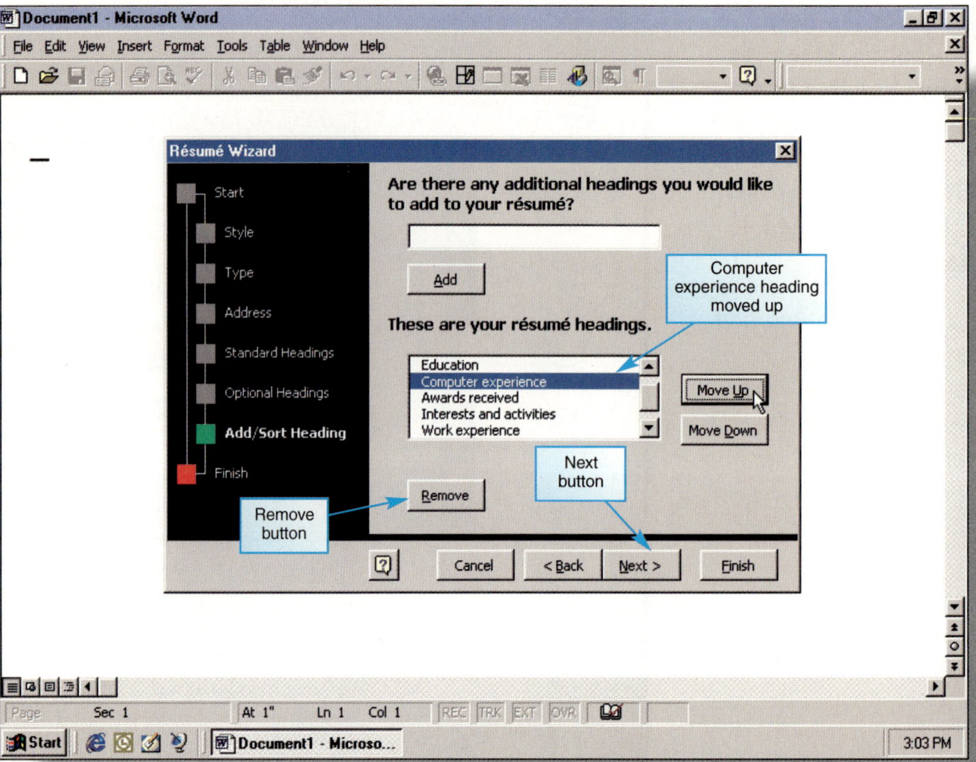

FIGURE 3-13

13 Click the Next button. When the Finish panel displays, point to the Finish button.

Word displays the Finish panel in the Resume Wizard dialog box, which indicates the wizard is ready to create your document (Figure 3-14).

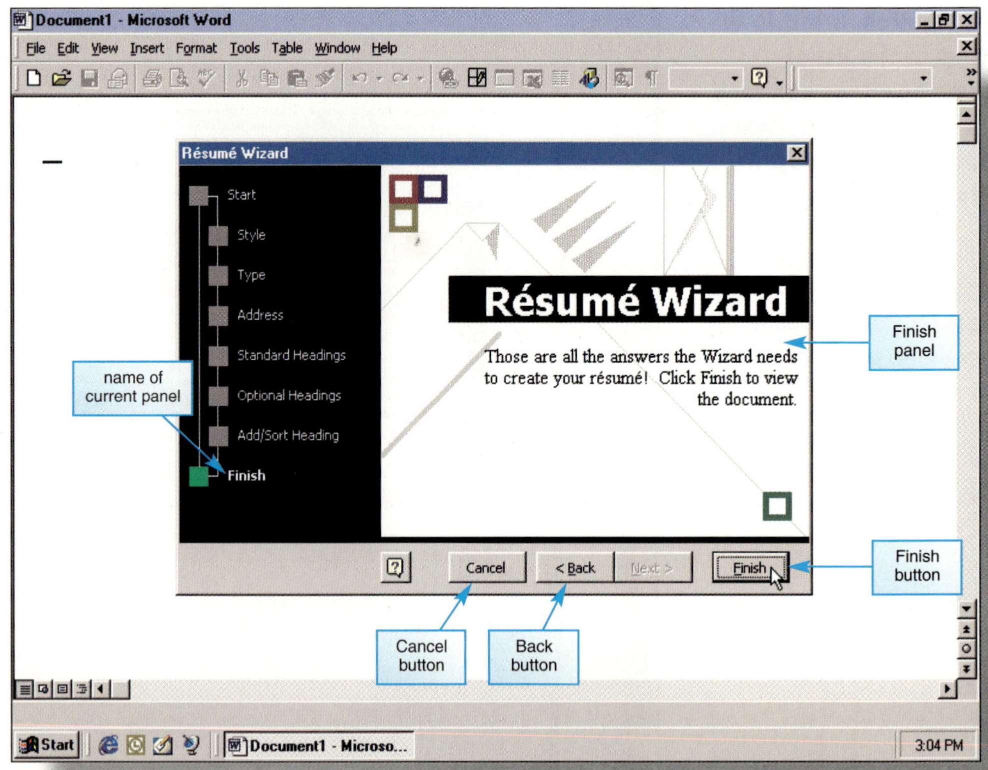

FIGURE 3-14

14 **Click the Finish button. If the Word window is not maximized, click its Maximize button. If the Office Assistant displays, click its Cancel button. To close the Office Assistant, if necessary, right-click it and then click Hide on the shortcut menu.**

Word creates an entry-level contemporary style resume layout (Figure 3-15). You are to personalize the resume as indicated.

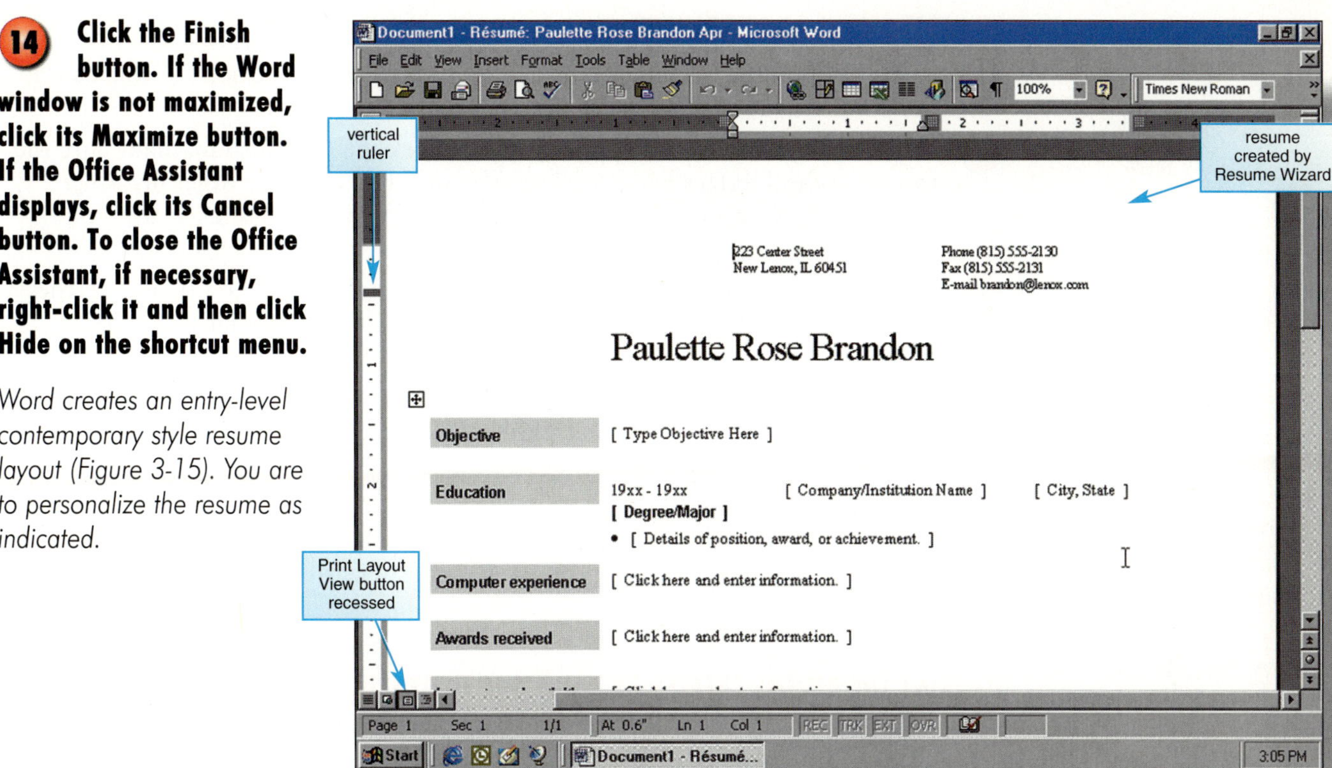

FIGURE 3-15

When you create a resume using the Resume Wizard (see Figure 3-14), you can click the Back button in any panel of the Resume Wizard dialog box to change any of the previous options you selected. To exit from the Resume Wizard and return to the document window without creating the resume, click the Cancel button in any panel of the Resume Wizard dialog box.

In addition to the Resume Wizard, Word provides many other wizards to assist you in creating documents: agenda for a meeting, calendar, envelope, fax cover sheet, legal pleading, letter, mailing label, memorandum, and Web page.

Word displays the resume in the document window in print layout view. You can tell you are in print layout view by looking at the Word window (Figure 3-15). Notice that in print layout view, the **Print Layout View button** on the horizontal scroll bar is recessed. Also, notice that a **vertical ruler** displays at the left edge of the document window, in addition to the horizontal ruler at the top of the window.

Your screen was in normal view when you created documents in Project 1 and for most of Project 2. In Project 2, when you created the header, you were in print layout view. In both normal view and print layout view, you can type and edit text. The difference is that **print layout view** shows you exactly how the printed page will print. That is, in print layout view, Word places the entire piece of paper in the document window, showing precisely the positioning of the text, margins, headers, footers, and footnotes on the printed page.

Other Ways

1. Right-click Start button, click Open, double-click New Office Document, click Other Documents tab, double-click Resume Wizard icon
2. Click New Office Document button on Microsoft Office Shortcut Bar, click Other Documents tab, double-click Resume Wizard icon
3. In Microsoft Word, on File menu click New, click Other Documents tab, double-click Resume Wizard icon

Resetting Menus and Toolbars

To set the menus and toolbars so they appear exactly as shown in this book, you should reset your menus and toolbars as outlined in Appendix C or follow the steps on the next page.

TO RESET MENUS AND TOOLBARS

1. Click View on the menu bar and then point to Toolbars. Click Customize on the Toolbars submenu.
2. When the Customize dialog box displays, click the Options tab, make sure the top three check boxes have check marks and then click the Reset my usage data button. When the Microsoft Word dialog box displays, click the Yes button.
3. Click the Toolbars tab. Click Standard in the Toolbars list and then click the Reset button. When the Reset Toolbar dialog box displays, click the OK button.
4. Click Formatting in the Toolbars list and then click the Reset button. When the Reset Toolbar dialog box displays, click the OK button. Click the Close button.

Word resets the menus and toolbars.

To see the entire resume created by the Resume Wizard, you should print the resume.

TO PRINT THE RESUME CREATED BY THE RESUME WIZARD

1. Double-click the move handle on the Standard toolbar to display the entire toolbar. Ready the printer and then click the Print button on the Standard toolbar.
2. When the printer stops, retrieve the hard copy resume from the printer.

The printed resume is shown in Figure 3-16.

Resume Contents

Omit the following items from a resume: social security number, marital status, age, height, weight, gender, physical appearance, health, citizenship, references, previous pay rates, reasons for leaving a prior job, current date, and high school information (if you are a college graduate).

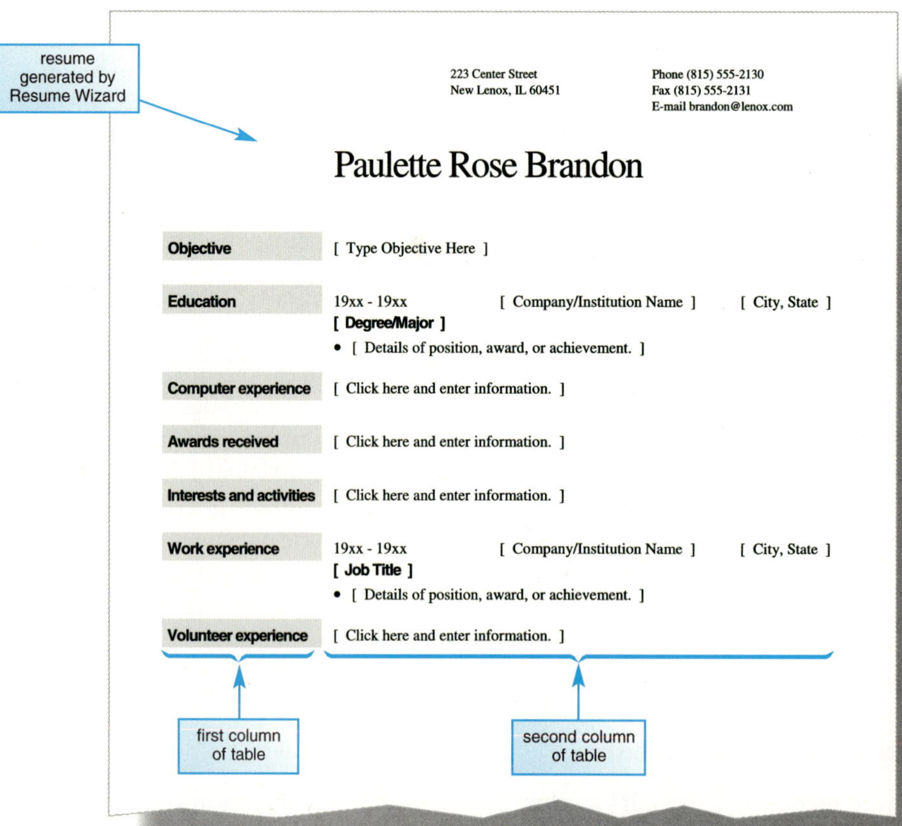

FIGURE 3-16

Personalizing the Resume

The next step is to personalize the resume. Where Word has indicated, you type the objective, education, computer experience, awards received, interests and activities, work experience, and volunteer experience next to the respective headings. In the education and work experience sections, you select and replace text to customize these sections. The following pages show how to personalize the resume generated by the Resume Wizard.

More About 2000

Job Searches

The World Wide Web has several sites that assist you in locating a job. For a list of Web links to sites on job searches, visit the Word 2000 More About Web page (www.scsite.com/wd2000/more.htm) and then click Links to Sites on Job Searches.

Displaying Formatting Marks

As you have learned, it is helpful to display **formatting marks** that indicate where in the document you pressed the ENTER key, SPACEBAR, and other keys. If formatting marks do not display already on your screen, follow this step to display them.

TO DISPLAY FORMATTING MARKS

 If the Show/Hide ¶ button on the Standard toolbar is not already recessed, click it.

Word displays formatting marks in the document window, and the Show/Hide ¶ button on the Standard toolbar is recessed (see Figure 3-17 on the next page).

Tables

When the Resume Wizard prepares a resume, it arranges the body of the resume as a table. A Word **table** is a collection of rows and columns. As shown in Figure 3-16, the section headings (Objective, Education, Computer experience, Awards received, Interests and activities, Work experience, and Volunteer experience) are placed in the first column of the table; the details for each of these sections are placed in the second column of the table. Thus, this table contains two columns (see Figure 3-17 on the next page). It also contains seven rows – one row for each section of the resume.

The intersection of a row and a column is called a **cell**, and cells are filled with text. Each cell has an **end-of-cell mark**, which is a formatting mark, that you use to select and format cells. You have learned that formatting marks do not print on a hard copy.

To see clearly the rows, columns, and cells in a Word table, some users prefer to show gridlines. As illustrated in Figure 3-17, **gridlines** help identify the rows and columns in a table. If you want to display gridlines in a table, position the insertion point somewhere in the table, click Table on the menu bar, and then click **Show Gridlines.** If you want to hide the gridlines, click somewhere in the table, click Table on the menu bar, and then click **Hide Gridlines**.

More About 2000

Tables

To select a single cell in a table, click to the left of the cell. To select an entire row, click to the left of the row. To select an entire column, click the column's top border. To add a row or column, click where you want to insert, click Table on the menu bar, point to Insert, and then click the appropriate command.

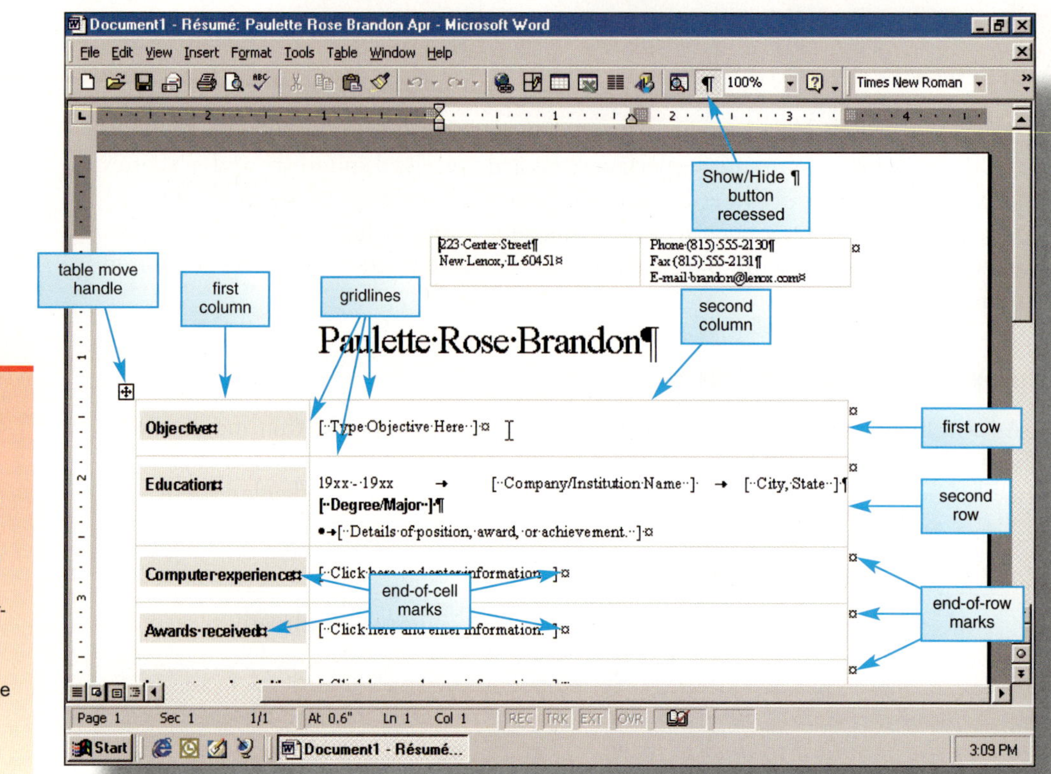

FIGURE 3-17

More About

The Ruler

When the insertion point is in a table, the ruler shows the boundaries of each column in the table. For example, in Figure 3-17, the address information at the top of the resume is a separate table of one row and two columns. The width of the two columns is shown on the ruler.

The upper-left corner of the table displays the **table move handle**, which you drag to move the table to a new location. You also can resize a table, add or delete rows or columns in a table, and format a table. These and other features of tables are discussed in more depth when you create the cover letter later in this project.

Zooming

If you have a Microsoft IntelliMouse, you can zoom in and out of a document by holding the CTRL key while rotating the wheel forward or backward. To learn other features of the IntelliMouse, click the Start button on the taskbar, point to Programs, point to Microsoft Hardware, point to Mouse, and then click Intellipoint Online User's Guide.

Zooming Text Width

In Projects 1 and 2, your screen was in normal view and you used the zoom page width command to display text on the screen as large as possible without extending the right margin beyond the right edge of the document window. When you are in print layout view, the zoom page width command extends the edges of the paper to the margins –making the text smaller on the screen. To make the text as large as possible on the screen in print layout view, you should **zoom text width** as shown in the following steps.

To Zoom Text Width

1 **Click the Zoom box arrow on the Standard toolbar and then point to Text Width in the Zoom list (Figure 3-18).**

2 **Click Text Width.**

Word extends the text to the right edge of the document window (see Figure 3-19 on the next page).

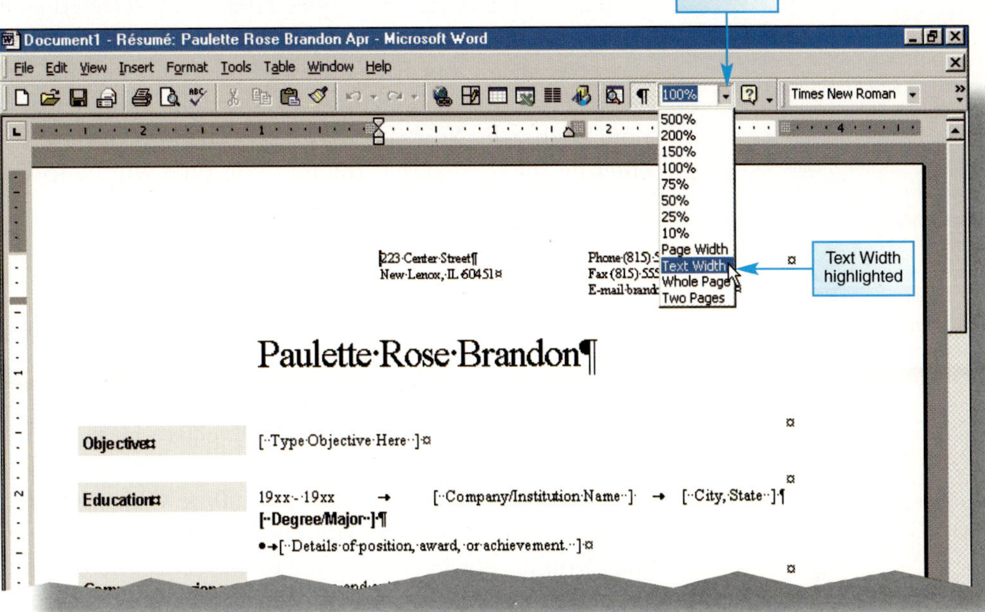

FIGURE 3-18

Other Ways

1. On View menu click Zoom, select Text Width, click OK button

Word computes a zoom percentage based on a variety of settings. The percentage that displays in your Zoom box may be different, depending on your system configuration. Notice in Figure 3-18 that the Zoom list contains more options when the Word window is in print layout view than in normal view.

The next step is to bold the name, Paulette Rose Brandon, in the resume as described in the following steps.

TO BOLD TEXT

1. Drag through the name, Paulette Rose Brandon, to select it.
2. Double-click the move handle on the Formatting toolbar to display the entire toolbar. Click the Bold button on the Formatting toolbar.

Word bolds the name, Paulette Rose Brandon (see Figure 3-19 on the next page).

Styles

When you use a wizard to create a document, Word formats the document using styles. You learned in Project 2 that a **style** is a customized format that you can apply to text. Recall that the formats defined by a style include character formatting, such as the font and font size, and paragraph formatting, such as line spacing and text alignment.

The Style box on the Formatting toolbar displays the name of the style associated with the location of the insertion point. You can identify many of the characteristics assigned to a style by looking at the Formatting toolbar. For example, in Figure 3-19 on the next page, the insertion point is in a paragraph formatted with the Objective style, which uses the 10-point Times New Roman font for the characters.

Styles

To apply a different style to a paragraph, click in the paragraph, click the Style box arrow on the Formatting toolbar, and then click the desired paragraph style. To apply a different style to characters, select the characters, click the Style box arrow on the Formatting toolbar, and then click the desired character style.

If you click the Style box arrow on the Formatting toolbar, the list of styles associated with the current document displays. Paragraph styles affect an entire paragraph, whereas character styles affect only selected characters. In the Style list, **paragraph style** names are followed by a proofreader's paragraph mark (¶), and **character style** names are followed by an underlined letter a (<u>a</u>).

In Project 2, you changed the formats assigned to a style by changing the Footnote Text style. You also may select the appropriate style from the Style list before entering the text so that the text you type will be formatted according to the selected style.

Selecting and Replacing Text

The next step in personalizing the resume is to select text that the Resume Wizard inserted into the resume and replace it with personal information. The first heading on the resume is the objective. You enter the objective where the Resume Wizard inserted the words, Type Objective Here, which is called **placeholder text.**

To replace text in Word, select the text to be removed and then type the desired text. To select the placeholder text, Type Objective Here, you click it. Then, you type the objective. As soon as you begin typing, the selected placeholder text is deleted; thus, you do not have to delete the selection before you begin typing. Perform the following steps to enter the objective into the resume.

To Select and Replace Placeholder Text

1 Click the placeholder text, Type Objective Here.

Word highlights the placeholder text in the resume (Figure 3-19). Notice the style is Objective in the Style box on the Formatting toolbar.

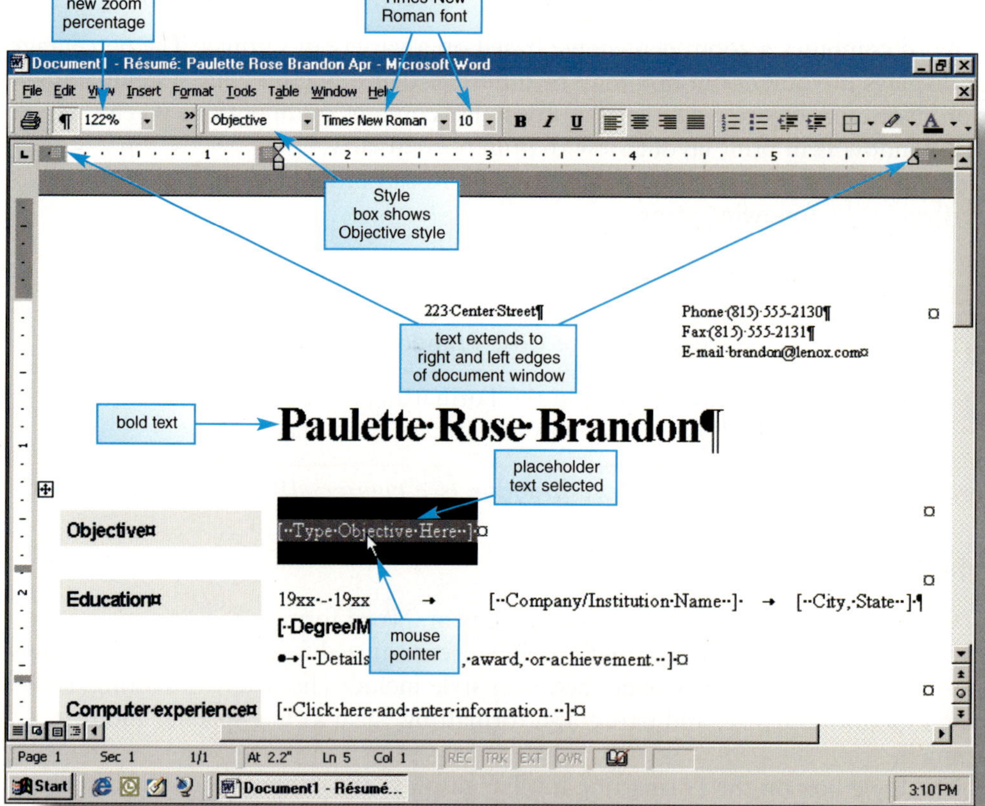

FIGURE 3-19

2 **Type** `To obtain a sales management position for personal computers and related hardware and software products.`

Word replaces the highlighted placeholder text, Type Objective Here, with the objective you type (Figure 3-20). Your document may wordwrap on a different word depending on the type of printer you are using.

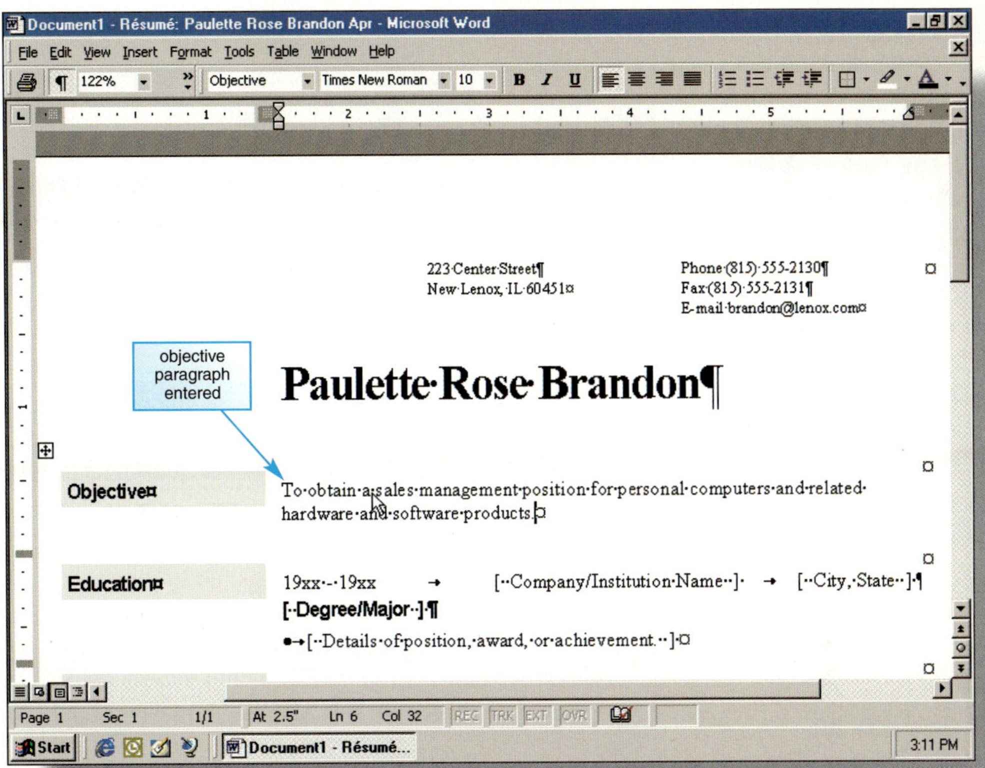

FIGURE 3-20

The next step in personalizing the resume is to replace the wizard's words and phrases in the education section of the resume with your own words and phrases as shown in the following steps.

To Select and Replace Resume Wizard Supplied Text

1 **If necessary, scroll down to display the entire education section of the resume. Drag through the xx in the first 19xx of the education section.**

Word selects the xx in the first year (Figure 3-21).

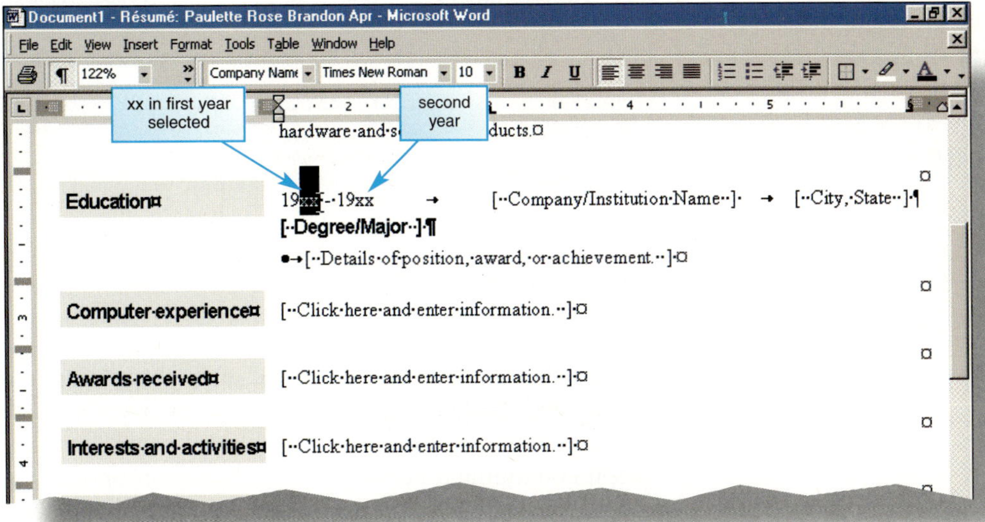

FIGURE 3-21

2 **Type** 97 **and then drag through the 19xx in the second year of the education section. Type** 2001 **and then click the placeholder text, Company/Institution Name.**

Word highlights the placeholder text, Company/ Institution Name (Figure 3-22). The years now display as 1997 - 2001 in the education section.

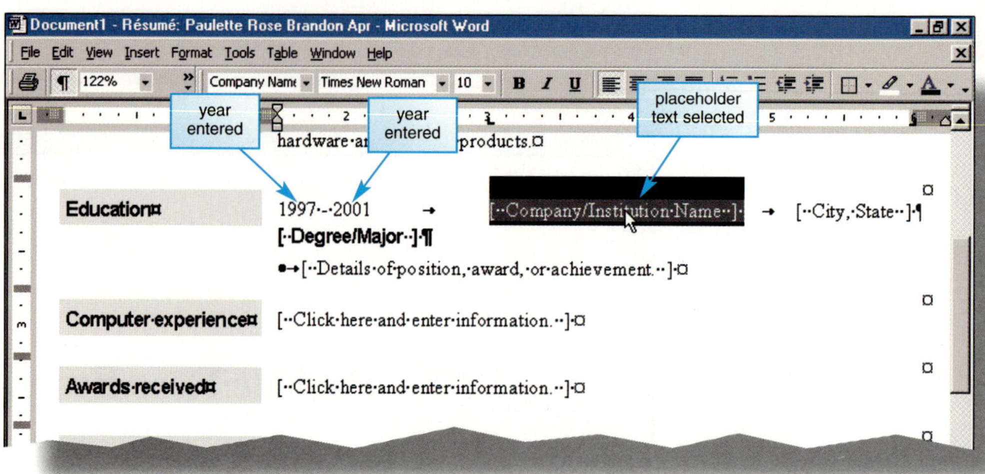

FIGURE 3-22

3 **Type** Illinois State College **and then click the placeholder text, City, State. Type** Springfield, IL **and then click the placeholder text, Degree/Major. Type** Marketing Management **and then click the placeholder text, Details of position, award, or achievement. Type** B.S. in Management, May 2001 **and then press the** ENTER **key. Type** A.S. in Business, May 1999 **and then press the** ENTER **key. Type** A.S. in Computer Technology, December 1999 **as the last item in the list (Figure 3-23).**

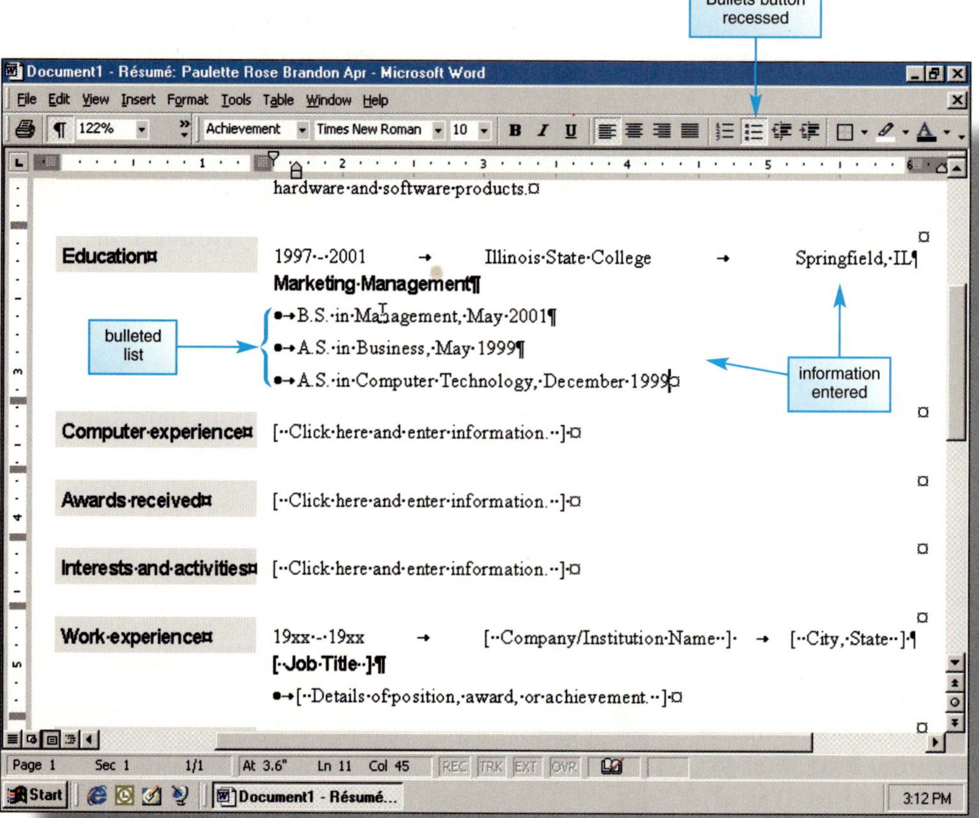

FIGURE 3-23

A **bullet** is a symbol positioned at the beginning of a paragraph. A list of paragraphs with bullets is called a **bulleted list**. The list of degrees in the education section of the resume, for example, is a bulleted list. When the insertion point is in a paragraph containing a bullet, the Bullets button on the Formatting toolbar is recessed. In a bulleted list, each time you press the ENTER key, a bullet displays at the beginning of the new paragraph.

The next step is to enter the computer experience section of the resume as described in the following steps.

TO ENTER PLACEHOLDER TEXT

1. If necessary, scroll down to display the computer experience section of the resume. Click the placeholder text, Click here and enter information, to select it.
2. Type the first paragraph of computer experience (software applications) as shown in Figure 3-24.
3. Press the ENTER key. Type the second paragraph of computer experience (hardware) as shown in Figure 3-24.
4. Press the ENTER key. Type the third paragraph of computer experience (programming languages) as shown in Figure 3-24.
5. Press the ENTER key. Type the fourth paragraph of computer experience (operating systems) as shown in Figure 3-24. Do not press the ENTER key at the end of this line.

The computer experience section of the resume is entered (Figure 3-24).

The Registered Trademark Symbol

To automatically enter the registered trademark symbol, type (r). Or, press ALT+CTRL+R. Or, click Insert on the menu bar, click Symbol, click the Special Characters tab, click Registered in the Character list, click the Insert button, and then click the Close button.

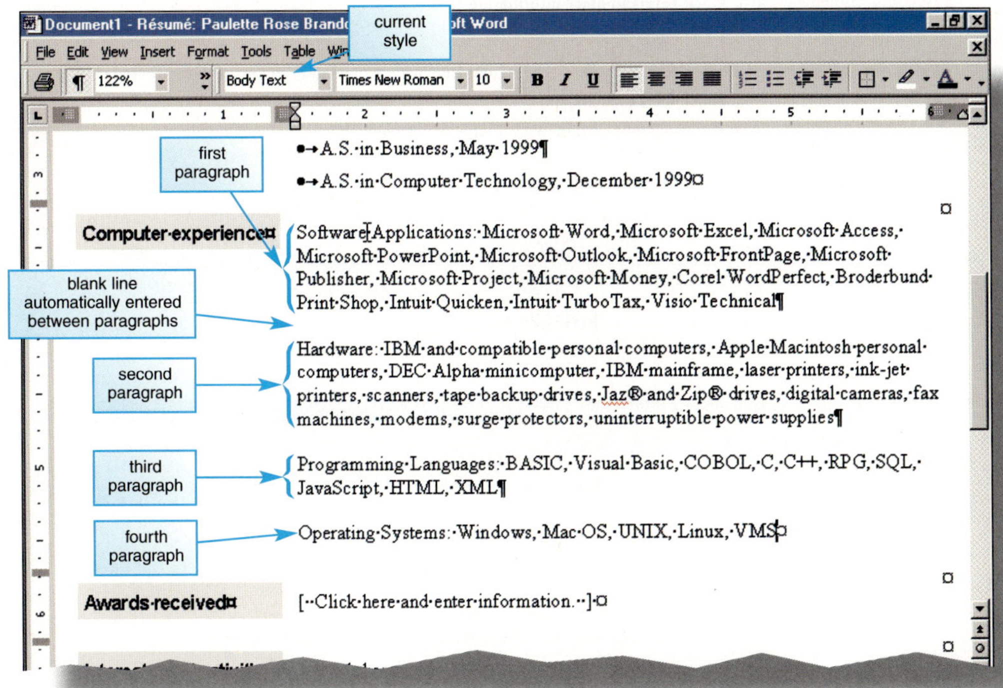

FIGURE 3-24

Entering a Line Break

The next step in personalizing the resume is to enter the awards received section. The style used for the characters in the awards received section of the resume is the Objective style. A paragraph formatting characteristic of the Objective style is that when you press the ENTER key, the insertion point advances downward at least 11 points, which leaves nearly an entire blank line between each paragraph. For example, each time you pressed the ENTER key in the computer experience section, Word placed a blank line between each paragraph (Figure 3-24).

You want the lines within the awards received section to be close to each other (see Figure 3-1 on page WD 3.5). Thus, you will not press the ENTER key between each award received. Instead, you will create a **line break**, which advances the insertion point to the beginning of the next physical line– ignoring any paragraph formatting instructions. Perform the following steps to enter the awards received section using a line break, instead of a paragraph break, between each line.

Steps To Enter a Line Break

1. **If necessary, scroll down to display the awards received section of the resume. In the awards received section, click the placeholder text, Click here and enter information. Type** `Dean's List, every semester` **and then press the SHIFT+ENTER keys.**

Word inserts a line break character, which is a formatting mark, after the named award and moves the insertion point to the beginning of the next physical line (Figure 3-25).

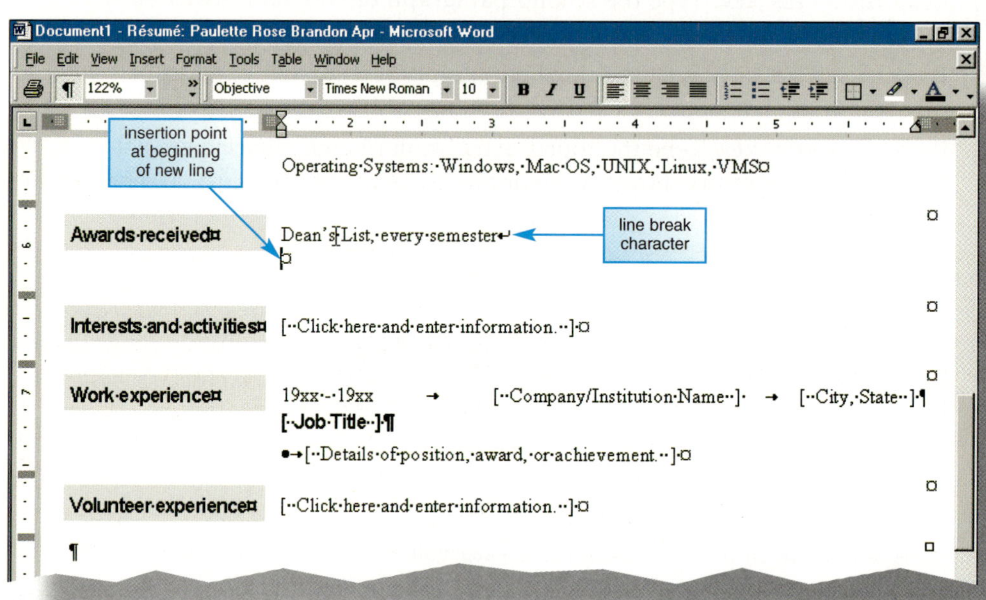

FIGURE 3-25

2. **Type** `Top Seller in Student Government Association Fund-raiser, 2001` **and then press the SHIFT+ENTER keys. Type** `Carmon Management Scholarship, 1997-2001` **and then press the SHIFT+ENTER keys. Type** `MOUS certification: Word and Excel` **as the last award. Do not press the SHIFT+ENTER keys at the end of this line.**

The awards received section is entered (Figure 3-26).

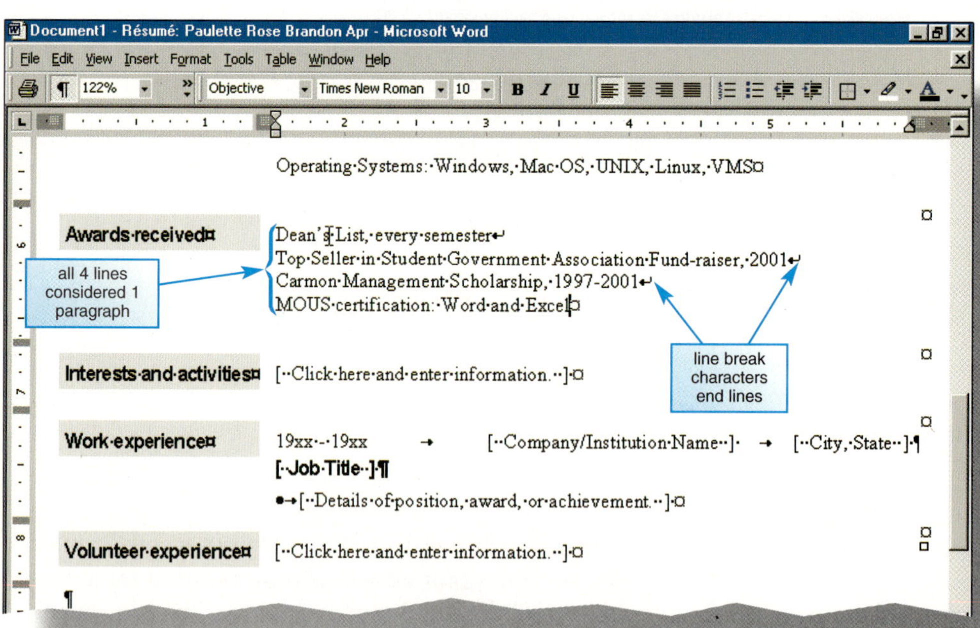

FIGURE 3-26

Enter the remaining text for the resume as described in the following steps.

TO ENTER THE REMAINING SECTIONS OF THE RESUME

1. If necessary, scroll down to display the interests and activities section of the resume. Click the placeholder text, Click here and enter information. Type `The Marketing Club, 1999-2001` and then press the SHIFT+ENTER keys.
2. Type `Student Government Association, 1998-2001` and then press the SHIFT+ENTER keys.
3. Type `Plan to pursue Master's degree beginning fall 2002` as the last activity. Do not press the SHIFT+ENTER keys at the end of this line.
4. If necessary, scroll down to display the work experience section of the resume. Drag through the xx in the first 19xx, type `99` and then drag through the 19xx in the second year. Type `2001` as the year.
5. Click the placeholder text, Company/Institution Name. Type `Illinois State College` as the new text. Click the placeholder text, City, State. Type `Springfield, IL` as the city and state.
6. Click the placeholder text, **Job Title**. Type `Help Desk Consultant` as the title.
7. Click the placeholder text, Details of position, award, or achievement. Type `Assist faculty and staff with software questions` and then press the ENTER key. Type `Log hardware problems` and then press the ENTER key. Type `Conduct software training sessions` as the last item in the list.
8. If necessary, scroll down to display the volunteer experience section of the resume. Click the placeholder text, Click here and enter information. Type `Assist in various fund-raising events for school, church, and the community. Examples include phone-a-thons, magazine sales, car washes, and used equipment sales.` Do not press the ENTER key at the end of this line.

The interests and activities, work experience, and volunteer experience sections of the resume are complete (Figure 3-27).

References

Do not state "References Available Upon Request" on your resume; nor should references be listed on the resume. Employers assume you will give references, if asked, and this information simply clutters a resume. Often you are asked to list references on your application. Be sure to give your references a copy of your resume.

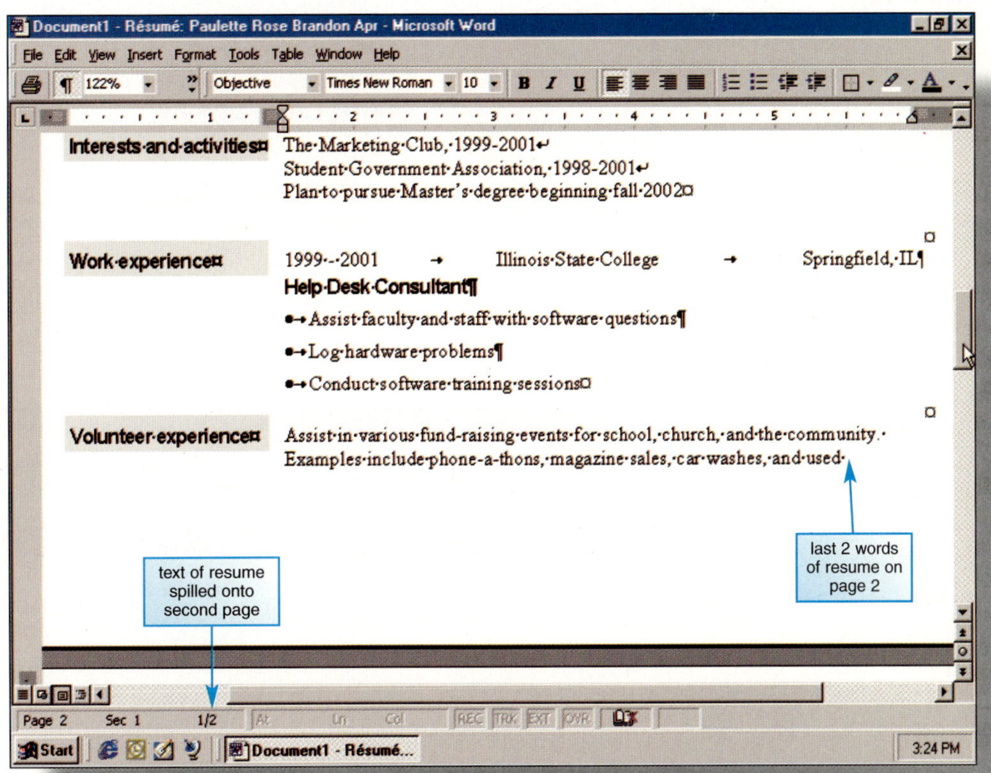

FIGURE 3-27

Print Preview

To magnify a page in print preview, be sure the Magnifier button is recessed on the Print Preview toolbar and then click in the document to zoom in or out. Magnifying a page has no effect on the printed document. To edit a document in print preview, be sure the Magnifier button is not recessed and then edit the text.

Notice in Figure 3-27 on the previous page that the last two words of the resume spilled onto a second page. The next section illustrates how to shrink the resume so it fits on a single page.

Viewing and Printing the Resume in Print Preview

To see exactly how a document will look when you print it, you should display it in **print preview**. Print preview displays the entire document in reduced size on the Word screen. In print preview, you can edit and format text, adjust margins, view multiple pages, reduce the document to fit on a single page, and print the document.

If a document *spills* onto a second page by just a line or two, you can try to shrink the document so it fits onto a single page using the **Shrink to Fit button** in print preview. In the previous steps, the last two words of the resume spilled onto a second page. Perform the following steps to view the resume, display both pages of the resume, shrink the resume, and finally print the resume in print preview.

To Print Preview a Document

1 Double-click the move handle on the Standard toolbar to display the entire toolbar. Point to the Print Preview button on the Standard toolbar (Figure 3-28).

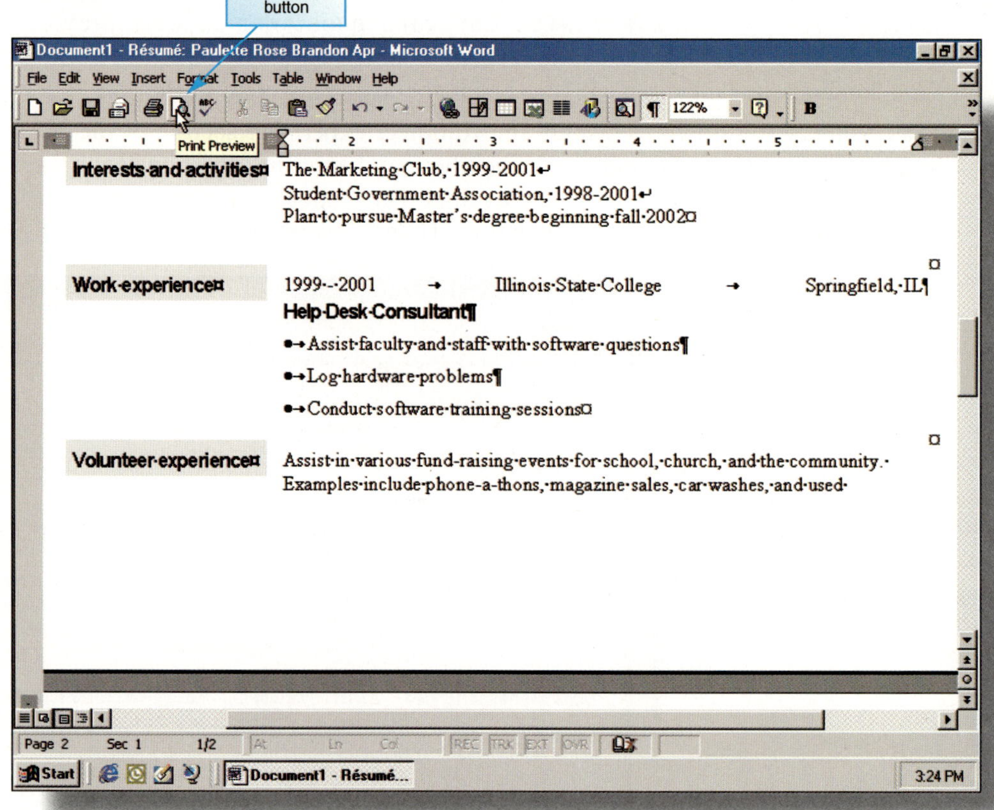

FIGURE 3-28

Click the Print Preview button.

Word displays the document in print preview. The *Print Preview toolbar* displays below the menu bar; the Standard and Formatting toolbars disappear from the screen. Depending on your settings, your screen may display one or two pages in the Preview window.

3 Click the Multiple Pages button on the Print Preview toolbar. Point to the icon in the first row and second column of the grid.

Word displays a *grid* so you can select the number of pages to display (Figure 3-29). With the current selection, Word will display one row of two pages (1 x 2) – or two pages side by side.

4 Click the icon in the first row and second column of the grid. Point to the Shrink to Fit button on the Print Preview toolbar.

Word displays the two pages of the resume side by side (Figure 3-30).

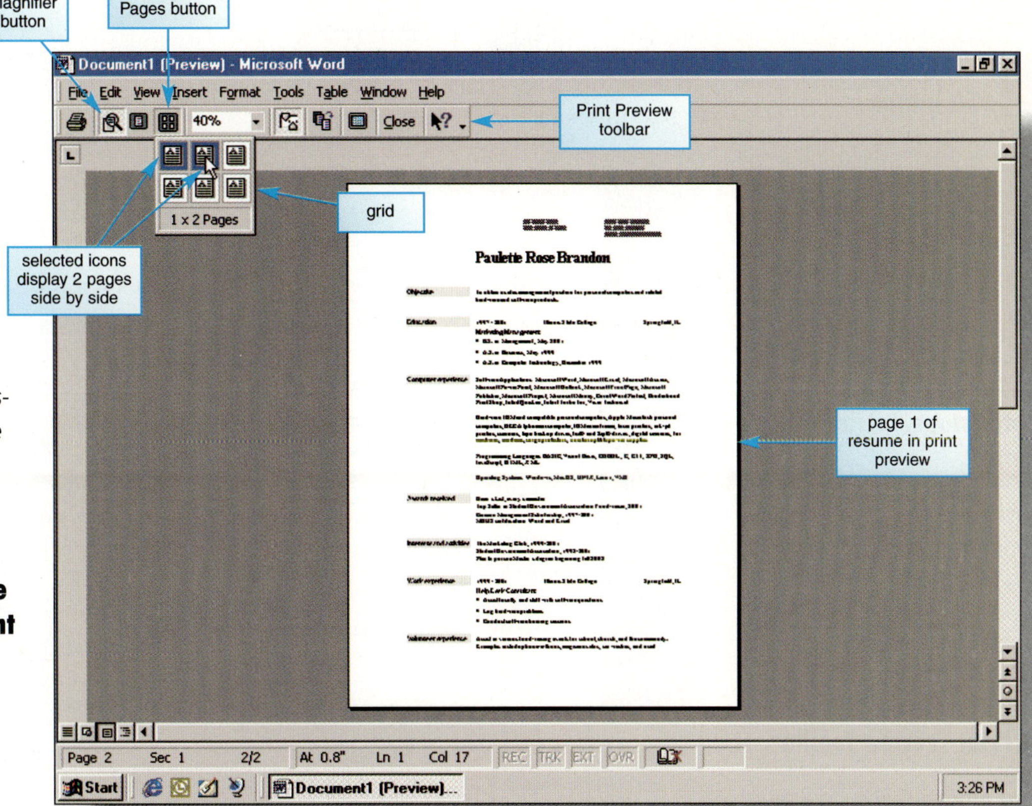

FIGURE 3-29

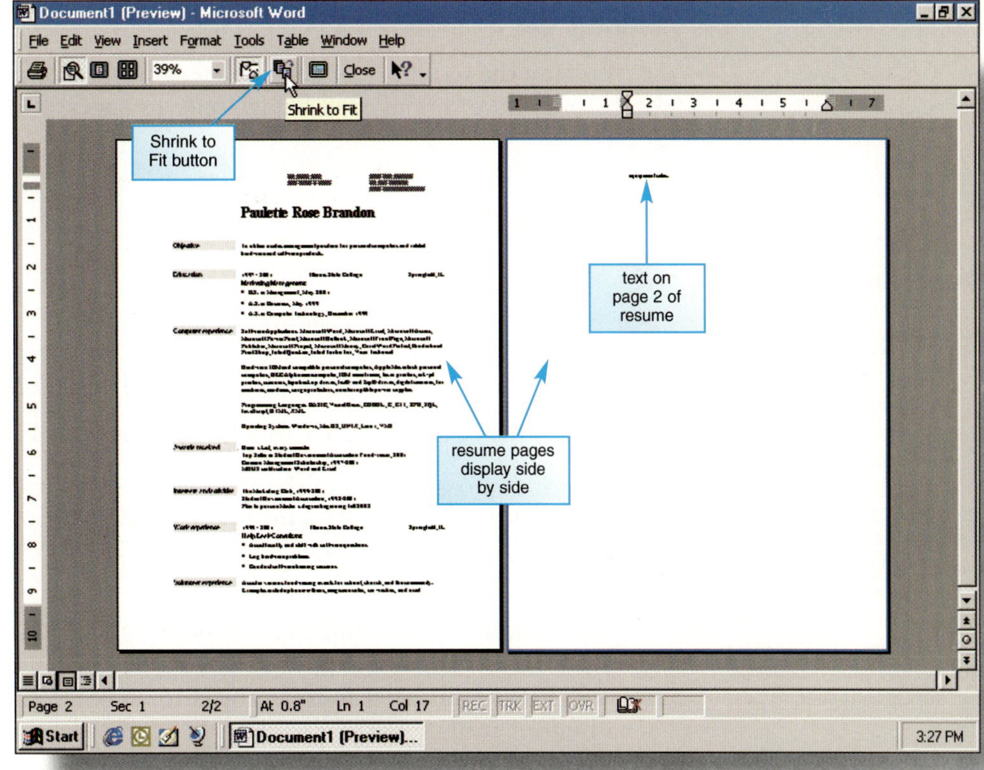

FIGURE 3-30

5 Click the Shrink to Fit button.

Word shrinks the resume to a single page by reducing font sizes (Figure 3-31).

6 Click the Print button on the Print Preview toolbar. When the printer stops, retrieve the printout.

Word prints the resume on the printer (see Figure 3-1 on page WD 3.5).

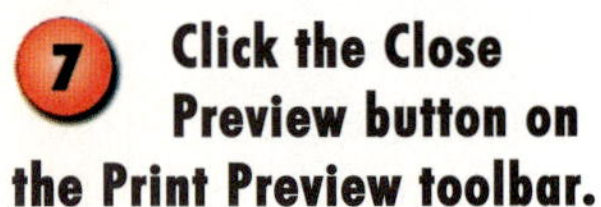

7 Click the Close Preview button on the Print Preview toolbar.

Word returns to the document window, displaying the resume.

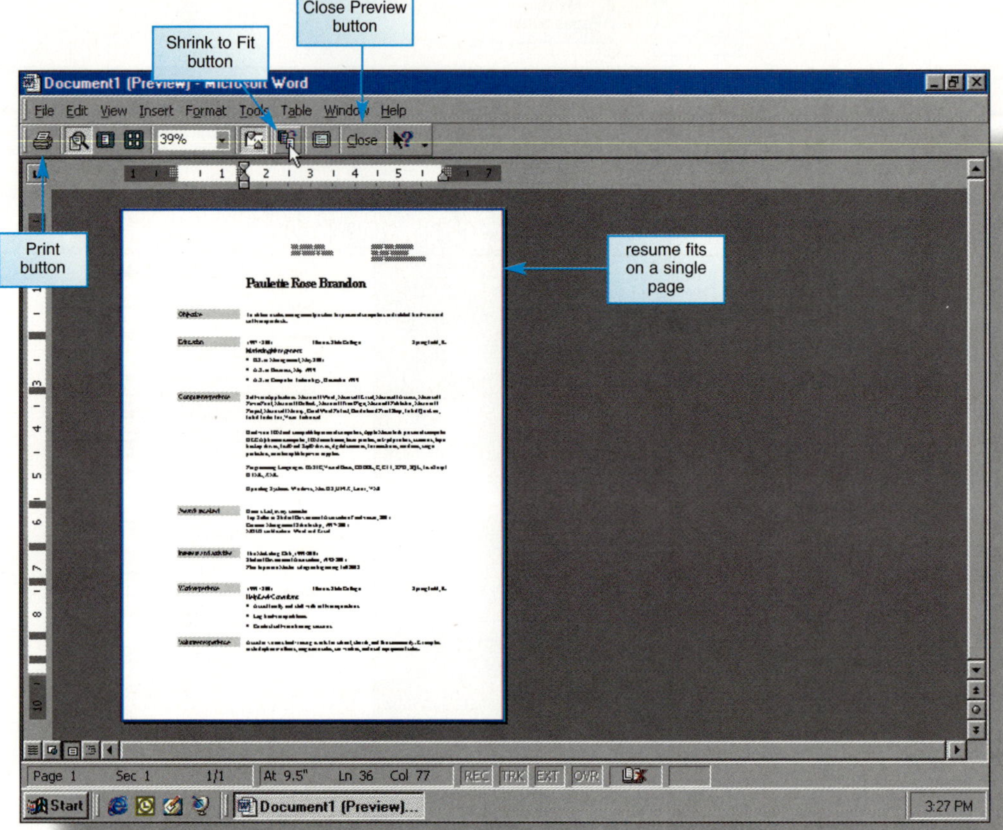

FIGURE 3-31

Other Ways

1. On File menu click Print Preview
2. Press CTRL+F2

Saving the Resume

Because the resume now is complete, you should save it. For a detailed example of the procedure summarized below, refer to pages WD 1.26 through WD 1.28 in Project 1.

TO SAVE A DOCUMENT

1. Insert your floppy disk into drive A.
2. Click the Save button on the Standard toolbar.
3. Type `Brandon Resume` in the File name text box. Do not press the ENTER key.
4. Click the Save in box arrow and then click 3½ Floppy (A:).
5. Click the Save button in the Save As dialog box.

Word saves the document on a floppy disk in drive A with the file name, Brandon Resume.

The resume now is complete. The next step in Project 3 is to create a cover letter to send with the resume to a potential employer. Do not close the Brandon Resume. You will use it again later in this project to copy the address, telephone, fax, and e-mail information.

More About

Printing

If you want to save ink, print faster, or decrease printer overrun errors, lower the printer resolution. Click File on the menu bar, click Print, click the Properties button in the Print dialog box, click the Graphics tab, click the Resolution box arrow, click a lower resolution than displayed currently, click the Apply button, click the OK button, and then click the Close button.

Creating a Letterhead

You have created a resume to send to prospective employers. Along with the resume, you will attach a personalized cover letter. You would like the cover letter to have a professional looking letterhead (see Figure 3-2a on page WD 3.6). The following pages describe how to use Word to create a letterhead.

In many businesses, letterhead is preprinted on stationery that is used by everyone throughout the corporation. For personal letters, the expense of preprinted letterhead can be costly. Thus, you can create your own letterhead and save it in a file. When you want to create a letter with the letterhead, you simply open the letterhead file and then save the file with a new name, preserving the original letterhead file.

The steps on the following pages illustrate how to create a personal letterhead file.

More About 2000

Letterhead Design

Letterhead designs vary. Some are centered at the top of the page, while others have text or graphics aligned with the left and right margins. Another style places the company's name and logo at the top of the page with the address and other information at the bottom. Well-designed letterheads add professionalism to correspondence.

Opening a New Document Window

The resume currently displays in the document window. You want to leave the resume open because you intend to use it again during this Word session. Thus, you want to work with two documents at the same time: the resume and the letterhead. Each of these documents will display in a separate document window. Perform the following steps to open a new document window for the letterhead file.

Steps To Open a New Document Window

1. **Point to the New Blank Document button on the Standard toolbar (Figure 3-32).**

2. **Click the New Blank Document button.**

Word opens a new document window (see Figure 3-33 on the next page).

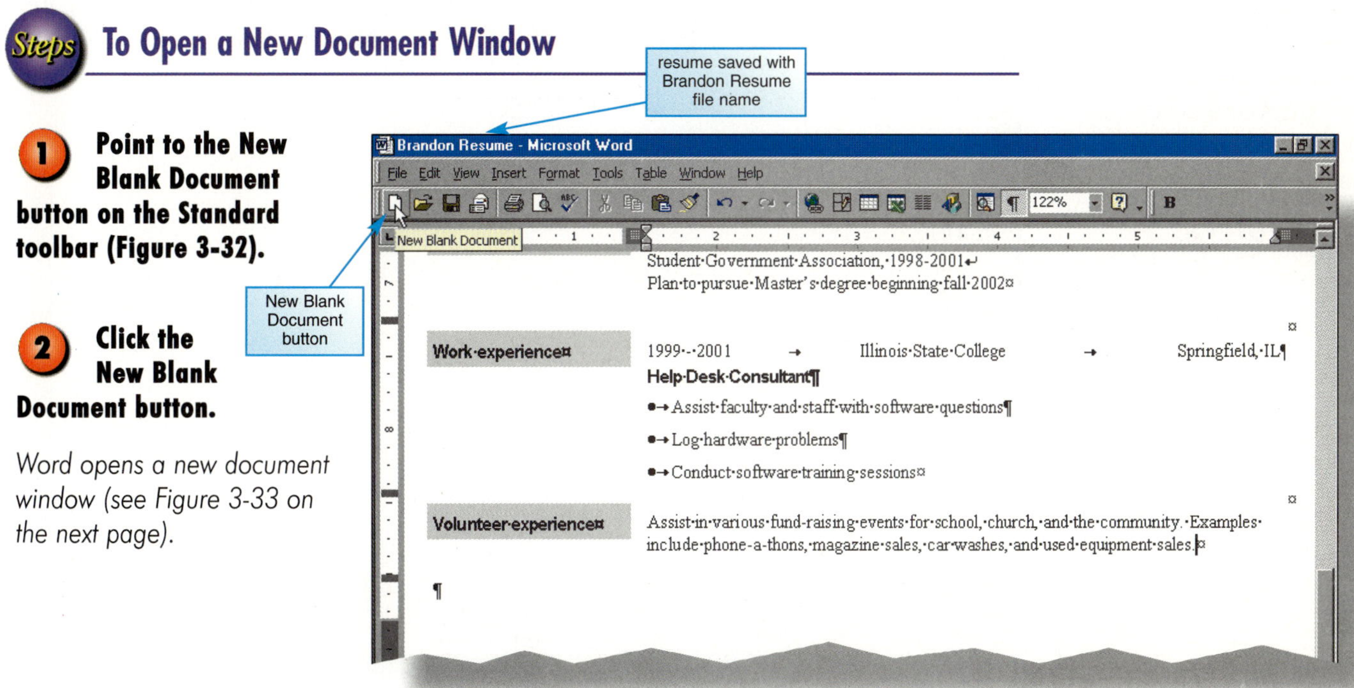

FIGURE 3-32

Other Ways

1. On File menu click New, click General tab, double-click Blank Document icon

The Brandon Resume document still is open. The program buttons on the taskbar display the names of the open Word document windows. In Figure 3-33 on the next page, the Brandon Resume is open and Document2 is open. The Document2 button on the taskbar is recessed, indicating that it is the active document displayed in the document window.

The name in the letterhead is to be a font size of 20. Perform the following steps to change the font size.

TO CHANGE THE FONT SIZE

1. Double-click the move handle on the Formatting toolbar to display the entire toolbar. Click the Font Size box arrow on the Formatting toolbar.
2. Scroll to and then click 20 in the Font Size list.

Word changes the displayed font size to 20 (Figure 3-33).

Adding Color to Characters

The characters in the letterhead are to be green. Perform the following steps to change the color of the characters before you enter them.

Steps To Color Characters

1 Point to the Font Color button arrow on the Formatting toolbar (Figure 3-33).

The color that displays below the letter A on the Font Color button is the most recently used color for characters; thus, the color on your button may differ from this figure.

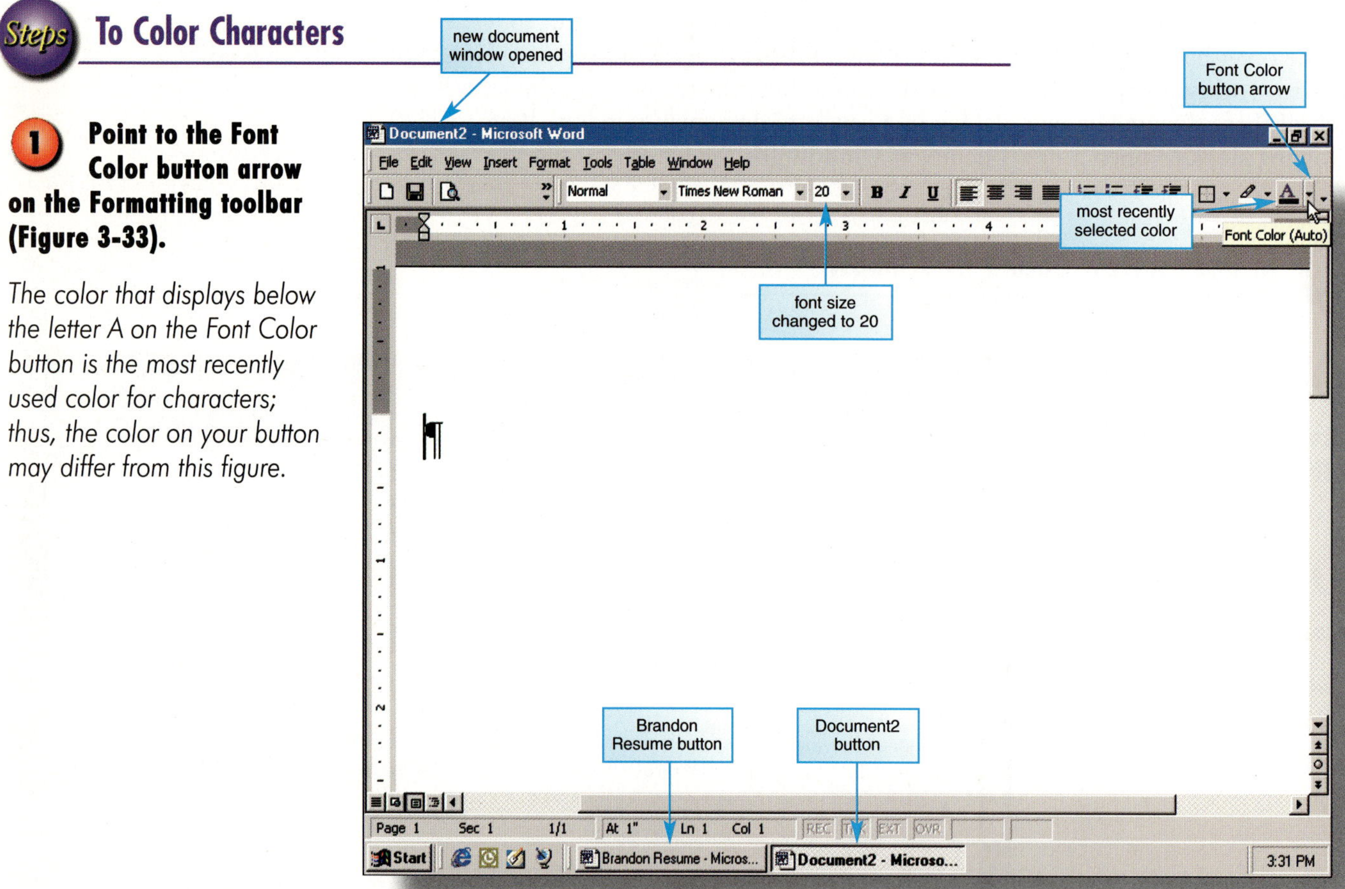

FIGURE 3-33

2 **Click the Font Color button arrow. Point to Green on the color palette.**

Word displays a list of available colors on the **color palette** *(Figure 3-34). Automatic is the default color, which usually is black.*

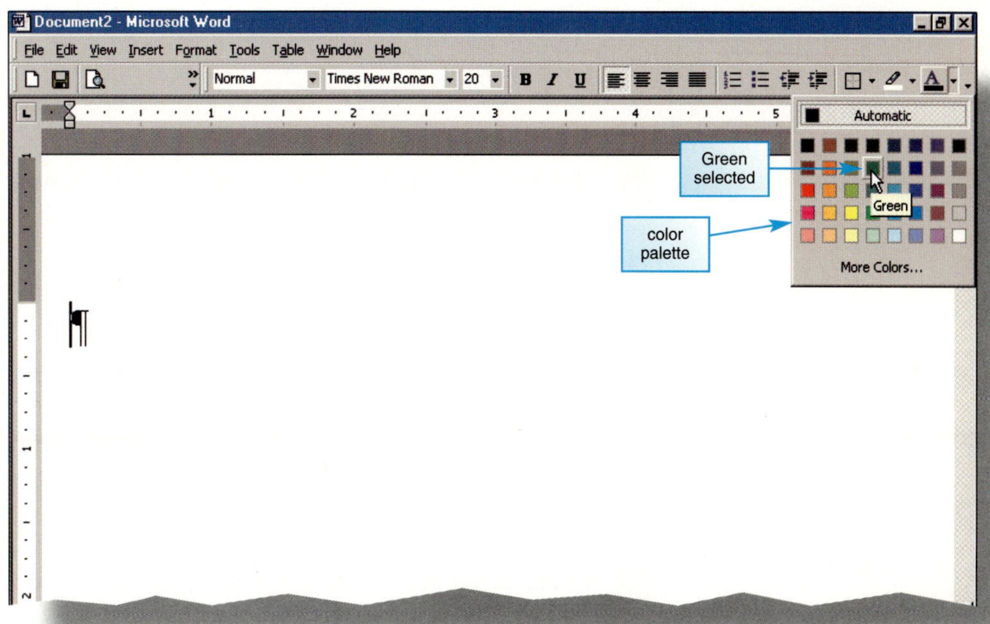

FIGURE 3-34

3 **Click Green. Type** `Paulette Rose Brandon` **and then press the ENTER key.**

Word displays the first line of the letterhead in green (Figure 3-35).

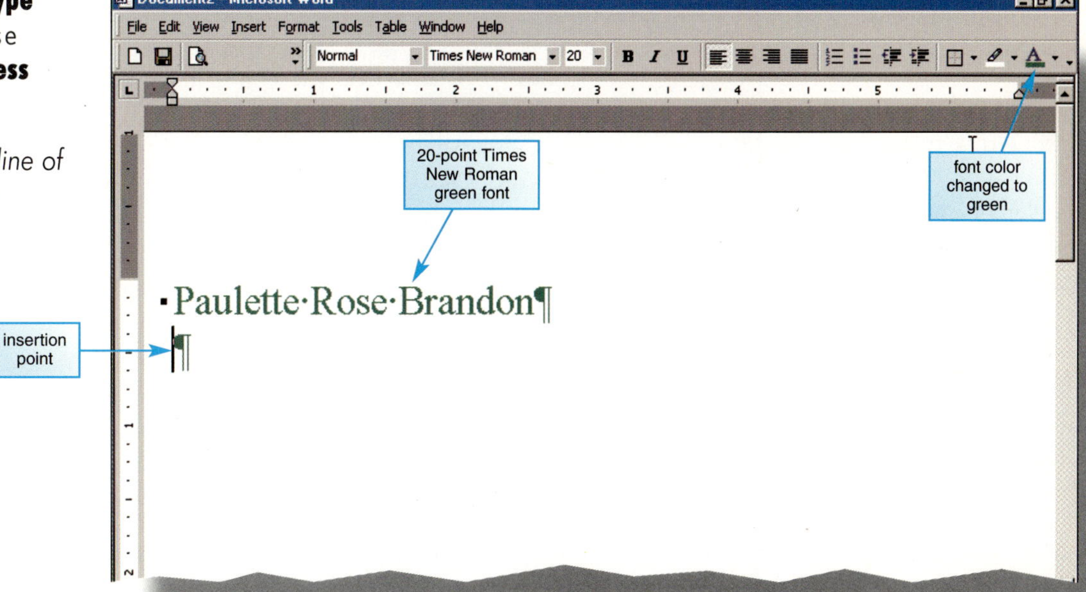

FIGURE 3-35

Notice the paragraph mark on line 2 is green. Recall that each time you press the ENTER key, formatting is carried forward to the next paragraph. If, for some reason, you wanted to change the text back to black at this point, you would click the Font Color button arrow on the Formatting toolbar and then click Automatic.

Other Ways

1. Right-click paragraph mark or selected text, click Font on shortcut menu, click Font tab, click Font Color box arrow, click desired color, click OK button
2. On Format menu click Font, click Font tab, click Font Color box arrow, click desired color, click OK button

The next step is to insert a graphic of a rose and resize it as described in the following steps.

TO ENTER AND RESIZE A GRAPHIC

1. If necessary, scroll up so that the name, Paulette Rose Brandon, is positioned at the top of the document window. With the insertion point below the name, click Insert on the menu bar, point to Picture, and then click Clip Art.
2. When the Insert ClipArt window opens, click the Search for clips text box. Type rose and then press the ENTER key.
3. Click the clip of the rose that matches the one shown in Figure 3-36. Click the Insert clip button on the Pop-up menu. Click the Close button on the Insert ClipArt window's title bar.
4. Click the graphic to select it. Drag the upper-right corner sizing handle diagonally toward the center of the graphic until the selection rectangle is positioned approximately as shown in Figure 3-36.
5. Click the paragraph mark to the right of the graphic to position the insertion point to the right of the graphic.

Word inserts the clip art and resizes it to approximately one-fourth of its original size (Figure 3-36).

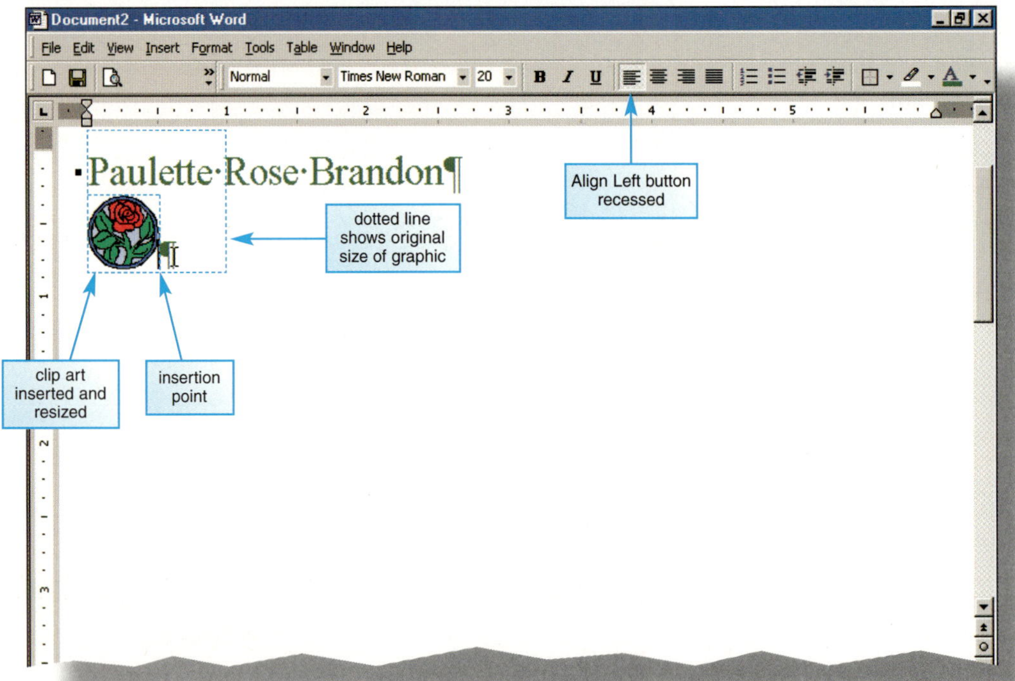

FIGURE 3-36

Setting Tab Stops Using the Tabs Dialog Box

The graphic of the rose is left-aligned (Figure 3-36). The address is to be positioned at the right margin of the same line. If you click the Align Right button, the graphic will be right-aligned. In Word, a paragraph cannot be both left-aligned and right-aligned. To place text at the right margin of a left-aligned paragraph, you set a tab stop at the right margin.

Word, by default, places **tab stops** at every .5" mark on the ruler (see Figure 3-38). These default tabs are indicated on the horizontal ruler by small **tick marks**. You also can set your own custom tab stops. When you set a **custom tab stop**, Word clears all default tab stops to the left of the custom tab stop. You also can specify how the text will align at a tab stop: left, centered, right, or decimal. Word stores tab settings in the paragraph mark at the end of each paragraph. Thus, each time you press the ENTER key, any custom tab stops are carried forward to the next paragraph.

In this letterhead, you want the tab stop to be right-aligned with the right margin; that is, at the 6" mark on the ruler. One method of setting custom tab stops is to click on the ruler at the desired location of the tab stop. You cannot, however, click at the right margin location. Thus, use the Tabs dialog box to set this custom tab stop as shown in the following steps.

The Tabs Dialog Box

You can use the Tabs dialog box to change an existing tab stop's alignment or position. You also can place leader characters in the empty space occupied by the tab. Leader characters, such as a series of dots, often are used in a table of contents to precede the page number. Simply click the desired leader in the Leader area of the Tabs dialog box.

To Set Custom Tab Stops Using the Tabs Dialog Box

1 **With the insertion point positioned between the paragraph mark and the graphic, click Format on the menu bar and then point to Tabs (Figure 3-37).**

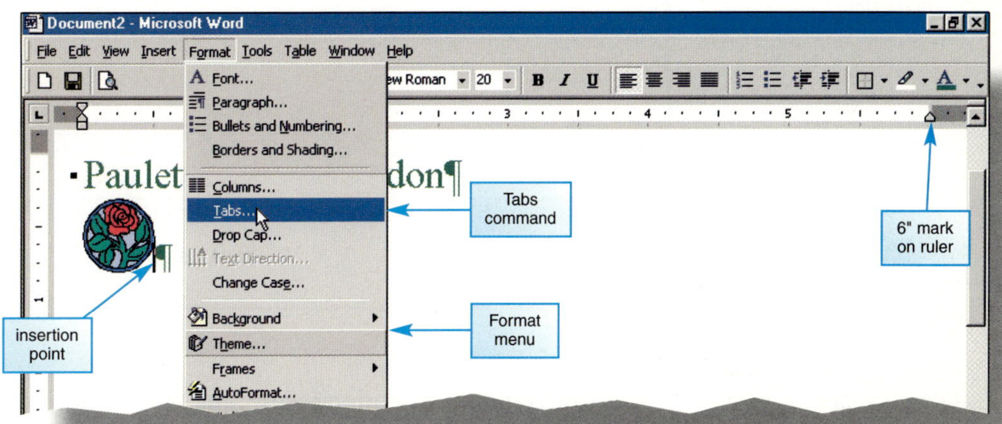

FIGURE 3-37

2 **Click Tabs. When the Tabs dialog box displays, type 6 in the Tab stop position text box and then click Right in the Alignment area. Point to the Set button.**

Word displays the Tabs dialog box (Figure 3-38).

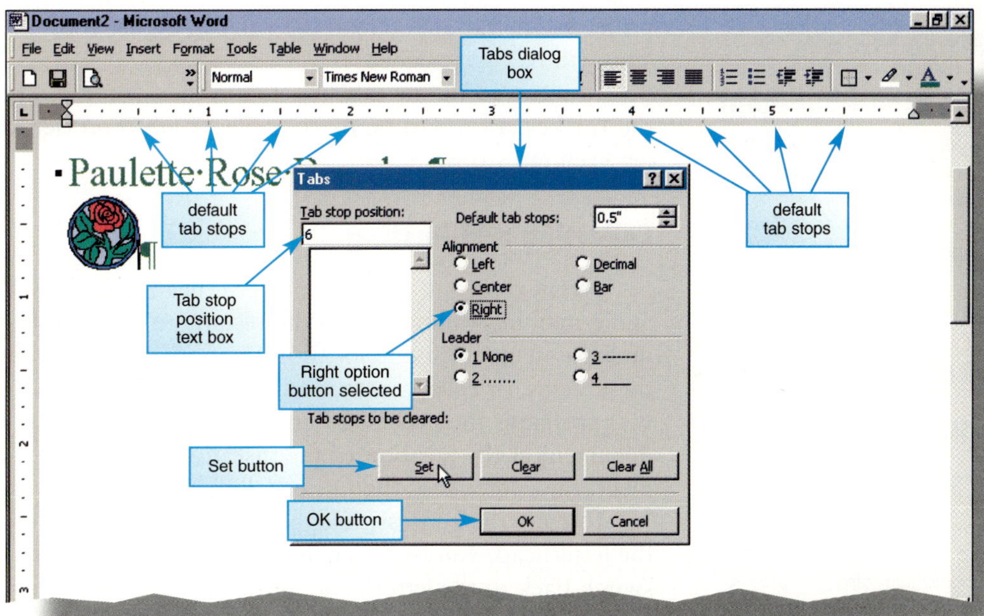

FIGURE 3-38

3 Click the Set button and then click the OK button.

Word places a ***tab marker*** *at the 6" mark on the ruler and removes all default tab stops to the left of the tab marker (Figure 3-39).*

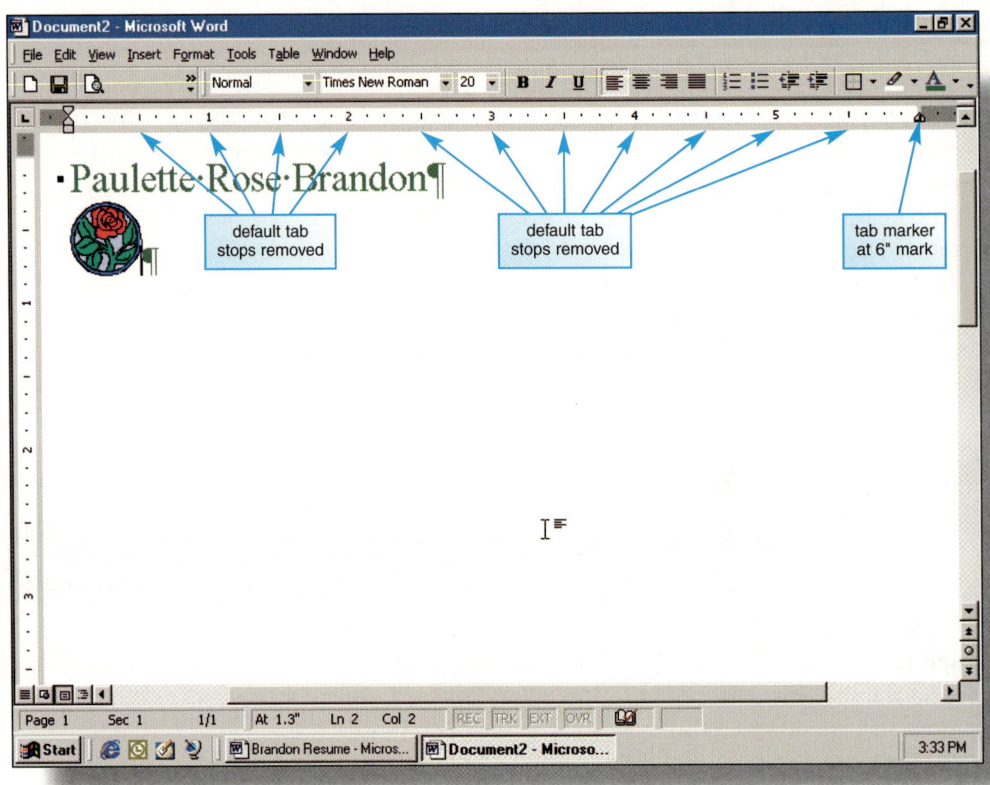

FIGURE 3-39

1. Click button on left of ruler until desired tab stop alignment displays and then click ruler

More About 2000

Tab Stop Alignment

If you have a series of numbers that you want aligned on the decimal point, such as dollar amounts, use a decimal-aligned tab stop for the data.

Clipboards

The Windows Clipboard holds only one item at a time. When you collect multiple items on the Office Clipboard, the last copied item also is copied to the Windows Clipboard. When you clear the Office Clipboard, the Windows Clipboard also is cleared.

When you set a custom tab stop, the tab marker on the ruler reflects the tab stop alignment. A capital letter L indicates a left-aligned tab stop; a mirror image of a capital letter L indicates a right-aligned tab stop; an upside down T indicates a centered tab stop; and an upside down T with a dot next to it indicates a decimal-aligned tab stop. The tab markers are discussed as they are presented in these projects. The tab marker on the ruler in Figure 3-39 indicates text entered at that tab stop will be right-aligned.

To move from one tab stop to another, you press the TAB key. When you press the TAB key, a formatting mark, called a **tab character**, displays in the empty space between tab stops.

Collecting and Pasting

The next step in creating the letterhead is to copy the address, telephone, fax, and e-mail information from the resume to the letterhead. When you want to copy multiple items from one location to another, you use the Office Clipboard to copy these items, or **collect** them, and then paste them in a new location. You have learned that **pasting** is the process of copying an item from the Office Clipboard into the document at the location of the insertion point. When you paste text into a document, the contents of the Office Clipboard are not erased.

To copy the address, telephone, fax, and e-mail information from the resume to the letterhead, you first switch to the resume, copy the items to the Office Clipboard, switch back to the letterhead, and then paste the information into the letterhead. The following pages illustrate this process.

Follow these steps to switch from the letterhead to the resume.

To Switch from One Open Document to Another

1 **Point to the Brandon Resume - Microsoft Word button on the taskbar (Figure 3-40).**

2 **Click the Brandon Resume - Microsoft Word button.**

Word switches from the cover letter to the resume (see Figure 3-41 below).

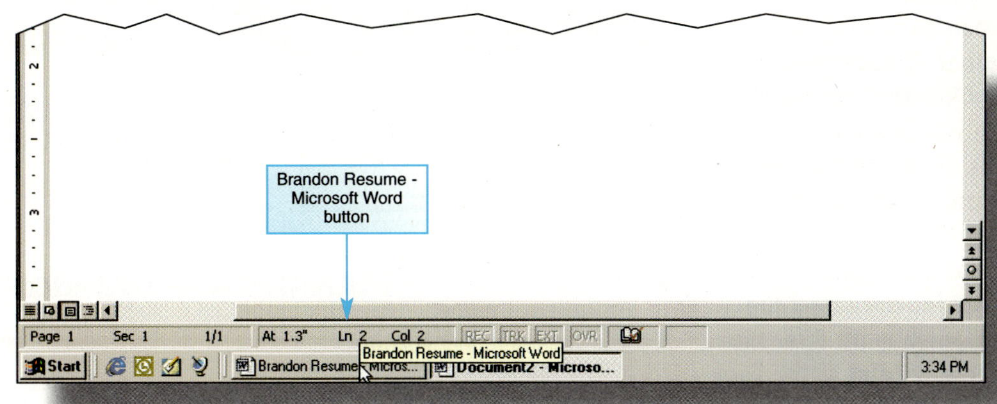

FIGURE 3-40

Other Ways

1. On Window menu click document name

You copy multiple items to the Office Clipboard so you can paste them later. Each copied item displays as an icon on the Clipboard toolbar, as shown in these steps.

To Collect Items

1 **Press CTRL+HOME to display the top of the resume. Click View on the menu bar, point to Toolbars, and then point to Clipboard (Figure 3-41).**

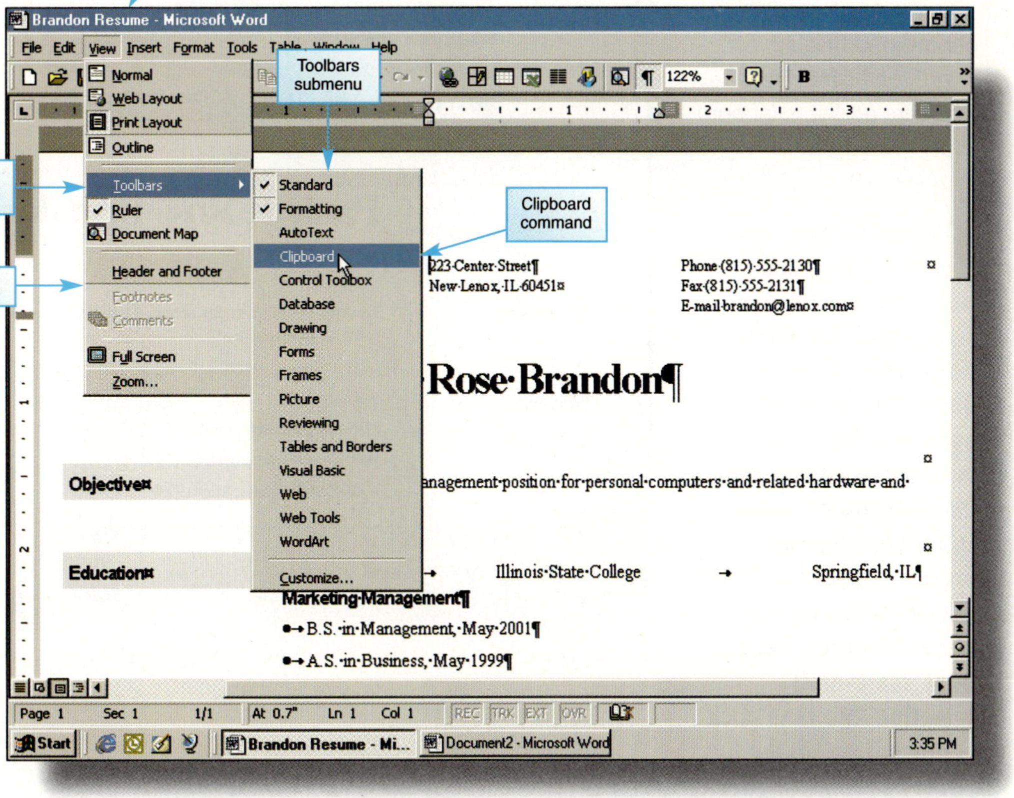

FIGURE 3-41

2 **Click Clipboard. If it is not dimmed, click the Clear Clipboard button on the Clipboard toolbar. If necessary, drag the Clipboard toolbar's title bar so the toolbar does not cover the address information in the resume. Drag through the street address, 223 Center Street (do not select the paragraph mark after the address). Point to the Copy button on the Clipboard toolbar.**

The Clipboard toolbar displays in the document window (Figure 3-42). The street address is selected.

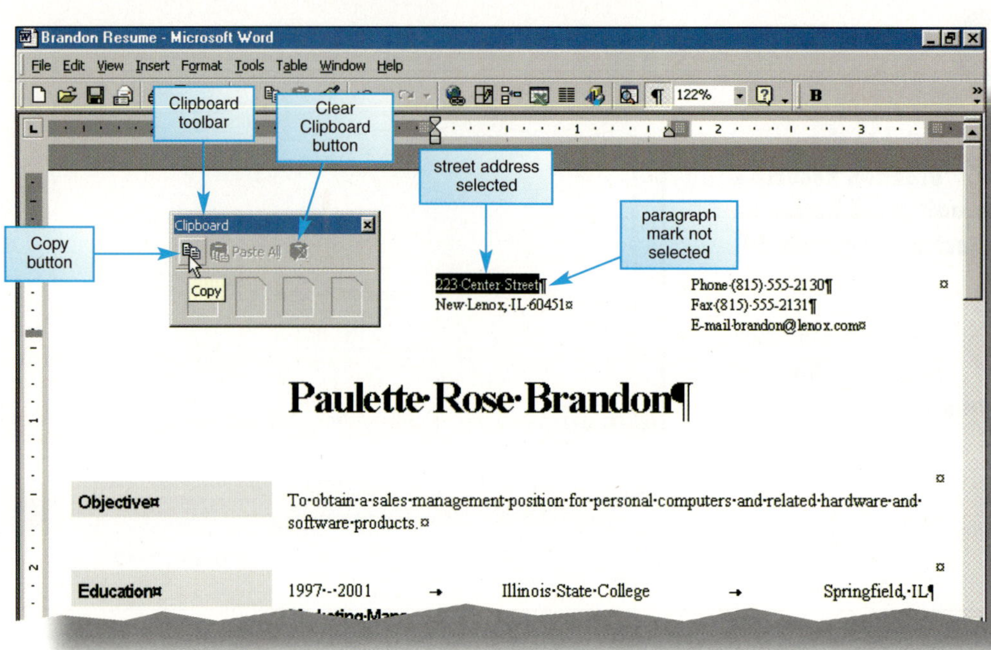

FIGURE 3-42

3 **Click the Copy button on the Clipboard toolbar.**

Word places a copy of the street address on the Office Clipboard and displays an icon that represents the copied item on the Clipboard toolbar.

4 **Drag through the city, state, and postal code information and then click the Copy button on the Clipboard toolbar. Drag through the telephone information and then click the Copy button on the Clipboard toolbar. Drag through the fax information and then click the Copy button on the Clipboard toolbar. Drag through the e-mail information and then click the Copy button on the Clipboard toolbar (Figure 3-43).**

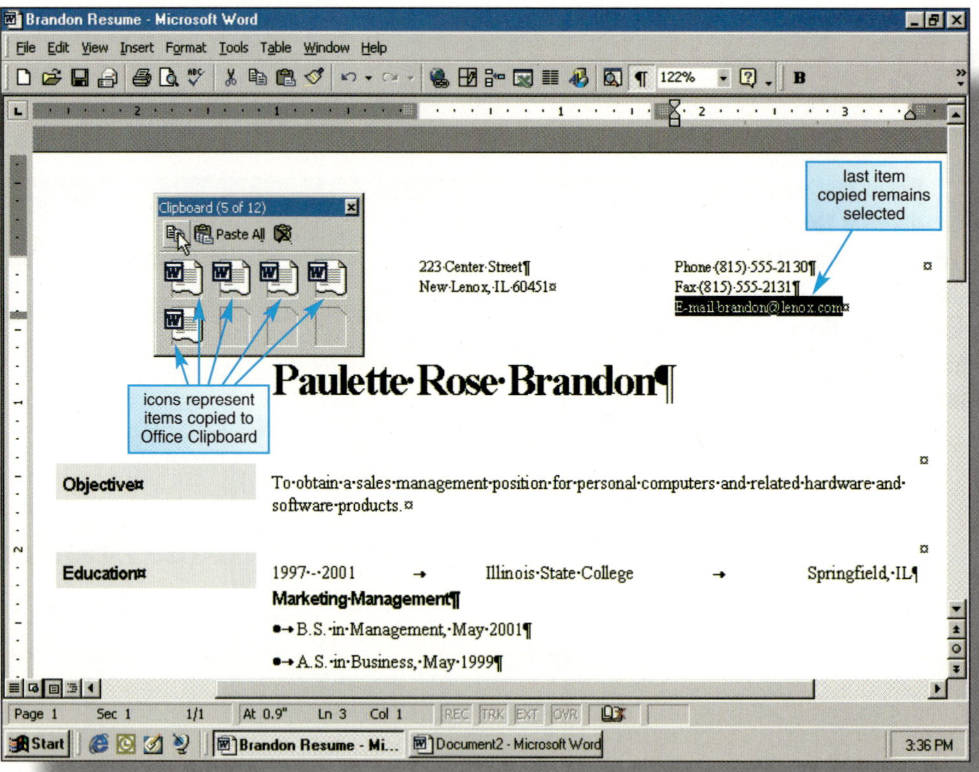

FIGURE 3-43

Other Ways

1. Click the Copy button on the Standard toolbar two consecutive times

The Office Clipboard can store up to 12 items at one time. When you copy a thirteenth item, Word deletes the first item to make room for the new item. When you point to the icons on the Clipboard toolbar, the first 50 characters of text in the item display as a ScreenTip.

Perform the following steps to paste the items from the Office Clipboard into the letterhead.

To Paste from the Office Clipboard

1 Click the Document2 - Microsoft Word button on the taskbar to display the letterhead document window.

2 With the insertion point between the paragraph mark and the rose graphic, press the TAB key.

Word displays the letterhead with the Clipboard toolbar in the middle of the Word window (Figure 3-44). The insertion point is positioned at the 6" mark on the ruler, which is the location of the right-aligned tab stop. The right-pointing arrow is a tab character that displays each time you press the TAB key.

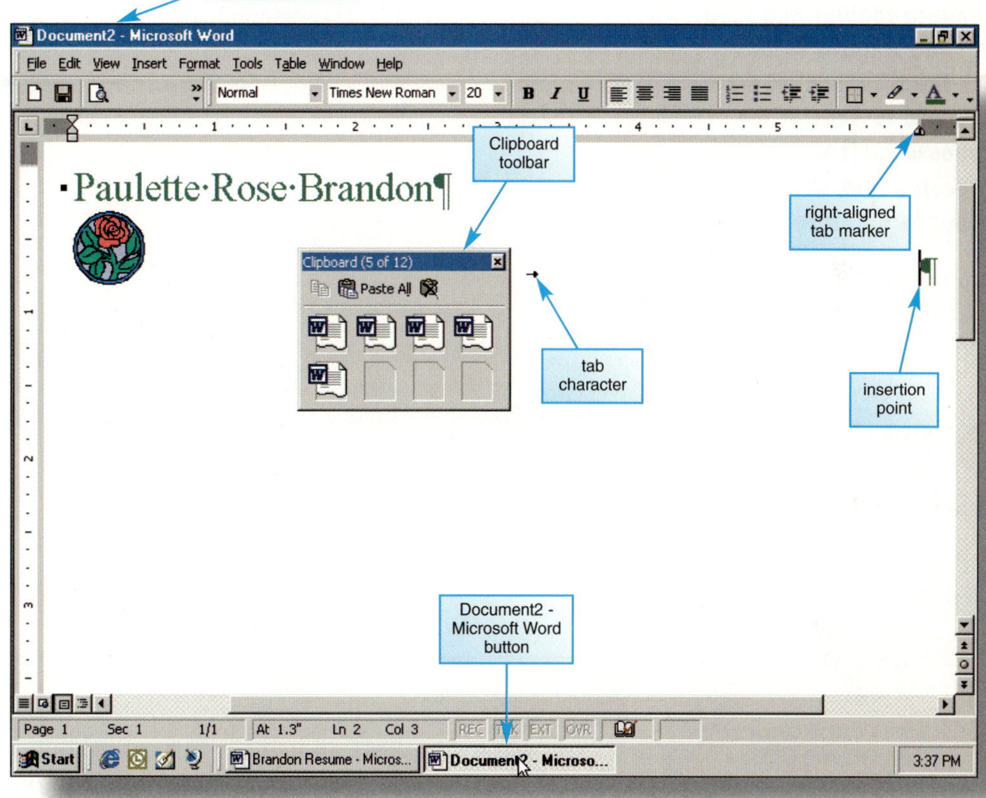

FIGURE 3-44

3 Click the first icon on the Clipboard toolbar.

Word pastes the contents of the clicked item at the location of the insertion point (Figure 3-45). Notice the text is aligned with the right margin because of the right-aligned tab stop.

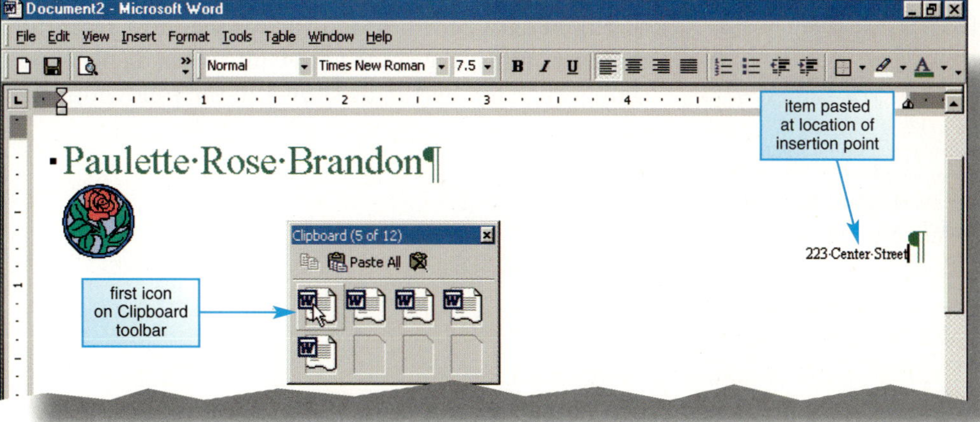

FIGURE 3-45

4 **Press the COMMA key and then the SPACEBAR. Click the second icon on the Clipboard toolbar and the press the ENTER key. Press the TAB key. Click the third icon on the Clipboard toolbar and then press the SPACEBAR twice. Click the fourth icon on the Clipboard toolbar and then press the SPACEBAR twice. Click the fifth icon on the Clipboard toolbar. If the Clipboard toolbar covers the pasted text, drag the toolbar to a new location.**

Word pastes all items from the Office Clipboard into the letterhead (Figure 3-46).

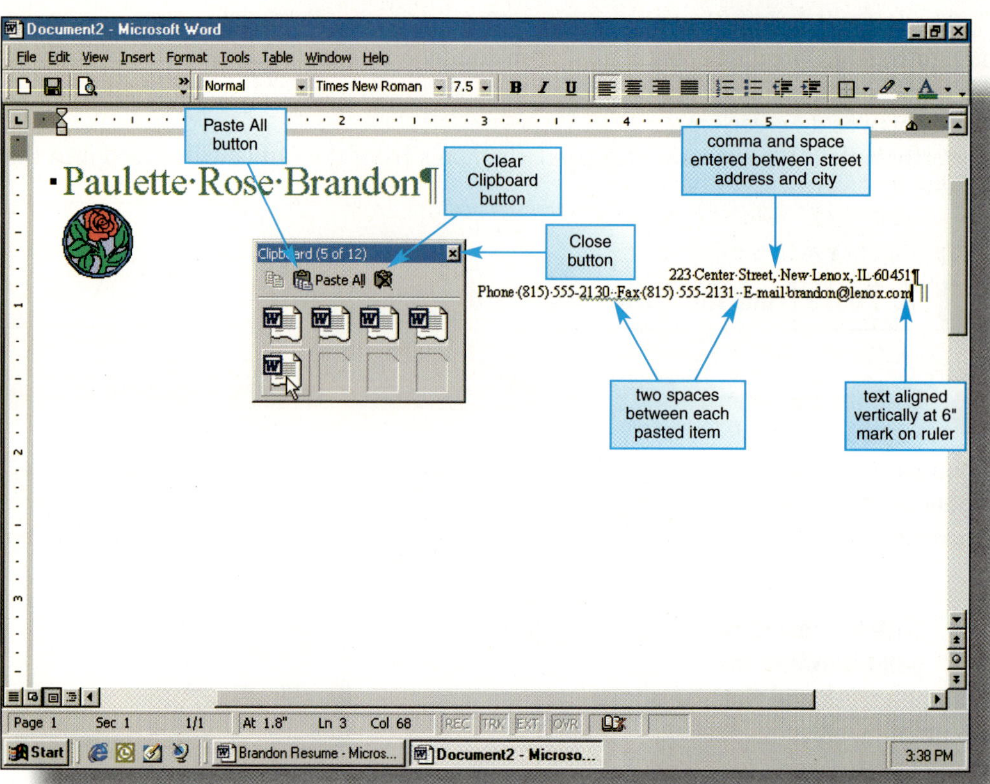

FIGURE 3-46

5 **Click the Close button on the Clipboard toolbar.**

Word removes the Clipboard toolbar from the window.

Other Ways

1. Click Items button arrow on docked Clipboard toolbar and then click item to paste

Office Clipboard

Depending on your Office Clipboard usage, clicking either the Copy button or the Cut button on the Standard toolbar twice in succession may display the Clipboard toolbar. You can click the Copy button on the Standard toolbar or the Copy button on the Clipboard toolbar to collect items on the Office Clipboard.

If you wanted to paste all items in a row without any characters or formatting in between them, you would click the Paste All button on the Clipboard toolbar. If, for some reason, you wanted to erase all items on the Office Clipboard, click the Clear Clipboard button on the Clipboard toolbar (Figure 3-46).

The next step is to change the font size to 9 and the color of the characters to green in the address, telephone, fax, and e-mail information in the letterhead. Recall that the Font Color button displays the most recently used color, which is green, in this case. When the color you want to use displays on the Font Color button, you simply click the button as shown in the following steps.

Steps To Color More Characters the Same Color

1 Drag through the address, telephone, fax, and e-mail information in the letterhead, including both paragraph marks at the end of the lines. Click the Font Size box arrow on the Formatting toolbar and then click 9 in the Font Size list. Point to the Font Color button on the Formatting toolbar (Figure 3-47).

2 Click the Font Color button. Click inside the selected text to remove the highlight.

Word changes the color of the selected characters to green (see Figure 3-48).

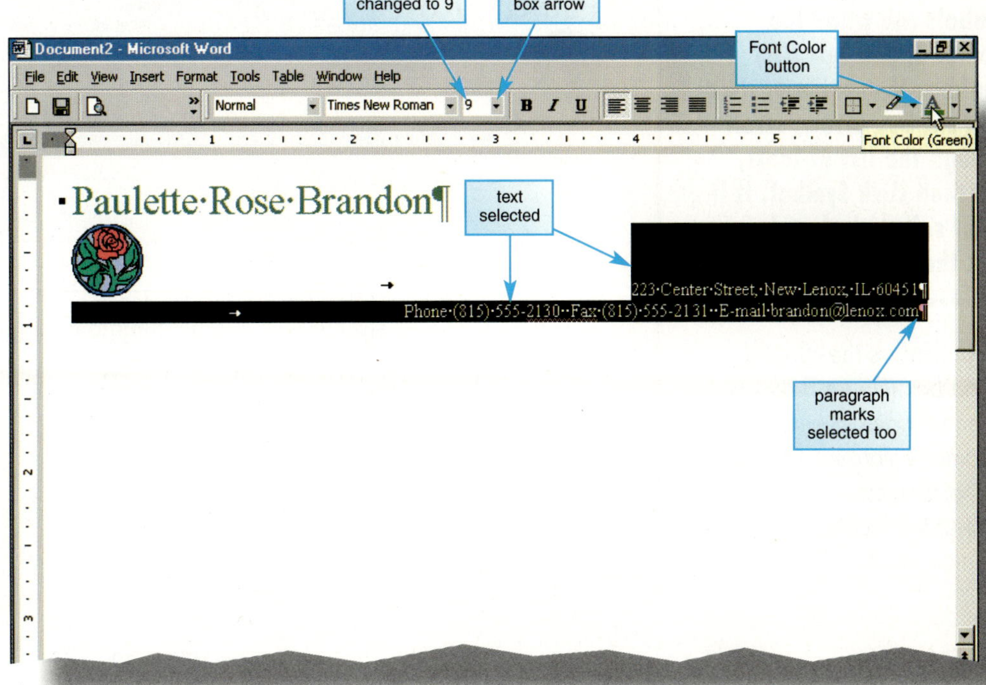

FIGURE 3-47

Other Ways

1. Right-click paragraph mark or selected text, click Font on shortcut menu, click Font tab, click Font Color box arrow, click desired color, click OK button
2. On Format menu click Font, click Font tab, click Font Color box arrow, click desired color, click OK button

Inserting Symbols into a Document

To visually separate the telephone and fax information in the letterhead, you want a small round dot to display between them. Likewise, you want a small round dot to display between the fax and e-mail information. To insert symbols, such as dots, letters in the Greek alphabet, and mathematical characters, you can use the Symbol dialog box, as shown in the following steps.

Steps To Insert a Symbol into Text

1 Click where you want to insert the symbol, in this case, the space between the telephone and fax information. Click Insert on the menu bar and then point to Symbol (Figure 3-48).

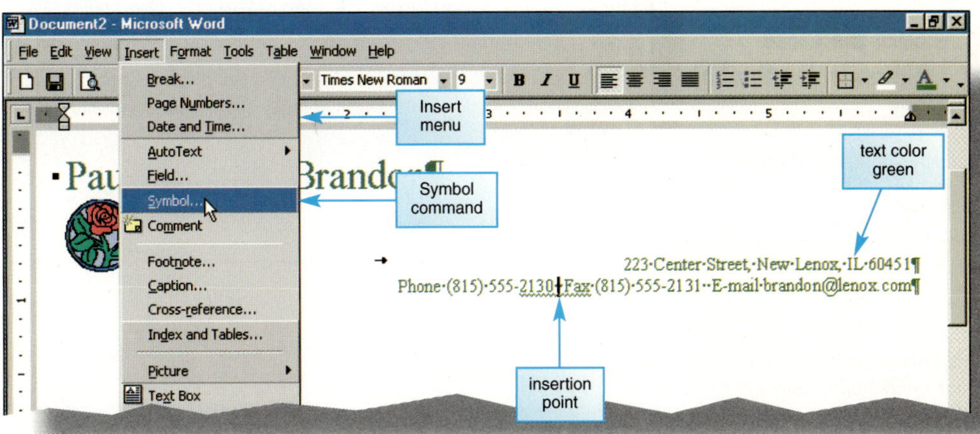

FIGURE 3-48

2 **Click Symbol. If necessary, click the Symbols tab when the Symbol dialog box first displays. If necessary, click the Font box arrow, scroll through the list of fonts, and then click Symbol. If it is not selected already, click the dot symbol. Click the Insert button.**

Word displays the Symbol dialog box (Figure 3-49). When you click a symbol, it becomes enlarged. The dot symbol displays in the document at the location of the insertion point.

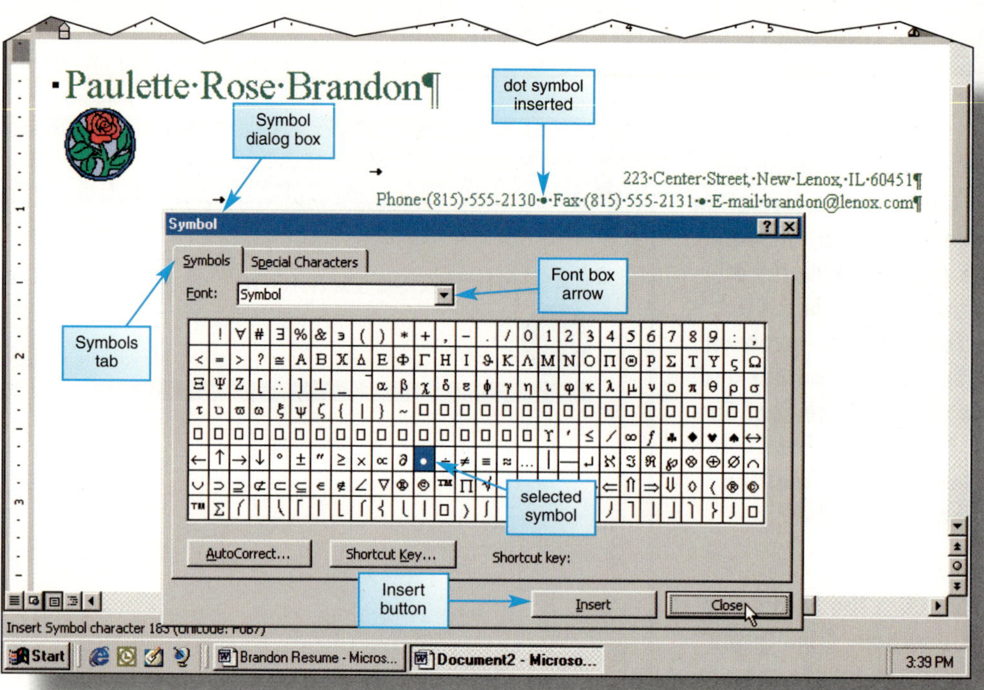

FIGURE 3-49

3 **Click where you want to insert the next symbol, in this case, the space between the fax and e-mail information in the document window. With the dot symbol still selected in the dialog box, click the Insert button. Point to the Close button in the Symbol dialog box.**

Word inserts the selected symbol at the location of the insertion point (Figure 3-50).

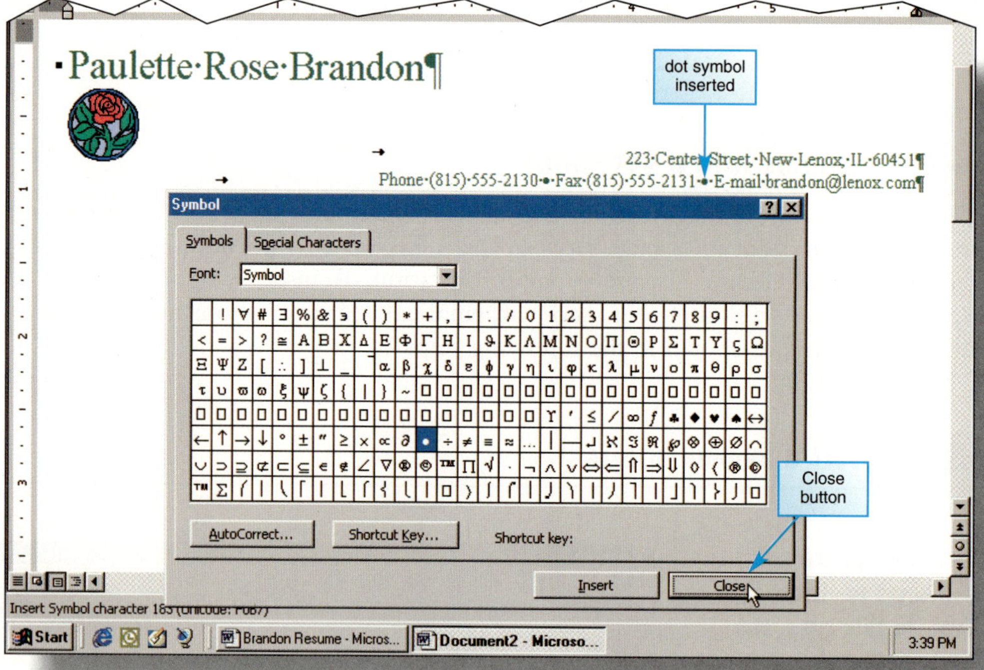

FIGURE 3-50

4 **Click the Close button in the Symbol dialog box.**

Word closes the Symbol dialog box.

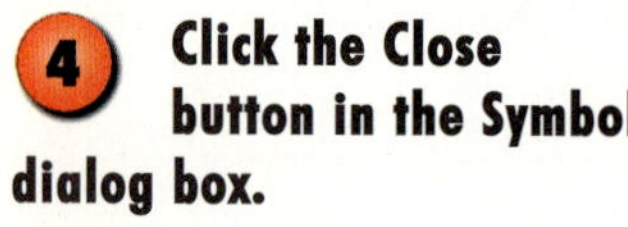

Other Ways

1. Type ALT+0 (zero) followed by ANSI character code for symbol using numeric keypad

You also can insert ANSI (American National Standards Institute) characters into a document by entering the ANSI code directly into the document. The **ANSI characters** are a predefined set of characters, including both characters on the keyboard and special characters, such as the dot symbol. To enter the ANSI code, make sure the NUM LOCK key is on. Press and hold the ALT key and then type the numeral zero followed by the ANSI code for the characters. You *must* use the numeric keypad when entering the ANSI code. For a complete list of ANSI codes, see your Microsoft Windows documentation.

Special Characters

In addition to symbols, you can insert special characters including a variety of dashes, hyphens, spaces, apostrophes, and quotation marks through the Symbol dialog box. Click Insert on the menu bar, click Symbol, click the Special Characters tab, click the desired character in the Insert Character list, click the Insert button, and then click the Close button.

Adding a Bottom Border to a Paragraph

To add professionalism to the letterhead, you would like to draw a horizontal line from the left margin to the right margin immediately below the telephone, fax, and e-mail information. In Word, you can draw a solid line, called a **border**, at any edge of a paragraph. That is, borders may be added above or below a paragraph, to the left or right of a paragraph, or any combination of these sides.

When adding a border to a paragraph, it is important that you have an extra paragraph mark below the paragraph you intend to border. Otherwise, each time you press the ENTER key, the border will be carried forward to each subsequent paragraph. If you forget to do this after you have added a border, simply click the Undo button on the Standard toolbar and begin again.

Perform the following steps to add a bottom border to the paragraph containing telephone, fax, and e-mail information.

To Add a Bottom Border to a Paragraph

1 Press the END key to move the insertion point to the end of the line and then press the ENTER key to create a paragraph mark below the line you want to border. Press CTRL+Z to undo the AutoFormat of the e-mail address. Press the UP ARROW key to reposition the insertion point in the paragraph that will contain the border. Point to the Border button arrow on the Formatting toolbar.

The name of this button changes depending on the last border type added. In this figure, it is the Outside Border button (Figure 3-51).

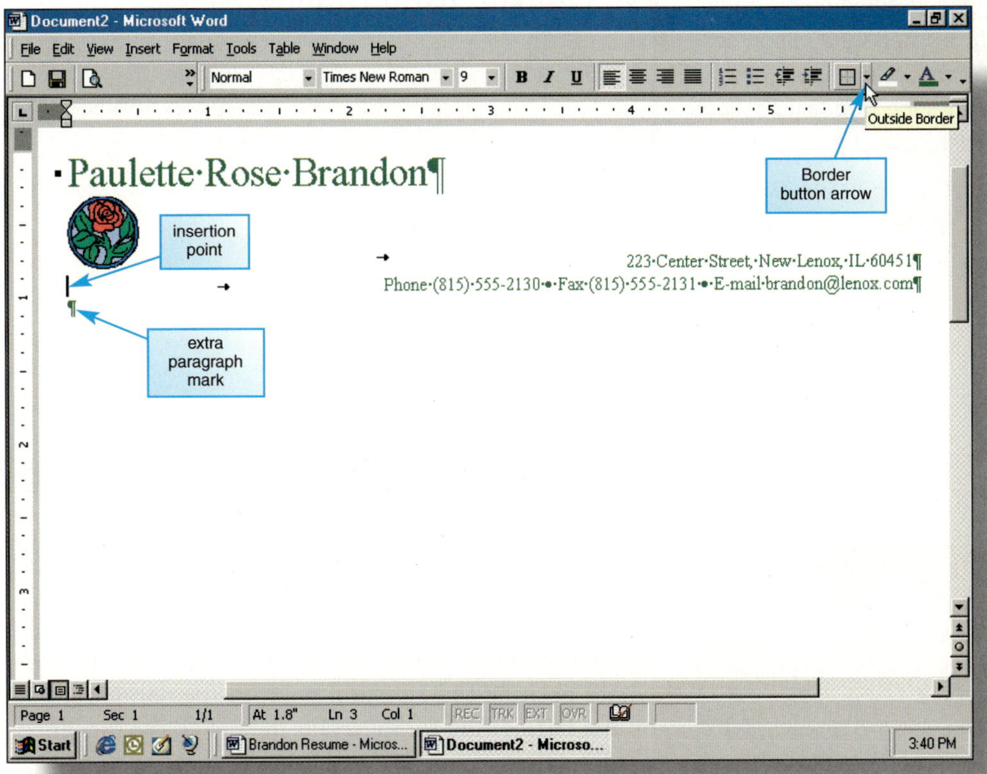

FIGURE 3-51

2 Click the Border button arrow and then point to the Bottom Border button.

Word displays the border palette (Figure 3-52). Using the ***border palette****, you can add a border to any edge of a paragraph.*

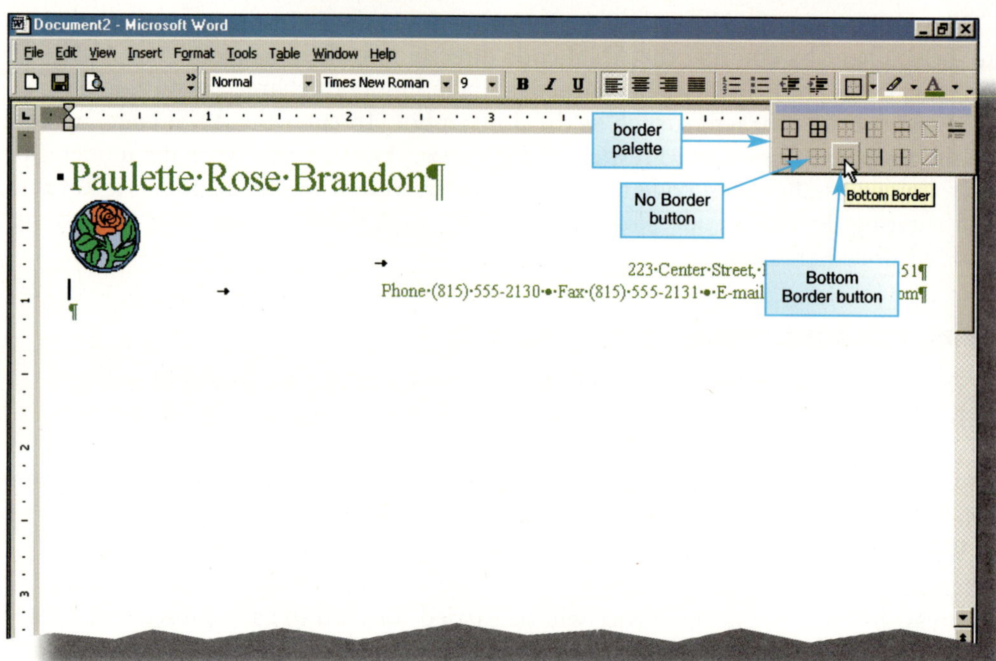

FIGURE 3-52

3 Click the Bottom Border button.

Word places a bottom border below the paragraph containing the insertion point (Figure 3-53). The Border button on the Formatting toolbar now displays the icon for a bottom border.

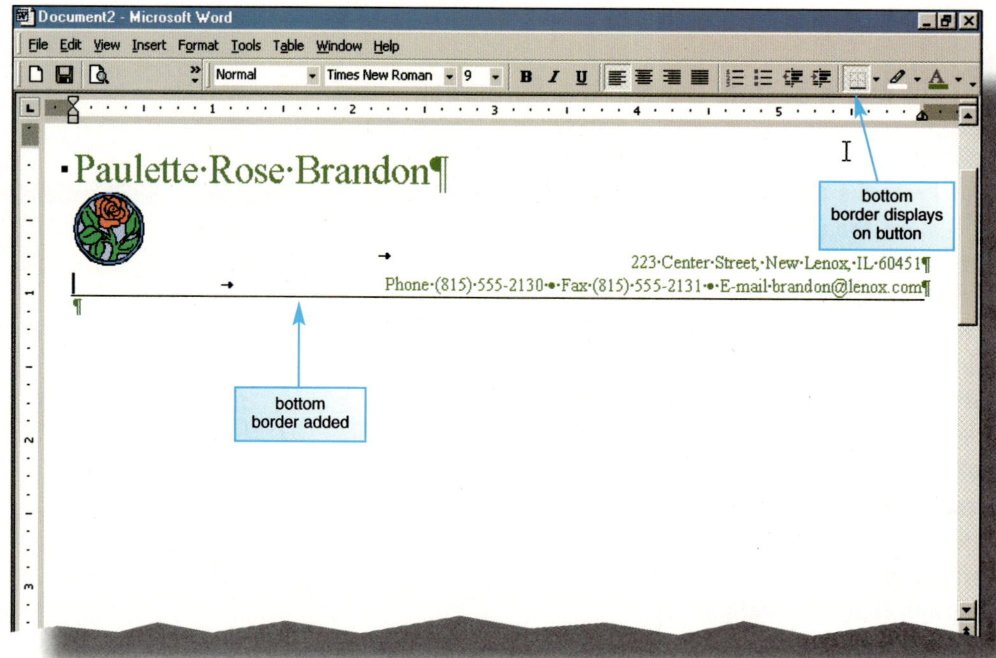

FIGURE 3-53

Other Ways

1. Click Border button on Tables and Borders toolbar
2. On Format menu click Borders and Shading, click Borders tab, click Bottom button in Preview area, click OK button

If, for some reason, you wanted to remove a border from a paragraph, you would position the insertion point in the paragraph, click the Border button arrow on the Formatting toolbar, and then click the No Border button (Figure 3-52) on the border palette.

Perform the following step to change the color of the text below the border back to Automatic (black).

Borders

If you do not want the border of the current paragraph to extend to the margins, drag the right or left indent markers inward on the ruler to narrow the border.

TO CHANGE COLOR OF TEXT

1. Press the DOWN ARROW key.
2. Click the Font Color button arrow and then click Automatic.

Word changes the color of the paragraph mark below the border to black (see Figure 3-54 on page WD 3.43).

Now that you have created your letterhead, you should save it in a file.

More About 2000

Letterhead Contents

All letterheads should contain the following items: complete legal name of company, group, or individual; full street address including any building, room, suite number, or post office box; city, state, and postal code. Other items sometimes found in a letterhead include a logo, department name, telephone number, fax number, e-mail address, and Web address.

TO SAVE THE LETTERHEAD

1. Insert your floppy disk into drive A.
2. Double-click the move handle on the Standard toolbar to display the entire toolbar. Click the Save button on the Standard toolbar.
3. Type the file name `Brandon Letterhead` in the File name text box.
4. If necessary, click the Save in box arrow and then click 3½ Floppy (A:).
5. Click the Save button in the Save As dialog box.

Word saves the document on a floppy disk in drive A with the file name, Brandon Letterhead.

Each time you wish to create a letter, you would open your letterhead file (Brandon Letterhead) and then immediately save it with a new file name. By doing this, your letterhead file will remain unchanged for future use.

Creating a Cover Letter

You have created a letterhead for your cover letter. The next step is to compose the cover letter. The following pages outline how to use Word to compose a cover letter with a bulleted list and a table.

Components of a Business Letter

Cover Letters

You should always send a personalized cover letter with a resume. A cover letter should highlight aspects of your background relevant to the position. Because it often is difficult to recall past achievements and activities, you should keep a personal file containing documents that outline your accomplishments.

During your professional career, you will create many business letters. A **cover letter** is one type of business letter. All business letters contain the same basic components. When preparing business letters, you should include all essential elements. **Essential business letter elements** include the date line, inside address, message, and signature block (see Figure 3-2a on the page WD 3.6). The **date line**, which consists of the month, day, and year, is positioned two to six lines below the letterhead. The **inside address**, placed three to eight lines below the date line, usually contains the addressee's courtesy title plus full name, business affiliation, and full geographical address. The **salutation**, if present, begins two lines below the last line of the inside address. The body of the letter, the **message**, begins two lines below the salutation. Within the message, paragraphs are single-spaced with double-spacing between paragraphs. Two lines below the last line of the message, the **complimentary close** displays. Capitalize only the first word in a complimentary close. Type the **signature block** at least four lines below the complimentary close, allowing room for the author to sign his or her name.

Table 3-1 Common Business Letter Styles

LETTER STYLES	FEATURES
Block	All components of the letter begin flush with the left margin.
Modified Block	The date, complimentary close, and signature block are centered, positioned approximately ½" to the right of center, or at the right margin. All other components of the letter begin flush with the left margin.
Modified Semi-Block	The date, complimentary close, and signature block are centered, positioned approximately ½" to the right of center, or at the right margin. The first line of each paragraph in the body of the letter is indented ½" to 1" fom the left margin. All other components of the letter begin flush with the left margin.

You can follow many different styles when you create business letters. The cover letter in this project follows the **modified block style**. Table 3-1 outlines the differences between three common styles of business letters.

Saving the Cover Letter with a New File Name

The document in the document window currently has the name Brandon Letterhead, the name of the personal letterhead. Because you want the letterhead to remain unchanged, save the document with a new file name as described in these steps.

Templates

As an alternative to saving the letterhead as a Word document, you could save it as a template by clicking the Save as type box arrow in the Save As dialog box and then clicking Document Template. To use the template, click File on the menu bar, click New, click the General tab, and then click the template icon or name.

TO SAVE THE DOCUMENT WITH A NEW FILE NAME

1. If necessary, insert your floppy disk into drive A.
2. Click File on the menu bar and then click Save As.
3. Type the file name `Brandon Cover Letter` in the File name text box.
4. If necessary, click the Save in box arrow and then click 3½ Floppy (A:).
5. Click the Save button in the Save As dialog box.

Word saves the document on a floppy disk in drive A with the file name, Brandon Cover Letter (see Figure 3-54).

The font size of characters in the resume is 10. You want the size of the characters in the cover letter to be slightly larger, yet close to the size of those in the resume. Perform the following steps to increase the font size of characters in the cover letter to 11.

TO INCREASE THE FONT SIZE

1. If necessary, click the paragraph mark below the border to position the insertion point below the border.
2. Double-click the move handle on the Formatting toolbar to display the entire toolbar. Click the Font Size box arrow on the Formatting toolbar and then click 11 in the Font Size list.

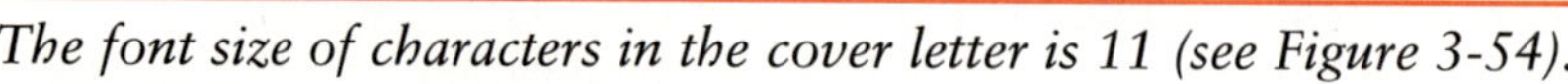

The font size of characters in the cover letter is 11 (see Figure 3-54).

Bar Tabs

To insert a vertical line at a tab stop, set a bar tab. To do this, click the button at the left edge of the horizontal ruler until its icon changes to a Bar Tab icon (a vertical bar) and then click the location on the ruler. Or, click Bar in the Alignment area of the Tabs dialog box.

Setting Tab Stops Using the Ruler

The first required element of the cover letter is the date line, which is positioned three lines below the letterhead. The month, day, and year in the date line begins 3.5 inches from the left margin, which is one-half inch to the right of center. Thus, you should set a custom tab stop at the 3.5" mark on the ruler.

Earlier you used the Tabs dialog box to set a tab stop because you could not use the ruler to set a tab stop at the right margin. In the following steps, you set a left-aligned tab stop using the ruler.

Steps To Set Custom Tab Stops Using the Ruler

1 Press the ENTER key twice. If necessary, click the button at the left edge of the horizontal ruler until it displays the left tab icon. Point to the 3.5" mark on the ruler.

Each time you click the button at the left of the horizontal ruler, its icon changes (Figure 3-54). The left tab icon looks like a capital letter L.

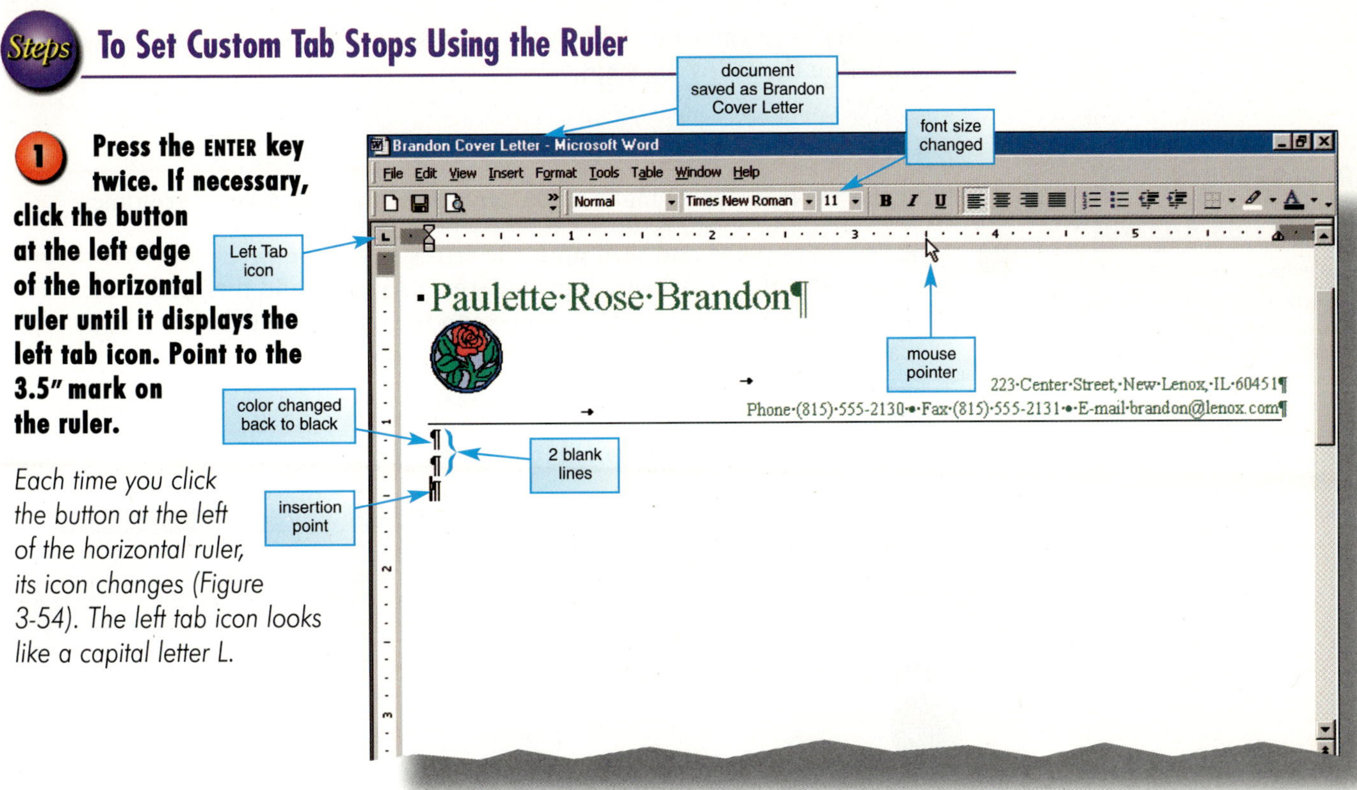

FIGURE 3-54

2 Click the 3.5" mark on the ruler.

Word places a left tab marker at the 3.5" mark on the ruler (Figure 3-55). The text you enter at this tab stop will be left-aligned.

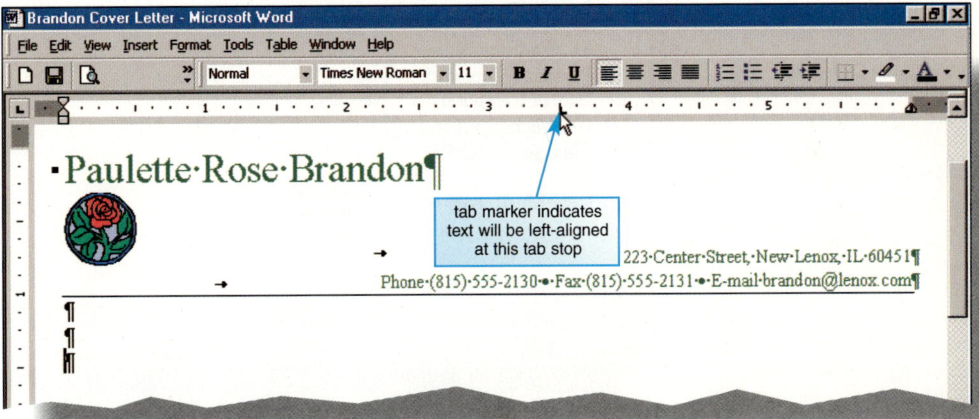

FIGURE 3-55

Other Ways

1. On Format menu click Tabs, enter tab stop position, click appropriate alignment, click OK button

If, for some reason, you wanted to move a custom tab stop, you would drag the tab marker to the desired location on the ruler. If you wanted to change the alignment of a custom tab stop, you could remove the existing tab stop and then insert a new one as described in the steps above. To remove a custom tab stop, point to the tab marker on the ruler and then drag the tab marker down and out of the ruler. You also could use the Tabs dialog box to change an existing tab stop's alignment or position. You have learned that you click Format on the menu bar and then click Tabs to display the Tabs dialog box.

The next step is to enter the date, inside address, and salutation in the cover letter as described in the following steps.

More About 2000

The Inside Address

Pay close attention to the spelling, punctuation, and official abbreviations of company names. For example, does the company name spell out the word, and, or does it use the ampersand (&) character? Is the word Company spelled out or abbreviated? If so, how is it abbreviated?

TO ENTER THE DATE, INSIDE ADDRESS, AND SALUTATION

1. Press the TAB key. Type `June 4, 2001` and press the ENTER key three times.
2. Type `Mr. Carl Reed` and then press the ENTER key. Type `Personnel Director` and then press the ENTER key. Type `Deluxe Computers` and then press the ENTER key. Type `100 Michigan Avenue` and then press the ENTER key. Type `Chicago, IL 60601` and then press the ENTER key twice.
3. Type `Dear Mr. Reed` and then press the COLON key (:).

The date, inside address, and salutation are entered (Figure 3-56).

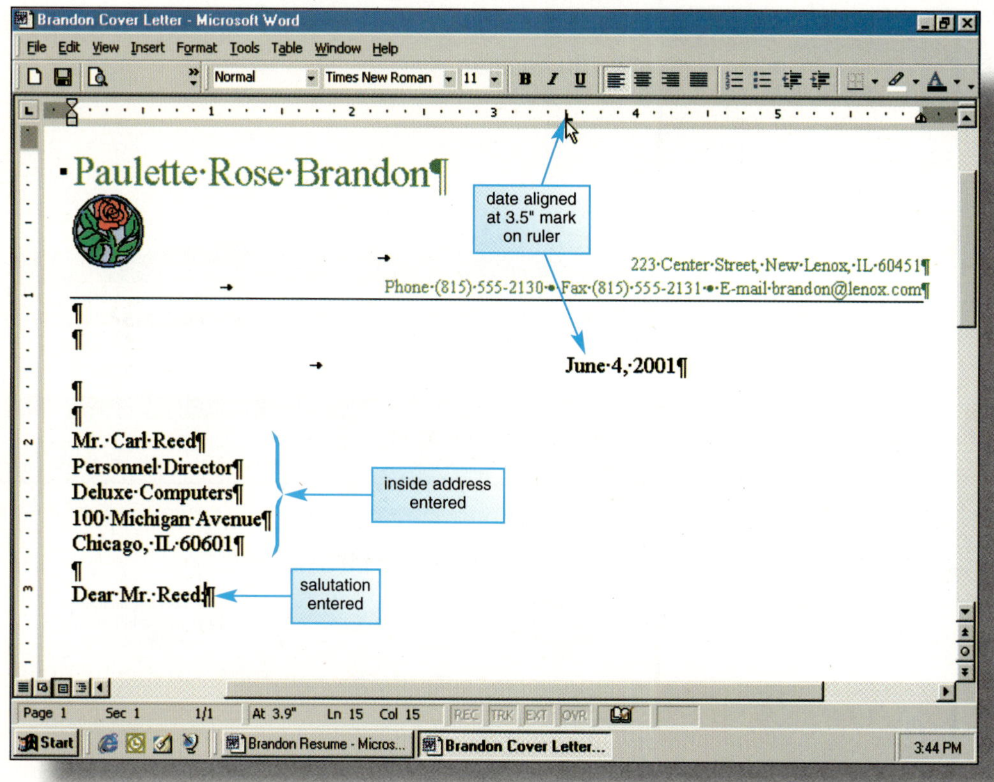

FIGURE 3-56

Salutations

The salutation "To whom it may concern" should be avoided - it is extremely impersonal. If you cannot obtain the name and gender of the company officer to which you are addressing your letter, then use the recipient's title in the salutation, e.g., Dear Personnel Supervisor.

Creating an AutoText Entry

If you use the same text frequently, you can store the text in an **AutoText entry** and then use the stored entry throughout this document, as well as future documents. That is, you type the entry only once, and for all future occurrences of the text, you access the stored entry as you need it. In this way, you avoid entering the text inconsistently or incorrectly in different locations throughout the same document. Follow these steps to create an AutoText entry for the prospective employer's company name.

Steps To Create an AutoText Entry

1 Drag through the text to be stored, in this case, Deluxe Computers. Be sure not to select the paragraph mark at the end of the text. Click Insert on the menu bar and then point to AutoText. Point to New on the AutoText submenu.

Word highlights the company name, Deluxe Computers, in the inside address (Figure 3-57). Notice the paragraph mark is not part of the selection.

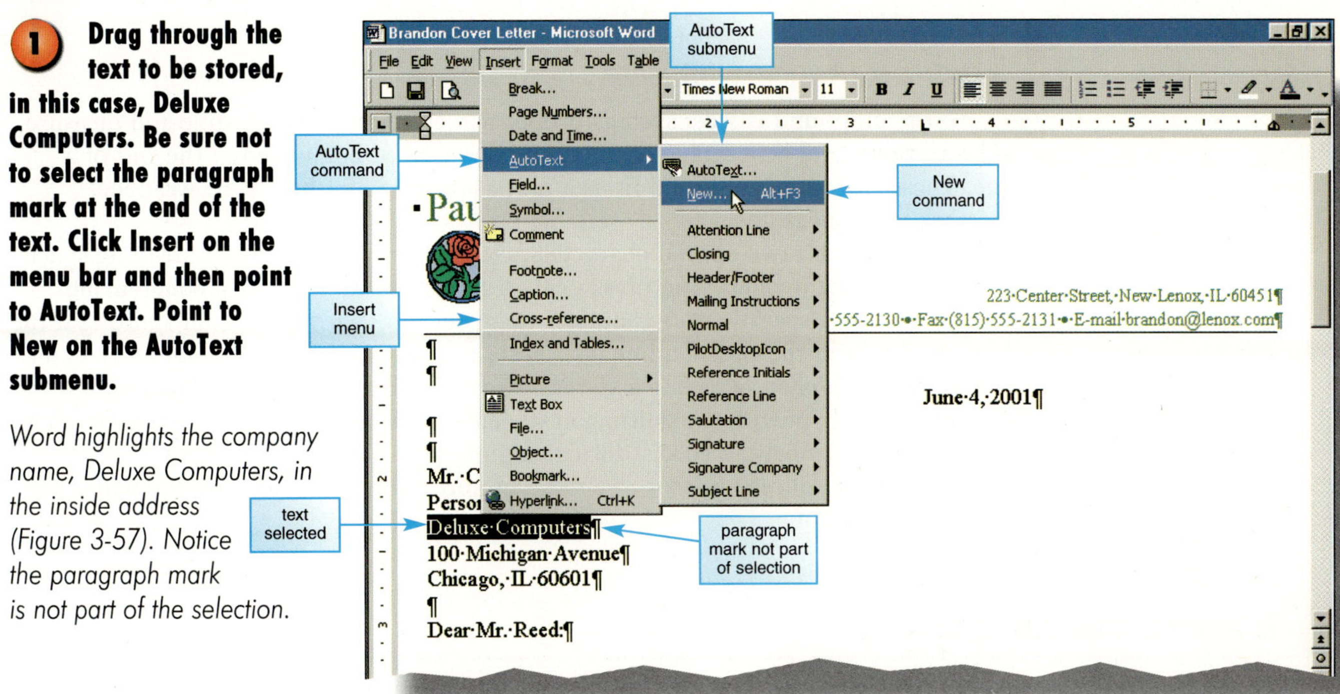

FIGURE 3-57

2 Click New on the AutoText submenu. When the Create AutoText dialog box displays, type dc **and then point to the OK button.**

Word displays the Create AutoText dialog box (Figure 3-58). In this dialog box, Word proposes a name for the AutoText entry, which usually is the first word(s) of the selection. You change it to a shorter name, dc.

3 Click the OK button. If Word displays a dialog box, click the Yes button.

Word stores the AutoText entry and closes the AutoText dialog box.

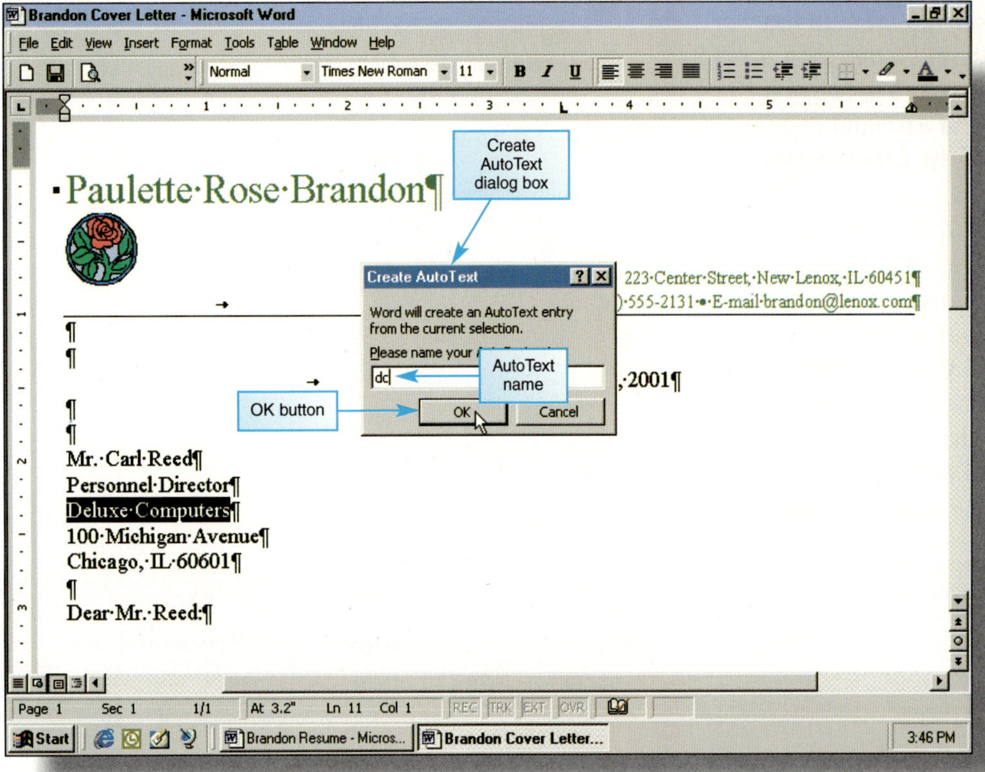

FIGURE 3-58

The name, dc, has been stored as an AutoText entry. Later in the project, you will use the AutoText entry, dc, instead of typing the company name, Deluxe Computers.

Entering a Nonbreaking Space

Some compound words, such as proper names, dates, units of time and measure, abbreviations, and geographic destinations, should not be divided at the end of a line. These words either should fit as a unit at the end of a line or be wrapped together to the next line.

Word provides two special characters to assist with this task: nonbreaking space and nonbreaking hyphen. You press CTRL+SHIFT+SPACEBAR to enter a **nonbreaking space**, which is a special space character that prevents two words from splitting if the first word falls at the end of a line. Likewise, you press CTRL+SHIFT+HYPHEN to enter a **nonbreaking hyphen**, which is a special type of hyphen that prevents two words separated by a hyphen from splitting at the end of a line. When you enter these characters into a document, a special formatting mark displays on the screen.

Perform the following steps to enter a nonbreaking space between the words in the newspaper name.

To Insert a Nonbreaking Space

1 Scroll the salutation to the top of the document window. Click after the colon in the salutation and then press the ENTER key twice. If the Office Assistant displays, click its Cancel button. Type `I am responding to your computer sales management trainee position advertised in the` **and then press the SPACEBAR. Press CTRL+I to turn on italics. Type** `Chicago` **and then press CTRL+SHIFT+SPACEBAR.**

Word enters a nonbreaking space after the word, Chicago (Figure 3-59).

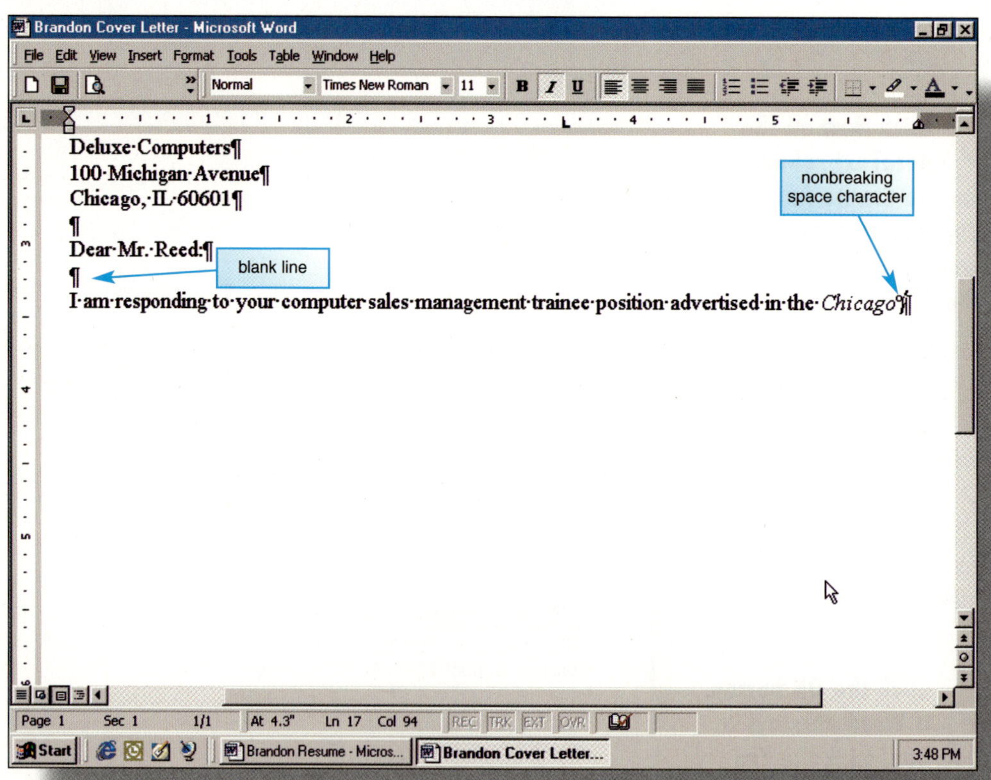

FIGURE 3-59

2 **Type** Times **and then press CTRL+I to turn off italics. Press the PERIOD key.**

Word wraps the two words in the newspaper title, Chicago Times, to the next line (Figure 3-60).

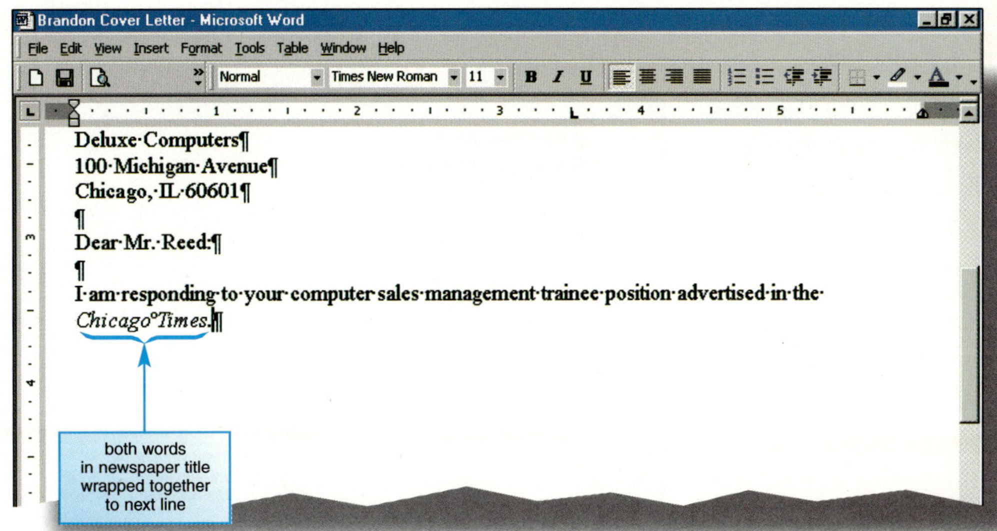

FIGURE 3-60

Other Ways

1. On Insert menu click Symbol, click Special Characters tab, click Nonbreaking Space in Character list, click Insert button, click Close button

Inserting an AutoText Entry

At the end of the next sentence in the body of the cover letter, you want to put the company name, Deluxe Computers. Recall that earlier in this project, you stored an AutoText entry name of dc for Deluxe Computers. Thus, you will type the AutoText entry's name and then instruct Word to replace the AutoText entry's name with the stored entry of Deluxe Computers. Perform the following steps to insert an AutoText entry.

To Insert an AutoText Entry

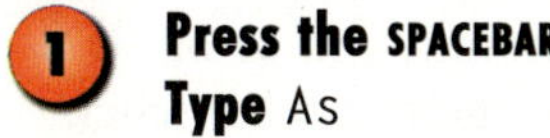

1 **Press the SPACEBAR. Type** As indicated in the enclosed resume, I have the credentials that you are seeking and believe I can be a valuable asset to dc **as shown in Figure 3-61.**

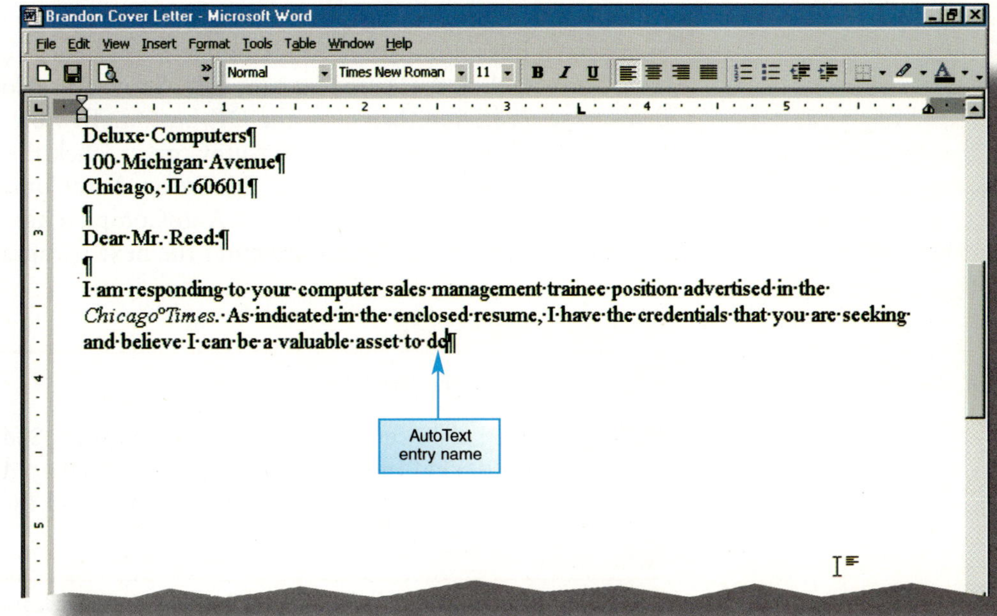

FIGURE 3-61

Press F3. Press the PERIOD key.

Word replaces the characters, dc, with the stored AutoText entry, Deluxe Computers (Figure 3-62).

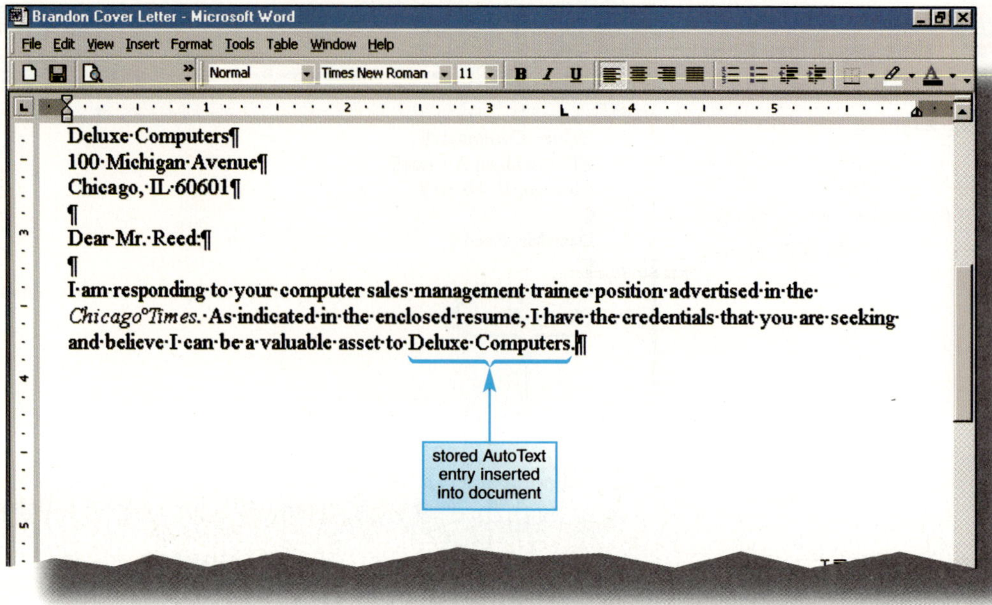

FIGURE 3-62

Other Ways

1. Type first few characters to display AutoComplete tip, press ENTER
2. On Insert menu point to AutoText, point to style linked to AutoText entry, click desired AutoText entry
3. On Insert menu point to AutoText, click AutoText, select desired AutoText entry name, click OK button

Pressing F3 instructs Word to replace the AutoText entry name with the stored AutoText entry. In Project 2, you learned how to use the AutoCorrect feature, which enables you to insert and also create AutoCorrect entries (just as you did for this AutoText entry). The difference between an AutoCorrect entry and an AutoText entry is that the AutoCorrect feature makes corrections for you automatically as soon as you press the SPACEBAR or a punctuation mark key, whereas you must press F3 or click the AutoText command to instruct Word to make an AutoText correction.

If you watch the screen as you type, you may discover that AutoComplete tips display on the screen. As you type, Word searches the list of AutoText entry names and if one matches your typing, Word displays its complete name above your typing as an **AutoComplete tip**. In addition to AutoText entries, Word proposes AutoComplete tips for the current date, a day of the week, a month, and so on. If your screen does not display AutoComplete tips, click Tools on the menu bar, click AutoCorrect, click the AutoText tab, click Show AutoComplete tip for AutoText and dates to select it, and then click the OK button. To view the complete list of entries, click Tools on the menu bar, click AutoCorrect, click the AutoText tab, and then scroll through the list of entries. To ignore an AutoComplete tip proposed by Word, simply continue typing to remove the AutoComplete tip from the screen.

Perform the following steps to enter the next paragraph into the cover letter.

TO ENTER A PARAGRAPH

1. Press the ENTER key twice.
2. Type `I am a recent graduate of Illinois State College with degrees in both marketing management and computer technology. My courses in each major included the following` and then press the COLON key.
3. Press the ENTER key twice.

The paragraph is entered (Figure 3-63 on page WD 3.50).

AutoFormat As You Type

As you type text into a document, Word automatically formats it for you. Table 3-2 outlines commonly used AutoFormat As You Type options and their results.

Table 3-2 Commonly Used AutoFormat As You Type Options

TYPED TEXT	AUTOFORMAT FEATURE	EXAMPLE
Quotation marks or apostrophes	Changes straight quotation marks or apostrophes to curly ones	"the" becomes “the”
Text, a space, one hyphen, one or no spaces, text, space	Changes the hyphen to an en dash	ages 20 - 45 becomes ages 20 – 45
Text, two hyphens, text, space	Changes the two hyphens to em dash	Two types--yellow and red becomes Two types—yellow and red
Web address followed by space or ENTER key	Formats address as a hyperlink	www.scsite.com becomes www.scsite.com
Three hyphens, underscores, equal signs, asterisks, tildes, or number signs and then ENTER key	Places a border above a paragraph	--- Hyphens converted to line becomes Hyphens converted to line
Number followed by a period, hyphen, right parenthesis, or greater than sign and then a space or tab followed by text	Creates a numbered list when you press the ENTER key	1. Word 2. Excel becomes 1. Word 2. Excel
Asterisk, hyphen, greater than sign and then a space or tab followed by text	Creates a bulleted list when you press the ENTER key	* Standard toolbar * Formatting toolbar becomes Standard toolbar Formatting toolbar
Fraction and then a space or hyphen	Converts the entry to a fraction-like notation	1/2 becomes ½
Ordinal and then a space or hyphen	Makes the original a superscript	3rd becomes 3rd

You can type a list and then place the bullets on the paragraphs at a later time, or you can use Word's AutoFormat As You Type feature to bullet the paragraphs as you type them. Because your fingers are on the keyboard already, perform the steps on the next page to add bullets automatically to a list as you type.

AutoFormat

For an AutoFormat option to work as expected, it must be turned on. To check if an AutoFormat option is enabled, click Tools on the menu bar, click AutoCorrect, click the AutoFormat As You Type tab, select the appropriate check boxes, and then click the OK button. For example, Format beginning of list item like the one before it and Automatic bulleted lists should both contain check marks for automatic bullets.

To Bullet a List as You Type

1 **Press the ASTERISK key (*) and then press the SPACEBAR. Type** `Marketing Management: Principles of Marketing, Promotions, Retailing, Sales, Advertising, Personal Selling, International Marketing, Consumer Behavior` **as the first list item (Figure 3-63).**

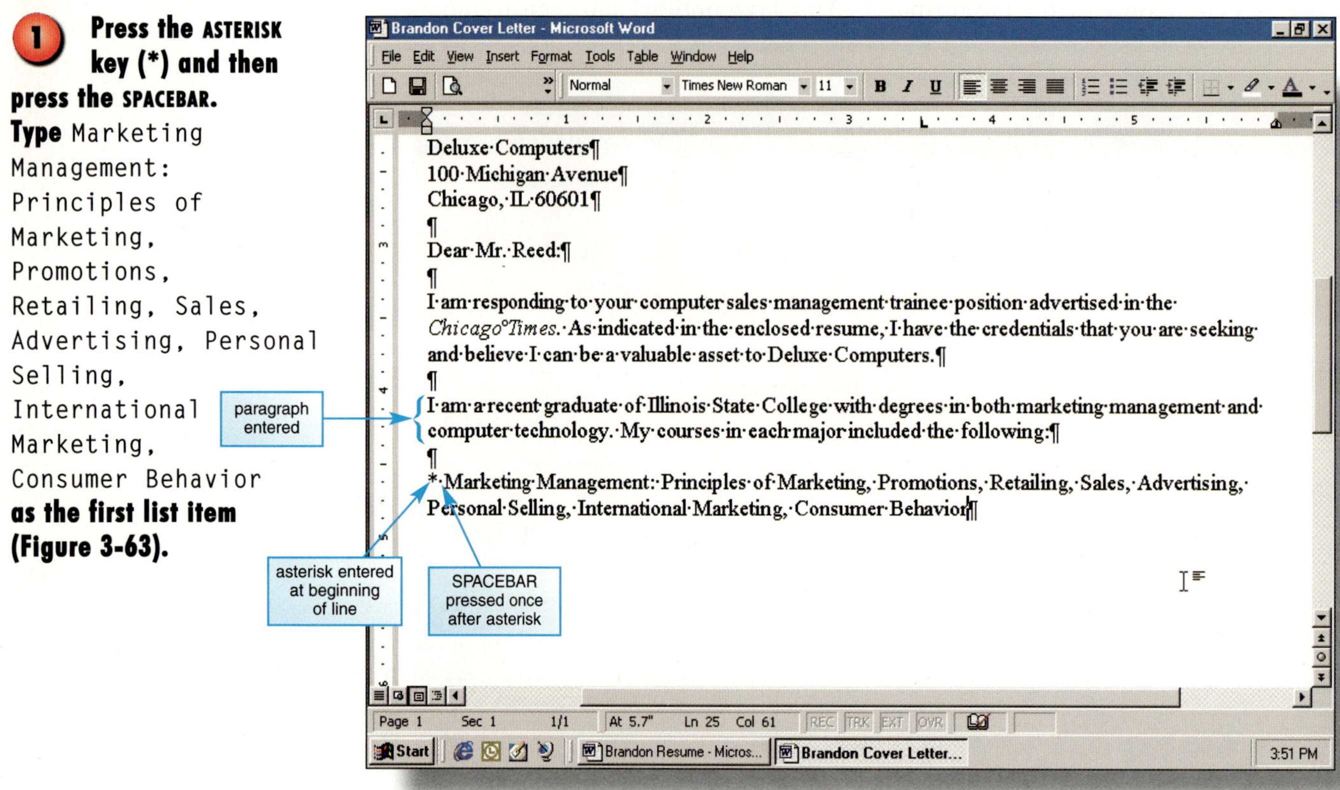

FIGURE 3-63

2 **Press the ENTER key.**

Word converts the asterisk to a bullet character, places another bullet on the second list item, and indents the two bulleted paragraphs.

3 **Type** `Computer Technology: Computer Concepts, PC Technology, Structured Programming, Object-Oriented Programming, Database Techniques, Web Design` **and then press the ENTER key.**

Word places a bullet on the next line (Figure 3-64).

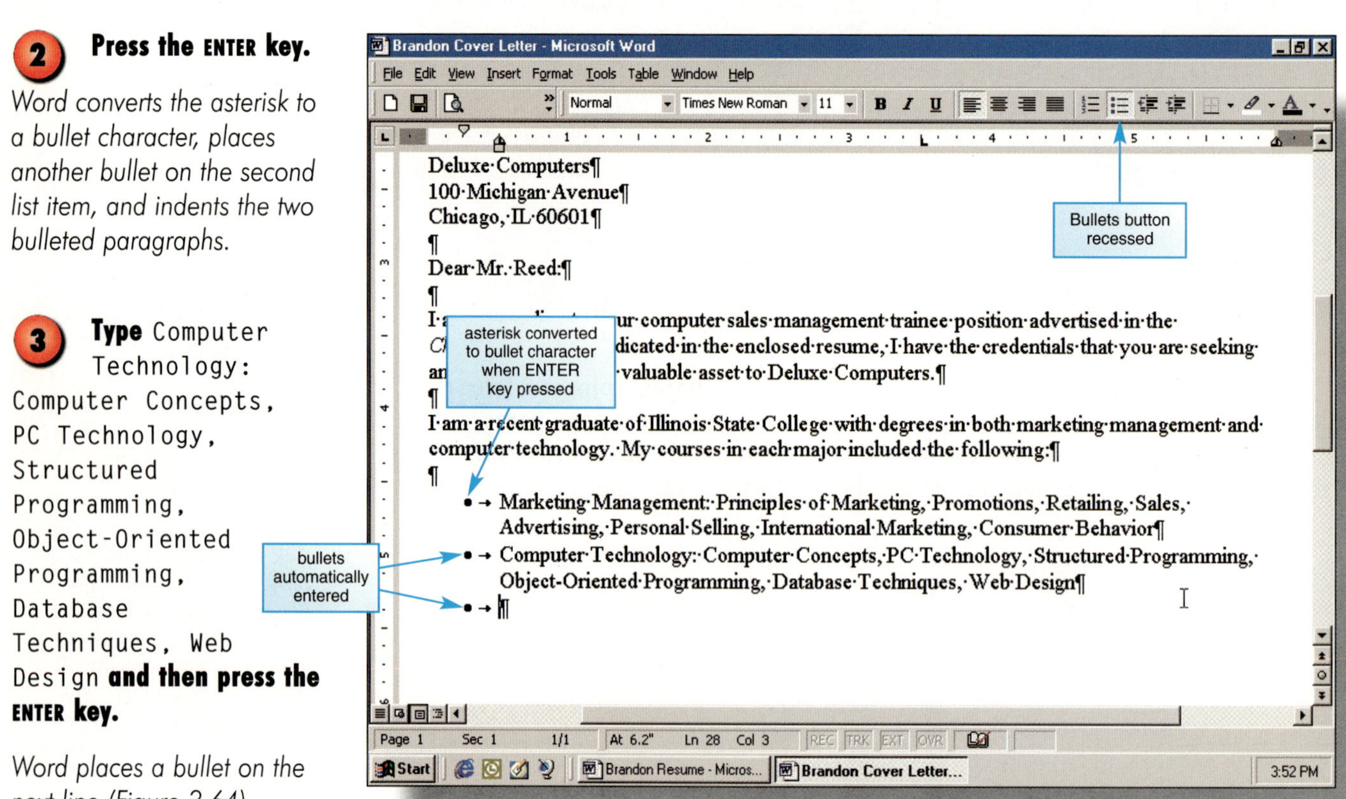

FIGURE 3-64

Press the ENTER key.

Word removes the lone bullet because you pressed the ENTER key twice (Figure 3-65). The Bullets button no longer is recessed.

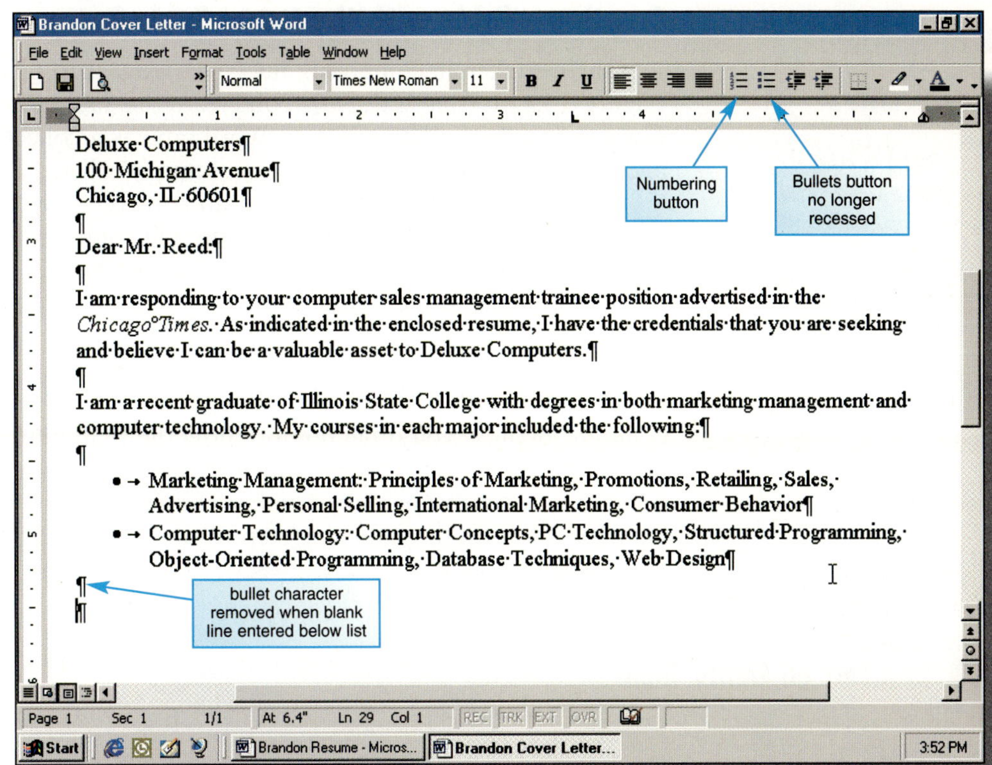

FIGURE 3-65

Other Ways

1. Select list, click Bullets button on Formatting toolbar
2. Select list, right-click selection, click Bullets and Numbering on shortcut menu, click Bulleted tab, click desired bullet type, click OK button
3. Select list, on Format menu click Bullets and Numbering, click Bulleted tab, click desired bullet type, click OK button

When the insertion point is in a bulleted list, the Bullets button on the Formatting toolbar is recessed. To instruct Word to stop bulleting paragraphs, you press the ENTER key twice or click the Bullets button.

If you know before you type a list that it is to be numbered, you can add numbers as you type, just as you can add bullets as you type. To number a list, type the number one followed by a period and then a space (1.) at the beginning of the first item and then type your text. When you press the ENTER key, Word places the number two (2.) at the beginning of the next line automatically. As with bullets, press the ENTER key twice at the end of the list or click the Numbering button on the Formatting toolbar to stop numbering (Figure 3-66).

Perform the following steps to enter the next paragraph into the cover letter.

TO ENTER A PARAGRAPH

1. Scroll up and then type `As shown in the following table, I earned exceptional grades in both marketing management and computer technology courses.`
2. Press the ENTER key twice.

The paragraph is entered (see Figure 3-66 on the next page).

More About 2000

Outline Numbered Lists

To create an outline numbered list, click Format on the menu bar, click Bullets and Numbering, click the Outline Numbered tab, and then click a style that does not contain the word 'Heading.' To promote or demote a list item to the next or previous levels, click the Increase Indent and Decrease Indent buttons on the Formatting toolbar.

Word Tables

Although you can use the TAB key to create a table, many Word users prefer to use its table feature. With a Word table, you can arrange numbers in columns. For emphasis, tables can be shaded and have borders. Word tables can be sorted, and you can have Word add the contents of an entire row or column.

Creating a Table with the Insert Table Button

The next step in composing the cover letter is to place a table listing your GPAs (Figure 3-2a on page WD 3.6). You create this table using Word's table feature. As discussed earlier in this project, a Word table is a collection of rows and columns, and the intersection of a row and a column is called a cell.

Within a Word table, you easily can rearrange rows and columns, change column widths, sort rows and columns, and sum the contents of rows and columns. You can use the Table AutoFormat dialog box to make the table display in a professional manner. You also can chart table data.

The first step in creating a table is to insert an empty table into the document. When inserting a table, you must specify the total number of rows and columns required, which is called the **dimension** of the table. The table in this project has two columns. Because you often do not know the total number of rows in a table, many Word users create one row initially and then add rows as they need them. The first number in a dimension is the number of rows, and the second is the number of columns. Perform the following steps to insert a 1 x 2 table; that is, a table with one row and two columns.

Steps To Insert an Empty Table

1 Double-click the move handle on the Standard toolbar. Click the Insert Table button on the Standard toolbar. Point to the cell in the first row and second column of the grid to highlight the first two cells in the first row of the grid.

*Word displays a **grid** to define the dimension of the desired table (Figure 3-66). Word will insert the table immediately above the insertion point.*

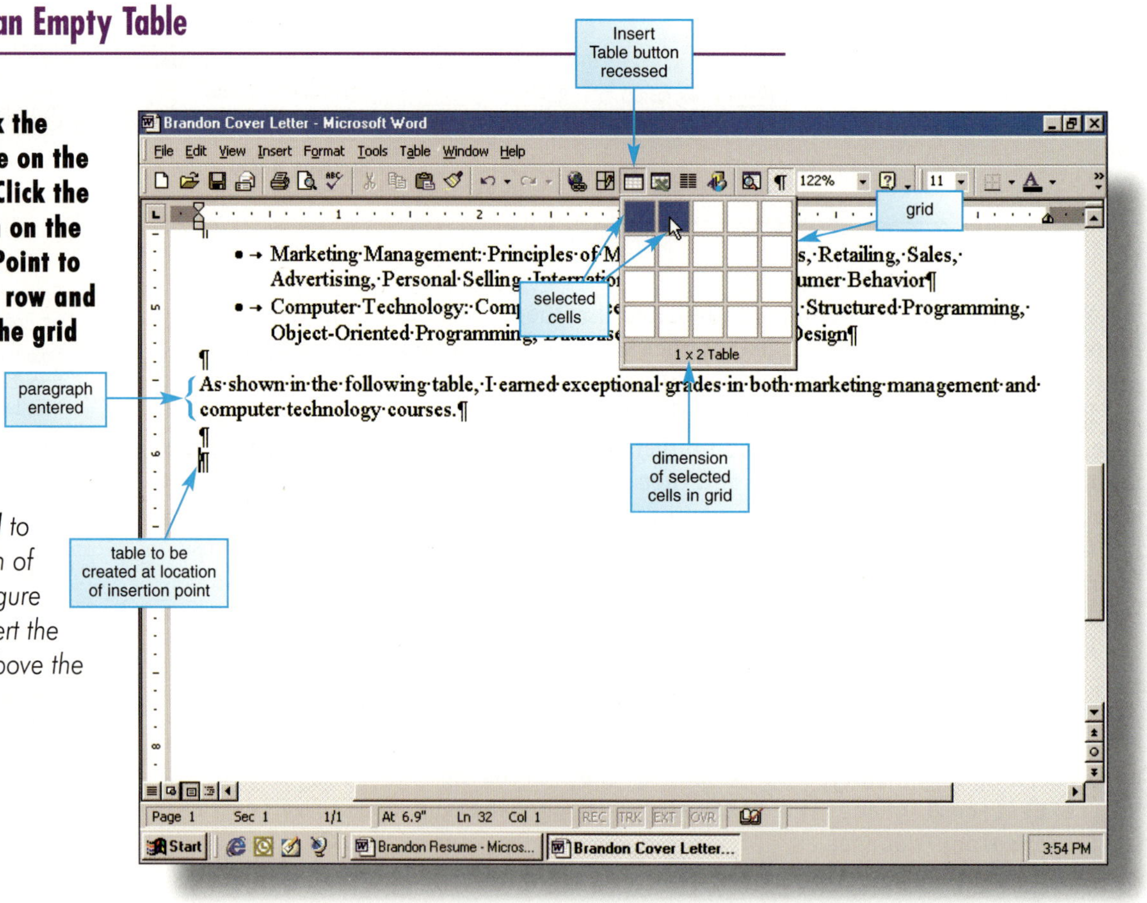

FIGURE 3-66

2 Click the cell in the first row and second column of the grid.

Word inserts an empty 1 × 2 table into the document (Figure 3-67). The insertion point is in the first cell (row 1 and column 1) of the table.

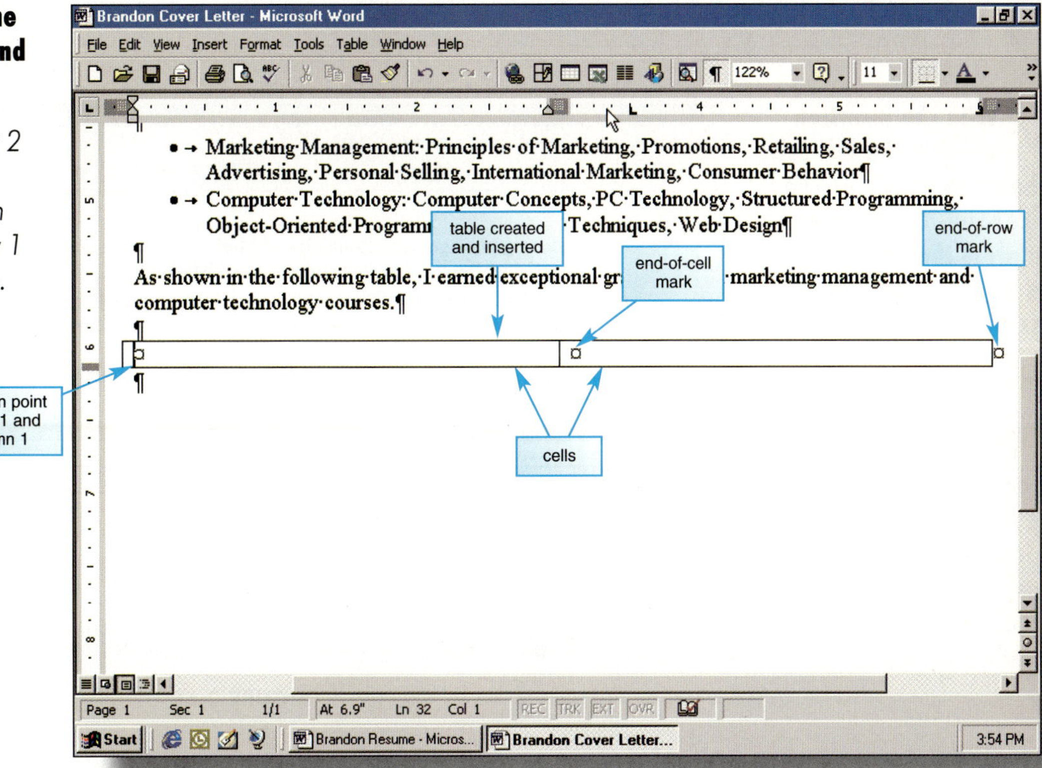

FIGURE 3-67

Other Ways

1. On Table menu point to Insert, click Table, enter number of columns, enter number of rows, click OK button

As you learned earlier in this project, each row of a table has an end-of-row mark, which you use to add columns to the right of a table. Each cell has an end-of-cell mark, which you use to select a cell. The end-of-cell mark currently is left-aligned; thus it is positioned at the left edge of each cell. You can use any of the paragraph formatting buttons on the Formatting toolbar to change the alignment of the text within the cells. For example, if you click the Align Right button on the Formatting toolbar, the end-of-cell mark and any entered text will display at the right edge of the cell.

For simple tables, such as the one just created, Word users click the Insert Table button to create a table. For more complex tables, such as one with a varying number of columns per row, Word has a Draw Table feature that allows you to use a pencil pointer to draw a table on the screen. Project 4 discusses the Draw Table feature.

More About 2000

Draw Table

To use Draw Table, click the Tables and Borders button on the Standard toolbar to change the mouse pointer to a pencil. Use the pencil to draw from one corner to the opposite diagonal corner to define the perimeter of the table. Then, draw the column and row lines inside the perimeter. To remove a line, use the Eraser button on the Tables and Borders toolbar.

Entering Data into a Word Table

The next step is to enter data into the empty table. Cells are filled with data. The data you enter within a cell wordwraps just as text does between the margins of a document. To place data into a cell, you click the cell and then type. To advance rightward from one cell to the next, press the TAB key. When you are at the rightmost cell in a row, also press the TAB key to move to the first cell in the next row; do not press the ENTER key. The ENTER key is used to begin a new paragraph within a cell.

To add new rows to a table, press the TAB key with the insertion point positioned in the bottom right corner cell of the table. Perform the steps on the next page to enter data into the table.

To Enter Data into a Table

1 **With the insertion point in the left cell of the table, type** GPA for Marketing Courses **and then press the TAB key. Type** 3.8/4.0 **and then press the TAB key.**

Word enters the table data into the first row of the table and adds a second row to the table (Figure 3-68). The insertion point is positioned in the first cell of the second row.

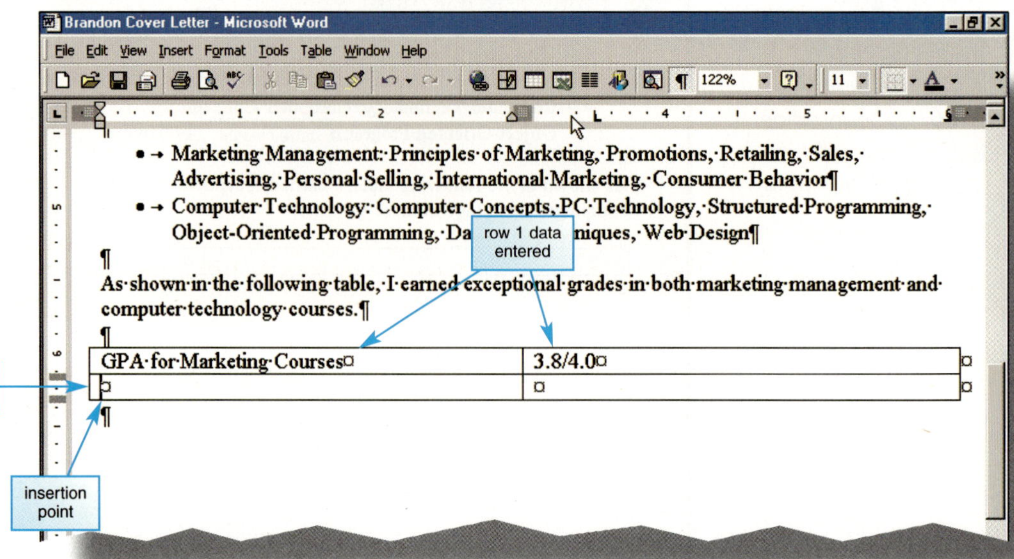

FIGURE 3-68

2 **Type** GPA for Computer Courses **and then press the TAB key. Type** 3.9/4.0 **and then press the TAB key. Type** Overall GPA **and then press the TAB key. Type** 3.8/4.0 **as shown in Figure 3-69.**

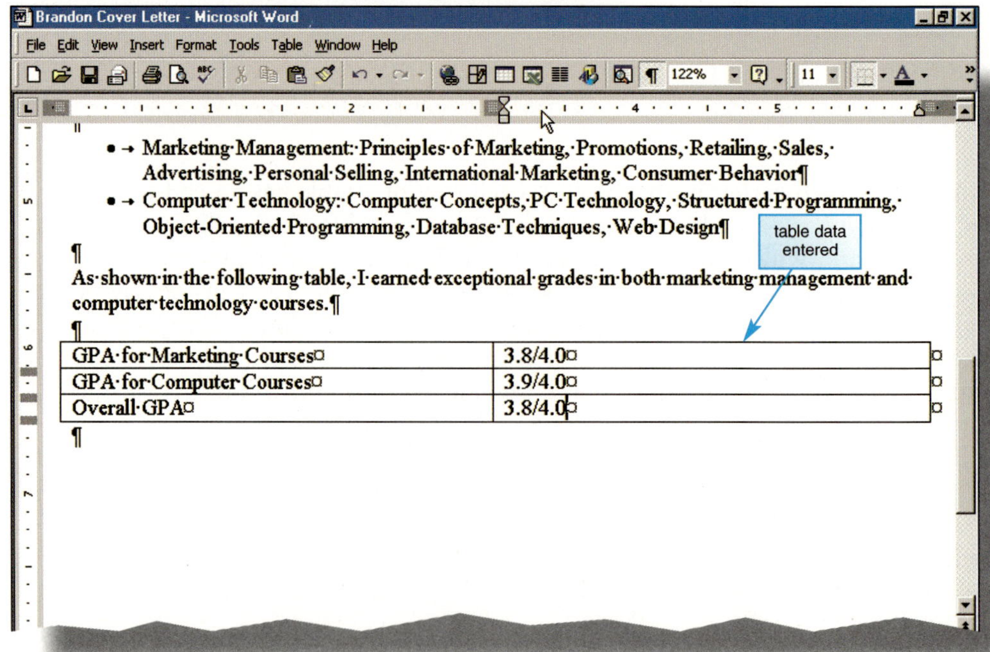

FIGURE 3-69

Tabs

Because the TAB key advances the insertion point from one cell to the next in a table, press the CTRL+TAB keys to insert a tab character into a cell.

You modify the contents of cells just as you modify text in a document. To delete the contents of a cell, select the cell contents by pointing to the left edge of a cell, clicking when the mouse pointer changes direction, and then pressing the DELETE key. To modify text in a cell, click in the cell and then correct the entry. You can double-click the OVR indicator on the status bar to toggle between insert and overtype modes. You also may drag and drop or cut and paste the contents of cells.

Formatting a Table

Although you can format each row, column, and cell of a table individually, Word provides a Table AutoFormat feature that contains predefined formats for tables. Perform the following steps to format the entire table using Table AutoFormat.

Table Commands

If a Table command is dimmed on the Table menu, it is likely that the insertion point is not in the table.

To AutoFormat a Table

1 With the insertion point in the table, click Table on the menu bar and then point to Table AutoFormat (Figure 3-70).

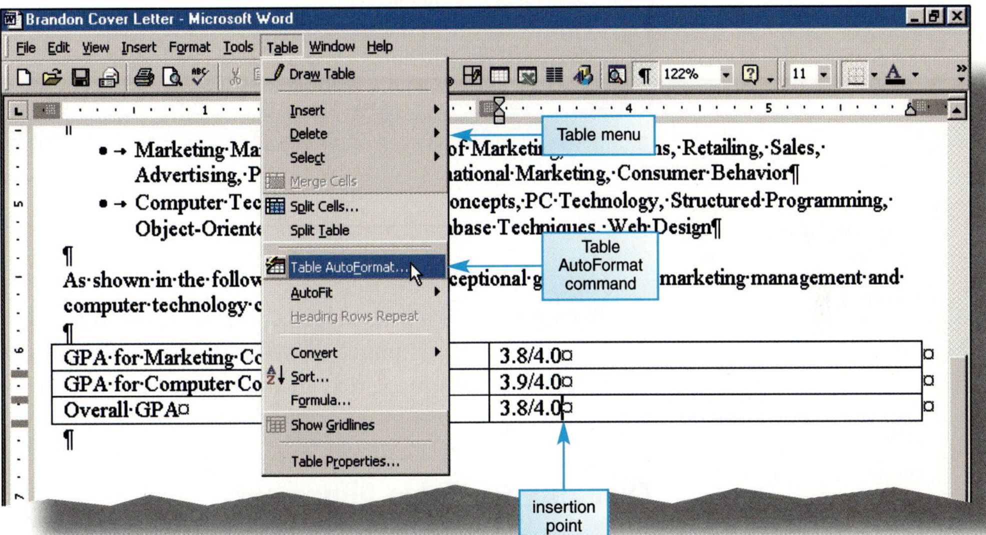

FIGURE 3-70

2 Click Table AutoFormat. When the Table AutoFormat dialog box displays, scroll through the Formats list and then click Contemporary. If necessary, click Heading rows in the Apply special formats to area to remove the check mark. Be sure the remaining check boxes match Figure 3-71.

Word displays the Table AutoFormat dialog box (Figure 3-71). This table does not have a heading row.

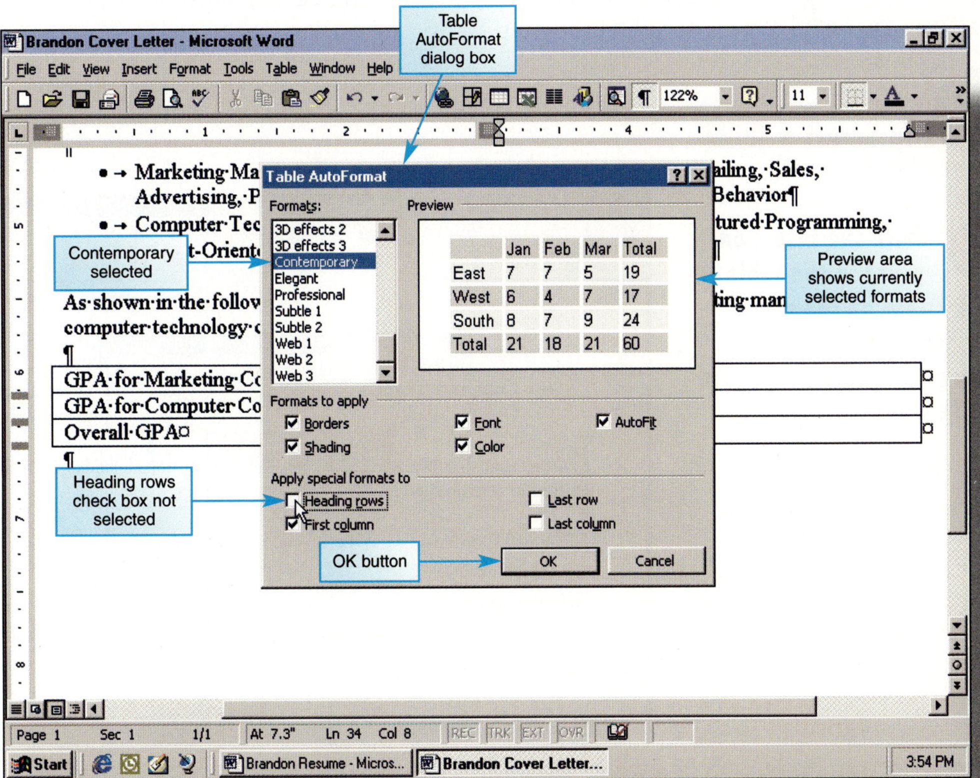

FIGURE 3-71

Click the OK button.

Word formats the table according to the Contemporary format (Figure 3-72).

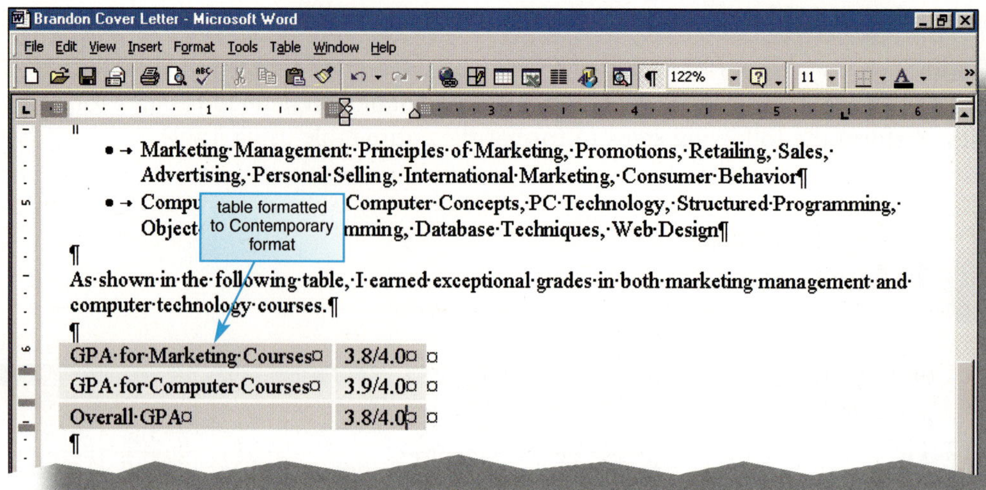

FIGURE 3-72

1. Click Table AutoFormat button on Tables and Borders toolbar

Because AutoFit was selected in the Table AutoFormat dialog box (see Figure 3-71 on the previous page), Word automatically adjusted the widths of the columns based on the amount of text in the table. In this case, Word reduced the size of the column widths.

Changing the Table Alignment

When you first create a table, it is left-aligned; that is, flush with the left margin. This table should be centered. To center a table, you first must select the entire table and then center it using the Center button on the Formatting toolbar, as shown in the following steps.

To Select a Table

1 With the insertion point in the table, click Table on the menu bar, point to Select, and then point to Table (Figure 3-73).

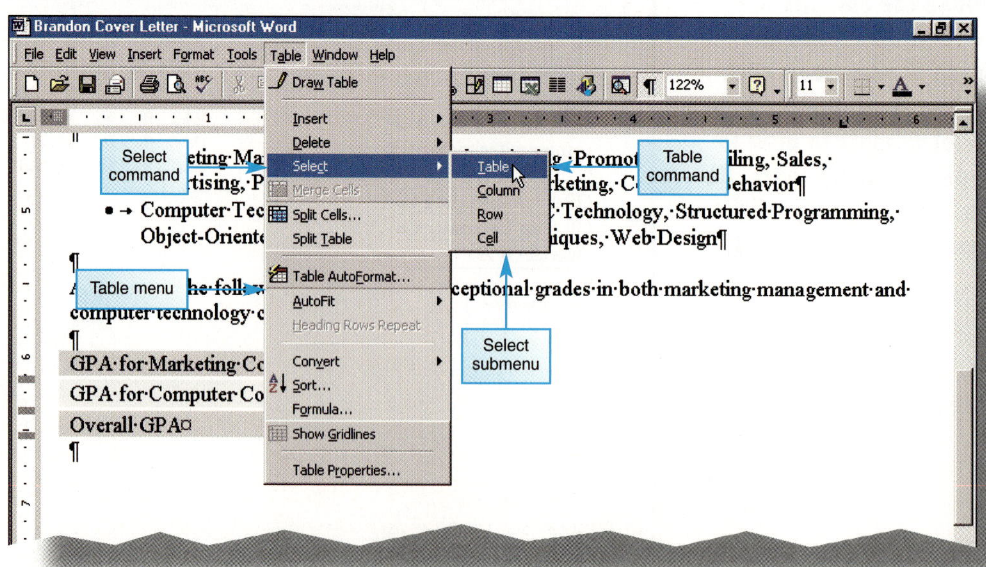

FIGURE 3-73

Click Table.

Word highlights the contents of the entire table.

Double-click the move handle on the Formatting toolbar. Click the Center button on the Formatting toolbar.

Word centers the table between the left and right margins (Figure 3-74).

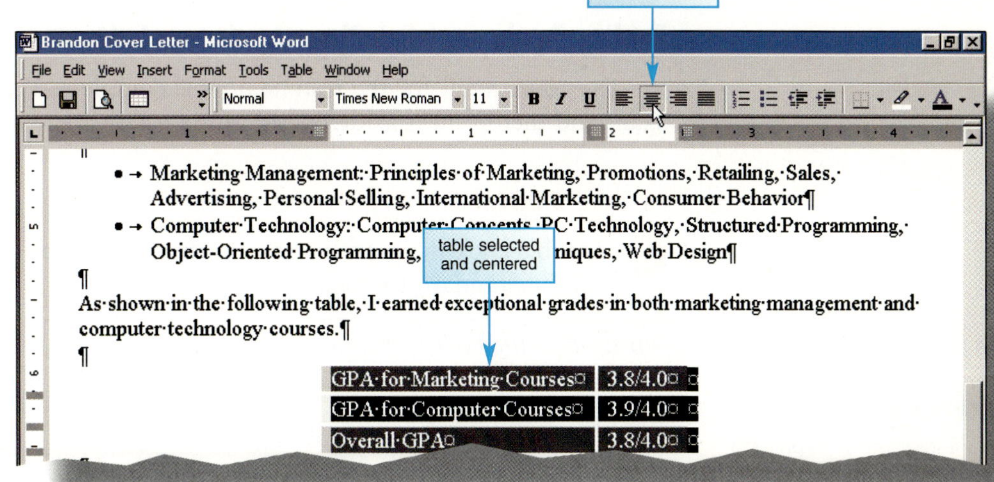

FIGURE 3-74

Other Ways

1. With insertion point in table, press ALT+5 (using the 5 on the numeric keypad with NUM LOCK off)

Perform the following steps to enter the remainder of the cover letter.

TO ENTER THE REMAINDER OF THE COVER LETTER

1. Click the paragraph mark below the table. Press the ENTER key. Type the paragraph shown in Figure 3-75, making certain you use the AutoText entry, dc, to insert the company name.
2. Press the ENTER key twice. Press the TAB key. Type `Sincerely` and then press the COMMA key.
3. Press the ENTER key four times. Press the TAB key. Type `Paulette Rose Brandon` and then press the ENTER key twice.
4. Type `Enclosure` as the final text.

The cover letter text is complete (Figure 3-75).

More About

Selecting Tables

If you use the keyboard shortcut to select a table, ALT+NUM5, you must be careful to press the 5 on the numeric keypad. You cannot use the 5 on the keyboard area. Also, be sure that NUM LOCK is off; otherwise, the keyboard shortcut will not work.

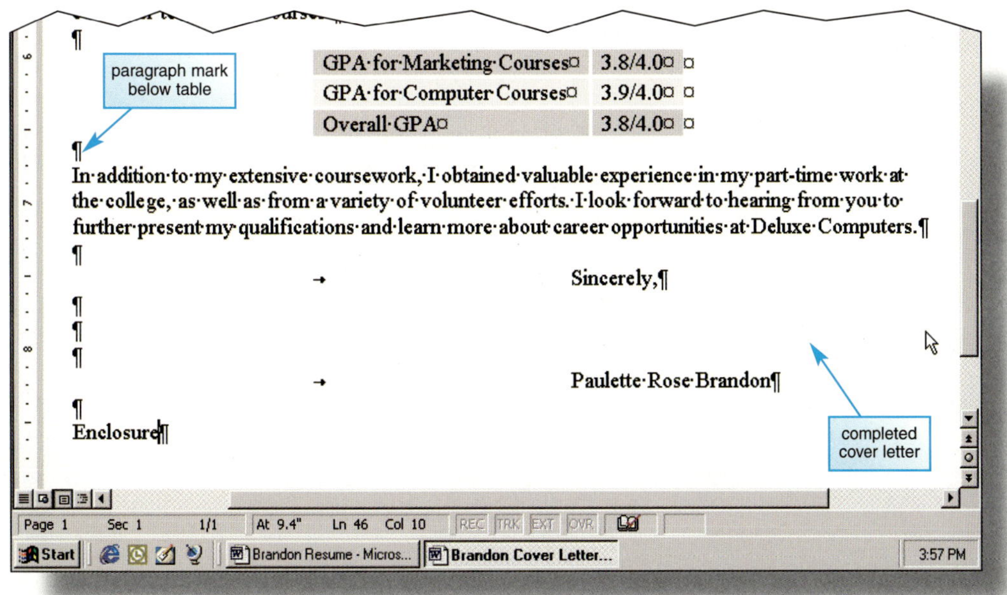

FIGURE 3-75

More About

Proofreading

You should be absolutely certain that your resume and accompanying cover letter are error free. Check spelling and grammar using Word. Proofread for grammatical errors. Set the resume and cover letter aside for a couple of days, and then proofread them again. Ask others, such as a friend or teacher, to proofread them also.

Saving Again and Printing the Cover Letter

The cover letter for the resume now is complete. You should save the cover letter again and then print it as described in the following steps.

TO SAVE A DOCUMENT AGAIN

1. Double-click the move handle on the Standard toolbar. Click the Save button on the Standard toolbar.

Word saves the cover letter with the same file name, Brandon Cover Letter.

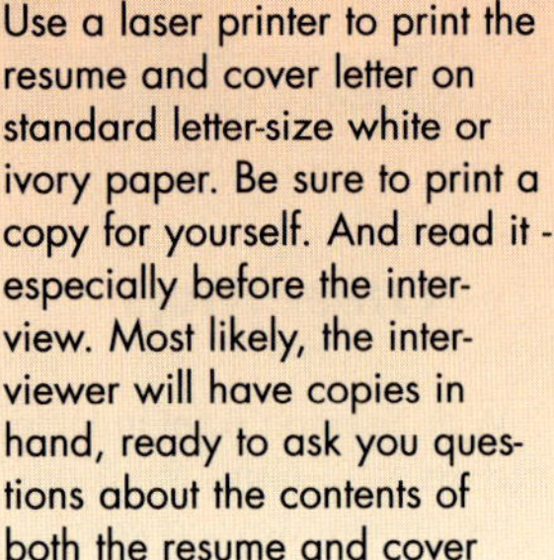

Printing

Use a laser printer to print the resume and cover letter on standard letter-size white or ivory paper. Be sure to print a copy for yourself. And read it - especially before the interview. Most likely, the interviewer will have copies in hand, ready to ask you questions about the contents of both the resume and cover letter.

TO PRINT A DOCUMENT

1. Click the Print button on the Standard toolbar.

The completed cover letter prints as shown in Figure 3-2a on page WD 3.6.

Preparing and Printing an Envelope Address

The final step in this project is to prepare and print an envelope address, as shown in the following steps.

Steps To Prepare and Print an Envelope Address

1. **Scroll through the cover letter to display the inside address in the document window. Drag through the inside address to select it. Click Tools on the menu bar and then point to Envelopes and Labels (Figure 3-76).**

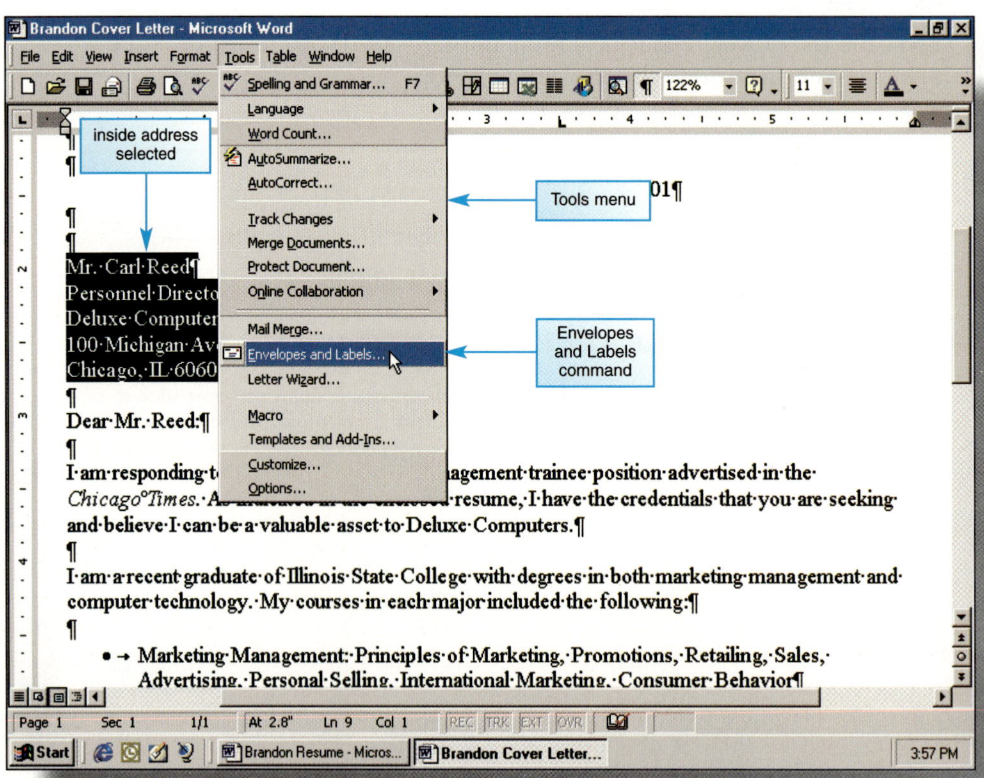

FIGURE 3-76

2 **Click Envelopes and Labels. When the Envelopes and Labels dialog box displays, if necessary, click the Envelopes tab. Click the Return address text box. Type** `Paulette R. Brandon` **and then press the ENTER key. Type** `223 Center Street` **and then press the ENTER key. Type** `New Lenox, IL 60451` **and then point to the Print button in the Envelopes and Labels dialog box.**

Word displays the Envelopes and Labels dialog box (Figure 3-77). The selected inside address displays in the Delivery address text box.

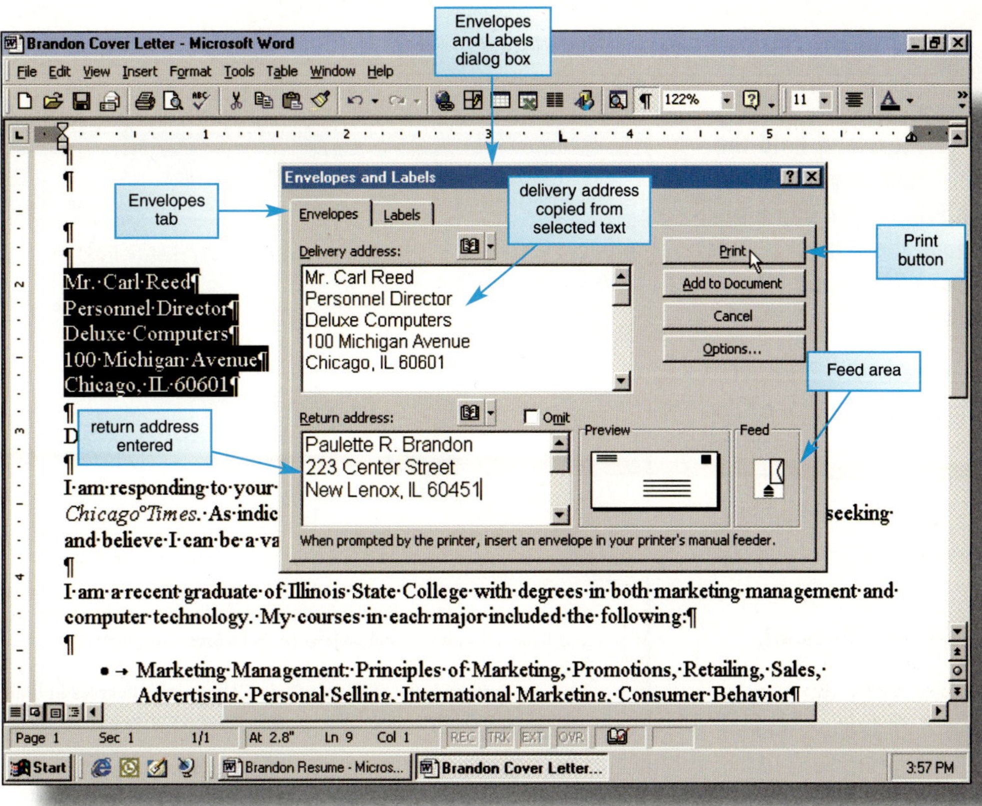

FIGURE 3-77

3 **Insert an envelope into your printer as shown in the Feed area of the Envelopes and Labels dialog box and then click the Print button in the dialog box. If a Microsoft Word dialog box displays, click the No button.**

Word prints the envelope (Figure 3-78).

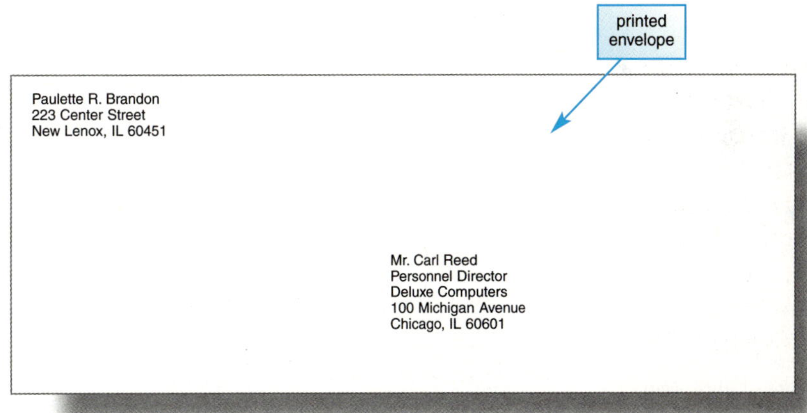

FIGURE 3-78

Instead of printing an envelope, you can print a mailing label. To do this, click the Labels tab in the Envelopes and Labels dialog box.

Currently, you have two documents open: the resume and cover letter. When you are finished with both documents, you may wish to close them. Instead of closing each one individually, you can close all open files at once as shown in the steps on the next page.

Office Supplies

For more information on where to obtain supplies for printing documents, visit the Word 2000 More About Web page (www.scsite.com/wd2000/more.htm) and then click Online Office Supplies.

To Close All Open Word Documents

1. **Press and hold the SHIFT key and then click File on the menu bar. Release the SHIFT key. Point to Close All on the File menu.**

   Word displays a Close All command, instead of a Close command, on the File menu because you pressed the SHIFT key when clicking the menu name (Figure 3-79).

2. **Click Close All.**

   Word closes all open documents and displays a blank document window. If at this point you wanted to begin a new document, you would click the New Blank Document button on the Standard toolbar.

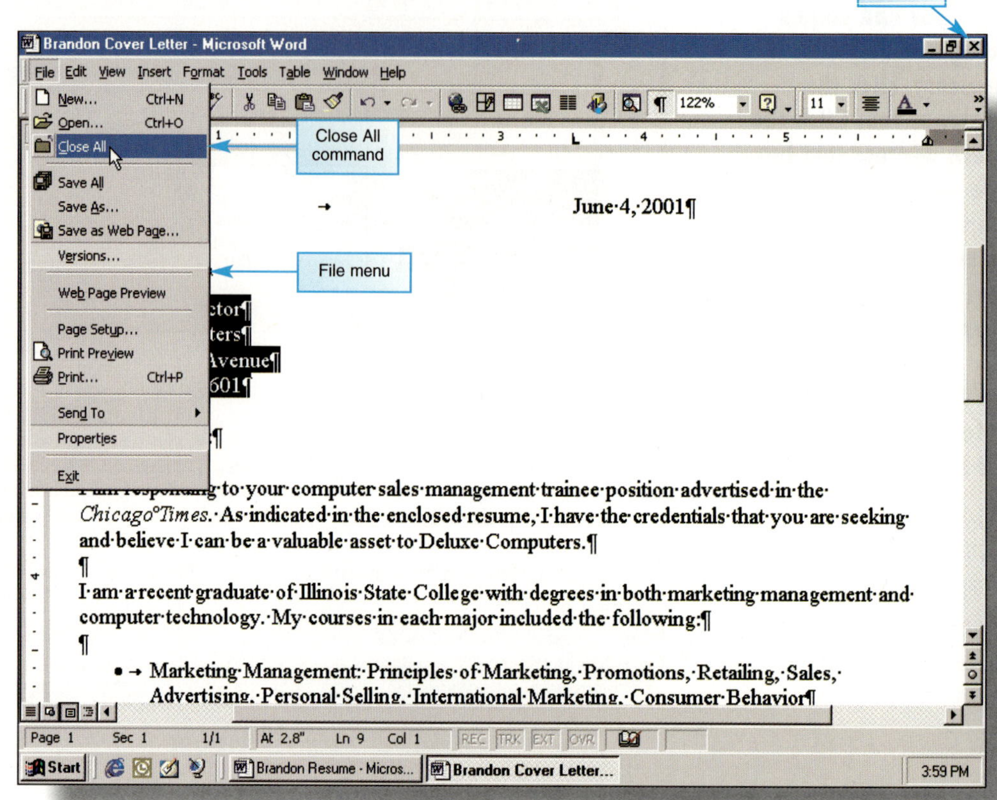

FIGURE 3-79

More About

Quick Reference

For a table that lists how to complete the tasks covered in this book using the mouse, menu, shortcut menu, and keyboard, visit the Shelly Cashman Series Office Web page (www.scsite.com/off2000/qr.htm) and then click Microsoft Word 2000.

The final step in this project is to quit Word as described in the step below.

TO QUIT WORD

1. Click the Close button in the Word window.

The Word window closes.

CASE PERSPECTIVE SUMMARY

With your resume writing expertise and Paulette's business sense, you have created an effective resume and cover letter. Paulette immediately staples the two documents together, places them in the envelope, adds necessary postage, and delivers the envelope to the post office. As she places her cover letter and resume in the mail, Paulette dreams about a career at Deluxe Computers. She plans to wait one week to hear from Mr. Reed, the personnel director at Deluxe Computers. If he has not contacted her in that time, Paulette plans to follow up with a telephone call to him.

Project Summary

Project 3 introduced you to creating a resume using a wizard and creating a cover letter with a letterhead, a bulleted list, and a table. You used the Resume Wizard to create a resume, and then used several formatting techniques to personalize the resume. You viewed, reduced the size of, and printed the resume in print preview. You created a letterhead and then created the cover letter. While creating the letterhead, you learned how to add color to characters, set custom tab stops, collect and paste between documents, add a symbol to a document, and add a border to a paragraph. You created an AutoText entry, which you used when you personalized the cover letter. Finally, you prepared and printed an envelope.

What You Should Know

Having completed this project, you now should be able to perform the following tasks:

- Add a Bottom Border to a Paragraph (*WD 3.39*)
- AutoFormat a Table (*WD 3.55*)
- Bold Text (*WD 3.17*)
- Bullet a List as You Type (*WD 3.50*)
- Change Color of Text (*WD 3.41*)
- Change the Font Size (*WD 3.28*)
- Close All Open Word Documents (*WD 3.60*)
- Collect Items (*WD 3.33*)
- Color Characters (*WD 3.28*)
- Color More Characters the Same Color (*WD 3.37*)
- Create a Resume Using Word's Resume Wizard (*WD 3.7*)
- Create an AutoText Entry (*WD 3.45*)
- Display Formatting Marks (*WD 3.15*)
- Enter a Line Break (*WD 3.22*)
- Enter a Paragraph (*WD 3.48, WD 3.51*)
- Enter and Resize a Graphic (*WD 3.30*)
- Enter Data into a Table (*WD 3.54*)
- Enter Placeholder Text (*WD 3.21*)
- Enter the Date, Inside Address, and Salutation (*WD 3.44*)
- Enter the Remainder of the Cover Letter (*WD 3.57*)
- Enter the Remaining Sections of the Resume (*WD 3.23*)
- Increase the Font Size (*WD 3.42*)
- Insert a Nonbreaking Space (*WD 3.46*)
- Insert a Symbol into Text (*WD 3.37*)
- Insert an AutoText Entry (*WD 3.47*)
- Insert an Empty Table (*WD 3.52*)
- Open a New Document Window (*WD 3.27*)
- Paste from the Office Clipboard (*WD 3.35*)
- Prepare and Print an Envelope Address (*WD 3.58*)
- Print a Document (*WD 3.58*)
- Print Preview a Document (*WD 3.24*)
- Print the Resume Created by the Resume Wizard (*WD 3.14*)
- Quit Word (*WD 3.60*)
- Reset Menus and Toolbars (*WD 3.14*)
- Save a Document (*WD 3.26*)
- Save a Document Again (*WD 3.58*)
- Save the Document with a New File Name (*WD 3.42*)
- Save the Letterhead (*WD 3.41*)
- Select a Table (*WD 3.56*)
- Select and Replace Placeholder Text (*WD 3.18*)
- Select and Replace Resume Wizard Supplied Text (*WD 3.19*)
- Set Custom Tab Stops Using the Ruler (*WD 3.43*)
- Set Custom Tab Stops Using the Tabs Dialog Box (*WD 3.31*)
- Switch From One Open Document to Another (*WD 3.33*)
- Zoom Text Width (*WD 3.17*)

More About 2000

Microsoft Certification

The Microsoft Office User Specialist (MOUS) Certification program provides an opportunity for you to obtain a valuable industry credential - proof that you have the Word 2000 skills required by employers. For more information, see Appendix D or visit the Shelly Cashman Series MOUS Web page at www.scsite.com/off2000/cert.htm.

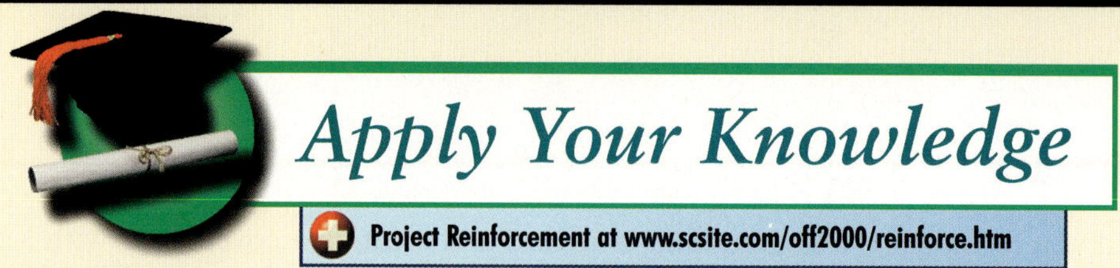

1 Working with a Table

Instructions: Start Word. Open the document, Expenses Table, on the Data Disk. If you did not download the Data Disk, see the inside back cover for instructions for downloading the Data Disk or see your instructor.

The document is a Word table that you are to edit and format. The revised table is shown in Figure 3-80.

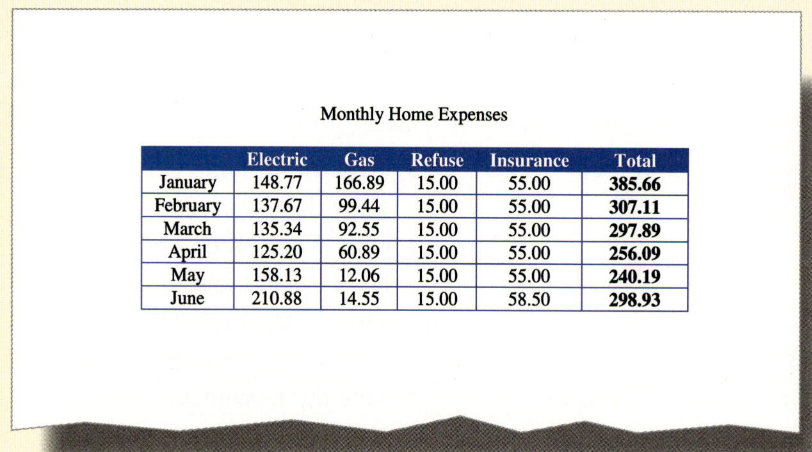

Monthly Home Expenses

	Electric	Gas	Refuse	Insurance	Total
January	148.77	166.89	15.00	55.00	**385.66**
February	137.67	99.44	15.00	55.00	**307.11**
March	135.34	92.55	15.00	55.00	**297.89**
April	125.20	60.89	15.00	55.00	**256.09**
May	158.13	12.06	15.00	55.00	**240.19**
June	210.88	14.55	15.00	58.50	**298.93**

FIGURE 3-80

Perform the following tasks:

1. With the insertion point in the table, click Table on the menu bar and then click Table AutoFormat. In the Table AutoFormat dialog box, scroll to and then click Grid 8 in the Formats list. All check boxes should have check marks except for these two: Last row and Last column. Click the OK button.
2. Select the Phone column by pointing to the top of the column until the mouse pointer changes to a downward pointing arrow and then clicking. Right-click in the selected column and then click Delete Columns on the shortcut menu to delete the Phone column.
3. Add a new row to the table for June as follows: Electric– 210.88; Gas– 14.55; Refuse– 15.00; Insurance – 58.50.
4. With the insertion point in the table, click Table on the menu bar, point to Select, and then click Table. Double-click the move handle on the Formatting toolbar. Click the Center button on the Formatting toolbar to center the table.
5. Click in the rightmost column, Insurance. Click Table on the menu bar, point to Insert, and then click Columns to the Right. Type `Total` as the new column's heading.
6. Position the insertion point in the January Total cell (second row, sixth column). Click Table on the menu bar and then click Formula. When the Formula dialog box displays, be sure the formula is =SUM(LEFT) and then click the OK button to place the Total expenses for January in the cell. Repeat for each month s total expense. For these expenses, you will need to edit the formula so it reads =SUM(LEFT) instead of =SUM(ABOVE).
7. Select the cells containing the total expense values and then click the Bold button on the Formatting toolbar.
8. Click File on the menu bar and then click Save As. Use the file name, Revised Expenses, to save the document on your floppy disk.
9. Print the revised table.

1 Using Word's Resume Wizard to Create a Resume

Problem: You are a student at University of Tennessee expecting to receive your Bachelor of Science degree in Restaurant/Hotel Management this May. As the semester end is approaching quickly, you are beginning a search for full-time employment upon graduation. You prepare the resume shown in Figure 3-81 using Word's Resume Wizard.

Instructions:

1. Use the Resume Wizard to create a resume. Select the Contemporary style for the resume. Use the name and address information in Figure 3-81 when the Resume Wizard requests it.
2. Personalize the resume as shown in Figure 3-81. When entering multiple lines in the Awards received, Memberships, Languages, and Hobbies sections, be sure to enter a line break at the end of each line, instead of a paragraph break.
3. Check the spelling of the resume.
4. Save the resume on a floppy disk with Schumann Resume as the file name.
5. View the resume from within print preview. If the resume exceeds one page, use print preview to shrink it to a page. Print the resume.

9-point font

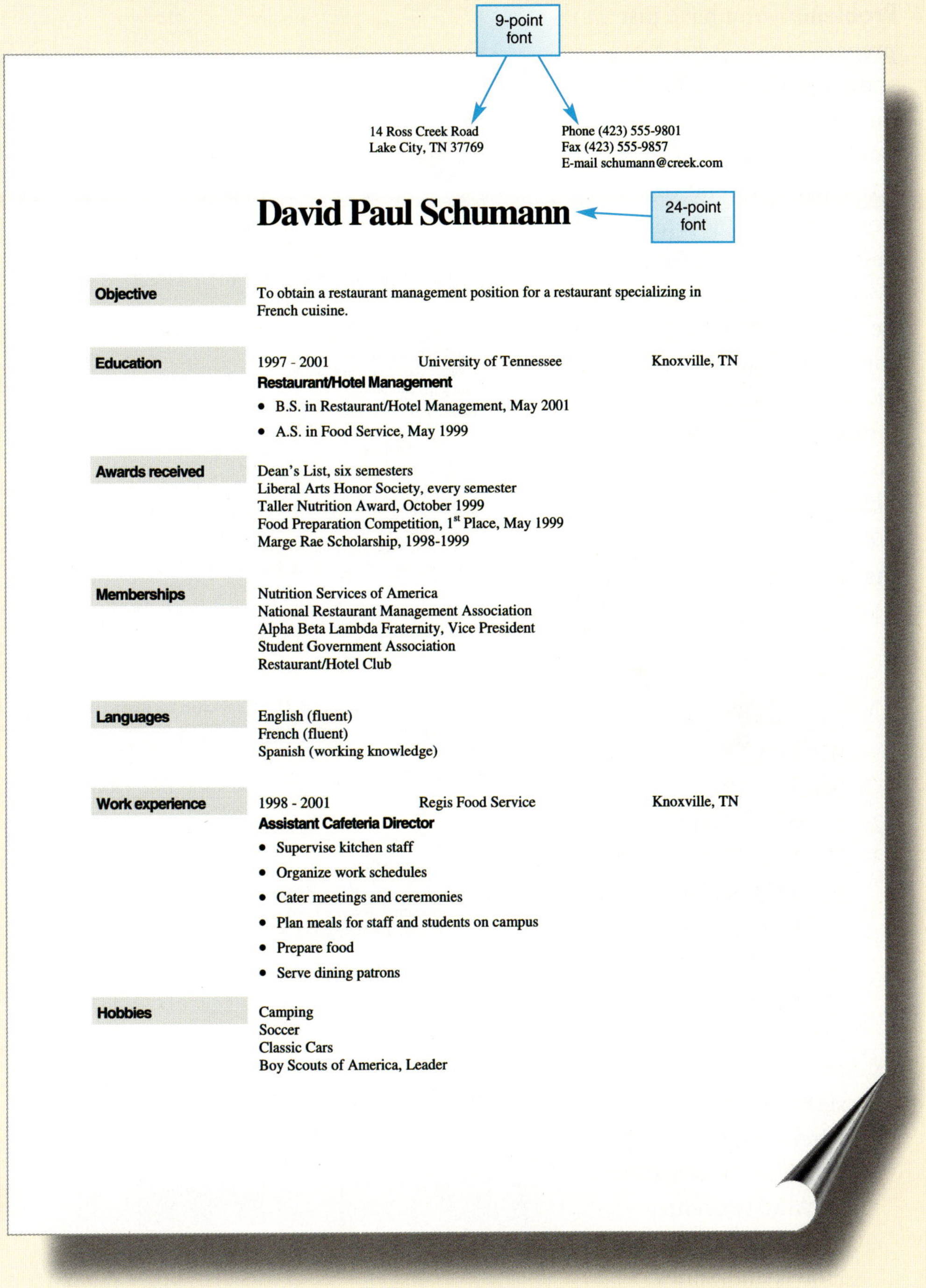

14 Ross Creek Road
Lake City, TN 37769

Phone (423) 555-9801
Fax (423) 555-9857
E-mail schumann@creek.com

David Paul Schumann ← 24-point font

Objective	To obtain a restaurant management position for a restaurant specializing in French cuisine.
Education	1997 - 2001 University of Tennessee Knoxville, TN **Restaurant/Hotel Management** • B.S. in Restaurant/Hotel Management, May 2001 • A.S. in Food Service, May 1999
Awards received	Dean's List, six semesters Liberal Arts Honor Society, every semester Taller Nutrition Award, October 1999 Food Preparation Competition, 1st Place, May 1999 Marge Rae Scholarship, 1998-1999
Memberships	Nutrition Services of America National Restaurant Management Association Alpha Beta Lambda Fraternity, Vice President Student Government Association Restaurant/Hotel Club
Languages	English (fluent) French (fluent) Spanish (working knowledge)
Work experience	1998 - 2001 Regis Food Service Knoxville, TN **Assistant Cafeteria Director** • Supervise kitchen staff • Organize work schedules • Cater meetings and ceremonies • Plan meals for staff and students on campus • Prepare food • Serve dining patrons
Hobbies	Camping Soccer Classic Cars Boy Scouts of America, Leader

FIGURE 3-81

2 Creating a Cover Letter with a Table

Problem: You have just prepared the resume shown in Figure 3-81 on the previous page and now are ready to create a cover letter to send to a prospective employer. In yesterday's edition of the *West Coast Tribune*, you noticed an advertisement for a restaurant manager at Worldwide Hotels and Suites. You prepare the cover letter shown in Figure 3-82 to send with your resume.

letterhead

20-point indigo font

9-point indigo font

clip keywords: hands on serving tray

11-point font

David Paul Schumann

14 Ross Creek Road, Lake City, TN 37769
Phone (423) 555-9801 • Fax (423) 555-9857 • E-mail schumann@creek.com

April 18, 2001

Ms. Amy Leonard
Food Service Director
Worldwide Hotels and Suites
202 Park Boulevard
Richmond, CA 98993

Dear Ms. Leonard:

I am responding to your advertisement in the *West Coast Tribune* for the restaurant manager position that will be opening in June. I have enclosed my resume for your consideration.

I will be graduating from the University of Tennessee in May. My courses in restaurant management and nutrition included the following:

- Restaurant Management: Introduction to Food Service, Restaurant Management, Food Service Marketing, Computers in Food Service, Food Production, Food Safety
- Nutrition: Food Planning and Preparation, Nutrition Essentials, Diet Planning, Nutrition Problems, Nutrition for Health

Through my part-time work for the university for Regis Food Service, I have first-hand experience with many aspects of food service. My annual reviews were outstanding. The following table lists my overall rating for each review.

Academic Year	Rating
2000-2001	5.0/5.0
1999-2000	4.8/5.0
1998-1999	4.5/5.0

Given my coursework and experience, I feel I would be a valuable asset to your organization. I look forward to hearing from you to schedule an interview and to discuss my career opportunities with Worldwide Hotels and Suites.

Sincerely,

David Paul Schumann

Enclosure

FIGURE 3-82

Instructions:

1. Create the letterhead shown at the top of Figure 3-82. Save the letterhead with the file name, Schumann Letterhead.
2. Create the letter shown in Figure 3-82 using the modified block style. Set a tab stop at the 3.5" mark on the ruler for the date line, complimentary close, and signature block. After entering the inside address, create an AutoText entry for Worldwide Hotels and Suites, and use the AutoText entry whenever you have to enter the company name, Worldwide Hotels and Suites. Center the table and format it using the Elegant format in the Table AutoFormat dialog box.
3. Save the letter on a floppy disk with Schumann Cover Letter as the file name.
4. Check the spelling of the cover letter. Save the cover letter again with the same file name.

5. View the cover letter from within print preview. If the cover letter exceeds one page, use print preview to shrink it to a single page. Print the cover letter.
6. Prepare and print an envelope address and mailing label using the inside address and return address in the cover letter.

3 Using Wizards to Compose a Personal Cover Letter and Resume

Problem: You are currently in the market for a new job and are ready to prepare a resume and cover letter.

Instructions: Obtain a copy of last Sunday's newspaper. Look through the classified section and cut out a want ad in an area of interest. Assume you are in the market for the position being advertised. Use the Resume Wizard to create a resume. Use the Letter Wizard to create the cover letter. Display the Letter Wizard by clicking Tools on the menu bar and then clicking Letter Wizard. *Hint:* Use Help for assistance in using the Letter Wizard. Use the want ad for the inside address and your personal information for the return address. Try to be as accurate as possible when personalizing the resume and cover letter. Submit the want ad with your cover letter and resume.

The difficulty of these case studies varies:
▶ are the least difficult; ▶▶ are more difficult; and ▶▶▶ are the most difficult.

1 ▶ Your boss has asked you to create a calendar for October so he can post it on the office bulletin board. Use the Calendar Wizard in the Other Documents sheet of the New Office Document dialog box. Use the following settings in the wizard: boxes & borders style, landscape print direction, leave room for a picture, October 2001 for both the start and end date. With the calendar on the screen, click the current graphic and delete it. Insert a clip art image of a haunted house or a similar seasonal graphic and then resize the image so it fits in the entire space for the graphic.

2 ▶ You have been asked to prepare the agenda for the next monthly department meeting. Use the Agenda Wizard in the Other Documents sheet of the New Office Document dialog box. Use the following settings in the wizard: style – modern; meeting date – 4/18/2001; meeting time – 2:00 p.m.; title – Monthly Meeting; meeting location – Conference Room B; headings – Please read and Please bring; names on agenda – Meeting called by, Note taker, and Attendees; Topics, People, and Minutes – Approve March Minutes, C. Dolby, 5; Department News, E. Jones, 10; Budget Status, J. Peterson, 15; Annual Kick-Off Dinner, T. Greeson, 15; New Business, Floor, 15; add a form for recording the minutes. On the agenda created by the wizard, add the following names in the appropriate spaces: C. Dolby called the meeting; R. Wilson will be the note taker; all people listed in this assignment will be attending – including you. Also, attendees should bring the 2001 Budget Report and read the March Minutes.

Cases and Places

3 ◗ You notice that Word has a Letter Wizard, which you can begin by clicking Tools on the menu bar and then clicking Letter Wizard. To assist you with letter preparation, you decide to prepare the letter shown in Figure 3-82 on page WD 3.64 using the Letter Wizard. How does the document prepared using the Letter Wizard differ from the one created from scratch? Do you prefer using a wizard or composing a letter from scratch?

4 ◗◗ A potential employer has asked you to fax your cover letter and resume so she may review it immediately. Use the Fax Wizard and the following settings: create the fax cover sheet with a note and print the fax so you can send it on a separate fax machine. It must be faxed to K. J. Buchham at Jade Enterprises (One Main Street, Cambridge, MA 02142; telephone 617-555-0098; fax 617-555-0099). Each is one page in length. Fax a copy to T. R. Green at the same number. In the fax, write a message informing K. J. Buchham that your cover letter and resume are attached and if she has any questions, she can contact you. Use your own name, address, and telephone information in the fax.

5 ◗◗ As chairperson of the Annual Company Picnic, you look for volunteers to assist with various activities. You have compiled a list of jobs for the picnic: prepare fliers, distribute fliers, plan meal and order food, plan and organize games, plan children's activities, reserve park pavilion, setup on day of picnic, and cleanup on day of picnic. You prepare a memorandum asking fellow employees for their assistance. A copy of the memo should be sent to Howard Bender. Use the Memo Wizard, together with the concepts and techniques presented in this project, to create and format the interoffice memorandum.

6 ◗◗◗ You have been asked to locate a speaker for this year's commencement address at your school. Locate the address of someone you feel would be a highly respected and enthusiastic speaker for the commencement address. Using Word's Letter Wizard, write the individual a letter inviting him or her to speak at the commencement. In the letter, present a background of your school, the student body, the staff, and any other aspects of your school that would make this speaker want to attend your commencement. Be sure to list the date, time, and location of the commencement in the letter. Apply the concepts and techniques presented in this project to personalize the letter.

7 ◗◗◗ Many individuals place their resumes on the World Wide Web for potential employers to see. Find a resume on the Web that you believe could be improved if it were designed differently. Print the resume. Using the text on the resume, Word's Resume Wizard, and the techniques presented in this project, create a new resume that would be more likely to catch a potential employer's attention. Turn in both the resume from the Web and your newly designed version of the resume.

Microsoft Word 2000

Creating Web Pages Using Word

CASE PERSPECTIVE

In Project 3, Paulette Rose Brandon created her resume (Figure 3-1 on page WD 3.5). Paulette graduated with you from Illinois State College. She was proficient in business, and you excelled at Internet skills. Recently, Paulette has been surfing the Internet on her own and has discovered that many people have their own personal Web pages with links to other Web sites and Web pages such as resumes and schedules. These personal Web pages are very impressive. To make herself more attractive to a potential employer, Paulette has asked you to help her create a personal Web page that contains a hyperlink to her resume. To do this, she must save her resume as a Web page. Paulette also wants her Web page to contain two more hyperlinks: one to her favorite Web site (www.scsite.com) and another to her e-mail address. This way, potential employers easily can send her a message.

To complete this Web Feature, you will need the resume created in Project 3 so you can save it as a Web page and then use the resulting Web page as a hyperlink destination. (If you did not create the resume, see your instructor for a copy.)

Introduction

Word provides two techniques for creating Web pages. If you have an existing Word document, you can save it as a Web page. If you do not have an existing Word document, you can create a new Web page by using a Web page template or the Web Page Wizard, which provides customized templates you can modify easily. In addition to these Web tools, Word has many other **Web page authoring** features. For example, you can include frames, hyperlinks, sounds, videos, pictures, scrolling text, bullets, horizontal lines, check boxes, option buttons, list boxes, text boxes, and scripts on Web pages.

In this Web Feature, you save the resume created in Project 3 as a Web page. You then use Word's Web Page Wizard to create another Web page that contains two frames (Figure 1a on the next page). A **frame** is a rectangular section of a Web page that can display another separate Web page. Thus, a Web page that contains multiple frames can display multiple Web pages simultaneously. Word stores all frames associated with a Web page in a single file called the **frames page**. The frames page is not visible on the screen; it simply is a container for all frames associated with a Web page. When you open the frames page in Word or a Web browser, all frames associated with the Web page display on the screen.

In this Web Feature, the file name of the frames page is Brandon Personal Web Page. When you initially open this frames page, the left frame contains the title Paulette Rose Brandon and two hyperlinks – My Resume and My Favorite Site; the right frame displays Paulette's resume (Figure 1a). You have learned that a hyperlink is a shortcut that allows a user to jump easily and quickly to another location in the same document or to other documents or Web pages. The My Resume hyperlink is a connection to the resume, and the My Favorite Site hyperlink is a connection to www.scsite.com.

When you click the My Favorite Site hyperlink, the www.scsite.com Web site displays in the right frame (Figure 1b). When you click the My Resume hyperlink, the resume displays in the right frame. The resume itself contains a hyperlink to an e-mail address. When you click the e-mail address, Word opens your e-mail program automatically with the recipient's address (brandon@lenox.com) already filled in (Figure 1c). You simply type a message and then click the Send button, which places the message in the Outbox or sends it if you are connected to an e-mail server.

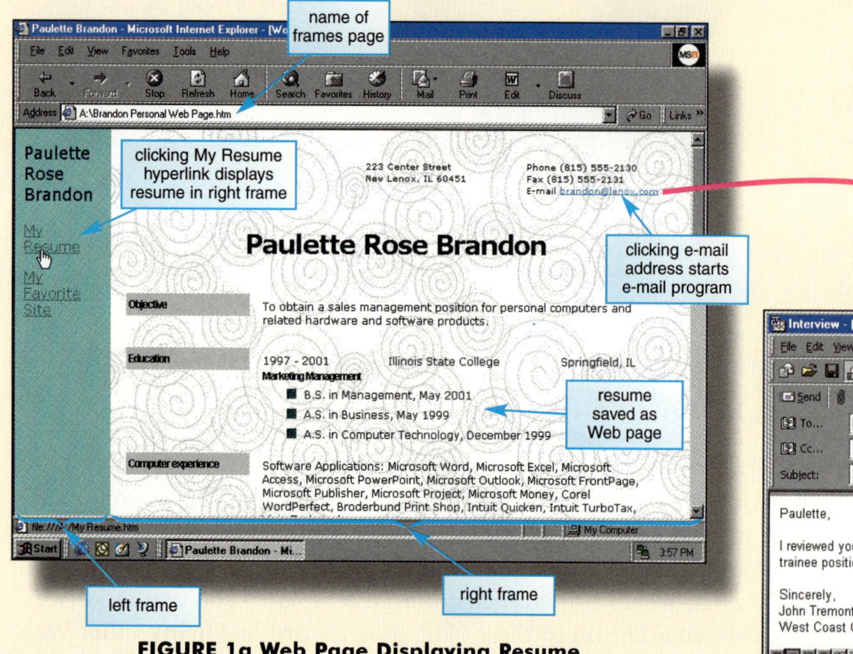

FIGURE 1a Web Page Displaying Resume

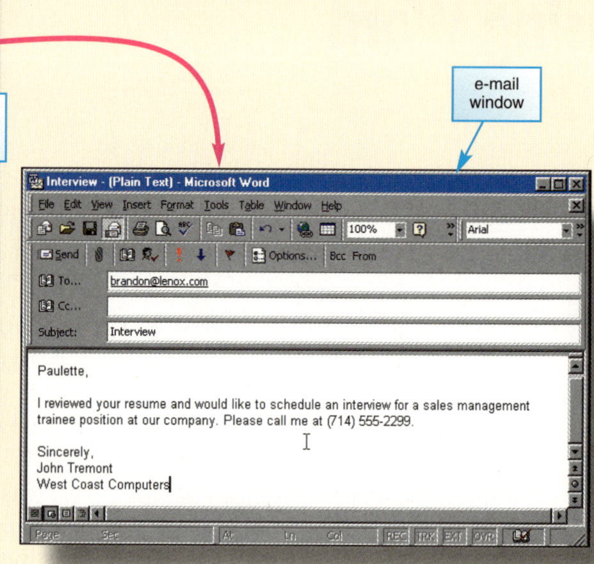

FIGURE 1c E-mail Program

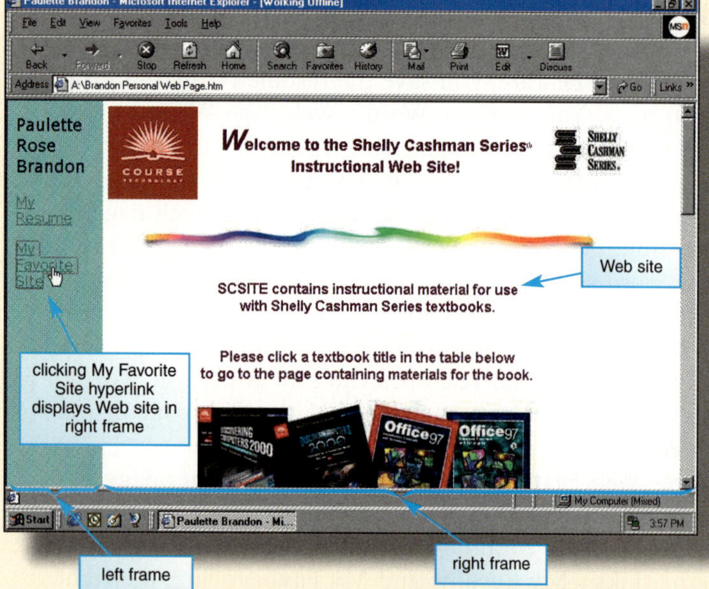

FIGURE 1b Web Page Displaying Web Site

Once you have created Web pages, you can publish them. **Publishing** is the process of making Web pages available to others, for example on the World Wide Web or on a company's intranet. In Word, you can publish Web pages by saving them to a Web folder or to an FTP location. The procedures for publishing Web pages in Microsoft Office are discussed in Appendix B.

Because this Web Feature is for instructional purposes, you create and save your frames page and associated Web pages on a floppy disk rather than to the Web. Saving these pages to the floppy disk may be a slow process – please be patient.

Saving a Word Document as a Web Page

Once you have created a Word document, you can save it as a Web page so that it can be published and then viewed by a Web browser, such as Internet Explorer. Perform the following steps to save the resume created in Project 3 as a Web page.

To Save a Word Document as a Web Page

1 Start Word and then open the Brandon Resume created in Project 3. Reset your toolbars as described in Appendix C. Click File on the menu bar and then point to Save as Web Page (Figure 2).

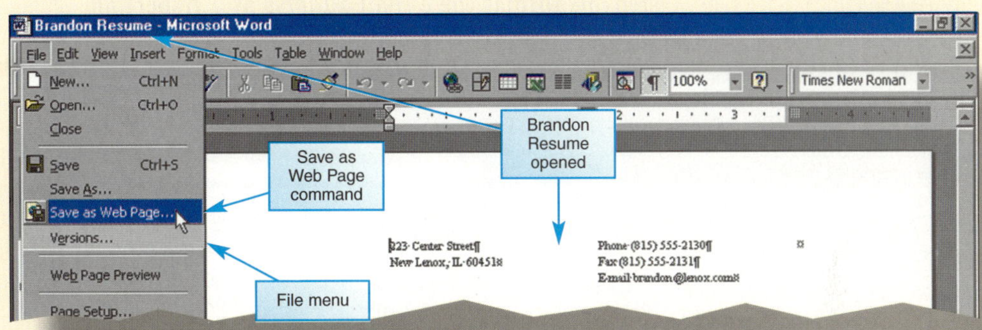

FIGURE 2

2 Click Save as Web Page. When the Save As dialog box displays, type Brandon Resume Web Page **in the File name text box and then, if necessary, change the Save in location to 3½ Floppy (A:) as shown in Figure 3.**

3 Click the Save button in the Save As dialog box.

Word displays the Brandon Resume Web Page in the Word window (see Figure 4 on the next page).

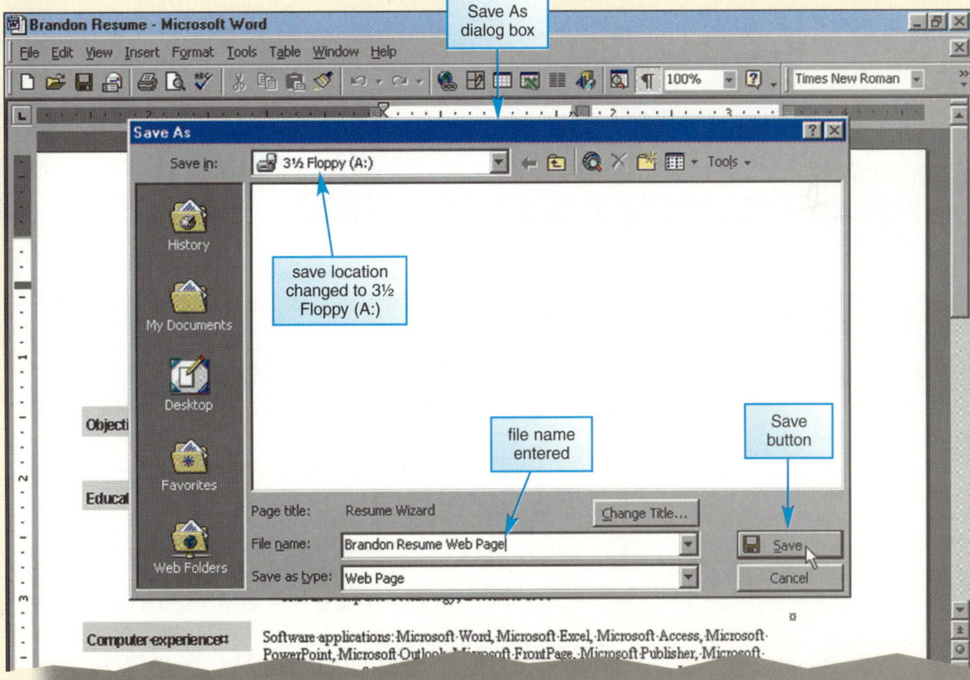

FIGURE 3

Word switches to Web layout view and also changes some of the toolbar buttons and menu commands to provide Web page authoring features. For example, the Standard toolbar now displays a New Web Page button (Figure 4 on the next page). The Web Layout View button on the horizontal scroll bar is recessed.

The resume displays on the Word screen similar to how it will display in a Web browser. Some of Word's formatting features are not supported by Web pages; thus, your Web page may display slightly different from the original Word document.

Formatting the E-mail Address as a Hyperlink

You want the e-mail address in your resume to be formatted as a hyperlink so that when someone clicks the e-mail address on your Web page, his or her e-mail program opens automatically with your e-mail address already filled in.

You have learned that when you press the SPACEBAR or ENTER key after a Web or e-mail address, Word automatically formats it as a hyperlink. Perform the following steps to format the e-mail address as a hyperlink.

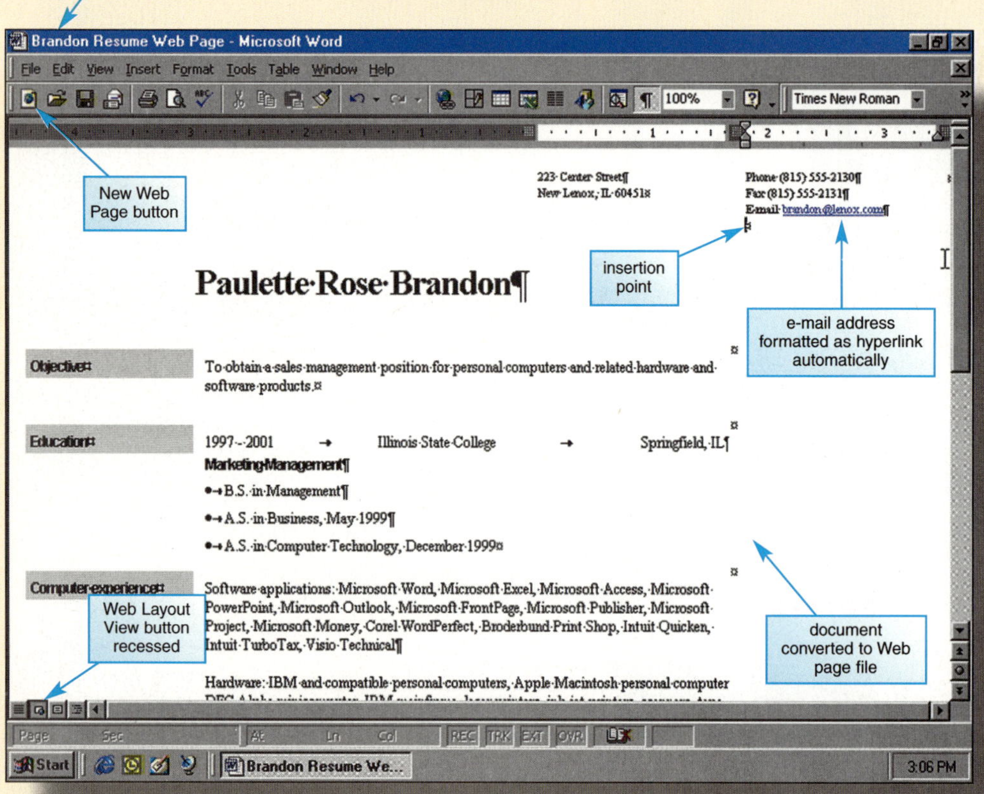

FIGURE 4

TO FORMAT A HYPERLINK AUTOMATICALLY

1. Position the insertion point immediately after the e-mail address; that is, after the m in com.
2. Press the ENTER key.

Word automatically formats the e-mail address as a hyperlink; that is, it is colored blue and underlined (Figure 4).

You are now finished modifying the Brandon Resume Web Page file. Thus, perform the following steps to save the file again and then close it.

TO SAVE AND CLOSE A WEB PAGE

1. Click the Save button on the Standard toolbar.
2. Click File on the menu bar and then click Close.

Word saves the file and closes it. The Word window is empty.

Web Page Design

For more information on guidelines for designing Web pages, visit the Word 2000 More About Web page (www.scsite.com/wd2000/more.htm) and then click Web Page Design.

Using Word's Web Page Wizard to Create a Web Page

In the previous section, you saved an existing Word document as a Web page. Next, you want to create a brand new Web page. You can create a Web page from scratch using a Web page template or you can use the **Web Page Wizard**. Because this is your first experience creating a new Web page with frames, you should use the Web Page Wizard as shown in the following steps.

To Create a Web Page Using the Web Page Wizard

1 Click File on the menu bar and then click New. If necessary, click the Web Pages tab when the New dialog box first displays. Point to the Web Page Wizard icon.

Word displays several Web page template icons and the Web Page Wizard in the Web Pages sheet (Figure 5).

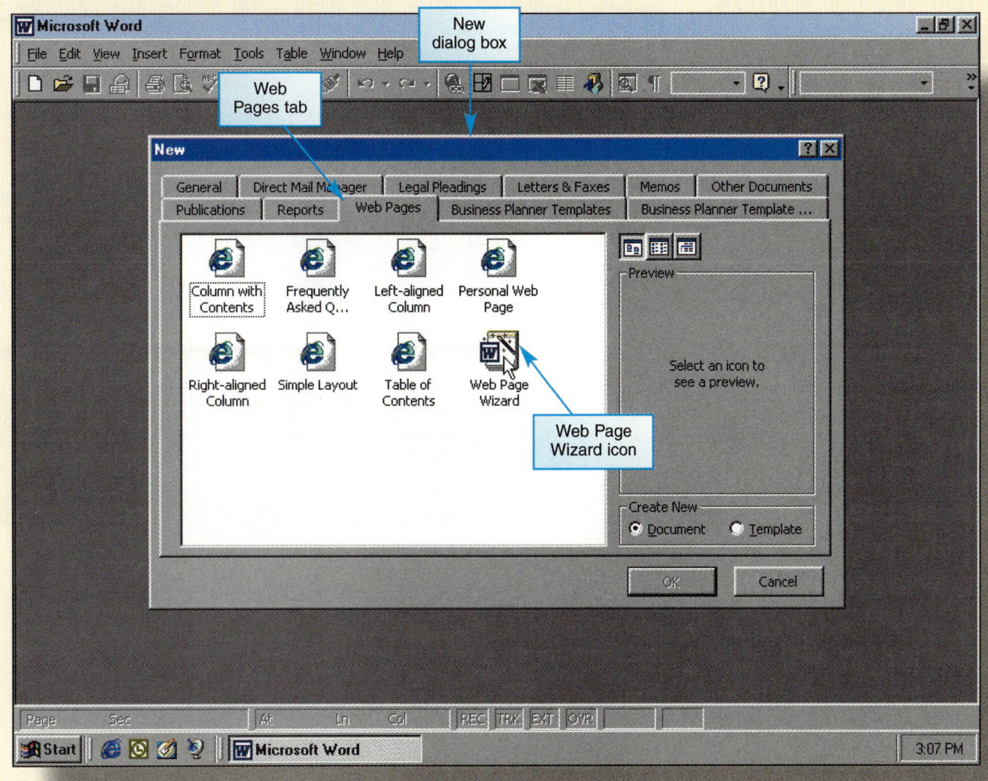

FIGURE 5

2 Double-click the Web Page Wizard icon. When the Start panel displays in the Web Page Wizard dialog box, click the Next button. When the Title and Location panel displays, type `Paulette Brandon` **in the Web site title text box. Press the TAB key and then type** `a:` **in the Web site location text box.**

*Word displays the **Title and Location panel** in the Web Page Wizard dialog box (Figure 6). In this dialog box, the title you enter displays in the Web browser's title bar.*

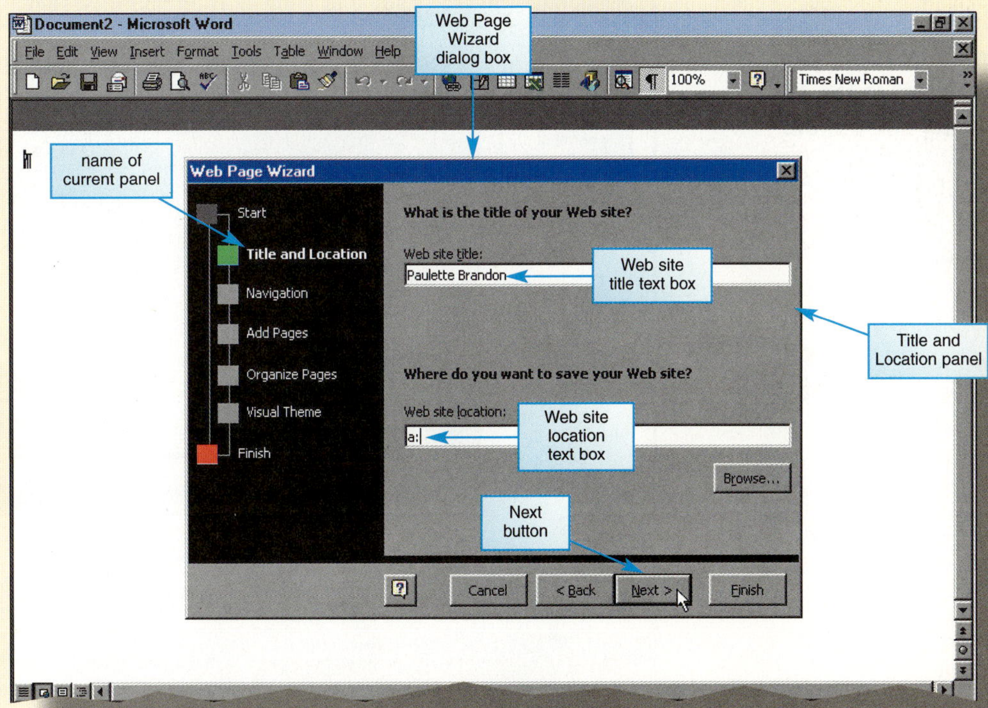

FIGURE 6

3 Click the Next button. When the Navigation panel displays, click Vertical frame, if necessary, and then point to the Next button.

Word displays the Navigation panel in the Web Page Wizard dialog box (Figure 7). In this dialog box, you select the placement of hyperlinks on your Web page(s).

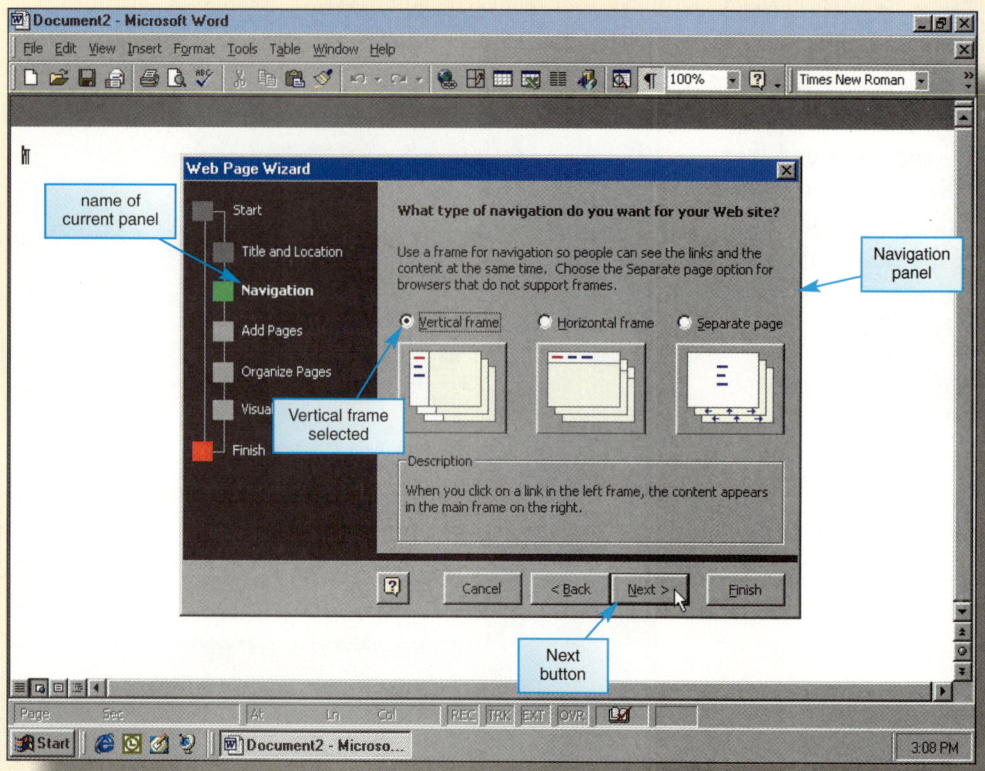

FIGURE 7

4 Click the Next button. When the Add Pages panel displays, click the Remove Page button three times and then point to the Add Existing File button.

Word displays the Add Pages panel that initially lists three Web page names: Personal Web Page, Blank Page 1, and Blank Page 2. You do not want any of these Web page names on your Web page; thus, you remove them (Figure 8). You will click the Add Existing File button to add Brandon Resume Web Page to the list.

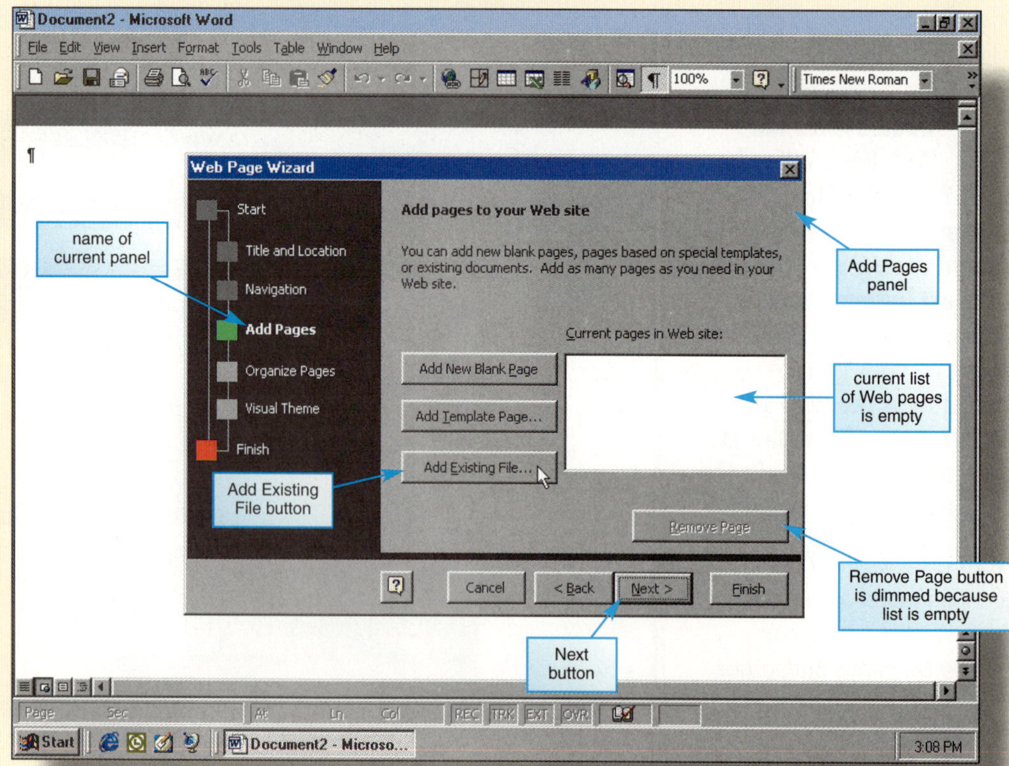

FIGURE 8

5 Click the Add Existing File button to display the Open dialog box. If necessary, change the Look in location to 3½ Floppy (A:). Click Brandon Resume Web Page and then point to the Open button in the Open dialog box (Figure 9).

6 Click the Open button in the Open dialog box.

The wizard adds Brandon Resume Web Page to the list in the Add Pages panel.

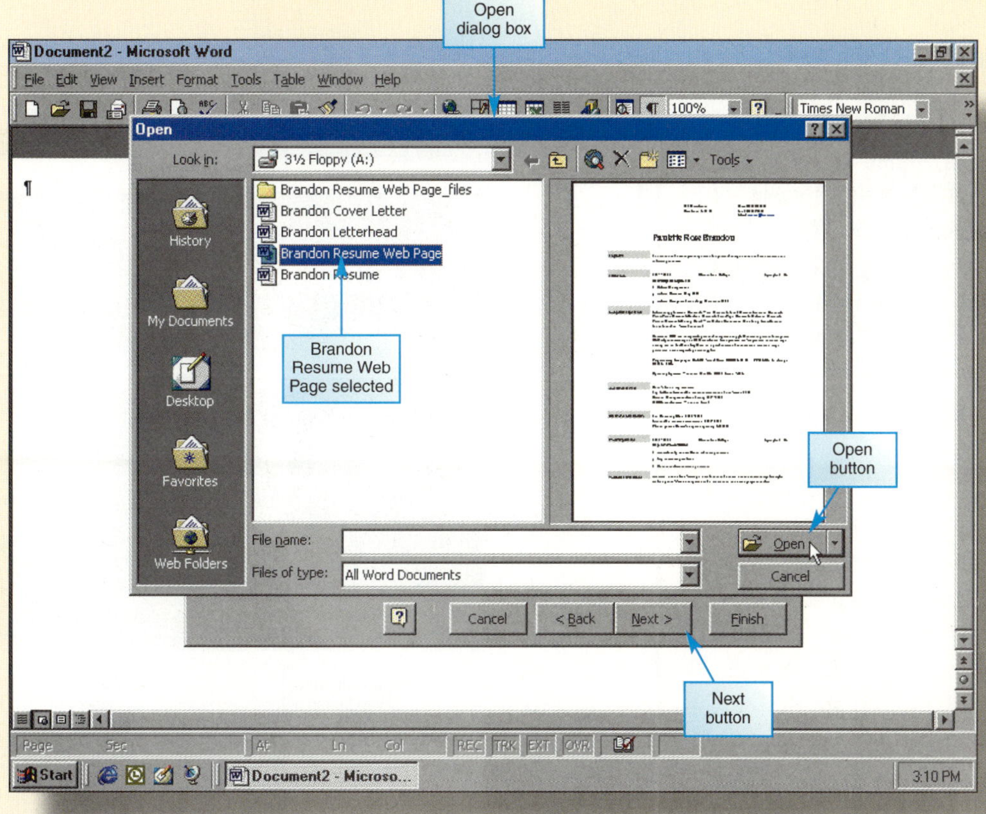

FIGURE 9

7 Click the Next button in the Add Pages panel. When the Organize Pages panel displays, click the Rename button. When the Rename Hyperlink dialog box displays, type `My Resume` **in the text box. Point to the OK button.**

In the Organize Pages panel *in the Web Page Wizard, you specify the sequence and names of the hyperlinks to be in the left frame of the Web page (Figure 10).*

8 Click the OK button.

Word renames the hyperlink to My Resume.

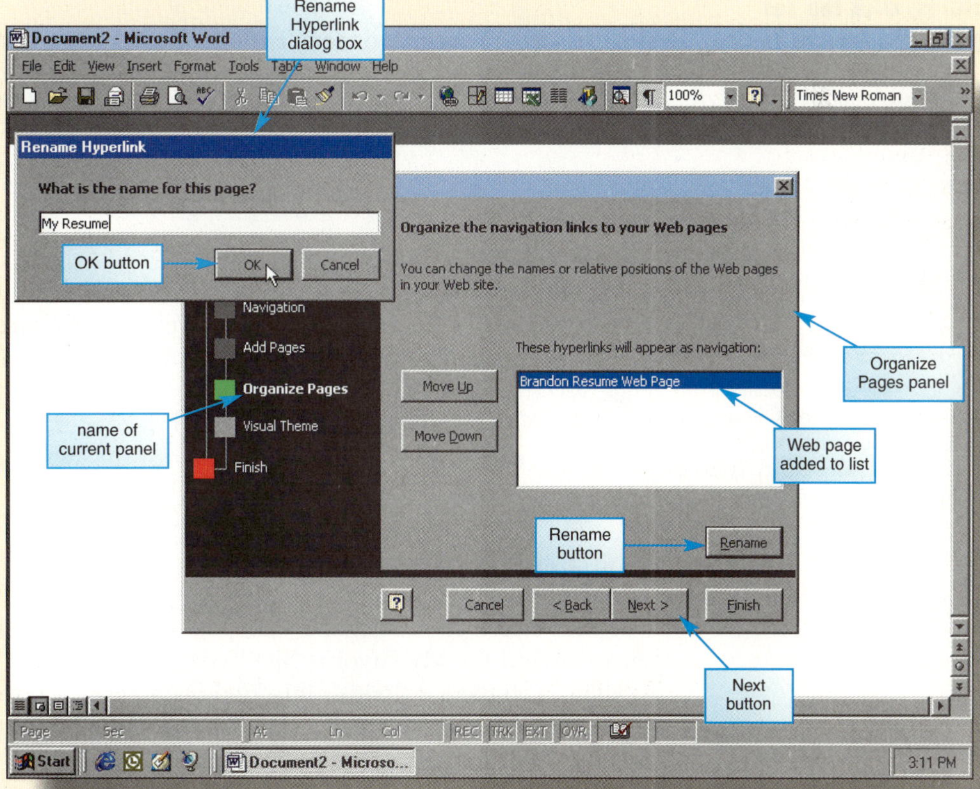

FIGURE 10

9 Click the Next button. If the displayed theme in the Visual Theme panel is not Spiral, click the Browse Themes button. When the Theme dialog box displays, scroll to and then click Spiral in the Choose a Theme list. Click the OK button.

*Word displays the **Visual Theme panel** in the Web Page Wizard dialog box (Figure 11). A **theme** is a collection of defined design elements and color schemes.*

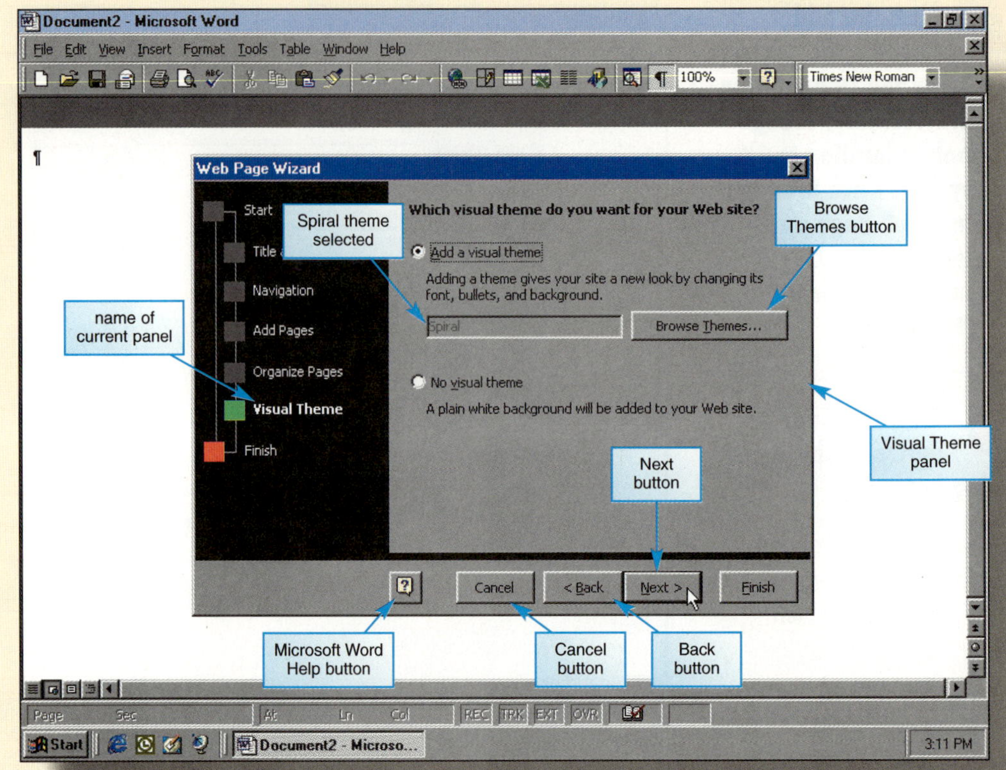

FIGURE 11

10 Click the Next button. When the Finish panel displays, click the Finish button. If the Office Assistant displays a message about navigation features, click the Yes button. If a Frames toolbar displays in your document window, click its Close button to remove it from the screen.

After about a minute, Word displays a layout of the Web pages (see Figure 12). The My Resume hyperlink displays in a frame on the left and the resume displays in a frame on the right.

Other Ways

1. On Start menu click New Office Document, click Web Pages tab, double-click Web Page Wizard icon
2. Click New Office Document button on Microsoft Office Shortcut Bar, click Web Pages tab, double-click Web Page Wizard icon

When creating a Web page using the Web Page Wizard, you can click the Back button (Figure 11) in any panel of the Web Page Wizard dialog box to change any previously entered information. For help with entering information into the Web Page Wizard, click the Microsoft Word Help button in the appropriate panel. To exit from the Web Page Wizard and return to the document window without creating the Web page, click the Cancel button in any of the Web Page Wizard dialog boxes.

Modifying a Web Page

The next step is to modify the Web pages. First, you make the left frame smaller and then you add the My Favorite Site hyperlink.

The Web page is divided into two frames, one on the left and one on the right. A **frame border** separates the frames. When you point to the frame border, the mouse pointer shape changes to a double-headed arrow.

You want to make the left frame narrower. To do this, you drag the frame border as illustrated in the following steps.

To Resize a Web Page Frame

Point to the frame border.

The mouse pointer shape changes to a double-headed arrow and Word displays the ScreenTip, Resize (Figure 12).

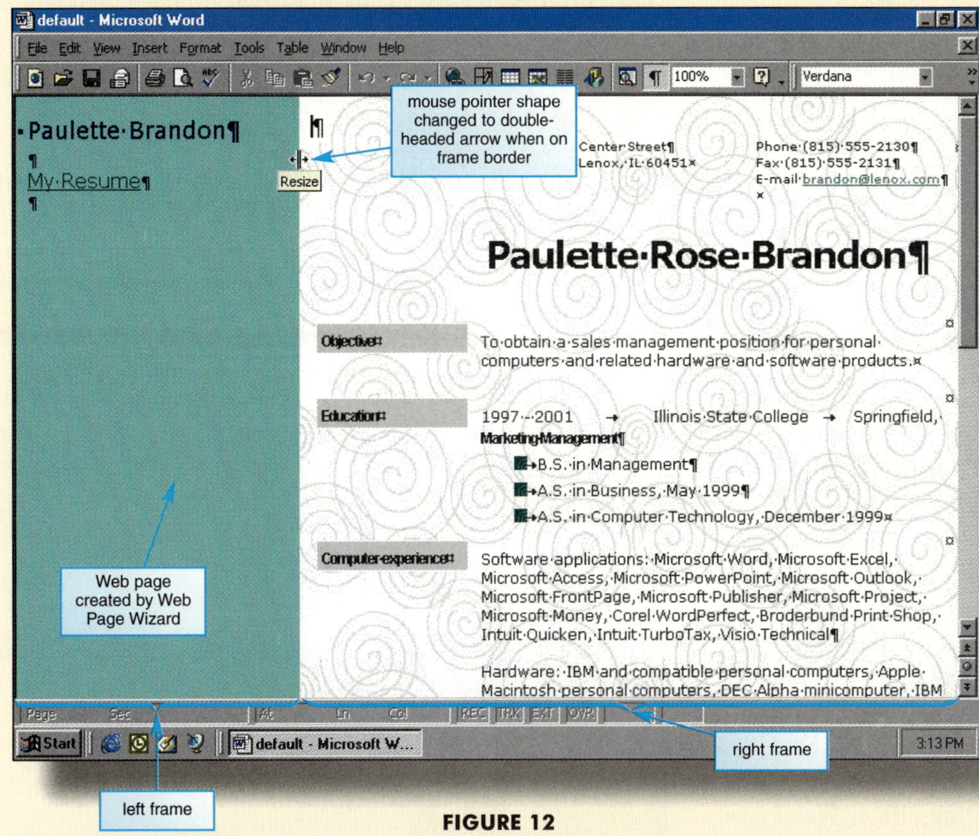

FIGURE 12

2 **Drag the frame border to the left until it is positioned under the r in Brandon (Figure 13).**

Word narrows the left frame and widens the right frame (see Figure 14 on the next page).

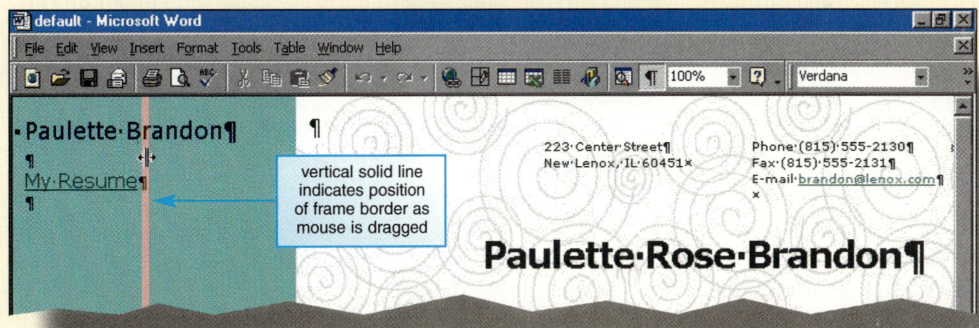

FIGURE 13

In the left frame, you want to add a My Favorite Site hyperlink. You used the Web Page Wizard to link the My Resume hyperlink to the Web page file called Brandon Resume Web Page, which means when you click the My Resume link in the left frame, the Brandon Resume Web Page file displays in the right frame. Similarly, when you click the My Favorite Site hyperlink, you want a Web site to display in the right frame.

The first step is to enter the hyperlink text into the left frame as described in the steps on the next page.

Highlighting

To add color to an online document or e-mail communication, highlight the text. Highlighting alerts the reader to the text's importance, much like a highlight marker does in a textbook. To highlight text, select it, click the Highlight button arrow on the Formatting toolbar, and then click the desired highlight color.

TO ENTER AND FORMAT TEXT

1. Click in the left frame of the Web page. Click the paragraph mark below the My Resume hyperlink and then press the ENTER key.
2. Double-click the move handle on the Formatting toolbar to display the entire toolbar. Click the Font Size box arrow and then click 12.
3. Type `My Favorite Site` as the text.

Word enters the text, My Favorite Site, in the left frame using a font size of 12.

Perform the following steps to link the My Favorite Site text to a Web site.

Steps To Add a Hyperlink

1 **Drag through the My Favorite Site text. Double-click the move handle on the Standard toolbar to display the entire toolbar. Click the Insert Hyperlink button on the Standard toolbar. When the Insert Hyperlink dialog box displays, if necessary, click Existing File or Web Page in the Link to list. Type** `http://www.scsite.com` **in the Type the file or Web page name text box (Figure 14).**

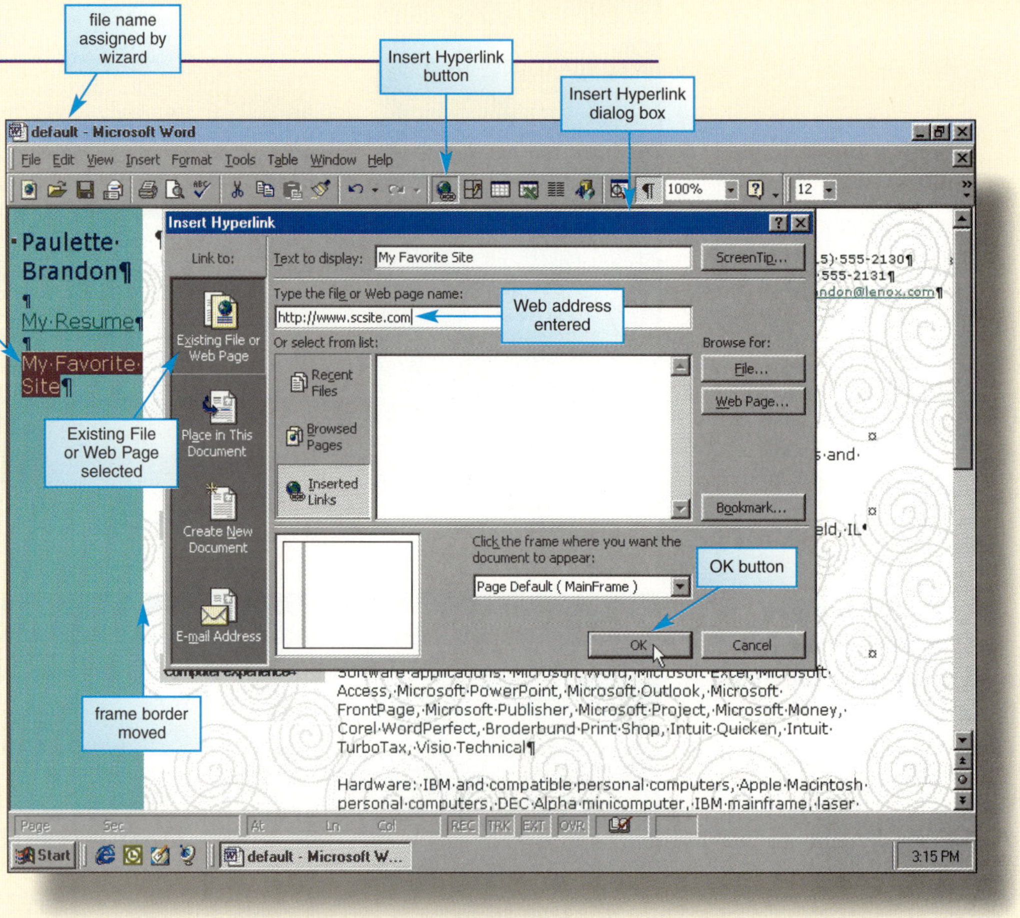

2 **Click the OK button.**

Word formats the My Favorite Site text as a hyperlink that when clicked displays the associated Web site in the right frame (see Figure 1b on page WDW 1.2).

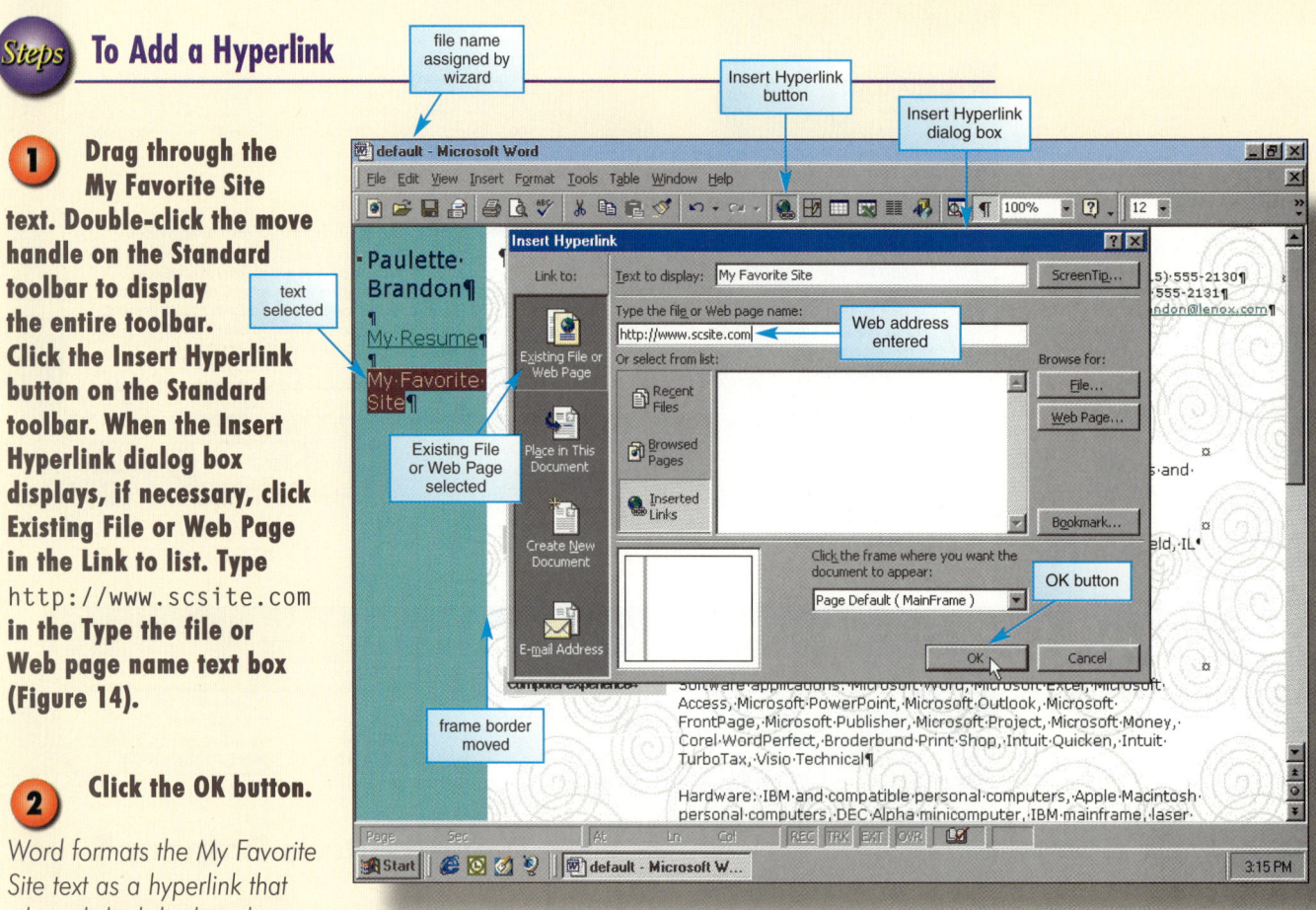

FIGURE 14

1. Right-click selected text, point to Hyperlink on shortcut menu, click Edit hyperlink on Hyperlink submenu

If you wanted to edit an existing hyperlink, you would drag through the hyperlink text and then click the Insert Hyperlink button on the Standard toolbar. Word will display the Edit Hyperlink dialog box instead of the Insert Hyperlink dialog box. Other than the title bar, these two dialog boxes are the same.

The Resume Wizard assigned the file name, default, to this frames page (Figure 14). Save the frames page with a new name as described in the following steps.

TO SAVE THE FRAMES PAGE WITH A NEW FILE NAME

1. Insert your floppy disk into drive A.
2. Click File on the menu bar and then click Save As.
3. Type the file name `Brandon Personal Web Page` in the File name text box. Do not press the ENTER key.
4. If necessary, click the Save in box arrow and then click 3½ Floppy (A:).
5. Click the Save button in the Save As dialog box.

Word saves the frames page and associated frames on a floppy disk in drive A with the file name Brandon Personal Web Page.

Viewing the Web Page in Your Default Browser

To see how the Web page looks in your default browser without actually connecting to the Internet, you use the **Web Page Preview command**. That is, if you click File on the menu bar and then click Web Page Preview, Word opens your Web browser in a separate window and displays the open Web page file in the browser window.

From the browser window, you can test your hyperlinks to be sure they work – before you publish them to the Web. For example, in the left frame, click the My Favorite Site link to display the Web site www.scsite.com in the right frame. (If you are not connected to the Internet, your browser will connect you and then display the Web site.) Click the My Resume link to display the Brandon Resume Web Page in the right frame. Click the e-mail address to open your e-mail program with the address, brandon@lenox.com, entered in the recipient's address box. When finished, close the browser window.

The next step is to quit Word.

TO QUIT WORD

1. Click the Close button at the right edge of Word's title bar.

The Word window closes.

Editing a Web Page from Your Browser

One of the powerful features of Office 2000 is the ability to edit a Web page directly from Internet Explorer. The steps on the next page illustrate how to open your Web page in Internet Explorer and then edit it from Internet Explorer.

Web Pages

Use horizontal lines to separate sections of a Web page. To add a horizontal line at the location of the insertion point, click Format on the menu bar, click Borders and Shading, click the Horizontal Line button, click the desired line type in the Horizontal Line dialog box, and then click the Insert Clip button on the Pop-up menu.

More About 2000

HTML

If you wish to view the HTML source code associated with the Web page you have created, click View on the menu bar and then click HTML Source, which starts the HTML Source Editor. To close the HTML Source Editor, click File on the menu bar and then click Exit.

Microsoft Certification

The Microsoft Office User Specialist (MOUS) Certification program provides an opportunity for you to obtain a valuable industry credential - proof that you have the Word 2000 skills required by employers. For more information, see Appendix D or visit the Shelly Cashman Series MOUS Web page at www.scsite.com/off2000/cert.htm.

To Edit a Web Page from Your Browser

1 **Click the Start button on the taskbar, point to Programs, and then click Internet Explorer. When the Internet Explorer window displays, type** `a:Brandon Personal Web Page.htm` **in the Address Bar and then press the ENTER key. Point to the Edit with Microsoft Word for Windows button on the toolbar.**

Internet Explorer opens the Brandon Personal Web Page and displays it in the browser window (Figure 15). Internet Explorer determines the Office program you used to create the Web page and associates that program with the Edit button.

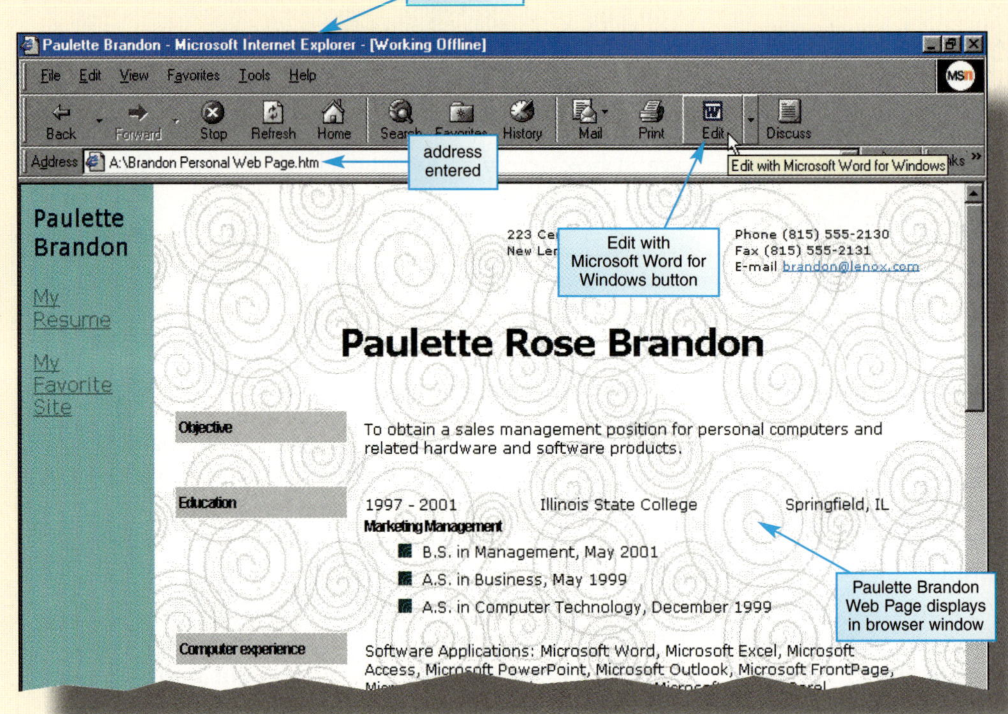

FIGURE 15

2 **Click the Edit with Microsoft Word for Windows button.**

Internet Explorer starts Microsoft Word and displays the Brandon Personal Web Page in the Word window.

3 **In the left frame, click immediately to the left of the B in Brandon. Type** Rose **and then press the SPACEBAR.**

Paulette's middle name displays in the left frame of the Web page (Figure 16).

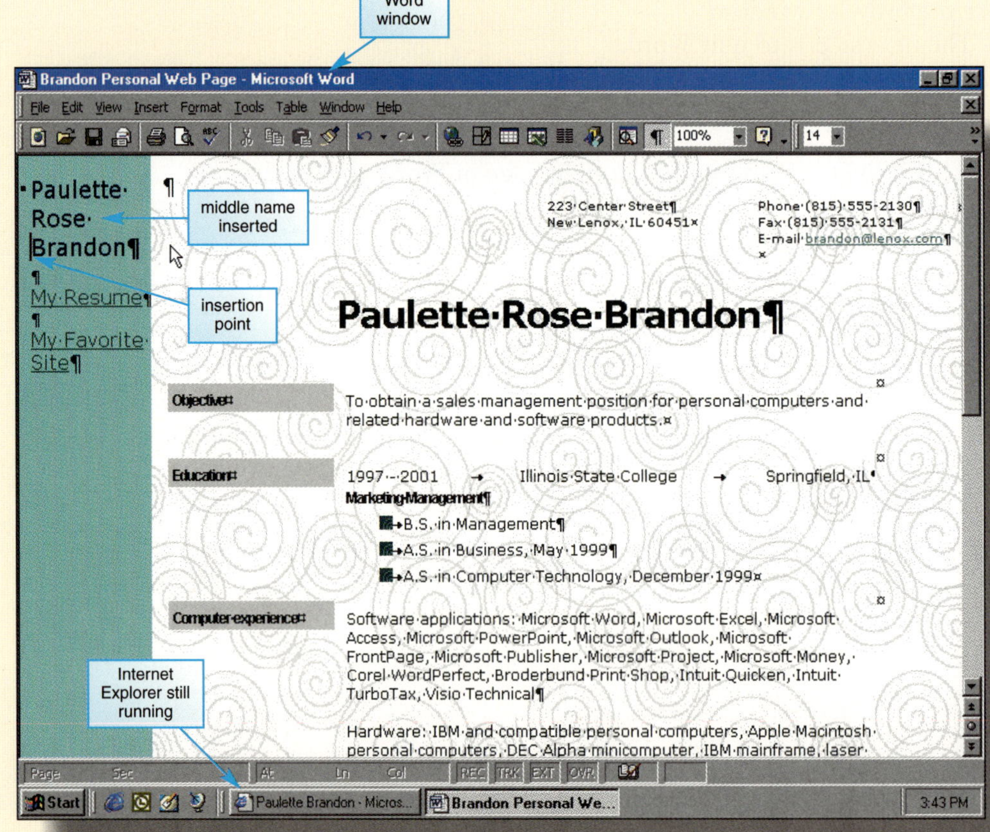

FIGURE 16

4 **Click the Save button on the Standard toolbar. Click the Close button at the right edge of Word's title bar.**

Word saves the revised Web page and, after about a minute, the Word window closes.

5 **When the Internet Explorer window redisplays, click the Refresh button on the toolbar.**

Internet Explorer displays the revised Web page (Figure 17).

6 **Click the Close button at the right edge of the Internet Explorer window.**

The Internet Explorer window closes.

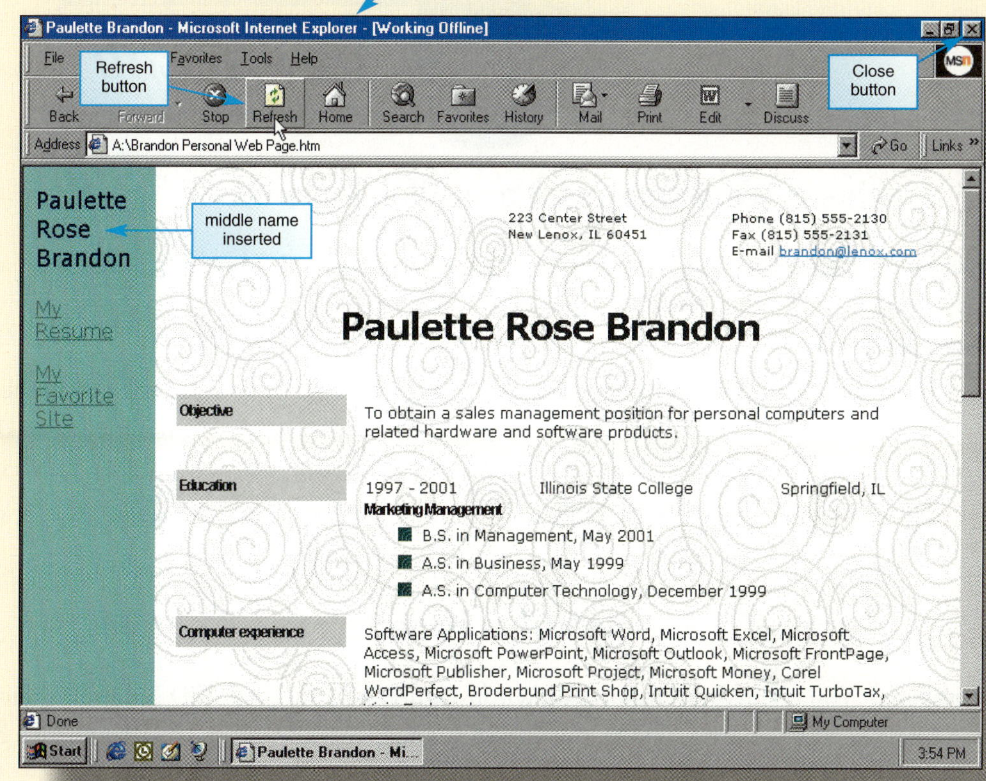

FIGURE 17

If the right edge of the resume wraps when you display it in the browser, you can follow the steps above to edit it in Word and drag the right border of the resume table to the right.

The final step is to make your Web pages and associated files available to others on your network, on an intranet, or on the World Wide Web. See Appendix B and then talk to your instructor about how you should do this for your system.

More About 2000

Quick Reference

For a table that lists how to complete the tasks covered in this book using the mouse, menu, shortcut menu, and keyboard, visit the Shelly Cashman Series Office Web page (www.scsite.com/off2000/qr.htm) and then click Microsoft Word 2000.

CASE PERSPECTIVE SUMMARY

Paulette is thrilled with her personal Web pages. They look so professional! Paulette now is ready to publish the Web pages and associated files to the World Wide Web. After talking with her ISP's technical support staff, she learns she can use Word to save a copy of her Web page files directly on her ISP's Web server. You are familiar with this feature of Word and assist Paulette with this task. Next, she connects to the Web and displays her personal Web pages from her browser. Paulette is quite impressed with herself!

Web Feature Summary

This Web Feature introduced you to creating a Web page by saving an existing Word document as a Web Page file. You also created a new Web page with frames using the Web Page Wizard and then modified this Web page. You created a hyperlink to an e-mail address, one to a Web page file, and another to a Web site.

1 Saving a Word Document as a Web Page

Problem: You created the research paper shown in Figure 2-74 on pages WD 2.57 and WD 2.58 in Project 2. You decide to save this research paper as a Web page.

Instructions:

1. Open the Digital Camera Paper shown in Figure 2-74. (If you did not create the research paper, see your instructor for a copy.) Then, save the paper as a Web page using the file name Digital Camera Web Page.
2. Print the Web page. Click File on the menu bar and then click Web Page Preview to view the Web page in your browser. Close the browser window. Quit Word.

2 Creating a Web Page with a Hyperlink to a Web Site

Problem: You created the resume shown in Figure 3-81 on page WD 3.63 in Project 3. You decide to create a personal Web page with a link to this resume. Thus, you also must save the resume as a Web page.

Instructions:

1. Open the Schumann Resume shown in Figure 3-81. (If you did not create the resume, see your instructor for a copy.) Then, save the resume as a Web page using the file name Schumann Resume Web Page. Convert the e-mail address to a Web page by clicking immediately to the right of the address and pressing the ENTER key. Save the Web page again.
2. Create a personal Web page with frames using the Web Page Wizard. Use the following settings as the wizard requests them: apply vertical frame navigation; create a hyperlink to the Schumann Resume Web Page; change the name of the hyperlink to My Resume; select a visual theme you like best.
3. Insert a hyperlink called My Favorite Site and link it to your favorite Web address.
4. Save the Web page. Test your Web page links. Print the Web page. Click File on the menu bar and then click Web Page Preview to view the Web page in your browser. Close the browser window. Quit Word.

3 Creating a Personal Web Page

Problem: You have decided to create your own personal Web page using the Personal Home Page template in the Web Page Wizard.

Instructions:

1. Create your own personal Web page using the Web Page Wizard. Use Horizontal frame as your navigation method. When the Add Pages panel displays, keep the Personal Web Page, and delete Blank Page 1 and Blank Page 2. Select a theme you like best.
2. Personalize the Personal Web Page as indicated on the template. For each bullet in the Favorite Links section, enter a URL of a site on the Web that interests you.
3. Save the Web page. Test your Web page links.
4. Ask your instructor for instructions on how to publish your Web page so that others may have access to it.

MICROSOFT

Excel 2000

Microsoft Excel 2000

Creating a Worksheet and Embedded Chart

OBJECTIVES

You will have mastered the material in this project when you can:

- Start Excel
- Describe the Excel worksheet
- Reset menus and toolbars
- Select a cell or range of cells
- Enter text and numbers
- Use the AutoSum button to sum a range of cells
- Copy a cell to a range of cells using the fill handle
- Change the size of the font in a cell
- Bold cell entries
- Apply the AutoFormat command to format a range
- Center cell contents across a series of columns
- Use the Name box to select a cell
- Create a Column chart using the Chart Wizard
- Save a workbook
- Print a worksheet
- Quit Excel
- Open a workbook
- Use the AutoCalculate area to determine totals
- Correct errors on a worksheet
- Use the Office Assistant and other online Help tools to answer your questions

Get Smart

Smart Cards Open Convenience Doors

What can pay for your laundry, open your dorm door, feed the parking meter, and withdraw money from an automatic teller machine? Need a hint? It is smart, but it never went to college. It is a smart card, and it is coming soon to your wallet.

This ingenious card resembles a credit card in size, but instead of a magnetic strip on the back, it has a microprocessor chip inside. This chip gives the card its brains, while it gives its owner convenience and security.

University of Michigan and University of Illinois students are familiar with the card, as are students at 25 other schools across the United States and Canada. They use it for everything from calling Mom back home to checking out library books to debiting their checking accounts.

The nonprofit Smart Card Forum (www.smartcardforum.org) has helped bring this technology to education. The 200 members of this organization represent a cross-section of technology experts and smart card users who are working to increase multiple-application smart cards in the government, private, and education sectors.

Some visionaries predict 3.75 billion smart cards will be issued by 2005, with owners using them to make 25 billion transactions yearly. The cost to manufacture one card ranges from 80 cents to 15 dollars depending on the application and complexity.

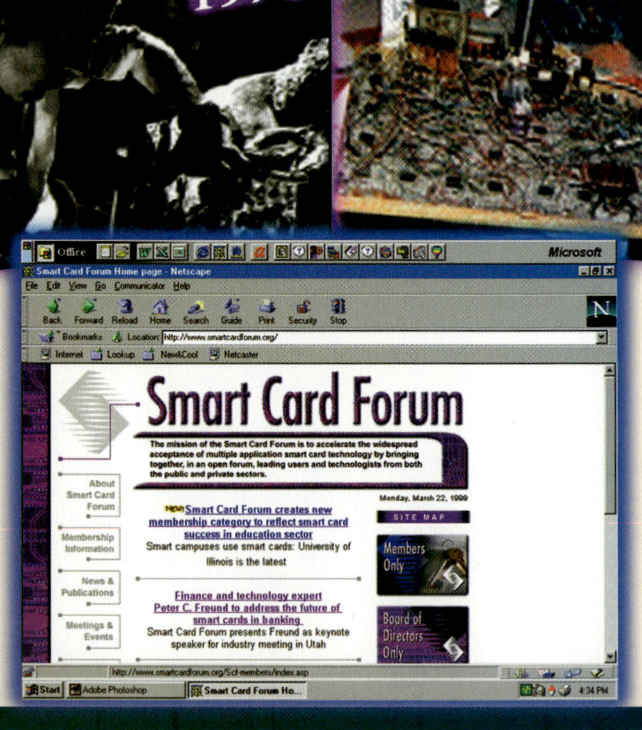

Two types of smart cards are available. One is a memory card. The memory card contains a stored value that the owner can spend on transactions such as paying bus fare or making a call from a public telephone. When the value is depleted, the card is useless.

The second is an intelligent card. The intelligent card contains a central processing unit that can store data and make decisions. Owners begin with a set monetary value, such as $100, and then they can make a purchase that does not exceed this figure. If the amount is insufficient, they can add money to the balance. These functions are similar to the activities you will perform using Microsoft Excel in this project for the Fun-N-Sun Sojourn company, where you will enter numbers in predefined storage areas, or cells, and then calculate a sum.

The smart card originated in 1974 when Roland Moreno, a reporter and self-taught inventor, secured a chip on an epoxy card. His vision was for merchants to accept electronic payments by inserting three cards in his Take the Money and Run (TMR) machine. One card identified the merchant, the second contained the customer's electronic money, and the third had a list of deadbeat accounts that could not be used to make a transaction. Pictures and descriptions of Moreno's invention and other smart card developments are found in the Smart Card Museum (www.cardshow.com/museum).

Today, chips for the cards are manufactured by such industry leaders as Motorola, Gemplus, and Schlumberger. These companies are working to meet the demand for the cards, which is increasing at a rate of 30 percent annually. With an ever-growing global marketplace, smart cards are a smart way of doing business.

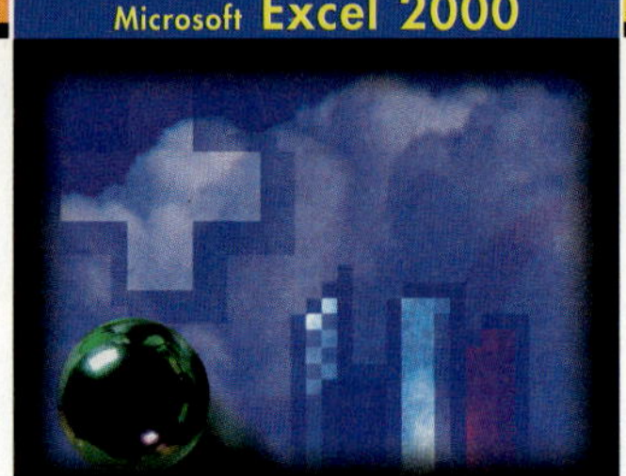

Microsoft Excel 2000

Creating a Worksheet and Embedded Chart

CASE PERSPECTIVE

While on spring break in the Bahamas four years ago, Kylie Waiter and three of her friends came up with the idea of creating a worldwide travel agency that catered to young adults. After graduation, they invested $3,000 each and started their dream company, Fun-N-Sun Sojourn. Thanks to their market savvy and the popularity of personal computers and the World Wide Web, the company has become the premier provider of student vacations.

As sales continue to grow, the management at Fun-N-Sun Sojourn has realized they need a better tracking system for first quarter sales. As a result, they have asked you to prepare a first quarter sales worksheet that shows the sales for the first quarter.

In addition, Kylie has asked you to create a graphical representation of the first quarter sales because she has little tolerance for lists of numbers.

What Is Microsoft Excel 2000?

Microsoft Excel is a powerful spreadsheet program that allows you to organize data, complete calculations, make decisions, graph data, develop professional looking reports, publish organized data to the Web, and access real-time data from Web sites. The four major parts of Excel are:

- **Worksheets** Worksheets allow you to enter, calculate, manipulate, and analyze data such as numbers and text. The term worksheet means the same as spreadsheet.
- **Charts** Charts pictorially represent data. Excel can draw a variety of two-dimensional and three-dimensional charts.
- **Databases** Databases manage data. For example, once you enter data onto a worksheet, Excel can sort the data, search for specific data, and select data that meets a criteria.
- **Web Support** Web support allows Excel to save workbooks or parts of a workbook in HTML format so they can be viewed and manipulated using a browser. You also can access real-time data using Web queries.

Project One — Fun-N-Sun Sojourn First Quarter Sales

From your meeting with Fun-N-Sun Sojourn's management, you have determined the following needs, source of data, calculations, and chart requirements.

Need: An easy-to-read worksheet (Figure 1-1) that shows Fun-N-Sun Sojourn's first quarter sales for each key vacation package (Bahamas Repose, Daytona Delight, Key West Haven, and South Padre Del Sol) by sales channel (Mail, Campus, Telephone, and Web). The worksheet also should include total sales for each vacation package, each sales channel, and total company sales for the first quarter.

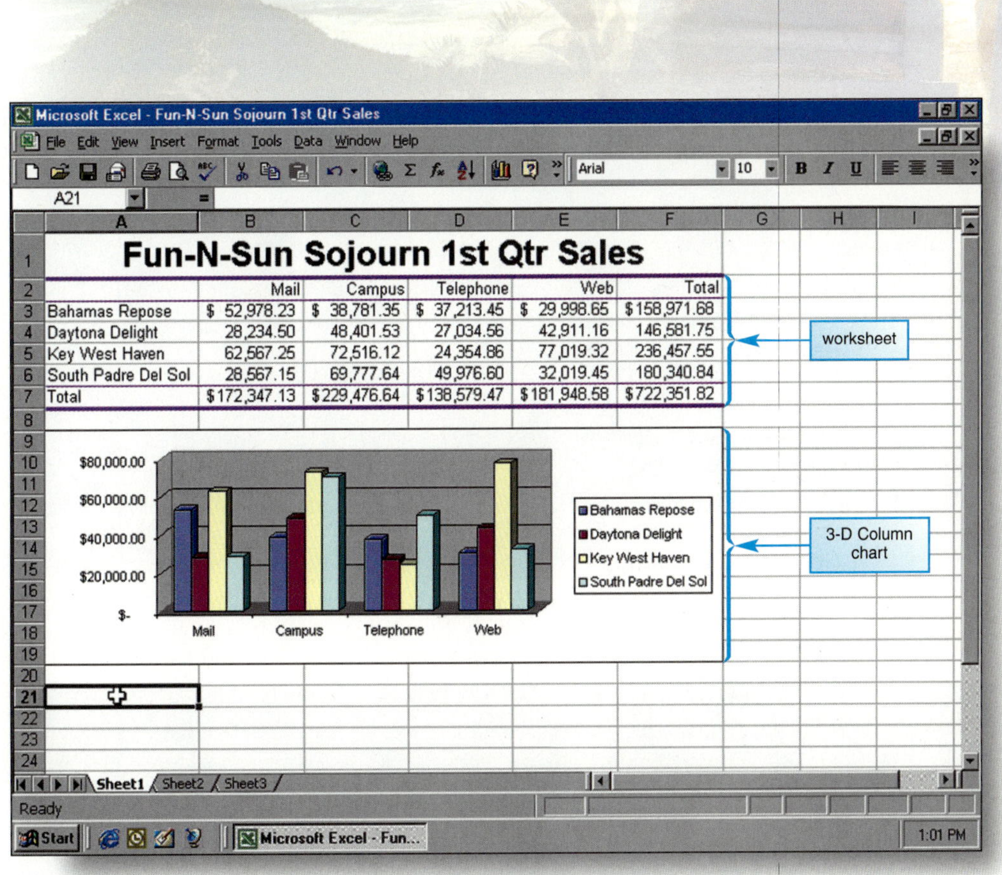

Fun-N-Sun Sojourn 1st Qtr Sales

	Mail	Campus	Telephone	Web	Total
Bahamas Repose	$ 52,978.23	$ 38,781.35	$ 37,213.45	$ 29,998.65	$158,971.68
Daytona Delight	28,234.50	48,401.53	27,034.56	42,911.16	146,581.75
Key West Haven	62,567.25	72,516.12	24,354.86	77,019.32	236,457.55
South Padre Del Sol	28,567.15	69,777.64	49,976.60	32,019.45	180,340.84
Total	$172,347.13	$229,476.64	$138,579.47	$181,948.58	$722,351.82

FIGURE 1-1

Source of Data: The data for the worksheet is available at the end of the first quarter from Eric Jacobs, chief financial officer (CFO) of Fun-N-Sun Sojourn.

Calculations: You have determined that the following calculations must be made for the worksheet: (a) total first quarter sales for each of the four vacation packages; (b) total first quarter sales for each of the four sales channels; and (c) total company first quarter sales.

Chart Requirements: Below the worksheet, construct a 3-D Column chart that compares the amount of sales to the four sales channels for each vacation package.

More About 2000

Excel 2000

With its shortcut menus, toolbars, what-if analysis tools, and Web capabilities, Excel 2000 is one of the easiest, and yet most powerful, worksheet packages available. Its easy-to-use formatting features allow you to produce professional looking worksheets. Its powerful analytical tools make it possible to answer complicated what-if questions with a few clicks of the mouse button. Its Web capabilities allow you to create, publish, view, and analyze data on an intranet or the World Wide Web.

More About 2000

Worksheet Development

The key to developing a useful worksheet is careful planning. Careful planning can reduce your effort significantly and result in a worksheet that is accurate, easy to read, flexible, and useful. When analyzing a problem and designing a worksheet solution, you should follow these steps: (1) define the problem, including need, source of data, calculations, and charting and Web requirements; (2) design the worksheet; (3) enter the data and formulas; and (4) test the worksheet.

Starting Excel

To start Excel, Windows must be running. Perform the following steps to start Excel.

To Start Excel

1 Click the Start button on the taskbar and then point to New Office Document.

The Start menu displays (Figure 1-2).

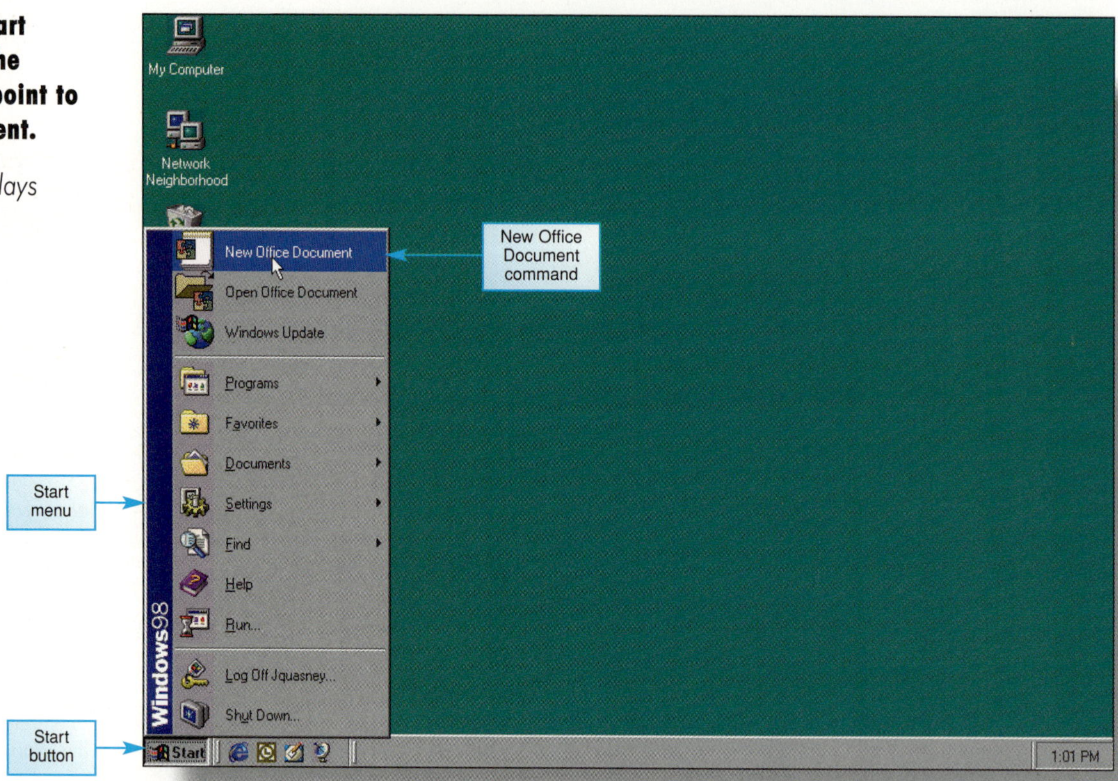

FIGURE 1-2

2 Click New Office Document. If necessary, click the General tab, and then point to the Blank Workbook icon.

The New Office Document dialog box displays (Figure 1-3).

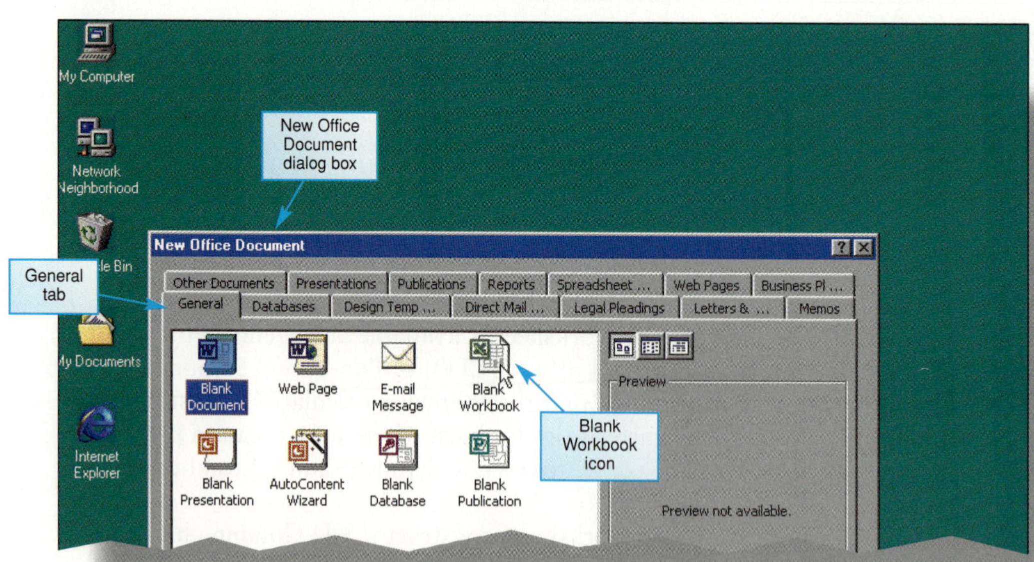

FIGURE 1-3

3 **Double-click the Blank Workbook icon. If necessary, maximize the Excel window by double-clicking its title bar.**

Excel displays an empty workbook titled Book1 (Figure 1-4).

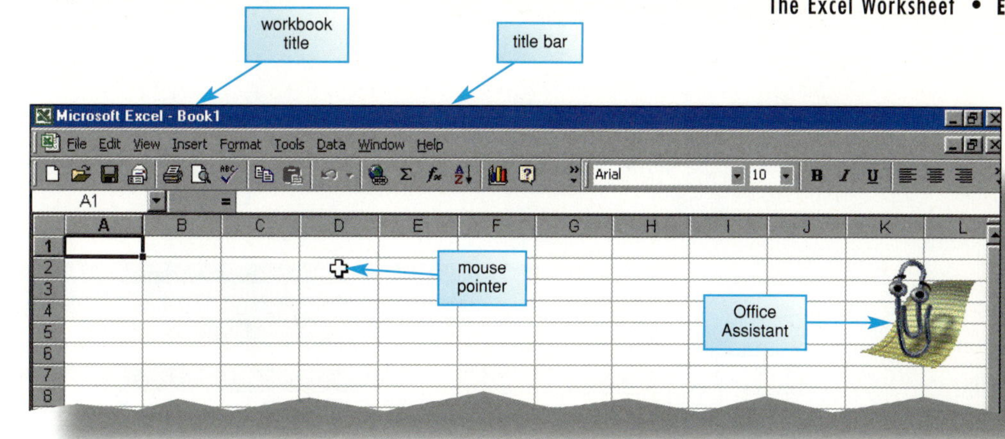

FIGURE 1-4

4 **If the Office Assistant displays (Figure 1-4), click Help on the menu bar and then click Hide the Office Assistant.**

Excel hides the Office Assistant (Figure 1-5). The purpose of the Office Assistant will be discussed later in this project.

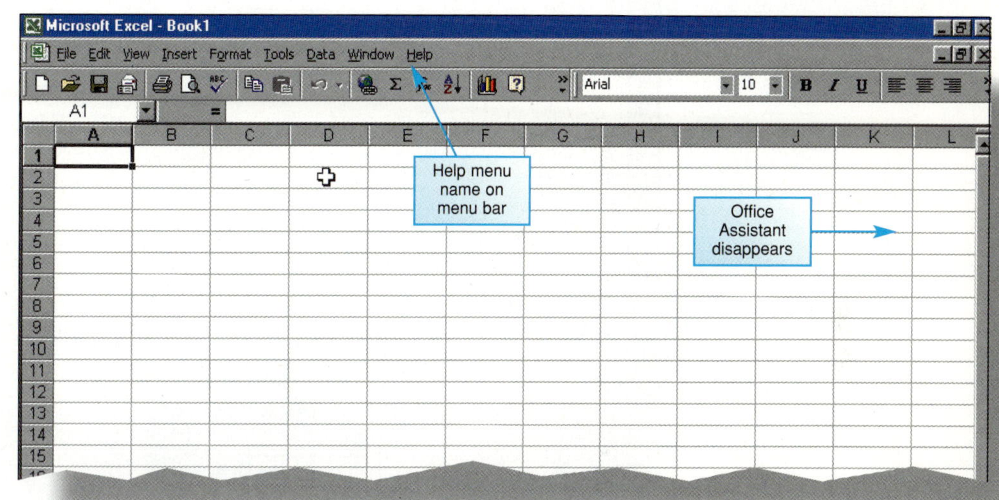

FIGURE 1-5

The Excel Worksheet

When Excel starts, it creates a new empty workbook, called Book1. The **workbook** (Figure 1-6 on the next page) is like a notebook. Inside the workbook are sheets, called **worksheets**. Each sheet name displays on a **sheet tab** at the bottom of the workbook. For example, Sheet1 is the name of the active worksheet displayed in the workbook called Book1. If you click the tab labeled Sheet2, Excel displays the Sheet2 worksheet. A new workbook opens with three worksheets. If necessary, you can add additional worksheets to a maximum of 255. This project uses only the Sheet1 worksheet. Later projects will use multiple worksheets in a workbook.

The Worksheet

The worksheet is organized into a rectangular grid containing columns (vertical) and rows (horizontal). A column letter above the grid, also called the **column heading**, identifies each **column**. A row number on the left side of the grid, also called the **row heading**, identifies each **row**. With the screen resolution set to 800 × 600, twelve columns (A through L) and twenty-five rows (1 through 25) of the worksheet display on the screen when the worksheet is maximized as shown in Figure 1-6 on the next page.

More About 2000

The Office Assistant

In Step 4 you were instructed to hide the Office Assistant. You may want to have it remain on the screen because it can be helpful. For example, the Office Assistant tracks your work. If you complete a task and the Office Assistant knows a better, alternative way to carry out the task, it will add the alternative to its tips list. You can view the most recent tip by clicking the light bulb when it displays above the Office Assistant.

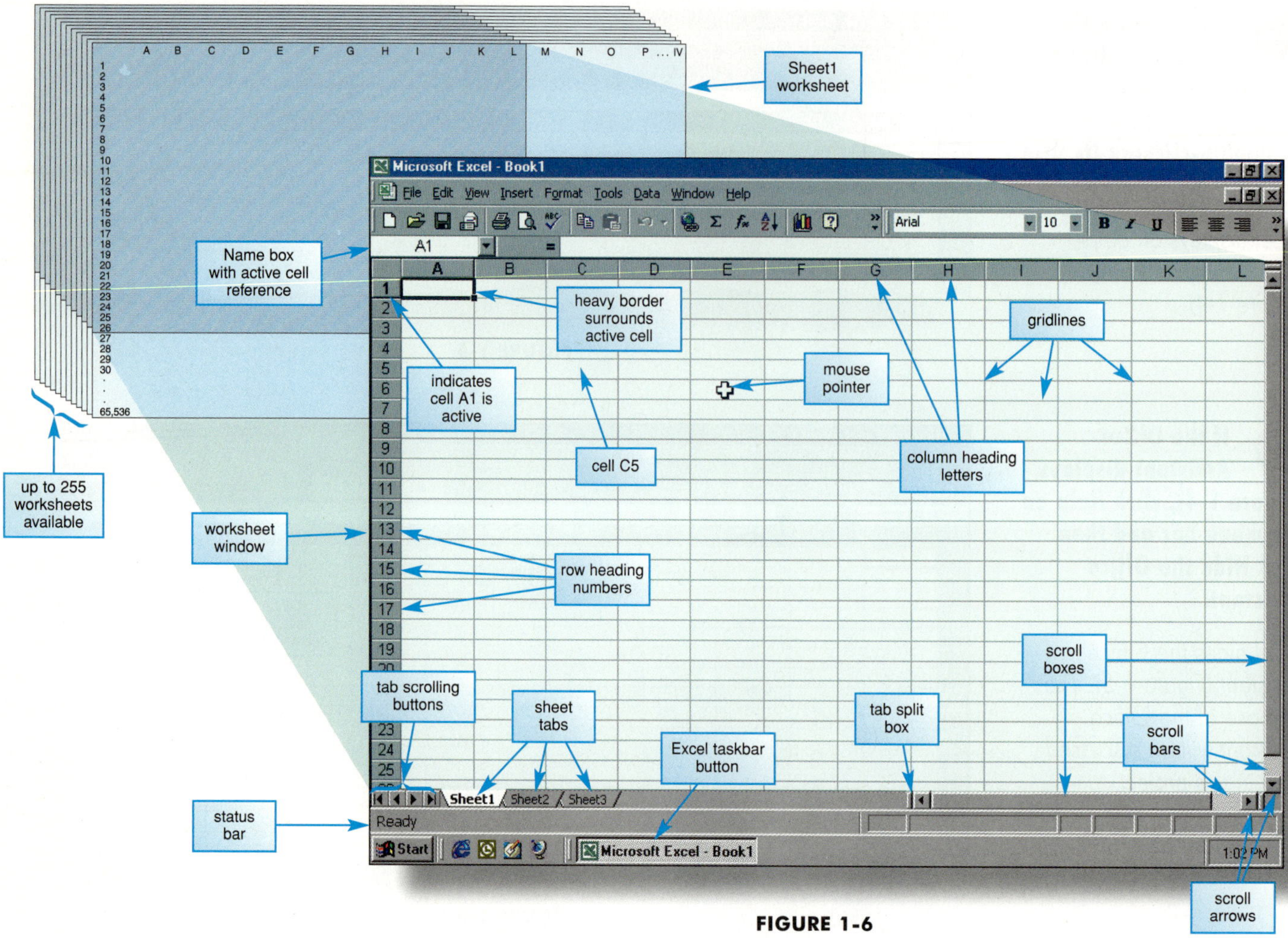

FIGURE 1-6

The Worksheet Size and Window

Excel's maximum 256 columns and 65,536 rows make for a gigantic worksheet — so big, in fact, that you might imagine it takes up the entire wall of a large room. Your computer screen, by comparison, is like a small window that allows you to view only a small area of the worksheet at one time. While you cannot see the entire worksheet, you can move the Excel window over the worksheet to view any part of it. To display the last row in a blank worksheet, press the END key and then press the DOWN ARROW key. Press CTRL+HOME to return to the top of the worksheet.

The intersection of each column and row is a cell. A **cell** is the basic unit of a worksheet into which you enter data. Each worksheet in a workbook has 256 columns and 65,536 rows for a total of 16,777,216 cells. The column headings begin with A and end with IV. The row headings begin with 1 and end with 65,536. Only a small fraction of the active worksheet displays on the screen at one time.

A cell is referred to by its unique address, or **cell reference**, which is the coordinates of the intersection of a column and a row. To identify a cell, specify the column letter first, followed by the row number. For example, cell reference C5 refers to the cell located at the intersection of column C and row 5 (Figure 1-6).

One cell on the worksheet, designated the **active cell**, is the one in which you can enter data. The active cell in Figure 1-6 is A1. Cell A1 is identified in three ways. First, a heavy border surrounds the cell; second, the **active cell reference** displays immediately above column A in the **Name box**; and third, the column heading A and row heading 1 light up so it is easy to see which cell is active (Figure 1-6).

The horizontal and vertical lines on the worksheet itself are called **gridlines**. Gridlines make it easier to see and identify each cell in the worksheet. If desired, you can turn the gridlines off so they do not display on the worksheet, but it is recommended that you leave them on.

The mouse pointer in Figure 1-6 has the shape of a block plus sign. The mouse pointer displays as a **block plus sign** whenever it is located in a cell on the worksheet. Another common shape of the mouse pointer is the block arrow. The mouse pointer turns into the **block arrow** whenever you move it outside the worksheet or when you drag cell contents between rows or columns. The other mouse pointer shapes are described when they display on the screen during this and subsequent projects.

The Mouse Pointer Shape

The mouse pointer can change to one of more than fifteen different shapes, such as an arrow, cross hair, or chart symbol, depending on the task you are performing in Excel and the mouse pointer's location on the screen.

Worksheet Window

You view the portion of the worksheet displayed on the screen through a **worksheet window** (Figure 1-6). Below and to the right of the worksheet window are **scroll bars**, **scroll arrows**, and **scroll boxes** that you can use to move the window around to view different parts of the active worksheet. To the right of the sheet tabs at the bottom of the screen is the **tab split box**. You can drag the tab split box (Figure 1-6) to increase or decrease the view of the sheet tabs. When you decrease the view of the sheet tabs, you increase the length of the horizontal scroll bar; and vice versa.

The menu bar, Standard toolbar, and Formatting toolbar display at the top of the screen just below the title bar (Figure 1-7a). The Standard toolbar and Formatting toolbar display on one row. Because both of these toolbars cannot fit entirely on a single row, a portion or all of the Standard toolbar displays on the left of the row and a portion or all of the Formatting toolbar displays on the right.

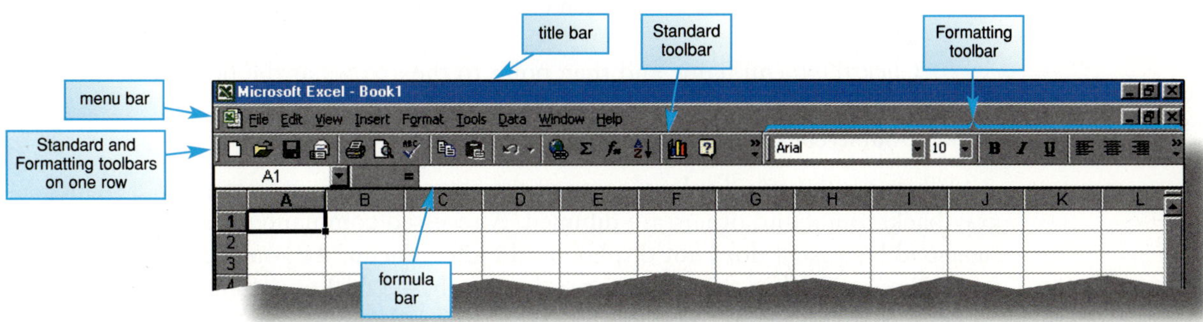

(a) Menu Bar and Toolbars

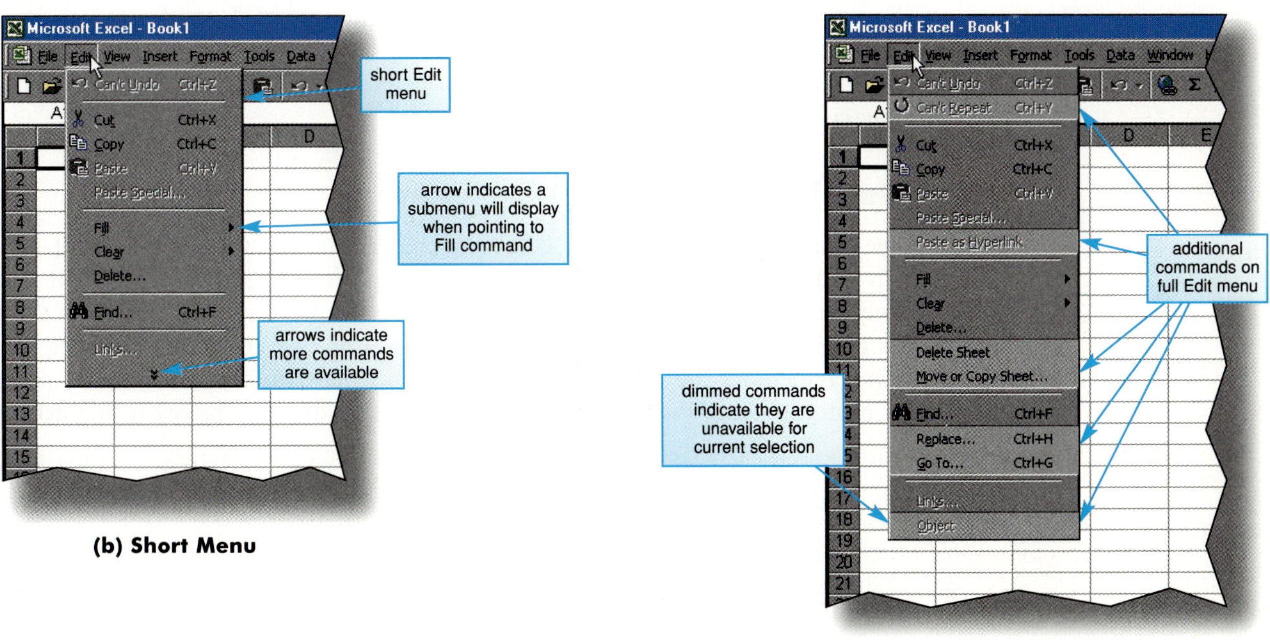

(b) Short Menu

(c) Full Menu

FIGURE 1-7

The Worksheet Window

If the buttons and toolbars on your screen are distracting to you, you can increase the number of rows and columns displayed by clicking Full Screen on the View menu. Excel immediately will hide the buttons and bars, thus increasing the size of the window. Excel also displays a small toolbar with the Full Screen button on it. Click the Full Screen button to return to the previous view.

Menu Bar

The menu bar is a special toolbar that includes the Excel menu names (Figure 1-7a on the previous page). The menu bar that displays when you start Excel is the **Worksheet menu bar**. Each menu name represents a menu of commands that you can use to retrieve, store, print, and manipulate data on the worksheet. When you point to a menu name on the menu bar, the area of the menu bar containing the name changes to a button. To display a menu, such as the Edit menu, click the Edit menu name on the menu bar (Figures 1-7b and 1-7c on the previous page). If you point to a command with an arrow on the right, a submenu displays from which you can choose a command.

When you click a menu name on the menu bar, a **short menu** displays listing the most recently used commands (Figure 1-7b). If you wait a few seconds or click the arrows at the bottom of the short menu (Figure 1-7b), the full menu displays. The **full menu** lists all the commands associated with a menu (Figure 1-7c). You also can display a full menu immediately by double-clicking the menu name on the menu bar. In this book, when you display a menu, always display the full menu using one of the following techniques.

1. Click the menu name on the menu bar and then wait a few seconds.
2. Click the menu name and then click the arrows at the bottom of the short menu.
3. Click the menu name and then point to the arrows at the bottom of the short menu.
4. Double-click the menu name.

When a full menu displays, some of the commands are recessed into a shaded gray background and others are dimmed. A recessed command is called a **hidden command** because it does not display on the short menu. As you use Excel, it automatically personalizes the short menus for you based on how often you use commands. That is, as you use hidden commands, Excel unhides them and places them on the short menu. A **dimmed command** displays in a faint type, which indicates it is not available for the current selection.

The menu bar can change to include other menu names depending on the type of work you are doing in Excel. For example, if you are working with a chart sheet rather than a worksheet, the **Chart menu bar** displays with menu names that reflect charting commands.

Standard Toolbar and Formatting Toolbar

The Standard toolbar (Figure 1-8a) and the Formatting toolbar (Figure 1-8b) contain buttons and list boxes that allow you to perform frequent tasks more quickly than when using the menu bar. For example, to print a worksheet, you click the Print button on the Standard toolbar. Each button has a picture on the button face that helps you remember the button's function. Also, when you move the mouse pointer over a button or box, the name of the button or box displays below it in a **ScreenTip**.

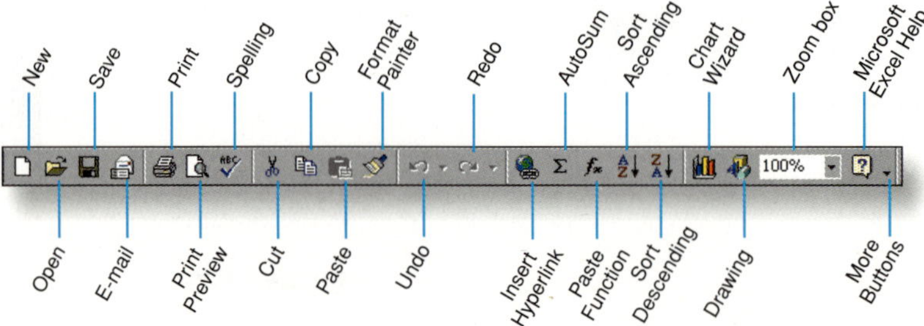

FIGURE 1-8a Standard Toolbar

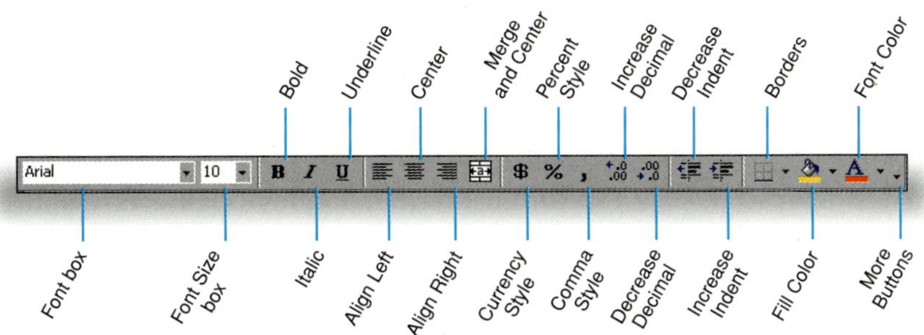

FIGURE 1-8b Formatting Toolbar

More About

Toolbars on Separate Rows

You can point to an empty location on the Formatting toolbar and drag it immediately below the Standard toolbar to display the toolbars on separate rows.

Figures 1-8a and 1-8b illustrate the Standard and Formatting toolbars and describe the functions of the buttons. Each of the buttons and list boxes will be explained in detail when they are used in the projects.

Both the Standard and Formatting toolbars are preset to display on the same row, immediately below the menu bar. To display the entire Standard toolbar, double-click the move handle on the left. Excel slides the Formatting toolbar to the right so the toolbars appear as shown in Figure 1-9a.

More About

Sizing Toolbar Buttons

If you have difficulty seeing the small buttons on the toolbars, you can increase their size by clicking View on the menu bar, pointing to Toolbars, clicking Customize on the Toolbars submenu, clicking the Options tab, clicking the Large icons check box, and clicking the Close button.

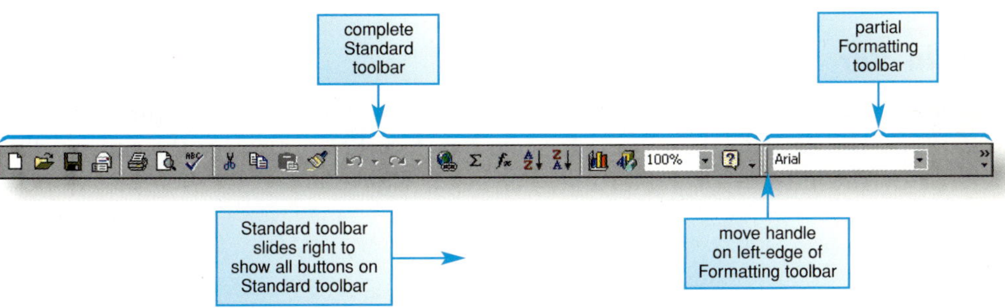

(a) Complete Standard Toolbar and Partial Formatting Toolbar

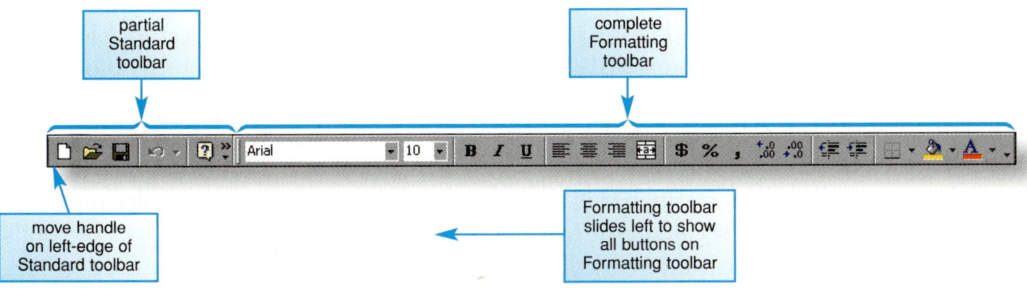

(b) Partial Standard Toolbar and Complete Formatting Toolbar

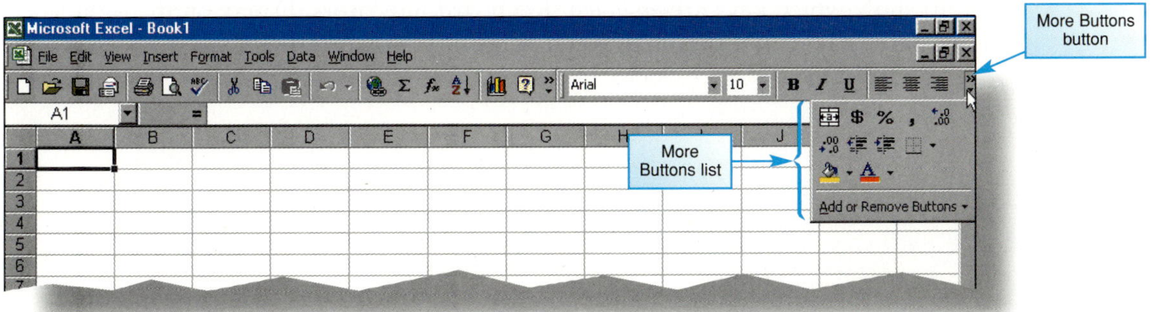

(c) More Buttons List

FIGURE 1-9

To display the entire Formatting toolbar, double-click the move handle on its left edge or drag the move handle to the left. When you display the complete Formatting toolbar, a portion of the Standard toolbar is hidden (Figure 1-9b on the previous page).

An alternative to sliding one toolbar over another is to use the **More Buttons button** on a toolbar to display the buttons that are hidden (Figure 1-9c on the previous page).

As with the menus, Excel will personalize the toolbars. That is, if you use a hidden button on a partially displayed toolbar, Excel will remove the button from the More Buttons list (Figure 1-9c) and promote it to the toolbar. For example, if you click the Bold button and then the Italic button on the Formatting toolbar in Figure 1-9c, Excel will promote these buttons to the Formatting toolbar and remove buttons from the Standard or Formatting toolbars to make room on the row.

More About 2000

Resetting Toolbars

If your toolbars have a different set of buttons than shown in Figures 1-8a and 1-8b on the previous page, it is likely that a prior user added or deleted buttons. To reset the Standard or Formatting toolbars, click View on the menu bar, point to Toolbars, click Customize on the Toolbars submenu, click the Toolbars tab, click the name of the toolbar to reset, click the Reset button, and click the OK button. To remove promoted buttons, click the Options tab, click the Reset my usage data button, click the Yes button, and click the Close button.

Resetting Menus and Toolbars

Each project in this book begins with resetting the menus and toolbars to the settings as they were at the initial installation of the software. To reset your menus and toolbars so they display exactly as shown in this book, follow the steps outlined in Appendix C.

Formula Bar

Below the Standard and Formatting toolbars is the formula bar (Figure 1-10). As you type, the data displays in the **formula bar**. Excel also displays the active cell reference on the left side of the formula bar in the **Name box**.

Status Bar

Immediately above the Windows taskbar at the bottom of the screen is the status bar. The **status bar** displays a brief description of the command selected (highlighted) in a menu, the function of the button the mouse pointer is pointing to, or the current activity (mode) in progress (Figure 1-10). **Mode indicators**, such as Enter and Ready, display on the status bar and specify the current mode of Excel. When the mode is **Ready**, Excel is ready to accept the next command or data entry. When the mode indicator reads **Enter**, Excel is in the process of accepting data through the keyboard into the active cell.

In the middle of the status bar is the AutoCalculate area. The **AutoCalculate area** can be used in place of a calculator to view the sum, average, or other types of totals of a group of numbers on the worksheet. The AutoCalculate area is discussed in detail later in this project.

Keyboard indicators, such as NUM (Num Lock), CAPS (Caps Lock), and SCRL (Scroll) show which keys are engaged. Keyboard indicators display on the right side of the status bar within the small rectangular boxes (Figure 1-10).

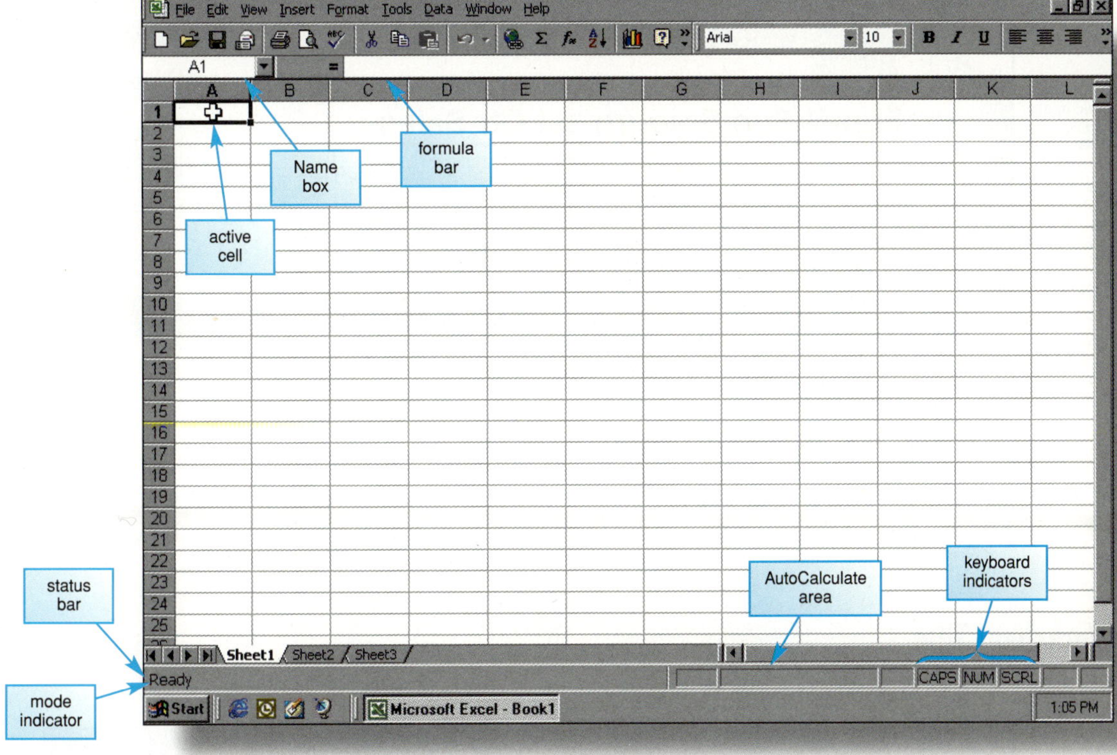

FIGURE 1-10

Selecting a Cell

To enter data into a cell, you first must select it. The easiest way to **select a cell** (make it active) is to use the mouse to move the block plus sign to the cell and then click.

An alternative method is to use the **arrow keys** that are located just to the right of the typewriter keys on the keyboard. An arrow key selects the cell adjacent to the active cell in the direction of the arrow on the key.

You know a cell is selected (active) when a heavy border surrounds the cell (cell A1 in Figure 1-10) and the active cell reference displays in the Name box on the left side of the formula bar.

More About 2000

Selecting a Cell

You can select any cell by typing the cell reference, such as B4, in the Name box on the left side of the formula bar.

Entering Text

In Excel, any set of characters containing a letter, hyphen (as in a telephone number), or space is considered **text**. Text is used to place titles on the worksheet, such as worksheet titles, column titles, and row titles. In Project 1 (Figure 1-11 on the next page), the worksheet title, Fun-N-Sun Sojourn 1st Qtr Sales, identifies the worksheet. The column titles in row 2 (Mail, Campus, Telephone, Web, and Total) identify the data in each column. The row titles in column A (Bahamas Repose, Daytona Delight, Key West Haven, South Padre Del Sol, and Total) identify the data in each row.

More About 2000

Text

A text entry in a cell can contain from 1 to 32,767 characters. Although text entries are used primarily to identify parts of the worksheet, other applications exist in which text entries are data that you dissect, string together, and manipulate using text functions.

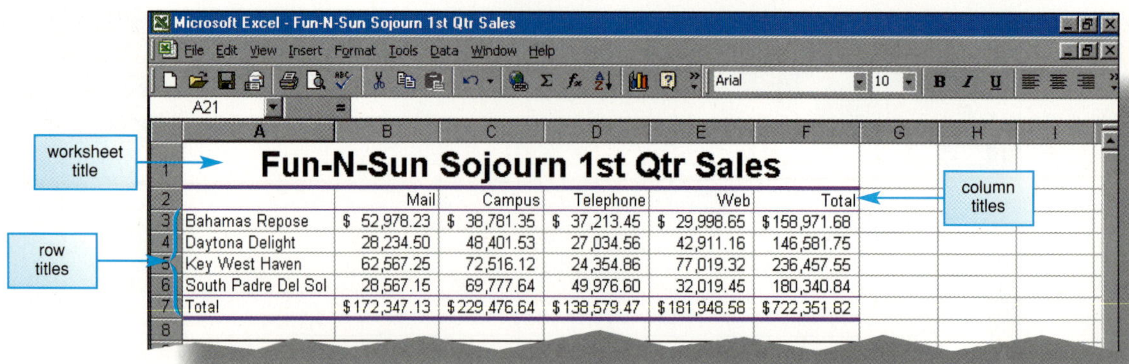

FIGURE 1-11

Entering the Worksheet Title

The following steps show how to enter the worksheet title in cell A1. Later in this project, the worksheet title will be formatted so it displays as shown in Figure 1-11.

To Enter the Worksheet Title

1 **Click cell A1.**

Cell A1 becomes the active cell and a heavy border surrounds it (Figure 1-12).

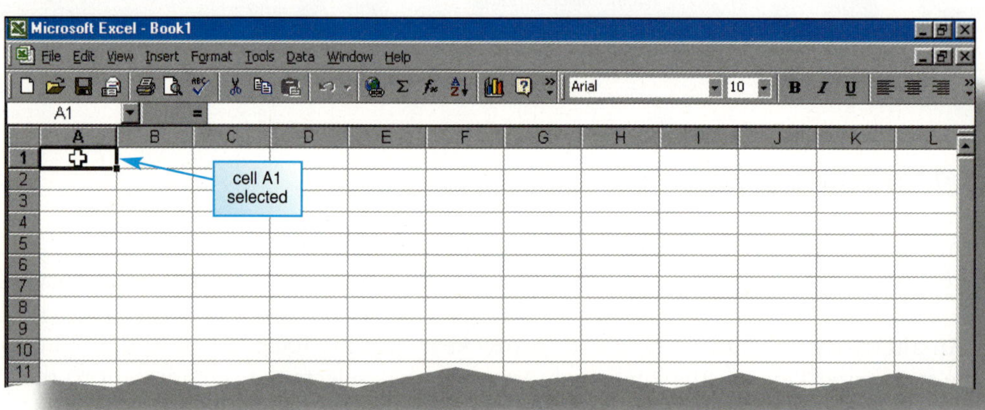

FIGURE 1-12

2 **Type** `Fun-N-Sun Sojourn 1st Qtr Sales` **in cell A1.**

The title displays in the formula bar and in cell A1. The text in cell A1 is followed by the insertion point (Figure 1-13). The ***insertion point*** *is a blinking vertical line that indicates where the next character typed will display.*

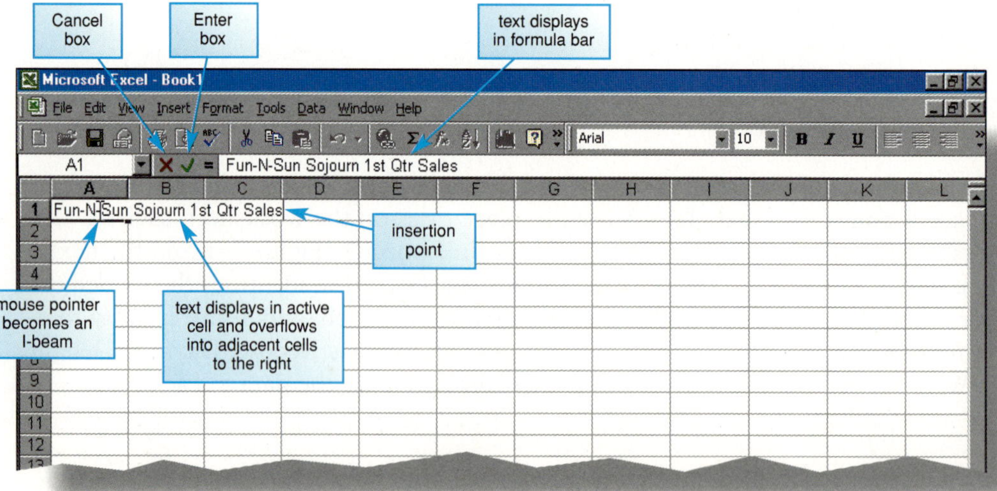

FIGURE 1-13

Point to the Enter box (Figure 1-14).

When you begin typing a cell entry, Excel displays two boxes in the formula bar: the Cancel box and the Enter box.

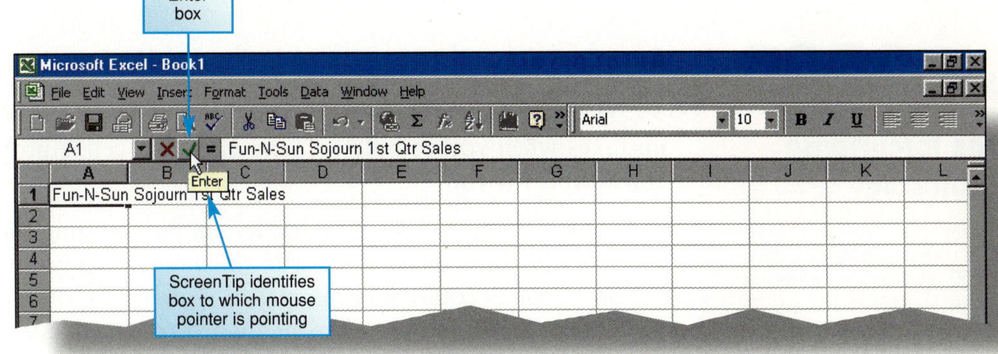

FIGURE 1-14

Click the Enter box to complete the entry.

Excel enters the worksheet title in cell A1 (Figure 1-15).

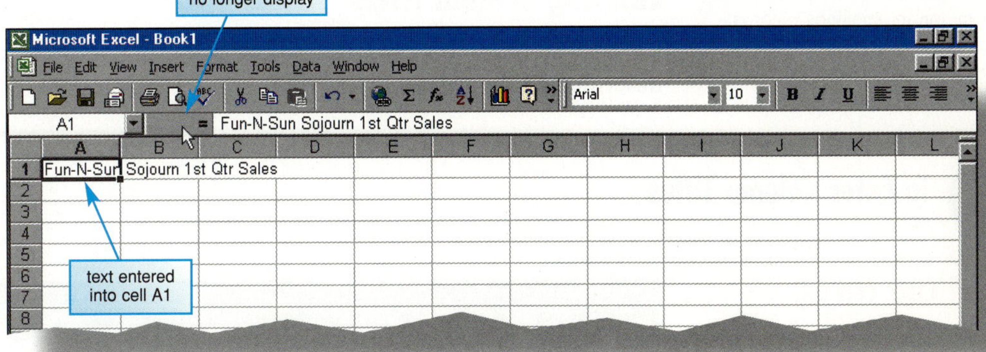

FIGURE 1-15

1. Click any cell other than active cell
2. Press ENTER
3. Press an arrow key
4. Press HOME, PAGE UP PAGE DOWN, or END

More About 2000

Entering Data

Unless you are entering large amounts of data into a worksheet, you probably will want to set the ENTER key to complete an entry without changing the active cell location. If pressing the ENTER key changes the active cell location, you can change it by clicking Options on the Tools menu, clicking the Edit tab, removing the check mark from the Move Selection after Enter check box, and then clicking the OK button. If you want the ENTER key to change the active cell location, click the desired direction in the Move Selection after Enter list box and then click the OK button.

In Step 3, clicking the **Enter box** completes the entry. Clicking the **Cancel box** cancels the entry.

When you complete a text entry into a cell, a series of events occurs. First, Excel positions the text left-aligned in the cell. **Left-aligned** means the cell entry is positioned at the far left in the cell. Therefore, the F in the worksheet title, Fun-N-Sun Sojourn 1st Qtr Sales, begins in the leftmost position of cell A1.

Second, when the text is longer than the width of a column, Excel displays the overflow characters in adjacent cells to the right as long as these adjacent cells contain no data. In Figure 1-15, the width of cell A1 is approximately nine characters. The text consists of 31 characters. Therefore, Excel displays the overflow characters from cell A1 in cells B1, C1, and D1 because these cells are empty. If cell B1 contained data, only the first nine characters in cell A1 would display on the worksheet. Excel would hide the overflow characters, but they still would remain stored in cell A1 and display in the formula bar whenever cell A1 is the active cell.

Third, when you complete an entry by clicking the Enter box, the cell in which the text is entered remains the active cell.

Correcting a Mistake While Typing

If you type the wrong letter and notice the error before clicking the Enter box or pressing the **ENTER key**, use the **BACKSPACE key** to erase all the characters back to and including the one that is wrong. To cancel the entire entry before entering it into the cell, click the Cancel box in the formula bar or press the **ESC key**. If you see an error in a cell, select the cell and retype the entry. Later in this project, additional error-correction techniques are covered.

The IntelliSense Technology

Microsoft's IntelliSense technology is built into all the Office 2000 applications. It tries to understand what you are doing and helps you do it. The smart toolbars, adaptive menus, Office Assistant, and AutoCorrect are part of the IntelliSense technology. For example, Excel can correct common misspellings automatically. When you press the ENTER key, the corrected text is entered in the cell.

AutoCorrect

The **AutoCorrect feature** of Excel works behind the scenes, correcting common mistakes when you complete a text entry in a cell. AutoCorrect makes three types of corrections for you:

1. Corrects two initial capital letters by changing the second letter to lowercase.
2. Capitalizes the first letter in the names of days.
3. Replaces commonly misspelled words with their correct spelling. For example, it will change the misspelled word *recieve* to *receive* when you complete the entry. AutoCorrect will correct the spelling automatically of more than 400 commonly misspelled words.

Entering Column Titles

To enter the column titles, select the appropriate cell and then enter the text, as described in the following steps.

To Enter Column Titles

1 Click cell B2.

Cell B2 becomes the active cell. The active cell reference in the Name box changes from A1 to B2 (Figure 1-16).

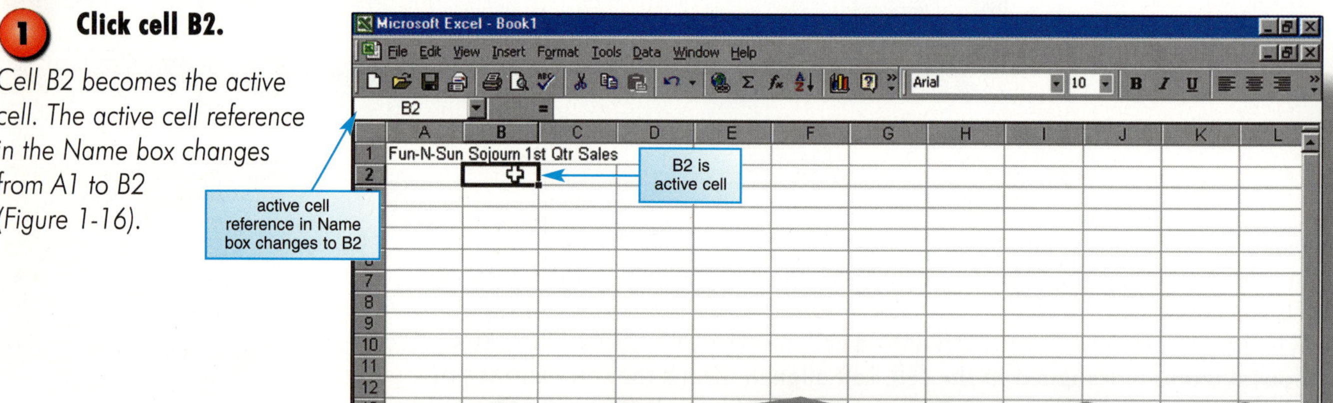

FIGURE 1-16

2 Type `Mail` **in cell B2.**

Excel displays Mail in the formula bar and in cell B2 (Figure 1-17).

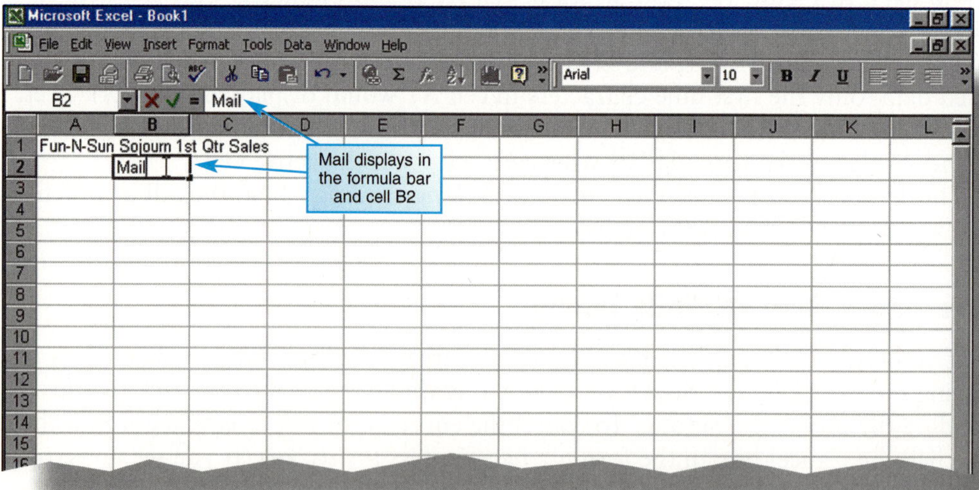

FIGURE 1-17

Press the RIGHT ARROW key.

Excel enters the column title, Mail, in cell B2 and makes cell C2 the active cell (Figure 1-18).

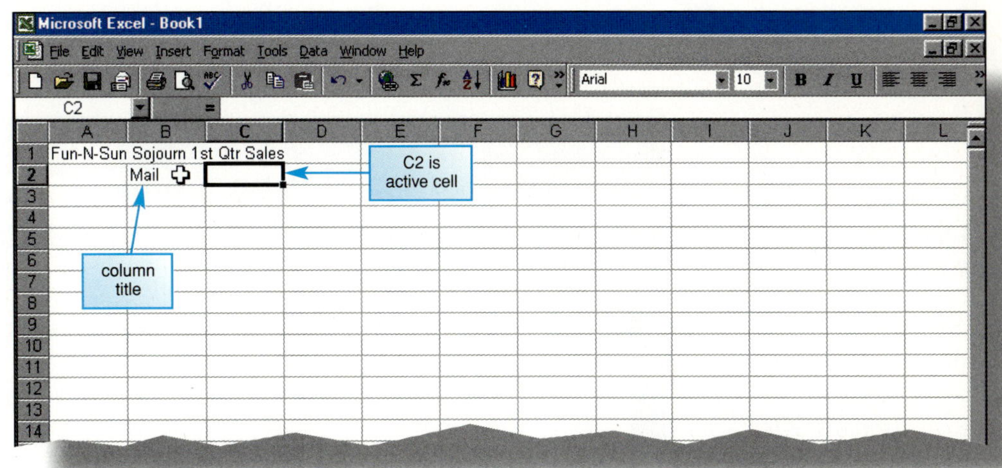

FIGURE 1-18

Repeat Steps 2 and 3 for the remaining column titles in row 2. That is, enter `Campus` **in cell C2,** `Telephone` **in cell D2,** `Web` **in cell E2, and** `Total` **in cell F2. Complete the last entry in cell F2 by pressing the ENTER key.**

The column titles display left-aligned as shown in Figure 1-19.

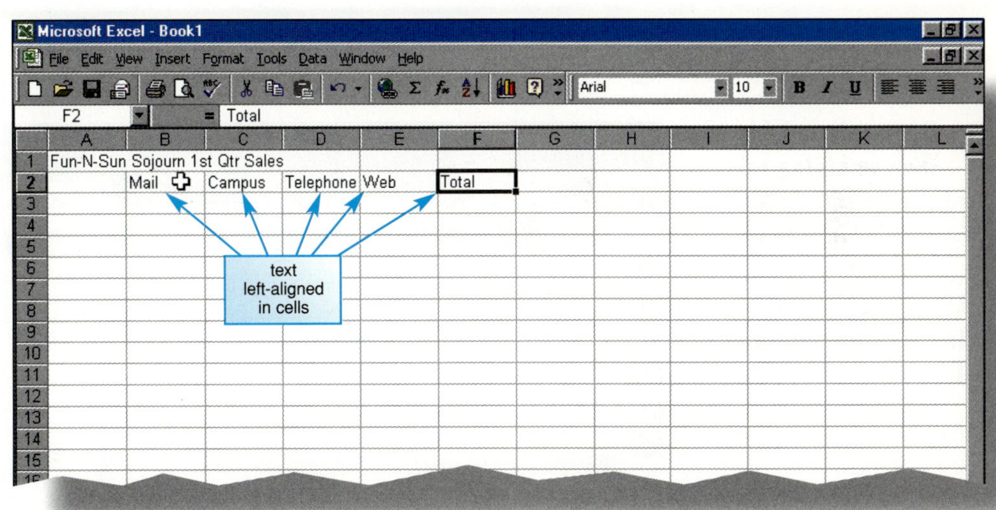

FIGURE 1-19

If the next entry is in an adjacent cell, use the arrow keys to complete the entry in a cell. When you press an arrow key to complete an entry, the adjacent cell in the direction of the arrow (up, down, left, or right) becomes the active cell. If the next entry is in a non-adjacent cell, click the next cell in which you plan to enter data, or click the Enter box, or press the ENTER key and then click the appropriate cell for the next entry.

Entering Row Titles

The next step in developing the worksheet in Project 1 is to enter the row titles in column A. This process is similar to entering the column titles and is described in the steps on the next page.

To Enter Row Titles

1 **Click cell A3. Type** `Bahamas Repose` **and then press the DOWN ARROW key.**

Excel enters the row title Bahamas Repose in cell A3 and cell A4 becomes the active cell (Figure 1-20).

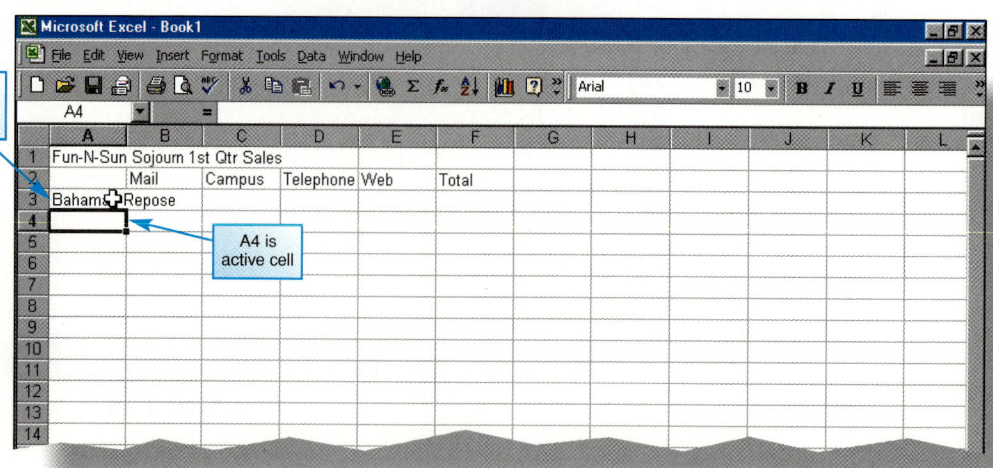

FIGURE 1-20

2 **Repeat Step 1 for the remaining row titles in column A. Enter** `Daytona Delight` **in cell A4,** `Key West Haven` **in cell A5,** `South Padre Del Sol` **in cell A 6, and** `Total` **in cell A7.**

The row titles display as shown in Figure 1-21.

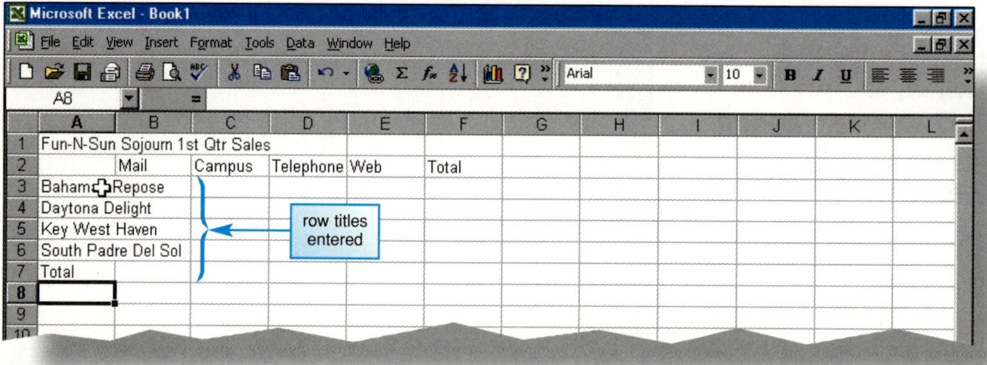

FIGURE 1-21

In Excel, text is left-aligned in a cell, unless you change it by realigning it. Excel treats any combination of numbers, spaces, and nonnumeric characters as text. For example, the following entries are text:

401AX21, 921-231, 619 321, 883XTY

Entering Data

When you type the first few letters of an entry in a cell, Excel can complete the entry for you, based on the entries already in that column. This is called the AutoComplete feature. If you want to pick an entry from a list of column entries, right-click a cell in the column and then click Pick from List on the shortcut menu.

Entering Numbers

In Excel, you can enter numbers into cells to represent amounts. **Numbers** can contain only the following characters:

0 1 2 3 4 5 6 7 8 9 + - ( ) , / . $ % E e

If a cell entry contains any other keyboard character (including spaces), Excel interprets the entry as text and treats it accordingly. The use of the special characters is explained when they are used in a project.

In Project 1, the Fun-N-Sun first quarter numbers are summarized in Table 1-1.

Table 1-1 Fun-N-Sun First Quarter Data				
	MAIL	CAMPUS	TELEPHONE	WEB
Bahamas Repose	52978.23	38781.35	37213.45	29998.65
Daytona Delight	28234.50	48401.53	27034.56	42911.16
Key West Haven	62567.25	72516.12	24354.86	77019.32
South Padre Del Sol	28567.15	69777.64	49976.60	32019.45

Entering Numbers as Text

Some times, you will want Excel to treat numbers, such as ZIP codes, as text. To enter a number as text, start the entry with an apostrophe (').

These numbers, which represent first quarter sales for each of the sales channels and vacation packages, must be entered in rows 3, 4, 5, and 6. The following steps illustrate how to enter these values one row at a time.

To Enter Numeric Data

1 Click cell B3. Type 52978.23 **and then press the RIGHT ARROW key.**

Excel enters the number 52978.23 in cell B3 and changes the active cell to cell C3 (Figure 1-22). The numbers are formatted with dollar signs and commas later in this project.

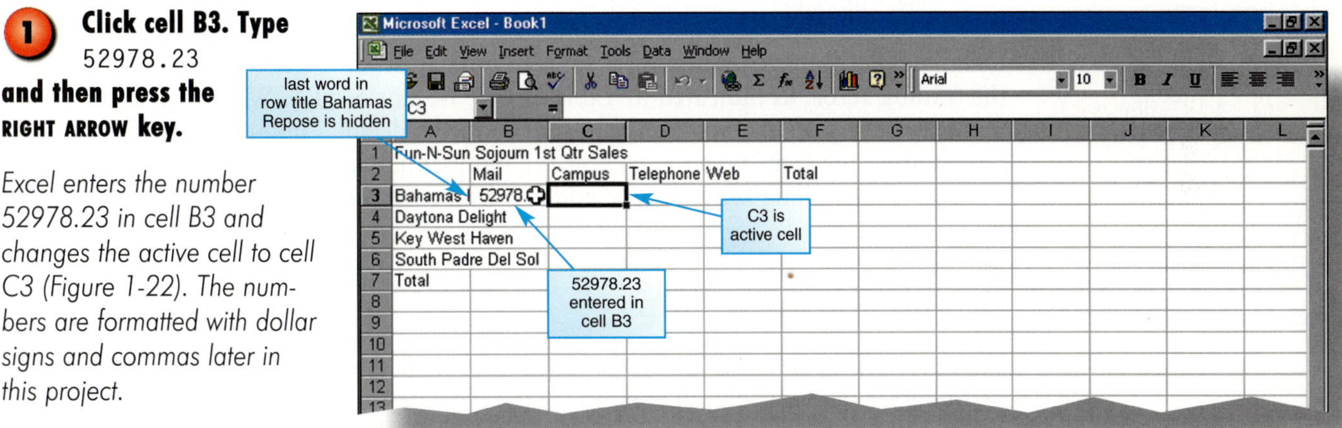

FIGURE 1-22

2 Enter 38781.35 **in cell C3,** 37213.45 **in cell D3, and** 29998.65 **in cell E3.**

Row 3 now contains the first quarter sales by sales channel for the vacation package Bahamas Repose (Figure 1-23). The numbers in row 3 are ***right-aligned****, which means Excel displays the cell entry to the far right in the cell.*

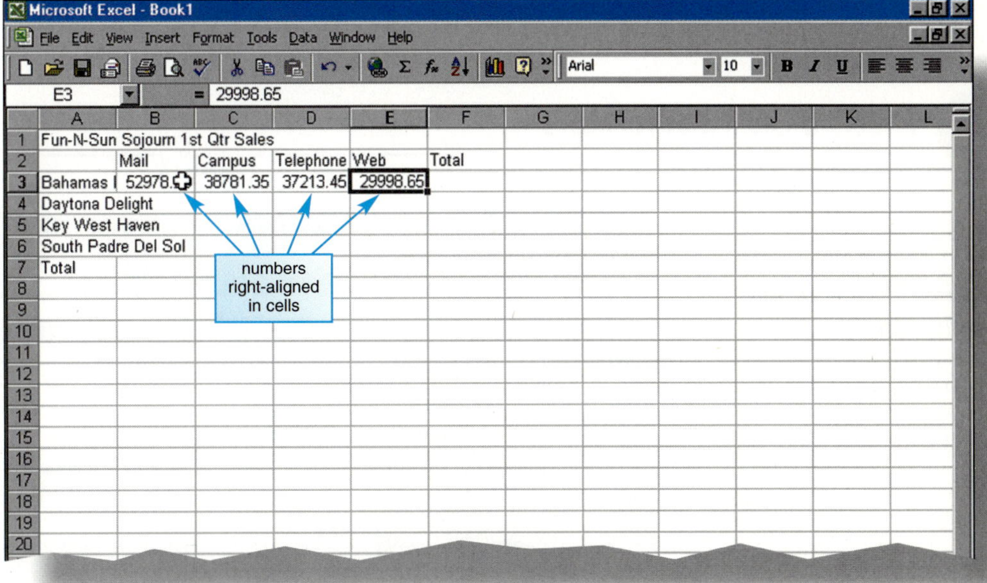

FIGURE 1-23

3 **Click cell B4. Enter the remaining first quarter sales provided on the previous page in Table 1-1 by sales channel for each of the three remaining vacation packages in rows 4, 5, and 6.**

The first quarter sales display as shown in Figure 1-24.

data entered on worksheet

row titles partially display

FIGURE 1-24

More About 2000

Number Limits

In Excel, a number can be between approximately -1 x 10^{308} and 1 x 10^{308}. That is, a negative 1 followed by 308 zeros or a positive 1 followed by 308 zeros. To enter a number such as 5,000,000,000,000, you can type 5,000,000,000,000 or you can type 5E12, which stands for 5 x 10^{12}.

As you can see in Figure 1-24, when you enter data into the cell in column B, the row titles in column A partially display. Later when the worksheet is formatted, the row titles will display in their entirety.

Steps 1 through 3 complete the numeric entries. You are not required to type dollar signs, commas, or trailing zeros. As you can see in Figure 1-24, if you typed the trailing zeros, as indicated in Table 1, they do not display. When you enter a number that has cents, however, you must add the decimal point and the numbers representing the cents when you enter the number. Later in this project, dollar signs, commas, and trailing zeros will be added to improve the appearance of the numbers.

Calculating a Sum

The next step in creating the first quarter sales worksheet is to determine the total first quarter sales by Mail in column B. To calculate this value in cell B7, Excel must add the numbers in cells B3, B4, B5, and B6. Excel's **SUM function** provides a convenient means to accomplish this task.

To use the SUM function, first you must identify the cell in which the sum will be stored after it is calculated. Then, you can use the **AutoSum button** on the Standard toolbar to enter the SUM function as shown in the following steps.

To Sum a Column of Numbers

1 **Click cell B7 and then point to the AutoSum button on the Standard toolbar.**

Cell B7 becomes the active cell (Figure 1-25).

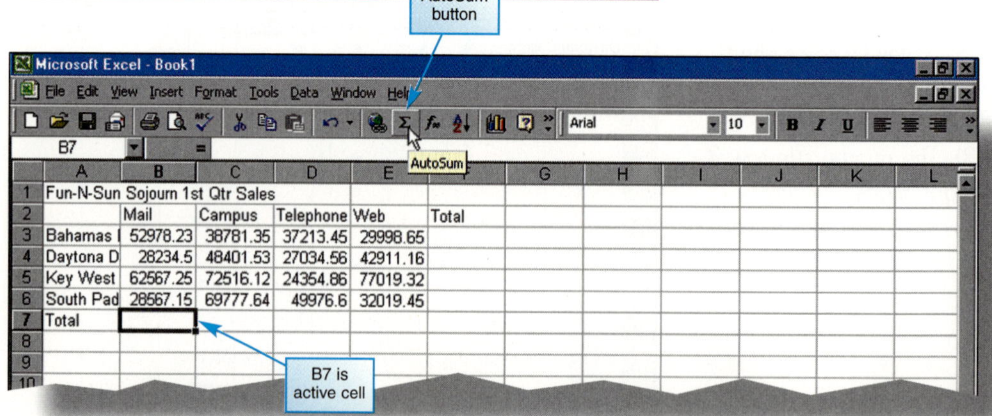

FIGURE 1-25

2 **Click the AutoSum button.**

Excel responds by displaying = SUM(B3:B6) in the formula bar and in the active cell B7 (Figure 1-26). The B3:B6 within parentheses following the function name SUM is Excel's way of identifying the cells B3 through B6. Excel also surrounds the proposed cells to sum with a moving border, called a ***marquee****.*

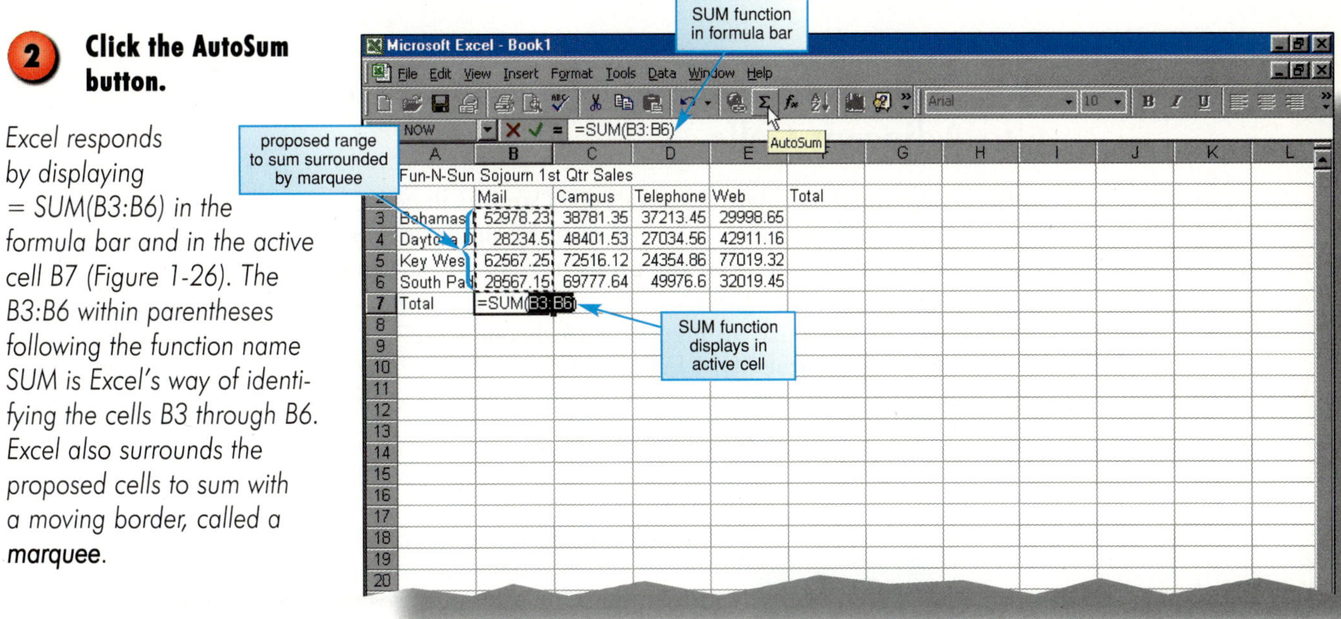

FIGURE 1-26

3 **Click the AutoSum button a second time.**

Excel enters the sum of the first quarter sales in cell B7 (Figure 1-27). The SUM function assigned to cell B7 displays in the formula bar when cell B7 is the active cell.

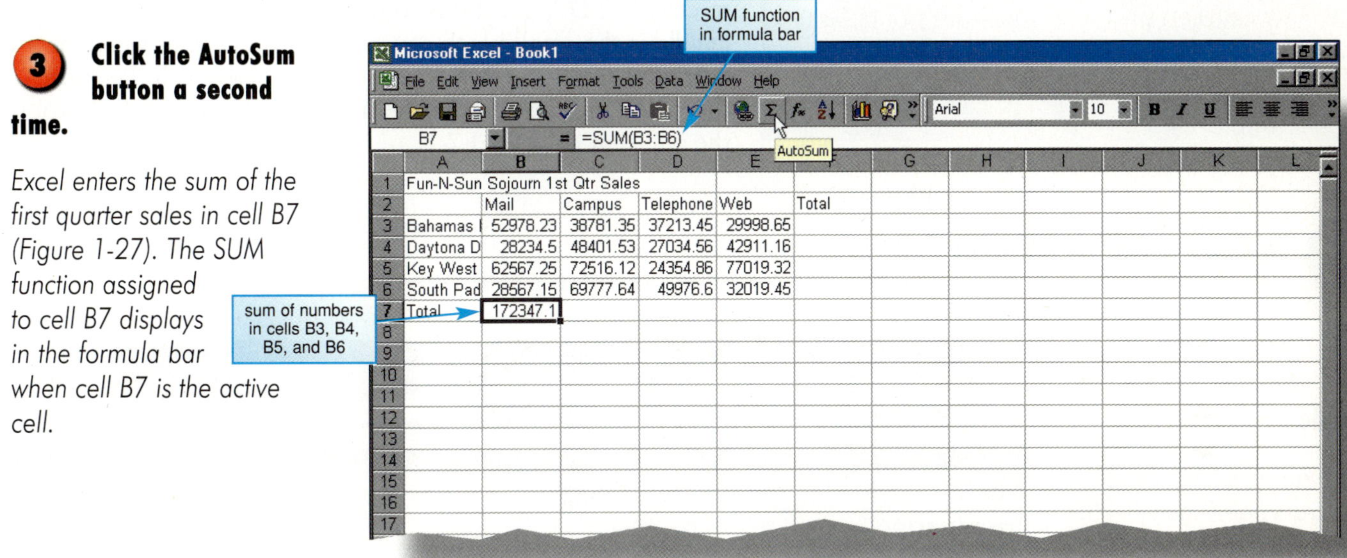

FIGURE 1-27

Other Ways

1. Press ALT+EQUAL SIGN (=) twice
2. Click Edit Formula (=) box in formula bar, select SUM in Functions list, click OK button

When you enter the SUM function using the AutoSum button, Excel automatically selects what it considers to be your choice of the group of cells to sum. The group of adjacent cells B3, B4, B5, and B6 is called a range. A **range** is a series of two or more adjacent cells in a column or row or a rectangular group of cells. Many Excel operations, such as summing numbers, take place on a range of cells.

When proposing the range to sum, Excel first looks for a range of cells with numbers above the active cell and then to the left. If Excel proposes the wrong range, you can drag through the correct range anytime prior to clicking the AutoSum button a second time. You also can enter the correct range by typing the beginning cell reference, a colon (:), and the ending cell reference.

Using the Fill Handle to Copy a Cell to Adjacent Cells

Excel also must calculate the totals for Campus in cell C7, Telephone in cell D7, and for Web in cell E7. Table 1-2 illustrates the similarities between the entry in cell B7 and the entries required for the totals in cells C7, D7, and E7.

To place the SUM functions in cells C7, D7, and E7, you can follow the same steps shown previously in Figures 1-25 through 1-27. A second, more efficient method is to copy the SUM function from cell B7 to the range C7:E7. The cell being copied is called the **copy area**. The range of cells receiving the copy is called the **paste area**.

Although the SUM function entries are similar in Table 1-2, they are not exact copies. The range in each SUM function entry to the right of cell B7 uses cell references that are one column to the right of the previous column. When you copy cell references, Excel automatically adjusts them for each new position, resulting in the SUM function entries illustrated in Table 1-2. Each adjusted cell reference is called a **relative reference.**

The easiest way to copy the SUM formula from cell B7 to cells C7, D7, and E7 is to use the fill handle. The **fill handle** is the small black square located in the lower-right corner of the heavy border around the active cell. Perform the following steps to use the fill handle to copy cell B7 to the adjacent cells C7:E7.

Table 1-2 SUM Function Entries in Row 7

CELL	*SUM FUNCTION ENTRIES*	*REMARK*
B7	=SUM(B3:B6)	Sums cells B3, B4, B5, and B6
C7	=SUM(C3:C6)	Sums cells C3, C4, C5, and C6
D7	=SUM(D3:D6)	Sums cells D3, D4, D5, and D6
E7	=SUM(E3:E6)	Sums cells E3, E4, E5, and E6

To Copy a Cell to Adjacent Cells in a Row

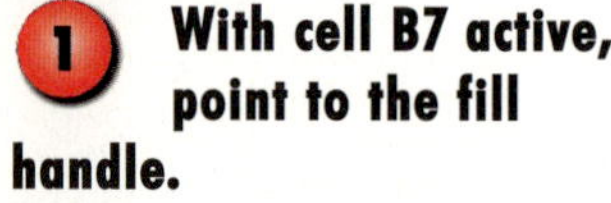

1 With cell B7 active, point to the fill handle.

The mouse pointer changes to a cross hair (Figure 1-28).

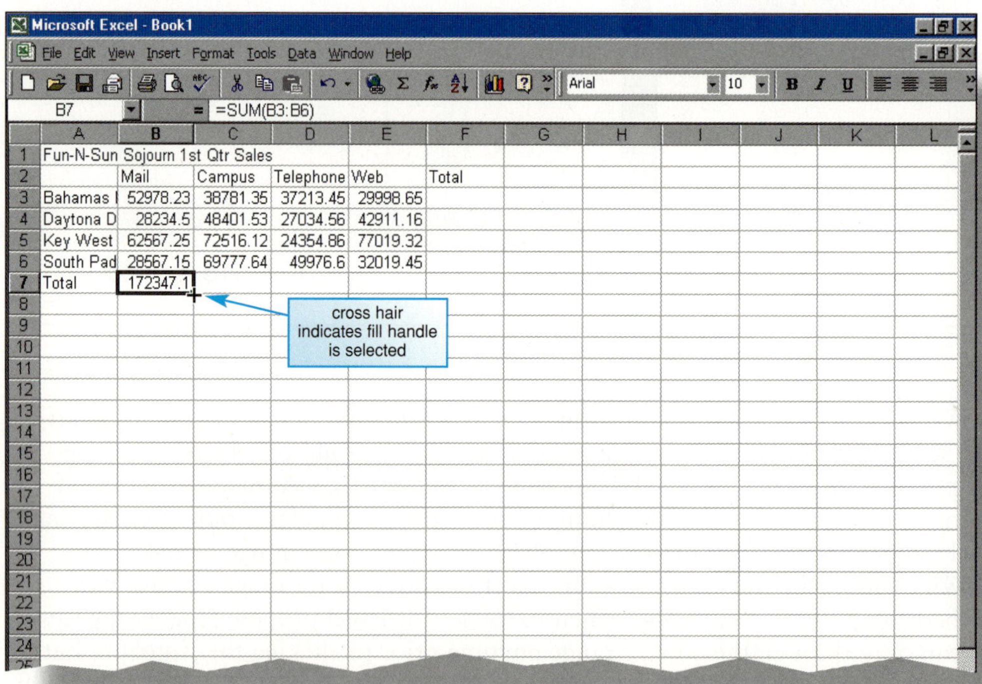

FIGURE 1-28

2 **Drag the fill handle to select the paste area, range C7:E7.**

Excel displays a shaded border around the paste area, range C7:E7, and the copy area, cell B7 (Figure 1-29).

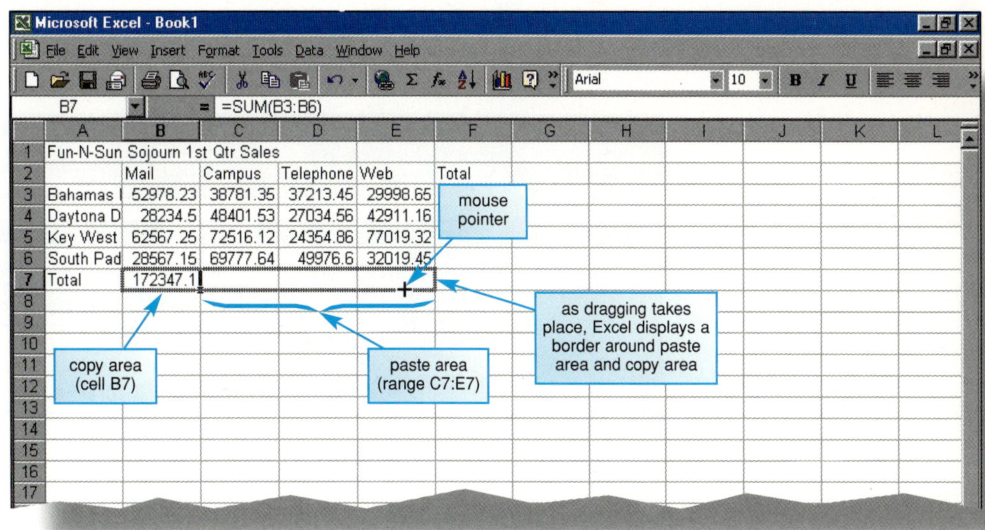

FIGURE 1-29

3 **Release the mouse button.**

Excel copies the SUM function in cell B7 to the range C7:E7 (Figure 1-30). In addition, Excel calculates the sums and enters the results in cells C7, D7, and E7.

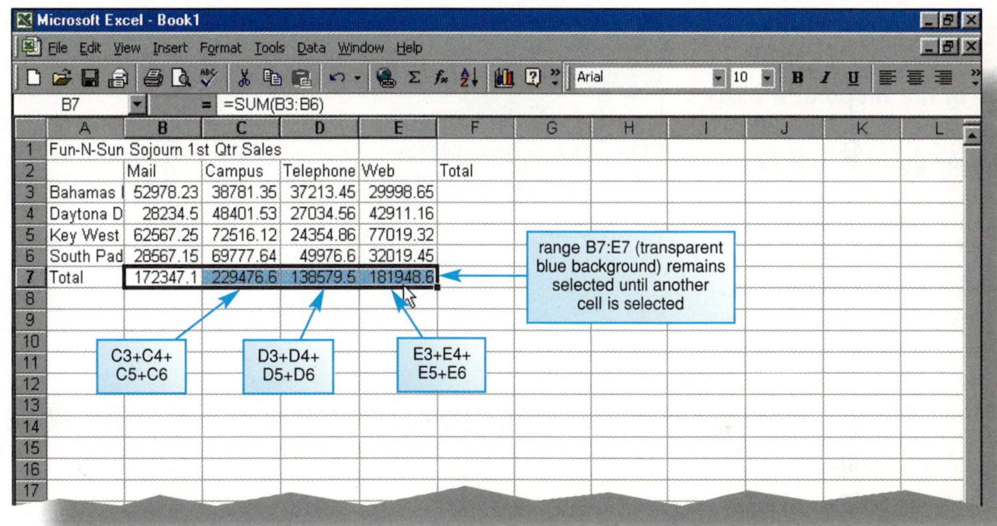

FIGURE 1-30

Once the copy is complete, Excel continues to display a heavy border and transparent (blue) background around cells B7:E7. The heavy border and transparent background indicate a selected range. Cell B7, the first cell in the range, does not display with the transparent background because it is the active cell. If you click any cell, Excel will remove the heavy border and transparent background. The heavy border and transparent (blue) background is called **see-through view**.

Using the Mouse to Copy

Another way to copy a cell or range of cells is to select the copy area, point to the border of the copy area, and then, while holding down the CTRL key, drag the copy area to the paste area. If you drag without holding down the CTRL key, Excel moves the data, rather than copying it.

Determining Row Totals

The next step in building the worksheet is to determine totals for each vacation package and total first quarter sales for the company in column F. Use the SUM function in the same manner as you did when the sales by sales channel were totaled in row 7. In this example, however, all the rows will be totaled at the same time. The steps on the next page illustrate this process.

To Determine Multiple Totals at the Same Time

Click cell F3.

Cell F3 becomes the active cell (Figure 1-31).

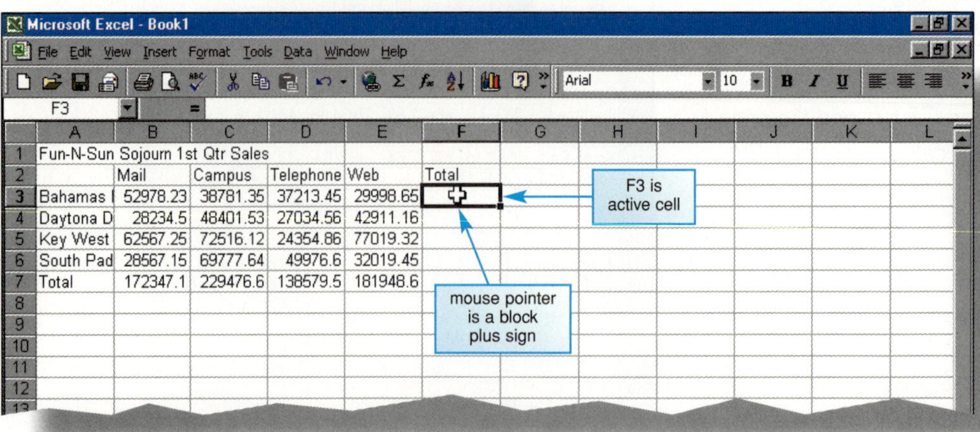

FIGURE 1-31

2 With the mouse pointer in cell F3 and in the shape of a block plus sign, drag the mouse pointer down to cell F7.

Excel highlights the range F3:F7 (Figure 1-32).

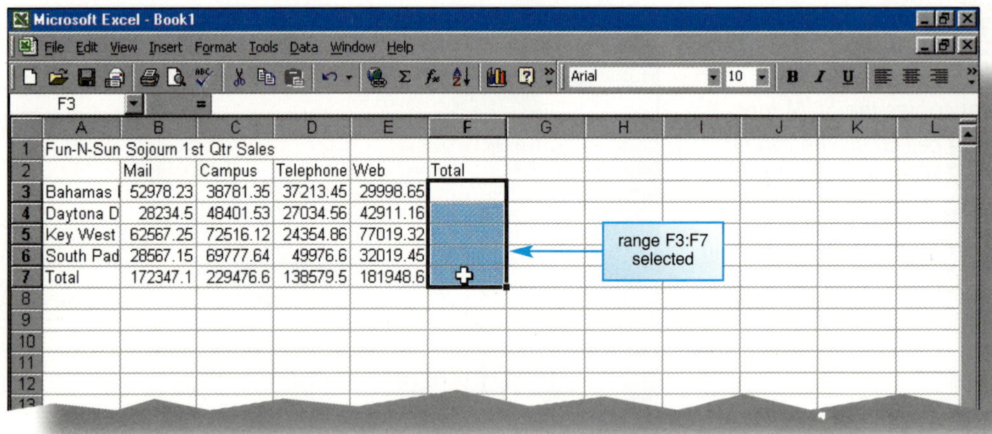

FIGURE 1-32

Click the AutoSum button on the Standard toolbar.

Excel assigns the appropriate SUM functions to cell F3, F4, F5, F6, and F7, and then calculates and displays the sums in the respective cells (Figure 1-33).

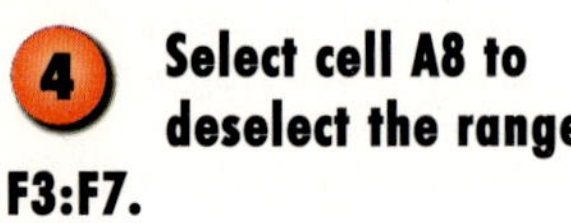

Select cell A8 to deselect the range F3:F7.

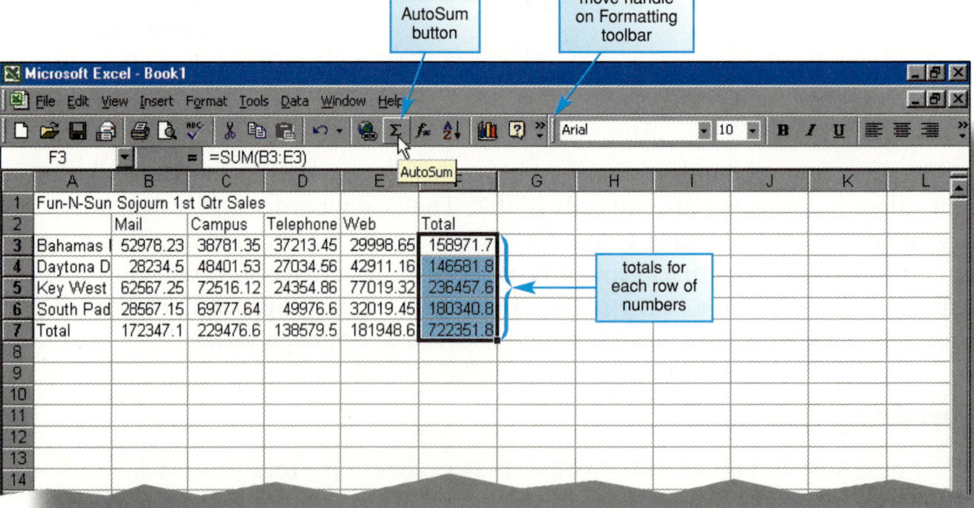

FIGURE 1-33

If each cell in the selected range is next to a row of numbers, Excel assigns the SUM function to each cell in the selected range when you click the AutoSum button. Thus, five SUM functions with different ranges were assigned to the selected range, one for each row. This same procedure could have been used earlier to sum the columns. That is, rather than selecting cell B7, clicking the AutoSum button twice, and then copying the SUM function to the range C7:E7, you could have selected the range B7:E7 and then clicked the AutoSum button once.

Summing Columns and Rows

A quick way to determine all of the totals in row 7 and column F shown in Figure 1-33 at once is to select the range (B3:F7) and then click the AutoSum button. The range B3:F7 includes the numbers to sum plus an additional row (row 7) and an additional column (column F), in which the totals will display.

Formatting the Worksheet

The text, numeric entries, and functions for the worksheet now are complete. The next step is to format the worksheet. You **format** a worksheet to emphasize certain entries and make the worksheet easier to read and understand.

Figure 1-34a shows the worksheet before formatting. Figure 1-34b shows the worksheet after formatting. As you can see from the two figures, a worksheet that is formatted not only is easier to read, but also looks more professional.

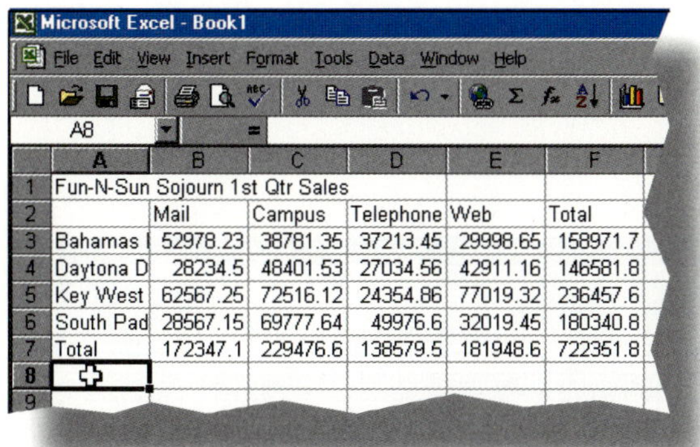

(a) Before Formatting

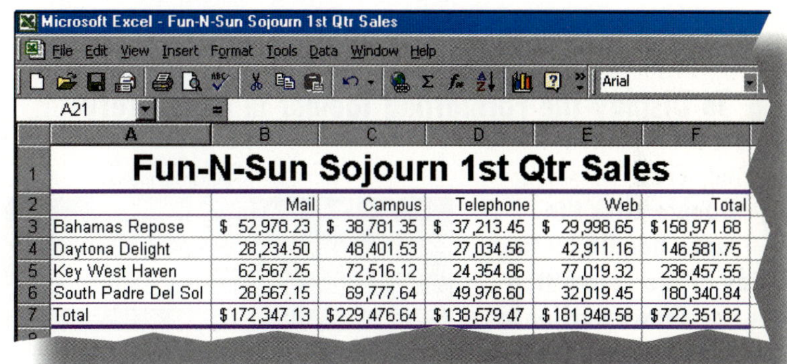

(b) After Formatting

FIGURE 1-34

To change the unformatted worksheet in Figure 1-34a to the formatted worksheet in Figure 1-34b, the following tasks must be completed:

1. Bold the worksheet title in cell A1.
2. Enlarge the worksheet title in cell A1.
3. Format the body of the worksheet. The body of the worksheet, range A2:F7, includes the column titles, row titles, and numbers. Formatting the body of the worksheet results in numbers represented in a dollars-and-cents format, dollar signs in the first row of numbers and the total row, underlines that emphasize portions of the worksheet, and modified column widths.
4. Center the worksheet title in cell A1 across columns A through F.

The process required to format the worksheet is explained in the remainder of this section. Although the format procedures will be carried out in the order described above, you should be aware that you can make these format changes in any order.

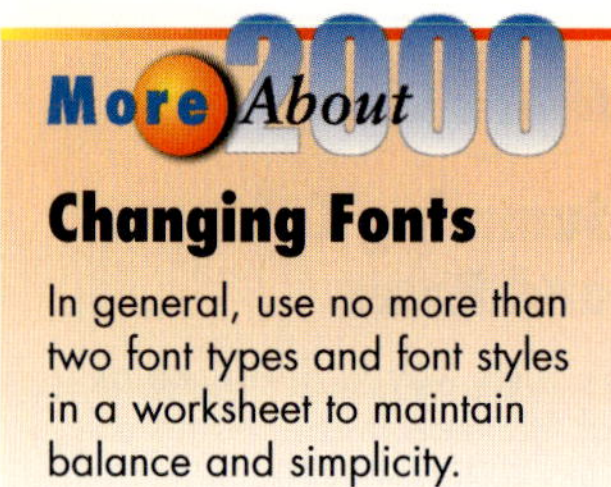

Changing Fonts

In general, use no more than two font types and font styles in a worksheet to maintain balance and simplicity.

Fonts, Font Size, and Font Style

Characters that display on the screen are a specific shape, size, and style. The **font type** defines the appearance and shape of the letters, numbers, and special characters. The **font size** specifies the size of the characters on the screen. Font size is gauged by a measurement system called points. A single **point** is about 1/72 of one inch in height. Thus, a character with a **point size** of 10 is about 10/72 of one inch in height.

Font style indicates how the characters are formatted. Common font styles include regular, bold, underlined, or italicized.

When Excel begins, the preset font type for the entire workbook is Arial with a size and style of 10-point regular. Excel allows you to change the font characteristics in a single cell, a range of cells, the entire worksheet, or the entire workbook.

Displaying the Formatting Toolbar in Its Entirety

Most of the formatting you will do in Excel can be accomplished using the buttons on the Formatting toolbar. Thus, before starting the formatting process display the Formatting toolbar in its entirety as shown in the following steps.

To Display the Formatting Toolbar in Its Entirety

1 Double-click the move handle on the left side of the Formatting toolbar as shown earlier in Figure 1-33 on page E1.26.

The entire Formatting toolbar displays and only a portion of the Standard toolbar displays (Figure 1-35).

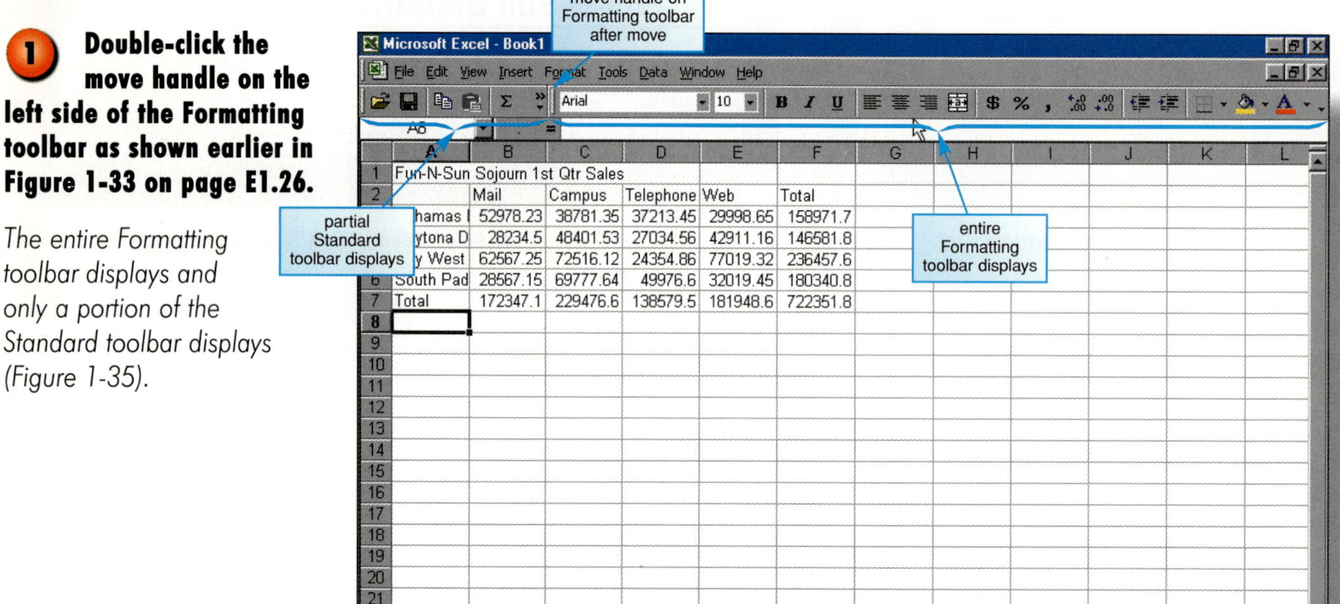

FIGURE 1-35

1. Drag move handle to left
2. Click More Buttons button on Standard toolbar to display hidden buttons

Bolding a Cell

You **bold** an entry in a cell to emphasize it or make it stand out from the rest of the worksheet. Perform the following steps to bold the worksheet title in cell A1.

Steps To Bold a Cell

1 Click cell A1 and then point to the Bold button on the Formatting toolbar.

The ScreenTip displays immediately below the Bold button to identify the function of the button (Figure 1-36).

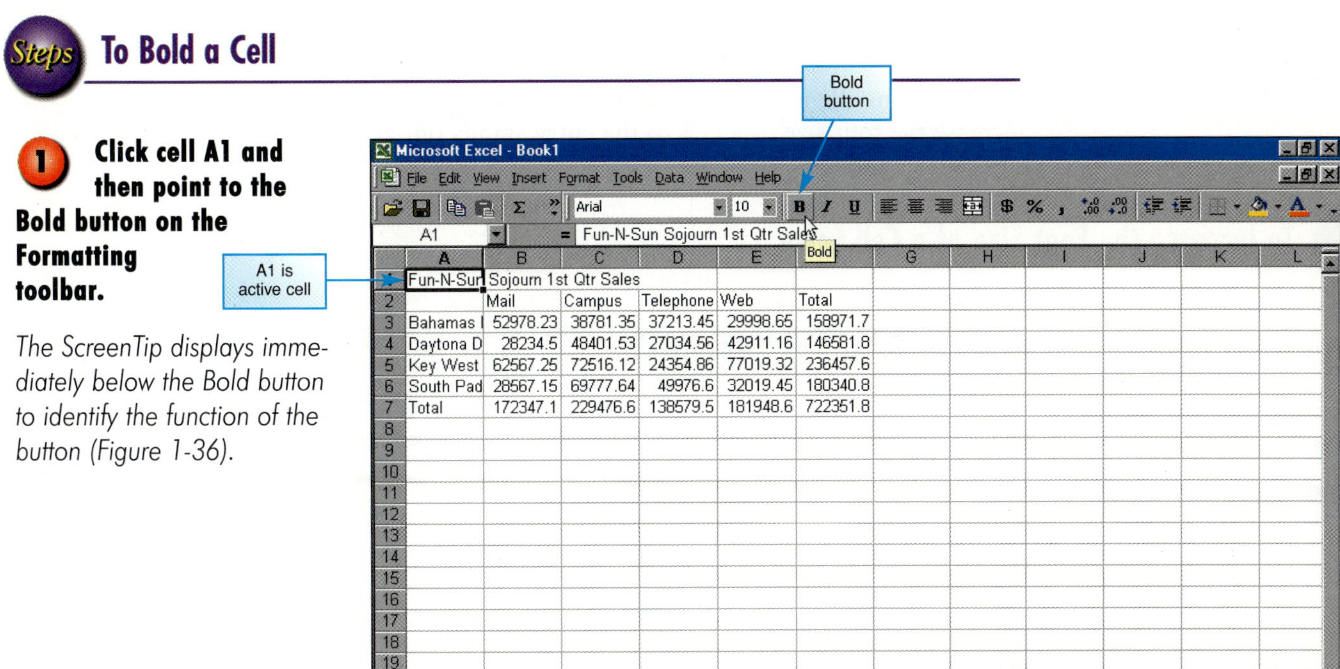

	A	B	C	D	E
1	Fun-N-Sun	Sojourn 1st Qtr Sales			
2		Mail	Campus	Telephone	Web	Total
3	Bahamas I	52978.23	38781.35	37213.45	29998.65	158971.7
4	Daytona D	28234.5	48401.53	27034.56	42911.16	146581.8
5	Key West	62567.25	72516.12	24354.86	77019.32	236457.6
6	South Pad	28567.15	69777.64	49976.6	32019.45	180340.8
7	Total	172347.1	229476.6	138579.5	181948.6	722351.8

FIGURE 1-36

2 Click the Bold button.

Excel applies a bold format to the worksheet title Fun-N-Sun Sojourn 1st Qtr Sales (Figure 1-37).

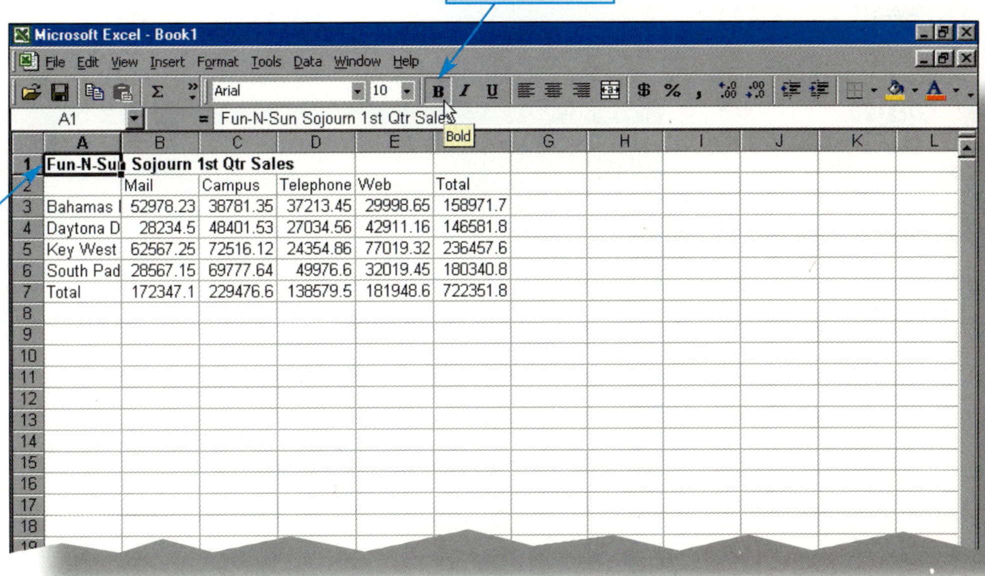

FIGURE 1-37

When the active cell is bold, the Bold button on the Formatting toolbar is recessed, or dimmed (Figure 1-37). Clicking the Bold button a second time removes the bold format.

Other Ways

1. Press CTRL+B
2. Right-click cell, click Format Cells on shortcut menu, click Font tab, click Bold, click OK button
3. On Format menu click Cells, click Font tab, click Bold, click OK button

Increasing the Font Size

Increasing the font size is the next step in formatting the worksheet title. You increase the font size of a cell so the entry stands out and is easier to read.

Steps To Increase the Font Size of a Cell Entry

1 With cell A1 selected, click the Font Size box arrow on the Formatting toolbar and then point to 20 in the Font Size list (Figure 1-38).

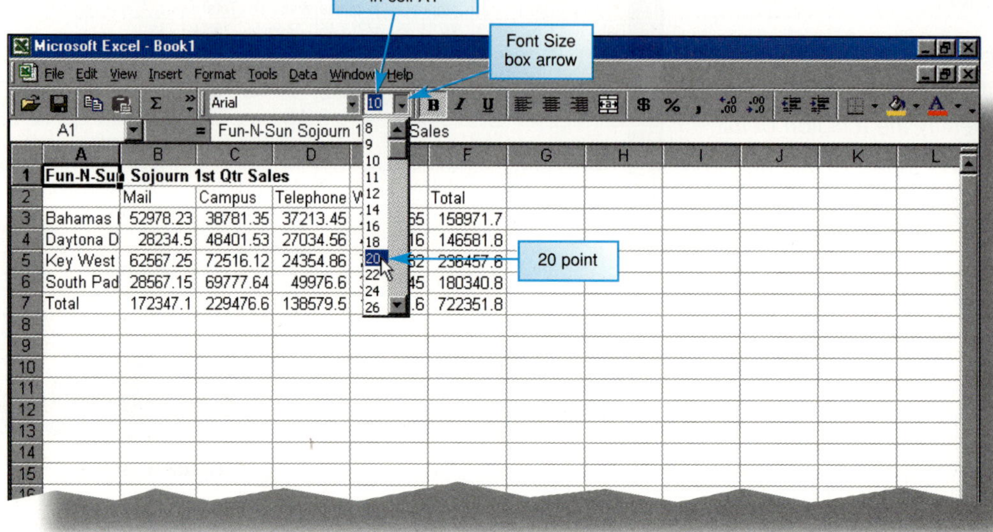

FIGURE 1-38

2 Click 20.

The font size of the characters in the worksheet title in cell A1 increase from 10 point to 20 point (Figure 1-39).

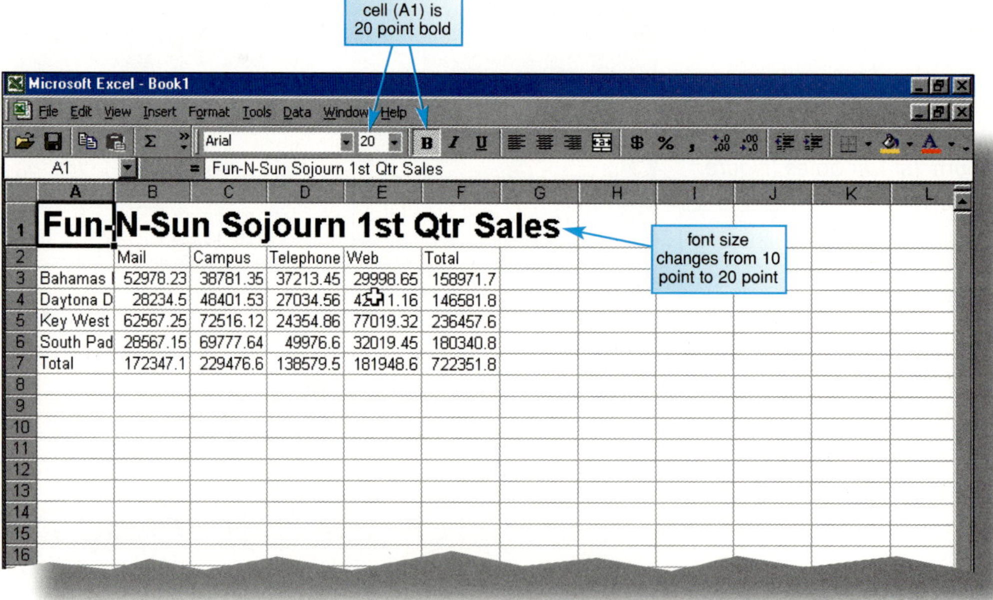

FIGURE 1-39

Other Ways

1. Press CTRL+1, click Font tab, select font size, click OK button
2. Right-click cell, click Format Cells on shortcut menu, click Font tab, select font size, click OK button
3. On Format menu click Cells, click Font tab, select font size, click OK button

An alternative to clicking a font size in the Font Size list is to type the font size in the Font Size box and then press the ENTER key. With cell A1 selected (Figure 1-39), the Font Size box shows the new font size 20 and the recessed Bold button shows the active cell is bold.

According to the requirements, the worksheet title must be centered across columns A through F. Because the increased font size causes the worksheet title to exceed the length of the combined columns (Figure 1-39), the centering will be done after the body of the worksheet is formatted.

Using AutoFormat to Format the Body of a Worksheet

Excel has several customized format styles called **table formats** that allow you to format the body of the worksheet. Using table formats can give your worksheet a professional appearance. Follow these steps to format the range A2:F7 automatically using the **AutoFormat command** on the Format menu.

To Use AutoFormat to Format the Body of a Worksheet

1 Select cell A2, the upper-left corner cell of the rectangular range to format. Drag the mouse pointer to cell F7, the lower-right corner cell of the range to format.

Excel highlights the range to format with a heavy border and blue background (Figure 1-40).

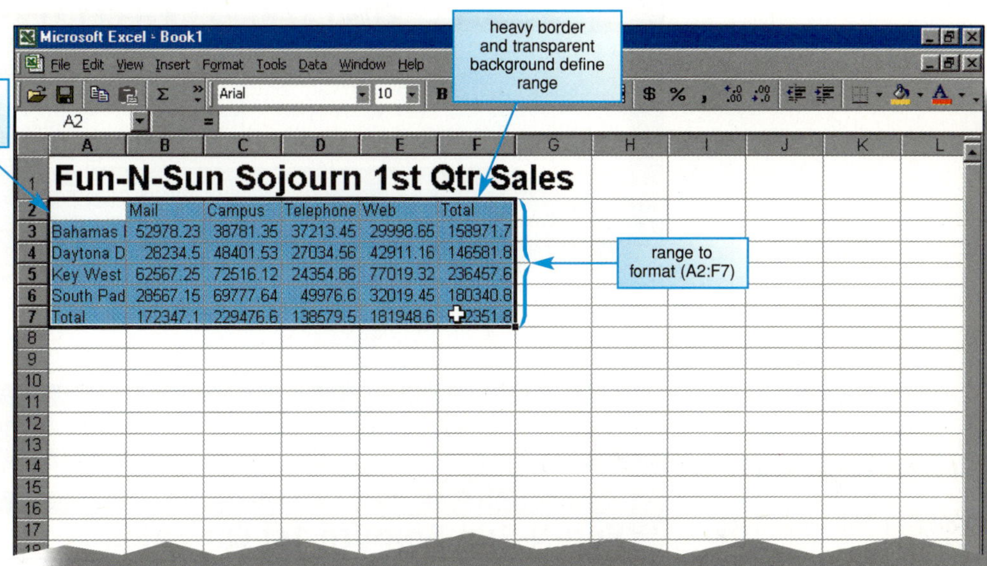

FIGURE 1-40

2 Click Format on the menu bar and then point to AutoFormat.

The Format menu displays (Figure 1-41).

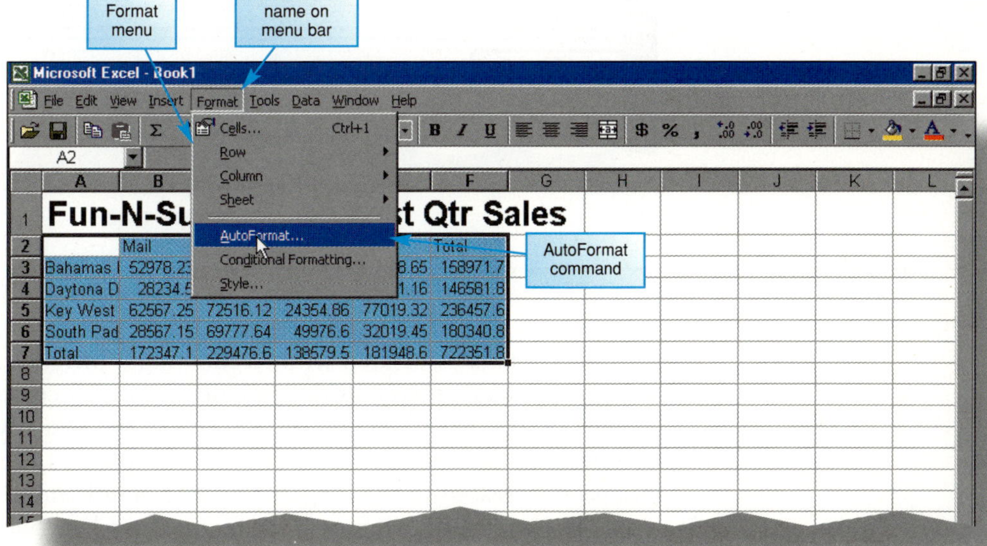

FIGURE 1-41

3 **Click AutoFormat. Click the Accounting 2 format (column 2, row 3) in the AutoFormat dialog box. Point to the OK button.**

The AutoFormat dialog box displays with a list of customized formats (Figure 1-42). Each format illustrates how the body of the worksheet will display if it is chosen.

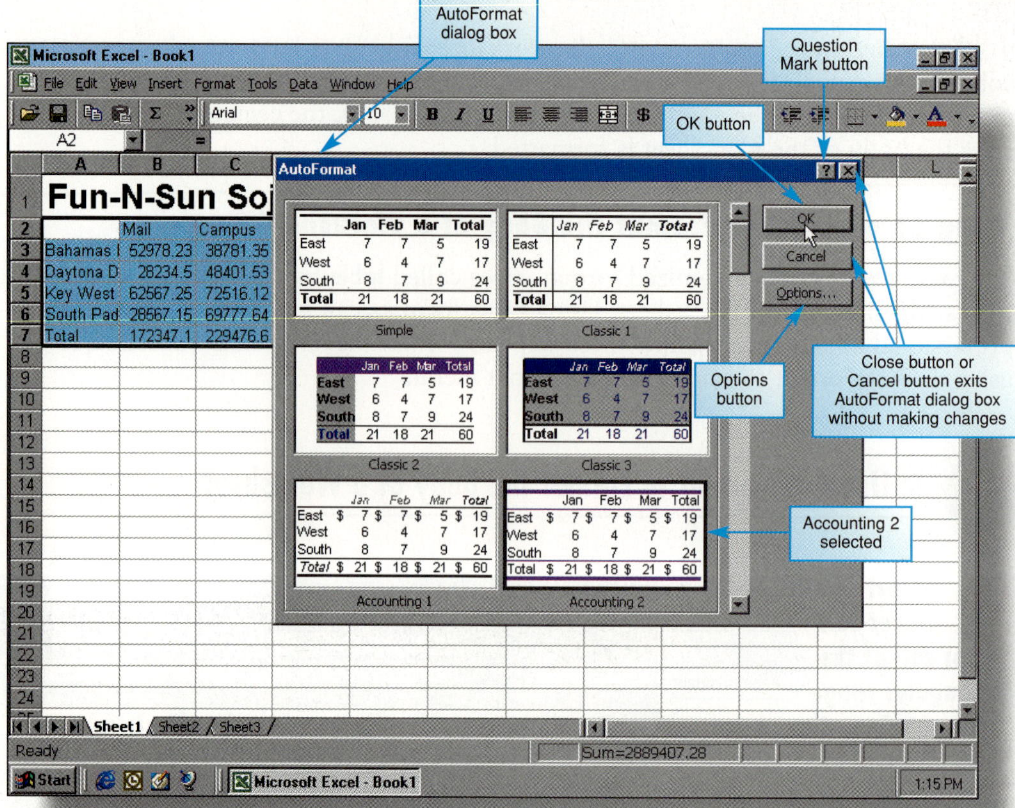

FIGURE 1-42

4 **Click the OK button. Select cell A9 to deselect the range A2:F7.**

Excel displays the worksheet with the range A2:F7 using the customized format, Accounting 2 (Figure 1-43).

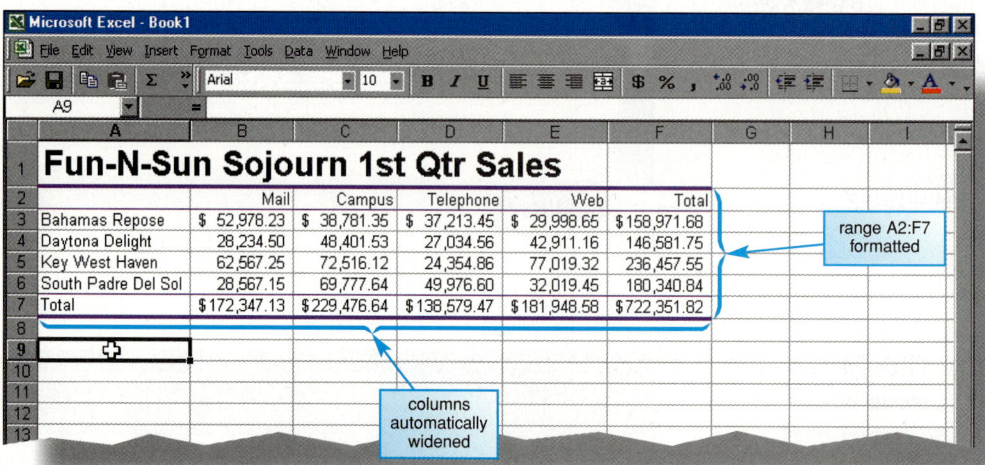

FIGURE 1-43

The formats associated with Accounting 2 include right-alignment of column titles, numbers displayed as dollars and cents with comma separators, numbers aligned on the decimal point, dollar signs in the first row of numbers and in the total row, and top and bottom rows display with borders. The width of column A also has been increased so the longest row title, South Padre Del Sol, just fits in the column. The widths of columns B through F have been increased so that the formatted numbers will fit in the cells.

The AutoFormat dialog box shown in Figure 1-42 includes 17 customized formats and five buttons. Use the scroll bar to view the 11 customized formats that do not display in the dialog box. Each one of these customized formats offers a different look. The one you choose depends on the worksheet you are creating.

The five buttons in the dialog box allow you to cancel, complete the entries, get Help, and adjust a customized format. The **Close button** terminates current activity without making changes. You also can use the **Cancel button**, immediately below the **OK button**, for this purpose. Use the **Question Mark button**, to obtain Help on any box or button located in the dialog box. The **Options button** allows you to select additional formats to assign as part of the selected customized format.

Customizing the AutoFormat

It is not uncommon to apply two or more of the customized formats shown in Figure 1-42 to the same range. If you assign two customized formats to a range, Excel does not remove the original format from the range; it simply adds the second customized format to the first. Thus, if you decide to change a customized format, first select the range, and then, in the AutoFormat dialog box, assign it the customized format titled None.

Centering the Worksheet Title Across Columns

With the column widths increased, the final step in formatting the worksheet title is to center it across columns A through F. Centering a worksheet title across the columns used in the body of the worksheet improves the worksheet's appearance.

To Center a Cell's Contents Across Columns

1 **Click cell A1. Drag the block plus sign to the rightmost cell (F1) of the range to center (A1:F1). Point to the Merge and Center button on the Formatting toolbar.**

When you drag through the range A1:F1, Excel highlights the cells (Figure 1-44).

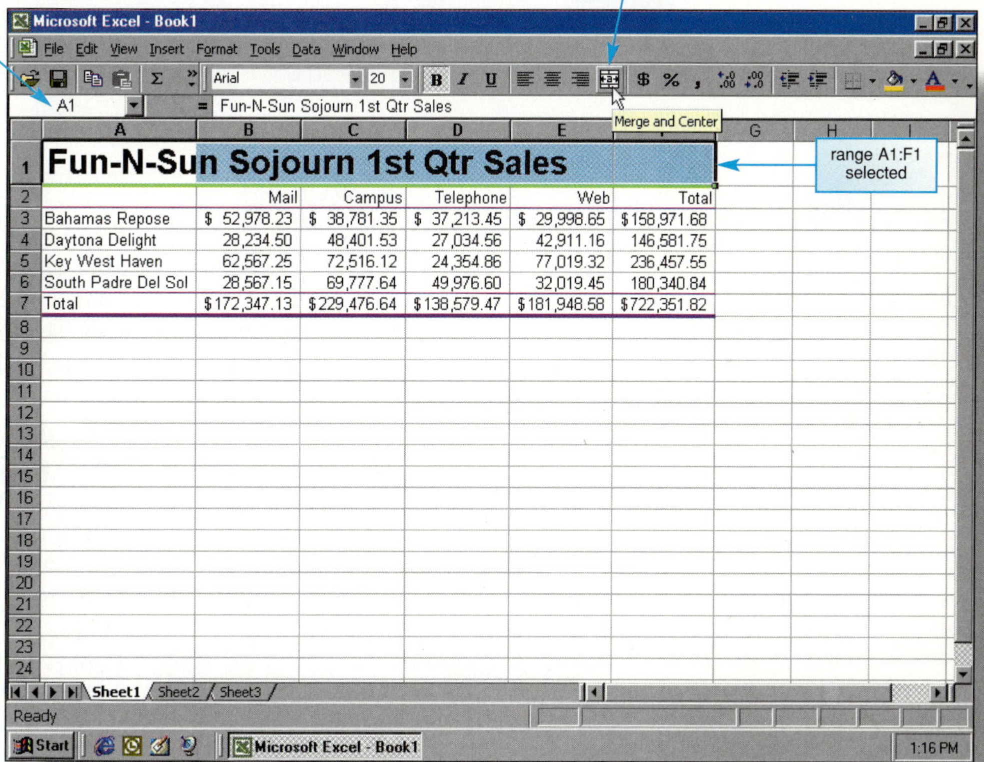

FIGURE 1-44

2 **Click the Merge and Center button.**

Excel merges the cells A1 through F1 to create a new cell A1 and centers the contents of cell A1 across columns A through F (Figure 1-45). After the merge, cells B1 through F1 no longer exist on the worksheet.

3 **Click cell A9 to deselect cell A1.**

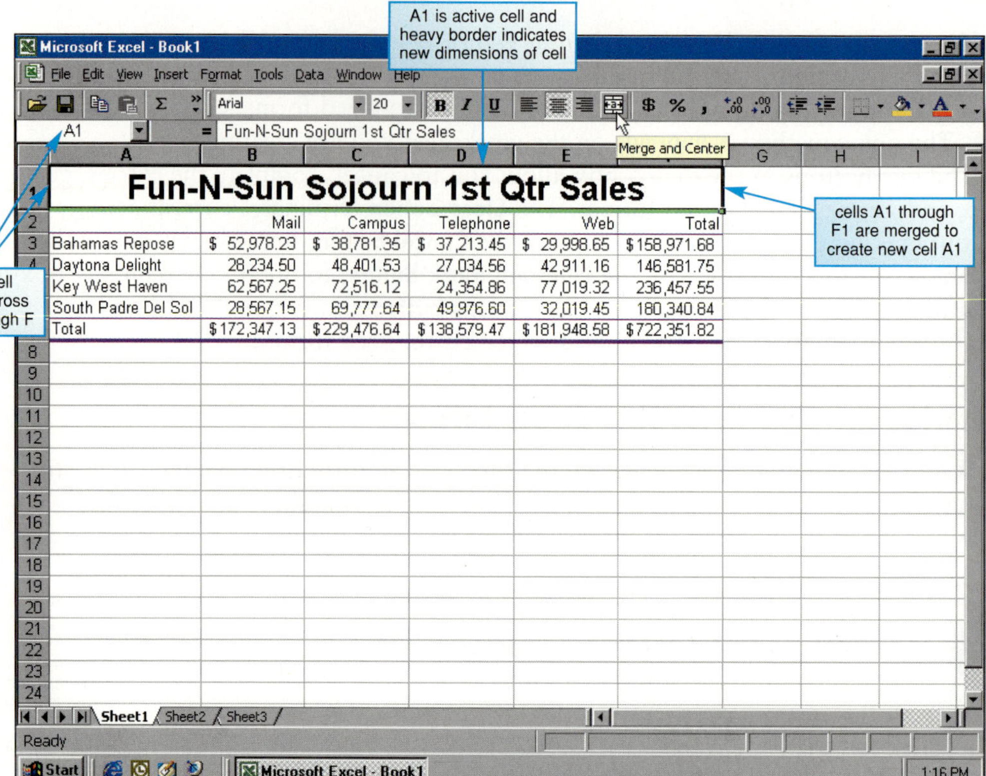

FIGURE 1-45

Other Ways

1. Right-click cell, click Format Cells on shortcut menu, click Alignment tab, select Center Across Selection in Horizontal list, click OK button
2. On Format menu click Cells, click Alignment tab, select Center Across Selection in Horizontal list, click OK button

More About 2000

The Name Box

If you repeatedly select certain cells in a worksheet, consider naming the cells in the Name box. Select the cells one at a time and then type a name in the Name box for each, such as Company Total, for cell F7 shown in Figure 1-48. Then, when you want to select one of the named cells, click the Name box arrow and click the cell name in the Name box list.

Excel not only centers the worksheet title, but also merges cells A1 through F1 into one cell, cell A1. Thus, the heavy border that defines the active cell in Figure 1-45 covers what originally was cells A1 through F1. For the Merge and Center button to work properly, all the cells except the leftmost cell in the range of cells must be empty.

Most formats assigned to a cell will display on the Formatting toolbar when the cell is selected. For example, the font type and font size display in their appropriate boxes. Recessed buttons indicate an assigned format. To determine if less frequently used formats are assigned to a cell, point to the cell and right-click. Next, click Format Cells, and then click each of the tabs in the Format Cells dialog box.

The worksheet now is complete. The next step is to chart the first quarter sales for the four vacation packages by sales channel. To create the chart, you must select the cell in the upper-left corner of the range to chart (cell A2). Rather than clicking cell A2 to select it, the next section describes how to use the Name box to select the cell.

Using the Name Box to Select a Cell

The **Name box** is located on the left side of the formula bar. To select any cell, click the Name box and enter the cell reference of the cell you want to select. Perform the following steps to select cell A2.

To Use the Name Box to Select a Cell

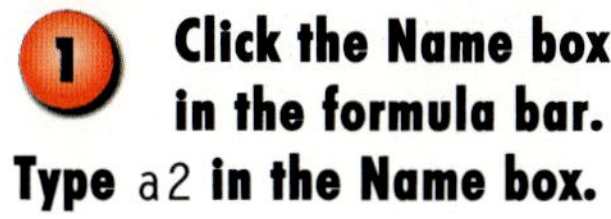

Click the Name box in the formula bar. Type a2 **in the Name box.**

Even though cell A9 is the active cell, the Name box displays the typed cell reference a2 (Figure 1-46).

a2 typed in Name box

A9 is active cell

FIGURE 1-46

Press the ENTER key.

Excel changes the active cell from cell A9 to cell A2 (Figure 1-47).

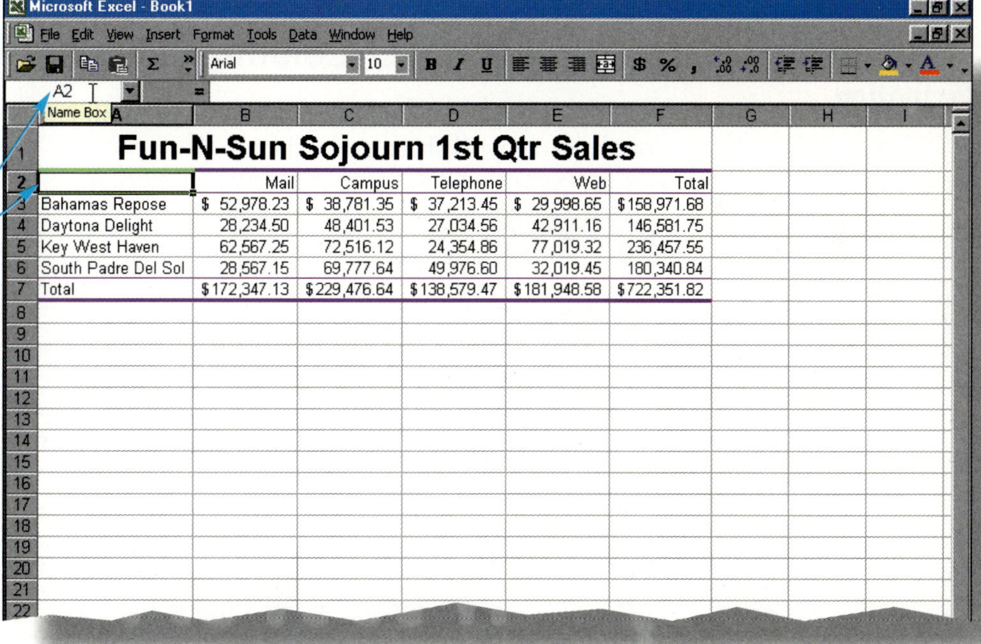

FIGURE 1-47

As you will see in later projects, besides using the Name box to select any cell in a worksheet, you also can use it to assign names to a cell or range of cells.

Excel supports several additional ways to select a cell, as summarized on the next page in Table 1-3.

Table 1-3 Selecting Cells in Excel

KEY, BOX, OR COMMAND	FUNCTION
ALT+PAGE DOWN	Selects the cell one window to the right and moves the window accordingly.
ALT+PAGE UP	Selects the cell one window to the left and moves the window accordingly.
ARROW	Selects the adjacent cell in the direction of the arrow on the key.
CTRL+ARROW	Selects the border cell of the worksheet in combination with the arrow keys and moves the window accordingly. For example, to select the rightmost cell in the row that contains the active cell, press CTRL+RIGHT arrow. You also can press the END key, release it, and then press the arrow key to accomplish the same task.
CTRL+HOME	Selects cell A1 or the cell one column and one row below and to the right of frozen titles and moves the window accordingly.
Find command on Edit menu	Finds and selects a cell that contains specific contents that you enter in the Find dialog box. If necessary, Excel moves the window to display the cell. You can press SHIFT+F5 or CTRL+F to display the Find dialog box.
F5 or Go To command on Edit menu	Selects the cell that corresponds to the cell reference you enter in the Go To dialog box and moves the window accordingly. You can press CTRL+G to display the Find dialog box.
HOME	Selects the cell at the beginning of the row that contains the active cell and moves the window accordingly.
Name box	Selects the cell in the workbook that corresponds to the cell reference you enter in the Name box.
PAGE DOWN	Selects the cell down one window from the active cell and moves the window accordingly.
PAGE UP	Selects the cell up one window from the active cell and moves the window accordingly.

Navigation

For more information on selecting cells that contain certain entries, such as constants or formulas, visit the Excel 2000 More About Web page (www.scsite.com/ex2000/more.htm) and click Using Go To Special.

Adding a 3-D Column Chart to the Worksheet

The 3-D Column chart (Figure 1-48) is called an **embedded chart** because it is drawn on the same worksheet as the data.

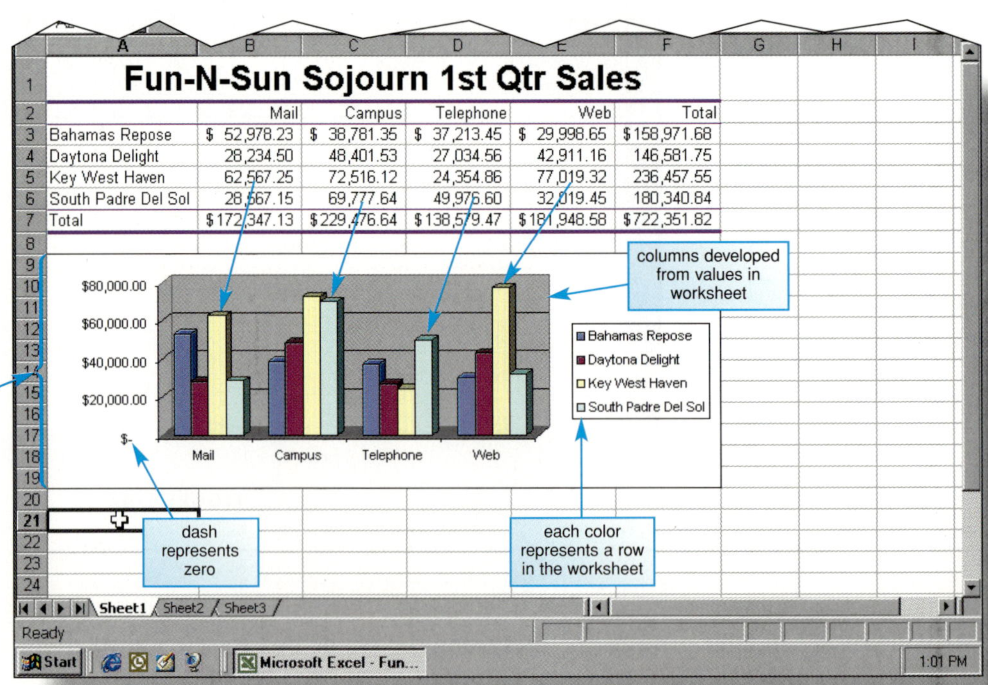

FIGURE 1-48

For the sales channel Mail, the light blue column represents the first quarter sales for the Bahamas Repose vacation package ($52,978.23); the purple column represents the first quarter sales for Daytona Delight ($28,234.50); the light yellow column represents the first quarter sales for Key West Haven ($62,567.25); and the turquoise column represents the first quarter sales for South Padre Del Sol ($28,567.15). For the sales channels Campus, Telephone, and Web, the columns follow the same color scheme to represent the comparable first quarter sales. The totals from the worksheet are not represented because the totals were not in the range specified for charting.

Excel derives the scale along the vertical axis (also called the **y-axis** or **value axis**) of the chart on the basis of the values in the worksheet. For example, no value in the range B3:E6 is less than zero or greater than $80,000.00. Excel also determines the $20,000.00 increments along the y-axis automatically. The format used by Excel for the numbers along the y-axis includes representing zero (0) with a dash (Figure 1-48).

With the range to chart selected, you click the **Chart Wizard button** on the Standard toolbar to initiate drawing the chart. The area on the worksheet where the chart displays is called the **chart location**. The chart location is the range A9:F19, immediately below the worksheet data.

Follow the steps below to draw a 3-D Column chart that compares the first quarter sales by vacation package for the four sales channels.

Steps To Add a 3-D Column Chart to the Worksheet

1 Double-click the move handle on the left side of the Standard toolbar to display the entire toolbar. With cell A2 selected, position the block plus sign within the cell's border and drag the mouse pointer to the lower-right corner cell (cell E6) of the range to chart (A2:E6). Point to the Chart Wizard button on the Standard toolbar.

Excel highlights the range to chart (Figure 1-49).

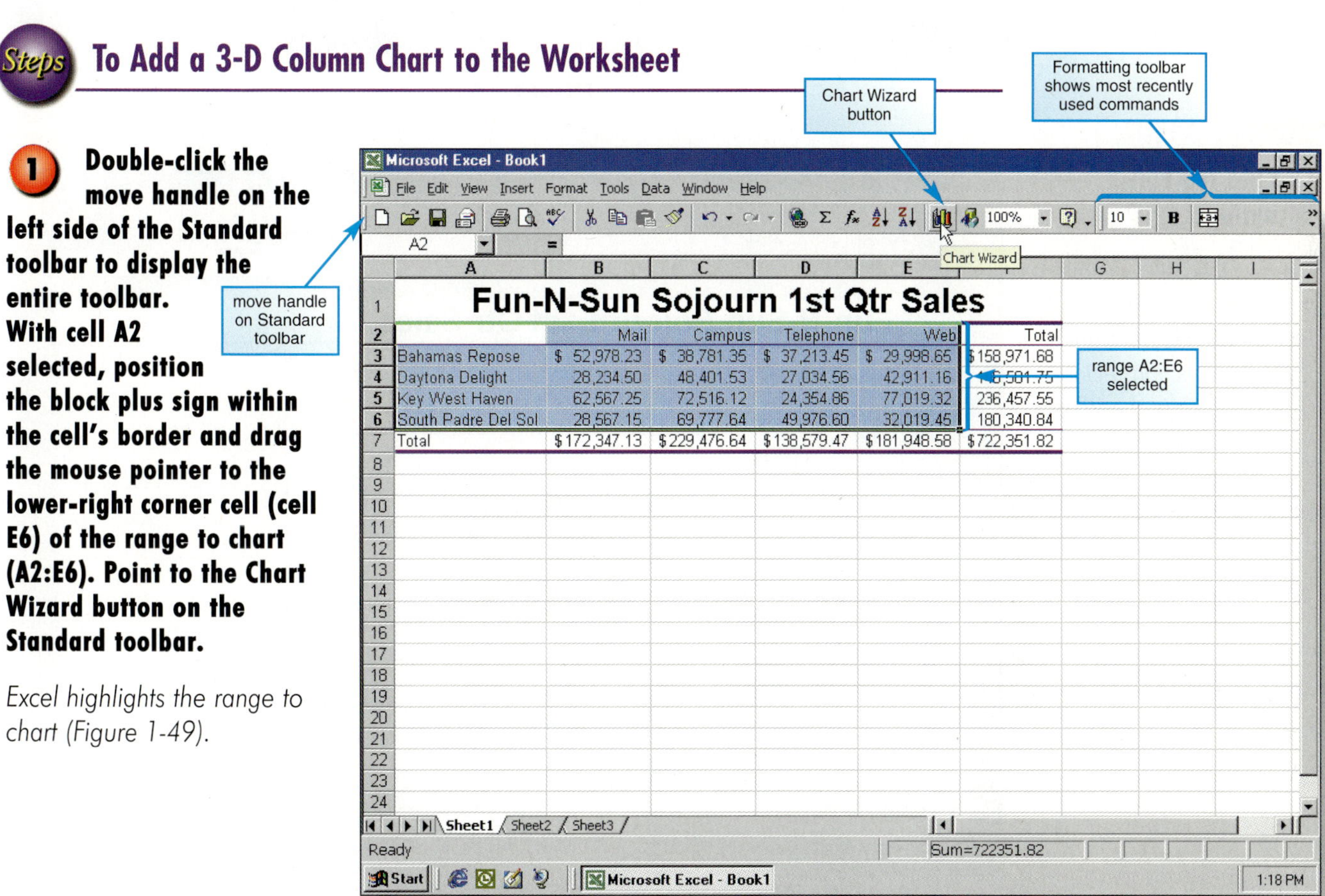

FIGURE 1-49

2 Click the Chart Wizard button.

The Chart Wizard – Step 1 of 4 – Chart Type dialog box displays.

3 With Column selected in the Chart type list, click the 3-D Column chart sub-type (column 1, row 2) in the Chart sub-type area. Point to the Finish button.

Column is highlighted in the Chart type list and Clustered column with a 3-D visual effect is highlighted in the Chart sub-type area (Figure 1-50).

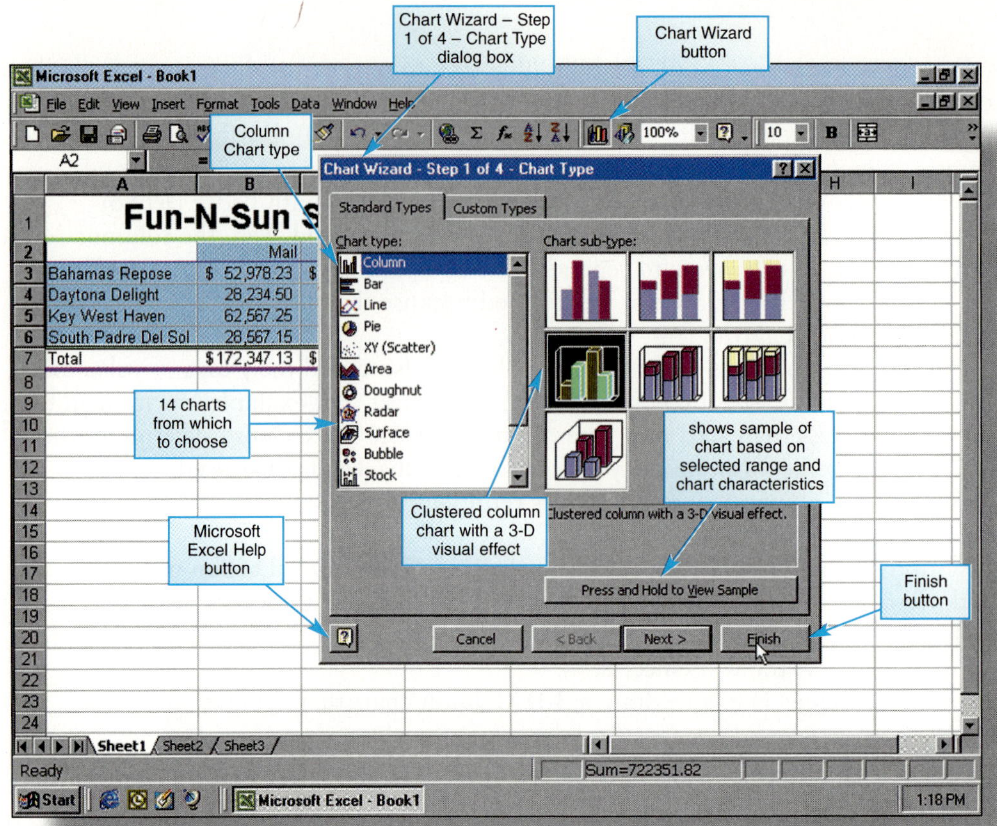

FIGURE 1-50

4 Click the Finish button.

Excel draws the 3-D Column chart (Figure 1-51). The chart displays in the middle of the window in a selection rectangle. The small **sizing handles** *at the corners and along the sides of the selection rectangle indicate the chart is selected.*

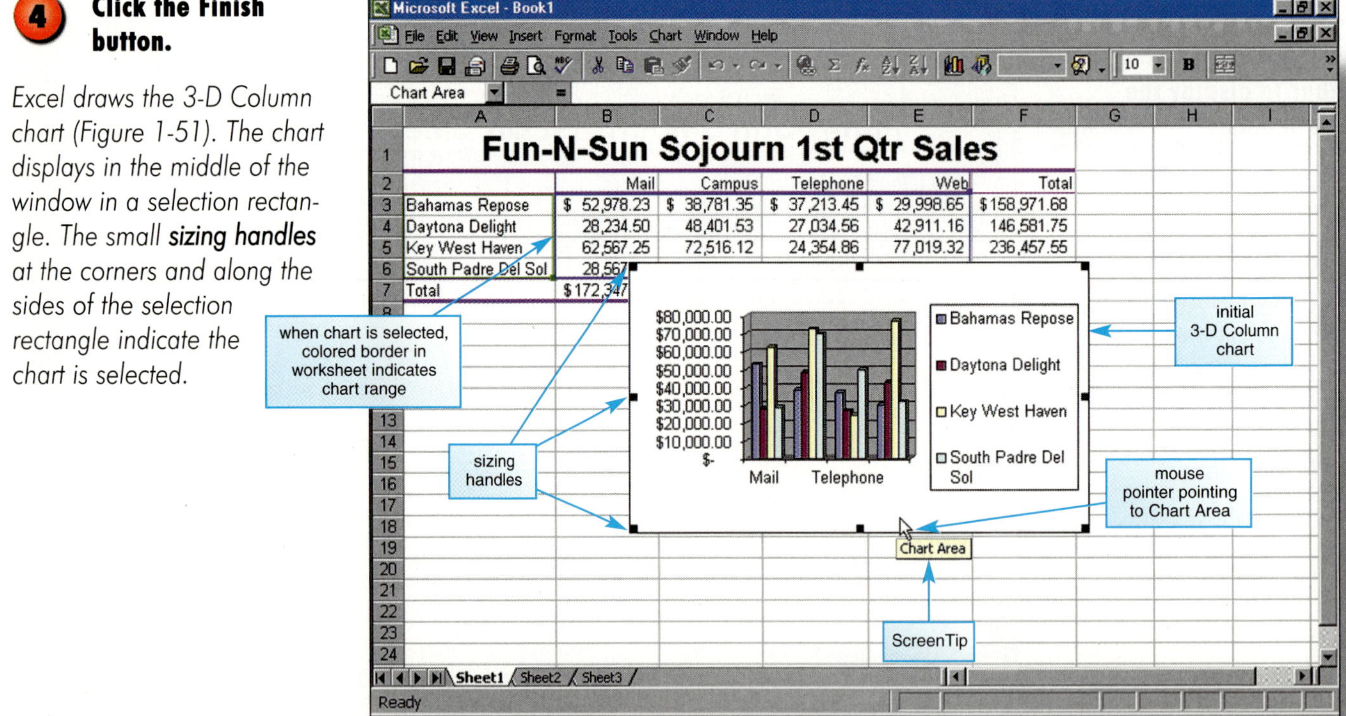

FIGURE 1-51

5 **Point to an open area in the lower-right section of the Chart Area so the ScreenTip, Chart Area, displays (Figure 1-51). The ScreenTip defines the area of the chart that the mouse pointer is pointing to. Drag the chart down and to the left to position the upper-left corner of the dotted line rectangle over the upper-left corner of cell A9 (Figure 1-52).**

Excel displays a dotted line rectangle showing the new chart location. As you drag the selected chart, the mouse pointer changes to a cross hair with four arrowheads.

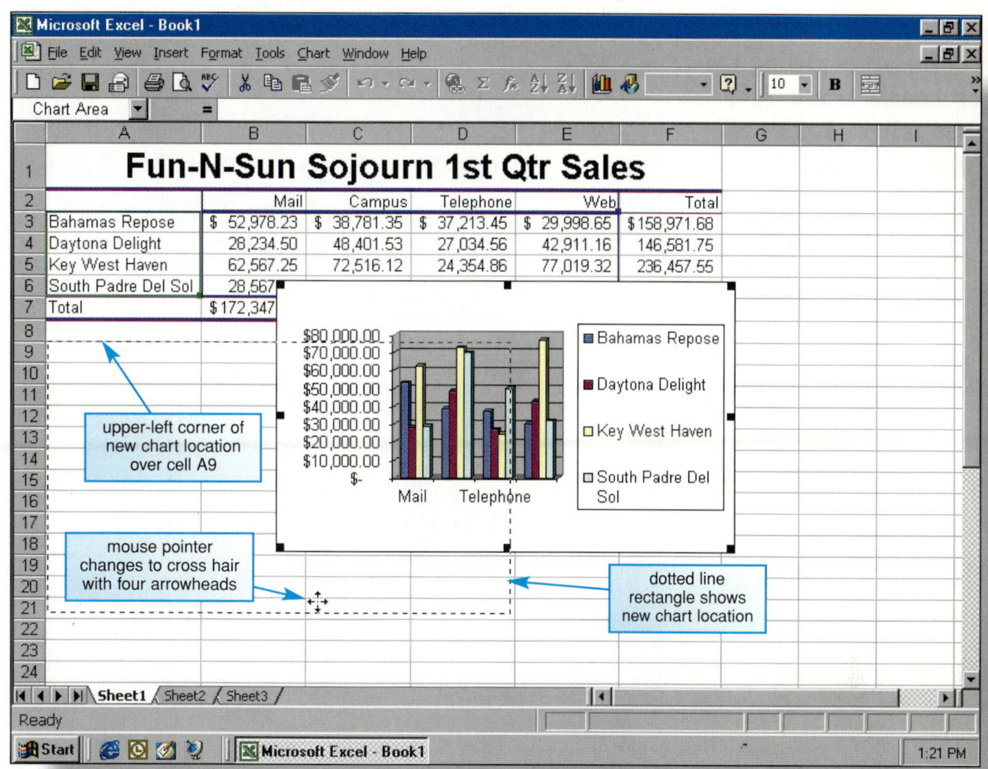

FIGURE 1-52

6 **Release the mouse button. Point to the middle sizing handle on the right edge of the selection rectangle.**

The chart displays in a new location (Figure 1-53). The mouse pointer changes to a horizontal line with two arrowheads when it points to a sizing handle.

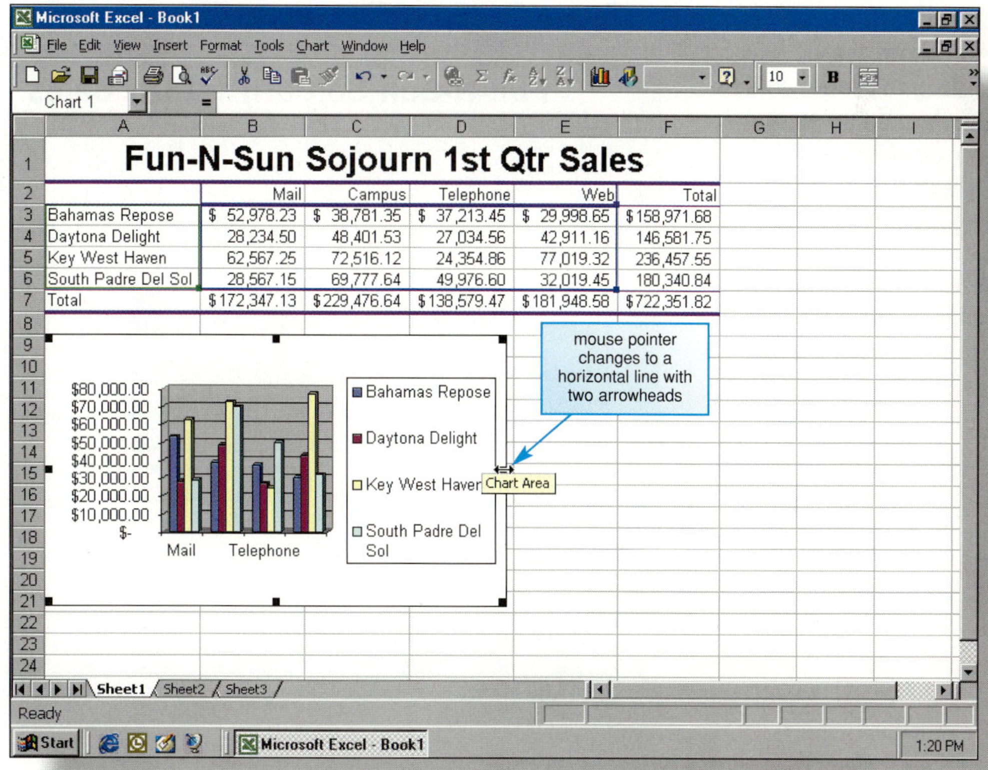

FIGURE 1-53

7 **While holding down the ALT key, drag the sizing handle to the right edge of column F. Release the mouse button.**

While you drag, the dotted line rectangle shows the new chart location (Figure 1-54). Holding down the ALT key while you drag a chart snaps (aligns) the new border to the worksheet gridlines.

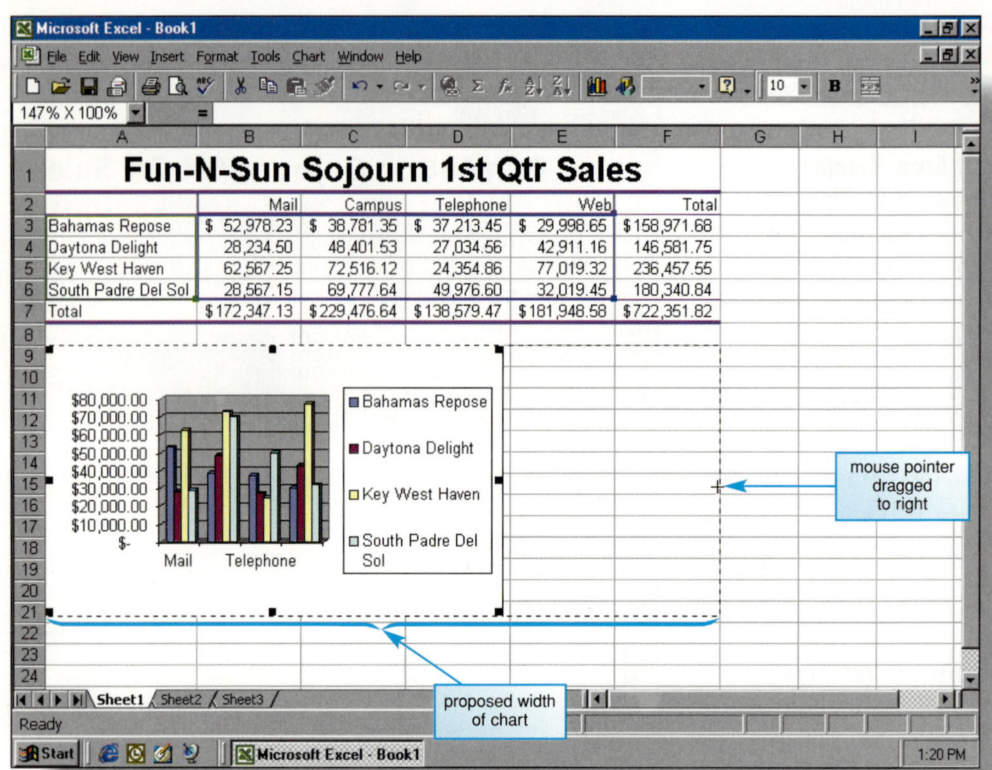

FIGURE 1-54

8 **If necessary, hold down the ALT key and drag the lower-middle sizing handle up to the lower edge of row 19. Click cell A21 to deselect the chart.**

The new chart location extends from the top of cell A9 to the bottom of cell F19 (Figure 1-55).

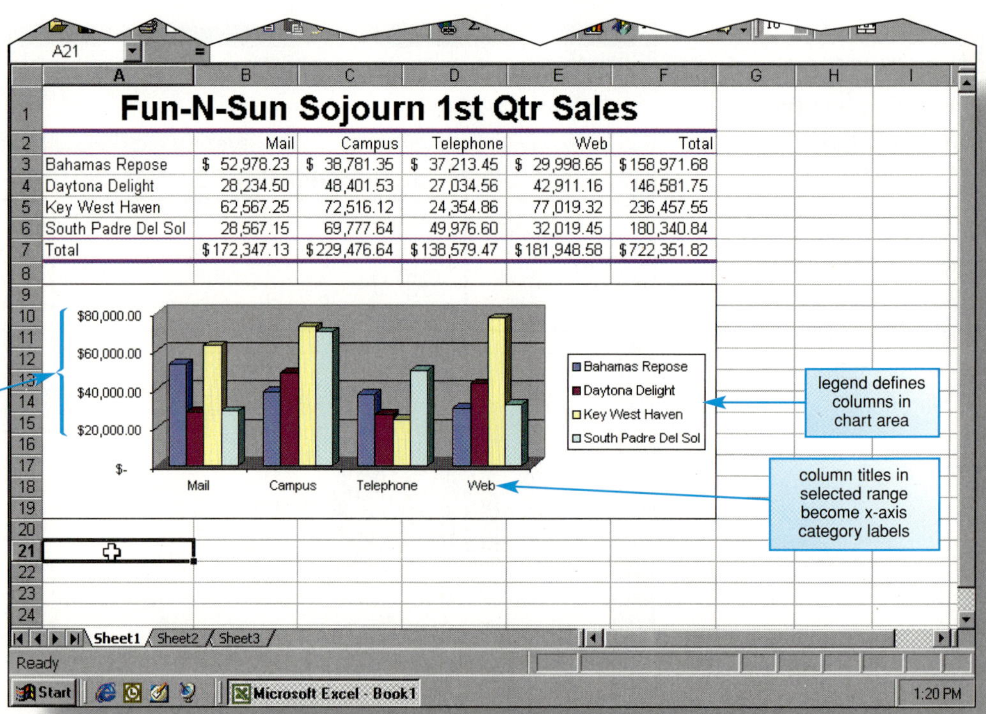

FIGURE 1-55

Other Ways

1. Select range, press F11
2. Select range, on Insert menu click Chart

The embedded 3-D Column chart in Figure 1-55 compares the first quarter sales for the four vacation packages within each sales channel. It also allows you to compare first quarter sales among the sales channels.

Excel automatically selects the entries in the topmost row of the range (row 2) as the titles for the horizontal axis (also called the **x-axis** or **category axis**) and draws a column for each of the 16 cells in the range containing numbers. The small box to the right of the column chart in Figure 1-55 contains the legend. The **legend** identifies each bar in the chart. Excel automatically selects the leftmost column of the range (column A) as titles within the legend. As indicated earlier, it also automatically scales the y-axis on the basis of the magnitude of the numbers in the chart range.

Excel offers 14 different chart types (Figure 1-50 on page E 1.38). The **default chart type** is the chart Excel draws if you click the Finish button in the first Chart Wizard dialog box. When you install Excel on a computer, the default chart type is the 2-D (two-dimensional) Column chart.

Changing the Chart Type

Excel has fourteen chart types from which to choose. You can change the embedded 3-D Column chart to another type by double-clicking the chart location. When a heavy gray border surrounds the chart location, right-click the chart and then click Chart Type on the shortcut menu. You also can use the shortcut menu to format the chart to make it look more professional. Subsequent projects will discuss changing charts, sizing charts, adding text to charts, and drawing a chart on a chart sheet.

Saving a Workbook

While you are building a workbook, the computer stores it in memory. If the computer is turned off or if you lose electrical power, the workbook is lost. Hence, you must save on a floppy disk or hard disk any workbook that you will use later. A saved workbook is referred to as a **file** or **workbook.** The following steps illustrate how to save a workbook on a floppy disk in drive A using the Save button on the Standard toolbar.

Steps To Save a Workbook

1 With a floppy disk in drive A, click the Save button on the Standard toolbar.

The Save As dialog box displays (Figure 1-56). The preset Save in folder is My Documents, the preset file name is Book1, and the file type is Microsoft Excel Workbook. The buttons on the top and on the side are used to select folders and change the display of file names and other information.

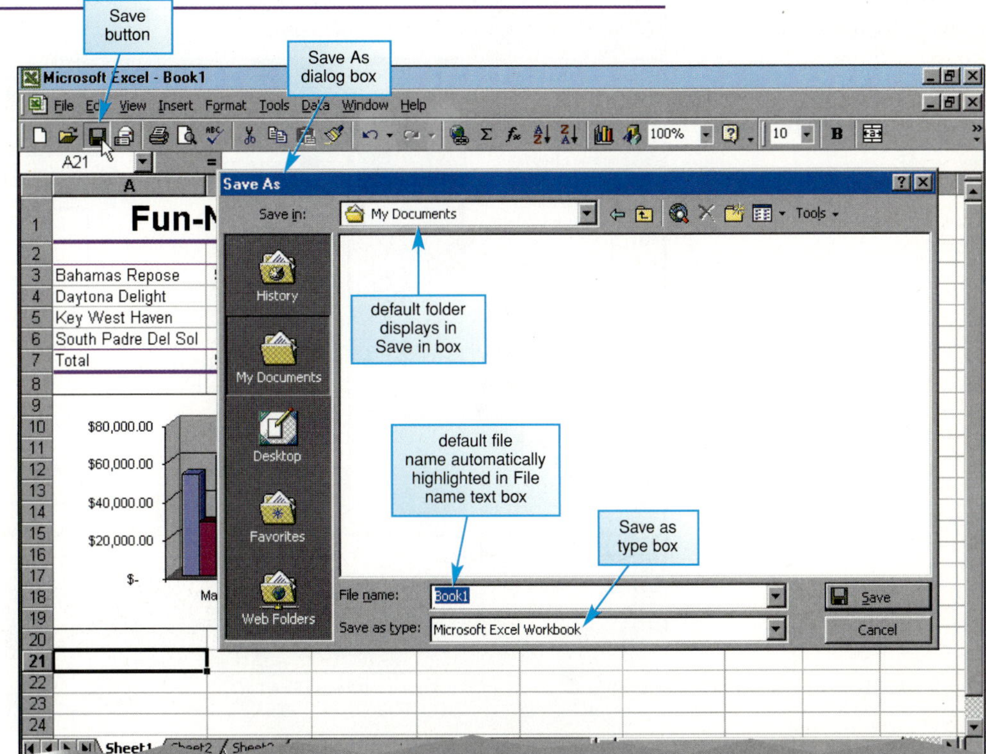

FIGURE 1-56

2 **Type** `Fun-N-Sun Sojourn 1st Qtr Sales` **in the File name text box.**

The new file name replaces Book1 in the File name text box (Figure 1-57). A file name can be up to 255 characters and can include spaces.

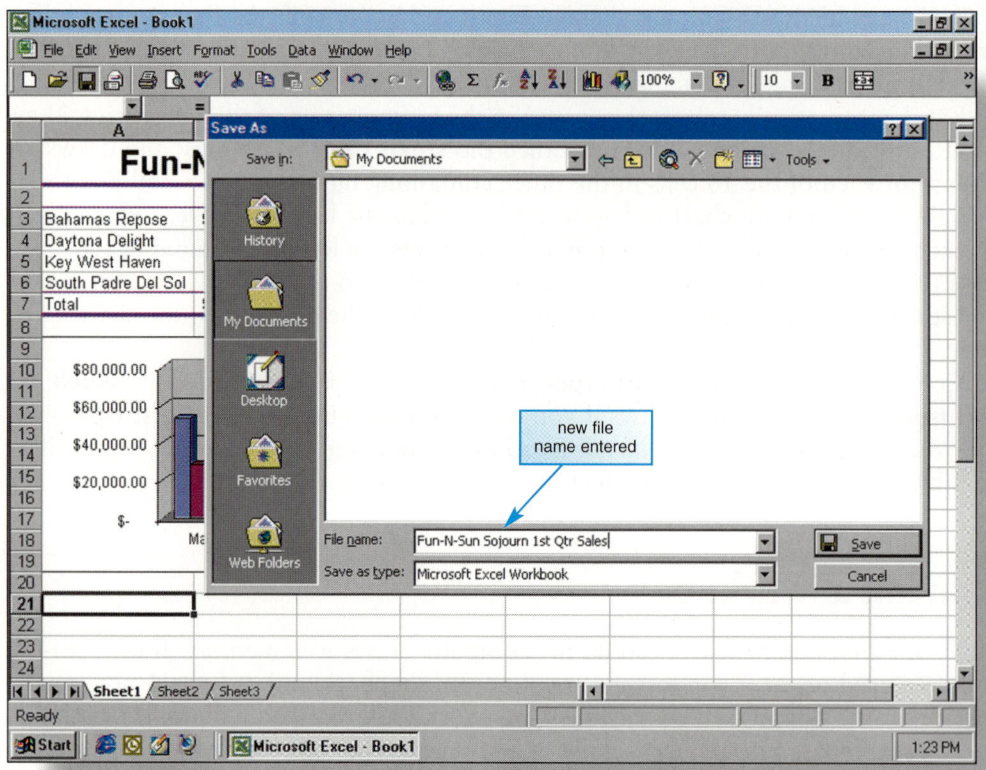

FIGURE 1-57

3 **Click the Save in box arrow and then point to 3½ Floppy (A:).**

A list of available drives and folders displays (Figure 1-58).

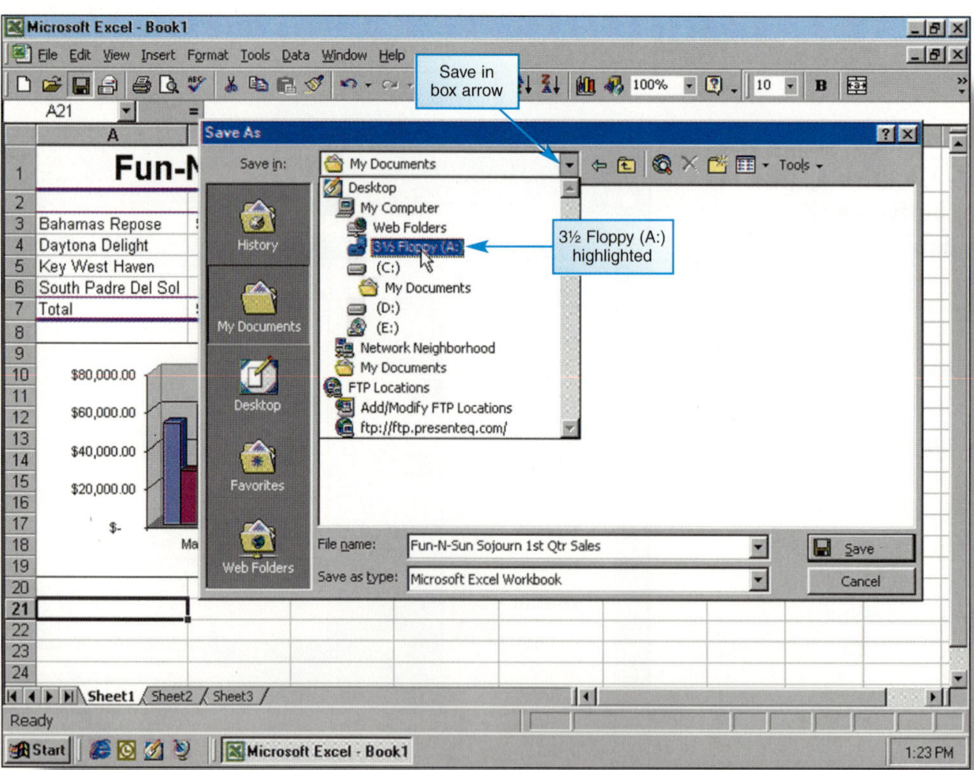

FIGURE 1-58

Click 3½ Floppy (A:) and then point to the Save button in the Save As dialog box.

Drive A becomes the selected drive (Figure 1-59).

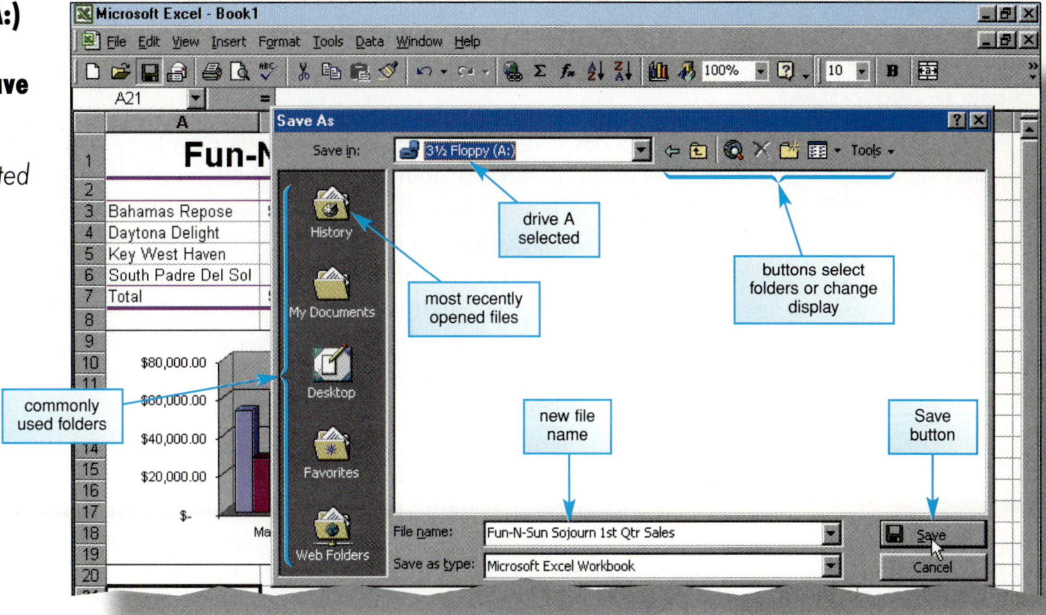

FIGURE 1-59

5 Click the Save button.

Excel saves the workbook on the floppy disk in drive A using the file name Fun-N-Sun Sojourn 1st Qtr Sales. Excel automatically appends the extension **.xls** *to the file name you entered in Step 2, which stands for Excel workbook. Although the workbook is saved on a floppy disk, it also remains in memory and displays on the screen (Figure 1-60). Notice the file name in the title bar.*

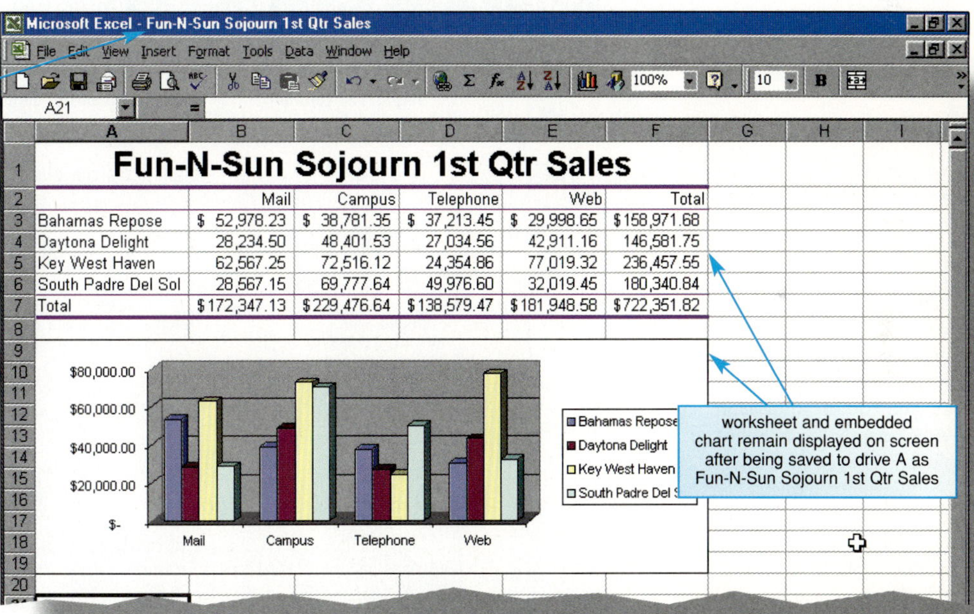

FIGURE 1-60

Other Ways

1. Press CTRL+S, type `file name`, select drive or folder, click OK button
2. Right-click workbook Control-menu icon on menu bar, click Save As on shortcut menu, type `file name`, select drive of folder, click OK button
3. On File menu click Save As, type `file name`, select drive of folder, click OK button

Saving a Worksheet as a Web Page

Excel allows you to save a worksheet in HTML format so you can publish it to the World Wide Web. Click Save as Web Page on the File menu. You have the option to save the worksheet as a static Web page or as a dynamic Web page. A static Web page means you can view the worksheet on the World Wide Web, but you cannot change cell contents. A dynamic Web page means you can modify the worksheet using a browser.

AutoSave

Are you worried about losing your work because your computer might crash? If so, you can use the AutoSave command on the Tools menu. The AutoSave command automatically saves your work every 10 minutes. If you prefer to change the time between saves, you can do so through the AutoSave dialog box that displays when you invoke the AutoSave command. AutoSave is an add-in program. If the AutoSave command does not display on your Tools menu, use the Add-Ins command on the Tools menu to add it.

While Excel is saving the workbook, it momentarily changes the word Ready on the status bar to Saving. It also displays a horizontal bar on the status bar indicating the amount of the workbook saved. After the save operation is complete, Excel changes the name of the workbook in the title bar from Book1 to Fun-N-Sun Sojourn 1st Qtr Sales (Figure 1-60 on the previous page).

When you click the **Tools button** in the Save As dialog box (Figure 1-59 on the previous page), a list box displays. The **General Options command** in the list allows you to save a backup copy of the workbook, create a password to limit access to the workbook, and carry out other functions that will be discussed later. Saving a **backup workbook** means that each time you save a workbook, Excel copies the current version of the workbook on disk to a file with the same name, but with the words, Backup of, appended to the front of the file name. In the case of a power failure or some other problem, use the backup version to restore your work.

You also can use the General Options command on the Tools list to assign a **password** to a workbook so others cannot open it. A password is case sensitive and can be up to 15 characters long. **Case sensitive** means Excel can differentiate between uppercase and lowercase letters. If you assign a password and forget the password, you cannot access the workbook.

The seven buttons at the top and to the right in the Save As dialog box (Figure 1-59) and their functions are summarized in Table 1-4.

Table 1-4 Save As Dialog Box Toolbar Buttons

BUTTON	BUTTON NAME	FUNCTION
	Default File Location	Displays contents of default file location
	Up One Level	Displays contents of next level up folder
	Search the Web	Starts browser and displays search engine
	Delete	Deletes selected file or folder
	Create New Folder	Creates new folder
	Views	Changes view of files and folders
Tools	Tools	Lists commands to print or modify file names and folders

The five buttons on the left of the Save As dialog box in Figure 1-59 allow you to select frequently used folders. The **History button** displays a list of shortcuts (pointers) to the most recently used files in a folder titled Recent. You can not save workbooks to the Recent folder.

Printing the Worksheet

Once you have created the worksheet and saved it on a floppy disk or hard disk, you might want to print it. A printed version of the worksheet is called a **hard copy** or **printout.**

You might want a printout for several reasons. First, to present the worksheet and chart to someone who does not have access to a computer, it must be in printed form. A printout, for example, can be handed out in a management meeting about first quarter sales. In addition, worksheets and charts often are kept for reference by people other than those who prepare them. In many cases, worksheets and charts are printed and kept in binders for use by others. This section describes how to print a worksheet and an embedded chart.

Saving Paper

If you are an environmentalist interested in saving trees, you can preview the printout on your screen, make adjustments to the worksheet, and then print it only when it appears exactly as you desire. The Print Preview button is immediately to the right of the Print button on the Standard toolbar. Clicking it displays an onscreen image of how the printout will appear. Each time you preview rather than print, you save paper destined for the wastepaper basket, which, in turn, saves trees.

To Print a Worksheet

1 **Ready the printer according to the printer instructions. Point to the Print button on the Standard toolbar (Figure 1-61).**

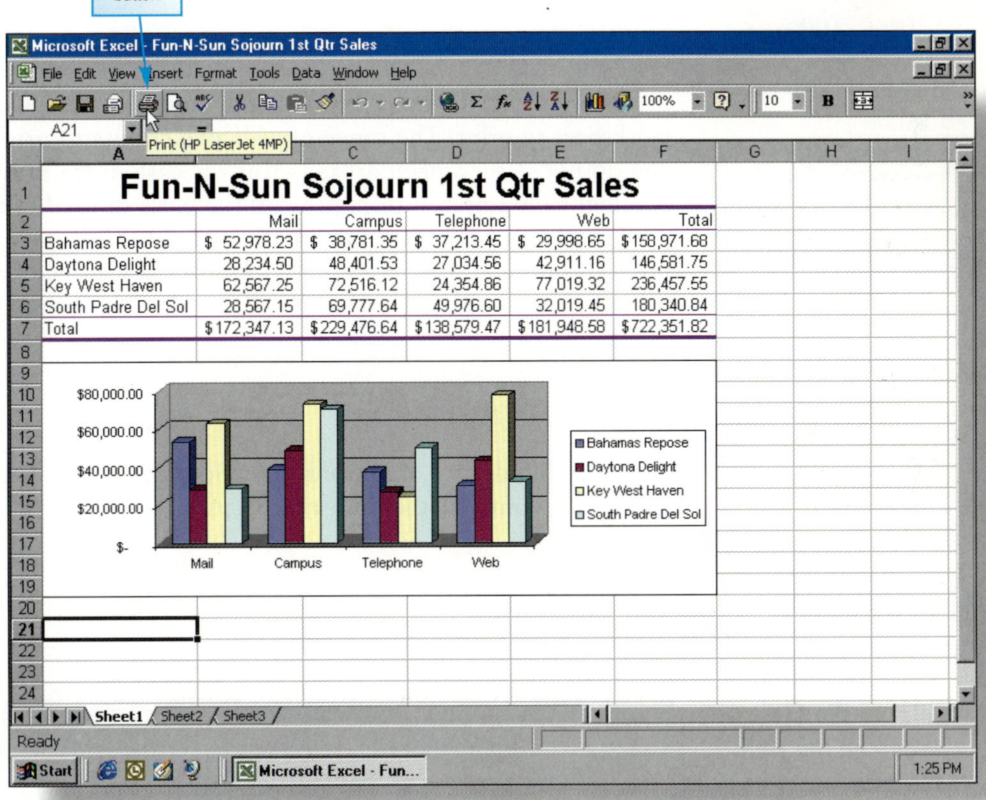

FIGURE 1-61

2 **Click the Print button. When the printer stops printing the worksheet and the chart, retrieve the printout (Figure 1-62).**

Excel displays the Printing dialog box that allows you to cancel the print job while the system is sending the worksheet and chart image to the printer.

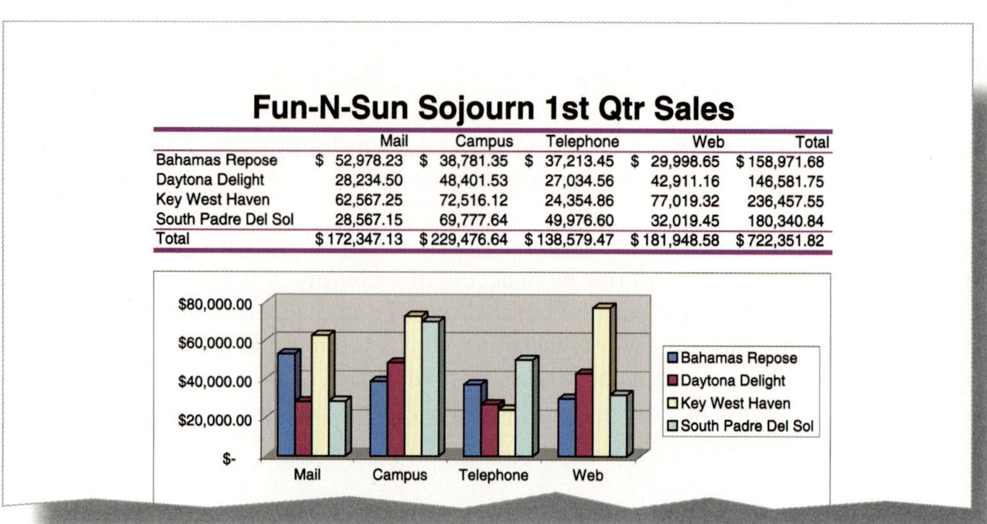

Fun-N-Sun Sojourn 1st Qtr Sales

	Mail	Campus	Telephone	Web	Total
Bahamas Repose	$ 52,978.23	$ 38,781.35	$ 37,213.45	$ 29,998.65	$ 158,971.68
Daytona Delight	28,234.50	48,401.53	27,034.56	42,911.16	146,581.75
Key West Haven	62,567.25	72,516.12	24,354.86	77,019.32	236,457.55
South Padre Del Sol	28,567.15	69,777.64	49,976.60	32,019.45	180,340.84
Total	$ 172,347.13	$ 229,476.64	$ 138,579.47	$ 181,948.58	$ 722,351.82

FIGURE 1-62

Other Ways

1. Press CTRL+P, click OK button
2. On File menu click Print, click OK button
3. Right-click workbook Control-menu icon on menu bar, click Print on shortcut menu, click OK button

Prior to clicking the Print button, you can select which columns and rows in the worksheet to print. The range of cells you choose to print is called the **print area**. If you do not select a print area, as was the case in the previous set of steps, Excel automatically selects a print area on the basis of used cells. As you will see in future projects, Excel has many different print options, such as allowing you to preview the printout on the screen to see if the printout is satisfactory prior to sending it to the printer. Several of these print options are discussed in Project 2.

Quitting Excel

After you build, save, and print the worksheet and chart, Project 1 is complete. To quit Excel, complete the following steps.

Steps To Quit Excel

1 **Point to the Close button on the right side of the title bar (Figure 1-63).**

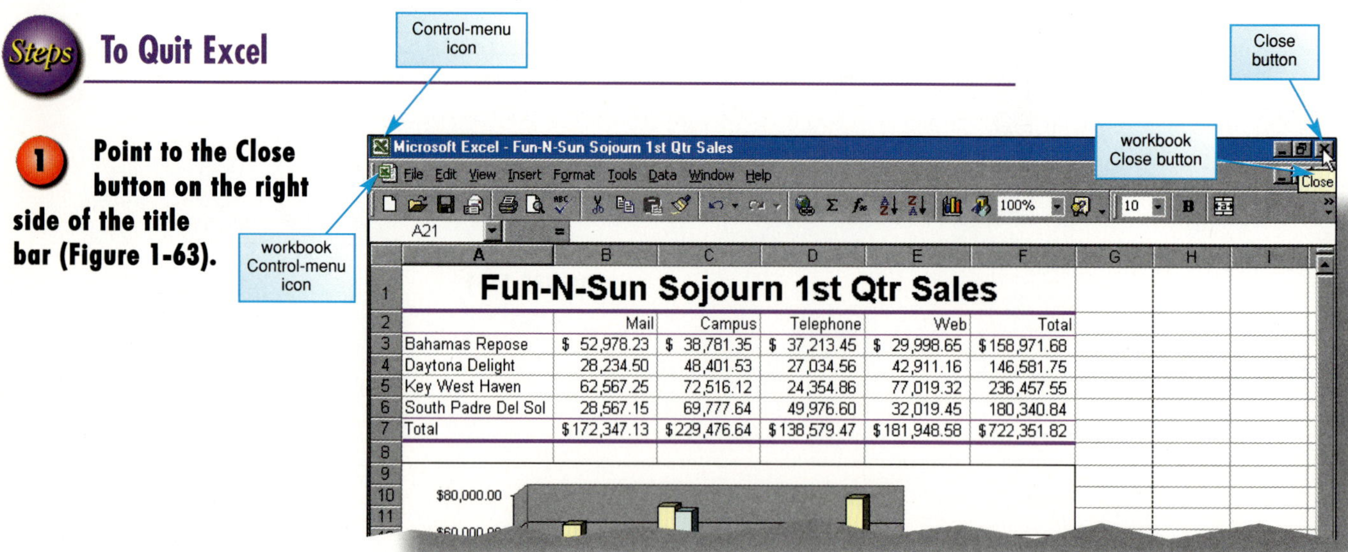

FIGURE 1-63

Click the Close button.

If you made changes to the workbook, the Microsoft Excel dialog box displays the question, Do you want to save the changes you made to 'Fun-N-Sun Sojourn 1st Qtr Sales.xls'? (Figure 1-64). Clicking the Yes button saves the changes before quitting Excel. Clicking the No button quits Excel without saving the changes. Clicking the Cancel button stops the Exit command and returns to the worksheet.

3 **Click the No button.**

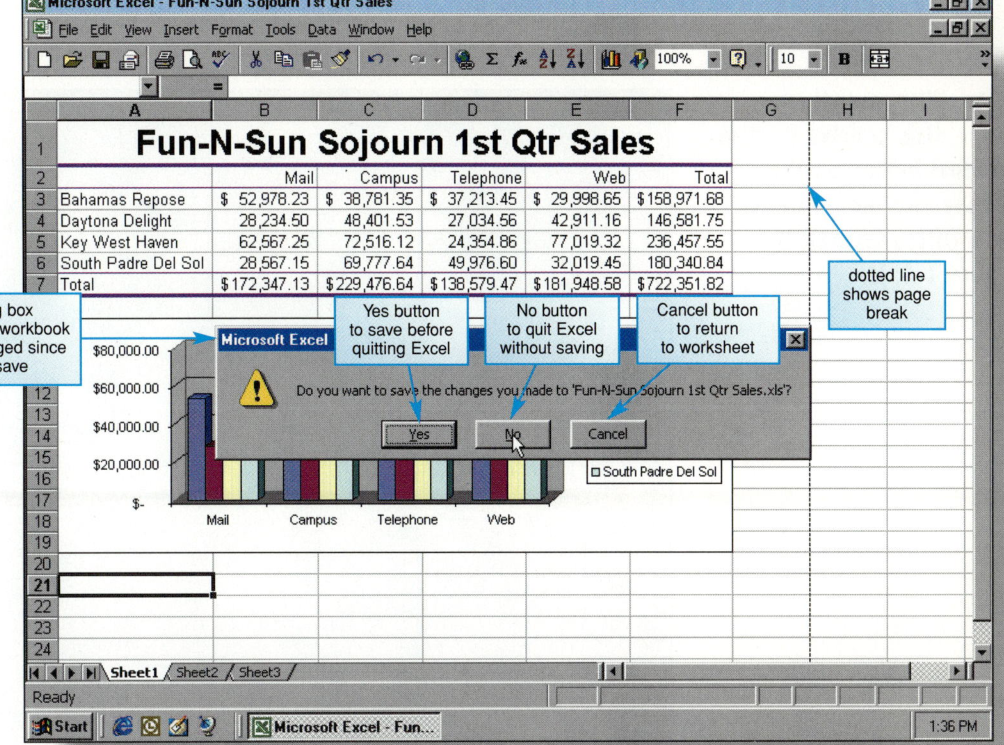

FIGURE 1-64

Other Ways

1. Double-click Control-menu icon
2. Right-click Microsoft Excel button on taskbar, click Close on shortcut menu
3. On File menu click Exit

In Figure 1-63, you can see that two Close buttons and two Control-menu icons display. The Close button and Control-menu icon on the title bar close Excel. The Close button and Control-menu icon on the menu bar close the workbook.

Starting Excel and Opening a Workbook

Once you have created and saved a workbook, you often will have reason to retrieve it from a floppy disk. For example, you might want to review the calculations on the worksheet and enter additional or revised data on it. The steps on the next page assume Excel is not running.

To Start Excel and Open a Workbook

1 With your floppy disk in drive A, click the Start button on the taskbar and then point to Open Office Document (Figure 1-65).

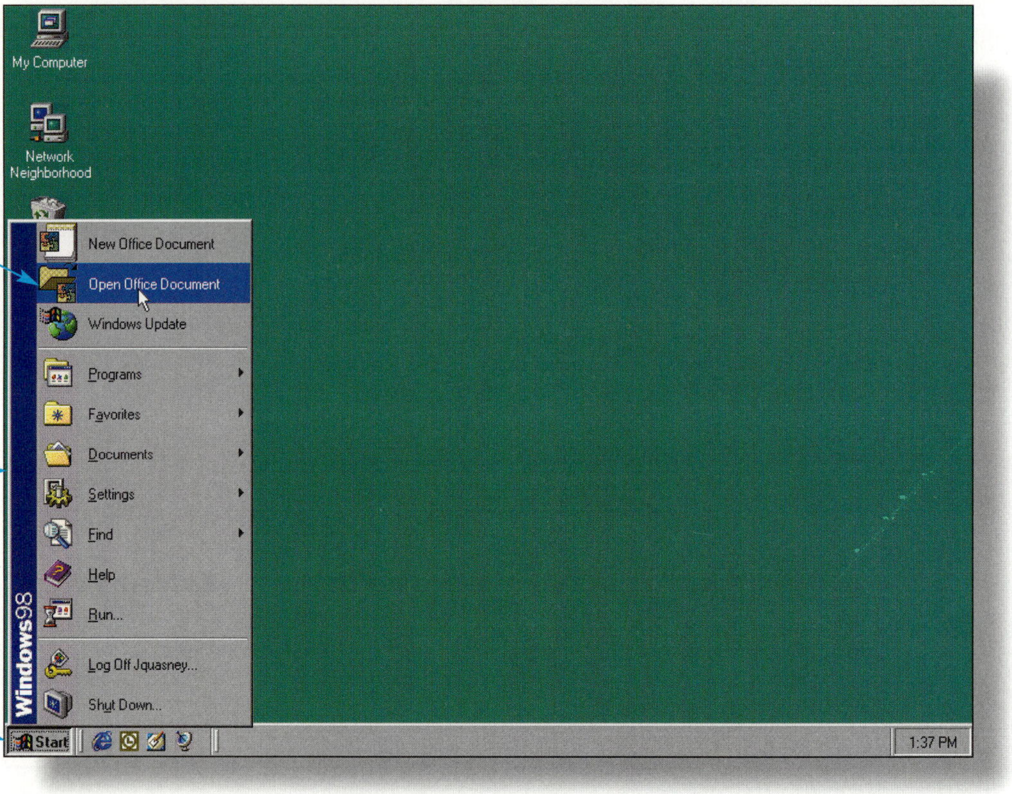

Open Office Document command

Start menu

Start button

My Computer

Network Neighborhood

New Office Document

Open Office Document

Windows Update

Programs

Favorites

Documents

Settings

Find

Help

Run...

Log Off Jquasney...

Shut Down...

Windows98

Start

1:37 PM

FIGURE 1-65

2 Click Open Office Document. If necessary, click the Look in box arrow and then click 3½ Floppy (A:).

The Open Office Document dialog box displays (Figure 1-66).

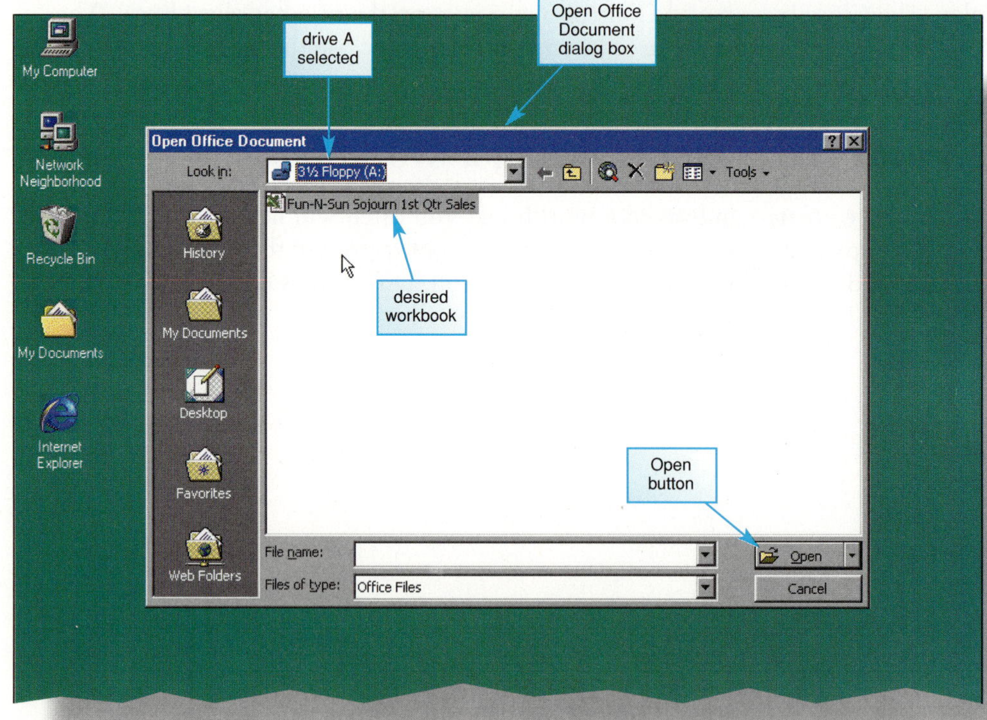

FIGURE 1-66

3 Double-click the file name Fun-N-Sun Sojourn 1st Qtr Sales.

Excel starts, opens the workbook Fun-N-Sun Sojourn 1st Qtr Sales.xls from drive A, and displays it on the screen (Figure 1-67). An alternative to double-clicking the file name is to click it and then click the Open button in the Open Office Document dialog box.

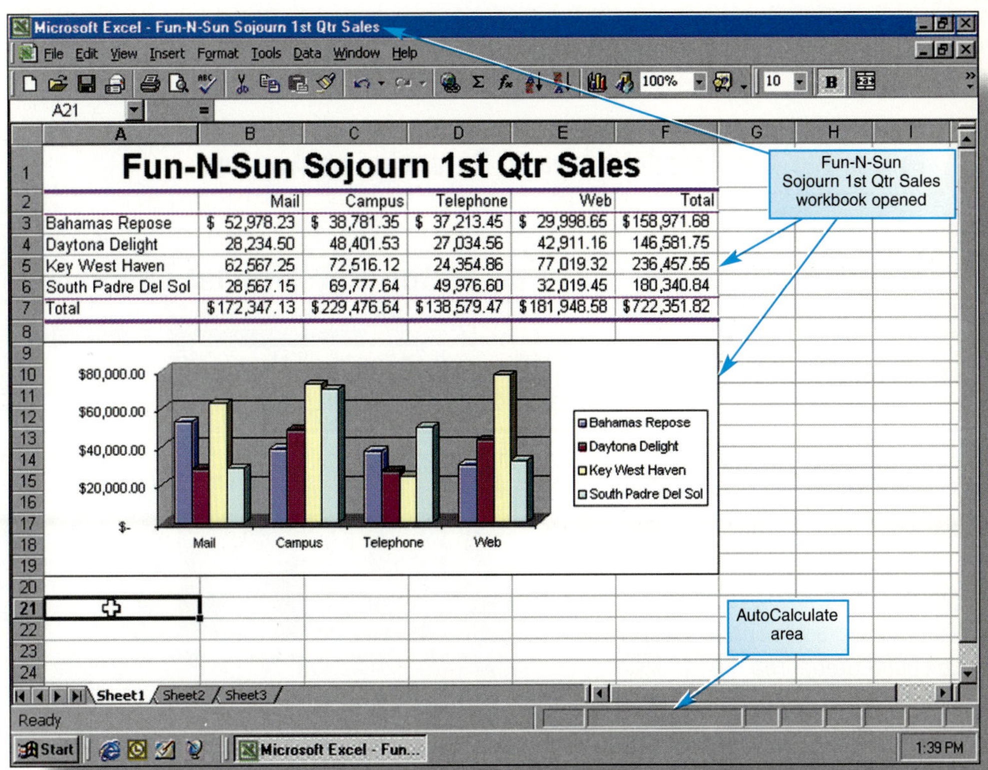

FIGURE 1-67

AutoCalculate

You easily can obtain a total, an average, or other information about the numbers in a range by using the **AutoCalculate area** on the status bar (bottom of Figure 1-67). All you need do is select the range of cells containing the numbers you want to check. Next, right-click the AutoCalculate area to display the shortcut menu (Figure 1-68 on the next page). The recessed check mark to the left of the active function (Sum) indicates that the sum of the selected range displays. The function commands on the AutoCalculate shortcut menu are described in Table 1-5.

Table 1-5 AutoCalculate Shortcut Menu Commands

COMMAND	FUNCTION
Average	Displays the average of the numbers in the selected range
Count	Displays the number of nonblank cells in the selected range
Count Nums	Displays the number of cells containing numbers in the selected range
Max	Displays the highest value in the selected range
Min	Displays the lowest value in the selected range
Sum	Displays the sum of the numbers in the selected range

The following steps show how to display the average first quarter sales by sales channel for the Bahamas Repose vacation package.

To Use the AutoCalculate Area to Determine an Average

1. **Select the range B3:E3. Right-click the AutoCalculate area on the status bar.**

The sum of the numbers in the range B3:E3 displays ($158,971.68) as shown in Figure 1-68 because Sum is active in the AutoCalculate area (you may see a total other than the Sum in your AutoCalculate area). The shortcut menu listing the various types of functions displays over the AutoCalculate area.

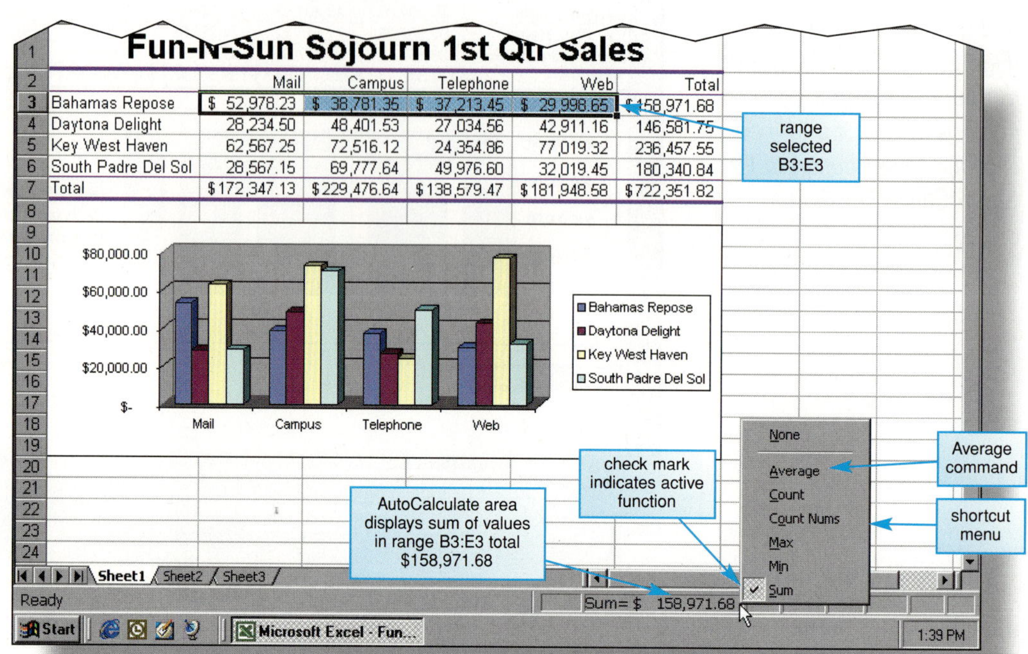

FIGURE 1-68

2. **Click Average on the shortcut menu.**

The average of the numbers in the range B3:E3 displays in the AutoCalculate area (Figure 1-69).

3. **Right-click the AutoCalculate area and then click Sum on the shortcut menu.**

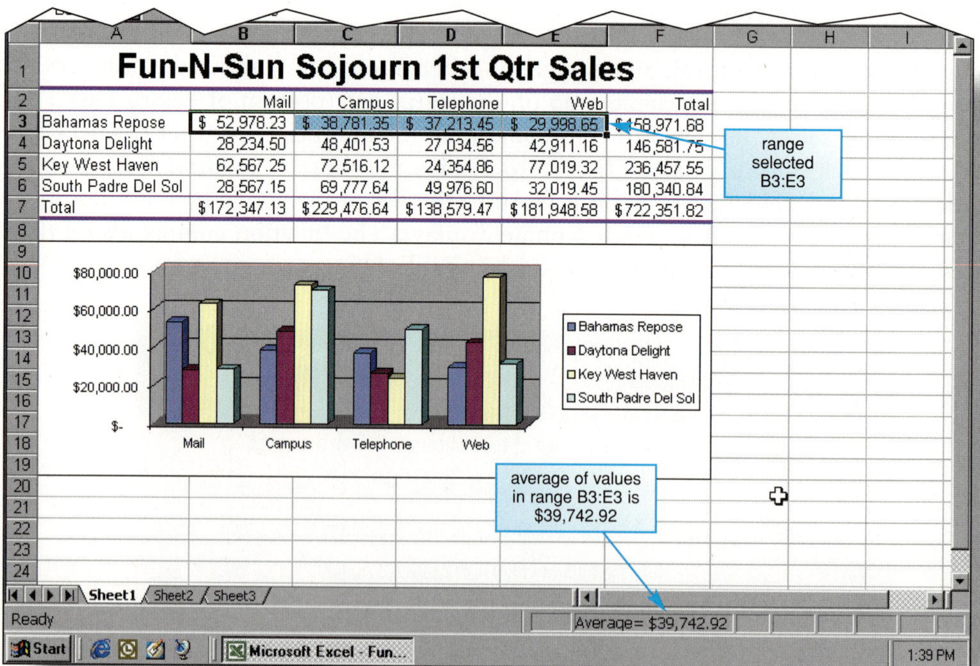

FIGURE 1-69

To change to any one of the other five functions for the range B3:E3, right-click the AutoCalculate area. Then click the desired function.

Shortcut Menus

Shortcut menus display frequently used commands related to an object that the mouse pointer points to. To display a shortcut menu, right-click the object as shown in Step 1. In some cases, you also can display the shortcut menu by selecting the object, such as a cell or range of cells, and pressing SHIFT+F10. To hide a shortcut menu, click outside the shortcut menu or press the ESC key.

Correcting Errors

You can correct errors on a worksheet using one of several methods. The one you choose will depend on the extent of the error and whether you notice it while typing the data or after you have entered the incorrect data into the cell.

Correcting Errors While You Are Typing Data into a Cell

If you notice an error while you are typing data into a cell, press the BACKSPACE key to erase the portion in error and then type the correct characters. If the error is a major one, click the Cancel box in the formula bar or press the ESC key to erase the entire entry and then reenter the data from the beginning.

In-Cell Editing

If you find an error in the worksheet after entering the data, you can correct the error in one of two ways:

1. If the entry is short, select the cell, retype the entry correctly, and click the Enter box or press the ENTER key. The new entry will replace the old entry.
2. If the entry in the cell is long and the errors are minor, the **Edit mode** may be a better choice. Use the Edit mode as described below.
   a. Double-click the cell containing the error. Excel switches to Edit mode, the active cell contents display in the formula bar, and a flashing insertion point displays in the active cell (Figure 1-70). This editing procedure is called **in-cell editing** because you can edit the contents directly in the cell. The active cell contents also display in the formula bar.

Correcting Errors

Learning how to correct errors in a worksheet is critical to becoming proficient in Excel. Thus, carefully review this section on how to correct errors prior to entering data in a cell, how to perform in-cell editing, how to undo the last entry, and how to clear cells.

contents of cell E2 display in formula bar

insertion point displays in cell after double-clicking

FIGURE 1-70

b. Make your changes, as specified below.
   (1) To insert between two characters, place the insertion point between the two characters and begin typing. Excel inserts the new characters at the location of the insertion point.
   (2) To delete a character in the cell, move the insertion point to the left of the character you want to delete and then press the DELETE key, or place the insertion point to the right of the character you want to delete and then press the BACKSPACE key. You also can use the mouse to drag through the character or adjacent characters you want to delete and then press the DELETE key or click the **Cut button** on the Standard toolbar.

In-Cell Editing

An alternative to double-clicking the cell to edit is to select the cell and then press F2.

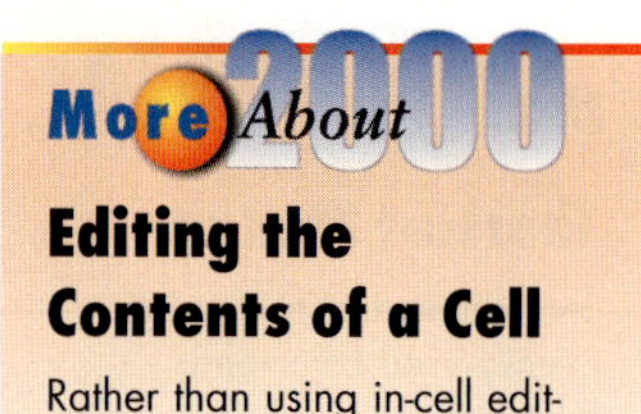

Editing the Contents of a Cell

Rather than using in-cell editing, you can select the cell and then click the formula bar to edit the contents.

(3) When you are finished editing an entry, click the Enter box or press the ENTER key.

When Excel enters the Edit mode, the keyboard usually is in Insert mode. In **Insert mode**, as you type a character, Excel inserts the character and moves all characters to the right of the typed character one position to the right. You can change to Overtype mode by pressing the INSERT key. In **Overtype mode,** Excel overtypes the character to the right of the insertion point. The INSERT key toggles the keyboard between Insert mode and Overtype mode.

While in Edit mode, you may have reason to move the insertion point to various points in the cell, select portions of the data in the cell, or switch from inserting characters to overtyping characters. Table 1-6 summarizes the most common tasks used during in-cell editing.

Table 1-6 Summary of In-Cell Editing Tasks

TASK	*MOUSE*	*KEYBOARD*
Move the insertion point to the beginning of data in a cell	Point to the left of the first character and click	Press HOME
Move the insertion point to the end of data in a cell	Point to the right of the last character and click	Press END
Move the insertion point anywhere in a cell	Point to the appropriate position and click the character	Press RIGHT ARROW or LEFT ARROW
Highlight one or more adjacent characters	Drag the mouse pointer through adjacent characters	Press SHIFT+RIGHT ARROW or SHIFT+LEFT ARROW
Select all data in a cell	Double-click the cell with the insertion point in the cell	
Delete selected characters	Click the Cut button on the Standard toolbar	Press DELETE
Toggle between Insert and Overtype modes		Press INSERT

Undoing the Last Entry

Excel provides the **Undo command** on the Edit menu and the **Undo button** on the Standard toolbar (Figure 1-71) that you can use to erase the most recent cell entry. Thus, if you enter incorrect data in a cell and notice it immediately, click the Undo command or Undo button and Excel changes the cell contents to what they were prior to entering the incorrect data.

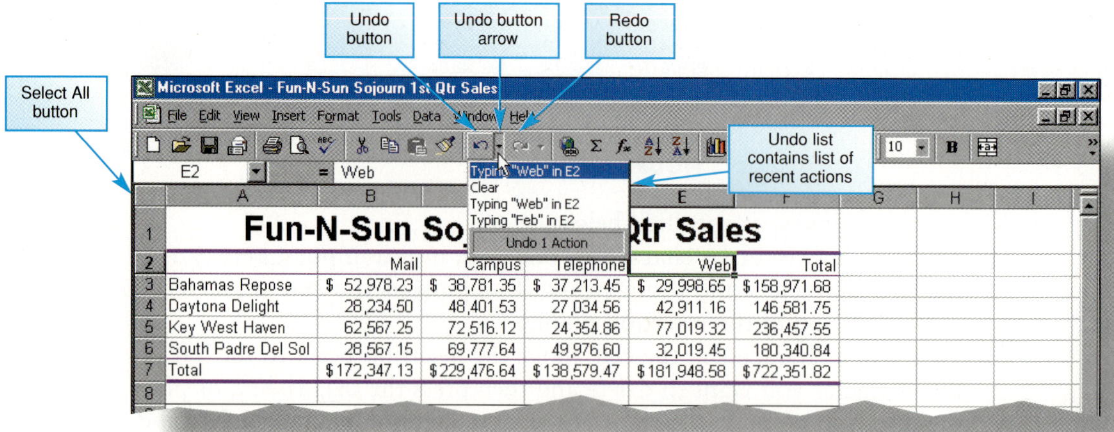

FIGURE 1-71

If Excel cannot undo an action, then the Undo button is inoperative. Excel remembers the last 16 actions you have completed. Thus, you can undo up to 16 previous actions by clicking the Undo box arrow to display the Undo list and clicking the action to be undone (Figure 1-71). You also can click Undo on the Edit menu rather than using the Undo button.

Next to the Undo button on the Standard toolbar is the Redo button. The **Redo button** allows you to repeat previous actions. You also can click Redo on the Edit menu rather than using the Redo button.

The Undo Button

The Undo button can undo far more complicated worksheet activities than just removing the latest entry from a cell. In fact, most commands can be undone if you click the Undo button before you make another entry or issue another command. You cannot undo a save or print command, but, as a general rule, the Undo button can restore the worksheet data and settings to their same state as the last time Excel was in Ready mode. With Excel 2000, multiple-level undo and redo capabilities are available.

Clearing a Cell or Range of Cells

If you enter data into the wrong cell or range of cells, you can erase, or clear, the data using one of several methods. **Never press the SPACEBAR to clear a cell.** Pressing the SPACEBAR enters a blank character. A blank character is text and is different from an empty cell, even though the cell may appear empty.

Excel provides four methods to clear the contents of a cell or a range of cells.

TO CLEAR CELL CONTENTS USING THE FILL HANDLE

1. Select the cell or range of cells and point to the fill handle so the mouse pointer changes to a cross hair.
2. Drag the fill handle back into the selected cell or range until a shadow covers the cell or cells you want to erase. Release the mouse button.

TO CLEAR CELL CONTENTS USING THE SHORTCUT MENU

1. Select the cell or range of cells to be cleared.
2. Right-click the selection.
3. Click Clear Contents on the shortcut menu.

TO CLEAR CELL CONTENTS USING THE DELETE KEY

1. Select the cell or range of cells to be cleared.
2. Press the DELETE key.

TO CLEAR CELL CONTENTS USING THE CLEAR COMMAND

1. Select the cell or range of cells to be cleared.
2. Click Edit on the menu bar and then click Clear.
3. Click All on the submenu.

You also can select a range of cells and click the Cut button on the Standard toolbar or click Cut on the Edit menu. Be aware, however, that the **Cut button** or **Cut command** not only deletes the contents from the range, but also copies the contents of the range to the Office Clipboard.

Clearing Formats

If you accidentally assign unwanted formats to a range of cells, you can use the Clear command on the Edit menu to delete the formats of a selected range. Doing so changes the format to normal. To view the characteristics of the normal format, click Style on the Format menu or press ALT+APOSTROPHE (').

Quick Reference

For a table that lists how to complete the tasks covered in this book using the mouse, menu, shortcut menu, and keyboard, visit the Shelly Cashman Series Office Web page (www.scsite.com/off2000/qr.htm), and then click Microsoft Excel 2000.

Clearing the Entire Worksheet

Sometimes, everything goes wrong. If this happens, you may want to clear the worksheet entirely and start over. To clear the worksheet, follow these steps.

TO CLEAR THE ENTIRE WORKSHEET

1. Click the Select All button on the worksheet (Figure 1-71 on page E 1.52).
2. Press the DELETE key or on the Edit menu click Clear and then click All on the submenu.

The **Select All button** selects the entire worksheet. Instead of clicking the Select All button, you also can press CTRL+A. You also can clear an unsaved workbook by clicking the workbook's Close button or by clicking **Close** on the File menu. If you close the workbook, click the **New button** on the Standard toolbar or click **New** on the File menu to begin working on the next workbook.

TO DELETE AN EMBEDDED CHART

1. Click the chart to select it.
2. Press the DELETE key.

Excel Help System

At any time while you are using Excel, you can get answers to questions by using the **Excel Help system**. Used properly, this form of online assistance can increase your productivity and reduce your frustrations by minimizing the time you spend learning how to use Excel.

The following section shows how to get answers to your questions using the Office Assistant. For additional information on using the Excel Help system, see Appendix A and Table 1-7 on page E1.57.

The Office Assistant

The Office Assistant unifies Excel Help, allows users to ask questions in their own words, and interactively provides tips and suggestions to let users discover the power of Excel 2000.

Using the Office Assistant

The **Office Assistant** answers your questions and suggests more efficient ways to complete a task. With the Office Assistant active, for example, you can type a question, word, or phrase in a text box and the Office Assistant provides immediate help on the subject. Also, as you create a worksheet, the Office Assistant accumulates tips that suggest more efficient ways to do the tasks you completed while building a worksheet, such as formatting, printing, and saving. This tip feature is part of the **IntelliSense™ technology** that is built into Excel, which understands what you are trying to do and suggests better ways to do it. When the light bulb displays above the Office Assistant, click it to see a tip.

The following steps show how to use the Office Assistant to obtain information on formatting a worksheet.

To Obtain Help Using the Office Assistant

1 **If the Office Assistant is not on the screen, click Help on the menu bar and then click Show the Office Assistant. With the Office Assistant on the screen, click it. Type** formatting **in the What would you like to do? text box in the Office Assistant balloon. Point to the Search button (Figure 1-72).**

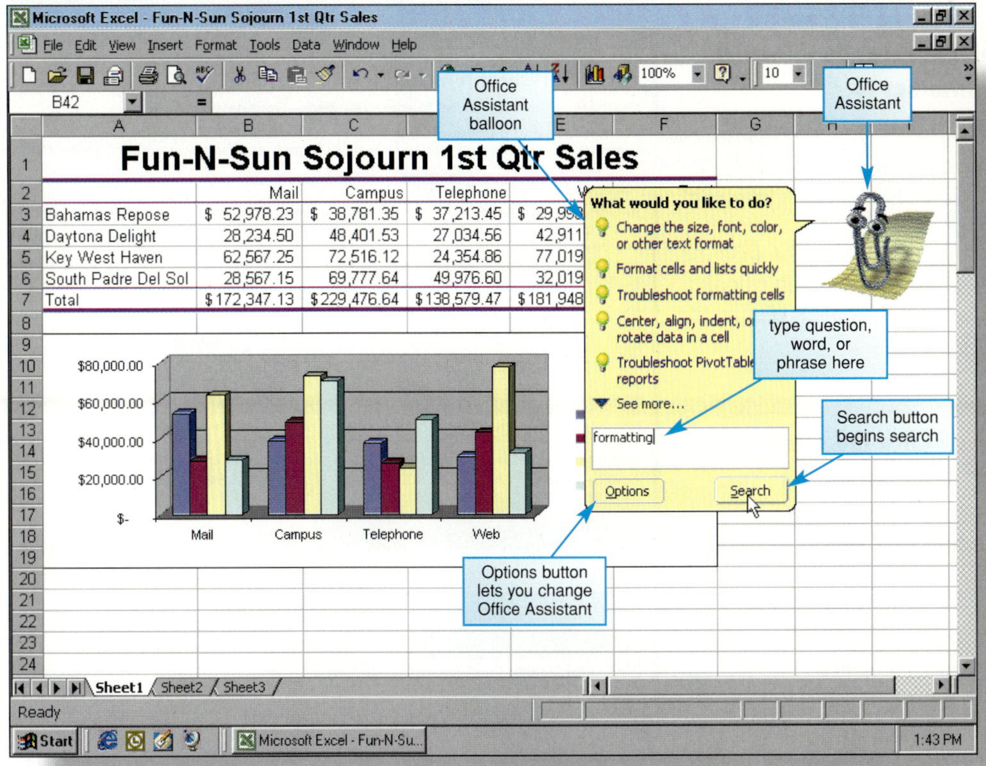

FIGURE 1-72

2 **Click the Search button. Point to the topic About worksheet formatting in the Office Assistant balloon.**

The Office Assistant displays a list of topics relating to the question, how do i format. The mouse pointer changes to a hand indicating it is pointing to a link (Figure 1-73).

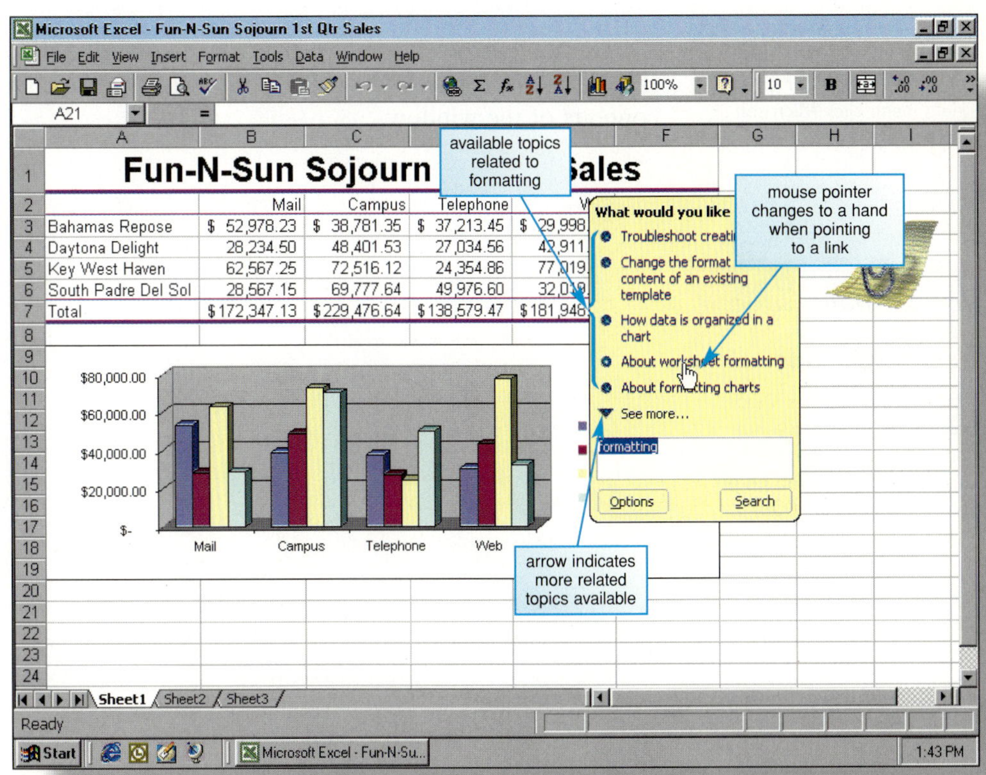

FIGURE 1-73

3 Click About worksheet formatting. When Excel displays the Microsoft Excel Help window, double-click its title bar to maximize it.

The Office Assistant displays a Microsoft Excel Help window that provides Help information about worksheet formatting (Figure 1-74).

4 Click the Close button on the Microsoft Excel Help window title bar.

The Microsoft Excel Help window closes and the worksheet is active.

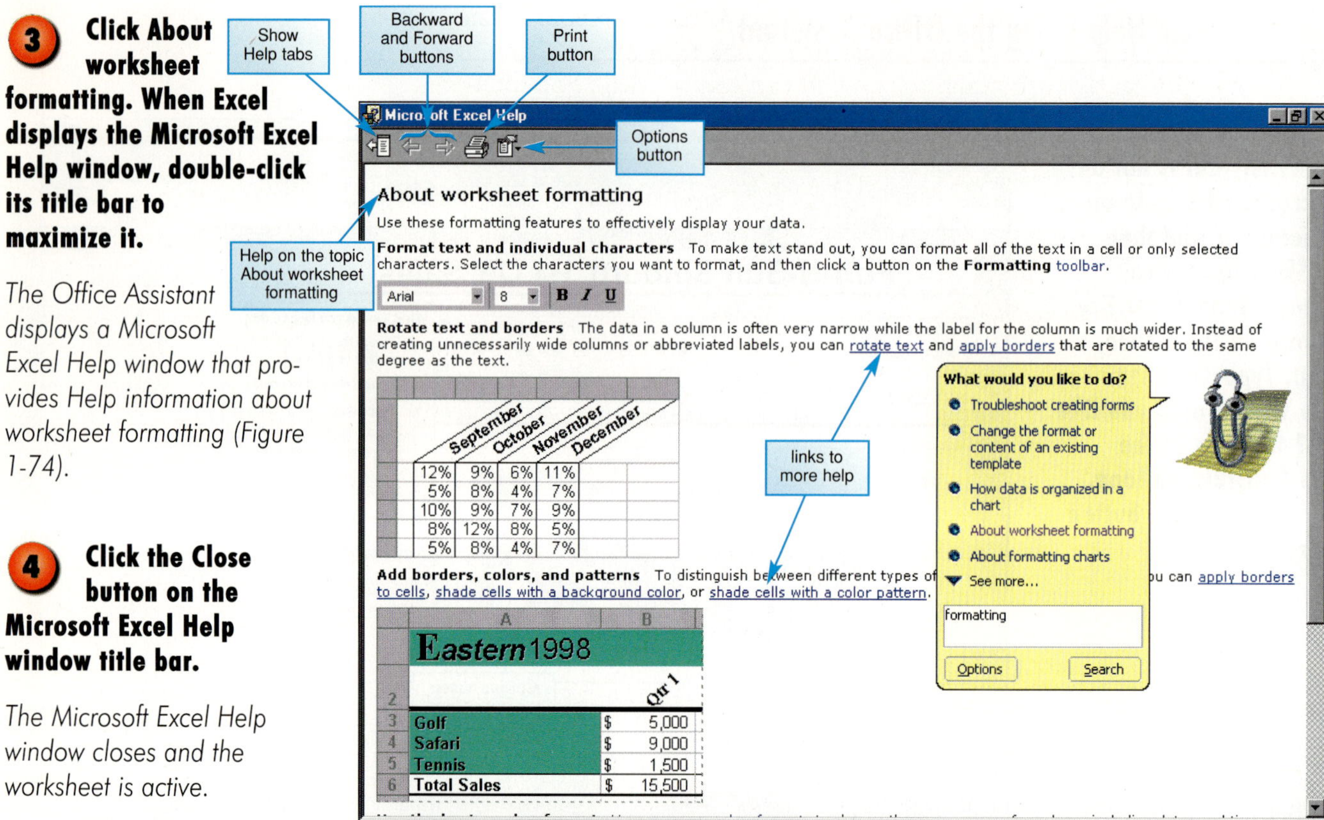

FIGURE 1-74

Other Ways

1. If Office Assistant is on, click Microsoft Excel Help button on Standard toolbar or on Help menu click Microsoft Excel Help

Use the buttons in the upper-left corner of the Microsoft Excel Help window (Figure 1-74) to navigate through the Help system, change the display, and print the contents of the window.

Excel 2000 Tips

To receive a newsletter titled *ExcelTips* regularly via e-mail at no charge, visit the Excel 2000 More About Web page (www.scsite.com/ex2000/more.htm) and click ExcelTips.

Table 1-7 summarizes the nine categories of Help available to you. Because of the way the Excel Help system works, please review the right most column of Table 1-7 if you have difficulties activating the desired category of Help. For additional information on using the Excel Help system, see Appendix A.

Table 1-7 Excel Help System

TYPE	*DESCRIPTION*	*HOW TO ACTIVATE*	*TURNING THE OFFICE ASSISTANT ON AND OFF*
Answer Wizard	Similar to the Office Assistant in that it answers questions that you type in your own words.	Click the Microsoft Excel Help button on the Standard toolbar. If necessary, maximize the Help window by double-clicking its title bar. Click the Answer Wizard tab.	If the Office Assistant displays, right-click it, click Options on the shortcut menu, click Use the Office Assistant to remove the check mark, click the OK button.
Contents sheet	Groups Help topics by general categories. Use when you know only the general category of the topic in question.	Click the Microsoft Excel Help button on the Standard toolbar. If necessary, maximize the Help window by double-clicking its title bar. Click the Contents tab.	If the Office Assistant displays, right-click it, click Options, click Use the Office Assistant to remove the check mark, click the OK button.
Detect and Repair	Automatically finds and fixes errors in the application.	Click Detect and Repair on the Help menu.	
Hardware and Software Information	Shows Product ID and allows access to system information and technical support information.	Click About Microsoft Excel on the Help menu and then click the appropriate button.	
Help for Lotus 1-2-3 Users	Used to assist Lotus 1-2-3 users who are learning Microsoft Excel.	Click Lotus 1-2-3 Help on the Help menu.	
Index sheet	Similar to an index in a book. Use when you know exactly what you want.	Click the Microsoft Excel Help button on the Standard toolbar. If necessary, maximize the Help window by double-clicking its title bar. Click the Index tab.	If the Office Assistant displays, right-click it, click Options, click Use the Office Assistant to remove the check mark, click the OK button.
Office Assistant	Answers questions that you type in your own words, offers tips, and provides Help for a variety of Excel features.	Click the Microsoft Excel Help button on the Standard toolbar or double-click the Office Assistant icon. Some dialog boxes also include the Microsoft Excel Help button.	If the Office Assistant does not display, click Show the Office Assistant on the Help menu.
Office on the Web	Used to access technical resources and download free product enhancements on the Web.	Click Office on the Web on the Help menu.	
Question Mark button and What's This? command	Used to identify unfamiliar items on the screen.	In a dialog box, click the Question Mark button and then click an item in the dialog box. Click What's This? on the Help menu, and then click an item on the screen.	

Quitting Excel

To quit Excel, complete the following steps.

TO QUIT EXCEL

1. Click the Close button on the right side of the title bar (see Figure 1-63 on page E 1.46).
2. If the Microsoft Excel dialog box displays, click the No button.

Quitting Excel 2000

Do not forget to remove the floppy disk from drive A after quitting Excel, especially if you are working in a laboratory environment. Nothing can be more frustrating than leaving all of your hard work behind on a floppy disk for the next user.

CASE PERSPECTIVE SUMMARY

The worksheet created in this project (Figure 1-1 on page E 1.7) allows the management of the Fun-N-Sun Sojourn company to examine the first quarter sales for the four key vacation packages. Furthermore, the 3-D Column chart should meet the needs of Kylie Waiter, who as you recall, has little tolerance for lists of numbers.

Project Summary

In creating the Fun-N-Sun Sojourn 1st Quarter Sales worksheet and chart in this project, you gained a broad knowledge about Excel. First, you were introduced to starting Excel. You learned about the Excel window and how to enter text and numbers to create a worksheet. You learned how to select a range and how to use the AutoSum button to sum numbers in a column or row. Using the fill handle, you learned how to copy a cell to adjacent cells.

Once the worksheet was built, you learned how to change the font size of the title, bold the title, and center the title across a range using buttons on the Formatting toolbar. Using the steps and techniques presented in the project, you formatted the body of the worksheet using the AutoFormat command, and you used the Chart Wizard to add a 3-D Column chart. After completing the worksheet, you saved the workbook on disk and printed the worksheet and chart. You learned how to edit data in cells. Finally, you learned how to use the Excel Help system to answer your questions.

What You Should Know

Having completed this project, you now should be able to perform the following tasks:

- Add a 3-D Column Chart to the Worksheet *(E 1.37)*
- Bold a Cell *(E 1.29)*
- Center a Cell's Contents Across Columns *(E 1.33)*
- Clear Cell Contents Using the Clear Command *(E 1.53)*
- Clear Cell Contents Using the DELETE Key *(E 1.53)*
- Clear Cell Contents Using the Fill Handle *(E 1.53)*
- Clear Cell Contents Using the Shortcut Menu *(E 1.53)*
- Clear the Entire Worksheet *(E 1.54)*
- Copy a Cell to Adjacent Cells in a Row *(E 1.24)*
- Delete an Embedded Chart *(E 1.54)*
- Determine Multiple Totals at the Same Time *(E 1.26)*
- Display the Formatting Toolbar in Its Entirety *(E 1.28)*
- Enter Column Titles *(E 1.18)*
- Enter Numeric Data *(E 1.21)*
- Enter Row Titles *(E 1.20)*
- Enter the Worksheet Title *(E 1.16)*
- Increase the Font Size of a Cell Entry *(E 1.30)*
- Obtain Help Using the Office Assistant *(E 1.55)*
- Print a Worksheet *(E 1.45)*
- Quit Excel *(E 1.46, E 1.57)*
- Save a Workbook *(E 1.41)*
- Start Excel *(E 1.8)*
- Start Excel and Open a Workbook *(E 1.48)*
- Sum a Column of Numbers *(E 1.22)*
- Use AutoFormat to Format the Body of a Worksheet *(E 1.31)*
- Use the AutoCalculate Area to Determine an Average *(E 1.50)*
- Use the Name Box to Select a Cell *(E 1.35)*

More About 2000

Microsoft Certification

The Microsoft Office User Specialist (MOUS) Certification program provides an opportunity for you to obtain a valuable industry credential — proof that you have the Excel 2000 skills required by employers. For more information, see Appendix D or visit the Shelly Cashman Series MOUS Web page at www.scsite.com/off2000/cert.htm.

1 Changing Data in a Worksheet

Instructions: Start Excel. Open the workbook Trevor's Shady Tree Service from the Data Disk. See the inside back cover of this book for instructions for downloading the Data Disk or see your instructor for information on accessing the files required in this book.

Make the changes to the worksheet described in Table 1-8 so it appears as shown in Figure 1-75. As you edit the values in the cells containing numeric data, watch the values in the total income (row 6), the total expenses (row 11), and the profit (row 12). The numbers in these three rows are based on formulas. When you enter a new value, Excel automatically recalculates the formulas. After you have successfully made the changes listed in the table, the profits in cells C12 through F12 should equal $18,580.17, $45,452.34, $44,101.35, and $26,996.44, respectively.

Save the workbook. Use the file name, Eric's Arborescent Service. Print the revised worksheet in landscape orientation and hand in the printout to your instructor. Use the Excel Help system to learn how to print in landscape orientation.

Microsoft Excel - Eric's Arborescent Service

	A	B	C	D	E	F
1	Eric's Arborescent Service					
2	INCOME:		Jan-Mar	Apr-June	July-Sept	Oct-Dec
3		Removal	$62,613.25	$95,324.56	$63,235.25	$95,324.56
4		Trimming	32,341.40	31,721.97	32,341.40	29,213.78
5		Treatment	26,945.30	32,090.21	42,982.90	14,213.75
6	TOTAL INCOME:		$121,899.95	$159,136.74	$138,559.55	$138,752.09
7	EXPENSES:					
8		Salaries	$54,430.00	$52,875.40	$48,430.00	$52,875.40
9		Rent	15,235.00	15,235.00	15,235.00	15,235.00
10		Cost of Goods	33,654.78	45,574.00	30,793.20	43,645.25
11	TOTAL EXPENSES:		$103,319.78	$113,684.40	$94,458.20	$111,755.65
12	PROFIT:		$18,580.17	$45,452.34	$44,101.35	$26,996.44

FIGURE 1-75

Table 1-8 New Worksheet Data

CELL	CHANGE CELL CONTENTS TO
A1	Eric's Arborescent Service
C3	62,613.25
D4	31,721.97
E5	42,982.90
F5	14,213.75
C8	54,430.00
E10	30,793.20
F10	43,645.25

1 Marvin's Music & Movie Mirage Sales Analysis Worksheet

Problem: The chief financial officer (CFO) of Marvin's Music & Movie Mirage needs a sales analysis worksheet similar to the one shown in Figure 1-76. Your task is to develop the worksheet. Table 1-9 provides the sales figures for the worksheet.

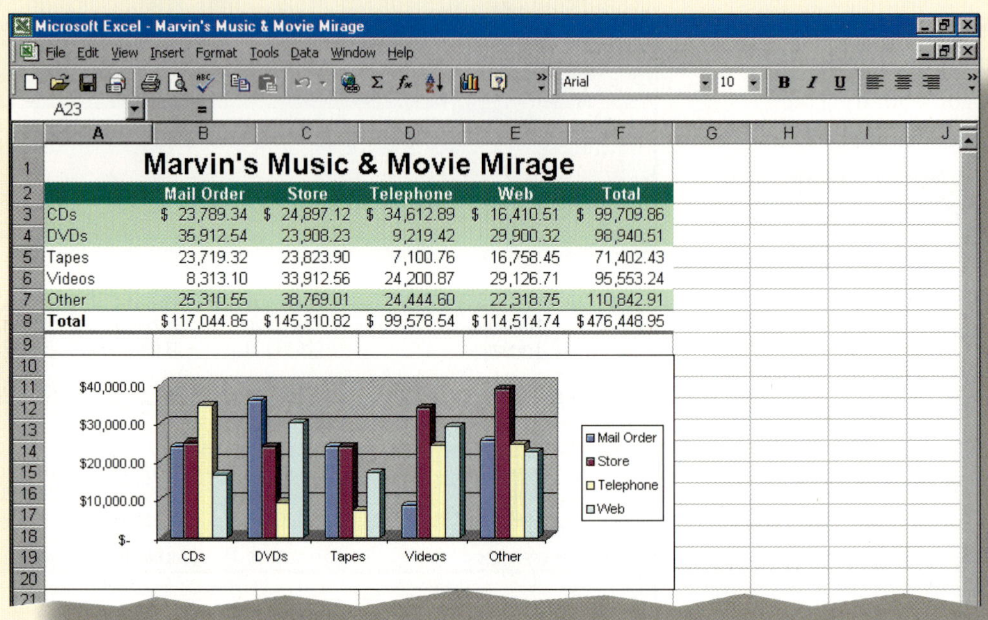

FIGURE 1-76

Instructions: Perform the following tasks.

1. Create the worksheet shown in Figure 1-76 using the title, sales amounts, and categories in Table 1-9.
2. Determine the totals for the types of products, sales channels, and company totals.
3. Format the worksheet title, Marvin's Music & Movie Mirage, in 18-point Arial, bold font, centered across columns A through F.
4. Format the range A2:F8 using the AutoFormat command on the Format menu as follows: (a) Select the range A2:F8 and then apply the table format Accounting 1; and (b) with the range A2:F8 still selected, apply the table format List 2. Excel 2000 appends the formats of List 2 to the formats of Accounting 1.
5. Select the range A2:E7 and then use the Chart Wizard button on the Standard toolbar to draw a Clustered column with a 3-D visual effect chart (column 1, row 2 in Chart sub-type list). Move the chart to the upper-left corner of cell A10 and then drag the lower-right corner of the chart location to cell F20.
6. Enter your name, course, laboratory assignment number, date, and instructor name in cells A24 through A28.
7. Save the workbook using the file name Marvin's Music & Movie Mirage.
8. Print the worksheet.
9. Make the following two corrections to the sales amounts: $35,987.99 for DVDs sold in a store and $36,498.33 for Videos sold over the telephone. After you enter the corrections, the company totals should equal $157,390.58 in cell C8 and $111,876.00 in cell D8.
10. Print the revised worksheet. Close the workbook without saving the changes.

Table 1-9 Marvin's Music & Movie Mirage Data

	MAIL ORDER	STORE	TELEPHONE	WEB
CDs	$23,789.34	$24,897.12	$34,612.89	$16,410.51
DVDs	35,912.54	23,908.23	9,219.42	29,900.32
Tapes	23,719.32	23,823.90	7,100.76	16,758.45
Videos	8,313.10	33,912.56	24,200.87	29,126.71
Other	25,310.55	38,769.01	24,444.60	22,318.75

2 Dollar Bill's Annual Software Sales Worksheet

Problem: As the assistant financial manager for Dollar Bill's Software, Inc., your supervisor has asked you to create a workbook to analyze the annual sales for the company by product group and store location. The software sales for the year are shown in Table 1-10.

Table 1-10 Dollar Bill's Data

	SAN ANTONIO	SAN FRANCISCO	CLEVELAND	CHARLOTTE
Business	35,102.15	18,231.56	31,012.40	12,012.00
Database	42,970.50	57,210.00	29,089.12	29,765.23
Education	21,892.70	18,329.34	26,723.15	22,914.50
Graphics	9,312.45	12,923.21	9,012.56	8,910.32
Games	13,453.30	22,134.45	13,908.55	9,143.75

Instructions: Perform the following tasks.

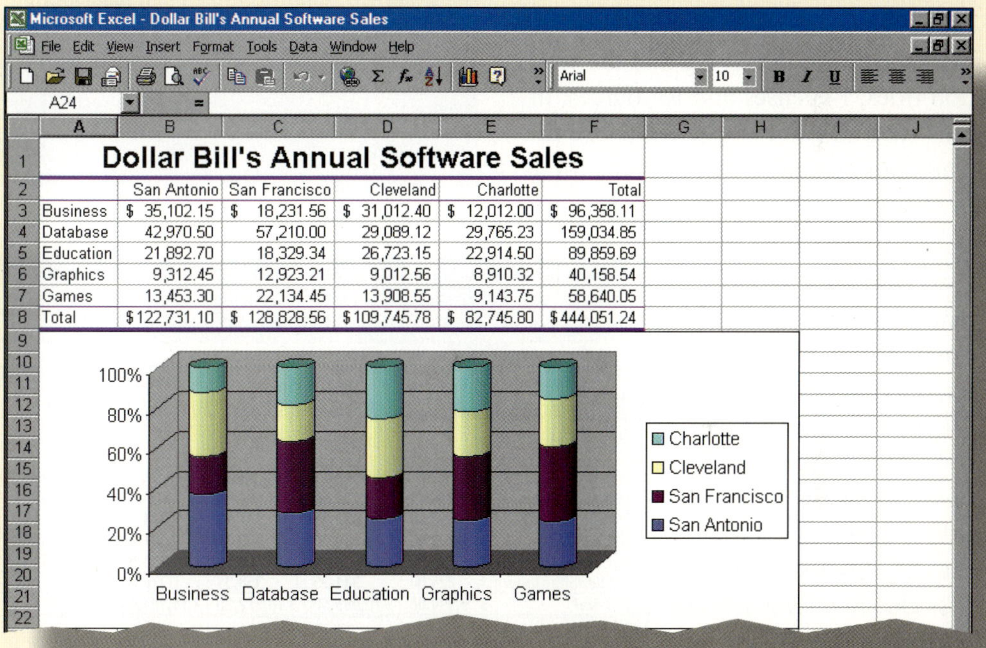

FIGURE 1-77

1. Create the worksheet shown in Figure 1-77 using the sales amounts in Table 1-10.
2. Direct Excel to determine the totals for the four store locations, the product categories, and the company.
3. Format the worksheet title, Dollar Bill's Annual Software Sales, in 18-point Arial bold font, and centered across columns A through F.
4. Use the AutoFormat command on the Format menu to format the range A2:F8. Use the table format Accounting 2.
5. Use the ChartWizard button on the Standard toolbar to draw the 3-D Stacked Cylinder chart (column 3, row 1 in the Chart sub-type list), as shown in Figure 1-77. Chart the range A2:E7 and use the chart location A9:H22. Extend the chart location to the right, if necessary.
6. Enter your name in cell A25. Enter your course, computer laboratory assignment number, date, and instructor name in cells A26 through A29.
7. Save the workbook using the file name, Dollar Bill's Annual Software Sales. Print the worksheet.
8. Two corrections to the sales amounts were sent in from the accounting department. The correct sales amounts are $16,453.21 for Games in San Antonio and $42,781.50 for Database software in Charlotte. Enter the two corrections. After you enter the two corrections, the company total should equal $460,067.42 in cell F8. Print the revised worksheet.
9. Use the Undo button to change the worksheet back to the original numbers in Table 1-10.
10. Use the Redo button to change the worksheet back to the revised state.
11. Hand in all printouts to your instructor. Close the workbook without saving the changes.

3 Projected College Cash Flow Analysis

Problem: Attending college is an expensive proposition and your resources are limited. To plan for your four-year college career, you have decided to organize your anticipated expenses and resources in a worksheet. The data required to prepare your worksheet is shown in Table 1-11.

Table 1-11 College Expenses and Resources

EXPENSES	*FRESHMAN*	*SOPHOMORE*	*JUNIOR*	*SENIOR*
Room & Board	$3,290.00	$3,454.50	$3,627.23	$3,808.59
Tuition & Books	4,850.00	5,092.50	5,347.13	5,614.48
Clothes	490.00	514.50	540.23	567.24
Entertainment	635.00	666.75	700.09	735.09
Miscellaneous	325.00	341.25	358.31	376.23
RESOURCES	*FRESHMAN*	*SOPHOMORE*	*JUNIOR*	*SENIOR*
Savings	$1,600.00	$1,680.00	$1,764.00	$1,852.20
Parents	2,340.00	2,457.00	2,579.85	2,708.84
Job	1,450.00	1,522.50	1,598.64	1,678.56
Financial Aid	4,200.00	4,410.00	4,630.50	4,862.03

Part 1 Instructions: Using the numbers in Table 1-11, create the worksheet shown in Figure 1-78. Enter the worksheet title in cell A1 and the section titles, Expenses and Resources, in cells A2 and A10, respectively. Use the AutoSum button to calculate the totals in rows 9 and 16 and column F.

To format the worksheet, use the table format Accounting 1 for the range A3:F9 and again for the range A11:F16. Increase the font size of the worksheet title to 18 point and the section titles to 16 point. Bold the entire worksheet by first clicking the Select All button on the worksheet and then clicking the Bold button on the Formatting toolbar. Center the title across columns A through F. Enter your name in cell A19 and your course, laboratory assignment number, date, and instructor name in cells A20 through A23. Use Help to determine how to use the Font Color button on the Formatting toolbar to change the font color of the worksheet title and section titles as shown in Figure 1-78.

Microsoft Excel - College Expenses and Resources

	A	B	C	D	E	F
1	Projected College Cash Flow Analysis					
2	Expenses					
3		*Freshman*	*Sophomore*	*Junior*	*Senior*	*Total*
4	Room & Board	$ 3,290.00	$ 3,454.50	$ 3,627.23	$ 3,808.59	$14,180.32
5	Tuition & Books	4,850.00	5,092.50	5,347.13	5,614.48	20,904.11
6	Clothes	490.00	514.50	540.23	567.24	2,111.97
7	Entertainment	635.00	666.75	700.09	735.09	2,736.93
8	Miscellaneous	325.00	341.25	358.31	376.23	1,400.79
9	*Total*	$ 9,590.00	$10,069.50	$10,572.99	$11,101.63	$41,334.12
10	Resources					
11		*Freshman*	*Sophomore*	*Junior*	*Senior*	*Total*
12	Savings	$ 1,600.00	$ 1,680.00	$ 1,764.00	$ 1,852.20	$ 6,896.20
13	Parents	2,340.00	2,457.00	2,579.85	2,708.84	10,085.69
14	Job	1,450.00	1,522.50	1,598.64	1,678.56	6,249.70
15	Financial Aid	4,200.00	4,410.00	4,630.50	4,862.03	18,102.53
16	*Total*	$ 9,590.00	$10,069.50	$10,572.99	$11,101.63	$41,334.12

FIGURE 1-78

Save the workbook using the file name, College Expenses and Resources. Print the worksheet. Use the Office Assistant to learn how to print only a specific area of a worksheet and then print the selection A1:F9 of the worksheet.

Increment all Junior-year expenses in column D by $500. Increment the financial aid for the Junior year by the amount required to cover the increase. The totals in cells F9 and F16 should equal $43,834.12. Print the worksheet. Close the workbook without saving changes. Hand in the three printouts to your instructor.

Part 2 Instructions: Open the workbook College Expenses and Resources created in Part 1. A close inspection of Table 1-11 shows a 5% increase each year over the previous year. Use the Office Assistant to determine how to enter the data for the last three years using a formula and the Copy command. For example, the formula to enter in cell C4 is =B4 * 1.05. Enter formulas to replace all the numbers in the range C4:E8 and C12:E15. If necessary, reformat the tables using Accounting 1 as you did in Part 1. The worksheet should appear as shown in Figure 1-78, except that some of the totals will be off by 0.01 due to round-off errors. Save the worksheet using the file name, College Expenses and Resources2. Print the worksheet. Press CTRL+` (left single quotation mark) to display the formulas. Print the formulas version. Hand in both printouts to your instructor.

The difficulty of these case studies varies:
◗ are the least difficult; ◗◗ are more difficult; and ◗◗◗ are the most difficult.

1 ◗ You just started as a summer intern at the Blue Suede Music Company. Your manager, Elma Presley, has asked you to prepare a worksheet and chart to help her analyze the yearly guitar sales by region and by guitar type (Table 1-12). Use the concepts and techniques presented in this project to create the worksheet and chart.

Table 1-12 Blue Suede Music Company Data

	NORTH	EAST	WEST	SOUTH
Classical	6734	7821	4123	7989
Steel String	5423	2134	6574	3401
Electric	3495	6291	7345	7098
Bass	5462	2923	8034	5135

2 ◗ The number of new cars and trucks has increased each year from 1996 through 2000, as indicated in Table 1-13. Create a worksheet and 3-D Column chart that illustrates these increases. Show model year and type car and truck totals. Use the concepts and techniques presented in this project to create the worksheet and chart.

Table 1-13 1996 - 2000 New Cars and Trucks Data

YEAR	DOMESTIC CARS*	IMPORT CARS*	DOMESTIC TRUCKS*	IMPORT TRUCKS*
1996	7,323	2,231	6,125	225
1997	7,498	2,356	6,315	257
1998	7,615	2,489	6,727	313
1999	7,734	2,501	6,501	407
2000	7,944	2,578	6,623	661

* in thousands

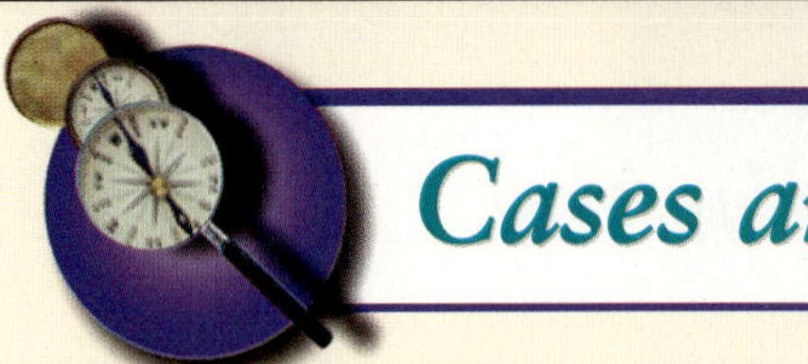

Cases and Places

3 ▸ You are a teaching assistant for the Computer Information Systems department. The department head has asked you to take her grade ledger (Table 1-14), which shows her grade distributions for all her spring classes, and separate them into categories based on the class and the grade. She wants a worksheet and 3-D Column chart to make it easier to view the grades as well as the totals at a glance. Use the concepts and techniques presented in this project to create the worksheet and chart.

Table 1-14 Semester Grade Summary

GRADE	CIS 104	CIS 205	CIS 299	CIS 331
A	2	1	4	2
B	22	7	2	3
C	15	10	11	9
D	20	5	15	6
F	11	8	19	3

4 ▸ The CheeseHeads restaurant in Green Bay, Wisconsin is trying to decide whether it is feasible to open another restaurant in the neighboring community of Oshkosh, Wisconsin. The owner, G. B. Pack, has asked you to develop a worksheet totaling all the revenue received last year. The revenue by quarter is: Quarter 1, $94,342.98; Quarter 2, $81,500.65; Quarter 3, $158,220.09; and Quarter 4, $225,435.50. Create a 3-D Pie chart to illustrate revenue contribution by quarter. Use the AutoCalculate area to find the average quarterly revenue.

5 ▸▸ The Palace Theater is a small movie house that shows almost-current releases at weekday evening, weekend matinee, and weekend evening screenings. Three types of tickets are sold at each presentation: general admission, senior citizen, and children. The theater management has asked you to prepare a worksheet, based on the revenue from a typical week, that can be used in reevaluating its ticket structure. During an average week, weekday evening shows generate $7,540 from general admission ticket sales, $3,575 from senior citizen ticket sales, and $1,375 from children ticket sales. Weekend matinee shows make $5,500 from general admission ticket sales, $1,950 from senior citizen ticket sales, and $2,500 from children ticket sales. Weekend evening shows earn $8,540 from general admission ticket sales, $7,350 from senior citizen ticket sales, and $1,100 from children ticket sales. Use the concepts and techniques presented in this project to prepare a worksheet that includes total revenues for each type of ticket and for each presentation time, and a Bar chart illustrating ticket revenues.

6 ▸▸▸ Some academic disciplines appear to attract more students of one gender than the other. Visit the Registrar's office at your school and find out how many males and how many females have declared majors in five disciplines. Using this information, create a worksheet showing the number of male, female, and total number of majors in each discipline. Include totals for each numeric column. Include a Column chart to illustrate your data.

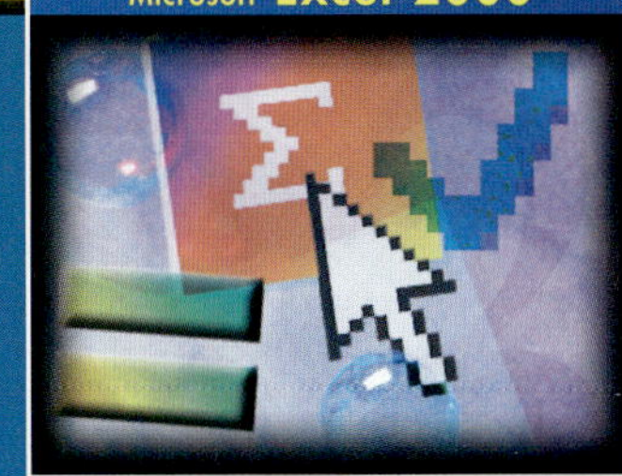

Microsoft Excel 2000

Formulas, Functions, Formatting, and Web Queries

OBJECTIVES

You will have mastered the material in this project when you can:

- Enter multiple lines of text in the same cell
- Enter a formula using the keyboard
- Enter formulas using Point mode
- Identify the arithmetic operators +, –, *, /, %, and ^
- Apply the AVERAGE, MAX, and MIN functions
- Determine a percentage
- Verify a formula
- Change the font of a cell
- Color the characters and background of a cell
- Add borders to a range
- Format numbers using the Format Cells dialog box
- Add conditional formatting to a range of cells
- Align text in cells
- Change the width of a column and height of a row
- Check the spelling of a worksheet
- Preview how a printed copy of the worksheet will look
- Distinguish between portrait and landscape orientation
- Print a partial or complete worksheet
- Display and print the formulas version of a worksheet
- Print to fit
- Use a Web query to get real-time data from a Web site
- Rename sheets
- E-mail the active workbook from within Excel

Windy City Pedal Pushers

Riding L.A.T.E. into the Morning

Mountain bikes, helmets, and reflectors ready, very early morning cyclists do whatever it takes to prepare themselves to pedal their bikes 25 miles in Chicago during the annual Friends of the Parks' L.A.T.E. Ride. The event is aptly named. L.A.T.E. is an acronym for Long After Twilight Ends. The moonstruck ride occurs from 1:30 A.M. to sunrise and weaves through Chicago's downtown and north side neighborhoods and parks.

Friends of the Parks' mission is to preserve and improve Chicago's neighborhood, regional, and lakefront parks in addition to children's playlots. Every year, volunteers contribute time, funds, and effort to clean and maintain the park grounds. Friends of the Parks' has been representing Chicago citizens since 1975, and the L.A.T.E. Ride is one event, in addition to the annual Earth Day clean-up, that promotes its causes.

So how does the Friends of the Parks' organization attempt to manage and organize information about the more than 9,000 participants who take part in the L.A.T.E. Ride event each year? Staff, many of whom volunteer their time and expertise, use worksheets to organize, chart, and present all types of

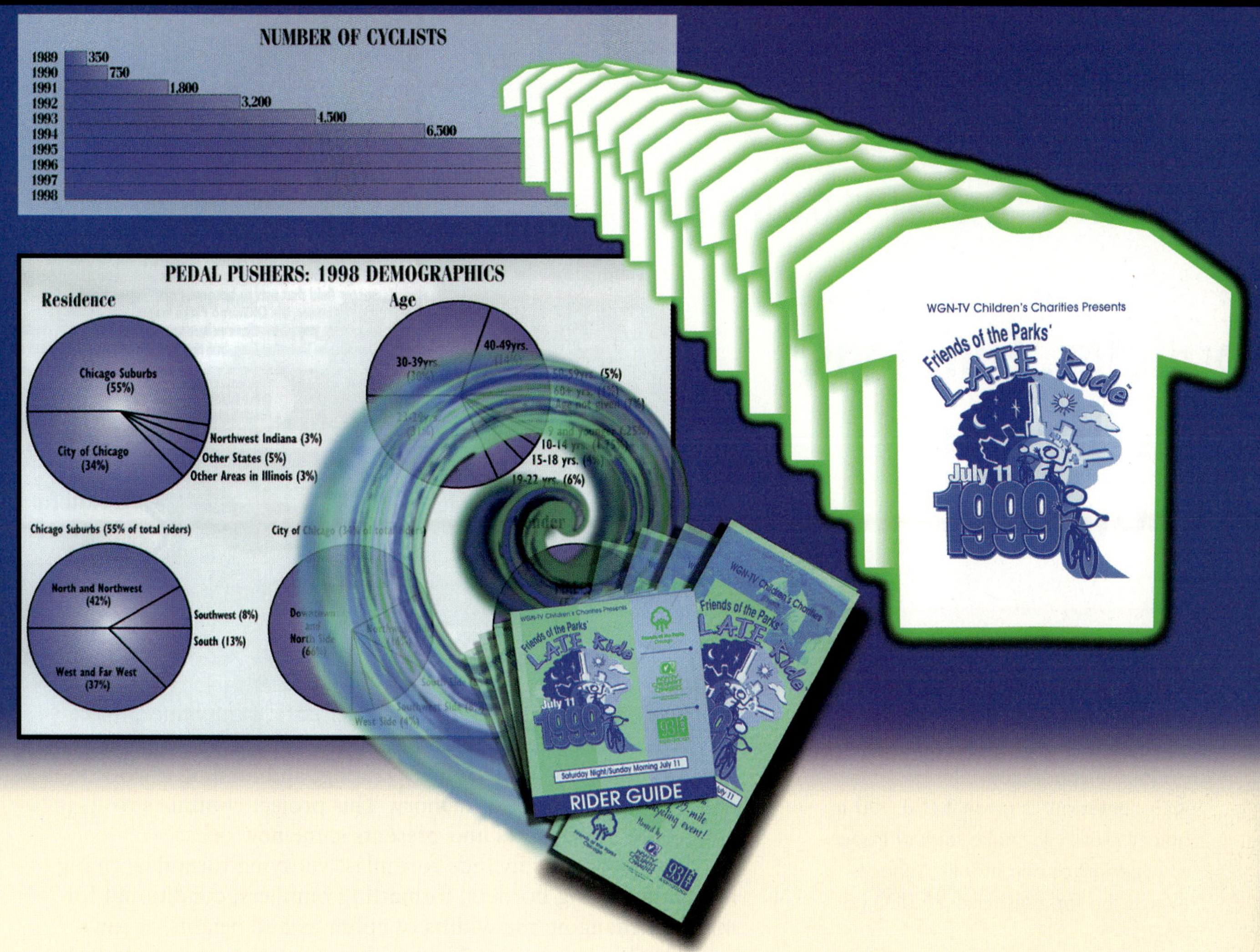

data with relative ease. They analyze and manipulate data; specifically, they input numbers and enter formulas to determine averages and percentages, as well as find the minimum and maximum numbers in a series. In addition, they create traditional Pie charts, Column charts, and other chart forms to represent the data visually.

If they want to determine, for example, the demographics of the L.A.T.E. bike riders, they can input participants' ages taken from a Friends of the Parks' survey and then allow the worksheet to generate Pie charts depicting the age breakdowns in a matter of seconds. Moreover, they can create a Column chart showing the number of participants from year to year. The Friends of the Parks' also can track how many participants live in Chicago, the suburbs, or other states and the number of male and female cyclists.

You will perform similar tasks in this project when you create a worksheet for the BetNet Stock Club. You will enter formulas, use the AVERAGE, MAX, and MIN functions, and then verify the formulas for accuracy.

The L.A.T.E. Ride was established in 1989 with 350 cyclists; most recently nearly 10,000 bike riders have participated. It is not by sheer coincidence that the numbers have escalated dramatically. Once the staff at the Friends of the Parks' collects survey data, they then input the numbers into worksheets using ranges of numbers, enter formulas, and apply formats for appropriate charts. Such data is important to determine marketing strategies or finalize the total number of glow-in-the-dark T-shirts and number tags needed for the participants to don for the ride.

So, if you are up for a challenge in the middle of the night in mid-July in the Windy City, grab your bike and head to the shores of Lake Michigan for the start of a L.A.T.E. night, pedal-pushing experience.

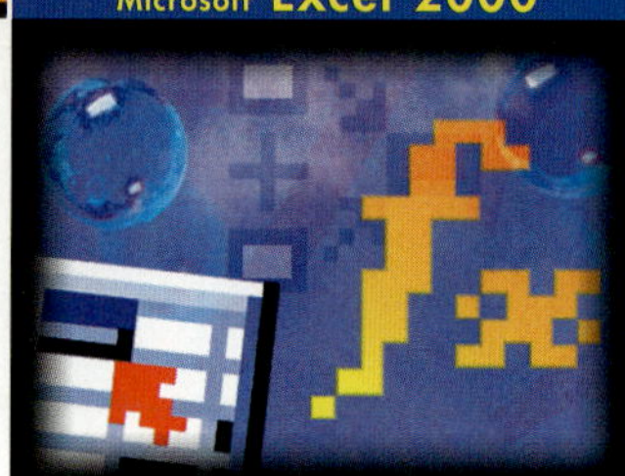

Microsoft Excel 2000

Formulas, Functions, Formatting, and Web Queries

PROJECT 2

CASE PERSPECTIVE

During their Freshman year in college, Michael Santos and six classmates began playing the Investment Challenge game on the Yahoo! Web site (quote.yahoo.com). In the game, each contestant is given $100,000 in fantasy money to make fantasy trades for a period of one month. Yahoo! awards the top finisher a $5,000 cash prize.

Recently, Michael and his classmates won the contest. With their newly gained confidence in investing, they used the prize money to start the BetNet Stock Club. They decided to invest in only the high-flying Internet stocks.

Each month, Michael summarizes the month-end financial status. As the club members approach graduation from college, the value of the club's portfolio has grown to nearly $900,000. As a result, the members voted to buy a new computer and Microsoft Office 2000 for Michael. With Office 2000, he plans to create a worksheet summarizing the club's stock activities that he can e-mail to the members. Michael has asked you to show him how to create the workbook and access real-time stock quotes over the Internet using Excel 2000.

Introduction

In Project 1, you learned how to enter data, sum values, make the worksheet easier to read, and draw a chart. You also learned about online Help and saving, printing, and loading a workbook from a floppy disk into memory. This project continues to emphasize these topics and presents some new ones.

The new topics include formulas, verifying formulas, changing fonts, adding borders, formatting numbers, conditional formatting, changing the widths of columns and heights of rows, spell checking, e-mailing from within an application, and alternative types of worksheet displays and printouts. One alternative display and printout shows the formulas rather than the values in the worksheet. When you display the formulas in the worksheet, you see exactly what text, data, formulas, and functions you have entered into it. Finally, this project covers Web queries to obtain real-time data from a Web site.

Project Two — BetNet Stock Club

The summary notes from your meeting with Michael include the following: need, source of data, calculations, and Web requirements.

Need: An easy-to-read worksheet that summarizes the club's investments (Figure 2-1a). For each stock, the worksheet is to include the name, symbol, date acquired, number of shares, initial price, initial cost, current price, current value, gain/loss, and percent gain/loss. Michael also has requested that the worksheet include totals and the average, highest value, and lowest value for each column of numbers. Finally, Michael wants to use Excel to access real-time stock quotes using Web queries (Figure 2-1b).

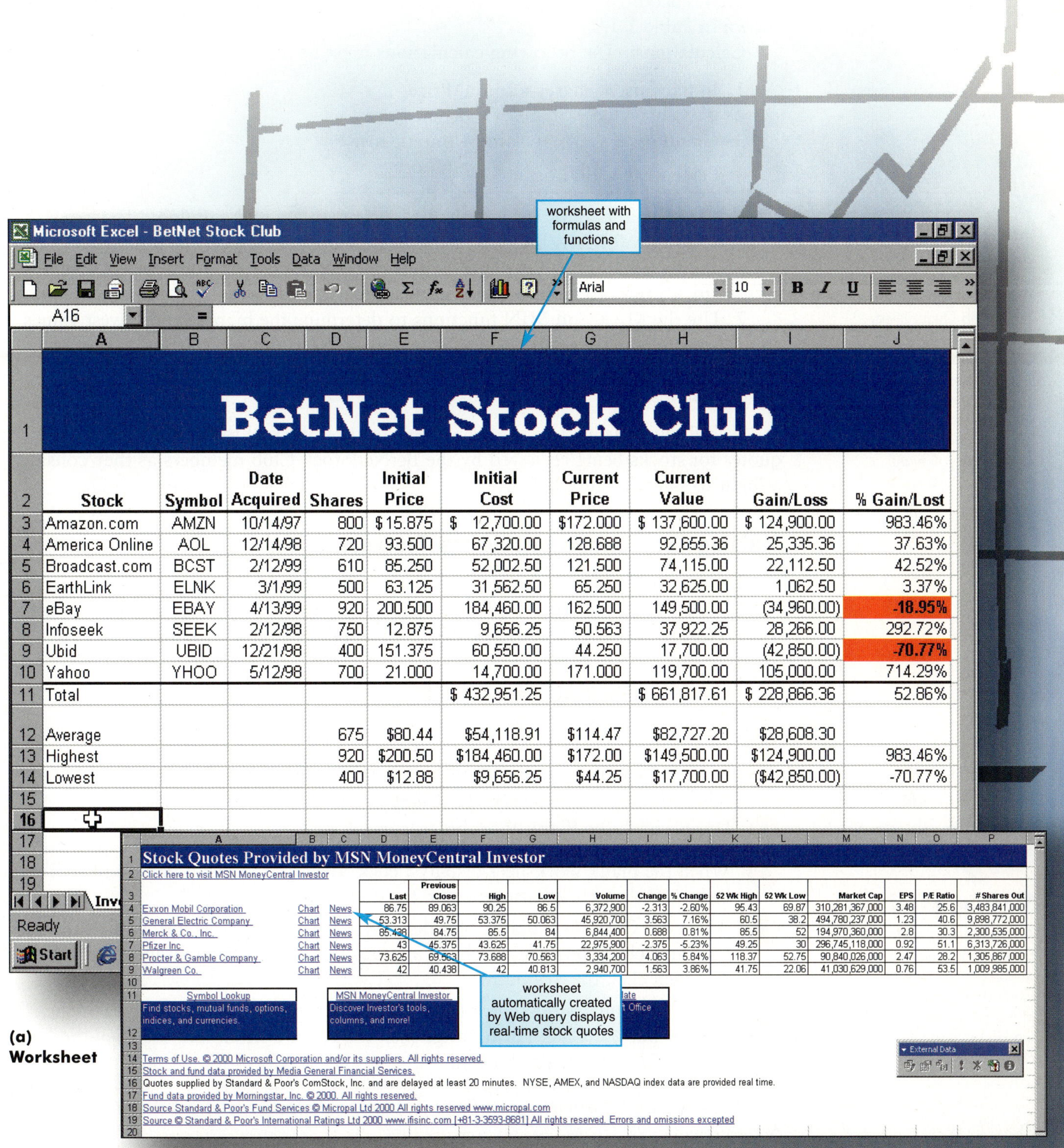

BetNet Stock Club

Stock	Symbol	Date Acquired	Shares	Initial Price	Initial Cost	Current Price	Current Value	Gain/Loss	% Gain/Lost
Amazon.com	AMZN	10/14/97	800	$15.875	$ 12,700.00	$172.000	$ 137,600.00	$ 124,900.00	983.46%
America Online	AOL	12/14/98	720	93.500	67,320.00	128.688	92,655.36	25,335.36	37.63%
Broadcast.com	BCST	2/12/99	610	85.250	52,002.50	121.500	74,115.00	22,112.50	42.52%
EarthLink	ELNK	3/1/99	500	63.125	31,562.50	65.250	32,625.00	1,062.50	3.37%
eBay	EBAY	4/13/99	920	200.500	184,460.00	162.500	149,500.00	(34,960.00)	-18.95%
Infoseek	SEEK	2/12/98	750	12.875	9,656.25	50.563	37,922.25	28,266.00	292.72%
Ubid	UBID	12/21/98	400	151.375	60,550.00	44.250	17,700.00	(42,850.00)	-70.77%
Yahoo	YHOO	5/12/98	700	21.000	14,700.00	171.000	119,700.00	105,000.00	714.29%
Total					$ 432,951.25		$ 661,817.61	$ 228,866.36	52.86%
Average			675	$80.44	$54,118.91	$114.47	$82,727.20	$28,608.30	
Highest			920	$200.50	$184,460.00	$172.00	$149,500.00	$124,900.00	983.46%
Lowest			400	$12.88	$9,656.25	$44.25	$17,700.00	($42,850.00)	-70.77%

(a) Worksheet

Stock Quotes Provided by MSN MoneyCentral Investor

Click here to visit MSN MoneyCentral Investor

			Last	Previous Close	High	Low	Volume	Change	% Change	52 Wk High	52 Wk Low	Market Cap	EPS	P/E Ratio	# Shares Out
Exxon Mobil Corporation	Chart	News	86.75	89.063	90.25	86.5	6,372,900	-2.313	-2.60%	95.43	69.87	310,281,367,000	3.48	25.6	3,483,841,000
General Electric Company	Chart	News	53.313	49.75	53.375	50.063	45,920,700	3.563	7.16%	60.5	38.2	494,780,237,000	1.23	40.6	9,898,772,000
Merck & Co., Inc.	Chart	News	85.438	84.75	85.5	84	6,844,400	0.688	0.81%	85.5	52	194,970,360,000	2.8	30.3	2,300,535,000
Pfizer Inc	Chart	News	43	45.375	43.625	41.75	22,975,900	-2.375	-5.23%	49.25	30	296,745,118,000	0.92	51.1	6,313,726,000
Procter & Gamble Company	Chart	News	73.625	69.563	73.688	70.563	3,334,200	4.063	5.84%	118.37	52.75	90,840,026,000	2.47	28.2	1,305,867,000
Walgreen Co.	Chart	News	42	40.438	42	40.813	2,940,700	1.563	3.86%	41.75	22.06	41,030,629,000	0.76	53.5	1,009,985,000

Symbol Lookup
Find stocks, mutual funds, options, indices, and currencies.

MSN MoneyCentral Investor
Discover Investor's tools, columns, and more!

Terms of Use. © 2000 Microsoft Corporation and/or its suppliers. All rights reserved.
Stock and fund data provided by Media General Financial Services.
Quotes supplied by Standard & Poor's ComStock, Inc. and are delayed at least 20 minutes. NYSE, AMEX, and NASDAQ index data are provided real time.
Fund data provided by Morningstar, Inc. © 2000. All rights reserved.
Source Standard & Poor's Fund Services © Micropal Ltd 2000 All rights reserved www.micropal.com
Source © Standard & Poor's International Ratings Ltd 2000 www.ifisinc.com [+81-3-3593-8681] All rights reserved. Errors and omissions excepted

(b) Web Query

FIGURE 2-1

Source of Data: The data supplied by Michael includes the stock names, symbols, dates acquired, number of shares, initial prices, and current prices. This data is shown in Table 2-1.

Calculations: The following calculations must be made for each of the stocks:

1. Initial Cost = Shares × Initial Price
2. Current Value = Shares × Current Price
3. Gain/Loss = Current Value – Initial Cost
4. Percentage Gain/Loss = $\frac{\text{Gain/Loss}}{\text{Initial Cost}}$
5. Compute the totals for initial cost, current value, and gain/loss.
6. Use the AVERAGE function to determine the average for the number of shares, initial price per share, initial stock cost, current stock price, current stock value, and gain/loss for each stock.
7. Use the MAX and MIN functions to determine the highest and lowest values for the number of shares, initial price per share, initial stock cost, current stock price, current stock value, gain/loss for each stock, and percent gain/loss.

Web Requirements: Use the Web query feature of Excel to get real-time stock quotes for stocks being reviewed by the BetNet Stock Club members as they consider a flight to safety (Figure 2-1b).

Web Queries

Thinking about being a day trader of stocks? If so, you will find Excel's Web Queries to be an invaluable tool. The Excel Web Query titled, Microsoft Investor Stock Quotes, can return near real-time stock quotes and links to breaking news for up to 20 stocks almost instantaneously. And you can refresh the results as often as you want.

Starting Excel and Resetting the Toolbars

To start Excel, Windows must be running. Perform the following steps to start Excel. Once Excel displays, steps 4 through 6 reset the toolbars to their default. Step 6 is necessary only if you added or deleted new buttons on the toolbars.

TO START EXCEL AND RESET THE TOOLBARS

1. Click the Start button on the taskbar.
2. Click New Office Document on the Start menu. If necessary, click the General tab in the New Office Document dialog box.
3. Double-click the Blank Workbook icon.
4. When the blank worksheet displays, click View on the menu bar, point to Toolbars, and then click Customize on the Toolbars submenu.
5. When the Customize dialog box displays, click the Options tab, make sure the top three check boxes have check marks, click the Reset my usage data button, and then click the Yes button.
6. Click the Toolbars tab. Click Standard, click the Reset button, and then click the OK button. Click Formatting, click the Reset button, and the click the OK button. Click the Close button.

The Standard and Formatting toolbars display as shown in Figure 2-1a on the previous page.

An alternative to Steps 1 through 3 is to click the Start button, point to Programs, and then click Microsoft Excel on the Programs submenu.

Starting Excel

An alternative way to start Excel when you want to open a workbook is to start Explorer, display the contents of the folder containing the workbook, and then double-click the workbook name.

Entering the Titles and Numbers into the Worksheet

The worksheet title in Figure 2-1a is centered across columns A through J in row 1. Because the centered text first must be entered into the leftmost column of the area across which it is centered, it will be entered into cell A1.

TO ENTER THE WORKSHEET TITLE

1. Select cell A1. Type `BetNet Stock Club` in the cell.
2. Press the DOWN ARROW key.

The worksheet title displays in cell A1 as shown in Figure 2-2 on the next page.

The column titles in row 2 begin in cell A2 and extend through cell J2. As shown in Figure 2-1a, the column titles in row 2 include multiple lines of text. To start a new line in a cell, press ALT+ENTER after each line, except for the last line, which is completed by clicking the Enter box, pressing the ENTER key, or pressing one of the arrow keys. When you see ALT+ENTER in a step, while holding down the ALT key, press the ENTER key and then release both keys.

The stock names and the row titles Total, Average, Highest, and Lowest in column A begin in cell A3 and continue down to cell A14.

The stock club's investments are summarized in Table 2-1. These numbers are entered into rows 3 through 10. The steps required to enter the column titles, stock names and symbols, total row titles, and numbers as shown in Figure 2-2 are explained in the remainder of this section.

Table 2-1 BetNet Stock Club Portfolio

STOCK	SYMBOL	DATE ACQUIRED	SHARES	INITIAL PRICE	CURRENT PRICE
Amazon.com	AMZN	10/14/97	800	15.875	172.00
America Online	AOL	12/14/98	720	93.50	128.688
Broadcast.com	BCST	2/2/99	610	85.25	121.5
EarthLink	ELNK	3/1/99	500	63.125	65.25
eBay	EBAY	4/13/99	920	200.50	162.50
Infoseek	SEEK	2/12/98	750	12.875	50.563
UBid	UBID	12/21/98	400	151.375	44.25
Yahoo	YHOO	5/12/98	700	21.00	171.00

TO ENTER THE COLUMN TITLES

1. With cell A2 active, type `Stock` and then press the RIGHT ARROW key.
2. Type `Symbol` and then press the RIGHT ARROW key.
3. Type `Date` and then press ALT+ENTER. Type `Acquired` and then press the RIGHT ARROW key.
4. Type `Shares` and then press the RIGHT ARROW key.
5. Type `Initial` and then press ALT+ENTER. Type `Price` and then press the RIGHT ARROW key.
6. Type `Initial` and then press ALT+ENTER. Type `Cost` and then press the RIGHT ARROW key.
7. Type `Current` and then press ALT+ENTER. Type `Price` and then press the RIGHT ARROW key.

More About 2000

Wrapping Text

If you have a long text entry, such as a paragraph, you can instruct Excel to wrap the text in a cell, rather than pressing ALT+ENTER to end a line. To wrap text, click Format Cells on the shortcut menu, click the Alignment tab, and click the Wrap Text check box. Excel will increase the height of the cell automatically so the additional lines will fit. If you want to control the contents of a line in a cell instead of letting Excel wrap based on the width of a cell, then you must end a line by pressing ALT+ENTER.

Formatting a Worksheet

With early spreadsheet packages, users often skipped rows to improve the appearance of the worksheet. With Excel, it is not necessary to skip rows because you can increase the height of rows to add white space between information.

Entering Two-Digit Years

When you enter a two-digit year value, Excel interprets the year as follows: (1) 00 through 29 as the years 2000 through 2029 and (2) 30 through 99 as the years 1930 through 1999. You may use four-digit years to ensure that Excel interprets year values the way you intend.

Entering Numbers into a Range

An efficient way to enter data into a range of cells is first to select the range. Enter the number that you want to assign to the upper-left cell. Excel responds by entering the value and moving the active cell selection down one cell. When you enter the last value in the first column, Excel moves to the top of the next column.

8. Type `Current` and then press ALT+ENTER. Type `Value` and then press the RIGHT ARROW key.
9. Type `Gain/Loss` and press the RIGHT ARROW key.
10. Type `% Gain/Loss` and then click cell A3.

The column titles display as shown in row 2 of Figure 2-2 below. When you press ALT+ENTER *to add more lines to a cell, Excel automatically increases the height of the entire row.*

The stock data in Table 2-1 on the previous page includes a date on which each stock was acquired. Excel considers a date to be a number and, therefore, displays it right-aligned in the cell. When you enter a date, Excel automatically formats the date so it resembles the way you entered it. For example, if you enter May 20, 1999, Excel displays it as 20-May-99. If you enter the same date in the format 5/20/99, then Excel displays it as 5/20/99. The following steps describe how to enter the stock data shown in Table 2-1, which includes dates.

TO ENTER THE STOCK DATA

1. With cell A3 selected, type `Amazon.com` and then press the RIGHT ARROW key. Type `AMZN` and then press the RIGHT ARROW key.
2. With cell C3 selected, type `10/14/97` and then press the RIGHT ARROW key. Type `800` and then press the RIGHT ARROW key.
3. With cell E3 selected, type `15.875` and then press the RIGHT ARROW key twice. Type `172` and then press the ENTER key.
4. Click cell A4. Enter the data in Table 2-1 for the seven remaining stocks in rows 4 through 10.

The stock data displays in rows 3 through 10 as shown in Figure 2-2.

TO ENTER THE TOTAL ROW TITLES

1. Click cell A11. Type `Total` and then press the DOWN ARROW key. With cell A12 selected, type `Average` and then press the DOWN ARROW key.
2. With cell A13 selected, type `Highest` and then press the DOWN ARROW key. With cell A14 selected, type `Lowest` and then press the ENTER key. Click cell F3.

The total row titles display as shown in Figure 2-2.

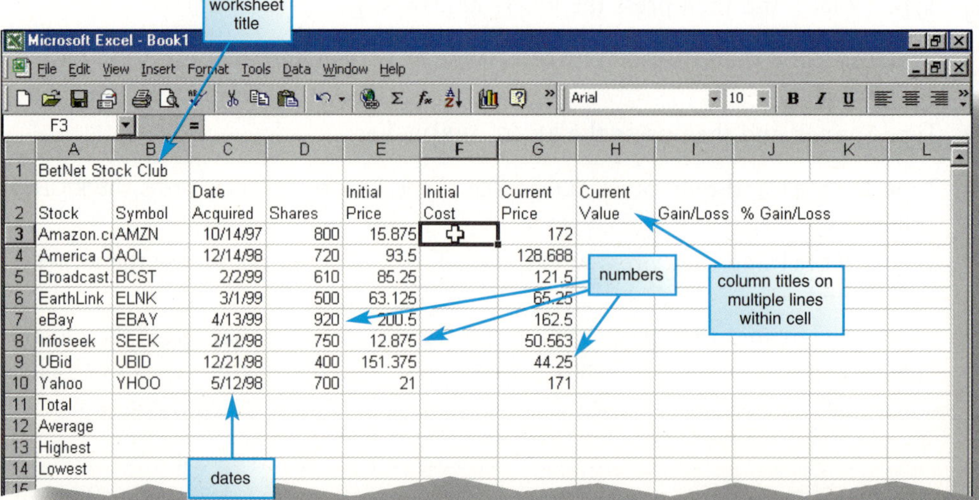

FIGURE 2-2

Entering Formulas

The initial cost for each stock, which displays in column F, is equal to the number of shares in column D times the initial price in column E. Thus, the initial cost for Amazon.com in row 3 is obtained by multiplying 800 (cell D3) times 15.875 (cell E3).

One of the reasons Excel is such a valuable tool is that you can assign a **formula** to a cell and Excel will calculate the result. Consider, for example, what would happen if you had to multiply 800 × 15.875 and then manually enter the result, 12700, in cell F3. Every time the values in cells D3 and E3 changed, you would have to recalculate the product and enter the new value in cell F3. By contrast, if you enter a formula in cell F3 to multiply the values in cells D3 and E3, Excel recalculates the product whenever new values are entered into those cells and displays the result in cell F3. Complete the following steps to enter the formula using the keyboard.

Recalculation of Formulas

Every time you enter a value into a cell in the worksheet, Excel recalculates all formulas. It makes no difference whether the worksheet contains one formula or hundreds of formulas. Excel recalculates the formulas instantaneously. This is one of the reasons why a spreadsheet package, such as Excel, is so powerful.

To Enter a Formula Using the Keyboard

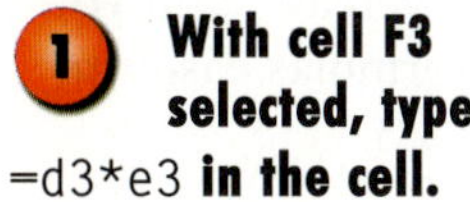

1 **With cell F3 selected, type** =d3*e3 **in the cell.**

The formula displays in the formula bar and in cell F3 (Figure 2-3).

formula begins with equal sign

as formula is typed, it displays in formula bar and in cell F3

Microsoft Excel - Book1

MIN =d3*e3

	A	B	C	D	E	F	G	H	I	J	K	L
1	BetNet Stock Club											
2	Stock	Symbol	Date Acquired	Shares	Initial Price	Initial Cost	Current Price	Current Value	Gain/Loss	% Gain/Loss		
3	Amazon.c	AMZN	10/14/97	800	15.875	=d3*e3	172					
4	America O	AOL	12/14/98	720	93.5		128.688					
5	Broadcast	BCST	2/2/99	610	85.25		121.5					
6	EarthLink	ELNK	3/1/99	500	63.125		65.25					
7	eBay	EBAY	4/13/99	920	200.5		162.5					
8	Infoseek	SEEK	2/12/98	750	12.875		50.563					
9	UBid	UBID	12/21/98	400	151.375		44.25					
10	Yahoo	YHOO	5/12/98	700	21		171					
11	Total											

FIGURE 2-3

2 **Press the** RIGHT ARROW **key twice to select cell H3.**

Instead of displaying the formula in cell F3, Excel completes the arithmetic operation indicated by the formula and displays the result, 12700 (Figure 2-4).

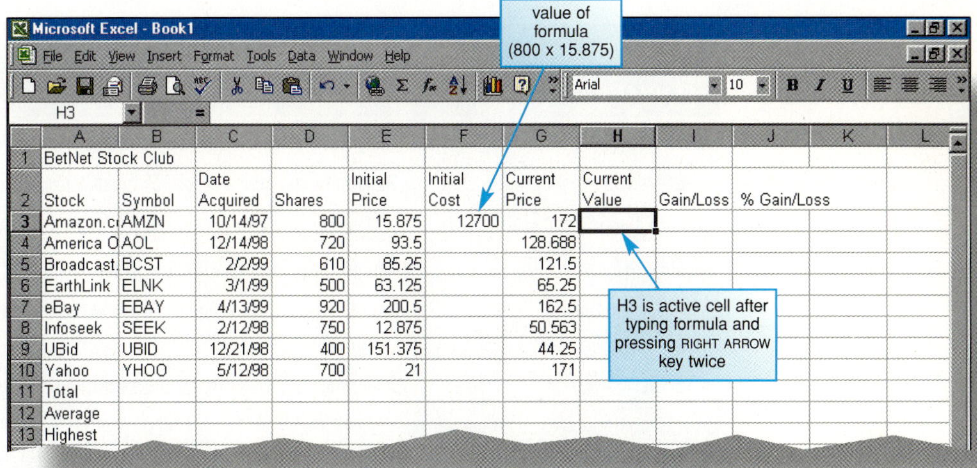

FIGURE 2-4

Entering Formulas

Besides the equal sign (=), you can start a formula with a plus sign (+) or a minus sign (-). If you do not begin with one of these characters, Excel interprets the formula as text.

The equal sign (=) preceding d3*e3 is an important part of the formula, it alerts Excel that you are entering a formula or function and not text. The asterisk (*) following d3 is the arithmetic operator that directs Excel to perform the multiplication operation. The valid Excel arithmetic operators are described in Table 2-2.

Table 2-2 Summary of Arithmetic Operators

ARITHMETIC OPERATOR	MEANING	EXAMPLE OF USAGE	MEANING
–	Negation	–10	Negative 10
%	Percentage	=30%	Multiplies 30 by 0.01
^	Exponentiation	=2 ^ 3	Raises 2 to the third power, which in this example is equal to 8
*	Multiplication	=6.1 * A1	Multiplies the contents of cell A1 by 6.1
/	Division	=H3 / H5	Divides the contents of cell H3 by the contents of cell H5
+	Addition	=4 + 8	Adds 4 and 8
–	Subtraction	=D34 – 35	Subtracts 35 from the contents of cell D34

More About

Troubling Formulas

If Excel does not accept a formula, remove the equal sign from the left side and complete the entry as text. Later, after entering additional data or after you have determined the error, reinsert the equal sign.

You can enter the cell references in formulas in uppercase or lowercase, and you can add spaces before and after arithmetic operators to make the formulas easier to read. That is, =d3*e3 is the same as =d3 * e3, =D3 * e3, or =D3 * E3.

Order of Operations

When more than one operator is involved in a formula, Excel follows the same basic order of operations that you use in algebra. Moving from left to right in a formula, the **order of operations** is as follows: first negation (–), then all percentages (%), then all exponentiations (^), then all multiplications (*) and divisions (/), and finally, all additions (+) and subtractions (–).

You can use **parentheses** to override the order of operations. For example, if Excel follows the order of operations, 10 * 6 – 3 equals 57. If you use parentheses, however, to change the formula to 10 * (6 – 3), the result is 30, because the parentheses instruct Excel to subtract 3 from 6 before multiplying by 10. Table 2-3 illustrates several examples of valid formulas and explains the order of operations.

Table 2-3 Examples of Excel Formulas

FORMULA	REMARK
=F6	Assigns the value in cell F6 to the active cell.
=6 + – 3^2	Assigns the sum of 6 + 9 (or 15) to the active cell.
=2 * K4 or =K4 * 2 or =(2 * K4)	Assigns two times the contents of cell K4 to the active cell.
=50% * 16	Assigns the product of 0.5 times 16 (or 8) to the active cell.
=– (J12 * S23)	Assigns the negative value of the product of the values contained in cells J12 and S23 to the active cell.
=5 * (L14 – H3)	Assigns the product of five times the difference between the values contained in cells H3 and L14 to the active cell.
=D1 / X6 – A3 * A4 + A5 ^ A6	From left to right: first exponentiation (A5 ^ A6), then division (D1 / X6), then multiplication (A3 * A4), then subtraction (D1 / X6) – (A3 * A4), and finally addition (D1 / X6 – A3 * A4) + (A5 ^ A6). If cells D1 = 10, A3 = 6, A4 = 2, A5 = 5, A6 = 2, and X6 = 2, then Excel assigns the active cell the value 18 (10 / 2 - 6 * 2 + 5 ^ 2 = 18).

The first formula (=d3*e3) in the worksheet was entered into cell F3 using the keyboard. The next section shows you how to enter the formulas in cells H3 and I3 using the mouse to select cell references in a formula.

Using Point Mode

Point mode allows you to create formulas using the mouse. Rather than typing a cell reference in a formula, simply click a cell and Excel appends the corresponding cell reference at the location of the insertion point. You also can use the Customize command on the shortcut menu that displays when you right-click a toolbar to create a Custom toolbar consisting of buttons that represent the operators. Thus, with Excel, you can enter entire formulas without ever touching the keyboard.

Entering Formulas Using Point Mode

In the worksheet shown in Figure 2-1a on page E 2.5, the current value of each stock displays in column H. The current value for Amazon.com in cell H3 is equal to the number of shares in cell D3 times the current price in cell G3. The gain/loss for Amazon.com in cell I3 is equal to the current value in cell H3 minus the initial cost in cell F3. The percentage gain loss for Amazon.com in cell J3 is equal to the gain/loss in cell I3 divided by the initial cost in cell F3.

Instead of using the keyboard to enter the formulas =D3*G3 in cell H3, =H3 – F3 in cell I3, and =I3/F3 in cell J3, you can use the mouse and Point mode to enter these three formulas. **Point mode** allows you to select cells for use in a formula by using the mouse.

To Enter Formulas Using Point Mode

1 **With cell H3 selected, type = (equal sign) to begin the formula and then click cell D3.**

Excel surrounds cell D3 with a marquee and appends D3 to the equal sign (=) in cell H3 (Figure 2-5).

Microsoft Excel - Book1

marquee surrounds selected cell D3

MIN =D3

	A	B	C	D	E	F	G	H	I	J	K	L
1	BetNet Stock Club											
2	Stock	Symbol	Date Acquired	Shares	Initial Price	Initial Cost	Current Price	Current Value	Gain/Loss	% Gain/Loss		
3	Amazon.c	AMZN	10/14/97	800	15.875	12700	172	=D3				
4	America O	AOL	12/14/98	720	93.5		128.688					
5	Broadcast.	BCST	2/2/99	610	85.25		121.5					
6	EarthLink	ELNK	3/1/99	500	63.125		65.25					
7	eBay	EBAY	4/13/99	920	200.5		162.5					
8	Infoseek	SEEK	2/12/98	750	12.875		50.563					
9	UBid	UBID	12/21/98	400	151.375		44.25					
10	Yahoo	YHOO	5/12/98	700	21		171					
11	Total											
12	Average											
13	Highest											

cell reference D3 appended to formula

FIGURE 2-5

2 **Type * (asterisk) and then click cell G3.**

Excel surrounds cell G3 with a marquee and appends G3 to the asterisk (*) in cell H3 (Figure 2-6).

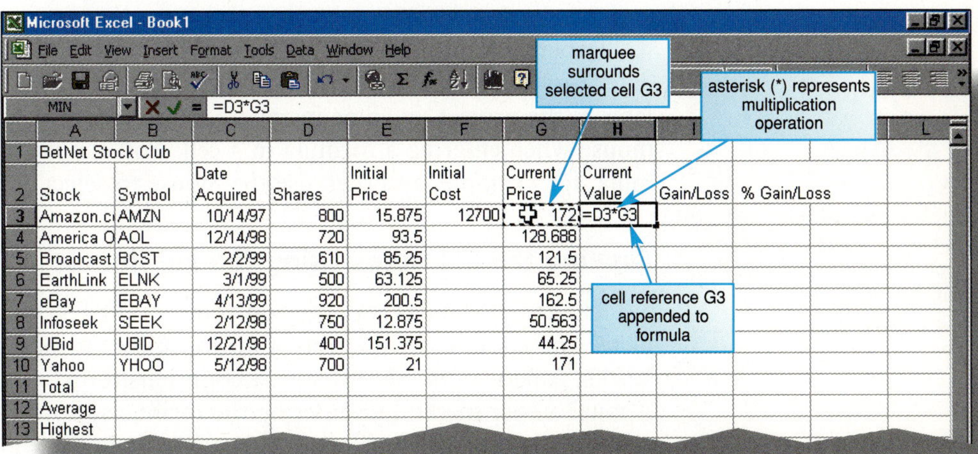

FIGURE 2-6

3 **Click the Enter box. Click cell I3. Type = (equal sign) and then click cell H3. Type – (minus sign) and then click cell F3.**

*Excel determines the product of =D3*G3 and displays the result, 137600, in cell H3. The formula =H3 – F3 displays in cell I3 and in the formula bar (Figure 2-7).*

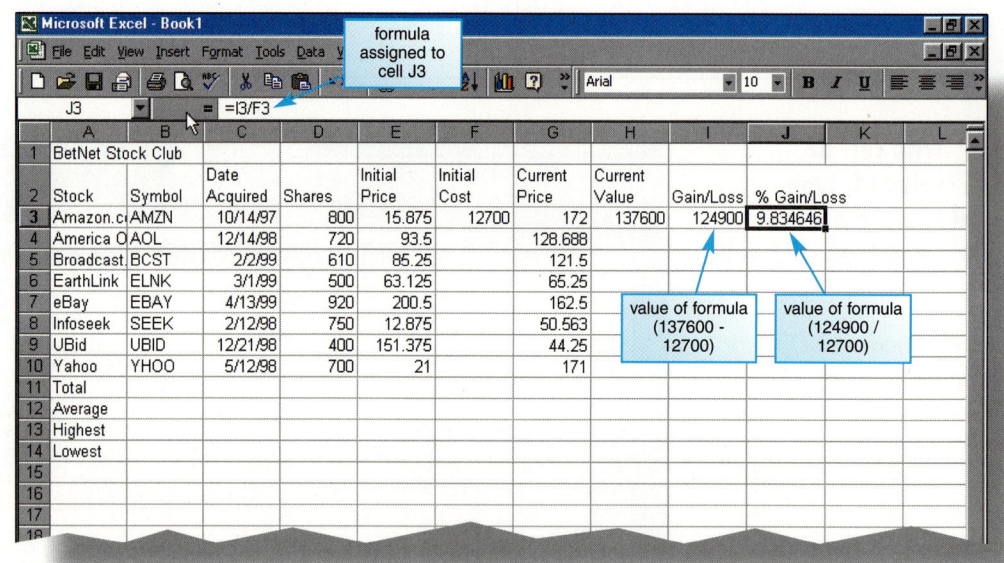

FIGURE 2-7

4 **Click the Enter box. Click cell J3. Type = (equal sign) and then click cell I3. Type / (division sign) and then click cell F3. Click the Enter box.**

The Gain/Loss for Amazon.com, 124900, displays in cell I3 and the % Gain/Loss for Amazon.com, 9.834646, displays in cell J3 (Figure 2-8). The 9.834646 represents 983.4646%.

FIGURE 2-8

Formulas

To change a formula to a number (constant), select the cell, click the Copy button on the Standard toolbar, on the Edit menu click Paste Special, click Values, and click the OK button.

Depending on the length and complexity of the formula, using Point mode to enter formulas often is faster and more accurate than using the keyboard. As shown later in the project, in some instances, you may want to combine the keyboard and mouse when entering a formula in a cell. You can use the keyboard to begin the formula, for example, and then use the mouse to select a range of cells.

Copying the Formulas Using the Fill Handle

The four formulas for Amazon.com in cells F3, H3, I3, and J3 now are complete. You could enter the same four formulas one at a time for the seven remaining stocks, America Online, Broadcast.com, EarthLink, eBay, Infoseek, UBid, and Yahoo. A much easier method of entering the formulas, however, is to select the formulas in row 3 and then use the fill handle to copy them through row 10. Recall from Project 1 that the fill handle is a small rectangle in the lower-right corner of the active cell. Perform the following steps to copy the formulas.

To Copy Formulas Using the Fill Handle

1 **Click cell F3 and then point to the fill handle. Drag the fill handle down through cell F10 and continue to hold down the mouse button.**

A border surrounds the copy and paste areas (range F3:F10) and the mouse pointer changes to a cross hair (Figure 2-9).

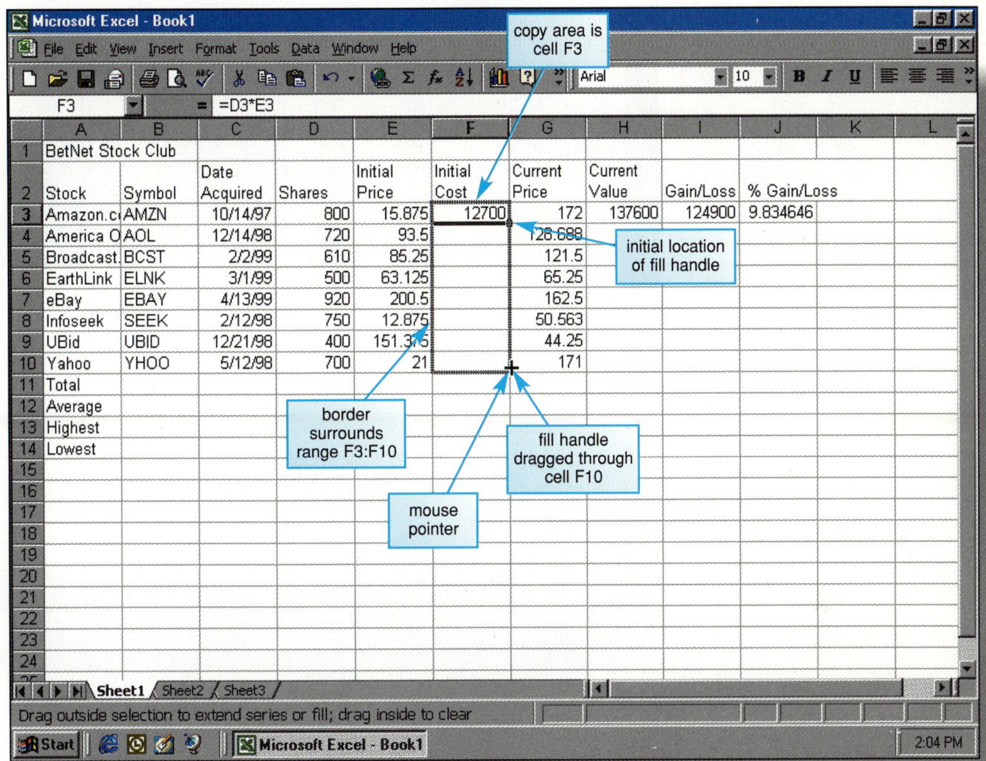

FIGURE 2-9

2 **Release the mouse button. Select the range H3:J3 and then point to the fill handle.**

*Excel copies the formula =D3*E3 to the range F4:F10 and displays the initial costs for the remaining seven stocks. The range H3:J3 is selected (Figure 2-10).*

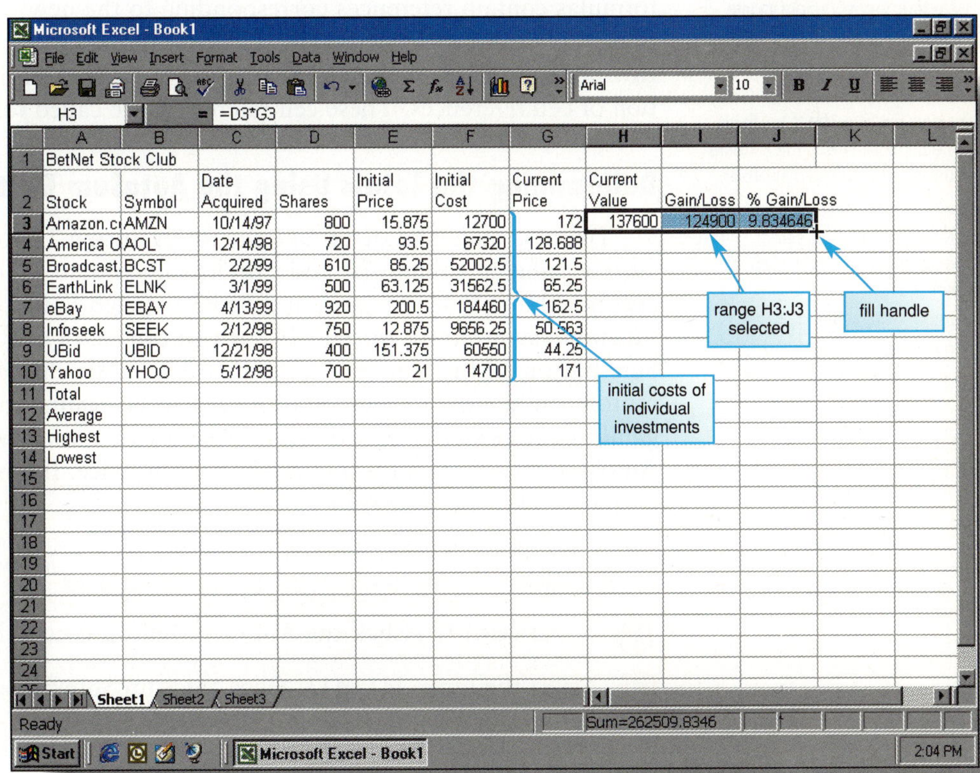

FIGURE 2-10

3 Drag the fill handle down through the range H4:J10.

*Excel copies the three formulas =D3*G3 in cell H3, =H3-F3 in cell I3, and =I3/F3 in cell J3 to the range H4:J10 and displays the current value, gain/loss, and percentage gain/loss for the remaining seven stocks (Figure 2-11).*

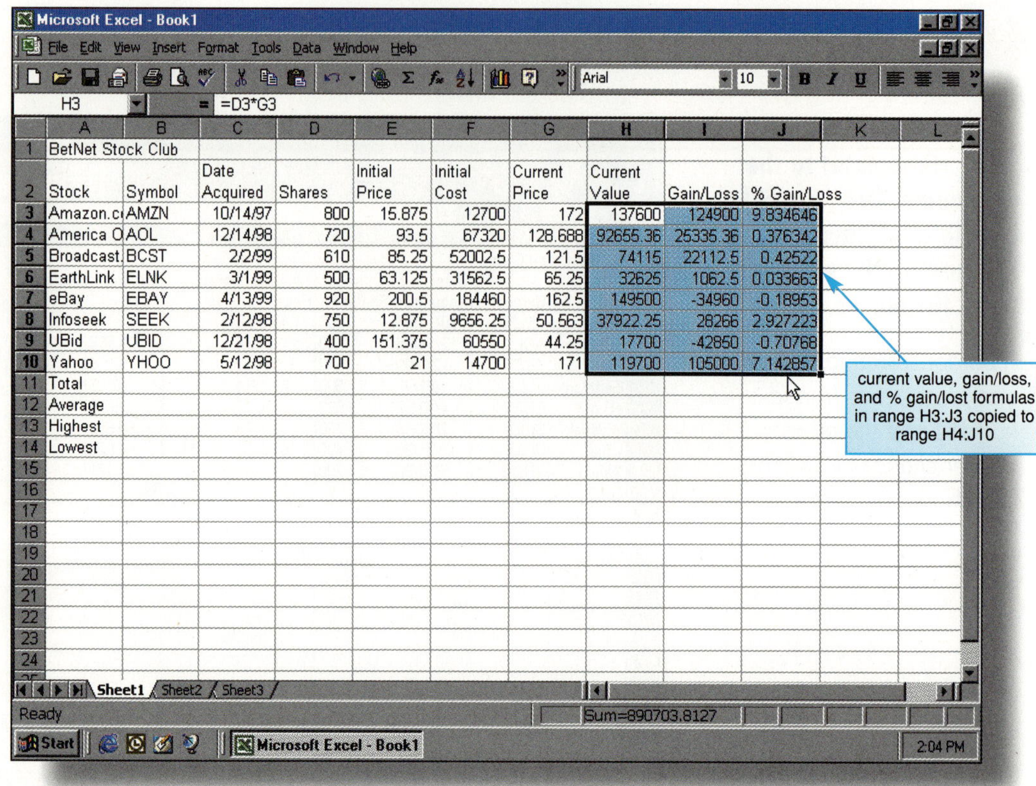

	A	B	C	D	E	F	G	H	I	J
1	BetNet Stock Club									
2	Stock	Symbol	Date Acquired	Shares	Initial Price	Initial Cost	Current Price	Current Value	Gain/Loss	% Gain/Loss
3	Amazon.c	AMZN	10/14/97	800	15.875	12700	172	137600	124900	9.834646
4	America O	AOL	12/14/98	720	93.5	67320	128.688	92655.36	25335.36	0.376342
5	Broadcast.	BCST	2/2/99	610	85.25	52002.5	121.5	74115	22112.5	0.42522
6	EarthLink	ELNK	3/1/99	500	63.125	31562.5	65.25	32625	1062.5	0.033663
7	eBay	EBAY	4/13/99	920	200.5	184460	162.5	149500	-34960	-0.18953
8	Infoseek	SEEK	2/12/98	750	12.875	9656.25	50.563	37922.25	28266	2.927223
9	UBid	UBID	12/21/98	400	151.375	60550	44.25	17700	-42850	-0.70768
10	Yahoo	YHOO	5/12/98	700	21	14700	171	119700	105000	7.142857
11	Total									
12	Average									
13	Highest									
14	Lowest									

FIGURE 2-11

Other Ways

1. Select copy area, right-click copy area, click Copy on shortcut menu, select paste area, right-click paste area, click Paste on shortcut menu
2. Select copy area, click Copy button on Standard toolbar, select paste area, click Paste button on Standard toolbar
3. Select copy area, on Edit menu click Copy, select paste area, on Edit menu click Paste
4. Select copy area, press CTRL+C, select paste area, press CTRL+V

Recall that when you copy a formula, Excel adjusts the cell references so the new formulas contain references corresponding to the new location and performs calculations using the appropriate values. Thus, if you copy downward, Excel adjusts the row portion of cell references. If you copy across, then Excel adjusts the column portion of cell references. These cell references are called **relative references.**

Determining the Totals Using the AutoSum Button

The next step is to determine the totals in row 11 for the initial cost in column F, current value in column H, and gain/loss in column I. To determine the total initial cost in column F, you must sum cells F3 through F10. To do so, you can enter the function =sum(f3:f10) in cell F11, or you can select cell F11 and then click the AutoSum button on the Standard toolbar twice. Similar SUM functions or the AutoSum button can be used in cells H11 and I11 to determine total current value and total gain/loss, respectively. Recall from Project 1 that when you select one cell and use the AutoSum button, you must click the button twice. If you select a range, then you need only click the AutoSum button once.

TO DETERMINE TOTALS USING THE AUTOSUM BUTTON

1. Select cell F11. Click the AutoSum button twice. (Do not double-click.)
2. Select the range H11:I11. Click the AutoSum button.

The three totals display in row 11 as shown in Figure 2-12.

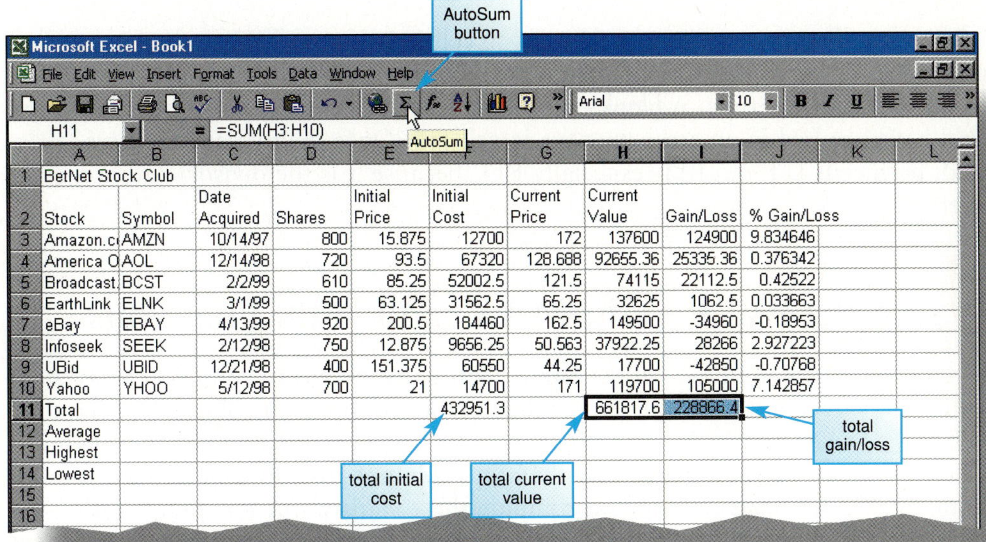

FIGURE 2-12

Rather than using the AutoSum function to calculate column totals individually, you can select all three cells before clicking the AutoSum button to calculate all three column totals at one time. To select the nonadjacent range F11, H11, and I11, select cell F11, and then, while holding down the CTRL key, drag through the range H11:I11. Next, click the AutoSum button.

Selecting a Range

If you dislike dragging to select a range, press F8 and use the arrow keys to select one corner of the range and then the cell diagonally opposite it in the proposed range. Make sure you press F8 to turn the selection off after you are finished with the range or you will continue to select ranges.

Determining the Total Percentage Gain/Loss

With the totals in row 11 determined, you can copy the percentage gain/loss formula in cell J10 to cell J11 as shown in the following steps.

TO DETERMINE THE TOTAL PERCENTAGE GAIN/LOSS

1. Select cell J10 and then point to the fill handle.
2. Drag the fill handle down through cell J11.

The formula, =I10/F10, is copied to cell J11. The resultant formula in cell J11 is =I11/F11, which shows a total club gain on the club's holdings of 0.528619 or 52.8619% (Figure 2-13).

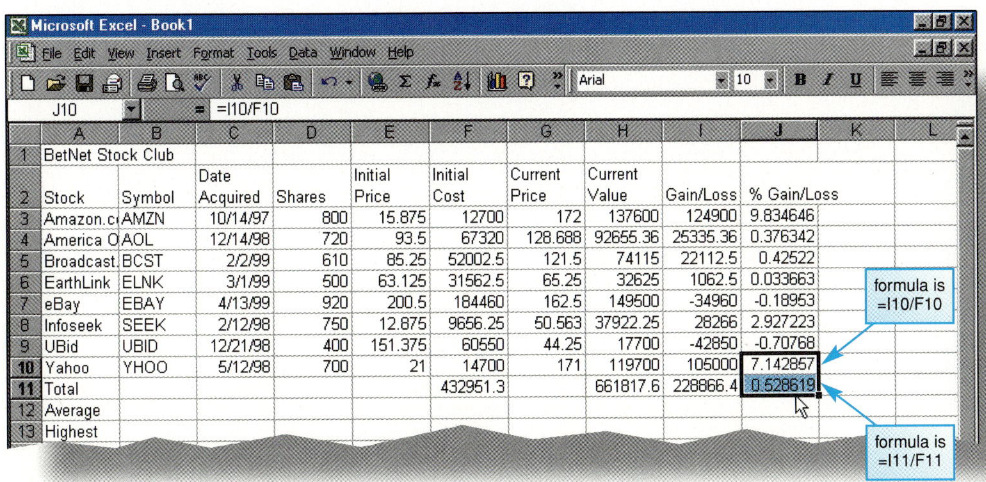

FIGURE 2-13

Formulas and Functions

For more information on entering formulas and functions, visit the Excel 2000 More About Web page (www.scsite.com/ex2000/more.htm) and click Using Formulas and Functions.

The formula was not copied originally to cell J11 when cell J3 was copied to the range J4:J10 because both cells involved in the computation (I11 and F11) were blank, or zero, at the time. A **blank cell** in Excel has a numerical value of zero, which would have resulted in an error message in cell J11. Once the totals were determined, both cells I11 and F11 (especially F11, because it is the divisor) had non-zero numerical values.

Using the AVERAGE, MAX, and MIN Functions

The next step in creating the BetNet Stock Club worksheet is to compute the average, highest value, and lowest value for the number of shares in column D using the AVERAGE, MAX, and MIN functions. Once the values are determined for column D, the entries can be copied across to the other columns. Excel includes prewritten formulas called **functions** to help you compute these statistics. A function takes a value or values, performs an operation, and returns a result to the cell. The values that you use with a function are called **arguments**. All functions begin with an equal sign and include the arguments in parentheses after the function name. For example, in the function =AVERAGE(D3:D10), the function name is AVERAGE and the argument is the range D3:D10.

With Excel, you can enter functions using one of three methods: (1) the keyboard or mouse; (2) the Edit Formula box and Functions box; and (3) the Paste Function button on the Standard toolbar. The method you choose will depend on whether you can recall the function name and required arguments. In the following pages, each of the three methods will be used. The keyboard and mouse will be used to determine the average number of shares (cell D12). The Edit Formula box and Functions box will be used to determine the highest number of shares (cell D13). The Paste Function button will be used to determine the lowest number of shares (cell D14).

Determining the Average of a Range of Numbers

The **AVERAGE function** sums the numbers in the specified range and then divides the sum by the number of non-zero cells in the range. To determine the average of the numbers in the range D3:D10, use the AVERAGE function as shown in the following steps.

The AVERAGE Function

A blank cell usually is considered to be equal to zero. The statistical functions, however, ignore blank cells. Thus, in Excel, the average of three cells with values of 2, blank, and 4 is 3 or (2 + 4) / 2, and not 2 or (2 + 0 + 4) / 3.

To Determine the Average of a Range of Numbers Using the Keyboard and Mouse

1 **Select cell D12. Type** =average(**in the cell. Click cell D3, the first endpoint of the range to average. Drag through cell D10, the second endpoint of the range to average.**

A marquee surrounds the range D3:D10. When you click cell D3, Excel appends cell D3 to the left parenthesis in the formula bar and surrounds cell D3 with a marquee. When you begin dragging, Excel appends to the argument a colon (:) and the cell reference of the cell where the mouse pointer is located (Figure 2-14).

	A	B	C	D	E	F	G	H	I	J
1	BetNet Stock Club									
2	Stock	Symbol	Date Acquired	Shares	Initial Price	Initial Cost	Current Price	Current Value	Gain/Loss	% Gain/Loss
3	Amazon.c	AMZN	10/14/97	800	15.875	12700	172	137600	124900	9.834646
4	America O	AOL	12/14/98	720	93.5	67320	128.688	92655.36	25335.36	0.376342
5	Broadcast.	BCST	2/2/99	610	85.25	52002.5	121.5	74115	22112.5	0.42522
6	EarthLink	ELNK	3/1/99	500	63.125	31562.5	65.25	32625	1062.5	0.033663
7	eBay	EBAY	4/13/99	920	200.5	184460	162.5	149500	-34960	-0.18953
8	Infoseek	SEEK	2/12/98	750	12.875	9656.25	50.563	37922.25	28266	2.927223
9	UBid	UBID	12/21/98	400	151.375	60550	44.25	17700	-42850	-0.70768
10	Yahoo	YHOO	5/12/98	700	21	14700	171	119700	105000	7.142857
11	Total					432951.3		661817.6	228866.4	0.528619
12	Average			=average(D3:D10						
13	Highest									
14	Lowest									

FIGURE 2-14

Click the Enter box.

Excel computes the average of the eight numbers in the range D3:D10 and displays the result, 675, in cell D12 (Figure 2-15). Thus, the average number of shares owned in the eight companies is 675.

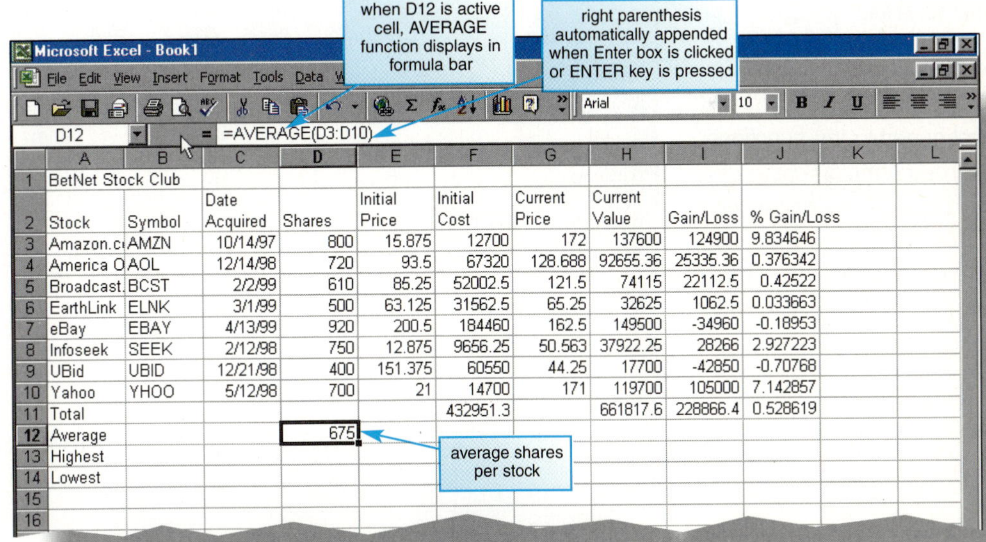

	A	B	C	D	E	F	G	H	I	J
1	BetNet Stock Club									
2	Stock	Symbol	Date Acquired	Shares	Initial Price	Initial Cost	Current Price	Current Value	Gain/Loss	% Gain/Loss
3	Amazon.c	AMZN	10/14/97	800	15.875	12700	172	137600	124900	9.834646
4	America O	AOL	12/14/98	720	93.5	67320	128.688	92655.36	25335.36	0.376342
5	Broadcast.	BCST	2/2/99	610	85.25	52002.5	121.5	74115	22112.5	0.42522
6	EarthLink	ELNK	3/1/99	500	63.125	31562.5	65.25	32625	1062.5	0.033663
7	eBay	EBAY	4/13/99	920	200.5	184460	162.5	149500	-34960	-0.18953
8	Infoseek	SEEK	2/12/98	750	12.875	9656.25	50.563	37922.25	28266	2.927223
9	UBid	UBID	12/21/98	400	151.375	60550	44.25	17700	-42850	-0.70768
10	Yahoo	YHOO	5/12/98	700	21	14700	171	119700	105000	7.142857
11	Total					432951.3		661817.6	228866.4	0.528619
12	Average			675						
13	Highest									
14	Lowest									

FIGURE 2-15

Other Ways

1. Click Edit Formula box in formula bar, click AVERAGE in Functions box
2. Click Paste Function button on Standard toolbar, click AVERAGE function

The AVERAGE function requires that the range (the argument) be included within parentheses following the function name. Excel thus automatically appends the right parenthesis to complete the AVERAGE function when you click the Enter box or press the ENTER key. When you use Point mode, as in the previous steps, you cannot use the arrow keys to complete the entry. While in Point mode, the arrow keys change the selected cell reference in the formula you are creating.

Determining the Highest Number in a Range of Numbers

The next step is to select cell D13 and determine the highest (maximum) number in the range D3:D10. Excel has a function called the **MAX function** that displays the highest value in a range. Although you could enter the MAX function using the keyboard and Point mode as you did in the previous steps, an alternative method to entering the function is to use the Edit Formula box and Functions box.

To Determine the Highest Number in a Range of Numbers Using the Edit Formula Box and Functions Box

1 Select cell D13. Click the Edit Formula box in the formula bar. Click the Functions box arrow and then point to MAX.

*The Name box in the formula bar changes to the **Functions box**. The **Formula Palette** displays immediately below the formula bar (Figure 2-16). An equal sign displays in the formula bar and the active cell, D13.*

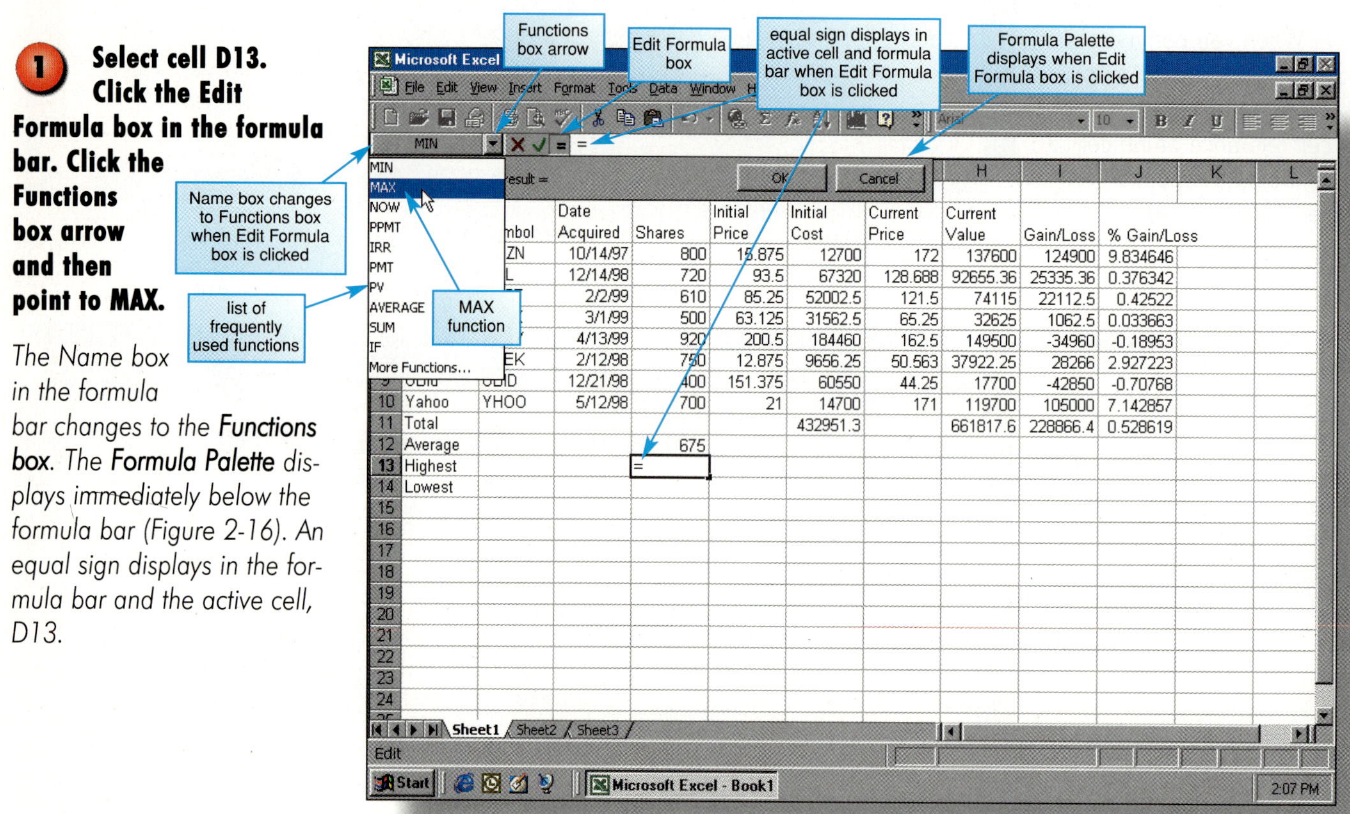

FIGURE 2-16

2 **Click MAX. When the MAX Formula Palette displays, type** `d3:d10` **in the Number 1 edit box. Point to the OK button.**

The MAX Formula Palette displays with the range d3:d10 entered in the Number 1 edit box (Figure 2-17). The completed MAX function displays in the formula bar, and the end of the function displays in the active cell, D13.

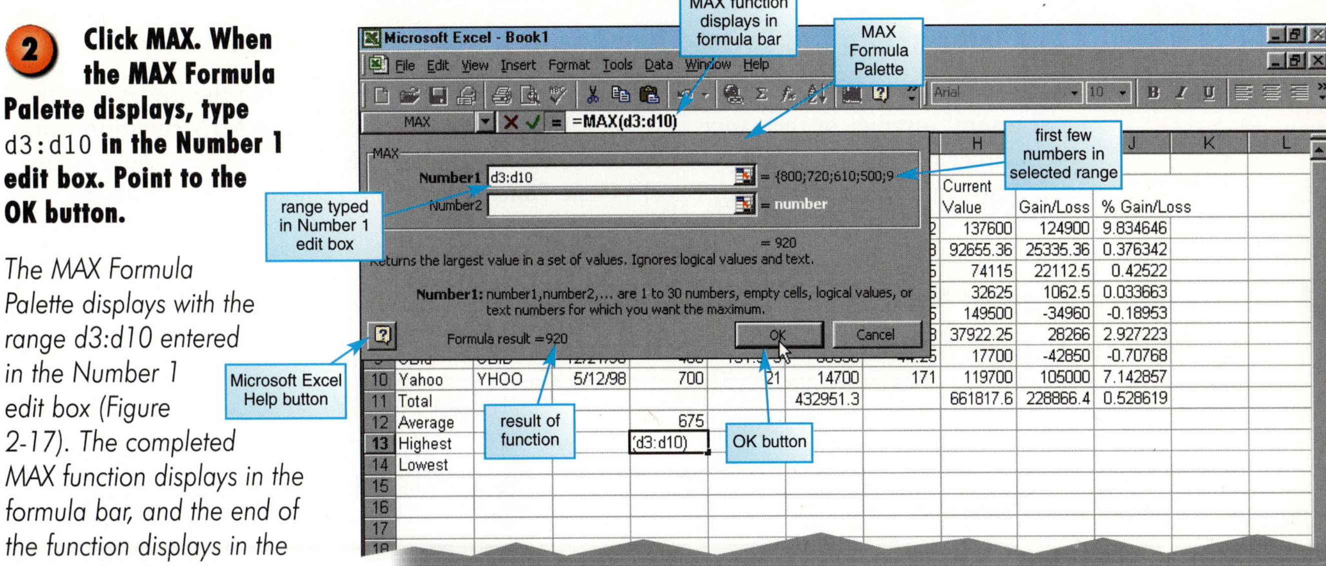

FIGURE 2-17

3 **Click the OK button.**

Excel determines that the highest value in the range D3:D10 is 920 (cell D7) and displays it in cell D13 (Figure 2-18).

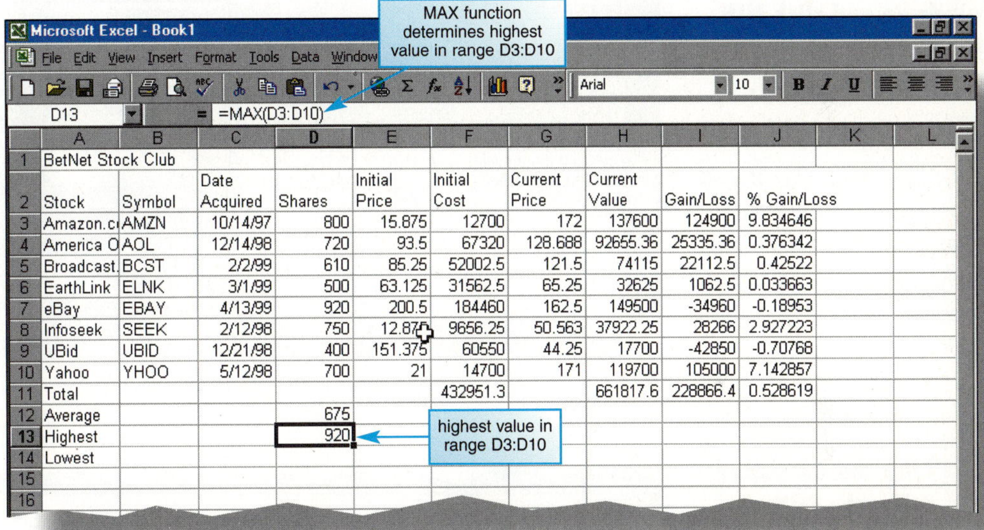

FIGURE 2-18

Other Ways

1. Click Paste Function button on Standard toolbar, click MAX function
2. Type MAX function in cell

As shown in Figure 2-17, the MAX Formula Palette displays the value the MAX function will return to cell D13. It also lists the first few numbers in the selected range, next to the Number 1 edit box.

In this example, rather than entering the MAX function, you easily could scan the range D3:D10, determine that the highest number of shares is 920, and enter the number as a constant in cell D13. The display would be the same as Figure 2-18. Because it contains a constant, cell D13 will continue to display 920, even if the values in the range D3:D10 change. If you use the MAX function, however, Excel will recalculate the highest value in the range D3:D10 each time a new value is entered into the worksheet. Manually determining the highest value in the range also would be more difficult if the club owned more stocks.

Determining the Lowest Number in a Range of Numbers

Next, you will enter the **MIN function** in cell D14 to determine the lowest (minimum) number in the range D3:D10. Although you can enter the MIN function using either of the methods used to enter the AVERAGE and MAX functions, these steps show an alternative using Excel's **Paste Function button** on the Standard toolbar.

To Determine the Lowest Number in a Range of Numbers Using the Paste Function Button

1 **Select cell D14. Click the Paste Function button on the Standard toolbar. When the Paste Function dialog box displays, click Statistical in the Function category list. Scroll down and click MIN in the Function name list. Point to the OK button.**

The Paste Function dialog box displays (Figure 2-19). Statistical and MIN are selected. An equal sign displays in the formula bar and in the active cell, D14.

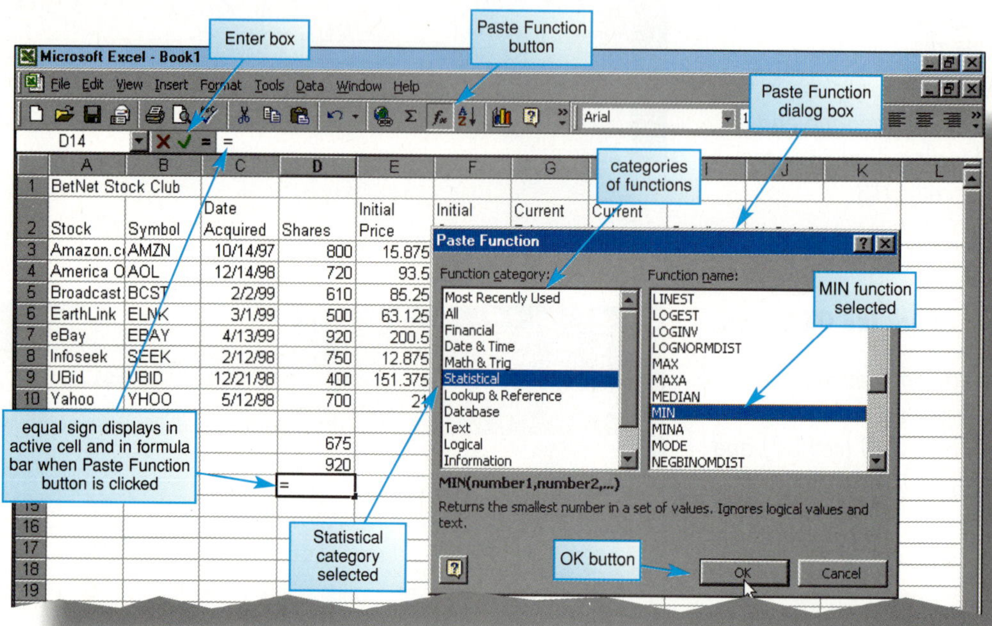

FIGURE 2-19

2 **Click the OK button. When the MIN Formula Palette displays, drag it to the bottom of the screen. Click cell D3 and then drag through cell D10.**

The MIN Formula Palette displays at the bottom of the screen (Figure 2-20). The range D3:D10 displays in the Number 1 edit box. The MIN function displays in the formula bar and the end of the MIN function displays in the active cell, D14.

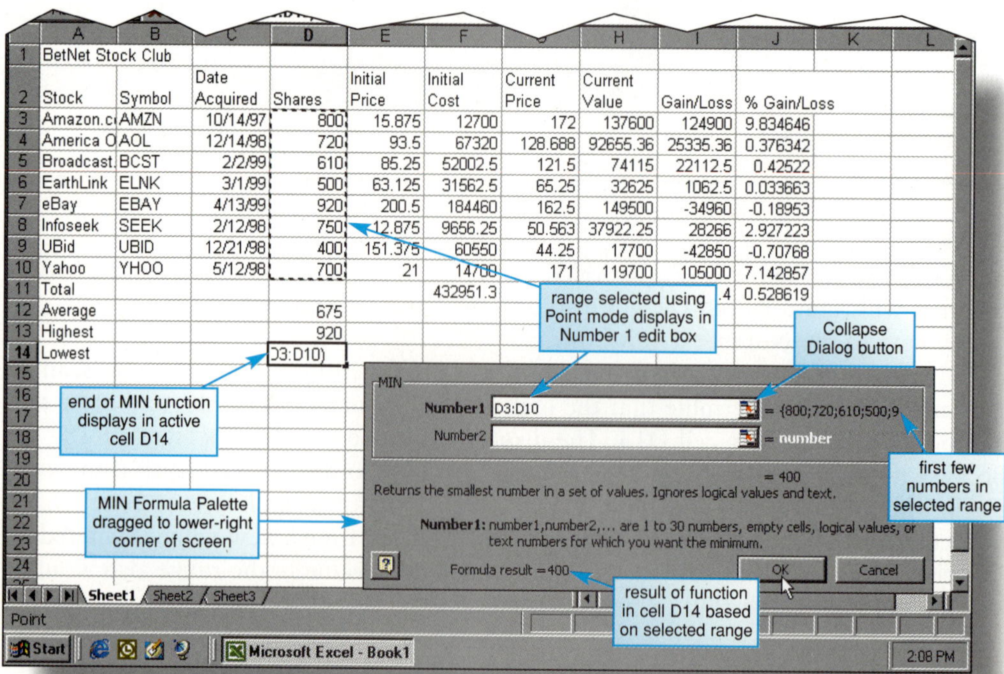

FIGURE 2-20

3 Click the Enter box.

Excel determines that the lowest value in the range D3:D10 is 400 and displays it in cell D14 (Figure 2-21).

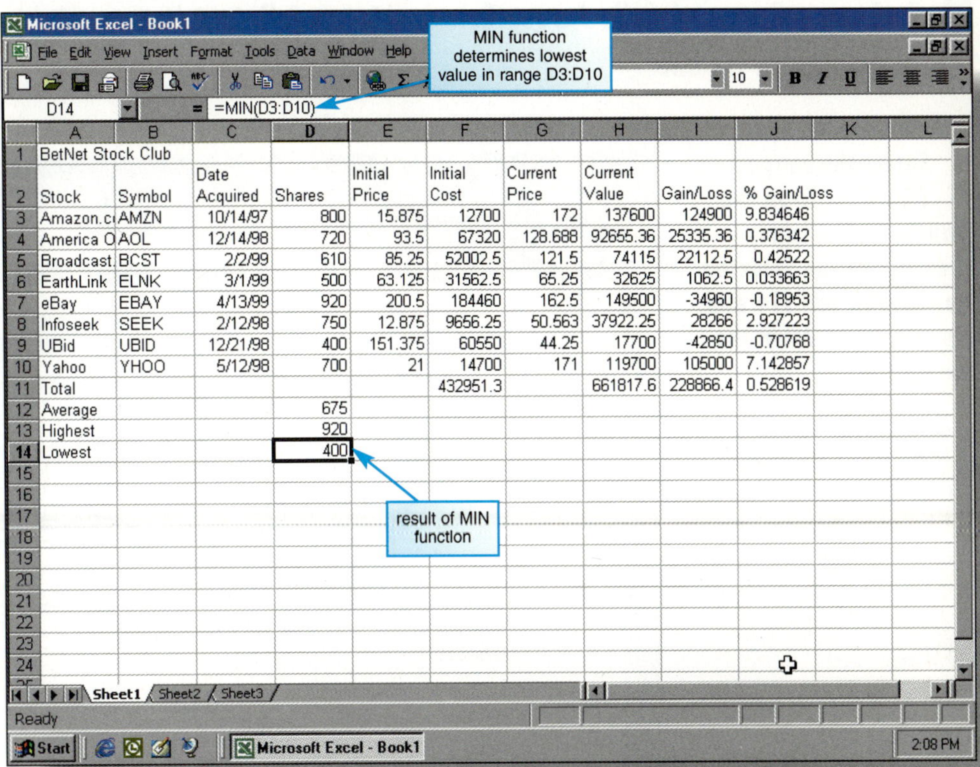

FIGURE 2-21

1. Click Edit Formula box in formula bar, click MIN function in Functions box
2. Type MIN function in cell

You can see from the previous example that using the Paste Function button on the Standard toolbar allows you to enter a function into a cell easily without requiring you to memorize its name or the required arguments. Anytime you desire to enter a function, but cannot remember the function name or the required arguments, simply click the Paste Function button on the Standard toolbar, select the desired function, and enter the arguments in the Formula Palette.

Thus far, you have learned to use the SUM, AVERAGE, MAX, and MIN functions. In addition to these four functions, Excel has more than 400 additional functions that perform just about every type of calculation you can imagine. These functions are categorized as shown in the Function category list box shown in Figure 2-19. To obtain a description of a selected function, select the Function name in the Paste Function dialog box. The description displays below the two list boxes in the dialog box.

The Formula Palette

Rather than dragging the Formula Palette out of the way to use Point mode to select a range as was done in Step 2 on the previous page, you can click the Collapse Dialog button to the right of the Number 1 or Number 2 boxes to hide the Formula Palette. Once you select the range, click the button a second time to re-display the Formula Palette.

Copying the AVERAGE, MAX, and MIN Functions

The next step is to copy the AVERAGE, MAX, and MIN functions in the range D12:D14 to the range E12:J14. The fill handle again will be used to complete the copy. The steps on the next page illustrate this procedure.

To Copy a Range of Cells Across Columns to an Adjacent Range Using the Fill Handle

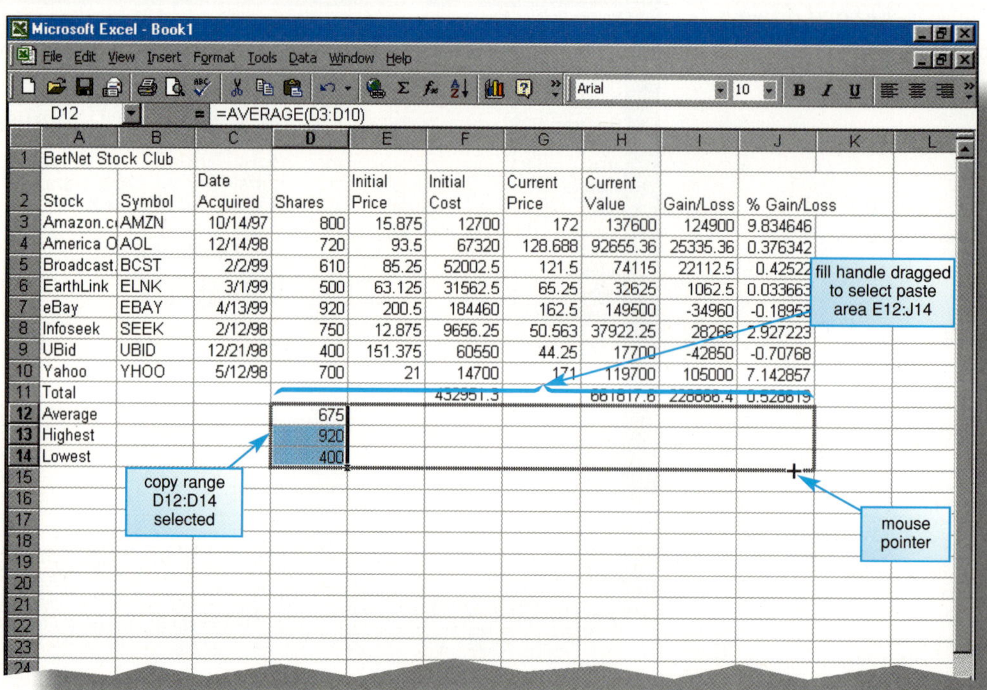

1 **Select the range D12:D14. Drag the fill handle in the lower-right corner of the selected range through cell J14 and continue to hold down the mouse button.**

Excel displays an outline around the paste area (range D12:J14) as shown in Figure 2-22.

FIGURE 2-22

2 **Release the mouse button.**

Excel copies the three functions to the range E12:J14 (Figure 2-23).

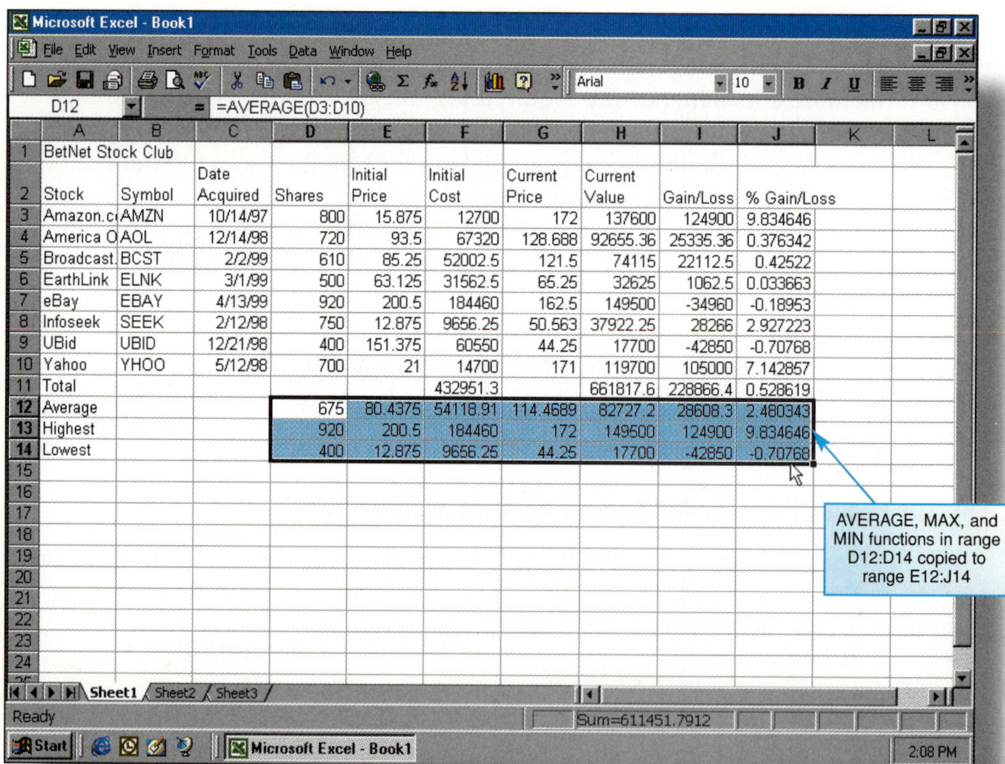

FIGURE 2-23

3 **Select cell J12 and press the DELETE key to delete the average of the percentage gain/loss.**

Cell J12 is blank (Figure 2-24).

4 **Click the Save button on the Standard toolbar. Type** `BetNet Stock Club` **in the File name text box. If necessary, click 3½ Floppy (A:) in the Save in box. Click the Save button in the Save As dialog box.**

The file name in the title bar changes to BetNet Stock Club (Figure 2-24).

Save button

BetNet Stock Club in title bar

percents in range J3:J10 cannot be averaged

	A	B	C	D	E	F	G	H	I	J
1	BetNet Stock Club									
2	Stock	Symbol	Date Acquired	Shares	Initial Price	Initial Cost	Current Price	Current Value	Gain/Loss	% Gain/Loss
3	Amazon.c	AMZN	10/14/97	800	15.875	12700	172	137600	124900	9.834646
4	America O	AOL	12/14/98	720	93.5	67320	128.688	92655.36	25335.36	0.376342
5	Broadcast.	BCST	2/2/99	610	85.25	52002.5	121.5	74115	22112.5	0.42522
6	EarthLink	ELNK	3/1/99	500	63.125	31562.5	65.25	32625	1062.5	0.033663
7	eBay	EBAY	4/13/99	920	200.5	184460	162.5	149500	-34960	-0.18953
8	Infoseek	SEEK	2/12/98	750	12.875	9656.25	50.563	37922.25	28266	2.927223
9	UBid	UBID	12/21/98	400	151.375	60550	44.25	17700	-42850	-0.70768
10	Yahoo	YHOO	5/12/98	700	21	14700	171	119700	105000	7.142857
11	Total					432951.3		661817.6	228866.4	0.528619
12	Average			675	80.4375	54118.91	114.4689	82727.2	28608.3	
13	Highest			920	200.5	184460	172	149500	124900	9.834646
14	Lowest			400	12.875	9656.25	44.25	17700	-42850	-0.70768

FIGURE 2-24

The average of the percentage gain/loss in cell J12 was deleted in Step 3 because an average of percents of this type is mathematically invalid.

Remember that Excel adjusts the ranges in the copied functions so each function refers to the column of numbers above it. Review the numbers in rows 12 through 14 in Figure 2-24. You should see that the functions in each column return the appropriate values, based on the numbers in rows 3 through 10 of that column.

This concludes entering the data and formulas into the worksheet. After saving the file, the worksheet remains on the screen with the file name, BetNet Stock Club, in the title bar. You immediately can continue with the next activity.

Verifying Formulas

One of the most common mistakes made with Excel is to include a wrong cell reference in a formula. Excel has two methods, the Auditing commands and Range Finder, to verify that a formula references the cells you want it to reference. The **Auditing commands** allow you to trace precedents and trace dependents. The **Trace Precedents command** highlights the cells in the worksheet that are referenced by the formula in the active cell. The **Trace Dependents command** highlights the cells with formulas in the worksheet that reference the active cell. The **Remove all Arrows command** removes the highlights.

As with the Trace Precedents command, **Range Finder** can be used to check which cells are being referenced in the formula assigned to the active cell. One of the advantages of Range Finder is that it allows you to make immediate changes to the cells referenced in a formula.

Verifying Formulas

If you lack confidence in your mathematical abilities, then you will find Range Finder and the Auditing commands to be useful to ensure the formulas you enter reference the correct cells.

Verifying a Formula Using Range Finder

To use Range Finder to verify that a formula contains the intended cell references, double-click the cell with the formula you want to check. Excel responds by highlighting the cells referenced in the formula so you can check that the correct cells are being used. The following steps use Range Finder to check the formula in cell J3.

To Verify a Formula Using Range Finder

Double-click cell J3.

Excel responds by displaying the cells in the worksheet referenced by the formula in cell J3 using different color borders (Figure 2-25). The different colors allow you to see easily which cells are being referenced by the formula in cell J3.

2 Click any cell or press the ESC key to quit Range Finder.

Microsoft Excel - BetNet Stock Club

cells referenced in formula in active cell are highlighted with corresponding colors

color of cell references corresponds to color of highlighted cells

	A	B	C	D	E	F	G	H	I	J
1	BetNet Stock Club									
2	Stock	Symbol	Date Acquired	Shares	Initial Price	Initial Cost	Current Price	Current Value	Gain/Loss	% Gain/Loss
3	Amazon.c	AMZN	10/14/97	800	15.875	12700	172	137600	124900	=I3/F3
4	America O	AOL	12/14/98	720	93.5	67320	128.688	92655.36	25335.36	0.376342
5	Broadcast	BCST	2/2/99	610	85.25	52002.5	121.5	74115	22112.5	0.42522
6	EarthLink	ELNK	3/1/99	500	63.125	31562.5	65.25	32625	1062.5	0.033663
7	eBay	EBAY	4/13/99	920	200.5	184460	162.5	149500	-34960	-0.18953
8	Infoseek	SEEK	2/12/98	750	12.875	9656.25	50.563	37922.25	28266	2.927223
9	UBid	UBID	12/21/98	400	151.375	60550	44.25	17700	-42850	-0.70768
10	Yahoo	YHOO	5/12/98	700	21	14700	171	119700	105000	7.142857
11	Total					432951.3		661817.6	228866.4	0.528619
12	Average			675	80.4375	54118.91	114.4689	82727.2	28608.3	
13	Highest			920	200.5	184460	172	149500	124900	9.834646
14	Lowest			400	12.875	9656.25	44.25	17700	-42850	-0.70768

FIGURE 2-25

Not only does Range Finder show you the cells referenced in the formula in cell J3, but you can drag the colored borders to other cells and Excel will change the cell references in the formula to the newly selected cells. If you use Range Finder to change cells referenced in a formula, press the ENTER key to complete the edit.

Verifying a Formula Using the Auditing Commands

The following steps show how to use the Trace Precedent and Trace Dependent commands to verify a formula is referencing the correct cells and to determine the cells that reference the active cell.

To Verify a Formula Using the Auditing Commands

1 If necessary, click cell J3. Click Tools on the menu bar and then click the down arrows at the bottom of the Tools menu to display the full menu. Point to Auditing. When the Auditing submenu displays, point to Trace Precedents.

The Auditing submenu displays as shown in Figure 2-26.

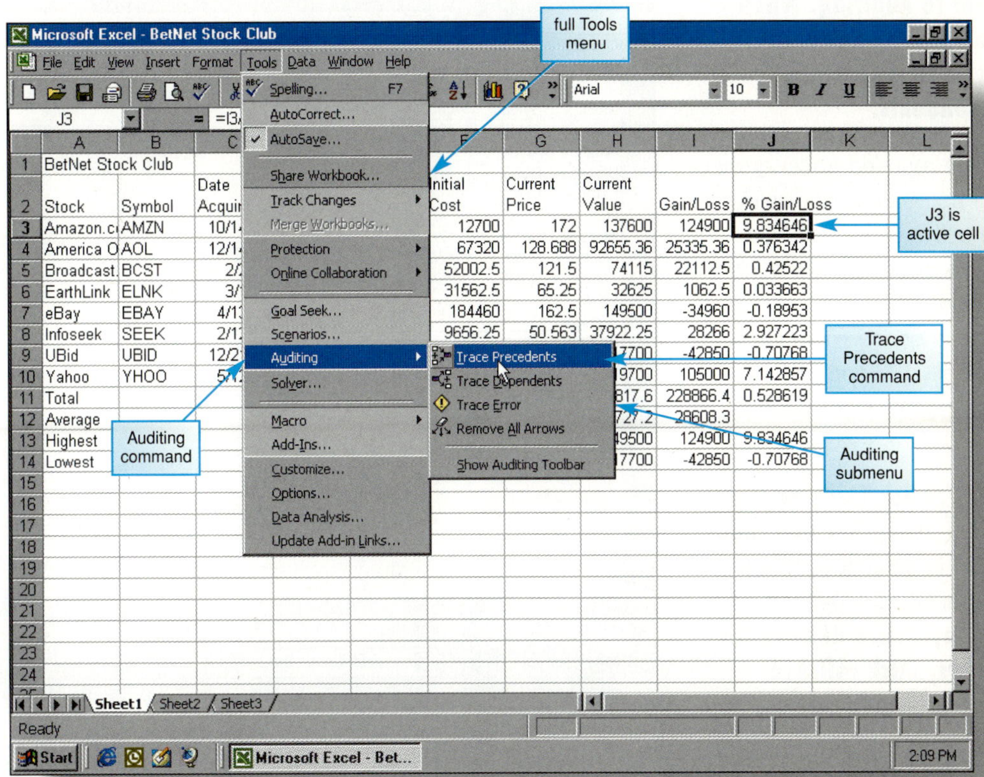

FIGURE 2-26

2 Click Trace Precedents.

Blue rounded tracer arrows that point upward display along a blue line in the cells (F3 and I3) that are used by the formula in the active cell, J3 (Figure 2-27). The horizontal arrow in cell J3 at the right end of the blue line indicates the active cell. You can use the blue line and arrows to verify that the correct cells are being used in the formula.

tracer arrows along line indicate the cells used in the formula assigned to active cell

arrowhead indicates tracing precedents for this cell

FIGURE 2-27

3 **Click Tools on the menu bar and then point to Auditing. When the Auditing submenu displays, click Trace Dependents.**

A blue rounded tracer arrow that points upward displays in the active cell, J3. A blue line extends downward to the two cells, J13 and J14 that depend on the value in cell J3. Cells J13 and J14 have arrowheads (Figure 2-28).

4 **Click Tools on the menu bar and then point to Auditing. When the Auditing submenu displays, click Remove All Arrows. Click cell A16.**

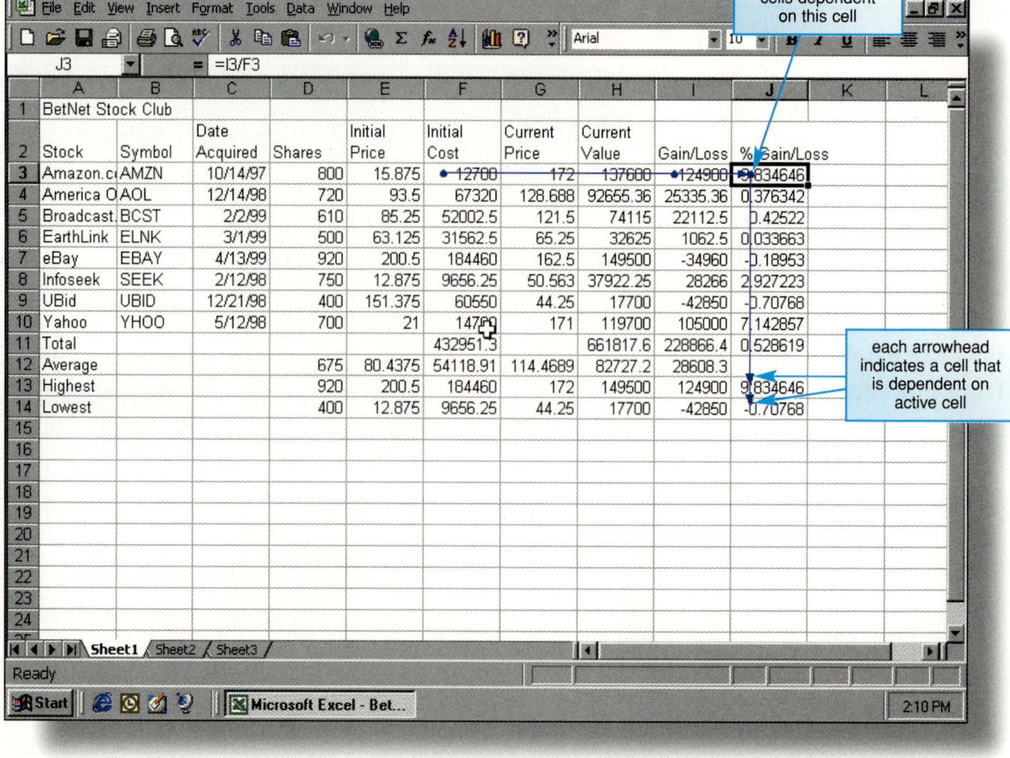

FIGURE 2-28

Other Ways

1. On Tools menu point to Auditing, click Show Auditing Toolbar, click buttons on Auditing toolbar

To change the active cell to the one at the other end of the blue line, double-click the blue line. This technique gives you a quick way to move from the active cell to one that provides data to the active cell. This is especially helpful in large worksheets.

If you click the Trace Precedents command a second time, Excel displays tracer arrows that show a second level of cells that are indirectly supplying data to the active cell. The same applies to the Trace Dependents command, only it shows the next level of cells that are dependent on the active cell.

Formatting the Worksheet

Although the worksheet contains the appropriate data, formulas, and functions, the text and numbers need to be formatted to improve their appearance and readability.

In Project 1, you used the AutoFormat command to format the majority of the worksheet. This section describes how to change the unformatted worksheet in Figure 2-29a to the formatted worksheet in Figure 2-29b using the Formatting toolbar and Format Cells command.

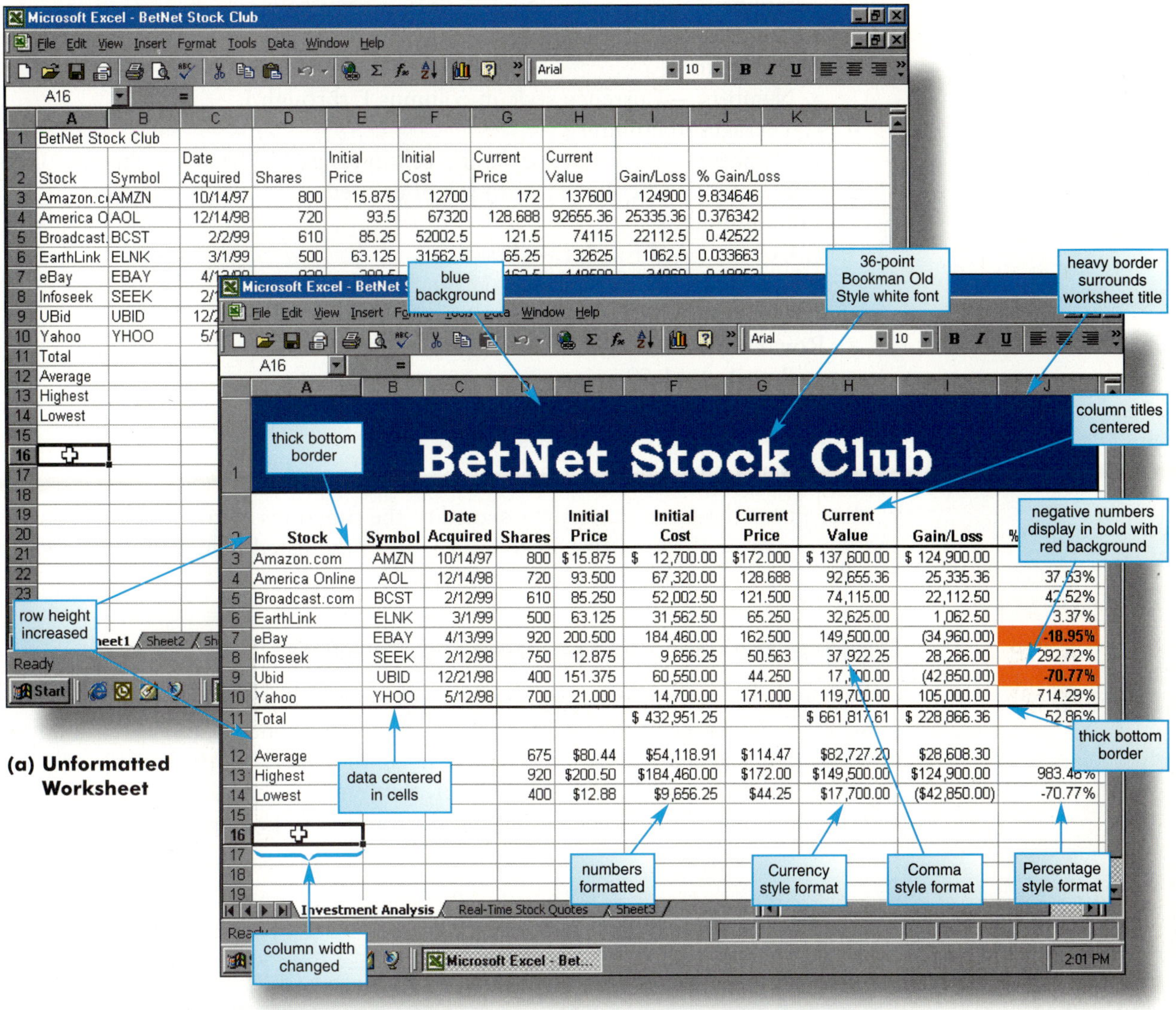

(a) Unformatted Worksheet

(b) Formatted Worksheet

FIGURE 2-29

The following outlines the type of formatting that is required in Project 2:

1. Worksheet title
   a. Font type — bold Bookman Old Style
   b. Font size — 36
   c. Font style — bold
   d. Alignment — center across columns A through J
   e. Background color (range A1:J1) — dark blue
   f. Font color — white
   g. Border — thick box border around range A1:J1
2. Column titles
   a. Font style — bold
   b. Alignment — center
   c. Border — thick bottom border on row 2
3. Data
   a. Alignment — center data in column B
   b. Numbers in top row (columns E through I in row 3) — Currency style
   c. Numbers below top row (rows 4 through 10) — Comma style
   d. Border — thick bottom border on row 10

Choosing Colors

Knowing how people perceive colors helps you emphasize parts of your worksheet. Warmer colors (red and orange) tend to reach toward the reader. Cooler colors (blue, green, and violet) tend to pull away from the reader. Bright colors jump out of a dark background and are easiest to see. White or yellow text on a dark blue, green, purple, or black background is ideal.

4. Total line
   a. Numbers — Currency style
5. Function lines
   a. Numbers — Currency style in columns E through I
6. Percentages in column J
   a. Numbers — Percentage style; if a cell in range J3:J10 is less than zero, then bold font and color background of cell red
7. Column widths
   a. Columns A through E — best fit
   b. Columns F, H through J — 12.00 characters
   c. Column G — 8.71 characters
8. Row heights
   a. Row 1 — 61.50 points
   b. Rows 2 — 36.00 points
   c. Row 12 —24.00 points
   d. Remaining rows — default

Except for the Currency style assigned to the functions in rows 12 through 14 and the conditional formatting in column J, all of the listed formats can be assigned to cells using the Formatting toolbar and mouse.

Changing the Font and Centering the Worksheet Title

When developing presentation-quality worksheets, different fonts often are used in the same worksheet. Excel allows you to change the font of individual characters in a cell or all the characters in a cell, in a range of cells, or in the entire worksheet. To emphasize the worksheet title in cell A1, the font type, size, and style are changed and the worksheet title is centered as described in the following steps.

To Change the Font and Center the Worksheet Title

1 Click cell A1. Double-click the move handle on the left side of the Formatting toolbar to display it in its entirety. Click the Font box arrow on the Formatting toolbar and then point to Bookman Old Style (or Courier New if your system does not have Bookman Old Style).

The Font list displays with Bookman Old Style highlighted (Figure 2-30).

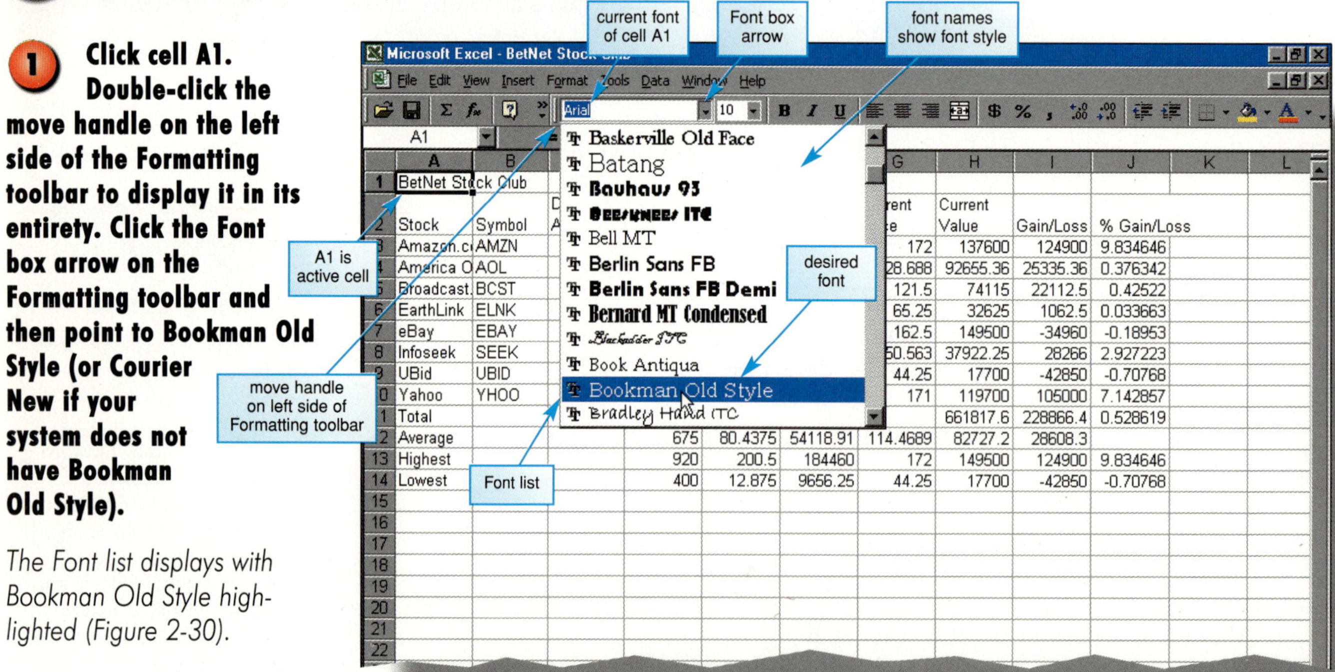

FIGURE 2-30

2 Click Bookman Old Style (or Courier New). Click the Font Size box arrow on the Formatting toolbar and then point to 36.

The characters in cell A1 display using Bookman Old Style (or Courier New). The font size 36 is highlighted in the Font Size list (Figure 2-31).

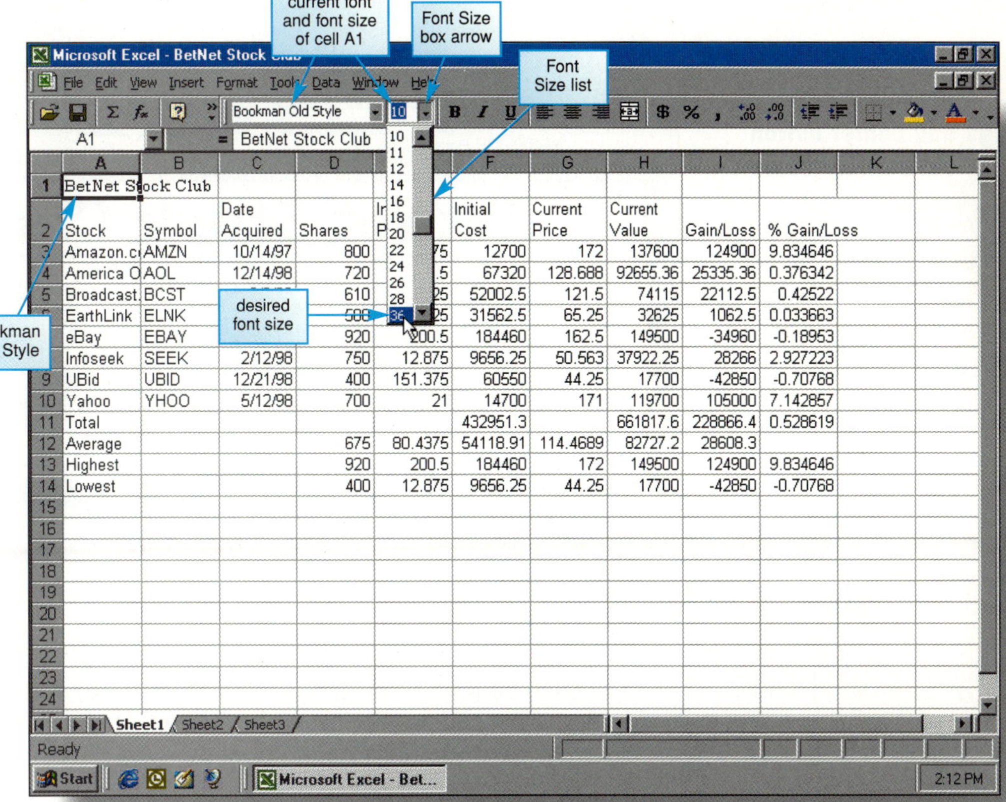

FIGURE 2-31

3 Click 36. Click the Bold button on the Formatting toolbar.

The text in cell A1 displays in 36-point Bookman Old Style bold font. Excel automatically increases the height of row 1 so that the larger characters fit in the cells (Figure 2-32).

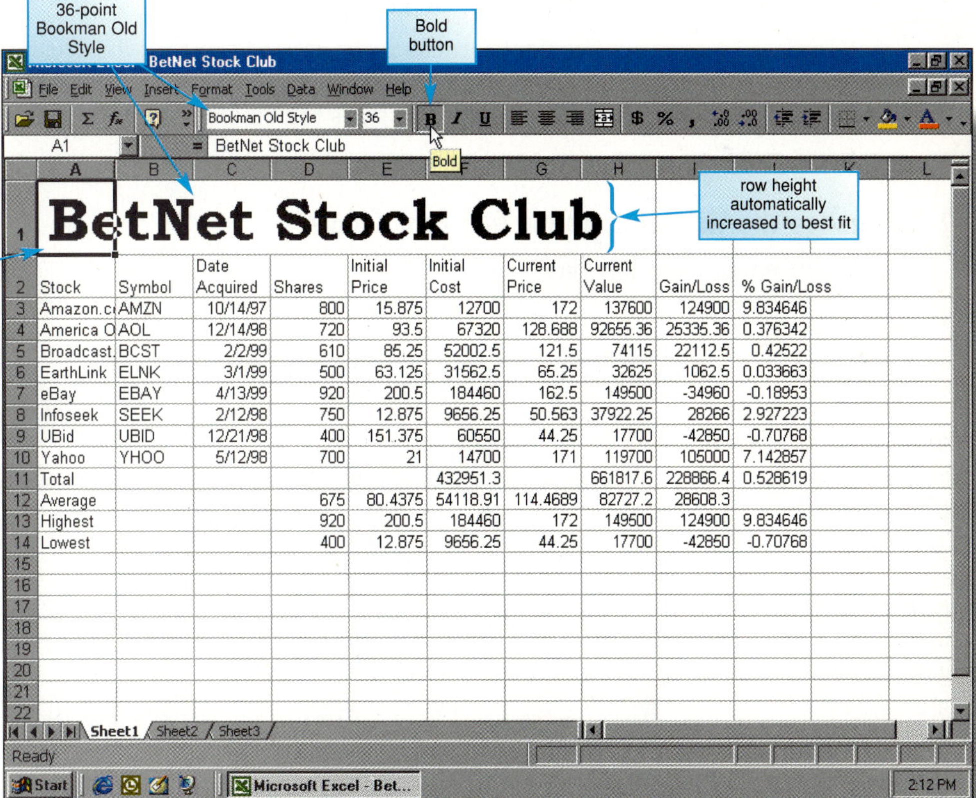

FIGURE 2-32

4 **Select the range A1:J1. Click the Merge and Center button on the Formatting toolbar.**

Excel merges the cells A1 through J1 to create a new cell A1 and centers the worksheet title across columns A through J (Figure 2-33).

FIGURE 2-33

Other Ways

1. Right-click cell, click Format Cells on shortcut menu, click Font tab, select font formats, click OK button
2. On the Format menu click Cells, click Font tab, select font formats, click OK button
3. Press CTRL+1, click Font tab, select font formats, click OK button

You can change a font type, size, or style at any time while the worksheet is active. Some Excel users prefer to change fonts before they enter any data. Others change the font while they are building the worksheet or after they have entered all the data.

Changing the Worksheet Title Background and Font Colors and Applying an Outline Border

The final formats to be assigned to the worksheet title are the dark blue background color, white font color, and thick box border (Figure 2-29b on page E 2.27). Perform the following steps to complete the formatting of the worksheet title.

To Change the Title Background and Font Colors and Apply an Outline Border

1 **With cell A1 selected, click the Fill Color button arrow on the Formatting toolbar and then point to the color Dark Blue (column 6, row 1) on the Fill Color palette.**

The Fill Color palette displays (Figure 2-34).

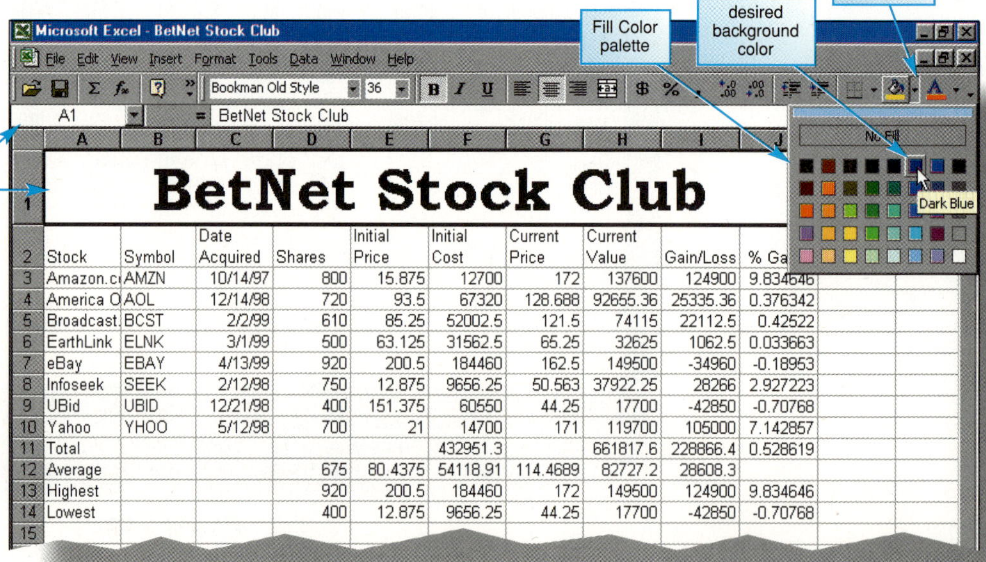

FIGURE 2-34

2 **Click the color Dark Blue. Click the Font Color button arrow on the Formatting toolbar. Point to the color White (column 8, row 5) on the Font Color palette.**

The background color of cell A1 changes from white to dark blue. The Font Color palette displays (Figure 2-35).

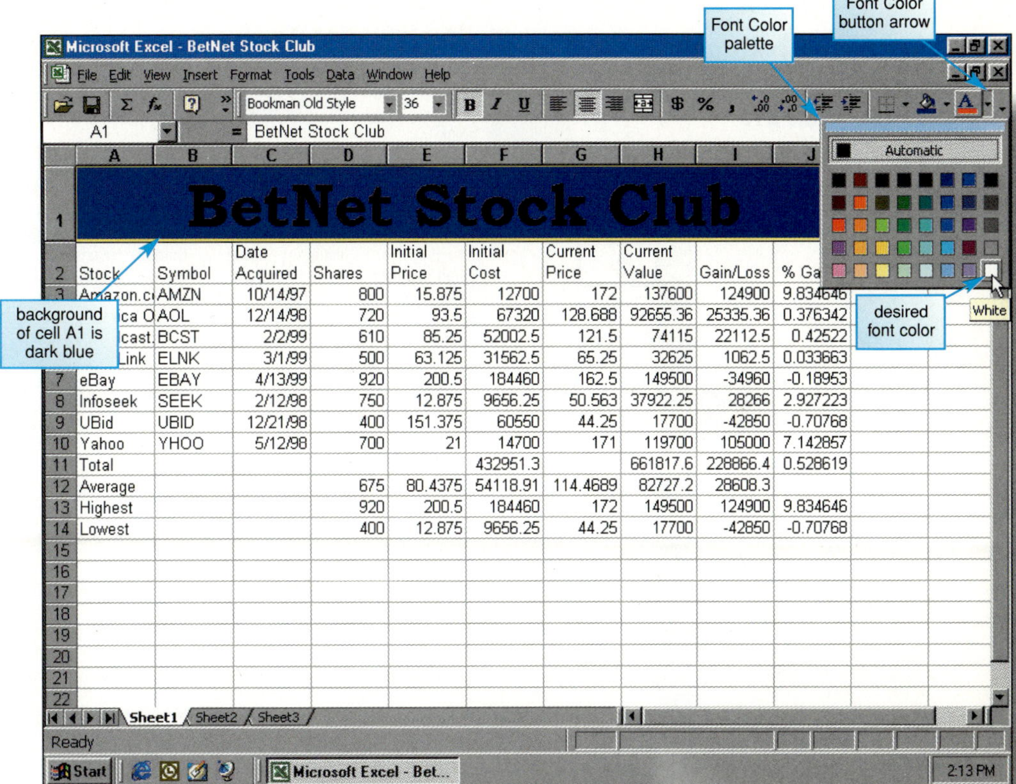

FIGURE 2-35

3 **Click the color White. Click the Borders button arrow on the Formatting toolbar and then point to the Thick Box Border button (column 4, row 3) on the Borders palette.**

The font in the worksheet title changes from black to white. The Borders palette displays (Figure 2-36).

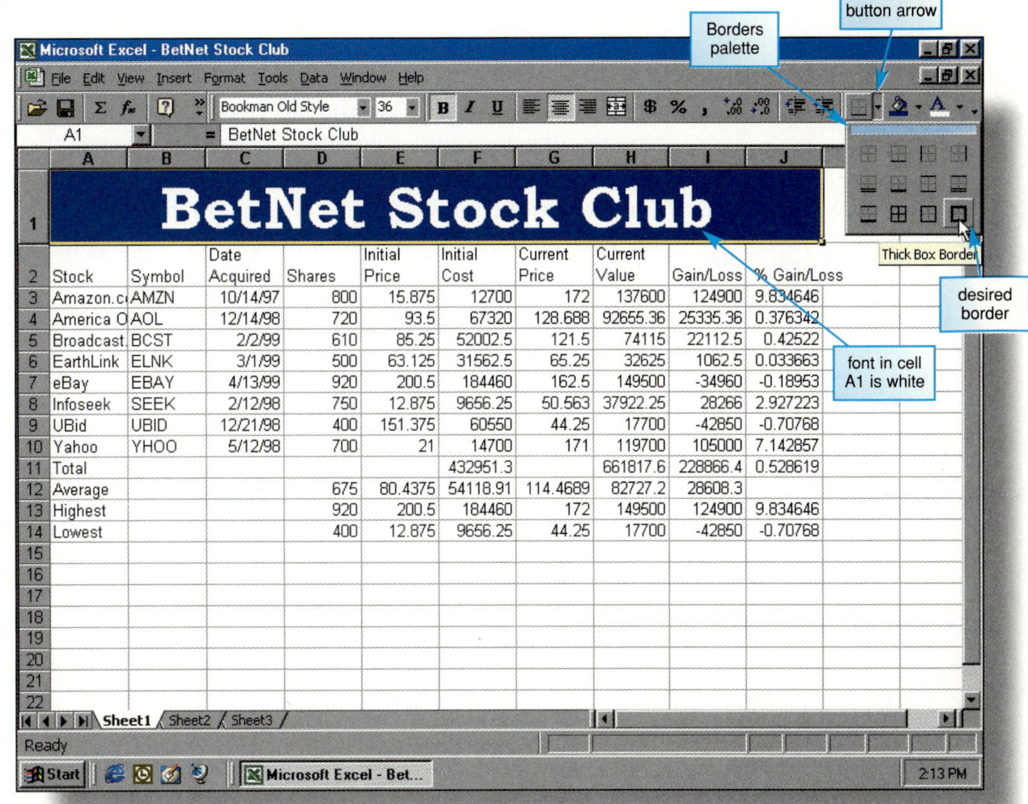

FIGURE 2-36

4 **Click the Thick Box Border button. Click cell A2 to deselect cell A1.**

Excel displays a thick box border around cell A1 (Figure 2-37).

Microsoft Excel - BetNet Stock Club

BetNet Stock Club

	A	B	C	D	E	F	G	H	I	J
2	Stock	Symbol	Date Acquired	Shares	Initial Price	Initial Cost	Current Price	Current Value	Gain/Loss	% Gain/Loss
3	Amazon.c	AMZN	10/14/97	800	15.875	12700	172	137600	124900	9.834646
4	America O	AOL	12/14/98	720	93.5	67320	128.688	92655.36	25335.36	0.376342
5	Broadcast.	BCST	2/2/99	610	85.25	52002.5	121.5	74115	22112.5	0.42522
6	EarthLink	ELNK	3/1/99	500	63.125	31562.5	65.25	32625	1062.5	0.033663
7	eBay	EBAY	4/13/99	920	200.5	184460	162.5	149500	-34960	-0.18953
8	Infoseek	SEEK	2/12/98	750	12.875	9656.25	50.563	37922.25	28266	2.927223
9	UBid	UBID	12/21/98	400	151.375	60550	44.25	17700	-42850	-0.70768
10	Yahoo	YHOO	5/12/98	700	21	14700	171	119700	105000	7.142857
11	Total					432951.3		661817.6	228866.4	0.528619
12	Average			675	80.4375	54118.91	114.4689	82727.2	28608.3	
13	Highest			920	200.5	184460	172	149500	124900	9.834646
14	Lowest			400	12.875	9656.25	44.25	17700	-42850	-0.70768

thick box border surrounds worksheet title in cell A1

FIGURE 2-37

Other Ways

1. Right-click range, click Format Cells on shortcut menu, click Patterns tab, click desired background color, click OK button
2. On Format menu click Cells, click Patterns tab, click desired background color, click OK button
3. Right-click range, click Format Cells on shortcut menu, click Border tab, click desired style, click desired border, click OK button
4. On Format menu click Cells, click Border tab, click desired style, click desired border, click OK button

You can remove borders, such as the thick box border around cell A1, by selecting the range and clicking the No Border button on the Borders palette. You can remove a background color by selecting the range, clicking the Fill Color button arrow on the Formatting toolbar, and clicking No Fill on the Fill Color palette. The same technique allows you to change the font color back to Excel's default, except you use the Font Color button arrow and click Automatic.

Applying Formats to the Column Titles

According to Figure 2-29b on page E 2.27, the column titles are bold, centered, and have a thick bottom border (underline). The following steps assign these formats to the column titles.

Adding Colors and Borders

Colors and borders can change a boring worksheet into an interesting and easy-to-read worksheet. Colors and borders also can be used to make important information stand out.

To Bold, Center, and Underline the Column Titles

1 **Select the range A2:J2. Click the Bold button on the Formatting toolbar. Click the Center button on the Formatting toolbar. Click the Borders button arrow on the Formatting toolbar and then point to the Thick Bottom Border button (column 2, row 2) on the Borders palette.**

The column titles in row 2 are bold and centered. The Borders palette displays (Figure 2-38).

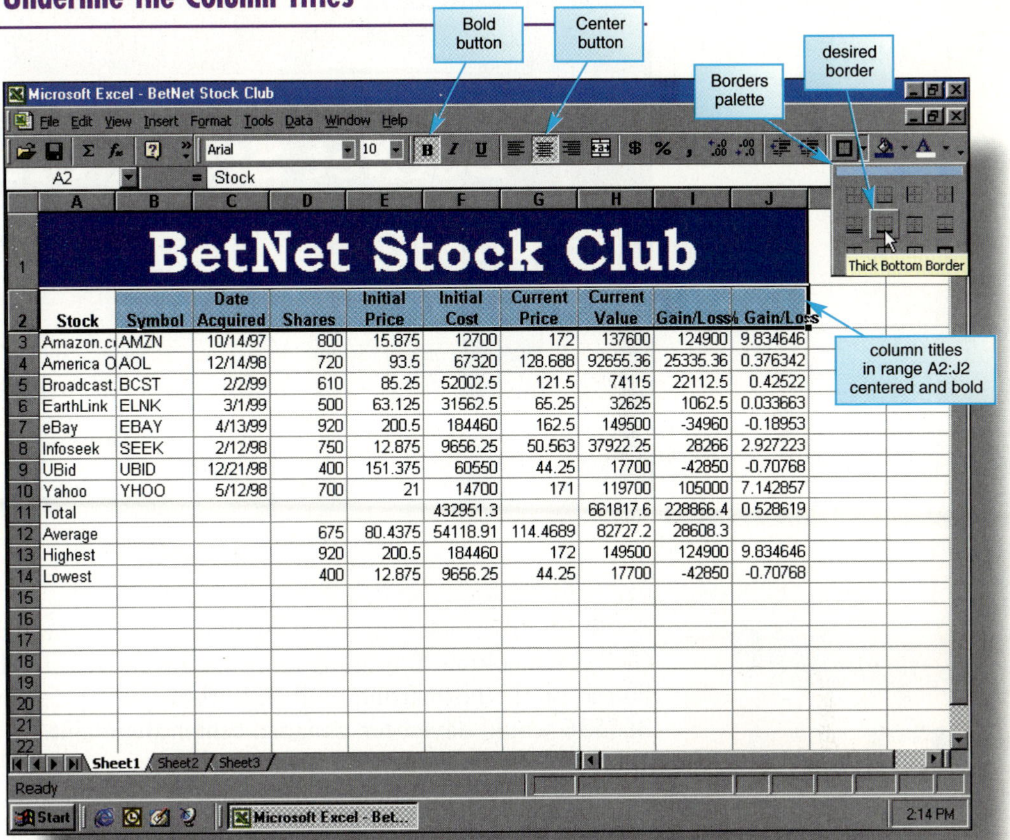

2 **Click the Thick Bottom Border button.**

Excel adds a thick bottom border to the range A2:J2.

Bold button

Center button

Borders palette

desired border

Thick Bottom Border

column titles in range A2:J2 centered and bold

FIGURE 2-38

Other Ways

1. Right-click cell, click Format Cells on shortcut menu, click Alignment tab, click Center in Horizontal list, click Font tab, click Bold in Font style list, click Border tab, click desired border, click OK button
2. On Format menu click Cells, click Alignment tab, click Center in Horizontal list, click Font tab, click Bold in Font style list, click Border tab, click desired border, click OK button
3. Press CTRL+1, click Alignment tab, click Center in Horizontal list, click Font tab, click Bold in Font style list, click Border tab, click desired border, click OK button

You can align the contents of cells in several different ways. Left alignment, center alignment, and right alignment are the more frequently used alignments. In fact, these three alignments are used so often that Excel has Left Align, Center, and Right Align buttons on the Formatting toolbar. In addition to aligning the contents of a cell horizontally, you also can align the contents of a cell vertically. You even can rotate the contents of a cell to various angles. For more information on alignment, on the Format menu click Cells and then click the Alignment tab.

Centering the Stock Symbols and Formatting the Numbers in the Worksheet

With the column titles formatted, the next step is to center the stock symbols in column B and format the numbers. If a cell entry is short, such as the stock symbols in column B, centering the entries within their respective columns improves the appearance of the worksheet. The following steps center the data in cells B3 to B10.

TO CENTER DATA IN CELLS

1. Select the range B3:B10. Click the Center button on the Formatting toolbar.

The stock symbols in column B are centered (Figure 2-39 on the next page).

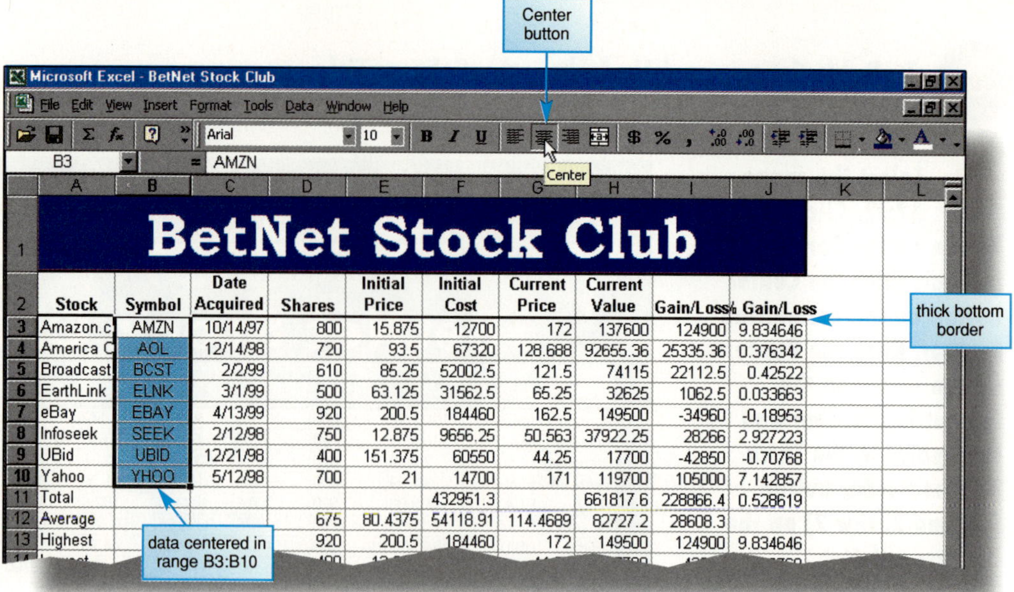

	A	B	C	D	E	F	G	H	I	J
2	Stock	Symbol	Date Acquired	Shares	Initial Price	Initial Cost	Current Price	Current Value	Gain/Loss	Gain/Loss
3	Amazon.c	AMZN	10/14/97	800	15.875	12700	172	137600	124900	9.834646
4	America C	AOL	12/14/98	720	93.5	67320	128.688	92655.36	25335.36	0.376342
5	Broadcast	BCST	2/2/99	610	85.25	52002.5	121.5	74115	22112.5	0.42522
6	EarthLink	ELNK	3/1/99	500	63.125	31562.5	65.25	32625	1062.5	0.033663
7	eBay	EBAY	4/13/99	920	200.5	184460	162.5	149500	-34960	-0.18953
8	Infoseek	SEEK	2/12/98	750	12.875	9656.25	50.563	37922.25	28266	2.927223
9	UBid	UBID	12/21/98	400	151.375	60550	44.25	17700	-42850	-0.70768
10	Yahoo	YHOO	5/12/98	700	21	14700	171	119700	105000	7.142857
11	Total					432951.3		661817.6	228866.4	0.528619
12	Average			675	80.4375	54118.91	114.4689	82727.2	28608.3	
13	Highest			920	200.5	184460	172	149500	124900	9.834646

FIGURE 2-39

Aligning and Rotating Text in Cells

Besides aligning text horizontally in a cell, you can align text vertically (top, center, bottom, or justify). You can also rotate text. To align vertically or rotate the text, click Format Cells on the shortcut menu, click the Alignment tab, and then select the type of alignment you want.

Rather than selecting the range B3:B10 in the previous step, you could have clicked the column B heading immediately above cell B1, and then clicked the Center button on the Formatting toolbar. In this case, all cells in column B down to cell B65536 would have been assigned center alignment.

When using Excel, you can use the buttons on the Formatting toolbar to format numbers as dollar amounts, whole numbers with comma placement, and percentages. Customized numeric formats also can be assigned using the **Cells command** on the Format menu or the **Format Cells command** on the shortcut menu.

As shown in Figure 2-29b on page E 2.27, the worksheet is formatted to resemble an accounting report. For example, in columns E through I, the first row of numbers (row 3), the totals (row 11), and the rows below the totals (rows 13 and 14) display with dollar signs, while the remaining numbers (rows 4 through 10) in these columns do not. To display a dollar sign in a number, you should use the Currency style format.

The **Currency style format** displays a dollar sign to the left of the number, inserts a comma every three positions to the left of the decimal point, and displays numbers to the nearest cent (hundredths place). The **Currency Style button** on the Formatting toolbar will assign the desired Currency style format. When you use the Currency Style button, Excel displays a **fixed dollar sign** to the far left in the cell, often with spaces between it and the first digit. To assign a **floating dollar sign** that displays immediately to the left of the first digit with no spaces, you must use the Cells command on the Format menu or the Format Cells command on the shortcut menu. The project specifications call for a fixed dollar sign to be assigned to the numbers in columns E through I in rows 3 and 11, and a floating dollar sign to be assigned to the monetary amounts in columns E through I in rows 12 through 14.

To display monetary amounts with commas and no dollar signs, you will want to use the Comma style format. The **Comma style format** inserts a comma every three positions to the left of the decimal point and displays numbers to the nearest hundredths (cents).

The remainder of this section describes how to format the numbers as shown in Figure 2-29b on page E 2.27.

Formatting Numbers Using the Formatting Toolbar

The following steps show how to assign formats using the Currency Style button and the Comma Style button on the Formatting toolbar.

Steps To Apply a Currency Style Format and Comma Style Format Using the Formatting Toolbar

1 **Select the range E3:I3. While holding down the CTRL key, select the nonadjacent range F11:I11. Point to the Currency Style button on the Formatting toolbar.**

The nonadjacent ranges display as shown in Figure 2-40.

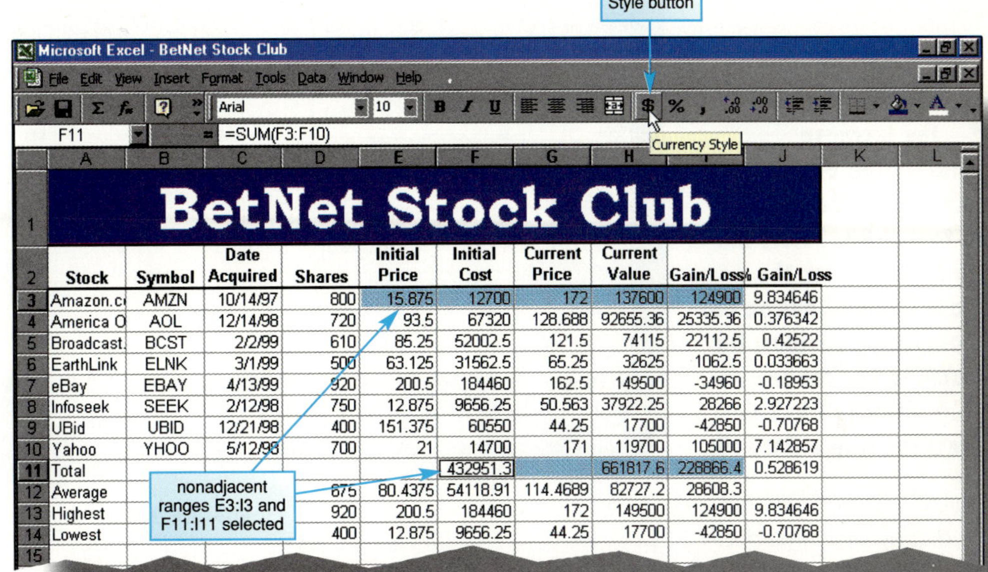

FIGURE 2-40

2 **Click the Currency Style button. Select the range E4:I10 and then point to the Comma Style button on the Formatting toolbar.**

Excel automatically increases the width of columns F, H, and I to best fit, so the numbers assigned the Currency style format will fit in the cells (Figure 2-41). The range E4:I10 is selected.

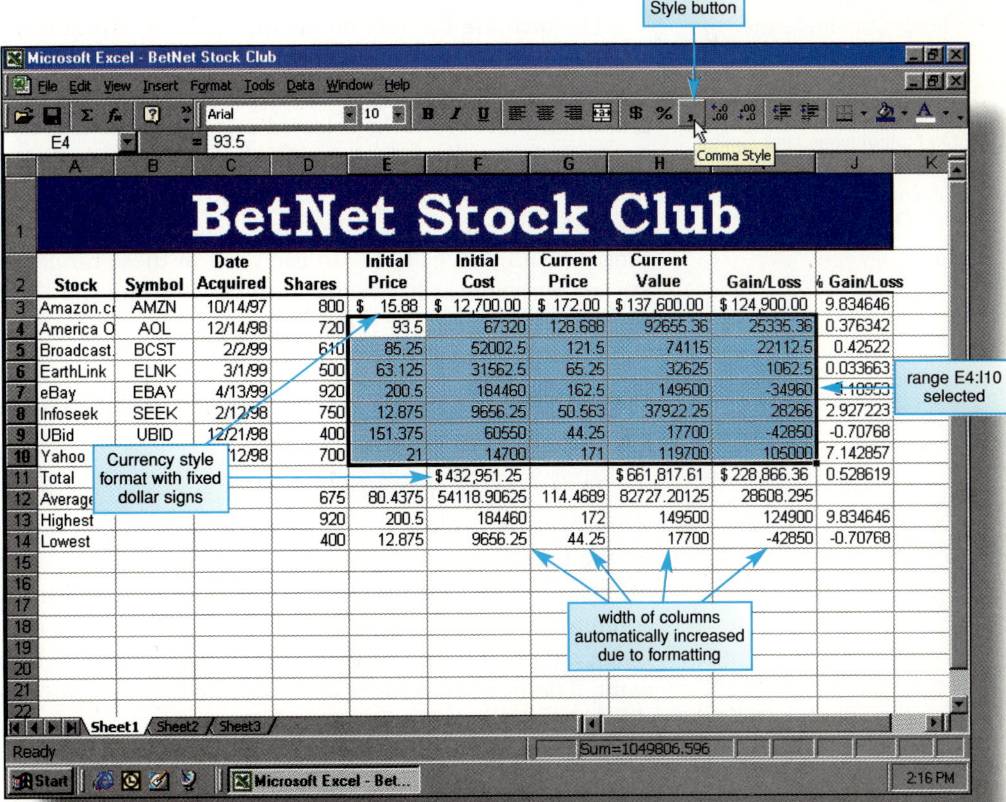

FIGURE 2-41

3 **Click the Comma Style button. Select the range A10:J10 and then click the Borders button on the Formatting toolbar.**

Excel assigns the Comma style format to the range E4:I10 and a thick bottom border to row 10.

4 **Click cell E3. Click the Increase Decimal button on the Formatting toolbar. Do the same to cell G3. Select the range E4:E10. Click the Increase Decimal button on the Formatting toolbar. Do the same to the range G4:G10. Click cell E12 to deselect the range G4:G10.**

The initial prices and current prices display with three decimal positions (Figure 2-42).

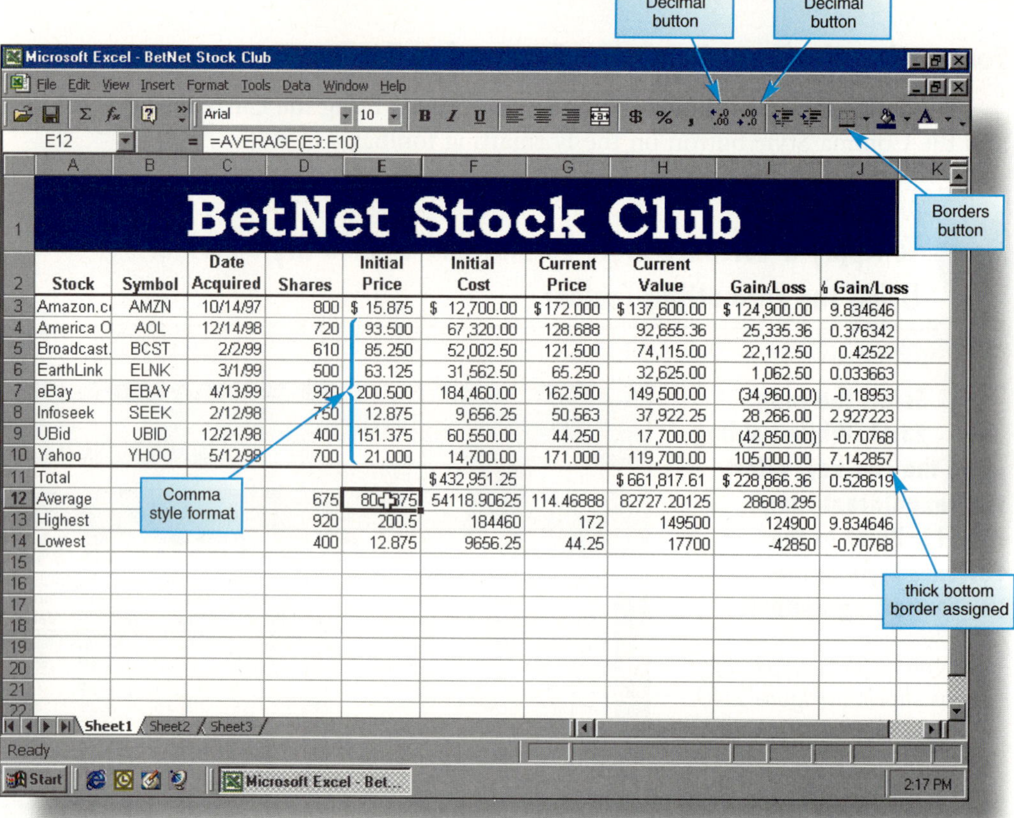

FIGURE 2-42

Other Ways

1. Right-click range, click Format Cells on shortcut menu, click Number tab, click Currency in Category list, click OK button
2. On Format menu click Cells, click Number tab, click Currency in Category list, click OK button

The **Increase Decimal button** on the Formatting toolbar is used to display additional decimal places in a cell. Each time you click the Increase Decimal button, Excel adds a decimal place to the selected cell. The **Decrease Decimal button** removes a decimal place from the selected cell each time it is clicked.

In Step 3, you clicked the Borders button on the Formatting toolbar because the Borders button is set to the thick bottom border that was assigned earlier to row 2.

The Currency Style button assigns a fixed dollar sign to the numbers in the ranges E3:I3 and F11:I11. In each cell in these ranges, the dollar sign displays to the far left with spaces between it and the first digit in the cell. Excel automatically rounds a number to fit the selected format.

Formatting Numbers Using the Format Cells Command on the Shortcut Menu

Thus far, you have been introduced to two ways of formatting numbers in a worksheet. In Project 1, you formatted the numbers using the AutoFormat command on the Format menu. In the previous section, you used the Formatting toolbar as a means of applying a format style. A third way to format numbers is to use the Cells command on the Format menu or the Format Cells command on the shortcut menu. Using either command allows you to display numbers in almost any format you want. The following steps show you how to use the Format Cells command to apply the Currency style format with a floating dollar sign to the totals in the range E12:I14.

To Apply a Currency Style Format with a Floating Dollar Sign Using the Format Cells Command

1 **Select the range E12:I14. Right-click the selected range. Point to Format Cells on the shortcut menu.**

The shortcut menu displays (Figure 2-43).

FIGURE 2-43

2 **Click Format Cells. Click the Number tab in the Format Cells dialog box. Click Currency in the Category list, click the third style ($1,234.10) in the Negative numbers list, and then point to the OK button.**

The Format Cells dialog box displays (Figure 2-44).

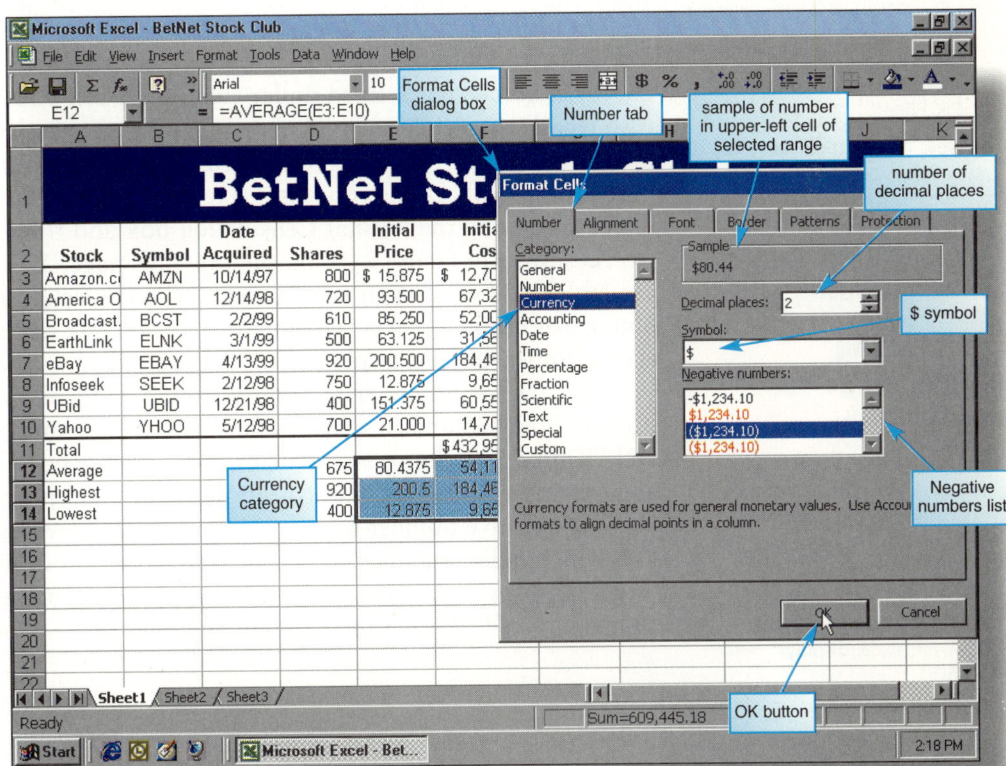

FIGURE 2-44

Click the OK button.

The worksheet displays with the totals in rows 12 through 14 assigned the Currency style format with a floating dollar sign (Figure 2-45).

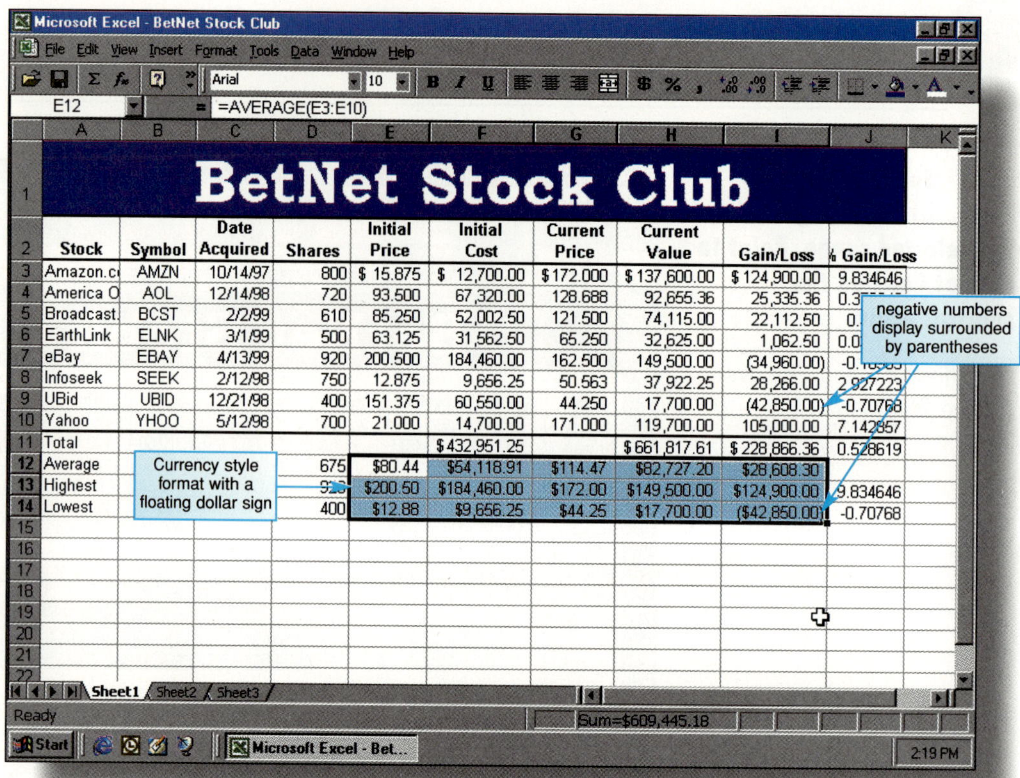

FIGURE 2-45

1. On Format menu click Cells, click Number tab, click Currency in Category list, select desired formats, click OK button
2. Press CTRL+SHIFT+DOLLAR SIGN

Formatting Numbers as You Enter Them

You can format numbers when you enter them by entering a dollar sign ($), comma (,), or percent sign (%) as part of the number. For example, if you enter 1500, Excel displays 1500. If you enter $1500, however, Excel displays $1,500.

Recall that a floating dollar sign always displays immediately to the left of the first digit, and the fixed dollar sign always displays on the left side of the cell. Cell E3, for example, has a fixed dollar sign, while cell E12 has a floating dollar sign. Also recall that, while cells E3 and E12 both were assigned a Currency style format, the Currency style was assigned to cell E3 using the Currency Style button on the Formatting toolbar. The result is a fixed dollar sign. The Currency style was assigned to cell E12 using the Format Cells dialog box and the result is a floating dollar sign.

As shown in Figure 2-44 on the previous page, 12 categories of formats are available from which you can choose. Once you select a category, you can select the number of decimal places, whether or not a dollar sign should display, and how negative numbers should display.

Selecting the appropriate negative numbers format in Step 2 is important, because doing so adds a space to the right of the number (as do the Currency Style and Comma Style buttons). Some of the available negative number formats do not align the numbers in the worksheet on the decimal points.

The negative number format selected in the previous set of steps displays in cell I14, which has a negative entry. The third selection in the Negative numbers list box (Figure 2-44) purposely was chosen to agree with the negative number format assigned to cell I9 using the Comma Style button.

Formatting Numbers Using the Percent Style Button and Increase Decimal Button

The last entry in the worksheet that needs to be formatted is the percent gain/loss in column J. Currently, the numbers in column J display as a decimal fraction (9.834646 in cell J3). Follow these steps to change to the Percent style format with two decimal places.

To Apply a Percent Style Format

1 **Select the range J3:J14. Click the Percent Style button on the Formatting toolbar.**

The numbers in column J display as a rounded whole percent.

2 **Click the Increase Decimal button on the Formatting toolbar twice.**

The numbers in column J display with two decimal places (Figure 2-46).

Percent Style button

Increase Decimal button

Decrease Decimal button

Percent style format with two decimal places

Microsoft Excel - BetNet Stock Club

J3 = =I3/F3

Increase Decimal

BetNet Stock Club

Stock	Symbol	Date Acquired	Shares	Initial Price	Initial Cost	Current Price	Current Value	Gain/Loss	% Gain/Loss
Amazon.c	AMZN	10/14/97	800	$ 15.875	$ 12,700.00	$172.000	$137,600.00	$124,900.00	983.46%
America O	AOL	12/14/98	720	93.500	67,320.00	128.688	92,655.36	25,335.36	37.63%
Broadcast.	BCST	2/2/99	610	85.250	52,002.50	121.500	74,115.00	22,112.50	42.52%
EarthLink	ELNK	3/1/99	500	63.125	31,562.50	65.250	32,625.00	1,062.50	3.37%
eBay	EBAY	4/13/99	920	200.500	184,460.00	162.500	149,500.00	(34,960.00)	-18.95%
Infoseek	SEEK	2/12/98	750	12.875	9,656.25	50.563	37,922.25	28,266.00	292.72%
UBid	UBID	12/21/98	400	151.375	60,550.00	44.250	17,700.00	(42,850.00)	-70.77%
Yahoo	YHOO	5/12/98	700	21.000	14,700.00	171.000	119,700.00	105,000.00	714.29%
Total					$432,951.25		$661,817.61	$228,866.36	52.86%
Average			675	$80.44	$54,118.91	$114.47	$82,727.20	$28,608.30	
Highest			920	$200.50	$184,460.00	$172.00	$149,500.00	$124,900.00	983.46%
Lowest			400	$12.88	$9,656.25	$44.25	$17,700.00	($42,850.00)	-70.77%

Sheet1 / Sheet2 / Sheet3

Ready Sum=2949.83%

Start Microsoft Excel - Bet... 2:19 PM

FIGURE 2-46

The **Percent Style button** on the Formatting toolbar is used to display a value determined by multiplying the cell entry by 100, rounding the result to the nearest percent, and adding a percent sign. For example, when cell J3 is formatted using the Increase Decimal button, the value 9.834646 displays as 983.46%. While they do not display, Excel does maintain all the decimal places for computational purposes. Thus, if cell J3 is used in a formula, the value used for computational purposes is 9.834646.

The last formatting requirement is to display the negative percents in column J in bold with a red background so they stand out. The **Conditional Formatting command** on the Format menu will be used to complete this task.

Rounding Numbers

When you instruct Excel to display a certain number of digits, it does maintain all the decimal places for computational purposes. For this reason, you may find a column sum to be off by a penny, because it is displaying data rounded to a specified number of digits, but it is using all the decimal places in the computation.

Conditional Formatting

Conditional Formatting

You can conditionally assign any format to a cell, a range of cells, the worksheet, or an entire workbook. If the value of the cell changes and no longer meets the specified condition, Excel temporarily suppresses the formats that highlight that condition.

Excel lets you apply formatting that appears only when the value in a cell meets conditions that you specify. This type of formatting is called **conditional formatting**. You can apply conditional formatting to a cell, a range of cells, the entire worksheet, or the entire workbook. Usually, you apply it to a range of cells that contains values you want to highlight if conditions warrant. For example, you can instruct Excel to bold and change the color of the background of a cell if the value in the cell meets a condition, such as being less than zero. For example, assume you assign the range J3:J10 the following condition:

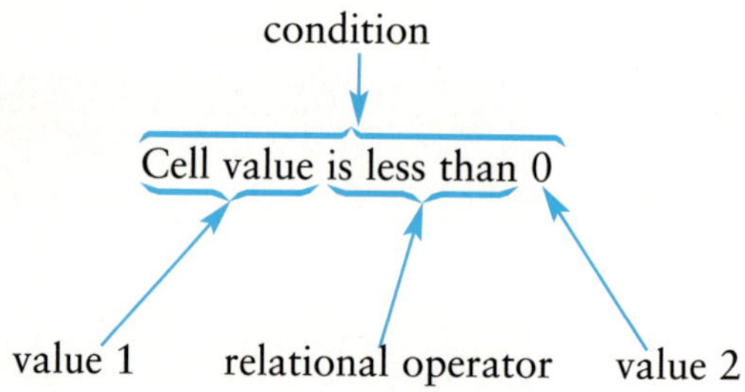

A **condition,** which is made up of two values and a relational operator, is true or false for each cell in the range. If the condition is true, then Excel applies the formatting. If the condition is false, then Excel suppresses the formatting. What makes conditional formatting so powerful is that the cell's appearance can change as you enter new values in the worksheet.

The following steps show how to assign conditional formatting to the range J3:J10. In this case, any cell value less than zero will cause the number in the cell to display in bold with a red background.

To Apply Conditional Formatting

1 Select the range J3:J10. Click Format on the menu bar and then point to Conditional Formatting.

The Format menu displays (Figure 2-47).

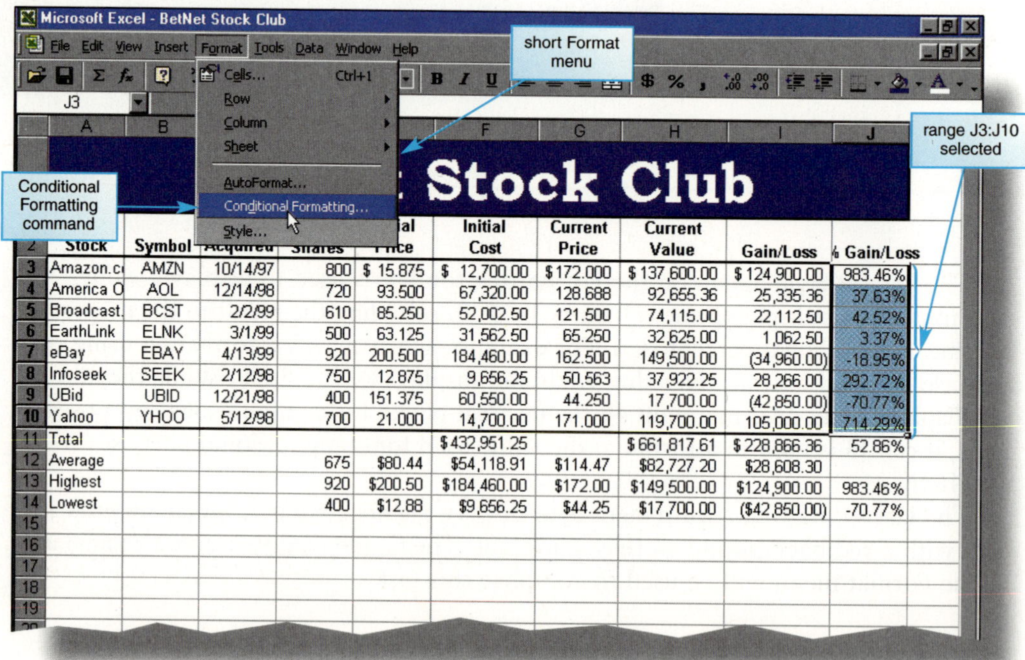

FIGURE 2-47

2 **Click Conditional Formatting. If necessary, click the leftmost text box arrow and then click Cell Value is. Click the middle text box arrow and then click less than. Type 0 in the rightmost text box. Point to the Format button.**

The Conditional Formatting dialog box displays as shown in Figure 2-48.

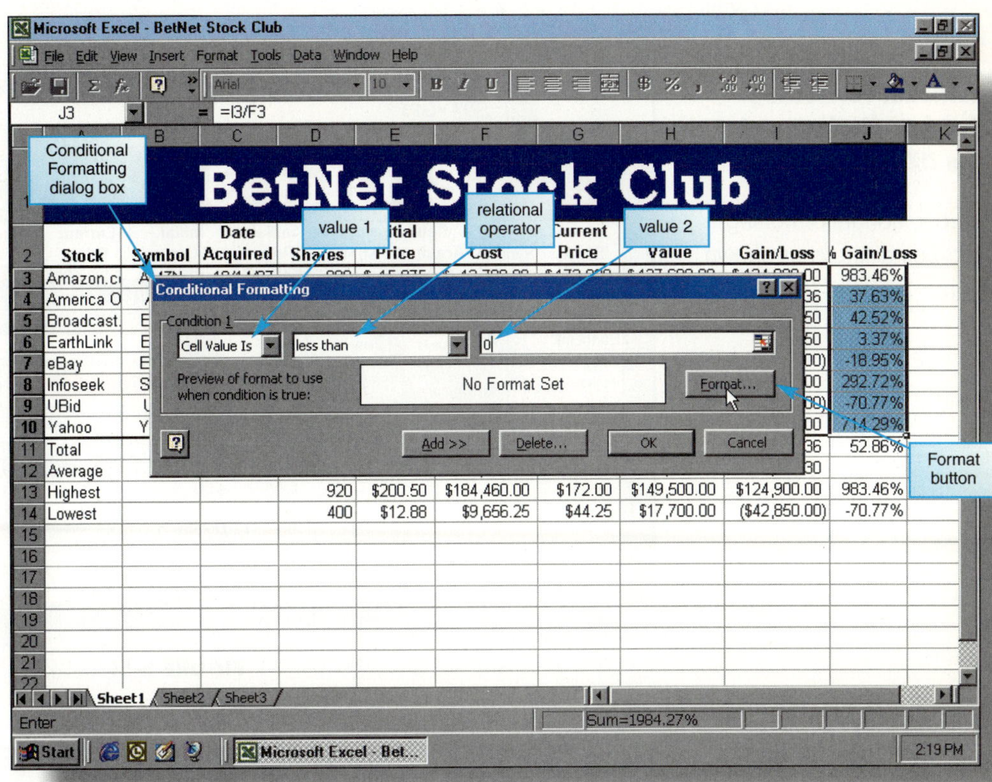

FIGURE 2-48

3 **Click the Format button. When the Format Cells dialog box displays, click the Font tab and then click Bold in the Font style list. Click the Patterns tab. Click the color red (column 1, row 3). Point to the OK button.**

The Patterns sheet in the Format Cells dialog box displays as shown in Figure 2-49.

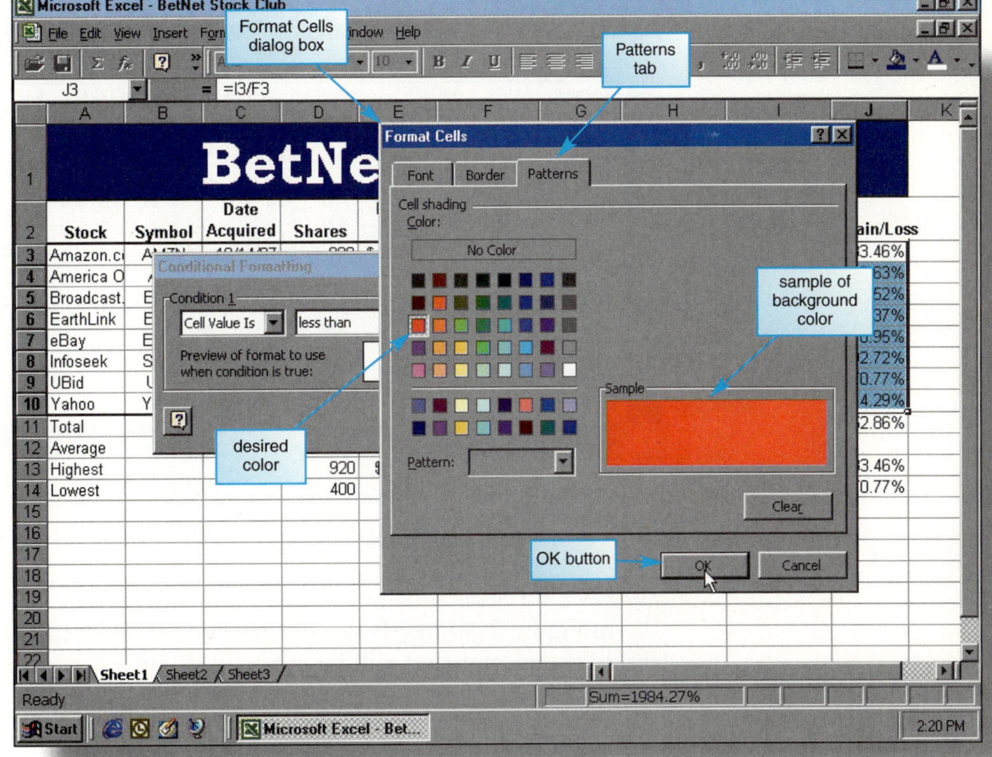

FIGURE 2-49

4 **Click the OK button. When the Conditional Formatting dialog box displays, point to the OK button.**

The Conditional Formatting dialog box displays as shown in Figure 2-50.

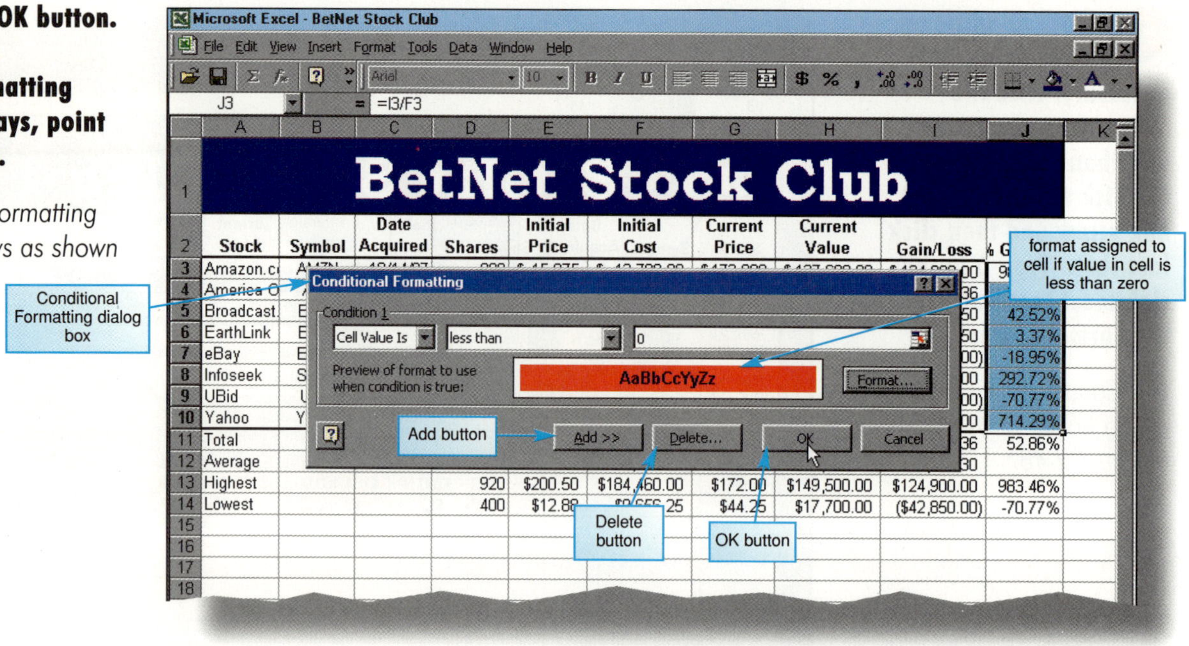

Conditional Formatting dialog box

format assigned to cell if value in cell is less than zero

Add button

Delete button

OK button

FIGURE 2-50

5 **Click the OK button. Click cell A16 to deselect the range J3:J10.**

Excel assigns the conditional format to the range J3:J10. Any negative value in this range displays in bold with a red background (Figure 2-51).

positive numbers display in black

negative numbers display in bold with red background

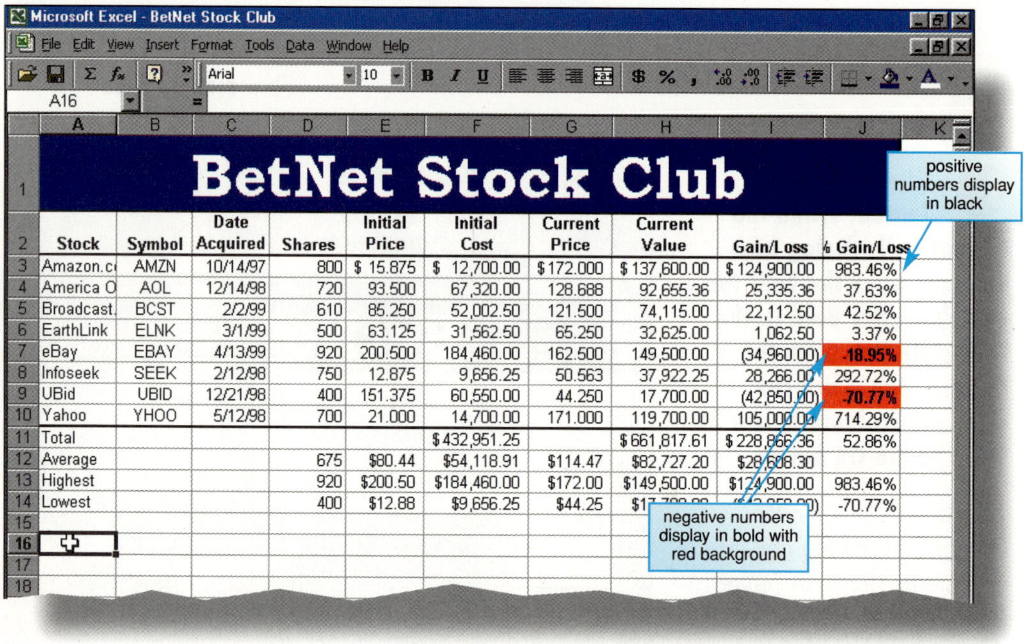

FIGURE 2-51

In Figure 2-50, the **Preview window** in the Conditional Formatting dialog box shows the format that will be assigned to any cells in the range J3:J10 that have a value less than zero. This preview allows you to modify the format before you click the OK button. The **Add button** in the Conditional Formatting dialog box allows you to add up to two additional conditions. The **Delete button** allows you to delete one or more active conditions.

The middle text box in the Conditional Formatting dialog box contains the relational operator. The eight different relational operators from which you can choose are summarized in Table 2-4

Table 2-4 Summary of Conditional Formatting Relational Operators

RELATIONAL OPERATOR	*DESCRIPTION*
Between	Cell value is between two numbers
Not between	Cell value is not between two numbers
Equal to	Cell value is equal to a number
Not equal to	Cell value is not equal to a number
Greater than	Cell value is greater than a number
Less than	Cell value is less than a number
Greater than or equal to	Cell value is greater than or equal to a number
Less than or equal to	Cell value is less than or equal to a number

Painting Formats

Painting is not an envious chore. In Excel, however, if you know how to paint, you can save yourself time and effort when formatting a worksheet. For example, if you see a cell that has the format you want to assign to another cell or range of cells, click the cell with the desired format, click the Format Painter button on the Standard toolbar, and then click the cell or drag through the cells you want to paint the format with.

With the number formatting complete, the next step is to change the column widths and row heights to make the worksheet easier to read.

Changing the Widths of Columns and Heights of Rows

When Excel starts and the blank worksheet displays on the screen, all of the columns have a default width of 8.43 characters, or 64 pixels. A **character** is defined as a letter, number, symbol, or punctuation mark in 10-point Arial font, the default font used by Excel. An average of 8.43 characters in this font will fit in a cell. Another measure is **pixels**, which is short for picture element. A pixel is a dot on the screen that contains a color. The size of the dot is based on your screen's resolution. At a common resolution of 800 × 600, 800 pixels display across the screen and 600 pixels display down the screen for a total of 480,000 pixels. It is these 480,000 pixels that form the font and other items you see on the screen.

The default row height in a blank worksheet is 12.75 points (or 17 pixels). Recall from Project 1 that a point is equal to 1/72 of an inch. Thus, 12.75 points is equal to about one-sixth of an inch. You can change the width of the columns or height of the rows at any time to make the worksheet easier to read or to ensure that an entry displays properly in a cell.

Changing the Widths of Columns

When changing the column width, you can set the width manually or you can instruct Excel to size the column to best fit. **Best fit** means that the width of the column will be increased or decreased so the widest entry will fit in the column. When the format you assign to a cell causes the entry to exceed the width of a column, Excel automatically changes the column width to best fit. This happened earlier when the Currency style format was used (Figure 2-41 on page E 2.35). If you do not assign a cell in a column a format, the width will remain 8.43 characters as is the case in columns A through D. To set a column width to best fit, double-click the right boundary of the column heading above row 1.

Sometimes, you may prefer more or less white space in a column than best fit provides. Excel thus allows you to change column widths manually. The following changes will be made to the column widths: columns A through E to best fit; column F to 12.00 characters, column G to 8.71 characters; and columns H through J to 12.00 characters.

More About 2000

Best Fit

Although Excel automatically increases the width of a column or the height of a row when you assign a format to a cell, it will not increase the column width or row height when a cell contains a formula and you change the value of a cell that is referenced in the formula. For example, if you change the number of shares in cell D3 from 800 to 10,0000, Excel will recalculate the formulas and display number signs (#) for the initial cost and gain/lost because the results of the formulas have more digits than can fit in the cell. You can fix the problem by double-clicking the right boundary of the column heading to change to best fit.

To Change the Widths of Columns

1 Drag through column headings A through E above row 1. Point to the boundary on the right side of column heading E.

The mouse pointer becomes a split double arrow (Figure 2-52).

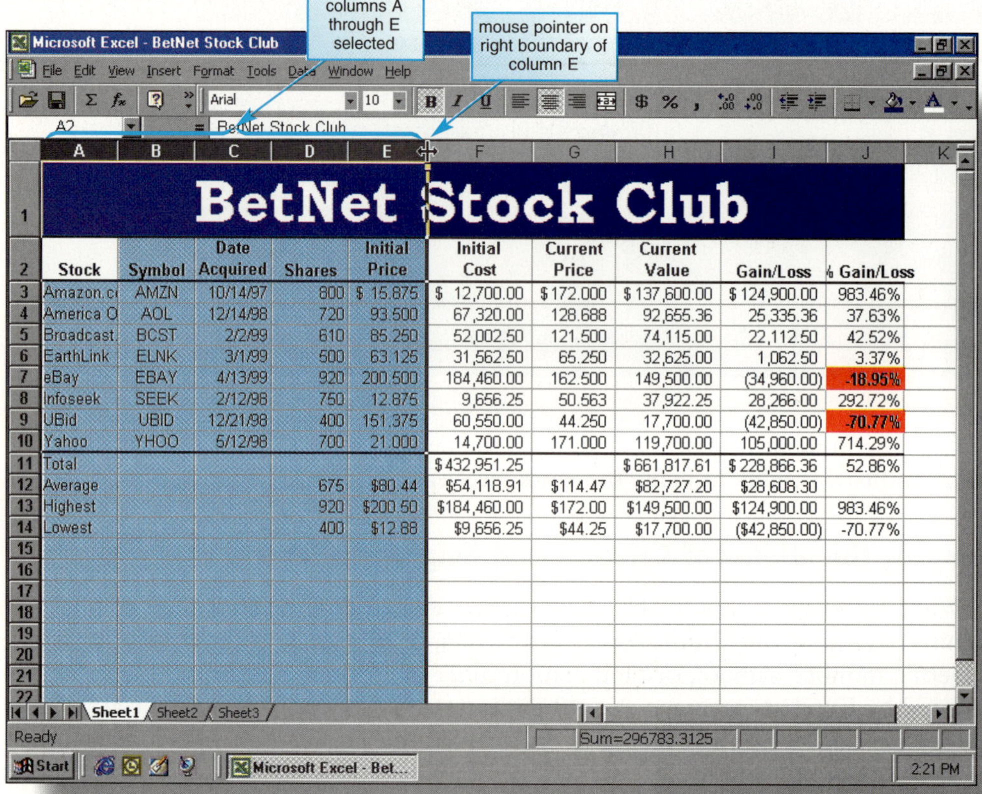

FIGURE 2-52

2 Double-click the right boundary of column heading E. Click cell A16 to deselect columns A through E. Point to the boundary on the right side of the column F heading above row 1. Drag to the right until the ScreenTip, Width: 12.00 (89 pixels), displays.

A dotted line shows the proposed right border of column F (Figure 2-53).

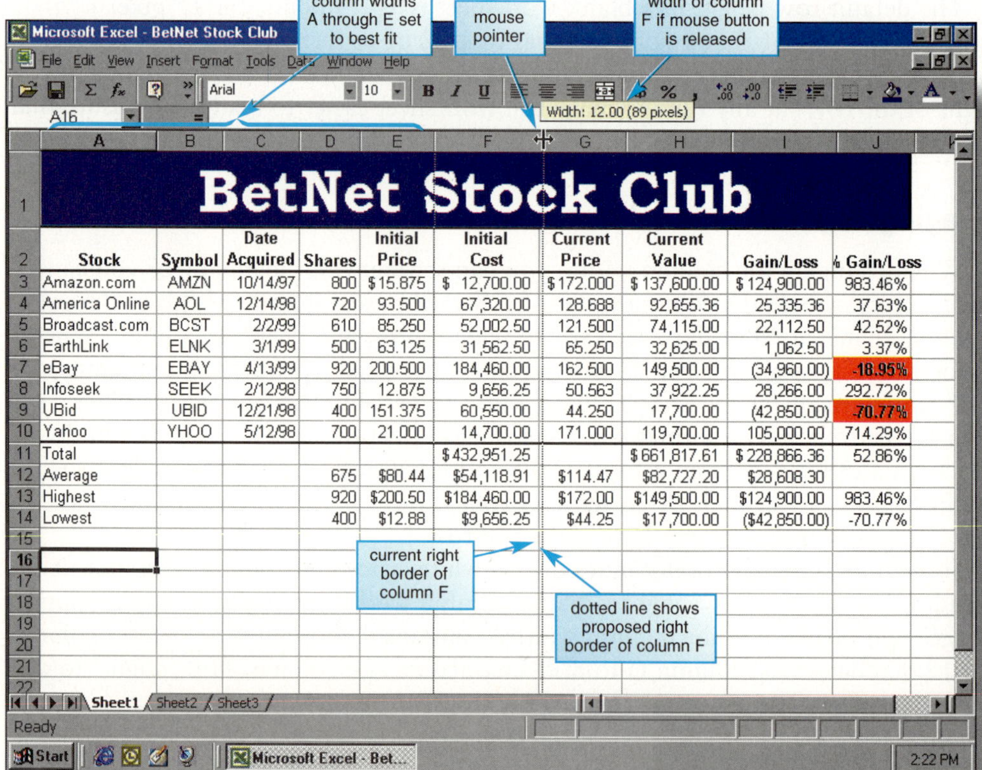

FIGURE 2-53

3 **Release the mouse button. Point to the boundary on the right side of the column G heading above row 1. Drag to the left until the ScreenTip, Width: 8.71 (66 pixels), displays.**

A dotted line shows the proposed right border of column G (Figure 2-54).

new column F width
mouse pointer
width of column G if mouse button is released

Microsoft Excel - BetNet Stock Club
Width: 8.71 (66 pixels)

BetNet Stock Club

	Stock	Symbol	Date Acquired	Shares	Initial Price	Initial Cost	Current Price	Current Value	Gain/Loss	% Gain/Loss
3	Amazon.com	AMZN	10/14/97	800	$15.875	$ 12,700.00	$172.000	$137,600.00	$124,900.00	983.46%
4	America Online	AOL	12/14/98	720	93.500	67,320.00	128.688	92,655.36	25,335.36	37.63%
5	Broadcast.com	BCST	2/2/99	610	85.250	52,002.50	121.500	74,115.00	22,112.50	42.52%
6	EarthLink	ELNK	3/1/99	500	63.125	31,562.50	65.250	32,625.00	1,062.50	3.37%
7	eBay	EBAY	4/13/99	920	200.500	184,460.00	162.500	149,500.00	(34,960.00)	-18.95%
8	Infoseek	SEEK	2/12/98	750	12.875	9,656.25	50.563	37,922.25	28,266.00	292.72%
9	UBid	UBID	12/21/98	400	151.375	60,550.00	44.250	17,700.00	(42,850.00)	-70.77%
10	Yahoo	YHOO	5/12/98	700	21.000	14,700.00	171.000	119,700.00	105,000.00	714.29%
11	Total					$432,951.25		$661,817.61	$228,866.36	52.86%
12	Average			675	$80.44	$54,118.91	$114.47	$82,727.20	$28,608.30	
13	Highest			920	$200.50	$184,460.00	$172.00	$149,500.00	$124,900.00	983.46%
14	Lowest			400	$12.88	$9,656.25	$44.25	$17,700.00	($42,850.00)	-70.77%

FIGURE 2-54

4 **Release the mouse button. Drag through column headings H through J above row 1. Point to the boundary on the right side of column J. Drag to the right until the ScreenTip, Width: 12.00 (89 pixels), displays.**

A dotted line shows the proposed right border of columns H through J (Figure 2-55).

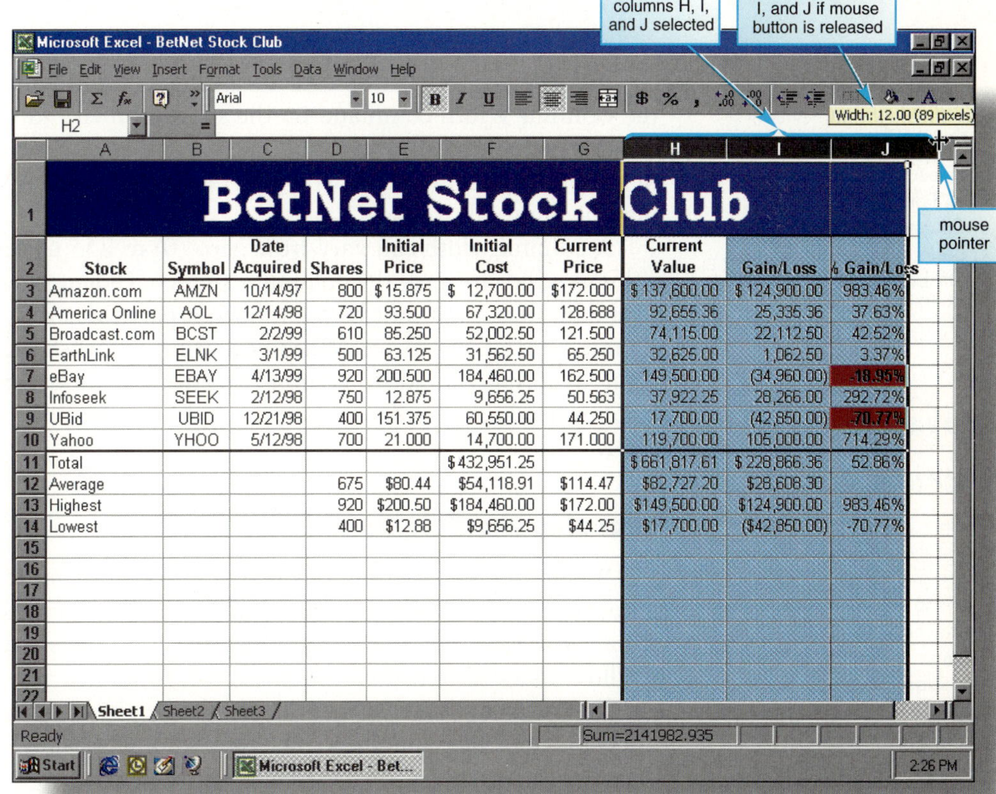

FIGURE 2-55

5 **Release the mouse button. Click cell A16 to deselect columns H through J.**

The worksheet displays with the new columns widths (Figure 2-56).

width of columns A through E set to best fit

width of column F set to 12.00

width of column G set to 8.71

width of columns H through J set to 12.00

	A	B	C	D	E	F	G	H	I	J
1	BetNet Stock Club									
2	Stock	Symbol	Date Acquired	Shares	Initial Price	Initial Cost	Current Price	Current Value	Gain/Loss	% Gain/Loss
3	Amazon.com	AMZN	10/14/97	800	$15.875	$ 12,700.00	$172.000	$ 137,600.00	$ 124,900.00	983.46%
4	America Online	AOL	12/14/98	720	93.500	67,320.00	128.688	92,655.36	25,335.36	37.63%
5	Broadcast.com	BCST	2/2/99	610	85.250	52,002.50	121.500	74,115.00	22,112.50	42.52%
6	EarthLink	ELNK	3/1/99	500	63.125	31,562.50	65.250	32,625.00	1,062.50	3.37%
7	eBay	EBAY	4/13/99	920	200.500	184,460.00	162.500	149,500.00	(34,960.00)	-18.95%
8	Infoseek	SEEK	2/12/98	750	12.875	9,656.25	50.563	37,922.25	28,266.00	292.72%
9	UBid	UBID	12/21/98	400	151.375	60,550.00	44.250	17,700.00	(42,850.00)	-70.77%
10	Yahoo	YHOO	5/12/98	700	21.000	14,700.00	171.000	119,700.00	105,000.00	714.29%
11	Total					$432,951.25		$ 661,817.61	$ 228,866.36	52.86%
12	Average			675	$80.44	$54,118.91	$114.47	$82,727.20	$28,608.30	
13	Highest			920	$200.50	$184,460.00	$172.00	$149,500.00	$124,900.00	983.46%
14	Lowest			400	$12.88	$9,656.25	$44.25	$17,700.00	($42,850.00)	-70.77%

FIGURE 2-56

Other Ways

1. Right-click column heading, click Column Width, enter desired column width, click OK button
2. Select cell or range of cells, on Format menu click Column, click Width, enter desired column width, click OK button

Hidden Columns

It often gets frustrating trying to use the mouse to unhide a range of columns. An alternative is to unhide columns using the keyboard. First select the columns to the right and left of the hidden ones and then press CTRL+SHIFT+RIGHT PARENTHESIS. To use the keyboard to hide a range of columns, press CTRL+O.

If you want to increase or decrease the column width significantly, you can use the Column Width command on the shortcut menu to change a column's width. To use this command, however, you must select one or more entire columns. As shown in the previous set of steps, you select entire columns by dragging through the column headings above row 1.

A column width can vary from zero (0) to 255 characters. If you decrease the column width to zero, the column is hidden. **Hiding** is a technique you can use to hide data that might not be relevant to a particular report or sensitive data that you do not want others to see. When you print a worksheet, hidden columns do not print. To display a hidden column, position the mouse pointer to the left of the column heading boundary where the hidden column is located and then drag to the right.

Changing the Heights of Rows

When you increase the font size of a cell entry, such as the title in cell A1, Excel automatically increases the row height to best fit so the characters display properly. Recall that Excel did this earlier (Figure 2-2 on page E 2.8) when you entered multiple lines in a cell in row 2.

You also can increase or decrease the height of a row manually to improve the appearance of the worksheet. The following steps show how to improve the appearance of the worksheet by increasing the height of row 1 to 61.50 points, row 2 to 36.00 points, and row 12 to 24.00 points. Perform the following steps to change the heights of these three rows.

To Change the Height of a Row by Dragging

1 Point to the boundary below row heading 1. Drag down until the ScreenTip, Height: 61.50 (82 pixels), displays.

The mouse pointer changes to a split double arrow (Figure 2-57). The distance between the dotted line and the top of row 1 indicates the proposed row height for row 1.

height of row 1 if mouse button is released

mouse pointer

dotted line shows proposed bottom border of row 1

FIGURE 2-57

2 Release the mouse button. Point to the boundary below row heading 2. Drag down until the ScreenTip, Height: 36.00 (48 pixels), displays.

Excel displays a horizontal dotted line (Figure 2-58). The distance between the dotted line and the top of row 2 indicates the proposed height for row 2.

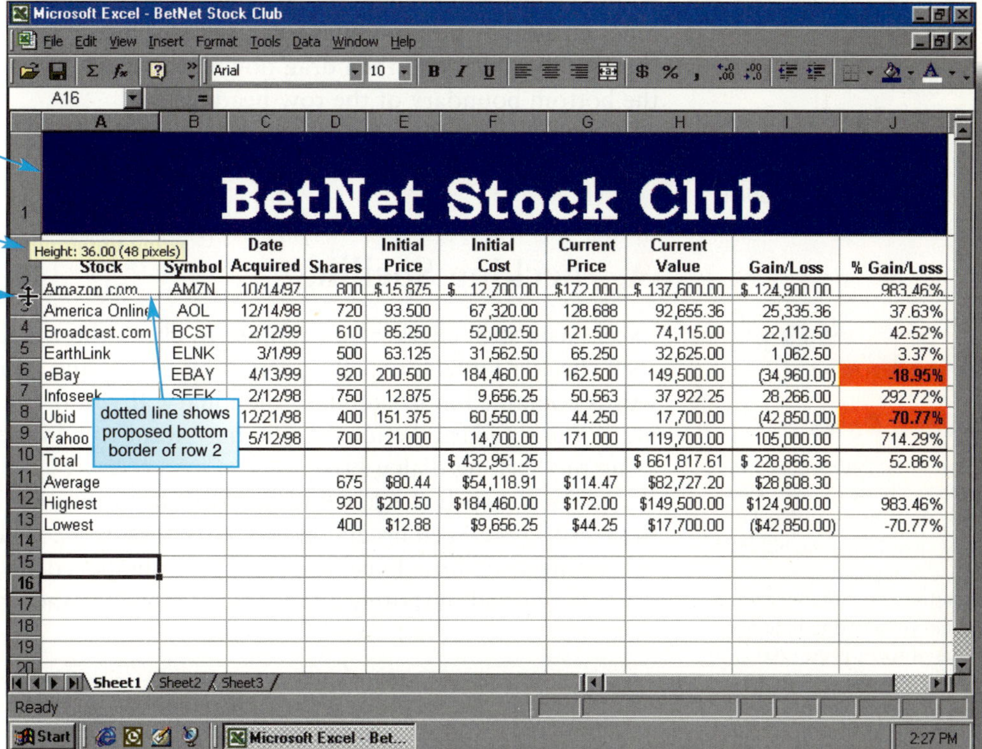

FIGURE 2-58

3 **Release the mouse button. Point to the boundary below row heading 12. Drag down until the ScreenTip, Height: 24.00 (32 pixels), displays. Release the mouse button.**

The Total row and the Average row have additional white space between them, which improves the appearance of the worksheet. The formatting of the worksheet is complete (Figure 2-59).

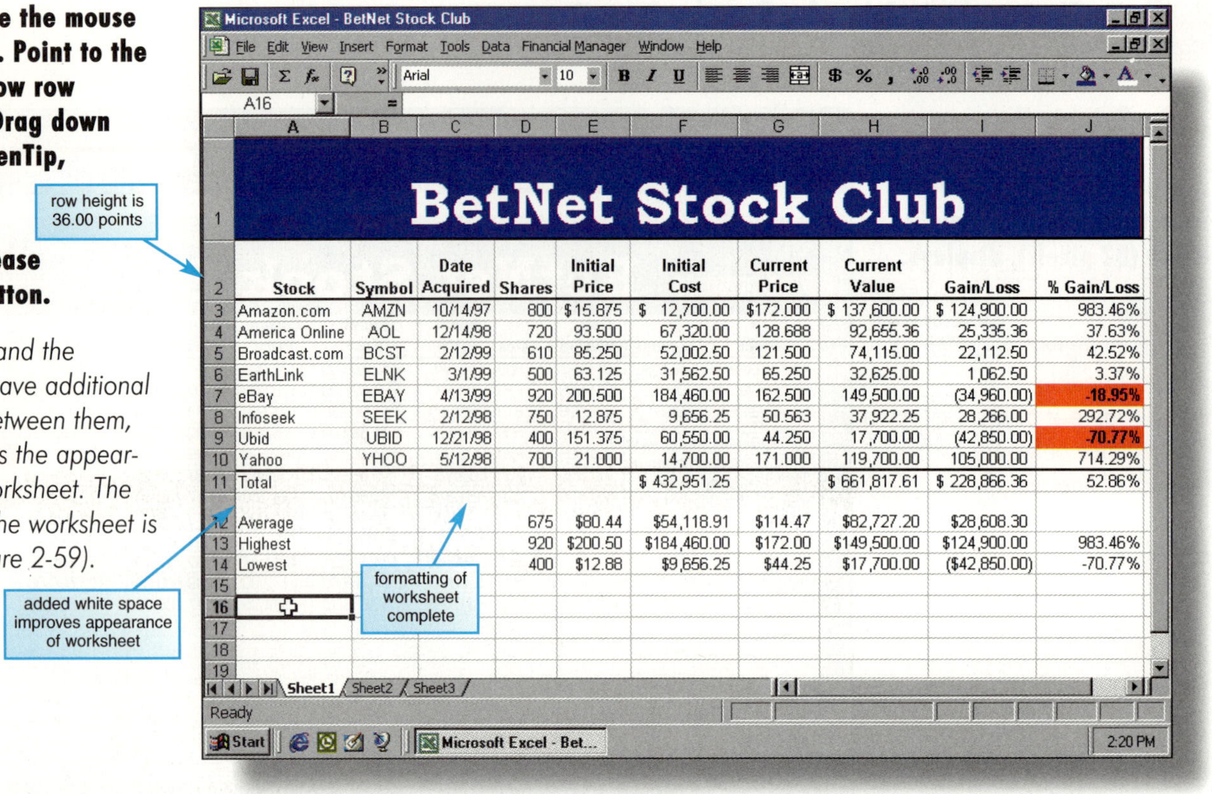
row height is 36.00 points
added white space improves appearance of worksheet
formatting of worksheet complete
Microsoft Excel - BetNet Stock Club
BetNet Stock Club
Stock | Symbol | Date Acquired | Shares | Initial Price | Initial Cost | Current Price | Current Value | Gain/Loss | % Gain/Loss
Amazon.com | AMZN | 10/14/97 | 800 | $ 15.875 | $ 12,700.00 | $172.000 | $ 137,600.00 | $ 124,900.00 | 983.46%
America Online | AOL | 12/14/98 | 720 | 93.500 | 67,320.00 | 128.688 | 92,655.36 | 25,335.36 | 37.63%
Broadcast.com | BCST | 2/12/99 | 610 | 85.250 | 52,002.50 | 121.500 | 74,115.00 | 22,112.50 | 42.52%
EarthLink | ELNK | 3/1/99 | 500 | 63.125 | 31,562.50 | 65.250 | 32,625.00 | 1,062.50 | 3.37%
eBay | EBAY | 4/13/99 | 920 | 200.500 | 184,460.00 | 162.500 | 149,500.00 | (34,960.00) | -18.95%
Infoseek | SEEK | 2/12/98 | 750 | 12.875 | 9,656.25 | 50.563 | 37,922.25 | 28,266.00 | 292.72%
Ubid | UBID | 12/21/98 | 400 | 151.375 | 60,550.00 | 44.250 | 17,700.00 | (42,850.00) | -70.77%
Yahoo | YHOO | 5/12/98 | 700 | 21.000 | 14,700.00 | 171.000 | 119,700.00 | 105,000.00 | 714.29%
Total | $ 432,951.25 | $ 661,817.61 | $ 228,866.36 | 52.86%
Average | 675 | $80.44 | $54,118.91 | $114.47 | $82,727.20 | $28,608.30
Highest | 920 | $200.50 | $184,460.00 | $172.00 | $149,500.00 | $124,900.00 | 983.46%
Lowest | 400 | $12.88 | $9,656.25 | $44.25 | $17,700.00 | ($42,850.00) | -70.77%
Sheet1
Sheet2
Sheet3
Ready
Start
Microsoft Excel - Bet...
2:20 PM

FIGURE 2-59

Other Ways

1. Right-click row heading or drag through multiple row headings and right-click, click Row Height on shortcut menu, enter desired row height, click OK button
2. Select cell or range of cells in column, on Format menu click Row, click Height on row submenu, enter desired row height, click OK button

The row height can vary between zero (0) and 409 points. As with column widths, when you decrease the row height to zero, the row is hidden. To display a hidden row, position the mouse pointer just below the row heading boundary where the row is hidden and then drag down. To set a row height to best fit, double-click the bottom boundary of the row heading.

The task of formatting the worksheet is complete. The next step is to check the spelling of the worksheet.

Checking Spelling

Excel has a spell checker you can use to check the worksheet for spelling errors. The spell checker looks for spelling errors by comparing words on the worksheet against words contained in its standard dictionary. If you often use specialized terms that are not in the standard dictionary, you may want to add them to a custom dictionary using the Spelling dialog box.

When the spell checker finds a word that is not in either dictionary, it displays the word in the Spelling dialog box. You then can correct it if it is misspelled.

To illustrate how Excel responds to a misspelled word, the word, Stock, in cell A2 is misspelled purposely as the word, Stpck, as shown in Figure 2-60.

More About 2000

Hidden Rows

You can use the keyboard to unhide a range of rows. First select the rows immediately above and below the hidden ones and then press CTRL+SHIFT+LEFT PARENTHESIS. To use the keyboard to hide a range of rows, press CTRL+9.

To Check Spelling on the Worksheet

1. **Double-click the move handle on the left side of the Standard toolbar to display the toolbar in its entirety. Select cell A2 and enter Stpck to misspell the word Stock. Select cell A1. Click the Spelling button on the Standard toolbar. When the spell checker stops on BetNet, click the Ignore button. When the spell checker stops on cell A2, click the word Stock in the Suggestions list.**

When the spell checker identifies the misspelled word, Stpck, the Spelling dialog box displays (Figure 2-60).

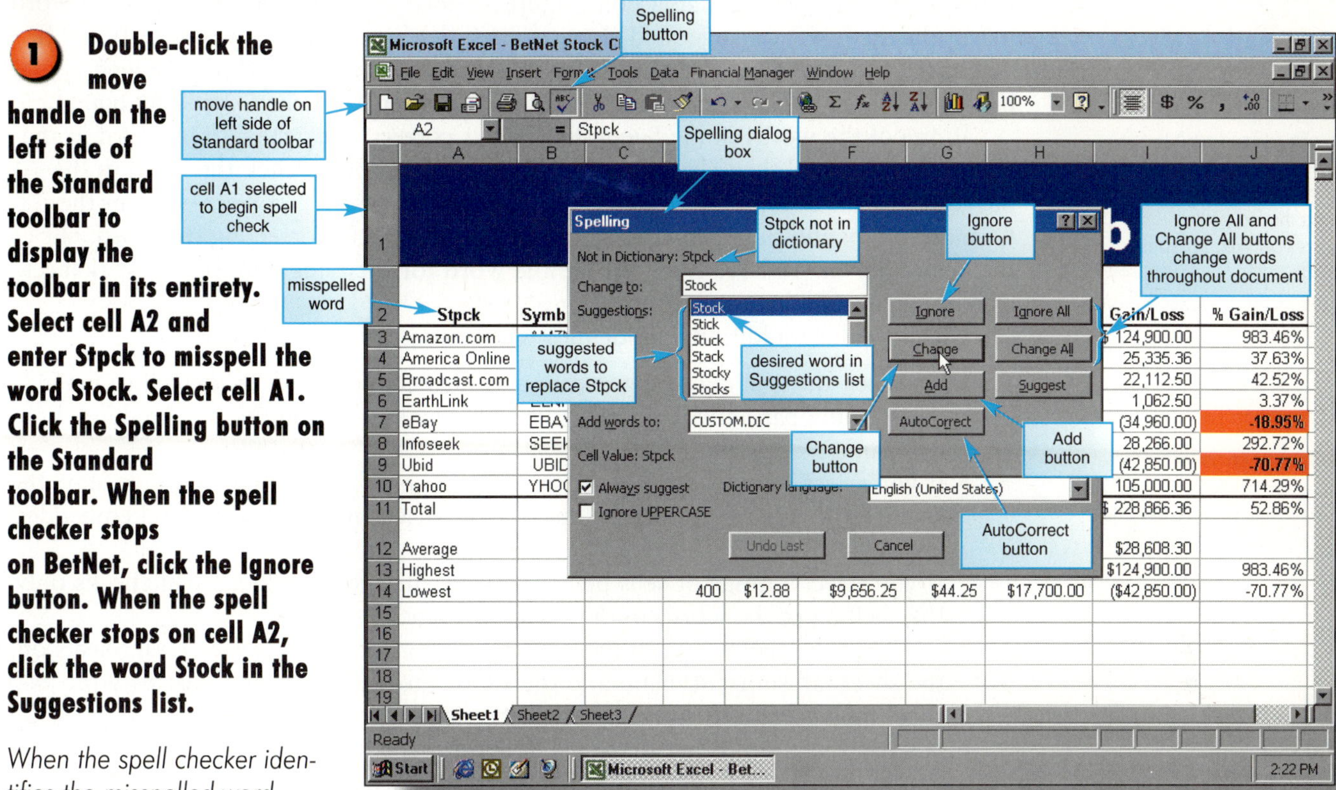

FIGURE 2-60

2. **Click the Change button. As the spell checker checks the remainder of the worksheet, click the Ignore and Change buttons as needed.**

The spell checker changes the misspelled word, Stpck, to the correct word, Stock, and continues spell checking the worksheet. When the spell checker is finished, it displays the Microsoft Excel dialog box with a message indicating that the spell check is complete for the entire sheet (Figure 2-61).

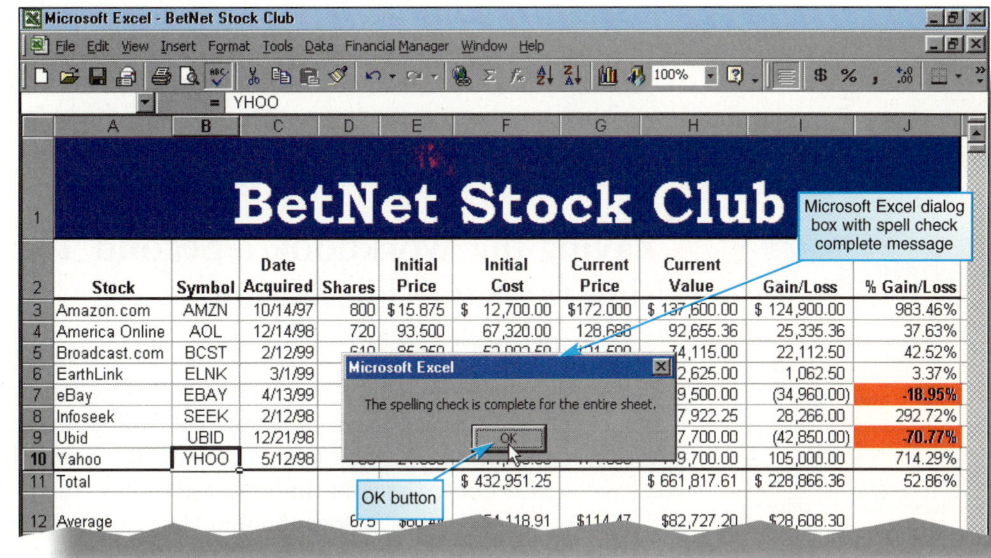

FIGURE 2-61

3. **Click the OK button.**

Other Ways

1. On the Tools menu click Spelling
2. Press F7

Checking Spelling

Always take the time to check the spelling of a worksheet before submitting it to your supervisor or instructor. Nothing deflates an impression more than a professional looking report with misspelled words.

When the spell checker identifies that a cell contains a word not in its standard or custom dictionary, it selects that cell as the active cell and displays the Spelling dialog box. The Spelling dialog box (Figure 2-60 on the previous page) lists the word not in the dictionary, a suggested correction, and a list of alternative suggestions. If you agree with the suggested correction in the **Change to box**, click the **Change button**. To change the word throughout the worksheet, click the **Change All button.**

If one of the words in the **Suggestions list** is correct, click the correct word in the Suggestions list and then click the Change button, or double-click the word in the Suggestions list. If none of the suggestions is correct, type the correct word in the Change to box and then click the Change button. To skip correcting the word, click the **Ignore button**. To have Excel ignore the word for the remainder of the worksheet, click the **Ignore All button.**

Consider these additional guidelines when using the spell checker:

- To check the spelling of the text in a single cell, double-click the cell to make the formula bar active and then click the Spelling button on the Standard toolbar.
- If you select a single cell so that the formula bar is not active and then start the spell checker, Excel checks the entire worksheet, including notes and embedded charts.
- If you select a range of cells before starting the spell checker, Excel checks only the spelling of the words in the selected range.
- To check the spelling of all the sheets in a workbook, click Select All Sheets on the sheet tab shortcut menu and then start the spell checker. To display the sheet tab shortcut menu, right-click the sheet tab.
- If you select a cell other than cell A1 before you start the spell checker, a dialog box will display when the spell checker reaches the end of the worksheet, asking if you want to continue checking at the beginning.
- To add words to the dictionary, click the **Add button** in the Spelling dialog box (Figure 2-60) when Excel identifies the word as not in the dictionary.
- Click the **AutoCorrect button** (Figure 2-60) to add the misspelled word and the correct version of the word to the AutoCorrect list. For example, suppose you misspell the word, do, as the word, dox. When the Spelling dialog box displays the correct word, do, in the Change to box, click the AutoCorrect button. Then, anytime in the future that you type the word, dox, Excel will change it to the word, do.

More About

Saving

If you want to save the workbook under a new name, click the Save As command on the File menu. Some Excel users feel better if they save workbooks on two different drives. They use the Save button on the Standard toolbar to save the latest version of the workbook on the default drive. Then, they use the Save As command to save a second copy on another drive.

Saving the Workbook a Second Time Using the Same File Name

Earlier in this project, you saved an intermediate version of the workbook using the file name, BetNet Stock Club. To save the workbook a second time using the same file name, click the Save button on the Standard toolbar. Excel automatically stores the latest version of the workbook using the same file name, BetNet Stock Club. When you save a workbook a second time using the same file name, Excel will not display the Save As dialog box as it does the first time you save the workbook. You also can click **Save** on the File menu or press SHIFT+F12 or CTRL+S to re-save a workbook.

If you want to save the workbook using a new name or on a different drive, click **Save As** on the File menu. Some Excel users, for example, use the Save button to save the latest version of the workbook on the default drive. Then, they use the Save As command to save a copy on another drive.

Previewing and Printing the Worksheet

In Project 1, you printed the worksheet without previewing it on the screen by clicking the Print button on the Standard toolbar. You can print the BetNet Stock Club worksheet the same way. By previewing the worksheet, however, you see exactly how it will look without generating a printout. Previewing allows you to see if the worksheet will print on one page in portrait orientation. **Portrait orientation** means the printout is printed across the width of the page. **Landscape orientation** means the printout is printed across the length of the page. Previewing a worksheet using the **Print Preview command** on the File menu or **Print Preview button** on the Standard toolbar can save time, paper, and the frustration of waiting for a printout only to discover it is not what you want.

Print Preview

A popular button in the preview window (Figure 2-63) is the Margins button. The Margins button allows you to drag the top, bottom, left, and right margins to center a worksheet or add room to fit a wide or long worksheet on a page. You even can change the column widths.

To Preview and Print a Worksheet

1 Point to the Print Preview button on the Standard toolbar (Figure 2-62).

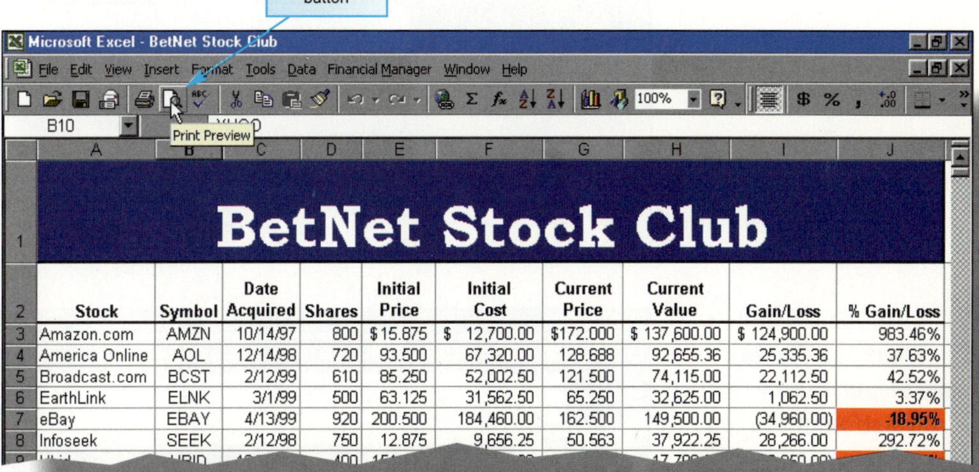

FIGURE 2-62

2 Click the Print Preview button. When the Preview window displays, point to the Setup button.

Excel displays a preview of the worksheet in portrait orientation. In portrait orientation, the worksheet does not fit on one page (Figure 2-63).

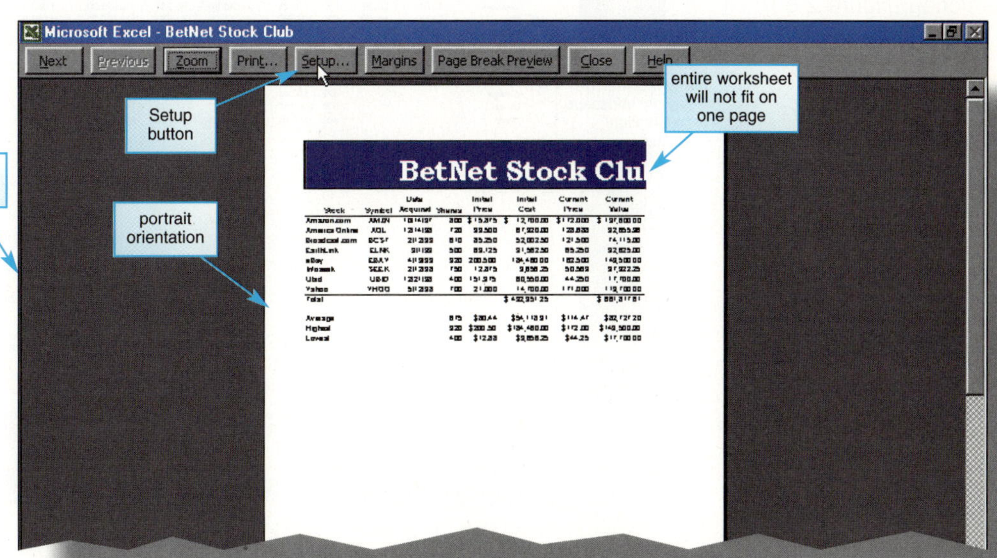

FIGURE 2-63

3 **Click the Setup button. When the Page Setup dialog box displays, click the Page tab and then click Landscape. Point to the OK button.**

The Page Setup dialog box displays. You have two choices in the Orientation area, Portrait or Landscape (Figure 2-64).

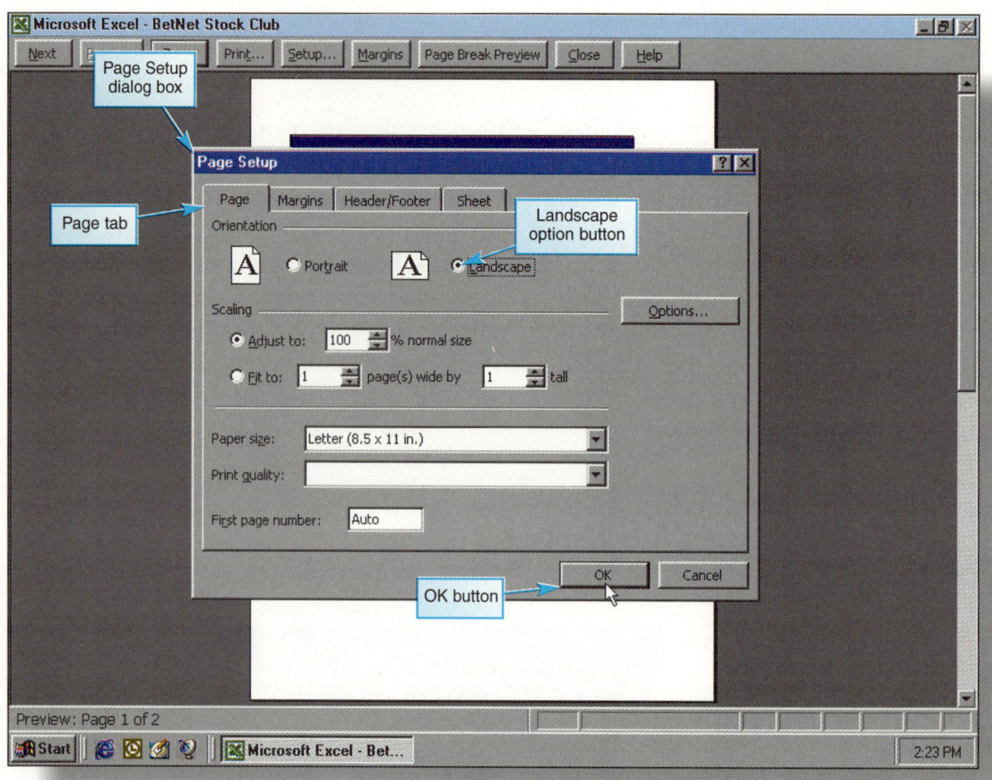

FIGURE 2-64

4 **Click the OK button. When the Preview window displays, point to the Print button at the top of the Preview window.**

The worksheet displays in the Preview window in landscape orientation (Figure 2-65)

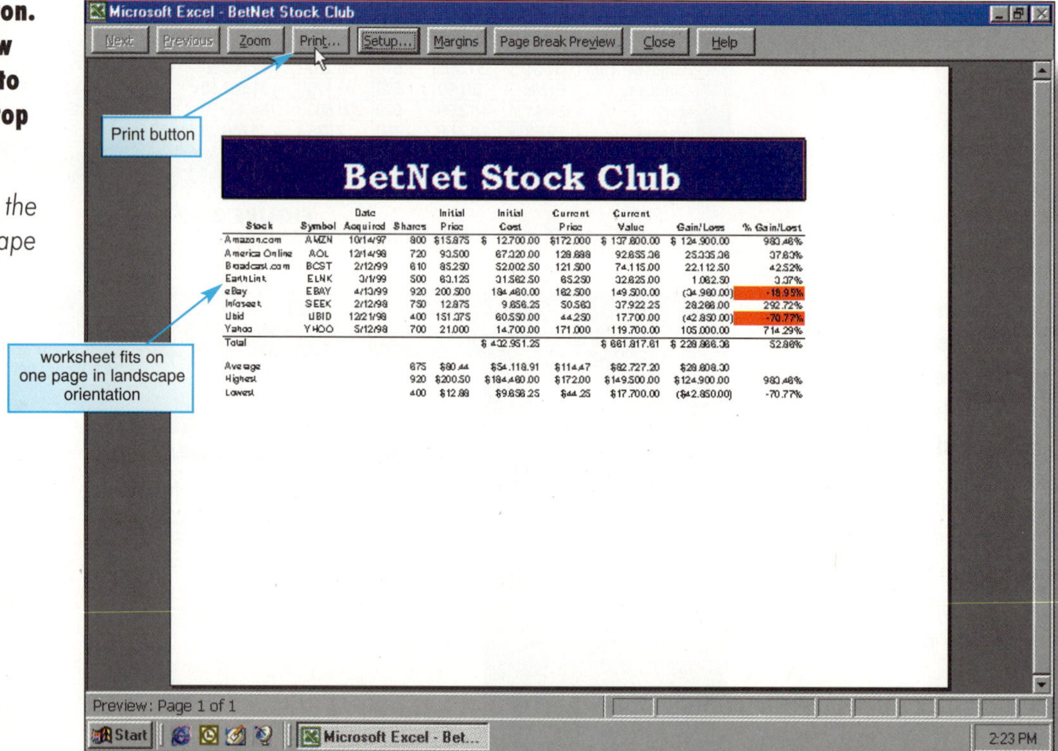

FIGURE 2-65

5 **Click the Print button. When the Print dialog box displays, point to the OK button.**

The Print dialog box displays as shown in Figure 2-66.

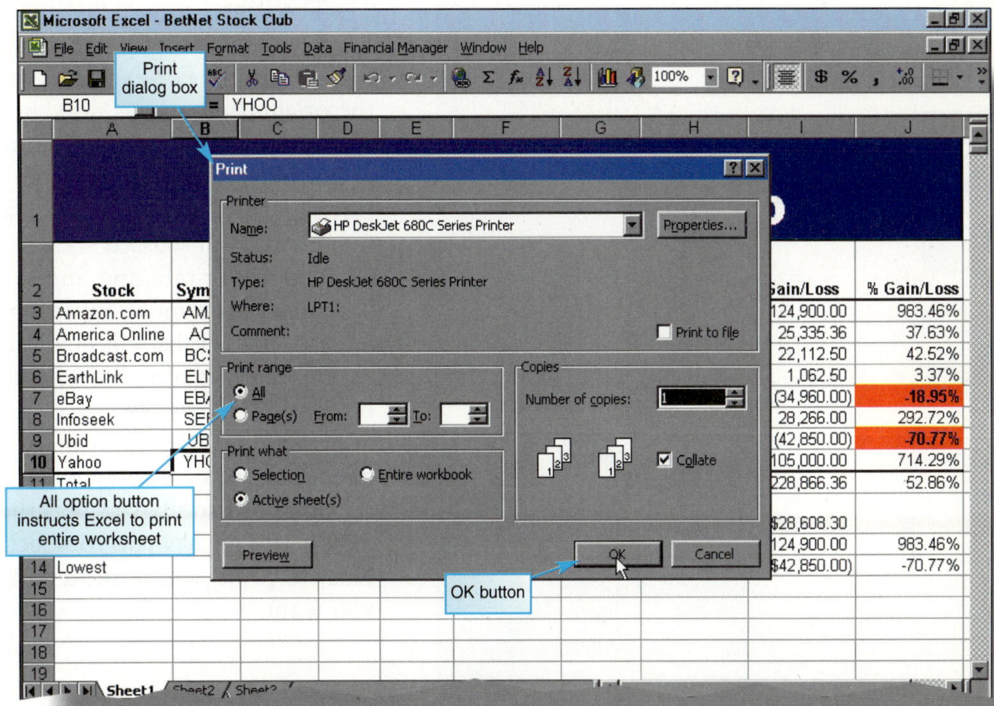

FIGURE 2-66

6 **Click the OK button. Click the Save button on the Standard toolbar.**

Excel prints the worksheet (Figure 2-67). The workbook is saved with the landscape orientation.

landscape orientation

BetNet Stock Club

Stock	Symbol	Date Acquired	Shares	Initial Price	Initial Cost	Current Price	Current Value	Gain/Loss	% Gain/Loss
Amazon.com	AMZN	10/14/97	800	$ 15.875	$ 12,700.00	$172.000	$ 137,600.00	$ 124,900.00	983.46%
America Online	AOL	12/14/98	720	93.500	67,320.00	128.688	92,655.36	25,335.36	37.63%
Broadcast.com	BCST	2/12/99	610	85.250	52,002.50	121.500	74,115.00	22,112.50	42.52%
EarthLink	ELNK	3/1/99	500	63.125	31,562.50	65.250	32,625.00	1,062.50	3.37%
eBay	EBAY	4/13/99	920	200.500	184,460.00	162.500	149,500.00	(34,960.00)	-18.95%
Infoseek	SEEK	2/12/98	750	12.875	9,656.25	50.563	37,922.25	28,266.00	292.72%
Ubid	UBID	12/21/98	400	151.375	60,550.00	44.250	17,700.00	(42,850.00)	-70.77%
Yahoo	YHOO	5/12/98	700	21.000	14,700.00	171.000	119,700.00	105,000.00	714.29%
Total					$ 432,951.25		$ 661,817.61	$ 228,866.36	52.86%
Average			675	$80.44	$54,118.91	$114.47	$82,727.20	$28,608.30	
Highest			920	$200.50	$184,460.00	$172.00	$149,500.00	$124,900.00	983.46%
Lowest			400	$12.88	$9,656.25	$44.25	$17,700.00	($42,850.00)	-70.77%

FIGURE 2-67

Other Ways

1. On the File menu click Print Preview
2. On the File menu click Page Setup, click Print Preview button
3. On File menu click Print, click Preview button

Once you change the orientation and save the workbook, it will remain until you change it. Excel sets the orientation for a new workbook to portrait.

There are several buttons at the top of the Preview window (Figure 2-65). The functions of these buttons are summarized in Table 2-5 on the next page.

Rather than click the Next and Previous buttons to move from page to page as described in Table 2-5, you can press the PAGE UP and PAGE DOWN keys. You also can click the previewed page in the Preview window when the mouse pointer shape is a magnifying glass to carry out the function of the Zoom button.

Table 2-5 Print Preview Buttons

BUTTON	FUNCTION
Next	Previews the next page
Previous	Previews the previous page
Zoom	Magnifies or reduces the print preview
Print...	Prints the worksheet
Setup...	Displays the Print Setup dialog box
Margins	Changes the print margins
Page Break Preview	Previews page breaks
Close	Closes the Preview window
Help	Displays Help about the Preview window

The Page Setup dialog box in Figure 2-64 on page E 2.52 allows you to make changes to the default settings for a printout. For example, on the Page tab, you can set the orientation as was done in the previous set of steps, scale the printout so it fits on one page, set the page size, and print quality. Scaling is an alternative to changing the orientation to fit a wide worksheet on one page. This technique will be discussed shortly. The Margins tab, Header/Footer tab, and Sheet tab in the Page Setup dialog box allow even more control of the way the printout will appear. These tabs will be discussed in later projects.

The Print dialog box shown in Figure 2-66 on the previous page displays when you use the Print command on the File menu or a Print button in a dialog box or Preview window. It does not display when you use the Print button on the Standard toolbar as was the case in Project 1. The Print dialog box allows you to select a printer, instruct Excel what to print, and indicate how many copies of the printout you want.

Printing a Section of the Worksheet

You might not always want to print the entire worksheet. You can print portions of the worksheet by selecting the range of cells to print and then clicking the Selection option button in the Print what area in the Print dialog box. The following steps show how to print the range A2:F11.

To Print a Section of the Worksheet

1 Select the range A2:F11. Click File on the menu bar and then click Print. Click Selection in the Print what area. Point to the OK button.

The Print dialog box displays (Figure 2-68). Because the Selection option button is selected, Excel will print only the selected range.

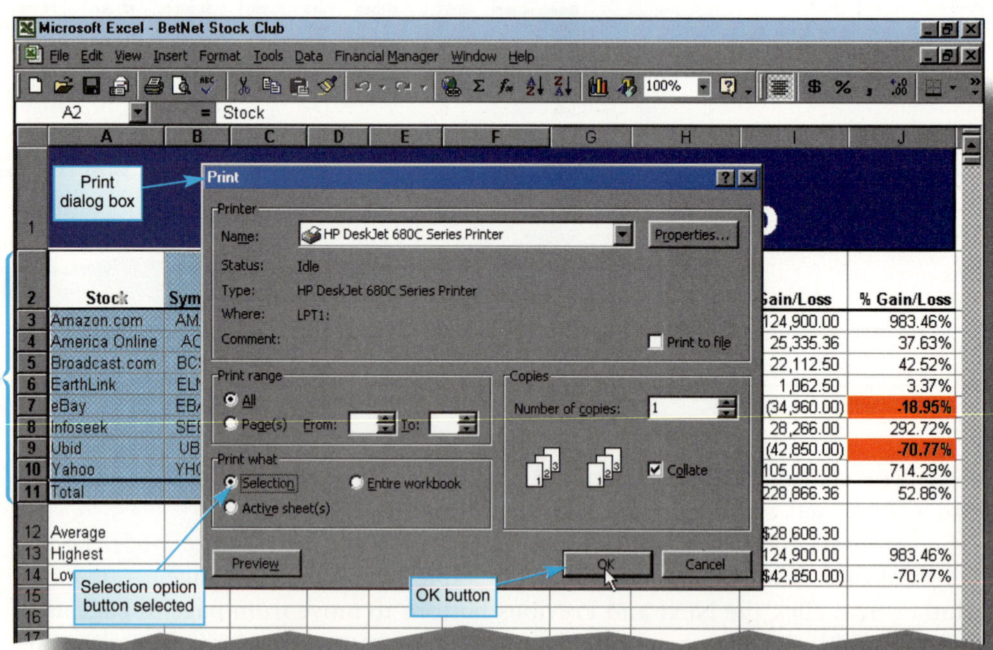

FIGURE 2-68

2 **Click the OK button. Click cell A16 to deselect the range A2:F11.**

Excel prints the selected range of the worksheet on the printer (Figure 2-69).

only selected range prints

Stock	Symbol	Date Acquired	Shares	Initial Price	Initial Cost
Amazon.com	AMZN	10/14/97	800	$ 15.875	$ 12,700.00
America Online	AOL	12/14/98	720	93.500	67,320.00
Broadcast.com	BCST	2/12/99	610	85.250	52,002.50
EarthLink	ELNK	3/1/99	500	63.125	31,562.50
eBay	EBAY	4/13/99	920	200.500	184,460.00
Infoseek	SEEK	2/12/98	750	12.875	9,656.25
Ubid	UBID	12/21/98	400	151.375	60,550.00
Yahoo	YHOO	5/12/98	700	21.000	14,700.00
Total					$ 432,951.25

FIGURE 2-69

Other Ways

1. Select range to print, on File menu click Print Area, click Set Print Area, click Print button on Standard toolbar; on File menu click Print Area, click Clear Print Area

Three option buttons display in the Print what area in the Print dialog box (Figure 2-68). As shown in the previous steps, the **Selection option button** instructs Excel to print the selected range. The **Active sheet(s) option button** instructs Excel to print the active sheet (the one displaying on the screen) or the selected sheets. Finally, the **Entire workbook option button** instructs Excel to print all the sheets with content in the workbook.

Displaying and Printing the Formulas Version of the Worksheet

Thus far, you have been working with the **values version** of the worksheet, which shows the results of the formulas you have entered, rather than the actual formulas. Excel also allows you to display and print the **formulas version** of the worksheet, which displays the actual formulas you have entered, rather than the resulting values. You can toggle between the values version and formulas version by pressing CTRL+LEFT SINGLE QUOTATION MARK (` to the left of the number 1 key).

The formulas version is useful for debugging a worksheet. **Debugging** is the process of finding and correcting errors in the worksheet. Because the formula version displays and prints formulas and functions, rather than the results, it makes it easier to see if any mistakes were made in the formulas.

When you change from the values version to the formulas version, Excel increases the width of the columns so the formulas and text do not overflow into adjacent cells on the right. The formulas version of the worksheet thus usually is significantly wider than the values version. To fit the wide printout on one page, you can use landscape orientation and the **Fit to option** on the Page tab in the Page Setup dialog box. To change from the values version to the formulas version of the worksheet and print the formulas on one page, perform the steps on the next page.

More About 2000

Printing

A dark font on a dark background, such as a red font on a blue background, will not print properly on a black and white printer. For black and white printing, use a light colored font on a dark background and a dark font on a light colored background.

More About 2000

Values versus Formulas

When completing class assignments, do not enter numbers in cells that require formulas. Most instructors require their students to hand in both the values version and formulas version of the worksheet. The formulas version verifies that you entered formulas, rather than numbers in formula-based cells.

To Display the Formulas in the Worksheet and Fit the Printout on One Page

1 **Press CTRL+LEFT SINGLE QUOTATION MARK (`). Click the right horizontal scroll arrow until column J displays.**

Excel changes the display of the worksheet from values to formulas (Figure 2-70). The formulas in the worksheet display showing unformatted numbers, formulas, and functions that were assigned to the cells. Excel automatically increases the column widths.

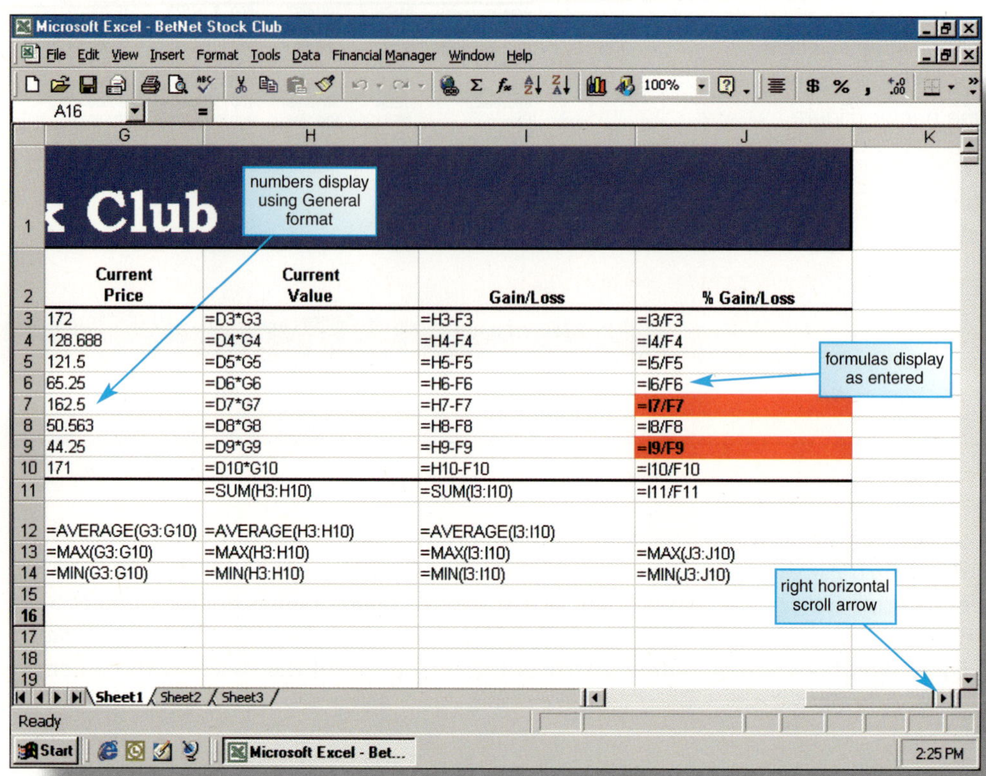

FIGURE 2-70

2 **Click File on the menu bar, and then click Page Setup. When the Page Setup dialog box displays, click the Page tab. If necessary, click Landscape, and then click Fit to. Point to the Print button in the Page Setup dialog box.**

Excel displays the Page Setup dialog box with the Landscape and Fit to option buttons selected (Figure 2-71).

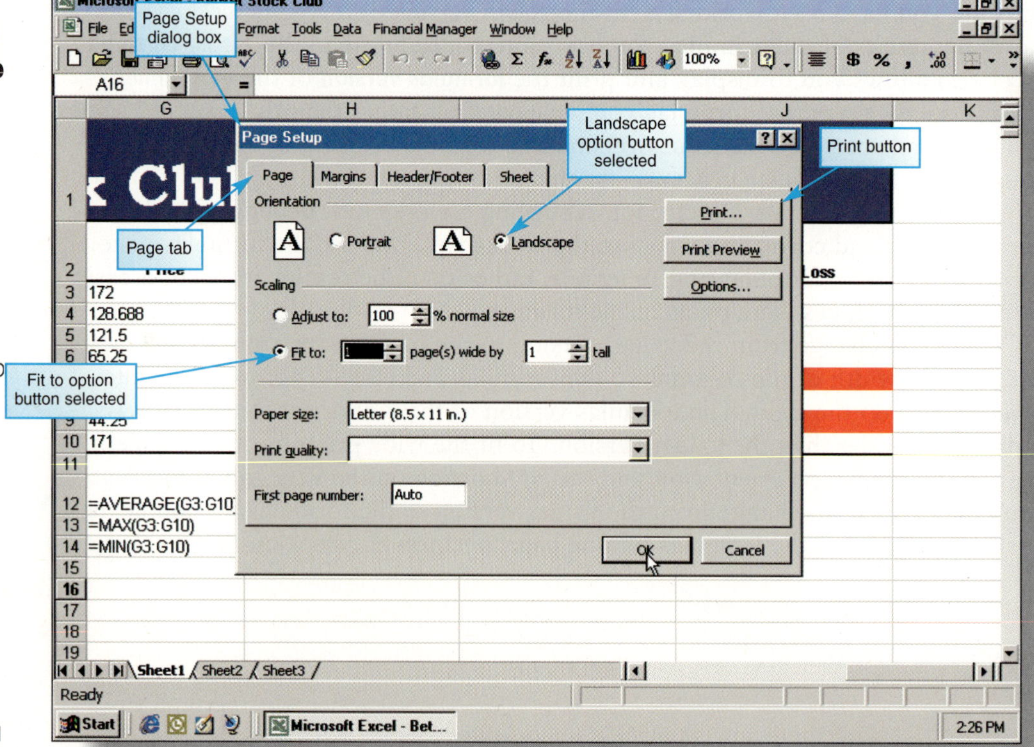

FIGURE 2-71

3 Click the Print button. When the Print dialog box displays, click the OK button. When you are done viewing and printing the formulas version, press CTRL+ LEFT SINGLE QUOTATION MARK (`) to display the values version.

Excel prints the formulas in the worksheet on one page in landscape orientation (Figure 2-72).

BetNet Stock Club

Stock	Symbol	Date Acquired	Shares	Initial Price	Initial Cost	Current Price	Current Value	Gain/Loss
Amazon.com	AMZN	35717	800	15.875	=D3*E3	172	=D3*G3	=H3-F3
America Online	AOL	36143	720	93.5	=D4*E4	128.688	=D4*G4	=H4-F4
Broadcast.com	BCST	36203	610	85.25	=D5*E5	121.5	=D5*G5	=H5-F5
EarthLink	ELNK	36220	500	63.125	=D6*E6	65.25	=D6*G6	=H6-F6
eBay	EBAY	36263	920	200.5	=D7*E7	162.5	=D7*G7	=H7-F7
Infoseek	SEEK	35838	750	12.875	=D8*E8	50.563	=D8*G8	=H8-F8
Ubid	UBID	36150	400	151.375	=D9*E9	44.25	=D9*G9	=H9-F9
Yahoo	YHOO	35927	700	21	=D10*E10	171	=D10*G10	=H10-F10
Total					=SUM(F3:F10)		=SUM(H3:H10)	=SUM(I3:I10)
Average			=AVERAGE(D3:D10)	=AVERAGE(E3:E10)	=AVERAGE(F3:F10)	=AVERAGE(G3:G10)	=AVERAGE(H3:H10)	=AVERAGE(I3:I10)
Highest			=MAX(D3:D10)	=MAX(E3:E10)	=MAX(F3:F10)	=MAX(G3:G10)	=MAX(H3:H10)	=MAX(I3:I10)
Lowest			=MIN(D3:D10)	=MIN(E3:E10)	=MIN(F3:F10)	=MIN(G3:G10)	=MIN(H3:H10)	=MIN(I3:I10)

FIGURE 2-72

1. On Tools menu click Options, click View tab, click Formulas, click OK button

Although the formulas version of the worksheet was printed in the previous example, you can see from Figure 2-72 that the display on the screen also can be used for debugging the worksheet.

Changing the Print Scaling Option Back to 100%

Depending on your printer driver, you may have to change the Print Scaling option back to 100% after using the Fit to option. Complete the following steps to reset the Print Scaling option so future worksheets print at 100%, instead of being squeezed on one page.

TO CHANGE THE PRINT SCALING OPTION BACK TO 100%

1. Click File on the menu bar and then click Page Setup.
2. Click the Page tab in the Page Setup dialog box. Click Adjust to in the Scaling area.
3. If necessary, type 100 in the Adjust to box.
4. Click the OK button.

The print scaling is set to normal.

The **Adjust to box** allows you to specify the percentage of reduction or enlargement in the printout of a worksheet. The default percentage is 100%. When you click the Fit to option, this percentage automatically changes to the percentage required to fit the printout on one page.

The Fit To Option

Do not take the Fit To option lightly. Most applications involve worksheets that extend well beyond the 8½-by-11-inch page. Most users, however, want the information on one page, at least with respect to the width of the worksheet. Thus, the Fit To option is a common choice among Excel users.

Getting External Data from a Web Source Using a Web Query

One of the major features of Excel 2000 is its capability of obtaining external data from sites on the World Wide Web. To get external data from a World Wide Web site, you must have access to the Internet. You then can run a **Web query** to retrieve data stored on a World Wide Web site. When you run a Web query, Excel returns the external data in the form of a worksheet. As described in Table 2-6, four Web queries are available when you first install Excel. Three of the four Web queries available relate to investment and stock market activities.

Table 2-6 Excel Web Queries

QUERY	EXTERNAL DATA RETURNED
Get More Web	Download additional Web queries
Microsoft Investor Currency Rates	Currency rates
Microsoft Investor Major Indices	Major Indices
Microsoft Investor Stock Quotes	Up to 20 stocks of your choice

The data returned by the stock-related Web queries is real-time in the sense that it is no more than 20 minutes old during the business day. The steps below show how to get the most recent stock quotes for the following six stocks being reviewed by the BetNet Stock Club members as they consider a flight to safety — Exxon Mobil (XOM), General Electric (GE), Merck (MRK), Pfizer (PFE), Proctor & Gamble (PG), and Walgreen (WAG). Although you can have a Web query return data to a blank workbook, the following steps have the data returned to a blank worksheet in the BetNet Stock Club workbook.

To Get External Data from a Web Source Using a Web Query

1. **With the BetNet Stock Club workbook open, click the Sheet2 tab at the bottom of the window. Click cell A1. Click Data on the menu bar, point to Get External Data and then point to Run Saved Query on the Get External Data submenu.**

The Get External Data submenu displays as shown in Figure 2-73.

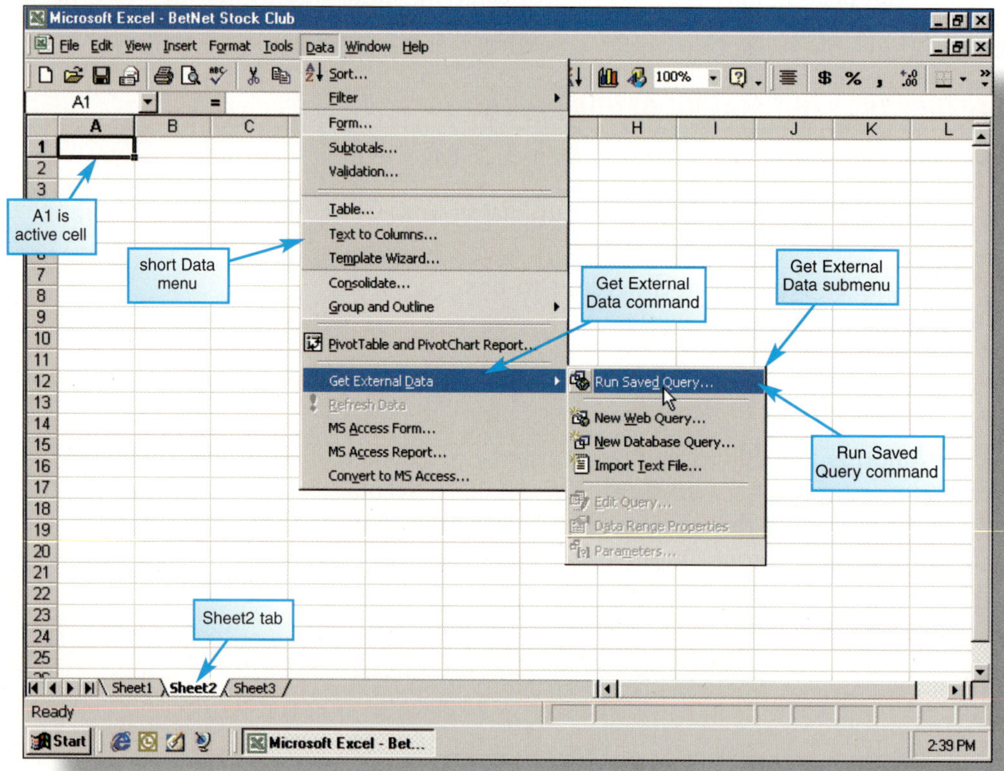

FIGURE 2-73

2 **Click Run Saved Query. When the Run Query dialog box displays, click Microsoft Investor Stock Quotes. Point to the Get Data button.**

The Run Query dialog box displays (Figure 2-74). If your display is different, ask your instructor for the folder location of the Web queries.

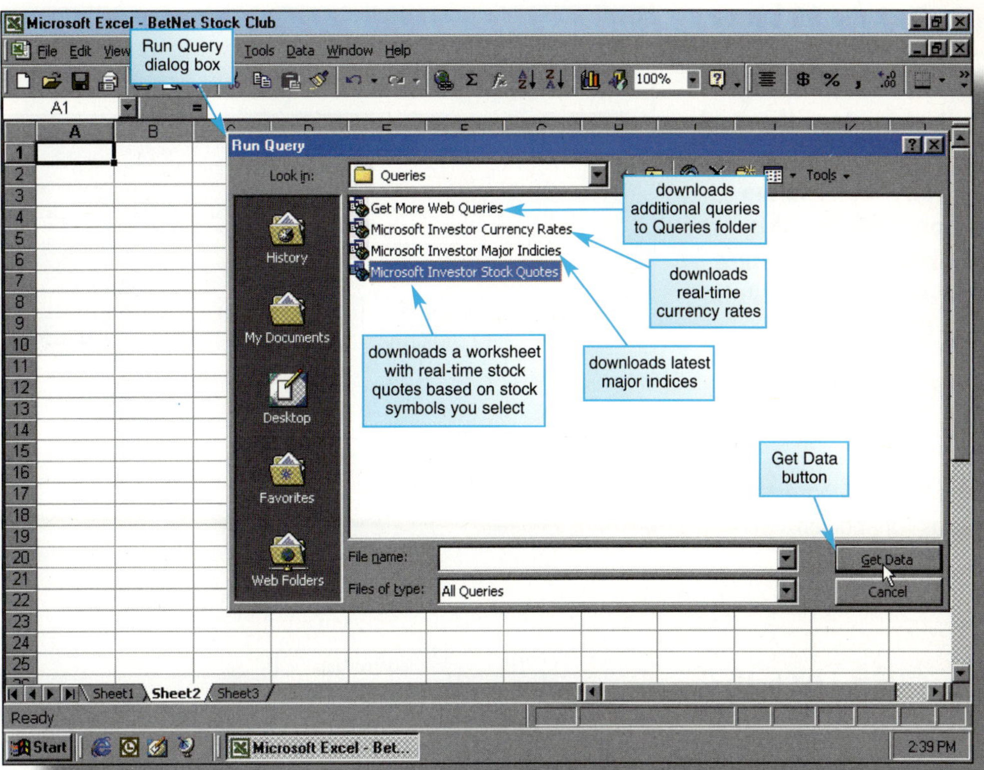

FIGURE 2-74

3 **Click the Get Data button. When the Returning External Data to Microsoft Excel dialog box displays, click Existing worksheet, if necessary, to select it. Point to the OK button.**

The Returning External Data to Microsoft Excel dialog box displays (Figure 2-75).

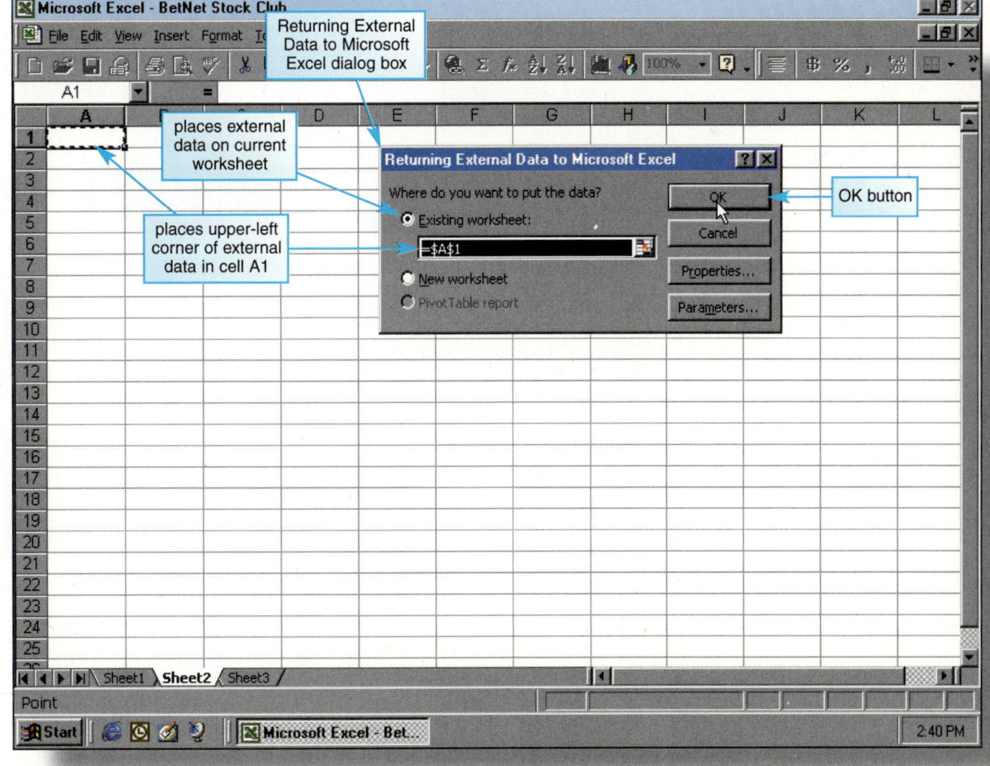

FIGURE 2-75

4 Click the OK button. When the Enter Parameter Value dialog box displays, type the stock symbols `xom, ge, mrk, pfe, pg, wag,` **in the text box. Click Use this value/reference for future refreshes to select it. Point to the OK button.**

The Enter Parameter Value dialog box displays (Figure 2-76). You can enter up to 20 stock symbols separated by commas (or spaces).

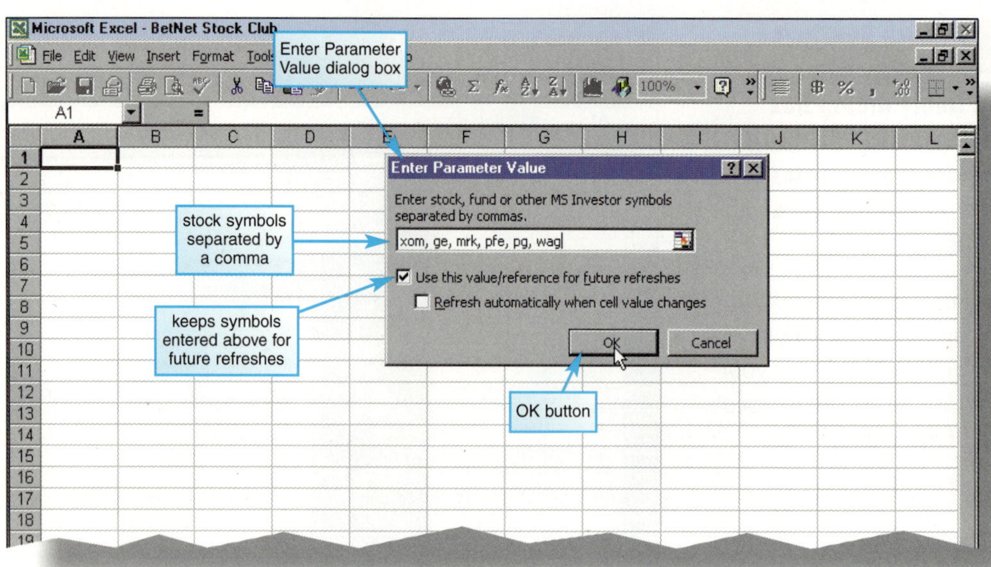

FIGURE 2-76

5 Click the OK button.

Once your computer connects to the Internet, a message displays to inform you that Excel is getting external data. After a short period, Excel displays a new worksheet with the desired data (Figure 2-77).

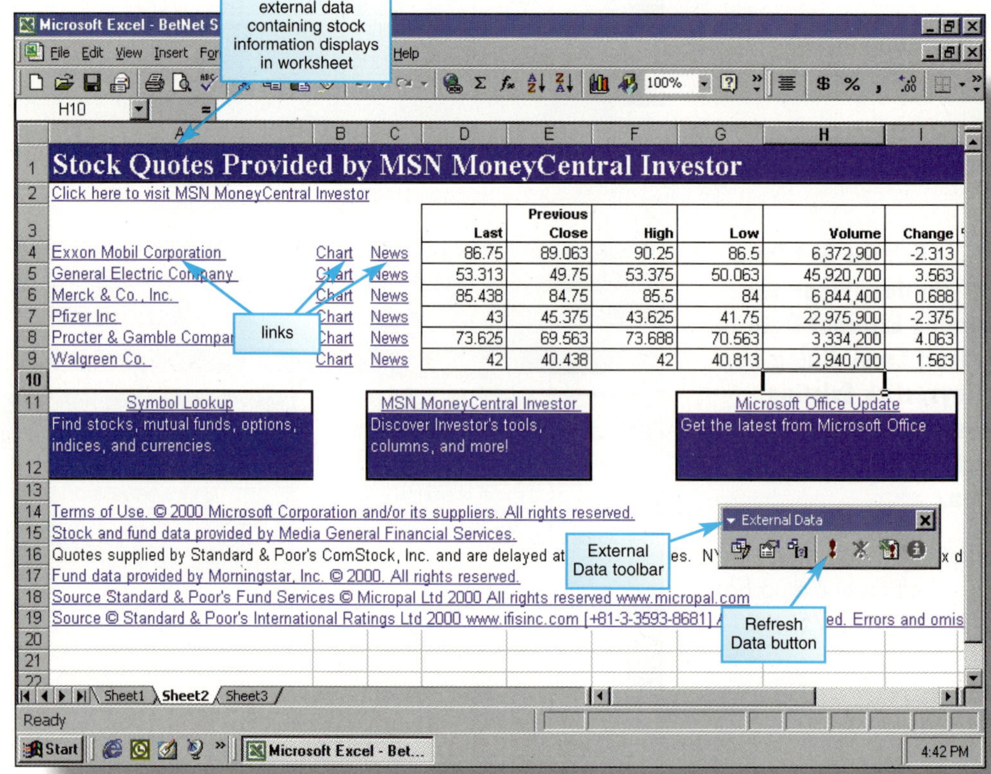

FIGURE 2-77

As shown in Figure 2-77, Excel displays the data returned from the Web query in an organized, formatted worksheet, which has a worksheet title, column titles, and a row of data for each stock symbol entered. Other than the first column, which contains the stock name and stock symbol, you have no control over the remaining columns of data returned. The latest price of each stock displays in column D.

Once the worksheet displays, you can refresh the data as often as you want. To refresh the data for all the stocks, click the **Refresh All button** on the **External Data toolbar** (Figure 2-78). Because the Use this value/reference for future refreshes check box was selected (Figure 2-76), Excel will continue to use the same stock symbols each time it refreshes. You can change the symbols by clicking the **Query Parameters button** on the External Data toolbar.

If the External Data toolbar does not display, right-click any toolbar and then click External Data. You also can invoke any Web query command by right-clicking the returned worksheet to display a shortcut menu.

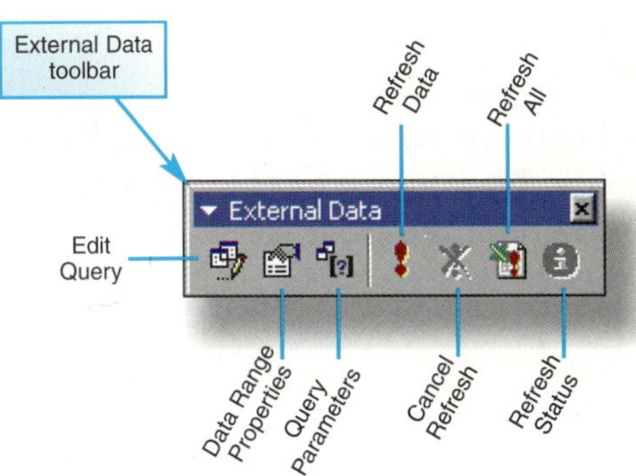

FIGURE 2-78

This section gives you an idea of the potential of Web queries by having you use just one of Excel's many available Web queries. To reinforce the topics covered here, work through In the Lab 3 at the end of this project.

The workbook is nearly complete. The final step is to change the names of the sheets located on the sheet tabs at the bottom of the Excel window.

Changing the Sheet Names

At the bottom of the window (Figure 2-79) are the tabs that allow you to display any sheet in the workbook. You click the tab of the sheet you want to display. The names of the sheets are preset to Sheet1, Sheet2, and so on. These names become increasingly important as you move towards more sophisticated workbooks, especially those in which you reference cells between sheets. The following steps show how to rename sheets by double-clicking the sheet tabs.

More About 2000

Web Queries

Most Excel specialists who perform Web queries use the worksheet returned from the Web query as an engine that supplies data to another worksheet in the workbook. With 3-D cell references, you can create a worksheet similar to the BetNet Stock Club, which feeds the Web query stock symbols and gets refreshed stock prices in return.

To Rename the Sheets

1 **Double-click the tab labeled Sheet2 in the lower-left corner of the window. Type** `Real-Time Stock Quotes` **as the sheet name and then click a cell on the worksheet.**

The new sheet name displays on the tab (Figure 2-79).

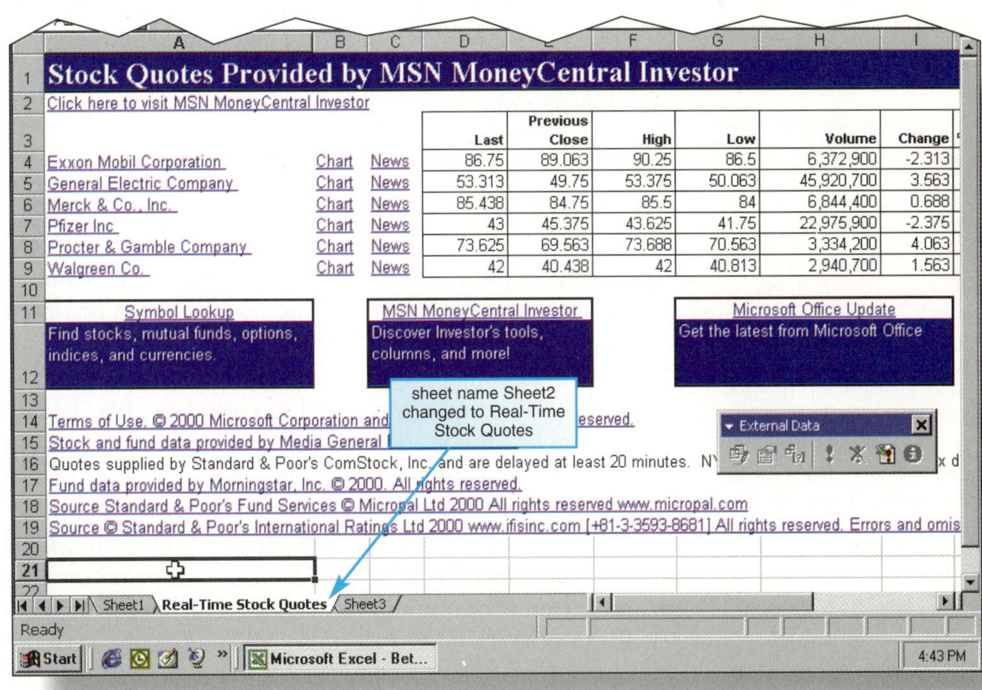

FIGURE 2-79

2 **Double-click the tab labeled Sheet1 in the lower-left corner of the window. Type** `Investment Analysis` **as the sheet name and then press the ENTER key.**

The sheet name changes from Sheet1 to Investment Analysis (Figure 2-80).

3 **Click the Save button on the Standard toolbar.**

	A	B	C	D	E	F	G	H	I	J
1	BetNet Stock Club									
2	Stock	Symbol	Date Acquired	Shares	Initial Price	Initial Cost	Current Price	Current Value	Gain/Loss	% Gain/Loss
3	Amazon.com	AMZN	10/14/97	800	$15.875	$ 12,700.00	$172.000	$ 137,600.00	$ 124,900.00	983.46%
4	America Online	AOL	12/14/98	720	93.500	67,320.00	128.688	92,655.36	25,335.36	37.63%
5	Broadcast.com	BCST	2/12/99	610	85.250	52,002.50	121.500	74,115.00	22,112.50	42.52%
6	EarthLink	ELNK	3/1/99	500	63.125	31,562.50	65.250	32,625.00	1,062.50	3.37%
7	eBay	EBAY	4/13/99	920	200.500	184,460.00	162.500	149,500.00	(34,960.00)	-18.95%
8	Infoseek	SEEK	2/12/98	750	12.875	9,656.25	50.563	37,922.25	28,266.00	292.72%
9	Ubid	UBID	12/21/98	400	151.375	60,550.00	44.250	17,700.00	(42,850.00)	-70.77%
10	Yahoo	YHOO	5/12/98	700	21.000	14,700.00	171.000	119,700.00	105,000.00	714.29%
11	Total					$ 432,951.25		$ 661,817.61	$ 228,866.36	52.86%
12	Average			675	$80.44	$54,118.91	$114.47	$82,727.20	$28,608.30	
13	Highest			920	$200.50	$184,460.00	$172.00	$149,500.00	$124,900.00	983.46%
14	Lowest				$12.88	$9,656.25	[illegible]	[illegible]	($42,850.00)	-70.77%

FIGURE 2-80

Other Ways

1. To rename, right-click sheet tab, click Rename on shortcut menu
2. To move, right-click sheet tab, click Move or Copy on shortcut menu
3. To move, on Edit menu click Move or Copy

Sheet names can contain up to 31 characters (including spaces) in length. Longer sheet names, however, mean that fewer tabs will display. To display more sheet tabs, you can drag the **tab split box** (Figure 2-80) to the right. This will reduce the size of the scroll bar at the bottom of the screen. Double-click the tab split box to reset it to its normal position.

You also can use the **tab scrolling buttons** to the left of the sheet tabs (Figure 2-80) to move between sheets. The leftmost and rightmost scroll buttons move to the first or last sheet in the workbook. The two middle scroll buttons move one sheet to the left or right.

Sheets Tabs

To move from sheet to sheet in a workbook, you click the sheet tabs at the bottom of the window. The name of the active sheet always is bold on a white background. Through the shortcut menu, you can rename the sheets, reorder the sheets, add and delete sheets, and move or copy sheets within a workbook or to another workbook.

E-mailing a Workbook from within Excel

The most popular service on the Internet is electronic mail, or e-mail. Using **e-mail**, you can converse with friends across the room or on another continent. One of the features of e-mail is the ability to attach Office files, such as Word documents or Excel workbooks to an e-mail and send it to a co-worker. In the past, if you wanted to send a workbook you saved it, closed the file, launched your e-mail program, and then attached the workbook to the e-mail before sending it. A new feature of Office 2000 is the capability of e-mailing the worksheet or workbook directly from within Excel. For these steps to work properly, you must have an e-mail address and one of the following as your e-mail program: Outlook, Outlook Express, Microsoft Exchange Client, or another 32-bit e-mail program compatible with Messaging Application Programming Interface. The following steps show how to e-mail the workbook from within Excel to Michael Santos. Assume his e-mail address is michael_santos@hotmail.com.

To E-mail a Workbook from within Excel

1 **With the BetNet Stock Club workbook open, click File on the menu bar, point to Send To, and then point to Mail Recipient (as Attachment).**

The File menu and Send To submenu display as shown in Figure 2-81.

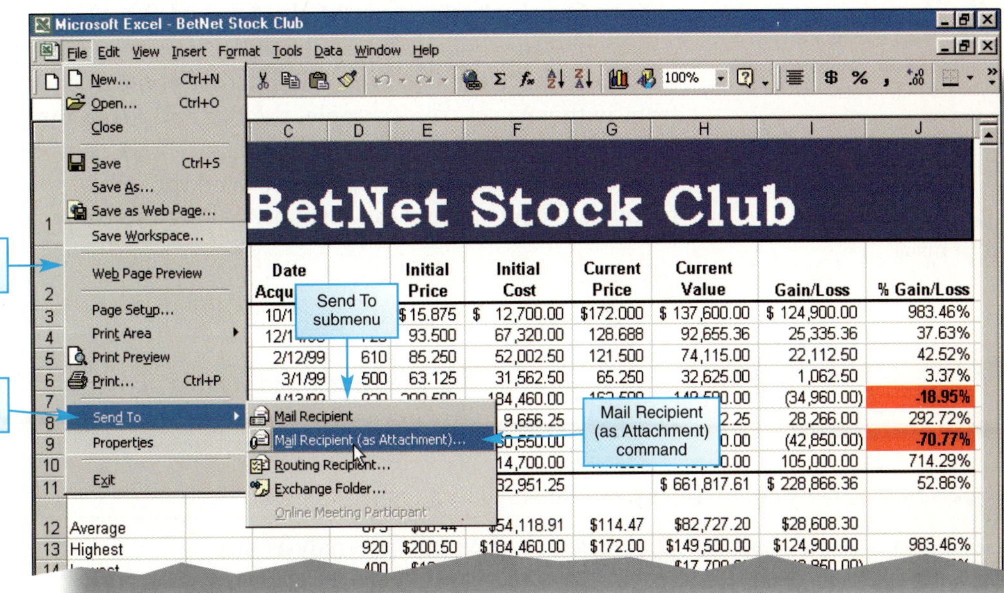

FIGURE 2-81

2 **Click Mail Recipient (as Attachment). When the e-mail Message window displays, type** michael_santos@hotmail.com **in the To text box. Type** BetNet Stock Club workbook **in the Subject text box. Point to the Send button.**

Excel displays the e-mail Message window (Figure 2-82).

3 **Click the Send button.**

The e-mail with the attached workbook is sent to michael_santos@hotmail.com.

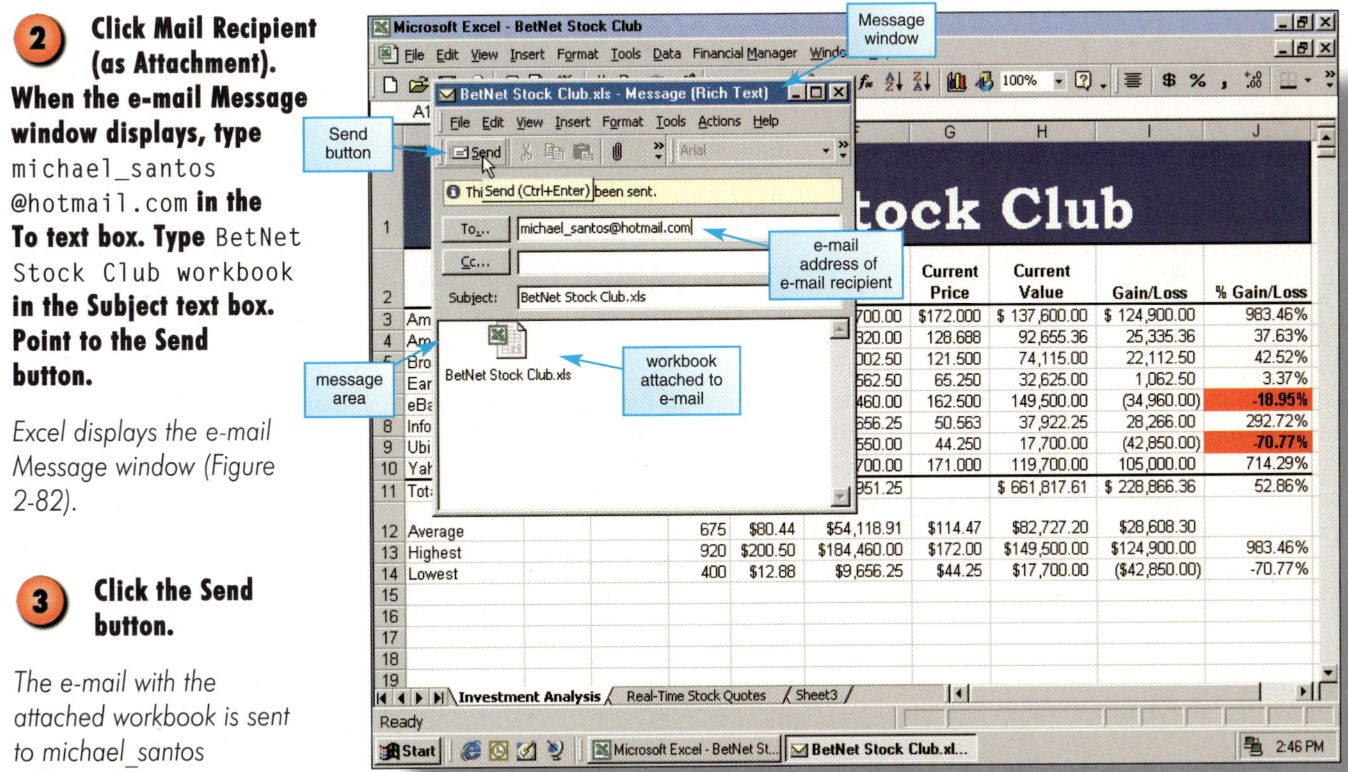

FIGURE 2-82

Other Ways

1. Click E-mail button on Standard toolbar

E-mail

Several Web sites are available that allow you to sign up for free e-mail. For more information on signing up for free e-mail, visit the Excel 2000 More About Web page (www.scsite.com/ex2000/more.htm) and click Signing Up for E-mail.

Quick Reference

For a table that lists how to complete the tasks covered in this book using the mouse, menu, shortcut menu, and keyboard, visit the Office 2000 Web page (www.scsite.com/off2000/qr.htm), and then click Microsoft Excel 2000.

Because the workbook was sent as an attachment, Michael Santos can save the attachment and then open the workbook in Excel. The alternative in the E-mail dialog box in Figure 2-81 on the previous page is to send a copy of the worksheet in HTML format. In this case, Michael would be able to read the worksheet in the e-mail message, but would not be able to open it in Excel.

Many more options are available that you can choose when you send an e-mail from within Excel. For example, the Bcc and From buttons on the toolbar in the Message window give you the same capabilities as an e-mail program. The Options button on the toolbar allows you to send the e-mail to a group of people in a particular sequence and get responses along the route.

Quitting Excel

After completing the workbook and related activities, you can quit Excel by performing the following steps.

TO QUIT EXCEL

1. Click the Investment Analysis tab.
2. Click the Close button on the upper-right corner of the title bar.
3. When the Microsoft Excel dialog box displays, click the Yes button.

CASE PERSPECTIVE SUMMARY

The worksheet and Web query (Figure 2-1 on page E 2.5) you created for Michael Santos will serve his purpose well. The worksheet, which he plans to e-mail to the club members, contains valuable information in an easy-to-read format. Finally, the Web query allows Michael to obtain the latest stock prices to keep the workbook as up to date as possible.

Project Summary

In creating the BetNet Stock Club workbook, you learned how to enter formulas, calculate an average, find the highest and lowest numbers in a range, audit formulas, change fonts, draw borders, format numbers, change column widths and row heights, and add conditional formatting to a range of numbers. You learned how to spell check a worksheet, preview a worksheet, print a worksheet, print a section of a worksheet and display and print the formulas in the worksheet using the Fit to option. You also learned how to complete a Web query to generate a worksheet using external data obtained from the World Wide Web and rename sheet tabs. Finally, you learned how to send an e-mail directly from within Excel with the opened workbook attached.

What You Should Know

Having completed this project, you now should be able to perform the following tasks:

- Apply a Currency Style Format and Comma Style Format Using the Formatting Toolbar *(E 2.35)*
- Apply a Currency Style Format with a Floating Dollar Sign Using the Format Cells Command *(E 2.37*
- Apply a Percent Style Format *(E 2.39)*
- Apply Conditional Formatting *(E 2.40)*
- Bold, Center, and Underline the Column Titles *(E 2.33)*
- Center Data in Cells *(E 2.33)*
- Change the Title Background and Font Colors and Apply an Outline Border *(E 2.30)*
- Change the Font and Center the Worksheet Title *(E 2.28)*
- Change the Height of a Row by Dragging *(E 2.47)*
- Change the Print Scaling Option Back to 100% *(E 2.57)*
- Change the Widths of Columns *(E 2.44)*
- Check Spelling on the Worksheet *(E 2.49)*
- Copy a Range of Cells Across Columns to an Adjacent Range Using the Fill Handle *(E 2.22)*
- Copy Formulas Using the Fill Handle *(E 2.13)*
- Determine the Average of a Range of Numbers Using the Keyboard and Mouse *(E 2.17)*
- Determine the Highest Number in a Range of Numbers Using the Edit Formula Box and Function Box *(E 2.18)*
- Determine the Lowest Number in a Range of Numbers Using the Paste Function Button *(E 2.20)*
- Determine the Total Percentage Gain/Loss *(E 2.15)*
- Determine Totals Using the AutoSum Button *(E 2.14)*
- Display the Formulas in the Worksheet and Fit the Printout on One Page *(E 2.56)*
- Enter a Formula Using the Keyboard *(E 2.9)*
- Enter Formulas Using Point Mode *(E 2.11)*
- Enter the Column Titles *(E 2.7)*
- Enter the Stock Data *(E 2.8)*
- Enter the Total Row Titles *(E 2.8)*
- Enter the Worksheet Title *(E 2.7)*
- E-mail a Workbook from within Excel *(E 2.63)*
- Get External Data from a Web Source Using a Web Query *(E 2.58)*
- Preview and Print a Worksheet *(E 2.51)*
- Print a Section of the Worksheet *(E 2.54)*
- Quit Excel *(E 2.64)*
- Rename the Sheets *(E 2.61)*
- Start Excel and Reset the Toolbars *(E 2.6)*
- Verify a Formula Using the Auditing Commands *(E 2.25)*
- Verify a Formula Using Range Finder *(E 2.24)*

Microsoft Certification

The Microsoft Office User Specialist (MOUS) Certification program provides an opportunity for you to obtain a valuable industry credential —- proof that you have the Excel 2000 skills required by employers. For more information, see Appendix D or visit the Shelly Cashman Series MOUS Web page at www.scsite.com/off2000/cert.htm.

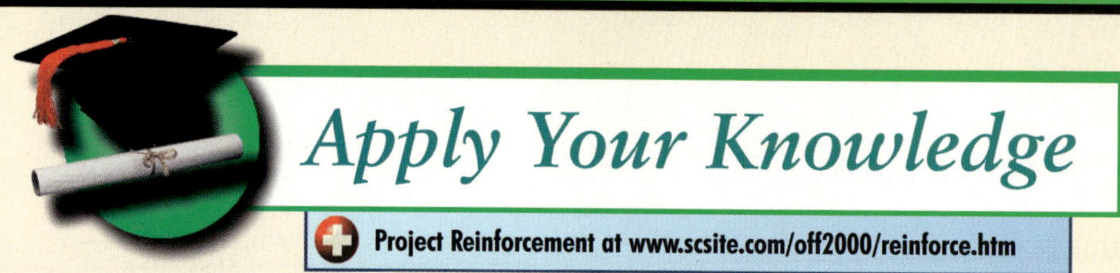

1 Sizes Galore and Much More Profit Analysis Worksheet

Instructions: Start Excel. Open the workbook Sizes Galore and Much More from the Data Disk. See the inside back cover of this book for instructions for downloading the Data Disk or see your instructor. The purpose of this exercise is to have you open a partially completed workbook, enter formulas and functions, copy the formulas and functions, and then format the numbers. As shown in Figure 2-83, the completed worksheet analyzes profits by product.

Sizes Galore and Much More
Profit Analysis

Product	Description	Cost	Profit	Units Sold	Total Sales	Profit	% Profit
T211	Sweater	$ 92.95	$ 9.25	52,435	$ 5,358,857.00	$ 485,023.75	9.051%
C215	Dress	175.99	15.65	16,534	3,168,575.76	258,757.10	8.166%
D212	Jacket	110.60	11.58	32,102	3,922,222.36	371,741.16	9.478%
K214	Coat	160.50	26.82	43,910	8,225,221.20	1,177,666.20	14.318%
Q213	Suit	121.35	13.21	34,391	4,627,652.96	454,305.11	9.817%
X216	Custom	200.23	38.35	23,910	5,704,447.80	916,948.50	16.074%
D342	Sleepwear	50.65	8.45	45,219	2,672,442.90	382,100.55	14.298%
H567	Hat	34.20	5.83	63,213	2,530,416.39	368,531.79	14.564%
C289	Shirt	43.00	6.75	52,109	2,592,422.75	351,735.75	13.568%
K451	Slacks	38.25	7.25	76,145	3,464,597.50	552,051.25	15.934%
Totals				439,968	$ 42,266,856.62	$ 5,318,861.16	
Lowest		$34.20	$5.83	16,534	$2,530,416.39	$258,757.10	8.166%
Highest		$200.23	$38.35	76,145	$8,225,221.20	$1,177,666.20	16.074%
Average		$102.77	$14.31	43,997	$4,226,685.66	$531,886.12	

FIGURE 2-83

Perform the following tasks.

1. Complete the following entries in row 3:
   a. Total Sales (cell F3) = Units Sold * (Cost + Profit) or =E3 * (C3+D3)
   b. Profit (cell G3) = Units Sold * Profit or = E3 * D3
      % Profit (cell H3) = Profit / Total Sales or = G3 / F3
2. Use the fill handle to copy the three formulas in the range F3:H3 to the range F4:H12.
3. Determine the Total Sales, and Profit column totals in row 13.
4. In the range C14:C16, determine the lowest value, highest value, and average value, respectively for the range C3:C12. Use the fill handle to copy the three functions to the range D14:H16. Delete the average from cell H16, because you can not average percents.
5. Use the Currency Style button on the Formatting toolbar to format the numbers in the ranges C3:D3, F3:G3, and F13:G13. Use the Comma Style button on the Formatting toolbar to format the numbers in cell E3 and the range C4:G12. Use the Decrease Decimal button on the Formatting toolbar to display the numbers in the range E3:E16 as whole numbers. Use the Percent Style and the Increase Decimal buttons on the Formatting toolbar to format the range H3:H15. Increase the decimal positions in this range to 3. Use the Format Cells command on the shortcut menu to format the numbers in the ranges C14:D16 and F14:G16 to a floating dollar sign.

Apply Your Knowledge

Project Reinforcement at www.scsite.com/off2000/reinforce.htm

6. Use Range Finder and then the Auditing commands to verify the formula in cell G3. Check both precedents and dependents (Figure 2-83) using the Auditing commands. Use the Remove Arrows command on the Auditing submenu to remove the arrows.
7. Enter your name, course, laboratory assignment number (Apply 2-1), date, and instructor name in the range A20:A24.
8. Preview and print the worksheet in landscape orientation. Save the workbook. Use the file name, Sizes Galore and Much More 2.
9. Print the range A1:H13. Print the formulas version (press CTRL+LEFT QUOTATION MARK) of the worksheet in landscape orientation (Figure 2-84) using the Fit to option on the Page tab in the Page Setup dialog box.
10. In column D, use the keyboard to add manually $1.00 to the profit of each product whose profit is less than $10.00, or else add $2.00. You should end up with $5,909,676.16 in cell G13. Print the worksheet. Do not save the workbook. Hand in the printouts to your instructor.

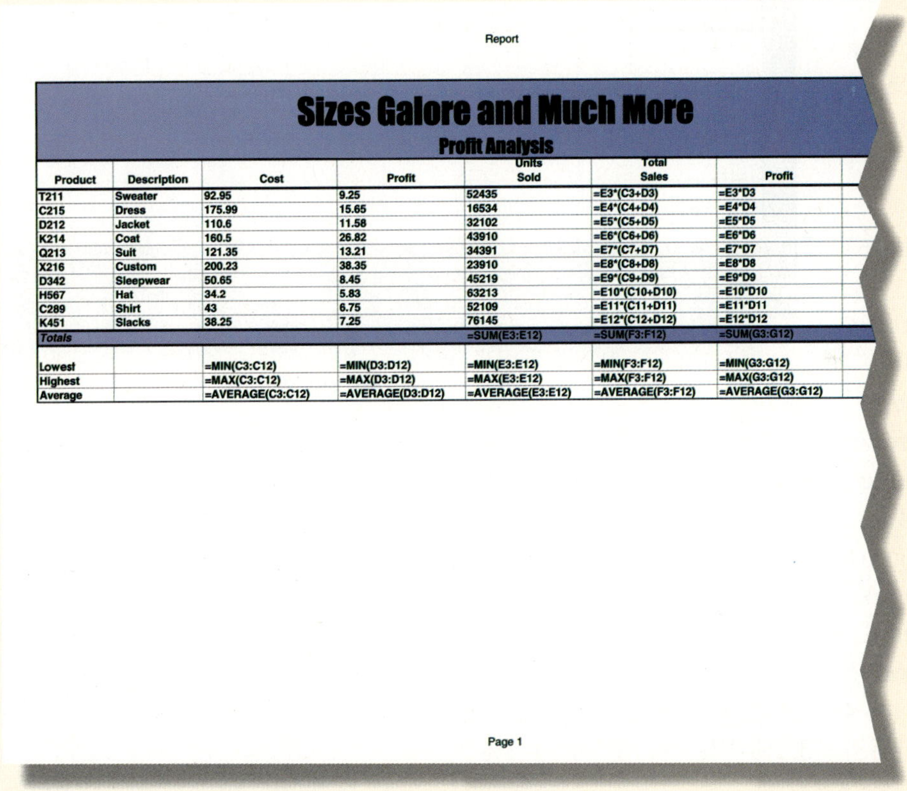

Report

Sizes Galore and Much More

Profit Analysis

Product	Description	Cost	Profit	Units Sold	Total Sales	Profit
T211	Sweater	92.95	9.25	52435	=E3*(C3+D3)	=E3*D3
C215	Dress	175.99	15.65	16534	=E4*(C4+D4)	=E4*D4
D212	Jacket	110.6	11.58	32102	=E5*(C5+D5)	=E5*D5
K214	Coat	160.5	26.82	43910	=E6*(C6+D6)	=E6*D6
Q213	Suit	121.35	13.21	34391	=E7*(C7+D7)	=E7*D7
X216	Custom	200.23	38.35	23910	=E8*(C8+D8)	=E8*D8
D342	Sleepwear	50.65	8.45	45219	=E9*(C9+D9)	=E9*D9
H567	Hat	34.2	5.83	63213	=E10*(C10+D10)	=E10*D10
C289	Shirt	43	6.75	52109	=E11*(C11+D11)	=E11*D11
K451	Slacks	38.25	7.25	76145	=E12*(C12+D12)	=E12*D12
Totals				=SUM(E3:E12)	=SUM(F3:F12)	=SUM(G3:G12)
Lowest		=MIN(C3:C12)	=MIN(D3:D12)	=MIN(E3:E12)	=MIN(F3:F12)	=MIN(G3:G12)
Highest		=MAX(C3:C12)	=MAX(D3:D12)	=MAX(E3:E12)	=MAX(F3:F12)	=MAX(G3:G12)
Average		=AVERAGE(C3:C12)	=AVERAGE(D3:D12)	=AVERAGE(E3:E12)	=AVERAGE(F3:F12)	=AVERAGE(G3:G12)

Page 1

FIGURE 2-84

1 Stars and Stripes Automotive Weekly Payroll Worksheet

Problem: The Stars and Stripes Automotive Company has hired you as a summer intern in its software applications area. Because you took an Excel course last semester, the assistant manager has asked you to prepare a weekly payroll report for the six employees listed in Table 2-7.

Instructions: Perform the following tasks to create a worksheet similar to the one shown in Figure 2-85.

Microsoft Excel - Stars and Stripes Automotive

	A	B	C	D	E	F	G	H
1	Stars and Stripes Automotive Weekly Payroll							
2	Employee	Rate	Hours	Dep.	Gross Pay	Fed. Tax	State Tax	Net Pay
3	Breeze, Linus	27.50	40.25	4.00	1,106.88	190.61	35.42	880.85
4	Santiago, Juan	18.75	56.00	1.00	1,050.00	202.31	33.60	814.09
5	Webb, Trevor	28.35	38.00	3.00	1,077.30	192.38	34.47	850.44
6	Sabol, Kylie	21.50	46.50	6.00	999.75	153.80	31.99	813.96
7	Ali, Abdul	19.35	17.00	2.00	328.95	50.41	10.53	268.02
8	Goldstein, Kevin	17.05	28.00	5.00	477.40	57.02	15.28	405.10
9	Totals		225.75		5,040.28	846.52	161.29	4,032.46
10	Average	22.08	37.63	3.50	840.05	141.09	26.88	672.08
11	Highest	28.35	56.00	6.00	1,106.88	202.31	35.42	880.85
12	Lowest	17.05	17.00	1.00	328.95	50.41	10.53	268.02

FIGURE 2-85

1. Enter the worksheet title `Stars and Stripes Automotive Weekly Payroll` in cell A1. Enter the column titles in row 2, the row titles in column A, and the data from Table 2-7 in columns B through D as shown in Figure 2-85.
2. Use the following formulas to determine the gross pay, federal tax, state tax, and net pay for the first employee
   a. Gross Pay (cell E3) = Rate*Hours or =B3*C3.
   b. Federal Tax (cell F3) = 20% * (Gross Pay – Dependents * 38.46) or =20% *(E3 – D3 * 38.46)
   c. State Tax (cell G3) = 3.2% * Gross Pay or =3.2% * E3
   d. Net Pay (cell H3) = Gross Pay – (Federal Tax + State Tax) or =E3 – (F3 + G3)

   Copy the formulas for the first employee to the remaining employees.
3. Calculate totals for hours, gross pay, federal tax, state tax, and net pay in row 9.
4. Use the appropriate functions to determine the average, highest, and lowest values of each column in rows 10 through 12.
5. Use Range Finder and then the Auditing commands to verify the formula entered in cell F3. Check both precedents and dependents with the Auditing commands. Remove all arrows.

Table 2-7 Payroll Data

EMPLOYEE	RATE	HOURS	DEPENDENTS
Breeze, Linus	27.50	40.25	4
Santiago, Juan	18.75	56.00	1
Webb, Trevor	28.35	38.00	3
Sabol, Kylie	21.50	46.50	6
Ali, Abdul	19.35	17.00	2
Goldstein, Kevin	17.05	28.00	5

6. Bold the worksheet title. Use buttons on the Formatting toolbar to assign the Comma style with two decimal places to the range B3:H12. Bold, italicize, and assign a thick bottom border (column 4, row 3 on the Borders palette) to the range A2:H2. Right-align the column titles in the range B2:H2. Italicize the range A9:A12. Assign a top border and double-line bottom border to the range A9:H9.
7. Change the width of column A to 15.00 characters. If necessary, change the widths of columns B through H to best fit. Change the height of rows 2 and 10 to 24.00 points.
8. Use the Conditional Formatting command on the Format menu to display bold font on a green background for any gross pay greater than $1,050.00 in the range E3:E8.
9. Enter your name, course, laboratory assignment number (Lab 2-1), date, and instructor name in the range A14:A18.
10. Save the workbook using the file name Stars and Stripes Automotive.
11. Preview and then print the worksheet.
12. Press CTRL+LEFT SINGLE QUOTATION MARK (`) to change the display from the values version to the formulas version. Print the formulas version of the worksheet in landscape orientation using the Fit to option on the Page tab in the Page Setup dialog box. After the printer is finished, press CTRL+LEFT SINGLE QUOTATION MARK (`) to reset the worksheet to display the values version. Reset the Scaling option to 100% by clicking the Adjust to option button in the Page sheet in the Page Setup dialog box and then setting the percent value to 100%.
13. Use the keyboard to increase manually the number of hours worked for each employee by 8 hours. The total net pay in cell H9 should equal $4,846.54. If necessary, increase the width of column F to best fit to view the new federal tax total. Preview and print the worksheet with the new values. Close the workbook without saving the changes. Hand in the printouts to your instructor.

2 Mortimer's Seaside Emporium Monthly Accounts Receivable Balance Sheet

Problem: You were recently hired as a part-time assistant in the Accounting department of Mortimer's Seaside Emporium, a popular Biloxi-based general merchandise company with several outlets along the Gulf coast. You have been asked to use Excel to generate a report (Figure 2-86 on the next page) that summarizes the monthly accounts receivable balance. A graphic breakdown of the data also is desired. The customer accounts receivable data in Table 2-8 is available for test purposes.

Table 2-8 Accounts Receivable Data

CUSTOMER NUMBER	CUSTOMER NAME	BEGINNING BALANCE	PURCHASES	PAYMENTS	CREDITS
27839	Patel, Nipul	$2,356.15	$739.19	$175.00	$435.10
31982	Jaworski, Stanley	6,291.74	1,098.35	250.00	0.00
45012	Portugal, Juanita	4,103.75	620.75	4,000.00	25.00
56341	Country, James	5,691.45	4,352.12	250.00	35.25
76894	Santiago, Carlos	1,045.23	542.10	750.00	189.95

(continued)

Mortimer's Seaside Emporium Monthly Accounts Receivable Balance Sheet *(continued)*

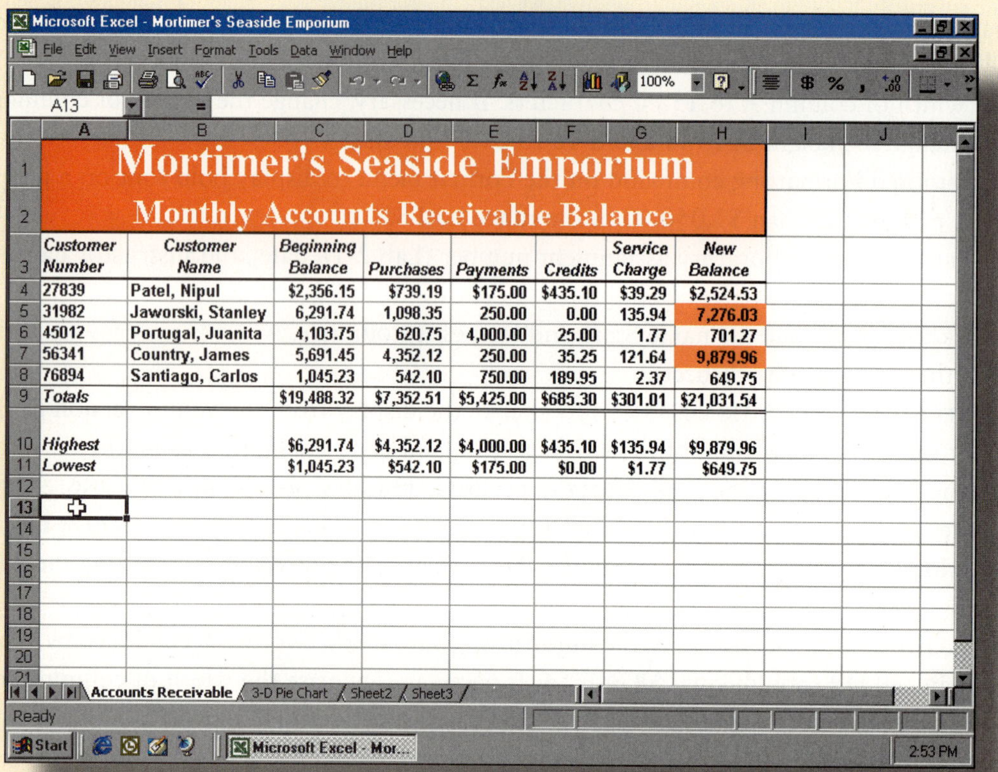

	A	B	C	D	E	F	G	H
1	Mortimer's Seaside Emporium							
2	Monthly Accounts Receivable Balance							
3	Customer Number	Customer Name	Beginning Balance	Purchases	Payments	Credits	Service Charge	New Balance
4	27839	Patel, Nipul	$2,356.15	$739.19	$175.00	$435.10	$39.29	$2,524.53
5	31982	Jaworski, Stanley	6,291.74	1,098.35	250.00	0.00	135.94	7,276.03
6	45012	Portugal, Juanita	4,103.75	620.75	4,000.00	25.00	1.77	701.27
7	56341	Country, James	5,691.45	4,352.12	250.00	35.25	121.64	9,879.96
8	76894	Santiago, Carlos	1,045.23	542.10	750.00	189.95	2.37	649.75
9	Totals		$19,488.32	$7,352.51	$5,425.00	$685.30	$301.01	$21,031.54
10	Highest		$6,291.74	$4,352.12	$4,000.00	$435.10	$135.94	$9,879.96
11	Lowest		$1,045.23	$542.10	$175.00	$0.00	$1.77	$649.75

FIGURE 2-86

Instructions Part 1: Create a worksheet similar to the one shown in Figure 2-86. Include all six items in Table 2-8 on the previous page in the report, plus a service charge and a new balance for each customer. Assume no negative unpaid monthly balances. Perform the following tasks.

1. Click the Select All button (to the left of column heading A) and then click the Bold button on the Standard toolbar to bold the entire worksheet.
2. Assign the worksheet title, `Mortimer's Seaside Emporium`, to cell A1. Assign the worksheet subtitle, `Monthly Accounts Receivable Balance`, to cell A2.
3. Enter the column titles in the range A3:H3 as shown in Figure 2-86. Change the width of column A to 9.57. Change the widths of columns B through H to best fit.
4. Enter the customer numbers and row titles in column A. Enter the customer numbers as text, rather than numbers. To enter the customer numbers as text, begin each entry with an apostrophe ('). Enter the remaining data in Table 2-8.
5. Use the following formulas to determine the monthly service charge in column G and the new balance in column H for customer 27839. Copy the two formulas down through the remaining customers.
   a. Service Charge = 2.25% * (Beginning Balance – Payments – Credits)
   b. New Balance = Beginning Balance + Purchases – Payments – Credits + Service Charge

6. Calculate totals for beginning balance, purchases, payments, credits, service charge, and new balance in row 9.
7. Assign cell C10 the appropriate function to calculate the maximum value in the range C4:C8. Copy cell C10 to the range D10:H10.
8. Assign cell C11 the appropriate function to calculate the minimum value in the range C4:C8. Copy cell C11 to the range D11:H11.
9. Change the worksheet title in cell A1 to 28-point CG Times font. Format the worksheet subtitle in cell A2 to 20-point CG Times font. Center the worksheet titles in cells A1 and A2 across column A through H. Change the heights of rows 1 through 3 and row 10 to 27.75. Add a heavy outline to the range A1:H2 using the Borders button on the Formatting toolbar.
10. Select the range A1:H2 and then change the background color to Orange (column 2, row 2) on the Fill Color palette. Change the font color in the range A1:H2 to White (column 8, row 5) on the Font Color palette.
11. Italicize the column titles in row 3. Use the Borders button to add a thick bottom border to the column titles in row 3. Center the column titles in the range B3:H3. Italicize the titles in rows 9, 10, and 11. Use the Borders button to add a single top border and double-line bottom border to the range A9:H9 (column 4, row 2) on the Borders palette.
12. Use the Format Cells command on the shortcut menu to assign the Currency style with a floating dollar sign to the cells containing numeric data in row 4 and rows 9 through 11. Use the same command to assign the Comma style (currency with no dollar sign) to the range C5:H8. The Format Cells command is preferred over the Comma Style button because the worksheet specifications call for displaying zero as 0.00 rather than as a dash (-), as shown in Figure 2-86.
13. Use the Conditional Formatting command on the Format menu to bold the font and color the background orange of any cell in the range H4:H8 that contains a value greater than or equal to 3000.
14. Change the widths of columns B through H again to best fit, if necessary.
15. Rename the sheet Accounts Receivable.
16. Enter your name, course, laboratory assignment number (Lab 2-2), date, and instructor name in the range A13:A17.
17. Save the workbook using the file name Mortimer's Seaside Emporium. Preview and then print the worksheet. Print the range A3:C9.
18. Press CTRL+LEFT SINGLE QUOTATION MARK (`) to change the display from the values version to the formulas version and then print the worksheet to fit on one page in landscape orientation. After the printer is finished, press CTRL+LEFT SINGLE QUOTATION MARK (`) to reset the worksheet to display the values version. Reset the Scaling option to 100% by clicking the Adjust to option button on the Page tab in the Page Setup dialog box and then setting the percent value to 100%. Hand in the printouts to your instructor.

(continued)

Mortimer's Seaside Emporium Monthly Accounts Receivable Balance Sheet *(continued)*

Instructions Part 2: This part requires that you use the Chart Wizard button on the Standard toolbar to draw a Pie chart. If necessary, use the Office Assistant to obtain information on drawing a Pie chart.

Draw the 3-D Pie chart showing the contribution of each customer to the total new balance as shown in Figure 2-87. Select the nonadjacent chart ranges B4:B8 and H4:H8. That is, select the range B4:B8 and then hold down the CTRL key and select the range H4:H8. The category names in the range B4:B8 will identify the slices, while the data series in the range H4:H8 will determine the size of the slices. Click the Chart Wizard button on the Standard toolbar. Draw the 3-D Pie chart on a new chart sheet. Use the 3-D Pie chart sub-type (column 2, row 1). Add the chart title Contributions to Accounts Receivable.

Rename the Chart1 sheet 3-D Pie Chart. Drag the Accounts Receivable tab to the left of the 3-D Pie Chart tab. Save the workbook using the same file name as in Part 1. Preview and print the chart.

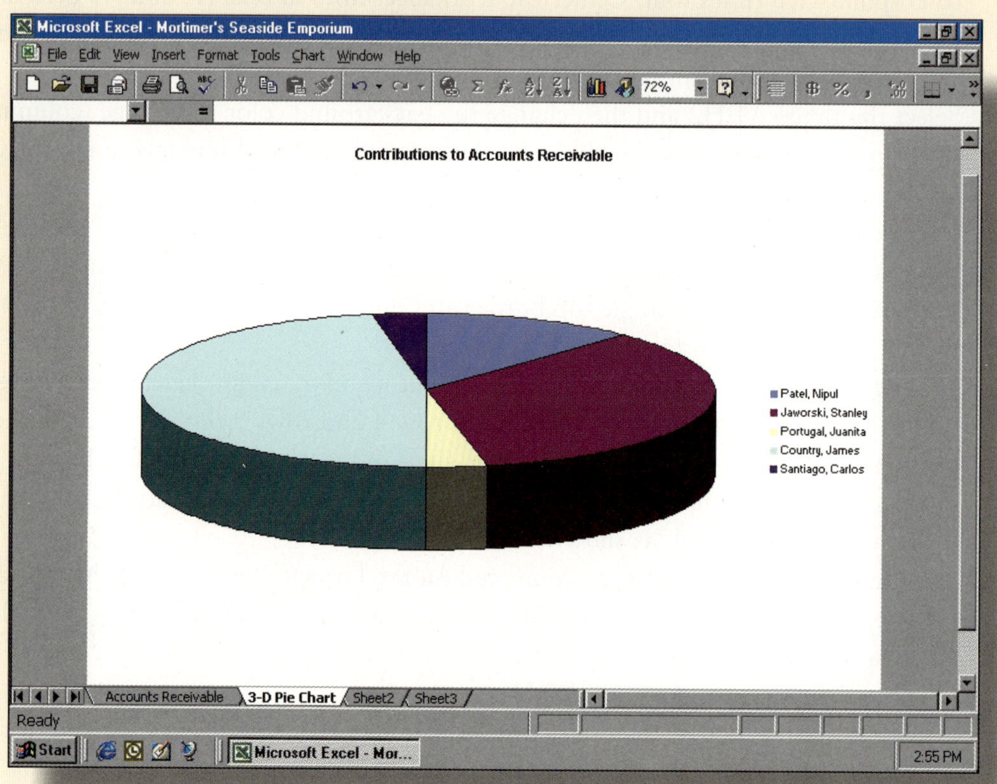

FIGURE 2-87

Instructions Part 3: Change the following purchases: account number 31982 to $3000.00; account number 76894 to $2500.00. The total new balance in cell H9 should equal $24,891.09. Select both sheets by holding down the SHIFT key and clicking the 3-D Pie Chart tab. Preview and print the selected sheets. Hand in the printouts to your instructor.

Instructions Part 4: With your instructor's permission, e-mail the workbook as an attachment to your instructor. Close the workbook without saving the changes.

3 Equity Web Queries

Problem: The chief accountant at Rhine.com recently attended a Microsoft seminar and learned that Microsoft Excel 2000 can connect to the World Wide Web, download real-time stock data into a worksheet, and then refresh the data as often as needed. Because you have had courses in Excel and the Internet, she has hired you as a consultant to develop a stock analysis workbook. Her portfolio is listed in Table 2-9.

Table 2-9 Portfolio

COMPANY	STOCK SYMBOL
Dell	DELL
IBM	IBM
Caterpillar	CAT
Wal-Mart	WMT

Instructions Part 1: If necessary, connect to the Internet. Open a new Excel workbook and select cell A1. Perform the following steps to run a Web query to obtain multiple stock quotes, using the stock symbols in Table 2-9.

1. Point to Get External Data on the Data menu and then click Run Saved Query.
2. Double-click Microsoft Investor Stock Quotes in the Run Query dialog box. If the Queries folder does not display, see your instructor for its location.
3. Click the OK button in the Returning External Data to Microsoft Excel dialog box.
4. When the Enter Parameter Value dialog box displays, enter the stock symbols in Table 2-9 into the text box, being sure to separate them by a comma or space. Click the Use this value/reference for future refreshes check box, click the Refresh automatically when cell value changes, and then click the OK button. After several seconds, the stock data returned by the Web query displays in a worksheet as shown in Figure 2-88 on the next page. Because the stock data returned is real-time, the numbers on your worksheet may be different.
5. Enter your name, course, laboratory assignment number (Lab 2-3a), date, and instructor name in the range A20:A24.
6. Rename the sheet Multiple Quotes. Save the workbook using the file name Equities Online. Preview and then print the worksheet in landscape orientation using the Fit to option.
7. Click the following links and print each: Microsoft Investor, Dell Computer Corporation, Dell Chart, and Dell News. After printing each Web page, close the browser and click the Microsoft Excel button on the taskbar to activate Excel. Hand in the printouts to your instructor.

(continued)

Equity Web Queries *(continued)*

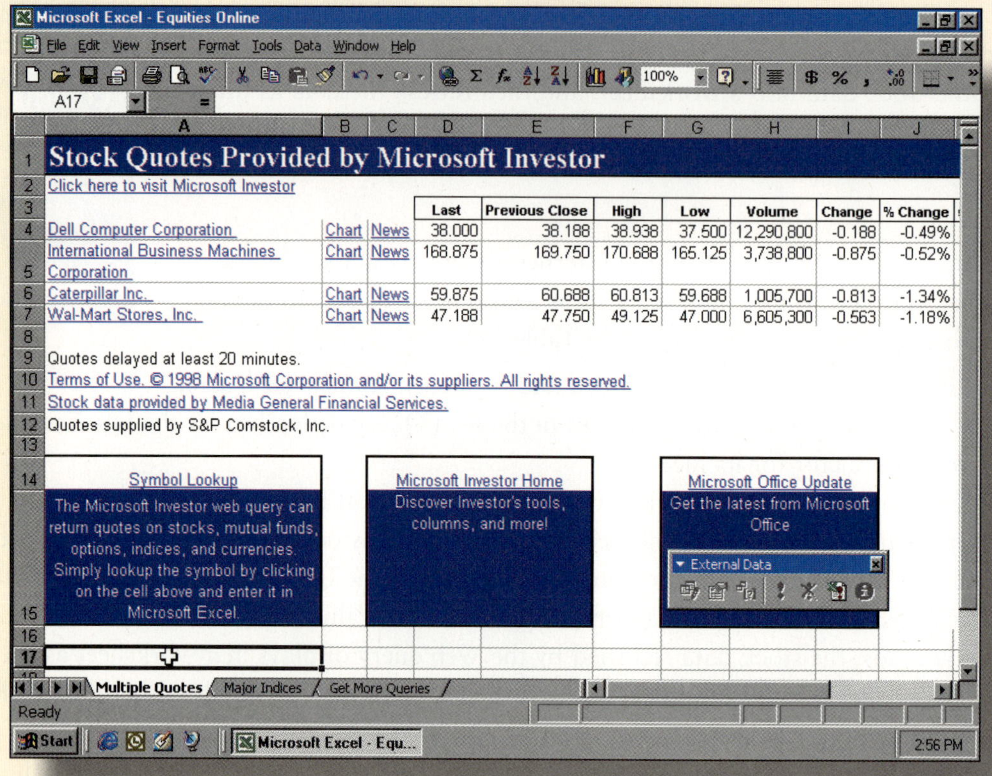

FIGURE 2-88

Instructions Part 2: Do the following to create a worksheet listing the major indices and their current values as shown in Figure 2-89.

1. With the workbook created in Part 1 open, click the Sheet2 tab. Point to Get External Data on the Data menu and then click Run Saved Query.
2. Double-click Microsoft Investor Major Indices in the Run Query dialog box.
3. Click the OK button in the Returning External Data to Microsoft Excel dialog box, starting the data in cell A1 of the existing worksheet.
4. The Web query returns the worksheet shown in Figure 2-89. Your results may differ.
5. Enter your name, course, laboratory assignment number (Lab 2-3b), date, and instructor name in the range A24:A28.
6. Rename the sheet Major Indices. Save the workbook using the same file as in Part 1. Preview and then print the worksheet in landscape orientation using the Fit to option. Hand in the printouts to your instructor.

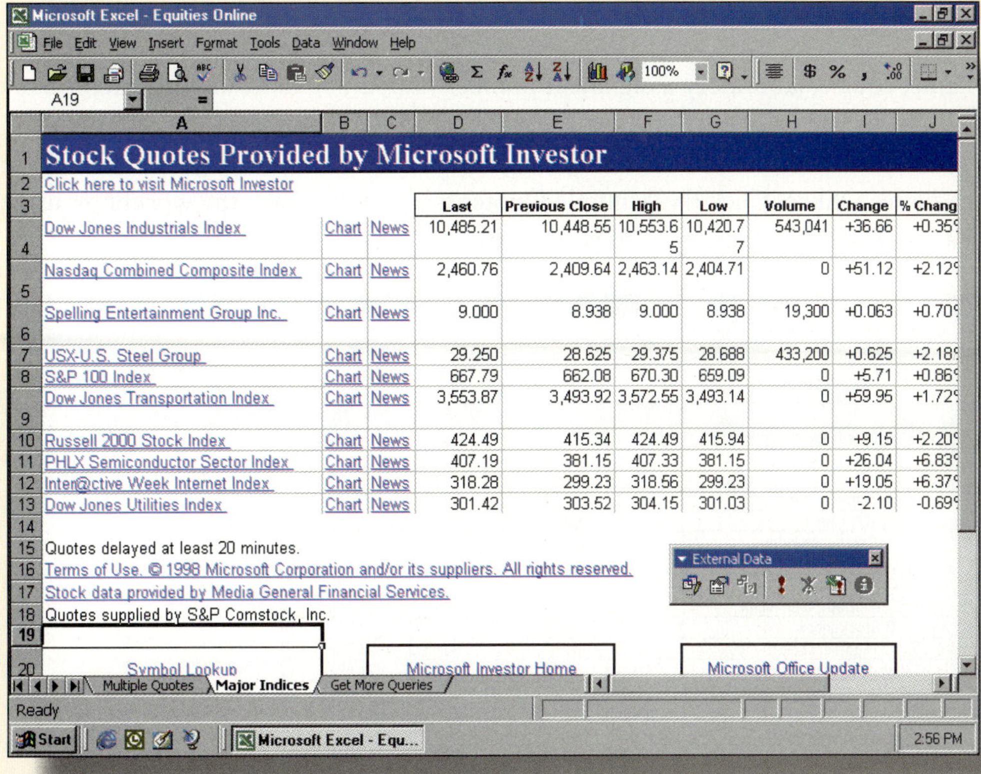

FIGURE 2-89

Instructions Part 3: Create a worksheet showing the latest commodity prices (Figure 2-90 on the next page). The Web query for commodity prices is not one of the queries available in the Queries folder by default. Thus, you must download it from the World Wide Web.

Perform the following tasks.

1. With the workbook Equities Online created in Parts 1 and 2 open, click Sheet3. Rename the Sheet3 tab Get More Queries.
2. Point to Get External Data on the Data menu, and then click Run Saved Query. Double-click Get More Web Queries in the Run Query dialog box.
3. Click the OK button in the Returning External Data to Microsoft Excel dialog box, starting the data in cell A1 of the existing worksheet.
4. When the worksheet titled Microsoft Excel Web Queries displays, scroll down and click the link DBC Major Markets under Stock Market Reports.
5. If the File in Use dialog box displays, click the Notify button. If the File Now Available dialog box displays, click the Read-Write button. The query creates a Read-Only workbook (Book2) and a Read-Write workbook (Book3).
6. With Book3 active, scroll down and over so cell B5 displays in the top left corner of your screen (Figure 2-90).

(continued)

Equity Web Queries *(continued)*

7. Enter your name, course, laboratory assignment number (Lab 2-3c), date, and instructor name in the range B1:B4.
8. After viewing the DBC Major Markets worksheet, preview and print the range B1:H33. On the Windows menu, click Equities Online. Click the Multiple Quotes tab and then save the workbook using the same name as in Part 1. Hand in the printout to your instructor.

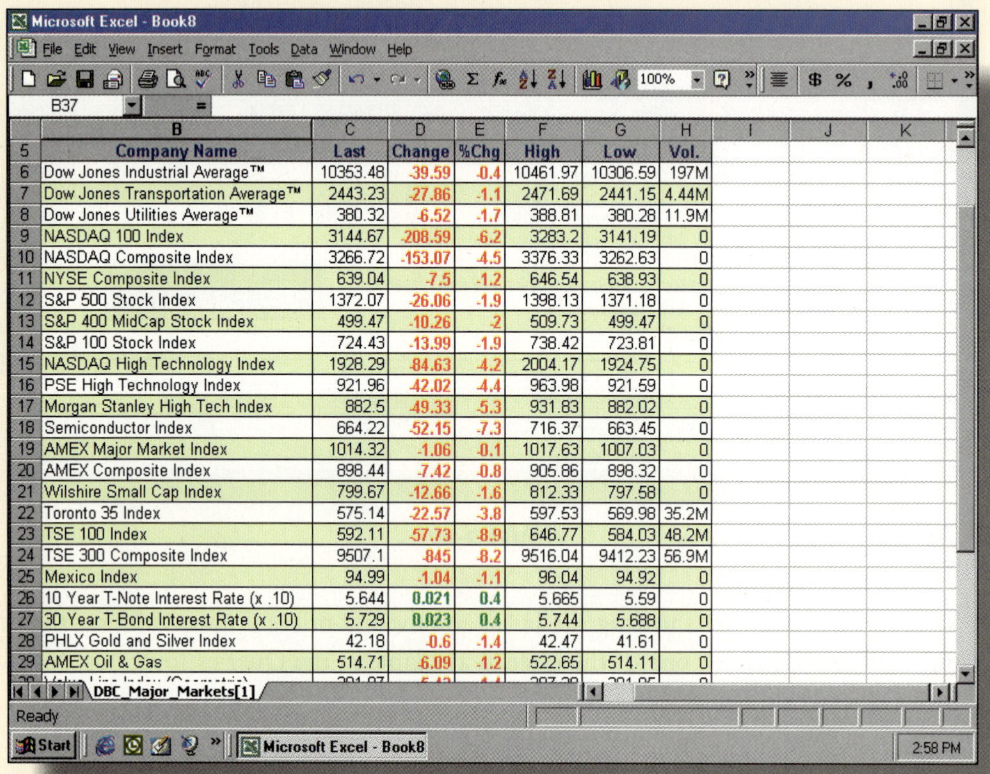

	Company Name	Last	Change	%Chg	High	Low	Vol.
6	Dow Jones Industrial Average™	10353.48	-39.59	-0.4	10461.97	10306.59	197M
7	Dow Jones Transportation Average™	2443.23	-27.86	-1.1	2471.69	2441.15	4.44M
8	Dow Jones Utilities Average™	380.32	-6.52	-1.7	388.81	380.28	11.9M
9	NASDAQ 100 Index	3144.67	-208.59	-6.2	3283.2	3141.19	0
10	NASDAQ Composite Index	3266.72	-153.07	-4.5	3376.33	3262.63	0
11	NYSE Composite Index	639.04	-7.5	-1.2	646.54	638.93	0
12	S&P 500 Stock Index	1372.07	-26.06	-1.9	1398.13	1371.18	0
13	S&P 400 MidCap Stock Index	499.47	-10.26	-2	509.73	499.47	0
14	S&P 100 Stock Index	724.43	-13.99	-1.9	738.42	723.81	0
15	NASDAQ High Technology Index	1928.29	-84.63	-4.2	2004.17	1924.75	0
16	PSE High Technology Index	921.96	-42.02	-4.4	963.98	921.59	0
17	Morgan Stanley High Tech Index	882.5	-49.33	-5.3	931.83	882.02	0
18	Semiconductor Index	664.22	-52.15	-7.3	716.37	663.45	0
19	AMEX Major Market Index	1014.32	-1.06	-0.1	1017.63	1007.03	0
20	AMEX Composite Index	898.44	-7.42	-0.8	905.86	898.32	0
21	Wilshire Small Cap Index	799.67	-12.66	-1.6	812.33	797.58	0
22	Toronto 35 Index	575.14	-22.57	-3.8	597.53	569.98	35.2M
23	TSE 100 Index	592.11	-57.73	-8.9	646.77	584.03	48.2M
24	TSE 300 Composite Index	9507.1	-845	-8.2	9516.04	9412.23	56.9M
25	Mexico Index	94.99	-1.04	-1.1	96.04	94.92	0
26	10 Year T-Note Interest Rate (x .10)	5.644	0.021	0.4	5.665	5.59	0
27	30 Year T-Bond Interest Rate (x .10)	5.729	0.023	0.4	5.744	5.688	0
28	PHLX Gold and Silver Index	42.18	-0.6	-1.4	42.47	41.61	0
29	AMEX Oil & Gas	514.71	-6.09	-1.2	522.65	514.11	0

FIGURE 2-90

Instructions Part 4: Click the Multiple Quotes tab. Right-click a toolbar and click External Data on the shortcut menu. Refresh the data by clicking the Refresh All button on the External Data toolbar. Click the Click here to visit Microsoft Investor link. When the MSN Money Central investor page displays, find the latest prices for the following symbols: MSFT, INTC, YHOO, and GE. Print the Web page for each. Hand in the printouts to your instructor.

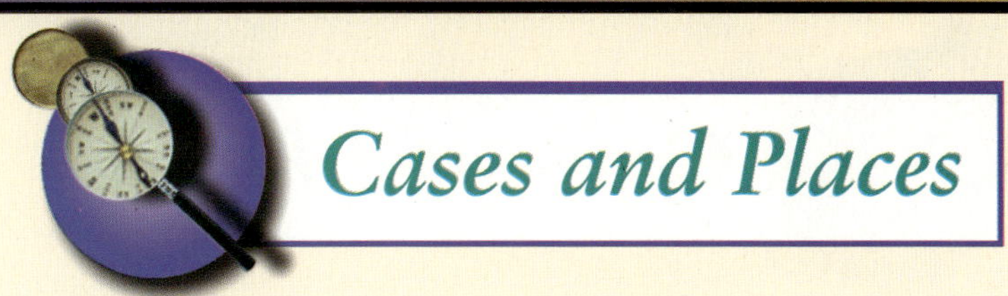

The difficulty of these case studies varies:
◗ are the least difficult; ◗◗ are more difficult; and ◗◗◗ are the most difficult.

1 ◗ The household electric bill has just arrived in the mail, and you have been accused of driving up the total by burning the midnight oil. You are convinced your late-night studying has little effect on the total amount due. You obtain a brochure from the electric company that lists the typical operating costs of appliances based on average sizes and local electricity rates (Figure 2-91).

With this data, you produce a worksheet to share with your family. Use the concepts and techniques presented in this project to create and format the worksheet.

APPLIANCE	COST PER HOUR	HOURS USED DAILY	TOTAL COST PER DAY	TOTAL COST PER MONTH (30 DAYS)
Clothes dryer	$0.5331	2		
Iron	$0.1173	0.5		
Light bulb (150 watt)	$0.0160	5		
Personal computer	$0.0213	3		
Radio	$0.0075	2		
Refrigerator	$0.0113	24		
Stereo	$0.0053	4		
Television	$0.0128	6		
VCR	$0.0032	2		

FIGURE 2-91

2 ◗ In order to determine the effectiveness of their endangered species recovery plan, the Fish and Wildlife Department traps and releases red wolves in selected areas and records how many are pregnant. To obtain a representative sample, the department tries to trap approximately 20% of the population. The sample for 5 sections is shown in Table 2-10.

Use the following formula to determine the total red wolf population for each section:

Wolves in a Section = 5 * (Total Catch + Pregnant Wolves) – 5 * Death Rate * (Total Catch + Pregnant Wolves)

Table 2-10 Red Wolf Catch Data

SECTION	WOLVES CAUGHT	WOLVES PREGNANT	ANNUAL DEATH RATE
1	55	21	19%
2	32	7	22%
3	26	8	32%
4	29	17	8%
5	72	28	29%

Use the concepts and techniques presented in this project to create the worksheet. Determine appropriate totals. Finally, estimate the total state red wolf population if 898 sections are in the state.

Cases and Places

3 ▶ The Student Loan Office has a special assistance program that offers emergency short-term loans at simple interest. The five types of emergency loans, end-of-year principal, rate, and time are shown in Table 2-11.

Create a worksheet that includes the information in Table 2-11, the interest, and amount due. Use the following formulas:

Interest = Principal x Rate x Time

Amount Due = Principal + Interest

Also include a total, maximum value, and minimum value for Principal, Interest, and Amount Due. Format the worksheet using the techniques presented in this project.

Table 2-11 Emergency Loans

LOAN TYPE	PRINCIPAL	RATE	TIME IN YEARS
Tuition Assistance	$96,000	9%	0.4
Academic Supplies	$32,000	11%	0.3
Room and Board	56,250	8%	0.2
Personal Emergency	$7,500	7%	0.17
Travel Expenses	$6,275	15%	0.33

4 ▶ Rich's Oil Production Company drills oil in six states. The management has asked you to develop a worksheet for the company's next meeting from the data in Table 2-12. The worksheet should determine the gross value of the oil, the taxes, and the net value for each state, as well as the net value for all the states. Use these formulas:

Gross Value = Barrels of Oil Produced × Price Per Barrel

Taxes = Gross Value * 7%

Net Value = Gross Value – Taxes

Include appropriate totals, averages, minimums, and maximums. Draw a pie chart on a separate sheet that shows the barrels of oil contribution of each state.

Table 2-12 Oil Production Data

STATE	BARRELS OF OIL PRODUCED	PRICE PER BARREL
Alaska	12,890	$14.25
California	4,321	$13.50
Louisiana	8,500	$15.25
Montana	4,250	$13.50
Oklahoma	9,705	$11.75
Texas	7,543	$14.25

5 ▶▶ Use the concepts and techniques described in this project to run the Web queries titled Microsoft Investor Dow30 and Microsoft Investor Currency Rates on separate worksheets shortly after the stock market opens. Print each worksheet to fit on one page in landscape orientation. Refresh the worksheets later in the day near the stock market close. Print the worksheets and compare them.

Run Get More Web Queries through the Run Saved Query command. Print the list on queries available on the Web. Download three of the queries. Run each one and print the results. For more information, see In the Lab Part 3 on page E 2.75.

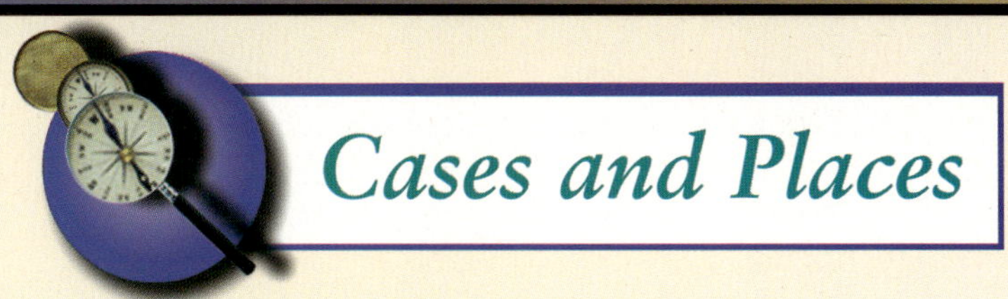

Cases and Places

6 ▸▸ The Woodbridge Furniture Company has decided to pay a 5% commission to its salespeople to stimulate sales. The company currently pays each employee a base salary. The management has projected each employee's sales for the next quarter. This information - employee name, employee base salary, and projected sales - follows: Baker, Tim, $6,000.00, $225,456.00; Learner, Joseph, $7,500.00, $264,888.00; Albright, Barbara, $8,500.00, $235,250.00; Mourissee, Lynn, $7,250.00, $258,450.00; Noble, Richard, $4,250.00, $325,456.00.

With this data, you have been asked to develop a worksheet calculating the amount of commission and the quarterly salary for each employee. The following formulas can be used to obtain this information:

Commission Amount = 5% x Projected Sales

Quarterly Salary = Employee Base Salary + Commission Amount

Include a total, Average Value, Highest Value, and Lowest Value for Employee Base Salary, Commission Amount, and Quarterly Salary. Create an appropriate chart illustrating the portion each employee's quarterly salary contributes to the total quarterly salary. Use the concepts and techniques presented in this project to create and format the worksheet and chart.

7 ▸▸▸ Regular, moderate exercise lowers cholesterol and blood pressure, reduces stress, controls weight, and increases bone strength. Fitness experts recommend individuals who need to lose weight do so at the rate of 1½ to 2 pounds per week. If an individual maintains a regular, sensible diet and burns 750 extra calories each day, he or she will lose about 1½ pounds of fatty tissue a week. Visit a fitness center at your school or in your community to discuss various exercise options. Find out the types of activities offered (for example, aerobics, swimming, jogging, tennis, racquetball, and basketball). Then, list how many calories are burned per hour when performing each of these activities. Using this information, create a worksheet showing the activities offered, the number of calories burned per hour performing these activities, the number of calories burned and pounds lost if you exercise two hours, four hours, and seven hours a week while performing each of these activities.

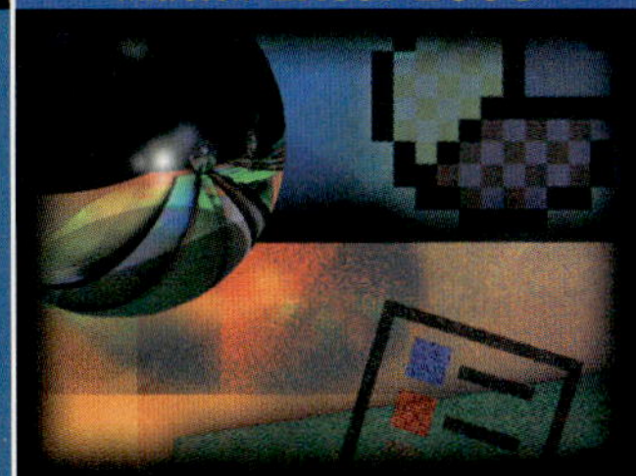

Microsoft Excel 2000

What-If Analysis, Charting, and Working with Large Worksheets

OBJECTIVES

You will have mastered the material in this project when you can:

- Rotate text in a cell
- Use the fill handle to create a series of month names
- Copy a cell's format to another cell using the Format Painter button
- Copy a range of cells to a nonadjacent paste area
- Freeze column and row titles
- Insert and delete cells
- Format numbers using format symbols
- Use the NOW function to display the system date
- Format the system date
- Use absolute cell references in a formula
- Use the IF function to enter one value or another in a cell on the basis of a logical test
- Copy absolute cell references
- Display and dock toolbars
- Add a drop shadow to a range of cells
- Create a 3-D Pie chart on a separate chart sheet
- Format a 3-D Pie chart
- Rearrange sheets in a workbook
- Preview and print multiple sheets
- Use the Zoom box to change the appearance of the worksheet
- View different parts of the worksheet through window panes
- Use Excel to answer what-if questions
- Use the Goal Seek command to analyze worksheet data

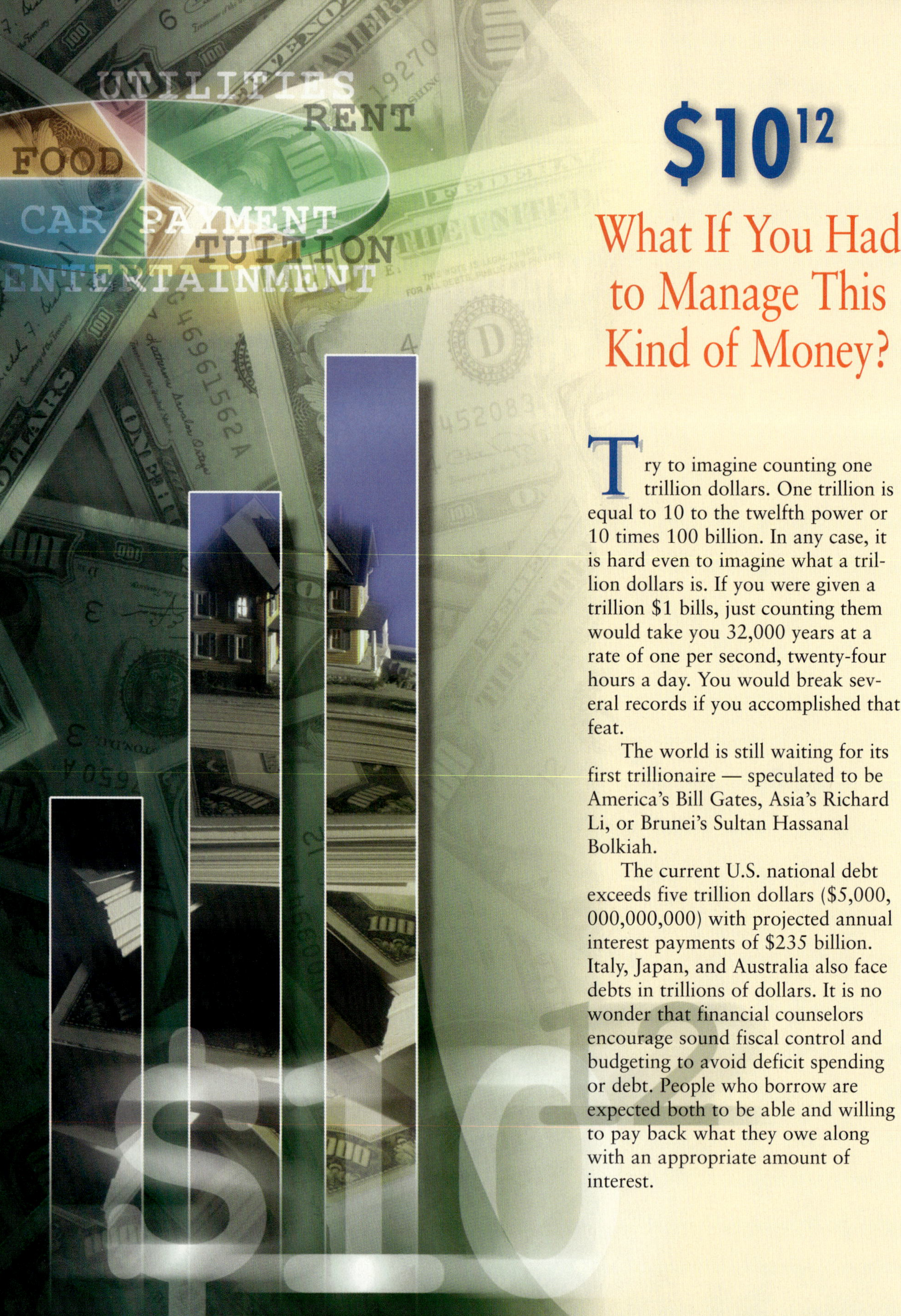

$\$10^{12}$

What If You Had to Manage This Kind of Money?

Try to imagine counting one trillion dollars. One trillion is equal to 10 to the twelfth power or 10 times 100 billion. In any case, it is hard even to imagine what a trillion dollars is. If you were given a trillion $1 bills, just counting them would take you 32,000 years at a rate of one per second, twenty-four hours a day. You would break several records if you accomplished that feat.

The world is still waiting for its first trillionaire — speculated to be America's Bill Gates, Asia's Richard Li, or Brunei's Sultan Hassanal Bolkiah.

The current U.S. national debt exceeds five trillion dollars ($5,000, 000,000,000) with projected annual interest payments of $235 billion. Italy, Japan, and Australia also face debts in trillions of dollars. It is no wonder that financial counselors encourage sound fiscal control and budgeting to avoid deficit spending or debt. People who borrow are expected both to be able and willing to pay back what they owe along with an appropriate amount of interest.

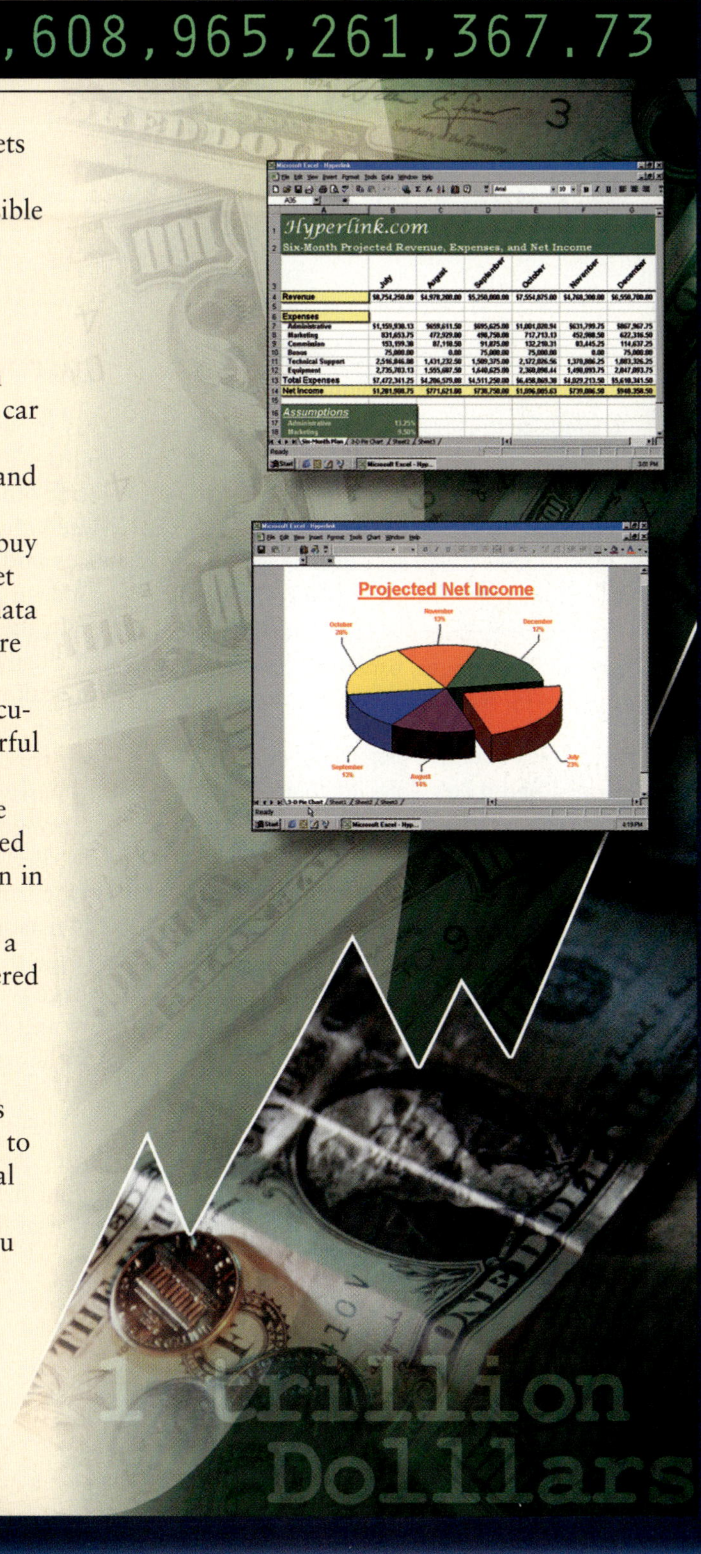

When working with any sum of money — whether an individual's thousands, the more than 125 American billionaires' billions, or even the nation's trillions — creating a realistic budget indeed can be difficult. Budgets provide a sense of perspective that makes it possible to keep debt at a minimum. Although you are not responsible for preparing a national $1.64 trillion budget, knowing where your money goes is the first step in planning a sound personal budget.

Budgeting using worksheets helps reconcile income and expenses. For example, based on a loan calculation and a budget, you can determine a reasonable monthly car payment. Your living expenses may include rent, food, utilities, car and loan payments, credit card payments, and entertainment. Developing a solid budget for these expenses can help you determine if you will be able to buy a future home. Budgets track your income, expenses, net worth, and cash flow, while organizing your financial data in a logical format. Using electronic spreadsheet software makes it easy to show exactly how you spend money.

In this project, you will use Excel's automatic recalculation feature to complete what-if analysis. It is a powerful tool used to analyze worksheet data. It allows you to scrutinize the impact of changing values in cells that are referenced by a formula in another cell. What if you need to know how much money to put down on a home loan in order to find a manageable monthly payment? What if your income changes or you add a new expense or pay a final payment? These questions and more can be answered easily with Excel's what-if capabilities. Excel not only recalculates all the formulas in a worksheet when new data is entered, it also redraws any associated charts.

Just as the nation must examine line by line how its money is spent, personal budget calculations allow you to do the same. Appearing somewhat restrictive, a personal budget is a necessity to avoid the alternative — if you exceed the average debt-to-asset ratio of 30 percent, you could end up joining the world's trillionaire debt club.

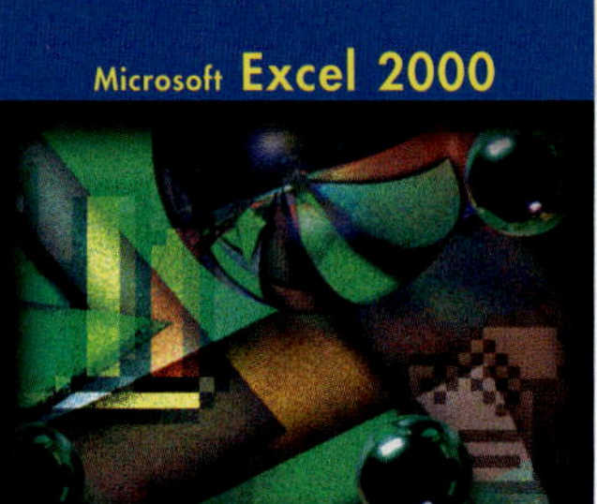

Microsoft Excel 2000

What-If Analysis, Charting, and Working with Large Worksheets

CASE PERSPECTIVE

Hyperlink.com is a global provider of routers, LAN switches, dial-up access servers, and network management software for the Internet. These products link geographically dispersed networks. Each June and December, the chief executive officer (CEO) of Hyperlink.com, Frances Collins, submits a plan to the board of directors to show projected revenues, expenses, and net income for the next six months.

Last December, Frances used pencil, paper, and a calculator to complete the report and draw a 3-D Pie chart. When she presented her report, the directors asked for the effect on the projected net income if the administrative expense allocation was changed. While the directors waited impatiently, Frances took several minutes to calculate the answers. Once she changed the projected expenses, the 3-D Pie chart no longer matched the projections. Frances now wants to use a computer and spreadsheet software to address what-if questions so she can take advantage of its instantaneous recalculation feature. As lead spreadsheet specialist for Hyperlink.com, you are to meet with Frances, determine her needs, and create the worksheet and chart.

Introduction

This project introduces you to techniques that will enhance your abilities to create worksheets and draw charts. You will learn about other methods for entering values in cells and formatting these values. You also will learn how to use absolute cell references and how to use the IF function to assign a value to a cell based on a logical test.

In the previous projects, you learned how to use the Standard and Formatting toolbars. Excel has several other toolbars that can make your work easier. One such toolbar is the **Drawing toolbar**, which allows you to draw shapes and arrows and add drop shadows to cells you want to emphasize.

Worksheets normally are much larger than those created in the previous projects, often extending beyond the size of the window. Because you cannot see the entire worksheet on the screen at one time, working with a large worksheet can be difficult. For this reason, Excel provides several commands that allow you to change the display on the screen so you can view critical parts of a large worksheet at one time. One command lets you freeze the row and column titles so they always display on the screen. Another command splits the worksheet into separate window panes so you can view different parts of a worksheet.

From your work in Project 1, you are aware of how easily charts can be created. This project covers additional charting techniques that allow you to convey your message in a dramatic pictorial fashion.

When you set up a worksheet, you should use as many cell references in formulas as possible, rather than constant values. The cell references in a formula often are called assumptions. **Assumptions** are values in cells you can change to determine new values for formulas. This project emphasizes the use of assumptions and introduces you to answering what-if questions such as, what if you decrease the marketing expenses assumption (cell B18 in Figure 3-1a) by 1% — how would the decrease affect the projected six-month net income (cell H14 in Figure 3-1a)? Being able to quickly analyze the effect of changing values in a worksheet is an important skill in making business decisions.

More About 2000

Why Business People Use Excel

The capability of Excel to instantaneously answer what-if questions is the single most important reason why millions of business people use this software. Just a few short years ago, only large expensive computers programmed by highly paid computer professionals could answer what-if questions of any complexity. And then you might have to wait days for the turnaround. Excel and its equivalents give the non-computer professional the ability to get complex business-related questions answered quickly and economically.

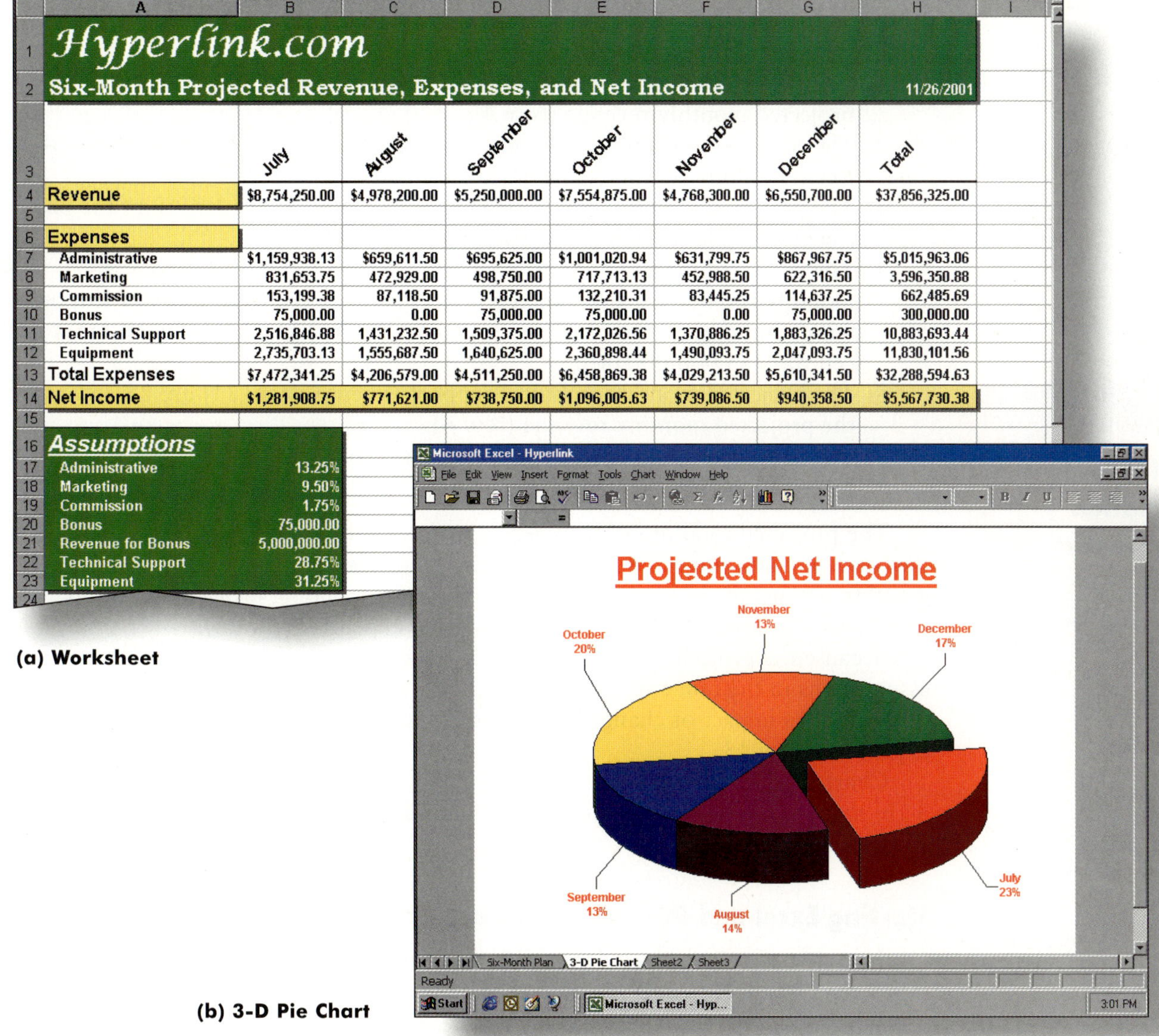

Hyperlink.com
Six-Month Projected Revenue, Expenses, and Net Income 11/26/2001

	July	August	September	October	November	December	Total
Revenue	$8,754,250.00	$4,978,200.00	$5,250,000.00	$7,554,875.00	$4,768,300.00	$6,550,700.00	$37,856,325.00
Expenses							
Administrative	$1,159,938.13	$659,611.50	$695,625.00	$1,001,020.94	$631,799.75	$867,967.75	$5,015,963.06
Marketing	831,653.75	472,929.00	498,750.00	717,713.13	452,988.50	622,316.50	3,596,350.88
Commission	153,199.38	87,118.50	91,875.00	132,210.31	83,445.25	114,637.25	662,485.69
Bonus	75,000.00	0.00	75,000.00	75,000.00	0.00	75,000.00	300,000.00
Technical Support	2,516,846.88	1,431,232.50	1,509,375.00	2,172,026.56	1,370,886.25	1,883,326.25	10,883,693.44
Equipment	2,735,703.13	1,555,687.50	1,640,625.00	2,360,898.44	1,490,093.75	2,047,093.75	11,830,101.56
Total Expenses	$7,472,341.25	$4,206,579.00	$4,511,250.00	$6,458,869.38	$4,029,213.50	$5,610,341.50	$32,288,594.63
Net Income	$1,281,908.75	$771,621.00	$738,750.00	$1,096,005.63	$739,086.50	$940,358.50	$5,567,730.38

Assumptions	
Administrative	13.25%
Marketing	9.50%
Commission	1.75%
Bonus	75,000.00
Revenue for Bonus	5,000,000.00
Technical Support	28.75%
Equipment	31.25%

(a) Worksheet

(b) 3-D Pie Chart

FIGURE 3-1

Project Three — Hyperlink.com Six-Month Projected Revenue, Expenses, and Net Income

Garbage In Garbage Out

Studies have shown that more than 25 percent of all business worksheets have errors. If your data or formulas are in error, then the results are in error. You can ensure accuracy of your formulas by using the Auditing command on the Tools menu. The Auditing command indicates relationships among formulas.

Formulas and Recalculation

Excel automatically recalculates all formulas in the workbook when you enter a value in a cell. If a workbook has many formulas, you can grow impatient waiting for the recalculation to take place, even though it seldom takes more than a few seconds with hundreds of formulas in a workbook. You can switch Excel to manual recalculation by clicking Tools on the menu bar, clicking Options, clicking the Calculation tab, and then clicking the Manual option button. You press F9 to recalculate when you have entered all of the values.

You took the following notes about the required worksheet and chart in your meeting with the CEO, Frances Collins.

Need: A worksheet (Figure 3-1a on the previous page) and 3-D Pie chart (Figure 3-1b on the previous page) are required. The worksheet is to show Hyperlink.com's projected monthly revenue, expenses, and net income for a six-month period. The 3-D Pie chart is to show the contribution of each projected month's net income to the projected seven-month total net income.

Source of Data: The six projected monthly revenues (row 4 of Figure 3-1a) and the seven assumptions (range B17:B23) that are used to determine the projected monthly expenses are based on the company's historical data. All the remaining numbers in Figure 3-1a are determined from these twelve numbers using formulas.

Calculations: Each of the projected monthly expenses in the range B7:G12 of Figure 3-1a — administrative, marketing, commission, bonus, technical support, and equipment — is determined by taking an assumed percentage of the corresponding projected monthly revenue in row 4. The assumptions in the range B17:B23 are as follows:

1. The projected monthly administrative expenses (row 7) are 13.25% of the projected monthly revenue (row 4).
2. The projected monthly marketing expenses (row 8) are 9.50% of the projected monthly revenue (row 4).
3. The projected monthly commission expenses (row 9) are 1.75% of the projected monthly revenue (row 4).
4. The projected monthly bonus (row 10) is $75,000.00, if the projected monthly revenue (row 4) exceeds the revenue for bonus to be awarded, otherwise the projected monthly bonus is zero. The revenue for bonus value is in cell B21 ($5,000,000.00).
5. The projected monthly technical support expenses (row 11) are 28.75% of the projected monthly revenue (row 4).
6. The projected monthly equipment expenses (row 12) are 31.25% of the projected monthly revenue (row 4).

The projected total monthly expenses in row 13 of Figure 3-1a are the sum of the corresponding projected monthly expenses in rows 7 through 12. The projected monthly net income in row 14 is equal to the corresponding projected monthly revenue (row 4) minus the projected monthly total expenses (row 13).

Because the projected expenses in rows 7 through 12 are dependent on the assumptions in the range B17:B23, you can use the what-if capability of Excel to determine the impact of changing these assumptions on the projected monthly total expenses in row 13.

Chart Requirements: A 3-D Pie chart is required on a separate sheet (Figure 3-1b) that shows the contribution of each month to the projected net income for the six-month period.

Starting Excel and Resetting Toolbars and Menus

To start Excel, Windows must be running. Perform the following steps to start Excel. Once Excel displays, Steps 4 through 6 reset the toolbars and menus to their original settings.

TO START EXCEL AND RESET TOOLBARS AND MENUS

1. Click the Start button on the taskbar.
2. Click New Office Document. If necessary, click the General tab in the New Office Document dialog box.
3. Double-click the Blank Workbook icon.
4. When the blank worksheet displays, click View on the menu bar, click the arrows at the bottom of the menu to display the full menu, point to Toolbars, and click Customize on the Toolbars submenu.
5. When the Customize dialog box displays, click the Options tab, make sure the top three check boxes contain check marks, click the Reset my usage data button, and then click the Yes button.
6. Click the Toolbars tab. Click Standard, click the Reset button, and then click the OK button. Click Formatting, click the Reset button, and the click the OK button. Click the Close button.
7. Double-click the move handle on the far left side of the Formatting toolbar so it displays in its entirety.

The Standard and Formatting toolbars should display as shown in Figure 3-2 on the next page.

See Appendix B for additional information on resetting the toolbars and menus.

Changing the Font of the Entire Worksheet to Bold

After starting Excel, the next step is to change the font of the entire worksheet to bold so all entries will be emphasized.

TO BOLD THE FONT OF THE ENTIRE WORKSHEET

1. Click the Select All button immediately above row heading 1 and to the left of column heading A.
2. Click the Bold button on the Formatting toolbar.

No immediate change takes place on the screen. As you enter text and numbers into the worksheet, however, Excel will display them in bold.

Readability

Formatting the entire worksheet in bold makes it easier for people with less than average eyesight to read the worksheet. An alternative is to increase the font size of the entire worksheet to 12 or 14 point or increase the percentage in the Zoom box.

Entering the Worksheet Titles

The worksheet contains two titles, one in cell A1, and another in cell A2. In the previous projects, titles were centered across the worksheet. With large worksheets that extend beyond the size of a window, it is best to enter titles in the upper-left corner as shown in Figure 3-1a on page E 3.5.

TO ENTER THE WORKSHEET TITLES

1. Select cell A1 and then type `Hyperlink.com` to enter the title.
2. Select cell A2 and then type `Six-Month Projected Revenue, Expenses, and Net Income` to enter the second title.
3. Select cell B3.

Excel responds by displaying the worksheet titles in cells A1 and A2 in bold (Figure 3-2).

Rotating Text

If you enter 90° in the Degrees box in the Alignment tab of the Format Cells dialog box, the text will display vertically and read from bottom to top in the cell. You can rotate the text clockwise by entering a number between -1° and -90°. If you enter -90°, the text will display vertically and read from top to bottom in the cell.

Rotating Text and Using the Fill Handle to Create a Series

When you first enter text, its angle is zero degrees (0°), and it reads from left to right in a cell. You can **rotate text** counterclockwise by entering a number between 1° and 90° on the Alignment sheet in the Format Cells dialog box. An example of rotating the text is shown in the next set of steps.

In Projects 1 and 2, you used the fill handle to copy a cell or a range of cells to adjacent cells. You also can use the fill handle to create a series of numbers, dates, or month names automatically. Perform the following steps to enter the month name, July, in cell B3, format cell B3 (including rotating the text), and then enter the remaining month names in the range C3:G3 using the fill handle.

Steps To Rotate Text and Use the Fill Handle to Create a Series of Month Names

1 With cell B3 active, type `July` **and then press the ENTER key. On the Formatting toolbar, click the Font Size box arrow and then click 11 in the Font Size list. Click the Borders button arrow and then click the Thick Bottom Border button on the Borders palette. Right-click cell B3 and then point to Format Cells on the shortcut menu.**

The text, July, displays in cell B3 using the assigned formats (Figure 3-2). The shortcut menu displays.

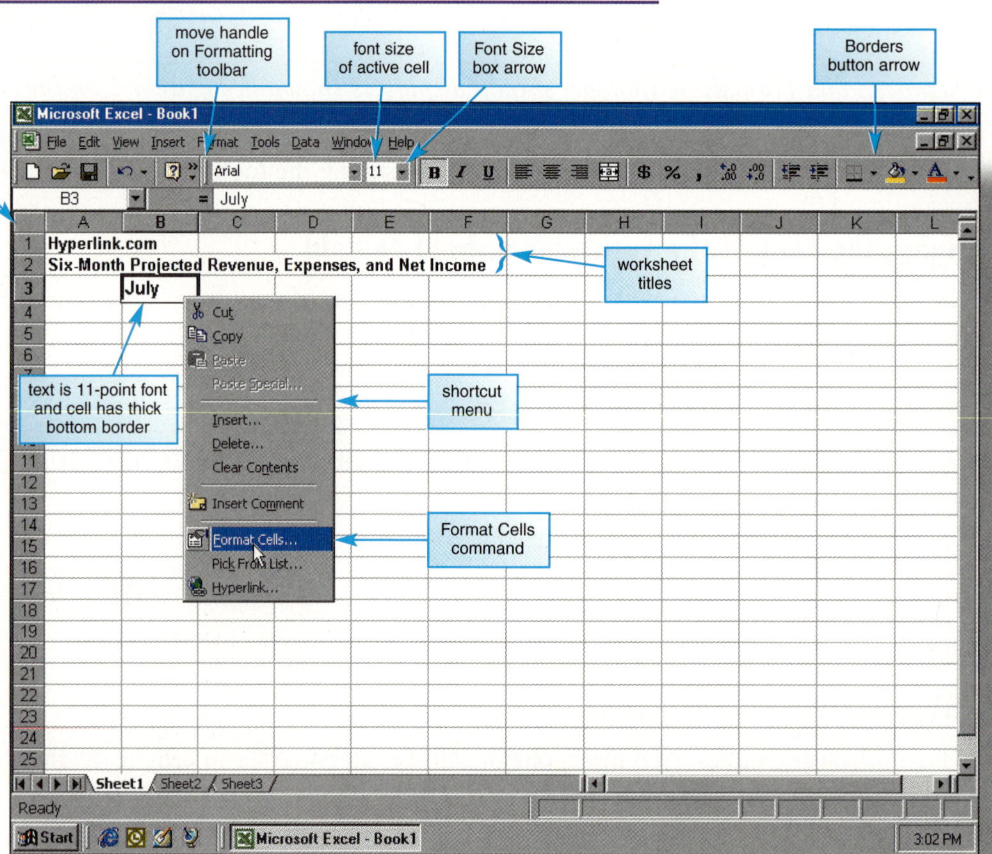

FIGURE 3-2

2 Click Format Cells. When the Format Cells dialog box displays, click the Alignment tab. Click the 45° point in the Orientation area and point to the OK button.

The Alignment sheet in the Format Cells dialog box displays. The Text hand in the Orientation area points to the 45° point and 45 displays in the Degrees box (Figure 3-3).

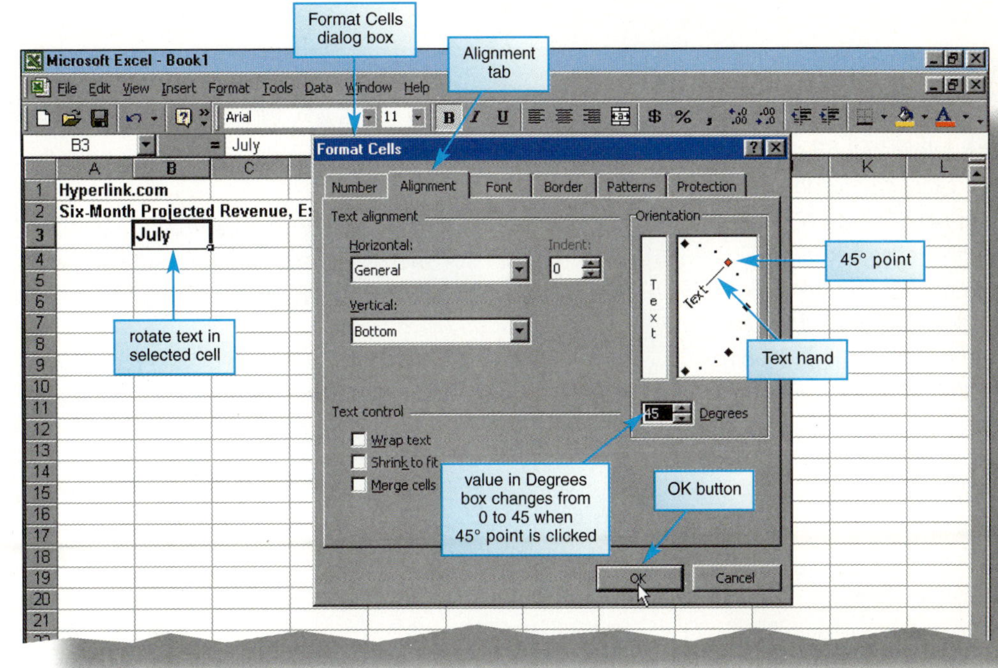

FIGURE 3-3

3 Click the OK button. Point to the fill handle on the lower-right edge of cell B3.

The text, July, in cell B3 displays at a 45° angle (Figure 3-4). Excel automatically increases the height of row 3 to best fit to display the rotated text. The mouse pointer changes to a cross hair.

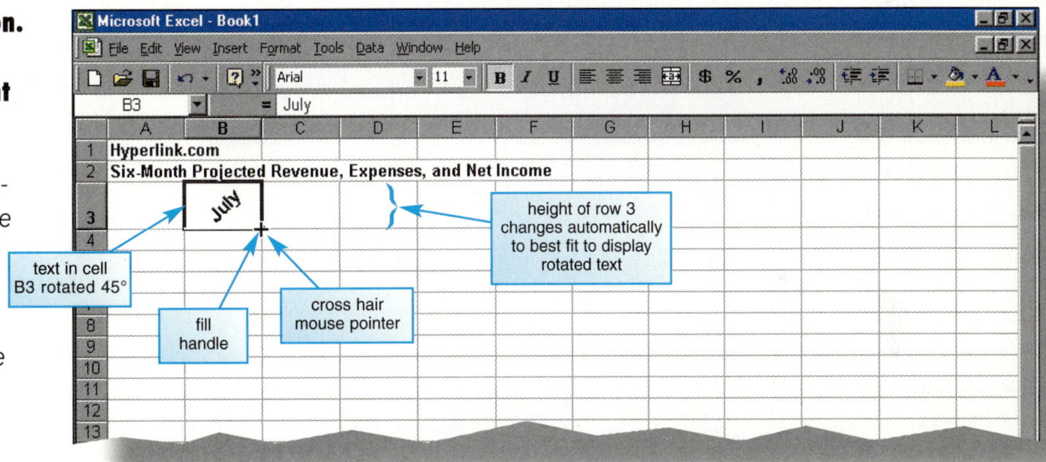

FIGURE 3-4

4 Drag the fill handle to the right to select the range C3:G3.

Excel displays a light border that surrounds the selected range (Figure 3-5).

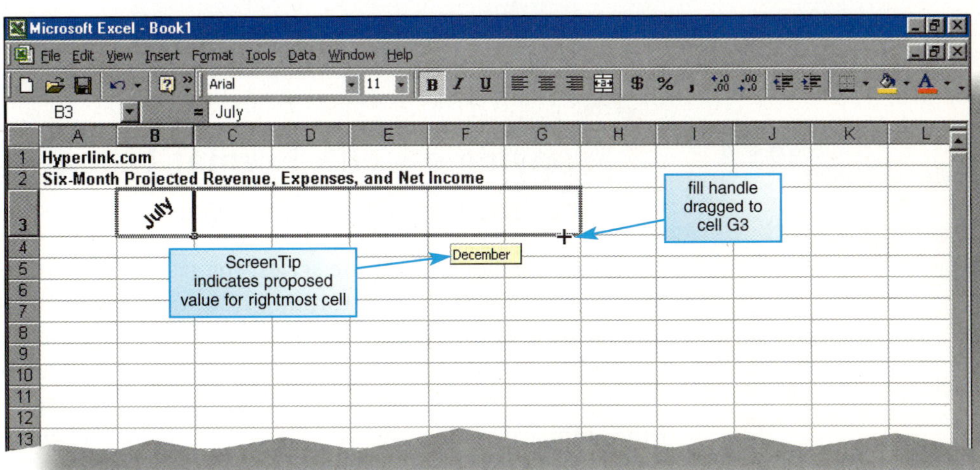

FIGURE 3-5

5 Release the mouse button.

Using July in cell B3 as the basis, Excel creates the month name series August through December in the range C3:G3 (Figure 3-6). The formats assigned to cell B3 earlier in Step 1 (11-point font, thick bottom border, text rotated 45°) also are copied to the range C3:G3.

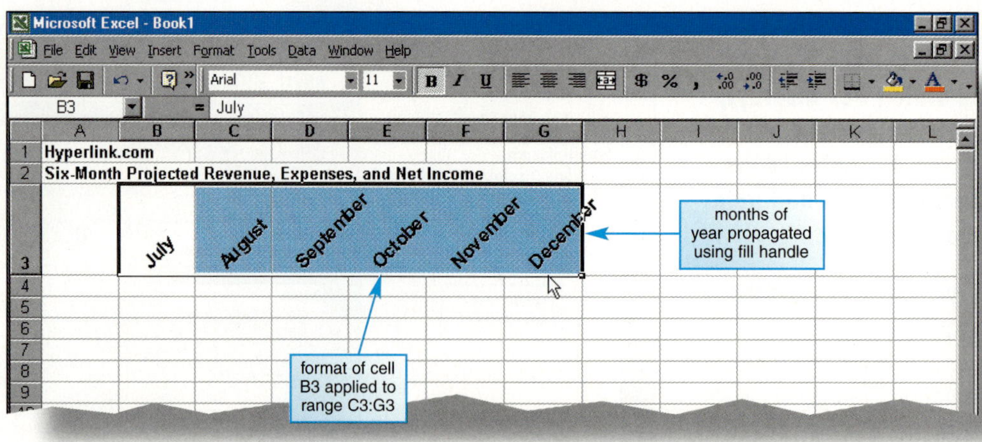

FIGURE 3-6

Other Ways

1. Enter start month in cell, right-drag fill handle in direction to fill, click Fill Months on shortcut menu

Besides creating a series of values, the fill handle also copies the format of cell B3 (11-point font, thick bottom border, text rotated 45°) to the range C3:G3. You can use the fill handle to create longer series than the one shown in Figure 3-6. If you drag the fill handle past cell G3 in Step 4, Excel continues to increment the months and logically will repeat July, August, and so on, if you extend the range far enough to the right.

You can create several different types of series using the fill handle. Table 3-1 illustrates several examples. Notice in Examples 4 through 7 that, if you use the fill handle to create a series of numbers or non-sequential months, you must enter the first item in the series in one cell and the second item in the series in an adjacent cell. Next, select both cells and drag the fill handle through the paste area.

Table 3-1 Examples of Series Using the Fill Handle

EXAMPLE	CONTENTS OF CELL(S) COPIED USING THE FILL HANDLE	NEXT THREE VALUES OF EXTENDED SERIES
1	3:00	4:00, 5:00, 6:00
2	Qtr3	Qtr4, Qtr1, Qtr2
3	Quarter 1	Quarter 2, Quarter 3, Quarter 4
4	Jul-2001, Oct-2001	Jan-2002, Apr-2002, Jul-2002
5	2000, 2001	2002, 2003, 2004
6	1, 2	3, 4, 5
7	600, 580	560, 540, 520
8	Sun	Mon, Tue, Wed
9	Saturday, Monday	Wednesday, Friday, Sunday
10	1st Section	2nd Section, 3rd Section, 4th Section
11	-99, -101	-103, -105, -107

More About 2000

The Magical Fill Handle

If you drag the fill handle to the left or up, Excel decrements the series. To use the fill handle to copy a potential series initiator, such as the word January, to a paste area, hold down the CTRL key while you drag.

Copying a Cell's Format Using the Format Painter Button

Because it is not part of the series, the last column title, Total, must be entered separately in cell H3 and formatted to match the other column titles. Imagine how many steps it would take, however, to assign the formatting of the other column titles to this cell — first, you have to change the font to 11 point, then add a thick bottom border, and finally, rotate the text 45°. Using the **Format Painter button** on the Standard toolbar, however, you can format a cell quickly by copying a cell's format to another cell. The following steps enter the column title, Total, in cell H3 and format the cell using the Format Painter button.

To Copy a Cell's Format Using the Format Painter Button

1 **Double-click the move handle on the Standard toolbar to display it in its entirety. Click cell H3. Type** `Total` **and then press the LEFT ARROW key. With cell G3 selected, click the Format Painter button on the Standard toolbar. Point to cell H3.**

The mouse pointer changes to a block plus sign with a paint brush (Figure 3-7).

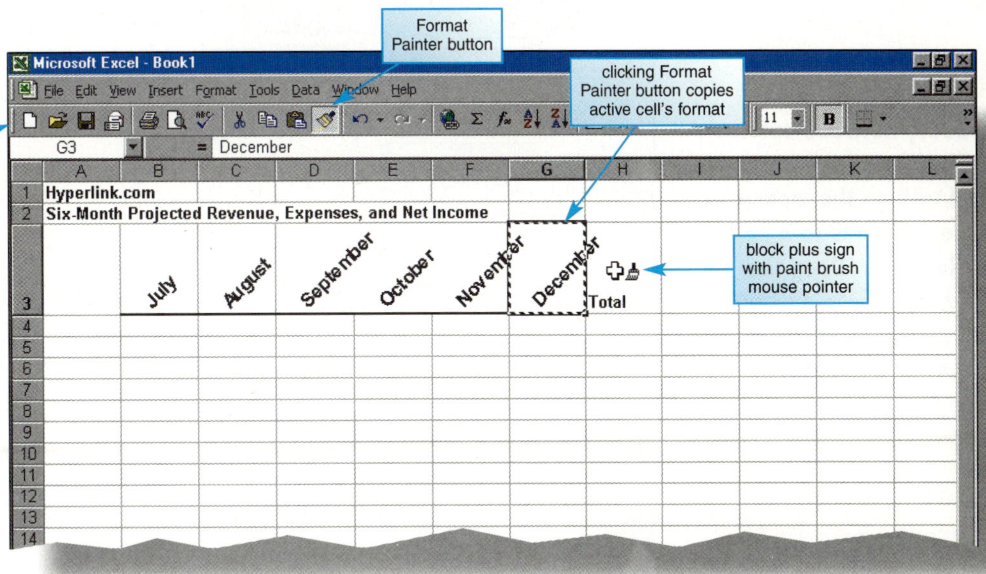

FIGURE 3-7

2 **Click cell H3 to assign the format of cell G3 to cell H3. Click cell A4.**

Excel copies the format of cell G3 (11-point font, thick bottom border, text rotated 45°) to cell H3 (Figure 3-8).

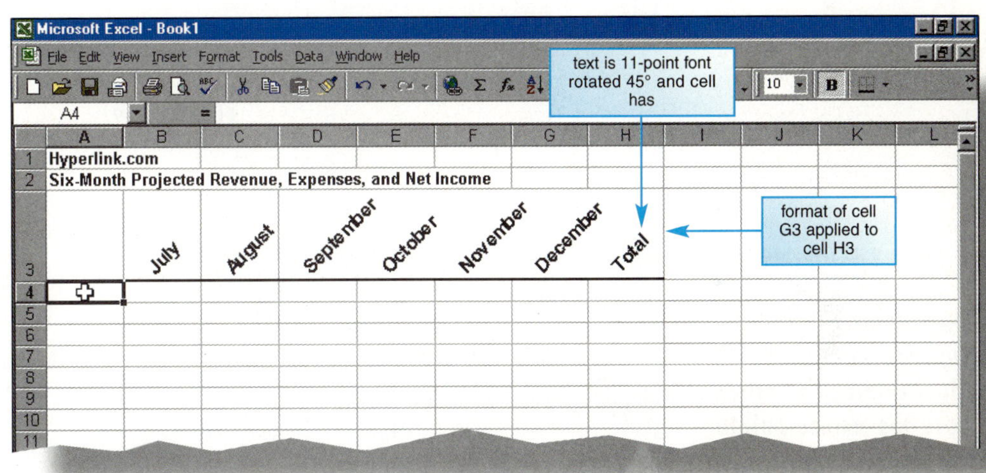

FIGURE 3-8

1. Click Copy button, on Edit menu click Paste Special, click Formats, click OK button

The Format Painter Button

Double-click the Format Painter button on the Standard toolbar to copy the formats to nonadjacent ranges. Click the Format Painter button to deactivate it.

The Format Painter button also can be used to copy the formats of a cell to a range of cells. To copy formats to a range of cells, select the cell or range with the desired format, click the Format Painter button on the Standard toolbar, and then drag through the range to which you want to paste the formats.

Increasing the Column Widths and Entering Row Titles

In Project 2, the column widths were increased after the values were entered into the worksheet. Sometimes, you may want to increase the column widths before you enter the values and then, if necessary, adjust them later. The steps on the next page increase the column widths and add the row titles in column A down to the Assumptions in cell A16.

To Increase Column Widths and Enter Row Titles

1 Move the mouse pointer to the boundary between column heading A and column heading B so the mouse pointer changes to a split double arrow. Drag the mouse pointer to the right until the ScreenTip displays, Width: 25.00 (180 pixels).

The ScreenTip and distance between the left edge of column A and the vertical dotted line below the mouse pointer shows the proposed column width (Figure 3-9).

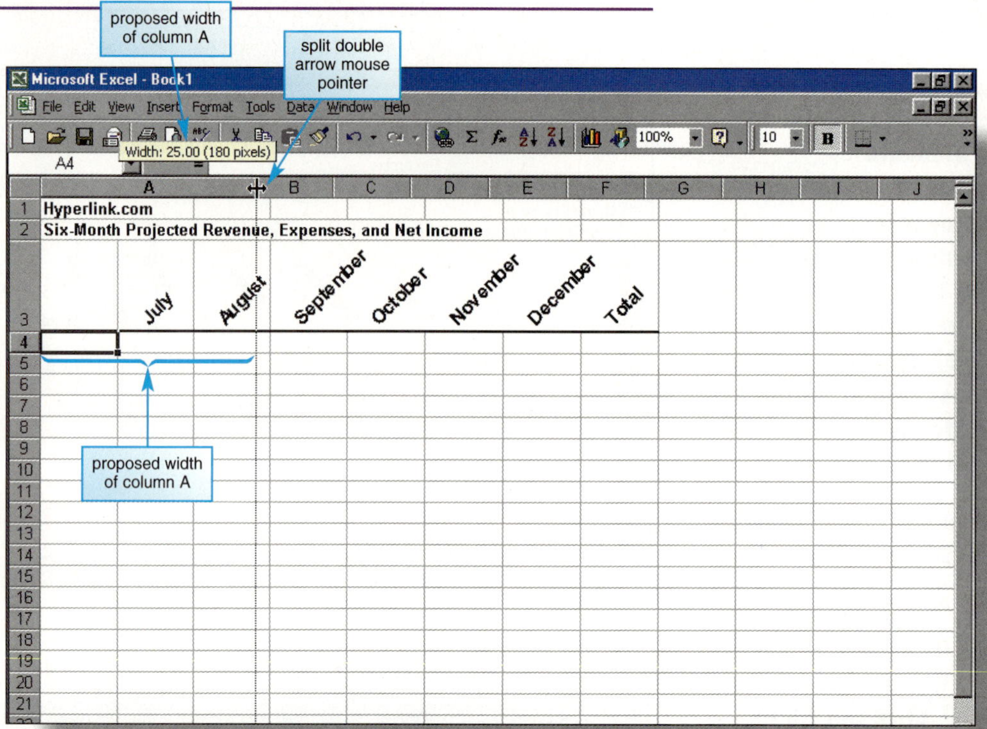

FIGURE 3-9

2 Release the mouse button. Click column heading B and drag through column heading G to select columns B through G. Move the mouse pointer to the boundary between column headings B and C and then drag the mouse to the right until the ScreenTip displays, Width: 13.00 (96 pixels).

The distance between the left edge of column B and the vertical line below the mouse pointer shows the proposed width of columns B through G (Figure 3-10).

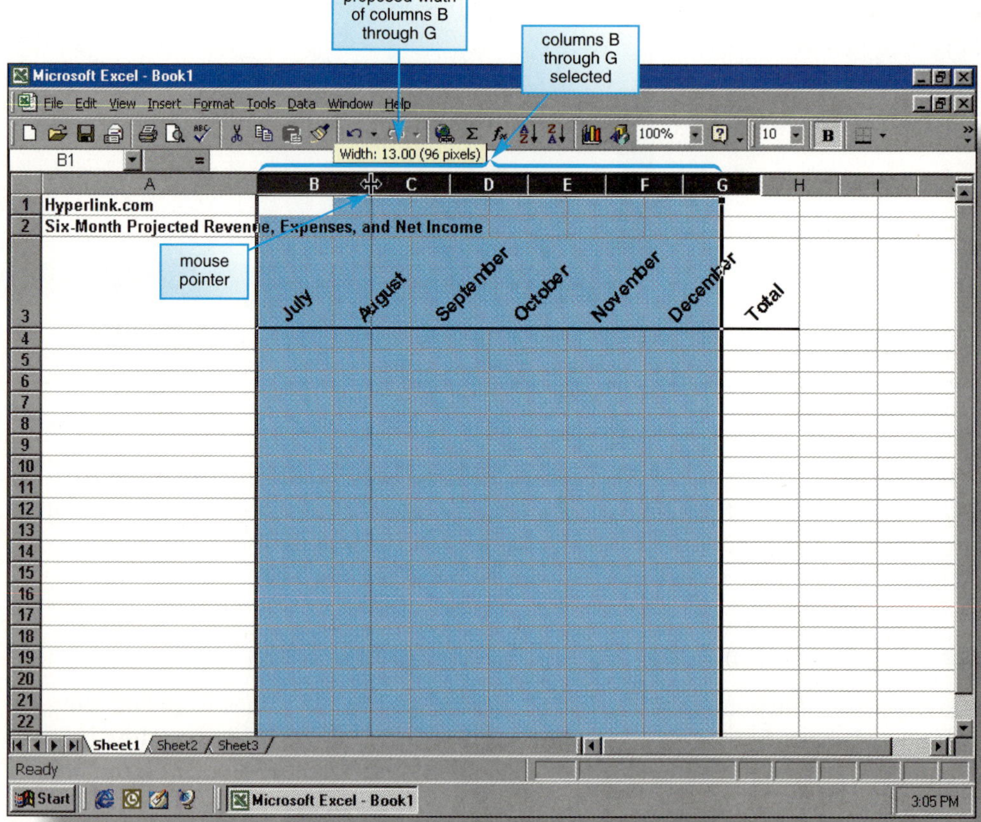

FIGURE 3-10

3 **Release the mouse button. Use the technique described in Step 1 to increase the width of column H to 15.00. Enter** Revenue **in cell A4,** Expenses **in cell A6,** Administrative **in cell A7,** Marketing **in cell A8, and** Commission **in cell A9. Enter** Bonus **in cell A10,** Technical Support **in cell A11,** Equipment **in cell A12,** Total Expenses **in cell A13,** Net Income **in cell A14, and** Assumptions **in cell A16. Select the range A7:A12. Double-click the move handle on the Formatting toolbar to display it in its entirety. Click the Increase Indent button on the Formatting toolbar. Click cell A17.**

The row titles display as shown in Figure 3-11.

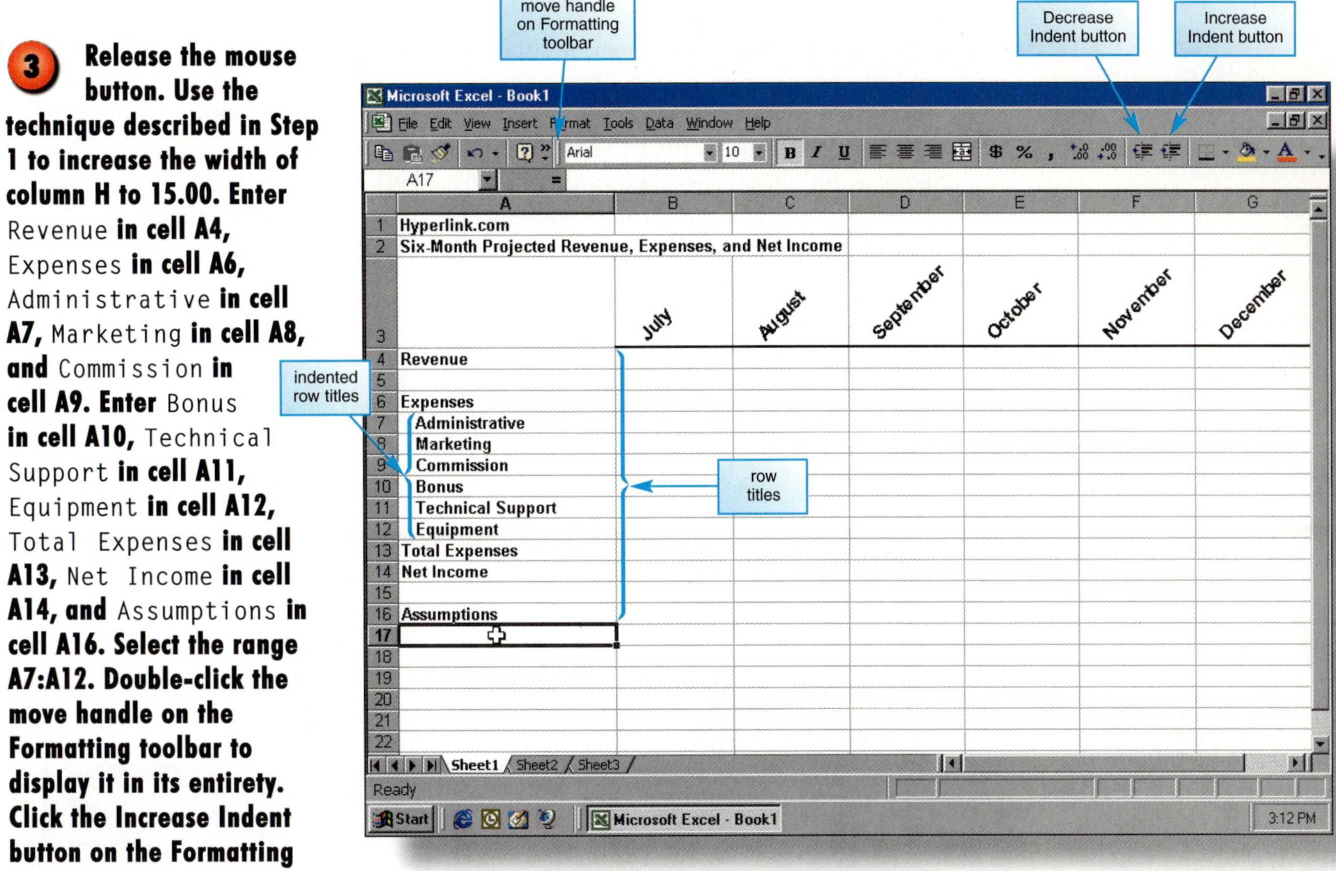

FIGURE 3-11

The **Increase Indent button** indents the contents of a cell to the right by three spaces each time you click it. The **Decrease Indent button** decreases the indent by three spaces each time you click it.

Other Ways

1. Right-click range, click Format cells, click Alignment tab, click Left (Indent) in Horizontal list, type number of spaces to indent in Indent text box, click OK button

Copying a Range of Cells to a Nonadjacent Paste Area

As shown in Figure 3-1a on page E 3.5, the row titles in the Assumptions table in the range A17:A23 are the same as the row titles in the range A7:A12, with the exception of the additional entry in cell A21. Hence, you can create the Assumptions table row titles by copying the range A7:A12 to the range A17:A23 and inserting the additional entry in cell A21. The range to copy (range A7:A12) is not adjacent to the paste area (range A17:A22). In the first two projects, you used the fill handle to copy a range of cells to an adjacent paste area. To copy a range of cells to a nonadjacent paste area, however, you cannot use the fill handle.

A more versatile method of copying a cell or range of cells is to use the Copy button and Paste button on the Standard toolbar. You can use these two buttons to copy a range of cells to an adjacent or nonadjacent paste area.

More About 2000

Shrink to Fit

An alternative to increasing the column widths is to shrink the characters in the cell to fit the current width of the column. To shrink to fit, click Format on the menu bar, click Cells, click the Alignment tab, and click the Shrink to fit check box in the Text control area.

Copying Across Workbooks

If you have a range of cells in another workbook that you want to copy into the current workbook, open the source workbook, select the range, and then click the Copy button to place the range of cells on the Office Clipboard. Next, activate the destination workbook by clicking its file name on the Window menu. Finally, select the paste area and then click the Paste button.

When you click the **Copy button**, it copies the contents and format of the selected range and places the copy on the Office Clipboard. The **Copy command** on the Edit menu or shortcut menu works the same as the Copy button. The **Office Clipboard** allows you to collect up to twelve different items from any Office application. When you copy a second item, the **Clipboard toolbar** displays with icons representing the different items copied to the Office Clipboard. You also can display the Clipboard toolbar by clicking View on the menu bar, pointing to Toolbars, and clicking Clipboard.

The **Paste button** copies the newest item on the Office Clipboard to the paste area. The **Paste command** on the Edit menu or shortcut menu works the same as the Paste button. If you want to copy an older item on the Office Clipboard, click the icon representing the item on the Clipboard toolbar. When you are copying the most recently copied item to more than one nonadjacent cell or range, use the Paste button. When you are copying to a single cell or range, complete the copy by pressing the ENTER key.

Steps To Copy a Range of Cells to a Nonadjacent Paste Area

Double-click the move handle on the Standard toolbar to display it in its entirety. Select the range A7:A12 and then click the Copy button on the Standard toolbar. Click cell A17, the top cell in the paste area.

Excel surrounds the range A7:A12 with a marquee when you click the Copy button (Figure 3-12). Excel also copies the values and formats of the range A7:A12 onto the Office Clipboard.

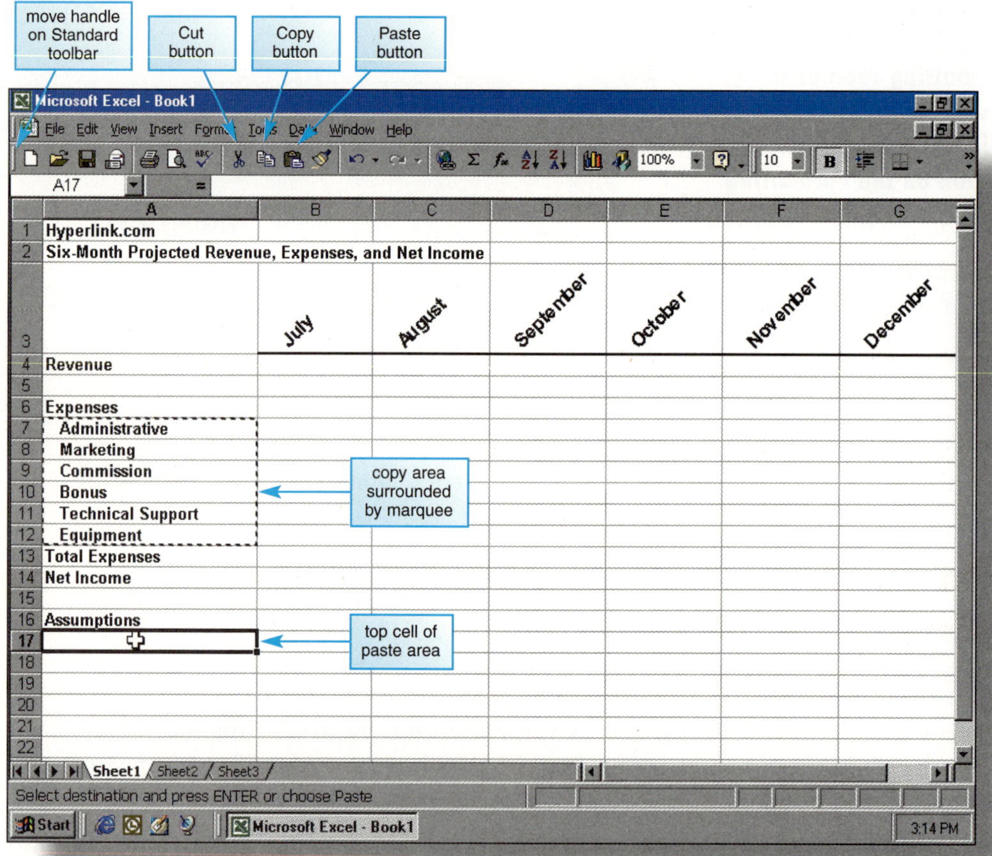

FIGURE 3-12

Press the ENTER key to complete the copy.

Excel copies the contents of the Office Clipboard (range A7:A12) to the paste area A17:A22 (Figure 3-13).

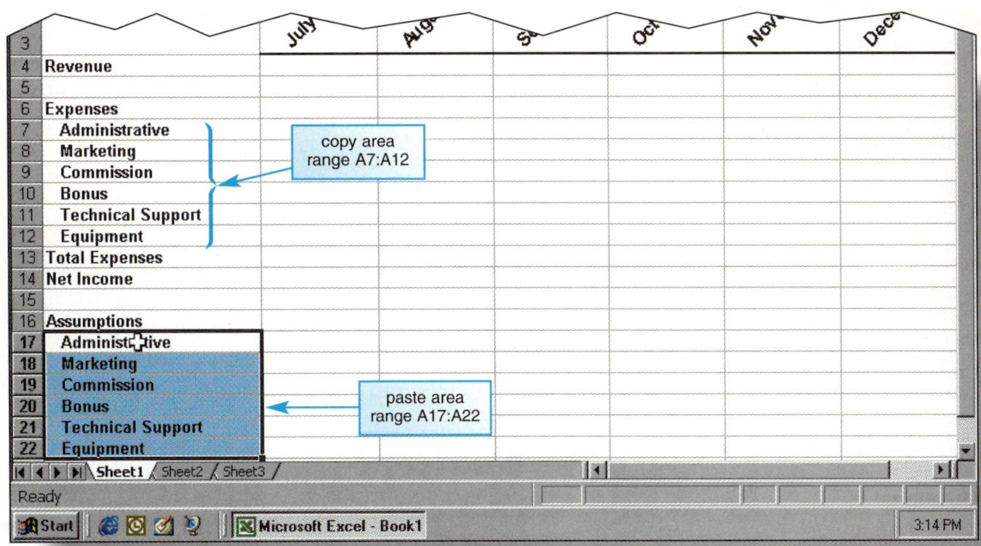

FIGURE 3-13

In Step 1 and Figure 3-12, you can see that you are not required to select the entire paste area (range A17:A22) before pressing the ENTER key to complete the copy. Because the paste area is exactly the same size as the range you are copying, you have to select only the top left cell of the paste area. In the case of a single column range such as A17:A22, the top cell of the paste area (cell A17) also is the upper-left cell of the paste area.

When you complete a copy, the values and formats in the paste area are replaced with the values and formats on the Office Clipboard. Any data contained in the paste area prior to the copy and paste is lost. If you accidentally delete valuable data, immediately click the Undo button on the Standard toolbar or click the **Undo Paste command** on the Edit menu to undo the paste.

When you press the ENTER key to complete a copy, the contents on the Office Clipboard are not available unless you display the Clipboard toolbar. When you paste using the Paste button or the Paste command on the Edit menu or shortcut menu, the contents of the Office Clipboard remain available for additional copying via the Paste button or Paste command. Hence, if you plan to copy the cells to more than one paste area, click the Paste button or click Paste on the Edit menu or shortcut menu instead of pressing the ENTER key. Then, select the next paste area and invoke the Paste command again. If you paste using the Paste button or the Paste command on the Edit menu or shortcut menu, the marquee remains around the copied range to remind you that this range is still on the Office Clipboard. To remove the marquee, press the ESC key.

Using Drag and Drop to Move or Copy Cells

You also can use the mouse to move or copy cells. First, you select the copy area and point to the border of the cell or range. You know you are pointing to the border of the cell or range when the mouse pointer changes to a **block arrow**. To move the selected cell or cells, drag the selection to its new location. To copy a selection, hold down the CTRL key while dragging the selection to its new location. Be sure to release the mouse button before you release the CTRL key. Using the mouse to move or copy cells is called **drag and drop**.

Other Ways

1. Select copy area and point to border of range; while holding down CTRL key, drag copy area to paste area
2. Right-click copy area, click Copy on shortcut menu, right-click paste area, click Paste
3. Select copy area, on Edit menu click Copy, select paste area, on Edit menu click Paste
4. Select copy area, press CTRL+C, select paste area, press CTRL+V

Copying versus Moving

You may hear someone say, "move it or copy it, it is all the same." No, it is not the same! When you move cells, the original location is blanked and the format is reset to the default. When you copy cells, the copy area remains intact. In short, copy cells to duplicate and move cells to rearrange.

Using the Cut Command

When you cut a cell or range of cells using the Cut command or Cut button on the Standard toolbar, it is copied to the Office Clipboard. It is not removed from the worksheet until you paste it in its new location by clicking the Paste button or pressing the ENTER key.

Another way to move cells is to select them, click the Cut button on the Standard toolbar (Figure 3-12 on page E 3.14) to remove them from the worksheet and copy them to the Office Clipboard, select the new area, and then click the Paste button on the Standard toolbar or press the ENTER key. You also can use the Cut command on the Edit menu or shortcut menu.

Inserting and Deleting Cells in a Worksheet

At any time while the worksheet is on the screen, you can insert cells to enter new data or delete cells to remove unwanted data. You can insert or delete individual cells, a range of cells, entire rows, entire columns, or entire worksheets.

Inserting Rows

The **Rows command** on the Insert menu or the **Insert command** on the shortcut menu allows you to insert rows between rows that already contain data. In the Assumptions table at the bottom of the worksheet, a row must be inserted between rows 20 and 21 so the Revenue for Bonus assumption can be added (see Figure 3-1a on page E 3.5). The following steps show how to accomplish the task of inserting a new row into the worksheet.

To Insert Rows

1 **Right-click row heading 21 and then point to Insert on the shortcut menu.**

Row 21 is selected, and the shortcut menu displays (Figure 3-14).

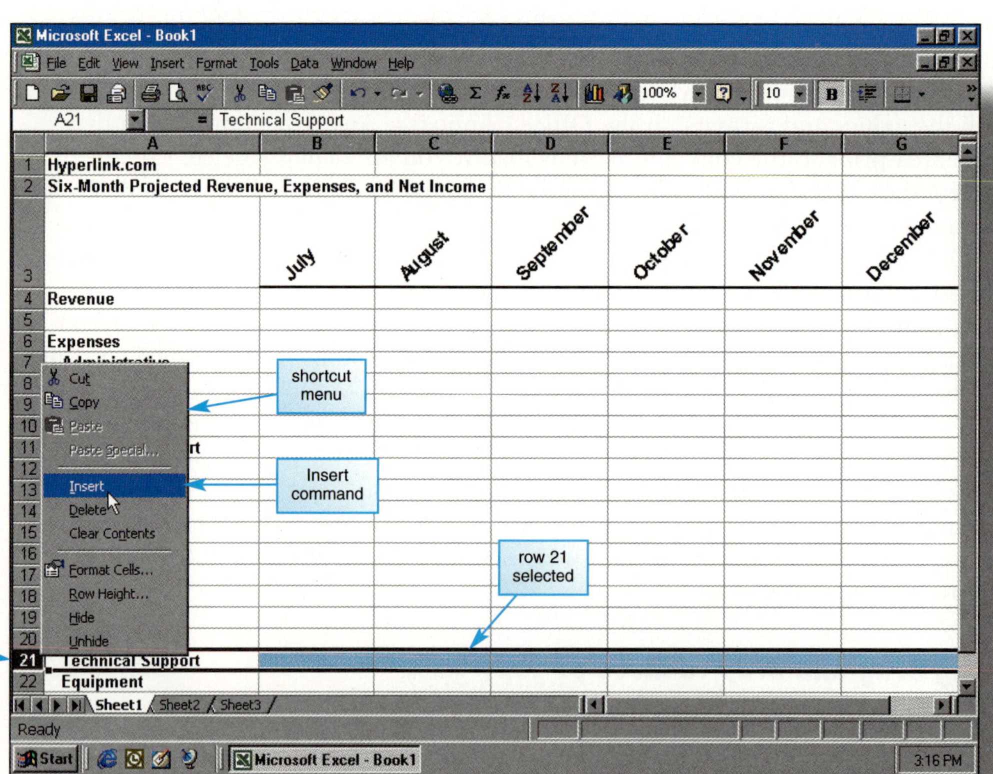

FIGURE 3-14

Click Insert. Click cell A21.

Excel inserts a new row by shifting down all rows below and including row 21, the one originally selected (Figure 3-15).

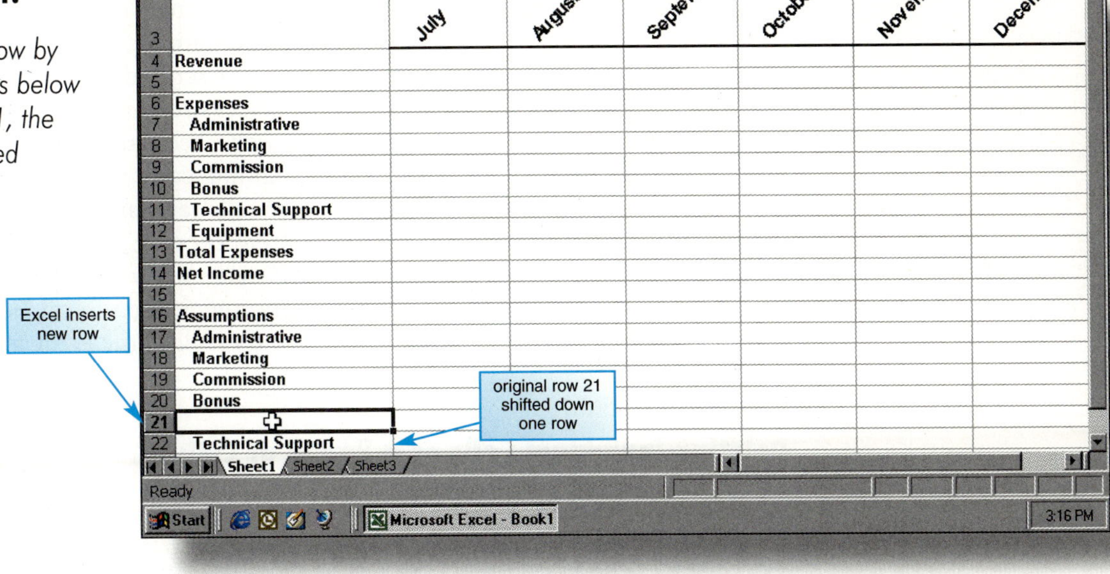

FIGURE 3-15

Other Ways

1. On the Insert menu click Rows
2. Press CTRL+SHIFT+PLUS SIGN, click Entire Row, click OK button

If the rows that are shifted down include any formulas, Excel adjusts the cell references to the new locations. Thus, if a formula in the worksheet references a cell in row 21 before the insert, then the cell reference in the formula is adjusted to row 22 after the insert.

The primary difference between the Insert command on the shortcut menu and the Rows command on the Insert menu is this: The Insert command on the shortcut menu requires that you select an entire row (or rows) in order to insert a row (or rows). The Rows command on the Insert menu requires that you select a single cell in a row to insert one row or a range of cells to insert multiple rows.

Inserting Columns

You insert columns into a worksheet in the same way you insert rows. To insert columns, begin your column selection immediately to the right of where you want Excel to insert the new blank columns. Select the number of columns you want to insert. Next, click Columns on the Insert menu or click Insert on the shortcut menu. Again, the primary difference between these two commands is this: The **Columns command** on the Insert menu requires that you select a single cell in a column to insert one column or a range of cells to insert multiple columns. The Insert command on the shortcut menu, however, requires that you select an entire column (or columns) to insert a column (or columns).

Inserting Individual Cells or a Range of Cells

The Insert command on the shortcut menu or the **Cells command** on the Insert menu allows you to insert a single cell or a range of cells. You should be aware that if you shift a single cell or a range of cells, however, they no longer may be lined up with their associated cells. To ensure that the values in the worksheet do not get out of order, it is recommended that you insert only entire rows or entire columns.

More About 2000

Moving and Inserting

You can move and insert between existing cells by holding down the SHIFT key while you drag the selection to the gridline where you want to insert. You also can copy and insert by holding down the CTRL and SHIFT keys while you drag the selection to the desired gridline.

Undo

Copying, deleting, inserting, and moving have the potential to render a worksheet useless. Carefully review these actions before continuing to the next task. If you are not sure the action is correct, click the Undo button on the Standard toolbar.

Deleting Columns and Rows

The Delete command on the Edit menu or shortcut menu removes cells (including the data and format) from the worksheet. Deleting cells is not the same as clearing cells. The Clear command, which was described earlier in Project 1 on page E 1.53, clears the data from the cells, but the cells remain in the worksheet. The **Delete command** removes the cells from the worksheet and shifts the remaining rows up (when you delete rows) or shifts the remaining columns to the left (when you delete columns). If formulas located in other cells reference cells in the deleted row or column, Excel does not adjust these cell references. Excel displays the error message **#REF!** in those cells to indicate a cell reference error. For example, if cell A7 contains the formula =A4+A5 and you delete row 5, then Excel assigns the formula =A4+#REF! to cell A6 (originally cell A7) and displays the error message #REF! in cell A6.

Deleting Individual Cells or a Range of Cells

Although Excel allows you to delete an individual cell or range of cells, you should be aware that if you shift a cell or range of cells on the worksheet, they no longer may be lined up with their associated cells. For this reason, it is recommended that you delete only entire rows or entire columns.

Entering Numbers with a Format Symbol

The next step in creating the Six-Month Projected Revenue, Expenses, and Net Income worksheet is to enter the row title, Revenue for Bonus, in cell A21 and enter the assumption values in the range B17:B23. You can enter the assumption numbers with decimal places and then format them later, as you did in Projects 1 and 2, or you can enter them with format symbols. When you enter a number with a **format symbol**, Excel immediately displays the number with the assigned format. Valid format symbols include the dollar sign ($), comma (,), and percent sign (%).

If the number entered is a whole number, then it displays without any decimal places. If the number entered with a format symbol has one or more decimal places, then Excel displays the number with two decimal places. Table 3-2 illustrates several examples of numbers entered with format symbols. The number in parentheses in column 4 indicates the number of decimal places.

Table 3-2 Numbers Entered with Format Symbols

FORMAT SYMBOL	TYPED IN FORMULA BAR	DISPLAYS IN CELL	COMPARABLE FORMAT
,	2,934	2,934	Comma (0)
	7,912.5	7,912.50	Comma (2)
$	$777	$777	Currency (0)
	$9281.12	$9,281.12	Currency (2)
	$48,103.6	$48,103.60	Currency (2)
%	32%	32%	Percent (0)
	89.2%	89.20%	Percent (2)
	16.31%	16.31%	Percent (2)

The following steps describe how to complete the entries in the Assumptions table and save an intermediate version of the workbook.

To Enter a Number with a Format Symbol

1 **Click cell A21 and enter** Revenue for Bonus **in the cell. Enter** 13.25% **in cell B17,** 9.5% **in cell B18,** 1.75% **in cell B19,** 75,000.00 **in cell B20,** 5,000,000.00 **in cell B21,** 28.75% **in cell B22, and** 31.25% **in cell B23.**

The entries display in a format based on the format symbols entered with the numbers (Figure 3-16).

2 **With a floppy disk in drive A, click the Save button on the Standard toolbar. Type** Hyperlink **in the File name text box. Click the Save in box arrow and then click 3½ Floppy (A:). Click the Save button in the Save As dialog box.**

The workbook name in the title bar changes from Book1 to Hyperlink.

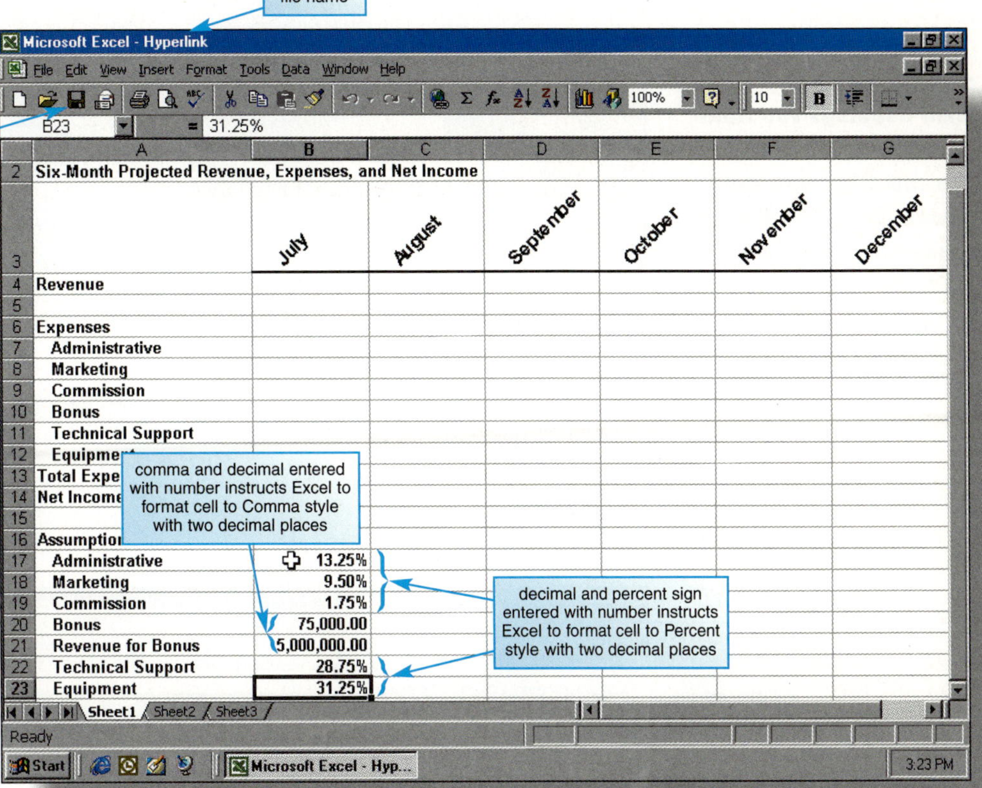

FIGURE 3-16

Other Ways

1. Enter numbers without format symbols, right-click range, click Format cells on shortcut menu
2. Enter numbers without format symbols, on Format menu click Cells

Freezing Worksheet Titles

Freezing worksheet titles is a useful technique for viewing large worksheets that extend beyond the window. For example, when you scroll down or to the right, the column titles in row 3 and the row titles in column A that define the numbers no longer display on the screen. This makes it difficult to remember what the numbers represent. To alleviate this problem, Excel allows you to freeze the titles so they display on the screen no matter how far down or to the right you scroll.

Complete the steps on the next page to freeze the worksheet title and column titles in rows 1, 2, and 3, and the row titles in column A using the **Freeze Panes command** on the **Window menu.**

To Freeze Column and Row Titles

1 **Click cell B4, the cell below the column headings you want to freeze and to the right of the row titles you want to freeze. Click Window on the menu bar and then point to Freeze Panes (Figure 3-17).**

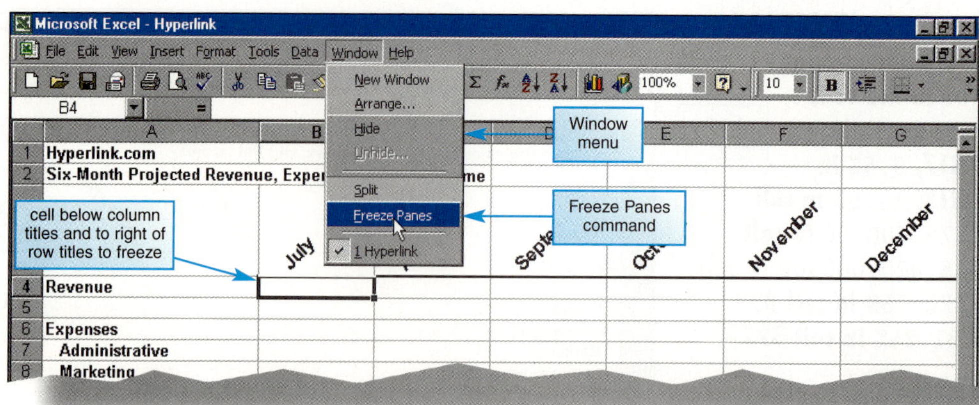

FIGURE 3-17

2 **Click Freeze Panes.**

Excel splits the window into two parts. The right border of column A changes to a thin black line indicating the split between the frozen row titles in column A and the rest of the worksheet. The bottom border of row 3 changes to a thin black line indicating the split between the frozen column titles in rows 1 through 3 and the rest of the worksheet (Figure 3-18).

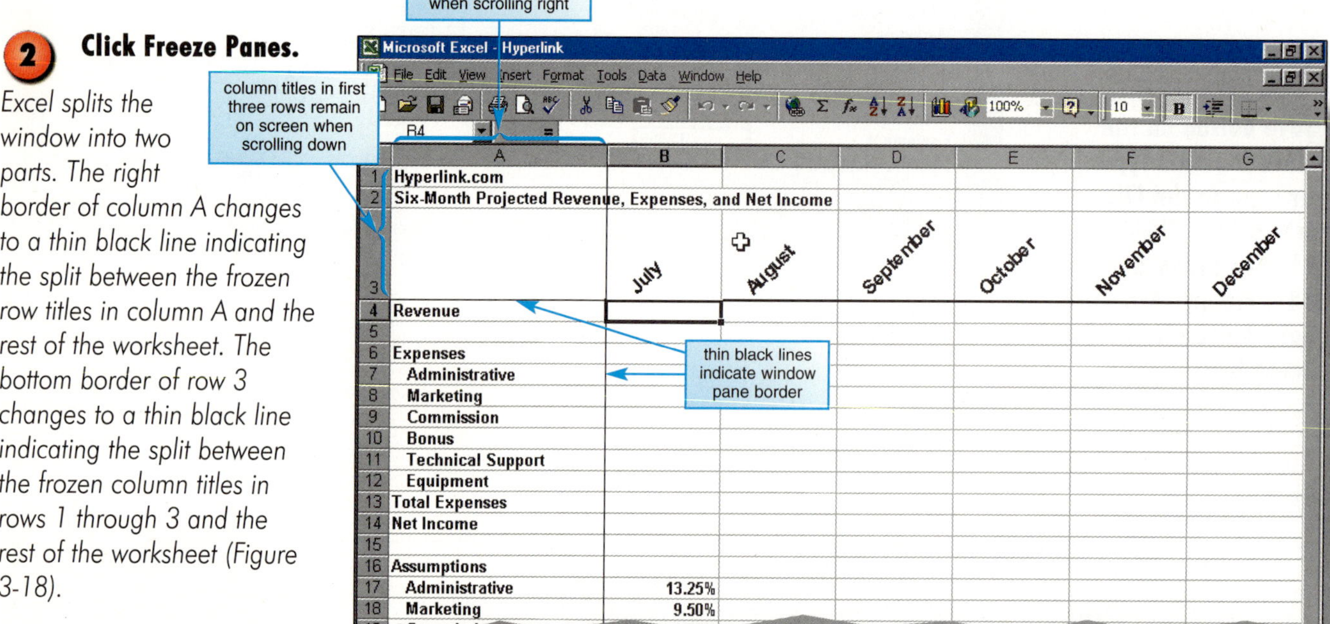

FIGURE 3-18

More About

Freezing Titles

If you want to freeze only column headings, select the appropriate cell in column A before you click Freeze Panes on the Window menu. If you only want to freeze row titles, then select the appropriate cell in row 1. To freeze both column and row titles, select the cell that is the intersection of the column and row titles.

Once frozen, the row titles in column A will remain on the screen even when you scroll to the right to display column H.

The titles remain frozen until you unfreeze them. You unfreeze the titles by clicking the **Unfreeze Panes command** on the Window menu. Later steps in this project show you how to use the Unfreeze Panes command.

Entering the Projected Revenue

The next step is to enter the projected monthly revenue and projected six-month total revenue in row 4. Enter these numbers without any format symbols as shown in the following steps.

TO ENTER THE PROJECTED REVENUE

1. Enter 8754250 in cell B4, 4978200 in cell C4, 5250000 in cell D4, 7554875 in cell E4, 4768300 in cell F4, and 6550700 in cell G4.
2. Click cell H4 and then click the AutoSum button on the Standard toolbar twice.

The projected six-month total revenue (37856325) displays in cell H4 (Figure 3-19). Columns B and C have scrolled off the screen, but column A remains because it was frozen earlier.

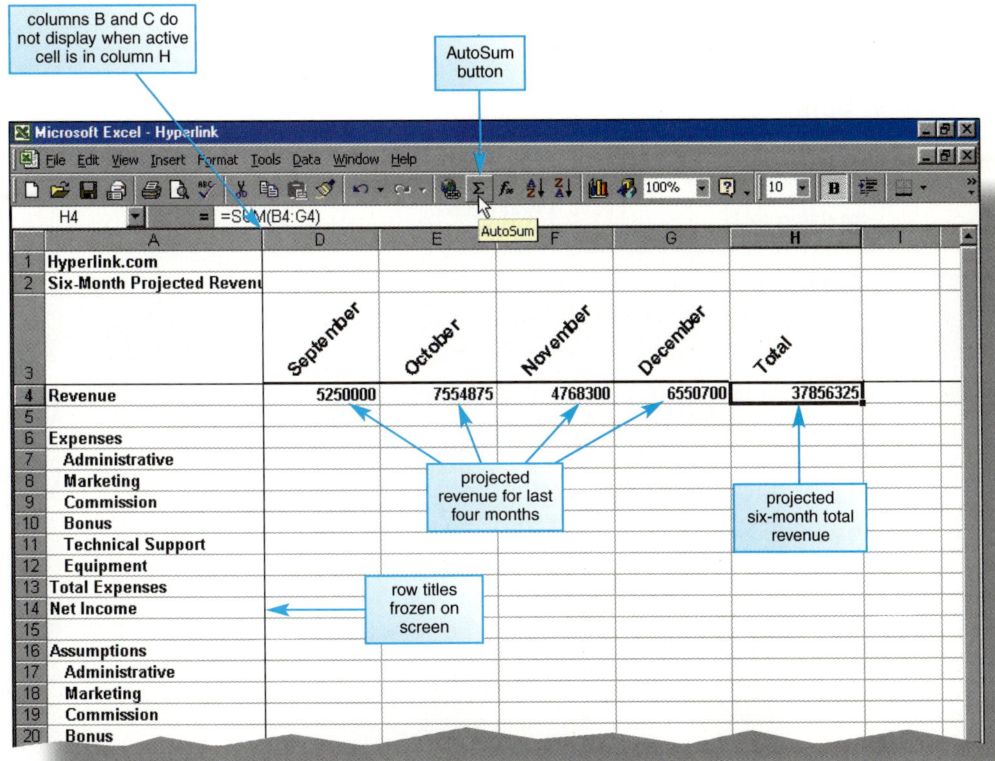

FIGURE 3-19

Range Finder

After entering a formula, verify the cells used by double-clicking the cell containing the formula. Range Finder will verify which cells you referenced by drawing colored outlines around them.

Recall from Projects 1 and 2 that if you select a single cell below or to the right of a range of numbers, then you must click the AutoSum button twice to display the sum. If you select a range of cells below or to the right of a range of numbers, then you only have to click the AutoSum button once to display the sums.

Excel's Intellisense™ Technology

When you enter a formula, Excel automatically checks for the 15 more common formula-building errors, including double operators, double parentheses, and transposed cell references. In addition, it usually offers a fix to the problem.

Displaying the System Date

The worksheet in Figure 3-1a on page E 3.5 includes a date stamp in cell H2. A **date stamp** shows the system date of which your computer keeps track. If the computer's system date is set to the current date, which normally it is, then the date stamp is equivalent to the current date.

In information processing, a report often is meaningless without a date stamp. For example, if a printout of the worksheet in this project was distributed to the company's analysts, the date stamp would show when the six-month projections were made.

To enter the system date in a cell in the worksheet, use the **NOW function**. The NOW function is one of twenty date and time functions available in Excel. When assigned to a cell, the NOW function returns a number that corresponds to the date and time for the days January 1, 1900 through December 31, 9999. Excel automatically formats the date stamp to the date and time format, m/d/yy h:mm, where the first m is the month, d is the day of the month, yy is the last two digits of the year, h is the hour of the day, and mm is the minutes past the hour.

The following steps show how to enter the NOW function and change the from m/d/yy h:mm to m/d/yyyy, where m is the month number, d is the day of the month, and yyyy is the year. With the recent turn of the century, it is recommended that you display all dates with a four-digit year.

To Enter and Format the System Date

1 Click cell H2 and then click the Paste Function button on the Standard toolbar. When the Paste Function dialog box displays, click Date & Time in the Function category list box. Scroll down in the Function name list box and then click NOW. Point to the OK button.

Excel displays an equal sign in the active cell and in the formula bar. The Paste Function dialog box displays (Figure 3-20).

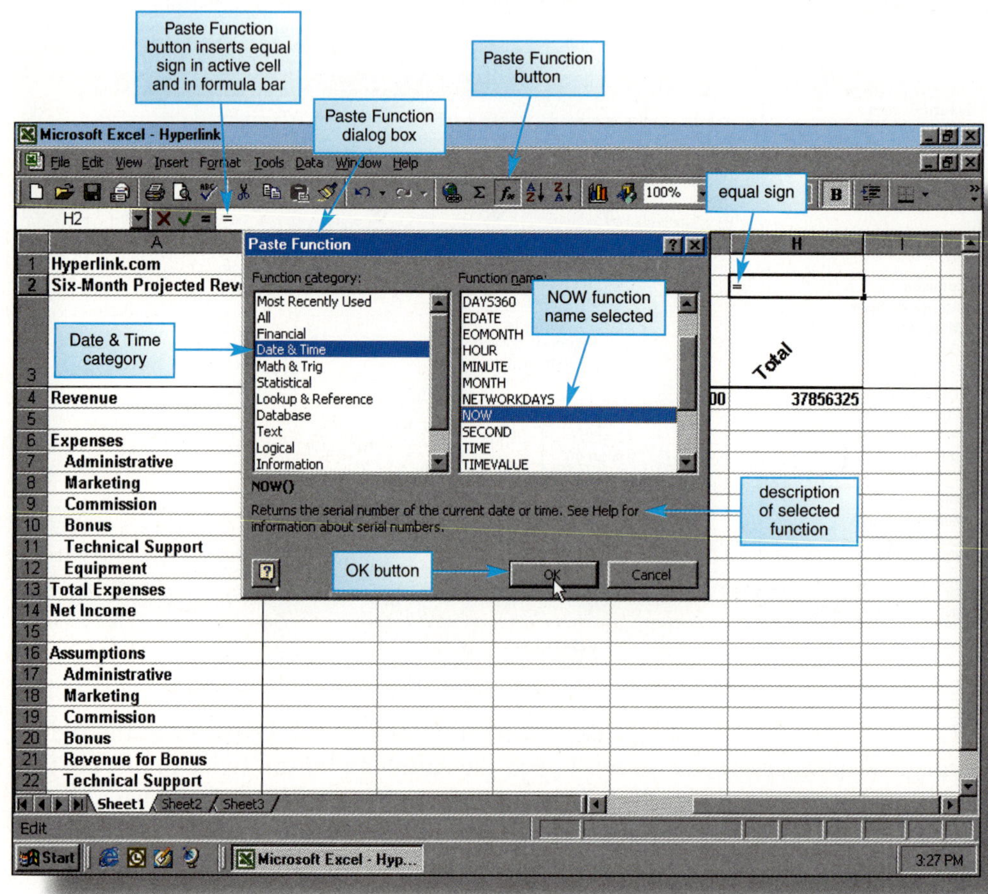

FIGURE 3-20

2 **Click the OK button. When the NOW Formula Palette displays, click the OK button. Right-click cell H2 and point to Format Cells.**

Excel displays the system date and time in cell H2 using the default date and time format m/d/yy h:mm. The date on your computer may be different. The shortcut menu displays (Figure 3-21).

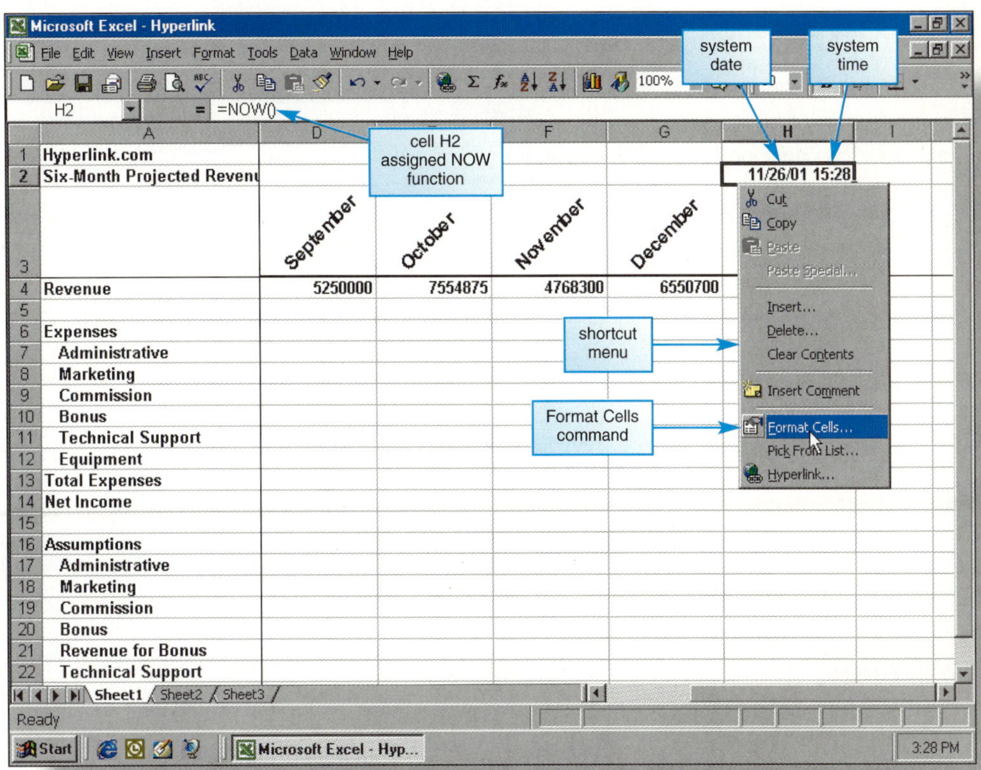

FIGURE 3-21

3 **Click Format Cells on the shortcut menu. If necessary, click the Number tab in the Format Cells dialog box. Click Date in the Category list box. Scroll down in the Type list box and then click 3/14/1998. Point to the OK button.**

Excel displays the Format Cells dialog box with Date and 3/14/1998 (m/dd/yyyy) highlighted (Figure 3-22). A sample of the format using the data in the active cell (H2) displays in the Sample area.

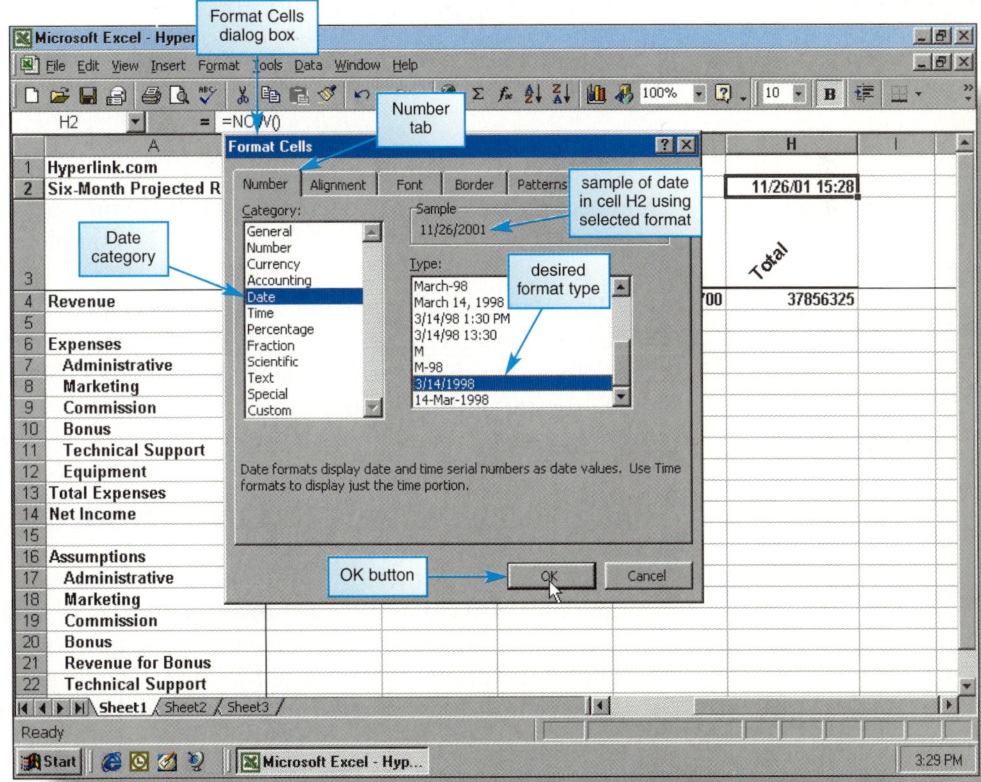

FIGURE 3-22

 **Click the OK button.**

Excel displays the system date in the form m/d/yyyy (Figure 3-23). The date on your computer may be different.

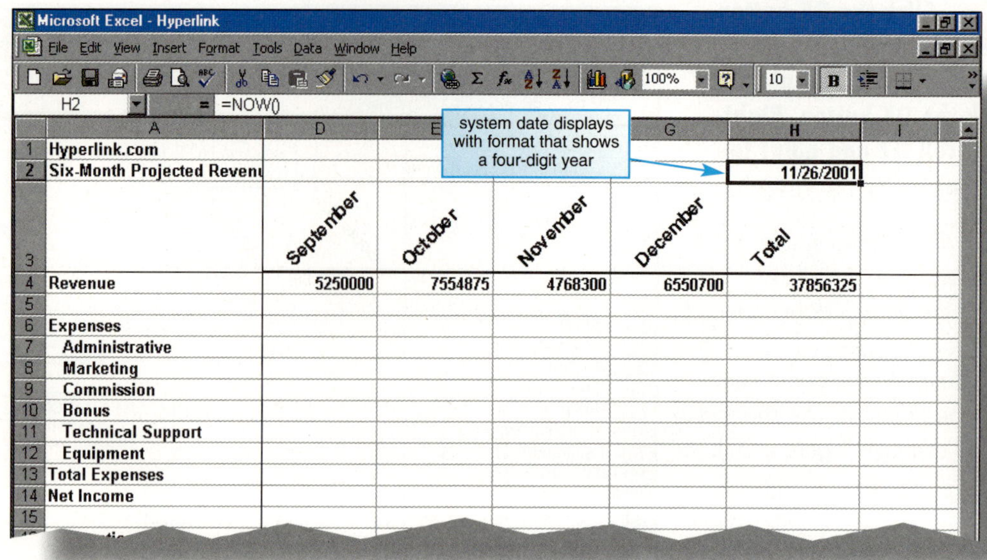

FIGURE 3-23

Other Ways

1. On Insert menu click Function, click Date & Time, click NOW, click Next button, click OK button
2. Press CTRL+SEMICOLON (not a volatile date)
3. Press CTRL+SHIFT+POUND SIGN to format date to day-month-year

In Figure 3-23, the date displays right-aligned in the cell because Excel treats a date as a number. If you assign the **General format** (Excel's preset, or default, format for numbers) to a date in a cell, the date displays as a number. For example, if the system time and date is 6:00 P.M. on June 29, 2001 and the cell containing the NOW function is assigned the General format, then Excel displays the following number in the cell:

37071.75

number of days since December 31, 1899 — time of day is 6:00 P.M. (¾ of day complete)

More About 2000

Date Manipulation

How many days have you been alive? Enter today's date (i.e., 12/5/2001) in cell A1. Next, enter your birth date (i.e., 6/22/1982) in cell A2. Select cell A3 and enter the formula =A1 - A2. Format cell A3 to the General style. Cell A3 will display the number of days you have been alive.

The whole number portion of the number (37071) represents the number of days since December 31, 1899. The decimal portion .75 represents the time of day (6:00 P.M.). To assign the General format to a cell, click General in the Category list box in the Format Cells dialog box.

Absolute Versus Relative Addressing

The next step is to enter the formulas that calculate the projected monthly expenses in the range B7:G13 and the net incomes in row 14 (Figure 3-1a on page E 3.5). The projected monthly expenses are based on the projected monthly revenue in row 4 and the assumptions in the range B17:B23. The formulas for each column are the same, except for the reference to the projected monthly revenues in row 4, which varies according to the month (B4 for July, C4 for August, and so on). Thus, the formulas can be entered for July in column B and copied to columns C through G. The formulas for determining the projected July expenses and net income in column B are shown in Table 3-3.

If you enter the formulas shown in the third column in Table 3-3 in column B for July and then copy them to columns C through G (August through December) in the worksheet, Excel will adjust the cell references for each column automatically. Thus, after the copy, the August administrative expense in cell C7 would be =C17*C4. While the cell reference C4 (August Revenue) is correct, the cell reference C17 references an empty cell. The formula for cell C7 should read =B17*C4 rather than =C17*C4. In this instance, you need a way to keep a cell reference in a formula the same when it is copied.

Table 3-3 Formulas for Determining July Expenses and Net Income

CELL	EXPENSE/INCOME	FORMULA	COMMENT
B7	Administrative	=B17 * B4	Administrative % times July Revenue
B8	Marketing	=B18 * B4	Marketing % times July Revenue
B9	Commission	=B19 * B4	Commission % times July Revenue
B10	Bonus	=IF(B4 >= B21, B20, 0)	Bonus equals value in B20 or zero
B11	Technical Support	=B22 * B4	Technical Support % times July Revenue
B12	Equipment	=B23 * B4	Equipment % times July Revenue
B13	Total Expenses	=SUM(B7:B12)	Sum of July expenses
B14	Net Income	=B4 - B13	July Revenue minus July Expenses

To keep a cell reference constant when it copies a formula or function, Excel uses a technique called **absolute referencing**. To specify an absolute reference in a formula, enter a dollar sign ($) before any column letters or row numbers you want to keep constant in formulas you plan to copy. For example, $B$17 is an absolute reference, while B17 is a relative reference. Both reference the same cell. The difference shows when they are copied. A formula using the absolute reference $B$17 instructs Excel to keep the cell reference B17 constant (absolute) as it copies the formula to a new location. A formula using the relative cell reference B17 instructs Excel to adjust the cell reference as it copies. Table 3-4 gives some additional examples of absolute references. A cell reference with only one dollar sign before either the column or the row is called a **mixed cell reference**.

Absolute Referencing

Absolute referencing is one of the more difficult worksheet concepts to understand. One point to keep in mind is that the Copy command is the only command affected by an absolute cell reference. An absolute cell reference instructs Excel to keep the same cell reference as it copies a formula from one cell to another.

Table 3-4 Additional Examples of Absolute References

CELL REFERENCE	TYPE OF REFERENCE	MEANING
$B$17	Absolute reference	Both column and row references remain the same when you copy this cell reference because they are absolute.
B$17	Mixed reference	This cell reference is mixed. The column reference changes when you copy this cell reference to another column because it is relative. The row reference does not change because it is absolute.
$B17	Mixed reference	This cell reference is mixed. The row reference changes when you copy this cell reference to another row because it is relative. The column reference does not change because it is absolute.
B17	Relative reference	Both column and row references are relative. When copied to another row and column, both the row and column in the cell reference are adjusted to reflect the new location.

Entering the July Administrative, Marketing, and Commission Formulas

The following steps show how to enter the Administrative formula (=$B$17*B4) in cell B7, the Marketing formula (=$B$18*B4) in cell B8, and the Commissions formula (=$B$19*B4) in cell B9 for the month of July using Point mode. To enter an absolute reference, you can type the dollar sign ($) or you can place the insertion point in or to the right of the cell reference you want to change to absolute and press then F4.

To Enter Formulas Containing Absolute Cell References

1 **Click cell B7. Type = (equal sign) and then click cell B17. Press F4 to change B17 to an absolute reference in the formula. Type * (asterisk) and then click cell B4.**

*The formula =$B$17*B4 displays in cell B7 and in the formula bar (Figure 3-24). A marquee surrounds cell B4.*

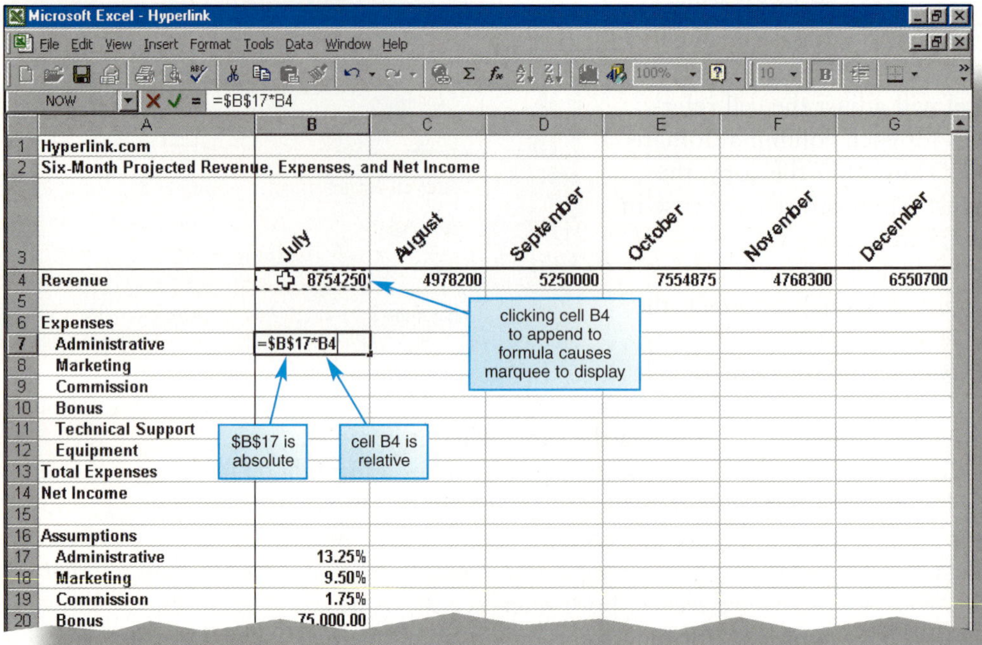

FIGURE 3-24

2 **Click the Enter box.**

3 **Click cell B8. Type = (equal sign) and then click cell B18. Press F4 to change B18 to an absolute reference in the formula. Type * (asterisk) and then click cell B4. Click the Enter box. Click cell B9. Type = (equal sign) and then click cell B19. Press F4 to change B19 to an absolute reference in the formula. Type * (asterisk) and then click cell B4. Click the Enter box.**

Excel displays the results in cells B7, B8, and B9 as shown in Figure 3-25.

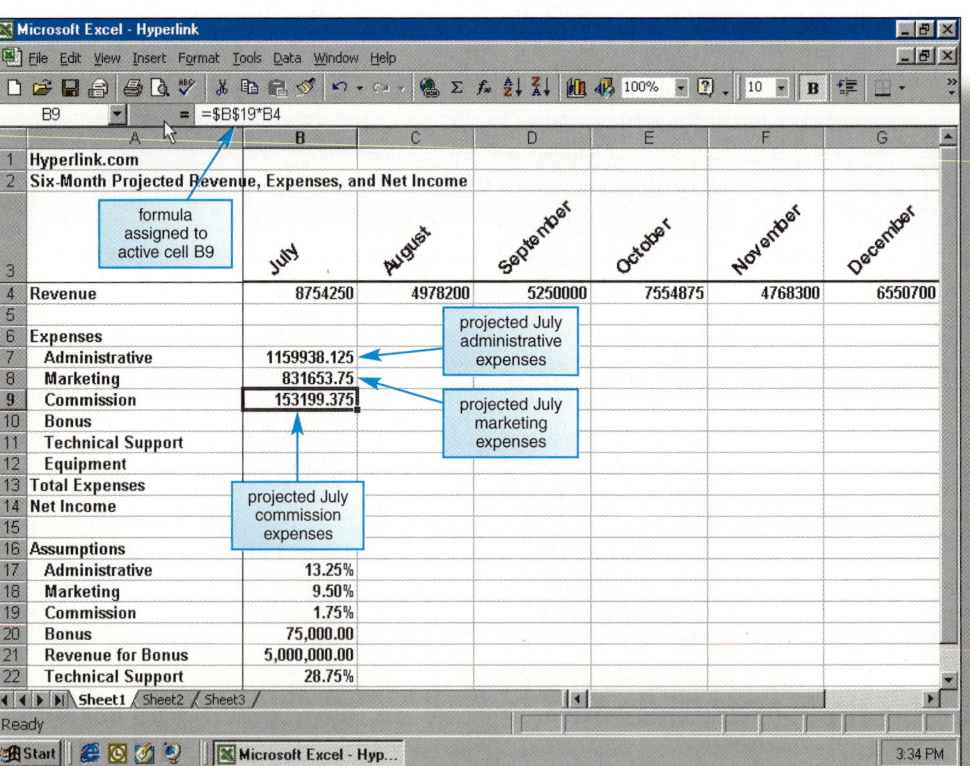

FIGURE 3-25

Other Ways

1. Enter formulas using keyboard

Making Decisions – The IF Function

If the projected July revenue in cell B4 is greater than or equal to the revenue for bonus in cell B21 (5,000,000.00), then the projected July bonus in cell B10 is equal to the amount in cell B20 (75,000.00); otherwise, cell B10 is equal to zero. One way to assign the projected monthly bonus in row 10 is to check each month individually to see if the projected revenue in row 4 equals or exceeds the revenue for bonus amount in cell B21 and, if so, then to enter 75,000.00 in row 10 for the corresponding month. Because the data in the worksheet changes each time you prepare the report or adjust the figures, however, you will find it preferable to have Excel assign the projected monthly bonus to the entries in the appropriate cells automatically. To do so, you need a formula or function in cell B10 that displays 75,000.00 or 0.00 (zero), depending on whether the projected July revenue in cell B4 is greater than or equal to or less than the number in cell B21.

The Excel **IF function** is useful when the value you want to assign to a cell is dependent on a logical test. For example, assume you assign cell B10 the IF function:

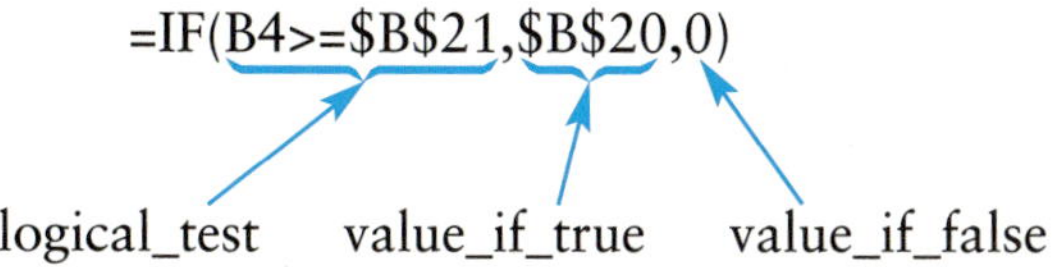

If the projected July revenue in cell B4 is greater than or equal to the value in cell B21, then the value in cell B20, 75000, displays in cell B10. If the projected July revenue in cell B4 is less than the value in cell B21, then cell B10 displays 0 (zero).

The general form of the IF function is:

=IF(logical_test, value_if_true, value_if_false)

The argument, value_if_true, is the value you want displayed in the cell when the logical test is true. The argument, value_if_false, is the value you want displayed in the cell when the logical test is false.

The leftmost entry in the general form of the IF function, **logical_test**, is made up of two expressions and a comparison operator. Each expression can be a cell reference, a number, text, a function, or a formula. Valid **comparison operators**, their meaning, and examples of their use in IF functions are shown in Table 3-5.

More About 2000

The IF Function

Assume you want to assign the formula =A4+B6 to the active cell, but display an empty cell (blank) when the formula is equal to zero. Try this: enter =IF(A4+B6 = 0, " ", A4+B6) into the cell. This IF function assigns the blank between the quotation marks to the cell when A4+B6 is equal to zero, otherwise, it assigns the formula to the cell.

Table 3-5 Comparison Operators

COMPARISON OPERATOR	*MEANING*	*EXAMPLE*
=	Equal to	=IF(A4 = G6, S12 ^ R3, J4 + K3)
<	Less than	=IF(C23 * Q2 < 534, $F$3, U23 - 3)
>	Greater than	=IF(=AVERAGE(F3:F5) > 70, 1, 0)
>=	Greater than or equal to	=IF(V4 >= $D$2, K8 * P4, 7)
<=	Less than or equal to	=IF(Y6 + H2 <= 25, $K13, 10 * L2)
<>	Not equal to	=IF(H4 <> C$3, "No", "Yes")

The steps on the next page assign the IF function =IF(B4>=$B$21,$B$20,0) to cell B10. This IF function will determine whether or not the worksheet assigns a bonus for July.

Steps To Enter an IF Function

1 Click cell B10. Type `=if(b4>=$b$21, $b$20,0` **in the cell. Click the Edit Formula box in the formula bar to display the IF Formula Palette to view the function arguments.**

The IF function displays in the formula bar and in the active cell B10. The IF Formula Palette displays that shows the logical_test, value_if_true, value_if_false, results of each part of the IF function, and the value that will be assigned to the cell based on the logical test (Figure 3-26).

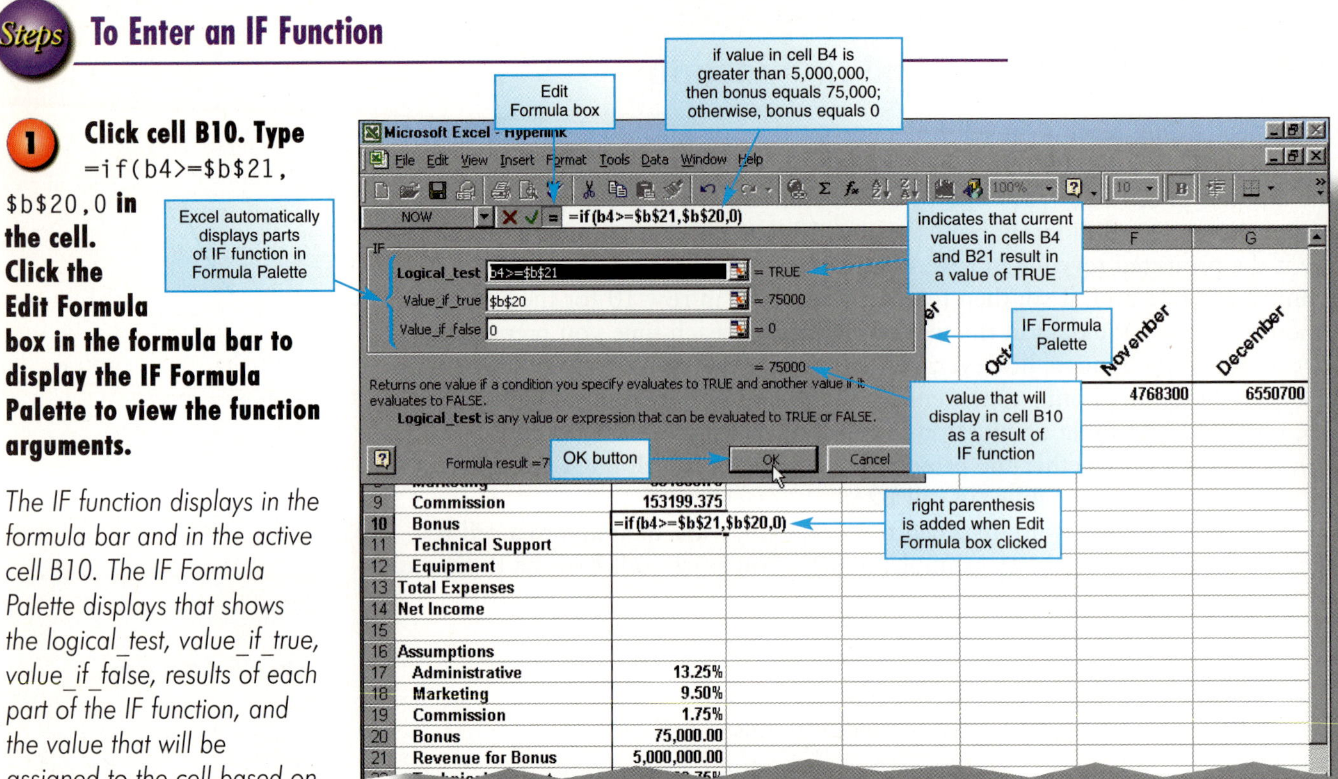

FIGURE 3-26

2 Click the OK button.

Excel displays 75000 in cell B10 because the value in cell B4 (8754250) is greater than or equal to the value in cell B21 (5,000,000.00) (Figure 3-27).

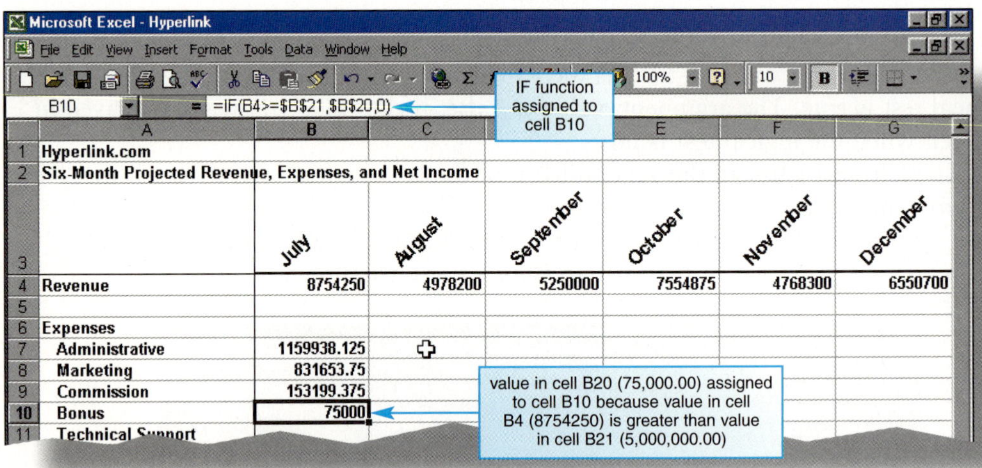

FIGURE 3-27

Other Ways

1. Click Paste Function button on Standard toolbar, click Logical category, click IF
2. Click Edit Formula box, click Functions box arrow, click IF

In Step 1, you could have clicked the Enter box or pressed the ENTER key to complete the entry rather than clicking the Edit Formula box. The Edit Formula box was clicked so you could see the IF function arguments on the IF Formula Palette before assigning the function to cell B10.

The value that Excel displays in cell B10 depends on the values assigned to cells B4, B20, and B21. For example, if the projected revenue in cell B4 is reduced below 5,000,000.00, then the IF function in cell B10 will change the display to zero. Increasing the revenue for bonus in cell B21 so that it exceeds the projected monthly revenue has the same effect.

Entering the Remaining Projected Expense and Net Income Formulas for July

The projected July technical support expense in cell B11 is equal to the technical support assumption in cell B22 (28.75%) times the projected July revenue in cell B4. Likewise, the projected July equipment expense in cell B12 is equal to the equipment assumption in cell B23 (31.25%) times the projected July revenue in cell B4. The projected total expenses for July in cell B13 is equal to the sum of the July expenses in the range B7:B12. The projected July net income in cell B14 is equal to the projected July revenue in cell B4 minus the projected July expenses in cell B13. The formulas are short and therefore they will be typed in, rather than entered using Point mode.

More About 2000

Changing a Formula to Its Result

You can replace a formula with its result so it remains constant. Do the following: (1) click the cell with the formula; (2) press F2 or click in the formula bar; (3) press F9 to display the value in the formula bar; and (4) press the ENTER key.

TO ENTER THE REMAINING PROJECTED JULY EXPENSE AND NET INCOME FORMULAS

1. Click cell B11. Type =b22*b4 and then press the DOWN ARROW key.
2. Type =b23*b4 and then press the DOWN ARROW key.
3. With cell B13 selected, click the AutoSum button on the Standard toolbar twice.
4. Click cell B14. Type =b4-b13 and then press the ENTER key.

The projected July technical support, manufacturing, total expenses, and net income display in cells B11, B12, B13, and B14, respectively (Figure 3-28a).

You can view the formulas in the worksheet by pressing CTRL+LEFT QUOTATION MARK (`). The display shown in Figure 3-28a changes to the display shown in Figure 3-28b. You can see that Excel converts all the formulas to uppercase. Press CTRL+LEFT QUOTATION MARK (`) to display the values again.

		July	August	Septe	Octobe	Novembe	Decembe
3							
4	Revenue	8754250	4978200	5250000	7554875	4768300	6550700
5							
6	Expenses						
7	Administrative	1159938.125					
8	Marketing	831653.75					
9	Commission	153199.375					
10	Bonus	75000					
11	Technical Support	2516846.875					
12	Equipment	2735703.125					
13	Total Expenses	7472341.25					
14	Net Income	1281908.75					
15							
16	Assumptions						
17	Administrative	13.25%					
18	Marketing	9.50%					
19	Commission	1.75%					
20	Bonus	75,000.00					
21	Revenue for Bonus	5,000,000.00					
22	Technical Support	28.75%					

values display

Sheet1 / Sheet2 / Sheet3 — Ready — Start — Microsoft Excel - Hyp... — 3:38 PM

(a) Values Version

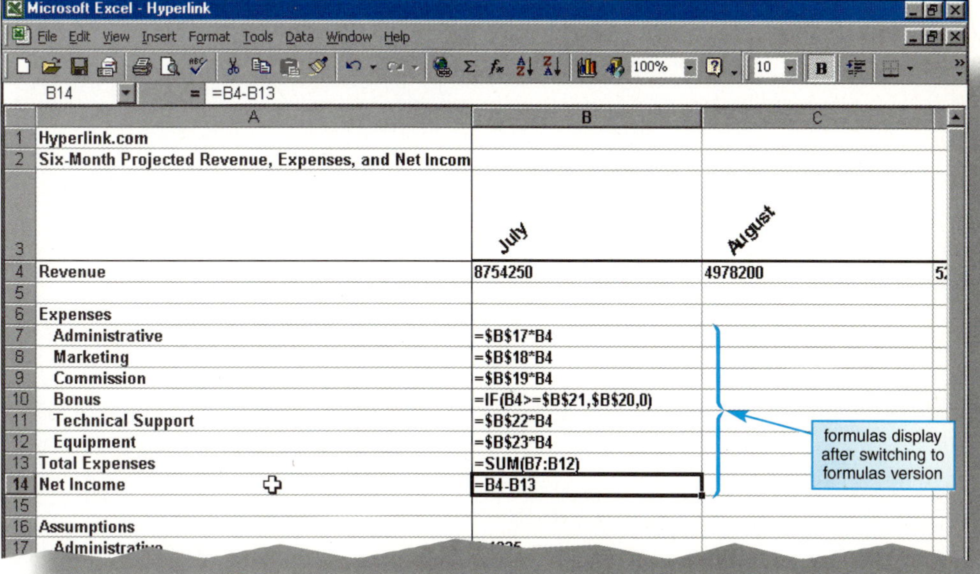

	A	B	C
1	Hyperlink.com		
2	Six-Month Projected Revenue, Expenses, and Net Incom		
3		July	August
4	Revenue	8754250	4978200
5			
6	Expenses		
7	Administrative	=$B$17*B4	
8	Marketing	=$B$18*B4	
9	Commission	=$B$19*B4	
10	Bonus	=IF(B4>=$B$21,$B$20,0)	
11	Technical Support	=$B$22*B4	
12	Equipment	=$B$23*B4	
13	Total Expenses	=SUM(B7:B12)	
14	Net Income	=B4-B13	
15			
16	Assumptions		
17	Administrative		

(b) Formulas Version

FIGURE 3-28

Copying the Projected July Expenses and Net Income Formulas to the Other Months

To copy the projected expenses and totals for July to the other five months, complete the following steps using the fill handle.

To Copy the Projected July Expenses and Net Income Using the Fill Handle

1 Select the range B7:B14. Point to the fill handle in the lower-right corner of cell B14.

The range B7:B14 is selected and the mouse pointer changes to a cross hair (Figure 3-29).

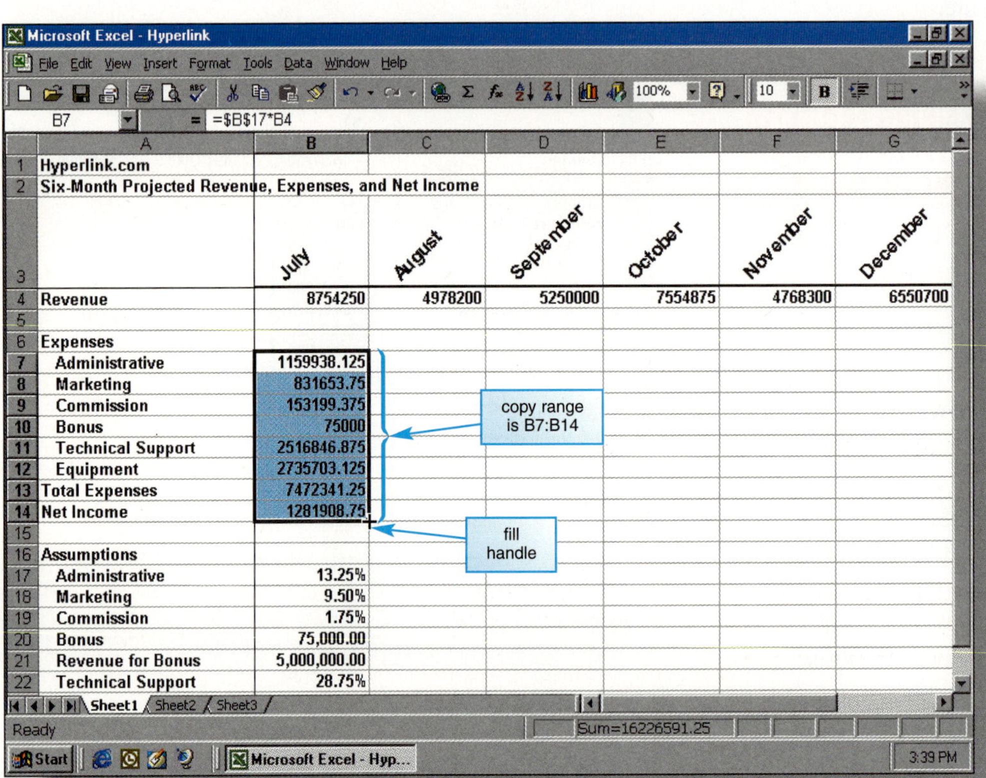

FIGURE 3-29

2 Drag the fill handle to select the paste area range C7:G14.

Excel copies the formulas in the range B7:B14 to the paste area range C7:G14 and displays the calculated amounts (Figure 3-30).

		July	August	September	October	November	December
3							
4	Revenue	8754250	4978200	5250000	7554875	4768300	6550700
5							
6	Expenses						
7	Administrative	1159938.125	659611.5	695625	1001020.938	631799.75	867967.75
8	Marketing	831653.75	472929	498750	717713.125	452988.5	622316.5
9	Commission	153199.375	87118.5	91875	132210.3125	83445.25	114637.25
10	Bonus	75000	0	75000	75000	0	75000
11	Technical Support	2516846.875	1431232.5	1509375	2172026.563	1370886.25	1883326.25
12	Equipment	2735703.125	1555687.5	1640625	2360898.438	1490093.75	2047093.75
13	Total Expenses	7472341.25	4206579	4511250	6458869.375	4029213.5	5610341.5
14	Net Income	1281908.75	771621	738750	1096005.625	739086.5	940358.5
15							
16	Assumptions						
17	Administrative	13.25%					
18	Marketing	9.50%					
19	Commission	1.75%					
20	Bonus	75,000.00					
21	Revenue for Bonus	5,000,000.00					
22	Technical Support	28.75%					

copy area range B7:B14 copied to paste area range C7:G14

projected December expenses based on projected December revenue (cell G4) and assumptions in range B17:B23

Sheet1 / Sheet2 / Sheet3 /

Ready Sum=70144919.63

Start Microsoft Excel - Hyp... 3:39 PM

FIGURE 3-30

Determining the Projected Total Expenses by Category and Total Net Income

Follow the steps below to determine the total projected expenses by category and net income in the range H7:H14.

TO DETERMINE THE PROJECTED EXPENSES BY CATEGORY AND NET INCOME

1. Select the range H7:H14.
2. Click the AutoSum button on the Standard toolbar.

The projected total expenses by category and total net income display in the range H7:H14 (Figure 3-31).

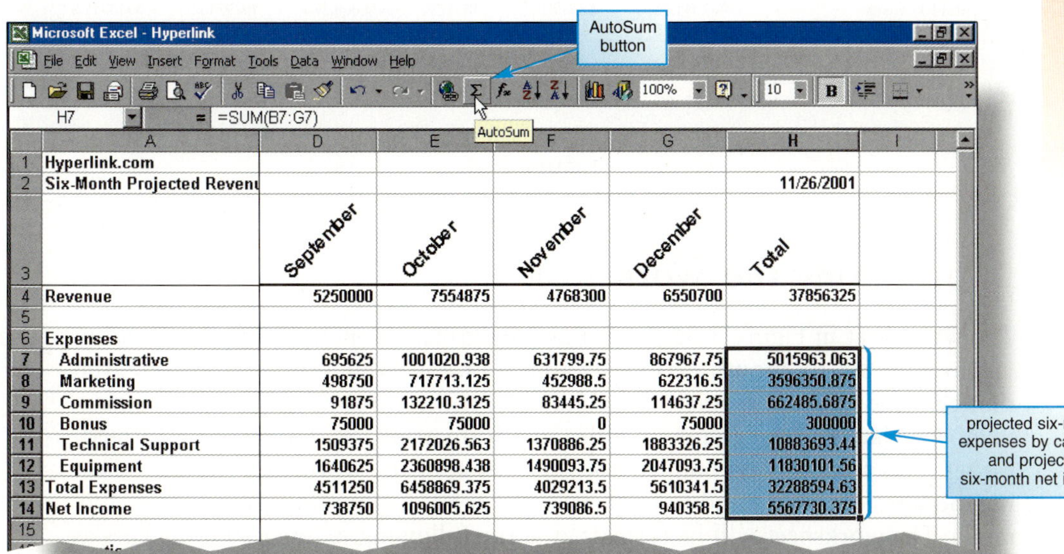

	A	D	E	F	G	H
1	Hyperlink.com					
2	Six-Month Projected Revenu					11/26/2001
3		September	October	November	December	Total
4	Revenue	5250000	7554875	4768300	6550700	37856325
5						
6	Expenses					
7	Administrative	695625	1001020.938	631799.75	867967.75	5015963.063
8	Marketing	498750	717713.125	452988.5	622316.5	3596350.875
9	Commission	91875	132210.3125	83445.25	114637.25	662485.6875
10	Bonus	75000	75000	0	75000	300000
11	Technical Support	1509375	2172026.563	1370886.25	1883326.25	10883693.44
12	Equipment	1640625	2360898.438	1490093.75	2047093.75	11830101.56
13	Total Expenses	4511250	6458869.375	4029213.5	5610341.5	32288594.63
14	Net Income	738750	1096005.625	739086.5	940358.5	5567730.375
15						

FIGURE 3-31

Error Values

Excel displays an error value in a cell when it cannot calculate the formula. Error values always begin with a number sign #. The more common occurring error values are: #DIV/0! (trying to divide by zero); #NAME? (use of a name Excel does not recognize); #N/A (refers to a value not available); #NULL! (specifies an invalid intersection of two areas); #NUM! (uses a number incorrectly); #REF (refers to a cell that is not valid); #VALUE! (uses an incorrect argument or operand); and ##### (cell not wide enough).

Unfreezing Worksheet Titles and Saving the Workbook

All the text, data, and formulas have been entered into the worksheet. The next step is to improve the appearance of the worksheet. Before modifying the worksheet's appearance, complete the following steps to unfreeze the titles and save the workbook under its current file name, Hyperlink.

Menu Commands

Many of the commands on the menus are toggle commands. For example, if you invoke the Freeze Panes command, the command changes to Unfreeze Panes the next time you display the Windows menu. These types of commands work like an on-off switch, or toggle.

TO UNFREEZE THE WORKSHEET TITLES AND SAVE THE WORKBOOK

1. Click cell B4 to clear the range selection from the previous steps.
2. Click Window on the menu bar and then point to Unfreeze Panes (Figure 3-32).
3. Click Unfreeze Panes.
4. Click the Save button on the Standard toolbar.

Excel unfreezes the titles so that column A scrolls off the screen when you scroll to the right and the first three rows scroll off the screen when you scroll down. The latest changes to the workbook are saved on disk using the file name Hyperlink.

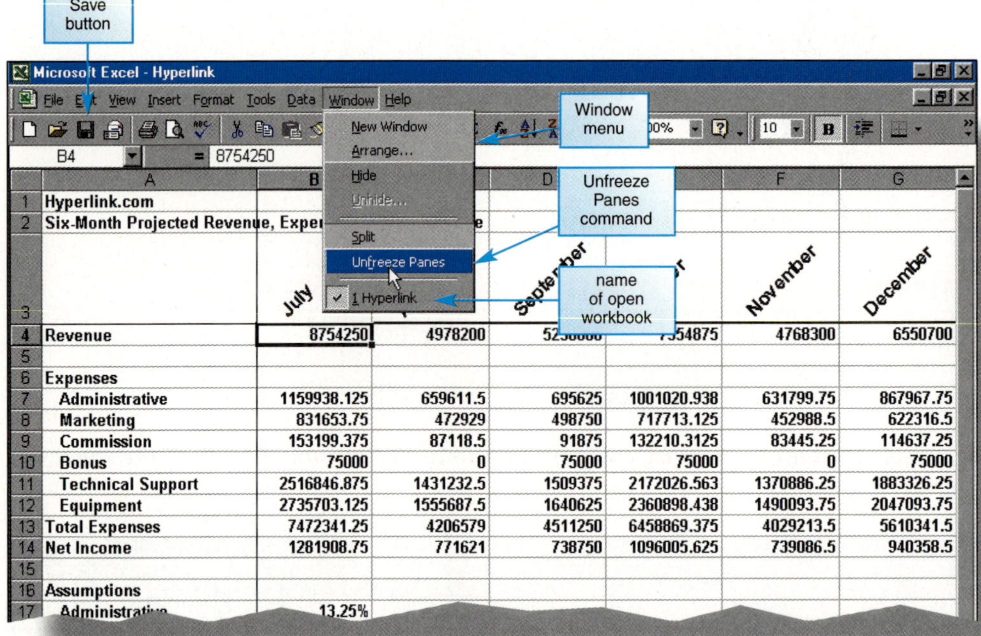

FIGURE 3-32

Formatting the Worksheet

The worksheet in Figure 3-32 determines the projected monthly expenses and net incomes for the six-month period. Its appearance is uninteresting, however, even though some minimal formatting (bolding worksheet, formatting assumptions' numbers, changing the column widths, and formatting the date) was performed earlier. This section will complete the formatting of the worksheet to make the numbers easier to read and to emphasize the titles, assumptions, categories, and totals. The worksheet will be formatted in the following manner so it appears as shown in Figure 3-33: (1) format the numbers; (2) format the worksheet title, column title, row titles, and net income row; and (3) format the assumptions table.

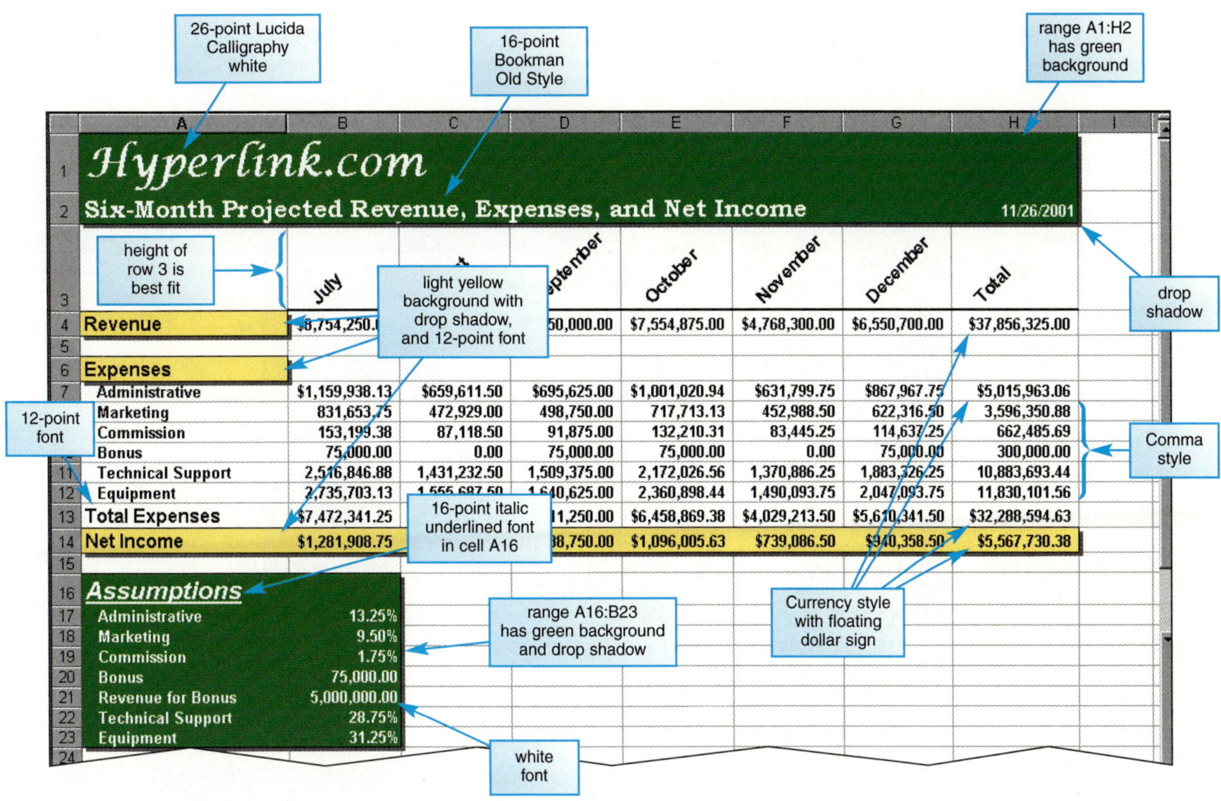

FIGURE 3-33

Formatting the Numbers

Format the projected monthly revenue and expenses in the range B4:H13 as follows:

1. Assign the Currency style with a floating dollar sign to rows 4, 7, 13, and 14.
2. Assign a customized Comma style to rows 8 through 12.

To assign a Currency style with a floating dollar sign, you must use the **Format Cells command** rather than the Currency Style button on the Formatting toolbar, which assigns a fixed dollar sign. The Comma style also must be assigned using the Format Cells command, because the Comma Style button on the Formatting toolbar displays a dash (-) when a cell has a value of zero. The specifications for this worksheet call for displaying a value of zero as 0.00 (see cell C10 in Figure 3-33), rather than as a dash. To create a Comma style using the Format Cells command, you can assign a Currency style with no dollar sign. The steps on the next two pages format the numbers in rows 4 and 7 through 14.

Number Formats

To view all the number formats available with Excel, click Custom in the Category list in the Number tab of the Format Cells dialog box.

To Assign Formats to the Projected Revenue, Expenses, and Net Income

1 Select the range B4:H4. While holding down the CTRL key, select the nonadjacent ranges B7:H7 and B13:H14. Use the horizontal scroll button to display cells to select, if necessary. Release the CTRL key. Right-click the selected range and then point to Format Cells on the shortcut menu.

Excel highlights the selected nonadjacent ranges and the shortcut menu displays as shown in Figure 3-34.

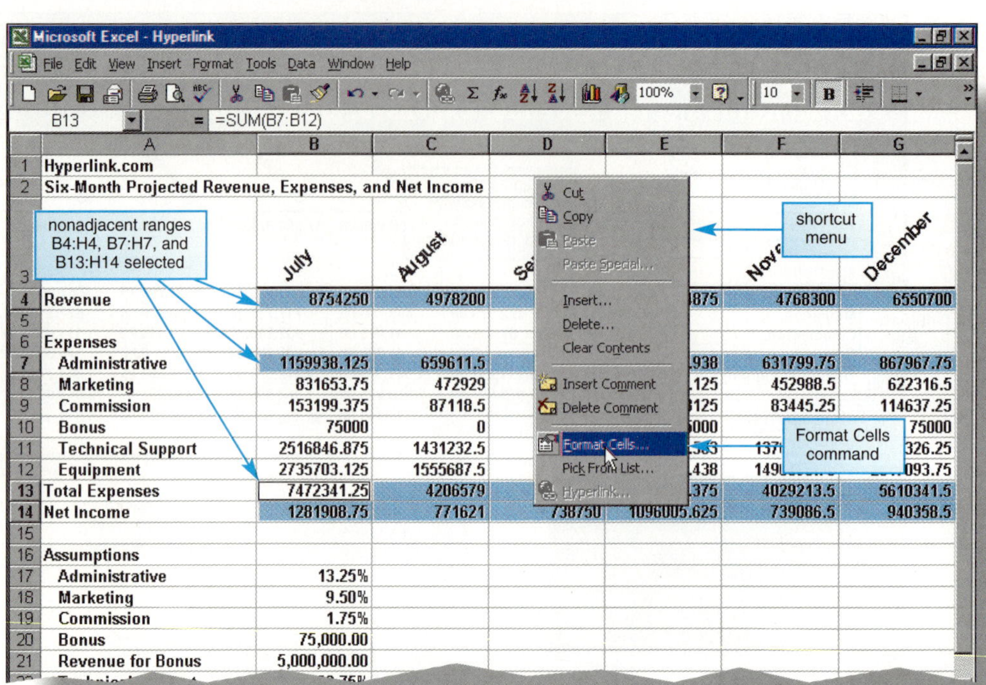

FIGURE 3-34

2 Click Format Cells. When the Format Cells dialog box displays, click the Number tab, click Currency in the Category list, select 2 in the Decimal places box, click $ in the Symbol list to ensure a dollar sign displays, and click ($1,234.10) in the Negative numbers list. Point to the OK button.

The cell format settings display in the Number sheet of the Format Cells dialog box (Figure 3-35).

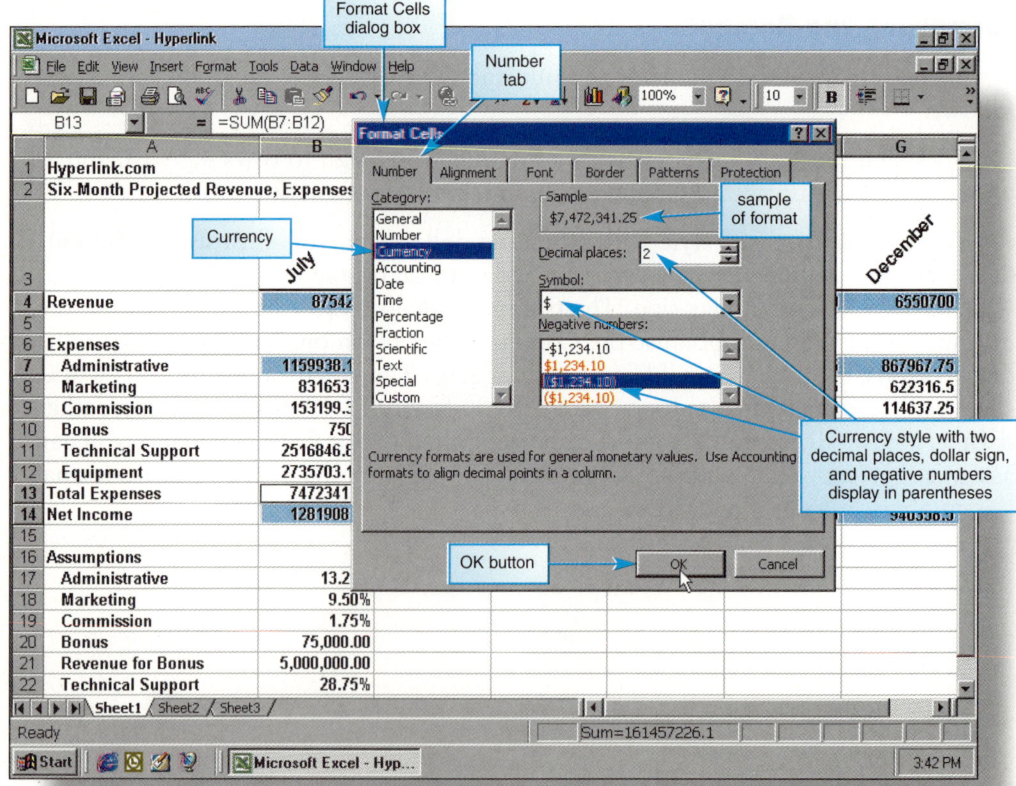

FIGURE 3-35

3 **Click the OK button. Select the range B8:H12. Right-click the selected range. Click Format Cells on the shortcut menu. Click Currency in the Category list, click 2 in the Decimal places box, click None in the Symbol list so a dollar sign does not display, click (1,234.10) in the Negative numbers list. Point to the OK button.**

The format settings display in the Format Cells dialog box as shown in Figure 3-36.

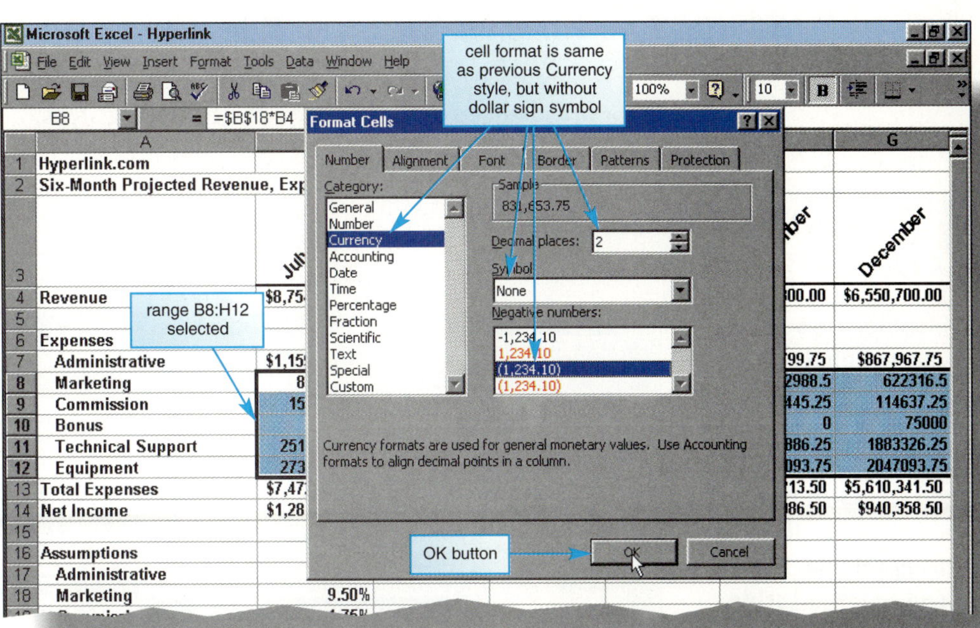

FIGURE 3-36

4 **Click the OK button. Select cell A1 to deselect the range B8:H12.**

The cell formats display as shown in Figure 3-37.

Microsoft Excel - Hyperlink

	A	B	C	D	E	F	G
1	Hyperlink.com						
2	Six-Month Projected Revenue, Expenses, and Net Income						
3		July	August	September	October	November	December
4	Revenue	$8,754,250.00	$4,978,200.00	$5,250,000.00	$7,554,875.00	$4,768,300.00	$6,550,700.00
5							
6	Expenses						
7	Administrative	$1,159,938.13	$659,611.50	$695,625.00	$1,001,020.94	$631,799.75	$867,967.75
8	Marketing	831,653.75	472,929.00	498,750.00	717,713.13	452,988.50	622,316.50
9	Commission	153,199.38	87,118.50	91,875.00	132,210.31	83,445.25	114,637.25
10	Bonus	75,000.00	0.00	75,000.00	75,000.00	0.00	75,000.00
11	Technical Support	2,516,846.88	1,431,232.50	1,509,375.00	2,172,026.56	1,370,886.25	1,883,326.25
12	Equipment	2,735,703.13	1,555,687.50	1,640,625.00	2,360,898.44	1,490,093.75	2,047,093.75
13	Total Expenses	$7,472,341.25	$4,206,579.00	$4,511,250.00	$6,458,869.38	$4,029,213.50	$5,610,341.50
14	Net Income	$1,281,908.75	$771,621.00	$738,750.00	$1,096,005.63	$739,086.50	$940,358.50
15							

FIGURE 3-37

In accounting, negative numbers often are displayed with parentheses surrounding the value rather than with a negative sign preceding the value. Thus, in Step 3 the format (1,234.10) in the Negative numbers list box was clicked. With the data being used in this project there are no negative numbers. You must, however, select a format for negative numbers and you must be consistent if you are choosing different formats in a column or the decimal points may not line up.

Instead of selecting Currency in the Category list in Step 3 (Figure 3-36), you could have selected Accounting to generate the same format. You should review the formats available below each category title. Thousands of combinations of format styles can be created using the options in the Format Cells dialog box.

Formatting the Worksheet Titles

To emphasize the worksheet titles in cells A1 and A2, the font type, size, and color are changed as described in the following steps.

To Format the Worksheet Titles

1 **Double-click the move handle on the Formatting toolbar to display it in its entirety. Click cell A1. Click the Font box arrow on the Formatting toolbar. Scroll down and point to Lucida Calligraphy (or a similar font in the Font list).**

The Font list displays as shown in Figure 3-38. The names of the fonts in the Font list display in the font style they represent, allowing you to view the style before you assign it to a cell or range of cells.

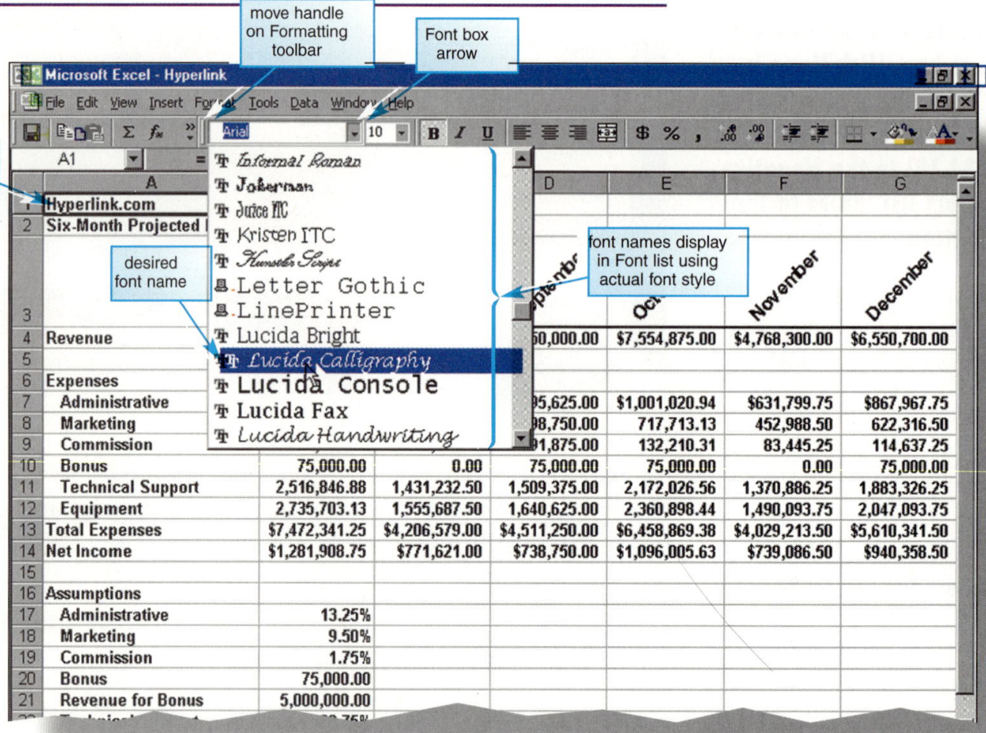

FIGURE 3-38

2 **Click Lucida Calligraphy. Click the Font Size box arrow on the Formatting toolbar and then click 26.**

3 **Click cell A2. Click the Font box arrow. Scroll down and click Bookman Old Style (or a similar font). Click the Font Size box arrow and then click 16.**

The worksheet titles in cells A1 and A2 display (Figure 3-39).

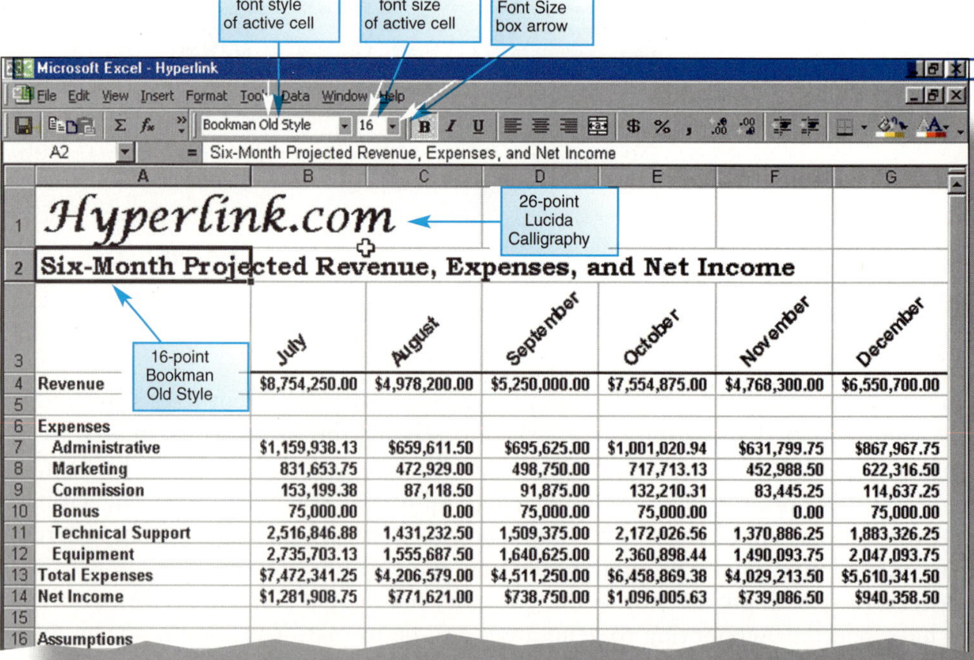

FIGURE 3-39

4 **Select the range A1:H2. Click the Fill Color button arrow on the Formatting toolbar. Click Green (column 4, row 2) on the Fill Color palette. Click the Font Color button arrow on the Formatting toolbar. Point to White (column 8, row 5) on the Font Color palette).**

Excel assigns a green background to the selected range and the Font Color palette displays (Figure 3-40).

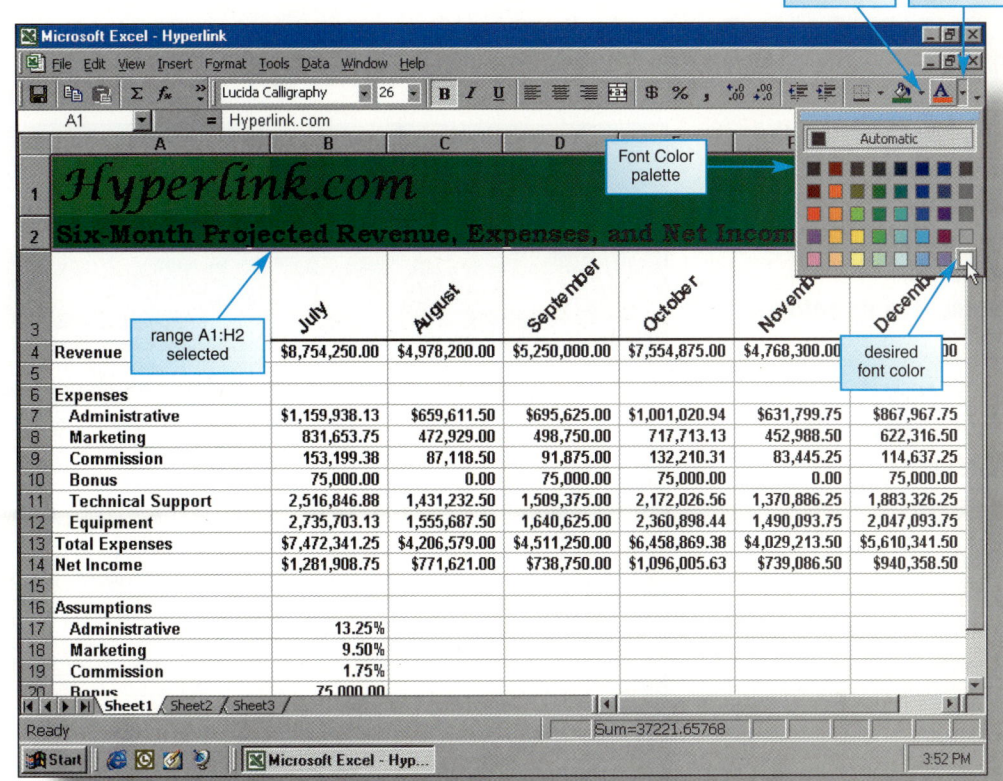

Click White.

Excel changes the color of the font in the range A1:H2 from black to white (see Figure 3-33 on page E 3.33).

Fill Color button arrow

Font Color button arrow

Microsoft Excel - Hyperlink

Font Color palette

range A1:H2 selected

desired font color

	A	B	C	D	E	F	G
1	Hyperlink.com						
2	Six-Month Projected Revenue, Expenses, and Net Incom						
3		July	August	September	October	Novemb	Decemb
4	Revenue	$8,754,250.00	$4,978,200.00	$5,250,000.00	$7,554,875.00	$4,768,300.00	00
5							
6	Expenses						
7	Administrative	$1,159,938.13	$659,611.50	$695,625.00	$1,001,020.94	$631,799.75	$867,967.75
8	Marketing	831,653.75	472,929.00	498,750.00	717,713.13	452,988.50	622,316.50
9	Commission	153,199.38	87,118.50	91,875.00	132,210.31	83,445.25	114,637.25
10	Bonus	75,000.00	0.00	75,000.00	75,000.00	0.00	75,000.00
11	Technical Support	2,516,846.88	1,431,232.50	1,509,375.00	2,172,026.56	1,370,886.25	1,883,326.25
12	Equipment	2,735,703.13	1,555,687.50	1,640,625.00	2,360,898.44	1,490,093.75	2,047,093.75
13	Total Expenses	$7,472,341.25	$4,206,579.00	$4,511,250.00	$6,458,869.38	$4,029,213.50	$5,610,341.50
14	Net Income	$1,281,908.75	$771,621.00	$738,750.00	$1,096,005.63	$739,086.50	$940,358.50
15							
16	Assumptions						
17	Administrative	13.25%					
18	Marketing	9.50%					
19	Commission	1.75%					
20	Bonus	75,000.00					

Sum=37221.65768

FIGURE 3-40

The next step is to add a drop shadow to the selected range A1:H2 using the Shadow button on the Drawing toolbar. First, the Drawing toolbar must display on the screen. The following section describes how to display and dock an inactive (hidden) toolbar.

Displaying the Drawing Toolbar

Excel has more than 200 toolbar buttons, most of which display on sixteen built-in toolbars. Two of these sixteen built-in toolbars are the Standard toolbar and Formatting toolbar, which usually display at the top of the screen. Another built-in toolbar is the Drawing toolbar. The **Drawing toolbar** provides tools that can simplify adding lines, boxes, and other geometric figures to a worksheet. You also can create customized toolbars containing the buttons that you use often.

You can use the shortcut menu or the **Toolbars command** on the View menu to display or hide any one of the sixteen toolbars. The Drawing toolbar also can be displayed or hidden by clicking the Drawing button on the Standard toolbar. Perform the steps on the next page to display the Drawing toolbar.

Other Ways

1. Right-click range, click Format cells on shortcut menu, click Patterns tab to color background or click Font tab to color font
2. On Format menu click Cells, click Patterns tab to color background or click Font tab to color font

Color Palettes

If your Color palette contains fewer colors than shown on the Color palette in Figure 3-40, then your system is using a different Color palette setting. The figures in this book were created using High Color (16 bit). To check your Color palette setting, return to the desktop, right-click the desktop, click Properties on the shortcut menu, click the Settings tab, and locate the Color palette box.

To Display the Drawing Toolbar

1 Double-click the move handle on the Standard toolbar to display it in its entirety.

2 Click the Drawing button on the Standard toolbar.

The Drawing toolbar displays (Figure 3-41). Excel displays the Drawing toolbar on the screen in the same location and with the same shape as it displayed the last time it was used.

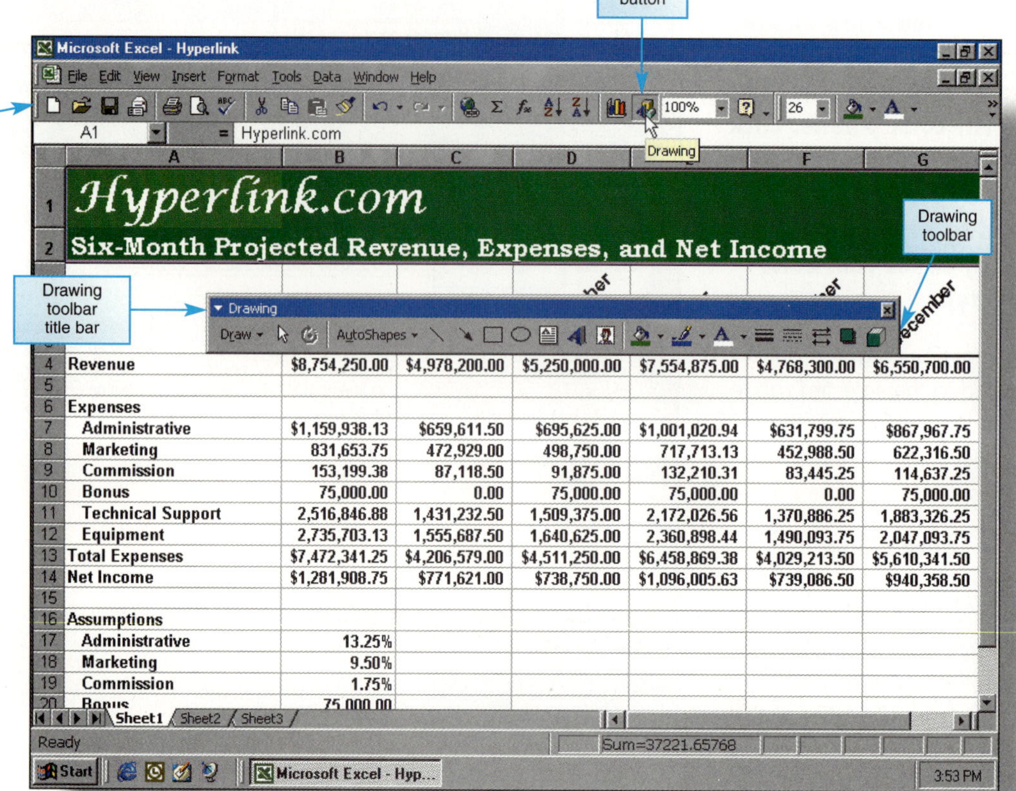

FIGURE 3-41

1. Right-click Standard or Formatting toolbar, click Drawing or shortcut menu
2. On View menu point to Toolbars, click Drawing

Moving and Docking a Toolbar

The Drawing toolbar in Figure 3-41 is called a **floating toolbar** because it displays in its own window with a title bar and can be moved anywhere in the Excel window. You move the toolbar by pointing to the toolbar title bar or to a blank area within the toolbar window (not on a button) and then dragging the toolbar to its new location. As with any window, you also can resize the toolbar by dragging the toolbar window borders. To hide a floating toolbar, click the Close button on the toolbar title bar. Sometimes a floating toolbar gets in the way no matter where you move it or how you resize it. Hiding the toolbar is one solution. At times, however, you will want to keep the toolbar available for use. For this reason, Excel allows you to position toolbars on the edge of its window. If you drag the toolbar close to the edge of the window, Excel positions the toolbar in a **toolbar dock**.

Excel has four toolbar docks, one on each of the four sides of the window. You can add as many toolbars to a dock as you want. Each time you dock a toolbar, however, the Excel window slightly decreases in size to compensate for the room taken up by the toolbar. The following steps show how to dock the Drawing toolbar at the bottom of the screen below the scroll bar.

More About 2000

Docking Toolbars

If you dock a toolbar on the left or right edge of the window that includes a box or a button with a list associated with it, the list will not be available.

To Dock a Toolbar at the Bottom of the Screen

1 **Point to the Drawing toolbar title bar or to a blank area in the Drawing toolbar.**

2 **Drag the Drawing toolbar over the status bar at the bottom of the screen.**

Excel docks the Drawing toolbar at the bottom of the screen (Figure 3-42).

8	Marketing	831,653.75	472,929.00	498,750.00	717,713.13	452,988.50	622,316.50
9	Commission	153,199.38	87,118.50	91,875.00	132,210.31	83,445.25	114,637.25
10	Bonus	75,000.00	0.00	75,000.00	75,000.00	0.00	75,000.00
11	Technical Support	2,516,846.88	1,431,232.50	1,509,375.00	2,172,026.56	1,370,886.25	1,883,326.25
12	Equipment	2,735,703.13	1,555,687.50	1,640,625.00	2,360,898.44		
13	Total Expenses	$7,472,341.25	$4,206,579.00	$4,511,250.00	$6,458,869.38		
14	Net Income	$1,281,908.75	$771,621.00	$738,750.00	$1,096,005.63		
15							
16	Assumptions						
17	Administrative	13.25%					
18	Marketing	9.50%					

Drawing toolbar docked horizontally across bottom of screen

FIGURE 3-42

Compare Figure 3-42 with Figure 3-41. Excel automatically resizes the Drawing toolbar to fit across the window and between the scroll bar and status bar. Also notice that the heavy window border that surrounded the floating toolbar has changed to a light border. To move a toolbar to any of the other three docks, drag the toolbar from its current position to the desired side of the window.

Toolbars

You can create your own toolbar and assemble the buttons you want on it by using the Customize command on the shortcut menu that displays when you right-click a toolbar.

Adding a Drop Shadow to the Title Area

With the Drawing toolbar docked at the bottom of the screen, the next step is to add the drop shadow to the range A1:H2.

To Add a Drop Shadow

1 **With the range A1:H2 selected, click the Shadow button on the Drawing toolbar. Point to Shadow Style 14 (column 2, row 4) on the Shadow palette.**

Excel displays the Shadow palette of drop shadows with varying shadow depths (Figure 3-43).

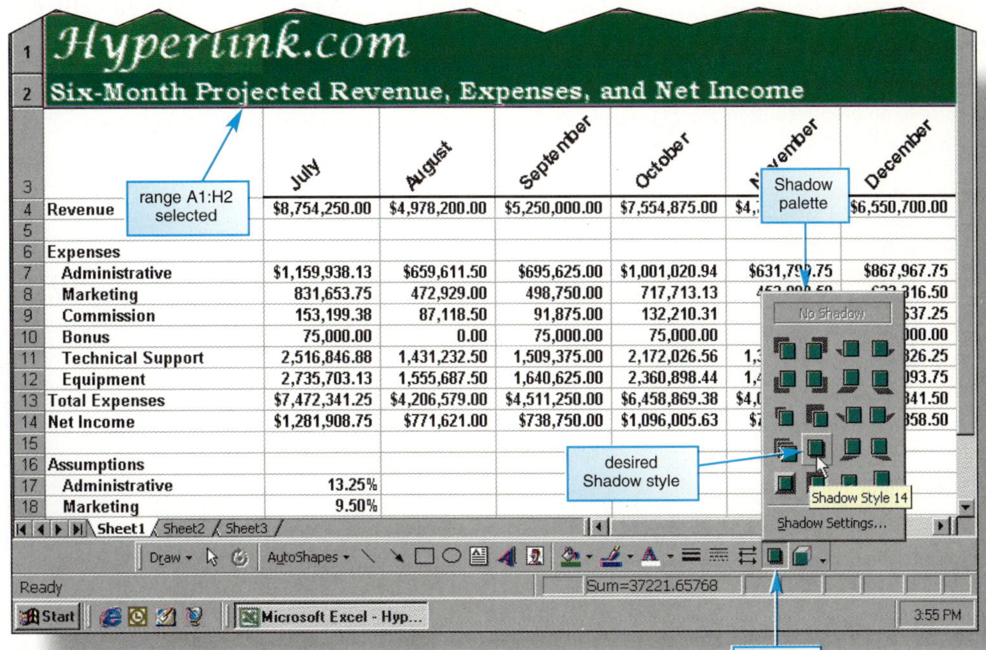

FIGURE 3-43

2 Click Shadow Style 14. Click cell A4 to deselect the range A1:H2.

Excel adds a drop shadow to the range A1:H2 (Figure 3-44).

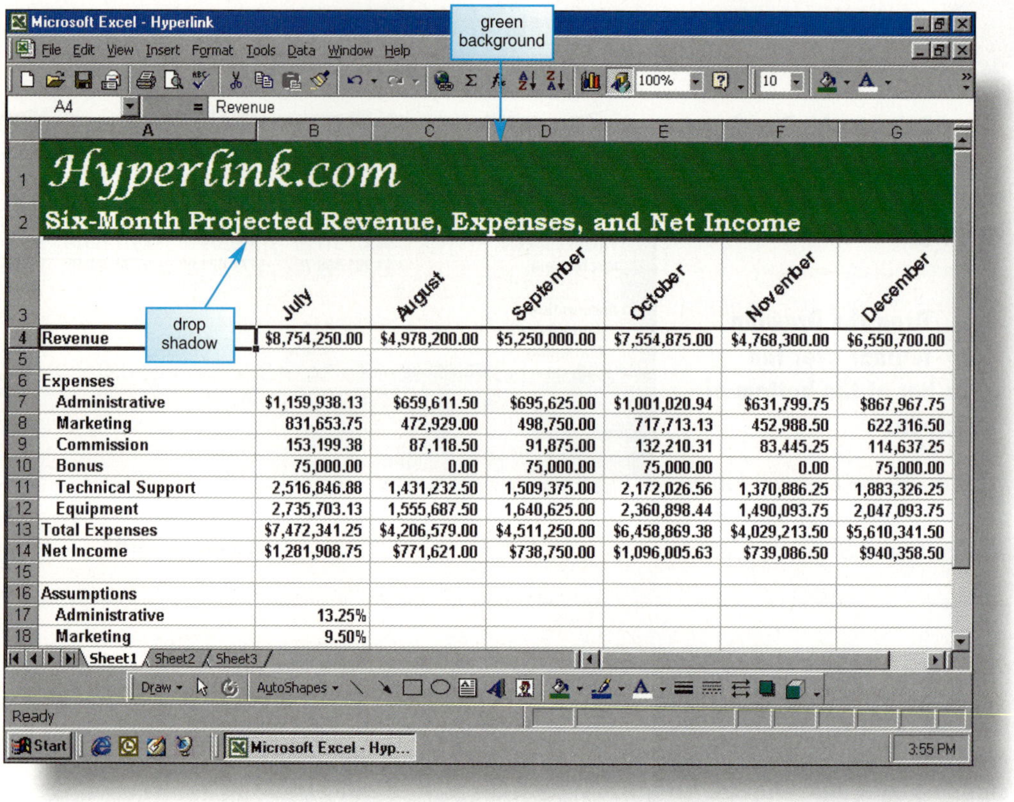

	A	B	C	D	E	F	G
3		July	August	September	October	November	December
4	Revenue	$8,754,250.00	$4,978,200.00	$5,250,000.00	$7,554,875.00	$4,768,300.00	$6,550,700.00
5							
6	Expenses						
7	Administrative	$1,159,938.13	$659,611.50	$695,625.00	$1,001,020.94	$631,799.75	$867,967.75
8	Marketing	831,653.75	472,929.00	498,750.00	717,713.13	452,988.50	622,316.50
9	Commission	153,199.38	87,118.50	91,875.00	132,210.31	83,445.25	114,637.25
10	Bonus	75,000.00	0.00	75,000.00	75,000.00	0.00	75,000.00
11	Technical Support	2,516,846.88	1,431,232.50	1,509,375.00	2,172,026.56	1,370,886.25	1,883,326.25
12	Equipment	2,735,703.13	1,555,687.50	1,640,625.00	2,360,898.44	1,490,093.75	2,047,093.75
13	Total Expenses	$7,472,341.25	$4,206,579.00	$4,511,250.00	$6,458,869.38	$4,029,213.50	$5,610,341.50
14	Net Income	$1,281,908.75	$771,621.00	$738,750.00	$1,096,005.63	$739,086.50	$940,358.50
15							
16	Assumptions						
17	Administrative	13.25%					
18	Marketing	9.50%					

FIGURE 3-44

When you add a drop shadow to a range of cells, Excel also selects the drop shadow and surrounds it with handles. To deselect the drop shadow, select any cell, as described in Step 2 above.

More About 2000

Deleting Drop Shadows

To remove an unwanted drop shadow, click it so the handles appear on the drop shadow, and then press the DELETE key. A drop shadow is a shape (object) and not a format. Thus, if you used the Format Painter button to apply formats from a range with a drop shadow, then the drop shadow will not be copied.

Formatting the Category Row Titles and Net Income Row

The following steps change the font size in cells A4, A6, A13, and A14 to 12 point; and then adds the light yellow background color and drop shadows to cells A4, A6, and the range A14:H14.

To Change Font Size, Add Background Colors, and Add Drop Shadows to Nonadjacent Selections

1 Double-click the move handle on the Formatting toolbar to display it in its entirety. With cell A4 selected, hold down the CTRL key, click cells A6, A13, and A14. Click the Font Size box arrow on the Formatting toolbar and then click 12.

The font size in cells A4, A6, A13, and A14 changes to 12 point.

2 Click cell A4. While holding down the CTRL key, click cell A6 and then select the range A14:H14. Click the Fill Color button arrow on the Formatting toolbar. Click Yellow (column 3, row 5) on the Fill Color palette. Click the Shadow button on the Drawing toolbar and point to Shadow Style 14 (column 2, row 4) in the Shadow palette.

The nonadjacent ranges are selected and the background color is changed to yellow (Figure 3-45). The Shadow palette displays.

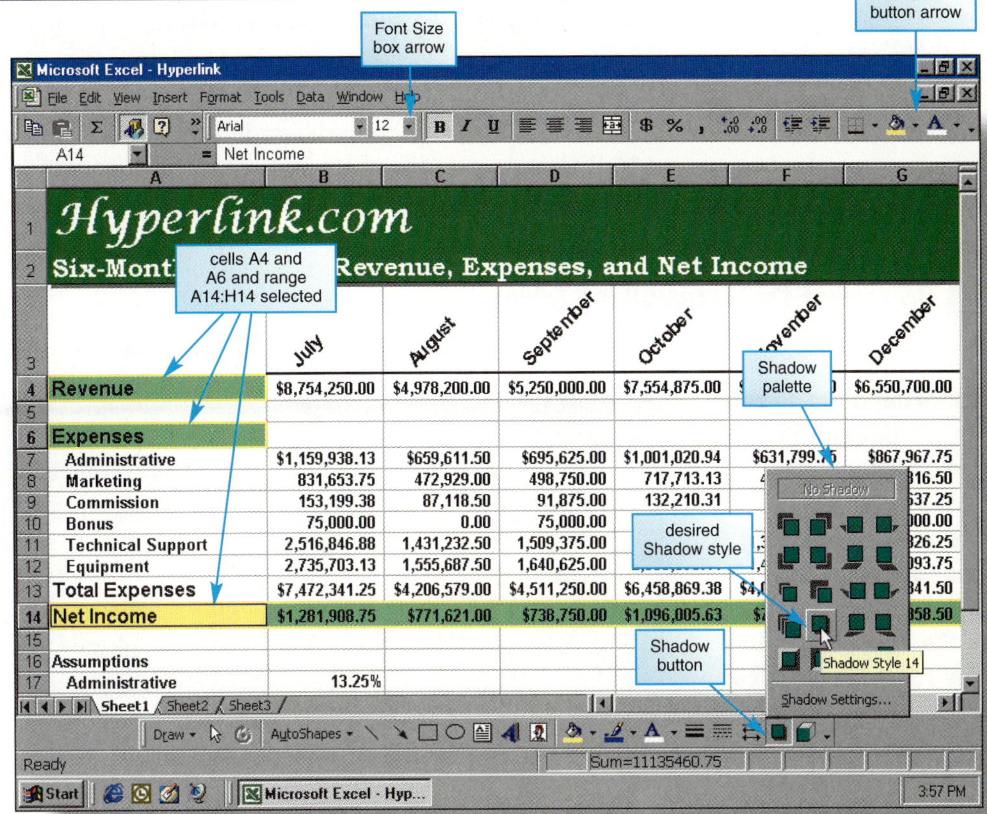

FIGURE 3-45

3 Click Shadow Style 14.

Excel adds a drop shadow to cells A4, A6, and the range A14:H14 (Figure 3-46).

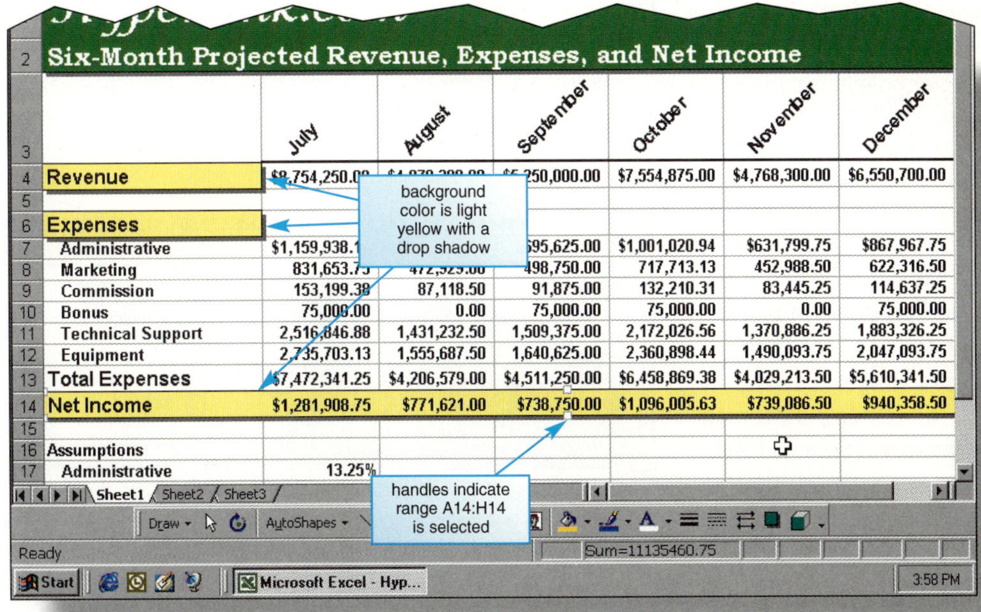

FIGURE 3-46

An alternative to formatting all three areas (cell A4, cell A6, and the range A14:H14) at once is to select each one separately and apply the formats.

Formatting the Assumptions Table

The last step to improving the appearance of the worksheet is to format the Assumptions table in the range A16:B23. The specifications in Figure 3-33 on page E 3.33 require a 16-point italic underlined font for the title in cell A16. The range A16:B23 has a green background color, white font, and a drop shadow that surrounds it. The following steps format the Assumptions table.

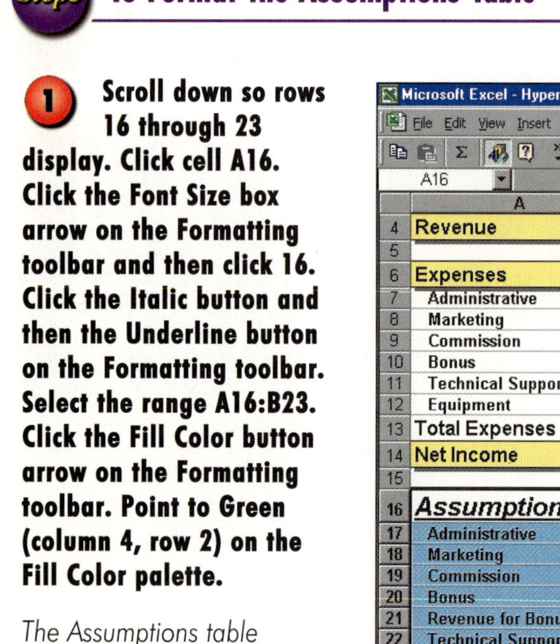

Steps To Format the Assumptions Table

1 **Scroll down so rows 16 through 23 display. Click cell A16. Click the Font Size box arrow on the Formatting toolbar and then click 16. Click the Italic button and then the Underline button on the Formatting toolbar. Select the range A16:B23. Click the Fill Color button arrow on the Formatting toolbar. Point to Green (column 4, row 2) on the Fill Color palette.**

The Assumptions table heading displays with the new formats. The range A16:B23 is selected and the Fill Color palette displays (Figure 3-47).

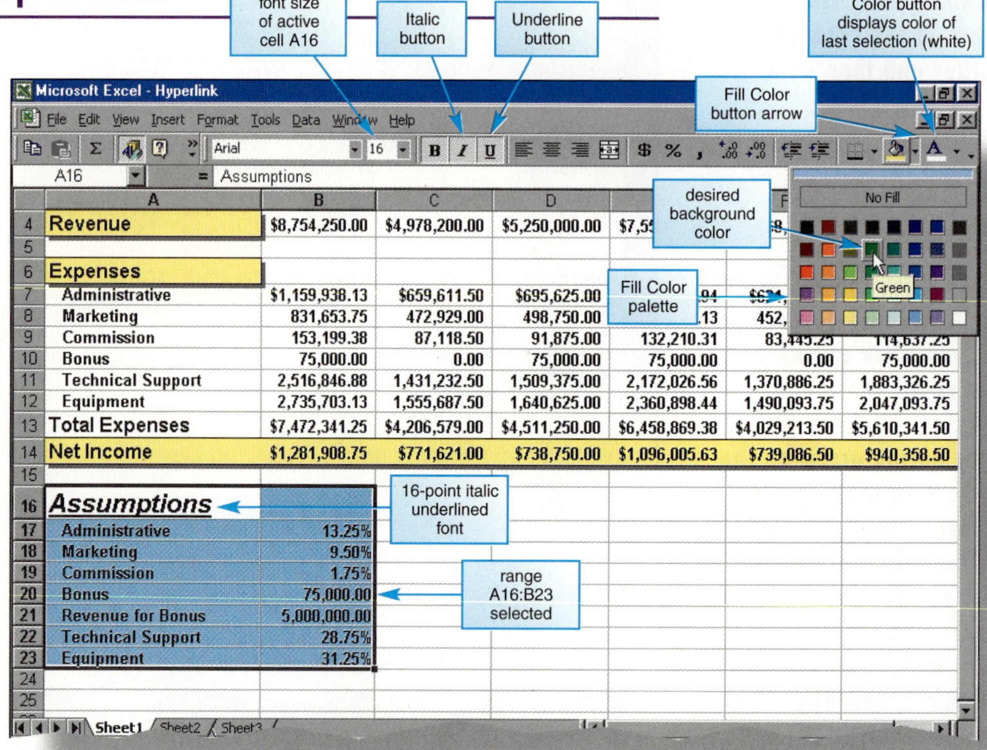

FIGURE 3-47

2 **Click Green on the Fill Color palette. Click the Font Color button on the Formatting toolbar to change the font in the selected range to white. Click the Shadow button on the Drawing toolbar. Click Shadow Style 14 on the Shadow palette. Select cell D23 to deselect the range A16:B23.**

The Assumptions table displays as shown in Figure 3-48.

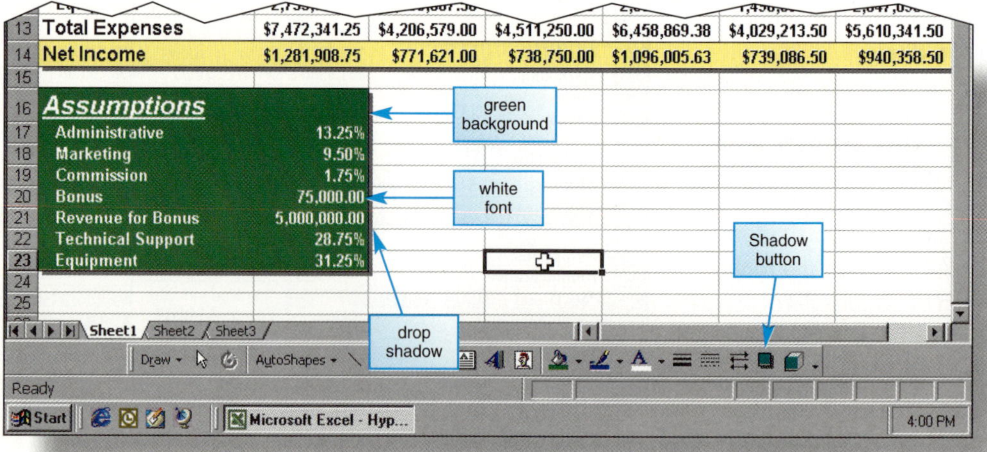

FIGURE 3-48

3 **Double-click the move handle on the Standard toolbar to display it in its entirety. Click the Drawing button on the Standard toolbar. Click the Save button on the Standard toolbar.**

Excel hides the Drawing toolbar and saves the workbook using the file name Hyperlink.

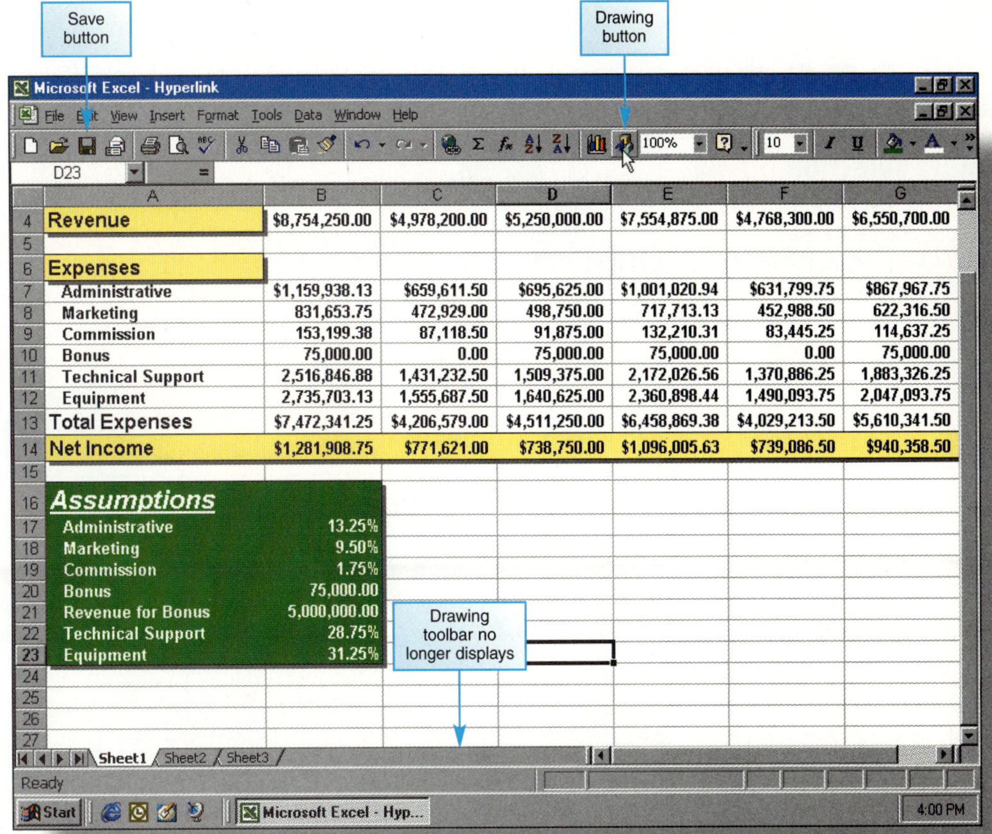

FIGURE 3-49

Other Ways

1. Right-click toolbar, click toolbar name on shortcut menu
2. On View menu click Toolbars, click toolbar name

The previous steps introduced you to two new formats, italic and underline. When you assign the **italic** font style to a cell, Excel slants the characters slightly to the right as shown in cell A16 in Figure 3-49. The **underline** format underlines only the characters in the cell rather than the entire cell as is the case when you assign a cell a bottom border.

The formatting of the worksheet is complete.

Adding a 3-D Pie Chart to the Workbook

The next step in the project is to draw the 3-D Pie chart on a separate sheet in the workbook Hyperlink, as shown in Figure 3-50 on the next page. A **Pie chart** is used to show the relationship or proportion of parts to a whole. Each slice (or wedge) of the pie shows what percent that slice contributes to the total (100%). The 3-D Pie chart in Figure 3-50 shows the contribution of each projected month's net income to the projected six-month net income. The Pie chart makes it easy to see that the month of July represents the largest contribution to the projected six-month net income.

Chart Selection

Line chart, Bar chart, Pie chart – which chart will best describe my worksheet data? For answers, click the Contents tab in the Microsoft Excel Help window. Double click the Changing the Type of Chart book. Click the Examples of chart types link, and then click the graphic.

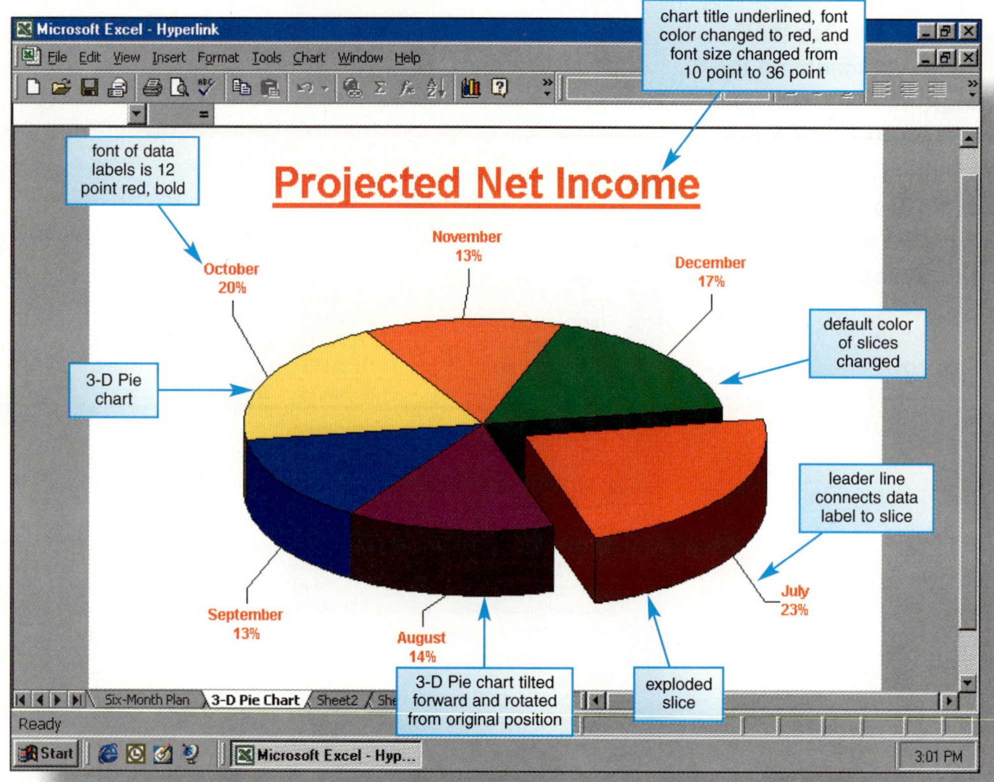

FIGURE 3-50

Nonadjacent Ranges

One of the more difficult tasks to learn is selecting nonadjacent ranges. To complete this task, do not hold down the CTRL key when you select the first range because Excel will consider the current active cell to be the first selection. Once the first range is selected, then hold down the CTRL key and drag through the ranges. If a desired range is not in the window, use the scroll arrows to move the window over the range. It is not necessary to hold down the CTRL key while you move the window.

Unlike the 3-D Column chart in Project 1, the 3-D Pie chart in Figure 3-50 is not embedded in the worksheet. This Pie chart resides on a separate sheet called a **chart sheet**.

The ranges in the worksheet to chart are the nonadjacent ranges B3:G3 and B14:G14 (Figure 3-51). The month names in the range B3:G3 will identify the slices; these entries are called **category names**. The range B14:G14 contains the data that determines the size of the slices in the pie; these entries are called the **data series**. Because there are six months, the 3-D Pie chart contains six slices.

This project also calls for emphasizing the month with the greatest contribution to the total projected net income (July) by offsetting its slice from the main portion. A Pie chart with one or more slices offset is called an **exploded Pie chart**.

As shown in Figure 3-50, the default 3-D Pie chart also has been enhanced by rotating and tilting the pie forward, changing the colors of the slices, and modifying the chart title and labels that identify the slices.

Drawing a 3-D Pie Chart on a Separate Chart Sheet

To draw the 3-D Pie chart on a separate chart sheet, select the nonadjacent ranges and then click the Chart Wizard button on the Standard toolbar. Once the chart is created, you can format it as shown in Figure 3-50.

To Draw a 3-D Pie Chart on a Separate Chart Sheet

1 **Select the range B3:G3. While holding down the CTRL key, select the range B14:G14. Point to the Chart Wizard button on the Standard toolbar.**

The nonadjacent ranges are selected (Figure 3-51).

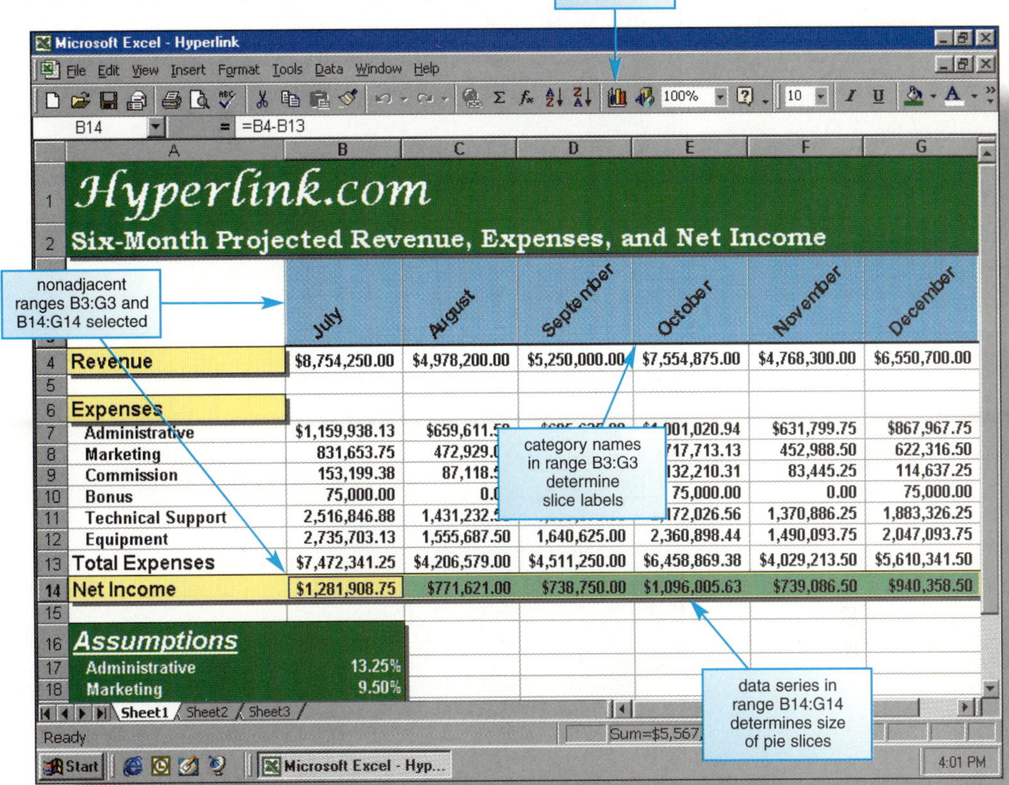

FIGURE 3-51

2 **Click the Chart Wizard button. When the Chart Wizard – Step 1 of 4 – Chart Type dialog box displays, click Pie in the Chart type list and then click the 3-D Pie chart (column 2, row 1) in the Chart sub-type box. Point to the Next button.**

The Chart Wizard—Step 1 of 4—Chart Type dialog box displays, which allows you to select one of the fourteen types of charts available in Excel (Figure 3-52).

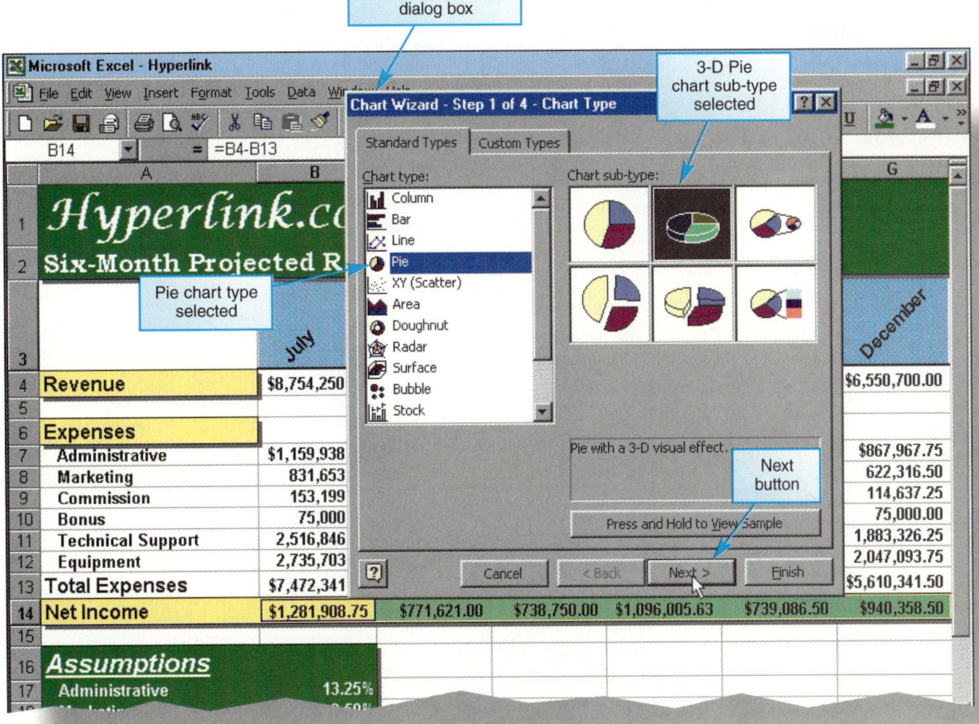

FIGURE 3-52

3 **Click the Next button.**

The Chart Wizard – Step 2 of 4 – Chart Source Data dialog box displays showing a sample of the 3-D Pie chart and the chart data range. A marquee surrounds the nonadjacent ranges on the worksheet (Figure 3-53).

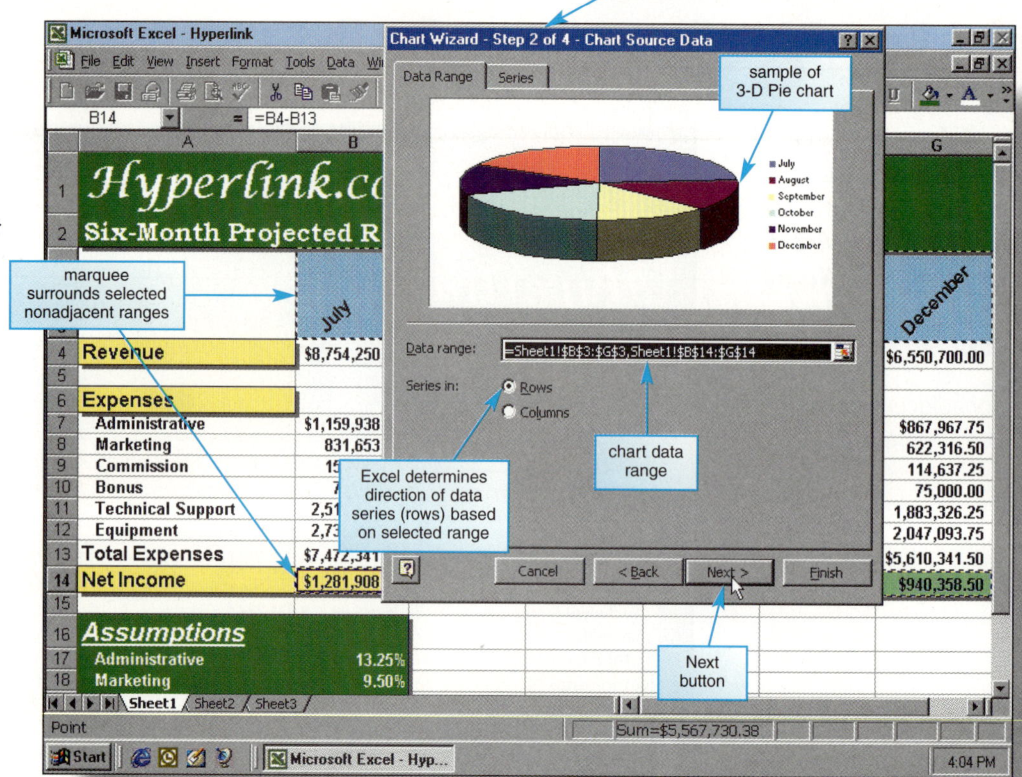

FIGURE 3-53

4 **Click the Next button. When the Chart Wizard – Step 3 of 4 – Chart Options dialog box displays, type** `Projected Net Income` **in the Chart title text box. Point to the Legend tab.**

Excel redraws the sample 3-D Pie chart with the chart title, Projected Net Income (Figure 3-54).

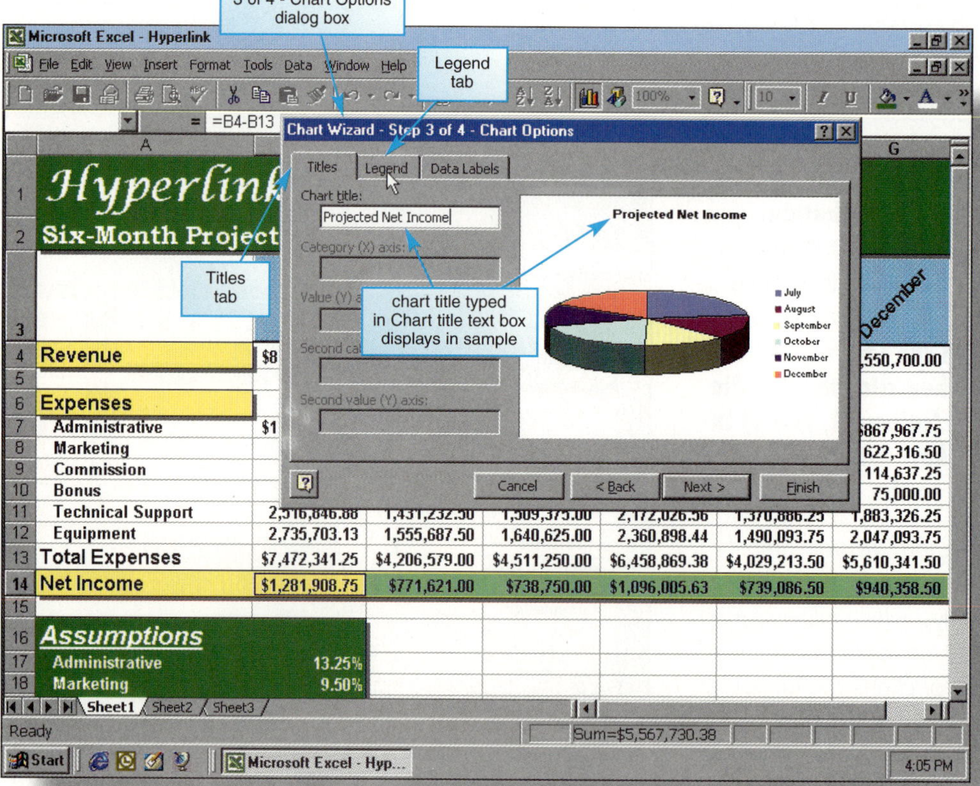

FIGURE 3-54

5 Click the Legend tab and then click Show legend to remove the check mark. Point to the Data Labels tab.

The Legend tab displays. Excel redraws the sample 3-D Pie chart without the legend. (Figure 3-55).

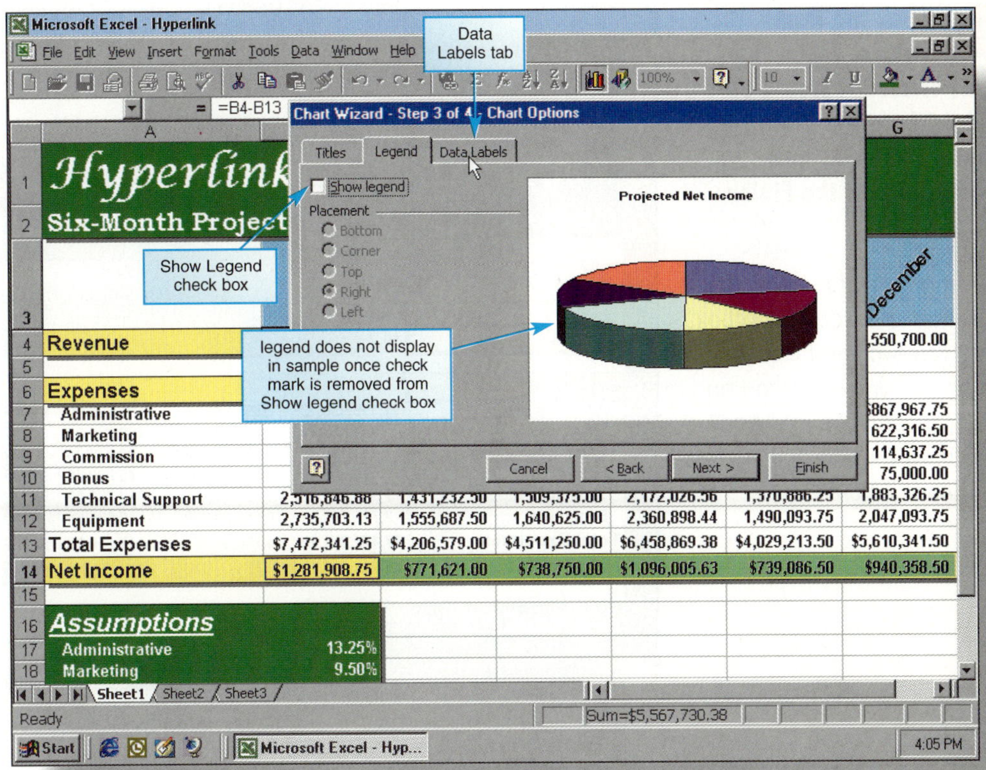

FIGURE 3-55

6 Click the Data Labels tab. Click Show label and percent in the Data labels area. Point to the Next button.

The Data Labels sheet displays. Excel redraws the sample 3-D Pie chart with data labels and percents (Figure 3-56).

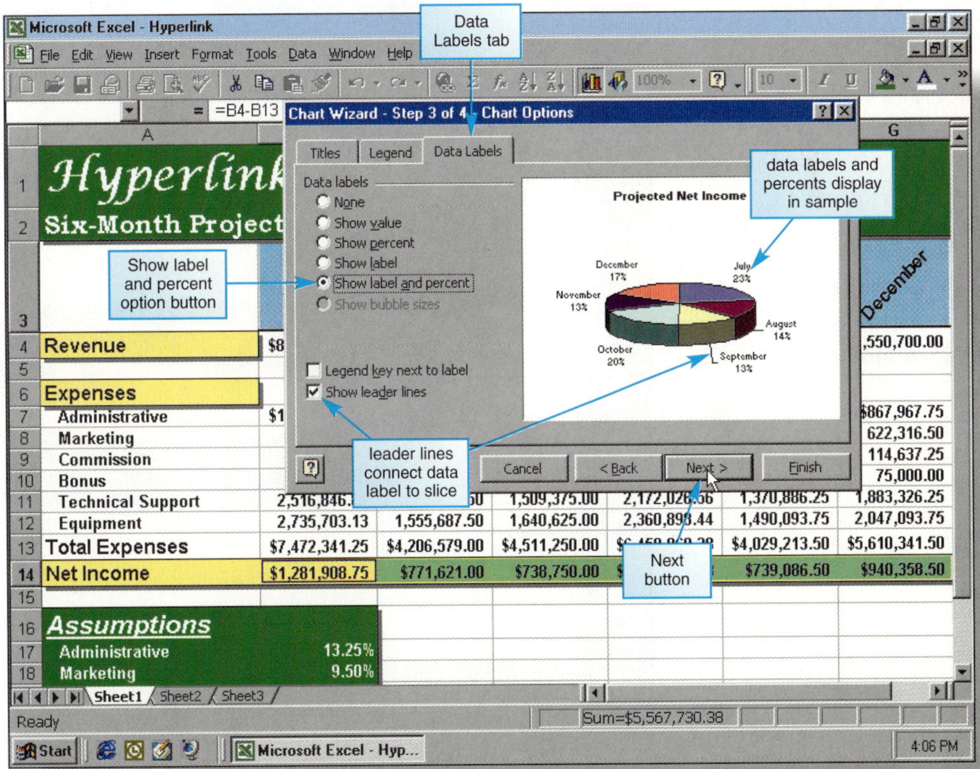

FIGURE 3-56

7 **Click the Next button. When the Chart Wizard – Step 4 of 4 – Chart Location dialog box displays, click As new sheet. Point to the Finish button.**

The Chart Wizard Step 4 of 4 Chart Location dialog box gives you two chart location options: to draw the chart on a new sheet in the workbook or to draw it as an object in a worksheet (Figure 3-57).

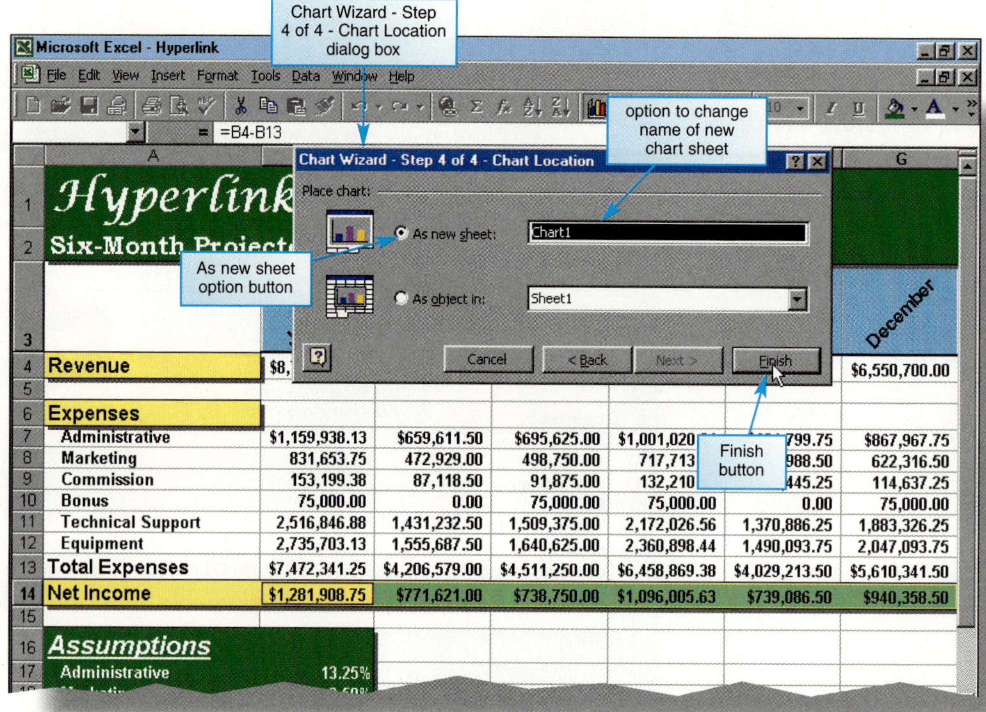

FIGURE 3-57

8 **Click the Finish button.**

Excel draws the 3-D Pie chart on a separate chart sheet (Chart1) in the Hyperlink workbook (Figure 3-58).

9 **Click the Save button on the Standard toolbar.**

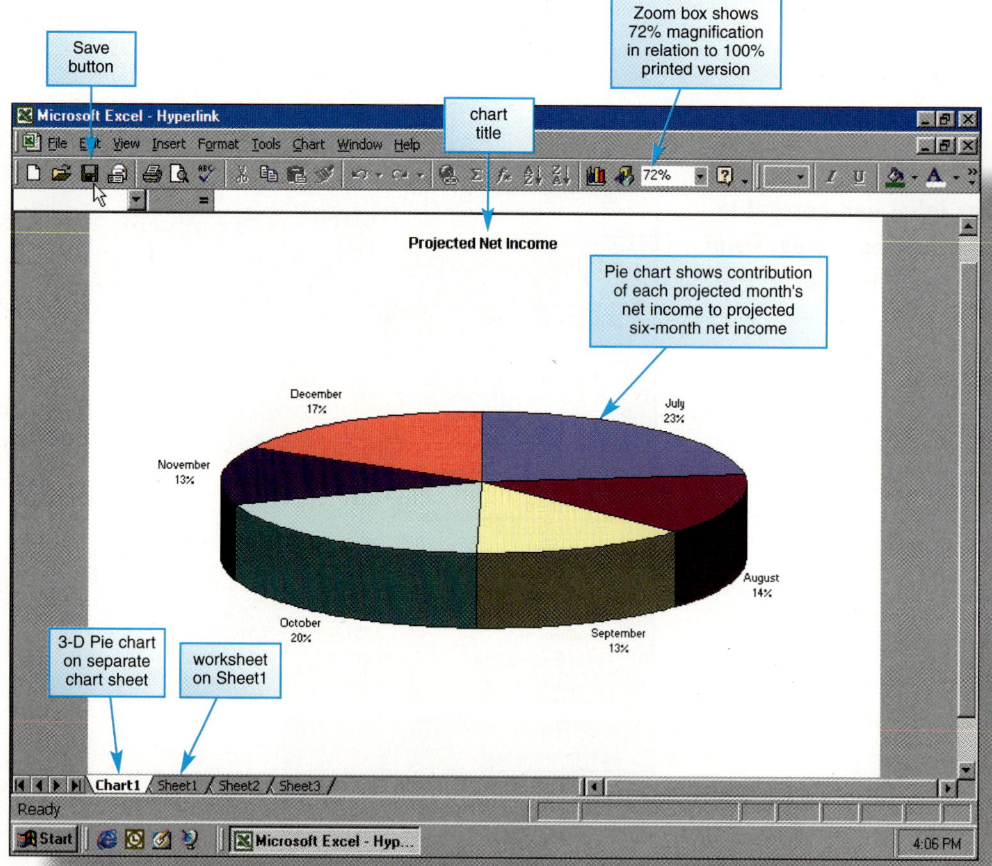

FIGURE 3-58

Other Ways

1. Select range to chart, press F11

Each slice of the 3-D Pie chart in Figure 3-58 represents one of the six months – July, August, September, October, November, and December. The names of the months and the percent contribution to the total value display outside the slices. The chart title, Projected Net Income, displays immediately above the 3-D Pie chart.

Excel determines the direction of the data series range (down a column or across a row) on the basis of the selected range. Because the selection for the 3-D Pie chart is across the worksheet (ranges B3:G3 and B14:G14), Excel automatically selects the Rows option button in the Data Range sheet as shown in Figure 3-53 on page E 3.46.

In any of the four Chart Wizard dialog boxes (Figure 3-53 through Figure 3-57), you can click the Back button to return to the previous Chart Wizard dialog box. You also can click the Finish button in any of the dialog boxes to create the chart with the options selected thus far.

Formatting the Chart Title and Chart Labels

The next step is to format the chart title and labels that identify the slices. Before you can format a **chart item**, such as the chart title or labels, you must select it. Once a chart item is selected, you can format it using the Formatting toolbar, shortcut menu, special keys, or the Format menu. In the following sections, you will use the Formatting toolbar to format chart items much like you formatted the cell entries earlier. Complete the following steps to format the chart title and labels.

Steps To Format the Chart Title and Labels

1 Double-click the move handle on the Formatting toolbar to display it in its entirety. Click the chart title. On the Formatting toolbar, click the Font Size box arrow, click 36, click the Underline button, click the Font Color button arrow, and then point to Red (column 1, row 3) on the Font Color palette.

Excel displays a box with handles around the chart title, increases the font size of the chart title, and underlines the chart title (Figure 3-59). The Font Color palette displays.

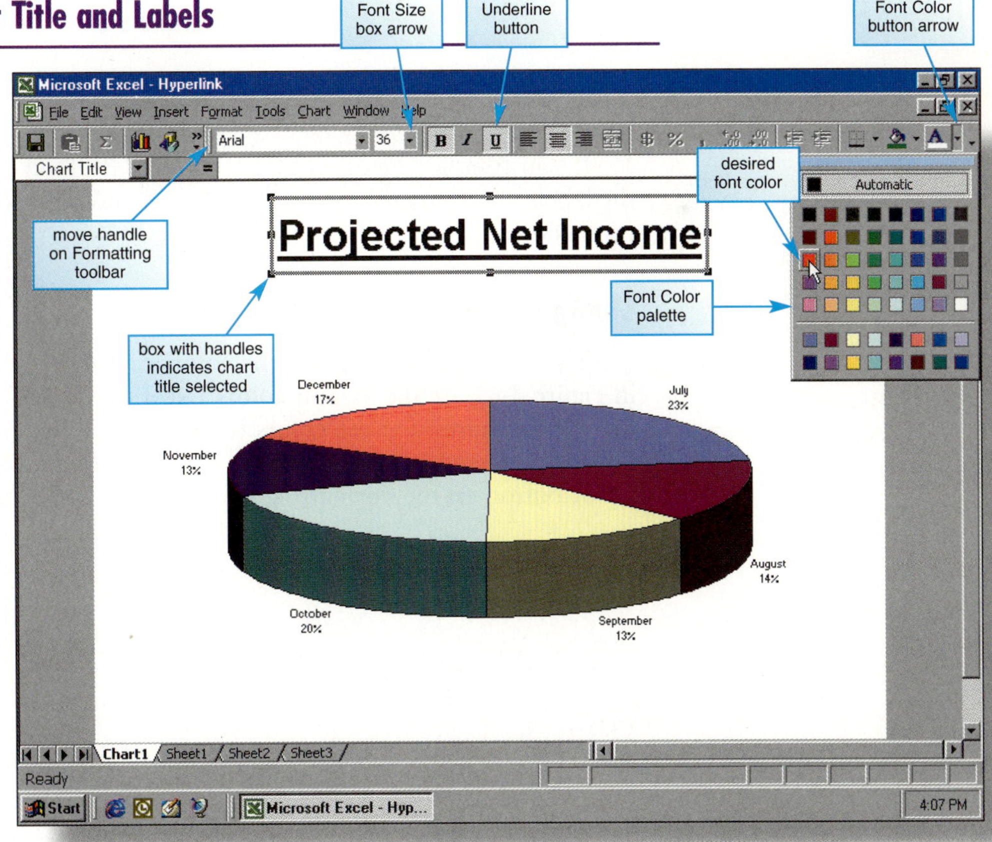

FIGURE 3-59

2 **Click Red. Right-click one of the five data labels that identify the slices. On the Formatting toolbar, click the Font Size box arrow, click 12, click the Bold button, and then click the Font Color button to change the font to the color red.**

The chart title and data labels display in red as shown in Figure 3-60. The data labels are selected.

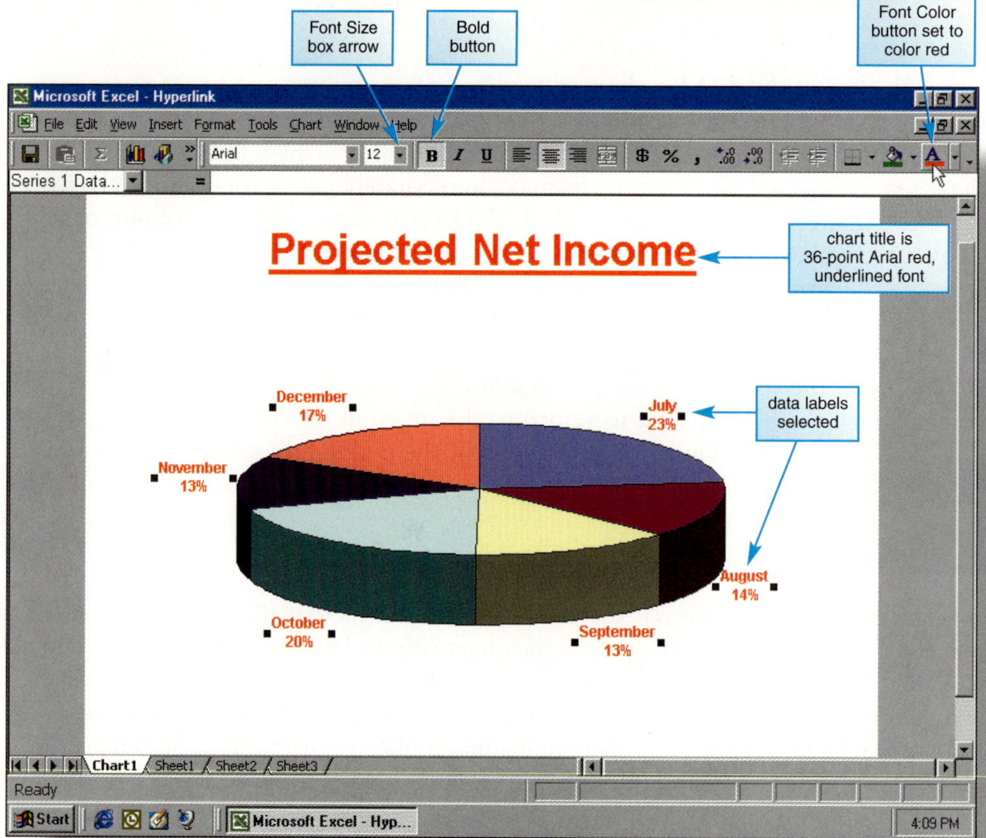

FIGURE 3-60

1. Right-click title or labels, click Format Title or click Format Data Labels on shortcut menu
2. Press CTRL+B to bold
3. Press CTRL+U to underline

If you compare Figure 3-60 with Figure 3-58 on page E 3.48, you can see that the labels and chart title are easier to read and make the chart sheet look more professional.

Changing the Colors of the Slices

The next step is to change the colors of the slices of the pie. The colors shown in Figure 3-61 are the default colors Excel uses when you first create a Pie chart. Project 3 requires that the colors be changed to those shown in Figure 3-50 on page E 3.44. To change the colors of the slices, select them one at a time and use the Fill Color button on the Formatting toolbar as shown in the following steps.

Steps To Change the Colors of the Pie Slices

1 Click the July slice twice, once to select all the slices and once to select the individual slice. (Do not double-click.) Click the Fill Color button arrow on the Formatting toolbar and then point to Red (column 1, row 3) on the Fill Color palette.

Excel displays resizing handles around the July slice and the Fill Color palette displays (Figure3-61).

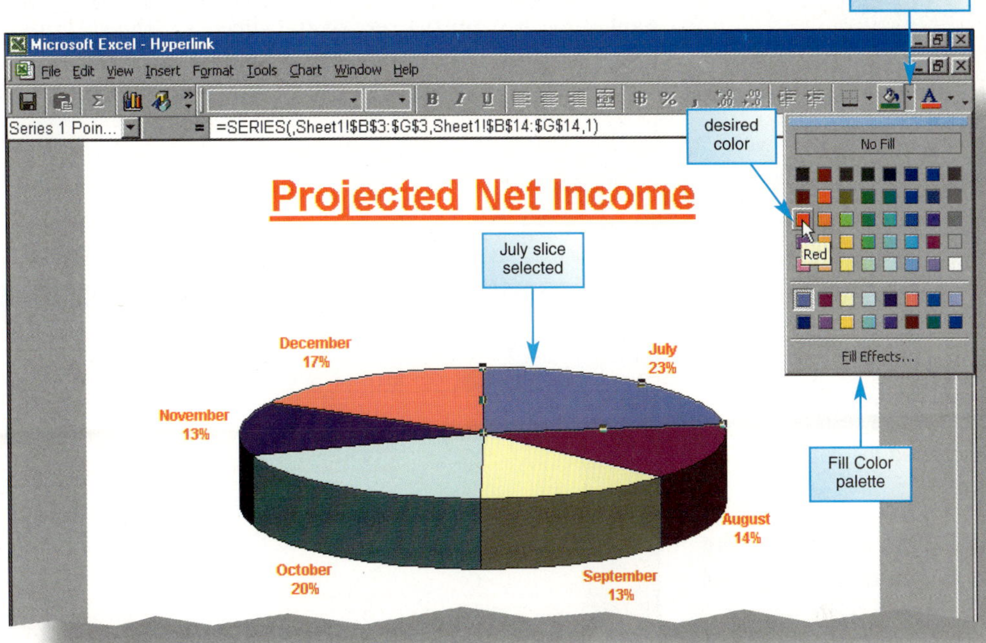

FIGURE 3-61

2 Click Red. One at a time, click the remaining slices and then use the Fill Color palette to change each slice to the following colors: December – Green (column 4, row 2); November – Orange (column 2, row 2); October – Yellow (column 3, row 4); September – Blue (column 6, row 2), and August – Plum (column 7, row 4). Click outside the Chart Area.

The Pie chart displays with colors assigned to the slices as shown in Figure 3-62.

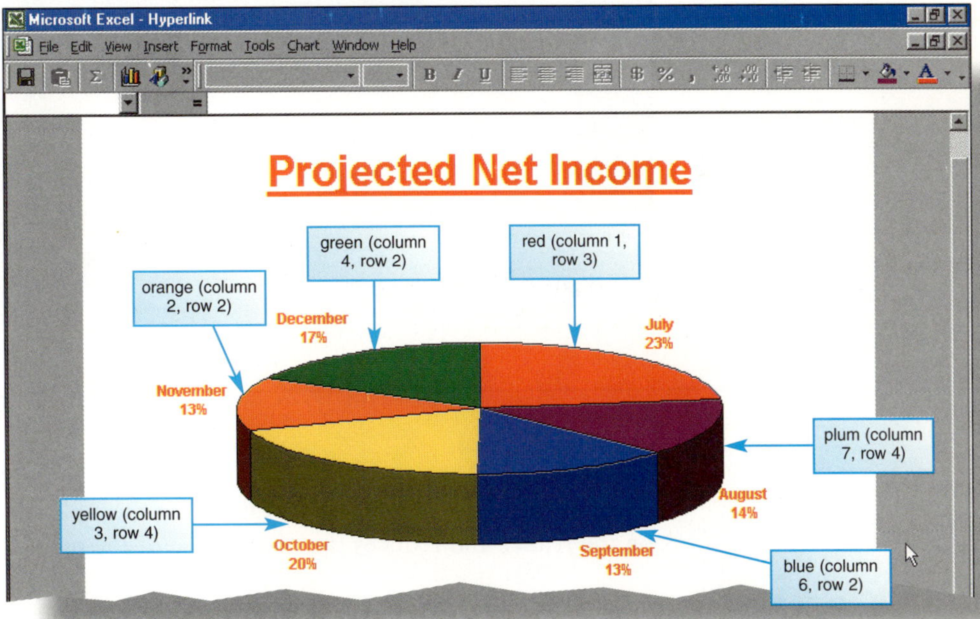

FIGURE 3-62

Other Ways

1. Click slice twice, right-click selected slice, click Format Data Point on shortcut menu, click Patterns tab, click color, click OK button
2. Click slice twice, on Format menu click Selected Data Point, click Patterns tab, click color, click OK button

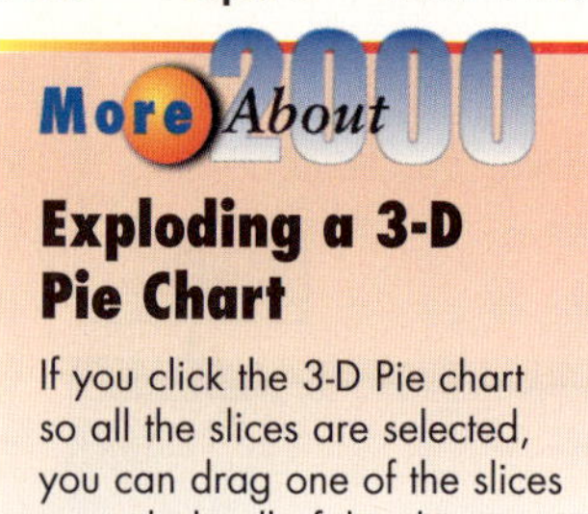

Exploding a 3-D Pie Chart

If you click the 3-D Pie chart so all the slices are selected, you can drag one of the slices to explode all of the slices.

Exploding the 3-D Pie Chart

The next step is to emphasize the slice representing July by offsetting, or **exploding**, it from the rest of the slices. Of the six months, July represents the greatest net income contributor; by exploding it, you can make this slice stand out from the rest. Perform the following steps to explode a slice of the 3-D Pie chart.

Steps To Explode the 3-D Pie Chart

1 Click the slice labeled July twice. (Do not double-click.)

Excel displays resizing handles around the July slice.

2 Drag the slice to the desired position and then release the mouse button.

Excel redraws the 3-D Pie chart with the July slice offset from the rest of the slices (Figure 3-63).

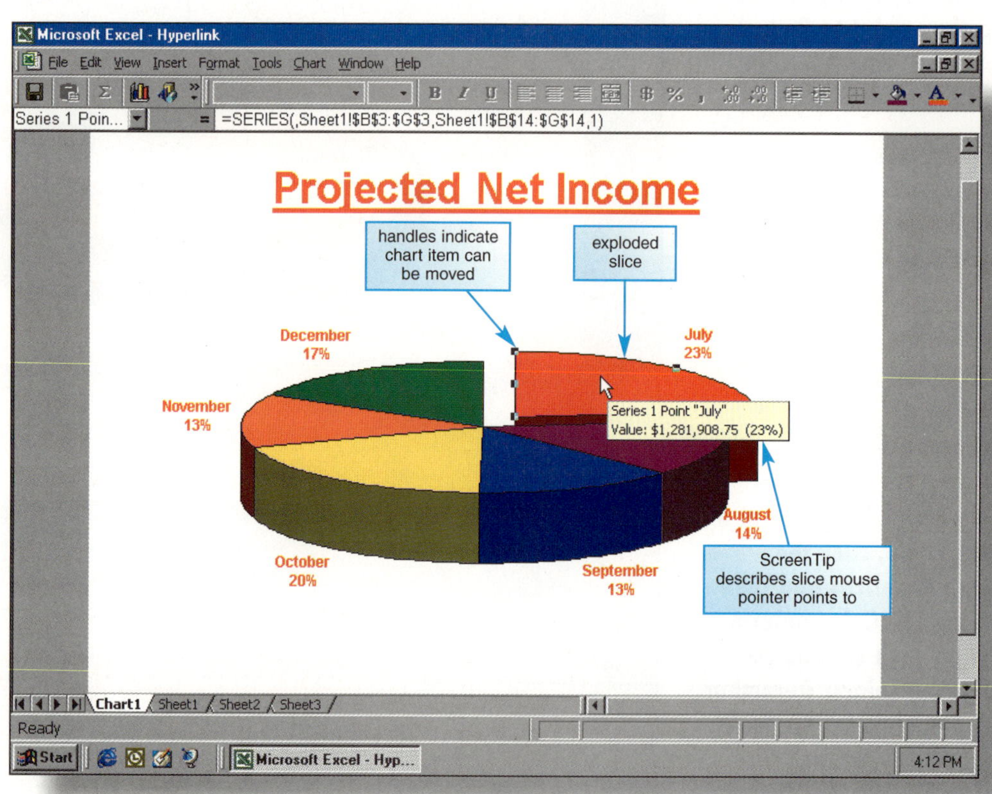

FIGURE 3-63

You can offset as many slices as you want, but remember that the reason for offsetting a slice is to emphasize it. Offsetting multiple slices tends to reduce the impact on the reader and reduces the overall size of the pie chart.

More About 2000

Changing a Pie Chart's Perspective

You can increase or decrease the base height (thickness) of the Pie chart by changing the height to base ratio in the Format 3-D View dialog box.

Rotating and Tilting the 3-D Pie Chart

With a three-dimensional chart, you can change the view to better display the section of the chart you are trying to emphasize. Excel allows you to control the rotation angle, elevation, perspective, height, and angle of the axes by using the **3-D View command** on the Chart menu.

To obtain a better view of the offset July slice, you can rotate the 3-D Pie chart 80° to the left. The rotation angle of the 3-D Pie chart is defined by the line that divides the July and December slices. When Excel initially draws a Pie chart, it always points one of the dividing lines between two slices to twelve o'clock (or zero degrees). Besides rotating the 3-D Pie chart, the following steps also change, or tilt, the elevation so the 3-D Pie chart is at less of an angle to the viewer.

To Rotate and Tilt the 3-D Pie Chart

1 **With the July slice selected, click Chart on the menu bar and then point to 3-D View.**

The Chart menu displays (Figure 3-64).

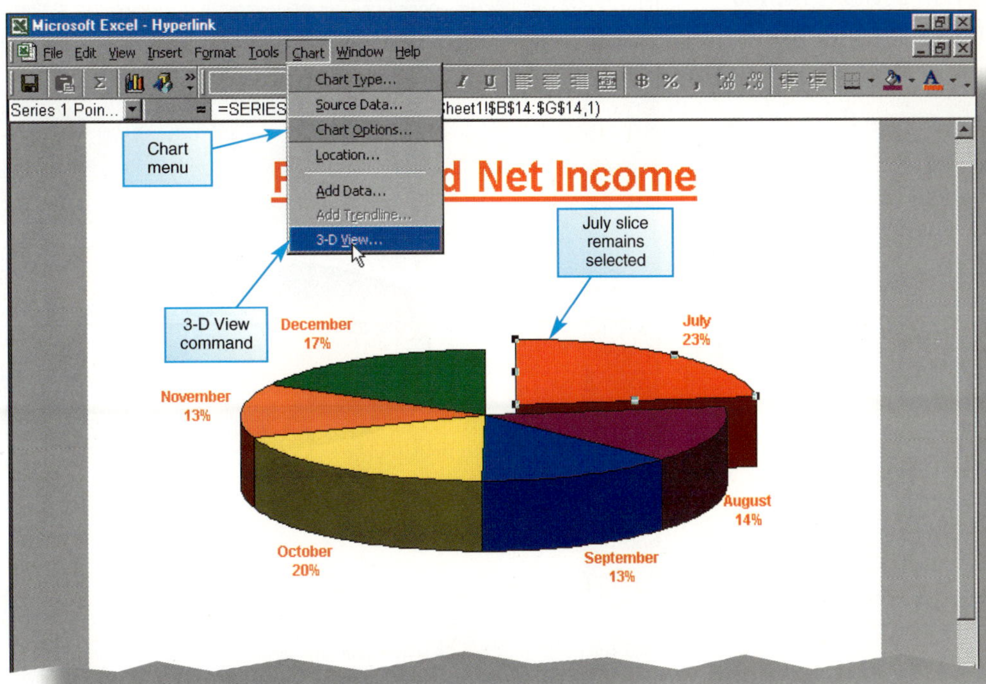

FIGURE 3-64

2 **Click 3-D View. When the 3-D View dialog box displays, click the up arrow button in the 3-D View dialog box until 25 displays in the Elevation box.**

The 3-D View dialog box displays (Figure 3-65). A sample of the 3-D Pie chart displays in the dialog box. The result of increasing the elevation of the 3-D Pie chart is to tilt it forward.

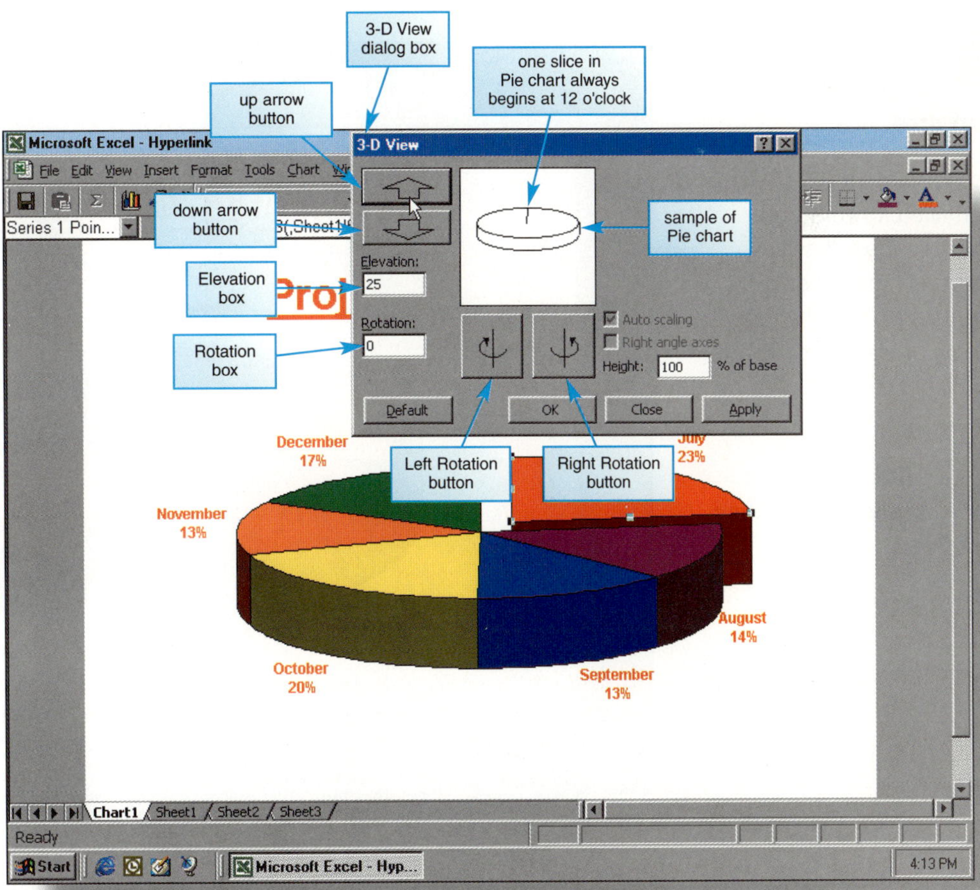

FIGURE 3-65

3 **Rotate the Pie chart by clicking the Left Rotation button until the Rotation box displays 80.**

The new rotation setting (80) displays in the **Rotation box** *as shown in Figure 3-66. A sample of the rotated Pie chart displays in the dialog box.*

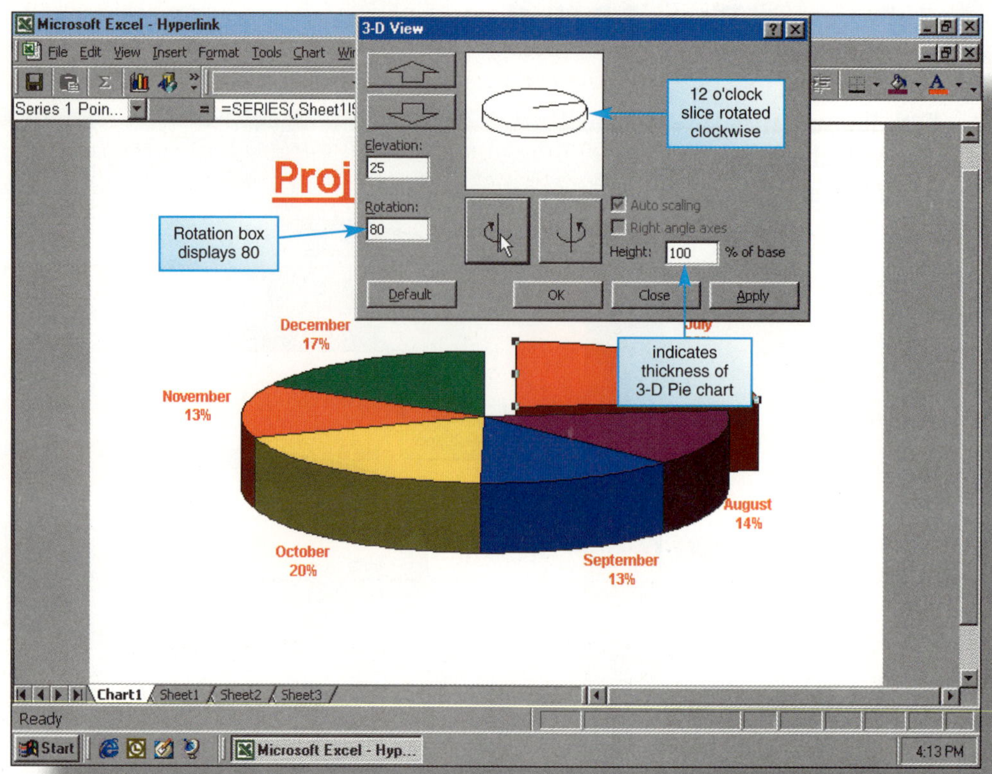

FIGURE 3-66

4 **Click the OK button. Click outside the chart area.**

Excel displays the 3-D Pie chart tilted forward and rotated to the left, which makes the space between the July slice and the main portion of the pie more prominent (Figure 3-67).

5 **Click File on the menu bar and then click Save.**

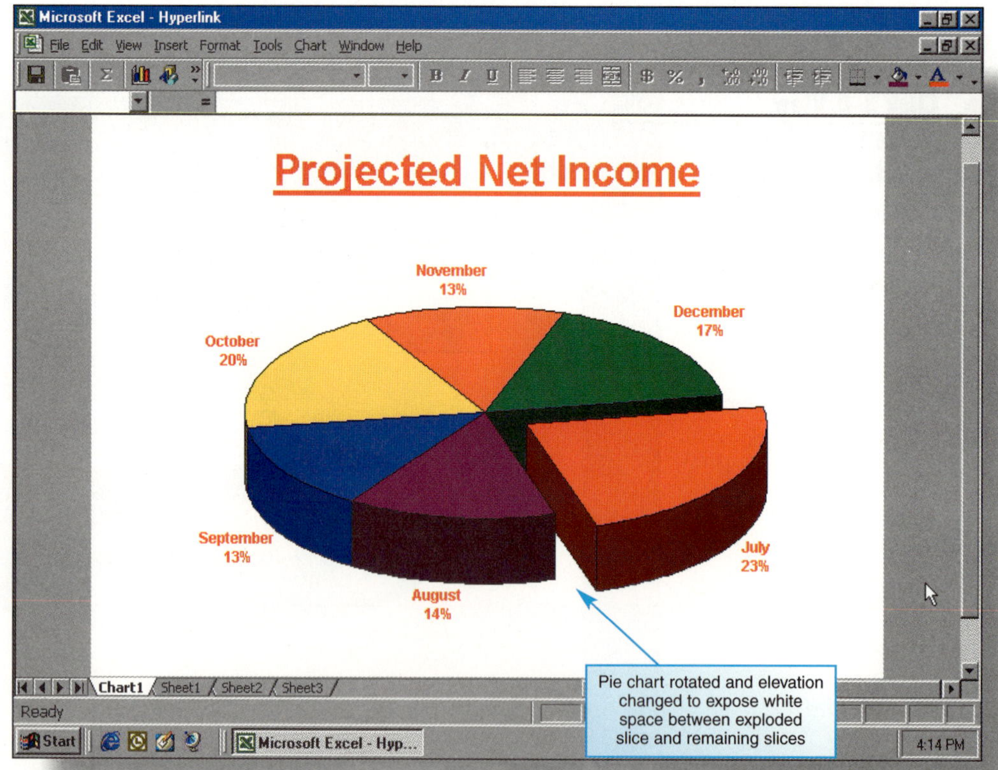

FIGURE 3-67

Compare Figure 3-67 with Figure 3-64 on page E 3.53. The offset of the July slice is more noticeable in Figure 3-67 because the Pie chart has been tilted and rotated to expose the white space between the July slice and the main portion of the 3-D Pie chart.

In addition to controlling the rotation angle and elevation, you also can control the thickness of the 3-D Pie chart by entering a percent smaller or larger than the default 100% in the **Height box** (Figure 3-66).

More About 2000

Charting

Press the ESC key to deselect a chart item.

Adding Leader Lines to the Data Labels

If you drag the data labels away from each slice, Excel draws thin **leader lines** that connect each data label to its corresponding slice. If the leader lines do not display, click Chart Options on the Chart menu and click the Show leader lines option button (see Figure 3-56 on page E 3.47).

To Add Leader Lines to the Data Labels

1 **Click the July data label twice. (Do not double-click.)**

Excel displays a box with handles around the July data label.

2 **Point to the upper-left handles on the box border and drag the July data label away from the July slice. Select and drag the remaining data labels away from their corresponding slices as shown in Figure 3-68. Click outside the chart area.**

The data labels display with leader lines as shown in Figure 3-68.

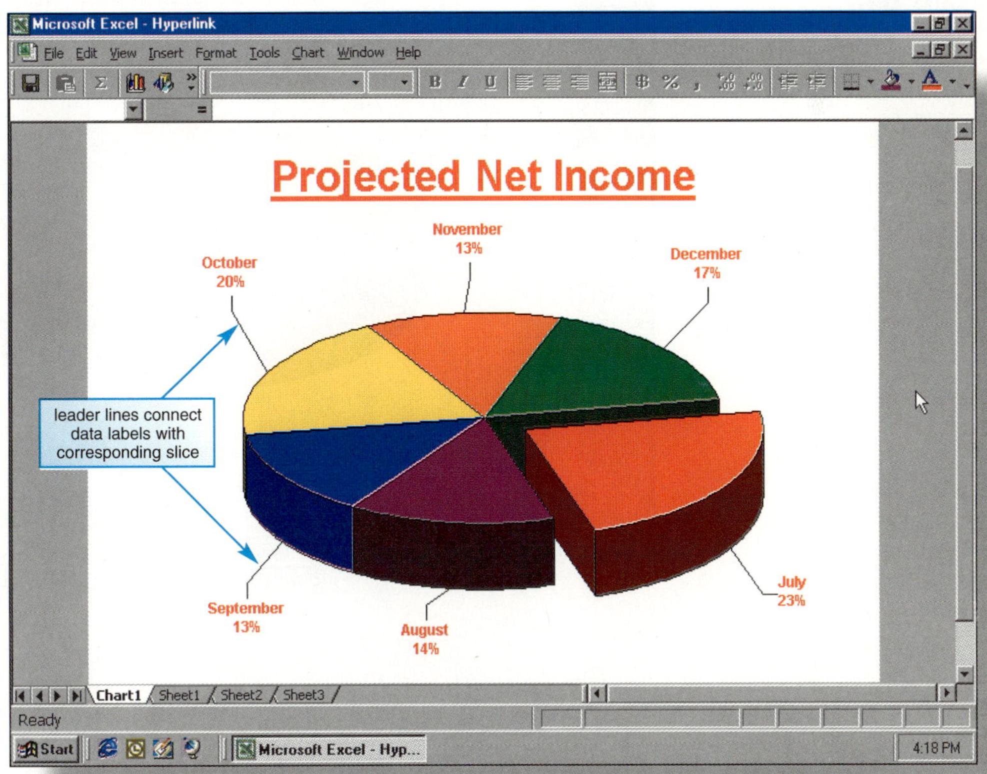

FIGURE 3-68

You also can select and format individual labels by clicking a specific data label after all the data labels have been selected. Making an individual data label larger or a different color, for example, helps you emphasize a small or large slice in a Pie chart.

Changing the Names of the Sheets and Rearranging the Order of the Sheets

The final step in creating the workbook is to change the names of the sheets at the bottom of the screen. The following steps show you how to rename the sheets and reorder the sheets so the worksheet comes before the chart sheet.

To Rename the Sheets and Rearrange the Order of the Sheets

1 Double-click the tab labeled Chart1 at the bottom of the screen. Type `3-D Pie Chart` **as the new tab label. Press the ENTER key.**

The label on the Chart1 tab changes to 3-D Pie Chart (Figure 3-69).

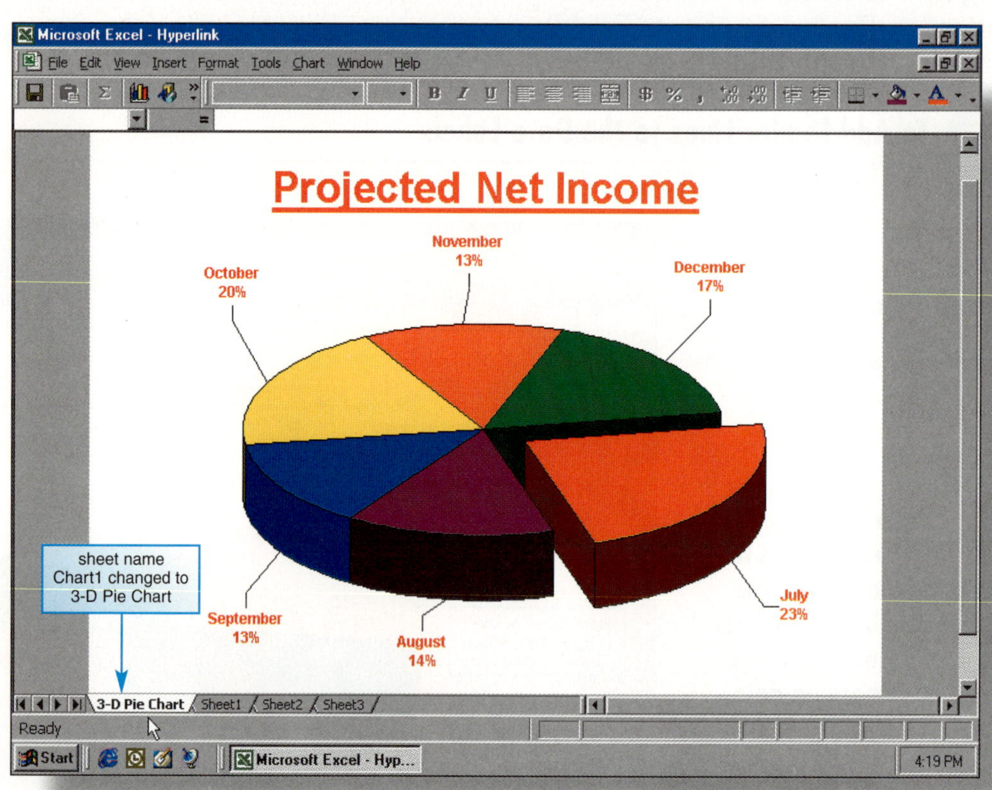

FIGURE 3-69

2 Double-click the tab labeled Sheet1 at the bottom of the screen. Type `Six-Month Plan` **as the new tab label and then press the ENTER key. Drag the Six-Month Plan tab to the left in front of the 3-D Pie Chart tab. Click cell D17 to deselect the chart ranges.**

Excel rearranges the sequence of the sheets and displays the worksheet (Figure 3-70).

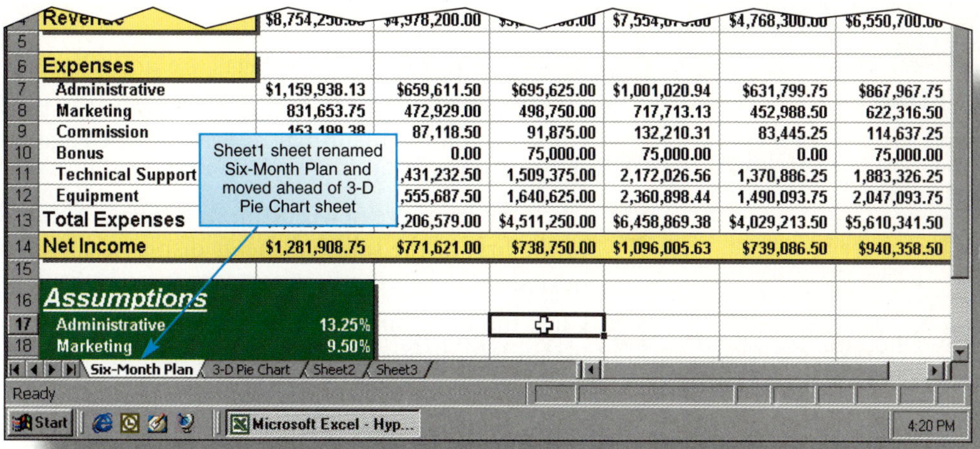

Sheet1 sheet renamed Six-Month Plan and moved ahead of 3-D Pie Chart sheet

FIGURE 3-70

Other Ways

1. To rename, right-click sheet tab, click Rename on shortcut menu
2. To move, right-click sheet tab, click Move or Copy on shortcut menu
3. To move, on the Edit menu click Move or Copy on shortcut menu

Checking Spelling, Saving, Previewing, and Printing the Workbook

With the workbook complete, the next sequences of steps check spelling, save, preview, and print the workbook. Each sequence of steps concludes with saving the workbook to ensure that the latest changes are saved on disk.

Checking Spelling in Multiple Sheets

The spelling checker checks the spelling only in the selected sheets. It will check all the cells in the selected sheets unless you select a range of two or more cells. Before checking the spelling, select the 3-D Pie Chart sheet as described in the following steps.

More About 2000

Checking Spelling

Unless a range of cells or an object is selected when you check spelling, Excel checks the selected worksheet, including all cell values, cell comments, embedded charts, text boxes, buttons, and headers and footers.

TO CHECK SPELLING IN MULTIPLE SHEETS

1. Double-click the move handle on the Standard toolbar to display it in its entirety. With the Six-Month Plan sheet active, hold down the CTRL key and then click the 3-D Pie Chart tab.
2. Click the Spelling button on the Standard toolbar. Correct any errors.
3. Click the Save button on the Standard toolbar.

Previewing and Printing the Workbook

After checking the spelling, the next step is to preview and print the sheets. As with spelling, Excel previews and prints only selected sheets. Also, because the worksheet is too wide to print in portrait orientation, you must change the orientation to landscape. Perform the steps on the next page to preview and print the workbook.

Printing

Is it taking too long and using too much ink to print colored worksheets? You can speed up the printing process and save ink if you do the following before printing a worksheet with color: click File on the menu bar, click Page Setup, click the Sheet tab, click the Black and white check box, and then click the OK button.

TO PREVIEW AND PRINT THE WORKBOOK IN LANDSCAPE ORIENTATION

1. Ready the printer. If both sheets are not selected, select the inactive one by holding down the CTRL key and then clicking the tab of the inactive sheet.
2. Click File on the menu bar and then click Page Setup. Click the Page tab and then click Landscape.
3. Click the Print Preview button in the Page Setup dialog box. When the preview of the first of the selected sheets displays, click the Next button to view the next sheet. Click the Previous button to redisplay the first sheet.
4. Click the Print button at the top of the Print Preview window. When the Print dialog box displays, click the OK button.
5. Right-click the Six-Month Plan tab. Click Ungroup Sheets on the shortcut menu to deselect the 3-D Pie Chart tab.
6. Click the Save button on the Standard toolbar.

The worksheet and 3-D Pie chart print as shown in Figures 3-71a and 3-71b.

(a) Worksheet

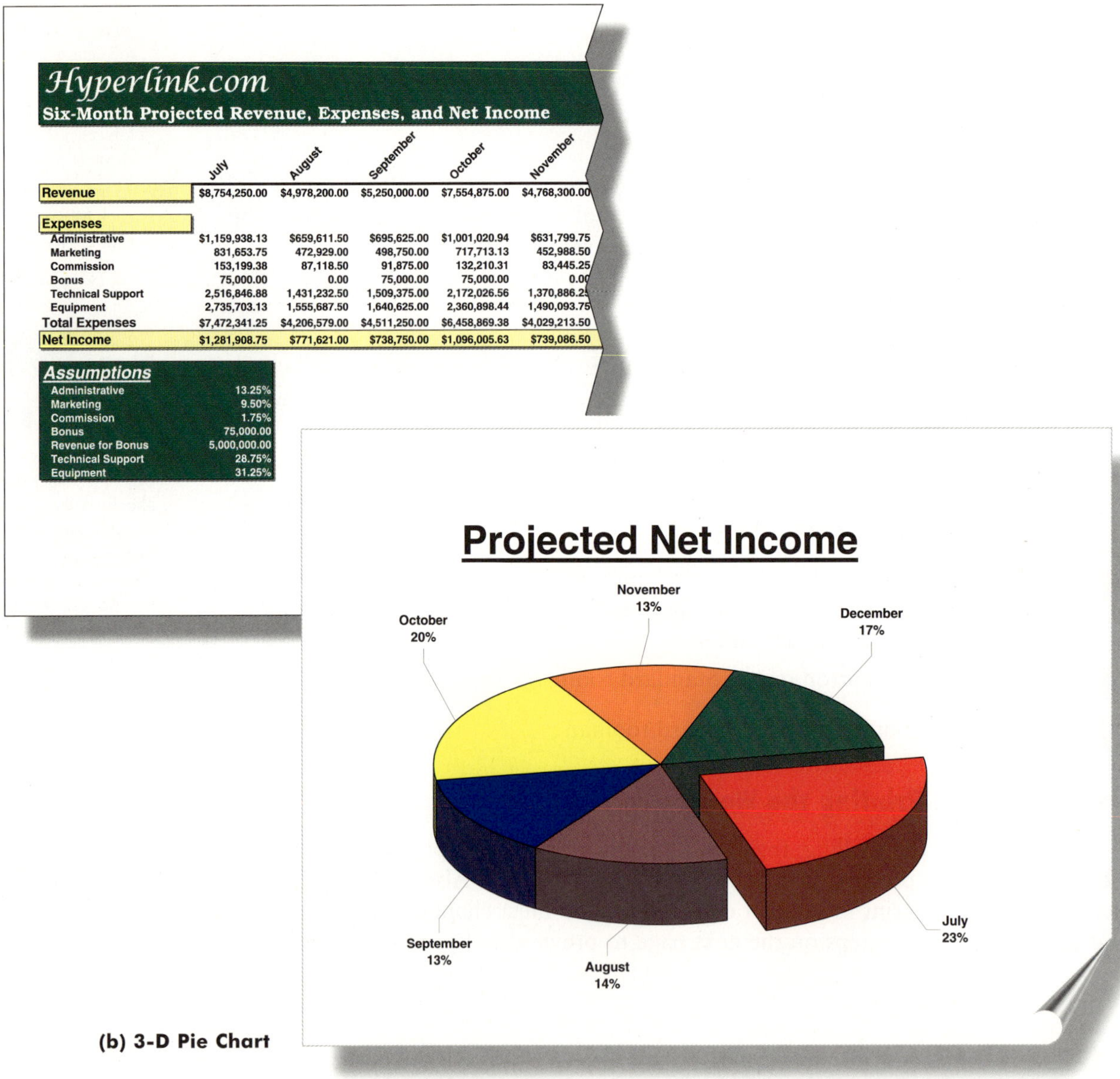

Hyperlink.com

Six-Month Projected Revenue, Expenses, and Net Income

	July	August	September	October	November
Revenue	$8,754,250.00	$4,978,200.00	$5,250,000.00	$7,554,875.00	$4,768,300.00
Expenses					
Administrative	$1,159,938.13	$659,611.50	$695,625.00	$1,001,020.94	$631,799.75
Marketing	831,653.75	472,929.00	498,750.00	717,713.13	452,988.50
Commission	153,199.38	87,118.50	91,875.00	132,210.31	83,445.25
Bonus	75,000.00	0.00	75,000.00	75,000.00	0.0
Technical Support	2,516,846.88	1,431,232.50	1,509,375.00	2,172,026.56	1,370,886.2
Equipment	2,735,703.13	1,555,687.50	1,640,625.00	2,360,898.44	1,490,093.75
Total Expenses	$7,472,341.25	$4,206,579.00	$4,511,250.00	$6,458,869.38	$4,029,213.50
Net Income	$1,281,908.75	$771,621.00	$738,750.00	$1,096,005.63	$739,086.50

Assumptions	
Administrative	13.25%
Marketing	9.50%
Commission	1.75%
Bonus	75,000.00
Revenue for Bonus	5,000,000.00
Technical Support	28.75%
Equipment	31.25%

(b) 3-D Pie Chart

FIGURE 3-71

An alternative to using the Ungroup Sheets command on the tab shortcut menu is to hold down the SHIFT key and then click the tab of the sheet you want active.

Changing the View of the Worksheet

With Excel, you easily can change the view of the worksheet. For example, you can magnify or shrink the worksheet on the screen. You also can view different parts of the worksheet through **window panes**.

Zooming

You can type any number between 10 and 400 in the Zoom box on the Standard toolbar.

Shrinking and Magnifying the View of a Worksheet or Chart

You can magnify (zoom in) or shrink (zoom out) the display of a worksheet or chart by using the **Zoom box** on the Standard toolbar. When you magnify a worksheet, the characters on the screen become large and fewer columns and rows display. Alternatively, when you shrink a worksheet, more columns and rows display. Magnifying or shrinking a worksheet affects only the view; it does not change the window size or printout of the worksheet or chart. Perform the following steps to shrink and magnify the view of the worksheet.

Steps To Shrink and Magnify the View of a Worksheet or Chart

1 Click the Zoom box arrow on the Standard toolbar. Point to 75% in the Zoom list.

A list of percentages displays (Figure 3-72).

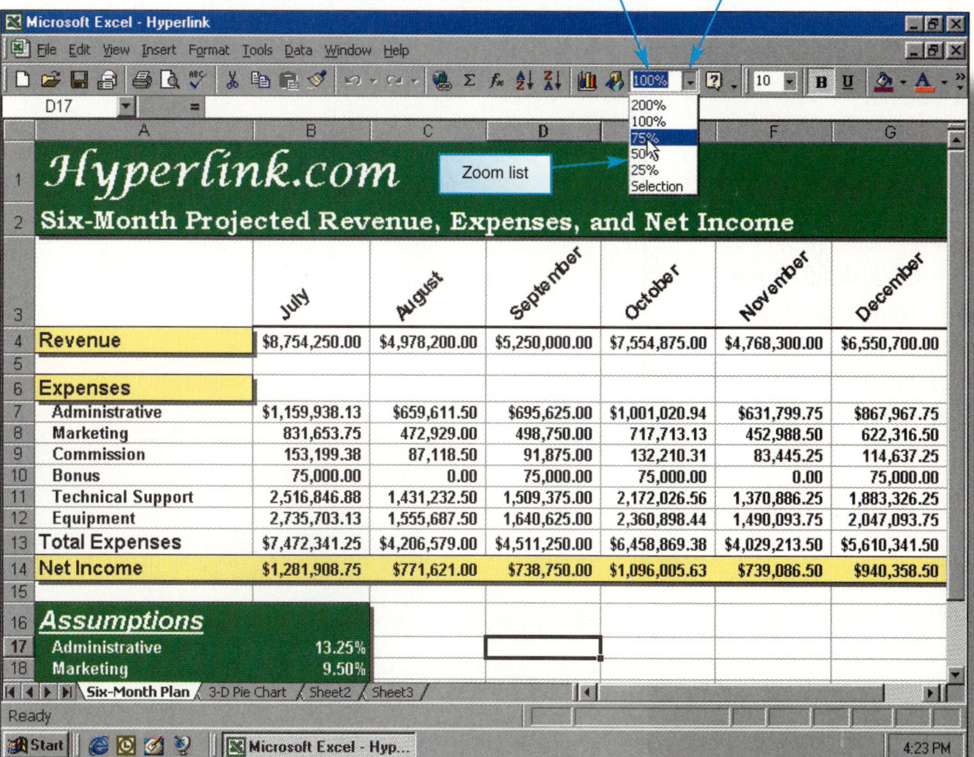

FIGURE 3-72

Click 75%.

Excel shrinks the display of the worksheet to 75% of its normal display (Figure 3-73). With the worksheet zoomed out to 75%, you can see more rows and columns than you did at 100% magnification. Many of the numbers, however, display as a series of number signs (#) because the columns are not wide enough to display the formatted numbers.

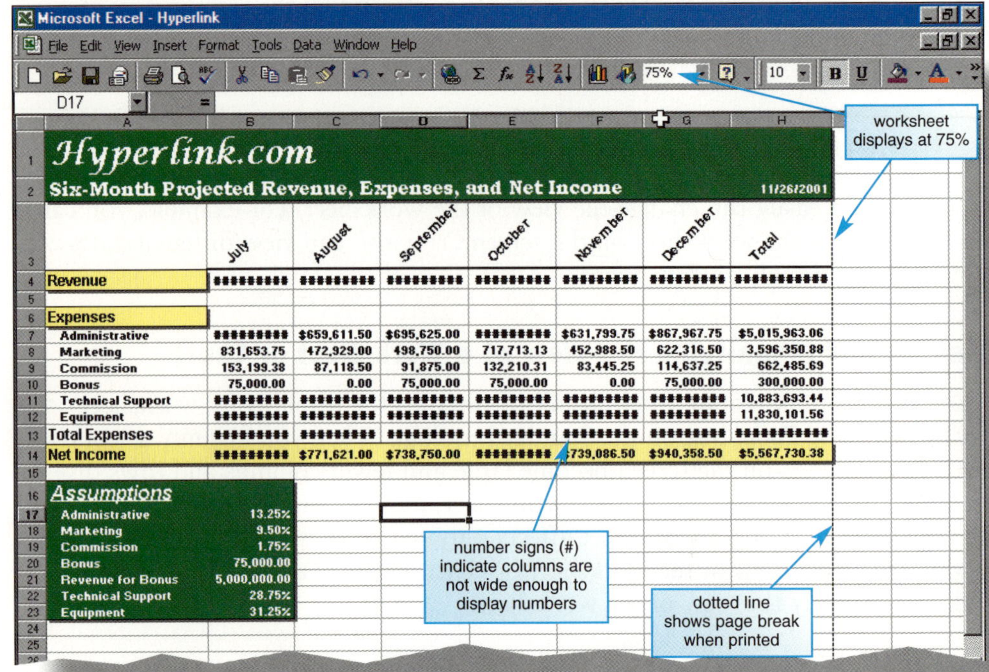

FIGURE 3-73

3 Click the Zoom box arrow on the Standard toolbar and then click 100%.

Excel returns to the default display of 100%.

4 Click the 3-D Pie Chart tab at the bottom of the screen. Click the Zoom box arrow on the Standard toolbar and then click 100%.

Excel changes the magnification of the chart from 72% (see Figure 3-69 on page E 3.56) to 100% (Figure 3-74). The chart displays at the same size as the printout of the chart.

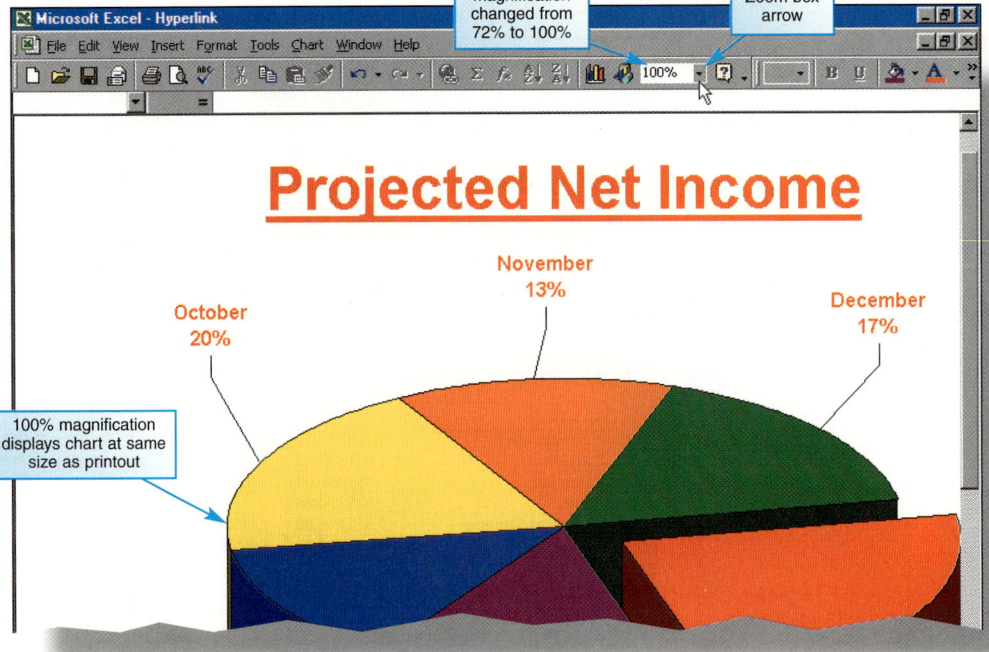

FIGURE 3-74

5 Enter 72 **in the Zoom box to return the chart to its original magnification.**

Other Ways

1. On View menu click Zoom, click desired magnification, click OK button
2. Type desired percent magnification in Zoom box on Standard toolbar

Excel normally displays a chart at approximately 75% magnification at 800 x 600 resolution so that the entire chart displays on the screen. By changing the magnification to 100%, you can see only a part of the chart, but at a magnification that corresponds with the chart's size on a printout. Excel allows you to enter a percent magnification in the Zoom box between 10 and 400 for worksheets and chart sheets.

Splitting the Window into Panes

Previously in this project, you used the Freeze Panes command to freeze worksheet titles on a large worksheet so they always would display on the screen. When working with a large worksheet, you also can split the window into two or four window panes to view different parts of the worksheet at the same time. To split the window into four panes, select the cell where you want the four panes to intersect. Next, click the **Split command** on the Window menu. Follow the steps below to split the window into four panes.

To Split a Window into Four Panes

1 Click the Six-Month Plan tab. Click cell D5, the intersection of the four proposed panes. Click Window on the menu bar and then point to Split.

The Window menu displays (Figure 3-75).

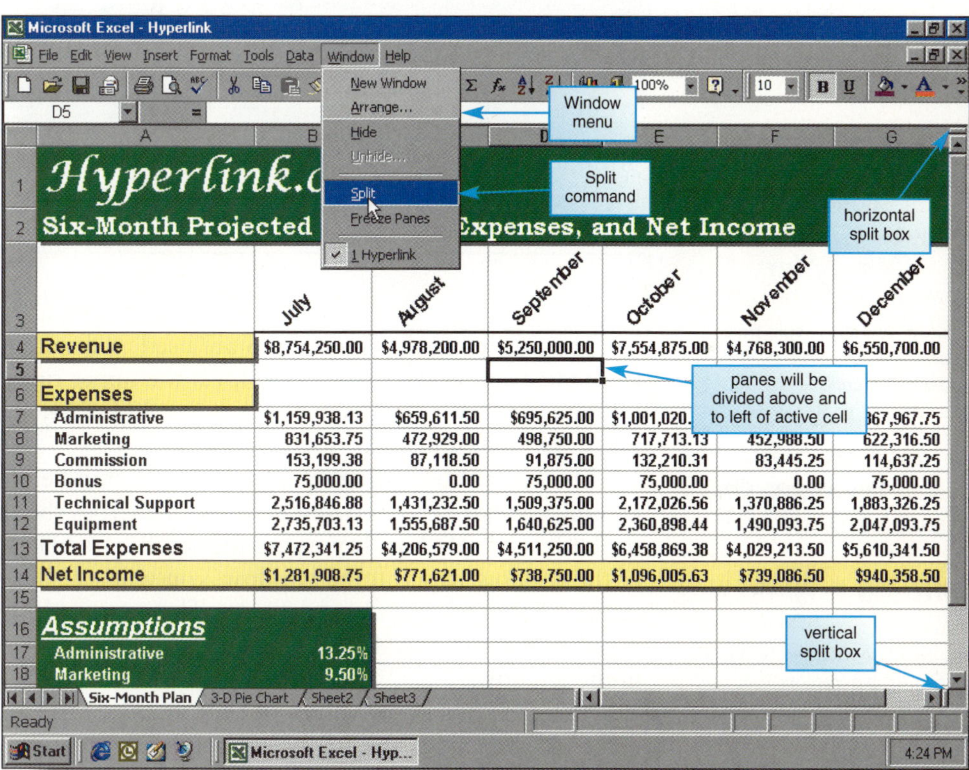

FIGURE 3-75

Click Split. Use the scroll arrows to display the four corners of the worksheet.

Excel divides the window into four panes, and the four corners of the worksheet display (Figure 3-76).

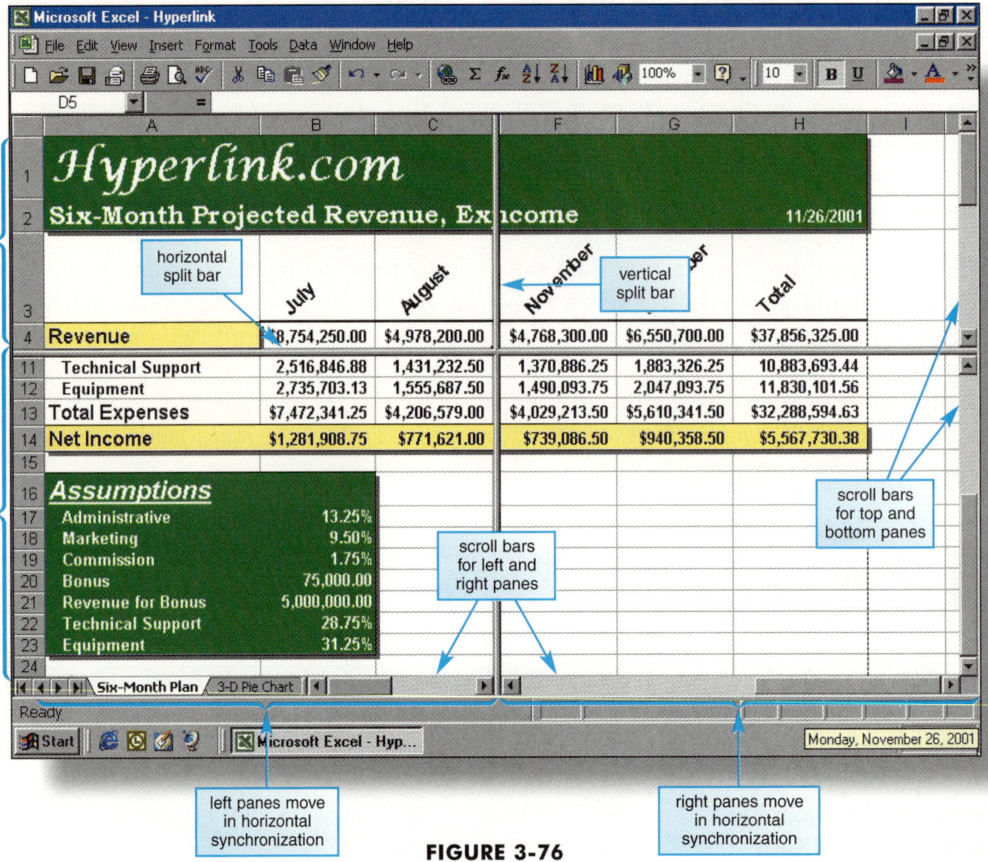

FIGURE 3-76

1. Drag horizontal split box and vertical split box to desired locations

More About

Splitting a Window

If you want to split the window into two panes, rather than four, drag the vertical split box or horizontal split box (Figure 3-75) to the desired location.

The four panes in Figure 3-76 are used to display the following: (1) the upper-left pane displays the range A1:C4; (2) the upper-right pane displays the range F1:I4; (3) the lower-left pane displays the range A11:C24; and (4) the lower-right pane displays the range F11:I24.

The vertical bar going up and down the middle of the window is called the **vertical split bar**. The horizontal bar going across the middle of the window is called the **horizontal split bar**. If you use the scroll bars below the window and to the right of the window to scroll the window, you will see that the panes split by the horizontal split bar scroll together vertically. The panes split by the vertical split bar scroll together horizontally. To resize the panes, drag either split bar to the desired location in the window.

You can change the values of cells in any of the four panes. Any change you make in one pane also takes effect in the other panes. To remove one of the split bars from the window, drag the split box to the edge of the window or double-click the split bar. Follow these steps to remove both split bars.

TO REMOVE THE FOUR PANES FROM THE WINDOW

1. Position the mouse pointer at the intersection of the horizontal and vertical split bars.
2. Double-click the split four-headed arrow.

Excel removes the four panes from the window.

What-If Analysis

The automatic recalculation feature of Excel is a powerful tool that can be used to analyze worksheet data. Recall from the Case Perspective on page E 3.4 the problem Frances Collins had when members of the board of directors suggested she change her assumptions to generate new projections. Because she had to calculate these values manually, it took her several minutes. The recalculations then rendered her chart useless.

Using Excel to scrutinize the impact of changing values in cells that are referenced by a formula in another cell is called **what-if analysis** or **sensitivity analysis**. Excel not only recalculates all formulas in a worksheet when new data is entered, but also redraws any associated charts.

In Project 3, the projected monthly expenses and net incomes in the range B7:G14 are dependent on the assumptions in the range B17:B23. Thus, if you change any of the assumption values, Excel immediately recalculates the projected monthly expenses in rows 7 through 13 and the projected monthly net incomes in row 14. Finally, because the projected monthly net incomes in row 14 change, Excel redraws the 3-D Pie chart, which is based on these numbers.

A what-if question for the worksheet in Project 3 might be, what if the first two and the fourth assumptions in the Assumptions table are changed as follows: Administrative 13.25% to 11.50%; Marketing 9.50% to 8.00%; and Bonus $75,000.00 to $50,000.00 — how would these changes affect the projected six-month net income in cell H14? To answer a question like this, you need to change only the first two and fourth values in the Assumptions table. Excel instantaneously recalculates the worksheet and redraws the 3-D Pie chart to answer the question regarding the projected six-month net income in cell H14.

The steps on the next page change the three assumptions as indicated in the previous paragraph and determine the new projected six-month net income in cell H14. To ensure that the Assumptions table and the projected six-month net income in cell H14 display on the screen at the same time, the steps on the next page also divide the window into two vertical panes.

What-If Analysis

Besides manually changing assumptions in a worksheet, Excel has additional methods for answering what-if questions, including Goal Seeking, Solver, Pivot Tables, Scenario Manager, and the Analysis ToolPak.

To Analyze Data in a Worksheet by Changing Values

1 **Use the vertical scroll bar to move the window so cell A4 is in the upper-left corner of the screen.**

2 **Drag the vertical split box (see Figure 3-75 on page E 3.61) from the lower-right corner of the screen to the left so that the vertical split bar is positioned in the middle of column F. Use the right scroll arrow to display the totals in column H in the right pane. Click cell B17.**

Excel divides the window into two vertical panes and shows the totals in column H in the pane on the right side of the window (Figure 3-77).

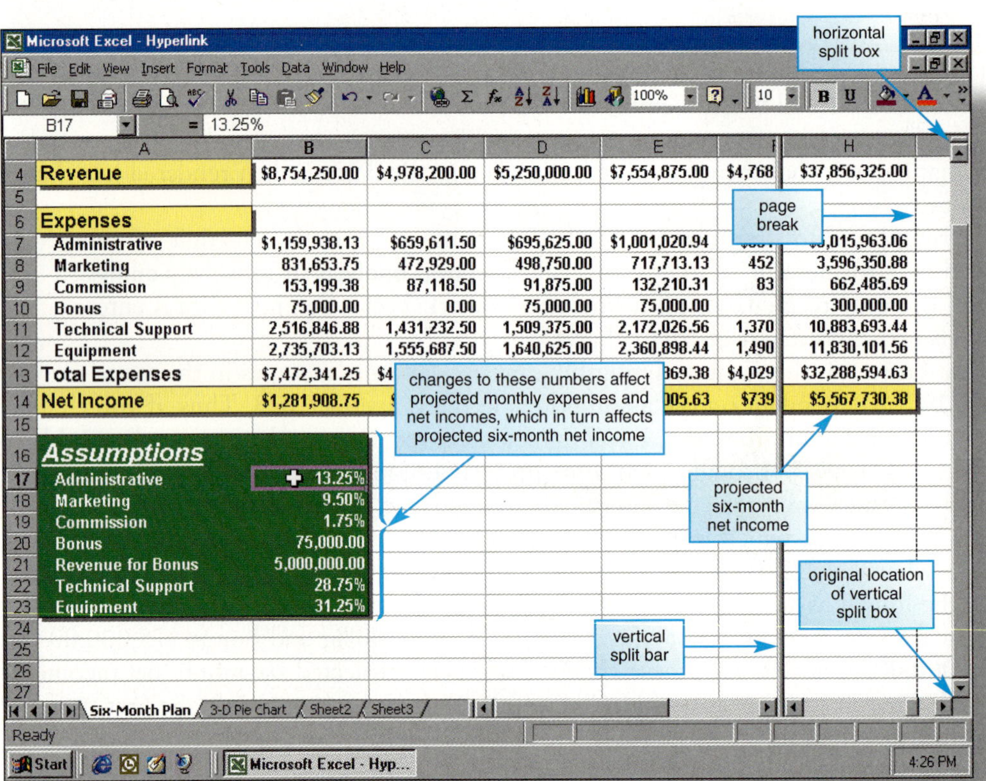

FIGURE 3-77

3 **Enter** `11.5` **in cell B17,** `8` **in cell B18, and** `50000` **in cell B20.**

Excel immediately recalculates all the formulas in the worksheet, including the projected six-month net income in cell H13 (Figure 3-78).

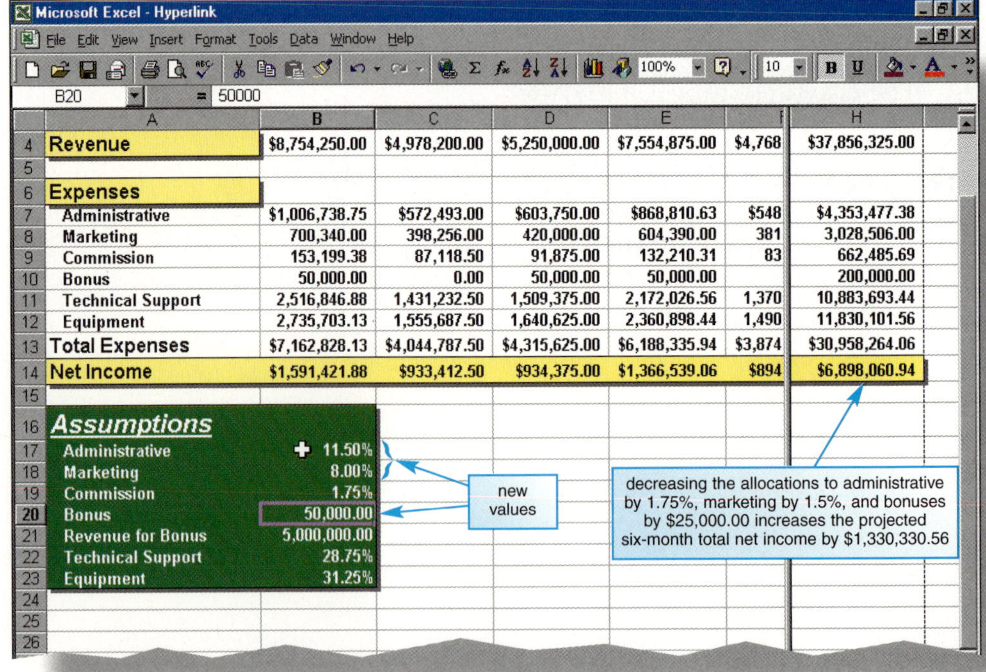

FIGURE 3-78

Each time you enter a new assumption, Excel recalculates the worksheet and redraws the 3-D Pie chart. This process usually takes less than one second, depending on how many calculations must be performed and the speed of your computer. Compare the projected six-month net incomes in Figures 3-77 and 3-78. By changing the values of the three assumptions (Figure 3-78), the projected six-month net income in cell H14 increases from $5,567,730.38 to $6,898,060.94. This translates into an increase of $1,330,330.56 for the projected six-month net income.

More About 2000

Undo

The Undo button is ideal for returning the worksheet to its original state after you have changed the value of a cell to answer a what-if question.

Goal Seeking

If you know the result you want a formula to produce, you can use **goal seeking** to determine the value of a cell on which the formula depends. The following example closes and reopens the Hyperlink workbook and uses the **Goal Seek command** on the Tools menu to determine what projected marketing percentage in cell B18 will yield a projected six-month net income of $7,000,000.00 in cell H14, rather than $5,567,730.38.

Steps To Goal Seek

1. **Close the Hyperlink workbook without saving changes. Click the Open button on the Standard toolbar and then reopen Hyperlink.**

2. **Drag the vertical split box to the middle of column F. Scroll down so row 4 is at the top of the screen. Display column H in the right pane. Click cell H14, the cell that contains the projected six-month net income. Click Tools on the menu bar and then point to Goal Seek.**

The vertical split bar displays in the middle of column F, and the Tools menu displays (Figure 3-79).

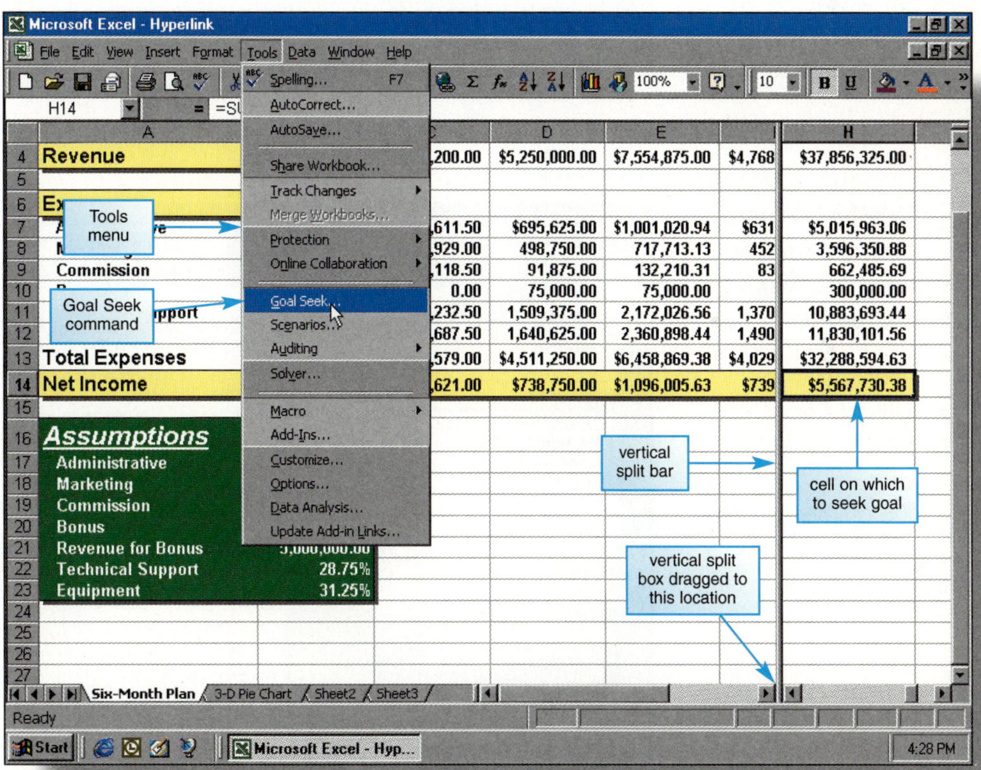

FIGURE 3-79

3 Click Goal Seek.

The Goal Seek dialog box displays. The Set cell box is assigned the cell reference of the active cell in the worksheet (cell H14) automatically.

4 Click the To value text box. Type 7,000,000 **and then click the By changing cell box. Click cell B18 on the worksheet.**

The Goal Seek dialog box displays as shown in Figure 3-80. A marquee displays around cell B18.

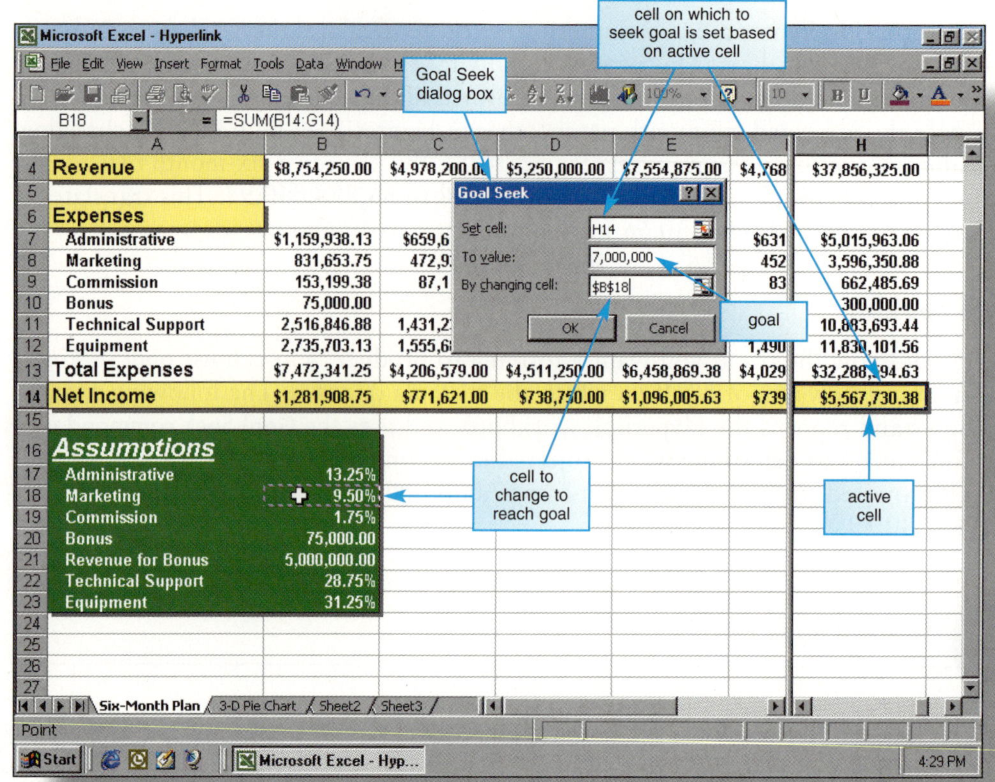

FIGURE 3-80

5 Click the OK button. When the Goal Seek Status dialog box displays, click the OK button.

Excel immediately changes cell H14 from $5,567,730.38 to the desired value of $7,000,000.00. More importantly, Excel changes the marketing assumption in cell B18 from 9.50% to 5.72% (Figure 3-81).

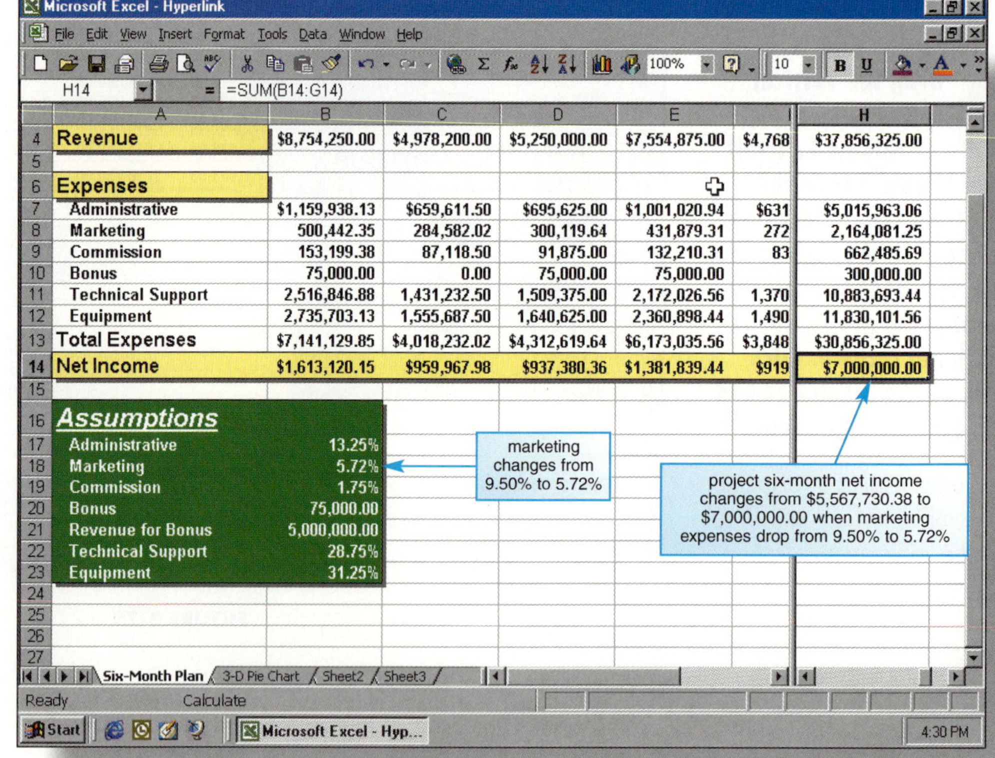

FIGURE 3-81

Goal seeking assumes you can change the value of only one cell referenced directly or indirectly. In this example, to change the projected six-month net income in cell H14 to $7,000,000.00, the marketing percentage in cell B18 must decrease by 3.78% from 9.50% to 5.72%.

You can see from this goal seeking example that the cell to change (cell B18) does not have to be referenced directly in the formula or function. For example, the projected six-month net income in cell H14 is calculated by the function =SUM(B14:G14). Cell B18 the marketing, is not referenced in the function. Instead, cell B18 is referenced in the formulas in rows 7 through 12, on which the projected monthly net incomes in row 13 are based. Excel is capable of goal seeking on the projected six-month net income by varying the marketing assumption.

More About 2000

Goal Seeking

Goal seeking is a methodology in which you know what answer you want a formula in a cell to be, but you do not know the value to place in a cell that is involved in the formula. You can goal seek by changing the value in a cell that is indirectly used in the formula as illustrated in Figures 3-80 and 3-81.

Quitting Excel

To quit Excel, complete the following steps.

TO QUIT EXCEL

1. Click the Close button on the title bar.
2. If the Microsoft Excel dialog box displays, click the No button.

CASE PERSPECTIVE SUMMARY

With the worksheet and chart developed in this project, the CEO of Hyperlink.com, Frances Collins, easily can respond to any what-if questions the board members ask the next time she presents her six-month plan. Questions that took several minutes to answer with paper and pencil now can be answered in a few seconds. Furthermore, computational errors are less likely to occur.

Project Summary

In creating the Hyperlink.com workbook, you learned how to work with large worksheets that extend beyond the window and how to use the fill handle to create a series. You learned to display hidden toolbars, dock a toolbar at the bottom of the screen, and hide an active toolbar. You learned about the difference between absolute cell references and relative cell references and how to use the IF function. You also learned how to rotate text in a cell, generate a series, freeze titles, change the magnification of the worksheet, display different parts of the worksheet through panes, and improve the appearance of a chart. Finally, this project introduced you to using Excel to do what-if analyzes by changing values in cells and goal seeking.

More About 2000

Quick Reference

For a table that lists how to complete the tasks covered in this book using the mouse, menu, shortcut menu, and keyboard, visit the Office 2000 Web page (www.scsite.com/office2000/qr.htm), and then click Microsoft Excel 2000.

What You Should Know

Having completed this project, you now should be able to perform the following tasks:

- Add a Drop Shadow *(E 3.39)*
- Add Leader Lines to the Data Labels *(E 3.55)*
- Analyze Data in a Worksheet by Changing Values *(E 3.64)*
- Assign Formats to the Projected Revenue, Expenses, and Net Income *(E 3.34)*
- Bold the Font of the Entire Worksheet *(E 3.7)*
- Change Font Size, Add Background Colors, and Add Drop Shadows to Nonadjacent Selections *(E 3.41)*
- Change the Colors of the Pie Slices *(E 3.51)*
- Check Spelling in Multiple Sheets (E 3.57)
- Copy a Cell's Format Using the Format Painter Button *(E 3.11)*
- Copy a Range of Cells to a Nonadjacent Paste Area *(E 3.14)*
- Copy the Projected July Expenses and Net Income Using the Fill Handle *(E 3.30)*
- Determine the Projected Expenses by Category and Net Income *(E 3.31)*
- Display the Drawing Toolbar *(E 3.38)*
- Dock a Toolbar at the Bottom of the Screen *(E 3.39)*
- Draw a 3-D Pie Chart on a Separate Chart Sheet *(E 3.45)*
- Enter a Number with a Format Symbol *(E 3.19)*
- Enter an IF Function *(E 3.28)*
- Enter and Format the System Date *(E 3.22)*
- Enter Formulas Containing Absolute Cell References *(E 3.26)*
- Enter the Projected Revenue *(E 3.21)*
- Enter the Remaining Projected Expense and Net Income Formulas *(E 3.29)*
- Enter the Worksheet Titles *(E 3.7)*
- Explode the 3-D Pie Chart *(E 3.52)*
- Format the Assumptions Table *(E 3.42)*
- Format the Chart Title and Labels *(E 3.49)*
- Format the Worksheet Titles *(E 3.36)*
- Freeze Column and Row Titles *(E 3.20)*
- Goal Seek *(E 3.65)*
- Increase Column Widths and Enter Row Titles *(E 3.12)*
- Insert Rows *(E 3.16)*
- Preview and Print the Workbook in Landscape Orientation *(E 3.58)*
- Quit Excel *(E 3.67)*
- Remove the Four Panes from the Window *(E 3.62)*
- Rename the Sheets and Rearrange the Order of the Sheets *(E 3.56)*
- Rotate and Tilt the 3-D Pie Chart *(E 3.53)*
- Rotate Text and Use the Fill Handle to Create a Series of Month Names *(E 3.8)*
- Shrink and Magnify the View of a Worksheet or Chart *(E 3.59)*
- Split a Window into Four Panes *(E 3.61)*
- Start Excel and Reset Toolbars and Menus *(E 3.7)*
- Unfreeze the Worksheet Titles and Save the Workbook *(E 3.32)*

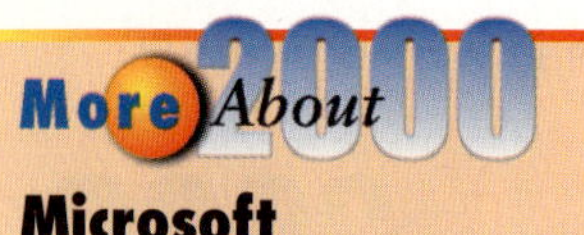

Microsoft Certification

The Microsoft Office User Specialist (MOUS) Certification program provides an opportunity for you to obtain a valuable industry credential - proof that you have the Excel 2000 skills required by employers. For more information, see Appendix D or visit the Shelly Cashman Series MOUS Web page at www.scsite.com/off2000/cert.htm.

Apply Your Knowledge

Project Reinforcement at www.scsite.com/off2000/reinforce.htm

1 Understanding the IF Function and Absolute Referencing

Instructions: Fill in the correct answers.

1. Determine the truth value (true or false) of the following logical tests, given the following cell values. A5 = 40; B6 = 29; C3 = 110; D7 = 10; and F4 = 125. Enter true or false.
   a. B6 < A5 Truth value: ____________________
   b. F4 = C3 Truth value: ____________________
   c. A5 + 15 * D7 / 5 <> C3 Truth value: ____________________
   d. C3 / D7 > A5 – B6 Truth value: ____________________
   e. F4 < (A5 + B6) * 2 -12 Truth value: ____________________
   f. C3 + 300 <= A5 * D7 + 10 Truth value: ____________________
   g. F4 + C3 > 2 * (F4 + 25) Truth value: ____________________
   h. A5 + D7 <> 2 * (F4 / 5) Truth value: ____________________
2. Write an IF function for cell C3 that assigns the value of cell D5 to cell C3 if the value in cell F2 is greater than the value in cell F3; otherwise the IF function assigns zero (0) to cell C3.
   Function: ____
3. Write an IF function for cell H5 that assigns the text "Eligible" if the value in cell H12 is three times greater than the value in cell H13; otherwise the IF function assigns the text "Not Eligible".
   Function: ____
4. A nested IF function is an IF function that contains another IF function in the value_if_true or value_if_false arguments. For example, =IF(D1 = "IN","Region 1", IF(D1 = "OH", "Region 2", "Not Applicable")) is a valid nested IF function. Start Excel and enter this IF function in cell C1 and then use the fill handle to copy the function down through cell C7. Enter the following data in the cells in the range D1:D7 and then write down the results that display in cells C1 through C7 for each set. Set 1: D1 = IL; D2 = IN; D3 = OH; D4 = MI; D5 = OH; D6 = IN; D7 = OH. Set 2: D1= WI; D2 = KY; D3 = IN; D4 = IL; D5 = IN; D6 = IN; D7 = OH.
   Function: ____
5. Write cell K5 as a relative reference, absolute reference, mixed reference with the row varying, and mixed reference with the column varying.

   ____________ ____________ ____________ ____________
6. Write the formula for cell B3 that divides cell F2 by the sum of cells A4 through A7. Write the formula so that when it is copied to cells C3 and D3, cell F2 remains absolute.
   Formula: ____
7. Write the formula for cell H5 that multiplies cell L8 times the sum of cells C4, D4, and E4. Write the formula so that when it is copied to cells H6, H7, and H8, cell L8 remains absolute.
   Formula: ____
8. Write the formula for cell J1 that multiplies cell P2 times the sum of cells Q10 through Q13. Write the formula so that when it is copied to cells K1 and L1, Excel adjusts all the cell references according to the new location.
   Formula: ____

1 R&R Hotel Indirect Expense Allocation

Problem: You are a work-study student at the local five-star R&R Hotel. Your work-study advisor at school and your supervisor at R&R Hotel have agreed on a challenging Excel project for you to do. They want you to create an indirect expense allocation worksheet (Figure 3-82) that will help the hotel administration better evaluate the profit centers described in Table 3-6.

R&R Hotel

INDIRECT EXPENSE ALLOCATION — 11/26/2001

	Dining Room	Banquet Room	Lounge	Fitness Center	Business Center	Conference Rooms	Snack Shop	Arcade	Total
Revenue	$625,900.00	$478,350.00	$392,775.00	$53,230.00	$133,125.00	$78,450.00	$85,350.00	$17,435.00	$1,864,615.00
Cost of Sales	213,450.00	123,900.00	105,630.00	34,945.00	12,600.00	42,500.00	34,000.00	8,550.00	575,575.00
Direct Costs	145,750.00	62,000.00	48,460.00	12,500.00	6,345.00	18,750.00	30,200.00	6,200.00	330,205.00
Indirect Expenses									
Administrative	$26,182.46	$20,010.19	$16,430.44	$2,226.70	$5,568.84	$3,281.70	$3,570.33	$729.34	$78,000.00
Marketing	18,797.66	14,366.29	11,796.22	1,598.66	3,998.14	2,356.09	2,563.32	523.63	56,000.00
Energy	11,748.54	8,978.93	7,372.63	999.16	2,498.84	1,472.56	1,602.07	327.27	35,000.00
Maintenance	2,727.27	9,090.91	2,181.82	3,272.73	545.45	4,181.82	909.09	1,090.91	24,000.00
Depreciation	7,613.64	25,378.79	6,090.91	9,136.36	1,522.73	11,674.24	2,537.88	3,045.45	67,000.00
Insurance	1,136.36	3,787.88	909.09	1,363.64	227.27	1,742.42	378.79	454.55	10,000.00
Total Indirect Expenses	$68,205.93	$81,612.99	$44,781.11	$18,597.25	$14,361.28	$24,708.83	$11,561.48	$6,171.14	$270,000.00
Net Income	$198,494.07	$210,837.01	$193,903.89	($12,812.25)	$99,818.72	($7,508.83)	$9,588.52	($3,486.14)	$688,835.00
Square Footage	1,500	5,000	1,200	1,800	300	2,300	500	600	13,200

Planned Indirect Expenses	
Administrative	$78,000.00
Marketing	$56,000.00
Energy	$35,000.00
Maintenance	$24,000.00
Depreciation	$67,000.00
Insurance	$10,000.00

FIGURE 3-82

Table 3-6 R&R Hotel Worksheet Data

	DINING ROOM	BANQUET ROOM	LOUNGE	FITNESS CENTER	BUSINESS CENTER	CONFERENCE ROOMS	SNACK SHOP	ARCADE
Revenue	625900	478350	392775	53230	133125	78450	85350	17435
Cost of Sales	213450	123900	105630	34945	12600	42500	34000	8550
Direct Costs	145750	62000	48460	12500	6345	18750	30200	6200
Square Footage	1500	5000	1200	1800	300	2300	500	600

Instructions Part 1: Do the following to create the worksheet shown in Figure 3-82.

1. Use the Select All button and Bold button to bold the entire worksheet. Enter the worksheet titles `R&R Hotel` in cell A1 and `Indirect Expense Allocation` in cell A2. Enter the system date in cell J2 using the NOW function. Format the date to the 3/4/1998 format style.
2. Enter the first four rows of data in Table 3-6 in rows 3 through 6. In row 3, use ALT+ENTER to display the column titles on two lines in a cell. Select the range J4:J6 and click the AutoSum button. Add a thick bottom border to the range B3:J3.
3. Enter the Square Footage row in Table 3-6 in row 16. Select cell J16 and use the AutoSum button to determine the sum of the values in the range B16:I16.
4. Change the following column widths: A = 26.00; B through I = 12.00, and J = 13.00. Change the height of row 16 to 39.00.
5. Enter the remaining row titles in the range A7:A17 as shown in Figure 3-82. Use the Indent button on the Formatting toolbar to indent the row titles in the range A8:A13.
6. Copy the range A8:A13 to the range A18:A23. Enter the numbers shown in the range B18:B23 of Figure 3-82 with format symbols.
7. The planned indirect expenses in the range B18:B23 are to be prorated across the profit center as follows: Administrative (row 8), Marketing (row 9), and Energy (row 10) on the basis of revenue volume; Maintenance (row 11), Depreciation (row 12), and Insurance (row 13) on the basis of square feet. Complete the following entries:
   a. Dining Room Administrative (cell B8) = Administrative Expenses * Dining Room Revenue / Total Revenue or =$B$18 * B4 / $J$4
   b. Marketing Administrative (cell B9) = Marketing Expenses * Dining Room Revenue / Total Revenue or =$B$19 * B4 / $J$4
   c. Energy Administrative (cell B10) = Energy Expenses * Dining Room Revenue / Total Revenue or =$B$20 * B4 / $J$4
   d. Maintenance Administrative (cell B11) = Maintenance Expenses * Dining Room Square Feet / Total Square Feet or =$B$21 * B16 / $J$16
   e. Depreciation Administrative (cell B12) = Depreciation Expenses * Dining Room Square Feet / Total Square Feet or =$B$22 * B16 / $J$16
   f. Insurance Administrative (cell B13) = Insurance Expenses * Dining Room Square Feet / Total Square Feet or =$B$23 * B16 / $J$16
   g. Total Indirect Expenses (cell B14) = SUM(B8:B13)
   h. Net Income (cell B15) = Revenue – (Cost of Sales + Direct Costs + Indirect Expenses) or =B4 – (B5 + B6 + B14)
   i. Use the fill handle to copy the range B8:B15 to the range C8:I15.
   j. Select the range J8:J15 and click the Auto Sum button on the Standard toolbar.
   k. Add a thick bottom border to the range B13:J13.
8. Use the Format Cells dialog box to format to Currency style with two decimal places and display negative numbers in parentheses to the following ranges: B4:J4; B8:J8; and B14:J15. Format to Comma style with two decimal places and display negative numbers in parentheses to the following ranges: B5:J6; B9:J13; and B16:J16.

(continued)

In the Lab

R&R Hotel Indirect Expense Allocation *(continued)*

9. Change the font in cell A1 to 48-point Brush Script MT (or a similar font). Change the font in cell A2 to 26-point Algerian (or a similar font). Change the font in cell A17 to 14-point italic and underlined.
10. Use the background color Blue-Gray (column 7, row 2) on the Fill Color palette, the foreground color White (column 8, row 5) on the Font Color palette, and a drop shadow (Shadow Type 6) for the following ranges: A1:J2; A7; A15:J15; and A17:B23. The Shadow button is on the Drawing toolbar.
11. Enter your name, course, laboratory assignment (Lab 3-1), date, and instructor name in the range A27:A31. Save the workbook using the file name, R&R Hotel.
12. Preview and print the worksheet. Preview and print the formulas version (CTRL+LEFT QUOTATION MARK) of the worksheet in landscape orientation using the Fit to option button in the Page Setup dialog box. After printing the formulas version, reset the print scaling to 100%. Press CTRL+LEFT QUOTATION MARK to display the values version of the worksheet. Save the workbook again.

Instructions Part 2: Draw a 3-D Pie chart (Figure 3-83) that shows the contribution of each category of indirect expense to the total indirect expenses. That is, chart the nonadjacent ranges A8:A13 (category names) and J8:J13 (data series). Show labels and percents. Do not show the legend. Do the following to the Pie chart:

1. Add the chart title and format it to 36-point Arial red, underlined font.
2. Explode the Administrative slice.
3. Select a slice and use the 3-D View command on the shortcut menu to change the elevation to 35° and the rotation to 80°.
4. Change the color of the slices as shown in Figure 3-83.
5. Drag the data labels away from the 3-D Pie chart so the leader lines from the data labels to the corresponding slices display.
6. Rename the sheets as follows: Chart1 to 3-D Pie Chart; Sheet1 to Planned Indirect Expenses. Rearrange the sheets so the Planned Indirect Expenses sheet is to the left of the 3-D Pie Chart sheet. Click the Planned Indirect Expenses tab.

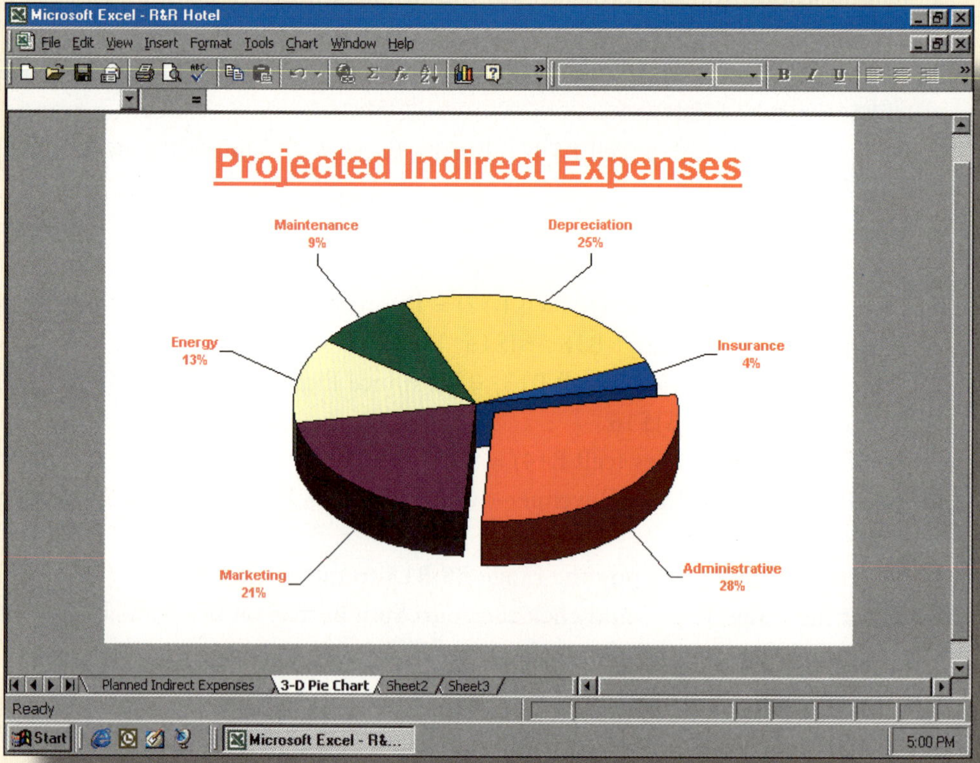

FIGURE 3-83

7. Save the workbook using the file name R&R Hotel. Print both sheets.

Instructions Part 3: Using the numbers in Table 3-7, analyze the effect of changing the planned indirect expenses in the range B18:B23 on the net incomes for each profit center. Print the worksheet for each case. You should end with the following totals in cell J15: Case 1 = $639,335.00 and Case 2 = $745,335.00

Table 3-7 What-If Data

	CASE 1	*CASE 2*
Administrative	92,000.00	56,000.00
Marketing	65,000.00	47,000.00
Energy	42,000.00	32,000.00
Maintenance	36,000.00	20,000.00
Depreciation	72,000.00	51,000.00
Insurance	12,500.00	7,500.00

2 E-Book.com Seven-Year Projected Financial Statement

Problem: You were recently certified at the Expert level in Excel by the Microsoft Office User Specialist program. Following certification, you were promoted to spreadsheet specialist at E-Book.com, an e-commerce Web site on the Internet that sells books, videos, and CDs. Your manager has asked you to create a worksheet that will project the revenue, expenses, taxes, and income for the next seven years based on the assumptions in Table 3-8. The desired worksheet is shown in Figure 3-84.

Table 3-8 Data for Assumptions

ASSUMPTIONS	
Units Sold in Year 2000	8,492,016
Unit Cost	9.27
Annual Sales Growth	7.00%
Annual Price Decrease	5.00%
Margin	40.00%

	A	B	C	D	E	F	G	H
1	E-Book.com							
2	Seven-Year Projected Financial Statement							11/26/2001
3		2001	2002	2003	2004	2005	2006	2007
4	Revenue	131,201,647	133,366,474	135,567,021	137,803,877	140,077,641	142,388,922	144,738,339
5	Cost of Goods Sold	78,720,988	80,019,885	81,340,213	82,682,326	84,046,585	85,433,353	86,843,004
6	Gross Margin	52,480,659	53,346,590	54,226,808	55,121,551	56,031,056	56,955,569	57,895,336
7	Expenses							
8	Advertising	19,681,247	20,005,971	20,336,053	20,671,582	21,012,646	21,359,338	21,711,751
9	Rent	1,800,000	1,980,000	2,178,000	2,395,800	2,635,380	2,898,918	3,188,810
10	Salaries	23,616,296	24,005,965	24,402,064	24,804,698	25,213,975	25,630,006	26,052,901
11	Supplies	1,968,025	2,000,497	2,033,505	2,067,058	2,101,165	2,135,834	2,171,075
12	Maintenance	2,100,000	5,450,000	3,900,000	5,350,000	2,750,000	2,950,000	3,100,000
13	Total Expenses	49,165,568	53,442,434	52,849,622	55,289,138	53,713,166	54,974,096	56,224,537
14								
15	Income Before Taxes	3,315,091	(95,844)	1,377,186	(167,587)	2,317,890	1,981,473	1,670,799
16	Income Taxes	1,326,036	0	550,874	0	927,156	792,589	668,320
17	Net Income	1,989,054	(95,844)	826,312	(167,587)	1,390,734	1,188,884	1,002,479
18								
19	Assumptions							
20	Units Sold in Year 2000	8,492,016						
21	Unit Cost	9.27						
22	Annual Sales Growth	7.00%						
23	Annual Price Decrease	5.00%						
24	Margin	40.00%						
25								

FIGURE 3-84

(continued)

E-Book.com Seven-Year Projected Financial Statement *(continued)*

Instructions Part 1: Do the following to create the worksheet shown in Figure 3-84.

1. Use the Select All button and Bold button to bold the entire worksheet. Enter the worksheet titles in cells A1 and A2. Enter the system date in cell H2 using the NOW function. Format the date to the 3/14/1998 style.
2. Enter the seven column titles 2001 through 2007 in the range B3:H3. Begin each year with an apostrophe so that the years are entered as text. Text headings are required for the charting in Part 2. Center and italicize cell B3. Rotate its contents 45°. Use the Format Painter button to copy the format assigned to cell B3 to the range C3:H3.
3. Enter the row titles in the range A4:A24. Change the font size in cells A7, A13, A15, and A17 to 12 point. Change the font size in cell A19 to 14 point and underline the characters in the cell. Add a heavy bottom border to the range A3:H3.
4. Change the following column widths: A = 23.43; B through H = 11.00. Change the heights of rows 7, 13, 15, 16, and 17 to 24.00.
5. Enter the assumptions values in Table 3-8 in the range B20:B24. Use format symbols.
6. Assign the Comma style format with no decimal places to the range B4:H17.
7. Complete the following entries:
   a. 2001 Revenue (cell B4) = Units Sold 2000 * (Unit Cost / (1 – Margin)) or =B20 * (B21 / (1 – B24))
   b. 2002 Revenue (cell C4) = 2001 Revenue * (1 + Annual Sales Growth) * (1 – Annual Price Decrease) or =B4 * (1 + $B$22) * (1 – $B$23)
   c. Copy cell C4 to the range D4:H4.
   d. 2001 Cost of Goods Sold (cell B5) = 2001 Revenue – (2001 Revenue * Margin) or =B4 * (1 - $B$24)
   e. Copy cell B5 to the range C5:H5.
   f. 2001 Gross Margin (cell B6) = 2001 Revenue – 2001 Cost of Goods Sold or =B4 – B5
   g. Copy cell B6 to the range C6:H6.
   h. 2001 Advertising (cell B8) = 1000 + 15% * 2001 Revenue or =1000 + 15% * B4
   i. Copy cell B8 to the range C8:H8.
   j. 2001 Rent (cell B9) = 1,800,000
   k. 2002 Rent (cell C9) = 2001 Rent + 10% * 2001 Rent or =B9 + (10% * B9)
   l. Copy cell C9 to the range D9:H9.
   m. 2001 Salaries (cell B10) = 18% * 2001 Revenue or =18% * B4
   n. Copy cell B10 to the range C10:H10.
   o. 2001 Supplies (cell B11) = 1.5% * 2001 Revenue or =1.5% * B4
   p. Copy cell B11 to the range C11:H11.
   q. Maintenance: 2001 = 2,100,000; 2002 = 5,450,000; 2003 = 3,900,000; 2004 = 5,350,000; 2005 = 2,750,000; 2006 = 2,950,000; 2007 = 3,100,000
   r. 2001 Total Expenses (cell B13) = SUM(B8:B12)
   s. Copy cell B13 to the range C13:H13.
   t. 2001 Income Before Taxes (cell B15) = 2001 Gross Margin – 2001 Total Expenses or =B6 – B13
   u. Copy cell B15 to the range C15:H15.

v. 2001 Income Taxes (cell B16): If 2001 Income Before Taxes is less than zero, then 2001 Income Taxes equal zero; otherwise 2001 Income Taxes equal 40% * 2001 Income Before Taxes or =IF(B15 < 0, 0, 40% * B15)

w. Copy cell B16 to the range C16:H16.

x. 2001 Net Income (cell B17) = 2001 Income Before Taxes – 2001 Income Taxes or =B15 – B16

y. Copy cell B17 to the range C17:H17.

8. Change the font in cell A1 to 26-point Book Antiqua (or a similar font). Change the font in cell A2 to 16-point Book Antiqua (or a similar font). Change the font in cell H2 to 10-point Century Gothic (or a similar font). Change the background and font colors and add drop shadows as shown in Figure 3-84.
9. Enter your name, course, laboratory assignment (Lab 3-1), date, and instructor name in the range A27:A31. Save the workbook using the file name, e-book.
10. Preview and print the worksheet. Preview and print the formulas version (CTRL+LEFT QUOTATION MARK) of the worksheet in landscape orientation using the Fit to option button in the Page Setup dialog box. After printing the formulas version, reset the print scaling to 100%. Press CTRL+LEFT QUOTATION MARK to display the values version of the worksheet. Save the workbook again.

Instructions Part 2: Draw a 3-D Column chart (Figure 3-85) that compares the projected net incomes for the years 2001 through 2007. Use the nonadjacent ranges B3:H3 and B17:H17. Add the chart title and format it as shown in Figure 3-85. Rename and rearrange the sheets as shown in Figure 3-85. Save the workbook using the same file name (e-book) as defined in Part 1. Print both sheets.

Instructions Part 3: If the 3-D Column chart is on the screen, click the Seven-Year Plan tab to display the worksheet. Divide the window into two panes by dragging the horizontal split bar between rows 6 and 7. Use the scroll bars to display both the top and bottom of the worksheet.

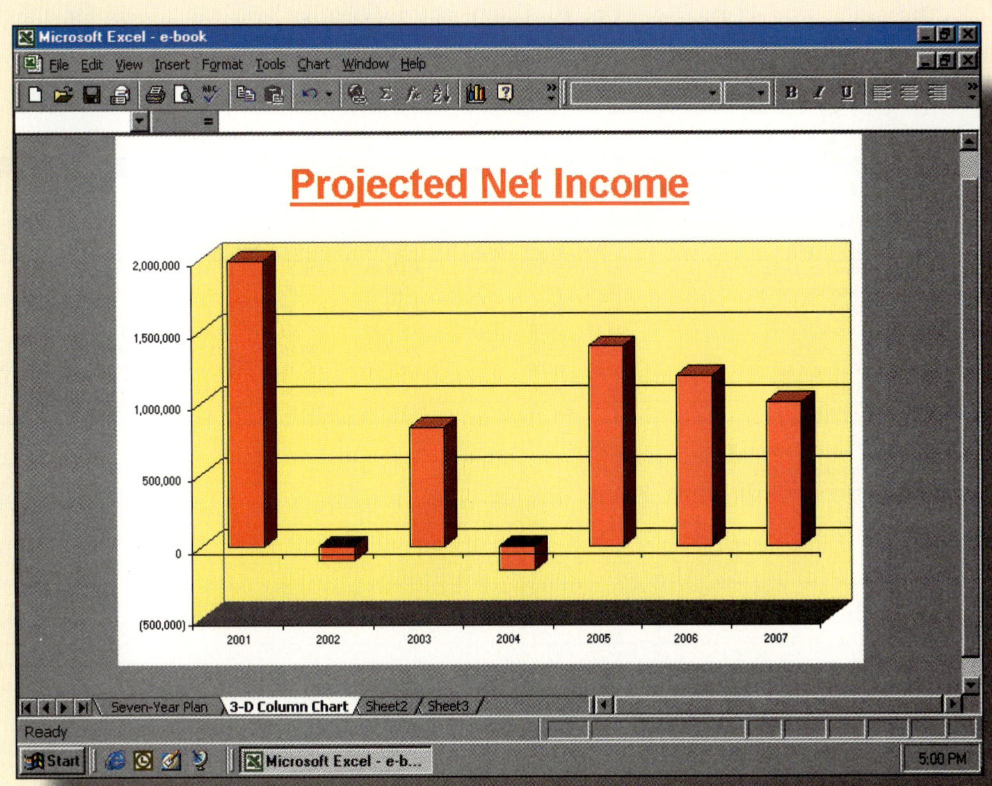

FIGURE 3-85

(continued)

E-Book.com Seven-Year Projected Financial Statement *(continued)*

Using the numbers in columns 2 and 3 of Table 3-9, analyze the effect of changing the annual sales growth (cell B22) and annual price decrease (cell B23) on the annual net incomes in row 17. The resulting answers are in column 4 of Table 3-9. Print both the worksheet and chart for each case.

Close the workbook without saving it, and then reopen it. Use the Goal Seek command to determine a margin (cell B24) that would result in a net income in 2007 of $5,000,000 (cell H17). You should end up with a margin of 43.94% in cell B24. After you complete the goal seeking, print only the worksheet. Do not save the workbook with the latest changes.

Table 3-9 Data to Analyze and Results

CASE	ANNUAL SALES GROWTH	ANNUAL PRICE DECREASE	2007 RESULTING NETINCOME
1	12.55%	2.15%	$3,950,985
2	15.25%	-5.50	$10,215,981
3	25.50%	9.35%	$5,613,019

3 Modifying the Stars and Stripes Automotive Weekly Payroll Worksheet

Problem: Your supervisor in the Payroll department has asked you to modify the payroll workbook developed in Exercise 1 of the Project 2 In the Lab section on page E 2.68, so that it displays as shown in Figure 3-86. If you did not complete Exercise 1 in Project 2, ask your instructor for a copy of the Stars and Stripes Automotive workbook or complete that exercise before you begin this one.

	A	B	C	D	E	F	G	H	I	J	K
1	**Stars and Stripes Automotive**										
2	Weekly Payroll Report for	1/5/2002									
3	Employee	Rate	Hours	Dep.	YTD Soc. Sec.	Gross Pay	Soc. Sec.	Medicare	Fed. Tax	State Tax	Net Pay
4	Breeze, Linus	27.50	40.25	4	4,974.00	1,110.31	68.84	16.10	191.29	35.53	798.55
5	Santiago, Juan	18.75	56.00	1	5,540.20	1,200.00	13.70	17.40	232.31	38.40	898.19
6	Webb, Trevor	28.35	38.00	3	4,254.00	1,077.30	66.79	15.62	192.38	34.47	768.03
7	Sabol, Kylie	21.50	46.50	6	5,553.90	1,069.63	0.00	15.51	167.77	34.23	852.11
8	Ali, Abdul	19.35	15.00	9	3,447.60	290.25	18.00	4.21	0.00	9.29	258.76
9	Chung, Lee	17.05	28.00	5	4,825.50	477.40	29.60	6.92	57.02	15.28	368.58
10	Fritz, Albert	28.35	38.75	3	5,553.90	1,098.56	0.00	15.93	196.64	35.15	850.84
11	Totals		262.50		34,149.10	6,323.45	196.93	91.69	1,037.42	202.35	4,795.07
12											
13	Social Security Tax	6.20%									
14	Medicare Tax	1.45%									
15	Maximum Social Security	$5,553.90									

FIGURE 3-86

In the Lab

The major modifications requested by your supervisor include: (1) reformatting the worksheet; (2) adding computations of time and a half for hours worked greater than 40; (3) removing the conditional formatting assigned to the range E3:E8; (4) charging no federal tax in certain situations; (5) adding Social Security and Medicare deductions; (6) adding and deleting employees; and (7) changing employee information. The Stars and Stripes Automotive workbook, as created in Project 2, is shown in Figure 2-85 on page E 2.68.

Instructions Part 1: Open the workbook, Stars and Stripes Automotive, created in Project 2. Perform the following tasks.

1. Use the Select All button and the Clear command on the Edit menu to clear all formats.
2. Bold the entire worksheet. Delete rows 10 through 12. Insert a row above row 2. Modify the wording in the worksheet title in cell A1 and change its point size to 14 so it appears as shown in Figure 3-86. Enter the worksheet subtitle, Weekly Payroll Report for, in cell A2. Assign the NOW function to cell B2 and format it to the 3/14/1998 style.
3. Insert a new column between columns D and E by right-clicking the column E heading and inserting a column. Enter the new column E title, `YTD Soc. Sec`, in cell E3. Insert two new columns between columns F and G. Enter the new column G title, `Soc. Sec.`, in cell G3. Enter the new column H title, `Medicare`, in cell H3. Freeze the panes (titles) in column A and rows 1 through 3.
4. Change the column widths and row heights as follows: A = 25.00; B = 9.43; C = 6.43; D = 6.00; E = 13.14; F through K = 9.71; and row 3 = 18.00. Right-align the column titles in the range B3:K3.
5. Delete row 9 (Goldstein, Kevin). Change Abdul Ali's hours worked to 15 and number of dependents to 9.
6. In column E, enter the YTD Social Security values listed in Table 3-10.
7. Insert two new rows immediately above the Totals row. Add the new employee data as listed in Table 3-11.
8. Use the Format Cells dialog box to assign a Comma style and two decimal places to the ranges B4:C11 and E4:K11. Center the range D4:D10.
9. Enter the Social Security and Medicare tax information headings in the range A13:A15. Enter the values in the range B13:B15. Use format symbols to format the numbers as shown in Figure 3-86.
10. Change the formulas to determine the gross pay in column F and the federal tax in column I.
    a. In cell F4, enter an IF function that applies the following logic: If Hours <= 40, then Gross Pay = Rate * Hours, otherwise Gross Pay = Rate * Hours + 0.5 * Rate * (Hours – 40)
    b. Copy the IF function in cell F4 to the range F5:F10.
    c. In cell I4, enter the IF function that applies the following logic: If (Gross Pay – Dependents * 38.46) > 0, then Federal Tax = 20% * (Gross Pay – Dependents * 38.46), otherwise Federal Tax = 0
    d. Copy the IF function in cell I4 to the range I5:I10.

Table 3-10 YTD Social Security Values

NAME	YTD SOC. SEC.
Breeze, Linus	4,974.00
Santiago, Juan	5,540.20
Webb, Trevor	4,254.00
Sabol, Kylie	5,553.90
Ali, Abdul	3,447.60

Table 3-11 New Employee Data

EMPLOYEE	RATE	HOURS	DEPENDENTS	YTD SOC.SEC.
Chung, Lee	17.05	28	5	4,825.50
Fritz, Albert	28.35	38.75	3	5,553.90

(continued)

Modifying the Stars and Stripes Automotive Weekly Payroll Worksheet *(continued)*

11. An employee pays Social Security tax only if his or her YTD Social Security is less than the maximum Social Security in column E. Use the following logic to determine the Social Security tax for Linus Breeze in cell G4:
    If Soc. Sec. Tax * Gross Pay + YTD Soc. Sec. > Maximum Soc. Sec., then Maximum Soc. Sec. – YTD Soc. Sec., otherwise Soc. Sec. Tax * Gross Pay
12. Make sure references to the values in the social security tax table (B13:B15) are absolute, and then copy the IF function to the range G5:G10.
13. In cell H4, enter the following formula and then copy it to the range H5:H10:
    Medicare = Medicare Tax * Gross Pay
14. Copy the state tax in cell J4 to the range J5:J10.
15. In cell K4, enter the following formula and copy it to the range K5:K10:
    = Gross Pay – (Soc. Sec. + Medicare + Fed. Tax + State Tax)
16. Determine any new totals as shown in row 11 of Figure 3-86.
17. Enter your name, course, laboratory assignment (Lab 3-2), date, and instructor name in the range A18:A22.
18. Unfreeze the panes (titles). Save the workbook using the file name, Stars and Stripes Automotive 2.
19. Use the Zoom box on the Standard toolbar to change the view of the worksheet. One by one, select all the percents in the Zoom list. When you are done, return the worksheet to 100% magnification.
20. Preview the worksheet. If number signs display in place of numbers in any columns, adjust the column widths. Print the worksheet in landscape orientation. Save the worksheet using the same file name.
21. Preview and print the formulas version (CTRL+LEFT QUOTATION MARK) in landscape orientation using the Fit to option button in the Page Setup dialog box. Close the worksheet without saving the latest changes.

Instructions Part 2: Using the numbers in Table 3-12, analyze the effect of changing the Social Security tax in cell B13 and the Medicare tax in cell B14. Print the worksheet for each case. The first case should result in a total Social Security tax in cell G11 of $250.12. The second case should result in a total Social Security tax of $324.00.

Table 3-12 Social Security and Medicare Taxes

CASE	SOCIAL SECURITY TAX	MEDICARE TAX
1	8%	2.75%
2	10.5%	2.25%

Cases and Places

The difficulty of these case studies varies:
◗ are the least difficult; ◗◗ are more difficult; and ◗◗◗ are the most difficult.

1 ◗ You are a managing editor for Swain Publishers, a company that produces paperback books sold worldwide. One of your responsibilities is to submit income projections to your publisher for the books you plan to sign. The projected first year net sales for the books you plan to do are shown in Table 3-13. Also included in the table are the percent of net sales for payment of royalties and manufacturing costs. Use the concepts and techniques presented in this project to create and format a worksheet that shows the projected royalties, projected manufacturing cost, net income for each book, and totals for the four numeric columns in Table 3-13. The net income for a book is equal to the net sales less the royalty and manufacturing costs.

Table 3-13 Projected 1st Year Net Sales

BOOK TITLE	NET SALES	ROYALTY	MANU. COSTS	NET INCOME
1	975,270.50	----	----	----
2	597,825.25	----	----	----
3	752,913.37	----	----	----
TOTAL	----	----	----	----
ASSUMPTIONS				
ROYALTIES	15.5%			
MANU. COSTS	21.5%			

Your publisher reviewed your plan and returned it, requesting printouts of the worksheet for the following set of values: Set 1 – Royalty 13.5%; Manufacturing Costs 31%; Set 2 – Royalty 14%; Manufacturing Costs 29%.

2 ◗ Lite Power Company is a large utility company in the Southwest. The company earns revenues from the sale of natural gas and electricity. A fixed percentage of this revenue is spent on marketing, payroll, equipment, production costs, and administrative expenses. Lite Power's president has summarized the company's receipts and expenditures over the past year on a quarterly basis as shown in Table 3-14.

Table 3-14 Quarterly Company Receipts and Expenditures

REVENUES	QUARTER 1	QUARTER 2	QUARTER 3	QUARTER 4
NATURAL GAS	52,349,812	67,213,943	55,329,781	51,690,655
ELECTRICITY	42,812,562	55,392,887	52,932,856	50,278,541
EXPENDITURES				
MARKETING	12.75%			
PAYROLL	32.65%			
EQUIPMENT	14.30%			
PRODUCTION	19.50%			
ADMINISTRATIVE	4.5%			

With this data, you have been asked to prepare a worksheet similar to Figure 3-1a on page E 3.5 for the next shareholders' meeting. The worksheet should show total revenues, total expenditures, and net income for each quarterly period. Include a chart that illustrates quarterly net income. Use the concepts and techniques presented in this project to create and format the worksheet and chart. During the meeting, one shareholder lobbied to reduce marketing expenditures by 2% and payroll costs by 6%. Perform a what-if analysis reflecting the proposed changes in expenditures.

3 Candie's sweet shop is open year round, but most of the shop's production revolves around four holidays: Valentine's Day (6,125 lbs.), Easter (4,250 lbs.), Halloween (8,825 lbs.), and Christmas (5,975 lbs.). On these days 31% of the store's output is fudge, 13% is caramel, 43% is boxed chocolate, and the remaining 13% is holiday-specific candy (such as chocolate hearts or candy canes). The fudge sells for $6.55 per pound, the caramel for $4.95 per pound, the boxed chocolate for $7.25 per pound, and holiday-specific candy for $3.75 per pound. Candie's management is considering revising its production figures. They have asked you to create a worksheet they can use in making this decision. The worksheet should show the amount of each candy produced for each holiday, potential sales for each type of candy, total potential sales for each holiday, total candy produced for the four holidays, and total potential sales from each type of candy. Include an appropriate chart illustrating total potential sales for each candy type. Use the concepts and techniques presented in this project to create and format the worksheet.

4 Your uncle, Dollar Bill, wants to save enough money to send his little girl to a private school. He has job orders at his custom drapery shop for the next six months: $800 in January, $750 in February, $550 in March, $665 in April, $388 in May, and $767 in June. Each month, Uncle Dollar Bill spends 40.25% of the orders on material, 3.5% on patterns, 3.25% on his retirement account, and 44% on food and clothing. The remaining profits (orders – expenses) will be put aside for the girl's education. Aunt Penny has agreed to provide an additional $25 whenever Uncle Dollar Bill's monthly profit exceeds $50. Your uncle has asked you to create a worksheet that shows orders, expenses, profits, and savings for the next six months, and totals for each category. Uncle Dollar Bill would like you to (a) goal seek to determine what percentage of profits to spend on food and clothing if $800 is needed for the school, and (b) perform a what-if analysis to determine the effect of reducing the percentage spent on material to 25%. Use the concepts and techniques presented in this project to create and format the worksheet.

5 Balancing a budget is a significant challenge for many students attending college. Whether you work part-time or simply draw on a sum of money while going to school, you must equalize income and expenditures to maintain your budget. Use the concepts and techniques presented in this project to create and format a worksheet that reflects your monthly budget throughout the school year. Indicate the amount of money you have available each month. Hypothesize percentages for monthly expenditures (tuition, books, entertainment, and so on). On the basis of these assumptions, determine expenditures for each month. Include a row for occasional miscellaneous expenses (such as travel). Ascertain the amount of money remaining at the end of each month; this amount will become part or all of the money available for the subsequent month. Perform at least one what-if analysis to examine the effect of changing one or more of the values in the worksheet, and goal-seek to determine how an expenditure must be modified to have $500 more available at the end of the school year.

Microsoft Excel 2000

Creating Static and Dynamic Web Pages Using Excel

CASE PERSPECTIVE

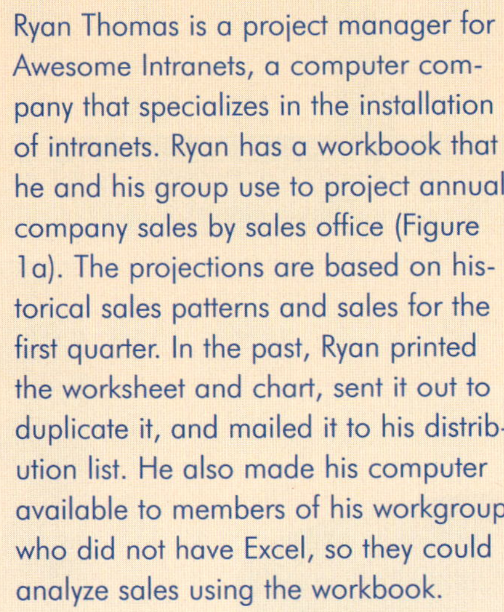

Ryan Thomas is a project manager for Awesome Intranets, a computer company that specializes in the installation of intranets. Ryan has a workbook that he and his group use to project annual company sales by sales office (Figure 1a). The projections are based on historical sales patterns and sales for the first quarter. In the past, Ryan printed the worksheet and chart, sent it out to duplicate it, and mailed it to his distribution list. He also made his computer available to members of his workgroup who did not have Excel, so they could analyze sales using the workbook.

Awesome Intranets recently upgraded to Office 2000 because of its Web and collaboration capabilities. After attending an Office 2000 training session, Ryan had a great idea and called you for help. He would like to save the Excel workbook (Figure 1a) on the company's intranet as a Web page (Figure 1b) so members on the distribution list could display it using their browser. He also suggested publishing the same workbook on the company's intranet as a dynamic (interactive) Web page (Figure 1c) so his workgroup could use its browser to manipulate the formulas and Pie chart without requiring Excel 2000.

Introduction

Excel 2000 provides fast and easy methods for saving workbooks as Web pages that can be stored on the World Wide Web, a company's intranet, or a local hard drive. A user then can display the workbook using a browser, rather than Excel.

You can save a workbook, or a portion of a workbook, as a static Web page or a dynamic Web page. A **static (noninteractive) Web page** is a snapshot of the workbook. It is similar to a printed report in that you can view it through your browser, but you cannot modify it. A **dynamic (interactive) Web page** includes the interactivity and functionality of the workbook, such as formulas, charting, and the recalculation features of Excel.

As shown in Figure 1 on the next page, in this Web Feature you will save a workbook (Figure 1a) as a static Web page (Figure 1b) and view it using your browser. Then you will take the same workbook and save it as a dynamic Web page (Figure 1c) and view it using your browser. After displaying the dynamic Web page in your browser, you will change certain values to test the Web page's interactivity and functionality.

The Save as Web Page command on the File menu allows you to **publish** workbooks, which is the process of making them available to others; for example, on the World Wide Web or on a company's intranet. If you have access to a Web server, you can publish Web pages by saving them to a Web folder or to an FTP location. The procedures for publishing Web pages to a Web folder or FTP location using Microsoft Office applications are discussed in Appendix B.

In this Web Feature, for instructional purposes, you will create and save the Web pages and associated folders on a floppy disk.

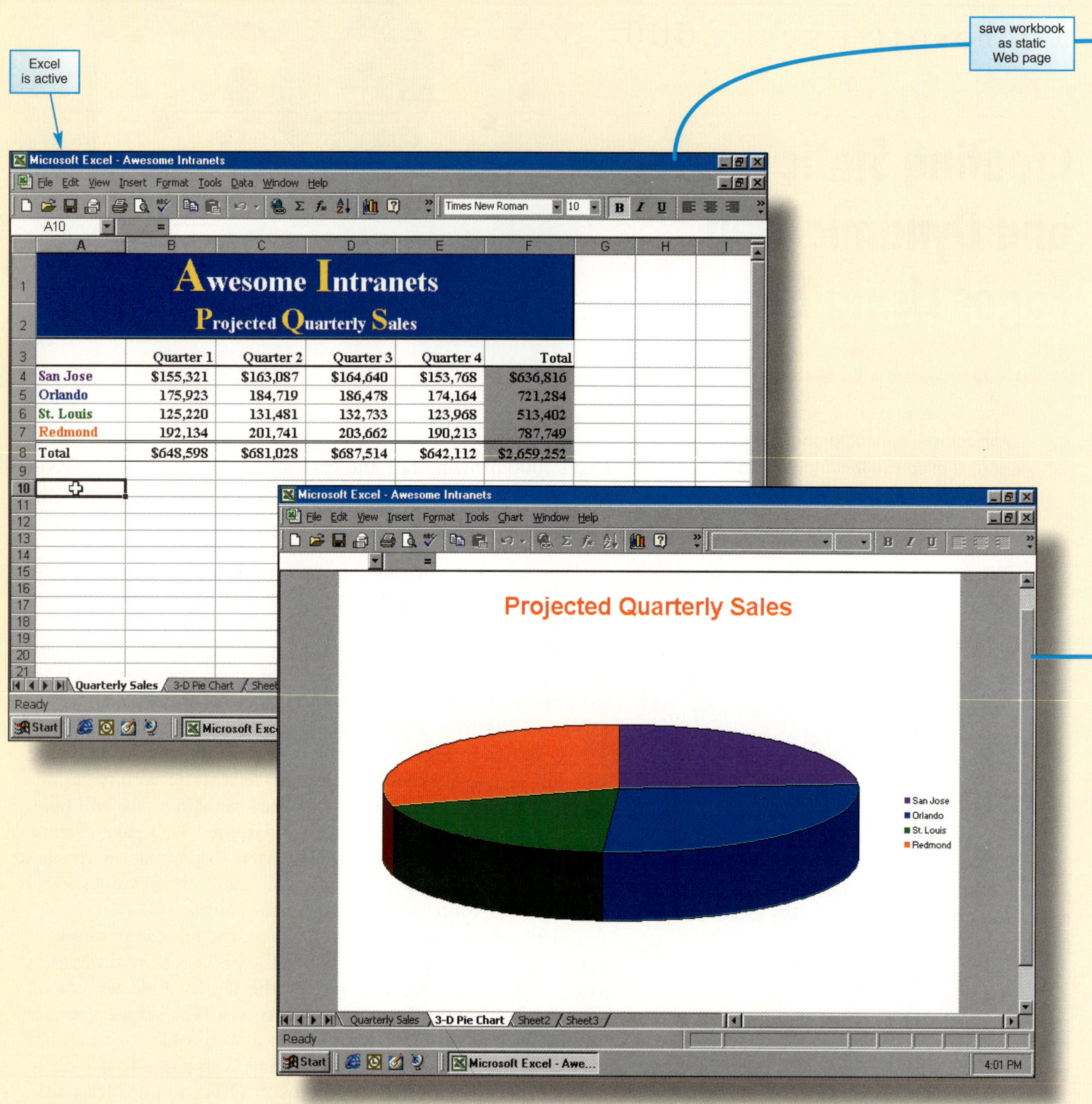

(a) Workbook Viewed in Excel

FIGURE 1

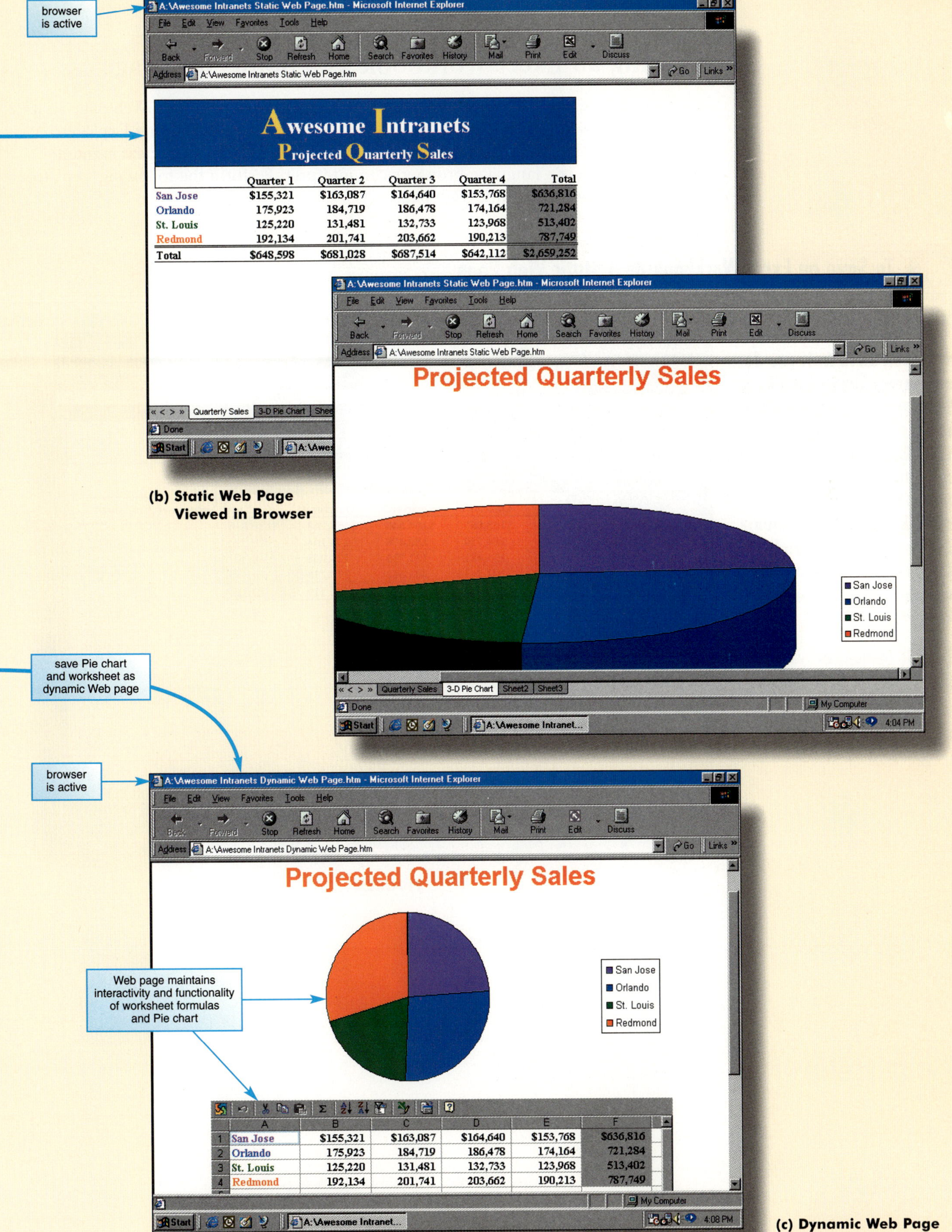

(b) Static Web Page Viewed in Browser

(c) Dynamic Web Page Viewed in Browser

Saving an Excel Workbook as a Static Web Page

Once you have created an Excel workbook, you can save it as a static Web page so it can be published and then viewed using a Web browser, such as Internet Explorer. The file format that Excel saves the workbook in is called **HTML (hypertext markup language)**, which is a language browsers can interpret. Perform the following steps to save the workbook as a static Web page.

To Save an Excel Workbook as a Static Web Page

1 Insert the Data Disk in drive A. If you do not have a copy of the Data Disk, see the inside back cover of this book. Start Excel and then open the workbook, Awesome Intranets, on drive A. Reset your toolbars as described in Appendix C. Click File on the menu bar and then point to Save as Web Page.

The File menu displays (Figure 2).

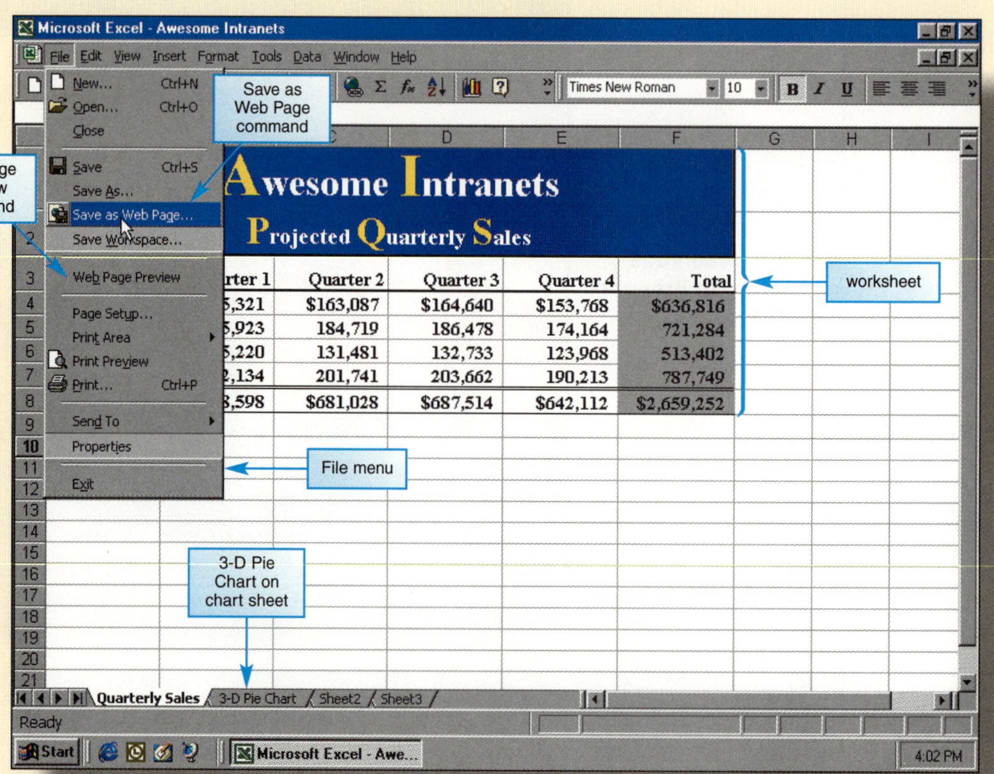

FIGURE 2

2 **Click Save as Web Page. When the Save As dialog box displays, type** `Awesome Intranets Static Web Page` **in the File name text box and then, if necessary, click the Save in box arrow and select 3½ Floppy (A:). Point to the Save button in the Save As dialog box.**

The Save As dialog box displays (Figure 3).

3 **Click the Save button. Click the Close button on the right side of the title bar to close Excel.**

Excel saves the workbook in HTML format on drive A using the file name, Awesome Intranets Static Web page.htm (see Figure 4 on the next page). Excel shuts down.

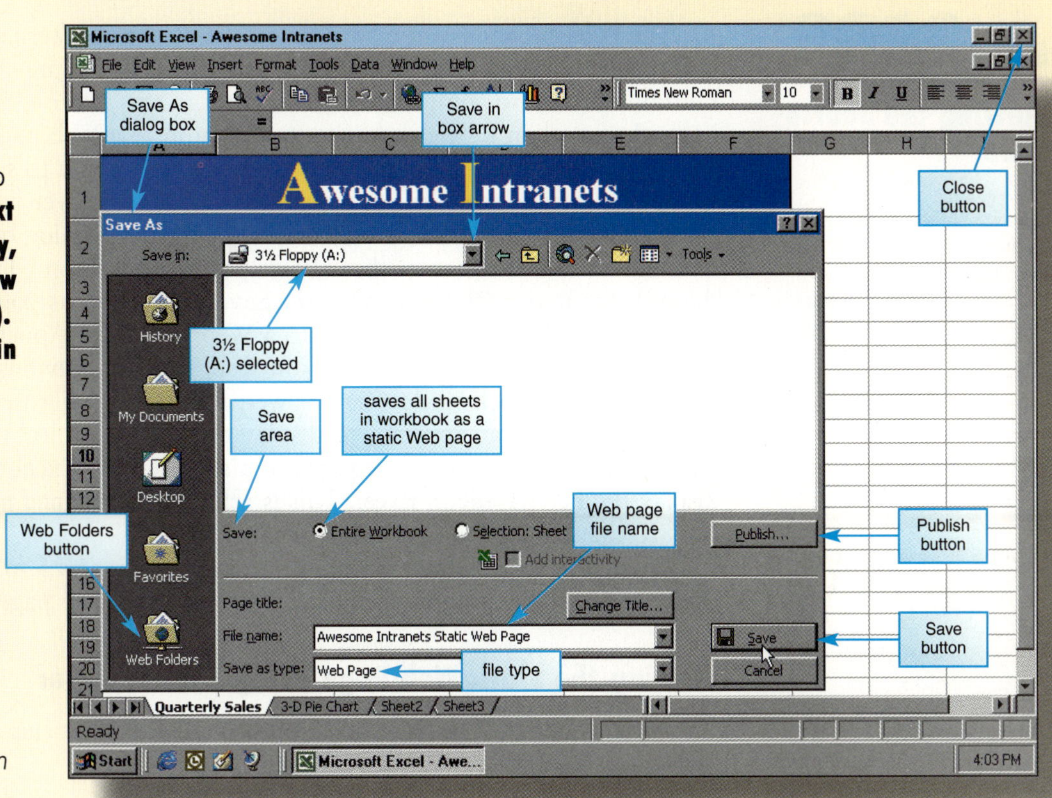

FIGURE 3

If you want to see how the workbook will display as a static Web page before you save it, you can click the **Web Page Preview command** on the File menu (Figure 2). This command will start your browser and display the static Web page. The Web Page Preview command is similar to the Print Preview command, which previews a printout of a workbook.

The Save As dialog box that displays when you use the Save as Web Page command is slightly different from the Save As dialog box that displays when you use the Save As command. When you use the Save as Web Page command, a **Save area** displays in the dialog box. Within the Save area are two option buttons, a check box, and a Publish button (Figure 3). You can select only one of the option buttons. The **Entire Workbook option button** is selected by default. This indicates Excel will save all the active sheets (Quarterly Sales and 3-D Pie Chart) in the workbook as a static Web page if you click the Save button. The alternative is the **Selection Sheet option button**. If you select this option, Excel will save only the active sheet (the one that is displaying in the Excel window) in the workbook. If you add a check mark to the **Add interactivity check box**, then Excel saves the sheet as a dynamic Web page. If you leave the Add interactivity check box unchecked, Excel saves the active sheet as a static Web page.

Publishing Web Pages

For more information on publishing Web pages using Excel, visit the Excel 2000 More About Web page (www.scsite.com/ex2000/more.htm) and click Publishing Web Pages Using Excel.

Viewing the Source Code

To view the HTML source code for the static Web page created in Excel, display the Web page in your browser, click View on the menu bar, and then click Source. If you are familiar with HTML, you will notice embedded XML (Extensible Markup Language) code. The XML code is used to hold the Excel formats so you can round-trip or open the HTML file in Excel.

The **Publish button** in the Save As dialog box is an alternative to the Save button. It allows you to customize the Web page further. In the previous set of steps, the Save button was used to complete the save. Later in this feature, the Publish button will be used to explain further how you can customize a Web page.

If you have access to a Web server and it allows you to save files to a Web folder, then you can save the Web page directly to the Web server by clicking the **Web Folders button** in the lower left corner of the Save As dialog box (Figure 3). If you have access to a Web server that allows you to save to an FTP, then you can select the FTP site under **FTP locations** in the Save in box just as you select any folder to save a file to. To save a workbook to a Web server, see Appendix B.

After Excel saves the workbook in Step 3 on the previous page, the HTML file displays in the Excel window as if it were saved as a Microsoft Excel workbook (.xls extension). Excel can continue to display the workbook in HTML format because within the HTML file that it created, it also saved the Excel formats that allow it to display the HTML file in Excel. This is referred to as **round tripping** the HTML file back to the application in which it was created.

When you save a static Web page, Excel also creates a folder on drive A. The folder contains the graphics required to display the Web page.

Viewing the Static Web Page Using Your Browser

With the static Web page saved on drive A, the next step is to view it using your browser as shown in the following steps.

To View the Static Web Page Using Your Browser

1. **Click the Start button on the taskbar, point to Programs, and then click Internet Explorer.**

2. **When the Internet Explorer window displays, type** `a:\awesome intranets static web page.htm` **in the Address bar and then press the ENTER key.**

The Web page, Awesome Intranets Static Web Page.htm, displays with the Quarterly Sales sheet active (Figure 4).

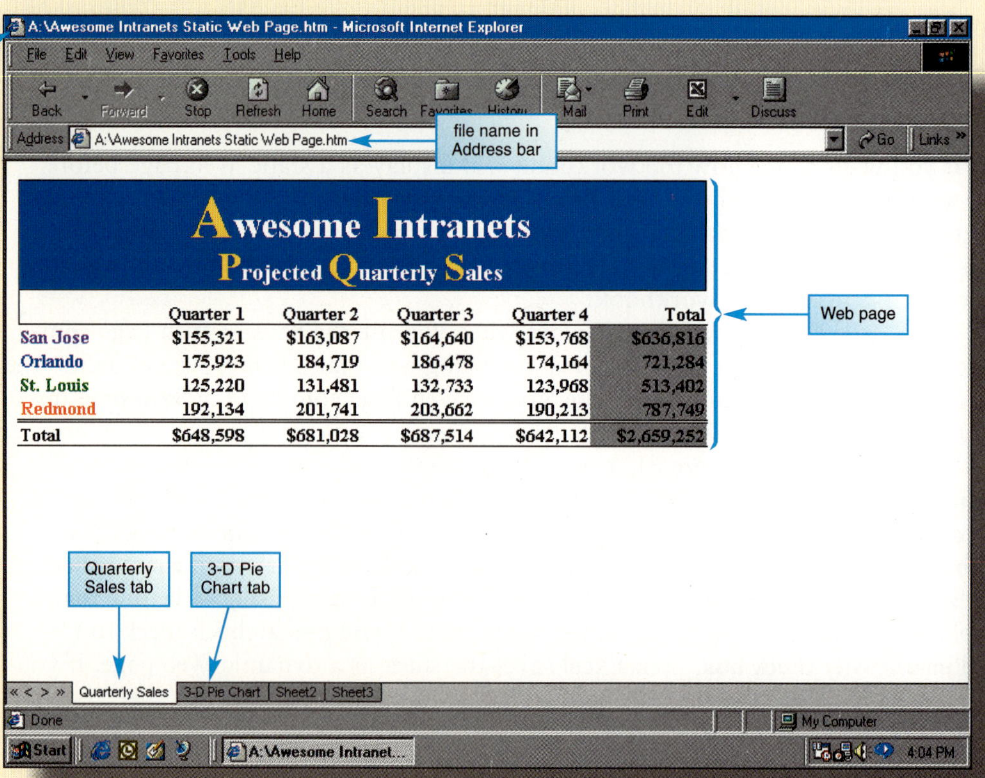

	Quarter 1	Quarter 2	Quarter 3	Quarter 4	Total
San Jose	$155,321	$163,087	$164,640	$153,768	$636,816
Orlando	175,923	184,719	186,478	174,164	721,284
St. Louis	125,220	131,481	132,733	123,968	513,402
Redmond	192,134	201,741	203,662	190,213	787,749
Total	$648,598	$681,028	$687,514	$642,112	$2,659,252

FIGURE 4

3 **Click the 3-D Pie Chart tab at the bottom of the window. Use the scroll arrows to display the legend.**

The 3-D Pie chart displays as shown in Figure 5.

4 **Click the Close button at the right side of the Internet Explorer title bar.**

The Internet Explorer window closes.

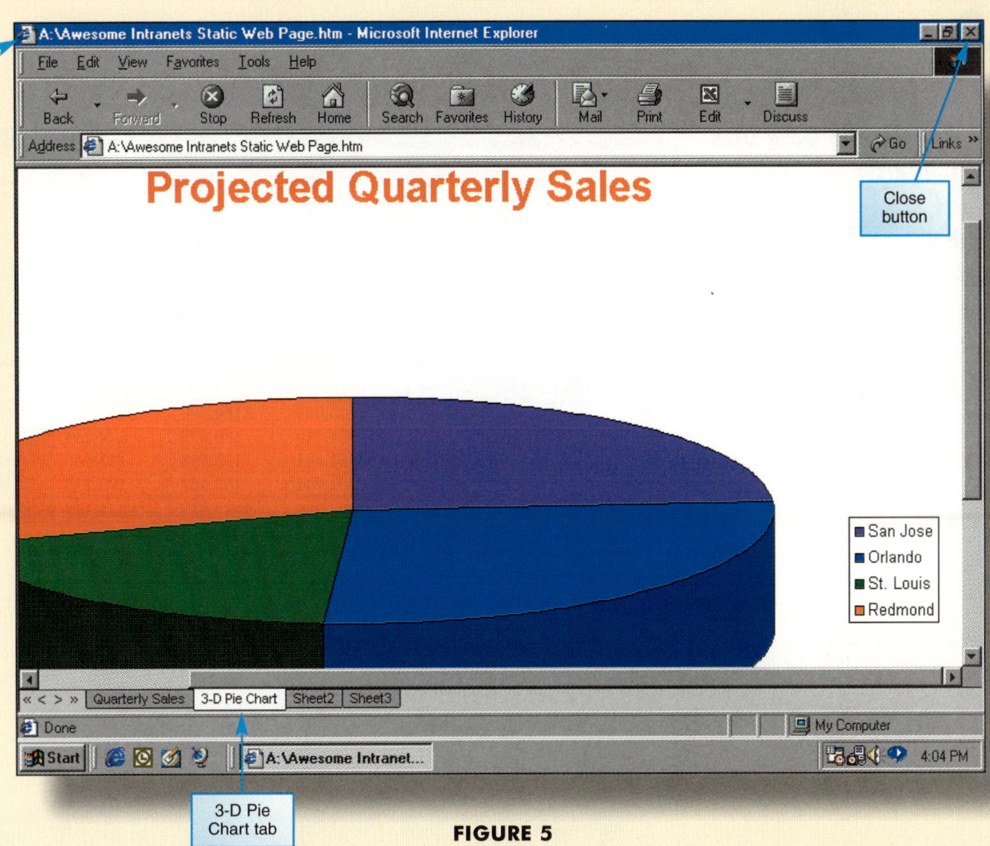

FIGURE 5

You can see from Figures 4 and 5 that the static Web page is an ideal media for distributing information to a large group of people. For example, the static Web page could be published to a Web server connected to the Internet and made available to anyone with a computer, browser, and the address of the Web page. Thus, publishing a static Web page of a workbook is an alternative to distributing printed copies of the workbook.

Figures 4 and 5 show that when you instruct Excel to save the entire workbook (see Figure 3 on page EW 1.5), it creates a Web page with tabs for each sheet in the workbook. Clicking a tab displays the corresponding sheet. If you want, you can use the Print command on the File menu in your browser to print the sheets one at a time.

Saving an Excel Chart as a Dynamic Web Page

This section publishes a dynamic Web page that includes Excel functionality and interactivity. The objective is to publish the 3-D Pie chart that is on the chart sheet in the Awesome Intranets workbook. The following steps use the Publish button in the Save As dialog box, rather than the Save button, to illustrate the additional publishing capabilities of Excel.

More About 2000

Viewing Web Pages Created in Excel

To view static Web pages created in Excel, you can use any browser. To view dynamic Web pages created in Excel, your computer must have the Microsoft Office Web Components and Microsoft Internet Explorer 4.01 or later installed. The Microsoft Office Web Components and Microsoft Internet Explorer 5 come with Microsoft Office 2000.

To Save an Excel Chart as a Dynamic Web Page

1 Insert the Data Disk in drive A. Start Excel and then open the workbook, Awesome Intranets, on drive A. Click File on the menu bar and then point to Save as Web Page.

The File menu displays (Figure 6).

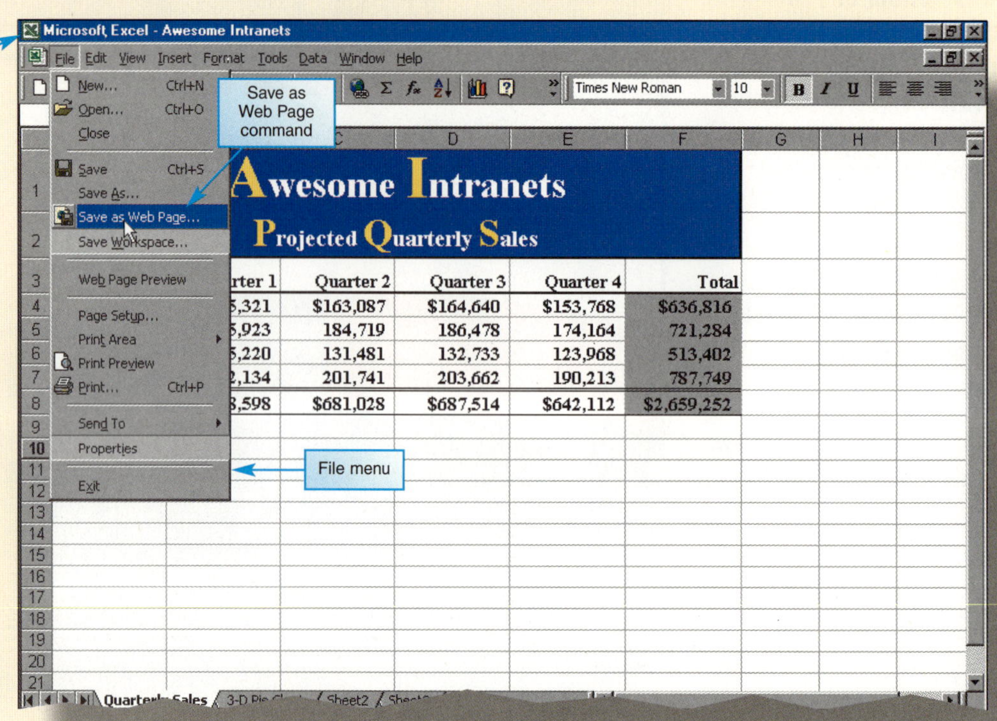

FIGURE 6

2 Click Save as Web Page. When the Save As dialog box displays, type `Awesome Intranets Dynamic Web Page` **in the File name text box and then, if necessary, click the Save in box arrow and select 3½ Floppy (A:). Point to the Publish button.**

The Save As dialog box displays (Figure 7). When you use the Publish button, you do not have to concern yourself with the option buttons and check box in the Save area.

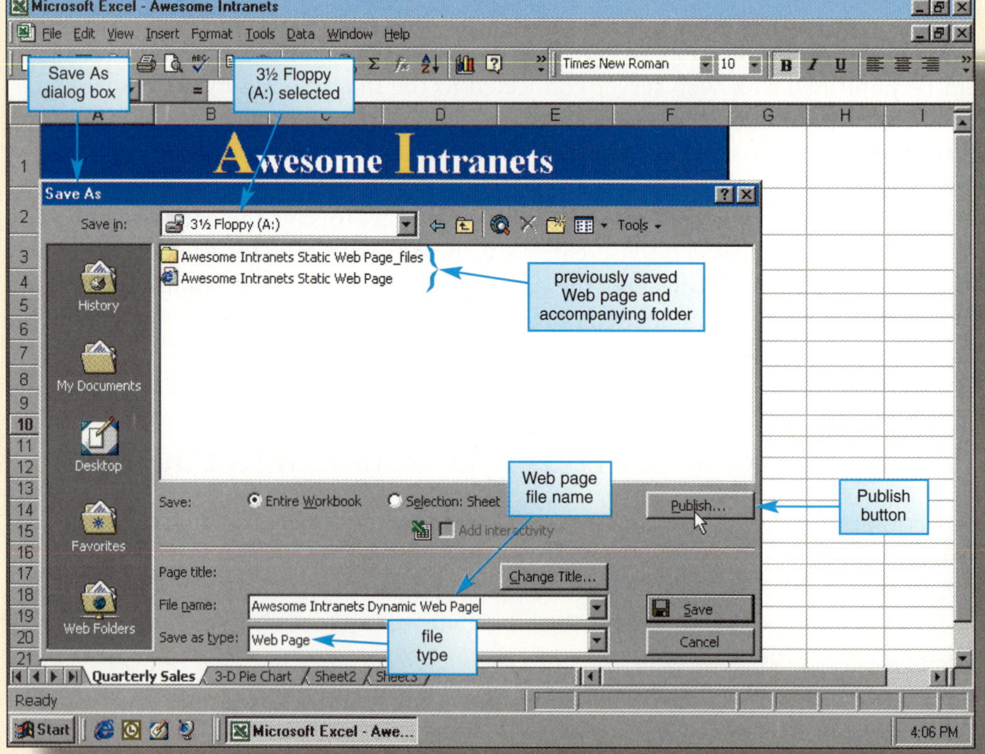

FIGURE 7

3 **Click the Publish button. When the Publish as Web Page dialog box displays, click the Choose box arrow and then click Items on 3-D Pie Chart. Click Add interactivity with in the Viewing options area. If necessary, select Chart functionality in the list box in the Viewing options area. Point to the Publish button.**

The Publish as Web page dialog box displays (Figure 8). When you select Items on 3-D Pie Chart, Excel immediately displays the 3-D Pie Chart sheet in the Excel window.

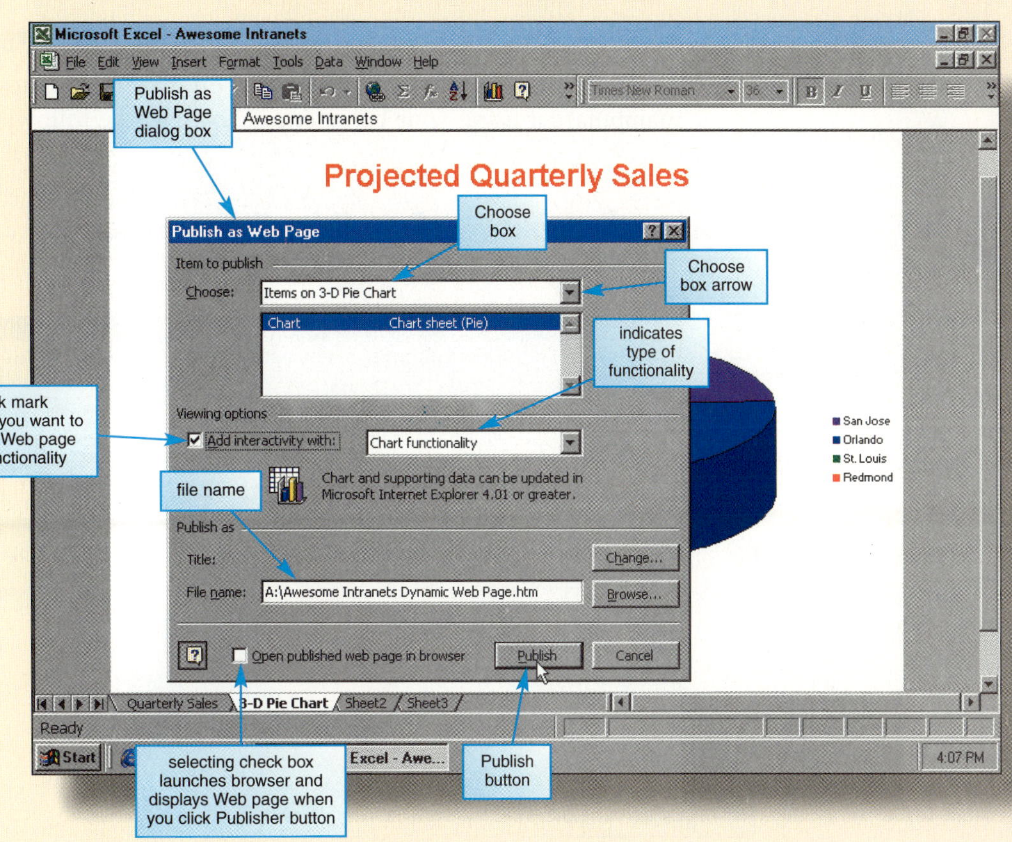

FIGURE 8

4 **Click the Publish button. Click the Close button on the right side of the Excel toolbar to close Excel.**

Excel saves the dynamic Web page on the Data Disk in drive A using the file name, Awesome Intranets Dynamic Web Page.htm. Excel shuts down.

Excel allows you to save an entire workbook, a sheet in the workbook, or a range on a sheet as a Web page. In Figure 7, you have the option in the Save area to save the entire workbook or a sheet. These option buttons are used with the Save button. If you want to be more selective in what you save, then you can disregard the option buttons in the Save area in Figure 7 and click the Publish button as described in Step 3. The **Choose box** in the **Publish as Web Page dialog box** in Figure 8 allows you more options in what to include on the Web page. You also may save the Web page as a dynamic Web page (interactive) or a static Web page (noninteractive). The check box at the bottom of the dialog box gives you the opportunity to start your browser automatically and display the newly created Web page after you click the Publish button.

How Excel Saves Web Pages

A saved static (noninteractive) Web page includes an htm file and an additional folder to hold the graphics that display as part of the Web page. All the components of a dynamic (interactive) Web page are saved in a single HTML file.

Viewing and Manipulating the Dynamic Web Page Using Your Browser

With the dynamic Web page saved on drive A, the next step is to view it and manipulate it using your browser as shown in the following steps.

To View and Manipulate the Static Web Page Using Your Browser

1 **Click the Start button on the taskbar, point to Programs, and then click Internet Explorer.**

2 **When the Internet Explorer window displays, type** `a:\awesome intranets dynamic web page.htm` **in the Address bar and then press the ENTER key.**

The Web page, Awesome Intranets Dynamic Web Page.htm, displays as shown in Figure 9. This Web page contains the information from the Awesome Intranets workbook. The 3-D Pie chart displays as a 2-D Pie chart with the rows and columns of the worksheet that determine the Pie chart immediately below it.

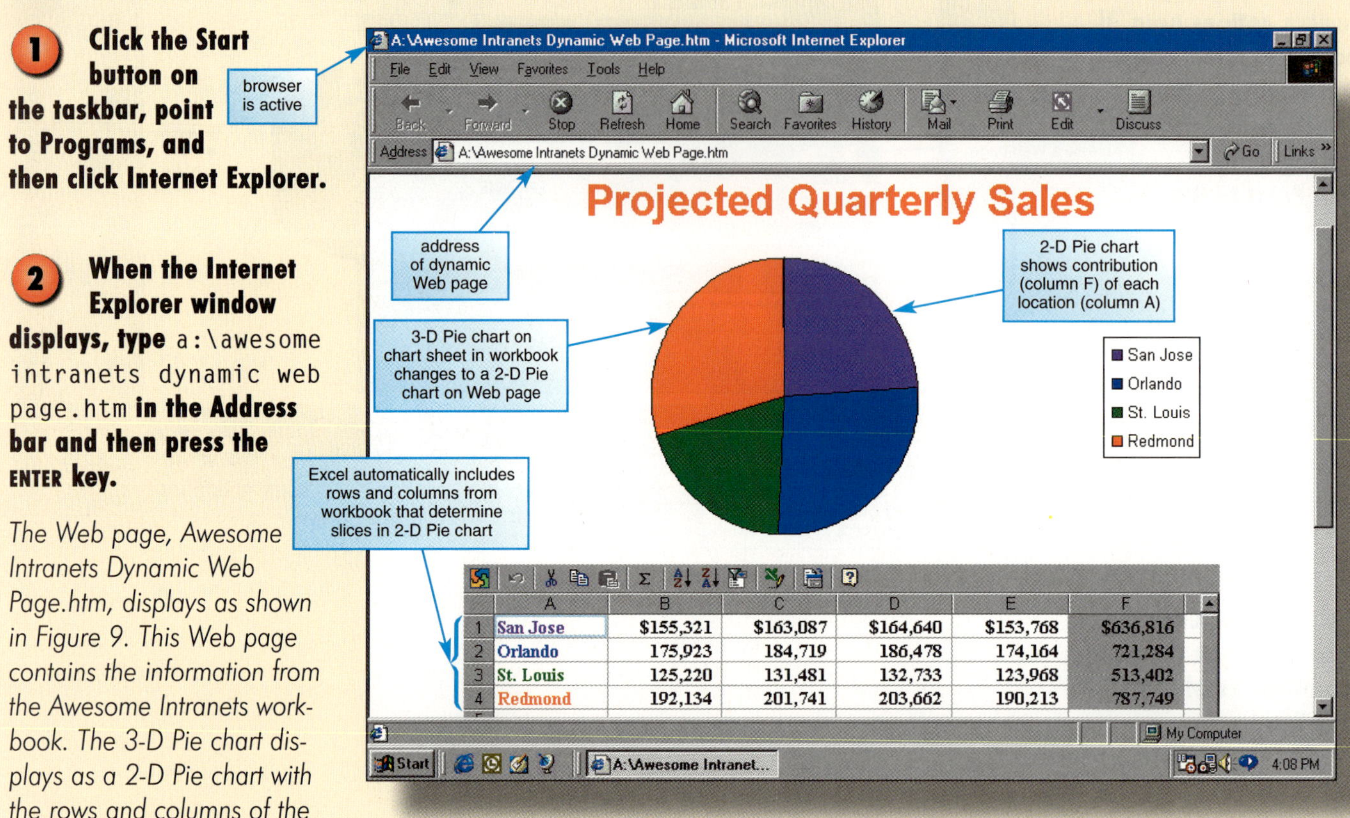

FIGURE 9

Click cell B4 and then enter 450000.

The formulas in the worksheet portion are recalculated and the size of the slices in the 2-D Pie chart change to agree with the new totals in column F (Figure 10).

4 **Click the Close button at the right side of the Internet Explorer title bar.**

The Internet Explorer window closes.

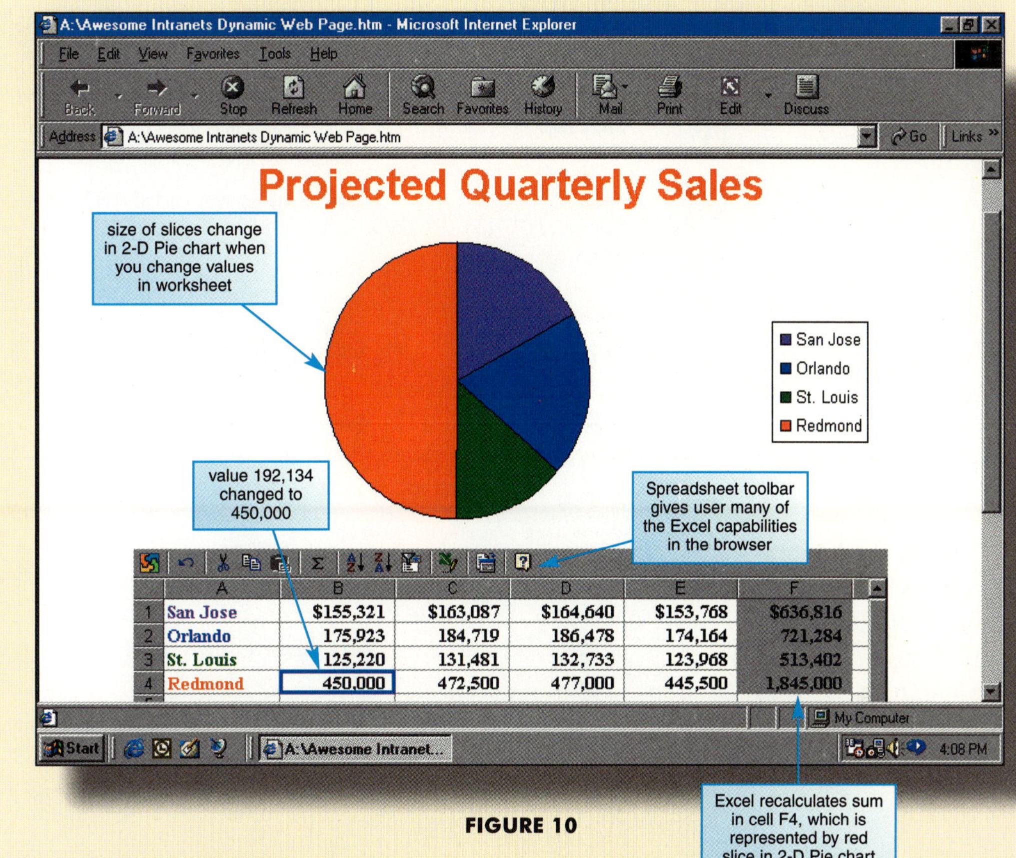

FIGURE 10

Figure 9 shows the result of saving the 3-D Pie chart as a dynamic Web page. Excel automatically changes the 3-D Pie chart to a 2-D Pie chart and adds the columns and rows from the worksheet below the chart. As shown in Figure 10, you can change the numbers in the worksheet that determine the size of the slices in the 2-D Pie chart and the Web page instantaneously recalculates all formulas and redraws the 2-D Pie chart. When cell B4 is changed from 192,134 to 450,000, the Web page recalculates the formulas in cells C4, D4, E4, and F4. The red slice in the 2-D Pie chart represents the value in cell F4. Thus, when the number in cell F4 changes from 787,749 to 1,845,000, the red slice in the 2-D Pie chart changes to a much larger slice of the pie. This interactivity and functionality allow you to share a workbook's formulas and charts with others who may not have access to Excel, but do have access to a browser.

Dynamic Web Pages

When you change a value in a dynamic Web page, it does not affect the saved workbook or the saved HTML file. If you save a modified Web page using the Save As command on the browser's File menu, it will save the original version and not the modified one you see on the screen.

Modifying the Worksheet on a Dynamic Web Page

Immediately above the rows and columns in the worksheet in Figure 10 is the **Spreadsheet toolbar**. The toolbar allows you to invoke the most commonly used worksheet commands. For example, you can select a cell immediately below a column of numbers and click the AutoSum button to sum the numbers in the column. Cut, copy, and paste capabilities also are available. The functions of the buttons on the Spreadsheet toolbar in Figure 10 are summarized in Table 1 on the next page.

Table 1 Spreadsheet Toolbar Buttons

BUTTON	NAME OF BUTTON	FUNCTION
	Office Logo	Displays information about the Microsoft Office Web Component, including the version number you have installed
	Undo	Reverses the last command or actions, or deletes the last entry you typed
	Cut	Removes the selection and places it on the Clipboard
	Copy	Copies the selection to the Clipboard
	Paste	Inserts the contents of the Clipboard
	AutoSum	Adds a column or row of numbers automatically
	Sort Ascending	Sorts the selected items in ascending sequence
	Sort Descending	Sorts the selected items in descending sequence
	AutoFilter	Selects specific items you want to display in a list
	Export to Excel	Opens the Web page as a workbook in Excel
	Property Toolbox	Displays the Spreadsheet Property Toolbox so you can modify the worksheet
	Help	Displays Microsoft Spreadsheet Help

In general, you can add formulas, format, sort, and export the Web page to Excel. Many additional Excel capabilities are available through the **Spreadsheet Property Toolbox** (Figure 11). You display the Spreadsheet Property Toolbox by clicking the Property Toolbox button on the Spreadsheet toolbar. When the Spreadsheet Property Toolbox displays, click the Format section bar. You can see in Figure 11, that many of the common formats, such as bold, italic, underline, font color, font style, and font size, are available through your browser for the purpose of formatting cells in the worksheet below the 2-D Pie chart on the Web page.

Creating Links

You can add hyperlinks to an Excel workbook before you save it as a Web page. You can add hyperlinks that link to a Web page, a location in a Web page, or to an e-mail address that automatically starts the viewer's e-mail program.

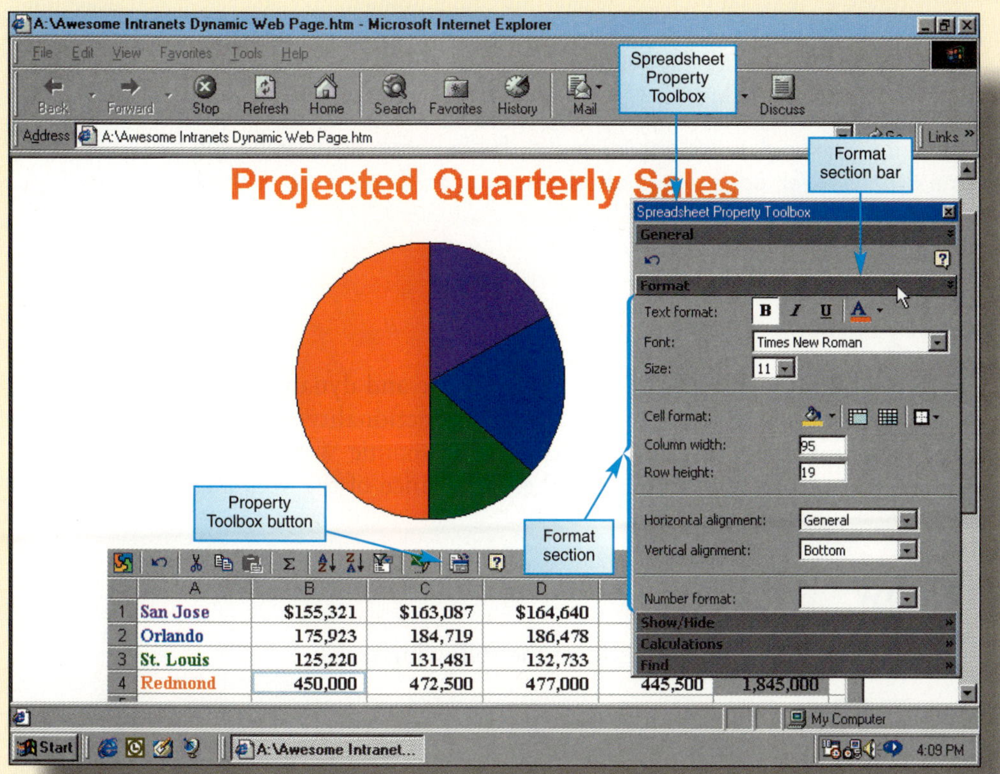

FIGURE 11

Modifying the dynamic Web page does not change the makeup of the original workbook or the Web page stored on disk, even if you use the Save As command on the browser's File menu. If you do use the Save As command in your browser, it will save the original htm file without any changes you made. You can, however, use the Export to Excel button on the toolbar to create a workbook that will include any changes you made in your browser. The Export to Excel button only saves the worksheet and not the 3-D Pie chart.

Quick Reference

For a table that lists how to complete the tasks covered in this book using the mouse, menu, shortcut menu, and keyboard, visit the Office 2000 Web page (www.scsite.com/office 2000/qr.htm), and then click Microsoft Excel 2000.

Microsoft Certification

The Microsoft Office User Specialist (MOUS) Certification program provides an opportunity for you to obtain a valuable industry credential - proof that you have the Excel 2000 skills required by employers. For more information, see Appendix D or visit the Shelly Cashman Series MOUS Web page at www.scsite.com/off2000/ cert.htm.

CASE PERSPECTIVE SUMMARY

Ryan is pleased with the two Web pages you created. By publishing the static Web page on the company s intranet, he no longer has to mail printouts of the workbook to his distribution list. Furthermore, because he can make the worksheet and chart available as a dynamic Web page, members of his group no longer need to use his computer.

Web Feature Summary

This Web Feature introduced you to publishing two types of Web pages: static and dynamic. Whereas the static Web page is a snapshot of the workbook, a dynamic Web page adds functionality and interactivity to the Web page. Besides changing the data and generating new results with a dynamic Web page, you also can add formulas and change the formats in your browser to improve the appearance of the Web page.

What You Should Know

Having completed this project, you now should be able to perform the following tasks:

- Save an Excel Chart as a Dynamic Web Page *(EW 1.8)*
- Save an Excel Workbook as a Static Web Page *(EW 1.4)*
- View and Manipulate the Static Web Page Using Your Browser *(EW 1.10)*
- View the Static Web Page Using Your Browser *(EW 1.6)*

1 Shocking Sound International Web Page

Problem: You are employed as a spreadsheet analyst by Shocking Sound International. Your supervisor has asked you to create a static Web page and dynamic Web page from the company's annual sales workbook.

Instructions Part 1: Start Excel and open the Shocking Sound International workbook from the Data Disk. If you do not have a copy of the Data Disk, see the inside back cover of this book. Do the following:

1. Review the worksheet and chart so you have an idea of what the workbook contains.
2. Save the workbook as a Web page on drive A using the file name, Shocking Sound International Static Web Page. Make sure you select Entire Workbook in the Save area before you click the Save button. Close Excel.
3. Start your browser. Type `a:\shocking sound international static web page.htm` in the Address bar. When the Web page displays, click the tabs at the bottom of the window to view the sheets. As you view each sheet, print it in landscape orientation. Quit your browser.

Instructions Part 2: Start Excel and open the Shocking Sound International workbook from the Data Disk. Do the following:

1. Click File on the menu bar and then click Save as Web Page. Use the Publish button to save the workbook as a Web page on drive A using the file name, Shocking Sound International Dynamic Web Page. In the Publish as Web Page dialog box, select Items on Bar Chart in the Choose box, click the Add Interactivity with check box and add chart functionality. Click the Publish button. Close Excel.
2. Start your browser. Type `a:\shocking sound international dynamic web page.htm` in the Address bar. When the Web page displays, click cell B6 and then click the AutoSum button on the Spreadsheet toolbar twice. Cell B6 should equal $2,806,007. Print the Web page.
3. Enter the following gross sales: Asia = 235,000; Canada = 542,500; Europe = 300,500; Latin America = 200,000; and United States = 1,500,000. Cell B6 should equal $2,778,000. Print the Web page. Quit your browser.

2 Microprocessor Plus Web Page

Problem: You are a Web consultant for Microprocessor Plus. You have been asked to create a static Web page and dynamic Web page from the workbook that the company uses to project sales and payroll expenses.

Instructions Part 1: Start Excel and open the Microprocessor workbook from the Data Disk. If you do not have a copy of the Data Disk, see the inside back cover of this book. Do the following:

1. Display the 3-D Pie Chart sheet. Redisplay the Projected Budget sheet.
2. Save the workbook as a Web page on drive A using the file name, Microprocessor Plus Static Web Page. Make sure you select Entire Workbook in the Save area before you click the Save button. Close Excel.
3. Start your browser. Type `a:\microprocessor plus static web page.htm` in the Address bar. When the Web page displays, click the tabs at the bottom of the window to view the sheets. Print each sheet in landscape orientation. Quit your browser.

(continued)

Microprocessor Plus Web Page *(continued)*

Instructions Part 2: Start Excel and open the Microprocessor workbook from the Data Disk. Do the following:

1. Click File on the menu bar and then click Save as Web Page. Use the Publish button to save the workbook as a Web page on drive A using the file name, Microprocessor Plus Dynamic Web Page. In the Publish as Web Page dialog box, select Items on 3-D Pie Chart in the Choose box, click the Add Interactivity with check box with chart functionality. Click the Publish button. Close Excel.
2. Start your browser. Type `a:\microprocessor plus dynamic web page.htm` in the Address bar. When the Web page displays, print it in landscape.
3. Scroll down and change the values of the following cells: cell B15 = 15%; cell B16 = 5%; cell B17 = 25,000; cell B19 = 20.75%; and cell B20 = 6.75%. Cell H12 should equal $1,008,561.47. The 3-D Pie chart should change to display the new contributions to the projected payroll expenses. Print the Web page. Quit your browser.

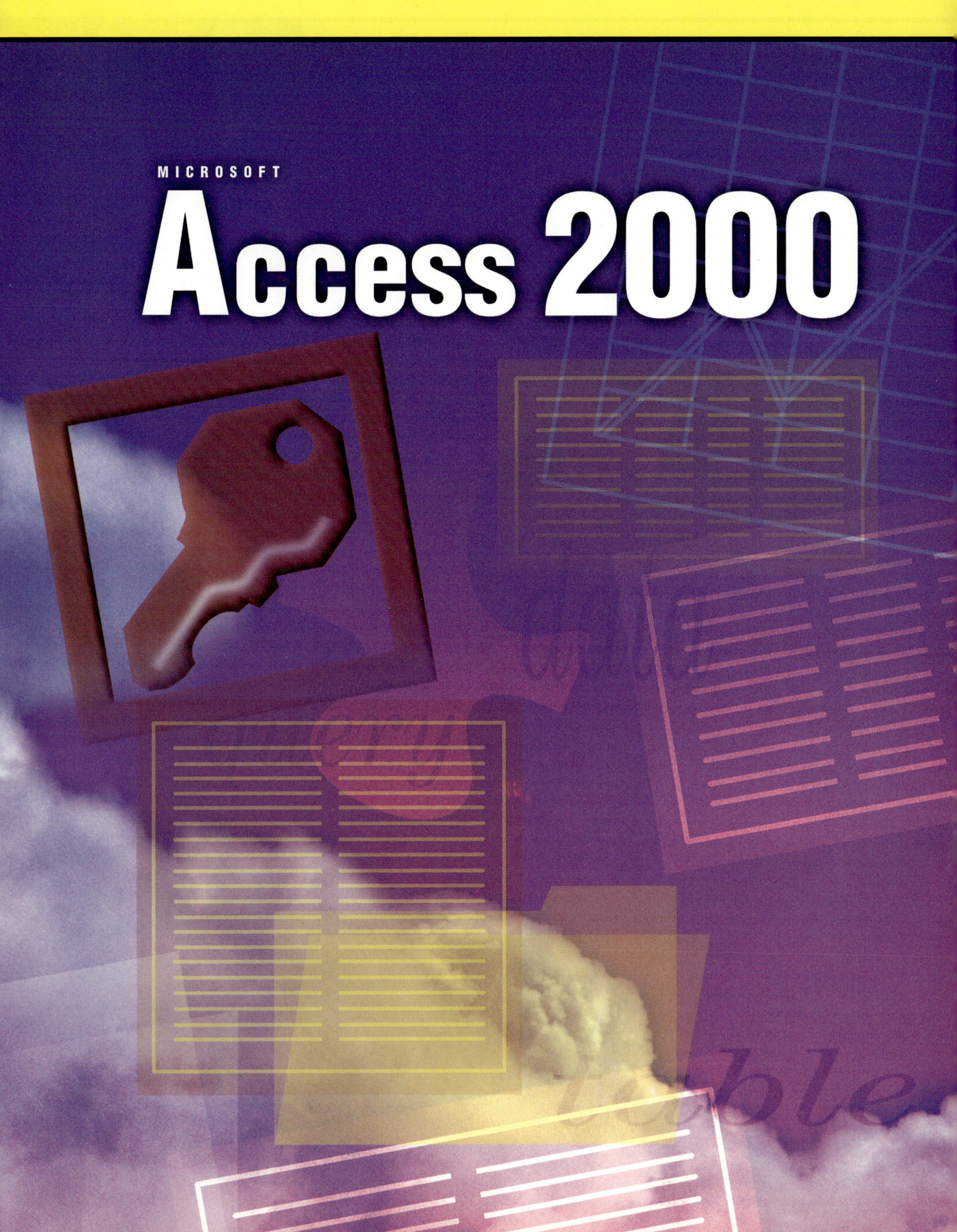
MICROSOFT
Access 2000

Microsoft Access 2000

Creating a Database Using Design and Datasheet Views

OBJECTIVES

You will have mastered the material in this project when you can:

- Describe databases and database management systems
- Start Access
- Describe the features of the Access screen
- Create a database
- Create a table
- Define the fields in a table
- Open a table
- Add records to an empty table
- Close a table
- Close a database and quit Access
- Open a database
- Add records to a nonempty table
- Print the contents of a table
- Use a form to view data
- Create a custom report
- Use Microsoft Access Help
- Design a database to eliminate redundancy

A Match Made in Computer Heaven

Mentoring Unites Experts and Schools

Educational issues dominate the airwaves and print media. From decorum in the classroom to equal access to the Internet, school-related topics are broadcast on the evening news and published in the morning newspapers. Then discussions take place around family dinner tables and at study sessions. Often these dialogues focus on improving the classroom experience by strengthening the relationship among educators, students, community members, and funding sources.

One effective way of enriching the learning process is to involve various groups in education. For example, college students are earning federal work-study funds by helping students in elementary grades learn to read and do math in the America Reads and the America Counts programs. More than 900 public schools have received grants in the 21st Century Community Learning Centers program to provide safe places for children to gather. Business leaders critique middle school students' writing samples as part of the National School Network Exchange, a

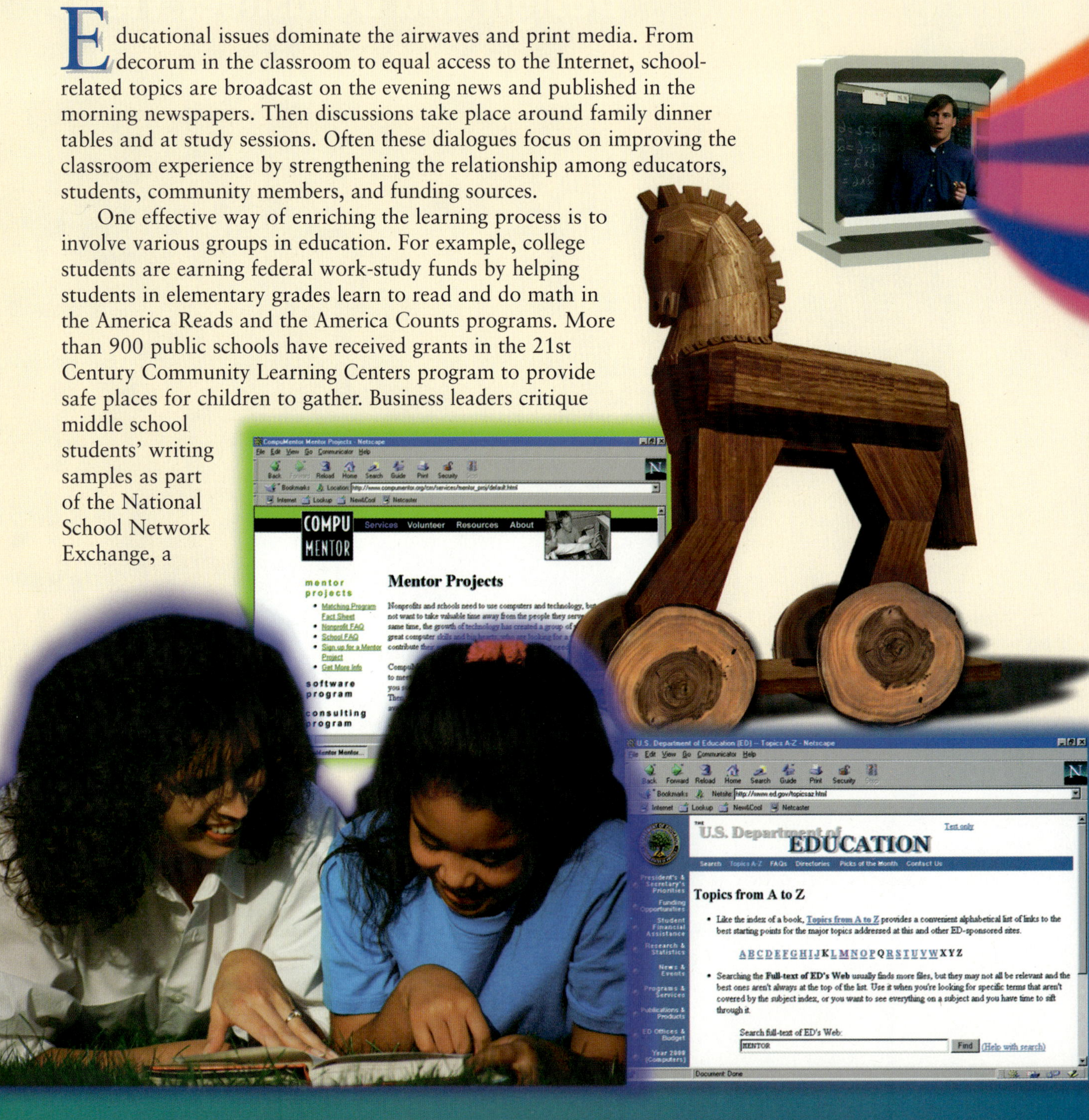

grant-funded program that links more than 500 schools, companies, museums, and governmental agencies via the Internet.

In mythology, Mentor advised Odysseus, who lead the Greeks in the Trojan War. In today's world, mentors advise people needing direction and coaching. These partnerships are common in the computer field. For example, network experts collaborate with a culturally diverse school district to network classrooms throughout the region. Technology buffs develop a distance education program for students living in remote areas. Software experts install donated copies of Microsoft Office in computer labs and then train teachers.

Building these partnerships requires superb technological and organizational skills, strong marketing, and dedicated staff members. Various local, regional, and national organizations have the right mix of technology expertise and qualified personnel to meet these requirements. The nation's largest nonprofit computerization assistance center, CompuMentor, is one of these successful partnering organizations. CompuMentor has linked its staff with more than 6,000 schools and other nonprofit organizations since 1987.

The heart of its success is matching computer experts with the appropriate school or organization. Some mentors volunteer long term, while others agree to work intensively for a few days, particularly in telecommunications areas. Potential mentors complete an application at CompuMentor's Web site (www.compumentor.org) by entering specific information in boxes, called fields, pertaining to their knowledge of operating systems, networking, and hardware repair. They give additional information about their available working hours, training experience, and special skills in office and accounting applications, databases, and desktop publishing.

This information structures records in the CompuMentor database. The staff then can search these records to find a volunteer whose skills match the school's or organization's needs. Similarly, in Project 1, you will use the Access database management system to enter records in the Bavant Marine Services database so the marina staff can match service technicians with boat owners whose vessels need repairs.

Uniting schools with appropriate experts increases awareness of educational issues and ultimately improves the learning process. For more information on building mentoring relationships, visit the U.S. Department of Education Web site (www.ed.gov) or call 1-800-USA-LEARN.

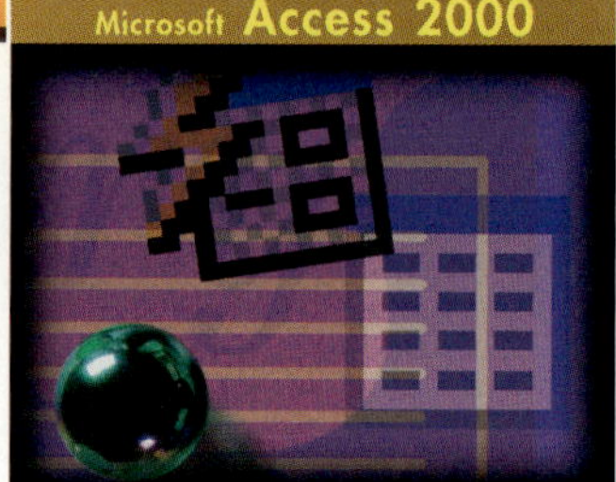

Microsoft Access 2000

Creating a Database Using Design and Datasheet Views

CASE PERSPECTIVE

With the popularity of water sports increasing, the number of recreational boaters has risen dramatically! Boats come in all shapes and sizes and are often stored at a marina.

Larger, full-service marinas typically have a service department. The department performs the requested work, such as engine repair, and bills the owner's account. Smaller marinas usually cannot provide on-site service departments, but can offer the same convenience to boat owners by contracting with Bavant Marine Services. A boat owner requiring service notifies the marina, which then contacts Bavant. Bavant sends a technician to perform the required labor and bills the marina.

To ensure operations run smoothly, Bavant Marine Services needs to maintain data on its technicians and their assigned marinas. Bavant wants to organize the data in a database, managed by a database management system such as Access. In this way, Bavant can keep its data current and accurate while management can analyze the data for trends and produce a variety of useful reports. Your task is to help Bavant Marine Services in creating and using their database.

What Is Microsoft Access 2000?

Microsoft Access 2000 is a powerful database management system (DBMS) that functions in the Windows environment and allows you to create and process data in a database. Some of the key features are:

- **Data entry and update** Access provides easy mechanisms for adding data, changing data, and deleting data, including the ability to make mass changes in a single operation.
- **Queries** (questions) Using Access, it is easy to ask complex questions concerning the data in the database and receive instant answers.
- **Forms** In Access, you can produce attractive and useful forms for viewing and updating data.
- **Reports** Access contains a feature to allow you to easily create sophisticated reports for presenting your data.
- **Web Support** Access allows you to save objects (reports, tables) in HTML format so they can be viewed using a browser. You also can create data access pages to allow real-time access to data in the database via the Internet.

Project One — Bavant Marine Services Database

Creating, storing, sorting, and retrieving data are important tasks. In their personal lives, many people keep a variety of records such as names, addresses, and telephone numbers of friends and business associates, records of investments, records of expenses for tax purposes, and so on. These records must be arranged for quick access. Businesses also must be able to store and access information quickly and easily. Personnel and inventory records, payroll information, client records, order data, and accounts receivable information all are crucial and must be available readily.

The term **database** describes a collection of data organized in a manner that allows access, retrieval, and use of that data. A database management system, such as Access, allows you to use a computer to create a database; add, change, and delete data in the database; sort the data in the database; retrieve data in the database; and create forms and reports using the data in the database.

In Access, a database consists of a collection of tables. Figure 1-1 shows a sample database for Bavant Marine Services. It consists of two tables. The Marina table contains information about the marinas that Bavant Marine Services provides service for. Each marina is assigned to a specific technician. The Technician table contains information about the technicians to whom these marinas are assigned.

fields

marinas of technician Trista Anderson

Marina table

MARINA NUMBER	NAME	ADDRESS	CITY	STATE	ZIP CODE	WARRANTY	NON-WARRANTY	TECH NUMBER
AD57	Alan's Docks	314 Central	Burton	MI	49611	$1,248.00	$597.75	23
AN75	Afton's Marina	21 West 8th	Glenview	MI	48121	$1,906.50	$831.25	36
BL72	Brite's Landing	281 Robin	Burton	MI	49611	$217.00	$0.00	36
EL25	Elend Marina	462 River	Torino	MI	48268	$413.50	$678.75	49
FB96	Fenton's Boats	36 Bayview	Cavela	MI	47926	$923.20	$657.50	23
FM22	Fedder Marina	283 Waterfront	Burton	MI	49611	$432.00	$0.00	36
JB92	JT Boat Club	28 Causeway	Torino	MI	48268	$0.00	$0.00	36
NW72	Nelson's Wharf	27 Lake	Masondale	MI	49832	$608.50	$520.00	23
SM72	Solton's Marine	867 Bay Ridge	Glenview	MI	48121	$462.50	$295.00	49
TR72	The Reef	92 East Bay	Woodview	MI	47212	$219.00	$0.00	36

records

technician Trista Anderson

Technician table

TECH NUMBER	LAST NAME	FIRST NAME	ADDRESS	CITY	STATE	ZIP CODE	HOURLY RATE	YTD EARNINGS
23	Anderson	Trista	283 Belton	Port Anton	MI	47989	$24.00	$17,862.00
36	Nichols	Ashton	978 Richmond	Hewitt	MI	47618	$21.00	$19,560.00
49	Gomez	Teresa	2855 Parry	Ashley	MI	47711	$22.00	$21,211.50

FIGURE 1-1

The rows in the tables are called **records**. A record contains information about a given person, product, or event. A row in the Marina table, for example, contains information about a specific marina.

The columns in the tables are called fields. A **field** contains a specific piece of information within a record. In the Marina table, for example, the fourth field, City, contains the city where the marina is located.

Databases in Access 2000

In some DBMS's, every table, query, form, or report is stored in a separate file. This is not the case in Access 2000, in which a database is stored in a single file on disk. The file contains all the tables, queries, forms, reports, and programs that you create for this database.

The first field in the Marina table is the Marina Number. This is a code assigned by Bavant Marine Services to each marina. Like many organizations, Bavant Marine Services calls it a *number* although it actually contains letters. The marina numbers have a special format. They consist of two uppercase letters followed by a two-digit number.

These numbers are unique; that is, no two marinas will be assigned the same number. Such a field can be used as a **unique identifier**. This simply means that a given marina number will appear only in a single record in the table. Only one record exists, for example, in which the marina number is BL72. A unique identifier also is called a **primary key**. Thus, the Marina Number field is the primary key for the Marina table.

The next eight fields in the Marina table are Name, Address, City, State, Zip Code, Warranty, Non-warranty, and Tech Number. The Warranty field contains the amount billed to the Marina that should be covered by the boat owner's warranty. The Non-warranty field contains the amount that is not covered by warranty.

For example, marina AD57 is Alan's Docks. It is located at 314 Central in Burton, Michigan. The zip code is 49611. The marina has been billed $1,248.00 that should be covered by warranty and $597.75 that will not be covered by warranty.

Each marina is assigned to a single technician. The last field in the Marina table, Tech Number, gives the number of the marina's technician.

The first field in the Technician table, Tech Number, is the number assigned by Bavant Marine Services to the technician. These numbers are unique, so Tech Number is the primary key of the Technician table.

The other fields in the Technician table are Last Name, First Name, Address, City, State, Zip Code, Hourly Rate, and YTD Earnings. The Hourly Rate field gives the technician's hourly billing rate, and the YTD Earnings field contains the total amount that has been paid to the technician for services so far this year.

For example, Technician 23 is Trista Anderson. She lives at 283 Belton in Port Anton, Michigan. Her zip code is 47989. Her hourly billing rate is $24.00 and her YTD earnings are $17,862.00.

The tech number displays in both the Marina table and the Technician table. It is used to relate marinas and technicians. For example, in the Marina table, you see that the tech number for marina AD57 is 23. To find the name of this technician, look for the row in the Technician table that contains 23 in the Tech Number field. Once you have found it, you know the marina is assigned to Trista Anderson. To find all the marinas assigned to Trista Anderson, on the other hand, look through the Marina table for all the marinas that contain 23 in the Tech Number field. Her marinas are AD57 (Alan's Docks), FB96 (Fenton's Boats), and NW72 (Nelson's Wharf).

Together with the management of Bavant Marine Services, you have determined the data that must be maintained in the database is that shown in Figure 1-1 on page A 1.7. You first must create the database and the tables it contains. In the process, you must define the fields included in the two tables, as well as the type of data each field will contain. You then must add the appropriate records to the tables. You also must print the contents of the tables. Finally, you must create a report with the Marina Number, Name, Warranty, and Non-warranty fields for each marina served by Bavant Marine Services. Other reports and requirements for the database at Bavant Marine Services will be addressed with the Bavant Marine Services management in the future.

Creating a Database

Access 2000 includes a Database Wizard that can guide you by suggesting some commonly used databases. If you already know the tables and fields you need, however, you simply create the database yourself. For more information, visit the Access 2000 More About Web page (www.scsite.com/ac2000/more.htm) and then click Database Wizard.

Starting Access and Creating a New Database

In Access, all the tables, reports, forms, and queries that you create are stored in a single file called a database. Thus before creating any of these objects, you must first start Access and create the database that will hold them. To start Access, first make sure that Windows is running. Once you have done so, perform the following steps to start Access, create a new database, and save the database on a floppy disk.

To Start Access

1 Place a formatted floppy disk in drive A, click the Start button, and then point to New Office Document on the Start menu.

The Start menu displays (Figure 1-2).

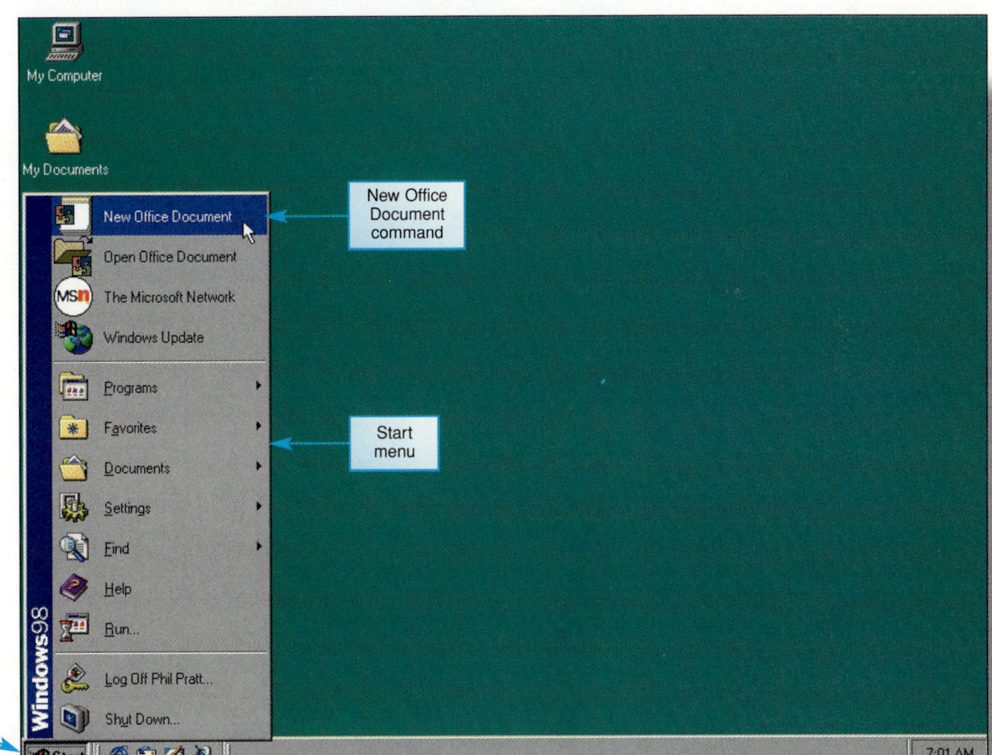

FIGURE 1-2

2 **Click New Office Document. If the General tab is not selected, that is, if it does not display in front of the other tabs, click the General tab. Click the Blank Database icon and then point to the OK button.**

The New Office Document dialog box displays (Figure 1-3). The Blank Database icon is selected.

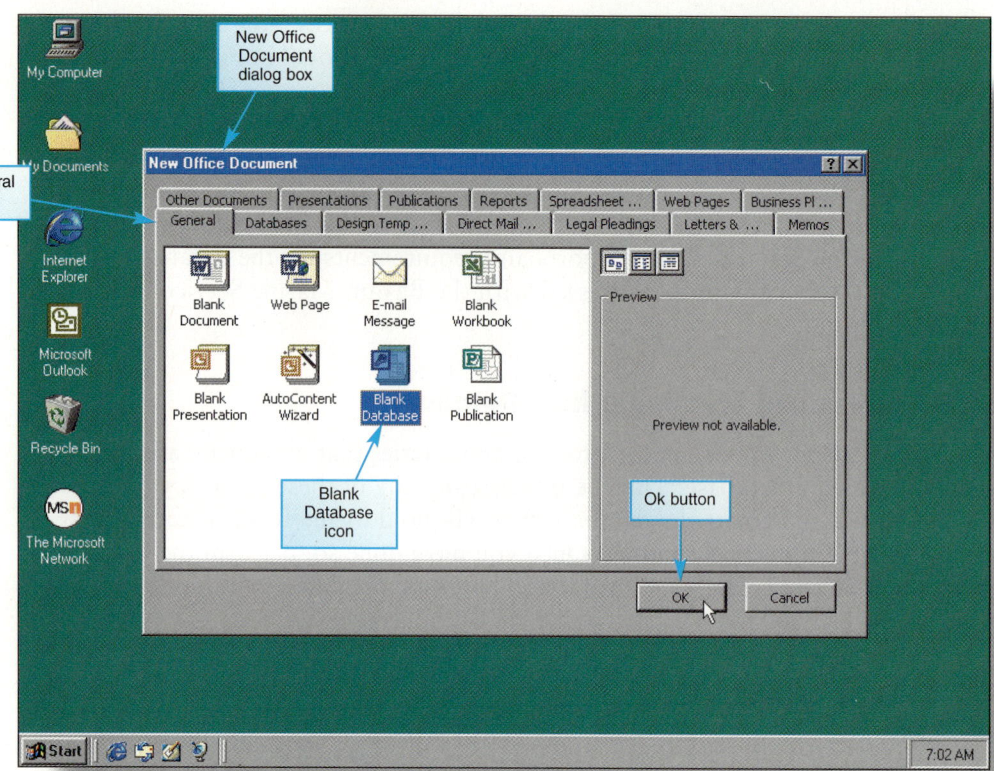

FIGURE 1-3

3 **Click the OK button and then point to the Save in box arrow.**

The File New Database dialog box displays (Figure 1-4).

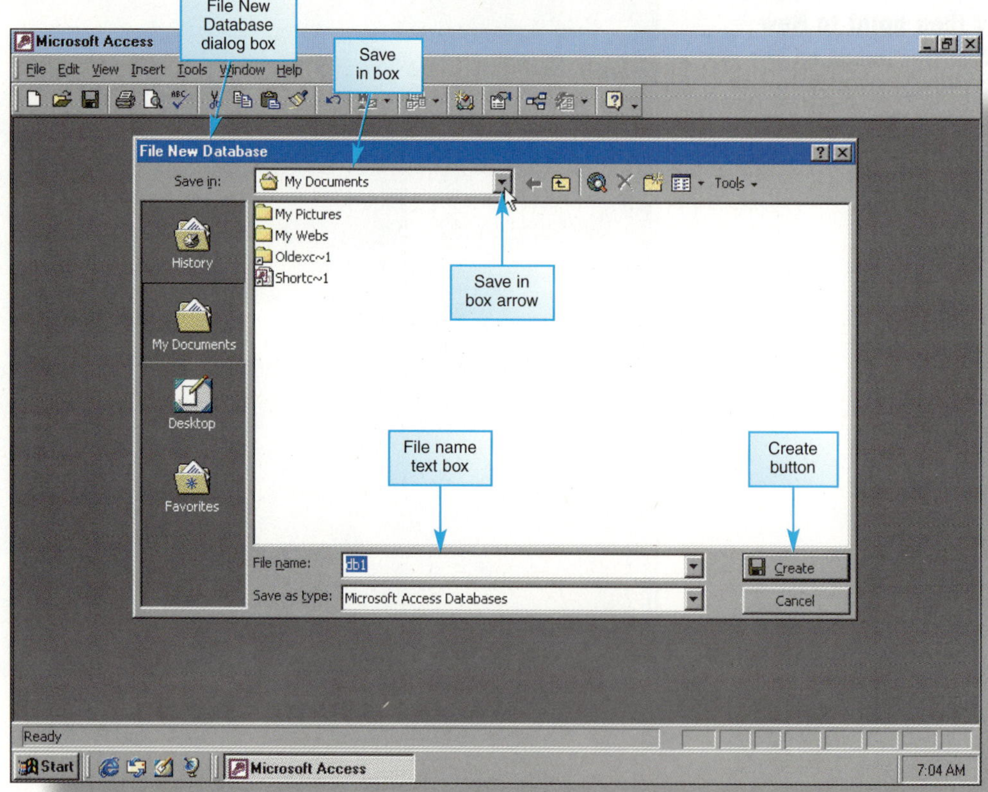

FIGURE 1-4

4 Click the Save in box arrow and then point to 3½ Floppy (A:).

The Save in list displays (Figure 1-5).

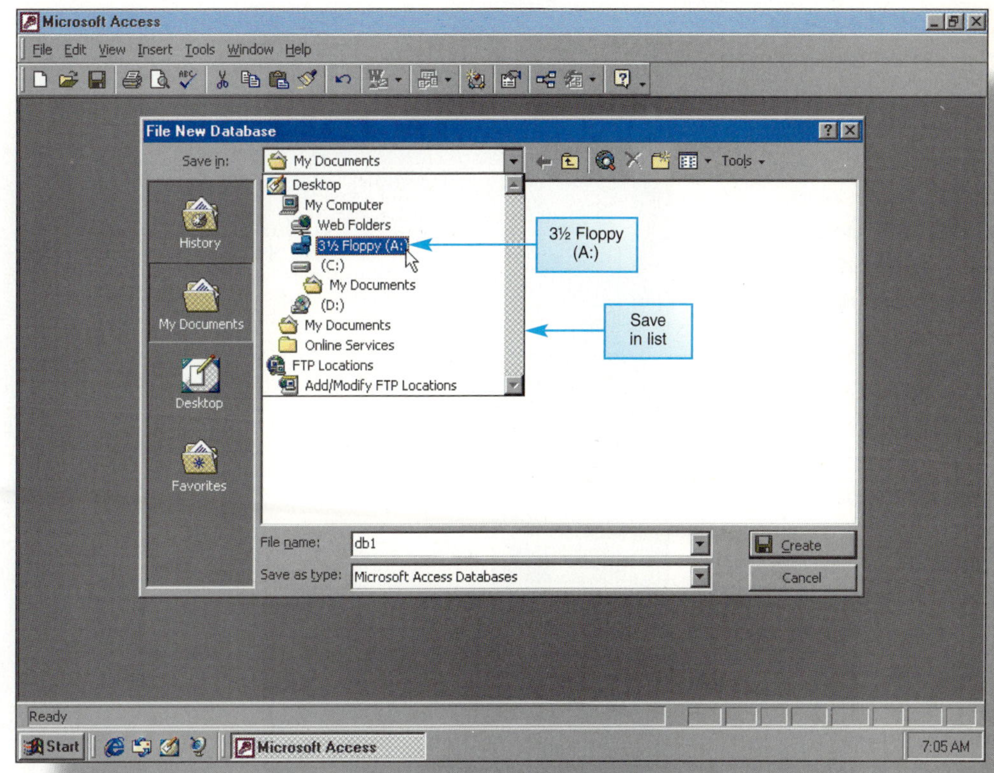

FIGURE 1-5

5 Click 3½ Floppy (A:). Click the File name text box. Repeatedly press the BACKSPACE key to delete db1 (your number may be different) and then type `Bavant Marine Services` **as the file name. Point to the Create button.**

The file name is changed to Bavant Marine Services (Figure 1-6).

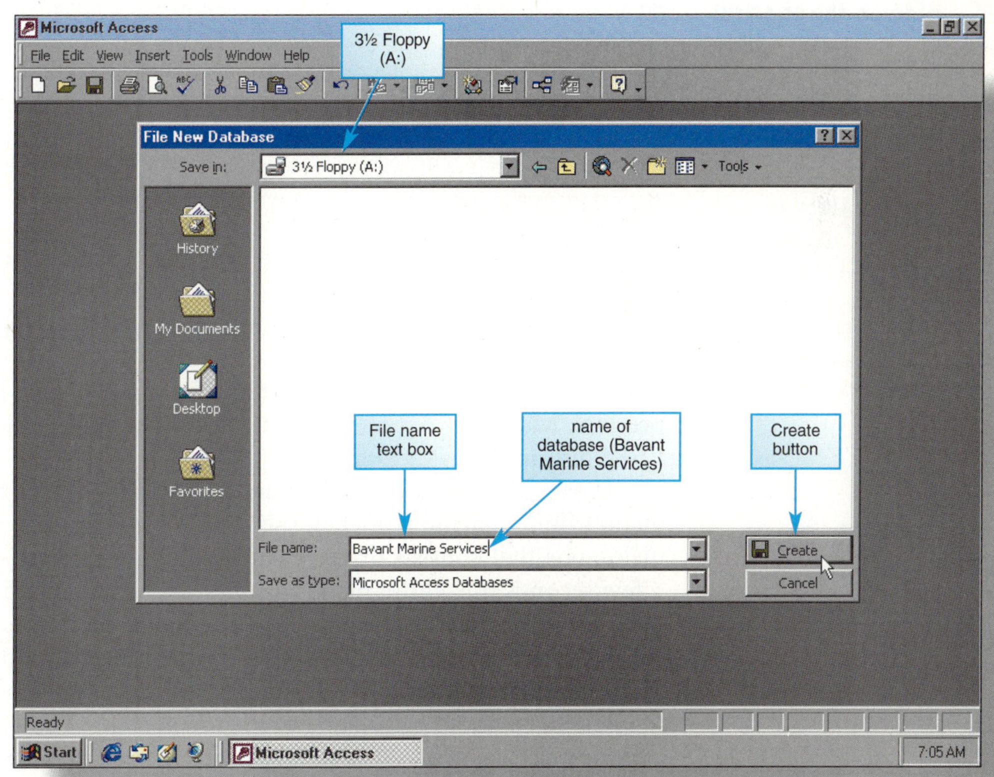

FIGURE 1-6

6 Click the Create button to create the database. If the Office Assistant displays, right-click the Office Assistant and then point to Hide on the shortcut menu.

The Bavant Marine Services database is created. The Bavant Marine Services : Database window displays on the desktop (Figure 1-7). The **Office Assistant***, a tool you can use to obtain help while working with Microsoft Access may display. (You will see how to use the Office Assistant later in this project.)*

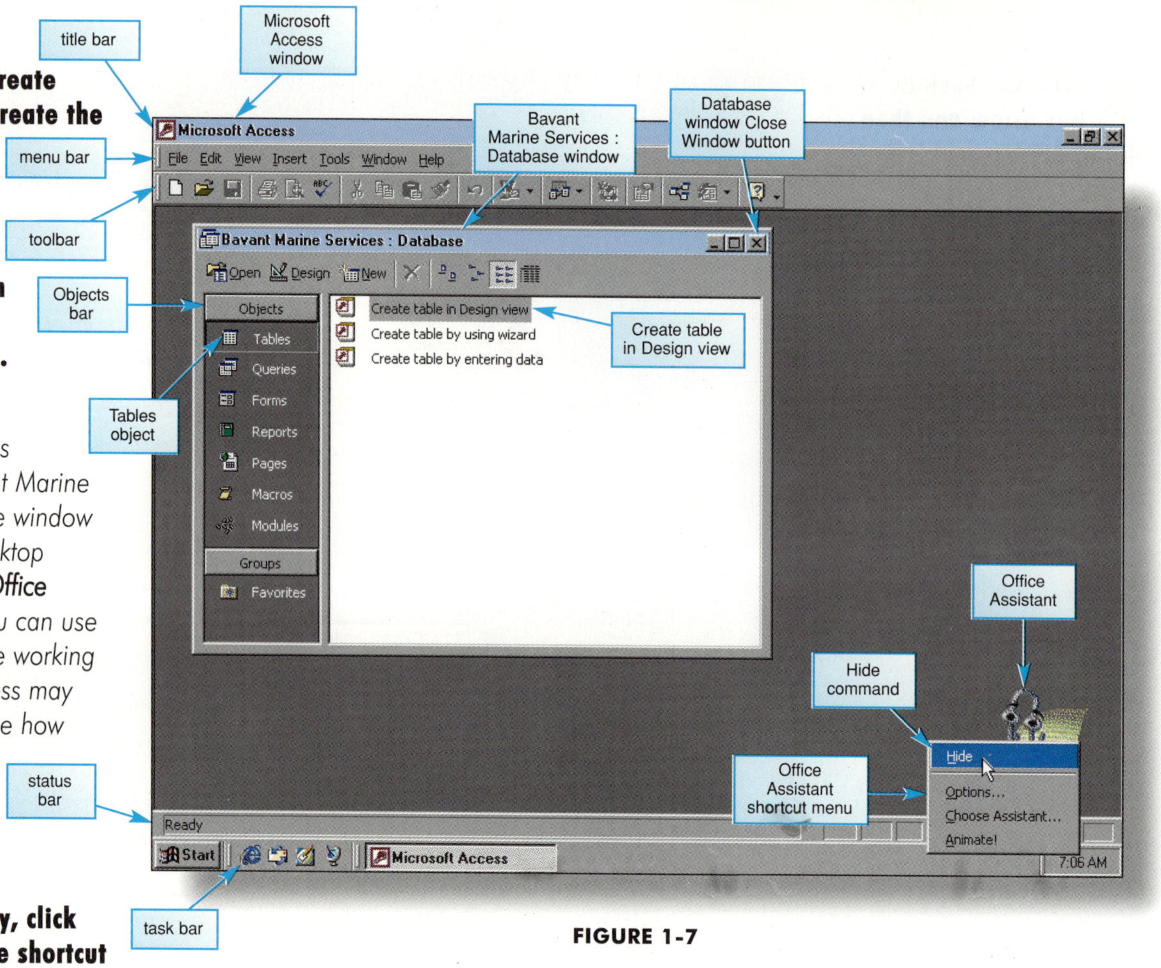

7 If necessary, click Hide on the shortcut menu.

The Office Assistant no longer displays.

FIGURE 1-7

Other Ways

1. Right-click Start button, click Open, double-click New Office Document
2. On Start menu click Programs, click Microsoft Access

More About

Toolbars

Normally, the correct Access 2000 toolbar automatically will display. If it does not, click View on the menu bar, and then click Toolbars. Click the toolbar for the activity in which you are engaged. See Appendix C for additional details.

The Access Desktop and the Database Window

The first bar on the desktop (Figure 1-7) is the **title bar**. It displays the title of the product, Microsoft Access. The button on the right is the **Close button**. Clicking the Close button closes the window.

The second bar is the **menu bar**. It contains a list of menu names. To open a menu from the menu bar, click the menu name. Initially a personalized version of the menu, one that consists of commands you have selected most recently, displays. After a few seconds, the entire menu displays. If the command you wish to select is on the personalized menu, you can select it immediately. If not, wait a few seconds to view the entire menu. (The menus shown throughout this book are the full menus, the ones that display after a few seconds.)

The third bar is the **Database window toolbar**. The Database window toolbar contains buttons that allow you to perform certain tasks more quickly than using the menu bar. Each button contains a picture, or **icon**, depicting its function. The specific buttons on the Database window toolbar will vary, depending on the task on which you are working.

The **taskbar** at the bottom of the screen displays the Start button, any active windows, and the current time.

Immediately above the Windows taskbar is the **status bar** (Figure 1-7). It contains special information that is appropriate for the task on which you are working. Currently, it contains the word, Ready, which means Access is ready to accept commands.

The **Database window**, referred to in Figure 1-7 as the Bavant Marine Services : Database window, is a special window that allows you to access easily and rapidly a variety of objects such as tables, queries, forms, and reports. To do so, you will use the various components of the window.

More About 2000

Creating a Table

Access 2000 includes **Table Wizards** that guide you by suggesting some commonly used tables and fields. If you already know the fields you need, however, it usually is easier to simply create the table yourself. For more information, visit the Access 2000 More About Web page (www.scsite.com/ac2000/more.htm) and then click Table Wizards.

Creating a Table

An Access database consists of a collection of tables. Once you have created the database, you must create each of the tables within it. In this project, for example, you must create both the Marina and Technician tables shown in Figure 1-1 on page A 1.7.

To create a table, you describe the **structure** of the table to Access by describing the fields within the table. For each field, you indicate the following:

1. **Field name** — Each field in the table must have a unique name. In the Marina table (Figure 1-8), for example, the field names are Marina Number, Name, Address, City, State, Zip Code, Warranty, Non-warranty, and Tech Number.

Structure of Marina table

FIELD NAME	DATA TYPE	FIELD SIZE	PRIMARY KEY?	DESCRIPTION
Marina Number	Text	4	Yes	Marina Number (Primary Key)
Name	Text	20		Marina Name
Address	Text	15		Street Address
City	Text	15		City
State	Text	2		State (Two-Character Abbreviation)
Zip Code	Text	5		Zip Code (Five-Character Version)
Warranty	Currency			Current Warranty Amount
Non-warranty	Currency			Current Non-warranty Amount
Tech Number	Text	2		Number of Marina's Technician

Data for Marina table

MARINA NUMBER	NAME	ADDRESS	CITY	STATE	ZIP CODE	WARRANTY	NON-WARRANTY	TECH NUMBER
AD57	Alan's Docks	314 Central	Burton	MI	49611	$1,248.00	$597.75	23
AN75	Afton's Marina	21 West 8th	Glenview	MI	48121	$1,906.50	$831.25	36
BL72	Brite's Landing	281 Robin	Burton	MI	49611	$217.00	$0.00	36
EL25	Elend Marina	462 River	Torino	MI	48268	$413.50	$678.75	49
FB96	Fenton's Boats	36 Bayview	Cavela	MI	47926	$923.20	$657.50	23
FM22	Fedder Marina	283 Waterfront	Burton	MI	49611	$432.00	$0.00	36
JB92	JT Boat Club	28 Causeway	Torino	MI	48268	$0.00	$0.00	36
NW72	Nelson's Wharf	27 Lake	Masondale	MI	49832	$608.50	$520.00	23
SM72	Solton's Marine	867 Bay Ridge	Glenview	MI	48121	$462.50	$295.00	49
TR72	The Reef	92 East Bay	Woodview	MI	47212	$219.00	$0.00	36

FIGURE 1-8

Data Types (General)

Different database management systems have different available data types. Even data types that are essentially the same can have different names. The Access 2000 Text data type, for example, is referred to as Character in some systems and Alpha in others.

Data Types (Access 2000)

Access 2000 offers a wide variety of data types, some of which have special options associated with them. For more information on data types, visit the Access 2000 More About Web page (www.scsite.com/ac2000/more.htm) and then click Data Types.

2. **Data type** — Data type indicates to Access the type of data the field will contain. Some fields can contain letters of the alphabet and numbers. Others contain only numbers. Others, such as Warranty and Non-warranty, can contain numbers and dollar signs.
3. **Description** — Access allows you to enter a detailed description of the field.

You also can assign field widths to text fields (fields whose data type is Text). This indicates the maximum number of characters that can be stored in the field. If you do not assign a width to such a field, Access assumes the width is 50.

You also must indicate which field or fields make up the **primary key**; that is, the unique identifier, for the table. In the sample database, the Marina Number field is the primary key of the Marina table and the Tech Number field is the primary key of the Technician table.

The rules for field names are:

1. Names can be up to 64 characters in length.
2. Names can contain letters, digits, and spaces, as well as most of the punctuation symbols.
3. Names cannot contain periods, exclamation points (!), or square brackets ([ ]).
4. The same name cannot be used for two different fields in the same table.

Each field has a **data type**. This indicates the type of data that can be stored in the field. The data types you will use in this project are:

1. **Text** — The field can contain any characters.
2. **Number** — The field can contain only numbers. The numbers either can be positive or negative. Fields are assigned this type so they can be used in arithmetic operations. Fields that contain numbers but will not be used for arithmetic operations usually are assigned a data type of Text. The Tech Number field, for example, is a text field because the tech numbers will not be involved in any arithmetic.
3. **Currency** — The field can contain only dollar amounts. The values will be displayed with dollar signs, commas, decimal points, and with two digits following the decimal point. Like numeric fields, you can use currency fields in arithmetic operations. Access assigns a size to currency fields automatically.

The field names, data types, field widths, primary key information, and descriptions for the Marina table are shown in Figure 1-8. With this information, you are ready to begin creating the table. To create the table, use the following steps.

To Create a Table

1 Right-click Create table in Design view and then point to Open on the shortcut menu.

The shortcut menu for creating a table in Design view displays (Figure 1-9).

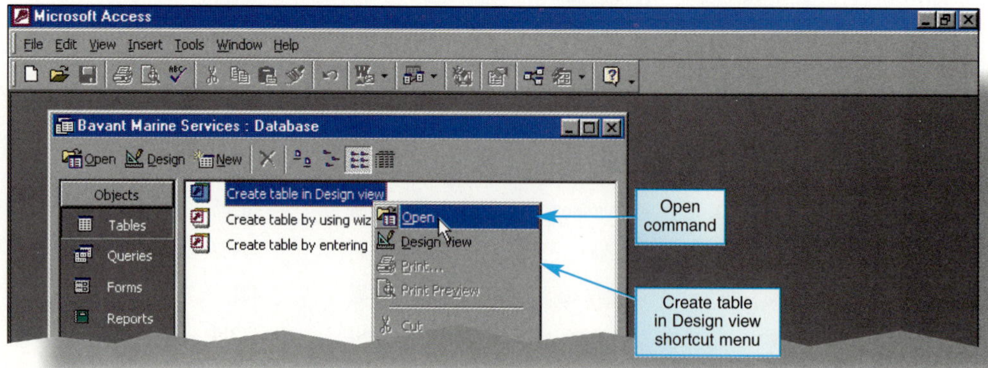

FIGURE 1-9

2 **Click Open.**

The Table1 : Table window displays (Figure 1-10).

3 **Click the Maximize button for the Table1 : Table window.**

A maximized Table1 : Table window displays.

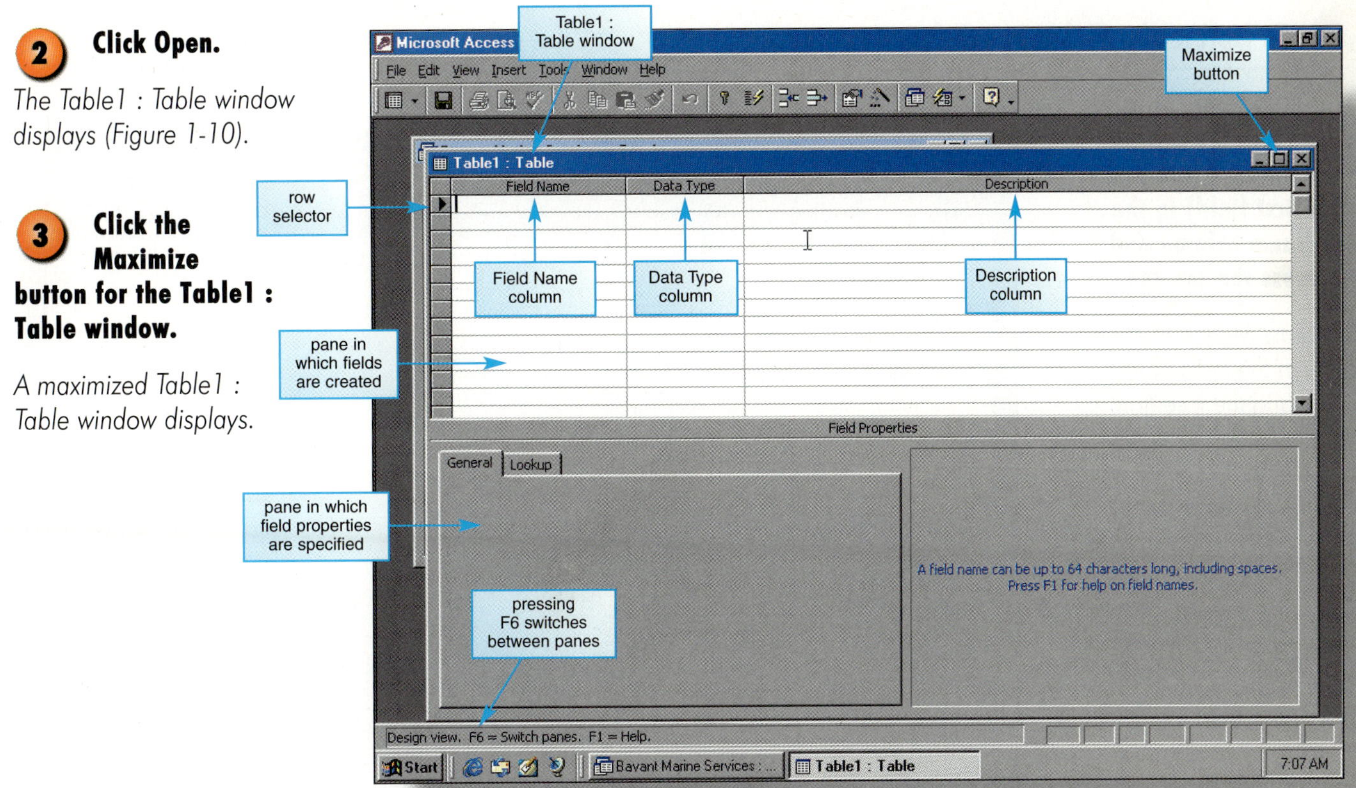

FIGURE 1-10

Defining the Fields

The next step in creating the table is to define the fields by specifying the required details in the Table window. Make entries in the Field Name, Data Type, and Description columns. Enter additional information in the Field Properties box in the lower portion of the Table window. Press the F6 key to move from the upper **pane** (portion of the screen), the one where you define the fields, to the lower pane, the one where you define field properties. Enter the appropriate field size and then press the F6 key to return to the upper pane. As you define the fields, the row selector (Figure 1-10) indicates the field you currently are describing. The **row selector** is a small box or bar that, when clicked, selects the entire row. It is positioned on the first field, indicating Access is ready for you to enter the name of the first field in the Field Name column.

Perform the steps on the next page to define the fields in the table.

1. Click New Object: AutoForm button arrow on Database window toolbar, click Table
2. On Insert menu click Table
3. Double-click Create table in Design view
4. Press ALT+N

Primary Keys

In some cases, the primary key consists of a combination of fields rather than a single field. For more information on determining primary keys in such situations, visit the Access 2000 More About Web page (www.scsite.com/ac2000/more.htm) and then click Primary Key.

Steps To Define the Fields in a Table

1 **Type** `Marina Number` **(the name of the first field) in the Field Name column and then press the TAB key.**

The words, Marina Number, display in the Field Name column and the insertion point advances to the Data Type column, indicating you can enter the data type (Figure 1-11). The word, Text, one of the possible data types, currently displays. The arrow in the Data Type column indicates a list of data types is available by clicking the arrow.

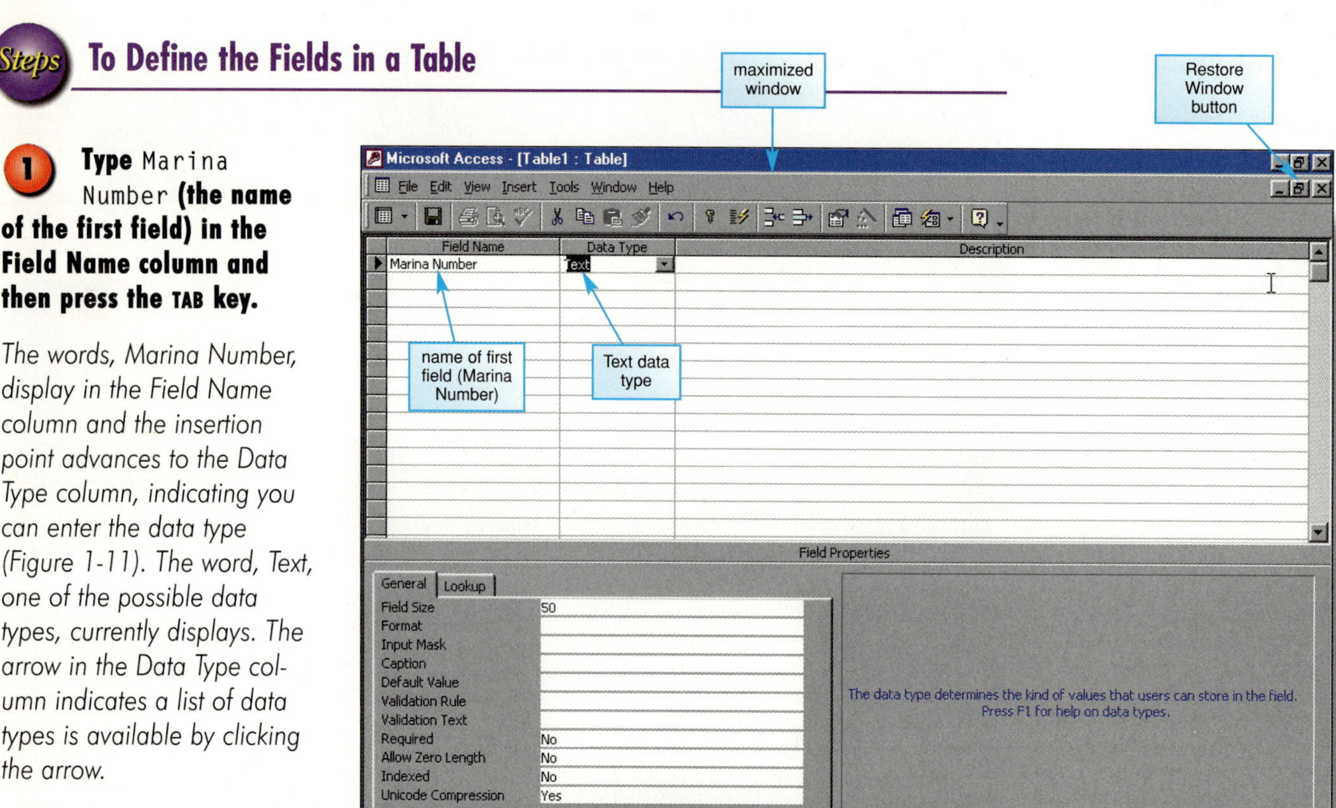

FIGURE 1-11

2 **Because Text is the correct data type, press the TAB key to move the insertion point to the Description column, type** `Marina Number (Primary Key)` **as the description and then point to the Primary Key button on the Database window toolbar.**

A ScreenTip, which is a description of the button, displays partially obscuring the description of the first field (Figure 1-12).

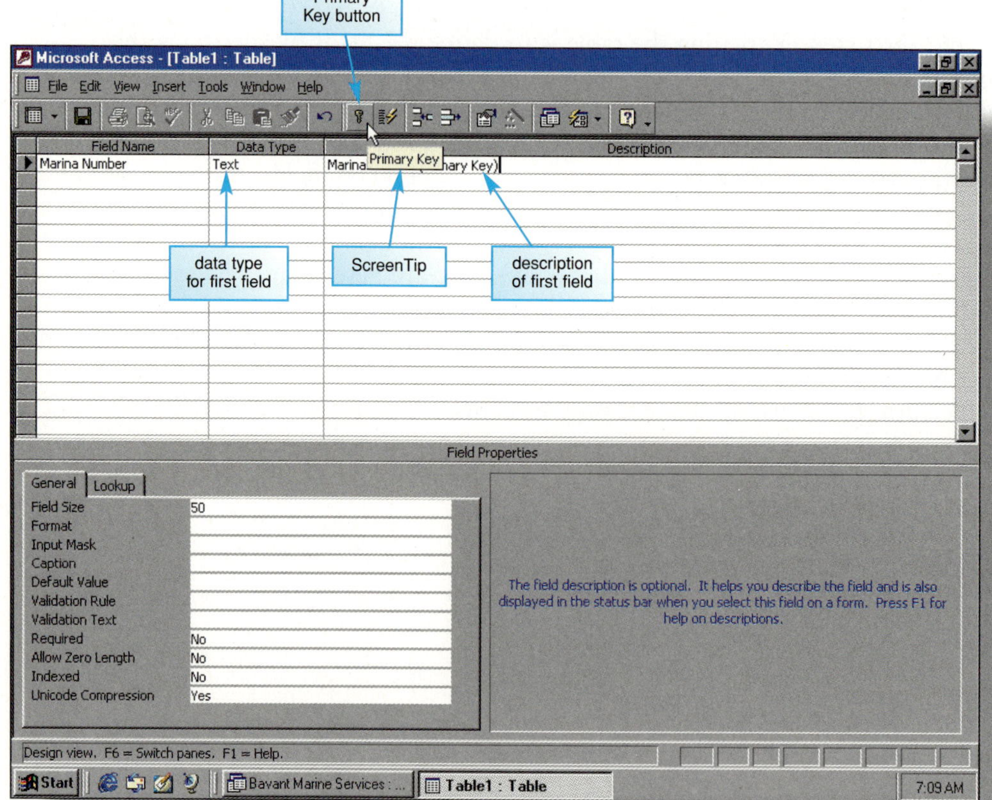

FIGURE 1-12

3 **Click the Primary Key button to make Marina Number the primary key and then press the F6 key to move the insertion point to the Field Size text box.**

The Marina Number field is the primary key as indicated by the key symbol that displays in the row selector (Figure 1-13). The current entry in the Field Size text box (50) is selected.

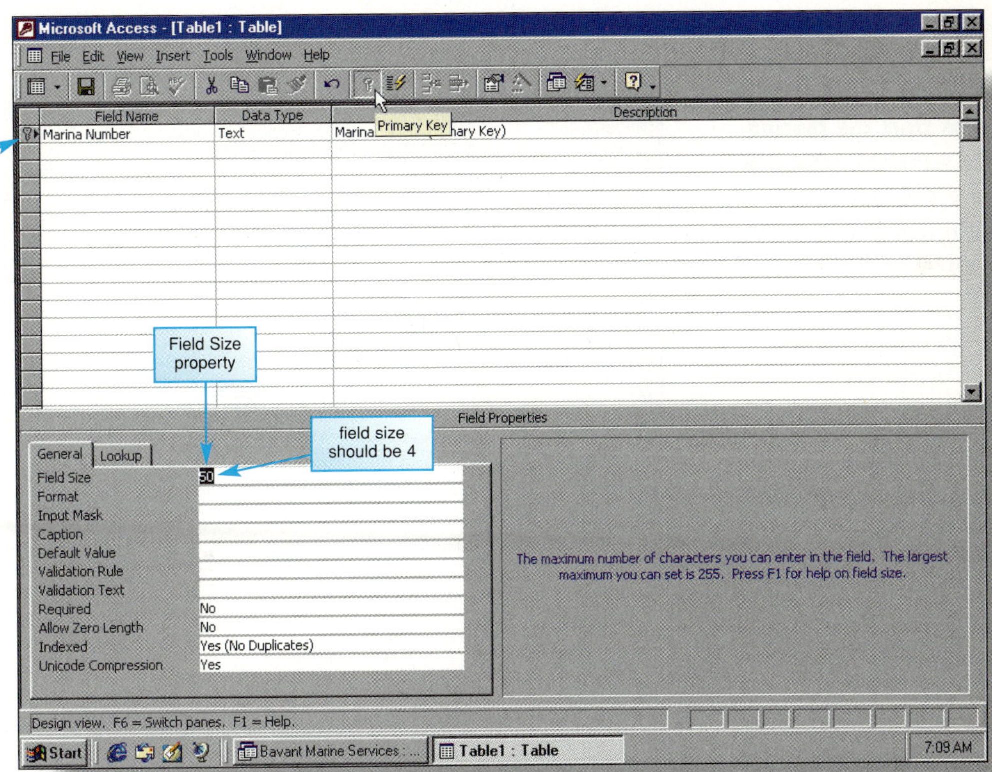

FIGURE 1-13

4 **Type 4 as the size of the Marina Number field. Press the F6 key to return to the Description column for the Marina Number field and then press the TAB key to move to the Field Name column in the second row.**

The row selector moves to the second row just below the field name Marina Number (Figure 1-14).

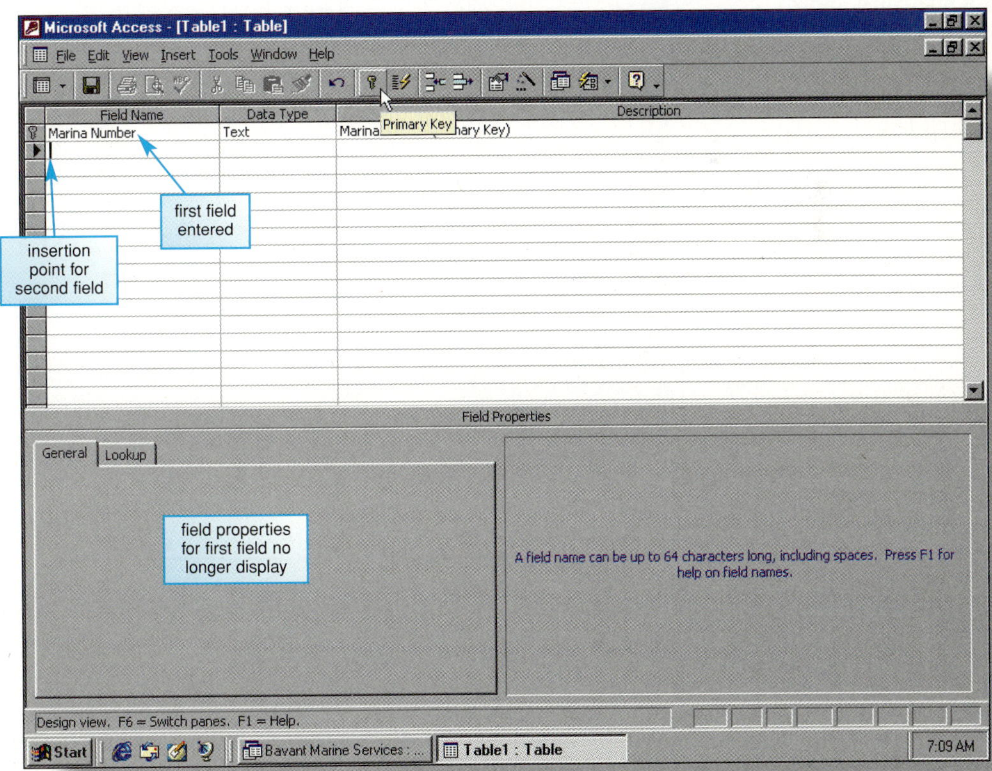

FIGURE 1-14

5 **Use the techniques illustrated in Steps 1 through 4 to make the entries from the Marina table structure shown in Figure 1-8 on page A 1.13 up through and including the name of the Warranty field. Click the Data Type column arrow and then point to Currency.**

The additional fields are entered (Figure 1-15). A list of available data types displays in the Data Type column for the Warranty field.

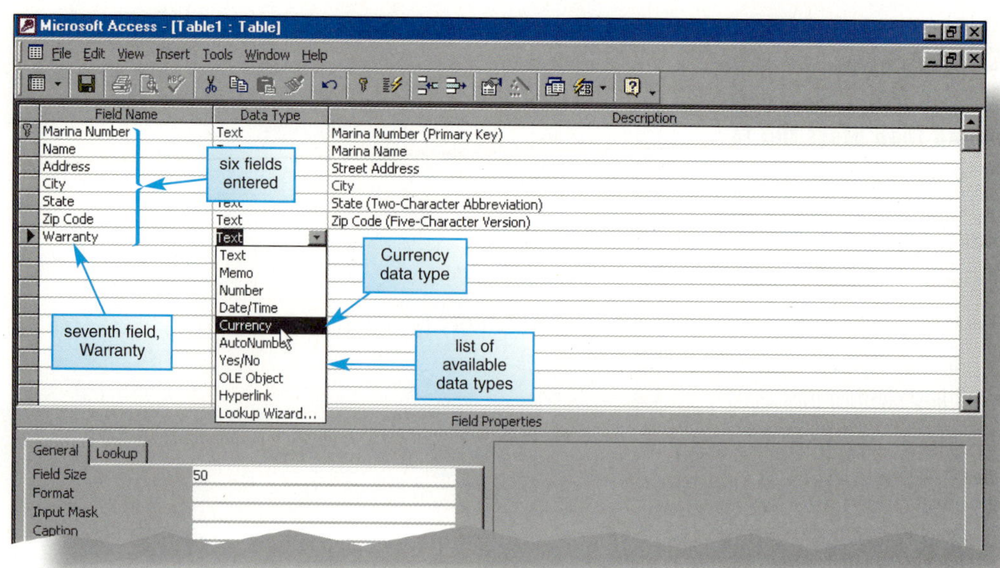

FIGURE 1-15

6 **Click Currency and then press the TAB key. Make the remaining entries from the Marina table structure shown in Figure 1-8.**

The fields are all entered (Figure 1-16).

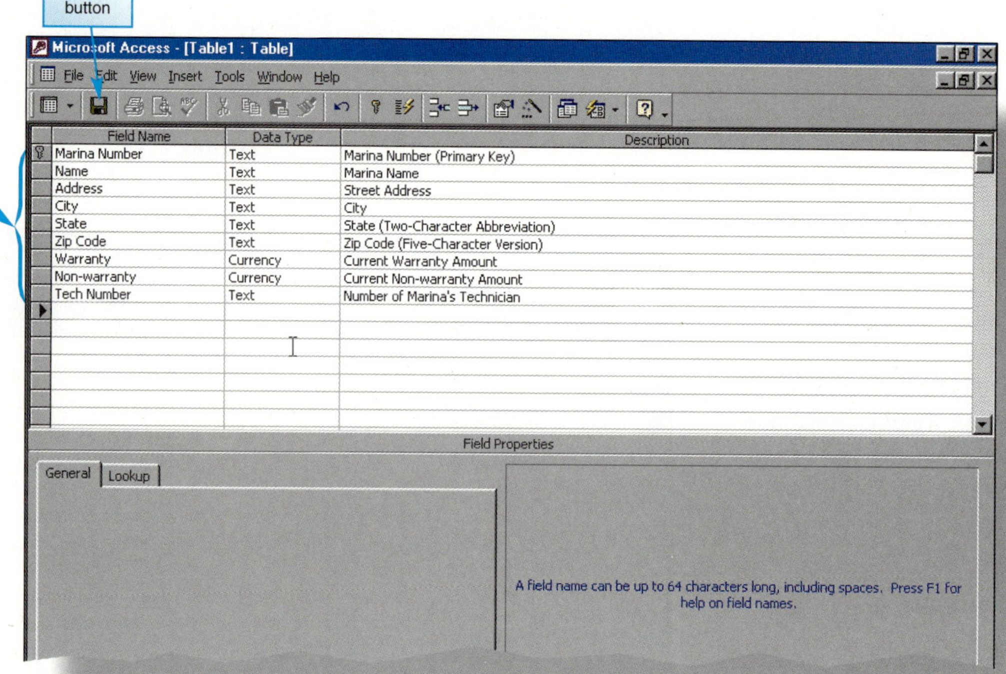

FIGURE 1-16

Correcting Errors in the Structure

When creating a table, check the entries carefully to ensure they are correct. If you make a mistake and discover it before you press the TAB key, you can correct the error by repeatedly pressing the BACKSPACE key until the incorrect characters are removed. Then, type the correct characters. If you do not discover a mistake until later, you can click the entry, type the correct value, and then press the ENTER key.

If you accidentally add an extra field to the structure, select the field by clicking the row selector (the leftmost column on the row that contains the field to be deleted). Once you have selected the field, press the DELETE key. This will remove the field from the structure.

If you forget a field, select the field that will follow the field you wish to add by clicking the row selector, and then press the INSERT key. The remaining fields move down one row, making room for the missing field. Make the entries for the new field in the usual manner.

If you made the wrong field a primary key field, click the correct primary key entry for the field and then click the Primary Key button on the Database window toolbar.

As an alternative to these steps, you may want to start over. To do so, click the Close button for the Table1 : Table window and then click No. The original desktop displays and you can repeat the process you used earlier.

More About 2000

Correcting Errors

Even after you have entered data, it still is possible to correct errors in the structure. Access 2000 will make all the necessary adjustments to the table structure of the table as well as to the data within it. (It is simplest to make the correction, however, before any data is entered.)

Saving a Table

The Marina table structure now is complete. The final step is to save the table within the database. At this time, you should give the table a name.

Table names are from one to 64 characters in length and can contain letters, numbers, and spaces. The two table names in this project are Marina and Technician.

To save the table, complete the following steps.

Steps To Save a Table

1 Click the Save button on the Database window toolbar (see Figure 1-16 on page A 1.18). Type `Marina` as the name of the table in the Table Name text box and then point to the OK button.

The Save As dialog box displays (Figure 1-17). The name of the table displays in the Table Name text box.

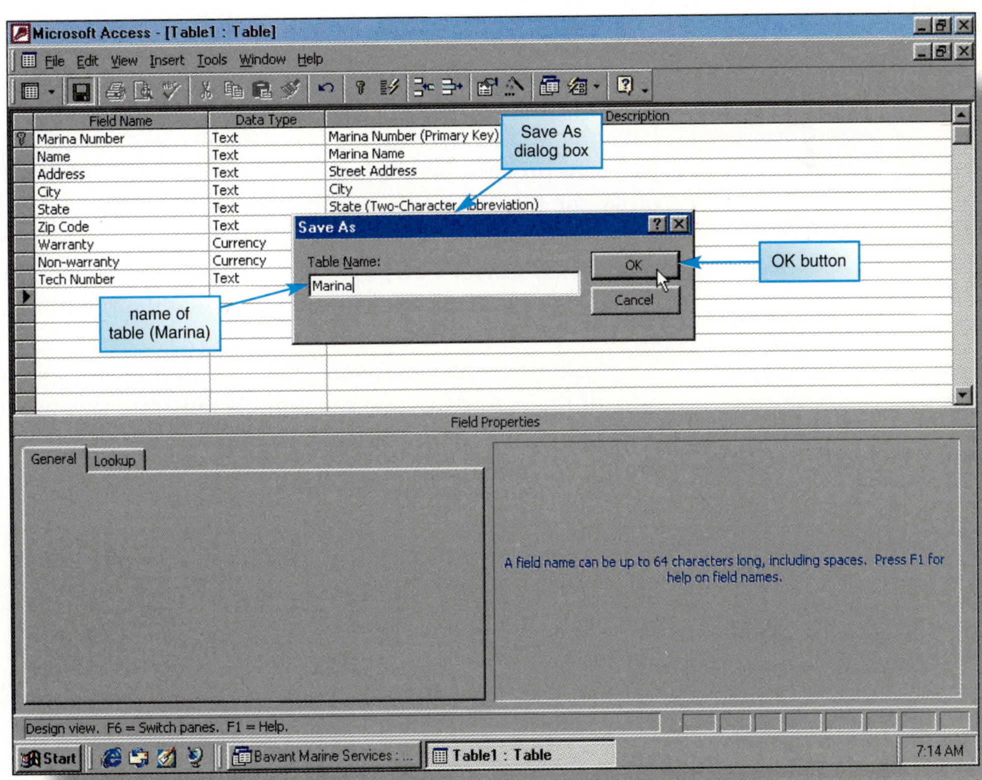

FIGURE 1-17

2 **Click the OK button and then point to the Close Window button for the Marina : Table window.**

The table is saved on the floppy disk in drive A. The name of the table is now Marina as indicated on the title bar (Figure 1-18).

3 **Click the Close Window button for the Marina : Table window. (Be sure not to click the Close button on the Microsoft Access title bar, because this would close Microsoft Access.)**

The Marina : Table window no longer displays.

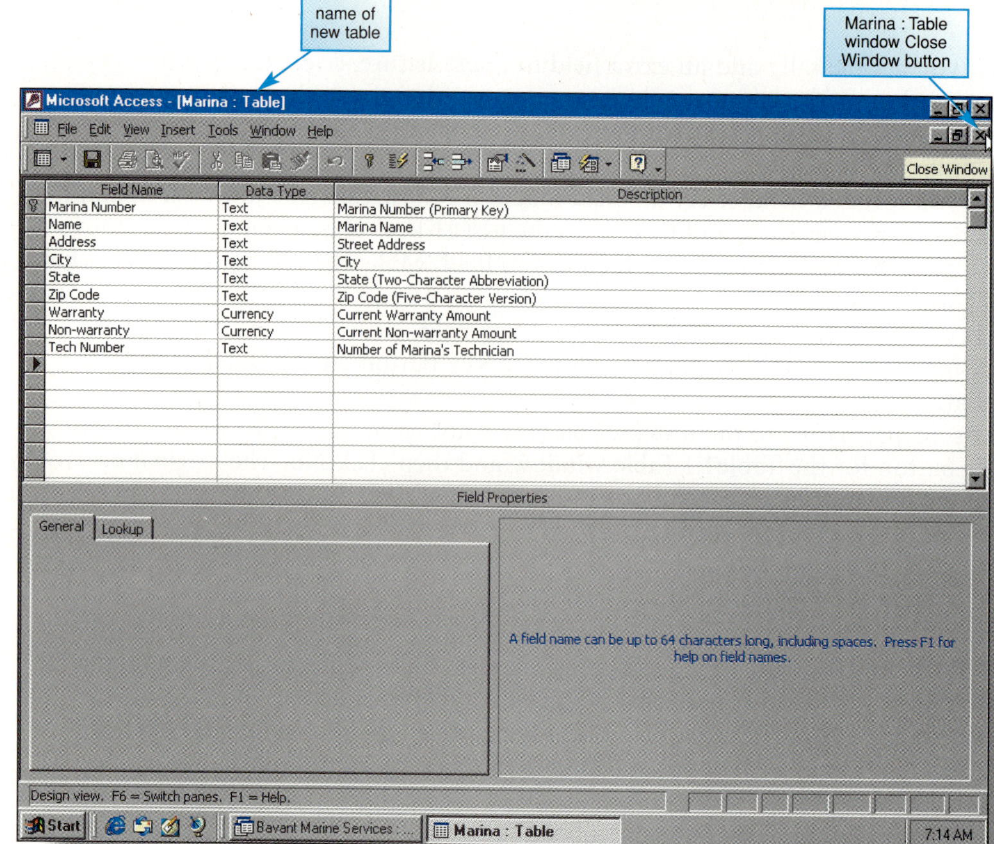

FIGURE 1-18

Other Ways

1. On File menu click Save
2. Press CTRL+S

More About 2000

Adding Records

As soon as you have entered or modified a record and moved to another record, the original record is saved. This is different from other tools. The rows entered in a spreadsheet, for example, are not saved until the entire spreadsheet is saved.

Adding Records to a Table

Creating a table by building the structure and saving the table is the first step in a two-step process. The second step is to add records to the table. To add records to a table, the table must be open. To open a table, right-click the table in the Database window and then click Open on the shortcut menu. The table displays in Datasheet view. In **Datasheet view**, the table is represented as a collection of rows and columns called a **datasheet**. It looks very much like the tables shown in Figure 1-1 on page A 1.7.

You often add records in phases. You may, for example, not have enough time to add all the records in one session. To illustrate this process, this project begins by adding the first two records in the Marina table (Figure 1-19). The remaining records are added later.

Marina table (first 2 records)

MARINA NUMBER	NAME	ADDRESS	CITY	STATE	ZIP CODE	WARRANTY	NON-WARRANTY	TECH NUMBER
AD57	Alan's Docks	314 Central	Burton	MI	49611	$1,248.00	$597.75	23
AN75	Afton's Marina	21 West 8th	Glenview	MI	48121	$1,906.50	$831.25	36

FIGURE 1-19

To open the Marina table and then add records, use the following steps.

Steps To Add Records to a Table

1 Right-click Marina in the Bavant Marine Services : Database window and then point to Open on the shortcut menu.

The shortcut menu for the Marina table displays (Figure 1-20). The Bavant Marine Services : Database window is maximized because the previous window, the Marina : Table window, was maximized. (If you wanted to restore the Database window to its original size, you would click the Restore Window button.)

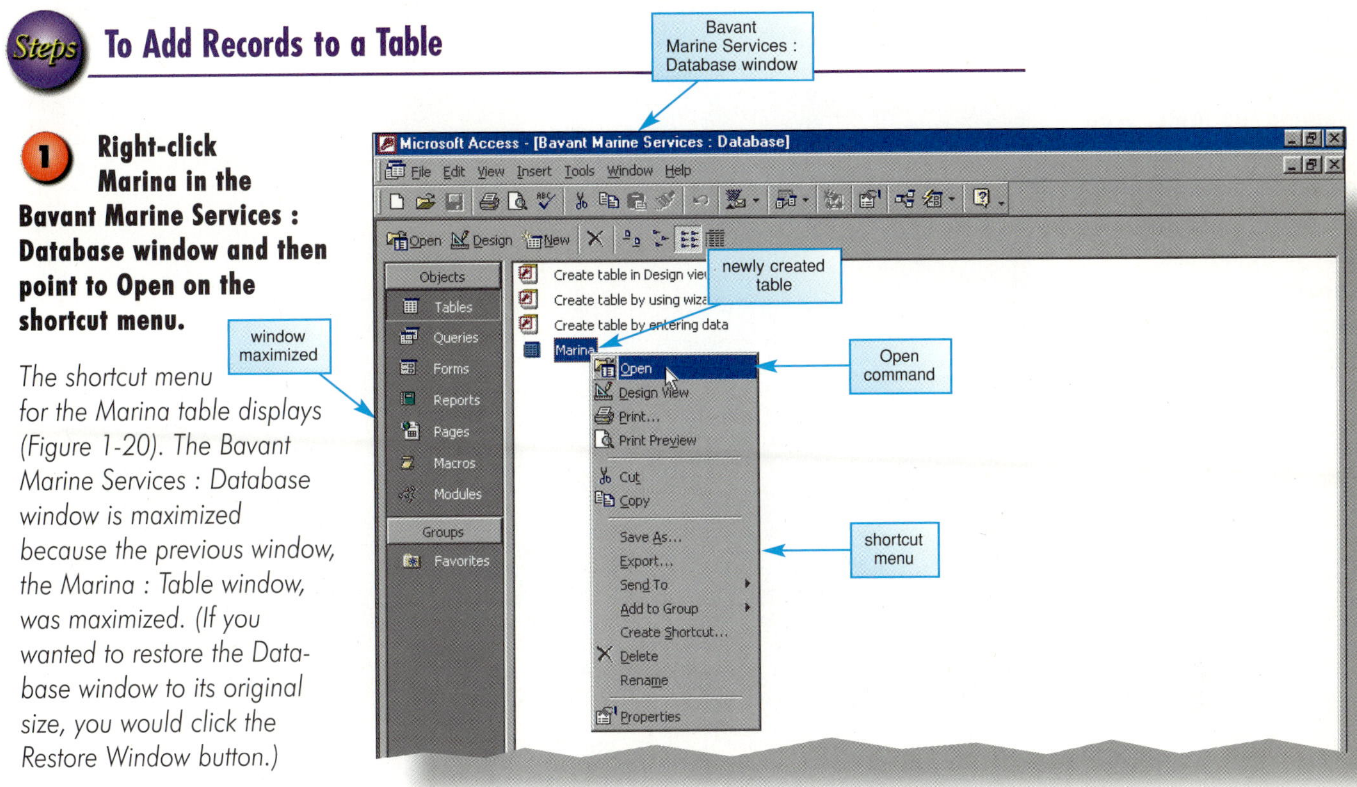

FIGURE 1-20

2 Click Open on the shortcut menu.

*The Marina : Table window displays (Figure 1-21). The window contains the Datasheet view for the Marina table. The **record selector** is positioned on the first record. The record selector is the small box or bar to the left of the record. The status bar at the bottom of the window also indicates that the record selector is positioned on record 1.*

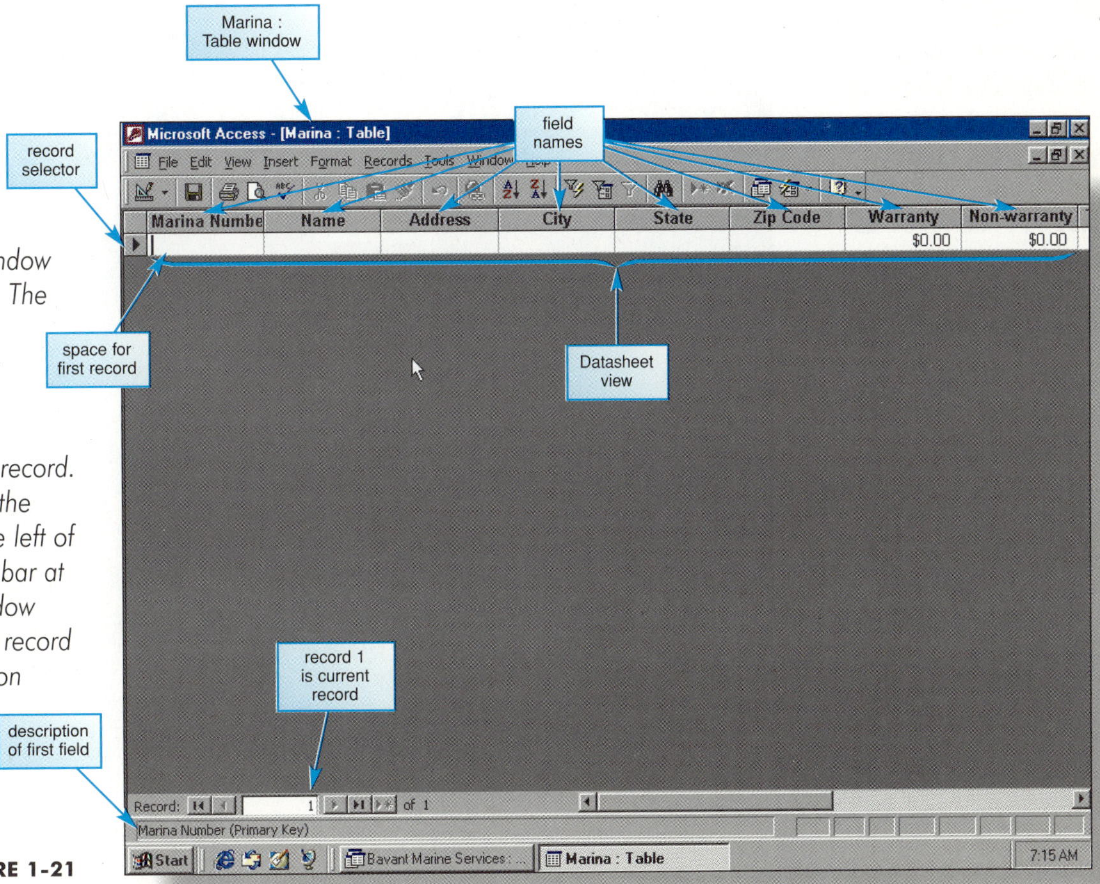

FIGURE 1-21

3 **If your window is not already maximized, click the Maximize button to maximize the window containing the table. Type** AD57 **as the first marina number, as shown in Figure 1-19. Be sure you type the letters in uppercase, because that is the way they are to be entered in the database.**

The marina number is entered, but the insertion point is still in the Marina Number field (Figure 1-22).

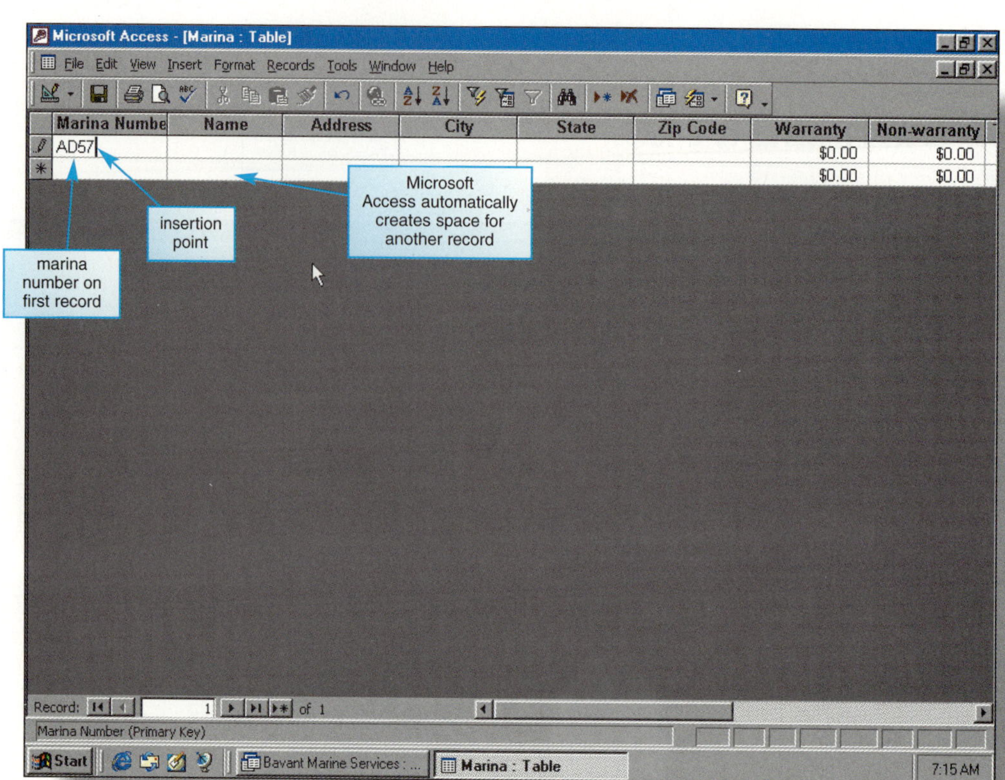

FIGURE 1-22

4 **Press the TAB key to complete the entry for the Marina Number field. Type the following entries, pressing the TAB key after each one:** Alan's Docks **as the name,** 314 Central **as the address,** Burton **as the city,** MI **as the state, and** 49611 **as the zip code.**

The Name, Address, City, State, and Zip Code fields are entered (Figure 1-23).

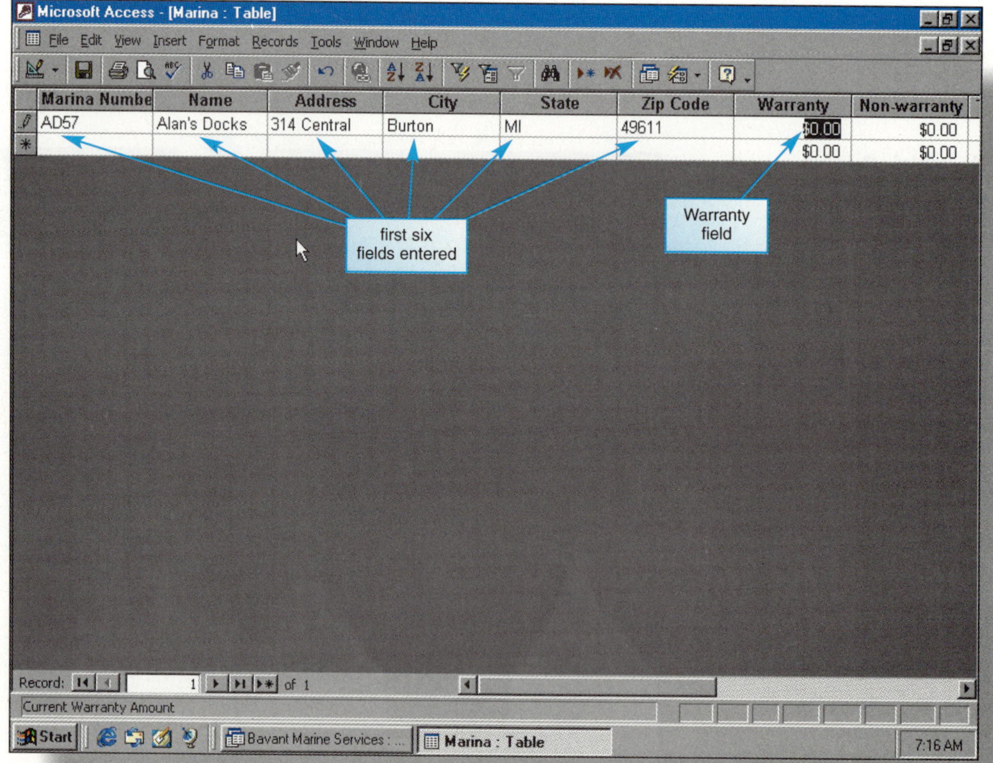

FIGURE 1-23

5 **Type** 1248 **as the warranty amount and then press the TAB key. (You do not need to type dollar signs or commas. In addition, because the digits to the right of the decimal point were both zeros, you did not need to type the decimal point.) Type** 597.75 **as the non-warranty amount and then press the TAB key. Type** 23 **as the tech number to complete the record.**

The fields have shifted to the left (Figure 1-24). The Warranty and Non-warranty values display with dollar signs and decimal points. The insertion point is positioned in the Tech Number field.

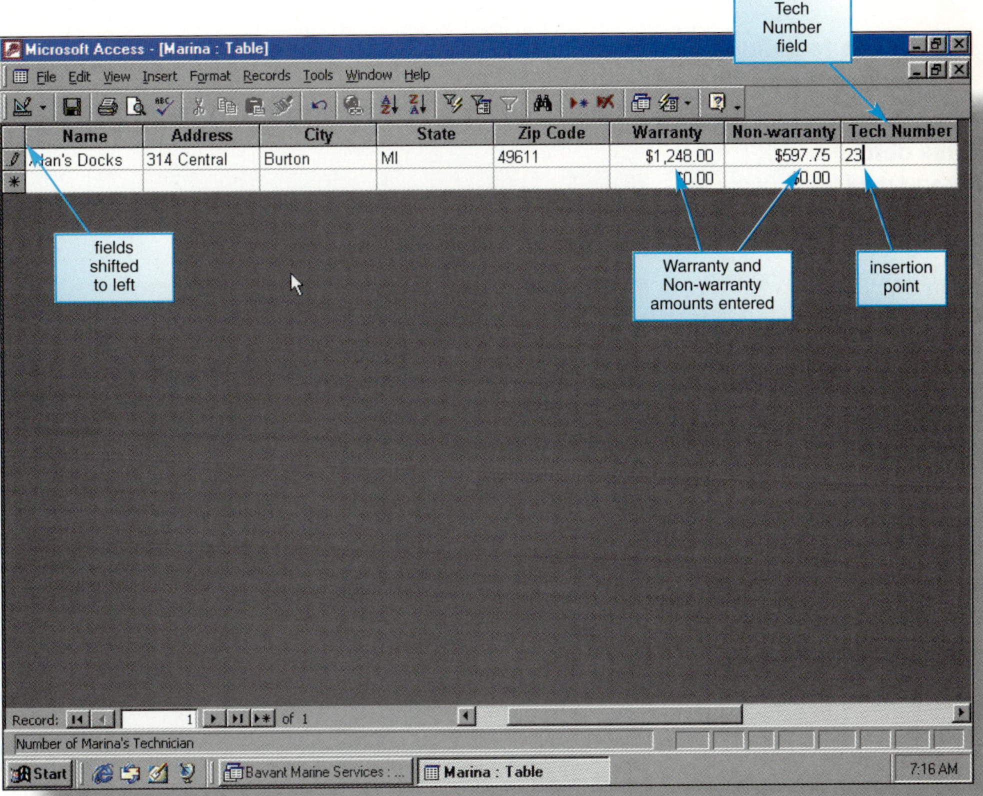

FIGURE 1-24

6 **Press the TAB key.**

The fields shift back to the right, the record is saved, and the insertion point moves to the marina number on the second row (Figure 1-25).

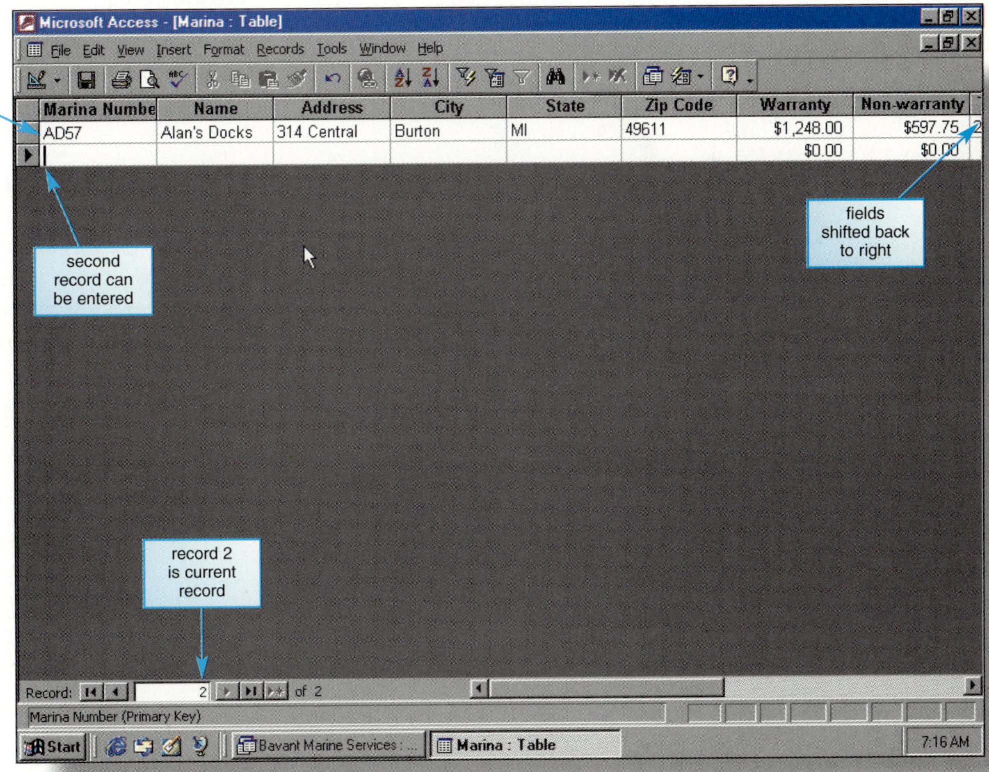

FIGURE 1-25

7 Use the techniques shown in Steps 3 through 6 to add the data for the second record in Figure 1-19.

The second record is added and the insertion point moves to the marina number on the third row (Figure 1-26).

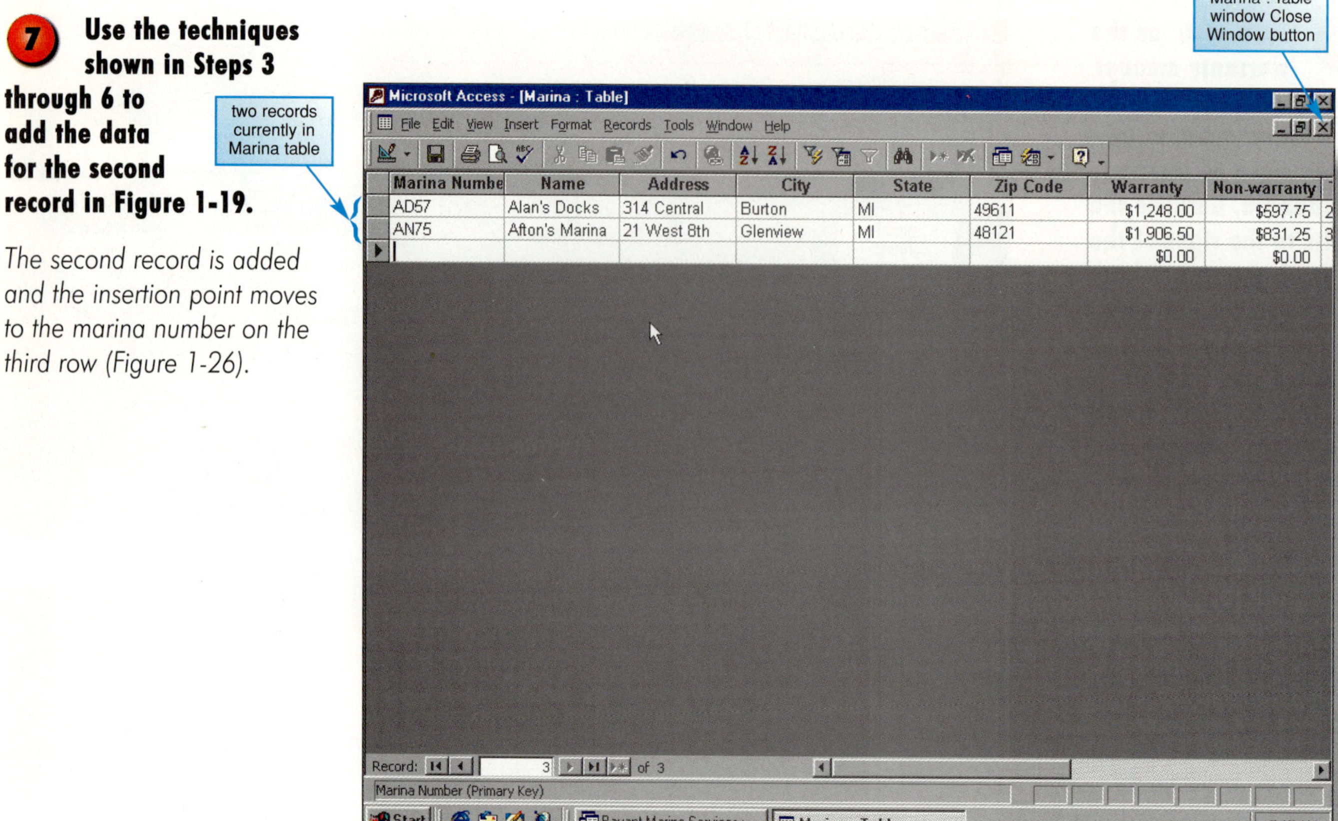

FIGURE 1-26

Closing a Table and a Database and Quitting Access

It is a good idea to close a table as soon as you have finished working with it. It keeps the screen from getting cluttered and prevents you from making accidental changes to the data in the table. If you no longer will work with the database, you should close the database as well. With the creation of the Marina table complete, you can quit Access at this point.

Perform the following steps to close the table and the database and then quit Access.

To Close a Table and Database and Quit Access

1 Click the Close Window button for the Marina : Table window (see Figure 1-26 on page A 1.24).

The datasheet for the Marina table no longer displays (Figure 1-27).

2 Click the Close button for the Bavant Marine Services : Database window (see Figure 1-27).

The Bavant Marine Services : Database window no longer displays.

3 Click the Close button for the Microsoft Access window.

The Microsoft Access window no longer displays.

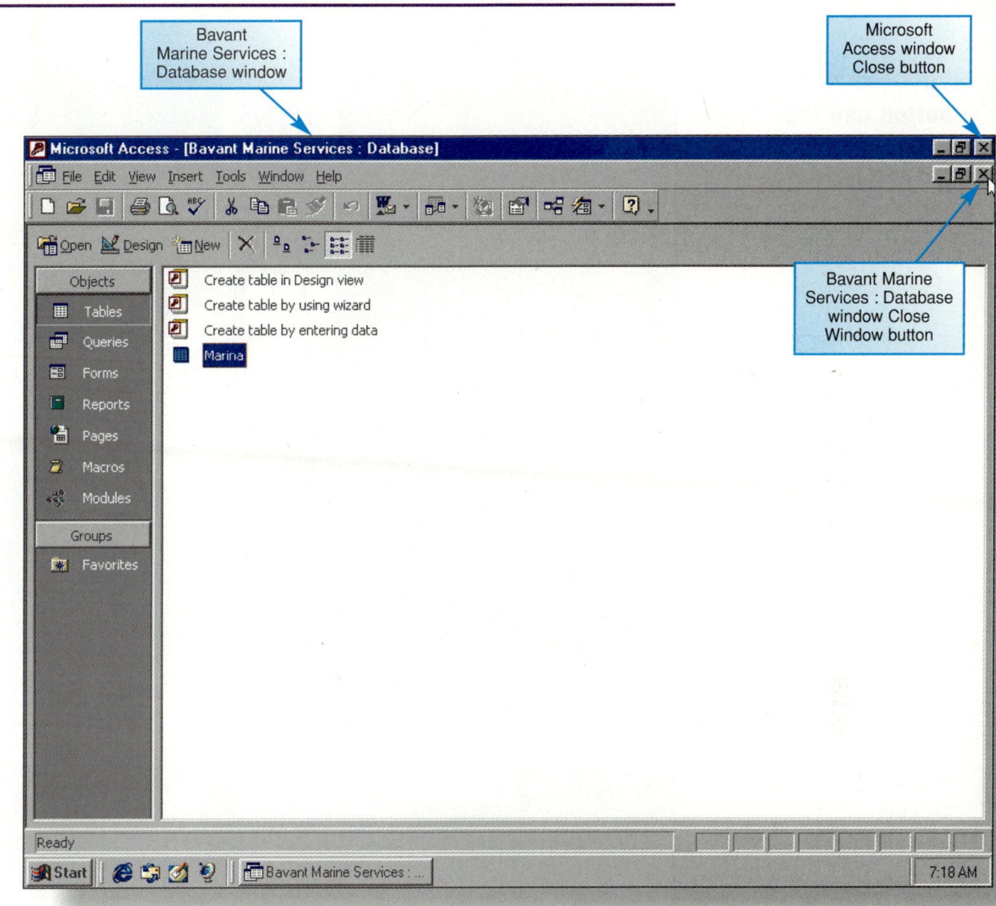

FIGURE 1-27

Opening a Database

To work with any of the tables, reports, or forms in a database, the database must be open. To open a database from the Windows desktop, click Open Office Document on the Start menu by performing the following steps. (The Other Ways box indicates ways to open a database from within Access.)

To Open a Database

1 Click the Start button and then point to Open Office Document (Figure 1-28).

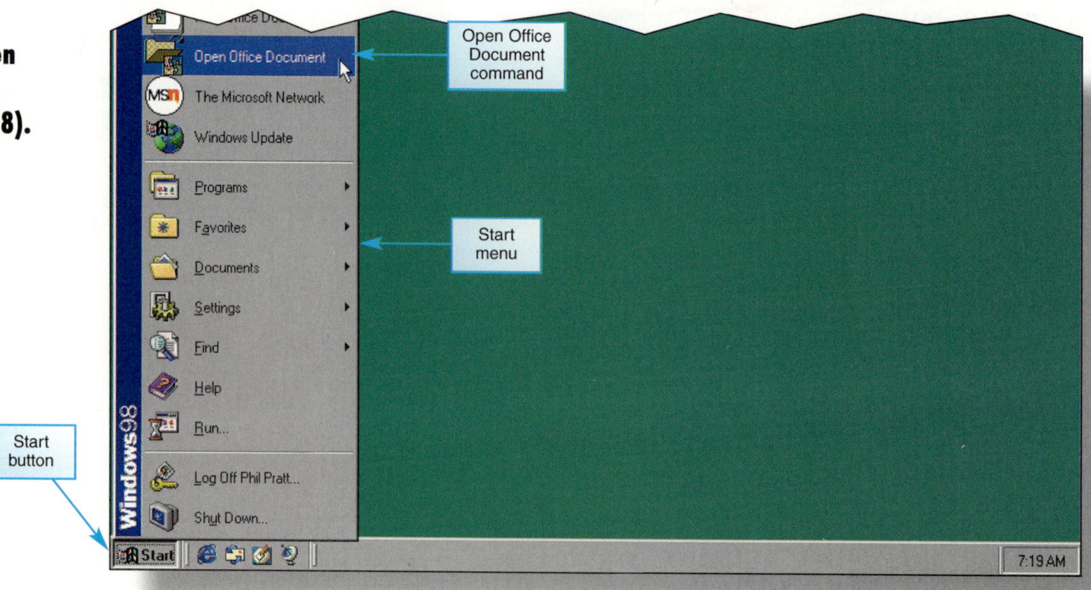

FIGURE 1-28

2 Click Open Office Document. If necessary, click the Look in box arrow and then click 3½ Floppy (A:) in the Look in box. If it is not already selected, click the Bavant Marine Services database name. Point to the Open button.

The Open Office Document dialog box displays (Figure 1-29). The 3½ Floppy (A:) folder displays in the Look in box and the files on the floppy disk in drive A display. Your list may be different.

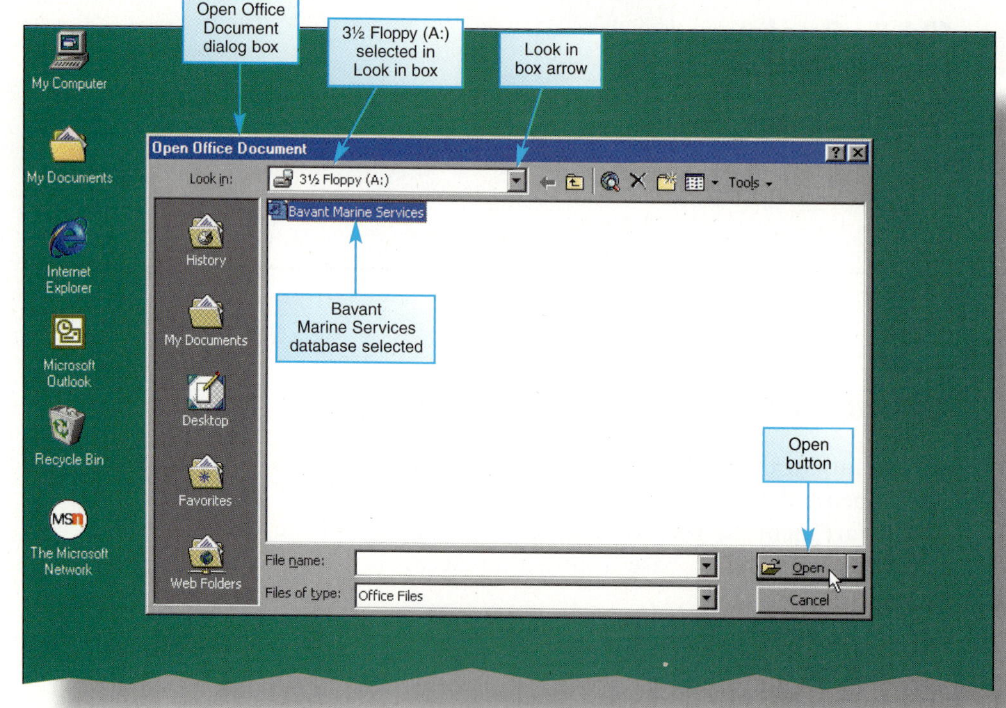

FIGURE 1-29

3 Click the Open button.

The database opens and the Bavant Marine Services : Database window displays.

Other Ways

1. Click Open button on Database window toolbar
2. On File menu click Open
3. Press CTRL+O

Adding Additional Records

You can add records to a table that already contains data using a process almost identical to that used to add records to an empty table. The only difference is that you place the insertion point after the last data record before you enter the additional data. To do so, use the **Navigation buttons** found near the lower-left corner of the screen. The purpose of each of the Navigation buttons is described in Table 1-1.

Table 1-1 Navigation Buttons in Datasheet View

BUTTON	PURPOSE
First Record	Moves to the first record in the table
Previous Record	Moves to the previous record
Next Record	Moves to the next record
Last Record	Moves to the last record in the table
New Record	Moves to the end of the table to a position for entering a new record

Complete the following steps to add the remaining records (Figure 1-30) to the Marina table.

Marina table (last 8 records)

MARINA NUMBER	NAME	ADDRESS	CITY	STATE	ZIP CODE	WARRANTY	NON-WARRANTY	TECH NUMBER
BL72	Brite's Landing	281 Robin	Burton	MI	49611	$217.00	$0.00	36
EL25	Elend Marina	462 River	Torino	MI	48268	$413.50	$678.75	49
FB96	Fenton's Boats	36 Bayview	Cavela	MI	47926	$923.20	$657.50	23
FM22	Fedder Marina	283 Waterfront	Burton	MI	49611	$432.00	$0.00	36
JB92	JT Boat Club	28 Causeway	Torino	MI	48268	$0.00	$0.00	36
NW72	Nelson's Wharf	27 Lake	Masondale	MI	49832	$608.50	$520.00	23
SM72	Solton's Marine	867 Bay Ridge	Glenview	MI	48121	$462.50	$295.00	49
TR72	The Reef	92 East Bay	Woodview	MI	47212	$219.00	$0.00	36

FIGURE 1-30

Steps To Add Additional Records to a Table

1 **Right-click Marina in the Bavant Marine Services : Database window and then click Open on the shortcut menu.**

2 **When the Marina table displays, maximize the window by clicking the Maximize button. Point to the New Record button.**

The datasheet displays (Figure 1-31).

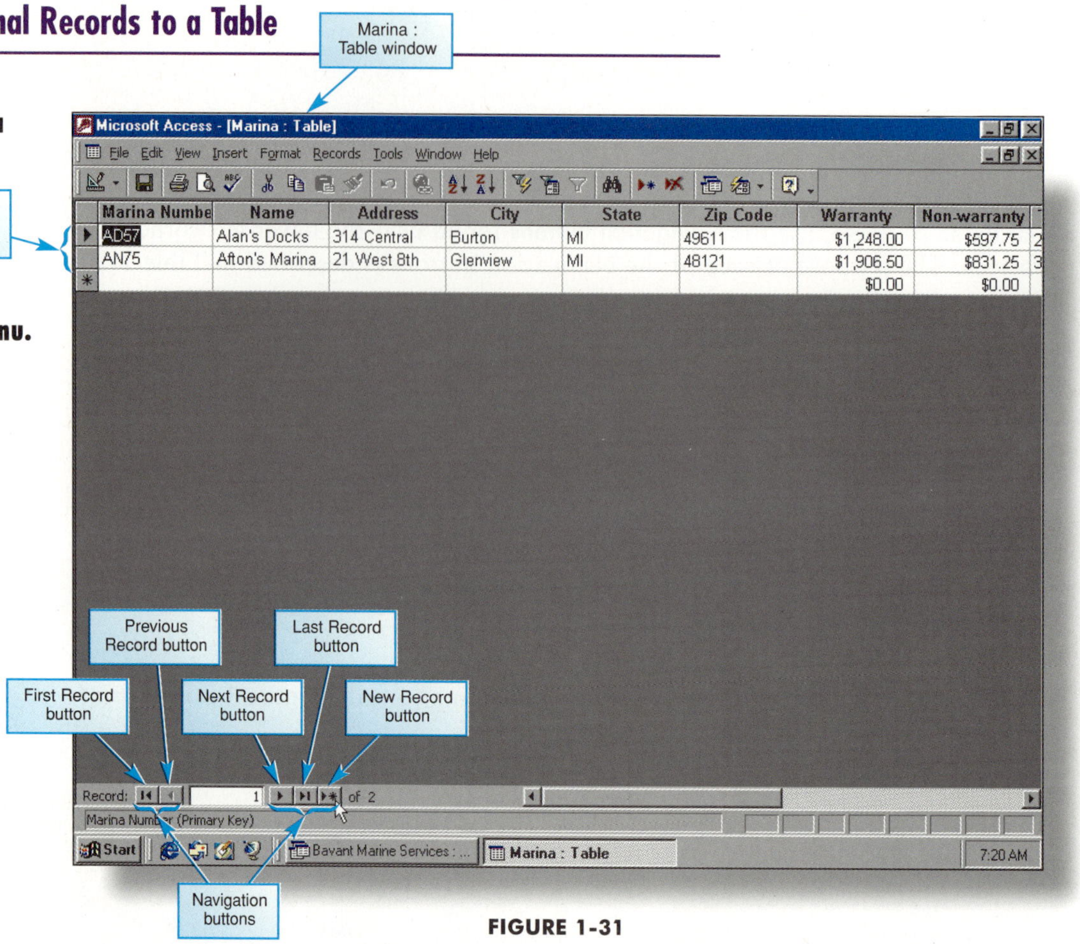

Marina : Table window
two records currently in table
Microsoft Access - [Marina : Table]
File Edit View Insert Format Records Tools Window Help
Marina Numbe
Name
Address
City
State
Zip Code
Warranty
Non-warranty
AD57 Alan's Docks 314 Central Burton MI 49611 $1,248.00 $597.75
AN75 Afton's Marina 21 West 8th Glenview MI 48121 $1,906.50 $831.25
$0.00 $0.00
Previous Record button
Last Record button
First Record button
Next Record button
New Record button
Record: 1 of 2
Marina Number (Primary Key)
Start
Bavant Marine Services : ...
Marina : Table
7:20 AM
Navigation buttons

FIGURE 1-31

3 **Click the New Record button.**

Access places the insertion point in position to enter a new record (Figure 1-32).

Microsoft Access - [Marina : Table]
File Edit View Insert Format Records Tools Window Help
Marina Numbe
Name
Address
City
State
Zip Code
Warranty
Non-warranty
AD57 Alan's Docks 314 Central Burton MI 49611 $1,248.00 $597.75
AN75 Afton's Marina 21 West 8th Glenview MI 48121 $1,906.50 $831.25
$0.00 $0.00
insertion point positioned on new record
Record: 3 of 3
Marina Number (Primary Key)
Start
Bavant Marine Services : ...
Marina : Table
7:20 AM

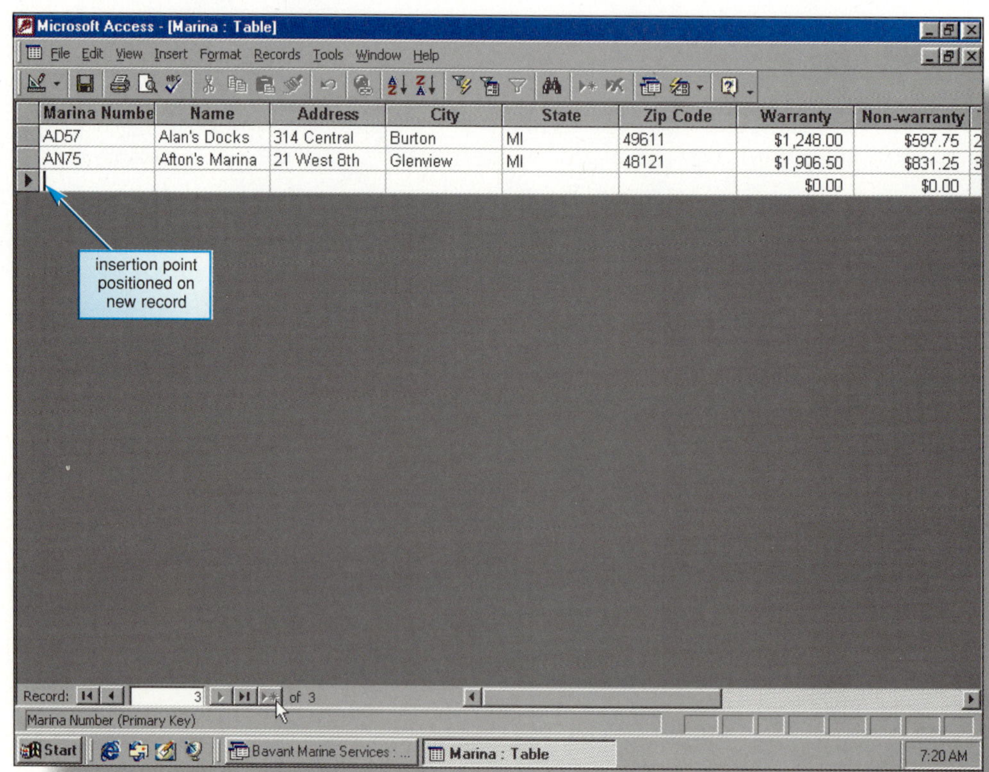

FIGURE 1-32

4 **Add the remaining records from Figure 1-30 on page A 1.27 using the same techniques you used to add the first two records. Point to the Close Window button.**

The additional records are added (Figure 1-33).

5 **Click the Close Window button.**

The window containing the table closes.

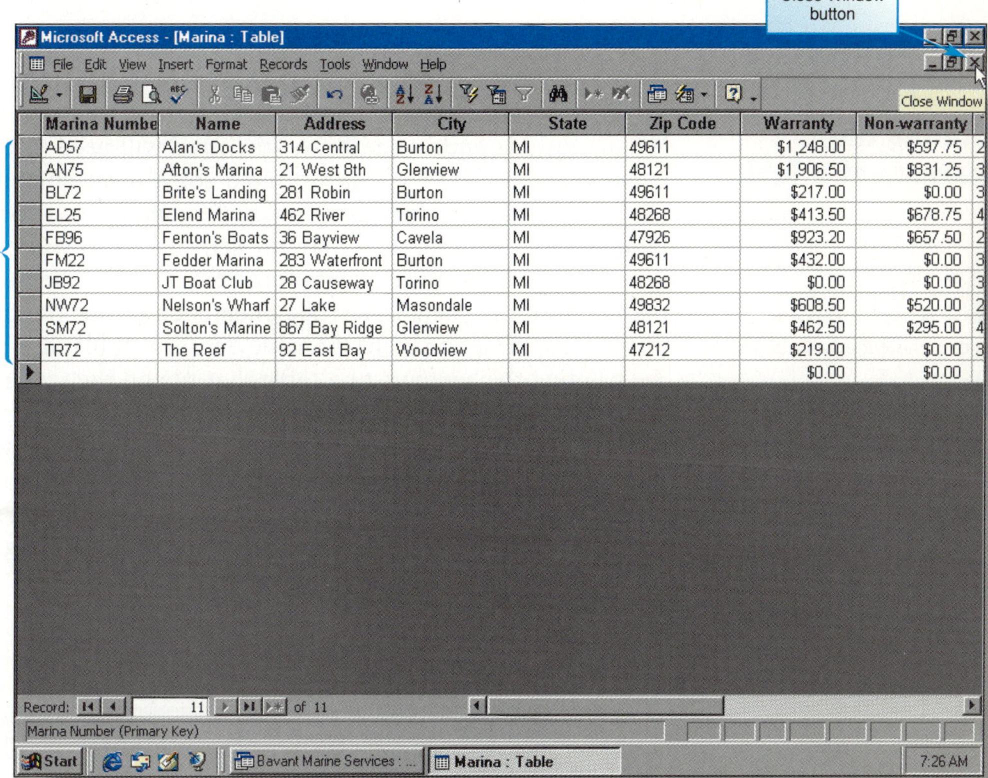

Marina Numbe	Name	Address	City	State	Zip Code	Warranty	Non-warranty	
AD57	Alan's Docks	314 Central	Burton	MI	49611	$1,248.00	$597.75	2
AN75	Afton's Marina	21 West 8th	Glenview	MI	48121	$1,906.50	$831.25	3
BL72	Brite's Landing	281 Robin	Burton	MI	49611	$217.00	$0.00	3
EL25	Elend Marina	462 River	Torino	MI	48268	$413.50	$678.75	4
FB96	Fenton's Boats	36 Bayview	Cavela	MI	47926	$923.20	$657.50	2
FM22	Fedder Marina	283 Waterfront	Burton	MI	49611	$432.00	$0.00	3
JB92	JT Boat Club	28 Causeway	Torino	MI	48268	$0.00	$0.00	3
NW72	Nelson's Wharf	27 Lake	Masondale	MI	49832	$608.50	$520.00	2
SM72	Solton's Marine	867 Bay Ridge	Glenview	MI	48121	$462.50	$295.00	4
TR72	The Reef	92 East Bay	Woodview	MI	47212	$219.00	$0.00	3
						$0.00	$0.00	

FIGURE 1-33

1. Click New Record button on Database window toolbar
2. On Insert menu click New Record

Correcting Errors in the Data

Check your entries carefully to ensure they are correct. If you make a mistake and discover it before you press the TAB key, correct it by pressing the BACKSPACE key until the incorrect characters are removed and then typing the correct characters.

If you discover an incorrect entry later, correct the error by clicking the incorrect entry and then making the appropriate correction. If the record you must correct is not on the screen, use the Navigation buttons (Next Record, Previous Record, and so on) to move to it. If the field you want to correct is not visible on the screen, use the horizontal scroll bar along the bottom of the screen to shift all the fields until the one you want displays. Then make the correction.

If you add an extra record accidentally, select the record by clicking the record selector that immediately precedes the record. Then, press the DELETE key. This will remove the record from the table. If you forget a record, add it using the same procedure as for all the other records. Access will place it in the correct location in the table automatically.

If you cannot determine how to correct the data, you are, in effect, stuck on the record. Access neither allows you to move to any other record until you have made the correction, nor allows you to close the table. If you encounter this situation, simply press the ESC key. Pressing the ESC key will remove from the screen the record you are trying to add. You then can move to any other record, close the table, or take any other action you desire.

Printing the Contents of a Table

You can change the paper size, paper source, or the printer that will be used to print the report. To change any of these, select the Page sheet in the Page Setup dialog box.

Previewing and Printing the Contents of a Table

When working with a database, you often will need to print a copy of the table contents. Figure 1-34 shows a printed copy of the contents of the Marina table. (Yours may look slightly different, depending on your printer.) Because the Marina table is wider substantially than the screen, it also will be wider than the normal printed page in portrait orientation. **Portrait orientation** means the printout is across the width of the page. **Landscape orientation** means the printout is across the length of the page. Thus, to print the wide database table, use landscape orientation. If you are printing the contents of a table that fits on the screen, you will not need landscape orientation. A convenient way to change to landscape orientation is to **preview** what the printed copy will look like by using Print Preview. This allows you to determine whether landscape orientation is necessary and, if it is, to change easily the orientation to landscape. In addition, you also can use Print Preview to determine whether any adjustments are necessary to the page margins.

Marina 9/7/2001

Marina Numbe	Name	Address	City	State	Zip Code	Warranty	Non-warranty	Tech Number
AD57	Alan's Docks	314 Central	Burton	MI	49611	$1,248.00	$597.75	23
AN75	Afton's Marina	21 West 8th	Glenview	MI	48121	$1,906.50	$831.25	36
BL72	Brite's Landing	281 Robin	Burton	MI	49611	$217.00	$0.00	36
EL25	Elend Marina	462 River	Torino	MI	48268	$413.50	$678.75	49
FB96	Fenton's Boats	36 Bayview	Cavela	MI	47926	$923.20	$657.50	23
FM22	Fedder Marina	283 Waterfront	Burton	MI	49611	$432.00	$0.00	36
JB92	JT Boat Club	28 Causeway	Torino	MI	48268	$0.00	$0.00	36
NW72	Nelson's Wharf	27 Lake	Masondale	MI	49832	$608.50	$520.00	23
SM72	Solton's Marina	867 Bay Ridge	Glenview	MI	48121	$462.50	$295.00	49
TR72	The Reef	92 East Bay	Woodview	MI	47212	$219.00	$0.00	36

Page 1

FIGURE 1-34

Perform the following steps to use Print Preview to preview and then print the Marina table.

To Preview and Print the Contents of a Table

1 Right-click Marina and then point to Print Preview on the shortcut menu.

The shortcut menu for the Marina table displays (Figure 1-35).

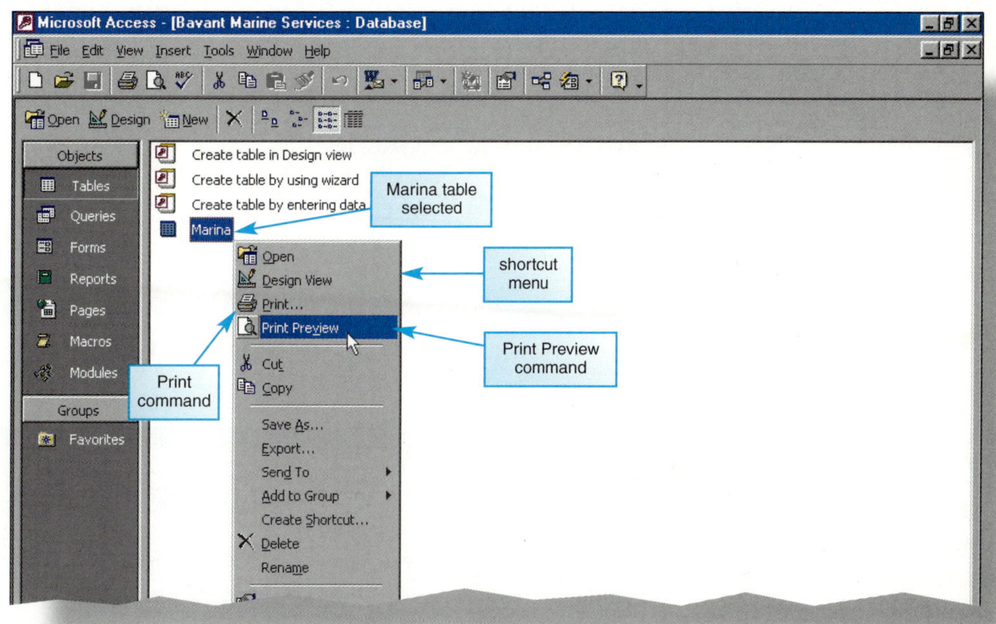

FIGURE 1-35

2 Click Print Preview on the shortcut menu. Point anywhere in the upper-right portion of the report.

The preview of the report displays (Figure 1-36).

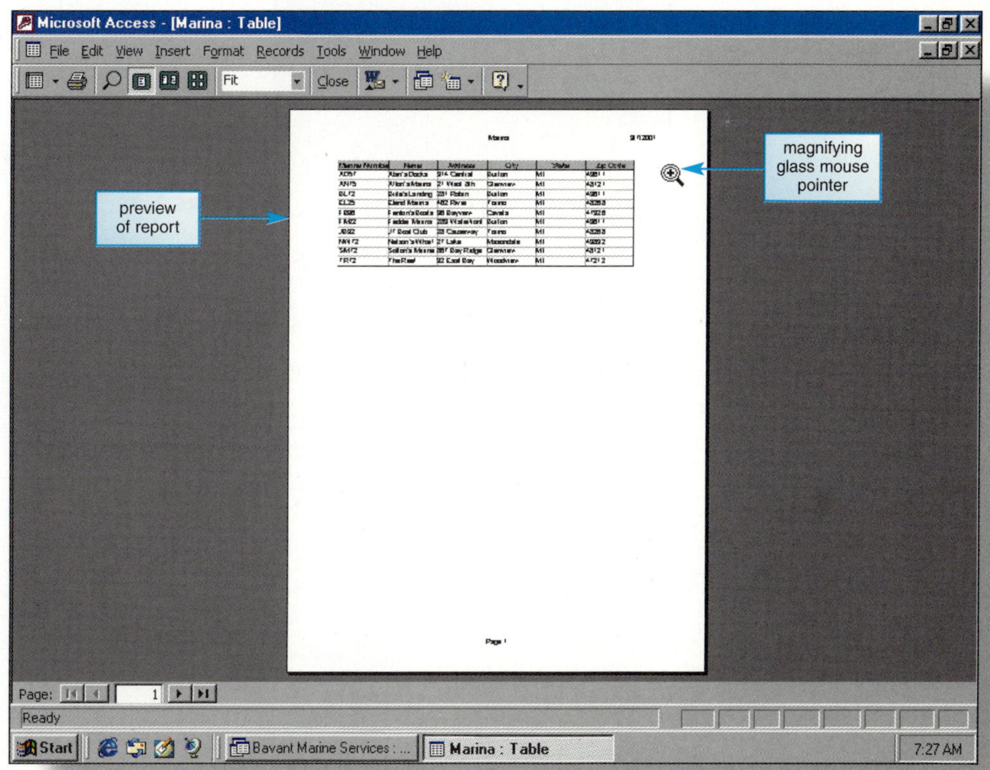

FIGURE 1-36

3 **Click the magnifying glass mouse pointer in the approximate position shown in Figure 1-36.**

The portion surrounding the mouse pointer is magnified (Figure 1-37). The last field that displays is the Zip Code field. The Warranty, Non-warranty, and Tech Number fields do not display. To display the additional fields, you will need to switch to landscape orientation.

Microsoft Access - [Marina : Table]

Marina 9/7/2001

Name	Address	City	State	Zip Code
Alan's Docks	314 Central	Burton	MI	49611
Afton's Marina	21 West 8th	Glenview	MI	48121
Brite's Landing	281 Robin	Burton	MI	49611
Elend Marina	462 River	Torino	MI	48268
Fenton's Boats	36 Bayview	Cavela	MI	47926
Fedder Marina	283 Waterfront	Burton	MI	49611
JT Boat Club	28 Causeway	Torino	MI	48268
Nelson's Wharf	27 Lake	Masondale	MI	49832
Solton's Marine	867 Bay Ridge	Glenview	MI	48121
The Reef	92 East Bay	Woodview	MI	47212

not all fields display

FIGURE 1-37

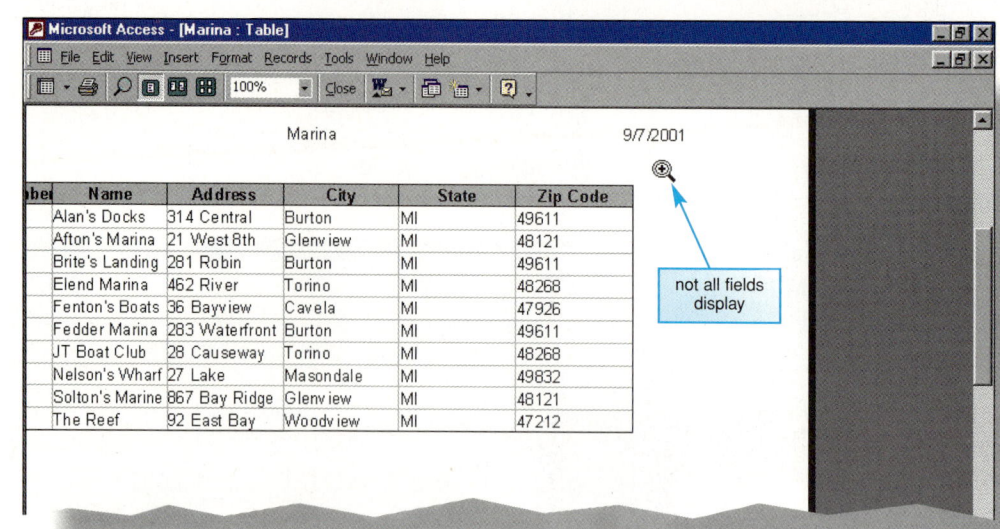

4 **Click File on the menu bar and then point to Page Setup. (Remember that you might have to wait a few seconds for the entire menu to display.)**

The File menu displays (Figure 1-38).

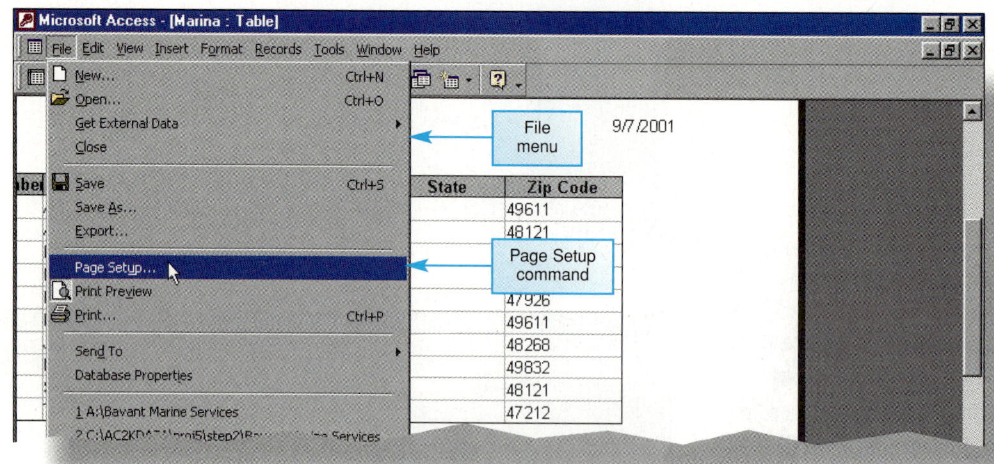

FIGURE 1-38

5 **Click Page Setup and then point to the Page tab.**

The Page Setup dialog box displays (Figure 1-39).

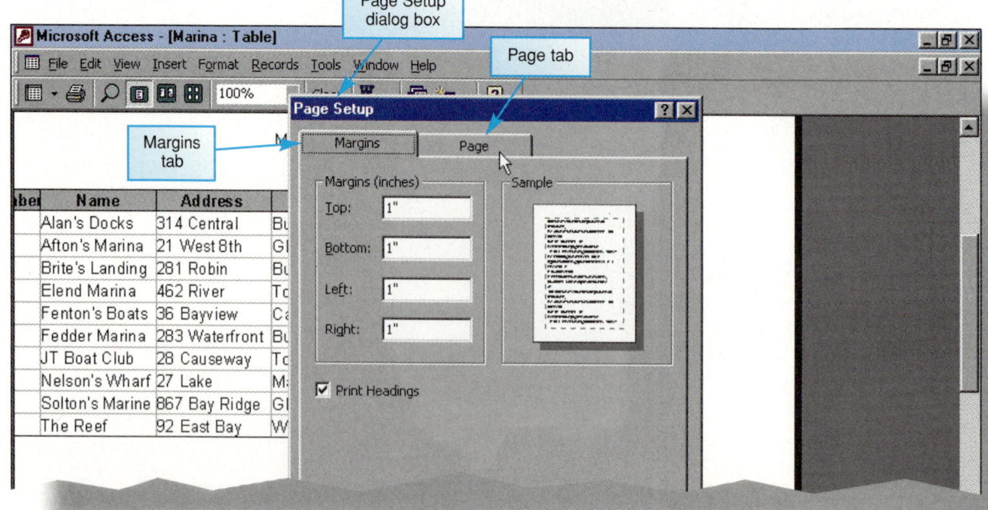

FIGURE 1-39

6 **Click the Page tab and then point to the Landscape option button.**

*The Page sheet displays (Figure 1-40). The Portrait option button currently is selected. (**Option button** refers to the round button that indicates choices in a dialog box. When the corresponding option is selected, the button contains within it a solid circle. Clicking an option button selects it, and deselects all others.)*

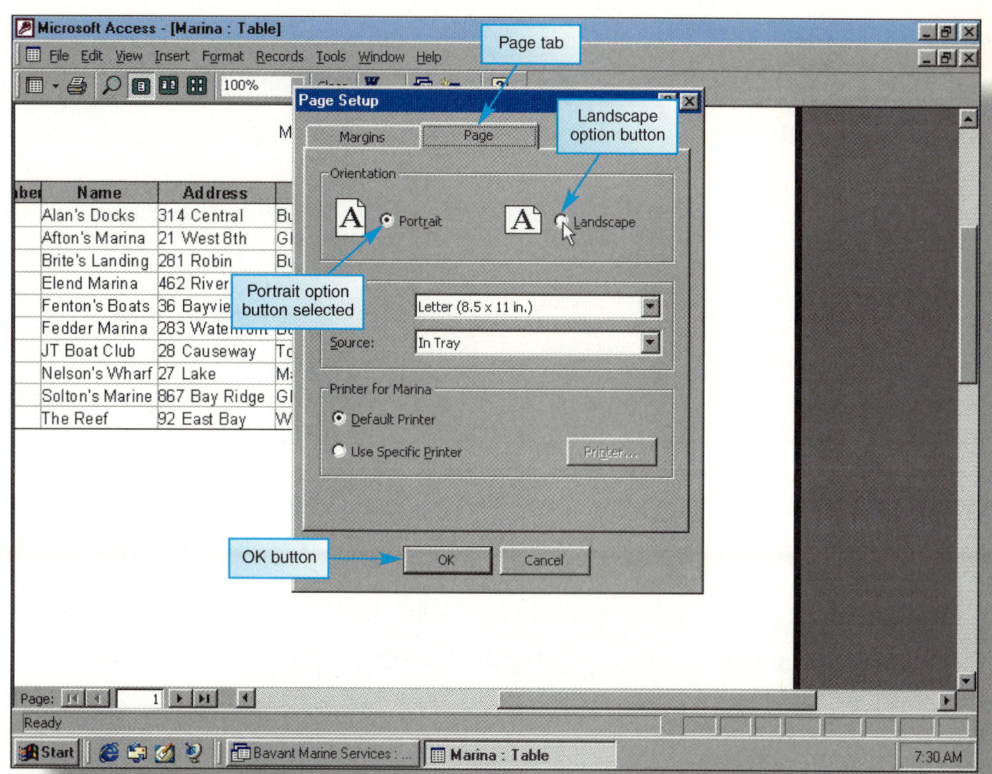

FIGURE 1-40

7 **Click Landscape and then click the OK button. Click the mouse pointer anywhere within the report to view the entire report.**

The orientation is changed to landscape as shown by the report that displays on the screen (Figure 1-41). The characters in the report are so small that it is difficult to determine whether all fields currently display. To zoom in on a portion of the report, click the desired portion of the report.

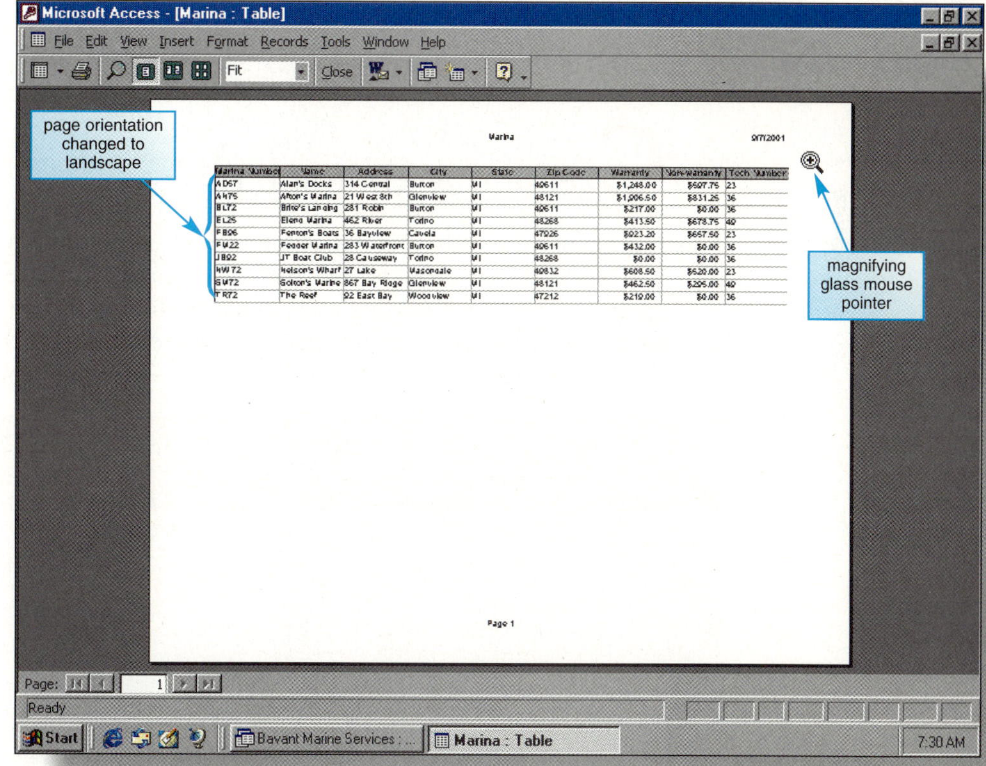

FIGURE 1-41

8 **Click the magnifying glass mouse pointer in the approximate position shown in Figure 1-41.**

The portion surrounding the mouse pointer is magnified (Figure 1-42). The last field that displays is the Tech Number field, so all fields currently display. If they did not, you could decrease the left and right margins; that is, the amount of space left by Access on the left and right edges of the report.

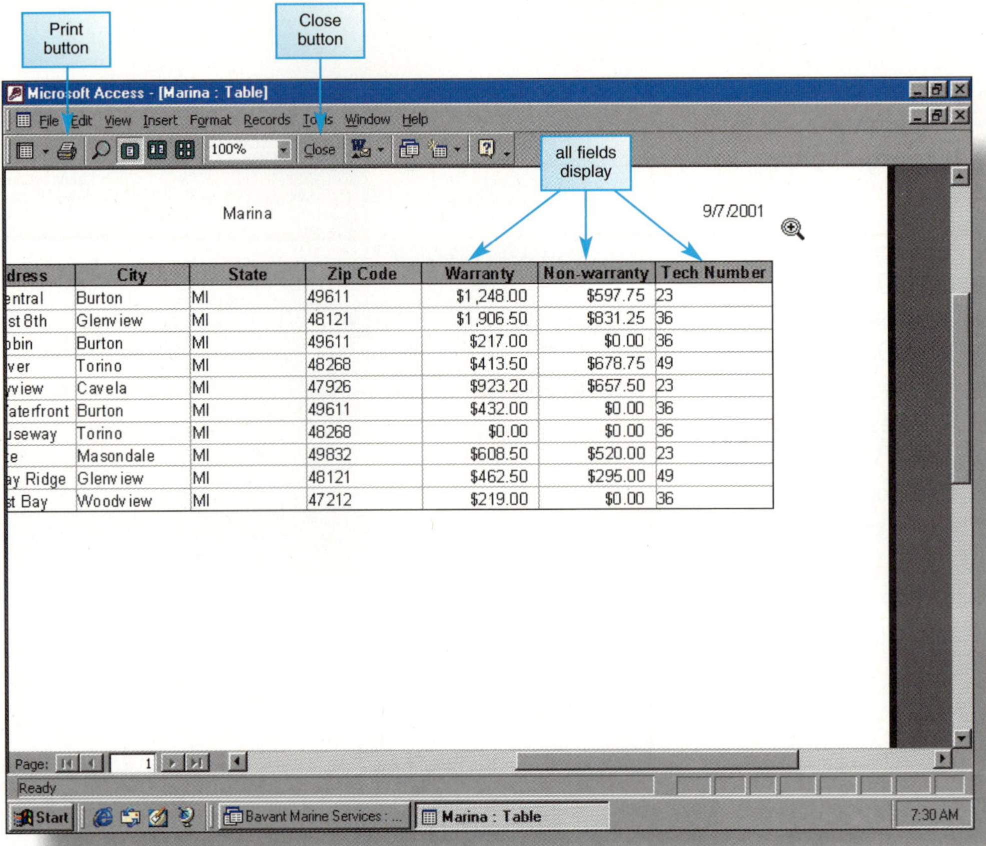

FIGURE 1-42

9 **Click the Print button to print the report. Click the Close button when the report has been printed to close the Print Preview window.**

The Print Preview window no longer displays.

Other Ways

1. On File menu click Print Preview to preview
2. On File menu click Print to print
3. Press CTRL+P to print

Creating Additional Tables

A database typically consists of more than one table. The sample database contains two, the Marina table and the Technician table. You need to repeat the process of creating a table and adding records for each table in the database. In the sample database, you need to create and add records to the Technician table. The structure and data for the table are given in Figure 1-43. The steps to create the table follow.

Structure of Technician table

FIELD NAME	DATA TYPE	FIELD SIZE	PRIMARY KEY?	DESCRIPTION
Tech Number	Text	2	Yes	Technician Number (Primary Key)
Last Name	Text	10		Last Name of Technician
First Name	Text	8		First Name of Technician
Address	Text	15		Street Address
City	Text	15		City
State	Text	2		State (Two-Character Abbreviation)
Zip Code	Text	5		Zip Code (Five-Character Version)
Hourly Rate	Currency			Hourly Rate of Technician
YTD Earnings	Currency			YTD Earnings of Technician

FIGURE 1-43

Data for Technician table

TECH NUMBER	LAST NAME	FIRST NAME	ADDRESS	CITY	STATE	ZIP CODE	HOURLY RATE	YTD EARNINGS
23	Anderson	Trista	283 Belton	Port Anton	MI	47989	$24.00	$17,862.00
36	Nichols	Ashton	978 Richmond	Hewitt	MI	47618	$21.00	$19,560.00
49	Gomez	Teresa	2855 Parry	Ashley	MI	47711	$22.00	$21,211.50

FIGURE 1-43 ***(continued)***

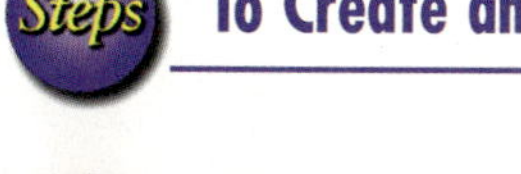

To Create an Additional Table

1 Make sure the Bavant Marine Services database is open. Right-click Create table in Design view and then click Open on the shortcut menu. Enter the data for the fields for the Technician table from Figure 1-43. Be sure to click the Primary Key button when you enter the Tech Number field. Point to the Save button on the Database window toolbar after you have entered all the fields.

The entries display (Figure 1-44).

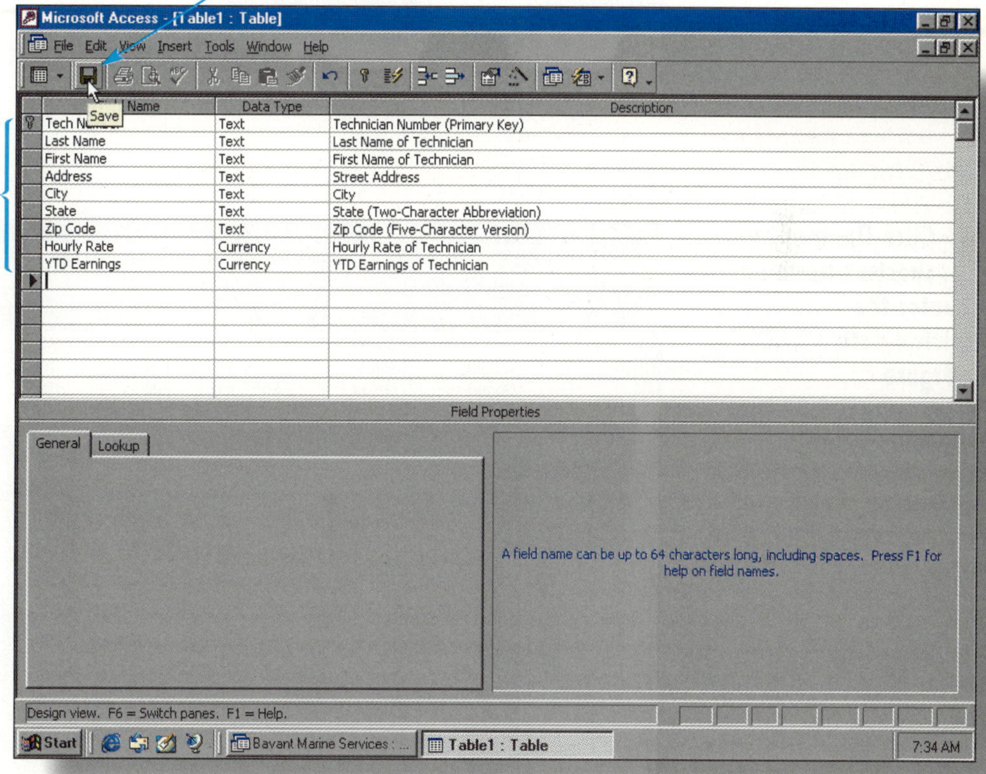

FIGURE 1-44

2 Click the Save button, type `Technician` **as the name of the table, and then click the OK button. Click the Close Window button.**

The table is saved in the Bavant Marine Services database. The Technician : Table window no longer displays.

Adding Records to the Additional Table

Now that you have created the Technician table, use the steps on the next page to add records to it.

To Add Records to an Additional Table

1 Right-click Technician and point to Open on the shortcut menu.

The shortcut menu for the Technician table displays (Figure 1-45).

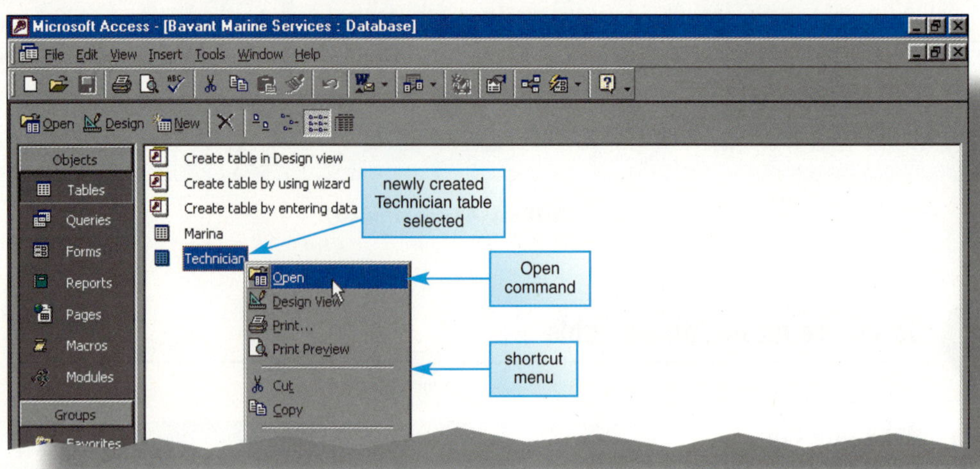

FIGURE 1-45

2 Click Open on the shortcut menu and then enter the Technician data from Figure 1-43 on page A 1.34 into the Technician table.

The datasheet displays with three records entered (Figure 1-46).

3 Click the Close Window button for the Technician : Table window.

Access closes the table and removes the datasheet from the screen.

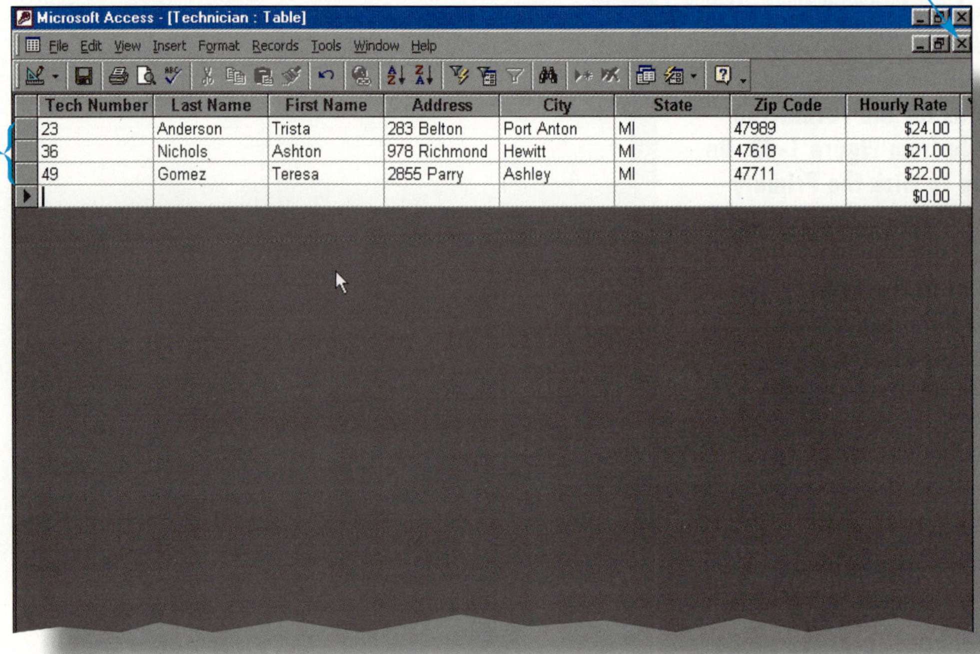

FIGURE 1-46

Using a Form to View Data

In creating tables, you have used Datasheet view; that is, the data on the screen displayed as a table. You also can use **Form view**, in which you see a single record at a time.

The advantage with Datasheet view is you can see multiple records at once. It has the disadvantage that, unless you have few fields in the table, you cannot see all the fields at the same time. With Form view, you see only a single record, but you can see all the fields in the record. The view you choose is a matter of personal preference.

Forms

Attractive and functional forms can improve greatly the data entry process. Forms are not restricted to data from a single table, but can incorporate data from multiple tables as well as special types of data like pictures and sounds. A good DBMS like Access 2000 furnishes an easy way to create sophisticated forms.

Creating a Form

To use Form view, you first must create a form. The simplest way to create a form is to use the New Object: AutoForm button on the Database window toolbar. To do so, first select the table for which the form is to be created in the Database window and then click the New Object: AutoForm button. A list of available objects displays. Click AutoForm in the list to select it.

Perform the following steps using the New Object: AutoForm button to create a form for the Marina table.

To Use the New Object: AutoForm Button to Create a Form

1 Make sure the Bavant Marine Services database is open, the Database window displays, and the Marina table is selected. Point to the New Object: AutoForm button arrow on the Database window toolbar (Figure 1-47).

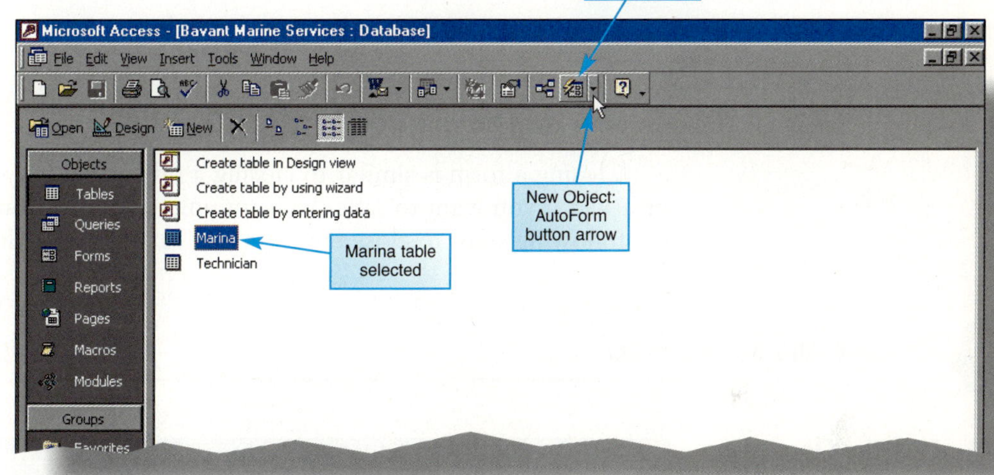

FIGURE 1-47

2 Click the New Object: AutoForm button arrow and then point to AutoForm.

A list of objects that can be created displays (Figure 1-48).

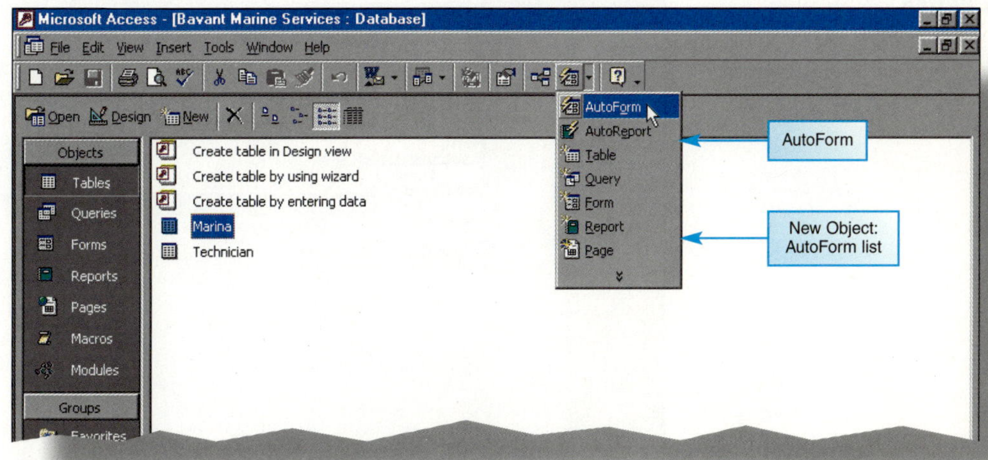

FIGURE 1-48

3 Click AutoForm in the New Object: AutoForm list.

The form displays (Figure 1-49). An additional toolbar, the Formatting toolbar, also displays. (When you close the form, this toolbar no longer displays.)

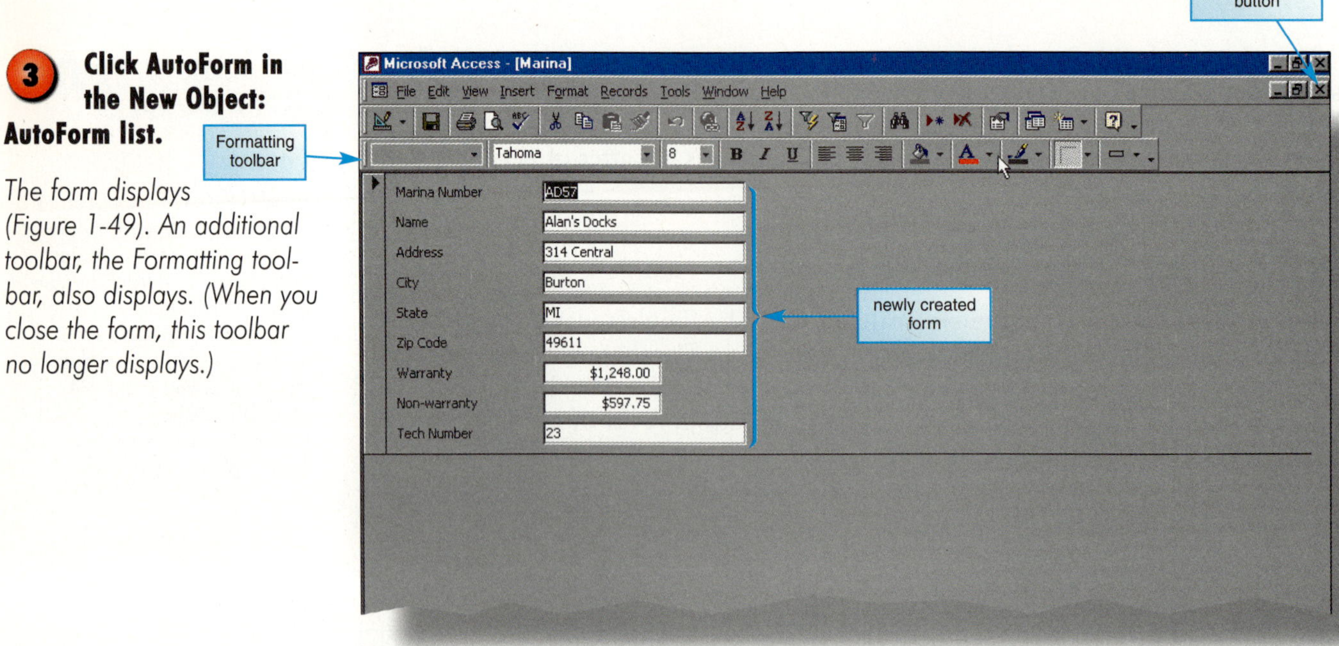

FIGURE 1-49

Closing and Saving the Form

Closing a form is similar to closing a table. The only difference is that you will be asked if you want to save the form unless you previously have saved it. Perform the following steps to close the form and save it as Marina.

To Close and Save a Form

1 Click the Close Window button for the Marina window (see Figure 1-49). Point to the Yes button.

The Microsoft Access dialog box displays (Figure 1-50).

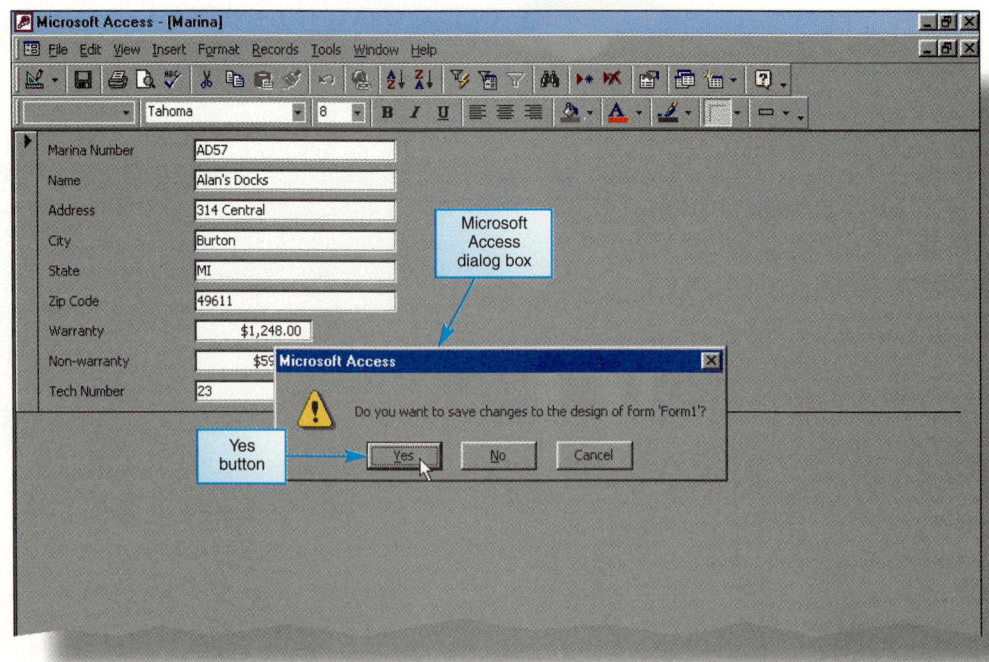

FIGURE 1-50

2 Click the Yes button and then point to the OK button.

The Save As dialog box displays (Figure 1-51). The name of the table (Marina) becomes the name of the form automatically. This name can be replaced with any name.

3 Click the OK button in the Save As dialog box.

The form is saved as part of the database and is removed from the screen. The Bavant Marine Services : Database window again displays.

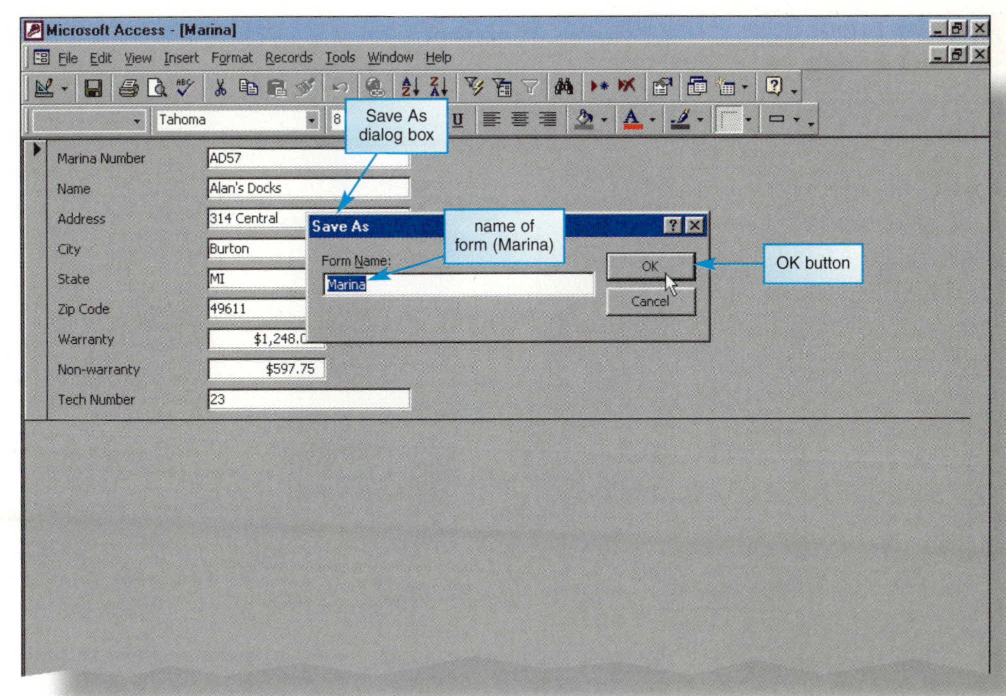

FIGURE 1-51

1. On File menu click Close

Opening the Saved Form

Once you have saved a form, you can use it at any time in the future by opening it. Opening a form is similar to opening a table; that is, make sure the form to be opened is selected, right-click, and then click Open on the shortcut menu. Before opening the form, however, the Forms object, rather than the Tables object, must be selected.

Perform the following steps to open the Marina form.

To Open a Form

1 With the Bavant Marine Services database open and the Database window on the screen, point to Forms on the Objects bar (Figure 1-52).

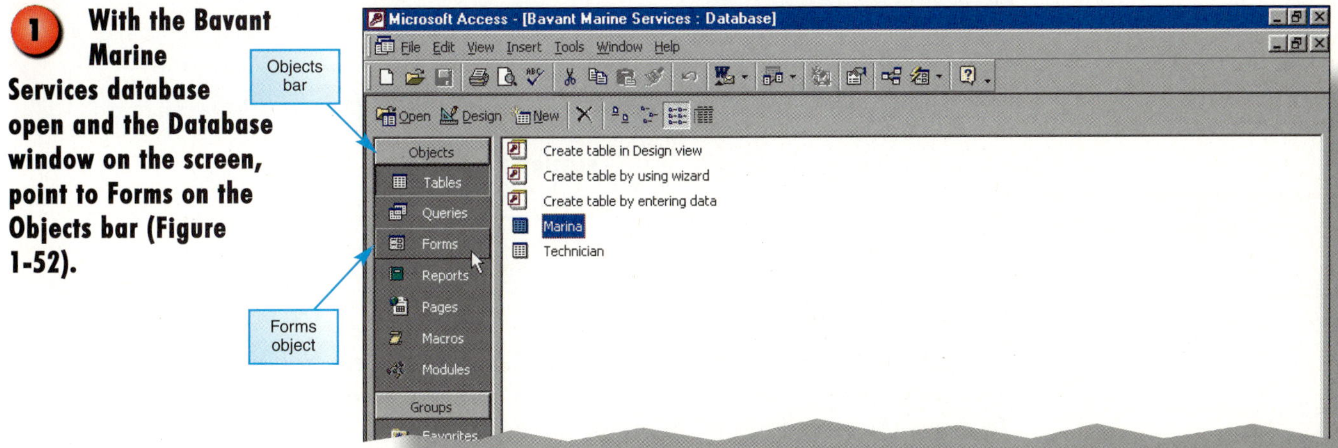

FIGURE 1-52

2 Click Forms, right-click Marina, and then point to Open on the shortcut menu.

The Forms object is selected and the list of available forms displays (Figure 1-53). Currently, the Marina form is the only form. The shortcut menu for the Marina form displays.

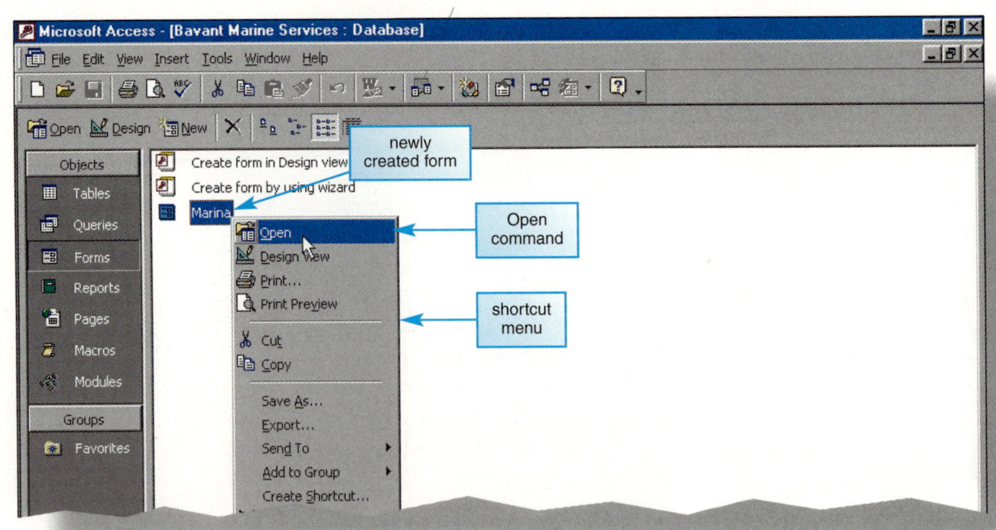

FIGURE 1-53

3 Click Open on the shortcut menu.

The Marina form displays (Figure 1-54).

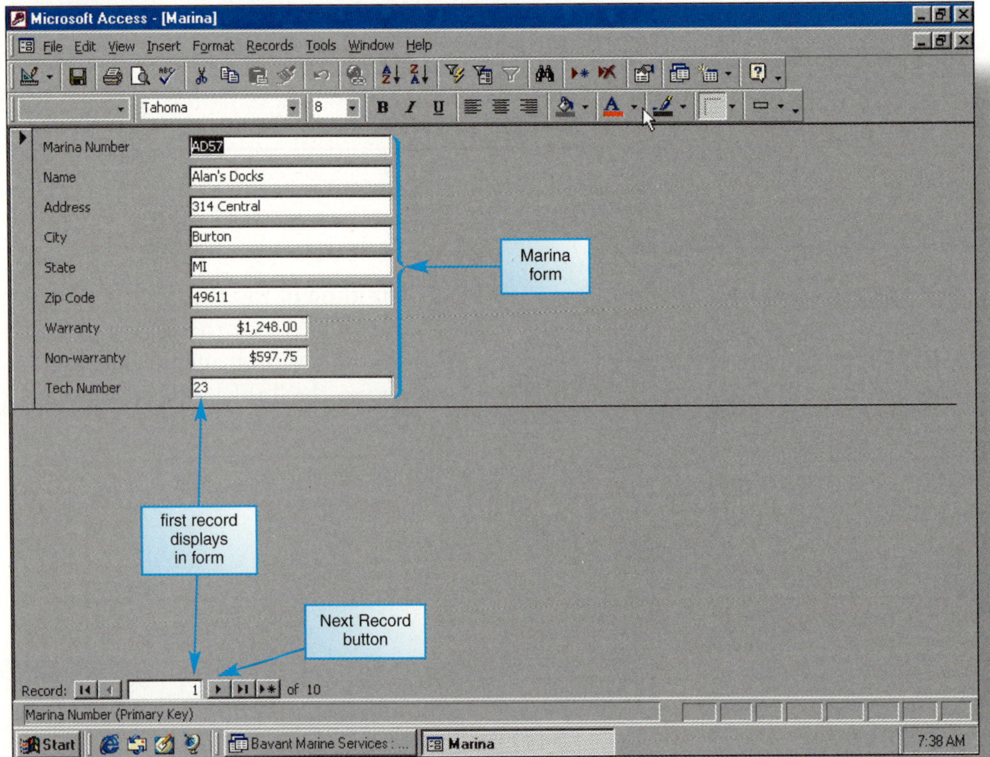

FIGURE 1-54

Other Ways

1. Click Forms object, double-click desired form
2. Click desired form, click Open button
3. Click desired from, press ALT+O

Using the Form

You can use the form just as you used Datasheet view. You use the Navigation buttons to move between records. You can add new records or change existing ones. To delete the record displayed on the screen, after selecting the record by clicking its record selector, press the DELETE key. Thus, you can perform database operations using either Form view or Datasheet view.

Because you can see only one record at a time in Form view, to see a different record, such as the fifth record, use the Navigation buttons to move to it. To move from record to record in Form view, perform the following step.

Steps To Use a Form

1 Click the Next Record button four times.

The fifth record displays on the form (Figure 1-55).

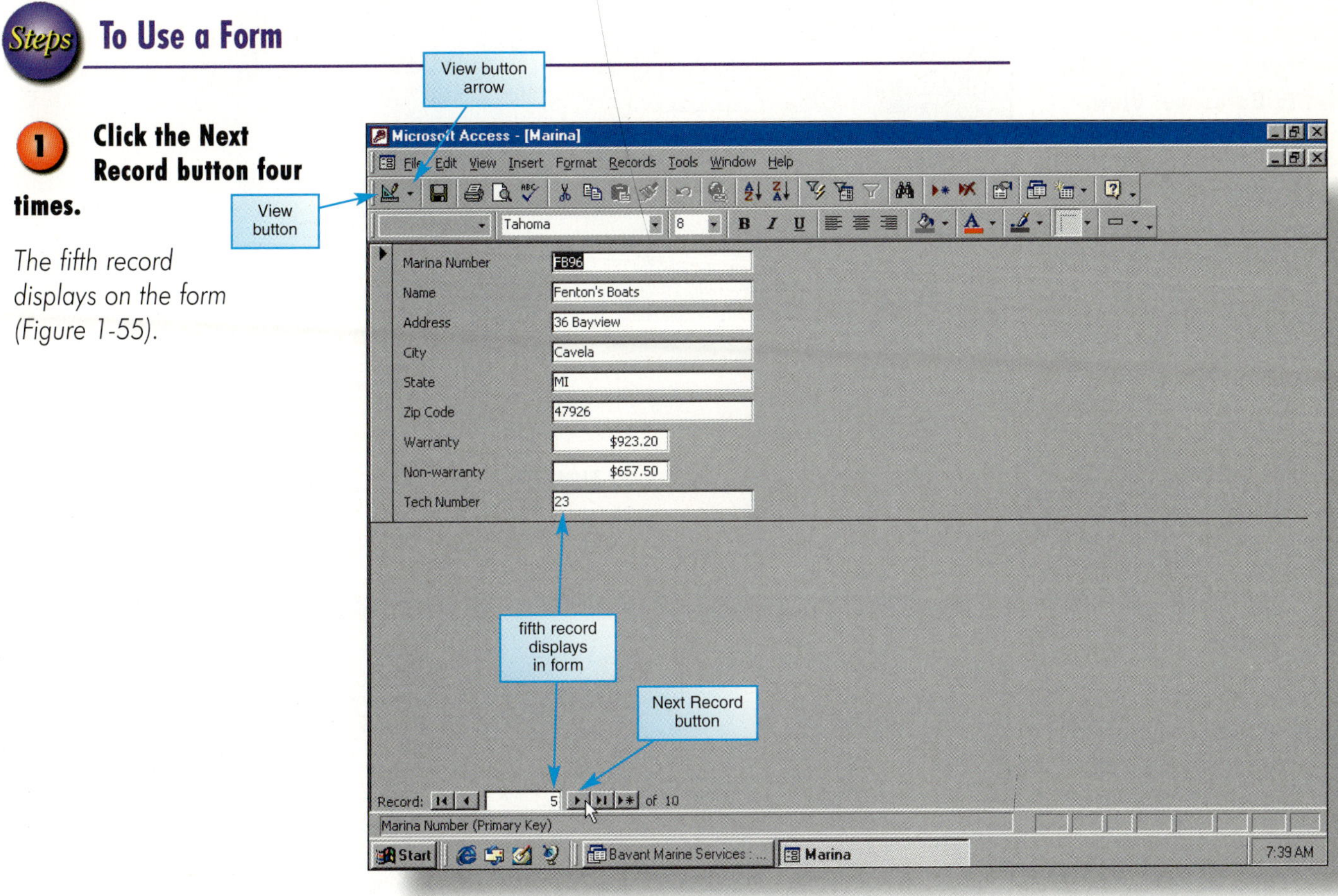

FIGURE 1-55

Switching Between Form View and Datasheet View

In some cases, once you have seen a record in Form view, you will want to move to Datasheet view to again see a collection of records. To do so, click the View button arrow on the Database window toolbar and then click Datasheet View in the list that displays.

Perform the steps on the next page to switch from Form view to Datasheet view.

To Switch from Form View to Datasheet View

Click the View button arrow on the Database window toolbar (see Figure 1-55) and then point to Datasheet View.

The list of available views displays (Figure 1-56).

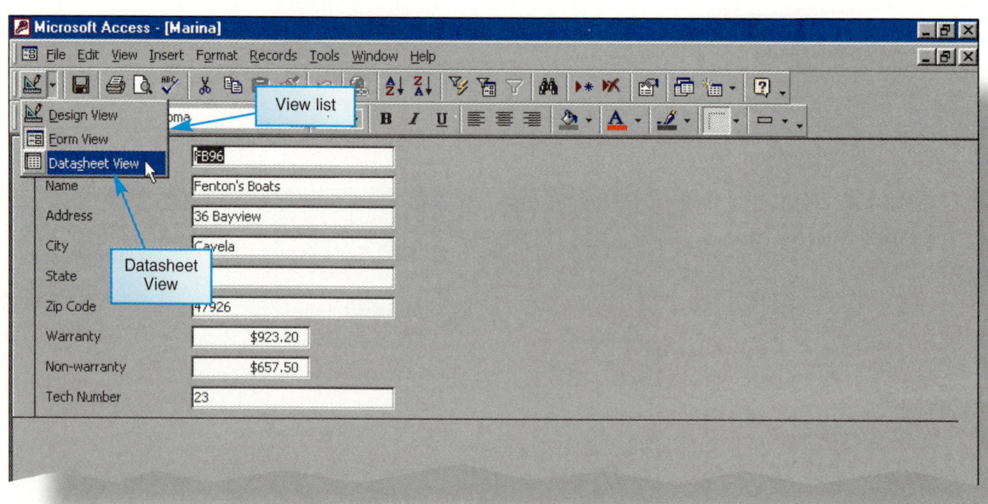

FIGURE 1-56

Click Datasheet View.

The table displays in Datasheet view (Figure 1-57). The record selector is positioned on the fifth record.

Click the Close Window button.

The Marina window closes and the datasheet no longer displays.

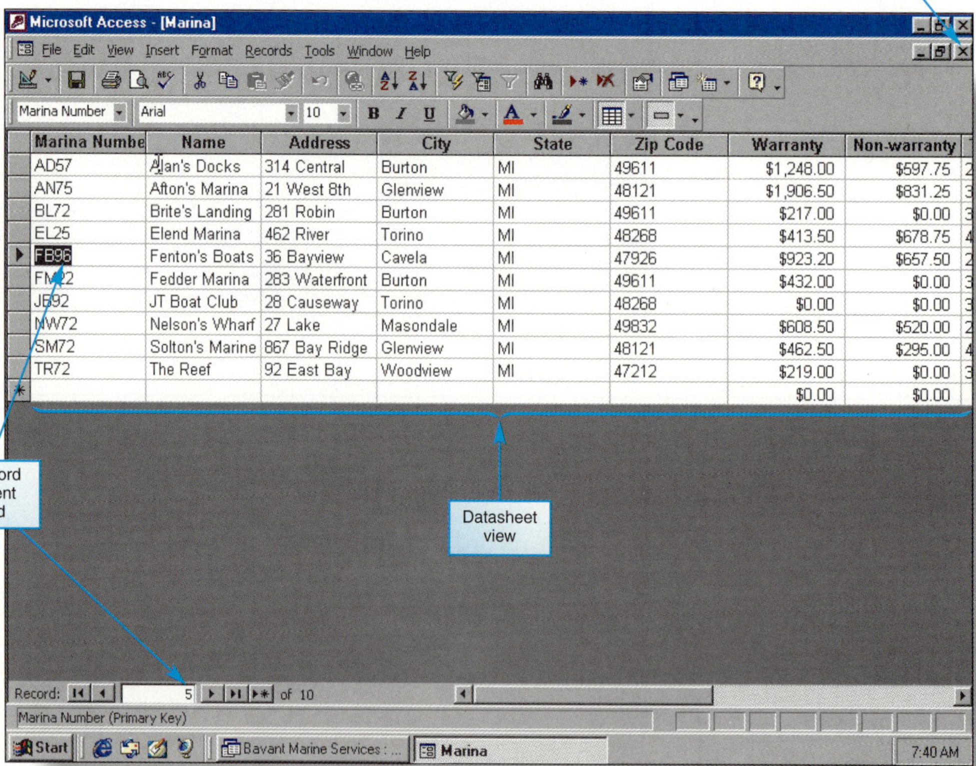

FIGURE 1-57

Other Ways

1. On View menu click Datasheet View

Creating a Report

Earlier in this project, you printed a table using the Print button. The report you produced was shown in Figure 1-34 on page A 1.30. While this type of report presented the data in an organized manner, it was not very flexible. It included all the fields, but in precisely the same order in which they occurred in the table. A way to change the title was not presented; it remained Marina.

In this section, you will create the report shown in Figure 1-58. This report features significant differences from the one in Figure 1-34 on page A 1.30. The portion at the top of the report in Figure 1-58, called a **page header**, contains a custom title. The contents of this page header display at the top of each page. The **detail lines**, which are the lines that are printed for each record, contain only those fields you specify and in the order you specify.

Perform the following steps to create the report in Figure 1-58.

More About 2000

Reports

Custom reports represent one of the more important ways of presenting the data in a database. Reports can incorporate data from multiple tables and can be formatted in a wide variety of ways. The ability to create sophisticated custom reports is one of the major benefits of a DBMS like Access 2000.

Billing Summary Report

Marina Number	*Name*	*Warranty*	*Non-warranty*
AD57	Alan's Docks	$1,248.00	$597.75
AN75	Afton's Marina	$1,906.50	$831.25
BL72	Brite's Landing	$217.00	$0.00
EL25	Elend Marina	$413.50	$678.75
FB96	Fenton's Boats	$923.20	$657.50
FM22	Fedder Marina	$432.00	$0.00
JB92	JT Boat Club	$0.00	$0.00
NW72	Nelson's Wharf	$608.50	$520.00
SM72	Solton's Marina	$462.50	$295.00
TR72	The Reef	$219.00	$0.00

FIGURE 1-58

Steps To Create a Report

1. Click Tables on the Objects bar. Make sure the Marina table is selected. Click the New Object: AutoForm button arrow on the Database window toolbar.

The list of available objects displays (Figure 1-59).

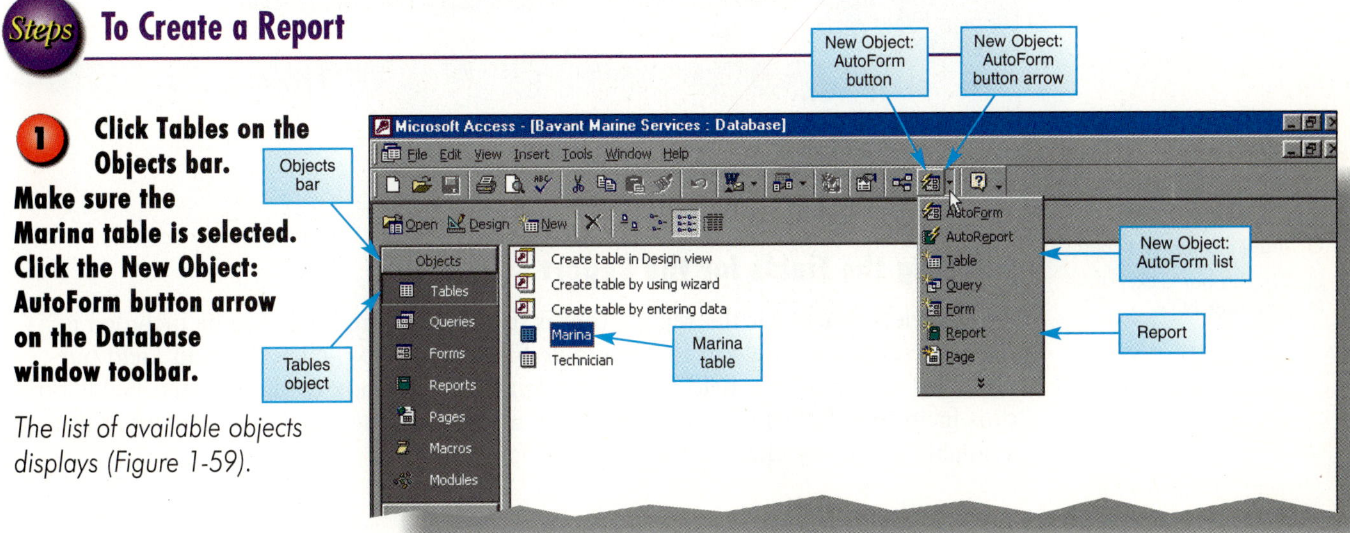

FIGURE 1-59

2 **Click Report and then point to Report Wizard.**

The New Report dialog box displays (Figure 1-60).

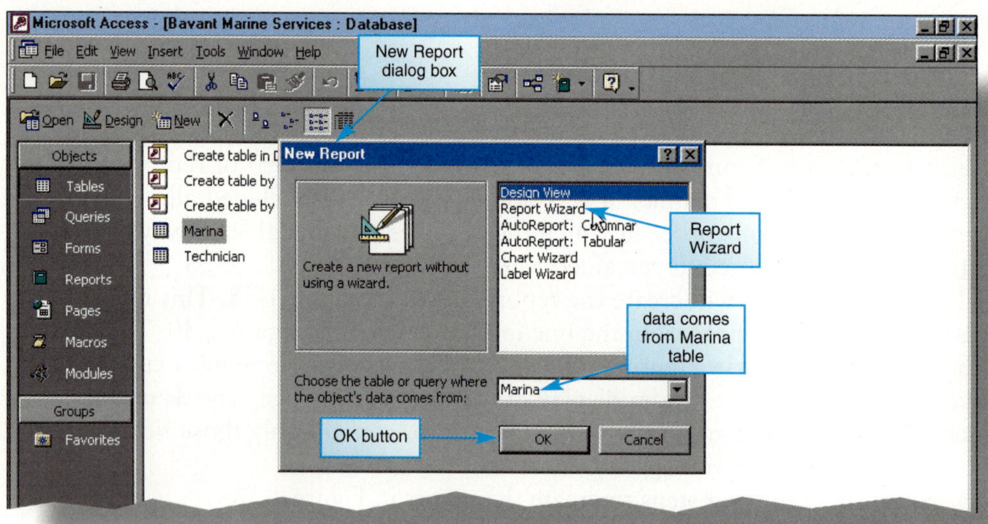

FIGURE 1-60

3 **Click Report Wizard and then click the OK button. Point to the Add Field button.**

The Report Wizard dialog box displays (Figure 1-61).

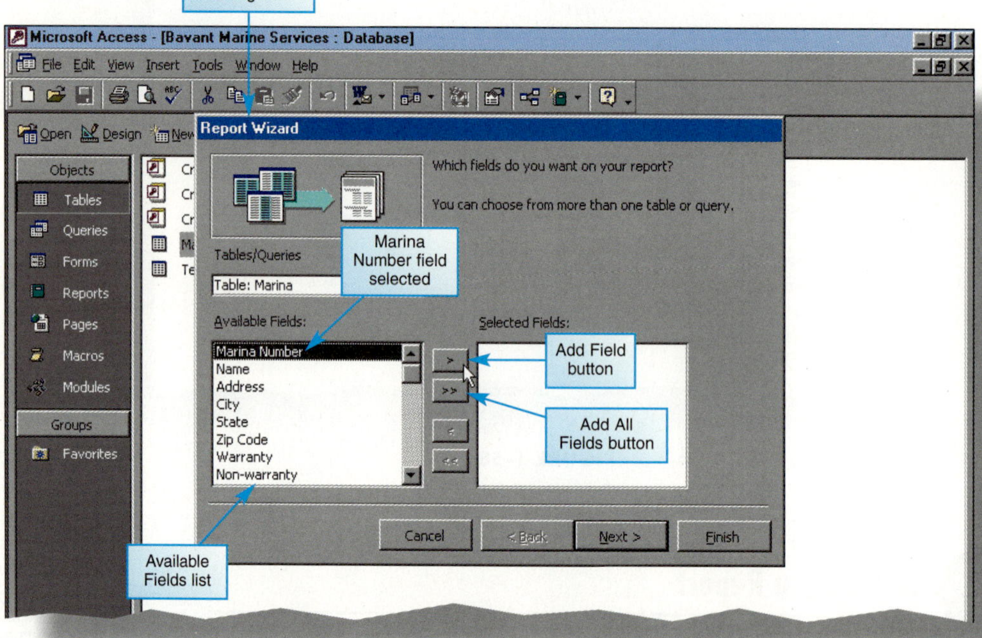

FIGURE 1-61

1. On Insert menu click Report
2. On Objects bar click Reports, click New

Selecting the Fields for the Report

To select a field for the report; that is, to indicate the field is to be included in the report, click the field in the Available Fields list. Next, click the Add Field button. This will move the field from the Available Fields box to the Selected Fields box, thus including the field in the report. If you wanted to select all fields, a shortcut is available simply by clicking the Add All Fields button.

To select the Marina Number, Name, Warranty, and Non-warranty fields for the report, perform the following steps.

To Select the Fields for a Report

1 Click the Add Field button to add the Marina Number field. Add the Name field by clicking it and then clicking the Add Field button. Add the Warranty and Non-warranty fields just as you added the Marina Number and Name fields.

The fields for the report display in the Selected Fields box (Figure 1-62).

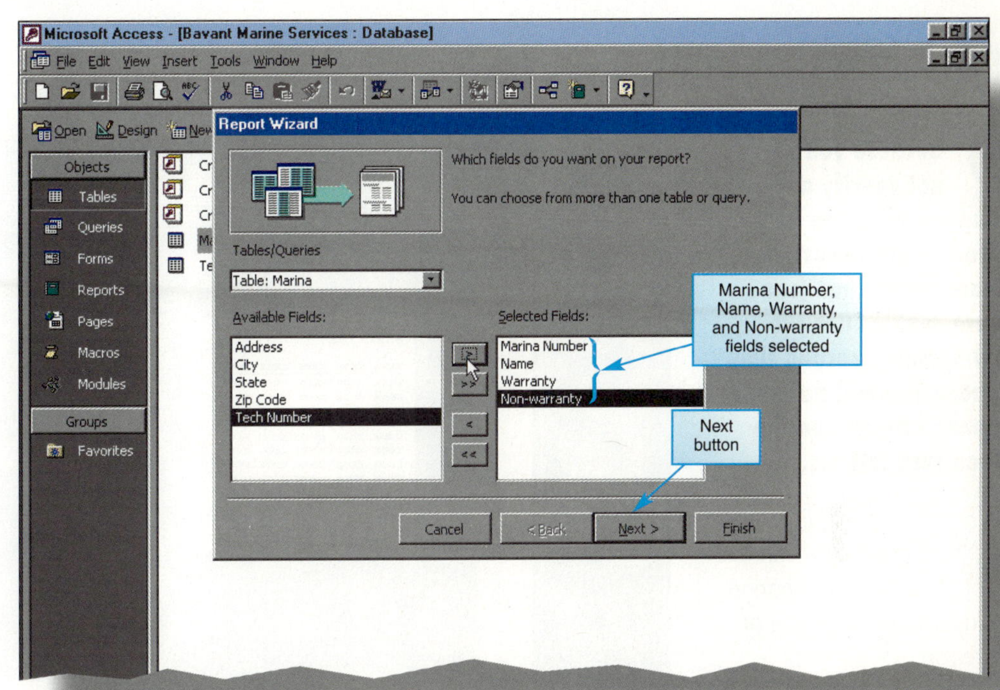

FIGURE 1-62

2 Click the Next button.

The Report Wizard dialog box displays (Figure 1-63).

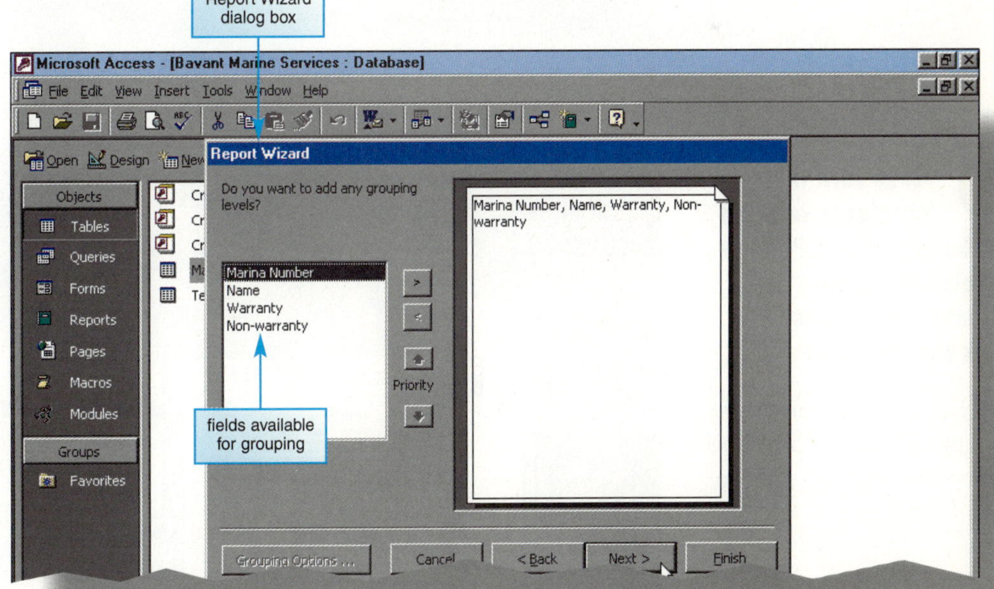

FIGURE 1-63

1. Double-click field

Completing the Report

Several additional steps are involved in completing the report. With the exception of changing the title, the Access selections are acceptable, so you simply will click the Next button.

Perform the following steps to complete the report.

To Complete a Report

1 Because you will not specify any grouping, click the Next button in the Report Wizard dialog box (see Figure 1-63). Click the Next button a second time because you will not need to make changes on the screen that follows.

The Report Wizard dialog box displays (Figure 1-64). In this dialog box, you can change the layout or orientation of the report.

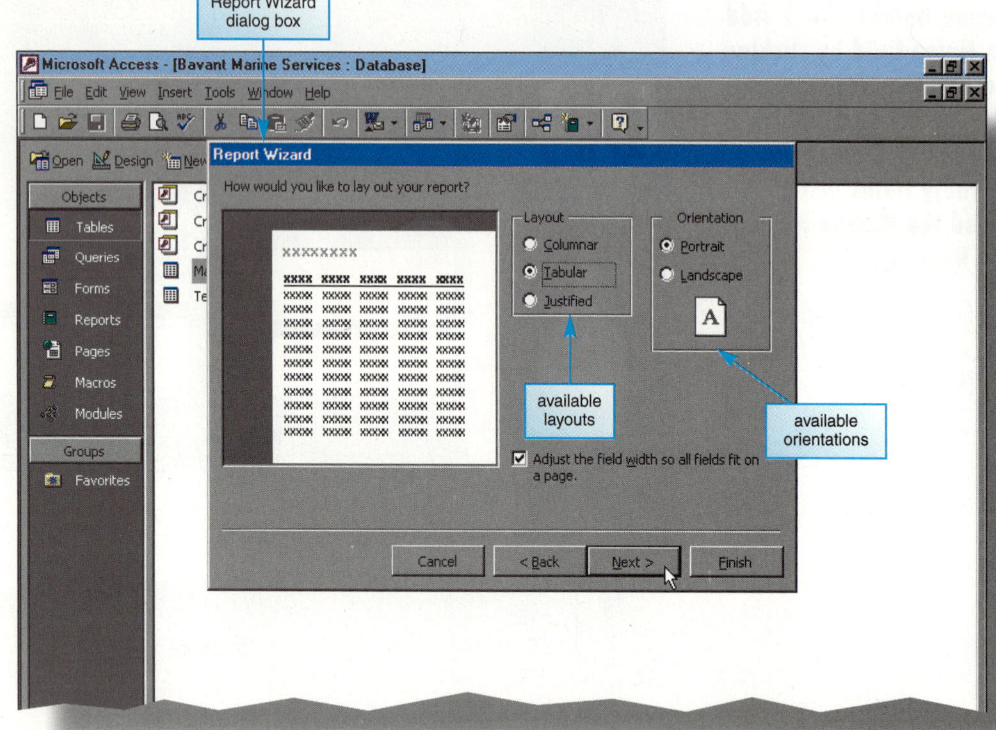

FIGURE 1-64

2 Make sure that Tabular is selected as the layout and Portrait is selected as the orientation and then click the Next button.

The Report Wizard dialog box displays (Figure 1-65). In this dialog box, you can select a style for the report.

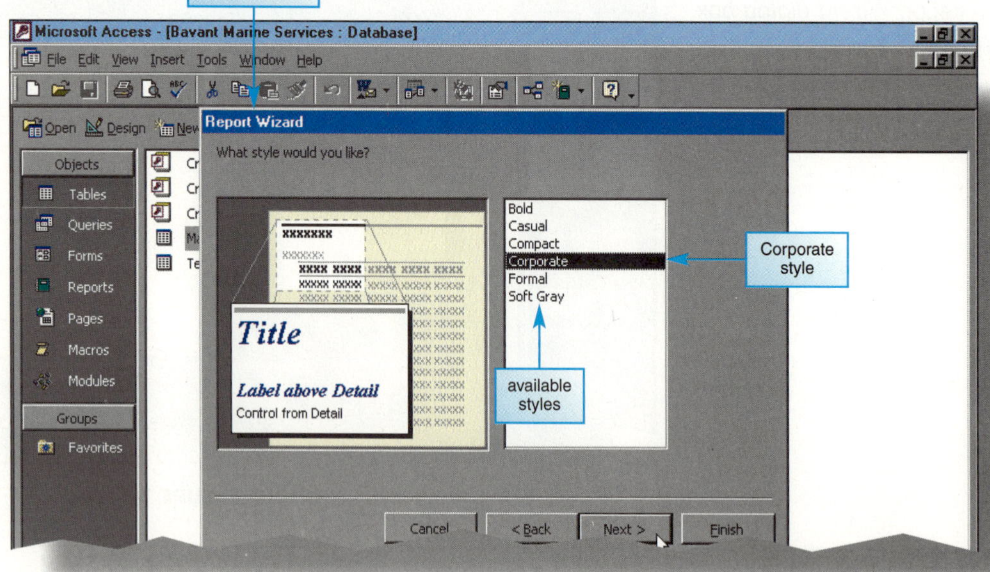

FIGURE 1-65

3 Be sure that the Corporate style is selected and then click the Next button.

The Report Wizard dialog box displays (Figure 1-66). In this dialog box, you can specify a title for the report.

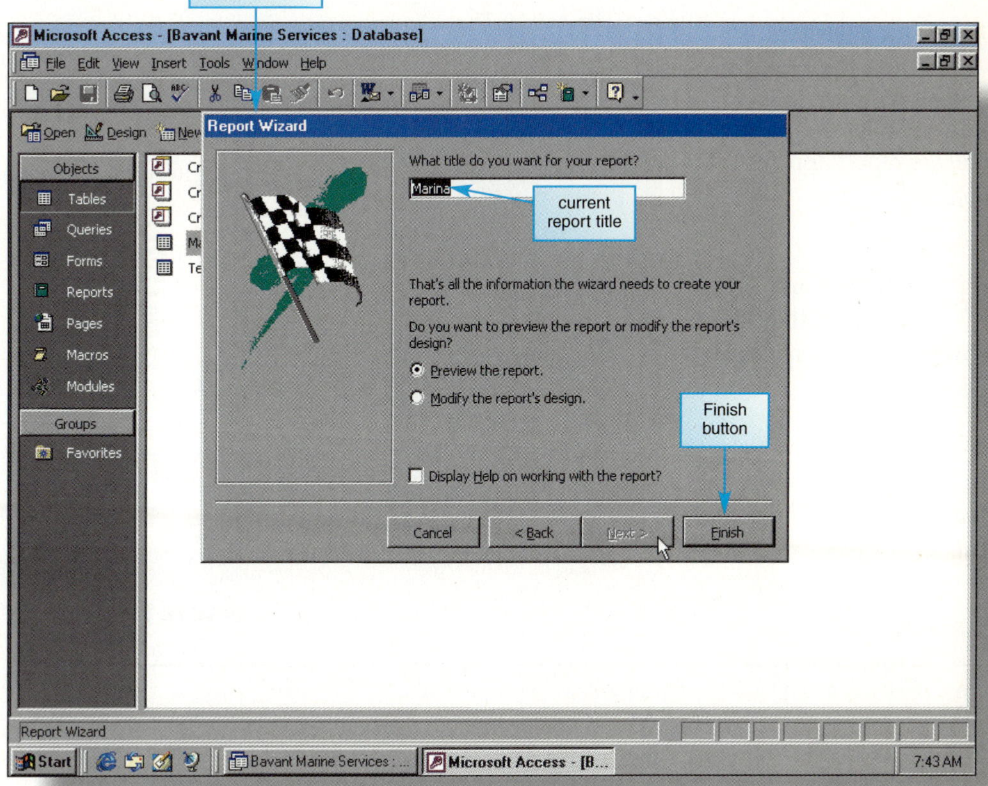

FIGURE 1-66

4 Type `Billing Summary Report` **as the new title and then click the Finish button.**

A preview of the report displays (Figure 1-67). Yours may look slightly different, depending on your printer.

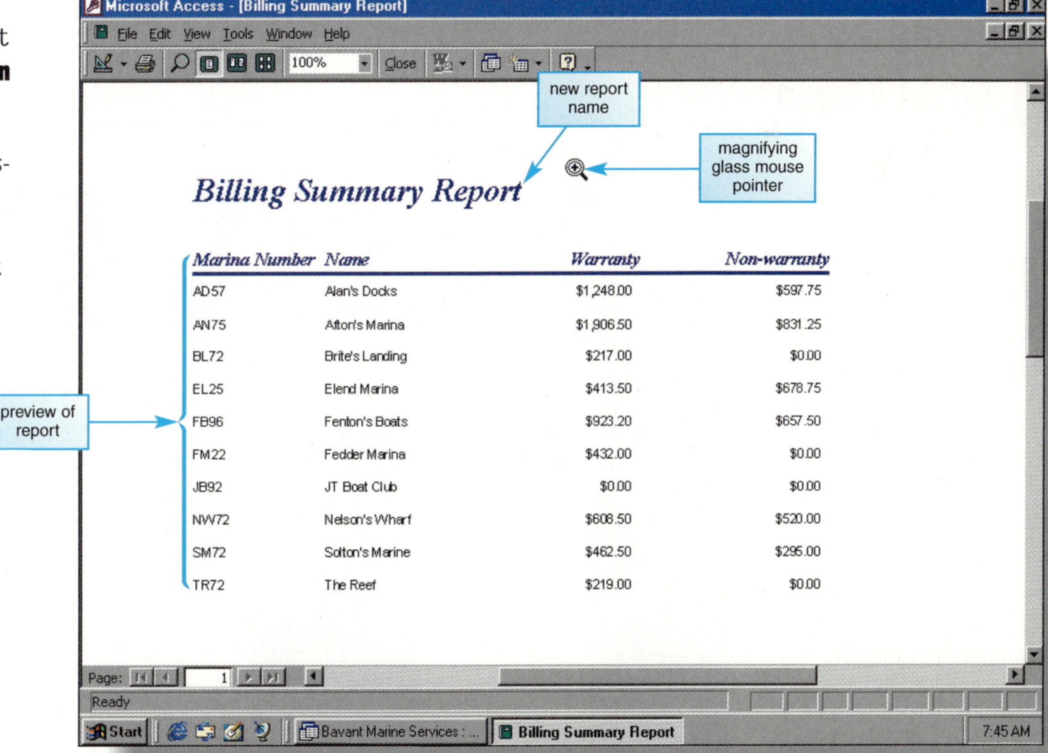

Marina Number	Name	Warranty	Non-warranty
AD57	Alan's Docks	$1,248.00	$597.75
AN75	Afton's Marina	$1,906.50	$831.25
BL72	Brite's Landing	$217.00	$0.00
EL25	Elend Marina	$413.50	$678.75
FB96	Fenton's Boats	$923.20	$657.50
FM22	Fedder Marina	$432.00	$0.00
JB92	JT Boat Club	$0.00	$0.00
NW72	Nelson's Wharf	$608.50	$520.00
SM72	Solton's Marine	$462.50	$295.00
TR72	The Reef	$219.00	$0.00

FIGURE 1-67

5 **Click anywhere within the report to see the entire report.**

The entire report displays (Figure 1-68).

6 **Click the Close Window button in the Billing Summary Report window.**

The report no longer displays. It has been saved automatically using the name Billing Summary Report.

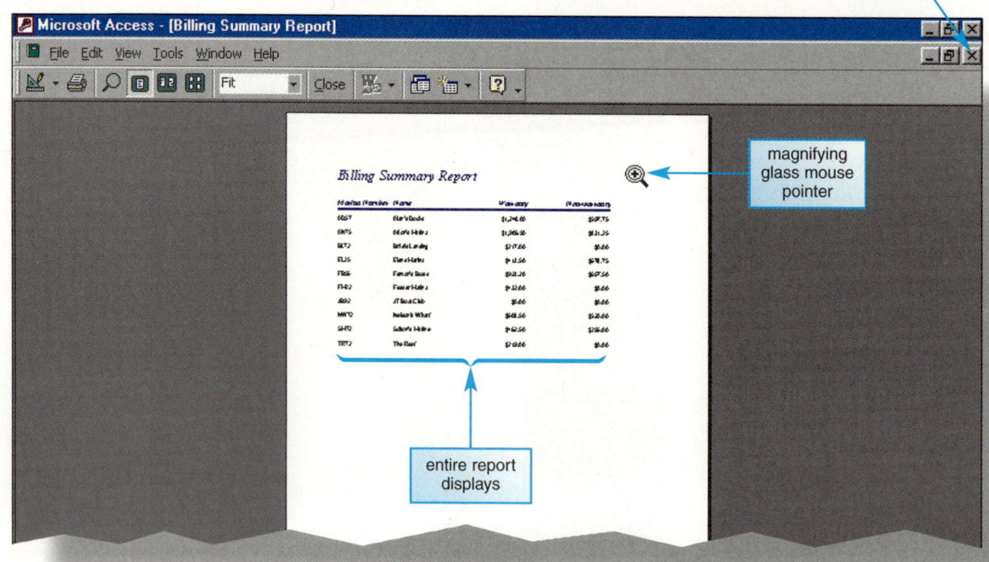

FIGURE 1-68

Printing the Report

To print a report from the Database window, first right-click the report. Then click Print on the shortcut menu to print the report or click Print Preview on the shortcut menu to see a preview of the report on the screen.

Perform the following steps to print the report.

Steps To Print a Report

1 **If necessary, click Reports on the Objects bar in the Database window, right-click Billing Summary Report, and then point to Print on the shortcut menu.**

The shortcut menu for the Billing Summary Report displays (Figure 1-69).

2 **Click Print on the shortcut menu.**

The report prints. It should look similar to the one shown in Figure 1-58 on page A 1.43.

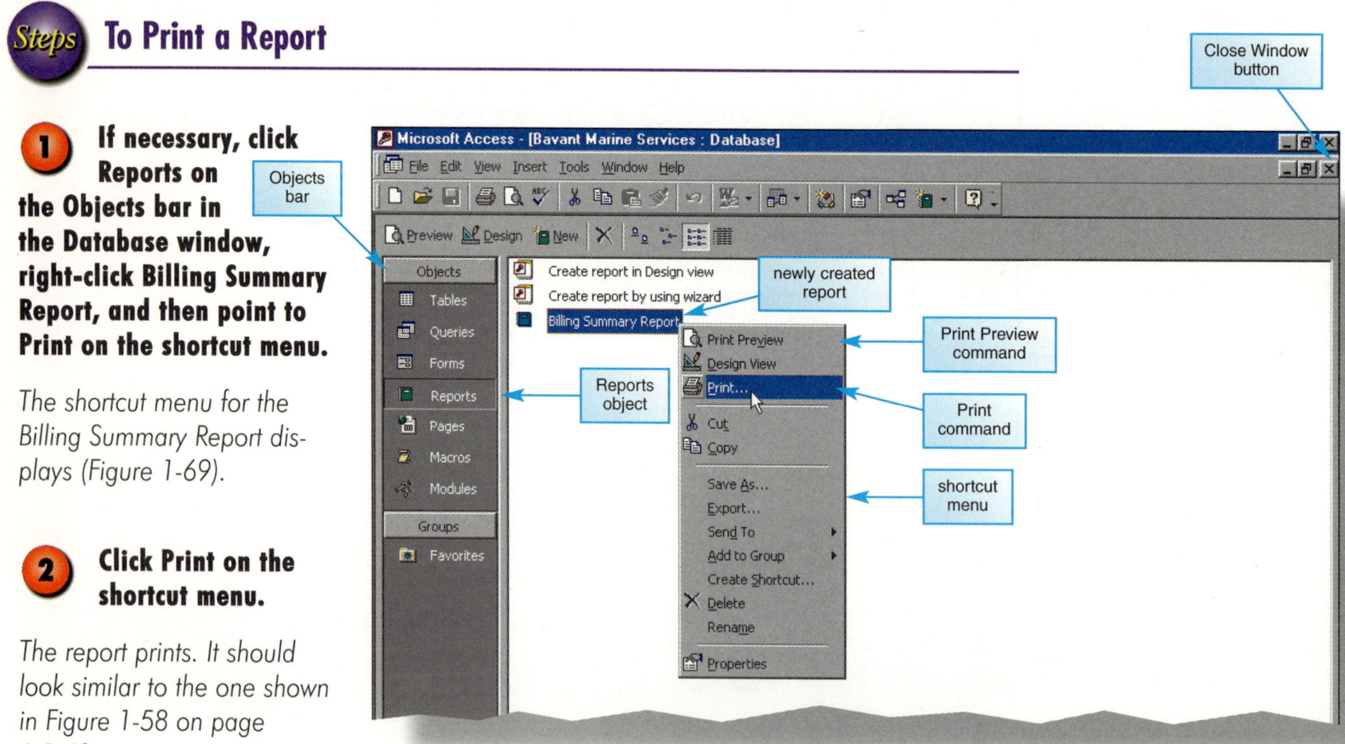

FIGURE 1-69

Closing the Database

Once you have finished working with a database, you should close it. The following step closes the database by closing its Database window.

TO CLOSE A DATABASE

 Click the Close Window button for the Bavant Marine Services : Database window.

Access Help System

At any time while you are using Access, you can get answers to questions by using the **Access Help system**. Used properly, this form of online assistance can increase your productivity and reduce your frustrations by minimizing the time you spend learning how to use Access. Table 1-2 on page A 1.51, summarizes the eight categories of help available to you. Because of the way the Access Help system works, please review the rightmost column of Table 1-2 if you have difficulties activating the desired category of help.

The following section shows how to get answers to your questions using the Office Assistant. For additional information on using the Access Help system, see Appendix A.

More About 2000

Quick Reference

For a table that lists how to complete the tasks covered in this book using the mouse, menu, shortcut menu, and keyboard, visit the Shelly Cashman Series Office Web page (www.scsite.com/off2000/qr.htm), and then click Microsoft Access 2000.

Using the Office Assistant

The **Office Assistant** answers your questions and suggests more efficient ways to complete a task. With the Office Assistant active, for example, you can type a question, word, or phrase in a text box and the Office Assistant provides immediate help on the subject. Also, as you create a database, the Office Assistant accumulates tips that suggest more efficient ways to do the tasks you completed while creating a database, such as printing and saving. This tip feature is part of the **IntelliSense™ technology** built into Access, which understands what you are trying to do and suggests better ways to do it. When the light bulb displays above the Office Assistant, click it to see a tip.

The steps on the next page show how to use the Office Assistant to obtain information on setting and changing the primary key.

Steps To Obtain Help Using the Office Assistant

1 If the Office Assistant does not display, click Show the Office Assistant on the Help menu. With the Office Assistant on the screen, click it. Type `how do i set the primary key` **in the What would you like to do? text box in the Office Assistant balloon. Point to the Search button (Figure 1-70).**

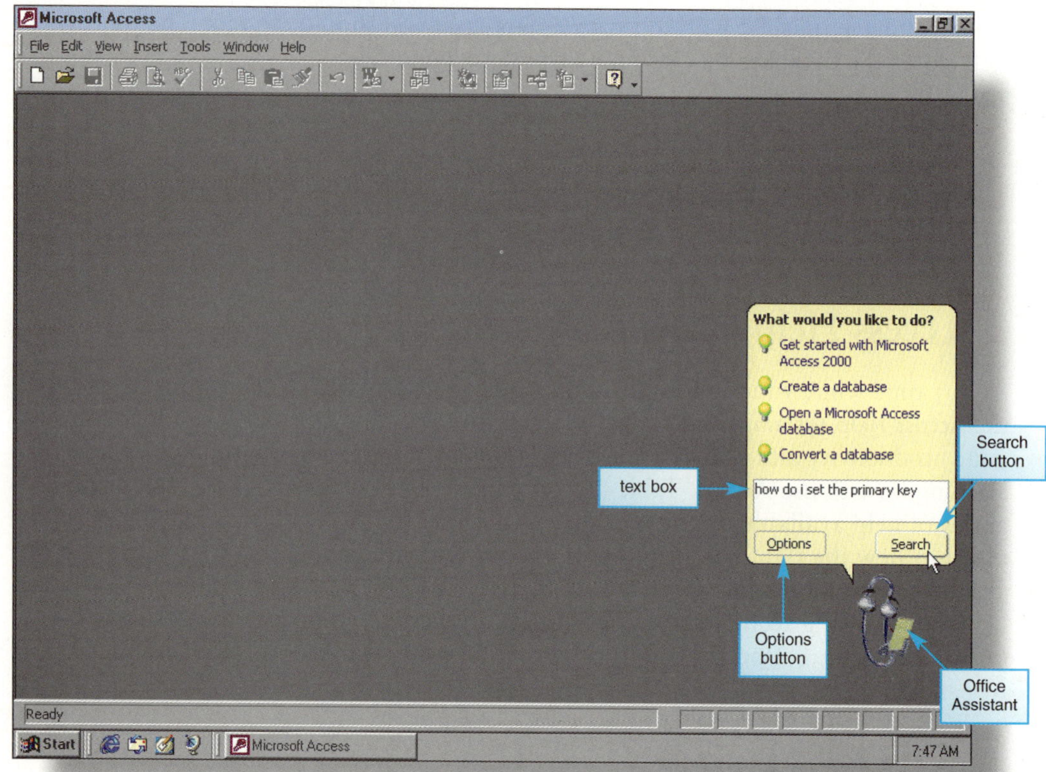

FIGURE 1-70

2 Click the Search button. Point to the topic Set or change the primary key.

The Office Assistant displays a list of topics relating to the question, "how do i set the primary key." (Your list may be different.) The mouse pointer changes to a hand (Figure 1-71).

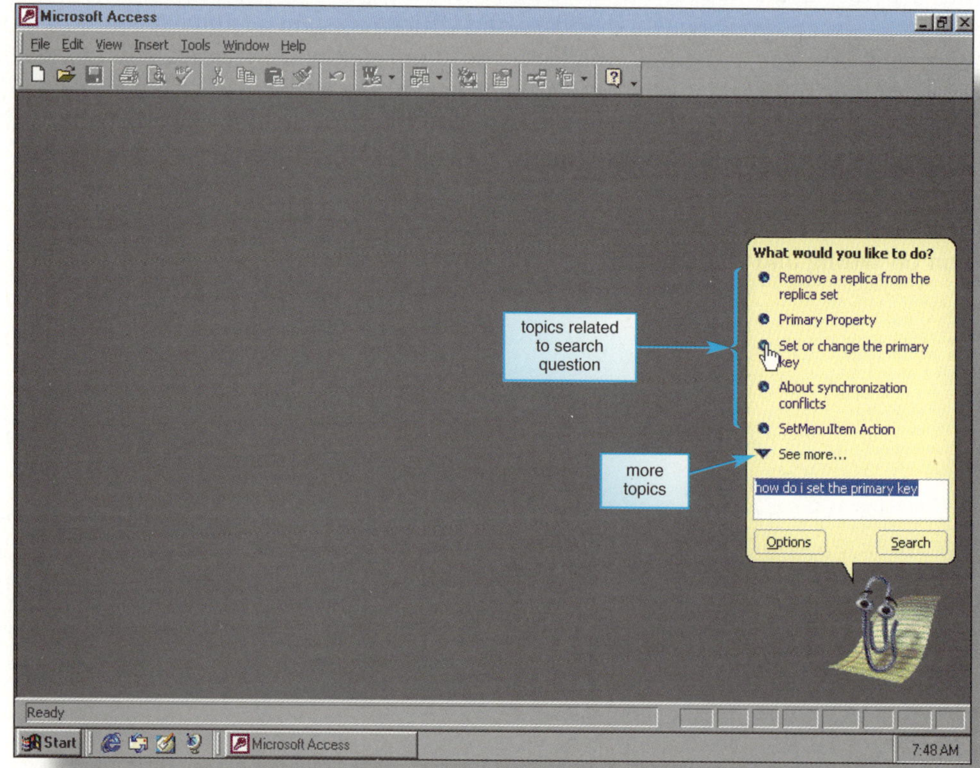

FIGURE 1-71

Click Set or change the primary key.

The Office Assistant displays a Microsoft Access Help window that provides Help information on setting or changing the primary key (Figure 1-72).

4 **Click the Close Window button on the Microsoft Access Help window title bar.**

The Microsoft Access Help window closes.

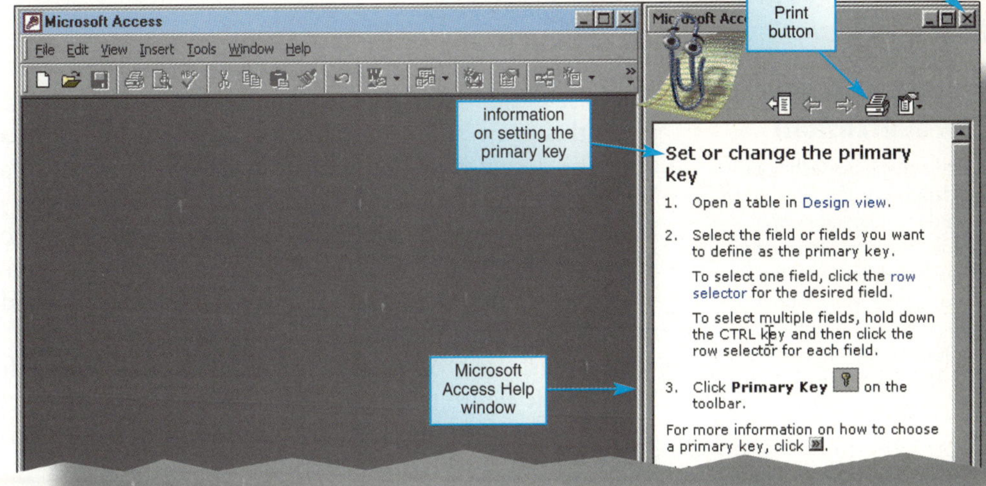

FIGURE 1-72

Table 1-2 summarizes the eight categories of Help available in Access 2000.

Table 1-2 Access Help System

TYPE	DESCRIPTION	HOW TO ACTIVATE	TURNING THE OFFICE ASSISTANT ON AND OFF
Answer Wizard	Similar to the Office Assistant in that it answers questions that you type in your own words.	Click the Microsoft Access Help button on the Database window toolbar. If necessary, maximize the Help window by double-clicking its title bar. Click the Answer Wizard tab.	If the Office Assistant displays, right-click it, click Options, click the Use the Office Assistant check box, and click the OK button.
Contents sheet	Groups Help topics by general categories. Use when you know only the general category of the topic in question.	Click the Microsoft Access Help button on the Database window toolbar. If necessary, maximize the Help window by double-clicking its title bar. Click the Contents tab.	If the Office Assistant displays, right-click it, click Options, click the Use the Office Assistant check box, and then click the OK button.
Detect and Repair	Automatically finds and fixes errors in the application.	Click Detect and Repair on the Help menu.	
Hardware and Software Information	Shows Product ID and allows access to system information and technical support information.	Click About Microsoft Access on the Help menu and then click the appropriate button.	
Index sheet	Similar to an index in a book; use when you know exactly what you want.	Click the Microsoft Access Help button on the Database window toolbar. If necessary, maximize the window by double-clicking its title bar. Click the Index tab.	If the Office Assistant displays, right-click it, click Options, click the Use the Office Assistant check box, and then click the OK button.
Office Assistant	Answers questions that you type in your own words, offers tips, and provides Help for a variety of Access features.	Click the Microsoft Access Help button on the Database window toolbar.	If the Office Assistant does not display, close the Microsoft Access Help window and then click Show the Office Assistant on the Help menu.
Office on the Web	Used to access technical resources and download free product enhancements on the Web.	Click Office on the Web on the Help menu.	
Question Mark button and What's This? command	Used to identify unfamiliar items on the screen.	Click the Question Mark button and click an item in the dialog box. Click What's This? on the Help menu, and then click an item on the screen.	

Database Design (Normalization)

There is a special technique for identifying and eliminating redundancy, called **normalization**. For more information on normalization, visit the Access 2000 More About Web page (www.scsite.com/ac2000/more.htm) and then click Normalization.

Designing a Database

Database design refers to the arrangement of data into tables and fields. In the example in this project, the design is specified, but in many cases, you will have to determine the design based on what you want the system to accomplish.

With large, complex databases, the database design process can be extensive. Major sections of advanced database textbooks are devoted to this topic. Often, however, you should be able to design a database effectively by keeping one simple principle in mind: Design to remove redundancy. **Redundancy** means storing the same fact in more than one place.

To illustrate, you need to maintain the following information shown in Figure 1-73. In the figure, all the data is contained in a single table. Notice that the data for a given technician (number, name, and so on) occurs on more than one record.

Marina table

MARINA NUMBER	NAME	ADDRESS	CITY	STATE	ZIP CODE	WARRANTY	NON WARRANTY	TECH NUMBER	LAST NAME	FIRST NAME
AD57	Alan's Docks	314 Central	Burton	MI	49611	$1,248.00	$597.75	23	Anderson	Trista
AN75	Afton's Marina	21 West 8th	Glenview	MI	48121	$1,906.50	$831.25	36	Nichols	Ashton
BL72	Brite's Landing	281 Robin	Burton	MI	49611	$217.00	$0.00	36	Nichols	Ashton
EL25	Elend Marina	462 River	Torino	MI	48268	$413.50	$678.75	49	Gomez	Teresa
FB96	Fenton's Boats	36 Bayview	Cavela	MI	47926	$923.20	$657.50	23	Anderson	Trista
FM22	Fedder Marina	283 Waterfront	Burton	MI	49611	$432.00	$0.00	36	Nichols	Ashton
JB92	JT Boat Club	28 Causeway	Torino	MI	48268	$0.00	$0.00	36	Nichols	Ashton
NW72	Nelson's Wharf	27 Lake	Masondale	MI	49832	$608.50	$520.00	23	Anderson	Trista
SM72	Solton's Marine	867 Bay Ridge	Glenview	MI	48121	$462.50	$295.00	49	Gomez	Teresa
TR72	The Reef	92 East Bay	Woodview	MI	47212	$219.00	$0.00	36	Nichols	Ashton

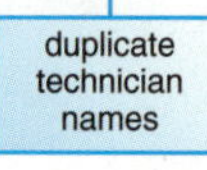

FIGURE 1-73

Database Design (Design Method)

There are a variety of methods that have been developed for designing complex databases given a set of input and output requirements. For more information on database design methods, visit the Access 2000 More About Web page (www.scsite.com/ac2000/more.htm) and then click Database Design.

Storing this data on multiple records is an example of redundancy, which causes several problems, including:

1. Redundancy wastes space on the disk. The address of technician 23 (Trista Anderson), for example, should be stored only once. Storing this fact several times is wasteful.
2. Redundancy makes updating the database more difficult. If, for example, Trista Anderson moves, her address would need to be changed in several different places.
3. A possibility of inconsistent data exists. Suppose, for example, that you change the address of Trista Anderson on marina FB96's record to 146 Valley, but do not change it on marina AD57's record. In both cases, the tech number is 23, but the addresses are different. In other words, the data is inconsistent.

The solution to the problem is to place the redundant data in a separate table, one in which the data will no longer be redundant. If, for example, you place the data for technicians in a separate table (Figure 1-74), the data for each technician will appear only once.

technician data is in separate table

Technician table

TECH NUMBER	LAST NAME	FIRST NAME	ADDRESS	CITY	STATE	ZIP CODE	HOURLY RATE	YTD EARNINGS
23	Anderson	Trista	283 Belton	Port Anton	MI	47989	$24.00	$17,862.00
36	Nichols	Ashton	978 Richmond	Hewitt	MI	47618	$21.00	$19,560.00
49	Gomez	Teresa	2855 Parry	Ashley	MI	47711	$22.00	$21,211.50

Marina table

MARINA NUMBER	NAME	ADDRESS	CITY	STATE	ZIP CODE	WARRANTY	NON-WARRANTY	TECH NUMBER
AD57	Alan's Docks	314 Central	Burton	MI	49611	$1,248.00	$597.75	23
AN75	Afton's Marina	21 West 8th	Glenview	MI	48121	$1,906.50	$831.25	36
BL72	Brite's Landing	281 Robin	Burton	MI	49611	$217.00	$0.00	36
EL25	Elend Marina	462 River	Torino	MI	48268	$413.50	$678.75	49
FB96	Fenton's Boats	36 Bayview	Cavela	MI	47926	$923.20	$657.50	23
FM22	Fedder Marina	283 Waterfront	Burton	MI	49611	$432.00	$0.00	36
JB92	JT Boat Club	28 Causeway	Torino	MI	48268	$0.00	$0.00	36
NW72	Nelson's Wharf	27 Lake	Masondale	MI	49832	$608.50	$520.00	23
SM72	Solton's Marine	867 Bay Ridge	Glenview	MI	48121	$462.50	$295.00	49
TR72	The Reef	92 East Bay	Woodview	MI	47212	$219.00	$0.00	36

FIGURE 1-74

Notice that you need to have the tech number in both tables. Without it, no way exists to tell which technician is associated with which marina. All the other technician data, however, was removed from the Marina table and placed in the Technician table. This new arrangement corrects the problems of redundancy in the following ways:

1. Because the data for each technician is stored only once, space is not wasted.
2. Changing the address of a technician is easy. You have only to change one row in the Technician table.
3. Because the data for a technician is stored only once, inconsistent data cannot occur.

Designing to omit redundancy will help you to produce good and valid database designs.

CASE PERSPECTIVE SUMMARY

In Project 1, you assisted Bavant Marine Service in their efforts to place their data in a database. You created the database that Bavant will use. Within this database, you created the Marina and Technician tables by defining the fields within them. You then added records to these tables. Once you created the tables, you printed the contents of the tables. You also used a form to view the data in the table. Finally, you used the Report Wizard to create a report containing the Marina Number, Name, Warranty, and Non-warranty fields for each marina served by Bavant Marine Services.

Project Summary

In Project 1, you learned about databases and database management systems. You learned how to create a database and how to create the tables within a database. You saw how to define the fields in a table by specifying the characteristics of the fields. You learned how to open a table, how to add records to it, and how to close it. You also printed the contents of a table. You created a form to view data on the screen and also created a custom report. You learned how to use Microsoft Access Help. Finally, you learned how to design a database to eliminate redundancy.

What You Should Know

Having completed this project, you now should be able to perform the following tasks:

- Add Additional Records to a Table *(A 1.27)*
- Add Records to a Table *(A 1.20)*
- Add Records to an Additional Table *(A 1.35)*
- Close a Database *(A 1.49)*
- Close a Table and Database and Quit Access *(A 1.24)*
- Close and Save a Form *(A 1.38)*
- Complete a Report *(A 1.46)*
- Create a Report *(A 1.43)*
- Create a Table *(A 1.13)*
- Create an Additional Table *(A 1.34)*
- Define the Fields in a Table *(A 1.15)*
- Obtain Help Using the Office Assistant *(A 1.50)*
- Open a Database *(A 1.25)*
- Open a Form *(A 1.39)*
- Preview and Print the Contents of a Table *(A 1.30)*
- Print a Report *(A 1.48)*
- Save a Table *(A 1.19)*
- Select the Fields for a Report *(A 1.45)*
- Start Access *(A 1.9)*
- Switch from Form View to Datasheet View *(A 1.41)*
- Use a Form *(A 1.36)*
- Use the New Object: AutoForm Button to Create a Form *(A 1.37)*

More About 2000

Microsoft Certification

The Microsoft Office User Specialist (MOUS) Certification program provides an opportunity for you to obtain a valuable industry credential — proof that you have the Access 2000 skills required by employers. For more information, see Appendix D or visit the Shelly Cashman Series MOUS Web page at www.scsite.com/off2000/cert.htm.

1 Changing Data and Creating Reports

Instructions: Start Access. Open the Sidewalk Scrapers database from the Access Data Disk. See the inside back cover for instructions for downloading the Access Data Disk or see your instructor for information on accessing the files required for this book. Sidewalk Scrapers is a snow removal service that was started by two high school juniors looking for ways to earn money for college. Sidewalk Scrapers provides snow removal to residences and businesses in a city that receives lots of snow during the winter months. The business has expanded rapidly and now employs high school and college students to shovel sidewalks, steps, and driveways. Sidewalk Scrapers has a database that keeps track of its workers and customers. The database has two tables. The Customer table contains data on the customers who use the services of Sidewalk Scrapers. The Worker table contains data on the students employed by Sidewalk Scrapers. The structure and data are shown for the Customer table in Figure 1-75 and for the Worker table in Figure 1-76.

Structure of Customer table

FIELD NAME	DATA TYPE	FIELD SIZE	PRIMARY KEY?	DESCRIPTION
Customer Number	Text	4	Yes	Customer Number (Primary Key)
Name	Text	20		Customer Name
Address	Text	15		Street Address
Telephone	Text	8		Telephone Number (999-9999 Version)
Balance	Currency			Amount Owed by Customer
Worker Id	Text	2		Id of Customer's Worker

Data for Customer table

CUSTOMER NUMBER	NAME	ADDRESS	TELEPHONE	BALANCE	WORKER ID
AL25	Arders, Lars	205 Norton	555-2050	$45.00	03
AT43	Atari Cleaners	147 Main	555-7410	$80.00	10
BH81	Bond, Laura	407 Scott	555-0704	$0.00	10
CH65	Chan's Bootery	154 Main	555-0504	$70.00	14
CI05	Cinco Gallery	304 Secord	555-1304	$29.00	03
JB51	Jordach, Ben	203 Norton	555-0213	$60.00	10
LK44	Lee, Kim	605 Thurston	555-5061	$0.00	10
MD60	Martinez, Dan	410 Orange	555-4110	$95.00	03
ME02	Meat Shoppe	75 Edgewater	555-7557	$0.00	14
ST21	Styling Salon	406 Secord	555-6454	$40.00	10

FIGURE 1-75

(continued)

Apply Your Knowledge

Project Reinforcement at www.scsite.com/off2000/reinforce.htm

Changing Data and Creating Reports *(continued)*

Structure of Worker table

FIELD NAME	DATA TYPE	FIELD SIZE	PRIMARY KEY?	DESCRIPTION
Worker Id	Text	2	Yes	Worker Identification Number (Primary Key)
Last Name	Text	15		Last Name of Worker
First Name	Text	10		First Name of Worker
Address	Text	20		Street Address
Telephone	Text	8		Telephone Number (999-9999 Version)
Pay Rate	Currency			Hourly Pay Rate

Data for Worker table

WORKER ID	LAST NAME	FIRST NAME	ADDRESS	TELEPHONE NUMBER	PAY RATE
03	Carter	Chris	467 Norton	555-7641	$4.50
10	Lau	John	56 Parker	555-5656	$4.25
14	Sanchez	Elena	211 Thurston	555-1122	$4.75

FIGURE 1-76

Perform the following tasks.

1. Open the Worker table in Datasheet view and add the following record to the table:

07	Ferrens	Louis	24 Scott	555-2442	4.25

   Close the Worker table.
2. Open the Worker table again. Notice that the record you just added has been moved. It is no longer at the end of the table. The records are in order by the primary key, Worker Id.
3. Print the Worker table.
4. Open the Customer table.
5. Change the Worker Id for customer LK44 to 07.
6. Print the Customer table.
7. Create the report shown in Figure 1-77 for the Customer table.
8. Print the report.

Balance Due Report

Customer Number	Name	Balance
AL25	Arders, Lars	$45.00
AT43	Atari Cleaners	$80.00
BH81	Bond, Laura	$0.00
CH65	Chan's Bootery	$70.00
CI05	Cinco Gallery	$29.00
JB51	Jordach, Ben	$60.00
LK44	Lee, Kim	$0.00
MD60	Martinez, Dan	$95.00
ME02	Meat Shoppe	$0.00
ST21	Styling Salon	$40.00

FIGURE 1-77

1 Creating the School Connection Database

Problem: The Booster's Club at the local high school raises money by selling merchandise imprinted with the school logo to alumni. The Booster's Club purchases products from vendors that deal in school specialty items. The database consists of two tables. The Item table contains information on items available for sale. The Vendor table contains information on the vendors.

Instructions: Perform the following tasks.

1. Create a new database in which to store all the objects related to the merchandise data. Call the database School Connection.
2. Create the Item table using the structure shown in Figure 1-78. Use the name Item for the table.
3. Add the data shown in Figure 1-78 to the Item table.
4. Print the Item table.
5. Create the Vendor table using the structure shown in Figure 1-79. Use the name Vendor for the table.
6. Add the data shown in Figure 1-79 on the next page to the Vendor table.
7. Print the Vendor table.
8. Create a form for the Item table. Use the name Item for the form.

Structure of Item table

FIELD NAME	DATA TYPE	FIELD SIZE	PRIMARY KEY?	DESCRIPTION
Item Id	Text	4	Yes	Item Id Number (Primary Key)
Description	Text	25		Description of Item
On Hand	Number	Long Integer		Number of Units On Hand
Cost	Currency			Cost of Item
Selling Price	Currency			Selling Price of Item
Vendor Code	Text	2		Code of Item Vendor

Data for Item table

ITEM ID	DESCRIPTION	ON HAND	COST	SELLING PRICE	VENDOR CODE
BA02	Baseball Cap	15	$12.50	$15.00	AL
CM12	Coffee Mug	20	$3.75	$5.00	GG
DM05	Doormat	5	$14.25	$17.00	TM
OR01	Ornament	25	$2.75	$4.00	GG
PL05	Pillow	8	$13.50	$15.00	TM
PN21	Pennant	22	$5.65	$7.00	TM
PP20	Pen and Pencil Set	12	$16.00	$20.00	GG
SC11	Scarf	17	$8.40	$12.00	AL
TT12	Tie	10	$8.90	$12.00	AL
WA34	Wastebasket	3	$14.00	$15.00	GG

FIGURE 1-78

(continued)

Creating the School Connection Database *(continued)*

Structure of Vendor table

FIELD NAME	DATA TYPE	FIELD SIZE	PRIMARY KEY?	DESCRIPTION
Vendor Code	Text	2	Yes	Vendor Code (Primary Key)
Name	Text	30		Name of Vendor
Address	Text	20		Street Address
City	Text	20		City
State	Text	2		State (Two-Character Abbreviation)
Zip Code	Text	5		Zip Code (Five-Character Version)
Telephone Number	Text	12		Telephone Number (999-999-9999 Version)

Data for Vendor table

VENDOR CODE	NAME	ADDRESS	CITY	STATE	CODE	TELEPHONE NUMBER
AL	Alum Logo Inc.	1669 Queen	Aurora	WI	53595	608-555-9753
GG	GG Gifts	5261 Stream	Brisbane	NM	88061	505-555-8765
TM	Trinkets 'n More	541 Maple	Kentwood	VA	20147	804-555-1234

FIGURE 1-79

9. Create and print the report shown in Figure 1-80 for the Item table. In this report, items are sorted by Description. To sort the report by Description, specify Description as the field on which to sort when the Report Wizard dialog box asks what sort order you want for your records.

Inventory Report

Item Id	*Description*	*On Hand*	*Cost*
BA02	Baseball Cap	15	$12.50
CM12	Coffee Mug	20	$3.75
DM05	Doormat	5	$14.25
OR01	Ornament	25	$2.75
PP20	Pen and Pencil Set	12	$16.00
PN21	Pennant	22	$5.65
PL05	Pillow	8	$13.50
SC11	Scarf	17	$8.40
TT12	Tie	10	$8.90
WA34	Wastebasket	3	$14.00

FIGURE 1-80

2 Creating the City Area Bus Company Database

Problem: Like many urban transportation companies, the City Area Bus Company sells advertising. Local firms buy advertising from ad sales representatives who work for the bus company. Ad sales representatives receive a commission based on the advertising revenues they generate. The database consists of two tables. The Advertiser table contains information on the organizations that advertise on the buses. The Sales Rep table contains information on the representative assigned to the advertising account.

Instructions: Perform the following tasks.

1. Create a new database in which to store all the objects related to the advertising data. Call the database City Area Bus Company.
2. Create the Advertiser table using the structure shown in Figure 1-81. Use the name Advertiser for the table.
3. Add the data shown in Figure 1-81 to the Advertiser table.

Structure of Advertiser table

FIELD NAME	DATA TYPE	FIELD SIZE	PRIMARY KEY?	DESCRIPTION
Advertiser Id	Text	4	Yes	Advertiser Id (Primary Key)
Name	Text	20		Name of Advertiser
Address	Text	15		Street Address
City	Text	15		City
State	Text	2		State (Two-Character Abbreviation)
Zip Code	Text	5		Zip Code (Five-Character Version)
Balance	Currency			Amount Currently Owed
Amount Paid	Currency			Amount Paid Year-to-Date
Sales Rep Number	Text	2		Number of Advertising Sales Representative

Data for Advertiser table

ADVERTISER ID	NAME	ADDRESS	CITY	STATE	ZIP CODE	BALANCE	AMOUNT PAID	SALES REP NUMBER
AC25	Alia Cleaners	223 Michigan	Crescentville	MA	05431	$85.00	$585.00	24
BB99	Bob's Bakery	1939 Jackson	Richmond	MA	05433	$435.00	$1,150.00	29
CS46	Cara's Salon	787 Ottawa	Cheltenham	CT	06470	$35.00	$660.00	29
FS78	Franz and Sons	3294 Campeau	Richmond	MA	05434	$185.00	$975.00	31
GR75	G's Restaurant	1632 Shue	Manyunk	CT	06471	$0.00	$1,500.00	24
HC11	Hilde's Cards	3140 Main	Crescentville	MA	05431	$250.00	$500.00	29
MC34	Mom's Cookies	1805 Broadway	Crescentville	MA	05431	$95.00	$1,050.00	29
NO10	New Orient	2200 Lawrence	Manyunk	CT	06471	$150.00	$350.00	24
PJ24	Pajama Store	13 Monroe	Cheltenham	CT	06470	$0.00	$775.00	31
TM89	Tom's Market	39 Albert	Richmond	MA	05433	$50.00	$500.00	24

FIGURE 1-81

(continued)

Creating the City Area Bus Company Database (continued)

4. Print the Advertiser table.
5. Create the Sales Rep table using the structure shown in Figure 1-82. Use the name Sales Rep for the table. Be sure that the field size for the Comm Rate field is Double.
6. Add the data shown in Figure 1-82 to the Sales Rep table.
7. Print the Sales Rep table.
8. Create a form for the Advertiser table. Use the name Advertiser for the form.

Structure of Sales Rep table

FIELD NAME	DATA TYPE	FIELD SIZE	PRIMARY KEY?	DESCRIPTION
Sales Rep Number	Text	2	Yes	Advertising Sales Rep Number (Primary Key)
Last Name	Text	15		Last Name of Advertising Sales Rep
First Name	Text	10		First Name of Advertising Sales Rep
Address	Text	15		Street Address
City	Text	15		City
State	Text	2		State (Two-Character Abbreviation)
Zip Code	Text	5		Zip Code (Five-Character Version)
Comm Rate	Number	Double		Commission Rate
Commission	Currency			Year-to-Date Total Commissions

Data for Sales Rep table

SALES REP NUMBER	LAST NAME	FIRST NAME	ADDRESS	CITY	STATE	ZIP CODE	COMM RATE	COMMISSION
24	Chou	Peter	34 Second	Crescentville	MA	05431	0.09	$7,500.00
29	Ortiz	Elvia	45 Belmont	Cheltenham	CT	06470	0.09	$8,450.00
31	Reed	Pat	78 Farmwood	Richmond	MA	05433	0.08	$7,225.00

FIGURE 1-82

9. Open the form you created and change the address for Advertiser Number HC11 to 340 Mainline.
10. Change to Datasheet view and delete the record for Advertiser Number GR75.
11. Print the Advertiser table.
12. Create and print the report shown in Figure 1-83 for the Advertiser table.

Advertiser Status Report

Advertiser Id	Name	Balance	Amount Paid
AC25	Alia Cleaners	$85.00	$585.00
BB99	Bob's Bakery	$435.00	$1,150.00
CS46	Cara's Salon	$35.00	$660.00
FS78	Franz and Sons	$185.00	$975.00
HC11	Hilde's Cards	$250.00	$500.00
MC34	Mom's Cookies	$95.00	$1,050.00
NO10	New Orient	$150.00	$350.00
PJ24	Pajama Store	$0.00	$775.00
TM89	Tom's Market	$50.00	$500.00

FIGURE 1-83

3 Creating the Resort Rental Database

Problem: A real estate company located in an ocean resort community provides a rental service for apartment/condo owners. The company rents units by the week to interested tourists and "snowbirds" (people who spend their winters in warmer climates). The database consists of two tables. The Rental Unit table contains information on the units available for rent. The Owner table contains information on the owners of the rental units.

Instructions: Perform the following tasks.

1. Create a new database in which to store all the objects related to the rental data. Call the database Resort Rentals.
2. Create the Rental Unit table using the structure shown in Figure 1-84. Use the name Rental Unit for the table. Note that the table uses a new data type, Yes/No for the Pool and Ocean View fields.
3. Add the data shown in Figure 1-84 to the Rental Unit table.

Structure of Rental Unit table

FIELD NAME	DATA TYPE	FIELD SIZE	PRIMARY KEY?	DESCRIPTION
Rental Id	Text	3	Yes	Rental Id (Primary Key)
Address	Text	20		Street Address of Rental Unit
City	Text	20		City
Bedrooms	Number			Number of Bedrooms
Bathrooms	Number			Number of Bathrooms
Sleeps	Number			Maximum Number that can sleep in rental unit
Pool	Yes/No			Does the rental unit have a pool?
Ocean View	Yes/No			Does the rental unit have an ocean view?
Weekly Rate	Currency			Weekly Rental Rate
Owner Id	Text	4		Id of Rental Unit's Owner

Data for Rental Unit table

RENTAL ID	ADDRESS	CITY	BED-ROOMS	BATH-ROOMS	SLEEPS	POOL	OCEAN VIEW	WEEKLY RATE	OWNER ID
101	521 Ocean	Hutchins	2	1	4	Y	Y	$750.00	ML10
103	783 First	Gulf Breeze	3	3	8	Y		$1,000.00	FH15
105	684 Beach	San Toma	1	1	3		Y	$700.00	PR23
108	96 Breeze	Gulf Breeze	1	1	2		Y	$650.00	PR23
110	523 Ocean	Hutchins	2	2	6	Y		$900.00	LD45
112	345 Coastal	Shady Beach	2	2	5		Y	$900.00	LD45
116	956 First	Gulf Breeze	2	2	6	Y	Y	$1,100.00	ML10
121	123 Gulf	San Toma	3	2	8	Y	Y	$1,300.00	FH15
134	278 Second	Shady Beach	2	1	4		Y	$1,000.00	FH15
144	24 Plantation	Hutchins	1	1	2	Y		$650.00	PR23

FIGURE 1-84

(continued)

Creating the Resort Rental Database *(continued)*

4. Use Microsoft Access Help to learn how to resize column widths in Datasheet view and then reduce the size of the Rental Id, Bedrooms, Bathrooms, Sleeps, Pool, Ocean View, Weekly Rate, and Owner Id columns.
5. Print the Rental Unit table.
6. Create the Owner table using the structure shown in Figure 1-85. Use the name Owner for the table.
7. Add the data shown in Figure 1-85 to the Owner table.
8. Print the Owner table.

Structure of Owner table

FIELD NAME	DATA TYPE	FIELD SIZE	PRIMARY KEY?	DESCRIPTION
Owner Id	Text	4	Yes	Owner Id (Primary Key)
Last Name	Text	15		Last Name of Owner
First Name	Text	10		First Name of Owner
Address	Text	15		Street Address
City	Text	15		City
State	Text	2		State (Two-Character Abbreviation)
Zip Code	Text	5		Zip Code (Five-Character Version)
Telephone	Text	12		Telephone Number (999-999-9999 Version)

Data for Owner table

OWNER ID	LAST NAME	FIRST NAME	ADDRESS	CITY	STATE	ZIP CODE	TELEPHONE NO
FH15	Franco	Hilda	1234 Oakley	Middleville	PA	19063	610-555-7658
LD45	Lakos	Daniel	45 Fanshawe	Grenard	MI	49441	616-555-9080
ML10	Manuel	Larry	78 Unruh	Dalute	CA	95518	916-555-8787
PR23	Peoples	Rita	5489 South	Johnson	LA	58345	504-555-9845

FIGURE 1-85

9. Create a form for the Rental Unit table. Use the name Rental Unit for the form.
10. Open the form you created and change the weekly rate for Rental Id 144 to $675.00.
11. Print the Rental Unit table.
12. Create and print the report shown in Figure 1-86 for the Rental Unit table.

Available Rental Units Report

Rental Id	Address	City	Weekly Rate
101	521 Ocean	Hutchins	$750.00
103	783 First	Gulf Breeze	$1,000.00
105	684 Beach	San Toma	$700.00
108	96 Breeze	Gulf Breeze	$650.00
110	523 Ocean	Hutchins	$900.00
112	345 Coastal	Shady Beach	$900.00
116	956 First	Gulf Breeze	$1,100.00
121	123 Gulf	San Toma	$1,300.00
134	278 Second	Shady Beach	$1,000.00
144	24 Plantation	Hutchins	$675.00

FIGURE 1-86

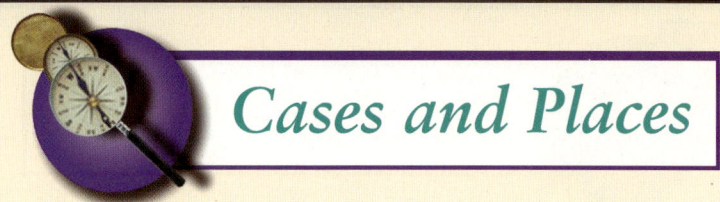

Cases and Places

The difficulty of these case studies varies:
◗ are the least difficult; ◗◗ are more difficult; and ◗◗◗ are the most difficult.

1 ◗ As a fund-raising project, the local college's Computer Science Club sells small computer accessories to students. Disks, disk cases, and mouse pads are some of the items that the club sells from a small kiosk in the student computer lab. The club has asked you to create a database that keeps track of their inventory and suppliers. The current inventory is shown in Figure 1-87.

Design and create a database to store the club's inventory. Then create the necessary tables, enter the data from Figure 1-87, and print the tables.

ITEM ID	DESCRIPTION	UNITS ON HAND	COST	SELLING PRICE	SUPPLIER CODE	SUPPLIER NAME	SUPPLIER TELEPHONE
1663	Antistatic Wipes	30	$0.15	$0.25	ER	Ergonomics Ltd.	517-555-3853
1683	CD Wallet	12	$3.45	$4.00	HI	Human Interface	317-555-4747
2563	Desktop Holder	4	$3.85	$4.75	ER	Ergonomics Ltd.	517-555-3853
2593	Disks	175	$0.20	$.75	HI	Human Interface	317-555-4747
3923	Disk Cases	12	$2.20	$2.75	HI	Human Interface	317-555-4747
3953	Mouse Holder	10	$0.80	$1.00	MT	Mouse Tracks	616-555-9228
4343	Mouse Pad	25	$2.25	$3.00	MT	Mouse Tracks	616-555-9228
5810	PC Tool Kit	9	$7.80	$9.00	ER	Ergonomics Ltd.	517-555-3853
5930	Wrist Rest	3	$2.90	$3.25	ER	Ergonomics Ltd.	517-555-3853

FIGURE 1-87

2 ◗ Sci-Fi Scene is a local bookstore that specializes in Science Fiction. The owner has asked you to create and update a database that she can use to keep track of the books she has in stock. You gather the information shown in Figure 1-88.

Design and create a database to store the book data. Then create the necessary tables, enter the data from Figure 1-88, and print the tables.

Cases and Places

BOOK CODE	TITLE	AUTHOR	UNITS ON HAND	PRICE	YEAR PUBLISHED	PUBLISHER CODE	PUBLISHER NAME
0488	Robot Wars	H Brawley	1	$5.95	1997	SI	Simpson-Ivan
0533	Albert's Way	H Brawley	2	$4.75	1999	SI	Simpson-Ivan
1019	Stargaze	G Chou	3	$5.50	1996	BB	Bertrand Books
128X	Comet Dust	R Eaton	2	$5.95	2000	PB	Peabody Books
1668	Android	E Dearling	3	$6.95	1999	VN	VanNester
3495	Dark Wind	G Chou	4	$4.95	1998	BB	Bertrand Books
3859	Infinity	R Torres	1	$4.75	1997	VN	VanNester
4889	The Galaxy	E Dearling	2	$6.75	2000	VN	VanNester
6517	Strange Alien	R Eaton	2	$9.95	1998	PB	Peabody Books
7104	Secret City	R Torres	1	$5.75	1997	VN	VanNester

FIGURE 1-88

3 ▶▶ The marching band director of your school has asked you to create a database of band members. He wants to keep track of the following data on each band member: name, address, telephone number, age, sex, emergency contact name, emergency telephone number, type of band instrument, band instrument number, whether the student owns or leases the instrument, and number of years in the band.

Design and create a database to meet the band director's needs. Create the necessary tables, enter some sample data, and print the tables to show the director.

4 ▶▶ You have been hired as an intern by the local humane society. The humane society would like you to computerize their adoption files. Currently, they keep all the information about animals that are placed for adoption on index cards. The cards include information on the family, for example, name, address, telephone number, number of children, any previous animal adoptions, and other family pets. Information on the animal also is kept, for example, type of animal, sex, age, name, and any medical problems.

Design and create a database to meet the humane society's needs. Create the necessary tables, enter some sample data, and print the tables to show the director of the humane society.

5 ▶▶▶ The Intramural Sports Club has decided that a good way to make money and help students would be to set up a used sports equipment co-operative similar to the secondhand sporting goods stores. As a member of the club, you are asked to create a database that can store data related to the sports equipment and the students who wish to sell their items.

Determine the type of data you will need, then design and create a database to meet the club's needs. Create the necessary tables, enter some sample data, and print the tables.

Microsoft Access 2000

Querying a Database Using the Select Query Window

OBJECTIVES

You will have mastered the material in this project when you can:

- State the purpose of queries
- Create a new query
- Use a query to display all records and all fields
- Run a query
- Print the answer to a query
- Close a query
- Clear a query
- Use a query to display selected fields
- Use text data in criteria in a query
- Use wildcards in criteria
- Use numeric data in criteria
- Use comparison operators
- Use compound criteria involving AND
- Use compound criteria involving OR
- Sort the answer to a query
- Join tables in a query
- Restrict the records in a join
- Use calculated fields in a query
- Calculate statistics in a query
- Use grouping with statistics
- Save a query
- Use a saved query

Where Have All the Children Gone?

National Database Helps Search for Missing Youngsters

All parents fear this situation: One minute their children are within eyesight; the next minute they have vanished, never to be seen again.

Nearly 4,600 children are abducted by non-family members each year, according to the U.S. Justice Department. Another 438,200 children are lost, injured, or otherwise missing. Yet, thousands of these children's records appear in a database maintained by the National Center for Missing and Exploited Children (NCMEC). Through this organization, the children, while they may be missing physically, appear in photo images.

NCMEC was created in 1984 as a public and private partnership to help the public search for missing children. Since the nonprofit Center opened, more than 1.3 million calls have been channeled through its national hotline (1-800-THE-LOST). In addition, NCMEC has partnered with the U.S. Department of

Justice's Office of Juvenile Justice and Delinquency Prevention (www.ncjrs.org) to promote and raise public awareness of this crime.

Since its inception, NCMEC has evolved into a high-tech resource for family, friends, and loved ones of missing and abused children. With nearly 114,600 attempted abductions reported each year, such a resource desperately is needed. Because of these alarming rates, NCMEC has established sophisticated databases that contribute to recovery rates, which are termed child case completions. Currently, the completion rate is 90 percent, dramatically up from 66 percent, which was the norm in 1989. Through partnerships with Intel, IBM, and Tektronix, to name a few, NCMEC has grown into a solid force for solving child cases.

One example of the advanced technology utilized by NCMEC is a database that contains photographs of missing children. Investigators and Web users are able to open the database and create a precise query based on such fields as the child's name, age, eye color, and weight. Then they run the query, and within a matter of seconds they have answers to the requested information. You can create queries and view some of these images at the NCMEC Web site (www.ncmec.org). Similarly, you will query the Bavant Marine Services Database in this project to obtain answers to questions regarding warranty amounts and marina names and locations.

Moreover, NCMEC's imaging specialists can alter a child's photograph to show how he might appear many years after he has disappeared. Subsequently, these images are stored in corresponding fields in the computerized imaging database. Many children who may not have been located otherwise have been found using this enhancement technology.

A recent technological development is the Multimedia Kiosk Program, which IBM donated to NCMEC. In this program, 50 kiosks have been placed in high pedestrian traffic areas such as LaGuardia Airport in New York and in large shopping malls throughout the country. They provide a functional database for the general public to learn about missing children and a means to transfer information quickly to affected friends and family.

Through the efforts of NCMEC, the nation now has a solid weapon and resource for the fight against child endangerment.

Microsoft Access 2000

Querying a Database Using the Select Query Window

CASE PERSPECTIVE

Now that Bavant Marine Services has created a database with marina and technician data, the management and staff of the organization hope to gain the benefits they expected when they set up the database. One of the more important benefits is the capability of easily asking questions concerning the data in the database and rapidly obtaining the answers. Among the questions they want answered are the following:

1. What are the warranty and non-warranty amounts for marina EL25?
2. Which marinas' names begin with Fe?
3. Which marinas are located in Burton?
4. What is the total amount (warranty amount plus non-warranty amount) for each marina?
5. Which marinas of technician 36 have warranty amounts of more than $1,000?

Your task is to assist Bavant Marine Services in obtaining answers to these questions as well as any other questions they deem important.

Introduction

A database management system such as Access offers many useful features, among them the capability of answering questions such as those posed by the management of Bavant Marine Services (Figure 2-1). The answers to these questions, and many more, are found in the database, and Access can find the answers quickly. When you pose a question to Access, or any other database management system, the question is called a query. A **query** is simply a question represented in a way that Access can understand.

Thus, to find the answer to a question, you first create a corresponding query using the techniques illustrated in this project. Once you have created the query, you instruct Access to run the query; that is, to perform the steps necessary to obtain the answer. When finished, Access will display the answer to your question in the format shown at the bottom of Figure 2-1.

Project Two — Querying the Bavant Marine Services Database

You must obtain answers to the questions posed by the management of Bavant Marine Services. These include the questions shown in Figure 2-1, as well as any other questions that the management deems important.

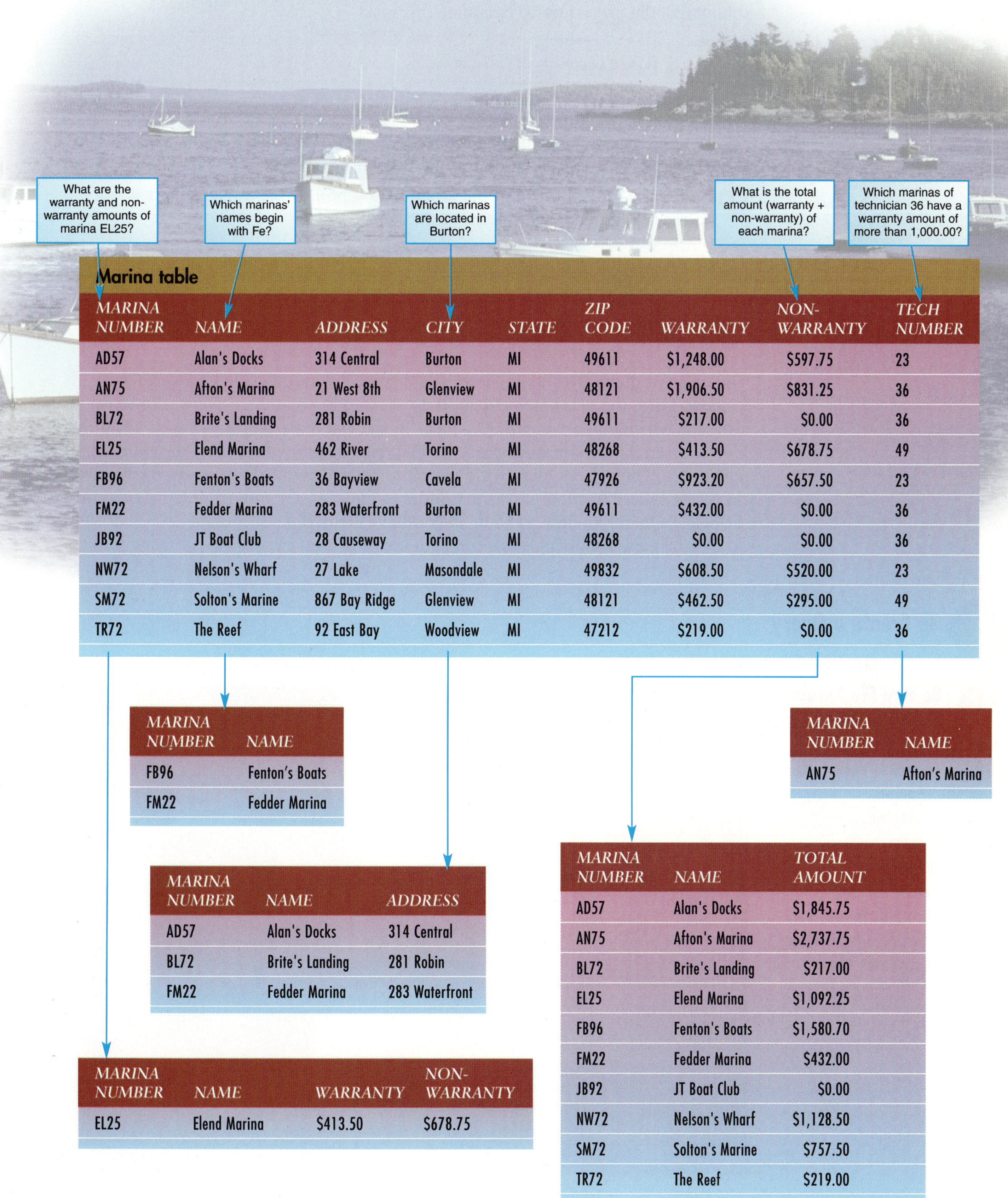

Marina table

MARINA NUMBER	NAME	ADDRESS	CITY	STATE	ZIP CODE	WARRANTY	NON-WARRANTY	TECH NUMBER
AD57	Alan's Docks	314 Central	Burton	MI	49611	$1,248.00	$597.75	23
AN75	Afton's Marina	21 West 8th	Glenview	MI	48121	$1,906.50	$831.25	36
BL72	Brite's Landing	281 Robin	Burton	MI	49611	$217.00	$0.00	36
EL25	Elend Marina	462 River	Torino	MI	48268	$413.50	$678.75	49
FB96	Fenton's Boats	36 Bayview	Cavela	MI	47926	$923.20	$657.50	23
FM22	Fedder Marina	283 Waterfront	Burton	MI	49611	$432.00	$0.00	36
JB92	JT Boat Club	28 Causeway	Torino	MI	48268	$0.00	$0.00	36
NW72	Nelson's Wharf	27 Lake	Masondale	MI	49832	$608.50	$520.00	23
SM72	Solton's Marine	867 Bay Ridge	Glenview	MI	48121	$462.50	$295.00	49
TR72	The Reef	92 East Bay	Woodview	MI	47212	$219.00	$0.00	36

MARINA NUMBER	NAME
FB96	Fenton's Boats
FM22	Fedder Marina

MARINA NUMBER	NAME
AN75	Afton's Marina

MARINA NUMBER	NAME	ADDRESS
AD57	Alan's Docks	314 Central
BL72	Brite's Landing	281 Robin
FM22	Fedder Marina	283 Waterfront

MARINA NUMBER	NAME	TOTAL AMOUNT
AD57	Alan's Docks	$1,845.75
AN75	Afton's Marina	$2,737.75
BL72	Brite's Landing	$217.00
EL25	Elend Marina	$1,092.25
FB96	Fenton's Boats	$1,580.70
FM22	Fedder Marina	$432.00
JB92	JT Boat Club	$0.00
NW72	Nelson's Wharf	$1,128.50
SM72	Solton's Marine	$757.50
TR72	The Reef	$219.00

MARINA NUMBER	NAME	WARRANTY	NON-WARRANTY
EL25	Elend Marina	$413.50	$678.75

FIGURE 2-1

Opening the Database

Before creating queries, first you must open the database. The following steps summarize the procedure to complete this task.

More About

Queries: Query Languages

Prior to the advent of query languages in the mid 1970s, obtaining answers to questions concerning data in a database was very difficult, requiring that someone write lengthy (several hundred line) programs in languages like COBOL. Query Languages made it easy to obtain answers to such questions.

TO OPEN A DATABASE

1. Click the Start button on the taskbar.
2. Click Open Office Document and then click 3½ Floppy (A:) in the Look in box. Make sure the database called Bavant Marine Services is selected.
3. Click the Open button in the Open dialog box. If the Tables object is not already selected, click Tables on the Objects bar.

The database is open and the Bavant Marine Services : Database window displays.

Creating a New Query

You create a query by making entries in a special window called a **Select Query window**. Once the database is open, the first step in creating a query is to select the table for which you are creating a query in the Database window. Next, using the New Object: AutoForm button on the Database window toolbar, you will design the new query. The Select Query window will display. It typically is easier to work with the Select Query window if it is maximized. Thus, as a standard practice, maximize the Select Query window as soon as you have created it.

Perform the following steps to begin creating a query.

Steps To Create a Query

1. **Be sure the Bavant Marine Services database is open, the Tables object is selected, and the Marina table is selected. Click the New Object: AutoForm button arrow on the Database window toolbar. Point to Query on the New Object: AutoForm menu.**

The list of available objects displays (Figure 2-2).

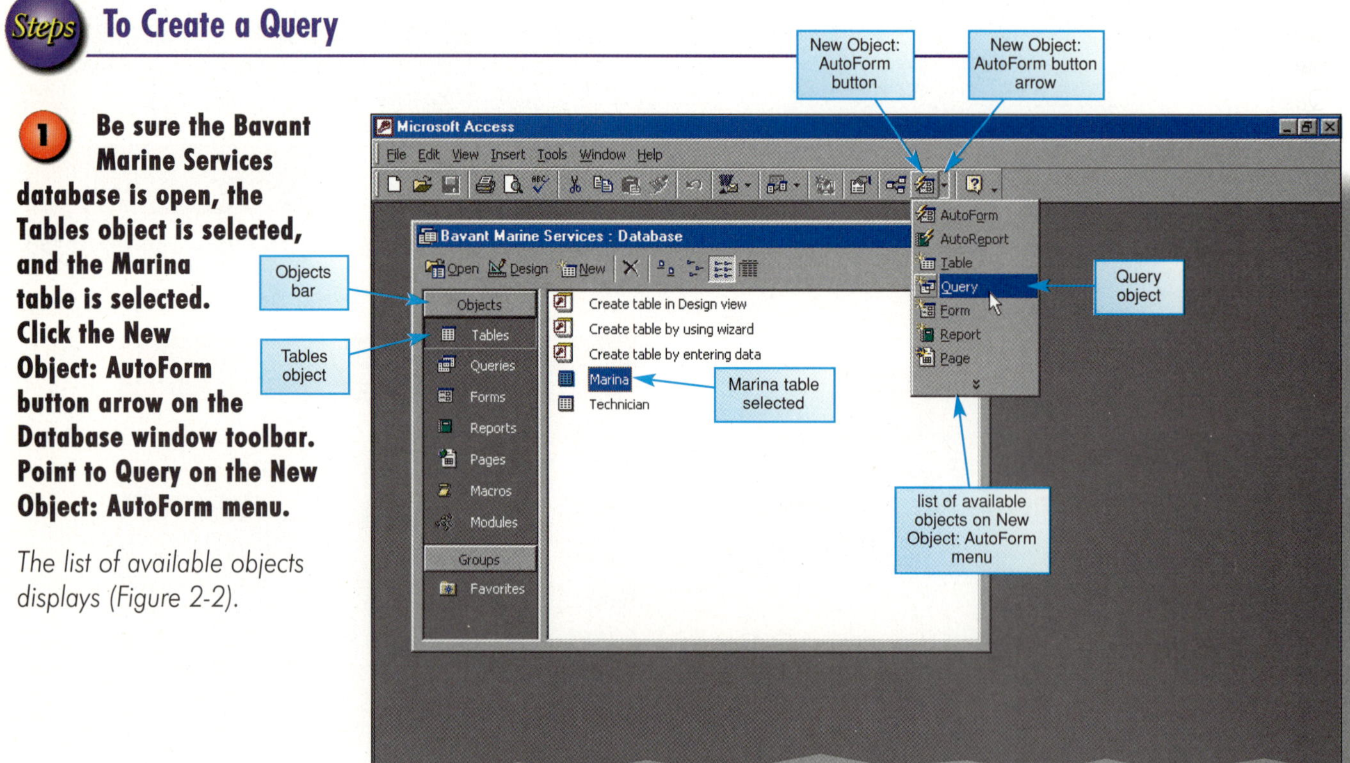

FIGURE 2-2

2 Click Query. Be sure Design View is selected and point to the OK button.

The New Query dialog box displays (Figure 2-3).

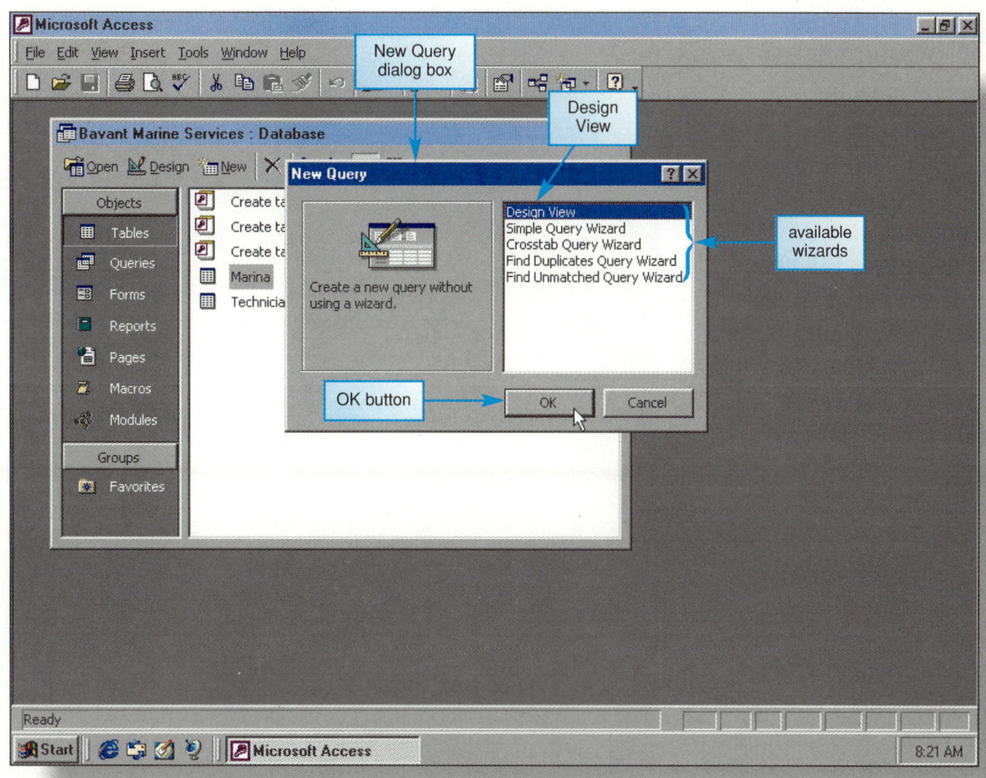

FIGURE 2-3

3 Click the OK button.

The Query1 : Select Query window displays (Figure 2-4). The Query Design toolbar has replaced the Database window toolbar.

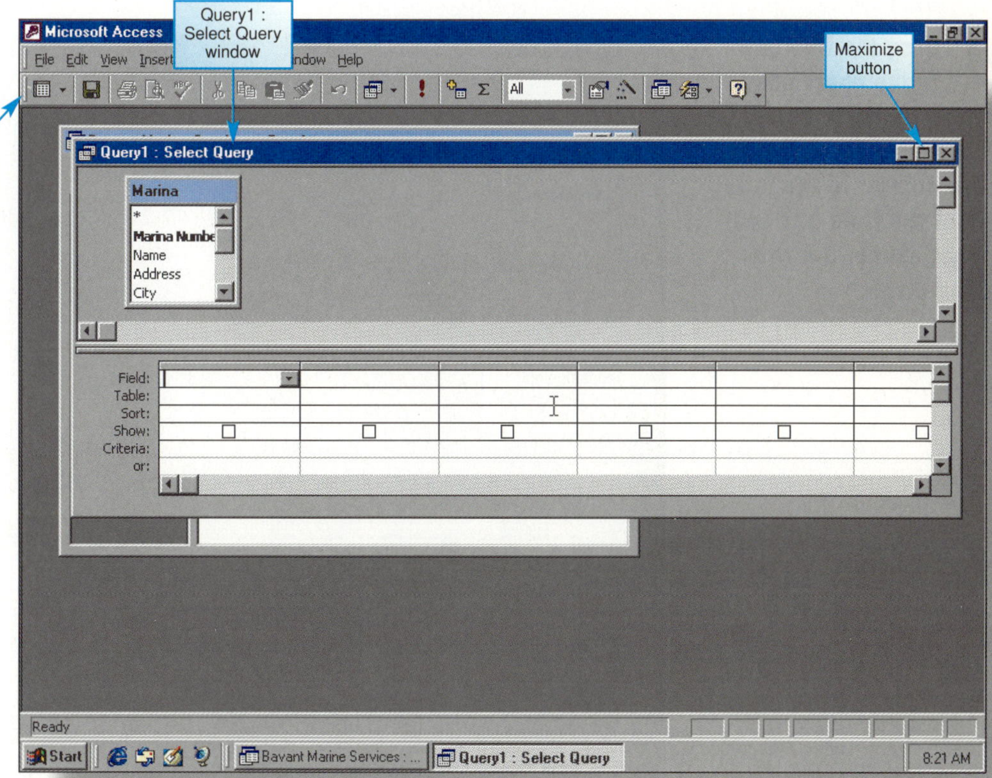

FIGURE 2-4

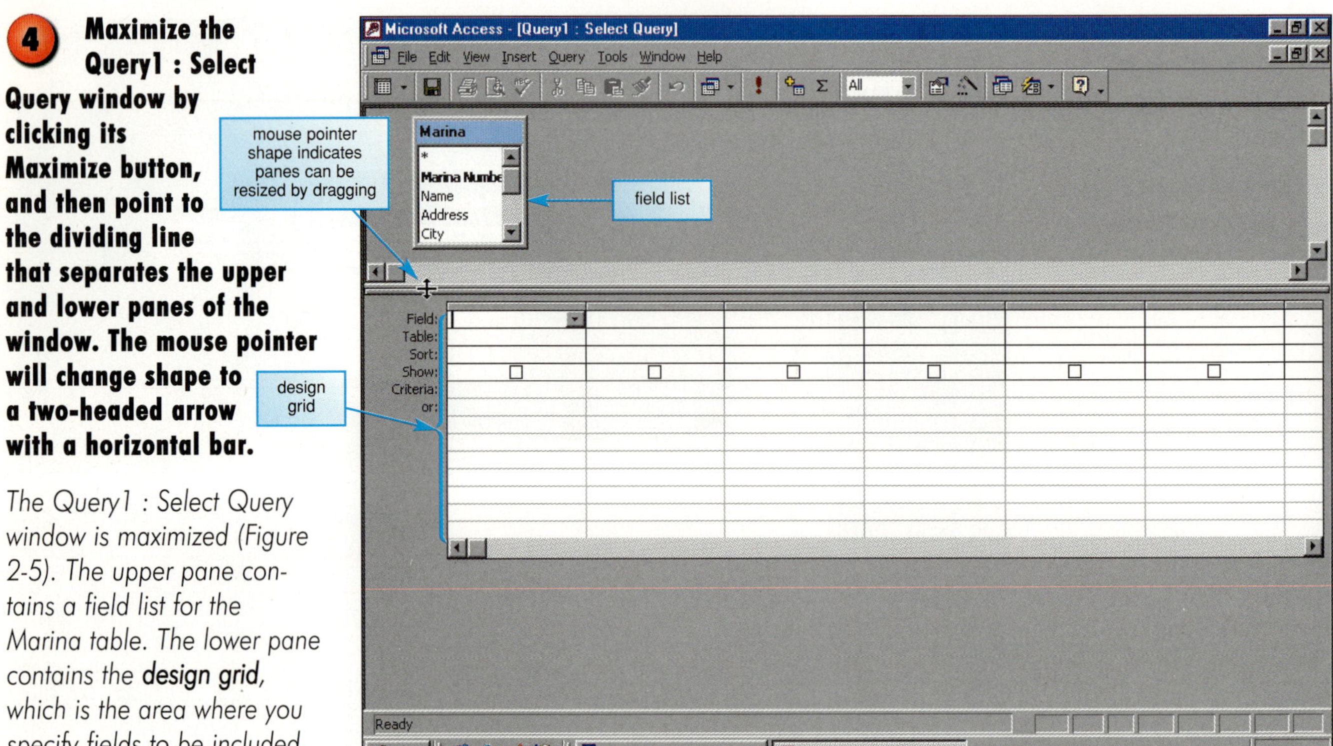

4 **Maximize the Query1 : Select Query window by clicking its Maximize button, and then point to the dividing line that separates the upper and lower panes of the window. The mouse pointer will change shape to a two-headed arrow with a horizontal bar.**

The Query1 : Select Query window is maximized (Figure 2-5). The upper pane contains a field list for the Marina table. The lower pane contains the **design grid**, *which is the area where you specify fields to be included, sort order, and the criteria the records you are looking for must satisfy.*

FIGURE 2-5

5 **Drag the line down to the approximate position shown in Figure 2-6 and then move the mouse pointer to the lower edge of the field box so it changes shape to a two-headed arrow.**

The two panes have been resized.

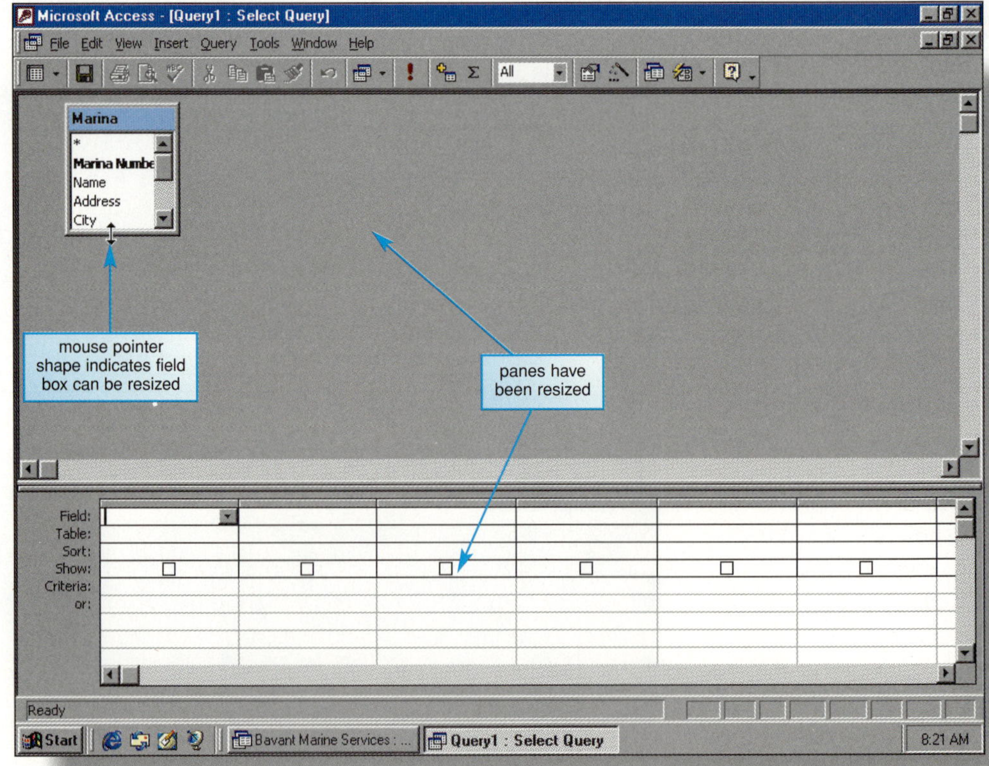

FIGURE 2-6

6 Drag the lower edge of the field box down far enough so all fields in the Marina table are visible.

All fields in the Marina table display (Figure 2-7).

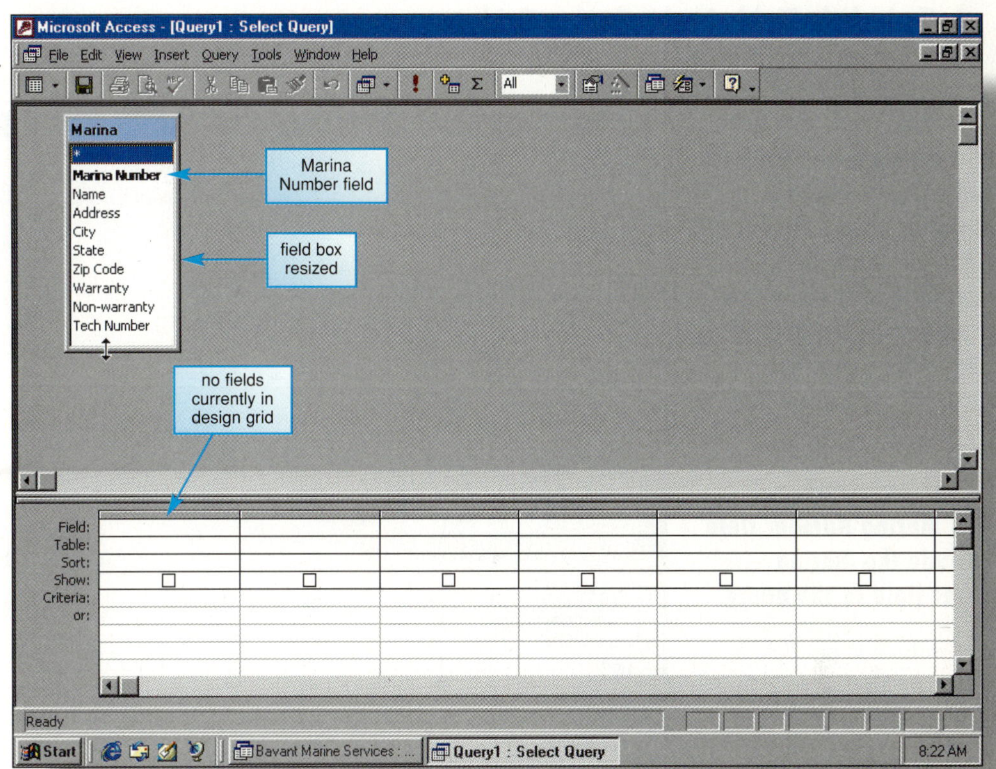

FIGURE 2-7

Other Ways

1. Click Queries object, double-click Create query in Design view
2. On Insert menu click Query

Using the Select Query Window

Once you have created a new Select Query window, you are ready to create the actual query by making entries in the design grid in the lower pane of the window. You enter the names of the fields you want included in the Field row in the grid. You also can enter criteria, such as the fact that the marina number must be EL25, in the Criteria row of the grid. When you do so, only the record or records that match the criterion will be included in the answer.

Displaying Selected Fields in a Query

Only the fields that appear in the design grid will be included in the results of the query. Thus, to display only certain fields, place only these fields in the grid, and no others. If you place the wrong field in the grid inadvertently, click Edit on the menu bar and then click Delete to remove it. Alternatively, you could click Clear Grid to clear the entire design grid and then start over.

The steps on the next page create a query to show the marina number, name, and technician number for all marinas by including only those fields in the design grid.

More About 2000

Queries: Query-by-Example

Query-by-Example, often referred to as QBE, was a query language first proposed in the mid 1970s. In this approach, users asked questions by filling in a table on the screen. The approach to queries taken by several DBMSs is based on Query-by-Example. For more information, visit the Access 2000 More About Web page (www.scsite.com/ac2000/more.htm) and click QBE.

To Include Fields in the Design Grid

1 **Make sure you have a maximized Query1 : Select Query window containing a field list for the Marina table in the upper pane of the window and an empty design grid in the lower pane (see Figure 2-7 on page A 2.9).**

2 **Double-click the Marina Number field to include the Marina Number field in the query.**

The Marina Number field is included as the first field in the design grid (Figure 2-8).

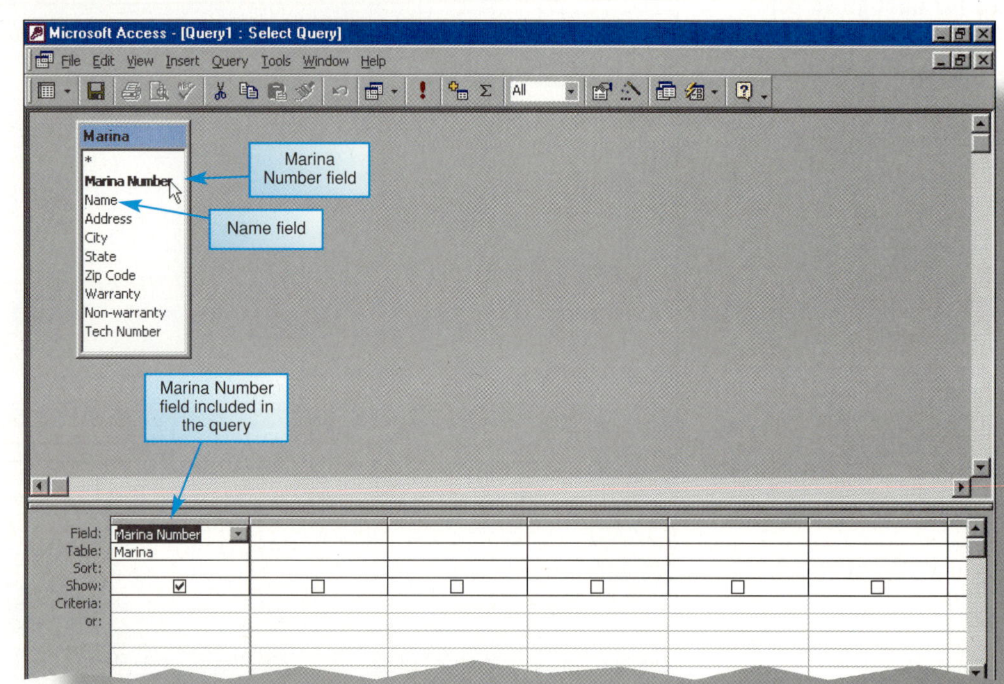

FIGURE 2-8

3 **Double-click the Name field to include it in the query. Include the Tech Number field using the same technique. Point to the Run button on the Query Design toolbar.**

The Marina Number, Name, and Tech Number fields are included in the query (Figure 2-9).

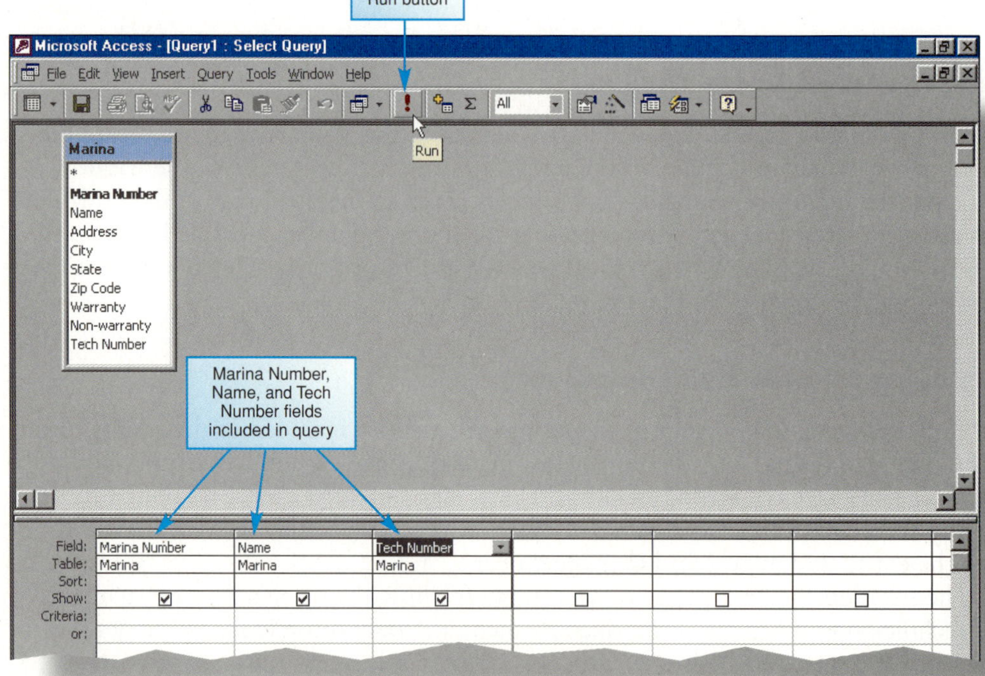

FIGURE 2-9

Other Ways

1. Drag field from field list to design grid
2. Click column in grid, click arrow, click field

Running a Query

Once you have created the query, you need to run the query to produce the results. To do so, click the Run button. Access then will perform the steps necessary to obtain and display the answer. The set of records that makes up the answer will be displayed in Datasheet view. Although it looks like a table that is stored on your disk, it really is not. The records are constructed from data in the existing Marina table. If you were to change the data in the Marina table and then rerun this same query, the results would reflect the changes.

To Run the Query

Click the Run button.

The query is executed and the results display (Figure 2-10). The Query Datasheet toolbar replaces the Query Design toolbar. The Sort Ascending button on the Query Datasheet toolbar now occupies the position of the Run button. If you do not move the mouse pointer after clicking a button, the ScreenTip for the button may obscure a portion of the first record, such as the ScreenTip for the Sort Ascending button. Moving the mouse pointer away from the toolbar after running the Query eliminates this problem.

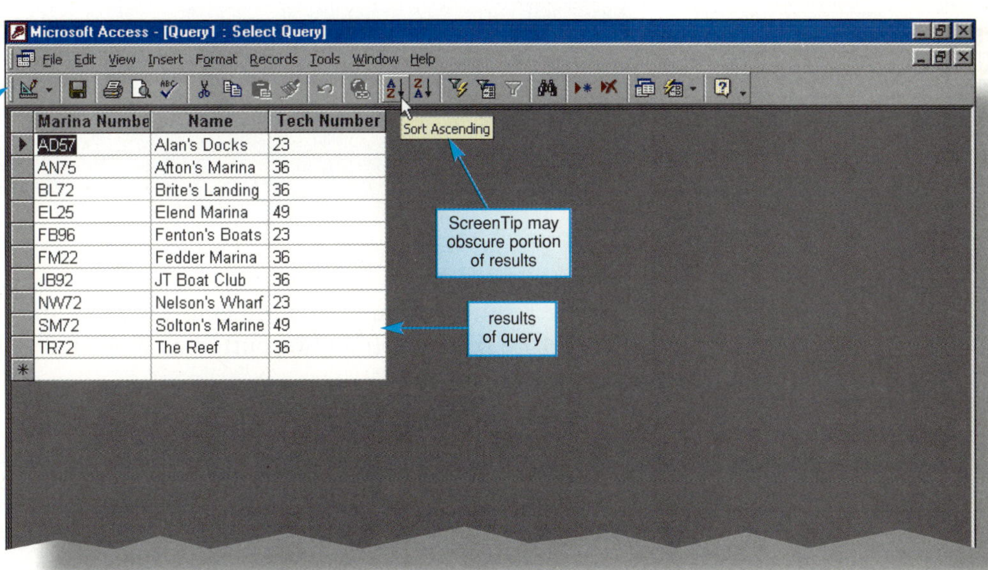

FIGURE 2-10

Move the mouse pointer to a position that is outside of the data and is not on the Query Datasheet toolbar.

The data displays without obstruction (Figure 2-11). Notice that an extra blank row, marking the end of the table, displays at the end of the results.

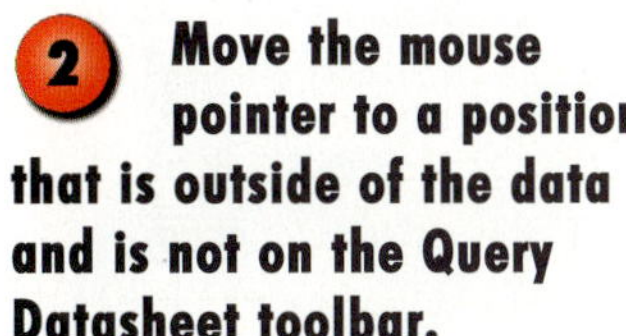

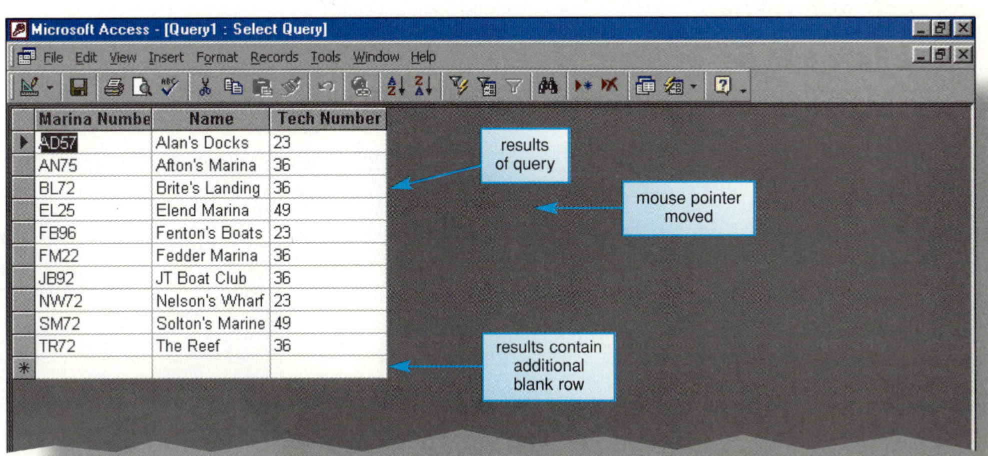

FIGURE 2-11

More About

Queries: SQL

The most widespread of all the query languages is a language called SQL. Many database management systems, including Access, offer SQL as one option for querying databases. For more information, visit the Access 2000 More About Web page (www.scsite.com/ac2000/more.htm) and click SQL.

Other Ways

1. On Query menu click Run
2. On View menu click Datasheet View

In all future examples, after running a query, move the mouse pointer so the table displays without obstruction.

Printing the Results of a Query

To print the results of a query, click the Print button on the toolbar. Complete the following steps to print the query results that currently display on the screen.

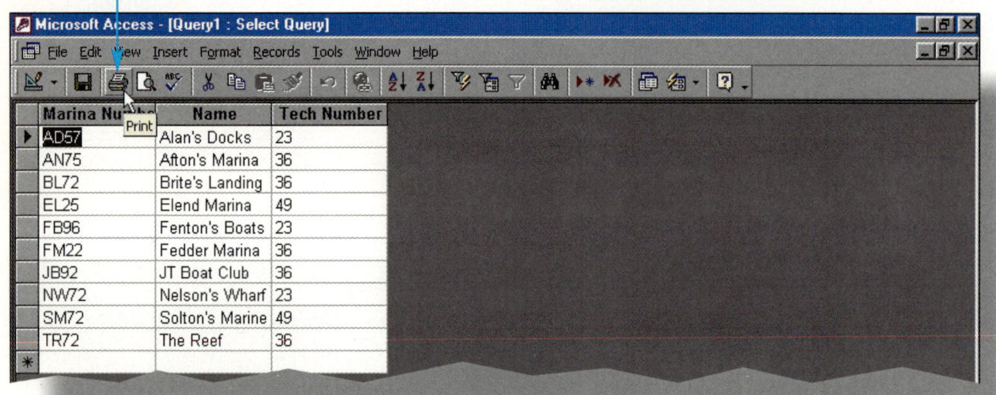

FIGURE 2-12

TO PRINT THE RESULTS OF A QUERY

1. Ready the printer and then point to the Print button on the Query Datasheet toolbar (Figure 2-12).
2. Click the Print button.

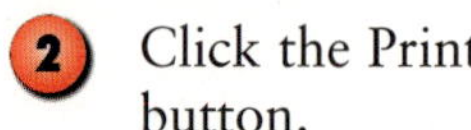

The results print.

If the results of a query require landscape orientation, switch to landscape orientation before you click the Print button as indicated in Project 1 on page A 1.30.

Returning to Design View

You can examine the results of a query on your screen to see the answer to your question. You can scroll through the records, if necessary, just as you scroll through the records of any other table. You also can print a copy of the table. In any case, once you are finished working with the results, you can return to Design view to ask another question. To do so, use the View button arrow on the Query Datasheet toolbar as shown in the following steps.

To Return to Design View

1. **Point to the View button arrow on the Query Datasheet toolbar (Figure 2-13).**

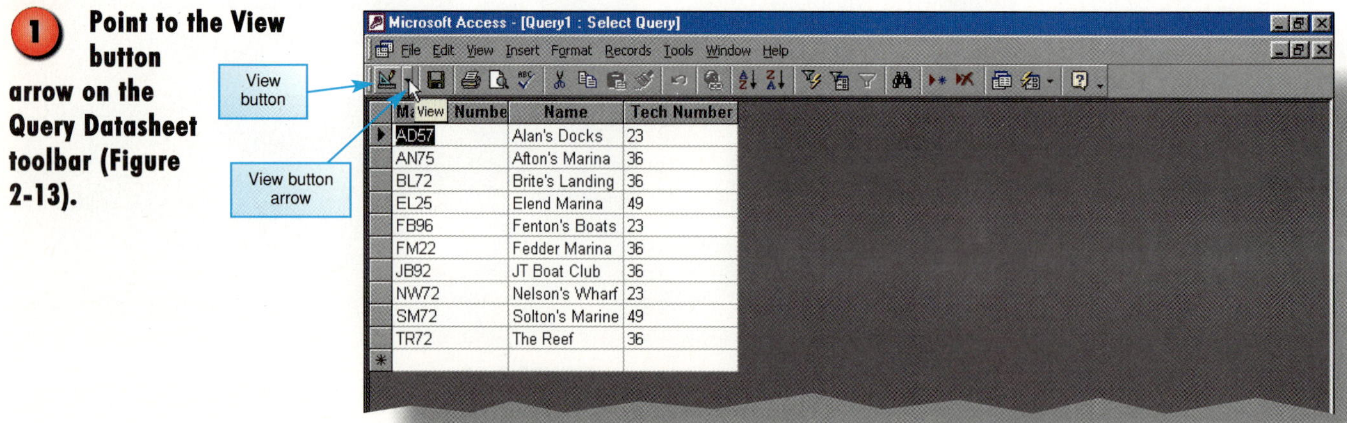

FIGURE 2-13

Click the View button arrow and then point to Design View.

The View button menu displays (Figure 2-14).

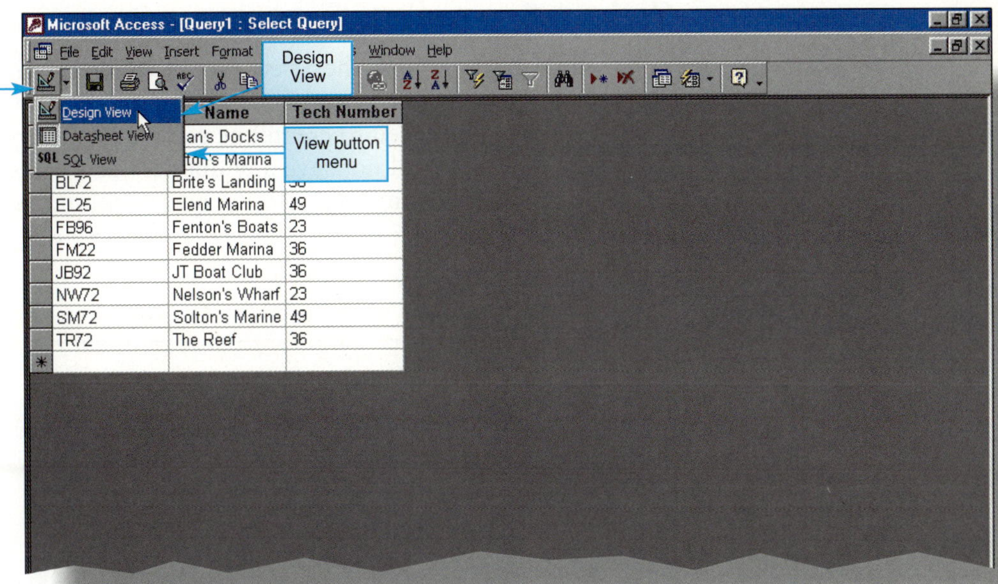

FIGURE 2-14

3 Click Design View.

The Query1 : Select Query window displays (Figure 2-15).

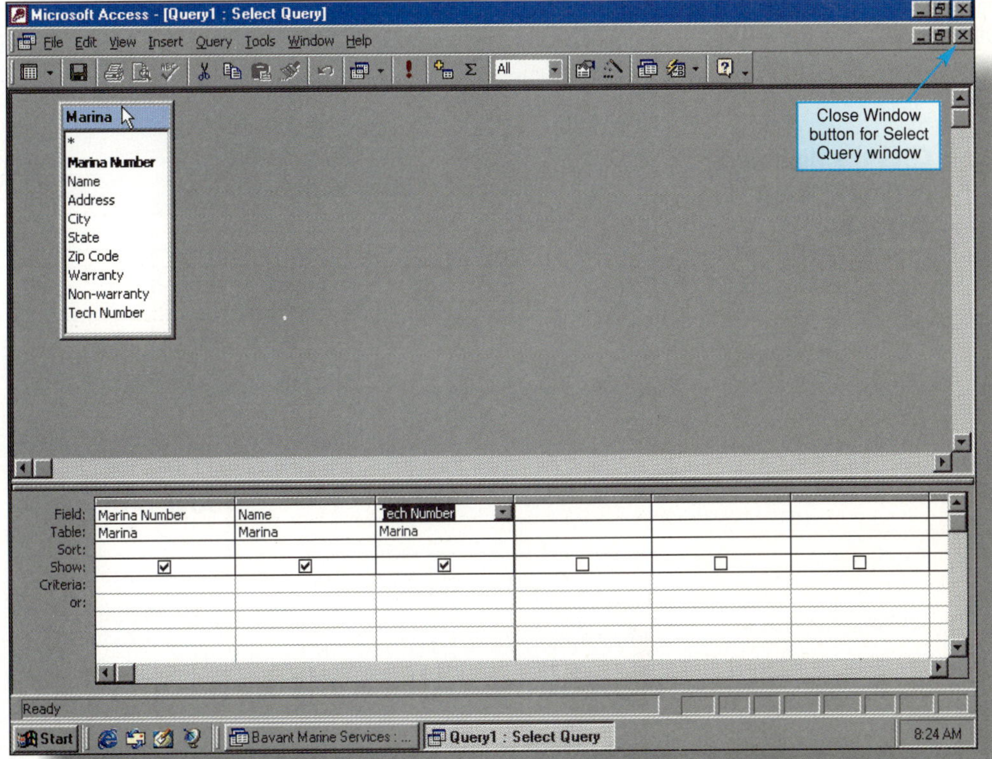

FIGURE 2-15

1. On View menu click Design View

Because Design View is the first command on the View button menu, you do not have to click the View button arrow and then click Design View. You simply can click the View button itself.

Closing a Query

To close a query, close the Select Query window. When you do so, Access displays the Microsoft dialog box asking if you want to save your query for future use. If you think you will need to create the same exact query often, you should save the query. For now, you will not save any queries. You will see how to save them later in the project. The following steps close a query without saving it.

To Close the Query

1 Click the Close Window button for the Query1 : Select Query window. (See Figure 2-15 on page A 2.13.)

The Microsoft Access dialog box displays (Figure 2-16). Clicking the Yes button saves the query and clicking the No button closes the query without saving.

2 Click the No button in the Microsoft Access dialog box.

The Query1 : Select Query window closes and is removed from the desktop.

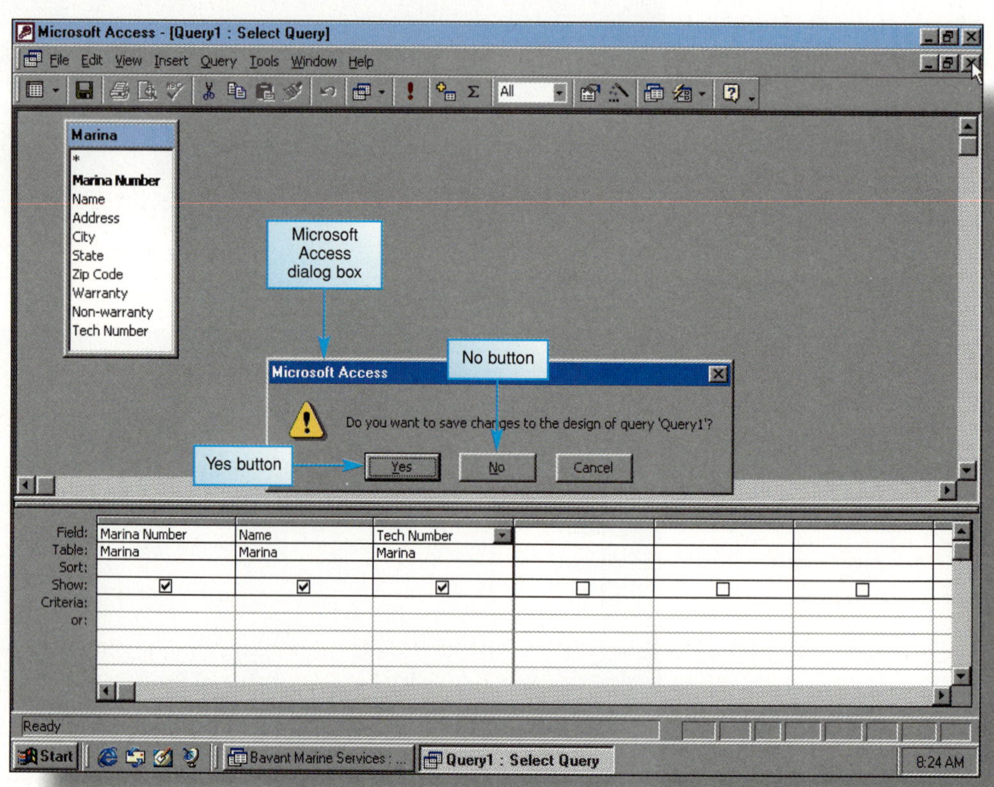

FIGURE 2-16

Other Ways

1. On File menu click Close

Including All Fields in a Query

If you want to include all fields in a query, you could select each field individually. A more simplified way exists to include all fields, however. By selecting the **asterisk (*)** in the field list, you are indicating that all fields are to be included. Complete the following steps to use the asterisk to include all fields.

To Include All Fields in a Query

1 **Be sure you have a maximized Query1 : Select Query window containing a field list for the Marina table in the upper pane and an empty design grid in the lower pane. (See Steps 1 through 6 on pages A 2.6 through A 2.9 to create the query and resize the window.) Point to the asterisk at the top of the field list.**

A maximized Query1 : Select Query window displays (Figure 2-17). The two panes have been resized.

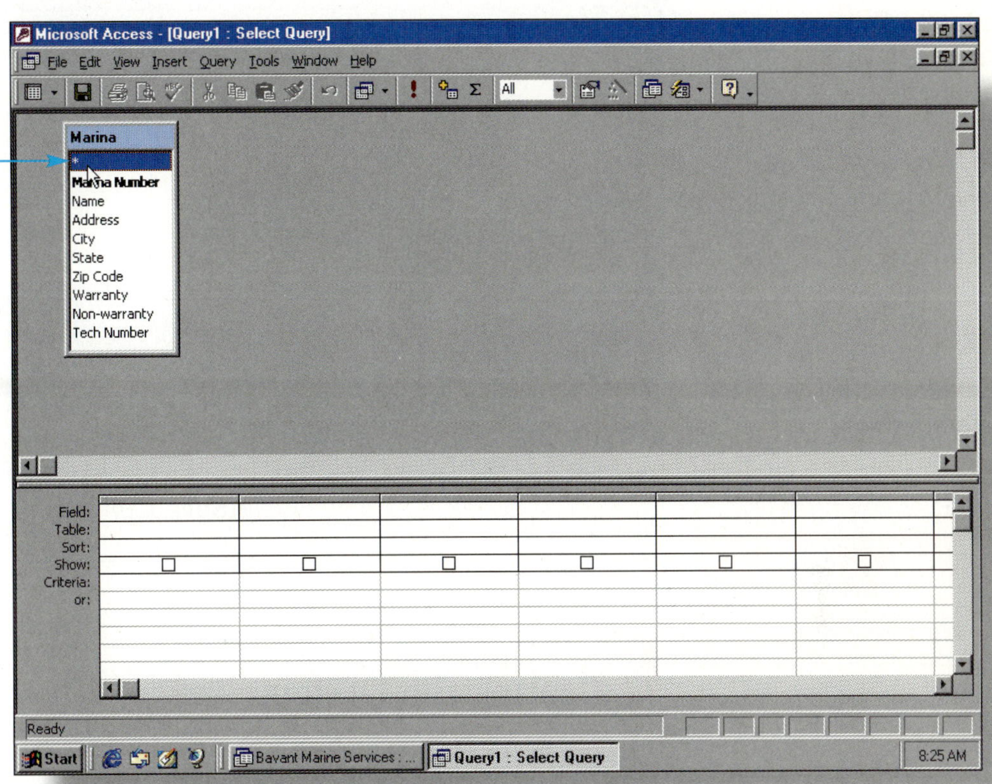

FIGURE 2-17

2 **Double-click the asterisk in the field list and then point to the Run button on the Query Design toolbar.**

The table name, Marina, followed by a period and an asterisk is added to the design grid (Figure 2-18), indicating all fields are included.

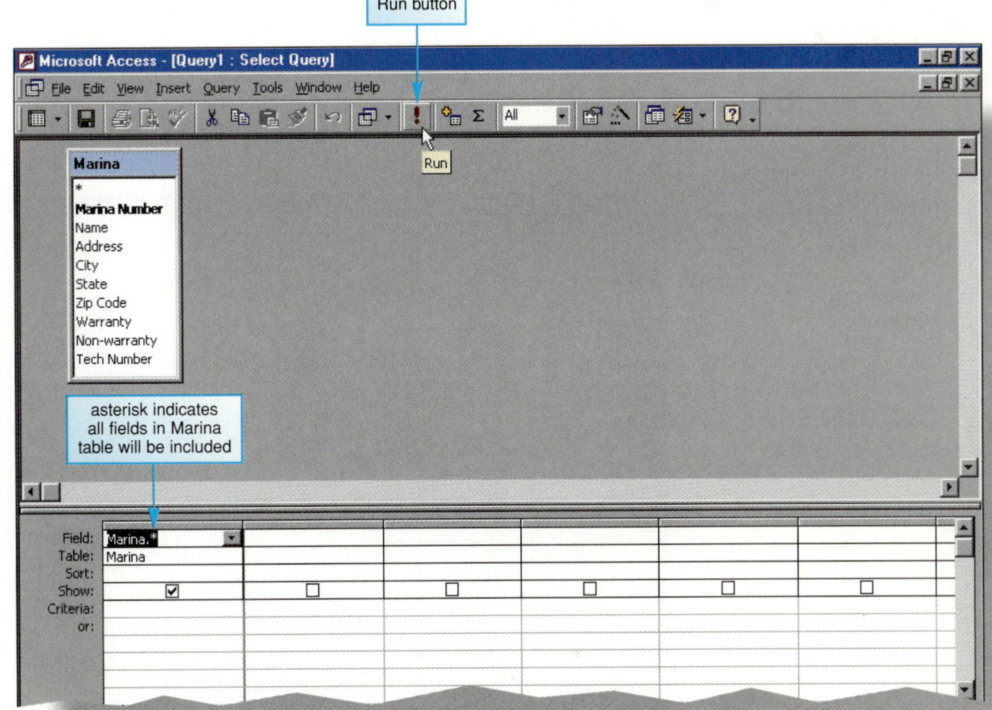

FIGURE 2-18

3 Click the Run button.

The results display and all fields in the Marina table are included (Figure 2-19). The Tech Number field does not display, because it does not fit on the screen.

4 Click the View button on the Query Datasheet toolbar to return to Design view.

Microsoft Access - [Query1 : Select Query]

View button

Marina Numbe	Name	Address	City	State	Zip Code	Warranty	Non-warranty
AD57	Alan's Docks	314 Central	Burton	MI	49611	$1,248.00	$597.75
AN75	Afton's Marina	21 West 8th	Glenview	MI	48121	$1,906.50	$831.25
BL72	Brite's Landing	281 Robin	Burton	MI	49611	$217.00	$0.00
EL25	Elend Marina	462 River	Torino	MI	48268	$413.50	$678.75
FB96	Fenton's Boats	36 Bayview	Cavela	MI	47926	$923.20	$657.50
FM22	Fedder Marina	283 Waterfront	Burton	MI	49611	$432.00	$0.00
JB92	JT Boat Club	28 Causeway	Torino	MI	48268	$0.00	$0.00
NW72	Nelson's Wharf	27 Lake	Masondale	MI	49832	$608.50	$520.00
SM72	Solton's Marine	867 Bay Ridge	Glenview	MI	48121	$462.50	$295.00
TR72	The Reef	92 East Bay	Woodview	MI	47212	$219.00	$0.00
						$0.00	$0.00

all fields included

FIGURE 2-19

Other Ways

1. Drag asterisk from field list to design grid
2. Click column in grid, click arrow, click Marina.

Clearing the Design Grid

If you make mistakes as you are creating a query, you can fix each one individually. Alternatively, you simply may want to **clear the query**; that is, clear out the entries in the design grid and start over. One way to clear out the entries is to close the Select Query window and then start a new query just as you did earlier. A simpler approach, however, is to click Clear Grid on the Edit menu.

Steps To Clear a Query

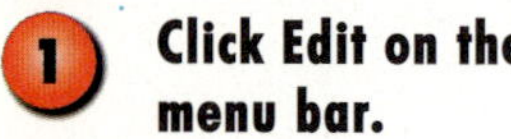

1 Click Edit on the menu bar.

The Edit menu displays (Figure 2-20).

2 Click Clear Grid.

Access clears the design grid so you can enter your next query.

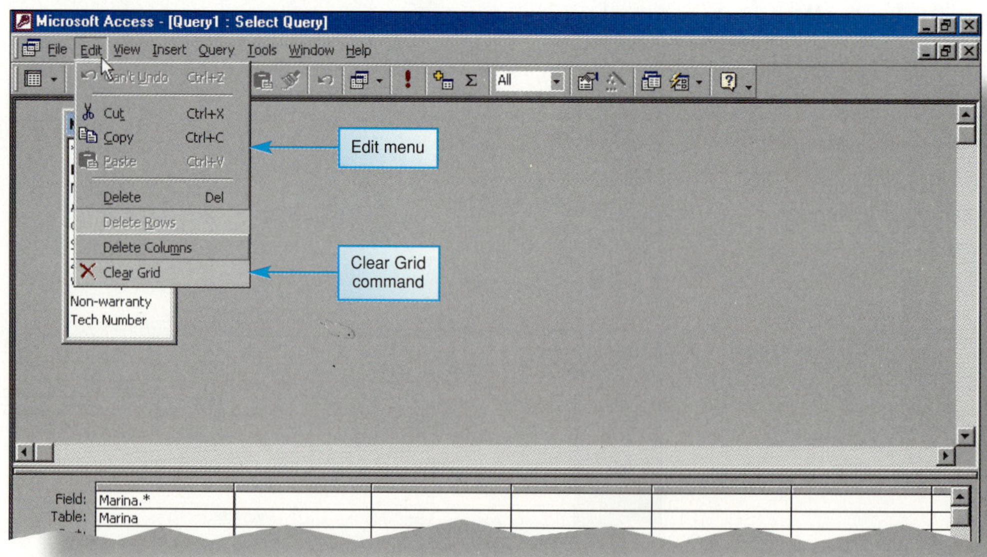

FIGURE 2-20

Entering Criteria

When you use queries, usually you are looking for those records that satisfy some criterion. You might want the name, warranty, and non-warranty amounts of the marina whose number is EL25, for example, or of those marinas whose names start with the letters, Fe. To enter criteria, enter them on the Criteria row in the design grid below the field name to which the criterion applies. For example, to indicate that the marina number must be EL25, you would type EL25 in the Criteria row below the Marina Number field. You first must add the Marina Number field to the design grid before you can enter the criterion.

The next examples illustrate the types of criteria that are available.

Using Text Data in Criteria

Some database systems require that text data must be enclosed in quotation marks. For example, to find customers in Michigan, "MI" would be entered as the criterion for the State field. In Access this is not necessary, because Access will insert the quotation marks automatically.

Using Text Data in Criteria

To use **text data** (data in a field whose type is text) in criteria, simply type the text in the Criteria row below the corresponding field name. The following steps query the Marina table and display the marina number, name, warranty amount, and non-warranty amount of marina EL25.

To Use Text Data in a Criterion

1 One by one, double-click the Marina Number, Name, Warranty, and Non-warranty fields to add them to the query. Point to the Criteria row for the first field in the design grid.

The Marina Number, Name, Warranty, and Non-warranty fields are added to the design grid (Figure 2-21). The mouse pointer on the Criteria entry for the first field (Marina Number) has changed shape to an I-beam.

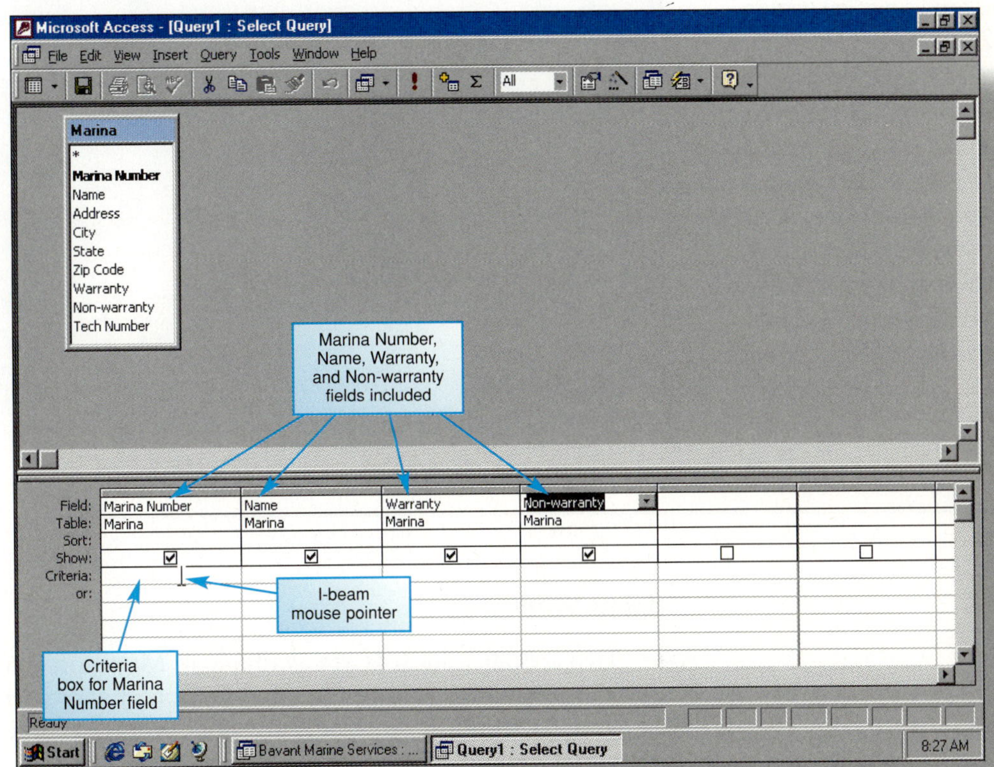

FIGURE 2-21

2 **Click the Criteria row, type** EL25 **as the criterion for the Marina Number field.**

The criterion is entered (Figure 2-22).

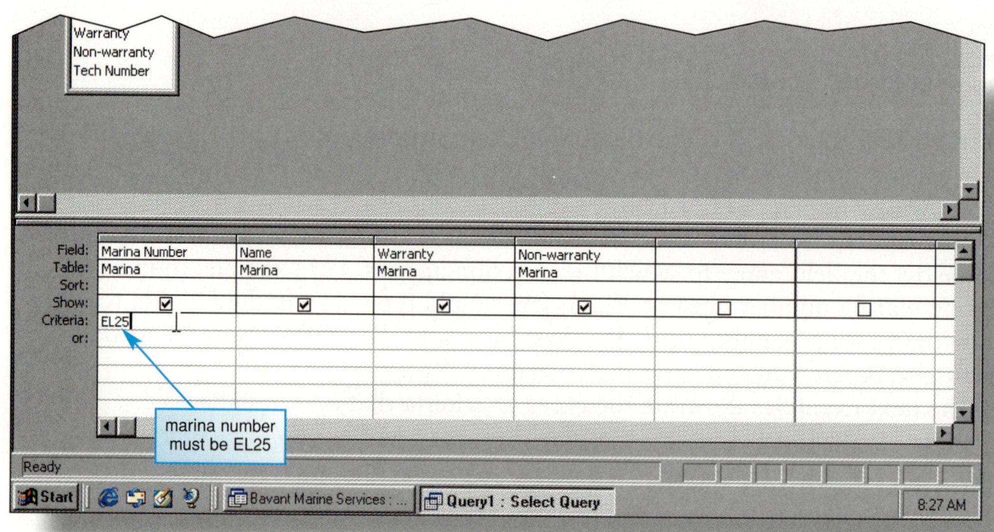

FIGURE 2-22

3 **Click the Run button to run the query.**

The results display (Figure 2-23). Only marina EL25 is included. (The extra blank row contains $0.00 in the Warranty and Non-warranty fields. Unlike text fields, which are left blank, number and currency fields in the extra row contain 0. Because the Warranty and Non-warranty fields are currency fields, the values display as $0.00.)

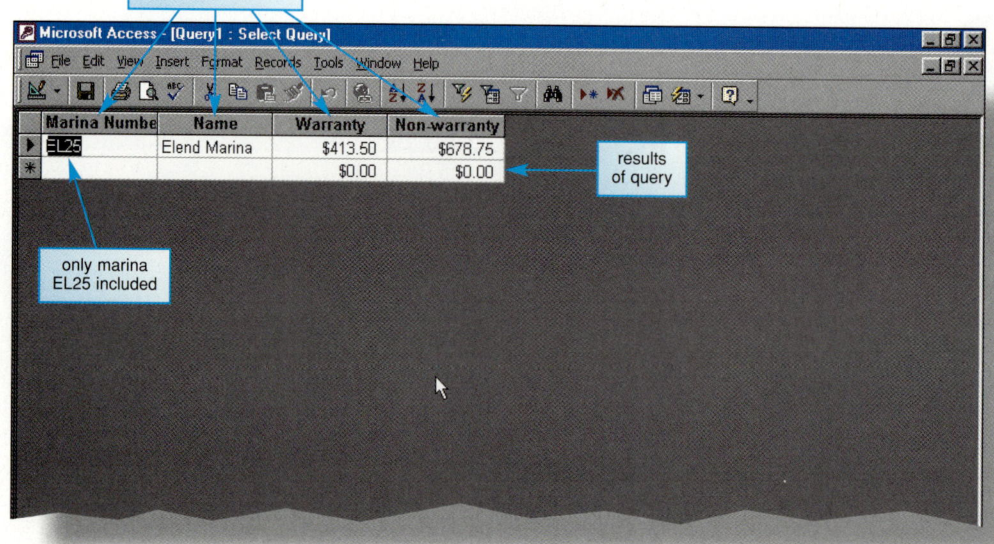

FIGURE 2-23

Using Wildcards

Two special wildcards are available in Microsoft Access. **Wildcards** are symbols that represent any character or combination of characters. The first of the two wildcards, the **asterisk (*)**, represents any collection of characters. Thus Gr* represents the letters, Gr, followed by any collection of characters. The other wildcard symbol is the **question mark (?)**, which represents any individual character. Thus t?m represents the letter, T, followed by any single character followed by the letter, m, such as Tim or Tom. To use a wildcard, begin the criterion with the special word LIKE.

The following steps use a wildcard to find the number, name, and address of those marinas whose names begin with Fe. Because you do not know how many characters will follow the Fe, the asterisk is appropriate.

To Use a Wildcard

1 Click the View button to return to Design view. Click the Criteria row under the Marina Number field and then use the DELETE or BACKSPACE key to delete the current entry (EL25). Click the Criteria row under the Name field. Type `LIKE Fe*` **as the entry.**

The criterion is entered (Figure 2-24).

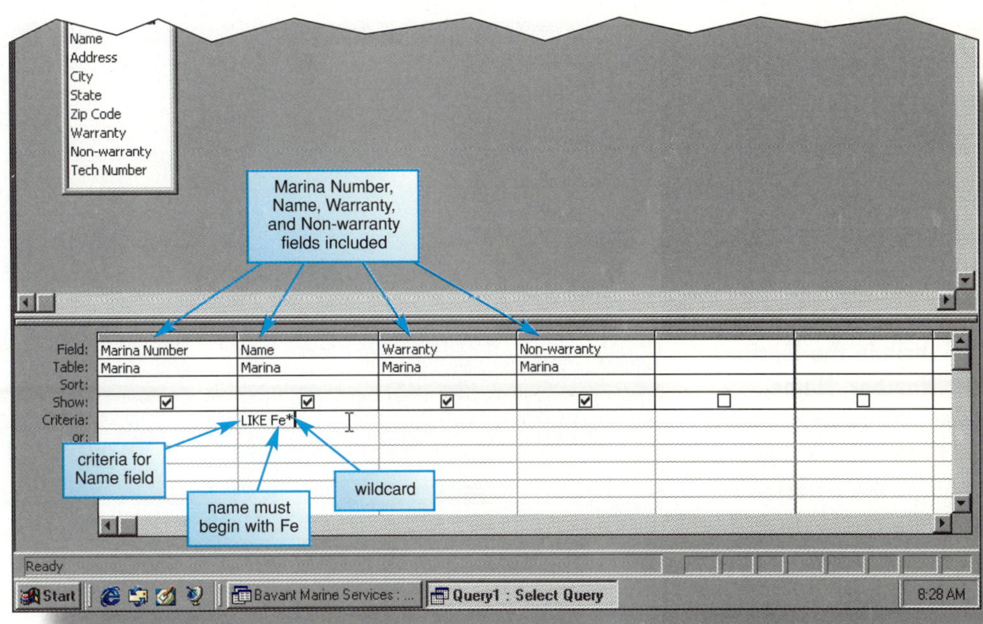

FIGURE 2-24

2 Click the Run button.

The results display (Figure 2-25). Only the marinas whose names start with Fe are included.

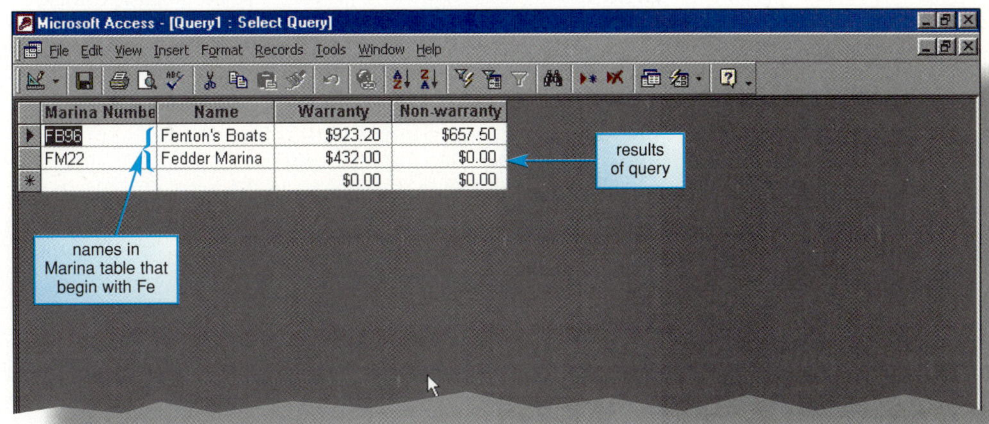

FIGURE 2-25

Criteria for a Field Not in the Result

In some cases, you may have criteria for a particular field that should not appear in the results of the query. For example, you may wish to see the marina number, name, address, and warranty amounts for all marinas located in Burton. The criteria involve the City field, which is not one of the fields to be included in the results.

To enter a criterion for the City field, it must be included in the design grid. Normally, this also would mean it would appear in the results. To prevent this from happening, remove the check mark from its Show check box in the Show row of the grid. The following steps illustrate the process by displaying the marina number, name, and warranty amounts for marinas located in Burton.

To Use Criteria for a Field Not Included in the Results

1 **Click the View button to return to Design view. On the Edit menu, click Clear Grid.**

Access clears the design grid so you can enter the next query.

2 **Include the Marina Number, Name, Address, Warranty, and City fields in the query. Type** `Burton` **as the criterion for the City field and then point to the City field's Show check box.**

The fields are included in the grid, and the criterion for the City field is entered (Figure 2-26).

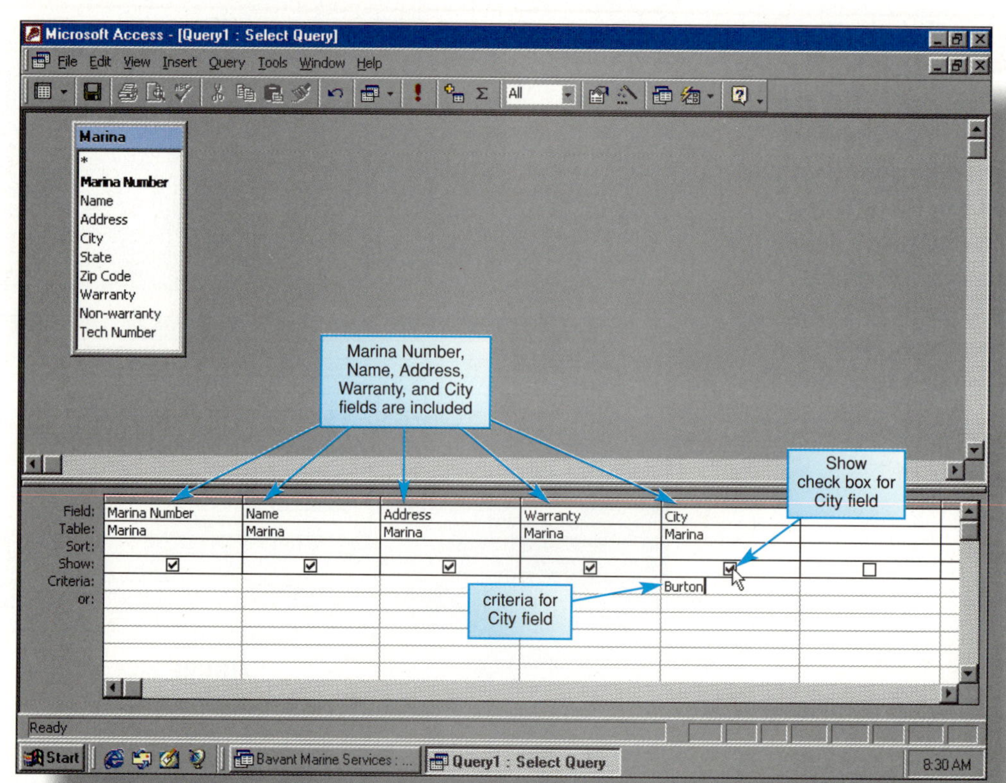

FIGURE 2-26

3 **Click the Show check box to remove the check mark.**

The check mark is removed from the Show check box for the City field (Figure 2-27), indicating it will not show in the result. Access has added quotation marks before and after Burton automatically.

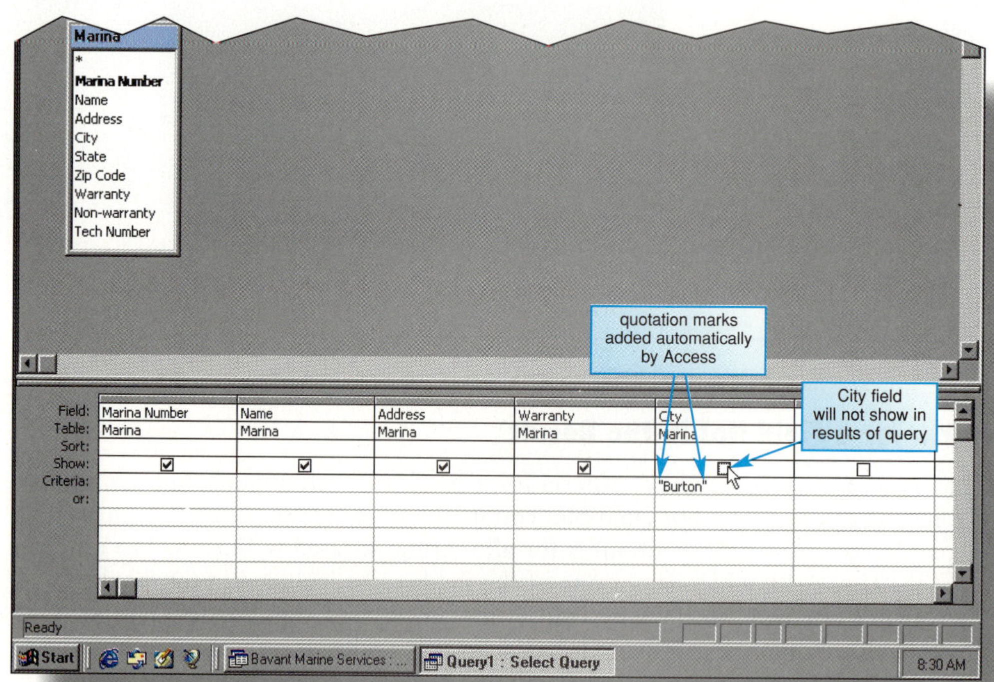

FIGURE 2-27

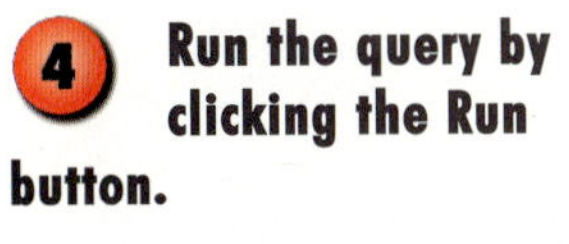

4 **Run the query by clicking the Run button.**

The results display (Figure 2-28). The City field does not display. The only marinas included are those located in Burton.

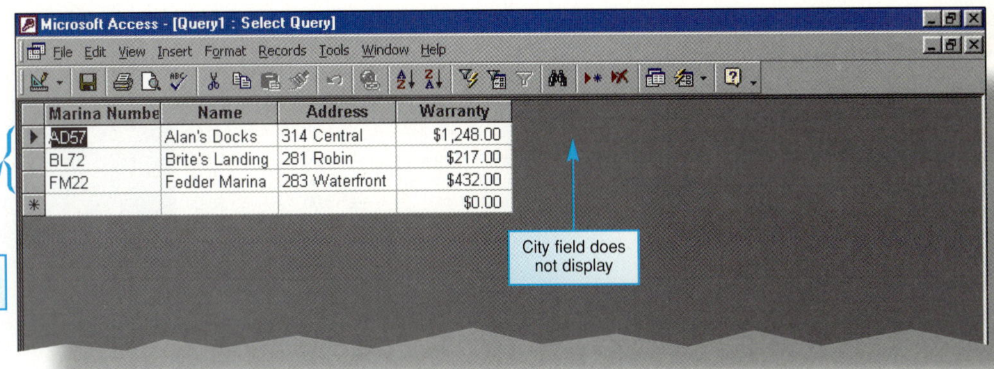

FIGURE 2-28

Using Numeric Data in Criteria

To enter a number in a criterion, type the number without any dollar signs or commas. Complete the following steps to display all marinas whose non-warranty amount is $0.00. To do so, you will need to type a 0 (zero) as the criterion for the Non-warranty field.

To Use a Number in a Criterion

1 **Click the View button to return to Design view. On the Edit menu, click Clear Grid.**

Access clears the design grid so you can enter the next query.

2 **Include the Marina Number, Name, Warranty, and Non-warranty fields in the query. Type** 0 **as the criterion for the Non-warranty field. You need not enter a dollar sign or decimal point in the criterion.**

The fields are selected and the criterion is entered (Figure 2-29).

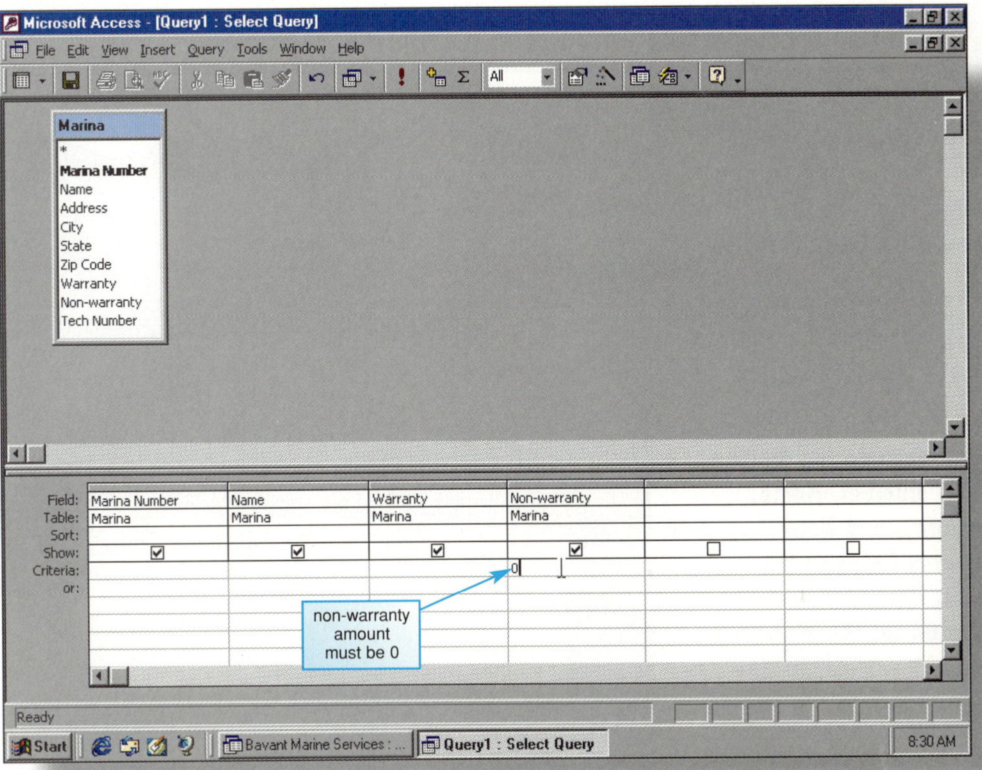

FIGURE 2-29

3 **Run the query by clicking the Run button.**

The results display (Figure 2-30). Only those marinas that have a non-warranty amount of $0.00 are included.

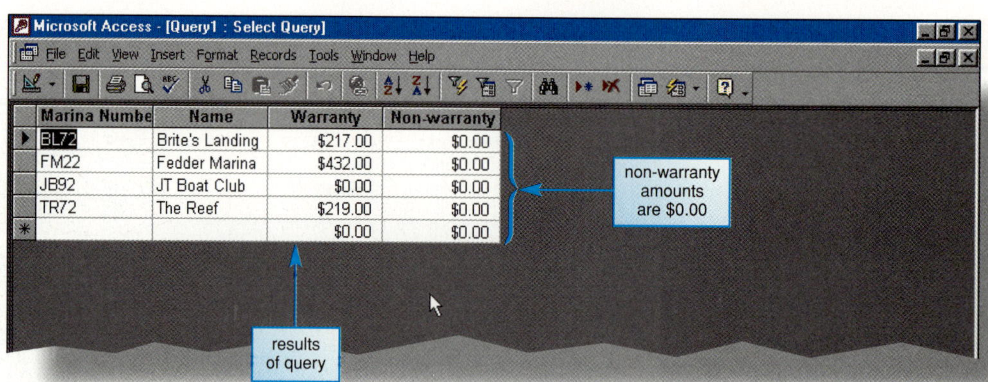

FIGURE 2-30

Using Comparison Operators

Unless you specify otherwise, Access assumes that the criteria you enter involve equality (exact matches). In the last query, for example, you were requesting those marinas whose non-warranty amount is equal to 0 (zero). If you want something other than an exact match, you must enter the appropriate **comparison operator**. The comparison operators are > (greater than), < (less than), >= (greater than or equal to), <= (less than or equal to), and NOT (not equal to).

Perform the following steps to use the > operator to find all marinas whose warranty amount is more than $1,000.

To Use a Comparison Operator in a Criterion

1 **Click the View button to return to Design view. On the Edit menu, click Clear Grid.**

Access clears the design grid so you can enter the next query.

2 **Include the Marina Number, Name, Warranty, and Non-warranty fields in the query. Type** >1000 **as the criterion for the Warranty field.**

The fields are selected and the criterion is entered (Figure 2-31).

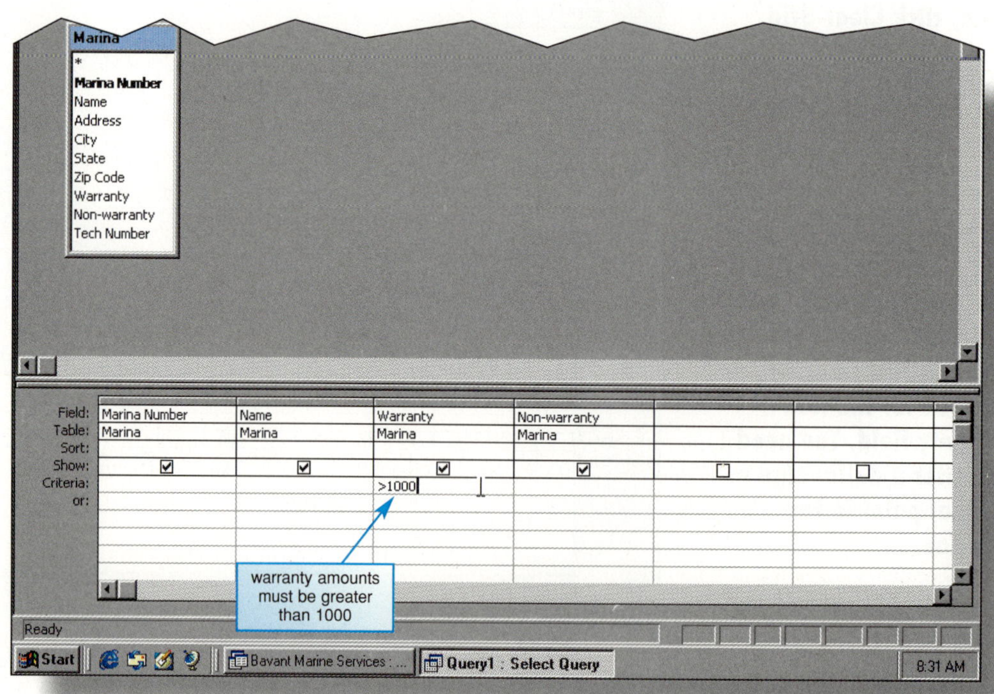

FIGURE 2-31

3 Run the query.

The results display (Figure 2-32). Only those marinas that have a warranty amount greater than $1,000 are included.

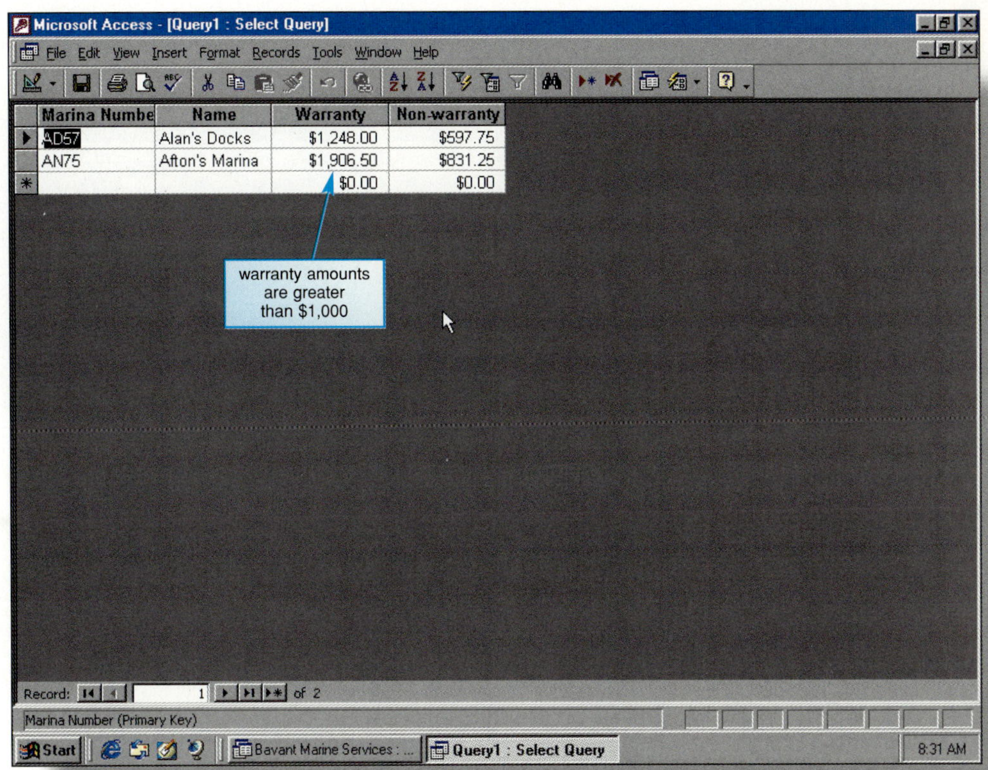

FIGURE 2-32

Using Compound Criteria

Often you will have more than one criterion that the data for which you are searching must satisfy. This type of criterion is called a **compound criterion**. Two types of compound criteria exist.

In **AND criterion**, each individual criterion must be true in order for the compound criterion to be true. For example, an AND criterion would allow you to find those marinas that have a warranty amount greater than $1,000 and whose technician is technician 36.

Conversely, an **OR criterion** is true provided either individual criterion is true. An OR criterion would allow you to find those marinas that have a warranty amount more than $1,000 or whose technician is technician 36. In this case, any marina whose warranty amount is greater than $1,000 would be included in the results whether or not the marina's technician is technician 36. Likewise, any marina whose technician is technician 36 would be included whether or not the marina had a warranty amount greater than $1,000.

Using AND Criteria

To combine criteria with AND, place the criteria on the same line. Perform the following steps to use an AND criterion to find those marinas whose warranty amount is greater than $1,000 and whose technician is technician 36.

To Use a Compound Criterion Involving AND

1 Click the View button to return to Design view. Include the Tech Number field in the query. If necessary, click the Criteria entry for the Warranty field, and then type >1000 as the criterion for the Warranty field. Click the Criteria entry for the Tech Number field and then type 36 as the criterion for the Tech Number field.

Criteria have been entered for the Warranty and Tech Number fields (Figure 2-33).

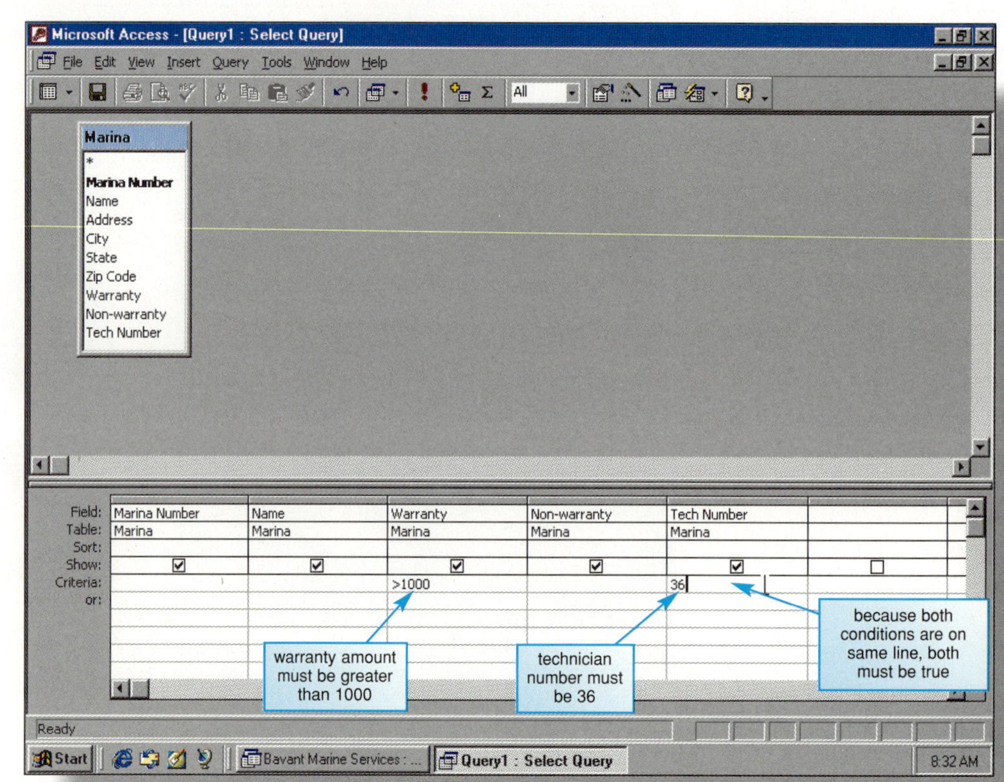

FIGURE 2-33

2 Run the query.

The results display (Figure 2-34). Only the single marina whose warranty amount is greater than $1,000.00 and whose technician number is 36 is included.

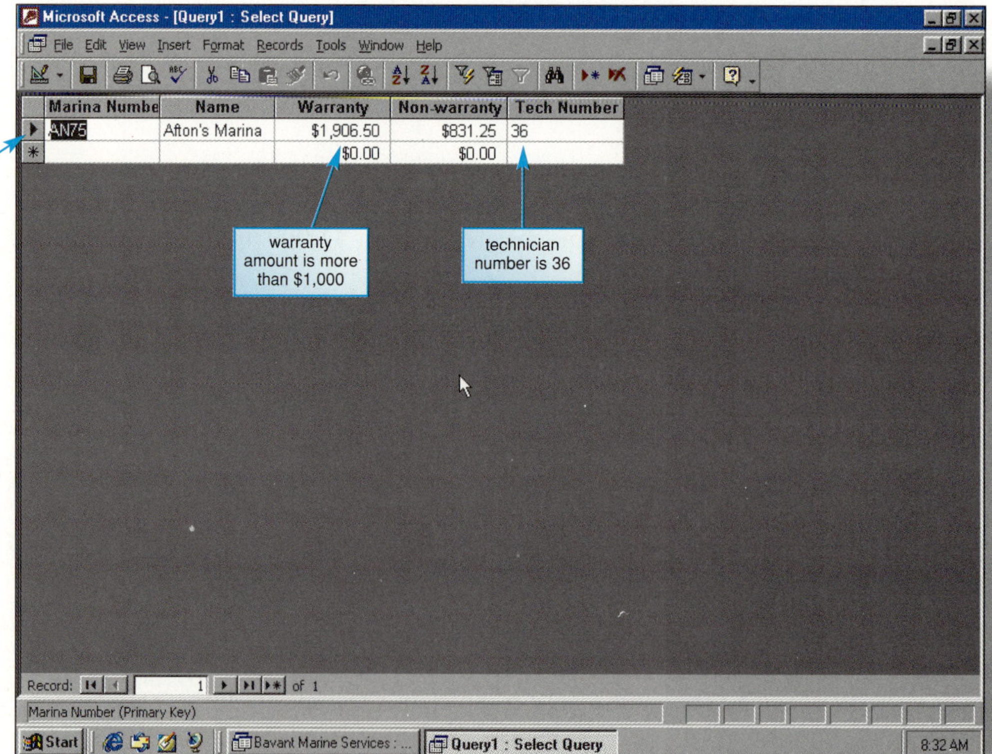

FIGURE 2-34

Using OR Criteria

To combine criteria with OR, the criteria must go on separate lines in the Criteria area of the grid. The following steps use an OR criterion to find those marinas whose warranty amount is greater than $1,000.00 or whose technician is technician 36 (or both).

To Use a Compound Criterion Involving OR

1 Click the View button to return to Design view.

2 Click the Criteria entry for the Tech Number field. Use the BACKSPACE key to delete the entry ("36"). Click the or row (below the Criteria row) for the Tech Number field and then type 36 **as the entry.**

The criteria are entered for the Warranty and Tech Number fields on different lines (Figure 2-35).

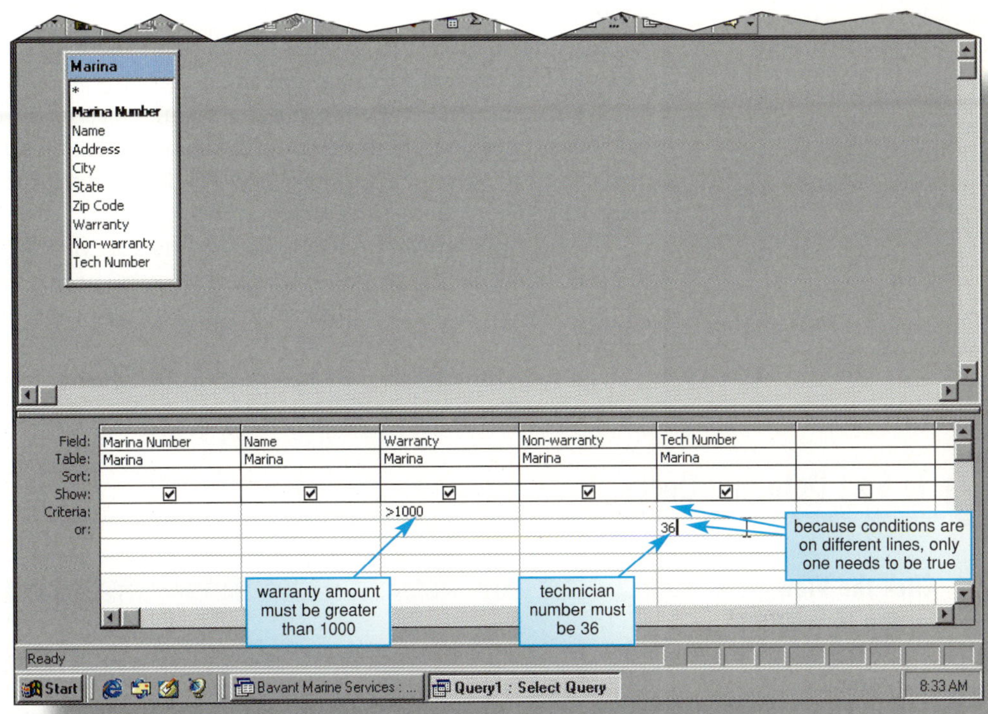

FIGURE 2-35

3 Run the query.

The results display (Figure 2-36). Only those marinas whose warranty amount is greater than $1,000.00 or whose technician number is 36 are included.

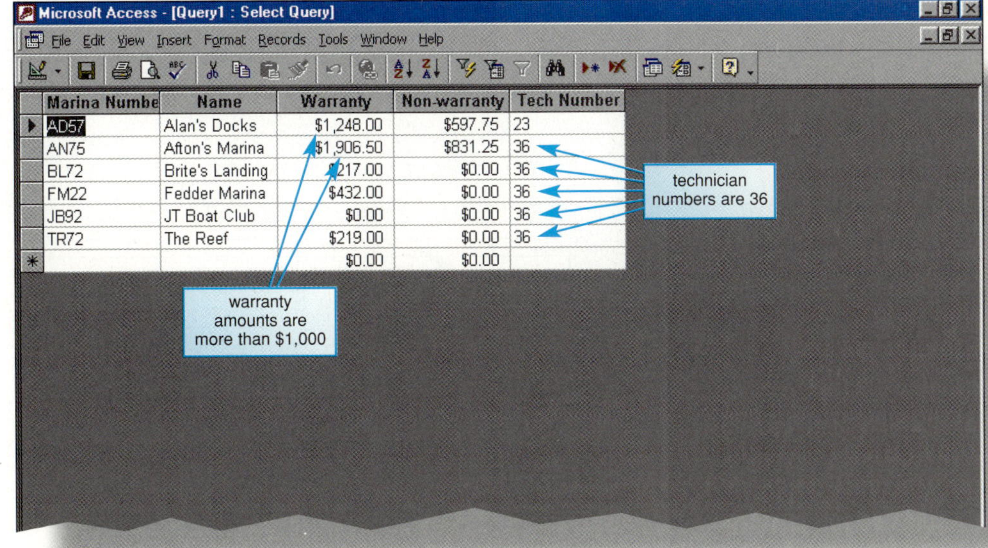

Marina Numbe	Name	Warranty	Non-warranty	Tech Number
AD57	Alan's Docks	$1,248.00	$597.75	23
AN75	Afton's Marina	$1,906.50	$831.25	36
BL72	Brite's Landing	$217.00	$0.00	36
FM22	Fedder Marina	$432.00	$0.00	36
JB92	JT Boat Club	$0.00	$0.00	36
TR72	The Reef	$219.00	$0.00	36
		$0.00	$0.00	

FIGURE 2-36

Sorting Data in a Query

In some queries, the order in which the records are displayed really does not matter. All you need be concerned about are the records that appear in the results. It does not matter which one is first or which one is last.

In other queries, however, the order can be very important. You may want to see the cities in which marinas are located and would like them arranged alphabetically. Perhaps you want to see the marinas listed by technician number. Further, within all the marinas of any given technician, you would like them to be listed by warranty amount.

To order the records in the answer to a query in a particular way, you **sort** the records. The field or fields on which the records are sorted is called the **sort key**. If you are sorting on more than one field (such as sorting by warranty amount within technician number), the more important field (Tech Number) is called the **major key** (also called the **primary sort key**) and the less important field (Warranty) is called the **minor key** (also called the **secondary sort key**).

To sort in Microsoft Access, specify the sort order in the Sort line of the design grid below the field that is the sort key. If you specify more than one sort key, the sort key on the left will be the major sort key and the one on the right will be the minor key.

The following steps sort the cities in the Marina table.

Compound Criteria

Access to compound criteria is precisely the approach that was proposed for Query-by-Example. (Placing criteria on the same line indicates they are connected by the word AND. Placing them on separate lines indicates they are connected by the word OR.)

To Sort Data in a Query

1 **Click the View button to return to Design view. On the Edit menu, click Clear Grid.**

2 **Include the City field in the design grid. Click the Sort row below the City field, and then click the Sort row arrow that displays.**

The City field is included (Figure 2-37). A list of available sort orders displays.

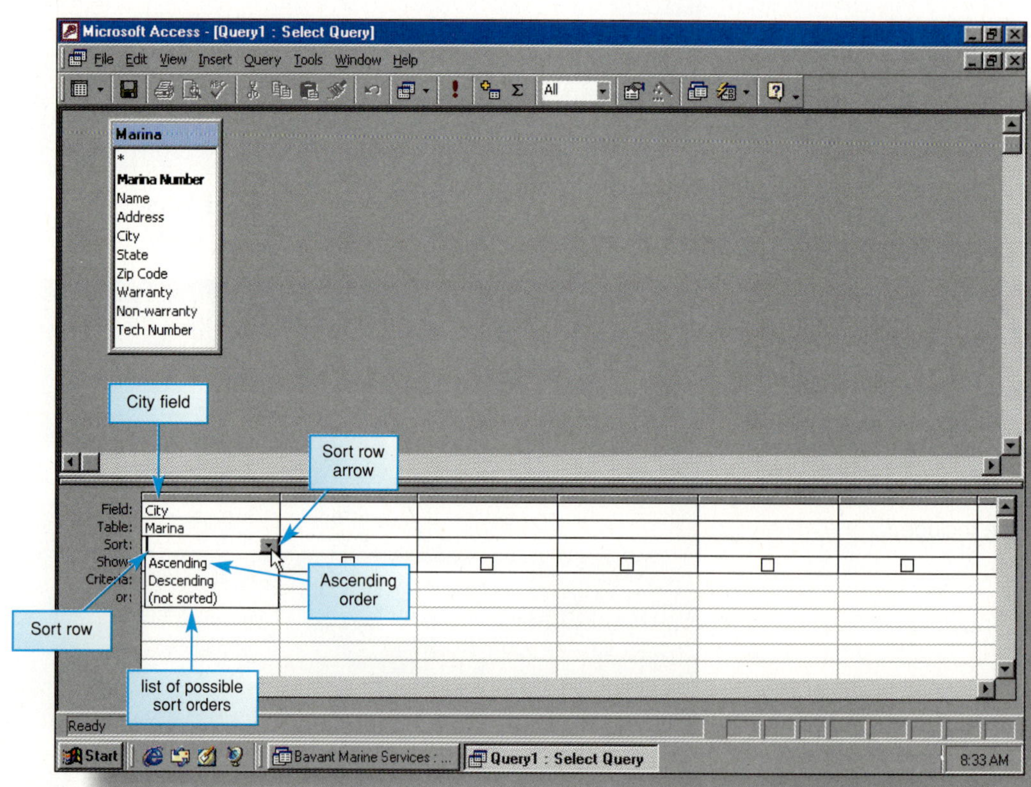

FIGURE 2-37

Click Ascending.

Ascending is selected as the order (Figure 2-38).

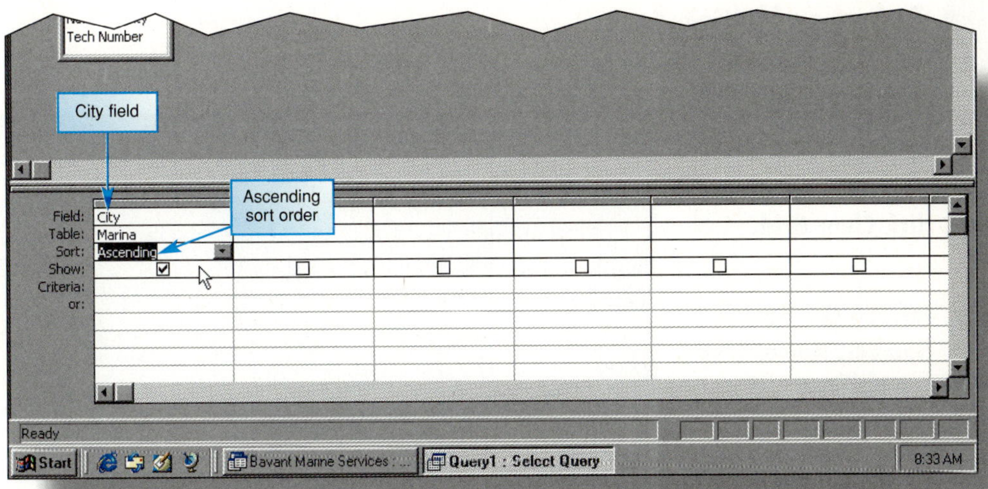

FIGURE 2-38

Run the query.

The results contain the cities from the Marina table (Figure 2-39). The cities display in alphabetical order. Duplicates, that is, identical rows, are included.

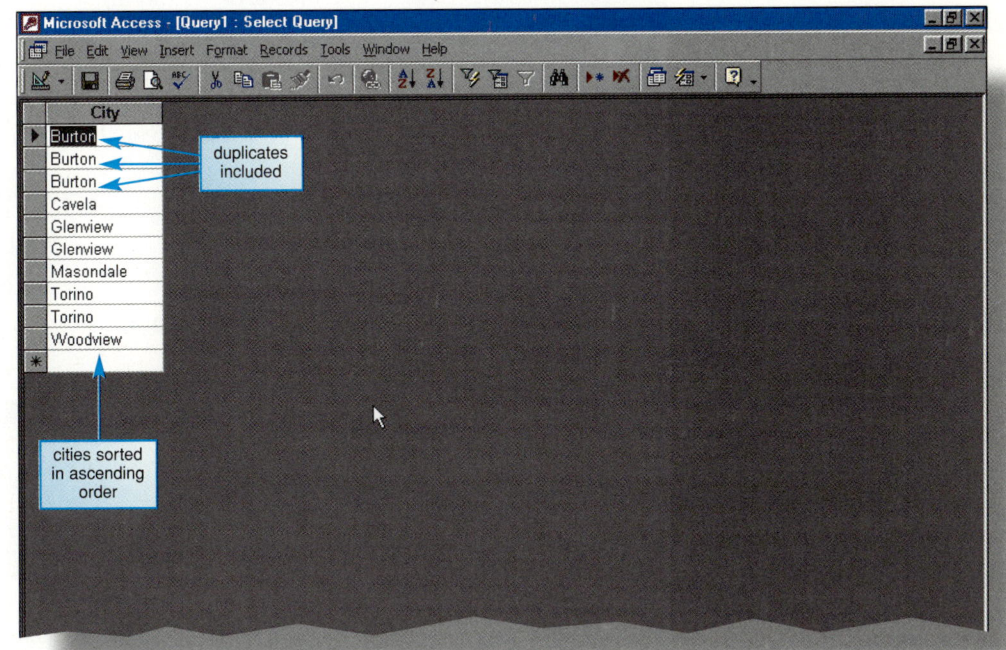

FIGURE 2-39

Sorting on Multiple Keys

The next example lists the number, name, technician number, and warranty amount for all marinas. The data is to be sorted by descending warranty amount (high to low) within technician number, which means that the Tech Number field is the major key and the Warranty field is the minor key. It also means that the Warranty field should be sorted in descending order.

The following steps accomplish this sorting by specifying the Tech Number and Warranty fields as sort keys and by selecting Descending as the sort order for the Warranty field.

To Sort on Multiple Keys

1 **Click the View button to return to Design view. On the Edit menu, click Clear Grid.**

2 **Include the Marina Number, Name, Tech Number, and Warranty fields in the query in this order. Select Ascending as the sort order for the Tech Number field and Descending as the sort order for the Warranty field (Figure 2-40).**

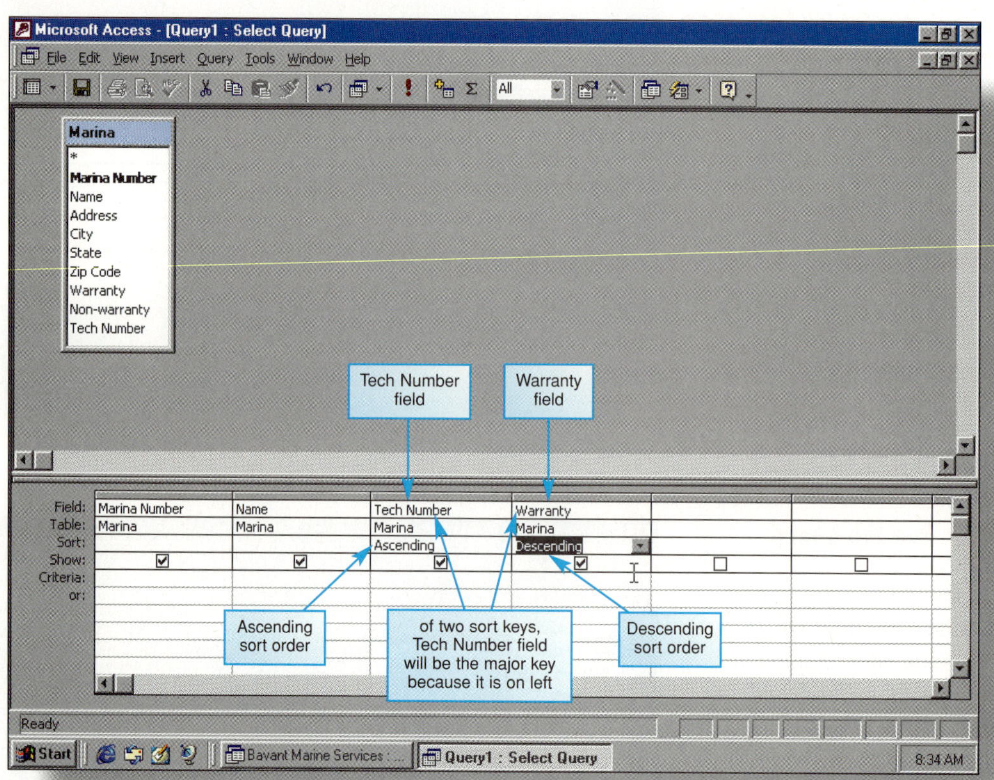

FIGURE 2-40

3 **Run the query.**

The results display (Figure 2-41). The marinas are sorted by technician number. Within the collection of marinas having the same technician, the marinas are sorted by descending warranty amount.

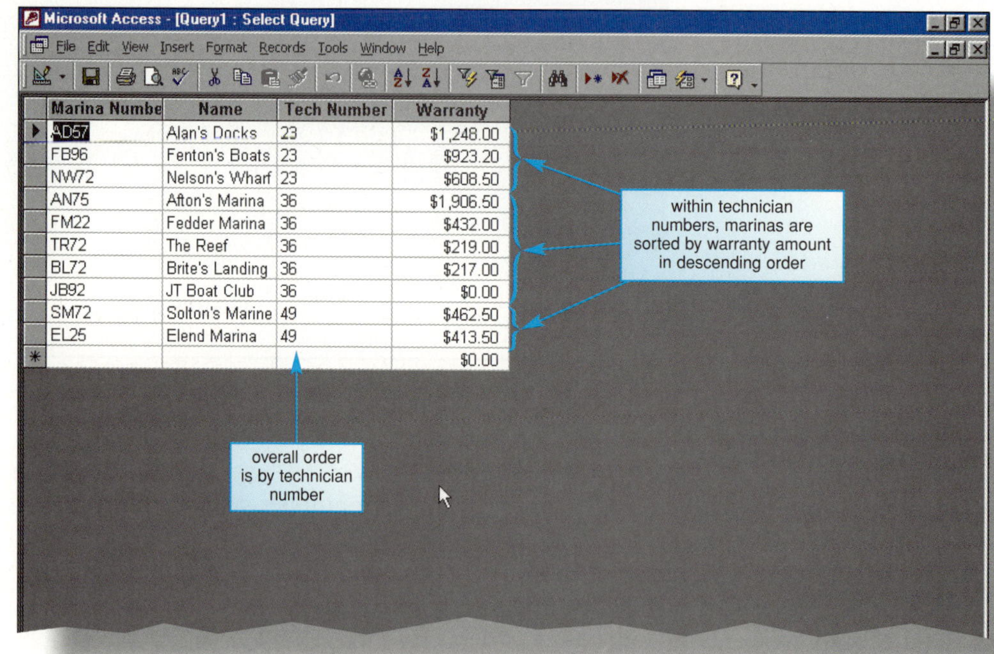

Marina Numbe	Name	Tech Number	Warranty
AD57	Alan's Docks	23	$1,248.00
FB96	Fenton's Boats	23	$923.20
NW72	Nelson's Wharf	23	$608.50
AN75	Afton's Marina	36	$1,906.50
FM22	Fedder Marina	36	$432.00
TR72	The Reef	36	$219.00
BL72	Brite's Landing	36	$217.00
JB92	JT Boat Club	36	$0.00
SM72	Solton's Marine	49	$462.50
EL25	Elend Marina	49	$413.50
			$0.00

FIGURE 2-41

It is important to remember that the major sort key must appear to the left of the minor sort key in the design grid. If you attempted to sort by warranty amount within technician number, but placed the Warranty field to the left of the Tech Number field, your results would be incorrect.

Sorting Data in a Query

When sorting data in a query, the records in the underlying tables (the tables on which the query is based) are not actually rearranged. Instead, the DBMS will determine the most efficient method of simply displaying the records in the requested order. The records in the underlying tables remain in their original order.

Omitting Duplicates

As you saw earlier, when you sort data, duplicates are included. In Figure 2-39 on page A 2.27, for example, Glenview appeared twice, Burton appeared three times, and Torino appeared twice. If you do not want duplicates included, use the Properties command and change the Unique Values property to Yes. Perform the following steps to produce a sorted list of the cities in the Marina table in which each city is listed only once.

To Omit Duplicates

1 **Click the View button to return to Design view. On the Edit menu, click Clear Grid.**

2 **Include the City field, click Ascending as the sort order, and right-click the second field in the design grid (the empty field following City). (You must right-click the second field or you will not get the correct results.)**

The shortcut menu displays (Figure 2-42).

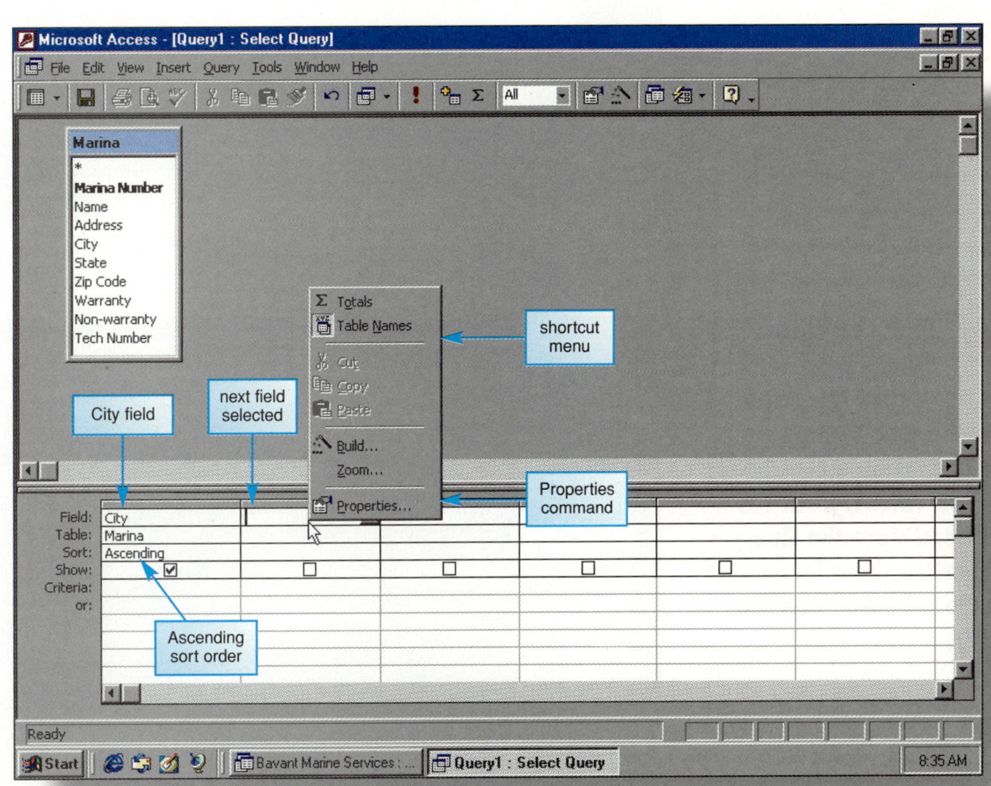

FIGURE 2-42

Click Properties on the shortcut menu.

The Query Properties sheet displays (Figure 2-43). (If your sheet looks different, you right-clicked the wrong place. Close the sheet that displays and right-click the second field in the grid.)

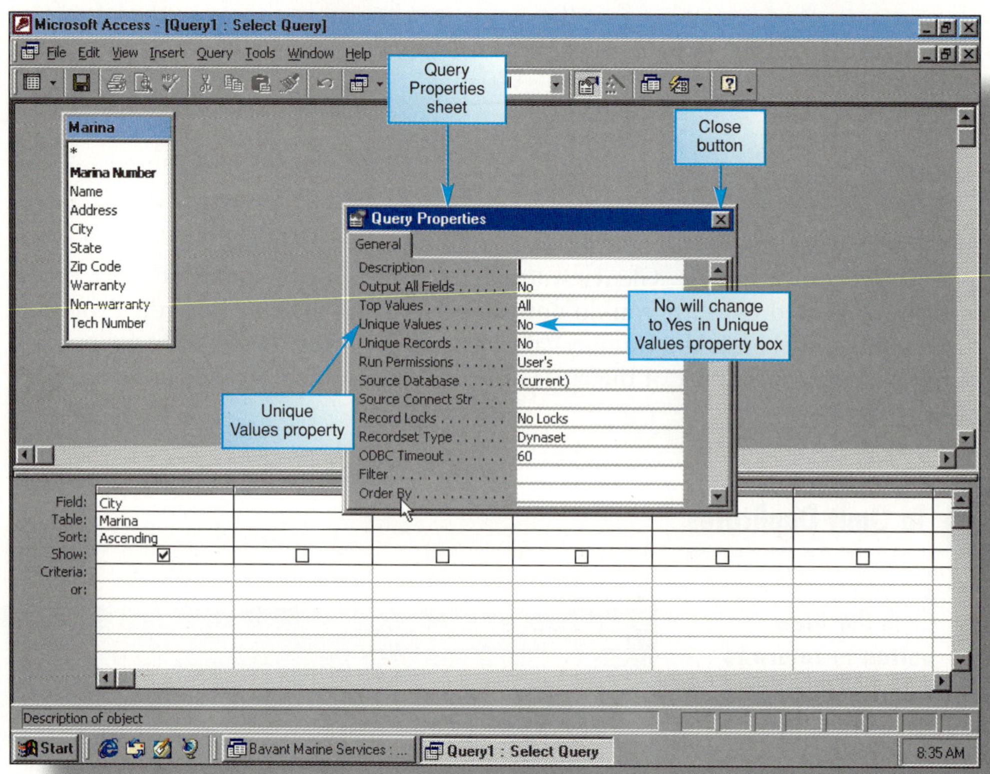

FIGURE 2-43

4 Click the Unique Values property box, and then click the arrow that displays to produce a list of available choices for Unique Values. Click Yes and then close the Query Properties sheet by clicking its Close button. Run the query.

The results display (Figure 2-44). The cities are sorted alphabetically. Each city is included only once.

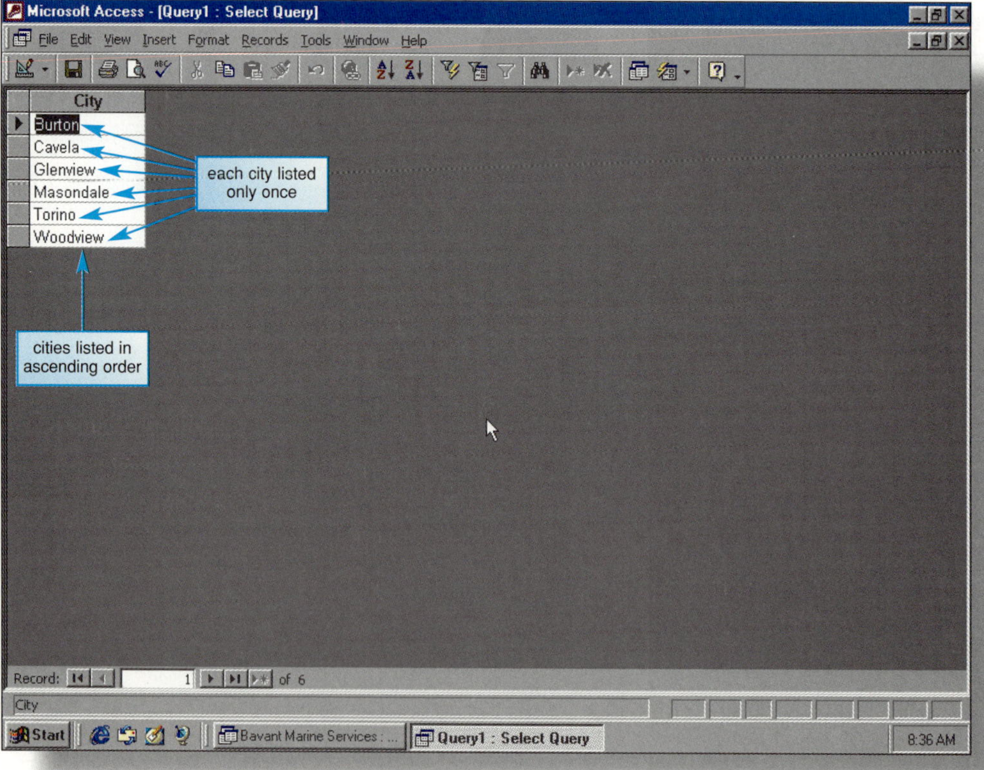

FIGURE 2-44

Other Ways

1. Click Properties button on toolbar
2. On View menu click Properties

Joining Tables

Bavant Marine Services needs to list the number and name of each marina along with the number and name of the marina's technician. The marina's name is in the Marina table, whereas the technician's name is in the Technician table. Thus, this query cannot be satisfied using a single table. You need to **join** the tables; that is, to find records in the two tables that have identical values in matching fields (Figure 2-45). In this example, you need to find records in the Marina table and the Technician table that have the same value in the Tech Number fields.

More About 2000

Joining Tables

One of the key features that distinguishes database management systems from file systems is the ability to join tables, that is, to create queries that draw data from two or more tables. Several types of joins are available. For more information, visit the Access 2000 More About Web page (www.scsite.com/ac2000/more.htm) and click Join Types.

give me the number and name of each Marina along with the number and name of the marina's technician

Marina table

MARINA NUMBER	NAME	. . .	TECH NUMBER
AD57	Alan's Docks	. . .	23
AN75	Afton's Marina	. . .	36
BL72	Brite's Landing	. . .	36
EL25	Elend Marina	. . .	49
FB96	Fenton's Boats	. . .	23
FM22	Fedder Marina	. . .	36
JB92	JT Boat Club	. . .	36
NW72	Nelson's Wharf	. . .	23
SM72	Solton's Marine	. . .	49
TR72	The Reef	. . .	36

Technician table

TECH NUMBER	LAST NAME	FIRST NAME	. . .
23	Anderson	Trista	. . .
36	Nichols	Ashton	. . .
49	Gomez	Teresa	. . .

MARINA NUMBER	NAME	. . .	TECH NUMBER	LAST NAME	FIRST NAME	. . .
AD57	Alan's Docks	. . .	23	Anderson	Trista	. . .
AN75	Afton's Marina	. . .	36	Nichols	Ashton	. . .
BL72	Brite's Landing	. . .	36	Nichols	Ashton	. . .
EL25	Elend Marina	. . .	49	Gomez	Teresa	. . .
FB96	Fenton's Boats	. . .	23	Anderson	Trista	. . .
FM22	Fedder Marina	. . .	36	Nichols	Ashton	. . .
JB92	JT Boat Club	. . .	36	Nichols	Ashton	. . .
NW72	Nelson's Wharf	. . .	23	Anderson	Trista	. . .
SM72	Solton's Marine	. . .	49	Gomez	Teresa	. . .
TR72	The Reef	. . .	36	Nichols	Ashton	. . .

FIGURE 2-45

To join tables in Access, first you bring field lists for both tables to the upper pane of the Select Query window. Access will draw a line, called a **join line**, between matching fields in the two tables indicating that the tables are related. You then can select fields from either table. Access will join the tables automatically.

The first step is to add an additional table, the Technician table, to the query. A join line will display connecting the Tech Number fields in the two field lists. This join line indicates how the tables are related; that is, linked through these matching fields. (If you fail to give the matching fields the same name, Access will not insert the line. You can insert it manually, however, by clicking one of the two matching fields and dragging the mouse pointer to the other matching field.)

The following steps add the Technician table and then select the appropriate fields.

To Join Tables

1 Click the View button to return to Design view. On the Edit menu, click Clear Grid.

2 Right-click any open area in the upper pane of the Query1 : Select Query window.

The shortcut menu displays (Figure 2-46).

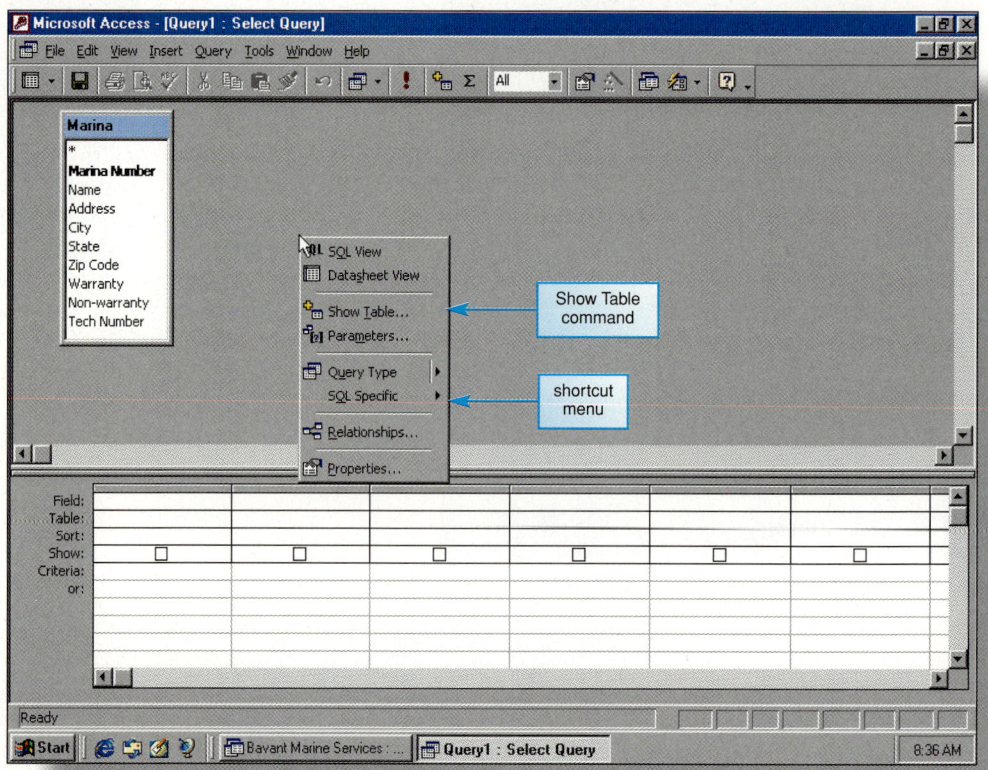

FIGURE 2-46

3 **Click Show Table on the shortcut menu.**

The Show Table dialog box displays (Figure 2-47).

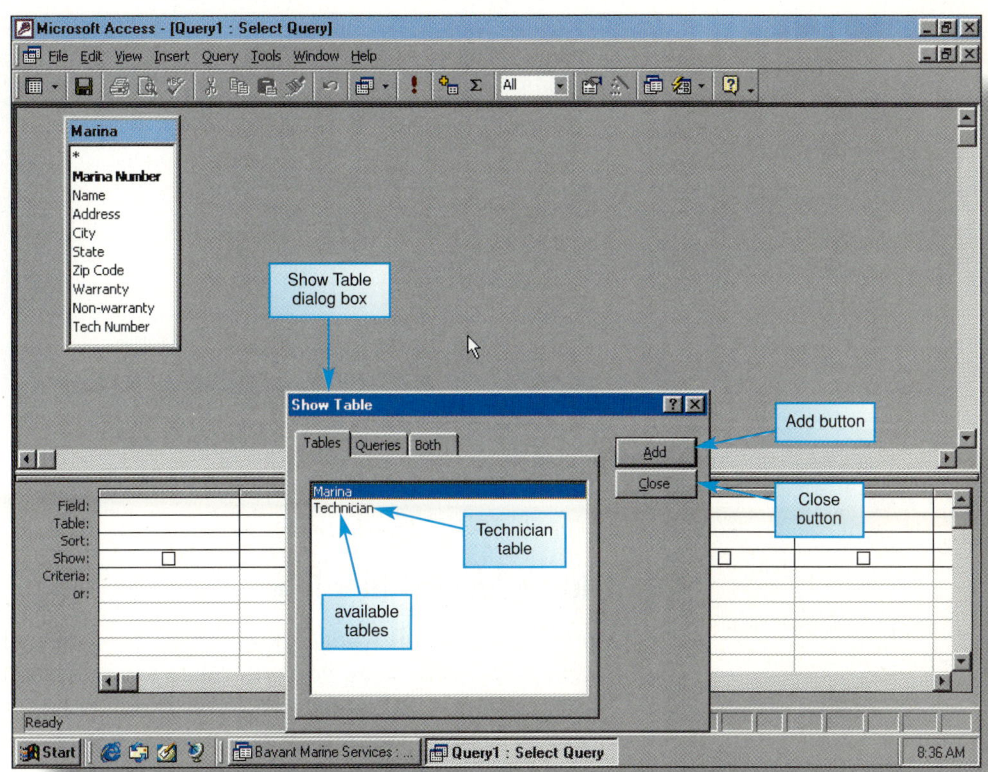

FIGURE 2-47

4 **Click Technician to select the Technician table and then click the Add button. Close the Show Table dialog box by clicking the Close button. Expand the size of the field list so all the fields in the Technician table display. Include the Marina Number, Name, and Tech Number fields from the Marina table and the Last Name and First Name fields from the Technician table.**

The fields from both tables are included (Figure 2-48).

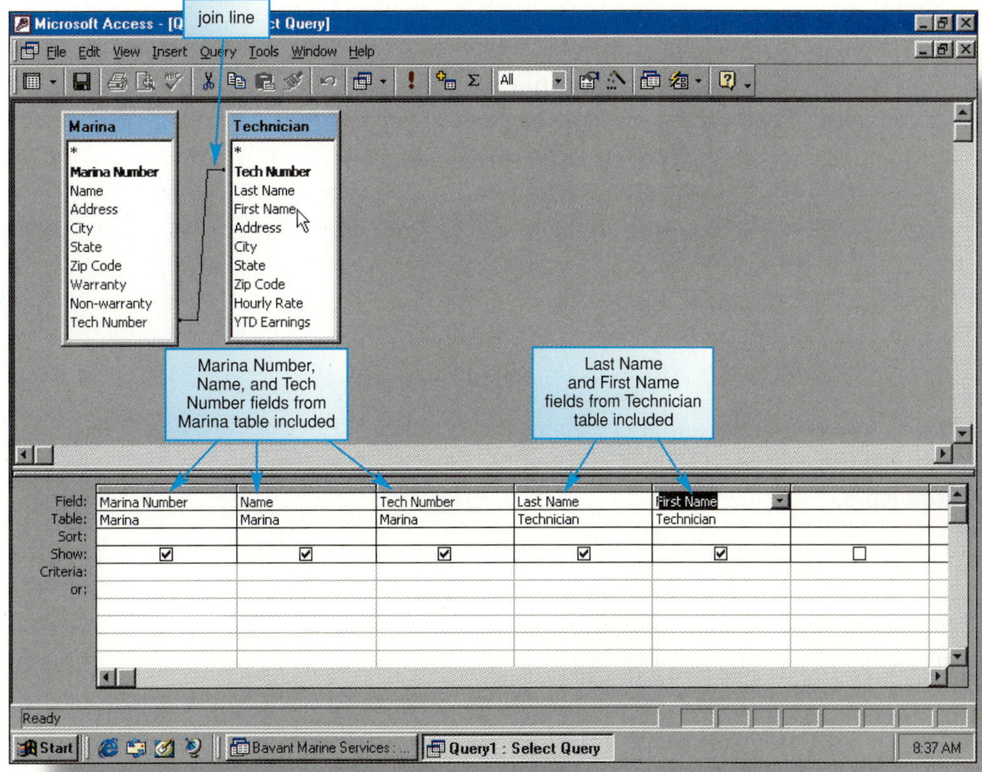

FIGURE 2-48

Run the query.

The results display (Figure 2-49) and contain data from both the Marina and the Technician tables.

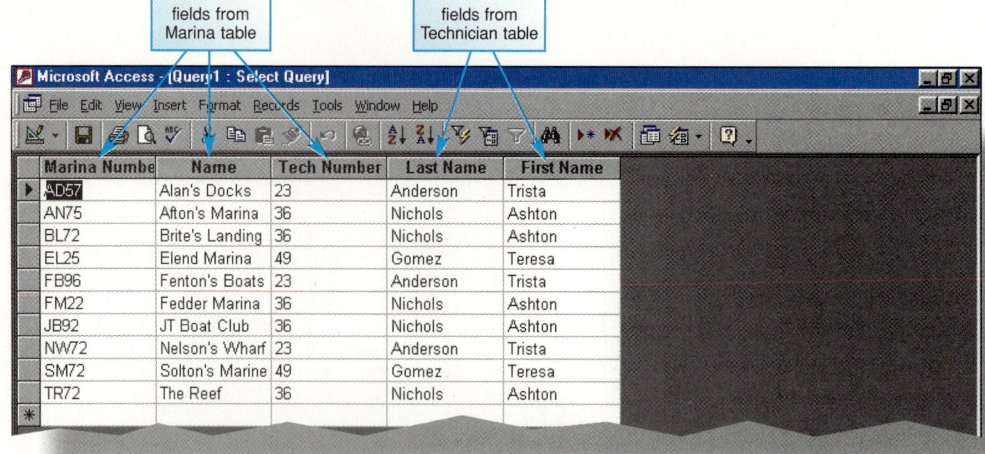

fields from Marina table
fields from Technician table
Microsoft Access - [Query1 : Select Query]
File Edit View Insert Format Records Tools Window Help
Marina Number | Name | Tech Number | Last Name | First Name
AD57 | Alan's Docks | 23 | Anderson | Trista
AN75 | Afton's Marina | 36 | Nichols | Ashton
BL72 | Brite's Landing | 36 | Nichols | Ashton
EL25 | Elend Marina | 49 | Gomez | Teresa
FB96 | Fenton's Boats | 23 | Anderson | Trista
FM22 | Fedder Marina | 36 | Nichols | Ashton
JB92 | JT Boat Club | 36 | Nichols | Ashton
NW72 | Nelson's Wharf | 23 | Anderson | Trista
SM72 | Solton's Marine | 49 | Gomez | Teresa
TR72 | The Reef | 36 | Nichols | Ashton

FIGURE 2-49

1. Click Show Table button on toolbar
2. On Query menu click Show Table

Restricting Records in a Join

Sometimes you will want to join tables, but you will not want to include all possible records. In such cases, you will relate the tables and include fields just as you did before. You also will include criteria. For example, to include the same fields as in the previous query, but only those marinas whose warranty amount is more than $1,000, you will make the same entries as before and then also type >1000 as a criterion for the Warranty field.

The following steps modify the query from the previous example to restrict the records that will be included in the join.

To Restrict the Records in a Join

Click the View button to return to Design view. Add the Warranty field to the query. Type >1000 as the criterion for the Warranty field and then click the Show check box for the Warranty field to remove the check mark.

The Warranty field displays in the design grid (Figure 2-50). A criterion is entered for the Warranty field and the Show check box is empty, indicating that the field will not display in the results of the query.

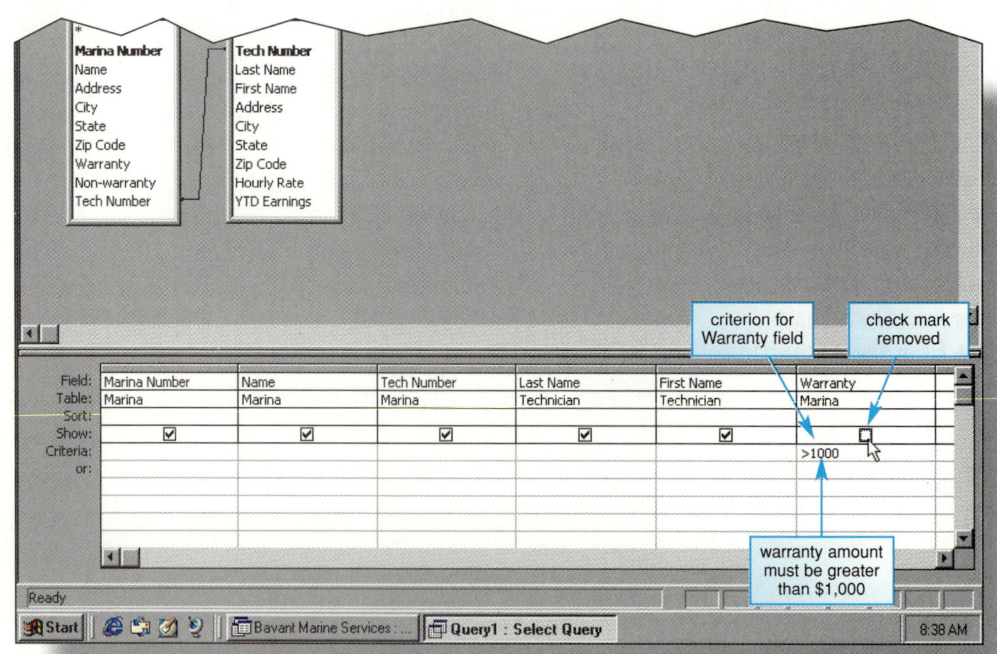

FIGURE 2-50

2 **Run the query.**

The results display (Figure 2-51). Only those marinas with a warranty amount greater than $1,000 display in the result. The Warranty field does not display.

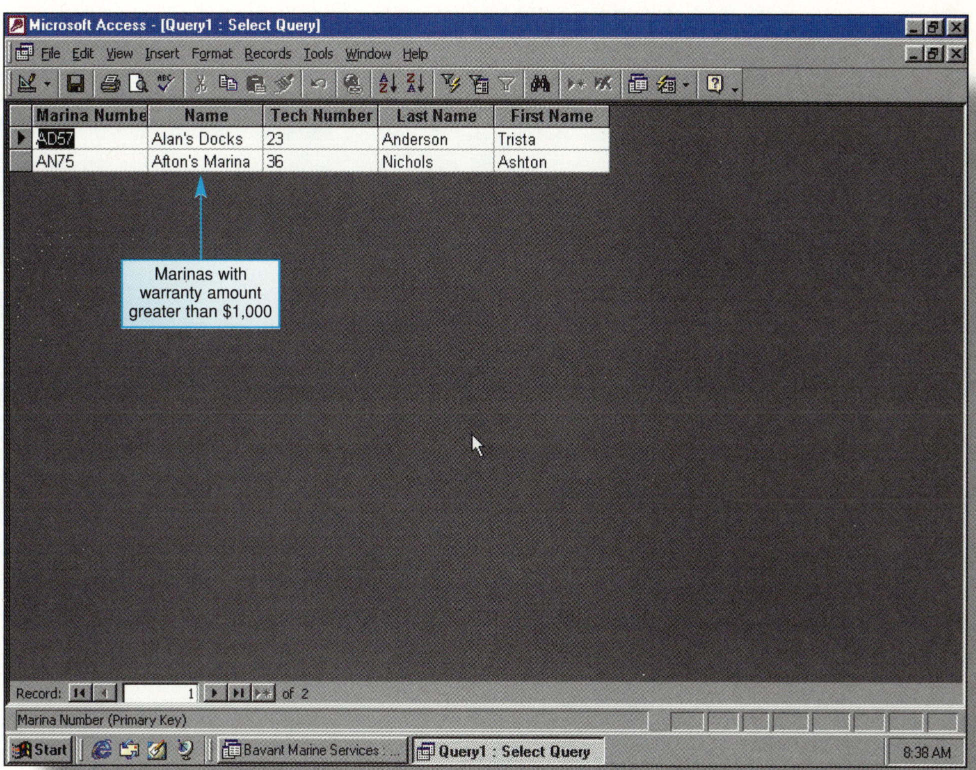

FIGURE 2-51

Using Calculated Fields in a Query

It is important to Bavant Marine Services to know the total amount for each marina; that is, the warranty amount plus the non-warranty amount. This poses a problem because the Marina table does not include a field for total amount. You can calculate it, however, because the total amount is equal to the warranty amount plus the non-warranty amount. Such a field is called a **calculated field**.

To include calculated fields in queries, you enter a name for the calculated field, a colon, and then the expression in one of the columns in the Field row. Any fields included in the expression must be enclosed in square brackets ([ ]). For the total amount, for example, you will type `Total Amount:[Warranty]+[Non-warranty]` as the expression.

You can type the expression directly into the Field row. You will not be able to see the entire entry, however, because the Field row is not large enough. The preferred way is to select the column in the Field row, right-click to display the shortcut menu, and then click Zoom. The Zoom dialog box displays where you can type the expression.

You are not restricted to addition in calculations. You can use subtraction (-), multiplication (*), or division (/). You also can include parentheses in your calculations to indicate which calculations should be done first.

Perform the following steps to remove the Technician table from the query (it is not needed), and then use a calculated field to display the number, name, and total amount of all marinas.

Calculated Fields

Because it is easy to compute values in a query, there is no need to store calculated fields, also called computed fields, in a database. There is no need, for example, to store the total amount (the warranty amount plus the non-warranty amount), because it can be calculated whenever it is required.

To Use a Calculated Field in a Query

1 **Click the View button to return to Design view. Right-click any field in the Technician table field list.**

The shortcut menu displays (Figure 2-52).

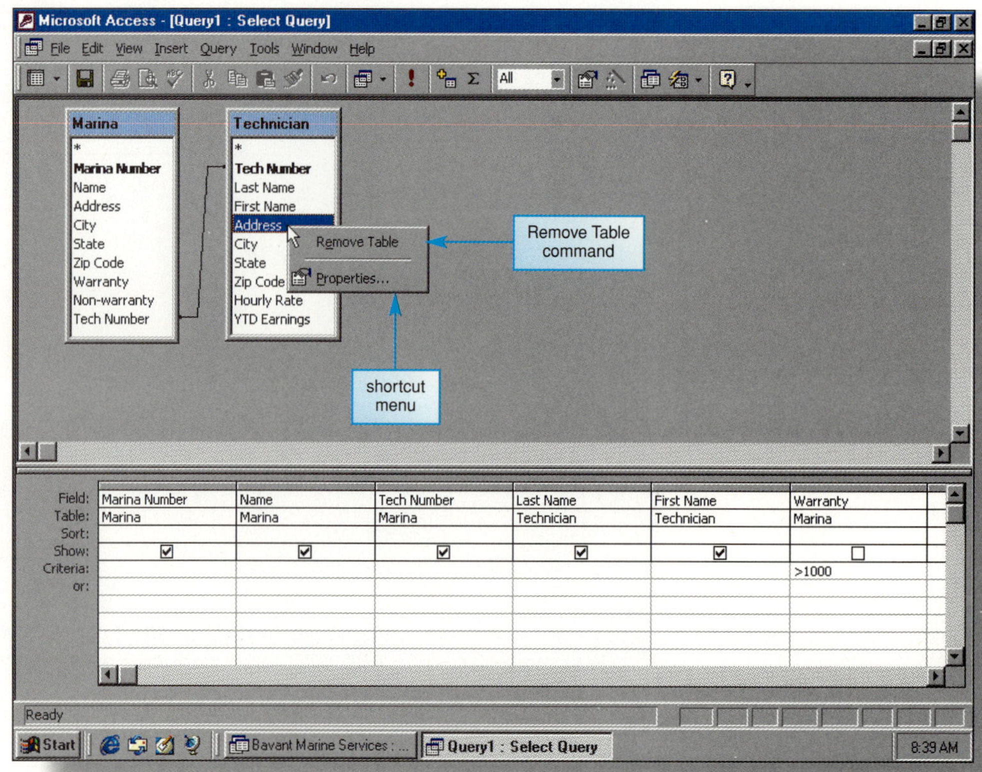

FIGURE 2-52

2 **Click Remove Table to remove the Technician table from the Query1 : Select Query window. On the Edit menu, click Clear Grid.**

3 **Include the Marina Number and Name fields. Right-click the Field row in the third column in the design grid and then click Zoom on the shortcut menu. Type** `Total Amount:[Warranty]+[Non-warranty]` **in the Zoom dialog box that displays.**

The Zoom dialog box displays (Figure 2-53). The expression you typed displays within the dialog box.

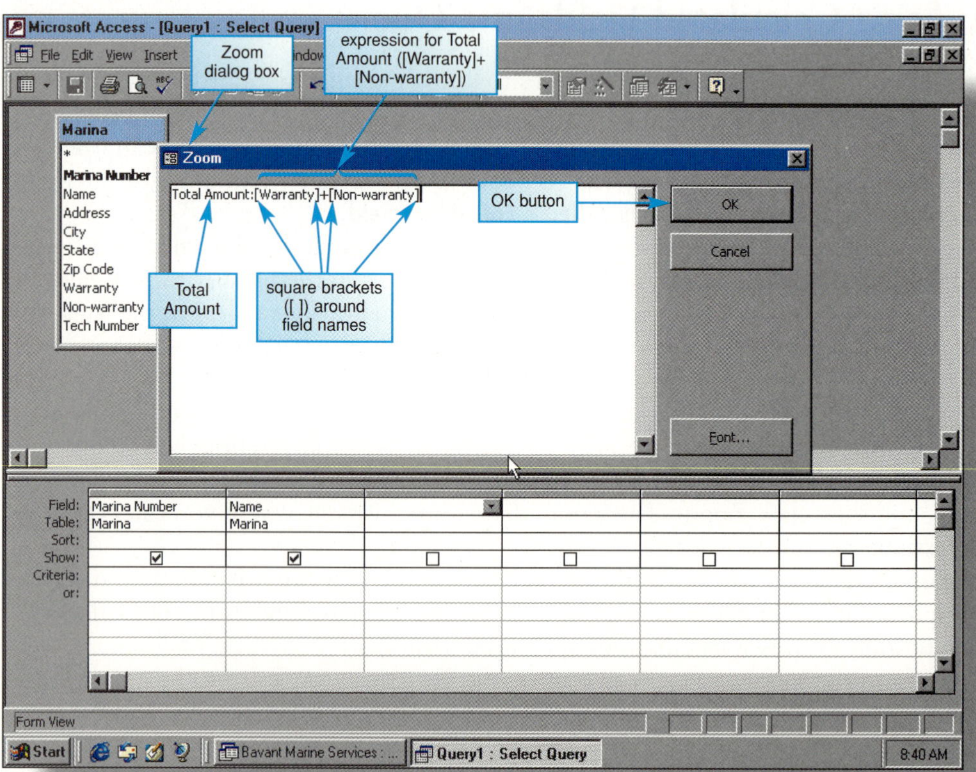

FIGURE 2-53

4 Click the OK button.

The Zoom dialog box no longer displays (Figure 2-54). A portion of the expression you entered displays in the third field in the design grid.

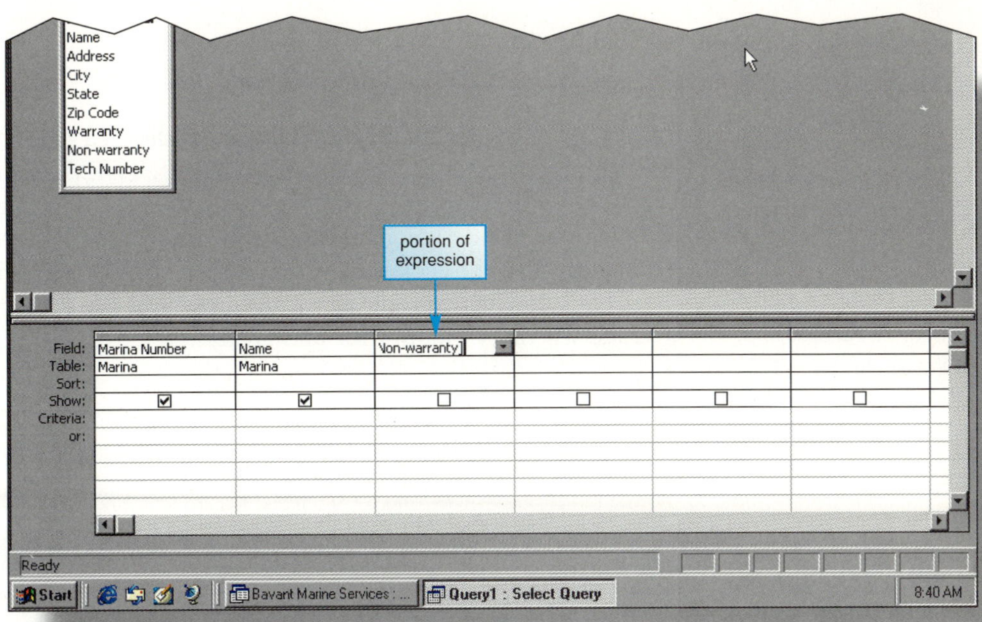

FIGURE 2-54

Run the query.

The results display (Figure 2-55). Microsoft Access has calculated and displayed the total amounts.

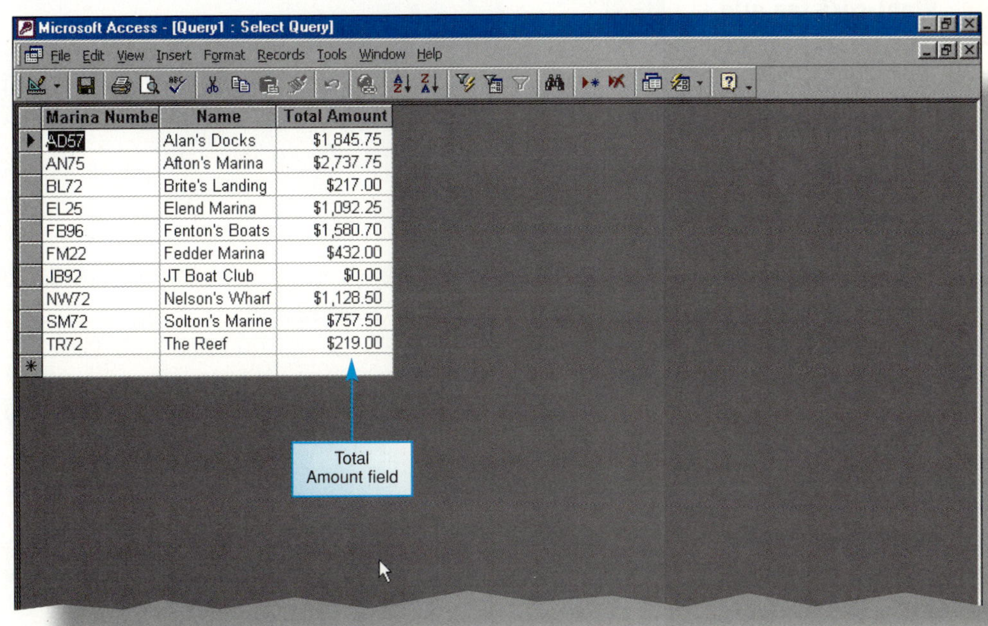

Marina Numbe	Name	Total Amount
AD57	Alan's Docks	$1,845.75
AN75	Afton's Marina	$2,737.75
BL72	Brite's Landing	$217.00
EL25	Elend Marina	$1,092.25
FB96	Fenton's Boats	$1,580.70
FM22	Fedder Marina	$432.00
JB92	JT Boat Club	$0.00
NW72	Nelson's Wharf	$1,128.50
SM72	Solton's Marine	$757.50
TR72	The Reef	$219.00

FIGURE 2-55

Rather than clicking Zoom on the shortcut menu, you can click Build. The Build dialog box then will display. This dialog box provides assistance in creating the expression. If you know the expression you will need, however, it usually is easier to enter it using Zoom.

1. Press SHIFT+F2

Calculating Statistics

Virtually all database management systems support the basic set of statistical calculations: sum, average, count, maximum, and minimum as part of their query feature. Some systems, including Access, add several more, such as standard deviation, variance, first, and last.

Calculating Statistics

Microsoft Access supports the built-in **statistics**: COUNT, SUM, AVG (average), MAX (largest value), MIN (smallest value), STDEV (standard deviation), VAR (variance), FIRST, and LAST. To use any of these in a query, you include it in the Total row in the design grid. The Total row routinely does not appear in the grid. To include it, right-click the grid, and then click Totals on the shortcut menu.

The following example illustrates how you use these functions by calculating the average warranty amount for all marinas.

To Calculate Statistics

1 Click the View button to return to Design view. On the Edit menu, click Clear Grid.

2 Right-click the grid.

The shortcut menu displays (Figure 2-56).

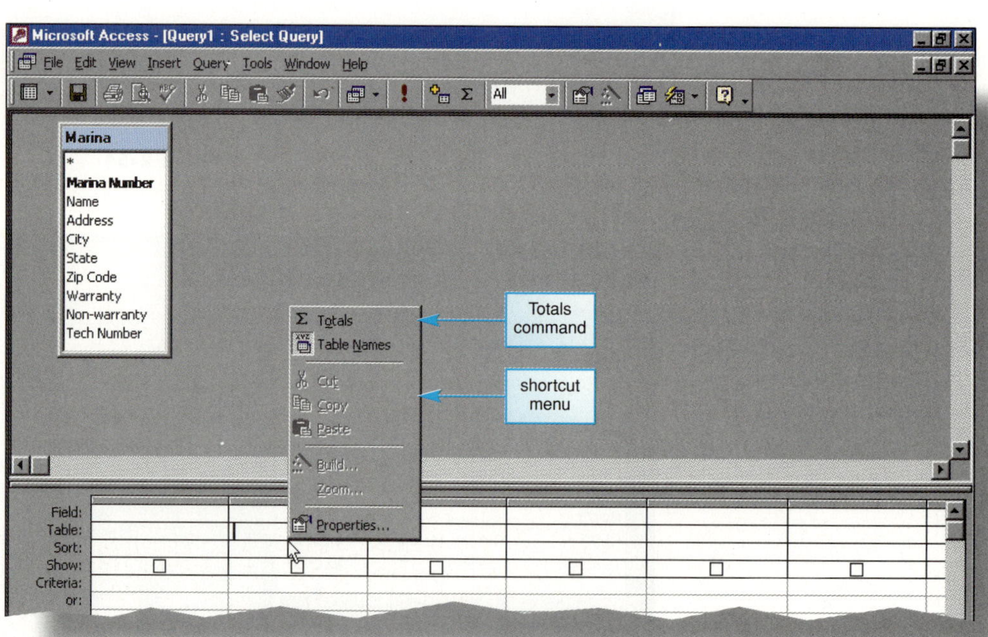

FIGURE 2-56

3 Click Totals on the shortcut menu and then include the Warranty field. Point to the Total row in the Warranty column.

The Total row now is included in the design grid (Figure 2-57). The Warranty field is included, and the entry in the Total row is Group By. The mouse pointer, which has changed shape to an I-beam, is positioned on the Total row under the Warranty field.

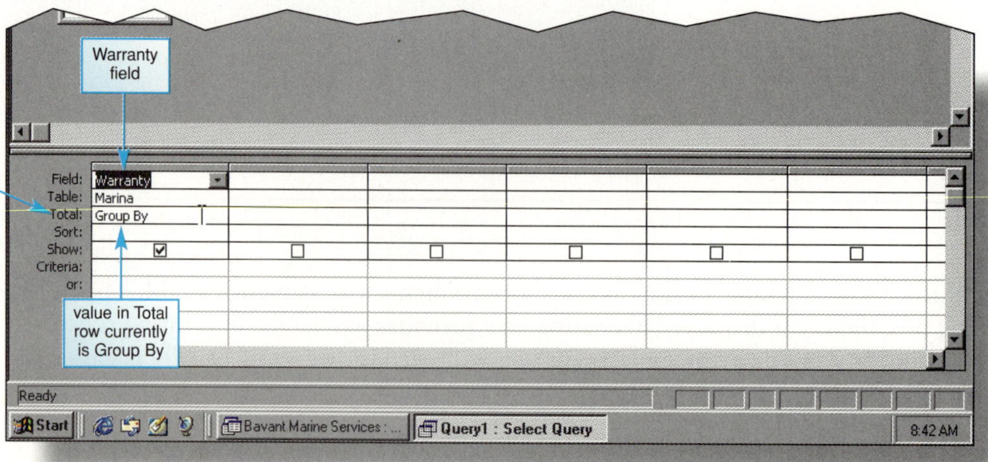

FIGURE 2-57

4 Click the Total row in the Warranty column, and then click the arrow that displays.

The list of available selections displays (Figure 2-58).

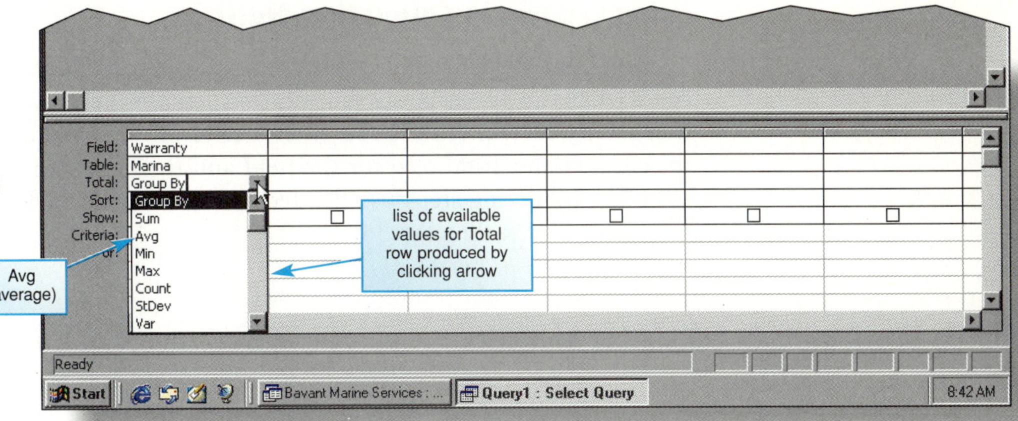

FIGURE 2-58

5 Click Avg.

Avg is selected (Figure 2-59).

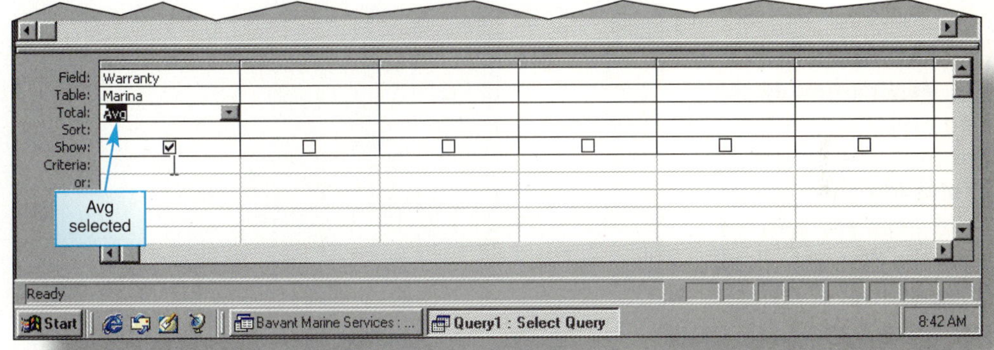

FIGURE 2-59

6 Run the query.

The result displays (Figure 2-60), showing the average warranty amount for all marinas.

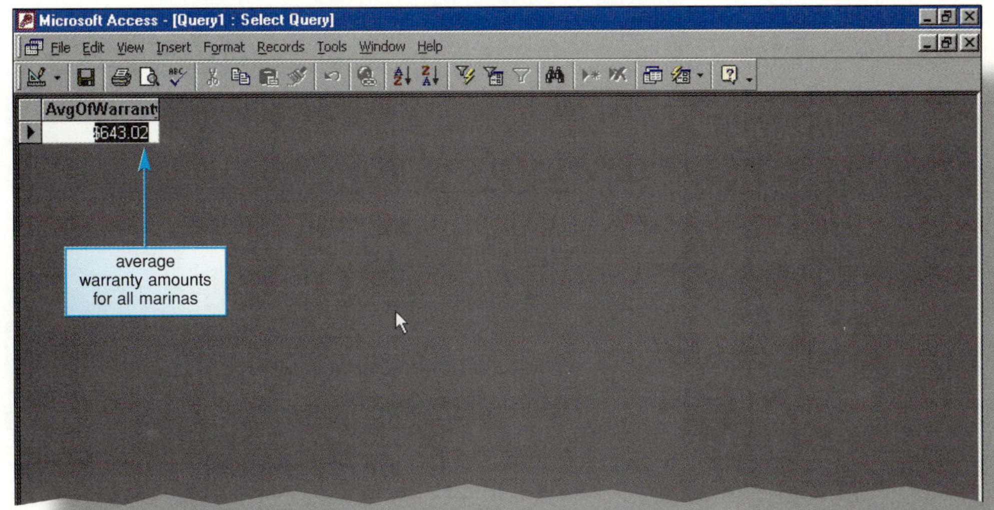

FIGURE 2-60

Other Ways

1. Click Totals button on toolbar
2. On View menu click Totals

Using Criteria in Calculating Statistics

Sometimes calculating statistics for all the records in the table is appropriate. In other cases, however, you will need to calculate the statistics for only those records that satisfy certain criteria. To enter a criterion in a field, first you select Where as the entry in the Total row for the field and then enter the criterion in the Criteria row. The following steps use this technique to calculate the average warranty amount for marinas of technician 36.

To Use Criteria in Calculating Statistics

1 Click the View button to return to Design view.

2 Include the Tech Number field in the design grid. Produce the list of available options for the Total row entry just as you did when you selected Avg for the Warranty field. Use the vertical scroll bar to move through the options until the word, Where, displays.

The list of available selections displays (Figure 2-61). The Group By entry in the Tech Number field may not be highlighted on your screen depending on where you clicked in the Total row.

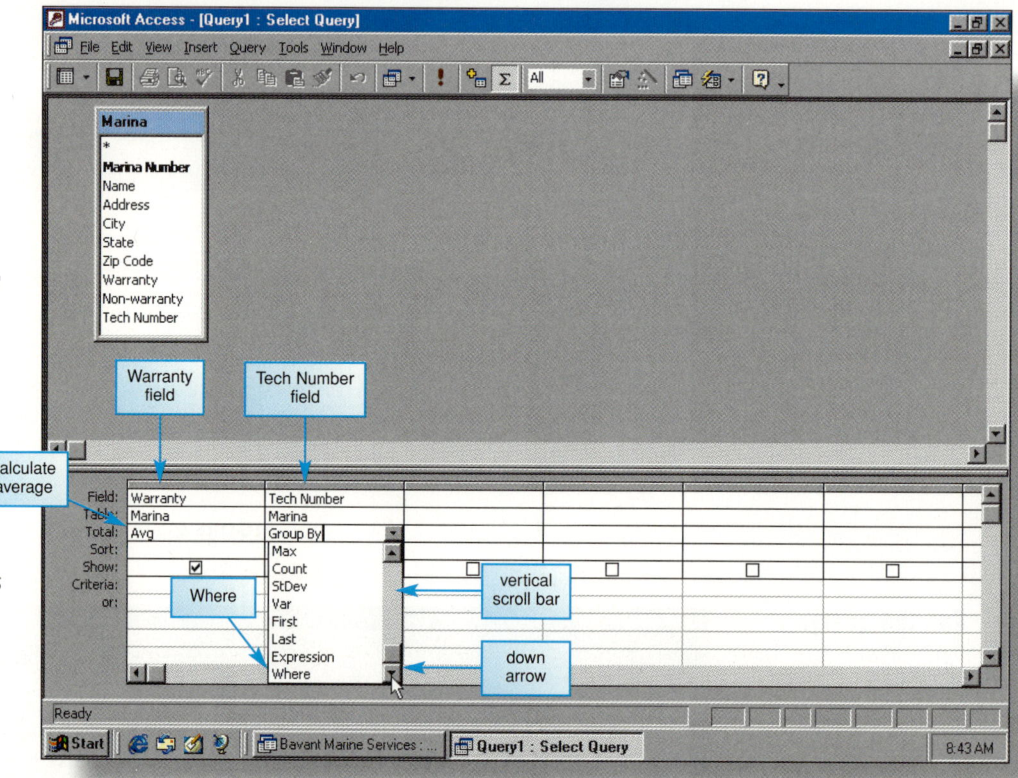

FIGURE 2-61

3 Click Where. Type 36 as the criterion for the Tech Number field.

Where is selected as the entry in the Total row for the Tech Number field (Figure 2-62) and 36 is entered as the Criterion.

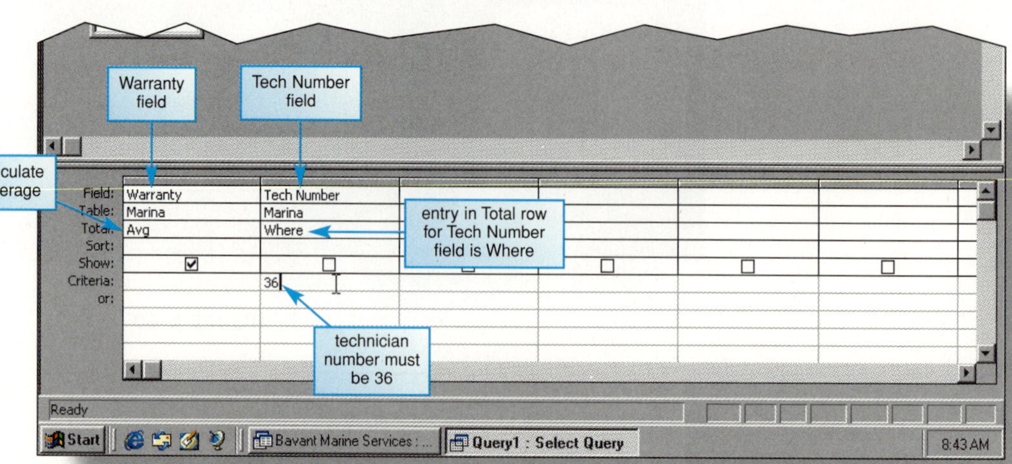

FIGURE 2-62

Run the query.

The result displays (Figure 2-63), giving the average warranty amount for marinas of technician 36.

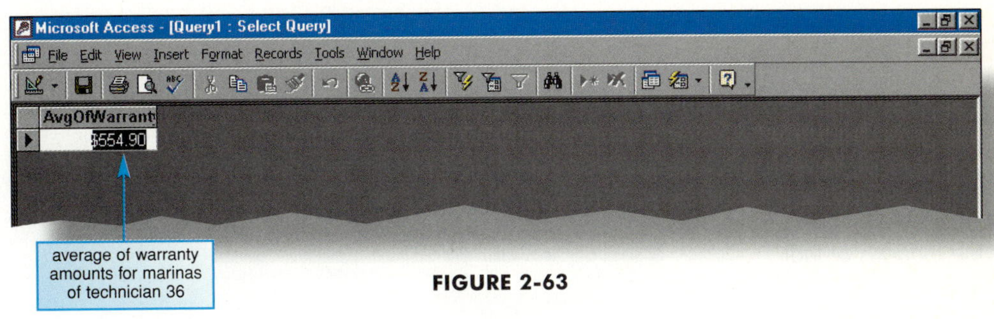

FIGURE 2-63

Grouping

Another way statistics often are used is in combination with grouping; that is, statistics are calculated for groups of records. You may, for example, need to calculate the average warranty amount for the marinas of each technician. You will want the average for the marinas of technician 23, the average for marinas of technician 36, and so on.

Grouping means creating groups of records that share some common characteristic. In grouping by Tech Number, for example, the marinas of technician 23 would form one group, the marinas of technician 36 would be a second, and the marinas of technician 49 form a third. The calculations then are made for each group. To indicate grouping in Access, select Group By as the entry in the Total row for the field to be used for grouping.

Perform the following steps to calculate the average warranty amount for marinas of each technician.

Quick Reference

For a table that lists how to complete the tasks covered in this book using the mouse, menu, shortcut menu, and keyboard, visit the Office 2000 Web page (www.scsite.com/off2000/qr.htm), and then click Microsoft Access 2000.

To Use Grouping

1 **Click the View button to return to Design view. On the Edit menu, click Clear Grid.**

2 **Include the Tech Number field. Include the Warranty field, and then select Avg as the calculation in the Total row.**

The Tech Number and Warranty fields are included (Figure 2-64). Group By currently is the entry in the Total row for the Tech Number field, which is correct; thus, it was not changed.

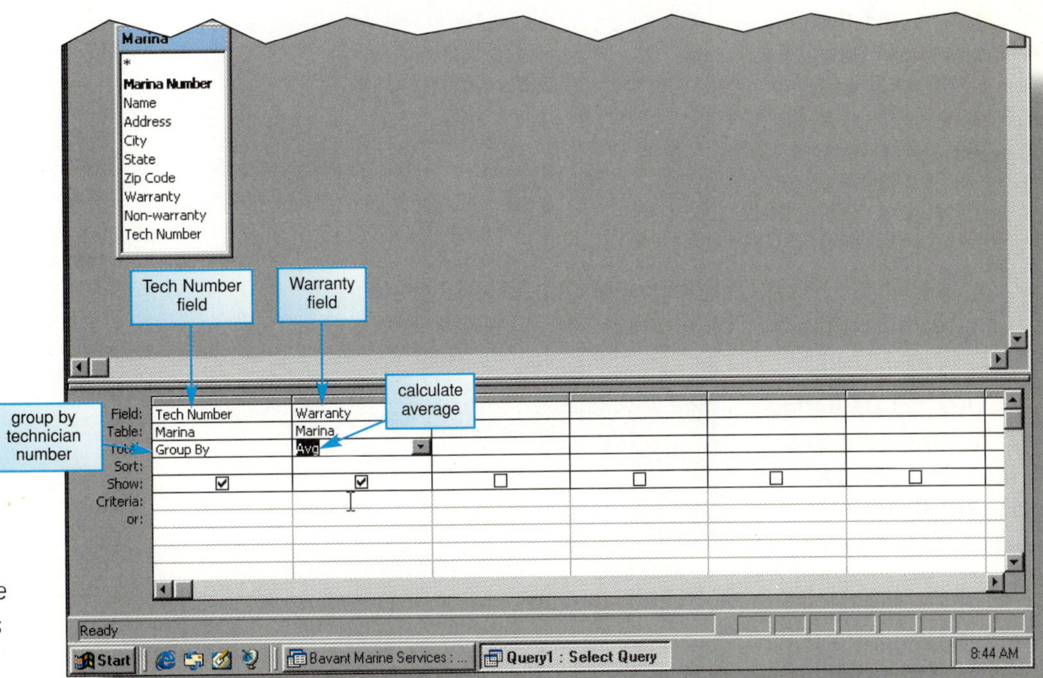

FIGURE 2-64

3 **Run the query.**

The result displays (Figure 2-65), showing each technician's number along with the average warranty amount for the marinas of that technician.

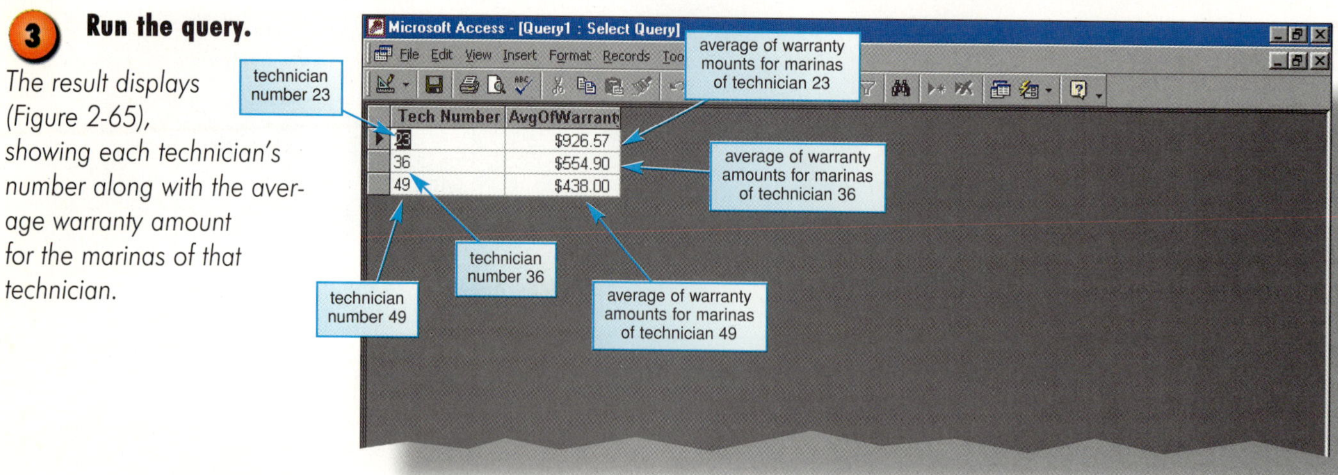

FIGURE 2-65

Saving a Query

In many cases, you will construct a query you will want to use again. By saving the query, you will eliminate the need to repeat all your entries. The following steps illustrate the process by saving the query you just have created and assigning it the name Average Warranty Amount by Technician.

To Save a Query

1 **Click the View button and then click the Save button. Type** `Average Warranty Amount by Technician` **and then point to the OK button.**

The Save As dialog box displays with the query name you typed (Figure 2-66).

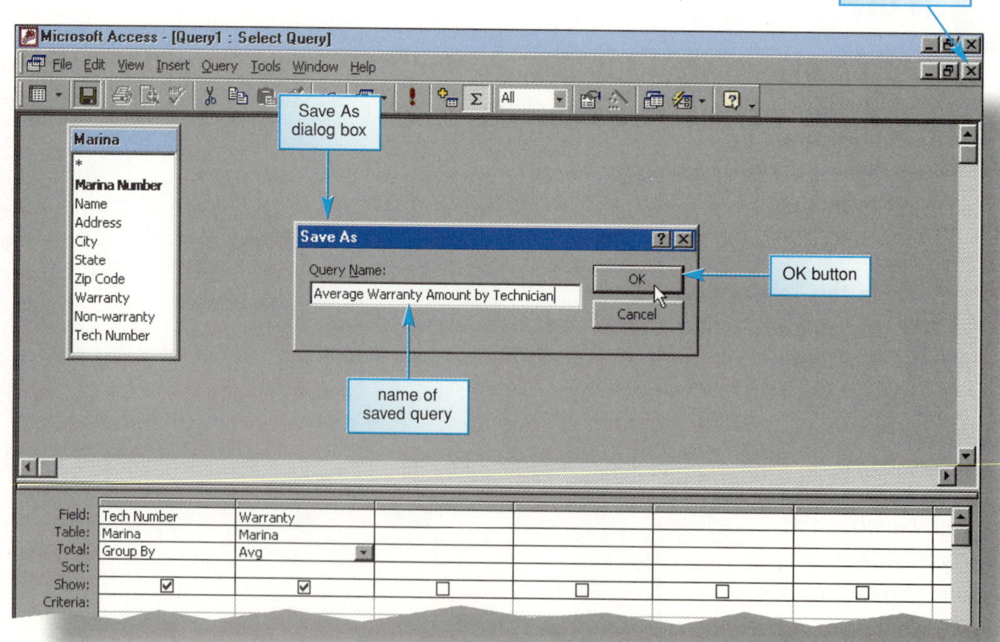

FIGURE 2-66

2 **Click the OK button to save the query, and then close the query by clicking the Query window's Close Window button.**

Access saves the query and closes the Query1 : Select Query window.

Other Ways

1. On File menu click Save
2. Press CTRL+S

Once you have saved a query, you can use it at any time in the future by opening it. Opening a query produces the same results as running the query from Design view. To open a saved query, click the Queries object in the Database window, right-click the query, and then click Open on the shortcut menu. You then could print the results by clicking the Print button. If you wish to change the design of the query, you would click Design View on the shortcut menu rather than Open. If you wanted to print it *without first opening it*, you would click Print on the shortcut menu.

The query is run against the current database. Thus, if changes have been made to the data since the last time you ran it, the results of the query may be different.

More About 2000

Microsoft Certification

The Microsoft Office User Specialist (MOUS) Certification program provides an opportunity for you to obtain a valuable industry credential — proof that you have the Access 2000 skills required by employers. For more information, see Appendix D or visit the Shelly Cashman Series MOUS Web page at www.scsite.com/off2000/cert.htm.

Closing a Database

The following step closes the database by closing its Database window.

TO CLOSE A DATABASE

 Click the Close Window button for the Bavant Marine Services : Database window.

CASE PERSPECTIVE SUMMARY

You have been successful in assisting the management of Bavant Marine Services by creating and running queries to obtain answers to important questions. You used various types of criteria in these queries. You joined tables in some of the queries. Some Bavant Marine Services queries used calculated fields and statistics. Finally, you saved one of the queries for future use.

Project Summary

In Project 2, you created and ran a variety of queries. You learned how to select fields in a query. You used text data and wildcards in criteria. You also used comparison operators in criteria involving numeric data. You combined criteria with both AND and OR. You learned how to sort the results of a query, how to join tables, and how to restrict the records in a join. You created computed fields and calculated statistics. You learned how to use grouping as well as how to save a query for future use.

What You Should Know

Having completed this project, you now should be able to perform the following tasks:

- Calculate Statistics *(A 2.38)*
- Clear a Query *(A 2.16)*
- Close the Database *(A 2.43)*
- Close a Query *(A 2.14)*
- Create a Query *(A 2.6)*
- Include All Fields in a Query *(A 2.15)*
- Include Fields in the Design Grid *(A 2.10)*
- Join Tables *(A 2.32)*
- Omit Duplicates *(A 2.29)*
- Open a Database *(A 2.6)*
- Print the Results of a Query *(A 2.12)*
- Restrict the Records in a Join *(A 2.34)*
- Return to the Design View *(A 2.12)*
- Run the Query *(A 2.11)*
- Save a Query *(A 2.42)*
- Sort Data in a Query *(A 2.26)*
- Sort on Multiple Keys *(A 2.28)*
- Use a Comparison Operator in a Criterion *(A 2.22)*
- Use a Compound Criterion Involving AND *(A 2.24)*
- Use a Compound Criterion Involving OR *(A 2.25)*
- Use a Calculated Field in a Query *(A 2.36)*
- Use a Number in a Criterion *(A 2.21)*
- Use a Wildcard *(A 2.18)*
- Use Criteria for a Field Not Included in the Results *(A 2.20)*
- Use Criteria in Calculating Statistics *(A 2.40)*
- Use Grouping *(A 2.41)*
- Use Text Data in a Criterion *(A 2.17)*

1 Querying the Sidewalk Scrapers Database

Instructions: Start Access. Open the Sidewalk Scrapers database from the Access Data Disk. See the inside back cover for instructions for downloading the Access Data Disk or see your instructor for information on accessing the files required for this book. Perform the following tasks.

1. Create a new query for the Customer table.
2. Add the Customer Number, Name, and Address fields to the design grid.
3. Restrict retrieval to only those records where the customer has an address on Secord.
4. Run the query and print the results.
5. Return to Design view and clear the grid.
6. Add the Customer Number, Name, Telephone, and Balance fields to the design grid.
7. Restrict retrieval to only those records where the balance is greater than $50.
8. Run the query and print the results.
9. Return to Design view and clear the grid.
10. Add the Customer Number, Name, Address, and Worker Id fields to the design grid.
11. Restrict retrieval to only those records where the Worker Id is either 03 or 07.
12. Run the query and print the results.
13. Return to Design view and clear the grid.
14. Join the Customer and Worker tables. Add the Customer Number, Name, and Worker Id fields from the Customer table and the First Name and Last Name fields from the Worker table.
15. Sort the records in ascending order by Worker Id.
16. Run the query and print the results.

1 Querying the School Connection Database

Problem: The Booster's Club has determined a number of questions they want the database management system to answer. You must obtain answers to the questions posed by the club.

Instructions: Use the database created in the In the Lab 1 of Project 1 for this assignment.

Perform the following tasks.

1. Open the School Connection database and create a new query for the Item table.
2. Display and print the Item Id, Description, and Selling Price fields for all records in the table as shown in Figure 2-67.
3. Display all fields and print all the records in the table.

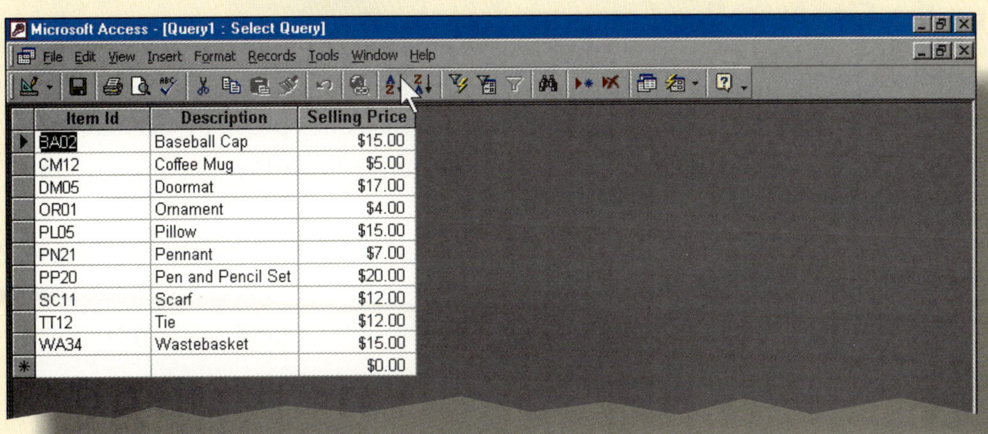

Item Id	Description	Selling Price
BA02	Baseball Cap	$15.00
CM12	Coffee Mug	$5.00
DM05	Doormat	$17.00
OR01	Ornament	$4.00
PL05	Pillow	$15.00
PN21	Pennant	$7.00
PP20	Pen and Pencil Set	$20.00
SC11	Scarf	$12.00
TT12	Tie	$12.00
WA34	Wastebasket	$15.00
		$0.00

FIGURE 2-67

4. Display and print the Item Id, Description, Cost, and Vendor Code fields for all items where the Vendor Code is TM.
5. Display and print the Item Id and Description fields for all items where the Description begins with the letters, Pe.
6. Display and print the Item Id, Description, and Vendor Code fields for all items with a cost greater than $10.
7. Display and print the Item Id and Description for all items that have a selling price of $10 or less.
8. Display and print all fields for those items with a cost greater than $10 and where the number on hand is less than 5.
9. Display and print all fields for those items that have a vendor code of TM or have a selling price less than $10.
10. Join the Item table and the Vendor table. Display the Item Id, Description, Cost, Name, and Telephone Number fields. Run the query and print the results.
11. Restrict the records retrieved in task 10 above to only those items where the number on hand is less than 10. Display and print the results.
12. Remove the Vendor table and clear the design grid.
13. Include the Item Id and Description fields in the design grid. Calculate the on-hand value (on hand * cost) for all records in the table. Display and print the results.
14. Display and print the average selling price of all items.
15. Display and print the average selling price of items grouped by vendor code.
16. Join the Item and Vendor tables. Include the Vendor Code and Name fields from the Vendor table. Include the Item Id, Description, Cost, and On Hand fields from the Item table. Save the query as Vendors and Items. Run the query and print the results.

2 Querying the City Area Bus Company Database

Problem: The advertising sales manager has determined a number of questions that he wants the database management system to answer. You must obtain answers to the questions posed by the manager.

Instructions: Use the database created in the In the Lab 2 of Project 1 for this assignment. Perform the following tasks.

1. Open the City Area Bus Company database and create a new query for the Advertiser table.
2. Display and print the Advertiser Id, Name, Balance, and Amount Paid fields for all the records in the table.
3. Display and print the Advertiser Id, Name, and Balance fields for all advertisers where the sales rep number is 24.
4. Display and print the Advertiser Id, Name, and Balance fields for all advertisers where the balance is greater than $200.
5. Display and print the Advertiser Id, Name, and Amount Paid fields for all advertisers where the sales rep number is 29 and the amount paid is greater than $1,000.
6. Display and print the Advertiser Id, Name, and City fields of all advertisers where the city begins with C.
7. Display and print the Advertiser Id, Name, and Balance fields for all advertisers where the sales rep number is 29 or the balance is less than $50.
8. Include the Advertiser Id, Name, City, and State fields in the design grid. Sort the records in ascending order by city within state. Display and print the results. The City field should display in the result to the left of the State field. (*Hint:* Use Microsoft Access Help to solve this problem.)
9. Display and print the cities in ascending order. Each city should display only once.
10. Display and print the Advertiser Id, Name, Balance, and Amount Paid fields from the Advertiser table and the First Name, Last Name, and Comm Rate fields from the Sales Rep table.
11. Restrict the records retrieved in task 10 above to only those advertisers that are in MA. Display and print the results.
12. Clear the design grid and add the First Name, Last Name, and Comm Rate fields from the Sales Rep table to the grid. Add the Name and Balance fields from the Advertiser table. Calculate the pending commission (balance * comm rate) for the Sales Rep table. Sort the records in ascending order by last name and format pending commission as currency. (*Hint:* Use Microsoft Access Help to solve this problem.) Run the query and print the results.
13. Display and print the following statistics: the total balance and total amount paid for all advertisers; the total balance for advertisers of sales rep 29; and the total amount paid for each sales rep.
14. Display and print the Sales Rep Number, Last Name, First Name, Advertiser Id, Name, Balance, and Amount Paid fields. Save the query as Sales Reps and Advertisers.

3 Querying the Resort Rentals Database

Problem: The real estate company has determined a number of questions that they want the database management system to answer. You must obtain answers to the questions posed by the company.

Instructions: Use the database created in the In the Lab 3 of Project 1 for this assignment. Perform the following tasks.

1. Open the Resort Rentals database and create a new query for the Rental Unit table.

2. Display and print the Rental Id, Address, City, and Owner Id fields for all the records in the table as shown in Figure 2-68.

Microsoft Access - [Query1 : Select Query]

Rental Id	Address	City	Owner Id
101	521 Ocean	Hutchins	ML10
103	783 First	Gulf Breeze	FH15
105	684 Beach	San Toma	PR23
108	96 Breeze	Gulf Breeze	PR23
110	523 Ocean	Hutchins	LD45
112	345 Coastal	Shady Beach	LD45
116	956 First	Gulf Breeze	ML10
121	123 Gulf	San Toma	FH15
134	278 Second	Shady Beach	FH15
144	24 Plantation	Hutchins	PR23

FIGURE 2-68

3. Display and print the Rental Id, Address, City, and Weekly Rate fields for all units that rent for less than $1,000 per week.
4. Display and print the Rental Id, Address, and Weekly Rate fields for all units that sleep more than four people and have a pool.
5. Display and print the Rental Id, Address, City, and Weekly Rate fields for all units that are either in Hutchins or Gulf Breeze, have more than one bedroom and an ocean view. (*Hint:* Use Microsoft Access Help to solve this problem.)
6. Display and print the Rental Id, Address, and City fields of all units where the city begins with S.
7. Display and print the Rental Id, Address, and Weekly Rate fields for all units that have more than one bedroom and more than one bathroom.
8. Include the Rental Id, Address, City, Bedrooms, Sleeps, and Weekly Rate fields in the design grid. Sort the records in descending order by bedrooms within sleeps. The Bedrooms field should display in the result to the left of the Sleeps field. Display and print the results. (*Hint:* Use Microsoft Access Help to solve this problem.)
9. Display and print the weekly rates in descending order. Each rate should display only once.
10. Display and print the Rental Id, Address, City, and Weekly Rate fields from the Rental Unit table and the First Name, Last Name, and Phone Number fields from the Owner table.
11. Restrict the records retrieved in task 10 above to only those units that rent for more than $1,000 per week. Display and print the results.
12. Clear the design grid and remove the Owner table from the query. Owner ML10 offers a 15% discount on the weekly rate if renters rent for more than one week at a time. What is the discounted weekly rental rate for his units? Display the rental id, address, city, and discounted weekly rate in your result. Format the discounted weekly rate as currency. (*Hint:* Use Microsoft Access Help to solve this problem.) Run the query and print the results.
13. Display and print the average weekly rate for each owner.
14. Display and print the Owner Id, First Name, Last Name, Rental Id, Address, City, and Weekly Rate fields. Save the query as Owners and Rental Units.

Cases and Places

The difficulty of these case studies varies:
▶ are the least difficult; ▶▶ are more difficult; and ▶▶▶ are the most difficult.

1 ▶ Use the Computer Accessories database you created in Case Study 1 of Project 1 for this assignment. Perform the following: (a) The Computer Science Club has been unhappy with the supplier, Mouse Tracks. Display and print the description, units on hand, and cost of all items supplied by Mouse Tracks. (b) The club is considering raising the selling price of items costing less than one dollar. Find the current profit (selling price – cost) of these items and display and print the item id, description, cost, selling price, and current profit. (c) The faculty advisor for the club needs to know the on-hand value of the club's inventory. Display and print the item id, description, and on-hand value (units on hand * cost) for all items. (d) The club needs to replenish its stock. Display and print the item id, description, units on hand, supplier name, and supplier telephone for all items where there are less than 10 items on hand. (e) The club would like to display a list of items for sale. Display and print the description and selling price. Sort the list in ascending order by selling price.

2 ▶ Use the Bookstore database you created in Case Study 2 of Project 1 for this assignment. The owner of the bookstore has put together a list of the most common type of questions she would like to ask the database. She wants to know if the database you created can answer these questions. Perform the following: (a) Display and print the book code, title, price, and year published for all books written by H Brawley. (b) Display and print the authors in ascending order. List each author only once. (c) Display and print a count of the books grouped by author. (d) Display and print the book code, title, author, and price for all books published in the year 2000. (e) Display and print the book code, title, units on hand, price, and on-hand value (units on hand * price) for all books. (f) Display and print the book code, title, price, and publisher name for all books where the number of units on hand is less than two.

3 ▶▶ Use the Band database you created in Case Study 3 of Project 1 for this assignment. Perform the following: (a) The band director would like a telephone list of all band members. List the name and telephone number of all band members. (b) The band is going to a marching band competition this weekend and it is important that school officials be able to reach a parent/guardian in case of emergency. List the name and emergency contact information for all band members. (c) The local college is offering a special weekend camp for clarinet players. Identify all band members that play the clarinet. (d) Students who have been band members for two years or more are eligible for special recognition. List the name, age, sex, band instrument, and number of years in the band for these band members. (e) The school has just negotiated a new lease arrangement with a local music store. List the name, telephone number, and type of band instrument for those band members that lease their instrument. (f) The band needs an updated directory. List the band instrument type, member name, age, sex, and years in band for each member. The list should be in order by last name within band instrument type.

4 ▶▶ Use the Humane Society database you created in Case Study 4 of Project 1 for this assignment. Display and print the following: (a) The name, address, and telephone number of all families that have adopted pets. (b) A list of all animals that have been adopted. The list should include the animal's name, type, age, and sex. (c) A list of all adoptions. The list should include the name of the family, telephone number, the animal's name and type. (d) The average number of other pets owned by families that have adopted animals. (e) A list of the different types of animals that have been adopted. Each animal type should display only once.

Microsoft Access 2000

Maintaining a Database Using the Design and Update Features of Access

OBJECTIVES

You will have mastered the material in this project when you can:

- Open a database
- Add, change, and delete records in a table
- Locate records
- Filter records
- Change the structure of a database
- Restructure a table
- Change field characteristics
- Add a field
- Save the changes to the structure
- Update the contents of a single field
- Make changes to groups of records
- Delete groups of records
- Specify a required field
- Specify a range
- Specify a default value
- Specify legal values
- Specify a format
- Save rules, values, and formats
- Update a table with validation rules
- Specify referential integrity
- Use subdatasheets
- Order records
- Create single-field and multiple-field indexes
- Close a database

Database Upkeep

An Ounce of Maintenance Is Worth a Pound of Restoration

Early on the morning of April 13, 1992, the Chicago River crashed through the roof of an abandoned railroad tunnel built in the 1800s. Water from Lake Michigan roared into the basements of Chicago's downtown office buildings, ruining computers, irreplaceable paper files, and environmental equipment. Due to lack of maintenance, what started as a small crack grew into a hemorrhage that city workers desperately tried to shore up while officials sent out for competitive bids. Unfortunately, the river would not wait the several months required for the bid process. If the city had acted immediately, a repair job estimated at $75,000 could have saved the ultimate $1 billion loss. In another, more recent example, the quality of a $44 million seismic retrofit on the freeway overpasses in San Diego came into question because of faulty welds.

Individuals are seldom faced with problems that have such massive financial impact. Unlike the Maytag repairman, however, people must contend with maintenance issues on a regular basis: cars, homes, dental

work, even personal computers. All are issues important to health, safety, and well-being. How a person handles these can make the difference between a happy life and a trying one. Likewise, for many business people, scientific researchers, and self-employed individuals, professional survival depends on maintaining their computer databases.

Information flows in today's world like the waters of all the rivers combined. From telephone lines, customer service terminals, satellite feeds, the mail, and so on, literally billions of pieces of data enter daily into the databases of entities such as insurance companies, banks, mail-order firms, astronomical observatories, medical research labs, doctors' offices, automobile dealerships, home-based businesses, and multitudes of others. Based on the content of this information, decisions are made and actions taken, often triggering a corresponding flow of information to other interested users. The process of handling this data — the lifeblood of today's information-based society — is known as database maintenance.

Microsoft Access 2000 is a powerful tool that facilitates designing the database and then maintaining it with ease. Effective design and update features in Access allow you to add, change, and delete records in a table, change the size of or add new fields to the database, and then quickly update the restructured database. In this project, you will learn the techniques to maintain any type of database with which you might work in your academic or professional life.

During college, you may use a personal database to organize and maintain information such as names, addresses, and telephone numbers of friends, family, and club members, or possessions such as a CD or tape collection, videos, or books. As a club member, you may be asked to design, update, and maintain a database of club members and information.

Your first use for a database may come when you start your search for the right graduate school or as you begin your mailing campaign for future employment opportunities. Once employed, you will be exposed to the use of databases in all facets of business. Learning the important skills associated with database maintenance will pave the way for opportunity in the workplace.

Maintenance might seem mundane, but certainly, an ounce of maintenance is worth a pound of restoration.

Microsoft Access 2000

Maintaining a Database Using the Design and Update Features of Access

CASE PERSPECTIVE

Bavant Marine Services now has created and loaded their database. The management and staff have received many benefits from the database, including the ability to ask a variety of questions concerning the data in the database. They now face the task of keeping the database up to date. They must add new records as they take on new marinas and technicians. They must make changes to existing records to reflect additional billings, payments, changes of address, and so on. Bavant Marine Services also found that it needed to change the structure of the database in two specific ways. The management decided they needed to categorize the marinas by the type of storage they offer, so they need to add a Marina Type field to the Marina table. They also discovered the Name field was too short to contain the name of one of the marinas so they need to enlarge the field. In addition, they wish to establish rules for the data entered in the database to ensure that users only can enter valid data. Finally, they determined they want to improve the efficiency of certain types of processing, specifically sorting and retrieving data. Your task is to help Bavant Marine Services in all these activities.

Introduction

Once a database has been created and loaded with data, it must be maintained. **Maintaining the database** means modifying the data to keep it up to date, such as adding new records, changing the data for existing records, and deleting records. **Updating** can include **mass updates** or **mass deletions**; that is, updates to, or deletions of, many records at the same time.

In addition to adding, changing, and deleting records, maintenance of a database periodically can involve the need to **restructure** the database; that is, to change the database structure. This can include adding new fields to a table, changing the characteristics of existing fields, and removing existing fields. It also can involve the creation of **indexes**, which are similar to indexes found in the back of books and used to improve the efficiency of certain operations.

Figure 3-1 summarizes some of the various types of activities involved in maintaining a database.

• Add new records
• Change records
• Delete records
• Change field width
• Add new field
• Use update and delete queries
• Create validations rules
• Specify default values
• Specify relationships
• Sort records
• Create indexes to improve performance

FIGURE 3-1

Project Three — Maintaining the Bavant Marine Services Database

You are to make the changes to the data in the Bavant Marine Services database as requested by the management of Bavant Marine Services. You must restructure the database to meet the current needs of Bavant Marine. This includes adding an additional field as well as increasing the width of one of the existing fields. You must modify the structure of the database in a way that prevents users from entering invalid data. Finally, management is concerned that some operations, for example, those involving sorting the data, are taking longer than they would like. You are to create indexes to attempt to address this problem.

Opening the Database

Before carrying out the steps in this project, first you must open the database. To do so, perform the following steps.

TO OPEN A DATABASE

1. Click the Start button on the taskbar.
2. Click Open Office Document and then click 3½ Floppy (A:) in the Look in box. If necessary, click the Bavant Marine Services database name.
3. Click the Open button.

The database opens and the Bavant Marine Services : Database window displays.

Maintaining a Database: Backup

Before making changes to the database, it is a good idea to make a copy of the database (called a **backup** or a **save** copy). To do so, use the copy features in Windows to copy the database to another file with a different name (for example, Bavant Marine Backup).

Adding, Changing, and Deleting Records in a Table

Keeping the data in a database up to date requires three tasks: adding new records, changing the data in existing records, and deleting existing records.

Adding Records in a Table

In Project 1, you added records to a database using Datasheet view; that is, as you were adding records, the records were displayed on the screen in the form of a datasheet, or table. When you need to add additional records, you can use the same techniques.

In Project 1, you used a form to view records. This is called **Form view**. You also can use Form view to update the data in a table. To add new records, change existing records, or delete records, you will use the same techniques you used in Datasheet view. To add a record to the Marina table with a form, for example, use the following steps. These steps use the Marina form you created in Project 1.

To Use a Form to Add Records

1. With the Bavant Marine Services database open, point to Forms on the Objects bar (Figure 3-2).

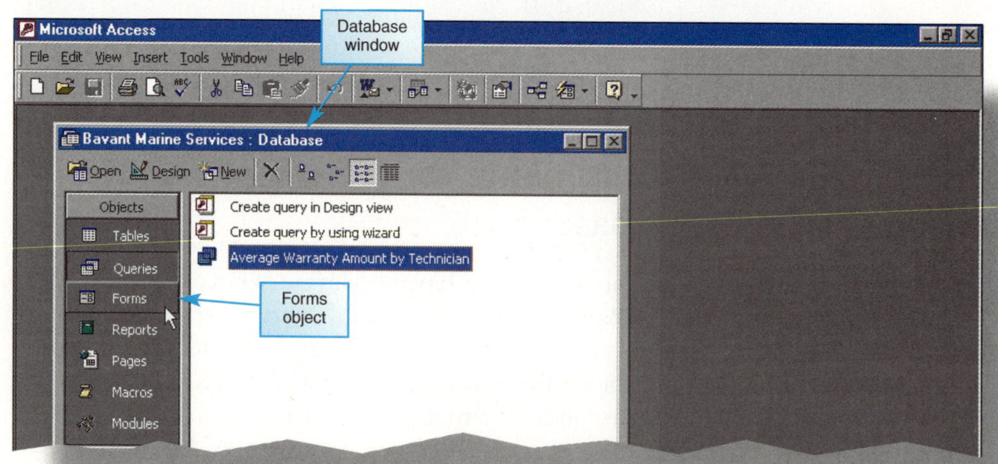

FIGURE 3-2

2 Click Forms. Right-click Marina.

The shortcut menu displays (Figure 3-3).

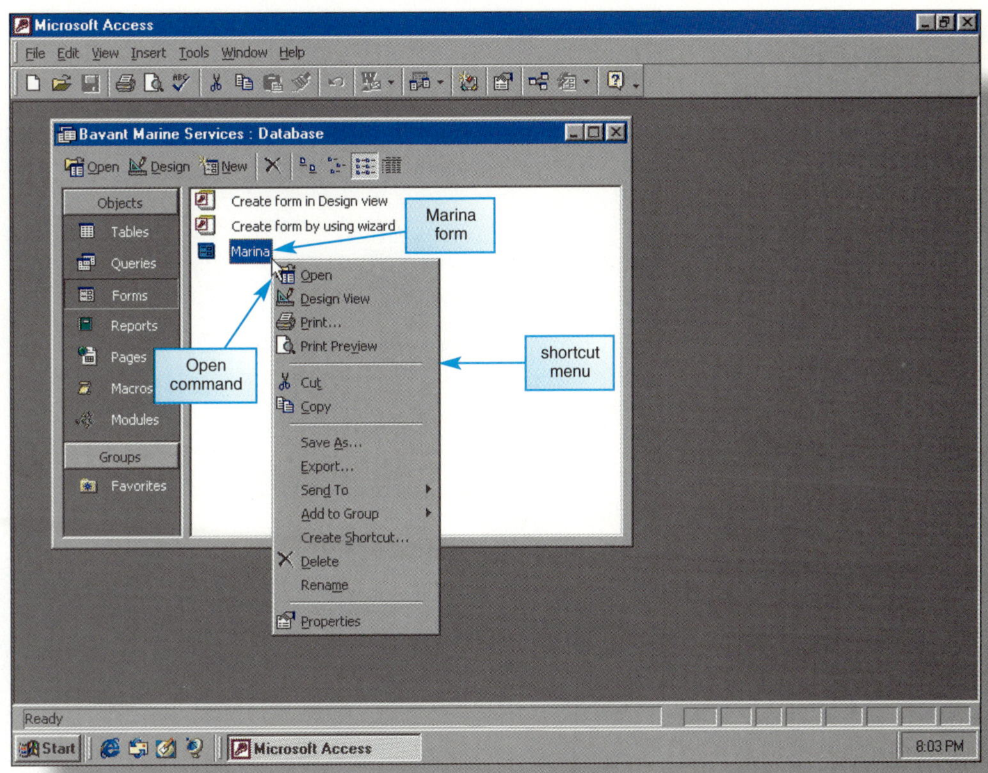

FIGURE 3-3

3 Click Open on the shortcut menu.

The form for the Marina table displays (Figure 3-4).

4 Click the New Record navigation button at the bottom of the Form view window.

The contents of the form are erased in preparation for a new record.

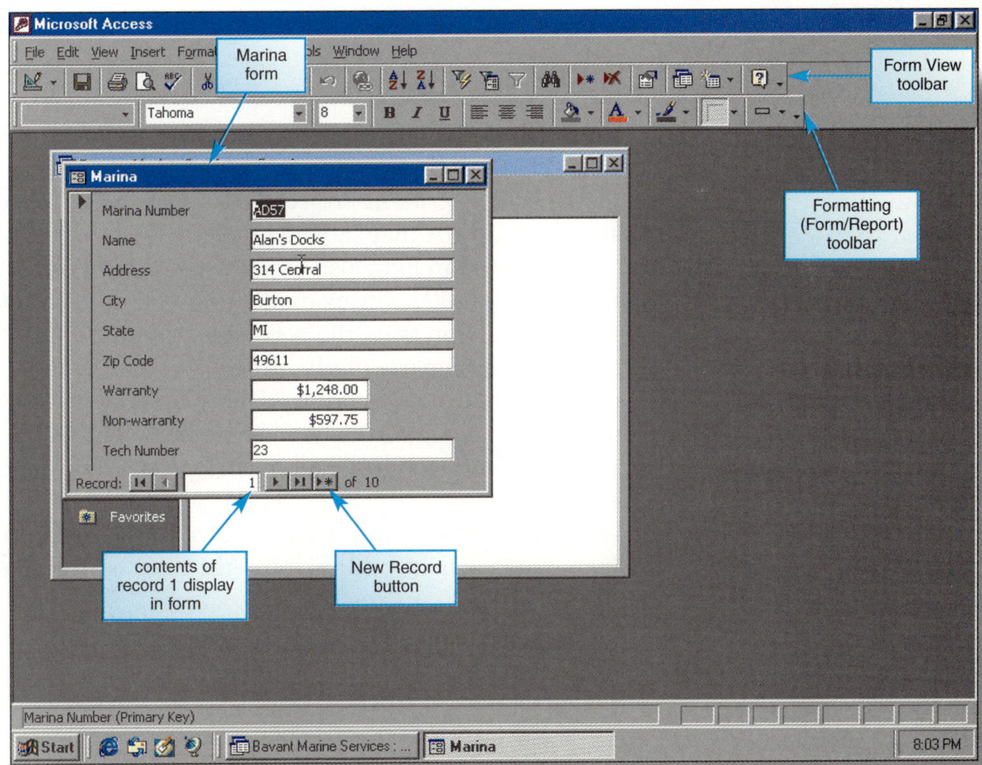

FIGURE 3-4

Using Figure 3-5, type the data for the new record. Press the TAB key after typing the data in each field, except after typing the final field (Tech Number).

The record displays.

6 Press the TAB key.

The record now is added to the Marina table and the contents of the form erased.

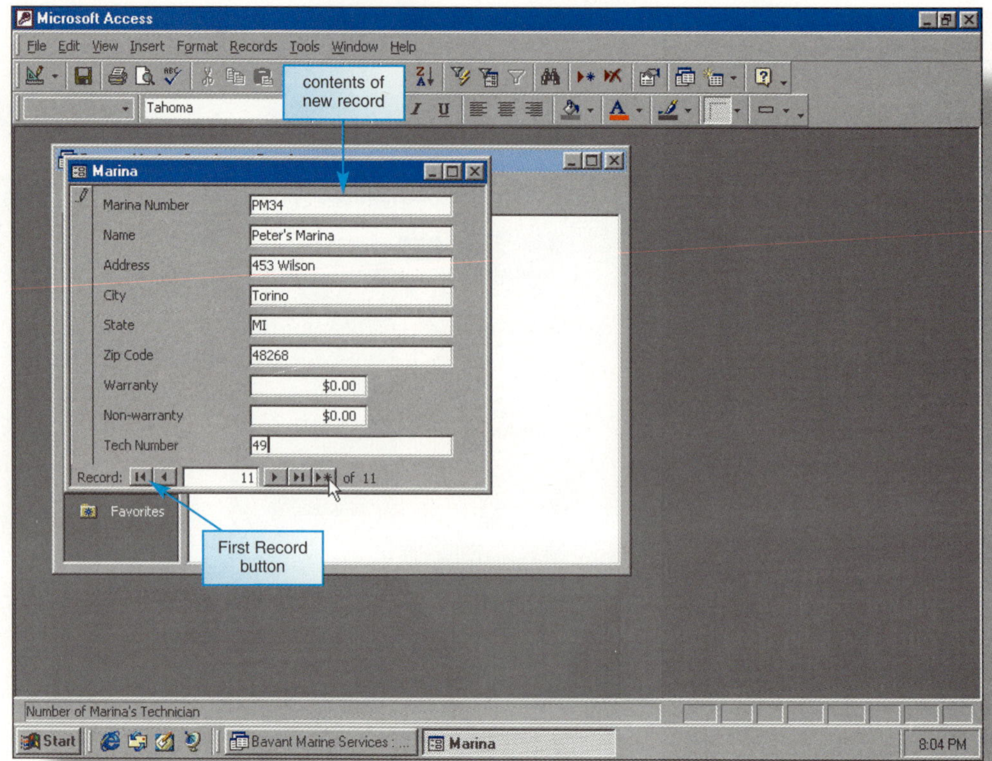

FIGURE 3-5

1. Click New Record button on the Form View toolbar
2. On Insert menu click New Record

Maintaining a Database: Recovery

If a problem occurs that damages either the data in the database or the structure of the database, the database is recovered by copying the backup copy over it. To do so, use the copy features of Windows to copy the backup version (for example, Bavant Marine Backup) over the actual database (for example, Bavant Marine Services). This will return the database to the state it was in when the backup was made.

Searching for a Record

In the database environment, **searching** means looking for records that satisfy some criteria. Looking for the marina whose number is FM22 is an example of searching. The queries in Project 2 also were examples of searching. Access had to locate those records that satisfied the criteria.

A need for searching also exists when using Form view or Datasheet view. To update marina FM22, for example, first you need to find the marina. In a small table, repeatedly pressing the Next Record button until marina FM22 is on the screen may not be particularly difficult. In a large table with many records, however, this would be extremely cumbersome. You need a way to be able to go directly to a record just by giving the value in some field. This is the function of the **Find button** on the Form View toolbar. Before clicking the Find button, select the field for the search.

Perform the following steps to move to the first record in the file, select the Marina Number field, and then use the Find button to search for the marina whose number is FM22.

Steps To Search for a Record

1 Make sure the form for the Marina table displays. Click the First Record navigation button at the lower-left corner of the Form view window (see Figure 3-5 on page A 3.8) to display the first record. If the Marina Number field currently is not selected, select it by clicking the field name. Point to the Find button on the Form View toolbar.

The first record displays in the form (Figure 3-6).

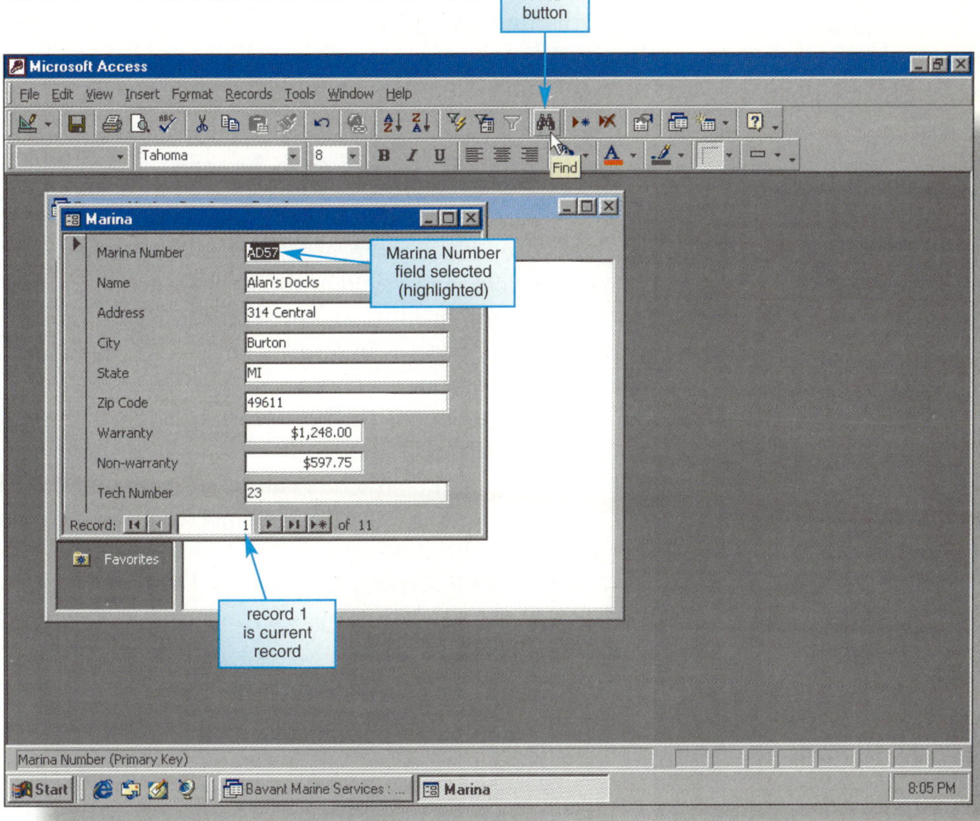

FIGURE 3-6

2 Click the Find button on the toolbar. Type FM22 in the Find What text box in the Find and Replace dialog box.

The Find and Replace dialog box displays (Figure 3-7). The Find What text box contains the entry, FM22.

3 Click the Find Next button and then click the Close button.

Access locates the record for marina FM22.

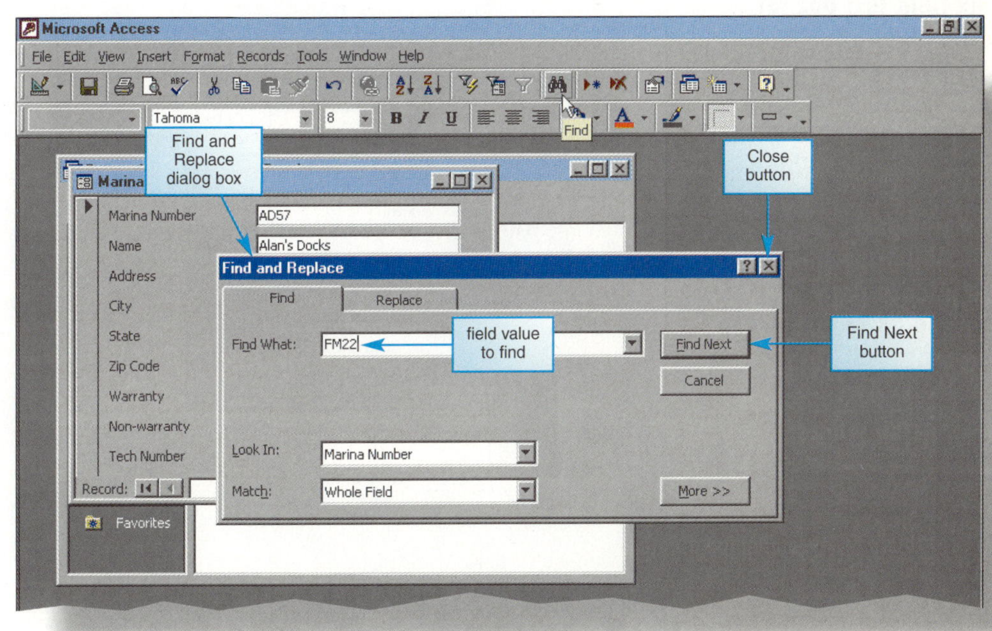

FIGURE 3-7

Other Ways

1. On Edit menu click Find
2. Press CTRL+F

In some cases, after locating a record that satisfies a criterion, you might need to find the next record that satisfies the same criterion. For example, if you have just found the first marina whose technician number is 23, you then may want to find the second such marina, then the third, and so on. To do so, repeat the same process. You will not need to retype the value, however.

More About 2000

Changing the Contents of a Record

To change data within a field, click within the field to display the insertion point. To replace the entire value, move the pointer to the leftmost part of the field until it changes into the plus pointer and then click. Type the new entry to replace the previous entry.

Changing the Contents of a Record

After locating the record to be changed, select the field to be changed by clicking the field. You also can repeatedly press the TAB key. Then make the appropriate changes. (Clicking the field automatically produces an insertion point. If you use the TAB key, you will need to press F2 to produce an insertion point.)

Normally, Access is in **Insert mode**, so the characters typed will be inserted at the appropriate position. To change to **Overtype mode**, press the INSERT key. The letters, OVR, will display near the bottom right edge of the status bar. To return to Insert mode, press the INSERT key. In Insert mode, if the data in the field completely fills the field, no additional characters can be inserted. In this case, you would need to increase the size of the field before inserting the characters. You will see how to do this later in the project.

Perform the following steps to use Form view to change the name of marina FM22 to Fedder's Marina by inserting an apostrophe (') and the letter, s, after Fedder. Sufficient room exists in the field to make this change.

To Update the Contents of a Field

1 Position the mouse pointer in the Name field text box for marina FM22 after the word, Fedder.

The mouse pointer shape is an I-beam (Figure 3-8).

2 Click to produce an insertion point and then type 's **to correct the name.**

The name is now Fedder's Marina.

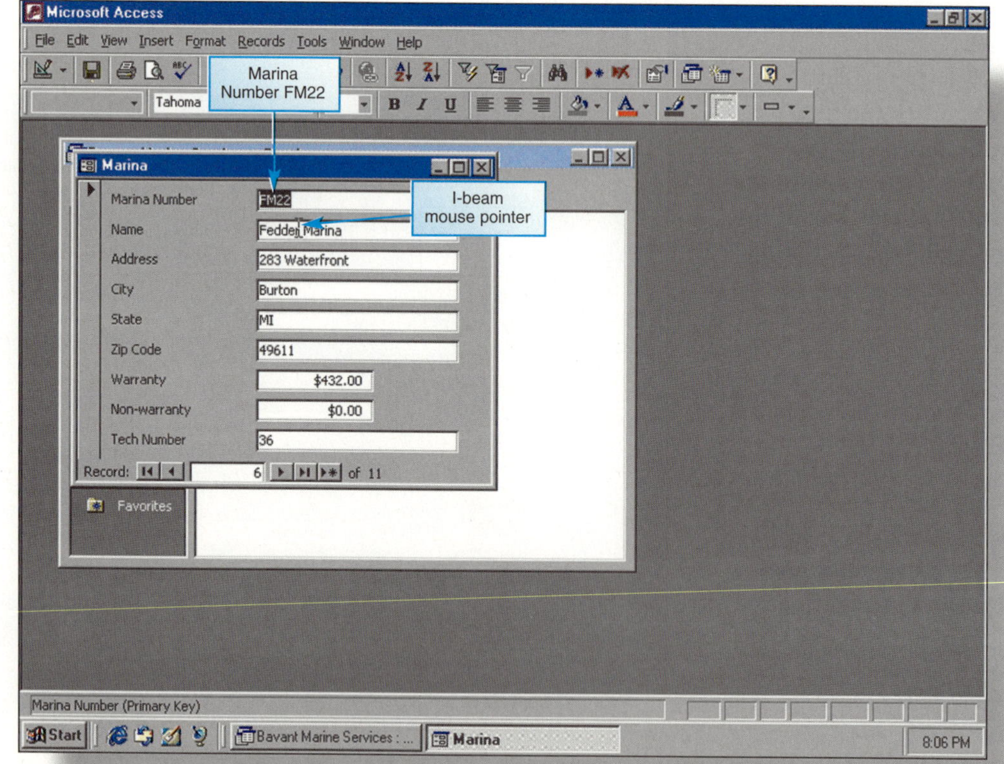

FIGURE 3-8

Switching Between Views

Sometimes, after working in Form view where you can see all fields, but only one record, it would be helpful to see several records at a time. To do so, switch to Datasheet view by clicking the View button arrow on the Form View toolbar and then clicking Datasheet View. Perform the following steps to switch from Form view to Datasheet view.

The View Button

You can use the View button to easily transfer between viewing the form (Form view) and reviewing the design of the form (Design view). To move to Datasheet view, you must click the down arrow, and then click Datasheet view in the drop-down list that displays.

Steps To Switch from Form View to Datasheet View

1 Point to the View button arrow on the Form View toolbar toolbar (Figure 3-9).

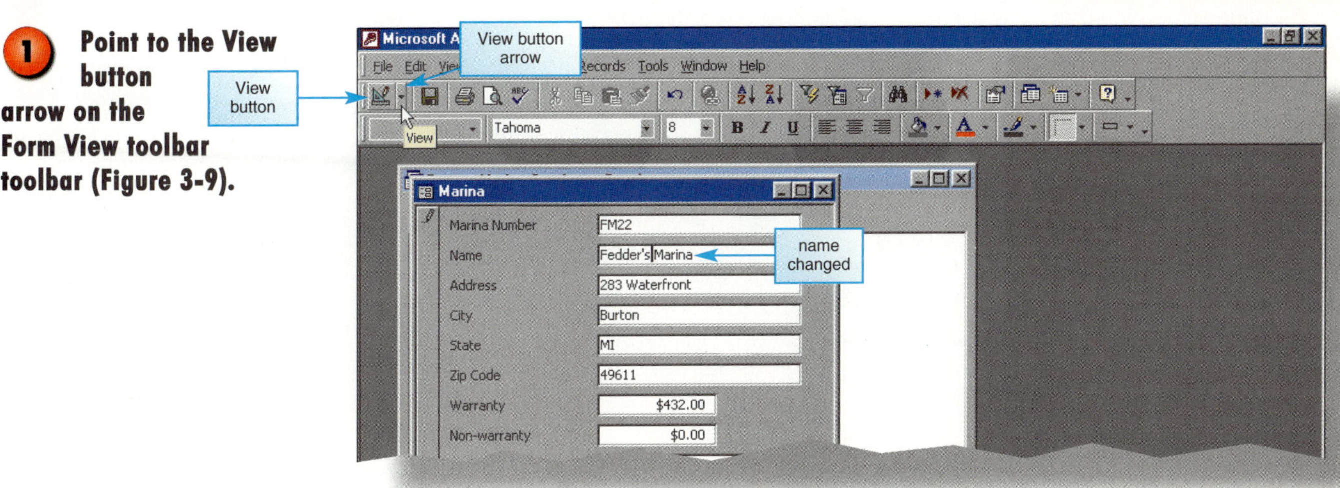

FIGURE 3-9

2 Click the View button arrow on the toolbar. Point to Datasheet View in the list.

The View list displays (Figure 3-10).

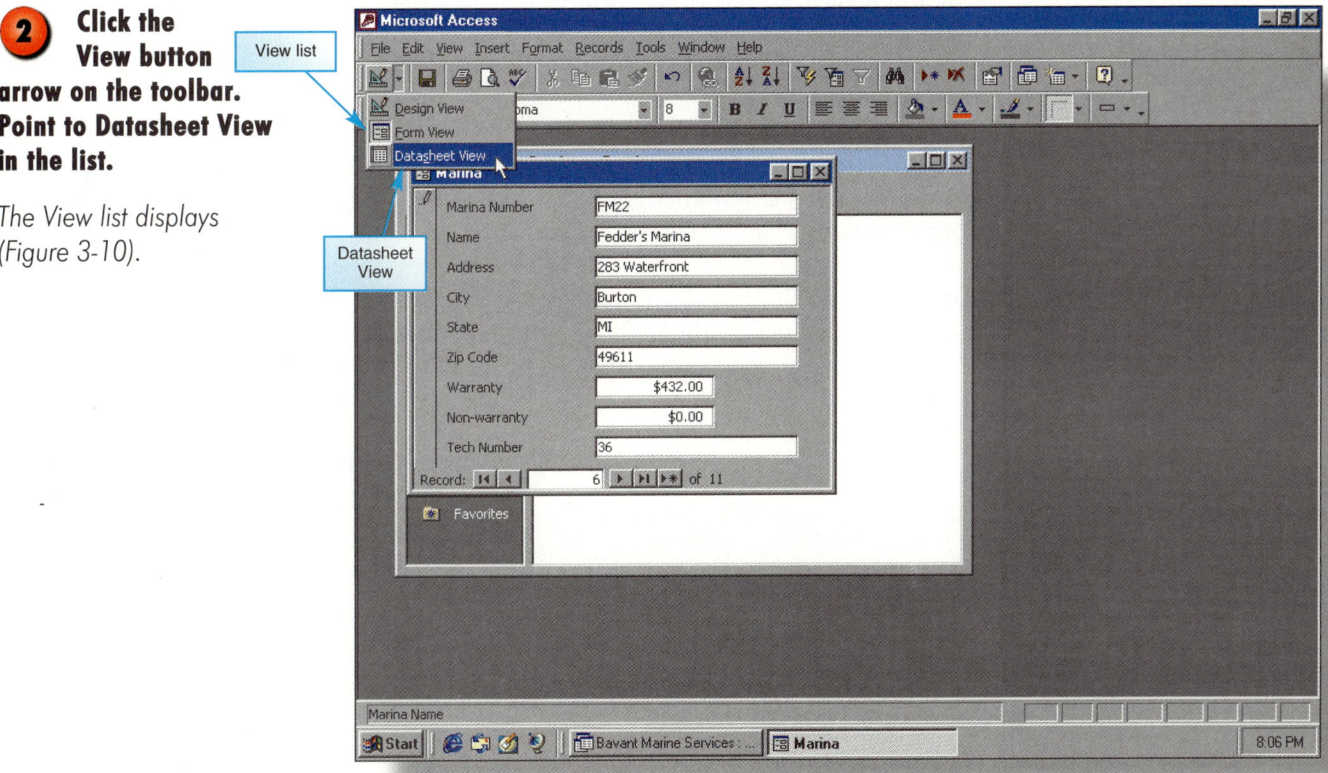

FIGURE 3-10

3 Click Datasheet View, and then maximize the window containing the datasheet.

The datasheet displays (Figure 3-11). The position in the table is maintained. The current record selector points to marina FM22, which is the marina that displayed on the screen in Form view. The Name field, the field in which the insertion point is displayed, is selected. The new record for marina PM34 is the last record in the table. When you close the table and open it later, marina PM34 will be in its appropriate location.

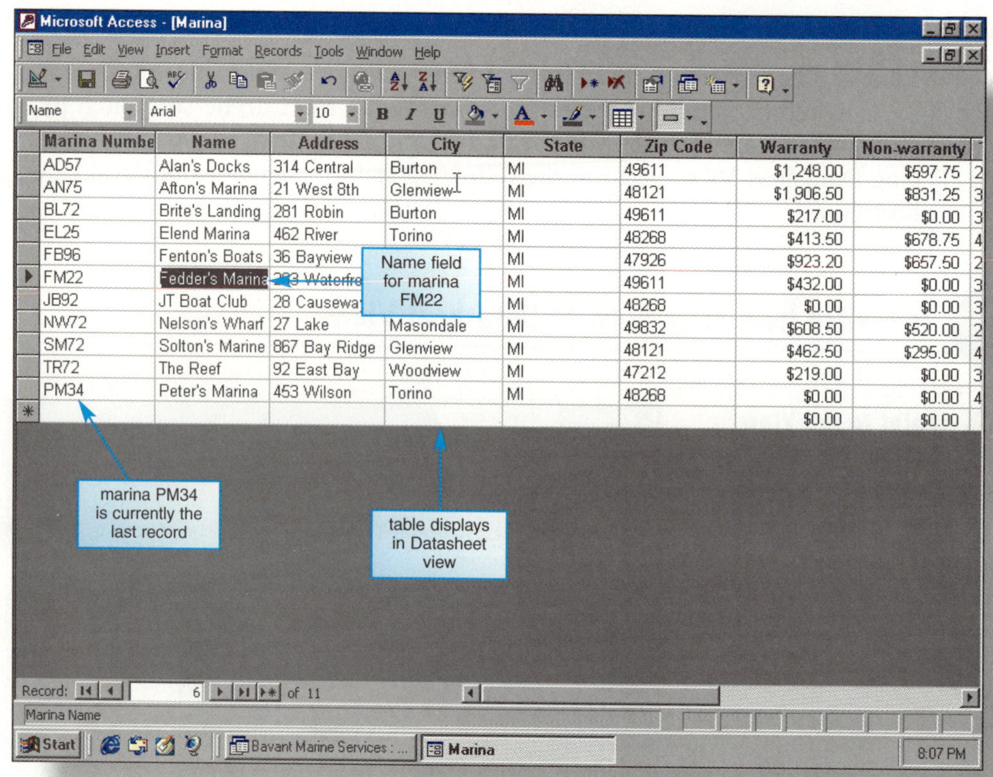

FIGURE 3-11

1. On View menu click Datasheet View

If you wanted to return to Form view, you would use the same process. The only difference is that you would click Form View instead of Datasheet View.

Filtering Records

You can use the Find button to locate a record quickly that satisfies a criterion (for example, the Marina Number is FM22). All records display, however, not just the record or records that satisfy the criterion. To have only the record or records that satisfy the criterion display, use a filter. The simplest type of filter is called **filter by selection**. To use filter by selection, give Access an example of the data you want by selecting the data within the table and then clicking the Filter By Selection button on the Form View toolbar. For example, if only the record or records on which the marina name is Fedder's Marina are to be included, you would select the Name field on the record for marina FM22, because the name on that record is Fedder's Marina. The following steps use filter by selection to display only the record for Fedder's Marina.

More About 2000

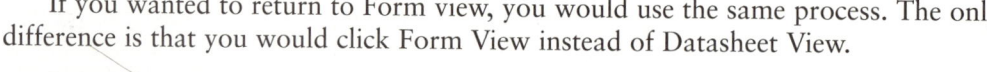

Filters: Filter by Form

If you want to filter records based on values in more than one field, click the Filter by Form button rather than the Filter by Selection button. You will then be able to fill in values in as many fields as you want. Once you are finished, click the Apply Filter button. Only those records containing all the values you entered will display. For more information, visit the Access 2000 Project 3 More About page (www.scsite.com/ac2000/more.htm) and click Filters.

To Filter Records

1 **Make sure the name for marina FM22 (Fedder's Marina) is selected and then point to the Filter By Selection button on the Form View toolbar (Figure 3-12).**

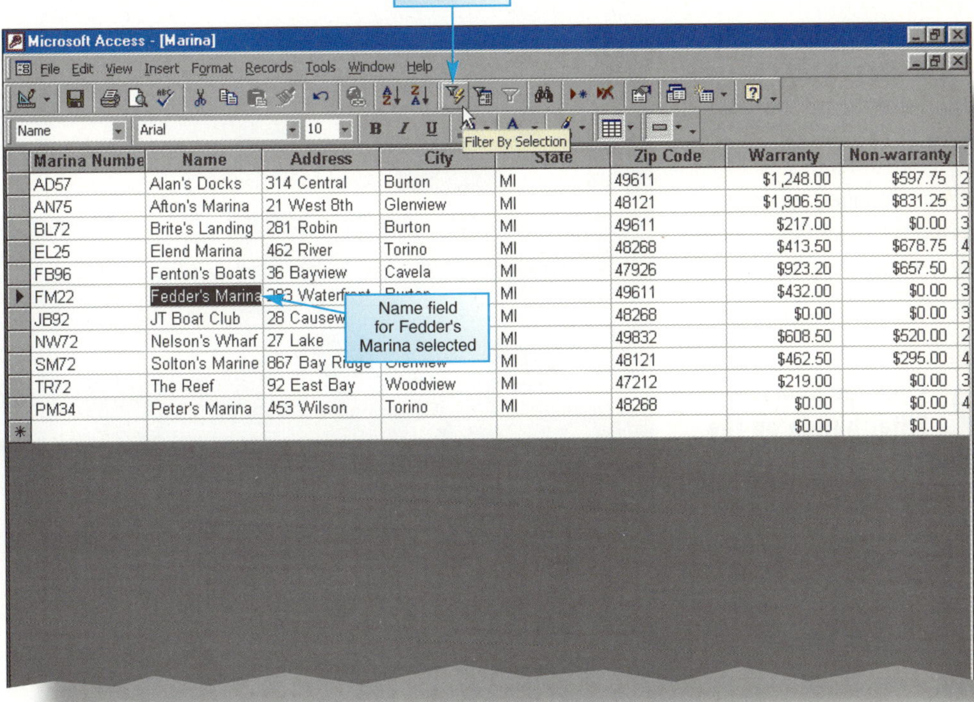

FIGURE 3-12

2 **Click the Filter By Selection button on the toolbar.**

Only the marina whose name is Fedder's Marina display (Figure 3-13).

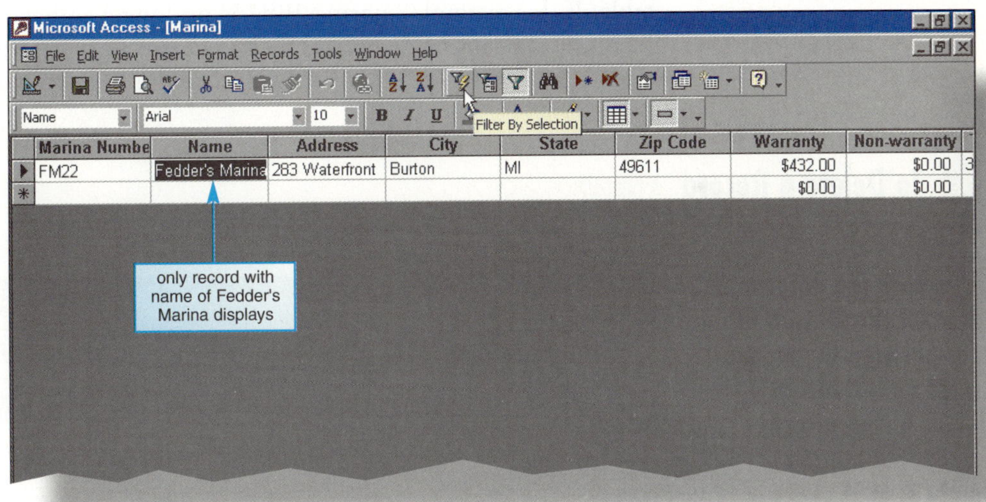

FIGURE 3-13

Because there only is one marina in the database with the name Fedder's Marina, only one marina displays. If you had instead selected the City field on the same record (Burton) before clicking the Filter By Selection button, three marinas would display, because there are currently three marinas located in Burton (marinas AD57, BL72, and FM22).

In order to have all records once again display, remove the filter by clicking the Remove Filter button on the Form View toolbar as in the following steps.

To Remove a Filter

1 **Point to the Remove Filter button on the Form View toolbar (Figure 3-14).**

The Remove Filter button is recessed because there currently is a filter applied to the table.

2 **Click the Remove Filter button on the toolbar.**

All records once again will display.

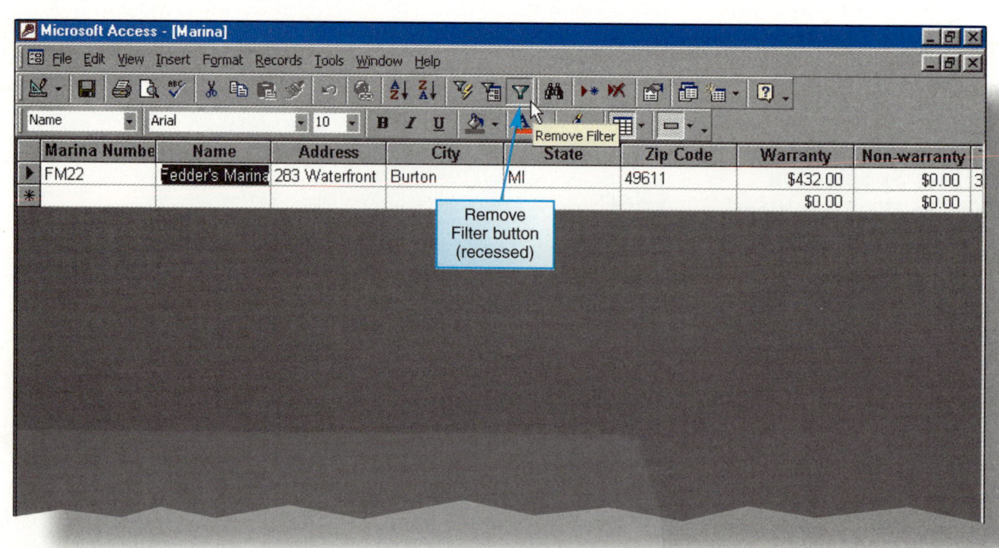

FIGURE 3-14

Other Ways

1. On Records menu click Filter, then click Filter By Selection

Deleting Records

When records are no longer needed, **delete the records** (remove them) from the table. If, for example, marina JB92 is no longer in business and already has settled its final bill, that marina's record should be deleted. To delete a record, first locate it and then press the DELETE key. Complete the following steps to delete marina JB92.

To Delete a Record

1 **With the datasheet for the Marina table open, position the mouse pointer on the record selector of the record in which the marina number is JB92 (Figure 3-15).**

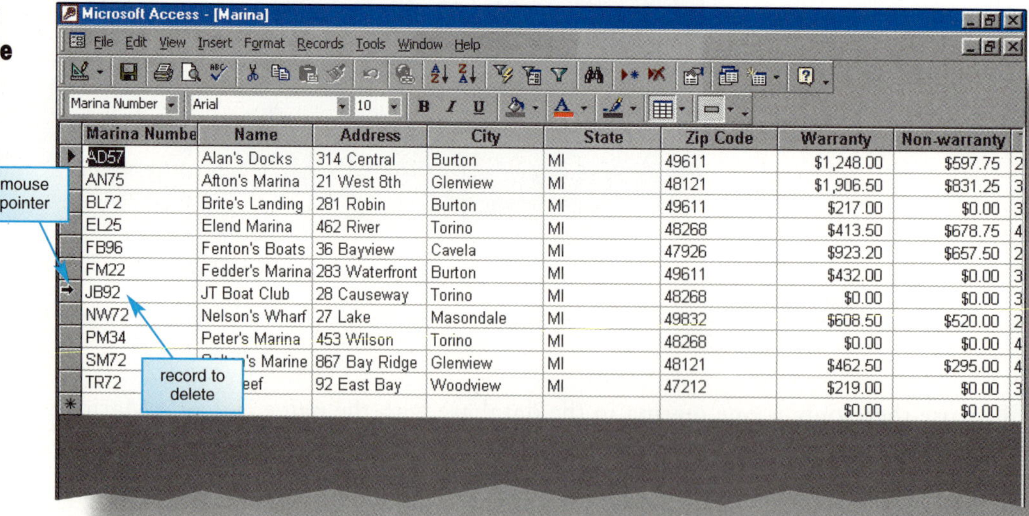

FIGURE 3-15

2 **Click the record selector to select the record, and then press the DELETE key to delete the record.**

The Microsoft Access dialog box displays (Figure 3-16). The message indicates that one record will be deleted.

3 **Click the Yes button to complete the deletion. Close the window containing the table by clicking its Close button on the title bar.**

The record is deleted and the Marina table window closes.

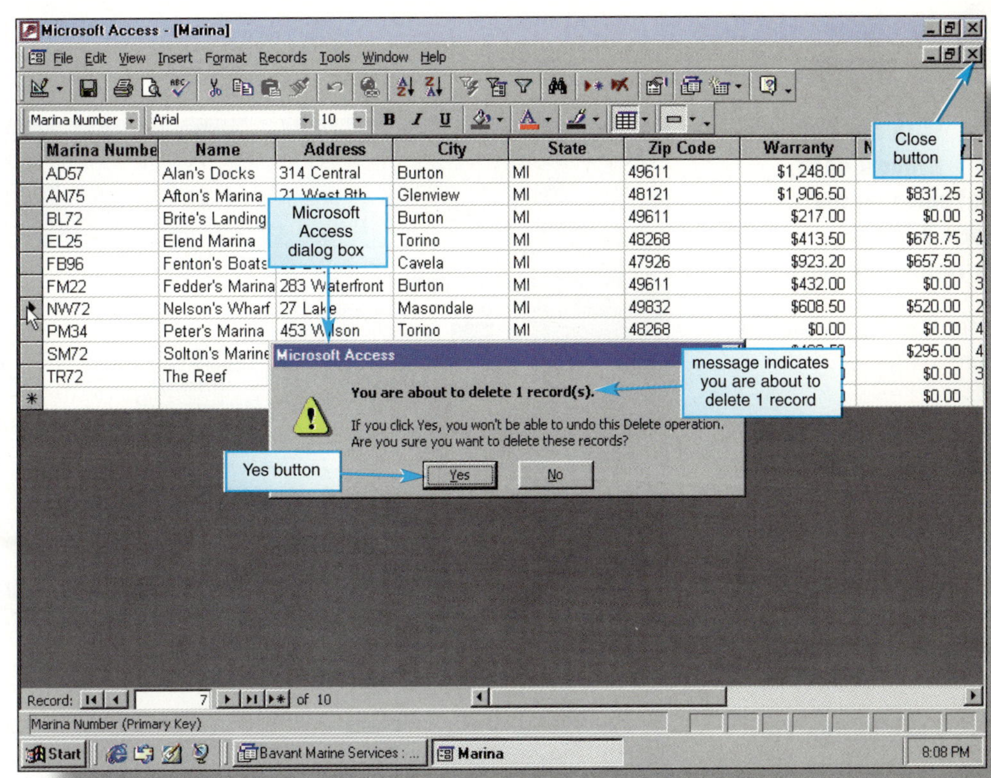

FIGURE 3-16

Changing the Structure of a Database

When you initially create a database, you define its **structure**; that is, you indicate the names, types, and sizes of all the fields. In many cases, the structure you first defined will not continue to be appropriate as you use the database. A variety of reasons exist why the structure of a table might need to change. Changes in the needs of users of the database may require additional fields to be added. In the Marina table, for example, if it is important to store a code indicating the marina type, you need to add such a field.

Characteristics of a given field may need to change. For example, the marina Alan's Docks's name is stored incorrectly in the database. It actually should be Alan's Docks Boat Works. The Name field is not large enough, however, to hold the correct name. To accommodate this change, you need to increase the width of the Name field.

It may be that a field currently in the table no longer is necessary. If no one ever uses a particular field, it is not needed in the table. Because it is occupying space and serving no useful purpose, it should be removed from the table. You also would need to delete the field from any forms, reports, or queries that include it.

To make any of these changes, click Design View on the shortcut menu.

More About 2000

Changing the Structure

A major advantage of using a full-featured database management system is the ease with which you can change the structure of the tables that make up the database. In a non-database environment, changes to the structure can be very cumbersome, requiring difficult and time-consuming changes to many programs.

Changing the Size of a Field

The steps on the next page change the size of the Name field from 20 to 25 to accommodate the change of name from Alan's Docks to Alan's Docks Boat Works.

To Change the Size of a Field

1 With the Database window open, click Tables on the Objects bar, and then right-click Marina.

The shortcut menu displays (Figure 3-17).

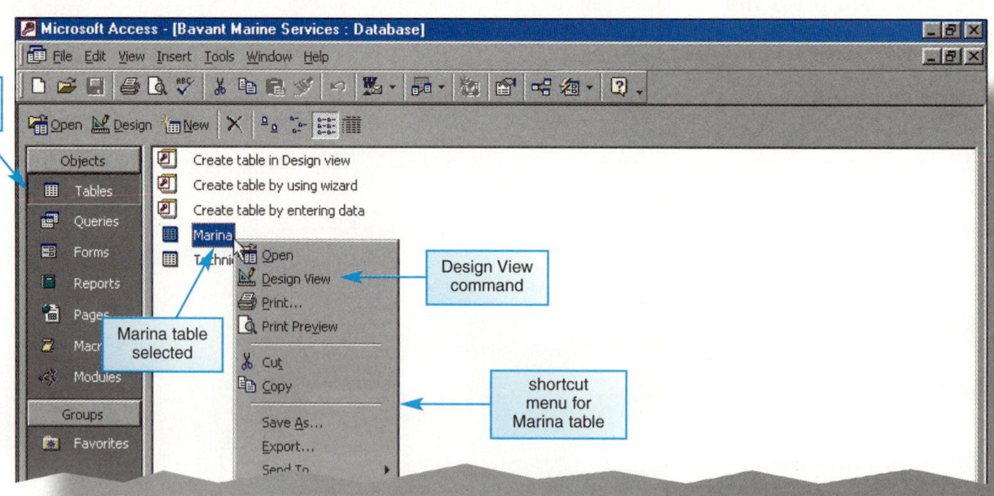

FIGURE 3-17

2 Click Design View on the shortcut menu and then point to the row selector for the Name field.

The Marina : Table window displays (Figure 3-18).

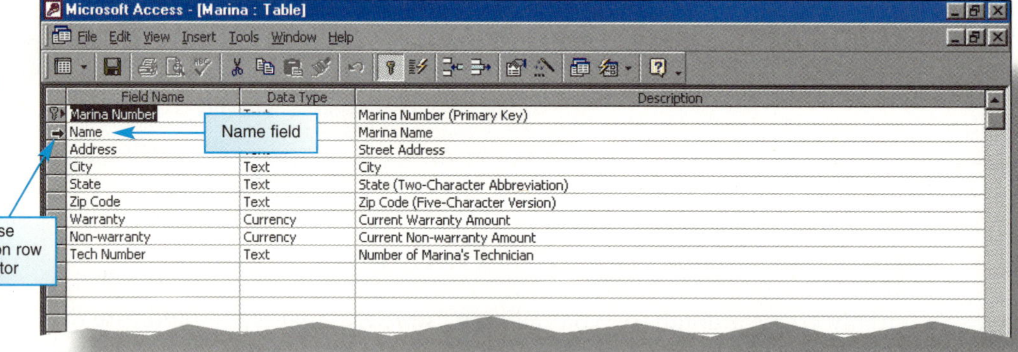

FIGURE 3-18

3 Click the row selector for the Name field.

The Name field is selected (Figure 3-19).

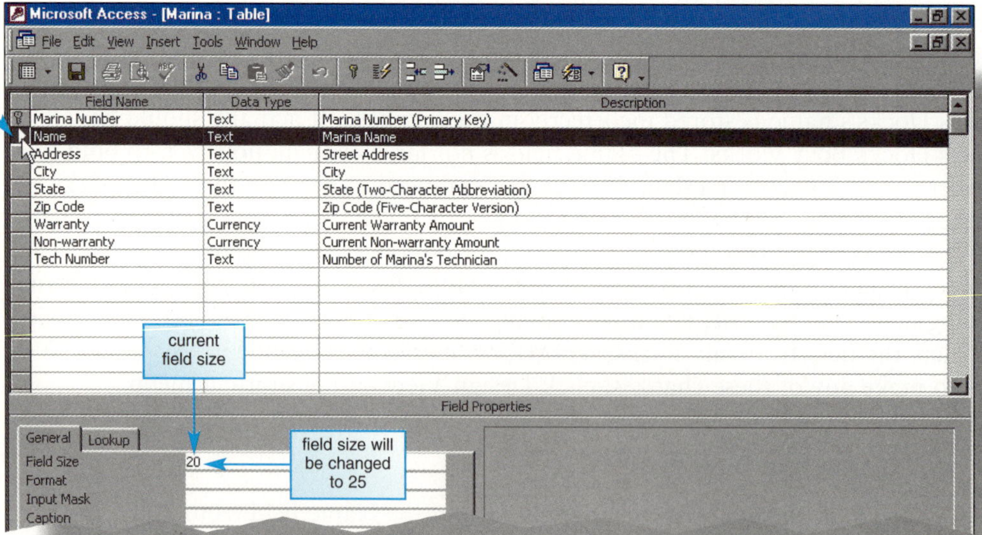

FIGURE 3-19

4 **Press F6 to select the field size, type** 25 **as the new size, and press F6 again.**

The size is changed (Figure 3-20).

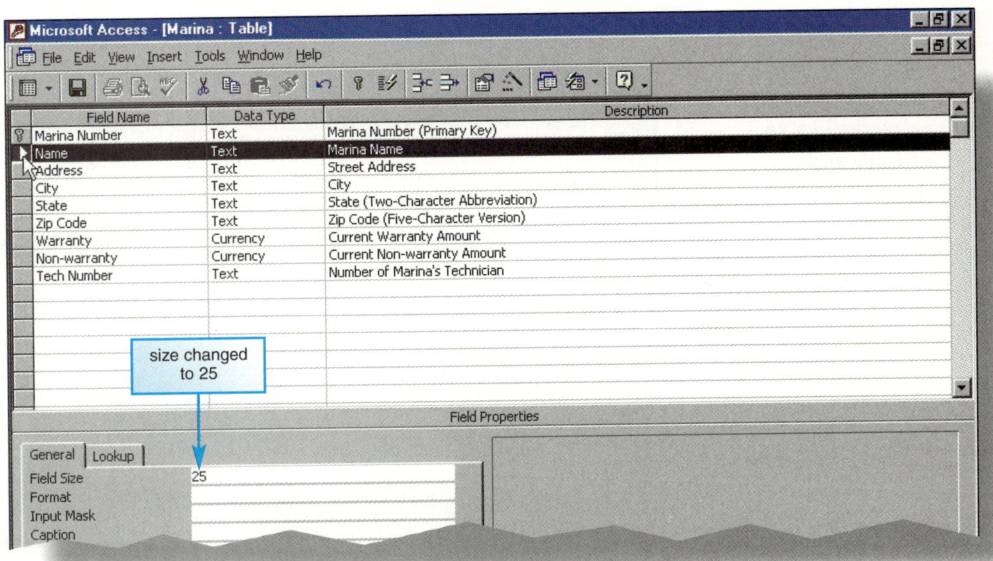

FIGURE 3-20

Adding a New Field

The management of Bavant decided they needed to categorize the marinas by the type of storage they offer. (Some marinas only support storing boats in the water. Others offer only rack storage where each boat is stored in a rack. When the owner wishes to use it, the marina places the boat in the water. As soon as the owner is done, the marina places the boat back on the rack. Still others offer both in-water and rack storage.)

To be able to store the marina type, the following steps add a new field, called Marina Type, to the table. The possible entries in this field are BIR (both in-water and rack storage), IWO (in-water only), and RSO (rack storage only). The new field will follow the zip code in the list of fields; that is, it will be the seventh field in the restructured table. The current seventh field (Warranty) will become the eighth field, Non-warranty will become the ninth field, and so on. Complete the following steps to add the field.

Adding a New Field

Tables frequently need to be expanded to include additional fields for a variety of reasons. Users needs can change. The field may have been omitted by mistake when the table was first created. Government regulations may change in such a way that the organization needs to maintain additional information.

To Add a Field to a Table

1 **Point to the row selector for the Warranty field (Figure 3-21).**

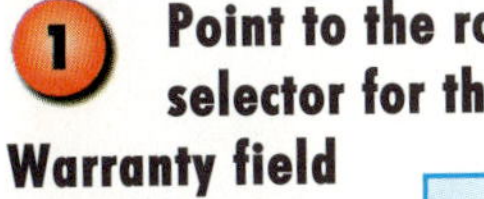

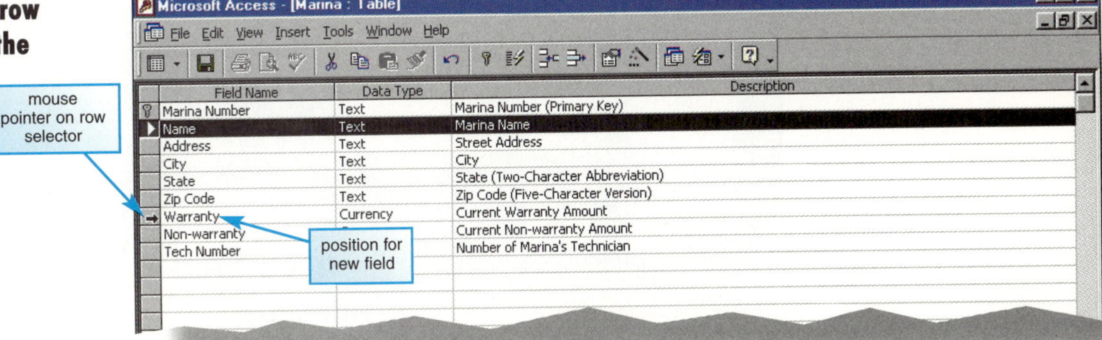

FIGURE 3-21

2 **Click the row selector for the Warranty field and then press the INSERT key to insert a blank row.**

A blank row displays in the position for the new field (Figure 3-22).

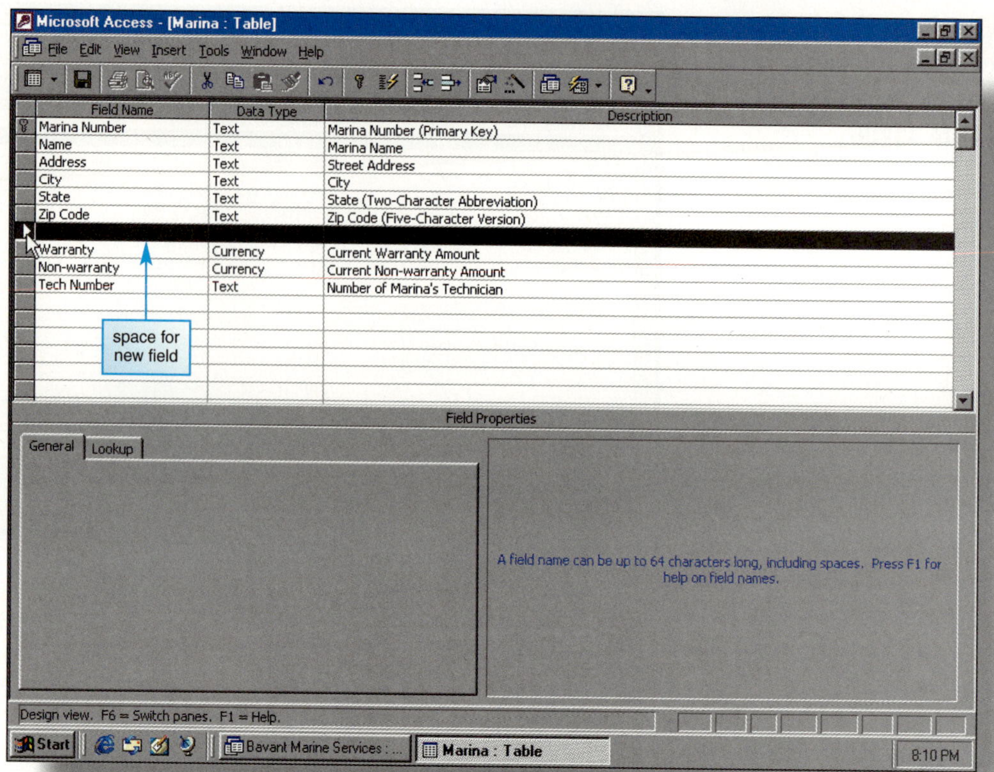

FIGURE 3-22

3 **Click the Field Name column for the new field. Type** `Marina Type` **as the field name and then press the TAB key. Select the Text data type by pressing the TAB key. Type** `Marina Type (BIR, IWO, or RSO)` **as the description. Press F6 to move to the Field Size text box, type** `3` **(the size of the Marina Type field), and then press F6 again.**

The entries for the new field are complete (Figure 3-23).

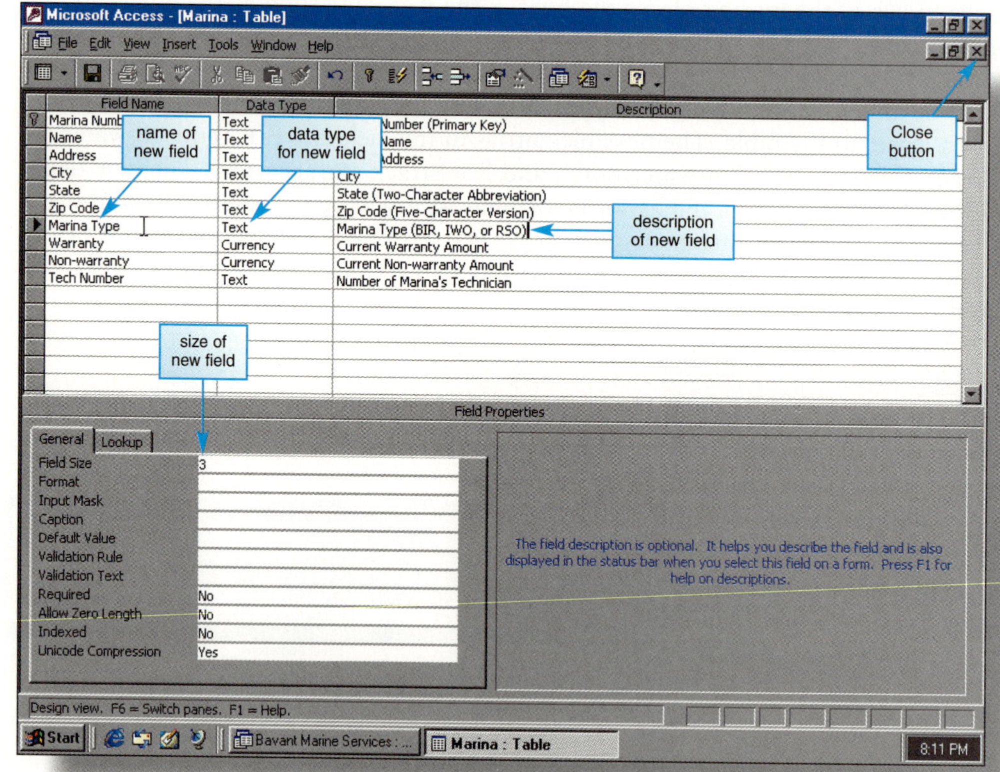

FIGURE 3-23

4 **Close the Marina : Table window by clicking its Close button on the title bar.**

The Microsoft Access dialog box displays (Figure 3-24) asking whether or not to save changes to the table s design.

5 **Click the Yes button to save the changes.**

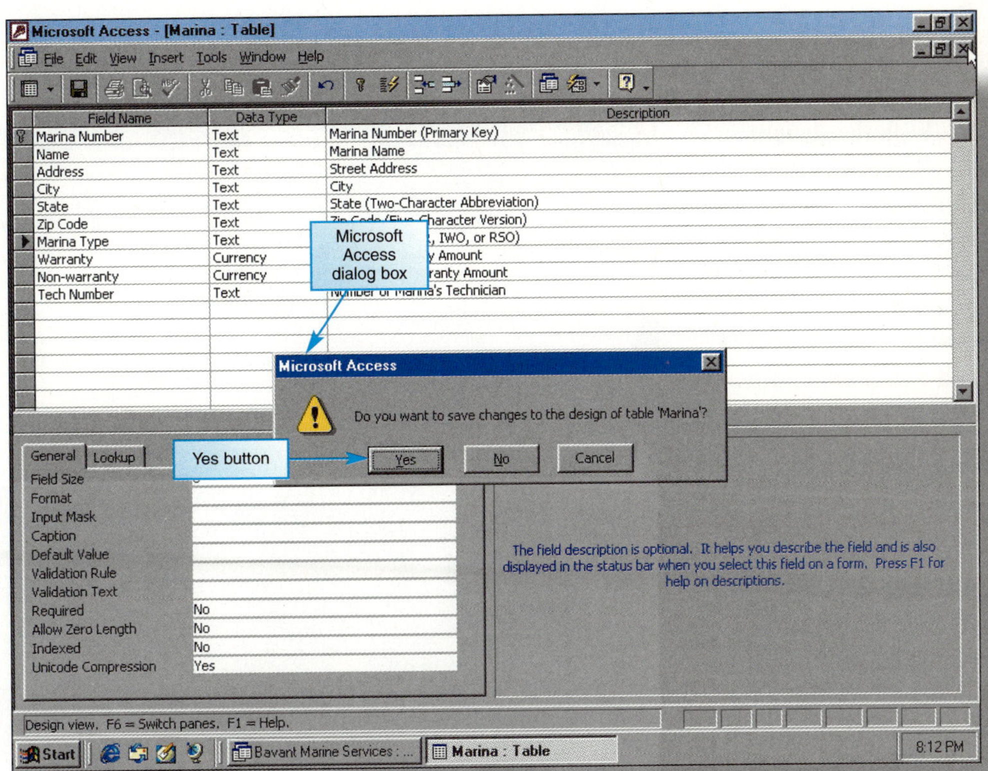

FIGURE 3-24

Deleting a Field from a Table

It is possible to find that a field in one of your tables is no longer needed. It may no longer serve a useful purpose or it may have been included by mistake. In such a case, you should delete the field. To do so, you first would open the table in Design view and then click the row selector for the field to select it. You then would press the DELETE key to delete the field. Access would request confirmation that you do indeed wish to delete the field. If you click the Yes button and then save your changes, the field will be removed from the table.

Updating the Restructured Database

Changes to the structure are available immediately. The Name field is longer, although it does not display that way on the screen, and the new Marina Type field is included.

To make a change to a single field, such as changing the name from Alan's Docks to Alan's Docks Boat Works, click the field to be changed, and then type the new value. If the record to be changed is not on the screen, use the Next Record or Previous Record navigation button to move to it. If the field to be corrected simply is not visible on the screen, use the horizontal scroll bar along the bottom of the screen to shift all the fields until the correct one displays. Then make the change.

Perform the steps on the next page to change the name of Alan's Docks to Alan's Docks Boat Works.

To Update the Contents of a Field

1 **With the Bavant Marine Services : Database window open, right-click Marina. Click Open on the shortcut menu. Position the I-beam mouse pointer to the right of the second s in Alan's Docks (marina AD57).**

The datasheet displays (Figure 3-25).

2 **Click immediately to the right of the second s in Alan's Docks, press the spacebar, and then type Boat Works to change the name.**

The name is changed from Alan's Docks to Alan's Docks Boat Works.

FIGURE 3-25

Resizing Columns

When you change the size of a field, the forms you previously created will not reflect your changes. If you used the AutoForm command, you can change the field sizes by simply recreating the form. To do so, right-click the form, click Delete, and create the form as you did in Project 1.

Resizing Columns

The default column sizes provided by Access do not always allow all the data in the field to display. You can correct this problem by **resizing the column** (changing its size) in the datasheet. In some instances, you actually may want to reduce the size of a column. The City field, for example, is short enough that it does not require all the space on the screen that is allotted to it.

Both types of changes are made the same way. Position the mouse pointer on the right boundary of the column's **field selector** (the line in the column heading immediately to the right of the name of the column to be resized). The mouse pointer will change to a two-headed arrow with a vertical bar. You then can drag the line to resize the column. In addition, you can double-click in the line, in which case Access will determine the best size for the column.

The following steps illustrate the process for resizing the Name column to the size that best fits the data.

To Resize a Column

1 Point to the right boundary of the field selector for the Name field (Figure 3-26).

field selector for Name field

right boundary of field selector

mouse pointer shape indicates column can be resized

name has been changed

FIGURE 3-26

2 Double-click the right boundary of the field selector for the Name field.

The Name column has been resized (Figure 3-27).

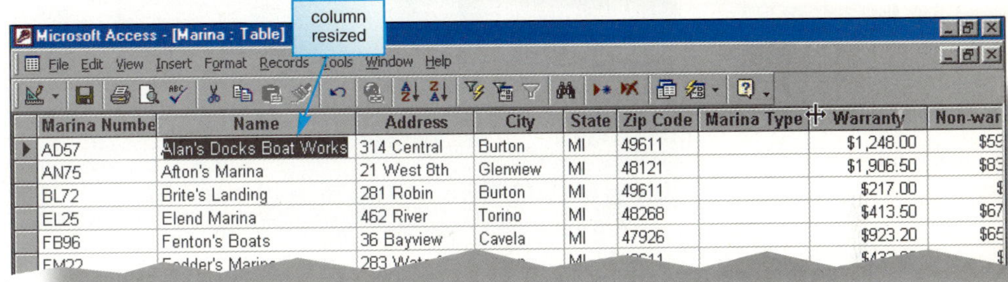

FIGURE 3-27

3 Use the same technique to resize the Address, City, State, Zip Code, and Warranty field columns to best fit the data.

The columns have been resized (Figure 3-28).

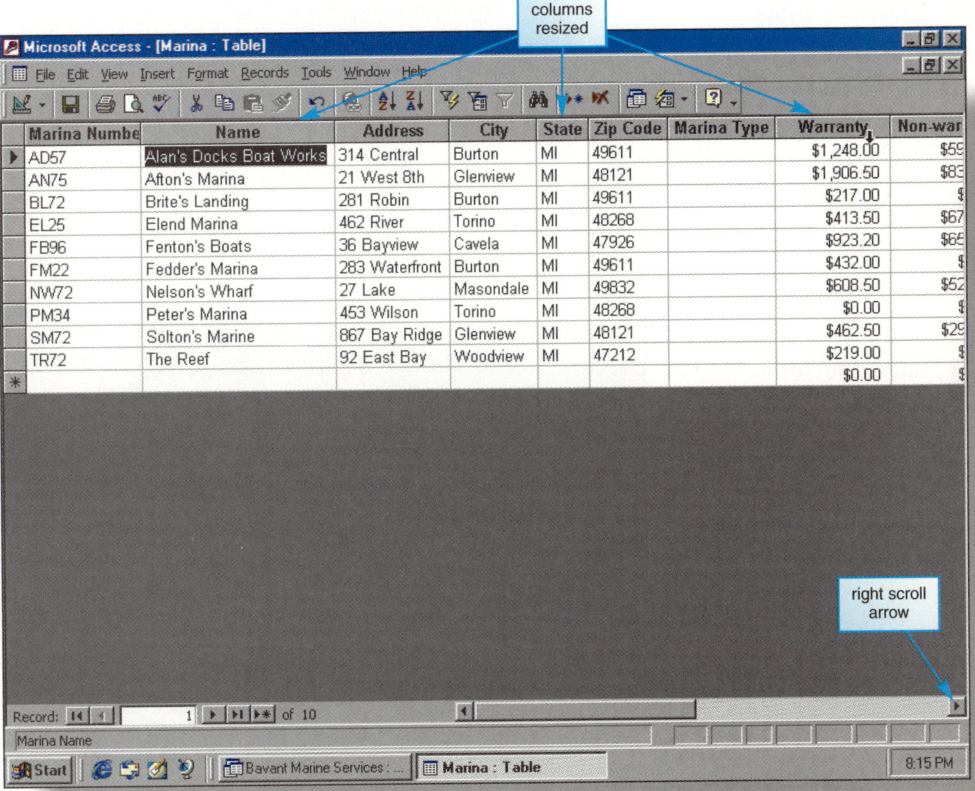

FIGURE 3-28

4 **Click the right scroll arrow to display the Non-warranty and Tech Number field columns, and then resize the Non-warranty and Tech Number field columns to best fit the data.**

All the columns have been resized (Figure 3-29).

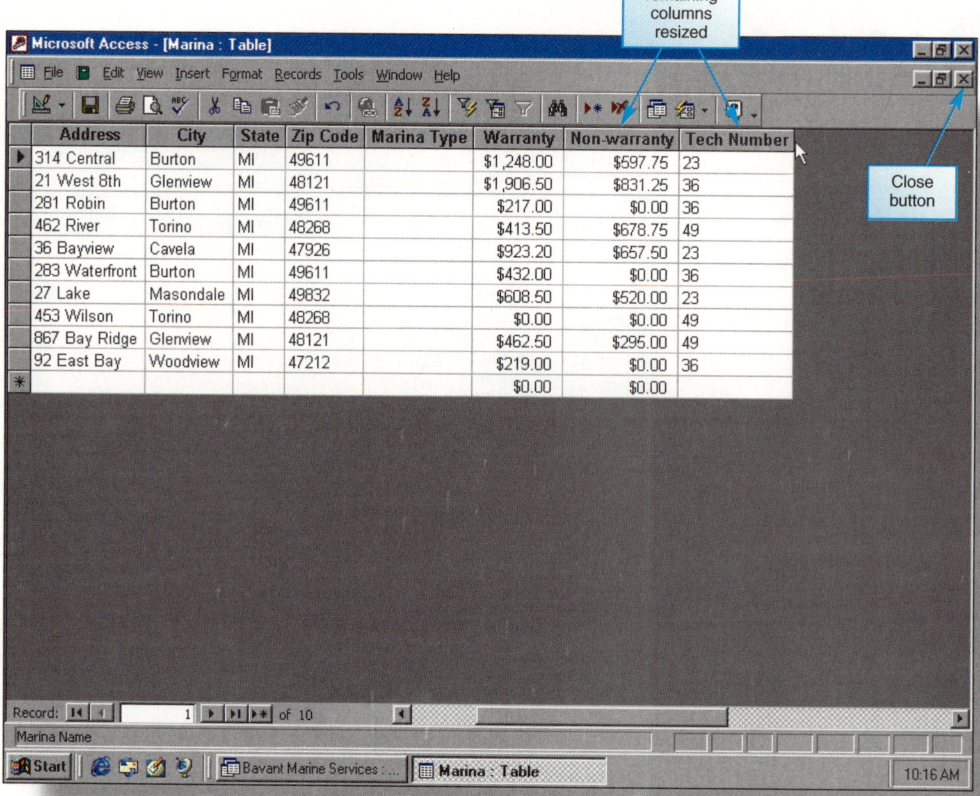

FIGURE 3-29

5 **Close the Marina : Table window by clicking its Close button on the title bar.**

The Microsoft Access dialog box displays (Figure 3-30) asking whether or not to save changes to the table's layout.

6 **Click the Yes button.**

The changes are saved. The next time the datasheet displays, the columns will have the new widths.

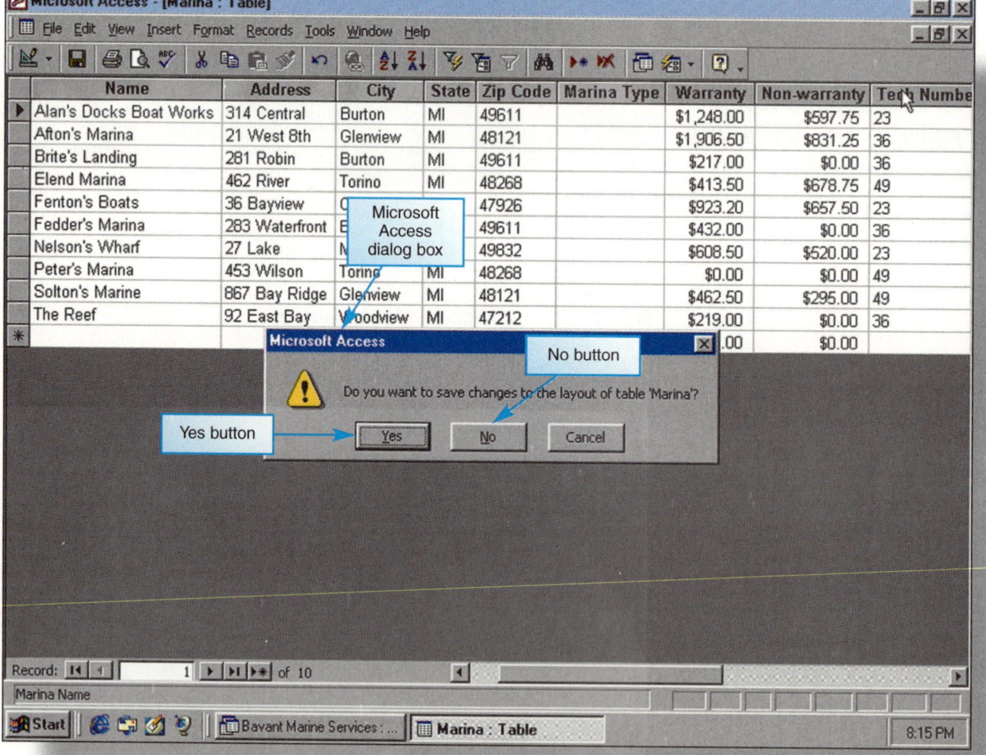

FIGURE 3-30

Other Ways

1. On Format menu click Column Width

Using an Update Query

The Marina Type field is blank on every record. One approach to entering the information for the field would be to step through the entire table, assigning each record its appropriate value. If most of the marinas have the same type, a simpler approach is available.

At Bavant, for example, most marinas are type BIR. Initially, you can set all the values to BIR. To accomplish this quickly and easily, you use a special type of query called an **update query**. Later, you can change the type for those marinas that only offer in-water storage (IWO) or only offer rack storage (RSO).

The process for creating an update query begins the same as the process for creating the queries in Project 2. After selecting the table for the query, right-click any open area of the upper pane, click Query Type on the shortcut menu, and then click Update Query on the menu of available query types. An extra row, Update To:, displays in the design grid. Use this additional row to indicate the way the data will be updated. If a criterion is entered, then only those records that satisfy the criterion will be updated.

Perform the following steps to change the value in the Marina Type field to BIR for all the records. Because all records are to be updated, no criterion will be entered.

Update Queries

Any full-featured database management system will offer some mechanism for updating multiple records at a time, that is, for making the same change to all the records that satisfy some criterion. Some systems, including Access, accomplish this through the query tool by providing a special type of query for this purpose.

Steps To Use an Update Query to Update All Records

1. **With the Marina table selected, click the New Object: AutoForm button arrow on the Database window toolbar.**

The New Object: AutoForm list displays (Figure 3-31).

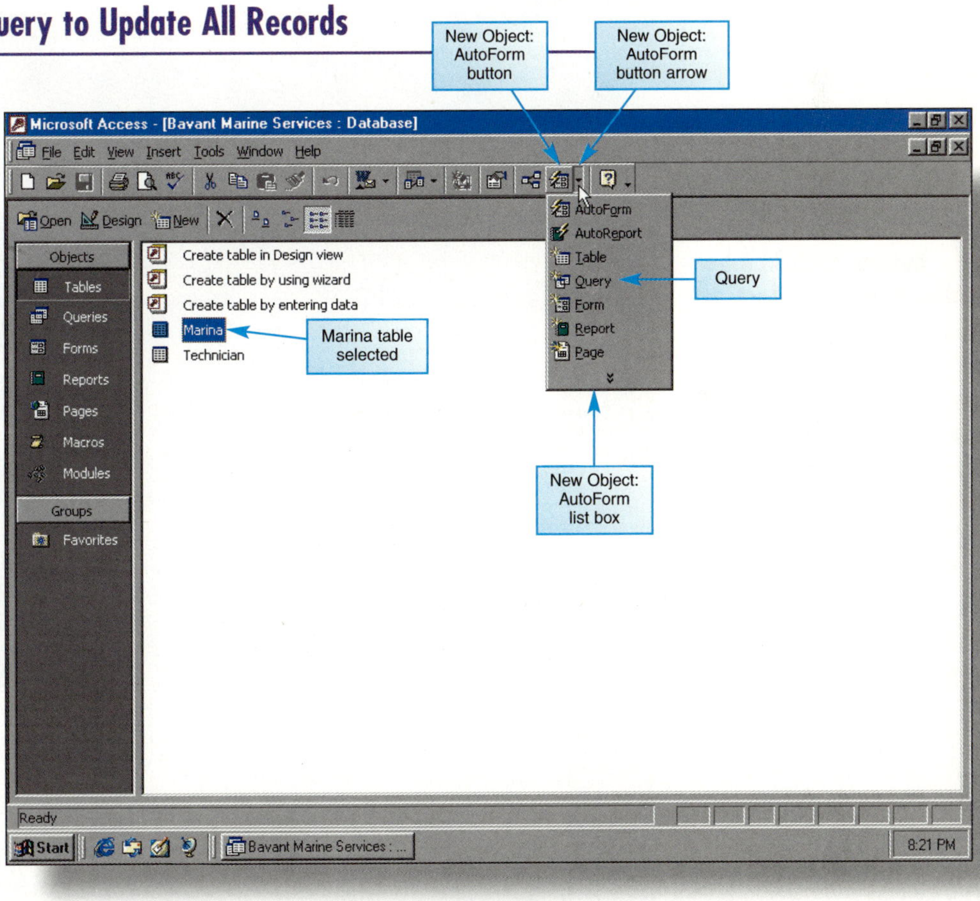

FIGURE 3-31

Click Query in the list.

The New Query dialog box displays (Figure 3-32). Design View is selected.

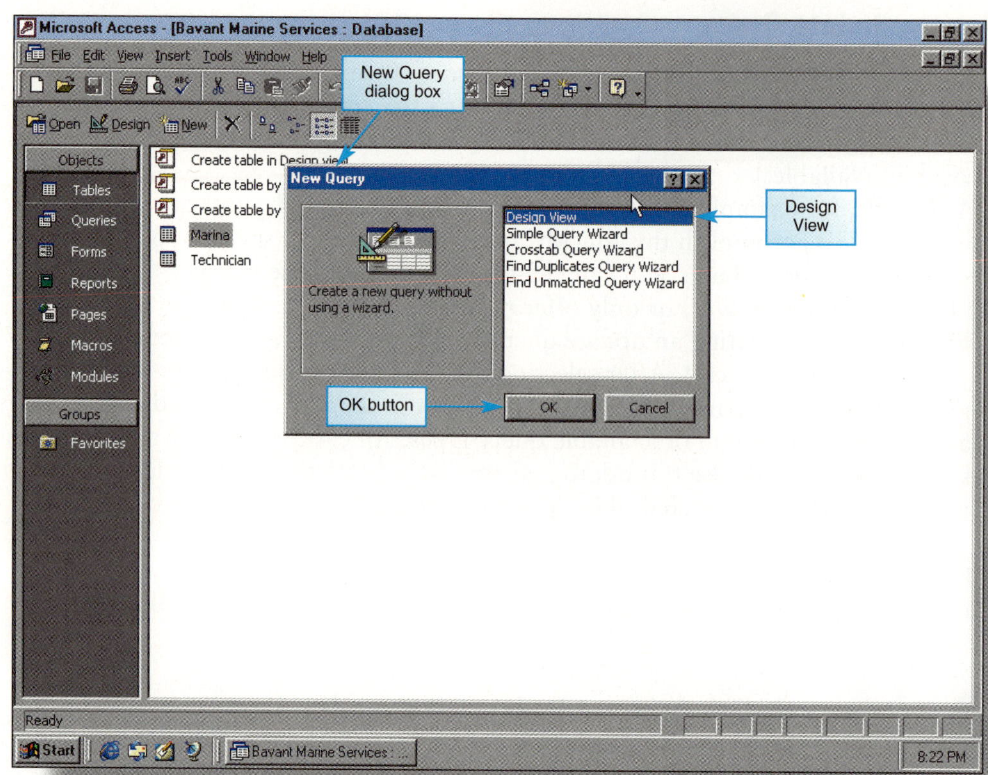

FIGURE 3-32

Click the OK button, and then be sure the Query1 : Select Query window is maximized. Resize the upper and lower panes of the window as well as the Marina field list box so all fields in the Marina table field list display (see page A 2.9 in Project 2). Right-click the upper pane and point to Query Type on the shortcut menu.

The shortcut menu displays (Figure 3-33). The Query Type submenu displays, showing available query types.

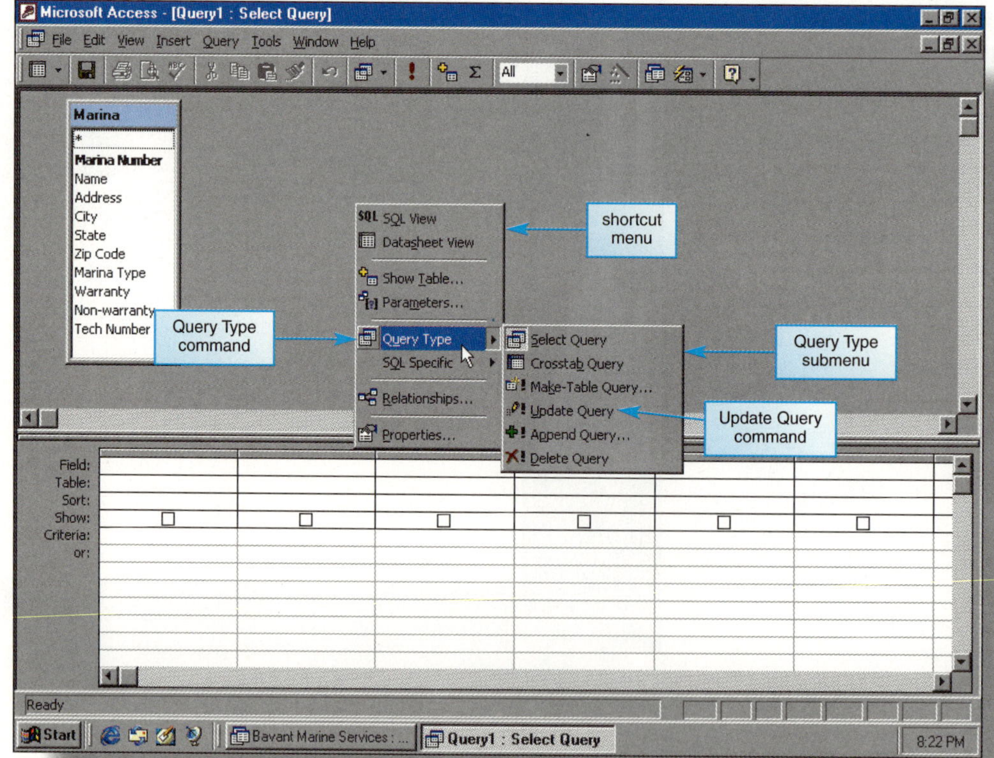

FIGURE 3-33

4 Click Update Query on the submenu, double-click the Marina Type field in the Marina table field list to select the field, click the Update To text box in the first column of the design grid, and then type `BIR` **as the new value.**

The Marina Type field is selected (Figure 3-34). In an Update Query, the Update To row displays in the design grid. The value to which the field is to be changed is entered as BIR. Because no criteria are entered, the Marina Type value on every row will be changed to BIR.

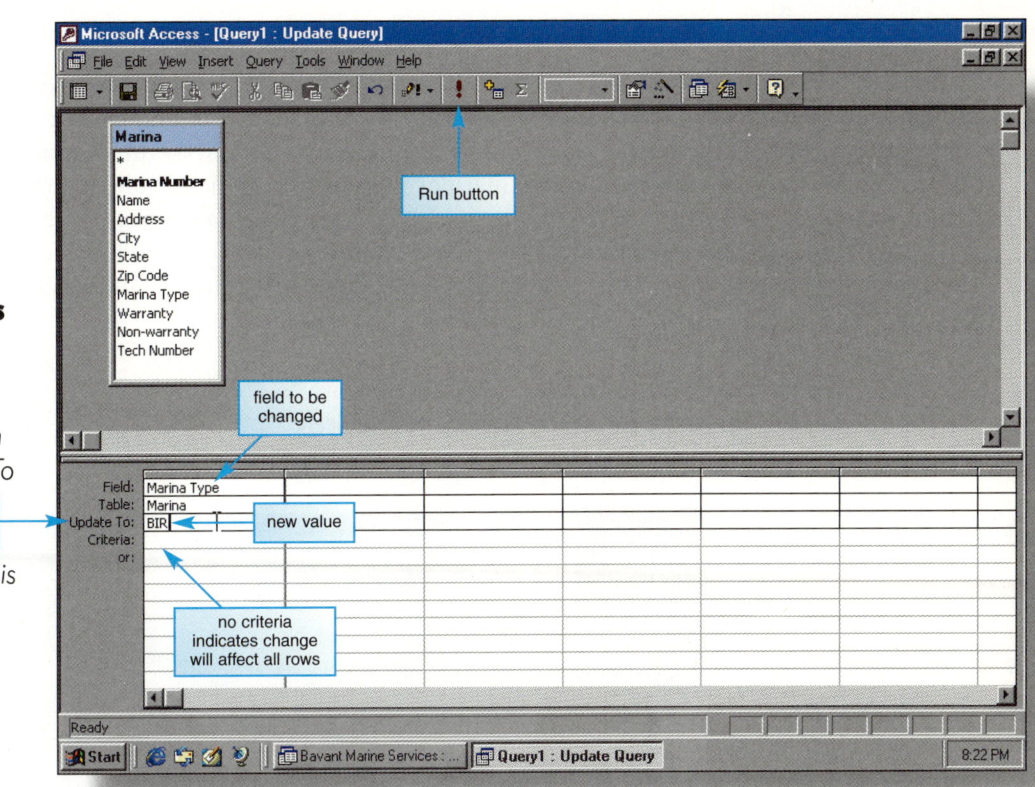

FIGURE 3-34

5 Click the Run button on the Query Design toolbar.

The Microsoft Access dialog box displays (Figure 3-35). The message indicates that 10 rows will be updated by the query.

6 Click the Yes button.

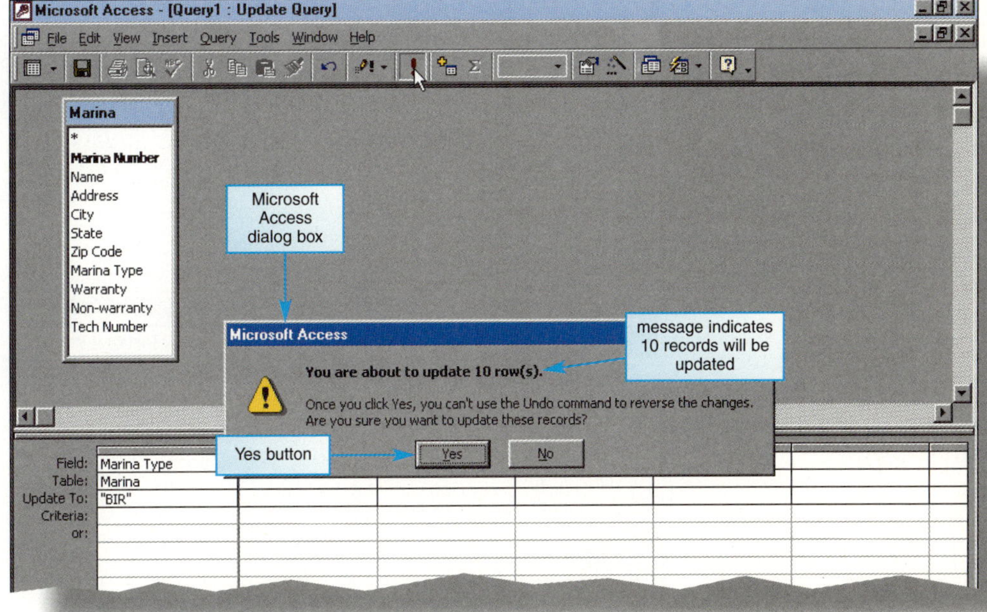

FIGURE 3-35

1. Click Query Type button arrow on Query Design toolbar, click Update Query
2. On Query menu click Update Query

Delete Queries

Any full-featured database management system will offer some means of deleting multiple records at one time, that is, deleting all the records that satisfy a given criterion. Access accomplishes this by providing a special type of query for this purpose.

Using a Delete Query to Delete a Group of Records

In some cases, you may need to delete several records at a time. If, for example, all marinas in a particular zip code are to be serviced by another firm, the marinas with this zip code can be deleted from the Bavant Marine Services database. Instead of deleting these marinas individually, which could be very cumbersome, you can delete them in one operation by using a **delete query**, which is a query that will delete all the records satisfying the criteria entered in the query.

Perform the following steps to use a delete query to delete all marinas whose zip code is 48121.

To Use a Delete Query to Delete a Group of Records

1 Click Edit on the menu bar and then click Clear Grid to clear the grid. Right-click the upper pane and then point to Query Type on the shortcut menu.

The shortcut menu displays (Figure 3-36). The Query Type submenu displays the available query types.

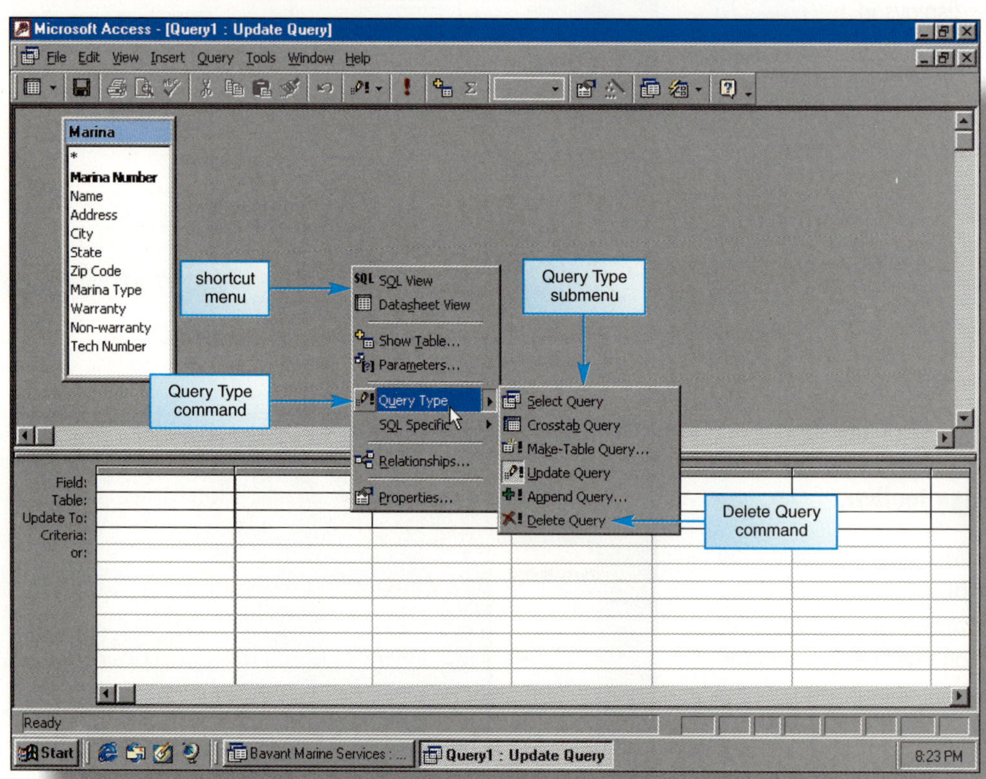

FIGURE 3-36

2 **Click Delete Query on the submenu, double-click the Zip Code field in the Marina table field list to select the field, and then click the Criteria entry. Type** 48121 **as the criterion.**

The criterion is entered in the Zip Code field (Figure 3-37). In a Delete Query, the Delete row displays in the design grid.

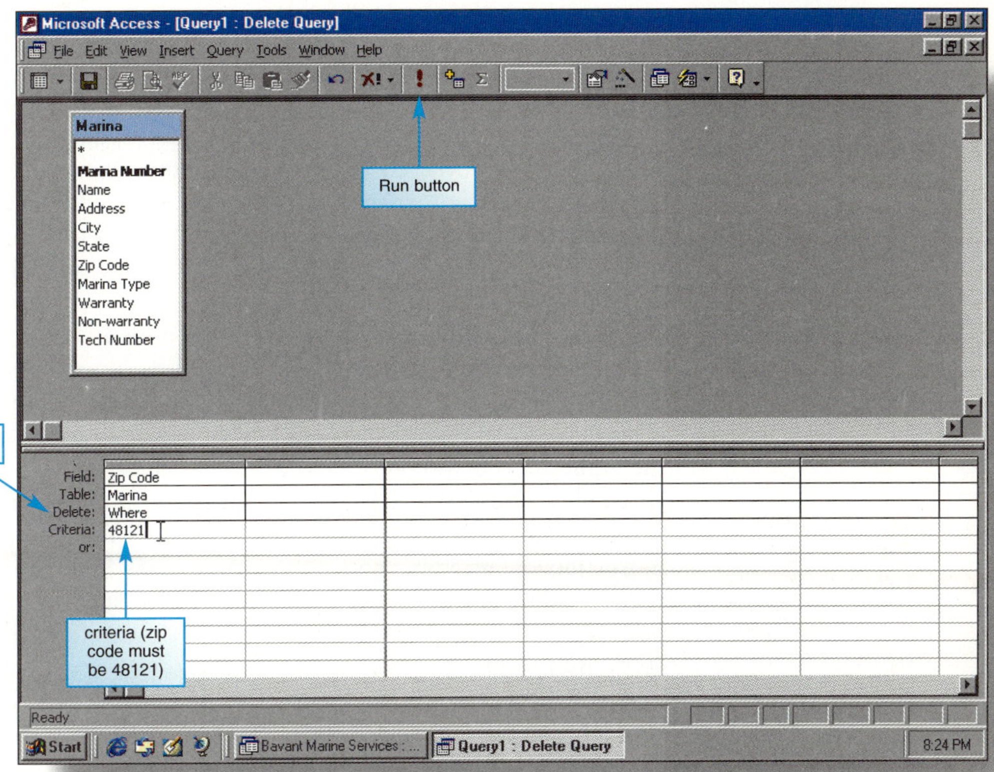

FIGURE 3-37

3 **Click the Run button on the Query Design toolbar to run the query.**

The Microsoft Access dialog box displays (Figure 3-38). The message indicates the query will delete 2 rows (records).

4 **Click the Yes button. Close the Query window by clicking its Close button on the title bar. Do not save the query.**

The two marinas with zip code 48121 have been removed from the table.

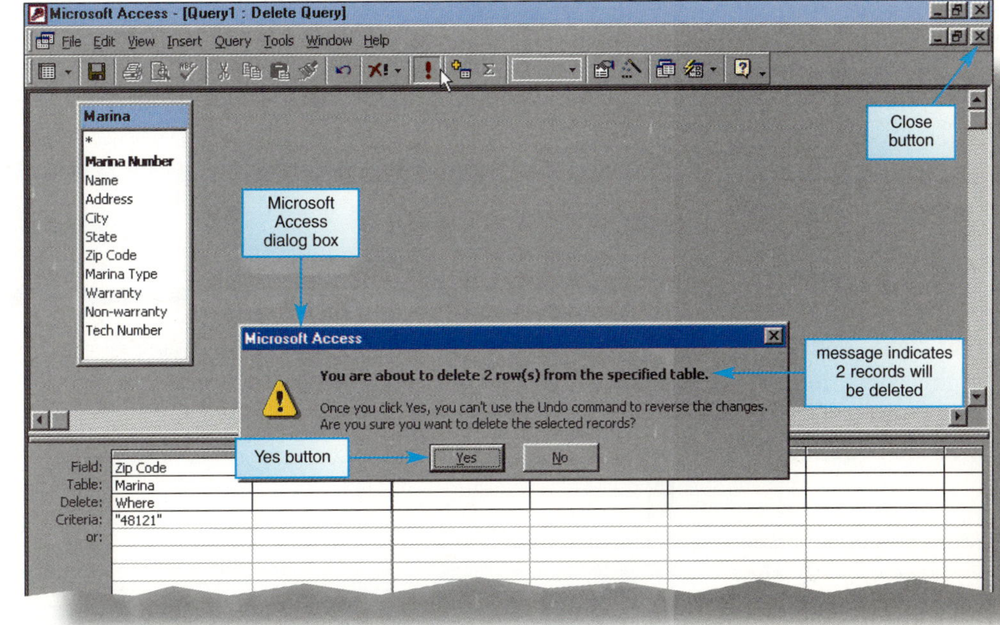

FIGURE 3-38

Other Ways

1. Click Query Type button arrow on Query Design toolbar, click Delete Query
2. On Query menu click Delete Query

Creating Validation Rules

You now have created, loaded, queried, and updated a database. Nothing you have done so far, however, ensures that users enter only valid data. To do so, you create **validation rules**; that is, rules that the data entered by a user must follow. As you will see, Access will prevent users from entering data that does not follow the rules. The steps also specify **validation text**, which is the message that will be displayed if a user violates the validation rule.

Validation rules can indicate a **required field**, which is a field in which the user actually must enter data. For example, by making the Name field a required field, a user actually must enter a name (that is, the field cannot be blank). Validation rules can make sure a user's entry lies within a certain **range of values**; for example, that the values in the Warranty field are between $0.00 and $10,000.00. They can specify a **default value**; that is, a value that Access will display on the screen in a particular field before the user begins adding a record. To make data entry of marina numbers more convenient, you also can have lowercase letters displayed automatically as uppercase letters. Finally, validation rules can specify a collection of acceptable values; for example, that the only legitimate entries for the Marina Type field are BIR, IWO, and RSO.

Specifying a Required Field

To specify that a field is to be required, change the value in the Required text box from No to Yes. The following steps specify that the Name field is to be a required field.

To Specify a Required Field

1 **With the Database window open and the Tables object selected, right-click Marina. Click Design View on the shortcut menu, and then select the Name field by clicking its row selector. Point to the Required text box.**

The Marina : Table window displays (Figure 3-39). The Name field is selected.

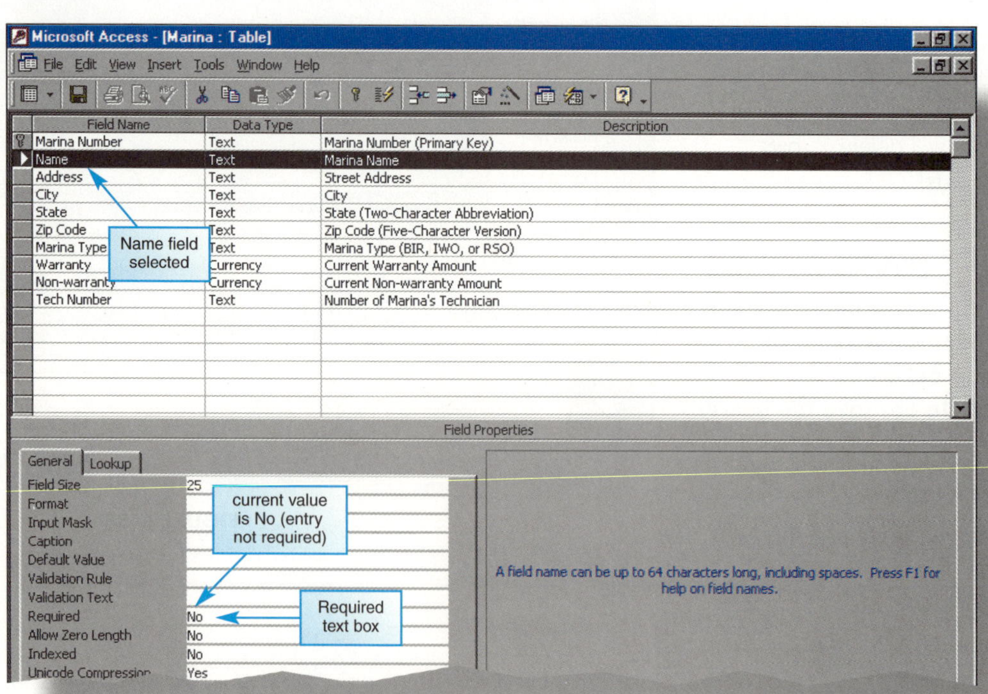

FIGURE 3-39

2 Click the Required text box in the Field Properties pane, and then click the down arrow that displays. Click Yes in the list.

The value in the Required text box changes to Yes (Figure 3-40). It now is required that the user enters data into the Name field when adding a record.

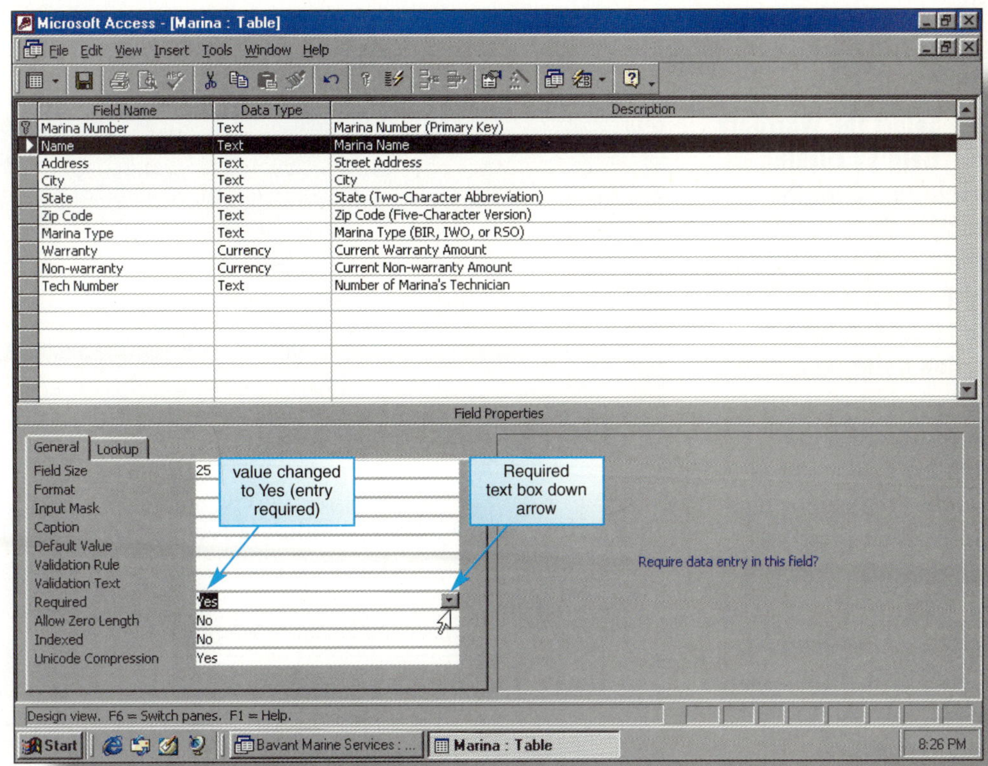

FIGURE 3-40

Specifying a Range

The following step specifies that entries in the Warranty field must be between $0.00 and $10,000.00. To indicate this range, you will enter a condition that specifies that the warranty amount must be both >= 0 (greater than or equal to zero) and <= 10000 (less than or equal to 10000).

To Specify a Range

1 **Select the Warranty field by clicking its row selector. Click the Validation Rule text box in the Field Properties pane to produce an insertion point, and then type** `>=0 and <=10000` **as the rule. Click the Validation Text text box in the Field Properties pane to produce an insertion point, and then type** `Must be between $0.00 and $10,000.00` **as the text. You must type all the text, including the dollar signs in this text box.**

The validation rule and text are entered (Figure 3-41). In the Validation Rule text box, Access automatically changed the lowercase letter, a, to uppercase in the word, and.

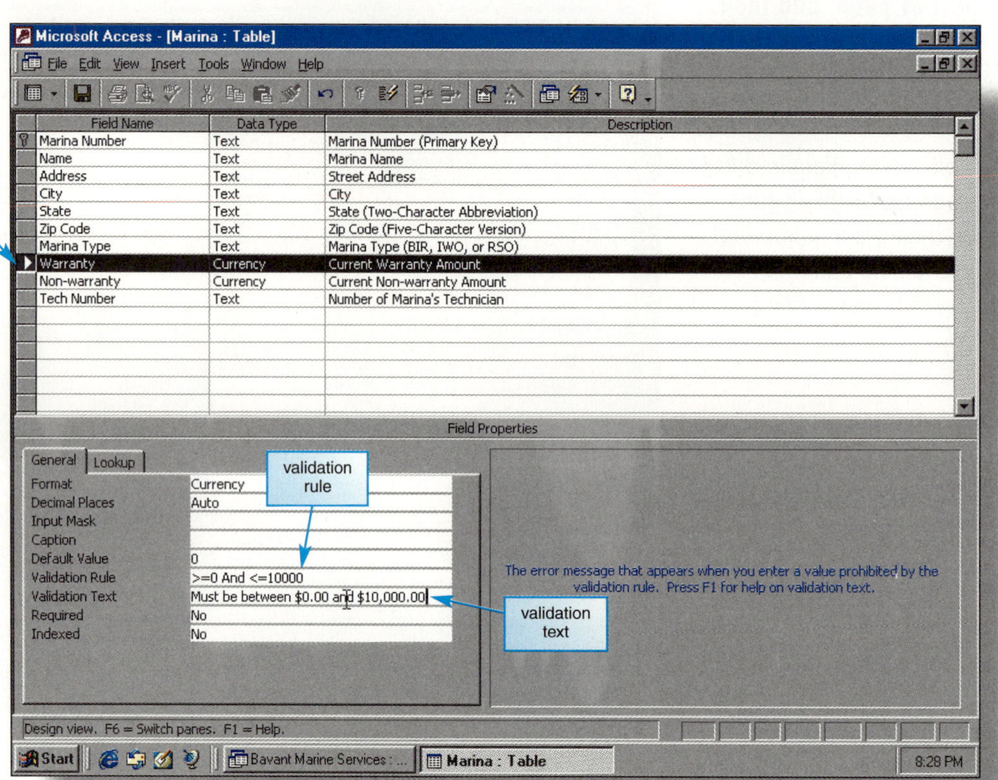

FIGURE 3-41

Users now will be prohibited from entering a warranty amount that either is less than $0.00 or greater than $10,000.00 when they add records or change the value in the Warranty field.

Specifying a Default Value

To specify a default value, enter the value in the Default Value text box in the Field Properties pane. The following step specifies BIR as the default value for the Marina Type field. This simply means that if users do not enter a marina type, the type will be BIR.

To Specify a Default Value

1 Select the Marina Type field by clicking its row selector. Click the Default Value text box in the Field Properties pane and then type =BIR **as the value.**

The Marina Type field is selected. The default value is entered in the Default Value text box (Figure 3-42).

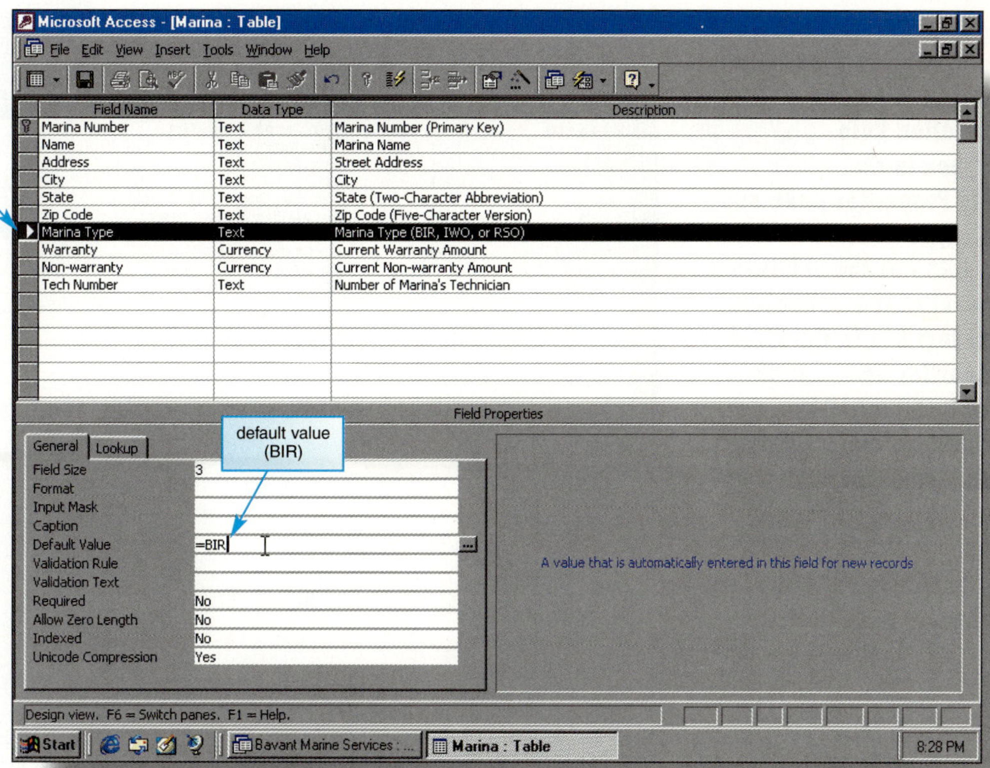

FIGURE 3-42

From this point on, if users do not make an entry in the Marina Type field when adding records, Access will set the value to BIR.

Specifying a Collection of Legal Values

The only **legal values** for the Marina Type field are BIR, IWO, and RSO. An appropriate validation rule for this field can direct Access to reject any entry other than these three possibilities. Perform the step on the next page to specify the legal values for the Marina Type field.

To Specify a Collection of Legal Values

1 Make sure the Marina Type field is selected. Click the Validation Rule text box in the Field Properties pane and then type `=BIR or =IWO or =RSO` **as the validation rule. Click the Validation Text text box in the Field Properties pane and then type** `Must be BIR, IWO, or RSO` **as the validation text.**

The Marina Type field is selected. The validation rule and text have been entered (Figure 3-43). In the Validation Rule text box, Access automatically inserted quotation marks around the BIR, IWO, and RSO values and changed the lowercase letter, o, to uppercase in the word, or.

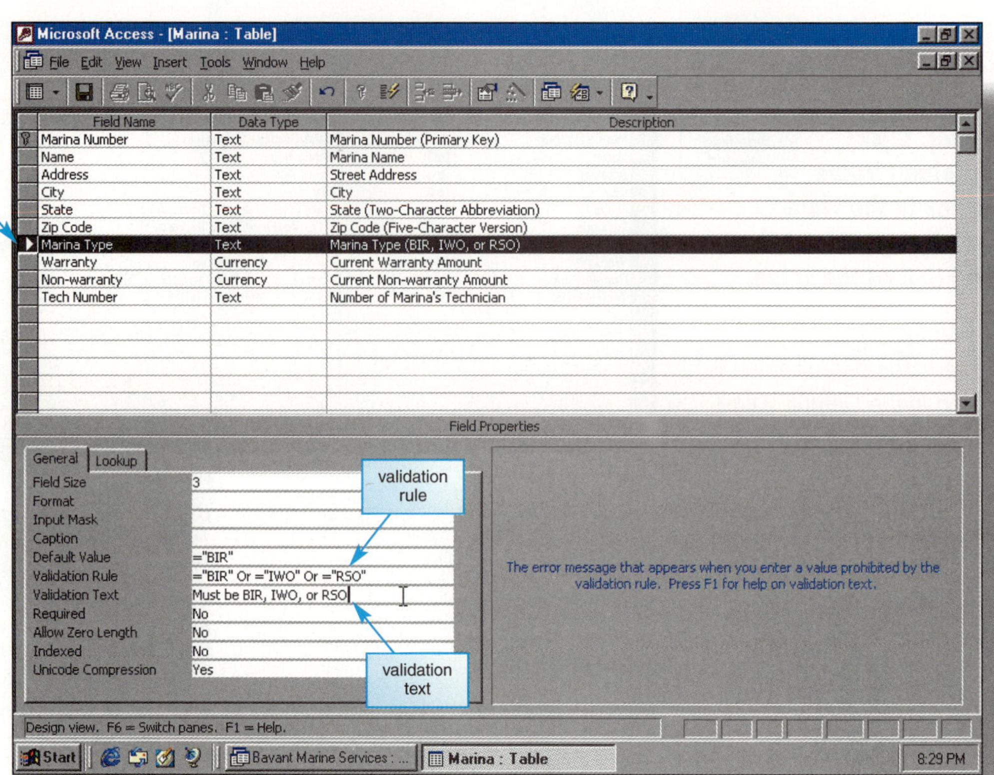

FIGURE 3-43

Users now will be allowed to enter only BIR, IWO, or RSO in the Marina Type field when they add records or make changes to this field.

Using a Format

To affect the way data is displayed in a field, you can use a **format**. To use a format, you enter a special symbol, called a **format symbol**, in the field's Format text box in the Field Properties pane. The following step specifies a format for the Marina Number field in the Marina table. The format symbol used in the example is >, which causes Access to display lowercase letters automatically as uppercase. The format symbol < would cause Access to display uppercase letters automatically as lowercase.

To Specify a Format

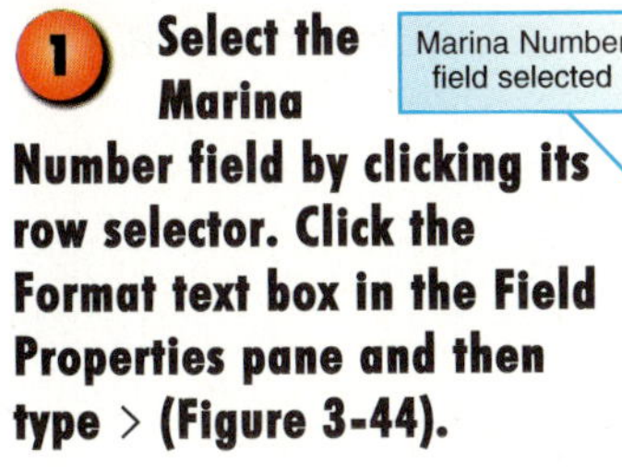

1 Select the Marina Number field by clicking its row selector. Click the Format text box in the Field Properties pane and then type > (Figure 3-44).

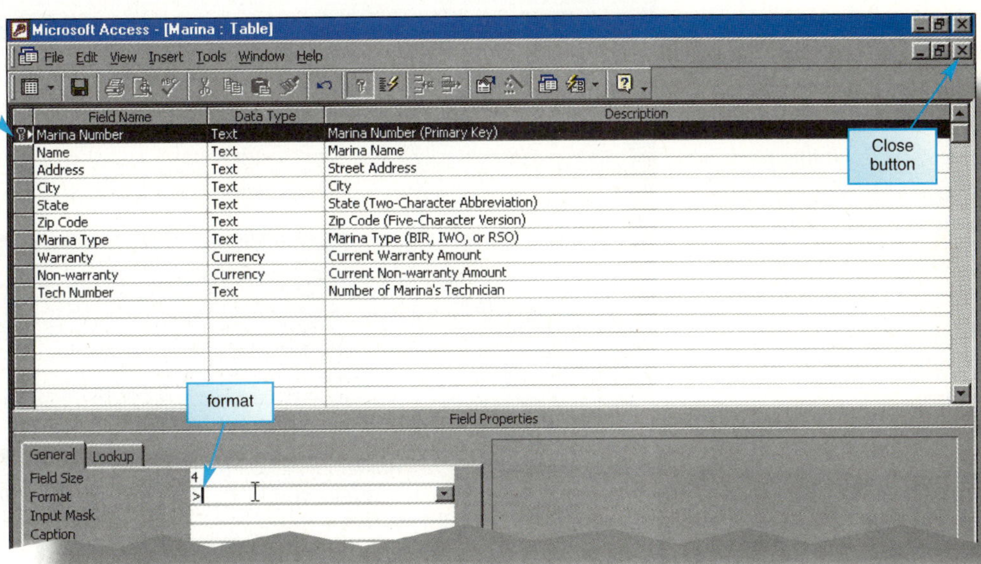

FIGURE 3-44

From this point on, any lowercase letters will be displayed automatically as uppercase when users add records or change the value in the Marina Number field.

Saving Rules, Values, and Formats

To save the validation rules, default values, and formats, perform the following steps.

To Save the Validation Rules, Default Values, and Formats

1 Click the Close button on the Marina: Table window title bar to close the window.

The Microsoft Access dialog box displays, asking if you want to save your changes (Figure 3-45).

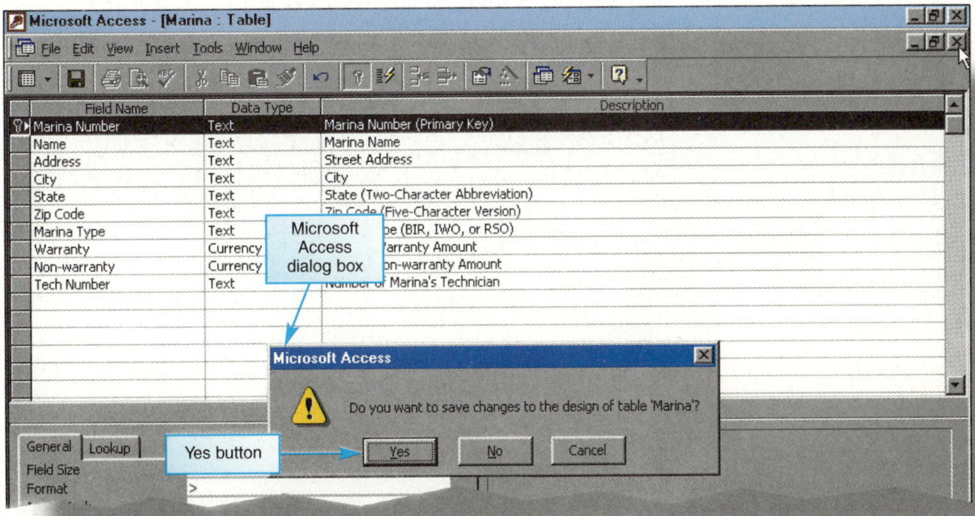

FIGURE 3-45

Click the Yes button to save the changes.

The Microsoft Access dialog box displays (Figure 3-46). This message asks if you want the new rules applied to current records. If this were a database used to run a business or to solve some other critical need, you would click Yes. You would want to be sure that the data already in the database does not violate the rules.

Click the No button.

The changes are made.

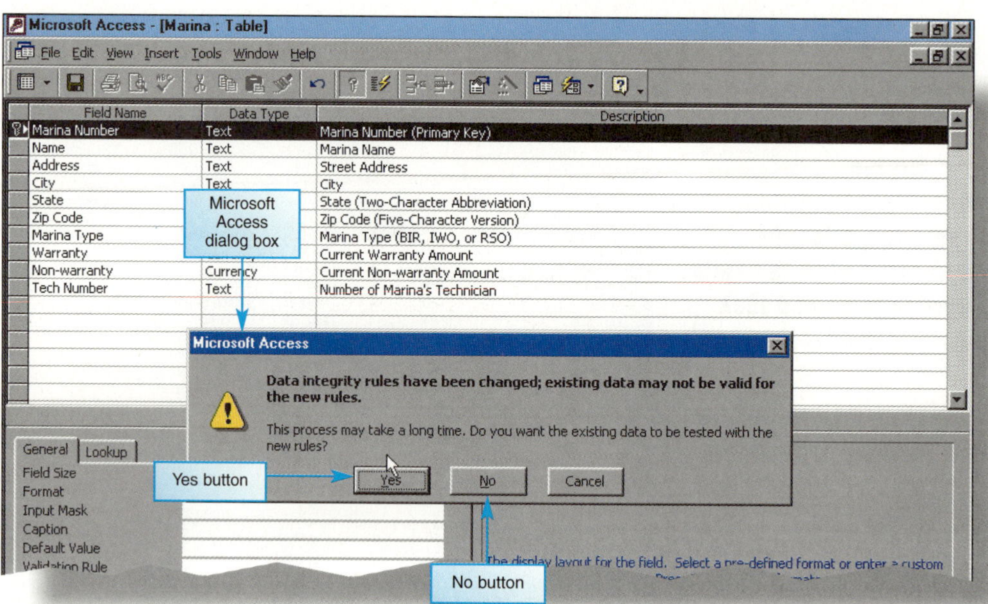

FIGURE 3-46

Updating a Table that Contains Validation Rules

When updating a table that contains validation rules, Access provides assistance in making sure the data entered is valid and formatted correctly. Access also will not accept invalid data. Entering a number that is out of the required range, for example, or entering a value that is not one of the possible choices, will produce an error message in the form of a dialog box. The database will not be updated until the error is corrected.

If the marina number entered contains lowercase letters, such as es21 (Figure 3-47), Access will display the data automatically as ES21 (Figure 3-48).

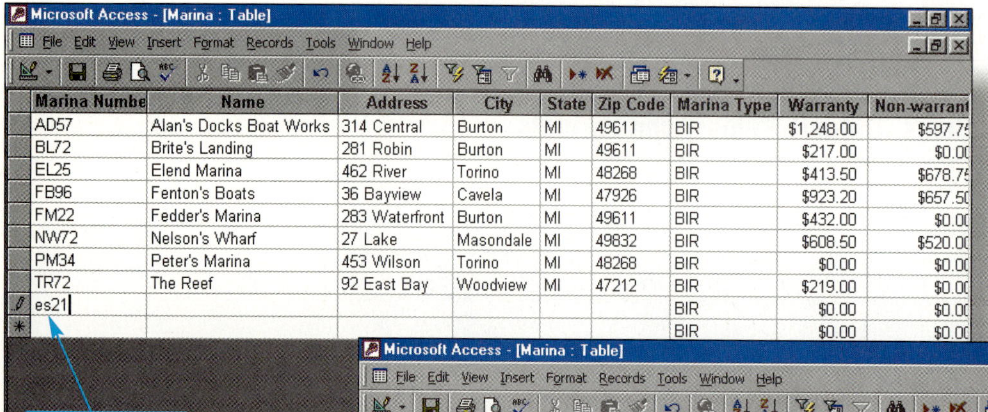

FIGURE 3-47

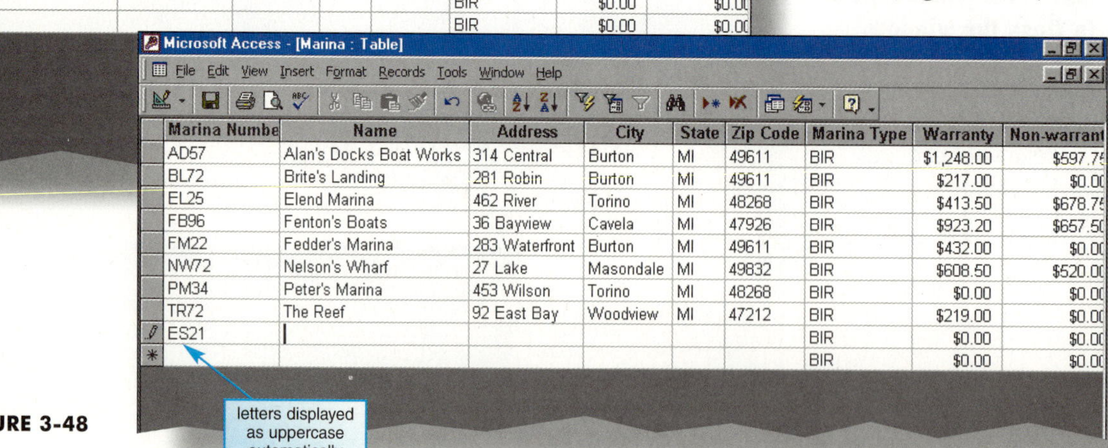

FIGURE 3-48

Instead of the Marina Type field initially being blank, it now contains the value BIR, because BIR is the default value. Thus, for any marina whose type is BIR, it is not necessary to enter the value. By pressing the TAB key, the value BIR is accepted.

If the marina type is not valid, such as ABX, Access will display the text message you specified (Figure 3-49) and not allow the data to enter the database.

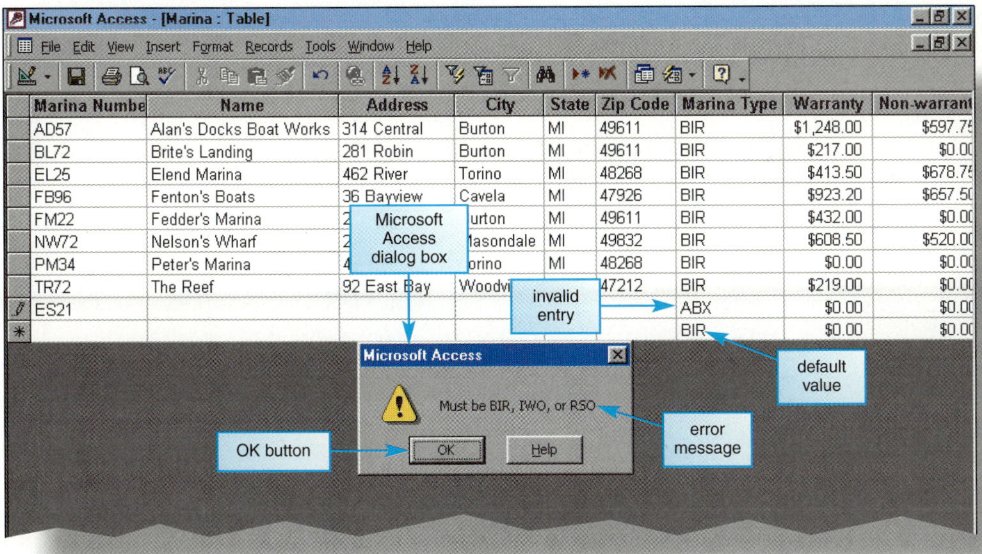

FIGURE 3-49

If the Warranty value is not valid, such as 22500, Access also displays the appropriate message (Figure 3-50) and refuses to accept the data.

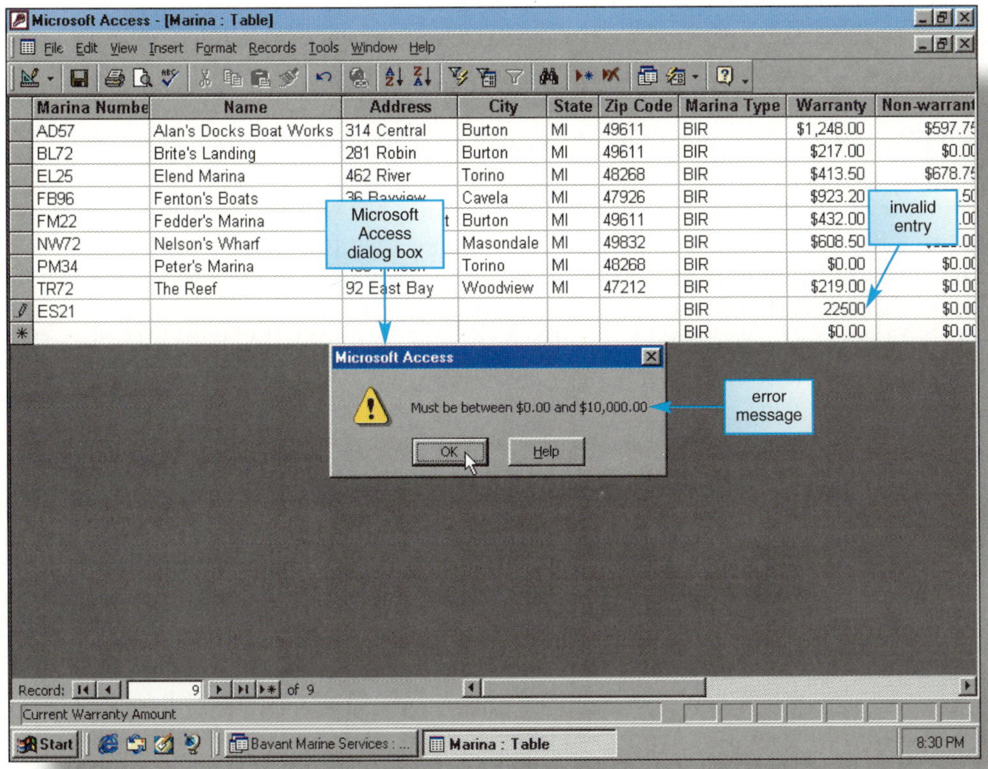

FIGURE 3-50

If a required field contains no data, Access indicates this by displaying an error message as soon as you attempt to leave the record (Figure 3-51). The field must contain a valid entry before Access will move to a different record.

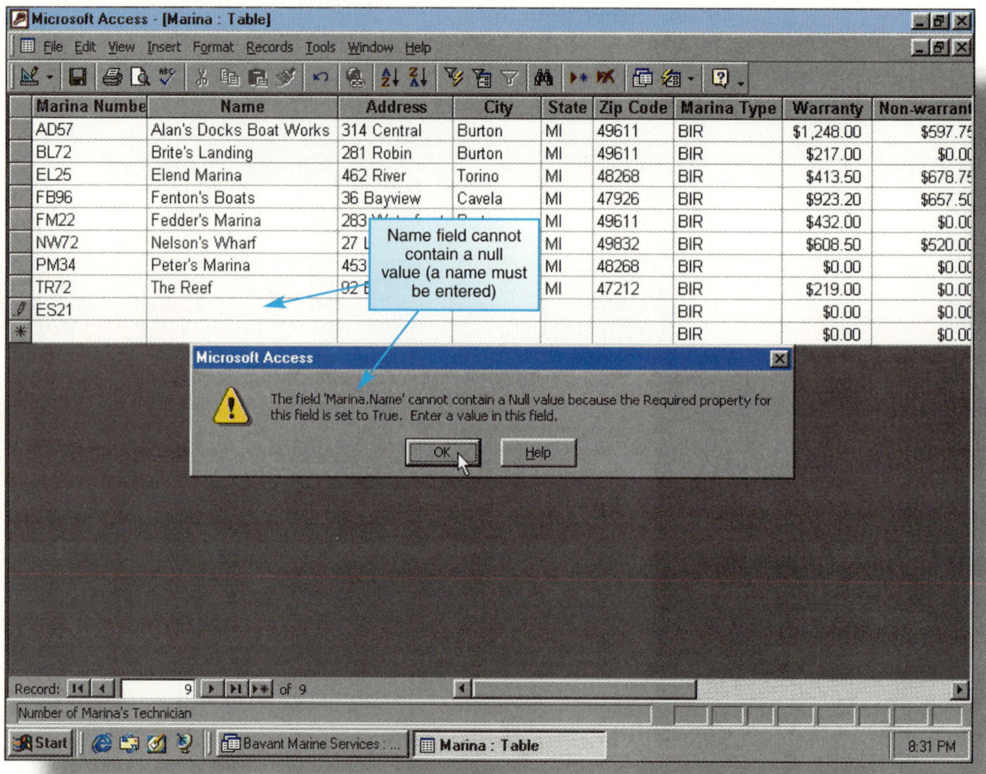

FIGURE 3-51

Take care when creating validation rules as you may come to an impasse where you neither can leave the field nor close the table because you have entered data into a field that violates the validation rule. It may be that you cannot remember the validation rule you created or it was created incorrectly.

First, try to type an acceptable entry. If this does not work, repeatedly press the BACKSPACE key to erase the contents of the field and then try to leave the field. If you are unsuccessful using this procedure, press the ESC key until the record is removed from the screen. The record will not be added to the database.

Should the need arise to take this drastic action, you probably have a faulty validation rule. Use the techniques of the previous sections to correct the existing validation rules for the field.

Making Individual Changes to a Field

Earlier, you changed all the entries in the Marina Type field to BIR. You now have created a rule that will ensure that only legitimate values (BIR, IWO, or RSO) can be entered in the field. To make a change, click the field to be changed to produce an insertion point, use the BACKSPACE or DELETE key to delete the current entry, and then type the new entry.

Complete the following steps to change the Marina Type value on the second and eighth records to IWO and on the fifth record to RSO.

To Make Individual Changes

1 Make sure the Marina table displays in Datasheet view (Figure 3-52).

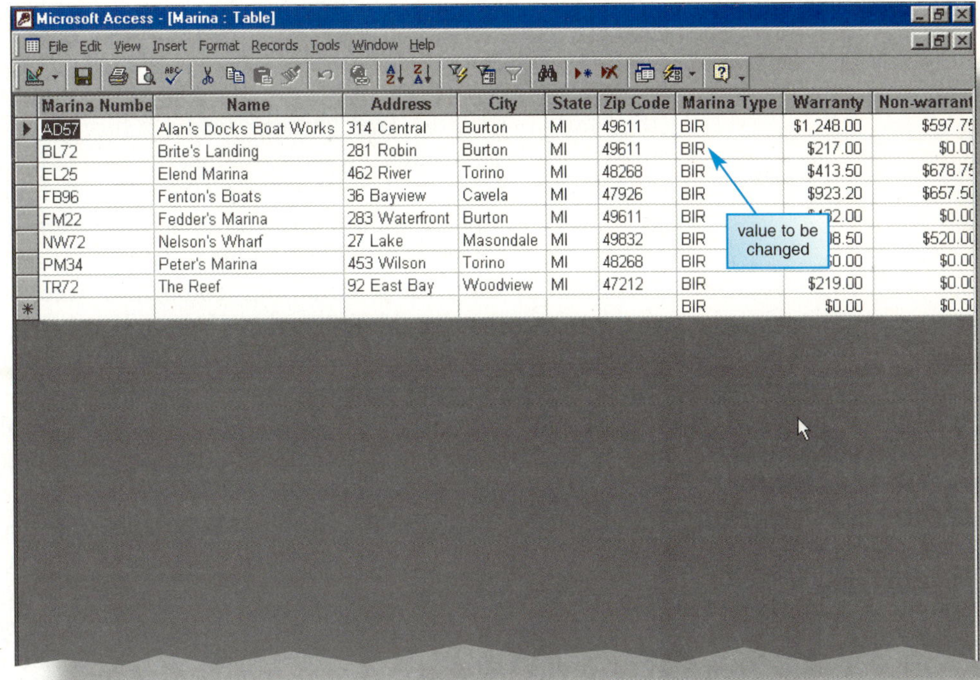

Marina Numbe	Name	Address	City	State	Zip Code	Marina Type	Warranty	Non-warrant
AD57	Alan's Docks Boat Works	314 Central	Burton	MI	49611	BIR	$1,248.00	$597.7
BL72	Brite's Landing	281 Robin	Burton	MI	49611	BIR	$217.00	$0.0
EL25	Elend Marina	462 River	Torino	MI	48268	BIR	$413.50	$678.7
FB96	Fenton's Boats	36 Bayview	Cavela	MI	47926	BIR	$923.20	$657.5
FM22	Fedder's Marina	283 Waterfront	Burton	MI	49611	BIR	2.00	$0.0
NW72	Nelson's Wharf	27 Lake	Masondale	MI	49832	BIR	8.50	$520.0
PM34	Peter's Marina	453 Wilson	Torino	MI	48268	BIR	0.00	$0.0
TR72	The Reef	92 East Bay	Woodview	MI	47212	BIR	$219.00	$0.0
*						BIR	$0.00	$0.0

FIGURE 3-52

2 Click to the right of the BIR entry in the Marina Type field on the second record to produce an insertion point. Press the BACKSPACE key three times to delete BIR and then type `IWO` as the new value. In a similar fashion, change the BIR entry on the fifth record to `RSO` and on the eighth record to `IWO` (Figure 3-53).

Microsoft Access - [Marina : Table]

File Edit View Insert Format Records Tools Window Help

Marina Numbe	Name	Address	City	State	Zip Code	Marina Type	Warranty	Non-warrant
AD57	Alan's Docks Boat Works	314 Central	Burton	MI	49611	BIR	$1,248.00	
BL72	Brite's Landing	281 Robin	Burton	MI	49611	IWO	$217.00	
EL25	Elend Marina	462 River	Torino	MI	48268	BIR	$413.50	
FB96	Fenton's Boats	36 Bayview	Cavela	MI	47926	BIR	$923.20	$657.5
FM22	Fedder's Marina	283 Waterfront	Burton	MI	49611	RSO		$0.0
NW72	Nelson's Wharf	27 Lake	Masondale	MI	49832	BIR		$520.0
PM34	Peter's Marina	453 Wilson	Torino	MI	48268	BIR		$0.0
TR72	The Reef	92 East Bay	Woodview	MI	47212	IWO	$219.00	$0.0
*						BIR	$0.00	$0.0

Close button

values changed

Record: 8 of 8

Marina Type (BIR, IWO, or RSO)

Start | Bavant Marine Services : ... | Marina : Table | 8:32 PM

FIGURE 3-53

3 Close the Marina : Table window by clicking its Close button on the title bar.

The Marina Type field changes now are complete.

Specifying Referential Integrity

Referential Integrity

Referential integrity is an essential property for databases, but providing support for it proved to be one of the most difficult tasks facing the developers of relational database management systems. For more information, visit the Access 2000 Project 3 More About page (www.scsite.com/ac2000/more.htm) and click Referential Integrity.

The property that ensures that the value in a foreign key must match that of another table's primary key is called **referential integrity**. A **foreign key** is a field in one table whose values are required to match the *primary key* of another table. In the Marina table, the Tech Number field is a foreign key that must match the primary key of the Technician table; that is, the technician number for any marina must be a technician currently in the Technician table. A marina whose technician number is 02, for example, should not be stored because technician 02 does not exist.

In Access, to specify referential integrity, you must define a relationship between the tables by using the Relationships command. Access then prohibits any updates to the database that would violate the referential integrity. Access will not allow you to store a marina with a technician number that does not match a technician currently in the Technician table. Access also will prevent you from deleting a technician who currently has marinas. Technician 36, for example, currently has several marinas in the Marina table. If you deleted technician 36, these marinas technician numbers would no longer match anyone in the Technician table.

The type of relationship between two tables specified by the Relationships command is referred to as a **one-to-many relationship**. This means that *one* record in the first table is related to (matches) *many* records in the second table, but each record in the second table is related to only *one* record in the first. In the Bavant Marine database, for example, a one-to-many relationship exists between the Technician table and the Marina table. *One* technician is associated with *many* marinas, but each marina is associated with only a single technician. In general, the table containing the foreign key will be the *many* part of the relationship.

The following steps use the Relationships command to specify referential integrity by specifying a relationship between the Technician and Marina tables.

To Specify Referential Integrity

1 **Close any open datasheet by clicking its Close button on the title bar. Then point to the Relationships button on the Database window toolbar (Figure 3-54).**

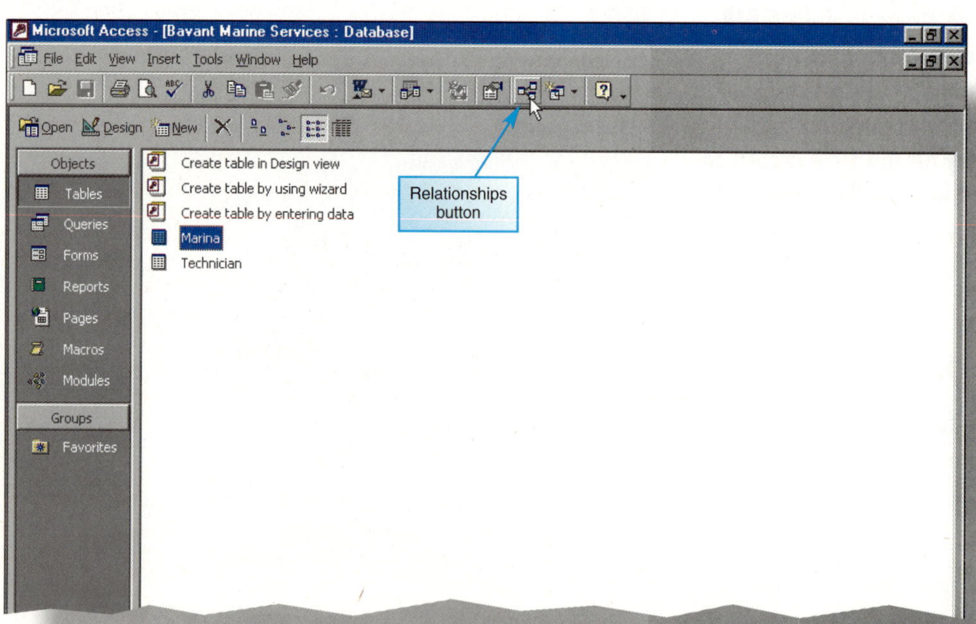

FIGURE 3-54

2 Click the Relationships button on the toolbar.

The Show Table dialog box displays (Figure 3-55).

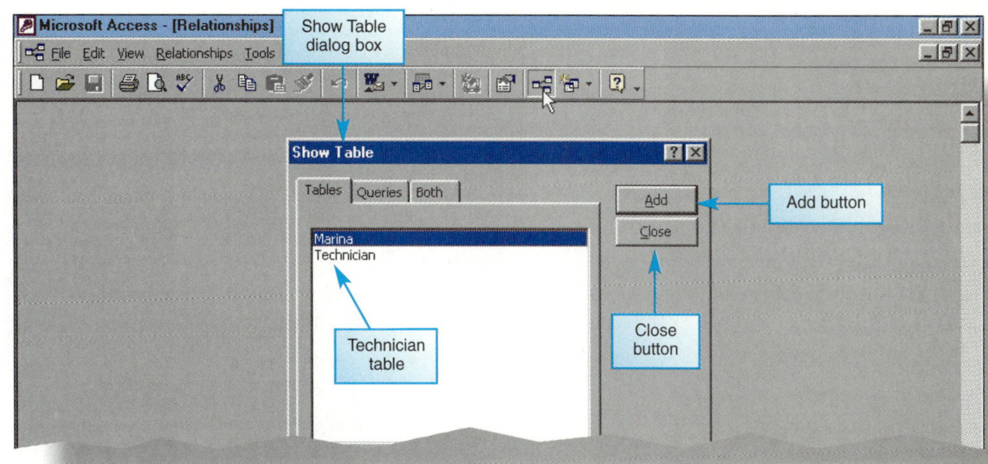

FIGURE 3-55

3 Click the Technician table, click the Add button, click the Marina table, click the Add button again, and then click the Close button. Resize the field list boxes that display so all fields are visible. Point to the Tech Number field in the Technician table field list.

Field list boxes for the Technician and Marina tables display (Figure 3-56). The list boxes have been resized so all fields are visible.

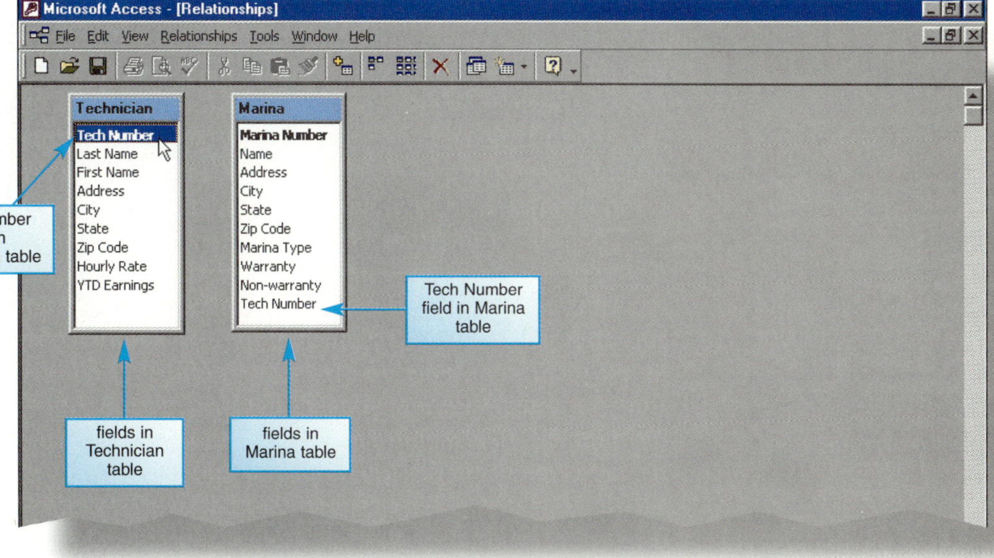

FIGURE 3-56

4 Drag the Tech Number field in the Technician table field list to the Tech Number field in the Marina table field list.

The Edit Relationships dialog box displays (Figure 3-57). The correct fields (the Tech Number fields) have been identified as the matching fields.

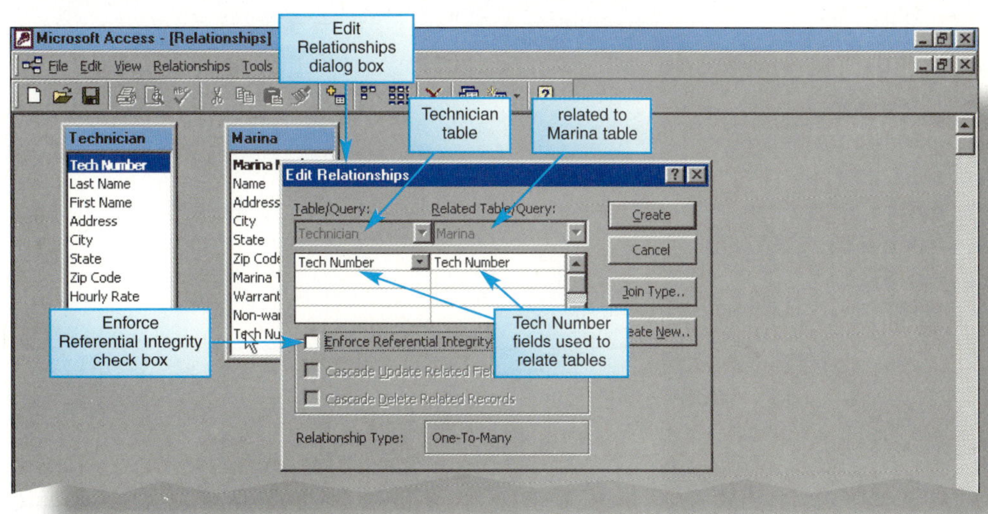

FIGURE 3-57

5 Click Enforce Referential Integrity.

Enforce Referential Integrity is selected (Figure 3-58). With Enforce Referential Integrity selected, Access will reject any update that would violate referential integrity.

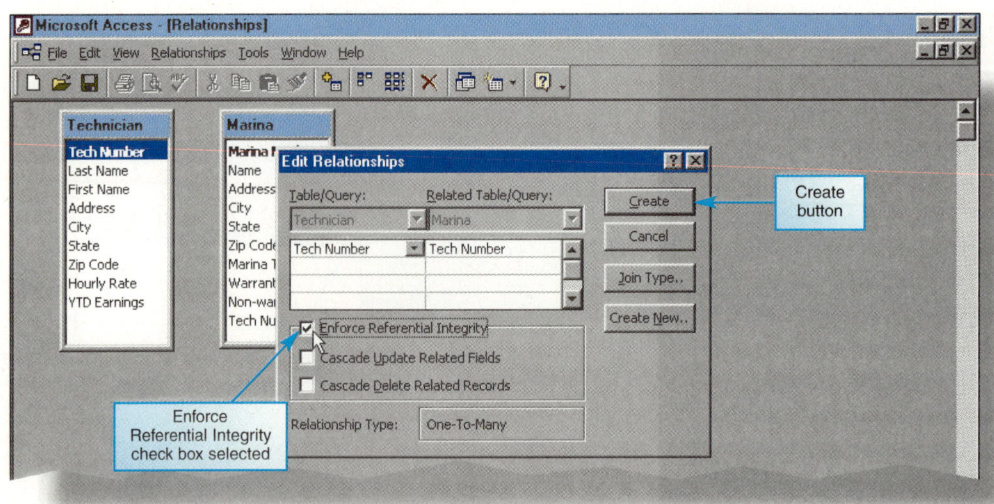

FIGURE 3-58

6 Click the Create button.

Access creates the relationship and displays it visually with the ***relationship line*** *joining the two Tech Number fields (Figure 3-59). The number 1 at the top of the relationship line close to the Tech Number field in the Technician table indicates that the Technician table is the one part of the relationship. The infinity symbol at the other end of the relationship line indicates that the Marina table is the many part of the relationship.*

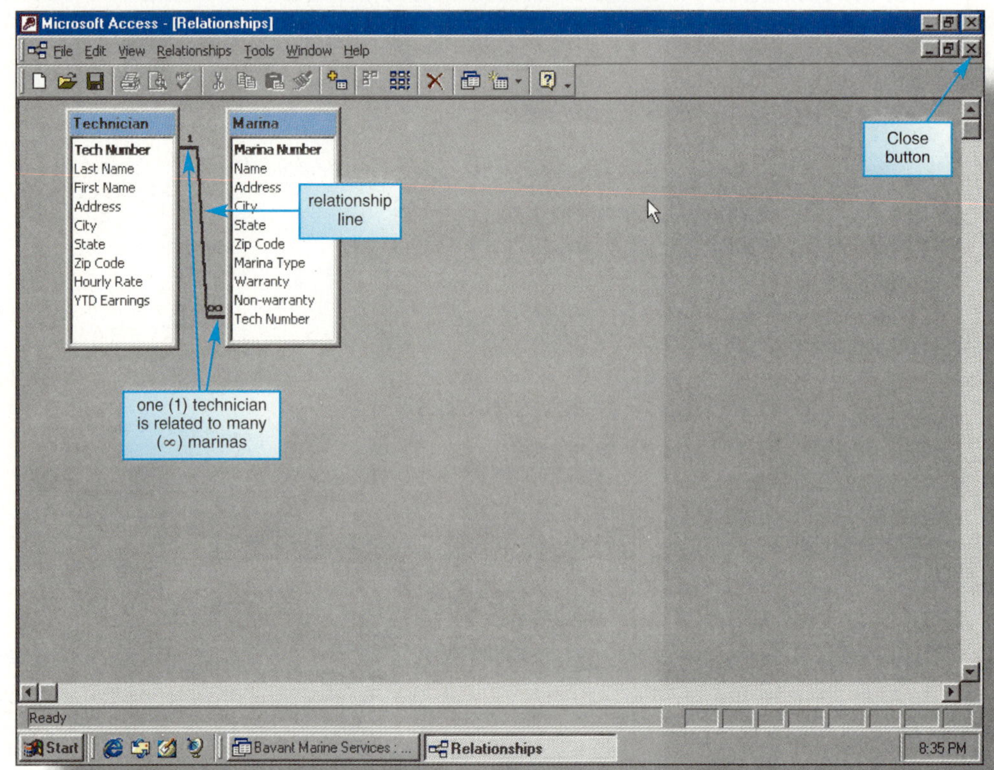

FIGURE 3-59

7 Close the Relationships window by clicking its Close button on the title bar. Click the Yes button to save your work.

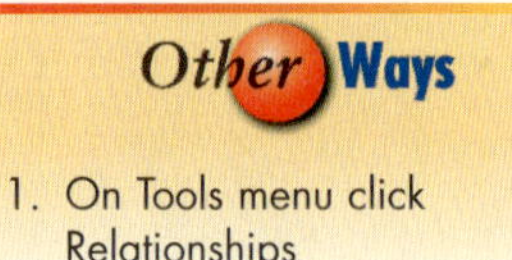

Other Ways

1. On Tools menu click Relationships

Access now will reject any number in the Tech Number field in the Marina table that does not match a technician number in the Technician table. Trying to add a marina whose Tech Number field does not match would result in the error message shown in Figure 3-60.

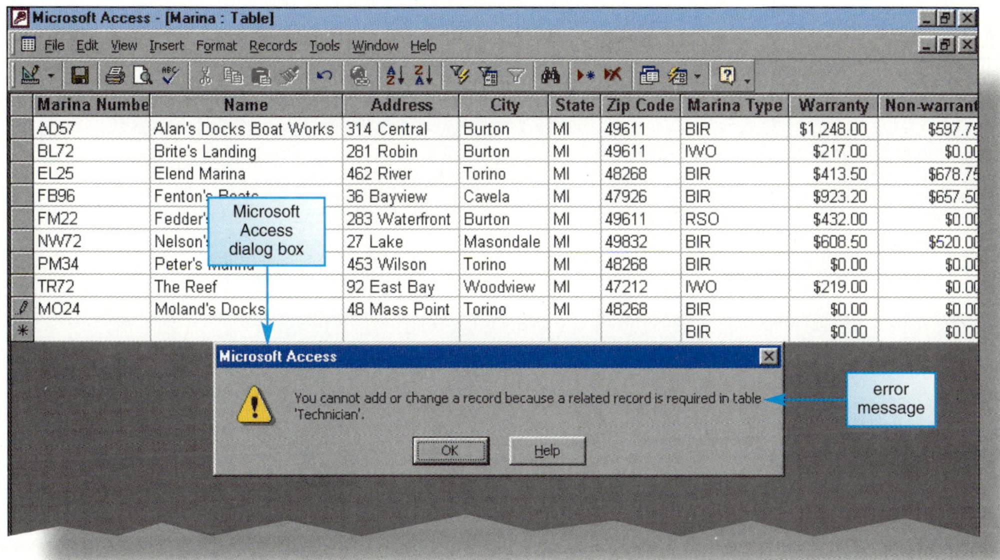

FIGURE 3-60

More About

Relationships: Printing Relationships

You can obtain a printed copy of your relationships within a database once you have created them. To do so, first click the Relationships button to display the relationships. Next, click File on the menu bar and then click Print Relationships. When the Print Preview window displays, click the Print button on the Print Preview toolbar.

A deletion of a technician for whom related marinas exist also would be rejected. Attempting to delete technician 36 from the Technician table, for example, would result in the message shown in Figure 3-61.

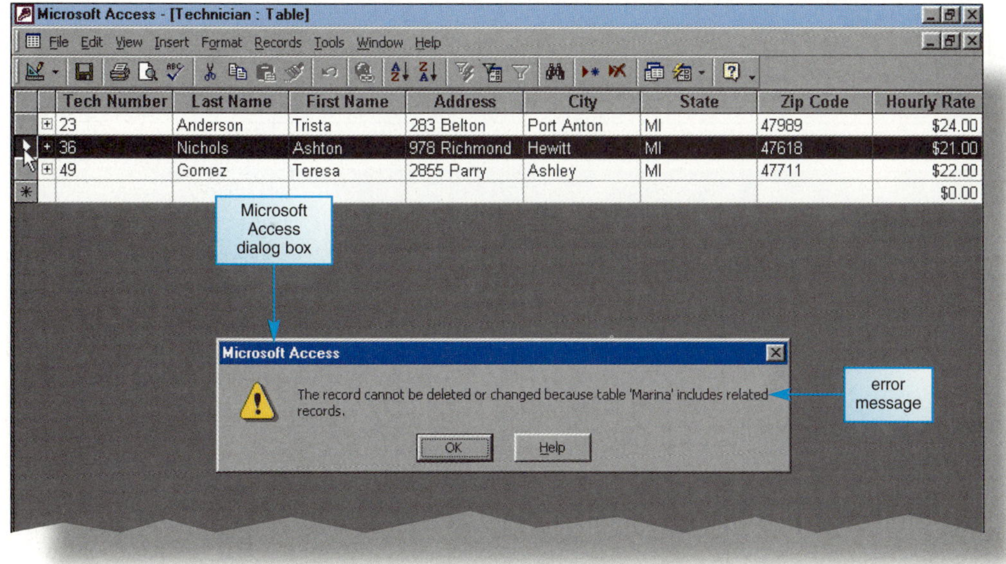

FIGURE 3-61

Using Subdatasheets

Now that the Technician table is related to the Marina table, it is possible to view the marinas of a given technician when you are viewing the datasheet for the Technician table. The marinas for the technician will display right under the technician in a **subdatasheet**. The fact that such a subdatasheet is available is indicated by a plus symbol that displays in front of the rows in the Technician table. To display the subdatasheet, click the plus symbol. The steps on the next page display the subdatasheet for technician 36.

To Use a Subdatasheet

1 **With the Database window open and the Tables object selected, right-click Technician. Click Open on the shortcut menu. Point to the plus symbol in front of the row for technician 36 (Figure 3-62).**

+ sign indicates subdatasheet available

FIGURE 3-62

2 **Click the plus symbol in front of the row for technician 36.**

The subdatasheet displays (Figure 3-63). It contains only those marinas that are assigned to technician 36.

3 **Click the minus symbol to remove the subdatasheet and then close the datasheet for the Technician table by clicking its Close button on the title bar.**

The datasheet no longer displays.

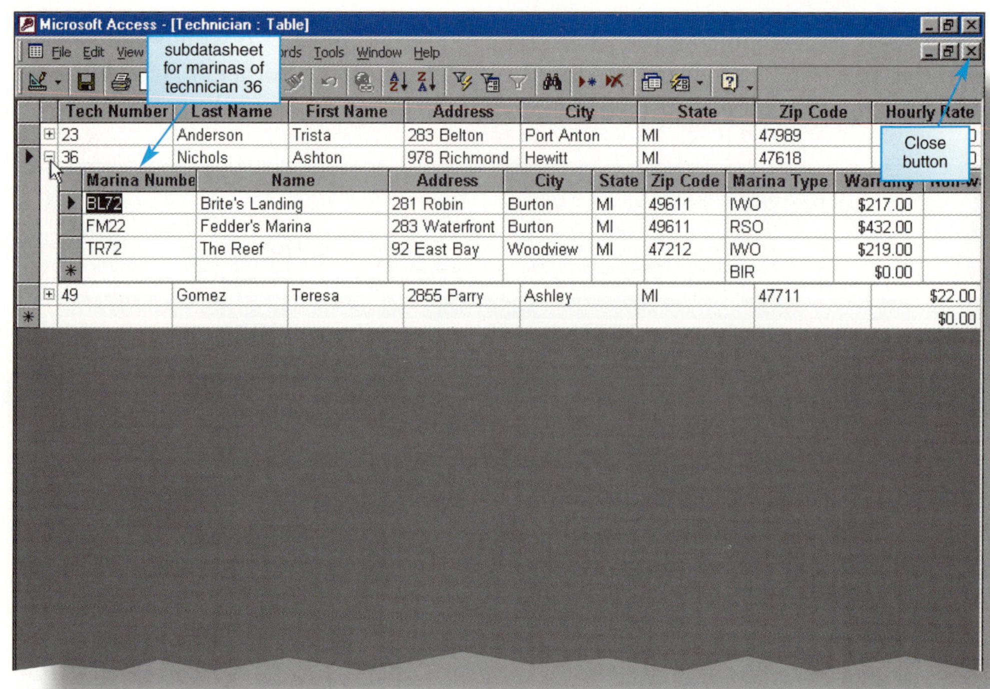

FIGURE 3-63

Ordering Records

Recall from previous discussions that Access sequences the records by marina number whenever listing them because the Marina Number field is the primary key. To change the order in which records display, use the Sort Ascending or Sort Descending buttons on the Table Datasheet toolbar. Either button reorders the records based on the field in which the insertion point is located.

Perform the following steps to order the records by marina name using the Sort Ascending button.

To Use the Sort Ascending Button to Order Records

1 **Open the Marina table in Datasheet view, and then click the Name field on the first record (any other record would do as well). Point to the Sort Ascending button on the Table Datasheet toolbar (Figure 3-64).**

FIGURE 3-64

2 **Click the Sort Ascending button on the toolbar.**

The rows now are ordered by name (Figure 3-65).

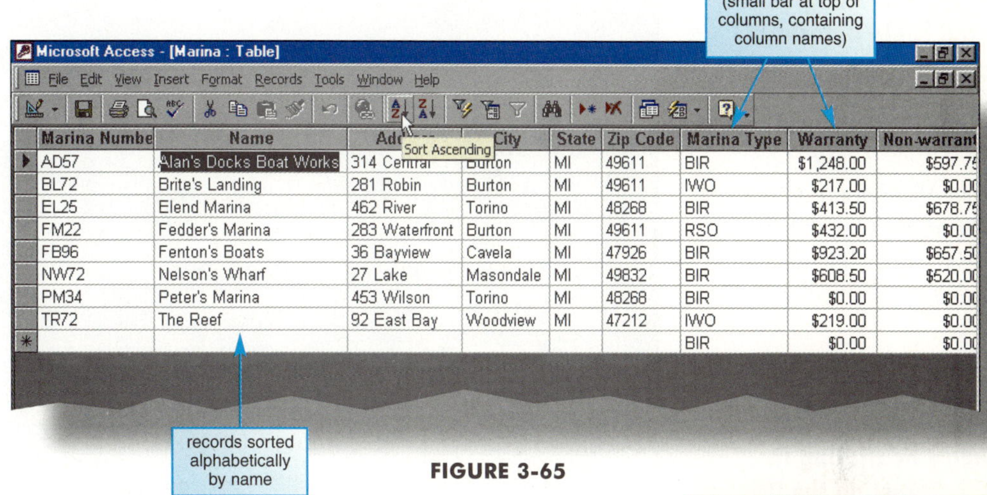

FIGURE 3-65

Other Ways

1. On Records menu click Sort, then click Sort Ascending

If you wanted to sort the data in reverse order, you would click the Sort Descending button on the Table Datasheet toolbar instead of the Sort Ascending button.

Ordering Records on Multiple Fields

Just as you are able to sort the answer to a query on multiple fields, you also can sort the data that displays in a datasheet on multiple fields. To do so, the major and minor keys must be next to each other in the datasheet with the major key on the left. (If this is not the case, you can drag the columns into the correct position. Instead of dragging, however, usually it will be easier to use a query that has the data sorted in the desired order.)

Given that the major and minor keys are in the correct position, select both fields and then click the Sort Ascending button on the Table Datasheet toolbar. To select the fields, click the **field selector** for the first field (the major key). Next, hold down the SHIFT key and then click the field selector for the second field (the minor key). A **field selector** is the small bar at the top of the column that you click to select an entire field in a datasheet.

Order records on the combination of the Marina Type and Warranty fields using the Sort Ascending button on the Table Datasheet toolbar by completing the following steps.

To Use the Sort Ascending Button to Order Records on Multiple Fields

1 Click the field selector at the top of the Marina Type field column to select the entire column. Hold down the SHIFT key and then click the field selector for the Warranty field column. Release the SHIFT key. Click the Sort Ascending button on the Table Datasheet toolbar.

The rows are ordered by marina type (Figure 3-66). Within each group of marinas of the same type, the rows are ordered by the warranty amount.

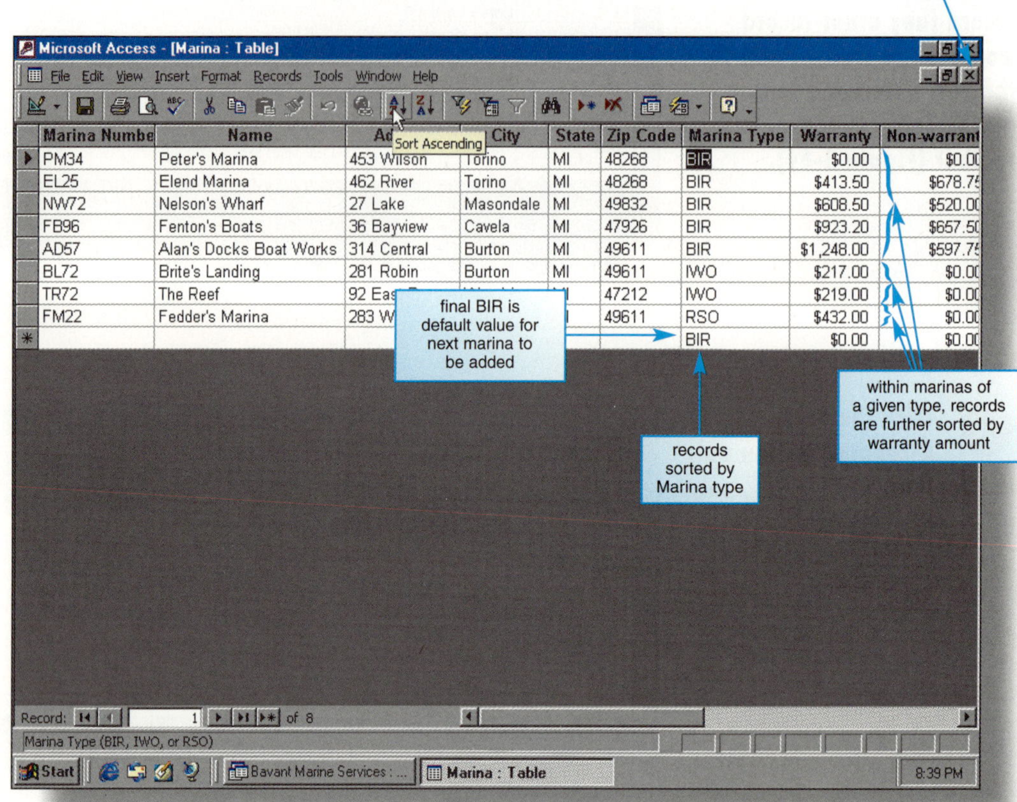

FIGURE 3-66

2 Close the Marina : Table window by clicking its Close button on the title bar. Click the No button to abandon changes.

The next time the table is open, the records will display in their original order.

Creating and Using Indexes

You already are familiar with the concept of an index. The index in the back of a book contains important words or phrases together with a list of pages on which the given words or phrases can be found. An **index** for a table is similar. Figure 3-67, for example, shows the Marina table along with an index built on names. In this case, the items of interest are names instead of keywords or phrases as is the case in the back of this book. The field or fields on which the index is built is called the **index key**. Thus, in Figure 3-67, the Name field is the index key.

Index on Name	
NAME	RECORD NUMBER
Alan's Docks Boat Works	1
Brite's Landing	2
Elend Marina	3
Fedder's Marina	5
Fenton's Boasts	4
Nelson's Wharf	6
Peter's Marina	7
The Reef	8

Marina Table							
RECORD NUMBER	MARINA NUMBER	NAME	ADDRESS	CITY	STATE	ZIP CODE	. . .
1	AD57	Alan's Docks Boat Works	314 Central	Burton	MI	49611	. . .
2	BL72	Brite's Landing	281 Robin	Burton	MI	49611	. . .
3	EL25	Elend Marina	462 River	Torino	MI	48268	. . .
4	FB96	Fenton's Boats	36 Bayview	Cavela	MI	47926	. . .
5	FM22	Fedder's Marina	283 Waterfront	Burton	MI	49611	. . .
6	NW72	Nelson's Wharf	27 Lake	Masondale	MI	48268	. . .
7	PM34	Peter's Marina	453 Wilson	Torino	MI	48268	. . .
8	TR72	The Reef	92 East Bay	Woodview	MI	47212	. . .

FIGURE 3-67

Each name occurs in the index along with the number of the record on which the corresponding marina is located. Further, the names appear in the index in alphabetical order. If Access were to use this index to find the record on which the name is Fenton's Boats, for example, it could scan rapidly the names in the index to find Fenton's Boats. Once it did, it would determine the corresponding record number (4) and then go immediately to record 4 in the Marina table, thus finding this marina more quickly than if it had to look through the entire Marina table one record at a time. Indexes make the process of retrieving records very fast and efficient. (With relatively small tables, the increased efficiency associated with indexes will not be apparent readily. In practice, it is common to encounter tables with thousands, tens of thousands, or even hundreds of thousands, of records. In such cases, the increase in efficiency is dramatic. In fact, without indexes, many operations in such databases would simply not be practical. They would take too long to complete.)

Because no two marinas happen to have the same name, the Record Number column contains only single values. This may not always be the case. Consider the index on the Zip Code field shown in Figure 3-68 on the next page. In this index, the Record Number column contains several values, namely all the records on which the corresponding zip code displays. The first row, for example, indicates that zip code 47212 is found only on record 8; whereas, the fourth row indicates that zip code 49611 is found on records 1, 2, and 5. If Access were to use this index to find all marinas in zip code 49611, it could scan rapidly the zip codes in the index to find 49611. Once it did, it would determine the corresponding record numbers (1, 2, and 5) and then go immediately to these records. It would not have to examine any other records in the Marina table.

Indexes

The most common structure for high-performance indexes is called a B-tree. It is a highly efficient structure that supports very rapid access to records in the database as well as a rapid alternative to sorting records. Virtually all systems use some version of the B-tree structure. For more information, visit the Access 2000 Project 3 More About page (www.scsite.com/ac2000/more.htm) and click B-tree.

Index on Zip Code	
ZIP CODE	RECORD NUMBER
47212	8
47926	4
48268	3, 7
49611	1, 2, 5
49832	6

Marina Table							
RECORD NUMBER	MARINA NUMBER	NAME	ADDRESS	CITY	STATE	ZIP CODE	. . .
1	AD57	Alan's Docks Boat Works	314 Central	Burton	MI	49611	. . .
2	BL72	Brite's Landing	281 Robin	Burton	MI	49611	. . .
3	EL25	Elend Marina	462 River	Torino	MI	48268	. . .
4	FB96	Fedder's Landing	36 Bayview	Cavela	MI	47926	. . .
5	FM22	Fedder's Boasts	283 Waterfront	Burton	MI	49611	. . .
6	NW72	Nelson's Wharf	27 Lake	Masondale	MI	48268	. . .
7	PM34	Peter's Marina	453 Wilson	Torino	MI	48268	. . .
8	TR72	The Reef	92 East Bay	Woodview	MI	47212	. . .

FIGURE 3-68

Another benefit of indexes is that they provide an efficient way to order records. That is, if the records are to display in a certain order, Access can use an index instead of physically having to rearrange the records in the database file. Physically rearranging the records in a different order, which is called **sorting**, can be a very time-consuming process.

To see how indexes can be used for alphabetizing records, look at the record numbers in the index (see Figure 3-67 on page A 3.45) and suppose you used these to list all marinas. That is, simply follow down the Record Number column, listing the corresponding marinas. In this example, first you would list the marina on record 1 (Alan's Docks Boat Works), then the marina on record 2 (Brite's Landing), then the marina on record 3 (Elend Marina), then the marina on record 5 (Fedder's Marina), then the Marina on record 4 (Fenton's Boats), and so on. The marinas would be listed alphabetically by name without actually sorting the table.

To gain the benefits from an index, you first must create one. Access automatically creates an index on the primary key as well as some other special fields. If, as is the case with both the Marina and Technician tables, a table contains a field called Zip Code, for example, Access will create an index for it automatically. You must create any other indexes you feel you need, indicating the field or fields on which the index is to be built.

Although the index key usually will be a single field, it can be a combination of fields. For example, you may want to sort records by warranty within marina type. In other words, the records are ordered by a combination of fields: Marina Type and Warranty. An index can be created for this purpose by using a combination of fields for the index key. In this case, you must assign a name to the index. It is a good idea to assign a name that represents the combination of fields. For example, an index whose key is the combination of the Marina Type and Warranty fields, might be called TypeWarranty.

How Does Access Use an Index?

Access creates an index whenever you request that it do so. Access takes care of all the work in setting up and maintaining the index. In addition, Access will use the index automatically.

If you request that data be sorted in a particular order and Access determines that an index is available that it can use to make the process efficient, it will do so. If no index is available, it still will sort the data in the order you requested; it will just take longer.

Similarly, if you request that Access locate a particular record that has a certain value in a particular field, Access will use an index if an appropriate one exists. If not, it will have to examine each record until it finds the one you want.

In both cases, the added efficiency provided by an index will not be apparent readily in tables that have only a few records. As you add more records to your tables, however, the difference can be dramatic. Even with only 50 to 100 records, you will notice a difference. You can imagine how dramatic the difference would be in a table with 50,000 records.

When Should You Create an Index?

An index improves efficiency for sorting and finding records. On the other hand, indexes occupy space on your disk. They also require Access to do extra work. Access must maintain all the indexes that have been created up to date. Thus, both advantages and disadvantages exist to using indexes. Consequently, the decision as to which indexes to create is an important one. The following guidelines should help you in this process.

Create an index on a field (or combination of fields) if one or more of the following conditions are present:

1. The field is the primary key of the table (Access will create this index automatically)
2. The field is the foreign key in a relationship you have created
3. You frequently will need your data to be sorted on the field
4. You frequently will need to locate a record based on a value in this field

Because Access handles condition 1 automatically, you only need to concern yourself about conditions 2, 3, and 4. If you think you will need to see marina data arranged in order of warranty amounts, for example, you should create an index on the Warranty field. If you think you will need to see the data arranged by warranty within technician number, you should create an index on the combination of the Tech Number field and the Warranty field. Similarly, if you think you will need to find a marina given the marina s name, you should create an index on the Name field.

More About 2000

Microsoft Certification

The Microsoft Office User Specialist (MOUS) Certification program provides an opportunity for you to obtain a valuable industry credential - proof that you have the Access 2000 skills required by employers. For more information, see Appendix D or visit the Shelly Cashman Series MOUS Web page at www.scsite.com/off2000/cert.htm.

Creating Single-Field Indexes

A **single-field index** is an index whose key is a single field. In this case, the index key is to be the Name field. In creating an index, you need to indicate whether to allow duplicates in the index key; that is, two records that have the same value. For example, in the index for the Name field, if duplicates are not allowed, Access would not allow the addition of a marina whose name is the same as the name of an existing marina in the database. In the index for the Name field, duplicates will be allowed. Perform the following steps to create a single-field index.

To Create a Single-Field Index

1 Right-click Marina. Click Design View on the shortcut menu, and then, if necessary, maximize the Marina : Table window. Click the row selector to select the Name field. Click the Indexed text box in the Field Properties pane. Click the Indexed text box down arrow.

The Indexed list displays (Figure 3-69). The items in the list are No (no index), Yes (Duplicates OK) (create an index and allow duplicates), and Yes (No Duplicates) (create an index but reject (do not allow) duplicates).

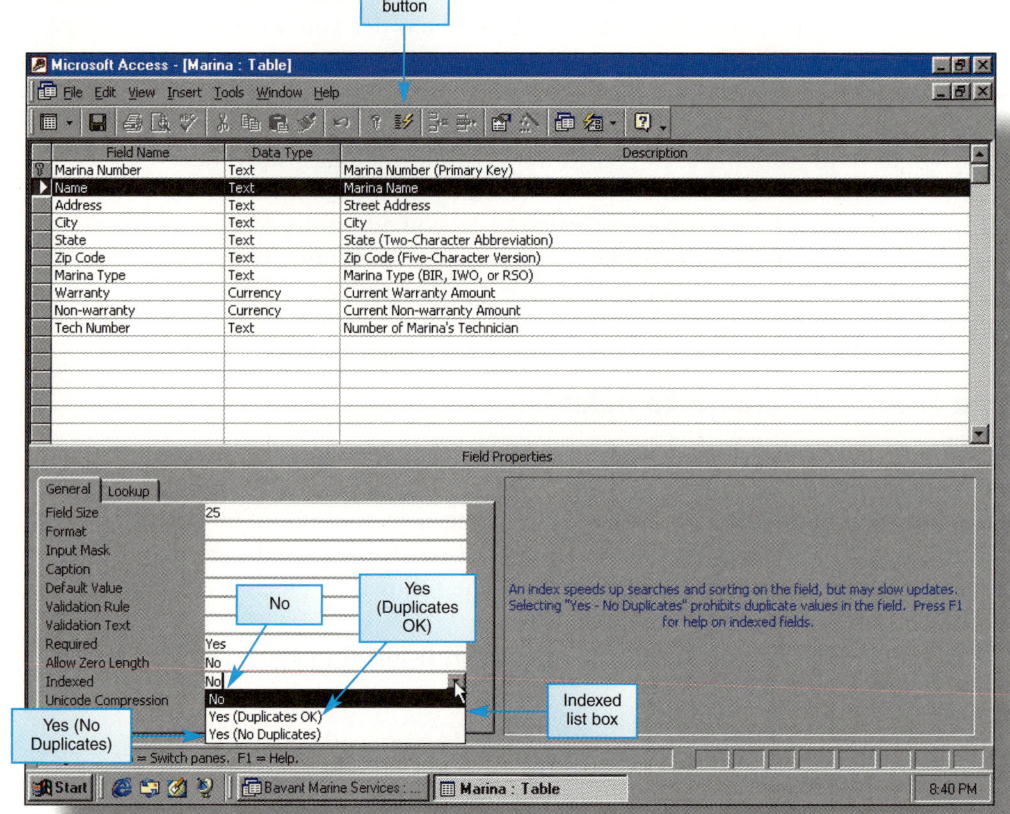

FIGURE 3-69

2 Click the Yes (Duplicates OK) item in the list.

The index on the Name field now will be created and is ready for use as soon as you save your work.

Quick Reference

For a table that lists how to complete the tasks covered in this book using the mouse, menu, shortcut menu, and keyboard, visit the Office 2000 Web page (www.scsite.com/off2000/qr.htm), and then click Microsoft Access 2000.

Creating Multiple-Field Indexes

Creating **multiple-field indexes**, that is, indexes whose key is a combination of fields, involves a different process than creating single-field indexes. To create multiple-field indexes, you will use the **Indexes button** on the Table Design toolbar, enter a name for the index, and then enter the combination of fields that make up the index key. The following steps create a multiple-field index with the name TypeWarranty. The key will be the combination of the Marina Type field and the Warranty field.

To Create a Multiple-Field Index

1 **Point to the Indexes button on the Table Design toolbar (Figure 3-70).**

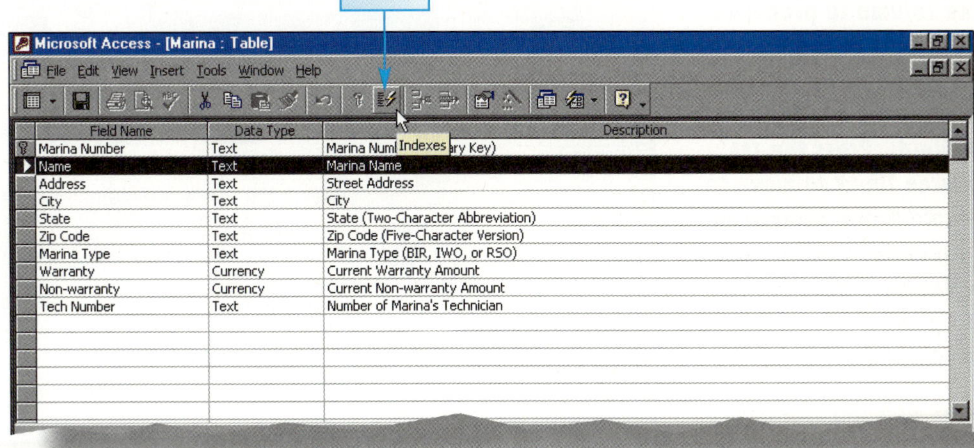

FIGURE 3-70

2 **Click the Indexes button on the toolbar. Click the blank row (the row following Name) in the Index Name column in the Indexes: Marina window. Type** `TypeWarranty` **as the index name and then press the TAB key. Point to the down arrow in the Field Name column.**

The Indexes: Marina dialog box displays. It shows the indexes that already have been created and allows you to create additional indexes (Figure 3-71). The index name has been entered as TypeWarranty. An insertion point displays in the Field Name column. The index on the Marina Number field is the primary index and was created automatically by Access. The index on the Name field is the one just created. Access created other indexes (for example, on the Zip Code field) automatically. In this dialog box, you can create additional indexes.

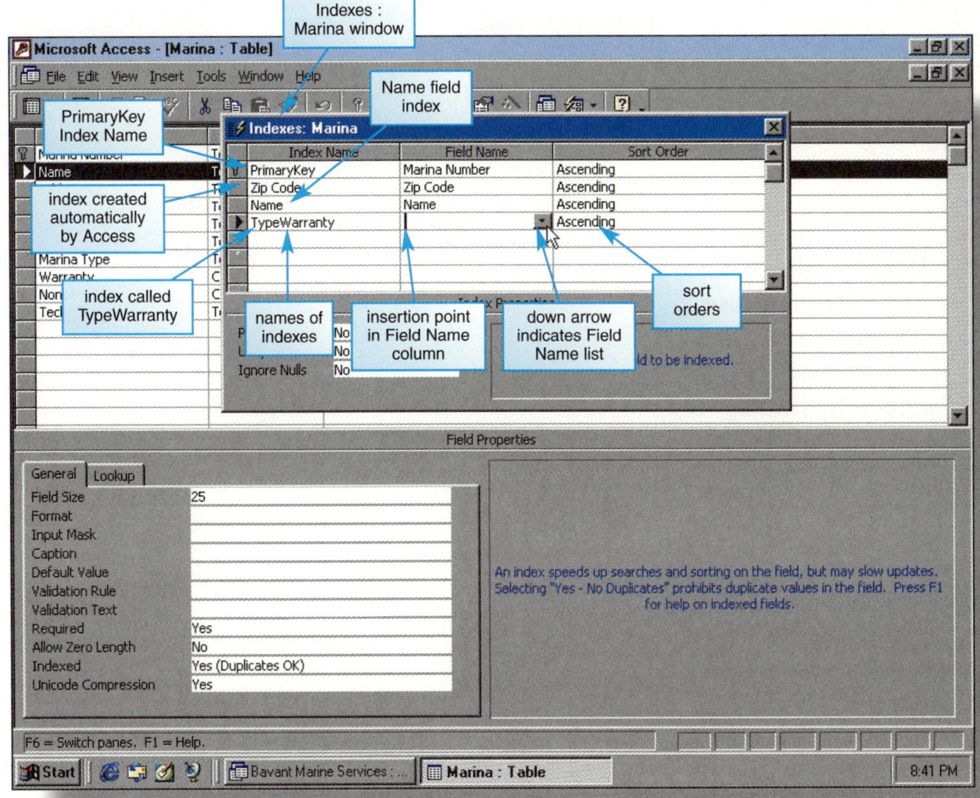

FIGURE 3-71

3 **Click the down arrow in the Field Name column to produce a list of fields in the Marina table, scroll down the list, and then select the Marina Type field . Press the TAB key three times to move to the Field Name column on the following row. Select the Warranty field in the same manner as the Marina Type field.**

Marina Type and Warranty are selected as the two fields for the TypeWarranty index (Figure 3-72). The absence of an index name on the row containing the Warranty field indicates that it is part of the previous index named, TypeWarranty.

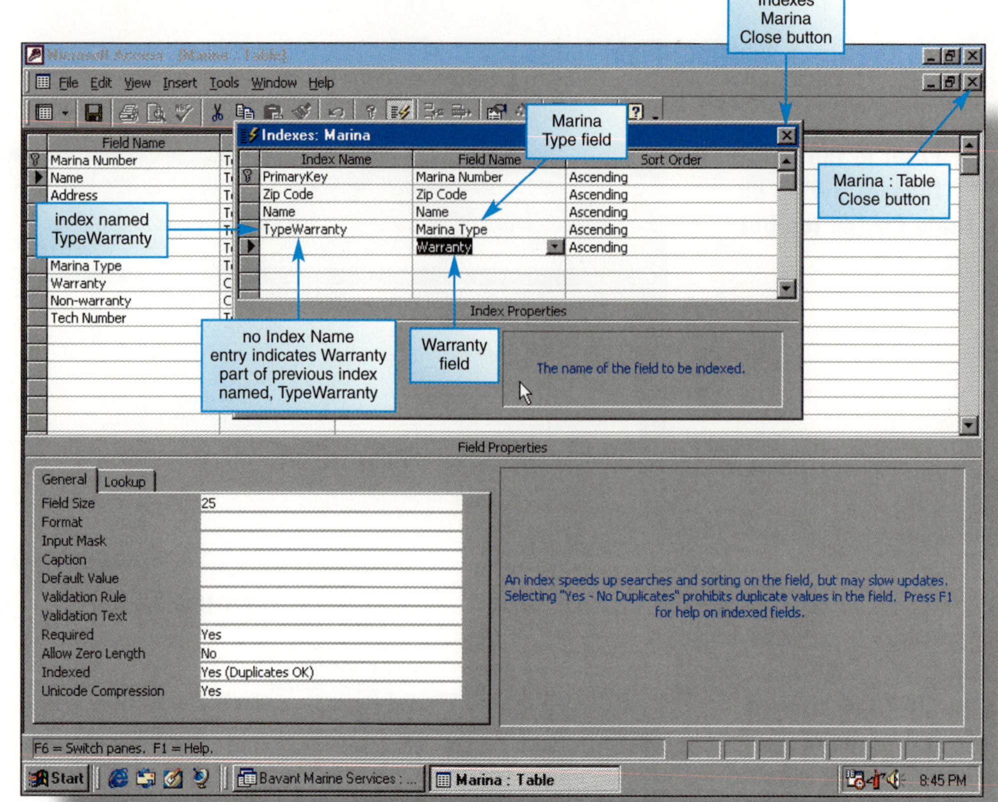

FIGURE 3-72

4 **Close the Indexes: Marina dialog box by clicking its Close button on the title bar, and then close the Marina : Table window by clicking its Close button on the title bar. When the Microsoft Access dialog box displays, click the Yes button to save your changes.**

The indexes are created and the Database window displays.

1. On View menu click Indexes

Closing the Database

The following step closes the database by closing the Database window.

TO CLOSE A DATABASE

Click the Close button on the Bavant Marine Services : Database window title bar.

The database closes.

The indexes now have been created. Access will use them automatically whenever possible to improve efficiency of ordering or finding records. Access also will maintain them automatically. That is, whenever the data in the Marina table is changed, Access will make appropriate changes in the indexes automatically.

CASE PERSPECTIVE SUMMARY

In Project 3, you assisted Bavant Marine Service in the maintenance of the database. You used Form view to add a record to the database and searched for a record satisfying a criterion. You used a filter so you could view only the record you needed. You changed and deleted records. You changed the structure of the Marina table in the Bavant Marine Services database, created validation rules, and specified referential integrity. You used a subdatasheet to view the marinas assigned to a technician while viewing technician data. You made mass changes and created indexes to improve performance.

Project Summary

In Project 3, you learned how to maintain a database. You saw how to use Form view to add records to a table. You learned how to locate and filter records. You saw how to change the contents of records in a table and how to delete records from a table. You restructured a table, both by changing field characteristics and by adding a new field. You saw how to make changes to groups of records and how to delete groups of records. You learned how to create a variety of validation rules to specify a required field, specify a range, specify a default value, specify legal values, and specify a format. You examined the issues involved in updating a table with validation rules. You also saw how to specify referential integrity. You learned how to view related data by using subdatasheets. You learned how to order records. Finally, you saw how to improve performance by creating single-field and multiple-field indexes.

What You Should Know

Having completed this project, you now should be able to perform the following tasks:

- Add a Field to a Table *(A 3.17)*
- Change the Size of a Field *(A 3.16)*
- Close a Database *(A 3.50)*
- Create a Multiple-Field Index *(A 3.49)*
- Create a Single-Field Index *(A 3.48)*
- Delete a Record *(A 3.14)*
- Filter Records *(A 3.13)*
- Make Individual Changes *(A 3.36)*
- Open a Database *(A 3.6)*
- Remove a Filter *(A 3.14)*
- Resize a Column *(A 3.21)*
- Save the Validation Rules, Default Values, and Formats *(A 3.33)*
- Search for a Record *(A 3.9)*
- Specify a Collection of Legal Values *(A 3.32)*
- Specify a Default Value *(A 3.31)*
- Specify a Format *(A 3.33)*
- Specify a Range *(A 3.30)*
- Specify a Required Field *(A 3.28)*
- Specify Referential Integrity *(A 3.38)*
- Switch from Form View to Datasheet View *(A 3.11)*
- Update the Contents of a Field *(A 3.10, A 3.20)*
- Use a Delete Query to Delete a Group of Records *(A 3.26)*
- Use a Form to Add Records *(A 3.6)*
- Use a Subdatasheet *(A 3.42)*
- Use an Update Query to Update All Records *(A 3.23)*
- Use the Sort Ascending Button to Order Records *(A 3.43)*
- Use the Sort Ascending Button to Order Records on Multiple Fields *(A 3.44)*

Project Reinforcement at www.scsite.com/off2000/reinforce.htm

1 Maintaining the Sidewalk Scrapers Database

Instructions: Start Access. Open the Sidewalk Scrapers database from the Data Disk. See the inside back cover of this book for instructions for downloading the Data Disk or see your instructor for information on accessing the files required for this book. Perform the following tasks.

1. Open the Customer table in Design view as shown in Figure 3-73.

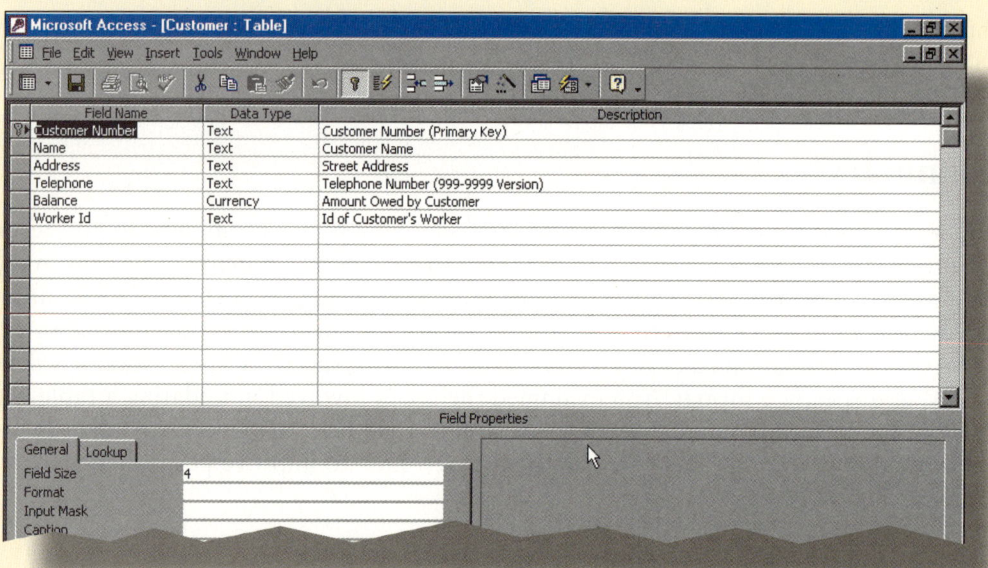

FIGURE 3-73

2. Increase the size of the Name field to 25.
3. Format the Customer Number field so any lowercase letters display in uppercase.
4. Make the Name and Address fields required fields.
5. Specify that Balance amounts must be less than or equal to $125.00. Include validation text.
6. Create an index that allows duplicates for the Name field.
7. Save the changes to the structure.
8. Open the Customer table in Datasheet view.
9. Change the name of customer ST21 to Styling Salon and Tanning.
10. Resize the Name column so the complete name for customer ST21 displays. Resize the Telephone, Balance, and Worker Id field columns to the best size.
11. Close the table and click Yes to save the changes to the layout of the table.
12. Print the table.
13. Open the Customer table and use Filter by Selection to find the record for customer BH81. Delete the record.
14. Print the table.
15. Sort the data in descending order by balance.
16. Print the table. Close the table. If you are asked to save changes to the design of the table, click the No button.
17. Establish referential integrity between the Worker table (the one table) and the Customer table (the many table). Print the relationships window by making sure the relationships window is open, clicking File on the menu bar, and then clicking Print Relationships.

1 Maintaining the School Connection Database

Problem: The Booster's club would like to make some changes to the School Connection database structure. They need to increase the size of the Description field and add an additional index. Because several different individuals update the data, the club also would like to add some validation rules to the database. Finally, some new items must be added to the database.

Instructions: Use the database created in the In the Lab 1 of Project 1 for this assignment. Perform the following tasks.

1. Open the School Connection database and open the Item table in Design view as shown in Figure 3-74.

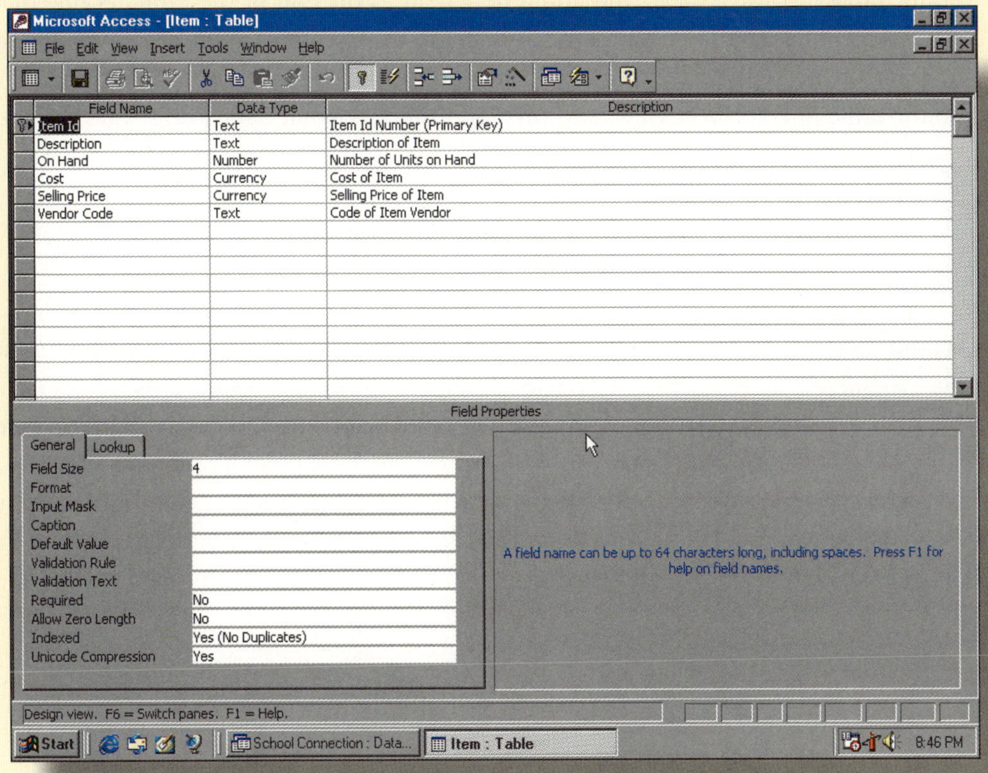

FIGURE 3-74

2. Create an index for the Description field. Be sure to allow duplicates.
3. Create and save the following validation rules for the Item table. List the steps involved on your own paper.
   a. Make the Description field a required field.
   b. Ensure that any lowercase letters entered in the Item Id field are displayed as uppercase.
   c. Specify that the on hand units must be between 0 and 50. Include validation text.
4. Save the changes.
5. Open the Item form you created in Project 1, and then add the following record to the Item table:

MN04	Mouse Pad	5	$9.10	$11.00	AL

(continued)

Maintaining the School Connection Database *(continued)*

6. Switch to Datasheet view and sort the records in ascending order by description.
7. Print the table. Close the table. If you are asked to save changes to the design of the table, click the No button.
8. Create a new query for the Item table.
9. Using a query, delete all records in the Item table where the description starts with the letter T. (*Hint*: Use online Help to solve this problem.) Close the query without saving it.
10. Print the Item table.
11. Open the Vendor table in Design view, and add a new field to the end of the table. Name the field, Fax Number. This new field has the same data type and length as Telephone Number. Enter the same comment as Telephone Number but replace Telephone with Fax. Save the change to the table design.
12. Open the Vendor table in Datasheet view, and then add the following data to the Fax Number field.

AL	608-555-6574
GG	505-555-8766
TM	804-555-1235

13. Resize the Vendor Code, City, State, Zip Code, Telephone Number, and Fax Number columns to the best size.
14. Print the table. If necessary, change the margins so the table prints on one page in landscape orientation. Save the change to the layout of the table.
15. Specify referential integrity between the Vendor table (the one table) and the Item table (the many table). Print the Relationships window by making sure the Relationships window is open, clicking File on the menu bar, and then clicking Print Relationships.

2 Maintaining the City Area Bus Company Database

Problem: The Advertising Sales Manager of the City Area Bus Company would like to make some changes to the database structure. Another field must be added to the database, and the size of the First Name field must be increased. Because several different individuals update the data, the manager also would like to add some validation rules to the database. Finally, some additions and deletions are to be made to the database.

Instructions: Use the database created in the In the Lab 2 of Project 1 for this assignment. Perform the following tasks.

1. Open the City Area Bus Company database and open the Advertiser table in Design view as shown in Figure 3-75.

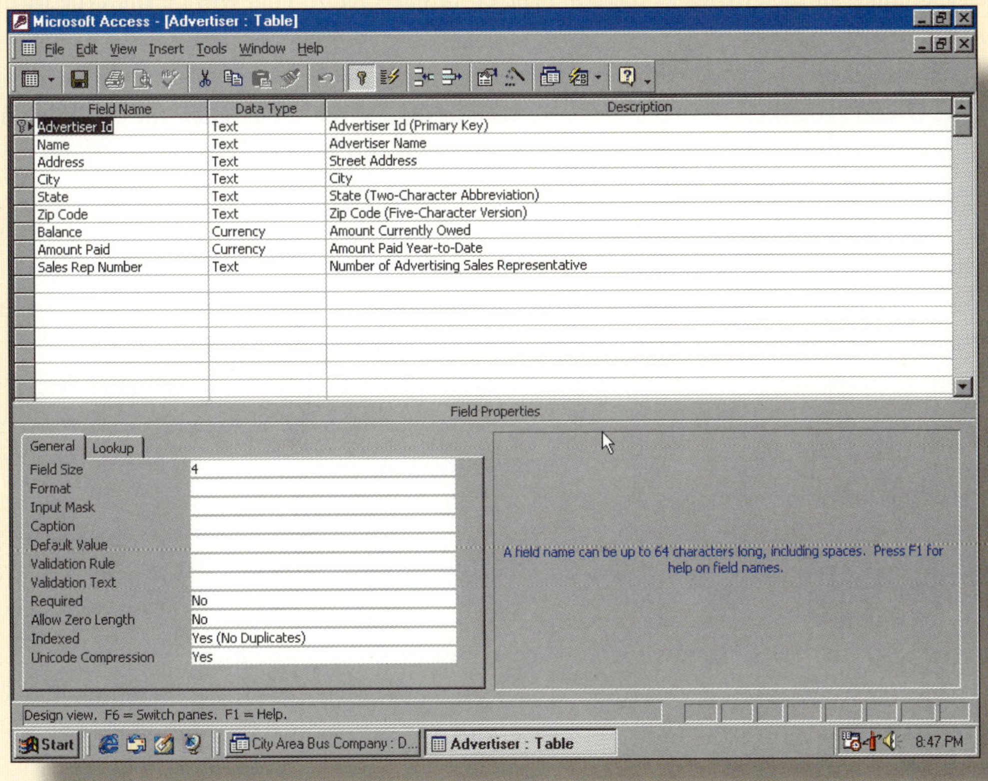

FIGURE 3-75

2. Create an index for the Name field. Be sure to allow duplicates. Create an index on the combination of the State and Zip Code fields. Name the index Statezip. Save these changes.
3. Display the Advertiser table in Datasheet view and order the records by zip code within state.
4. Print the table. If necessary, change the margins so the table prints on one page in landscape orientation. Close the table. If you are asked to save changes to the design of the table, click the No button.
5. Open the Advertiser table in Design view and change the field width of the Name field to 22.

(continued)

Maintaining the City Area Bus Company Database *(continued)*

6. Add the field, Ad Type, to the Advertiser table. Define the field as Text with a width of 3. Insert the Ad Type field after the Zip Code field. This field will contain data on the type of advertising account. Advertisers are classified as retail (RET), service (SER), and dining (DIN).
7. Save these changes and display the Advertiser table in Datasheet view.
8. Change the name of account HC11 to Hilde's Cards & Gifts.
9. Resize the Name column to fit the changed entry. Adjust the width of the remaining columns to best fit the size of the data.
10. Print the table. If necessary, change the margins so the table prints on one page in landscape orientation. Close the table. Save the layout changes to the table.
11. Using a query, change all the entries in the Ad Type column to RET. This will be the type of most accounts. Do not save the query.
12. Open the Advertiser table and order the records in descending order by balance. Print the table and then close the table. If you are asked to save changes to the design of the table, click the No button.
13. Create the following validation rules for the Advertiser table and save the changes to the table. List the steps involved on your own paper.
    a. Make the Name field a required field.
    b. Specify the legal values RET, SER, and DIN for the Ad Type field. Include validation text.
    c. Ensure that any letters entered in the Advertiser Id and State fields are displayed as uppercase.
    d. Specify that balance must be less than or equal $450.00. Include validation text.
14. You can use either Form view or Datasheet view to add records to a table. To use Form view, you must replace the form you created in Project 1 with a form that includes the new field, Ad Type. With the Advertiser table selected, click the New Object: AutoForm button arrow on the Database Window toolbar. Click AutoForm. Use this form that contains ad type to add the following record:

PP24	Pia's Pizza	113 Main	Richmond	MA	05434	DIN	$50.00	$0.00	31

15. Close the form. Click the Yes button when asked if you want to save the form. Save the form as Advertiser. Click the Yes button when asked if you want to replace the Advertiser form you created in Project 1.
16. Open the Advertiser form and locate the advertiser with advertiser NO10 and then change the ad type for the record to DIN. Change the ad type for advertisers AC25 and CS46 to SER.
17. Change to Datasheet view and print the table.
18. Use Filter by Form to find all records in the table where the account has the ad type of RET and a zip code of 05434. Delete these records. (*Hint:* Read the More About on page A 3.12 to solve this problem.)
19. Print the Advertiser table. Specify referential integrity between the Sales Rep table (the one table) and the Advertiser table (the many table). Print the Relationships window by making sure the Relationships window is open, clicking File on the menu bar, and then clicking Print Relationships.

3 Maintaining the Resort Rentals Database

Problem: The real estate company has determined that some changes must be made to the database structure. Another field must be added and the size of the Name field must be increased. Because several different individuals update the data, the company also would like to add some validation rules to the database. Finally, some additions and deletions are required to the database.

Instructions: Use the database created in the In the Lab 3 of Project 1 for this assignment. Perform the following tasks.

1. Open the Resort Rentals database and open the Rental Unit table in Design view as shown in Figure 3-76.

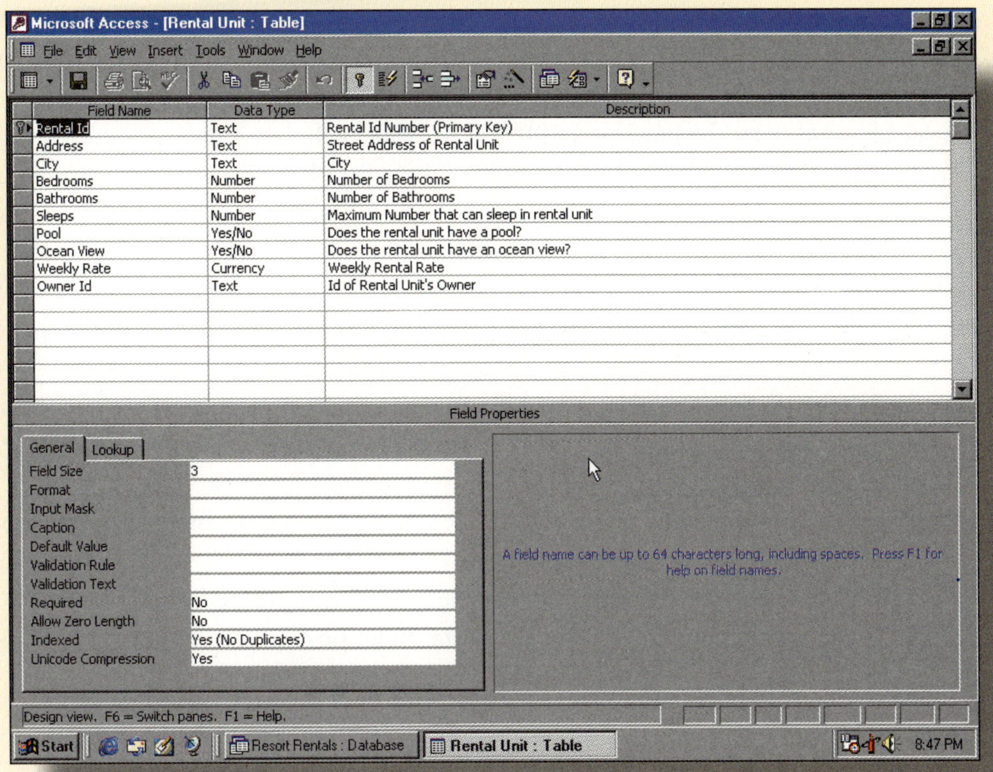

FIGURE 3-76

2. Create an index for the City field. Be sure to allow duplicates. Create an index on the combination of the Bedrooms and Bathrooms fields. Name the index Bedbath. Create an index on the combination of the Pool and Ocean View fields. Name the index PoolView. Save these changes.
3. Display the Rental Unit table and order the records by bathrooms within bedrooms.
4. Print the table and then close the table. If you are asked to save changes to the design of the table, click the No button.
5. Add the field, For Sale, to the Rental Unit table. Define the field as a Yes/No field. Insert the field after the Weekly Rate field. This field will indicate whether or not the rental unit is for sale.
6. Save these changes and display the Rental Unit table in Datasheet view.

(continued)

Maintaining the Resort Rentals Database *(continued)*

7. Units 101, 108, and 134 are for sale. Update the records for these rental units. Decrease the width of the For Sale column.
8. Print the table. If necessary, change the margins so the table prints on one page in landscape orientation. Close the table. Save the layout changes to the table.
9. Create the following validation rules for the Rental Unit table and save the changes to the table. List the steps involved on your own paper.
   a. Make the Address, City, Bedrooms, Bathrooms, and Sleeps fields required fields.
   b. Assign a default value of 1 to the Bedrooms and Bathrooms fields. Assign a default value of 2 to the Sleeps field.
   c. Specify that the Bedrooms and Bathrooms fields must be at least one and the Sleeps field must be at least 2. Include validation text.
   d. Specify that weekly rate must be between $500 and $2,000. Include validation text.
10. The real estate office has just received a new listing from Rita Peoples. The unit has been assigned the id 148. It is located at 123 Second in San Toma. The unit sleeps 10, has 3 bedrooms, 3 bathrooms, a pool but no ocean view. The weekly rate is $1,400 and the owner is interested in selling the unit. Add this record to the database. Remember that you can use either Form view or Datasheet view to add records to a table. If you use Form view, you must replace the form you created in Project 1 with a form that includes the new field, For Sale.
11. If necessary, close the form. Click Yes when asked if you want to save the form. Save the form as Rental Unit. Click the Yes button when asked if you want to replace the Rental Unit you created in Project 1.
12. Change to Datasheet view and print the table.
13. Using a query, delete all records in the table where the rental unit is in Gulf Breeze and has one bedroom.
14. Print the Rental Unit table.
15. Specify referential integrity between the Owner table (the one table) and the Rental Unit table (the many table). Print the Relationships window by making sure the Relationships window is open, clicking File on the menu bar, and then clicking Print Relationships.

Cases and Places

The difficulty of these case studies varies:
◗ are the least difficult; ◗◗ are more difficult; and ◗◗◗ are the most difficult.

1 ◗ Use the Computer Science Club database you created in Case Study 1 of Project 1 for this assignment. Execute each of these tasks and then print the results:

(a) Antistatic Wipes are now called Antistatic Cloths.
(b) The club has sold all the desktop holders and decided to delete this item from inventory.
(c) Mouse Tracks has increased the cost of their items by 10%. The club also has raised the selling price by 10% for these items.
(d) The club sold 25 disks.
(e) Human Interface has a new telephone number, 317-555-5847.
(f) The description for item 4343 should really be Mouse Pad with Logo.
(g) Specify referential integrity between the two tables in the database.

2 ◗ Use the Sci-Fi Scene database you created in Case Study 2 of Project 2 for this assignment. Execute each of these tasks and then print the results:

(a) The bookstore has added a used book section. The owner would like to add these books to the database but she must know whether a book is used or new. Add a field to the database to indicate whether a book is used or new. All books currently in the database are new books.
(b) The title for book 0533 is really Albert s Truth & Way.
(c) Add the used book, Martian Politics to the database and use 9867 as the book code. Martian Politics was written by E Dearling in 1995. It was published by VanNester and will sell for $2.50.
(d) Dark Wind was published in 1996.
(e) The owner sold the last copy of Infinity and the book is now out of print.
(f) Specify referential integrity between the two tables in the database.

3 ◗◗ Use the band database created in Case Study 3 of Project 1 for this assignment:

(a) Determine and create the appropriate validity checks for the sex, number of years in band, own or lease instrument, and age fields.
(b) Ensure that data always is entered in the name, telephone number, emergency contact name, and emergency contact number fields.
(c) Add three records to the database.

Cases and Places

4 ▸▸ Use the humane society database created in Case Study 4 of Project 1 for this assignment:

(a) Add a field to the database to store the date the pet was adopted and enter some sample data for this field.
(b) Determine and create appropriate validity checks for the fields in your database.
(c) Add two records to the database.
(d) Determine and create appropriate indexes for your database. Use the indexes to sort the data.
(e) Analyze the database and determine if you have a one-to-many relationship between any tables. If so, specify referential integrity between the one table and the many table.

5 ▸▸▸ Use the Intramural Sports Club database you created in Case Study 5 of Project 1 for this assignment:

(a) Analyze the database and determine if you need any additional fields. Do you have a field for the date you received a sports item? Do you have e-mail addresses for each student? Add any fields that you now think would be useful to the database.
(b) Determine and create appropriate validity checks for the fields in your database.
(c) Add two records to the database.
(d) Determine and create appropriate indexes for your database. Use the indexes to sort the data.
(e) Analyze the database and determine if you have a one-to-many relationship between any tables. If so, specify referential integrity between the one table and the many table.

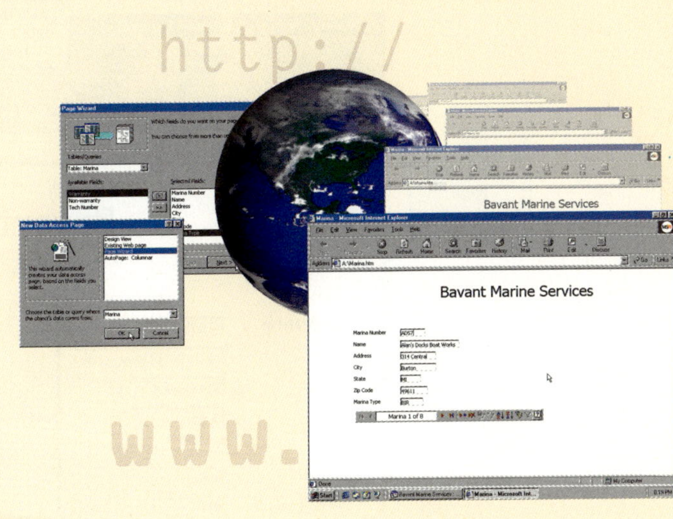

Microsoft Access 2000

Publishing to the Internet Using Data Access Pages

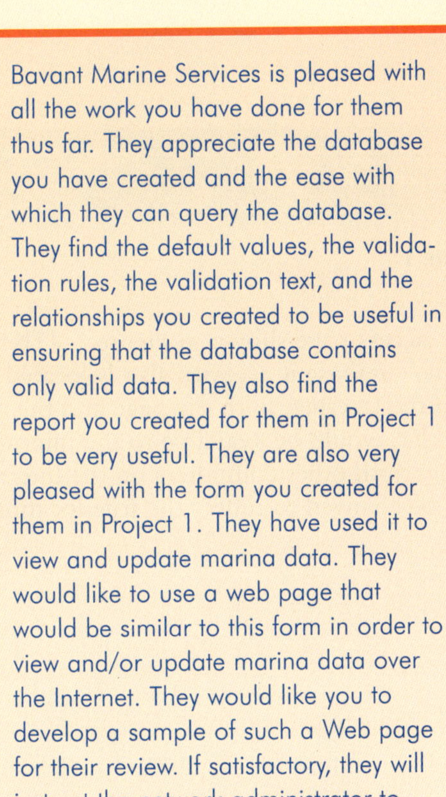

CASE PERSPECTIVE

Bavant Marine Services is pleased with all the work you have done for them thus far. They appreciate the database you have created and the ease with which they can query the database. They find the default values, the validation rules, the validation text, and the relationships you created to be useful in ensuring that the database contains only valid data. They also find the report you created for them in Project 1 to be very useful. They are also very pleased with the form you created for them in Project 1. They have used it to view and update marina data. They would like to use a web page that would be similar to this form in order to view and/or update marina data over the Internet. They would like you to develop a sample of such a Web page for their review. If satisfactory, they will instruct the network administrator to make both the database and your Web page accessible on the Internet.

Introduction

Microsoft Access 2000 supports data access pages. A **data access page** is an HTML (hypertext markup language) document that can be bound directly to data in the database. The fact that it is an **HTML (hypertext markup language) document** means that it can be run on the Internet. Data access pages can be run only in the Microsoft Internet Explorer browser. The fact that it is bound directly to the database means that it can access data in the database directly.

Figure 1 on the next page shows a sample data access page run in the Internet Explorer browser. Notice that it is similar to the form created in Project 1 (see page A 1.38). Although running in the browser, the data access page is displaying data from the Bavant Marine Services database. Furthermore, the page can be used to change this data. You can use it to change the contents of existing records, to delete records, and to add new records.

More About 2000

Publishing to the Internet: Saving Other Objects

You also can publish other objects such as reports and datasheets to the Internet. To publish a datasheet or a report to the Internet, save the object as a Web page in HTML format. To do so, select the name of the object in the Database window, click File on the menu bar, and then click Export. In the Save As Type box, click HTML Documents.

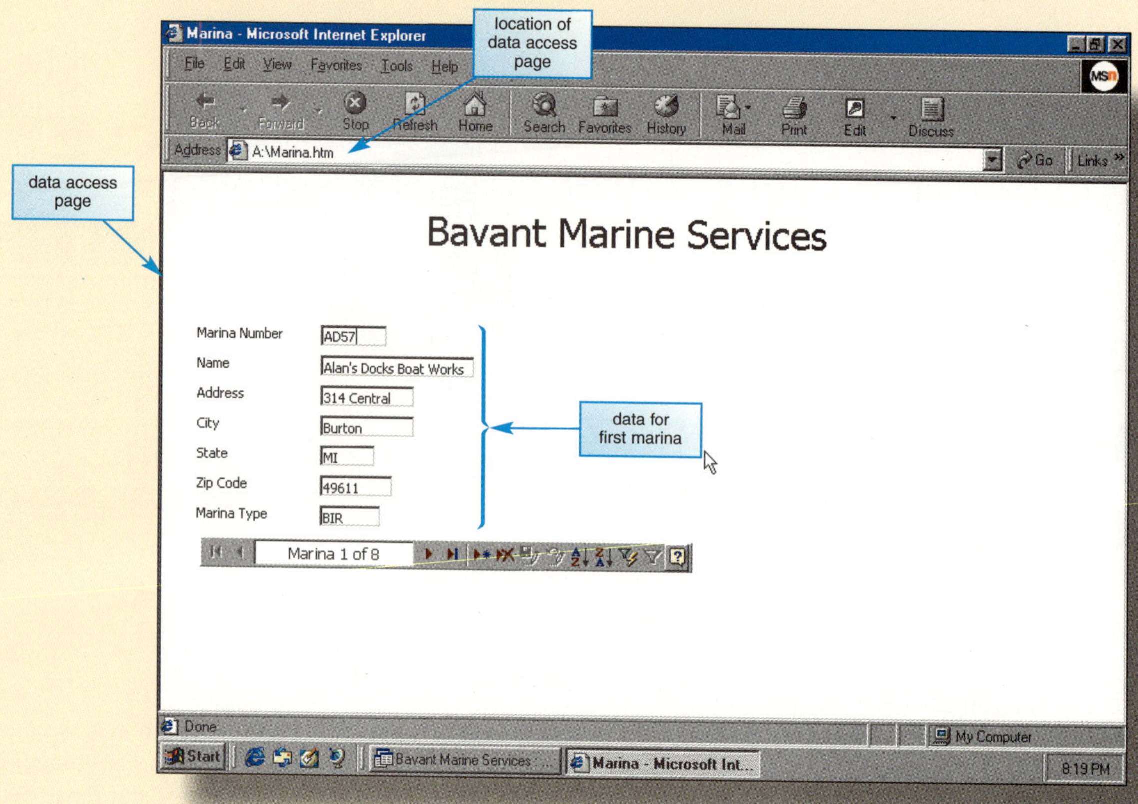

FIGURE 1

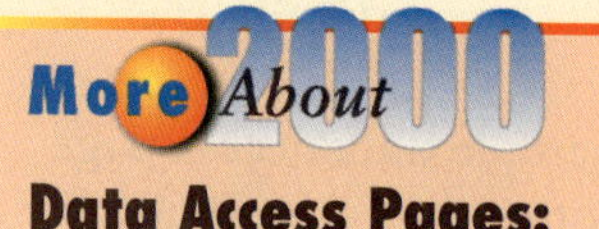

Data Access Pages: Reporting

Data Access Pages can be used for interactive reporting. They are especially helpful in reports that involve grouping. Expand indicators let users see various levels of detail. For more information, visit the Access 2000 Project 3 More About page (www.scsite.com/ac2000/more.htm) and click Data Access Page.

In this project, you will create the data access page shown in Figure 1. (This data access page is located on the Data Disk. The database it accesses also is located on the Data Disk. In order to use this page on the Internet, both the page and the database would need to be located on a server that would be available to the Internet. A **server** is a computer that shares its resources with other computers on the Internet. The address entered in the browser would be changed to reflect the true location of the page.)

Opening the Database

Before carrying out the steps in this project, you first must open the database. To do so, perform the following steps.

Data Access Pages: Analysis

Data Access Pages can be used to analyze data in a variety of ways. The tool for doing so is a PivotTable list, an interactive table that allows dynamic analysis of data. For more information, visit the Access 2000 Project 3 More About page (www.scsite.com/ac2000/more.htm) and click Data Access Page.

TO OPEN A DATABASE

1. Click the Start button on the taskbar.
2. Click Open Office Document and then click 3½ Floppy (A:) in the Look in box. If necessary, click the Bavant Marine Services database name in the list.
3. Click the Open button.

The database opens and the Bavant Marine Services : Database window displays.

Creating a Data Access Page

To create a data access page, use the Page Wizard as shown in the following steps.

Steps To Create a Data Access Page

1. **With the Marina table selected, click the New Object: AutoForm button arrow on the Database window toolbar.**

The list of available objects displays (Figure 2).

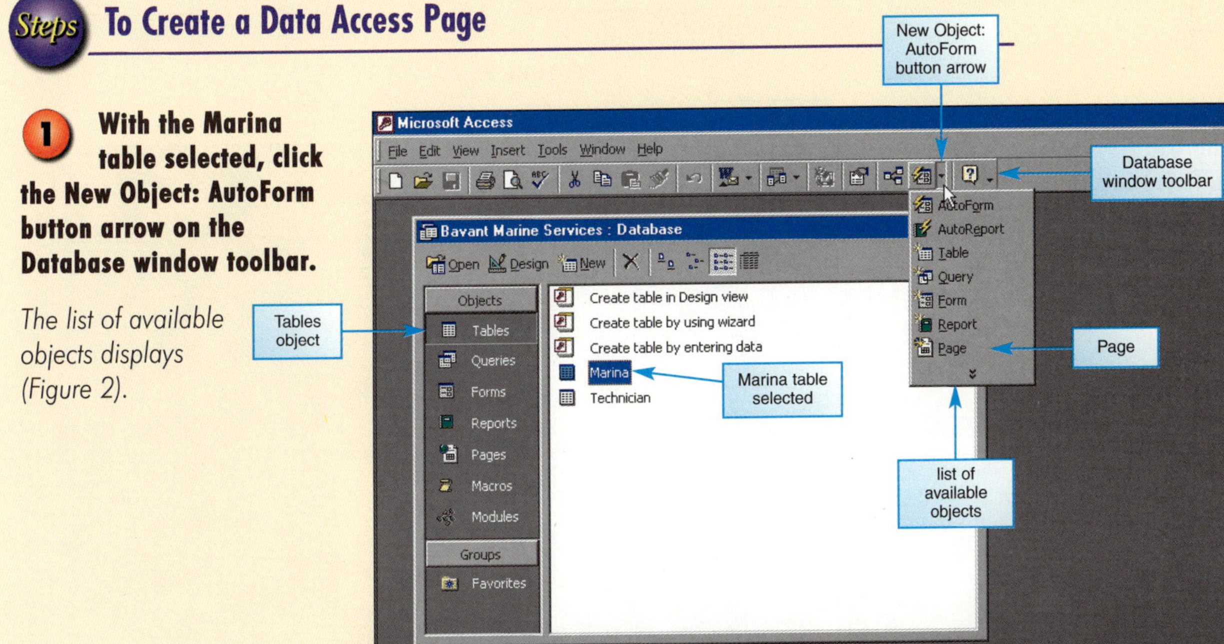

FIGURE 2

2 **Click Page. When the New Data Access Page dialog box displays, click Page Wizard and then point to the OK button.**

The New Data Access Page dialog box displays with Page Wizard selected (Figure 3).

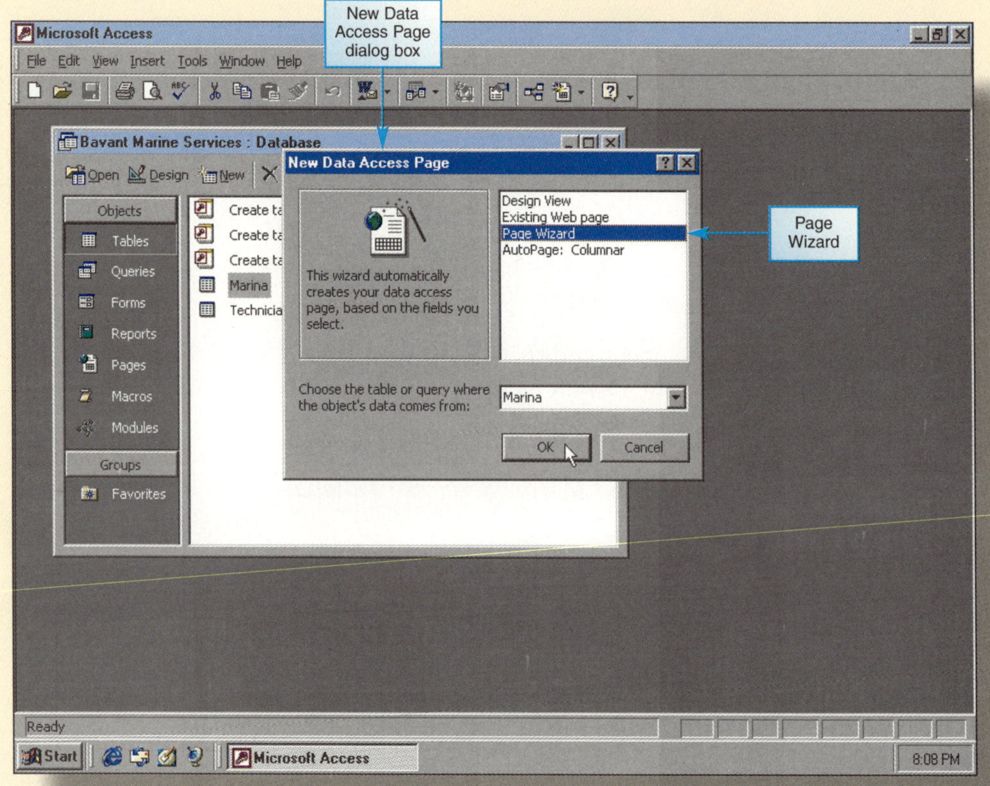

FIGURE 3

3 **Click the OK button. Point to the Add Field button.**

The Page Wizard dialog box displays (Figure 4). The fields in the Marina table display in the Available Fields box. The Marina Number field currently is selected.

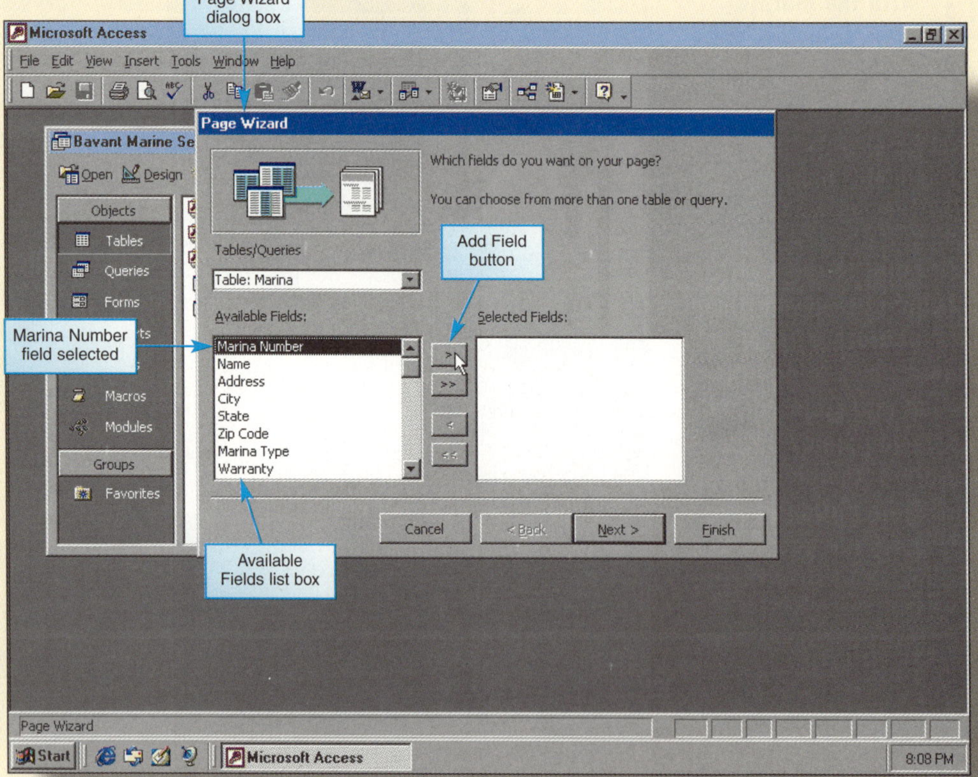

FIGURE 4

4 Click the Add Field button to add the Marina Number field to the Selected Fields box. Click the Add Field button six more times to add the Name, Address, City, State, Zip Code, and Marina Type fields. Point to the Next button.

The Marina Number, Name, Address, City, State, Zip Code, and Marina Type fields are added to the Selected Fields box (Figure 5).

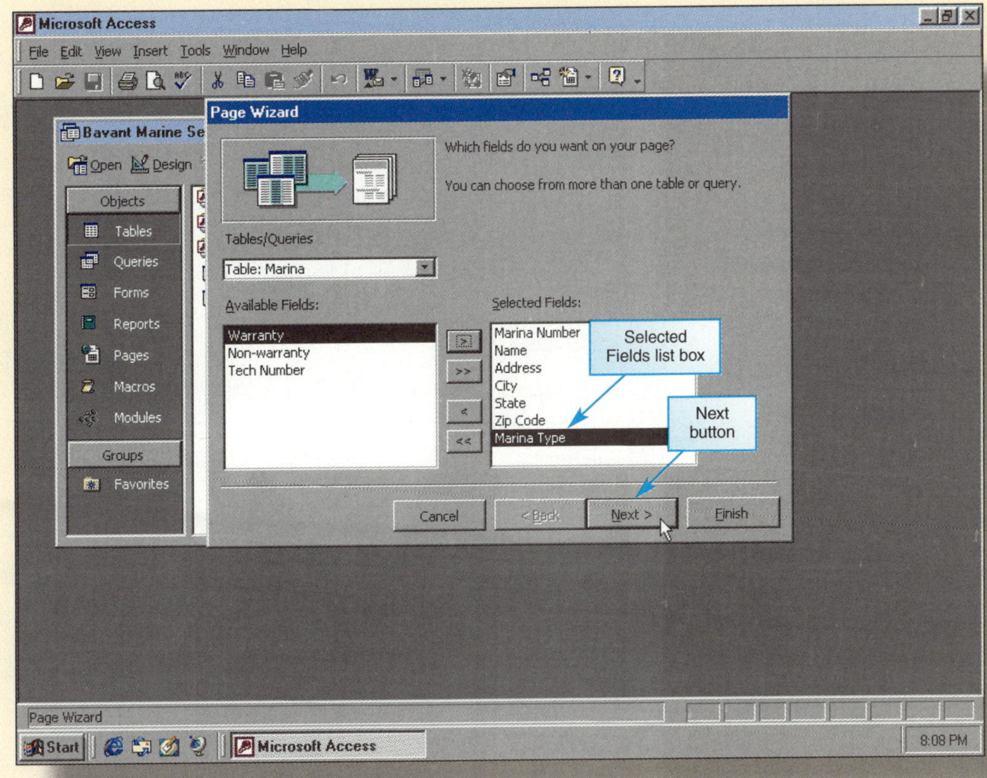

FIGURE 5

5 Click the Next button.

The next Page Wizard dialog box displays (Figure 6).

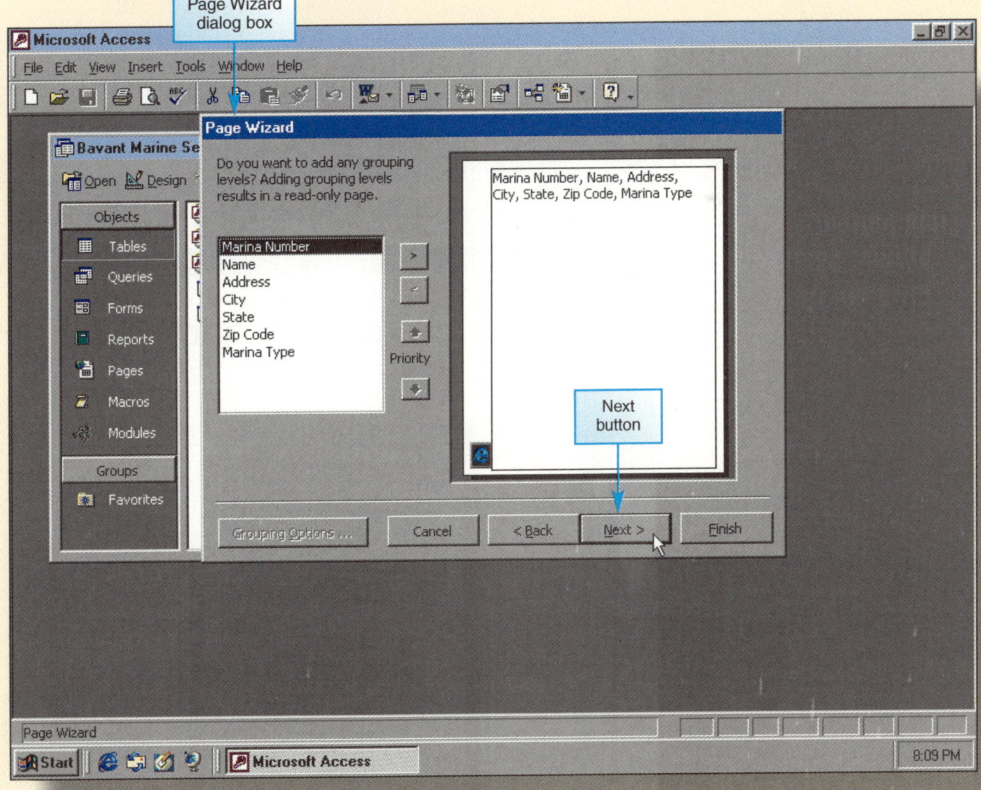

FIGURE 6

6 Click the Next button because no grouping levels are needed. Click the Next button a second time because no changes are needed to the sort order. Point to the Finish button.

The next Page Wizard dialog box displays (Figure 7).

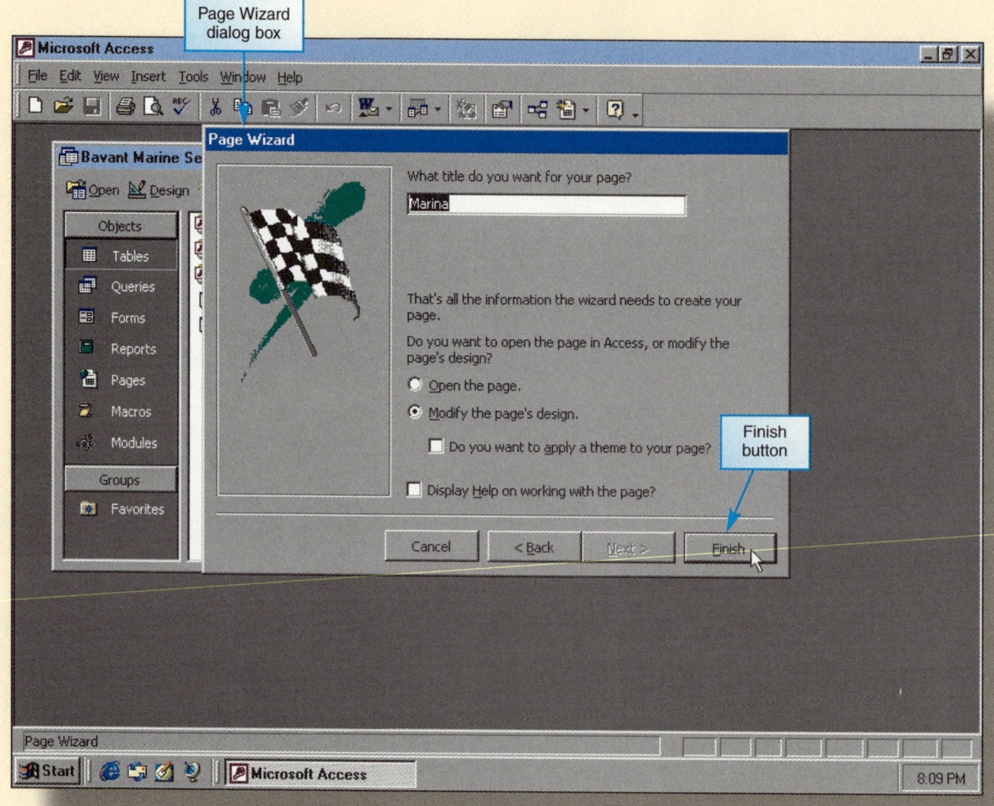

FIGURE 7

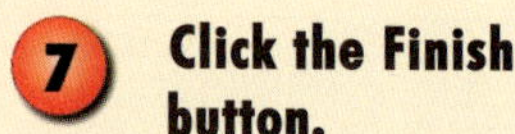

7 Click the Finish button.

The Page1: Data Access Page displays (Figure 8). The process of creating a data access page may take several seconds.

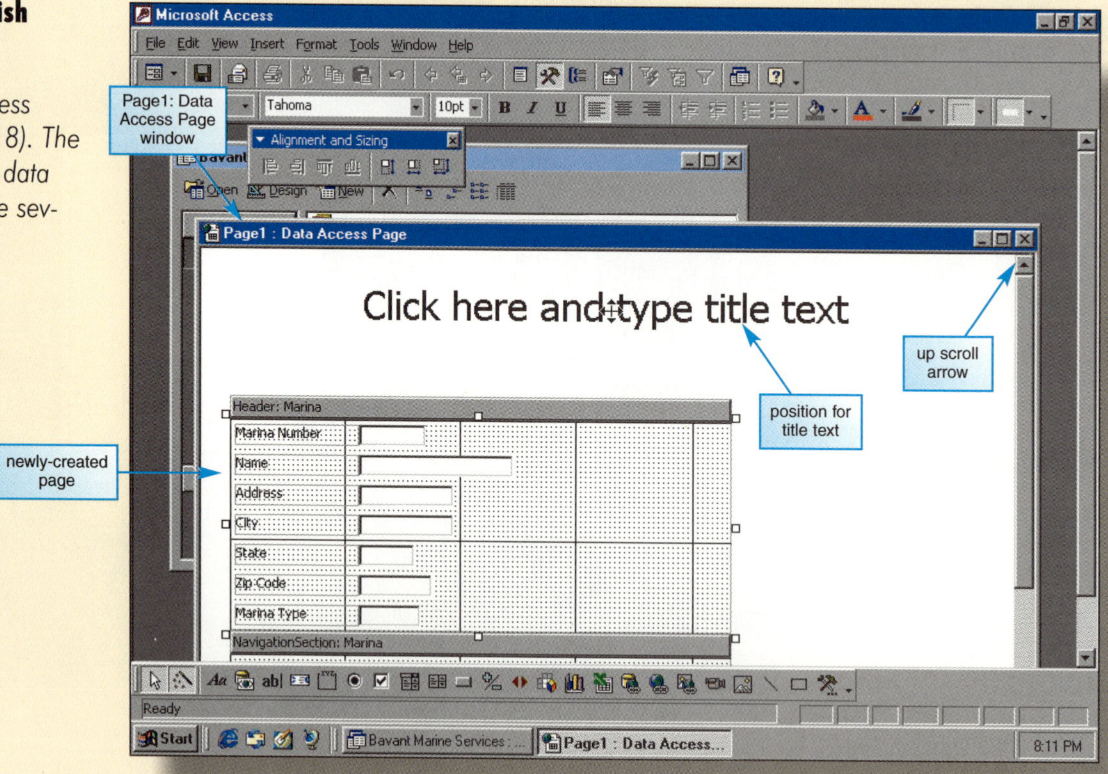

FIGURE 8

8 **If necessary, click the up arrow on the vertical scroll bar to display the top of the screen. Click anywhere on the portion of the screen labeled "Click here and type title text" and then type** `Bavant Marine Services` **as the title text.**

The data access page displays (Figure 9). The title is changed to Bavant Marine Services.

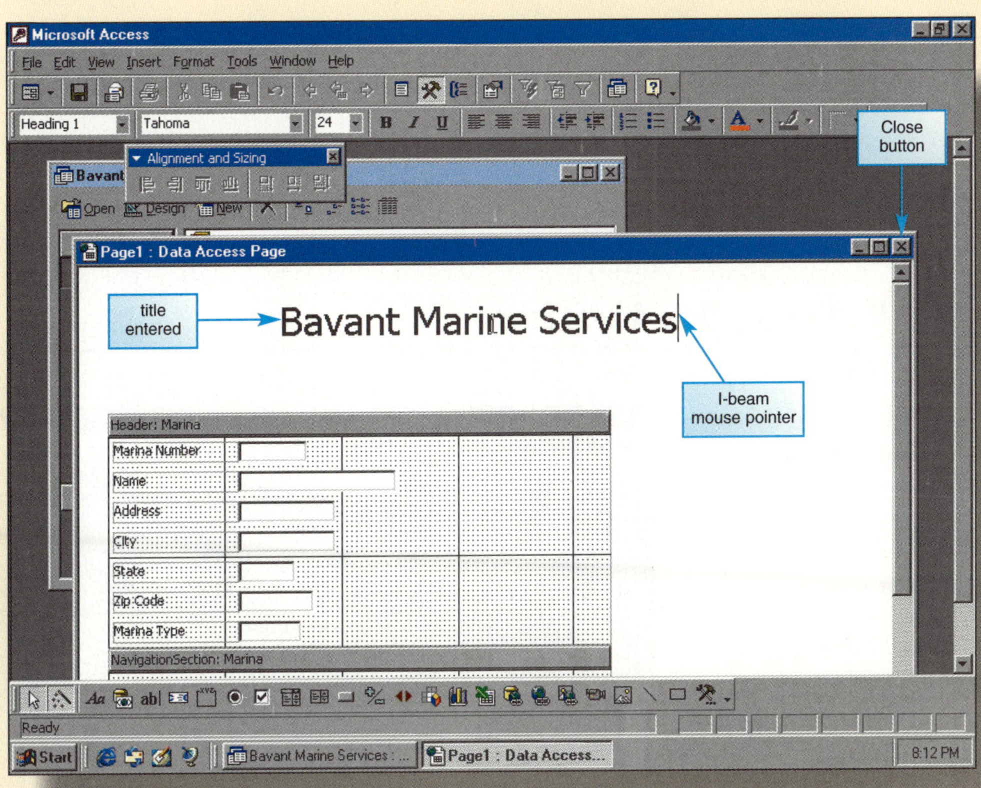

FIGURE 9

9 **Click the Close button on the Page1: Data Access Page title bar to close the window. When the Save As Data Access Page dialog box displays, type** `Marina` **as the name of the page and click Save. If necessary, click 3½ Floppy (A:) in the Save in box to save your page to the same location as your database.**

The data access page is created and saved as Marina.

Microsoft Certification

The Microsoft Office User Specialist (MOUS) Certification program provides an opportunity for you to obtain a valuable industry credential - proof that you have the Access 2000 skills required by employers. For more information, see Appendix D or visit the Shelly Cashman Series MOUS Web page at www.scsite.com/off2000/cert.htm.

Previewing the Data Access Page

While in Access, you can preview what the page will look like in the browser by using Web Page Preview on the shortcut menu. The following steps preview the data access page that was just created.

To Preview the Data Access Page

1 With the Database window open, click the Pages object. Right-click Marina and then point to Web Page Preview on the shortcut menu.

The shortcut menu displays (Figure 10).

2 Click Web Page Preview on the shortcut menu.

The page displays in the maximized Internet Explorer window, similarly to Figure 1 on page AW 1.2.

3 Click the Close button on the Internet Explorer window title bar to quit Internet Explorer. Click the Close button on the Microsoft Access window title bar to quit Access.

The page no longer displays. The database is closed.

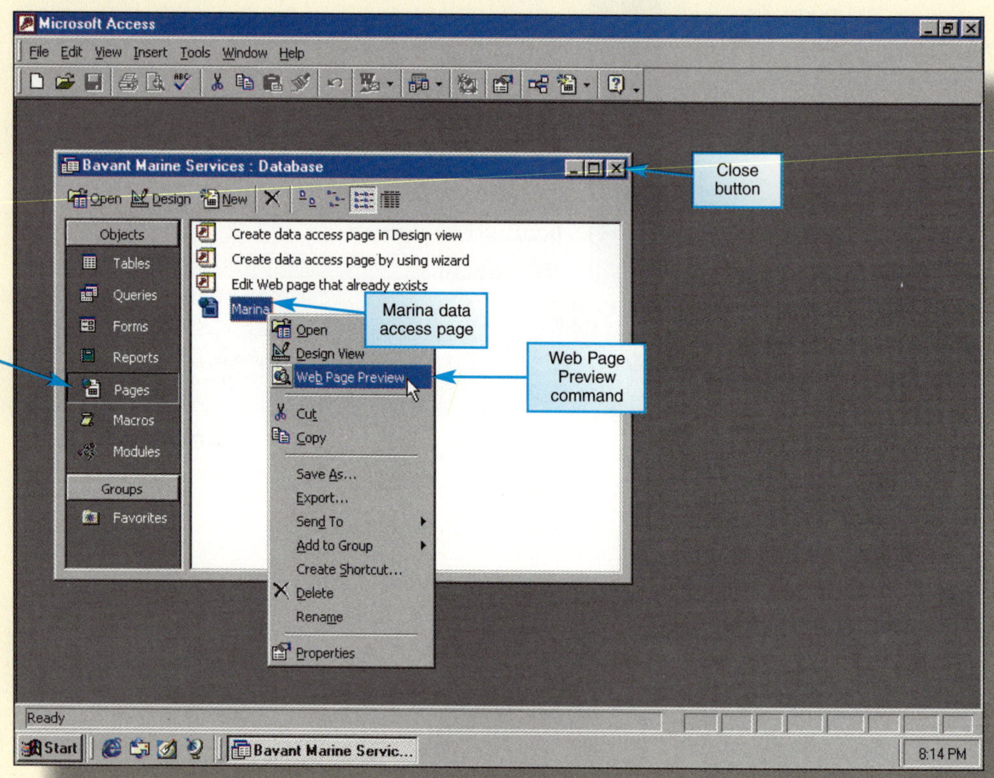

FIGURE 10

Using the Data Access Page

To use the data access page, start Internet Explorer, type the location of the data access page (for example, a:\marina.htm if you created the page on your Data Disk), and then press the ENTER key. The page then will display (Figure 11). To ensure that the data displays in marina number order, click the Sort Ascending button on the record navigation toolbar.

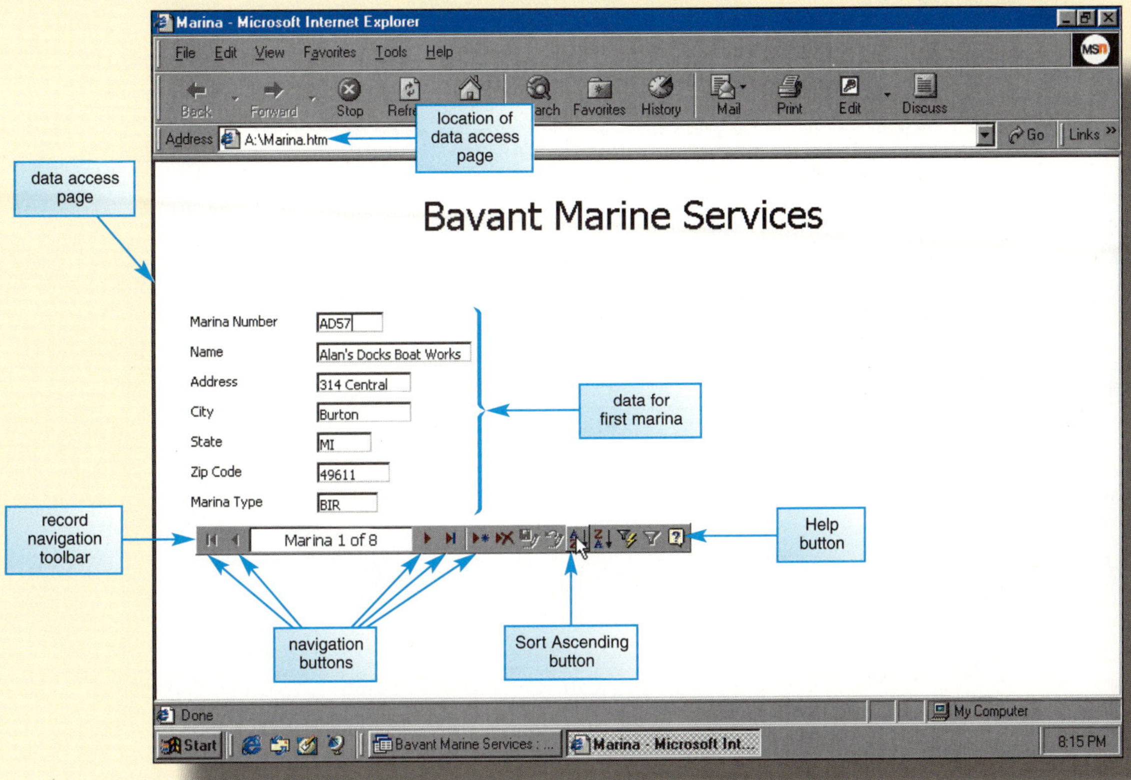

FIGURE 11

You can use the navigation buttons just as you do when viewing a datasheet or a form in Access. You can get help on the way you use the page by clicking the Help button (see Figure 11). Details concerning the use of the page then will display (Figure 12 on the next page). Clicking the plus symbol (+) in front of a category will change the plus symbol to a minus symbol (-) and display all the topics within the category. Clicking the question mark symbol (?) in front of a topic will display details concerning the topic. In Figure 12 on the next page, the plus symbol that was originally in front of the Working with Data access pages category has been changed to a minus symbol and the Data Access pages: What they are and how they work Help information displays. In addition, the Microsoft Access Data Pages Help window has been maximized, which makes it easier to read the help information.

Quick Reference

For a table that lists how to complete the tasks covered in this book using the mouse, menu, shortcut menu, and keyboard, visit the Shelly Cashman Series Office site (www.scsite.com/off2000/qr.htm), and then click the application name.

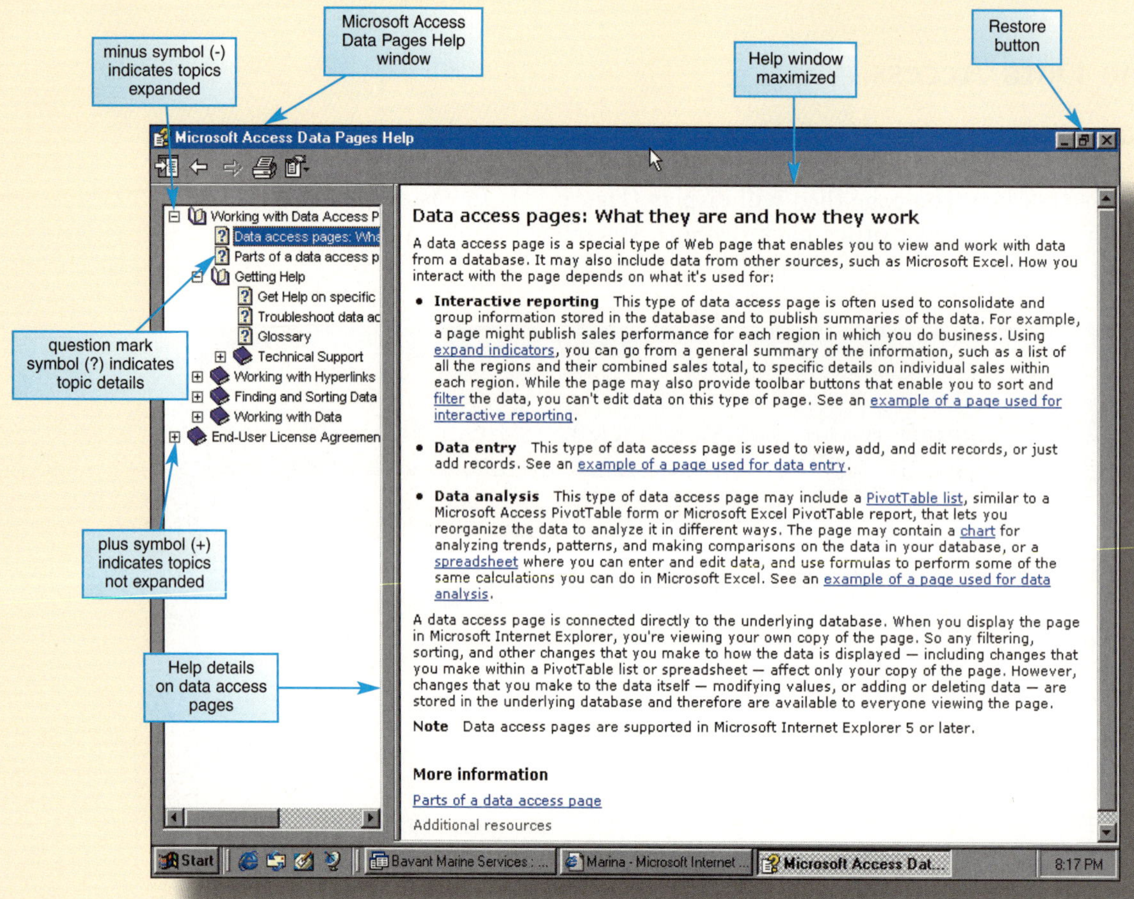

FIGURE 12

CASE PERSPECTIVE SUMMARY

In this Web Feature, you created a data access page for the Marina table in the Bavant Marine Services database. This page will enable Bavant to access their database using the Internet.

Web Feature Summary

In this Web Feature, you learned how to create a data access page to enable users to access the data in a database via the Internet. You worked with the Page Wizard to create such a page. You then previewed the data access page from within Access. Finally, you saw how to use the data access page.

What You Should Know

Having completed this Web Feature, you now should be able to perform the following tasks:

- Create a Data Access Page *(AW 1.3)*
- Open a Database *(AW 1.3)*
- Preview the Data Access Page *(AW 1.8)*
- Use a Data Access Page *(AW 1.9)*

1 Creating a Data Access Page for the Sidewalk Scrapers Database

Instructions: Start Access. Open the Sidewalk Scrapers database from the Data Disk. See the inside back cover of this book for instructions for downloading the Data Disk or see your instructor for information on accessing the files required for this book. Perform the following tasks.

1. Create a data access page for the Worker table (Figure 13).

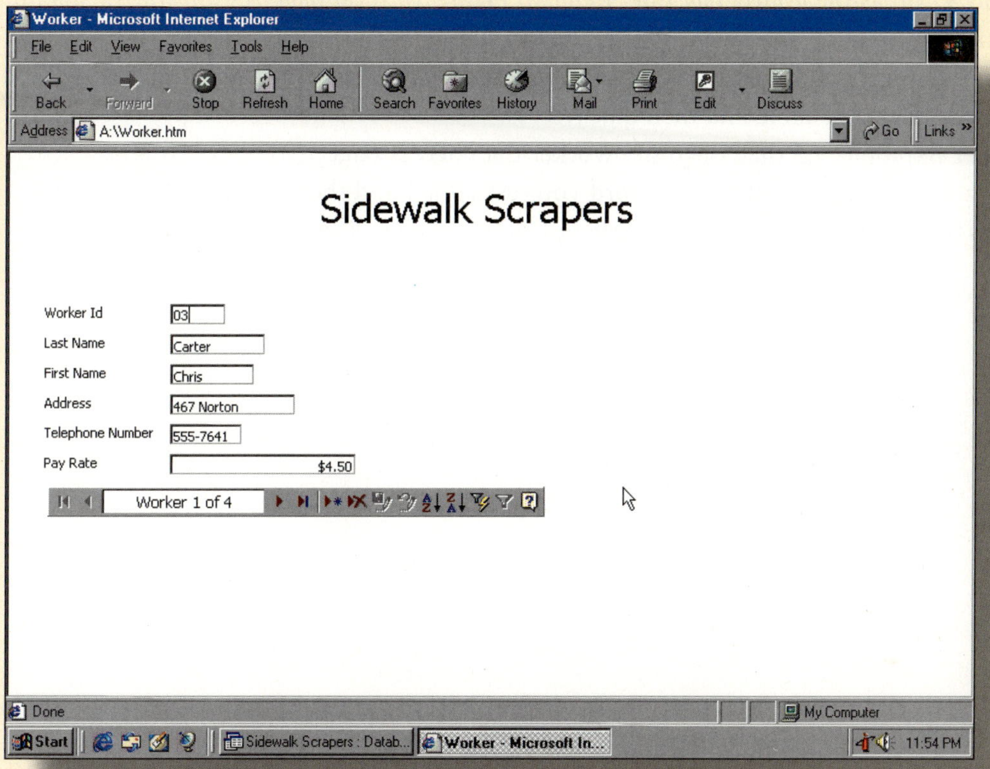

FIGURE 13

2. Print the data access page. To print the page, preview the page, click File on the menu bar, and then click Print.

2 Using a Data Access Page

Instructions: Make sure the Data Disk containing the Sidewalk Scrapers database and the data access page you created in In the Lab 1 is in drive A. Perform the following tasks.

1. Start Internet Explorer and then open the Worker data access page.
2. Use the data access page to add yourself as a new record to the Worker table. Use 99 as the worker id number and $7.00 as the hourly pay rate. Refer to Figure 1-76 on page A 1.56 for the maximum field sizes for the remaining fields.
3. Quit Internet Explorer and then start Access. Open the Worker table in Datasheet view. You now should have 5 records. Print the table and then quit Access.
4. Start Internet Explorer and then open the Worker data access page.
5. Use the data access page to delete the record you just added and then quit Internet Explorer.
6. Start Access and then open the Worker table in Datasheet view. Print the table and then quit Access.

MICROSOFT

PowerPoint 2000

1

2

3

4

5

6

Microsoft PowerPoint 2000

Using a Design Template and AutoLayouts to Create a Presentation

OBJECTIVES

You will have mastered the material in this project when you can:

- Start a presentation as a New Office document
- Describe the PowerPoint window
- Select a design template
- Create a title slide
- Describe and use text attributes such as font size and font style
- Save a presentation
- Add a new slide
- Create a multi-level bulleted list slide
- Move to another slide in normal view
- End a slide show with a black slide
- View a presentation in slide show view
- Quit PowerPoint
- Open a presentation
- Check the spelling and consistency of a presentation
- Edit a presentation
- Change line spacing on the slide master
- Display a presentation in black and white
- Print a presentation in black and white
- Use the PowerPoint Help system

Puttin' on the Glitz

Presentations Help COMDEX Shine

Microsoft's Bill Gates will be there. So will thousands of the world's computer industry executives. And they will be joined by hundreds of thousands of curious technology affectionados seeking the latest trends in hardware, software, and the Internet.

They will be attending COMDEX, North America's largest trade show. COMDEX/Fall is held in Las Vegas each November, and COMDEX/Spring is held in Chicago in April. Both shows feature speeches by industry leaders, tutorials on the latest technologies, and thousands of square feet of exhibits showcasing the latest in computer technology.

Information technology (IT) experts headline COMDEX as the premier IT event in the world. Indeed, more than 10,000 new products are unveiled at the Fall show. Since COMDEX's inception in 1979, some of the more notable product launches have been the IBM PC in 1981, COMPAQ's suitcase-sized portable computer, Microsoft's first version of Windows, Apple's original Macintosh computer, and CD-ROM drives.

Attendance and industry representation have grown steadily. The first show featured 150 exhibitions seen by 4,000 curious visitors. Six years later, more than 1,000 companies displayed their wares for more than 100,000 techies. Recent shows have produced as many as 2,400 booths visited by 250,000-plus attendees.

Computer companies realize their sales forces need to capture their audiences' attention, so they add sensory cues to their exhibits. They treat the trade show visitors to a multimedia blitz of sound, visuals, and action with the help of presentation software such as Microsoft PowerPoint 2000. This program enhances the presenters' speeches by highlighting keywords in the presentation, displaying graphs, pictures, and diagrams, and playing sound and video clips.

In this project, you will learn to use PowerPoint 2000 to create a presentation, which also is called a slide show, concerning effective study skills. You then will run the slide show and print handouts for the audience. In later projects you will add animation, pictures, and sound.

PowerPoint's roots stem from the innovative work performed by a small company called Forethought, Inc. Programmers at this pioneering business coined the phrase, desktop presentation graphics, for formal slide shows and created a complete software package that automated creating slides containing text, charts, and graphics. Microsoft liked the visual appeal of the software and acquired Forethought in 1987. Company executives decided to market the software to Apple Macintosh users because Mac computers were considered clearly superior to IBM-based personal computers for graphics applications.

Microsoft PowerPoint became a favorite among Mac users. Meanwhile, Lotus Freelance Graphics and Software Publishing Harvard Graphics were popular within the PC community. This division ceased, however, when Microsoft released Windows 3.0 in 1990 and subsequently developed a Windows version of PowerPoint to run on PCs.

Since that time, Macintosh and PC users alike have utilized the presentation power of PowerPoint. The package has grown to include animation, audio and video clips, and Internet integration. Certainly the technology gurus at COMDEX have realized PowerPoint's dazzling visual appeal. So will you as you complete the exercises in this textbook.

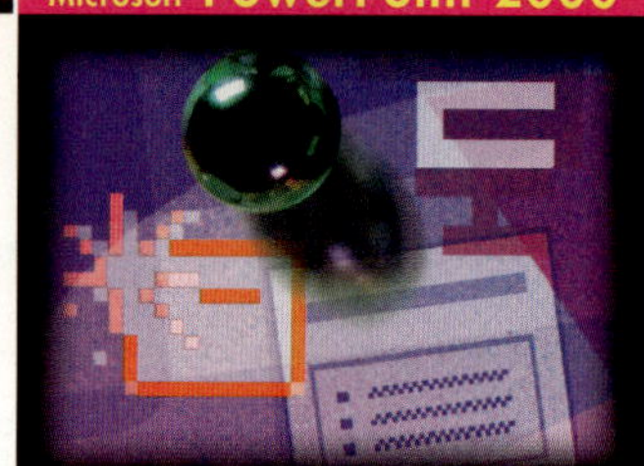

Microsoft PowerPoint 2000

Using a Design Template and AutoLayouts to Create a Presentation

CASE PERSPECTIVE

Excellent study habits are the keys to college success. What matters is not how long people study — it is how well they use their time. Students who study well can maximize their hours, have time for other activities, make the highest grades, and have a better chance to get accepted to their desired school. Ultimately, they generally earn higher incomes because their good study habits carry over to the working environment.

Advisers in Seaview College's Counseling Department spend many hours each semester helping students organize their study times, maximize their classroom experiences, and read their textbooks for ultimate comprehension. Dr. Ramon Martinez, the dean of counseling, has asked you to develop a short presentation to run at next semester's Freshmen Orientation sessions. You agree to create the presentation using a computer and PowerPoint software with the theme of effective study habits. In addition, you will print handouts of the presentation for the incoming students and also print a copy of the presentation on transparency film to enable the advisers to project the slides using an overhead projector.

What Is Microsoft PowerPoint 2000?

Microsoft PowerPoint 2000 is a complete presentation graphics program that allows you to produce professional-looking presentations. A PowerPoint **presentation** also is called a **slide show.** PowerPoint gives you the flexibility to make presentations using a projection device attached to a personal computer (Figure 1-1a) and using overhead transparencies (Figure 1-1b). In addition, you can take advantage of the World Wide Web and run virtual presentations on the Internet (Figure 1-1c). PowerPoint also can create paper printouts of the individual slides, outlines, and speaker notes.

PowerPoint contains several features to simplify creating a slide show. For example, you can instruct PowerPoint to create a predesigned presentation, and then you can modify the presentation to fulfill your requirements. You quickly can format a slide show using one of the professionally designed presentation design templates. To make your presentation more impressive, you can add tables, charts, pictures, video, sound, and, animation effects. You also can check the spelling of your slide show as you type or after you have completed designing the presentation. For example, you can instruct PowerPoint to restrict the number of bulleted items on a slide or limit the number of words in each paragraph. Additional PowerPoint features include the following:

- **Word processing** — create bulleted lists, combine words and images, find and replace text, and use multiple fonts and type sizes.
- **Outlining** — develop your presentation using an outline format. You also can import outlines from Microsoft Word or other word processing programs.
- **Charting** — create and insert charts into your presentations. The two chart types are: standard, which includes bar, line, pie, and xy (scatter) charts; and custom, which displays floating bars, colored lines, and three-dimensional cones.

(a) Projection Device Connected to a Personal Computer

(b) Overhead Transparencies

FIGURE 1-1

(c) PowerPoint Presentation Over the World Wide Web

- **Drawing** — form and modify diagrams using shapes such as arcs, arrows, cubes, rectangles, stars, and triangles.
- **Inserting multimedia** — insert artwork and multimedia effects into your slide show. Clip Gallery 5.0 contains hundreds of clip art images, pictures, photos, sounds, and video clips. You can search for clips by entering words or phrases that describe the subject you want, by looking for clips with similar artistic styles, colors, or shapes, or by connecting to a special Web site reserved for Clip Gallery users. You also can import art from other applications.
- **Web support** — save presentations or parts of a presentation in HTML format so they can be viewed and manipulated using a browser. You can publish your slide show to the Internet or to an intranet. You also can insert action buttons and hyperlinks to create a self-running or interactive Web presentation.
- **E-mailing** — send an individual slide as an e-mail message or your entire slide show as an attachment to an e-mail message.
- **Using Wizards** — quickly and efficiently create a presentation by answering prompts for specific content criteria. For example, the **AutoContent Wizard** gives prompts for the type of slide show you are planning, such as communicating bad news or motivating a team, and the type of output, such as an on-screen presentation or black and white overheads. If you are planning to run your presentation on another computer, the **Pack and Go Wizard** helps you bundle everything you need, including any objects associated with that presentation. If you cannot confirm that this other computer has PowerPoint installed, you also can include the **PowerPoint Viewer**, a program that allows you to run, but not edit, a PowerPoint slide show.

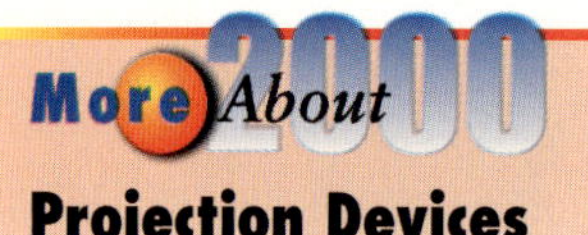

Projection Devices

Multimedia projectors have become the standard for today's presenters. The newest devices are about the size of a deli sandwich, weigh just five pounds, and fill the room with brilliant, clear images. For more information, visit the PowerPoint 2000 More About Web page (www.scsite.com/pp2000/more.htm) and click Projection.

Project One — Effective Study Skills

This book presents a series of projects using PowerPoint to produce slides similar to those you would develop in an academic or business environment. Project 1 uses PowerPoint to create the presentation shown in Figures 1-2a through 1-2d. The objective is to produce a presentation, called Effective Study Skills, to be displayed using an overhead projector. As an introduction to PowerPoint, this project steps you through the most common type of presentation, which is a bulleted list. A **bulleted list** is a list of paragraphs, each preceded by a bullet. A **bullet** is a symbol such as a heavy dot (•) or other character that precedes text when the text warrants special emphasis.

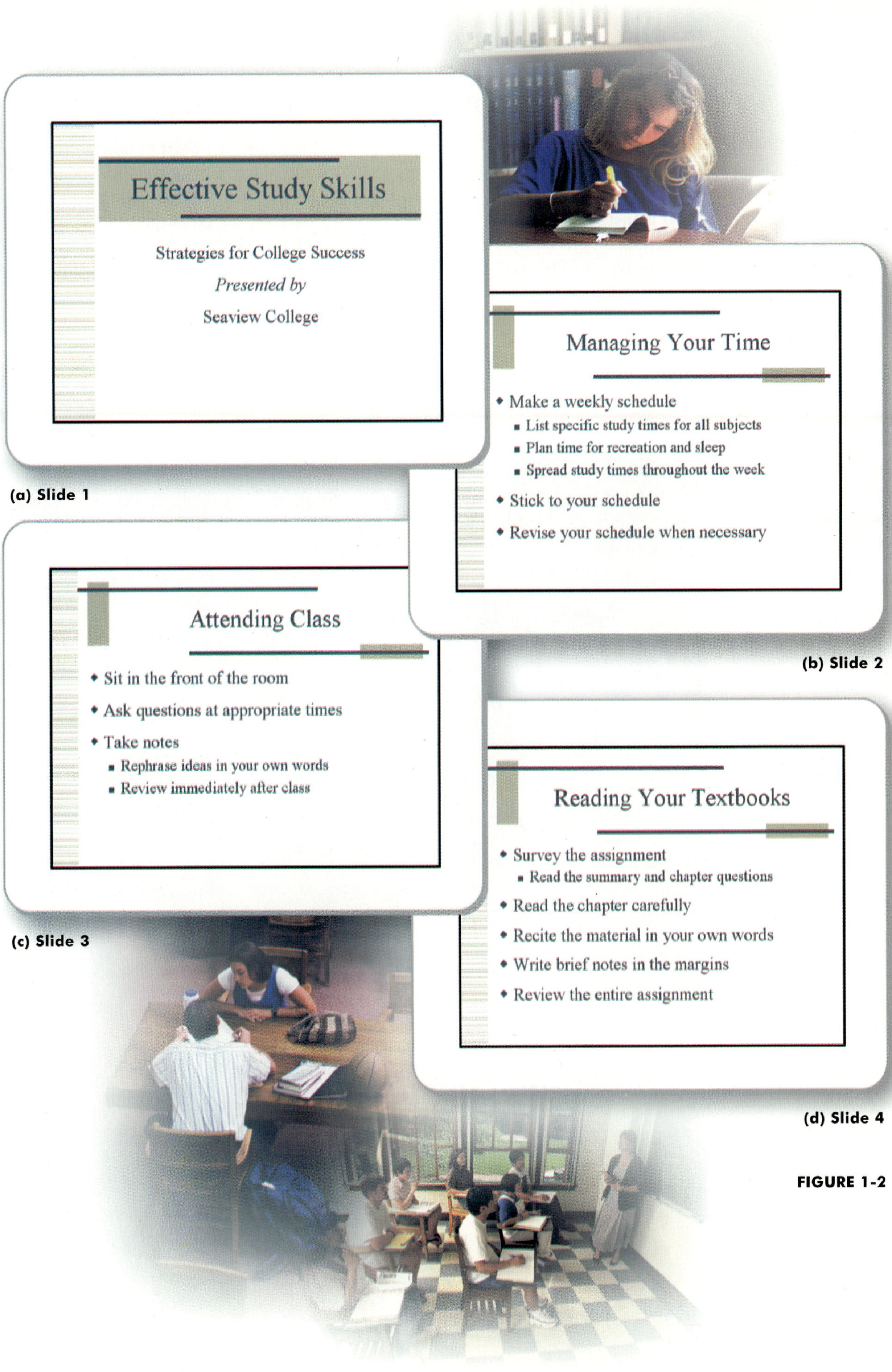

Effective Study Skills

Strategies for College Success

Presented by

Seaview College

(a) Slide 1

Managing Your Time

- Make a weekly schedule
  - List specific study times for all subjects
  - Plan time for recreation and sleep
  - Spread study times throughout the week
- Stick to your schedule
- Revise your schedule when necessary

(b) Slide 2

Attending Class

- Sit in the front of the room
- Ask questions at appropriate times
- Take notes
  - Rephrase ideas in your own words
  - Review immediately after class

(c) Slide 3

Reading Your Textbooks

- Survey the assignment
  - Read the summary and chapter questions
- Read the chapter carefully
- Recite the material in your own words
- Write brief notes in the margins
- Review the entire assignment

(d) Slide 4

FIGURE 1-2

Starting a Presentation as a New Office Document

The quickest way to begin a new presentation is to use the **Start button** on the **taskbar** at the bottom of your screen. When you click the Start button, the **Start menu** displays several commands for simplifying tasks in Windows. When Microsoft Office 2000 is installed, the Start menu displays the New Office Document and Open Office Document commands. You use the **New Office Document command** to designate the type of Office document you are creating. The Open Office Document command is discussed later in this project. Perform these steps to start a new presentation, or ask your instructor how to start PowerPoint on your system.

To Start a New Presentation

1 Click the Start button on the taskbar and then point to New Office Document.

The programs on the Start menu display above the Start button (Figure 1-3). The New Office Document command is highlighted on the Start menu. Your computer system displays the time on the clock in the tray status area on the taskbar.

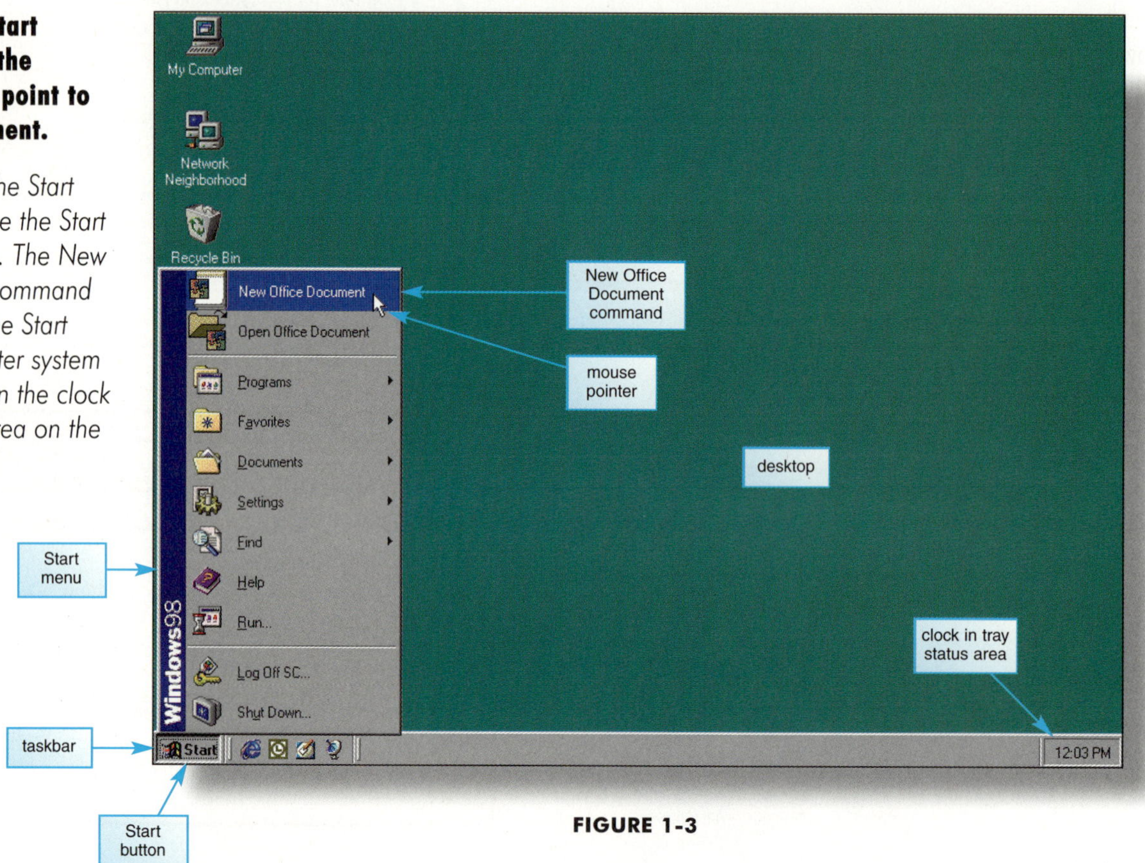

FIGURE 1-3

2 Click New Office Document. If necessary, click the General tab in the New Office Document dialog box, and then click the Blank Presentation icon.

Office displays several icons on the General sheet in the New Office Document dialog box (Figure 1-4). Each icon represents a different type of document you can create in Microsoft Office. In this project, you will create a new presentation using Microsoft PowerPoint, starting with a blank presentation.

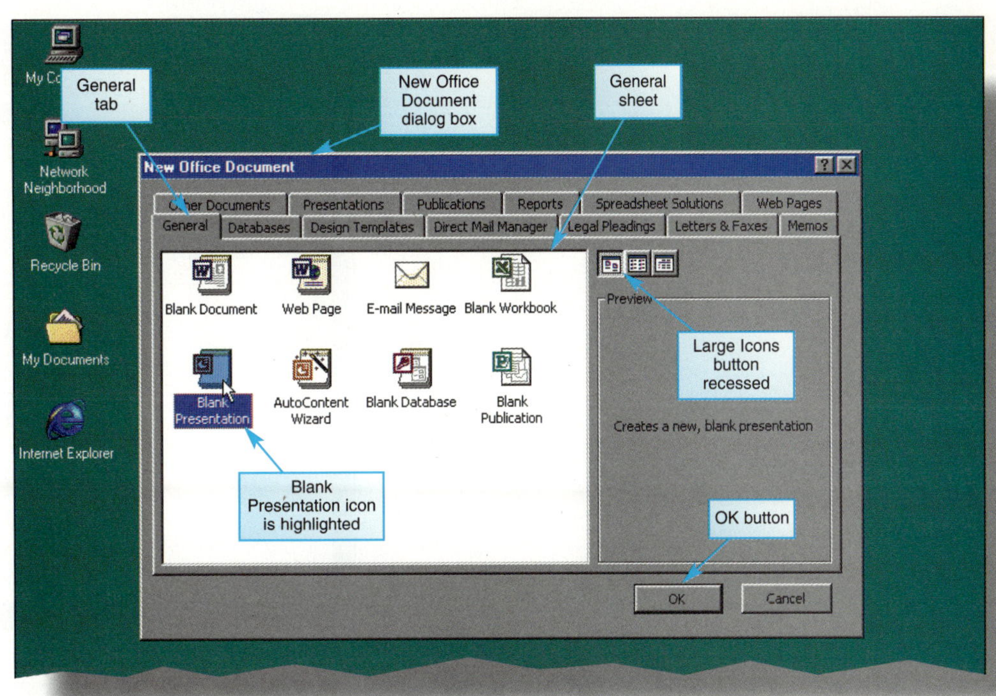

FIGURE 1-4

3 Click the OK button. If necessary, enlarge the PowerPoint window by double-clicking its title bar. If the Office Assistant displays, right-click the Office Assistant and then click Hide on the shortcut menu. Point to the OK button in the New Slide dialog box.

The New Slide dialog box displays (Figure 1-5). The Title Slide AutoLayout is selected, and its name displays in the lower-right corner of the New Slide dialog box. The Office Assistant will be discussed later in this project.

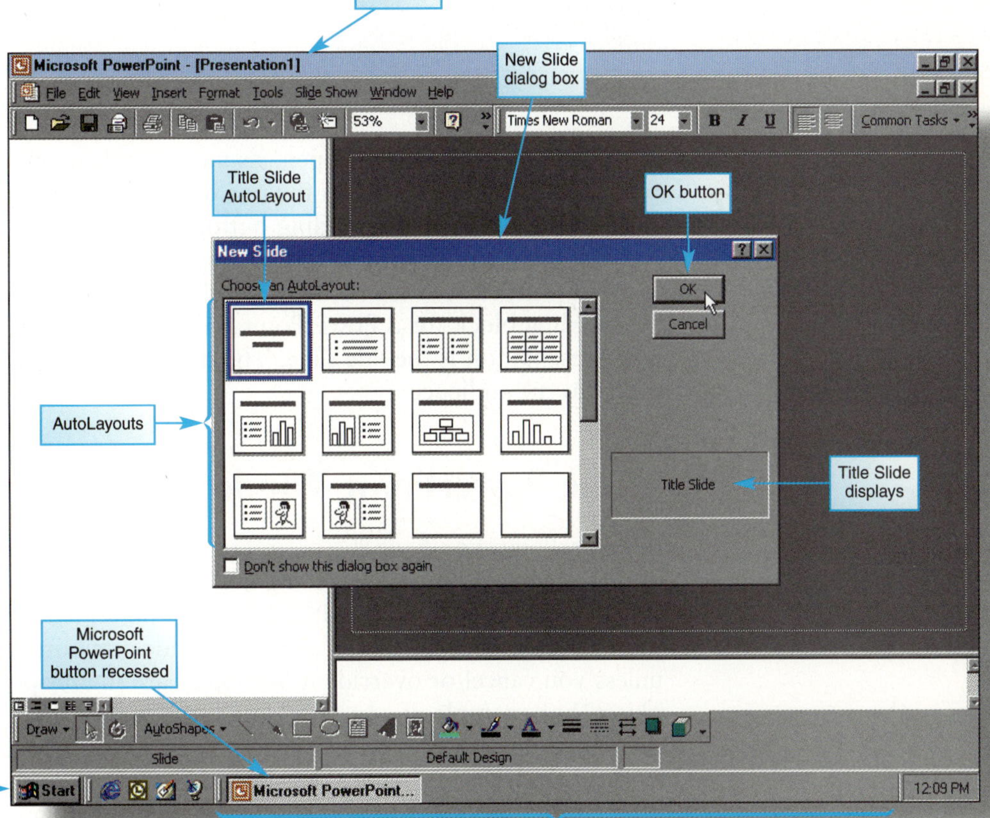

FIGURE 1-5

4 Click the OK button.

PowerPoint displays the Title Slide AutoLayout and the Default Design template on Slide 1 (Figure 1-6). The title bar identifies this window as a Microsoft PowerPoint presentation currently titled [Presentation1]. The status bar displays information about the current slide: the slide number and the name of the current design template.

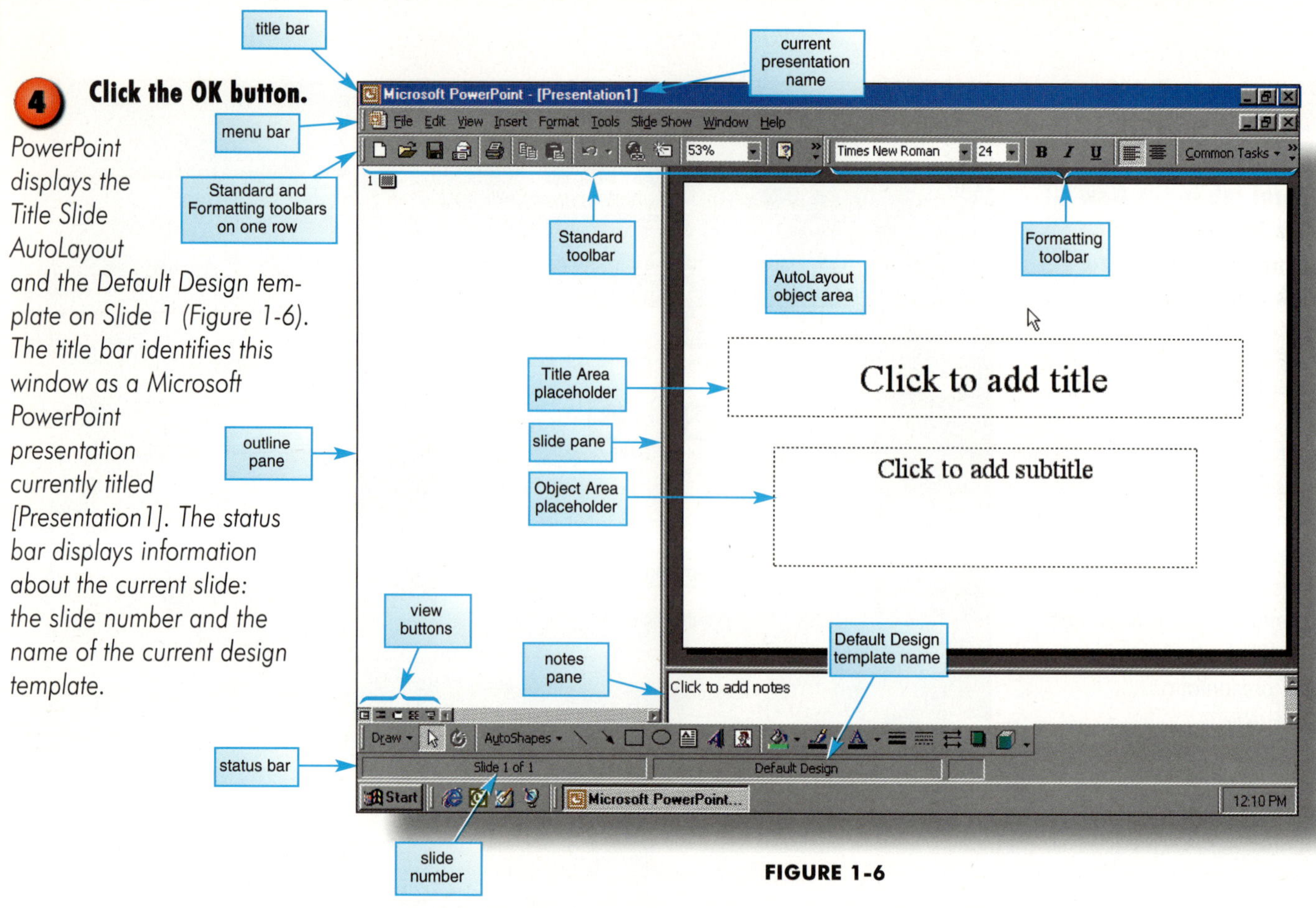

FIGURE 1-6

When an application is open, its name displays on a button in the **taskbar button area**. The **active application** is the one displaying on the foreground of the desktop. That application's corresponding button in the taskbar button area displays recessed.

The basic unit of a PowerPoint presentation is a **slide**. A slide contains one or many **objects**, such as a title, text, graphics, tables, charts, and drawings. An object is the building block for a PowerPoint slide. PowerPoint assumes the first slide in a new presentation is the **title slide**. The title slide's purpose is to introduce the presentation to the audience.

The PowerPoint Window

In PowerPoint, you have the option of using the PowerPoint default settings or establishing your own. A **default setting** is a particular value for a variable that PowerPoint assigns initially. It controls the placement of objects, the color scheme, the transition between slides, and other slide attributes, and it remains in effect unless you cancel or override it. **Attributes** are the properties or characteristics of an object. For example, if you underline the title of a slide, the title is the object, and the underline is the attribute. When you start PowerPoint, the default **slide layout** is **landscape orientation**, where the slide width is greater than its height. In landscape orientation, the slide size is preset to 10 inches wide and 7.5 inches high. The slide layout can be changed to **portrait orientation**, so that the slide height is greater than its width, by clicking Page Setup on the File menu. In portrait orientation, the slide width is 7.5 inches, and the height is 10 inches.

PowerPoint Views

PowerPoint has five views: normal view, outline view, slide view, slide sorter view, and slide show. A **view** is the mode in which the presentation displays on the screen. You may use any or all views when creating your presentation, but you can use only one at a time. Change views by clicking one of the view buttons found in the lower-left of the PowerPoint window above the status bar (Figure 1-6). The PowerPoint window display is dependent on the view. Some views are graphical while others are textual.

You generally will use normal view and slide sorter view when you are creating your presentation. Normal view is composed of three panes, which are the **outline pane**, **slide pane**, and **notes pane**. You can drag the pane borders to adjust the size of the panes. They allow you to work on various aspects of your presentation simultaneously (Figure 1-6). You can type the text of your presentation in the outline pane and easily rearrange bulleted lists, paragraphs, and individual slides. As you type in the outline pane, you can view this text in the slide pane. You also can enter text, graphics, animations, and hyperlinks directly in the slide pane. You can type notes and additional information in the notes pane. This text can consist of notes to yourself or remarks to share with your audience. After you have created at least two slides, **scroll bars**, **scroll arrows**, and **scroll boxes** will display below and to the right of the windows, and you can use them to view different parts of the panes.

Slide sorter view is helpful when you want to see all the slides in your presentation simultaneously. A miniature version of each slide displays, and you can rearrange their order, add transitions and timings to switch from one side to the next in your presentation, add and delete slides, and preview animations.

Table 1-1 identifies the view buttons and provides an explanation of each view.

PowerPoint Views

The three panes in normal, outline, and slide views allow you to work on all aspects of your presentation simultaneously. You can drag the pane borders to make each area larger or smaller.

Table 1-1 View Buttons and Functions

BUTTON	NAME	FUNCTION
	Normal View	Displays three panes: the outline pane, the slide pane, and the notes pane.
	Outline View	Displays a presentation in an outline format showing slide titles and text. It is best used for organizing and developing the content of your presentation. You can rearrange paragraphs and bullet points in this view.
	Slide View	Displays a single slide as it appears in your presentation. Slide view is used to incorporate text, graphics, video, audio, hyperlinks, and animation and also to create line-by-line progressive disclosure, called build effects. Use slide view to create or edit a presentation.
	Slide Sorter View	Displays miniature versions of all slides in your presentation. You then can copy, cut, paste, or otherwise change slide position to modify your presentation. Slide sorter view also is used to add timings, to select animated transitions, and to preview animations.
	Slide Show View	Displays your slides as an electronic presentation on the full screen of your computer's monitor. Looking much like a slide projector display, you can see the effect of transitions, build effects, slide timings, and animations.

Placeholders, Title Area, Object Area, Mouse Pointer, and Scroll Bars

The PowerPoint window contains elements similar to the document windows in other Microsoft Office 2000 applications. Other features are unique to PowerPoint. The main elements are the Title Area and Object Area placeholders, the mouse pointer, and scroll bars.

PLACEHOLDERS **Placeholders** are boxes that display when you create a new slide. All AutoLayouts except the Blank AutoLayout contain placeholders. Depending on the particular slide layout selected, placeholders display for the slide title, text, charts, tables, organization charts, media clips, and clip art. You type titles, body text, and bulleted lists in **text placeholders**; you place graphic elements in chart placeholders, table placeholders, organizational chart placeholders, and clip art placeholders. A placeholder is considered an **object**, which is a single element of your slide. An empty placeholder is called an **unfilled object**; a placeholder containing text or graphics is called a **filled object**. When a filled object contains text, it is called a **text object**.

TITLE AREA Surrounded by a dotted outline, the **Title Area** is the location of the text placeholder where you will type the main heading of a new slide (Figure 1-6 on page PP 1.12).

OBJECT AREA Surrounded by a dotted outline, the **Object Area** is the empty area that displays below the Title Area on a slide. It can contain various placeholders for displaying subtitle or supporting information such as clip art and charts (Figure 1-6).

MOUSE POINTER The **mouse pointer** can have a different shape depending on the task you are performing in PowerPoint and the pointer's location on the screen. The different shapes are discussed when they display in subsequent projects.

The Mouse Pointer

The Microsoft IntelliMouse® pointing device can help you build presentations efficiently. For example, you can roll the wheel forward or backward instead of clicking a scroll bar. You also can have your document scroll automatically. For more information, visit the PowerPoint 2000 More About Web page (www.scsite.com/pp2000/more.htm) and click IntelliMouse.

SCROLL BARS When you add a second slide to your presentation, **vertical scroll bars** display on the right side of the outline and slide panes. PowerPoint allows you to use the scroll bars to move forward or backward through your presentation.

The **horizontal scroll bar** also displays when you add a second slide to your presentation. It is located on the bottom of the slide pane and allows you to display a portion of the slide when the entire slide does not fit on the screen.

Menu Bar, Standard Toolbar, Formatting Toolbar, Drawing Toolbar, and Status Bar

The menu bar, Standard toolbar, and Formatting toolbar display at the top of the screen just below the title bar (Figure 1-6). The Standard and Formatting toolbars are by default on one row. The Drawing toolbar and status bar display at the bottom of the screen above the Windows taskbar.

MENU BAR The menu bar displays the PowerPoint menu names (Figure 1-7a). Each menu name represents a menu of commands that you can use to retrieve, store, print, and manipulate objects in your presentation. When you point to a menu name on the menu bar, the area of the menu bar containing the name changes to a button. To display a menu, such as the Insert menu, click the Insert menu name on the menu bar (Figures 1-7b and 1-7c). If you point to a command with an arrow on the right, a submenu displays from which you can choose a command.

When you click a menu name on the menu bar, a **short menu** displays listing the most recently used commands (Figure 1-7b). If you wait a few seconds or click the arrows at the bottom of the short menu (Figure 1-7b), the full menu displays. The **full menu** shows all the commands associated with a menu (Figure 1-7c). As you use PowerPoint, it automatically personalizes the menus for you based on how often you use commands. In this book, when you display a menu, wait a few seconds or click the arrows at the bottom of the menu so the long menu displays. The **hidden commands** that display on the full menu are recessed. **Dimmed commands** (gray background) indicate they are not available for the current selection.

The menu bar can change to include other menu names depending on the type of work you are doing. For example, if you are adding a chart to a slide, Data and Chart menu names are added to the menu bar with commands that reflect charting options.

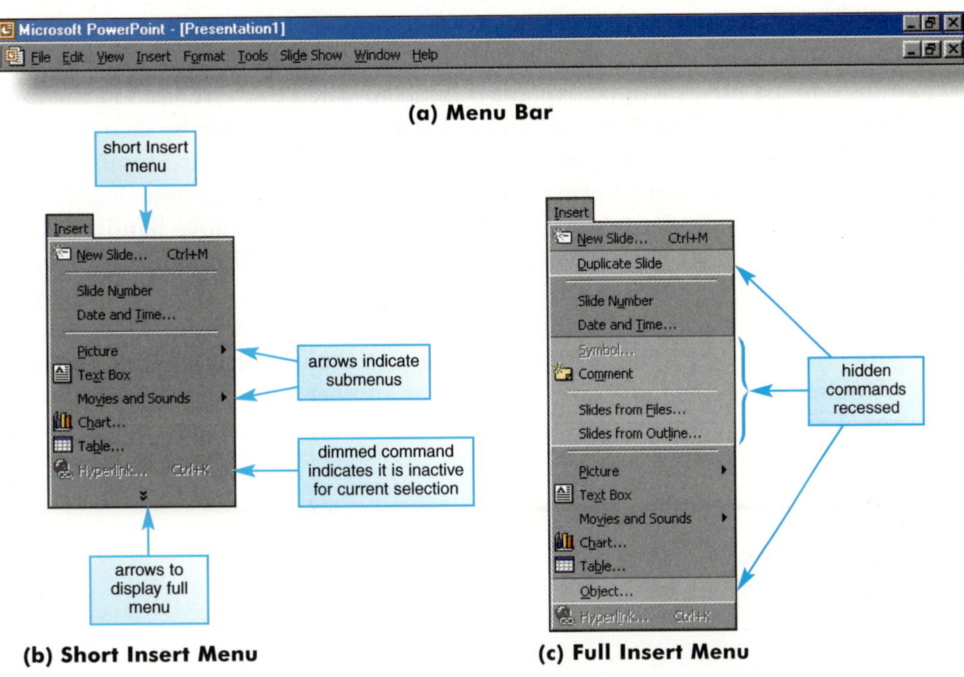

(a) Menu Bar

(b) Short Insert Menu

(c) Full Insert Menu

FIGURE 1-7

STANDARD, FORMATTING, AND DRAWING TOOLBARS The Standard toolbar (Figure 1-8a), Formatting toolbar (Figure 1-8b), and Drawing toolbar (Figure 1-8c) contain buttons and list boxes that allow you to perform frequent tasks more quickly than when using the menu bar. For example, to print a slide show, you click the Print button on the Standard toolbar. Each button has an image on the button that helps you remember the button's function. When you move the mouse pointer over a button or box, the name of the button or box also displays below it. This name is called a **ScreenTip**.

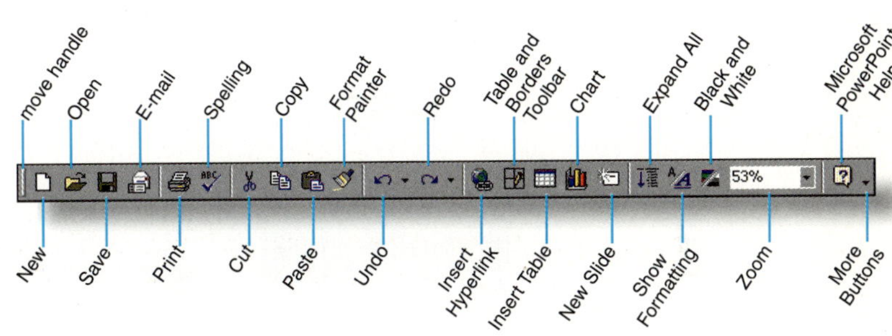

(a) Standard Toolbar

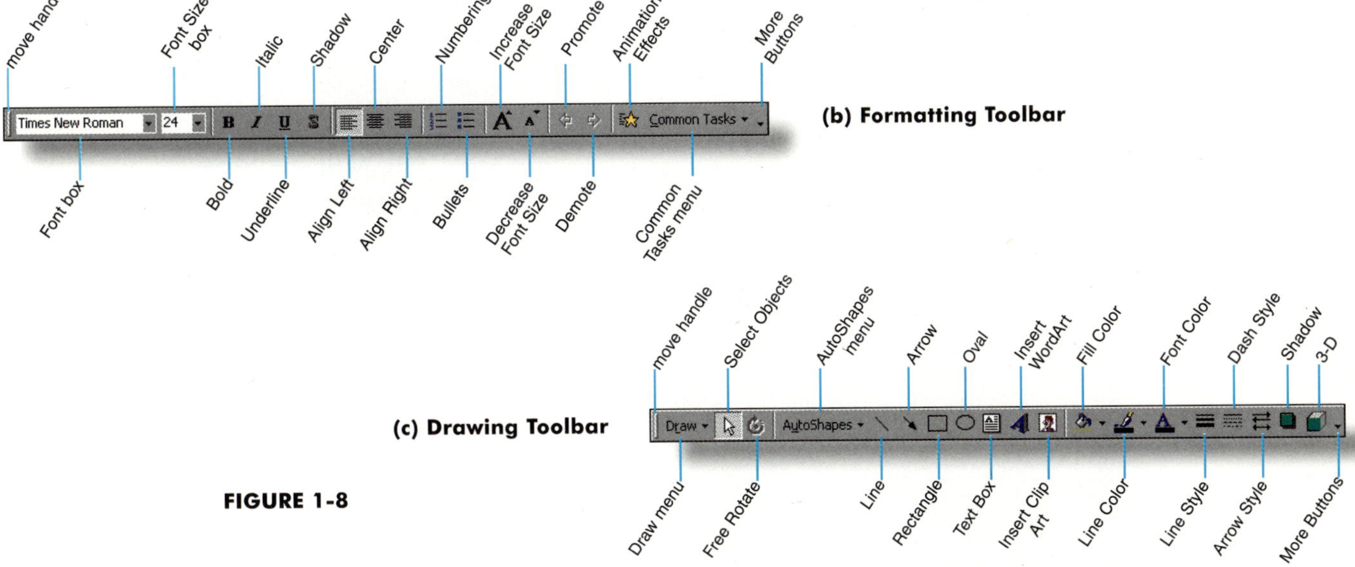

(b) Formatting Toolbar

(c) Drawing Toolbar

FIGURE 1-8

Toolbars

To display more of the PowerPoint window, you can hide a toolbar you no longer need. To hide a toolbar, right-click any toolbar and then click the check mark next to the toolbar you want to hide.

Figures 1-8a, 1-8b, and 1-8c on the previous page illustrate the Standard, Formatting, and Drawing toolbars and describe the functions of the buttons. Each of the buttons and list boxes will be explained in detail when they are used in the projects.

Remember, both the Standard and Formatting toolbars are by default on the same row immediately below the menu bar. Usually, the Standard toolbar displays on the left of the row and the Formatting toolbar displays on the right (Figure 1-9a).

To view the entire Formatting toolbar, double-click the move handle on its left edge or drag the move handle to the left. When you show the complete Formatting toolbar, a portion of the Standard toolbar is hidden (Figure 1-9b). To display the entire Standard toolbar, double-click its move handle. PowerPoint slides the Formatting toolbar to the right so the toolbars return to the way they look in Figure 1-9a.

An alternative to sliding one toolbar over another is to use the More Buttons button on a toolbar to display the buttons that are hidden (Figure 1-9c).

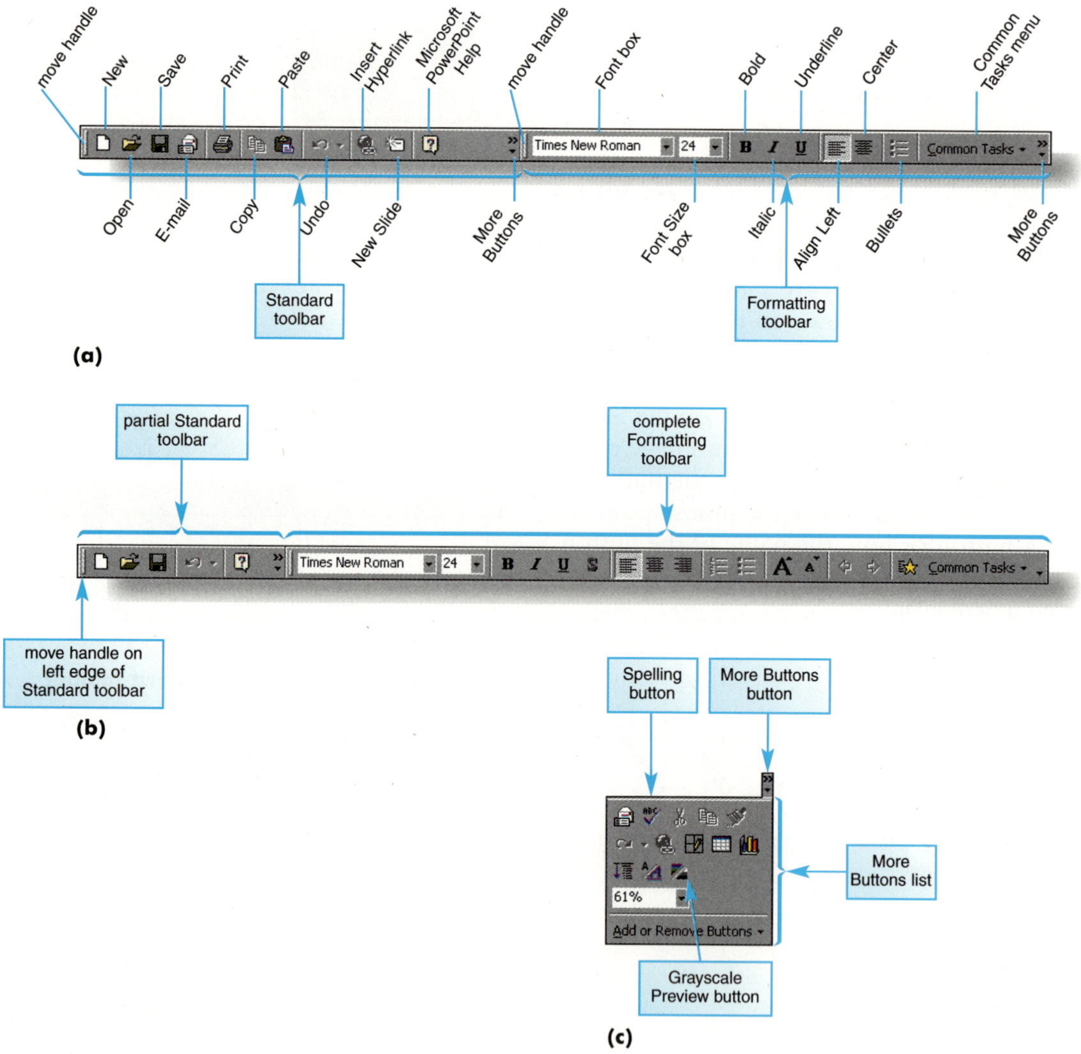

FIGURE 1-9

As with the menus, PowerPoint will personalize the toolbars. That is, if you use a hidden button on a partially displayed toolbar, PowerPoint will remove the button from the More Buttons list (Figure 1-9c) and place it on the toolbar. For example, if you click the Spelling button and then the Grayscale Preview button on the Standard toolbar (Figure 1-9c), PowerPoint will display these buttons on the Standard toolbar and remove buttons from the Standard or Formatting toolbars to make room on the row.

STATUS BAR Immediately above the Windows taskbar at the bottom of the screen is the status bar. The **status bar** consists of a message area and a presentation design template identifier (Figure 1-11 on page PP 1.18). Generally the message area displays the current slide number and the total number of slides in the slide show. For example, in Figure 1-11 the message area displays Slide 1 of 1. Slide 1 is the current slide, and of 1 indicates the slide show contains only 1 slide. The template identifier displays Default Design, which is the template PowerPoint uses initially.

PowerPoint has several additional toolbars you can display by pointing to Toolbars on the View menu and then clicking the respective name on the Toolbars submenu. You also can display a toolbar by pointing to a toolbar and right-clicking to display a shortcut menu, which lists the available toolbars. A **shortcut menu** contains a list of commands or items that relate to the item to which you are pointing when you right-click.

Personalizing

Have some fun building your presentation by adding sound cues. You can download files from the Microsoft Web site that play sounds when you scroll, open dialog boxes, and zoom in or out. For more information, visit the PowerPoint 2000 More About Web page (www.scsite.com/pp2000/more.htm) and click Personalizing.

Resetting Menus and Toolbars

Each project in this book begins with the menu bars and toolbars appearing as they did at initial installation of the software. To reset your toolbars and menus so they appear exactly as shown in this book, follow the steps outlined in Appendix C.

Displaying the Formatting Toolbar in Its Entirety

Perform the following steps to display the entire Formatting toolbar.

To Display the Formatting Toolbar in Its Entirety

1 Point to the move handle on the Formatting toolbar (Figure 1-10).

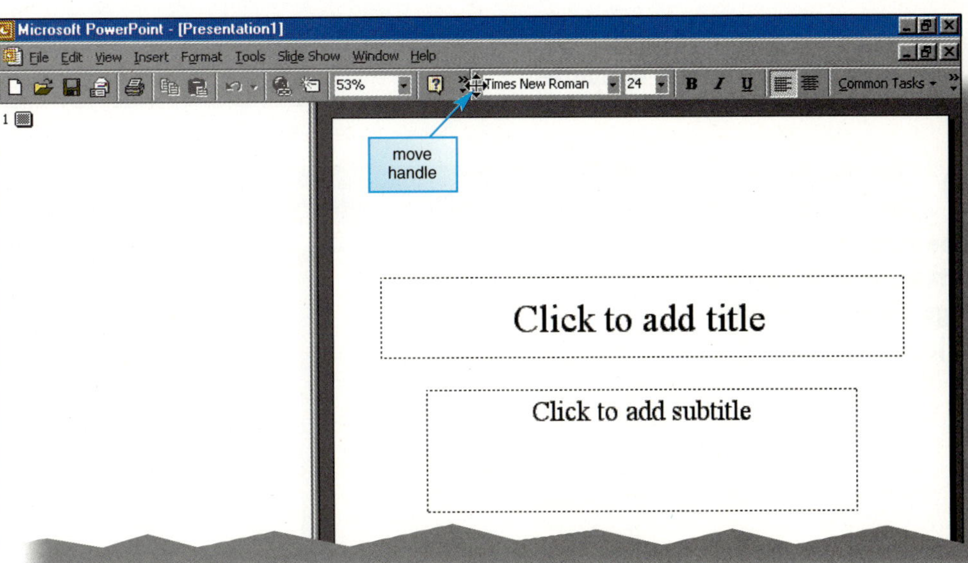

FIGURE 1-10

2 Double-click the move handle on the Formatting toolbar.

The entire Formatting toolbar displays (Figure 1-11).

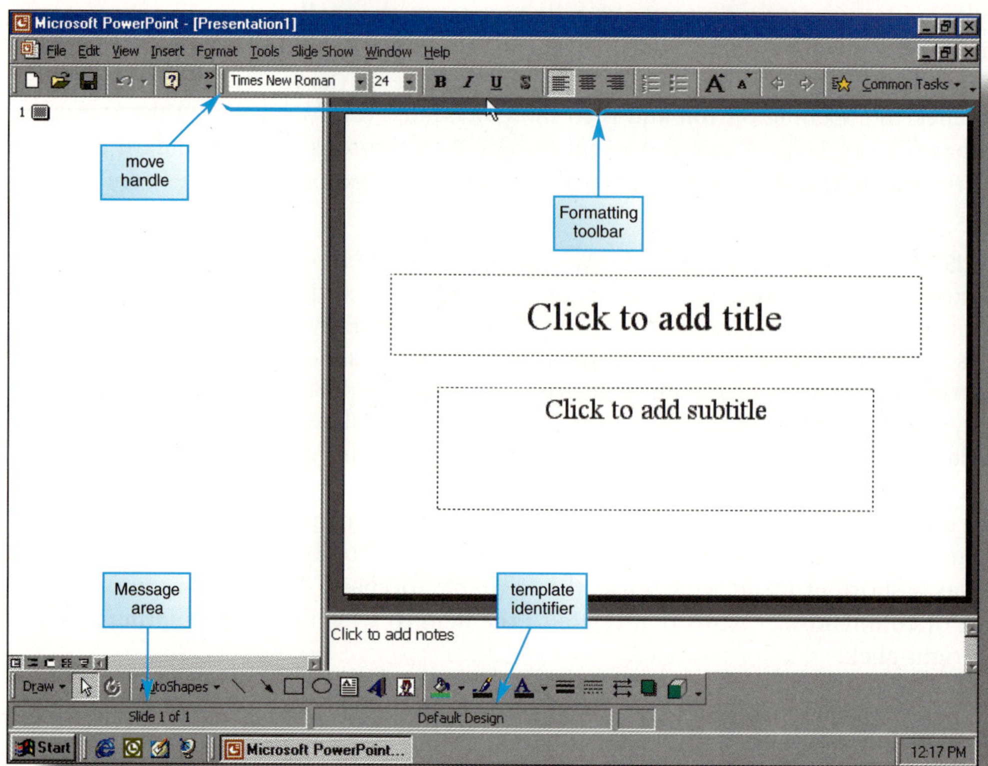

FIGURE 1-11

Choosing a Design Template

A **design template** provides consistency in design and color throughout the entire presentation. It determines the color scheme, font and font size, and layout of your presentation. Perform the following steps to choose a design template.

To Choose a Design Template

1 Click the Common Tasks menu button on the Formatting toolbar and then point to Apply Design Template (Figure 1-12).

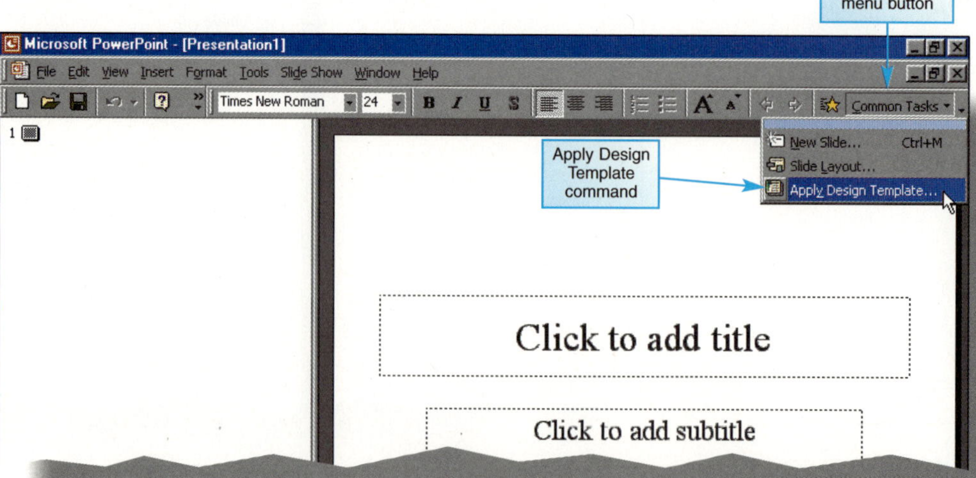

FIGURE 1-12

2 Click Apply Design Template.

The Apply Design Template dialog box displays (Figure 1-13). Numerous design template names display in the list box. Artsy is highlighted in the list, and a thumbnail view of the Artsy design template displays in the preview area. If the preview area does not display, click the Views button arrow and then click Preview. The Cancel button or the Close button can be used to close the Apply Design Template dialog box if you do not want to apply a new template.

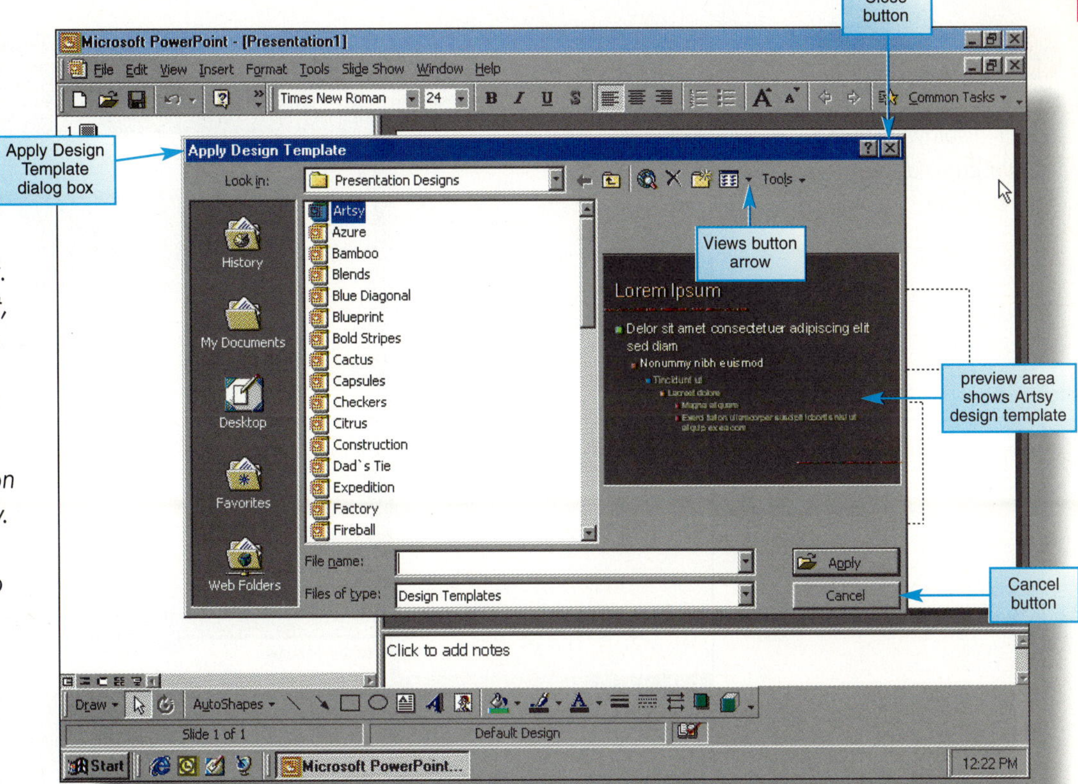

FIGURE 1-13

3 Click the down scroll arrow to scroll down the list of design templates until Straight Edge appears. Click Straight Edge. Point to the Apply button.

A preview of the Straight Edge design template displays in the preview area (Figure 1-14).

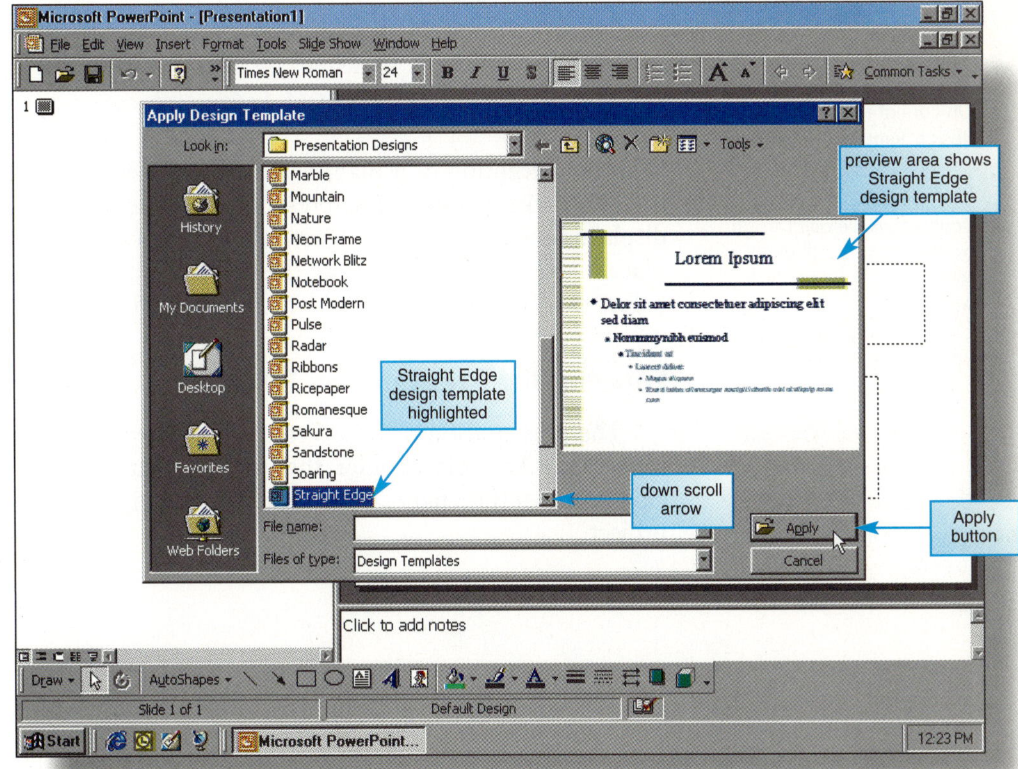

FIGURE 1-14

Click the Apply button.

Slide 1 displays with the Straight Edge design template (Figure 1-15).

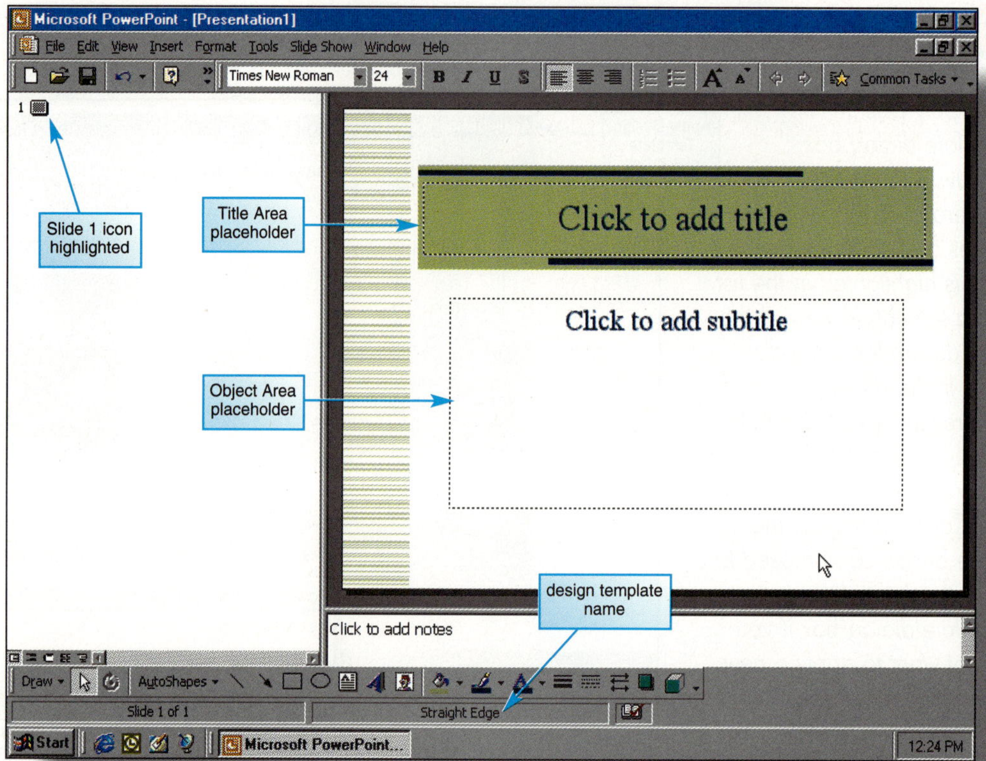

FIGURE 1-15

Other Ways

1. Double-click Straight Edge in list
2. On Format menu click Apply Design Template, scroll down to select Straight Edge, click Apply
3. Double-click Default Design on status bar, scroll down to select Straight Edge, click Apply

Creating a Title Slide

With the exception of a blank slide, PowerPoint also assumes every new slide has a title. To make creating your presentation easier, any text you type after a new slide displays becomes the title object. The AutoLayout for the title slide has a Title Area placeholder near the middle of the window and an Object Area placeholder directly below the Title Area placeholder (Figure 1-15).

Entering the Presentation Title

The presentation title for Project 1 is Effective Study Skills. As you begin typing in the Title Area placeholder, the title text displays immediately after the Slide 1 icon in the outline pane. Perform the following steps to create the title slide for this project.

Steps To Enter the Presentation Title

1 Click the label, Click to add title, located inside the Title Area placeholder.

*The insertion point is in the Title Area placeholder (Figure 1-16). The **insertion point** is a blinking vertical line (|), which indicates where the next character will display. The mouse pointer changes to an I-beam. A **selection rectangle** displays around the Title Area placeholder. The placeholder is selected as indicated by the border and sizing handles displaying on the edges.*

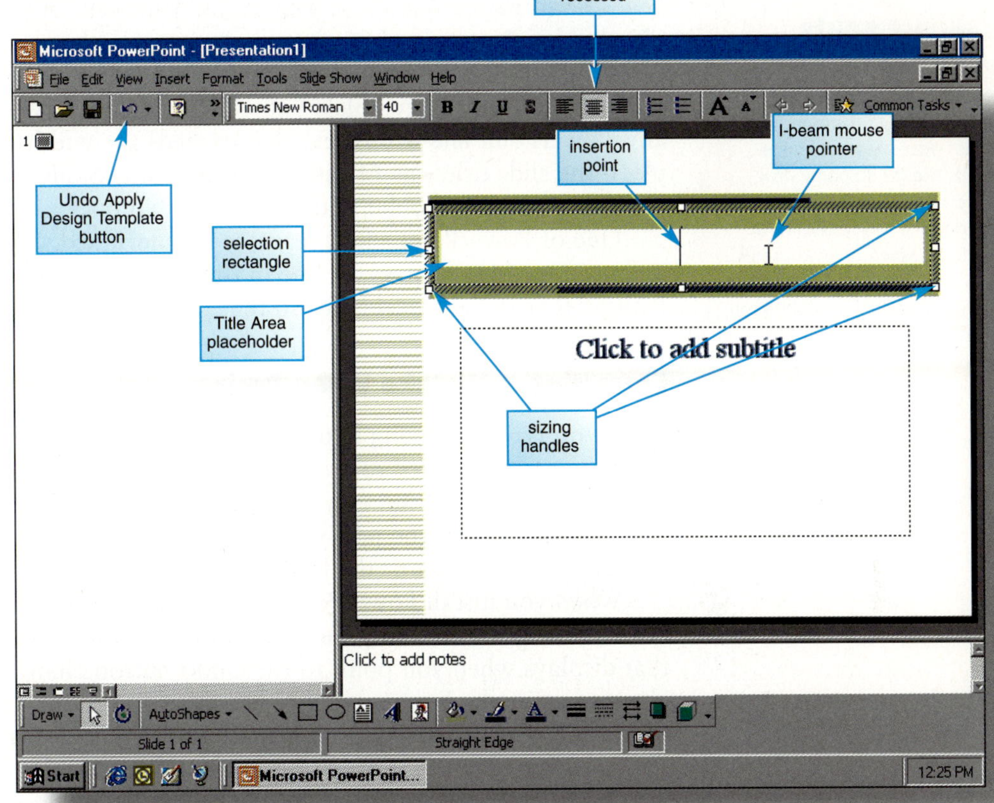

FIGURE 1-16

2 Type `Effective Study Skills` **in the Title Area placeholder. Do not press the ENTER key.**

The title text, Effective Study Skills, displays in the Title Area placeholder and in the outline pane (Figure 1-17). The current title text displays with the default font (Times New Roman) and default font size (40).

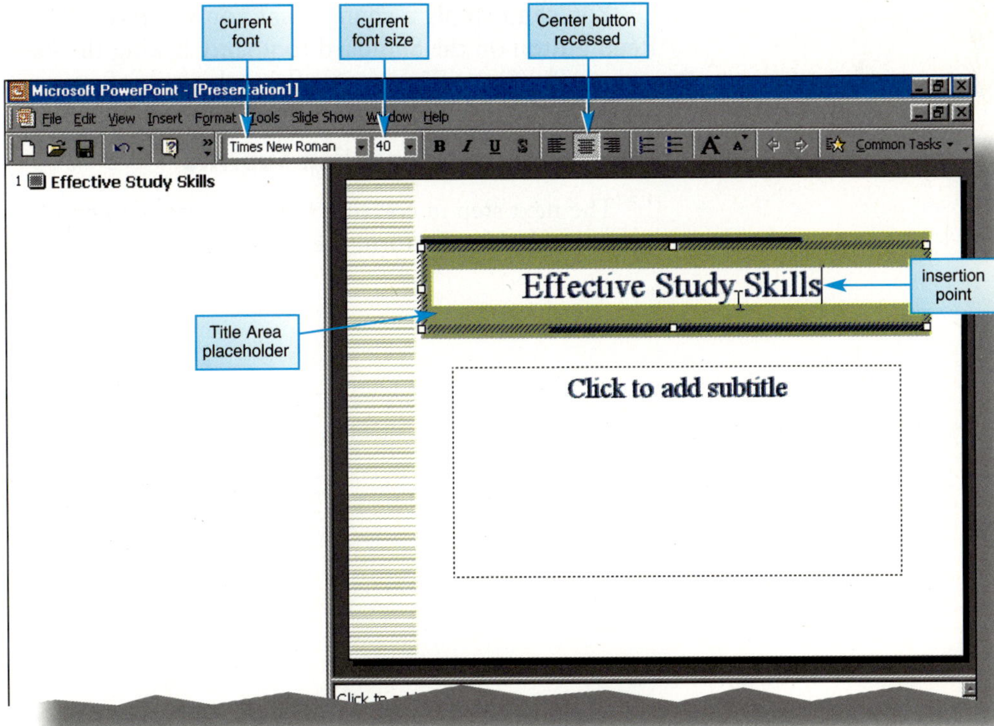

FIGURE 1-17

Enhancements

Microsoft touts the AutoFit text feature as an important PowerPoint 2000 upgrade. Other ease-of-use enhancements are the tri-pane view, the ability to create tables easily, and the self-paced introduction, which gives a useful overview of PowerPoint's key features. For more information, visit the PowerPoint 2000 More About Web page (www.scsite.com/pp2000/more.htm) and click Enhancements.

Notice that you do not press the ENTER key after the word Skills. If you press the ENTER key after typing the title, PowerPoint creates a new line, which would be a new second paragraph in the Title Area. You want only one paragraph in this text placeholder. A **paragraph** is a segment of text with the same format that begins when you press the ENTER key and ends when you press the ENTER key again. Therefore, do not press the ENTER key unless you want to create a two-paragraph title. Additionally, PowerPoint **line wraps** text that exceeds the width of the placeholder. For example, if the slide title was Effective College Study Skills, it would exceed the width of the Title Area placeholder and display on two lines.

One of PowerPoint's new features is **AutoFit text.** If you are creating your slide and need to squeeze an extra line in the text placeholder, PowerPoint will resize the existing text in the placeholder so that this extra line will fit on the screen.

Correcting a Mistake When Typing

If you type the wrong letter and notice the error before pressing the ENTER key, press the BACKSPACE key to erase all the characters back to and including the one that is incorrect. If you mistakenly press the ENTER key after entering the title and the insertion point is on the new line, simply press the BACKSPACE key to return the insertion point to the right of the letter s in the word Skills.

When you install PowerPoint, the default setting allows you to reverse up to the last 20 changes by clicking the **Undo button** on the Standard toolbar. The ScreenTip that displays when you point to the Undo button changes to indicate the type of change just made. For example, if you type text in the Title Area placeholder and then point to the Undo button, the ScreenTip that displays is Undo Typing. For clarity, when referencing the Undo button in this project, the name displaying in the ScreenTip is referenced. Another way to reverse changes is to click the Undo command on the Edit menu. Like the Undo button, the Undo command reflects the last type of change made to the presentation.

You can reapply a change that you reversed with the Undo button by clicking the Redo button on the Standard toolbar. Clicking the **Redo button** reverses the last undo action. The ScreenTip name reflects the type of reversal last performed.

Entering the Presentation Subtitle

The next step in creating the title slide is to enter the subtitle text into the Object Area placeholder. Perform the following steps to enter the presentation subtitle.

To Enter the Presentation Subtitle

1 Click the label, Click to add subtitle, located inside the Object Area placeholder.

The insertion point is in the Object Area placeholder (Figure 1-18). The mouse pointer changes to an I-beam indicating the mouse is in a text placeholder. The selection rectangle indicates the placeholder is selected. The default Object Area text font size is 32.

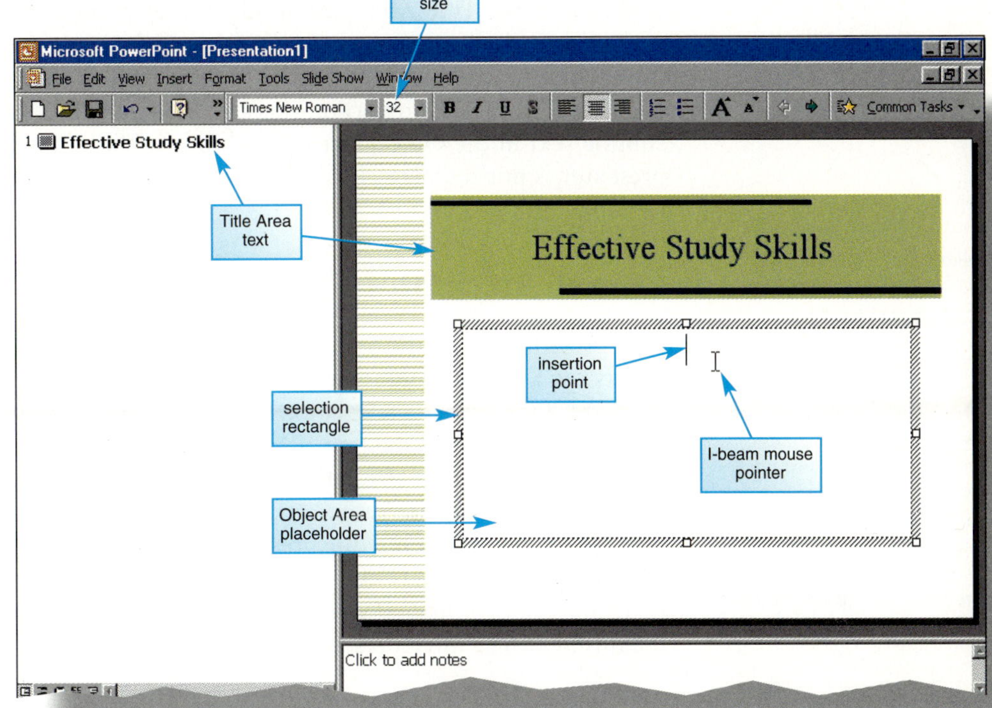

FIGURE 1-18

2 Type Strategies for College Success **and then press the ENTER key. Type** Presented by **and then press the ENTER key. Type** Seaview College **but do not press the ENTER key.**

The text displays in the Object Area placeholder and the outline pane (Figure 1-19). The insertion point displays after the letter e in College. A red wavy line displays under the word, Seaview, to indicate a possible spelling error. A light bulb may display in the top-left corner of the text placeholder, depending on your computer's settings. The Office Assistant generates this light bulb to give you design tips.

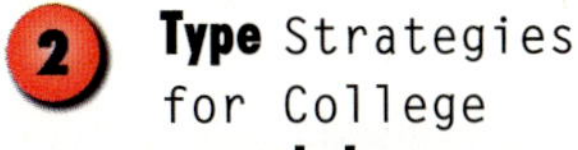

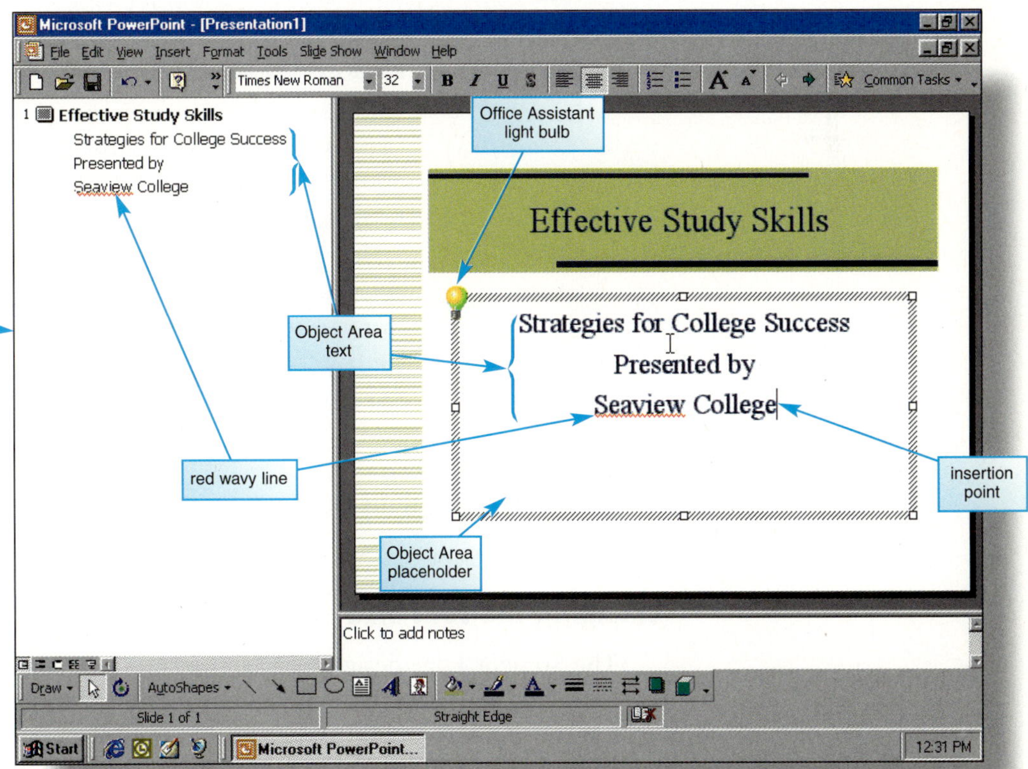

FIGURE 1-19

The previous section created a title slide using an AutoLayout for the title slide. PowerPoint displayed the title slide layout because you created a new presentation. You clicked the Title Area placeholder to select it and then typed your title. In general, to type text in any text placeholder, click the text placeholder and begin typing. You could, however, enter text in the Title Area placeholder without selecting this placeholder because PowerPoint assumes every slide has a title. You also added subtitle text in the Object Area placeholder. While this information identifying the presenter is not required, it often is useful for the audience.

More About 2000

Text Attributes

An extensive glossary of typography terms is available at the Microsoft Web site. The information includes a diagram illustrating the text attributes. For more information, visit the PowerPoint 2000 More About Web page (www.scsite.com/pp2000/more.htm) and click Attributes.

Text Attributes

This presentation is using the Straight Edge design template. Each design template has its own text attributes. A **text attribute** is a characteristic of the text, such as font, font size, font style, or text color. You can adjust text attributes any time before, during, or after you type the text. Recall that a design template determines the color scheme, font and font size, and layout of your presentation. Most of the time, you use the design template's text attributes and color scheme. Occasionally you may want to change the way your presentation looks, however, and still keep a particular design template. PowerPoint gives you that flexibility. You can use the design template and change the text's color, font size, font, and font style. Table 1-2 explains the different text attributes available in PowerPoint.

Table 1-2 Design Template Text Attributes

ATTRIBUTE	DESCRIPTION
Color	Defines the color of text. Displaying text in color requires a color monitor. Printing text in color requires a color printer or plotter.
Font	Defines the appearance and shape of letters, numbers, and special characters.
Font size	Specifies the size of characters on the screen. Character size is gauged by a measurement system called points. A single point is about 1/72 of an inch in height. Thus, a character with a point size of eighteen is about 18/72 (or 1/4) of an inch in height.
Font style	Defines text characteristics. Font styles include plain, italic, bold, shadowed, and underlined. Text may have one or more font styles at a time.
Subscript	Defines the placement of a character in relationship to another. A subscript character displays or prints slightly below and immediately to one side of another character.
Superscript	Defines the placement of a character in relationship to another. A superscript character displays or prints above and immediately to one side of another character.

The next two sections explain how to change the font size and font style attributes.

Changing the Font Size

The Straight Edge design template default font size is 40 points for title text and 32 points for body text. A point is 1/72 of an inch in height. Thus, a character with a point size of 40 is about 40/72 (or 5/9) of an inch in height. Slide 1 requires you to increase the font size for the paragraph, Effective Study Skills. Perform the following steps to increase the font size.

Steps To Increase Font Size

1 Position the mouse pointer in the Title Area placeholder and then triple-click.

PowerPoint selects the entire line (Figure 1-20). You select an entire line quickly by triple-clicking any area within the Title Area placeholder.

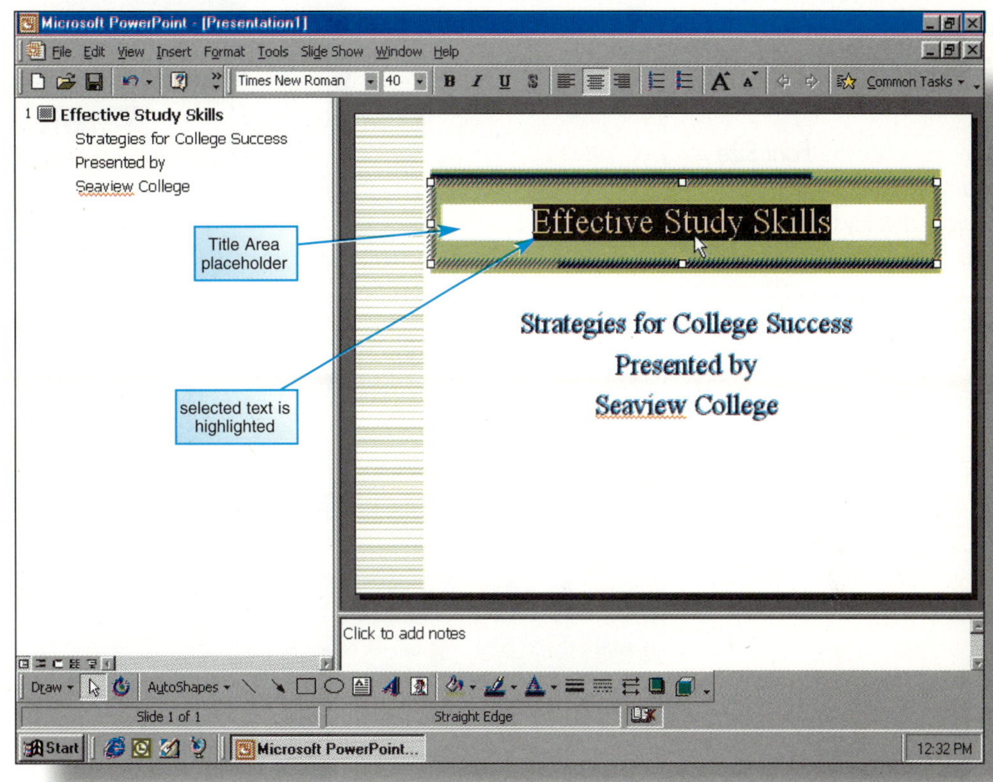

FIGURE 1-20

3 With Effective Study Skills highlighted, point to the Font Size box arrow in the Font Size box on the Formatting toolbar.

When you point to a button or other areas on a toolbar, PowerPoint displays a ScreenTip. A ***ScreenTip*** *contains the name of the tool to which you are pointing. When pointing to the Font Size box or the Font Size box arrow, the ScreenTip displays the words, Font Size (Figure 1-21). The* ***Font Size box*** *indicates that the title text is 40 points.*

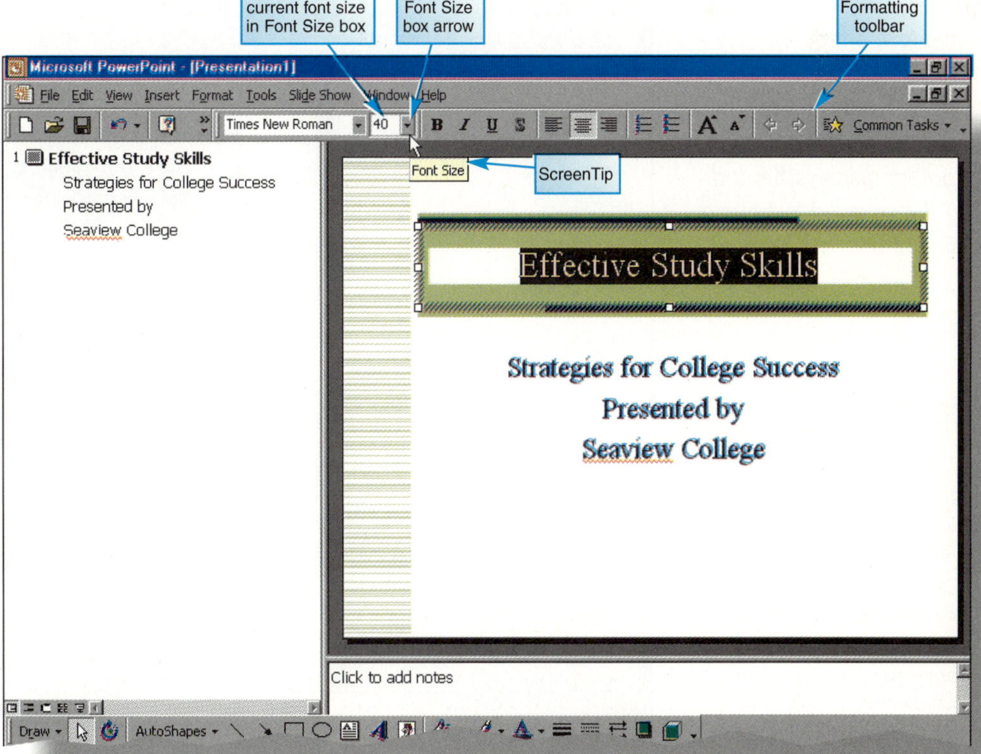

FIGURE 1-21

4 **Click the Font Size box arrow, click the down scroll arrow on the Font Size scroll bar until 54 appears, and then point to 54.**

When you click the **Font Size box arrow***, a list of available font sizes displays in the Font Size list box. The font sizes displayed depend on the current font, which is Times New Roman. Font size 54 is highlighted (Figure 1-22).*

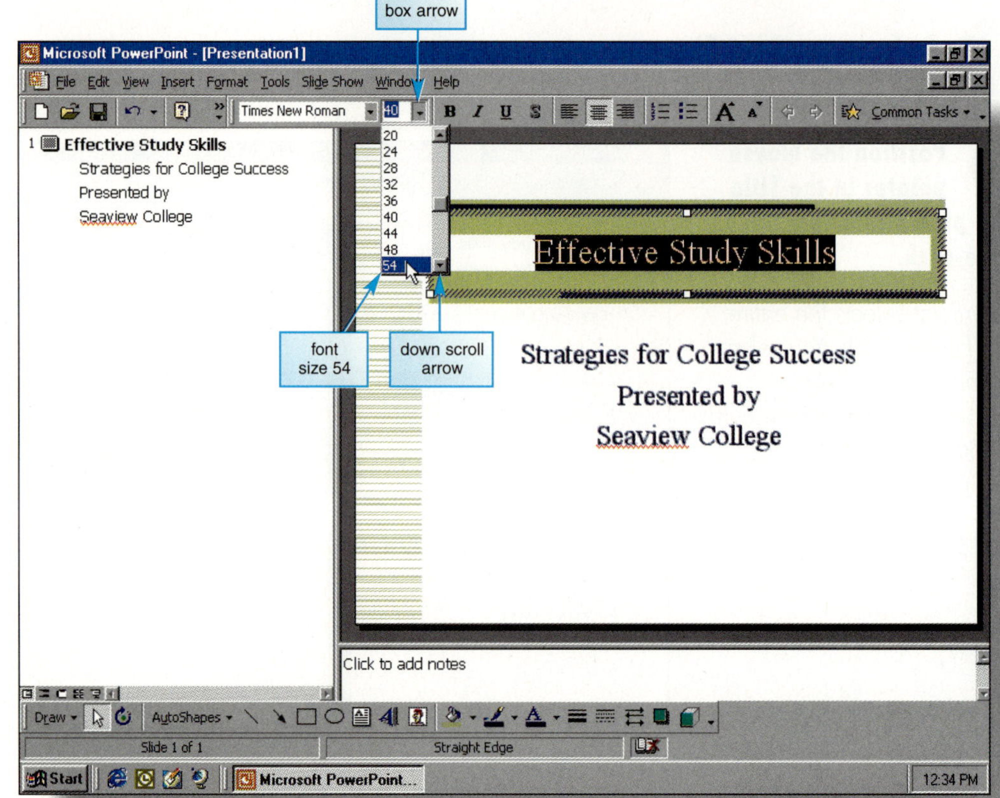

FIGURE 1-22

5 **Click 54.**

The title text, Effective Study Skills, increases in font size to 54 points (Figure 1-23). The Font Size box on the Formatting toolbar displays 54, indicating the selected text has a font size of 54.

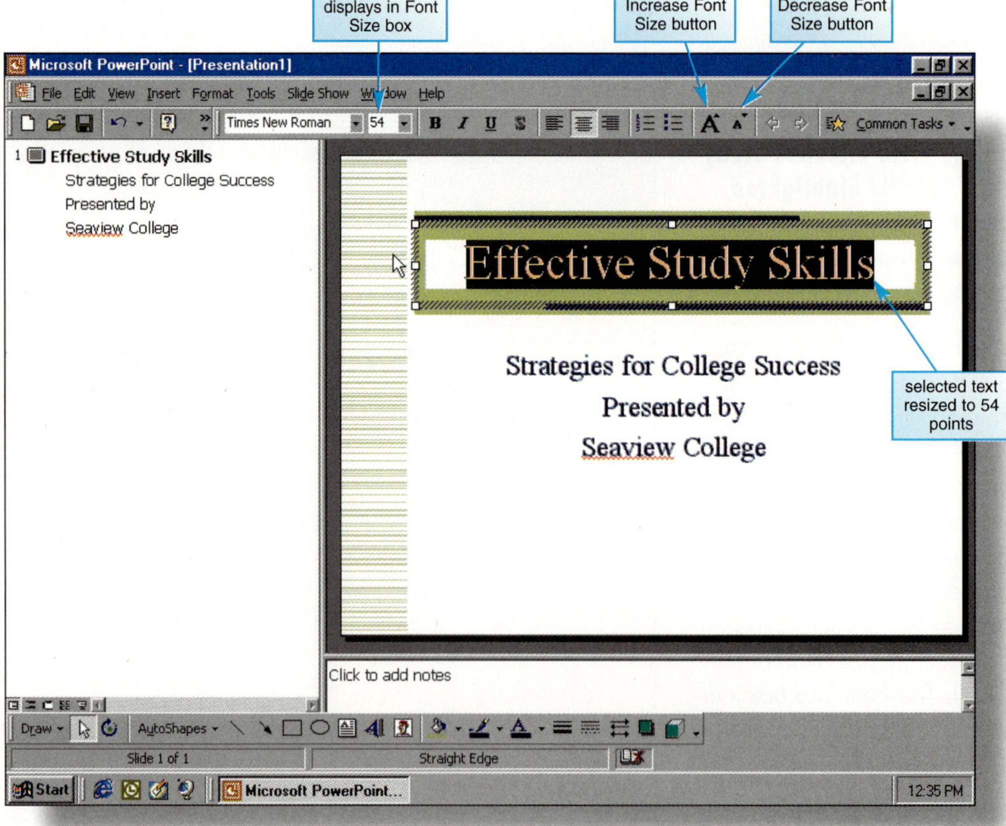

FIGURE 1-23

Other Ways

1. Right-click selected text, click Font on shortcut menu, type new font size in Size box
2. Click Increase Font Size button on Formatting toolbar
3. Click Font Size box on Formatting toolbar, type font size between 1 and 4000
4. On Format menu click Font, click new font size in Size box, or type font size between 1 and 4000

You also can use the **Increase Font Size button** on the Formatting toolbar to increase the font size. Each time you click the button, the font size becomes larger in preset increments. If you need to decrease the font size, click the Font Size box arrow and select a size smaller than 40. Another method is to click the **Decrease Font Size button** on the Formatting toolbar. The font size will become smaller in preset increments each time you click the button.

Changing the Style of Text to Italic

Text font styles include plain, italic, bold, shadowed, and underlined. PowerPoint allows you to use one or more text font styles in your presentation. Perform the following steps to add emphasis to the title slide by changing plain text to italic text.

To Change the Text Font Style to Italic

1 Triple-click the paragraph, Presented by, in the Object Area text placeholder, and then point to the Italic button on the Formatting toolbar.

The paragraph, Presented by, is highlighted (Figure 1-24). The **Italic button** *is three-dimensional.*

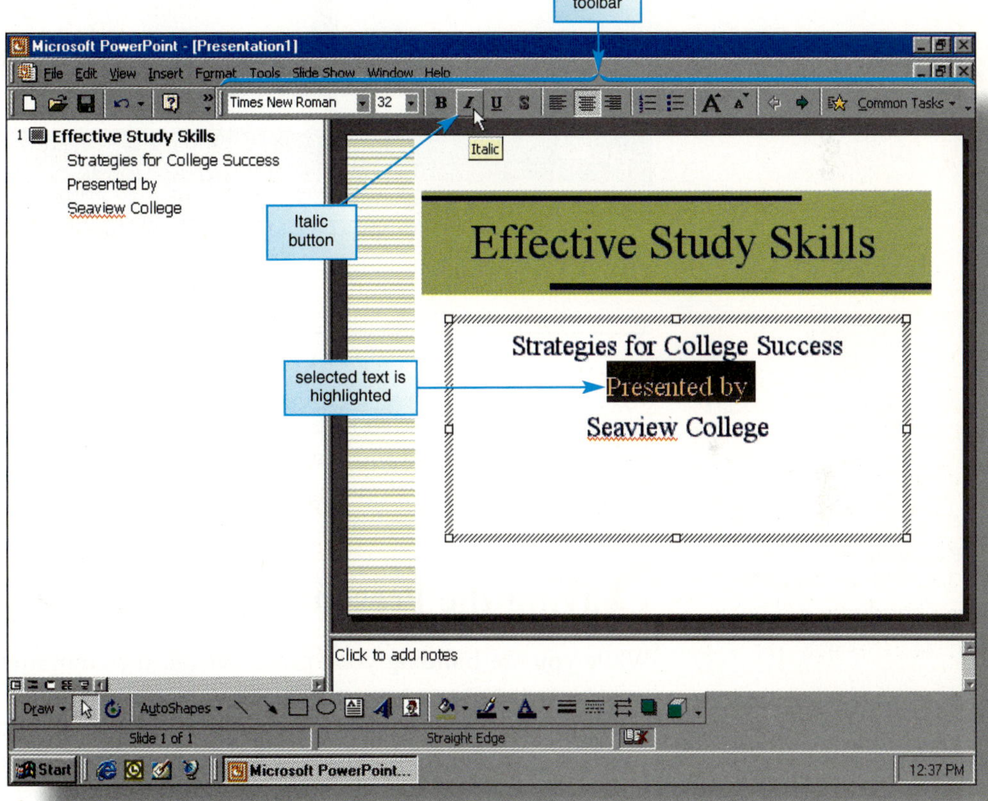

FIGURE 1-24

Click the Italic button.

The text is italicized in both the slide and outline panes, and the Italic button is recessed on the Formatting toolbar (Figure 1-25).

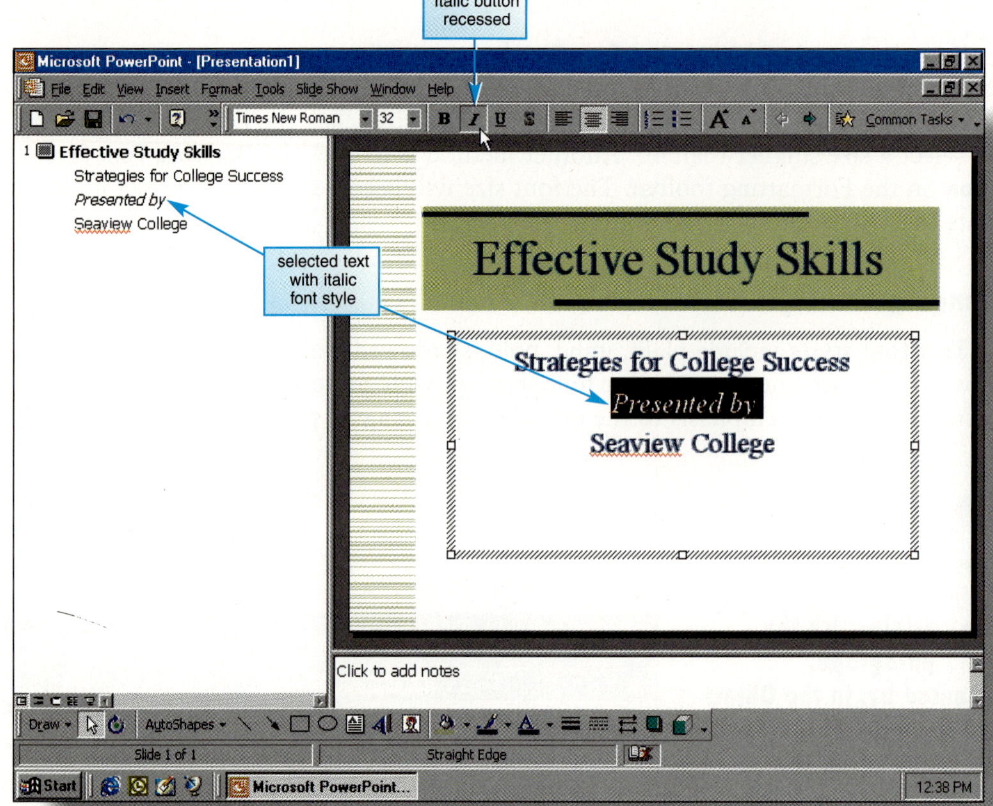

FIGURE 1-25

Other Ways

1. Right-click selected text, click Font on shortcut menu, click Italic in Font style list
2. On Format menu click Font, click Italic in Font style list
3. Press CTRL+I

To remove italics from text, select the italicized text and then click the Italic button. As a result, the Italic button is not recessed, and the text does not have the italic font style.

Saving the Presentation on a Floppy Disk

While you are building your presentation, the computer stores it in main memory. It is important to save your presentation frequently because the presentation will be lost if the computer is turned off or you lose electrical power. Another reason to save your work is that if you run out of lab time before completing your project, you may finish the project later without starting over. You must, therefore, save any presentation you will use later. Before you continue with Project 1, save the work completed thus far. Perform the following steps to save a presentation on a floppy disk using the Save button on the Standard toolbar.

Steps To Save a Presentation on a Floppy Disk

1. **Insert a formatted floppy disk in drive A and then click the Save button on the Standard toolbar.**

The Save As dialog box displays (Figure 1-26). The default folder, My Documents, displays in the Save in box. Effective Study Skills displays highlighted in the File name box because PowerPoint uses the words in the Title Area placeholder as the default file name. Presentation displays in the Save as type box. Clicking the Cancel button closes the Save As dialog box.

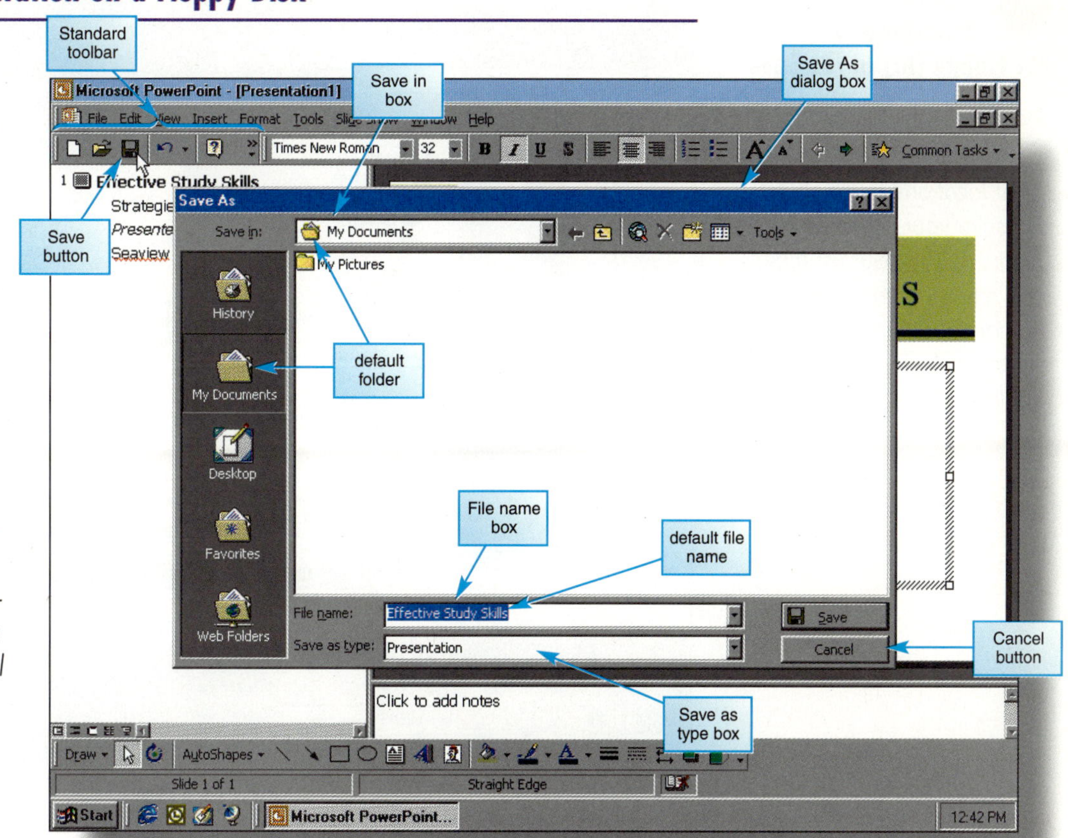

FIGURE 1-26

2. **Type Studying in the File name box. Do not press the ENTER key after typing the file name.**

The name, Studying, displays in the File name box (Figure 1-27).

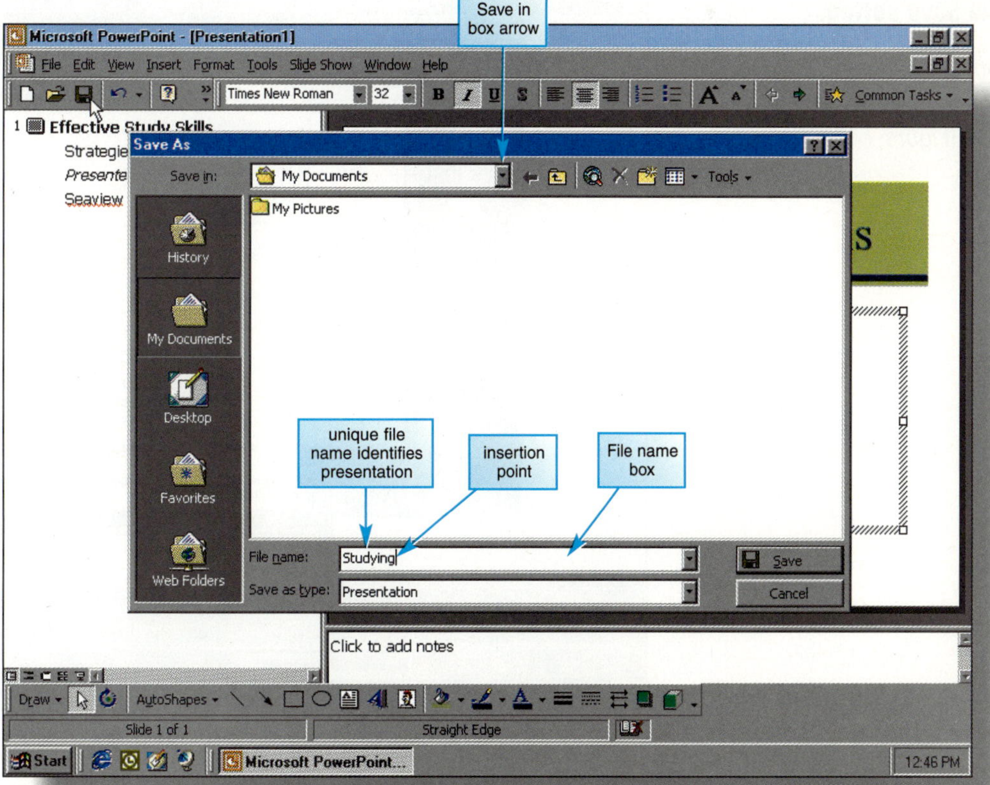

FIGURE 1-27

3 Click the Save in box arrow. Point to 3½ Floppy (A:) in the Save in list.

The Save in list displays a list of locations to which you can save your presentation (Figure 1-28). Your list may look different depending on the configuration of your system. 3½ Floppy (A:) is highlighted.

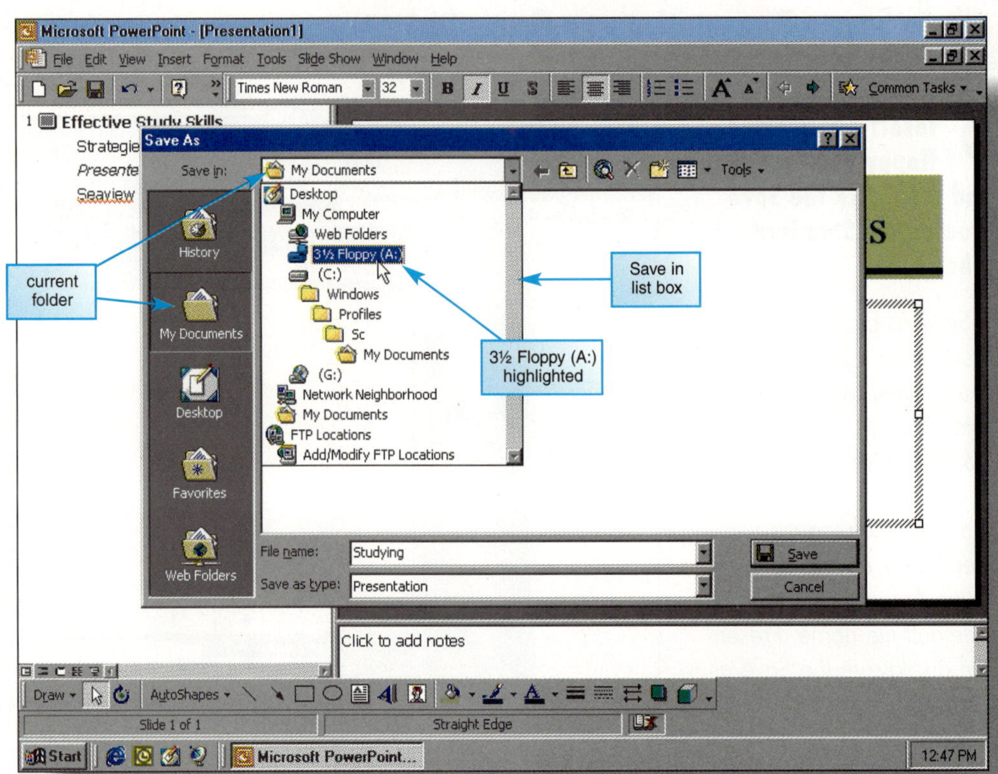

FIGURE 1-28

4 Click 3½ Floppy (A:) and then point to the Save button.

Drive A becomes the destination location for the presentation (Figure 1-29).

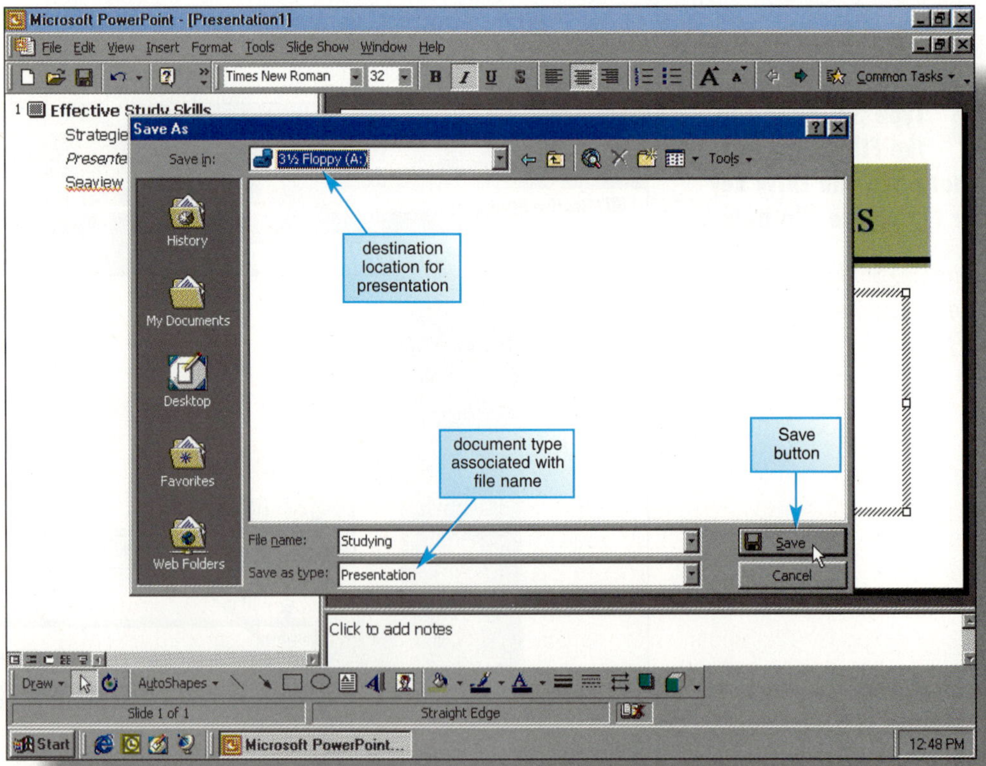

FIGURE 1-29

Click the Save button.

PowerPoint saves the presentation to your floppy disk in drive A. The title bar displays the file name, Studying, used to save the presentation (Figure 1-30).

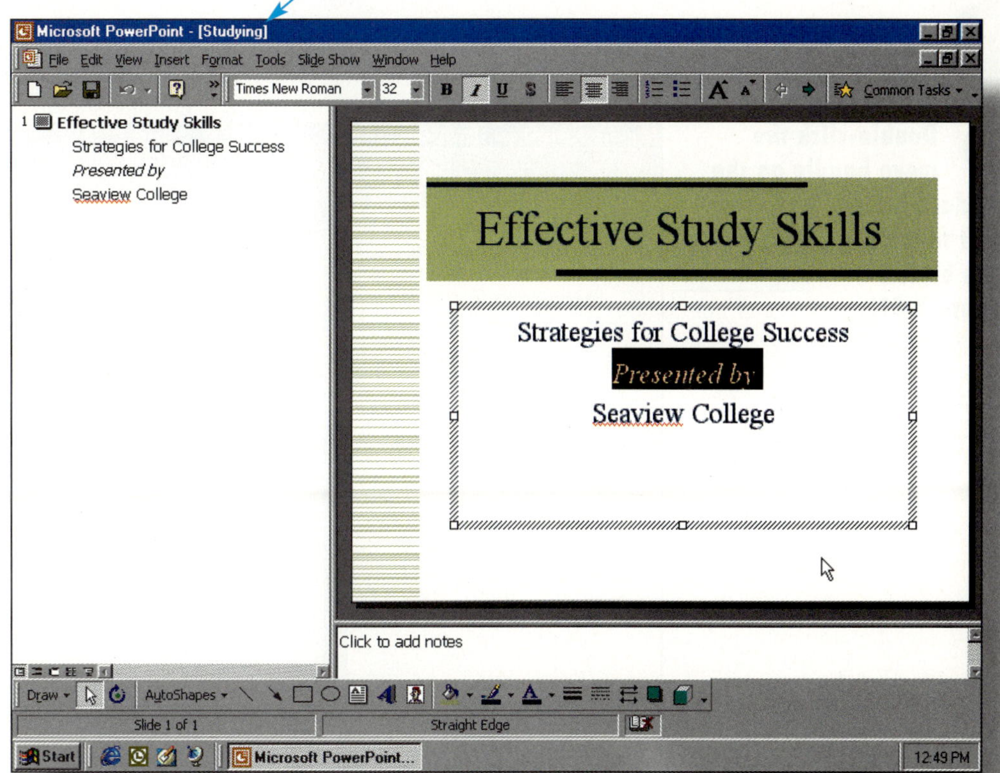

FIGURE 1-30

1. On File menu click Save As
2. Press CTRL+S or press SHIFT+F12

PowerPoint automatically appends the extension .ppt to the file name, Studying. The **.ppt** extension stands for **P**ower**P**oin**t**. Although the slide show, Studying, is saved on a floppy disk, it also remains in main memory and displays on the screen.

It is a good practice to save periodically while you are working on a project. By doing so, you protect yourself from losing all the work you have done since the last time you saved.

Adding a New Slide to a Presentation

The title slide for your presentation is created. The next step is to add the first bulleted list slide immediately after the current slide in Project 1. Usually when you create your presentation, you add slides with text, graphics, or charts. When you add a new slide, PowerPoint displays a dialog box for you to choose one of the 24 different AutoLayouts. These AutoLayouts have placeholders for various objects. Some placeholders allow you to double-click the placeholder and then access other PowerPoint objects. More information about using AutoLayout placeholders to add graphics follows in subsequent projects. Perform the steps on the next page to add a new slide using the Bulleted List AutoLayout.

Steps To Add a New Slide Using the Bulleted List AutoLayout

1 Double-click the move handle on the Standard toolbar and then point to the New Slide button (Figure 1-31).

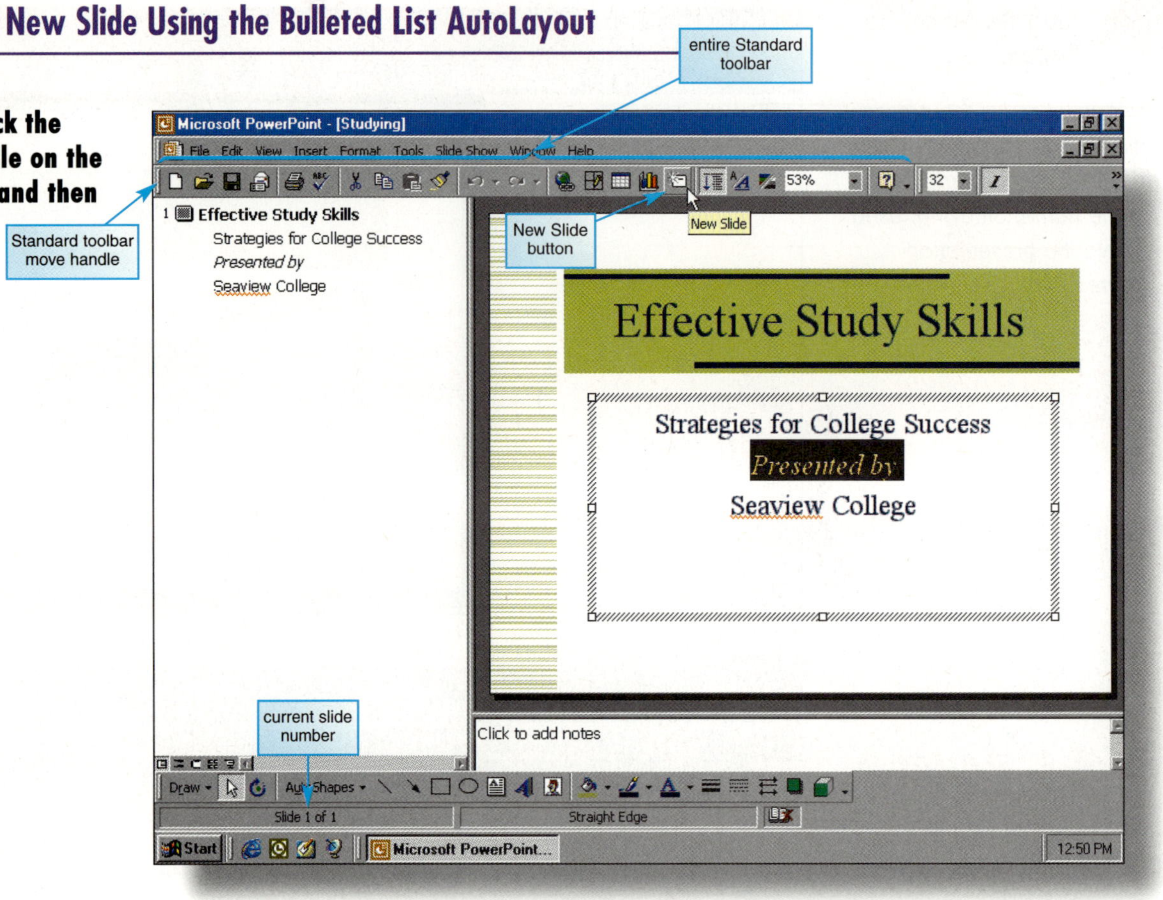

FIGURE 1-31

2 Click the New Slide button. When the New Slide dialog box displays, point to the OK button.

The New Slide dialog box displays (Figure 1-32). The Bulleted List AutoLayout is selected, and the AutoLayout title, Bulleted List, displays at the bottom-right corner of the New Slide dialog box.

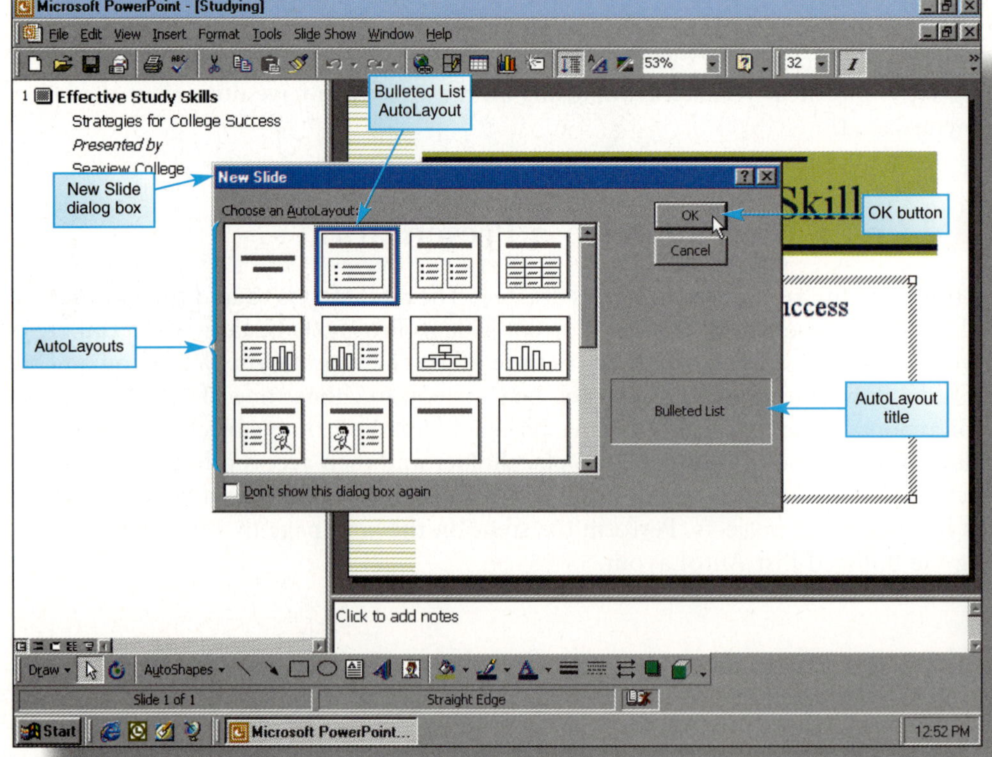

FIGURE 1-32

Click the OK button.

Slide 2 displays keeping the attributes of the Straight Edge design template using the Bulleted List AutoLayout (Figure 1-33). Slide 2 of 2 displays on the status bar. The vertical scroll bar displays in the slide pane. The bullet appears as a diamond.

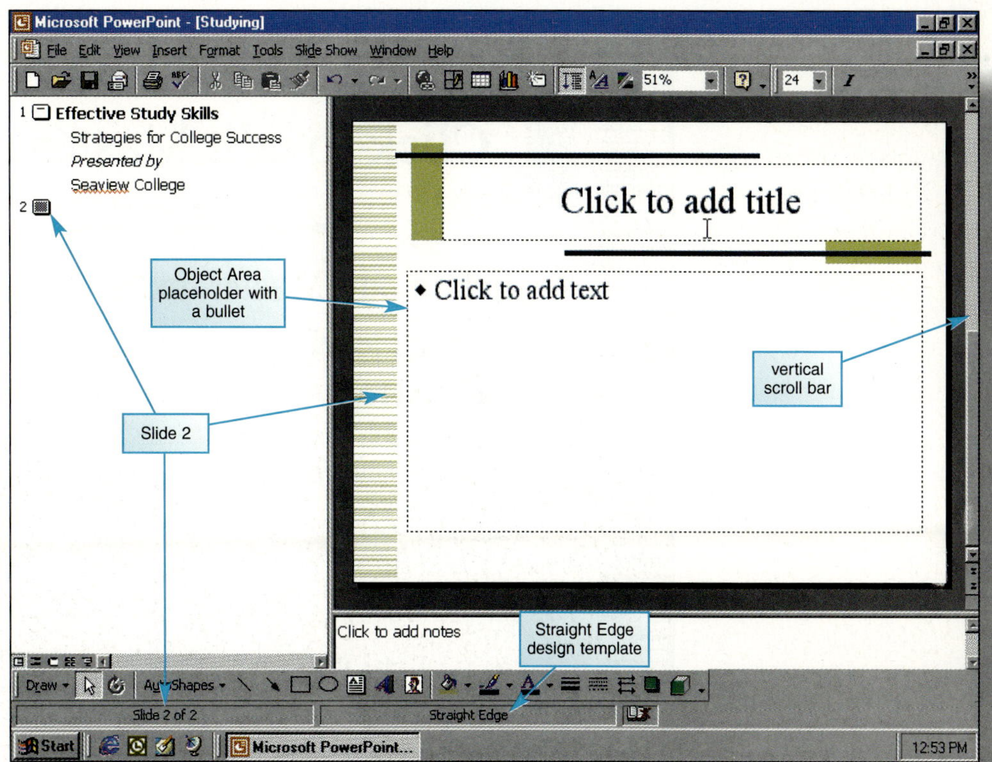

FIGURE 1-33

Other Ways

1. Click Common Tasks menu button on Formatting toolbar, click New Slide
2. On Insert menu click New Slide
3. Press CTRL+M

Because the Bulleted List AutoLayout was selected, PowerPoint displays Slide 2 with a Title Area placeholder and an Object Area placeholder with a bullet. You can change the layout for a slide at any time during the creation of your presentation by clicking the Common Tasks menu button on the Formatting toolbar and then clicking the Slide Layout button. You then can double-click the AutoLayout of your choice.

Creating a Bulleted List Slide

The bulleted list slides in Figure 1-2 on page PP 1.9 contain more than one level of bulleted text. A slide with more than one level of bulleted text is called a **multi-level bulleted list slide**. A **level** is a position within a structure, such as an outline, that indicates a magnitude of importance. PowerPoint allows for five paragraph levels. Each paragraph level has an associated bullet. The bullet font is dependent on the design template. Figure 1-34 on the next page identifies the five paragraph levels and the bullet fonts for the Straight Edge design template. Beginning with the Second level, each paragraph indents to the right of the preceding level.

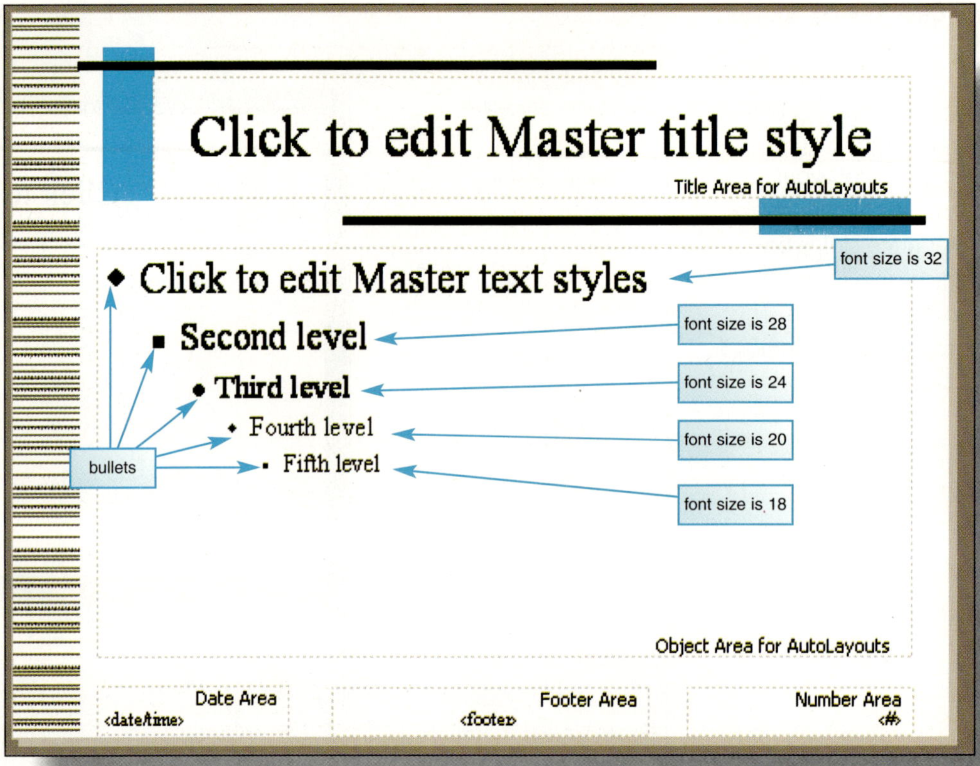

FIGURE 1-34

An indented paragraph is **demoted**, or pushed down to a lower level. For example, if you demote a First level paragraph, it becomes a Second level paragraph. This lower-level paragraph is a subset of the higher-level paragraph. It usually contains information that supports the topic in the paragraph immediately above it. You demote a paragraph by clicking the **Demote button** on the Formatting toolbar.

When you want to raise a paragraph from a lower level to a higher level, you **promote** the paragraph by clicking the **Promote button** on the Formatting toolbar.

Creating a multi-level bulleted list slide requires several steps. Initially, you enter a slide title in the Title Area placeholder. Next, you select the Object Area text placeholder. Then you type the text for the multi-level bulleted list, demoting and promoting paragraphs as needed. The next several sections explain how to add a multi-level bulleted list slide.

Entering a Slide Title

PowerPoint assumes every new slide has a title. The title for Slide 2 is Managing Your Time. Perform the following step to enter this title.

More About 2000

Slide Masters

Each design template has a corresponding slide master designed by Microsoft graphic artists. The text attributes and color schemes are developed to coordinate with each other and to evoke audience reactions, such as excitement or relaxation.

To Enter a Slide Title

1 If necessary, click the Title Area placeholder and then type `Managing your Time` **as the title. Do not press the ENTER key.**

The title, Managing Your Time, displays in the Title Area placeholder and in the outline pane (Figure 1-35). The insertion point displays after the e in Time.

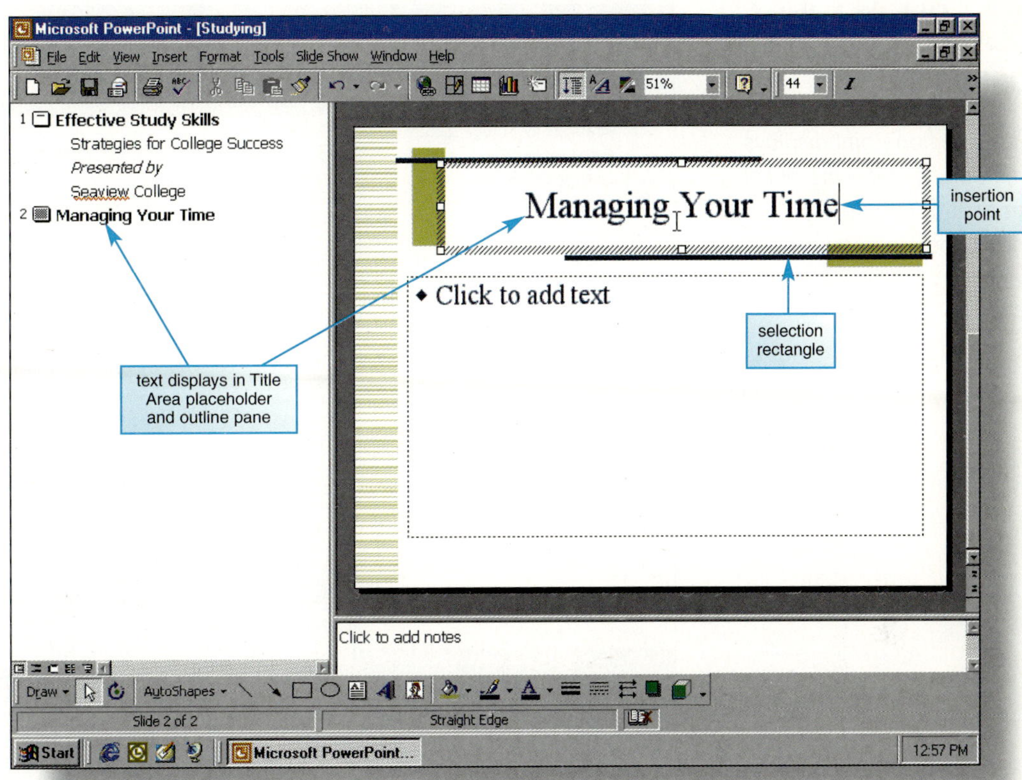

FIGURE 1-35

Selecting an Object Area Placeholder

Before you can type text in the Object Area placeholder, you first must select it. Perform the step on the next page to select the Object Area placeholder on Slide 2.

To Select an Object Area Placeholder

1 Click the bulleted paragraph labeled, Click to add text.

The insertion point displays immediately after the bullet on Slide 2 (Figure 1-36). The mouse pointer may change shape if you move it away from the bullet.

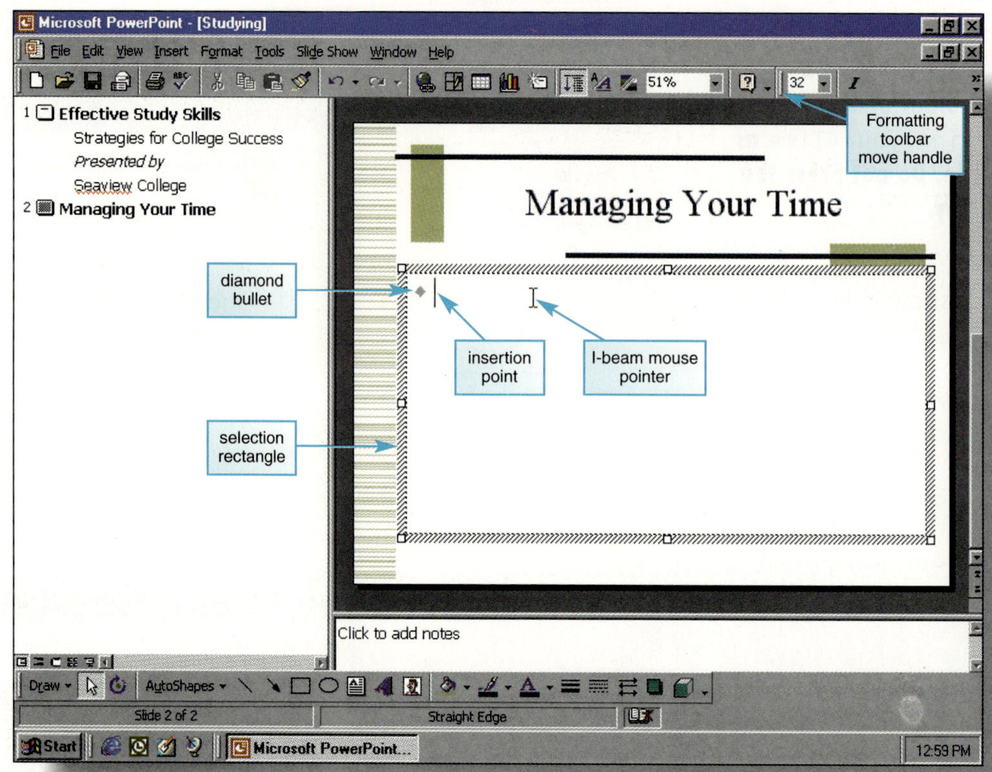

FIGURE 1-36

Other Ways

1. Press CTRL+ENTER

Typing a Multi-level Bulleted List

Recall that a bulleted list is a list of paragraphs, each of which is preceded by a bullet. Also recall that a paragraph is a segment of text ended by pressing the ENTER key. The next step is to type the multi-level bulleted list, which consists of the six entries (Figure 1-2 on page PP 1.9). Perform the following steps to type a multi-level bulleted list.

Steps To Type a Multi-level Bulleted List

1 **Double-click the move handle on the Formatting toolbar. Type** `Make a weekly schedule` **and then press the ENTER key.**

The paragraph, Make a weekly schedule, displays (Figure 1-37). The font size is 32. The insertion point displays after the second bullet. When you press the ENTER key, PowerPoint ends one paragraph and begins a new paragraph. Because you are using the Bulleted List AutoLayout, PowerPoint places a diamond bullet in front of the new paragraph.

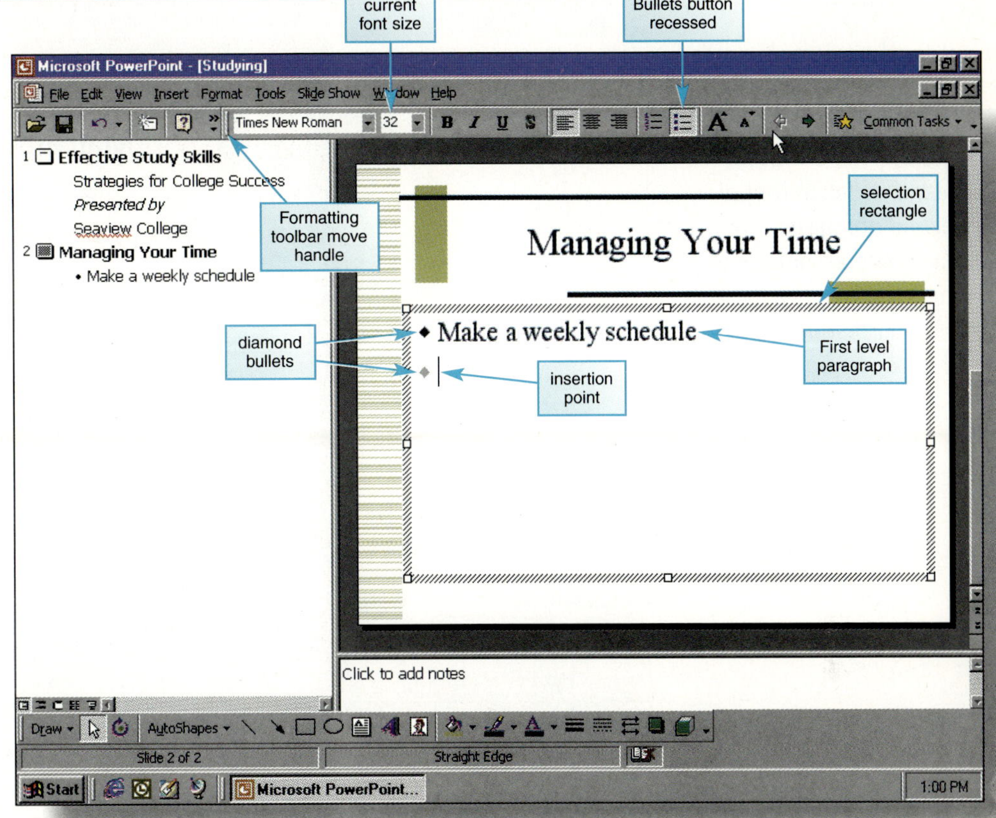

FIGURE 1-37

2 **Point to the Demote button (Figure 1-38).**

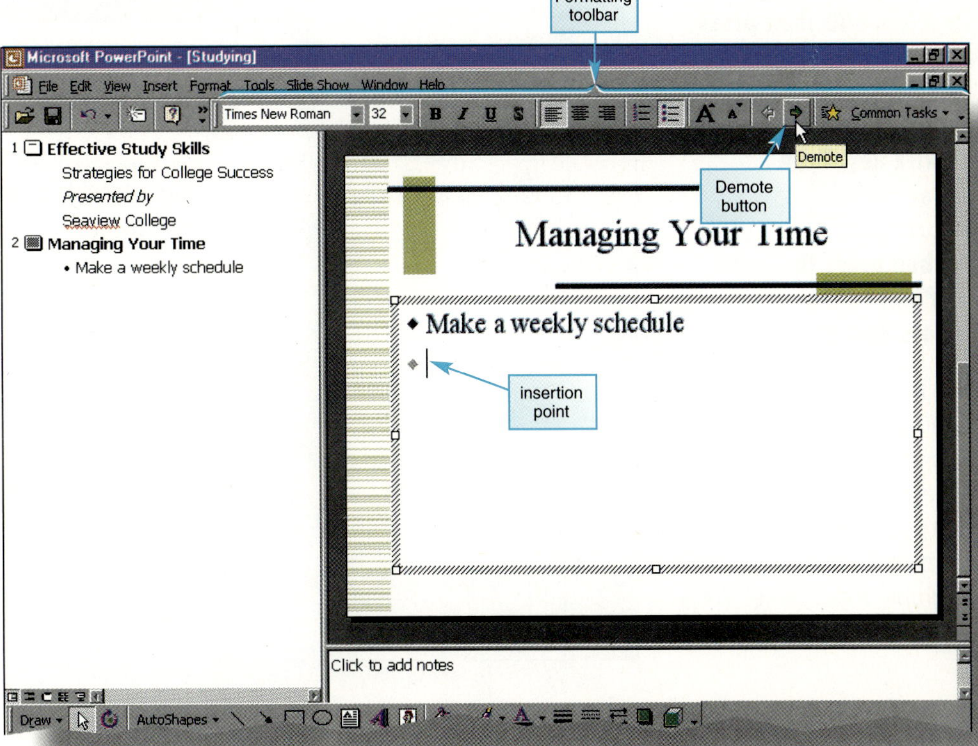

FIGURE 1-38

Click the Demote button.

The second paragraph indents under the first and becomes a Second level paragraph (Figure 1-39). Notice the bullet in front of the second paragraph changes from a diamond to a box, and the font size for the demoted paragraph now is 28. The insertion point displays after the box.

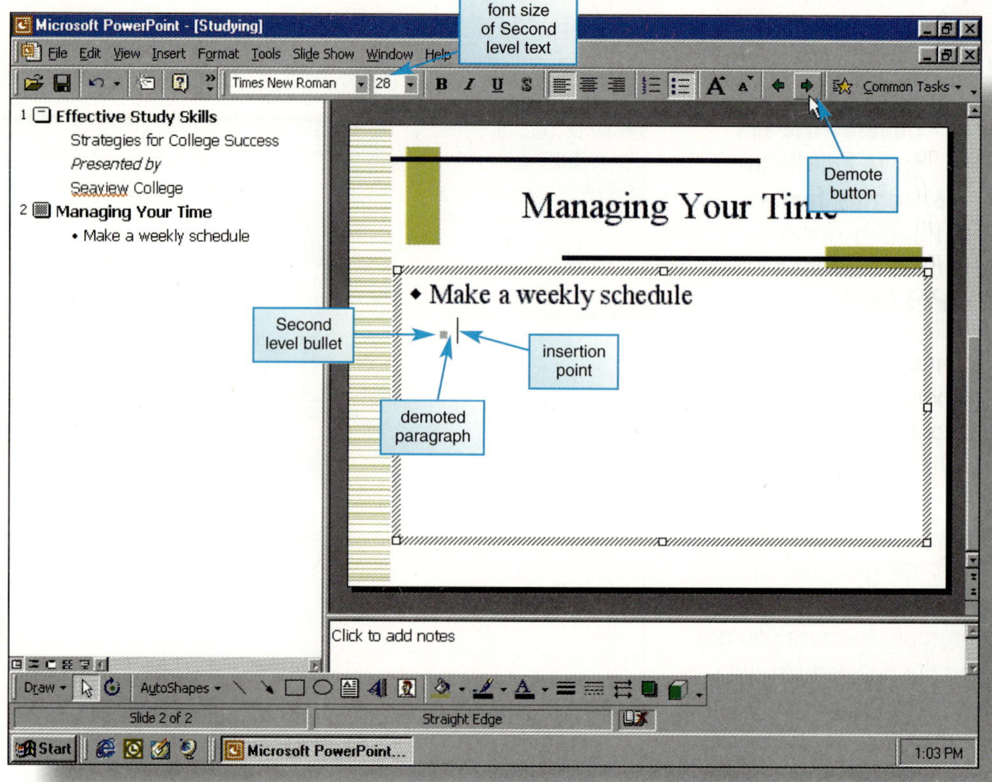

FIGURE 1-39

Type `List specific study times for all subjects` **and then press the ENTER key. Type** `Plan time for recreation and sleep` **and then press the ENTER key. Type** `Spread study times throughout the week` **and then press the ENTER key. Point to the Promote button.**

Three new Second level paragraphs display with boxes in both the slide and outline panes (Figure 1-40). When you press the ENTER key, PowerPoint adds a new paragraph at the same level as the previous paragraph.

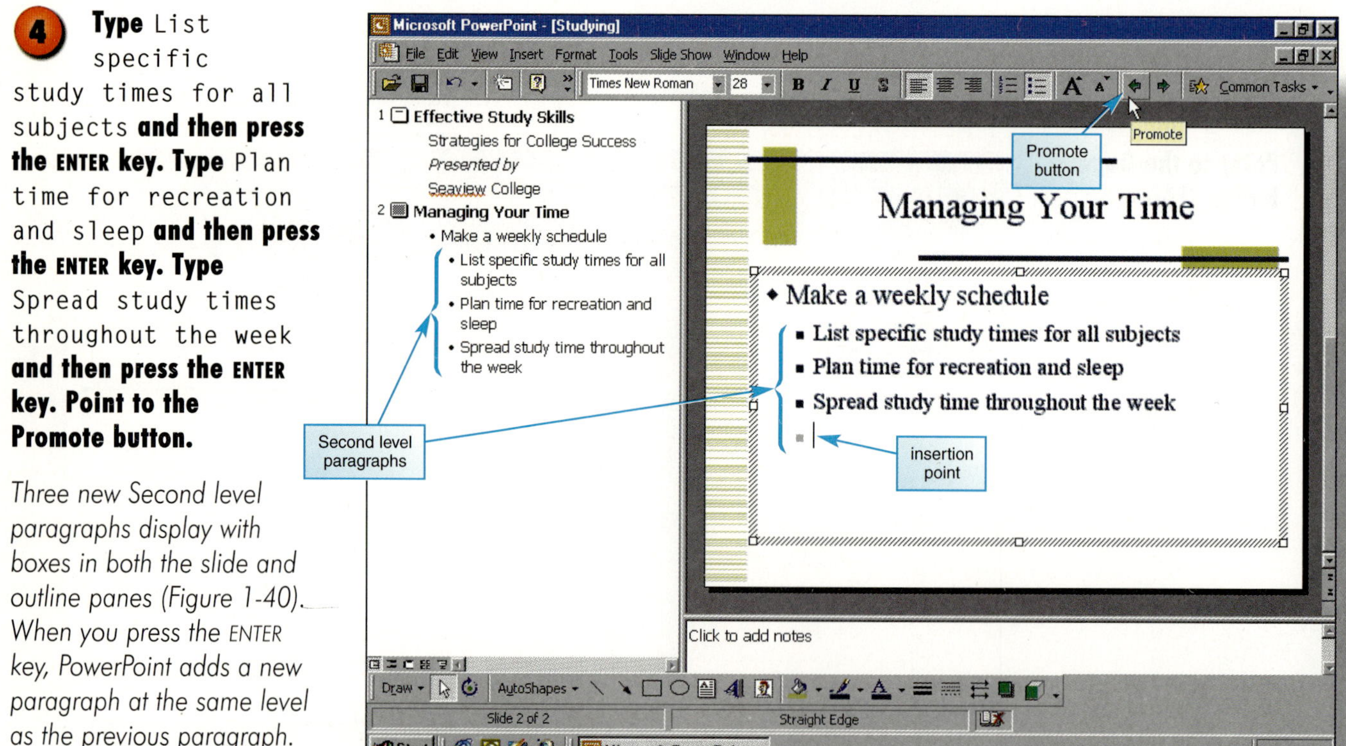

FIGURE 1-40

5 Click the Promote button.

The Second level paragraph becomes a First level paragraph (Figure 1-41). The bullet in front of the new paragraph changes from a box to a diamond, and the font size for the promoted paragraph is 32. The insertion point displays after the diamond bullet.

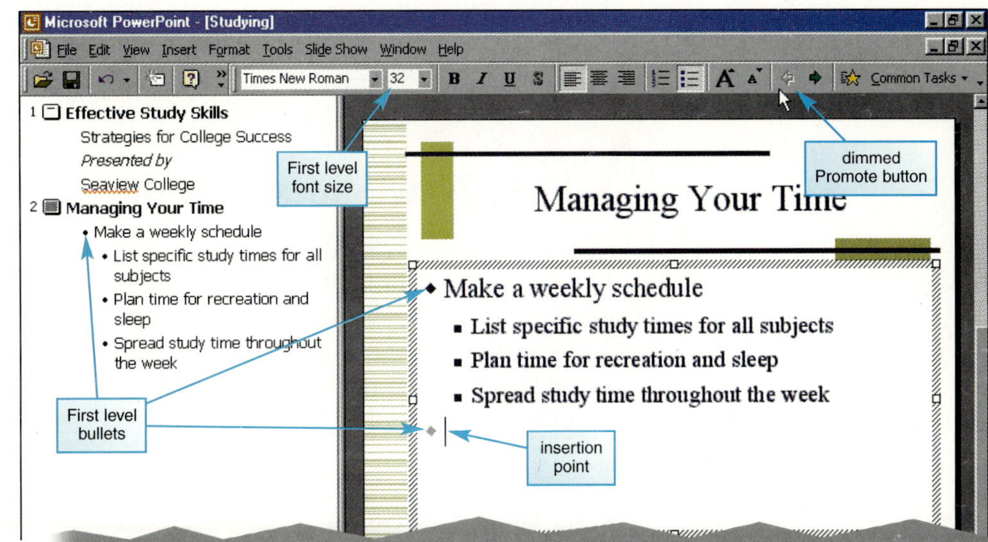

FIGURE 1-41

Perform the following steps to complete the text for Slide 2.

TO TYPE THE REMAINING TEXT FOR SLIDE 2

1. Type `Stick to your schedule` and then press the ENTER key.
2. Type `Revise your schedule when necessary` but do not press the ENTER key.

The insertion point displays after the y in necessary (Figure 1-42).

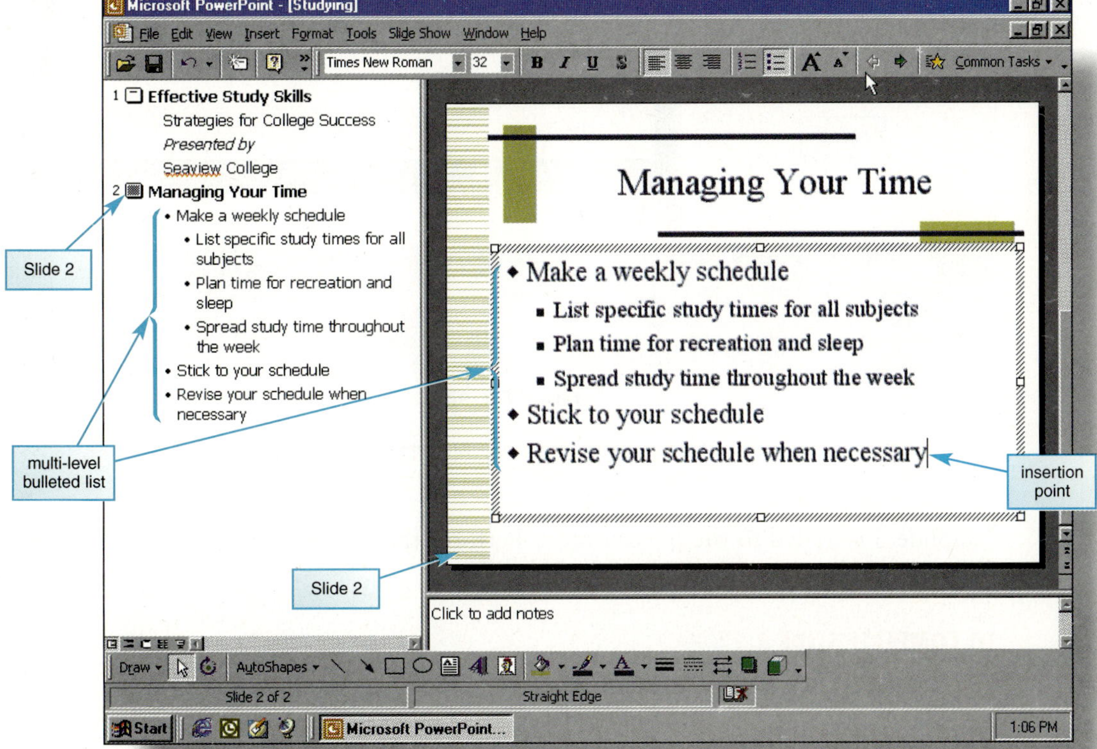

FIGURE 1-42

Notice that you did not press the ENTER key after typing the last bullet line in Step 2. If you press the ENTER key, a new bullet displays after the last entry on this slide. To remove an extra bullet, press the BACKSPACE key.

Adding New Slides with the Same AutoLayout

When you add a new slide to a presentation and want to keep the same AutoLayout used on the previous slide, PowerPoint gives you a shortcut. Instead of clicking the New Slide button and clicking an AutoLayout in the New Slide dialog box, you can press and hold down the SHIFT key and then click the New Slide button. Perform the following step to add a new slide (Slide 3) and keep the Bulleted List AutoLayout used on the previous slide.

To Add a New Slide with the Same AutoLayout

1 Press and hold down the SHIFT key, click the New Slide button on the Standard toolbar, and then release the SHIFT key.

Slide 3 displays the Bulleted List AutoLayout (Figure 1-43). Slide 3 of 3 displays on the status bar.

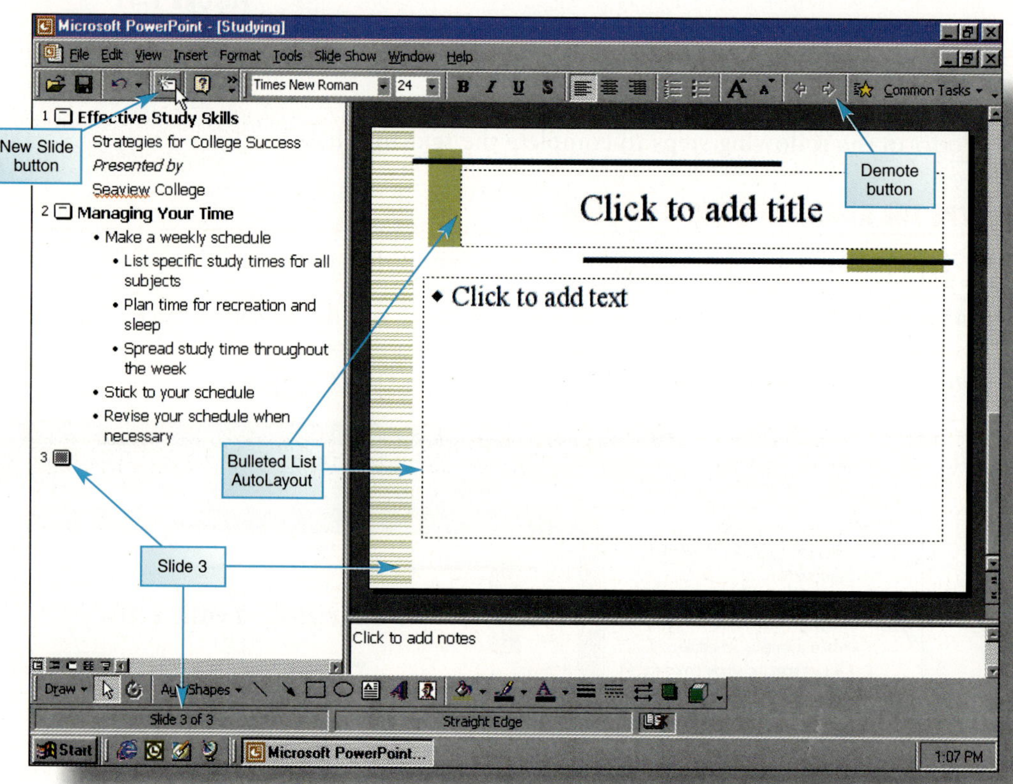

FIGURE 1-43

Other Ways

1. Press SHIFT+CTRL+M

Slide 3 is added to the presentation. Perform the following steps to add text to Slide 3 and to create a multi-level bulleted list.

TO COMPLETE SLIDE 3

1. Type `Attending Class` in the Title Area placeholder.
2. Press CTRL+ENTER to move the insertion point to the Object Area placeholder.

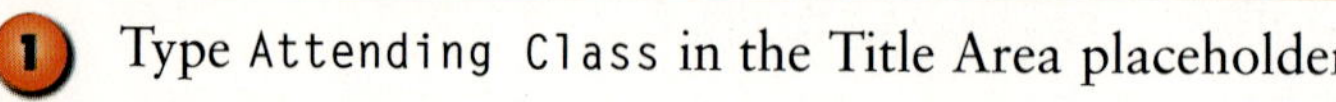

3. Type `Sit in the front of the room` and then press the ENTER key.
4. Type `Ask questions at appropriate times` and then press the ENTER key.
5. Type `Take notes` and then press the ENTER key.
6. Click the Demote button.
7. Type `Rephrase ideas in your own words` and then press the ENTER key.
8. Type `Review immediately after class` but do not press the ENTER key.

Slide 3 displays as shown in Figure 1-44. The Office Assistant light bulb may display to offer design help. If so, you may click the light bulb next to the Office Assistant to see a tip. For additional help on using the Office Assistant, refer to Appendix A.

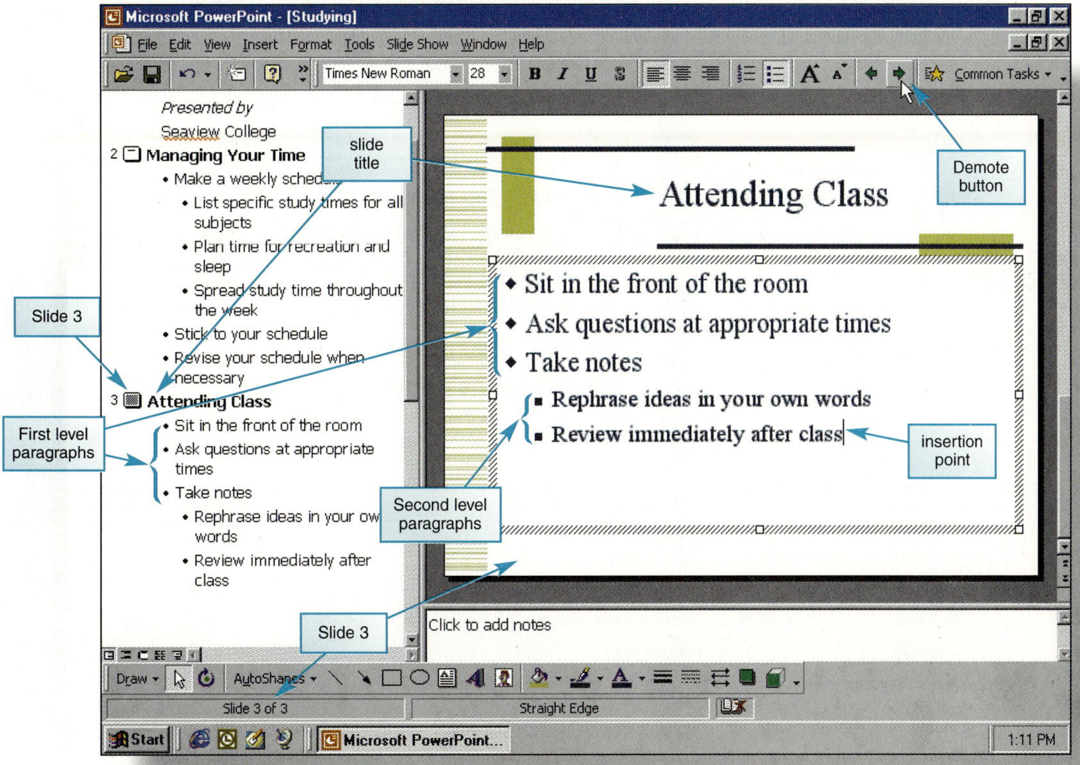

FIGURE 1-44

Slide 4, also a multi-level bulleted list, is the last slide in this presentation. Perform the following steps to create Slide 4.

TO CREATE SLIDE 4

1. Press and hold down the SHIFT key, click the New Slide button on the Standard toolbar, and then release the SHIFT key.
2. Type `Reading Your Textbooks` in the Title Area placeholder.
3. Press CTRL+ENTER to move the insertion point to the Object Area placeholder.
4. Type `Survey the assignment` and then press the ENTER key.
5. Click the Demote button. Type `Read the summary and chapter questions` and then press the ENTER key.

6. Click the Promote button. Type `Read the chapter carefully` and then press the ENTER key.
7. Type `Recite the material in your own words` and then press the ENTER key.
8. Type `Write brief notes in the margins` and then press the ENTER key.
9. Type `Review the entire assignment` but do not press the ENTER key.

The Title Area and Object Area text objects display in the slide and outline panes (Figure 1-45). The Office Assistant light bulb may display to offer design help.

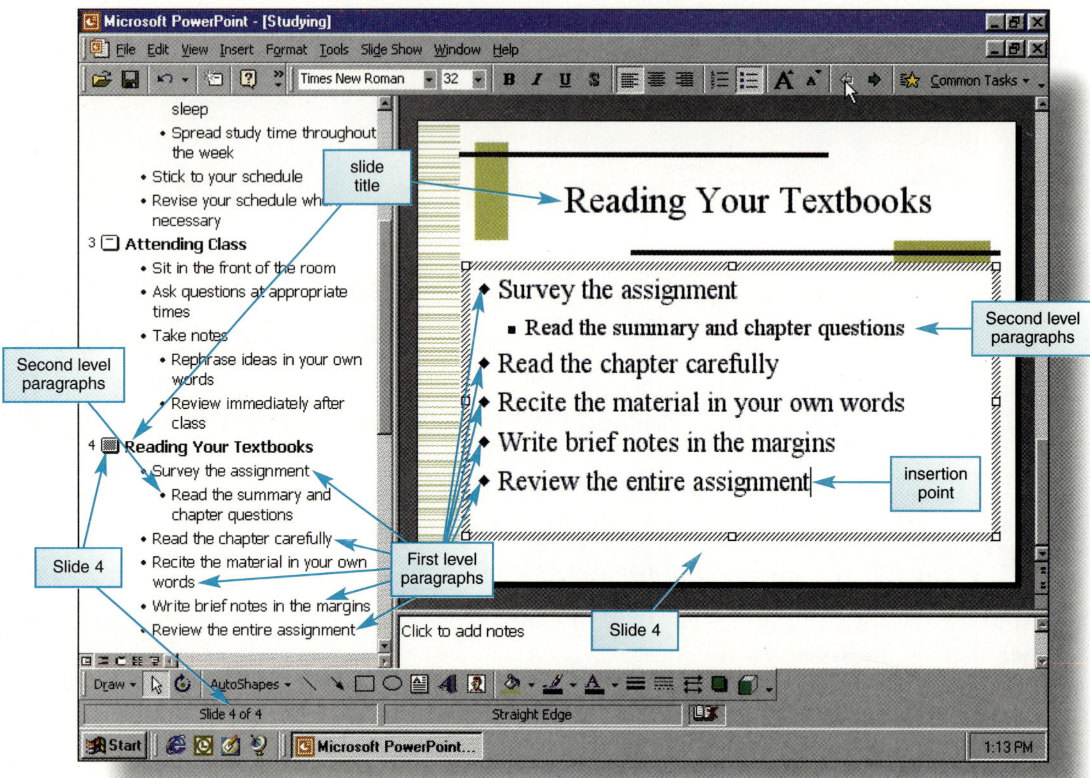

FIGURE 1-45

All slides for the Studying presentation are created. This presentation consists of a title slide and three multi-level bulleted list slides.

Black Slides

Insert a blank, black slide between sections of a large presentation or when you want to pause for discussion. The black slide focuses the audience's attention on you, the speaker, and away from the screen display.

Ending a Slide Show with a Black Slide

After the last slide in the slide show displays, the default PowerPoint setting is to end your presentation with a black slide. This black slide displays only when the slide show is running and concludes your slide show gracefully so your audience never sees the PowerPoint window. A black slide ends all slide shows until the option setting is deactivated. Perform the following steps to verify the End with black slide option is activated.

Steps To End a Slide Show with a Black Slide

1 Click Tools on the menu bar and then point to Options (Figure 1-46).

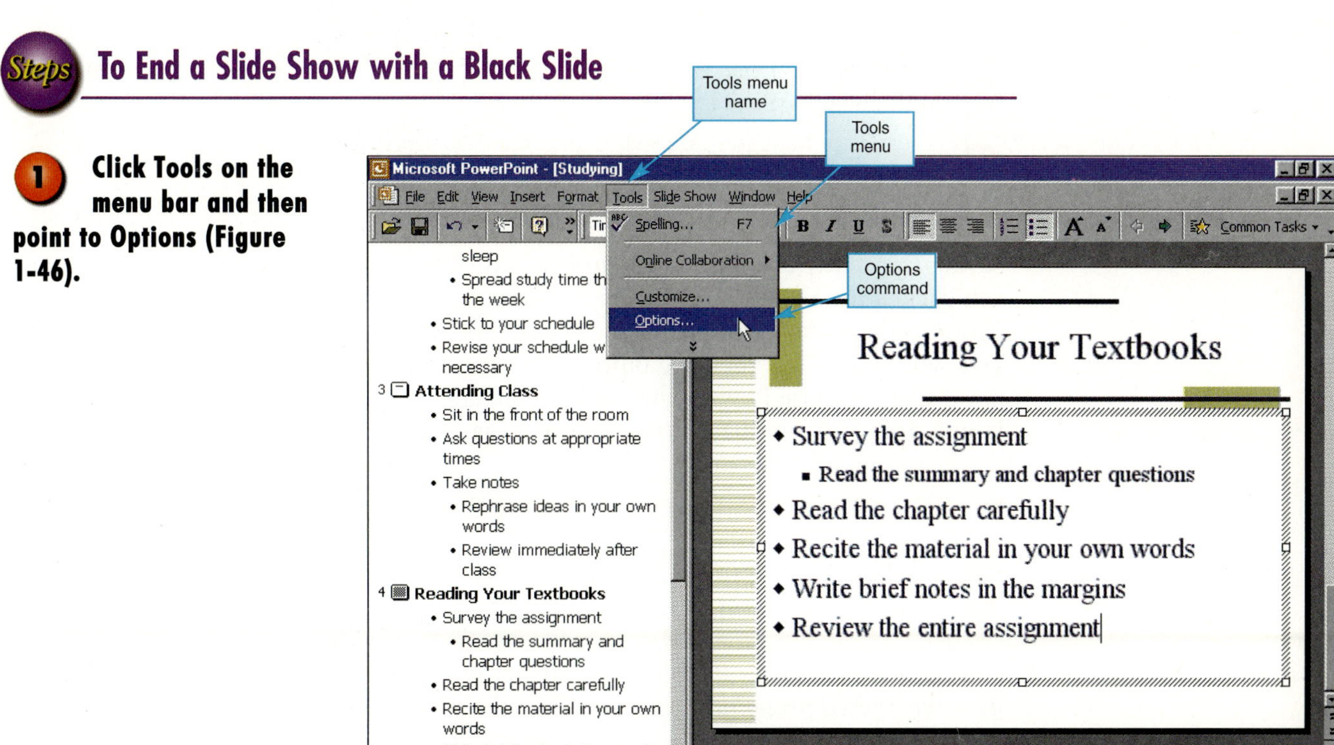

FIGURE 1-46

2 Click Options. If necessary, click the View tab when the Options dialog box opens. Verify a check mark displays in the End with black slide check box. If a check mark does not display, click the End with black slide check box.

The Options dialog box displays (Figure 1-47). The View sheet contains settings for the overall PowerPoint display and for a particular slide show.

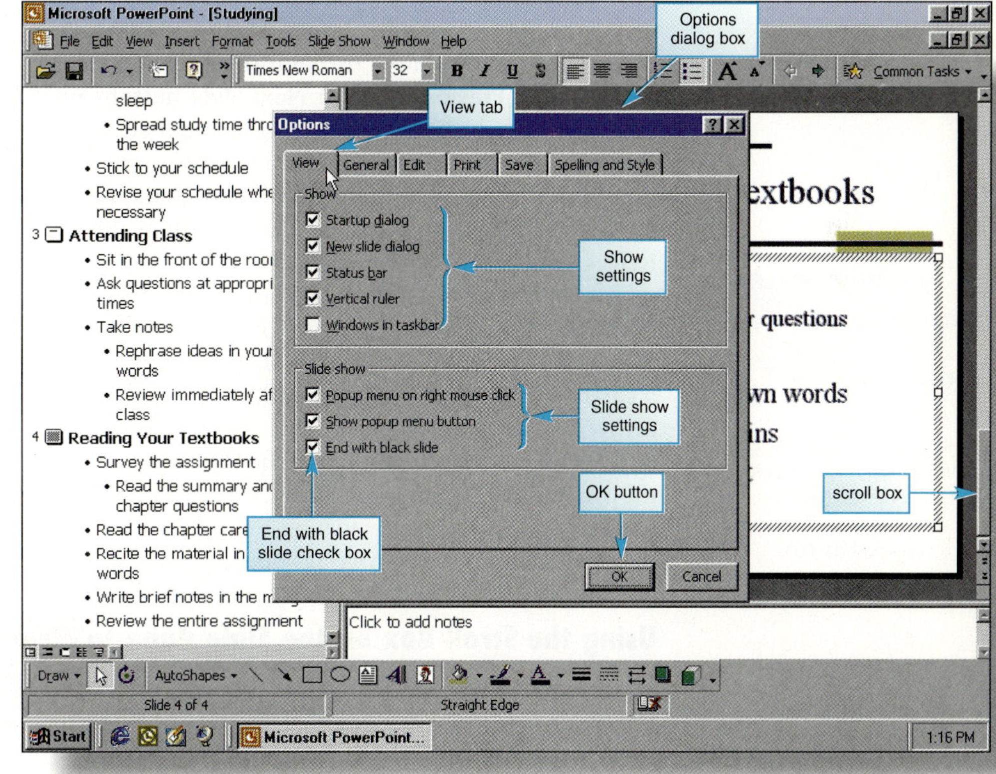

FIGURE 1-47

3 Click the OK button.

The End with black slide option is activated.

Now that all aspects of the presentation are complete, you need to save the additions and changes you have made to your Studying presentation.

Saving a Presentation with the Same File Name

Saving frequently cannot be overemphasized. When you first saved the presentation, you clicked the Save button on the Standard toolbar and the Save dialog box displayed. When you want to save the changes made to the presentation after your last save, you again click the Save button. This time, however, the Save dialog box does not display because PowerPoint updates the document called Studying.ppt on your floppy disk. Perform the following steps to save the presentation again.

TO SAVE A PRESENTATION WITH THE SAME FILE NAME

1. Be sure your floppy disk is in drive A.
2. Click the Save button on the Standard toolbar.

PowerPoint overwrites the old Studying.ppt document on the floppy disk in drive A with the revised presentation document. Slide 4 displays in the PowerPoint window.

Moving to Another Slide in Normal View

When creating or editing a presentation in normal view, you often want to display a slide other than the current one. You can move to another slide using several methods. In the outline pane, you can point to any of the text in a particular slide to display that slide in the slide pane, or you can drag the scroll box on the vertical scroll bar up or down to move through the text in your presentation. In the slide pane, you can click the **Previous Slide** or **Next Slide** buttons on the vertical scroll bar. Clicking the Next Slide button advances to the next slide in the presentation. Clicking the Previous Slide button backs up to the slide preceding the current slide. You also can drag the scroll box on the vertical scroll bar. When you drag the scroll box, the **slide indicator** displays the number and the title of the slide you are about to display. Releasing the mouse button displays the slide.

A slide's **Zoom setting** affects the portion of the slide displaying in the slide pane. PowerPoint defaults to a setting of approximately 50% so the entire slide displays. This percentage depends on the size and type of your monitor. If you want to display a small portion of the current slide, you would zoom in by clicking the Zoom box arrow and then clicking the desired magnification. You can display the entire slide in the slide pane by clicking Fit in the Zoom list. The Zoom setting affects the action of the vertical and horizontal scroll bars. If Zoom is set so that the entire slide is not visible in the slide pane, clicking the up scroll arrow on the vertical scroll bar displays the next portion of your slide, not the previous slide.

Zoom

You can increase your Zoom setting to as large as 400% when you want to see details on small objects. Likewise, you can decrease your Zoom setting to as small as 10%.

Using the Scroll Box on the Slide Pane to Move to Another Slide

Before continuing with Project 1, you want to display the title slide. Perform the following steps to move from Slide 4 to the Slide 1 using the scroll box on the slide pane vertical scroll bar.

To Use the Scroll Box on the Slide Pane to Move to Another Slide

1. **Position the mouse pointer on the scroll box. Press and hold down the left mouse button.**

Slide: 4 of 4 Reading Your Textbooks displays in the slide indicator (Figure 1-48). The Slide 4 icon is shaded in the outline pane.

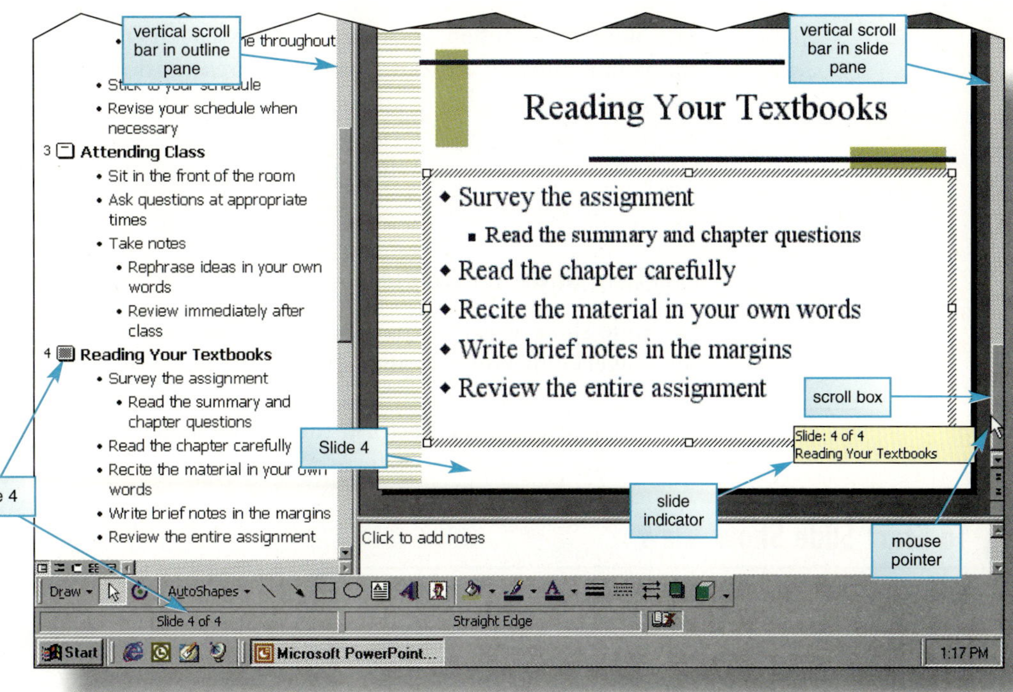

FIGURE 1-48

2. **Drag the scroll box up the vertical scroll bar until Slide: 1 of 4 Effective Study Skills displays in the slide indicator.**

Slide: 1 of 4 Effective Study Skills displays in the slide indicator (Figure 1-49). Slide 4 still displays in the PowerPoint window, and the Slide 4 icon is shaded in the outline pane.

3. **Release the left mouse button.**

Slide 1, titled Effective Study Skills, displays in the PowerPoint window. The Slide 1 icon is shaded in the outline pane.

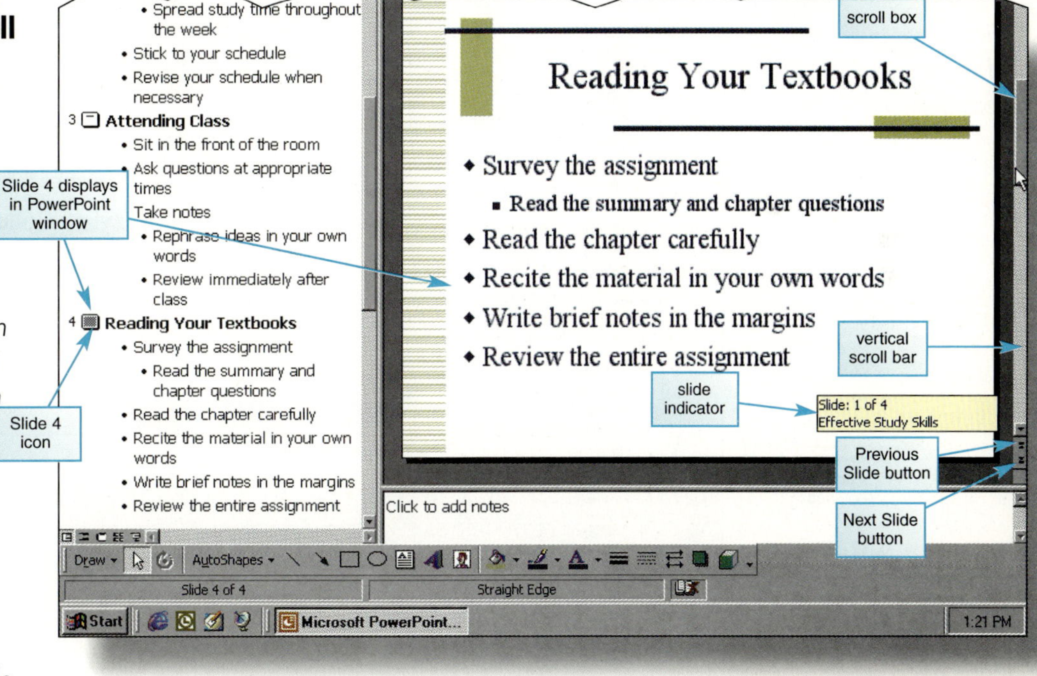

FIGURE 1-49

Other Ways

1. Click Next Slide button or Previous Slide button to move forward or back one slide
2. Press PAGE DOWN or PAGE UP to move forward or back one slide

Viewing the Presentation Using Slide Show

The **Slide Show button**, located at the lower-left of the PowerPoint window above the status bar, allows you to display your presentation electronically using a computer. The computer acts like a slide projector, displaying each slide on a full screen. The full screen slide hides the toolbars, menus, and other PowerPoint window elements. Slide show view is used when making a presentation. You can start slide show view from any view: normal view, outline view, slide view, or slide sorter view.

Starting Slide Show View

Slide show view begins when you click the Slide Show button in the lower-left of the PowerPoint window above the status bar. PowerPoint then displays the current slide on the full screen without any of the PowerPoint window objects, such as the menu bar or toolbars. Perform the following steps to start slide show view.

To Start Slide Show View

1 Point to the Slide Show button in the lower-left of the PowerPoint window above the status bar.

The Normal View button is recessed because you still are in normal view (Figure 1-50).

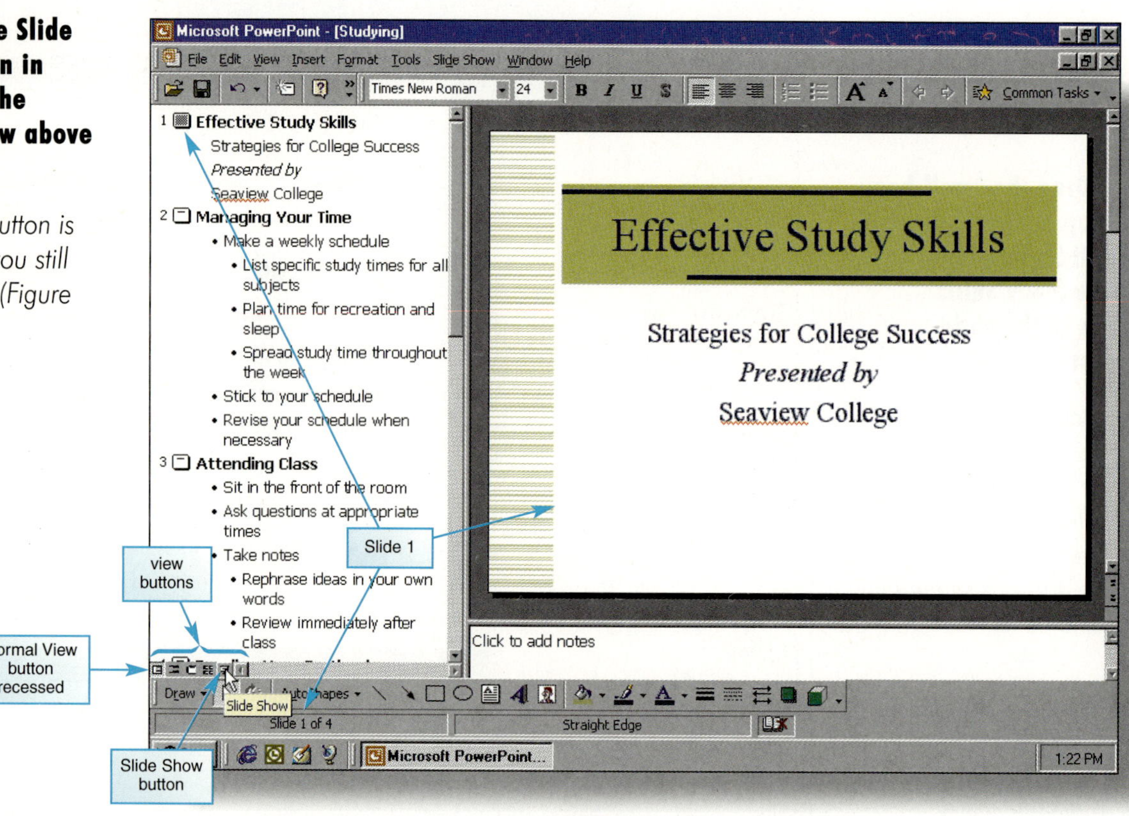

FIGURE 1-50

Click the Slide Show button.

The title slide fills the screen (Figure 1-51). The PowerPoint window is hidden.

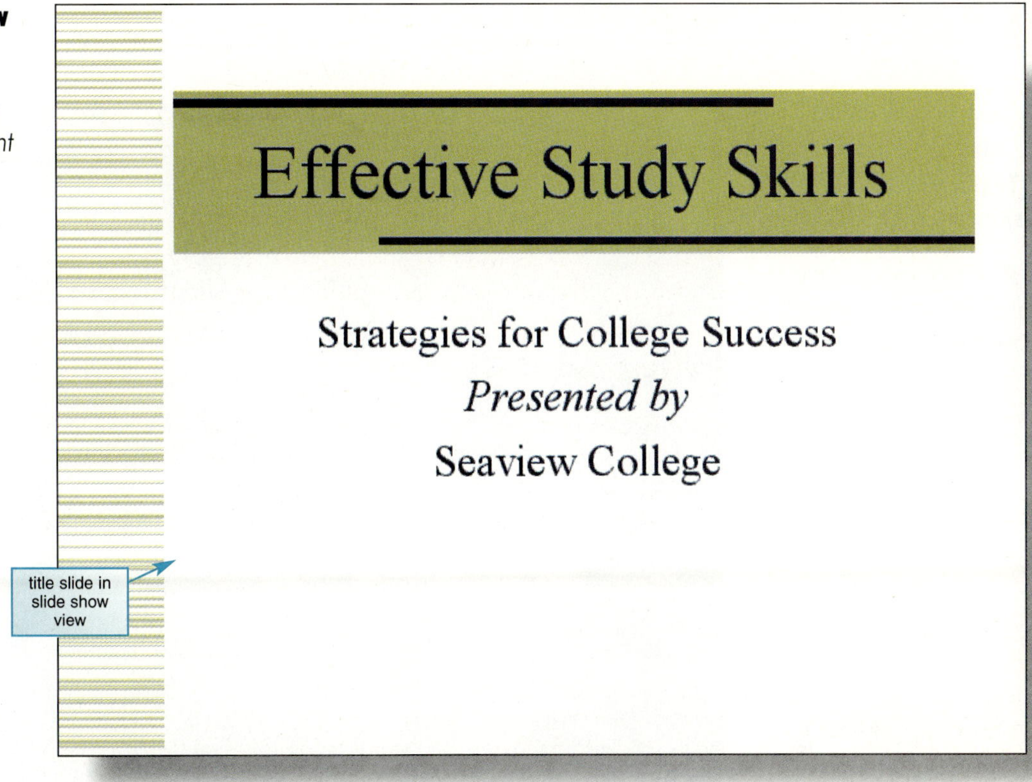
Effective Study Skills
Strategies for College Success
Presented by
Seaview College
title slide in slide show view

FIGURE 1-51

Other Ways

1. On View menu click Slide Show
2. Press F5

Advancing Through a Slide Show Manually

After you begin slide show view, you can move forward or backward through your slides. PowerPoint allows you to advance through your slides manually or automatically. Automatic advancing is discussed in a later project. Perform the steps on the next page to move manually through your slides.

To Move Manually Through Slides in a Slide Show

Click each slide until the Reading Your Textbooks slide (Slide 4) displays.

Each slide in your presentation displays on the screen, one slide at a time. Each time you click the mouse button, the next slide displays.

2 Click Slide 4.

The black slide displays (Figure 1-52). The message at the top of the slide announces the end of the slide show. To return to normal view, click the black slide.

FIGURE 1-52

Other Ways

1. Press PAGE DOWN to advance one slide at a time, or press PAGE UP to go backward one slide at a time
2. Press RIGHT ARROW key to advance one slide at a time, or press LEFT ARROW key to go backward one slide at a time

Using the Popup Menu to Go to a Specific Slide

Slide show view has a shortcut menu, called **Popup menu**, that displays when you right-click a slide in slide show view. This menu contains commands to assist you during a slide show. For example, clicking the **Next command** moves you to the next slide. Clicking the **Previous command** moves you to the previous slide. You can go to any slide in your presentation by pointing to the **Go command** and then clicking Slide Navigator. The **Slide Navigator dialog box** contains a list of the slides in your presentation. Go to the requested slide by double-clicking the name of that slide.

Perform the following steps to go to the title slide (Slide 1) in your presentation.

To Display the Popup Menu and Go to a Specific Slide

1 With the black slide displaying in slide show view, right-click the slide. Point to Go on the Popup menu, and then point to Slide Navigator on the Go submenu.

The Popup menu displays on the black slide, and the Go submenu displays (Figure 1-53). Your screen may look different because the Popup menu displays near the location of the mouse pointer at the time you right-click.

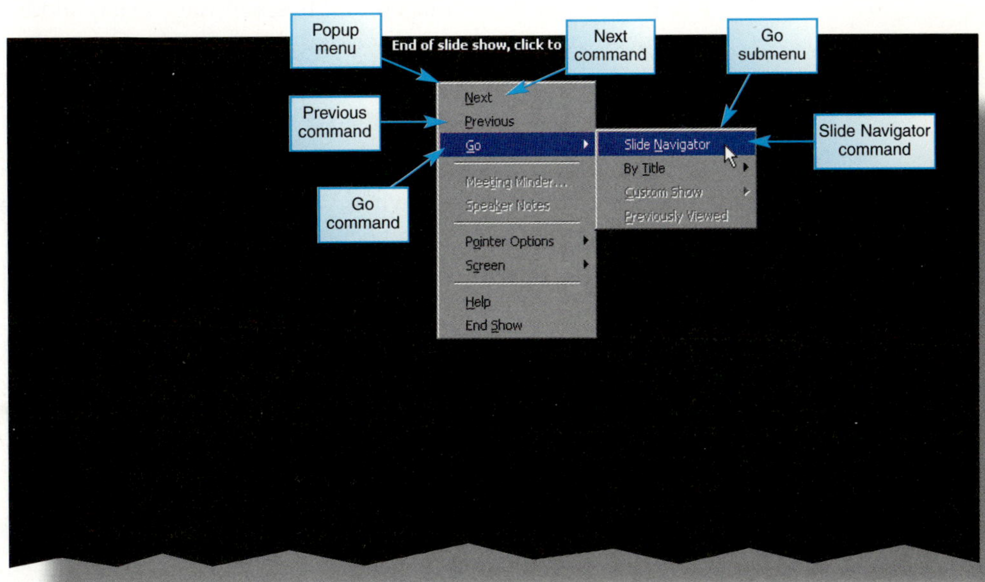

FIGURE 1-53

2 Click Slide Navigator. When the Slide Navigator dialog box displays, point to 1. Effective Study Skills in the Slide titles list.

The Slide titles list contains the title text of the slides in your presentation (Figure 1-54). You want to go to Slide 1 in your presentation. Slide 4 is the last slide viewed during your slide show.

3 Double-click 1. Effective Study Skills.

The title slide, Effective Study Skills, displays.

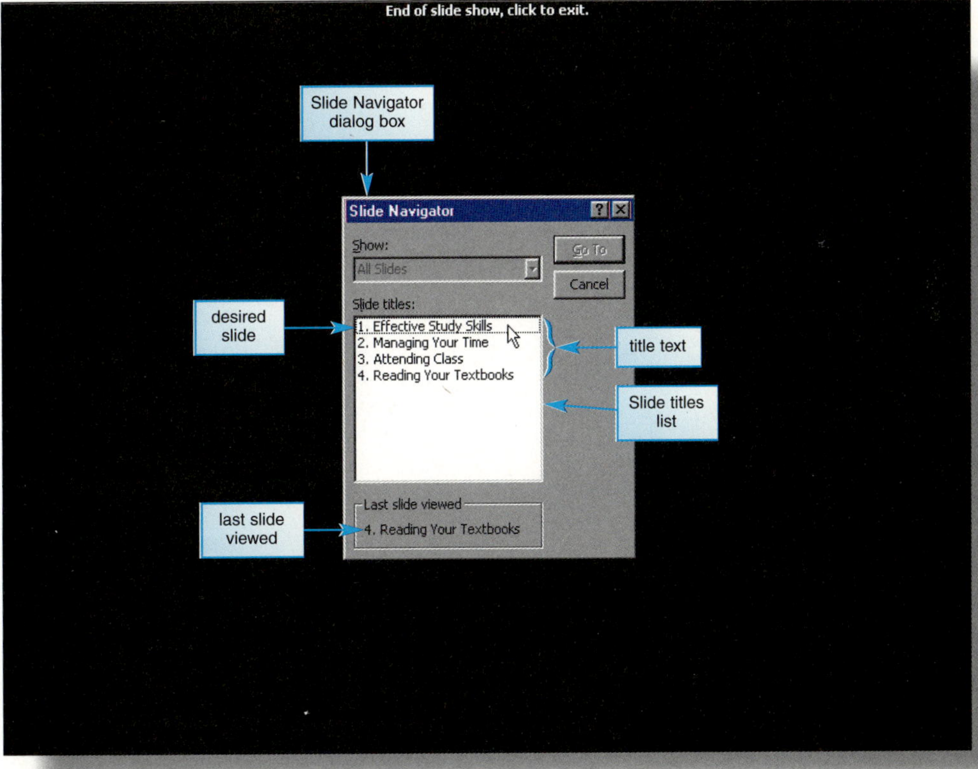

FIGURE 1-54

Other Ways

1. Right-click, point to Go, click Slide Navigator, type slide number, press ENTER

Additional Popup menu commands allow you to write meeting minutes or to create a list of action items during a slide show, change the mouse pointer to a pen that draws in various colors, blacken the screen, and end the slide show. Popup menu commands are discussed in subsequent projects.

Using the Popup Menu to End a Slide Show

The **End Show command** on the Popup menu exits slide show view and returns to the view you were in when you clicked the Slide Show button. Perform the following steps to end slide show view and return to normal view.

Steps To Use the Popup Menu to End a Slide Show

1 Right-click the title slide.

The Popup menu displays on Slide 1.

2 Point to End Show on the Popup menu.

Your Popup menu may display in a different location (Figure 1-55).

3 Click End Show.

PowerPoint exits slide show view and returns to normal view. Slide 1 displays because it is the last slide displayed in slide show view.

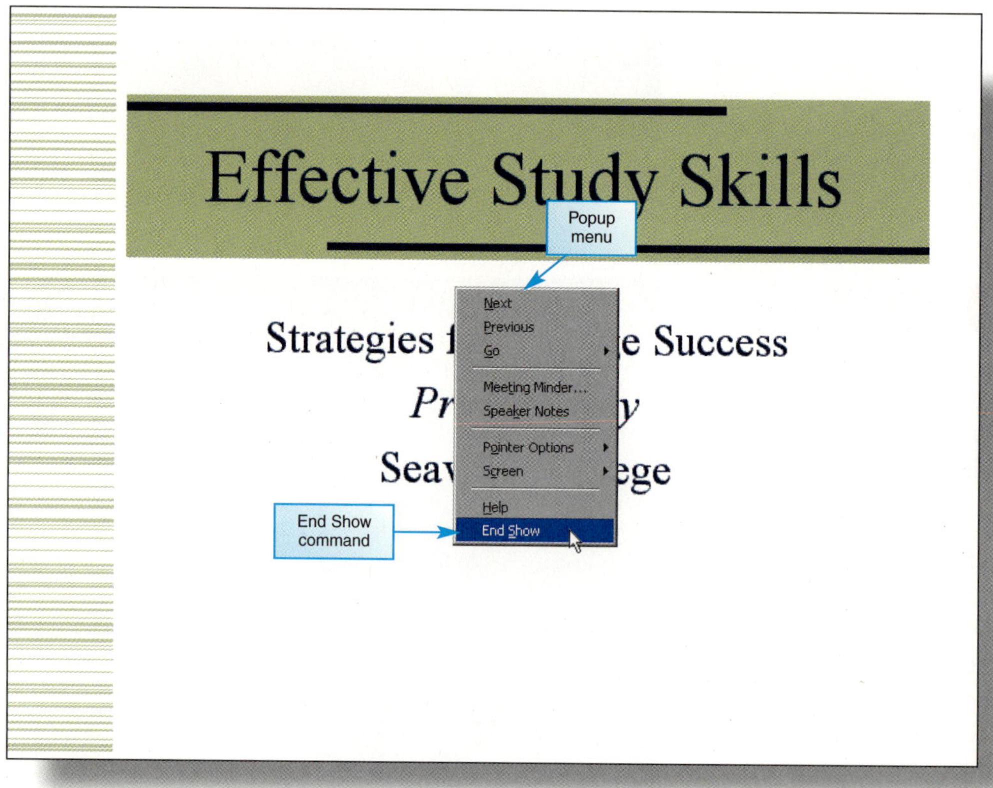

FIGURE 1-55

Other Ways

1. Click last slide in presentation to return to slide at which you began slide show view
2. Press ESC to display slide last viewed in slide show view

Quitting PowerPoint

The Studying presentation now is complete. When you quit PowerPoint, PowerPoint prompts you to save any changes made to the presentation since the last save, closes all PowerPoint windows, and then quits PowerPoint. Closing PowerPoint returns control to the desktop. Perform the following steps to quit PowerPoint.

Steps To Quit PowerPoint

1 **Point to the Close button on the title bar (Figure 1-56).**

2 **Click the Close button.**

PowerPoint closes and the Windows desktop displays. If you made changes to the presentation since your last save, a Microsoft PowerPoint dialog box displays the question, Do you wish to save the changes you made to Studying?. Click the Yes button to save the changes to the presentation before closing PowerPoint. Click the No button to quit PowerPoint without saving the changes. Click the Cancel button to return to the presentation.

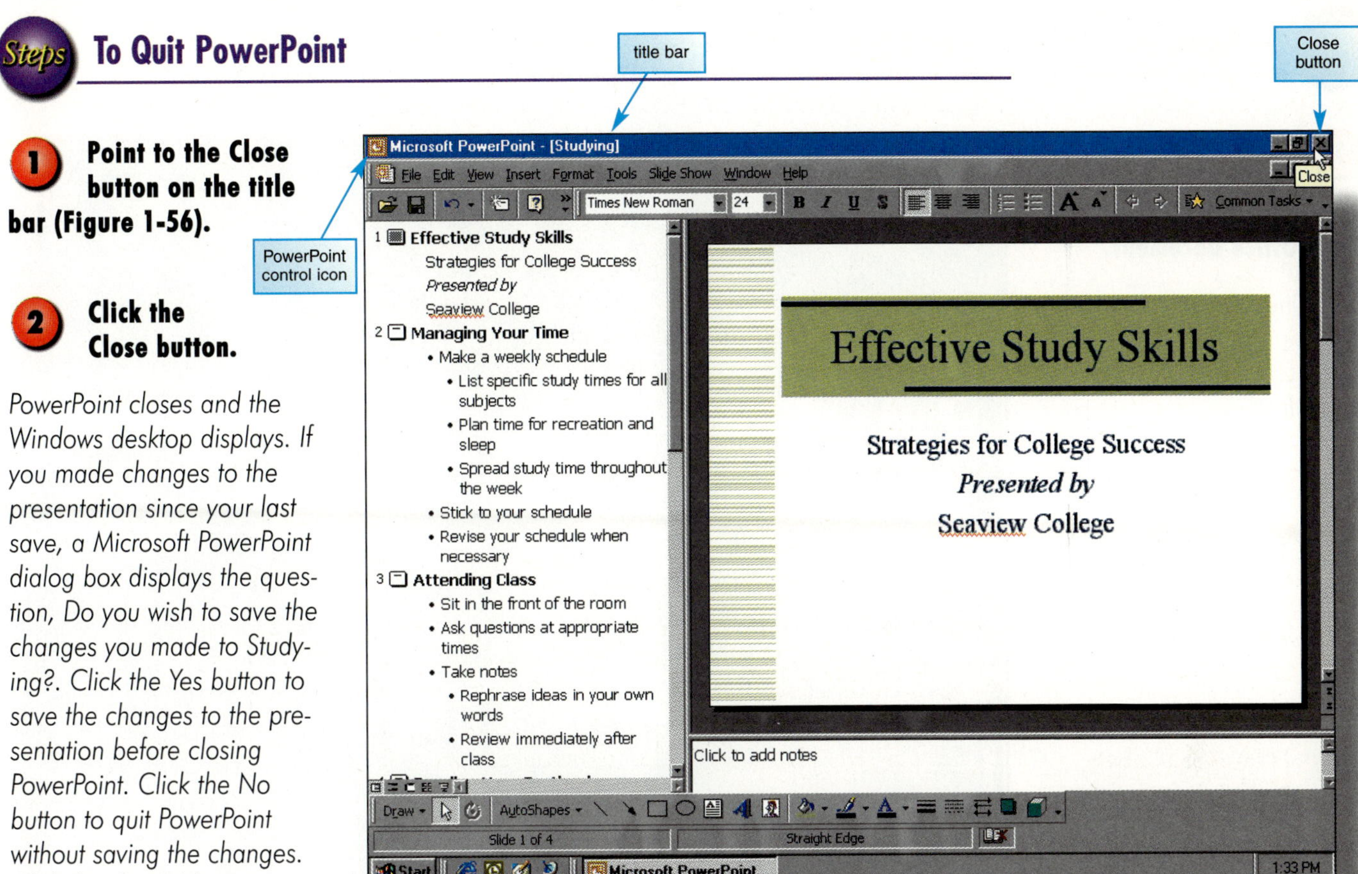

FIGURE 1-56

Other Ways

1. On title bar double-click PowerPoint control icon; or on title bar click PowerPoint control icon, click Close
2. On File menu click Exit
3. Press CTRL+Q or press ALT+F4

Opening a Presentation

Earlier, you saved the presentation on a floppy disk using the file name, Studying.ppt. Once you create and save a presentation, you may need to retrieve it from the floppy disk to make changes. For example, you may want to replace the design template or modify some text. Recall that a presentation is a PowerPoint document. Use the **Open Office Document command** to open an existing presentation.

Opening an Existing Presentation

Ensure that the floppy disk used to save Studying.ppt is in drive A. Then perform the steps on the next page to open the Studying presentation using the Open Office Document command on the Start menu.

To Open an Existing Presentation

1 Click the Start button on the taskbar and then point to Open Office Document.

The Windows Start menu displays (Figure 1-57). Open Office Document is highlighted.

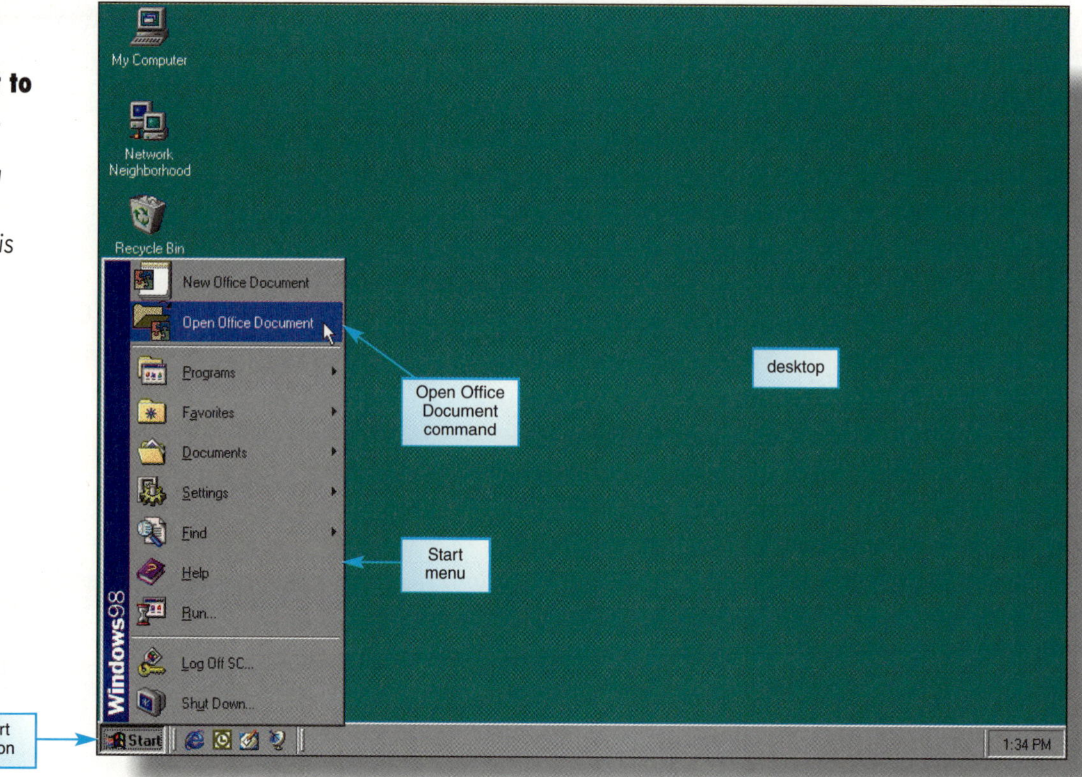

FIGURE 1-57

2 **Click Open Office Document. When the Open Office Document dialog box displays, if necessary, click the Look in box arrow and then click 3½ Floppy (A:) (see Figures 1-28 and 1-29 on page 1.30 to review this process).**

The Open Office Document dialog box displays (Figure 1-58). A list of existing files on drive A displays because your floppy disk is in drive A. Notice that Office Files displays in the Files of type box. The file, Studying, is highlighted. Your list of existing files may be different depending on the files saved on your floppy disk.

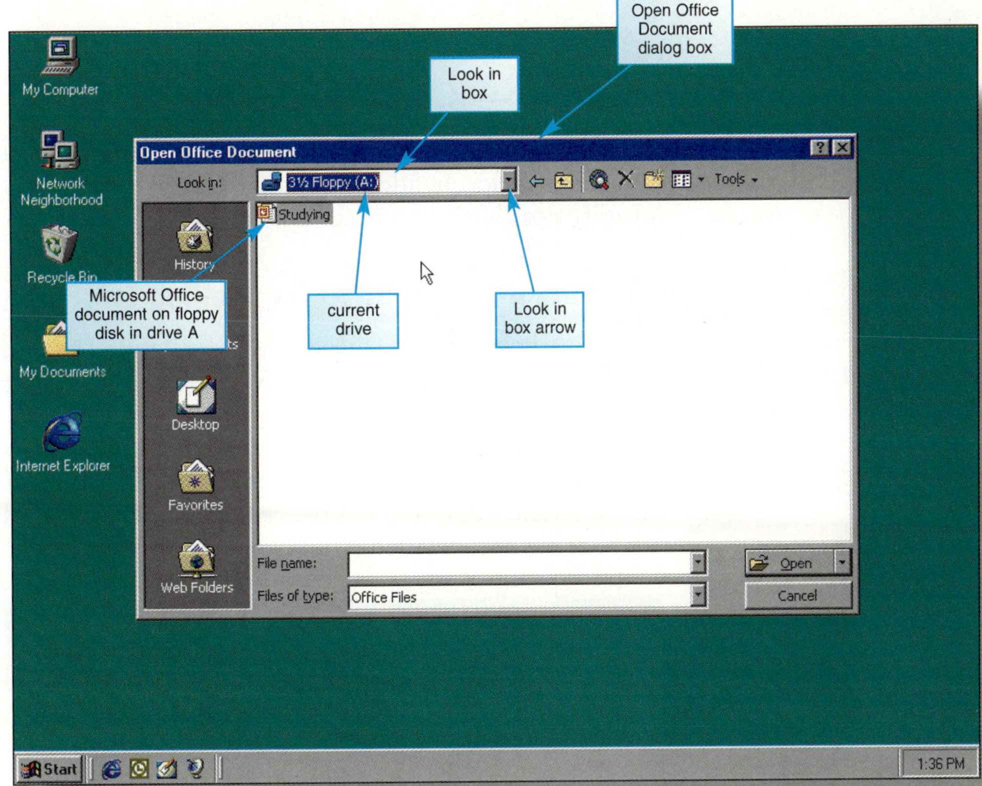

FIGURE 1-58

3 **Double-click Studying.**

PowerPoint starts, opens Studying.ppt from drive A into main memory, and displays the first slide on the screen. The presentation displays in normal view because PowerPoint opens a presentation in the same view in which it was saved.

Other Ways

1. Click Open Office Document button on Microsoft Office Shortcut Bar, click folder or drive name in Look in list, double-click document name
2. On Start menu click Documents, click document name

When you start PowerPoint and open Studying.ppt, this application and the file name display on a recessed button in the taskbar button area. When more than one application is open, you can switch between applications by clicking the button labeled with the name of the application to which you want to switch.

Checking a Presentation for Spelling and Consistency

After you create a presentation, you should check it visually for spelling errors and style consistency. In addition, you can use PowerPoint's Spelling and Style tools to identify possible misspellings and inconsistencies.

More About 2000

Dictionaries

Microsoft has partnered with publishing companies to produce the world's first global dictionary. More than 250 people worked to compile the three million English words contained in this work. The terms are used worldwide, for more than 80 percent of the world's computer-based communication uses the English language.

Checking a Presentation for Spelling Errors

PowerPoint checks your entire presentation for spelling mistakes using a standard dictionary contained in the Microsoft Office group. This dictionary is shared with the other Microsoft Office applications such as Word and Excel. A **custom dictionary** is available if you want to add special words such as proper names, cities, and acronyms. When checking a presentation for spelling errors, PowerPoint opens the standard dictionary and the custom dictionary file, if one exists. When a word displays in the Spelling dialog box, you perform one of the actions listed in Table 1-3.

Table 1-3 Summary of Spelling Checker Actions

FEATURE	DESCRIPTION
Ignore the word	Click Ignore when the word is spelled correctly but not found in the dictionaries. PowerPoint continues checking the rest of the presentation.
Ignore all occurrences of the word	Click Ignore All when the word is spelled correctly but not found in the dictionaries. PowerPoint ignores all occurrences of the word and continues checking the rest of the presentation.
Select a different spelling	Click the proper spelling of the word from the list in the Suggestions box. Click Change. PowerPoint corrects the word and continues checking the rest of the presentation.
Change all occurrences of the misspelling to a different spelling	Click the proper spelling of the word from the list in the Suggestions box. Click Change All. PowerPoint changes all occurrences of the misspelled word and continues checking the rest of the presentation.
Add a word to the custom dictionary	Click Add. PowerPoint opens the custom dictionary, adds the word, and continues checking the rest of the presentation.
View alternative spellings	Click Suggest. PowerPoint lists suggested spellings. Click the correct word from the Suggestions box or type the proper spelling. Then click Change. PowerPoint continues checking the rest of the presentation.
Add spelling error to AutoCorrect list	Click AutoCorrect. PowerPoint adds the spelling error and its correction to the AutoCorrect list. Any future misspelling of the word is corrected automatically as you type.
Close	Click Close to exit from the spelling checker and to return to the PowerPoint window.

The standard dictionary contains commonly used English words. It does not, however, contain proper names, abbreviations, technical terms, poetic contractions, or antiquated terms. PowerPoint treats words not found in the dictionaries as misspellings.

Starting the Spelling Checker

Start the Spelling checker by clicking the Spelling command on the Tools menu. Perform the following steps to start the Spelling checker and check your entire presentation.

Steps To Start the Spelling Checker

1 Double-click the move handle on the Standard toolbar. Point to the Spelling button on the Standard toolbar (Figure 1-59).

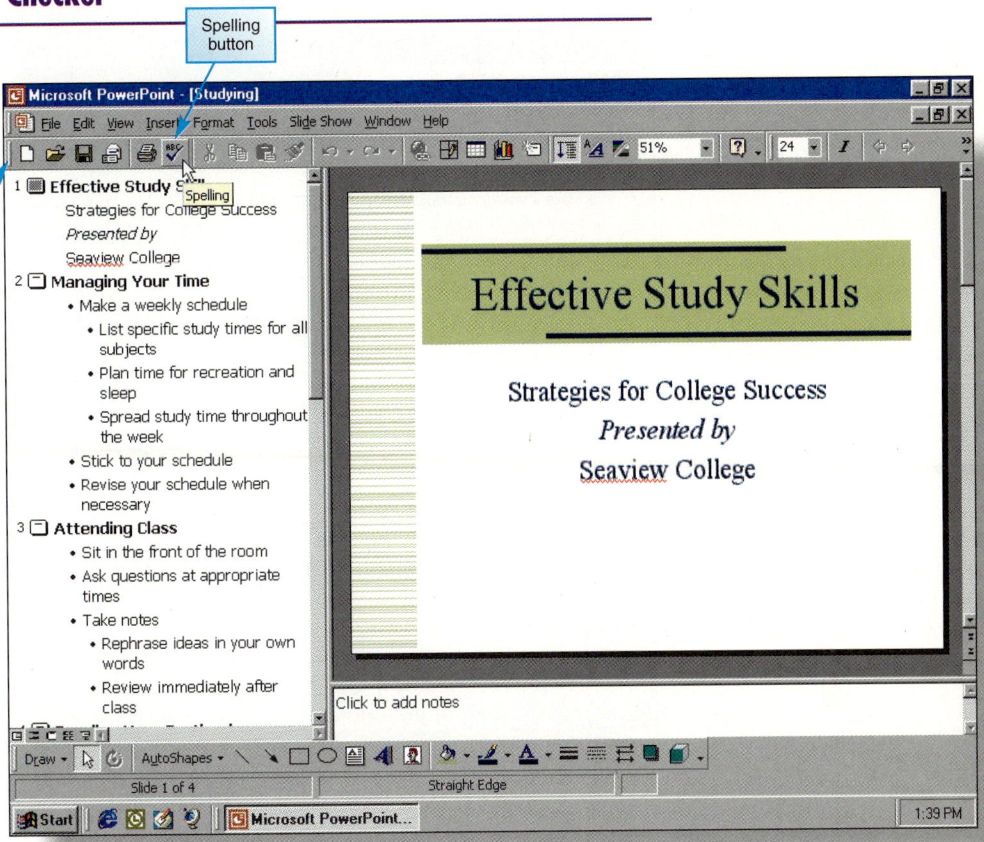

FIGURE 1-59

2 Click the Spelling button. When the Spelling dialog box displays, point to the Ignore button.

PowerPoint launches the Spelling checker and displays the Spelling dialog box (Figure 1-60). The word, Seaview, displays in the Not in Dictionary box. Depending on your custom dictionary, Seaview may not be recognized as a misspelled word.

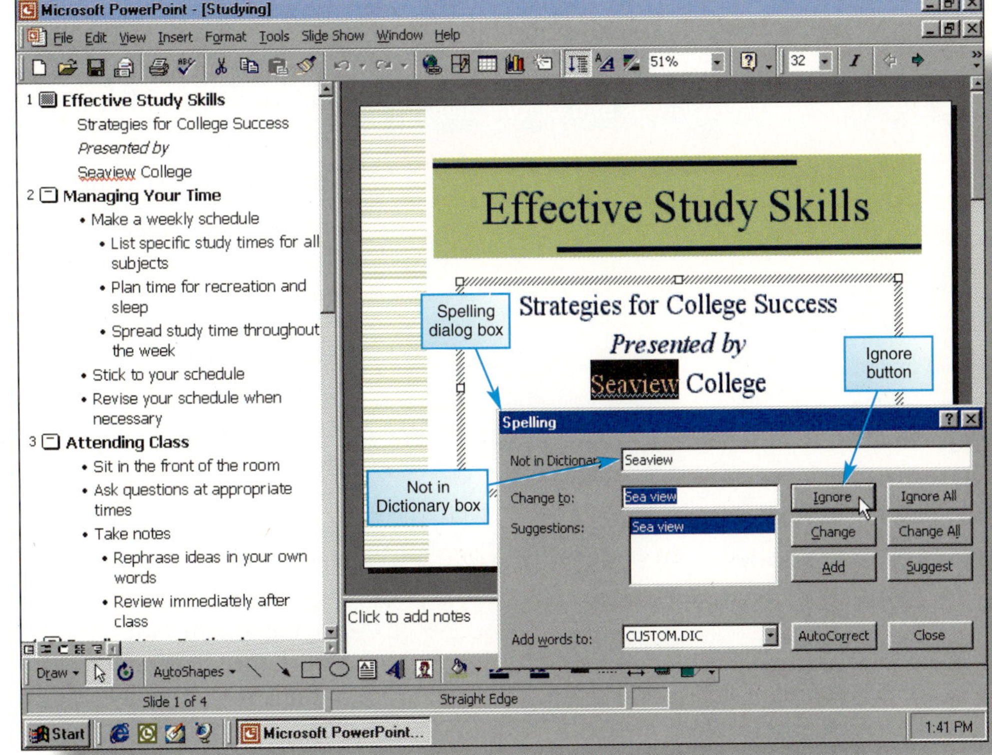

FIGURE 1-60

Click the Ignore button.

PowerPoint ignores the word, Seaview, and continues searching for additional misspelled words. PowerPoint may stop on additional words depending on your typing accuracy. When PowerPoint has checked all slides for misspellings, it displays the Microsoft PowerPoint dialog box informing you that the spelling check is complete (Figure 1-61).

Click the OK button.

PowerPoint closes the Spelling checker and returns to the current slide, Slide 1, or to the slide where a possible misspelled word appeared.

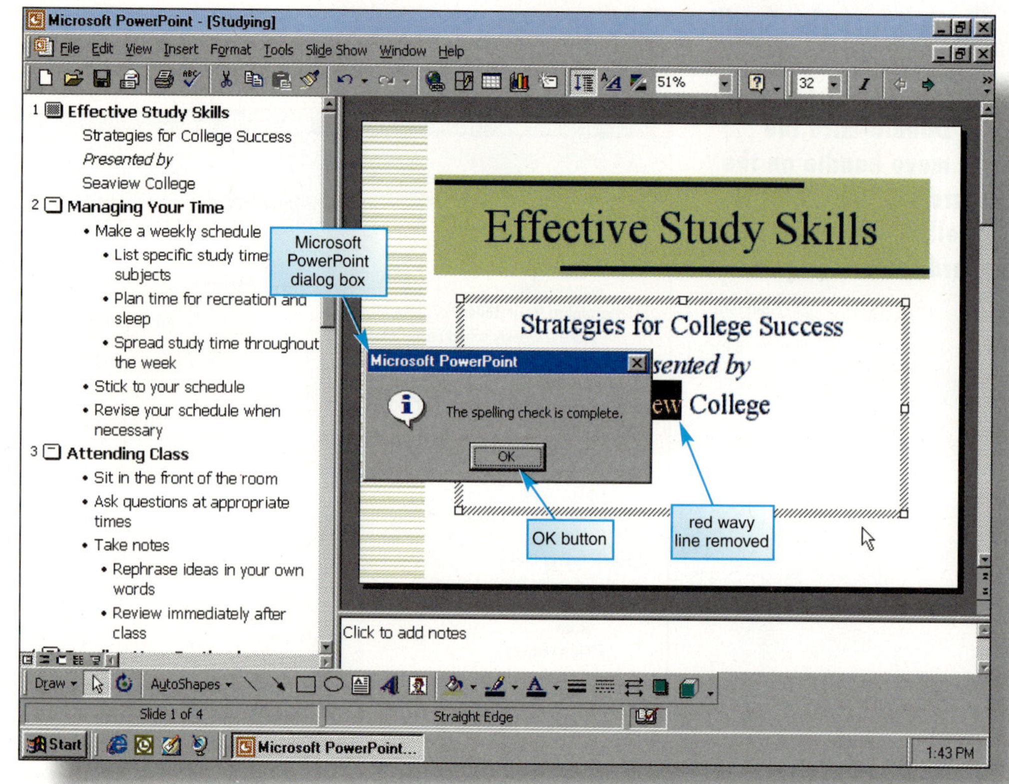

FIGURE 1-61

1. Press ALT+T, press S; when finished, press ENTER

The red wavy line under the word, Seaview, is gone because you instructed PowerPoint to ignore that word, which does not appear in the standard dictionary. You also could have added that word to the dictionary so it would not be flagged as a possible misspelled word in subsequent presentations you create using that word.

Table 1-4 Style Checker Options and Default Settings

OPTION	SETTING
CASE	
Slide title style	Title Case
Body text style	Sentence case
END PUNCTUATION	
Slide title punctuation	Paragraphs have punctuation
Body punctuation	Paragraphs have consistent punctuation
VISUAL CLARITY	
Number of fonts should not exceed	3
Title text size should be at least	36
Body text size should be at least	20
Number of bullets should not exceed	6
Number of lines per title should not exceed	2
Number of lines per bullet should not exceed	2

Checking a Presentation for Style Consistency

Recall that the Office Assistant may have generated a light bulb in the text placeholder when you were typing your title slide (see Figure 1-19 on page PP 1.23). The Office Assistant recognized you were starting to prepare a slide show and offered design tips. These tips can range from suggesting clip art to ensuring your presentation meets predefined criteria for style consistency. For example, in this Studying presentation the first word in each line of text begins with a capital letter, and each line does not end with a period. The Office Assistant automatically checks for case and end punctuation consistency and for visual clarity. It identifies problems on a screen by displaying a light bulb. You then can choose to correct or to ignore the elements PowerPoint flags. You can change the options to suit your design specifications. Table 1-4 identifies each option available in the Style checker and each default setting.

Correcting Errors

After creating a presentation and running the Spelling checker, you may find that you must make changes. Changes may be required because a slide contains an error, the scope of the presentation shifts, or the style is inconsistent. This section explains the types of errors that commonly occur when creating a presentation.

Correcting Errors

While PowerPoint's Spelling checker and Style checker are valuable tools, they are not infallible. You should proofread your presentation carefully by saying each word aloud and pointing to each word as you say it. Be mindful of commonly misused words such as its and it's, their and they're, and you're and your

Types of Corrections Made to Presentations

You generally make three types of corrections to text in a presentation: additions, deletions, and replacements.

- **Additions** — are necessary when you omit text from a slide and need to add it later. You may need to insert text in the form of a sentence, word, or single character. For example, you may want to add the rest of the presenter's first name on your title slide.
- **Deletions** — are required when text on a slide is incorrect or is no longer relevant to the presentation. For example, one of your slides may look cluttered. Therefore, you may want to remove one of the bulleted paragraphs to add more space.
- **Replacements** — are needed when you want to revise the text in your presentation. For example, you may want to substitute the word, their, for the word, there.

Editing text in PowerPoint is basically the same as editing text in a word process ing package. The following sections illustrate the most common changes made to text in a presentation.

Deleting Text

You can delete text using one of three methods. One is to use the BACKSPACE key to remove text just typed. The second is to position the insertion point to the left of the text you wish to delete and then press the DELETE key. The third method is to drag through the text you wish to delete and then press the DELETE key. (Use the third method when deleting large sections of text.)

Replacing Text in an Existing Slide

When you need to correct a word or phrase, you can replace the text by selecting the text to be replaced and then typing the new text. As soon as you press any key on the keyboard, the highlighted text is deleted and the new text displays.

PowerPoint inserts text to the left of the insertion point. The text to the right of the insertion point moves to the right (and shifts downward if necessary) to accommodate the added text.

Changing Line Spacing

The bulleted lists on Slides 2, 3, and 4 look crowded; yet, there is ample blank space that could be used to separate the paragraphs. You can adjust the spacing on each slide, but when several slides need to be changed, you should change the slide master. Each PowerPoint component (slides, title slides, audience handouts, and speaker's notes) has a **master**, which controls its appearance. Slides have two masters, title master and slide master. The **title master** controls the appearance of the title slide. The **slide master** controls the appearance of the other slides in your presentation.

Table 1-5 Summary of Slide Master Components

ELEMENT	DESCRIPTION
Background items	Any object other than the title object or text object. Typical items include borders and graphics such as a company logo, page number, date, and time.
Color scheme	A coordinated set of eight colors designed to complement each other. Color schemes consist of background color, line and text color, shadow color, title text color, object fill color, and three different accent colors.
Date	Inserts the special symbol used to print the date the presentation was printed.
Font	Defines the appearance and shape of letters, numbers, and special characters.
Font size	Specifies the size of the characters on the screen. Character size is gauged by a measurement system called points. A single point is about 1/72 of an inch in height. Thus, a character with a point size of eighteen is about 18/72 of an inch in height.
Font style	Font styles include plain, italic, bold, shadowed, and underlined. Text may have more than one font style at a time.
Slide number	Inserts the special symbol used to print the slide number.
Text alignment	Position of text in a paragraph is left-aligned, right-aligned, centered, or justified. Justified text is proportionally spaced across the object.
Time	Inserts the special symbol used to print the time the presentation was printed.

Each design template has a specially designed slide master. If you select a design template but want to change one of its components, you can override that component by changing the slide master. Any change to the slide master results in changing every slide in the presentation, except the title slide. For example, if you change the line spacing to .5 inches before each paragraph on the slide master, each slide (except the title slide) changes line spacing after each paragraph to .5 inches. The slide master components more frequently changed are listed in Table 1-5.

Additionally, each view has its own master. You can access the master by holding down the SHIFT key while clicking the appropriate view button. For example, holding down the SHIFT key and clicking the Slide View button displays the slide master. To exit a master, click the view button to which you wish to return. To return to slide view, for example, click the Slide View button.

Displaying the Slide Master

Before you can change line spacing on the slide master, you first must display it. Perform the following steps to display the slide master.

Steps To Display the Slide Master

1 Click the Next Slide button on the slide pane to display Slide 2. Press and hold down the SHIFT key and then point to the Slide View button.

When you hold down the SHIFT key, the ScreenTip displays Slide Master View (Figure 1-62).

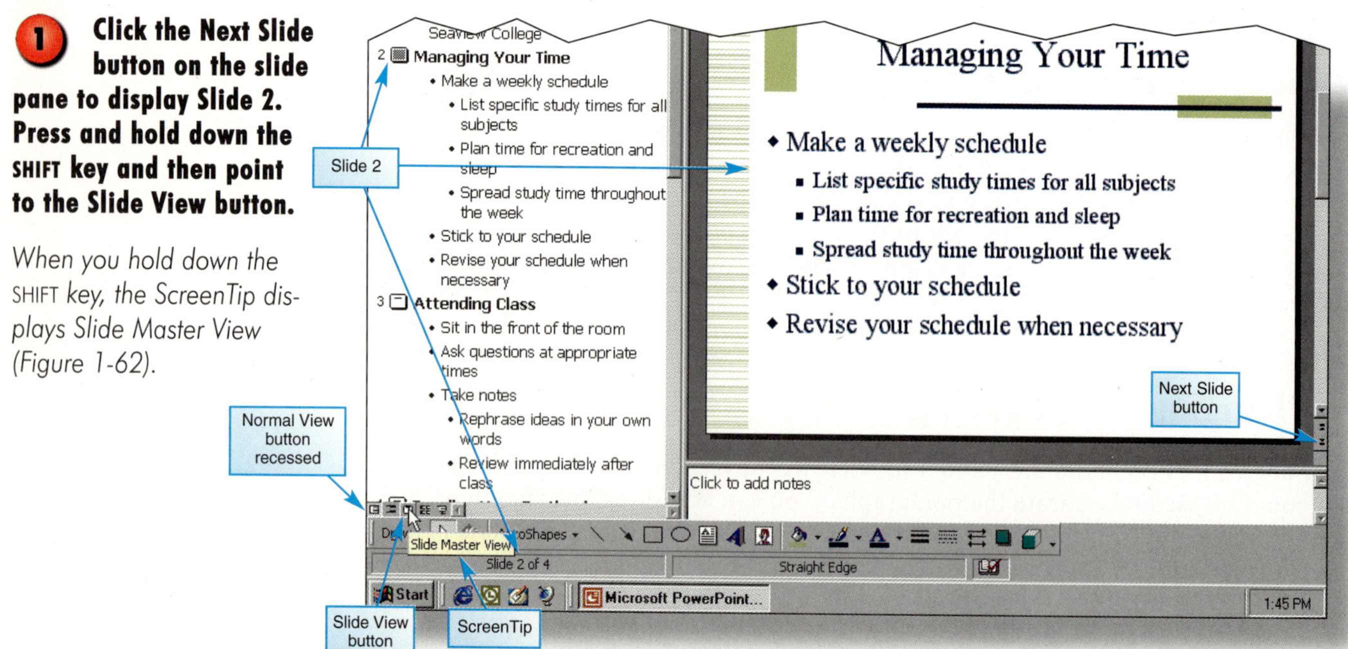

FIGURE 1-62

2 **While holding down the SHIFT key, click the Slide Master View button. Then release the SHIFT key.**

The slide master and Master toolbar display (Figure 1-63).

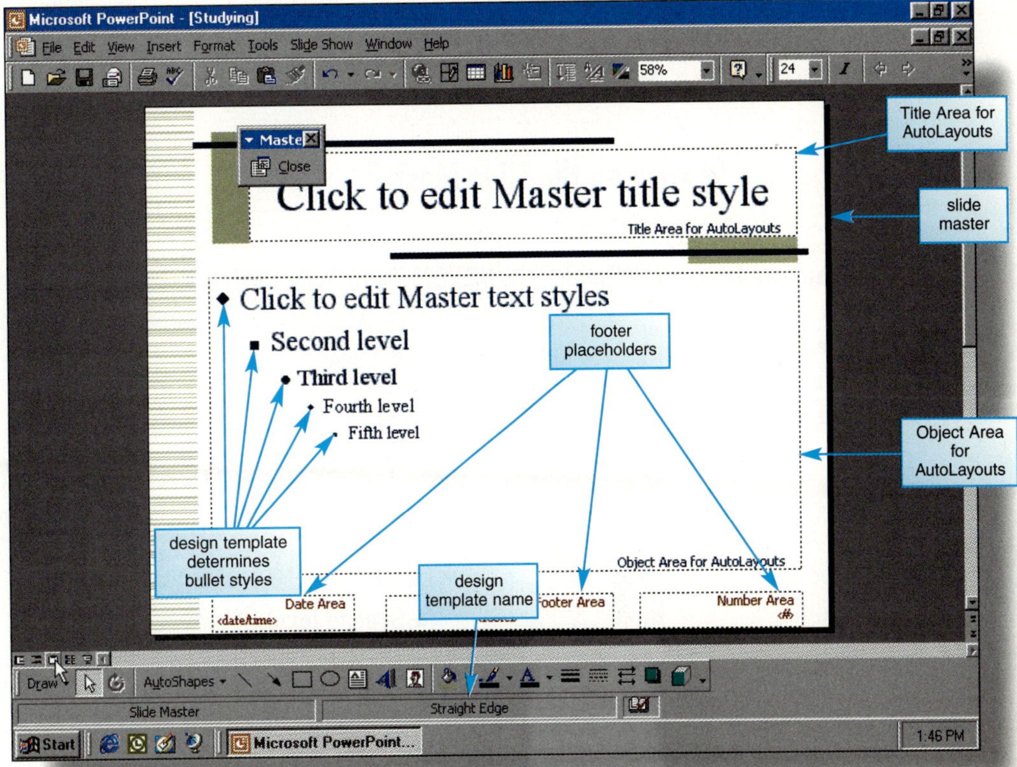

FIGURE 1-63

1. On View menu point to Master, click Slide Master

Changing Line Spacing on the Slide Master

Change line spacing by clicking the Line Spacing command on the Format menu. When you click the **Line Spacing command**, the Line Spacing dialog box displays. The Line Spacing dialog box contains three boxes, Line spacing, Before paragraph, and After paragraph, which allow you to adjust line spacing within a paragraph, before a paragraph, and after a paragraph, respectively.

Before paragraph line spacing is controlled by establishing the number of units before a paragraph. Units are either lines or points; lines are the default unit. Points may be selected by clicking the down arrow next to the Before paragraph box (see Figure 1-66 on page PP 1.61). Recall from page PP 1.24 that a single point is about 1/72 of an inch in height.

The Line spacing, Before paragraph, and After paragraph boxes each contain an amount of space box and a unit of measure box. To change the amount of space displaying between paragraphs, click the amount of space box up arrow or down arrow in the Line spacing box. To change the amount of space displaying before a paragraph, as you did in this project, click the amount of space box up arrow or down arrow in the Before paragraph box. To change the amount of space displaying after a paragraph, click the amount of space box up arrow or down arrow in the After paragraph box. To change the unit of measure from Lines to Points in the Line Spacing dialog box, click the arrow next to the appropriate unit of measure box and then click Points in the list.

In this project, you change the number in the amount of space box to increase the amount of space that displays before every paragraph, except the first paragraph, on every slide. For example, increasing the amount of space box to 0.5 lines increases the amount of space that displays before each paragraph.

Line Spacing

Blank space on a slide can be advantageous. The absence of text, called white space, helps the viewer focus attention on the presenter. Do not be afraid to increase line spacing to give your text some breathing room.

The first paragraph on every slide, however, does not change because of its position in the Object Area placeholder. Perform the following steps to change the line spacing.

To Change Line Spacing on the Slide Master

1 **Click the bulleted paragraph in the Object Area placeholder labeled, Click to edit Master text styles.**

The insertion point displays at the point you clicked (Figure 1-64). The Object Area placeholder is selected.

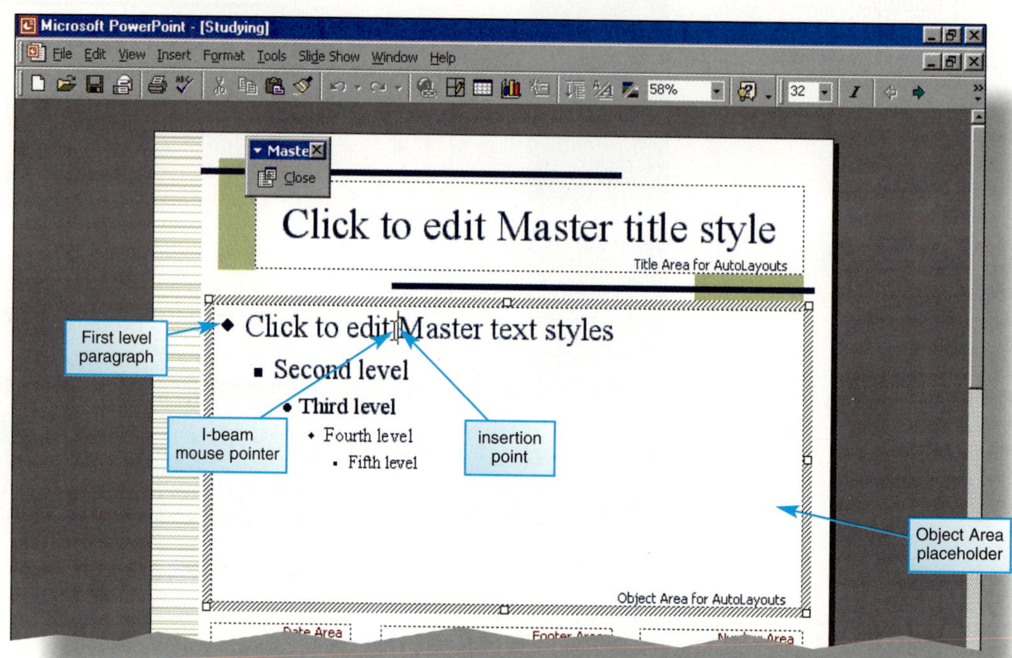

FIGURE 1-64

2 **Click Format on the menu bar and then point to Line Spacing. (Remember that you might have to wait a few seconds for the entire menu to display.)**

The Format menu displays (Figure 1-65).

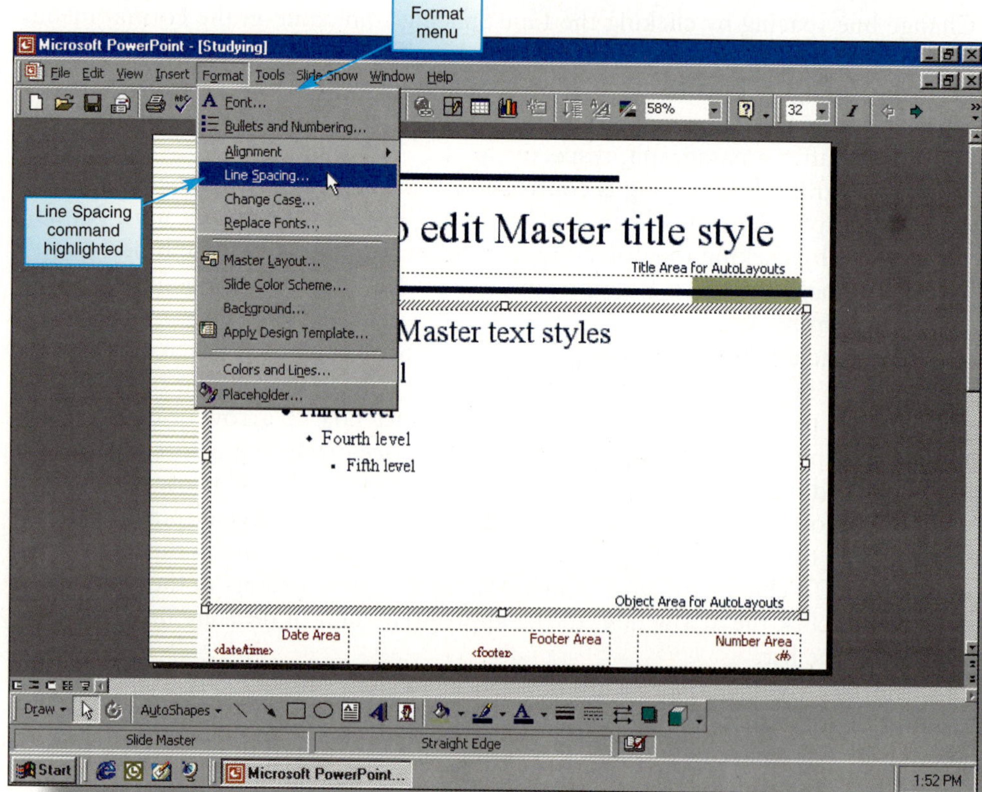

FIGURE 1-65

3 Click Line Spacing. Point to the Before Paragraph amount of space box up arrow.

PowerPoint displays the Line Spacing dialog box (Figure 1-66). The default Before paragraph line spacing is set at 0.2 Lines.

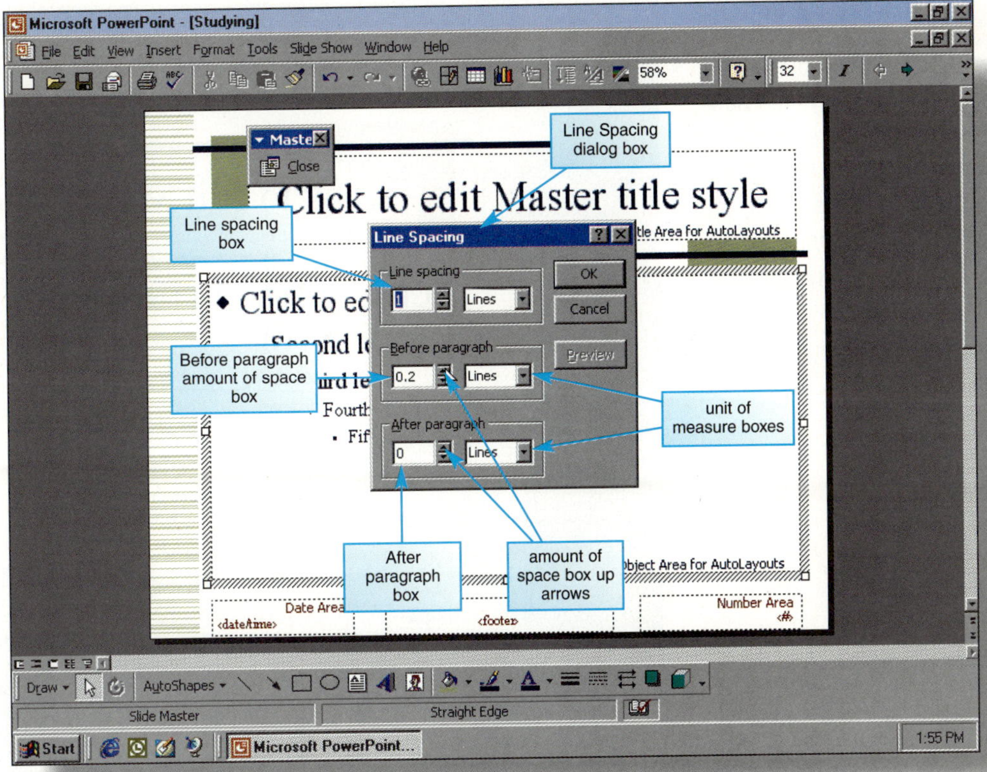

FIGURE 1-66

4 Click the Before paragraph amount of space box up arrow six times.

The Before paragraph amount of space box displays 0.5 (Figure 1-67). The Preview button is available after this change is made in the Line Spacing dialog box. If you click the Preview button, PowerPoint temporarily updates your presentation with the new amount of space setting. This new setting is not actually applied until you click the OK button.

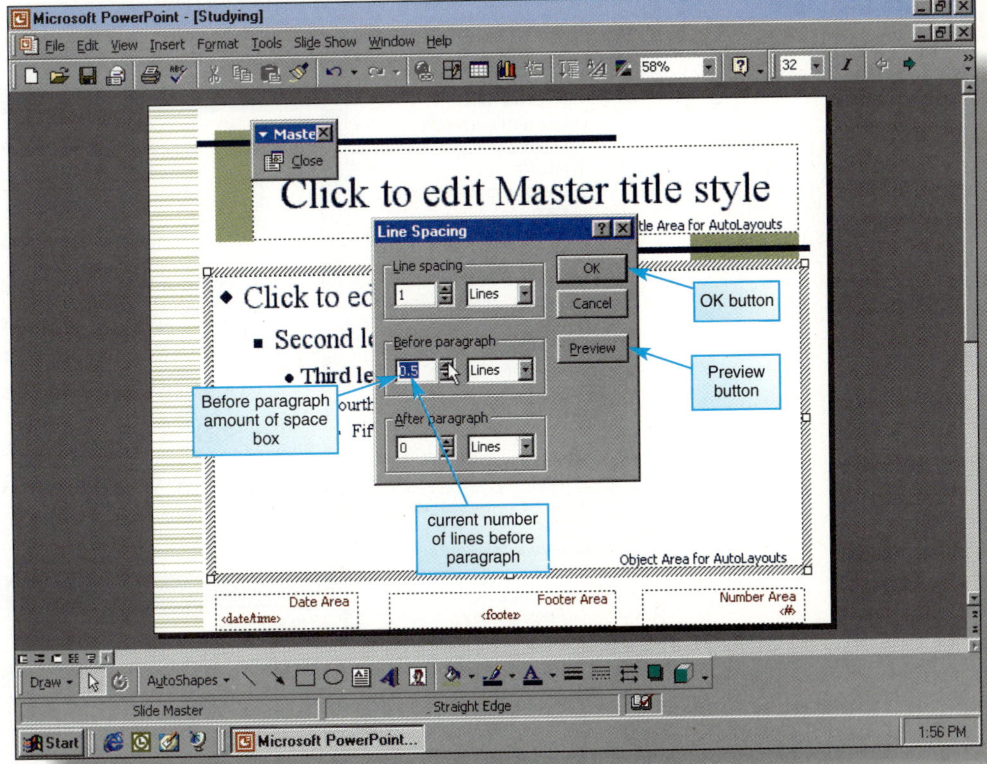

FIGURE 1-67

5 **Click the OK button.**

The slide master Object Area placeholder displays the new line spacing (Figure 1-68). Depending on the video drivers installed, the spacing on your screen may appear slightly different than this figure.

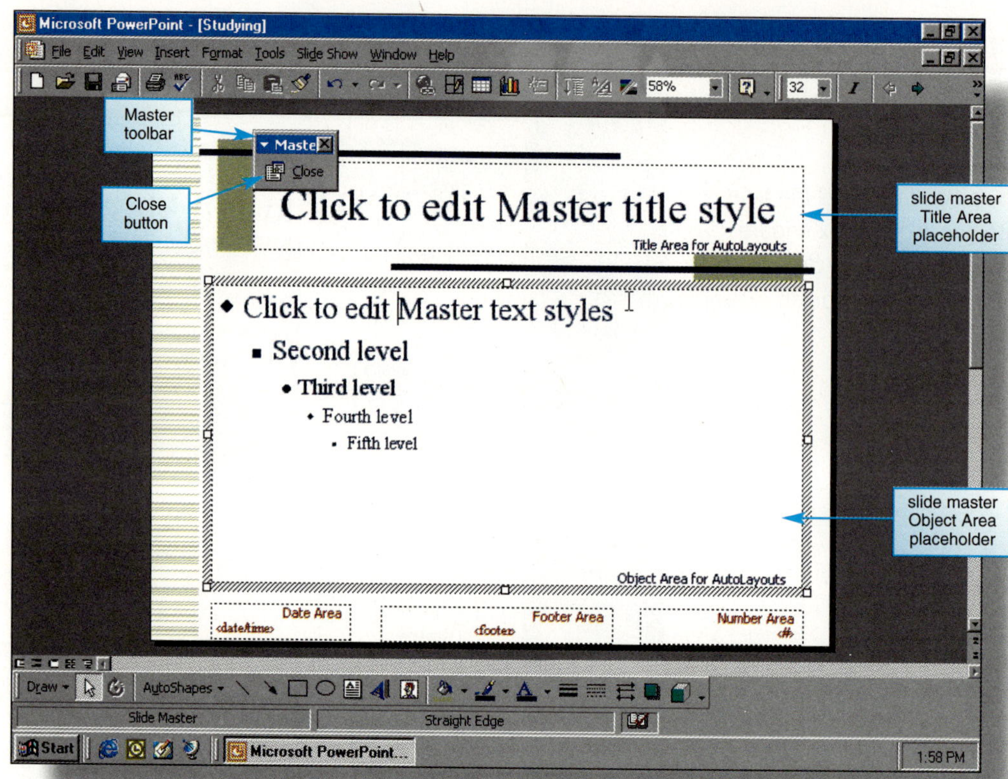

FIGURE 1-68

6 **Click the Close button on the Master toolbar to return to normal view.**

Slide 2 displays with the Before paragraph line spacing set to 0.5 Lines (Figure 1-69).

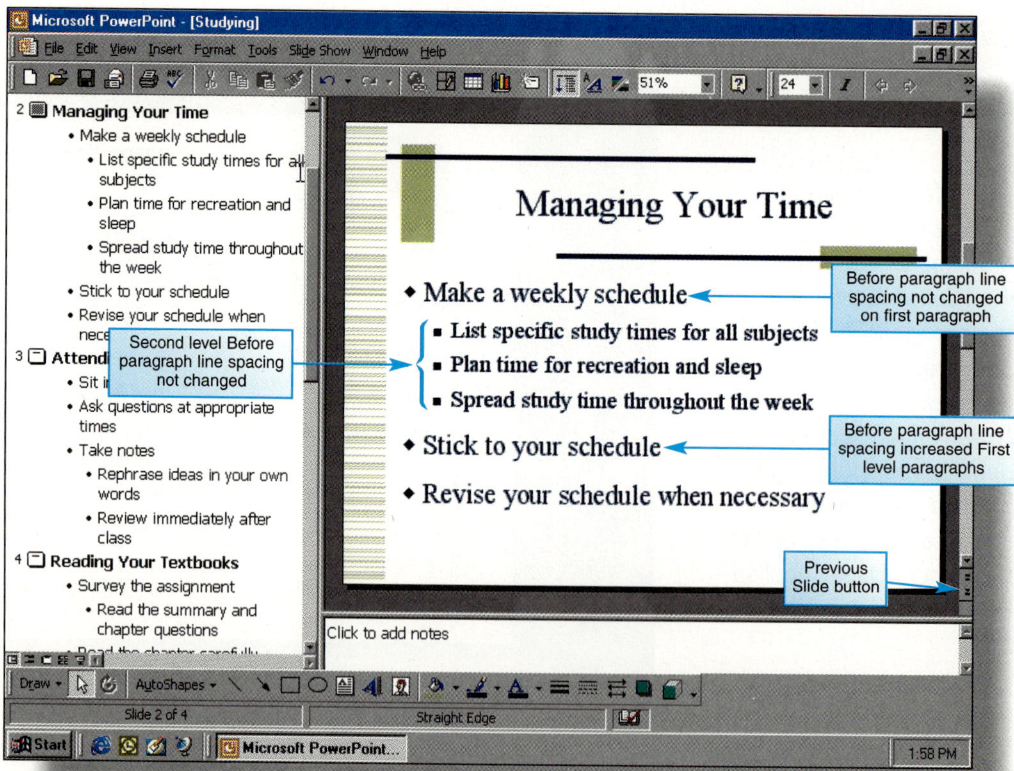

FIGURE 1-69

To display line spacing changes without making them permanent, click the Preview button in the Line Spacing dialog box. If you want to close the Line Spacing dialog box without applying the changes, click the Cancel button.

The placeholder at the top of the slide master (Figure 1-68) is used to edit the Master title style. The Object Area placeholder under the Master Title Area placeholder is used to edit the Master text styles. Here you make changes to the various bullet levels. Changes can be made to line spacing, bullet font, text and line color, alignment, and text shadow.

Table 1-6 Appearance in Black and White View

OBJECT	DISPLAY
Text	Black
Text shadows	Hidden
Embossing	Hidden
Fills	Grayscale
Frame	Black
Pattern fills	Grayscale
Lines	Black
Object shadows	Grayscale
Bitmaps	Grayscale
Slide backgrounds	White

Displaying a Presentation in Black and White

You want to print handouts of your presentation and create overhead transparencies. The **Grayscale Preview button** allows you to display the presentation in black and white before you print. Table 1-6 identifies how PowerPoint objects display in black and white.

Perform the following steps to display the presentation in black and white.

To Display a Presentation in Black and White

1 Click the Previous Slide button to display Slide 1. Point to the Grayscale Preview button on the Standard toolbar.

Slide 1 displays. The Grayscale Preview ScreenTip displays (Figure 1-70).

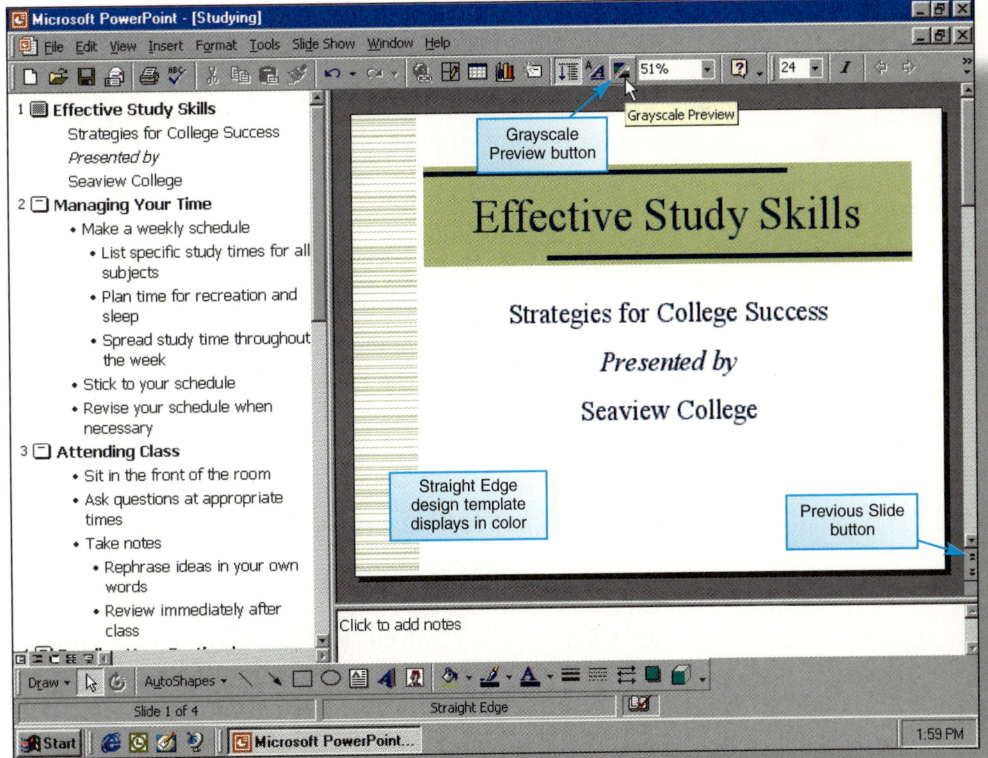

FIGURE 1-70

Click the Grayscale Preview button.

Slide 1 displays in black and white (Figure 1-71). The Grayscale Preview button is recessed on the Standard toolbar.

3 Click the Next Slide button three times to view all slides in the presentation in black and white.

Click the Grayscale Preview button.

Slide 4 displays with the default Straight Edge color scheme.

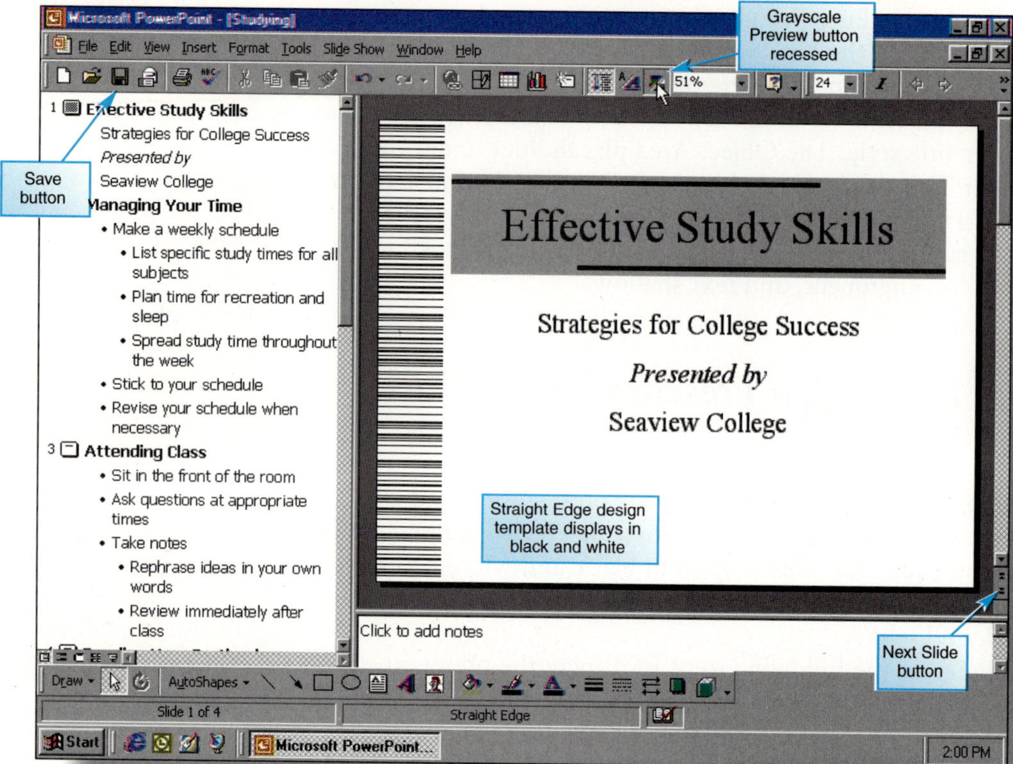

FIGURE 1-71

1. On View menu click Black and White

After you view the text objects in your presentation in black and white, you can make any changes that will enhance printouts produced from a black and white printer or photocopier.

Printing a Presentation

After you create a presentation, you often want to print it. A printed version of the presentation is called a **hard copy**, or **printout**. The first printing of the presentation is called a **rough draft**. The rough draft allows you to proofread the presentation to check for errors and readability. After correcting errors, you print the final copy of your presentation.

Saving a Presentation Before Printing

Prior to printing your presentation, you should save your work in the event you experience difficulties with the printer. You occasionally may encounter system problems that can be resolved only by restarting the computer. In such an instance, you will need to reopen your presentation. As a precaution, always save your presentation before you print. Perform the following steps to save the presentation before printing.

TO SAVE A PRESENTATION BEFORE PRINTING

1. Verify that your floppy disk is in drive A.
2. Click the Save button on the Standard toolbar.

All changes made after your last save now are saved on a floppy disk.

Printing the Presentation

After saving the presentation, you are ready to print. Clicking the **Print button** on the Standard toolbar causes PowerPoint to print all slides in the presentation. Perform the following steps to print the presentation slides.

To Print a Presentation

1. **Ready the printer according to the printer instructions. Then click the Print button on the Standard toolbar.**

The printer icon in the tray status area on the taskbar indicates a print job is processing (Figure 1-72). After several moments, the slide show begins printing on the printer. When the presentation is finished printing, the printer icon in the tray status area on the taskbar no longer displays.

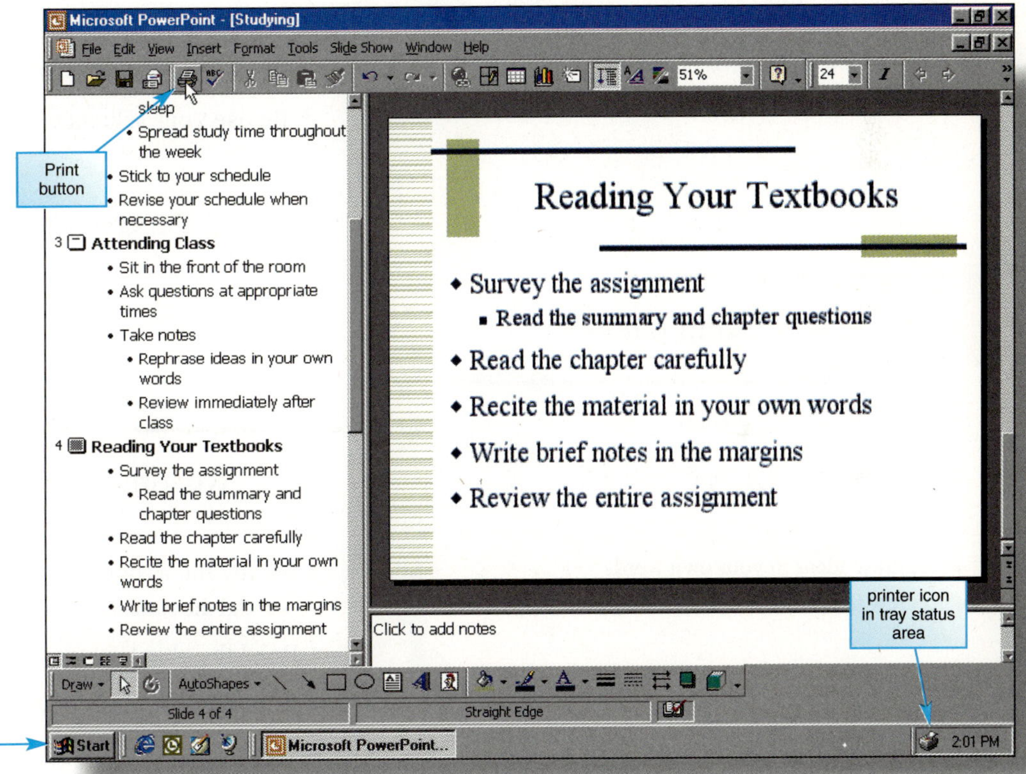

FIGURE 1-72

2 **When the printer stops, retrieve the printouts of the slides.**

The presentation, Studying, prints on four pages (Figures 1-73a through 1-73d).

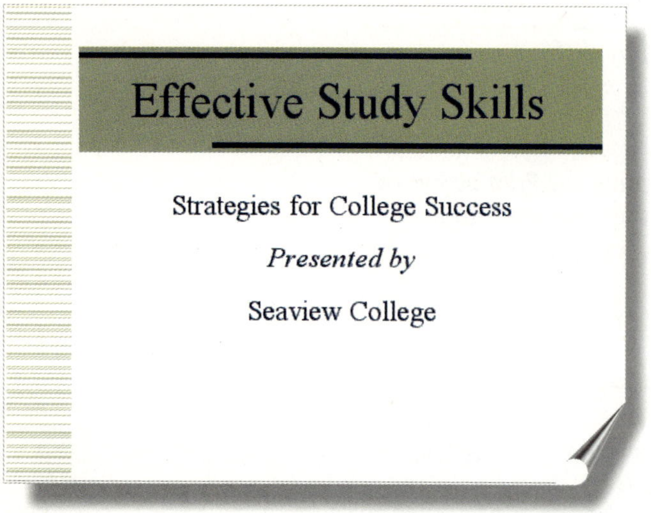

Effective Study Skills

Strategies for College Success

Presented by

Seaview College

(a) Slide 1

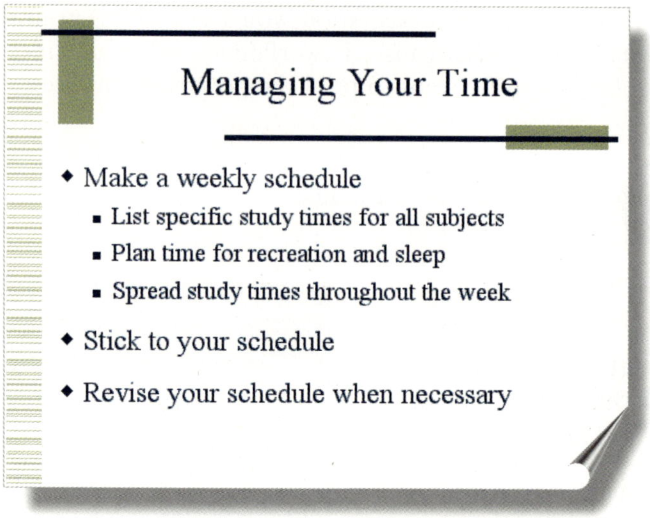

Managing Your Time

- Make a weekly schedule
  - List specific study times for all subjects
  - Plan time for recreation and sleep
  - Spread study times throughout the week
- Stick to your schedule
- Revise your schedule when necessary

(b) Slide 2

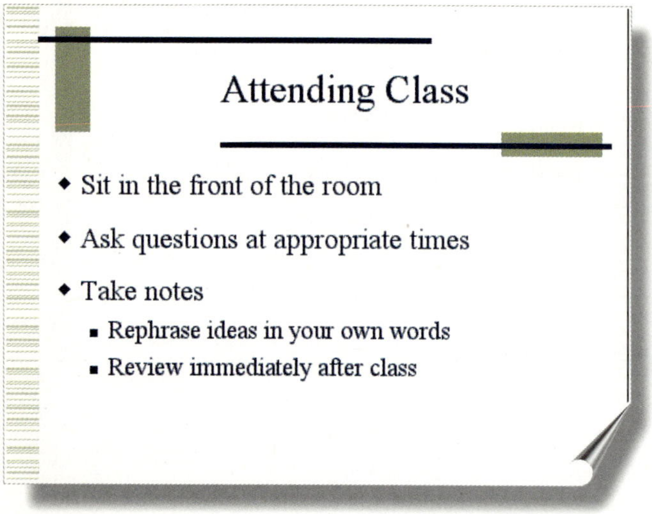

Attending Class

- Sit in the front of the room
- Ask questions at appropriate times
- Take notes
  - Rephrase ideas in your own words
  - Review immediately after class

(c) Slide 3

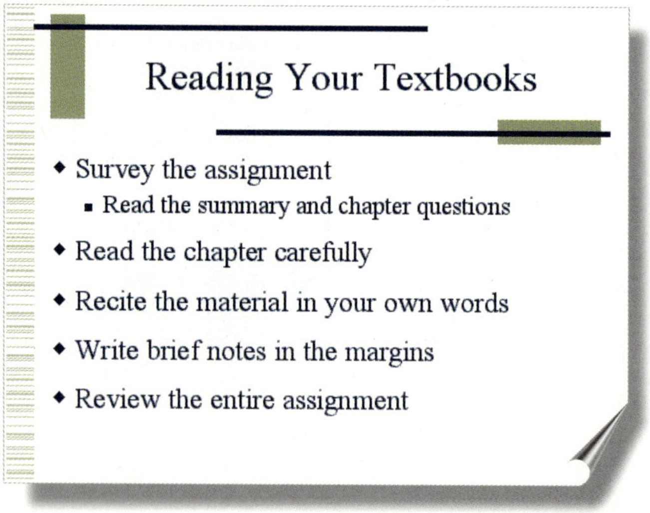

Reading Your Textbooks

- Survey the assignment
  - Read the summary and chapter questions
- Read the chapter carefully
- Recite the material in your own words
- Write brief notes in the margins
- Review the entire assignment

(d) Slide 4

FIGURE 1-73

1. On File menu click Print
2. Press CTRL+P or press CTRL+SHIFT+F12

You can click the printer icon next to the clock in the tray status area on the taskbar to obtain information about the presentations printing on your printer and to delete files in the print queue that are waiting to be printed.

Making a Transparency

Now that you have printed handouts, you want to make overhead transparencies. You can make transparencies using one of several devices. One device is a printer attached to your computer, such as an ink-jet printer or a laser printer. Transparencies produced on a printer may be in black and white or color, depending on the printer. Another device is a photocopier. Because each of these devices requires a special transparency film, check the user's manual for the film requirement of your specific device, or ask your instructor.

PowerPoint Help System

You can get answers to PowerPoint questions at any time by using the **PowerPoint Help system**. Used properly, this form of online assistance can increase your productivity and reduce your frustrations by minimizing the time you spend learning how to use PowerPoint. The following section shows how to get answers to your questions using the Office Assistant.

More About 2000

Help

In previous versions of Microsoft PowerPoint and other software, users had to spend hours pouring through thick reference manuals to find relevant information. This task was particularly difficult for novice computer users. Today, the Office Assistant helps you search for relevant information instantly and easily.

Using the Office Assistant

The **Office Assistant** answers your questions and suggests more efficient ways to complete a task. With the Office Assistant active, for example, you can type a question, word, or phrase in a text box and the Office Assistant provides immediate help on the subject. Also, as you create a worksheet, the Office Assistant accumulates tips that suggest more efficient ways to do the tasks you completed while building a presentation, such as formatting, printing, and saving. This tip feature is part of the **IntelliSense™ technology** that is built into PowerPoint, which understands what you are trying to do and suggests better ways to do it. When the light bulb displays above the Office Assistant, click it to see a tip.

The following steps show how to use the Office Assistant to obtain information on formatting a presentation.

Steps To Obtain Help Using the Office Assistant

1 If the Office Assistant is not on the screen, click Show the Office Assistant on the Help menu. With the Office Assistant on the screen, click it. Type `how do i take meeting minutes` **in the What would you like to do? text box in the Office Assistant balloon. Point to the Search button (Figure 1-74).**

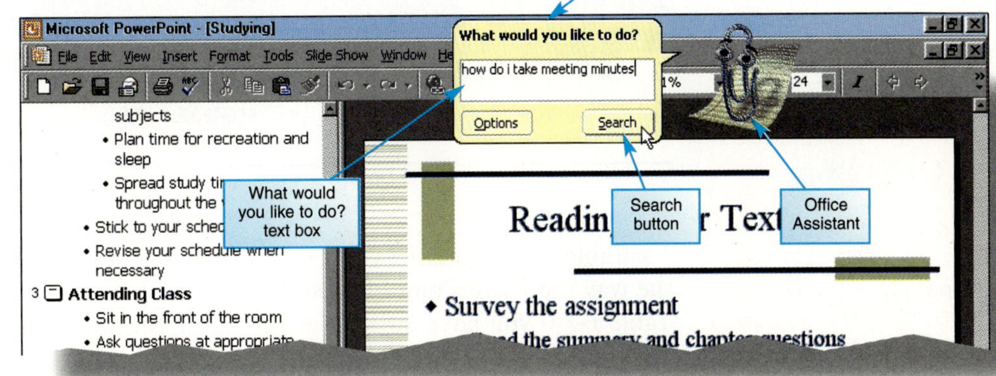

FIGURE 1-74

2 **Click the Search button. Point to the topic Take notes or meeting minutes during a slide show in the Office Assistant balloon.**

The Office Assistant displays a list of topics relating to the question how do i take meeting minutes (Figure 1-75). The mouse pointer changes to a hand.

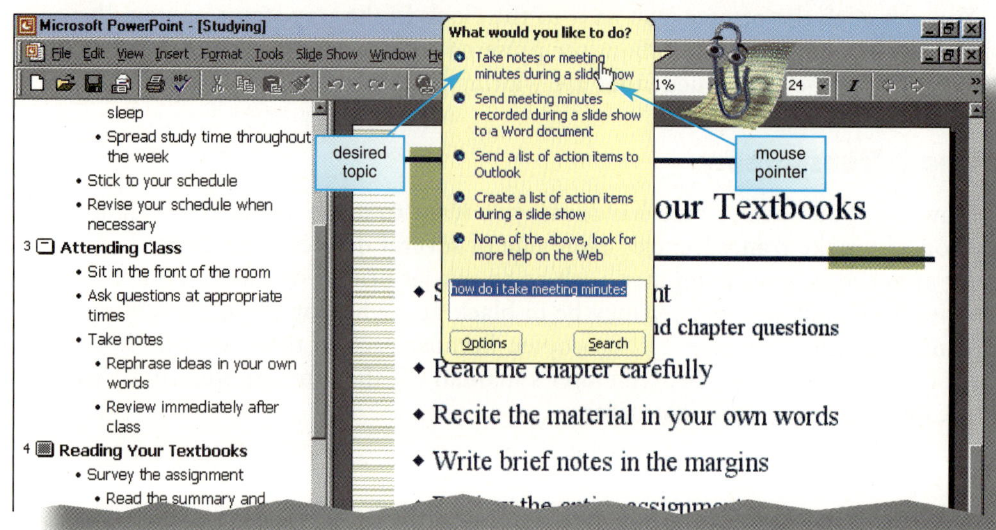

FIGURE 1-75

3 **Click Take notes or meeting minutes during a slide show.**

The Office Assistant displays a Microsoft PowerPoint Help window that provides Help information on taking notes or meeting minutes during a slide show (Figure 1-76).

4 **Click the Close button on the Microsoft PowerPoint Help window title bar.**

The Microsoft PowerPoint Help window closes, and the worksheet again is active.

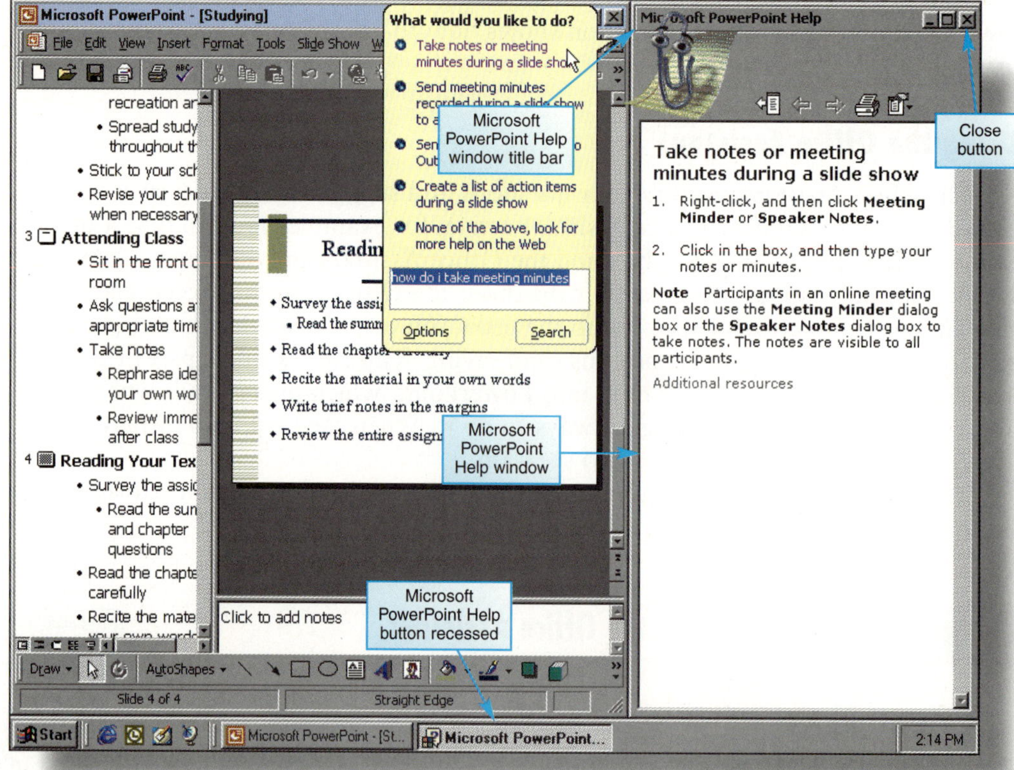

FIGURE 1-76

Other Ways

1. With Office Assistant on, click Microsoft PowerPoint Help button; or on Help menu click Microsoft PowerPoint Help
2. Press F1

Table 1-7 summarizes the eight categories of help available to you. Because of the way the PowerPoint Help system works, please review the right-most column of Table 1-7 if you have difficulties activating the desired category of help.

Table 1-7 PowerPoint Help System

TYPE	DESCRIPTION	HOW TO ACTIVATE	TURNING THE OFFICE ASSISTANT ON AND OFF
Answer Wizard	Similar to the Office Assistant in that it answers questions that you type in your own words.	Click the Microsoft PowerPoint Help button on the Standard toolbar. If necessary, maximize the Help window by double-clicking its title bar. Click the Answer Wizard tab.	If the Office Assistant displays, right-click it, click Options, click the Use the Office Assistant check box, and then click the OK button.
Contents sheet	Groups Help topics by general categories. Use when you know only the general category of the topic in question.	Click the Office Assistant button on the Standard toolbar. If necessary, maximize the Help window by double-clicking its title bar. Click the Contents tab.	If the Office Assistant displays, right-click it, click Options, click the Use the Office Assistant check box, and then click the OK button.
Detect and Repair	Automatically finds and fixes errors in the application.	Click Detect and Repair on the Help menu.	
Hardware and Software Information	Shows Product ID and allows access to system information and technical support information.	Click About Microsoft PowerPoint on the Help menu and then click the System Information or Technical Information button.	
Index sheet	Similar to an index in a book; use when you know exactly what you want.	Click the Microsoft PowerPoint Help button on the Standard toolbar. If necessary, maximize the Help window by double-clicking its title bar. Click the Index tab.	If the Office Assistant displays, right-click it, click Options, click Use the Office Assistant check box, and then click the OK button.
Office Assistant	Answers questions that you type in your own words, offers tips, and provides Help for a variety of PowerPoint features.	Click the Microsoft PowerPoint Help button on the Standard toolbar.	If the Office Assistant does not display, close the Microsoft PowerPoint Help window and then click Show the Office Assistant on the Help menu.
Office on the Web	Accesses technical resources and download free product enhancements on the Web.	Click Office on the Web on the Help menu.	
Question Mark button and What's This? command	Identifies unfamiliar items on the screen.	Click the Question Mark button and then click an item in the dialog box. Click What's This? on the Help menu, and then click an item on the screen.	

You can use the Office Assistant to search for Help on any topic concerning PowerPoint. For additional information on using the PowerPoint Help system, see Appendix A.

More About 2000

Quick Reference

For a table that lists how to complete the tasks covered in this book using the mouse, menu, shortcut menu, and keyboard, visit the Shelly Cashman Series Office Web page (www.scsite.com/off2000/qr.htm) and then click Microsoft PowerPoint 2000.

Quitting PowerPoint

Project 1 is complete. The final task is to close the presentation and quit PowerPoint. Perform the following steps to quit PowerPoint.

TO QUIT POWERPOINT

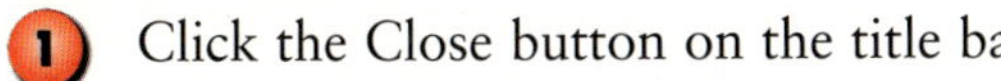

1. Click the Close button on the title bar.
2. If prompted to save the presentation before quitting PowerPoint, click the Yes button in the Microsoft PowerPoint dialog box.

CASE PERSPECTIVE SUMMARY

Your Effective Study Skills PowerPoint slide show should help Dr. Martinez and the counseling staff present essential college survival skills to incoming freshmen attending orientation sessions at your school. The four slides display the key study habits all students need to succeed throughout college. The title slide identifies the topic of the presentation, and the next three slides give key pointers regarding time management, class attendance, and textbook usage. The counselors will use your overhead transparencies to organize their speeches, and the students will keep handouts of your slides for future reference.

Project Summary

Project 1 introduced you to starting PowerPoint and creating a multi-level bulleted list presentation. You learned about PowerPoint design templates, objects, and attributes. This project illustrated how to create an interesting introduction to a presentation by changing the text font style to italic and increasing font size on the title slide. Completing these tasks, you saved your presentation. Then, you created three multi-level bulleted list slides to explain how to study effectively in college. Next, you learned how to view the presentation in slide show view. Then you learned how to quit PowerPoint and how to open an existing presentation. You used the Spelling checker to search for spelling errors and learned how the Office Assistant Style checker identifies inconsistencies in design specifications. Using the slide master, you quickly adjusted the Before paragraph line spacing on every slide to make better use of white space. You learned how to display the presentation in black and white. Then, you learned how to print hard copies of your slides in order to make overhead transparencies. Finally, you learned how to use the PowerPoint Help system.

What You Should Know

Having completed this project, you now should be able to perform the following tasks:

- Add a New Slide Using the Bulleted List AutoLayout *(PP 1.32)*
- Add a New Slide with the Same AutoLayout *(PP 1.40)*
- Change Line Spacing on the Slide Master *(PP 1.60)*
- Change the Text Font Style to Italic *(PP 1.27)*
- Choose a Design Template *(PP 1.18)*
- Complete Slide 3 *(PP 1.40)*
- Create Slide 4 *(PP 1.41)*
- Display a Presentation in Black and White *(PP 1.63)*
- Display the Formatting Toolbar in its Entirety *(PP 1.17)*
- Display the Popup Menu and Go to a Specific Slide *(PP 1.49)*
- Display the Slide Master *(PP 1.58)*
- End a Slide Show with a Black Slide *(PP 1.43)*
- Enter a Slide Title *(PP 1.35)*
- Enter the Presentation Subtitle *(PP 1.23)*
- Enter the Presentation Title *(PP 1.21)*
- Increase Font Size *(PP 1.25)*
- Move Manually Through Slides in a Slide Show *(PP 1.48)*
- Obtain Help Using the Office Assistant *(PP 1.67)*
- Open an Existing Presentation *(PP 1.52)*
- Print a Presentation *(PP 1.65)*
- Quit PowerPoint *(PP 1.51, 1.69)*
- Save a Presentation Before Printing *(PP 1.65)*
- Save a Presentation on a Floppy Disk *(PP 1.29)*
- Save a Presentation with the Same File Name *(PP 1.44)*
- Select an Object Area Placeholder *(PP 1.36)*
- Start a New Presentation *(PP 1.10)*
- Start Slide Show View *(PP 1.46)*
- Start the Spelling Checker *(PP 1.55)*
- Type a Multi-level Bulleted List *(PP 1.37)*
- Type the Remaining Text for Slide 2 *(PP 1.39)*
- Use the Popup Menu to End a Slide Show *(PP 1.50)*
- Use the Scroll Box on the Slide Pane to Move to Another Slide *(PP 1.45)*

More About 2000

Microsoft Certification

You can prove to your employer that you have essential PowerPoint 2000 skills. The Microsoft Office User Specialist (MOUS) Certification program allows you to obtain this valuable credential known throughout the computer industry. For more information, see Appendix D or visit the Shelly Cashman Series MOUS Web page at www.scsite.com/off2000/cert.htm.

1 Computer Buying Basics

Instructions: Start PowerPoint. Open the presentation Apply-1 from the PowerPoint Data Disk. See the inside back cover for instructions for downloading the PowerPoint Data Disk or see your instructor for information on accessing the files required for this book. This slide lists questions to consider when buying a computer. Perform the following tasks to change the slide so it looks like the one in Figure 1-77.

Buying a Computer?
Ask these questions:
Hardware
How fast is the microprocessor?
How large is the hard drive?
How much RAM is included?
Software
Will I be using graphics?
Will I be computing my finances and taxes?

FIGURE 1-77

1. Click the Common Tasks menu button on the Formatting toolbar, and then click the Apply Design Template command. Choose the Blends design template.
2. Press and hold down the SHIFT key, and then click the Slide Master View button to display the slide master. Click the paragraph, Click to edit Master text styles. Click Format on the menu bar and then click Line Spacing. Increase the Before paragraph line spacing to 1 Lines. Click the OK button. Then click the Close button on the Master toolbar to return to normal view.
3. Select the text in the Title Area placeholder. Click the Bold button on the Formatting toolbar.
4. If necessary, select the text in the Title Area placeholder. Click the Font Size box arrow on the Font Size button on the Formatting toolbar. Click the down scroll arrow and then scroll down and click font size 48.
5. Click the paragraph in the Object Area placeholder, How fast is the microprocessor?. Click the Demote button on the Formatting toolbar.
6. Demote the four other paragraphs that end with a question mark.
7. Click File on the menu bar and then click Save As. Type `Buying a Computer` in the File name box. If drive A is not already displaying in the Save in box, click the Save in box arrow, and then click 3½ Floppy (A:). Click the Save button.
8. Click the Grayscale Preview button on the Standard toolbar to display the presentation in black and white.
9. Click the Print button on the Standard toolbar.
10. Click the Close button on the menu bar to quit PowerPoint.
11. Write your name on the printout, and hand it in to your instructor.

NOTE: These labs require you to create presentations based on notes. When you design these slide shows, use the 7 x 7 rule, which states that each line should have a maximum of seven words, and each slide should have a maximum of seven lines.

1 Financial Freedom at Community Savings & Loan

Problem: You work at the Community Savings & Loan. The institution's vice president wants you to help her prepare a presentation for an upcoming seminar for the community regarding achieving financial freedom. She hands you the notes in Figure 1-78, and you create the presentation shown in Figures 1-79a through 1-79d.

I) Money Sense –
Gaining Financial Freedom
- A) Presented by:
- B) Rich Jackson
- C) Community Savings & Loan

II) Start Saving Now
- A) Use the benefits of compounding interest
  - 1) Search for investments with high returns
  - 2) Consider stocks and stock mutual funds
- B) Have an emergency money fund
  - 1) Try to save six months' living expenses
  - 2) Put in easily liquidated accounts

III) Spend Within Your Means
- A) Make a budget and stick to it
- B) Watch for bargains
  - 1) Shop at pre-season and post-season sales
- C) Buy classic clothes and furnishings
  - 1) They will not seem dated years later

IV) Pay Yourself First
- A) You are your primary financial obligation
  - 1) Be completely committed to saving regularly
- B) Save 10 percent of your gross income
  - 1) As your salary grows, increase this amount
- C) Use direct deposit to ensure a transaction

FIGURE 1-78

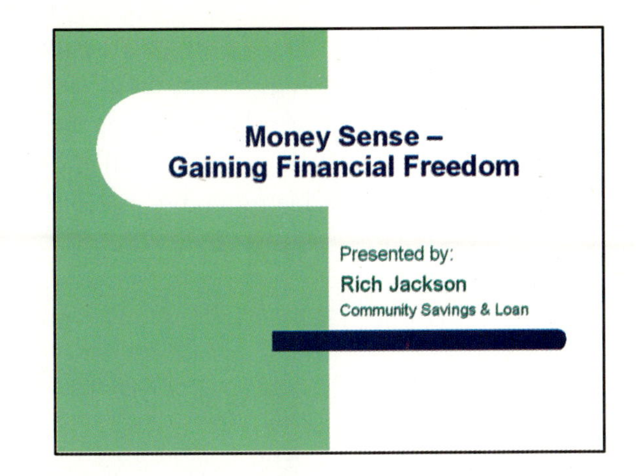

Money Sense –
Gaining Financial Freedom
Presented by:
Rich Jackson
Community Savings & Loan

(a) Slide 1

Start Saving Now

- Use the benefits of compounding interest
  - Search for investments with high returns
  - Consider stocks and stock mutual funds
- Have an emergency money fund
  - Try to save six months' living expenses
  - Put in easily liquidated accounts

(b) Slide 2

Spend Within Your Means

- Make a budget and stick to it
- Watch for bargains
  - Shop at pre-season and post-season sales
- Buy classic clothes and furnishings
  - They will not seem dated years later

(c) Slide 3

Pay Yourself First

- You are your primary financial obligation
  - Be completely committed to saving regularly
- Save 10 percent of your gross income
  - As your salary grows, increase this amount
- Use direct deposit to ensure a transaction

(d) Slide 4

FIGURE 1-79

Instructions: Perform the following tasks.

1. Create a new presentation using the Capsules design template.
2. Using the typed notes illustrated in Figure 1-78, create the title slide shown in Figure 1-79a using your name in place of Rich Jackson. Decrease the font size of the paragraph, Presented by:, to 24. Decrease the font size of the paragraph, Community Savings & Loan, to 20.
3. Using the typed notes in Figure 1-78, create the three bulleted list slides shown in Figures 1-79b through 1-79d. Increase the Before paragraph spacing to .8 Lines.
4. Click the Spelling button on the Standard toolbar. Correct any errors.
5. Save the presentation on a floppy disk using the file name, Money Freedom.
6. Display the presentation in black and white.
7. Print the black and white presentation. Quit PowerPoint.

2 Lake Shore Mall Fashion Show

Problem: You work in a clothing store at Lake Shore Mall, and your manager has asked you to participate in the annual fashion show. You decide to get involved with the segment promoting clothing to wear on job interviews. You determine that a PowerPoint presentation would help the commentator present key points as the models display accompanying clothing. You interview fashion coordinators at various stores in the mall and organize the list in Figure 1-80. Then you select a PowerPoint design template and decide to modify it. *Hint*: Use the PowerPoint Help system to solve this problem.

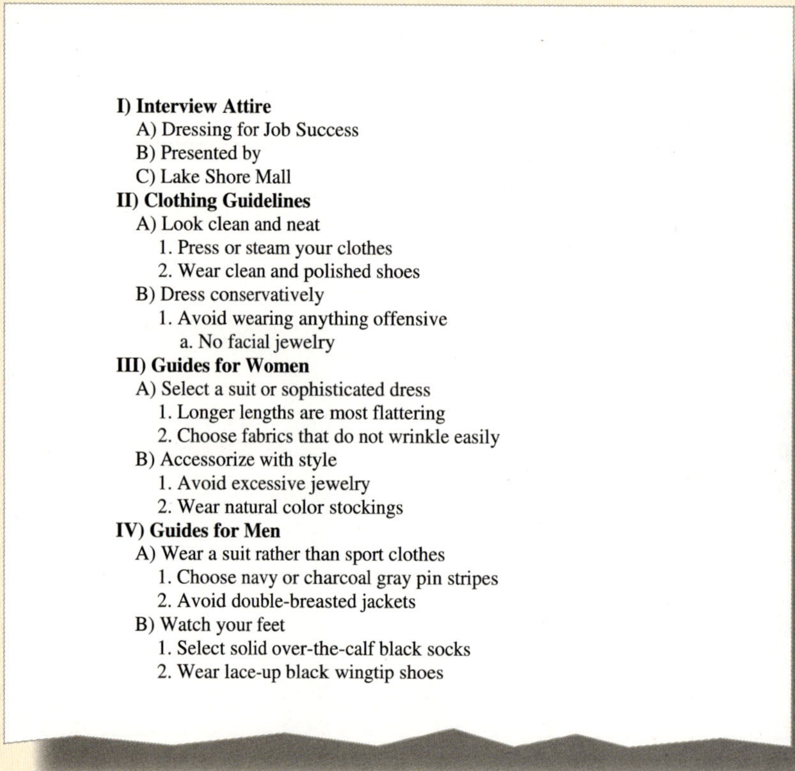

I) Interview Attire
- A) Dressing for Job Success
- B) Presented by
- C) Lake Shore Mall

II) Clothing Guidelines
- A) Look clean and neat
  - 1. Press or steam your clothes
  - 2. Wear clean and polished shoes
- B) Dress conservatively
  - 1. Avoid wearing anything offensive
    - a. No facial jewelry

III) Guides for Women
- A) Select a suit or sophisticated dress
  - 1. Longer lengths are most flattering
  - 2. Choose fabrics that do not wrinkle easily
- B) Accessorize with style
  - 1. Avoid excessive jewelry
  - 2. Wear natural color stockings

IV) Guides for Men
- A) Wear a suit rather than sport clothes
  - 1. Choose navy or charcoal gray pin stripes
  - 2. Avoid double-breasted jackets
- B) Watch your feet
  - 1. Select solid over-the-calf black socks
  - 2. Wear lace-up black wingtip shoes

FIGURE 1-80

Instructions: Perform the following tasks.

1. Create a new presentation using the Post Modern design template.
2. Using the notes in Figure 1-80, create the title slide shown in Figure 1-81a. Increase the font size of the paragraph, Dressing for Job Success, to 36. Decrease the font size of the paragraph, Presented by, to 28.
3. Using the notes in Figure 1-80, create the three multi-level bulleted list slides shown in Figures 1-81b through 1-81d.
4. Display the slide master. Click the paragraph, Click to edit Master title style. Click the Bold button on the Formatting toolbar.
5. Click the paragraph, Click to edit Master text styles. On the Format menu, click Line Spacing, and then increase the Before paragraph line spacing to 0.75 Lines. Click the paragraph, Second level. On the Format menu, click Line Spacing, and then increase the After paragraph spacing to 0.25 Lines.

(a) Slide 1

Clothing Guidelines
- Look clean and neat
  - Press or steam your clothes
  - Wear clean and polished shoes
- Dress conservatively
  - Avoid wearing anything offensive
    - No facial jewelry

9/12/01 Student Name 2

(b) Slide 2

Guides for Women
- Select a suit or sophisticated dress
  - Longer lengths are most flattering
  - Choose fabrics that do not wrinkle easily
- Accessorize with style
  - Avoid excessive jewelry
  - Wear natural color stockings

9/12/01 Student Name 3

(c) Slide 3

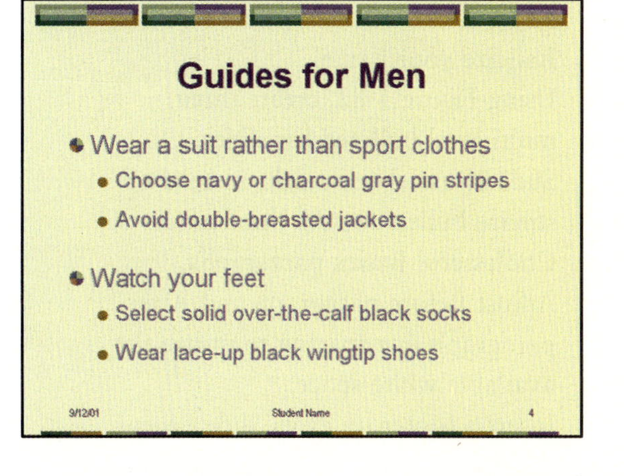

(d) Slide 4

FIGURE 1-81

6. Drag the scroll box in the slide pane down to display the title master. Click the paragraph, Click to edit Master title style. Click the Bold button on the Formatting toolbar.
7. Return to normal view. On the View menu, click Header and Footer. If necessary, click the Slide tab. Add the date (so it updates automatically), a slide number, and your name to the footer. Display the footer on all slides.
8. Drag the scroll box to display Slide 1. Click the Slide Show button to start slide show view. Then click to display each slide.
9. Save the presentation on a floppy disk using the file name, Interview Attire. Display and print the presentation in black and white. Quit PowerPoint.

3 Cholesterol Basics at the Community Wellness Center

Problem: At your visit to the South Suburban Community Wellness Center last week, staff nurse Debbie Ortiz explained the fundamentals of cholesterol to you and several other patients. You decide she can use a presentation and handouts to better educate clinic visitors. *Hint*: Use the PowerPoint Help system to solve this problem.

Instructions: Using the list in Figure 1-82, design and create a presentation. The presentation must include a title slide and three bulleted list slides. Perform the following tasks.

1. Create a new presentation using the Dad's Tie design template.
2. Create a title slide titled, Cholesterol Highs and Lows. Include a subtitle, using your name in place of Debbie Ortiz. Decrease the font size for paragraphs Presented by: and South Suburban Wellness Center to 32. Italicize your name.
3. Using Figure 1-82, create three multi-level bulleted list slides. On Slide 2, use check marks instead of square bullets for the three main Cholesterol Basics paragraphs.
4. Adjust Before paragraph and After paragraph line spacing to utilize the available white space.
5. Insert a footer on every slide except the title slide that includes the current date, your name, and the slide number.
6. View the presentation in slide show view to look for errors. Correct any errors.
7. Check the presentation for spelling errors.
8. Save the presentation to a floppy disk with the file name, Cholesterol Basics. Print the presentation slides in black and white. Quit PowerPoint.

I) Cholesterol Highs and Lows
- A) Presented by:
- B) Debbie Ortiz
- C) South Suburban Wellness Center

II) Cholesterol Basics
- A) Needed by:
  - 1) Every cell in your body
- B) Builds:
  - 1) Brain and nerve tissues; bile
- C) Manufactured by:
  - 1) Liver and small intestine

III) HDL (high density lipids)
- A) H stands for "Healthy"
- B) Good for your heart
  - 1) Delivers cholesterol deposits in body to liver
    - a) Liver disposes or recycles these deposits

IV) LDL (low density lipoproteins)
- A) L stands for "Lethal"
- B) Enemy of the heart
  - 1) Transports needed cholesterol to cells
  - 2) Dumps excess on arterial walls and tissues

FIGURE 1-82

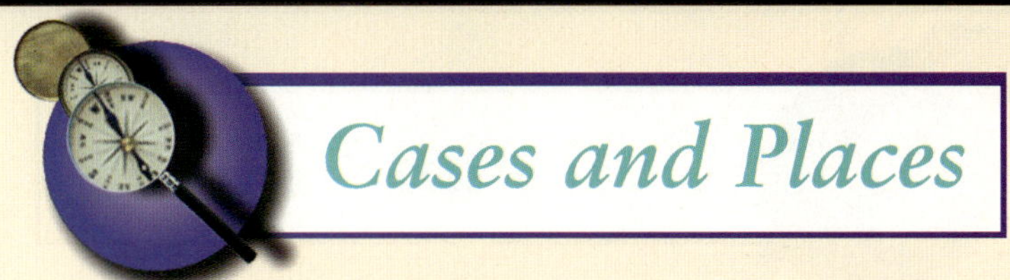

Cases and Places

The difficulty of these case studies varies:
◗ are the least difficult; ◗◗ are more difficult; and ◗◗◗ are the most difficult.

1 ◗ Dr. Doug Gordon, chief ophthalmologist at the North Shore Eye Clinic, knows that many people take their eyesight for granted. They visit an eye doctor only when they are having difficulties, such as eye pain or extreme redness. He urges everyone, from newborns to senior citizens, to preserve their eyesight by scheduling regular eye exams. The times for these checkups varies by age. Dr. Gordon has contacted you to help him prepare a presentation that will be delivered at community fairs and at the local shopping mall. He has prepared the notes in Figure 1-83 and has asked you to use them to develop a title slide and additional slides that can be used on an overhead projector. Use the concepts and techniques introduced in this project to create the presentation.

The Eyes Have It
When Is Checkup Time?
Dr. Doug Gordon
North Shore Eye Clinic

Children
- Newborns
  - When: In nursery
  - Potential problems: infections, abnormalities
- Infants (to 6 months)
  - When: once
  - Potential problems: eye misalignment
- Youngsters (ages 1 to 6)
  - When: every 1 to 3 years
  - Potential problems: nearsightedness, farsightedness, astigmatism, lazy eye
- School-age children (ages 7 to 17)
  - When: every 1 to 2 years
  - Potential problems: nearsightedness, farsightedness, astigmatism

Adults
- Ages 18 to 40
  - When: every 1 to 2 years
  - Potential problems: needing reading glasses, early stages of glaucoma
- Ages 41 – 64
  - When: every 1 to 2 years
  - Potential problems: glaucoma, cataracts, macular degeneration

Seniors (ages 65+)
- When: annually
- Potential problems: glaucoma, cataracts, macular degeneration

FIGURE 1-83

Cases and Places

2 ▸▸ This past holiday season, the Highland Shores police and fire departments experienced an unusually high number of calls for assistance. Many of these problems were the result of mishaps that easily could have been prevented. Police Chief Victor Halen and Fire Chief Norton Smits want to inform community residents at local block parties next summer about how they can follow a few safety precautions to reduce their chances of injuries. The chiefs want you to help them prepare a slide show and handouts for the community. They have typed safety tips for you (Figure 1-84), and they have asked you to prepare five slides that can be used on an overhead projector and as handouts. They want the title slide to introduce them and their topic. Use the concepts and techniques introduced in this project to create the presentation.

Seasonal Safety

Using Candles
- Never burn unattended or in drafts
- Burn on a heat-resistant surface
- Trim wick to ¼ inch before lighting
  - Do not drop wick trimming into candle
- Burn for 2 – 3 hours at a time
  - Allow to cool before relighting

Decorating
- Be mindful of children
  - Hang ornaments, tinsel on high branches
  - Keep dangerous plants out of reach
    - Mistletoe, poinsettia, and holly contain toxic substances

Lighting
- Use the right lights
  - Choose lights with the UL label
  - Check for defects
    - Cracked sockets, frayed wires, loose connections
  - Turn off lights before leaving house

Cooking
- Reduce the risk of bacterial growth
  - Keep food on table two hours maximum
    - Egg dishes should be refrigerated hourly
    - Rotate foods occasionally
- Do not leave food unattended on stovetops

FIGURE 1-84

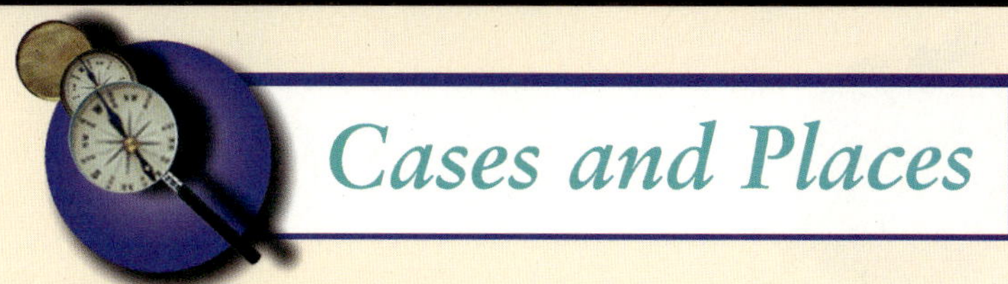

Cases and Places

3 ▶▶ CPU-4-U is a computer repair store near campus that specializes in repairing computer systems and building custom computers. The co-owners, Warren Shilling and Mary Burg, want to attract new customers, and they have asked you to help them design a PowerPoint advertising campaign. Having graduated from your college, they are familiar with the hardware and software students need for their classes. Computer users can make appointments to bring their computers to the shop or to arrange for on-site service 24 hours a day. CPU-4-U also carries a complete line of supplies, including toner cartridges, paper, and labels. Many students consult with the technicians to plan for future computer purchases and to arrange financing for their new systems. The store is located in Tinley Mall, 6302 South State Street, Ypsilanti, Michigan. For more information call 555-2297. Using the techniques presented in this project, prepare a title slide and three bulleted list slides to be used for their presentation and for handouts.

4 ▶▶ The Poochy Humane Society in your town wants to increase community awareness of its services and facilities. The society's director, Jennifer Durkin, has decided that one way she can promote the shelter is by informing community residents on how they should react when a loose dog approaches them. She decides to address residents who regularly participate in activities at the local park district and who are walking, jogging, and biking in the community park. She wants to inform them that they can react in one of three ways when a stray dog approaches. They can be friendly by talking softly and by extending one of their hands palm down. Another behavior is to assert dominance. Using this approach, they should look at the dog sternly and yell, "Go away!" A third reaction is to act submissively by relaxing their muscles and glancing to the side. This technique is especially useful for an encounter with a big dog that thinks it is in control. The Poochy Humane Society is located at 10836 Windy Terrace; the telephone number is 555-DOGS. Using the concepts and techniques presented in this project, prepare a title slide and three bulleted list slides to be used on an overhead projector and as handouts for community residents.

5 ▶▶ Fat is one of the three essential components your body needs. The other two are protein and carbohydrates. Unfortunately, many people throughout the world consume too much fat in their diets. Although fat intake needs vary based on age and weight, following a low-fat diet can reduce the risk of heart disease. Some fats are healthy and actually help give energy, prevent blood clotting, and reduce cholesterol and triglyceride levels. These fats, commonly called essential fatty acids (EFAs) or Vitamin F, are found in cold-water fish and cold-temperature plant oils, such as flax seed and black currant. Monounsaturated fats also are healthy for the body. They are found in olive, almond, and canola oils, they all are liquid at room temperature, and they generally come from plant seeds. Although polyunsaturated fats can decrease cholesterol levels, they also can decrease the percentage of healthy HDL cholesterol (see In the Lab Project 3). Like monounsaturated fats, they come from plant seeds and are liquid at room temperature. They are found in safflower oil and corn oil. Saturated fats and hydrogenated fats are unhealthy because they can clog arteries and elevate cholesterol levels. They are found in animal foods, such as butter, margarine, and meat. Using the concepts and techniques presented in this project, prepare a presentation describing the various type of fats in our foods and their benefits or dangers to our health. Create a title slide and at least three additional slides that can be used with an overhead projector and as handouts.

Cases and Places

6 ▶▶ Every day, two Americans are killed in collisions between trains and cars or between trains and pedestrians. Many more people suffer serious injuries from these accidents. Lighting is not a significant factor, for more than 50 percent of these accidents occur at crossings marked with gates and flashing lights, and more than 70 percent occur during the day. People involved in train accidents have one or more of these three personality traits: impatient, and not wanting to wait for a train; inattentive, and daydreaming or listening to loud music; or ignorant, and not aware of the impending danger. Drivers and pedestrians can reduce the risk of train accidents by looking both ways before crossing the tracks, never walking down a track, and assuming that a train can come at any time in either direction on any track. If your car stalls on a railroad track when a train is approaching, get out immediately and run away from the track in the same direction from which the train is coming. (If you run in the same direction the train is traveling, the train will hit your car, which can potentially hit you.) Using the concepts and techniques presented in this project, prepare a presentation to warn drivers and pedestrians of the dangers involved in crossing railroad tracks. Create a title slide and at least three additional slides that can be used with an overhead projector and as handouts.

7 ▶▶▶ In the Lab Project 1 discusses the need for developing techniques to achieve financial freedom. One of the suggestions is to invest in stocks or in stock mutual funds. These mutual funds pool shareholders' money and invest in a diversified portfolio of funds. Interview a financial planner or research the Internet for information on the various types of mutual funds and how they are managed. Determine the fees and expenses involved in this type of investment. Then, using the concepts and techniques presented in this project, prepare a presentation to report your findings. Create a title slide and at least three additional slides that can be used with an overhead projector and as handouts.

Microsoft PowerPoint 2000

Using Outline View and Clip Art to Create a Slide Show

OBJECTIVES

You will have mastered the material in this project when you can:

- Create a presentation from an outline
- Start a presentation as a new PowerPoint document
- Use outline view
- Create a presentation in outline view
- Add a slide in outline view
- Create multi-level bulleted list slides in outline view
- Create a closing slide in outline view
- Save and review a presentation
- Change the slide layout
- Insert clip art from Microsoft Clip Gallery 5.0
- Move clip art
- Change clip art size
- Add a header and footer to outline pages
- Add animation and slide transition effects
- Apply animation effects to bulleted slides
- Animate clip art objects
- Format and animate a title slide
- Run an animated slide show
- Print a presentation outline
- E-mail a slide show from within PowerPoint

No Sweat

Deliver Your Presentation with Ease

What two words strike panic in the hearts of millions of people across the world? Public speaking.

Countless surveys throughout the decades have asked people to list their greatest fears. Going to the dentist always is near the top of the dreaded-events list. So are contracting a fatal disease and losing a job. The mere thought of standing in front of a group of people and trying to say something coherent, however, tops their lists every time. The memories of dry mouths, sweaty palms, queasy stomachs, and shaky

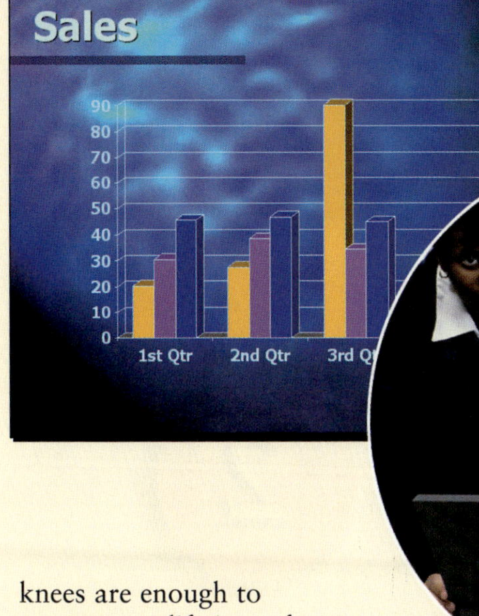

present

knees are enough to guarantee a lifetime of nightmares.

Fortunately, PowerPoint has eased the pain of speechmaking somewhat. As you learned in Project 1, this software helps you organize your thoughts and present your information in an orderly, attractive manner. In Project 2, you will add to your knowledge base by learning to change layouts and then insert drawings and photos in your slides. Ultimately, your slide shows will have visual appeal and ample content.

While the PowerPoint slide shows help you plan your speeches, they also help your audience absorb your message. People learn most effectively when their five senses are involved. Researchers have determined that individuals remember 10 percent of what they read, 20 percent of what they hear, 30 percent of what they see, and an amazing 70 percent when they both see and hear. That is why it is important to attend class instead of copying your classmate's notes. When you see and hear your instructor deliver a lecture and write your own notes, you are apt to interpret the concepts correctly and recall this information at the ever-important final exam.

The synergy of the speech-graphics combo is recognized in a variety of venues. For example, some college administrators and instructors are requiring students to register for their communications and PowerPoint classes concurrently. Bill Clinton's maps and Ross Perot's charts are staples in their speech repertoires.

The theories of structuring effective communication presentations are deep rooted. Dale Carnegie wrote *How to Win Friends and Influence People* in 1936, and the millions of people who have read that book have learned practical advice on achieving success through communication. He formed the Dale Carnegie Institute, which has taught 4.5 million graduates worldwide the techniques of sharing ideas effectively and persuading others. Microsoft has included Carnegie's four-step process — plan, prepare, practice, and present — in the PowerPoint Help system.

In the days prior to PowerPoint, slides and overhead transparencies were the domain of artists in a corporation's graphic communications department. With the influx of Microsoft Office on desktops throughout a company, however, employees from all departments now develop the slide shows. According to Microsoft, the average PowerPoint user now creates nine presentations each month, which is double the number produced in 1995.

With all these presentations, that means a lot of sweaty palms and shaky knees. But with planning and practice — and powerful PowerPoint presentations — these speakers can deliver their messages confidently and successfully.

Microsoft PowerPoint 2000

Using Outline View and Clip Art to Create a Slide Show

CASE PERSPECTIVE

A college education no longer is considered an extravagance; instead, it is essential for landing and advancing in many jobs. The college experience has a price, however. Students often find their budgets maximized and their bank accounts drained. Financial aid in the form of scholarships, loans, and grants can help ease this burden. Each year millions of dollars of scholarship money go unclaimed because students do not know where or how to find these funds. Fortunately, a little effort can uncover an assortment of scholarship sources.

Many financially strapped students at your college visit the Office of Financial Aid in hopes of finding some relief. Dr. Mary Halen, the director of financial aid, has asked you to help prepare a student lecture on the topic of searching for scholarships. You suggest developing a short PowerPoint presentation to accompany her talk. The slide show will give an overview of researching scholarship sources, applying for the funds, considering merit scholarships and private sources, and surfing the Internet for additional information. You decide to add clip art and animation to increase visual interest. Then you e-mail the completed presentation to her.

Creating a Presentation from an Outline

At some time during either your academic or business life, you probably will make a presentation. The presentation may be informative by providing detailed information about a specific topic. Other presentations may be persuasive by selling a proposal or a product to a client, convincing management to approve a new project, or persuading the board of directors to accept the new fiscal budget. As an alternative to creating your presentation in the slide pane in normal view, as you did in Project 1, PowerPoint provides an outlining feature to help you organize your thoughts. When the outline is complete, it becomes the foundation for your presentation.

You can create your presentation outline using outline view. When you create an outline, you type all the text at one time, as if you were typing an outline on a sheet of paper. This technique differs from creating a presentation in the slide pane in normal view, where you type text as you create each individual slide and the text displays in both the slide and outline panes. PowerPoint creates the presentation as you type the outline by evaluating the outline structure and displaying a miniature view of the slide. Regardless of the view in which you build a presentation, PowerPoint automatically creates the five views discussed in Project 1: normal, outline, slide, slide sorter, and slide show.

The first step in creating a presentation in outline view is to type a title for the outline. The **outline title** is the subject of the presentation and later becomes the presentation title slide. Then you type the remainder of the outline, indenting appropriately to establish a structure or hierarchy. Once the outline is complete, you make your presentation more persuasive by adding graphics. This project uses outlining to create the presentation and clip art graphics to support the text visually.

Project Two — Searching for Scholarships

Project 2 uses PowerPoint to create the six-slide Searching for Scholarships presentation shown in Figures 2-1a through 2-1f. You create the presentation from the outline in Figure 2-2 on the next page.

(a) Slide 1

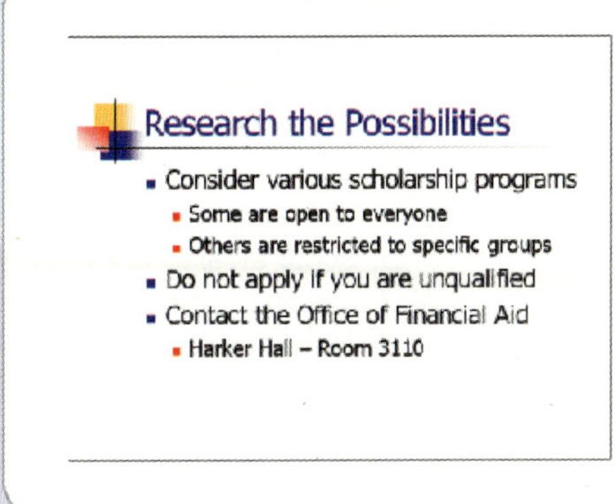

(b) Slide 2

(c) Slide 3

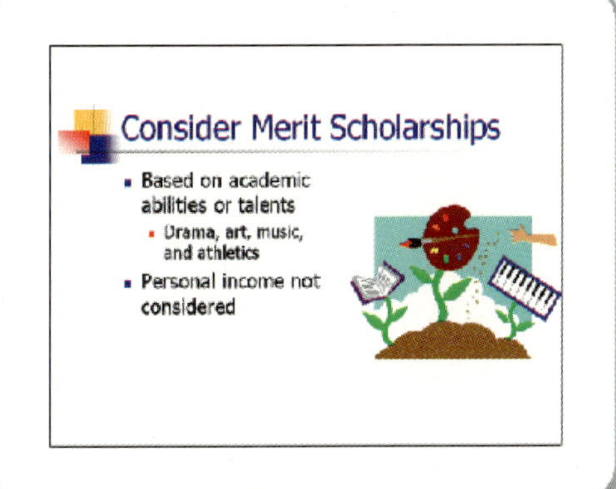

(d) Slide 4

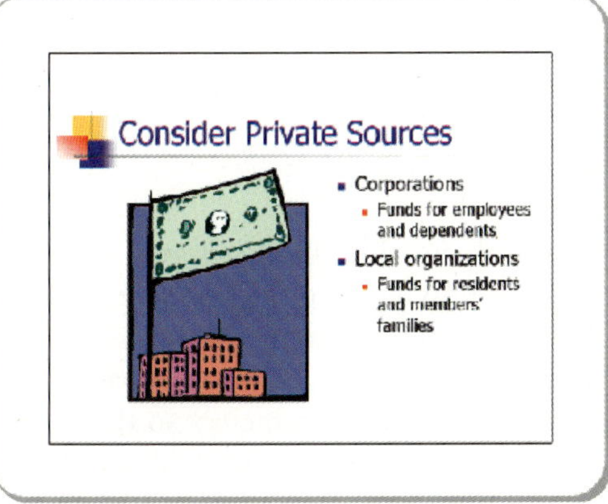

(e) Slide 5

Additional Information
- College Board Online
  - www.collegeboard.org
- U.S. Department of Education
  - www.ed.gov
- Financial Aid Information Page
  - www.finaid.org

(f) Slide 6

FIGURE 2-1

I. Searching for Scholarships
   A. Finding Cash for College
   B. Presented by
   C. The Office of Financial Aid
II. Research the Possibilities
   A. Consider various scholarship programs
      1. Some are open to everyone
      2. Others are restricted to specific groups
   B. Do not apply if you are unqualified
   C. Contact the Office of Financial Aid
      1. Harker Hall – Room 3110
III. Start Searching Early
   A. Allow for deadlines
      1. References may need to write letters
   B. Some awards are made to first applicants
IV. Consider Merit Scholarships
   A. Based on academic abilities or talents
      1. Drama, art, music, and athletics
   B. Personal income not considered
V. Consider Private Sources
   A. Corporations
      1. Funds for employees and dependents
   B. Local organizations
      1. Funds for residents and members' families
VI. Additional Information
   A. College Board Online
      1. www.collegeboard.org
   B. U.S. Department of Education
      1. www.ed.gov
   C. Financial Aid Information Page
      1. www.finaid.org

FIGURE 2-2

Using PowerPoint

The word "PowerPoint" traditionally is used as a noun to refer to the software you are using in these projects to create presentations. With our ever-changing language, however, the word has evolved into a synonym for the term presentation. You now can ask your instructor, Did you grade my PowerPoint?

Starting a New Presentation

Project 1 introduced you to starting a presentation document, choosing an AutoLayout, and applying a design template. The following steps summarize how to start a new presentation, choose an AutoLayout, apply a design template, and display the entire Formatting toolbar. For a more detailed explanation, see pages PP 1.10 through PP 1.20 in Project 1. To reset your toolbars and menus so they display exactly as shown in this book, follow the steps outlined in Appendix C. Perform the following steps to start a new presentation.

TO START A NEW PRESENTATION

1. Click the Start button on the taskbar.
2. Click New Office Document. If necessary, click the General tab in the New Office Document dialog box.
3. Double-click the Blank Presentation icon.
4. Click the OK button when the New Slide dialog box displays to select the Title Slide AutoLayout.
5. Double-click Default Design on the status bar. Double-click the Blends design template in the Presentation Designs list in the Apply Design template dialog box.
6. If the Office Assistant displays, right-click the Office Assistant and then click Hide on the shortcut menu.
7. Double-click the move handle on the Formatting toolbar in the Microsoft PowerPoint window to display it in its entirety.

PowerPoint displays the Title Slide AutoLayout and the Blends design template on Slide 1 in normal view (Figure 2-3).

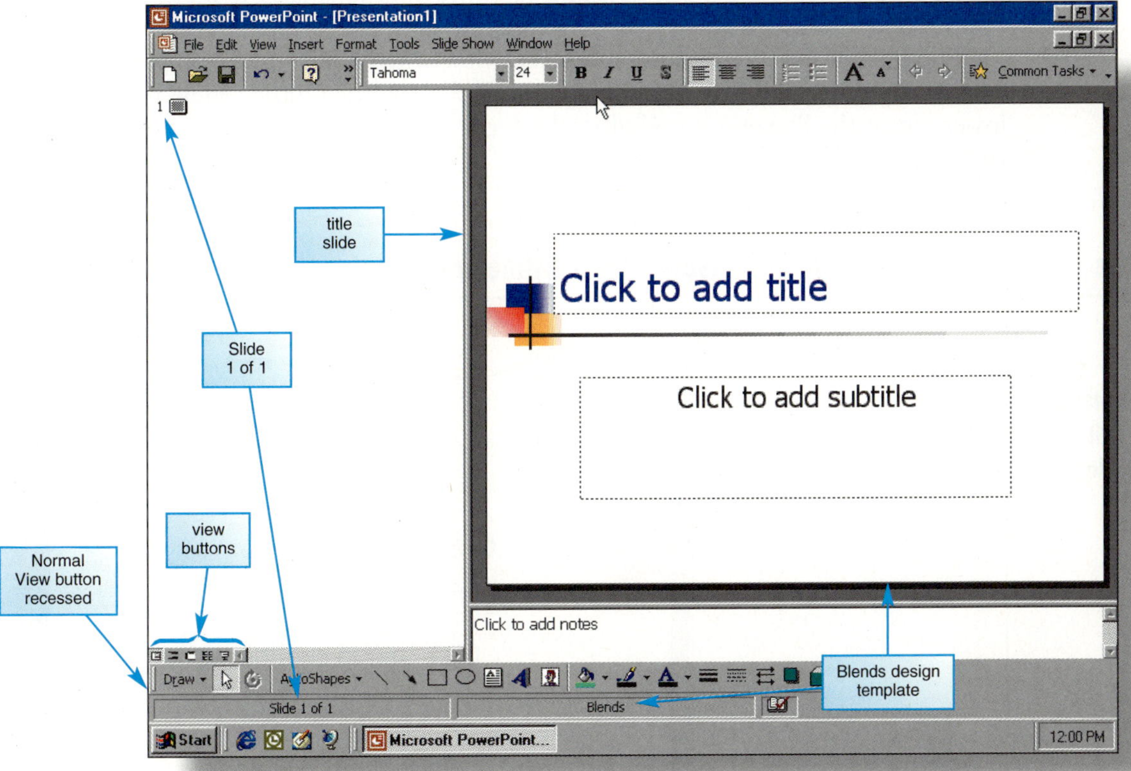

FIGURE 2-3

Using Outline View

Outline view provides a quick, easy way to create a presentation. Outlining allows you to organize your thoughts in a structured format. An outline uses indentation to establish a hierarchy, which denotes levels of importance to the main topic. An **outline** is a summary of thoughts, presented as headings and subheadings, often used as a preliminary draft when you create a presentation.

The three panes — outline, slide, and notes — shown in normal view also display in outline view. In outline view, however, the outline pane occupies the largest area on the left side of the window, and the slide pane shrinks to the upper-right corner to display how the current slide will look in normal view, slide view, slide sorter view, and slide show view. The notes pane displays under the slide pane. In the outline pane, the slide text displays along with a slide number and a slide icon. Body text is indented under the title text. Graphic objects, such as pictures, graphs, or tables, do not display in outline view. The slide icon is blank when a slide does not contain graphics. The attributes for text in outline view are the same as in normal view except for color and paragraph style.

Heading Levels

While PowerPoint gives you six heading levels to use on each slide, graphic designers suggest you limit your slides to three levels. The details on all six levels may overwhelm audiences. If you find yourself needing more than three levels, consider combining content in one level or using two different slides.

PowerPoint limits the number of heading levels to six. The first heading level is the slide title and is not indented. The remaining five heading levels are the same as the five indent levels in slide view. Recall from Project 1 that PowerPoint allows for five indent levels and that each indent level has an associated bullet.

The outline begins with a title on **heading level 1**. The title is the main topic of the slide. Text supporting the main topic begins on **heading level 2** and indents under heading level 1. **Heading level 3** indents under heading level 2 and contains text to support heading level 2. **Heading level 4, heading level 5**, and **heading level 6** indent under heading level 3, heading level 4, and heading level 5, respectively. Use heading levels 4, 5, and 6 as required. They generally are used for very detailed scientific and engineering presentations. Business and sales presentations usually focus on summary information and use heading level 1, heading level 2, and heading level 3.

PowerPoint initially displays in normal view when you start a new presentation. Change from normal view to outline view by clicking the Outline View button at the lower left of the PowerPoint window. Perform the following steps to change the view from normal view to outline view.

Steps To Change the View to Outline View and Display the Outline Toolbar

1 Point to the Outline View button located at the lower left of the PowerPoint window (Figure 2-4).

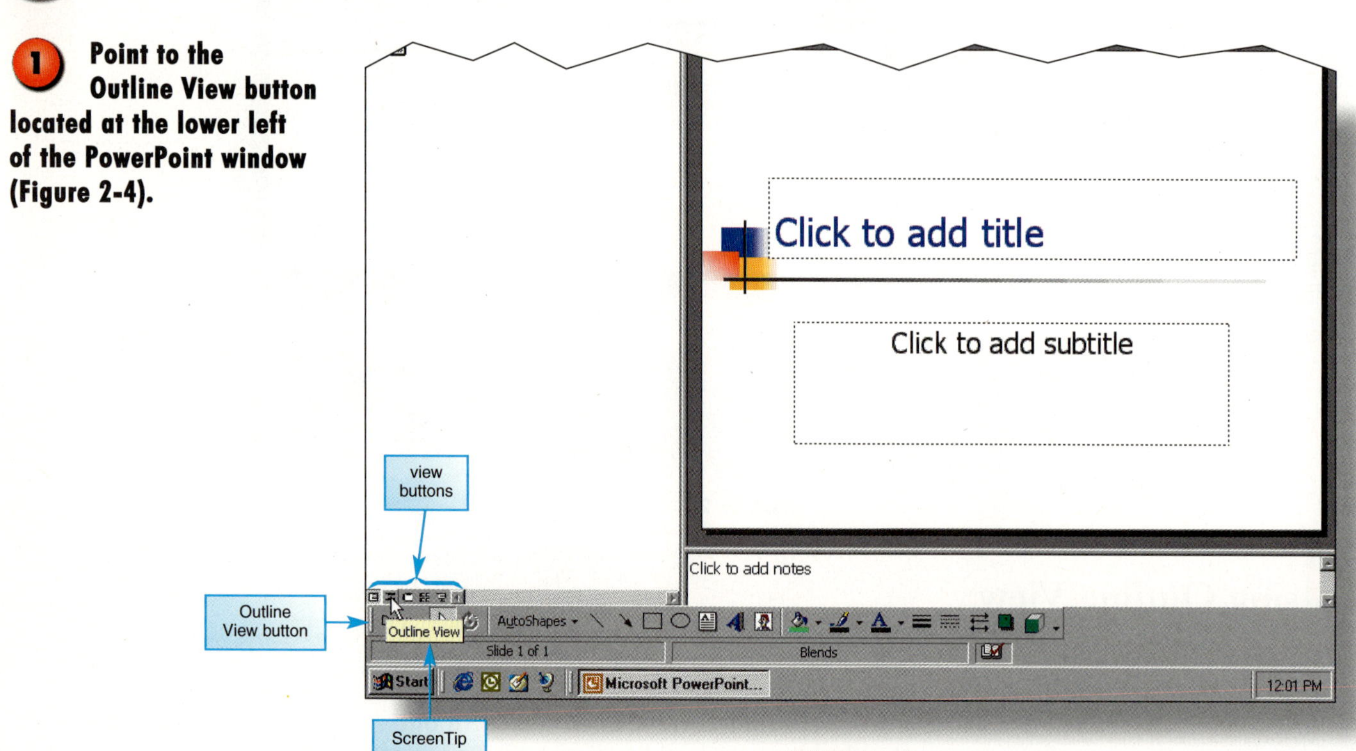

FIGURE 2-4

2 **Click the Outline View button.**

3 **Click View on the menu bar and then point to Toolbars. Point to Outlining on the Toolbars submenu.**

PowerPoint displays in outline view and the Toolbars submenu displays (Figure 2-5).

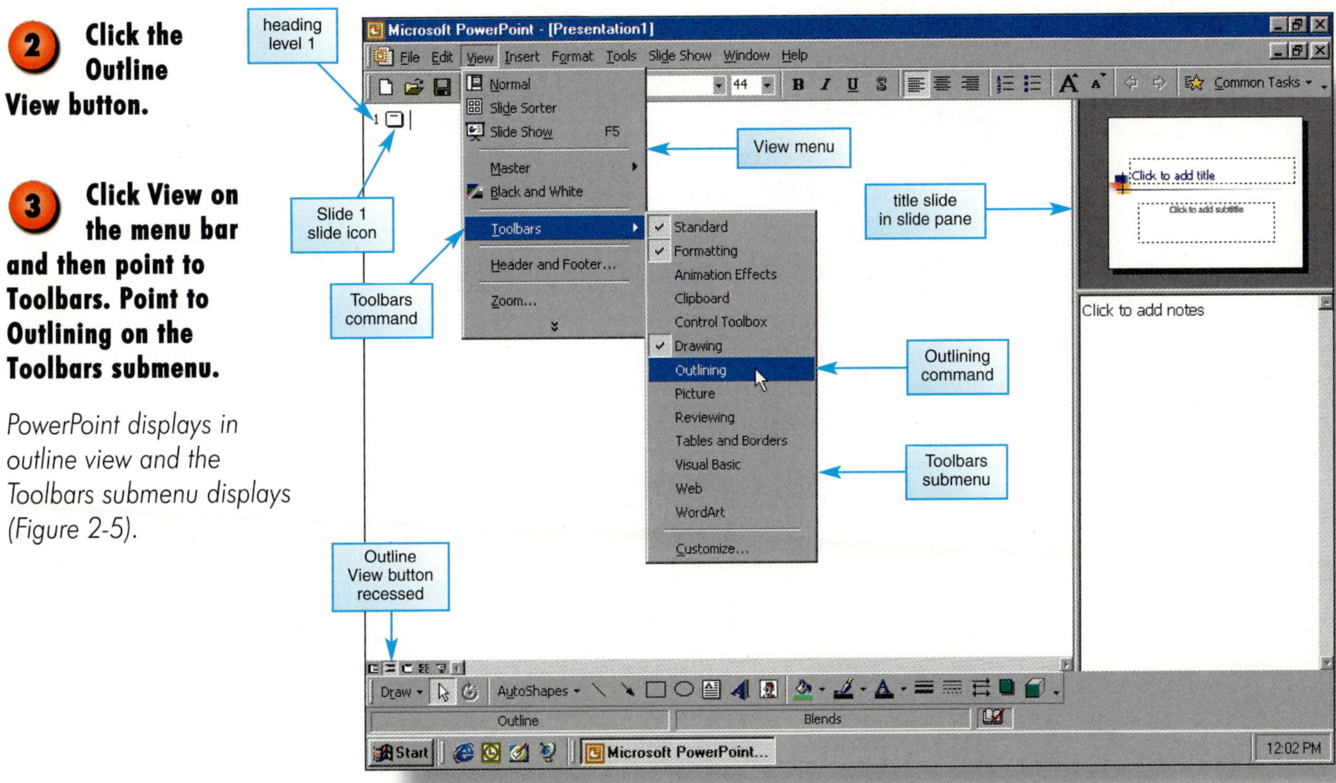

FIGURE 2-5

4 **Click Outlining.**

PowerPoint displays in outline view with the Outlining toolbar (Figure 2-6). PowerPoint displays the color view of Slide 1 in the slide pane.

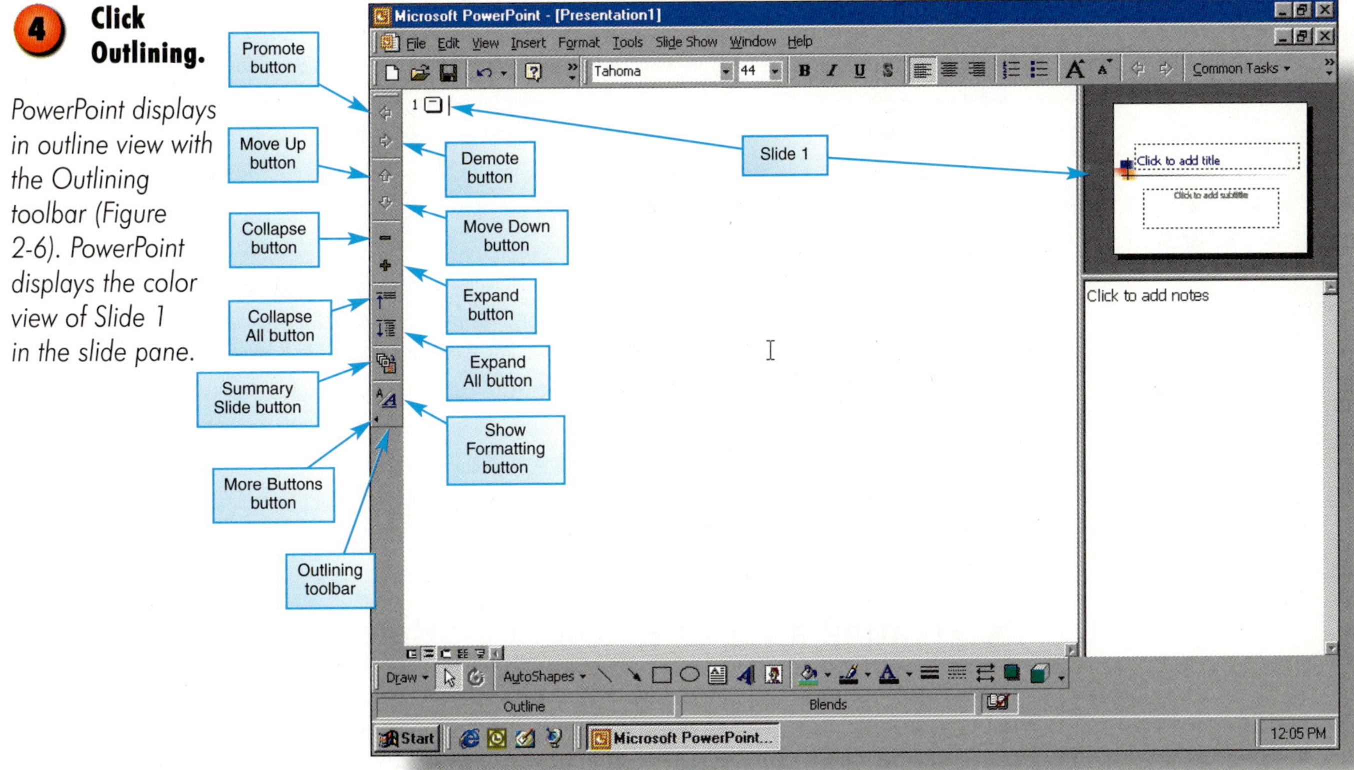

FIGURE 2-6

You can create and edit your presentation in outline view. Outline view also makes it easy to sequence slides and to relocate title text and body text from one slide to another. In addition to typing text to create a new presentation in outline view, PowerPoint can produce slides from an outline created in Microsoft Word or another word processor, if you save the outline as an RTF file or as a plain text file. The file extension **RTF** stands for **R**ich **T**ext **F**ormat.

The PowerPoint Window in Outline View

The PowerPoint window in outline view differs from the window in normal view because the Outlining toolbar displays, the outline pane occupies the majority of the window, and the slide pane displays a miniature version of the current slide. Table 2-1 describes the buttons on the Outlining toolbar.

Table 2-1 Buttons on the Outlining Toolbar

BUTTON	BUTTON NAME	DESCRIPTION
	Promote	Moves the selected paragraph to the next-higher heading level (up one level, to the left).
	Demote	Moves the selected paragraph to the next-lower heading level (down one level, to the right).
	Move Up	Moves a selected paragraph and its collapsed (temporarily hidden) subordinate text above the preceding displayed paragraph.
	Move Down	Moves a selected paragraph and its collapsed (temporarily hidden) subordinate text down, below the following displayed paragraph.
	Collapse	Hides all but the title of selected slides. Collapsed text is represented by a gray line.
	Expand	Displays the titles and all collapsed text of selected slides.
	Collapse All	Displays only the title of each slide. Text other than the title is represented by a gray line below the title.
	Expand All	Displays the titles and all the body text for each slide.
	Summary Slide	Creates a new slide from the titles of the slides you select in slide sorter or normal view. The summary slide creates a bulleted list from the titles of the selected slides. PowerPoint inserts the summary slide in front of the first selected slide.
	Show Formatting	Shows or hides character formatting (such as bold and italic) in normal view. In slide sorter view, switches between showing all text and graphics on each slide and displaying titles only.
	More Buttons	Allows you to select the particular buttons you want to display on the toolbar.

Creating a Presentation in Outline View

Outline view enables you to view title and body text, add and delete slides, drag and drop slide text, drag and drop individual slides, promote and demote text, save a presentation, print an outline, print slides, copy and paste slides or text to and from other presentations, apply a design template, and import an outline. When you **drag and drop** slide text or individual slides, you change the order of the text or the slides by selecting the text or slide you want to move or copy and then dragging the text or slide to its new location.

Developing a presentation in outline view is quick because you type the text for all slides on one screen. Once you type the outline, the presentation fundamentally is complete. If you choose, you then can go to normal view or slide view to enhance your presentation with graphics.

Design Templates

You can change design templates easily, even when you have completed creating each slide in your presentation. Each design template changes the color scheme, font attributes, and graphic objects throughout the entire file. For more information, visit the PowerPoint 2000 More About Web page (www.scsite.com/pp2000/more.htm) and click Design Templates.

Creating a Title Slide in Outline View

Recall from Project 1 that the title slide introduces the presentation to the audience. In addition to introducing the presentation, Project 2 uses the title slide to capture the attention of the students in your audience by using a design template with colorful graphics. Perform the following steps to create a title slide in outline view.

Steps To Create a Title Slide in Outline View

1 **Type** `Searching for Scholarships` **and then press the ENTER key.**

Searching for Scholarships is the title for Slide 1 and is called heading level 1. A slide icon displays to the left of each slide title. The font for heading level 1 is Tahoma and the font size is 44 points. Pressing the ENTER key moves the insertion point to the next line and maintains the same heading level. The insertion point is in position for typing the title for Slide 2 (Figure 2-7).

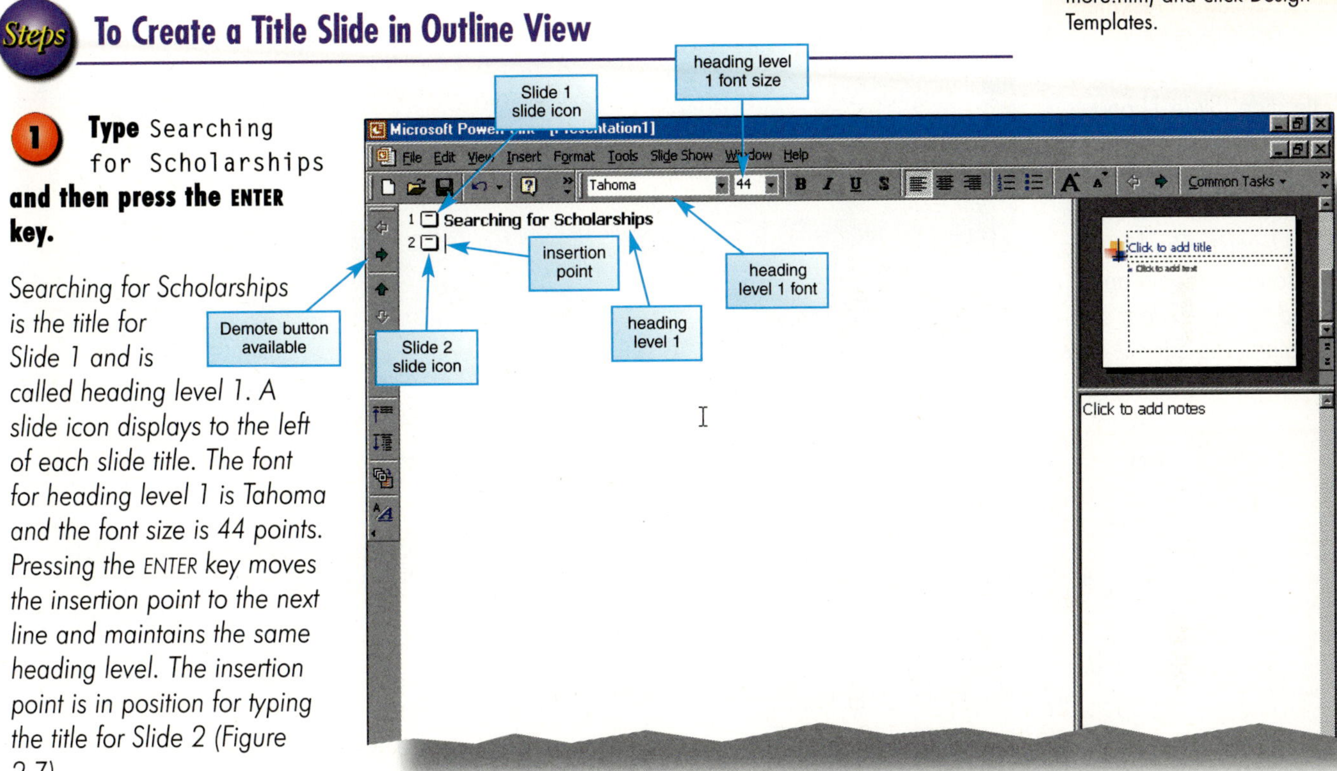

FIGURE 2-7

2 **Point to the Demote button.**

The Demote ScreenTip displays (Figure 2-8).

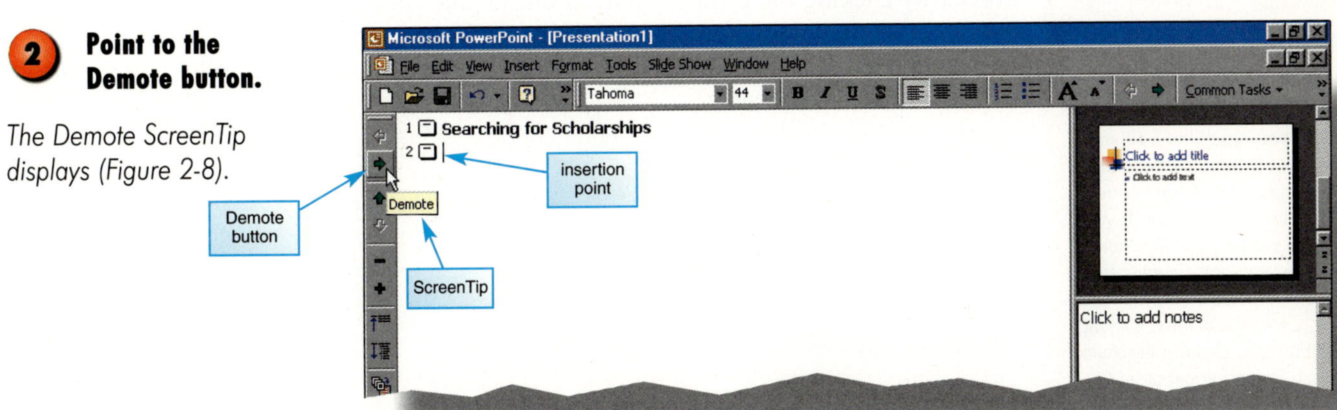

FIGURE 2-8

3 Click the Demote button on the Outlining toolbar. Type Finding Cash for College **and then press the ENTER key. Type** Presented by **and then press the ENTER key. Type** The Office of Financial Aid **and then press the ENTER key.**

The paragraphs, Finding Cash for College, Presented by, and The Office of Financial Aid, are subtitles on the title slide (Slide 1) and demote to heading level 2 (Figure 2-9). Heading level 2 is indented to the right under heading level 1. The heading level 2 font is Tahoma and the heading level 2 font size is 32 points. The Slide 2 slide icon does not display.

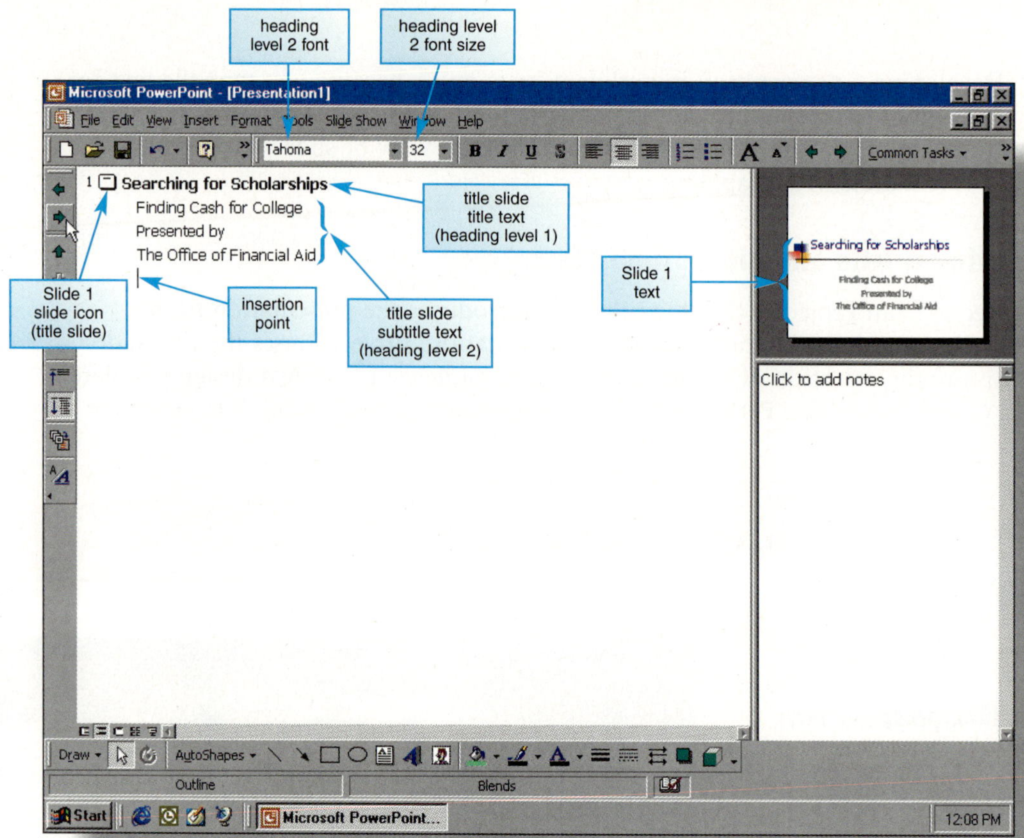

FIGURE 2-9

Other Ways

1. Type title text, press ENTER, click Demote button on Formatting toolbar, type subtitle text, press ENTER
2. Type title text, press ENTER, press TAB, type subtitle text, press ENTER

More About 2000

Auto-Fit Text

PowerPoint will reduce the point size of text automatically when you reach the bottom of the Object Area placeholder and need to squeeze an additional line on the slide. If you do not want to use this Auto-Fit feature, you can deactivate it by clicking Tools on the menu bar, clicking Options, clicking the Edit tab, clicking the Autofit text to text placeholder check box, and clicking OK.

The title slide text for the Searching for Scholarships presentation is complete. The next section explains how to add a slide in outline view.

Adding a Slide in Outline View

Recall from Project 1 that when you add a new slide in normal view, PowerPoint defaults to the Bulleted List AutoLayout. This action occurs in outline view as well. One way to add a new slide in outline view is to promote a paragraph to heading level 1 by clicking the Promote button on the outlining toolbar until the insertion point or the paragraph displays at heading level 1. A slide icon displays when the insertion point or paragraph reaches heading level 1. Perform the following steps to add a slide in outline view.

To Add a Slide in Outline View

1 Point to the Promote button on the Outlining toolbar.

The insertion point still is positioned at heading level 2 (Figure 2-10).

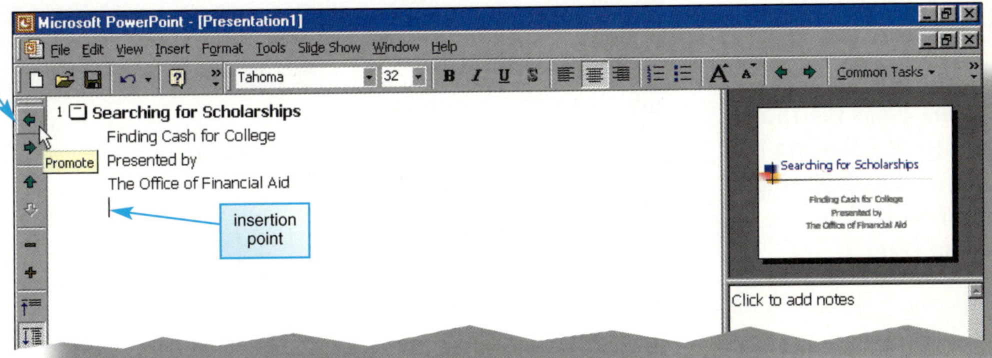

FIGURE 2-10

2 Click the Promote button.

The Slide 2 slide icon displays indicating a new slide is added to the presentation (Figure 2-11). The insertion point is in position to type the title for Slide 2 at heading level 1.

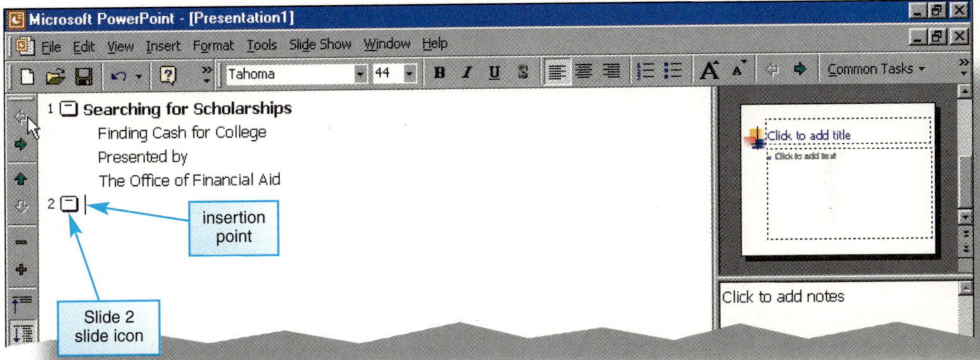

FIGURE 2-11

Other Ways

1. Click New Slide button on Standard toolbar, click OK button
2. On Insert menu click New Slide, click OK button
3. Press ALT+I, press N, press ENTER
4. Press CTRL+M, press ENTER
5. Press and hold SHIFT, press TAB until paragraph or insertion point displays at heading level 1, release TAB

After you add a slide, you are ready to type the slide text. The next section explains how to create a multi-level bulleted list slide in outline view.

Creating Multi-level Bulleted List Slides in Outline View

To create a multi-level bulleted list slide, you demote or promote the insertion point to the appropriate heading level and then type the paragraph text. Recall from Project 1 that when you demote a paragraph, PowerPoint adds a bullet to the left of each heading level. Depending on the design template, each heading level has a different bullet font. Also recall that the design template determines font attributes, including the bullet font.

Slide 2 is the first **informational slide** for Project 2. Slide 2 introduces the main topic: students can conduct searches to find many scholarships available to them. Each of the three major points regarding finding scholarship information displays as heading level 2, and the first and third points have two supporting paragraphs, which display as heading level 3. The steps on the next page explain how to create a multi-level bulleted list slide in outline view.

To Create a Multi-level Bulleted List Slide in Outline View

1 **Type** Research the Possibilities **and then press the ENTER key. Click the Demote button on the Outlining toolbar to demote to heading level 2.**

The title for Slide 2, Research the Possibilities, displays and the insertion point is in position to type the first bulleted paragraph (Figure 2-12). A bullet displays to the left of the insertion point.

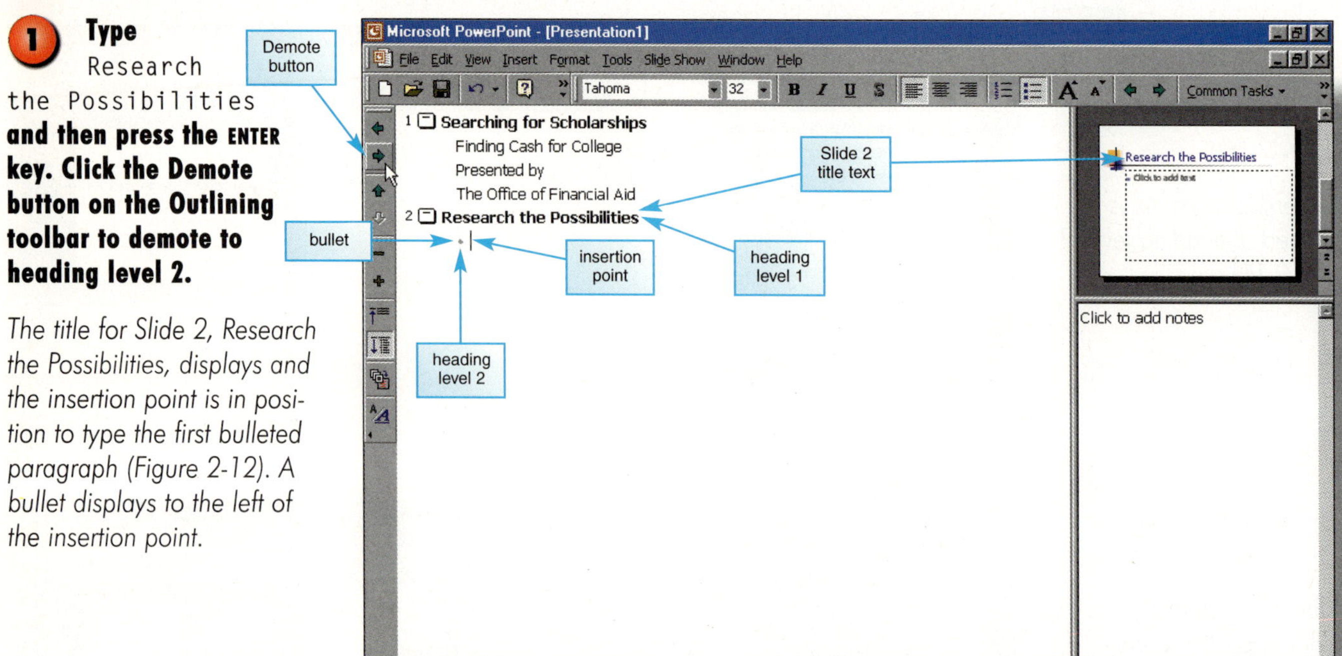

FIGURE 2-12

2 **Type** Consider various scholarship programs **and then press the ENTER key. Click the Demote button on the Outlining toolbar to demote to heading level 3. Type** Some are open to everyone **and then press the ENTER key.**

Slide 2 displays three heading levels: the title, Research the Possibilities, on heading level 1, the first bulleted paragraph on heading level 2, and the third bulleted paragraph and insertion point on heading level 3 (Figure 2-13). The heading level 3 font is Tahoma and the font size is 28 points.

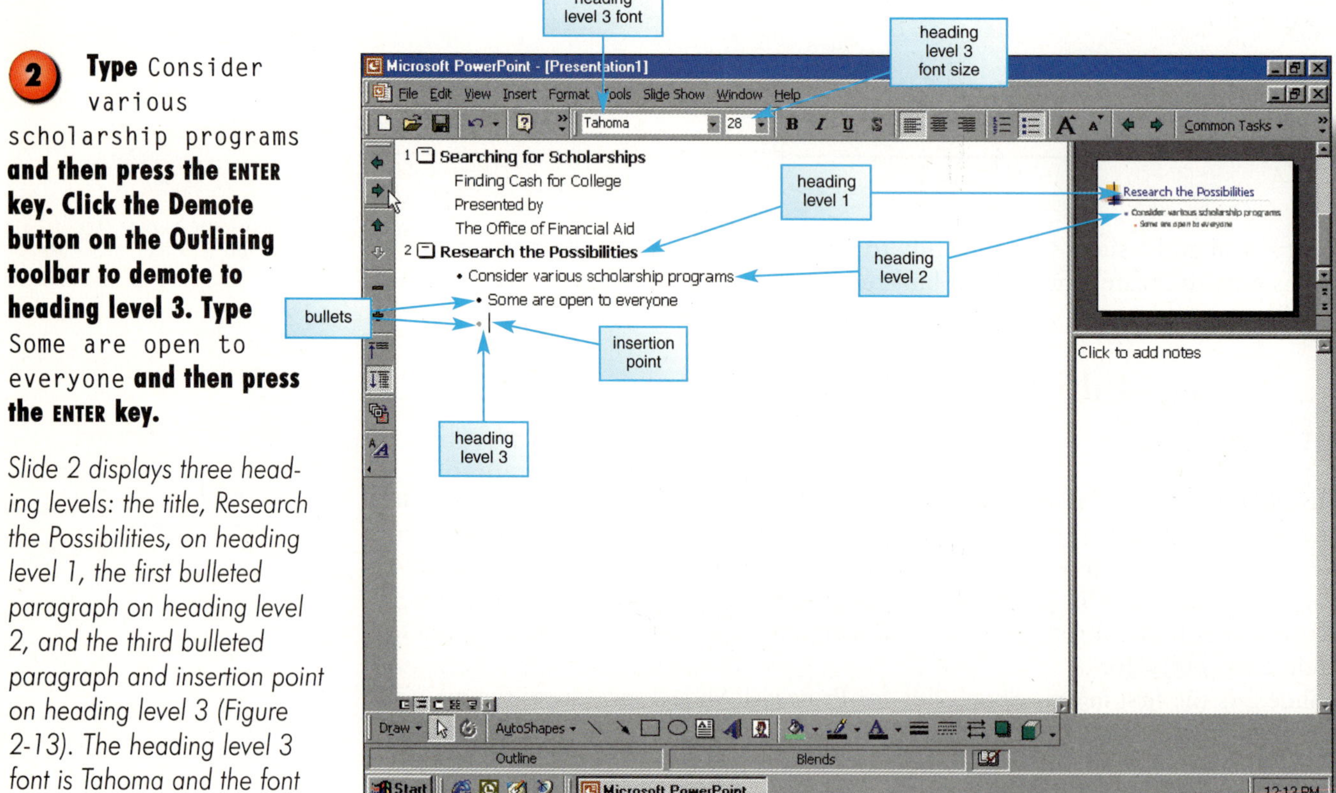

FIGURE 2-13

3 **Type** `Others are restricted to specific groups` **and then press the ENTER key. Click the Promote button on the Outlining toolbar to promote to heading level 2. Type** `Do not apply if you are unqualified` **and then press the ENTER key. Type** `Contact the Office of Financial Aid` **and then press the ENTER key. Click the Demote button on the Outlining toolbar to demote to heading level 3. Type** `Harker Hall – Room 3110` **and then press the ENTER key.**

The text for Slide 2 is complete (Figure 2-14). Pressing the ENTER key begins a new paragraph at the same heading level as the previous paragraph. A red wavy line displays under the word Harker to indicate that particular word is not found in the Microsoft main dictionary or open custom dictionaries.

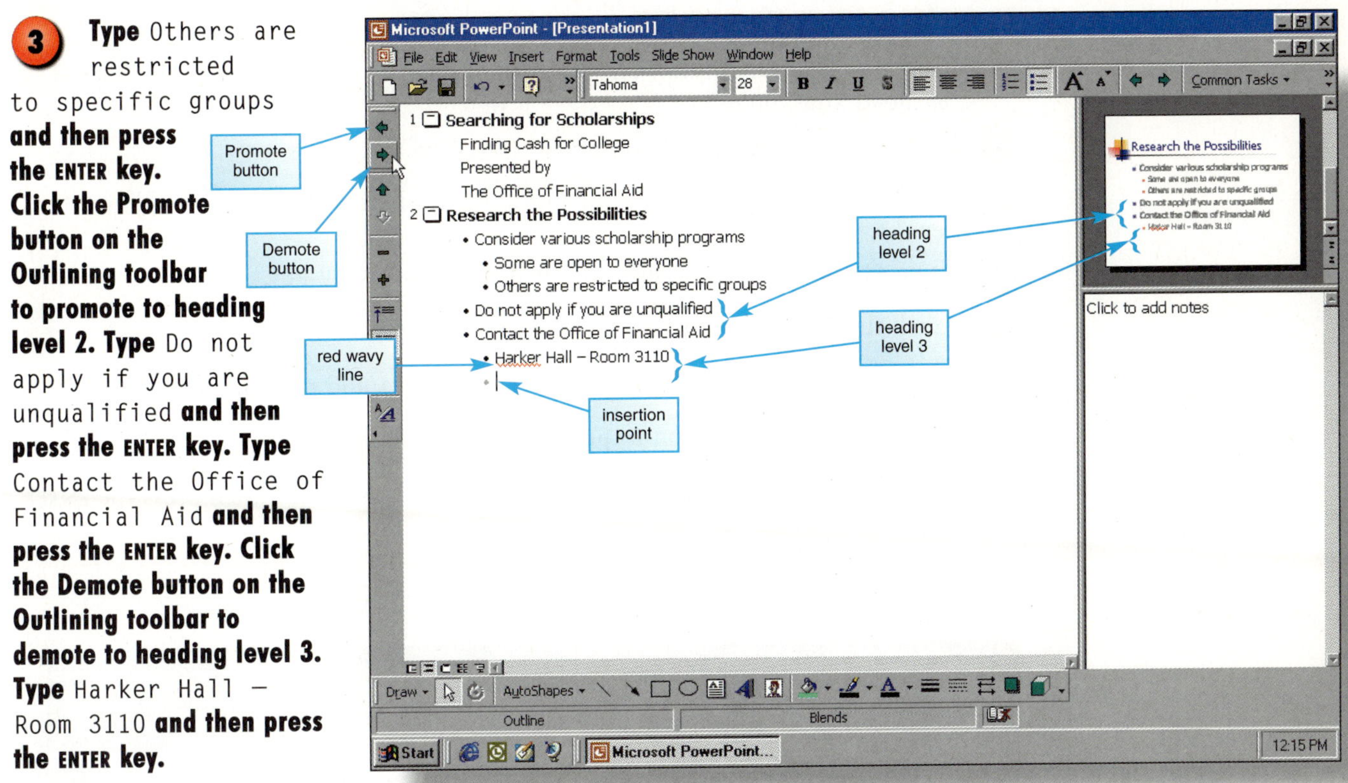

FIGURE 2-14

Creating Subordinate Slides

When developing your presentation, begin with a main topic and follow with **subordinate slides**, which are slides to support the main topic. Placing all your information on one slide may overwhelm your audience. In Project 1 you learned about the 7 × 7 rule, which recommends that each line should have a maximum of seven words, and each slide should have a maximum of seven lines. The steps on the next page use this 7 × 7 rule and explain how to create subordinate slides giving techniques for finding scholarships. The information on the next slide, Slide 3, provides information explaining the importance of looking for scholarships in a timely manner. Slides 4 and 5 list information on merit and private scholarships.

TO CREATE A SUBORDINATE SLIDE

1. Click the Promote button on the Outlining toolbar two times so that Slide 3 is added after Slide 2.
2. Type `Start Searching Early` and then press the ENTER key.
3. Click the Demote button on the Outlining toolbar to demote to heading level 2.
4. Type `Allow for deadlines` and then press the ENTER key.
5. Click the Demote button to demote to heading level 3.
6. Type `References may need to write letters` and then press the ENTER key.
7. Click the Promote button to promote to heading level 2.
8. Type `Some awards are made to first applicants` and then press the ENTER key.

The completed Slide 3 displays (Figure 2-15).

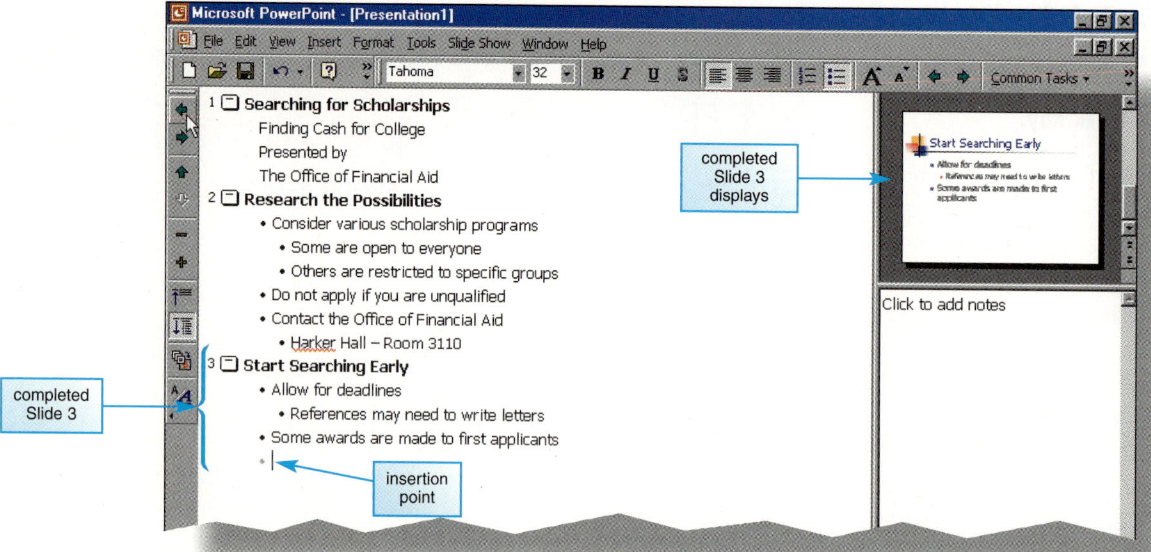

FIGURE 2-15

Creating a Second Subordinate Slide

The next step is to create Slide 4, which discusses merit scholarships. Perform the following steps to create this subordinate slide.

TO CREATE A SECOND SUBORDINATE SLIDE

1. Click the Promote button on the Outlining toolbar to add Slide 4 after Slide 3. Type `Consider Merit Scholarships` and then press the ENTER key.
2. Click the Demote button on the Outlining toolbar to demote to heading level 2. Type `Based on academic abilities or talents` and then press the ENTER key.
3. Click the Demote button to demote to heading level 3. Type `Drama, art, music, and athletics` and then press the ENTER key.

4. Click the Promote button to promote to heading level 2. Type `Personal income not considered` and then press the ENTER key.

The completed Slide 4 displays (Figure 2-16).

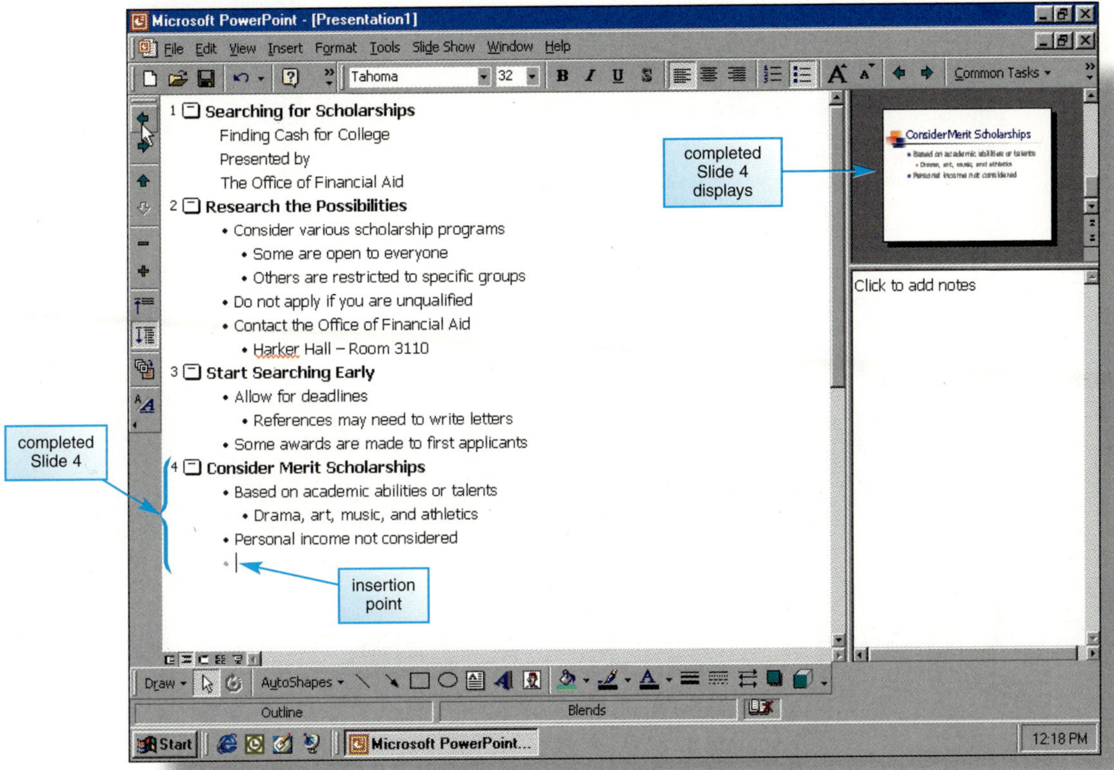

FIGURE 2-16

Creating a Third Subordinate Slide

The next step is to create Slide 5, which gives details on private sources of scholarship funds. Perform the following steps to create this subordinate slide.

TO CREATE A THIRD SUBORDINATE SLIDE

1. Click the Promote button on the Outlining toolbar to add Slide 5 after Slide 4. Type `Consider Private Sources` and then press the ENTER key.
2. Click the Demote button on the Outlining toolbar to demote to heading level 2. Type `Corporations` and then press the ENTER key.
3. Click the Demote button to demote to heading level 3. Type `Funds for employees and dependents` and then press the ENTER key.
4. Click the Promote button to promote to heading level 2. Type `Local organizations` and then press the ENTER key.
5. Click the Demote button to demote to heading level 3. Type `Funds for residents and members' families` and then press the ENTER key.

The completed Slide 5 displays (Figure 2-17 on the next page).

More About 2000

Smart Quotes

When you type an apostrophe and quotation marks, PowerPoint automatically converts these symbols to smart quotes, which also are called curly quotes. These symbols are in the shape of a dot and curved line (' " ' ") instead of a straight line (' "). If you want to use straight quotes instead, click Options on the Tools menu, click the Edit tab, and the click the Replace straight quotes with smart quotes check box.

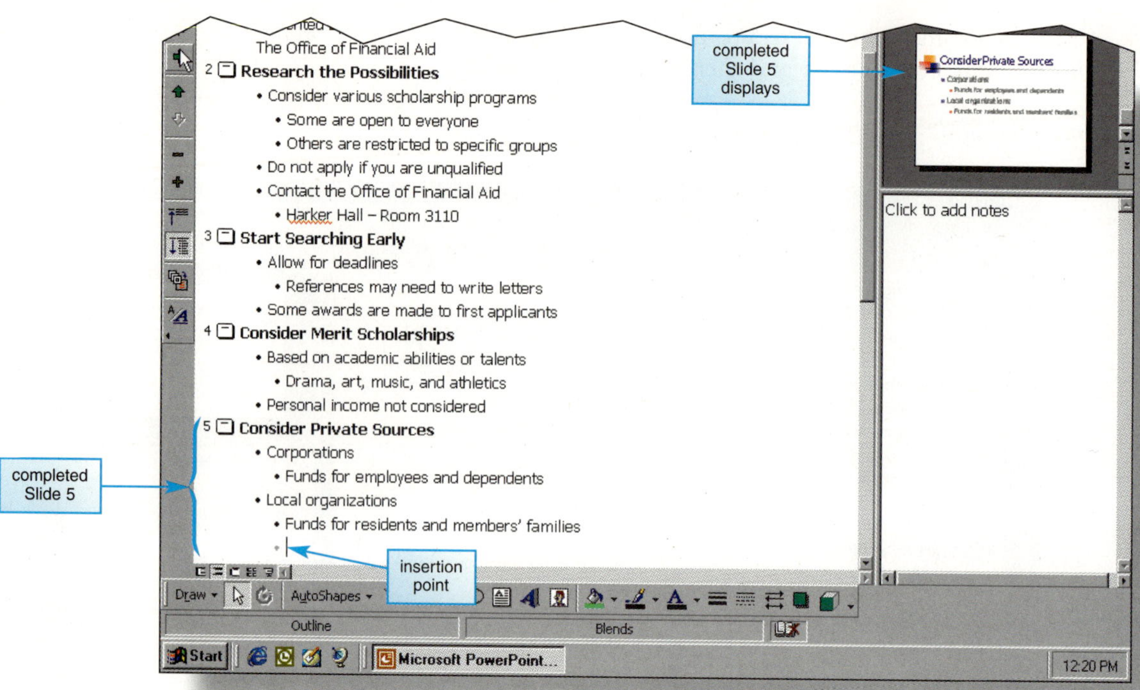

FIGURE 2-17

Creating a Closing Slide in Outline View

The last slide in your presentation is the closing slide. A **closing slide** gracefully ends a presentation. Often used during a question and answer session, the closing slide usually remains on the screen to reinforce the message delivered during the presentation. Professional speakers design the closing slide with one or more of these methods.

1. List important information. Tell the audience what to do next.
2. Provide a memorable illustration or example to make a point.
3. Appeal to emotions. Remind the audience to take action or accept responsibility.
4. Summarize the main points of the presentation.
5. Cite a quotation that directly relates to the main points of the presentation. This technique is most effective if the presentation started with a quotation.

Starting Presentations

When faced with constructing a new PowerPoint presentation, you may find it helpful to start by designing your closing slide first. Knowing how you want the slide show to end helps you focus on reaching this conclusion. You can create each slide in the presentation with this goal in mind.

The closing slide in this project lists three links to sites on the World Wide Web that have additional information on scholarships. Perform the following steps to create this closing slide.

TO CREATE A CLOSING SLIDE IN OUTLINE VIEW

1. Click the Promote button on the Outlining toolbar two times so that Slide 6 is added to the end of the presentation. Type `Additional Information` as the slide title and then press the ENTER key.
2. Click the Demote button on the Outlining toolbar to demote to heading level 2. Type `College Board Online` and then press the ENTER key.
3. Click the Demote button to demote to heading level 3. Type `www.collegeboard.org` and then press the ENTER key.
4. Click the Promote button to promote to heading level 2. Type `U.S. Department of Education` and then press the ENTER key.

5. Click the Demote button to demote to heading level 3. Type `www.ed.gov` and then press the ENTER key.
6. Click the Promote button to promote to heading level 2. Type `Financial Aid Information Page` and then press the ENTER key.
7. Click the Demote button to demote to heading level 3. Type `www.finaid.org` but do not press the ENTER key.

The completed Slide 6 displays (Figure 2-18). PowerPoint automatically displays the first two Internet addresses underlined and with a font color of red.

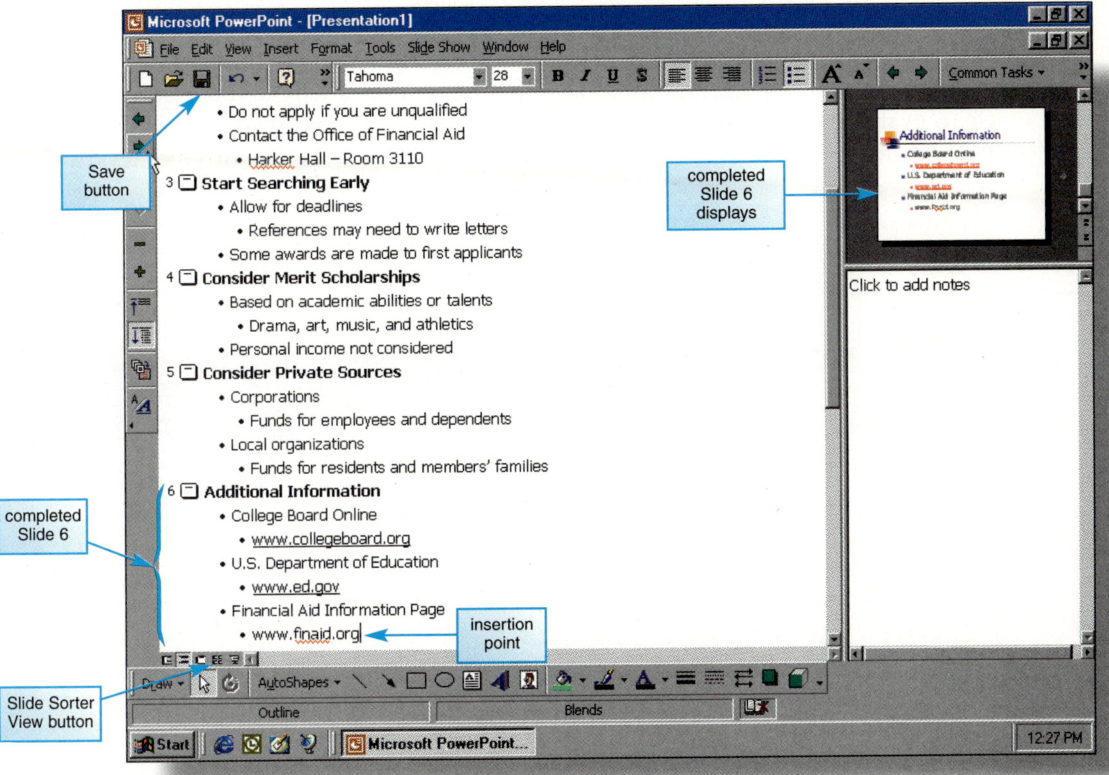

FIGURE 2-18

The outline now is complete and the presentation should be saved. The next section explains how to save the presentation.

Saving a Presentation

Recall from Project 1 that it is wise to save your presentation frequently. Now that you have created all the text for your presentation, you should save your presentation. For a detailed explanation of the following summarized steps, refer to pages PP 1.28 through PP 1.31 in Project 1.

TO SAVE A PRESENTATION

1. Insert a formatted floppy disk in drive A and then click the Save button on the Standard toolbar.
2. Click the Save in box arrow. Click 3½ Floppy (A:) in the Save in list.

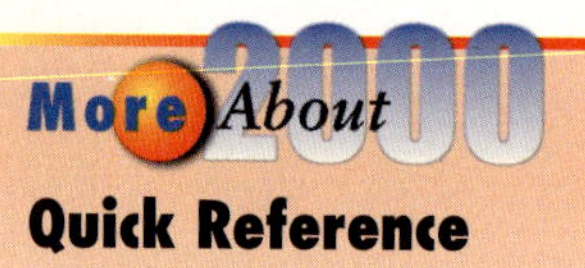

Quick Reference

For a table that lists how to complete the tasks covered in this book using the mouse, menu, shortcut menu, and keyboard, visit the Office 2000 Web page (www.scsite.com/off2000/qr.htm) and then click Microsoft PowerPoint.

3. Click the Save button in the Save As dialog box.

The presentation is saved on the floppy disk in drive A under the file name Searching for Scholarships. PowerPoint uses the first text line in your presentation as the default file name. The file name displays on the title bar.

Reviewing a Presentation in Slide Sorter View

In Project 1, you displayed slides in slide show view to evaluate the presentation. Slide show view, however, restricts your evaluation to one slide at a time. Outline view is best for quickly reviewing all the text for a presentation. The slide sorter view allows you to look at several slides at one time, which is why it is the best view to use to evaluate a presentation for content, organization, and overall appearance. Perform the following step to change from outline view to slide sorter view.

To Change the View to Slide Sorter View

1. **Click the Slide Sorter View button at the lower left of the PowerPoint window.**

PowerPoint displays the presentation in slide sorter view (Figure 2-19). Slide 6 is selected because it was the current slide in outline view.

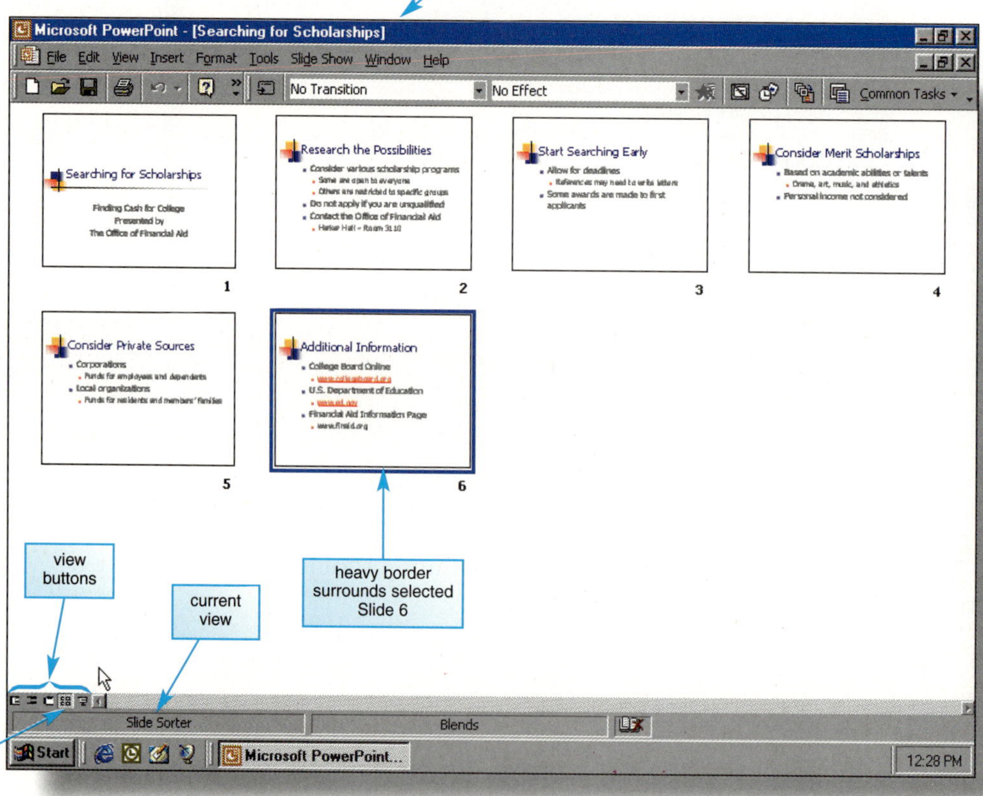

FIGURE 2-19

1. On View menu click Slide Sorter
2. Press ALT+V, press D

You can review the six slides in this presentation all in one window. Notice the slides have a significant amount of white space and look drab. These observations indicate a need to add visual interest to the slides by using graphics, such as clip art. The next several sections explain how to improve the presentation by changing slide layouts and adding clip art.

You can make changes to text in normal view, outline view, and slide view. It is best, however, to change the view to slide view when altering the slide layouts so you can see the result of your changes. Perform the following steps to change the view from slide sorter view to slide view.

To Change the View to Slide View

1 **Point to the Slide 3 slide miniature (Figure 2-20).**

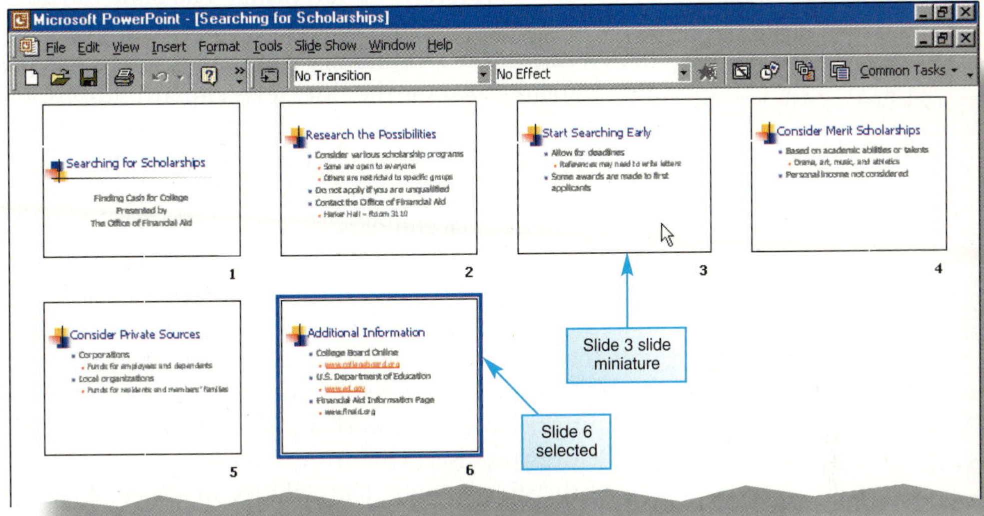

FIGURE 2-20

2 **Click the Slide 3 slide miniature. Click the Slide View button at the lower left of the PowerPoint window.**

Slide 3 displays in slide view (Figure 2-21). The Slide View button is recessed at the lower left of the PowerPoint window. The Slide 3 icon is highlighted in the outline pane.

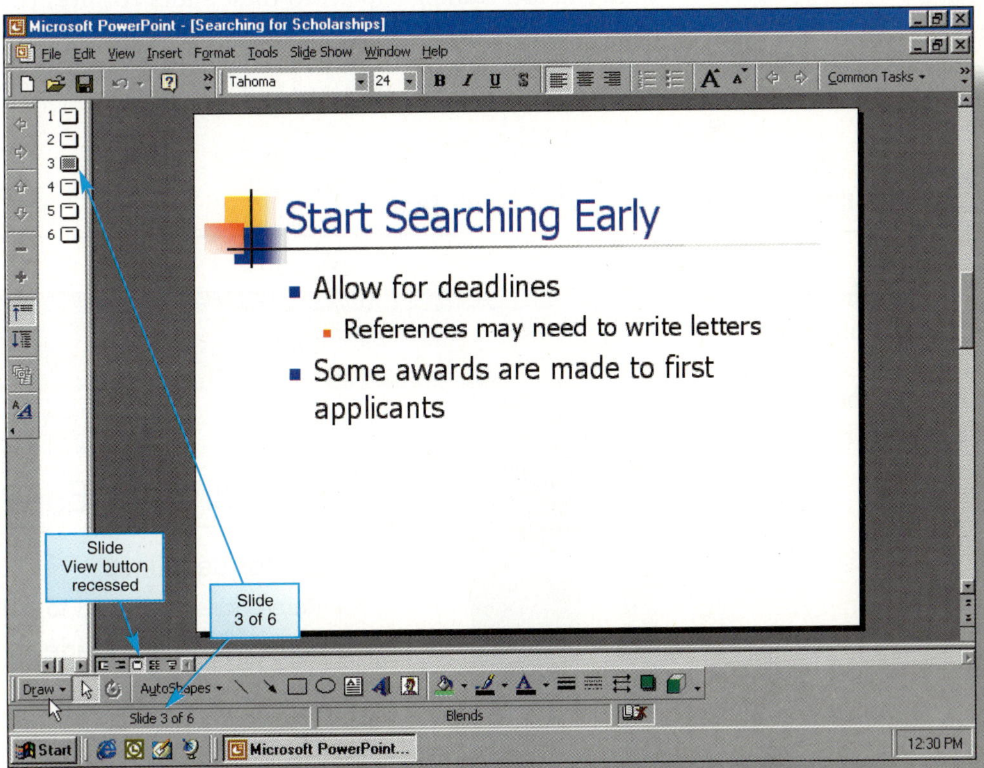

FIGURE 2-21

Changing Slide Layout

Toolbar Buttons

You can customize your toolbars by using buttons that are larger than the ones normally displayed. To enlarge the buttons, click Customize on the Tools menu, click the Options tab, and then select the Large icons check box. This setting will affect all of your Microsoft Office programs.

When you began developing this presentation, PowerPoint displayed the New Slide dialog box with the default Title Slide AutoLayout selected. When you added the five new slides to your presentation, PowerPoint used the default Bulleted List AutoLayout. After creating a slide, you can change its layout by clicking the **Common Tasks button** on the Formatting toolbar and then clicking the Slide Layout command on the Common Tasks button menu. The Slide Layout dialog box then displays.

Like the AutoLayout dialog box, the **Slide Layout dialog box** allows you to choose one of the 24 different AutoLayouts that has placeholders arranged in various configurations for the title, text, clip art, graphs, tables, and media clips. The placement of the text, in relationship to nontext objects, depends on the slide layout. The nontext Object Area placeholder may be to the right or left of the text, above the text, or below the text. Additionally, some slide layouts are constructed with two nontext object placeholders.

When you change the layout of a slide, PowerPoint retains the text and graphics and repositions them into the appropriate placeholders. Using slide layouts eliminates the need to resize objects and the font size because PowerPoint automatically sizes the objects and text to fit the placeholders. If the objects are in landscape orientation, PowerPoint sizes them to the width of the placeholders. If the objects are in portrait orientation, PowerPoint sizes them to the height of the placeholder.

Before you insert clip art into an AutoLayout placeholder, you first must select one of the slide layouts that includes an Object Area placeholder with a clip art region. This Object Area placeholder contains instructions to open Microsoft Clip Gallery 5.0. Double-clicking the clip art region in the Object Area placeholder activates the instructions. The Object Area placeholders on Slides 3, 4, and 5 will hold clip art. Adding clip art to these slides requires two steps. First, change the slide layout to Clip Art & Text or Text & Clip Art. Then insert clip art into the Object Area placeholder. Perform the following steps to change the slide layout on Slide 3 from a bulleted list to Clip Art & Text.

To Change Slide Layout to Clip Art & Text

1. **Click the Common Tasks button on the Formatting toolbar and then point to Slide Layout (Figure 2-22).**

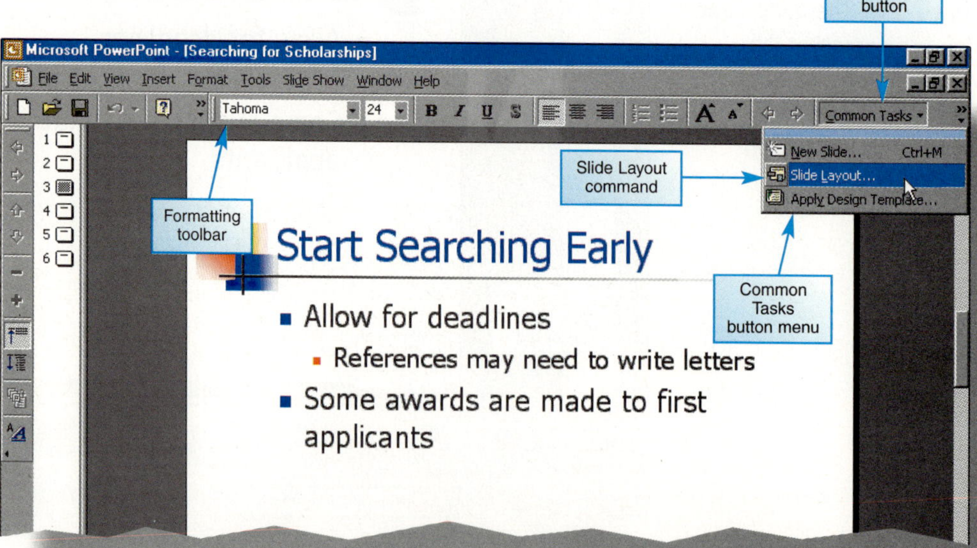

FIGURE 2-22

2 Click Slide Layout on the Common Tasks button menu. Click the Clip Art & Text slide layout located in row three, column two when the Slide Layout dialog box displays. Point to the Apply button.

The Slide Layout dialog box displays (Figure 2-23). The Clip Art & Text slide layout is selected. When you click a slide layout, its name displays in the box at the lower-right corner of the Slide Layout dialog box.

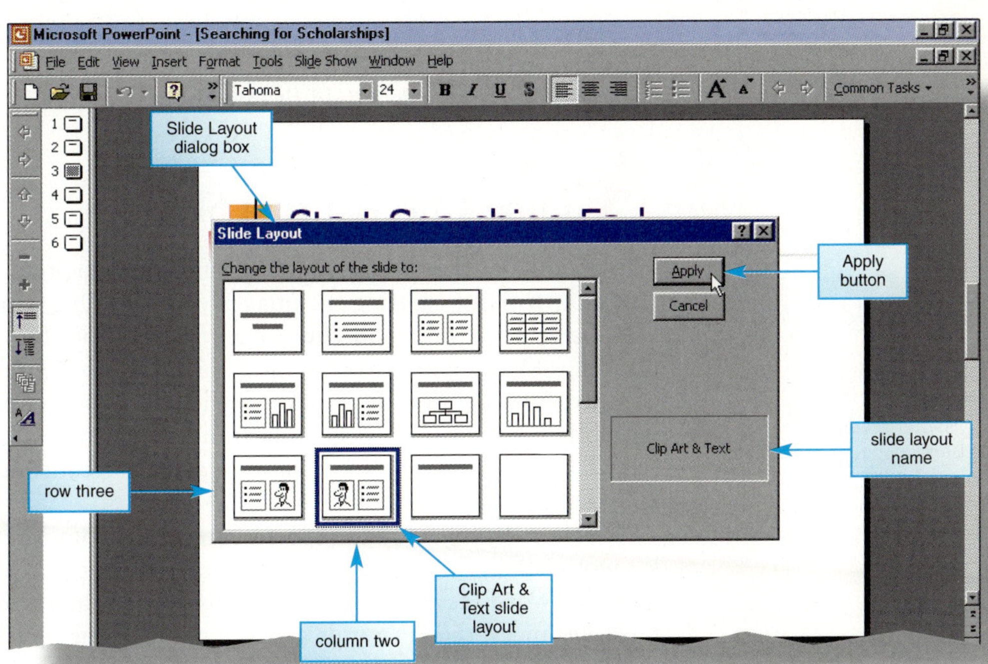

FIGURE 2-23

3 Click the Apply button.

Slide 3 displays the Clip Art & Text AutoLayout (Figure 2-24). PowerPoint moves the text object containing the bulleted list to the right side of the slide and automatically resizes the text to fit the object. The left side of the Object Area placeholder displays the message, Double click to add clip art.

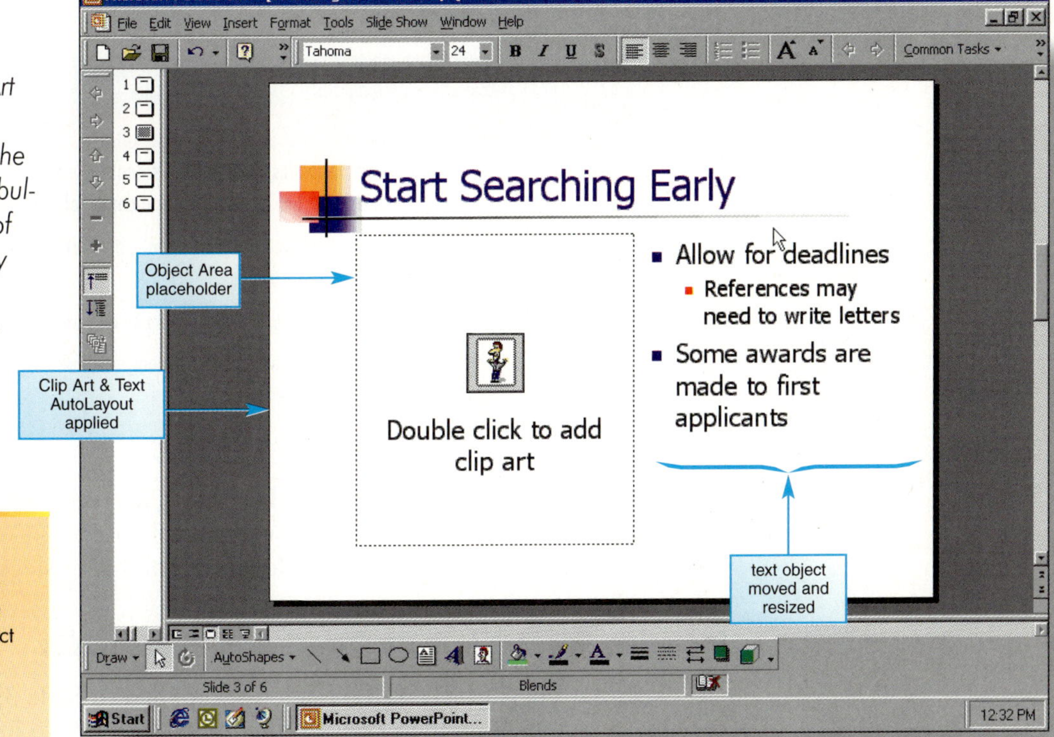

FIGURE 2-24

Other Ways

1. Right-click slide anywhere except Title Area or Object Area placeholders, click Slide Layout, double-click desired slide layout
2. Click Common Tasks menu button, click Slide Layout, double-click desired slide layout
3. On Format menu click Slide Layout, double-click desired slide layout
4. Press ALT+O, press L, press arrow keys to select desired slide layout, press ENTER

PowerPoint reduced the heading level 2 text in the Slide 3 placeholder from a font size of 32 points to 28 points and the heading level 3 text from 28 points to 24 points so all the words would fit into the text object.

Adding Clip Art to a Slide

Legal Use of Clip Art

Be certain you have the legal right to use clip art, photographs, sounds, and movies in your slide show. Read the copyright notices that accompany clip art software and are posted on Web sites. The owners of these images and files often ask you to give them credit for using their work, which may be accomplished by stating where you obtained the images.

Clip art offers a quick way to add professional-looking graphic images to your presentation without creating the images yourself. One clip art source is the Microsoft Clip Gallery 5.0. **Microsoft Clip Gallery 5.0** is a tool that accompanies Microsoft Office 2000 and allows you to insert pictures, photographs, audio clips, and video clips to a presentation. It contains a wide variety of clip art images and is shared with other Microsoft Office applications. Microsoft Clip Gallery 5.0 combines topic-related clip art images into categories, such as Academic, Business, Entertainment, and Healthcare & Medicine.

Table 2-2 shows four of the 51 categories from Microsoft Clip Gallery 5.0 and keywords of various clip art files in those categories. Clip art images have one or more keywords associated with various entities, activities, labels, and emotions. In most instances, the keywords give the name of the physical object and related categories. For example, an image of a horse in the Animals category has the keywords, animals, nature, creatures, mammals, domestic animals, and horses. You can enter these keywords in the Search for clips text box to find clip art when you know one of the words associated with the clip art image. Otherwise, you may find it necessary to scroll through several categories to find an appropriate picture.

Table 2-2 Microsoft Clip Gallery 5.0 Category and Keyword Examples

CATEGORY	CLIP ART KEYWORDS
Academic	Books; activities; graduations; schools; academic, music, school bells; academic, books, education; academic, office, office
Business	Risks; decisions; light bulbs; goals; motivation; challenges; workers; teamwork; activities
Entertainment	Musicians; musical notes; magic; dance; motion pictures; juggling priorities
Healthcare & Medicine	Research; vaccinations; equipment; medical; surgery; nursing; chiropractors; veterinary medicine; dentistry

Depending on the installation of Microsoft Clip Gallery 5.0 on your computer, you may not have the clip art pictures used in this project. Contact your instructor if you are missing clip art when you perform the following steps.

Inserting Clip Art into an Object Area Placeholder

Now that the Clip Art & Text layout is applied to Slide 3, you insert clip art into the Object Area placeholder. Perform the following steps to insert clip art to the Object Area placeholder on Slide 3.

To Insert Clip Art into an Object Area Placeholder

1 Position the mouse pointer anywhere within the clip art region of the Object Area placeholder.

The mouse pointer is positioned inside the clip art region of the Object Area placeholder (Figure 2-25). The mouse pointer becomes a four-headed arrow. It is not necessary to point to the picture inside the placeholder.

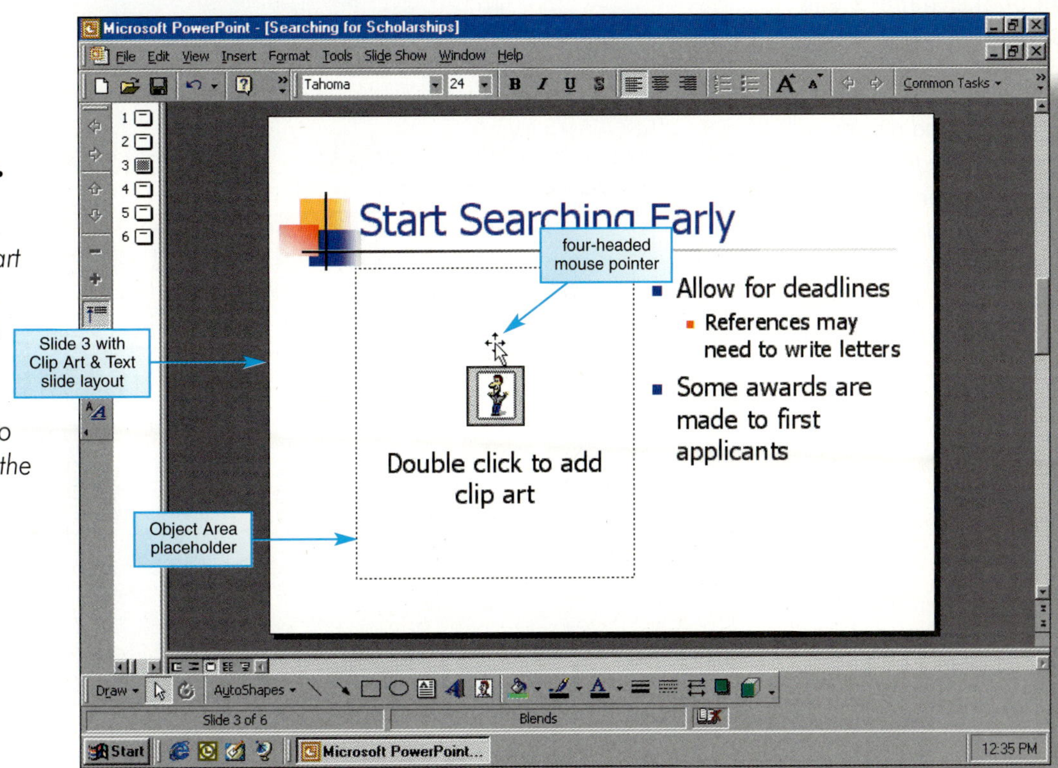

FIGURE 2-25

2 Double-click the left side of the Object Area placeholder on Slide 3.

PowerPoint displays the Microsoft Clip Gallery dialog box (Figure 2-26). The Pictures sheet displays clip art images by category, and New Category is the selected category. The Search for clips text box displays, Type one or more words. . . , as the entry.

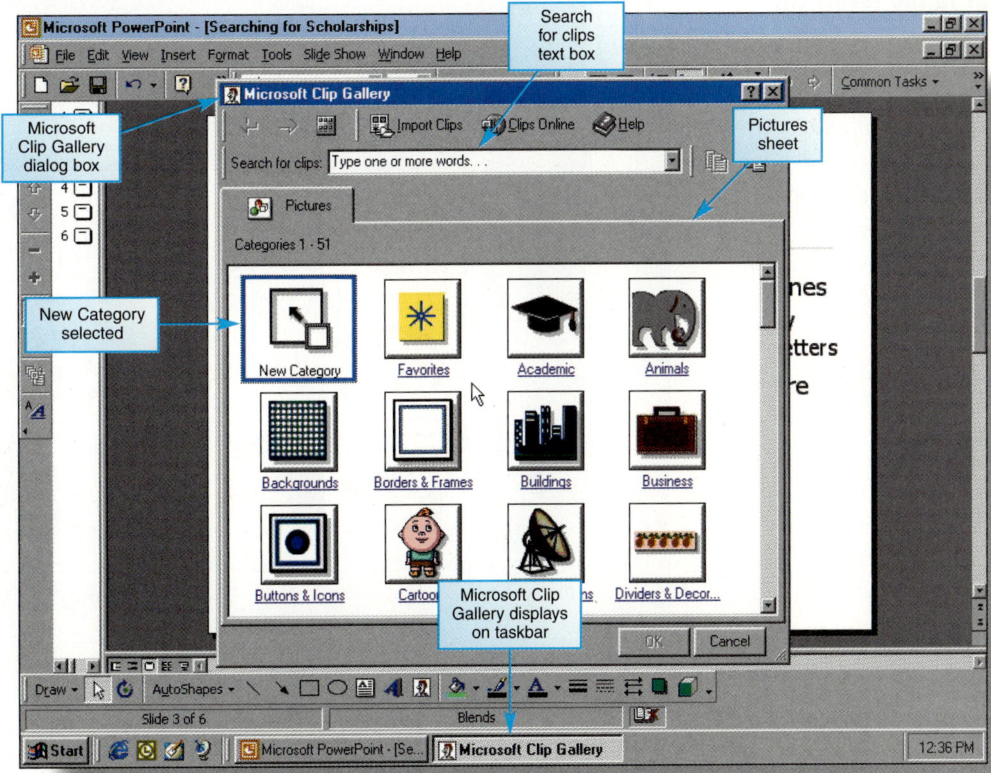

FIGURE 2-26

3 **Click the Search for clips text box. Type** books papers **and then press the ENTER key.**

The Microsoft Clip Gallery searches for and displays all pictures having the keywords, books and papers (Figure 2-27). The desired clip art image of a man looking in a book displays. Your images may be different depending on the clip art installed on your computer.

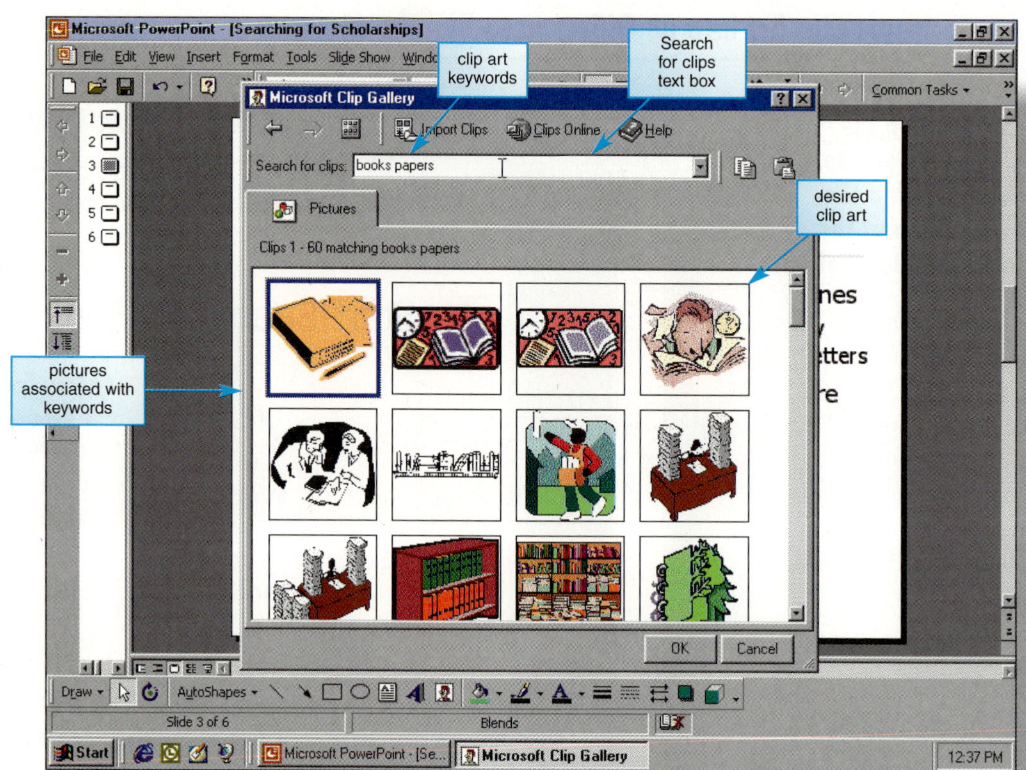

FIGURE 2-27

4 **Click the desired picture and then point to the Insert clip button.**

When you click the desired picture, a Pop-up menu displays (Figure 2-28). If you want to see a larger image of the selected image, you would click Preview clip on the Pop-up menu.

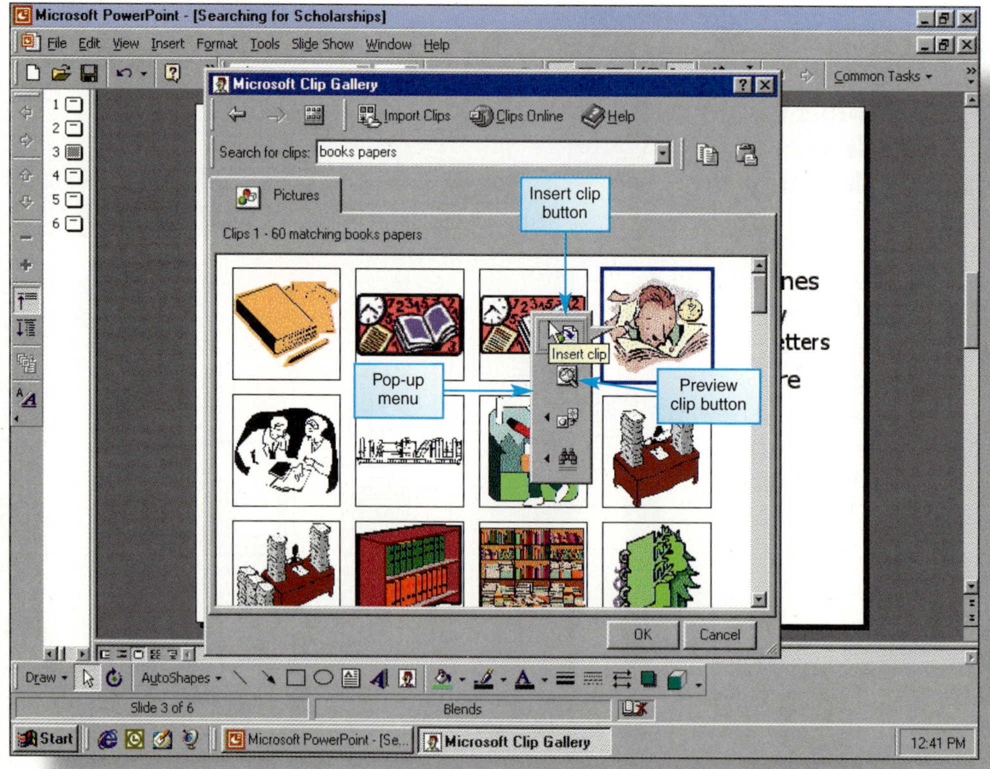

FIGURE 2-28

5 Click the Insert clip button on the Pop-up menu.

The selected picture is inserted into the Object Area placeholder on Slide 3 (Figure 2-29). PowerPoint automatically sizes the picture to fit the placeholder.

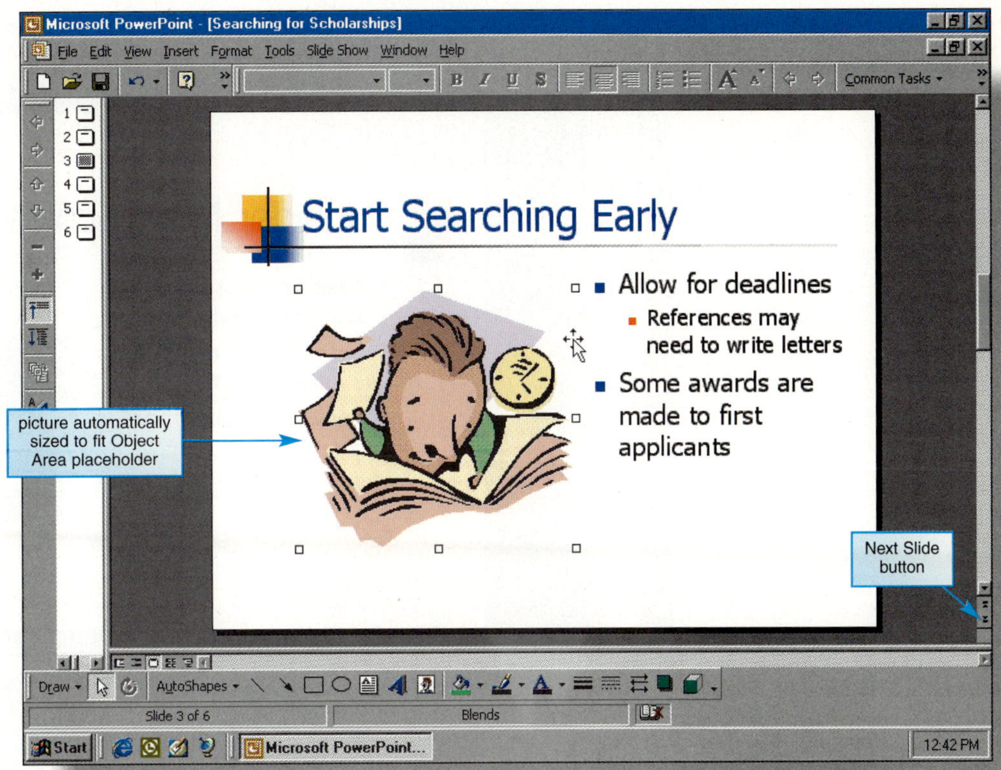

FIGURE 2-29

Inserting Clip Art on Other Slides

Slide 3 is complete, and you now want to add other clip art to Slides 4 and 5. Slide 5 also uses the Clip Art & Text slide layout, but Slide 4 uses the Text & Clip Art slide layout so the text displays on the left side of the slide and the clip art displays on the right side. Perform the following steps to change the slide layouts and then add clip art to Slide 4.

TO CHANGE THE SLIDE LAYOUT TO TEXT & CLIP ART AND INSERT CLIP ART

1. Click the Next Slide button on the vertical scroll bar to display Slide 4.
2. Click the Common Tasks menu button on the Formatting toolbar and then click Slide Layout.
3. Double-click the Text & Clip Art slide layout located in row three, column one.
4. Double-click the clip art region of the Object Area placeholder on the right side of Slide 4.
5. Type `art music` in the Search for clips text box and then press the ENTER key.
6. If necessary, scroll to display the desired clip art displaying a book, an artist's palette, and a keyboard. Click the desired clip art and then click Insert clip on the Pop-up menu.

The selected picture is inserted into the Object Area placeholder on Slide 4 (Figure 2-30 on the next page). PowerPoint automatically sizes the picture to fit the placeholder.

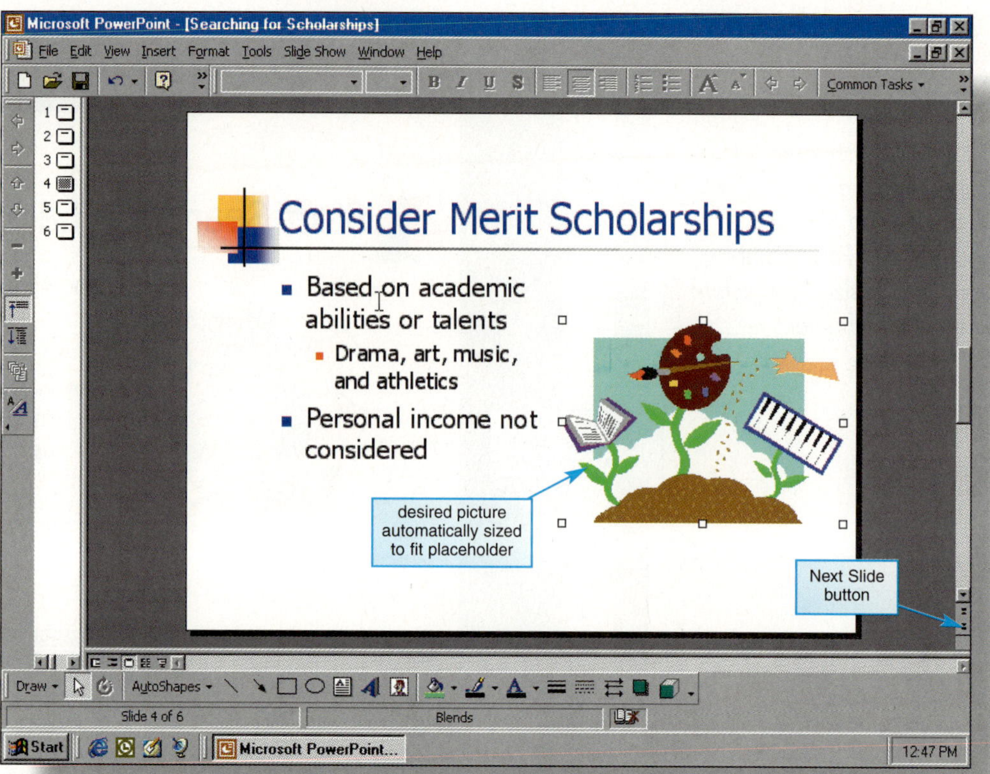

FIGURE 2-30

Slide 4 is complete. Your next step is to add other clip art to Slide 5, which also uses the Clip Art & Text slide layout you used in Slide 3. Perform the following steps to change the slide layouts and then add clip art to Slide 5.

TO CHANGE THE SLIDE LAYOUT TO CLIP ART & TEXT AND INSERT CLIP ART

1. Click the Next Slide button on the vertical scroll bar to display Slide 5.
2. Click the Common Tasks menu button on the Formatting toolbar and then click Slide Layout.
3. Double-click the Clip Art & Text slide layout located in row three, column two.
4. Double-click the clip art region of the Object Area placeholder on the left side of Slide 5.
5. Type `buildings money` in the Search for clips text box and then press the ENTER key.
6. If necessary, scroll to display the desired clip art displaying buildings with money on a flagpole. Click the desired clip art and then click Insert clip on the Pop-up menu.

The selected picture is inserted into the Object Area placeholder on Slide 5 (Figure 2-31). PowerPoint automatically sizes the picture to fit the placeholder.

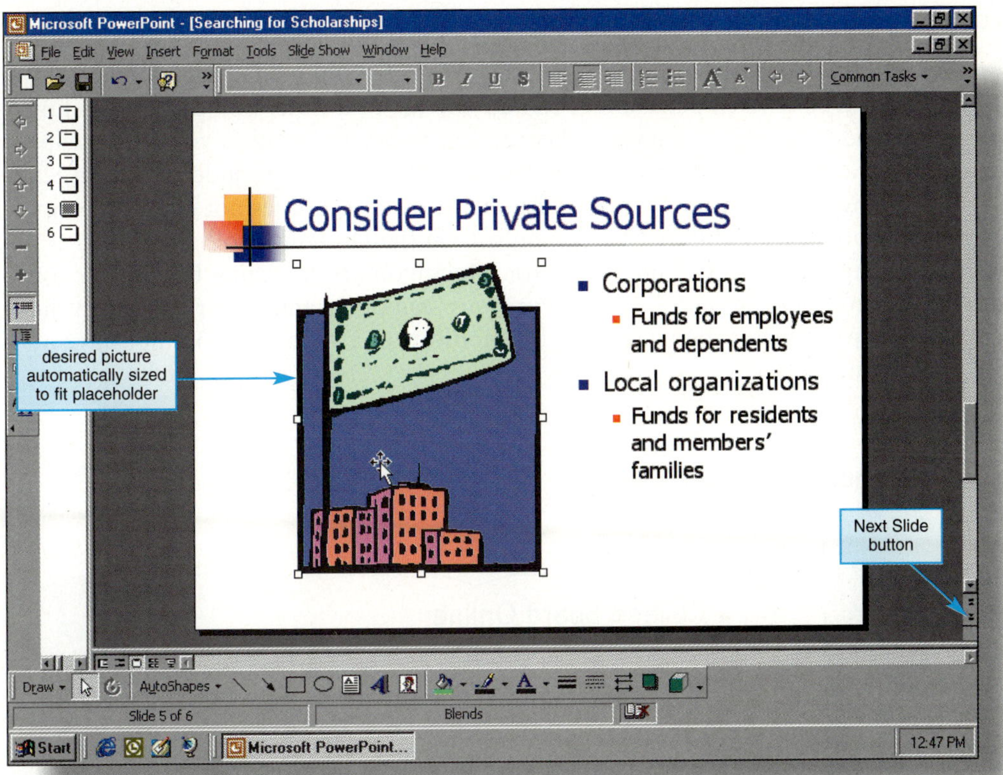

FIGURE 2-31

In addition to the clip art images in Microsoft Clip Gallery 5.0, other sources for clip art include retailers specializing in computer software, the Internet, bulletin board systems, and online information systems. Some popular online information systems are The Microsoft Network, America Online, CompuServe, and Prodigy. A **bulletin board system** is a computer system that allows users to communicate with each other and share files. Microsoft has created Clip Gallery Live, a special page on its World Wide Web site with new clips you can review and add to your Clip Gallery.

Besides clip art, you can insert pictures into your presentation. These may include scanned photographs, line art, and artwork from compact discs. To insert a picture into a presentation, the picture must be saved in a format that PowerPoint can recognize. Table 2-3 identifies some of the formats PowerPoint recognizes.

You can import files saved with the .emf, .gif, .jpg, .png, .bmp, .rle, .dib, and .wmf formats directly into your presentations. All other file formats require separate filters that are shipped with the PowerPoint installation software and must be installed. You can download additional graphics filters from the Microsoft Office Update Web site.

Table 2-3 Primary File Formats Recognized by PowerPoint

FORMAT	FILE EXTENSION
Computer Graphics Metafile	*.cgm
CorelDRAW	*.cdr, .cdt, .cmx, and .pat
Encapsulated PostScript	*.eps
Enhanced Metafile	*.emf
FlashPix	*.fpx
Graphics Interchange Format	*.gif
Hanako	*.jsh, .jah, and .jbh
Joint Photographic Experts Group (JPEG)	*.jpg
Kodak Photo CD	*.pcd
Macintosh PICT	*.pct
PC Paintbrush	*.pcx
Portable Network Graphics	*.png
Tagged Image File Format	*.tif
Windows Bitmap	*.bmp, .rle, .dib
Microsoft Windows Metafile	*.wmf
WordPerfect Graphics	*.wpg

Design

Graphic artists suggest designing a presentation in black and white and then adding color to emphasize particular areas on the slide. By starting with black letters on a white background, basic design principles, such as balance, contrast, rhythm, and harmony, are evident.

Inserting Clip Art on a Slide without a Clip Art Region

PowerPoint does not require you to use an AutoLayout containing a clip art region in the Object Area placeholder to add clip art to a slide. You can insert clip art on any slide regardless of its slide layout. On Slides 3, 4, and 5, you added clip art images that enhanced the message in the text. Recall that the slide layout on Slide 6 is the Bulleted List AutoLayout. Because this AutoLayout does not contain a clip art region, you click the Insert Clip Art button on the Drawing toolbar to start Microsoft Clip Gallery 5.0. The picture for which you are searching has money coming out of a computer monitor. Its keywords are computer and dollars. Perform the following steps to insert the picture of this monitor on a slide that does not have a clip art region.

To Insert Clip Art on a Slide without a Clip Art Region

1 **Click the Next Slide button on the vertical scroll bar to display Slide 6.**

2 **Point to the Insert Clip Art button on the Drawing toolbar.**

Clicking the Insert Clip Art button on the Drawing toolbar performs the same action as double-clicking an Object Area placeholder (Figure 2-32).

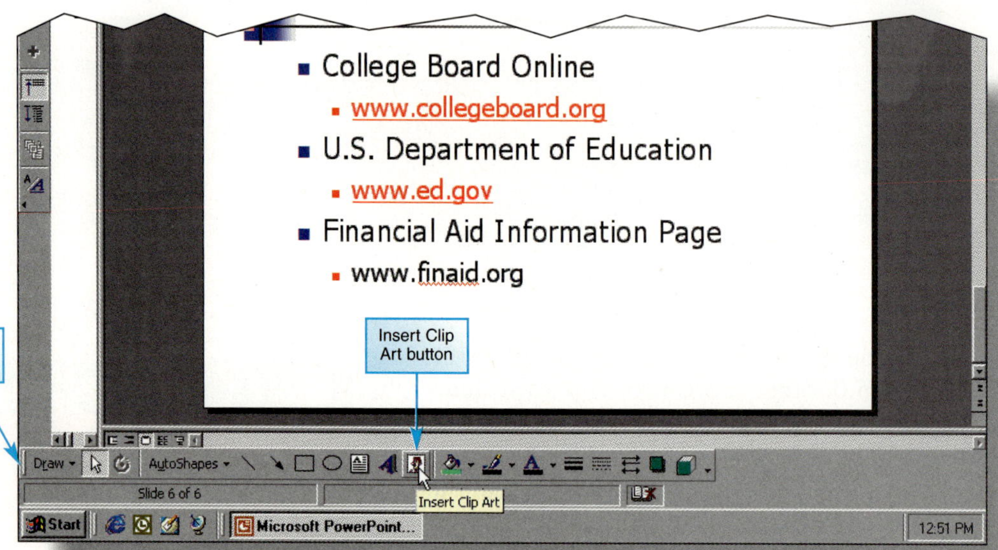

FIGURE 2-32

3 **Click the Insert Clip Art button.**

4 **Type** computer dollars **in the Search for clips text box and then press the ENTER key. If necessary, scroll to display the desired clip art displaying a computer monitor with money.**

The clip art image of money floating out of a computer monitor displays (Figure 2-33).

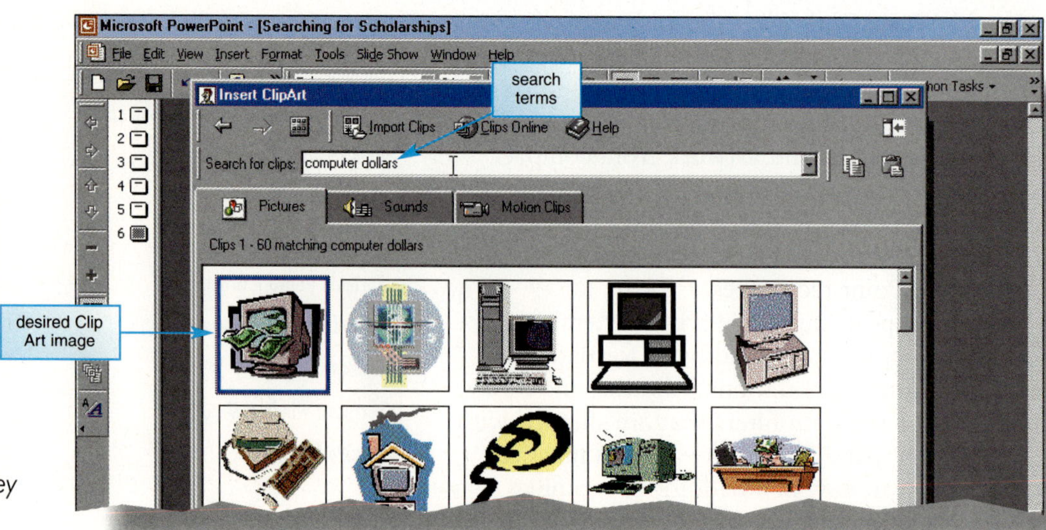

FIGURE 2-33

5 Click the desired clip art and then click Insert clip on the shortcut menu. Point to the Close button on the Insert Clip Art title bar.

PowerPoint inserts the desired clip art on Slide 6. Slide 6, however, is not visible until you close the Insert ClipArt dialog box (Figure 2-34).

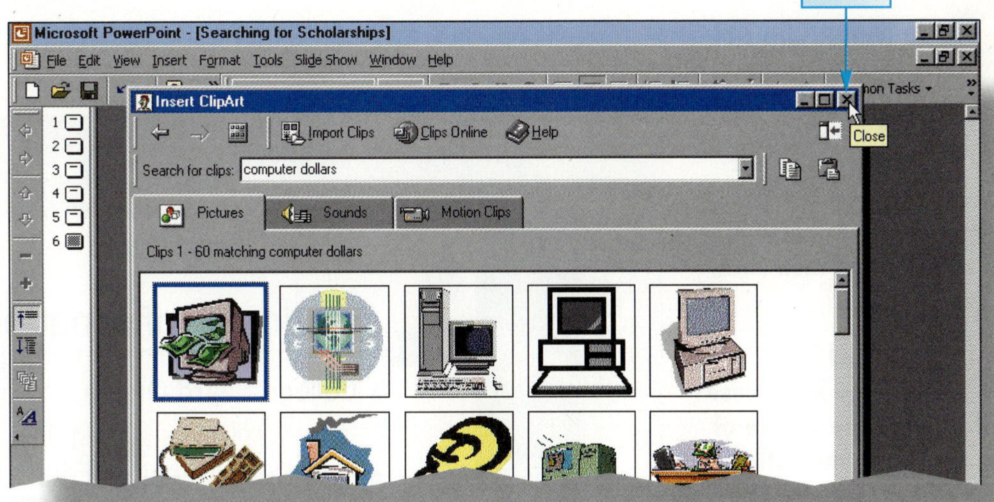

FIGURE 2-34

6 Click the Close button on the Insert ClipArt title bar.

The selected picture is inserted on Slide 6 (Figure 2-35). Sizing handles indicate the clip art is selected.

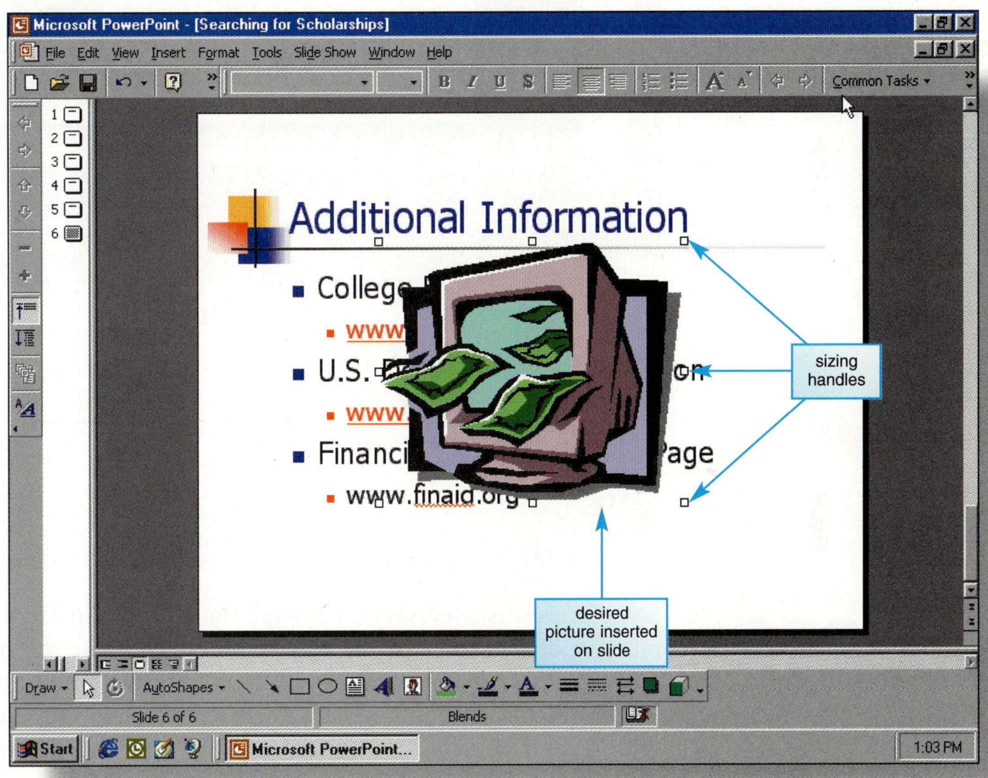

FIGURE 2-35

Moving Clip Art

After you insert clip art on a slide, you may want to reposition it. The picture of the monitor on Slide 6 overlays the bulleted list. You want to move the picture away from the text to the bottom-right corner of the slide. First move the picture and then change its size. Perform the steps on the next page to move the monitor to the bottom-right side of the slide.

To Move Clip Art

1 **If the picture of the monitor is not already selected, use the mouse pointer to point to the monitor and then click.**

2 **Press and hold down the left mouse button. Drag the picture of the monitor to the bottom-right corner of the slide. Release the left mouse button.**

When you drag an object, a dotted box displays. The dotted box indicates the new position of the object. When you release the left mouse button, the picture of the monitor displays in the new location (Figure 2-36). Sizing handles display at the corners and along the edges of the monitor.

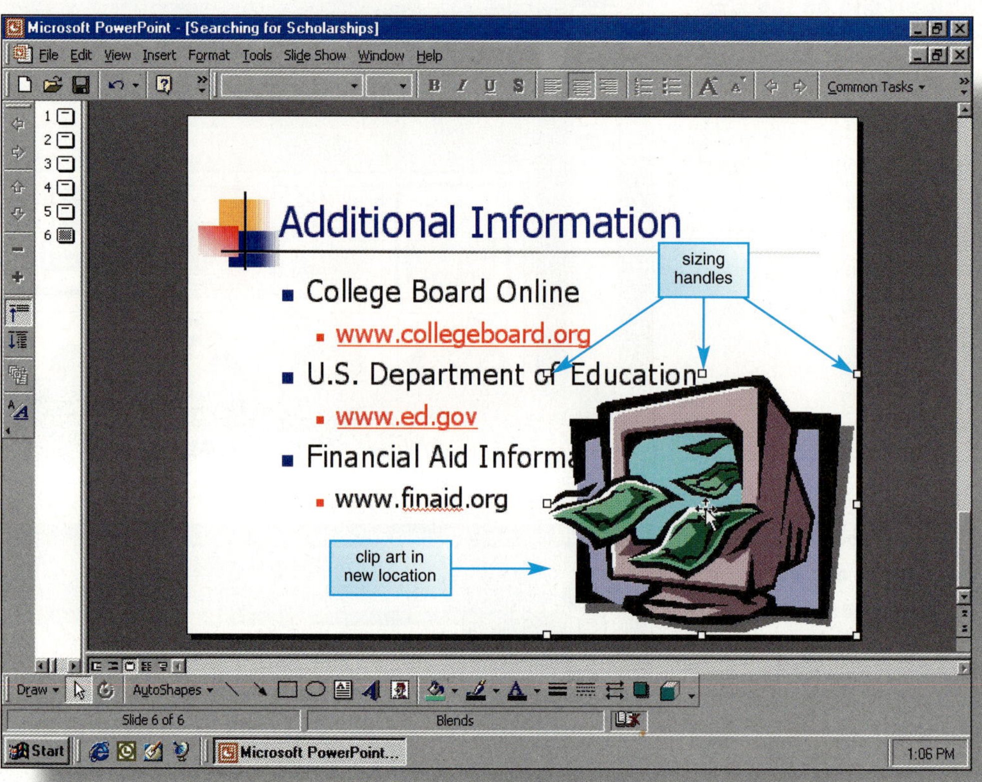

FIGURE 2-36

1. Select clip art, press arrow keys to move to new position

Changing Clip Art

If you alter a clip art image, be certain you have the legal right to make these modifications. For example, corporate logos are designed using specific colors and shapes and often cannot be changed. Photographs and illustrations cannot damage a person's reputation by casting them in a "false light," such as inserting a photograph of your teacher on the FBI's Top Ten Most Wanted list.

Changing the Size of Clip Art

Sometimes it is necessary to change the size of clip art. For example, on Slide 6, the monitor covers some of the bulleted text. To make the picture fit onto the slide, you reduce its size. To change the size of a clip art picture by an exact percentage, use the **Format Picture command.** The Format Picture dialog box contains six tabbed sheets with several options for formatting a picture. The **Size sheet** contains options for changing the size of a picture. You either enter the exact height and width in the Size and rotate area, or enter the height and width as a percentage of the original picture in the Scale area. When the **Lock aspect ratio check box** displays a check mark, the height and width settings change to maintain the aspect ratio of the original picture. **Aspect ratio** is the relationship between the height and width of an object. For example, a 3-by-5-inch picture scaled to 50 percent would become a 1½-by-2½-inch picture. Perform the following steps to reduce the size of the monitor.

To Change the Size of Clip Art

1 **Right-click the monitor picture. Point to Format Picture (Figure 2-37).**

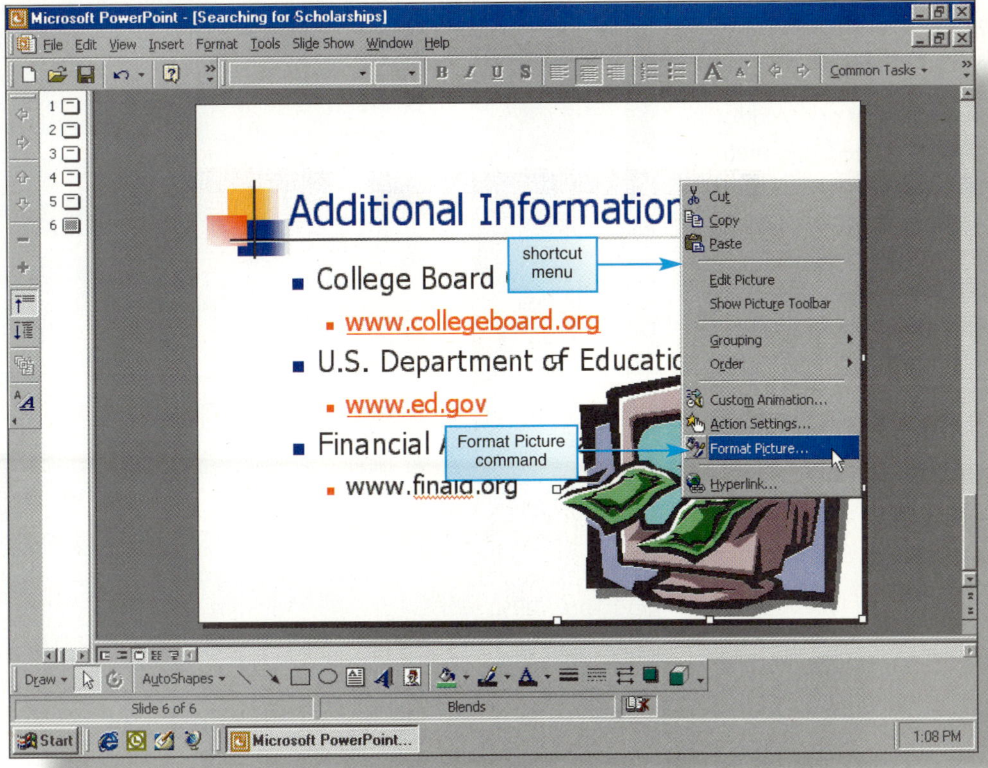

FIGURE 2-37

2 **Click Format Picture on the shortcut menu. Click the Size tab when the Format Picture dialog box displays.**

The Size sheet in the Format Picture dialog box displays (Figure 2-38). The Height and Width text boxes in the Scale area display the current percentage of the monitor picture, 100. Check marks display in the Lock aspect ratio and Relative to original picture size check boxes.

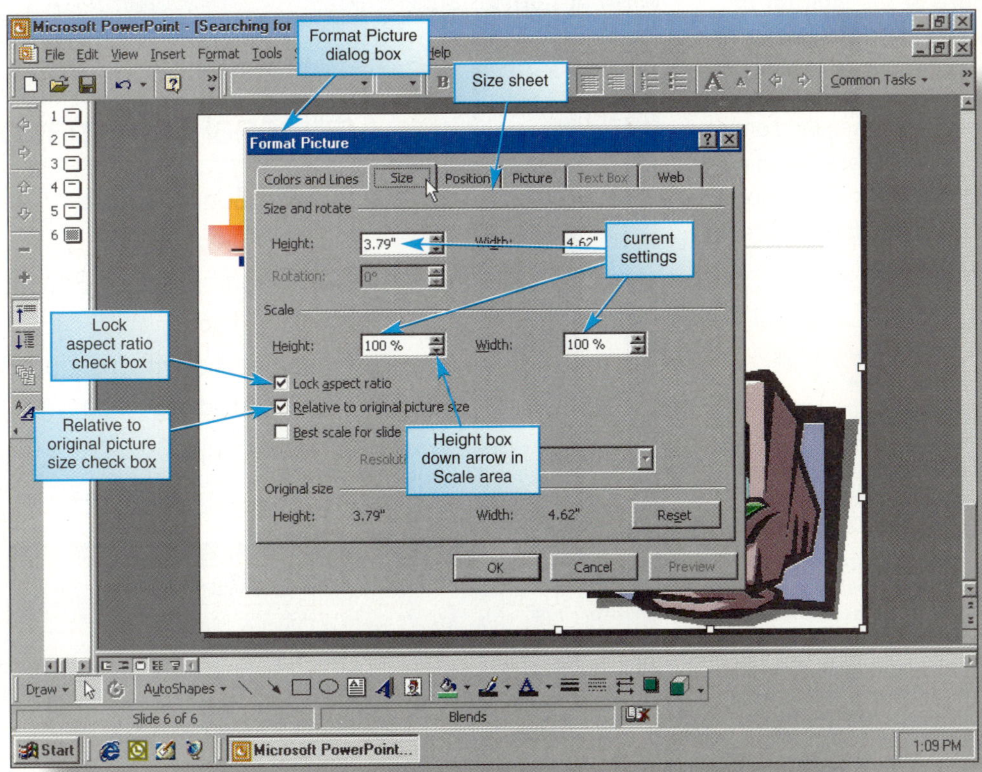

FIGURE 2-38

3 Click the Height box down arrow in the Scale area until 65% displays and then point to the OK button.

Both the Height and Width text boxes in the Scale area display 65% (Figure 2-39). PowerPoint automatically changes the Height and Width text boxes in the Size and rotate area to reflect changes made in the Scale area.

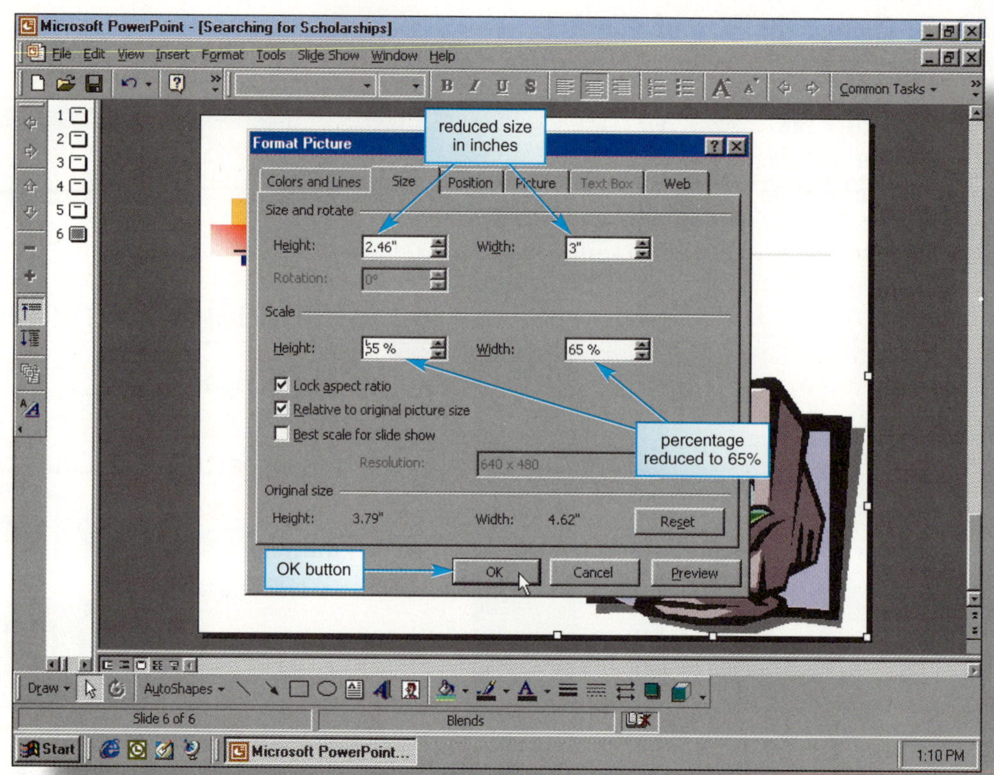

FIGURE 2-39

4 Click the OK button. Drag the picture of the monitor to the bottom-right corner of the slide.

PowerPoint closes the Format Picture dialog box and displays the reduced monitor picture in the desired location (Figure 2-40).

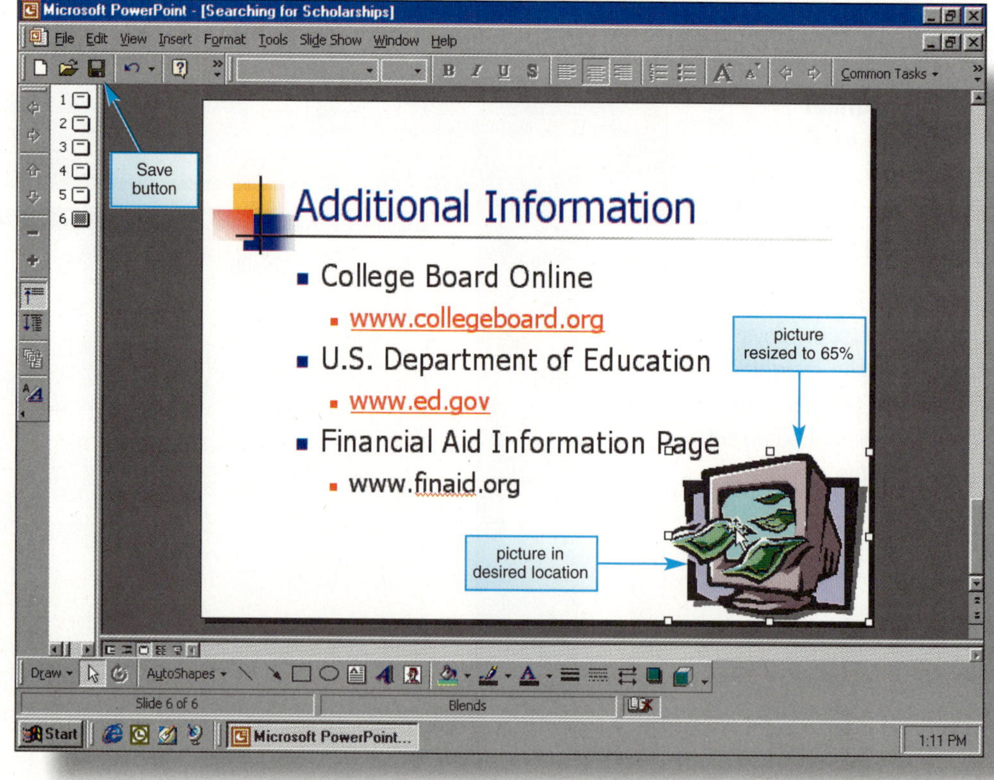

FIGURE 2-40

Other Ways

1. Click clip art object, on Format menu click Picture, click Size tab, click Height box up or down arrow in Scale area, click OK
2. Press ALT+O, press I, press CTRL+TAB three times to select Size tab, press TAB to select Height text box in Scale area, press up or down arrow keys to increase or decrease size, press ENTER
3. Click clip art object, drag a sizing handle until object is desired shape and size

Creating a Hyperlink

The Internet address in the last bulleted item on Slide 6 does not appear underlined and with a font color of red. When you were creating that slide, you typed the first two Web page addresses for the College Board Online and the U.S. Department of Education and then pressed the ENTER key after each address. When you performed this action, PowerPoint enabled the **AutoFormat as you type** option and changed the addresses' appearances to display as **hyperlinks**. A hyperlink is a shortcut that allows a user to jump from the presentation to another destination, such as a Web page on the Internet or another document on your computer. You did not press the ENTER key after you typed the address for the Financial Aid Information Web site, so the text did not change appearance and become a hyperlink. You can check to see if the AutoFormat as you type option is enabled by clicking Tools on the menu bar, clicking Options, and then verifying the AutoFormat as you type check box is selected.

To change the last bulleted line to a hyperlink, perform the following steps.

TO CREATE A HYPERLINK

1. Click the end of the last bulleted line, www.finaid.org.
2. Press the ENTER key.
3. Press the BACKSPACE key twice.

The last Internet address displays underlined and with a font color of red.

Saving the Presentation Again

To preserve the work completed, perform the following step to save the presentation again.

TO SAVE A PRESENTATION

1. Click the Save button on the Standard toolbar.

The changes made to the presentation after the previous save are saved on a floppy disk.

A default setting in PowerPoint allows for fast saves, which save only the changes made since the last time you saved. If you want to full save a copy of the complete presentation, click Tools on the menu bar, click Options on the Tools menu, and then click the Save tab. Remove the check mark in the Allow fast saves check box by clicking the check box and then click the OK button.

Adding a Header and Footer to Outline Pages

A printout of the presentation outline often is used as an audience handout. Distributing a copy of the outline provides the audience with paper on which to write notes or comments. Another benefit of distributing a copy of the outline is to help the audience see the text on the slides when lighting is poor or the room is too large. To help identify the source of the printed outline, add a descriptive header and footer. A **header** displays at the top of the sheet of paper or slide, and a **footer** displays at the bottom. Both contain specific information, such as the presenter's name or the company's telephone number. In addition, the current date and time and the slide or page number can display beside the header or footer information.

Footers

If you are going to turn your PowerPoint slides into overhead transparencies, consider using page numbers and the presentation name in the footer. This information will help keep the transparencies organized.

Using the Notes and Handouts Sheet to Add Headers and Footers

You add headers and footers to outline pages by clicking the Notes and Handouts sheet in the Header and Footer dialog box and entering the information you wish to print. Perform the following steps to add the current date, header information, the page number, and footer information to the printed outline.

Steps To Use the Notes and Handouts Sheet to Add Headers and Footers

1 Click View on the menu bar and then point to Header and Footer (Figure 2-41).

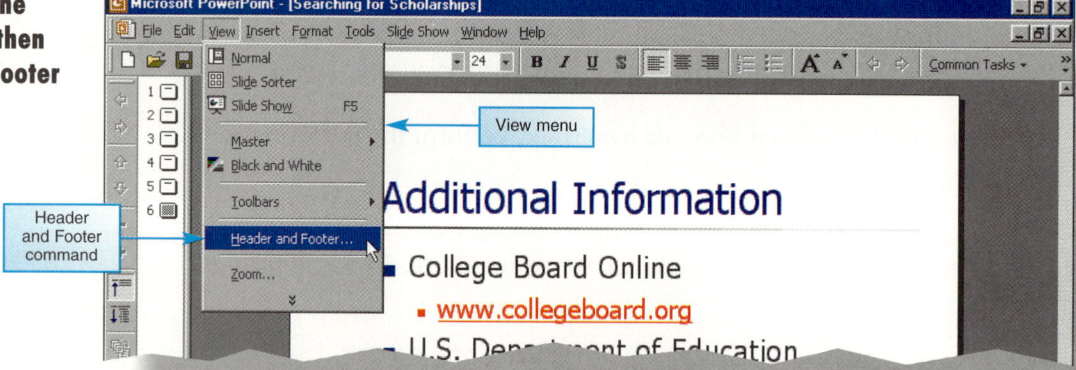

FIGURE 2-41

2 Click Header and Footer on the View menu. Click the Notes and Handouts tab when the Header and Footer dialog box displays.

The Notes and Handouts sheet in the Header and Footer dialog box displays (Figure 2-42). Check marks display in the Date and time, Header, Page number, and Footer check boxes. The Fixed option button is selected.

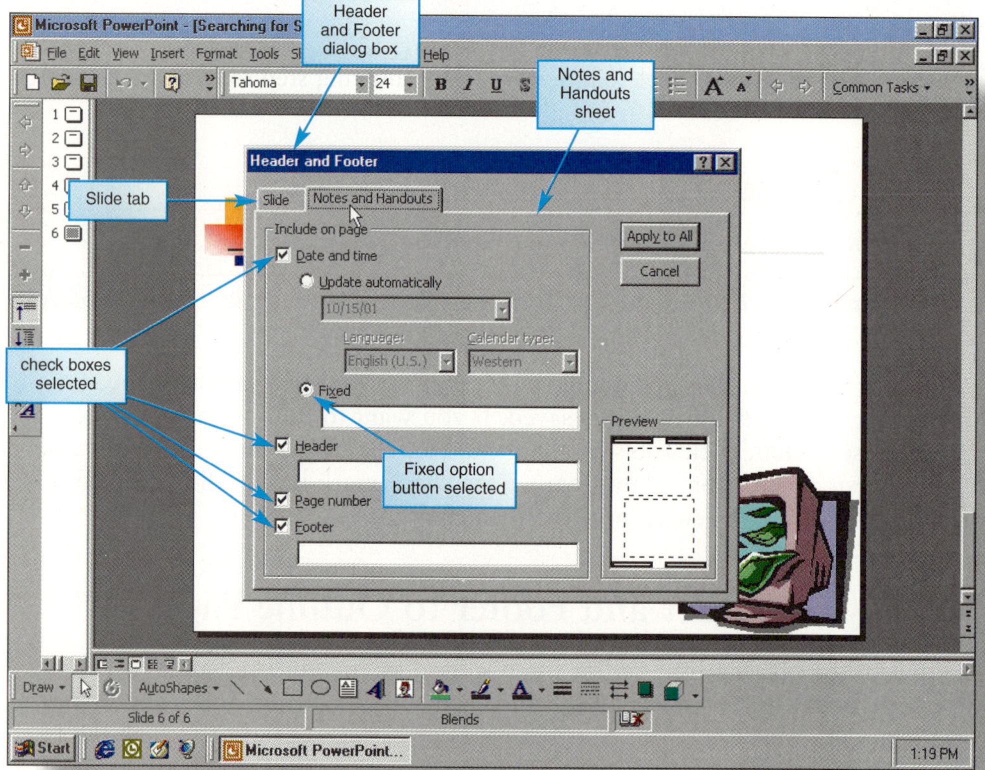

FIGURE 2-42

3 Click the Update automatically option button and then click the Header text box. Type `Searching for Scholarships` **in the Header text box. Click the Footer text box. Type** `Office of Financial Aid` **in the Footer text box and then point to the Apply to All button (Figure 2-43).**

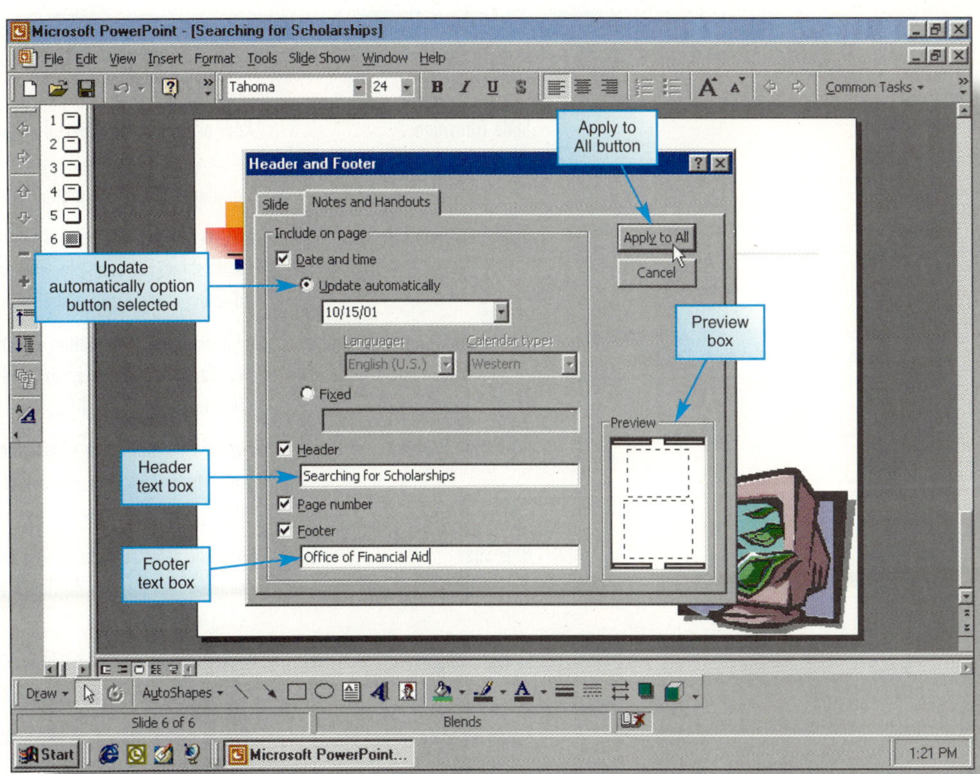

FIGURE 2-43

Click the Apply to All button.

PowerPoint applies the header and footer text to the outline, closes the Header and Footer dialog box, and displays Slide 6. You cannot see header and footer text until you print the outline (see Figure 2-67 on page PP 2.53).

Adding Animation Effects

PowerPoint provides many animation effects to make your slide show presentation look professional. In this project you use slide transition and custom animation. A **slide transition** is a special effect used to progress from one slide to the next in a slide show. **Custom animation effects** define animation types and speeds and sound effects on a slide. The following pages discuss each of these animation effects in detail.

Slide Sorter Toolbar

PowerPoint provides you with multiple methods for accomplishing most tasks. Generally, the fastest method is to right-click to display a shortcut menu. Another frequently used method is to click a toolbar button. For example, you can apply slide transition effects by clicking the Slide Transition Effects list box on the Slide Sorter toolbar.

The Slide Sorter toolbar displays only when you are in slide sorter view. It displays to the right of the Standard toolbar, in place of the Formatting toolbar. The Slide Sorter toolbar contains tools to help you quickly add animation effects to your slide show. Table 2-4 on the next page explains the function of the buttons and boxes on the Slide Sorter toolbar.

Table 2-4 Buttons and Boxes on the Slide Sorter Toolbar

BUTTON/BOX	BUTTON/BOX NAME	FUNCTION
	Slide Transition	Adds or changes the special effect that introduces a slide during a slide show. For example, you can play a sound when the slide displays, or you can make the slide fade from black.
Split Vertical Out	Slide Transition Effects	Adds or changes the special effect that introduces a slide during a slide show. For example, you can play a sound when the slide displays, or you can make the slide fade from black.
Zoom In From Screen Center	Animation Effects	Adds or changes animation effects on the current slide. Animation effects include sounds, text and object movements, and movies that occur during a slide show.
	Animation Preview	Runs all the animation effects for the current slide in a slide-miniature window so you can see how the animation will work during the slide show.
	Hide Slide	Hides the selected slide. If you are in slide view, hides the current slide so that it is not displayed automatically during an electronic slide show.
	Rehearse Timings	Runs your slide show in rehearsal mode, in which you can set or change the timing of your electronic slide show.
	Summary Slide	Creates a new slide from the titles of the slides you select in slide sorter view or normal view. The summary slide creates a bulleted list from the titles of the selected slides. PowerPoint inserts the summary slide in front of the first selected slide.
	Speaker Notes	Displays the speaker notes for the current slide. You can include speaker notes on your printed handouts, or you can print them to remember key points during a presentation.
Common Tasks	Common Tasks	Contains the three more frequently used commands: New Slide, Slide Layout, and Apply Design Template.
	More Buttons	Allows you to select the particular buttons you want to display on the toolbar.

Adding Slide Transitions to a Slide Show

Slide Transitions

Graphic designers suggest using a maximum of two different slide transition effects in one presentation. Any more than two can cause audience members to fixate on the visual effects and not on the slide content or the speaker.

PowerPoint allows you to control the way you advance from one slide to another by adding slide transitions to a slide show. PowerPoint has 42 different slide transitions, and you can vary the speed of each in your presentation. The name of the slide transition characterizes the visual effect that displays. For example, the slide transition effect, Split Vertical Out, displays the next slide by covering the previous slide with two vertical boxes moving from the center of the screen until the two boxes reach the left and right edges of the screen. The effect is similar to opening draw drapes over a window.

PowerPoint requires you to select at least one slide before applying slide transition effects. In this presentation, you apply slide transition effects to all slides except the title slide. Because Slide 6 already is selected, you must select Slides 2, 3, 4, and 5. The technique used to select more than one slide is the **SHIFT+click technique**. To perform the SHIFT+click technique in slide sorter view, press and hold down the SHIFT key as you click the starting and ending range of desired slides. After you click the slides to which you want to add animation effects, release the SHIFT key.

In the Searching for Scholarships presentation, you wish to display the Wipe Down slide transition effect between slides. That is, all slides begin stacked on top of one another, like a deck of cards. As you click the mouse to view the next slide, the new slide enters the screen by starting at the top of the slide and gliding down to the bottom of the slide. This effect resembles pulling down a window shade. Perform the following steps to apply the Wipe Down slide transition effect to the Searching for Scholarships presentation.

Steps To Add Slide Transitions to a Slide Show

1 Click the Slide Sorter View button at the lower left of the PowerPoint window.

PowerPoint displays the presentation in slide sorter view (Figure 2-44). Slide 6 is selected. Slide 6 currently does not have a slide transition effect, as noted in the Slide Transition Effects box on the Slide Sorter toolbar.

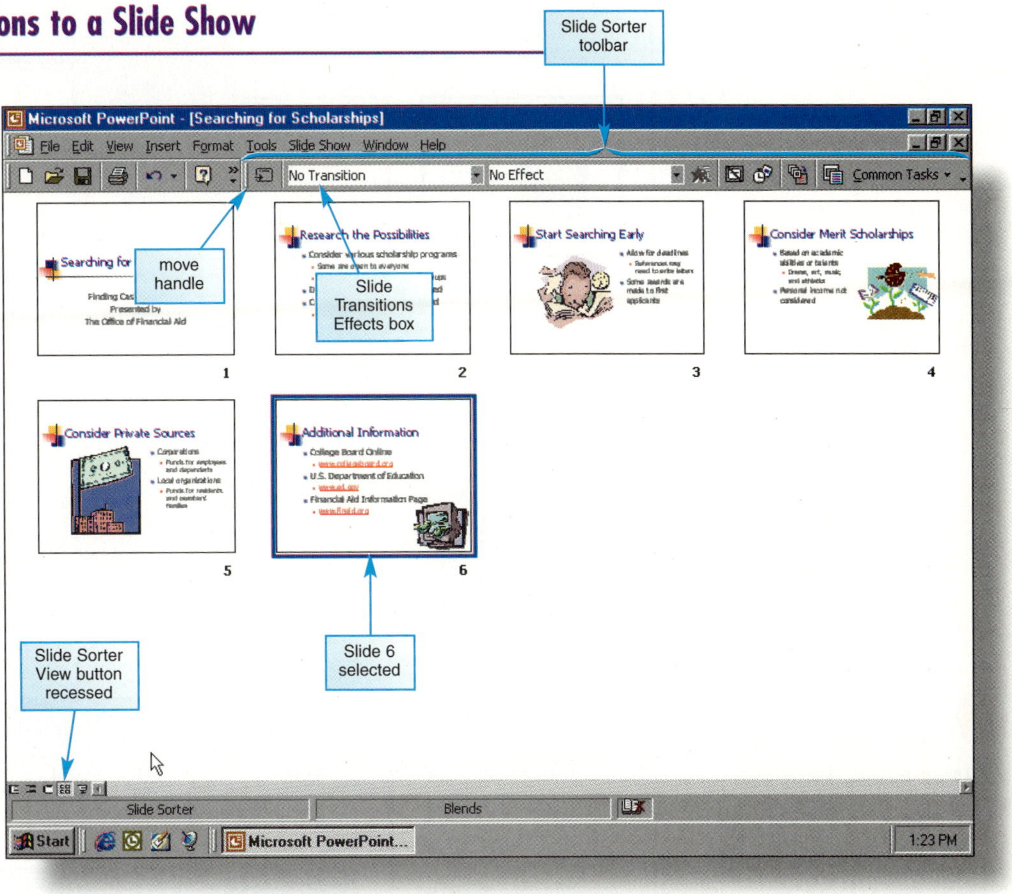

Slide Sorter toolbar
move handle
Slide Transitions Effects box
Slide 6 selected
Slide Sorter View button recessed

FIGURE 2-44

2 Press and hold down the SHIFT key and then click Slide 2. Release the SHIFT key.

Slides 2 through 6 are selected, as indicated by the heavy border around each slide (Figure 2-45).

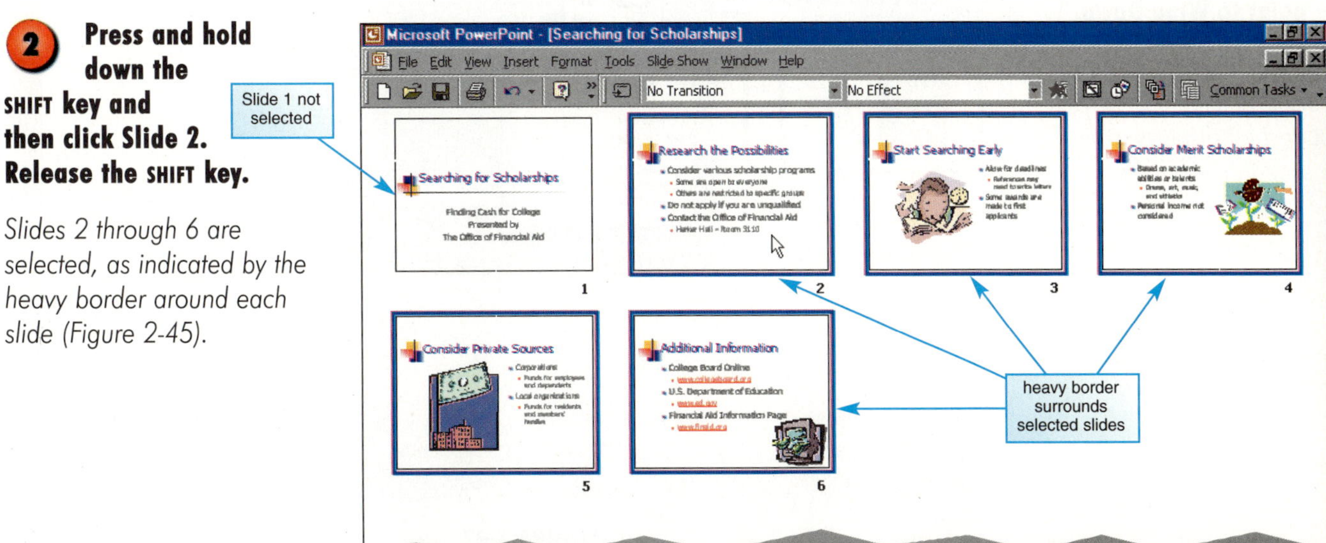

FIGURE 2-45

3 **Point to Slide 2 and right-click. Point to Slide Transition (Figure 2-46).**

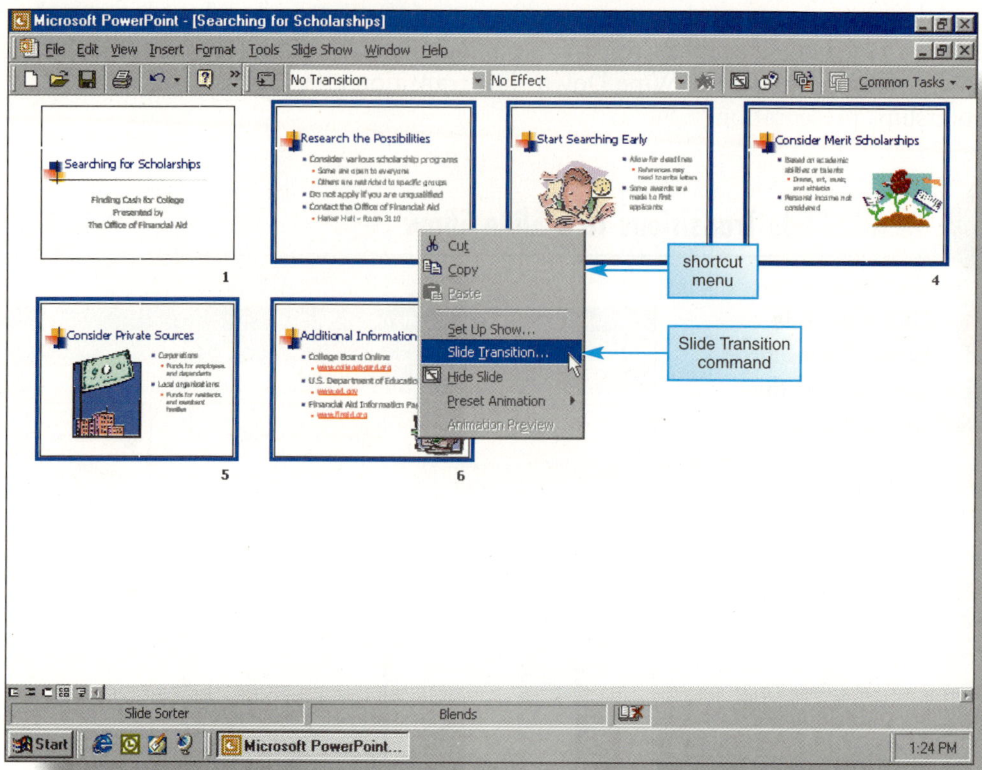

FIGURE 2-46

4 **Click Slide Transition on the shortcut menu. Click the Effect box arrow when the Slide Transition dialog box displays. Scroll down to display the Wipe Down effect in the Effect list, and then point to Wipe Down.**

The Slide Transition dialog box displays (Figure 2-47). The Effect list displays available slide transition effects.

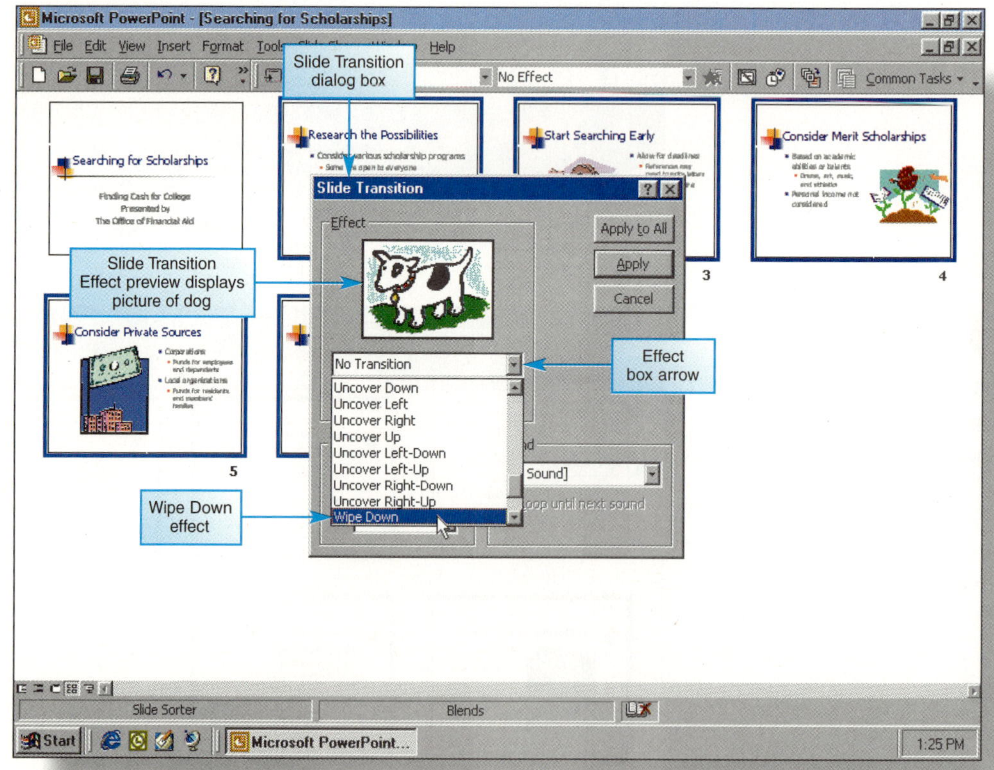

FIGURE 2-47

5 Click Wipe Down in the list. Point to the Apply button.

The Slide Transition Effect preview demonstrates the Wipe Down effect (Figure 2-48). To see the demonstration again, click the picture in the Slide Transition Effect preview.

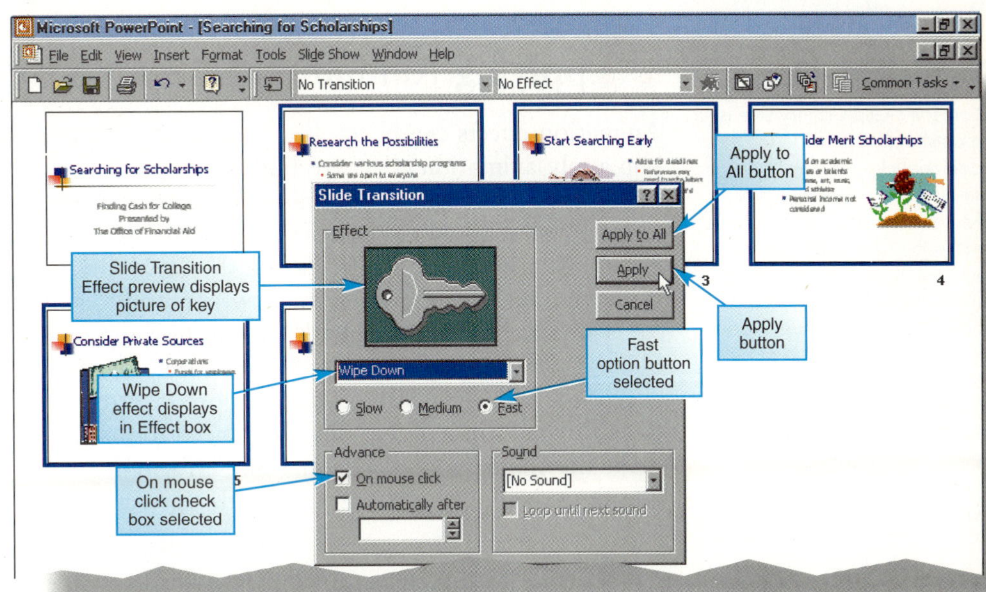

FIGURE 2-48

6 Click the Apply button.

PowerPoint displays the presentation in slide sorter view (Figure 2-49). A slide transition icon displays under each selected slide, which indicates that a slide transition effect has been added to those slides. The current slide transition effect, Wipe Down, displays in the Slide Transition Effects box.

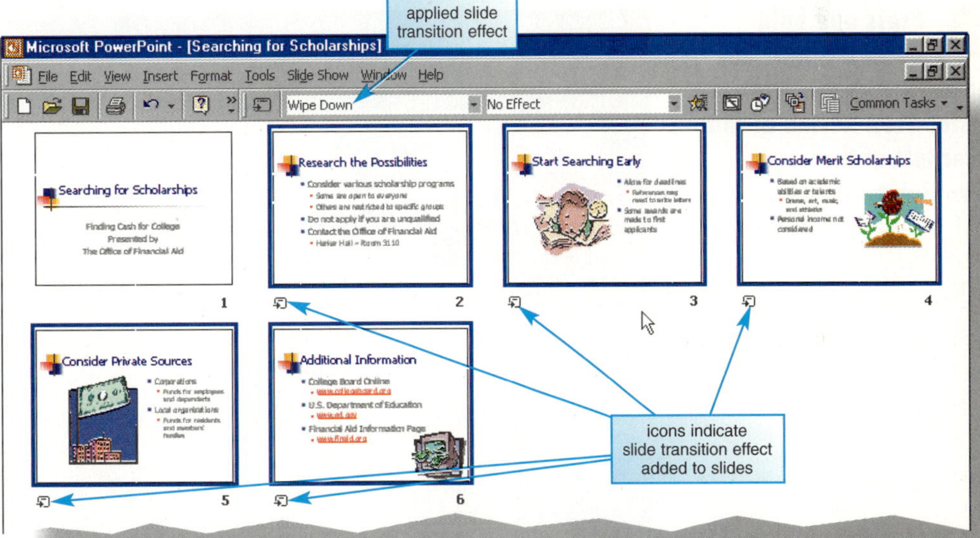

FIGURE 2-49

Other Ways

1. Select slide, right-click selected slide, click Slide Transition, click Effect box arrow, select desired effect, click Apply button
2. Select slide, on Slide Show menu click Slide Transition, click Effect box arrow, select desired effect, click Apply button

To adjust the speed at which the special effect runs during the slide show, click Slow, Medium, or Fast in the Effect area in the Slide Transition dialog box. When you click a particular speed option, PowerPoint runs that effect in the sample picture.

To apply slide transition effects to every slide in the presentation, right-click a slide, click Slide Transition on the shortcut menu, choose the desired slide transition effect, and then click the Apply to All button.

To remove slide transition effects when displaying the presentation in slide sorter view, select the slides to which slide transition effects are applied, click the Slide Transition Effects box arrow, and select No Transition.

The Wipe Down slide transition effect has been applied to the presentation. The next step in creating this slide show is to add animation effects to individual slides.

Clip Gallery Live

Microsoft's Clip Gallery Live is an outstanding place to locate additional clip art. This Web site also contains movie clips, pictures, and sounds. To connect to the Clip Gallery Live site, click the Insert Clip Art button on the Drawing toolbar and then click the Clips Online button. Another method of connecting to this area is to visit the PowerPoint 2000 More About Web page (www.scsite.com/pp2000/more.htm) and click Clip Gallery Live.

Applying Animation Effects to Bulleted Slides

Animation effects can be applied to text as well as to objects, such as clip art. When you apply animation effects to bulleted text, you progressively disclose each bulleted paragraph. As a result, you build the slide paragraph by paragraph during the running of a slide show to control the flow of information. PowerPoint has a wide variety of custom animation effects and the capability to dim the paragraphs already displaying on the slide when the new paragraph is displayed.

The next step is to apply the Zoom In From Screen Center animation effect to Slides 2, 3, 4, 5, and 6 in the Searching for Scholarships presentation. All slides, except the title slide, will have the Zoom In From Screen Center animation effect. Recall from Project 1 that when you need to make a change that affects all slides, make the change to the slide master. Perform the following steps to apply animation effects to the bulleted paragraphs in this presentation.

To Use the Slide Master to Apply Animation Effects to All Bulleted Slides

1 **Press and hold down the SHIFT key and then click the Slide Master View button at the lower left of the PowerPoint window.**

The slide master displays (Figure 2-50).

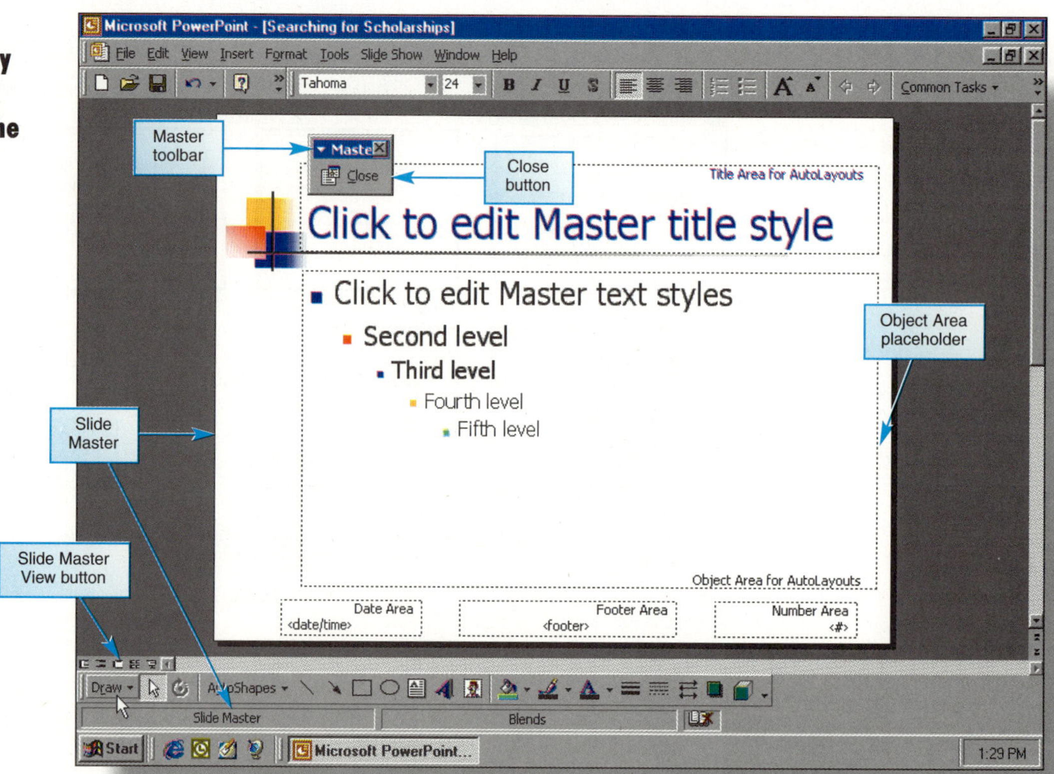

FIGURE 2-50

5 Click Wipe Down in the list. Point to the Apply button.

The Slide Transition Effect preview demonstrates the Wipe Down effect (Figure 2-48). To see the demonstration again, click the picture in the Slide Transition Effect preview.

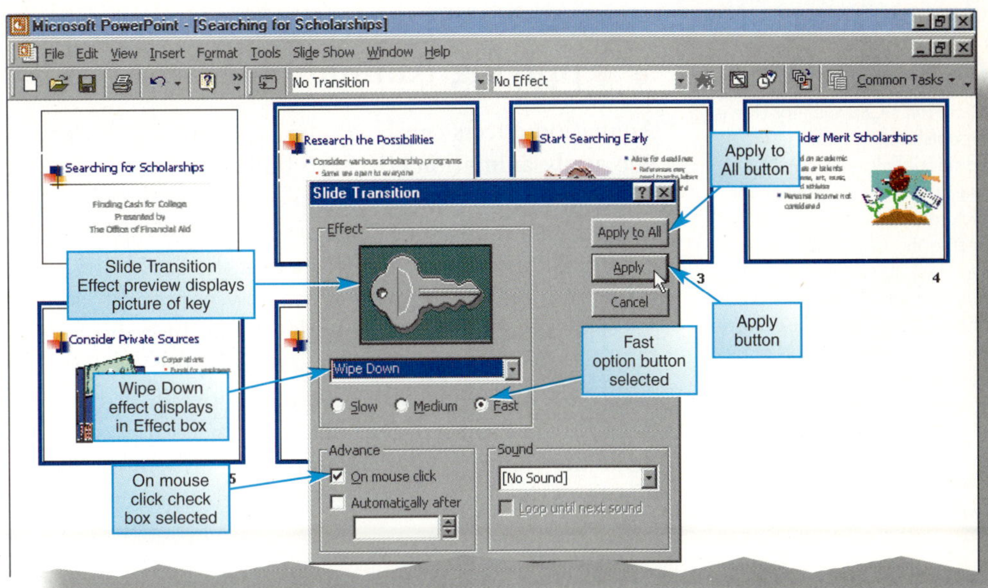

FIGURE 2-48

Click the Apply button.

PowerPoint displays the presentation in slide sorter view (Figure 2-49). A slide transition icon displays under each selected slide, which indicates that a slide transition effect has been added to those slides. The current slide transition effect, Wipe Down, displays in the Slide Transition Effects box.

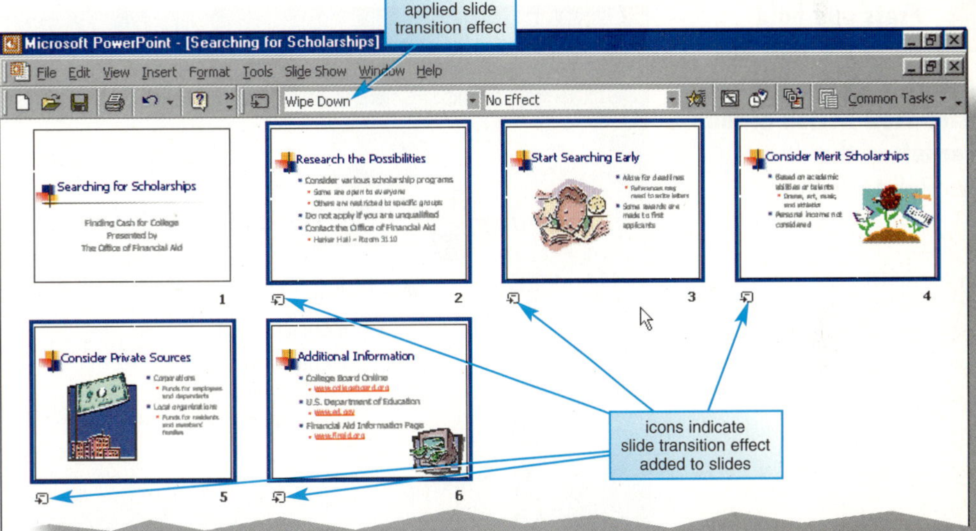

FIGURE 2-49

To adjust the speed at which the special effect runs during the slide show, click Slow, Medium, or Fast in the Effect area in the Slide Transition dialog box. When you click a particular speed option, PowerPoint runs that effect in the sample picture.

To apply slide transition effects to every slide in the presentation, right-click a slide, click Slide Transition on the shortcut menu, choose the desired slide transition effect, and then click the Apply to All button.

To remove slide transition effects when displaying the presentation in slide sorter view, select the slides to which slide transition effects are applied, click the Slide Transition Effects box arrow, and select No Transition.

The Wipe Down slide transition effect has been applied to the presentation. The next step in creating this slide show is to add animation effects to individual slides.

1. Select slide, right-click selected slide, click Slide Transition, click Effect box arrow, select desired effect, click Apply button
2. Select slide, on Slide Show menu click Slide Transition, click Effect box arrow, select desired effect, click Apply button

Clip Gallery Live

Microsoft's Clip Gallery Live is an outstanding place to locate additional clip art. This Web site also contains movie clips, pictures, and sounds. To connect to the Clip Gallery Live site, click the Insert Clip Art button on the Drawing toolbar and then click the Clips Online button. Another method of connecting to this area is to visit the PowerPoint 2000 More About Web page (www.scsite.com/pp2000/more.htm) and click Clip Gallery Live.

Applying Animation Effects to Bulleted Slides

Animation effects can be applied to text as well as to objects, such as clip art. When you apply animation effects to bulleted text, you progressively disclose each bulleted paragraph. As a result, you build the slide paragraph by paragraph during the running of a slide show to control the flow of information. PowerPoint has a wide variety of custom animation effects and the capability to dim the paragraphs already displaying on the slide when the new paragraph is displayed.

The next step is to apply the Zoom In From Screen Center animation effect to Slides 2, 3, 4, 5, and 6 in the Searching for Scholarships presentation. All slides, except the title slide, will have the Zoom In From Screen Center animation effect. Recall from Project 1 that when you need to make a change that affects all slides, make the change to the slide master. Perform the following steps to apply animation effects to the bulleted paragraphs in this presentation.

Steps To Use the Slide Master to Apply Animation Effects to All Bulleted Slides

1 Press and hold down the SHIFT key and then click the Slide Master View button at the lower left of the PowerPoint window.

The slide master displays (Figure 2-50).

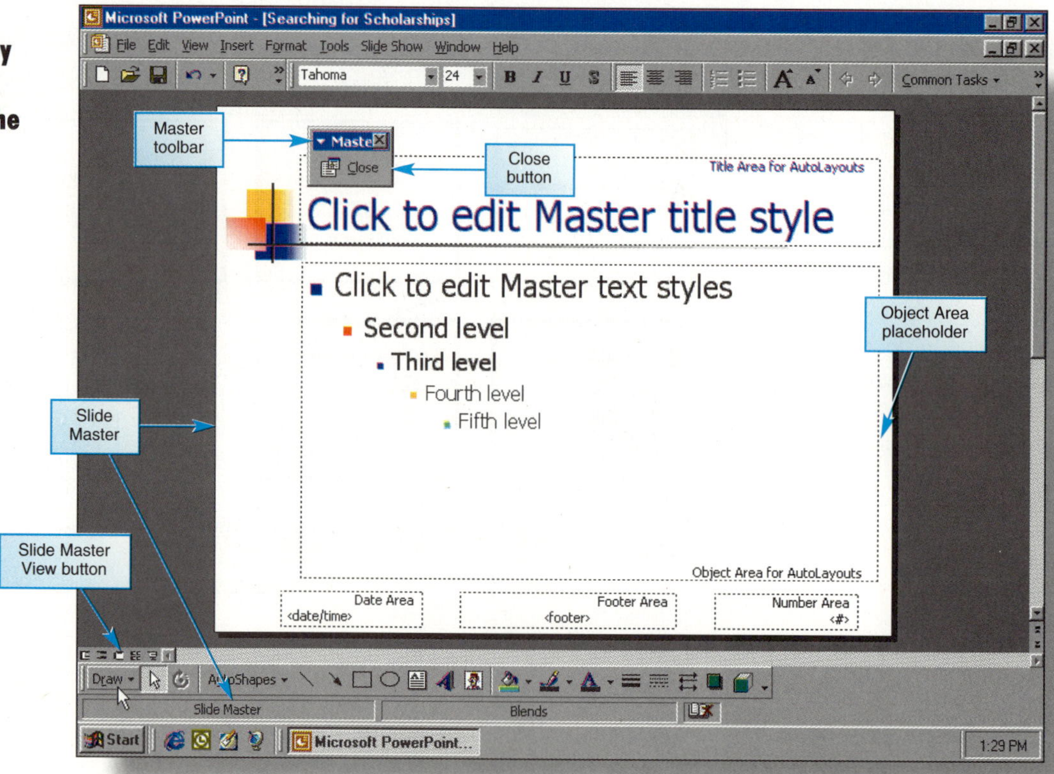

FIGURE 2-50

2 **Right-click the Object Area placeholder in the slide master. Point to Custom Animation (Figure 2-51).**

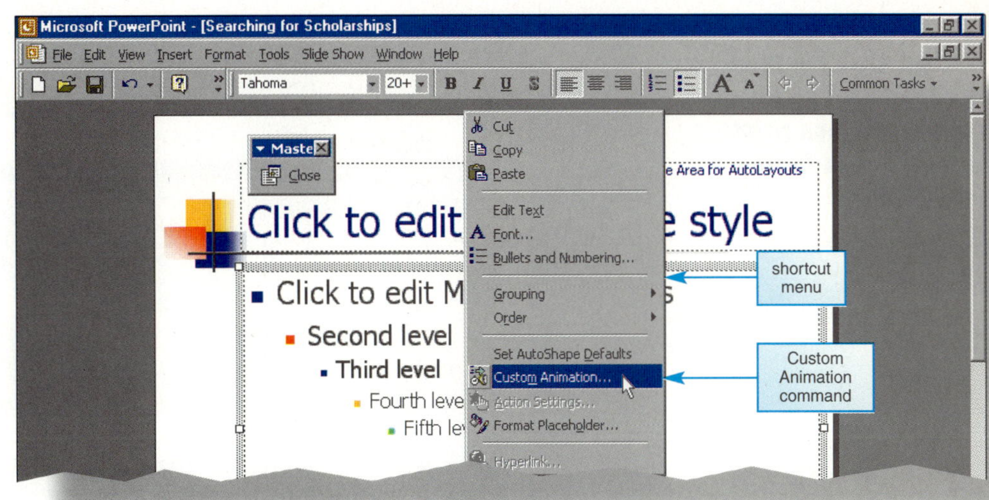

FIGURE 2-51

3 **Click Custom Animation on the shortcut menu. If necessary, click the Effects tab when the Custom Animation dialog box displays.**

The Custom Animation dialog box displays (Figure 2-52).

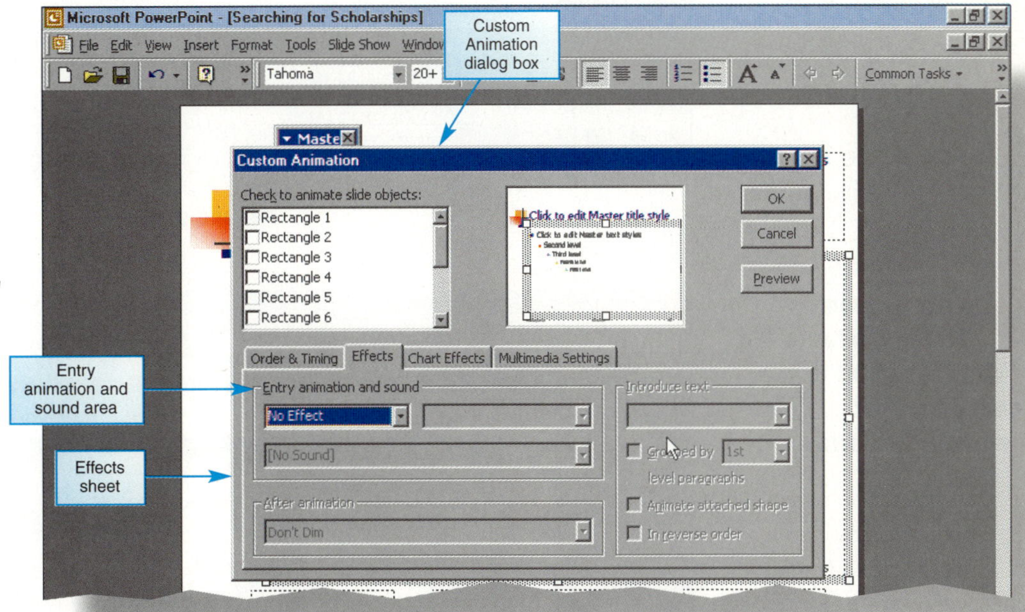

FIGURE 2-52

4 **Click the left Entry animation and sound box arrow. Scroll down the list until Zoom displays and then point to Zoom (Figure 2-53).**

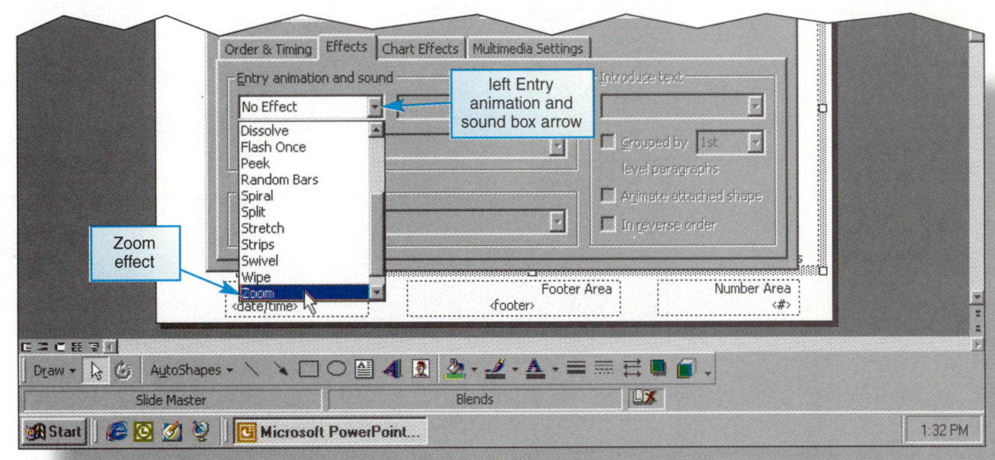

FIGURE 2-53

5 Click Zoom in the list. Click the right Entry animation and sound box arrow and then point to In From Screen Center (Figure 2-54).

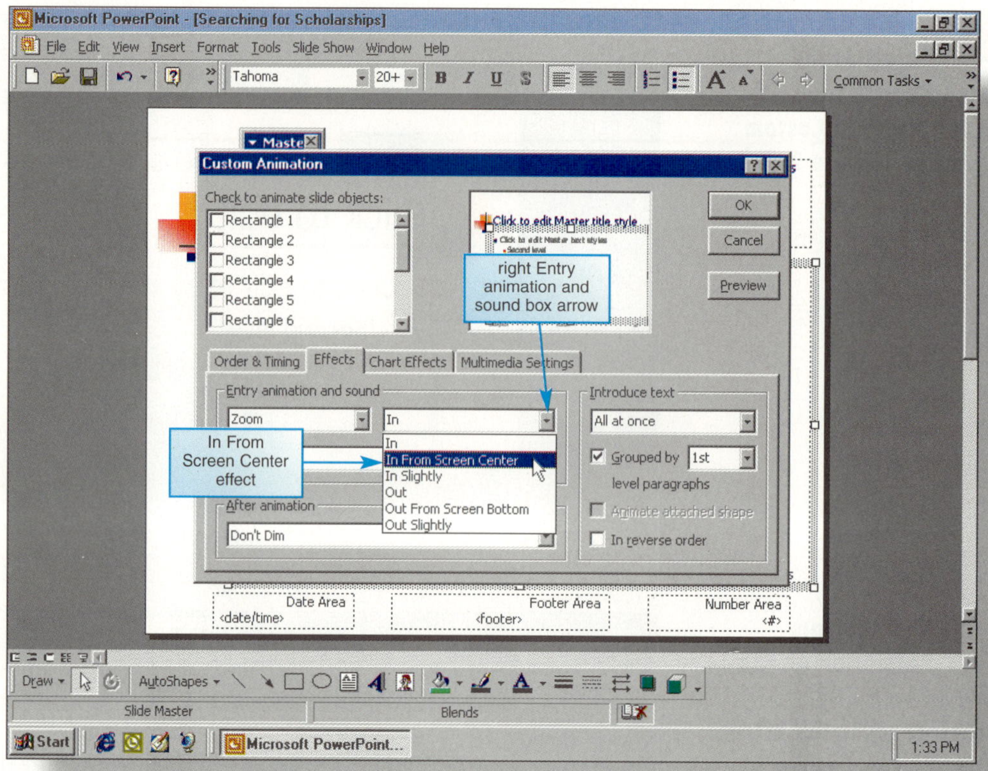

FIGURE 2-54

6 Click In From Screen Center in the list and then point to the Grouped by level paragraphs box arrow.

The Entry animation and sound boxes display Zoom and In From Screen Center, respectively (Figure 2-55). A check mark displays in the Grouped by level paragraphs box, and 1st level paragraphs is the default setting.

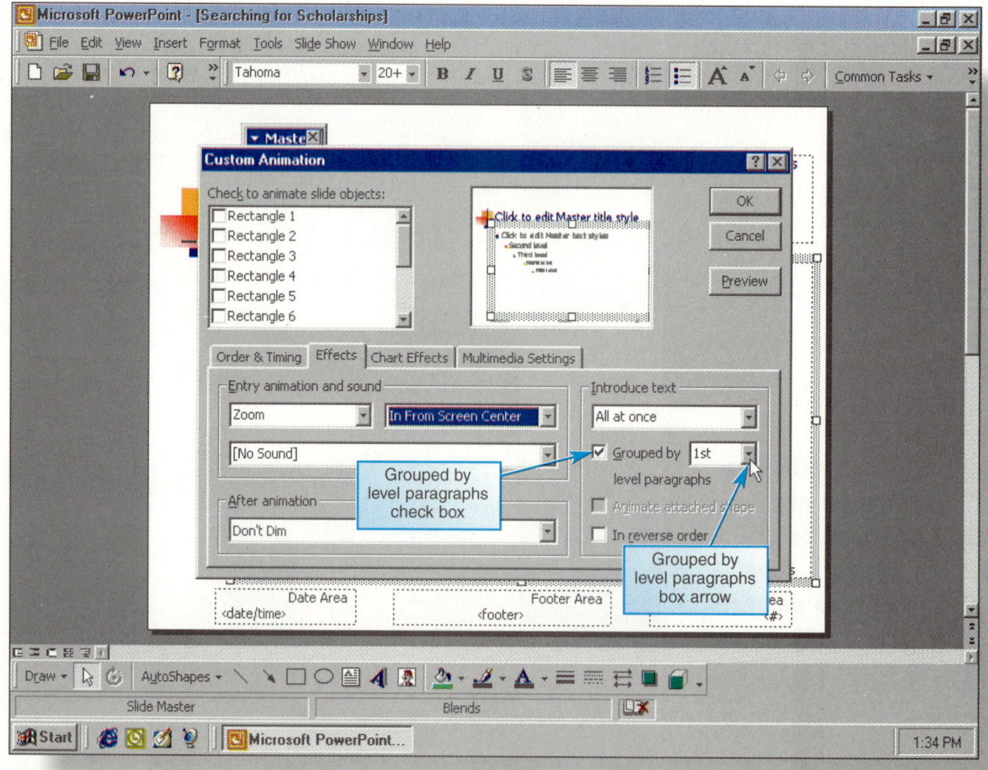

FIGURE 2-55

7 Click the Grouped by level paragraphs box arrow and then point to 3rd.

3rd is highlighted in the Grouped by level paragraphs list (Figure 2-56).

8 Click 3rd in the list and then click the OK button.

PowerPoint applies the animation effects to the slide master, closes the Custom Animation dialog box, and then displays the slide master.

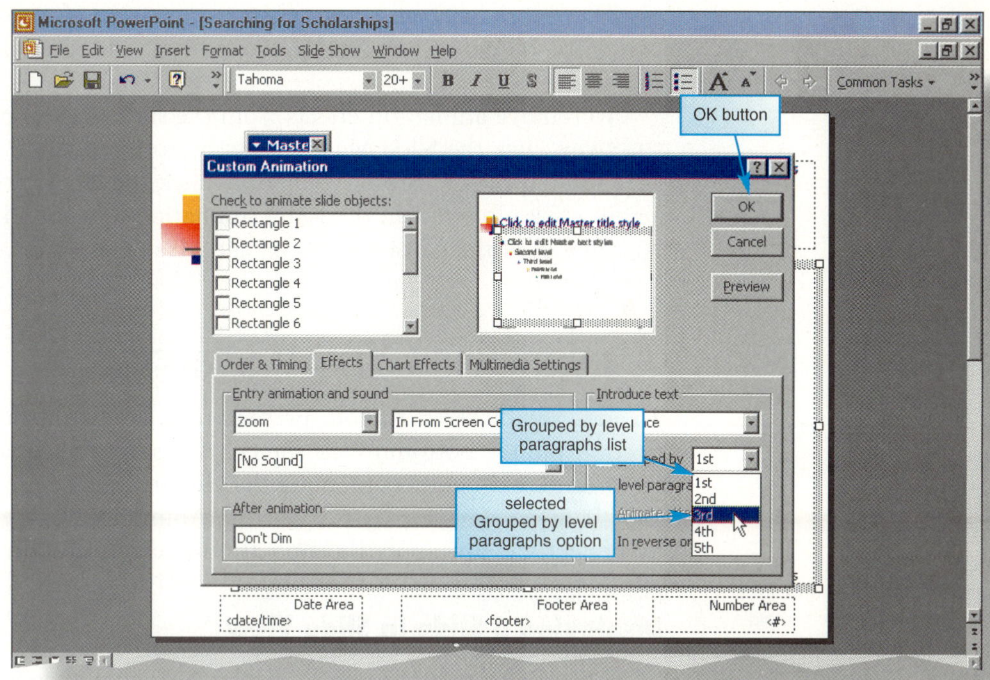

FIGURE 2-56

9 Click the Close button on the Master toolbar.

PowerPoint closes the slide master and returns to slide sorter view (Figure 2-57). The icons next to the slide transition effect icons indicate animation effects have been added to the slides.

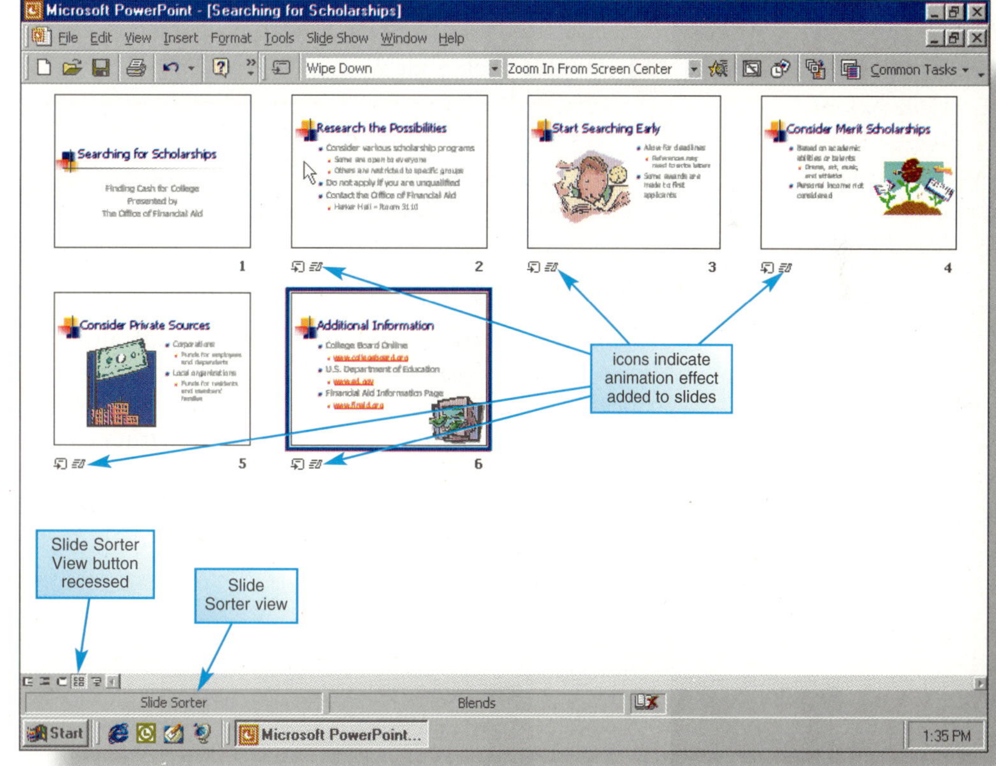

FIGURE 2-57

Other Ways

1. On View menu point to Master, click Slide Master, right-click Object Area placeholder, on Slide Show menu click Custom Animation, click Effects tab, click Entry animation and sound box arrow, click desired animation effect, click Grouped by level paragraphs box arrow, click appropriate paragraph level, click OK

The Zoom In From Screen Center animation effect displays for each bulleted paragraph on paragraph level 1, 2, or 3 on Slides 2 through 6 when the slide show is running.

To remove animation effects from the slide master, press and hold down the SHIFT key, click the Slide Master View button, release the SHIFT key, right-click the slide master, click Custom Animation, click the left Entry animation and sound box arrow, click No effect in the Entry animation and sound list, click the OK button, and then click the Close button on the Master toolbar.

Animating Clip Art Objects

Finding Clip Art

Many Web sites offer thousands of clip art images that you can import directly into your presentations. Along with pictures sorted into easy-to-navigate categories, these sites contain bullets, lines, and buttons. Use a search engine to find public domain graphics for your presentations. Use the keywords clip art and clip+art.

To add visual interest to your presentation, you want the monitor clip art on Slide 6 to rise from the bottom of the screen. Animating a clip art object takes several steps. First, display the slide containing the clip art (Slide 6) in slide view. Then select the clip art object and display the Custom Animation dialog box. Next, select the animation effect. Finally, apply the animation effect as described in the following sections.

Displaying a Slide in Slide View

PowerPoint requires you to display a slide in slide view before adding animation effects to clip art. Before continuing with the animation of the monitor on Slide 6, display the slide in slide view as described in the following step.

TO DISPLAY A SLIDE IN SLIDE VIEW

 Double-click Slide 6.

Slide 6 displays in slide view.

With Slide 6 displaying in slide view, you are ready to animate the monitor clip art as explained in the next section.

Animating Clip Art

PowerPoint allows you to animate clip art along with animating text. Because Slide 6 lists three sources on the Internet for current scholarship information, you want to emphasize these sites by having the monitor clip art pass from the left side of the screen to the right. One way of animating clip art is to select options in the Custom Animation dialog box, similarly to what you did to animate text. A quicker way is to choose an animation option from the Preset Animation list. Perform the following steps to add the Flying animation effect to the monitor on Slide 6.

To Animate Clip Art

1 Click the monitor clip art object. Click Slide Show on the menu bar, point to Preset Animation, and then point to Flying.

Animation options display in the Preset Animation submenu (Figure 2-58). The monitor clip art is selected.

2 Click Flying on the Preset Animation submenu.

PowerPoint applies the Flying animation effect to the clip art. You will see this effect when you run your slide show.

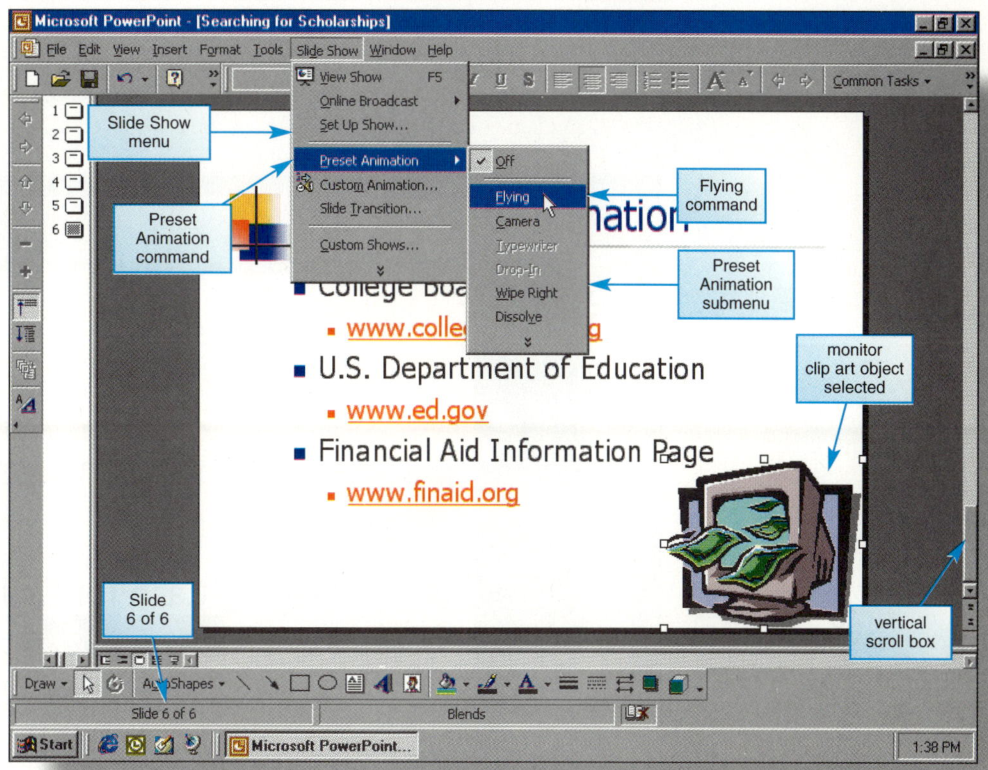

FIGURE 2-58

When you run the slide show, the names of each of the three Internet sites will display, and then the monitor clip art will begin moving from the left side of the slide and stop at the position where you inserted it onto Slide 6.

Other Ways

1. Click clip art, on Slide Show menu click Custom Animation, click Effects tab, click Entry animation and sound box arrows, click desired animation effects, click OK
2. Press TAB until clip art is selected, press ALT+D, press M, press DOWN ARROW key until desired animation effect selected, press ENTER

Formatting and Animating a Title Slide

The title slide of every presentation should seize the attention of the audience. In order to excite the audience with the Searching for Scholarships presentation, you want to intensify the subtitle object on the title slide. First, you italicize the words Presented by, and then you increase the size of the words, Finding Cash for College. Finally, you add animation effects to the subtitle.

The first step is to display Slide 1 and then format the title slide subtitle. Perform the following steps to format the subtitle object on Slide 1.

TO CHANGE TEXT FONT STYLE TO ITALIC AND INCREASE FONT SIZE

1. Drag the vertical scroll box to display Slide 1.
2. Triple-click the paragraph, Finding Cash for College.
3. Click the Font Size box arrow on the Formatting toolbar and then select the font size 40 in the list.

4. Triple-click the paragraph, Presented by, and then click the Italic button on the Formatting toolbar.

The formatted subtitle on Slide 1 displays (Figure 2-59). The paragraph, Finding Cash For College, displays in font size 40, and the words, Presented by, display the italic font style.

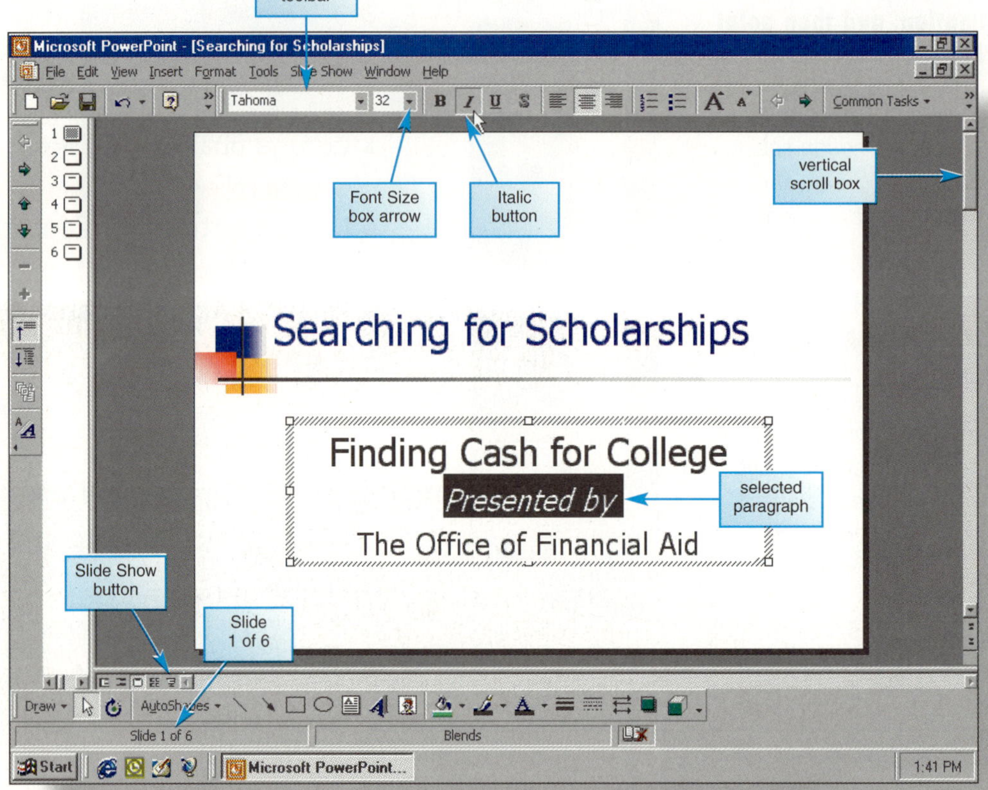

FIGURE 2-59

The next step is to apply the Dissolve animation effect to the subtitle text. Perform the following steps to animate the paragraphs in the subtitle object on Slide 1.

TO ANIMATE TEXT

1. Right-click the Object Area placeholder and then click Custom Animation on the shortcut menu.
2. If necessary, click the Effects tab in the Custom Animation dialog box.
3. Click the left Entry animation and sound box arrow.
4. Scroll down the list until Dissolve displays and then click Dissolve in the list.
5. Click the OK button.

The Object Area object, Text 2, is selected in the preview box and in the Check to animate slide objects box. Dissolve displays in the Entry animation and sound box. By default, the subtitle text is grouped by first level paragraphs. PowerPoint applies the animation effect, closes the Custom Animation dialog box, and then displays Slide 1.

Animation effects are complete for this presentation. You now are ready to review the presentation in slide show view.

Saving the Presentation Again

The presentation is complete. Perform the following step to save the finished presentation on a floppy disk before running the slide show.

TO SAVE A PRESENTATION ON A FLOPPY DISK

 Click the Save button on the Standard toolbar.

PowerPoint saves the presentation on your floppy disk by saving the changes made to the presentation since the last save.

Giving a Slide Show

PowerPoint's Projector Wizard automatically sets the optimum screen resolution for your monitor or projector when you are running your presentation in a large room. To start the Project Wizard, click Set Up Show on the Slide Show menu, click the Projector Wizard button, and follow the instructions. If you are using two monitors, you can display your slide show on one monitor and view your notes, outline, and slides on the second monitor.

Running an Animated Slide Show

Project 1 introduced you to using slide show view to look at your presentation one slide at a time. This project introduces you to running a slide show with slide transition effects and text and object animation effects. When you run a slide show with slide transition effects, PowerPoint displays the slide transition effect when you click the mouse button to advance to the next slide. When a slide has text animation effects, each paragraph level displays as determined by the animation settings. Animated clip art objects display the selected animation effect in the sequence established in the Custom Animation dialog box. Perform the following steps to run the animated Searching for Scholarships slide show.

To Run an Animated Slide Show

1 With Slide 1 displaying, click the Slide Show button at the lower left of the PowerPoint window. When Slide 1 displays in slide show view, click the slide anywhere.

PowerPoint first displays the title slide title object, Searching for Scholarships (Figure 2-60). When you click the slide, the first heading level 2 subtitle paragraph, Finding Cash for College, displays using the Dissolve animation effect.

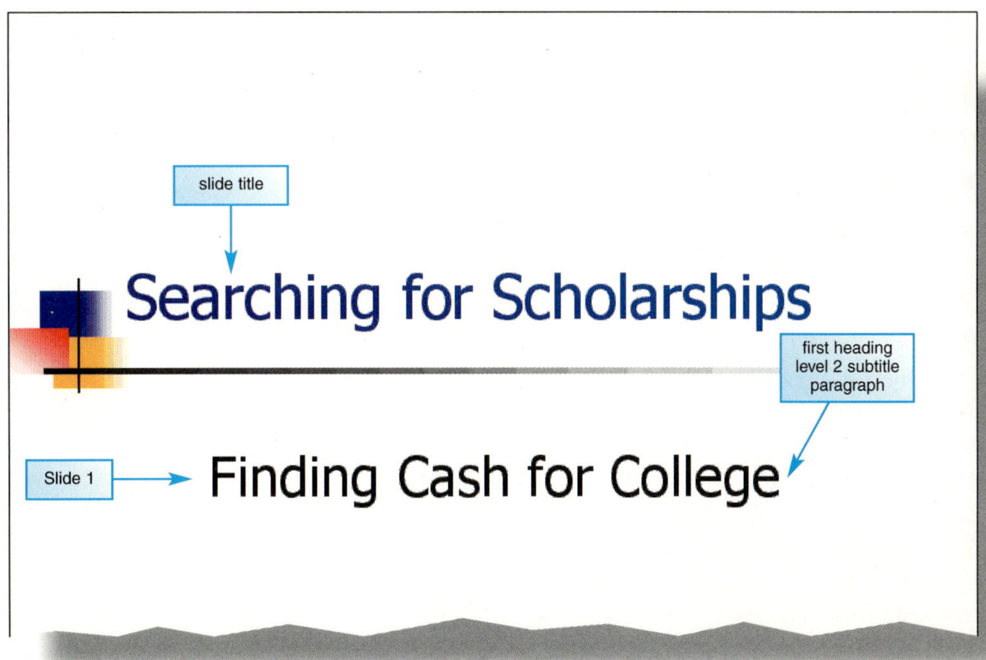

FIGURE 2-60

Click the slide again.

PowerPoint displays the second heading level 2 subtitle paragraph, Presented by, using the Dissolve animation effect (Figure 2-61). If the Popup Menu buttons display when you move the mouse pointer, do not click them.

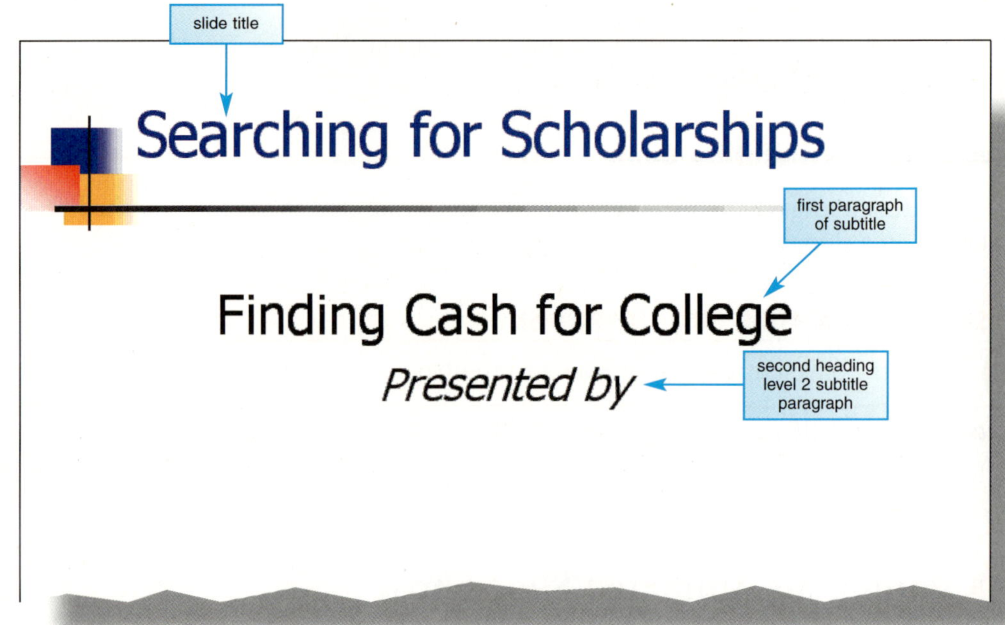

FIGURE 2-61

Click the slide again.

PowerPoint displays the third heading level 2 subtitle paragraph, The Office of Financial Aid, beneath the second heading level 2 subtitle paragraph. PowerPoint again uses the Dissolve animation effect (Figure 2-62).

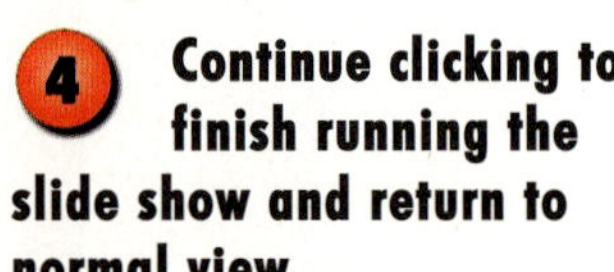

Continue clicking to finish running the slide show and return to normal view.

Each time a new slide displays, PowerPoint first displays the Wipe Down slide transition effect and then displays only the slide title. Then, PowerPoint builds each slide based on the animation settings. When you click the slide after the last paragraph displays on the last slide of the presentation, PowerPoint displays a blank slide. When you click again, PowerPoint exits slide show view and returns to normal view.

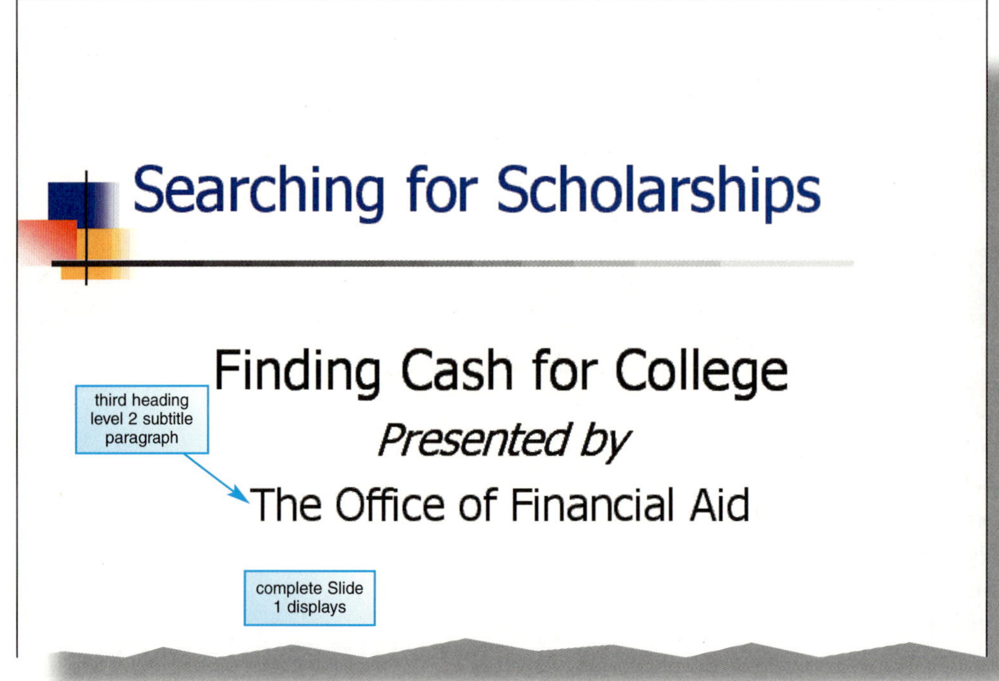

FIGURE 2-62

Other Ways

1. On Slide Show menu click View Show, click slide until slide show ends
2. Press ALT+D, press V, press ENTER until slide show ends

Now that the presentation is complete and you have tested the animation effects, the last step is to print the presentation outline and slides.

Printing in Outline View

When you click the Print button on the Standard toolbar, PowerPoint prints a hard copy of the presentation component last selected in the Print what box in the Print dialog box. To be certain to print the component you want, such as the presentation outline, use the Print command on the File menu. When the Print dialog box displays, you can select the appropriate presentation component in the Print what box. The next two sections explain how to use the Print command on the File menu to print the presentation outline and the presentation slides.

Outlines

You can send your PowerPoint outline to Microsoft Word and then create handouts and other documents using that text. To perform this action, click the Grayscale Preview button on the Standard toolbar, click File on the menu bar, point to Send To, click Microsoft Word, and then select the desired page layout.

Printing an Outline

During the development of a lengthy presentation, it often is easier to review your outline in print rather than on the screen. Printing your outline also is useful for audience handouts or when your supervisor or instructor wants to review your subject matter before you develop your presentation fully.

Recall that the Print dialog box displays print options. When you wish to print your outline, select Outline View in the Print what list located in the Print dialog box. The outline, however, prints as last viewed in outline view. This means that you must select the Zoom setting to display the outline text as you wish it to print. If you are uncertain of the Zoom setting, you should return to outline view and review it prior to printing. Perform the following steps to print an outline from slide view.

Steps To Print an Outline

1 Ready the printer according to the printer manufacturer's instructions. Click File on the menu bar and then point to Print.

*The File menu displays (Figure 2-63). The **Collapse All button** on the Outlining toolbar is recessed, so the entire outline will not print. If you want to print all the lines of text on the slides, you would click the **Expand All button**.*

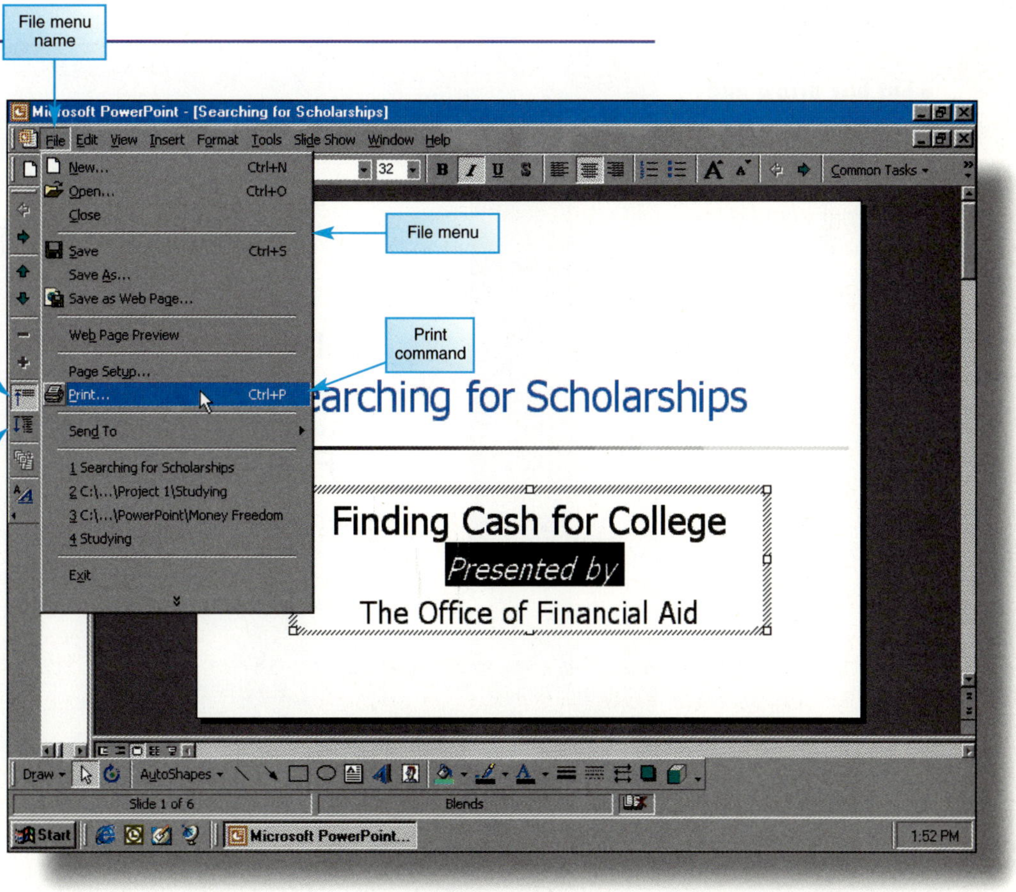

FIGURE 2-63

2 **Click Print on the File menu.**

The Print dialog box displays (Figure 2-64).

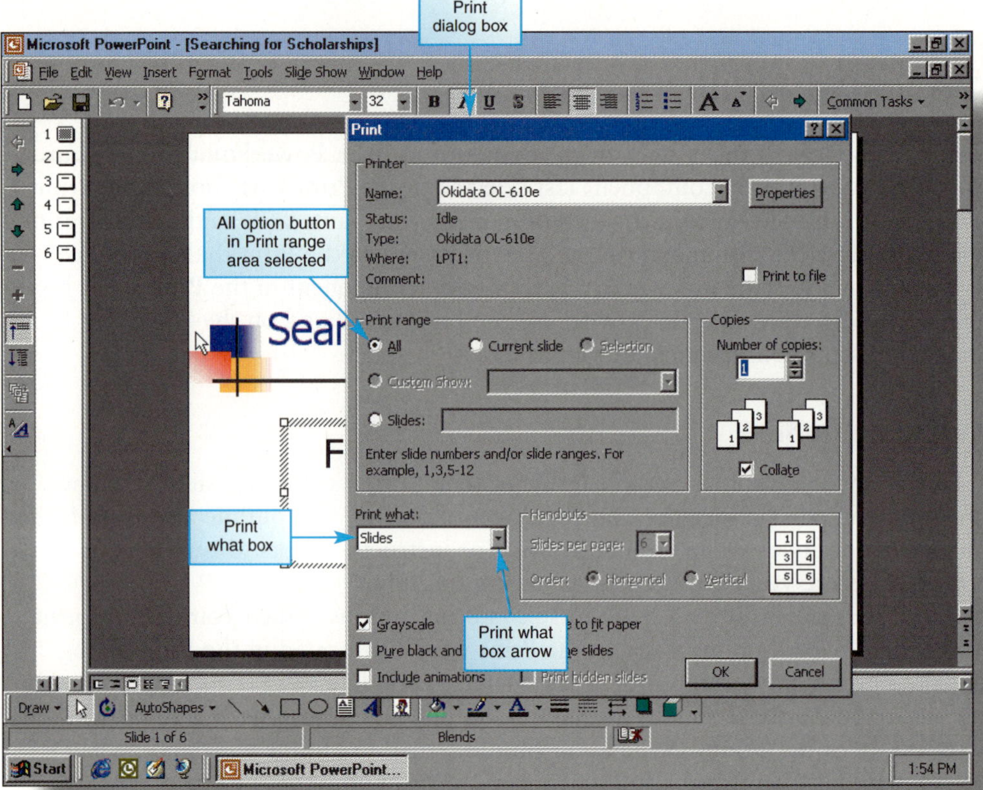

FIGURE 2-64

3 **Click the Print what box arrow and then point to Outline View.**

Outline View displays highlighted in the Print what list (Figure 2-65).

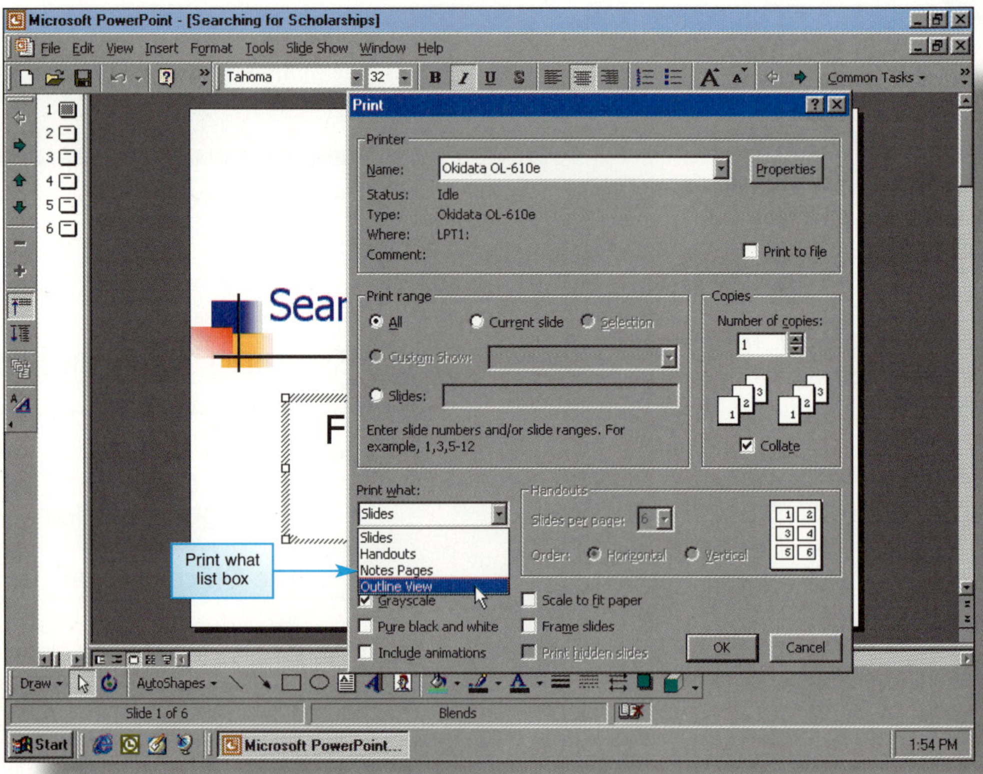

FIGURE 2-65

4 Click Outline View in the list and then point to the OK button (Figure 2-66).

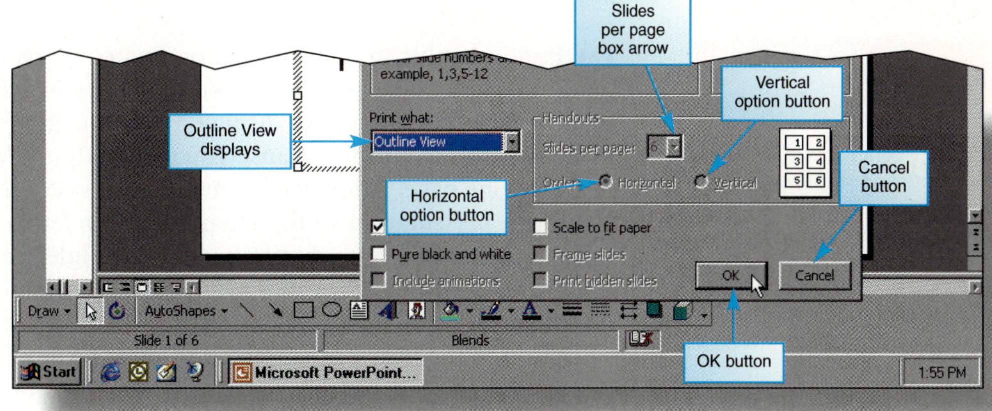

FIGURE 2-66

Click the OK button.

The outline prints. Clicking the Cancel button, cancels the printing request.

6 When the printer stops, retrieve the printout of the outline (Figure 2-67).

The six PowerPoint slides display in outline form. The words, Searching for Scholarships, and the current date display in the header, and the words, Office of Financial Aid, and the page number display in the footer.

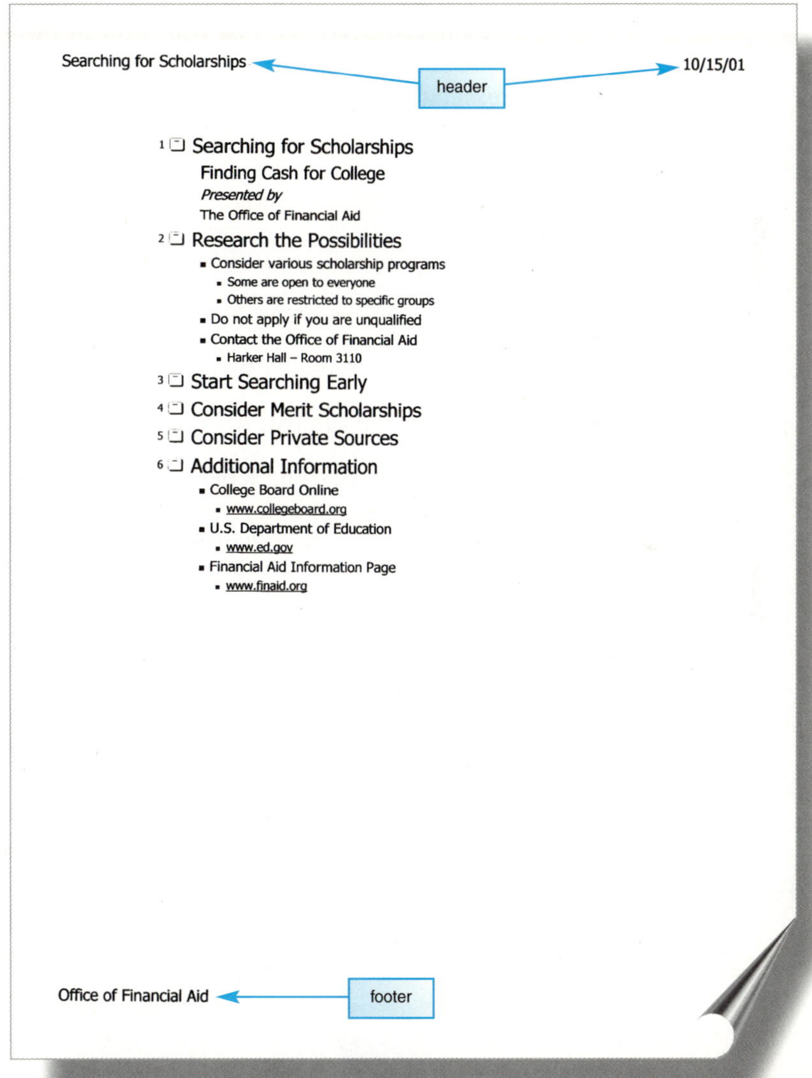

FIGURE 2-67

You may select the Print command from the File menu while in any view except slide show view.

Other Ways

1. Press ALT+F, press P, press TAB, press W, press down arrow until Outline View selected, press ENTER, press ENTER

Printing

If your printer seems to print slowly, Microsoft suggests clearing at least two megabytes of space on your hard drive and also closing any unnecessary programs that are running simultaneously.

The Print what list in the Print dialog box contains options for printing handouts, and the Handouts area allows you to specify whether you want two, three, four, six, or nine slide images to display on each page. Printing handouts is useful for reviewing a presentation because you can analyze several slides displaying simultaneously on one page. Additionally, many businesses distribute handouts of the slide show before a presentation so the attendees can refer to a copy. To print handouts, click Handouts in the Print what box, click the Slides per page box arrow in the Handouts area, and then click 2, 3, 4, 6, or 9. You can change the order in which the Searching for Scholarships slides display on a page by clicking the Horizontal option button in the Order area, which displays Slides 1 and 2, 3 and 4, and 5 and 6 adjacent to each other, or the Vertical option button in the Order area, which displays Slides 1 and 4, 2 and 5, and 3 and 6 adjacent to each other.

Printing Presentation Slides

After correcting errors, you will want to print a final copy of your presentation. If you made any changes to your presentation since your last save, be certain to save your presentation before you print.

Perform the following steps to print the presentation.

TO PRINT PRESENTATION SLIDES

1. Ready the printer according to the printer manufacturer's instructions.
2. Click File on the menu bar and then click Print on the File menu.
3. When the Print dialog box displays, click the Print what box arrow.
4. Click Slides in the list.
5. Click the OK button. When the printer stops, retrieve the slide printouts.

The printouts should resemble the slides shown in Figures 2-68a through 2-68f.

(a) Slide 1

(b) Slide 2

FIGURE 2-68

(c) Slide 3

Based on academic abilities or talents
- Drama, art, music, and athletics

Personal income not considered

(d) Slide 4

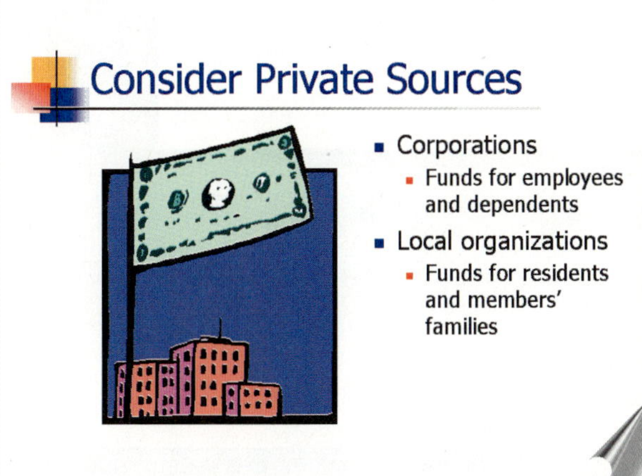

(e) Slide 5

- College Board Online
  - www.collegeboard.org
- U.S. Department of Education
  - www.ed.gov
- Financial Aid Information Page
  - www.finaid.org

(f) Slide 6

FIGURE 2-68 ***(continued)***

E-mailing a Slide Show from within PowerPoint

Billions of e-mail messages are sent throughout the world each year. Computer users use this popular service on the Internet to send and receive plain text e-mail or to send and receive rich e-mail content that includes graphics, links to other Web pages, and file attachments. These attachments can include Office files, such as Word documents or PowerPoint slide shows. Using Office 2000, you can e-mail the presentation directly from within PowerPoint. In previous versions of Microsoft Office, to send a presentation you would have had to save it, close the file, launch your e-mail program, and then attach the presentation to the e-mail before sending it.

For these steps to work properly, users need an e-mail address and a 32-bit e-mail program compatible with a Messaging Application Programming Interface, such as Outlook, Outlook Express, or Microsoft Exchange Client. Free e-mail accounts are available at www.hotmail.com. The steps on the next page show how to e-mail the slide show from within PowerPoint to Dr. Mary Halen. Assume her e-mail address is mary_halen@hotmail.com. If you do not have an E-mail button on the Standard toolbar, then this activity is not available to you.

E-mail

UCLA Professor Leonard Kleinrock sent the first e-mail message in 1969 to a colleague at Stanford University. Today, Americans send more than 2.2 billion e-mail messages daily, as compared to fewer than 300 million pieces of first-class mail.

To E-mail a Slide Show from within PowerPoint

1 Double-click the move handle on the Standard toolbar and then click the E-mail button on the Standard toolbar. If necessary, click the Send the entire presentation as an attachment option button or click the same message displayed by the Office Assistant. Point to the OK button.

The E-mail dialog box displays (Figure 2-69).

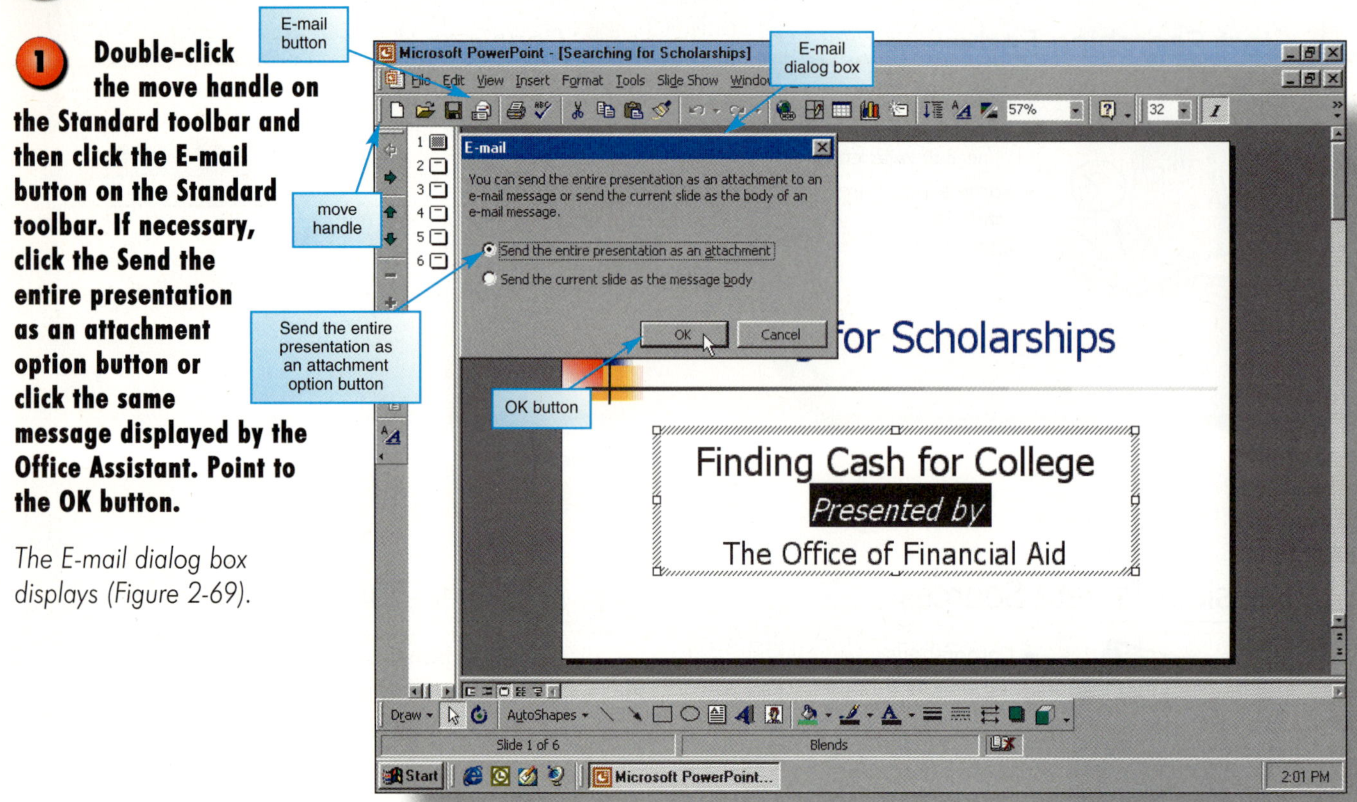

FIGURE 2-69

2 Click the OK button. When the New Message window displays, type `mary_halen@hotmail.com` **in the To box. Type** `Scholarships presentation` **in the Subject box. Click the Message box.**

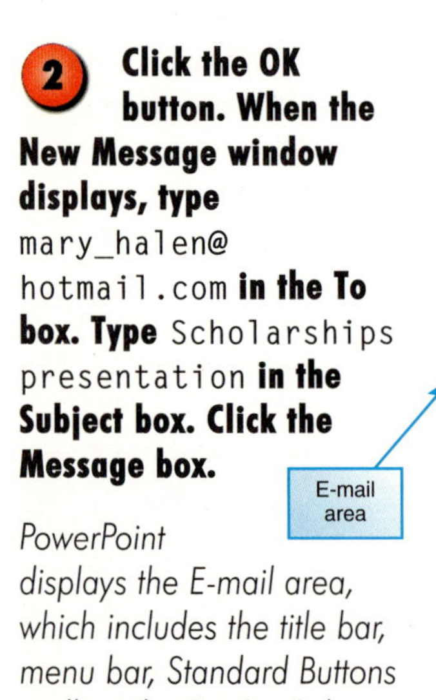

PowerPoint displays the E-mail area, which includes the title bar, menu bar, Standard Buttons toolbar, the To, Cc, Subject, and Attach boxes, and the Formatting Bar toolbar (Figure 2-70). The insertion point is in the Message box so you can type a message to Dr. Mary Halen.

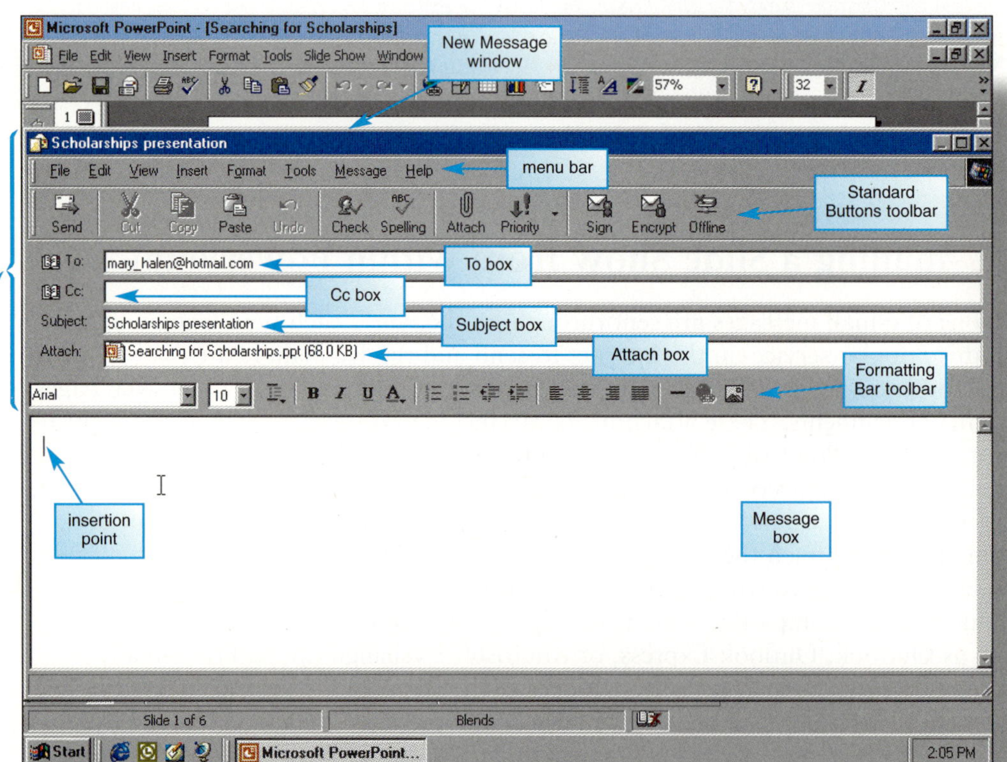

FIGURE 2-70

3 **Type** `Attached is the PowerPoint presentation you can use to accompany your lecture on scholarships.` **in the Message box. Point to the Send button.**

This message helps Dr. Halen understand the purpose of your e-mail when she opens her mail (Figure 2-71).

4 **Click the Send button on the Standard Buttons toolbar.**

The e-mail with the attached presentation is sent to mary_halen@hotmail.com.

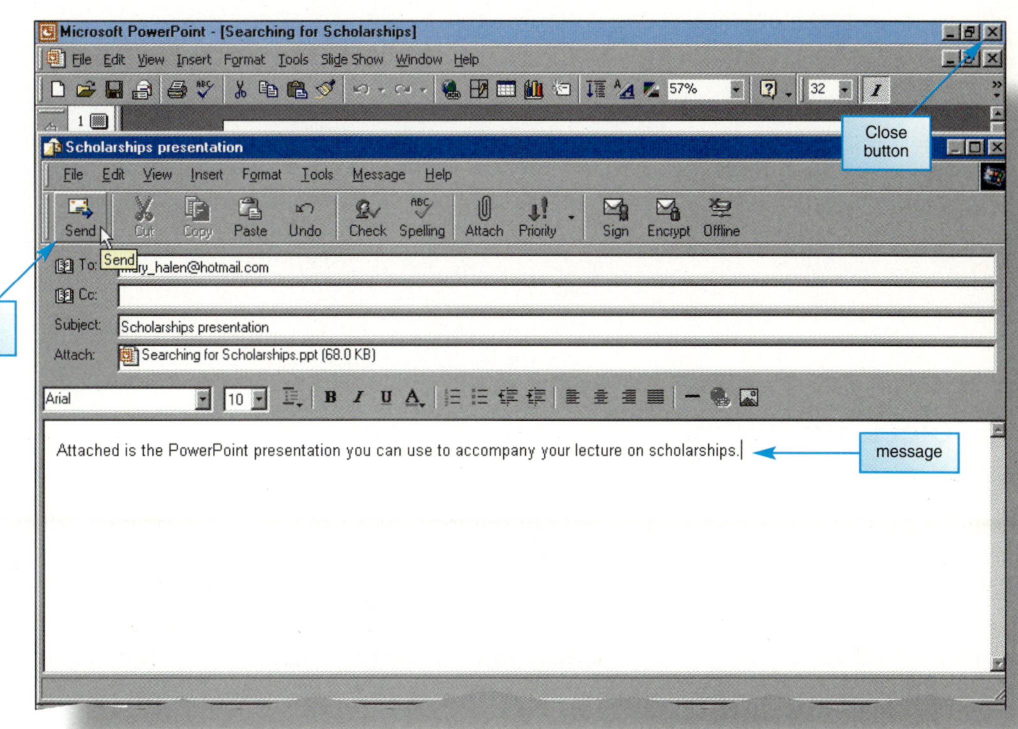

FIGURE 2-71

Because the slide show was sent as an attachment, Dr. Halen can save the attachment and then open the presentation in PowerPoint. The alternative in the E-mail dialog box in Figure 2-69 on page PP 2.56 is to send a copy of the current slide as the e-mail message. In this case, Mary would be able to see the slide in her e-mail, but she would not be able to open it in PowerPoint.

You can choose many more options when you send e-mail from within PowerPoint. For example, the Apply Stationery command on the Format menu in the Outlook Express window adds graphics to your message, such as colorful candles for a birthday message or chicken soup for a get well note. In addition, the Encrypt message on the Standard Buttons toolbar allows you to send secure messages that only your intended recipient can read.

Microsoft Certification

The Microsoft Office User Specialist (MOUS) Certification program allows you to prove your knowledge of essential PowerPoint 2000 skills. For more information, see Appendix D or visit the Shelly Cashman Series MOUS Web page at www.scsite.com/off2000/cert.htm.

Saving and Quitting PowerPoint

If you made any changes to your presentation since your last save, you should save it again before quitting PowerPoint. For more details on quitting PowerPoint, refer to pages PP 1.50 through PP 1.51 in Project 1. Perform the following steps to save changes to the presentation and quit PowerPoint.

TO SAVE CHANGES AND QUIT POWERPOINT

1. Click the Close button on the Microsoft PowerPoint window title bar.
2. If prompted, click the Yes button.

PowerPoint saves any changes made to the presentation since the last save and then quits PowerPoint.

CASE PERSPECTIVE SUMMARY

The Searching for Scholarships slide show should help some students at your school find sources of financial aid. These classmates viewing your presentation in the Office of Financial Aid will realize that many sources of scholarships are overlooked. When Dr. Halen runs your slide show, she will describe and expand upon the available scholarships you list in your slides. The audience members should have a better understanding of potential sources of scholarship money by knowing possible aid sources, the benefits of searching early, the difference between merit and private scholarships, and places to look on the Internet for more details.

Project Summary

Project 2 introduced you to outline view, clip art, and animation effects. You created a slide presentation in outline view where you entered all the text in the form of an outline. You arranged the text using the Promote and Demote buttons. Once your outline was complete, you changed slide layouts and added clip art to the Object Area placeholders. After adding clip art to another slide without a clip art region in the Object Area placeholder, you moved and sized the picture. You added slide transition effects and text animation effects. Then you applied animation effects to clip art. You learned how to run an animated slide show demonstrating slide transition and animation effects. Finally, you printed the presentation outline and slides using the Print command on the File menu and e-mailed the presentation.

What You Should Know

Having completed this project, you now should be able to perform the following tasks:

- Add a Slide in Outline View *(PP 2.13)*
- Add Slide Transitions to a Slide Show *(PP 2.39)*
- Animate Clip Art *(PP 2.47)*
- Animate Text *(PP 2.48)*
- Change the Size of Clip Art *(PP 2.33)*
- Change Slide Layout to Clip Art & Text *(PP 2.22)*
- Change the Slide Layout to Clip Art & Text and Insert Clip Art *(PP 2.28)*
- Change the Slide Layout to Text & Clip Art and Insert Clip Art *(PP 2.27)*
- Change the View to Outline View and Display the Outline Toolbar *(PP 2.8)*
- Change the View to Slide Sorter View *(PP 2.20)*
- Change the View to Slide View *(PP 2.21)*
- Change Text Font Style to Italic and Increase Font Size *(PP 2.47)*
- Create a Closing Slide in Outline View *(PP 2.18)*
- Create a Hyperlink *(PP 2.35)*
- Create a Multi-level Bulleted List Slide in Outline View *(PP 2.14)*
- Create a Second Subordinate Slide *(PP 2.16)*
- Create a Third Subordinate Slide *(PP 2.17)*
- Create a Subordinate Slide *(PP 2.16)*
- Create a Title Slide in Outline View *(PP 2.11)*
- Display a Slide in Slide View *(PP 2.46)*
- E-mail a Slide Show from within PowerPoint *(PP 2.56)*
- Insert Clip Art into an Object Area Placeholder *(PP 2.25)*
- Insert Clip Art on a Slide without a Clip Art Region *(PP 2.30)*
- Move Clip Art *(PP 2.32)*
- Print an Outline *(PP 2.51)*
- Print Presentation Slides *(PP 2.54)*
- Run an Animated Slide Show *(PP 2.49)*
- Save a Presentation *(PP 2.19, 2.35)*
- Save a Presentation on a Floppy Disk *(PP 2.49)*
- Save Changes and Quit PowerPoint *(PP 2.57)*
- Start a New Presentation *(PP 2.7)*
- Use the Notes and Handouts Sheet to Add Headers and Footers *(PP 2.36)*
- Use the Slide Master to Apply Animation Effects to All Bulleted Slides *(PP 2.42)*

1 Intensifying a Presentation by Applying a Design Template, Changing Slide Layout, Inserting Clip Art, and Applying Animation Effects

Instructions: Start PowerPoint. Open the presentation Antique from the Data Disk. See the inside back cover of this book for instructions for downloading the Data Disk or see your instructor for information on accessing the files required in this book. Perform the following tasks to change the presentation to look like Figures 2-72a through 2-72e.

1. Apply the Dad's Tie design template. Add the current date, slide number, and your name to the notes and handouts footer.
2. On Slide 1, italicize the paragraph, Midwest College Art Department, and then decrease the font size to 28 points. Insert the gramophone clip art image shown in Figure 2-72a. Scale the clip art to 90% using the Format Picture command on the shortcut menu. Drag the gramophone clip art image to align the upper-left corner of the dotted box below the letter w in the word Show, as shown in Figure 2-72a. Apply the Spiral custom animation effect to the clip art.

(a) Slide 1

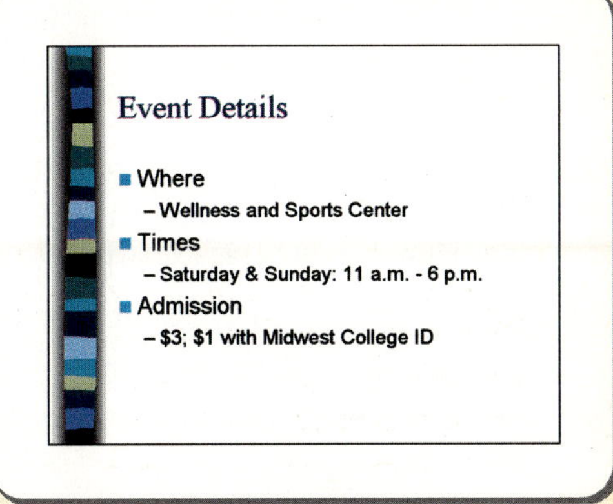

(b) Slide 2

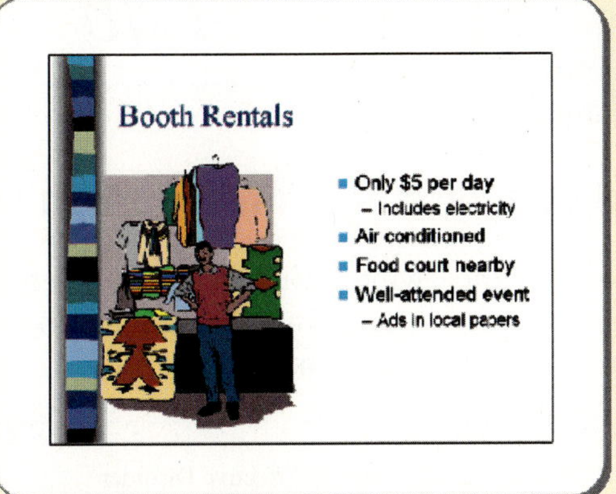

(c) Slide 3

(d) Slide 4

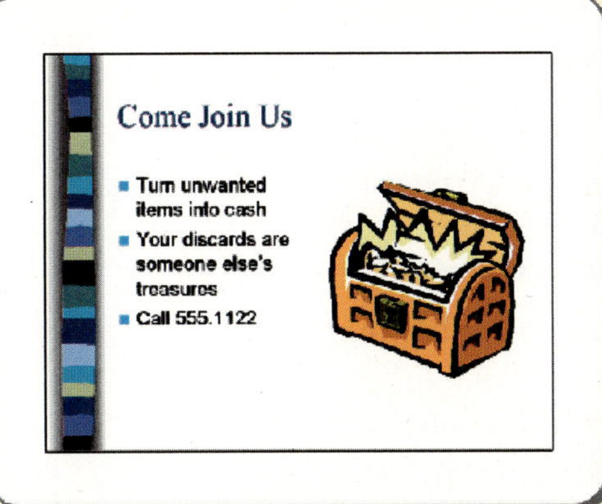

(e) Slide 5

FIGURE 2-72

(continued)

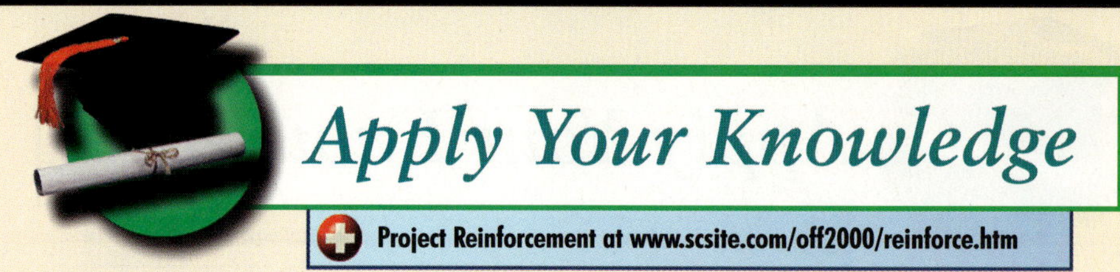

Intensifying a Presentation by Applying a Design Template, Changing Slide Layout, Inserting Clip Art, and Applying Animation Effect *(continued)*

3. Go to Slide 3. Change the slide layout to Clip Art & Text. Insert the vendor clip art image shown in Figure 2-72c. Change the size of the vendor clip art image to 275%. Move the vendor clip art image so the left edge of the selection rectangle aligns with the blue strip running down the slide.
4. Go to Slide 4. Change the slide layout to 2 Column Text. Select the bottom three categories (Furniture, Jewelry, Arts & Crafts), press and hold down the left mouse button, and drag the text to the right placeholder.
5. Go to Slide 5. Change the slide layout to Text & Clip Art. Insert the treasure chest clip art image shown in Figure 2-72e. Change the size of the treasure chest to 100%.
6. Add the Uncover Right slide transition effect to all slides except the title slide.
7. Save the presentation on a floppy disk using the file name, Antique Show.
8. Print the presentation in black and white. Print the presentation outline. Quit PowerPoint.

1 Adding Clip Art and Animation Effects to a Presentation Created in Outline View

Problem: Every fall and winter you experience the "winter blues." You feel depressed and lethargic, and you notice your friends are feeling the same symptoms. In the spring and summer months, however, these symptoms fade away. In your Health 101 class, you learn that these "winter blues" feelings are attributed to Seasonal Affective Disorder, commonly called SAD. They result from fewer hours of daylight, cold temperatures, and inclement weather. One of the assignments in this class is a research paper and accompanying five-minute presentation. You decide to conduct additional research on SAD and create the outline shown in Figure 2-73 to prepare your presentation. You use the outline to create the slide show shown in Figures 2-74a through 2-74d.

I. Seasonal Affective Disorder
  A. Jacob Heilman
  B. Health 101
II. Symptoms of SAD
  A. Frequent depression
  B. Increasing appetite
    1. Craving carbohydrates
  C. Oversleeping
  D. Being irritable
III. Causes of SAD
  A. Increased melatonin
    1. A natural tranquilizer
    2. Secreted in greater amounts in darkness
  B. Internal clock desynchronized
IV. Relief for SAD
  A. Use light therapy
    1. Use bright lights in the morning
    2. Take a walk outside
  B. Avoid overeating
  C. Think spring!

FIGURE 2-73

Instructions: Perform the following tasks.

1. Create a new presentation using the Sandstone design template.
2. Using the outline shown in Figure 2-73, create the title slide shown in Figure 2-74a.

Use your name instead of the name Jacob Heilman. Decrease the font size of the class name to 28 points. Insert the clip art that has the keywords, emotions, hearts, sadness, broken. Center the clip art under the class name.

3. Using the outline in Figure 2-73, create the three bulleted list slides shown in Figures 2-74b through 2-74d.
4. Change the slide layout on Slide 2 to Text & Clip Art. Using the Object Area placeholder, insert the clip art shown in Figure 2-74b that has the keywords, sorrow, grief, sadness, tears. Scale the clip art to 200%.
5. Change the slide layout on Slide 3 to Clip Art & Text. Using the Object Area placeholder, insert the clip art shown in Figure 2-74c that has the keywords, medicine, body parts, healthcare.
6. On Slide 4, change the slide layout to Text & Clip Art. Insert the clip art shown in Figure 2-74d that has the keywords, emotions, nature, seasons. Animate the sun clip art using the Spiral custom animation effect.
7. Add the slide number and your name to the slide footer. Display the footer on all slides except the title slide. Add your name to the outline header and your school's name to the outline footer.
8. Apply the Fade Through Black slide transition effect to Slides 2, 3, and 4.
9. Save the presentation on a floppy disk using the file name, SAD.
10. Print the presentation outline. Print the presentation. Quit PowerPoint.

(a) Slide 1

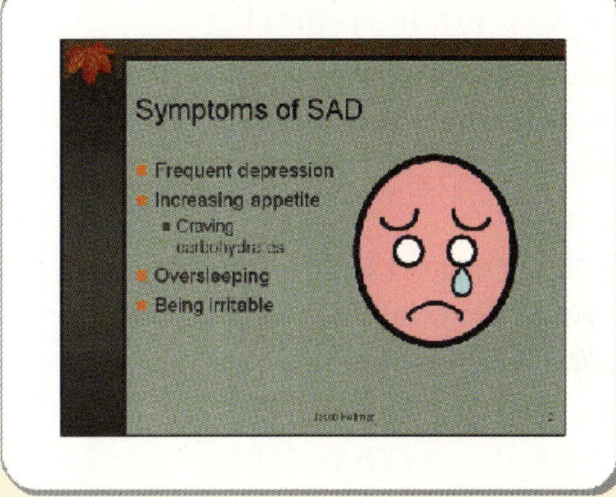

(b) Slide 2

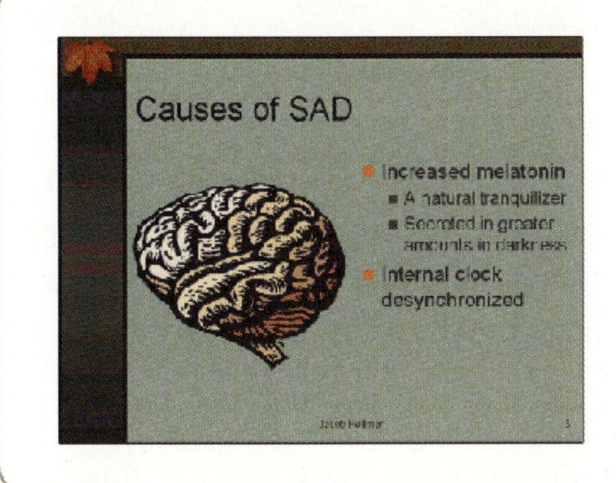

(c) Slide 3

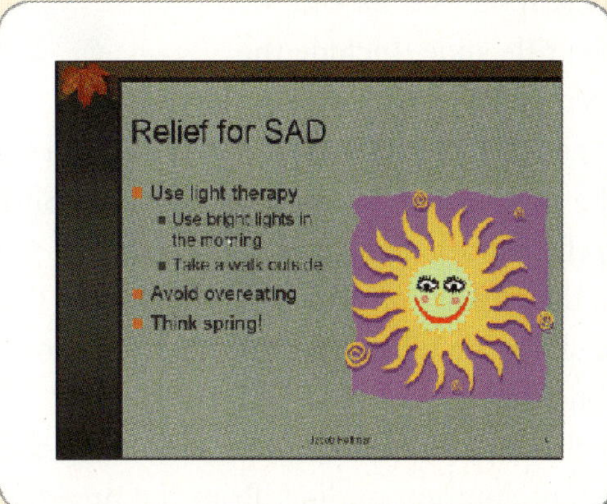

(d) Slide 4

FIGURE 2-74

2 Animating a Slide Show

Problem: The park district in your community wants to develop a PowerPoint presentation that encourages residents to consider Nordic skiing at South Shore Park for fun and recreation. You have been active in many park district activities, so the marketing director asks you for assistance. She approves the outline you developed in Figure 2-75. When you practice your presentation, you decide to add animation effects to the slide show. The completed slide show is shown in Figures 2-76a through 2-76d. *Hint*: Use Help to solve this problem.

Instructions: Perform the following tasks.

1. Create a new presentation using the Nature design template and the outline shown in Figure 2-75.
2. On the title slide, increase the font size of Fun and Fitness to 36 points. Decrease the font size of the word, at, to 28 points. Using Figure 2-76a as a reference, insert the clip art that has the keywords, people, person, sports. Scale the clip art to 95% and drag it to the upper-right corner of the slide.
3. On Slide 2, change the slide layout to 2 Column Text. Drag the text into the right column placeholder so your slide looks like Slide 2 in Figure 2-76b.
4. On Slide 3, change the slide layout to Text & Clip Art. Insert the clip art shown in Figure 2-76c that has the keywords, animals, cartoons, nature, birds. Scale the clip art to 115%.
5. On Slide 4, change the slide layout to Clip Art & Text. Insert the clip art shown in Figure 2-76d that has the keywords, household, hats, clothes. Scale the clip art to 200%.
6. Add the current date, slide number, and your name to the slide footer. Display the footer on all slides except the title slide. Include the current date and your name on the outline header. Include South Shore Park and the page number on the outline footer.
7. Apply the Box Out slide transition effect to Slide 2 through 4. Apply the Peek From Top custom animation effect to the subtitle text on Slides 1 through 4. On Slide 1, introduce text grouped by 3rd level paragraphs.
8. Animate the clip art on Slide 1 using the Fly From Right custom animation effect so it displays immediately after the slide title when you run the slide show. Animate clip art on Slide 3 using the Fly From Top custom animation effect.
9. Save the presentation on a floppy disk using the file name, Nordic Skiing.
10. Print the presentation outline. Print the presentation slides. Print a handout with all four slides arranged vertically on one page. Quit PowerPoint.

I. Nordic Skiing
    A. Fun and Fitness
    B. at
    C. South Shore Park
II. Have Fun
    A. Enjoy touring with friends and family
    B. Join enthusiasts in a race, or slip into solitude
    C. Snow conditions require quality gear
        1. No wax skis are convenient
        2. Waxable skis perform best
III. Get Fit
    A. Use a variety of styles
        1. Slow and easy
        2. Fast and hard
    B. Take lessons
        1. Qualified instructors have certification
IV. Dress Right
    A. Skiing builds heat and requires light clothing
    B. Dress in layers
    C. Always wear a hat
        1. 50% of heat may be lost through the head

FIGURE 2-75

In the Lab

(a) Slide 1

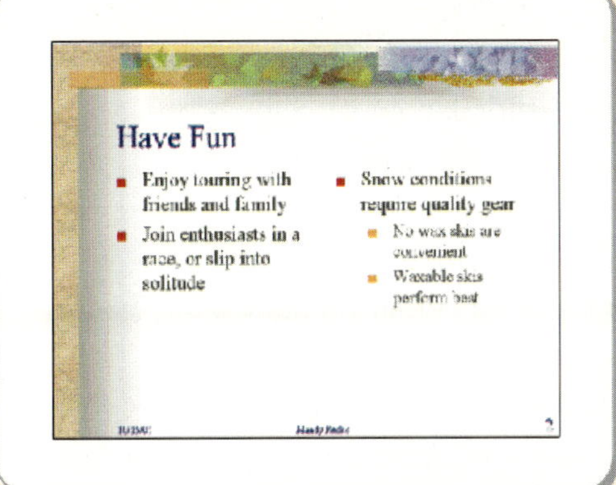

(b) Slide 2

(c) Slide 3

(d) Slide 4

FIGURE 2-76

3 Creating a Presentation in Outline View, Inserting Clip Art, and Applying Slide Transition and Animation Effects

Problem: Bernice Simpson, the director of student life at your school, has asked you to help her prepare a lecture for students on the topic of stress management. You suggest developing a short PowerPoint presentation to accompany her talk. The slide show will describe how stress develops, how it affects studying and sleeping patterns, and what techniques can combat stress. It will conclude with describing how combating stress will improve the students' overall health and outlook toward life. You create the presentation using the outline shown in Figure 2-77 on the next page. You then refine the presentation using clip art, slide transitions, and animation effects to create the slide show shown in Figures 2-78a through 2-78f on page PP 2.65. *Hint*: Use Help to solve this problem.

Instructions: Perform the following tasks.

1. Create a new presentation using the Notebook design template and the outline in Figure 2-77.
2. On the title slide, animate the three subtitles with the Dissolve custom animation effect.

(continued)

Creating a Presentation in Outline View, Inserting Clip Art, and Applying Slide Transition and Animation Effects *(continued)*

3. Use Figure 2-78c as a reference. Change the slide layout on Slide 3 to Clip Art & Text. Then insert clip art that has the keywords, office, people, people at work.
4. Change the slide layout on Slide 4 (Figure 2-78d) to Text & Clip Art. Insert clip art that has the keywords household, people, signs, symbols.
5. On Slide 5 (Figure 2-78e), change the slide layout to Clip Art & Text. Insert the clip art that has the keyword, graduations.
6. On Slide 6 (Figure 2-78f), change the slide layout to Text & Clip Art. Insert the clip art that has the keywords, academic, people, schools. Scale the clip art to 100%.

I. Dealing with Stress
    A. Managing Stress in Your Life
    B. Presented by
    C. The Office of Student Life
II. What Causes Stress
    A. You react physically and emotionally
    B. Positive stress helps you think and perform
    C. Negative stress makes you tense and frustrated – and will not go away
        1. 50% of you suffer negative stress regularly
        2. Symptoms include headaches, indigestion
III. How Can I Study Better?
    A. Keep good posture
    B. Take deep breaths
    C. Hide the clock
    D. Make a schedule
        1. Schedule time for homework and fun
IV. How Can I Sleep Better?
    A. Do not exercise at night
        1. Try morning workouts
    B. Avoid caffeine, alcohol, fried foods
    C. Turn off the phone
V. What Else Can I Do?
    A. Laugh and be flexible
    B. Imagine pleasant thoughts
        1. Graduating with honors
        2. Being with friends
VI. What Are the Benefits?
    A. You can improve immediately
    B. Changes will affect you forever
    C. You will be healthier and energized

FIGURE 2-77

7. Add the current date, your name, and slide number to the slide footer. Display the footer on all slides. Display your name and the current date on the outline header, and display the page number and the name of your school on the outline footer.
8. Apply the Wipe Down slide transition effect to Slides 2 through 6. Change the animation order so the clip art displays before the bulleted text. Apply the Split Horizontal In custom animation effect to all heading level 2 and 3 paragraphs on Slides 2 through 6. Apply the Fly From Right custom animation effect to the clip art on Slide 6.
9. Save the presentation on a floppy disk using the file name, Dealing With Stress.
10. Run the slide show.
11. Print the presentation outline. Print the presentation slides. Print a handout with all six slides arranged horizontally on one page. E-mail the presentation to Bernice using the address Bernice_Simpson@hotmail.com. Quit PowerPoint.

In the Lab

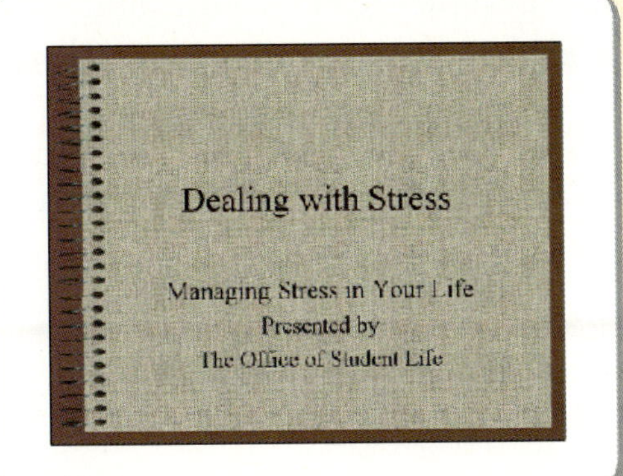

(a) Slide 1

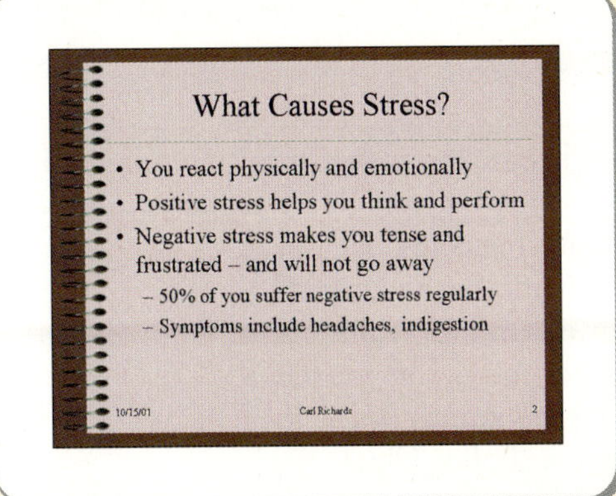

(b) Slide 2

(c) Slide 3

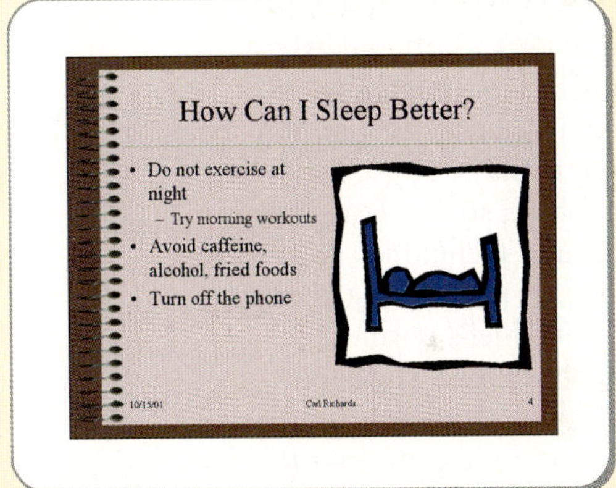

(d) Slide 4

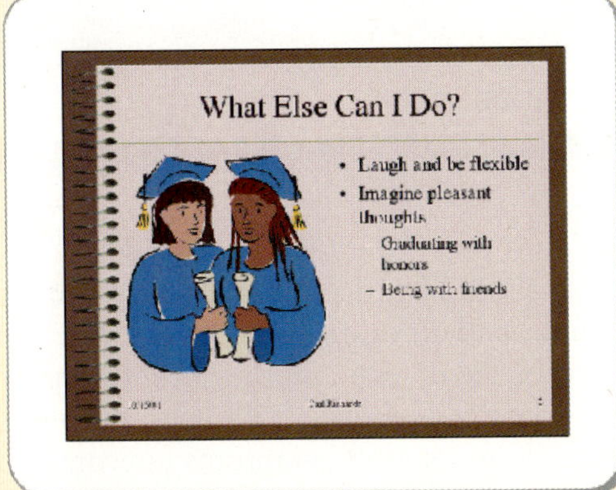

(e) Slide 5

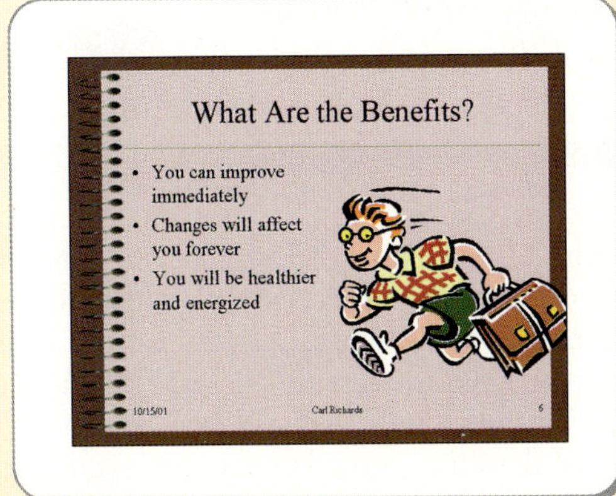

(f) Slide 6

FIGURE 2-78

Cases and Places

The difficulty of these case studies varies: ◗ is the least difficult; ◗◗ is more difficult.

1 ◗ The dispatcher at the Brook Highlands Police Station is noticing an increase in the number of calls made to the emergency 911 telephone number. These calls, unfortunately, are not always emergencies. Community residents have been calling the number to obtain information on everything from the times of movies at the local theatre to the names of the local city trustees. Police Chief Wilbur Thiel wants to inform homeowners of the importance of using the 911 service correctly. He created the following outline (Figure 2-79) and asks you to help him prepare an accompanying PowerPoint presentation to show at the local mall and food stores. Using the concepts and techniques introduced in this project, together with Chief Thiel's outline, develop slides for a slide show. Include clip art and animation effects to add interest. Print the outline and slides as a one-page handout so they can be distributed to residents at the conclusion of the presentation.

I. 911 A Call for Help
   A. Presented by
   B. Chief Wilbur Thiel
   C. Brook Highlands Police Department
II. What It Is For
   A. When you need an emergency response
      1. Fire
      2. Police
      3. Emergency Medical Personnel
   B. When disaster occurs
      1. Tornadoes, earthquakes, floods
III. How To Help
   A. Do not call for general information
      1. Consult local telephone directories
   B. If you call by mistake
      1. Tell the dispatcher you have misdialed
   C. Wait if you hear a recording
IV. Other Information
   A. Tell the telephone company if you change your name or address
      1. This info displays on the dispatcher s screen
      2. The dispatcher relies on this information
   B. Be certain your house number can be seen from the street

FIGURE 2-79

2 ◗◗ About 25 percent of the population suffers from the flu each year from October through May. Flu-related symptoms generally last for two weeks and include sudden headaches, chills, dry coughs, high fevers, and body aches. Serious complications are common, and an estimated 20,000 Americans die each year from the disease. Annual flu shots can help prevent the illness, and they are recommended for high-risk individuals such as the elderly and healthcare workers. Some drugs will help shorten the duration of the illness and decrease its severity if given within 48 hours after symptoms appear. General health tips include eating a balanced diet, getting enough rest, staying home when ill, exercising frequently, and washing hands frequently with warm, soapy water. Your campus' health services department wants to develop a presentation for students informing them about the flu and giving advice to stay healthy. Using the techniques introduced in the project, create a presentation about the flu. Include appropriate clip art and animation effects.

Microsoft PowerPoint 2000

Creating a Presentation on the Web Using PowerPoint

CASE PERSPECTIVE

The advisers at Lake View College's Counseling Department are pleased with the Effective Study Skills presentation you developed in Project 1. The results indicate that students who view the slide show and read the handouts gain helpful information about time management, class attendance, and textbook usage. The counselors realize, however, that students who often have difficulty in class are those who have poor listening skills. The counselors refer these students to the Tutoring Center for help.

Now the Tutoring Center wants you to develop a similar presentation describing how students can improve their listening skills. Dr. Rachel Sims, the Tutoring Center director, knows that students can improve their listening capability by practicing some techniques. Dr. Sims decides the most effective way to disseminate this information is to have you prepare a PowerPoint slide show highlighting these skills and then make the presentation available on the World Wide Web to all students. The slide show, called Listen Up, will contain this information along with clip art and animation effects for visual interest. Dr. Sims then wants you to publish the presentation on the World Wide Web.

Introduction

The graphic design power of PowerPoint allows you to create vibrant presentations that convey information in a clear, interesting manner. Some of these presentations are created for small, specific audiences, such as a subcommittee planning a department golf outing. In this case, the presentation may be shown in an office conference room. On the other hand, other presentations are designed for large, general audiences, such as workers at a corporation's various offices across the country learning about a new computer system being installed. These employees can view the presentation on their company's **intranet**, which is an internal network that uses Internet technologies. On a grand scale, you can inform the entire world about the contents of your presentation by posting your slide show to the World Wide Web. To publish to the World Wide Web, you need an **FTP (File Transfer Protocol)** program to copy your presentation and related files to an **Internet service provider (ISP)** computer.

PowerPoint allows you to create Web pages in three ways. First, you can start a new presentation, as you did in Projects 1 and 2 when you produced the Effective Study Skills and Searching for Scholarships presentations. PowerPoint provides a Web Presentation template in the **AutoContent Wizard** option when you start PowerPoint. The wizard provides design and content ideas to help you develop an effective slide show for an intranet or for the Internet by opening a sample presentation that you can alter by adding your own text and graphics.

Second, by using the **Save as Web Page** command, you can convert an existing presentation to a format compatible with popular Web browsers, such as Microsoft Internet Explorer. This command allows you to create a Web page from a single slide or from a multiple-slide presentation. This Web feature illustrates opening the Listen Up presentation on the Data Disk and then saving the presentation as a Web page. PowerPoint will start your default browser and open your HTML file so you can view the presentation (Figures 1a through 1e). Finally, you will edit the presentation, save it again, and view it in your default browser.

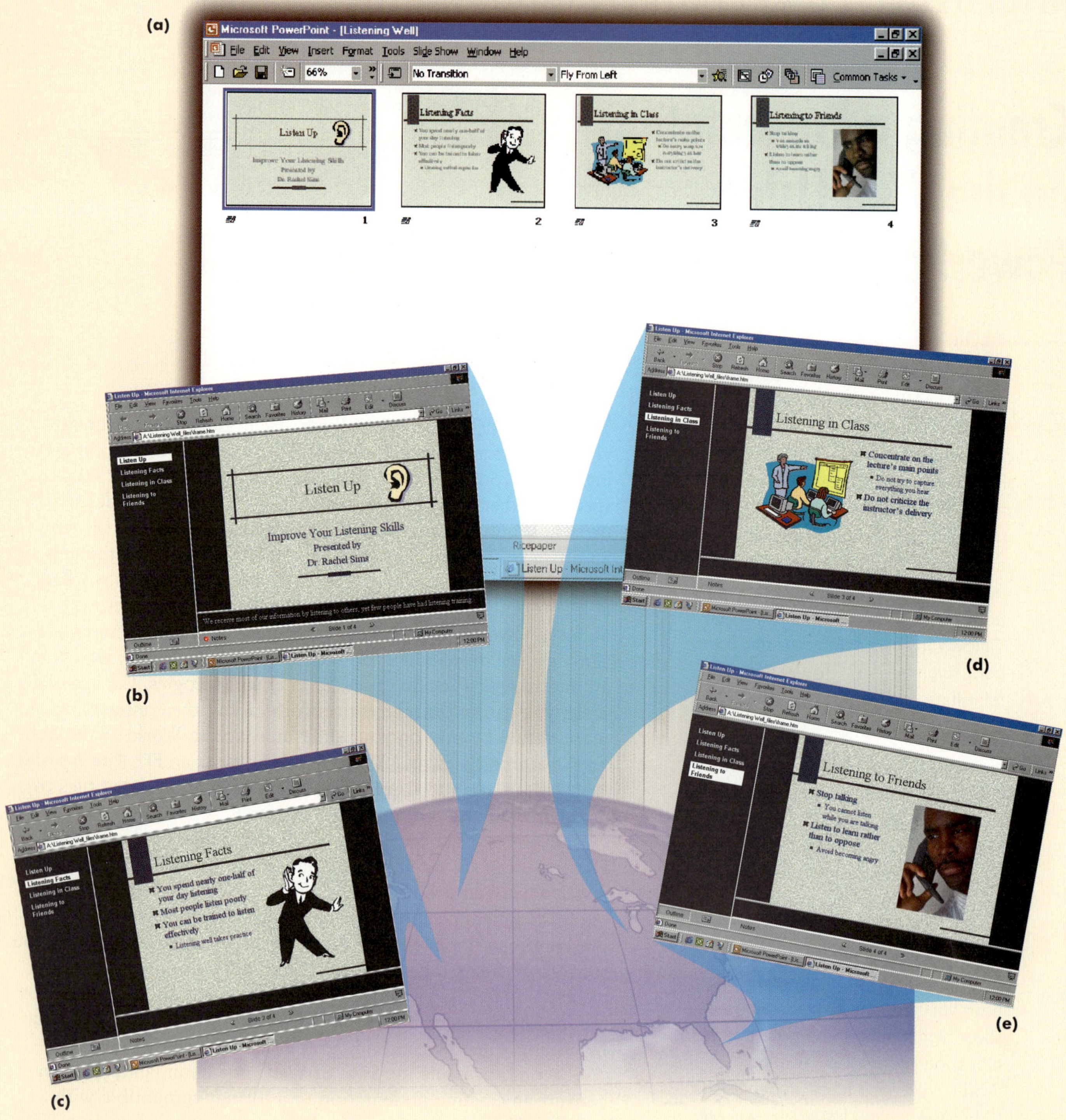

FIGURE 1

Third, in PowerPoint you can preview your presentation as a Web page. This action opens your presentation in your default Web browser without saving HTML files. You could use this feature to review and modify your work in progress until you develop a satisfactory presentation.

Because you are converting the Listen Up presentation on the Data Disk to a Web page, the first step in this project is to open the Listen Up file. Then you will save the file as a Web page and view the presentation in your default browser. For instructional purposes in this Web feature, you create and save your Web page on a floppy disk. At times, this saving process may be slow, so you must be patient.

The World Wide Web

More than three-fourths of college graduates use the World Wide Web for their job hunting efforts. They search for specific information on their careers, and then they turn to corporate Web sites for information on job vacancies and the annual report. They also e-mail their resumes to potential employers and post their resumes on online job services. For more information, visit the PowerPoint 2000 More About Web page (www.scsite.com/pp2000/more.htm) and click Jobs.

Saving a PowerPoint Presentation as a Web Page

Once a PowerPoint slide show is complete, you want to save it as a Web page so you can publish and then view it in a Web browser. PowerPoint allows you to **publish** the presentation by saving the pages to a Web folder or to an FTP location. The procedures for publishing Web pages to the World Wide Web in Microsoft Office are discussed in Appendix B. When you publish your presentation to the Web, it is available for other computer users to view on the Internet or through other means.

You can save and then view the presentation in two ways. First, you can save the entire presentation as a Web page, quit PowerPoint, open your browser, and open the Web page in your browser. Second, in this Web feature you will combine these steps by saving the presentation to drive A and then viewing the presentation. In this case, PowerPoint automatically will start the browser and display your presentation. Perform the steps on the next page to save and publish the Listen Up presentation as a Web page.

To Save a PowerPoint Presentation as a Web Page

1 Start PowerPoint and then open the Listen Up file on the Data Disk. Reset your toolbars as described in Appendix C. Click the notes pane and then type `We receive most of our information by listening to others, yet few people have had listening training.` **Click File on the menu bar and then point to Save as Web Page.**

PowerPoint opens and displays the presentation in normal view (Figure 2). The notes pane lets you type speaker notes to remind you of information you want to share with your audience. The File menu displays.

file name displays on title bar
File menu name
File menu
Save as Web Page command
Normal View button recessed
speaker notes in notes pane

FIGURE 2

2 Click Save as Web Page. When the Save As dialog box displays, type `Listening Well` **in the File name text box.**

PowerPoint displays the Save As dialog box (Figure 3). Web Page displays in the Save as type box.

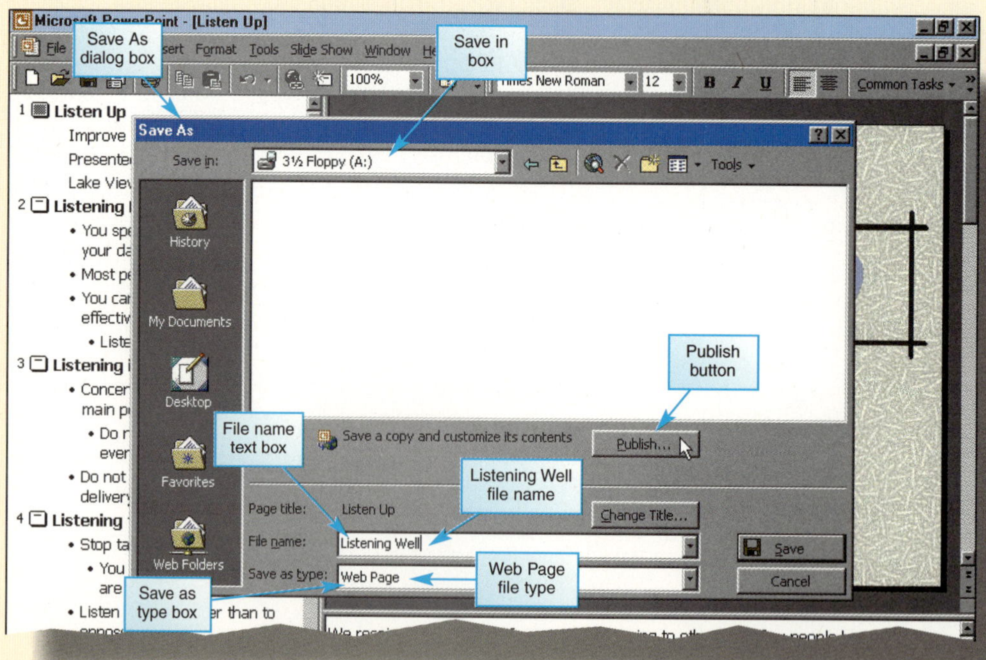

FIGURE 3

3 **Click the Publish button. If the Office Assistant displays, click No, don't provide help now. When the Publish as Web Page dialog box displays, triple-click the Publish a copy as File name text box and then type** `A:\Listening Well` **in the text box. Be certain the Open published Web page in browser check box is selected. Point to the Publish button.**

The Publish as Web Page dialog box displays (Figure 4). PowerPoint defaults to publishing the complete presentation, although you can choose to publish one or a range of slides. The Open published Web page in browser check box is selected, which means the Listening Well presentation will open in your default browser when you click the Publish button.

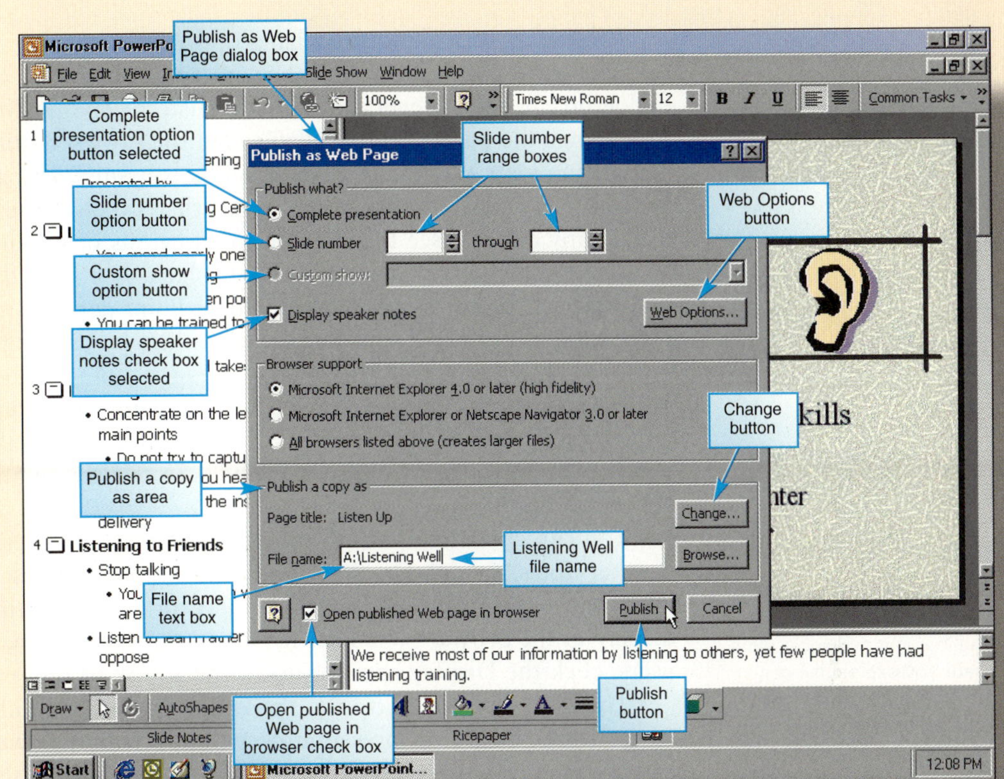

FIGURE 4

Click the Publish button.

PowerPoint saves the presentation as Listening Well.htm on your Data Disk in drive A. After a few seconds, PowerPoint opens your default Web browser in a separate window (Figure 5).

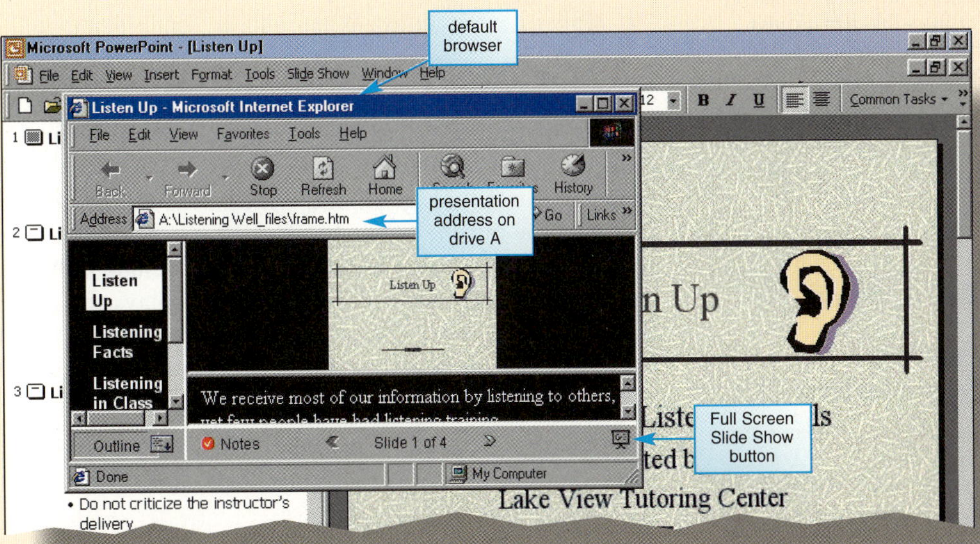

FIGURE 5

Other Ways

1. Press ALT+F, press G, type new file name, press SHIFT+TAB two times, press P, change file name in Publish copy as box, press ENTER

Publishing provides customizing options that are not available when you merely save the entire publication and then start your browser. The Publish as Web Page dialog box provides several options to customize your Web page. For example, you can change the page title that displays in the browser's title bar and history list. People visiting your Web site can store a link to your Web page, which will display in their favorites list. To change the page title, you click the Change button in the Publish a copy as area (see Figure 4 on the previous page) and then type a new title.

The Publish what? area of the Publish as Web Page dialog box allows you to publish parts of your presentation. PowerPoint defaults to publishing the complete presentation, but you can select specific slides by clicking the Slide number option button and then entering the range of desired slide numbers. In addition, you can publish a custom show you have created previously. A **custom show** is a subset of your presentation that contains slides tailored for a specific audience. For example, you may want to show Slides 1, 2, and 4 to one group and Slides 1, 3, and 4 to another group.

You can choose to publish only the publication slides, and not the accompanying speaker notes. By default, the **Display speaker notes check box** is selected in the Publish what? area. You typed speaker notes for Slide 1 of this presentation, so they will display in the browser window. If you do not want to make your notes available to users, click the Display speaker notes check box to remove the check mark.

The Web Options button in the Publish what? area allows you to select options to determine how your presentation will look when viewed in a Web browser. You can choose options such as allowing slide animation to show, selecting the screen size, and having the notes and outline panes display when viewing the presentation in a Web browser.

Now that you have opened the Listen Up file and saved the presentation as a Web page, you want to view the slide show using your default browser.

Speaker Notes

When you prepare speaker notes for your presentation, remember that audiences want to hear you explain the concepts on the slides. Each slide should list the key points, and your notes should guide you with the supplemental information you will deliver. Your listeners can retain a maximum of six major points you make, so these facts and your explanation should comprise the majority of your presentation. For more information, visit the PowerPoint 2000 More About Web page (www.scsite.com/pp2000/more.htm) and click Speaker Notes.

More About 2000

Viewing Presentations

The PowerPoint Viewer allows users to see your Web presentation without installing PowerPoint. This application is handy when you are going to deliver your slide show at a remote site on a computer other than your own. Microsoft distributes this software free of charge. For more information, visit the PowerPoint 2000 More About Web page (www.scsite.com/pp2000/more.htm) and click Viewer.

Viewing a Presentation as a Web Page

PowerPoint makes it easy to create a presentation and then view how it will display on an intranet or the World Wide Web. By viewing your slide show, you can decide which features look good and which need modification. The left side of the window contains the outline pane showing a table of contents consisting of each slide's title text. You can click the **Expand/Collapse Outline button** below the outline pane to view the complete slide text. The right side displays the complete slide in the slide pane. The speaker notes display in the notes pane under the slide pane. Perform the following steps to view your Listening Well presentation as a Web page.

Steps To View a Presentation as a Web Page

1 If necessary, double-click the Microsoft Internet Explorer title bar to maximize the browser window. Point to the Full Screen Slide Show button.

The title text and ear clip art of the first slide of the Listening Well presentation display in the slide pane in the browser window (Figure 6). The outline pane contains the table of contents, which consists of the title text of each slide. The notes pane displays the speaker notes.

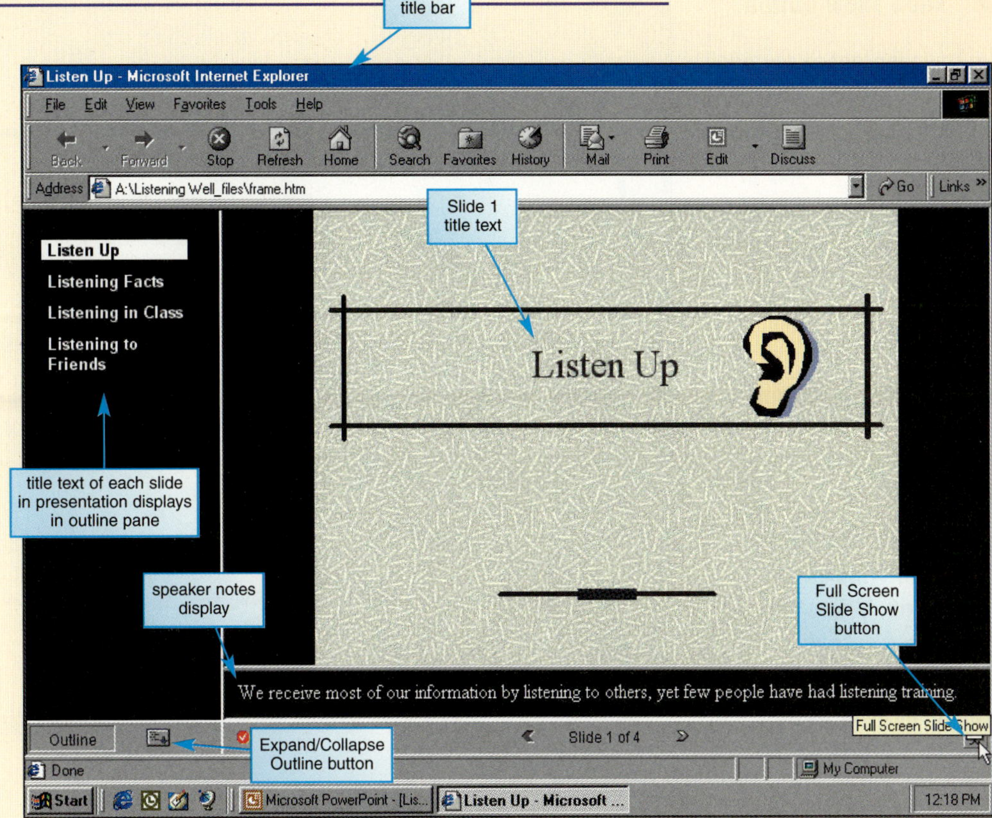

FIGURE 6

2 **Click the Full Screen Slide Show button.**

Slide 1 fills the entire screen (Figure 7). The Slide 1 title text and ear clip art display.

3 **Click to display the first line of the Object Area placeholder text.**

The first line of the Slide 1 Object Area placeholder text displays.

4 **Continue clicking each slide in the presentation. When the black slide displays, click it. Point to the Expand/Collapse Outline button below the outline pane.**

Each of the four slides in the Listening Well presentation displays. The message on the black slide, End of slide show, click to exit., indicates the conclusion of the slide show.

5 **Click the Expand/Collapse Outline button.**

The text of each slide displays in the outline pane (Figure 8). Lines display to the left and under the text of the current slide in this pane. To display only the title of each slide, you would click the Expand/Collapse Outline button again.

FIGURE 7

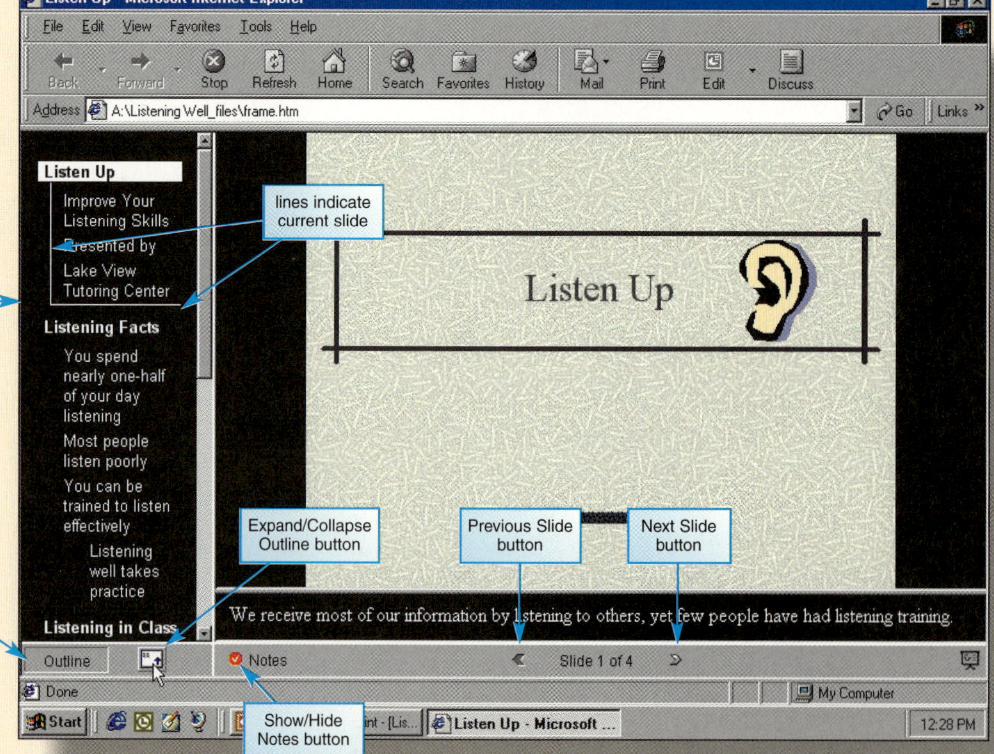

FIGURE 8

You can alter the browser window by choosing to display or hide the outline and notes panes. To eliminate the outline pane, click the **Show/Hide Outline button** below the outline pane. If you later want to display the outline pane, you would click the Show/Hide Outline button again. Similarly, the **Show/Hide Notes button** below the slide pane allows you to display or conceal the speaker notes on a particular slide.

To advance through the Web pages, click the **Next Slide button** below the slide pane. Likewise, to display a slide appearing earlier in the slide show, click the **Previous Slide button**.

Persuading Audiences

As you choose to show or hide your outline and notes, consider the needs of your audience. Some researchers believe listeners are more attentive on Sundays, Mondays, and Tuesdays because they are more relaxed than at the middle and end of a week. Thus, you may need to provide more information via the outline and notes when your audience is less focused.

Editing a Web Page through a Browser

Dr. Rachel Sims, the Tutoring Center director, informs you that she wants her name to display on the title slide so that students can contact her for further information. She suggests you change the last line of the Slide 1, Lake View Tutoring Center, to her name. Perform the following steps to modify Slide 1.

To Edit a Web Page through a Browser

1 Point to the Edit button on the Standard Buttons toolbar.

Slide 1 displays in the browser (Figure 9). The ScreenTip, Edit with Microsoft PowerPoint for Windows, indicates you can modify the presentation using PowerPoint directly from the browser window. Your computer may indicate other editing options, such as using Windows Notepad.

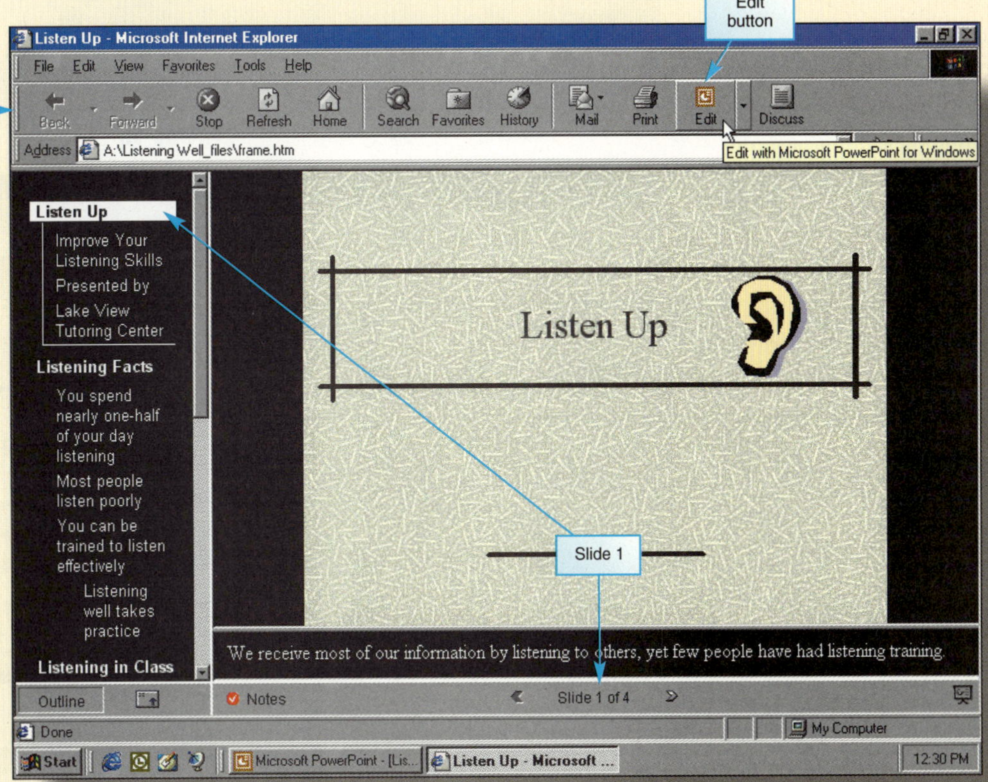

FIGURE 9

2 **Click the Edit button. Triple-click the last second level line, Lake View Tutoring Center.**

When you click the Edit button, PowerPoint returns control to the PowerPoint window, as indicated by the title bar and the recessed Microsoft PowerPoint – [Listening Well] button (Figure 10). A selection rectangle displays around the Object Area placeholder text. The last line is highlighted.

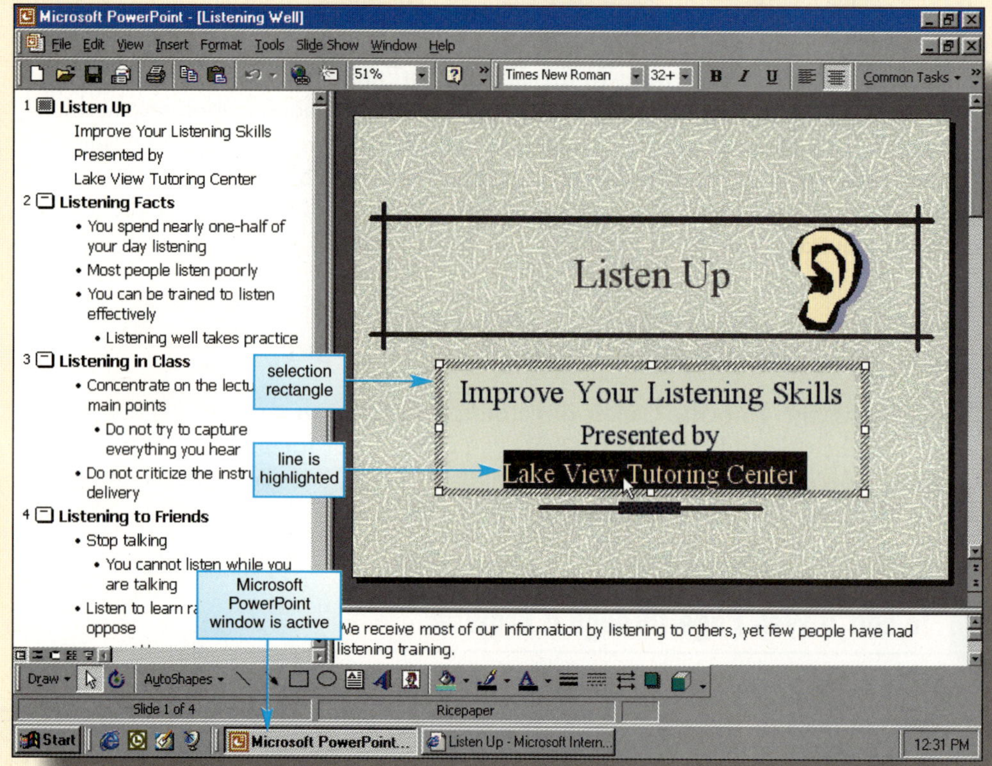

FIGURE 10

3 **Type** `Dr. Rachel Sims` **and then point to the Save button on the Standard toolbar.**

The last line is modified (Figure 11).

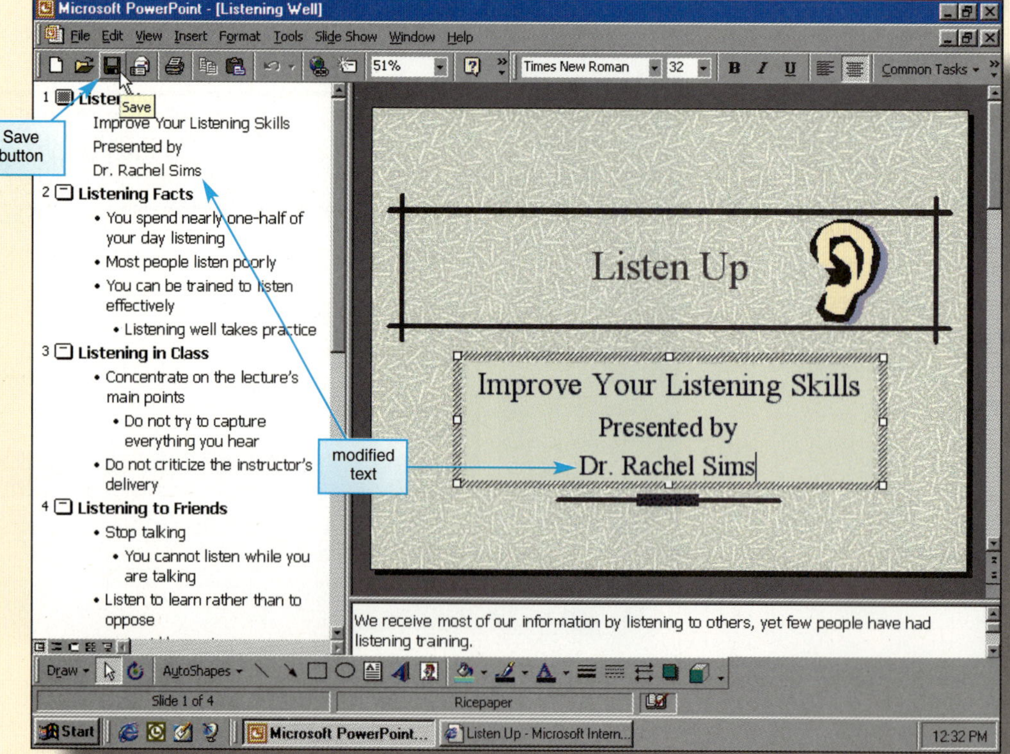

FIGURE 11

4 **Click the Save button. Point to the Listen Up – Microsoft Internet Explorer button on the taskbar.**

PowerPoint saves the changes to the Listening Well.htm file on the Data Disk. The buttons on the taskbar indicate that both PowerPoint and the browser are open (Figure 12).

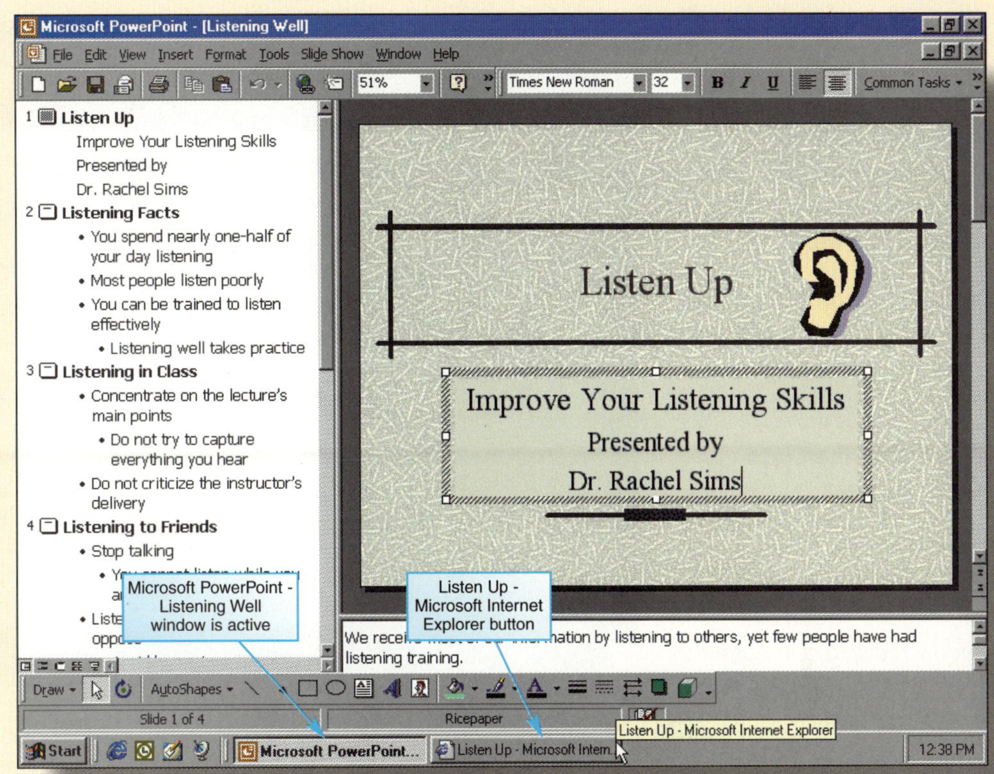

FIGURE 12

5 **Click the Listen Up – Microsoft Internet Explorer button and then point to the Refresh button on the Standard Buttons toolbar.**

The browser window displays the title text and clip art on Slide 1 (Figure 13). Clicking the **Refresh button** *displays the most current version of the Web page.*

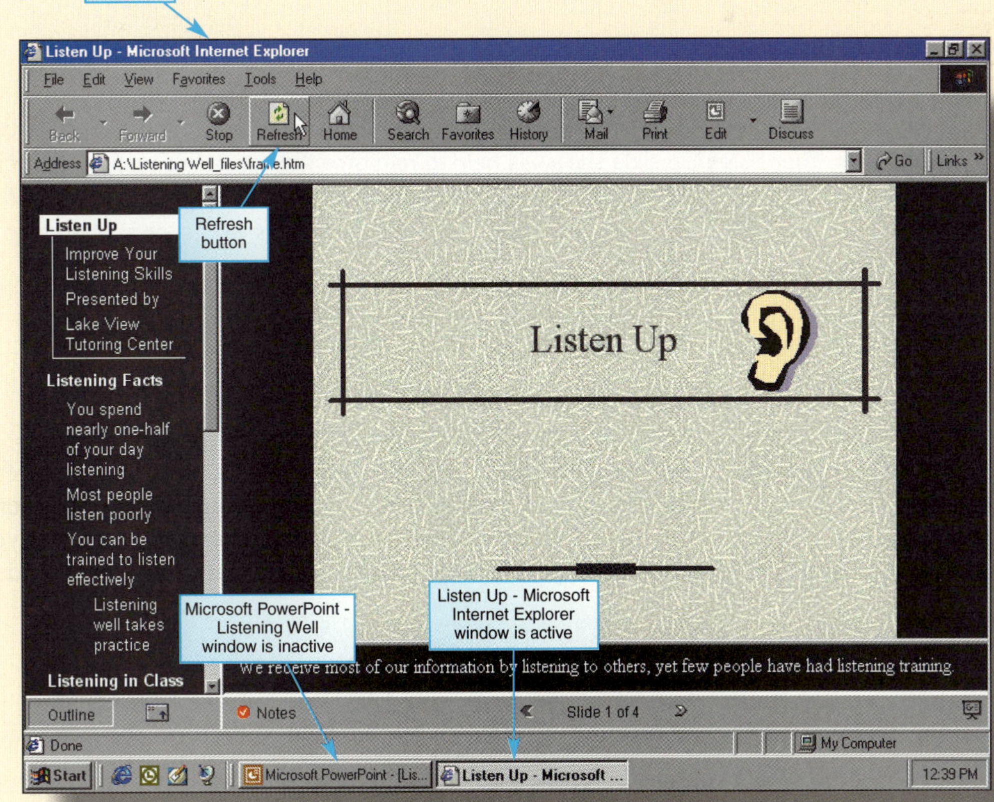

FIGURE 13

6 **Click the Refresh button. Click the slide three times to display all the Object Area placeholder text. Point to the Close button on the browser title bar.**

The complete Slide 1 displays (Figure 14). The last line reflects the editing changes.

7 **Click the Close button.**

PowerPoint closes the Listening Well Web presentation, and the PowerPoint window redisplays in normal view.

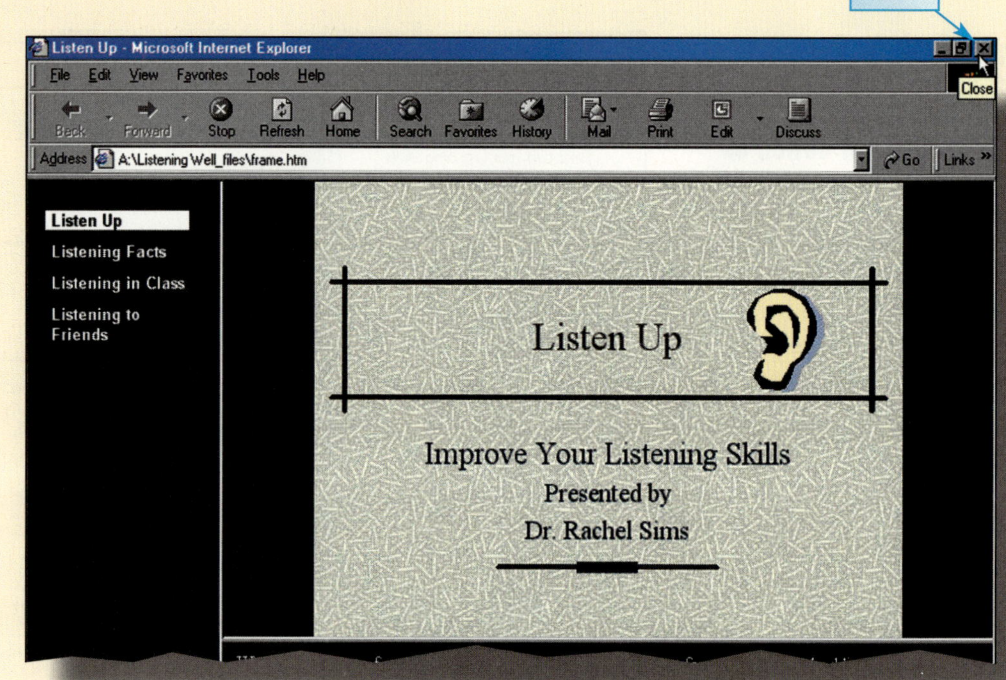

FIGURE 14

The Web page now is complete. The next step is to make your Web presentation available to others on your network, an intranet, or the World Wide Web. Ask your instructor how you can publish your presentation.

CASE PERSPECTIVE SUMMARY

Students attending Dr. Rachel Sims' lecture in the Tutoring Center should learn techniques that will improve their listening skills. Your Listen Up slide show will help to reinforce the key points presented, including facts about listening effectively. The students will be able to apply the theories when they are in class and with their friends. Dr. Sims can publish your presentation to the World Wide Web so that students who cannot attend the lecture also can gain the useful information presented.

Web Feature Summary

This Web feature introduced you to creating a Web page by saving an existing PowerPoint presentation as an HTML file. You then viewed the presentation as a Web page in your default browser. Next, you modified Slide 1. Finally, you reviewed your Slide 1 change using your default browser. Now that your Listen Up presentation is converted to a Web page, you can post the file to an intranet or to the World Wide Web.

What You Should Know

Having completed this Web feature, you now should be able to perform the following tasks:

- Edit a Web Page through a Browser *(PPW 1.9)*
- Save a PowerPoint Presentation as a Web Page *(PPW 1.4)*
- View a Presentation as a Web Page *(PPW 1.7)*

1 Creating a Web Page from the Studying Presentation

Problem: The advisers at Seaview College want to expand the visibility of the Effective Study Skills presentation created for them in Project 1. They believe the World Wide Web would be an excellent vehicle to help students throughout the campus and at other colleges, and they have asked you to help transfer the presentation to the Internet.

Instructions: Start PowerPoint and then perform the following steps with a computer.

1. Open the Studying presentation shown in Figures 1-2a through 1-2d on page PP 1.9 that you created in Project 1. (If you did not complete Project 1, see your instructor for a copy of the presentation.)
2. Use the Save as Web Page command on the File menu to convert and publish the presentation. Save the Web page using the file name, Effective Studying.
3. View the presentation in a browser.
4. Modify Slide 3 by adding a First level line that states, Arrive a few minutes before class starts, as the last line on the screen.
5. View the modified Web page in a browser.
6. Ask your instructor for instructions on how to post your Web page so others may have access to it.

2 Creating a Web Page from the Scholarship Presentation

Problem: The Searching for Scholarships presentation you developed in Project 2 for the Office of Financial Aid is generating much interest. Students are visiting the office, which has moved to Room 4321, and requesting a date to hear the lecture and to see the slide show. Dr. Mary Halen, the Financial Aid director, has asked you to post the presentation to the school's intranet.

Instructions: Start PowerPoint and then perform the following steps with a computer.

1. Open the Searching for Scholarships presentation shown in Figures 2-1a through 2-1f on page PP 2.5 that you created in Project 2. (If you did not complete Project 2, see your instructor for a copy of the presentation.)
2. Use the Save as Web Page command on the File menu to convert and publish the presentation. Save the Web page using the file name, Scholarship Sources.
3. View the presentation in a browser.
4. Modify Slide 2 by changing the room number to 4321.
5. Modify Slide 4 by changing the word, athletics, to the word, writing, in the Second level paragraph.
6. View the modified Web page in a browser.
7. Ask your instructor for instructions on how to post your Web page so others may have access to it.

3 Creating a Personal Presentation

Problem: You have decided to apply for a job at a company several hundred miles from your campus. You are preparing to send your resume and cover letter to the human resources department, and you want to develop a unique way to publicize your computer expertise. You decide to create a personalized PowerPoint presentation emphasizing your academic strengths and extra-curricular activities. You refer to this presentation in your cover letter and inform the company officials that they can view this presentation because you have saved the presentation as a Web page and posted the page to your school's server.

Instructions: Start PowerPoint and then perform the following steps with a computer.

1. Prepare a presentation highlighting your academic strengths. Create a title slide and at least three additional slides. Use appropriate clip art, animation effects, and slide transition effects.
2. Use the Save as Web Page command to convert and publish the presentation. Save the Web page using the file name, Supplemental Information.
3. View the presentation in a browser.
4. Ask your instructor for instructions on how to post your Web page so others may have access to it.

MICROSOFT

Outlook 2000

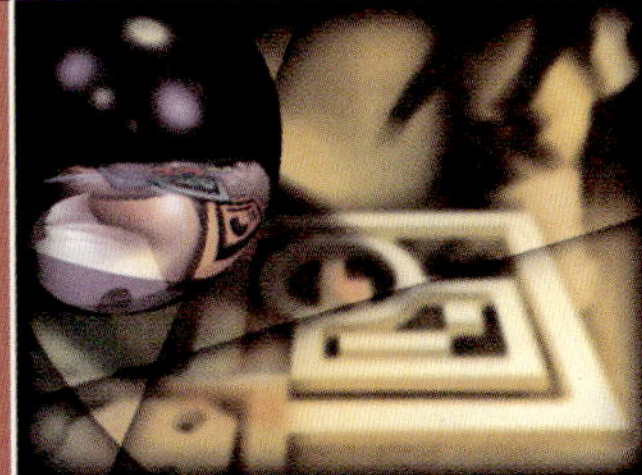

Microsoft Outlook 2000

Schedule and Contact Management Using Outlook

OBJECTIVES

You will have mastered the material in this project when you can:

- Start Outlook
- Open the Calendar folder
- Describe the components of the Calendar – Microsoft Outlook window
- Understand the elements of the Outlook Bar
- Create a personal subfolder
- Enter one-time and recurring appointments
- Use the Date Navigator to move to different days
- Use natural language phrases to enter appointment dates and times
- Move and edit appointments
- Create an event
- Display the calendar in Day, Work Week, Week, and Month views
- Print the calendar in Daily Style, Weekly Style, and Monthly Style
- Create and print a task list
- Create and print a contact list
- Use the find contact feature
- Create a category of contacts
- Import and export personal subfolders
- Delete personal subfolders from the hard disk
- Quit Outlook

A Positive Outlook

Managing Time and Information

Imagine the beginning of time: no electronic devices, very few engagements, and a slow-paced environment with regard to schedules and appointments. Now fast forward to the twenty-first century: cellular technology and satellite systems, the Internet and e-mail communications, and desktop information management (DIM) all at your fingertips every day without a second thought for the incredible advancements made in the primary fields of science and technology.

Although electronic devices are from this millennium, even prehistoric man was concerned with timekeeping and calendars. More than 20,000 years ago, ice-age hunters in Europe scratched lines and gouged holes in sticks and bones, possibly counting the days between phases of the moon. More than 4,000 years ago in England, Stonehenge's alignments show its purposes apparently included the determination of seasonal or celestial events. The Egyptians devised a 365-day calendar that seems to have begun in 4236 B.C. — the earliest recorded year in history.

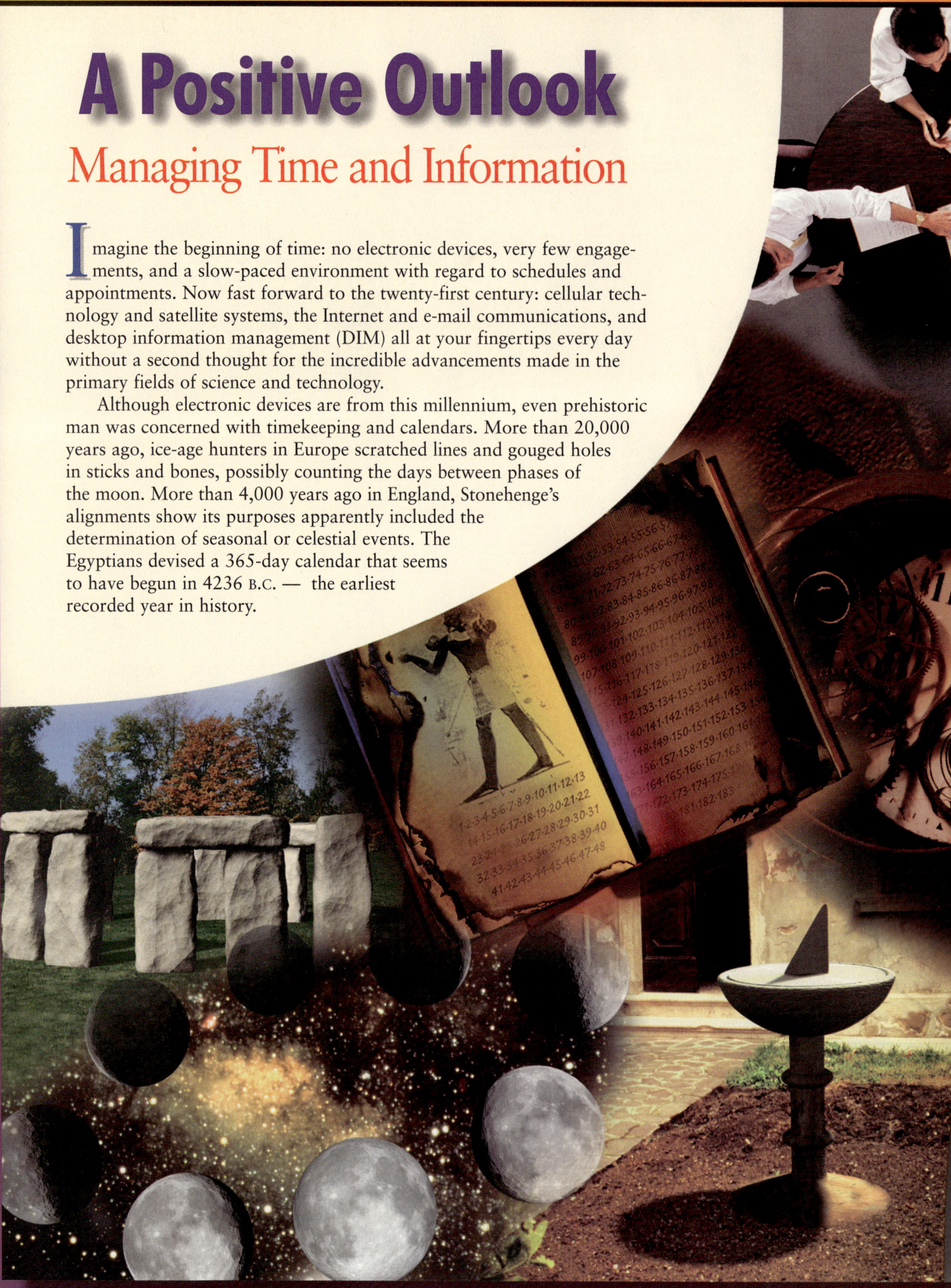

As far back as six thousand years ago, great Middle Eastern and North African civilizations introduced clock making. About 1500 B.C., sundials, the first portable timepieces, were designed, which led to the development of horology, or the science of measuring time.

The need to develop newer methods to organize and manage time more effectively continues to expand. Computer users today have no shortage of tools that combine the capabilities of accessing information and communications using e-mail, voice mail, facsimile, meetings, telephone, newsletters, reports, planners, browsers, and custom groupware.

With the tremendous quantities of electronic and paper communications bombarding individuals, the need to organize is a daunting task. The positive aspects of electronic information transmission, however, have helped to manage the paper flow and decrease the amount of time it takes to send information; for example, instantly through cyberspace rather than the U.S. Postal Service. This global electronic network is remaking daily life and forces individuals to prioritize their tasks.

Microsoft Outlook 2000 has been designed to answer the problem of electronic information overload. A desktop information management (DIM) system, Outlook is a central location from which you can create, view, and organize all of your information. The data is stored in folders. A shortcut stores the folder location and allows you to open it quickly using shortcuts on the Outlook Bar.

From Inbox, you can read and send e-mail messages. Calendar provides the tools to create appointments, plan meetings and events, and review tasks. Using Contacts, you are able to store names, addresses, and other data about your business and personal contacts. Tasks simplifies to-do lists and allows you to organize assignments. Journal presents a review of your work history. Notes is an area where you can formulate ideas and save reminders. With this integration, you eliminate the need for weekly planners, daily pocket calendars, sticky notes, and task lists. With its Internet browsing capabilities, Outlook also acts as a Web Address Book and allows you to store, manage, and navigate favorite sites.

Perhaps in the historic archives of the next millennium, our civilization's desktop information management systems will seem as obsolete as the Aztec calendar stone. Until then, however, the organization, efficiency, and timesavings they give to the information explosion of today are indeed a blessing.

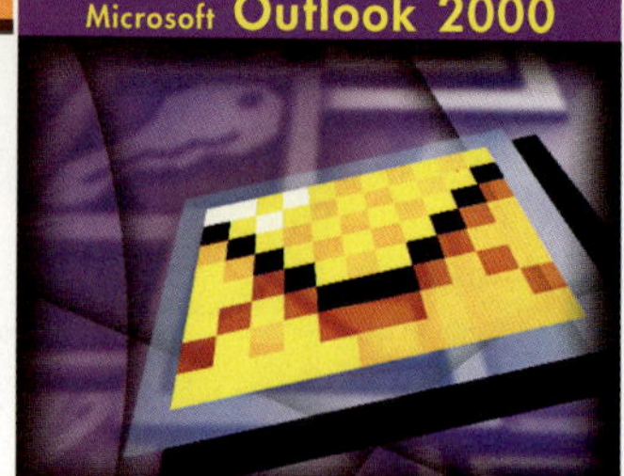

Microsoft Outlook 2000

Schedule and Contact Management Using Outlook

CASE PERSPECTIVE

Tamara Wilson is a student at Community College. Her busy schedule includes classes, studying, and social time. Tamara is concerned that she will forget something important if she does not keep track of her activities in an orderly manner. Tamara's parents bought her a laptop computer for college. The computer came with a number of software packages, including Microsoft Outlook. Tamara has read about Outlook and thinks it seems like a great tool to help her keep organized this semester. She decided to use Outlook to schedule all of her daily activities, including time that she is in class, time for studying, and social time.

You are a consultant in the college's computer lab. Tamara comes to you for help setting up her calendar. She would like to schedule all of her classes for the semester. She read that Outlook allows you to create a single calendar event and set a weekly recurrence pattern, which will help her with this task. Tamara also plans to schedule time and committee meetings. Tamara feels that having her time scheduled should help her to meet all important deadlines and appointments. With your help, she can accomplish this goal.

What Is Microsoft Outlook 2000?

Microsoft Outlook, an application contained in Microsoft Office 2000, is an effective **desktop information management (DIM)** program that helps you organize your busy schedule, keep track of your contacts, and communicate with others. Most individuals have multiple appointments to keep and tasks to accomplish in a day, week, or month. Outlook assists in maintaining a full schedule such as this, organizing the information in a structured, readable manner. Users easily can track meetings, e-mail messages, and notes with a particular contact. Outlook's Calendar, Contacts, Tasks, or Notes components aid in this organization. Contact information readily is available with the Find option, which can be accessed from the calendar, e-mail, and other Outlook components. DIMs such as Outlook provide a way for individuals and workgroups to organize, find, view, and share information easily.

Files created in Word, Excel, Access, and PowerPoint can be used in your Outlook folder or attached to an e-mail message. Outlook also makes it easy to share data between applications. For instance, your contact list can become the data source for a Word mail merge, or Word can be used as your editor for e-mail messages. Outlook's Inbox and Calendar folders make it easy to update, print, and fax your schedule to anyone, anywhere.

Project One — Tamara Wilson's DIM System

In Project 1, the basic features of Outlook are addressed in the creation of a calendar of classes and appointments. In addition to creating the Calendar, you will print it in three views: Day, Week, and Month. Figure 1-1 outlines the creation process. Then, you will create a task list for a given day and a contact list.

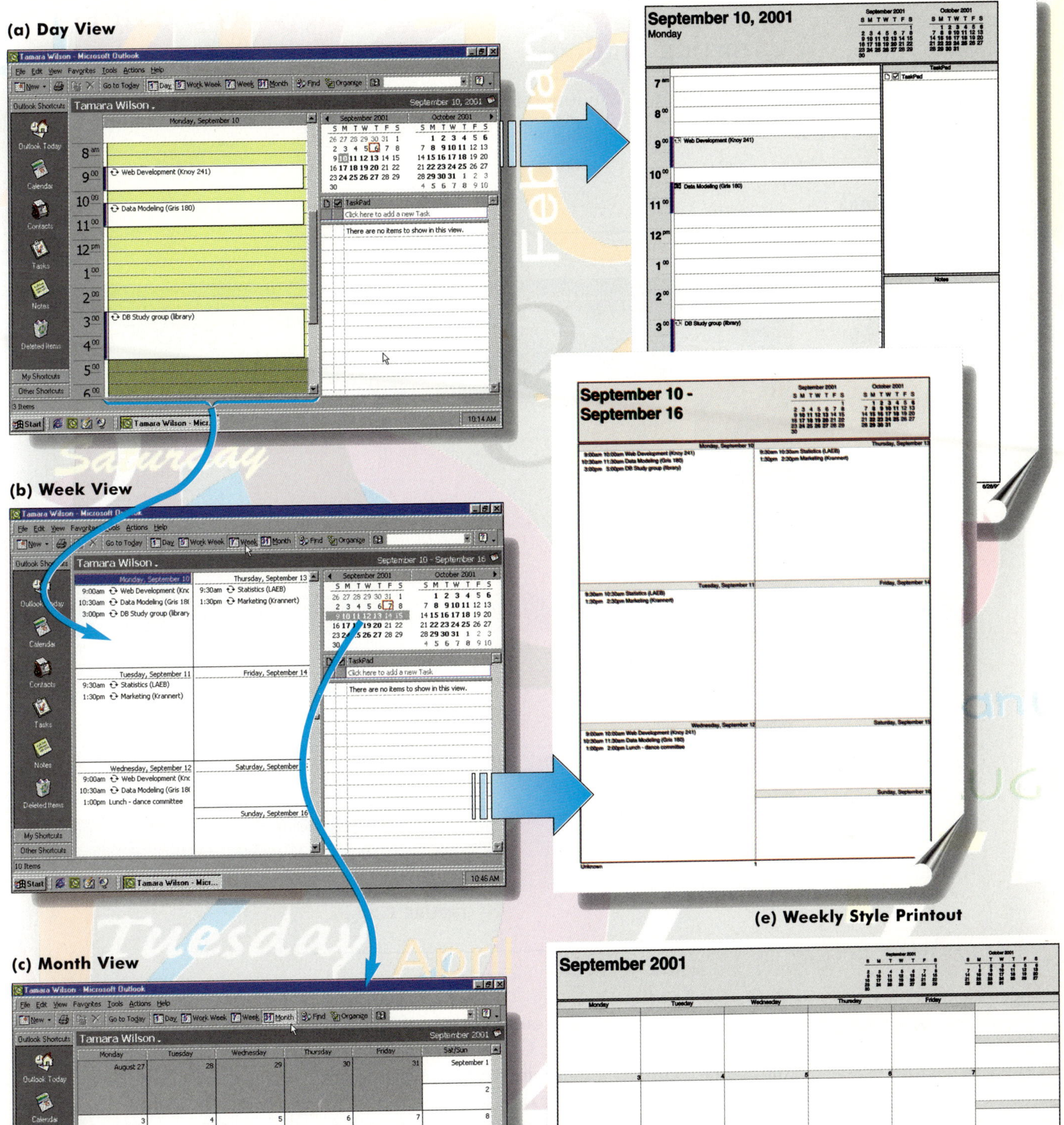
(a) Day View
(b) Week View
(c) Month View
(d) Daily Style Printout
(e) Weekly Style Printout
(f) Monthly Style Printout

FIGURE 1-1

Starting Outlook

To start Outlook, Windows must be running. Perform the following step to start Outlook.

Steps To Start Outlook

1 Click the Launch Microsoft Outlook icon on the Quick Launch toolbar.

Outlook displays the Inbox folder in the Inbox — Microsoft Outlook window (Figure 1-2).

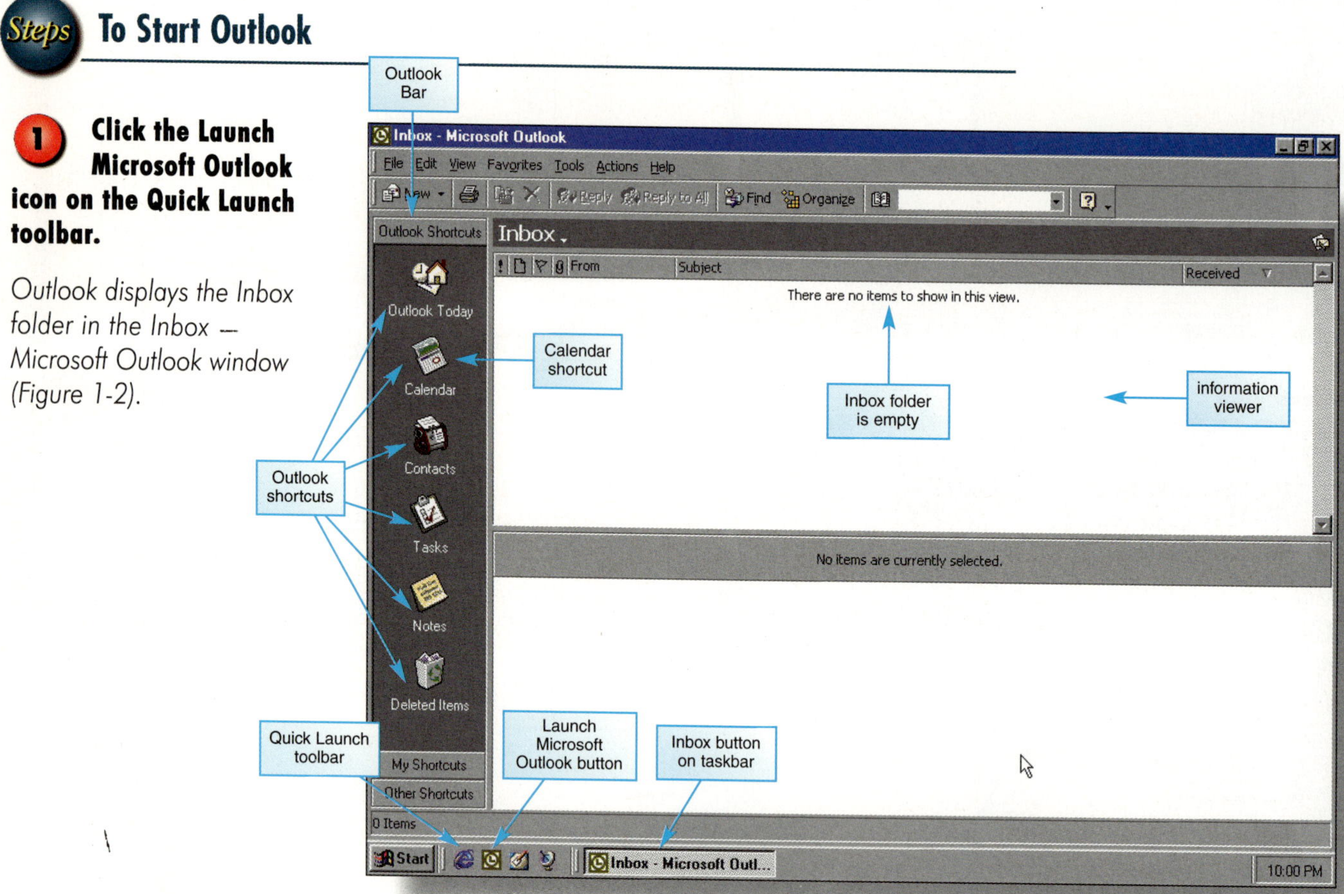

FIGURE 1-2

Other Ways

1. Click Start button on taskbar, point to Programs on Start menu, click Microsoft Outlook
2. Double-click Microsoft Outlook icon on desktop

Outlook is organized around groups of **items**, such as Outlook Today, Calendar, Contacts, Tasks, and Notes. Groups of the same type are stored in the same Outlook folder. For example, all appointments are stored in the Calendar folder, and all contact information is stored in the Contacts folder. When a folder is opened, the items in the selected folder display in the **information viewer** (Figure 1-2).

Opening the Calendar Folder

To begin entering items in Tamara Wilson's calendar, perform the following steps to open the Calendar folder.

Steps To Open the Calendar Folder

1 Click the Calendar shortcut on the Outlook Bar on the left side of the screen.

Outlook opens the Calendar folder and the Calendar – Microsoft Outlook window displays. When you open the Calendar folder, the Calendar displays in the default Day view (Figure 1-3). The Outlook ***Day view*** *allows you to enter information for one day at a time.*

2 If necessary, click the Maximize button on the title bar to maximize the Calendar – Microsoft Outlook window. If your screen displays a larger appointment area than the one in Figure 1-3, drag the appointment area border to the left.

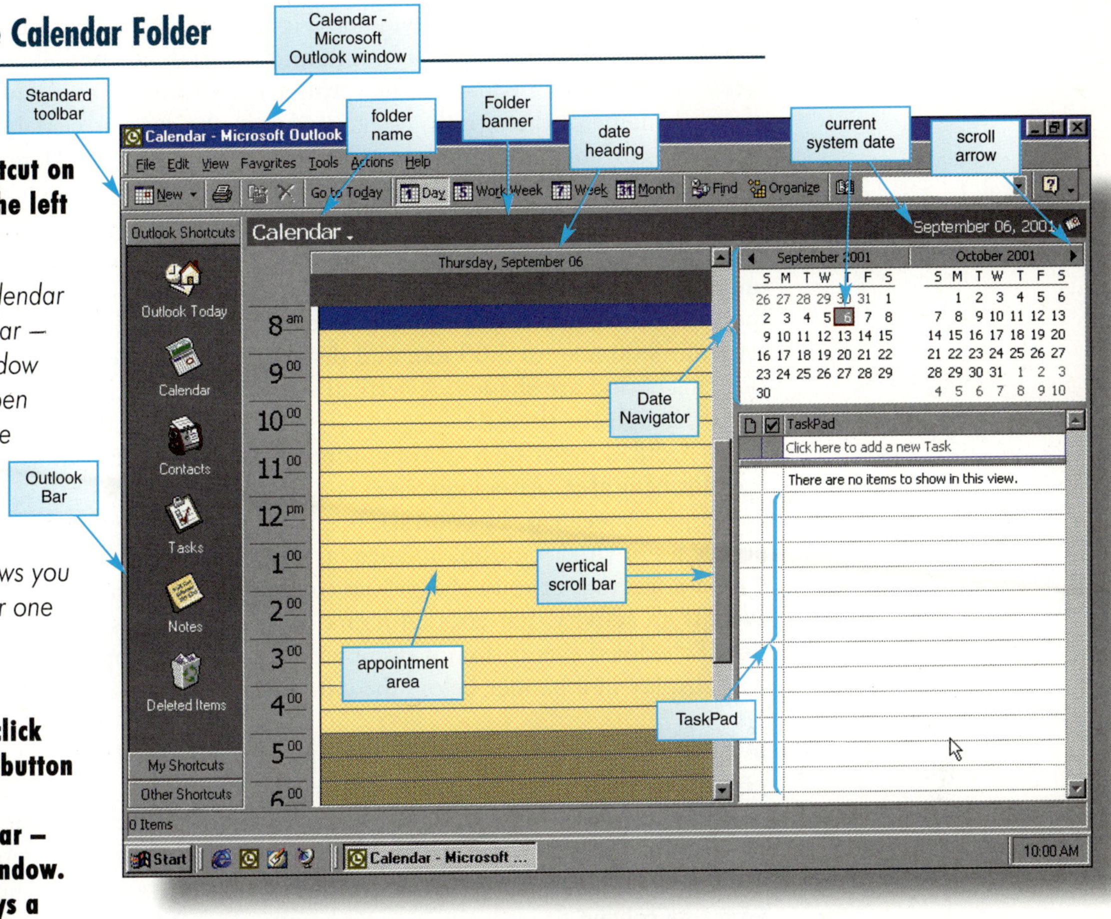

FIGURE 1-3

1. On View menu point to Go To, click Calendar on Go To submenu

The Calendar — Microsoft Outlook Window

The **Calendar – Microsoft Outlook window** (Figure 1-3) includes a variety of features to help you work efficiently. It contains many elements similar to the windows in other applications, as well as some that are unique to Outlook. The main elements of the Calendar – Microsoft Outlook window are the Outlook Bar, the Standard toolbar, the Folder banner, the Date Navigator, the appointment area, and the TaskPad. The following paragraphs explain some of the features of the Calendar – Microsoft Outlook window.

FOLDER BANNER The Folder banner (Figure 1-3) is the horizontal bar just below the Standard toolbar. The name of the active folder displays on the left side of the Folder banner; an icon for the active folder displays on the right. When the folder name is clicked, the Folder List showing available folders and subfolders displays.

DATE NAVIGATOR The **Date Navigator** (Figure 1-3 on the previous page) includes two monthly calendars (the current month and the previous or following month) and scroll arrows. When you click the scroll arrows to move to a new date, Calendar displays the name of the month, week, or day in the current view in the appointment area. The current system date has a square around it in the Date Navigator. Dates displayed in bold in the Date Navigator indicate days on which an item is scheduled.

APPOINTMENT AREA The **appointment area** (Figure 1-3) contains a date heading and, under the date heading, time slots for the current view. The date currently selected in the Date Navigator displays in the date heading. By default, workday time slots are set from 8:00 A.M. to 5:00 P.M. and display with a white background. Time slots outside this period are shaded. A vertical scroll bar allows backward and forward movement through the time slots.

Scheduled items such as appointments, meetings, or events, display in the appointment area. An **appointment** is an activity that does not involve other resources or people. A **meeting**, by contrast, is an appointment to which other resources or people are invited. Outlook's Calendar can be used to schedule several people to attend a meeting or only one person to attend an appointment (such as a class). An **event** is an activity that lasts 24 hours or longer, such as a seminar, birthday, or vacation. Scheduled events do not occupy time slots in the appointment area; instead, they display in a banner below the date heading.

TASKPAD The **TaskPad** (Figure 1-3) displays below the Date Navigator. **Tasks** are personal or work-related duties that need to be tracked through completion. The TaskPad displays your tasks and their status. You can change the way tasks appear by clicking TaskPad View on the View menu or add details to a task by double-clicking the **Tasks shortcut**. When a task is complete, select the check box in the **Complete column** to indicate its completion.

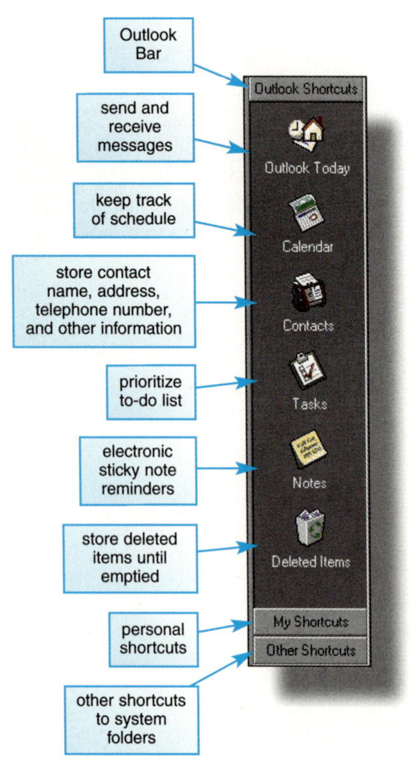

FIGURE 1-4

OUTLOOK SHORTCUTS On the left side of the Calendar – Microsoft Outlook window is a vertical bar called the **Outlook Bar** (Figure 1-4). The Outlook Bar contains shortcuts representing the standard items that are part of Microsoft Outlook. The Outlook Bar is divided into groups to help organize your information. The standard Outlook groups include shortcuts to folders for Outlook Today, Calendar, Contacts, Tasks, Notes, and Deleted Items; although the shortcuts in your Outlook Bar may include other shortcuts. When you click a shortcut, Outlook opens the folder. The function performed when you click each folder is illustrated in Figure 1-4.

MY SHORTCUTS Another shortcut bar available in Outlook is My Shortcuts. This bar contains shortcuts to Inbox, Drafts, and Journal. Outlook also prompts you to add shortcuts to this bar when creating new folders.

OTHER SHORTCUTS This bar contains shortcuts to My Computer, My Documents, and Favorites. Easy access to these important system components is available through the Other Shortcuts bar.

STANDARD TOOLBAR Figure 1-5 shows the Standard toolbar in the Calendar – Microsoft Outlook window. The button names indicate their functions. Each button can be clicked to perform a frequently used task, such as creating a new appointment, printing, or changing the current view.

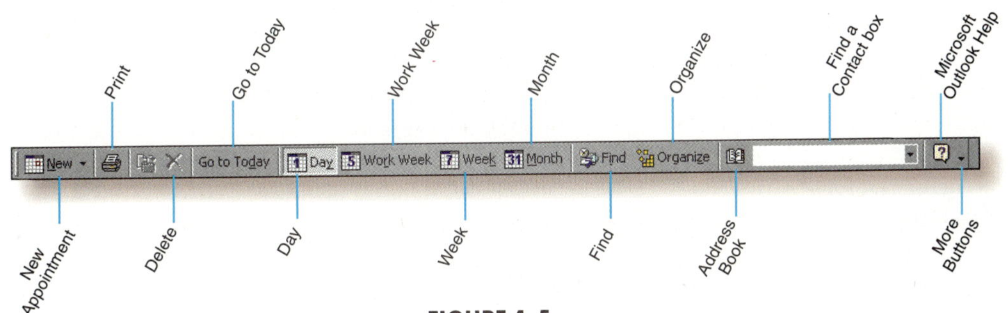

Standard Toolbar

FIGURE 1-5

Creating a Personal Subfolder in the Calendar Folder

If you were the only person using Outlook on a computer, you could enter appointments and events directly into the main Calendar folder, creating a daily, weekly, and monthly schedule. In many office and school situations, however, several people share one computer and therefore need to create separate folders in which to store appointments and events. With Outlook, you can create personal subfolders in which to store your personal calendar and other files. Subfolders then can be saved on the hard disk or a floppy disk. If working on a networked computer, check with your instructor or database manager for the policy on creating and saving subfolders. In this project, substitute your name in place of Tamara Wilson as you create the personal subfolders. Perform the following steps to create a personal subfolder to store Tamara Wilson's calendar.

Folders

The Outlook Bar can be used to open any files on your computer or any computer to which you are connected. Click the Other group on the Outlook Bar and then click My Computer to view or open any files. Files can be viewed as icons, in a table, or in a timeline.

To Create a Personal Subfolder in the Calendar Folder

1 Right-click the folder name Calendar in the Folder banner. Point to New Folder on the shortcut menu.

Outlook displays a shortcut menu of tasks associated with the Calendar folder (Figure 1-6).

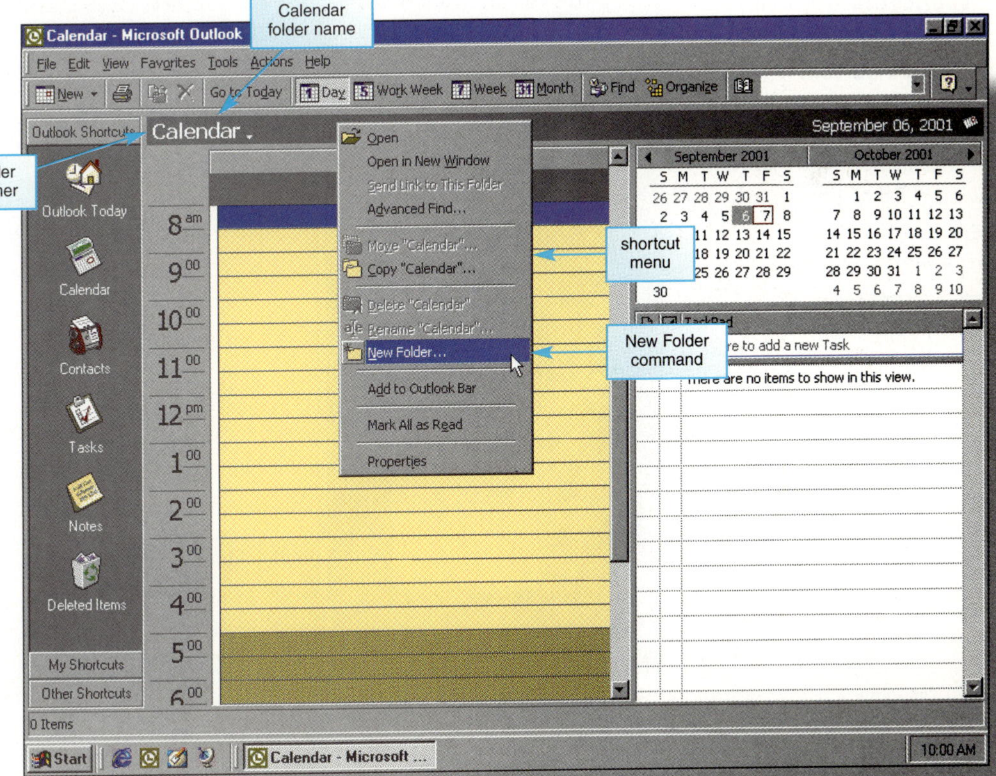

FIGURE 1-6

2 Click New Folder. Type `Tamara Wilson` **in the Name text box. Point to the OK button.**

The Create New Folder dialog box displays. It contains a text box for the folder name, a list box to indicate what type of items the folder will contain, and a list of folders and subfolders (Figure 1-7). Appointment Items is the default in the Folder contains list box.

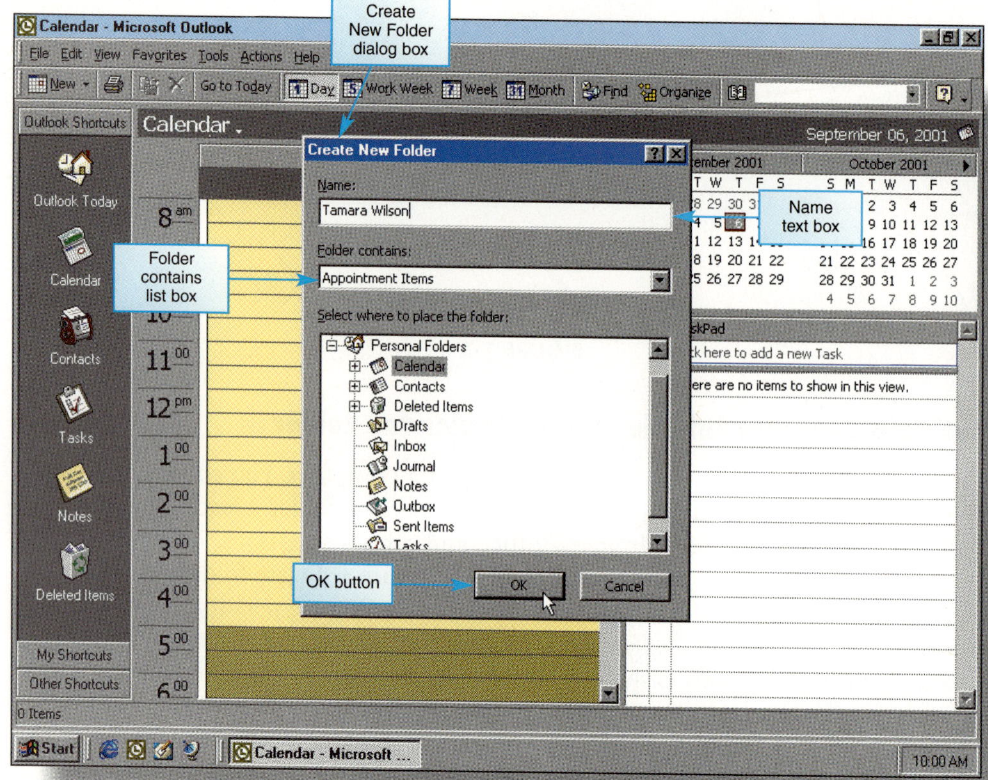

FIGURE 1-7

3 Click the OK button. When the Add shortcut to Outlook Bar? dialog box displays, click the No button.

A Folder List displays to the left of the appointment area, showing a list of available folders and subfolders. The new subfolder icon and name, Tamara Wilson, display (Figure 1-8).

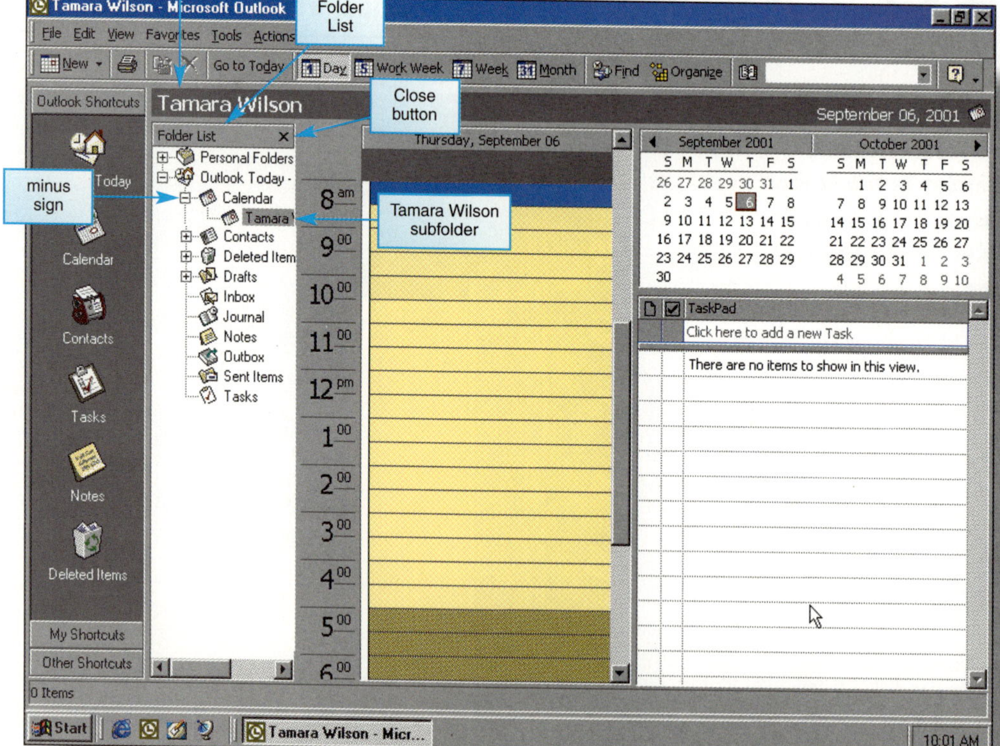

FIGURE 1-8

Other Ways

1. On File menu point to New, click Folder
2. On File menu point to Folder, click New Folder
3. Press CTRL+SHIFT+E

By clicking the No button in the Add shortcut to Outlook Bar? dialog box, a shortcut for this folder will not be added to the Outlook Bar. In the Folder List, the Calendar now displays with a minus sign to the left. The **minus sign** indicates that the folder is expanded. A **plus sign** to the left of a folder indicates that additional folders are below.

A personal folder now is created in which calendar information is stored. Perform the following step to change to that folder.

To Change to a Personal Folder

1 If necessary, click the plus sign (+) to the left of the Calendar icon in the Folder List to expand the folder list in the Calendar folder. Click the Tamara Wilson folder. Click the Close button to close the Folder List.

The Tamara Wilson folder displays (Figure 1-9). The folder name displays on the Outlook title bar and in the Folder banner.

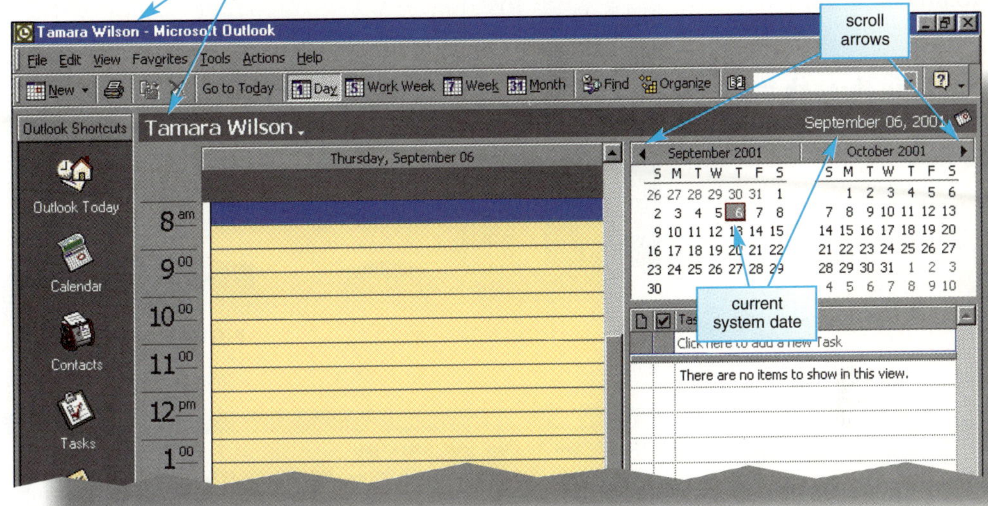

FIGURE 1-9

With the Tamara Wilson personal subfolder open, you can enter items into the schedule in the next steps.

Opening Calendars

Other users can give you access to their calendar. This allows you to make appointments, check their free times, schedule meetings, check or copy contacts, or anything else that you can do with your own calendar. This is useful if you are required to schedule meetings or events that depend on other people's schedules.

Entering Appointments Using the Appointment Area

Calendar allows you to schedule appointments, meetings, and events for yourself as well as for others who have given permission to open their subfolders. Students and business people will find that scheduling resources and people is easy to do with Outlook's Calendar application.

The next section describes how to enter appointments into Tamara Wilson's personal subfolder, starting with appointments for September 10, 2001. Classes and study hours are recurring appointments; meetings and lunch are one-time appointments.

When entering an appointment into a time slot that is not visible in the current view, use the vertical scroll bar to bring the time slot into view. Once you enter an appointment, you can perform ordinary editing actions. Perform the steps on the next page to enter appointments using the appointment area.

To Enter Appointments Using the Appointment Area

1 If necessary, click the scroll arrows in the Date Navigator to display September and October 2001. Click 10 in the September calendar in the Date Navigator to display it in the appointment area.

2 Drag through the 9:00 am - 10:00 am time slot.

The 9:00 am - 10:00 am time slot is highlighted (Figure 1-10).

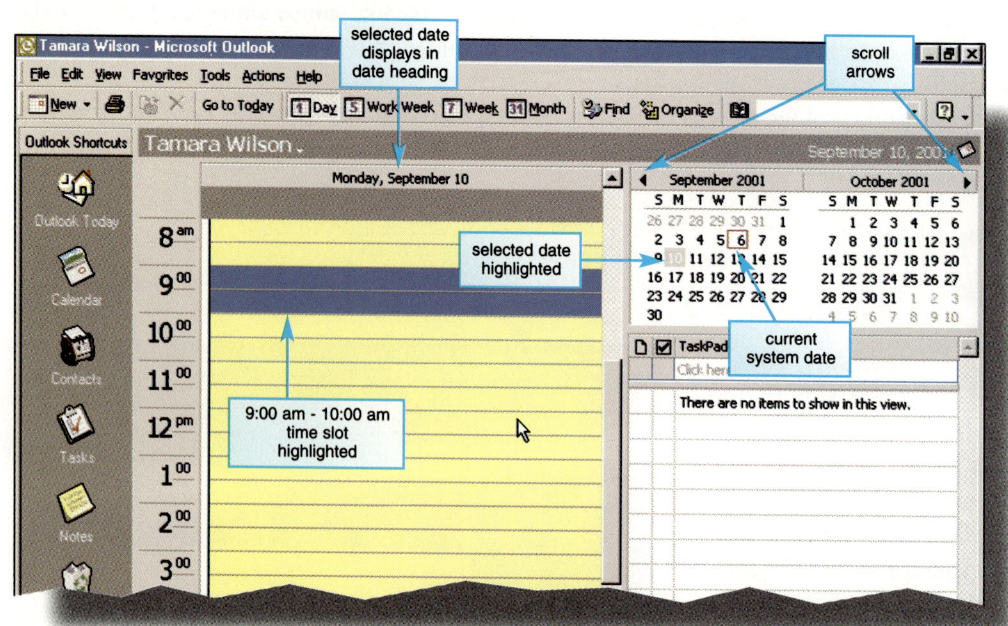

FIGURE 1-10

3 Type `Web Development` **as the first appointment.**

As soon as you begin typing, the highlighted time slot changes to a text box with blue top and bottom borders.

4 Drag through the 10:30 am - 11:30 am time slot. Type `Data Modeling` **as the second appointment.**

5 Drag through the 12 pm - 1:00 pm time slot. Type `Lunch - dance committee` **as the third appointment and then press the ENTER key.**

The three appointments display in the appointment area (Figure 1-11).

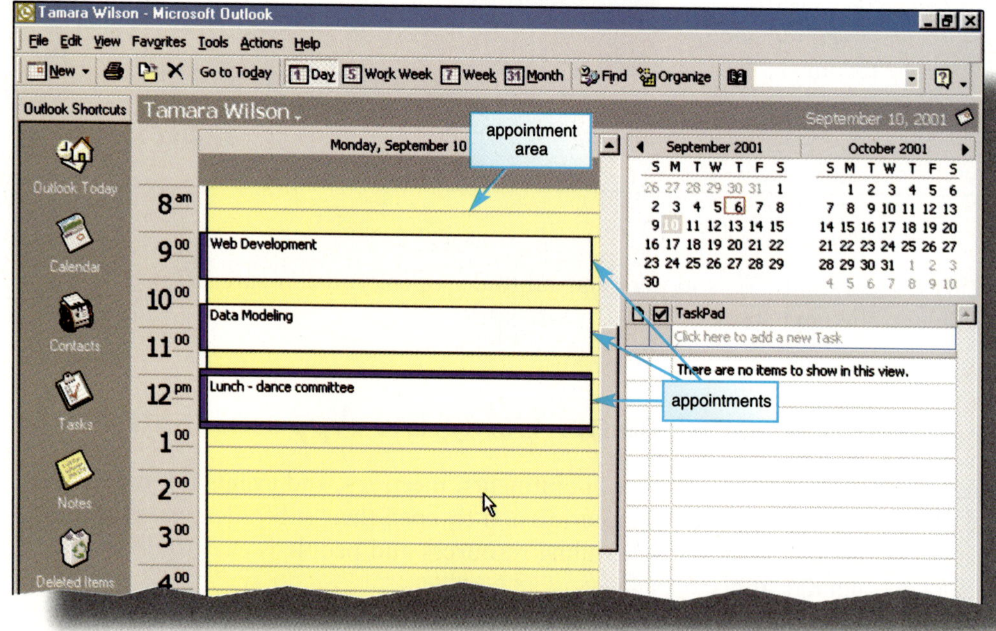

FIGURE 1-11

Other Ways

1. Double-click time slot
2. Right-click time slot, click New Appointment on shortcut menu
3. On Actions menu click New Appointment
4. Press ALT+A, press O
5. Press CTRL+N

If you make a mistake while typing and notice the error before clicking outside the appointment time slot or pressing **the ENTER key**, use the BACKSPACE key to erase all the characters back to and including the error. To cancel the entire entry before clicking outside the appointment time slot or pressing the ENTER key, press the ESC key. If you discover an error in an appointment after clicking outside the appointment or pressing the ENTER key, click the appointment and retype the entry. Later in this project, additional editing techniques are covered.

Entering Appointments Using the Appointment Window

You can enter appointments either by typing them directly into the appointment area as shown in the previous section, or you can enter them using the **Appointment window**. Using the Appointment window is a slightly more involved process, but it allows the specification of more details about the appointment. The following steps describe how to enter an appointment at 3:00 P.M. to 5:00 P.M. using the Appointment window.

More About

Appointments

Appointments can be designated as busy, free, tentative, or out of office. You also can schedule appointments as private, which prevents them from being seen by other users who have access to your calendar. The private check box is located in the bottom-right corner of the Appointment window. Once an appointment is marked as private, a key symbol displays next to the text in the appointment, indicating the information is private or "locked." This can be applied to appointments, tasks, meetings, or contacts.

To Enter and Save Appointments Using the Appointment Window

1 Drag through the 3:00 pm - 5:00 pm time slot and then click the New Appointment button on the Standard toolbar.

The Untitled Appointment window displays with the insertion point in the Subject text box on the Appointment tab (Figure 1-12).

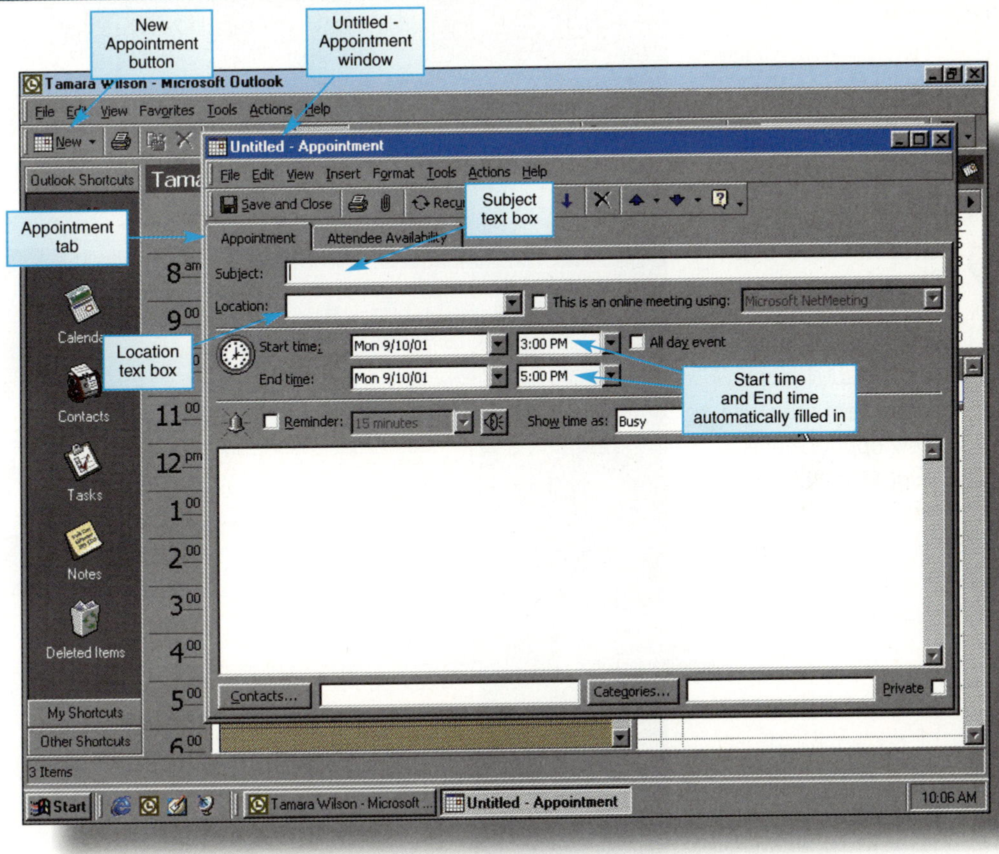

FIGURE 1-12

Type `DB Study group` **in the Subject text box and then press the TAB key to move the insertion point to the Location text box. Type** `library` **in the Location text box and then point to the Save and Close button on the Standard toolbar in the Appointment window.**

Both the subject and location of the appointment display in the appropriate text boxes. Once typed, the appointment subject displays on the Appointment window title bar and on the taskbar button (Figure 1-13).

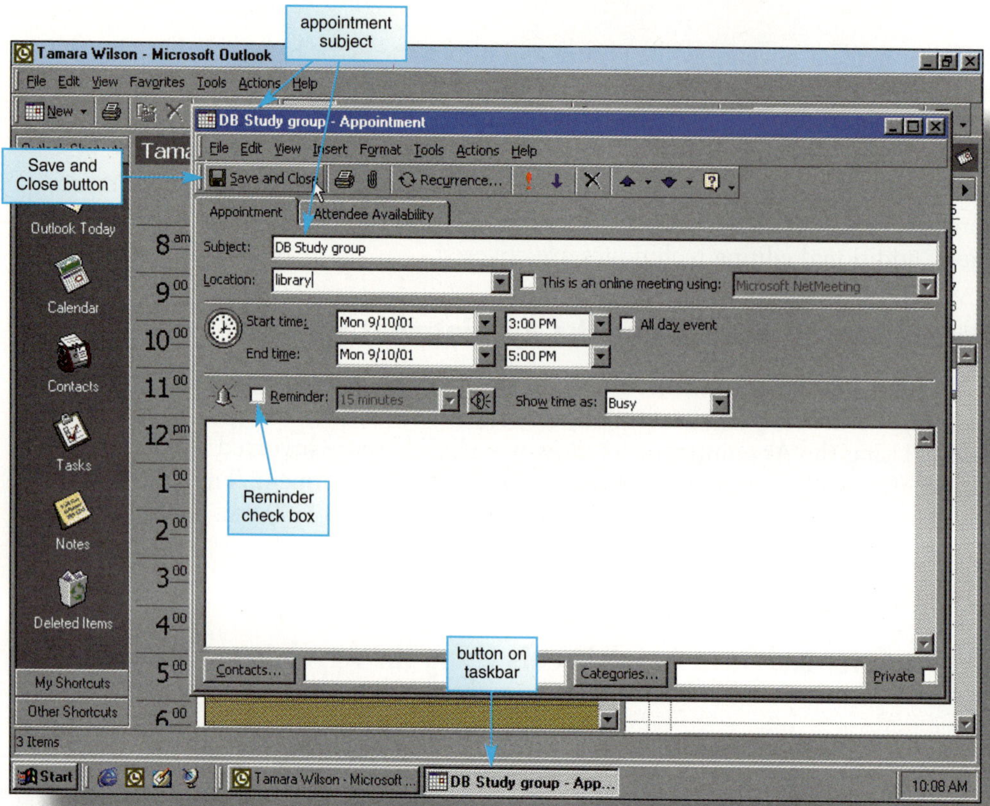

FIGURE 1-13

3 **Click the Save and Close button.**

The schedule for Monday, September 10, 2001 displays in the appointment area with the four new appointments entered (Figure 1-14).

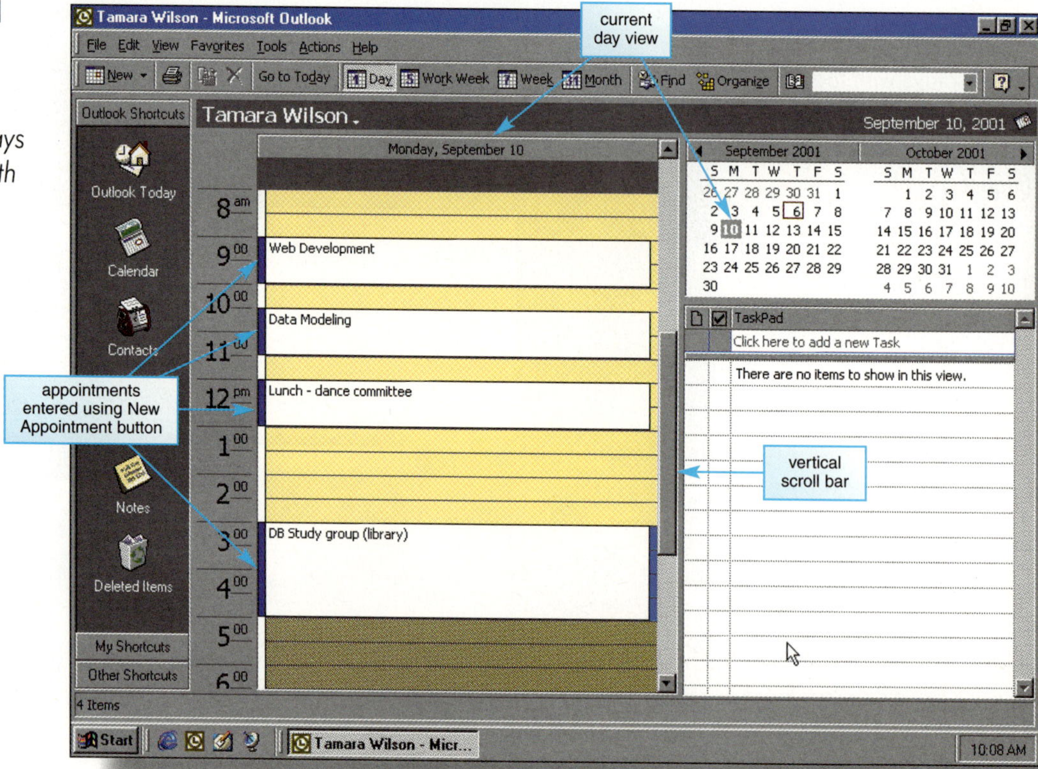

FIGURE 1-14

Click the Reminder check box (Figure 1-13) to instruct your computer to play a reminder sound before an appointment time. A bell icon, called the **Reminder symbol**, displays next to appointments with reminders.

Press the TAB key to move through the fields in the Appointment window, or click any text or list box to make a change. Normal editing techniques also can be used to make changes. In the next steps, recurrence is added to the appointments just entered.

Recurring Appointments

Many appointments are **recurring**, or occur at regular intervals. For example, a class held every Monday and Wednesday from 9:00 A.M. to 10:00 A.M. is a recurring meeting. In this project, Tamara Wilson's college classes and study hours occur at regular weekly intervals. Having to type these recurring appointments for each occasion would be very time-consuming. By designating an appointment as recurring, an appointment only needs to be added once and then recurrence is specified for the days on which it occurs. Table 1-1 lists Tamara's recurring appointments.

Table 1-1 Recurring Appointments

TIME	APPOINTMENT	OCCURRENCE
9:00 am - 10:00 am	Web Development (Knoy 241)	Every Monday and Wednesday (30 times)
10:30 am - 11:30 am	Data Modeling (Gris 180)	Every Monday and Wednesday (30 times)
12 m - 1:00 pm	Lunch – dance committee (cafeteria)	Monday, September 10, 2001
3:00 pm - 5:00 pm	DB Study group (library)	Every Monday (15 times)

Perform the following steps to set recurring appointments.

Steps To Set Recurring Appointments

1. **With Monday, September 10, 2001 displayed, use the vertical scroll bar to display the Web Development appointment in the appointment area. Double-click the words Web Development.**

The Web Development – Appointment window displays.

2. **Click the Location text box and then type** Knoy 241 **to set the location of the class. Point to the Recurrence button on the Standard toolbar.**

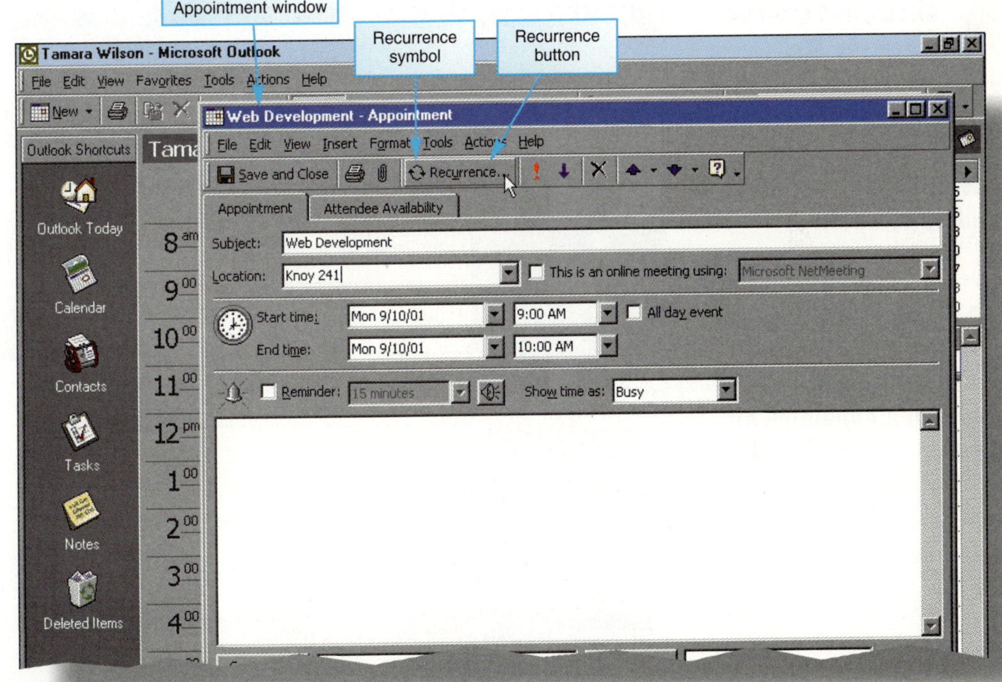

FIGURE 1-15

The symbol on the Recurrence button (Figure 1-15) will become the **Recurrence symbol** *that displays beside the appointment in the appointment area.*

3 **Click the Recurrence button on the Standard toolbar. Click the Wednesday check box to select the days this appointment will recur. Click End after, double-click in the End after text box, and then type** 30 **as the number of occurrences. Point to the OK button.**

The Appointment Recurrence dialog box displays (Figure 1-16). The Web Development appointment is set to recur on Mondays (selected as the default) and Wednesdays (selected in the step) and end after 30 occurrences.

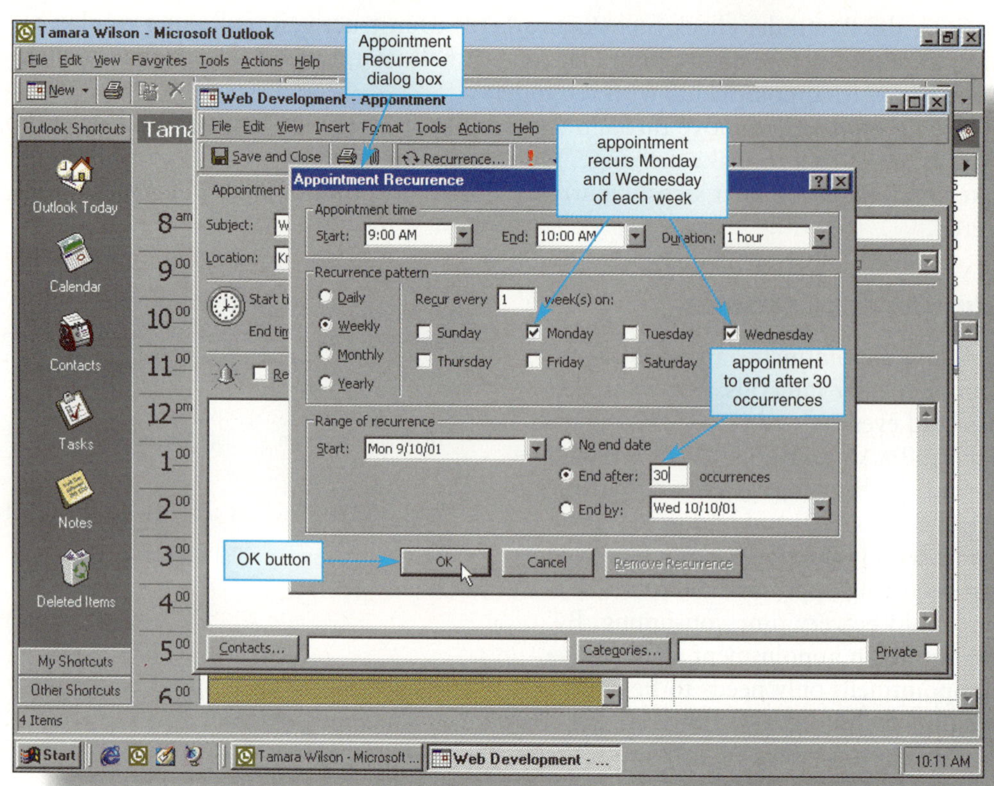

FIGURE 1-16

4 **Click the OK button. When the Web Development – Recurring Appointment window displays, click the Save and Close button on the Standard toolbar.**

5 **Repeat Steps 1 through 4 to make the Data Modeling and DB Study group appointments recurring. See Table 1-1 on the previous page for the location, range, and ending dates.**

The Monday, September 10, 2001 schedule is complete (Figure 1-17). A Recurrence symbol displays beside each recurring appointment.

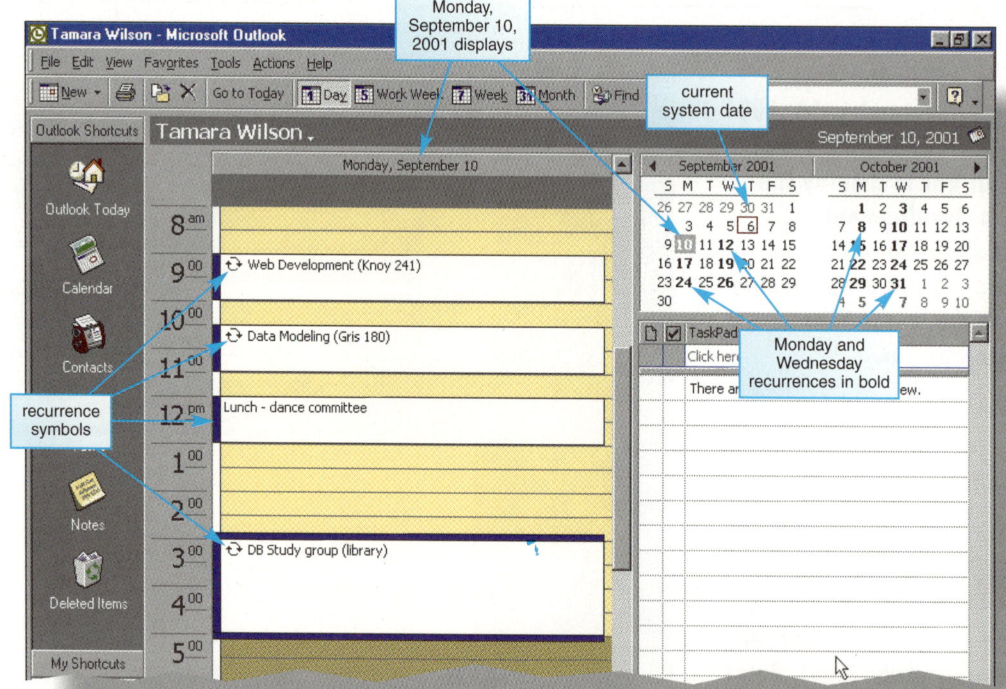

FIGURE 1-17

1. On Actions menu click New Recurring Appointment
2. Press ALT+A, press A

The Date Navigator serves several purposes when creating appointments. Recurring appointments are assigned to their appropriate dates automatically. Once an appointment is assigned to a date, it displays in bold in the Date Navigator (Figure 1-17). You can change these features using the **Format View command** on the View menu.

The Date Navigator also allows easy movement and display of a specific date in the appointment area. This allows appointments to be entered on that date. This technique of moving through the Calendar is demonstrated in the next section.

Recurring Icon

The recurring icon can be applied to appointments, events, meetings, and tasks. Double-click the item to open its dialog window and then click the Recurrence button.

Moving to the Next Day in Calendar

Now that the Monday schedule is complete, the next step is to enter appointments for Tuesday. To do so, Tuesday must display in the appointment area. The following steps show how to move to the next day using the Date Navigator.

To Move to the Next Day in the Appointment Area

1 Click 11 in the September 2001 calendar in the Date Navigator. Drag through the 9:30 am - 10:30 am time slot. Point to the New Appointment button on the Standard toolbar.

Tuesday, September 11, 2001 displays in the appointment area (Figure 1-18).

2 Click the New Appointment button.

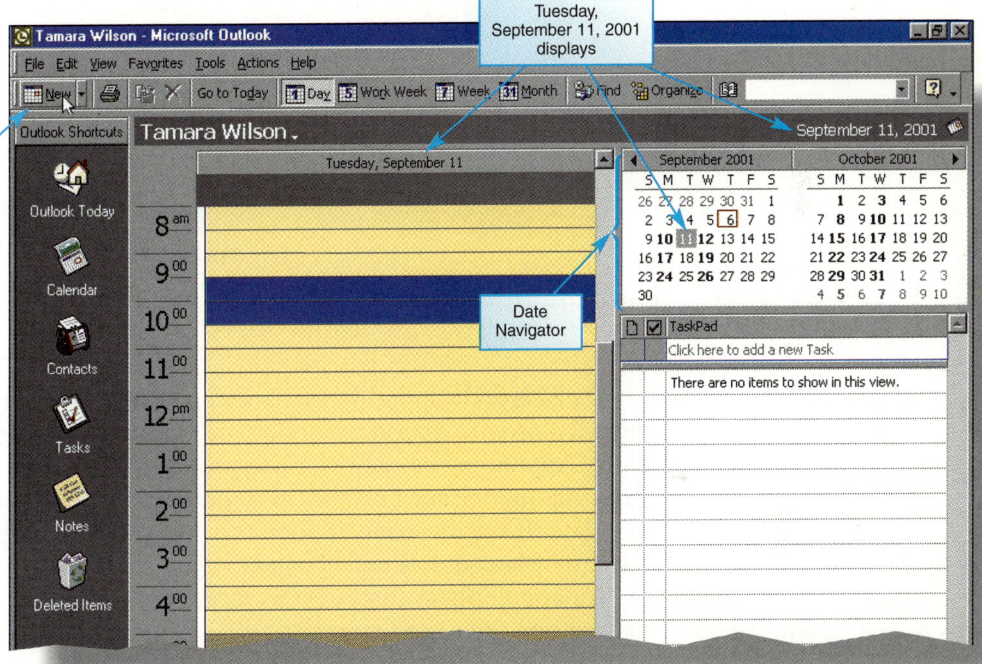

FIGURE 1-18

1. On View menu point to Go To, click Go to Date on Go To submenu
2. Press CTRL+G

Table 1-2 contains the additional recurring appointments for the steps on the next page.

Table 1-2 Additional Recurring Appointments

TIME	APPOINTMENT	OCCURRENCE
9:30 am - 10:30 am	Statistics (LAEB)	Every Tuesday and Thursday for 30 times
1:30 pm - 2:30 pm	Marketing (Krannert)	Every Tuesday and Thursday for 30 times

Perform the following steps to finish entering the recurring appointments.

To Complete the Recurring Appointments

1 Enter the additional recurring appointments provided in Table 1-2 on the previous page.

The schedule for Tuesday, September 11, 2001 displays (Figure 1-19).

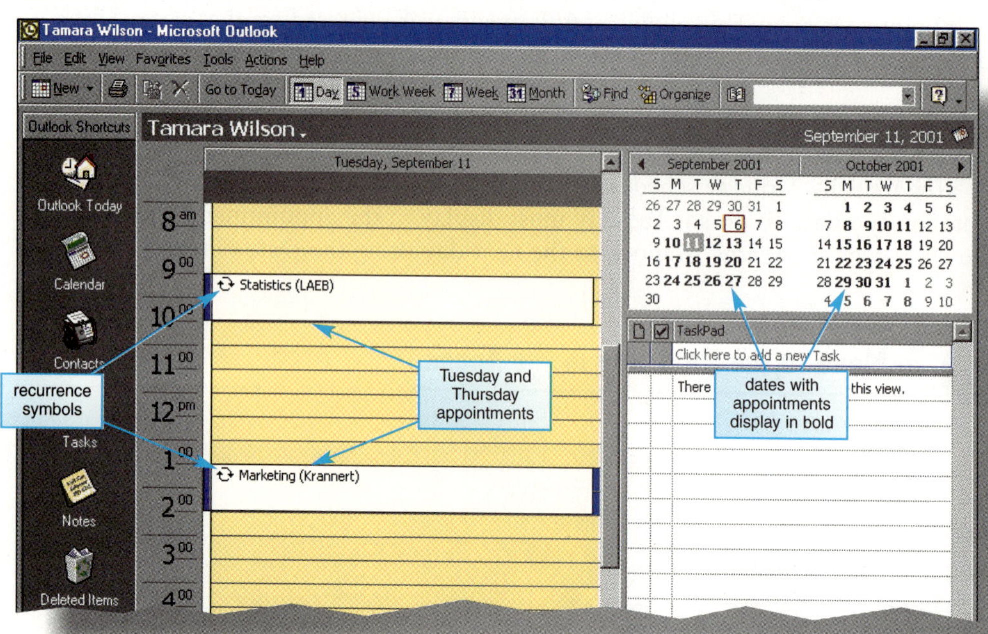

FIGURE 1-19

Daily, weekly, monthly, or yearly recurrence patterns are possible in the Appointment Recurrence options. Outlook also provides three options for the range of recurrence. Appointments can recur every week or choice of weeks for one or multiple days. An appointment can be set to occur a certain number of times or up to a certain date. If the recurring appointment is on-going, such as office hours, you can select the **No end date option button.**

An appointment can be set as recurring when first entered, or, if you decide to make a one-time appointment recurring later, double-click the appointment and then click the Recurrence button. You can edit recurring appointments to add new days, omit certain days, or change other recurrence details. Editing recurring appointments is covered in more detail later in the project.

More About 2000

Moving a Recurring Appointment

If a recurring appointment is moved, only the selected instance of the appointment is moved. If all instances of an appointment need to be moved, open the appointment, click Recurrence on the Appointment menu, and then change the recurrence pattern.

Using Natural Language Phrases to Enter Appointment Dates and Times

In the steps just completed, dates and times were entered in the Appointment window using standard numerical entries. Outlook's **AutoDate function**, however, provides the capability of specifing appointment dates and times using natural language phrases. For example, you can type phrases such as, next Tuesday, two weeks from yesterday, or midnight, and Outlook will calculate the correct date.

In this example, the Chi Omega/Sig Ep dance will be held one week from Saturday at the sorority house, on Saturday, September 22, 2001, from 7:00 P.M. to 11:30 P.M. The following steps describe how to enter the date and time for the dance using natural language phrases.

To Enter Appointment Dates and Times Using Natural Language Phrases

1 **With Tuesday, September 11, 2001 displayed in the appointment area, click the New Appointment button on the Standard toolbar.**

2 **Type** Chi Omega/Sig Ep dance **in the Subject text box and then press the TAB key. Type** Sorority house **in the Location text box and then press the TAB key twice.**

The appointment information is entered in the Appointment window. Tues 9/11/01 is highlighted in the Start time date box (Figure 1-20).

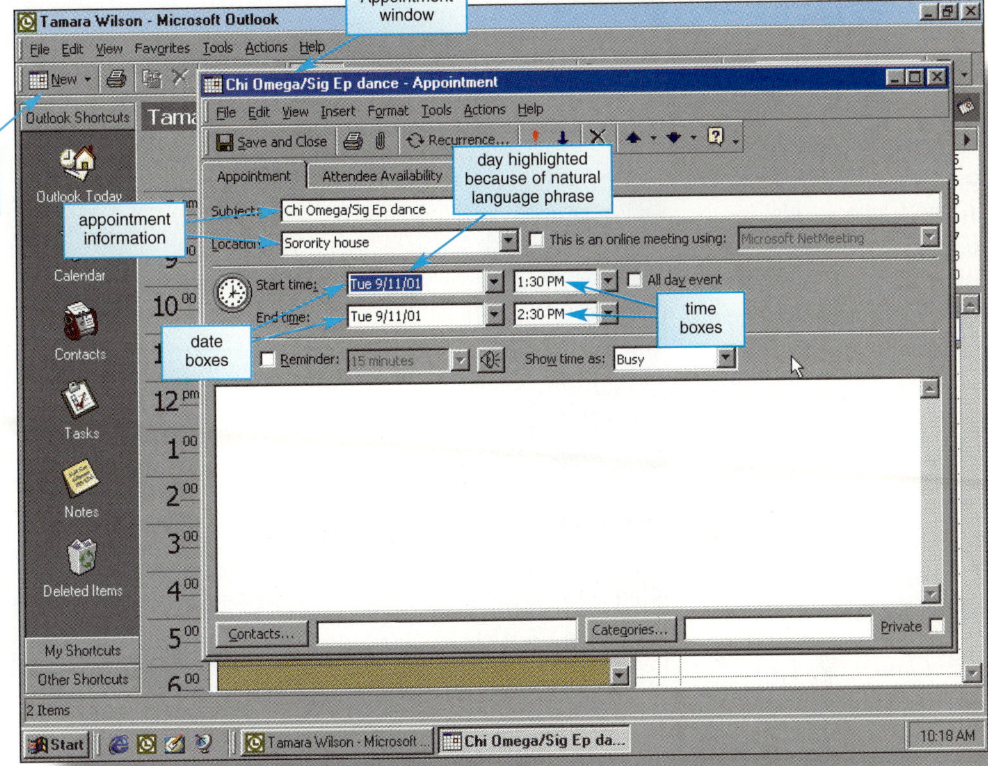

FIGURE 1-20

3 **Type** one week from Saturday **in the Start time date box for the date. Press the TAB key. Type** seven **in the Start time time box. Press the TAB key twice.**

Outlook automatically converts the phrase, one week from Saturday, into the date, Sat 9/22/01, the appropriate date in both the Start time date and End time date boxes and 7:00 PM in the time box (Figure 1-21).

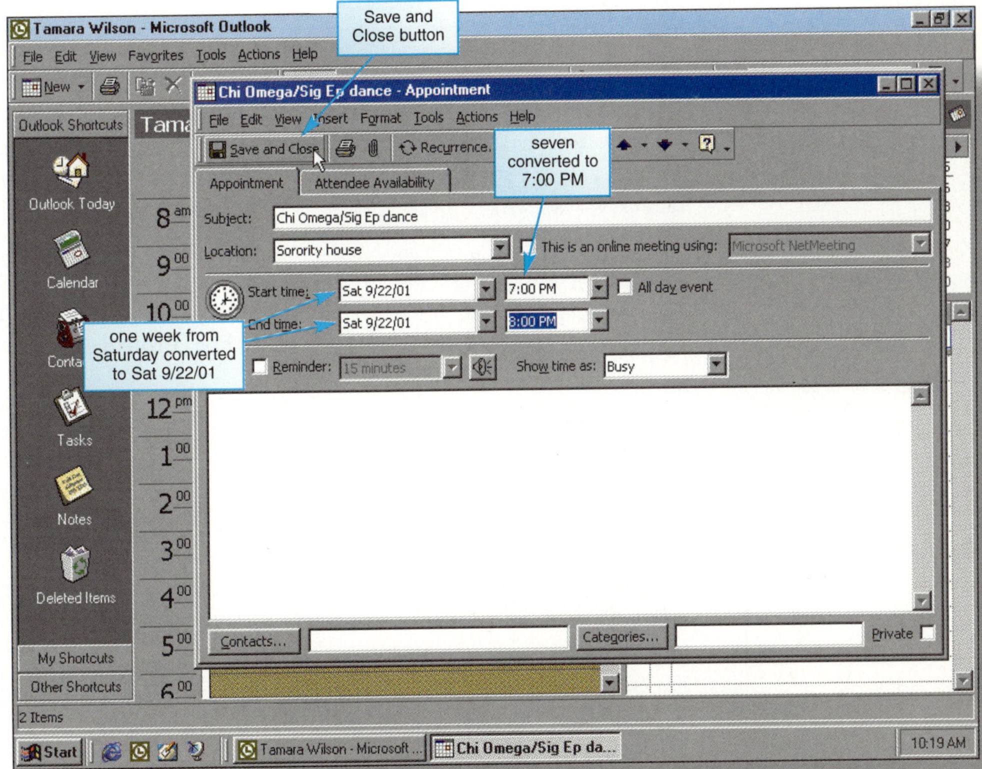

FIGURE 1-21

4 **Type** `eleven thirty` **in the End time time box and then press the ENTER key.**

Outlook automatically converts the word, eleven thirty, to 11:30 PM and sets the appointment end time for 11:30 PM. Outlook sets appointments for 30 minutes unless you enter a new End time or drag through a longer time slot in the appointment area before clicking the New Appointment button or changing the default setting.

5 **Click the Save and Close button on the Standard toolbar.**

The Chi Omega/Sig Ep dance – Appointment window closes and Tuesday, September 11, 2001 displays in the appointment area. The Chi Omega/Sig Ep dance is added to the calendar on Saturday, September 22, 2001 (Figure 1-22).

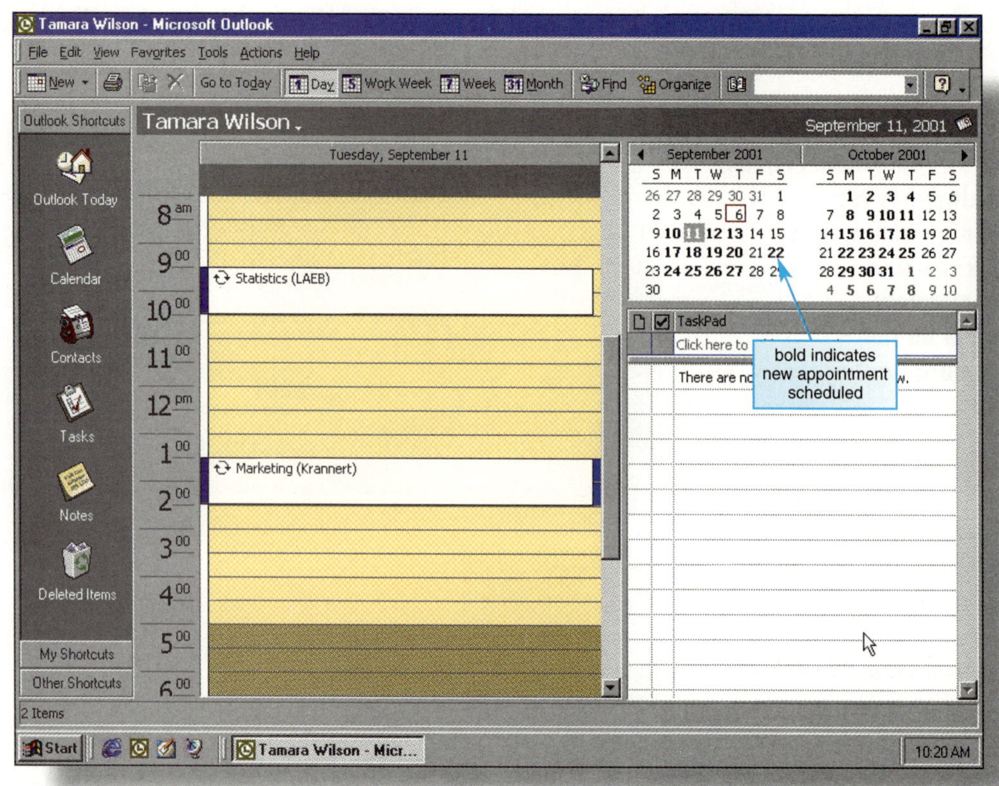

FIGURE 1-22

Table 1-3 AutoDate Options	
CATEGORY	*EXAMPLES*
Dates Spelled Out	July twenty-third, March 29th, first of December this Fri, next Sat, two days from now three wks ago, next week one month from today
Times Spelled Out	noon, midnight nine o'clock a.m., five twenty 7 pm
Descriptions of Times and Dates	now yesterday, today, tomorrow next, last ago, before, after ending, following for, from, that, this, till, through, until
Holidays	Cinco de Mayo Christmas, Christmas Day, Christmas Eve Halloween Independence Day New Year's Day, New Year's Eve St. Patrick's Day Valentine's Day Veterans Day

In addition to these natural language phrases, Outlook can convert abbreviations and ordinal numbers into complete words and dates. For example, type Feb instead of February or the first of September instead of 9/1. Outlook's Calendar application also will convert words such as yesterday, tomorrow, and the names of holidays that occur only once each year, such as Independence Day. Table 1-3 lists the various AutoDate options.

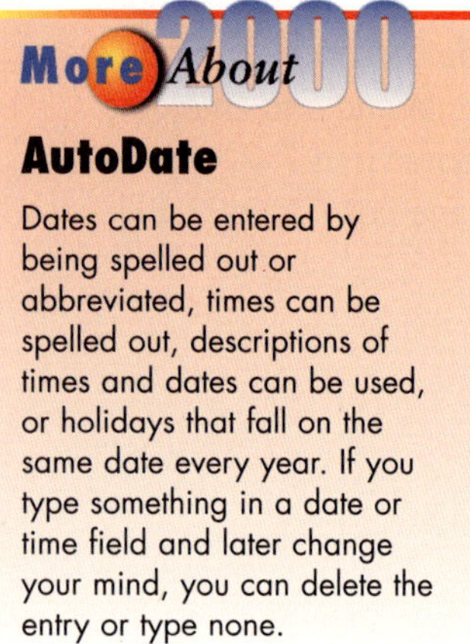

AutoDate

Dates can be entered by being spelled out or abbreviated, times can be spelled out, descriptions of times and dates can be used, or holidays that fall on the same date every year. If you type something in a date or time field and later change your mind, you can delete the entry or type none.

Editing Appointments

Because schedules often need to be rearranged, Outlook provides several ways of editing appointments. Edit the subject and location of an appointment by clicking the appointment and editing the information directly in the appointment area, or double-click the appointment and make corrections using the Appointment window. All occurrences in a series of a recurring appointment can be changed, or one occurrence can be altered.

Editing Appointments

Click Tools on the menu bar and then click Find to locate an appointment that you cannot remember. In the Look for box, click Appointments and meetings. You then may search for any word or subject.

Deleting Appointments

Appointments sometimes are canceled and must be deleted from the schedule. For example, the schedule created thus far in this project contains appointments on Thursday, November 22, 2001. Because November 22 is Thanksgiving Day, however, no classes will meet and the scheduled appointments need to be deleted. The following steps describe how to delete an appointment from the schedule.

To Delete an Appointment

1 Click 22 in the November 2001 calendar in the Date Navigator. Click the first appointment to be deleted, Statistics, and then point to the Delete button on the Standard toolbar (Figure 1-23).

Thursday, November 22 displays at the top of the appointment area (Figure 1-23). The blue top and bottom borders indicate the Statistics appointment is selected.

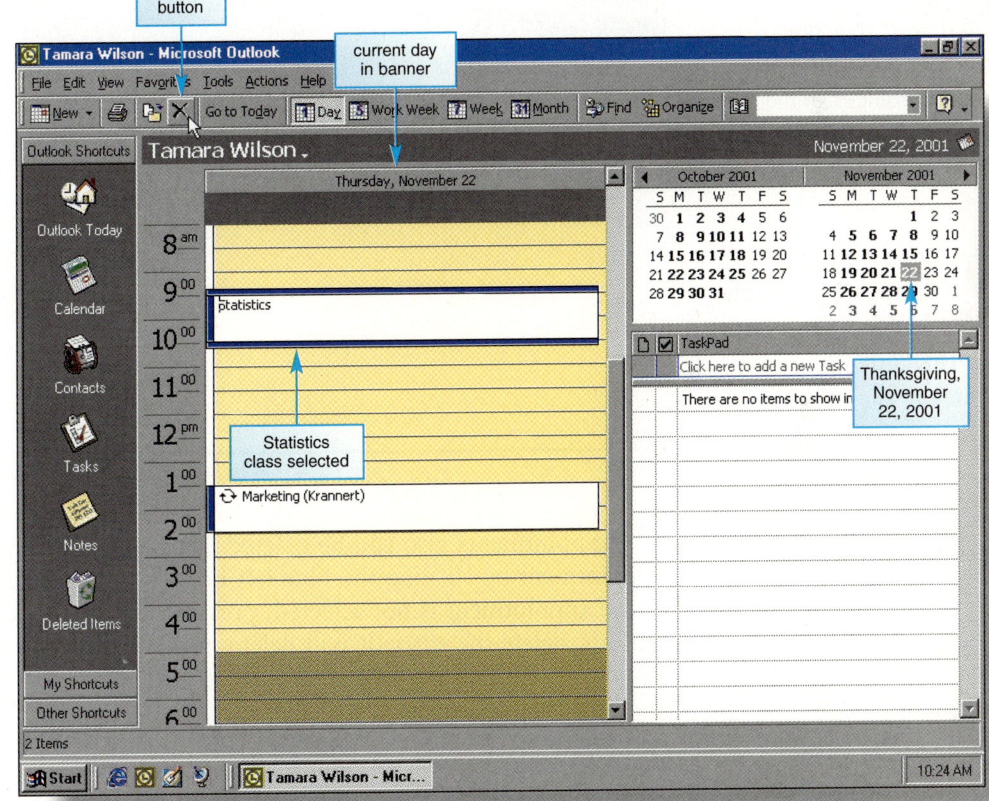

FIGURE 1-23

2 **Click the Delete button. When the Confirm Delete dialog box displays, point to the OK button.**

Because the appointment selected is a recurring appointment, a Confirm Delete dialog box displays, asking to delete all occurrences of the recurring appointment or just this one (Figure 1-24). The Delete this one option button is selected automatically.

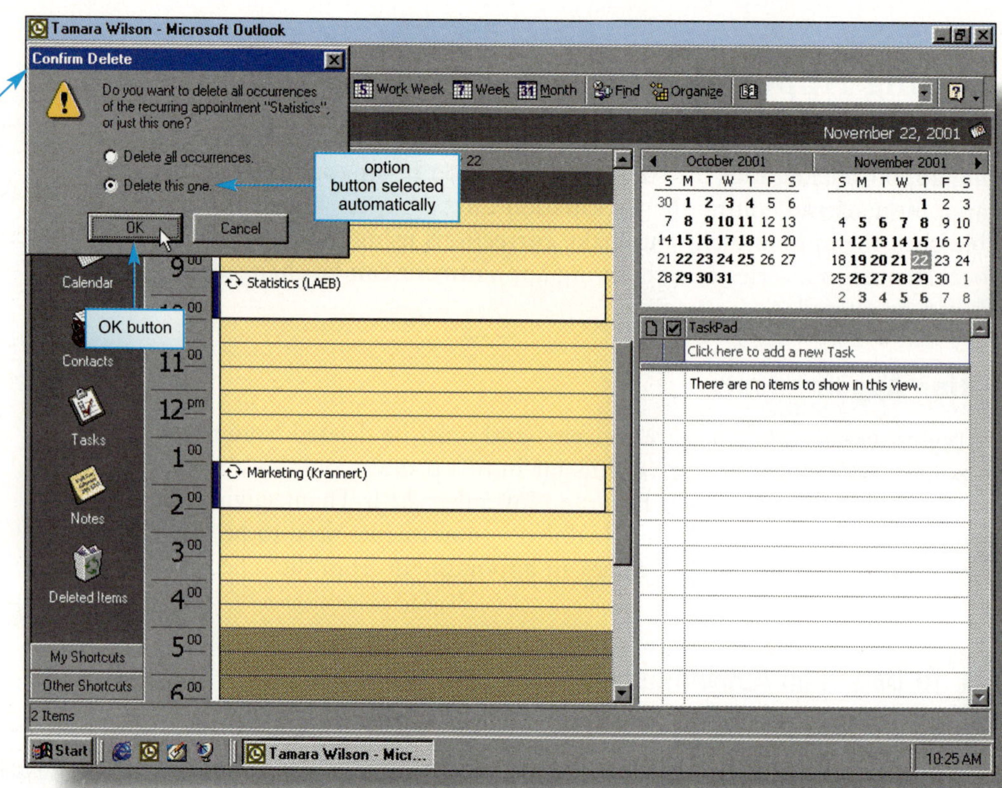

FIGURE 1-24

3 **Click the OK button.**

The Statistics appointment is deleted from Thursday, November 22, 2001. All other occurrences of the appointment remain in the schedule.

4 **Repeat Steps 1 through 3 to delete the Marketing appointment from Thursday, November 22, 2001.**

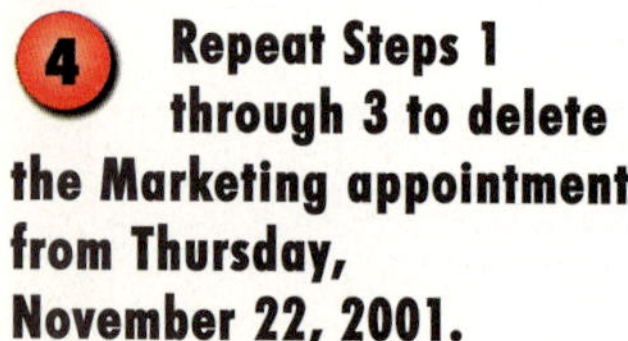

Other Ways

1. Right-click appointment to be deleted, click Delete on shortcut menu
2. Click blue left border of appointment, press DELETE

Appointments also can be deleted using the DELETE key. First, select the entire appointment by clicking the blue left border and then press the DELETE key. If the entire appointment is not selected, pressing the DELETE key (or the BACKSPACE key) will not delete the entry; it will delete only individual characters of the appointment subject. Even if all the characters are deleted, the time slot remains active and any symbols remain in place.

Moving Appointments to a New Time

Outlook also provides several ways to move appointments. Suppose for instance, that some students cannot make it to the dance committee lunch at noon on Monday, September 10, 2001. That lunch needs to be rescheduled to 1:00 P.M. - 2:00 P.M. Instead of deleting and then retyping the appointment in the new time slot, simply drag it to the new time slot. The following steps describe how to move an appointment to a new time.

To Move an Appointment to a New Time

1 Click 10 in the September 2001 calendar in the Date Navigator.

2 Position the mouse pointer on the blue left border of the Lunch - dance committee appointment.

The mouse pointer changes to a four-headed arrow (Figure 1-25).

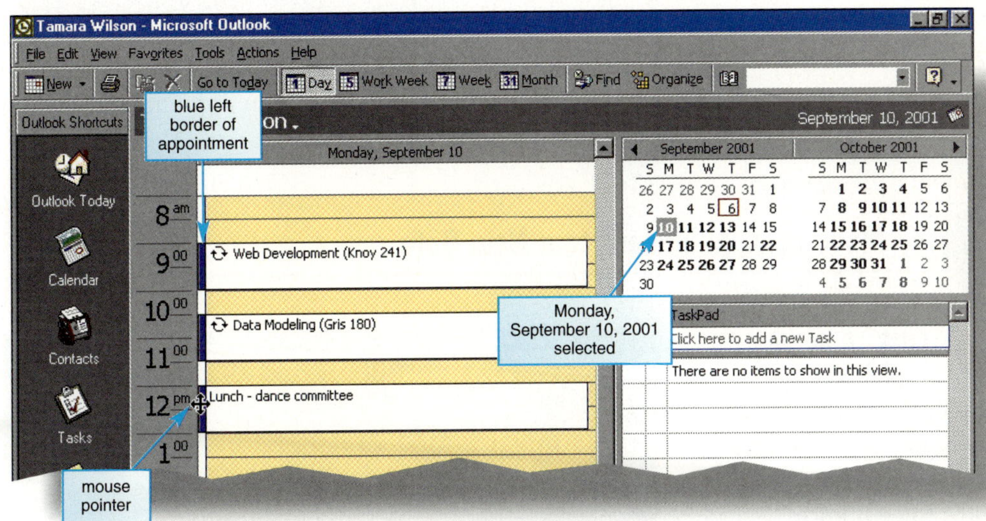

FIGURE 1-25

3 Drag the appointment down to the 1:00 pm – 2:00 pm time slot.

As the appointment is dragged, the mouse pointer changes to a pointer with a small dotted box below it. This is called the **drag icon**.

4 Release the mouse button to drop the appointment in the new time slot.

The appointment is placed in the 1:00 pm – 2:00 pm time slot (Figure 1-26). Outlook automatically allows adequate time for the moved appointment, in this case, one hour.

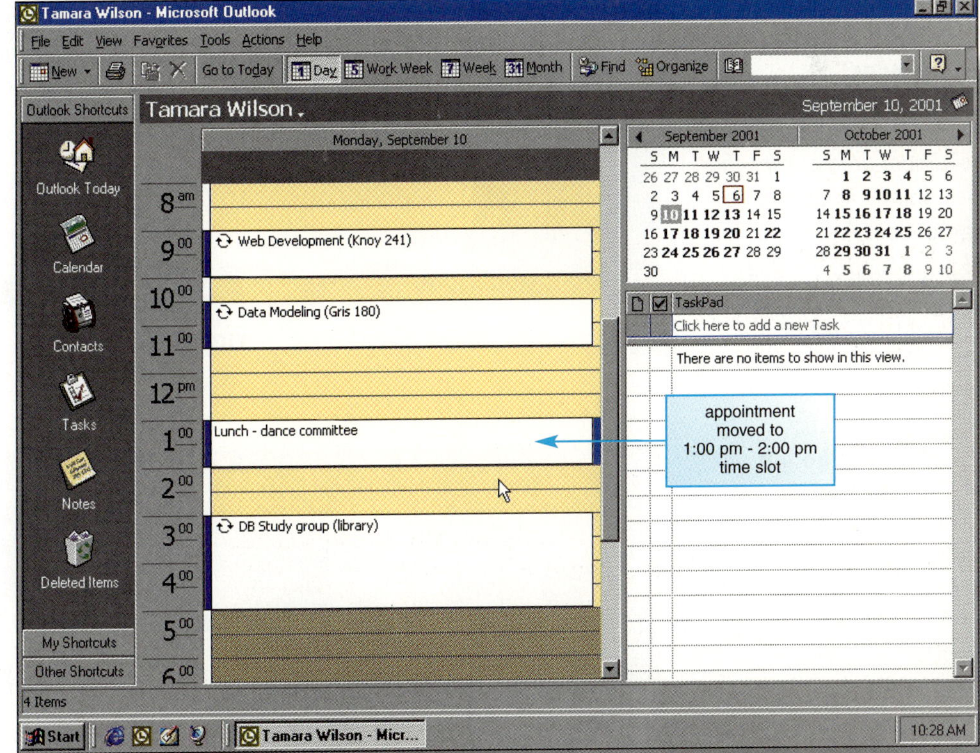

FIGURE 1-26

An appointment can be moved to a new time using the Appointment window as well. Simply type a different time in the Start time or End time list boxes or click one of the time box arrows and choose a different time from the list. Natural language phrases also can be used in the time box, which Outlook then converts to the appropriate times.

Other Ways

1. Double-click appointment, edit date in Start date box in Appointment window
2. Click left border of appointment, press CTRL+X, click new date in Date Navigator, click new time slot in appointment area, press CTRL+V

Moving Appointments to a New Date

If an appointment is being moved to a new date but remaining in the same time slot, simply drag the appointment to the new date in the Date Navigator. Using this method allows the movement of an appointment quickly and easily to a new date, as shown in the following steps.

To Move an Appointment to a New Date

1. **Click 10 in the September 2001 calendar in the Date Navigator. Click the blue left border of the Lunch - dance committee appointment to select it. Drag the appointment from the appointment area to the 12 in the September 2001 calendar.**

Dragging outside the appointment area causes the mouse pointer to change to the drag icon. A grey border displays around 12 in the September 2001 calendar in the Date Navigator (Figure 1-27).

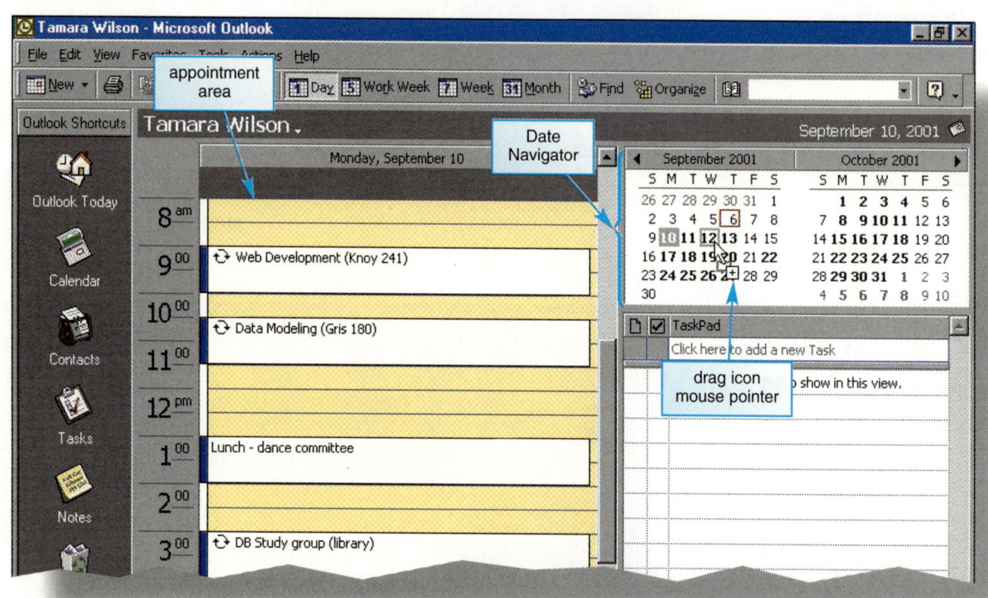

FIGURE 1-27

2. **Release the left mouse button.**

The appointment moves from Monday, September 10, 2001 to Wednesday, September 12, 2001 (Figure 1-28).

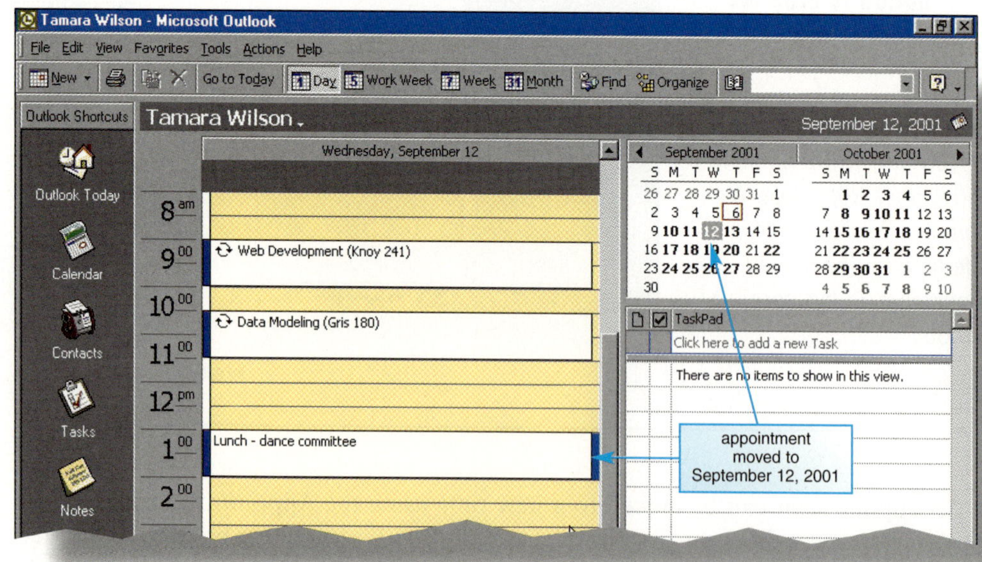

FIGURE 1-28

Outlook provides several ways to move appointments to new dates in addition to the drag and drop method used in the previous steps. Appointments can be moved to new dates by making changes in the Appointment window or by using the cut and paste method discussed in the following section.

Moving an Appointment to a New Month

If an appointment is being moved to a month not displayed in the Date Navigator, it simply cannot be dragged to a date not displayed. Cutting and pasting the appointment to a new date will work.

When you cut an item in other Office 2000 applications, the item that you cut disappears from the screen. In Outlook, the item remains on the screen until it is pasted to another location.

The members of the dance committee rescheduled lunch, and during their meeting, also decided to reschedule the dance to a date in October. The time of the dance is moved from Saturday, September 22, 2001 to Saturday, October 6, 2001. The following steps describe how to move an appointment to a new month using the cut and paste method.

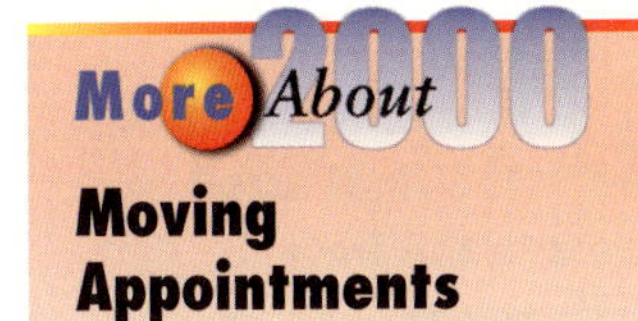

Moving Appointments

To send an appointment to a co-worker, right-click the appointment and choose Forward on the shortcut menu.

To Move an Appointment to a New Month

1 **Click 22 in the September 2001 calendar in the Date Navigator. Scroll down to the 7:00 pm time slot. Click the blue left border of the Chi Omega/Sig Ep dance appointment to select it. Click Edit on the menu bar and then point to Cut.**

The Edit menu displays (Figure 1-29).

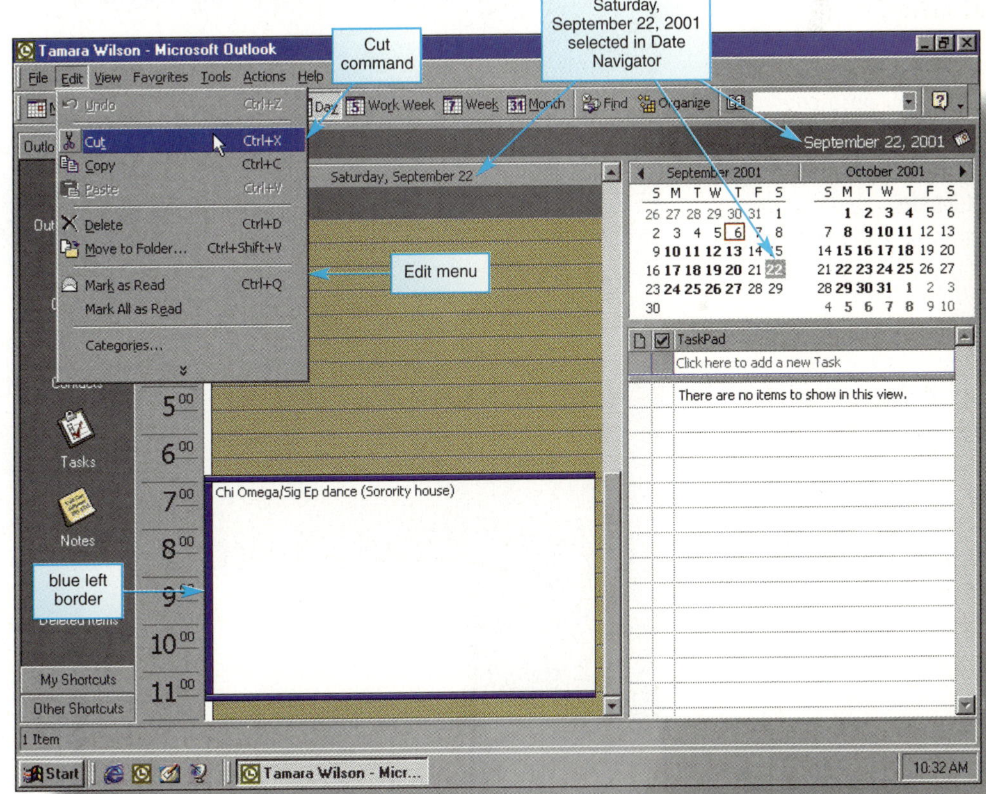

FIGURE 1-29

Click Cut.

The appointment is copied to the Clipboard. The appointment does not disappear, as expected.

3 If necessary, click the right scroll arrow in the Date Navigator to display October 2001. Click 6 in the October 2001 calendar in the Date Navigator.

Outlook displays Saturday, October 6, 2001 in the appointment area. The 7:00 pm - 11:30 pm time slot is highlighted (Figure 1-30).

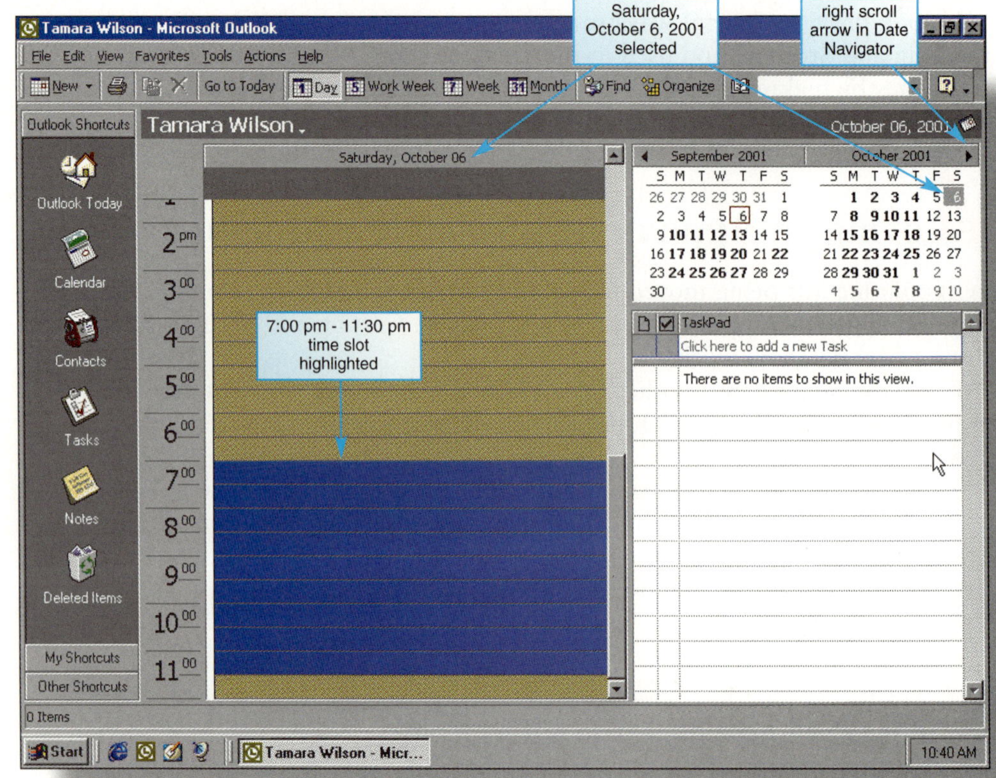

FIGURE 1-30

4 Click Edit on the menu bar and then click Paste.

The appointment now displays in the 7:00 pm – 11:30 pm time slot in the appointment area for Saturday, October 6, 2001 (Figure 1-31).

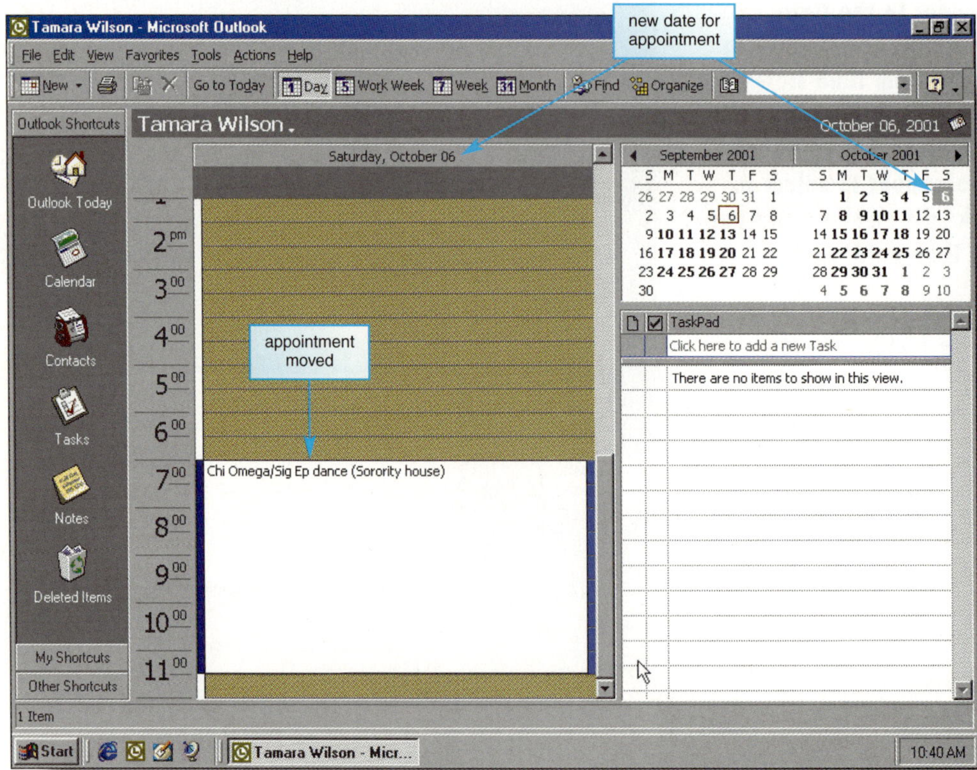

FIGURE 1-31

Either the drag and drop method or the cut and paste method is available for appointment movement. Regardless of the method, the results are the same. An appointment can be moved to a different time on the same day, to a different day, or to an entirely different month.

Creating an Event

Outlook's Calendar folder allows you to keep track of important events. **Events** are activities that last 24 hours or longer. Examples of events include birthdays, conferences, weddings, vacations, holidays, and so on; they can be one time or recurring. Events differ from appointments in one primary way — they do not display in individual time slots in the appointment area. When an event is scheduled, its description displays in a small **banner** below the date heading. The details of the event can be indicated as time that is free, busy, or out of the office during the event. The following steps show how to enter a birthday as an event.

Locations

As appointments or events are entered with specific locations, the locations automatically are accumulated in a list. This list is accessible through the arrow to the right of the Location text box. Frequently used locations can be selected from this list, thus saving typing time.

To Create an Event

1 Click the left scroll arrow to display September 2001 in the Date Navigator. Click 25 in the September 2001 calendar in the Date Navigator.

2 Double-click the date heading at the top of the appointment area. When the Untitled – Event window displays, type `Den's birthday` **in the Subject text box. Point to the Save and Close button on the Standard toolbar.**

The Untitled – Event window displays (Figure 1-32). Double-clicking the date heading allows all day events to be scheduled. The All day event check box thus is selected by default. The Show time as text box indicates Free.

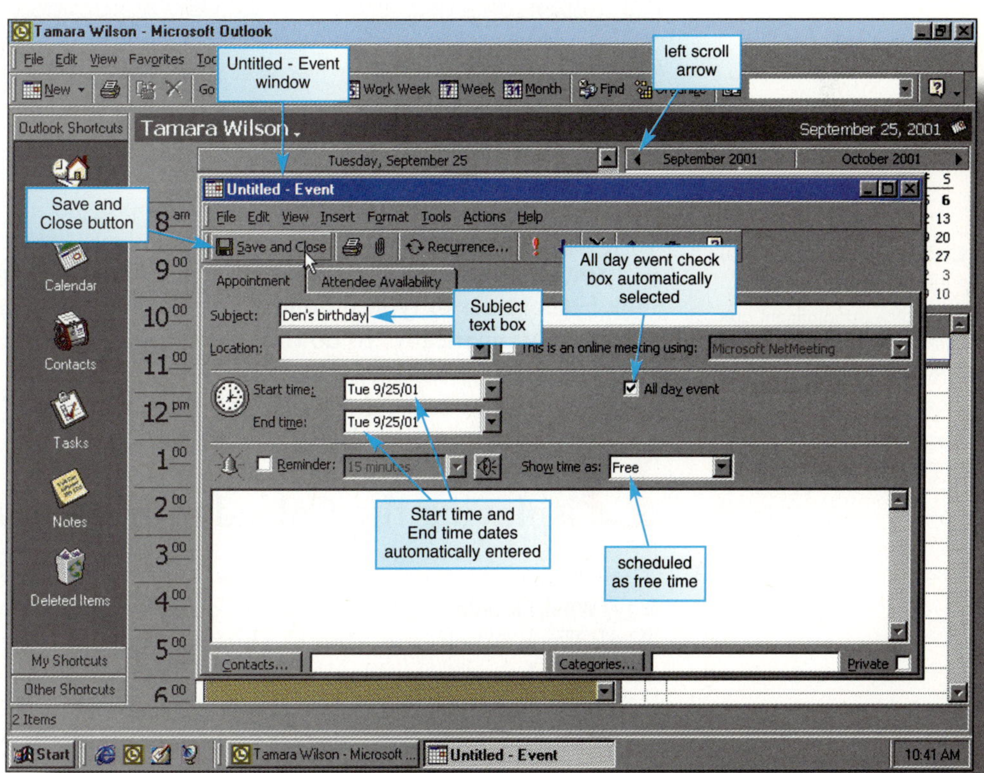

FIGURE 1-32

Click the Save and Close button.

The Event subject displays in a banner below the date heading (Figure 1-33).

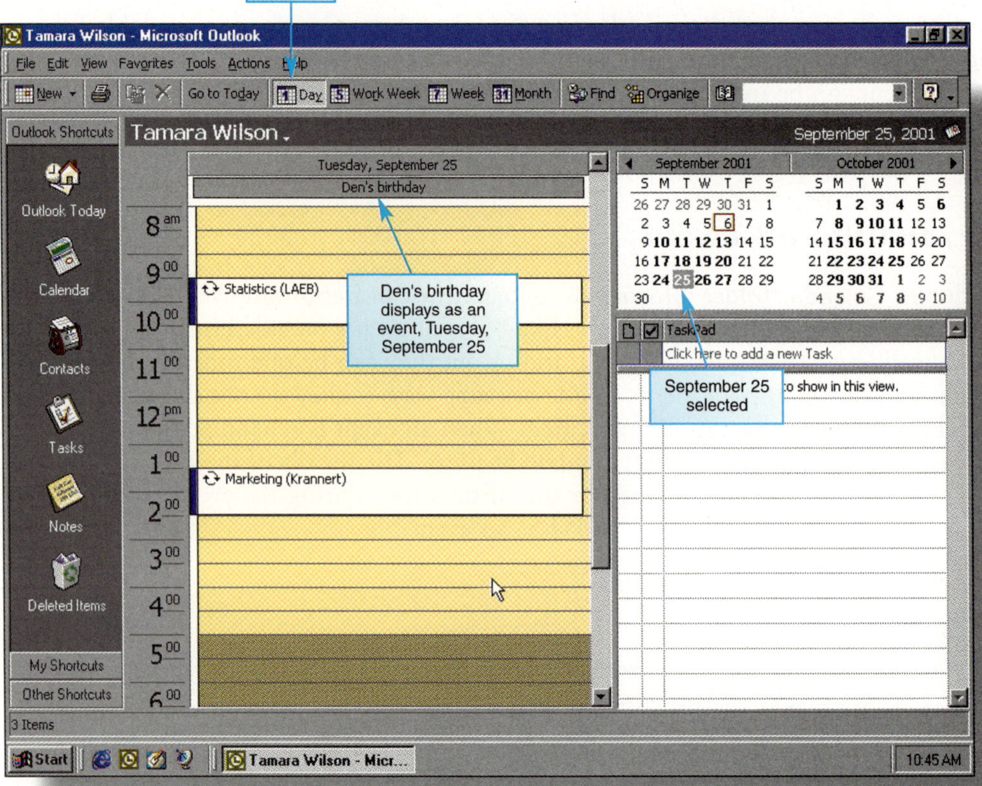

FIGURE 1-33

1. On Actions menu click New All Day Event
2. Right-click appointment area, click New All Day Event on shortcut menu
3. Press ALT+A, press E
4. Press CTRL+N, click All day event check box

You could use the same steps to enter holidays as annual events; however, Outlook has a folder of typical holidays for various countries that can be added to your calendar automatically. To do this, click Options on the Tools menu and then click Add Holidays in the Calendar sheet.

Now that the schedule is complete, the Calendar can be displayed in various views.

Displaying the Calendar in Week and Month Views

The default view type of the Calendar folder is the Day/Week/Month view. While in **Day/Week/Month view**, Outlook can display calendars in four different views: Day, Work Week, Week, and Month. Thus far in the project, you have used only the Day view, which is indicated by the recessed Day button on the Standard toolbar.

Now that the schedule is complete, it also can be displayed in Week or Month view. Although the screen displays quite differently in Week and Month views, the same tasks can be performed as in Day view: appointments and events can be added, edited, or deleted, and reminders can be set and removed.

Work Week View

A new feature in Outlook 2000 is the Work Week view. The **Work Week view** shows five work days (Monday through Friday) in columnar style. The advantage of displaying a calendar in this view is the ability to see how many appointments are scheduled for the Monday through Friday time frame, eliminating the weekends. The following step changes the Calendar view to Work Week view.

To Change to Work Week View

1 With Wednesday, September 12, 2001 selected in the Date Navigator, click the Work Week button on the Standard toolbar.

The calendar displays in Work Week view (Figure 1-34). Notice that September 10 through September 14 are all highlighted in the Date Navigator, and the Work Week button is recessed.

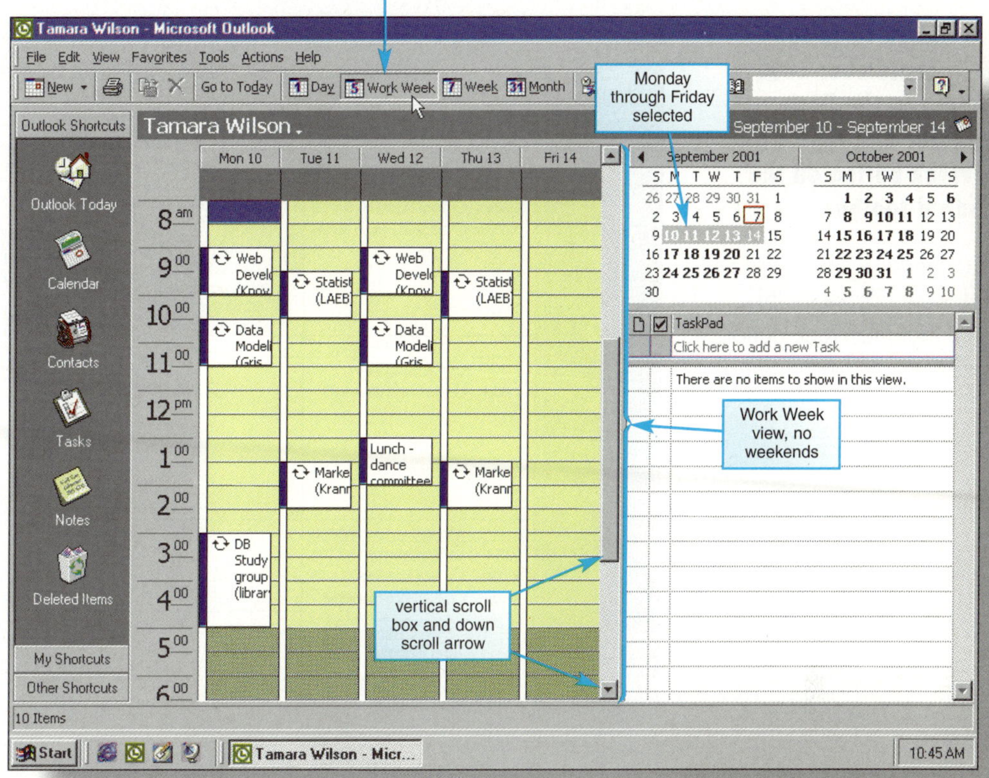

FIGURE 1-34

1. On View menu click Work Week
2. Press ALT+V, press R

The vertical scroll box and arrows allow backward or forward movement within the week selected. An individual appointment can be selected by double-clicking it. As shown in Figure 1-35 on the next page, some appointments may be too long to display horizontally in the appointment area. Dragging the border of the appointment area to the right will increase its width so that more of the appointments display.

Work Week

The Work Week is a new feature with Outlook 2000. The default work week days are Monday through Friday. You can select the days of your work week by clicking Tools on the menu bar and then click Options. On the Preferences tab, click Calendar Options.

Week View

The advantage of displaying a calendar in **Week view** is to see how many appointments are scheduled for any given week. In Week view, the seven days of the selected week display in the appointment area. The five days of the work week (Monday through Friday) display in individual frames, while Saturday and Sunday share a single frame. The step on the next page describes how to display the calendar in Week view.

To Change to Week View

1 Click 15 in the September 2001 calendar in the Date Navigator and then click the Week button on the Standard toolbar.

The calendar displays in Week view (Figure 1-35). Notice that the Week button is recessed on the Standard toolbar.

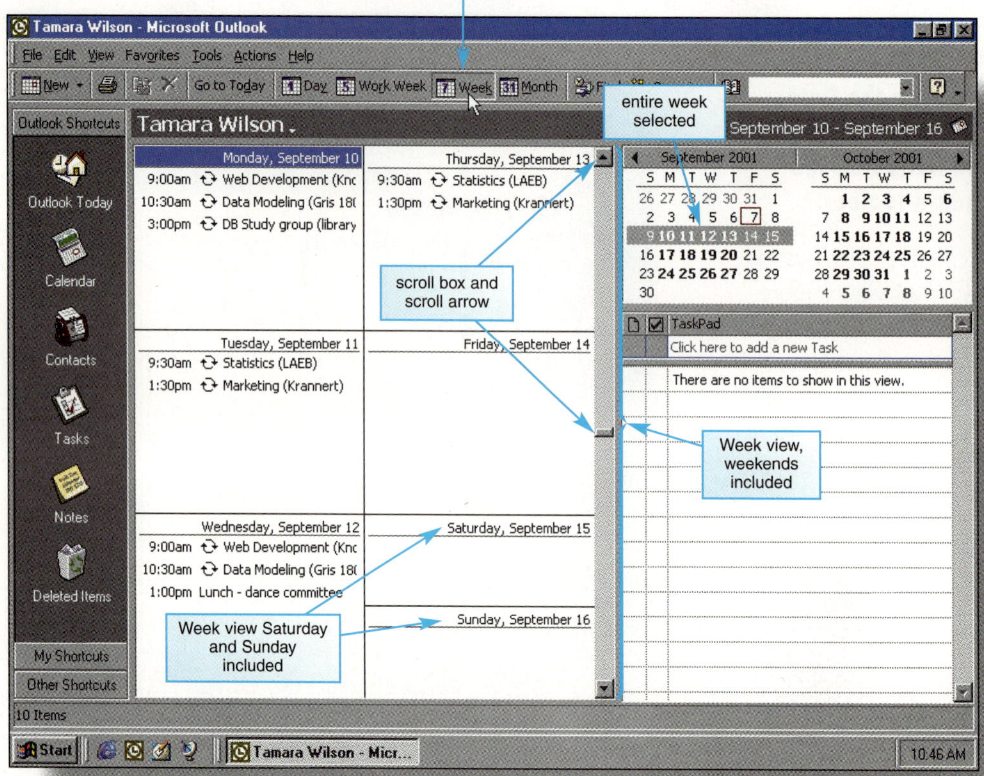

FIGURE 1-35

Other Ways

1. On View menu click Week
2. Press ALT+V, press K

The vertical scroll box and arrows allow backward or forward movement one week at a time. As in Day view, double-click an appointment to view and edit appointment details. As shown in Figure 1-35, some appointments may be too long to display horizontally in the appointment area. Dragging the border of the appointment area to the right will increase its width so more of the appointment descriptions display. The rest of the Week view is adjusted accordingly to display a single month in the Date Navigator and a more narrow TaskPad. If a day has too many items to display vertically, Outlook will display a down arrow in the bottom right-hand corner of the day frame. Clicking the down arrow returns the calendar to Day view so you can view the rest of the appointments for the day.

Month View

The **Month view** resembles a standard monthly calendar page and displays your schedule for an entire month. Appointments are listed in each date frame in the calendar. The following steps illustrate how to display the calendar in Month view.

Steps To Change to Month View

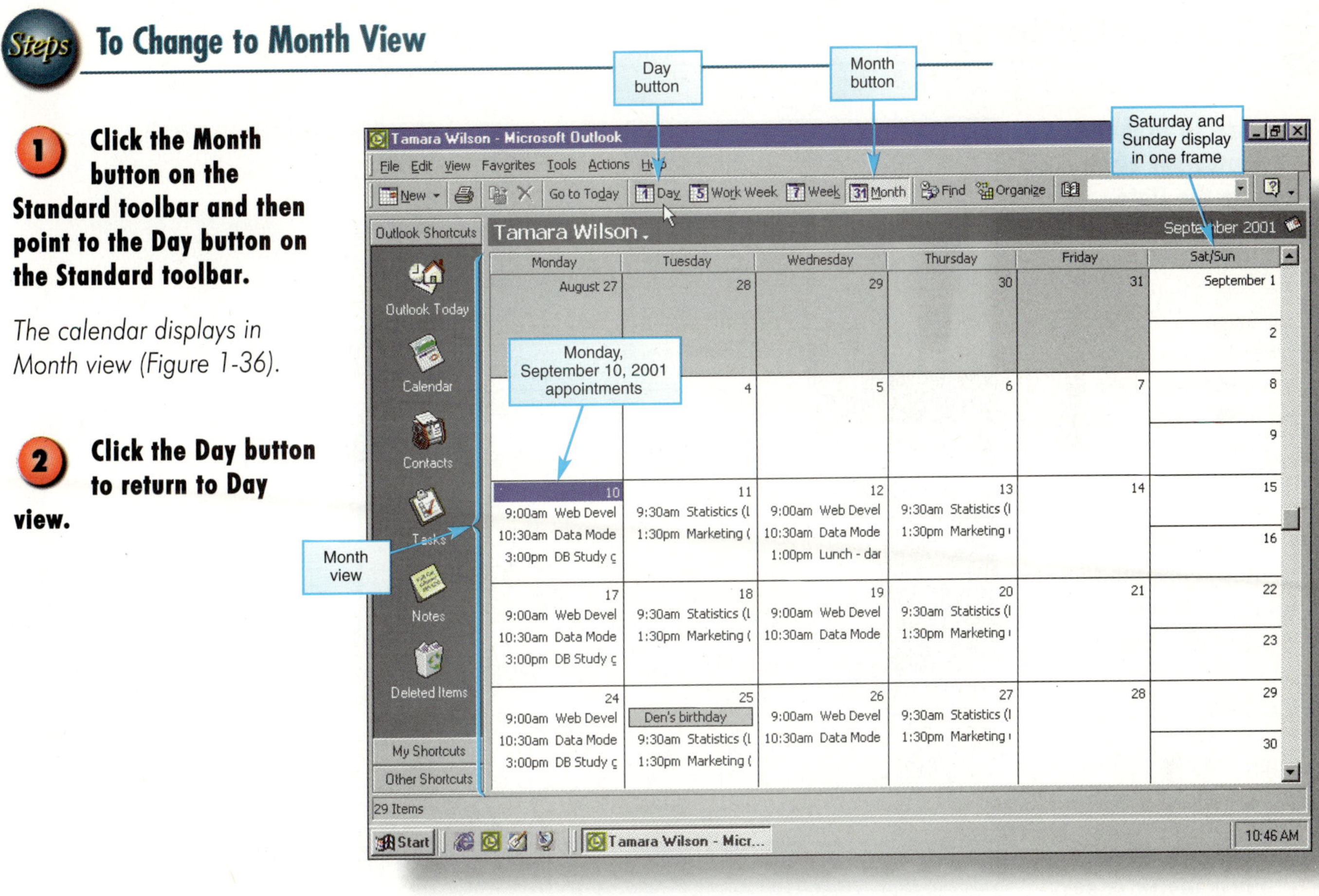

1 **Click the Month button on the Standard toolbar and then point to the Day button on the Standard toolbar.**

The calendar displays in Month view (Figure 1-36).

2 **Click the Day button to return to Day view.**

FIGURE 1-36

Other Ways

1. On View menu click Month
2. Press ALT+V, press M

Use the vertical scroll box and arrows to move the Month view forward and backward one week at a time. As you drag the vertical scroll box, Outlook displays the first day of the week in a ScreenTip beside the scroll box. As with Day and Week views, you can add, edit, or delete appointments in Month view. Because the appointments are abbreviated considerably in Month view, however, it is easier to switch back to Day view to make changes.

Creating a Task List Using the Taskpad

Now that your daily appointments are organized, you can use **TaskPad** in the Calendar window to organize the many duties and projects for each day. The TaskPad, which displays below the Date Navigator, in the Calendar window, allows creation of a **task list** of items that need to be tracked through completion. **Tasks** can be simple to do items, daily reminders, assignments with due dates, or business responsibilities. In this project, single-user tasks that occur once are entered, but a Tasks folder also can be created for recurring tasks, group tasks, and assigned or forwarded tasks. Perform the steps on the next page to create a task list using the TaskPad.

More About 2000

Tasks

A task is a personal or work-related duty or errand that you keep in your Outlook task list and track through completion. A task can occur only once or repeatedly as a recurring task. You can add a task to your Outlook task list from within Word. This is helpful if you have a document in Word that must be reviewed, and you want a reminder to review it. From Outlook, you also can assign tasks to other people and track the progress of tasks as they are completed.

To Create a Task List Using the TaskPad

1 **Click 10 in the September 2001 calendar in the Date Navigator.**

The TaskPad displays on the right below the Date Navigator in the Calendar window. The TaskPad is divided into two main sections, a new task area and the task list.

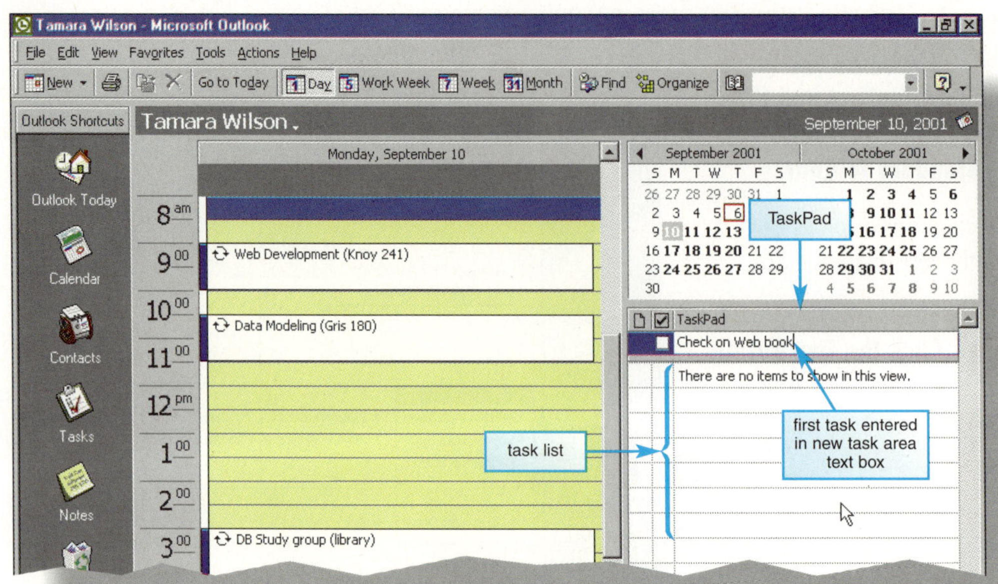

FIGURE 1-37

2 **In the new task area, click the text box labeled Click here to add a new task. Type** `Check on Web book` **in the text box.**

The screen displays (Figure 1-37).

3 **Press the ENTER key.**

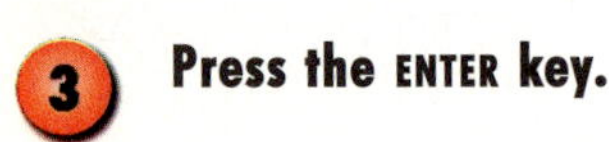

4 **Type** `Get new license` **in the text box and then press the ENTER key. Type** `Pick up dance decorations` **in the text box and then press the ENTER key.**

The task icon displays to the left of each task. As each task is entered, the previous task moves down the list. The insertion point is active in the text box.

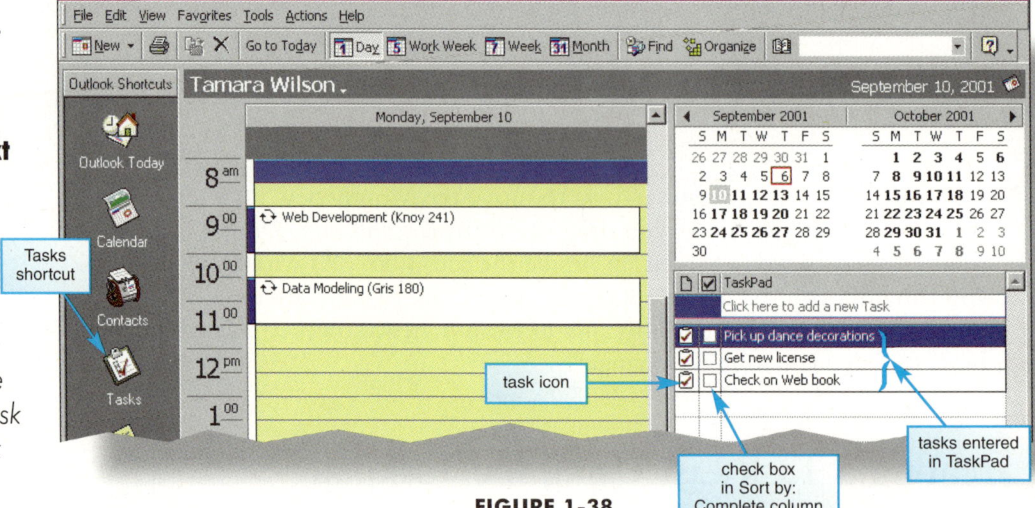

FIGURE 1-38

5 **Click outside the TaskPad.**

Your TaskPad now should look like the one shown in Figure 1-38.

Other Ways

1. On File menu point to New, click Tasks on New submenu
2. Click New Appointment button arrow on Standard toolbar, click Task
3. Press CTRL+SHIFT+K

To add details to tasks, such as due date, status, and priority, double-click a task on the TaskPad to open a Task window.

When a task is complete, click the check box in the Sort by: Complete column to the left of the task's subject. A check mark called a **Completed icon** will display in the Complete column and a line will be placed through the task indicating it is complete. To delete a task entirely from the TaskPad, select the task and then click the Delete button on the Standard toolbar.

If you have many tasks on various days, or if you assign tasks to others, it is advisable to create a personal Tasks subfolder for your task list, as created for your calendar. This also is true if you are working in a lab situation or on a shared computer.

More About 2000

Editing Tasks

You can drag a task from the TaskPad to a time slot in the appointment area, making the task an appointment.

Printing a Calendar

All or part of your calendar can be printed in a number of different layouts or **print styles**. The following section describes how to print the calendar created in Daily, Weekly, and Monthly Styles.

Daily Style

A printout of a single day of the calendar, called the **Daily Style**, shows the day's appointments, tasks, and a two-month calendar. Follow the steps to print the calendar in Daily Style.

To Print the Calendar in Daily Style

1 Ready the printer. Click 10 in the September 2001 calendar in the Date Navigator and then click the Print button on the Standard toolbar. Point to the OK button.

The Print dialog box displays (Figure 1-39). Because the Appointment window was in Day view when the Print button was clicked, Daily Style is selected in the Print style list by default.

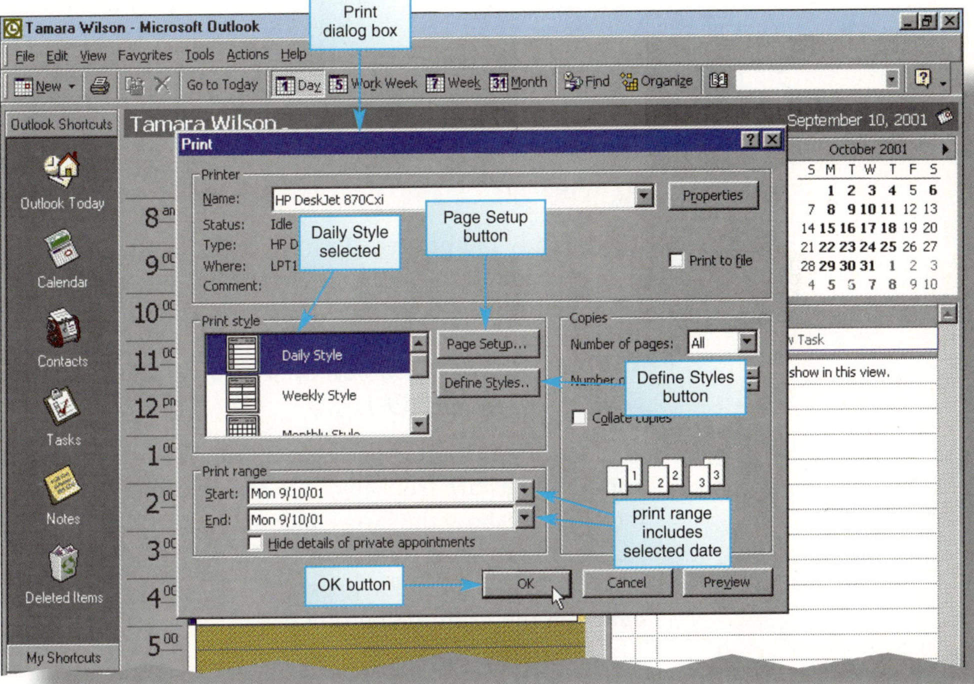

FIGURE 1-39

2 With Daily Style selected in the Print style list, click the OK button.

The daily schedule of appointments for Monday, September 10, 2001 prints on the printer. The printout should display as shown in Figure 1-1d on page O 1.7.

Other Ways

1. On File menu click Print
2. Press CTRL+P

The Daily Style printout includes features from the Day view of the Calendar, including appointments, events, tasks, and notes. Dates with appointments print in bold in the two-month calendar. Page numbers and current system dates display at the bottom of the page. The Page Setup button in the Print dialog box allows style modifications to include or omit various features, including TaskPad and the Notes area. Specific time ranges also can be printed, rather than the default 7:00 A.M. to 6:00 P.M.

Weekly Style

To print a calendar in the Weekly Style, click the Print button on the Standard toolbar while viewing the calendar in Week view or select the Weekly Style in the Print dialog box, as explained in the following step.

TO PRINT THE CALENDAR IN WEEKLY STYLE

Ready the printer. With Monday, September 10, 2001 selected in the Date Navigator, click the Print button on the Standard toolbar. Click Weekly Style in the Print style list and then click the OK button.

The calendar for the week of Monday, September 10, 2001 through Sunday, September 16, 2001 prints on the printer as shown in Figure 1-1e on page O 1.7.

Printing

The margins, page orientation, or paper size can be changed in the Page Setup dialog box.

Depending on the number of appointments, choose to print the weekly calendar on one or two pages. To change the number of pages in the printout, click the Page Setup button in the Print dialog box. Tasks and notes also can be added to the printout.

Monthly Style

The following step prints the calendar in Monthly Style.

TO PRINT THE CALENDAR IN MONTHLY STYLE

Ready the printer. With Monday, September 10, 2001 selected in the Date Navigator, click the Print button on the Standard toolbar. Click Monthly Style in the Print style list and then click the OK button.

The calendar for the month of September 2001 prints on the printer as shown in Figure 1-1f on page O 1.7.

Selecting Monthly Style prints the calendar in landscape orientation. Some appointments are truncated due to lack of space. The Monthly Style of printout is intended to show the larger picture rather than the detail of a Daily Style printout.

Another useful print style is **Tri-fold Style**, which prints a daily appointment list, a task list, and a calendar for the week. To save styles and setups, use the **Define Styles button** in the Print dialog box.

Printing the Task List

To print only the task list, first open the Tasks folder. The following steps describe how to print the task list by itself.

TO PRINT THE TASK LIST

1. Click the Tasks shortcut on the Outlook Bar to display the task list entered in the TaskPad.
2. Click the Print button on the Standard toolbar. When the Print dialog box displays, click the OK button.

The task list prints (Figure 1-40).

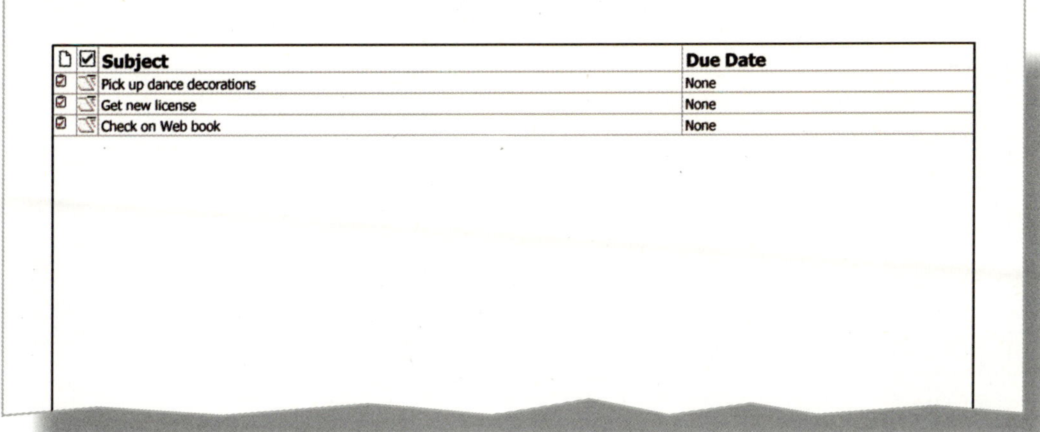

Subject	Due Date
Pick up dance decorations	None
Get new license	None
Check on Web book	None

FIGURE 1-40

Contacts

The **Contacts** component of Outlook allows you to store information about individuals or companies. Contacts are people with whom you communicate for school, business, or personal reasons. To help organize information about her personal contacts, Tamara keeps their names, addresses, and telephone numbers in a business card holder and in her address book. With Outlook, you can create and maintain important contact information in a **contact list**, which is stored in the Contacts folder. Your contact list is like an electronic address book that allows you to store names, addresses, e-mail addresses, and more. Once the information has been entered, your contact list can be retrieved, sorted, edited, organized, or printed. Outlook 2000 also includes a **Find option** that lets you search for a contact name in your address book while you are using the Calendar, Inbox, or other Outlook components.

When opening the Contacts folder, information about each contact displays on an address card in the default **Address Cards view**. Each address card includes fields such as name, address, various telephone numbers, as well as e-mail and Web page addresses. Choose which fields display on the cards using the View menu.

In addition to organizing your contacts, Outlook's Contacts can serve many other functions. Contacts can be used to assign a task, send a message, or schedule a meeting with a contact. A contact list also can be used as an e-mail address book or as a database for a mail merge using Microsoft Word 2000. An Internet URL can be accessed through Contacts by clicking a contact's Web page address. If you click your contact's e-mail address, an addressed message box comes up — ready for use.

Although her address book works fine, Tamara thinks she could communicate more efficiently if she entered her professors' addresses and telephone numbers into a contact list. The following sections describe how to create and print a contact list containing the contacts shown in Table 1-4 on page O 1.39.

The Internet

Outlook automatically creates a hyperlink when you type a Web page address or e-mail address in the text box of a Contact window. If you are connected to an Internet browser, you can click the hyperlink to quickly go to the destination or send an e-mail message.

Creating a Personal Subfolder in the Contacts Folder

The first step in creating the contact list is creating a personal subfolder. When only one person is working on a computer, a contact list can be stored in Outlook's Contacts folder. Tamara, however, shares her computer with a roommate and thus wants to store her contact list in a personal subfolder.

Steps To Create a Personal Subfolder in the Contacts Folder

1 **Click the Contacts shortcut on the Outlook Bar. When the Contacts folder opens, right-click the Folder banner and then click New Folder on the shortcut menu.**

The Contacts – Microsoft Outlook window and Create New Folder dialog box display (Figure 1-41).

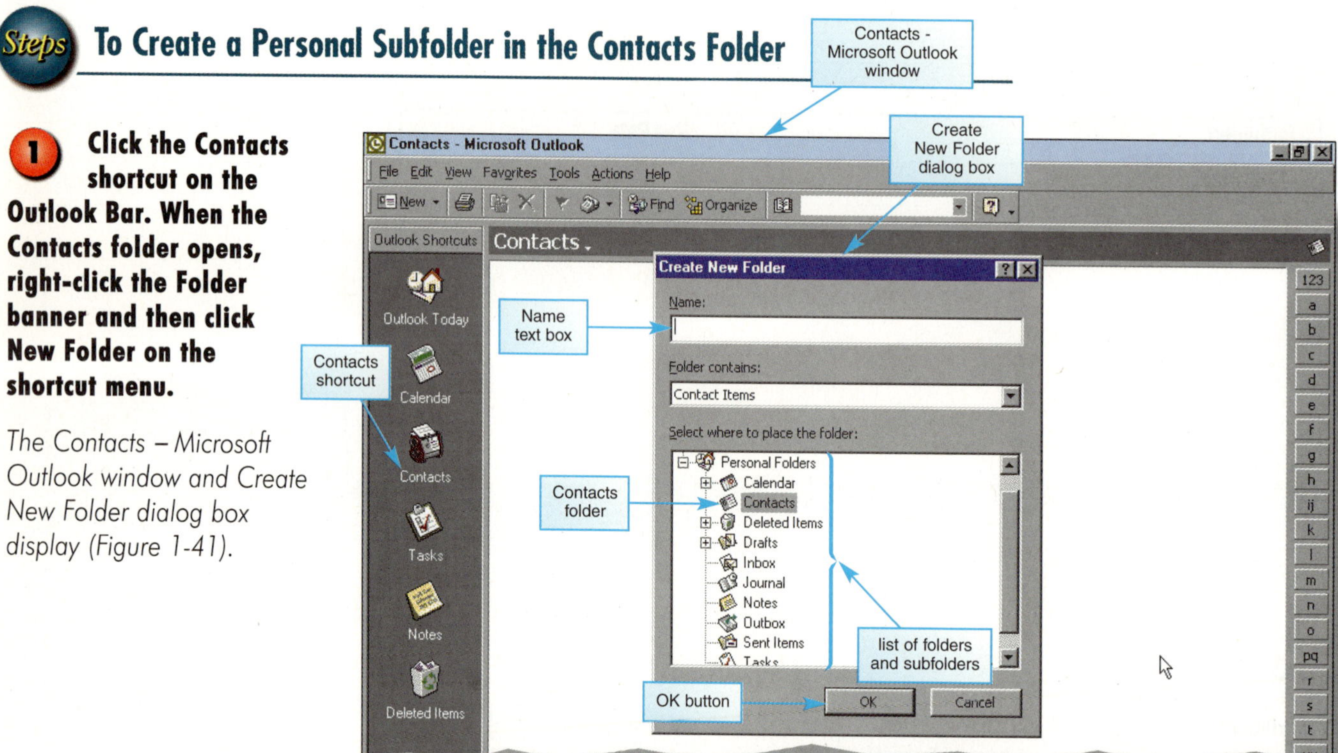

FIGURE 1-41

2 **Type** `Tamara's Contacts` **in the Name text box and then point to the OK button.**

The Create New Folder dialog box displays. The new subfolder, Tamara's Contacts, becomes a subfolder of the Contacts folder (Figure 1-42). Tamara's Contacts displays in the Name text box.

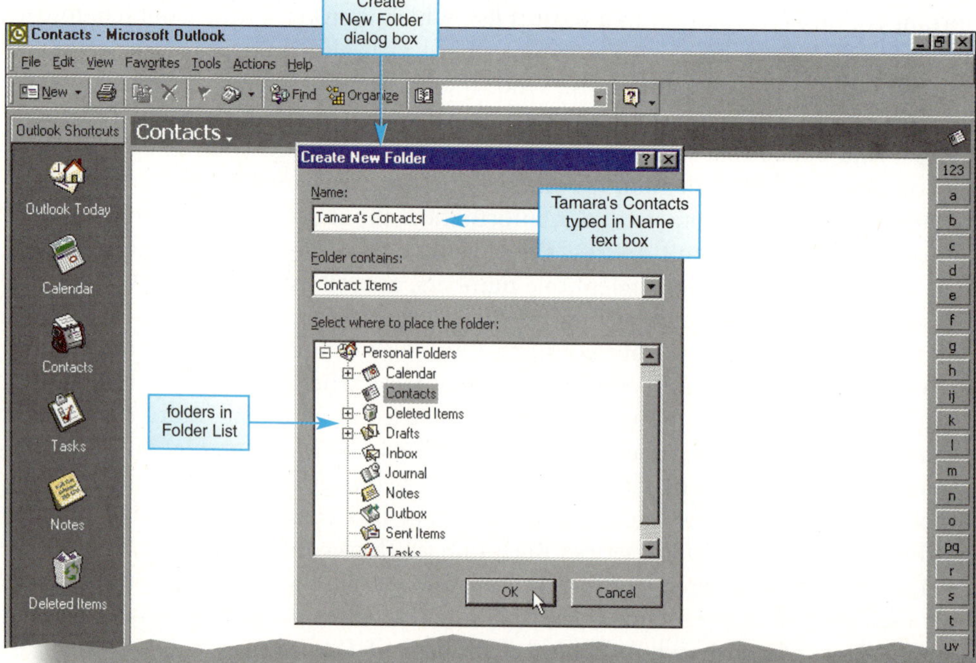

FIGURE 1-42

3 Click the OK button. When the Add shortcut to Outlook Bar? dialog box displays, click the No button.

The Folder List displays to the left of the contact area, showing a list of available folders and subfolders (Figure 1-43).

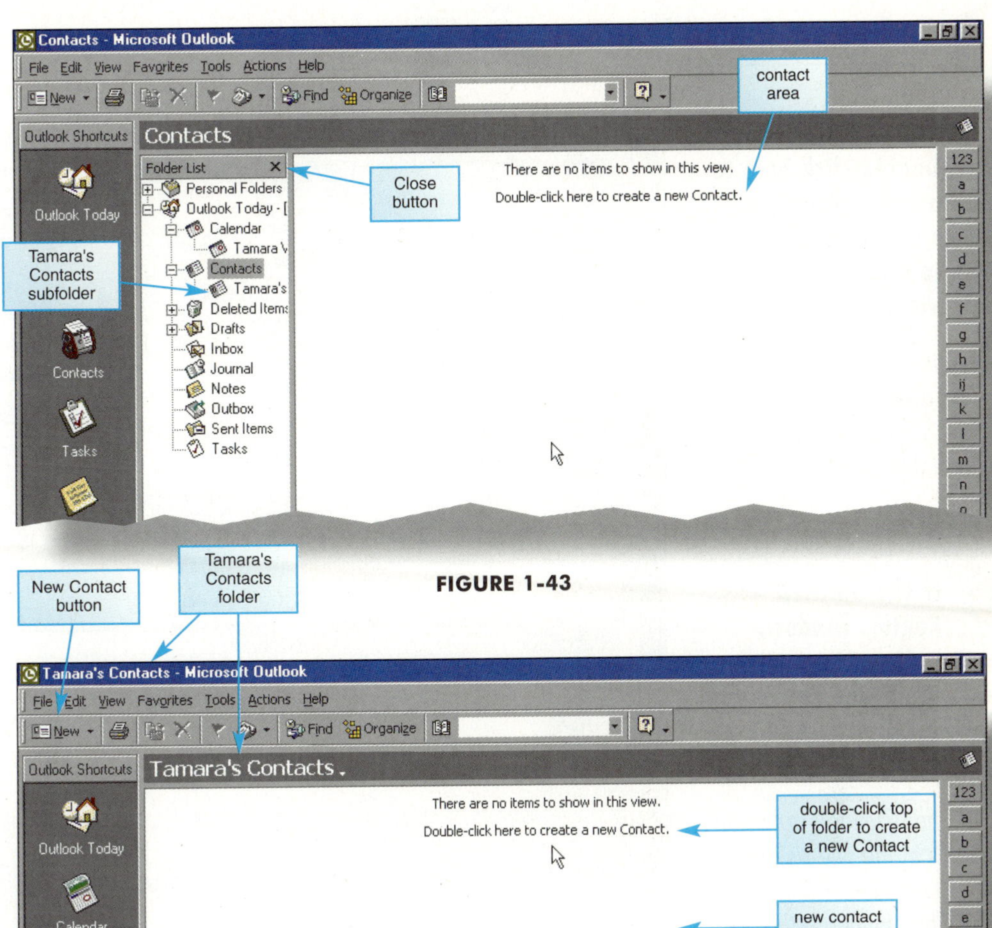

FIGURE 1-43

4 Click Tamara's Contacts in the Folder List and then click the Close button to close the Folder List.

The Tamara's Contacts – Microsoft Outlook window displays. Because no contacts have been entered, a message displays (Figure 1-44).

FIGURE 1-44

Other Ways

1. On File menu point to Folder, click New Folder on Folder submenu
2. Press CTRL+SHIFT+E

With the subfolder created in which to store the contact list, you can enter the contact names and other pertinent information provided in Table 1-4.

Creating a Contact List

The steps on the next page describe how to enter the data in Table 1-4 in the contact list.

Table 1-4 Contact Information

NAME	ADDRESS	BUSINESS TELEPHONE
Dr. Dennis Richards	1130 Muirfield Road Du Bois, PA 15801	(814) 555-0925
Dr. Margaret Bacher	301 Tyler Street Garden City, PA 19063	(814) 555-4508
Dr. Peter Konstant	2110 Hinsdale Blvd. Johnstown, PA 15901	(814) 555-1234
Dr. Donna Schwartz	8995 St. Andrews Chatham, PA 16935	(814) 555-1403

To Create a Contact List

1 **Double-click, Double-click here to create a new Contact., in the new contact area as shown in Figure 1-44 on the previous page.**

The Untitled – Contact window displays. This window allows general contact information to be entered.

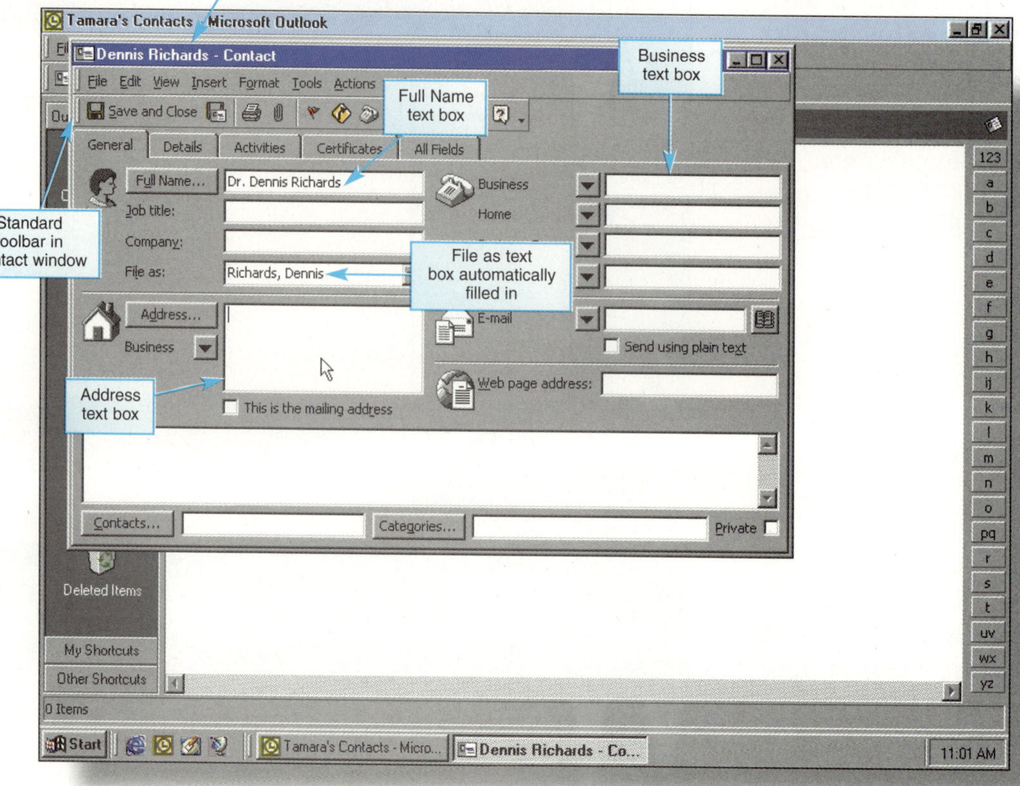

FIGURE 1-45

In the Untitled – Contact window, type `Dr. Dennis Richards` **in the Full Name text box. Click the Address text box.**

Notice that Outlook automatically fills in the File as text box, last name first (Figure 1-45). The Untitled – Contact window changes to the Dennis Richards – Contact window.

3 **In the Address text box, type** `1130 Muirfield Road` **and then press the ENTER key. Type** `Du Bois, PA 15801` **and then click the Business text box. Type** `(814) 555-0925` **in the Business text box. If necessary, click the Maximize button or drag the border of the window to the right until the entire telephone number displays. Point to the Save and Close button on the Standard toolbar in the Contact window.**

The Dennis Richards – Contact window displays (Figure 1-46).

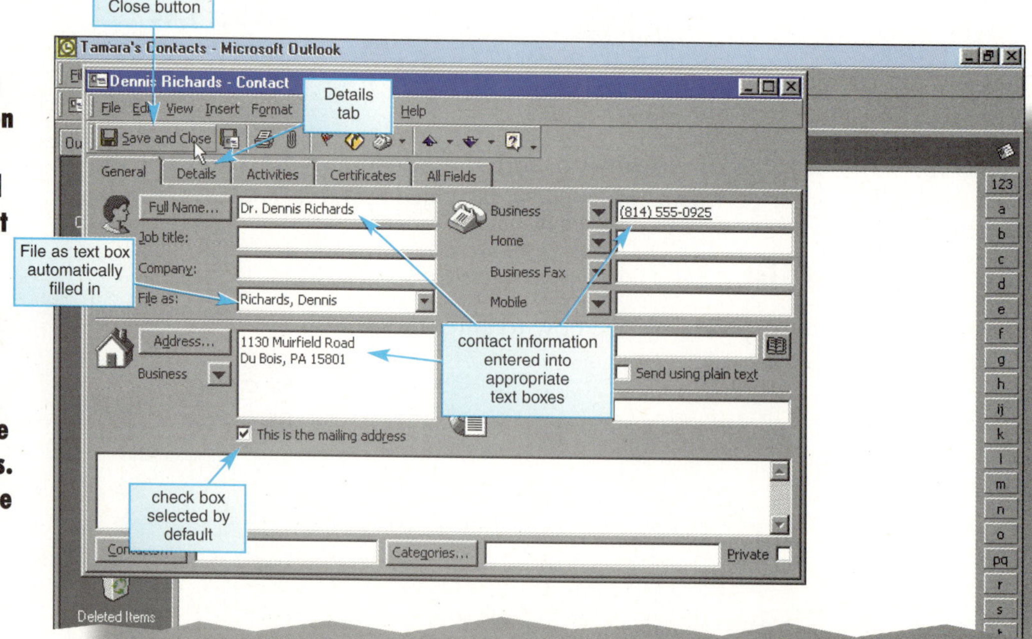

FIGURE 1-46

4 Click the Save and Close button.

The Dennis Richards address card displays in Address Cards view in the Tamara's Contacts – Microsoft Outlook window (Figure 1-47). Address Cards is the current view by default.

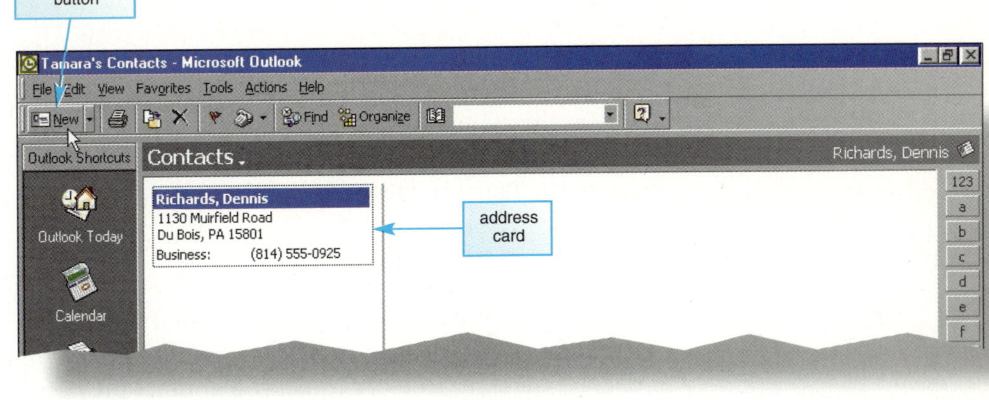

FIGURE 1-47

5 Click the New Contact button on the Standard toolbar. Repeat Steps 2 through 4 to enter the three remaining contacts in Table 1-4 on page O 1.39.

When complete, the contact list should look like Figure 1-48. Outlook automatically lists the contacts in alphabetical order. The phrase on the right side of the Folder banner, Bac – Sch, indicates the range of contacts currently displayed (Bacher to Schwartz).

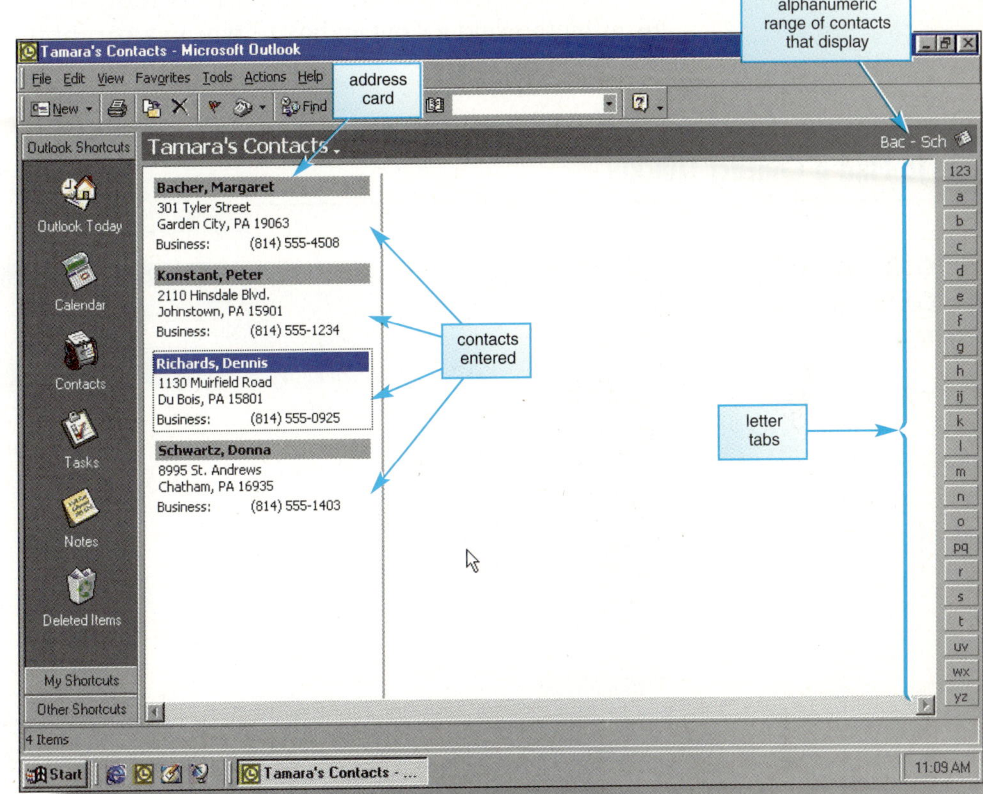

FIGURE 1-48

Other Ways

1. On File menu point to New, click Contact on New submenu
2. On Actions menu click New Contact
3. Press CTRL+SHIFT+C

Because this contact list is very short, all the names display in Address Cards view. With longer lists, however, you quickly can locate a specific contact by clicking the letter tab on the right side of the Microsoft Outlook – Contacts window (Figure 1-48).

Once the contact list is complete, it can be viewed, edited, or updated at any time. You can make some changes by typing inside the card itself. To display and edit all the information for a contact, double-click the address card to display the Contacts window. Use this window to enter information about a contact, such as e-mail and Web page addresses. Up to 18 different telephone numbers also can be stored for each contact and categorized by location and type (business, home, fax, mobile, pager, and so on). Clicking the **Details tab** (Figure 1-46) allows you to enter a contact's department, manager's name, nickname, and even birthday information.

Although the Contacts folder displays in Address Cards view by default (Figure 1-48 on the previous page), several other views are available. To change views, click View on the menu bar and highlight Current View. You can choose views such as Detailed Address Cards, Phone List, By Category, By Company, By Location, and By Follow-up Flag. The view also can be customized.

Finding a Contact Quickly

To find a contact quickly, use the **Find a Contact box** on the Standard toolbar. Enter a first or last name, in full or partially. An e-mail alias also can be used to find a contact quickly. To locate quickly a contact previously searched for, click the Find a Contact box arrow and select a name.

A contact record was created for Peter Konstant. This record can be found easily by using the Find a Contact box to type in a part of the contact name as shown in the following steps.

To Find a Contact Quickly

1 Click the Find a Contact box. Type kon **in the box.**

The letters display in the Find a Contact box (Figure 1-49). The letters, kon are used to find the contact beginning with those letters.

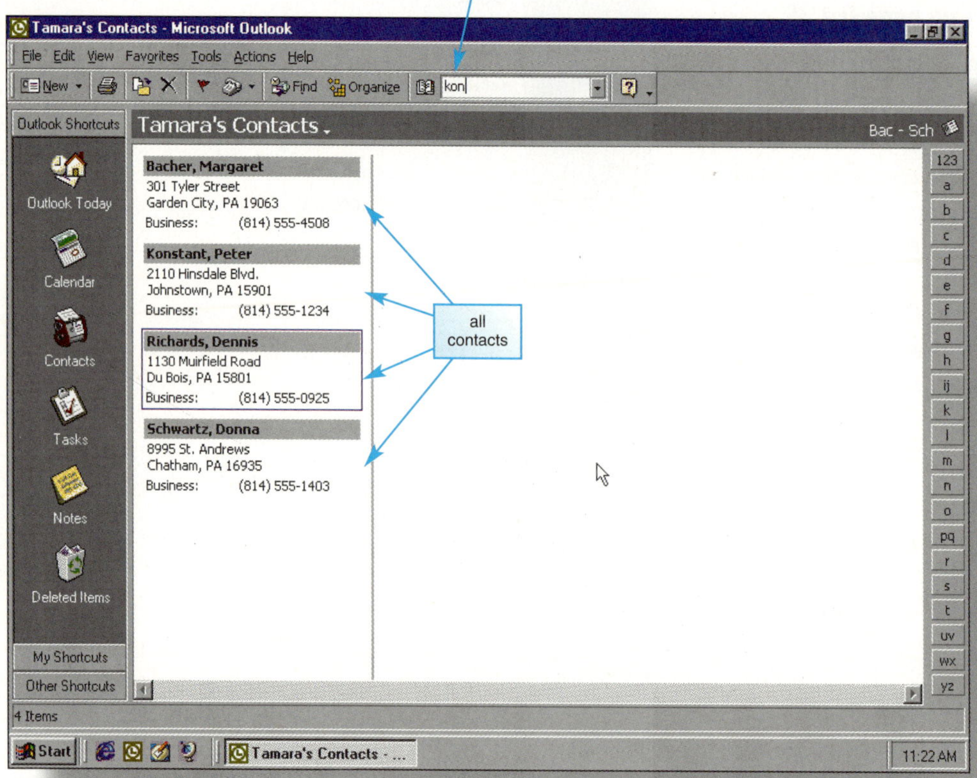

FIGURE 1-49

2 Press the ENTER key.

Outlook displays the Peter Konstant – Contact window (Figure 1-50). Currently, only one contact exists with the letters, kon, in its name.

3 Click the Close button in the Peter Konstant – Contact window.

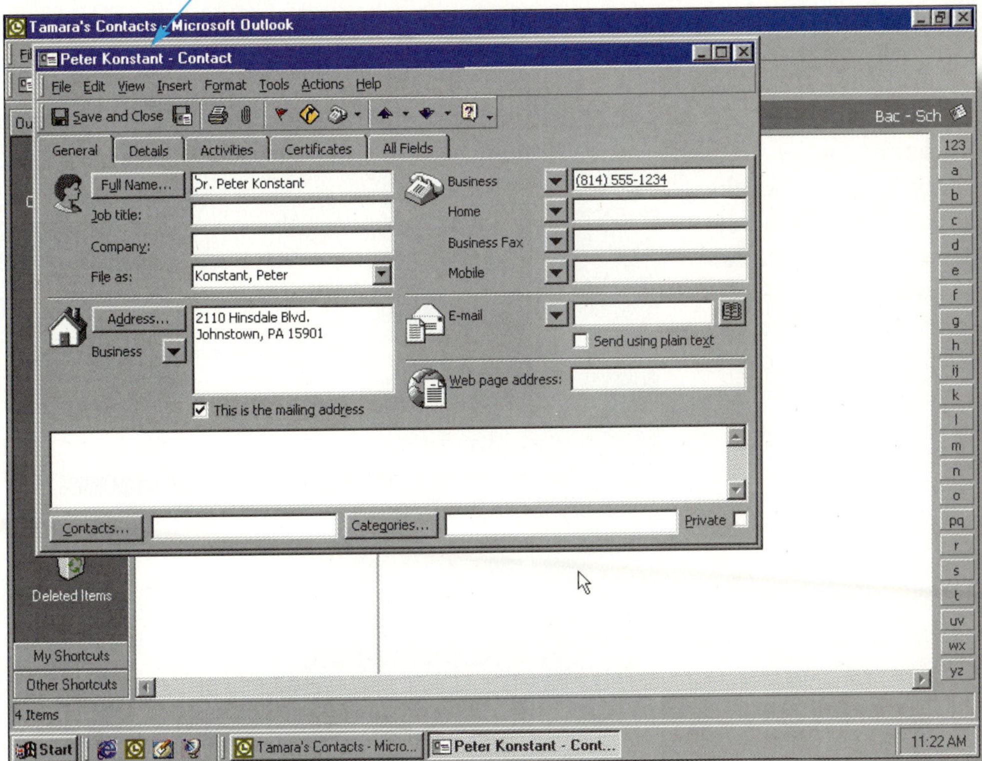

FIGURE 1-50

If more than one contact with the starting letters, kon, exists, a Choose Contact window displays with the list of all contacts beginning with the kon string. Then, you make a selection in this window.

Other Ways

1. On Tools menu click Find
2. Press CTRL+SHIFT+F

Organizing Contacts

To help manage your contacts further, the contact list can be categorized and sorted in any number of ways. For example, you can group contacts into categories such as Key Customer, Business, Hot Contact, or even Ideas, Competition, and Strategies. In addition, you may want to create your own categories to group contacts by company, department, a particular project, a specific class, and so on. You also can sort by any part of the address, for example, by postal code for bulk mailings.

For the contact list created in this project, it is appropriate to organize the contacts in a personal category. You can do this by selecting the contacts and then adding them to the personal category of the contact list. The steps on the next page illustrate this procedure.

More About 2000

Contacts

Outlook 2000 has many new features for contact organization. You can organize contacts from one or more Contacts folders in a personal distribution list. When adding new contacts, Outlook checks for duplicates, and if found, gives you the option to merge the new information automatically with the existing contact entry. For mail merging, you can use a subset of your Contacts folder, filter the contacts list, and then use the filtered list to begin a mail merge from Outlook.

To Organize Contacts

1 Click the Organize button on the Standard toolbar. Click the name bar of the Margaret Bacher contact record. Hold down the CTRL key and click the other three contact records. Release the CTRL key, and then point to the Add contacts box arrow.

The Ways to Organize Tamara's Contacts dialog box displays (Figure 1-51). All four records are selected.

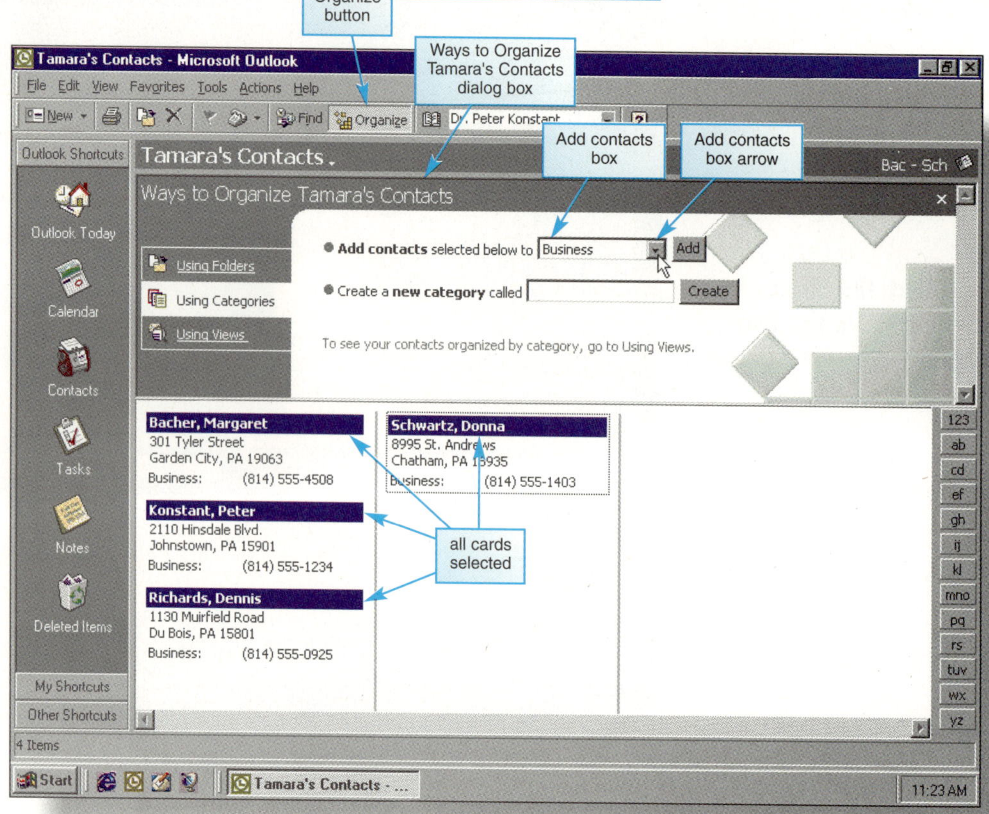

FIGURE 1-51

2 Click the Add contacts box arrow. Scroll down and point to the Personal category.

A list of categories displays (Figure 1-52). Personal is highlighted.

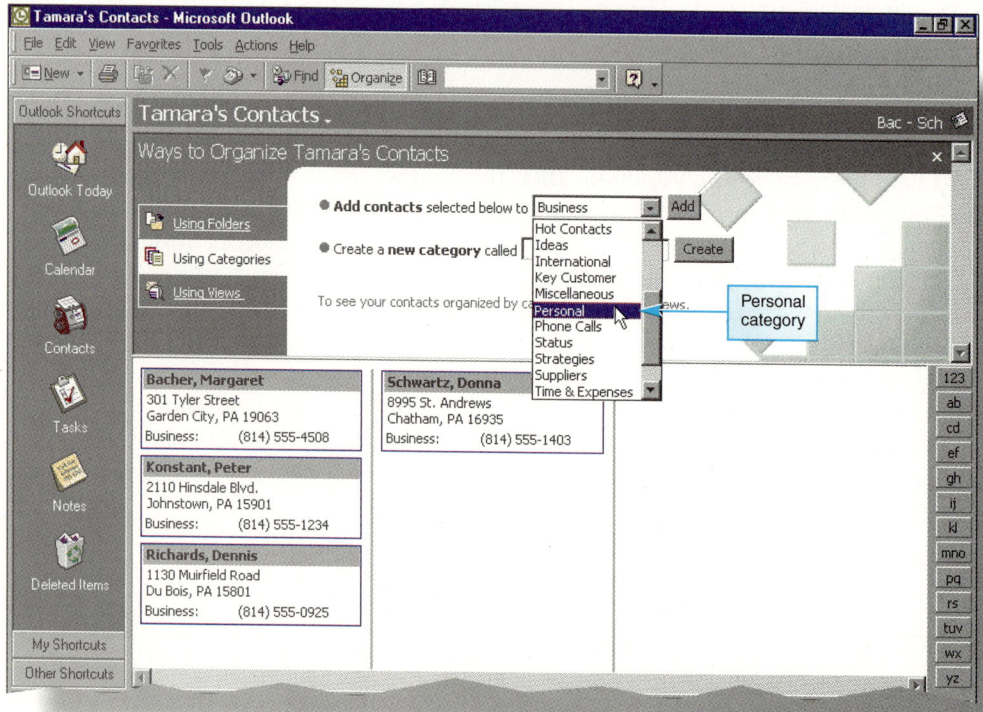

FIGURE 1-52

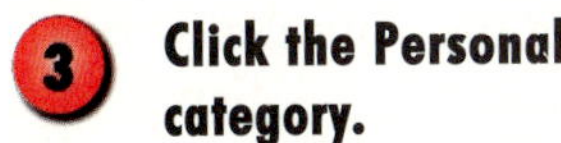

3 **Click the Personal category.**

Personal displays in the Add contacts box (Figure 1-53).

4 **Click the Add button. When the word Done! displays to the right of the Add button, click the Close button.**

The contacts are added to the Personal category.

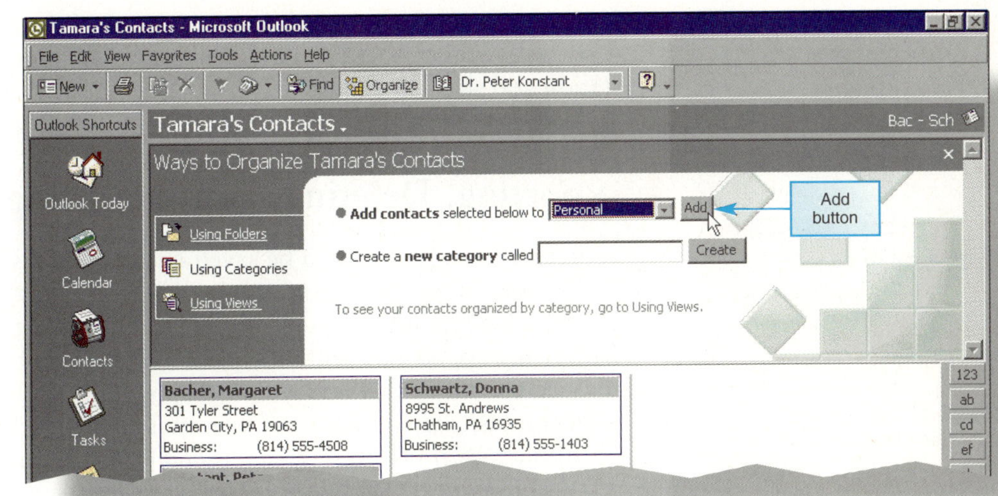

FIGURE 1-53

Other Ways

1. On Tools menu click Organize

The contacts now are organized into the Personal contacts list. Organizing contacts in different categories helps make searching for groups of names easier. Names in a contact list can be categorized and sorted into several different categories including Key Customer, Business, or custom categories that you create. By putting all professors into a personal category, it segregates them from all other contacts entered.

Printing the Contact List

Printing the contact list is an easy way to obtain a listing of people frequently contacted. The printed list can be used for business mailings, invitations to social gatherings, or even a telephone or Christmas card list. The following step describes how to print the contact.

TO PRINT THE CONTACT LIST

1 Ready the printer. Click the Print button on the Standard toolbar. When the Print dialog box displays, click the OK button.

The printed contact list should look like the list shown in Figure 1-54.

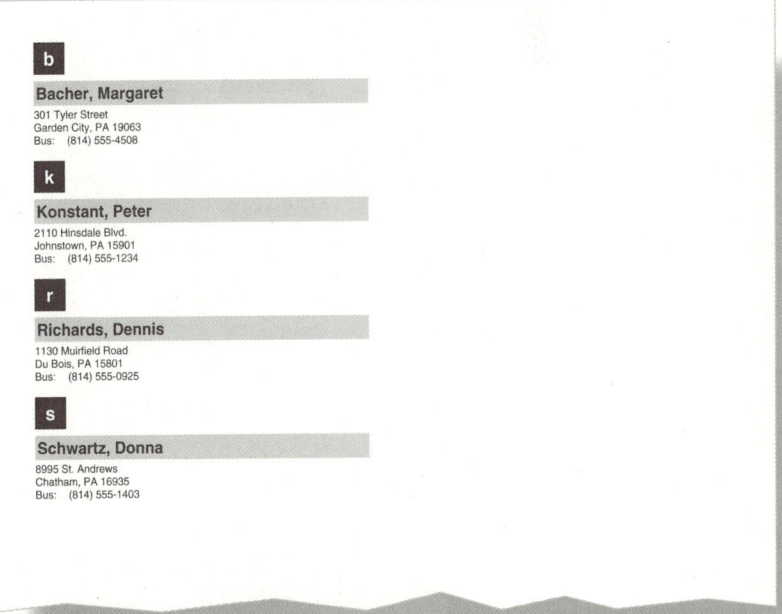

b

Bacher, Margaret
301 Tyler Street
Garden City, PA 19063
Bus: (814) 555-4508

k

Konstant, Peter
2110 Hinsdale Blvd.
Johnstown, PA 15901
Bus: (814) 555-1234

r

Richards, Dennis
1130 Muirfield Road
Du Bois, PA 15801
Bus: (814) 555-0925

s

Schwartz, Donna
8995 St. Andrews
Chatham, PA 16935
Bus: (814) 555-1403

FIGURE 1-54

A printout can be customized by changing the Print style in the Print dialog box. These styles let you choose from a variety of fields, along with choices for paper orientation and size.

Exporting, Deleting, and Importing Subfolders

Saving

All appointments, events, meetings, and tasks are saved as separate files on your disk. They therefore can be edited, moved, copied, or deleted. These items can be saved together as a group using the Import and Export Wizard.

The contact list now is ready to be saved on a floppy disk. Saving your work on a floppy disk allows you to take your schedule to another computer or to merge your contacts as a mailing list into another computer's word processor.

With many application software packages, a single file, such as a letter or spreadsheet, can be saved directly on a floppy disk. With Outlook, however, each appointment, task, or contact is a file in itself. Thus, rather than saving numerous individual files, Outlook uses an **Import and Export Wizard** to guide you through the process of saving an entire subfolder. Transferring a subfolder onto a floppy disk is called **exporting**. Moving a subfolder back to a computer is called **importing**. Subfolders can be imported and exported from any Outlook application. Outlook then saves the subfolder on a floppy disk, adding the extension **.pst**.

Exporting Subfolders

Because Tamara Wilson's contact list is completed, Tamara's Contacts subfolder is exported first. The following steps show how to export subfolders onto a floppy disk.

Steps To Export Subfolders onto a Floppy Disk

1. **Insert a floppy disk in your floppy disk drive. Click File on the menu bar and then click Import and Export.**

2. **When the Import and Export Wizard dialog box displays, click Export to a file in the Choose an action to perform list. Point to the Next button.**

The Import and Export Wizard dialog box displays (Figure 1-55). Using this Wizard allows you to perform one of seven import and export options available with Outlook.

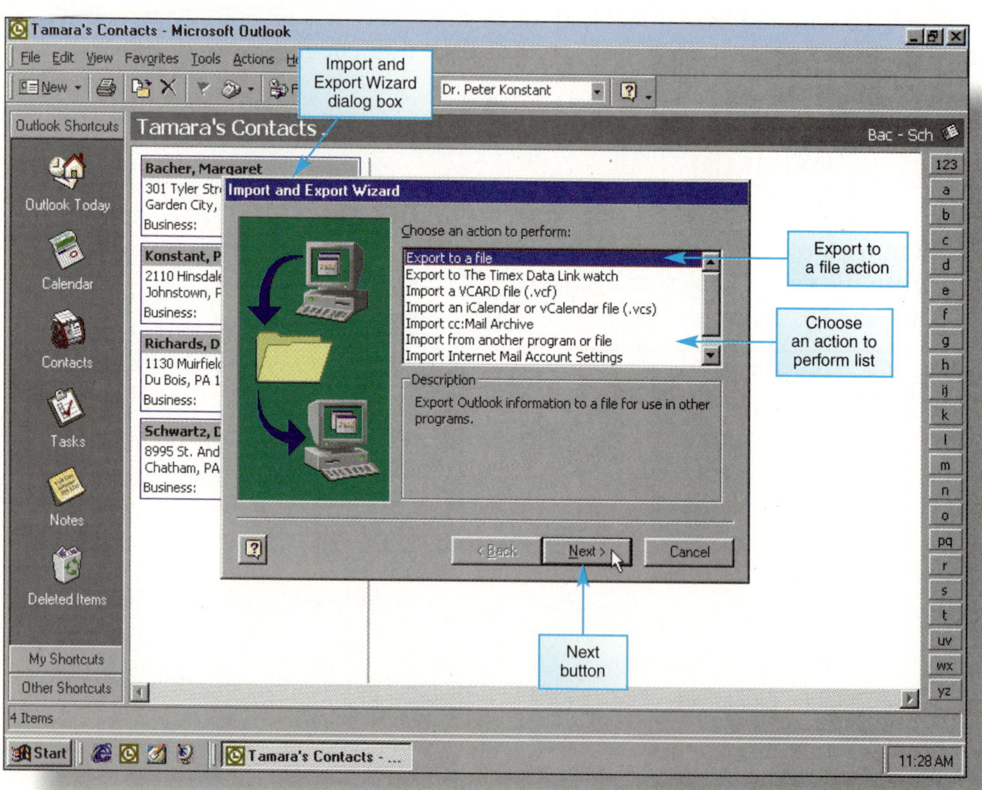

FIGURE 1-55

3 Click the Next button. In the Export to a File dialog box, click Personal Folder File (.pst) and then click the Next button. If necessary, click the plus sign (+) to the left of the Contacts icon in the Select a folder to export from list. Click Tamara's Contacts.

The Export Personal Folders dialog box displays (Figure 1-56). The Tamara's Contacts subfolder is selected as the folder from which to export.

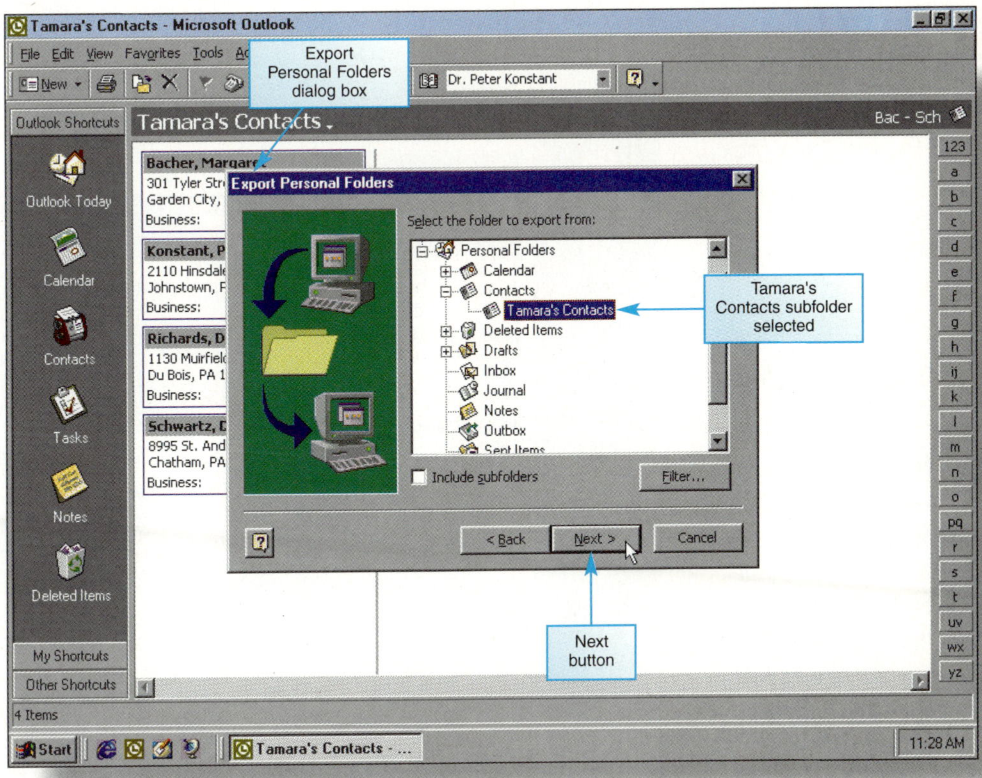

FIGURE 1-56

4 Click the Next button. Type `a:\Tamara's Contacts.pst` **in the Save exported file as text box. (If your floppy drive is not labeled A, type the drive letter accordingly.) Point to the Finish button.**

The last screen of the Import and Export Wizard, displays (Figure 1-57). The subfolder will be exported to drive A and saved as Tamara's Contacts.

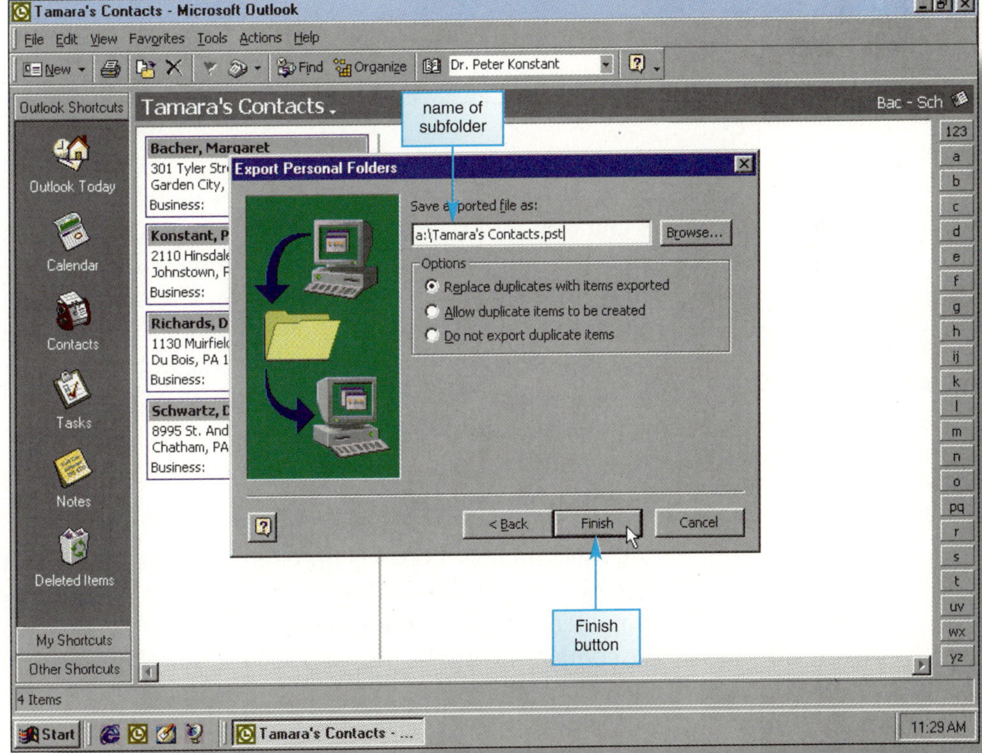

FIGURE 1-57

5 Click the Finish button.

The Create Microsoft Personal Folders dialog box displays as Outlook exports the folder. The subfolder is saved on your floppy disk (Figure 1-58).

6 Click the OK button.

7 To export a Calendar subfolder, repeat Steps 1 through 5. You do not have to open the Calendar folder to export the subfolder. Instead, when the Export Personal Folders dialog box displays, click the plus sign (+) next to the Calendar icon and then click the Tamara Wilson subfolder. Save the exported file on a floppy disk as Tamara Wilson.

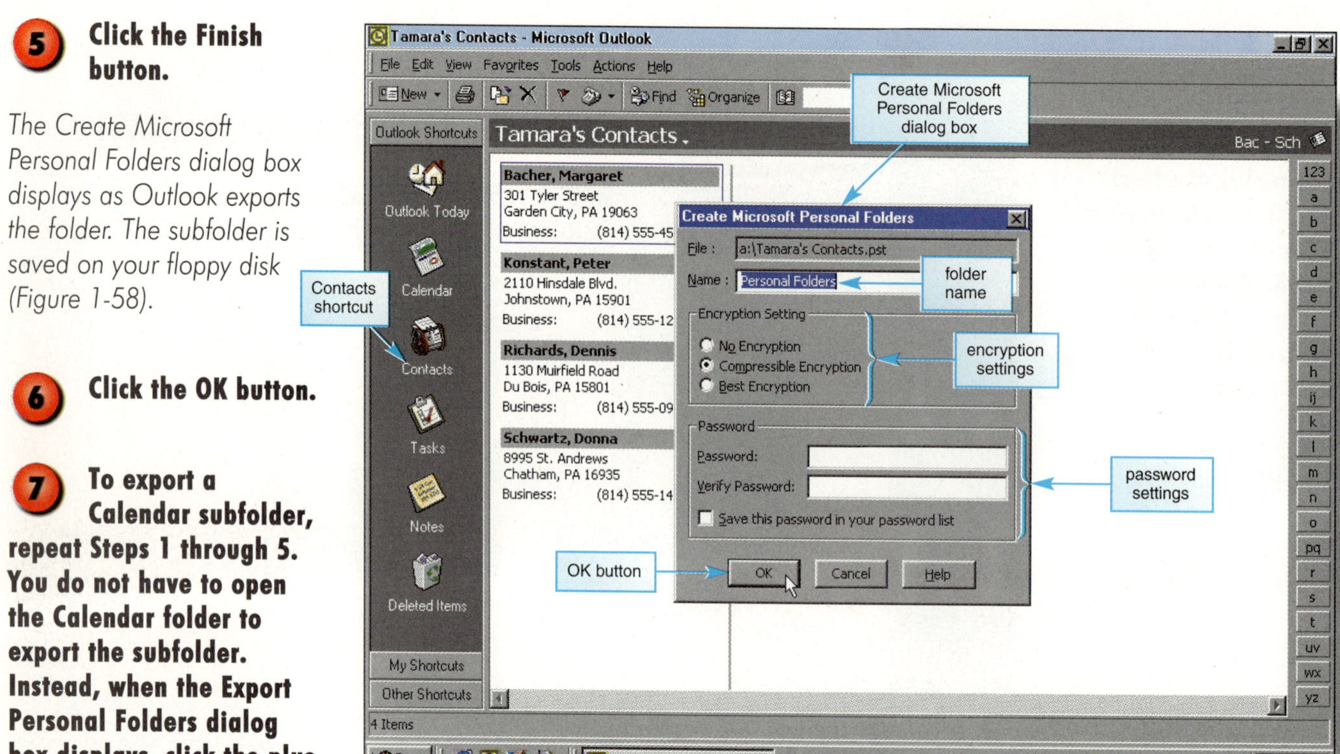

FIGURE 1-58

Folders

To locate quickly a folder or file, use the Folder List. If the Folder List is not visible, click View on the menu bar and then click Folder List.

Subfolders can be exported to a personal folder file, which can be viewed only in Outlook, or saved as another file type, such as a text file, which then can be imported into other programs. Importing and exporting folders allows Outlook items to be shared easily. For example, a company Calendar subfolder may be imported to publicize a company meeting, a group Contacts subfolder may be imported to make information about the people who work on a project available to everyone, or a team Tasks subfolder may be imported to help everyone track work on a project.

Deleting Subfolders

The Tamara's Contacts and Tamara Wilson Calendar subfolders now have been exported onto a floppy disk. A copy of each still is present on the hard disk of your computer, however, and displays in Outlook's Folder List. To delete a subfolder from the computer entirely, use the Delete command. Perform the following steps to delete a personal subfolder.

To Delete a Personal Subfolder

1 If necessary, click the Contacts shortcut on the Outlook Bar. Right-click the Tamara's Contacts folder banner. Point to Delete "Tamara's Contacts" on the shortcut menu (Figure 1-59).

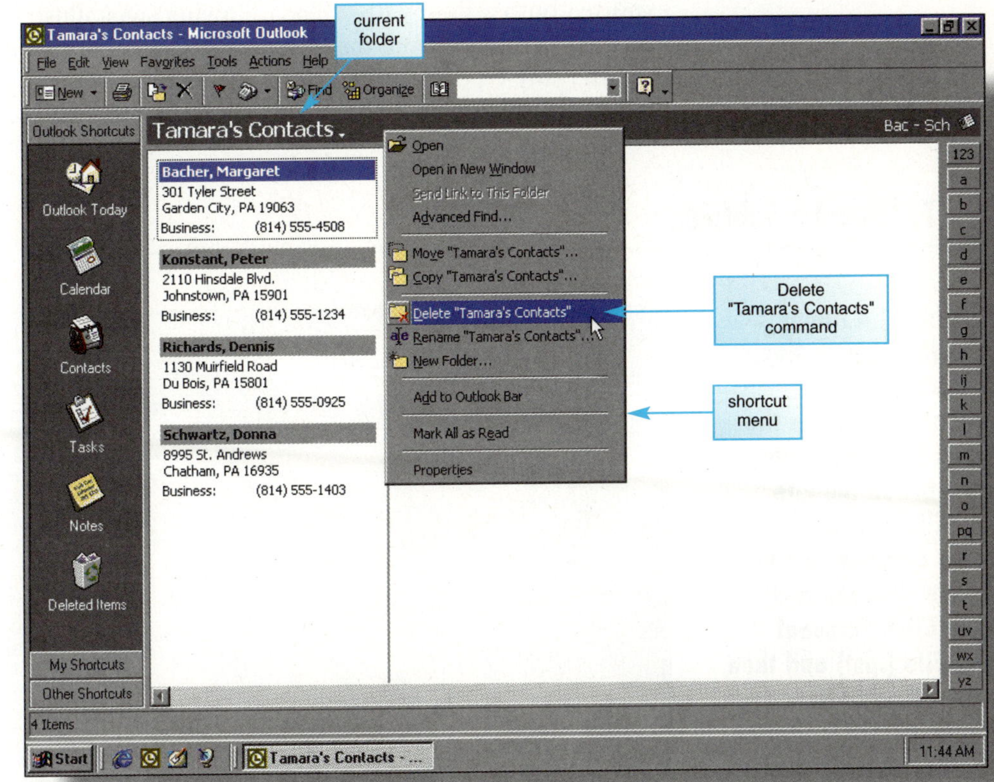

FIGURE 1-59

2 Click the Delete "Tamara's Contacts" command. Click Yes when the dialog box displays asking if you are sure you want to delete the folder.

3 Click the down arrow on the Contacts banner. If necessary, click the plus sign (+) to the left of the Calendar icon in the Folder List to expand the folder list in the Calendar folder. Click the Tamara Wilson folder.

4 Right-click the Tamara Wilson folder banner. Click Delete "Tamara Wilson" on the shortcut menu.

The Tamara Wilson folder no longer displays.

Other Ways

1. On Folder banner, right-click folder name, click Delete on Standard toolbar

Outlook sends the deleted subfolders to a special folder called Deleted Items. If you accidentally delete a subfolder without first exporting it onto a floppy disk, you still can open the subfolder by double-clicking it in the Folder List. To display the subfolder, you may need to click the plus sign (+) next to the Deleted Items. Once a subfolder no longer is needed, right-click the subfolder in the Folder List and click Delete on the shortcut menu. Deleting a subfolder from the Deleted Items folder permanently removes it from the hard disk. You can delete only subfolders; Outlook's main application folders, such as Calendar and Contacts, cannot be deleted.

Thus far in Project 1 you have created a schedule, a task list, and a contact list and exported your personal subfolders onto a floppy disk. Once a subfolder is created and exported, often it will need to be retrieved or imported from the disk. For example, you might want to revise your office hours, add exam dates to your schedule, or use your schedule on a different computer. To do so, you must import or retrieve the subfolder from the floppy disk.

Importing Subfolders

Earlier, the Calendar subfolder containing appointment and event files was exported onto a floppy disk. The following steps illustrate how to import the same Calendar subfolder from the floppy disk. To import a subfolder, Outlook must be running. Any type of subfolder then can be imported from any application within Outlook.

To Import a Subfolder

1 Insert a floppy disk in your floppy disk drive. Click the Calendar shortcut on the Outlook Bar. Click Import and Export on the File menu. Click Import from another program or file and then click the Next button. Click Personal Folder File (.pst) and then click the Next button. Type `a:\Tamara Wilson.pst` **in the File to import text box or click the Browse button to access your floppy drive and select the Tamara Wilson subfolder. Point to the Next button.**

The drive, subfolder name, and extension for the subfolder display in the File to import text box (Figure 1-60).

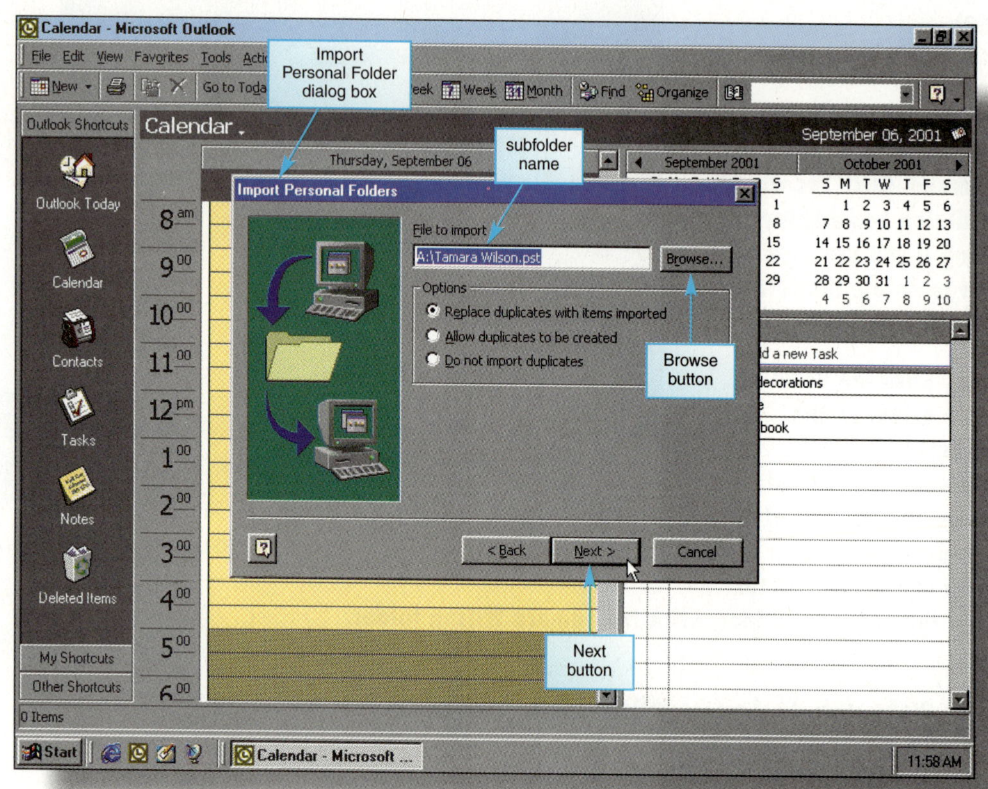

FIGURE 1-60

Importing

Other contact lists can be imported through the Import and Export Wizard on the File menu. The Wizard allows you to copy information that exists in other applications to Outlook.

 **Click the Next button. When the Import Personal Folders dialog box displays, click Calendar in the Select the folder to import from list. Point to the Finish button.**

The last screen of the Import and Export Wizard displays, allowing you to choose the Outlook application to import (Figure 1-61).

3 Click the Finish button.

The subfolder is imported into Outlook as a subfolder of Calendar.

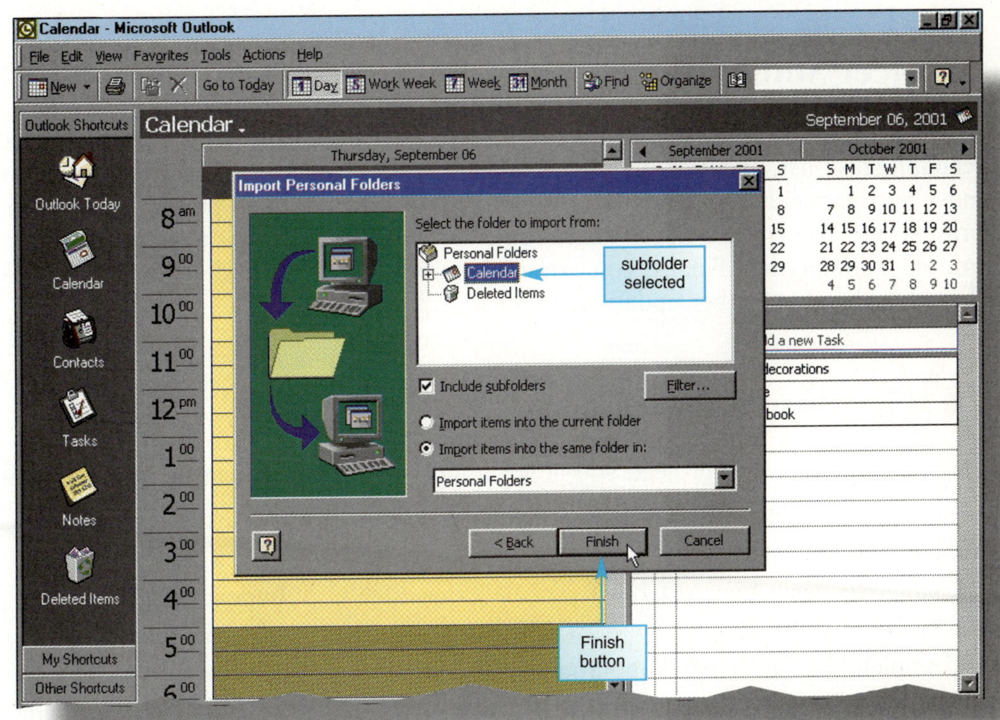

FIGURE 1-61

The Calendar subfolder now is available to be opened, edited, and printed as described earlier in this project. When changes are complete, the subfolder again can be exported and deleted from the hard disk. In addition to Outlook subfolders, Outlook's Import and Export Wizard allows the import of a Personal Address Book with contact names, addresses, and telephone numbers, or existing information to be brought in from other programs, such as Microsoft Mail or Schedule+.

Quitting Outlook

The project now is complete and you are ready to quit Outlook. The following step describes how to quit Outlook.

TO QUIT OUTLOOK

 Click the Close button on the Outlook title bar.

A dialog box displays, instructing you to please wait while Microsoft Outlook exits. Outlook closes and the Windows desktop displays.

CASE PERSPECTIVE SUMMARY

Tamara Wilson's school and meeting schedule, including all her classes and other engagements, are entered in her calendar and saved in a personal subfolder. With your help, she has identified and scheduled all of her recurring appointments, created a task list, and organized her contacts. Now she feels she is prepared to handle her busy workload.

Project Summary

In this project you learned about desktop information management by using Outlook to create a personal schedule, task list, and a contact list. You learned how to enter appointments, create recurring appointments, move appointments to new dates, schedule events, and view and print your calendar in different views and print styles. You created a task list to serve as a reminder of tasks to be completed. You also created and printed a contact list. Finally, you exported your personal subfolders onto a floppy disk and later imported the subfolders for further updating.

What You Should Know

Having completed this project, you now should be able to perform the following tasks:

- Change to Month View *(O 1.33)*
- Change to a Personal Folder *(O 1.13)*
- Change to Week View *(O 1.32)*
- Change to Work Week View *(O 1.31)*
- Complete the Recurring Appointments *(O 1.20)*
- Create an Event *(O 1.29)*
- Create a Contact List *(O 1.40)*
- Create a Personal Subfolder in the Calendar Folder *(O 1.11)*
- Create a Personal Subfolder in the Contacts Folder *(O 1.38)*
- Create a Task List Using the TaskPad *(O 1.34)*
- Delete an Appointment *(O 1.23)*
- Delete a Personal Subfolder *(O 1.49)*
- Enter Appointment Dates and Times Using Natural Language Phrases *(O 1.21)*
- Enter and Save Appointments Using the Appointment Window *(O 1.15)*
- Enter Appointments Using the Appointment Area *(O 1.14)*
- Export Subfolders onto a Floppy Disk *(O 1.46)*
- Find a Contact Quickly *(O 1.42)*
- Import a Subfolder *(O 1.50)*
- Move an Appointment to a New Date *(O 1.26)*
- Move an Appointment to a New Month *(O 1.27)*
- Move an Appointment to a New Time *(O 1.25)*
- Move to the Next Day in the Appointment Area *(O 1.19)*
- Open the Calendar Folder *(O 1.9)*
- Organize Contacts *(O 1.44)*
- Print the Contact List *(O 1.45)*
- Print the Calendar in Daily Style *(O 1.35)*
- Print the Calendar in Monthly Style *(O 1.36)*
- Print the Calendar in Weekly Style *(O 1.36)*
- Print the Task List *(O 1.37)*
- Quit Outlook *(O 1.51)*
- Set Recurring Appointments *(O 1.17)*
- Start Outlook *(O 1.8)*

1 Creating a Schedule

Problem: You recently accepted a job at a sporting goods store in the mall. You need to give your boss a schedule of your classes for the semester so she will know when you are available to work. You decide to schedule your time in Outlook and then will print a month view of the calendar. This calendar is for the Spring semester that begins Monday, January 8, 2001, and ends Friday, May 4, 2001.

Instructions: Perform the following tasks.

1. Create a personal Calendar subfolder called [Your name] Schedule. Using the information in Table 1-5, enter each of the classes as a recurring appointment.
2.

Table 1-5 Recurring Appointments

CLASS	DAYS	TIME
World History	M, W	8:00 am - 9:30 am
Biology	M, W, F	10:00 am - 11:00 am
English Literature	T, Th	9:00 am - 10:30 am
C++ Programming	T, Th	11:00 am - 12:30 pm

Add study time each week to the schedule as a recurring appointment occurring Mondays and Wednesdays from 1:00 P.M. - 3:00 P.M.

3. Schedule your Clothing Drive Committee meetings beginning January 11, 2001 for three Thursdays from 7:00 P.M. – 8:00 P.M.
4. Your parents' anniversary is January 24, 2001. This should be scheduled as a one-time event.
5. Add a hair cut appointment for February 6, 2001 from 4:00 P.M. - 4:30 P.M.
6. All classes are cancelled from February 19 - 23, 2001 for Spring break. Delete the occurrences of classes during this week, but not all recurring instances.
7. Print a copy of your calendar in Monthly Style for the months of January and February.
8. Export your subfolder onto a floppy disk and then delete it from the hard disk.

2 Creating a Contact List

Problem: You just have been elected as the secretary of the Student Computer Club. You want to be able to send out meeting notifications, surveys, and newsletters to all members of the club on a regular basis. To do this, you need to organize club members' names, addresses, e-mail addresses, and telephone numbers. You decide to use the Outlook Contacts component to create a contact list.

Instructions: Create a personal Contacts subfolder in which to store a contact list containing the club members' listed in Table 1-6. Add the Grade Level field to Address Cards view using the Show Fields on the View menu. In the Contacts window, enter the student's grade level in the Grade Level field. When the list is complete, export the subfolder onto a floppy disk and then delete it from the hard disk.

Table 1-6 Contact Information

NAME	ADDRESS	TELEPHONE	E-MAIL	GRADE LEVEL
Bessie Smith	111 S. Parkway	(708) 555-1128	bsmith@isp.com	Sophomore
Julius Vicarro	1023 Christina	(708) 555-0920	jvicarro@isp.com	Junior
Aisha Washburn	995 Softwood	(708) 555-1210	awashburn@isp.com	Junior
Ramay Illona	748 Vermont	(708) 555-9842	rillona@isp.com	Freshman
Bert Gately	400 N. Riverside	(708) 555-4001	bgately@isp.com	Senior
Michael Gallagher	897 Ridge Road	(708) 555-1983	mgallagher@isp.com	Sophomore

3 Creating a Calendar and a Task List

Problem: You are the newly named manager of software development for a small company in Chicago. In order to manage your staff successfully, you must be highly organized, tracking all meetings, tasks, project completion dates, and other important events. In addition to your work duties, you teach a class Monday nights from 7:00 P.M. to 9:30 P.M. at the local college.

Instructions: Perform the following tasks.

1. Create a personal Calendar subfolder called Innovative Software Company.
2. Enter the appointments in the calendar, using the information listed in Table 1-7.
3. Create a task list containing the following tasks:
    a. Send sales report to Bernie
    b. Schedule meeting to discuss IST software
    c. Call Friedel about Germany trip
    d. Sign maintenance contract on PowerSource
4. Print the calendar for the month of June.
5. Export the personal subfolder onto a floppy disk and then delete it from the hard disk.

Table 1-7 Appointment Information

DESCRIPTION	DATE	TIME
Staff meeting	Every Friday from May 4, 2001 - June 29, 2001	9:00 am - 10:00 am
Shipping system completion	June 8, 2001	
Customer training session	June 12 and 14, 2001	8:30 am - 4:30 pm
Manufacturing system due	June 18, 2001	
David's birthday	June 22, 2001	
Telephone meeting with Alicia	June 25, 2001	9:30 am - 10:00 am
Discuss new projects	June 27, 2001	11:30 am - 1:00 pm
Meeting with John	June 28, 2001	3:00 pm - 4:00 pm

Cases and Places

The difficulty of these case studies varies:
▶ are the least difficult; ▶▶ are more difficult; and ▶▶▶ are the most difficult.

1 ▶ Create a personal schedule for the next month. Include any work and class time, together with study time. Use recurring appointments when possible. All day activities should be scheduled as events.

2 ▶ You are in charge of scheduling for the month of April at work. Make up a schedule of work times for four employees. Adam works Mondays, Wednesdays, and Fridays from 9:00 A.M. to 5:00 P.M. Beth works Tuesdays, Thursdays, and Saturdays from 9:00 A.M. to 5:00 P.M. Abdul works from 12 noon until 9:00 P.M. on Mondays, Wednesdays, and Fridays. Elizabeth completes the schedule working from 12 noon until 9:00 P.M. on Tuesdays, Thursdays, and Saturdays.

3 ▶▶ You work at the school's Writing Lab. You need to create a week schedule of hours and print it. From Monday through Saturday, the lab is open from 8:00 A.M. - 9:00 P.M. The lab is reserved on Mondays and Wednesdays from 2:00 P.M. - 4:00 P.M. for a Beginning Writing class. It also is reserved on Tuesdays and Thursdays from 1:00 P.M. - 3:00 P.M. for an Advanced Writing class. The lab is closed all day Sunday.

4 ▶▶ Create journal entries from your personal schedule for the past week. Comment on activities in which you participated and tasks that you accomplished. Write when the activity was started and ended. Note the problems (if any) associated with the activity. When commenting on completed tasks, include notes about the results of having completed it. Specify what would have happened had the task not been completed when it was.

5 ▶▶ Create a contact list of your family, friends, and colleagues. Include their names, addresses, telephone numbers, and e-mail addresses (if any). Enter the name of the company each one works for, if appropriate. For family, list their birthdays and wedding anniversarys (if any) using the Details tab.

6 ▶▶ Use the natural language option in the Start date box to create a list of events for the year. Create a new calendar that contains the following holidays: Valentine's Day, St. Patrick's Day, Independence Day, Halloween, Veterans Day, Christmas Eve, Christmas Day, New Year's Eve, and New Year's Day. For the last five holidays, indicate that you will be out of the office all day. Also, add events for several family or friend birthdays or anniversaries, using the natural language option. For instance, schedule these events by utilizing the phrase, two weeks from today (or something similar) as a start date. Try different phrase options to schedule these.

7 ▶▶▶ You recently accepted a position with an international pharmaceutical company. Your first assignment is to make the main telephone and address file available to everyone in the firm. The file, which currently is maintained in a three-ring binder, contains names, addresses, telephone numbers, e-mail addresses and Web sites of your company's many subsidiaries and vendors. You decide to create a contact list using Outlook so everyone can access the same information and automatically dial and send e-mail and access Web sites. Create a contact list that includes at least the names, addresses, and Web sites of seven pharmaceutical companies. Make up some fictional company names and addresses or look up pharmaceutical companies on the Web using one of the Internet search engines. Create a Contacts subfolder in which to store the contact list.

Office 2000 Integration

Office 2000 Integration

PROJECT 1

Integrating Office 2000 Applications and the World Wide Web

OBJECTIVES

You will have mastered the material in this project when you can:

- Integrate the Office 2000 applications to create a Web site
- Add hyperlinks to a Word document
- Embed an Excel chart into a Word document
- Add scrolling text to a Web page created in Word
- Add a hyperlink to a PowerPoint slide
- Create Web pages from a PowerPoint presentation
- Create a data access page from an Access database

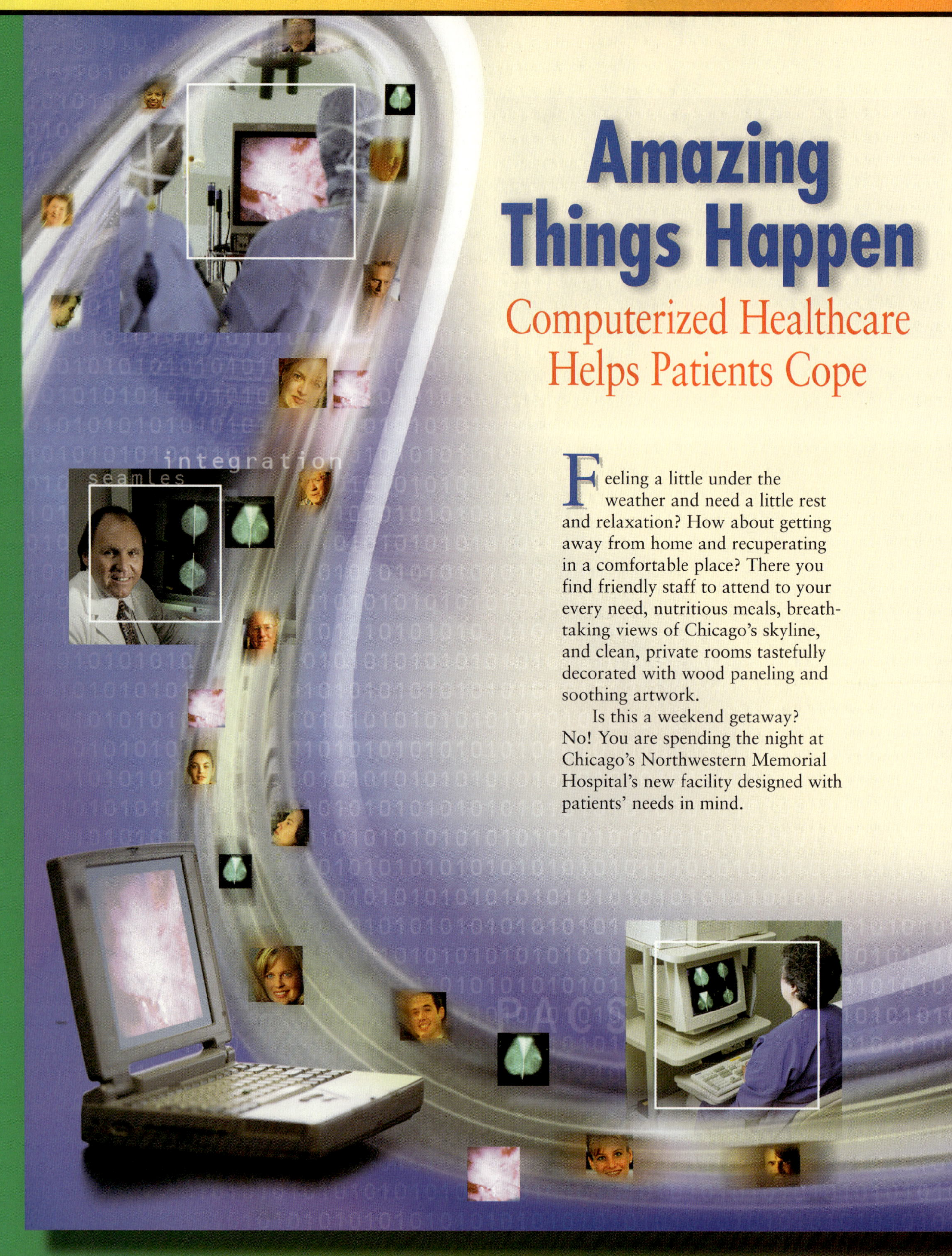

Amazing Things Happen

Computerized Healthcare Helps Patients Cope

Feeling a little under the weather and need a little rest and relaxation? How about getting away from home and recuperating in a comfortable place? There you find friendly staff to attend to your every need, nutritious meals, breathtaking views of Chicago's skyline, and clean, private rooms tastefully decorated with wood paneling and soothing artwork.

Is this a weekend getaway? No! You are spending the night at Chicago's Northwestern Memorial Hospital's new facility designed with patients' needs in mind.

The hospital's advertising slogan, Amazing Things Happen, certainly applies to the efforts of the 4,500 employees, 1,000 physicians, and 800 volunteers involved in planning the state-of-the-art building for more than a decade. The design team formed 125 user groups composed of staff, patients, and their families to develop an ideal patient encounter. They provided input on designing areas that facilitate communication and ergonomics and even staged a mock cardiac arrest to develop optimal working conditions.

The $580 million medical center opened in 1999 and contains the floor area of 44 football fields. Intertwined in this space are 600 miles of fiber-optic and high-speed copper cable that integrate computer functions. Patients are introduced to the innovative computerization techniques the minute they enter the medical center. Instead of registering at a central desk, they proceed directly to a nursing unit on a particular floor. Once the patients are settled in their beds, caregivers complete their registration forms by inputting personal data in notebook computers that are connected to the hospital's computer system through data connections in each private room.

Various medical personnel then can access this data. Doctors use notebook computers to retrieve the records as they make their rounds. Caregivers in the emergency room can retrieve laboratory reports seconds after the tests are complete, which enhances their ability to treat critical patients when seconds matter most. Billing department employees can generate comprehensive statements that detail specific procedures and charges. Students throughout the world can view the latest surgical procedures via teleconferences made possible by special cameras in each operating room.

Another aspect of computer integration throughout the hospital is the use of filmless X-rays. Instead of using the traditional method of exposing and then developing celluloid film, radiology technicians now use the picture archiving and communication system (PACS) to take a digital image. Each of the thousands of X-rays taken monthly is stored on an optical storage system, which eliminates the need to save physical hard copy film in a special room. Caregivers can retrieve these radiology images from workstations throughout the hospital, including intensive care units and the emergency room. When necessary, these files can be transmitted to other medical facilities throughout the world via the Internet.

In this Integration Feature, you will develop a Web site for Global Computers and use Microsoft Word, Excel, PowerPoint, Access, and Internet Explorer to help this business compete in a technologically skilled field. Likewise, Northwestern Memorial Hospital integrates its computer applications to maximize patients' convenience and to minimize costs. Overall, with this seamless integration, amazing things happen.

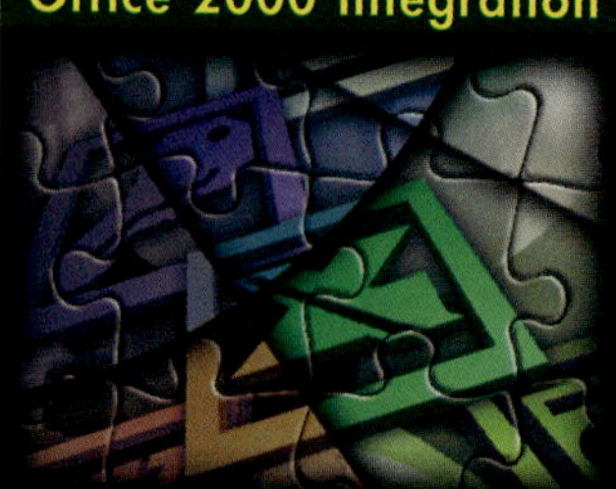

Integrating Office 2000 Applications and the World Wide Web

CASE PERSPECTIVE

Global Computers is a local computer store Dan Salvatori opened two years ago. Initially, business was good because Global Computers was the only company in the area that sold computer equipment. Recently, several new stores have opened, cutting into Global Computers' business.

Dan thinks that his business would increase if he implements a marketing strategy that advertises the advantages his store has over his competitors' stores. Global Computers offers the lowest hardware and software prices in town. In addition, Dan employs a highly trained sales and technical support staff. He is looking at ways to advertise these benefits in an efficient and cost-effective way. He thinks a Web site would be the answer, but he is inexperienced with the Internet. Dan knows that you are studying computer technology and asks you to help him create a Web site advertising Global Computers.

Introduction

From your meeting with Dan Salvatori, you were given four files of information to use to create the Web site for Global Computers.

1. A Word document that contains the company logo and company name (Figure 1-1a on page I 1.6).
2. An Excel workbook with a 3-D Pie chart graphically illustrating the company's breakdown by product (Figure 1-1b on page I 1.6).
3. A PowerPoint slideshow that contains general company information (Figure 1-1g on page I 1.7).
4. An Access database that contains product information (Figure 1-1c on page I 1.6).

The Global Computers Web site should include the following:

1. A home page with a 3-D Pie chart that contains sales information per product line (Figure 1-1e on page I 1.7). Three hypertext links also are included on the home page: About Us, Products, and E-Mail Comments.
2. The Products data access Web page (Figure 1-1d on page I 1.6) is created from the Access file. Clicking the Products link on the home page accesses this Web page. On this Web page, visitors can scroll through the products, categorized by product line.
3. The PowerPoint Web page (Figure 1-1g on page I 1.7) displays information about the company. Clicking the About Us link on the home page accesses this Web page.
4. Using the E-Mail Comments hyperlink, you can create an Outlook e-mail message (Figure 1-1f on page I 1.7). E-mail is sent to the e-mail address global@isp.com.

Integration Project — Global Computers Web Site

Many businesses today advertise their products on the Internet, as described in the Case Perspective. Companies find it easy to create Web pages using information already saved in spreadsheet, database, or presentation software formats. The Web page creation capabilities of Office 2000 make it simple for you to create an entire Web site using the information available. In Word, a document can be created and saved as a Web page. PowerPoint provides the same capability and adds a navigation structure for browsing. In addition, Access provides a Wizard to create data access pages that enables the Web page visitor to scroll through the database.

The following pages contain a detailed explanation of these tasks.

Web Pages

Making information available on the Internet is a key aspect of business today. To facilitate this trend, the Office 2000 applications allow you to generate Web pages easily from existing files. An entire Web site can be created with files from Word, Excel, PowerPoint, or Access, using the Save As Web Page feature.

Adding Hyperlinks to a Word Document

The Web site created for Global Computers consists of an initial Web page, called the **home page**, with two hyperlinks to other Web pages, an e-mail link, and a 3-D Pie chart. A **hyperlink** is a hot spot that allows you to jump to another location. Text is used (About Us, Products, E-mail Comments) for the three hyperlinks on the Global Computers home page (Figure 1-1e). The first hyperlink (About Us) jumps to a PowerPoint Web page that contains staff and general product information about the company. A second hyperlink (Products) jumps to a data access page that contains inquiry capabilities to the Global Computers' product database. This Web page is for inquiring only; updating the database is prohibited. The third hyperlink (E-mail Comments) creates an e-mail message. In order to organize the three hyperlinks to the left of the Pie chart, a table will be created in the Word document.

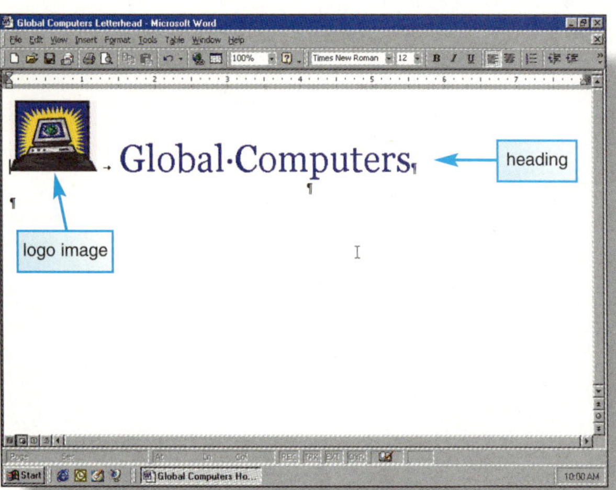

(a) Word Document

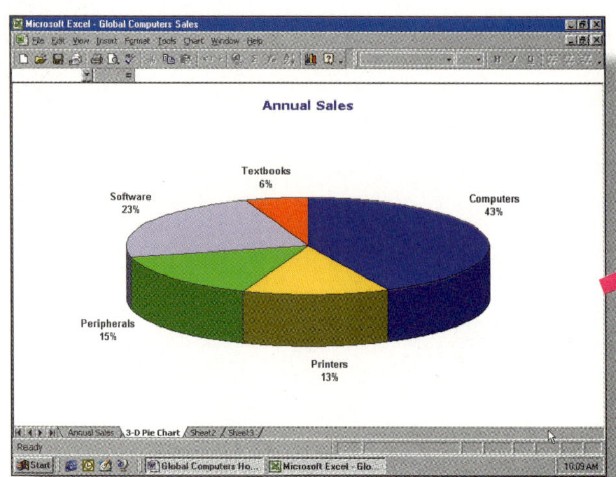

(b) 3-D Pie Chart

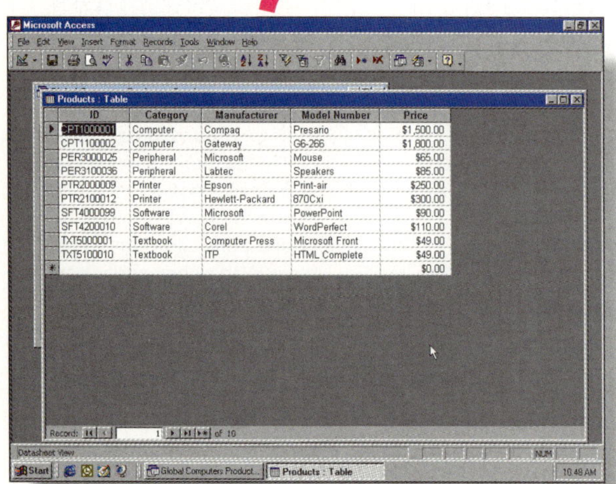

ID	Category	Manufacturer	Model Number	Price
CPT1000001	Computer	Compaq	Presario	$1,500.00
CPT1100002	Computer	Gateway	G6-266	$1,800.00
PER3000025	Peripheral	Microsoft	Mouse	$65.00
PER3100036	Peripheral	Labtec	Speakers	$85.00
PTR2000009	Printer	Epson	Print-air	$250.00
PTR2100012	Printer	Hewlett-Packard	870Cxi	$300.00
SFT4000099	Software	Microsoft	PowerPoint	$90.00
SFT4200010	Software	Corel	WordPerfect	$110.00
TXT5000001	Textbook	Computer Press	Microsoft Front	$49.00
TXT5100010	Textbook	ITP	HTML Complete	$49.00
				$0.00

(c) Access Table Used to Create Data Access Page

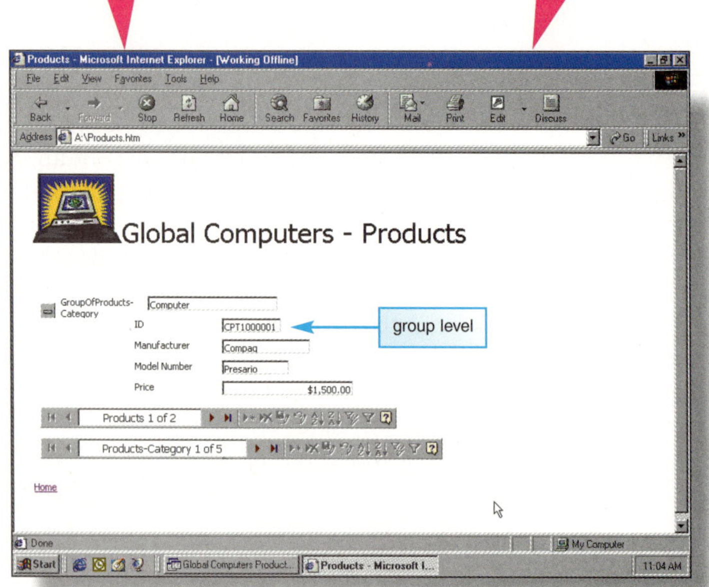

(d) Data Access Page

FIGURE 1-1

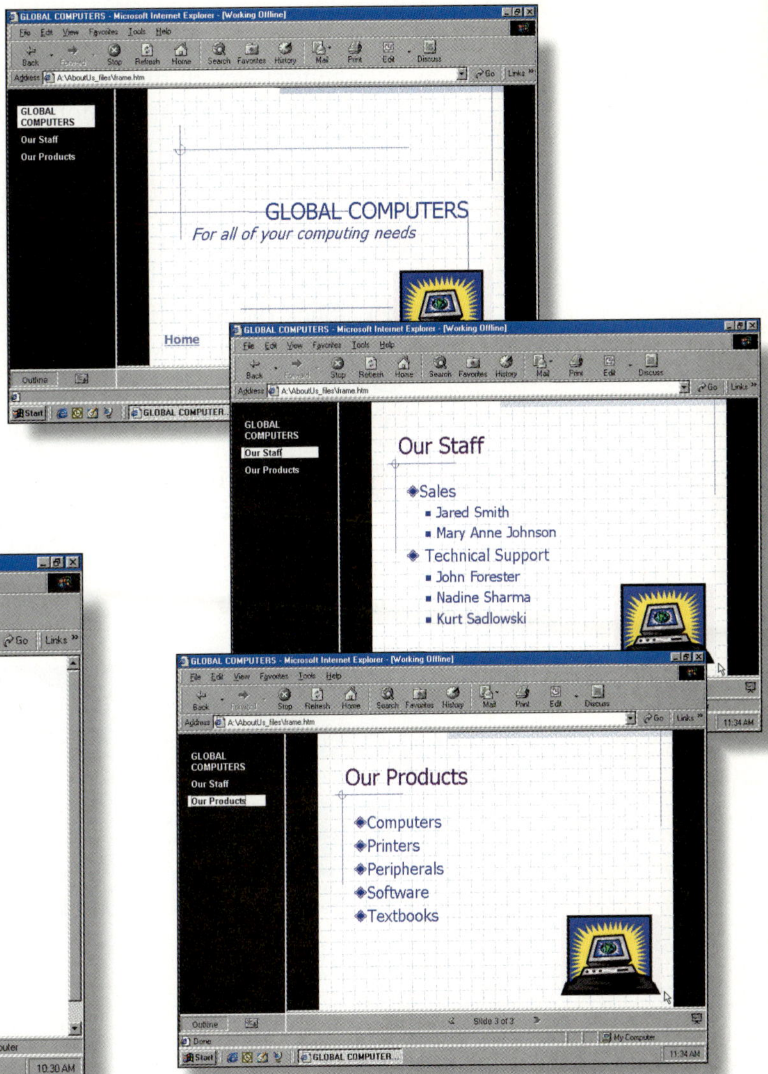

GLOBAL COMPUTERS
Our Staff
Our Products
GLOBAL COMPUTERS
For all of your computing needs
Home

GLOBAL COMPUTERS
Our Staff
Our Products
Our Staff
Sales
Jared Smith
Mary Anne Johnson
Technical Support
John Forester
Nadine Sharma
Kurt Sadlowski

GLOBAL COMPUTERS
Our Staff
Our Products
Our Products
Computers
Printers
Peripherals
Software
Textbooks

Global Computers
33 Ackmar, Sarasota, FL 34236 (941) 555-1242
About Us
Products
E-mail Comments
Annual Sales
Textbooks 6%
Software 23%
Computers 43%
Peripherals 15%
Printers 13%

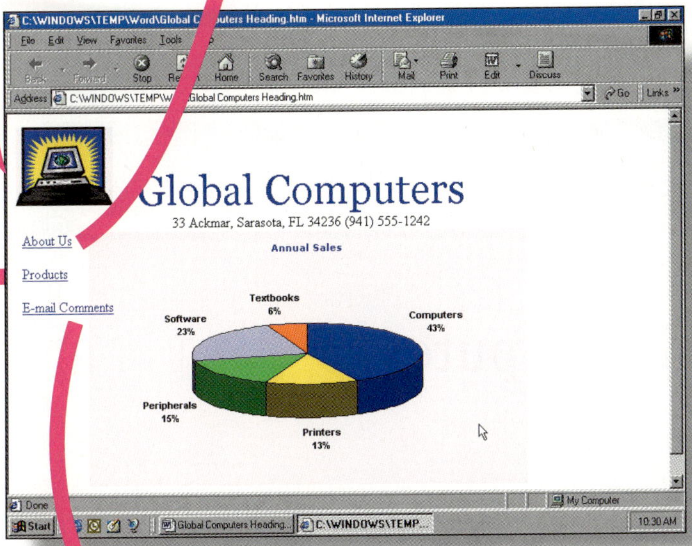

(e) Word Document Saved As a Web Page

(g) PowerPoint Presentation Saved As Web Pages

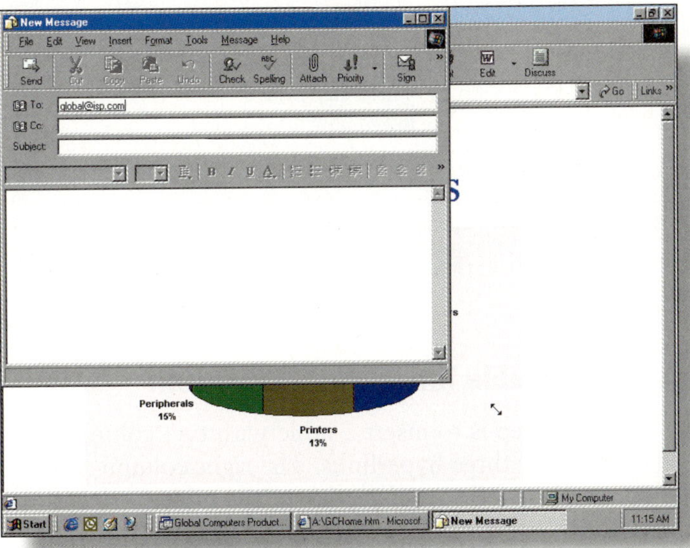

(f) New E-mail Message Created from Hyperlink

The first step in this project is to open the Word document Global Computers Letterhead and save it as Global Computers Home Page.

TO START WORD AND OPEN AN EXISTING DOCUMENT

1. Insert the Integration Data Disk in drive A. If you do not have the Integration Data Disk, see the inside back cover of this book.
2. Click the Start button on the taskbar. Click Open Office Document.
3. Click the Look in box arrow and then click 3½ Floppy (A:).
4. Double-click Global Computers Letterhead.
5. Click File on the menu bar and then click Save As. Type `Global Computers Home Page` in the File name text box and then click the Save button in the Save As dialog box.

The document is saved as Global Computers Home Page (Figure 1-2).

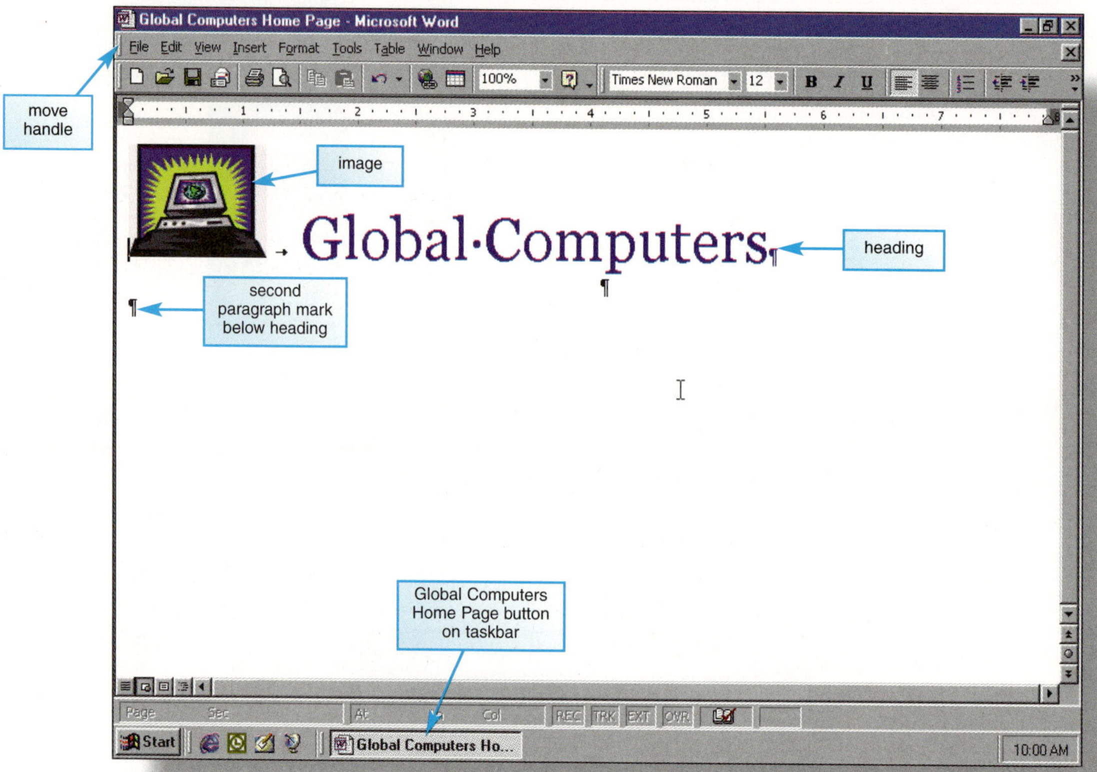

FIGURE 1-2

Tables

You can use tables to create page layouts, such as side-by-side paragraphs, or to create text, graphics, and nested tables on a Web page. Tables are used frequently on the World Wide Web to structure information and images.

Inserting a Table into a Word Document

The next step is to insert a table with two columns and one row. The left column will contain the three hyperlinks. The right column will contain the 3-D Pie chart.

Perform the following steps to add a table to the Global Computers Home Page document.

Steps To Insert a Table into a Word Document

1 Double-click the move handle on the Standard toolbar to display it in its entirety. Position the insertion point on the second paragraph mark after the header Global Computers. Click Table on the menu bar, point to Insert, and then click Table.

The Insert Table dialog box displays (Figure 1-3).

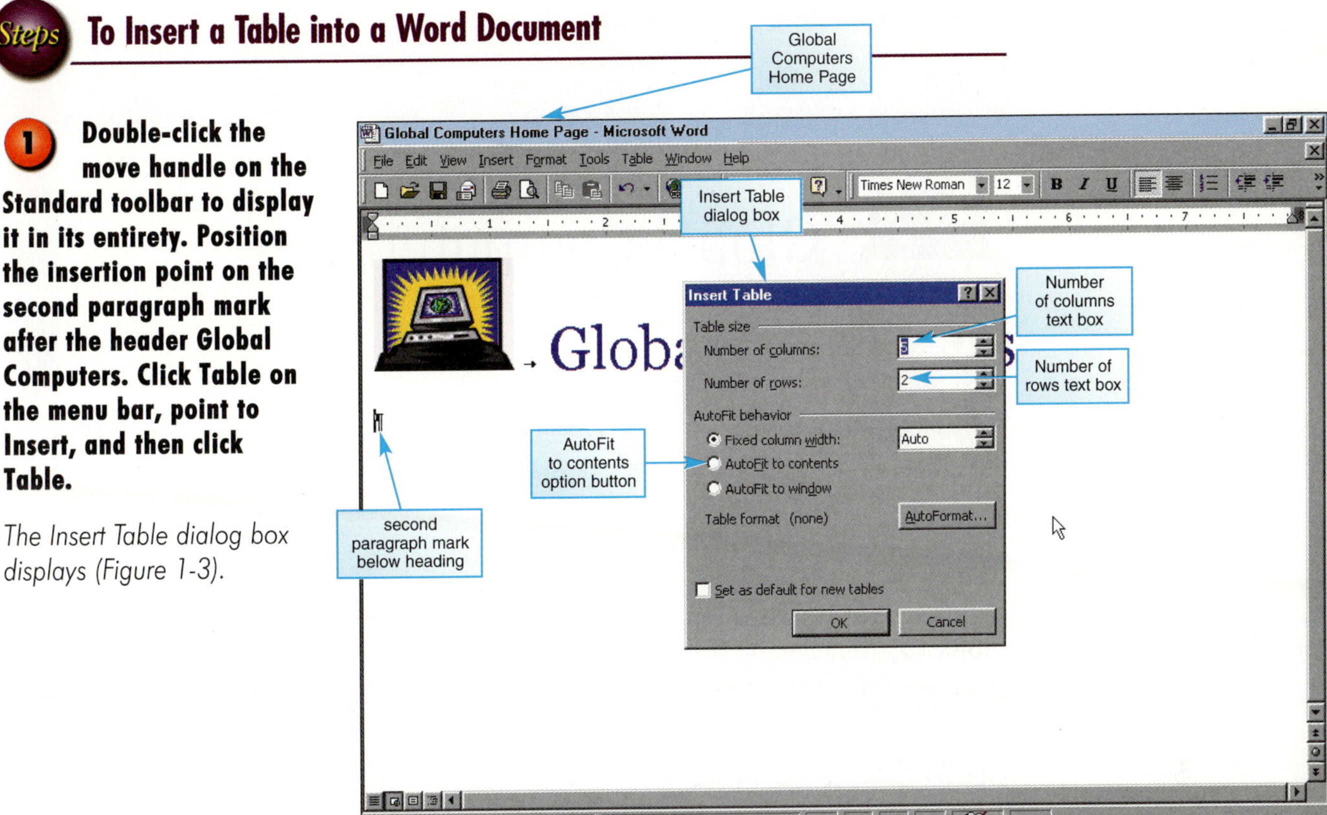

FIGURE 1-3

2 Type 2 in the Number of columns text box and then press the TAB key. Type 1 in the Number of rows text box and then click AutoFit to contents in the AutoFit behavior area. Point to the OK button.

The new settings display in the Insert Table dialog box (Figure 1-4).

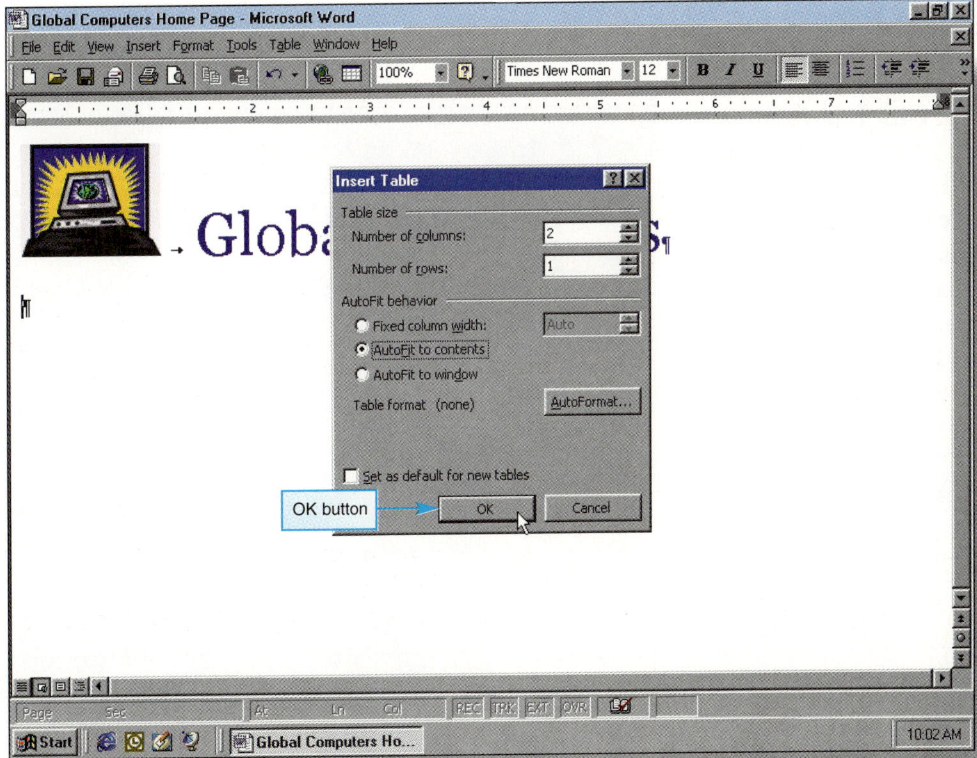

FIGURE 1-4

Click the OK button.

The table displays in the Word document (Figure 1-5).

FIGURE 1-5

1. Click Insert Table button on Standard toolbar, drag through one row and two columns, click mouse button

Step 2 instructed you to select AutoFit to contents. The **AutoFit to contents** option allows you to make the columns in a table automatically fit the contents. If you do not select AutoFit to contents, you can adjust the column widths manually using the sizing handles.

Eliminating the Table Border

The two-column, one-row table has been inserted into the Word document. The table border is not necessary for the Web page. The next steps instruct you how to remove the border of the table.

To Remove the Table Border

1. Click Table on the menu bar and then click Table Properties. Click the Borders and Shading button in the Table sheet. If necessary, click the Borders tab. Point to the None button in the Setting area of the Borders sheet.

The Borders and Shading dialog box displays (Figure 1-6).

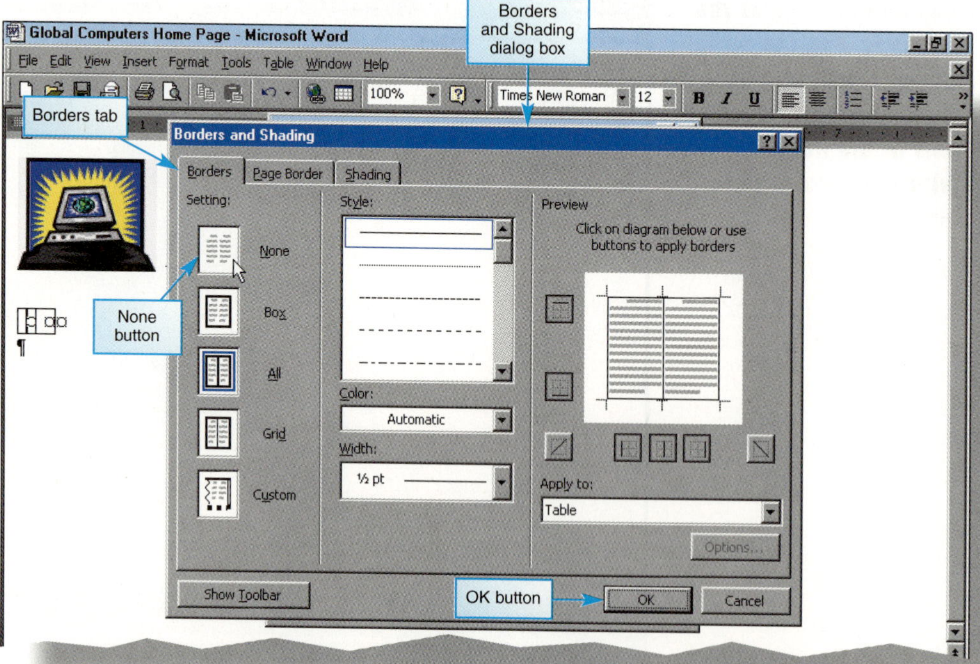

FIGURE 1-6

2 **Click None in the Setting area and then click the OK button in the Borders and Shading dialog box. Click the OK button in the Table Properties dialog box.**

The borderless table displays (Figure 1-7).

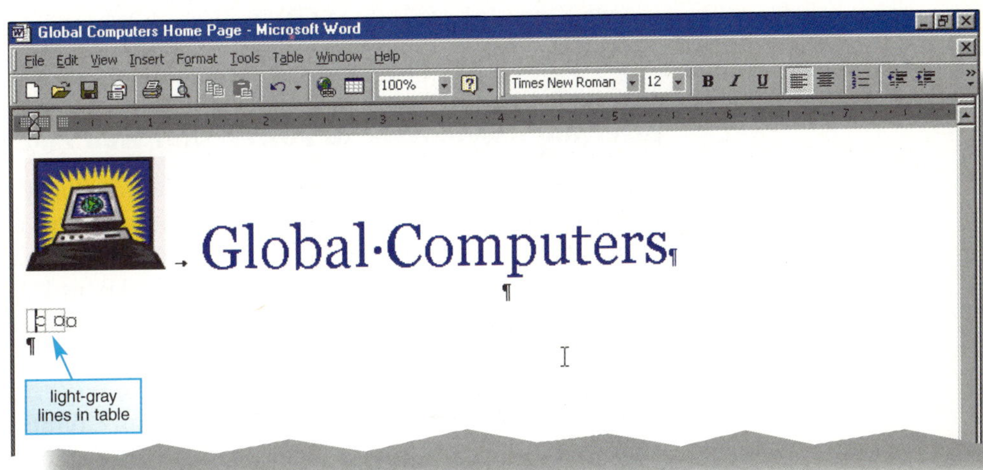

FIGURE 1-7

The border of the table still displays as light-gray lines in the Word document. This can be used as a guide when entering text or images. When the document is viewed in your browser or printed, the table border does not display or print.

Inserting the Text for the Hyperlinks

After creating the borderless table, you must insert the three text phrases that will be used as hyperlinks on the home page. These phrases (About Us, Products, and E-Mail Comments) allow you to jump to two other Web pages and create an e-mail message. Perform the steps below to add the text phrases that are used as hyperlinks.

More About 2000

Hyperlinks

In addition to the way in which the hyperlinks are created in this project, you can copy and paste text as a hyperlink. Copy the text you want to the Clipboard, click where you want to insert the text, and then click Paste as Hyperlink on the Edit menu.

To Insert Text for Hyperlinks

1 **If necessary, click the leftmost cell in the table.**

2 **Type** `About Us` **and then press the ENTER key twice. Type** `Products` **and then press the ENTER key twice. Type** `E-Mail Comments` **as the final text phrase.**

The table displays with the three text phrases that will be used as hyperlinks (Figure 1-8).

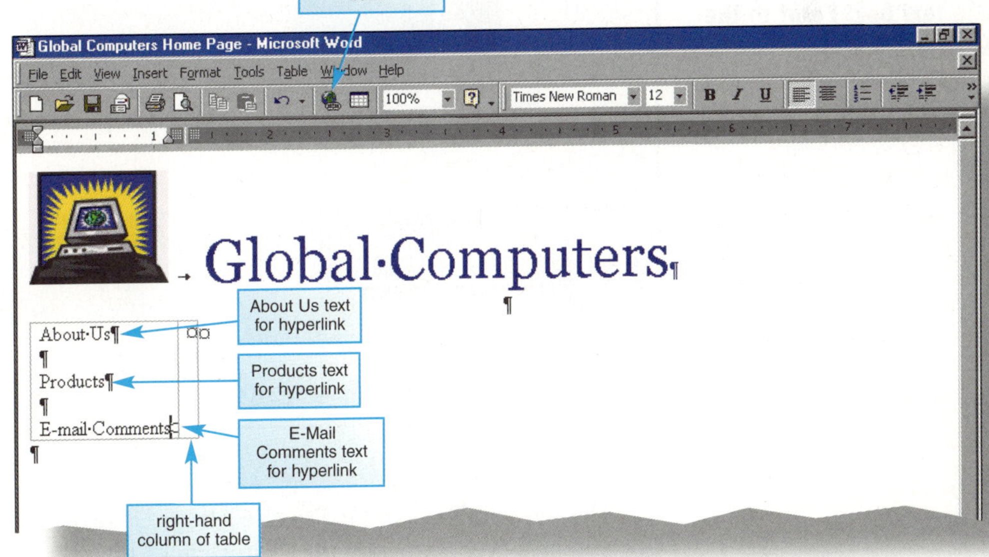

FIGURE 1-8

With the text phrases added, the next step is to select each text phrase and then insert the corresponding hyperlink.

Inserting a Hyperlink to PowerPoint Web Pages

The **Insert Hyperlink feature** provides the capability of linking to an existing file or Web page, to a place within the current document, to a newly created document, or to an e-mail address. In this project, two text phrases (About Us and Products) will be created that hyperlink to Web pages. The About Us hyperlink will jump to a PowerPoint presentation that is saved as a Web page using the Web page name About Us.htm. The Products hyperlink will jump to a data access page using the Web page name Products.htm. You will create the data access page later from an existing Access database. The third text phrase (E-Mail Comments) links to an e-mail address.

Perform the following steps to create a hyperlink for the first text phrase.

To Insert a Hyperlink to PowerPoint Web Pages

1 **Drag through the text, About Us, in the table. Click the Insert Hyperlink button on the Standard toolbar.**

2 **If necessary, click the Existing File or Web Page button on the Link to bar. Type** `a:\AboutUs.htm` **in the Type the file or Web page name text box. Point to the OK button.**

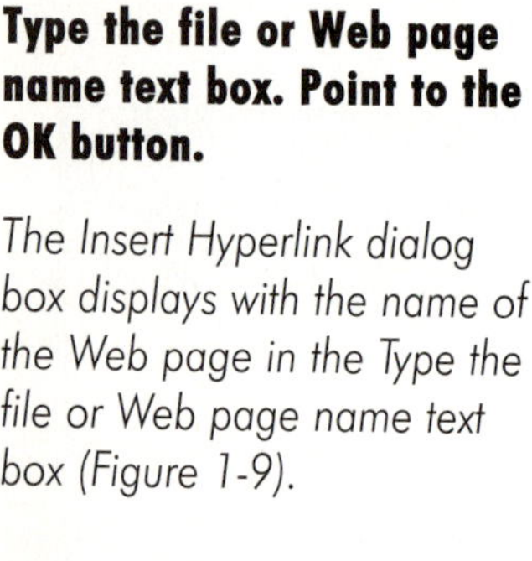

The Insert Hyperlink dialog box displays with the name of the Web page in the Type the file or Web page name text box (Figure 1-9).

FIGURE 1-9

3 **Click the OK button.**

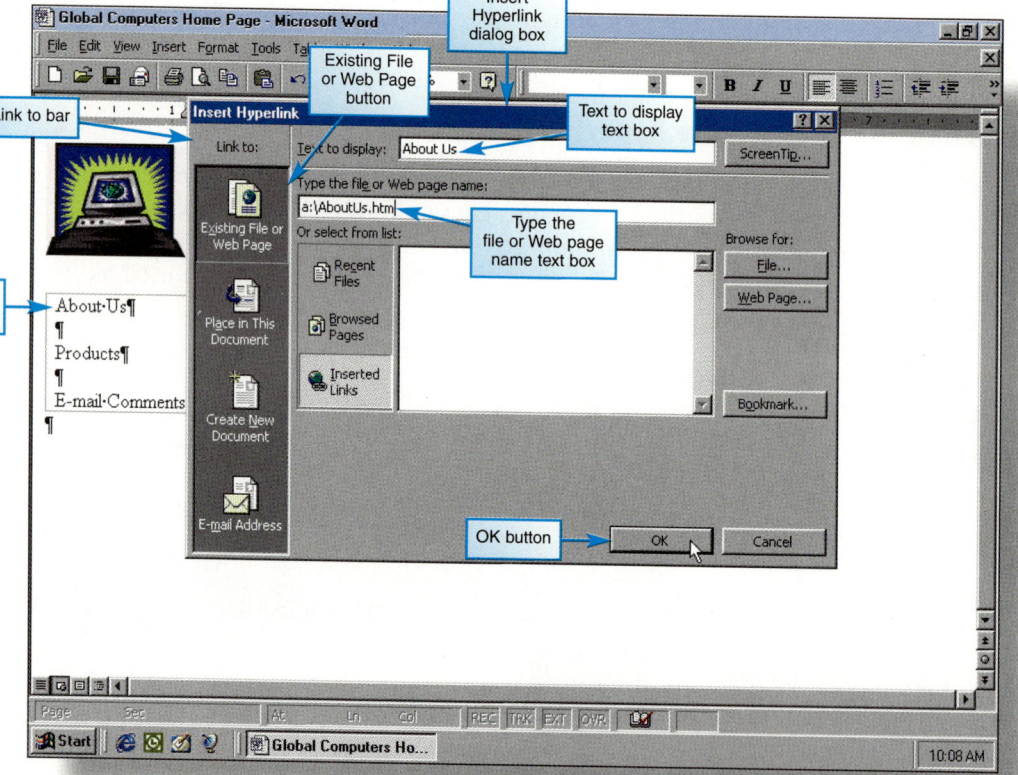

Other Ways

1. On Insert menu click Hyperlink
2. Right-click selected words, About Us, click Hyperlink on shortcut menu
3. Press CTRL+K

The hyperlink is assigned to the About Us text phrase. Once the Word document is saved as a Web page and the visitor clicks the text, About Us, the AboutUs.htm file on drive A displays. Perform the following steps to add the next two hyperlinks.

TO INSERT THE REMAINING HYPERLINKS

1. Double-click the word, Products. Click the Insert Hyperlink button on the Standard toolbar.
2. Type `a:\Products.htm` in the Type the file or Web page name text box and then click the OK button.
3. Drag through the text, E-Mail Comments. Click the Insert Hyperlink button on the Standard toolbar and then click E-Mail Address on the Link to bar.
4. Type `global@isp.com` in the E-Mail address text box and then click the OK button.

The table displays (Figure 1-10).

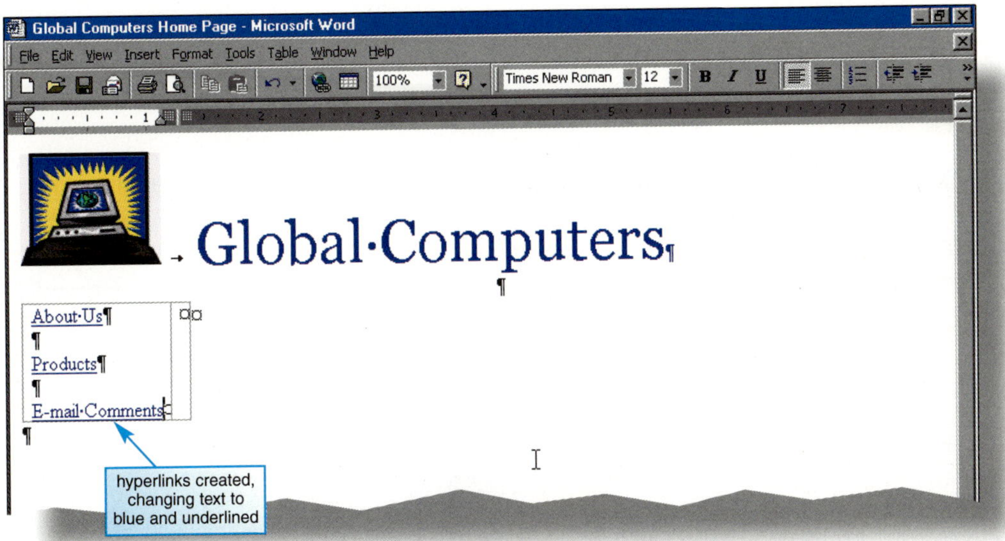

FIGURE 1-10

The three hyperlinks are created. When you click the e-mail hyperlink, it will create an e-mail message to global@isp.com. The other two hyperlinks (About Us and Products) will not work until the corresponding Web pages are created later in this project.

Embedding an Excel Chart into a Word Document

This project uses the **Object Linking and Embedding (OLE)** feature of Microsoft Office 2000 to insert the Excel chart into a Word document. OLE allows you to incorporate parts of a document or entire documents from one application into another.

The 3-D Pie chart in Excel is called a **source object** (Figure 1-1b on page I 1.6) and the Global Computers Home Page document is the **destination document**. Once an object is embedded, it becomes part of the destination document. This project illustrates using the **Paste Special command** on the Edit menu to embed the Excel object. The Paste Special command inserts an object into Word, but still recognizes the **source program**, the program in which the object was created. When you double-click an embedded object, such as the Annual Sales worksheet, the source program opens and allows you to make changes. In this example, Excel is the source program. With the hyperlinks added to the Word document, the next step is to embed the 3-D Pie chart.

More About 2000

Embedded Objects

The advantage of using an integrated set of applications, such as Microsoft Office 2000, is the ability to share information between applications. The Object Linking and Embedding (OLE) features of Office 2000 makes the integration process more efficient. A chart created in Excel can be included in a Word document using OLE. To edit the embedded object, double-click it. The source program then starts and opens the source object for editing.

TO OPEN AN EXCEL WORKBOOK

1. Insert the Integration Data Disk in drive A. If you do not have the Integration Data Disk, see the inside back cover of this book.
2. Click the Start button on the taskbar and then click Open Office Document.
3. Click the Look in box arrow and then click 3½ Floppy (A:).
4. Double-click the Global Computers Sales workbook.

The next two sections explain how to embed an Excel chart into a Word document and resize it. The first section explains embedding a chart into a Word document. Perform the following steps to embed the Excel 3-D Pie chart into the Word document.

To Embed an Excel Chart into a Word Document

1. **Double-click the move handle on the Standard toolbar to display it in its entirety. If necessary, click the 3-D Pie chart tab.**

The 3-D Pie chart is active and displays (Figure 1-11).

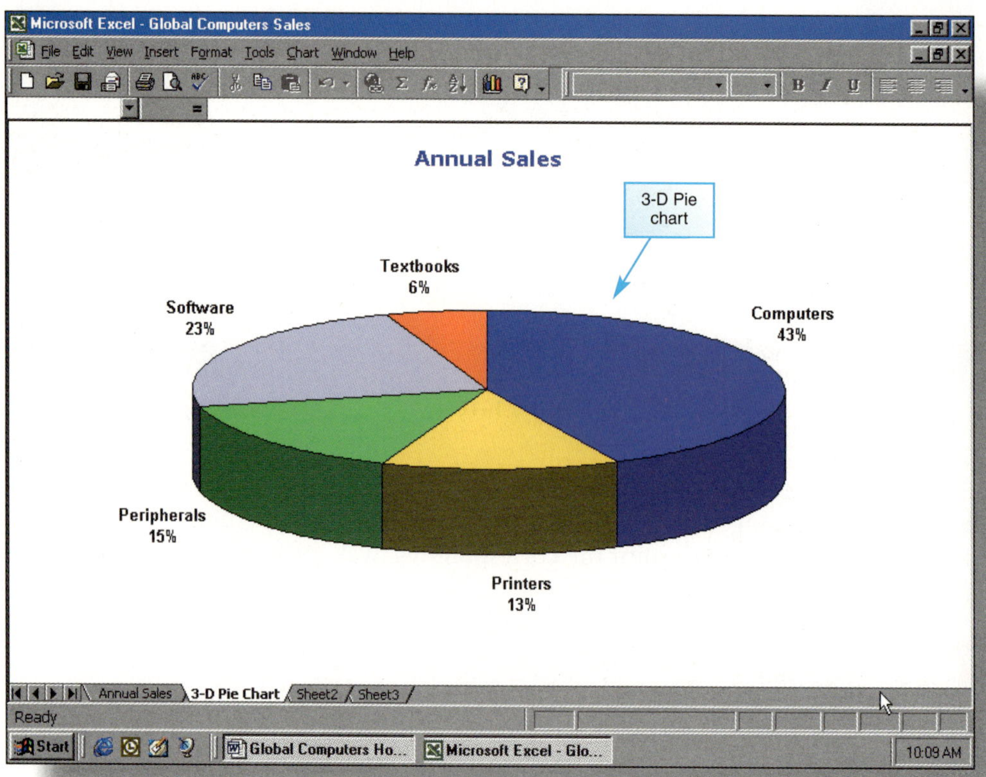

FIGURE 1-11

2 Click the Chart Area to select the chart and then click the Copy button on the Standard toolbar.

Excel places a copy of the 3-D Pie chart on the Office Clipboard. A scrolling marquee displays around the Chart Area (Figure 1-12).

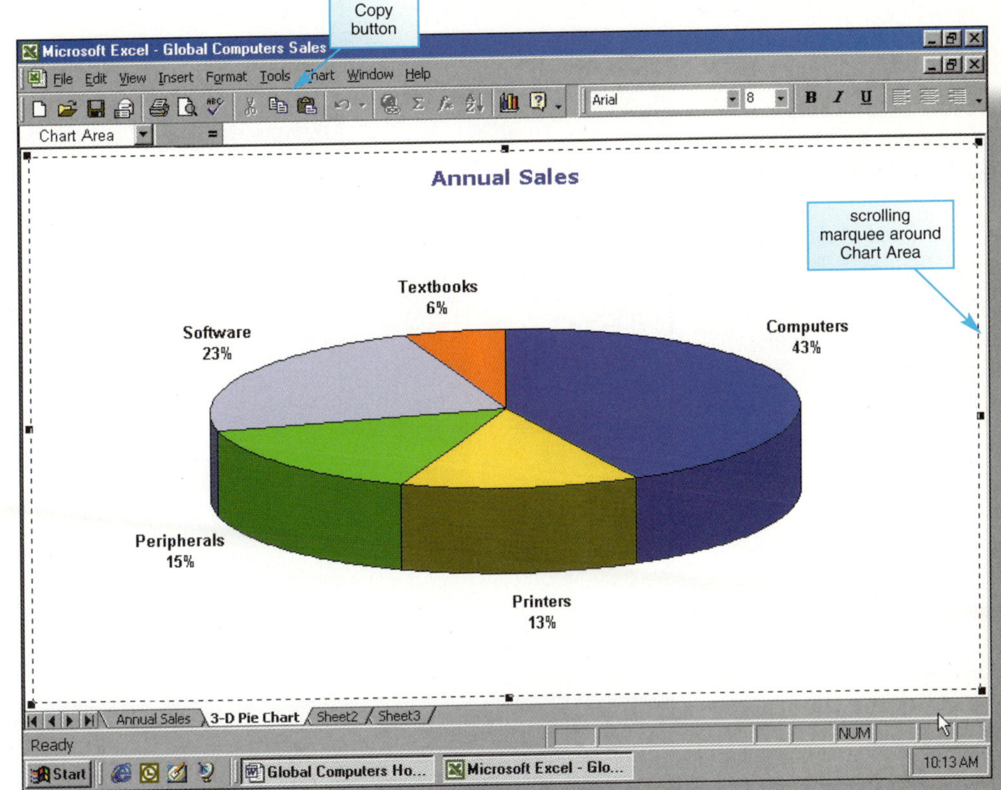

FIGURE 1-12

3 Click the Global Computers Home Page button on the taskbar. If necessary, click the right-hand column of the table.

4 Click Edit on the menu bar and then point to Paste Special.

The Edit menu displays and the Paste Special command is highlighted (Figure 1-13).

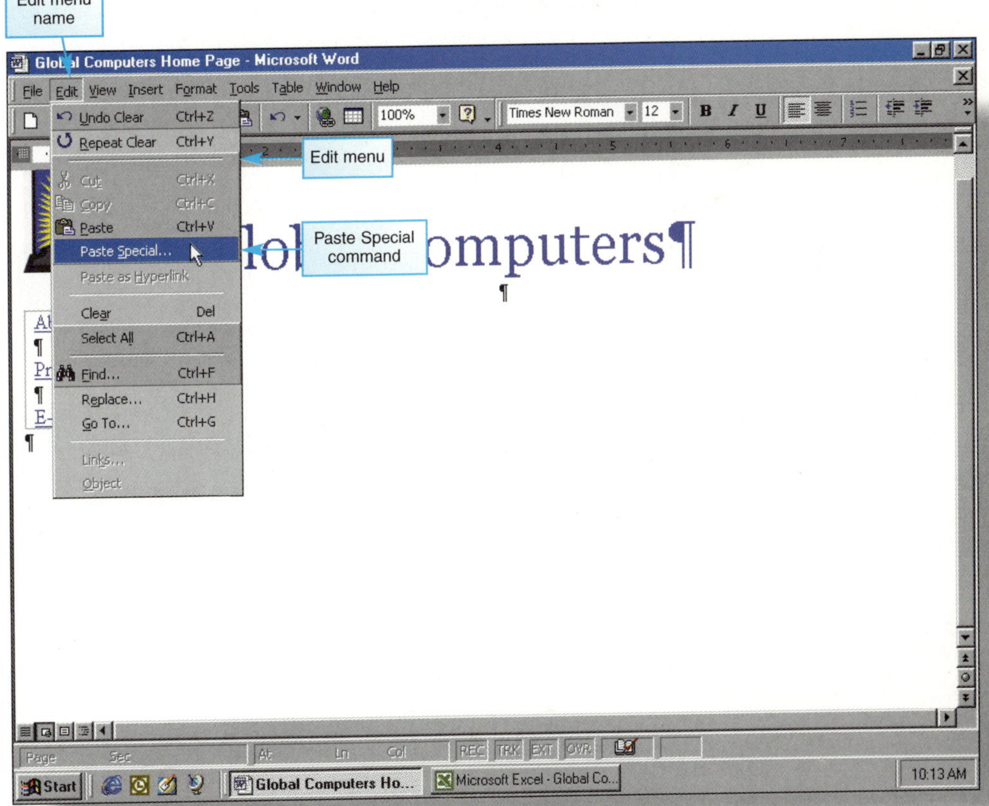

FIGURE 1-13

5 Click Paste Special. If necessary, click Microsoft Excel Chart Object in the As list box. Point to the OK button.

The Paste Special dialog box displays (Figure 1-14). The Paste option button is selected. Microsoft Excel Chart Object displays in the As list box.

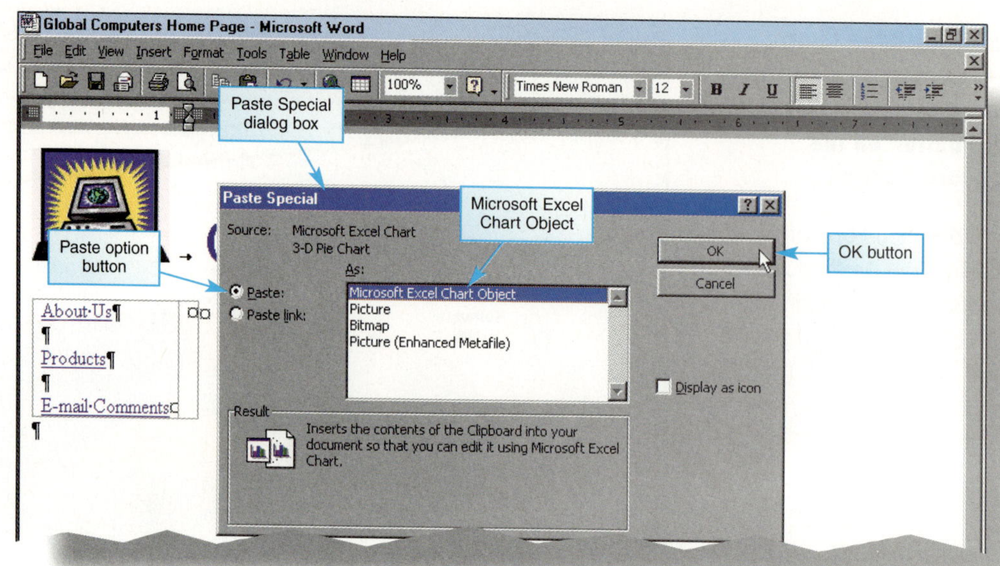

FIGURE 1-14

6 Click the OK button.

Word embeds the 3-D Pie chart into the document (Figure 1-15).

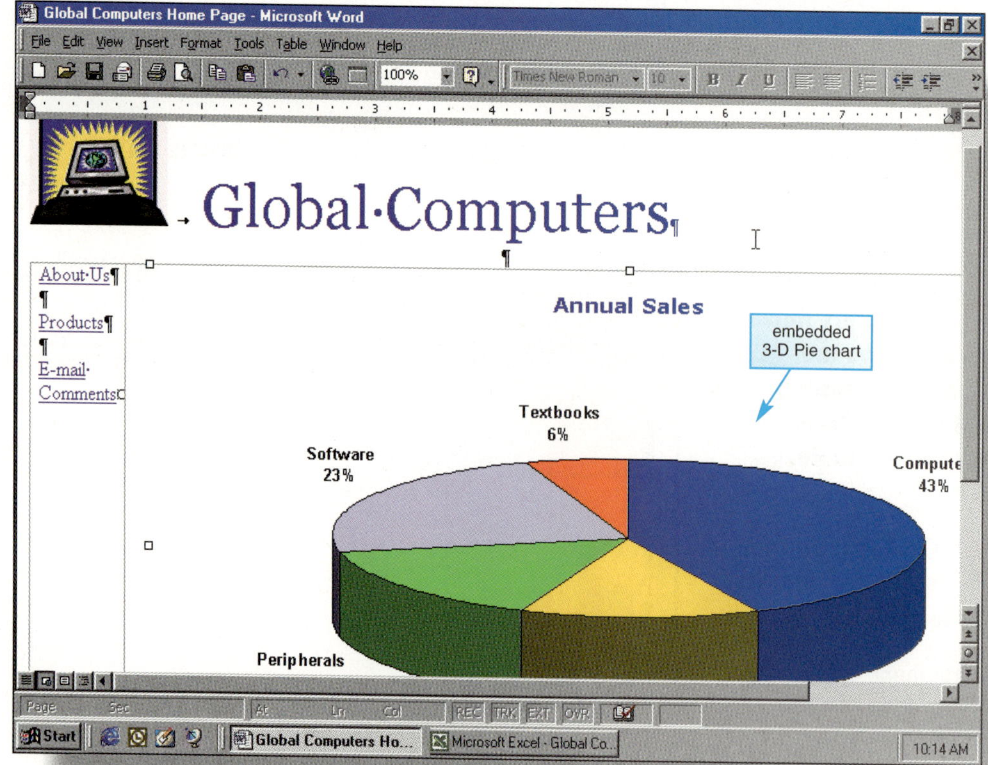

FIGURE 1-15

Other Ways

1. On Edit menu click Copy
2. Press CTRL+C

Changing the Size of an Embedded Object

The embedded Pie chart exceeds the margins of the Global Computers document. Reducing the size of the 3-D Pie chart will improve the layout of the document. In this project, you will use the Format Object dialog box to change the size of the chart.

All Microsoft Office applications allow you to use three methods to copy objects between applications: (1) copy and paste; (2) copy and embed; and (3) copy and link. The first method uses the Copy and Paste buttons. The latter two use the Paste Special command. Table 1-1 summarizes the differences among the three methods.

Perform the following steps to reduce the size of the chart using the Object command on the Format menu.

Table 1-1 Copy Methods

METHOD	CHARACTERISTICS
Copy and paste	The source document becomes part of the destination document. An object may be edited, but the editing features are limited to those of the destination application. An Excel worksheet becomes a Word table. If changes are made to values in the Word table, any original Excel formulas are not recalculated.
Copy and embed	The source document becomes part of the destination document. An object may be edited in the destination document using source editing features. The Excel worksheet remains a worksheet in Word. If changes are made to values in the worksheet with Word active, Excel formulas will be recalculated. If, however, you change the worksheet in Excel, without the document open in Word, these changes will not display in the Word document the next time you open it.
Copy and link	The source document does not become part of the destination document, even though it appears to be a part. Instead, a link is established between the two documents, so that when you open the Word document, the worksheet displays within the document, as though it were a part of it. When you attempt to edit a linked worksheet in Word, the system activates Excel. If you change the worksheet in Excel, the changes also will display in the Word document the next time you open it.

To Change the Size of an Embedded Object

1 If necessary, click the 3-D Pie chart to select it. Click Format on the menu bar and then point to Object.

The 3-D Pie chart is selected as indicated by sizing handles on the selection rectangle. The Format menu displays and the Object command is highlighted (Figure 1-16).

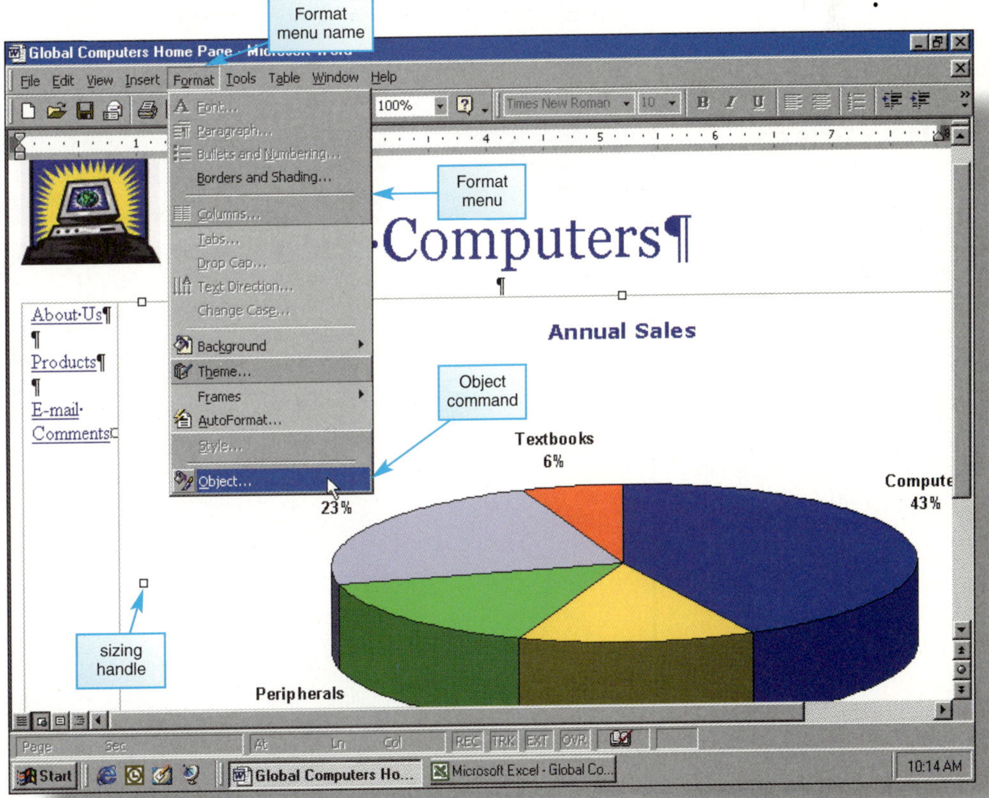

FIGURE 1-16

2 **Click Object. If necessary, click the Size tab.**

The Format Object dialog box and Size sheet display (Figure 1-17).

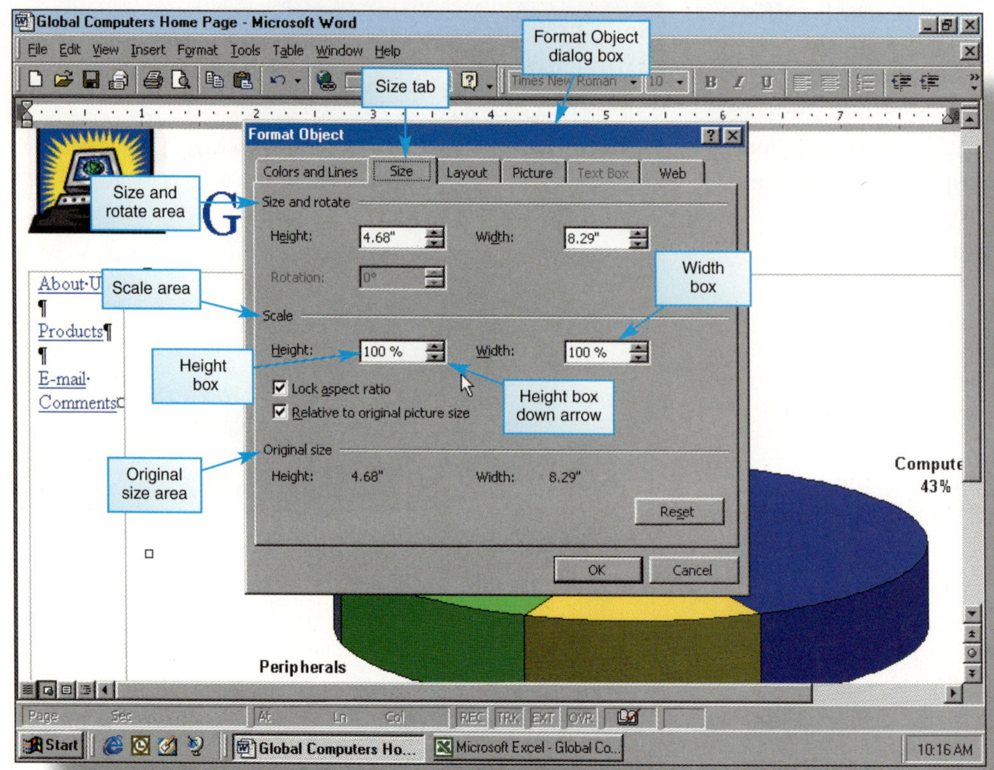

FIGURE 1-17

3 **In the Scale area, click the Height box down arrow until 65% displays. Point to the OK button.**

The Height box and the Width box both display 65% (Figure 1-18). When you change the percentage in the Height box, the percentage in the Width box also changes.

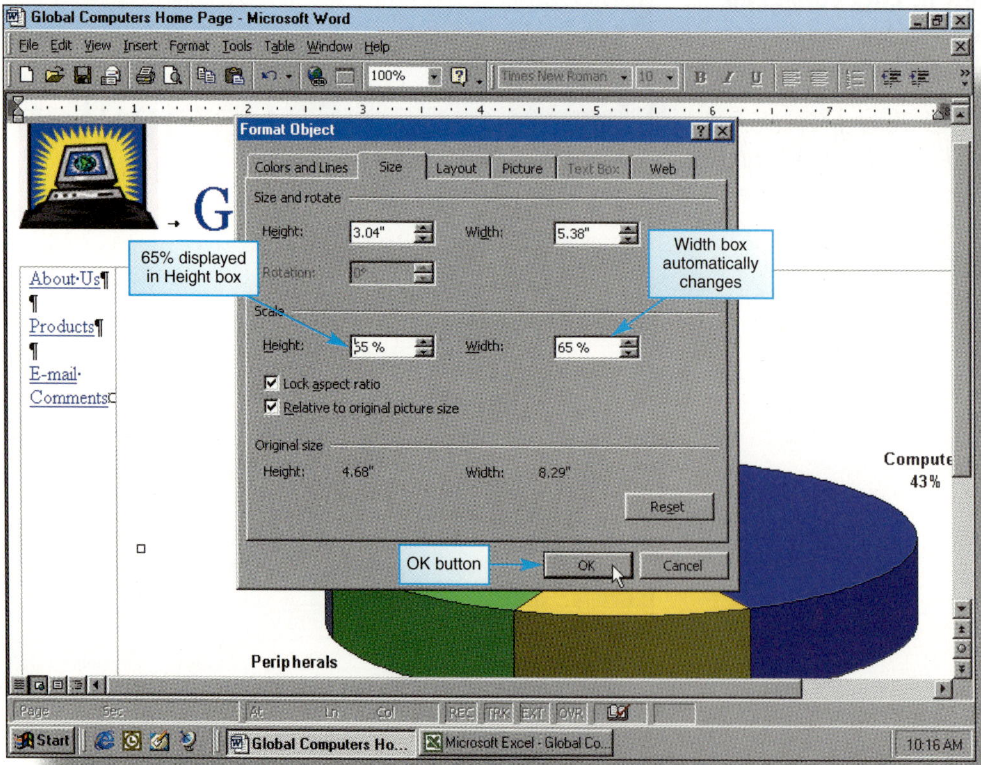

FIGURE 1-18

4 Click the OK button. If necessary, scroll to see the embedded chart.

Word reduces the size of the chart to 65% of its original size (Figure 1-19).

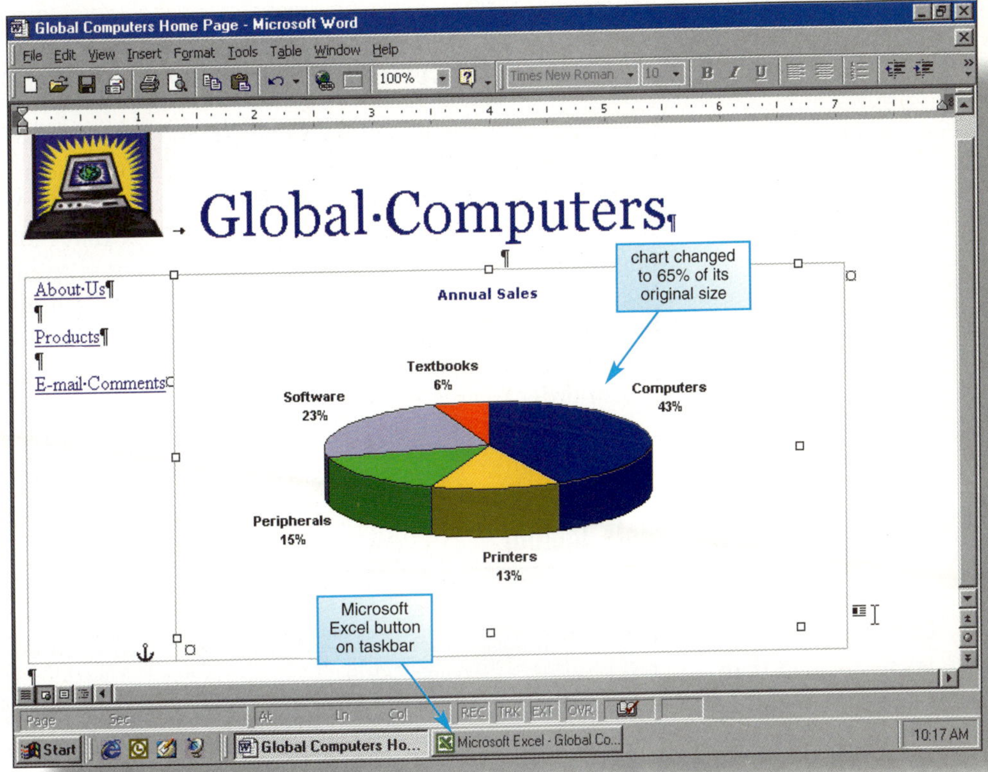

FIGURE 1-19

Other Ways

1. Right-click 3-D Pie chart, click Format Object on shortcut menu

The Format Object dialog box contains two areas with which to change the size of an object. The **Size and rotate area** allows you to increase or decrease the height or width of an object in inches. When available, it also allows you to rotate the object in degrees around an axis. The **Scale area** allows you to change the size of an object by a specific percentage while maintaining the height-to-width ratio. The height-to-width ratio is called **aspect ratio**. The **Original size area** at the bottom of the Format Object dialog box displays the original height and width of the selected object.

More About 2000

Resizing

To resize an image proportionally from a corner, you can press and hold the SHIFT key and drag a corner sizing handle. To resize vertically, horizontally, or diagonally from the center outward, press and hold CTRL and drag a sizing handle. To resize proportionally from the center outward, press and hold CTRL+SHIFT and drag a corner sizing handle.

Quitting Excel

With the 3-D Pie chart embedded in the Word document, you no longer need the Global Computers Sales workbook open. Perform the following steps to quit Excel.

TO QUIT EXCEL

1. Right-click the Microsoft Excel - Global Computers Sales button on the taskbar. Click Close on the shortcut menu. If prompted to save changes, click the No button.
2. If the Microsoft Excel dialog box displays regarding saving the large amount of information on the Clipboard, click the No button.

Adding Scrolling Text to a Word Document

The Word document is almost ready to be saved as a Web page. The final item that needs to be added is something that will capture the attention of your Web page visitor. One of the attention grabbing techniques that Web developers use is scrolling marquees. A **scrolling marquee** is a line of text that moves from one side of the Web page to the other. Generally, scrolling text is used to highlight information about the Web site. With Word 2000, you can create scrolling text using the **Scrolling Text button** on the Web Tools toolbar. A scrolling marquee will be created just below the Global Computers header.

In order to create scrolling text, the Web Tools toolbar must display. Perform the following steps to display the Web Tools toolbar.

To Display the Web Tools Toolbar

1. **Click View on the menu bar and then point to Toolbars. Point to Web Tools on the Toolbars submenu.**

2. **Click Web Tools. If necessary, drag the Web Tools toolbar to the center, right side of the window using the Web Tools toolbar title bar.**

The Web Tools toolbar displays (Figure 1-20).

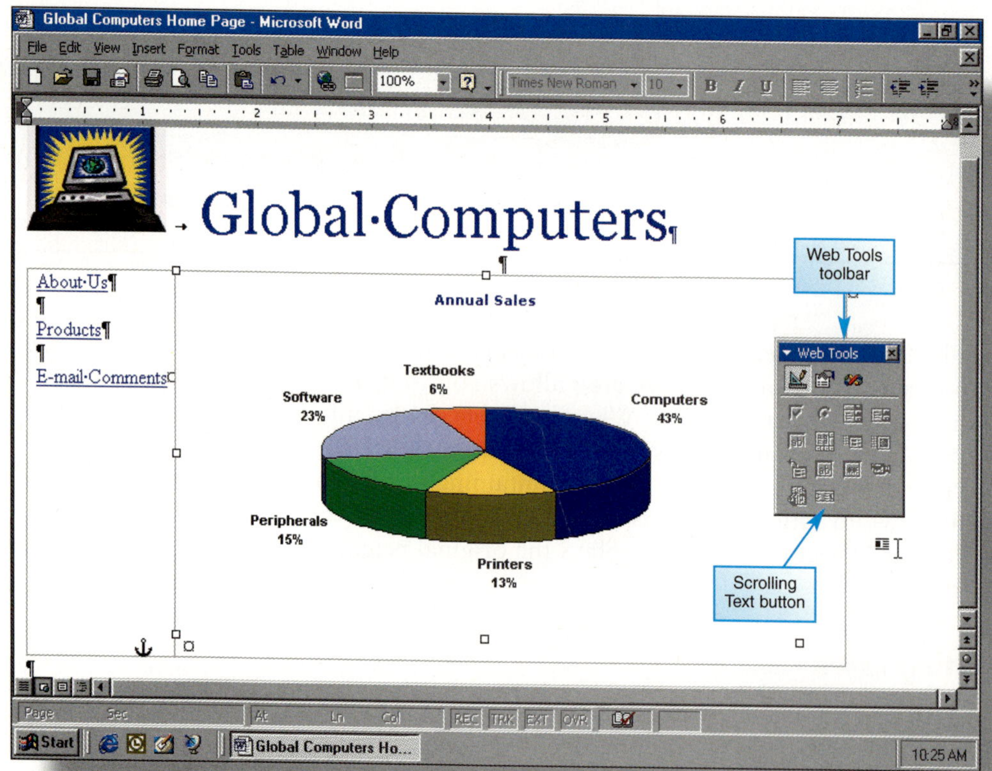

FIGURE 1-20

The Web Tools toolbar is used to create the scrolling text that moves under the Web page header.

Inserting Scrolling Text

A number of options exist for scrolling text. The **behavior** of the text specifies the manner in which the text moves on the Web page. By default, the behavior of the line of text is to scroll. **Scrolling** moves the text in from one side and off the other side of the Web page. Another behavior option is to slide the text. Setting the behavior to **slide** moves the text in from one side of the Web page and stops as soon as the text touches the opposite side. The third option is to set text behavior to alternate. **Alternate** bounces the text back and forth in the margins of the marquee. The default behavior is scrolling text. In this project, the scrolling text behavior is changed to slide.

To Insert Scrolling Text

1 Click the paragraph mark between the m and the p below the Global Computers title and then click the Scrolling Text button on the Web Tools toolbar.

The Scrolling Text dialog box displays (Figure 1-21).

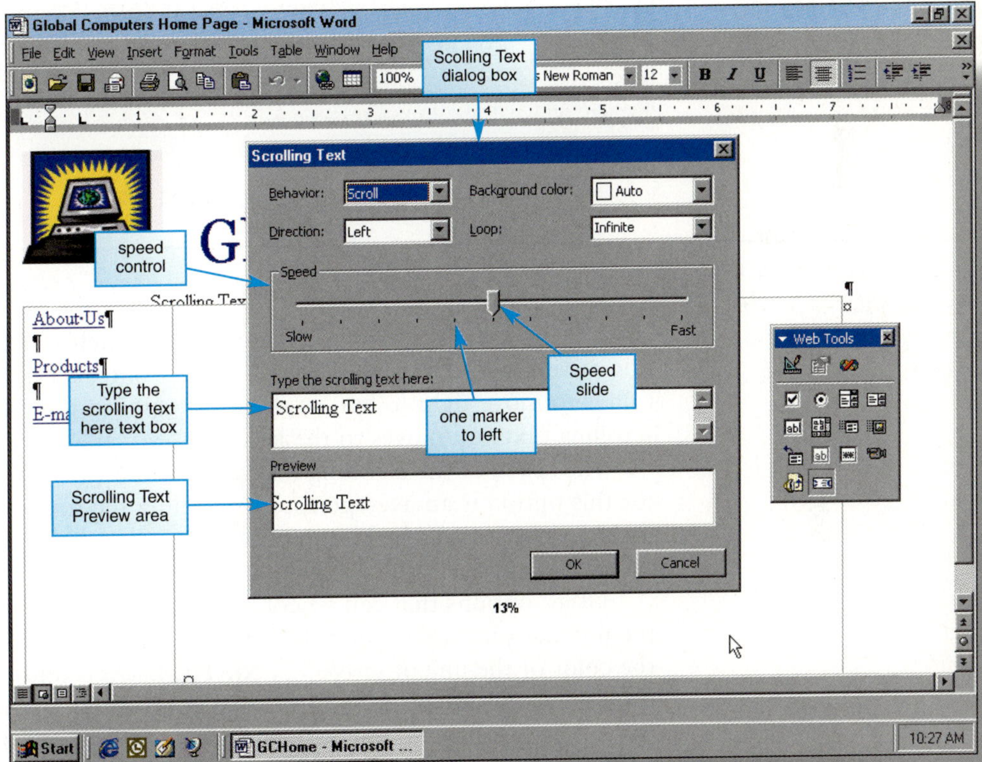

FIGURE 1-21

2 **Click the Behavior box arrow and then click Slide in the list.**

3 **Drag through the text, Scrolling Text, in the Type the scrolling text here text box. Type** `33 Ackmar, Sarasota, FL 34236 (941) 555-1242` **as the scrolling text.**

4 **Drag the Speed slide one speed marker to the left and then click the OK button.**

The scrolling text displays (Figure 1-22).

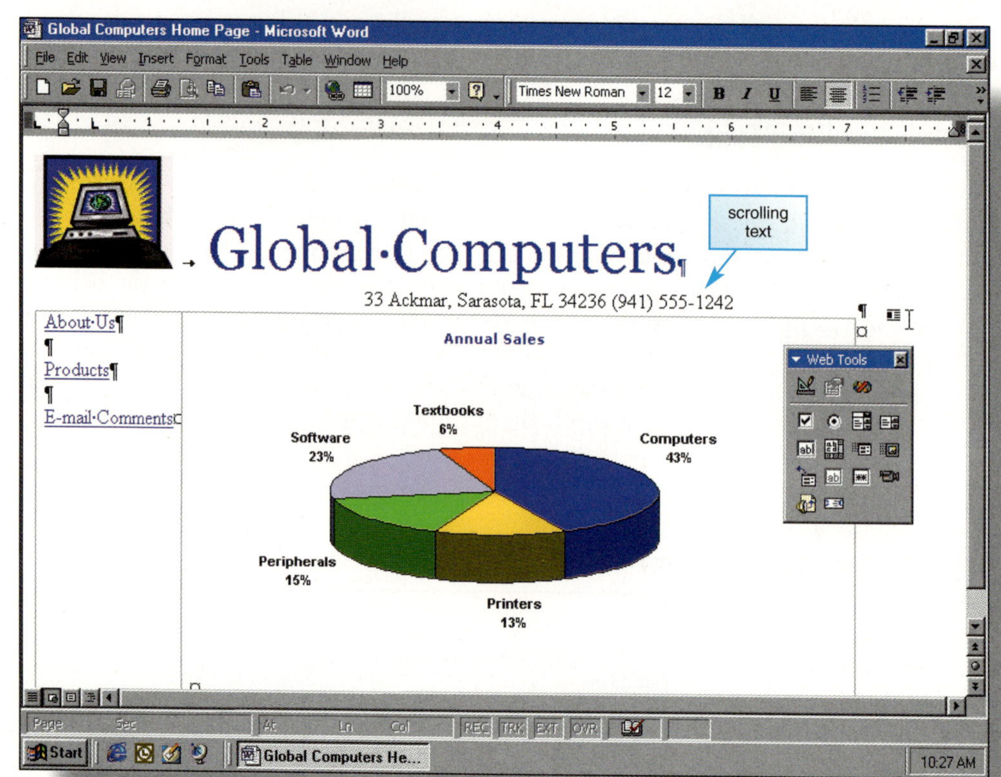

FIGURE 1-22

The **direction** of the text movement can be left to right or right to left. The direction attribute in the scrolling text options controls this movement. The default direction is to move right to left, so the text begins in the right margin of the line of scrolling text and moves to the left.

The **speed** of the scrolling text also can be varied from slow to fast. The default for this option is an average speed. Scrolling the text too fast cancels the benefits of the scrolling text. If the Web page visitor cannot read the text as it scrolls, the text serves no purpose.

Other options that can be controlled in scrolling text are background colors and the number of times to loop the scrolling text. The **background** attribute determines the color of the line of scrolling text. The background default is a transparent background, so the background of the line of scrolling text displays the background color of whatever is behind it. The **loop** attribute determines the number of times that the scrolling text moves across the Web page. The default is an infinite loop, but the loop can be set to a specific number of times.

The default direction, background color, and loop are used for the scrolling text that is inserted into the Word document. Slide was selected as the Behavior for the scrolling text. Because of that, the text scrolls from the right margin and stops scrolling when it reaches the left margin. The next section explains how to resize the scrolling text

Scrolling Text

To format the text, use the Font command in the Format menu while you are in Design mode. You turn off design mode to see the results. In browsers that do not support scrolling text, the text will appear but it will not be scrolling.

Resizing the Scrolling Text

The default is to move the text all the way across the Web page from the right margin of the page to the left margin. Sometimes it is better to shorten the distance of the scrolling text. In this project, the scrolling text is centered below the header of the Word document. The Web page visitor sees the company name with address and telephone number information below it. The Design Mode is used to change the size of the scrolling text.

Perform the following steps to change the size of the scrolling text.

To Resize the Scrolling Text

1 **Click the Design Mode button on the Web Tools toolbar.**

2 **If necessary, click anywhere within the scrolling text box to select the text. Point to the center resize handle on the right side of the text box.**

The text box displays as shown in Figure 1-23.

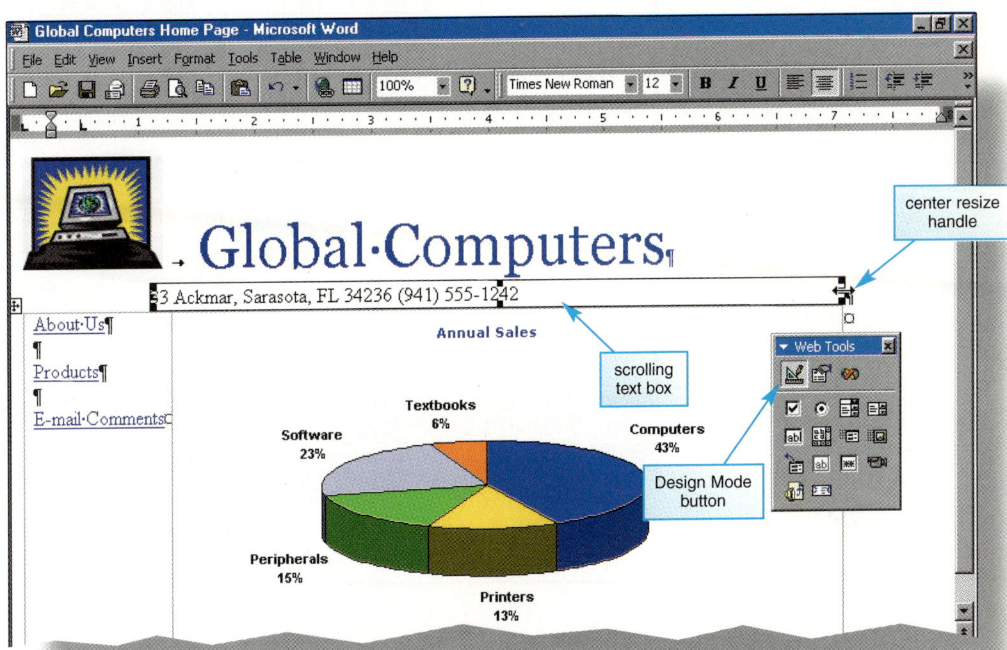

FIGURE 1-23

3 **Drag the center resize handle to the left, so it rests immediately below and in between the s in Computers and the paragraph mark in the Global Computers title.**

The text box displays (Figure 1-24).

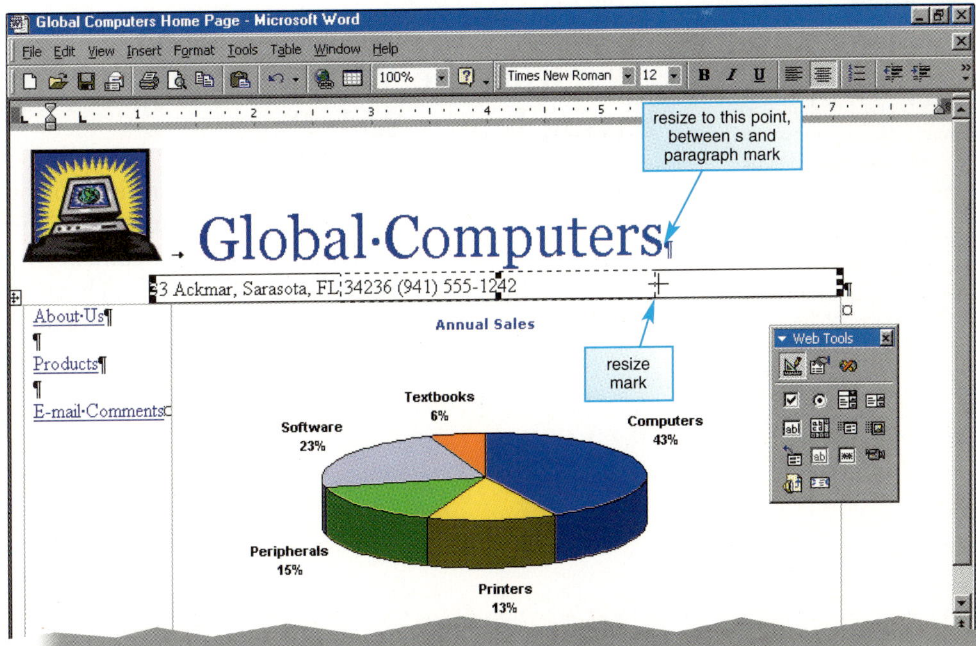

FIGURE 1-24

Release the mouse button.

The scrolling text box is repositioned (Figure 1-25).

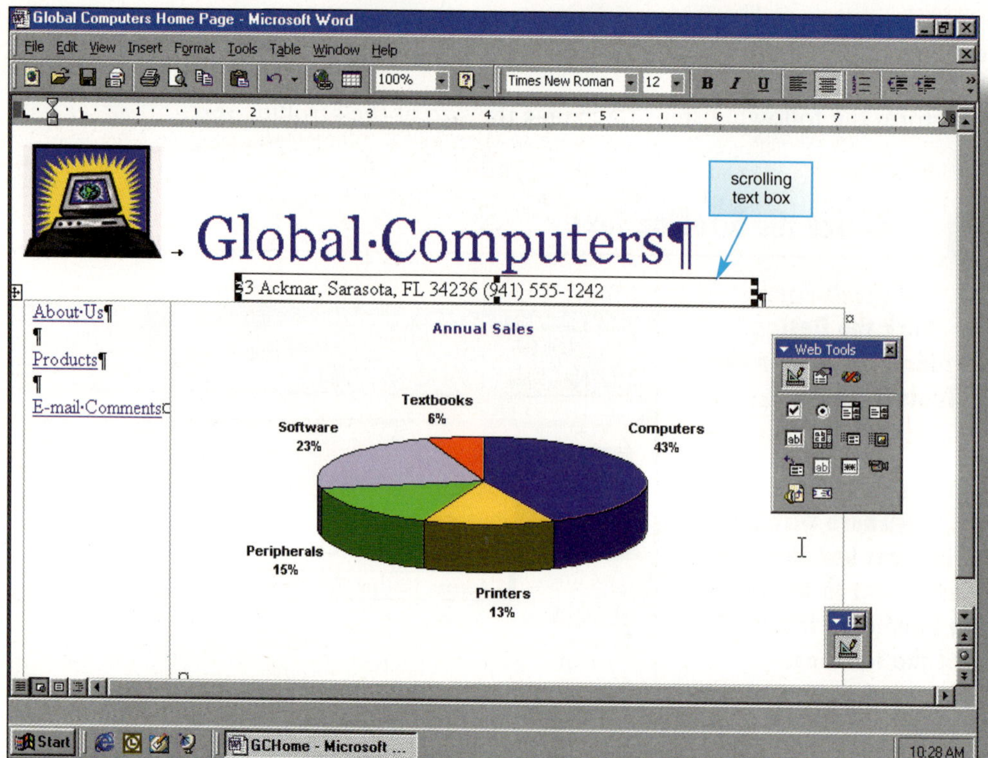

FIGURE 1-25

Web Page Formatting

Because Word provides formatting options that most Web browsers do not support, some text and graphics may look different when you view them on a Web page. When creating documents for the Web, using Web layout view will ensure that your graphics look the way you want them to when they are viewed as Web pages in a Web browser.

The home page for the Global Computers Web site is complete. The Web page should be viewed in your browser to verify that it is correct. Perform the following steps to view the Web page in your browser.

Viewing the Word Document in Your Browser and Saving It as a Web Page

The next step is to view the Word document in your browser to verify that all information is accurate. After verifying its accuracy, you then can save the Word document as an HTML file. Saving the Word document as an HTML file makes it possible for it to be viewed using a browser, such as Internet Explorer.

Perform the following steps to preview the document in your browser and then save the Word document as an HTML file.

Steps To Preview the Web Page

1. **Click File on the menu bar and then point to Web Page Preview.**

2. **Click Web Page Preview. If necessary, click the Maximize button on your browser.**

The Web page displays (Figure 1-26).

3. **Click the browser's Close button.**

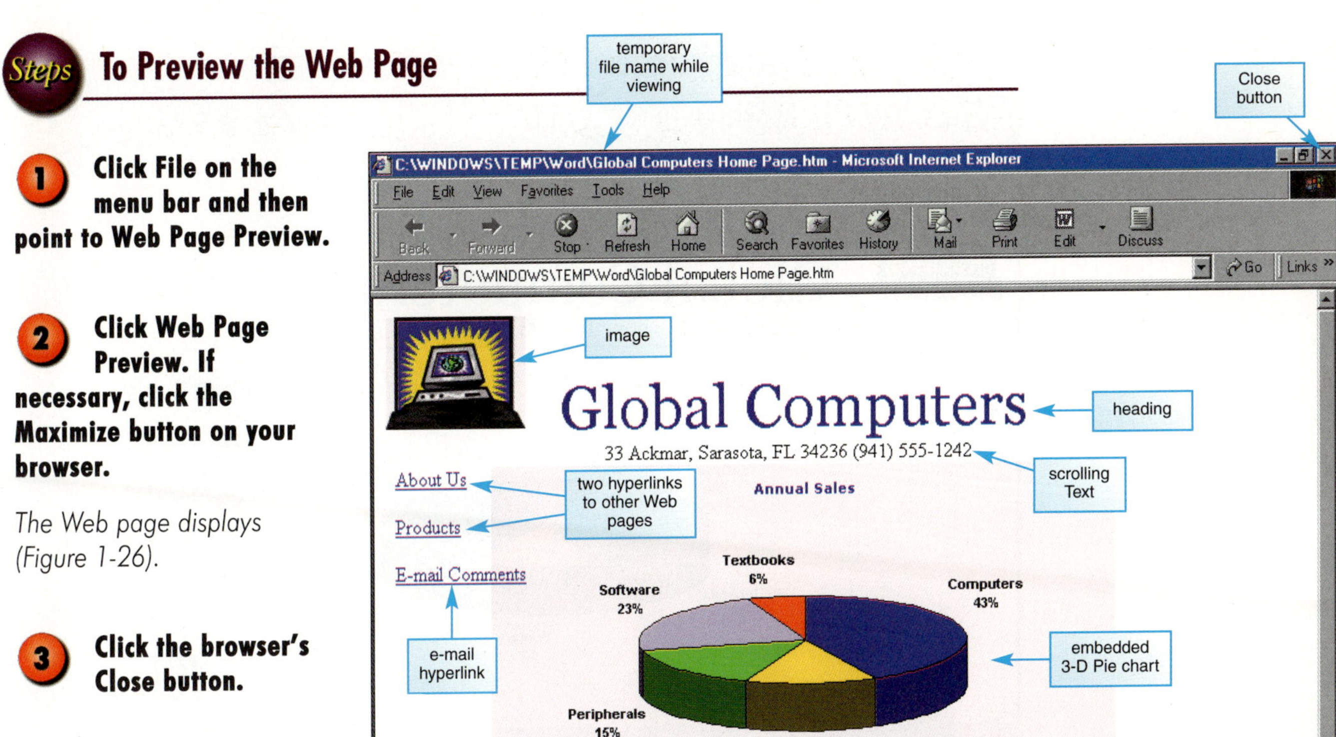

FIGURE 1-26

Other Ways

1. Click File on menu bar, press B

Verify that the Web page contains all information necessary and displays as shown in Figure 1-26. The Web page consists of a header with an image and the company name. Below that is a single line of scrolling text that scrolls in from the right margin and stops when it reaches the left margin. Next, is a borderless table with three hyperlinks in the left-hand column and a 3-D Pie chart in the right-hand column. The E-Mail Comments hyperlink should work appropriately when you click it, displaying a new message. The other two links, About Us and Products, do not work because the corresponding Web pages are not available until later in this project.

If the Web page is correct, save it on the Integration Data Disk as an HTML file. If changes need to be made to the Web page, return to the Word document and correct it. Perform the following steps to save the document as a Web page.

TO SAVE A DOCUMENT WITH A NEW FILE NAME

1. Click File on the menu bar and then click Save As Web page.
2. Type `GCHome` in the File name text box.
3. If necessary, click the Save in arrow and click 3½ Floppy (A:).
4. Click the Save button in the Save As dialog box.

The GCHome Web page displays in the Word window (Figure 1-27 on the next page).

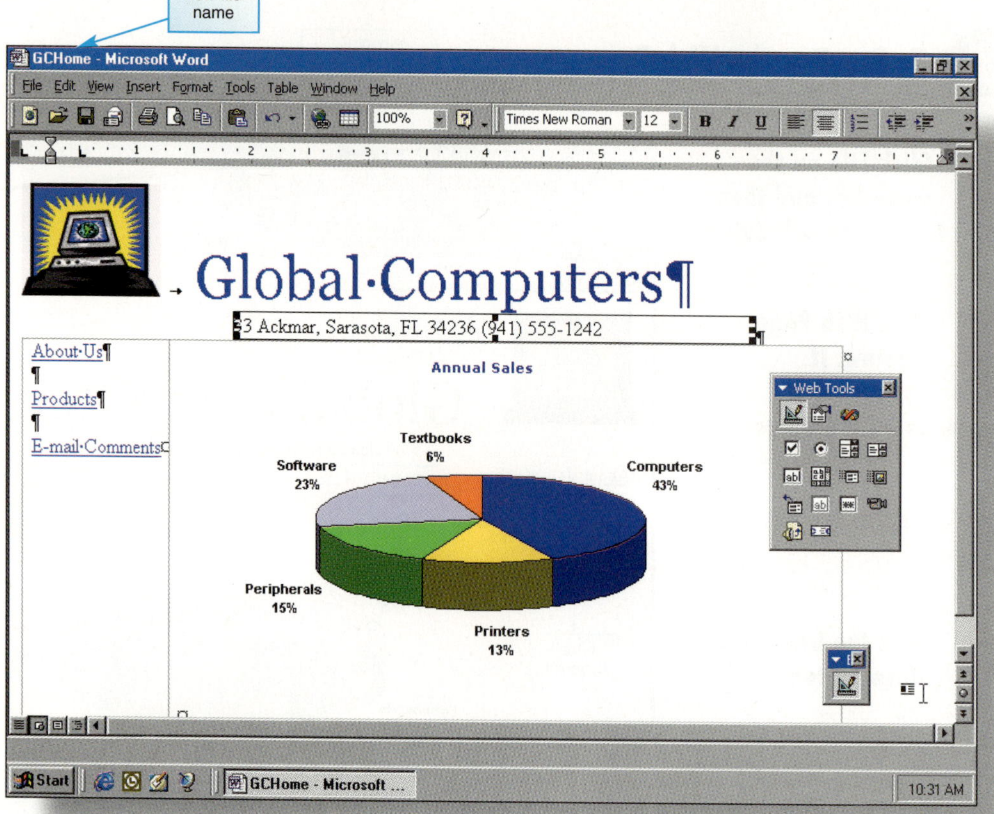

FIGURE 1-27

Saving an existing Word document as a Web page allows you quickly to get a Word document ready for copying to the Web or to an intranet. The alternative to this is using hypertext markup language (HTML) to develop the Web pages. **HTML** is a programming language used for Web page creation. The home page created earlier in this project could be created using HTML tags (code). For documents that already are in Word format, the easier method is to use the Save as Web Page feature of Word. Close Word using the following step.

TO QUIT WORD

1. Click the Close button on the Word title bar.

The next step in creating the Web site for Global Computers is to save a PowerPoint presentation as an HTML file. Perform the following steps to open a PowerPoint presentation, add a hyperlink to the first page, and save the presentation as an HTML file.

Creating a PowerPoint Presentation Web Page

PowerPoint is a powerful software tool used to present information about a company, school, or organization. **PowerPoint 2000** allows you to create Web pages from an existing PowerPoint presentation, using the Save as Web Page feature. The presentation then can be viewed using your browser.

The PowerPoint presentation used in this project consists of three slides (Figure 1-1g on page I 1.7). The first page is a header slide, containing the company name and a graphic. The second slide contains information about the Global Computers staff, with names and job responsibilities. The last slide contains information about the Global Computers product lines. This information can be used in its present format to enhance a presentation about the company. As Web pages, you can use this presentation to address a much wider, global audience on the World Wide Web.

Perform the following steps to open an existing PowerPoint presentation.

TO OPEN A POWERPOINT PRESENTATION

1. Click the Start button on the taskbar and then click Open Office Document.
2. Click the Look in box arrow and then click 3½ Floppy (A:).
3. Double-click the Global Computers Presentation name.

The first slide of the PowerPoint presentation displays (Figure 1-28).

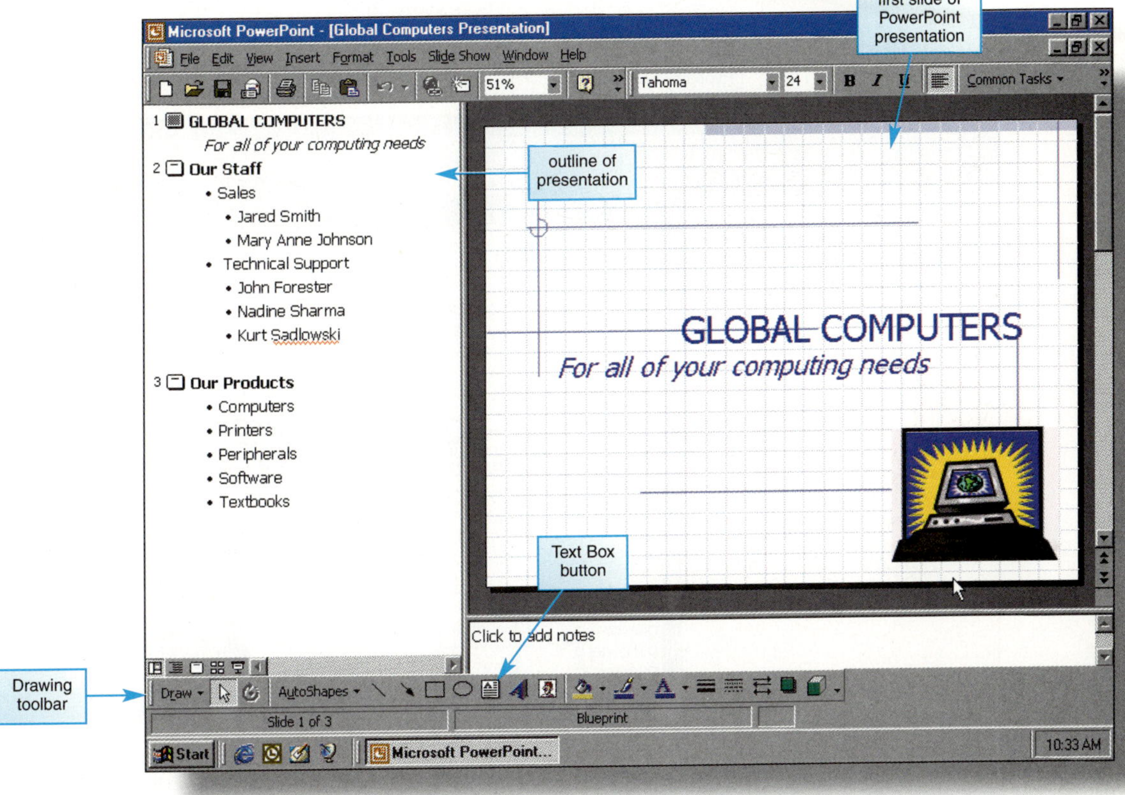

FIGURE 1-28

The PowerPoint presentation now is open. The next step is to add a hyperlink on the first page of the presentation that allows the Web page visitor to return to the Global Computers home page.

Adding Text for a Hyperlink

One of the most important features of Web sites is the capability of linking from one Web page to another using hyperlinks. In earlier steps in this project, you added three hyperlinks to the Global Computers home page. Once Web page visitors link to the PowerPoint Web pages, however, they cannot return to the home page without using the Back button on the browser's toolbar. This is not a convenient way for Web page visitors to navigate through the Web site. In this section, you will add a hyperlink (Home) to the first slide of the PowerPoint presentation (Figure 1-1e on page I 1.7).

Perform the following steps to add the text that will be used as a hyperlink on the PowerPoint Web page.

TO ADD TEXT FOR A HYPERLINK

1. Click the Text Box button on the Drawing toolbar.
2. Click in the lower, left-hand corner of the first page of the PowerPoint presentation.
3. Type `Home` as the hyperlink text.

The text box displays (Figure 1-29).

Other Ways

1. On Insert menu click Text Box
2. Click Insert on menu bar, press X

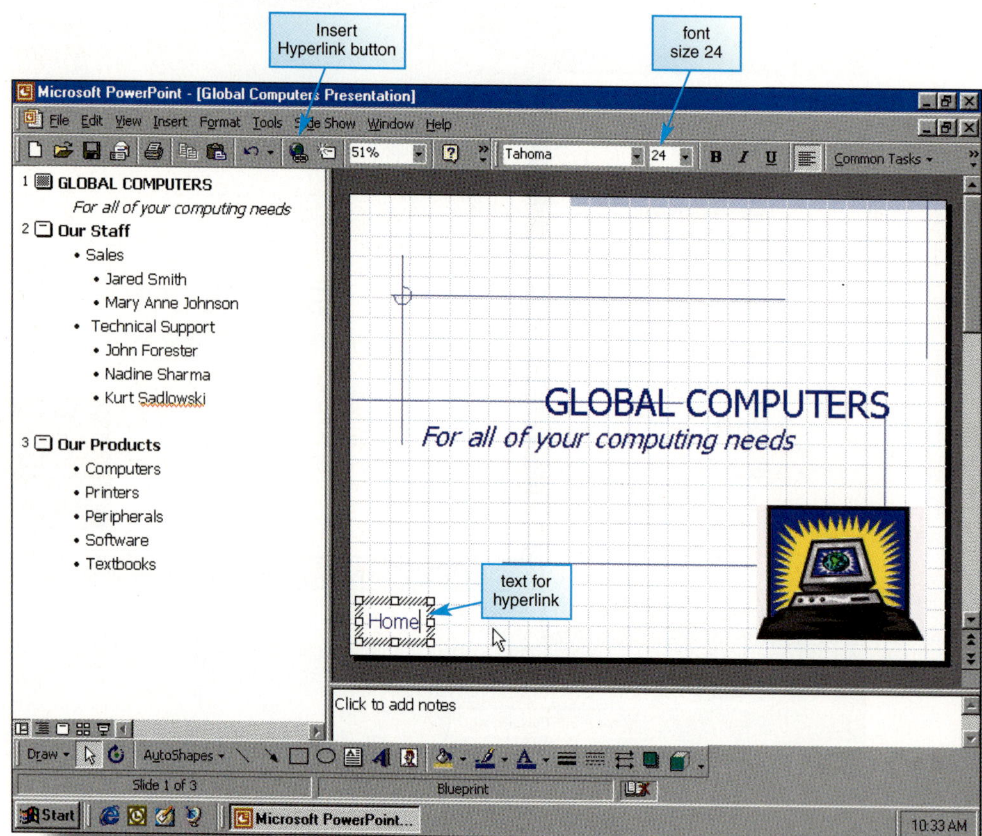

FIGURE 1-29

Creating a Hyperlink

After you enter the text for the hyperlink, you can create the hyperlink. When clicked, the hyperlink jumps to the Global Computers home page created previously in this project and saved on drive A. To create the hyperlink, you will use the Insert Hyperlink button on the Standard toolbar.

Perform the following steps to create the PowerPoint hyperlink.

TO CREATE A HYPERLINK IN A POWERPOINT PRESENTATION

1. Double-click the word, Home.
2. If necessary, click the Font Size box arrow and then click 24. Click the Bold button on the Formatting toolbar.
3. Click the Insert Hyperlink button on the Standard toolbar.
4. If necessary, click the Existing File or Web Page button on the Link to bar. Type `a:\GCHome.htm` in the Type the file or Web page name text box. Click the OK button.

Slide 1 of the presentation displays as shown in Figure 1-30.

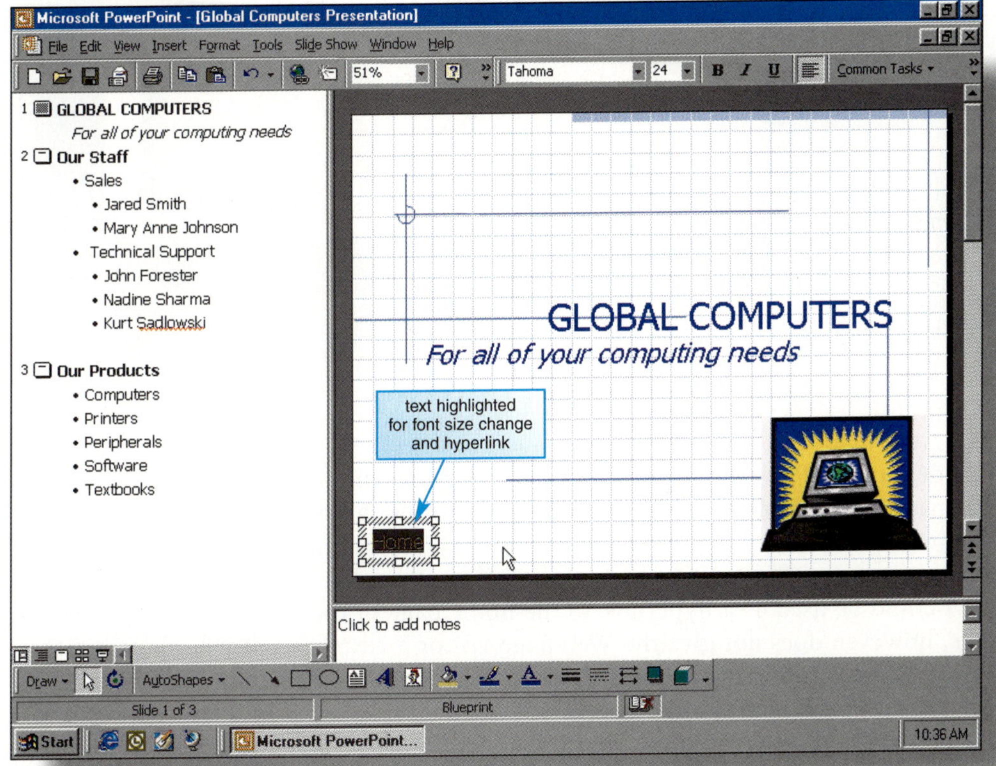

FIGURE 1-30

Other Ways

1. Right-click highlighted word, Home, click Hyperlink on shortcut menu
2. On Insert menu click Hyperlink
3. Press CTRL+K

Viewing and Saving the PowerPoint Web Page

Just as you did in the previous section of this project, view the Web page before saving it. It is important to verify all of the Web page navigation features before you save the file.

TO VIEW THE WEB PAGE IN YOUR BROWSER

1. Click File on the menu bar and then point to Web Page Preview.
2. Click Web Page Preview.
3. If necessary, click the Maximize button on your browser title bar.

The PowerPoint Web page displays (Figure 1-31 on the next page).

Other Ways

1. Click Insert on menu bar, press B

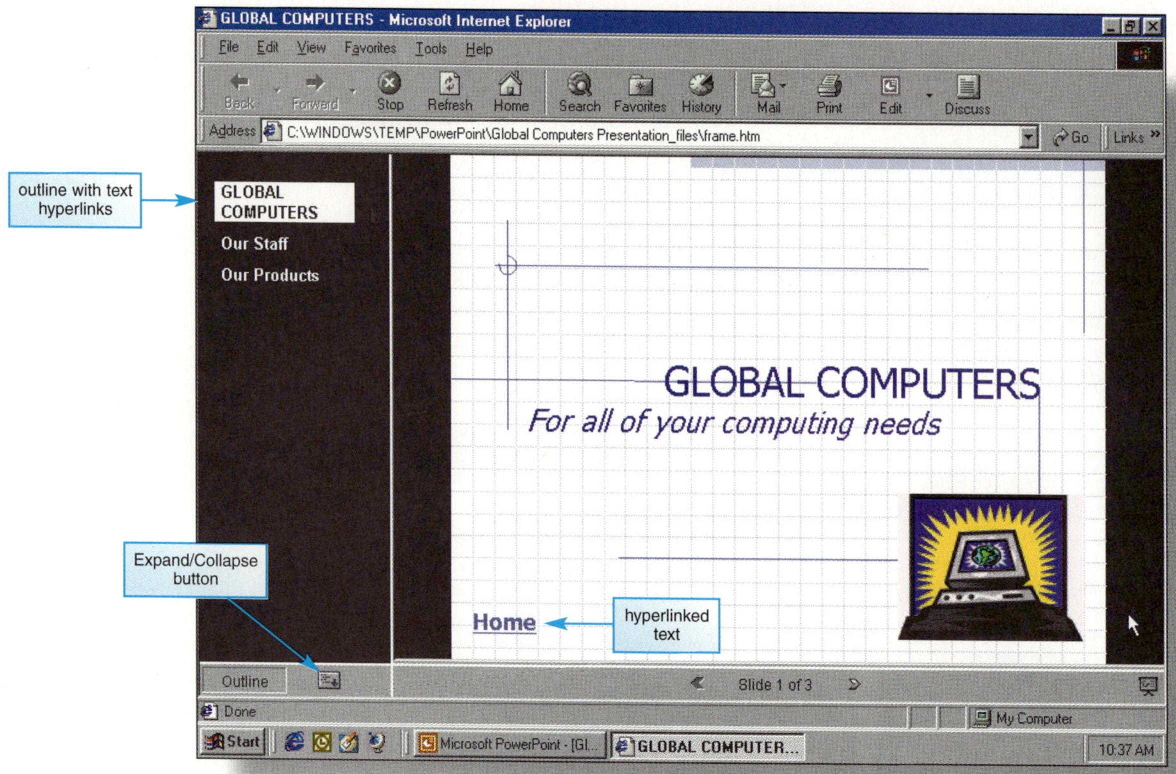

FIGURE 1-31

Outline

The outline pane is displayed by default when you view a presentation in a browser. To hide this pane, click the Outline button while in the browser. Click the Outline button again to redisplay the outline pane.

Slide 1 of the PowerPoint presentation Web page contains a hyperlink to the home page of the Global Computers Web site. Although you created this hyperlink by adding a text box to the first slide, you also can create hyperlinks from existing text or images in a PowerPoint presentation. For example, the computer image on slide 1 could be used as a hyperlink to the home page of the Web site. Using that image, however, does not give the Web page visitor a clear idea of where the hyperlink will go. It is more appropriate to create a hyperlink to the home page from text (Home) that makes sense to the visitor.

In addition to any hyperlinks that are added to the presentation, PowerPoint automatically creates hyperlinks in the left-hand column of the Web page, called the **outline**. This outline can be expanded or collapsed using the **Expand/Collapse Outline button** on the Standard toolbar and is used to navigate through the Web page presentation. The text in the heading of each slide is used as the phrases for these hyperlinks. When you click a link, the hyperlinks jump to the particular slide within the presentation. The ease of navigation within a PowerPoint Web page is valuable to the Web page visitor.

As well as being able to add your own hyperlink text, PowerPoint provides some ready-made action buttons that you can insert into your Web pages. **Action buttons** contain shapes, such as left and right arrows, that can be used to hyperlink to other Web pages within the presentation. You can insert symbols on the action buttons for going to the next (right arrow), previous (left arrow), first (beginning arrow), and last (end arrow) slides. PowerPoint also includes action buttons for playing movies or sounds. You insert these action buttons using the slide master feature of PowerPoint.

Saving the PowerPoint Presentation as a Web Page

The next step is to save the PowerPoint presentation as a Web page. When you save a PowerPoint presentation as a Web page, the Web page is saved in a default folder. All supporting files such as bullets, backgrounds, and images are organized in this folder automatically. The name of the PowerPoint slide show opened in this section is Global Computers Presentation. PowerPoint uses the name of the saved Web page and adds the string, _files, for the name of the new folder. When the current presentation is saved as a Web page, the folder name that PowerPoint Web creates is AboutUs_files. The default name for the first slide in the presentation is frame.htm. The structure used in the folder organization makes Web page publishing easier because you can keep track of all of the files associated with the Web page.

Perform the steps below to save the PowerPoint presentation as a Web page.

TO SAVE THE POWERPOINT PRESENTATION AS A WEB PAGE

1. Click the Microsoft PowerPoint button on the taskbar.
2. Click File on the menu bar and then click Save as Web Page.
3. Type `AboutUs` in the File name text box.
4. If necessary, click the Look in box arrow and then click 3½ Floppy (A:).
5. Click the Save button in the Save As dialog box.

The PowerPoint presentation is saved as a Web page.

The task of saving the PowerPoint presentation as a Web page is complete. The hyperlink has been added to the first page of the presentation that jumps to the Web site home page when clicked. Standard Web page navigation was added automatically to the presentation that allows the Web page visitor to jump to any slide in the Web page presentation. All of the files necessary for the Web page were saved in a folder named AboutUs_files.

After saving the PowerPoint presentation as a Web page, you can quit PowerPoint and close your browser as shown in the following steps.

TO QUIT POWERPOINT AND CLOSE YOUR BROWSER

1. Click the Close button on the PowerPoint title bar.
2. Click the Close button on the browser title bar.

Creating a Data Access Page from an Access Database

The next step in the Global Computers Web site creation is to use an Access database to create a data access page. A **data access page** is a special type of Web page that is designed for viewing and working with data. Similar to a form, a data access page is connected (bound) directly to an Access database.

Data access pages are used to analyze data, enter and edit data, make projections, and review data. You also can create a chart using the chart component to analyze trends, show patterns, and make comparisons on the data in the database. Then, you can add spreadsheet controls to allow the inclusion of formulas for calculations.

One of the more frequently used purposes for data access pages is for viewing records in a database via a company's intranet or the World Wide Web. Data access pages give you a way to inquire on large amounts of data in a selective way. Groups of records can be expanded or collapsed so that Web page visitors can view the data they want to see. This section presents steps and techniques to create this type of data access page.

TO OPEN AN ACCESS DATABASE

1. Click the Start button on the taskbar. Click Open Office Document.
2. If necessary, click the Look in box arrow and then click 3½ Floppy (A:).
3. Double-click the Global Computers Products database name.

Access starts and displays the Global Computers Products : Database window (Figure 1-32).

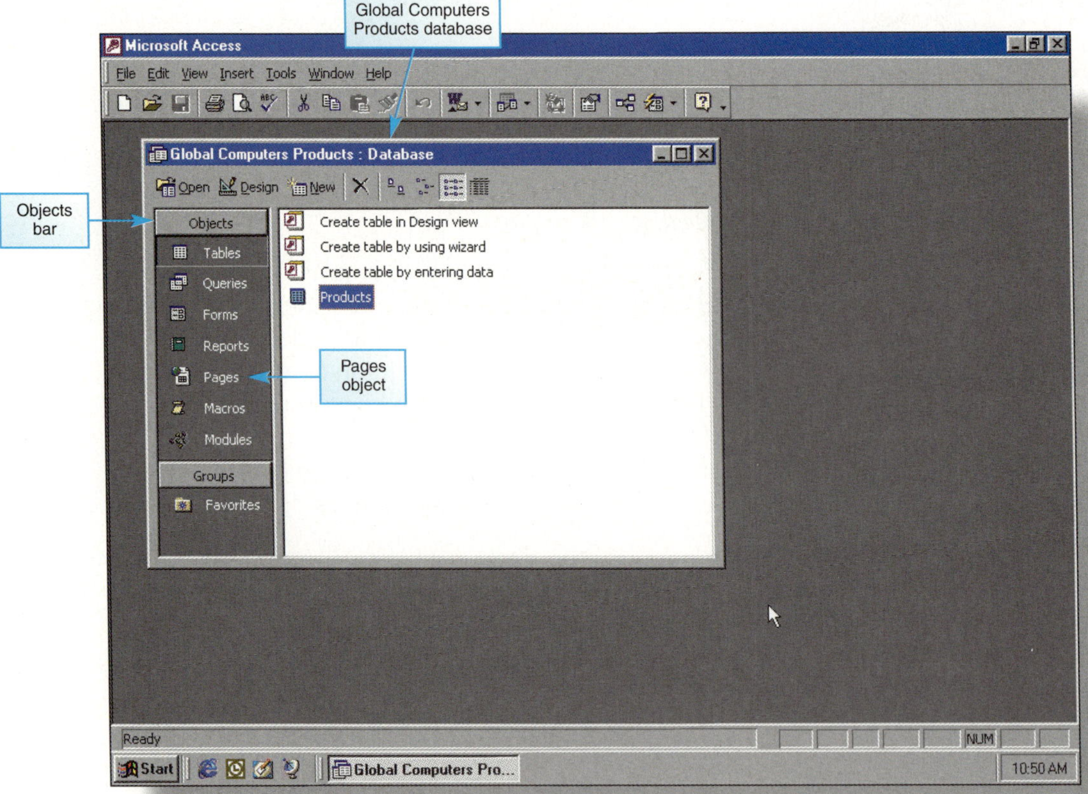

FIGURE 1-32

Creating a Data Access Page Using the Wizard

For the Global Computers Web site, you do not want the database to be altered by the Web page visitor in any way. The visitors should be allowed to view only the data. Because of this, you must add a group level to the data access page. Adding **group levels** results in a read-only page. The Web page visitors can view all data and alter that view, but they cannot change the data itself.

Perform the following steps to use the wizard to create a data access page.

To Create a Data Access Page Using the Wizard

1 Click the Pages object on the Objects bar.

2 Double-click the Create data access page by using wizard in the list box.

The Page Wizard dialog box displays (Figure 1-33). The Products table is selected automatically because it is the only table in the database. If more than one table exists, you would need to click the Tables object in the Objects bar and then select the appropriate table before clicking the Pages object in Step 1.

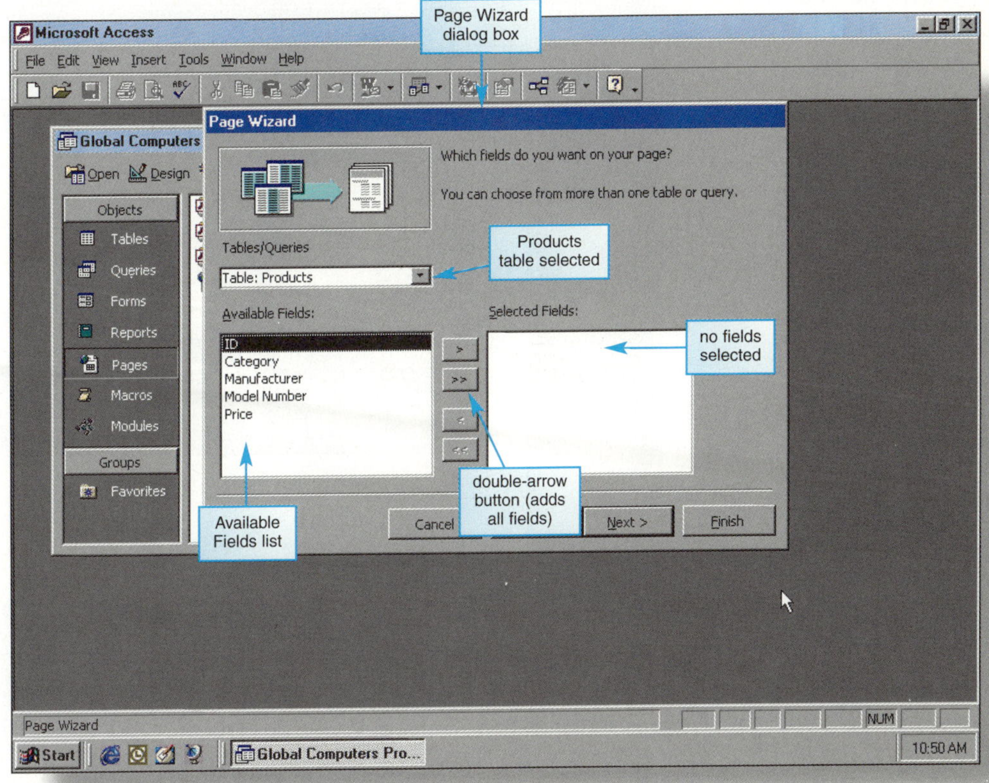

FIGURE 1-33

3 Click the double-arrow button to add all the fields. Point to the Next button.

All the fields in the table are listed in the Selected Fields box (Figure 1-34). This means you want to display all the fields on the data access page.

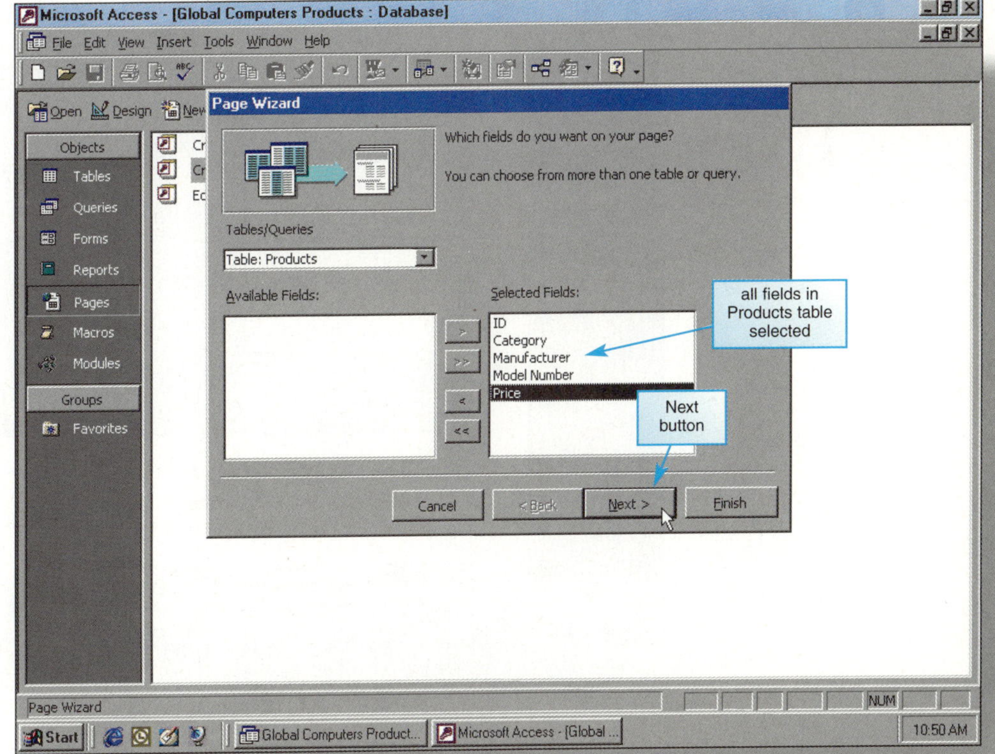

FIGURE 1-34

4 **Click the Next button. Double-click Category in the list box on the left. Point to the Next button.**

Adding a group level, such as Category, prohibits the data access page from being updated. Category displays in the upper-right box indicating it has been selected (Figure 1-35).

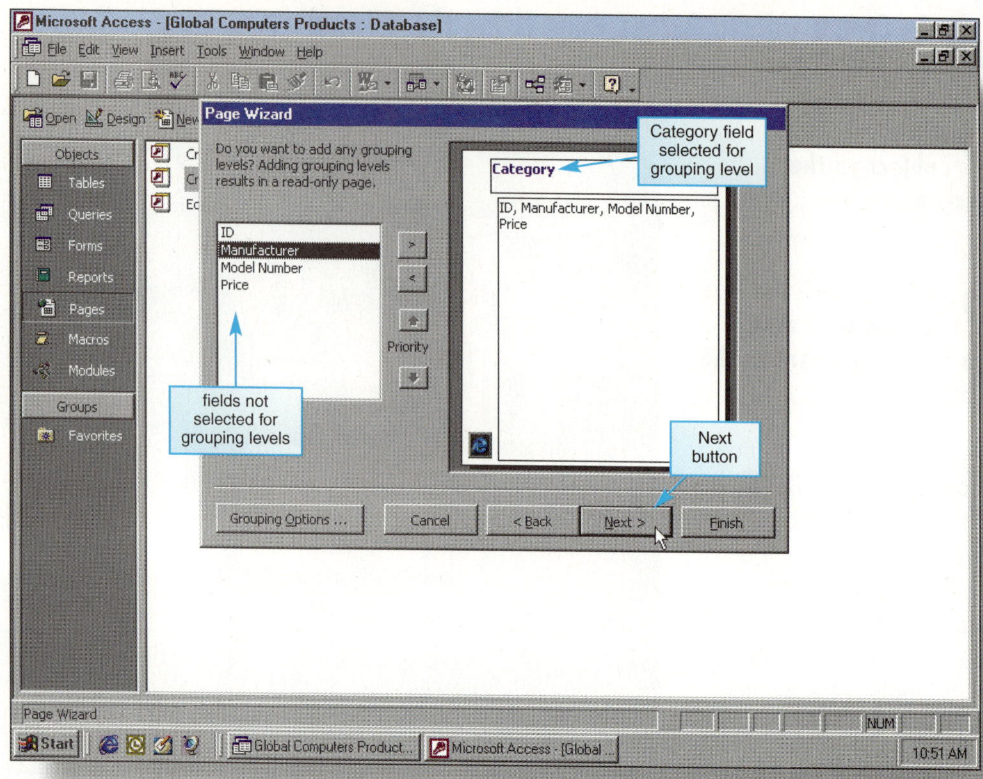

FIGURE 1-35

5 **Click the Next button. When the Page Wizard dialog box displays with the question, What sort order do you want for detail records?, point to the Next button.**

The Page Wizard dialog box displays (Figure 1-36).

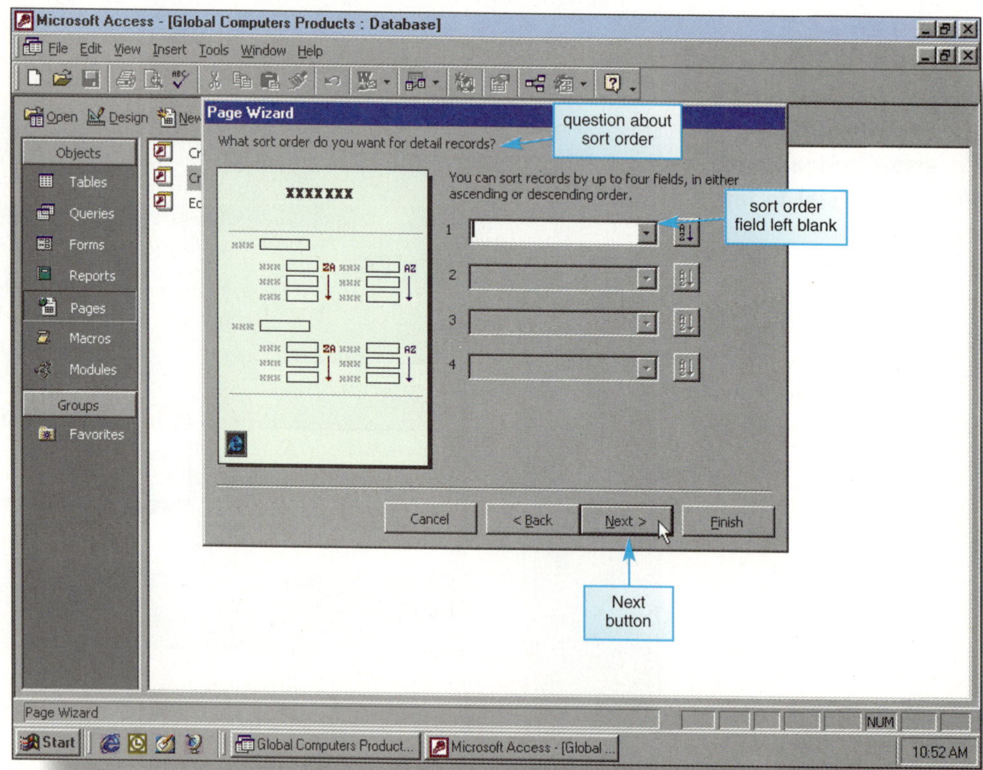

FIGURE 1-36

6 Click the Next button and then type `Products` **in the What title do you want for your page? text box. If necessary, click Modify the page's design to select it. Point to the Finish button.**

The Page Wizard dialog box displays with the title, Products, in the text box and the Modify the page s design option button selected (Figure 1-37).

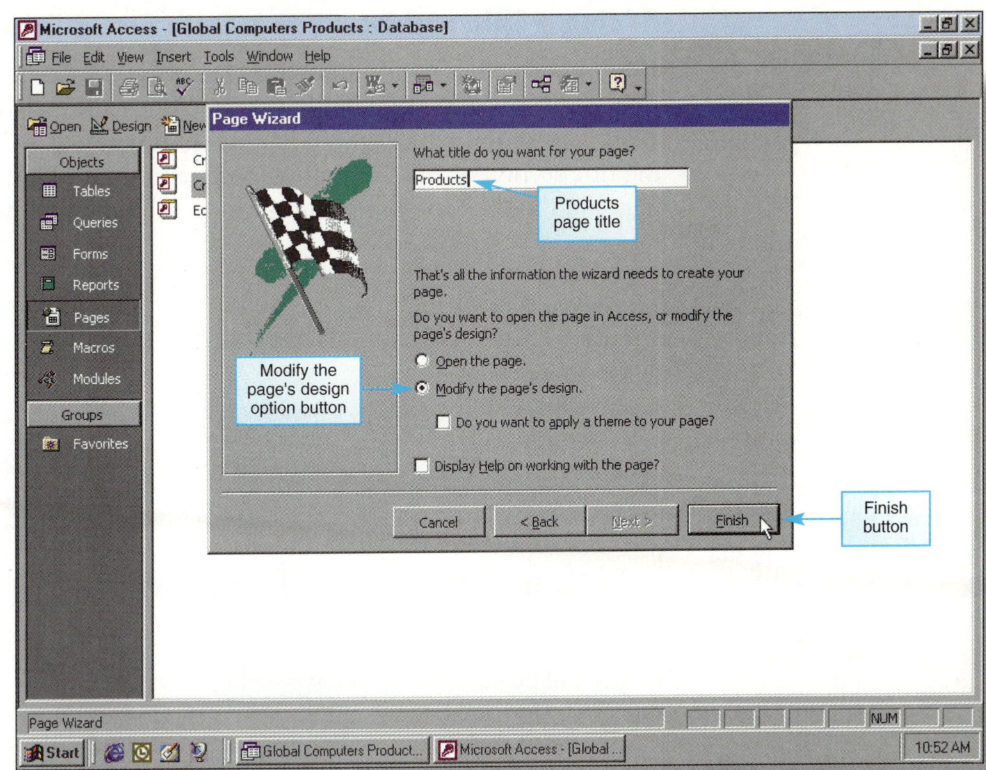

FIGURE 1-37

7 Click the Finish button.

Access displays the data access page in Design view (Figure 1-38).

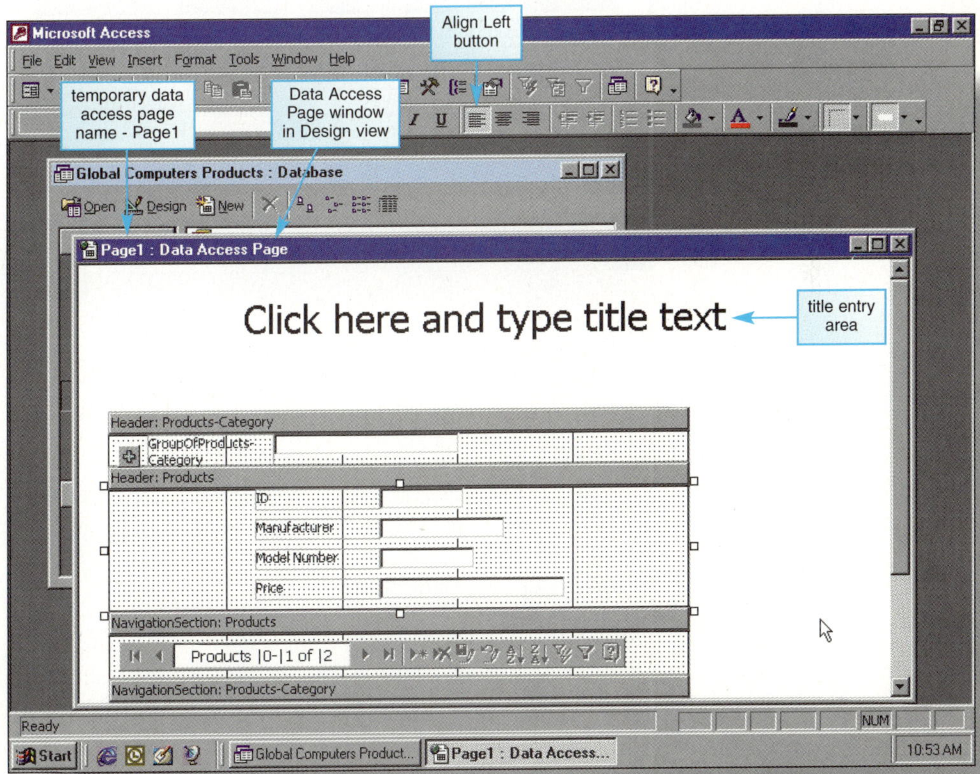

FIGURE 1-38

Adding a Title and Image to a Data Access Page

The data access page is created, but additional information can be helpful for the Web page visitor. It is appropriate to insert a title at the top of the page that tells the visitor the purpose of the Web page. Inserting the Global Computers logo image in the title section of the data access page maintains its consistency with the other Web pages in the site. The following steps explain how to add a title text and image.

To Add a Title and Image to a Data Access Page

1 If necessary, scroll to the top of the data access page. With the data access page in Design view, click anywhere in the Click here and type title text entry area. Click the Align Left button on the Standard toolbar. Type `Global Computers - Products` **as the title text.**

The data access page displays as shown in Figure 1-39.

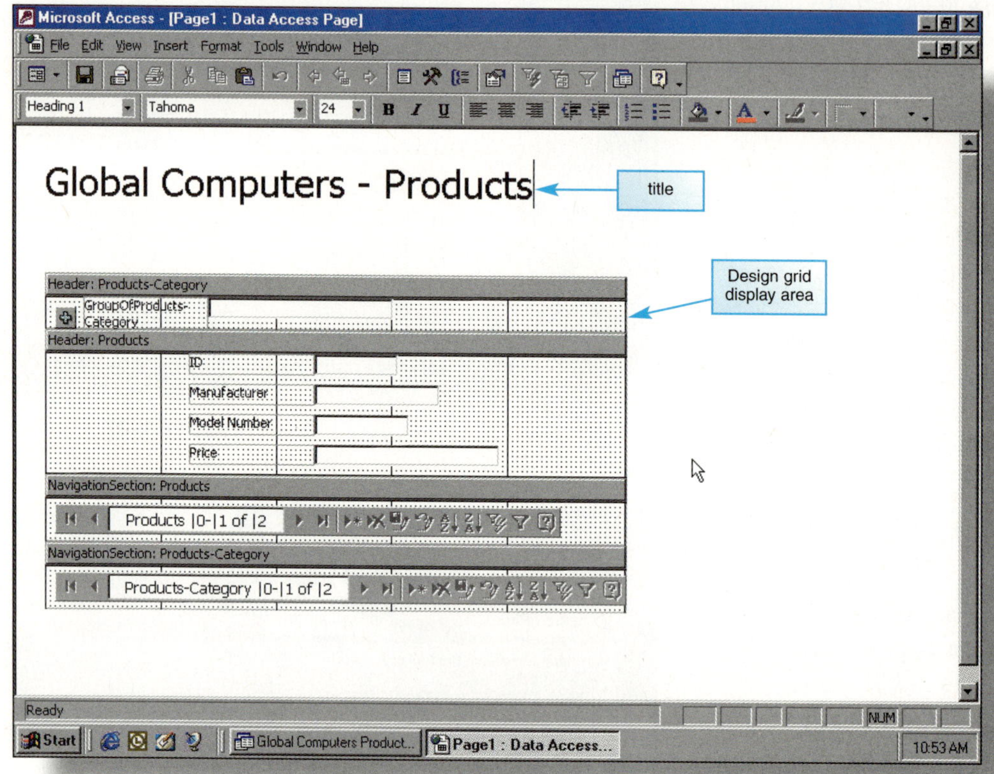

FIGURE 1-39

2 **Click to the left of the G in Global to position the insertion point. Click Insert on the menu bar and then click Picture.**

3 **If necessary, click 3½ Floppy (A:) in the Look in list. Double-click computer.gif.**

4 **If necessary, click the image to select it. Point to the sizing handle at the bottom-right corner of the image. Drag the sizing handle upward until the selection rectangle is positioned approximately to the position shown in Figure 1-40 and hold.**

The data access page displays as shown in Figure 1-40.

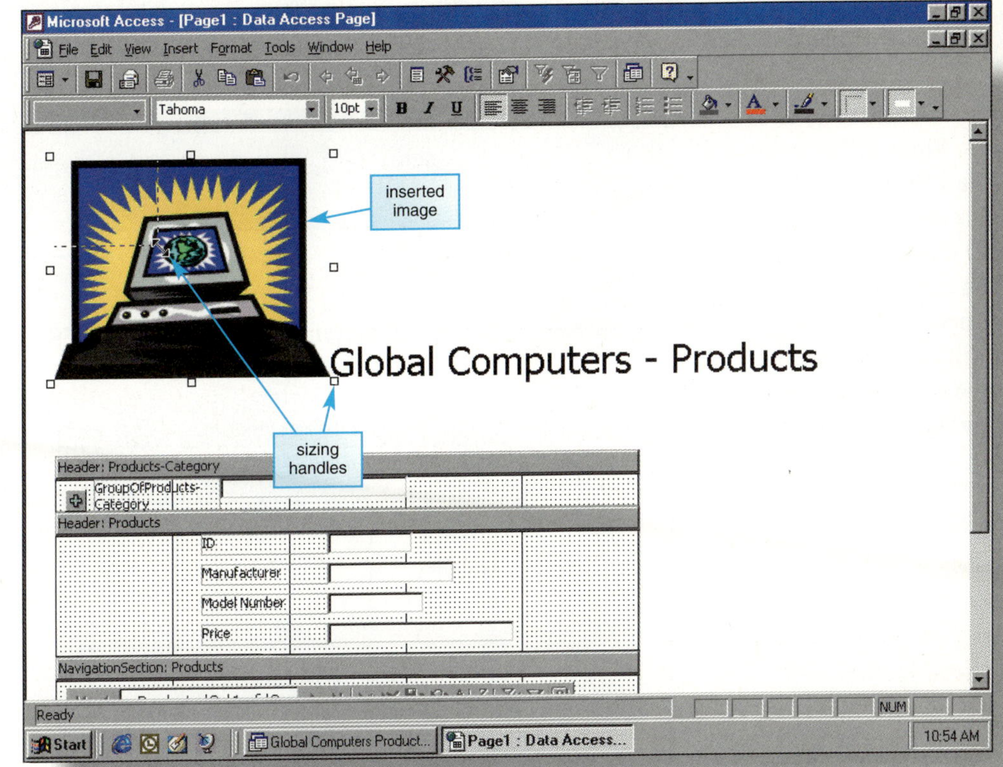

FIGURE 1-40

5 **Release the mouse button. Click outside the image.**

1. Click Insert on menu bar, press P

The data access page is created, and a heading and image are positioned in the header as shown in Figure 1-1d on page I 1.6. The next step is to add a hyperlink that jumps to the Web site home page.

Adding a Hyperlink to a Data Access Page

Just as you did on the PowerPoint Web page, a hyperlink to the home page should be added to the data access page. This allows the Web page visitor to jump to the Global Computers home page without having to use the Back button on the browser's toolbar.

Data Access Pages

In addition to using Data Access Pages in a browser, you also can work with a data access page in Page view in Microsoft Access. Data access pages can supplement the forms and reports that you use in your database application. When deciding whether to design a data access page, form, or report, consider the tasks that you want to perform.

To Add a Hyperlink to a Data Access Page

1 If necessary, click View on the menu bar and then click Toolbox to display the Toolbox. Scroll down so the bottom of the data access page displays. Click the Hyperlink button on the Toolbox and then point below the Design grid.

The hyperlink mouse pointer displays as shown in Figure 1-41.

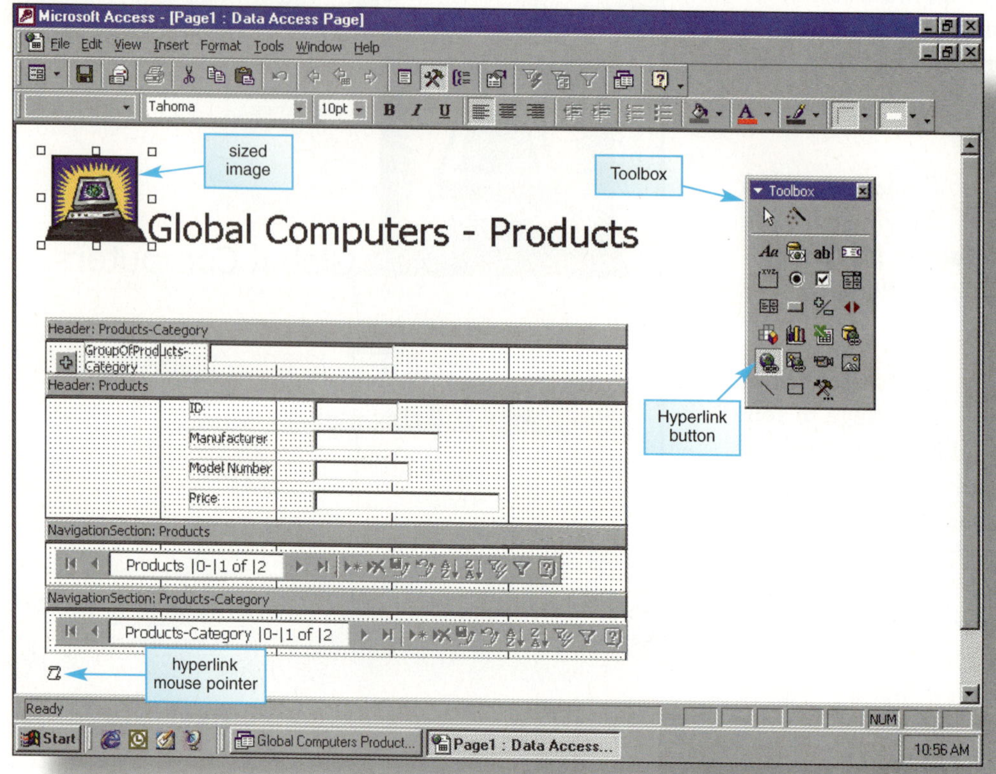

FIGURE 1-41

2 Click below the Design grid.

The Insert Hyperlink dialog box displays (Figure 1-42).

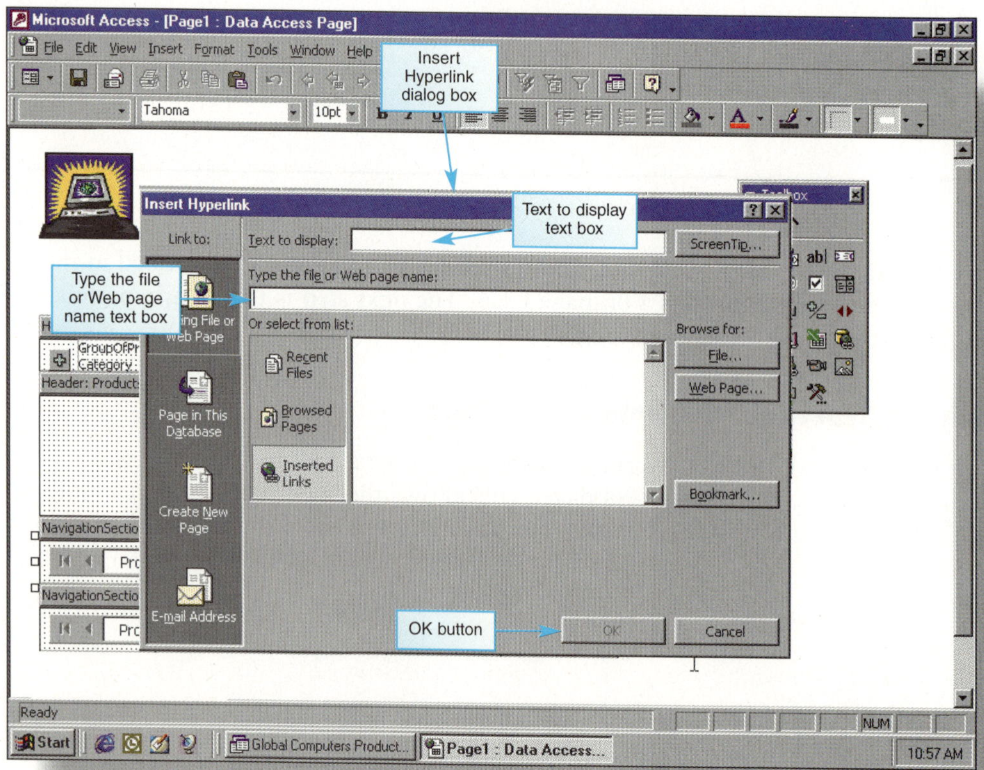

FIGURE 1-42

3 **If necessary, click the Existing File or Web Page button on the Link to bar. Type** `Home` **in the Text to display text box. Type** `a:\GCHome.htm` **in the Type the file or Web page name text box and then click the OK button.**

4 **Click anywhere on the data access page to deselect the hyperlink box.**

The data access page displays as shown in Figure 1-43.

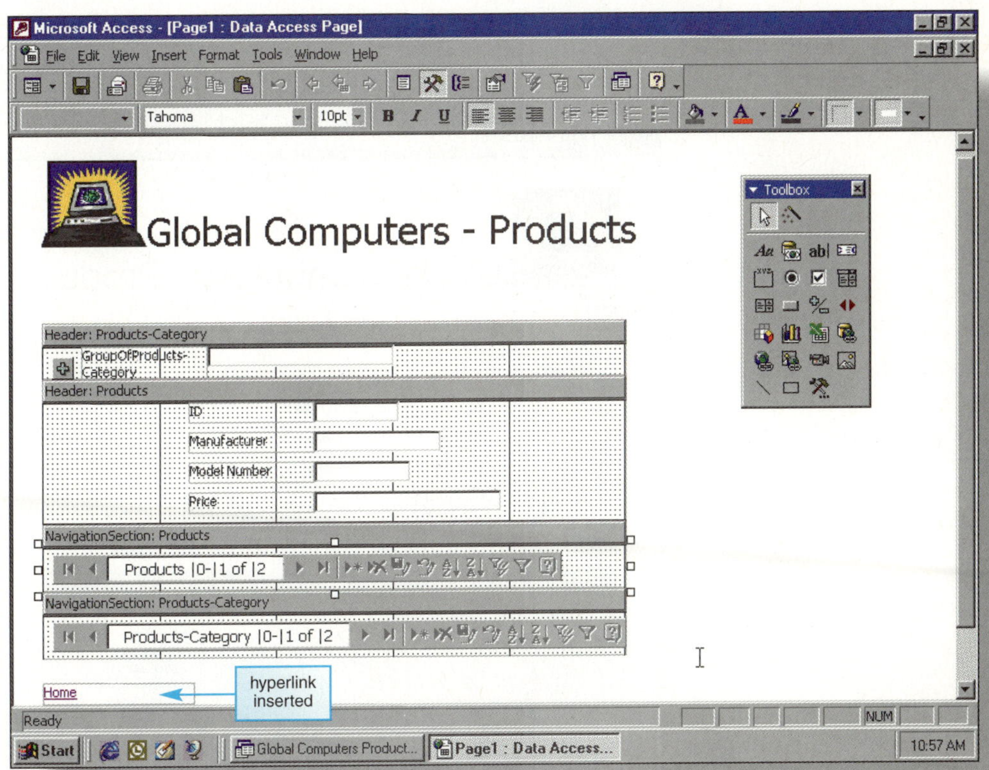

FIGURE 1-43

Other Ways

1. Right-click below Design grid, click Hyperlink on shortcut menu

The data access page is complete. In the next steps, you will save the page to the Integration Data Disk and view it in the browser.

Saving the Data Access Page and Viewing It

In other sections of this project, you have viewed the Web page, verified that it is correct, and then saved. Unlike Word and PowerPoint, you must save a data access page before you can preview it in your browser. Perform the following steps to save the file on the Integration Data Disk and then view it in your browser. As the Web page is being opened in your browser, a Databinding message displays on the status bar of your browser. This indicates that the data access page is connecting to the database that was open when the page was created (Global Computers Products).

TO SAVE THE DATA ACCESS PAGE AND VIEW IT IN YOUR BROWSER

1. Click File on the menu bar and then click Web Page Preview. When the Microsoft Access dialog box displays, click the Yes button.
2. Type `Products` in the File name text box. If necessary, select 3½ Floppy (A:) in the Look in list.
3. Click the Save button in the Save As Data Access Page dialog box.
4. Click the Expand indicator to the left of the GroupOfProducts-Category to expand the display.

The data access page displays in your browser (Figure 1-44 on the next page).

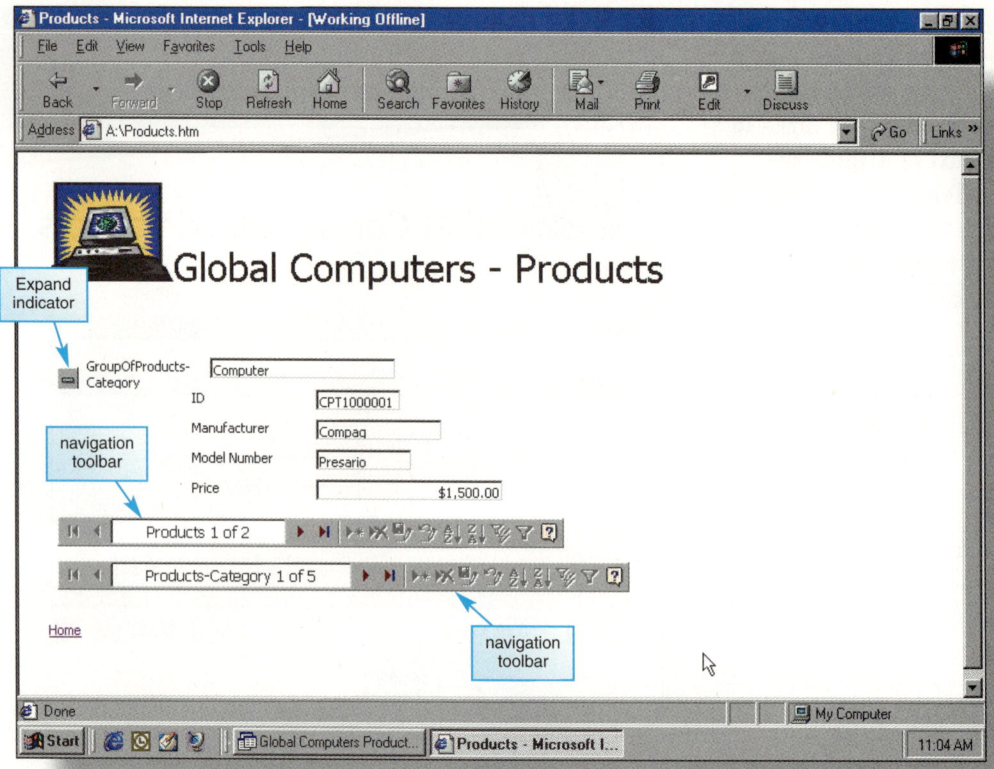

FIGURE 1-44

Once the data access page is saved, you can preview it and then quit Access and close your browser.

TO QUIT ACCESS AND CLOSE YOUR BROWSER

1. Right-click the Global Computer Products button on the taskbar and then click Close on the shortcut menu.

2. Click the Close button on the Access title bar to quit Access.

Grouping records on a data access page is similar to grouping records on a report. You can group the data on this data access page in different ways, but you cannot edit the data. The records in the data access page can be expanded or collapsed, using the Expand and Collapse indicators. Using the record **navigation toolbars** on the data access page, you can move, sort, and filter records and obtain Help.

Use the navigation toolbar to verify that the information in the database displays correctly. Click the link to the home page of the Web site to verify it.

Testing the Web Site

The Global Computers Web site is complete. To ensure that all the links in the site are viable, perform the following steps to open the home page and then thoroughly test the entire Web site.

TO TEST THE WEB SITE

1. Start your browser.
2. Click the Address bar of your browser.
3. Type `a:\GCHome.htm` in the text box.

The home page of the Global Computers Web site displays as shown in Figure 1-45.

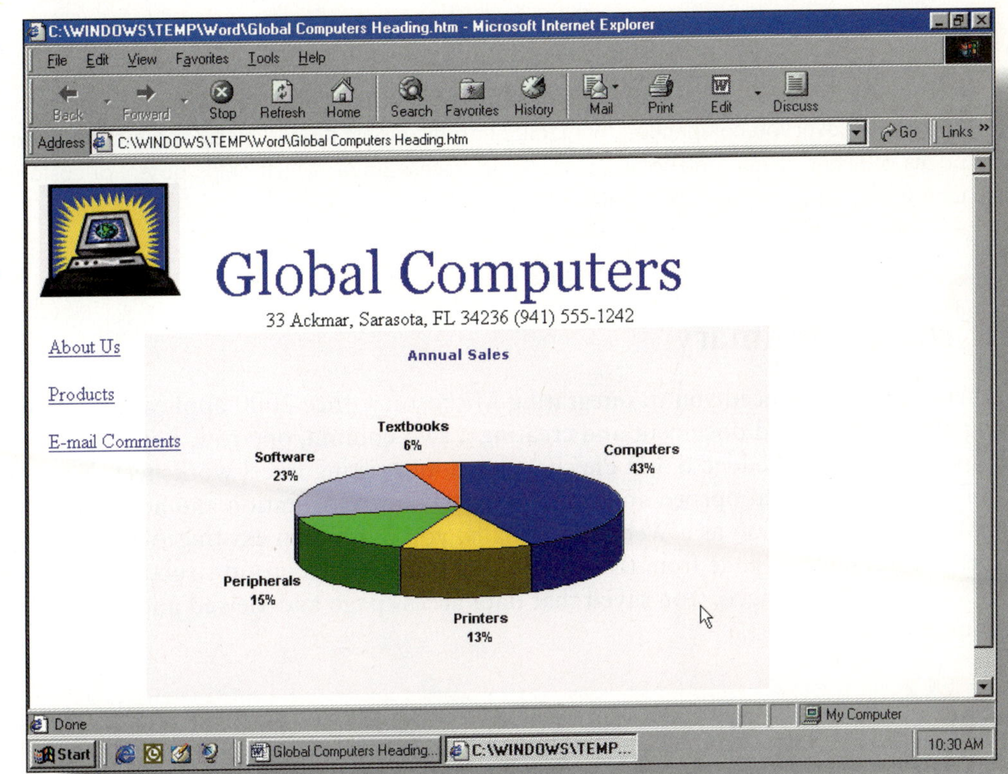

FIGURE 1-45

Verifying the Hyperlinks in Your Browser

All hyperlinks should be tested by clicking them and verifying that they jump to the correct Web page. There are three hyperlinks on the home page: About Us, Products, and E-Mail Comments. Perform the following steps to test the links.

TO VERIFY THE HYPERLINKS

1. Click the About Us hyperlink.
2. Click the navigation buttons to view all slides on the Web page.
3. On the first slide on the PowerPoint Web page, click Home.
4. Click the Products hyperlink. Click the Expand and Collapse indicators and then scroll through the database using the navigation toolbars.
5. On the data access page, click the Home hyperlink.
6. Click the E-Mail Comments link.

A new e-mail message displays with global@isp.com in the To text box.

With the hyperlinks verified, follow these steps to quit the e-mail program and your browser.

TO QUIT E-MAIL AND CLOSE YOUR BROWSER

1. Click the Close button on your e-mail program.
2. Click the Close button on your browser.

Discussions

The Discussions feature enables you and other people to insert remarks into a Web page. The discussions are threaded; that is, replies to a discussion remark are nested directly under it. You can have multiple discussions in progress simultaneously. You start a discussion from within your browser. The Discussions feature is available only with Microsoft Office Server Extensions, a feature that is set up by your system administrator. Learn more about discussions in Word Help.

CASE PERSPECTIVE SUMMARY

Dan is very happy with the Web site that you helped him create. He thinks it will stress the benefits of global Computers over the competition by highlighting his highly trained sales and technical staff. The site also lists the prices of his hardware and software in a data access page, which helps potential customers when they shop. Now Dan feels better prepared to compete.

Project Summary

This project introduced you to integrating Microsoft Office 2000 applications. You started this project by opening an existing Word document and creating a two-column, one-row, borderless table. You then inserted three hyperlinks and embedded a 3-D Pie chart from an existing Excel worksheet. You saved that document as an HTML file. You then opened an existing PowerPoint presentation and added a hyperlink to the first slide. You saved this presentation as a Web page. Finally, you opened an existing Access database. You used the Wizard to create a data access page from that database. You created a group structure so that the database could be viewed but not changed. You saved that data access page and viewed and tested all Web pages and hyperlinks in your browser.

What You Should Know

Having completed this project, you now should be able to perform the following tasks:

- Add a Hyperlink to a Data Access Page *(I 1.38)*
- Add a Title and Image to a Data Access Page *(I 1.36)*
- Add Text for a Hyperlink *(I 1.28)*
- Change the Size of an Embedded Object *(I 1.17)*
- Create a Data Access Page Using the Wizard *(I 1.33)*
- Create a Hyperlink in a PowerPoint Presentation *(I 1.29)*
- Display the Web Tools Toolbar *(I 1.20)*
- Embed an Excel Chart into a Word Document *(I 1.14)*
- Insert a Hyperlink to PowerPoint Web Pages *(I 1.12)*
- Insert a Table into a Word Document *(I 1.9)*
- Insert Scrolling Text *(I 1.21)*
- Insert Text for Hyperlinks *(I 1.11)*
- Insert the Remaining Hyperlinks *(I 1.13)*
- Open an Access Database *(I 1.32)*
- Open an Excel Workbook *(I 1.14)*
- Open a PowerPoint Presentation *(I 1.27)*
- Quit Access and Close Your Browser *(I 1.40)*
- Quit E-Mail and Close Your Browser *(I 1.41)*
- Quit Excel *(I 1.19)*
- Quit PowerPoint and Close Your Browser *(I 1.31)*
- Quit Word *(I 1.26)*
- Preview the Web Page *(I 1.25)*
- Remove the Table Border *(I 1.10)*
- Resize the Scrolling Text *(I 1.23)*
- Save a Document with a New File Name *(I 1.25)*
- Save the Data Access Page and View It in Your Browser *(I 1.39)*
- Save the PowerPoint Presentation as a Web Page *(I 1.31)*
- Start Word and Open an Existing Document *(I 1.8)*
- Test the Web Site *(I 1.41)*
- Verify the Hyperlinks *(I 1.41)*
- View the Web Page in Your Browser *(I 1.29)*

1 Creating a Web Page in Word with an Embedded Excel Chart

Problem: As president of Scientific Systems International, you have created a worksheet and chart in Excel. Create a Web page in Word and embed the chart from the Scientific Systems International workbook on the home page. Add a link to a second Web page and an e-mail link to ssi@isp.com below the chart. Create a second Web page in Word by embedding the Scientific Systems International worksheet.

Instructions: Perform the following tasks.

1. Start Excel by opening the Scientific Systems International workbook.
2. Start Word and create a new Web page. Add a title as shown in Figure 1-46. Select the Scientific Systems International chart, copy it, and use the Paste Special dialog box in Word to embed the Excel Worksheet Object. Be sure the Float over text check box is cleared in the Paste Special dialog box.
3. Add two hyperlinks to the bottom of the page in a centered, borderless table. The first hyperlink should jump to the Web page SSIsales.htm, which is created next. The second hyperlink creates an e-mail to ssi@isp.com.
4. Save this file as SSI.htm.
5. Create a new Web page in Word.
6. Embed the Excel worksheet into the Word page. That is, switch to Excel, select the worksheet, copy the worksheet to the Clipboard, switch to Word, and use the Paste Special dialog box in Word to embed the Excel Worksheet Object. Be sure the Float over text check box is cleared in the Paste Special dialog box.
7. Save this file as SSIsales.htm.
8. View the SSI.htm file in your browser (Figure 1-46). Print the Web page. Link to the SSIsales.htm page (Figure 1-47) and print it.

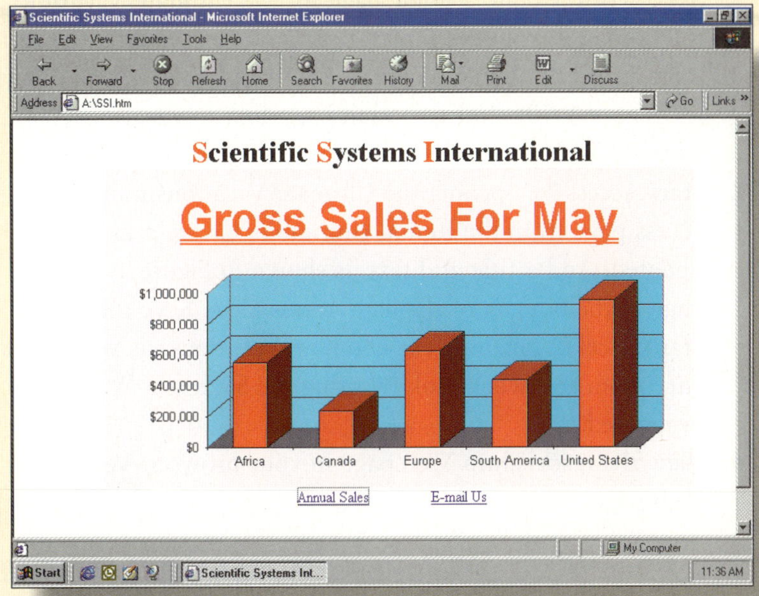

FIGURE 1-46

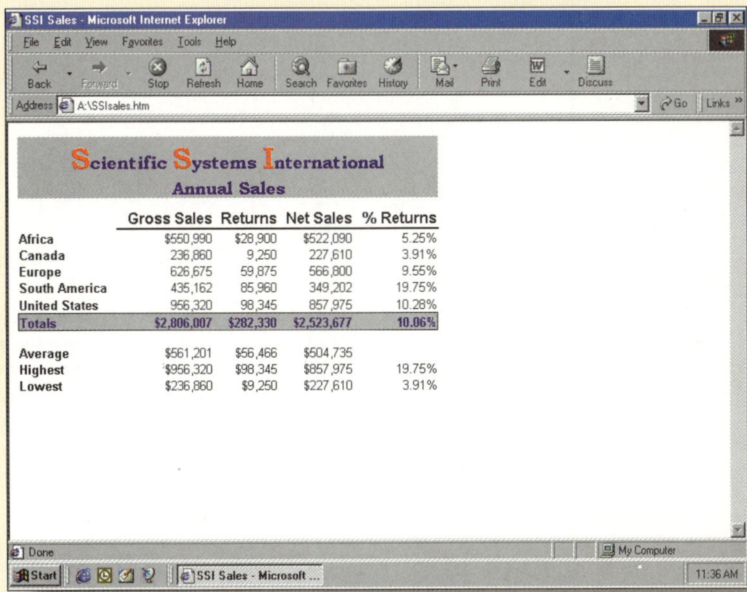

Scientific Systems International
Annual Sales

	Gross Sales	Returns	Net Sales	% Returns
Africa	$550,990	$28,900	$522,090	5.25%
Canada	236,860	9,250	227,610	3.91%
Europe	626,675	59,875	566,800	9.55%
South America	435,162	85,960	349,202	19.75%
United States	956,320	98,345	857,975	10.28%
Totals	$2,806,007	$282,330	$2,523,677	10.06%
Average	$561,201	$56,466	$504,735	
Highest	$956,320	$98,345	$857,975	19.75%
Lowest	$236,860	$9,250	$227,610	3.91%

FIGURE 1-47

2 Ultimate Vacations Web Site with Data Access Page and Excel Worksheet

Problem: Joanne Gately, owner of Ultimate Vacations, would like to advertise her rental agency over the World Wide Web. She has come up with a design idea that includes the database of rental units and their availability. She also wants an e-mail link for comments.

Instructions: Perform the following tasks.

1. Start Word. Create a home page for the Ultimate Vacations Web site (Figure 1-48). Add a title and insert the saling.gif from the Integration Data Disk. Add a borderless table below the title. In the left-hand column, insert three hyperlinks to Web pages rentals.htm (Rental Units, Figure 1-49), available.htm (Availability, Figure 1-50), and an e-mail hyperlink to vacations@isp.com. Type the text in the right-hand column. Save the Web page as resorts.htm.
2. Start Access by opening the Ultimate Vacations.mdb database on the Integration Data Disk. Create a data access page from the Rental Unit table. Create a group level using the City field so the database cannot be updated. Add a title and text as shown in Figure 1-49. Add a link named Home to the resorts.htm home page at the bottom of the data access page. Save the data access page as rentals.htm.
3. Start Excel by opening the Ultimate Vacations.xls workbook on the Integration Data Disk. Create a Web page from this workbook by using the Save as a Web Page command on the File menu. Use the file name, available.htm.
4. View the resorts.htm Web page in your browser. Verify that all links work by clicking each one. Print all Web pages.

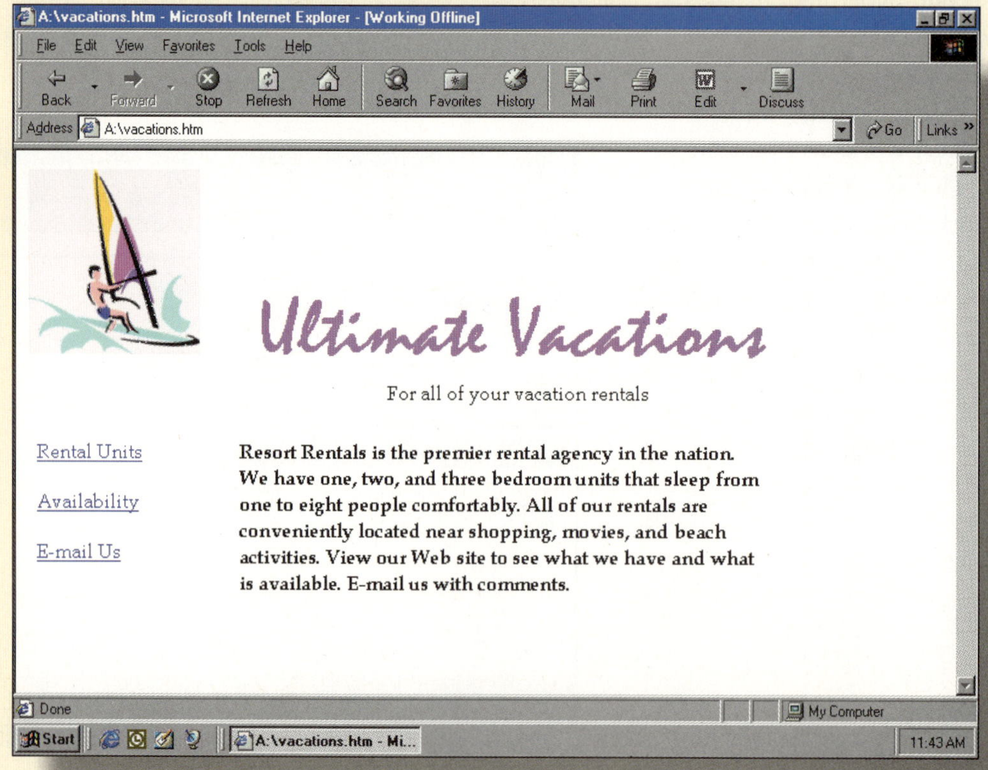

FIGURE 1-48

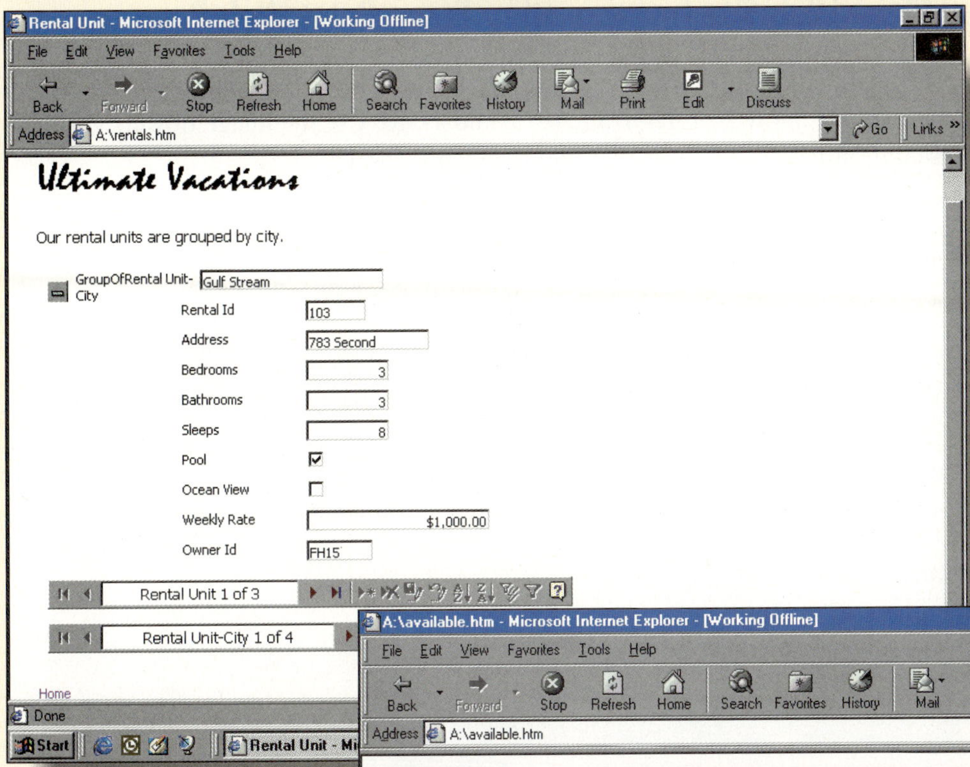

Rental Unit - Microsoft Internet Explorer - [Working Offline]

Address A:\rentals.htm

Ultimate Vacations

Our rental units are grouped by city.

GroupOfRental Unit-City: Gulf Stream

Rental Id	103
Address	783 Second
Bedrooms	3
Bathrooms	3
Sleeps	8
Pool	☑
Ocean View	☐
Weekly Rate	$1,000.00
Owner Id	FH15

Rental Unit 1 of 3

Rental Unit-City 1 of 4

Home

FIGURE 1-49

A:\available.htm - Microsoft Internet Explorer - [Working Offline]

Address A:\available.htm

Rental Units Available

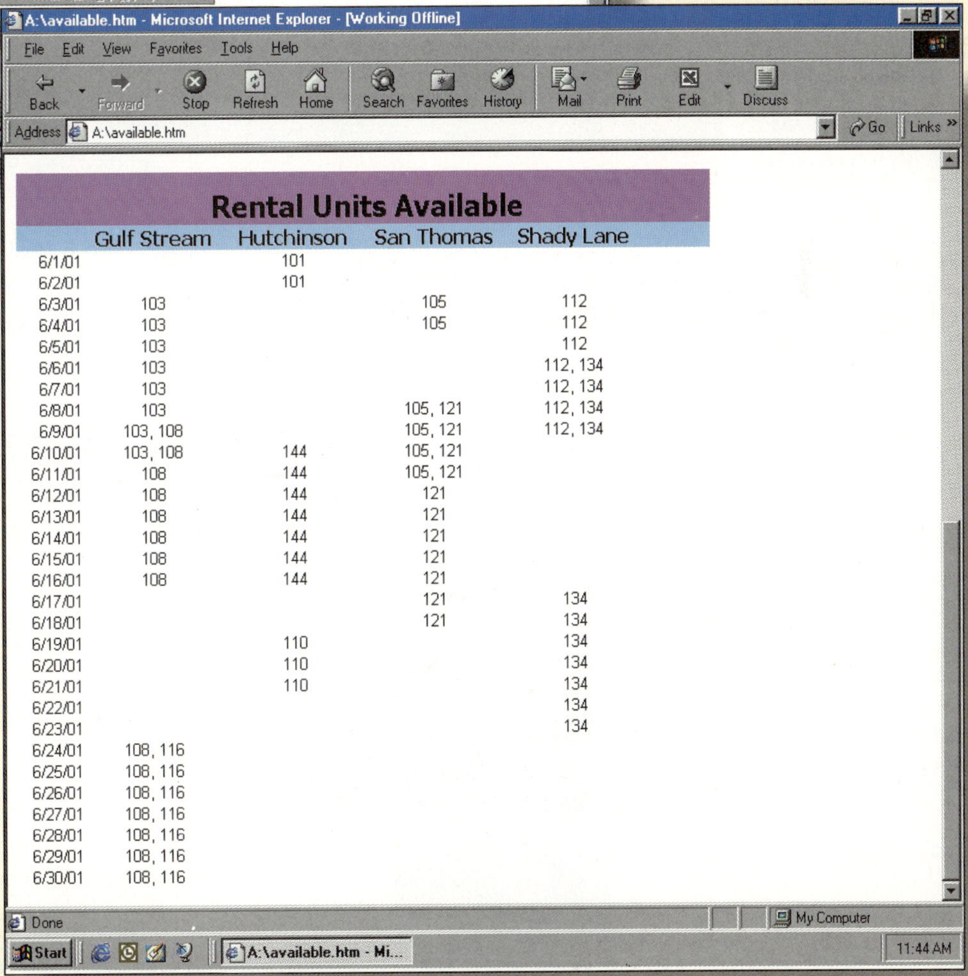

	Gulf Stream	Hutchinson	San Thomas	Shady Lane
6/1/01		101		
6/2/01		101		
6/3/01	103		105	112
6/4/01	103		105	112
6/5/01	103			112
6/6/01	103			112, 134
6/7/01	103			112, 134
6/8/01	103		105, 121	112, 134
6/9/01	103, 108		105, 121	112, 134
6/10/01	103, 108	144	105, 121	
6/11/01	108	144	105, 121	
6/12/01	108	144	121	
6/13/01	108	144	121	
6/14/01	108	144	121	
6/15/01	108	144	121	
6/16/01	108	144	121	
6/17/01			121	134
6/18/01			121	134
6/19/01		110		134
6/20/01		110		134
6/21/01		110		134
6/22/01				134
6/23/01				134
6/24/01	108, 116			
6/25/01	108, 116			
6/26/01	108, 116			
6/27/01	108, 116			
6/28/01	108, 116			
6/29/01	108, 116			
6/30/01	108, 116			

FIGURE 1-50

3 Creating an Antique Show Web Site Incorporating PowerPoint Web Pages

Problem: As the promotions specialist for the Midwest College Art Department, you are responsible for creating the Web site that advertises the Antique Show (Figures 1-51, 1-52, and 1-53). Use the image flowers.gif for Figure 1-51. The PowerPoint presentation has five Web pages, one of which is shown.

Instructions: Perform the following tasks.

1. Start Word. Create the Web page shown in Figure 1-51. Include scrolling text below the Web page title. Insert three text hyperlinks to the document; PowerPoint Web pages (Apply-2.htm), the map.htm page, and an e-mail link to mc@isp.com. Save this Web page as antiqueshow.htm.
2. Create a new Web page in Word (Figure 1-53). Insert the map.gif image from the Integration Data Disk. Add a text box to the Web page. Add an arrow to connect the text box to the area indicated on the map. Save the file as map.htm.
3. Open the PowerPoint presentation Apply-2.ppt. Apply Design Template Blends.ppt (or another colorful template). Save the PowerPoint presentation as Web pages on the Integration Data Disk. Name the Web pages Apply-2.htm.
4. View the Web pages in your browser. Print them all.

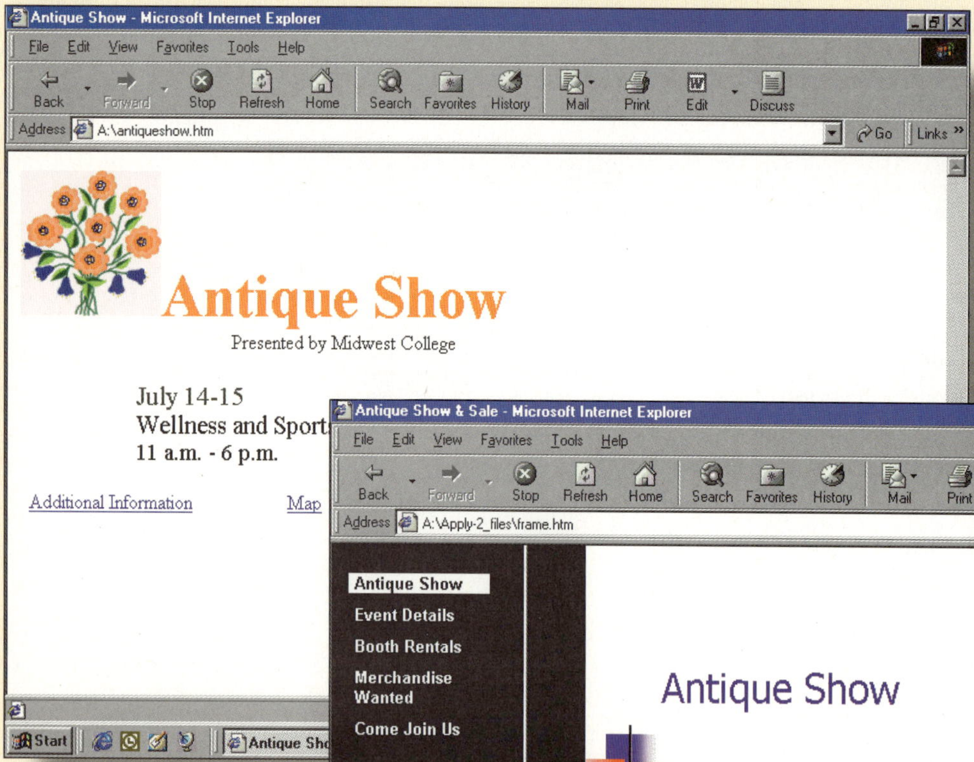

FIGURE 1-51

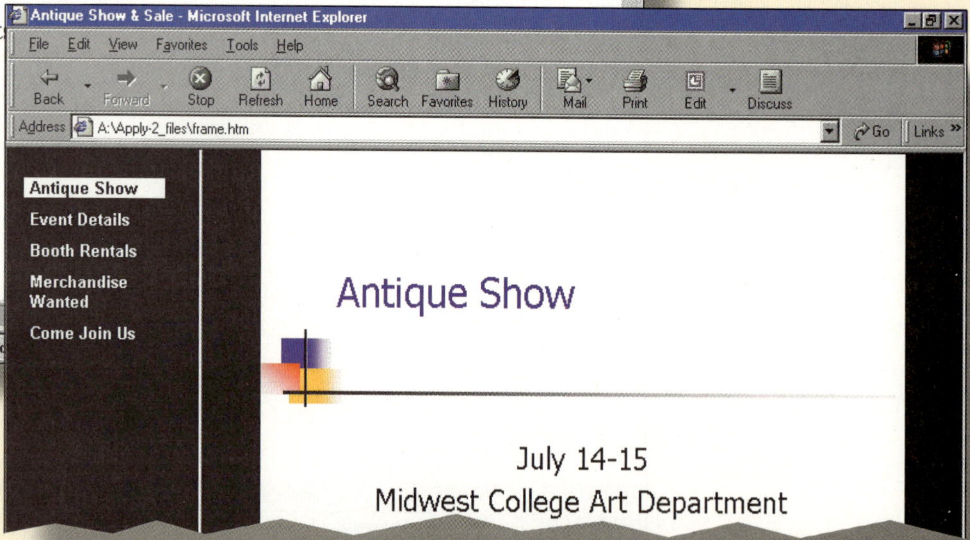

FIGURE 1-52

In the Lab

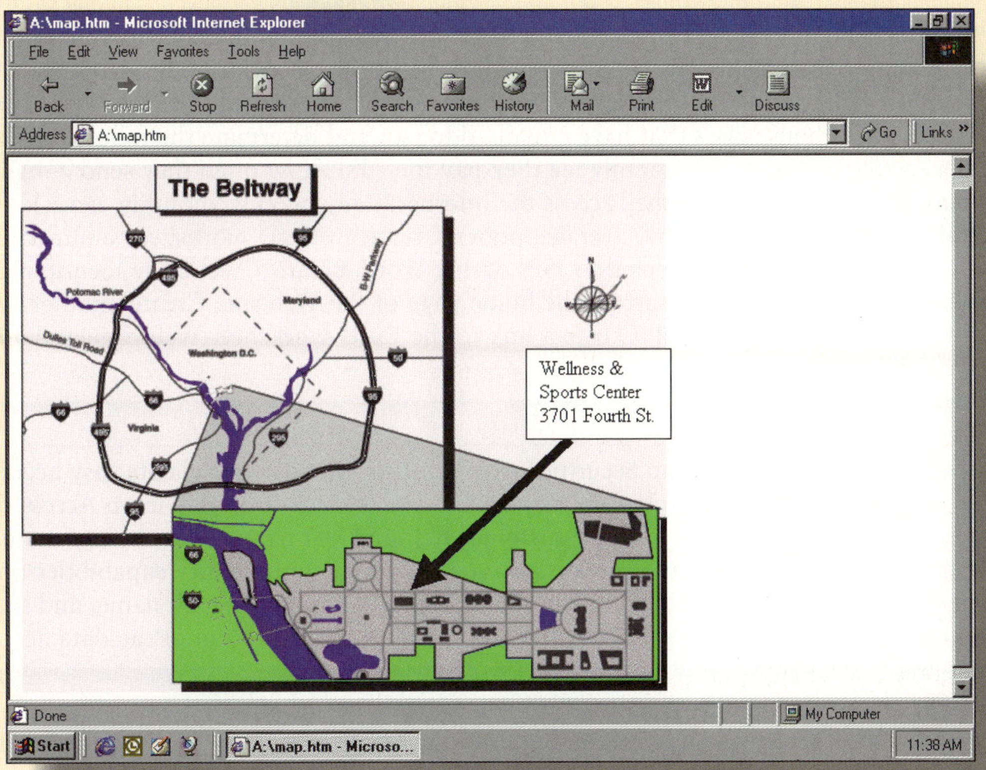

FIGURE 1-53

Cases and Places

The difficulty of these case studies varies:
◗ are the least difficult; ◗◗ are more difficult; and ◗◗◗ are the most difficult.

1 ◗ You are the membership director of the St. John Ice Rink, which has three membership plans. The Gold plan is good for a single membership, has an initial fee of $100 and a monthly charge of $25, and provides the member with unlimited access to club facilities. The Silver plan also is good for a single membership, has an initial fee of $35 and a monthly charge of $10, and restricts the member's admittance to nonprime-time hours. The Family plan is good for an entire family membership, has an initial fee of $250 and a monthly charge of $50, and provides each family member with unlimited access to club facilities. Create a worksheet in Excel that summarizes each of these plans. Create a Web page using Word that embeds the Excel worksheet; the goal of the Web site is to gain new members. Make sure an e-mail address is included.

2 ◗ You are preparing to teach a distance learning class at the community college. It is important for you to steer prospective students toward a reliable Internet service provider (ISP). It would be helpful for you to have information on the costs and service quality of the various ISPs in your area. Take a poll of 10 students in your in-house class that have e-mail addresses and determine the following: the name of their Internet service provider, the monthly fee they pay their ISP, how often they send e-mail (daily, weekly, monthly, never), how often they access the Internet (daily, weekly, monthly, never), and their rating of the ISPs service (excellent, good, average, poor). Create an Excel worksheet summarizing your data and a chart of the monthly fees paid to ISPs. Using Word, create a Web page identifying the local ISPs according to cost. Embed the chart on the home page of the Web site. Create another Web page, embedding the worksheet from Excel. Create a link to the Excel worksheet Web page and a link to the home page of each ISP.

3 ◗ As investment broker for Beyond Securities, you want to provide your clients easy access to the latest value of their portfolios. Using only four major stock names, create a table in an Access database that contains a unique customer ID number, customer first and last name, address, city, state, zip, stock name, and stock value. From this table, create a data access page with inquiry capabilities only, using the stock name as the group level. Include only the customer ID number, stock name, and stock value in the data access page. Create links to the four stock companies at the bottom of the data access page.

4 ◗◗ As chairperson of the Marketing committee for your Investment Club, you are responsible for distributing valuable information to the club members. You notice that Excel has a Web query called DBC Best Credit Cards, which lists the issuing institution, the telephone number, the interest rate, the fee, and the number of interest-free days for 10 to 15 companies. You decide this is extremely useful information. After running the Web query, create a worksheet that nicely organizes this information using 3-D references to the Web Query sheet. Then, create a Web page using Word that includes the Excel worksheet as an embedded object. If you do not have the DBC Best Credit Cards Web query, you will need to download it from the Get More Web Queries worksheet (see Excel Help for more detailed information on downloading Web queries).

5 ◗◗◗ As a member of the Student Government Association (SGA), you are delivering a five-minute presentation about the current student body at your school. Obtain statistics and interesting facts on your school's student body, e.g., percentage of male/female; number of freshman, sophomore, junior, senior students; ratio of part-time versus full-time students; age ranges; and so on. Create an Excel worksheet summarizing your findings. Create an Excel chart for one of the interesting statistics. Create a PowerPoint slide show containing at least seven slides, one of which is the title slide and one is a closing slide. Embed the Excel chart into one of the PowerPoint slides. Save the PowerPoint presentation as Web pages. Include a link at the bottom of the page to the school's home page. Also include links to other appropriate SGA sources on the World Wide Web.

Every two-to-three years, Microsoft Corporation introduces a new version of Office. The newest version, Microsoft Office XP (eXPerience), will be released in 2001.

If you know how to use Office 2000, then you will have no problem adapting quickly to Office XP. The purpose of this section is to introduce you to some of the new features.

Changes to the User Interface

The user interface changes described in this section pertain to most or all of the Office XP applications. These changes include a flatter look, the addition of task panes, speech recognition, easier access to the Help system, a command to display the Standard and Formatting toolbars on one or two rows, AutoCorrect Options buttons, Paste Options buttons, and an improved Office Clipboard.

Flatter Look

The applications have a smooth, flat, two-dimensional look (Figure 1), which is intended to give them a more pleasing appearance.

Task Panes

Microsoft has added task panes to all the Office XP applications. Word has seven task panes titled New Document, Clipboard, Search, Styles and Formatting, Reveal Formatting, Mail Merge, and Translate. Excel and Access have three task panes each – New Document, Clipboard, and Search. PowerPoint has a total of ten task panes. A task pane (Figure 1) enables you to carry out some tasks more quickly. You use these task panes to format documents, show the contents of the Office Clipboard, initiate new documents, and serve as an entry point for searches.

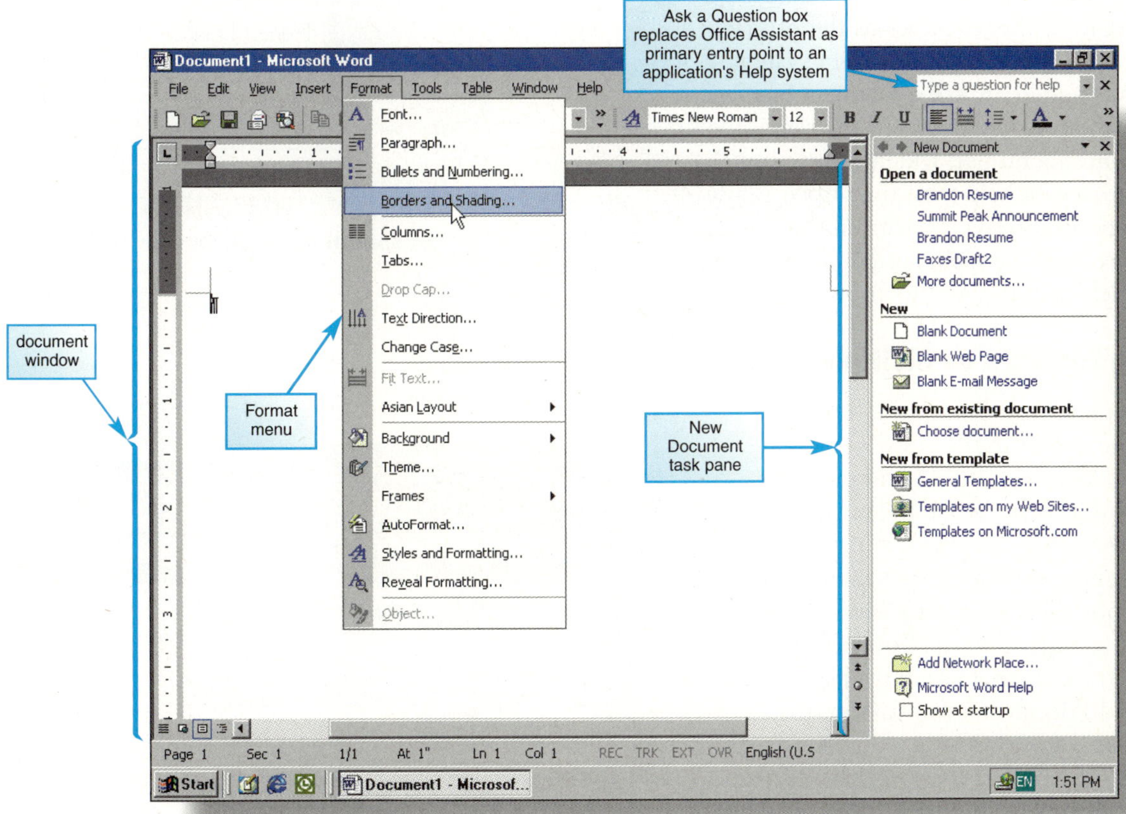

FIGURE 1

Speech Recognition and Text to Speech

With the **Office Speech Recognition software** installed and a microphone, you can speak the names of toolbar buttons, menus, menu commands, list items, alerts, and dialog box controls, such as OK and Cancel. You also can dictate text and numbers, delete text, and insert text. To indicate whether you want to speak commands or dictate cell entries, you use the **Language bar** Figure 2(a). You can display the Language bar in two ways: (1) click the Speech Recognition icon in the taskbar tray status area by the clock and then click Show the Language bar in the menu Figure 2(b), or (2) point to the **Speech command** on the **Tools menu** and then click the **Speech Recognition command** on the **Speech submenu**.

Through the Language bar, you also can display a **transparent keyboard** on the screen that allows you to use the mouse to enter text and numbers.

If you have speakers, you can instruct the computer to speak a document or worksheet to you. You can select either a male or female voice.

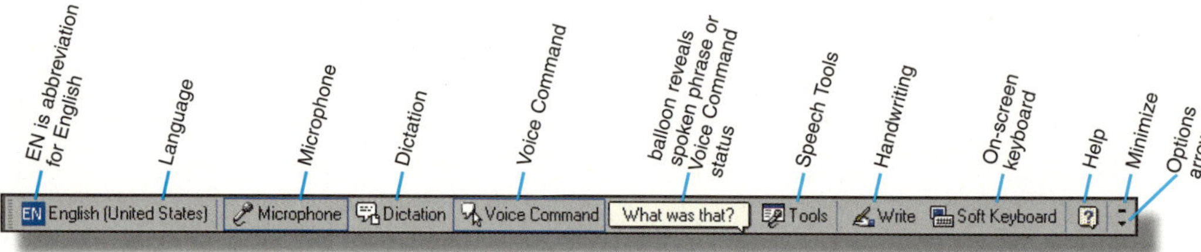

(a) Language Bar

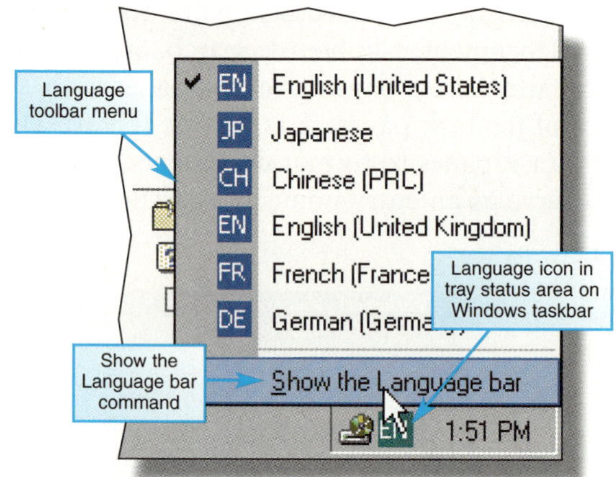

(b) Speech Recognition Icon Menu

FIGURE 2

Improved Help System

Although the Office Assistant remains available in Office XP, it no longer serves as the primary entry point into an application's Help system. Microsoft has added an **Ask a Question box** (see Figure 1 on the previous page) to the right side of an application's menu bar, which offers a much easier way to access help than the Office Assistant. You may enter questions or terms in the Ask a Question box, and the Help system immediately displays a Help window on the topic.

Displaying Toolbars on Multiple Rows

The Standard and Formatting toolbars display at the top of the window in most applications. They can display on the same row or separate rows. When the toolbars display on the same row, there is more room for the document to display, but many of the buttons do not show on the toolbars. Microsoft has added a command to the Toolbar Options list (Figure 3) to make it easier to display the Standard and Formatting toolbars on the same row or on separate rows. Also, the Standard and Formatting Toolbar Options lists display the hidden buttons belonging to both toolbars.

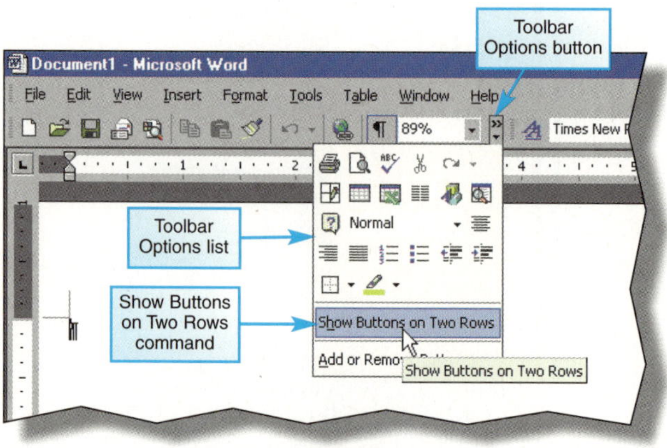

FIGURE 3

AutoCorrect Options Button

If the AutoCorrect feature of changes a misspelled word in your document, it tags it. When you later point to the tagged word, Office XP displays a small blue line under it. If you point to the blue line, it changes to the **AutoCorrect Options button** (Figure 4), which allows you to reject the change or update the AutoCorrect options.

If AutoCorrect makes a correction that you delete and retype the way it was originally, Office XP no longer will recorrect it a second time.

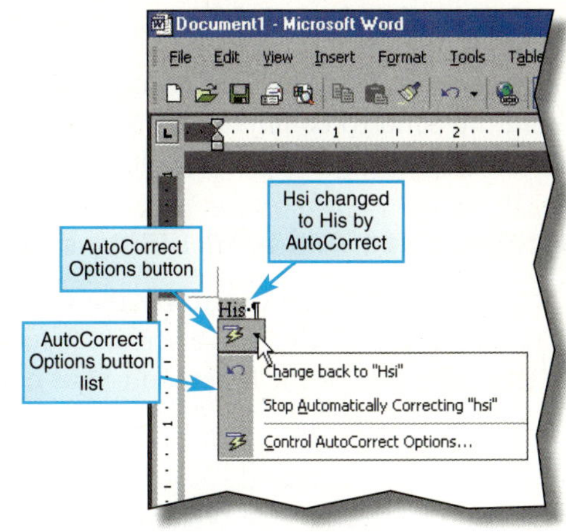

FIGURE 4

Paste Options Button

When you paste an item from the Office Clipboard into a document, a **Paste Options button** displays close to the pasted item (Figure 5). The Paste Options button lets you control how the pasted text will be formatted. Once you start a new task, such as entering text, the Paste Options button disappears.

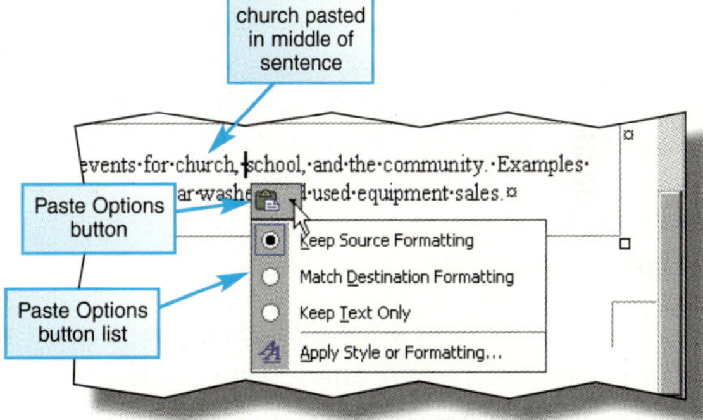

FIGURE 5

Office Clipboard

Office XP will let you accumulate up to 24 different copied items on its Office Clipboard. Once you copy the second item to the Office Clipboard, Office XP displays the Clipboard task pane. The Clipboard task pane previews both text and pictures (Figure 6). To paste any one of the items into a document, position the insertion point and click the preview text or picture in the Clipboard task pane.

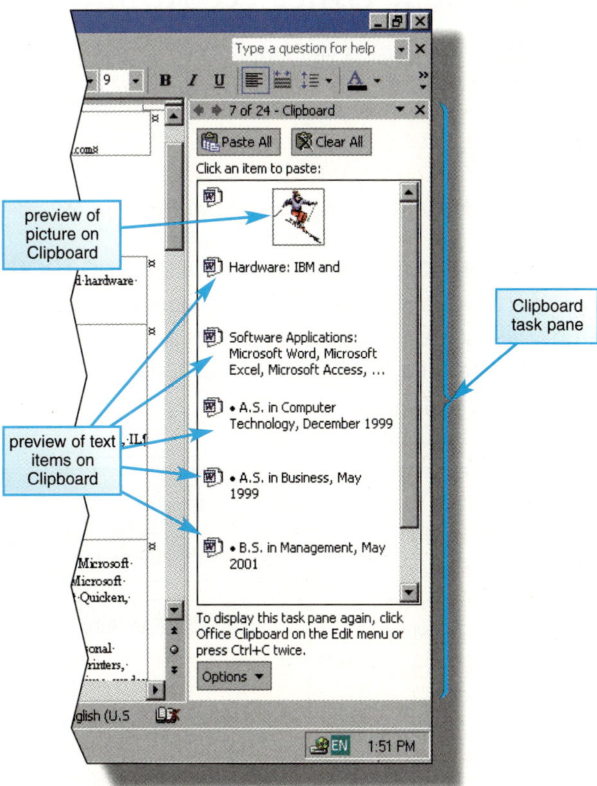

FIGURE 6

Other Office XP Enhancements

Office XP includes numerous enhancements beyond the user interface for most applications. Some of these enhancements are listed below.

Digital Signature

Office XP uses **Microsoft Authenticode technology** to enable you digitally to sign a file by using a digital certificate. A **digital certificate** confirms that the document originated from the signer, and the signature confirms that it has not been altered.

E-Mail Based Collaboration

The Send To command on the File menu lets you send a document to a group of reviewers. Office XP lets you better track the document and manage the changed versions.

E-Mail Introduction Field

If you send the active document via e-mail by clicking the E-mail button on the Standard toolbar or by clicking the Send to command on the File menu, an Introduction text box displays under the Subject text box. The Introduction text box allows you to append a message to the active document sent in the e-mail.

Resizable Open and Save Dialog Boxes

With Office XP, you can resize the Open and Save dialog boxes. If you double-click their title bars, they maximize to fill the entire screen. You also can add folders that you use often to the Places bar, which is on the right side of the Open and Save dialog boxes.

Web Services

The **Add Network Place Wizard** lets you add folders located on servers to your system. This wizard gives you easy access to the added folders through the Save and Open dialog boxes. Through the Microsoft Network (MSN), you also can share files with others without quitting an Office XP application.

Privacy

If you plan to share an Office XP file with others and prefer the author of the file be anonymous, the Security tab in the Options dialog box allows you to instruct Office XP to remove the personal information normally appended to the file.

Save My Settings

Office XP has a **Save My Settings Wizard** that lets you save your Office settings to a file or the Web. You later can restore the settings to the same personal computer or another personal computer. You activate the Save My Settings Wizard through the Microsoft Office Tools command on the Programs submenu.

Individual Office XP Applications

This section discusses the enhancements that are specific to the applications in Office XP. The individual applications use 2002 to refer to the next version, rather than XP.

Word 2002

The following changes are contained in Word 2002.

NEW BUTTONS ON STANDARD AND FORMATTING TOOLBARS Microsoft has added a Search button to the Word Standard toolbar (Figure 7). The **Search button** displays the Search pane and invokes Word's significantly improved search engine. The Styles and Formatting button, Distributed button, and Line Spacing button have been added to theFormatting toolbar. The **Styles and Formatting button** displays the Styles and Formatting task pane, which can be used to simplify formatting a document. The **Distributed button** spaces characters in a paragraph so the paragraph displays as a perfect rectangle. The **Line Spacing button** lets you adjust the amount of space between lines in a paragraph.

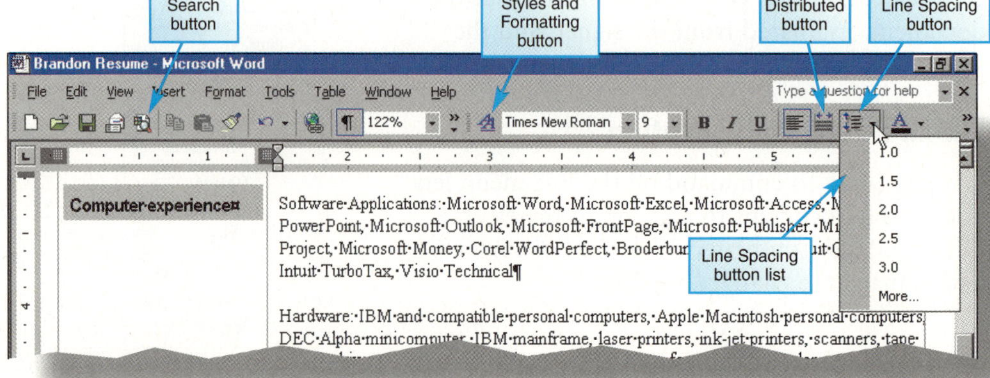

FIGURE 7

TRACKED CHANGES Word 2002 does a much better job tracking changes in a document than previous versions of Word did. No longer are the changes mixed with the original text. Instead, Word 2002 uses balloons in the margin to describe changes (Figure 8).

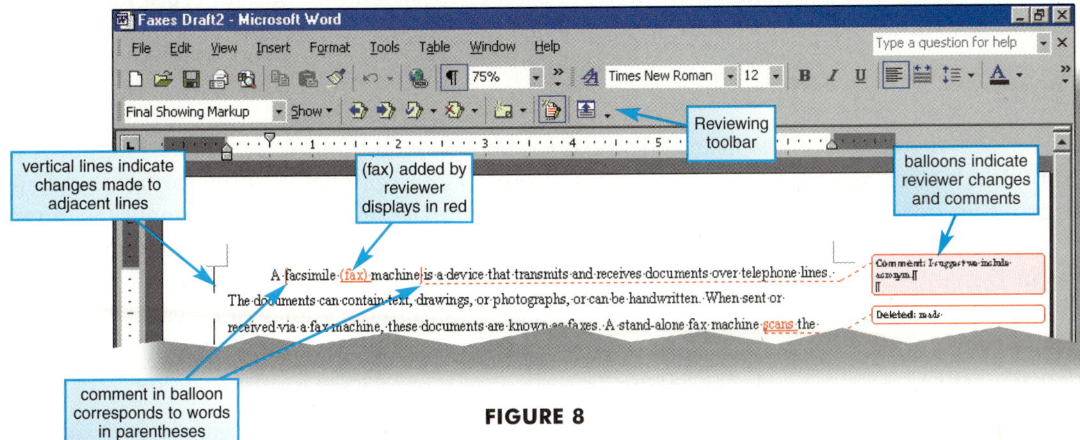

FIGURE 8

PERSISTENT WORD COUNT A new toolbar, the **Word Count toolbar**, includes a Word Count box and Recount button that allows you to maintain a persistent or continuous word count as you create a document (Figure 9).

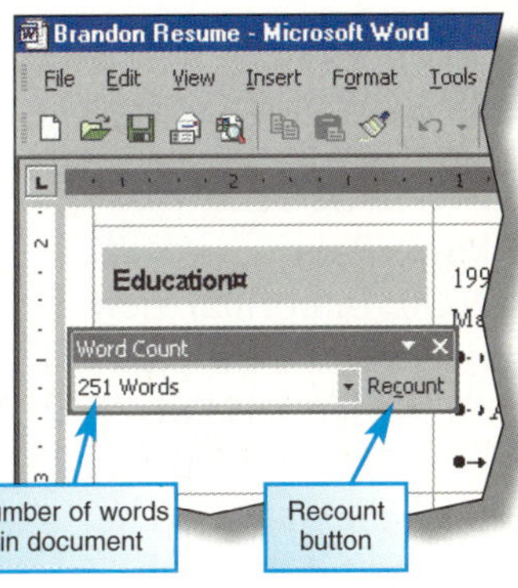

FIGURE 9

TURN HTML ROUND TRIPPING OFF This enhancement allows you to use Word 2002 to publish clean HTML, without all the extras required for Word to read back the HTML file.

OTHER CHANGES Significant improvements have been made to comparing and merging documents, revealing format codes, maintaining consistent formats, checking for format inconsistencies within a document, and easily selecting non-adjacent text in a document. Major improvements also have been made to how you handle bulleted and numbered lists, table support, proofing tools, mail merge, and the inclusion of watermarks. Finally, Word 2002 improves accessibility to disabled users.

Excel 2002

Microsoft has added several new minor features to Excel 2002, but in general it differs little from Excel 2000. The only new button added to the often-used Standard and Formatting toolbars is a **Search button** Figure 10(a), which can be used to search for text and numbers in cells. The Edit Formula box on the formula bar has been replaced by the **Insert Function button**. The AutoSum button now has an arrow that displays a list of often-used functions from which you can choose.

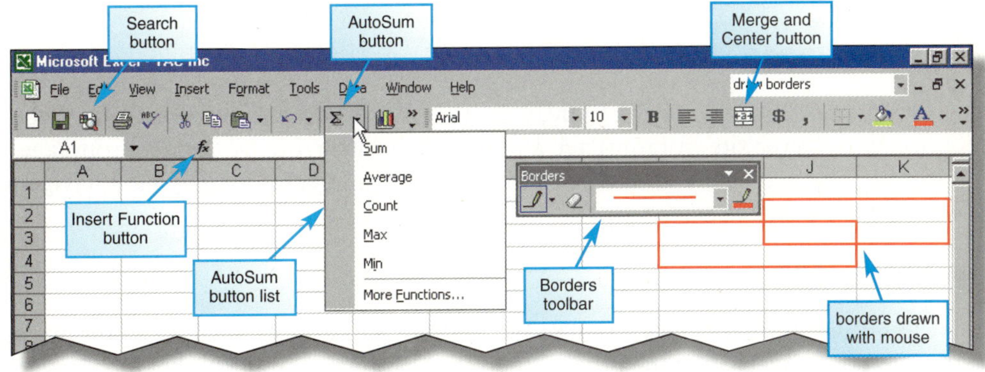

(a) Excel Toolbars

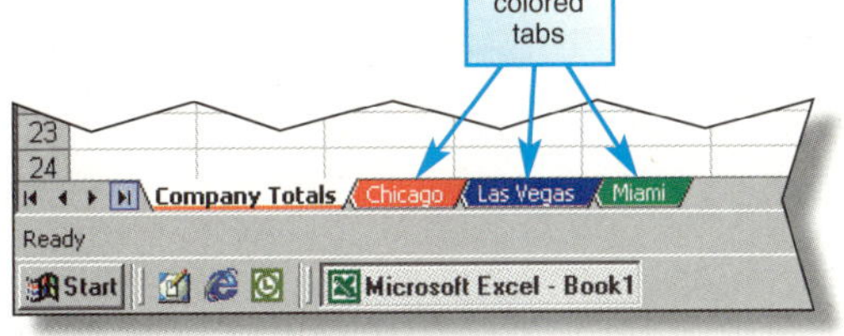

(b) Colored Tabs

FIGURE 10

You can use your mouse to draw borders by using buttons on the **Borders toolbar**. The Merge and Center button functions as a toggle between centering and left aligning. You also can change the colors of the worksheet tabs Figure 10(b) on the previous page through their shortcut menu.

Other features in Excel 2002 include protection by range, recognition of data types for sorting purposes, and new functionality for creating formulas and verifying spreadsheet accuracy.

Access 2002

The interface of Access 2002 is nearly identical to the Access 2000 interface. While supporting the Access 2000 file format, the next release of Access also offers an optional new file format that handles new properties and changes in an improved fashion. The compact and repair functionality is improved and is better able to recover files with broken forms and reports. Other new features include multiple undos and redos in Design view, improved PivotChart and PivotTable capabilities, new events for forms, new properties for both forms and reports, and new shortcut keys to make your work easier.

PowerPoint 2002

PowerPoint 2002 has three main views: normal, slide view, and slide show rather than the five views of PowerPoint 2000. In normal view (Figure 11), the pane on the left has two tabs. One tab lets you view the outline. The second tab lets you display slide thumbnails of the presentation. The right pane shows the current slide.

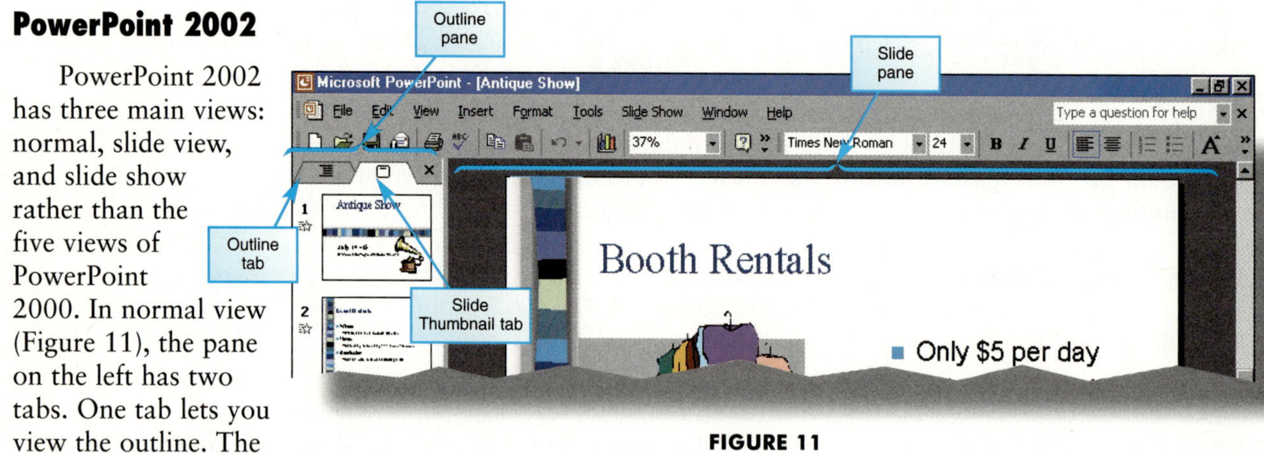

FIGURE 11

Microsoft has added, replaced, or moved a few of the buttons on the PowerPoint Standard and Formatting toolbars. The button lineup on these two toolbars should speed up the creation of presentations.

Other PowerPoint 2002 features make it easier to broadcast presentations over the Web, collaborate with others, preview presentations before you print, and apply multiple masters to the same presentation.

FrontPage 2002

FrontPage 2002 includes new features that allow you to customize your Web site by opening your Office Web Server site in FrontPage and changing the layout or theme. FrontPage 2002 will also give you improved site management, better editing features, and ease in applying a navigational structure to your Web site.

Publisher 2002

Publisher 2002 includes a tighter integration with other Office XP applications. For example, Publisher 2002 looks and feels like the other Office applications. With Publisher 2002, you can have more than one publication open simultaneously. Other features include coordinated font sets to give a publication a new look, improved mail merge, better print preview, superior handling of EPS files, and the ability to save and open HTML documents.

Outlook 2002

Outlook 2002 replaces the Personal Folders with Local Information Store Folders, which improve your ability to collaborate, replicate, and manage documents. Other new features of Outlook 2002 include completion of e-mail addresses, calendar coloring, an improved preview pane, and better synchronization.

Office 2000 Learn It Online

Instructions: To complete Exercises 1 through 5, start your browser, enter the URL `scsite.com/off2000/exs.htm`, and then follow the instructions in the exercise. For Exercises 6 through 8, you must have the application open.

1. Project Reinforcement – True/False, Multiple Choice and Short Answer

Click Project Reinforcement. Below the application title, click the Project title for which you want to take a quiz. Print the quiz by clicking Print on the File menu. Answer each question. Write your first and last name at the top of each page, and then hand in the printout to your instructor.

2. Practice Test

Click Practice Test. Below the application title, click the Project title for which you want to take a practice test. Answer each question, enter your first and last name at the bottom of the page, and then click the Grade Test button. When the graded practice test displays on your screen, click Print on the File menu to print a hard copy. Continue to take practice tests until you score 80% or better. Hand in a printout of the final practice test to your instructor.

3. Who Wants to Be a Computer Genius?

Click Computer Genius. Below the application title, click the Project title for which you want to become a computer genius. Read the instructions, enter your first and last name at the bottom of the page, and then click the PLAY button. Hand in your score to your instructor.

4. Wheel of Terms

Click Wheel of Terms. Below the application title, click the Project title for which you want to play Wheel of Terms. Read the instructions, and then enter your first and last name and your school name. Click VERY HIGH SCORES to see other student scores. Click the PLAY button. Hand in your score to your instructor.

5. Crossword Puzzle Challenge

Click Crossword Puzzle Challenge. Below the application title, click the Project title for which you want to complete the Crossword Puzzle challenge. Read the instructions, and then enter your first and last name. Click the PLAY button. Work the crossword puzzle. When you are finished, click the Submit button. When the crossword puzzle redisplays, click the Print button. Hand in the printout to your instructor.

6. Tips and Tricks

Start the application you are studying. On the Help menu, click Office on the Web. Click Assistance under the application title on the left side of the screen. Click the Tips and Tricks link. Click a topic that pertains to the project you are studying. Right-click the information and then click Print. Construct a brief example of what the information pertains to in the application to show you understand how to use the tip or trick. Hand in the example and printed information to your instructor.

7. Newsgroups

Start the application you are studying. On the Help menu, click Office on the Web. Click Assistance under the application title on the left side of the screen. Click the Newsgroups link. Click a topic that pertains to the project you are studying. Print three comments and hand them in to your instructor.

8. Expanding Your Horizons

Start the application you are studying. On the Help menu, click Office on the Web. Click Assistance under the application title on the left side of the screen. Click the Articles link. Click a topic that pertains to the project you are studying. Print the information. Construct a brief example of what the information pertains to in the application to show you understand the contents of the article. Hand in the example and printed information to your instructor.

Word 2000 Enhanced Project 1 Laboratory Exercises

For a sample result of an exercise, visit scsite.com/off2000enh/labs.htm.

1 Cabin for Rent

Your neighbor is renting his cabin. Because you are a Marketing Major, he has asked you to prepare an announcement that he can post at various locations around town. Use the following text and picture: first line of headline – EXPERIENCE NATURE...; second line of headline – ... GET AWAY FROM IT ALL; graphic of a cabin is located in the Clip Gallery using the keyword cabin; body title – CABIN FOR RENT; first paragraph text – Enjoy the great outdoors with all the comforts of home. Equipped with gas fireplace, two full baths, color television and VCR, fully equipped kitchen, telephone, and central heat and air conditioning.; second paragraph text – Located on Eastwood Lake, this two-bedroom log cabin offers fishing, boating, and swimming. Restaurants and unique shops are nearby.; last line – Call 555-6987 for more information. Use the following or similar fonts: headline – 36-point Andy; body title – 36-point Times New Roman; all other text – 22-point Times New Roman. Resize the graphic so the announcement fits on a single page. Use the concepts and techniques presented in Word Project 1 to create and format this announcement.

2 Lakefront Condominiums

You work as a computer specialist at Lancaster Development. Your manager has assigned you the task of preparing an announcement to mail to potential customers in several suburbs. The announcement should contain a graphic of lakefront condominiums. Use the following text and picture: first line of headline – Lakefront Condominiums...; second line of headline – ...A Dream Come True; picture of lakefront condominiums is located in the Clip Gallery using the keyword condominium; body title – LANCASTER DEVELOPMENT; first paragraph text – Looking for a quiet lakefront condominium? Let the qualified experts at Lancaster Development help you find that perfect place!; second paragraph text – To view these fine properties, e-mail us at lancaster@town.net or call 555-2685. Appointments are available seven days a week.; last line – Visit www.lancaster.com for more information. Use the following or similar fonts: headline – 36-point Harlow Solid Italic; body title – 26-point Algerian; all other text – 22-point Times New Roman. Resize the graphic so the announcement fits on a single page. Use the concepts and techniques presented in Word Project 1 to create and format this announcement.

3 Motorcycle

A co-worker is selling his motorcycle. Because of your extensive computer experience, he has asked you to prepare an announcement that he can post on the office bulletin boards. Use the following text and picture: first line of headline – For Sale...; second line of headline – ...Must See!; picture of a motorcycle is located in the Clip Gallery using the keyword motorcycle; body title – 1991 Custom Motorcycle; first paragraph text – This beautiful motorcycle has had only one owner. Must see. It is fully loaded with a chrome package and limited edition pipes; second paragraph – The motorcycle is in excellent condition and has low mileage. Asking $12,500.; last line – Call 555-0311 for more information. Use the following or similar fonts: headline – 48-point Arial Black; body title – 28-point Arial Rounded MT Bold; all other text – 22-point Times New Roman. Resize the graphic so the announcement fits on a single page. Use the concepts and techniques presented in Word Project 1 to create and format this announcement.

Word 2000 Enhanced Project 2 Laboratory Exercises

For a sample result of an exercise, visit scsite.com/off2000enh/labs.htm.

1 Help for the Spelling Challenged

This week's assignment in your introductory computer class is to prepare a short research paper on the use of word processing software as a spelling tool. The paper must be presented according to the MLA documentation style, contain one footnote (explanatory note), and have three references. Use the concepts and techniques presented in Word Project 2, along with the following information, to create and format the research paper.

Use the title, Help for the Spelling Challenged, for the research paper. To begin the paper, start with the second sentence of the second paragraph on page WD 1.4 and continue through the end of this paragraph. Use the third paragraph on page WD 1.4 as the text in the second paragraph of the research paper, except omit the last sentence. End the second paragraph of your paper by typing this sentence, `Microsoft Word will check your typing for possible spelling errors.`

Continue your research paper with text from the fourth, sixth, and seventh paragraphs of the article (on page WD 1.5). Use the first two sentences of the eighth paragraph of the article as the text in the last paragraph in your research paper. Type this sentence as the last sentence in the last paragraph of your research paper: `Microsoft Word and a good dictionary should enhance your spelling skills, and stop your words from Wobbling.`

You should use this textbook, the www.scsite.com/wd2000 Web site, and the book titled *Spelling Woes* by Terry Hoecker (The Berkley Publishing Group, New York, 2001) as your references. Reflecting on a personal experience, write an explanatory note as a footnote where you deem appropriate in the research paper.

2 Personalized Letters and Resumes

Your English composition instructor has assigned a research paper on resumes and cover letters. The paper must be presented according to the MLA documentation style, contain one footnote (explanatory note), and have three references. Use the concepts and techniques presented in Word Project 2, along with the following information, to create and format the research paper.

Use the title, Personalized Letters and Resumes, for the research paper. The first three paragraphs of your research paper are the same text as the first three paragraphs of the article on pages WD 3.2 and WD 3.3 in your textbook.

For the first sentence of the fourth paragraph, type `As you embark on your professional career, you have the advantage of using Word to prepare a resume and a personalized cover letter.` Continue the fourth paragraph by typing the two sentences in the fifth paragraph of the article (page WD 3.3). End the fourth paragraph by typing this sentence: `Word provides the tools that eliminate the need to start from scratch every time, while you provide responses and supply the substance.`

For the fifth paragraph in your research paper, use the second and third sentences of the seventh paragraph in the article (page WD 3.3). Use the last paragraph of the article on page WD 3.3 as the last paragraph of your research paper.

You should use this textbook, the www.scsite.com/wd2000 Web site, and the book titled *Computer Use and Your Career* by Kelly Dyrcz (William Morrow and Company, New York, 2001) as your references. Reflecting on a personal experience, write an explanatory note as a footnote where you deem appropriate in the research paper.

Word 2000 Enhanced Project 3 Laboratory Exercises

For a sample result of an exercise, visit scsite.com/off2000enh/labs.htm.

1 Kayla Lou Maxwell Resume

Because you are majoring in Computer Technology, your friend, Kayla, has asked you to assist her in preparing her resume. Use the concepts and techniques presented in Word Project 3, along with the following information, to create and format the resume.

Kayla's full name is Kayla Lou Maxwell, and she lives at Nine Keswick Court in Stafford, Virginia, 22554. Her telephone number is (540) 555-2862; fax number is (540) 555-2863, and e-mail address is maxwell@times.net. Her objective is to obtain a position at a commercial television station.

She attended Virginia University in Washington, D.C., from 1998 – 2002 and obtained her B.A. in Radio and Television in May 2002 with a major in Broadcasting. Relevant courses she took included Introduction to Mass Media, Mass Communication, Electronic Media, Radio Production, Television Production, Broadcast Journalism, Mass Communication Law, Radio-Television Performance, Script Writing, Advanced Television Production, News Writing and Editing, Voice and Diction, and Interviewing.

Kayla received the following awards while in college: 1998-2002 Academic All-Star; Dean's List, every semester; 2001 Volunteer of the Year – Forest Preserve Prairie People; and 2002 Scholarship, National Public Television Association. She worked from 1999-2002 at Virginia University as a Student Assistant for the University Cable Station performing the following tasks: developed scripts for community service announcements, designed on-air campus broadcasts, performed on-air talk shows, and organized and maintained the research library.

Her interests and activities included the following: Sigma Alpha Honor Society; Volunteer – Humanity Habitat, Prairie People; Speech Club, Member; and VU Symphonic Choir. Kayla speaks the following languages: English, fluent; Spanish, fluent. Her hobbies include swimming and backpacking.

2 Kayla Lou Maxwell Cover Letter

Your friend Kayla would like to prepare a cover letter for her resume. She has asked you to assist her with composing the letter using a Word template. Use the concepts and techniques presented in Word Project 3, along with the following information, to create and format the cover letter.

For the return address, Kayla's complete name is Kayla Lou Maxwell, and she lives at Nine Keswick Court in Stafford, Virginia, 22554. Use today's date and the following inside address: Mr. Eric Winder, WTTA Studios, 375 Benning Road in Washington, D.C. 20002.

Below the salutation, the text of the cover letter is as follows: first paragraph – I am responding to an advertisement for a television production assistant that appeared in Sunday's edition of the *Washington Daily*. I have enclosed my resume highlighting my background and feel I can be a valuable asset to WTTA Studios.; second paragraph – Through my part-time work for the University Cable Station, I have first-hand experience as a television production assistant. My field of study at Virginia University has focused heavily on broadcasting and communications. My courses are as follows:; first bulleted item – Broadcast Management: Broadcast Sales, Broadcast Journalism, Broadcast Programming, Radio and Television Writing; second bulleted item – Communication Arts: Principles of Persuasion, Fundamentals of Public Speaking, Interviewing, Voice and Diction; third paragraph – As shown in the following table, I have obtained exceptional grades in these areas.; first row of table – Broadcasting Courses GPA 4.0/4.0; second row – Communications Courses GPA 3.8/4.0; third row – Overall GPA 3.9/4.0; last paragraph – Given my extensive coursework and experience, I feel I can be a definite asset to your organization. I look forward to hearing from you to schedule an interview and to discuss my career opportunities with WTTA Studios.

Excel 2000 Project 1 Laboratory Exercises

For a sample result of an exercise, visit scsite.com/off2000enh/labs.htm.

1 Ryder's Global Golf 2nd Qtr Sales

Sam Ryder has hired you to create a quarterly sales report from the data in Table E-1 that shows totals for each store location, each catagory, and the entire company. Mr. Ryder also would like a Clustered column with a 3-D visual effect chart that compares the category sales within each store location. Use the title of this exercise as the worksheet title. Change the worksheet title to 18-point bold font. Merge and center the title across columns A through F. Use the AutoFormat command to format the body to the Accounting 3 type. Draw the chart in the range A9:H24. Save the workbook using the title of this exercise. Hand in a printout of the worksheet.

Table E-1 Ryder's Global Golf 2nd Qtr Sales Data

	LONDON	TOKYO	PHOENIX	MADRID
Clubs	$150,567.35	$221,734.00	$231,982.75	$193,141.00
Bags	28,526.50	43,582.40	67,340.75	48,965.25
Apparel	34,204.50	19,444.50	29,975.43	89,456.23
Accessories	17,436.25	19,657.43	27,634.90	29,087.50

2 Malcom's Music City Monthly Sales Report

You work as a spreadsheet specialist for Malcom's Music City. Your manager has assigned you the tasks of developing a monthly sales report that shows sales of CDs, cassettes, videos, and DVDs by city from the data in Table E-2. The report should contain totals for each city, each product category, and the entire company. Your manager also would like a stacked column with a cylindrical shaped chart that compares the product category sales within each city. Use Malcom's Music City as the worksheet title. Change it to 20-point bold font. Use Monthly Sales Report as the worksheet subtitle in cell A2. Change it to 14-point bold font. One at a time, merge and center both titles across columns A through G. Use the AutoFormat command to format the body to the Accounting 2 type. Draw the chart in the range A10:G23. Save the workbook using the title of this exercise. Hand in a printout of the worksheet.

Table E-2 Malcom's Music City Monthly Sales Data

	REDMOND	DETROIT	PEORIA	NASHVILLE	ATLANTA
CDs	$152,982.15	$164,110.55	$252,546.00	$139,623.50	$353,134.56
Cassettes	125,450.00	200,659.40	126,342.56	233,761.65	121,098.45
Videos	153,289.50	244,198.00	85,194.25	134,312.25	231,657.15
DVDs	96,539.50	134,567.35	49,451.75	78,012.50	104,300.75

Excel 2000 Project 2 Laboratory Exercises

For a sample result of an exercise, visit scsite.com/off2000enh/labs.htm.

1 Peek-a-Boo Supplies Annual Sales Analysis

You are a spreadsheet specialist for Peek-a-Boo Supplies. Your supervisor has requested that you create a worksheet that shows the annual sales by salesperson. The data and the format of the report she wants, including the totals, are shown in Figure E-1. The formulas in Figure E-1 are as follows: Formula A = Sales Amount – Sales Return; Formula B = Net Sales – Sales Quota; Formula C = Average function; Formula D = Total Net Sales / Total Sales Quota; Formula E = Max function; Formula F = Min function.

Use the concepts and techniques developed in Excel Project 2 to create and format the worksheet. Save the workbook using the title of this exercise. Hand in a printout of the values version and formulas version of the worksheet (see page E 2.57). Change Ali Raffari's sales amount to $24,000,000. The % of Quota Sold should be equal to 113.49%. Hand in a printout of the modified worksheet.

SALES REP NAME	SALES AMOUNT	SALES RETURNS	NET SALES	SALES QUOTA	ABOVE QUOTA
Juanita Santos	$12,125,007	$1,120,250	Formula A	$12,000,000	Formula B
Ahab Boyd	11,452,675	1,359,000	↓	10,000,000	↓
Zhu Bongjee	34,268,350	2,922,100	↓	30,000,000	↓
Ali Raffari	21,256,350	3,213,500	↓	15,000,000	↓
Nipul Gandi	33,960,000	4,430,000	↓	23,545,000	↓
Totals	—	—	—	—	—
Average	Formula C →	→	→	—	
% of Quota Sold	Formula D				
Max Net Sales	Formula E				
Min Net Sales	Formula F				

FIGURE E-1

2 CompSci Profit Potential

Mr. Rogers hired you as a student intern to develop worksheets for his computer parts business. Highest on his priority list is a Profit Potential worksheet. The data and the format of the report he wants are shown in Figure E-2. Also include a sum, average, highest, and lowest for each column. The formulas in Figure E-2 are as follows:

Formula A = Units on Hand * Average Unit Cost
Formula B = Average Unit Cost * (1 / (1 – .65))
Formula C = Units on Hand * Average Unit Price
Formula D = Total Value – Total Cost
Formula E = Average function
Formula F = Min function
Formula G = Max function

Use the concepts and techniques developed in Excel Project 2 to create and format the worksheet and chart. Save the workbook using the title of this exercise. Hand in a printout of the values version and formulas version of the worksheet (see page E 2.57). Mr. Rogers just received a shipment of 2,000 additional monitors. Change the Units on Hand to 8,313 and hand in a printout of the worksheet. The additional inventory yields a total profit potential of $2,353,764.86.

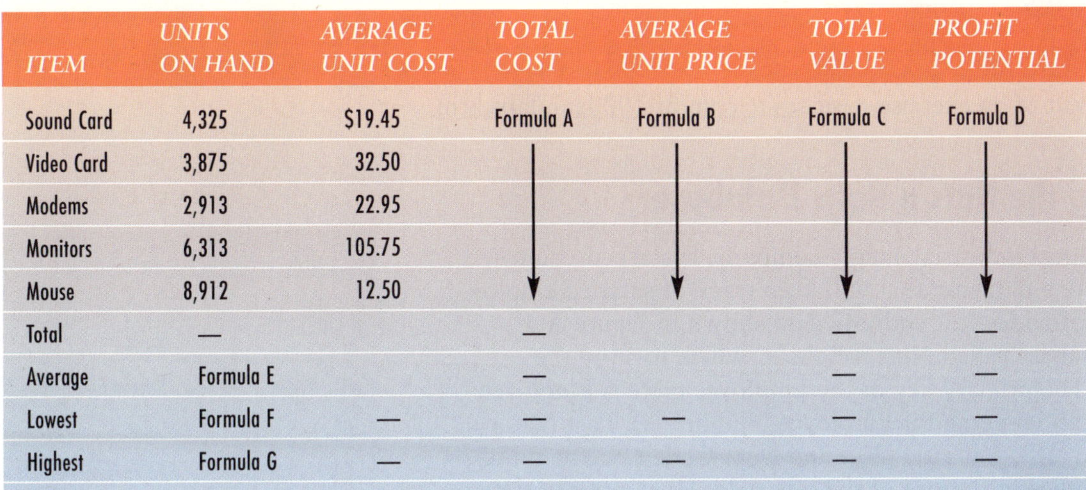

ITEM	UNITS ON HAND	AVERAGE UNIT COST	TOTAL COST	AVERAGE UNIT PRICE	TOTAL VALUE	PROFIT POTENTIAL
Sound Card	4,325	$19.45	Formula A	Formula B	Formula C	Formula D
Video Card	3,875	32.50	↓	↓	↓	↓
Modems	2,913	22.95	↓	↓	↓	↓
Monitors	6,313	105.75	↓	↓	↓	↓
Mouse	8,912	12.50	↓	↓	↓	↓
Total	—		—		—	—
Average	Formula E		—		—	—
Lowest	Formula F	—	—	—	—	—
Highest	Formula G	—	—	—	—	—

FIGURE E-2

Excel 2000 Project 3 Laboratory Exercises

For a sample result of an exercise, visit scsite.com/off2000enh/labs.htm.

1 Ruler Medical Quarterly Growth

You are a project leader in the Information Technology department at Ruler Medical Corporation. The planning committee has requested a workbook that shows quarterly growth based on Qtr 1 sales and growth data. The data and general layout of the worksheet, including the totals, are shown in Figure E-3. Enter the following formulas for Qtr 1 in the locations shown in Figure E-3 and then copy them to the remaining quarters.

Formula A = Qtr 1 Revenue
Formula B = IF(Qtr Growth Rate < 0, Revenue * (Qtr Cost Rate + Extra), Revenue * Qtr Cost Rate)
Formula C = Revenue – Cost

The total profit for the four quarters should equal $11,737,546.15. The planning committee also wants an embedded (on the same sheet with the data) 3-D Pie chart (column 2, row 1 in the Chart sub-type area) showing the profit contribution of each quarter to the total profit. The specifications also call for exploding Qtr 4 in the 3-D Pie chart. Use the concepts and techniques developed in the first three projects to create and format the worksheet and 3-D Pie chart.

Save the workbook using the title of this exercise. Hand in a printout of the values version and formulas version of the worksheet (see page E 2.57). Use the Goal Seek command to determine the Qtr 1 Revenue (first value in the Assumptions area) that will generate a total profit of $14,000,000.00. You should end up with a Qtr 1 Revenue of $6,959,458.22. Hand in a printout of the modified worksheet and 3-D Pie chart.

	QTR 1	QTR 2	QTR 3	QTR 4	TOTAL
Revenue	Formula A →	→	→	→	—
Cost	Formula B →	→	→	→	—
Profit	Formula C →	→	→	→	—
Assumptions					
Qtr 1 Revenue	$5,834,783.00				
Qtr Growth Rate	0.00%	-3.00%	5.00%	3.75%	
Qtr Cost Rate	48.00%	43.00%	66.00%	41.50%	
Extra	2.25%	2.65%	1.20%	2.65%	

FIGURE E-3

Microsoft Access 2000 Enhanced Exercises

Access 2000 Project 1 Laboratory Exercises

For a sample result of an exercise, visit scsite.com/off2000enh/labs.htm.

1 Creating the Nuts n Bolts Database

Nuts n Bolts, a local industrial supply company, has asked you to create and update a database that will keep track of salaried employees. The owner provides you with the data shown in Figure A-1.

Create a database called Nuts n Bolts in which to store the employee data. The primary key of the Employee table is Employee Number. Use Text data type for Employee Number (4), Last Name (15), First Name (10), Job Title (20), and Dept Code (2). The number in parentheses indicates the size of the text field. Use Currency data type for Salary. The primary key for the Department table is Dept Code. Use Text data type for both Dept Code (2) and Dept Name (18). Add the data shown in Figure A-1 to the database. Print the Employee table and the Department table. Create and print a report for the Employee table. Name the report, Salary Report. The report should include the employee's last name, first name, job title, and salary. Sort the report in ascending order by last name.

Data for Department Table

DEPT CODE	DEPT NAME
01	Accounting
02	Human Resources
03	Sales
04	Purchasing

Data for Employee Table

EMPLOYEE NUMBER	LAST NAME	FIRST NAME	JOB TITLE	SALARY	DEPT CODE
0031	Fitzpatrick	Luke	Materials Manager	$43,500.00	04
0043	Radel	Nancy	Buyer	$38,250.00	04
0056	McCoy	Mark	Accountant	$30,900.00	01
0067	Peng	Ung	Benefits Analyst	$34,500.00	02
0078	Alvarez	Elvira	Salesperson	$29,500.00	03
0230	Sampers	Gene	Shift Supervisor	$29,000.00	03
0233	Gerriston	Chandra	Financial Analyst	$36,000.00	01
0344	Novelli	Laura	Sales Manager	$44,000.00	03
0440	Evans	Michael	Trainer	$39,500.00	02
0551	Gierson	Kim	Buyer	$32,000.00	04

FIGURE A-1

2 Creating the Library Literacy Database

A local library is organizing a fund-raiser that will include an auction. The library will use the funds to expand its literacy outreach programs. The library has asked you to create a database to keep track of the donated goods and services as well as the businesses that donate them. The library already has received some donations and provides you with the data shown in Figure A-2.

Create a database called Library Literacy in which to store the auction items. The primary key of the Item table is Item Number. Use text data type for Item Number (3), Description (30), and Donor Number (2). The number in parentheses indicates the size of the text field. Use Currency data type for Item Value and Minimum Bid. The primary key for the Donor table is Donor Number. Use Text data type for Donor Number (2), Name (25), Address (15), City (15), State (2), Zip Code (5), and Telephone Number (12). Add the data shown in Figure A-2 to the database. Print the Item table and the Donor table. Create and print a report for the Item table that includes the description, item value, and minimum bid. Name the report, Auction Items List. Sort the report in ascending order by description.

Data for Item Table

ITEM NUMBER	DESCRIPTION	ITEM VALUE	MINIMUM BID	DONOR NUMBER
B08	Bird Feeder	$30.00	$8.00	04
B12	Beauty Makeover	$75.00	$10.00	03
C01	Crystal Bowl	$45.00	$9.00	03
C03	Cookware Set	$130.00	$40.00	03
D05	Dinner for 2	$80.00	$30.00	01
F04	Fresh Floral Arrangement	$50.00	$10.00	02
F06	Silk Floral Arrangement	$60.00	$15.00	02
G11	Gourmet Picnic	$90.00	$50.00	01
Q02	Handmade Quilt	$350.00	$100.00	04
T01	Terra Cotta Vase	$110.00	$70.00	04

Data for Donor Table

DONOR NUMBER	NAME	ADDRESS	CITY	STATE	ZIP CODE	TELEPHONE NUMBER
01	Meeker Foods	215 Watkins	Oakdale	MO	48101	710-555-6543
02	Ole Florist	266 Ralston	Allanson	IL	48102	530-555-9876
03	May's Dept Store	542 Prairie	Oakdale	MO	48101	710-555-7890
04	Liz's Whimsies	96 Prospect	Bishop	IL	48103	530-555-1298

FIGURE A-2

Access 2000 Project 2 Laboratory Exercises

For a sample result of an exercise, visit scsite.com/off2000enh/labs.htm.

1 Querying the Nuts n Bolts Database

Now that you have entered the data for the Nuts n Bolts database, the owner has several questions to pose to the database. Use the database to answer the following: (a) The employees in the Human Resources department have not had training on using the new accounting system. Display and print the first name, last name, and job title of all employees who work in the Human Resources department. (b) The organization chart for Nuts n Bolts needs to be updated. Display and print the job titles in ascending order. List the job titles only once.
(c) Employees who are paid less than $30,000 and work in the Sales department are eligible for a bonus equal to 5% of their annual salary. Display and print the first name, last name, salary, and bonus amount for these eligible employees. (d) The owner would like an updated department list. Display and print the department name, first name, last name, job title, and salary. Sort the output in order by salary (descending) within department name (ascending).

2 Calculating Statistics for the Nuts n Bolts Database

Nuts n Bolts has been asked to provide salary data for a national survey. Use the database to answer the following: (a) What is the average salary of all employees? (b) What is the highest salary? (c) What is the lowest salary? (d) What is the total salary of all employees? (e) What is the average salary by department?

3 Querying the Library Literacy Database

Now that you have entered the auction data, the library has several questions they would like answered. Use the database to answer the following: (a) Display and print the description, item value, and minimum bid of all items that are some type of floral arrangement (*Hint:* Use wildcards to solve this problem). (b) Display and print the item number, description, and minimum bid of all items that have a value greater than or equal to $100. (c) Display and print the donor name, item number, description and item value of all items. (d) Display and print the item number, item value, and minimum bid of all items with a minimum bid of $10 or less. (e) Display and print the item number, description, and minimum bid of all donated items. Sort the output in order by description (ascending) within minimum bid (descending). (*Hint:* Use Help to solve this problem.)

Access 2000 Project 3 Laboratory Exercises

For a sample result of an exercise, visit scsite.com/off2000enh/labs.htm.

1 Updating the Nuts n Bolts Database

Nuts n Bolts has had several personnel changes in the past few weeks and the database must be updated. In some cases, the table structure must be changed before the data can be updated. For example, the last name field is not large enough for Nancy Radel's married name. Execute each of these tasks: (a) Nancy Radel recently married and is now known as Nancy Radel-Machajewski. (b) Monica Sales has joined the company as a salesperson in the sales department. Monica's starting salary is $32,000. Her employee number is 0671. (c) Michael Evans is no longer employed by the company. (d) Chandra Gerriston has been promoted to controller at a salary of $40,000. Resize the columns in the Employee table to best fit the data. Print the updated Employee table.

2 Improving the Nuts n Bolts Database

Because the Nuts n Bolts database contains salary information, the owner wants to be sure that all data entered in the database is accurate. He also wants to improve the efficiency of the database by creating some additional indexes. The owner has asked you to do the following: (a) The company frequently needs to display employee data in order by last name within department code. Create an index to help with this task. (b) The Employee Number and Dept Code fields were defined as text. This is correct, but the owner wants to be sure that only numbers are entered in these fields. (*Hint:* Use Help and search for input mask to solve this problem.) (c) The Employee table should include the Dept Code for only those departments in the Department table. (d) No employee makes less than $20,000 or more than $65,000.

3 Updating the Library Literacy Database

The library would like to add another field to the database. They would like to know whether the donated item is a good or a service. Create a text field to store this information. Name the field, Item Type (3) and place it after the Description field. The field has the value GDS if the item is a good, and SER if the item is a service. Currently, the only items in the database that are service items are items B12 and D05. The library has received another item from May's Dept Store. The store is donating a leather briefcase (item number L01) worth $95. The minimum bid is $45. May's also has informed you that item C01 is really a crystal bud vase. Liz's Whimsies has withdrawn the terra cotta vase and replaced it with a tennis sweater. The item number, item value, and minimum bid remain the same. Resize the columns in the Item table to best fit the data. Print the Item table.

PowerPoint 2000 Project 1 Laboratory Exercises

For a sample result of an exercise, visit scsite.com/off2000enh/labs.htm.

1 Bike Rally and Rodeo

As publicity director for your community's bicycle club, you are responsible for creating a presentation for the club's fifth annual bike rally and rodeo. Use the data in Table P-1 to create this slide show. Choose an appropriate design template. Be certain to include a title slide. Save the presentation with the name of this exercise. Print the presentation slides.

2 Flu Blues and News

Every fall, the Health Clinic receives many telephone calls from students wondering if they should get a flu shot. You work in the clinic part time and volunteer to create a PowerPoint presentation that answers many of the common questions. Using the data in Table P-2, develop this slide show. Choose an appropriate design template. Include a title slide and four bulleted list slides. Check for spelling errors. Save the presentation with the name of this exercise. Print the presentation slides.

Table P-1 Bike Rally and Rodeo Data

CREST HEIGHTS BICYCLE CLUB
BIKE RALLY AND RODEO

Bike Rally Information
- Date
  - June 23
- Time
  - 10 a.m. - noon
- Leave from Crest Heights High School
- Tour 15 miles of historical Crest Heights

Bike Rodeo Information
- Designed for children
- Eight-station safety course
  - Sponsored by
    - First Insure Insurance Company
    - Crest Heights Police Department
- Participants receive food coupons

Registration Information
- Call
  - Jim Palmer
    - 555-1010
- Visit
  - Crest Heights Village Hall
    - Monday through Friday from 9 a.m. - 5 p.m.

Table P-2 Flu Blues and News Data

What Are the Flu Blues?
- Fever as high as 104 degrees
- Total body aches
- Severe weakness
- Loss of appetite
- Throat problems
  - Dry cough, sore throat

What Is the Flu News?
- Shot prevents 70% to 90% of cases
- Get shot in October and November
  - Flu season is December through March
- Shots safe for women more than three months pregnant during flu season
- New vaccine needed every year

Who Needs a Flu Shot?
- Health-care workers
- People with severe anemia, diabetes, and asthma
- People with chronic lung, heart, kidney, and immune diseases
- Anyone 65 years of age and older

What Is In the Vaccine?
- An inactive - or dead - virus
  - It is impossible to get the flu from vaccine
    - Some people get flu-like symptoms from vaccine
- Grown in hens' eggs
  - Tell your doctor if you are allergic to eggs

PowerPoint 2000 Project 2 Laboratory Exercises

For a sample result of an exercise, visit scsite.com/off2000enh/labs.htm.

1 Personal Training

Working out with a personal trainer is one of the first steps people can make toward enhancing their lives. Your school's Fitness Center has personal trainers available, and the Center's Director, Jesse Hernandez, asks you to create a PowerPoint presentation to help students maximize their personal training sessions. Use the outline in Figure P-1 to create a slide show for Jesse. Select an appropriate design template. Introduce the presentation with a title slide. Include clip art and animation effects. Display the presentation title in the outline header and your name in the outline footer. Save the presentation using the title, Personal Training. Print the slides and the presentation outline.

I. What to Expect From Your Trainer
- A. Explanation of current trends and techniques
  - 1. All trainers are nationally certified
    - a. Must attend continuing education programs
- B. Thorough fitness evaluation
- C. Supervised exercise sessions

II. Make the Commitment
- A. Set aside extra time
  - 1. In addition to training sessions
- B. Acquire healthy eating habits
  - 1. Reduce fats and cholesterol
- C. Use trainer's educational and motivational techniques

III. Be Realistic
- A. People fail due to unrealistic expectations
  - 1. They feel burned out and frustrated
- B. Work slowly
  - 1. Your body and mind need time to adjust
- C. Set achievable goals
  - 1. You know what you can achieve

IV. Make Trade-Offs
- A. Old habits are difficult to break
- B. Create list of possible barriers
  - 1. Be prepared to face these problems
- C. Plan to overcome these hurdles

V. Acquire Support
- A. Communicate your goals to your support system
  - 1. Will reinforce reasons for changing your lifestyle
  - 2. Might motivate others
- B. Commit yourself to you

FIGURE P-1

2 Babbling Brook Nature Center

The Babbling Brook Nature Center in your community offers a Speakers' Bureau composed of four scientists. Jessica Cantero, the Nature Center's director, has asked you to prepare a PowerPoint presentation, and she gives you the data shown in Table P-3. Select a design template and create a slide show using this data. Introduce the presentation with a title slide. For Slide 2, list information promoting the Speakers' Bureau benefits. Use the row headings in Table P-3 to create Slides 3 through 6. Modify the slide layouts. Choose appropriate clip art, add animation effects, and include slide transitions. Display the presentation title in the outline header and your name in the outline footer. Save the presentation using the name, Babbling Brook. Print the slides and the presentation outline. E-mail the presentation to Jessica_Cantero@hotmail.com.

Table P-3 Babbling Brook Speakers' Bureau Data

TOPICS	*PREFERRED AUDIENCE*	*SPEAKER*
Bird Populations	Grade school, conservation groups	Warren Scott
Insect Populations	Preschool through high school	Karen Williams
Native Vegetation	Conservation groups, service clubs, senior citizens	Sheryl Martinez
Small Mammals	Kindergarten through college	Vijay Patel

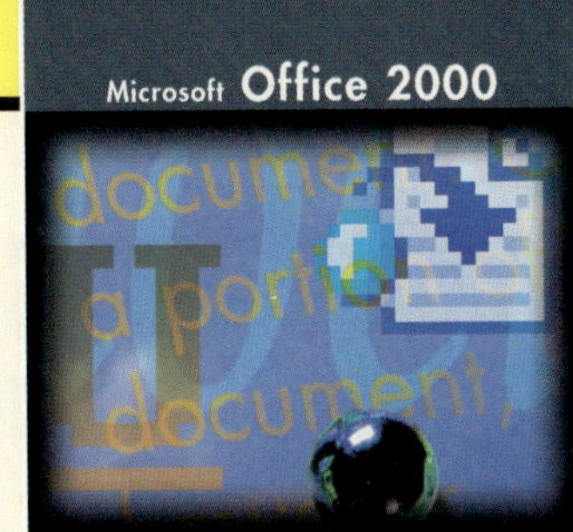

APPENDIX A
Microsoft Office 2000 Help System

Using the Microsoft Office Help System

This appendix demonstrates how you can use the Microsoft Office 2000 Help system to answer your questions. At any time while you are using one of the Microsoft Office 2000 applications, you can interact with the Help system to display information on any topic associated with the application. To illustrate the use of the Microsoft Office 2000 Help system, the Microsoft Word 2000 application will be used in this appendix. The Help systems in other Microsoft Office applications respond in a similar fashion.

The two primary forms of Help available in each Microsoft Office application are the Office Assistant and the Microsoft Help window. The one you use will depend on your preference. As shown in Figure A-1, you access either form of Help in Microsoft Word by pressing the F1 key, clicking Microsoft Word Help on the Help menu, or clicking the Microsoft Word Help button on the Standard toolbar. Word responds in one of two ways:

1. If the Office Assistant is turned on, then the Office Assistant displays with a balloon (lower-right side of Figure A-1).
2. If the Office Assistant is turned off, then the Microsoft Word Help window displays (lower-left side of Figure A-1)

Table A-1 on the next page summarizes the nine categories of Help available to you. Because of the way the Word Help system works, please review the rightmost column of Table A-1 if you have difficulties activating the desired category of Help.

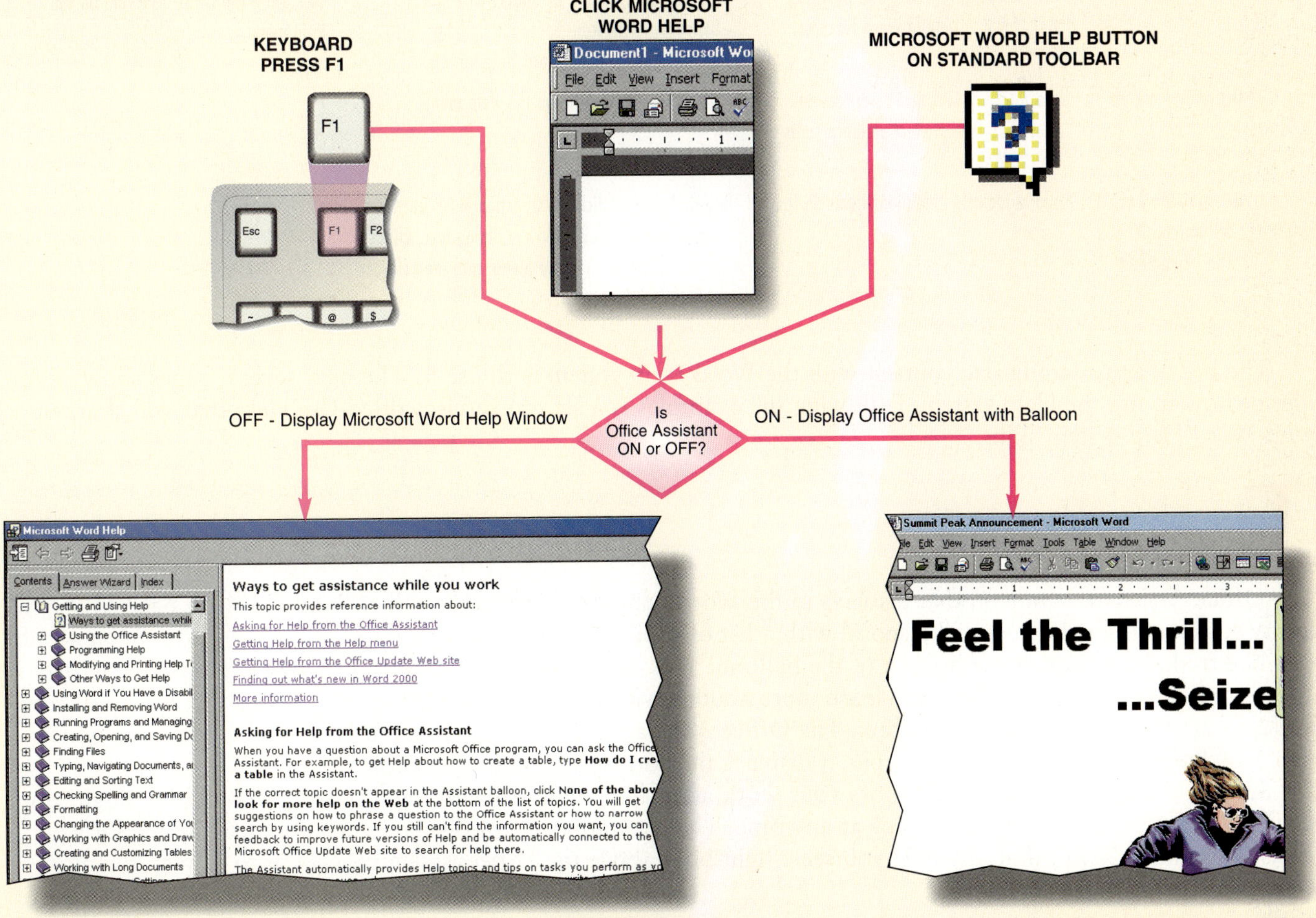

KEYBOARD
PRESS F1

HELP MENU
CLICK MICROSOFT
WORD HELP

MICROSOFT WORD HELP BUTTON
ON STANDARD TOOLBAR

Is
Office Assistant
ON or OFF?

OFF - Display Microsoft Word Help Window

ON - Display Office Assistant with Balloon

FIGURE A-1

Table A-1 Word Help System

TYPE	DESCRIPTION	HOW TO ACTIVATE	TURNING THE OFFICE ASSISTANT ON AND OFF
Answer Wizard	Similar to the Office Assistant in that it answers questions that you type in your own words.	Click the Microsoft Word Help button on the Standard toolbar. If necessary, maximize the Help window by double-clicking its title bar. Click the Answer Wizard tab.	If the Office Assistant displays, right-click it, click Options on the shortcut menu, click Use the Office Assistant to remove the check mark, click the OK button.
Contents sheet	Groups Help topics by general categories. Use when you know only the general category of the topic in question.	Click the Microsoft Word Help button on the Standard toolbar. If necessary, maximize the Help window by double-clicking its title bar. Click the Contents tab.	If the Office Assistant displays, right-click it, click Options, click Use the Office Assistant to remove the check mark, click the OK button.
Detect and Repair	Automatically finds and fixes errors in the application.	Click Detect and Repair on the Help menu.	
Hardware and Software Information	Shows Product ID and allows access to system information and technical support information.	Click About Microsoft Word on the Help menu and then click the appropriate button.	
Help for WordPerfect Users	Used to assist WordPerfect users who are learning Microsoft Word.	Click WordPerfect Help on the Help menu.	
Index sheet	Similar to an index in a book; use when you know exactly what you want.	Click the Microsoft Word Help button on the Standard toolbar. If necessary, maximize the Help window by double-clicking its title bar. Click the Index tab.	If the Office Assistant displays, right-click it, click Options, click Use the Office Assistant to remove the check mark, click the OK button.
Office Assistant	Answers questions that you type in your own words, offers tips, and provides Help for a variety of Word features.	Click the Microsoft Word Help button on the Standard toolbar or double-click the Office Assistant icon. Some dialog boxes also include the Microsoft Word Help button.	If the Office Assistant does not display, click Show the Office Assistant on the Help menu.
Office on the Web	Used to access technical resources and download free product enhancements on the Web.	Click Office on the Web on the Help menu.	
Question Mark button and What's This? command	Used to identify unfamiliar items on the screen.	In a dialog box, click the Question Mark button and then click an item in the dialog box. Click What's This? on the Help menu, and then click an item on the screen.	

The best way to familiarize yourself with the Word Help system is to use it. The next several pages show examples of how to use the Help system. Following the examples is a set of exercises titled Use Help that will sharpen your Word Help system skills.

The Office Assistant

The **Office Assistant** is an icon that displays in the Word window (lower-right side of Figure A-1 on page MO A.1). It has dual functions. First, it will respond with a list of topics that relate to the entry you make in the What would you like to do? text box at the bottom of the balloon. This entry can be in the form of a word, phrase, or written question. For example, if you want to learn more about saving a file, you can type, save, save a file, how do I save a file, or anything similar in the text box. The Office Assistant responds by displaying a list of topics from which you can choose. Once you choose a topic, it displays the corresponding information.

Second, the Office Assistant monitors your work and accumulates tips during a session on how you might do your work better. You can view the tips at any time. The accumulated tips display when you activate the Office Assistant balloon. Also, if at any time you see a light bulb above the Office Assistant, click it to display the most recent tip.

You may or may not want the Office Assistant to display on the screen at all times. You can hide it, and then show it at a later time. You may prefer not to use the Office Assistant at all. In this case, you use the Microsoft Word Help window (lower-left side of Figure A-1 on page MO A.1). Thus, not only do you need to know how to show and hide the Office Assistant, but you also need to know how to turn the Office Assistant on and off.

Showing and Hiding the Office Assistant

When Word is first installed, the Office Assistant displays in the Word window. You can move it to any location on the screen. You can click it to display the Office Assistant balloon, which allows you to request Help. If the Office Assistant is on the screen and you want to hide it, you click the **Hide the Office Assistant command** on the Help menu. You also can right-click the Office Assistant to display its shortcut menu and then click the **Hide command** to hide it. When the Office Assistant is hidden, then the **Show the Office Assistant command** replaces the Hide the Office Assistant command on the Help menu. Thus, you can show or hide the Office Assistant at any time.

Turning the Office Assistant On and Off

The fact that the Office Assistant is hidden, does not mean it is turned off. To turn the Office Assistant off, it must be displayed in the Word window. You right-click it to display its shortcut menu (right side of Figure A-2). Next, click Options on the shortcut menu. Invoking the **Options command** causes the Office Assistant dialog box to display (left side of Figure A-2).

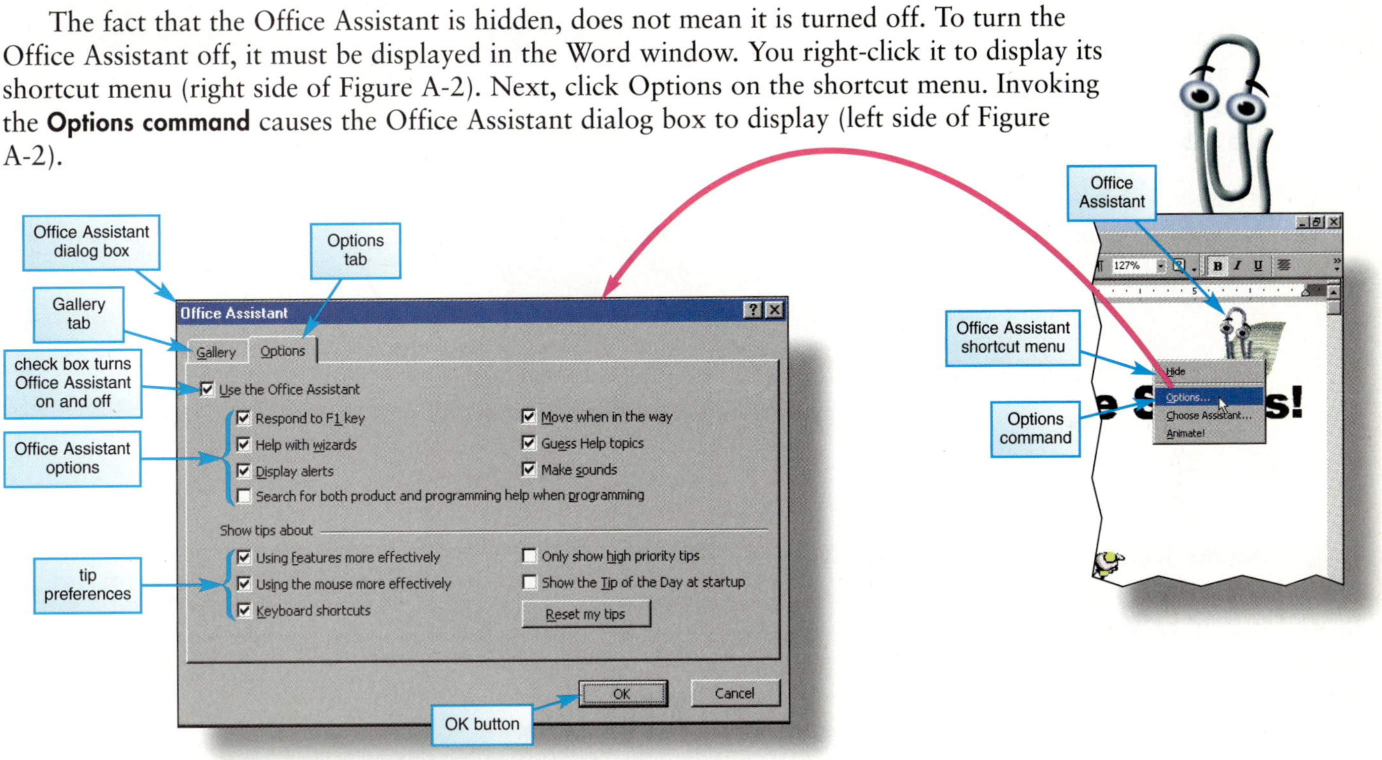

FIGURE A-2

The top check box in the Options sheet determines whether the Office Assistant is on or off. To turn the Office Assistant off, remove the check mark from the **Use the Office Assistant check box** and then click the OK button. As shown in Figure A-1 on page MO A.1, if the Office Assistant is off when you invoke Help, then the Microsoft Word Help window displays instead of the Office Assistant. To turn the Office Assistant on at a later time, click the Show the Office Assistant command on the Help menu.

Through the Options command on the Office Assistant shortcut menu, you can change the look and feel of the Office Assistant. For example, you can hide the Office Assistant, turn the Office Assistant off, change the way it works, choose a different Office Assistant icon, or view an animation of the current one. These options also are available by clicking the Options button that displays in the Office Assistant balloon (Figure A-3 on the next page).

The **Gallery sheet** (Figure A-2) in the Office Assistant dialog box allows you to change the appearance of the Office Assistant. The default is the paper clip (Clippit). You can change it to a bouncing red happy face (The Dot), a robot (F1), a professor (The Genius), the Microsoft Office logo (Office Logo), the earth (Mother Nature), a cat (Links), or a dog (Rocky).

Using the Office Assistant

As indicated earlier, the Office Assistant allows you to enter a word, phrase, or question and then responds by displaying a list of topics from which you can choose to display Help. The following steps show how to use the Office Assistant to obtain Help about online meetings.

Steps To Use the Office Assistant

1 **If the Office Assistant is not turned on, click Help on the menu bar and then click Show the Office Assistant. Click the Office Assistant. When the Office Assistant balloon displays, type** `what are online meetings` **in the text box. Point to the Search button.**

The Office Assistant balloon displays as shown in Figure A-3.

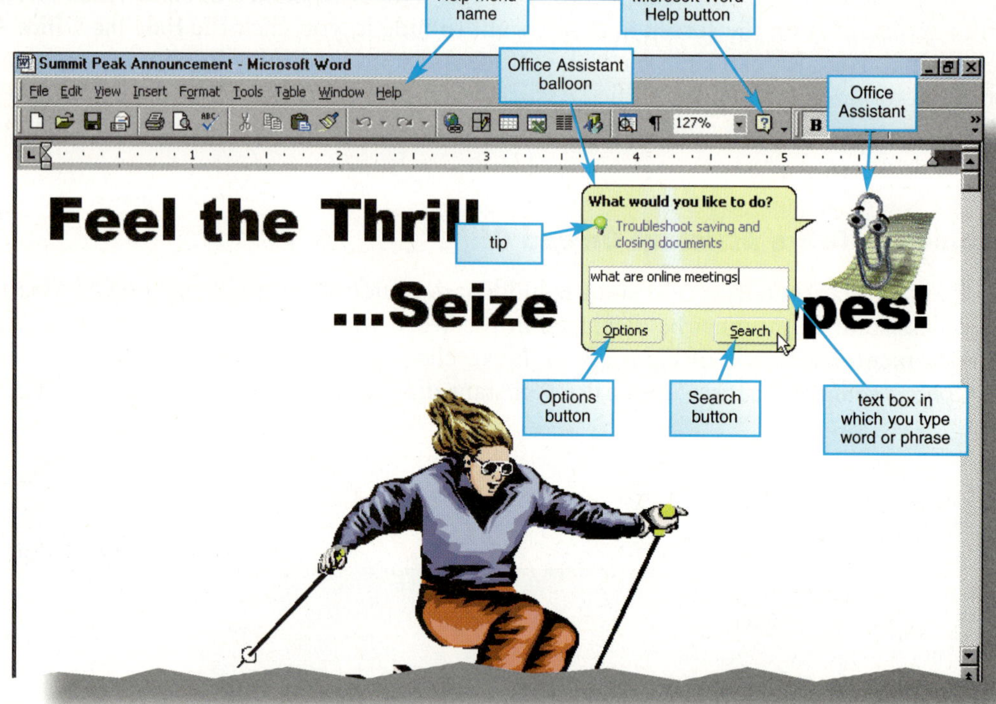

FIGURE A-3

2 **Click the Search button. When the Office Assistant balloon redisplays, point to the topic, About online meetings (Figure A-4).**

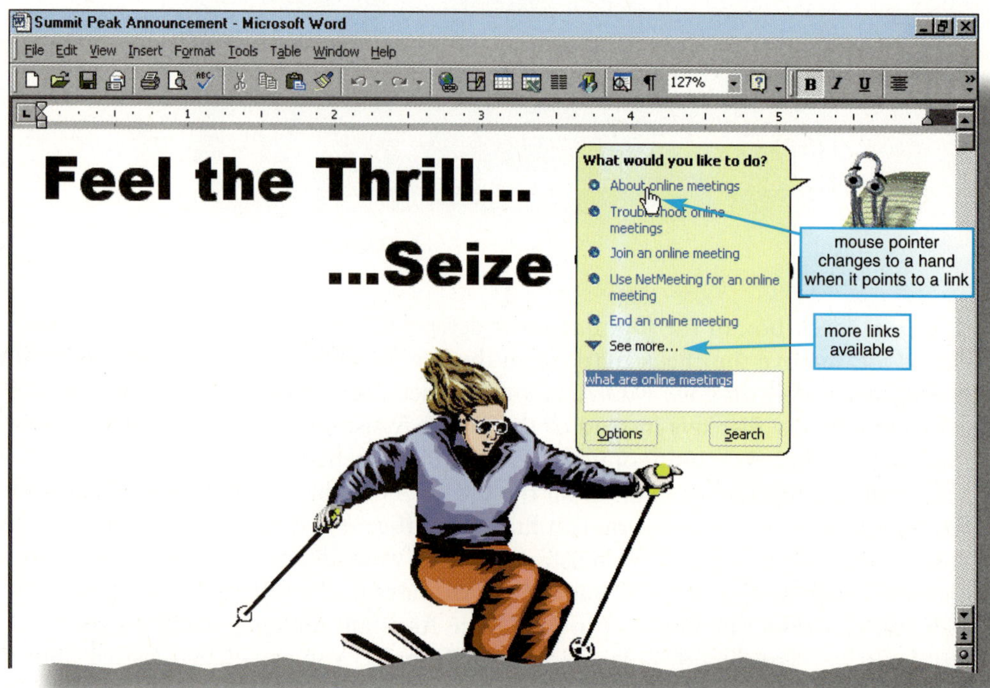

FIGURE A-4

3 Click the topic, About online meetings. Double-click the Microsoft Word Help window title bar to maximize it. If necessary, move or hide the Office Assistant so you can view all of the text in the Microsoft Word Help window.

The Microsoft Word Help window displays the information about online meetings (Figure A-5).

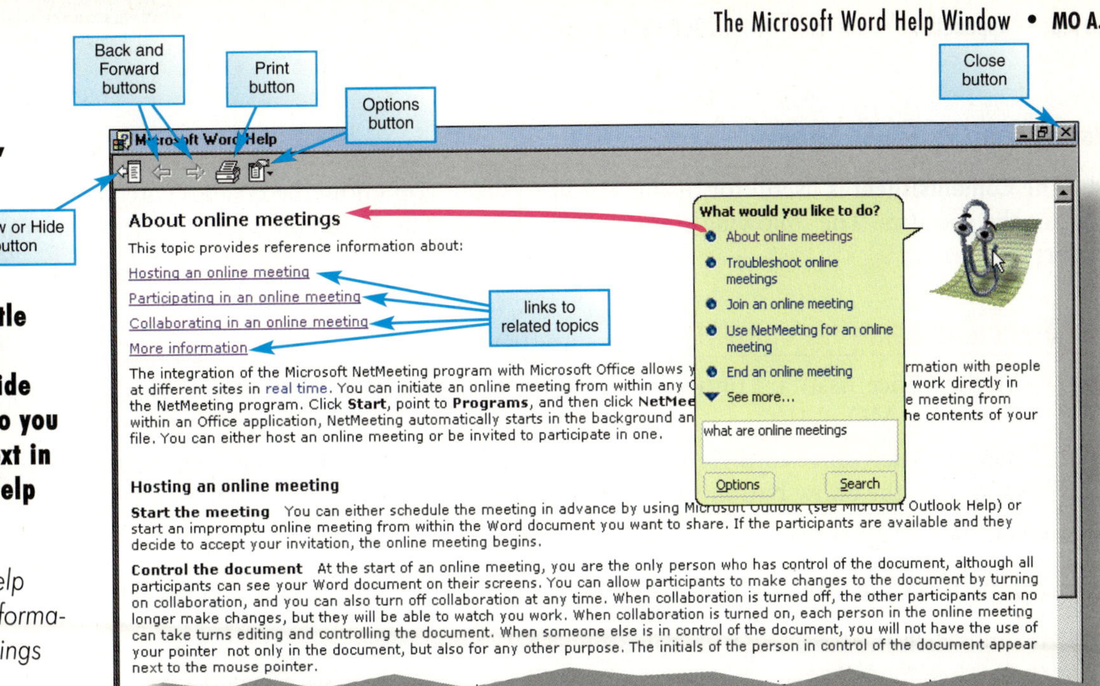

FIGURE A-5

When the Microsoft Word Help window displays, you can choose to read it or print it. To print the information, click the Print button on the Microsoft Word Help toolbar. Table A-2 lists the function of each button on the toolbar in the Microsoft Word Help window. To close the Microsoft Word Help window shown in Figure A-5, click the Close button on the title bar.

Table A-2 Microsoft Word Help Toolbar Buttons

BUTTON	NAME	FUNCTION
[icon] or [icon]	Show or Hide	Displays or hides the Contents, Answer Wizard, Index tabs
[icon]	Back	Displays the previous Help topic
[icon]	Forward	Displays the next Help topic
[icon]	Print	Prints the current Help topic
[icon]	Options	Displays a list of commands

Other Ways

1. If Office Assistant is turned on, on Help menu click Microsoft Word Help, or click Microsoft Word Help button on Standard toolbar to display Office Assistant balloon

The Microsoft Word Help Window

If the Office Assistant is turned off and you click the Microsoft Word Help button on the Standard toolbar, the **Microsoft Word Help window** displays (Figure A-6 on the next page). This window contains three tabs on the left side: Contents, Answer Wizard, and Index. Each tab displays a sheet with powerful look-up capabilities. Use the Contents sheet as you would a table of contents at the front of a book to look up Help. The Answer Wizard sheet answers your queries in the same manner as the Office Assistant. You use the Index sheet in the same manner as an index in a book.

Click the tabs to move from sheet to sheet. The five buttons on the toolbar, Show or Hide, Back, Forward, Print, and Options also are described in Table A-2.

Besides clicking the Microsoft Word Help button on the Standard toolbar, you also can click the Microsoft Word Help command on the Help menu or press the F1 key to display the Microsoft Word Help window to gain access to the three sheets. To close the Microsoft Word Help window, click the Close button in the upper-right corner on the title bar.

Using the Contents Sheet

The **Contents sheet** is useful for displaying Help when you know the general category of the topic in question, but not the specifics. The following steps show how to use the Contents sheet to obtain information about Web folders.

TO OBTAIN HELP USING THE CONTENTS SHEET

1. With the Office Assistant turned off, click the Microsoft Word Help button on the Standard toolbar (Figure A-3 on page MO A.4).
2. When the Microsoft Word Help window displays, double-click the title bar to maximize the window. If necessary, click the Show button to display the tabs.
3. Click the Contents tab.
4. Double-click the Working with Online and Internet Documents book on the left side of the window.
5. Double-click the Creating Web Pages book below the Working with Online and Internet Documents book.
6. Click the About Web Folders subtopic below the Creating Web Pages book.

Word displays Help on the subtopic, About Web Folders (Figure A-6).

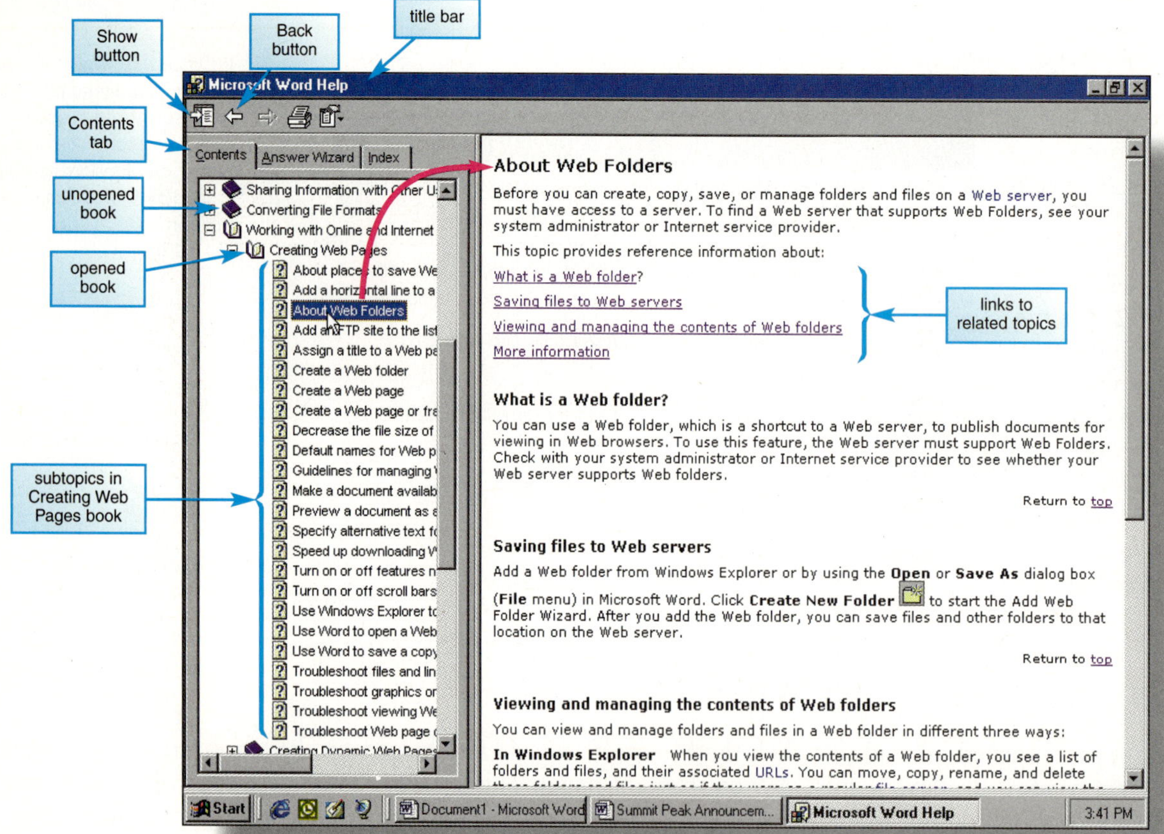

FIGURE A-6

Once the information on the subtopic displays, you can scroll through the window and read it or you can click the Print button to obtain a hard copy. If you decide to click another subtopic on the left or a link on the right, you can get back to the Help page shown in Figure A-6 by clicking the Back button as many times as necessary.

Each topic in the Contents list is preceded by a book icon or question mark icon. A **book icon** indicates subtopics are available. A **question mark icon** means information on the topic will display if you double-click the title. The book icon opens when you double-click the book (or its title) or click the plus sign (+) to the left of the book icon.

Using the Answer Wizard Sheet

The **Answer Wizard sheet** works like the Office Assistant in that you enter a word, phrase, or question and it responds with topics from which you can choose to display Help. The following steps show how to use the Answer Wizard sheet to obtain Help about discussions in a Word document.

TO OBTAIN HELP USING THE ANSWER WIZARD SHEET

1. With the Office Assistant turned off, click the Microsoft Word Help button on the Standard toolbar (Figure A-3 on page MO A.4).
2. When the Microsoft Word Help window displays, double-click the title bar to maximize the window. If necessary, click the Show button to display the tabs.
3. Click the Answer Wizard tab. Type `what are discussions` in the What would you like to do? text box on the left side of the window. Click the Search button.
4. When a list of topics displays in the Select topic to display list box, click About discussions in Word.

Word displays Help about discussions (Figure A-7).

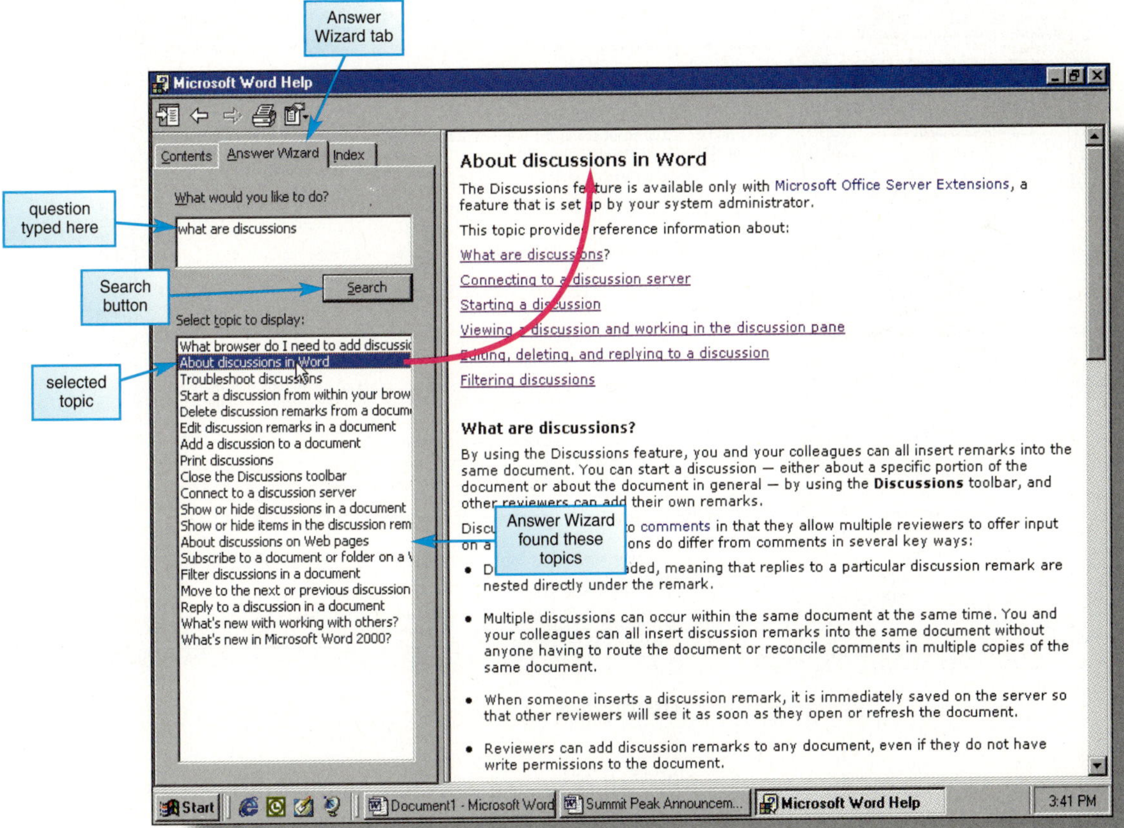

FIGURE A-7

If the topic, About discussions in Word, does not include the information you are searching for, click another topic in the list. Continue to click topics until you find the desired information.

Using the Index Sheet

The third sheet in the Microsoft Word Help window is the Index sheet. Use the **Index sheet** to display Help when you know the keyword or the first few letters of the keyword you want to look up. The following steps show how to use the Index sheet to obtain Help on understanding the readability statistics available to evaluate the reading level of a document.

TO OBTAIN HELP USING THE INDEX SHEET

1. With the Office Assistant turned off, click the Microsoft Word Help button on the Standard toolbar (Figure A-3 on page MO A.4).
2. When the Microsoft Word Help window displays, double-click the title bar to maximize the window. If necessary, click the Show button to display the tabs.
3. Click the Index tab. Type `readability` in the Type keywords text box on the left side of the window. Click the Search button.

Word highlights the first topic (Readability scores) on the left side of the window and displays information about two readability tests on the right side of the window (Figure A-8).

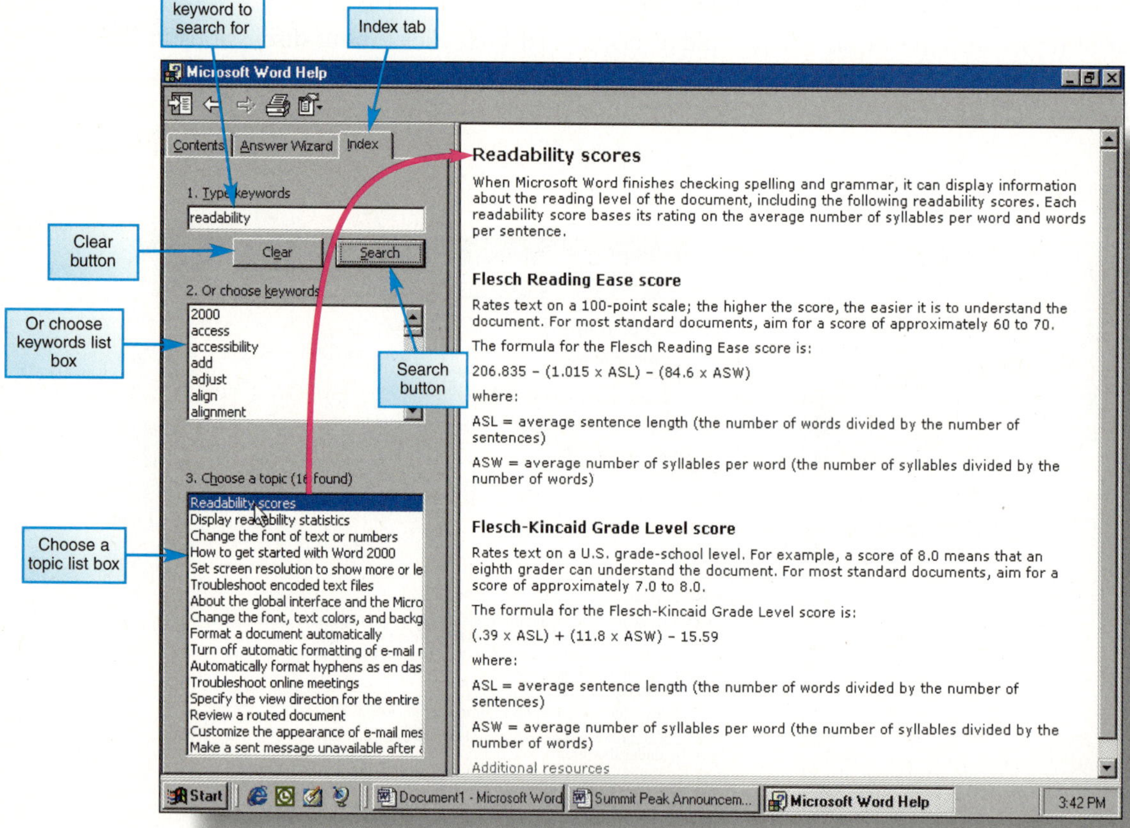

FIGURE A-8

In the Choose a topic list box on the left side of the window, you can click another topic to display additional Help.

An alternative to typing a keyword in the Type keywords text box is to scroll through the Or choose keywords list box (the middle list box on the left side of the window). When you locate the keyword you are searching for, double-click it to display Help on the topic. Also in the Or choose keywords list box, the Word Help system displays other topics that relate to the new keyword. As you begin typing a new keyword in the Type keywords text box, Word jumps to that point in the middle list box. To begin a new search, click the Clear button.

What's This? Command and Question Mark Button

Use the What's This command on the Help menu or the Question Mark button in a dialog box when you are not sure what an object on the screen is or what it does.

What's This? Command

You use the **What's This? command** on the Help menu to display a detailed ScreenTip. When you invoke this command, the mouse pointer changes to an arrow with a question mark. You then click any object on the screen, such as a button, to display the ScreenTip. For example, after you click the What's This? command on the Help menu and then click the Zoom box on the Standard toolbar, a description of the Zoom box displays (Figure A-9). You can print the ScreenTip by right-clicking it and clicking Print Topic on the shortcut menu.

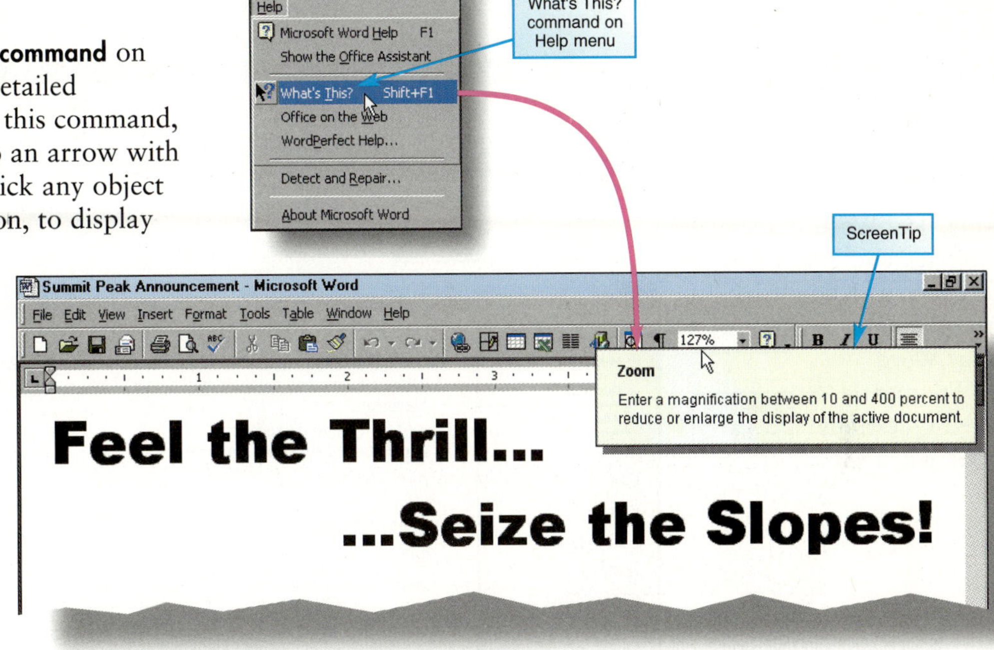

FIGURE A-9

Question Mark Button

In a response similar to the What's This? command, the **Question Mark button** displays a ScreenTip. You use the Question Mark button with dialog boxes. It is located in the upper-right corner on the title bar of dialog boxes, next to the Close button. For example, in Figure A-10, the Print dialog box displays on the screen. If you click the Question Mark button, and then click the Print to file check box, an explanation of the Print to file check box displays in a ScreenTip. You can print the ScreenTip by right-clicking it and clicking Print Topic on the shortcut menu.

If a dialog box does not include a Question Mark button, press the SHIFT+F1 keys. This combination of keys will change the mouse pointer to an arrow with a question mark. You then can click any object in the dialog box to display the ScreenTip.

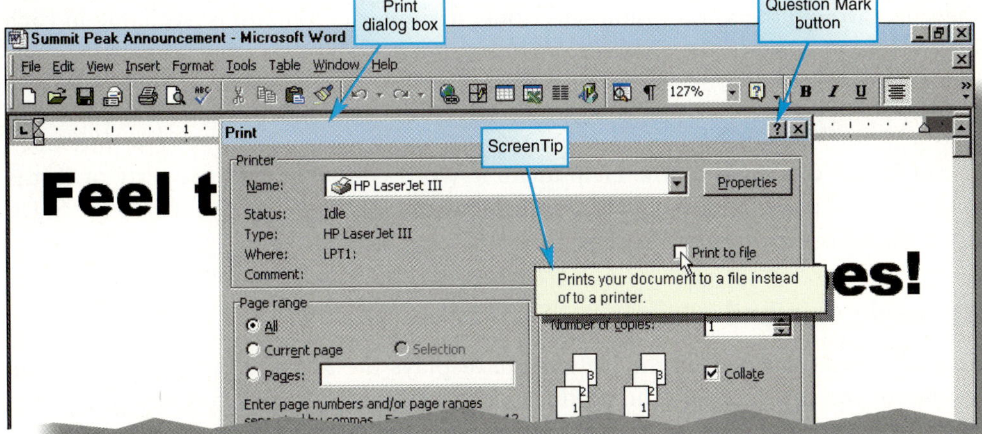

FIGURE A-10

Office on the Web Command

The **Office on the Web command** on the Help menu displays a Microsoft Web page containing up-to-date information on a variety of Office-related topics. To use this command, you must be connected to the Internet. Once the page displays, you can click the Word link on the left side of the window and then click the Assistance link (Figure A-11). The Word Assistance Web page contains several links such as Knowledge Base Articles about Word and Frequently Asked Questions about Word.

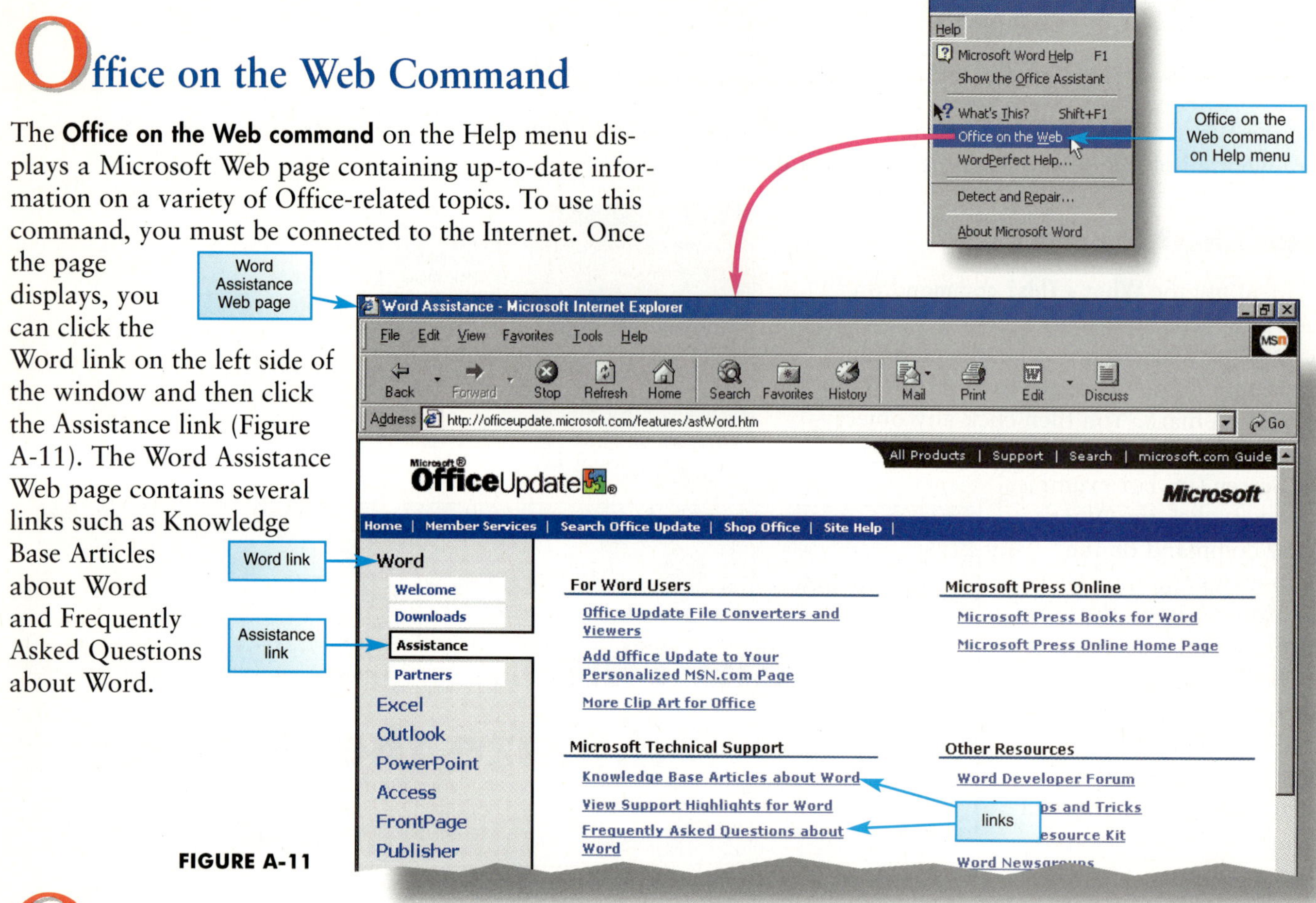

FIGURE A-11

Other Help Commands

Three additional commands available on the Help menu are WordPerfect Help, Detect and Repair, and About Microsoft Word. The WordPerfect Help command is available only if it was included as part of a Custom install of Word 2000. The Help menu of the other Office applications have similar commands that are useful when using each Office application.

WordPerfect Help Command

The **WordPerfect Help command** on the Help menu offers assistance to WordPerfect users switching to Word. When you choose this command, Word displays the Help for WordPerfect Users dialog box. The instructions in the dialog box step the user through the appropriate selections. A similar command is available in each of the other Office applications.

Detect and Repair Command

Use the **Detect and Repair command** on the Help menu if Word is not running properly or if it is generating errors. When you invoke this command, the Detect and Repair dialog box displays. Click the Start button in the dialog box to initiate the detect and repair process.

About Microsoft Word Command

The **About Microsoft Word command** on the Help menu displays the About Microsoft Word dialog box. The dialog box lists the owner of the software and the product identification. You need to know the product identification if you call Microsoft for assistance. The two buttons below the OK button are the System Info button and the Tech Support button. The **System Info button** displays system information, including hardware resources, components, software environment, and applications. The **Tech Support button** displays technical assistance information.

1 Using the Office Assistant

Instructions: Perform the following tasks using the Word Help system.

1. If the Office Assistant is turned on, click it to display the Office Assistant balloon. If the Office Assistant is not turned on, click Help on the menu bar, and click Show the Office Assistant.
2. Right-click the Office Assistant and then click Options on the shortcut menu. Click the Gallery tab in the Office Assistant dialog box and then click the Next button to view all the Office Assistants. Click the Options tab in the Office Assistant dialog box and review the different options for the Office Assistant. Click the Question Mark button and then display ScreenTips for the first two check boxes (Use the Office Assistant and Respond to F1 key). Right-click the ScreenTips to print them. Hand them in to your instructor. Close the Office Assistant dialog box.
3. Click the Office Assistant and then type `show me the keyboard shortcuts` in the What would you like to do? text box at the bottom of the balloon. Click the Search button.
4. Click Keyboard shortcuts in the Office Assistant balloon. If necessary, double-click the title bar to maximize the Microsoft Word Help window. Click the Function keys link and then click the SHIFT+Function key link to view the set of shortcut keys using the SHIFT key and function keys. Click the Print button on the Microsoft Word Help toolbar to print the list of shortcut keys. Hand in the printouts to your instructor.
5. Close all open Help windows.
6. Click the Office Assistant. If it is not turned on, click Show the Office Assistant on the Help menu. Search for the topic, what is a netmeeting. Click the Use NetMeeting for an online meeting link. When the Microsoft Word Help window displays, maximize the window and then click the the Start an impromptu online meeting with Microsoft Word link. Read and print the information. Close the Microsoft Word Help window.

2 Expanding on the Word Help System Basics

Instructions: Use the Word Help system to understand the topics better and answer the questions listed below. Answer the questions on your own paper, or hand in the printed Help information to your instructor.

1. Right-click the Office Assistant. If it is not turned on, click Show the Office Assistant on the Help menu. When the shortcut menu displays, click Options. Click Use the Office Assistant to remove the check mark, and then click the OK button.
2. Click the Microsoft Word Help button on the Standard toolbar. Maximize the Microsoft Word Help window. If the tabs are hidden on the left side, click the Show button. Click the Index tab. Type `undo` in the Type keywords text box. Click the Search button. Click Reset built-in menus and toolbars. Print the information. Click the Hide button and then the Show button. Click the four links below What do you want to do? Read and print the information for each link. Close the Microsoft Word Help window. Hand in the printouts to your instructor.
3. Press the F1 key. Maximize the Microsoft Word Help window. Click the Answer Wizard tab. Type `help` in the What would you like to do? text box, and then click the Search button. Click Ways to get assistance while you work. Read through the information that displays. Print the information. Click the first two links. Read and print the information for both.
4. Click the Contents tab. Click the plus sign (+) to the left of the Typing, Navigating Documents, and Selecting Text book. Click the plus sign (+) to the left of the Selecting Text book. One at a time, click the three topics below the Selecting Text book. Read and print each one. Close the Microsoft Word Help window. Hand in the printouts to your instructor.
5. Click Help on the menu bar and then click What's This? Click the E-mail button on the Standard toolbar. Right-click the ScreenTip to print the ScreenTip. Click Format on the menu bar and then click Paragraph. When the Paragraph dialog box displays, click the Question Mark button on the title bar. Click the Special box. Right-click the ScreenTip to print the ScreenTip. Hand in the printouts to your instructor. Close the Paragraph dialog box and the Microsoft Word window.

APPENDIX B

Publishing Office Web Pages to a Web Server

With a Microsoft Office 2000 program, such as Word, Excel, Access, or PowerPoint, you use the **Save as Web Page command** on the File menu to save the Web page to a Web server using one of two techniques: Web folders or File Transfer Protocol. A **Web folder** is an Office 2000 shortcut to a Web server. **File Transfer Protocol (FTP)** is an Internet standard that allows computers to exchange files with other computers on the Internet.

You should contact your network system administrator or technical support staff at your ISP to determine if their Web server supports Web folders, FTP, or both, and to obtain necessary permissions to access the Web server. If you decide to publish Web pages using a Web folder, you must have the Office Server Extensions (OSE) installed on your computer. OSE comes with the Standard, Professional, and Premium editions of Office 2000.

Using Web Folders to Publish Office Web Pages

If you are granted permission to create a Web folder (shortcut) on your computer, you must obtain the URL of the Web server, and a user name and possibly a password that allows you to access the Web server. You also must decide on a name for the Web folder. Table B-1 explains how to create a Web folder.

Office adds the name of the Web folder to the list of current Web folders. You can save to this folder, open files in the folder, rename the folder, or perform any operations you would to a folder on your hard disk. You can use your Office program or Windows Explorer to access this folder. Table B-2 explains how to save to a Web folder.

Using FTP to Publish Office Web Pages

When publishing a Web page using FTP, you first add the FTP location to your computer and then you can save to it. An **FTP location**, also called an **FTP site**, is a collection of files that resides on an FTP server. In this case, the FTP server is the Web server.

To add an FTP location, you must obtain the name of the FTP site, which usually is the address (URL) of the FTP server, and a user name and a password that allows you to access the FTP server. You save and open the Web pages on the Web server using the name of the FTP site. Table B-3 explains how to add an FTP site.

Office adds the name of the FTP site to the FTP locations in the Save As and Open dialog boxes. You can open and save files on this FTP location. Table B-4 explains how to save using an FTP location.

Table B-1 Creating a Web Folder
1. Click File on the menu bar and then click Save As; or click File on the menu bar and then click Open.
2. When the Save As dialog box or the Open dialog box displays, click the Web Folders shortcut on the Places Bar along the left side of the dialog box.
3. Click the Create New Folder button.
4. When the first dialog box of the Add Web Folder wizard displays, type the URL of the Web server and then click the Next button.
5. When the Enter Network Password dialog box displays, type the user name and, if necessary, the password in the respective text boxes and then click the OK button.
6. When the last dialog box of the Add Web Folder wizard displays, type the name you would like to use for the Web folder. Click the Finish button.
7. Close the Save As or the Open dialog box.

Table B-2 Saving to a Web Folder
1. Click File on the menu bar and then click Save As.
2. When the Save As dialog box displays, type the Web page file name in the File name text box. Do not press the ENTER key.
3. Click Web Folders shortcut on the Places Bar along the left side of the dialog box.
4. Double-click the Web folder name in the Save in list.
5. When the Enter Network Password dialog box displays, type the user name and password in the respective text boxes and then click the OK button.
6. Click the Save button in the Save As dialog box.

Table B-3 Adding an FTP Location
1. Click File on the menu bar and then click Save As; or click File on the menu bar and then click Open.
2. In the Save As dialog box, click the Save in box arrow and then click Add/Modify FTP Locations in the Save in list; or in the Open dialog box, click the Look in box arrow and then click Add/Modify FTP Locations in the Look in list.
3. When the Add/Modify FTP Locations dialog box displays, type the name of the FTP site in the Name of FTP site text box. If the site allows anonymous logon, click Anonymous in the Log on as area; if you have a user name for the site, click User in the Log on as area and then type the user name. Type the password in the Password text box. Click the OK button.
4. Close the Save As or the Open dialog box.

Table B-4 Saving to an FTP Location
1. Click File on the menu bar and then click Save As.
2. When the Save As dialog box displays, type the Web page file name in the File name text box. Do not press the ENTER key.
3. Click the Save in box arrow and then click FTP Locations.
4. Double-click the name of the FTP site you want to save to.
5. When the FTP Log On dialog box displays, type your user name and password and then click the OK button.
6. Click the Save button in the Save As dialog box.

APPENDIX C

Resetting the Menus and Toolbars

When you first install Microsoft Office 2000, the Standard and Formatting toolbars display on one row in some of the applications. As you use the buttons on the toolbars and commands on the menus, Office personalizes the toolbars and the menus based on their usage. Each time you start an application, the toolbars and menus display in the same settings as the last time you used the application. The following steps show how to reset the Word menus and toolbars to their installation settings.

Steps To Reset My Usage Data and Toolbar Buttons

1 Click View on the menu bar and then point to Toolbars. Point to Customize on the Toolbars submenu.

The View menu and Toolbars submenu display (Figure C-1).

Toolbars command

View menu

Toolbars submenu

buttons promoted to Formatting toolbar based on usage

Customize command

FIGURE C-1

2 Click Customize. When the Customize dialog box displays, click the Options tab. Make sure the three check boxes in the Personalized Menus and Toolbars area have check marks and then point to the Reset my usage data button.

The Customize dialog box displays as shown in Figure C-2.

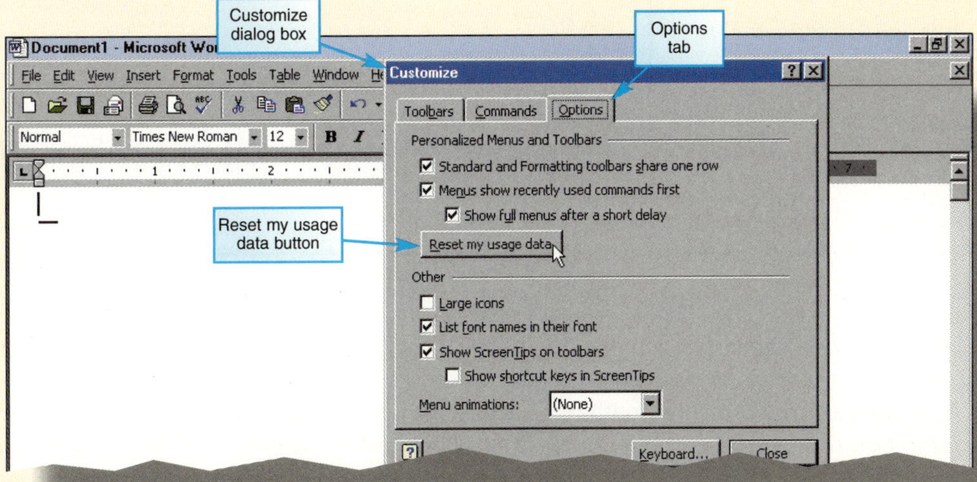

FIGURE C-2

3 Click the Reset my usage data button. When the Microsoft Word dialog box displays explaining the function of the Reset my usage data button, click the Yes button. In the Customize dialog box, click the Toolbars tab.

The Toolbars sheet displays (Figure C-3).

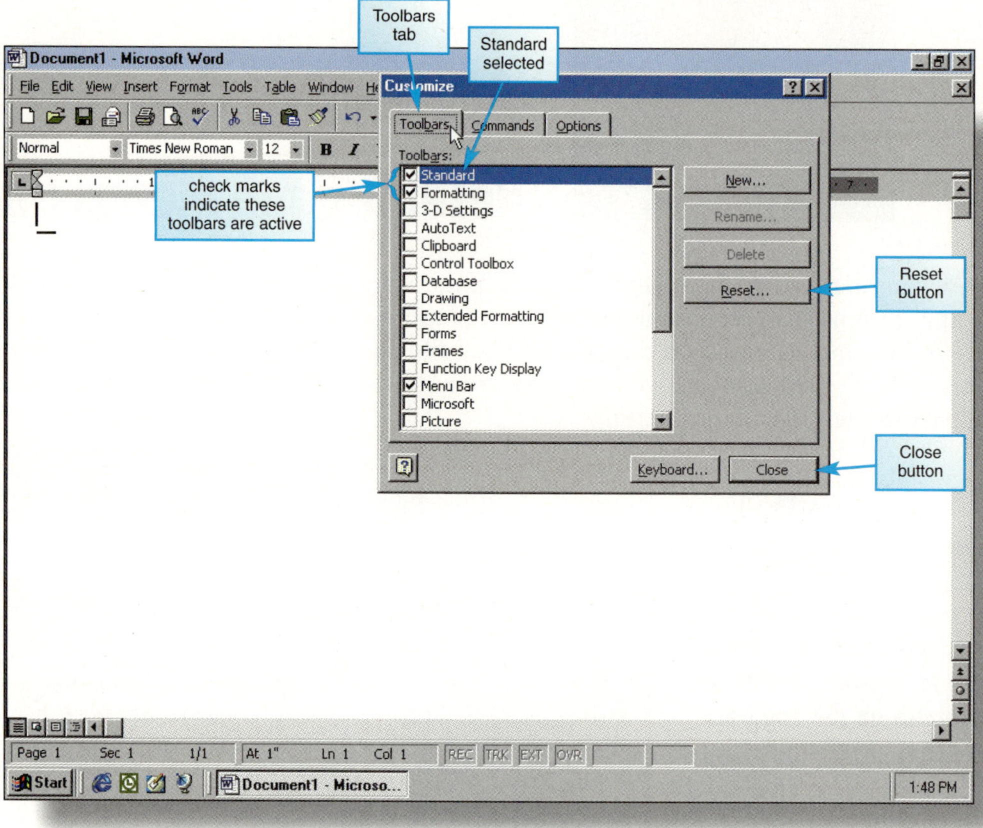

FIGURE C-3

4 Click Standard in the Toolbars list and then click the Reset button. When the Reset Toolbar dialog box displays, click the OK button. Click Formatting in the Toolbars list and then click the Reset button. When the Reset Toolbar dialog box displays, click the OK button.

5 Click the Close button in the Customize dialog box.

The toolbars display as shown in Figure C-4.

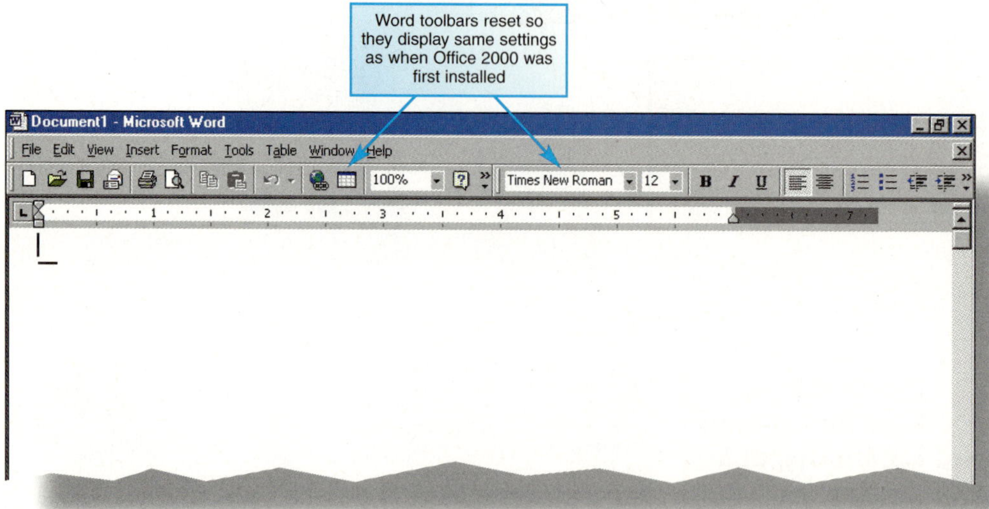

FIGURE C-4

Steps 3 and 4 display or remove any buttons that were added or deleted through the use of the Add or Remove Buttons button on the More Buttons menu.

You can turn off both the toolbars sharing a single row and the short menus by removing the check marks from the two top check boxes in the Options sheet in the Customize dialog box (Figure C-2 on the previous page). If you remove these check marks, Word will display the toolbars on two separate rows below the menu bar and will show only full menus.

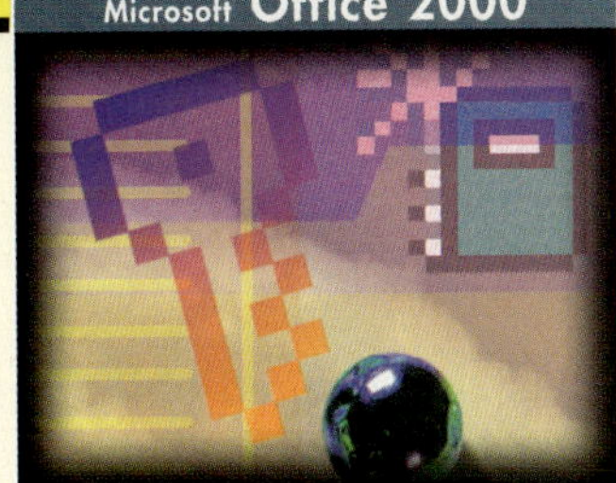

APPENDIX D

Microsoft Office User Specialist Certification Program

The Microsoft Office User Specialist (MOUS) Certification Program provides a framework for measuring your proficiency with the Microsoft Office 2000 applications, such as Word 2000, Excel 2000, Access 2000, and PowerPoint 2000. Three levels of certification are available — Master, Expert, and Core. The three levels of certification are described in Table D-1.

Table D-1 Three Levels of MOUS Certification

LEVEL	DESCRIPTION	REQUIREMENTS	CREDENTIAL AWARDED
Master	Indicates that you have a comprehensive understanding of Microsoft Office 2000	Pass all FIVE of the required exams: Microsoft Word 2000 Expert Microsoft Excel 2000 Expert Microsoft PowerPoint 2000 Core Microsoft Access 2000 Core Microsoft Outlook 2000 Core	Candidates will be awarded one certificate for passing all five of the required Microsoft Office 2000 exams: Microsoft Office User Specialist: Microsoft Office 2000 Master
Expert	Indicates that you have a comprehensive understanding of the advanced features in a specific Microsoft Office 2000 application	Pass any ONE of the Expert exams: Microsoft Word 2000 Expert Microsoft Excel 2000 Expert	Candidates will be awarded one certificate for each of the Expert exams they have passed: Microsoft Office User Specialist: Microsoft Word 2000 Expert Microsoft Office User Specialist: Microsoft Excel 2000 Expert
Core	Indicates that you have a comprehensive understanding of the core features in a specific Microsoft Office 2000 application	Pass any ONE of the Core exams: Microsoft Word 2000 Core Microsoft Excel 2000 Core Microsoft PowerPoint 2000 Core Microsoft Access 2000 Core Microsoft Outlook 2000 Core	Candidates will be awarded one certificate for each of the Core exams they have passed: Microsoft Office User Specialist: Microsoft Word 2000 Microsoft Office User Specialist: Microsoft Excel 2000 Microsoft Office User Specialist: Microsoft PowerPoint 2000 Microsoft Office User Specialist: Microsoft Access 2000 Microsoft Office User Specialist: Microsoft Outlook 2000

Why Should You Get Certified?

Being a Microsoft Office User Specialist provides a valuable industry credential — proof that you have the Office 2000 applications skills required by employers. By passing one or more MOUS certification exams, you demonstrate your proficiency in a given Office application to employers. With nearly 80 million copies of Office in use around the world, Microsoft is targeting Office certification to a wide variety of companies. These companies include temporary employment agencies that want to prove the expertise of their workers, large corporations looking for a way to measure the skill set of employees, and training companies and educational institutions seeking Microsoft Office teachers with appropriate credentials.

The MOUS Exams

You pay $50 to $100 each time you take an exam, whether you pass or fail. The fee varies among testing centers. The Expert exams, which you can take up to 60 minutes to complete, consist of between 40 and 60 tasks that you perform online. The tasks require you to use the application just as you would in doing your job. The Core exams contain fewer tasks, and you will have slightly less time to complete them. The tasks you will perform differ on the two types of exams.

How Can You Prepare for the MOUS Exams?

The Shelly Cashman Series® offers several Microsoft-approved textbooks that cover the required objectives on the MOUS exams. For a listing of the textbooks, visit the Shelly Cashman Series MOUS Web page at www.scsite.com/off2000/cert.htm and click the Shelly Cashman Office Series 2000 Microsoft-Approved MOUS Textbooks link (Figure D-1). After using any of the books listed in an instructor-led course, you will be prepared to take the MOUS exam indicated.

How to Find an Authorized Testing Center

You can locate a testing center by calling 1-800-933-4493 in North America or visiting the Shelly Cashman Series MOUS Web page at www.scsite.com/off2000/cert.htm and then clicking the Locate an Authorized Testing Center Near You link (Figure D-1). At this Web page, you can look for testing centers around the world.

Shelly Cashman Series MOUS Web Page

The Shelly Cashman Series MOUS Web page (Figure D-1) has more than fifteen Web pages you can visit to obtain additional information on the MOUS Certification Program. The Web page (www.scsite.com/off2000/cert.htm) includes links to general information on certification, choosing an application for certification, preparing for the certification exam, and taking and passing the certification exam.

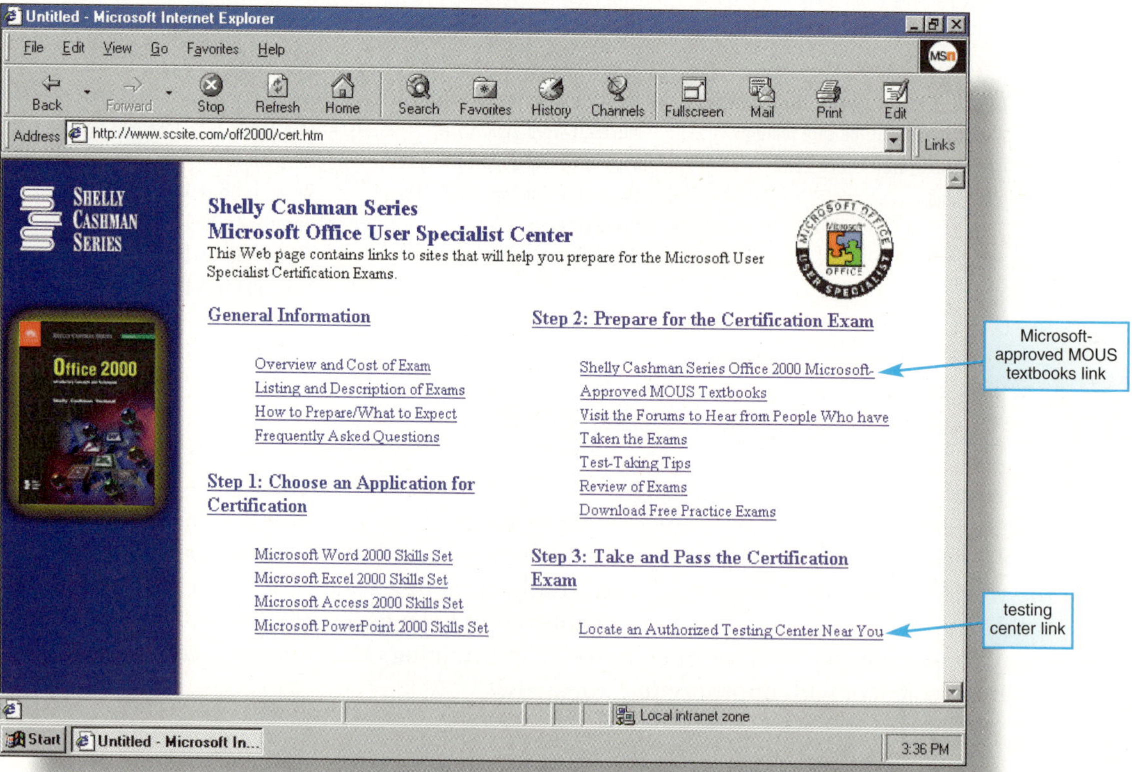

FIGURE D-1

Microsoft Office 2000 User Specialist Certification Map

The tables on the following pages list the skill sets and activities you should be familiar with if you plan to take the Microsoft Office User Specialist Certification examinations for Microsoft Word 2000, Microsoft Excel 2000, Microsoft Access 2000, or Microsoft PowerPoint 2000. Each activity is accompanied by page numbers on which the activity is illustrated in the book.

Microsoft Word 2000 User Specialist Certification Map

The Microsoft Word 2000 portion of *Microsoft Office 2000: Introductory Concepts and Techniques* (ISBN 0-7895-6251-0, 0-7895-6250-2, or 0-7895-5615-4) and *Microsoft Office 2000: Advanced Concepts and Techniques* (ISBN 0-7895-4649-3 or 0-7895-5629-4) used in combination in a two-sequence course has been approved by Microsoft as courseware for the Microsoft Office User Specialist (MOUS) program. After completing the Word 2000 projects and exercises in these two books, students will be prepared to take the Core-level Microsoft Office User Specialist Exam for Microsoft Word 2000. Table D-2 lists the skill sets, activities, and page number where the activity is discussed in the books. You should be familiar with each of the activities if you plan to take the Microsoft Word 2000 Core examination.

The Microsoft Word 2000 portion of *Microsoft Office 2000: Post Advanced Concepts and Techniques* (ISBN 0-7895-5691-X) used in combination with *Microsoft Office 2000: Introductory Concepts and Techniques* and *Microsoft Office 2000: Advanced Concepts and Techniques* in a third course has been approved by Microsoft as courseware for the Microsoft Office User Specialist (MOUS) program – Expert level. Table D-3 on the next page lists the skill sets, activities, and page number where the activity is discussed in the book for the Expert-level Microsoft Office User Specialist Exam for Microsoft Word 2000.

Table D-2 Microsoft Word 2000 MOUS Core Skill Sets, Activities, and Map

SKILL SETS	ACTIVITIES	PAGE NUMBERS
Working with text	Use the Undo, Redo, and Repeat command	WD 1.35, WD 1.36
	Apply font formats (Bold, Italic, and Underline)	WD 1.33, WD 1.39, WD 1.42
	Use the SPELLING feature	WD 1.22, WD 1.59, WD 2.50
	Use the THESAURUS feature	WD 2.48, WD 2.61
	Use the GRAMMAR feature	WD 1.22, WD 1.59, WD 2.50
	Insert page breaks	WD 2.31, WD 2.35, WD 4.21
	Highlight text in document	WDW 1.9, WD 6.61
	Insert and move text	WD 1.54, WD 2.46, WD 2.56
	Cut, Copy, Paste, and Paste Special using the Office Clipboard	WD 1.54, WD 2.45, WD 3.33, WD 3.35, WD 6.35
	Copy formats using the Format Painter	WD 6.57
	Select and change font and font size	WD 1.17, WD 1.31, WD 1.32
	Find and replace text	WD 2.43, WD 2.56
	Apply character effects (superscript, subscript, strikethrough, small caps, and outline)	WD 2.18, WD 4.16, WD 4.17
	Insert date and time	WD 6.17
	Insert symbols	WD 2.33, WD 3.37, WD 3.46
	Create and apply frequently used text with AutoCorrect	WD 2.20, WD 2.21
Working with paragraphs	Align text in paragraphs (Center, Left, Right, and Justified)	WD 1.33, WD 1.35, WD 2.17, WD 2.18, WD 6.26
	Add bullets and numbering	WD 3.50, WD 3.51, WD 4.40, WD 5.30, WD 6.63
	Set character, line, and paragraph spacing options	WD 2.9, WD 2.11, WD 2.18, WD 4.38, WD 6.42
Working with paragraphs (con't)	Apply borders and shading to paragraphs	WD 3.39, WD 4.8, WD 6.37, WD 6.45
	Use indentation options (Left, Right, First Line, and Hanging Indent)	WD 2.18, WD 2.19, WD 2.37, WD 6.43
	Use TABS command (Center, Decimal, Left, and Right)	WD 3.31, WD 3.32, WD 3.43, WD 6.49
	Create an outline style numbered list	WD 3.51, WD 5.30
	Set tabs with leaders	WD 3.31
Working with documents	Print a document	WD 1.50, WD 5.40, WD 6.47
	Use print preview	WD 3.24, WD 4.57
	Use Web Page Preview	WDW 1.11, WDW 1.14
	Navigate through a document	WD 1.25, WD 1.26, WD 1.40, WD 4.25
	Insert page numbers	WD 2.14
	Set page orientation	WD 5.24
	Set margins	WD 2.8, WD 6.7
	Use GoTo to locate specific elements in a document	WD 2.42, WD 2.43
	Create and modify page numbers	WD 2.14, WD 4.29
	Create and modify headers and footers	WD 2.12, WD 2.15, WD 4.28
	Align text vertically	WD 3.35, WD 3.36, WD 4.42
	Create and use newspaper columns	WD 6.23, WD 6.25
	Revise column structure	WD 6.30, WD 6.48, WD 6.51
	Prepare and print envelopes and labels	WD 3.58, WD 5.48, WD 5.54

(Table D-2 continued on the next page)

Table D-2 Microsoft Word 2000 MOUS Core Skill Sets, Activities, and Map

SKILL SETS	ACTIVITIES	PAGE NUMBERS
Working with documents (con't)	Apply styles	WD 2.26, WD 4.19, WD 6.33
	Create sections with formatting that differs from other sections	WD 4.21, WD 4.29, WD 6.24
	Use click & type	WD 2.13
Managing files	Use save	WD 1.26, WD 1.49
	Locate and open an existing document	WD 1.52, WD 4.23
	Use Save As (different name, location, or format)	WD 1.49, WD 3.42, WDW 1.11
	Create a folder	WD 1.49
	Create a new document using a Wizard	WD 3.7, WDW 1.5
	Save as Web Page	WDW 1.3
	Use templates to create a new document	WD 3.18, WD 5.6, WD 5.9
	Create Hyperlinks	WD 2.39, WD 2.53, WDW 1.10
Managing files (con't)	Use the Office Assistant	WD 1.55
	Send a Word document via e-mail	WD 2.54, WDI 1.7
Using tables	Create and format tables	WD 3.52, WD 3.55, WD 4.42, WD 4.49
	Add borders and shading to tables	WD 3.55, WD 4.59, WD 4.61
	Revise tables (insert and delete rows and columns, change cell formats)	WD 3.15, WD 3.62, WD 4.46, WD 4.53
	Modify table structure (merge cells, change height and width)	WD 4.47, WD 4.48, WD 4.53, WD 4.59
	Rotate text in a table	WD 4.50, WD 4.59
Working with pictures and charts	Use the Drawing toolbar	WD 4.15, WD 6.9, WD 6.40
	Insert graphics into a document (WordArt, ClipArt, Images)	WD 1.43, WD 4.12, WD 4.33, WD 4.54, WD 6.9

Table D-3 Microsoft Word 2000 MOUS Expert Skill Sets, Activities, and Map

SKILL SETS	ACTIVITIES	PAGE NUMBERS
Working with paragraphs	Apply paragraph and section shading	WD 4.10, WD 4.51, WD 6.45
	Use text flow options (Widows/Orphans options and keeping lines together)	WD 2.32, WD 7.33
	Sort lists, paragraphs, tables	WD 2.40, WD 5.45, WD 5.59
Working with documents	Create and modify page borders	WD 6.59, WD 8.48
	Format first page differently than subsequent pages	WD 4.7, WD 4.21, WD 4.28, WD 7.59, WD 9.47
	Use bookmarks	WD 7.59, WD 9.47
	Create and edit styles	WD 2.26, WD 9.17
	Create watermarks	WD 4.54, WD 6.44
	Use find and replace with formats, special characters, and non-printing elements	WD 2.45
	Balance column length (using column breaks appropriately)	WD 6.25, WD 6.51
	Create or revise footnotes and endnotes	WD 2.23, WD 2.30, WD 2.61
	Work with master documents and subdocuments	WD 7.36, WD 7.65
	Create and modify a table of contents	WD 7.57, WD 7.63, WD 7.67
	Create cross-reference	WD 7.29
	Create and modify an index	WD 7.31, WD 7.56, WD 7.63, WD 7.67
Using tables	Embed worksheets in a table	WD 7.23, WDI 2.6
	Perform calculations in a table	WD 3.62, WD 4.59
	Link Excel data as a table	WD 7.24, WDI 2.4, WDI 2.12
	Modify worksheets in a table	WD 7.22, WDI 2.12
Working with pictures and charts	Add bitmapped graphics	WD 6.53, WD 6.54, WD 9.22
	Delete and position graphics	WD 1.46, WD 5.12, WD 6.20, WD 6.46, WD 6.54
	Create and modify charts	WD 4.33, WD 4.35, WD 4.36, WD 4.37, WDI 2.6
	Import data into charts	WDI 2.8
Using mail merge	Create main document	WD 5.14, WD 5.25, WD 5.27, WD 5.29
	Create data source	WD 5.17
	Sort records to be merged	WD 5.45, WD 5.59
	Merge main document and data source	WD 5.41, WD 5.43, WD 5.59
	Generate labels	WD 5.48
	Merge a document using alternate data sources	WDI 1.4
Using advanced features	Insert a field	WD 5.34, WD 5.37, WD 8.17, WD 8.20, WD 8.28
	Create, apply, and edit macros	WD 9.26, WD 9.29, WD 9.39
	Copy, rename, and delete macros	WD 9.28, WD 9.64
	Create and modify form	WD 8.8, WD 8.15, WD 9.8
	Create and modify a form control (e.g., add an item to a drop-down list)	WD 8.17, WD 8.20, WD 8.28, WD 9.54, WD 9.57, WD 9.59
	Use advanced text alignment features with graphics	WD 5.13, WD 6.20, WD 6.28, WD 6.40, WD 6.54, WD 7.25
	Customize toolbars	WD 1.14, WD 9.30
Collaborating with workgroups	Insert comments	WD 7.10, WD 7.17
	Protect documents	WD 7.34, WD 7.42, WD 8.8, WD 8.47, WD 9.8
	Create multiple versions of a document	WD 7.15
	Track changes to a document	WD 7.13, WD 7.19
	Set default file location for workgroup templates	WD 8.56
	Round Trip documents from HTML	WDW 1.12

Microsoft Excel 2000 User Specialist Certification Map

The Microsoft Excel 2000 portion of *Microsoft Office 2000: Introductory Concepts and Techniques* (ISBN 0-7895-6251-0, 0-7895-6250-2, or 0-7895-5615-4) and *Microsoft Office 2000: Advanced Concepts and Techniques* (ISBN 0-7895-4649-3 or 0-7895-5629-4) used in combination in a two-sequence course has been approved by Microsoft as courseware for the Microsoft Office User Specialist (MOUS) program. After completing the Excel 2000 projects and exercises in these two books, students will be prepared to take the Core-level Microsoft Office User Specialist Exam for Microsoft Excel 2000. Table D-4 lists the skill sets, activities, and page number where the activity is discussed in the books. You should be familiar with each of the activities if you plan to take the Microsoft Excel 2000 Core examination.

The Microsoft Excel 2000 portion of *Microsoft Office 2000: Post Advanced Concepts and Techniques* (ISBN 0-7895-5691-X) used in combination with *Microsoft Office 2000: Introductory Concepts and Techniques* and *Microsoft Office 2000: Advanced Concepts and Techniques* in a third course has been approved by Microsoft as courseware for the Microsoft Office User Specialist (MOUS) program – Expert level. Table D-5 on the next page lists the skill sets, activities, and page number where the activity is discussed in the book for the Expert-level Microsoft Office User Specialist Exam for Microsoft Excel 2000.

Table D-4 Microsoft Excel 2000 MOUS Core Skill Sets, Activities, and Map

SKILL SETS	ACTIVITIES	PAGE NUMBERS
Working with cells	Use Undo and Redo	E 1.52, E 1.61
	Clear cell content	E 1.53
	Enter text, dates, and numbers	E 1.15, E 1.20, E 2.7, E 3.21
	Edit cell content	E 1.51, E 1.59
	Go to a specific cell	E 1.34, E 1.36
	Insert and delete selected cells	E 3.16, E 3.76
	Cut, copy, paste, paste special, and move selected cells, use the Office Clipboard	E 1.24, E 3.14, E 3.15
	Use Find and Replace	E 6.58
	Clear cell formats	E 1.53
	Work with series (AutoFill)	E 3.8-10
	Create hyperlinks	E 4.42
Working with files	Use Save	E 2.50, E 3.43
	Use Save As (different name, location, format)	E 1.41, E 3.19
	Locate and open an existing workbook	E 1.48, E 3.65
	Create a folder	E 1.44
	Use templates to create a new workbook	E 6.26
	Save a worksheet/workbook as a Web Page	EW 1.3
	Send a workbook via e-mail	E 2.62
	Use the Office Assistant	E 1.55
Formatting worksheets	Apply font styles (typeface, size, color, and styles)	E 2.28, E 2.30, E 3.36
	Apply number formats (currency, percent, dates, comma)	E 2.35, E 2.37, E 2.39, E 3.22
	Modify size of rows and columns	E 2.43, E 2.47, E 3.12
	Modify alignment of cell content	E 2.33
	Adjust the decimal place	E 2.36, E 2.39
	Use the Format Painter	E 3.10
	Apply AutoFormat	E 1.31
	Apply cell borders and shading	E 2.30, E 2.33, E 2.36
	Merge cells	E 1.33, E 2.30
	Rotate text and change indents	E 3.8
	Define, apply, and remove a style	E 6.22
Page setup and printing	Preview and print worksheets and workbooks	E 2.51, E 3.58
	Use Web Page Preview	EW 1.3
	Print a selection	E 2.54
	Change page orientation and scaling	E 2.56, E 3.58
	Set page margins and centering	E 6.49
	Insert and remove a page break	E 6.56
	Set print, and clear a print area	E 5.22
	Set up headers and footers	E 6.49
	Set print titles and options (gridlines, print quality, row and column headings)	E 6.55
Working with worksheets and workbooks	Insert and delete rows and columns	E 3.16
	Hide and unhide rows and columns	E 2.43, E 2.46
	Freeze and unfreeze rows and columns	E 3.19, E 3.32
	Change the zoom setting	E 3.59
	Move between worksheets in a workbook	E 2.61, E 3.58
	Check spelling	E 2.48, E 3.57
	Rename a worksheet	E 2.61, E 3.56
	Insert and delete worksheets	E 6.27
	Move and copy worksheets	E 6.28
	Link worksheets and consolidate data using 3-D references	E 6.61
Working with formulas and functions	Enter a range within a formula by dragging	E 2.17, E 2.20
	Enter formulas in a cell and using the formula bar	E 2.9, E 2.11, E 3.26
	Revise formulas	E 2.24
	Use references (absolute and relative)	E 3.24
	Use AutoSum	E 1.22, E 2.14, E 3.21, E 3.31, E 3.29
	Use Paste Function to insert a function	E 2.20
	Use basic functions (AVERAGE, SUM, COUNT, MIN, MAX)	E 1.22, E 2.16

(Table D-4 continued on the next page)

Table D-4 Microsoft Excel 2000 MOUS Core Skill Sets, Activities, and Map

SKILL SETS	ACTIVITIES	PAGE NUMBERS
Working with formulas and functions (con't)	Enter functions using the Formula Palette	E 2.18, E 2.20, E 3.28
	Use date functions (NOW and DATE)	E 3.21
	Use financial functions (FV and PMT)	E 4.16
	Use logical functions (IF)	E 3.27
Using charts and objects	Preview and print charts	E 2.51, E 3.58
	Use Chart Wizard to create a chart	E 1.36, E 3.45
	Modify charts	E 1.36, E 1.40, E 3.49
	Insert, move, and delete an object (picture)	E 4.42
	Create and modify lines and objects	E 6.45

Table D-5 Microsoft Excel 2000 MOUS Expert Skill Sets, Activities, and Map

SKILL SETS	ACTIVITIES	PAGE NUMBERS
Importing and exporting data	Import data from text files (insert, drag and drop)	E 9.9, E 9.13
	Import from other applications	E 9.13, E 9.18
	Import a table from an HTML file (insert, drag and drop – including HTML round tripping)	E 9.18
	Export to other applications	E 9.9
Using templates	Apply templates	E 6.26
	Edit templates	E 6.16
	Create templates	E 6.7
Using multiple workbooks	Use a workspace	E 6.62
	Link workbooks	E 6.61
Formatting numbers	Apply number formats (accounting, currency, number)	E 2.35, E 2.37, E 2.39, E 3.22
	Create custom number formats	E 6.20
	Use conditional formatting	E 2.40
Printing workbooks	Print and preview multiple worksheets	E 3.58, E 5.22
	Use Report Manager	E 8.48
Working with named ranges	Add and delete a named range	E 4.12, E 5.19
	Use a named range in a formula	E 4.14
	Use Lookup Functions (HLOOKUP or VLOOKUP)	E 5.15
Working with toolbars	Hide and display toolbars	E 1.14, E 3.37, E 3.43
	Customize a toolbar	E 7.18
	Assign a macro to a command button	E 7.18
Using macros	Record macros	E 7.11
	Run macros	E 7.15
	Edit macros	E 7.16, E 7.33
Auditing a worksheet	Work with the Auditing toolbar	E 8.10, E 8.15
	Trace errors (find and fix errors)	E 8.15
	Trace precedents (find cells referred to in a specific formula)	E 2.25
	Trace dependents (find formulas that refer to a specific cell)	E 2.25
Displaying and formatting data	Apply conditional formats	E 2.40, E 4.27
	Perform single and multi-level sorts	E 5.22, E 5.25
	Use grouping and outlines	E 5.30
	Use data forms	E 5.9
	Use subtotaling	E 5.27
	Apply data filters	E 5.35
	Extract data	E 5.43
	Query databases	E 5.32, E 5.35, E 5.40
	Use data validation	E 8.15
Using analysis tools	Use PivotTable AutoFormat	E 9.51
	Use Goal Seek	E 3.65, E 4.52, E 8.21
	Create pivot chart reports	E 9.42
	Work with Scenarios	E 8.35, E 8.48
	Use Solver	E 8.23
	Use data analysis and PivotTables	E 9.59
	Create interactive PivotTables for the Web	EW 1.1
	Add fields to a PivotTable using the Web browser	EW 2.13
Collaborating with workgroups	Create, edit, and remove a comment	E 6.47
	Apply and remove worksheet and workbook protection	E 4.49
	Change workbook properties	E 8.54
	Apply and remove file passwords	E 8.32
	Track changes (highlight, accept, and reject)	E 9.25
	Create a shared workbook	E 9.25
	Merge workbooks	E 9.61

Microsoft Access 2000 User Specialist Certification Map

The Microsoft Access 2000 portion of *Microsoft Office 2000: Introductory Concepts and Techniques* (ISBN 0-7895-6251-0, 0-7895-6250-2, or 0-7895-5615-4) and *Microsoft Office 2000: Advanced Concepts and Techniques* (ISBN 0-7895-4649-3 or 0-7895-5629-4) used in combination in a two-sequence course has been approved by Microsoft as courseware for the Microsoft Office User Specialist (MOUS) program. After completing the Access 2000 projects and exercises in these two books, students will be prepared to take the Core-level Microsoft Office User Specialist Exam for Microsoft Access 2000. Table D-6 lists the skill sets, activities, and page number where the activity is discussed in the books. You should be familiar with each of the activities if you plan to take the Microsoft Access 2000 Core examination.

The Microsoft Access 2000 portion of *Microsoft Office 2000: Post Advanced Concepts and Techniques* (ISBN 0-7895-5691-X) used in combination with *Microsoft Office 2000: Introductory Concepts and Techniques* and *Microsoft Office 2000: Advanced Concepts and Techniques* in a third course has been approved by Microsoft as courseware for the Microsoft Office User Specialist (MOUS) program – Expert level. Table D-7 on the next page lists the skill sets, activities, and page number where the activity is discussed in the book for the proposed Expert-level Microsoft Office User Specialist Exam for Microsoft Access 2000.

Table D-6 Microsoft Access 2000 MOUS Core Skill Sets, Activities, and Map

SKILL SETS	ACTIVITIES	PAGE NUMBERS
Planning and designing databases	Determine appropriate data inputs for your database	A 1.52
	Determine appropriate data outputs for your database	A 1.53
	Create table structure	A 1.15, A 1.34
	Establish table relationships	A 3.38
Working with Access	Use the Office Assistant	A 1.49
	Select an object using the Objects Bar	A 1.39, A 1.48, A 2.6
	Print database objects (tables, forms, reports, queries)	A 1.31, A 1.48, A 2.12
	Navigate through records in a table, query, or form	A 1.27, A 1.41
	Create a database (using a Wizard or in Design view)	A 1.9
Building and modifying tables	Create tables by using the Table Wizard	A 1.13
	Set primary keys	A 1.14, A 1.17
	Modify field properties	A 3.16, A 3.28
	Use multiple data types	A 1.14
	Modify tables using Design view	A 3.16
	Use the Lookup Wizard	A 6.7
	Use the Input Mask Wizard	A 6.10
Building and modifying forms	Create a form with the Form Wizard	A 4.31, A 5.21
	Use the Control Toolbox to add controls	A 4.34, A 4.37, A 4.43
	Modify format properties (font, style, font size, color, caption, etc.) of controls	A 4.36, A 4.45, A 5.42
	Use form sections (headers, footers, detail)	A 4.43, A 5.40
	Use a calculated control on a form	A 4.34
Viewing and organizing information	Use the Office Clipboard	A 6.36
	Switch between object views	A 1.42, A 3.11
	Enter records using a datasheet	A 1.21, A 1.28
Viewing and organizing information (con't)	Enter records using a form	A 3.8
	Delete records from a table	A 1.29, A 3.14, A 3.26
	Find a record	A 3.9
	Sort records	A 2.26, A 3.43
	Apply and remove filters (filter by form and filter by selection)	A 3.13, A 3.14
	Specify criteria in a query	A 2.17, A 2.19, A 2.21, A 2.24, A 3.26
	Display related records in a subdatasheet	A 3.42
	Create a calculated field	A 2.36
	Create and modify a multi-table select query	A 2.32, A 2.34
Defining relationships	Establish relationships	A 3.38
	Enforce referential integrity	A 3.38
Producing reports	Create a report with Report Wizard	A 1.43, A 4.9, A 4.19
	Preview and print a report	A 1.48
	Move and resize a control	A 4.27, A 6.16
	Modify format properties (font, style, font size, color, caption, etc.)	A 4.16, A 6.20
	Use the Control Toolbox to add controls	A 6.21
	Use report sections (headers, footers, detail)	A 4.14, A 4.25
	Use a calculated control in a report	A 6.20
Integrating with other applications	Import data to a new table	AI 1.3
	Save a table, query, form as a Web page	AW 1.1
	Add hyperlinks	A 5.6, A 5.18
Using Access tools	Print database relationships	A 3.41
	Backup and restore a database	A 3.6
	Compact and repair a database	A 5.48

Table D-7 Microsoft Access 2000 MOUS Expert Skill Sets, Activities, and Map

SKILL SETS	ACTIVITIES	PAGE NUMBERS
Building and modifying tables	Set validation text	A 3.31
	Define data validation criteria	A 3.28
	Modify an input mask	A 6.10, A 9.15
	Create and modify Lookup fields	A 6.7, A 7.13
	Optimize data type usage (double, long, int, byte, etc.)	A 9.12
Building and modifying forms	Create a form in Design view	A 8.35
	Insert a graphic on a form	A 8.56
	Modify control properties	A 4.16, A 5.36, A 5.37, A 5.38, A 8.14, A 8.33
	Customize form sections (headers, footers, detail)	A 4.43, A 5.40
	Modify form properties	A 4.45, A 5.33
	Use the subform control and synchronize forms	A 5.26, A 8.36
	Create a switchboard	A 6.40
Refining queries	Apply filters (filter by form and filter by selection) in a query's recordset	A 7.19
	Create a totals query	A 2.38
	Create a parameter query	A 7.20
	Specify criteria in multiple fields (AND vs. OR)	A 2.24, A 2.25
	Modify query properties (field formats, caption, input masks, etc.)	A 7.17
	Create an action query (update, delete, insert)	A 3.23, A 3.26
	Optimize queries using indexes	A 3.48, A 9.12
	Specify join properties for relationships	A 7.16
Producing reports	Insert a graphic on a report	A 7.56
	Modify report properties	A 4.15, A 7.26
	Create and modify a report in Design view	A 7.24
	Modify control properties	A 4.15, A 6.20, A 7.35
	Set section properties	A 4.15
	Use the subreport control and synchronize reports	A 7.29
Defining relationships	Establish one-to-one relationships	A 7.12
	Establish many-to-many relationships	A 7.12
	Set Cascade Update and Cascade Delete options	A 9.17
Utilizing Web capabilities	Create hyperlinks	A 5.6, A 5.18
	Use the group and sort features of data access pages	A 9.26
	Create a data access page	AW 1.3
Using Access tools	Set and modify a database password	A 9.22
	Set startup options	A 9.20
	Use Add-ins (Database Splitter, Analyzer, Link Table Manager)	A 9.8, A 9.11
	Encrypt and decrypt a database	A 9.24
	Use simple replication (copy for a mobile user)	A 9.32
	Run macros using controls	A 6.49
	Create a macro using the Macro Builder	A 6.29
	Convert a database to a previous version	A 9.7
Data integration	Export database records to Excel	AI 2.3
	Drag and drop tables and queries to Excel	AI 2.6
	Present information as a chart (MS Graph)	A 8.40
	Link to existing data	AI 1.3

Microsoft PowerPoint 2000 User Specialist Certification Map

The Microsoft PowerPoint 2000 portion of *Microsoft Office 2000: Introductory Concepts and Techniques* (ISBN 0-7895-6251-0, 0-7895-6250-2, or 0-7895-5629-4) used in combination in a two-sequence course has been approved by Microsoft as courseware for the Microsoft Office User Specialist (MOUS) program. After completing the PowerPoint 2000 projects and exercises in these two books, students will be prepared to take the Core-level Microsoft Office User Specialist Exam for Microsoft PowerPoint 2000. Table D-8 lists the skill sets, activities, and page number where the activity is discussed in the books. You should be familiar with each of the activities if you plan to take the Microsoft PowerPoint 2000 Core examination.

The Microsoft PowerPoint 2000 portion of *Microsoft Office 2000: Post Advanced Concepts and Techniques* (ISBN 0-7895-5691-X) used in combination with *Microsoft Office 2000: Introductory Concepts and Techniques* and *Microsoft Office 2000: Advanced Concepts and Techniques* in a third course has been approved by Microsoft as courseware for the Microsoft Office User Specialist (MOUS) program – Expert level. Table D-9 on the next page lists the skill sets, activities, and page number where the activity is discussed in the book for the Expert-level Microsoft Office User Specialist Exam for Microsoft PowerPoint 2000.

Table D-8 Microsoft PowerPoint 2000 MOUS Core Skill Sets, Activities, and Map

SKILL SETS	ACTIVITIES	PAGE NUMBERS
Creating a presentation	Delete slides	PP 4.53
	Create a specified type of slide	PP 1.33, PP 1.40-42, PP 2.7, PP 2.11, PP 2.13, PP 2.15, PP 2.18
	Create a presentation from a template and/or a Wizard	PP 1.8, PP 2.7, PPW 1.1
	Navigate among different views (slide, outline, sorter, tri-pane)	PP 1.13, PP 2.8, PP 2.20, PP 2.21, PP 2.46
	Create a new presentation from existing slides	PP 4.6
	Copy a slide from one presentation into another	PP 3.8
	Insert headers and footers	PP 2.35
	Create a blank presentation	PP 1.10, PP 2.6, PP 3.7
	Create a presentation using the AutoContent Wizard	PP 1.8
	Send a presentation via e-mail	PP 2.55
Modifying a presentation	Change the order of slides using Slide Sorter view	PP 4.50-51
	Find and replace text	PP 1.57, PPW 1.10, PP 4.7, PP 4.24
	Change the layout for one or more slides	PP 2.22, PP 2.27-28
	Change slide layout (modify the Slide Master)	PP 1.57-63, PP 2.42, PP 3.14-18, PP 4.8
	Modify slide sequence in the outline pane	PP 2.10, PP 4.25-26, PP 4.49, PP 4.54
	Apply a design template	PP 1.18, PP 2.7, PP 3.9
Working with text	Check spelling	PP 1.54
	Change and replace text fonts (individual slide and entire presentation)	PP 1.24, PP 1.27, PP 2.47, PP 3.10
	Enter text in tri-pane view	PP 1.21, PP 1.23, PP 1.35, PP 1.37-42, PP 2.11-12 PP 2.14-19
	Import text from Word	PP 3.7-8
	Change the text alignment	PP 1.59
	Create a text box for entering text	PP 4.35, PP 4.37
	Use the Wrap text in AutoShape feature	PP 4.59
	Use the Office Clipboard	PP 3.34
	Use the Format Painter	PP 4.64
Working with text (con't)	Promote and Demote text in slide and outline panes	PP 1.37-41, PP 2.11, PP 2.14-19
Working with visual elements	Add a picture from the ClipArt Gallery	PP 2.24, PP 2.27-30, PP 3.16-18, PP 3.52, PP 4.8
	Add and group shapes using WordArt or the Drawing toolbar	PP 3.53-58, PP 4.13-21
	Apply formatting	PP 1.25, PP 1.27, PP 2.47, PP 3.14, PP 3.45-49, PP 4.34-38
	Place text inside a shape using a text box	PP 4.35
	Scale and size an object including clip art	PP 2.32, PP 3.39, PP 3.53, PP 4.21, PP 4.33
	Create tables within PowerPoint	PP 3.41-49
	Rotate and fill an object	PP 4.19-20, PP 4.34
Customizing a presentation	Add AutoNumber bullets	PP 3.18
	Add speaker notes	PPW 1.4
	Add graphical bullets	PP 3.19-21
	Add slide transitions	PP 2.38, PP 3.58, PP 4.54
	Animate text and objects	PP 2.50-51, PP 3.58, PP 4.54
Creating output	Preview presentation in black and white	PP 1.63
	Print slides in a variety of formats	PP 1.64, PP 2.51, PP 2.54
	Print audience handouts	PP 1.64, PP 2.5, PP 3.59
	Print speaker notes in a specified format	PP 3.55
Delivering a presentation	Start a slide show on any slide	PP 1.46, PP 1.48, PP 2.49
	Use on-screen navigation tools	PP 1.48, PP 2.50, PP 3.40 PP 3.41, PP 4.38, PP 4.44
	Print a slide as an overhead transparency	PP 1.67
	Use the pen during a presentation	PP 4.60
Managing files	Save changes to a presentation	PP 1.51, PP 1.65, PP 1.69, PP 2.35, PP 2.49, PP 2.57, PPW 1.4, PP 3.12, PP 4.6
	Save as a new presentation	PP 1.28, PP 2.19
	Publish a presentation to the Web	PPW 1.3
	Use Office Assistant	PP 1.67
	Insert hyperlink	PP 2.35, PP 4.27-30

Table D-9 Microsoft PowerPoint 2000 MOUS Expert Skill Sets, Activities, and Map

SKILL SETS	ACTIVITIES	PAGE NUMBERS
Creating a presentation	Automatically create a summary slide	PP 4.52-53
	Automatically create slides from a summary slide	PP 4.51
	Design a template	PP 2.11, PP 6.56
	Format presentations for the Web	PPW 1.3
Modifying a presentation	Change tab formatting	PP 5.7
	Use the Wrap text in AutoShape feature	PP 4.16, PP 5.42
	Apply a template from another presentation	PP 3.9
	Customize a color scheme	PP 4.8, PP 6.55
	Apply animation effects	PP 2.37, PP 2.46-48, PP 3.58 PP 4.54, PP 5.45, PP 5.59
	Create a custom background	PP 3.12-18, PP 4.8, PP 5.45-48
	Add animated GIFs	PPI 2.8, PP 5.16-17, PP 6.52
	Add links to slides within the presentation	PP 4.64
	Customize clip art and other objects (resize, scale, etc.)	PP 2.33, PP 3.39, PP 3.53, PP 3.54-58, PP 5.18
	Add a presentation within a presentation	PP 5.9-13
	Add an action button	PP 4.27-30
	Hide slides	PP 4.49
	Set automatic slide timings	PP 5.54-58
Working with visual elements	Add textured backgrounds	PP 4.58
	Apply diagonal borders	PP 5.33
Using data from other sources	Export an outline to Word	PP 2.51, PP 6.70
	Add a table (from Word)	PP 5.36-38
	Insert an Excel chart	PP 5.19-33
	Add sound	PP 4.27-30, PPI 2.6-8
	Add video	PPI 2.1, PP 6.9
Creating output	Save slide as a graphic	PP 5.24
	Generate meeting notes	PP 5.60
	Change output format (Page setup)	PP 2.51, PP 3.59, PP 5.19, PP 6.16-19
	Export to 35mm slides	PP 4.53
Delivering a presentation	Save presentation for use on another computer (Pack 'N Go)	PPW 1.8, PP 6.12-13, PPW 2.2-6
	Electronically incorporate meeting feedback	PP 5.50
	Use presentations on demand	PP 5.48, PP 5.52
Managing files	Save embedded fonts in presentation	PPW 2.5
	Save HTML to a specific target browser	PPW 1.6
Working with PowerPoint	Customize the toolbar	PP 2.22, PP 6.9-14, PP 6.66
	Create a toolbar	PP 6.9-11
Collaborating with workgroups	Subscribe to a presentation	PPW 2.12
	View a presentation on the Web	PPW 1.6, PPW 2.6
	Use Net Meeting to schedule a broadcast	PP 5.50
	Use NetShow to deliver a broadcast	PP 5.52
Working with charts and tables	Build a chart or graph	PP 5.25-35
	Modify charts or graphs	PP 5.29-35
	Build an organization chart	PP 3.22-40
	Modify an organization chart	PP 4.38-43
	Modify PowerPoint tables	PP 4.44-46

Index

Microsoft Office 2000 Quick Reference Summary

In the Microsoft Office 2000 applications, you can accomplish a task in a number of ways. The following five tables (one for Word, Excel, Access, PowerPoint, and Outlook) provide a quick reference to each task presented in *Microsoft Office 2000: Introductory Concepts and Techniques* and its companion textbooks *Microsoft Office 2000: Advanced Concepts and Techniques* and *Microsoft Office 2000: Post Advanced Concepts and Techniques*. Any task with a page number reference beginning with 1, 2, or 3 is from *Microsoft Office 2000: Introductory Concepts and Techniques*. Any page number reference beginning with 4, 5, or 6 is from *Microsoft Office 2000: Advanced Concepts and Techniques*. Any page number reference beginning with 7, 8, or 9 is from *Microsoft Office 2000: Post Advanced Concepts and Techniques*. You can invoke the commands listed in the MENU BAR and SHORTCUT MENU columns using either the mouse or keyboard.

Table 1 Microsoft Word 2000 Quick Reference Summary

TASK	PAGE NUMBER	MOUSE	MENU BAR	SHORTCUT MENU	KEYBOARD SHORTCUT
1.5 Line Spacing	WD 2.18		Format | Paragraph | Indents and Spacing tab	Paragraph | Indents and Spacing tab	CTRL+5
ActiveX Control, Format	WD 9.55		Format | Control	Format Control	
ActiveX Control, Insert	WD 9.54	Desired button on Control Toolbox toolbar			
ActiveX Control, Set Properties	WD 9.57	Properties button on Control Toolbox toolbar		Properties	
ActiveX Control, Write Code	WD 9.60	View Code button on Control Toolbox toolbar		View Code	
Animate Text	WD 8.45		Format | Font | Text Effects tab	Font | Text Effects tab	
AutoCorrect Entry, Create	WD 2.21		Tools | AutoCorrect | AutoCorrect tab		
AutoShape, Add	WD 7.49	AutoShapes button on Drawing toolbar			
AutoText Entry, Create	WD 3.45		Insert | AutoText | New		ALT+F3
AutoText Entry, Insert	WD 3.47		Insert | AutoText		Type entry, then F3
Blank Line Above Paragraph	WD 2.18		Format | Paragraph | Indents and Spacing tab	Paragraph | Indents and Spacing tab	CTRL+0
Bold	WD 1.33	Bold button on Formatting toolbar	Format | Font | Font tab	Font | Font tab	CTRL+B
Bookmark, Add	WD 7.59		Insert | Bookmark		
Bookmark, Go To	WD 7.60	Select Browse Object button on vertical scroll bar	Edit | Go To		CTRL+G
Border, Bottom	WD 3.39	Border button arrow on Formatting toolbar	Format | Borders and Shading | Borders tab		
Border, Outside	WD 4.8	Border button arrow on Tables and Borders toolbar	Format | Borders and Shading | Borders tab		
Border, Page	WD 6.59		Format | Borders and Shading | Page Border tab	Borders and Shading | Page Border tab	
Bulleted List	WD 3.50	Bullets button on Formatting toolbar	Format | Bullets and Numbering | Bulleted tab	Bullets and Numbering | Bulleted tab	* and then space followed by text, then ENTER
Capitalize Letters	WD 2.18		Format | Font | Font tab	Font | Font tab	CTRL+SHIFT+A

(continued)

Table 1 Microsoft Word 2000 Quick Reference Summary *(continued)*

TASK	PAGE NUMBER	MOUSE	MENU BAR	SHORTCUT MENU	KEYBOARD SHORTCUT
Caption, Add	WD 7.26		Insert | Caption		
Caption, Update Caption Number	WD 7.27			Update Field	F9
Case of Letters	WD 2.18				SHIFT+F3
Center	WD 1.35	Center button on Formatting toolbar	Format | Paragraph | Indents and Spacing tab	Paragraph | Indents and Spacing tab	CTRL+E
Center Vertically	WD 4.17		File | Page Setup | Layout tab		
Character Formatting, Remove	WD 2.18		Format | Font	Font	CTRL+Q
Character Spacing	WD 6.42		Format | Font | Character Spacing tab	Font | Character Spacing tab	
Chart, Format Axis Numbers	WD 4.35	Click axis, Increase or Decrease Decimals button on Formatting toolbar	Click axis, Format | Format Axis	Right-click axis, click Format Axis	
Chart, Move Legend	WD 4.36		Click legend, Format | Format Legend	Right-click legend, click Format Legend	
Chart Table	WD 4.33		Insert | Picture | Chart		
Clip Art, Insert	WD 1.43		Insert | Picture | Clip Art		
Clip Gallery Live	WD 4.12		Insert | Picture | Clip Art		
Close All Documents	WD 3.60		SHIFT+File | Close All		
Close Document	WD 1.54	Close button on menu bar	File | Close		CTRL+W
Color Characters	WD 3.28	Font Color button arrow on Formatting toolbar	Format | Font | Font tab	Font | Font tab	
Column Break	WD 6.31		Insert | Break		CTRL+SHIFT+ENTER
Columns	WD 6.25	Columns button on Standard toolbar	Format | Columns		
Columns, Balance	WD 6.51		Insert | Break		
Columns, Format	WD 6.25		Format | Columns		
Comment, Delete	WD 7.18	Delete Comment button on Reviewing toolbar		Right-click comment reference mark in document window, click Delete Comment	
Comment, Insert	WD 7.10	Insert Comment button on Reviewing toolbar	Insert | Comment		
Comment, Modify	WD 7.12	Double-click comment reference mark in document window	View | Comments	Right-click comment reference mark in document window, click Edit Comment	
Comment, Review	WD 7.17	Next Comment button on Reviewing toolbar			
Comment, Print	WD 7.12		File | Print | Options button		
Copy	WD 3.33	Copy button on Standard toolbar or Clipboard toolbar	Edit | Copy	Copy	CTRL+C
Count Words	WD 2.49		Tools | Word Count		
Cross-Reference, Create	WD 7.29		Insert | Cross-reference		
Current Date, Insert	WD 6.17		Insert | Date and Time		
Data Source, Add Field	WD 5.23	Manage Fields button on Database toolbar			
Data Source, Add Record	WD 5.24	Add New Record button on Database toolbar			
Data Source, Change Designation	WDI 1.4	Mail Merge Helper button on Mail Merge toolbar	Tools | Mail Merge		
Data Source, Create	WD 5.17	Mail Merge Helper button on Mail Merge toolbar	Tools | Mail Merge		

Table 1 Microsoft Word 2000 Quick Reference Summary *(continued)*

TASK	PAGE NUMBER	MOUSE	MENU BAR	SHORTCUT MENU	KEYBOARD SHORTCUT
Data Source, Delete Record	WD 5.24	Delete Record button on Database toolbar			
Delete Text	WD 1.54	Cut button on Standard toolbar	Edit | Cut	Cut	DELETE or BACKSPACE
Demote List Item	WD 3.51	Decrease Indent button on Formatting toolbar			
Distribute Columns Evenly	WD 4.48	Distribute Columns Evenly button on Tables and Borders toolbar	Table | AutoFit | Distribute Columns Evenly		
Document Map	WD 7.66	Document Map button on Standard toolbar			
Distribute Rows Evenly	WD 4.47	Distribute Rows Evenly button on Tables and Borders toolbar	Table | AutoFit | Distribute Rows Evenly		
Document Window, Open New	WD 3.27	New Blank Document button on Standard toolbar	File | New | General tab		
Double Strikethrough, Characters	WD 4.17		Format | Font | Font tab	Font | Font tab	
Double-Space Text	WD 2.9		Format | Paragraph | Indents and Spacing tab	Paragraph | Indents and Spacing tab	CTRL+2
Double-Underline	WD 2.18		Format | Font | Font tab	Font | Font tab	CTRL+SHIFT+D
Drawing Object, 3-D Effect	WD 9.24	3-D button on Drawing toolbar			
Drawing Object, Fill	WD 8.43	Fill Color button on Drawing toolbar	Format | AutoShape | Colors and Lines tab	Format AutoShape | Colors and Lines tab	
Drawing Object, Order	WD 8.42	Draw button on Drawing toolbar, Order			
Drawing Object, Rotate	WD 7.51	Draw button on Drawing toolbar, Rotate or Flip			
Drawing Object, Shadow	WD 9.24	Shadow button on Drawing toolbar			
Drawing Objects, Group	WD 7.52	Select objects, Draw button on Drawing toolbar, Group		Right-click selected object, click Grouping	
Drop Cap	WD 6.28		Format | Drop Cap		
E-mail Document	WD 2.54	E-mail button on Standard toolbar	File | Send To | Mail Recipient		
Embed Excel Worksheet	WD 7.23		Insert | Object | Create from File tab		
Embedded Object, Convert to Word Graphic	WD 7.24				CTRL+SHIFT+F9
Emboss, Characters	WD 4.17		Format | Font | Font tab	Font | Font tab	
Engrave, Characters	WD 4.17		Format | Font | Font tab	Font | Font tab	
Envelope	WD 3.58		Tools | Envelopes and Labels		
Envelopes Using Data Source	WD 5.54	Mail Merge Helper button on Mail Merge toolbar	Tools | Mail Merge		
Erase Table Lines	WD 4.45	Eraser button on Tables and Borders toolbar			
Field Codes, Display	WD 5.39		Tools | Options | View tab		ALT+F9
Field Codes, Print	WD 5.40		Tools | Options | Print tab		
Fill-in Field	WD 5.37	Insert Word Field button on Mail Merge toolbar	Insert | Field		
Find	WD 2.45	Select Browse Object button on vertical scroll bar	Edit | Find		CTRL+F

(continued)

Table 1 Microsoft Word 2000 Quick Reference Summary *(continued)*

TASK	PAGE NUMBER	MOUSE	MENU BAR	SHORTCUT MENU	KEYBOARD SHORTCUT
Find and Replace	WD 2.43	Select Browse Object on vertical scroll bar	Edit | Replace		CTRL+H
First-Line Indent	WD 2.19	Drag First Line Indent marker on ruler	Format | Paragraph | Indents and Spacing tab	Paragraph | Indents and Spacing tab	
Floating Graphic	WD 6.20	Text Wrapping button on Picture toolbar	Format | Picture | Layout tab	Format Picture | Layout tab	
Folder, Create	WD 1.49		File | Save As		
Font	WD 1.31	Font button on Formatting toolbar	Format | Font | Font tab	Font | Font tab	CTRL+SHIFT+F
Font Size	WD 1.17	Font Size box arrow on Formatting toolbar	Format | Font | Font tab	Font | Font tab	CTRL+SHIFT+P
Footnote, Create	WD 2.23		Insert | Footnote		
Footnote, Delete	WD 2.30	Delete note reference mark in document window			
Footnote, Edit	WD 2.30	Double-click note reference mark in document window	View | Footnotes		
Footnotes to Endnotes, Convert	WD 2.30		Insert | Footnote		
Form, Add Help Text	WD 8.36	Double-click form field		Right-click form field, click Properties	
Form, Change Bookmark	WD 9.47	Double-click form field		Right-click form field, click Properties	
Form, Check Box Options	WD 8.29	Double-click check box form field		Right-click form field, click Properties	
Form, Drop-Down Form Field Options	WD 8.21	Double-click drop-down form field		Right-click form field, click Properties	
Form, Insert Check Box	WD 8.28	Check Box Form Field on Forms toolbar			
Form, Insert Drop-Down Form Field	WD 8.20	Drop-Down Form Field button on Forms toolbar			
Form, Insert Table	WD 8.15	Insert Table button on Forms toolbar	Table | Insert | Table		
Form, Insert Text Form Field	WD 8.17	Text Form Field button on Forms toolbar			
Form, Protect	WD 8.47	Protect Form button on Forms toolbar	Tools | Protect Document		
Form, Remove Field Shading	WD 8.39	Form Field Shading button on Forms toolbar			
Form, Save Data Only	WD 8.52		File | Save As | Tools | General Options		
Form, Text Form Field Options	WD 8.18	Double-click text form field		Right-click form field, click Properties	
Format Painter	WD 6.57	Format Painter button on Standard toolbar			
Formatting Marks	WD 1.20	Show/Hide ¶ button on Standard toolbar	Tools | Options | View tab		CTRL+SHIFT+*
Formatting Toolbar, Display Entire	WD 1.13	Double-click move handle on Formatting toolbar			
Full Menu	WD 1.12	Double-click menu name	Click menu name, wait few seconds		
Go To	WD 2.42	Select Browse Object button on vertical scroll bar	Edit | Go To		CTRL+G
Gridlines, Show	WD 8.16		Table | Show Gridlines		
Gutter Margin	WD 7.62		File | Page Setup | Margins tab		

Table 1 Microsoft Word 2000 Quick Reference Summary *(continued)*

TASK	PAGE NUMBER	MOUSE	MENU BAR	SHORTCUT MENU	KEYBOARD SHORTCUT
Hanging Indent, Create	WD 2.37	Drag Hanging Indent marker on ruler	Format | Paragraph | Indents and Spacing tab	Paragraph | Indents and Spacing tab	CTRL+T
Hanging Indent, Remove	WD 2.18	Drag Hanging Indent marker on ruler	Format | Paragraph | Indents and Spacing tab	Paragraph | Indents and Spacing tab	CTRL+SHIFT+T
Header, Different from Previous	WD 4.28	In print layout view, double-click header area	View | Header and Footer		
Header, Display	WD 2.12	In print layout view, double-click header area	View | Header and Footer		
Headers, Alternating	WD 7.60	Page Setup button on Header and Footer toolbar	File | Page Setup | Layout tab		
Help	WD 1.55	Microsoft Word Help button on Standard toolbar	Help | Microsoft Word Help		F1
Hidden Characters	WD 4.17		Format | Font | Font tab	Font | Font tab	
Highlight Text	WD 6.61	Highlight button on Formatting toolbar			
HTML Source	WDW 1.11		View | HTML Source		
Hyperlink, Add	WDW 1.10	Insert Hyperlink button on Standard toolbar		Hyperlink	
Hyperlink, Create	WD 2.39	Insert Hyperlink button on Standard toolbar		Hyperlink	Web address then ENTER or SPACEBAR
Hyperlink, Edit	WDW 1.10	Insert Hyperlink button on Standard toolbar		Hyperlink	
IF Field	WD 5.34	Insert Word Field button on Mail Merge toolbar	Insert | Field		
Index Entry, Mark	WD 7.31		Insert | Index and Tables | Index tab		ALT+SHIFT+X
Index, Build	WD 7.56		Insert | Index and Tables | Index tab		
Index, Update	WD 7.67			Right-click selected table of contents, click Update Field	Select table of contents, F9
Insert File	WD 4.23		Insert | File		
Insert Merge Fields	WD 5.27	Insert Merge Field button on Mail Merge toolbar			
Italicize	WD 1.39	Italic button on Formatting toolbar	Format | Font | Font tab	Font | Font tab	CTRL+I
Justify	WD 6.26	Justify button on Formatting toolbar	Format | Paragraph | Indents and Spacing tab	Paragraph | Indents and Spacing tab	CTRL+J
Landscape Orientation	WD 5.24		File | Page Setup | Paper Size tab		
Last Editing Location	WD 4.25				SHIFT+F5
Leader Characters	WD 3.31		Format | Tabs		
Left-Align	WD 2.17	Align Left button on Formatting toolbar	Format | Paragraph | Indents and Spacing tab	Paragraph | Indents and Spacing tab	CTRL+L
Line Break, Enter	WD 3.22				SHIFT+ENTER
Link	WD 6.34		Edit | Paste Special		
Link Excel Data to Word Chart	WDI 2.8		Edit | Paste Link		
Link Excel Worksheet	WDI 2.4		Insert | Object | Create from File		
List Item, Demote	WD 5.32	Increase Indent button on Formatting toolbar			SHIFT+TAB
List Item, Promote	WD 5.32	Decrease Indent button on Formatting toolbar			TAB
Macro, Copy	WD 9.64	In Visual Basic Editor, Copy button on Standard toolbar, then Paste button on Standard toolbar	In Visual Basic Editor, Edit | Copy; then Edit | Paste	In Visual Basic Editor, Copy then Paste	In Visual Basic Editor, CTRL+C then CTRL+V

(continued)

Table 1 Microsoft Word 2000 Quick Reference Summary *(continued)*

TASK	PAGE NUMBER	MOUSE	MENU BAR	SHORTCUT MENU	KEYBOARD SHORTCUT
Macro, Delete	WD 9.65		Tools | Macro | Macros		
Macro, Record	WD 9.26	Double-click REC status indicator on status bar	Tools | Macro | Record New Macro		
Macro, Run	WD 9.29	Run Macro button on Standard toolbar in Visual Basic Editor	Tools | Macro | Macros		ALT+F8
Macro, Run on Exit	WD 9.52	Double-click form field		Right-click form field, click Properties	
Macro, View VBA Code	WD 9.39		Tools | Macro | Macros		ALT+F11
Mailing Label	WD 3.58		Tools | Envelopes and Labels		
Mailing Labels Using Data Source	WD 5.48	Mail Merge Helper button on Mail Merge toolbar	Tools | Mail Merge		
Main Document, Identify	WD 5.14	Mail Merge Helper button on Mail Merge toolbar	Tools | Mail Merge		
Margins	WD 2.8	In print layout view, drag margin boundary	File | Page Setup | Margins tab		
Master Document, Open	WD 7.65	Open button on Standard toolbar, then Expand Subdocuments button on Outlining toolbar			
Menus and Toolbars, Reset	WD 2.7		View | Toolbars | Customize | Options tab		
Merge Certain Records	WD 5.43	Merge button on Mail Merge toolbar			
Merge to E-mail Addresses	WDI 1.4	Merge button on Mail Merge toolbar			
Merge to Printer	WD 5.40	Merge to Printer button on Mail Merge toolbar			
Merged Data, View	WD 5.47	View Merged Data button on Mail Merge toolbar			
Move Selected Text	WD 2.46	Drag and drop	Edit | Cut; Edit | Paste		CTRL+X; CTRL+V
Nonbreaking Hyphen	WD 3.46		Insert | Symbol | Special Characters tab		CTRL+SHIFT+HYPHEN
Nonbreaking Space	WD 3.46		Insert | Symbol | Special Characters tab		CTRL+SHIFT+SPACEBAR
Normal Style, Apply	WD 4.19	Style box arrow on Formatting toolbar	Format | Style		CTRL+SHIFT+N
Note Pane, Close	WD 2.29	Close button in note pane			
Numbered List	WD 3.51	Numbering button on Formatting toolbar	Format | Bullets and Numbering | Numbered tab	Bullets and Numbering | Numbered tab	1. and then space followed by text, then ENTER
Open Document	WD 1.52	Open button on Standard toolbar	File | Open		CTRL+O
Orphan	WD 2.32		Format | Paragraph | Line and Page Breaks tab	Paragraph | Line and Page Breaks tab	
Outline Numbered List	WD 5.30		Format | Bullets and Numbering | Outline Numbered tab		
Outline, Characters	WD 4.17		Format | Font | Font tab	Font | Font tab	
Outline, Create	WD 7.37	Outline View button on horizontal scroll bar	View | Outline		
Outline, Demote Heading	WD 7.45	Demote button on Outlining toolbar			TAB
Outline, Demote Heading to Body Text	WD 7.47	Demote to Body Text button on Outlining toolbar			TAB until style is body text
Outline, Promote Heading	WD 7.45	Promote button on Outlining toolbar			SHIFT+TAB

Table 1 Microsoft Word 2000 Quick Reference Summary *(continued)*

TASK	PAGE NUMBER	MOUSE	MENU BAR	SHORTCUT MENU	KEYBOARD SHORTCUT
Outline, Show First Line of Paragraphs	WD 7.46	Show First Line Only button on Outlining toolbar			
Page Break	WD 2.35		Insert | Break		CTRL+ENTER
Page Numbers, Insert	WD 2.14	Insert Page Number button on Header and Footer toolbar	Insert | Page Numbers		
Page Numbers, Modify	WD 4.29		Insert | Page Numbers		
Paragraph Formatting, Remove	WD 2.18		Format | Paragraph	Paragraph	CTRL+SPACEBAR
Paragraphs, Keep Together	WD 7.33		Format | Paragraph	Paragraph	
Password-Protect File	WD 7.34		File | Save As | Tools | General Options		
Paste	WD 3.35	Paste button on Standard toolbar or click icon on Clipboard toolbar	Edit | Paste	Paste	CTRL+V
Picture Bullets	WD 4.40		Format | Bullets and Numbering | Bulleted tab	Bullets and Numbering | Bulleted tab	
Picture, Insert	WD 6.53		Insert | Picture | From File		
Print Document	WD 1.50	Print button on Standard toolbar	File | Print		CTRL+P
Print Preview	WD 3.24	Print Preview button on Standard toolbar	File | Print Preview		CTRL+F2
Promote List Item	WD 3.51	Increase Indent button on Formatting toolbar			
Quit Word	WD 1.51	Close button on title bar	File | Exit		ALT+F4
Rectangle, Draw	WD 8.40	Rectangle button on Drawing toolbar			
Redo Action	WD 1.35	Redo button on Standard toolbar	Edit | Redo		
Repeat Command	WD 1.36		Edit | Repeat		
Resize Graphic	WD 1.47	Drag sizing handle	Format | Picture | Size tab		
Restore Graphic	WD 1.48	Format Picture button on Picture toolbar	Format | Picture | Size tab		
Reviewer Initials, Change	WD 7.12		Tools | Options | User Information tab		
Right-Align	WD 1.33	Align Right button on Formatting toolbar	Format | Paragraph | Indents and Spacing tab	Paragraph | Indents and Spacing tab	CTRL+R
Rotate Text in Table	WD 4.50	Change Text Direction button on Tables and Borders toolbar	Format | Text Direction	Text Direction	
Ruler, Show or Hide	WD 1.11		View | Ruler		
Save as Web Page	WDW 1.3		File | Save as Web Page		
Save Document – New Name	WD 1.49		File | Save As		F12
Save Document – Same Name	WD 1.49	Save button on Standard toolbar	File | Save		CTRL+S
Save New Document	WD 1.26	Save button on Standard toolbar	File | Save		CTRL+S
Save Version	WD 7.15	Save Version button on Reviewing toolbar	File | Versions		
Section Break, Continuous	WD 6.24		Insert | Break		
Section Break, Next Page	WD 4.21		Insert | Break		

(continued)

Table 1 Microsoft Word 2000 Quick Reference Summary *(continued)*

TASK	PAGE NUMBER	MOUSE	MENU BAR	SHORTCUT MENU	KEYBOARD SHORTCUT
Security Level	WD 9.10		Tools | Macro | Security | Security Level tab		
Select Document	WD 2.46	Point to left and triple-click	Edit | Select All		CTRL+A
Select Graphic	WD 1.46	Click graphic			CTRL+SHIFT+RIGHT ARROW
Select Group of Words	WD 1.41	Drag through words			CTRL+SHIFT+RIGHT ARROW
Select Line	WD 1.37	Point to left of line and click			SHIFT+DOWN ARROW
Select Multiple Paragraphs	WD 1.30	Point to left of paragraph and drag down			CTRL+SHIFT+ DOWN ARROW
Select Paragraph	WD 2.46	Triple-click paragraph			
Select Sentence	WD 2.45	CTRL+click in sentence			CTRL+SHIFT+RIGHT ARROW
Select Table	WD 3.56	Drag through table	Table | Select | Table		ALT+5 (on numeric keypad)
Select Word	WD 1.38	Double-click word			CTRL+SHIFT+ RIGHT ARROW
Shade Graphic	WD 6.21	Format Picture button on Picture toolbar	Format | Picture | Colors and Lines tab	Format Picture | Colors and Lines tab	
Shade Paragraph	WD 6.45	Shading Color button on Tables and Borders toolbar	Format | Borders and Shading | Shading tab	Borders and Shading | Shading tab	
Shadow, on Characters	WD 4.17		Format | Font | Font tab	Font | Font tab	
Single-Space Paragraph	WD 4.31		Format | Paragraph | Indents and Spacing tab	Paragraph | Indents and Spacing tab	CTRL+1
Small Uppercase Letters	WD 2.18		Format | Font | Font tab	Font | Font tab	CTRL+SHIFT+K
Sort Data Records	WD 5.45	Merge button on Mail Merge Merge toolbar			
Sort Paragraphs	WD 2.40		Table | Sort		
Spelling Check as You Type	WD 1.22	Double-click Spelling and Grammar Status icon on status bar		Right-click flagged word, click correct word	
Spelling Check At Once	WD 2.50	Spelling and Grammar button on Standard toolbar	Tools | Spelling and Grammar	Spelling	F7
Standard Toolbar, Display Entire	WD 1.15	Double-click move handle on Standard toolbar			
Strikethrough, Characters	WD 4.17		Format | Font | Font tab	Font | Font tab	
Style, Apply	WD 6.33	Style box arrow on Formatting toolbar	Format | Style		
Style, Create	WD 9.17		Format | Style		
Style, Modify	WD 2.26		Format | Style		
Subdocument, Break Connection	WD 7.46	Remove Subdocument icon on Outlining toolbar			
Subdocument, Create	WD 7.43	Create Subdocument button on Outlining toolbar			
Subdocument, Delete	WD 7.46	Click subdocument icon, press DELETE			
Subdocument, Insert	WD 7.40	Insert Subdocument button on Outlining toolbar			
Subdocuments, Collapse	WD 7.41	Collapse Subdocuments button on Outlining toolbar			
Subdocuments, Expand	WD 7.41	Expand Subdocuments button on Outlining toolbar			
Subscript	WD 2.18		Format | Font | Font tab	Font | Font tab	CTRL+=
Superscript	WD 2.18		Format | Font | Font tab	Font | Font tab	CTRL+SHIFT+PLUS SIGN
Switch from Data Source to Main Document	WD 5.25	Mail Merge Main Document button on Database toolbar			
Switch to Open Document	WD 3.33	Program button on taskbar	Window | document name		

Table 1 Microsoft Word 2000 Quick Reference Summary *(continued)*

TASK	PAGE NUMBER	MOUSE	MENU BAR	SHORTCUT MENU	KEYBOARD SHORTCUT
Symbol, Insert	WD 3.37		Insert | Symbol		ALT+0 (on numeric keypad)
Synonym	WD 2.48		Tools | Language | Thesaurus	Synonyms | desired word	SHIFT+F7
Tab Stops, Insert	WD 3.31	Click location on ruler	Format | Tabs		
Table AutoFormat	WD 3.55	AutoFormat button on Tables and Borders toolbar	Table | Table AutoFormat		
Table of Contents, Create	WD 7.57		Insert | Index and Tables | Table of Contents tab		
Table of Contents, Update	WD 7.67			Right-click selected table of contents, click Update Field	Select table of contents, F9
Table of Figures, Create	WD 7.54		Insert | Index and Tables | Table of Figures tab		
Table, Create	WD 3.52	Insert Table button on Standard toolbar	Table | Insert | Table		
Table, Draw	WD 4.42	Tables and Borders button on Standard toolbar	Table | Draw Table		
Template	WD 5.6		File | New		
Template, Create	WD 8.9		File | New		
Text Box, Convert to a Frame	WD 7.28	Double-click text box	Format | Text Box	Format Text Box	
Text Box, Format	WD 6.41	Double-click text box	Format | Text Box	Format Text Box	
Text Box, Insert	WD 6.40	Text Box button on Drawing toolbar	Insert | Text Box		
Toolbar, Customize	WD 9.30		Tools | Customize	Customize	
Top Alignment	WD 4.22		File | Page Setup | Layout tab		
Track Changes	WD 7.13	Double-click TRK status indicator on status bar	Tools | Track Changes | Highlight Changes		
Track Changes, Stop	WD 7.14	Double-click TRK status indicator on status bar	Tools | Track Changes | Highlight Changes		
Tracked Changes, Display	WD 7.14		Tools | Track Changes | Highlight Changes	Right-click TRK status indicator on status bar, click Highlight Changes	
Tracked Changes, Print	WD 7.21		Tools | Track Changes | Highlight Changes	Right-click TRK status indicator on status bar, click Highlight Changes	
Tracked Changes, Review	WD 7.29	Click Next Change button on Reviewing toolbar		Right-click TRK status indicator on status bar, click Accept or Reject Changes	
Underline	WD 1.42	Underline button on Formatting toolbar	Format | Font | Font tab	Font | Font tab	CTRL+U
Underline Words, not Spaces	WD 2.18		Format | Font | Font tab	Font | Font tab	CTRL+SHIFT+W
Undo Command or Action	WD 1.36	Undo button on Standard toolbar	Edit | Undo		CTRL+Z
Unlink a Field	WD 5.28				CTRL+SHIFT+F9
Unprotect Document	WD 9.8	Protect Form button on Forms toolbar	Tools | Unprotect Document		
Visual Basic Editor, Close	WD 9.45	Close button on title bar	File | Close and Return to Microsoft Word		ALT+Q
Visual Basic Editor, Insert Procedure	WD 9.48	Insert UserForm button arrow on Standard toolbar	Insert | Procedure		
Vertical Rule	WD 6.37		Format | Borders and Shading | Borders tab		
Watermark	WD 4.54	In print layout view, double-click header area	View | Header and Footer		
Web Page Frame, Resize	WDW 1.9	Drag frame border	Format | Frames | Frame Properties | Frame tab		

(continued)

Table 1 Microsoft Word 2000 Quick Reference Summary *(continued)*

TASK	PAGE NUMBER	MOUSE	MENU BAR	SHORTCUT MENU	KEYBOARD SHORTCUT
Web Page, View	WDW 1.11		File | Web Page Preview		
Web Page Wizard	WDW 1.5		File | New | Web Pages tab		
Widow	WD 2.32		Format | Paragraph | Line and Page Breaks tab	Paragraph | Line and Page Breaks tab	
Wizard, Resume	WD 3.7		File | New | Other Documents tab		
WordArt Drawing Object, Format	WD 6.12	Format WordArt button on WordArt toolbar	Format | WordArt	Format WordArt	
WordArt Drawing Object, Insert	WD 6.9	Insert WordArt button on Drawing toolbar	Insert | Picture | WordArt		
WordArt Drawing Object, Shape	WD 6.14	WordArt Shape button on WordArt toolbar			
Wrap Text Around Graphic	WD 6.54	Text Wrapping button on Picture toolbar	Format | Picture | Layout tab	Format Picture | Layout tab	
Zoom Page Width	WD 1.15	Zoom box arrow on Formatting toolbar	View | Zoom		
Zoom Text Width	WD 3.17	Zoom box arrow on Formatting toolbar	View | Zoom		
Zoom Whole Page	WD 6.32	Zoom box arrow on Formatting toolbar	View | Zoom		

Table 2 Microsoft Excel 2000 Quick Reference Summary

TASK	PAGE NUMBER	MOUSE	MENU BAR	SHORTCUT MENU	KEYBOARD SHORTCUT
Advanced Filter	E 5.41		Data | Filter | Advanced Filter		ALT+D | F | A
Arrow, Add	E 6.45	Arrow button on Drawing toolbar			
AutoFilter	E 5.35		Data | Filter | AutoFilter		ALT+D | F | F
Auditing Toolbar, Display	E 8.10		Tools | Auditing | Show Auditing Toolbar		ALT+T | U | S
AutoFormat	E 1.31		Format | AutoFormat		ALT + O | A
AutoSum	E 1.22	AutoSum button on Standard toolbar	Insert | Function		ALT+=
Bold	E 1.29	Bold button on Formatting toolbar	Format | Cells | Font tab	Format Cells | Font tab	CTRL+B
Borders	E 2.30	Borders button on Formatting toolbar	Format | Cells | Border tab	Format Cells | Border tab	CTRL+1 | B
Center	E 2.33	Center button on Formatting toolbar	Format | Cells | Alignment tab	Format Cells | Alignment tab	CTRL+1 | A
Center Across Columns	E 1.33	Merge and Center button on Formatting toolbar	Format | Cells | Alignment tab	Format Cells | Alignment tab	CTRL+1 | A
Chart	E 1.37	Chart Wizard button on Standard toolbar	Insert | Chart		F11
Clear Cell	E 1.53	Drag fill handle back	Edit | Clear | All	Clear Contents	DELETE
Close All Workbooks	E 1.46		SHIFT+File | Close All		SHIFT+ALT+F | C
Close Workbook	E 1.46	Close button on menu bar or workbook Control menu icon	File | Close		CTRL+W
Color Background	E 2.30	Fill Color button on Formatting toolbar	Format | Cells | Patterns tab	Format Cells | Patterns tab	CTRL+1 | P
Column Width	E 2.44	Drag column heading boundary	Format | Column | Width tab	Column Width	ALT+O | C | W
Comma Style Format	E 2.32	Comma Style button on Formatting toolbar	Format | Cells | Number tab | Accounting	Format Cells | Number tab | Accounting	CTRL+1 | N
Command Button	E 7.27	Command Button button on Control Toolbox toolbar			
Comment	E 6.47		Insert | Comment	Insert Comment	ALT+I | M
Conditional Formatting	E 2.40		Format | Conditional Formatting		ALT+O | D
Copy and Paste	E 3.14	Copy button and Paste button on Standard toolbar	Edit | Copy; Edit | Paste	Copy to copy | Paste to paste	CTRL+C; CTRL+V
Currency Style Format	E 2.35	Percent Style button on Formatting toolbar	Format | Cells | Number tab | Currency	Format Cells | Number tab | Accounting	CTRL+1 | N
Custom Formats	E 6.20		Format | Cells | Number tab | Custom	Format Cells | Number tab | Custom	CTRL+1 | N
Cut	E 3.16	Cut button on Standard toolbar	Edit | Cut	Cut	CTRL + X
Data Form	E 5.9		Data | Form		ALT+D | O
Data Map, Add Button	E 9.36		Tools | Customize	Customize	ALT+T | C
Data Map, Change Features	E 9.40		Map | Features	Features	
Data Map, Create	E 9.37	Map button on Standard toolbar	Insert | Object | Microsoft Map		ALT+I | O
Data Map, Format	E 9. 42	In Microsoft Map Control, drag button to work area	View		ALT+V
Data Table	E 4.19		Data | Table		

(continued)

Table 2 Microsoft Excel 2000 Quick Reference Summary *(continued)*

TASK	PAGE NUMBER	MOUSE	MENU BAR	SHORTCUT MENU	KEYBOARD SHORTCUT
Data Validation, Cell	E 8.16		Data | Validation		ALT+D | L
Date	E 3.22	Paste Function button on Standard toolbar	Insert | Function		CTRL+ SEMICOLON
Decimal Place, Decrease	E 2.36	Decrease Decimal button on Formatting toolbar	Format | Cells | Number tab | Currency	Format Cells | Number tab | Currency	CTRL+1 | N
Decimal Place, Increase	E 2.36	Increase Decimal button on Formatting toolbar	Format | Cells | Number tab | Currency	Format Cells | Number tab | Currency	CTRL+1 | N
Delete Rows or Columns	E 3.18		Edit | Delete	Delete	DELETE
Draft Quality	E 6.55		File | Page Setup | Sheet tab		ALT+F | U | S
Drop Shadow	E 3.39	Shadow button on Drawing toolbar			
Embed a Clip Art Graphic	E 4.44		Insert | Picture | Clip Art		ALT+I | P | C
E-mail from Excel	E 2.63	E-mail button on Standard toolbar	File | Send To | Mail Recipient		ALT+F | D | A
File Passwords, Saving	E 8.32		File | Save As | Tools | General Options		ALT+F | A | ALT+L | G
Find	E 6.58		Edit | Find		CTRL+F
Fit to Print	E 2.56		File | Page Setup | Page tab		
Font Color	E 2.30	Font Color button on Formatting toolbar	Format | Cells | Font tab	Format Cells | Font tab	CTRL+1 | F
Font Size	E 1.30	Font Size box arrow on Formatting toolbar	Format | Cells | Font tab	Format Cells | Font tab	CTRL+1 | F
Font Type	E 2.28	Font box on Formatting toolbar	Format | Cells | Font tab	Format Cells | Patterns tab	CTRL+1 | F
Footer	E 6.49		File | Page Setup | Header/Footer tab		ALT+F | U | H
Formula Palette	E 2.18	Edit Formula box in formula bar	Insert | Function		CTRL+A after typing function name
Formulas Version	E 2.56		Tools | Options | View | Formulas		CTRL+ SINGLE LEFT QUOTATION MARK
Freeze Worksheet Titles	E 3.20		Windows | Freeze Panes		ALT+W | F
Function	E 2.20	Paste Function button on Standard toolbar	Insert | Function		SHIFT+F3
Gridlines	E 6.55		File | Page Setup | Sheet tab		ALT+F | U | S
Go To	E 1.36	Click cell	Edit | Go To		F5
Goal Seek	E 3.65		Tools | Goal Seek		ALT+T | G
Header	E 6.49		File | Page Setup | Header/Footer tab		ALT+F | U | H
Help	E 1.54	Microsoft Excel Help button on Standard toolbar	Help | Microsoft Excel Help		F1
Hide Column	E 2.46	Drag column heading boundary	Format | Column	Column Height	CTRL+0 (zero) to hide CTRL+SHIFT+) to display
Hide Row	E 2.48	Drag row heading boundary	Format | Row	Row Height	CTRL+9 to hide CTRL+SHIFT+(to display
Import Data from Access Table	E 9.14		Data | Get External Data | New Database Query		ALT+D | D | N
Import Data from Text File	E 9.9		Data | Get External Data | Import Text File		ALT+D | D | T
Import Data from Web Page	E 9.18		Data | Get External Data | New Web Query		ALT+D | D | W
In-Cell Editing	E 1.51	Double-click cell			F2
Insert Rows or Columns	E 3.16		Insert | Rows or Insert | Columns	Insert	ALT+I | R or ALT+I | C

Table 2 Microsoft Excel 2000 Quick Reference Summary *(continued)*

TASK	PAGE NUMBER	MOUSE	MENU BAR	SHORTCUT MENU	KEYBOARD SHORTCUT
Italicize	E 3.42	Italic button on Formatting toolbar	Format | Cells | Font tab	Format Cells | Font tab	CTRL+I
Link Update	E 6.63		Edit | Links		ALT+E | K
Link Worksheet to Word Document	EI 1.4		Edit | Copy; Edit | Paste Special	Copy to copy | Paste Special to paste	CTRL+C; ALT+E | S
Macro, Execute	E 7.15	Run Macro button on Visual Basic toolbar	Tools | Macro | Macros		ALT+F8
Macro, Record	E 7.11		Tools | Macro | Record New Macro		ALT+T | M | R
Macro, View Code	E 7.16		Tools | Macro | Macros | Edit		ALT+F8
Margins	E 6.49		File | Page Setup | Margins		ALT+F | U | M
Menu, Customize	E 7.22		Tools | Customize | Commands tab	Customize | Commands tab	ALT+T | C | C
Move	E 3.15	Point to border and drag	Edit | Cut; Edit | Paste		CTRL+X; CTRL+V
Name Cells	E 4.12	Click in Name box and type name	Insert | Name | Create or Insert | Name | Define		CTRL+SHIFT+F3
Name Cells, Redefine	E 5.18		Insert | Name | Define		ALT+I | N | D
New Workbook	E 1.54	New button on Standard toolbar	File | New		CTRL+N
Open Workbook	E 1.48	Open button on Standard toolbar	File | Open		CTRL+O
Outline a Range	E 4.9	Borders button on Formatting toolbar	Format | Cells | Border tab	Format Cells | Border tab	CTRL+1 | B
Outline a Worksheet	E 5.30		Data | Group and Outline		ALT+D | G | A
Page Break	E 6.56		Insert | Page Break		ALT+I | B
Percent Style Format	E 2.39	Percent Style button on Formatting toolbar	Format | Cells | Number tab | Percentage	Format Cells | Number | Percentage	CTRL+1 | N
PivotChart, Add Data to	E 9.49	Drag button from PivotTable toolbar to PivotChart			
PivotChart, Change View	E 9.54	Click interactive buttons on PivotChart			
PivotChart, Create	E 9.46		Data | PivotTable and PivotChart Report		ALT+D | P
PivotChart, Format	E 9.51	Chart Wizard button on PivotTable toolbar	Chart | Chart Type	Chart Type	ALT+C | T
PivotTable, Change View	E 9.60	Drag buttons to different locations on PivotTable			
PivotTable, Format	E 9.57	Format Report button on PivotTable toolbar	Format | AutoFormat	Format Report	ALT+O | A
PivotTable List, Add Fields	EW 2.14	Drag field from PivotTable Field List window			
PivotTable List, Add Summary Totals	EW 2.6	AutoCalc button on toolbar in browser			
PivotTable List, Change View	EW 2.10	Drag data fields to Row Field area in browser			
PivotTable List, Create	EW 2.2		File | Save as Web Page		ALT+F | G
PivotTable List, Filter	EW 2.4	Click field drop-down arrow and remove check marks			
PivotTable List, Remove Field	EW 2.12			Remove Field	
PivotTable List, Sort	EW 2.8	Sort Ascending button or Sort Descending button on toolbar in browser			
Preview Worksheet	E 2.51	Print Preview button on Standard toolbar	File | Print Preview		ALT+F | V

(continued)

Table 2 Microsoft Excel 2000 Quick Reference Summary *(continued)*

TASK	PAGE NUMBER	MOUSE	MENU BAR	SHORTCUT MENU	KEYBOARD SHORTCUT
Print Row and Column Headings	E 6.55		File | Page Setup | Sheet tab		ALT+F | U | S
Print Row and Column Titles	E 6.55		File | Page Setup | Sheet tab		ALT+F | U | S
Print Worksheet	E 2.51	Print button on Standard toolbar	File | Print		CTRL+P
Properties, Set	E 7.30	Properties button on Control Toolbox toolbar			
Protect Worksheet	E 4.49		Tools | Protection | Protect Sheet		ALT+T | P | P
Quit Excel	E 1.46	Close button on title bar	File | Exit		ALT+F4
Redo	E 1.52	Redo button on Standard toolbar	Edit | Redo		ALT+E | R
Remove Auditing Arrows	E 2.23	Remove All Arrows button on Auditing toolbar	Tools | Auditing | Remove All Arrows		ALT+T | U | A
Remove Precedent Arrows, Audit	E 8.12	Remove Precedent Arrows button on Auditing toolbar			
Remove Splits	E 3.62	Double-click split bar	Window | Split		ALT+W | S
Rename Sheet Tab	E 2.61	Double-click sheet tab		Rename	
Replace	E 6.58		Edit | Replace		CTRL+H
Rotate Text	E 3.8		Format | Cells | Alignment tab	Format Cells | Alignment tab	ALT+O | E | A
Route Workbook	E 9.27		File | Send To | Routing Recipient		ALT+F | D | R
Row Height	E 2.47	Drag row heading boundary	Format | Row	Row Height	ALT+O | R | E
Save as Web Page	EW 1.3		File | Save as Web Page		ALT+F | G
Save Workbook – New Name	E 1.41		File | Save As		ALT+F | A
Save Workbook – Same Name	E 2.50	Save button on Standard toolbar	File | Save		CTRL+S
Scenario, Add	E 8.45	Add button in Scenario Manager dialog box	Tools | Scenarios		ALT+T | E | ALT+A
Scenario, Show	E 8.47	Show button in Scenario Manager dialog box	Tools | Scenarios		ALT+T | E | ALT+S
Scenario Manager	E 8.35		Tools | Scenarios		ALT+T | E
Scenario PivotTable	E 8.52	Summary button in Scenario Manager dialog box, choose Scenario PivotTable	Tools | Scenarios		ALT+T | E | ALT+U | ALT+P
Scenario Summary	E 8.50	Summary button in Scenario Manager dialog box, choose Scenario summary	Tools | Scenarios		ALT+T | E | ALT+U | ALT+S
Select All of Worksheet	E 1.54	Select All button on worksheet			CTRL+A
Select Multiple Sheets	E 3.57	CTRL and click tab or SHIFT and click tab	Select All Sheets		
Series	E 3.8	Drag fill handle	Edit | Fill | Series		ALT+E | I | S
Shortcut Menu	E 1.51	Right-click			SHIFT+F10
Solver	E 8.23		Tools | Solver		ALT+T | V
Solver, Solve Problem	E 8.25	Solve button in Solver Parameters dialog box	Tools | Solver		ALT+T | V | ALT+S
Sort	E 5.22	Click Sort Ascending or Sort Descending button on Standard toolbar	Data | Sort		ALT+D | S
Spell Check	E 2.49	Spelling button on Standard toolbar	Tools | Spelling		F7

Table 2 Microsoft Excel 2000 Quick Reference Summary *(continued)*

TASK	PAGE NUMBER	MOUSE	MENU BAR	SHORTCUT MENU	KEYBOARD SHORTCUT
Split Window into Panes	E 3.61	Drag vertical or horizontal split box	Window | Split		ALT+W | S
Stock Quotes	E 2.58		Data | Get External Data | Run Web Query		ALT+D | D | D
Style, Add	E 6.22		Format | Style | Add button		ALT+O | S
Style, Apply	E 6.25		Format | Style		ALT+O | S
Subtotals	E 5.27		Data | Subtotals		ALT+D | B
Subtotals, Remove	E 5.31		Data | Subtotals | Remove All button		ALT+D | B | R
Switch Summary Functions	E 9.59	Field Settings button on PivotTable toolbar		Field Settings	
Text Box, Add	E 6.45	Text Box button on Drawing toolbar			
Toolbar, Customize	E 7.18		Tools | Customize | Commands tab	Customize | Commands tab	ALT+T | C | C
Toolbar, Reset	E 1.14		View | ToolBars | Customize | Toolbars tab	Customize | Toolbars tab	ALT+V | T | C | B
Toolbar, Show Entire	E 1.28	Double-click move handle			
Toolbar, Show or Hide	E 3.38		View | Toolbars	Customize	ALT+V | T
Trace Dependents	E 2.25	Trace Dependents button on Auditing toolbar		Tools | Auditing | Trace Dependents	ALT+T | U | D
Trace Precedents	E 2.25	Trace Precedents button on Auditing toolbar	Tools | Auditing | Trace Precedents		ALT+T | U | T
Track Changes, Disable	E 9.35		Tools | Track Changes | Highlight Changes | remove check mark		ALT+T | T | H
Track Changes, Enable	E 9.26		Tools | Track Changes | Highlight Changes		ALT+T | T | H
Track Changes, Review	E 9.31	Point to blue triangle	Tools | Track Changes | Accept or Reject Changes		ALT+T | T | A
Underline	E 3.42	Underline button on Formatting toolbar	Format | Cells | Font tab	Format Cells | Font tab	CTRL+U
Undo	E 1.52	Undo button on Standard toolbar	Edit | Undo		CTRL+Z
Unfreeze Worksheet Titles	E 3.32		Windows | Unfreeze Panes		ALT+W | F
Unlock Cells	E 4.49		Format | Cells | Protection tab	Format Cells | Protection tab	CTRL+1 | SHIFT+P
Unprotect Worksheet	E 4.51		Tools | Protection | Unprotect Sheet		ALT+T | P | P
Visual Basic Editor	E 7.31	View Code button on Control Toolbox toolbar	Tools | Macro | Visual Basic Editor		ALT+F11
WordArt	E 6.41	Insert WordArt button on Drawing toolbar	Insert | Picture | WordArt		ALT+I | P | W
Web Page Preview	EW 1.3		File | Web Page Preview		ALT+F | B
Workbook Properties	E 8.54		File | Properties		ALT+F | I
Zoom	E 3.59	Zoom box on Standard toolbar	View | Zoom		ALT+V | Z

Table 3 Microsoft Access 2000 Quick Reference Summary

TASK	PAGE NUMBER	MOUSE	MENU BAR	SHORTCUT MENU	KEYBOARD SHORTCUT
Add Clip Art	A 7.56	Unbound Object Frame button	Insert | Object		
Add Chart	A 8.40		Insert | Chart		
Add Combo Box	A 4.37	Combo Box button			
Add Command Button	A 8.9	Command Button button			
Add Date	A 7.39		Insert | Date and Time		
Add Field	A 3.17	Insert Rows button	Insert | Rows	Insert Rows	INSERT
Add Fields Using Field List	A 7.27	Drag field			
Add Label	A 4.43	Label button			
Add Page Number	A 7.41		Insert | Page Number		
Add Record	A 1.21, A 1.28	New Record button	Insert | New Record	New Record	
Add Rectangle	A 8.30	Rectangle button			
Add Subform	A 8.36	Subform / Subreport button			
Add Subreport	A 7.29	Subform / Subreport button			
Add Switchboard Item	A 6.44	New button			
Add Switchboard Page	A 6.43	New button			
Add Table to Query	A 2.32	Show Table button	Query | Show Table	Show Table	
Add Text Box	A 4.34	Text Box button			
Apply Filter	A 3.13	Filter by Selection or Filter by Form button	Records | Filter | Filter by Selection or Records | Filter | Filter by Form	Filter by Selection or Filter For	
Calculate Statistics	A 2.40	Totals button	View | Totals	Totals	
Change Field Properties in Query	A 7.17	Properties button	View | Properties	Properties	
Change Group of Records	A 3.23	Query Type button arrow | Update Query	Query | Update Query	Query Type | Update Query	
Change Join Properties in Query	A 7.16		View | Join Properties	Join Properties	
Change Margins	A 7.41		File | Page Setup | Margins tab		
Change Property	A 4.16	Properties button	View | Properties	Properties	
Change Referential Integrity Options	A 9.16		Relationships | Edit Relationship	Edit Relationship	
Clear Query	A 2.16		Edit | Clear Grid		
Close Database	A 1.25	Close button	File | Close		
Close Form	A 1.38	Close button	File | Close		
Close Query	A 2.14	Close button	File | Close		
Close Table	A 1.25	Close button	File | Close		
Collapse Subdatasheet	A 3.42	Expand indicator (–)			
Compact a Database	A 5.48		Tools | Database Utilities | Compact and Repair		
Convert Database to Earlier Version	A 9.7		Tools | Database Utilities | Convert Database		
Copy Object to Clipboard	A 6.36	Copy button	Edit | Copy	Copy	CTRL+C
Create Calculated Field	A 2.36			Zoom	SHIFT+F2
Create Data Access Page	AW 1.3	New Object button arrow | Page	Insert | Page		
Create Database	A 1.9	Start button | New Office Document	File | New		CTRL+N
Create Form	A 1.37, A 4.31	New Object button arrow | AutoForm	Insert | Form		

Table 3 Microsoft Access 2000 Quick Reference Summary *(continued)*

TASK	PAGE NUMBER	MOUSE	MENU BAR	SHORTCUT MENU	KEYBOARD SHORTCUT
Create Form Using Design View	A 8.35	Double-click Create Form in Design View	Insert | Form | Design View		
Create Index	A 3.48	Indexes button	View | Indexes		
Create Input Mask	A 6.10	Input Mask text box			
Create Labels	A 7.47	New Object button arrow | Report | Label Wizard	Insert | Report | Label Wizard		
Create Lookup Wizard Field	A 6.8	Text arrow | Lookup Wizard			
Create Macro	A 6.27	New Object button arrow | Macro	Insert | Macro		
Create PivotTable	A 8.47	New Object button arrow | Form | PivotTable Wizard	Insert | Form | PivotTable Wizard		
Create Query	A 2.6	New Object button arrow | Query	Insert | Query		
Create Replica	A 9.32		Tools | Replication | Create Replica		
Create Report	A 1.43	New Object button arrow | Report	Insert | Report		
Create Report Using Design View	A 7.24	Double-click Create Report in Design View	Insert | Report | Design View		
Create Snapshot	AI 2.9		File | Export	Export	
Create SQL Query	A 9.36	View button arrow | SQL View	View | SQL View	SQL View	
Create Switchboard	A 6.40		Tools | Database Utilities | Switchboard Manager		
Create Table	A 1.14	Tables object | Create table in Design view or Create table by using Wizard	Insert | Table		
Default Value	A 3.31	Default Value box			
Delete Field	A 1.19, A 3.19	Delete Rows button	Edit | Delete Rows	Delete Rows	DELETE
Delete Group of Records	A 3.26	Query Type button arrow | Delete Query	Query | Delete Query	Query Type | Delete Query	
Delete Record	A 3.14	Delete Record button	Edit | Delete Record	Delete Record	DELETE
Display Field List	A 7.24	Field List button	View | Field List		
Encrypt Database	A 9.24		Tools | Security | Encrypt/Decrypt Database		
Exclude Duplicates	A 2.29	Properties button	View | Properties | Unique Values Only	Properties | Unique Values Only	
Exclude Field from Query Results	A 2.20	Show check box			
Expand Subdatasheet	A 3.42	Expand indicator (+)			
Export Data Using Drag-and-Drop	AI 2.6	Drag object to desired application			
Export Data Using Export Command	AI 2.3		File | Export	Export	
Field Size	A 1.17, A 3.16	Field Size text box			
Field Type	A 1.16	Data Type arrow | appropriate type, appropriate letter			
Filter Query's Recordset	A 7.19	Filter by Selection or Filter by Form button	Records | Filter | Filter by Selection or Records | Filter | Filter by Form	Filter by Selection or Filter For	
Format	A 3.33	Format box			
Import Worksheet	AI 1.3		File | Get External Data | Import	Import	

(continued)

Table 3 Microsoft Access 2000 Quick Reference Summary *(continued)*

TASK	PAGE NUMBER	MOUSE	MENU BAR	SHORTCUT MENU	KEYBOARD SHORTCUT
Include All Fields in Query	A 2.15	Double-click asterisk			
Include Field in Query	A 2.10	Double-click field in field list box			
Key Field	A 1.17	Primary Key button	Edit | Primary Key	Primary Key	
Link Worksheet	AI 1.3		File | Get External Data | Link Tables	Link Tables	
Modify Switchboard Page	A 6.44, A 6.46	Edit button			
Move Control	A 4.33	Drag control		Properties | All tab | Top and Properties | All tab | Left	
Move to Design View	A 5.39	View button	View | Design View	Design View	
Move to First Record	A 1.27	First Record button			CTRL+UP ARROW
Move to Last Record	A 1.27	Last Record button			CTRL+DOWN ARROW
Move to Next Record	A 1.27	Next Record button			DOWN ARROW
Move to Previous Record	A 1.27	Previous Record button			UP ARROW
Open Database	A 1.26	Start button | Open Office Document	File | Open Database		CTRL+O
Open Form	A 3.7	Forms object | Open button		Open	Use arrow keys to move highlight to name, then press ENTER key
Open Table	A 1.21	Tables object | Open button		Open	Use arrow keys to move highlight to name, then press ENTER key
Preview Table	A 1.31	Print Preview button	File | Print Preview	Print Preview	
Print Relationships	A 3.38		File | Print Relationships		
Print Report	A 1.48	Print button	File | Print	Print	CTRL+P
Print Results of Query	A 2.12	Print button	File | Print	Print	CTRL+P
Print Table	A 1.31	Print button	File | Print	Print	CTRL+P
Quit Access	A 1.25	Close button on title bar	File | Exit		ALT+F4
Relationships (Referential Integrity)	A 3.38	Relationships button	Tools | Relationships	Relationships	
Remove Control	A 4.24	Cut button	Edit | Cut	Cut	DELETE
Remove Filter	A 3.14	Remove Filter button	Records | Remove Filter/Sort	Remove Filter/Sort	
Remove Password	A 9.25		Tools | Security | Unset Database Password		
Resize Column	A 3.21, A 5.13	Drag right boundary of field selector	Format | Column Width	Column Width	
Resize Control	A 5.29	Drag sizing handle	View | Properties | All tab | Width and View | Properties | All tab | Height	Properties | All tab | Width and Properties | All tab | Height	
Resize Row	A 5.13	Drag lower boundary of row selector	Format | Row Height	Row Height	
Resize Section	A 4.43	Drag section boundary	View | Properties | All tab | Height	Properties | All tab | Height	
Restructure Table	A 3.16	Tables object | Design button		Design View	
Return to Design View	A 2.12	View button	View | Design View		
Run Query	A 2.11	Run button	Query | Run		
Save Form	A 1.38	Save button	File | Save		CTRL+S
Save Query	A 2.42	Save button	File | Save		CTRL+S
Save Table	A 1.19	Save button	File | Save		CTRL+S
Search for Record	A 3.9	Find button	Edit | Find		CTRL+F

Table 3 Microsoft Access 2000 Quick Reference Summary *(continued)*

TASK	PAGE NUMBER	MOUSE	MENU BAR	SHORTCUT MENU	KEYBOARD SHORTCUT
Select Fields for Report	A 1.45	Add Field button or Add All Fields button			
Set Password	A 9.22		Tools | Security | Set Database Password		
Set Startup Options	A 9.20		Tools | Startup		
Sort Data in Query	A 2.26	Sort row | arrow | type of sort			
Sort Records	A 3.43	Sort Ascending or Sort Descending button	Records | Sort | Sort Ascending or Sort Descending	Sort Ascending or Sort Descending	
Specify Sorting and Grouping in Report	A 7.25	Sorting and Grouping button	View | Sorting and Grouping	Sorting and Grouping	
Switch Between Form and Datasheet Views	A 1.42, A 3.11	View button	View | Datasheet View		
Synchronize Design Master and Replica	A 9.34		Tools | Replication | Synchronize Now		
Update Hyperlink Field	A 5.18		Insert | Hyperlink	Hyperlink | Edit Hyperlink	CTRL+K
Update OLE Field	A 5.15		Insert | Object	Insert Object	
Use AND Criterion	A 2.24				Type criteria on same line
Use Documenter	A 9.13	Analyze button arrow | Documenter	Tools | Analyze | Documenter		
Use OR Criterion	A 2.25				Type criteria on separate lines
Use Performance Analyzer	A 9.11	Analyze button arrow | Analyze Performance	Tools | Analyze | Performance		
Use Table Analyzer	A 9.8	Analyze button arrow | Analyze Table	Tools | Analyze | Table		
Validation Rule	A 3.30	Validation Rule box			
Validation Text	A 3.30	Validation Text box			

Table 4 Microsoft PowerPoint 2000 Quick Reference Summary

TASK	PAGE NUMBER	MOUSE	MENU BAR	SHORTCUT MENU	KEYBOARD SHORTCUT
Action Button, Add	PP 4.27	AutoShapes button on Drawing toolbar | Action Buttons	Slide Show | Action Buttons		ALT+D | I
Action Button, Add Caption (Text Box)	PP 4.35	Text Box button on Drawing toolbar	Insert | Text Box		ALT+I | X
Action Button, Fill Color	PP 4.34	Fill Color button on Drawing toolbar	Format | AutoShape | Colors and Lines tab	Format AutoShape | Colors and Lines tab	ALT+O | O | Colors and Lines tab
Action Button, Scale	PP 4.33	Drag sizing handle	Format | AutoShape | Size tab	Format AutoShape | Size tab	ALT+O | O | Size tab
Action Button, Shadow	PP 4.35	Shadow button on Drawing toolbar			
Animate Text	PP 2.48	Custom Animation button on Animation Effects toolbar	Slide Show | Custom Animation | Effects tab	Custom Animation | Effects tab	ALT+D | M
Animation Order, Set	PP 5.49	Animation Effects button on Formatting toolbar | Custom Animation button	Slide Show | Custom Animation	Custom Animation	ALT+D | M
Apply Design Template	PP 1.18	Apply Design Template button on Standard toolbar; Apply Design Template on Common Tasks button menu on Formatting toolbar	Format | Apply Design Template	Apply Design Template	ALT+O | Y
AutoShape, Add Shadow	PP 5.41	Shadow button on Drawing toolbar			
AutoShape, Add Text	PP 5.42	Drag sizing handle	Format | AutoShape | Text Box tab | Resize AutoShape to fit text	Format AutoShape | Text Box tab | Resize AutoShape to fit text	ALT+O | O | CTRL+TAB | TAB | SPACEBAR
AutoShape, Insert	PP 5.40	AutoShapes menu button on Drawing toolbar			ALT+U
AutoShape, Rotate	PP 5.44	Free Rotate button on Drawing toolbar; Draw button on Drawing toolbar | Rotate or Flip | Free Rotate	Format | AutoShape | Size tab | Rotation text box		ALT+R | P | T; ALT+O | O | CTRL+TAB
Bullets, Remove	PP 4.48	Bullets button on Formatting toolbar	Format | Bullets and Numbering | Bulleted tab | None	Bullets and Numbering | Bulleted tab | None	ALT+O | B | SPACEBAR
Change Design Templates	PP 3.9	Double-click design template name on status bar; Apply Design Template button on Standard toolbar	Format | Apply Design Template	Apply Design Template	ALT+O | Y
Change Font	PP 3.10	Font box arrow on Formatting toolbar	Format | Font	Font	ALT+O | F
Change Font Color	PP 1.24	Font Color button arrow on Drawing toolbar | color sample	Format | Font	Font | Color	ALT+O | F | ALT+C | DOWN ARROW
Change Slide Layout	PP 2.22	Slide Layout on Common Tasks button menu on Formatting toolbar	Format | Slide Layout	Slide Layout	ALT+O | L | RIGHT ARROW
Change Slide Order	PP 4.50, PP 4.54	Drag			
Change Slide Timing	PP 5.51		Slide Show | Custom Animation	Custom Animation	ALT+D | M
Chart, Add Title and Data Labels	PP 5.33		Chart | Chart Options | Titles or Data Labels tab	Chart Options	ALT+C | O
Chart, Insert Excel	PP 5.21		Insert | Object | Create from file		ALT+I | O | ALT+F
Chart, Select Different Type	PP 5.27		Chart | Chart Type	Chart Type	ALT+C | T
Check Spelling	PP 1.55	Spelling button on Standard toolbar	Tools | Spelling		F7

Table 4 Microsoft PowerPoint 2000 Quick Reference Summary *(continued)*

TASK	PAGE NUMBER	MOUSE	MENU BAR	SHORTCUT MENU	KEYBOARD SHORTCUT
Choose a Design Template	PP 1.18	Common Tasks button on Formatting toolbar | Apply Design Template	Format | Apply Design Template	Apply Design Template	ALT+C | Y
Clip Art, Animate	PP 2.47		Slide Show | Preset Animation		ALT+D | P
Clip Art, Change Size	PP 2.33	Format Picture button on Picture toolbar | Size tab	Format | Picture | Size tab	Format Picture | Size tab	ALT+O | I | Size tab
Clip Art, Insert	PP 2.25	Insert Clip Art button on Drawing toolbar	Insert | Picture | Clip Art		ALT+I | P | C
Clip Art, Move	PP 2.32	Drag			
Clip Art, Ungroup	PP 3.54	Draw button on Drawing toolbar | Ungroup		Grouping | Ungroup	SHIFT+F10 | G | U
Connect to Microsoft Clip Gallery Live Site	PPI 1.4	Insert Clip Art button on Drawing toolbar | Clips Online button on Insert ClipArt toolbar	Insert | Picture | Clip Art | Clips Online button on Insert ClipArt toolbar		ALT+I | P | C | ALT+C
Control, Add to Form	PP 6.31	Double-click Control in Toolbox			
Create a Table	PP 3.41	Insert Table button on Standard toolbar	Insert | Table		ALT+I | B
Custom Background, Insert Picture	PP 3.16		Format | Background	Background	ALT+O | K
Decrease Font Size	PP 1.25	Decrease Font Size button on Formatting toolbar	Format | Font	Font | Size	CTRL+SHIFT+<
Delete an Object	PP 3.56	Select object | Cut button on Standard toolbar	Edit | Clear or Edit | Cut	Cut	ALT+E | A or DELETE or CTRL+X
Delete Slide	PP 4.53	Click slide icon, press DELETE	Edit | Delete Slide		ALT+E | D
Delete Text	PP 4.9	Cut button on Standard toolbar	Edit | Cut	Cut	CTRL+X
Demote a Paragraph	PP 1.34	Demote button on Formatting toolbar			TAB or ALT+SHIFT+ RIGHT ARROW
Deselect a Clip Art Object	PP 3.55	Click outside clip art object area			
Discussions, Close	PPW 2.13	Close button on Discussions toolbar	Tools | Online Collaboration | Web Discussions		ALT+T | N | W
Discussions, Start	PPW 2.10	Discussions menu button on Discussions toolbar; Discussion Options	Tools | Online Collaboration | Web Discussions | Discussions menu button | Discussion Options		ALT+T | N | W
Display Guides	PP 4.11		View | Guides	Guides	ALT+V | G
Display Rulers	PP 4.10		View | Ruler	Ruler	ALT+V | R
Edit Web Page Through Browser	PPW 1.9	Edit button on Internet Explorer Standard Buttons toolbar			
E-mail from PowerPoint	PP 2.56	E-mail button on Standard toolbar	File | Send To | Mail Recipient		ALT+F | D | A
Export Outline to Microsoft Word	PP 6.70	Save button on Standard toolbar | Save as type | Outline/RTF	File | Save As | Save as type | Outline/RTF		ALT+F | A | ALT+T
Graphical Bullets, Add	PP 3.19	Bullets button on Formatting toolbar	Format | Bullets and Numbering | Bulleted tab | Character	Bullets and Numbering | Bulleted tab | Character	ALT+O | B | ALT+H
Group Objects	PP 3.57	Drag through objects | Draw button on Drawing toolbar | Group		Grouping | Group	
Header and Footer, Add to Page	PP 2.36		View | Header and Footer | Notes and Handouts tab		ALT+V | H

(continued)

Table 4 Microsoft PowerPoint 2000 Quick Reference Summary *(continued)*

TASK	PAGE NUMBER	MOUSE	MENU BAR	SHORTCUT MENU	KEYBOARD SHORTCUT
Header and Footer, Add to Slide	PP 1.75		View | Header and Footer | Slide tab		ALT+V | H
Help	PP 1.67	Microsoft PowerPoint Help button on Standard toolbar	Help		F1
Hide Guides	PP 4.38		View | Guides	Guides	ALT+V | G
Hide Rulers	PP 4.22		View | Ruler	Ruler	ALT+V | R
Hide Slide	PP 4.49	Hide Slide button on Slide Sorter toolbar	Slide Show | Hide Slide	Hide Slide	ALT+D | H
Increase Font Size	PP 1.25	Increase Font Size button on Formatting toolbar	Format | Font	Font | Size	CTRL+SHIFT+>
Increase Placeholder Width	PP 5.15	Drag sizing handle	Format | Placeholder | Size tab | Width box arrow	Format Placeholder | Size tab | Width box arrow	ALT+O | O | RIGHT ARROW | ALT+D
Increase Zoom Percentage	PP 4.13	Zoom box arrow on Standard toolbar	View | Zoom		ALT+V | Z
Insert Slide from Another Presentation	PP 5.10		Insert | Slides from Files | Find Presentation tab | Browse | Open | Insert | Close		ALT+I | F | ALT+B | ALT+O | ALT+S | I | ESC
Italicize Text	PP 1.27	Italic button on Formatting toolbar	Format | Font | Font style	Font | Font style	CTRL+I
Macro, Create by Using Macro Recorder	PP 6.16		Tools | Macro | Record New Macro		
Macro, View VBA Code	PP 6.24		Tools | Macro | Macros | Edit		ALT+T | M | V
Menu, Customize by Adding a Command	PP 6.20	More Buttons button on Standard toolbar | Add or Remove Buttons | Customize | Commands tab	View | Toolbars | Customize | Commands tab	Customize | Commands tab	
Microsoft Organization Chart, Add Co-worker Boxes	PP 4.41	Co-worker box tool on Microsoft Organization Chart icon bar			
Microsoft Organization Chart, Add Shadow Effects	PP 3.36		Boxes | Shadow	Shadow	ALT+B | W
Microsoft Organization Chart, Add Subordinate Boxes	PP 3.27	Subordinate box tool on Microsoft Organization Chart icon bar			
Microsoft Organization Chart, Change Border Style	PP 3.37		Boxes | Border Style	Border Style	ALT+B | B
Microsoft Organization Chart, Change Style	PP 3.29		Styles		ALT+S
Microsoft Organization Chart, Copy a Branch	PP 3.31		Edit | Copy	Copy	CTRL+C
Microsoft Organization Chart, Delete a Branch	PP 4.39		Edit | Select | Branch | Edit | Clear		CTRL+B | DELETE
Microsoft Organization Chart, Open	PP 3.24		Insert | Picture | Organization Chart		ALT+I | P | O
Microsoft Organization Chart, Paste a Branch	PP 3.32		Edit | Paste Boxes	Paste Boxes	CTRL+V
Microsoft Organization Chart, Quit	PP 3.38	Close button on Microsoft Organization Chart title bar	File | Close and Return to presentation		ALT+F | C
Microsoft Organization Chart, Scale	PP 3.39	Format Object button on Picture toolbar | Size tab	Format | Object | Size tab	Format Object | Size tab	ALT+O | O | Size tab
Move a Paragraph Down	PP 2.10	Move Down button on Outlining toolbar			ALT+SHIFT+ DOWN ARROW
Move a Paragraph Up	PP 2.10	Move Up button on Outlining toolbar			ALT+SHIFT+UP ARROW

Table 4 Microsoft PowerPoint 2000 Quick Reference Summary *(continued)*

TASK	PAGE NUMBER	MOUSE	MENU BAR	SHORTCUT MENU	KEYBOARD SHORTCUT
Move Paragraph in Outline View	PP 4.25	Drag			
New Slide	PP 1.32	New Slide on Common Tasks button menu on Formatting toolbar	Insert | New Slide		CTRL+M
Next Slide	PP 1.44	Next Slide button on vertical scroll bar			PAGE DOWN
Object Area Placeholder, Increase Width	PP 3.51	Select placeholder | Drag sizing handle			
Omit Background Graphics	PP 5.46		Format | Background | Omit background graphics from master	Background | Omit background graphics from master	ALT+O | K | ALT+G
Open an Outline	PP 3.7	Open button on Standard toolbar	File | Open		CTRL+O
Open Presentation	PP 1.52	Open button on Standard toolbar	File | Open		CTRL+O
Open Presentation and Print by Executing Macro	PP 6.23	Open button on Standard toolbar | double-click file name | Enable Macros | Print | Print Handout	File | Open | double-click file name | Enable Macros | File | Print Handout		
Previous Slide	PP 1.44	Previous Slide button on scroll bar			PAGE UP
Print a Presentation	PP 1.65	Print button on Standard toolbar	File | Print		CTRL+P
Print Handouts	PP 3.59		File | Print | Print what box arrow | Handouts		CTRL+P | TAB | TAB | DOWN ARROW
Promote a Paragraph	PP 1.34	Promote button on Outlining toolbar			SHIFT+TAB or ALT+SHIFT+LEFT ARROW
Quit PowerPoint	PP 1.51	Close button on title bar or double-click Control icon on title bar	File | Exit		ALT+F4
Redo Action	PP 1.22	Redo button on Standard toolbar	Edit | Redo		CTRL+Y or ALT+E | R
Save a Presentation	PP 1.29	Save button on Standard toolbar	File | Save		CTRL+S
Save as Web Page	PPW 1.4		File | Save as Web Page | Publish button		ALT+F | G | ALT+P
Self-Running Presentation, Create	PP 5.53		Slide Show | Set Up Show | Browsed at a kiosk (full screen)		ALT+D | S | K
Set Manual Slide Show Timings	PP 5.55		Slide Show | Slide Transition | Automatically after text box up arrow | Automatically after | Apply button	Slide Transition | On mouse click | Automatically after | Apply button	ALT+D | T | ALT+C | SPACEBAR
Slide Show	PP 1.46	Slide Show button in PowerPoint window	View | Slide Show		F5 or ALT+V | W
Slide Transitions, Add	PP 2.39		Slide Show | Slide Transition		ALT+D | T
Summary Slide, Add	PP 4.52	Summary Slide button on Slide Sorter toolbar			
Table, Delete Row	PP 4.45	Select row | Cut button on Standard toolbar			
Table, Format	PP 3.47	Table button on Tables and Borders toolbar | Select Table	Format | Table	Borders and Fill	
Table, Format Cell	PP 3.45	Click cell			
Table, Insert	PP 5.37		Insert | Object | Create from file		ALT+I | O | ALT+F
Text Preset Animation Effects	PP 3.58	Slide Sorter View button in PowerPoint window	View | Slide Sorter		ALT+V | D

(continued)

Table 4 Microsoft PowerPoint 2000 Quick Reference Summary *(continued)*

TASK	PAGE NUMBER	MOUSE	MENU BAR	SHORTCUT MENU	KEYBOARD SHORTCUT
Toolbar, Create	PP 6.10	More Buttons button on Standard toolbar | Add or Remove Buttons | Customize | Toolbars tab | New button	View | Toolbars | Customize | Toolbars tab | New button	Customize | Toolbars tab | New button	
Toolbar, Customize by Adding Button	PP 6.11	More Buttons button on Standard toolbar| Add or Remove Buttons | Customize | Commands tab	View | Toolbars | Customize | Commands tab	Customize | Commands tab	
Toolbar, Show Entire	PP 1.17	Double-click move handle			
Undo Action	PP 1.22	Undo button on Standard toolbar	Edit | Undo		CTRL+Z or ALT+E | U
Visual Basic Editor, Close and Return to Microsoft PowerPoint	PP 6.66		File | Return to Microsoft PowerPoint		ALT+Q
Visual Basic Editor, Start	PP 6.27		Tools | Macro | Visual Basic Editor		ALT+F11
WordArt, Fill Color	PP 4.19	Format WordArt button on WordArt toolbar | Colors and Lines tab	Format | WordArt | Colors and Lines tab	Format WordArt | Colors and Lines tab	ALT+O | O | Colors and Lines tab
WordArt, Height and Width	PP 4.17	Format WordArt button on WordArt toolbar | Size tab	Format | WordArt | Size tab	Format WordArt | Size tab	ALT+O | O | Size tab
WordArt, Scale	PP 4.21	Format WordArt button on WordArt toolbar | Size tab	Format | WordArt | Size tab	Format WordArt | Size tab	ALT+O | O | Size tab
WordArt, Style	PP 4.14	Insert WordArt button on WordArt toolbar	Insert | Picture | WordArt		ALT+I | P | W

Table 5 Microsoft Outlook 2000 Quick Reference Summary

TASK	PAGE NUMBER	MOUSE	MENU BAR	SHORTCUT MENU	KEYBOARD SHORTCUT
Change to Day View	O 1.33	Day button	View | Day		ALT+V, press Y
Change to Month View	O 1.33	Month button	View | Month		ALT+V, press M
Change to Week View	O 1.32	Week button	View | Week		ALT+V, press K
Change to Work Week View	O 1.31	Work Week button	View | Work Week		ALT+V, press R
Create a Task	O 1.34	New button			CTRL+SHIFT+K
Create an Event	O 1.29	New button	Actions | New All Day Event	New All Day Event	ALT+A, press E
Create Contact List	O 1.40	New butonn	Actions | New Contact	New Contact	CTRL+N
Create Subfolder	O 1.11		File | New | Folder	New Folder	CTRL+SHIFT+E
Delete an Appointment	O 1.23	Delete button	Edit | Delete	Delete	CTRL+D
Delete Folder	O 1.49	Delete button	File | Folder | Delete	Delete	
Enter Appointments	O 1.14	New Appointment button	Actions | New Appointment	New Appointment	CTRL+N, ALT+A, press O
Find a Contact	O 1.42	Find button		Tools | Find	CTRL+SHIFT+F
Import/Export Folders	O 1.46		File | Import and Export		
Move an Appointment	O 1.25		Edit | Copy Edit | Paste		CTRL+C, CTRL+V
Move to Next Day	O 1.19		View | Go To | Go to Date	Go to Date	CTRL+G
Open Calendar	O 1.9		View | Go To | Calendar		
Organize Contacts	O 1.44	Organize button		Tools | Organize	
Print Calendar	O 1.35	Print button		File | Print	CTRL+P
Print Contact List	O 1.45	Print button		File | Print	CTRL+P
Recurring Appointments	O 1.17	Recurrence button on Standard toolbar in Appointment window	Actions | Recurrence	New Recurring Appointment	ALT+A, press A